A CHRONOLOGY OF AMERICAN MUSICAL THEATER

A CHRONOLOGY OF
AMERICAN
MUSICAL THEATER

Richard C. Norton

VOLUME 3

OXFORD
UNIVERSITY PRESS
2002

OXFORD
UNIVERSITY PRESS

Oxford New York
Auckland Bangkok Buenos Aires Cape Town Chennai
Dar es Salaam Delhi Hong Kong Istanbul Karachi Kolkata
Kuala Lumpur Madrid Melbourne Mexico City Mumbai Nairobi
São Paulo Shanghai Singapore Taipei Tokyo Toronto

and an associated company in Berlin

Copyright © 2002 by Oxford University Press

Published by Oxford University Press, Inc.
198 Madison Avenue, New York, New York 10016
www.oup.com

Oxford is a registered trademark of Oxford University Press

Library of Congress Cataloging-in-Publication Data

Norton, Richard C , 1953-
A chronology of American musical theater / Richard C. Norton
Includes indexes
ISBN 978-0-19-515567-9   3
1. Musical theater — New York (State) — New York — Chronology I Title.
ML 1711.8.N3 N67 2002
782.1'4'097471 — dc21   2001055710

EDITORIAL AND PRODUCTION STAFF
Project Editor: Mark Mones
Production Director: John Sollami
Indexes: Prepared by Magic Fingers
Book Designer: Joan Greenfield
Composition: General Meador, Inc.
Publisher: Karen Day

CONTENTS

A CHRONOLOGY OF
AMERICAN MUSICAL THEATER

VOLUME 1: 1750–1912

VOLUME 2: 1912–1952

VOLUME 3: 1952–2001

A CHRONOLOGY OF AMERICAN MUSICAL THEATER

Rosalind Russell and two Brazilian cadets in WONDERFUL TOWN
(Photo: Vandamm Studio)
Billy Rose Theatre Collection, New York Public Library for the Performing Arts

1952–1953 SEASON

1952.10 ## WISH YOU WERE HERE

A Musical Comedy in Two Acts, 15 Scenes. Book by Arthur Kober and Joshua Logan. Based on Arthur Kober's play "Having Wonderful Time." Music and lyrics by Harold Rome. Direction and dances by Joshua Logan. Settings and lighting by Jo Mielziner. Costumes by Robert Mackintosh. Musical direction, Jay Blackton. Orchestrations by Don Walker. Musical continuity by Trude Rittman. Produced by Leland Hayward and Joshua Logan. Opened 25 June 1952 at the Imperial Theatre and closed 28 November 1953 after 598 performances.

CAST (in order of appearance): *Teddy Stern*: PATRICIA MARAND. *Chick Miller*: JACK CASSIDY. *Fay Fromkin*: SHEILA BOND. *Itchy Flexner*: SIDNEY ARMUS. *Pinky Harris*: PAUL VALENTINE. *Hatty "Muscles" Green*: JOHN PERKINS. *Lou Kandel*: SAMMY SMITH. *Herman Fabricant*: HARRY CLARK. *Marvin*: Fred Sadoff. *Sonja*: Elaine Gordon. *Schmutz*: Larry Blyden. *Eli*: Frank Aletter. *Barney*: Ray Hyson. *Sid*: Robert Dixon. *Lenny*: Richard France. *Sam*: Joe Milan. *Monty*: Tom Ayre. *Henrietta*: Mardi Bayne. *Gussie*: Leila Martin. *Wallflowers (4)*: *Irma*: Roslynd Lowe. *Shirley*: Sybil Lamb. *Lena*: Denise Griffin. *Judy*: Shirley Ann Prior. *Miriam, who has hay fever*: Nancy Franklin. *The New Girl*: Florence Henderson. *The Girl Diver*: Beverly Weston. *The Acrobat*: Steve Wiland. *Eccentric Diver*: Joseph Thomas.

Waiters: *Mel*: Gus Giordano. *Fred*: Stan [Stanley] Grover. *Morrie*: Bill Hogue. *Bill*: Leo Kayeworth. *Butch*: George Lenz. *Joe*: Reid Shelton. *Harry*: Harry Snow. *Phil*: Ray Steele. *Alex*: Tom Tryon. *Mac*: Don Wayne. *Bathing Beauties*: *Billie*: Sue Brin. *Kitty*: Norma Doggett. *Mildred*: Joan Johnston. *Sarah*: Phyllis Newman. *Felice*: Gloria Van Deweel. *Anna*: Jan Stuart. *Wilma*: Rain Winslow. *Athletes, Guests, Staff Members*: Nancy Baker, Joan Berke, Toni Parker, Candi Parsons, Inga Rode, Elliott Feder, Al Lawrence, Don Paterson, Wally Strauss.

The action takes place at Camp Karefree, a summer camp for adults, "where friendships are formed to last a whole lifetime through," located in the heart of Vacationland. It could be the Berkshires, the Adirondacks, the Poconos, the White Mountains—or even the Catskills.

Act 1, Scene 1: Outside Teddy's Cabin. *Scene 2*: Locker Room. *Scene 3*: Porch of the Social Hall. *Scene 4*: Social Hall. *Scene 5*: A Path through the Woods. *Scene 6*: Athletic Field. *Scene 7*: A Path through the Woods. *Scene 8*: Eagle Rock. *Scene 9*: The Boat House. *Scene 10*: The Lake Front.

Act 2, Scene 1: The Campfire. *Scene 2*: A Path through the Woods. *Scene 3*: Pinky's Cabin. *Scene 4*: Porch of the Social Hall. *Scene 5*: Basket Ball Court.

ACT 1
Scene 1
  "Camp Karefree"
    S. Smith, Waiters, Ensemble
  "Goodbye Love"[1]
    P. Marand, S. Bond, Girls
  "(Ballad of a) Social Director"
    S. Armus, Ensemble
  "Shopping Around"
    S. Bond
Scene 2
  "Bright College Days"
    Waiters
  "Mix and Mingle"
    J. Cassidy, Waiters
Scene 3
  "Could Be"
    P. Marand, Girls
Scene 4
  "Tripping the Light Fantastic"
    Ensemble

"(Ballad of a) Social Director" (reprise)
    S. Armus, Ensemble
Scene 5
  "Where Did the Night Go?"
    J. Cassidy, P. Marand, Ensemble
Scene 6
  "Certain Individuals"
    S. Bond, Ensemble
Scene 8
  "They Won't Know Me"
    J. Cassidy
Scenes 9 and 10
  "Summer Afternoon"
    P. Valentine, Ensemble

ACT 2
Scene 1
  "Where Did the Night Go?" (reprise)
    F. Aletter, Ensemble
  "Don José (of Far Rockaway)"
    S. Armus, Ensemble
  "Everybody Love Everybody"
    S. Bond, Ensemble
  "Wish You Were Here"
    J. Cassidy, Waiters
Scene 3
  "Relax"
    P. Valentine, P. Marand
Scene 4
  "Where Did the Night Go?" (Be-Bop Version)
    S. Bond, Ensemble
  "Flattery"
    P. Marand, S. Armus
Scene 5
  Finale
    Entire Company

AN EVENING WITH BEATRICE LILLIE

1952.11

A Musical Revue in Two Acts, 13 Scenes. Directed by Edward Duryea Dowling. Settings by Rolf Gerard. At the pianos, Eadie (Griffith) and Rack [Howard Godwin]. Produced by Edward Duryea Dowling. Opened 2 October 1952 at the Booth Theatre and closed 30 May 1953 after 275 performances.

CAST: BEATRICE LILLIE, REGINALD GARDINER, Florence Bray, Xenia Bank, John Philip.

ACT 1[2]
Scene 1
  Reginald Gardiner
Scene 2
  A Star's First Night (The Girl Friend from WALK A LITTLE FASTER, 1932)
    The Star: X. Bank. *The Maid*: F. Bray. *The Star's Friend*: B. Lillie.

---

[1]During run, replaced with:
  "(There's) Nothing Nicer Than People"
    P. Marand, S. Bond, Girls

[2]During the course of the run and subsequent tour, Beatrice Lillie interpolated other songs and sketches associated with her career including:
  "Kiss Me Again" (from MLLE. MODISTE, 1906)
    (*Music by* Victor Herbert. *Lyrics by* Henry Blossom.)

Scene 3

One in Three
R. Gardiner

Scene 4

Wind
B. Lillie

Scene 5

Trains (from AT HOME ABROAD, 1935)
R. Gardiner

Scene 6

Father and Son
Father: R. Gardiner. *Son*: B. Lillie.

Scene 7

Anesthesia
R. Gardiner

Scene 8

References (from THE NINE O'CLOCK REVUE,
London, 1922; THE CHARLOT REVUE OF 1926, New York,
1925)
Sybil: B. Lillie. *Mrs. Mason*: F. Bray. *Mrs. Barrowdale*: X. Bank.

Scene 9

The Conductor
R. Gardiner

ACT 2

Scene 1

Eadie and Rack at the Pianos

Scene 2

Reginald Gardiner

Scene 3

Beatrice Lillie, accompanied by Rack.
Singer: J. Phillip.

"Come into the Garden, Maud"
J. Phillip

"Rhythm" (from PLEASE!, London, 1933; THE SHOW IS ON, 1936;
HAPPY RETURNS, London, 1938)
(*Music by* Richard Rodgers. *Lyrics by* Lorenz Hart.)

"Paree" (from AT HOME ABROAD, 1935; HAPPY RETURNS,
London, 1938; BETTER LATE, London, 1946)
(*Music by* Arthur Schwartz. *Lyrics by* Howard Dietz.)

"I've Been to a Marvelous Party" (from SET TO MUSIC, 1939)
(*Music and Lyrics by* Nöel Coward.)

"Nanette" (from THE BANDWAGON)
(*Music by* Arthur Schwartz. *Lyrics by* Howard Dietz.)

"The Lesson With the Fan"
(*Music by* Guy d'Hardelot. *Lyrics by* Frederick E. Weatherly.)

"Please Be Kind"
(*Music by* Saul Chaplin. *Lyrics by* Sammy Cahn.)

"Maud"
(*Music by* Muriel Lillie. *Lyrics by* Nicholas Phipps.)

"Not Wanted on the Voyage"
(*Music by* Beatrice Lillie. *Lyrics by* Nicholas Phipps.)

"Wind 'Round My Heart" (from BIG TOP, London, 1942)
(*Music by* Harry Parr-Davies. *Lyrics by* Barbara Gordon and
Basil Thomas.)

"Zither Song"
(*Music by* Beatrice Lillie. *Lyrics by* Bud McCreery.)

"I'm So Weary of It All" (from SET TO MUSIC, 1939; ALL CLEAR,
London, 1939)
(*Music and Lyrics by* Noël Coward.)

World War I Medley:

"I Want to Go Back to Michigan" (interpolation, 5064 GERRARD,
London, 1915)
(*Music and Lyrics by* Irving Berlin.)

"Lazy"
(*Music and Lyrics by* Irving Berlin.)

"Susannah's Squeaking Shoes" (from THE NINE O'CLOCK REVUE,
London, 1922; THE CHARLOT REVUE OF 1926, New York)
(*Music by* Muriel Lillie. *Lyrics by* Arthur Weigall.)

"There Are Fairies at the Bottom of Our Garden" (interpolation, THE
THIRD LITTLE SHOW, 1931)
(*Music by* Liza Lehmann. *Lyrics by* Rose Fyleman.)

"The Party's Over Now" (from WORDS AND MUSIC, London,
1932)
(*Music and Lyrics by* Noël Coward.)

Scene 4

Finale

"Rocked in the Cradle of the Deep"
(*Music and Lyrics by* John Philip Knight, Emma Willard.)

"Take My Heart (and Do With It What You Please)"
(*Music by* Fred Ahlert. *Lyrics by* Joe Young.)

"I Got Rhythm" (from GIRL CRAZY, 1930)
(*Music by* George Gershwin. *Lyrics by* Ira Gershwin.)

"Sonny Boy" (from THE SINGING FOOL, film)
(*Music and Lyrics by* Al Jolson, Buddy G. DeSylva, Lew Brown,
Ray Henderson.)

"Blue Skies" (from BETSY, 1926; THE JAZZ SINGER,
film)
(*Music and Lyrics by* Irving Berlin.)

"On Your Toes" (from ON YOUR TOES, 1936)
(*Music by* Richard Rodgers. *Lyrics by* Lorenz Hart.)

"Rose of Washington Square" (from ZIEGFELD MIDNIGHT
FROLIC, 1920)
(*Music by* James Hanley. *Lyrics by* Ballard MacDonald.)

"The Star Spangled Banner" (traditional)
(Bea Lillie version from THE SHOW IS ON, 1936; DOCTOR
RHYTHM, film)

"Spinning Song"
(*Music and Lyrics by* Noël Coward.)

"The Irish Song" (Rosie O'Grady)
(*Music and Lyrics by* Noël Coward.)

"A Bar on the Piccola Marina"
(*Music and Lyrics by* Noël Coward.)

"There Are Times" (from A TO Z, London, 1921)
(*Music and Lyrics by* Ivor Novello.)

"Paint"
(*Music by* Norman Hackforth. *Lyrics by* Nicholas Phipps.)

"I Apologize" (Burlesque version introduced in WALK A LITTLE
FASTER, 1932; PLEASE!, London, 1933)
(*Music and Lyrics by* Al Hoffman, Al Goodhart, Ed Nelson.)

"Three Little Fishies"
(*Music and Lyrics by* Saxie Dowell.)

"Where the Black-Eyed Susans Grow" (from ROBINSON CRUSOE,
1916; CHEEP, London, 1917)
(*Music by* Richard A. Whiting. *Lyrics by* Dave Radford.)

"He Was a Gentleman"
(*Music by* Jay Gorney. *Lyrics by* E. Y. Harburg.)

The Fan
(*by* Fletcher)

1952.12　　　　THE CONSUL

A Revival of the Opera (Musical Drama) in Three Acts, 6 Scenes[3]. Libretto
and music by Gian-Carlo Menotti. Conductor, Thomas Schippers. Settings
and costumes by Horace Armistead. Lighting by Jean Rosenthal. Assistant
to Mr. Menotti, Bill Butler. Choreography by John Butler. Staged by

---

[3]Originally produced in New York 15 March 1950 at the Ethel Barrymore
Theatre for 269 performances. For Synopsis of Scenes, see original 1950
production. No individual musical numbers given.

Gian-Carlo Menotti. Produced by the New York City Opera Company (Joseph Rosenstock, General director). Opened 8 October 1952 at the New York City Center and closed 29 October 1952 after 3 performances in repertory.

CAST: (in order of appearance): *John Sorel*: RICHARD TORIGI. *Magda Sorel*: PATRICIA NEWAY. *The Mother*: MARY KRESTE. *Secret Police Agent*: EMILE RENAN. *First Plainclothesman*: Charles Kuestner. *Second Plainclothesman*: Thomas Powell. *The Secretary*: GLORIA LANE. *Mr. Kofner*: JON GEYANS [George Gaynes]. *The Foreign Woman*: MARIA MARLO. *Anna Gomez*: Vilma Georgiou. *Vera Boronel*: Edith Evans. *Nika Magadoff, The Magician*: NORMAN KELLEY. *Assan*: Arthur Newman. *Voice on the Record*: Mabel Mercer.

1952.13 BUTTRIO SQUARE

A Musical Play in Two Acts, 6 Scenes. Book by Billy Gilbert and Gen Genovese. Music by Arthur Jones and Fred Stamer. Lyrics by Gen Genovese. Based on a play by Hal Cranton from an original story by Gen Genovese. Settings and lighting by Samuel Leve. Costumes supervised by Sal Anthony. Choral arrangements and direction by Maurice Levine. Dance music composed and arranged by Roger Adams. Orchestrations by Don Walker. Musical director, Maurice Levine. Entire production choreographed and directed by Eugene Loring. Produced by Gen Genovese and Edward Woods. Opened 14 October 1952 at the Century Theatre and closed 18 October 1952 after 7 performances.

CAST (in order of appearance): *Michelino*: David Kurlan. *Padre*: Vincent Barbi. *Angela*: Rina Falcone. *Maria*: Joan Morton. *Elizabetta*: Ann Needham. *Dominic*: Lionel Ames. *Baron D'Alessandro*: Ernest Sarracino. *Rocco*: Ferdinand Hilt. *Vittorio*: James MacCracken. *Cassio*: Orville Sherman. *Pietro*: Ted Thurston. *Emelia*: Jane Harven. *Francesca*: Marie Gibson. *Pappa Mario*: BILLY GILBERT. *Norina*: Charlotte Jones. *Carlo*: Henry Hamilton. *Sgt. McKenzie*: Walter Black. *Capt. Steve Dickson*: LAWRENCE BROOKS. *Pvt. Poole*: James Tarbutton. *Tabulator*: Leon Daniels. *Marisa D'Alessandro*: LOIS HUNT. *Pvt. Burns*: Joe Mantell. *Corporal. Gower*: Al Checco. *Pvt. Whitfield*: George Reeder. *Pvt. Webster*: Don [Donald] Driver. *Terry Patterson*: SUSAN JOHNSON. *Joan Wellington*: Marti Stevens.

Dancing Group: Estelle Aza, Bettina Dearborn, Marcella Dodge, Vera Lee, Zoya Leporsky, Joan Morton, Ann Needham, Ann Olchoff, Sandra Zell, Alvin Bean, James Capp, Don Driver, George Foster, Loren Hightower, Rudy Mattise, Greg O'Brien, George Reeder, Lewis Schaw. *Singing Group*: Sara Bettis, Joyce Carol, Ann DeBella, Rina Falcone, Marie Gibson, Iona Noble, Noella Pelloquin, Jan Scott, Joannne Spiller, Lionel Ames, Vincent Barbi, Robert Gilson, Henry Hamilton, Gene Holman, Mike King, Henry Lawrence, James MacCracken, Ted Thurston, Joseph Tocci. *Children*: Barbara Karen, Babs Wood, Darryl Richards.

The action takes place in a small village in Northeast Italy. The time is the spring and fall, 1946.

Act 1, Scene 1: Road to the Village. Morning. *Scene 2*: Buttrio Square.

Act 2, Scene 1: G.I. Barracks. Several months later. *Scene 2*: Buttrio Square. *Scene 3*: Mario's Bakeshop. *Scene 4*: Buttrio Square.

ACT 1
Opening
    D. Kurlan, V. Barbi, E. Sarracino, F. Hilt, Village Dancers, Singers
"Every Day Is a Holiday"
    L. Brooks, Villagers
"Let's Make It Forever"
    L. Brooks
"I'll Tell the World"
    L. Hunt
"No Place Like This Country"
    L. Brooks, GIs
"Take It Away"
    GIs, Village Girls
    (*Music by* Roger Adams.)
"Get Me Out"
    S. Johnson
"I'm Gonna Be a Pop"
    B. Gilbert, Villagers
"One Is a Lonely Number"
    L. Brooks, Village Dancers
"One Is a Lonely Number" (reprise)
    L. Hunt

"Tarantula"
    Villagers
ACT 2
"Get Me Out" (reprise)
    S. Johnson
"Love Swept Like a Storm"
    J. MacCracken, Village Singers, Dancers
"Fraternization Ballet"
    A. Checco, V. Barbi, Villagers
"I Keep Telling Myself"
    S. Johnson
"More and More"
    L. Brooks, L. Hunt
"You're Mine, All Mine"
    S. Johnson, O. Sherman
Finale
    Entire Company

THE MIKADO,
1952.14 or The Town of Titipu

A Revival of the Comic Opera in Two Acts[4]. Libretto by William S. Gilbert. Music by Arthur Sullivan. Staged by S. M. Chartok. Musical director, Lehman Engel. Settings by Ralph Alswang. Costumes by Peggy Morrison. Assistant conductor, Eugene Kusmiak. Production consultant, Martyn Green. Produced by S. M. Chartok. Opened 20 October 1952 at the Mark Hellinger Theatre and closed 25 October 1952 after 8 performances.

CAST: *Nanki-Poo*: ROBERT ROUNSEVILLE. *Noble Lords (2)*: *Go-To*: Radley Flynn. *Pish-Tush*: FRANK ROGIER. *Pooh-Bah*: ROBERT ECKLES. *Ko-Ko*: MARTYN GREEN. *Three Sisters, Wards of Ko-Ko*: *Yum-Yum*: LILLIAN MURPHY. *Pitti-Sing*: MARY ROCHE. *Peep-Bo*: DOROTHY MacNEIL. *Katisha*: ELLA HALMAN. *The Mikado of Japan*: JOSEPH MACAULAY.

School Girls, Nobles, Guards: Mary Louise Beatie, Dolores DePuglia, Helen Dodge, Grace Lang, Stella Matthews, Eileen Moran, Shirley Pringle, Rita Schoen, Catherine Currie, Bonnie Grevatt, Glynn Hill, Jan Newby, Athena Pappas, Gloria Sacks, Jeanne Schlegel, Helen Whitfield, Don Kaplan, Don LaMon, Ray Morrissey, Feodore Tedick, Vincent Henry, Anthony Cerami, Michael Rich, Ken Smith, John Dorrin, Herbert Estrow, Radley Flynn, Roger Franklin, Irl Mowery, Bill Nuss, Stanley Propper, Chase Willard.

1952.15 MY DARLIN' AIDA

A Musical Play in Two Acts, 10 Scenes. Libretto by Charles Friedman, adapted from Giuseppe Verdi's opera 'Aida' (and its libretto by Antonio Ghislanzoni from a scenario by Auguste Mariette). Music by Giuseppe Verdi. Directed by Charles Friedman. Supervised and lighted by Hassard Short. Designed and costumed by Lemuel Ayers. Choreography by Hanya Holm. Musical director, Franz Allers. Choral director, Robert Shaw. New orchestral arrangements by Hans Spialek. Production associate, Shirley Bernstein. Associate producer, Paul Vroom. Produced by Robert L. Joseph. Opened 27 October 1952 at the Winter Garden and closed 10 January 1953 after 89 performances.

CAST (in order of appearance): *Rumford*: WILLIAM WALDERMAN. *Mayor Brad Sourby*: STANLEY CARLSON. *Aida*: ELAINE MALBIN (evenings), EILEEN SCHAULER (matinees). *Raymond Demarest*: WILLIAM OLVIS or HOWARD JARRATT. *Jason*: ALONZO BOSAN. *Morning Star*: Ida Johnson. *Zeporah*: Lavinia Williams. *Lolly*: OLIVE MOOREFIELD. *Wheat*: George Fisher. *Frog*: John Fleming. *Liz*: Fredye Marshall. *Rebecca*: Billie Allen. *Lucy*: Joyce Sellinger. *Yancey Hoyt*: William Sutherland. *Jessica Farrow*: DOROTHY SARNOFF (evenings), BETTE DUBRO (matinees). *General Farrow*: KENNETH SCHON. *Choir Soloist*: Theresa Green. *Sis*: Ruth Ann Fleming. *Dolly*: Ruth McVayne. *Bonnie*: Sue Dorris. *Maggie*: Muriel Birckhead. *Aggie*: Martha Flynn. *Laurie*: Lola Fisher. *Mary*: Ruth Schumacher. *Nellie*: Mary Ann Tomlinson. *Bettie*: Jane Copeland. *Onnie*: Carol Jones. *Maids*: Billie

---

[4]First presented in New York 20 July, 10-29 August 1885 at the Union Square and People's Theatres for 22 performances. First authorized production presented 19 August 1885 at the Fifth Avenue Theatre by Richard D'Oyly Carte for 250 performances. For Synopsis of Scenes and Musical Numbers, see 19 August 1885 D'Oyly Carte production.

Allen, Jacqueline Hairston, Lavinia Williams. *Magician*: Gordon Hamilton. *Mrs. Sourby*: Jo Anne Taylor. *Howie*: Walter Kelvin. *Bull*: Edward Wellman. *Steve*: Robert Busch. *Hutch*: Thornton Marker. *Adam Brown*: WILLIAM DILLARD. *Flower*: Jacqueline Hairston. *Rebecca*: Billie Allen. *Susie*: Gloria Davy. *Lilly*: Charlotte Holloman. *Liz*: Fredye Marshall. *Morning Star*: Ida Johnson. *Zeporah*: Lavinia Williams. *Pork*: Ned Wright. *Handy*: Calvin Dash. *Wheat*: George Fisher. *Major Stanhope*: William Sutherland. *Children*: Paula Anderson, Gail Culberson, Sharyn Kenney.

Singers: Muriel Birckhead, Dorothy Candee, Jane Copeland, Gloria Davy, Sue Dorris, Lola Fisher, Ruth Anne Fleming, Martha Flynn, Theresa Green, Charlotte Holloman, Ida Johnson, Carol Jones, Fredye Marshall, Ruth McVayne, Joyce Sellinger, Ruth Schumacher, Jo Anne Taylor, Mary Ann Tomlinson, Robert Baird, Gino Baldi, Robert Busch, Benjamin Cassidy, Jack Dabdoub, Calvin Dash, George Fisher, John Fleming, Arthur Hammond, Walter Kelvin, Thornton Marker, William Noble, Michael O'Carolan, Charles O'Neill, Robert Price, Michael Roberts, William Sutherland, Edgar Thompson, Casper Vecchione, Robert Watts, Edward Wellman, Ned Wright, Robert Yeager. *Dancers*: Billie Allen, Betty Buday, Nanci Darken, Bettye Griffin, Dody Goodman, Jacqueline Hairston, Erona Harris, Joan Kruger, Carmelita Lanza, Lavinia Williams, Doris Wright, Paul Gannon, Gordon Hamilton, Eddie Heim, Ed Holleman, Louis Johnson, Joe Nash, Walter Nicks, Paul Olson, Frank Seabolt, Claude Thompson.

The action of the play extends over the first year of the Civil War, on or about General Farrow's plantation, near Memphis, Tennessee.

Act 1, Scene 1: The Terrace of the Big House, May 7, 1861, evening. *Scene 2*: The Giant Oak, immediately afterwards. *Scene 3*: The Cemetery by the Negro Church, the following night. *Scene 4*: Jessica's Boudoir in the Big House, three months later. *Scene 5*: The Square at the Boat Landing, immediately afterwards.

Act 2, Scene 1: The Terrace of the Big House. Three weeks later, night. *Scene 2*: The Path to the Quarter, immediately afterwards. *Scene 3*: The Quarter, immediately afterwards. *Scene 4*: The Hallway in the Big House, toward dawn. *Scene 5*: The Negro Church and the Cemetary, immediately afterwards.

ACT 1

Scene 1

Prelude and Opening

"My Darlin' Aida"
W. Olvis

"Love Is Trouble"
D. Sarnoff, W. Olvis

"Love Is Trouble" (reprise)
E. Malbin, D. Sarnoff, W. Olvis

"Me and Lee"
K. Schon, W. Wilderman, W. Olvis, E. Malbin, D. Sarnoff,
Company

Scene 2

"Me and Lee" (reprise)
The Men

"March on for Tennessee"
E. Malbin

Scene 3

"Why We Ain't Free"
T. Green, Women's Choir

"Knights of the White Cross"
W. Wilderman, W. Olvis, the Knights

Scene 4

"A Jamboree"
D. Sarnoff, Girls

Dance
The Maids

"Letter Duet"
E. Malbin, D. Sarnoff

"Me and Lee" (reprise)
The Men

Scene 5

"Homecoming"
Company

"When You Grow Up"
Women, Children

"Soldiers' March"
Men

Ballet
Dancers

"King Called Cotton"
Company

"Gotta Live Free"
W. Dillard

"Master and Slave" — Sextette
W. Dillard, E. Malbin, W. Olvis, D. Sarnoff, W. Wilderman,
K. Schon, Company

"Sing! South! Sing!"
Company

ACT 2

Scene 1

Spiritual
The Choir

"I Want to Pray"
D. Sarnoff

"Alone"
E. Malbin

"Three Stones to Stand On"
E. Malbin, W. Dillard

"You're False"
E. Malbin, W. Dillard

"There'll Have To Be Changes Made"
E. Malbin, W. Olvis

"Away"
E. Malbin, W. Olvis

"Land of Mine"
E. Malbin, W. Olvis, W. Dillard

Scene 3

Ballet
Dancers, Singers

Scene 4

"I Don't Want You"
D. Sarnoff, W. Olvis

Scene 5

"The Trial"
D. Sarnoff, W. Wilderman, the Knights

"You Are My Darlin' Bride"
W. Olvis

"Oh, Sky, Goodbye"
E. Malbin

"Why Ain't We Free"
E. Malbin, W. Olvis, D. Sarnoff, the Choir

THE PIRATES OF PENZANCE,
1952.16 or The Slave of Duty

A Revival of the Comic Opera in Two Acts[5]. Libretto by William S. Gilbert. Music by Arthur Sullivan. Staged by S. M. Chartok. Musical director, Lehman Engel. Settings by Ralph Alswang. Costumes by Peggy Morrison. Assistant conductor, Eugene Kusmiak. Production consultant, Martyn Green. Produced by S. M. Chartok. Opened 27 October 1952 at the Mark Hellinger Theatre and closed 1 November 1952 after 8 performances.

CAST: *Samuel*: FRANK ROGIER. *Frederick*: ROBERT ROUNSEVILLE. *Ruth*: ELLA HALMAN. *Richard*: JOSEPH MACAULAY. *General Stanley's Daughters (4)*: *Kate*: MARY ROCHE. *Edith*: LILLIAN MURPHY. *Mabel*: SHIRLEY PRINGLE. *Isabel*: Shirley Pringle. *Major-General Stanley*: MARTYN GREEN. *Edward*: Robert Eckles.

General Stanley's Wards: Mary Louise Beatie, Dolores DePuglia, Helen Dodge, Grace Lang, Stella Matthews, Eileen Moran, Shirley Pringle, Rita Schoen, Catherine Currie, Bonnie Grevatt, Glynn Hill, Jan Newby, Athena Pappas, Gloria Sacks, Jeanne Schlegel, Helen Whitfield. *Pirates and Policemen*: Anthony Cerami, Vincent Henry, Don Kaplan, Don La Mon, Ray Morrissey, Michael Rich, Ken Smith, Feodore Tedick, John Dorrin, Herbert Estrow, Radley Flynn, Roger Franklin, Irl Mowery, Bill Nuss, Stanley Propper, Chase Willard.

---

[5]First presented in New York 31 December 1879 at the Fifth Avenue Theatre for a total of 91 performances in two engagements. For Synopsis of Scenes and Musical Numbers, see original 1879 production.

1952.17 TRIAL BY JURY

A Revival of the Comic Opera in One Act[6]. Libretto by William S. Gilbert. Music by Arthur Sullivan. Staged by S. M. Chartok. Musical director, Lehman Engel. Settings by Ralph Alswang. Costumes by Peggy Morrison. Assistant conductor, Eugene Kusmiak. Production consultant, Martyn Green. Produced by S. M. Chartok. Opened 3 November 1952 at the Mark Hellinger Theatre and closed 8 November 1952 after 8 performances.

CAST: *Foreman of the Jury*: ROBERT ECKLES. *Associate*: Robert Franklin. *Usher*: RADLEY FLYNN. *Defendant*: EARL WILLIAM. *The Learned Judge*: MARTYN GREEN. *Counsel for the Plaintiff*: FRANK ROGIER. *The Plaintiff*: AUDREY DEARDEN.
Bridesmaids: Mary Louise Beatie, Helen Dodge, Bonnie Grevatt, Glynn Hill, Grace Lang, Sheila Mathews, Eileen Moran, Shirley Pringle. *Spectators*: Catherine Currie, Dolores de Puglia, Jan Newby, Athena Pappas, Gloria Sacks, Jeanne Schlegel, Rita Schoen, Helen Whitfield, Stanley Propper, Michael Rich, Anthony Cerami. *Jurymen*: Don Kaplan, Don LaMon, Ray Morrissey, Feodore Tedick, Vincent Henry, Ken Smith, John Dorrin, Herbert Estrow, Roger Franklin, Irl Mowery, Bill Nuss, Chase Willard.

H.M.S. PINAFORE,
1952.18 or The Lass That Loved a Sailor

A Revival of the Comic Opera in Two Acts[7]. Libretto by William S. Gilbert. Music by Arthur Sullivan. Staged by S. M. Chartok. Musical director, Lehman Engel. Settings by Ralph Alswang. Costumes by Peggy Morrison. Assistant conductor, Eugene Kusmiak. Production consultant, Martyn Green. Produced by S. M. Chartok. Opened 3 November 1952 at the Mark Hellinger Theatre and closed 8 November 1952 after 8 performances.

CAST: *Tommy Tucker*: Bonnie Grevatt. *Bill Bobstay*, Boatswain: Robert Eckles. *Bob Beckett*: Radley Flynn. *Little Buttercup*, Mrs. Cripps, a Portsmouth bum-boat woman: ELLA HALMAN. *Dick Deadeye*, Able Seaman: JOSEPH MACAULAY. *Ralph Rackstraw*, Able Seaman: ROBERT ROUNSEVILLE. *Captain Corcoran*, Commander of the *H.M.S. Pinafore*: FRANK ROGIER. *Josephine*, the Captain's Daughter: LILLIAN MURPHY. *The Rt. Hon. Sir Joseph Porter, K.C.B.*, First Lord of the Admiralty: MARTYN GREEN. *Hebe*: Sir Joseph's First Cousin: Mary Roche.
First Lord's Sisters, His Cousins, His Aunts: Mary Lousie Beatie, Dolores de Puglia, Helen Dodge, Grace Lang, Sheila Mathews, Eileen Moran, Shirley Pringle, Rita Schoen, Glynn Hill, Catherine Currie, Jan Newby, Athena Pappas, Gloria Sacks, Jeanne Schlegel, Helen Whitfield. *Sailors*: Don Kaplan, Don LaMon, Ray Morrissey, Feodore Tedick, Vincent Henry, Anthony Cerami, Michael Rich, Ken Smith, John Dorrin, Herbert Estrow, Roger Franklin, Irl Mowery, Bill Nuss, Stanley Propper, Chase Willard. *Marines*: Edward Marshall, William Briggs, James Maroney, Lynn Allen.

IOLANTHE,
1952.19 or The Peer and the Peri

A Revival of the Comic Opera in Two Acts[8]. Libretto by William S. Gilbert. Music by Arthur Sullivan. Staged by S. M. Chartok. Musical director, Lehman Engel. Settings by Ralph Alswang. Costumes by Peggy Morrison. Assistant conductor, Eugene Kusmiak. Production consultant, Martyn Green. Produced by S. M. Chartok. Opened 10 November 1952 at the Mark Hellinger Theatre and closed 15 November 1952 after 8 performances.

CAST: *Leila*: Mary Roche. *Celia*: Audrey Dearden. *Fleta*: Eileen Moran. *The Fairy Queen*: ELLA HALMAN. *Iolanthe*: GLYNN HILL. *Strephon*: FRANK ROGIER. *Phyllis*: LILLIAN MURPHY. *Lord Chancellor*: MARTYN GREEN. *Earl of Tolloller*: EARL WILLIAM. *Earl of Mountararat*: JOSEPH MACAULAY. *Private Willis*: ROBERT ECKLES.
Fairies: Mary Louise Beatie, Dolores DePuglia, Helen Dodge, Grace Lang, Sheila Matthews, Shirley Pringle, Rita Schoen, Catherine Currie, Bonnie Grevatt, Glynn Hill, Jan Newby, Athena Pappas, Gloria Sacks, Jeanne Schlegel, Helen Whitfield.

---

[6]First presented in New York 15 November 1875 at the Eagle Theatre for 8 performances. For Synopsis of Scenes and Musical Numbers, see original 1875 production.
[7]First produced in New York 15 January 1879 at the Standard Theatre for 175 performances. For Synopsis of Scenes and Musical Numbers, see original 1879 production.
[8]First presented in New York 25 November 1882 at the Standard Theatre for 105 performances. For Synopsis of Scenes and Musical Numbers, see original 1882 production.

Peers: Anthony Cerami, Vincent Henry, Don LaMon, Ray Morrissey, Michael Rich, Ken Smith, Feodore Tedick, John Dorrin, Herbert Estrow, Radley Flynn, Roger Franklin, Irl Mowery, Bill Nuss, Stanley Propper, Chase Willard, Robert Driscoll.

1952.20 TWO'S COMPANY

A Musical Revue in Two Acts, 19 Scenes. Sketches by Charles Sherman, Peter DeVries, (Arnold B. Horwitt, Lee Rogow, Nat Hiken, Billy Friedberg, Mort Green, George Foster, Oliver Wakefield). Music by Vernon Duke, (Sheldon Harnick). Lyrics by Ogden Nash, (Sammy Cahn, Sheldon Harnick). Sketches directed by Jules Dassin. Additional lyrics by Sammy Cahn, (Sheldon Harnick). Musical supervisor and conductor, Milton Rosenstock. Scenery and lighting by Ralph Alswang. Costumes by Miles White. Ballet music by Genevieve Pitot and David Baker. Vocal arrangements by Milton Rosenstock. Associate producer, Clifford Hayman. Dances and musical numbers staged by Jerome Robbins. Entire production under the supervision of John Murray Anderson. Produced by James Russo and Michael Ellis. Opened 15 December 1952 at the Alvin Theatre and closed 8 March 1953 after 90 performances.

CAST: BETTE DAVIS, HIRAM SHERMAN, DAVID BURNS, BILL CALLAHAN, NORA KAYE, STANLEY PRAGER, ELLEN HANLEY, GEORGE S. IRVING, MARIA KARNILOVA, BUZZ MILLER, OLIVER WAKEFIELD, PETER KELLEY.
Singers: Art Carroll, Clifford Fearl, Bill Krach, Robert Neukum, Franklin Neil, Leonore Korman, Tina Louise, May Muth, Basha Regis, Deborah Remsen, (Sue Hight), Teddy Tavenner, Doris Wolin. *Dancers*: William Inglis, John Kelly, Ralph Linn, Job Sanders, Stanley Simmons, Florence Baum, Jeanna Belkin, Eleanor Boleyn, Barbara Heath, Dorothy Hill, Julie Marlowe, Helen Murielle. ROBERT ORTON'S TEEN ACES: Robert Orton, Francis Edwards, Henry Mallory, Gilbert Shipley, Armstead Shobey, Norman Shobey.

ACT 1[9]

Scene 1
Opening—"Theatre Is a Lady"
B. Callahan, Boys, Girls
(*Music by* Vernon Duke. *Lyrics by* Ogden Nash. *Orchestrated by* Don Walker.) *Introduced by* H. Sherman.

Scene 2
"Turn Me Loose on Broadway"
B. Davis, B. Miller, R. Pagent, J. Sanders, S. Simmons
(*Music by* Vernon Duke. *Lyrics by* Ogden Nash. *Orchestrated by* Clare Grundman.)

Scene 3
And a Little Child
(*by* Arnold B. Horwitt and Lee Rogow)
Producer: G. S. Irving. *Secretary*: T. Louise. *Dudley Dawson*: D. Burns. *Rollo*: M. Mann. *Butler*: F. Neil. *Mrs. Wilkins*: M. Muth.

Scene 4
"It Just Occurred to Me"
P. Kelley, D. Remsen, Singing Ensemble
(*Music by* Vernon Duke. *Lyrics by* Sammy Cahn. *Orchestrated by* Clare Grundman.)
Danced by F. Baum, B. Heath, H. Murielle, R. Linn, R. Pagent, J. Sanders.

Scene 5
Jealousy
(*by* Nat Hiken and Billy Friedberg)
Helen: B. Davis. *Stanley*: D. Burns.

Scene 6
"Baby Couldn't Dance"
(*Music by* Vernon Duke. *Lyrics by* Ogden Nash. *Orchestrated by* Clare Grundman.)
Girl: N. Kaye. *Boy*: B. Callahan. *Professor*: S. Simmons. *Pupils*: B. Heath, F. Baum.

Scene 7
"A Man's Home"
H. Sherman

---

[9]Act 1 running order revised after the opening; Hiram Sherman was given a featured specialty in Act 2, following "Esther."

(Music and Lyrics by Sheldon Harnick.
Orchestrated by Don Walker.)

Scene 8

One's a Crowd

(*by* Mort Green and George Foster)
That One: B. Davis. *Reggie:* H. Sherman. *J.C.:* G. S. Irving.
Harassed Gentleman: S. Prager. *Audience:* T. Tavenner,
E. Renard, T. Louise, C. Fearl, D. Hill, M. Muth,
E. Boleyn, D. Hill, S. Hight, R. Neukum.

Scene 9

"Roundabout"

E. Hanley
(*Music by* Vernon Duke. *Lyrics by* Ogden Nash.
Scenario by Horton Foote and Jerome Robbins. *Orchestrated
by* Don Walker.)
Danced by N. Kaye, R. Linn, R. Pagent, W. Inglis,
E. Boleyn, B. Heath, Dancing Ensemble.

Scene 10

The Voice of Inexperience

(*by* Oliver Wakefield)
O. Wakefield

Scene 11

"Roll Along, Sadie"

B. Davis, H. Sherman, B. Miller, R. Linn, Company
(*Music by* Vernon Duke. *Lyrics by* Ogden Nash. *Orchestrated by*
Phil Lang.)

ACT 2

Scene 1

"(It Came Out of the) Clear Blue Sky"

P. Kelley, S. Hight, Singers
(*Music by* Vernon Duke. *Lyrics by* Ogden Nash. *Orchestrated by*
Don Walker.)
Danced by M. Karnilova, R. Pagent, Dancers.

Scene 2

Street Scenes

(*by* Charles Sherman with Peter DeVries)
B. Davis, H. Sherman

Scene 3

"Esther"

(D. Burns)
(*Music by* Vernon Duke. *Lyrics by* Sammy Cahn. *Orchestrated by*
Don Walker.)
Melvin: D. Burns. *Esther:* M. Karnilova. *Native:* B. Miller.

Scene 4

When in Rome

(*by* Arnold B. Horwitt and Lee Rogow)
Strombolini: D. Burns. *Nina:* H. Murielle.
Thomaso: S. Prager. *Porter:* E. Renard. *Jezebela:* B. Davis.
Musician: G. S. Irving.

Scene 5

"Haunted Hot Spot"

E. Hanley
(*Music by* Vernon Duke. *Lyrics by* Ogden Nash. *Orchestrated by*
Don Walker.)
Danced by The Stripper: N. Kaye. *The Drummer:* B. Callahan.
The Pianist: B. Miller.

Scene 6

"Purple Rose"

(*Sketch by* Charles Sherman with Peter DeVries. *Music by* Vernon Duke.
Lyrics by Ogden Nash. *Orchestrated by* Phil Lang.)
Sybill: B. Davis. *Peter:* H. Sherman. *Horatio:* E. Renard.
Terrance: G. S. Irving. *Hilary:* C. Fearl. *Hortense:* M. Muth.
Ginger: D. Remsen. *Camera Man:* M. Brenner. *Butler:* F. Neil. *Maid:*
B. Regis. *Virgil:* R. Neukum. *Cicero:* B. Krach.

Scene 7

"Just Like a Man"

B. Davis
(*Music by* Vernon Duke. *Lyrics by* Ogden Nash.
Orchestrated by Phil Lang.)

Scene 8

Finale

The Company
(*Music by* Vernon Duke. *Lyrics by* Ogden Nash.
Orchestrated by Clare Grundman.)

1953.01   # HAZEL FLAGG

A Musical Satire in Two Acts, 15 Scenes. Book by Ben Hecht. Based on the story ("Letter to the Editor") by James Street and the film "Nothing Sacred" by Ben Hecht, (Ring Lardner, Jr.). Music by Jule Styne. Lyrics by Bob Hilliard. Dances and musical numbers staged by Robert Alton. Book directed by David Alexander. Production (settings) designed and lighted by Harry Horner. Costumes by Miles White. Musical director, Pembroke Davenport. Choral arrangements and direction by Hugh Martin. Orchestrations by Don Walker. Ballet arrangements by Oscar Kosarin. Entire production under the supervision of Robert Alton. Produced by Jule Styne in association with Anthony Brady Farrell. Opened 11 February 1953 at the Mark Hellinger Theatre, closing 4 July 1953; re-opened 7 September 1953 and closed 19 September 1953 after 190 performances.

CAST (in order of appearance): *An Editor:* Dean Campbell. *Oleander:* Jonathan Harris. *Laura Carew:* BENAY VENUTA. *Wallace Cook:* JOHN HOWARD. *Vermont Villagers:* Carol Hendricks, B. J. Keating, Joan Morton, Dorothy Love, Laurel Shelby. *Mr. Billings:* Lawrence Weber. *Mr. Jenkins:* Robert Lenn. *Hazel Flagg:* HELEN GALLAGHER. *Dr. Downer:* THOMAS MITCHELL. *Man on the Street:* George Reeder. *Bellboy:* Jerry Craig. *Maximilian Lavian:* John Pelletti. *Fireman:* Bill Heyer. *Miss Winterbottom:* Betsy Holland. *Mayor of New York:* JACK WHITING. *Whitey:* SHEREE NORTH. *Willie:* John Brascia. *Dr. Egelhofer:* Ross Martin. *Chorus Girls:* Lori Jon, Virginia Poe. *Committeemen:* Michael Spaeth, John Bartis. *Policeman:* Eric Schepard.

Dancers: Estelle Aza, Chris Carter, Marcella Dodge, Lillian Donau, Anna Friedland, Ruby Herndon, Lori Jon, Sherry McCutcheon, Betty McMillen, Barbara Michaels, Judy Miller, Joan Morton, Margot Meyers, Virginia Poe, Eva Ralf, Beryl Towbin, Toni Wheelis, Christopher Brown, Ronald Cecill, Don Crichton, Al Craine, Hugh Lambert, Gerard Leavitt, George Reeder, Eric Schepard, Michael Spaeth. *Singers:* Sara Dillon, Mary Harmon, Carol Hendricks, Betsy Holland, Dorsie Hollingsworth, B. J. Keating, Beverly McFadden, Laurel Shelby, John Bartis, Dean Campbell, David Carter, Jerry Craig, Bob Davis, Bill Heyer, Robert Lenn, David Randall.

Act 1, Scene 1: Conference Room of Everywhere Magazine. Late afternoon, 1930s. *Scene 2:* Dr. Downer's House. The next day. *Scene 3:* Railroad Depot, Stonyhead. That evening. *Scene 4:* A New York Street. The next day. *Scene 5:* Hazel's New York Hotel Suite. Later that day. *Scene 6:* Laura Carew's Office. Two weeks later. *Scene 7:* Hazel's Hotel Suite. Evening. A week later. *Scene 8:* (a) A Cross Section of New York City. Later that evening. (b) Roseland Ballroom.

Act 2, Scene 1: A Radio Station in the Hotel. The next morning. *Scene 2:* Hazel's Hotel Bedroom. The same morning. *Scene 3:* The same. Several hours later. *Scene 4:* The Mayor's Luncheon. That afternoon. *Scene 5:* Under the East River Bridge. Later that evening. *Scene 6:* A Barge on the River's edge. A little later. *Scene 7:* Finale.

ACT 1[10]

Scene 1

"A Little More Heart"

B. Venuta, J. Howard, Magazine Staff

Scene 2

"The World Is Beautiful Today"[11]

H. Gallagher

---

[10]During the first engagement of the show, substantial revisions were made in the book and score. For the September re-opening, the following songs were added:

"Money Burns a Hole in My Pocket" (added to Act 1, Scene 5)
Tony Bavaar (Wallace)

"Something in the Wind" (added to Act 2, Scene 5 before "Laura de Maupassant")
T. Bavaar

[11]During the first engagement replaced by:

"My Wild Imagination" (Act 1, Scene 2)
H. Gallagher

"I'm Glad I'm Leaving"
H. Gallagher

Scene 3

"The Rutland Bounce" (Dance)
J. Morton, G. Reeder, D. Crichton, Villagers

Scene 4

"Hello, Hazel"
B. Venuta, New Yorkers

Scene 5

"Paris Gown" (Ballet)
H. Gallagher, J. Pelletti,
R. Cecill, G. Leavitt, G. Reeder, Models, Attendants

"The World Is Beautiful Today"
(reprise)[12]
J. Howard, Editors

Scene 6

"Every Street's a Boulevard in Old New York"
J. Whiting

Scene 7

"How Do You Speak to an Angel?"
J. Howard

Scene 8A

"Autograph Chant"[13]
Autograph Hunters

"I Feel Like I'm Gonna Live Forever"
H. Gallagher

Scene 8B

"You're Gonna Dance With Me, Willie"
H. Gallagher, J. Brascia, Company

ACT 2

Scene 1

"Who Is the Bravest?"
University Glee Club

Scene 2

"Dream Parade" (Ballet)
H. Gallagher, Company

Scene 4

"Salome"
Dancing Girls
Salome: S. North. *Cowboy Singer*: D. Campbell.
Cowboy Dancers: G. Reeder, D. Crichton.

"Everybody Loves To Take a Bow"
B. Venuta, J. Whiting, Men

Scene 5

"Laura De Maupassant"
H. Gallagher

Scene 6

"Autograph Chant"
(reprise)
Autograph Hunters

Scene 7

"I Feel Like I'm Gonna Live Forever"
(reprise)
Company
followed by "How Do You Speak to an Angel?"
(earlier placement)
J. Howard

---

[12]During the first engagement replaced by:
"Make the People Cry" (Act 1, Scene 5)
B. Venuta, J. Harris, Editors

[13]During the first engagement moved to the end of Scene 7.

1953.02 # MAGGIE

A Musical Play in Two Acts, 9 Scenes. Book by Hugh Thomas. Based on James M. Barrie's comedy "What Every Woman Knows." Music and lyrics by William Roy. Directed by Michael Gordon. Sets and costumes by Raoul Pene du Bois. Choreography by June Graham. Lighting by Peggy Clark. Musical direction and choral arrangements by Maurice Levine. Orchestrations by Don Walker. Dance arrangements by Dean Fuller. Production associate, Harry Zevin. Produced by Franklin Gilbert and John Fearnley. Opened 18 February 1953 at the National Theatre and closed 21 February 1953 after 5 performances.

<u>CAST</u> (in order of appearance): *Alick Wylie*: BRAMWELL FLETCHER. *James Wylie*: JAMES BRODERICK. *David Wylie*: FRANK MAXWELL. *Maggie Wylie*: BETTY PAUL. *John Shand*: KETH ANDES. *Prof. Dubois*: Henry Hamilton. *Mrs. MacLaughlin*: Jenny Lou Law. *Madame Marstonne*: ODETTE MYRTIL. *Sybil Tenterdon*: CELIA LIPTON. *Williams*: Gene Holmann. *Venables*: JOHN HOYT. *John Shand (in ballet)*: MARC PLATT. *Maggie Wylie (in ballet)*: ALICIA KRUG. *Sybil Tenterdon (in ballet)*: KATHRYN LEE. *Porters*: Gene Holmann, Henry Hamilton, Oran Osburn. *Conductor*: Paul Ukena.

Singers: Marion Lauer, Jan Scott, Joanne Spiller, Gloria Van Dorpe, Robert Busch, John Ford, Henry Hamilton, Gene Holmann, James E. McCracken, Oran Osburn, Paul Ukena. *Dancers*: Adele Aron, Sura Gesben, Jeanne Jones, Patti Karkalits, Nata Lee, Ruby Ann Saber, J. Corky Geil, John George, Alan Howard, David Nillo, Bob St. Clair, Keith Willis.

Act 1, Scene 1: The Wylie Home in a small town near Glasgow, Scotland. Winter, 1899. *Scene 2*: Covering the years between 1899 and 1905. *Scene 3*: Lobby of the Bright Heather Hotel, Glasgow. Winter, 1905. *Scene 4*: Glasgow. The same night. *Scene 5*: garden of Mme. Marstonne's Country home. A late afternoon in Spring, 1906.

Act 1, Scene 1: Padding Station. Spring, 1906. *Scene 2*: John Shand's Study. The same day. *Scene 3*: Paddington Station. Later that Spring. *Scene 4*: Garden of Mme. Marstonne's Country Home. Summer, 1906.

ACT 1

"I Never Laughed in My Life"
K. Andes

"Long and Weary Wait"
K. Andes, B. Paul

"Thimbleful"
B. Fletcher, F. Maxwell, J. Broderick, K. Andes, B. Paul

"He's the Man"
K. Andes, Singers, Dancers

"What Every Woman Knows"
B. Paul

"Any Afternoon About Five"
O. Myrtil

"Smile For Me"
(Staged by Paul Godkin.) B. Paul

"You Become Me"
B. Paul, K. Andes

"He's the Man" (reprise)
Company

"It's Only Thirty Years"
O. Myrtil, J. Hoyt

"What Every Woman Knows" (reprise)
B. Paul

"The New Me" (Ballet)
B. Paul, B. Fletcher, F. Maxwell, J. Broderick, Singers, Dancers

ACT 2

"The Train With the Cushioned Seats"
F. Maxwell, B. Fletcher, J. Broderick
(Staged by Paul Godkin.)

"People in Love"
K. Andes, C. Lipton

"Practical"
B. Paul

"Charm"
B. Paul

"Fun in the Country"
O. Myrtil

"What Every Woman Knows" (reprise)
B. Paul

9

"Smile For Me" (reprise)
  B. Paul
"You Become Me" (reprise)
  K. Andes

1953.03 WONDERFUL TOWN

A Musical Comedy in Two Acts, 13 Scenes. Book by Joseph Fields and Jerome Chodorov. Based on the play "My Sister Eileen" by Joseph Fields and Jerome Chodorov and the stories of the same name by Ruth McKenney. Music by Leonard Bernstein. Lyrics by Betty Comden and Adolph Green. Dances and musical numbers staged by Donald Saddler. Sets and costumes by Raoul Pene du Bois. Lighting by Peggy Clark. Miss Russell's clothes by Main Bocher. Musical direction and vocal arrangements by Lehman Engel. Orchestrations by Don Walker. Production directed by George Abbott. Produced by Robert Fryer. Opened 25 February 1953 at the Winter Garden and closed 3 July 1954 after 559 performances.

CAST (in order of appearance): *Guide:* Warren Galjour. *Appopolous:* HENRY LASCOE. *Lonigan:* Walter Kelvin. *Helen:* Michele Burke. *Wreck:* JORDAN BENTLEY. *Violet:* Dody Goodman. *Valenti:* Ted Beniades. *Eileen:* EDITH ADAMS. *Ruth:* ROSALIND RUSSELL. *A Strange Man:* Nathaniel Frey. *Drunks:* Lee Papell, Delbert Anderson. *Robert Baker:* GEORGE GAYNES. *Associate Editors:* Warren Galjour, Albert Linville. *Mrs. Wade:* Isabella Hoopes. *Frank Lippencott:* CRIS ALEXANDER. *Chef:* Nathaniel Frey. *Waiter:* Delbert Anderson. *Delivery Boy:* Alvin Bean. *Chick Clark:* DORT CLARK. *Shore Patrolman:* Lee Papell. *First Cadet:* David Lober. *Second Cadet:* Ray Dorian. *Policemen:* Lee Papell, Albert Linville, Delbert Anderson, Chris Robinson, Nathaniel Frey, Warren Galjour, Robert Kole. *Ruth's Escort:* Chris Robinson.
  Greenwich Villagers: Jean Eliot, Carol Cole, Marta Becket, Maxine Berke, Helena Seroy, Geraldine Delaney, Margaret Cady, Dody Goodman, Ed Balin, Alvin Bean, Ray Dorian, Edward Heim, Joe Layton, David Lober, Victor Moreno, William Weslow, Pat Johnson, Evelyn Page, Libi Staiger, Patty Wilkes, Helen Rice, Delbert Anderson, Warren Galjour, Robert Kole, Lee Papell, Chris Robinson.

Act 1, Scene 1: Christopher Street, Greenwich Village, New York City, 1935. *Scene 2:* Ruth and Eileen's Studio Apartment. *Scene 3:* Christopher Street. *Scene 4:* Baker's Office at the "Madhatter." *Scene 5:* The Street. *Scene 6:* The Back Yard. *Scene 7:* The Navy Yard. *Scene 8:* The Back Yard.

Act 2, Scene 1: The Christopher Street Station House. *Scene 2:* The Street. *Scene 3:* The Studio Apartment. *Scene 4:* The Street in front of the Village Vortex. *Scene 5:* The Village Vortex.

ACT 1

Scene 1
  "Christopher Street"
    W. Galjour, Villagers
Scene 2
  "Ohio"
    R. Russell, E. Adams
  "Conquering New York" (Dance)
    R. Russell, E. Adams, D. Lober, D. Goodman,
    Villagers
Scene 3
  "One Hundred Easy Ways"
    R. Russell
Scene 4
  "What a Waste"
    G. Gaynes, W. Galjour, A. Linville
  "Story Vignettes"
    (by Betty Comden and Adolph Green)
      Rexford: C. Robinson. *Mr. Mallory:* D. Anderson. *Danny:* N. Frey.
      Trent: L. Papell.
Scene 5
  "Never Felt This Way Before"
  (A Little Bit in Love)
    E. Adams
Scene 6
  "Pass The Football"
    J. Bentley, Villagers

"Conversation Piece" (Nice People, Nice Talk)
  R. Russell, E. Adams, C. Alexander, G. Gaynes, D. Clark
"A Quiet Girl"
  G. Gaynes
Scene 7
  "Conga!"
    R. Russell
      Danced by the Cadets.
Scene 8
  (Finale—Act 1 Conga! reprise)
    (R. Russell, Ensemble)

ACT 2
Scene 1
  "My Darlin' Eileen"
    E. Adams, D. Anderson, Police
Scene 2
  "Swing!"
    R. Russell, Villagers
Scene 3
  "Ohio" (reprise)
    R. Russell, E. Adams
Scene 4
  "It's Love"
    G. Gaynes, (E. Adams), Villagers
Scene 5
  ("The Village Vortex Blues" dance)
  {Let It Come Down}
    Villagers
  "Wrong Note Rag"
    R. Russell, E. Adams, Villagers
  (Finale—Act 2 "It's Love" reprise)
    Entire Company

1953.04 PORGY AND BESS

A Revival of the Folk Opera in Three Acts, 9 Scenes[14]. Book by DuBose Heyward adapted from the play "Porgy" by DuBose and Dorothy Heyward. Music by George Gershwin. Lyrics by DuBose Heyward and Ira Gershwin. Directed by Robert Breen. Chorus directed by Eva Jessye. Settings by Wolfgang Roth. Costumes by Jed Mace. Musical director, Alexander Smallens. Assistant musical director, Samuel Matlowsky. Produced by Blevins Davis and Robert Breen. Opened 10 March 1953 at the Ziegfeld Theatre and closed 28 November 1953 after 305 performances.

CAST (in order of appearance): *Clara:* HELEN COLBERT. *Mingo:* Jerry Laws. *Sportin' Life:* CAB CALLOWAY. *Serena:* HELEN THIGPEN. *Jake:* JOSEPH JAMES. *Robbins:* Howard Roberts. *Jim:* Hugh Dilworth and Sherman Sneed. *Peter, the Honey Man:* Joseph Crawford. *Lily, the Strawberry Woman:* Helen Dowdy. *Maria:* GEORGIA BURKE. *Porgy:* LeVERN HUTCHERSON, LESLIE SCOTT or

---

[14]First produced in New York 10 October 1935 at the Alvin Theatre for 124 performances. For Synopsis of Scenes and Musical Numbers, see original 1935 production. Ella Gerbert assisted in the direction of the production. During the summer of 1953, the second intermission was dropped and the Second Act was played in 6 Scenes. Dropped from Act 2, Scene 3 was: "Oh, Doctor Jesus."
  Added to this production were the following:
  Crap Game Fugue ("Roll Them Bones")
  (End of Act 1, Scene 1)
    L. Hutcherson, C. Calloway, J. McCurry, Men
  "I Ain't Got No Shame" (Opening of Act 2, Scene 1)
    C. Calloway, Ensemble
  "Buzzard (Song)" (Act 3, Scene 3)
    L. Hutcherson

IRVING BARNES. *Crown:* JOHN McCURRY. *Annie:* Catherine Ayers. *Bess:* LEONTYNE PRICE or URYLEE LEONARDOS. *Policeman:* Sam Kasakoff. *Detective:* Walter Riemer. *Undertaker:* William Veasey. *Frazier:* Moses LaMarr. *Ruby:* Elizabeth Foster. *Crab Man:* Ray Yeates. *Coroner:* Sam Kasakoff. *Policeman:* Willis Daily. *Porgy's Goat:* Jebob.

Residents of Catfish Row: Joseph Attles, Irving Barnes, Lawson Bates, James Hawthorne Bey, Rhoda Boggs, Walter P. Brown, Miriam Burton, Sibol Cain, Elsie Clark, Charles Colman, Clarice Crawford, Helen Ferguson, Doris Galiber, Ruby Grene, Kenneth Hibbert, George A. Hill, Joy McLean, Pauline Phelps, Edna Ricks, Anabelle Ross, George A. Royston, Dolores Swan, Clyde Turner, Eloise C. Uggams, Barbara Ann Webb. *Children:* Jacqueline Barnes, George Royston, Jr.

1953.05   REGINA

A Revival of the Musical Drama (Opera) in Three Acts, Prologue and 4 Scenes[15]. Text and music by Marc Blitzstein. Based on the play "The Little Foxes" by Lillian Hellman. Production directed by Robert Lewis. Conductor, Julius Rudel. Settings designed by Horace Armistead. Costumes designed by Aline Bernstein. Choreographer, John Butler. Lighting by Jean Rosenthal. (Orchestrations by Marc Blitzstein.) Produced by the New York City Opera. Opened 2 April 1953 at the New York City Center and closed 29 April 1953 after 3 performances in repertory.

CAST: *Regina Giddens:* BRENDA LEWIS. *Horace Giddens,* her husband: WILLIAM WILDERMAN. *Alexandra Giddens (Zan),* their daughter: PRISCILLA GILLETTE. *Regina's Brothers* (2): *Ben Hubbard:* LEON LISHNER. *Oscar Hubbard:* EMILE RENAN. *Birdie Hubbard,* Oscar's wife: EILEEN FAULL. *Leo Hubbard,* their son: MICHAEL POLLOCK. *Jazz:* WILLIAM DILLARD. *Addie,* cook: LUCRETIA WEST. *Cal,* butler: LAWRENCE WINTERS. *Marshall:* LLOYD THOMAS LEECH. *Belle,* maid: Margaret Tynes. *Bagtry:* Russell Goodwin. *Manders:* Charles Kuestner. *Band: Banjo:* Bernard Addison. *Clarinet:* Eddie Barefield. *Trombone:* Theodore Donnelly. *Drums:* Sticks Evans. *Pianist:* Lucy Brown. *Violinist:* Eugene Bergen.

1953.06   DIE FLEDERMAUS

A Revival of the Operetta in Three Acts[16]. (Original libretto by Carl Haffner and Richard Genée. Lyrics by Richard Genée. Based on the comedy "Le Réveillon" by Henri Meilhac and Ludovic Halévy.) English libretto by Ruth and Thomas Martin. Music by Johann Strauss. Staged by William Westerfield. Costume supervisor, Robert Fletcher. Choreography, John Butler. Conducted by Thomas P. Martin. Produced by the New York City Opera. Opened 8 April 1953 at the New York City Center and closed 3 May 1953 after 4 performances in repertory.

CAST: *Eisenstein:* JACK RUSSELL. *Rosalinda:* LAUREL HURLEY. *Adele:* ELAINE MALBIN. *Alfred:* JON CRAIN. *Falke:* WILLIAM SHRINER. *Frank:* RICHARD WENTWORTH. *Blind:* Luigi Vellucci. *Prince Orlofsky:* DONALD GRAMM. *Sally:* Jeanne Beauvais. *Frosch:* Ernest Sarracino. *Ivan:* Michael Arshansky. *Solo Dancers:* Jamie Bauer, Glen Tetley. *Ensemble:* New York City Opera Chorus.

The action takes place in the fashionable suburbs of Vienna in the 1860s.

Act 1: Rosalinda's Boudoir.

Act 2: At the Villa of Orlovsky.

Act 3: The Town Jail.

---

[15] Originally produced in New York 31 October 1949 at the 46th Street Theatre for 56 performances. For Synopsis of Scenes and Musical Numbers, see original 1949 production. An Intermission was added between Act 1, Scenes 1 and 2. Restored to the production:
   "Blues"
     L. West, B. Lewis

[16] First English language production in New York 16 March 1885 at the Casino Theatre for 42 performances. First New York production of this version 20 December 1950 at the Metropolitan Opera. No list of musical numbers appears in the program for this production. For listing of Musical Numbers, see 19 May 1954 New York City Center Light Opera production.

1953.07   CAN-CAN

A Musical Comedy in Two Acts, 17 Scenes. Music and lyrics by Cole Porter. Book and direction by Abe Burrows. Dances and musical numbers staged by Michael Kidd. Settings and lighting by Jo Mielziner. Costumes by Motley. Musical direction by Milton Rosenstock. Orchestrations by Philip J. Lang. Dance music arranged by Genevieve Pitot. Produced by Cy Feuer and Ernest H. Martin. Opened 7 May 1953 at the Sam S. Shubert Theatre and closed 25 June 1955 after 892 performances.

CAST (in order of appearance): *Bailiff:* David Collyer. *Registrar:* Michael Cavallaro. *Policemen:* Joe Cusanelli, Jon Silo, Arthur Rubin, Ralph Beaumont, Michael DeMarco, Socrates Birsky. *Judge Paul Barriere:* C. K. ALEXANDER. *Court President, Henri Marceaux:* David Thomas. *Judge Aristede Forestier:* PETER COOKSON. *Claudine:* GWEN VERDON. *Gabrielle:* Mary Anne Cohan. *Marie:* Beverly Purvin. *Celestine:* Jean Kraemer. *Hilaire Jussac:* ERIK RHODES. *Boris Adzinidzinadze:* HANS CONRIED. *Hercule:* ROBERT PENN. *Theophile:* PHIL LEEDS. *Etienne:* RICHARD PURDY. *Waiter:* Clarence Hoffman. *La Mome Pistache:* LILO. *Second Waiter:* Ferdinand Hilt. *Cafe Waiter:* Jon Silo. *Cafe Customer:* Joe Cusanelli. *Jailer:* Deedee Wood. *Model:* Pat Turner. *Mimi:* Dania Krupska. *Customers:* Sheila Arnold, David Thomas, Ferdinand Hilt. *Doctor:* Michael Cavallaro. *Second:* Arthur Rubin. *Prosecutor:* Ferdinand Hilt.

Dancers: Meredith Baylis, Shelah Hackett, Ina Hahn, Dania Krupska, Vera Lee, Beverly Tassoni, Pat Turner, Ruth Vernon, Deedee Wood, Ralph Beaumont, Socrates Birsky, Michael DeMarco, Al Lanti, Bert May, Tom Panko, Arthur Partington, Eddie Phillips, Michael Scrittorale.

Act 1, Scene 1: Correctional Court, Paris, 1893. *Scene 2:* A Street in Montmartre. *Scene 3:* Bal du Paradis. *Scene 4:* Pistache's Office. *Scene 5:* Bal du Paradis. *Scene 6:* Sidewalk Cafe. *Scene 7:* Jail. *Scene 8:* The Atelier. *Scene 9:* The Street. *Scene 10:* Quatz' Arts Ball.

Act 1, Scene 1: The Atelier. *Scene 2:* The Cafe. *Scene 3:* 'La Blanchisserie.' *Scene 4:* The Street. *Scene 5:* Roof of 'La Blanchisserie.' *Scene 6:* Prison. *Scene 7:* Court of Assizes.

ACT 1

Scene 1
  "Maidens Typical of France"
    The Laundresses

Scene 3
  "Never Give Anything Away"
    Lilo

Scene 4
  "C'est Magnifique"
    Lilo, P. Cookson

Scene 5
  "Quadrille"
    G. Verdon, B. May, Laundresses, Friends

Scene 6
  "Come Along With Me"
    E. Rhodes, H. Conried

Scene 7
  "Live and Let Live"
    Lilo
  "I Am in Love"
    P. Cookson

Scene 8
  "If You Loved Me Truly"
    H. Conried, G. Verdon, P. Leeds,
    R. Penn, R. Purdy, M. A. Cohan, J. Kraemer, B. Purvin

Scene 10
  "Montmart'" (Montmartre)
    Singing Ensemble
  "The Garden of Eden" Ballet
    Eve: G. Verdon. *Inchworms:* I. Hahn, S. Birsky. *Flamingos:* S. Hackett, A. Partington. *Kangaroos:* B. Tassoni, M. Scrittorale. *Penguins:* E. Phillips, D. Wood. *Sea Horses:* R. Vernon, T. Panko. *Frogs:* V. Lee, A. Lanti. *Leopards:* P. Turner, R. Beaumont. *Snake:* B. May.
  "Allez-Vous-En" (Go Away)
    Lilo

ACT 2

Scene 1

"Never, Never Be an Artist"
    H. Conried, P. Leeds, R. Purdy, P. Turner

Scene 2

"It's All Right With Me"
    P. Cookson

"Every Man Is a Stupid Man"
    Lilo

Scene 3

"The Apaches" (Dance)
    G. Verdon, R. Beaumont, Dancers

Scene 5

"I Love Paris"
    Lilo

"C'est Magnifique" (reprise)
    P. Cookson, Lilo

Scene 7

"Can-Can"
    Lilo, G. Verdon, Laundresses
Finale
    Entire Company

1953.08   ME AND JULIET

A Musical Comedy in Two Acts, 17 Scenes. Book and lyrics by Oscar Hammerstein II. Music by Richard Rodgers. Scenery and lighting by Jo Mielziner. Costumes by Irene Sharaff. Vocal and orchestral arrangements by Don Walker. Musical director, Salvatore Dell'Isola. Dances and musical numbers staged by Robert Alton. Production directed by George Abbott. Produced by Richard Rodgers and Oscar Hammerstein II. Opened 28 May 1953 at the Majestic Theatre and closed 3 April 1954 after 358 performances.

CAST (in order of appearance): *George*, Second Assistant Stage Manager: Randy Hall. *Sidney*, Electrician: Edwin Phillips. *Jeanie*, Chorus Singer: ISABEL BIGLEY. *Herbie*, Candy Counter Boy: JACKIE KELK. *Trio: Chris*, Rehearsal Piano Player: BARBARA CARROLL. *Milton*, Drummer: Herb Wasserman. *Stu*, Bass Fiddle Player: Joe Shulman. *Michael*, A Chorus Boy: Michael King. *Bob*, Electrician: MARK DAWSON. *Larry*, Assistant Stage Manager: BILL HAYES. *Mac*, Stage Manager: RAY WALSTON. *Monica*, Chorus Dancer: Patty Ann Jackson. *Ruby*, Company Manager: Joe Lautner. *Charlie* (Me), Featured Lead: Arthur Maxwell. *Dario*, Conductor: GEORGE S. IRVING. *Lily* (Juliet), Singing Principal: Helena Scott. *Jim* (Don Juan), Principal Dancer: Bob Fortier. *Susie* (Susie), Principal Dancer: Svetlana McLee. *Voice of Mr. Harrison*, Producer: Henry Hamilton. *Voice of Miss Davenport*, Choreographer: Deborah Remsen. *Hilda*, an aspirant for a dancing part: Norma Thornton. *Marcia*, another aspirant for a dancing part: Thelma Tadlock. *Betty*, successor to Susie as Principal Dancer: JOAN McCRACKEN. *Buzz*, Principal Dancer: BUZZ MILLER. *Ralph*, Alley Dancer: Ralph Linn. *Miss Oxford*, a bit player: Gwen Harmon. *Sadie*, an usher: Francine Bond. *Mildred*, Another Usher: Lorraine Havercroft. *A Theatre Patron*: Barbara Lee Smith. *Another Theatre Patron*: Susan Lovell.

Dancing Ensemble: Francine Bond, Betty Buday, Penny Ann Green, Lorraine Havercroft, Patty Ann Jackson, Helene Keller, Lucia Lambert, Harriet Leigh, Sonya Lindgren [Sonja Tyven], Elizabeth Logue, Shirley MacLaine, Cheryl Parker, Dorothy Silverherz, Thelma Tadlock, Norma Thornton, Janyce Ann Wagner, Rosemary Williams, Lance Avant, Grant Delaney, John George, Jack Konzal, Ralph Linn, Eddie Pfeiffer, Augustine Rodriguez, Bob St. Clair, Bill Weber. Singing Ensemble: Adele Castle, Gwen Harmon, Susan Lovell, Theresa Mari, Georgia Reed, Deborah Remsen, Thelma Scott, Barbara Lee Smith, Jack Drummond, John Ford, Henry Hamilton, Richard Hermany, Warren Kemmerling, Michael King, Larry Laurence, Jack Rains.

The entire action takes place in and around the theatre in which 'Me and Juliet' is playing.

Act 1, Scene 1: Backstage. *Scene 2*: The Orchestra Pit. *Scene 3*: First Scene of 'Me and Juliet.' *Scene 4*: The Light Bridge. *Scene 5*: During performance of 'Me and Juliet.' *Scene 6*: Backstage. *Scene 7*: The Alley leading to the Stage Door. *Scene 8*: Betty's Dressing Room. *Scene 9*: The Light Bridge. *Scene 10*: Night Club Scene in 'Me and Juliet' and Backstage.

Act 2, Scene 1: Downstairs Lounge in the Theatre. *Scene 2*: The Bar across the Street. *Scene 3*: A Second Act Sequence of 'Me and Juliet.' *Scene 4*: Theatre Manager's

Office. *Scene 5*: The Orchestra Pit. *Scene 6*: Last Scene of 'Me and Juliet.' *Scene 7*: Backstage.

ACT 1

Scene 1

"A Very Special Day"
    I. Bigley, Trio

"That's the Way It Happens"
    I. Bigley, Trio

"That's the Way It Happens" (reprise)
    B. Hayes

Dance Impromptu
    Chorus, R. Hall, Trio

Scene 2

Overture to 'Me and Juliet'
    G. S. Irving, Orchestra

Scene 3

Opening of 'Me and Juliet'
    H. Scott, B. Fortier, S. Lee, A. Maxwell

"Marriage Type Love"
    A. Maxwell, H. Scott, Singers

Scene 4

"Keep It Gay"
    M. Dawson,

Scene 5

"Keep It Gay" (dance reprise)
    B. Fortier, Chorus

Scene 6

"Keep It Gay" (dance reprise)
    J. McCracken, B. Miller, (Chorus)

"The Big, Black Giant"
    B. Hayes

"No Other Love"
    I. Bigley, B. Hayes

Scene 7

Dance
    R. Linn, F. Bond, E. Logue

"The Big, Black Giant" (reprise)
    J. Lautner

Scene 8

"It's Me"
    J. McCracken, I. Bigley

Scene 10

("No Other Love") (reprise)
    (H. Scott)

First Act Finale of 'Me and Juliet'
    H. Scott, J. McCracken, A. Maxwell, B. Fortier,
    I. Bigley, Chorus

ACT 2

Scene 1

"Intermission Talk"
    J. Kelk, Chorus

Scene 2

"It Feels Good"
    M. Dawson

Scene 3

Opening Sequence in Second Act of 'Me and Juliet'
    A. Maxwell, B. Fortier, H. Scott, Dancers

"The Baby You Love"[17]
    H. Scott, Dancers

---

[17]Dropped after opening.

"We Deserve Each Other"
  J. McCracken, B. Fortier, Chorus
Scene 4
  "I'm Your Girl"
    I. Bigley, B. Hayes
Scene 5
  (Change Music of Last Scene of 'Me and Juliet')
    (G. S Irving, Orchestra)

Scene 6
  Second Act Finale of 'Me and Juliet'
    A. Maxwell, H. Scott, J. McCracken, B. Fortier, Chorus
Scene 7
  Finale (of Our Play)
    Entire Company

1953–1954 SEASON

Carol Haney and Reta Shaw in THE PAJAMA GAME
Billy Rose Theatre Collection, New York Public Library for the Performing Arts

1953–1954 SEASON

1953.09 ## OKLAHOMA!

A Revival of the Musical Comedy in Two Acts, 6 Scenes[1]. Book and lyrics by Oscar Hammerstein II. Music by Richard Rodgers. Based on the play "Green Grow the Lilacs" by Lynn Riggs. (Originally) Directed by Rouben Mamoulian. Dances by Agnes de Mille, reproduced by Betty Gour. Settings by Lemuel Ayers. Costumes by Miles White. Production reproduced (staged) by Jerome Whyte. Orchestrations by Robert Russell Bennett. Musical director, Peter Laurini. Produced by Richard Rodgers and Oscar Hammerstein II. Opened 31 August 1953 at the New York City Center and closed 3 October 3 1953 after 40 performances.

CAST: *Aunt Eller*: MARY MARLO. *Curly*: RIDGE BOND. *Laurey*: FLORENCE HENDERSON. *Cord Elam*: Charles Hart. *Fred*: Charles Scott. *Slim*: Charles Rule. *Will Parker*: HARRIS HAWKINS. *Jud Fry*: ALFRED CIBELLI, JR. *Ado Annie Carnes*: BARBARA COOK. *Ali Hakim*: DAVID LE GRANT. *Gertie Cummings*: Judy Rawlings. *Ellen*: MAGGI NELSON. *Kate*: Barbara Reisman. *Sylvie*: Patti Parsons. *Armina*: Lynne Broadbent. *Aggie*: Cathy Conklin. *Andrew Carnes*: OWEN MARTIN. *Chalmers*: GEORGE LAWRENCE. *Mike*: Bob Lord.

Singers: Lenore Arnold, Lois Barrodin, Marylin Hardy, Frances Irby, Heidi Palmer, Barbara Reisman, Jeanne Shea, William Ambler, Dino Dante, James Fox, Christopher Golden, Bob Lord, Charles Rule, Charles Scott. *Dancers*: Lynne Broadbent, Bette Burton, Cathy Conklin, Betty Koerber, Gayle Parmelee, Patti Parsons, Cynthia Price, Georganne Shaw, Louellen Sibley, Marguerite Stewart, Payne Converse, Nick Dana, Jack Ketcham, Ronnie Landry, John Pero, Jr., Tom Pickler, Joe Ribeau.

1953.10 ## ANNA RUSSELL AND HER LITTLE SHOW

An Intimate Revue in Two Acts, 15 Scenes. Music and lyrics by Anna Russell. Staged by Arthur Klein. Lighting by Ralph Alswang. Musical arrangements by Arthur Harris. Choreography by Lorenzo Fuller. Produced by Eastman Boomer and Arthur Klein. Opened 7 September 1953 at the Vanderbilt Theatre and closed 19 September 1953 after 16 performances.

CAST: ANNA RUSSELL, ARTHUR BARNETT, JEAN LEON DESTINÉ, PAUL DUKE, JOSEPH SCANDUR, Doris Haley, Yolande Gaffne. *Duo-Pianists*: JANE ASHLOCK, ARTHUR HARRIS. *Drummers*: Alphonse Cimber, Ti-Marcel.

ACT 1

Scene 1

Jane Ashlock and Arthur Harris: Duo-Pianists

Scene 2

Arthur Barnett

Scene 3

"The Spider and the Lady"
J. L. Destiné, Y. Gaffne, Company
Drummers: A. Cimber, Ti-Marcel.

Scene 4

"A Symphony in Smoke"
P. Duke, D. Haley

Scene 5

Arthur Barnett

Scene 6

Anna Russell:
"Habanera," "O Night! O Day!," "Da Nyet, Da Nyet!," "Anameia's Death Scene," "I Gave My Love a Cherry" or "How to Write Your Own Schubert Operetta" (assisted by J. Scandur),"The Prince of Philadelphia," "Les Cigarettes," "Trink."

ACT 2

Scene 1

Arthur Barnett

---

[1]Originally presented in New York 31 March 1943 at the St. James Theatre for 2212 performances. For Synopsis of Scenes and Musical Numbers, see original 1943 production.

Scene 2

Music Appreciation—"The Bagpipes"
A. Russell

Scene 3

"The Witch Doctor"
J. L. Destiné, Company
(Voodoo dance in which the evil spirits are exorcised from the body of the patient.)

Scene 4

"Magic in Rhythm"
P. Duke, D. Haley

Scene 5

Arthur Barnett

Scene 6

Anna Russell:
"Hello! Hello! Oh, A Jolly Good Show" (assisted by J. Scandur), "Guarda La Bella Tomato," "Night and Day."

Scene 7

Anna Russell
"The Decline and Fall of The Popular Song" (as witnessed by Miss Russell), "Feeling Grand," "I'd Be a Red Hot Momma," "Chlorophyll Solly," "Miserable," "Mad."

Scene 8

Jane Ashlock, Arthur Harris (Duo-Pianists)

Scene 9

Finale

1953.11 ## CARNIVAL IN FLANDERS

A Musical Comedy in Two Acts. Book by Preston Sturges. Based on the film "La Kermesse Héroïque," screenplay by C. Spaak, J. Feyder and B. Zimmer. Music by James Van Heusen. Lyrics by Johnny Burke. Scenery by Oliver Smith. Costumes by Lucinda Ballard. Musical director, Harold Hastings. Vocal arrangements by Elie Siegmeister. Orchestrations by Don Walker. Carnival Ballet and musical numbers staged by Helen Tamiris. Directed by Preston Sturges. Produced by Paula Stone and Mike Sloane in association with Burke and Van Heusen. Opened 8 September 1953 at the New Century Theatre and closed 12 September 1953 after 6 performances.

CAST (in order of appearance): *Siska*: PAT STANLEY. *Jan Breughel*: KEVIN SCOTT. *Tailor*: Paul Reed. *Butcher*: Paul Lipson. *Barber*: Bobby Vail. *Innkeeper*: LEE GOODMAN. *Mayor*: ROY ROBERTS. *Cornelia*: DOLORES GRAY. *Martha*: Dolores Kempner. *Courier*: Matt Mattox. *Mourning Women*: Sandra Devlin, Julie Marlowe, Lorna Del Maestro. *First Officer*: Ray Mason. *Second Officer*: George Martin. *Third Officer*: Jimmy Alex. *The Duke*: JOHN RAITT. *First Citizen*: Wesley Swails. *Second Citizen*: Norman Weise. *Lisa*: Jean Bradley. *Katherine*: Undine Forrest. *Orderly*: William Noble.

Dancers: Lorna Del Maestro, Sandra Devlin, Pat Ferrier, Patti Karkalits, Mary Alice Kubes, Julie Marlowe, Billie Shane, Emy St. Just, Elfrieda Zieger, Jimmy Alex, John Aristedes, Harry Day, Ronnie Field, Skeet Guenther, George Martin, Greg O'Brien, Paul Olson, Richard Reed, Michael Spaeth. *Singers*: Jean Bradley, Jean Cowles, Undine Forrest, Dolores Kempner, Mara Landi, Mary Stanton, Gloria Van Dorpe, Lee Barry, Fred Bryan, Bill Conlon, Stokley Gray, William Noble, Dick Stewart, Wesley Swails, Norman Weise.

The entire action takes place in and around the town of Flacksenburg in Flanders in 1616.

ACT 1

"Ring the Bell"
R. Roberts, P. Lipson, B. Vail, P. Reed, L. Goodman, K. Scott, P. Stanley, Ensemble

"The Very Necessary You"
K. Scott, P. Stanley

"It's a Fine Old Institution"
D. Gray

"I'm One of Your Admirers"
D. Gray

"The Plundering of the Town"
D. Gray, M. Mattox, G. Martin, E. St. Just, J. Aristedes, J. Marlowe, Ensemble

"The Stronger Sex"
D. Gray
"The Sudden Thrill"
J. Raitt
"It's an Old Spanish Custom"
D. Gray, J. Raitt
"A Seventeen Gun Salute"
D. Gray, J. Raitt, M. Mattox, R. Mason, G. Martin, Ensemble
ACT 2
"You're Dead!"
R. Roberts, P. Lipson, B. Vail, L. Goodman, P. Reed
"(Here's That) Rainy Day"
D. Gray
"Take the Word of a Gentleman"
J. Raitt
"The Carnival Ballet"
The Virgin: E. St. Just. *The Bats*: G. O'Brien, P. Olson. *The Monk*: J. Aristedes. *The Goat*: H. Day. *The Youngest One*: P. Stanley. *The Plumed Swains*: J. Alex, R. Field, S. Guenther, M. Spaeth, G. Martin, R. Reed. *The Seven Virgins*: S. Devlin, L. Del Maestro, P. Ferrier, J. Marlowe, P. Karkalits, M. A. Kubes, E. Zeiger. *The Spanish Trio*: M. Mattox, G. Martin, J. Alex, Singers of the Town.
"A Moment of Your Love"
D. Gray, J. Raitt
"How Far Can a Lady Go?"
D. Gray
"It's a Fine Old Institution" (reprise)
D. Gray

1953.12 AT HOME WITH ETHEL WATERS

A Musical Revue in Two Acts, 7 Scenes. Staged by Richard Barr. Setting by Oliver Smith. Costumes by Robert Mackintosh. Produced by Charles Bowden and Richard Barr. Opened 22 September 1953 at the 48th Street Theatre and closed 10 October 1953 after 23 performances.

CAST: ETHEL WATERS, REGINALD BEANE (at the piano).

ACT 1
Scene 1
"I Ain't Gonna Sin No More"
(*Music and Lyrics by* Con Conrad and Herb Magidson.)
"(When It's) Sleepy Time Down South"
(*Music and Lyrics by* Clarence Muse, Leon René, Otis René.)
"Throw Dirt"
(*Music and Lyrics by* Shelton Brooks.)
"Am I Blue" (from film ON WITH THE SHOW)
(*Music by* Harry Akst. *Lyrics by* Grant Clarke.)
"Half of Me"
(*Music and Lyrics by* Peter de Rose and Sam Lewis.)
"Washtub Rubsudy" (from RHAPSODY IN BLACK)
(*Music by* Alberta Nichols. *Lyrics by* Mann Holiner.)E. Waters
Scene 2
"Bread and Gravy"
E. Waters, R. Beane
(*Music by* Hoagy Carmichael.)
Scene 3
Moods from his own 'Jazzantasy Suite:'
Blues, Syncopation, Boogie
R. Beane
"Love For Sale"
(*Music by* Cole Porter, arr. R. Beane.)R. Beane
Scene 4
"Dinah" (introduced by Miss Waters in PLANTATION REVUE)
(*Music by* Harry Akst. *Lyrics by* Sam M. Lewis and Joe Young.)
"Go Back Where You Stayed Last Night"
(*Music and Lyrics by* Ethel Waters and Sidney Easton.)
"My Man" (from ZIEGFELD FOLLIES OF 1921)
(*Music by* Maurice Yvain. *French lyrics by* Albert Willemetz, Jacques Charles. *English Lyrics by* Channing Pollock.)
"St. Louis Blues"
(*Music and Lyrics by* W. C. Handy.)

"Suppertime" (from AS THOUSANDS CHEER)
(*Music and Lyrics by* Irving Berlin.)
E. Waters
ACT 2
Scene 1
"Dance Hall Hostess" (from RHAPSODY IN BLACK)
(*Music by* Alberta Nichols. *Lyrics by* Mann Holiner.)
E. Waters
Scene 2
"Odd Moments"
(*by* R Beane)
Jerome Kern Medley
R. Beane
Scene 3
"Takin' a Chance on Love" (from CABIN IN THE SKY)
(*Music by* Vernon Duke. *Lyrics by* John Latouche and Ted Fetter.)
"Somethin' Told Me Not to Trust That Man"
(*Music by* Alberta Nichols. *Lyrics by* Mann Holiner.)
"Happiness is Jes' a Thing Called Joe" (from CABIN IN THE SKY film)
(*Music by* Harold Arlen. *Lyrics by* E. Y. Harburg.)
"Lady Be Good" (from LADY, BE GOOD)
(*Music by* George Gershwin. *Lyrics by* Ira Gershwin.)
"Stormy Weather" (from COTTON CLUB PARADE-1933)
(*Music by* Harold Arlen. *Lyrics by* Ted Koehler.)
"Mammy"
(Original version by the late Will Marion Cook)
"Motherless Chile" (Spiritual)
"Crucifixion" (Spiritual)
"Cabin in the Sky" (from CABIN IN THE SKY)
(*Music by* Vernon Duke. *Lyrics by* John Latouche.)
E. Waters

1953.13 COMEDY IN MUSIC

A Solo Performance in Two Acts. Produced by Harry D. Squires. Opened 2 October 1953 at the John Golden Theatre, vacationed beginning 3 July 1954, resumed 2 August 1954, and closed 21 January 1956 after 849 performances.

CAST: VICTOR BORGE.

MUSICAL NUMBERS[2]

---

[2]Musical Numbers not listed in program. List below prepared from reviews and recordings. Mr. Borge chose from the following material during the course of the New York run and subsequent tour:

1. Variations on a Theme
2. Medley of Popular Songs
3. Warsaw Concerto
(*Music by* Richard Addinsell.)
4. "Auf Wiedersehn Sweetheart"
(*Music and Lyrics by* John Sexton, John Turner, Eberhard Storch.)
5. "Tea for Two" (from NO NO NANETTE)
(*Music and Lyrics by* Vincent Youmans and Irving Caesar.)
6. Malaguena
(*Music by* Ernesto Lecuona.)
7. "Stardust"
(*Music by* Hoagy Carmichael and. *Lyrics by* Mitchell Parish.)
8. Nola
(*Music by* Felix Arndt.)
9. Tales from the Vienna Woods
(*Music by* Johann Strauss.)
10. Third Man Theme
(*Music by* Anton Karas.)

(Program read as follows:)
1. Frankly
2. We
3. Don't
4. Know
5. What
6. Mr. Borge
7. Will
8. Do
9. But
10. We're
11. Sure
12. He'll
13. Keep
14. Us
15. Posted
16. From
17. Time
18. To
19. Time

P.S. There is also an intermission . . . but only Mr. Borge knows when.

1953.14   REGINA

A Revival of the Musical Drama (Opera) in Three Acts, a Prologue and 4 Scenes[3]. Text and music by Marc Blitzstein. Based on the play "The Little Foxes" by Lillian Hellman. Production directed by Robert Lewis. Conductor, Julius Rudel. Settings designed by Horace Armistead. Costumes designed by Aline Bernstein. Choreographer, John Butler. Lighting by Jean Rosenthal. (Orchestrations by Marc Blitzstein.) Produced by the New York City Opera. Opened 9 October 1953 at the New York City Center and closed 15 October 1953 after 2 performances in repertory.

CAST: *Regina Giddens*: BRENDA LEWIS. *Horace Giddens*, her husband: WILLIAM WILDERMAN. *Alexandra Giddens* (Zan), their daughter: DOROTHY MacNEIL. *Regina's Brothers* (2): *Ben Hubbard*: LEON LISHNER. *Oscar Hubbard*: EMILE RENAN. *Birdie Hubbard*, Oscar's wife: WILLABELLE UNDERWOOD. *Leo Hubbard*, their son: MICHAEL POLLOCK. *Jazz*: WILLIAM DILLARD. *Addie*, cook: LUCRETIA WEST. *Cal*, butler: LAWRENCE WINTERS. *Marshall*: LLOYD THOMAS LEECH. *Belle*, maid: Margaret Tynes. *Bagtry*: Russell Goodwin. *Manders*: Charles Kuestner.

---

11. Nocturne
    (*Music by* Frederic Chopin.)
12. Blue Danube Waltz
    (*Music by* Johann Strauss.)
13. "Trees"
    (*Music by* Oscar Rasbach. *Poem by* Joyce Kilmer)
14. "One Fine Day"
    (*Music by* Giacomo Puccini.)
15. "A Mozart Opera" by Victor Borge
16. Tango
    (*Music by* Isaac Albeniz.)
17. Minute Waltz
    (*Music by* Frederic Chopin.)
18. Liebestraum
    (*Music by* Franz Lizst.)
19. Family Background
20. Phonetic Punctuation

[3]Originally produced in New York 31 October 1949 at the 46th Street Theatre for 56 performances. For Synopsis of Scenes and Musical Numbers, see original 1949 production. An Intermission was added between Act 1, Scenes 1 and 2. Restored to the production for this revival: "Blues"

    L. West, B. Lewis

1953.15   DIE FLEDERMAUS

A Revival of the Operetta in Three Acts.[4] (Original Viennese libretto by Carl Haffner and Richard Genée. Based on the comedy "Le Réveillon" by Henri Meilhac and Ludovic Halévy.) English libretto by Ruth and Thomas Martin. Music by Johann Strauss. Staged by Glenn Jordan. Choreography, John Butler. Costume supervisor, Robert Fletcher. Lighting by Hans Sondheimer. Conducted by Thomas P. Martin. Produced by the New York City Opera. Opened 10 October 1953 at the New York City Center and closed 7 November 1953 after 2 performances in repertory; re-opened 27 March 1954 and closed 1 May 1954 after 3 additional performances. Total this season: 5 performances.[5]

CAST: *Eisenstein*: JACK RUSSELL. *Rosalinda*: JEAN FENN. *Adele*: ADELAIDE BISHOP. *Alfred*: LLOYD THOMAS LEECH. *Falke*: EARL REDDING. *Frank*: Richard Wentworth. *Blind*: Luigi Vellucci. *Prince Orlofsky*: DONALD GRAMM. *Sally*: Jennie Andrea. *Frosch*: Coley Worth. *Ivan*: Michael Arshansky. *Solo Dancers*: Felisa Conde, Glen Tetley. *Ensemble*: New York City Opera Chorus.

1953.16   KISMET

A Musical Arabian Night (Musical Comedy) in Two Acts, 14 Scenes. Book by Charles Lederer and Luther Davis. Based on the play of the same name by Edward Knoblock. Music from Alexander Borodin. Musical adaptation and lyrics by Robert Wright and George Forrest. Settings and costumes designed by Lemuel Ayers. Lighting by Peggy Clark. Orchestral and choral arrangements by Arthur Kay. Musical direction by Louis Adrian. Dances and musical numbers staged by Jack Cole. Production directed by Albert Marre. Produced by Charles Lederer in association with Edwin Lester. Opened 3 December 1953 at the Ziegfeld Theatre and closed 23 April 1955 after 583 performances.

CAST (in order appearance): *Imam of The Mosque*: Richard Oneto. *Muezzins*: Gerald Cardoni, Kirby Smith, Ralph Strane, Louis Polacek. *Doorman*: Jack Mei Ling. *First Beggar*: EARLE MACVEIGH. *Second Beggar*: Robert Lamont. *Third Beggar*: Rodolfo Silva. *Dervishes*: Jack Dodds, Marc Wilder. *Omar*: PHILIP COOLIDGE. *Public Poet, later called Hajj*: ALFRED DRAKE. *Marsinah, His Daughter*: DORETTA MORROW. *A Merchant*: Kirby Smith. *Hassan-Ben*: HAL HACKETT. *Jawan*: TRUMAN GAIGE. *Street Dancers*: FLORENCE LESSING, Ethel Martin. *Akbar*: Jack Dodds. *Assiz*: Marc Wilder. *Bangle Man*: Richard Oneto. *Chief Policeman*: TOM CHARLESWORTH. *Second Policeman*: HAL HACKETT. *The Wazir of Police*: HENRY CALVIN. *Wazir's Guards*: Stephen Ferry, Steve Reeves. *Lalume*: JOAN DIENER. *Attendants*: Mario Lamm, John Weidemann. *Princesses of Ababu*: Patricia Dunn, Bonnie Evans, Reiko Sato. *The Caliph*: RICHARD KILEY. *Slave Girls*: Carol Ohmart, Joyce Palmer, Sandra Stahl, Lila Jackson. *A Peddler*: EARLE MACVEIGH. *A Servant*: Richard Vine. *Princess Zubbediya of Damascus*: FLORENCE LESSING. *Ayah to Zubbediya*: Lucy Andonian. *Princess Samaris of Bangalore*: BEATRICE KRAFT. *Ayah to Samaris*: Thelma Dare. *Street Women*: Jo Ann O'Connell, Lynne Stuart. *Prosecutor*: EARLE MACVEIGH. *Widow Yussef*: Barbara Slate. *Diwan Dancers*: Neile Adams, Jack Woods, Marc Wilder.

Singers: Gerald Cardoni, Robert Lamont, Richard Oneto, Louis Polacek, Kirby Smith, Ralph Strane, Richard Vine, George Yarick, Anita Coulter, Thelma Dare, Lila Jackson, Jo Ann O'Connell, Barbara Slate, Sandra Stahl, Lynne Stuart, Erica Twiford. Dancers: Neile Adams, Patricia Dale, Devra Kline, Ania Romaine, Vida Ann Solomon, Roberta Stevenson.

The action takes place in one day in Bagdad, Act 1 from Dawn to Dusk, Act 2 from Dusk to Dawn.

Act 1, Scene 1: A tent just outside the city. Scene 2: On the steps of the Mosque. Scene 3: The Bazaar of the Caravans. Scene 4: A side street. Scene 5; A garden. Scene 6: A street near the Bazaar. Scene 7: The throne room of His Exalted Excellency, the Wazir of Police.

Act 2, Scene 1: Along the route of the Caliph's Procession. Scene 2: The garden. Scene 3: Ante-room to the Wazir's harem. Scene 4: A rooftop pavilion in the Wazir's palace. Scene 5: A corridor in the Wazir's palace. Scene 6: Ante-room to the Wazir's harem. Scene 7: The ceremonial hall of the Caliph's palace.

---

[4]First English language production in New York 16 March 1885 at the Casino Theatre for 42 performances. First New York production of this adaptation 20 December 1950 at the Metropolitan Opera House. No list of musical numbers appears in the program for this production. For Synopsis of Scenes and Musical Numbers, see May 1954 revival.
[5]Settings uncredited. Settings and costumes were assembled from various sources, a previous Sol Hurok tour of DIE FLEDERMAUS and the Broadway production of MY DARLIN' AIDA.

ACT 1

Scene 1

"Sands of Time"
R. Oneto

"Rhymes Have I"
A. Drake, D. Morrow

"Fate"
A. Drake

Scene 2

"Fate" (reprise)
A. Drake

Scene 3

"Bazaar of the Caravans"
F. Lessing, J. Dodds, M. Wilder, Merchants and Shoppers

"Not Since Ninevah"
J. Diener, H. Calvin, P. Dunn, B. Evans, R. Sato,
J. Dodds, M. Wilder, Merchants, Shoppers

"Baubles, Bangles and Beads"
D. Morrow

Scene 5

"Stranger in Paradise"
R. Kiley, D. Morrow

Scene 6

"He's in Love!"
T. Charlesworth, H. Hackett, E. MacVeigh, P. Dunn,
B. Evans, R. Sato, J. Dodds, M. Wilder, R. Kiley,
P. Coolidge

Scene 7

"Gesticulate"
A. Drake, Wazir's Council

"Fate" (reprise)
A. Drake, Ladies of Wazir's Harem

ACT 2

Scene 1

"Night of My Nights"
R. Kiley, Entourage

Scene 2

"Stranger in Paradise" (reprise)
D. Morrow

"Baubles, Bangles and Beads" (reprise)
R. Kiley

"He's in Love!" (reprise)
Entourage

Scene 3

"Was I Wazir?"
H. Calvin, T. Charlesworth, H. Hackett, Guards

Scene 4

"Rahadlakum"
A. Drake, J. Diener, F. Lessing, B. Kraft, P. Dunn, B. Evans,
R. Sato, Ladies of the Wazir's Harem

"And This Is My Beloved"
D. Morrow, R. Kiley, A. Drake, H. Calvin

Scene 5

"The Olive Tree"
A. Drake

Scene 7

"Ceremonial of the Caliph's Diwan"
Diwan Dancers

"Presentation of Princesses"

a. Damascus
F. Lessing, L. Andonian

b. Bangalore
B. Kraft, T. Dare

c. Ababu
P. Dunn, B. Evans, R. Sato

Finale
A. Drake, Ensemble

JOHN MURRAY ANDERSON'S ALMANAC

1953.17

A Musical Revue in Two Acts, Prologue and 25 Scenes. Sketches by Jean Kerr, Sumner Locke-Elliott, Arthur Macrae, Herbert Farjeon, Lauri Wylie, Billy K. Wells, (Leslie Julian Jones, Orson Bean, Phil Green). Music and lyrics by Richard Adler and Jerry Ross, Cy Coleman, Michael Grace, Joseph McCarthy, Henry Sullivan, John Rox, Bart Howard, (Sheldon Harnick, Harry Belafonte, John Murray Anderson, Michael Grace, Carl Tucker, Sammy Gallup, Charles Zwar, Alan Melville). Sketches directed by Cyril Ritchard. Dances and musical numbers staged by Donald Saddler. Scenery by Raoul Pene du Bois. Costumes by Thomas Becher. Musical direction, Buster Davis. Orchestrations by Ted Royal. Vocal arrangements by Buster Davis. Dance music arranged by Gerald Alters. Entire production devised and staged by John Murray Anderson. Produced by Michael Grace, Stanley Gilkey and Harry Rigby. Opened 10 December 1953 at the Imperial Theatre and closed 26 June 1954 after 229 performances.

CAST: HERMIONE GINGOLD, BILLY DE WOLFE, HARRY BELAFONTE, POLLY BERGEN, ORSON BEAN, NANCI CROMPTON, CARLETON CARPENTER, HARRY MIMMO, ELAINE DUNN, CELIA LIPTON, JAMES JEWELL, KAY MEDFORD, Lee Becker, Imelda DeMartin, Dorothy Dushock, Greb Lober, Illona Murai, Margot Myers, Gwen Neilson, Gloria Smith, Jimmy Albright, Hank Brunjes, Ronald Cecill, Dean Crane, Ralph McWilliams, Gerard Leavitt, Jacqueline Mickles, Colleen Hutchins, Monique Van Vooren, Tina Louise, Larry Kert, Bob Kole, George Reeder, Jay Harnick, Kenneth Urmston, Toni Wheelis, Siri, Millard Thomas.

PROLOGUE[6]

"Harlequinade"
(*Music and Lyrics by* Richard Adler and Jerry Ross.)
Harlequin: C. Carpenter. *Puncinello*: H. Mimmo. *Pierrot*: J. Jewell. *Pierrette*: C. Lipton. *Columbine*: N. Crompton. *Pierrettes*: L. Becker, I. DeMartin, D. Dushock, G. Lober, I. Murai, M. Myers, G. Neilson, G. Smith. *Pierrots*: J. Albright, H. Brunjes, R. Cecill, D. Crane, R. McWilliams, G. Leavitt.

ACT 1

Scene 1

The Coronation: "Queen for a Day"
(*Music and Lyrics by* Richard Adler and Jerry Ross.)
The Four Queens: J. Mickles, C. Hutchins, M. Van Vooren, T. Louise. *The Bridegrooms*: L. Kert, B. Kole, G. Reeder, J. Harnick, R. Cecill, R. McWilliams, H. Brunjes, G. Leavitt. *Miss Reingold*: H. Gingold.

Scene 2

My Cousin Who?
(*by* Jean Kerr)
David: B. DeWolfe. *Butlers*: J. Albright, K. Urmston, R. Cecill, R. McWilliams. *Witch Doctor*: D. Crane. *Maids*: T. Wheelis, G. Neilson. *Rebecca*: C. Lipton. *Louise*: I. Murai.

Scene 3

"You're So Much a Part of Me"
(*Music and Lyrics by* Richard Adler and Jerry Ross.)
The Pierrot of 1953: C. Carpenter. *The Pierrette of 1953*: E. Dunn.

Scene 4

"I Dare to Dream"
P. Bergen
(*Music by* Michael Grace and Carl Tucker. *Lyrics by* Sammy Gallup.)

Scene 5

"The Cello"
(*Music by* Charles Zwar. *Lyrics by* Leslie Julian Jones.)
The Cellist: H. Gingold.

---

[6]Added during the run:
Jonathan Winters (Comedian Specialty: Marine Corps sketch)
"Anema e Corre"
Tony Bavaar
(*Music and Lyrics by* Mann Curtis and Harry Akst.)
"With All My Heart and Soul"
(T. Bavaar)
(*Music and Lyrics by* Mann Curtis and Harry Akst.)
The Minstrel: T. Bavaar. *The Countess*: G. Neilson. *Courtiers*: J. Harnick, S. Guenther, H. Brunjes.

Scene 6

Don Brown's Body

(*by* Jean Kerr)

Mike Hammer: O. Bean. *Sally Duprey*: K. Medford. *Man*: C. Carpenter. *Chorus*: J. Harnick, C. Hutchins, J. Mickles, T. Louise, B. Kole, M. Van Vooren, Siri, 5. Reeder, L. 5Kert.

Scene 7

"Mark Twain"[7]

H. Belafonte

(*Music and Lyrics by* Harry Belafonte.)

Guitarist: M. Thomas.

Scene 8

The Nightingale and the Rose (*Adapted* from the story of Oscar Wilde *by* John Murray Anderson.)(from GREENWICH VILLAGE FOLLIES OF 1922)

"Nightingale, Bring Me a Rose"

J. Jewell

(*Music by* Henry Sullivan. *Lyrics by* John Murray Anderson.)

The Story Teller: C. Lipton. *The Student*: D. Crane. *The Prince*: G. Leavitt. *The Coquette*: M. Myers. *The Nightingale*: N. Crompton. *Guests at the Ball*: Siri, M. Van Vooren, T. Louise, C. Hutchins, G. Lober, D. Dushock, G. Smith, G. Neilson, H. Brunjes, R. McWilliams, R. Cecill, G. Reeder, J. Albright.

Note: "The Nightingale and the Rose" was first presented by John Murray Anderson in one of his early "Greenwich Village Follies" (1922). It established a new form of production number which has subsequently become known as a "Ballet Ballad." The music of the present version has been written in its entirety by Henry Sullivan.

Scene 9

European Express

Mrs. A: H. Gingold. *Mrs. B*: B. DeWolfe.

Scene 10

"My Love Is A Wanderer"[8]

P. Bergen

(*Music and Lyrics by* Bart Howard.)

Scene 11

"Tin Pan Alley"

(*Music by* Cy Coleman. *Lyrics by* Joseph McCarthy, Jr.)

The Song Plugger: C. Carpenter. And R. Cecill, J. Harnick, L. Kert, B. Kole.

"Mammy Songs"

R. McWilliams, K. Urmston

"Rhythm Songs"

G. Reeder, I. DeMartin, L. Becker, G. Lober, D. Dushock

"Torch Songs"

G. Smith, I. Murai, M. Myers, H. Brunjes, G. Leavitt, D. Crane

"Patriotic Songs"

E. Dunn

Scene 12

"Merry Little Minuet"[9]

O. Bean

(*Music and Lyrics by* Sheldon Harnick.)

Scene 13

"Hope You Come Back"

(*by* Sumner Locke-Elliot)

(*Music and Lyrics by* Richard Adler and Jerry Ross.)

Meg: P. Bergen. *Beth*: N. Crompton. *Jo*: E. Dunn. *Amy*: H. Gingold. *Marmee*: K. Medford. *Laurie*: B. DeWolfe. *Friends*: J. Jewell, Entire Company.

ACT 2

Scene 1

Ziegfeldiana: "If Every Month Were June"

C. Lipton

(*Music by* Henry Sullivan. *Lyrics by* John Murray Anderson.)

The Spring Bride: C. Hutchins. *The Summer Bride*: Siri. *The Autumn Bride*: J. Mickles. *The Winter Bride*: M. Van Vooren. *The Bouquet*: N. Crompton. *The Train Bearers*: I. DeMartin, L. Becker, D. Dushock, G. Neilson.

[7]Dropped during the run.

[8]Dropped during the run.

[9]Dropped during the run.

Scene 2

"Which Witch?"

H. Gingold

(*Music by* Charles Zwar. *Lyrics by* Alan Melville.)

Scene 3

La Loge (Renoir)

(*by* Herbert Farjeon)

"Fini"

P. Bergen

(*Music and Lyrics by* Richard Adler and Jerry Ross.)

The Man in the Box: J. Harnick.

Scene 4

Cartoon

(*by* Arthur Macrae)

First Secretary: K. Medford. *Second Secretary*: C. Hutchins. *The New Manager*: O. Bean.

Scene 5

"Acorn in the Meadow"

H. Belafonte

(*Music and Lyrics by* Richard Adler and Jerry Ross.)

Scene 6

Harry Mimmo[10]

The Ladies: T. Louise, J. Mickles, M. Van Vooren. *Sedan Chair Bearers*: J. Harnick, L. Kert.

Scene 7

"When Am I Going to Meet Your Mother?"

E. Dunn, C. Carpenter

(*Music and Lyrics by* Richard Adler and Jerry Ross.)

Scene 8

Dinner for One

(*by* Lauri Wylie)

The Lady: H. Gingold. *The Butler*: B. DeWolfe.

Scene 9

(Chinese Monologue) [American Town]

(*by* Orson Bean and Phil Green)

O. Bean

Scene 10

"Hold 'Em Joe"

H. Belafonte

(*Music and Lyrics by* Harry Belafonte.)

Danced by I. Murai, G. Reeder, G. Smith, M. Van Vooren, C. Hutchins, Dancers.

Scene 11

La Pistachio

(*by* Billy K. Wells, *adapted* for the Almanac by Sumner Locke-Elliot)

Bobo: H. Gingold. *Cornelius*: B. DeWolfe. *Fifi*: K. Medford.

Scene 12

"The Earth and the Sky"

P. Bergen

(*Music and Lyrics by* John Rox.)

Finale

Entire Company

1954.01 THE GIRL IN PINK TIGHTS

A Musical Extravaganza in Two Acts, 17 Scenes. Book by Jerome Chodorov and Joseph Fields. Music by Sigmund Romberg. Lyrics by Leo Robin. Music developed and orchestrated by Don Walker. Scenery and lighting by Eldon Elder. Costumes by Miles White. Musical direction by Sylvan Levin. Ballet music arranged by Trude Rittman. Dances and musical numbers staged by Agnes de Mille. Entire production directed by Shepard Traube. Produced by Shepard Traube in association with Anthony Brady Farrell. Opened 5 March 1954 at the Mark Hellinger Theatre and closed 12 June 1954 after 115 performances.

CAST (in order of appearance): *Boris*: Joshua Shelley. *Volodya Kuzentsov*: ALEXANDRE KALIOUJNY. *Lisette Gervais*: (Zizi) JEANMAIRE. *Maestro Gallo*: CHARLES GOLDNER. *Lotta Leslie*: BRENDA LEWIS. *Clyde Hallam*: DAVID ATKINSON. *Eddington*: David Aiken. *Hattie Hopkins*: Dania Krupska. *Van Beuren*:

[10]Dropped during the run.

ROBERT SMITH. *British Tars*: Tom Rieder, John Taliaferro. *Policeman*: John Stamford. *Newspaper Boy*: Maurice Hines. *Shoe Shine Boy*: Gregory Hines. *Mike*: Kalem Kermoyan. *Bruce*: John Stamford. *Nellie*: Lydia Fredericks. *Hollister*: Ray Mason. *Simone*: Katia Geleznova. *Mimi*: Eva Rubinstein. *Lucette*: Lynne Marcus. *Odette*: Nancy King. *Gisele*: Lila Popper. *Paulette*: Mickey Gunnersen. *Fire Chiefs*: Ted Thurston, John Taliaferro. *Jenny*: Jenny Workman. *Blanchette*: Beryl Towbin. *Emile*: Ted Thurston. *Sommelier*: John Taliaferro. *Gypsy Violinist*: Douglas Rideout.

Singers: Lydia Fredericks, Jane House, Deedy Irwin, Peggy Kinard, Marni Nixon, Michelle Reiner, Joanne Spiller, Beverly Weston, David Aiken, Herbert Banke, Robert Driscoll, Kalem Kermoyan, Ray Mason, Stas Pajenski, Douglas Rideout, Tom Rieder, James Schlader, John Stamford, John Taliaferro, Ted Thurston. *Dancers*: Meredith Baylis, Joan Bowman, Katia Geleznova, Mickey Gunnerson, Mary Haywood, Rhoda Kerns, Nancy King, Lynne Marcus, Julie Marlowe, Ellen Matthews, Lila Popper, Eva Rubinstein, Dorothy Scott, Beverly Simms, Beryl Towbin, Diana Turner, Jenny Workman, Harry Asmus, Louis Kosman, Paul Olson, Edward Stinnett, William Weslow.

The action of the play takes place immediately following the Civil War in the theatrical district of New York.

Act 1, Scene 1: A Rehearsal Hall, the Academy of Music. *Scene 2*: A Street near the Academy of Music and Niblo's Garden. *Scene 3*: Outside the Academy of Music and Niblo's Garden. *Scene 4*: A Street near the Theatrical District. *Scene 5*: Bowling Green. *Scene 6*: The Stage at Niblo's Garden. *Scene 7*: A Corridor, the Academy of Music. *Scene 8*: The Stage at the Academy of Music. Three days later. *Scene 9*: A Street. *Scene 10*: In front of the Academy of Music.

Act 2, Scene 1: A Pier at Battery park. A week later. *Scene 2*: A Theatrical Costumer's. Two weeks later. *Scene 3*: The Stage at Niblo's Garden. *Scene 4*: A Private Dining Room at the Hotel Brevoort. *Scene 5*: A Corridor Backstage at Niblo's Garden. *Scene 6*: Clyde's Dressing Room. *Scene 7*: The final scene of "The Soul of Dick the Renegade." "The Bill Is Due! It Must Be Paid."

ACT 1[11]

Scene 1

Ballet Class
Danced by the French Ballet Company
Lisette: Jeanmaire. *Volodya*: A. Kalioujny. *Solists*: D. Turner, W. Weslow, L. Marcus, H. Asmus, B. Simms, P. Olson, D. Scott, E. Stinnett.

Scene 2

"That Naughty Show from Gay Paree"
Singing Ensemble

Scene 3

"Lost in Loveliness"
D. Atkinson
Lisette: Jeanmaire. *First Lover*: P. Olson. *Second Lover*: H. Asmus. *Lovers*: E. Stinnett, L. Kosman.

Scene 4

"I Promised Their Mothers"
C. Goldner

Scene 5

"Up in the Elevated Railway"
Jeanmaire, D. Atkinson, A. Kalioujny, D. Krupska, M. Hines, G. Hines, Singing Ensemble
"In Paris and In Love"
D. Atkinson, Jeanmaire

Scene 6

"You've Got To be a Little Crazy"
B. Lewis, L. Fredericks, K. Kermoyan, J. Stamford

Scene 7

"When I Am Free to Love"
Jeanmaire

Scene 8

Pas de Deux
Danced by Jeanmaire, A. Kalioujny

Scene 9

"Out of the Way"/"Roll Out the Hose, Boys"
Singing Ensemble

Scene 10

Finale (Act 1)
Entire Company

ACT 2[12]

Scene 1

"My Heart Won't Say Goodbye"
D. Atkinson, Jeanmaire, Singing Ensemble
"We're All in the Same Boat"
Entire Company

Scene 2

"Lost in Loveliness" (reprise)
D. Atkinson

Scene 3

Bacchanale
Danced by the French Ballet Company
Dionysius: A. Kalioujny. *The Wayward Nymph*: J. Workman. *Nymphs*: M. Baylis, J. Bowman, D. Scott, D. Turner, B. Simms, D. Turner. *Satyrs*: H. Asmus, P. Olson, E. Stinnett, W. Weslow. *Messenger*: B. Towbin. *Attendants*: M. Hines, G. Hines.
"My Heart Won't Say Goodbye" (reprise)
B. Lewis
"Love Is the Funniest Thing"
B. Lewis, C. Goldner

Scene 6

"When I Am Free to Love" (reprise)
Jeanmaire

Scene 7

"The Cardinal's Guard Are We"
B. Lewis, Singing Ensemble

Grand Imperial Ballet
Lucifer: A. Kalioujny. *Hecate*: Jeanmaire. *Devils*: H. Asmus, P. Olson, E. Stinnett, W. Weslow. *Evil Spirits*: K. Geleznova, L. Marcus, D. Scott, B. Simms. *Bats*: M. Hayward, M. Baylis, J. Bowman, J. Marlowe, L. Popper, D. Turner. *Dancing Batlets*: N. King, E. Matthews, E. Rubinstein, J. Workman. *Batlets*: M. Gunnerson, R. Kerns, B. Towbin. *Attendants*: M. Hines, G. Hines.

Finale (Act 2)
Entire Company

1954.02 **BY THE BEAUTIFUL SEA**

A Musical in Two Acts, 15 Scenes. Book by Herbert and Dorothy Fields. Music by Arthur Schwartz. Lyrics by Dorothy Fields. Settings and lighting by Jo Mielziner. Costumes by Irene Sharaff. Choreography by Helen Tamiris. Directed by Marshall Jamison. Musical direction and vocal arrangements by Jay Blackton. Orchestrations by Robert Russell Bennett. Production associate, Simon P. Herman. Produced by Robert Fryer and Lawrence Carr. Opened 8 April 1954 at the Majestic Theatre, moved 4 October 1954 to the Imperial Theatre and closed 27 November 1954 after 270 performances.

CAST (in order of appearance): *Quartet*: John Dennis, Reid Shelton, Ray Hyson, Larry Laurence. *Acrobats*: Ray Kirchner, Rex Cooper. *Cora Belmont*: Mary Harmon. *Molly Belmont*: Cindy Robbins. *Lillian Belmont*: Gloria Smith. *Ruby Monk*: MAE BARNES. *Mrs. Koch*: Edith True Case. *Carl Gibson*: CAMERON PRUD'HOMME. *Lottie Gibson*: SHIRLEY BOOTH. *Half-Note*: Robert Jennings. *Diabolo*: Thomas Gleason. *Baby Betsy Busch*: CAROL LEIGH. *Mickey Powers*: RICHARD FRANCE. *Dennis Emery*: WILBUR EVANS. *Flora Busch*: ANNE FRANCINE. *Willie Slater*:

---

[11]Program Note (Warning to the Public!): The characters and events depicted in the extravaganza we are about to present are not altogether fictional and have more than a family resemblance to those characters and events which led to the production of the first American musical comedy.

" ... In consequence of the destruction , by fire, of the Academy of Music, this city, Jarrett & Palmer, who were to have produced 'La Biche au Bois' with a ballet troupe from Paris, had on their hands a number of artists. William Wheatley, who was to produce 'The Black Crook,' a melodrama, at Niblo's Garden, was persuaded to utilize the unfortunate ballet company ... Charles M. Barras, the author of 'The Black Crook,' objected to this desecration of his work. But a payment of the sum of $1500 for the run of the piece, no matter what its duration might be, overcame his objections." From "A History of the New York Stage" by T. Allston Brown

[12]Added during the run to Act 2, Scene 7 after "The Cardinal's Guard Are We," before the Ballet:
"Going to the Devil"
Jeanmaire

Warde Donovan. *Lenny:* Larry Howard. *Sidney:* Eddie Roll. *Mr. Curtis:* Paul Reed. *Burt Mayer:* Larry Laurence. *Viola:* Gaby Monet.

Dancers: Cathryn Damon, Dorothy Donau, Lillian Donau, Pat Ferrier, Sigyn, Mona Tritsch, Rex Cooper, Bob Haddad, Larry Howard, Ray Kirchner, Victor Reilly, Eddie Roll, Arthur Partington. *Singers:* Suzanne Easter, Lola Fisher, Colleen O'Connor, Pat Roe, Jean Sincere, Libi Staiger, John Dennis, Warde Donovan, Thomas Gleason, Ray Hyson, Franklin Kennedy, Larry Laurence, George Lenz, Reid Shelton.

Act 1, Scene 1: Backyard of Lottie Gibson's Boarding House. Coney Island, early 1900s. *Scene 2:* Seaside Street in Coney Island. *Scene 3:* The Midway at Coney Island. *Scene 4:* The Old Mill. *Scene 5:* Backyard of Lottie Gibson's Boarding House. *Scene 6:* Midway at Coney Island. *Scene 7:* Seaside Street in Coney Island. *Scene 8:* Bedroom of Lottie Gibson's Boarding House. *Scene 9:* The Pavillion of Fun.

Act 2, Scene 1: The Backyard of Lottie Gibson's Boarding House. *Scene 2:* Stage of the Brighton Beach Theatre. *Scene 3:* Dreamland Casino. *Scene 4:* Lottie's Bedroom. *Scene 5:* Seaside Street in Coney Island. *Scene 6:* Dreamland Casino.

ACT 1

Scene 1

"Mona from Arizona"
J. Dennis, R. Shelton, R. Hyson, L. Laurence

"The Sea Song"
S. Booth, Boarders, Neighbors

Scene 2

"Old Enough to Love"
R. France

Scene 3

"Coney Island Boat"
S. Booth, R. Jennings, Visitors
(Counter Melody "In the Good Old Summertime" by Ben Shields and George Evans.)

Scene 4

"Alone Too Long"
W. Evans

Scene 5

"Happy Habit"
M. Barnes

Scene 6

"Goodtime Charlie"
R. France, L. Howard, E. Roll, M. Harmon, C. Robbins, G. Smith
Sports: Male Dancers. *Spicy Pictures: The Vendor:* L. Laurence. *Wicked Women:* Sigyn, L. Donau, C. Damon. *The Iceman:* A. Partington, P. Ferrier. *Serpentina Sal:* G. Monet. *Finale:* Dancing Company.

Scene 7

"Goodtime Charlie" (reprise)
R. France, L. Howard, E. Roll, M. Harmon, C. Robbins, G. Smith

Scene 8

"I'd Rather Wake Up By Myself"
S. Booth

Scene 9

"Hooray for George the Third"
T. Gleason, L. Staiger, Visitors

ACT 2

Scene 1

"Hang Up"
M. Barnes, Boarders, Neighbors

"Alone Too Long" (reprise)
S. Booth

"More Love Than Your Love"
W. Evans

Scene 2

Vaudeville: Acts on the Bill:

1. The Three Clowns. 2. A Lady in Red. 3. Butterfly Wings.

"Lottie Gibson Specialty"
S. Booth

Scene 3

"Throw the Anchor Away"
L. Laurence, A. Partington, M. Harmon

Dance
G. Monet, A. Partington, R. France, R. Cooper, Patrons

"More Love Than Your Love" (reprise)
W. Evans

Scene 4

"Happy Habit" (reprise)
S. Booth

Scene 5

"Old Enough to Love" (reprise)
R. France, C. Leigh

Scene 6

Finale
Entire Company

1954.03 THE GOLDEN APPLE

A Musical in Two Acts, 10 Scenes[13]. Book and lyrics by John Latouche. (A contemporary adaptation of Homer's "The Iliad" and "The Odyssey.") Music by Jerome Moross. Settings by William and Jean Eckart. Costumes by Alvin Colt. Lighting by Klaus Holm. Musical director, Hugh Ross. Orchestral arrangements by Jerome Moross and Hershy Kay. Choreography and musical numbers staged by Hanya Holm. Directed by Norman Lloyd. Produced by Alfred DeLiagre Jr. and Roger L. Stevens in association with T. Edward Hambleton and Norris Houghton. Opened 20 April 1954 at the Alvin Theatre and closed 7 August 1954 after 125 performances. Total including Off-Broadway run: 173 performances.

CAST (in order of appearance): *Helen,* a Farmer's Daughter: KAYE BALLARD. *Lovey Mars,* the Local Matchmaker: BIBI OSTERWALD. *Mrs. Juniper,* the Mayor's Wife: SHANNON BOLIN. *Miss Minerva Oliver,* the Village School Marm: PORTIA NELSON. *Mother Hare,* the Local Mystic: Martha Larrimore. *Penelope,* Ulysses' Wife: PRISCILLA GILLETTE. *Menelaus,* the Old Sheriff: Dean Mitchener. *The Heroes (12): Captain Mars:* Frank Seabolt. *Ajax:* Marten Sameth. *Agamemnon:* Crandall Diehl. *Nestor:* Maurice Edwards. *Bluey:* Murray Gitlin. *Thirsty:* Don Redlich. *Silas:* Peter De Mayo. *Homer:* Barton Mumaw. *Diomede:* Robert Flavelle. *Achilles:* Julian Patrick. *Patroclus:* Martin Keane. *Doc MacCahan:* Gary Gordon. *Ulysses,* a Veteran: STEPHEN DOUGLASS. *Theron:* David Hooks. *Mayor Juniper:* Jerry Stiller. *Paris,* a Travelling Salesman: JONATHAN LUCAS. *Hector Charybdis,* Mayor of Rhododendron: JACK WHITING.

Local Girls: Sara Bettis, Dorothy Etheridge, Nelle Fisher, Dee Harless, Janet Hayes, Lois McCauley, Ann Needham, Joli Roberts, Jere Stevens, Tao Strong, Helen Ahola. *Local Boys:* Santo Anselmo, Bob Gay, Ed Grace, Bill Nuss, Charles Post, Arthur Schoep.

The entire action takes place in the State of Washington between 1900 and 1910.

Act 1: The township of Angel's Roost on the edge of Mt. Olympus. *Scene 1:* In the Orchard. *Scene 2:* The Village Green. *Scene 3:* The Church Social. *Scene 4:* At Helen's House.

Act 2, Scene 1: The Seaport of Rhododendron. *Scene 2:* The Main Street of Rhododendron. *Scene 3:* Back in Angel's Roost. Penelope's Home. *Scene 4:* The Main Street again. *Scene 5:* The Big Spree. (a) Madam Calypso's Parlour. (b) The Brokerage Office of Scylla and Charybdis. (c) A waterfront dive. (d) The Hall of Science. (e) The Wrong Side of the Tracks. *Scene 6:* Angel's Roost. In the back yard.

ACT 1[14]

"Nothing Ever Happens in Angel's Roost"
K. Ballard, B. Osterwald, S. Bolin, P. Nelson

Mother Hare's Seance
(M. Larrimore)

"My Love Is On the Way"
P. Gillette

"The Heroes Come Home"
Entire Company

---

[13] First produced Off-Broadway 11 March-18 April 1954 at the Phoenix Theatre for 48 performances prior to its Broadway transfer. Off-Broadway performers who originated roles but did not play Broadway run: *Mrs. Juniper,* the Mayor's Wife: GERALDINE VITI. *Patroclus:* Larry Chelsi.
[14] Dropped from Off-Broadway for Broadway transfer:
"Wildflowers" (replaced by "When We Were Young")
P. Gillette
"We've Just Begun" (replaced by "The Tirade"/Finale)
S. Douglass, P. Gillette

"It Was a Glad Adventure"
S. Douglass, Heroes

"Come Along Boys"
The Heroes, Ensemble

"It's the Going Home Together"
S. Douglass, P. Gillette

Mother Hare's Prophecy
(M. Larrimore)

"Helen Is Always Willing"
The Heroes

The Church Social
The Heroes, Ensemble

"Introducin' Mr. Paris"
J. Lucas, Ensemble

The Judgement of Paris
B. Osterwald, S. Bolin, P. Nelson, M. Larrimore, J. Lucas

"Lazy Afternoon"
K. Ballard, J. Lucas

The Departure for Rhododendron
Entire Company

ACT 2

"My Picture in the Papers"
P. Gillette, J. Lucas, Male Ensemble

The Taking of Rhododendron
S. Douglass, J. Whiting, J. Lucas

Hector's Song
(J. Whiting)

"Windflowers"
P. Gillette

"Store-bought Suit"
S. Douglass

Calypso
C. Rae

Scylla and Charybdis
D. Michener, J. Whiting

"(By 'Goona-Goona' Lagoon)"
(B. Osterwald)

"Doomed, Doomed, Doomed"
P. Nelson

"Circe, Circe"
M. Larrimore, Ensemble
Danced by A. Needham.

The Sewing Bee
P. Gillette, K. Ballard, P. Nelson, S. Bolin,
B. Osterwald, M. Larrimore, S. Douglass, The Suitors

The Tirade
P. Gillette

Finale
Entire Company

1954.04 SHOWBOAT

A Revival of the Musical Play in Two Acts, 14 Scenes[15]. Music by Jerome Kern. Book and lyrics by Oscar Hammerstein II. Based on the novel of the same name by Edna Ferber. Staged by William Hammerstein. Settings by Howard Bay. Costumes by John Boyt. Lighting by Jean Rosenthal. Conductor, Julius Rudel. Orchestrations by Robert Russell Bennett. Produced by The New York City Opera Company. Opened 8 April 1954 at the New York City Center for 3 performances in repertory, closing 2 May 1954; re-opened under the auspices of the New York City Center Light Opera Company 5 May 1954 at the New York City Center and closed 16 May 1954 after 15 additional performances.[16]

---

[15]First presented in New York 27 December 1927 at the Ziegfeld Theatre for 572 performances. This revised version first presented 5 January 1946 at the Ziegfeld Theatre for 418 performances. For Synopsis of Scenes and Musical Numbers, see 1946 revival. Act 1, Scenes 2 and 3 combined from 1946 production. Act 2, Scene 8 reset in the Auditorium and Stage of the "Cotton Blossom."
[16]Dances uncredited.

CAST[17] (in order of their appearance): *Windy McLain*: Arthur Newman. *Steve*: ROBERT GALLAGHER. *Pete*: Boris Aplon. *Queenie*: HELEN PHILLIPS. *Parthy Ann Hawkes*: MARJORIE GATESON. *Captain Andy*: STANLEY CARLSON. *Ellie*: DIANA DRAKE. *Frank*: JACK ALBERTSON. *Rubberface*: Thomas R. Powell. *Julie*: HELENA BLISS. *Gaylord Ravenal*: ROBERT ROUNSEVILLE. *Vallon*: Lawrence Haynes. *Magnolia*: LAUREL HURLEY. *Joe*: WILLIAM C. SMITH. *Backwoodsman*: Arthur Newman. *Jeb*: Lawrence Haynes. *Barker*: Thomas R. Powell. *Fatima*: Ann Barry. *Second Barker*: Charles Kuestner. *Sport*: Roland Miles. *Strong Woman*: Meri Miller. *Landlady*: SARA FLOYD. *Ethel*: Gloria Wynder. *Jake*: Milton Lyon. *Jim*: Boris Aplon. *Man With Guitar*: Charles Kuestner. *Doorman at Trocadero*: Bill Smith. *Mother Superior*: Ellen Gleason. *Nun*: Barbara Ford. *Kim, as a child*: Adele Newton. *Drunk*: Charles Kuestner. *Lottie*: Marilyn Bladd. *Dolly*: Dorothy Mirr. *Sally*: Gloria Sacks. *Old Lady on Levee*: Sara Floyd. *Kim, in her Twenties*: Greta Thormsen.

Congress of Beauties: Joanne Budill, DeAnn Mears, Peg Shirley, Barbara Sohmers. *Children*: Ginger Brooks, Georgianna Catal, Claudia Crawford, Dale Dennard, Leonard Grinnage, Joan Nickel, Bonnie Sawyer. *Singing Ensemble*: Benjamin Bajorck, Marilyn Bladd, Adelaide Boatner Eugene S. Brice, Doryce Brown, Walter P. Brown, Joseph E. Crawford, Dawin Emanuel, Rina Falcone, John Fleming, Barbara Ford, Mareda Gaither, Ellen Gleason, Russell Goodwin, Louise Hawthorne, Ida Frances Johnson, Charles Kuestner, Sheila Mathews, James Martindale, William McDaniel, Roland Miles, Dorothy Mirr, John Neilsen, Benjamin Plotkin, Madeline Porter, William W. Reynolds, Gloria Sacks, Christine Spencer, William Starling, Joseph Tanner, Frederick L. Thomas, Greta Thormsen, DeLoyd Tibbs, Rodester Timmons, Clyde S. Turner, Rose Virga, Gloria Wynder.

1954.05 THE PAJAMA GAME

A Musical Comedy in Two Acts, 17 Scenes. Book by George Abbott and Richard Bisssell. Based on the novel "7 1/2 Cents" by Richard Bissell. Music and lyrics by Richard Adler and Jerry Ross. Scenery and costumes by Lemuel Ayers. Choreography by Bob Fosse. Musical director, Hal Hastings. Orchestrations by Don Walker. Dance music arrangements by Roger Adams. Production directed by George Abbott and Jerome Robbins. Produced by Frederick Brisson, Robert E. Griffith and Harold S. Prince. Opened 13 May 1954 at the St. James Theatre, moved 12 November 1956 to the Sam S. Shubert Theatre, and closed 24 November 1956 after 1063 performances.

CAST (in order of appearance): *Hines*: EDDIE FOY, JR. *Prez*: STANLEY PRAGER. *Joe*: Ralph Farnsworth. *Hasler*: RALPH DUNN. *Gladys*: CAROL HANEY. *Sid Sorokin*: JOHN RAITT. *Mabel*: RETA SHAW. *First Helper*: Jack Drummond. *Second Helper*: BUZZ MILLER. *Charlie*: Ralph Chambers. *Babe Williams*: JANIS PAIGE. *Mae*: THELMA PELISH. *Brenda*: MARION COLBY. *Poopsie*: Rae Allen. *Salesman*: JACK WALDRON. *Eddie*: Jim Hutchison. *Pop*: William David. *Worker*: PETER GENNARO.

Dancers: Carmen Alvarez, Marilyn Gennaro, Lida Koehring, Shirley MacLaine, Marsha Reynolds, Ann Wallace, Robert Evans, Eric Kristen, Jim Hutchison, Dale Moreda, Augustin Rodriguez, Ben Vargas. *Singers*: Rae Allen, Sara Dillon, Mara Landi, Virginia Martin, Mary Roche, Mary Stanton, Rudy Adamo, Bob Dixon, Jack Drummond, Ralph Farnsworth, John Ford, Gordon Woodburn.

The action takes place in Cedar Rapids, Iowa at the present time.

Act 1, Scene 1: Pajama Game curtain. *Scene 2*: The Sleep-Tite Pajama Factory Shop Floor. *Scene 3*: A Hallway in the Factory. *Scene 4*: The Factory Office. *Scene 5*: A wooded path on the way to the Union picnic. *Scene 6*: The Picnic Grounds. *Scene 7*: The wooded path at twilight. *Scene 8*: The Kitchen of Babe's House. *Scene 9*: The Factory. *Scene 10*: The Factory Shop.

Act 2, Scene 1: Eagle Hall. *Scene 2*: The Kitchen of Babe's House. *Scene 3*: A Hall in the Factory. *Scene 4*: Morning in the Office. *Scene 5*: Hernando's Hideaway. *Scene 6*: The Office. *Scene 7*: A Street near the Park.

ACT 1

Scene 1
"The Pajama Game"
E. Foy, Jr.

Scene 2
"Racing With the Clock"
Girls, Boys

"A New Town Is a Blue Town"
J. Raitt

Scene 3
"I'm Not at All in Love"
J. Paige, Girls

---

[17]Cast changes for the New York City Opera engagement: *Captain Andy*: BURL IVES. *Frank*: DONN [Donald] DRIVER. *Joe*: LAWRENCE WINTERS.

Scene 4

"I'll Never Be Jealous Again"
E. Foy, Jr., R. Shaw

"Hey There"
J. Raitt

Scene 5

"Her Is"
S. Prager, C. Haney

Scene 6

"Sleep-Tite"
J. Paige, Boys, Girls

"Once a Year Day"
J. Raitt, J. Paige, Company
Danced by C. Haney, B. Miller, P. Gennaro.

Scene 7

("Her Is" reprise)
(S. Prager, T. Pelish)

Scene 8

"Small Talk"
J. Raitt, J. Paige

Scene 9

"There Once Was a Man"
J. Raitt, J. Paige

Scene 10

"Hey There" (reprise)
J. Raitt

ACT 2

Scene 1

"Steam Heat"
C. Haney, B. Miller, P. Gennaro

Scene 2

"Hey There" (reprise)
J. Paige

Scene 3

"Think of the Time I Save"
E. Foy, Jr., Girls

Scene 4

"Hernando's Hideaway"
C. Haney, J. Raitt, Company

Scene 5

"Jealousy Ballet"
E. Foy, Jr., C. Haney, R. Shaw, Boys

Scene 7

"7 1/2 Cents"
J. Paige, S. Prager, Girls, Boys

("There Once Was a Man" reprise)
(J. Raitt, J. Paige)

"The Pajama Game" (Finale)
Entire Company

1954.06   # FLEDERMAUS

A Revival of the Comic Opera ("Die Fledermaus") in Three Acts.[18] (Original Viennese libretto by Carl Haffner and Richard Genée. (Based on "Le Réveillon" by Henri Meilhac and Ludovic Halévy.) Music by Johann Strauss. English libretto by Ruth and Thomas Martin. Staged by Glenn Jordan. Conductor, Thomas Martin. Choreography by Robert Pagent. Costumes by John Boyt. Lighting by Jean Rosenthal. Produced by the New York City Center Light Opera Company (William Hammerstein, Director.) Opened 19 May 1954 at the New York City Center and closed 6 June 1954 after 15 performances.[19]

CAST[20] (in order of appearance): *Alfredo,* an operatic tenor: LLOYD THOMAS LEECH, HAROLD R. BROWN. *Adele,* chambermaid: ADELAIDE BISHOP. *Rosalinda,* Eisenstein's wife: GLORIA LIND, GUEN OMERON. *Gabriel Von Eisenstein,* a banker: JACK RUSSELL, LLOYD THOMAS LEECH. *Blind,* Eisenstein's lawyer: CARL NICHOLAS. *Dr. Falke,* a friend of the Eisensteins': JOHN TYERS. *Frank,* prison warden: STANLEY CARLSON. *Sally,* Adele's sister, a ballet dancer: LIDIJA FRANKLIN. *Prince Orlofsky,* a very wealthy Russina Prince: DONALD GRAMM. *Ivan,* servant to Orlofsky: Thomas R. Powell. *Boris,* a dancer: ROBERT PAGENT. *Frosch,* a jailor: COLEY WORTH.

Servants: Stanley Bakis, Hill Eller, Alan James, Don Ratka, James Spicer, George Tucker. *Guests:* Marilyn Bladd, Rina Falcone, Barbara Ford, Ellen Gleason, Sheila Mathews, Dorothy Mirr, Gloria Sacks, Greta Thormsen, Rose Virga, Benjamin Bajorek, Dawin Emanuel, Russell Goodwin, Charles Kuestner, James Martindale, Roland Miles, Benjamin Plotkin, William W. Reynolds, Joseph Tanner.

The action takes place in the fashionable suburbs of Vienna in the 1850s.

Act 1: Rosalinda's Boudoir.

Act 2: At the Villa of Orlofsky.

Act 3: The Town Jail.

ACT 1

Introduction:

a. "Darling Rosalinda"
L. T. Leech

b. "We Are Going to a Party"
A. Bishop

"When These Lawyers Don't Deliver" (Trio)
G. Lind, J. Russell, C. Nicholas

"Come Along to the Ball" (Duet)
J. Tyers, J. Russell

"Oh Dear, It Breaks My Heart" (Trio)
G. Lind, A. Bishop, J. Russell

Finale
G. Lind, L. T. Leech, S. Carlson

ACT 2

"What a Joy to Be Here"
Ensemble

"Chacun à Son Goût"
D. Gramm

"My Friends, Your Kind Attention"
J. Tyers, D. Gramm

"Laughing Song"
A. Bishop, Ensemble

"How Engaging, How Exciting"
G. Lind, J. Russell

"Emperor Waltz" (Ballet)
R. Pagent, L. Franklin

"Voice of My Homeland" (Csardas)
G. Lind

Finale
Principals, Ensemble
a. "The King of Effervescence," b. "Sing to Love," c. "Ah, Happy Day."

ACT 3

"Pantomime"
S. Carlson, C. Worth

"Ever Since I Was a Baby" (Audition Song)
A. Bishop

"Vengeance Is Mine"
G. Lind, L. T. Leech, J. Russell

Finale
Entire Company

---

[18]First English language production in New York 16 March 1885 at the Casino Theatre for 42 performances. First New York production of this adaptation 20 December 1950 at the Metropolitan Opera House.
[19]Settings uncredited.

[20]Alternates sang roles Saturday and Sunday Matinees, Thursday and Saturday Evenings.

1954–1955 SEASON

Mary Martin in PETER PAN
Billy Rose Theatre Collection, New York Public Library for the Performing Arts

1954–1955 SEASON

1954.07 ## CAROUSEL

A Revival of the Musical Play in Two Acts, 9 Scenes[1]. Book and lyrics by Oscar Hammerstein II. Based on Ferenc Molnar's play "Liliom" as adapted by Benjamin F. Glazer. Music by Richard Rodgers. Staged by William Hammerstein. Dances by Agnes de Mille, restaged by Robert Pagent. Settings by Oliver Smith. Costumes by John Boyt. Lighting by Jean Rosenthal. Musical director, Julius Rudel. (Orchestrations by Don Walker.) Produced by the New York City Center Light Opera Company (William Hammerstein, Director). Opened 2 June 1954 at the New York City Center and closed 8 August 1954 after 79 performances.

CAST (in order of appearance): *Carrie Pipperidge*: BARBARA COOK. *Julie Jordan*: JO SULLIVAN. *Mrs. Mullin*: WINIFRED HEIDT. *Billy Bigelow*: CHRIS ROBINSON. *First Policeman*: Russell Goodwin. *David Bascombe*: Stanley Carlson. *Nettie Fowler*: JEAN HANDZLIK. *June Girl*: Mavis Ray. *Enoch Snow*: DON BLACKEY. *Jigger Craigin*: JOHN CONTE. *Hannah*: DUSTY WORRALL. *Boatswain*: ROBERT PAGENT. *Arminy*: Marilyn Bladd. *Second Policeman*: William W. Reynolds. *Captain*: Boris Aplon. *Heavenly Friend (Brother Joshua)*: Jay Velie. *Starkeeper*: Daniel Reed. *Louise*: BAMBI LINN. *Carnival Boy*: ROBERT PAGENT. *Enoch Snow, Jr.*: James Martindale. *Principal*: Russell Goodwin.

Townspeople: Marilyn Bladd, Lila Caputo, Rina Falcone, Barbara Ford, Ellen Gleason, Sheila Mathews, Dorothy Mirr, Gloria Sacks, Greta Thornsen, Benjamin Bajorek, Dawin Emanuel, Russell Goodwin, Charles Kuestner, James Martindale, Roland Miles, Benjamin Plotkin, William W. Reynolds, Joseph Tanner. *Dancers*: Ann Barry, Ann Dunbar, Ruby Herndon, Anne Meislik, Meri Miller, Eloise Milton, Mavis Ray, Nadine Revene, Francine Savery, Gini Turner, Rudy Jenkins, Don Little, Don Martin, Dick Rogers, Philip Salem, Mark Ward, Mark West. *Children of the Prelude*: Claudia Crawford, Adele Newton, Chris Snell.

1954.08 ## HAYRIDE

A Hillbilly Folk Musical (Revue) in Two Acts. (Based on the Old Dominion Barn Dance Show, presented and broadcast weekly from the WRVA Theatre, Richmond, Virginia.) Settings by Art Guild, Jack Woodson, Jack Durrenberger of Richmond, Virginia. Produced by Barron Howard and Jack Stone. Opened 13 September 1954 at the 48th Street Theatre and closed 2 October 1954 after 24 performances.[2]

CAST: SUNSHINE SUE (Femcee), COUSIN JOE MAPHIS (Comedian and Wizard of stringed instruments) & ROSE (Ballads of the prairie country), LESTER FLATT & EARL SCRUGGS (mountain music) FOGGY MOUNTAIN BOYS, Paul Warren, Jake Tulloch, Curly Sechler, The Coon Creek (Kentucky) Girls (songs of the old hill "splinter-kickin" dances and parties), Lilly May, Rosie, Black Eyed Susan, The Trail Blazers, Ray Smith, Roy Horton, Johnny Newton, Eddy (Texas) Smith, Quincy Snodgrass (comedian), Mary Klick (songs of the song and bayou regions), Zeb Robinson, Sonny Day (accordionist from Kentucky), Fiddlin' Irving, Zag the Ozark Mountain Boy (lonesome cabin songs of his native Ozark hills), Gene Jenkins (guitarist), Jody Carver.

Acts 1 and 2: The barn at "Medley Grove" Saturday night.

MUSICAL NUMBERS[3]
  "Old MacDonald Had a Farm"
  "The Blue Tail Fly"
  "Jumbalaya"
  Stephen Foster songs
  Hank Williams songs

  "Little Things Mean a Lot"
    Sunshine Sue
    (*Music and Lyrics by* Carl Stutz and Edith Lindeman.)
  "Vegetable Love"
    Zag the Ozark Mountain Boy

1954.09 ## THE BOY FRIEND

A Musical Comedy of the 1920's in Three Acts. Book, music and lyrics by Sandy Wilson. Directed by Vida Hope. Choreography by John Heawood. Settings and costumes by Reginald Woolley. Supervisor for scenery and lighting, (Abe) Feder. Supervisor for costumes, Robert Mackintosh. Orchestra, Paul McCrane and His Bearcats. Musical director, Anton Coppola. Orchestrations by Ted Royal and Charles L. Cooke. Production by Vida Hope. Produced by Cy Feuer and Ernest Martin. Opened 30 September 1954 at the Royale Theatre and closed 26 November 1955 after 483 performances.

CAST (in order of appearance): *Hortense*: Paulette Girard. *Nancy*: MILLICENT MARTIN. *Maisie*: ANN WAKEFIELD. *Fay*: Stella Claire. *Dulcie*: DILYS LAY. *Polly*: JULIE ANDREWS. *Marcel*: Joe Milan. *Alphonse*: Buddy Schwab. *Pierre*: Jerry Newby. *Madame Dubonnet*: RUTH ALTMAN. *Bobby Van Husen*: BOB SCHEERER. *Percival Browne*: ERIC BERRY. *Tony*: JOHN HEWER. *Phillipe*: Jimmy Alex. *Monica*: Berkley Marsh. *Lord Brockhurst*: GEOFFREY HIBBERT. *Lady Brockhurst*: Moyna MacGill. *Susanne*: Lyn Connorty. *Guests*: Phoebe MacKay, Marge Ellis, Mickey Calin. *Gendarme*: Douglas Deane. *Waiter*: Lyn Robert. *Pepe*: Joe Milan. *Lolita*: Stella Claire.

Act 1: The Drawing-room of the Villa Caprice, Madame Dubonnet's finishing school on the outskirts of Nice. 1926.

Act 2: The Plage. That afternoon.

Act 3: The Terrace of the Cafe Pataplon. That night.

ACT 1
  "Perfect Young Ladies"
    P. Girard, M. Martin, A. Wakefield, S. Claire, D. Lay
  "The Boy Friend"
    J. Andrews, A. Wakefield, D. Lay, S. Claire, M. Martin, J. Milan, J. Newby, B. Schwab
  "Won't You Charleston With Me?"
    A. Wakefield, B. Scheerer
  "Fancy Forgetting"
    R. Altman, E. Berry
  "I Could Be Happy With You"
    J. Andrews, J. Hewer
  Finale (Act 1), "The Boy Friend" (reprise)
    (Ensemble)
ACT 2
  "Sur la Plage" (On the Beach)
    A. Wakfield, B. Scheerer, S. Claire, J. Milan, D. Lay, B. Schwab, M. Martin, J. Newby, B. Marsh, J. Alex
  "A Room in Bloomsbury"
    J. Andrews, J. Hewer
  "You Don't Want to Play With Me Blues"
    R. Altman, E. Berry, S. Claire, D. Lay, M. Martin, B. Marsh
  "Safety in Numbers"
    A. Wakefield, B. Scheerer, J. Milan, J. Newby, B. Schwab
  Finale (Act 2)
    Entire Company
ACT 3
  "(The) Riviera"
    A. Wakefield, B. Scheerer, S. Claire, J. Milan, D. Lay, B. Schwab, M. Martin, J. Newby, B. Marsh, J. Alex
  "It's Never Too Late to Fall in Love"
    G. Hibbert, D. Lay
  "Carnival Tango"
    Danced by J. Milan, S. Claire
  "Poor Little Pierrette"
    R. Altman, J. Andrews
  Finale (Act 3)
    Entire Company

---

[1]First produced in New York 19 April 1945 at the Majestic Theatre for 890 performances. For Synopsis of Scenes and Musical Numbers, see original 1945 production. For this production, the Prologue became Act 1, Scene 1 (Prelude)

[2]Direction, costumes uncredited.

[3]Neither the program nor extant press materials offer a complete list of songs. The artists listed above performed their specialties, which included those listed.

1954.10

DIE FLEDERMAUS

A Revival of the Operetta in Three Acts[4]. (Original Viennese libretto by Carl Haffner and Richard Genée. Lyrics by Richard Genée. Based on the comedy "Le Réveillon" by Henri Meilhac and Ludovic Halévy). English libretto by Ruth and Thomas Martin. Music by Johann Strauss. Staged by William Westerfield. Costume supervisor, Robert Fletcher. Choreographer, Sophie Maslow. Conductor, Thomas P. Martin. Produced by the New York City Opera. Opened 3 October 1954 at the New York City Center and closed 16 October 1954 after 2 performances in repertory; re-opened 19 March 1955 at the New York City Center and closed 9 April 1955 after 2 additional performances. Total this season: 4 performances.[5]

CAST: *Eisenstein:* ERNEST McCHESNEY. *Rosalinda:* SUSAN JAGER. *Adele:* LAUREL HURLEY. *Alfred:* LLOYD THOMAS LEECH. *Falke:* WILLIAM WILDERMAN. *Frank:* Richard Wentworth. *Blind:* Luigi Vellucci. *Prince Orlofsky:* DONALD GRAMM. *Sally:* Peggy Bonini. *Frosch:* Coley Worth. *Ivan:* Thomas Powell. *Solo Dancers:* Ethel Winter, Donald MacKayle, Alvin Schulman. *Ensemble:* New York City Opera Chorus.

1954.11

BLUES, BALLADS AND SIN SONGS

A One Woman Musical Revue in Two Acts, 4 Scenes. (Concept inspired by Carl Sandburg.) Pianist, Gerald Cook. Musical settings, Gerald Cook. Miss Holman's gowns by Mainbocher (Act 1) and Frank Stanley (Act 2). Opened 4 October 1954 at the Bijou Theatre and closed 16 October 1954 after 12 performances.[6]

CAST: LIBBY HOLMAN.

ACT 1

Scene 1

"Good Morning Blues"
　(Gerald Cook)
"Smokey"
"Go 'Way From My Window"
　(Gerald Cook)
"In the Evening" (Traditional, arr. Gerald Cook)
"Barbara Allen" (Traditional)
"Rolly Trudum"

Scene 2

"Yandro"
"Cindy"
"Baby, Baby"
"Fare Thee Well" (Traditional, arr. Gerald Cook)

ACT 2

Scene 1

"Careless Love"
　(*Music and Lyrics by* W. C. Handy and Spencer Williams.)
"Riddle Song"
"Four Marys"
"The Loathly Bride"
"Johnny Has Gone"

Scene 2

"The Blues"
　(*Music by* Duke Ellington.)

"You Can't Go to Heaven"

"Number 12 Train"

"Evil Hearted Me" (Traditional, arr. by Gerald Cook)

"House of the Rising Sun" (Traditional, arr. by Gerald Cook)

Encores:

"Moanin' Low" (from THE LITTLE SHOW)
　(*Music by* Ralph Rainger. *Lyrics by* Howard Dietz.)
"Body and Soul" (from THREE'S A CROWD)
　(*Music by* Johnny Green. *Lyrics by* Edward Heyman, Robert Sour, Frank Eyton.)
"Something to Remember You By" (from THREE'S A CROWD)
　(*Music by* Arthur Schwartz. *Lyrics by* Howard Dietz.)

1954.12

ON YOUR TOES

A Revival of the Musical Comedy in Two Acts, 13 Scenes[7]. Book by Richard Rodgers, Lorenz Hart and George Abbott. Lyrics by Lorenz Hart. Music by Richard Rodgers. Directed by George Abbott. Dances staged by George Balanchine. Settings by Oliver Smith. Costumes by Irene Sharaff. Musical director, Salvatore Dell'Isola. Orchestrations by Don Walker. Produced by George Abbott. Opened 11 October 1954 at the 46th Street Theatre and closed 4 December 1954 after 64 performances.

CAST (in order of appearance): *Phil Dolan II:* Jack Williams. *Lil Dolan:* Eleanor Williams. *Phil Dolan III:* David Winters. *Stage Manager:* George Church. *Lola:* Dorene Kilmer. *Phil Dolan III, Junior:* BOBBY VAN. *Frankie Frayne:* KAY COULTER. *Sidney Cohn:* Joshua Shelley. *Vera Barnova:* VERA ZORINA. *Anushka:* Patricia Wilkes. *Peggy Porterfield:* ELAINE STRITCH. *Sergei Alexandrovitch:* Ben Astar. *Konstantine Morrosine:* Nicolas Orloff. *Snoopy:* John Robb. *Thug:* Nathaniel Frey. *Mischka:* Patrick Welch. *Ivan:* John Nola. *Vassilli:* Edward Pfeiffer. *Dimitri:* Ted Adkins. *Leo:* Robert Lindgren. *Ballet Stage Manager:* Bertram Wood. *Cop:* Arthur Grahl. *On Your Toes Jitterbug Couple:* Dorene Kilmer, Timmy Everett. *Adagio Couple:* Katia Geleznova, Edward Pfeiffer.

　Chorus: Girls: Phyllis Campbell, Lillian D'Honau, Patricia Drylie, Katia Geneznova, Carolyn George, Marilyn Hale, Dorene Kilmer, Helen Kramer, Sonja Lindgren (Tyven), Paula Lloyd, Sigyn, Barbara Michaels, Lois Platt, Nina Popova, Ruth Sobotka, Mary Stanton, Carol Stevens, Wendy Winn. *Boys:* Ted Adkins, Marvin Arnold, Johnny Bowen, Timmy Everett, Arthur Grahl, Edward Kerrigan, Jack Leigh, Robert Lindgren, John Nola, Edward Pfeiffer.

1954.13

PETER PAN

A Musical in Three Acts, 9 Scenes. Book (adapted from the play) by James M. Barrie[8]. Music by Mark Charlap. Lyrics by Carolyn Leigh. Additional music by Jule Styne; additional lyrics by Betty Comden and Adolph Green. Scenery by Peter Larkin. Costumes by Motley. Lighting by Peggy Clark. Technical direction, Richard Rodda. Music conductor, Louis Adrian. Orchestral arrangements by Albert Sendrey. Incidental music by Trude Rittman and Elmer Bernstein. Assistant to the director, Mary Hunter. Directed and staged by Jerome Robbins. Produced by Richard Halliday. Opened 20 October 1954 at the Winter Garden and closed 26 February 1955 after 152 performances.

CAST (in order of appearance): *Wendy:* KATHY NOLAN. *John:* ROBERT HARRINGTON. *Liza:* HELLER HALLIDAY. *Michael:* Joseph Stafford. *Nana:* Norman Shelly. *Mrs. Darling:* MARGALO GILLMORE. *Mr. Darling:* CYRIL RITCHARD. *Peter Pan:* MARY MARTIN. *Lion:* Richard Wyatt. *Kangaroo:* Don Lurio. *Ostrich:* Joan Tewksbury. *Slightly:* David Bean. *Tootles:* Ian Tucker. *Curly:* Stanley Stenner. *Nibs:* Paris Theodore. *Crocodile:* Norman Shelly. *First Twin:* Alan Sutherland. *Second Twin:* Darryl Duran. *Captain Hook:* CYRIL RITCHARD. *Smee:* JOE E. MARKS. *Tiger Lily:* SONDRA LEE. *Cecco:* Robert Tucker. *Noodler:* Frank Lindsay.

---

[4]First English language production in New York 16 March 1885 at the Casino Theatre for 42 performances. First New York production of this adaptation 20 December 1950 at the Metropolitan Opera House. For Synopsis of Scenes and Musical Numbers, see May 1954 revival.
[5]Settings uncredited. Settings and costumes were assembled from various sources, a previous Sol Hurok tour of DIE FLEDERMAUS and the Broadway production of MY DARLIN' AIDA.
[6]Producer uncredited.

[7]Originally produced in New York 11 April 1936 at the Imperial Theatre for 315 performances. For Synopsis of Scenes and Musical numbers, see original 1936 production. Same as original production except:

　"Two-a-Day for Keith" (Act 1, Scenes 1 and 2 dropped after opening)

　"You Took Advantage of Me" (from PRESENT ARMS, added to Act 2, Scene 3)

　　E. Stritch
[8]Adaptation uncredited.

Starkey: Robert Vanselow. *Mullins*: James White. *Jukes*: Frank Bouley. *Wendy Grown-Up*: Sallie Brophy. *Jane*: KATHY NOLAN. *Tinker Bell's Voice*: Jaye Rubanoff.

Pirates: Robert Tucker, Frank Lindsay, Frank Marasco, James Whyte, William Burke, Chester Fisher, John Newton, Arthur Tookoian, Robert Vanselow, Richard Winter. *Indians*: Robert Banas, Don Lurio, Robert Piper, William Sumner, Richard Wyatt, Linda Dangcil, Lisa Lang, Suzanne Luckey, Joan Tewkesbury.

Act 1, Scene 1: The Nursery of the Darling Residence. *Scene 2*: Flight to Neverland.

Act 2, Scene 1: Neverland. *Scene 2*: Path through the Woods. *Scene 3*: Neverland Home Underground.

Act 3, Scene 1: The Pirate Ship. *Scene 2*: Path through the Woods. *Scene 3*: The Nursery of the Darling Residence. *Scene 4*: The Nursery many years later.

ACT 1

Scene 1

"Tender Shepherd"
   M. Gillmore, K. Nolan, R. Harrington, J. Stafford
"I've Got to Crow"
   M. Martin
"Neverland"
   M. Martin
   (*Music by* Jule Styne. *Lyrics by* Betty Comden and Adolph Green.)
"I'm Flying"
   M. Martin, K. Nolan, R. Harrington, J. Stafford

ACT 2

Scene 1

"Pirate Song"
   C. Ritchard, Pirates
"A Princely Scheme"
   C. Ritchard, Pirates
"Indians!"
   S. Lee, Indians
"Wendy"
   M. Martin, Boys
   (*Music by* Jule Styne. *Lyrics by* Betty Comden and Adolph Green.)
"Another Princely Scheme" (Tarantella)
   C. Ritchard, Pirates
"Neverland Waltz"
   H. Halliday
   (*Music by* Jule Styne. *Lyrics by* Betty Comden and Adolph Green.)

Scene 2

"I Won't Grow Up"
   M. Martin, Boys
"Mysterious Lady"
   M. Martin, C. Ritchard
   (*Music by* Jule Styne. *Lyrics by* Betty Comden and Adolph Green.)

Scene 3

"Ugg-aWugg"/"The Pow Wow Polka"
   M. Martin, S. Lee, Children, Indians
   (*Music by* Jule Styne. *Lyrics by* Betty Comden and Adolph Green.)
"Distant Melody"
   M. Martin
   (*Music by* Jule Styne. *Lyrics by* Betty Comden and Adolph Green.)

ACT 3

Scene 1

"To the Ship"
   M. Martin, Company
"(Captain) Hook's Waltz"
   C. Ritchard, Pirates
   (*Music by* Jule Styne. *Lyrics by* Betty Comden and Adolph Green.)
"The Battle"
   M. Martin, C. Ritchard, Company

Scene 2

"I've Got to Crow" (reprise)
   M. Martin, H. Halliday, Company

Scene 3

"Tender Shepherd" (reprise)
   K. Nolan, R. Harrington, J. Stafford
"I Won't Grow Up" (reprise)
   The Darling Family, Lost Boys

Scene 4

"Neverland" (reprise)
   M. Martin

1954.14   SHOWBOAT

A Return Engagement of the Musical Play in Two Acts, 14 Scenes[9]. Music by Jerome Kern. Book and lyrics by Oscar Hammerstein II. Based on the novel of the same name by Edna Ferber. Staged by William Hammerstein. Settings by Howard Bay. Costumes by John Boyt. Lighting by Jean Rosenthal. Conductor, Julius Rudel. Orchestrations by Robert Russell Bennett. Produced by The New York City Opera Company. Opened 28 October 1954 at the New York City Center and closed 31 October 1954 after 2 performances.[10]

<u>CAST</u>: *Captain Andy*: RICHARD WENTWORTH. *Parthy Ann Hawkes*: JEAN HANDZLIK. *Magnolia*: LAUREL HURLEY. *Gaylord Ravenal*: ROBERT ROUNSEVILLE. *Julie*: HELENA BLISS. *Steve*: ROBERT GALLAGHER. *Queenie*: BETTY ALLEN. *Joe*: LAWRENCE WINTERS. *Frank*: JACK BLAIR. *Ellie*: MARIAN NILES. *Jim*: Michael Pollock. *Windy McLain*: Arthur Newman. *Man With Guitar*: Charles Kuestner. *Piano player*: Milton Lyon. *Landlady*: SARA FLOYD. *Pete*: Michael Pollock. *Sheriff Vallon*: Roy Urhausen. *Doorman at Trocadero*: Walter Brown. *Old Lady on Levee*: Sara Floyd. *Ethel*: Gloria Wynder. *Kim, as a child*: Adele Newton. *Backwoodsmen*: Roy Urhausen, Arthur Newman. *Ensemble*: New York City Opera Chorus.

1954.15   FANNY

A Musical Play in Two Acts, 16 Scenes. Book by S. N. Behrman and Joshua Logan. Based on the trilogy of plays "Marius-César-Fanny" by Marcel Pagnol. Music and lyrics by Harold Rome. Directed by Joshua Logan. Scenery and lighting by Jo Mielziner. Costumes by Alvin Colt. Dances by Helen Tamiris. Musical direction and vocal arrangements by Lehman Engel. Orchestral arrangements by Philip J. Lang. Musical continuity by Trude Rittman. Produced by David Merrick and Joshua Logan. Opened 4 November 1954 at the Majestic Theatre, moved 4 December 1956 to the Belasco Theatre, and closed 16 December 1956 after 888 performances.

<u>CAST</u> (in order of appearance): *Arab Rug Seller*: Mohammed el Bakkar. *Marius, son of Cesar*: WILLIAM TABBERT. *Fanny, daughter of Honorine*: FLORENCE HENDERSON. *Maori Vendor*: Katherine Graves. *Lace Vendor*: Betty Carr. *Customers*: Toni Wheelis, Lindsay Kirkpatrick, Dolores Smith, Margaret Baxter. *Twin Sisters, friends of Fanny: Claudine*: Tani Seitz. *Claudette*: Dran Seitz. *Charles*: Wally Strauss. *His Friends*: Bill Pope, Dean Crane, Ronald Cecill, Michael de Marco. *Friends of Fanny (4): Nanette*: Norma Doggett. *Mimi*: Carolyn Maye. *Marie*: Ellen Matthews. *Michellette*: Jane House. *Panisse, wealthy sailmaker*: WALTER SLEZAK. *Sailor*: Herb Banke. *The Admiral, an eccentric waterfront character*: GERALD PRICE. *Moroccan Drummer*: Charles Blackwell. *Second Mate*: Henry Michel. *Fisherman*: Steve Wiland. *Sailmaker*: Jack Washburn. *Fish-Stall Woman*: Florence Dunlap. *An Arab*: Michael Scrittorale. *Cesar, proprietor of cafe on waterfront*: EZIO PINZA. *Honorine, Fanny's*

---

[9]First presented in New York 27 December 1927 at the Ziegfeld Theatre for 572 performances. This revised version first presented 5 January 1946 at the Ziegfeld Theatre for 418 performances; this production presented by the New York City Opera 8 April 1954 at the New York City Center for 3 performances in repertory; re-opened under the auspices of the New York City Center Light Opera Company 5 May 1954 at the New York City Center for 15 additional performances. For Synopsis of Scenes and Musical Numbers, see 1946 revival. Act 1, Scenes 2 and 3 combined from 1946 production. Act 2, Scene 8 reset in the Auditorium and Stage of the "Cotton Blossom."
[10]Dances uncredited.

mother, a fish-stall keeper: EDNA PRESTON. *Escartifique*, a ferryboat captain: ALAN CARNEY. *M. Brun*, customs inspector recently returned from Paris: DON McHENRY. *Arab Dancing Girl*: NEJLA ATES. *Nun*: Ruth Schumacher. *Cesario*: Lloyd Reese. *Butler*: Mike Mason. *Maid*: Pat Finch. *Garage Owner*: Tom Gleason. *Priest*: Ray Dorian. *Acolytes*: Gary Wright, Daniel Labeille.

The action takes place in and around the Old Port of Marseilles over a period of year, not so long ago.

Act 1, Scene 1: The Waterfront of Marseilles. *Scene 2*: Hakim's Cellar. *Scene 3*: César's Bar. *Scene 4*: The Dock. *Scene 5*: César's Bar. *Scene 6*: Honorine's Kiosk. *Scene 7*: Panisse's Sail Shop. *Scene 8*: The Wedding. *Scene 9*: The Waterfront of Marseilles.

Act 2, Scene 1: The Nursery. *Scene 2*: Panisse's Living Room. *Scene 3*: Vignettes, 1, 2, 3. *Scene 4*: Cesario's Room. *Scene 5*: The Circus. *Scene 6*: A Garage in Toulon. *Scene 7*: Panisse's Bedroom.

ACT 1[11]

Scene 1

"Never Too Late For Love"
W. Slezak, Ensemble
"Cold-Cream Jar Song"
W. Slezak
"Octopus Song"
G. Price
"Restless Heart"
W. Tabbert, Male Ensemble
"Why Be Afraid to Dance?"
E. Pinza
Danced by E. Pinza, W. Tabbert, F. Henderson, Ensemble.
"Never Too Late For Love" (reprise)
E. Pinza, W. Slezak, E. Preston

Scene 2

"Shika, Shika"
N. Ates, M. el Bakkar, Ensemble

Scene 3

"Welcome Home"
E. Pinza
"I Like You"
W. Tabbert, E. Pinza
"I Have To Tell You"
F. Henderson
"Fanny"
W. Tabbert

Scene 4

Montage: The Lovers; The Sailing
F. Henderson, W. Tabbert, E. Pinza, Ensemble

Scene 6

"Oysters, Cockles and Mussels"
Ensemble

Scene 7

"Panisse and Son"
W. Slezak

Scene 8

Wedding Dance
Danced by C. Blackwell, Ensemble

Scene 9

Finale Act 1
Ensemble

---

[11]After the opening the order of songs in Act 1 was revised, and the following song was added before "Why Be Afraid to Dance?":
"Does He Know?"
F. Henderson, W. Tabbert
For the West Coast tour, the following song was added:
"Every Night" (early in Act 1)
Doretta Morrow (Fanny)

ACT 2

Scene 1

"Birthday Song"
F. Henderson, E. Preston, Ensemble

Scene 2

"To My Wife"
W. Slezak
"The Thought of You"
W. Tabbert, F. Henderson
"Love Is a Very Light Thing"
E. Pinza
"Other Hands, Other Hearts"
F. Henderson, E. Pinza, W. Tabbert
"Fanny" (reprise)
E. Pinza, F. Henderson, W. Tabbert

Scene 3

Montage
Ensemble

Scene 4

"Be Kind to Your Parents"
F. Henderson, L. Reese

Scene 5

"Cesario's Party" (Cirque Français)
Acrobats: C. Blackwell, M. de Marco, R. Dorian, B. Pope, T. Wheelis. *Pony and Trainer*: W. Strauss, S. Wiland. *Trained Seals*: D. Seitz, T. Seitz. *Living Statues*: B. Carr, R. Cecill, N. Doggett, R. Dorian, E. Matthews, D. Smith. *Clowns*: H. Banke, M. Mason, H. Michel, J. Washburn. *Finale*: Aerialist, D. Crane, Ensemble.

Scene 7

"Welcome Home" (reprise)
E. Pinza, W. Slezak

MRS. PATTERSON

1954.16

A Play with Music in Three Acts. Play by Charles Sebree and Greer Johnson. Songs and incidental music by James Shelton. Settings and costumes by Raoul Pene du Bois. Orchestrations by George Siravo. Musical director, Abba Bogin. Directed by Guthrie McClintic. Produced by Leonard Sillman. Opened 1 December 1954 at the National Theatre and closed 26 February 1955 after 102 performances.

<u>CAST</u> (in order of appearance): *Anna Hicks*: RUTH ATTAWAY. *Selma Mae*: VINIE BURROWS. *Theodora Hicks*, Teddy: EARTHA KITT. *Willie B. Brayboy*: TERRY CARTER. *Aunt Matt Crossy*: Estelle Hemsley. *Mr. D*: AVON LONG. *Bessie Bolt*: HELEN DOWDY. *Sylvanus*: Emory Richardson. *Mrs. Patterson*: ENID MARKEY. *June Embree*: Mary Ann Hoxworth. *Rose Embree*: Mary Harmon. *Fern Embree*: Joan Morgan.

The play takes place in late summer, 1920, at the edge of a small town in Kentucky.

Act 1: Early evening.

Act 2: The following day.

Act 3: The next evening.

MUSICAL NUMBERS

"Mrs. Patterson"
E. Kitt
"If I Was a Boy"
E. Kitt
"I Wish I Was a Boy"
H. Dowdy
(*Lyrics by* Charles Sebree and Greer Johnson.)
"Be Good, Be Good, Be Good" (The Devil Song)
E. Kitt
"Tea in Chicago"
E. Kitt
"My Daddy Is a Dandy"
E. Kitt
Finale
E. Kitt, R. Attaway

1954.17 HIT THE TRAIL

A Musical in Two Acts, 13 Scenes. Book by Frank O'Neill. Music by Frederico Valerio. Lyrics by Elizabeth Miele. Directed by Charles W. Christenberry, Jr. and Byrle Cass. Dances and musical numbers staged by Gene Bayliss. Settings and lighting by Leo Kerz. Costumes by Michi. Orchestrations by Don Walker. Musical director and vocal arranger, Arthur Norris. Produced by Elizabeth Miele. Opened 2 December 1954 at the Mark Hellinger Theatre and closed 4 December 1954 after 4 performances.

CAST: *Jerry:* DONN [Donald] DRIVER. *Joan:* DIANA DRAKE. *Willie:* Fred Lightner. *Clayton Harrison:* PAUL VALENTINE. *Lucy Vernay:* IRRA PETINA. *Murph:* ROBERT WRIGHT. *Aggie July:* TOBY DEANE. *Miller:* Charles G. Martin. *Waiters:* Jack Purcell, Rene Miville.

Dancers: Jeanna Belkin, Lois Bewley, Sandy Bozoki, Diane Consoer, Patty Fitzsimmons, Nancy Hackenberg, Robert Bakanic, Paul Gannon, Jack Purcell, Alton Ruff, Buff Shurr, Fred Zoeter. Singers: Josephine Annunciata, Irene Carroll, Peggy Kinard, Dolores Micheline, Michelle Reiner, Martha Rich, Iris Sinding, Flavine Valentine, Lois Van Pelt, Paul Brown, Michael King, Rene Miville, Robert Price, James Schlader.

The action takes place in Virginia City, Nevada, during the late 19th century.

Act 1, Scene 1: Outside Virginia City. *Scene 2:* Lucy Vernay's Dressing Room. *Scene 3:* The Blue Sierra Casino. *Scene 4:* A Street in Virginia City. *Scene 5:* Stage of Piper's Opera House. *Scene 6:* A Park in Virginia City. *Scene 7:* The Blue Sierra Casino.

Act 2, Scene 1: Emporium. *Scene 2:* Gambling Room. *Scene 3:* A Street in Virginia City. *Scene 4:* The Blue Sierra Casino. *Scene 5:* A Street in Virginia City. *Scene 6:* Garden behind Murph's House.

ACT 1
Scene 1
 "On With the Show"
  D. Driver, D. Drake, Troupers
Scene 2
 "Mr. Right"
  I. Petina
 "Dynamic"
  I. Petina, R. Wright
Scene 3
 "Blue Sierras"
  T. Deane, Patrons
 "No! No! No!"
  P. Valentine
 "The Wide Open Spaces"
  P. Valentine, T. Deane, D. Drake, D. Driver
Scene 4
 "Gold Cannot Buy"
  Townspeople
 "Remember the Night"
  P. Valentine, I. Petina
 "Tell Me How"
  R. Wright
Scene 5
 "It Was Destiny"
  T. Deane, Girls
Scene 6
 "Just a Wonderful Time"
  D. Driver, D. Drake
Scene 7
 "Nevada Hoe Down"
  T. Deane, Patrons

ACT 2
Scene 1
 "New Look Feeling"
  I. Petina, D. Driver, D. Drake, Patrons
  (*Staged by* Donn Driver.)
 "Set Me Free"
  I. Petina
 "Somehow I've Always Known"
  R. Wright

Scene 2
 "Remember the Night" (reprise)
  P. Valentine
Scene 3
 "My Fatal Charm"
  P. Valentine
 "Men Are a Pain in the Neck"
  T. Deane
Scene 4
 "Wherever I May Go"
  I. Petina
Scene 5
 "Take Your Time"
  D. Driver, D. Drake
Scene 6
 "Happy Birthday"
  Company
 "Mr. Right" (reprise)
  I. Petina, R. Wright

1954.18 THE SAINT OF BLEECKER STREET

A Musical Drama (Opera) in Three Acts, 5 Scenes. Music and libretto by Gian-Carlo Menotti. Conducted by Thomas Schippers. Staged by Gian-Carlo Menotti. Scenery and costumes by Robert Randolph. Lighting by Jean Rosenthal. Associate musical director, Samuel Krachmalnick. Assistant director, Bill Butler. Production supervisor, Lincoln Kirstein. Produced by Chandler Cowles. Opened 27 December 1954 at the Broadway Theatre and closed 2 April 1955 after 92 performances[12].

CAST (in order of appearance): *Assunta:* Catherine Akos. *Carmela:* Maria Di Gerlando. *Maria Corona:* Maria Marlo. *Her Dumb Son:* Ernesto Gonzales. *Don Marco:* Leon Lishner. *Annina:* VIRGINIA COPELAND or GABRIELLE RUGGIERO. *Michele:* DAVID POLERI or DAVIS CUNNINGHAM. *Desideria:* GLORIA LANE. *Salvatore:* David Aiken. *Concettina:* Lucy Becque. *A Young Man:* Richard Cassilly. *An Old Woman:* Elizabeth Carron. *Bartender:* Russell Goodwin. *First Guest:* Keith Kaldenberg. *Second Guest:* John Reardon. *A Nun:* Dorothy Krebill. *A Young Priest:* Robert Barry.

Neighbors, Friends, Policemen, etc.: Theodora Brandon, Betsy Bridge, Lorraine Bridges, Elizabeth Carron, Doris Davis, Mignon Dunn, Elizabeth Dunning, Joyce Duskin, Elaine Galante, Jeanne Grant, Mary Hensley, Carol Jones, Dorothy Krebill, Leslie MacLennan, Bessie Mijanovich, Doris Okerson, Francesca Roberto, Donna Sanders, Robert Barry, Michael Bulzomi, Richard Cassilly, Rico Froelich, Russell Goodwin, Gary Gordon, Don Grobe, Fred Jones, Keith Kaldenberg, Chester Ludgin, William MacCully, Michael MacLennan, Dan Merriman, John Reardon, Reid Shelton, Alan Smith, Roberts Watts.

Act 1, Scene 1: A cold water flat on Bleecker Street, (New York City). Good Friday afternoon. The present. *Scene 2:* A vacant lot on Mulberry Street. San Gennaro Day.

Act 2: An Italian restaurant, the following May.

Act 3, Scene 1: A subway station, a few months later. *Scene 2:* The cold water flat, several days later.

1954.19 HOUSE OF FLOWERS

A Musical in Two Acts, 13 Scenes. Book by Truman Capote, based on his novela of the same name. Music by Harold Arlen. Lyrics by Truman Capote and Harold Arlen. Directed by Peter Brook. Dances and musical numbers by Herbert Ross. Sets and costumes by Oliver Messel. Lighting by Jean Rosenthal. Musical director, Jerry Arlen. Orchestrations by Ted Royal. Produced by (Arnold) Saint Subber. Opened 30 December 1954 at the Alvin Theatre and closed 21 May 1955 after 165 performances.

CAST (in order of appearance): *Tulip:* DOLORES HARPER. *Gladiola:* ADA MOORE. *Pansy:* ENID MOSIER. *Do:* Winston George Henriques. *Don't:* Solomon Earl Green. *Mother:* Miriam Burton. *Ottilie, alias Violet:* DIAHANN CARROLL. *Madame Fleur:* PEARL BAILEY. *Captain Jonas:* RAY WALSTON. *Madame Tango:*

---
[12]No individual musical numbers listed.

JUANITA HALL. *Mamselle Ibo-Lele*: Pearl Reynolds. *The Sisters Meringue*: Leu Comacho, Margot Small. *Mamselle Honolulu*: Mary Mon Toy. *Mamselle Cigarette*: Glory Van Scott. *Royal*: RAWN SPEARMAN. *The Champion*: GEOFFREY HOLDER. *Chief of Police*: Don Redman. *Carmen*: Carmen De Lavallade. *Alvin*: Alvin Ailey. *Monsieur Jamison*: Dino DiLuca. *The Houngan*: FREDERICK O'NEAL. *Baron of the Cemetary*: GEOFFREY HOLDER. *Duchess of the Sea*: Miriam Burton. *Steel Band*: Michel Alexander, Roderick Clavery, Alphonso Marshall.

Townspeople: Joseph Comadore, Hubert Dilworth, Phillip Hepburn, Louis Johnson, Mary Louise, Audrey Mason, Arthur Mitchell, Walter Nicks, Albert Popwell, Sabu, Herbert Stubbs.

The action takes place on an island in the West Indies during Mardi Gras weekend.

Act 1, Scene 1: Maison Des Fleurs. *Scene 2*: On the way to the Cockfight. *Scene 3*: At the Cockfight. *Scene 4*: Maison Des Fleurs. *Scene 5*: The Houngan's Hut. *Scene 6*: The harbor of the town.

Act 2, Scene 1: Maison Des Fleurs. *Scene 2*: Madame Fleur's Salon. *Scene 3*: The Houngan's Hut. *Scene 4*: Madame Tango's Salon. *Scene 5*: Madame Fleur's Salon. *Scene 6*: Maison Des Fleurs. *(Scene 7: Finale.)*

ACT 1

Scene 1

"Waitin'"
E. Mosier, D. Harper, A. Moore

"One Man Ain't Quite Enough"
P. Bailey

"Madame Tango's Tango"
J. Hall, Tango Belles

"A Sleepin' Bee"
D. Carroll, E. Mosier, D. Harper, A. Moore

Scene 2

"Bamboo Cage"
G. Holder, The Steel Band, W. G. Henriques, S. E. Green, E. Mosier, D. Harper, A. Moore, J. Hall, D. Redman, Ensemble

Scene 3

"House of Flowers"
R. Spearman, D. Carroll

Scene 4

"Two Ladies in de Shade of de Banana Tree"
E. Mosier, A. Moore
Danced by C. de Lavallade, D. Harper.

"What Is a Friend For?"
P. Bailey

Scene 5

"A Sleepin' Bee" (reprise)
D. Carroll, R. Spearman

Scene 6

"Mardi Gras"
M. Burton
Danced by C. de Lavallade, A. Ailey, Ensemble.

"I Never has Seen Snow"
D. Carroll

ACT 2[13]

Scene 1

"Husband Cage"
E. Mosier, D. Harper, A. Moore, Ensemble

Scene 2

"Has I Let You Down?"
P. Bailey, E. Mosier, D. Harper, A. Moore

Scene 3

Voudou
F. O'Neal, Ensemble
The Drummers: Sabu, J. Comadore, M. Alexander, A. Marshall. *Duchess of the Sea*: M. Burton. *Octopus*: A. Popwell. *Shark*: W. Nicks, A. Mitchell, A. Marshall. *Turtle*: J. Comadore, Ensemble. *Baron of the Cemetary*: G. Holder. (Banda Dance choreographed by Geoffrey Holder.)

---

[13]Added after opening to Act 2, Scene 1 after "Husband Cage:"
"I'm Gonna Leave Off Wearing My Shoes"
D. Carroll, Ensemble

Scene 4

"Slide, Boy, Slide"
J. Hall, Ensemble
Danced by A. Ailey, Ensemble.

Scene 5

"Don't Like Goodbyes"
P. Bailey

Scene 6

"Turtle Song"
R. Spearman, D. Carroll, Ensemble

Scene 7

Finale: "Bamboo Cage"/"Banana Tree"
Entire Company

1955.01 # PLAIN AND FANCY

A Musical Comedy in Two Acts, 17 Scenes. Book by Joseph Stein and Will Glickman. Music by Albert Hague. Lyrics by Arnold B. Horwitt. Production directed by Morton DaCosta. Dances and musical numbers staged by Helen Tamiris. Sets and costumes by Raoul Pene du Bois. Lighting by Peggy Clark. Orchestrations by Philip J. Lang. Vocal arrangements by Crane Calder. Orchestra and chorus directed by Franz Allers. Produced by Richard Kollmar and James W. Gardiner in association with Yvette Schumer. Opened 27 January 1955 at the Mark Hellinger Theatre, moved 28 February 1955 to the Winter Garden, moved 7 November 1955 to the Mark Hellinger Theatre, and closed 3 March 1956 after 461 performances.

CAST (in order of appearance): *Ruth Winters*: SHIRL CONWAY. *Dan King*: RICHARD DERR. *A Man*: John Dennis. *Another Man*: Chris Robinson. *Katie Yoder*: GLORIA MARLOWE. *Papa Yoder*: STEFAN SCHNABEL. *Isaac Miller*: SAMMY SMITH. *Emma Miller*: NANCY ANDREWS. *Ezra Reber*: DOUGLAS FLETCHER RODGERS. *Hilda Miller*: BARBARA COOK. *A Young Miller*: Scotty Engel. *Another Young Miller*: Elaine Lynn. *Peter Reber*: DAVID DANIELS. *Rachel*: Ethel May Cody. *Samuel Zook*: DANIEL NAGRIN. *Levi Stolzfuss*: William Weslow. *Jacob Yoder*: Will Able. *Samuel Lapp*: Chris Robinson. *Abner Zook*: Edgar Thompson. *Ike Pilersheim*: James S. Moore. *Moses Zook*: John Dennis. *Abner Zook*: Tim Worthington. *An Amishman*: Robert Lindgren. *Another Amishman*: Herbert Surface. *Bessie*: Faith Daltry. *Sarah*: Renee Orin. *Esther*: Sybil Lamb. *Rebecca*: Betty McGuire. *Mary*: Muriel Shaw. *State Trooper*: Ray Hyson.

Dancers: Sara Aman, Imelda DeMartin, Ina Hahn, Marcia Howard, Lucia Lambert, Joan Darby, Ann Needham, Tao Strong, Beryl Towbin, Saint Amant, Crandall Diehl, Ronnie Lee, Robert Lindgren, James S. Moore, Philip Nasta, Robert St. Clair, William Weslow, David Wood. *Singers*: Marilyn Bradley, Faith Daltry, Janet Hayes, Sybil Lamb, Renee Orin, Betty McGuire, Muriel Shaw, Betty Zollinger, Ray Hyson, Jack Irwin, Robert Kole, Chris Robinson, John Dennis, Herbert Surface, Edgar F. Thompson, Tim Worthington, Paul Brown, Jim Schlader.

The play takes place in and around Bird-in-Hand, a town in the Amish country of Pennsylvania.

Act 1, Scene 1: A section of road, outside Lancaster. *Scene 2*: Another part of the road. *Scene 3*: The Yoder barnyard. *Scene 4*: The Yoder parlor. *Scene 5*: Side porch of the Yoder house. *Scene 6*: Barnyard on the River Farm. *Scene 7*: A bedroom in the Yoder home. *Scene 8*: The Yoder barnyard. *Scene 9*: In the Yoder barn.

Act 2, Scene 1: The River Farm. *Scene 2*: Kitchen of the Yoder home. *Scene 3*: Back porch of the Yoder home. *Scene 4*: Bedroom of the Yoder home. *Scene 5*: A section of the road. *Scene 6*: A Carnival Grounds. *Scene 7*: Side porch of the Yoder house. *Scene 8*: The Yoder barnyard.

ACT 1

Scene 1

"You Can't Miss It"
R. Derr, S. Conway, Ensemble

"It Wonders Me"
G. Marlowe

Scene 3

"Plenty of Pennsylvania"
N. Andrews, D. F. Rodgers, E. Lynn, Ensemble

"Young and Foolish"
D. Daniels

Scene 4

"Why Not Katie?"
D. F. Rodgers, Men

Scene 6

"Young and Foolish" (reprise)
    G. Marlowe, D. Daniels

"By Lantern Light"
    Danced by D, Nagrin, A. Needham,
    S. Aman, L. Lambert, T. Strong, S. Amant, C. Diehl, B. St. Clair

Scene 7

"It's a Helluva Way to Run a Love Affair"
    S. Conway

"This Is All Very New to Me"
    B. Cook, R. Lindgren, W. Weslow, Ensemble

Scene 8

"Plain We Live"
    S. Schnabel, Ensemble

Scene 9

The Shunning
    The Company

ACT 2

Scene 1

"How Do You Raise a Barn?"
    S. Schnabel, D. F. Rodgers, N. Andrews, D. Nagrin, Ensemble

"Follow Your Heart"
    D. Daniels, G. Marlowe, B. Cook

Scene 2

"City Mouse, Country Mouse"
    N. Andrews,
    with R. Orin, S. Lamb, M. Shaw, E. M. Cody, B. McGuire

Scene 4

"I'll Show Him"
    B. Cook

Scene 5

("Young and Foolish" reprise)
    G. Marlowe

Scene 6

Carnival Ballet
    B. Cook, D. F. Rodgers, Company

On the Midway
    Mambo Joe: D. Nagrin. *Scranton Sal*: S. Aman. *Swami*: R. Lindgren. *Sailor*:
    W. Able. *Barkers*: P. Nasta, C. Robinson, E. F. Thompson.

Dance Hall
    The Company

Scene 8

"Take Your Time and Take Your Pick"
    B. Cook, R. Derr, S. Conway

Finale
    Entire Company

1955.02 **SILK STOCKINGS**

A Musical Comedy in Two Acts. Book by George S. Kaufman, Leueen MacGrath and Abe Burrows. Suggested by the film "Ninotchka" by Melchior Lengyel. Music and lyrics by Cole Porter. Settings and lighting by Jo Mielziner. Costumes by Lucinda Ballard. Additional costumes by Robert Mackintosh. Musical direction and vocal arrangements by Herbert Greene. Orchestrations by Don Walker. Dance music arranged by Tommy Goodman. Dances and musical numbers staged by Eugene Loring. Directed by Cy Feuer. Produced by Cy Feuer and Ernest H. Martin. Opened 24 February 1955 at the Imperial Theatre and closed 14 April 1956 after 478 performances.

CAST (in order of appearance): *Peter Ilyitch Boroff*: PHILIP STERLING. *Hotel Doorman*: Walter Kelvin. *Hotel Manager*: Stanley Simmonds. *Flower Girl*: Geraldine Delaney. *Ivanov*: HENRY LASCOE. *Brankov*: LEON BELASCO. *Bibinski*: DAVID OPATOSHU. *Steve Canfield*: DON AMECHE. *First Commissar*: Edward Becker. *Guards*: Lee Barry, Dick Humphrey. *Vera*: JULIE NEWMAR. *Commissar Markovitch*: GEORGE TOBIAS. *Choreographer*: Kenneth Chertok. *Ninotchka*: HILDEGARDE NEFF. *Reporters*: Edward Becker, Tony Gardell, Arthur Rubin. *Janice Dayton*: GRETCHEN WYLER. *Pierre Bouchard*: Marcel Hillaire. *Chief Commissar*: Forrest

Green. *Minister*: Tony Gardell. *President of Politburo*: Walter Kelvin. *Saleslady*: Ludie Claire. *M. Fabour*: Paul Best. *Bookstall Man*: Louis Polacek. *French Comrades*: Win Mayo, Arthur Ulisse. *Movie Director*: Paul Best. *Assistant Director*: Lee Barry. *Sonia*: Devra Kline. *Grisha*: Forrest Green. *Anna*: Alexandra Moss. *Musicians*: Maurice Kogan, Leon Merian, Mervin Gold. *Guard*: Edward Becker.
    Dancers: Estelle Aza, Barbara Bostock, Verna Cain, Geraldine Delaney, Devra Kline, Pat McBride, Carol Risser, Carol Stevens, Onna White, Martin Allen, Tommy [Thomas] Andrew, George Foster, Bruce Hoy, John Ray.

ACT 1

"Too Bad"
    H. Lascoe, L. Belasco, D. Opatoshu, Hotel Staff

"Paris Loves Lovers"
    D. Ameche, H. Neff

"Stereophonic Sound"
    G. Wyler

"It's a Chemical Reaction, That's All"
    H. Neff

"All of You"
    D. Ameche

"Satin and Silk"
    G. Wyler

"Without Love"
    H. Neff

"All of You" (reprise)
    D. Ameche

ACT 2

"Hail, Bibinski"
    H. Lascoe, L. Belasco, D. Opatoshu, French Comrades

"As On Through the Seasons We Sail"
    D. Ameche, H. Neff

"Josephine"
    G. Wyler, Chorus

"Siberia"
    H. Lascoe, L. Belasco, D. Opatoshu

"Silk Stockings"
    D. Ameche

"The Red Blues"
    The Russians

Finale
    Entire Company

1955.03 **3 FOR TONIGHT**

A Diversion in Song and Dance (Musical Revue) in Two Acts, 12 Scenes. Staged and directed by Gower Champion. Lyrics and special material by Robert Wells. Original music by Walter Schumann. Arrangements by Nathan Scott. Conductor, Richard Pribor. Costumes by Jack's of Hollywood. Production (settings) designed by R. L. Grosh & Sons. Produced by Paul Gregory. Opened 6 April 1955 at the Plymouth Theatre and closed 18 June 1955 after 85 performances.

CAST: MARGE and GOWER CHAMPION, HARRY BELAFONTE, HIRAM SHERMAN, BETTY BENSON, Millard Thomas (guitarist).
    THE VOICES OF WALTER SCHUMANN: John Bennett, Robert Brink, Andrew Case, Gina Christen, Diane Doxee, Elaine Drew, Joyce L. Foss, Dorothy Gill, Nancy Harp, Jimmy Harris, Mark Karl, Jerry Madison, Robert Miller, Ned Romero, Jack Steele, Brad Thomas, Robert Trevis, Karen Vonne, Richard Wessler.

ACT 1

Scene 1

Master of Ceremonies
    H. Sherman

Scene 2

Impressions
"All You Need Is a Song"
    Voices of Walter Schumann

Scene 3

Dance, Dance, Dance; The Clock; By-Play for Drums
    Danced by M. Champion, G. Champion

31

Scene 4

"Jerry" (Traditional)

"Sylvie"

(*Music and Lyrics by* Harry Belafonte.)

"Mark Twain"

(*Music and Lyrics by* Harry Belafonte.)

"When the Saints Go Marching In"

H. Belafonte, *accompanied by* M. Thomas

(*Music and Lyrics by* Huddie Ledbetter and C. C. Carter.)

Scene 5

"The Sunday Picnic Social;" "Summer in Fairview Falls;"
"It Couldn't Be a Better Day;" "Here I Stand;" "The Auction;"
Finale

Danced by M. Champion, G. Champion

ACT 2

Scene 1

"Fly Bird"

B. Benson, Voices of Walter Schumann

Scene 2

"Noah" (Traditional, arr. by Harry Belafonte and Bill Attaway)

"Take My Mother Home" (Traditional, arr. by Hall Johnson)

"In That Great Gettin' Up Mornin'"

(*Arrangement by* Jester Herston.)

H. Belafonte, *accompanied by* M. Thomas

Scene 3

The Lecture

Read by H. Sherman, *Demonstrated by* M. Champion, G. Champion

Scene 4

"Matilda"

(*Music and Lyrics by* Harry Thomas.)

"Scarlet Ribbons"

(*Music by* Evelyn Danzig. *Lyrics by* Jack Segal.)H. Belafonte

Scene 5

"Yesterday"

"By the Light of the Silvery Moon" (from ZIEGFELD FOLLIES OF 1909)

(*Music by* Gus Edwards. *Lyrics by* Edward Madden.)

"Shine On, Harvest Moon" (from ZIEGFELD FOLLIES OF 1908)

(*Music and Lyrics by* Jack Norworth and Nora Bayes.)

Danced by M. Champion, G. Champion

Scene 6

"Troubles"

H. Belafonte

(*Music and Lyrics by* Harry Belafonte)

Scene 7

Finale

Entire Company

1955.04   ANKLES AWEIGH

A Musical Comedy in Two Act, 9 Scenes. Book by Guy Bolton and Eddie Davis. Music by Sammy Fain. Lyrics by Dan Shapiro. Staged by Fred F. Finklehoffe. Assistant to the director, Edward Clarke Lilley. Choreography by Tony Charmoli. Scenery and lighting by George Jenkins. Costumes by Miles White. Vocal and orchestral arrangements by Don Walker. Musical and choral director, Salvatore Dell'Isola. Dance music devised by Roger Adams. Additional dance music by Donald Pippin. Produced by Howard Hoyt, Reginald Hammerstein and Fred F. Finklehoffe[14]. Opened 18 April 1955 at the Mark Hellinger Theatre and closed 17 September 1955 after 176 performances.

---

[14]When the three producers withdrew after the opening, Anthony Brady Farrell, the owner of the Mark Hellinger Theatre, took over as producer.

CAST (in order of appearance): *Russ:* Ed Hanley. *Camera Man:* Ray Mason. *Tommy:* Bill Costin. *Pizza Cart Man:* Frank Conville. *Elsey:* BETTY KEAN. *Wynne:* JANE KEAN. *Dinky:* LEW PARKER. *Spud:* GABRIEL DELL. *Lieut. Bill Kelley:* MARK DAWSON. *Native Girl:* Nancy Walters. *Captain Zimmerman:* Mark Allen. *Admiral Pottles:* Will Hussung. *Chipolata:* THELMA CARPENTER. *Joe Mancinni:* MIKE KELLIN. *Tony:* Herb Fields. *Lucia:* Betty George. *The Duchess:* Karen Shepard. *Shore Patrol:* Skeet Guenther.

Dancers: Dick Alderson, Sandi Bonner, Gene Carrons, Patty Fitzsimmons, Marilyn Marsh, Meri Miller, Marianne Olsen, Marsha Rivers, Nina Starkey, Gloria Stevens, Patricia White (Wilde), Ethel Winter, Hank Brunjes, Don Emmons, Skeet Guenther, Jack Purcell, John Smolko, Jack Timmers. *Singers:* Marilynn Bradley, Thelma Dare, Virginia Martin, Ellen McCown, Janet Pavek, Karen Shepard, Nancy Walters, Herb Fields, Henry Hamilton, Warren Kemmerling, Michael King, Ray Mason, Jack Rains, Hobe Streiford.

The action takes place with an American movie company on location in Sicily and French Morocco at the present time.

Act 1, Scene 1: Montefino, The Piazza—afternoon. *Scene 2:* USS Alamo, below decks—that night. *Scene 3:* El Dahli Night Spot, Morocco—early the next morning.*Scene 4:* A Bedroom in El Dahli. *Scene 5:* Montefino, the Piazza.

Act 2, Scene 1: Hotel Argento, Montefino—next day. *Scene 2:* A street in Montefino. *Scene 3:* Joe's Room. *Scene 4:* Aboard the USS Alamo—the following night.

ACT 1

Scene 1

"Italy"

Boys, Girls

"Old Fashioned Mothers"

B. Kean, J. Kean

"Skip the Build-Up"

B. Kean, L. Parker

"Nothing At All"

J. Kean, M. Dawson

"Walk Like a Sailor"

J. Kean, L. Parker, G. Dell, Girls, B. Kean, H. Brunjes, S. Guenther

Scene 3

"Headin' For the Bottom"

T. Carpenter, Girls, Patrons of Night Spot

"Nothing Can Replace a Man"

J. Kean, Boys

"Here's to Dear Old Us"

B. Kean, L. Parker, G. Dell

Scene 4

"His and Hers"

J. Kean, M. Dawson

Scene 5

"La Festa"

Natives, Boys, Girls

Soloist: R. Mason.

ACT 2

Scene 1

"Ready Cash"

Croupiers, Gamblers

"Kiss Me and Kill Me With Love"

J. Kean, M. Dawson

"Honeymoon"

B. Kean, Girls

"The Villain Always Gets It"

Boys, Girls

Scene 2

"The Code"

Joe's Henchmen

Scene 4

"Walk Like a Sailor" (reprise)

Dancing Boys, Girls

"Eleven O'Clock Song"

B. Kean, J. Kean

Finale

Entire Company

ALL IN ONE

1955.05

A Triple Bill of a One-Act Opera, a Dance Program, and a Drama. Settings and lighting by Eldon Elder. Costumes by Pat Campbell. Produced by Charles Bowden and Richard Barr. Opened 19 April 1955 at the Playhouse and closed 28 May 1955 after 49 performances.

ACT 1

TROUBLE IN TAHITI, an Opera in One Act, 7 Scenes[15]. Libretto and music by Leonard Bernstein. Directed by David Brooks. Pianists, Joseph D. Lewis, Urey Krasnopolsky. Drummer, Max Rich. Bass, Leonard Gaskin.

CAST: *Dinah*: ALICE GHOSTLEY. *Sam*: JOHN TYERS. *Trio*: CONSTANCE BRIGHAM, John Taliaferro, James Tushar.

Scene 1: Sam and Dinah's House. *Scene 2*: Sam's Office. *Scene 3*: The Psychiatrist's Office. *Scene 4*: A Street in the City. *Scene 5*: The Gym. *Scene 6*: The Hat Shop. *Scene 7*: Sam and Dinah's House.

ACT 2

Paul Draper, accompanied by John Colman:

On the Beat
(*Music by* François Couperin.)

Alcina Suite
(*Music by* Georg Friedrich Handel.)

Minuet; Sarabande; Musette; Tambourine

Tea for Two
(*Music by* Vincent Youmans.)

Dance Without Music

In a Dance Hall
(*Music by* Cole Porter.)

Satire on a Political Speech

Improvisation

ACT 3

27 WAGONS FULL OF COTTON, a Drama in One Act, 3 Scenes, by Tennessee Williams. Directed by Vincent J. Donohue.

CAST: *Flora Meighan*: MAUREEN STAPLETON. *Jake Meighan*: MYRON McCORMICK. *Silva Vicarro*: FELICE ORLANDI.

All the action takes place on the front porch of the Meighan's residence near Blue Mountain, Mississippi.

Scene 1: Early evening. *Scene 2*: Noon, the next day. *Scene 3*: Nine o'clock that evening.

GUYS AND DOLLS

1955.06

A Revival of the Musical Fable (Comedy) in Two Acts, 17 Scenes[16]. Book by Jo Swerling and Abe Burrows. Based on a story and characters by Damon Runyon. Music and lyrics by Frank Loesser. Choreography by Onna White (after the original by Michael Kidd). Settings by Jo Mielziner. Costumes by Alvin Colt; Costume supervisor, Franck Spencer. Orchestral arrangements by George Bassman and Ted Royal. Vocal arrangements and direction by Herbert Greene. Musical director, Frederick Dvonch. Directed by Philip Mathias. Produced by the New York City Center Light Opera Company (William Hammerstein, General director). Opened 20 April 1955 at the New York City Center, closing 1 May 1955 after 15 performances; re-opened 31 May 1955 at the New York City Center and closed 12 June 1955 after an additional 16 performances. Total: 31 performances.

CAST (in order of appearance): *Nicely-Nicely Johnson*: OGGIE SMALL. *Benny Southstreet*: AL NESOR. *Rusty Charlie*: Murray Vines. *Sarah Brown*: LEILA MARTIN. *Arvide Abernathy*: MARTIN WOLFSON. *Mission Band*: Michelle Reiner, Paul Migan, Elaine Spaulding. *Harry the Horse*: TOM PEDI. *Lieut. Brannigan*: TOM AHEARNE. *Nathan Detroit*: WALTER MATTHAU. *Angie the Ox*: Ralph Vucci. *Miss Adelaide*: HELEN GALLAGHER. *Sky Masterson*: RAY SHAW. *Joey Biltmore*: Joe Bernard. *Mimi*: Norma Kaiser. *General Matilda B. Cartwright*: KATE TOMLINSON. *Big Jule*: LOU NOVA. *Drunk*: Robert Karl. *Waiter*: Seth Riggs.

---

[15]No individual musical numbers listed; performed as an opera.
[16]First presented in New York 24 November 1950 at the 46th Street Theatre for 1200 performances. For Synopsis of Scenes and Musical Numbers, see original 1950 production. "Travelling Light" omitted for this and all future productions.

Dancers: Ellen Beach, Sonya Besant, Louise Golden, Diana Hunter, Norma Kaiser, Loys Lozano, Marcia Maier, Kirsten Valbor, Albert Fiorella, Robert Karl, Frank Marasco, Tom Panko, Regis Powers, Victor Reilly, Harry Lee Rogers, Marc West. *Singers*: Ken Emery, Clifford Fearl, Tom Powell, Seth Riggs, Bob Rippy, Evans Thornton, Murray Vines, Ralph Vucci. *Sightseers*: Sheila Hayden, Rosemary Shein, Jane Wagner.

SOUTH PACIFIC

1955.07

A Revival of the Musical Play in Two Acts, 23 Scenes[17]. Book by Oscar Hammerstein II and Joshua Logan. Adapted from James A. Michener's novel "Tales of the South Pacific." Music by Richard Rodgers. Lyrics by Oscar Hammerstein II. Directed by Charles Atkin. Scenery by Jo Mielziner. Costumes by Motley; Costume supervisor, Frank Spencer. Musical director, Frederick Dvonch. Orchestrations by Robert Russell Bennett. Produced by the New York City Center Light Opera Company (William Hammerstein, General director). Opened 4 May 1955 at the New York City Center and closed 15 May 1955 after 15 performances.

CAST (in order of appearance): *Ngana*: Margaret Sokal. *Jerome*: Antonio Obregon. *Henry*: Richard Silvera. *Ensign Nellie Forbush*: SANDRA DEEL. *Emile DeBecque*: RICHARD COLLETT. *Bloody Mary*: SYLVIA SYMS. *Bloody Mary's Assistant*: Julie Winston. *Abner*: J. J. Riley. *Stewpot*: FRANK MAXWELL. *Luther Billis*: HENRY SLATE. *Professor*: GENE SAKS. *Lt. Joseph Cable, U.S.M.C.*: HERB BANKE. *Capt. George Brackett, U.S.N.*: MARTIN WOLFSON. *Cmdr. William Harbison, U.S.N.*: Warren J. Brown. *Yeoman Herbert Quale*: Seth Riggs. *Sgt. Kenneth Johnson*: Howard Lear. *Seabee Richard West*: Evans Thornton. *Seabee Morton Wise*: Murray Vines. *Seaman Tom O'Brien*: Dick Armbrust. *Radio Operator Bob McCaffrey*: Clifford Fearl. *Staff Sgt. Thomas Hassinger*: Ralph Vucci. *Lt. Genevieve Marshall*: Eileen Moran. *Ensign Dinah Murphy*: Edith Lane. *Ensign Janet MacGregor*: Janice Samarie. *Ensign Cora MacRae*: Louise Pearl. *Ensign Bessie Noonan*: Michelle Reiner. *Ensign Connie Walewska*: Helen Baisley. *Ensign Pamela Whitmore*: Elaine Spaulding. *Ensign Sue Yaeger*: Theresa Mari. *Liat*: CAROL LAWRENCE. *Marcel*, Henry's Assistant: Nick Gentile. *Lt. Buzz Adams*: Don Fellows. *Shore Patrol Officer*: Bob Rippy. *Sailors*: Richard Hildebrand, Raymond Wearer. *Islander*: Emy Boselli.

DAMN YANKEES

1955.08

A Musical in Two Acts, 22 Scenes. Book by George Abbott and Douglass Wallop. Based on the novel "The Year the Yankees Lost the Pennant" by Douglass Wallop. Music and lyrics by Richard Adler and Jerry Ross. Dances and musical numbers staged by Bob Fosse. Scenery and costumes designed by William and Jean Eckart. Musical direction by Hal Hastings. Orchestrations by Don Walker. Dance music arrangements by Roger Adams. Production directed by George Abbott. Produced by Frederick Brisson, Robert E. Griffith and Harold S. Prince in association with Albert B. Taylor. Opened 5 May 1955 at the 46th Street Theatre, moved 7 May 1957 to the Adelphi Theatre, and closed 19 October 1957 after 1019 performances.

CAST (in order of appearance): *Meg*: SHANNON BOLIN. *Joe Boyd*: ROBERT SHAFER. *Applegate*: RAY WALSTON. *Sister*: JEAN STAPLETON. *Doris*: Elizabeth Howell. *Joe Hardy*: STEPHEN DOUGLASS. *Henry*: Al Lanti. *Sohovik*: Eddie Phillips. *Smokey*: NATHANIEL FREY. *Vernon*: Albert Linville. *Van Buren*: RUSS BROWN. *Rocky*: JIMMIE KOMACK. *Gloria*: RAE ALLEN. *Teen-Ager*: Del Horstmann. *Welch*: RICHARD BISHOP. *Lola*: GWEN VERDON. *Miss Weston*: Janie Janvier. *Guard*: George Marcy. *Commissioner*: Del Horstmann. *Postmaster*: Albert Linville.

Dancers: Betty Carr, Patricia Ferrier, Marilyn Greer, Marie Kolin, Julia Marlowe, Svetlana McLee, Robert Evans, Timmy Everett, William Joyce, Harvey Jung, Al Lanti, George Marcy, Eddie Phillips, Mark Ward. *Singers*: Cherry Davis, Jeanne Grant, Janet Hayes, Janie Janvier, Joan Keenan, Suzanne Lovell, Frank Bouley, Fred Bryan, Del Horstmann, Ralph Lowe, Albert Linville, Ralph Strane. *Children*: Ronn Cummins, Jackie Scholle.

The action takes place some time in the future—Washington, D.C.

Act 1, Scene 1: Joe and Meg Boyd's Front Porch and Living Room. *Scene 2*: A Corridor under the stands of the Washington Baseball Park. *Scene 3*: The Dugout of the Washington Baseball Park. *Scene 4*: A Billboard near the Ballpark. *Scene 5*: Welch's Office. *Scene 6*: A Bench in front of the Joe hardy Billboard. *Scene 7*: Meg's House.

---

[17]First produced in New York 7 April 1949 at the Majestic Theatre for 1925 performances. For Synopsis of Scenes and Musical Numbers, see original 1949 production.

Scene 8: Corridor at the Ball Park. *Scene 9*: The Locker Room. *Scene 10*: In front of black curtain. *Scene 11*: The Stage of the Hotel Ballroom.

Act 2, Scene 1: The Locker Room. *Scene 2*: A Park at dusk. *Scene 3*: Applegate's Apartment. *Scene 4*: The Commissioner's Office. *Scene 5*: A Bench. *Scene 6*: A Night Club. *Scene 7*: The Joe Hardy Billboard. *Scene 8*: The Billboard. *Scene 9*: The Dugout and Stands. *Scene 10*: Corridor at Ballpark. *Scene 11*: Meg's House.

ACT 1

Scene 1

"Six Months Out of Every Year"
S. Bolin, R. Shafer, Baseball Fans, Baseball Widows
"Goodbye, Old Girl"
R. Shafer, S. Douglass

Scene 2

"Heart"
R. Brown, J. Kommack, N. Frey, A. Linville

Scene 3

"Shoeless Joe from Hannibal, Mo."
R. Allen, Baseball Players

Scene 5

"A Man Doesn't Know"
S. Douglass

Scene 6

"A Little Brains — A Little Talent"
G. Verdon

Scene 7

"A Man Doesn't Know" (reprise)
S. Douglass, S. Bolin

Scene 9

"Whatever Lola Wants"
G. Verdon

Scene 10

"Not Meg"[18]
R. Walston, Gossips

Scene 11

"Who's Got the Pain?"
G. Verdon, E. Phillips
(*Dance staged by* Bob Fosse and Gwen Verdon.)
"The American League"[19]
The Downtown Fan Club

ACT 2

Scene 1

"The Game"
J. Kommack, N. Frey, Baseball Players
"Heart" (reprise)[20]
J. Stapleton, R. Cummins, J. Scholle, C. Davis

Scene 2

"Near To You"
S. Douglass, S. Bolin

Scene 3

"Those Were the Good Old Days"
R. Walston

Scene 6

"Two Lost Souls"
G. Verdon, S. Douglass, Guys, Dolls

Scene 11

"A Man Doesn't Know" (reprise)
S. Bolin, R. Shafer

---

[18]Dropped shortly after opening and replaced by:
"Heart" (reprise)
J. Stapleton, R. Cummins, J. Scholle, C. Davis
[19]Dropped shortly after opening.
[20]Dropped shortly after opening.

1955.09   FINIAN'S RAINBOW

A Revival of the Musical in Two Acts, 10 Scenes[21]. Book by E.Y. Harburg and Fred Saidy. Lyrics by E. Y. Harburg. Music by Burton Lane. Directed by William Hammerstein. Scenery and lighting by Howard Bay. Costume supervision, Frank Spencer. Choreography by Onna White after the original by Michael Kidd. Costumes by Alvin Colt. Orchestrations by Robert Russell Bennett and Don Walker. Conducted by Julius Rudel. Musical director, Frederick Dvonch. Produced by the New York City Center Light Opera Company (William Hammerstein, General director). Opened 18 May 1955 at the New York City Center and closed 29 May 1955 after 15 performances.

CAST (in order of appearance): *Buzz Collins*: Eddie Bruce. *Sheriff*: Jack Bryan. *First Sharecropper*: Evans Thornton. *Second Sharecropper*: Seth Riggs. *Susan Mahoney*: ANITA ALVAREZ. *Henry*: Michael Gilford. *Third Sharecropper*: Rosetta LeNoire. *Finian McLonergan*: WILL MAHONEY. *Sharon McLonergan*: HELEN GALLAGHER. *Woody Mahoney*: MERV GRIFFIN. *Og, A Leprechaun*: DONN [Donald] DRIVER. *Howard*: Terry Carter. *Senator Billboard Rawkins*: Frank Borgman. *First Geologist*: Walter P. Brown. *Second Geologist*: Emory Knight. *Diane*: Lynn-Rose Kohan. *Honey Lou*: Jonelle Allen. *John, the Preacher*: Rodester Timmons. *Mr. Robust*: Oggie Small. *Mr. Shears*: James Elward. *First Passion Pilgrim Gospeller*: John Bouie. *Second Passion Pilgrim Gospeller*: Elwood Smith. *Third Passion Pilgrim Gospeller*: Jay J. Riley. *First Deputy*: Howard Lear. *Second Deputy*: Richard Blofson. *Third Deputy*: Emory Knight.

Dancers: Albert Fiorella, Robert Karl, Tom Panko, Charles Queenan, Jay J. Riley, Harry Lee Rogers, Marc West, Erona Harris, Norma Kaiser, Loys Lozano, Mary Martinet, Vera McNichols, Nadine Revene, Kirsten Valbor, Elizabeth Williamson. *Singers*: John Bouie, Walter P. Brown, Clifford Fearl, Howard Lear, Seth Riggs, Jay J. Riley, Robert Rippy, Elwood Smith, Evans Thornton, Rodester Timmons, Murray Vines, Helen Baisley, Theresa Mari, Rosalie Maxwell, Eileen Moran, Louise Pearl, Michelle Reiner, Janice Samarie, Christine Spencer.

1955.10   SEVENTH HEAVEN

A Musical Play in Two Acts, 16 Scenes. Book by Victor Wolfson and Stella Unger. Based on the play of the same name by Austin Strong. Music by Victor Young. Lyrics by Stella Unger. Scenery and costumes by Vertis. Lighting by Feder. Choreography by Peter Gennaro. Musical director, Max Meth. Orchestral arrangements by David Terry. Choral director, Crane Calder. Entire production staged by John C. Wilson. Produced by Gant Gaither and William Bacher. Opened 26 May 1955 at the ANTA Theatre and closed 2 July 1955 after 44 performances.

CAST (in order of appearance): *Boule*: KURT KASZNAR. *Camille*: GERRIANNE RAPHAEL. *Collette*: PATRICIA HAMMERLEE. *Fifi*: CHITA RIVERA. *Mme. Suze*: BEATRICE ARTHUR. *Father Chevillon*: Malcolm Lee Beggs. *Diane*: GLORIA DE HAVEN. *First Sailor*: Philip Cook. *Second Sailor*: Leo Kayworth. *Policeman*: Walter Brandin. *First Nun*: Nanette Vezina. *Second Nun*: Joy Marlene. *Street Cleaner*: Ralph Quist. *Organ Grinder*: William Carson. *First Senegalese*: Ray Saint Jacques. *Second Senegalese*: James E. Wall. *Dandy*: John Carter. *Baker Boy*: Joseph Flynn. *Housewife*: Jeanne Schegel. *Artist*: Jimmy White. *Streetwalkers*: Lee Becker (Theodore), Bonnie Evans, Helena Seroy. *Midinette*: Nancy Lynch. *Fleegle*: ROBERT CLARY. *Inspector*: Scott Merrill. *Gobin*: David Collyer. *Vulmir*: Ferdi Hoffman. *Chico*: RICARDO MONTALBAN. *Children*: Betty Jane Seagle, Barbara Stabile, Barclay Hodges. *French Official*: George Burles. *Flower Vendor*: Winifred Ainslee. *First French Soldier*: Ray Saint Jacques. *Second French Soldier*: James E. Wall. *First American Soldier*: Ralph Quist. *Second American Soldier*: Joseph Flynn. *Apaches*: Edmund Hall, Ralph Flynn. *Accordionist*: Dominic Cortese.

Dancers: Lee Becker (Theodore), Bonnie Evans, Nancy Lynch, Helena Seroy, Rebecca Vorno, Philip Cook, Victor Duntiere, William Guske, Philip Salem, Jimmy White. *Singers*: Winifred Ainslee, Gwen Harmon, Joy Marlene, Alexandra Moss, Jeanne Schlegel, Nanette Vezina, Walter Brandin, George Burles, William Carson, John Carter, Joseph Flynn, Edmund Hall, Leo Kayworth, Ralph Quist, Ray Saint Jacques, James E. Wall, Ralph Wayne.

The action takes places in and around Paris, 1914-1918.

Act 1, Scene 1: A Cul-de-Sac. *Scene 2*: A Street in Paris. *Scene 3*: Chico's Sewer. *Scene 4*: Rue Notre Dame de Lorette. *Scene 5*: Chico's Attic. *Scene 6*: The Street. *Scene 7*: 'Heaven'—four days later. *Scene 8*: Rue Notre Dame de Lorette. *Scene 9*: Fete Montmartre.

Act 2, Scene 1: Railroad Station. *Scene 2*: The Street. *Scene 3*: In the Trenches. *Scene 4*: No Man's Land. *Scene 5*: Behind the Lines—a Canteen. *Scene 6*: The Search. *Scene 7*: The Cul-de-Sac.

---

[21]First produced 10 January 1947 at the 46th Street Theatre for 725 performances. For Synopsis of Scenes and Musical Numbers, see original 1947 production.

ACT 1

"C'Est La Vie"
R. Clary, K. Kasznar, B. Arthur, Company

"Where Is That Someone For Me?"
G. DeHaven

"Camille, Collette, Fifi"
C. Rivera, P. Hammerlee, G. Raphael

"Man With a Dream"
R. Montalban

"Remarkable Fellow"
R. Montalban, C. Rivera, S. Merrill, Company

"If It's a Dream"
G. DeHaven

"Happy Little Crook"
R. Clary

"Sun at My Window, Love at My Door"
G. DeHaven, R. Montalban, Company

"Where Is That Someone For Me?" (reprise)
G. DeHaven

"Glove Dance"
B. Evans, N. Lynch, H. Seroy, R. Vorno, P. Cook, V. Duntiere, P. Salem, J. White

ACT 2

"A Miss You Kiss"
R. Montalban, Company

"Camille, Collette, Fifi" (reprise)
C. Rivera, P. Hammerlee, G. Raphael

"Chico's Reverie" (White and Gold Ballet)
Company

"Love, Love, Love"
G. Raphael, P. Hammerlee, C. Rivera, J. White

"If It's A Dream" (reprise)
G. DeHaven

"Love Sneaks Up on You"
R. Clary, P. Hammerlee

Finale
Entire Company

Julie Andrews and Rex Harrison in MY FAIR LADY
Museum of the City of New York

1955–1956 SEASON

1955.11

ALMOST CRAZY

A Musical Revue in Two Acts, 27 Scenes. Sketches mostly by James Shelton, Hal Hackady and Robert A. Bernstein, (Lester Judson, Kay Medford). Music and lyrics mostly by Portia Nelson, Raymond Taylor and James Shelton, (Lew Kesler, Joyce Geary, Ed Scott, Sam Rosen, Hal Hackady, Lenny Adelson, Jim Kaye, Carley Mills, Bill Russell, Stan Hagler, Helen Bragdon, Gene DePaul, Don Raye). Choreography by William Skipper. Sketches directed by Christopher Hewett. Scenery and lighting by John Robert Lloyd. Costumes by Stanley Simmons. Musical director, Al Rickey. Orchestral arrangements by Ted Royal. Entire production staged by Lew Kesler. Produced by John S. Cobb. Opened 20 June 1955 at the Longacre Theatre and closed 2 July 1955 after 16 performances.

CAST: KAY MEDFORD, JAMES SHELTON, BABE HINES, BETTY COLBY, KAREN ANDERS, KEVIN SCOTT, Alvin Beam, Vincent Beck, Ron Cecill, Nick Dana, Lorna Del Maestro, Phyllis Dorne, Mildred Hughes, Joan Morton, William Skipper, Gloria Smith, Rita Tanno, Richard Towers, Ann York.

ACT 1

Scene 1

"Everything's Gonna Be Much Worse Next Year"
(*Music by* Lew Kesler. *Lyrics by* James Shelton.)
Ladies of the Ensemble: R. Tanno, B. Colby, K. Anders, M. Hughes, J. Morton, L. Del Maestro, A. York, K. Medford. *Quartette*: W. Skipper, A. Beam, K. Scott, N. Dana.

Scene 2

"Mother's Day"
M. Hughes, K. Anders, A. York
(*Music by* Portia Nelson. *Lyrics by* Joyce Geary.)

Scene 3

"Why Not Me?"
P. Dorne, R. Cecill
(*Music by* Ed Scott. *Lyrics by* Sam Rosen.)

Scene 4

Fort Knox, New York
(*by* Lester Judson)

Scene 5

"But It's Love"
G. Smith, A. York, L. Del Maestro,
R. Tanno, J. Morton, W. Skipper, A. Beam, N. Dana, R. Cecill
(*Music by* Ray Taylor. *Lyrics by* Hal Hackady.)

Scene 6

"Don't Bait for Fish You Can't Fry"
B. Hines
(*Music and Lyrics by* Portia Nelson.)

Scene 7

This Is a Living
(*by* Hal Hackady)
Ralph Deadwood: K. Scott. *Mary Smiles Winter*: K. Medford. *A Model*: M. Hughes. *The Husband*: J. Shelton. *Maxine Madison*: K. Anders.

Scene 8

"Where Is the Girl?"
B. Colby, K. Scott
(*Music and Lyrics by* James Shelton.)

Scene 9

"Mother's Day"
M. Hughes, K. Anders, A. York
(*Music by* Portia Nelson. *Lyrics by* Joyce Geary.)

Scene 10

"Goin' to the Moon"
R. Tanno, J. Shelton, V. Beck, K. Medford, R. Towers
(*Music by* Ed Scott. *Lyrics by* Lenny Adelson.)

Scene 11

"Down to Eartha"
B. Colby
(*Music and Lyrics by* Ray Taylor.)

Scene 12

"Chat Noire"
K. Scott
(*Music by* Ray Taylor. *Lyrics by* Jim Kaye.)
Chat Noire: J. Morton. *Bartender*: F. Nay. *Cop*: N. Dana. *Sailor*: R. Cecill. *Street Cleaner*: F. Nay. *The Mouse*: A. Beam.

Scene 13

"I Can Live Without It"
K. Anders
(*Music and Lyrics by* Ray Taylor.)

Scene 14

If I Knew You Were Coming
(*by* Robert A. Bernstein)
Announcer: K. Anders. *Wife*: K. Medford. *Husband*: J. Shelton.

Scene 15

"Come and Get Cozy With Me"
(*Music by* Lew Kesler. *Lyrics by* Carley Mills.)
Lifeguard: K. Scott. *His Girl*: K. Anders. *Kitty's Roommate*: K. Medford. *Kitty's Beau*: J. Shelton. *Lovers*: B. Colby, V. Beck, Company.

ACT 2

Scene 1

"As We Told You"
(*Music by* Lew Kesler. *Lyrics by* James Shelton.)
Ladies of the Ensemble: R. Tanno, B. Colby, K. Anders, M. Hughes, J. Morton, A. York, L. Del Maestro, G. Smith. *Quartette*: W. Skipper, A. Beam, N. Dana, R. Cecill.

Scene 2

"Burlesque"
(*Music by* Bill Russell. *Lyrics by* Stan Hagler.)
Queenie: G. Smith. *Big Queenie*: K. Medford. *Barker*: F. Nay. *The Baritone*: K. Scott.

Scene 3

"Vertigo"
(*Music by* Ray Taylor. *Lyrics by* Helen Bragdon.)
Mistress of the Villa: B. Colby. *Tender of the Grapes*: V. Beck.

Scene 4

I Thought So Too
(*by* James Shelton)
Doctor: R. Towers. *First Woman*: L. Del Maestro. *First Man*: K. Scott. *Second Man*: J. Shelton. *Second Woman*: R. Tanno. *Third Woman*: K. Medford.

Scene 5

"Easy"
B. Hines
(*Music and Lyrics by* James Shelton.)

Scene 6

"Always Tell the Truth"
(*Dialogue by* Hal Hackady. *Music and Lyrics by* Portia Nelson.)
Truth: J. Morton. *Veracity*: K. Medford.

Scene 7

"Mother's Day"
M. Hughes, A. York, K. Anders
(*Music by* Portia Nelson. *Lyrics by* Joyce Geary.)

Scene 8

"Here Come the Blues"
W. Skipper
(*Music by* Gene DePaul. *Lyrics by* Don Raye.)
Danced by W. Skipper, J. Morton, L. Del Maestro, M. Hughes, 'The Leg' P. Dorne.

Scene 9

"More Fish"
K. Anders

Scene 10

"Love in the Barnyard"
B. Hines
(*Music and Lyrics by* Ray Taylor.)
Danced by G. Smith, L. Del Maestro, R. Tanno, P. Dorne, R. Cecill, A. Beam, N. Dana, W Skipper.

Scene 11

Love Me or Leave Me
(by Kay Medford and James Shelton)
The Grump: J. Shelton. Ruth: K. Medford.

Scene 12

Finale
Entire Company

1955.12 ## CATCH A STAR

A Musical Revue in Two Acts, 23 Scenes. Sketches by Danny and Neil Simon, (Mike Stewart). Music by Sammy Fain and Phil Charig. Lyrics by Paul (Francis) Webster and Ray Golden. Additional material by Lee Adams. (Additional music by Hal Borne, Sy Kleinman, Jerry Bock, Jay Navarro. Additional lyrics by Dave Ormont, Danny Shapiro, Milton Pascal, Larry Holofcener, Bernie Wayne, Lee Norris, I.A.L. Diamond, Norman Martin.) Sketches directed by Danny Simon. Dances and musical numbers staged by Lee Sherman. Settings devised and designed by Ralph Alswang. Costumes designed by Thomas Becher. Orchestrations and musical direction by Milton Greene. Ballet music composed by Herb Schutz. Revue co-ordinated by Robert Nesbitt. Entire production conceived and supervised by Ray Golden. Produced by Sy Kleinman. Opened 6 September 1955 at the Plymouth Theatre and closed 24 September 1955 after 23 performances.

CAST: PAT CARROLL, DAVID BURNS, ELAINE DUNN, JACK WAKEFIELD, HELEN HALPIN, MARC BREAUX, UNDINE FORREST, SONNY SPARKS, WAYNE SHERWOOD, KAY MALONE, DENNY DESMOND, CALVIN HOLT, TRUDE ADAMS, Lillian D'Honau, Kay Kingston, Mickey Calin, Louise Golden, Carl Jeffrey, Sigyn, Carol Field, Rhoda Kerns.

ACT 1

Scene 1

"Catch a Star!"
W. Sherwood
(Music by Sammy Fain. Lyrics by Paul Francis Webster.)

Scene 2

"Everybody Wants to Be in Show Business"
(Music by Phil Charig. Lyrics by Ray Golden, Bud Burtson.)
Producer: D. Burns. Stage Doorman: J. Wakefield. Thief: C. Jeffrey.
Policeman: W. Sherwood. Magician: C. Holt. Magician's Assistant: R. Kerns.
Model: U. Forrest. Woman With Baby Carriage: K. Malone. Ambulance
Attendants: M. Breaux, D. Desmond. Patient: M. Calin. Chorus Girls: L.
D'Honau, Sigyn. Waitress: H. Halpin. Secretaries: L. Golden, E. Dunn.
Charity Collector: K. Kingston.

Scene 3

New Styles in Acting
(by Danny Simon)
Producer: D. Burns. Secretary: C. Field. Military Pilot: J. Wakefield. Tennis
Player: D. Desmond. Professor: S. Sparks. The Ingenue: P. Carroll.

Scene 4

"A Little Travelling Music"
(Music by Hal Borne. Lyrics by Paul Francis Webster and Ray Golden.)
The Traveler: E. Dunn. Three Improper Bostonians: L. Golden, Sigyn,
L. D'Honau.

Scene 5

Matinee Idles
(by Danny and Neil Simon)
Hawker: D. Desmond. Pete: W. Sherwood. Man: J. Wakefield.
Trixie: P. Carroll. Dorothy: H. Halpin. Martha: C. Field. Lucille: U. Forrest.
Hazel: R. Kerns. Harriett: K. Malone. Florence: K. Kingston. Actor: S. Sparks.
Actress: L. D'Honau.

Scene 6

"One Hour Ahead of the Posse"
(Music by Phil Charig. Lyrics by Ray Golden and Dave Ormont.)
Killer: W. Sherwood. Girl: L. D'Honau. Sheriff: M. Breaux.
Posse: C. Holt, C. Jeffrey, M. Calin, D. Desmond. Folk Singers:
C. Field, R. Kerns, K. Malone.

Scene 7

And Then I Wrote
(by Danny and Neil Simon)
Harry: J. Wakefield. Kitty: H. Halpin. Max Dillingbert: D. Burns. Labonza:
S. Sparks. Gus: M. Breaux. Phoebe: U. Forrest. Customer: D. Desmond.

Scene 8

"Las Vegas"
(Music by Sy Kleinman. Lyrics by Ray Golden and Lee Adams.)
Girl: P. Carroll. Bellhops: W. Sherwood, C. Jeffrey, M. Calin, D. Desmond.

Scene 9

"To Be or Not To Be in Love"
(Music by Phil Charig. Lyrics by Ray Golden, Danny Shapiro,
Milton Pascal.)
Girl: T. Adams. Boy: M. Breaux.

Scene 10

"The Story of Alice"
(Music by Jerry Bock. Lyrics by Larry Holofcener.)
Quartet: H. Halpin, W. Sherwood, C. Holt, U. Forrest.

Scene 11

Room for Rent
(by Danny and Neil Simon)
Southern Belle: P. Carroll. First Man: D. Burns. First Roomer: J. Wakefield.
Second Roomer: S. Sparks. Third Roomer: K. Kingston. Second Man:
W. Sherwood.

Scene 12

"What a Song Can Do"
H. Halpin
(Music and Lyrics by Bernie Wayne and Lee Norris.)

Scene 13

"Carnival in Court"
(Music by Jay Navarro. Lyrics by Ray Golden and I. A. L. Diamond.)
Town Crier: D. Burns. Bailiff: C. Holt. Two Girls: Sigyn, L. Golden.
Judge: J. Wakefield. Plaintiff: H. Halpin. Defendant: S. Sparks.
Private Eye: M. Breaux. Private Eye's Wife: E. Dunn. Co-respondent:
P. Carroll. Three Belles: L. D'Honau, U. Forrest, K. Malone.
Two Sailors: M. Calin, D. Desmond. Basketman: W. Sherwood.
Basketwoman: C. Field.

ACT 2

Scene 1

Theatre Piece
Three Male Dancers: M. Breaux, M. Calin, C. Holt. Three Female Dancers:
Sigyn, E. Dunn, L. Golden. Character: C. Jeffrey. Glamour Girls: U. Forrest,
K. Malone, R. Kerns, L. D'Honau (Harlequin).

Scene 2

Arty
(by Danny and Neil Simon)
Mom: P. Carroll. Arty: J. Wakefield. First Man: D. Desmond. Second Man:
S. Sparks.

Scene 3

"Twist My Arm"
(Music by Sammy Fain. Lyrics by Paul Francis Webster.)
Girl: E. Dunn. Boy: M. Breaux.

Scene 4

"New Hollywood Plots"[1]
D, Burns, D. Desmond, C. Holt
(Music by Sammy Fain. Lyrics by Paul Francis Webster.)

Scene 5

"Foreign Cars"
T. Adams
(Music and Lyrics by Norman Martin)

Scene 6

"Gruntled"
(Music and Lyrics by Phil Charig, Ray Golden and Sy Kleinman.)
Girl: H. Halpin. Boy: D. Desmond. Three Couples: M. Breaux, E. Dunn,
C. Holt, L. D'Honau, M. Calin, Sigyn.

Scene 7

Matrimonial Agency
(by Danny and Neil Simon)
First Woman: U. Forrest. Second Woman: K. Malone. Adrian: D. Burns.
First Shopper: K. Kingston. First Man: M. Calin. Mrs. Ennis: P. Carroll. Miss
B.: C. Field. The Frenchman: M. Breaux. The Reject: J. Wakefield. The Body:
S. Sparks.

---

[1]Dropped during run.

Scene 8

"Fly Little Heart"
E. Dunn
(*Music by* Jerry Bock. *Lyrics by* Larry Holofcener.)

"Bachelor Hoedown"
E. Dunn, M. Breaux, Sigyn, L. Golden, C. Field, L. D'Honau,
R. Kerns, M. Calin, C. Holt, D. Desmond, C. Jeffrey, W. Sherwood
(*Music by* Jerry Bock. *Lyrics by* Larry Holofcener.)

Scene 9

Gift of the Magi
(*by* Mike Stewart)
P. Carroll

Scene 10

"Boffola"
Entire Cast
(*Music by* Phil Charig. *Lyrics by* Danny Shapiro, Milton Pascal, Ray Golden.)

1955.13   HEAR! HEAR!

A Musical Revue in Two Acts, 16 Scenes. Special songs and material, Tom
Waring, Charles Henderson, Lumpy Brannum, Jack Dolph, Buddy Bernier,
Phyllis Williams. Staged and directed by Fred Waring. Scenery by Sam
Leve. Costumes by Jeanne Partington. Stage director, Ray Sax. Choral direc-
tor, Jack Best. Orchestra director, Fred Culley. Produced by Fred Waring.
Opened 27 September 1955 at the Ziegfeld Theatre and closed 23 October
1955 after 38 performances.

CAST: FRED WARING AND ALL THE PENNSYLVANIANS: *Singers:* Dorothy
Arms (Soprano), Norma Barnes (Contralto), Patti Beems (Soprano), Ruth Best
(Soprano), Jack Best (Bass), Bill Caniff (Tenor), FRANK DAVIS (Bass baritone),
Norma Douglas (Alto), EDDIE ERICKSEN (Tenor), George Geyer (Baritone),
GORDON GOODMAN (Tenor), Ralph Isbell (Bass), LEONARD KRANENDONK
(Baritone), Bob Kranendonk (Baritone), JOE MARINE (Baritone), Preshy Marker
(Mezzo-Soprano), T. J. Marker (Bass), George Pilon (Tenor), BOB SANDS (Tenor),
Fred Waring, Jr. (Tenor). *Players:* Hawley Ades (Piano), Lamar Alsop (Viola), Lou Bode
(Clarient, Saxophone), LUMPY BRANNUM (String Bass), Ward Cole (Trumpet),
Fred Culley (Violin, Orchestral Director), Buss Dillon (Drums), Mike Doty (Clarinet),
Julius Ehrenworth (Cello), JEAN ELEY (Violin), LOU ELEY (Violin), Charles Evans
(Trombone), Ben Feldham (Violin), George Guggisberg (Trumpet), Nelson Keller
(Trumpet), Marvin Long (Trombone), POLEY McCLINTOCK (Drums), ROSALIE
RANDALL (Harp), Norman Ronemus (Saxophone, Clarinet), RAY SAX (Saxophone,
Clarinet).

ACT 1

Scene 1

Thanks for Coming:

"Your Song"
Your Hosts

"Hear! Hear!"
We! We!
(*Music and Lyrics by* Fred Waring.)

Scene 2

Let Freedom Sing:

"America Our Heritage"
The People
(*Music and Lyrics by* Helen Steele.)

"Where in the World But America"
The Same
(*Music and Lyrics by* Glenn Rowell, Fred Waring, Jack Dolph.)

"Paul Revere's Ride"
The Patriots

"Give Me Your Tired, Your Poor" (from MISS LIBERTY)
The People
(*Music by* Irving Berlin. *Lyrics by* Emma Lazarus.)

"Pledge of Allegiance"
US
(*Music by* Fred Waring.)

Scene 3

The Song Is the Thing:

"Say It With Music" (from THE MUSIC BOX REVUE OF 1921)
Singers, Players
(*Music and Lyrics by* Irving Berlin.)

"So Beats My Heart"
P. Beems, Singers, Players
(*Music and Lyrics by* Pat Ballard, Charles Henderson,
Tom Waring.)

Scene 4

Long Hair, Horse Hair, Cat Gut and Wire:

"Hora Staccato"
The No-Sing String Section

Scene 5

Rock and Roll:

"I Want You To Be My Baby"
J. Marine, the Beat Boys

Scene 6

Plain and Fancy Folk Songs

"Black Is the Color of My True Love's Hair"
R. Randall, Friends

"Across the Wide Missouri"
B. Kranendonk

"He's Gone Away"
The Girls He Left Behind

"Double Ring Ceremony"
Mountain Lovers
(*Music and Lyrics by* Buddy Bernier and Phyllis Williams.)

"Barefoot"
N. Douglas, J. Best, R. Best, E. Ericksen, P. Marker,
F. Waring, Jr.
(*Music and Lyrics by* Buddy Bernier, Charles Naylor,
Hugh Brannum.)

Scene 7

Songs of All Faiths:

"No Man Is an Island"
The Men

"Come, Come Ye Saints"
P. Beems, T. J. Marker, N. Barnes, G. Pilon

"I Wonder as I Wander"
D. Arms
(*Music and Lyrics by* John Jacob Niles.)

"Salve Regina"
The Chanters

"Work For the Night Is Coming"
J. Eley, R. Randall, M. Long, N. Keller

"Song of Galilee"
The Folks

"God of Our Fathers"
The People
(*Music and Lyrics by* George William Warren, Daniel Crane Roberts,
arranged by Livingston Gearhart.)

Scene 8

Negro Spiritual Inspiration:

"Deep River"
The Congregation

"The Creation" (Sermon from "God's Trombones")
F. Davis
(*Music and Lyrics by* Roy Ringwald and James Weldon Johnson.)

"He's Got the Whole World in His Hands"
The Preacher

Scene 9

Miniature Mammoth Minstrel Show:

"Rampart Street"
Marching Band

"Angels Meet Me at the Crossroads"
The Minstrels

"I'll Be Dar"
L. Kranendonk

"(I Dream of) Jeannie With the Light Brown Hair"
E. Ericksen
(*Music and Lyrics by* Stephen Foster, arranged by
Hawley Ades.)

"For Me and My Gal"
G. Geyer
(*Music by* George W. Meyer. *Lyrics by* Edgar Leslie and E. Ray Goetz.)
"Camptown Races"
R. Sax
"My L'ndy Lou"
G. Goodman
"Oh, Susanna"
The Minstrels
(*Music and Lyrics by* Stephen Foster, arranged by Hawley Ades.)
"Dixie"
Marching Band
Take Five (Intermission)
Unsung Dixieland Interlude
Junior's Jumpin' Jivers
(F. Waring, Jr., W. Cole, M. Doty, L. Bode, R. Sax, H. Ades, L. Brannum, B. Dillon.)

ACT 2
Scene 1
Primary Mathematics:
"Inchworm" (from HANS CHRISTIAN ANDERSEN film)
J. Marine, Friends
(*Music and Lyrics by* Frank Loesser.)
Scene 2
Collegiate Conviviality:
"A Toast to Michigan"
Convivial Collegians
(*Music and Lyrics by* Richard Kirk and Louis Elbel.)
"A Toast to All Colleges"
Same later
"Everybody's Alma Mater"
Alumni Association
Scene 3
High-Fidelity:
"My Old High School"
J. Marine, Old Grads
(*Music and Lyrics by* Tom Waring.)
Scene 4
Songs by New Young Pennsylvanians:
"Granada"
B. Sands
"Unchained Melody"
D. Arms
(*Music by* Alex North. *Lyrics by* Hy Zaret.)
"If I Love You" (from CAROUSEL)
P. Beems
(*Music by* Richard Rodgers. *Lyrics by* Oscar Hammerstein II.)
Piano Session (Title to be announced)
N. Douglas
Scene 5
Choral Symphony and Opera
"The Nutcracker Suite"
Choral Symphony Orchestra
(*Music by* Pyotor Tchaikovsky, arranged by Johnson-Cunkle-Simeone-Bernier-Waring.)
"Rigoletto"
Swanee River Quartet (R. Sands, P. Marker, R. Isbell, P. Beems)
Scene 6
The Ever-Shining Old Stars
L. Eley, J. Eley, L. Kranendonk, J. Marine, G. Goodman, L. Brannum, F. Davis
Scene 7
Songs You'd Hope to Hear, Hear and See, See:
"Dry Bones"
The Singers
"Dancing Tambourines"
The Singers, Players
(*Music by* W. C. Polla. *Lyrics by* Phil Ponce.)

"Over the Rainbow" (from THE WIZARD OF OZ film)
Everybody Sings
(*Music by* Harold Arlen. *Lyrics by* E. Y. Harburg.)
"Dear Old Donegal"
"Dark Town Strutters Ball"
(*Music and Lyrics by* Shelton Brooks.)
"Jesus Walked This Lonesome Valley"
"Joshua Fit the Battle of Jericho"
"The Happy Wanderer" (Val-De-Ri, Val-De-Ra)
(*Music by* Friedrich Wilhelm Möller. *Lyrics by* Antonia Ridge.)
"Carry Me Back to Old Virginny"
"Way Back Home"
(*Music and Lyrics by* Al Lewis and Tom Waring.)
"We'll Go a Long, Long Way Together"
(*Music and Lyrics by* Jimmy Kennedy, A. Fragna)
"With a Song in My Heart" (from SPRING IS HERE)
(*Music by* Richard Rodgers. *Lyrics by* Lorenz Hart.)
"You'll Never Walk Alone" (from CAROUSEL)
(*Music by* Richard. Rodgers. *Lyrics by* Oscar Hammerstein II.)
"Battle Hymn of the Republic"
(*Music and Lyrics by* Julia Ward Howe.)
Hear, Hear the People

1955.14 MAURICE CHEVALIER

Songs and Impressions (A Solo Musical Revue) in Two Acts. At the Piano, Fred Freed. Produced by Gilbert Miller. Opened 28 September 1955 at the Lyceum Theatre and closed 6 November 1955 after 47 performances.

ACT 1
Introduction—Fred Freed
"Ca Va, Ca Va"
(*Music by* Fred Freed. *Lyrics by* Maurice Chevalier.)
"Paris Oui Oui"
(*Music by* Henri Betti. *Lyrics by* André Hornez.)
"I Wonder Who's Kissing Her Now" (from THE PRINCE OF TONIGHT)
(*Music by* Joseph E. Howard, Harold Orlob. *Lyrics by* Will M. Hough, Frank R. Adams)
"Les Pas Perdus"
(*Music by* Henri Bourtayre. *Lyrics by* Robert Lamoureux and Maurice Chevalier.)
"L'Orientale"
(*Music by* Henri Betti. *Lyrics by* André Hornez.)
"C'Est Fort la Musique"
(*Music by* Fred Freed. *Lyrics by* Maurice Chevalier.)
ACT 2
Introduction—Fred Freed
"A Boy and a Girl"
(*Music by* Henri Betti. *English Lyrics by* Ben Smith.)
"L'Illusioniste"
(*Music by* Jean Constantin. *Lyrics by* Vittonet.)
"Un Gentleman"
(*Music and Lyrics by* Maurice Chevalier.)
"She and He"
(*Music by* Henri Betti. *English Lyrics by* Ben Smith.
"À Las Vegas"
(*Music by* Louiguy. *English Lyrics by* Maurice Chevalier.)
"Folies-Bergère"
(*Music by* Francis Lopez. *Lyrics by* Maurice Chevalier.)
"À Barcelone"
(*Music by* Henri Betti. *Lyrics by* Maurice Chevalier.)
"Accents Melodiques"
(*Sketch by* Maurice Chevalier.)
"Louise" (from INNOCENTS OF PARIS film)
(*Music by* Richard A. Whiting. *Lyrics by* Leo Robin.)
"Seems Like Old Times"
(*Music by* John Jacob Loeb. *Lyrics by* Carmen Lombardo.)

THE YEOMEN OF THE GUARD,
1955.15 or The Merryman and His Maid

A Revival of the Comic Opera in Two Acts[2]. Libretto by William S. Gilbert. Music by Arthur Sullivan. Scenery and costumes by Peter Goffin. Directed by Robert A. Gibson. Musical director, Isidore Godfrey. Produced by the D'Oyly Carte Opera Company. Opened 3 October 1955 at the Sam S. Shubert Theatre, closing 5 October 1955; re-opened 3 November 1955 and closed 5 November 1955 after 8 performances in repertory.

CAST: *Sir Richard Cholmondeley,* Lieutenant of the Tower: ALAN STYLER. *Colonel Fairfax* under sentence of death: LEONARD OSBORN. *Sergeant Meryll* of the Yeomen of the Guard: DONALD ADAMS. *Leonard Meryll,* his Son: John Fryatt. *Jack Point,* a Strolling Jester: PETER PRATT. *Wilfred Shadbolt,* Head Jailor and Assistant Tormentor: FISHER MORGAN. *First Yeoman:* Frederick Sinden. *Second Yeoman:* John Banks. *First Citizen:* Lawson Johnson. *Second Citizen:* John Reed. *Elsie Maynard,* a Strolling Player: MURIEL HARDING. *Phoebe Meryll,* Sergeant Meryll's Daughter: JOYCE WRIGHT. *Dame Carruthers,* Housekeeper to the Tower: ANN DRUMMOND-GRANT. *Kate,* her Niece: MAUREEN MELVIN. *Chorus of Yeomen of the Guard, Gentlemen, Citizens, etc.*

THE PIRATES OF PENZANCE,
1955.16 or The Slave of Duty

A Revival of the Comic Opera in Two Acts[3]. Libretto by William S. Gilbert. Music by Arthur Sullivan. Costumes designed by George Sheringham. Directed by Robert A. Gibson. Musical director, Isidore Godfrey. Produced by the D'Oyly Carte Opera Company. Opened 6 1955 at the Sam S. Shubert Theatre, closing 8 October 1955; re-opened 27 October 1955, and closed 29 October 1955 after 8 performances in repertory.[4]

CAST: *Major General Stanley:* PETER PRATT. *The Pirate King:* DONALD ADAMS. *Samuel,* his Lieutenant: Trevor Hills. *Frederic,* the Pirate Apprentice: NEVILLE GRIFFITHS. *Sergeant of Police:* FISHER MORGAN. *Mabel, Edith Kate,Isabel,* General Stanley's Daughters: MURIEL HARDING, JOYCE WRIGHT, JOY MORNAY, Margaret Dobson. *Ruth,* Pirate Maid-of-all-work: ANN DRUMMOND-GRANT. *Chorus of Pirates, Police and General Stanley's Daughters.*

DIE FLEDERMAUS
1955.17

A Revival of the Operetta in Three Acts[5]. (Original Viennese libretto by Carl Haffner and Richard Genée. Lyrics by Richard Genée. Based on the comedy "Le Réveillon" by Henri Meilhac and Ludovic Halévy.) English libretto by Ruth and Thomas Martin. Music by Johann Strauss. Staged by William Westerfield. Costume supervisor, Robert Fletcher. Choreographed by Ray Harrison. Conducted by Joseph Rosenstock. Produced by the New York City Opera. Opened 8 October 1955 at the New York City Center and closed 29 October 1955 after 3 performances in repertory; re-opened 31 March 1956 at the New York City Center and closed 7 April 1956 after 2 additional performances. Total this season: 5 performances.[6]

CAST: *Eisenstein:* JACK RUSSELL. *Rosalinda:* PHYLLIS CURTIN. *Adele:* PEGGY BONINI. *Alfred:* LLOYD THOMAS LEECH. *Falke:* JOHN EARDON. *Frank:* Richard Wentworth. *Blind:* Luigi Vellucci. *Prince Orlofsky:* MICHAEL POLLOCK. *Sally:* Jennie Andrea. *Frosch:* COLEY WORTH. *Ivan:* Thomas Powell. *Ensemble:* New York City Opera Chorus.

THE MIKADO,
1955.18 or The Town of Titipu

A Revival of the Comic Opera in Two Acts[7]. Libretto by William S. Gilbert. Music by Arthur Sullivan. Scenery designed by Peter Goffin. Costumes designed by Charles Ricketts. Directed by Robert A. Gibson. Musical director, Isidore Godfrey. Produced by the D'Oyly Carte Opera Company. Opened 10 October 1955 at the Sam S. Shubert Theatre, closing 12 October 1955; re-opened 31 October 1955-2 November 1955, 17 November 1955 and closed 19 November 1955 after 12 performances in repertory.

CAST: *The Mikado of Japan:* DONALD ADAMS. *Nanki-Poo,* his son, disguised as a wandering minstrel in love with YUM-YUM: NEVILLE GRIFFITHS. *Ko-Ko,* Lord High Executioner of Titipu: PETER PRATT. *Pooh-Bah,* Lord High Everything Else: FISHER MORGAN. *Pish-Tush, Go-To,* Noble Lords: Jeffrey Skitch, John Banks. *Yum-Yum, Pitti-Sing, Peep-Bo,* three sisters, wards of Ko-Ko: CYNTHIA MOREY, JOYCE WRIGHT, BERYL DIXON. *Katisha:* ANN DRUMMOND-GRANT. *Chorus of School Girls, Nobles, Guards and Coolies.*

JOYCE GRENFELL
1955.19 REQUESTS THE PLEASURE

A Musical Revue in Two Acts, 26 Scenes. Book and lyrics by Joyce Grenfell. Music by Richard Addinsell. (Additional music by George Bauer, William Blezard, Joan Chorlton, Douglas Gamlin, Terry Stanford, A. Reif, Donald Swann, Malcolm Arnold, Dennis Holloway and Ralph Freed. Additional lyrics by Oliver Bernard.) Directed by Laurier Lister. Musical director, George Bauer. Scenic supervision and lighting by Paul Morrison. Decor by Joan and David de Bethel, Victor Stiebel, Stanley Moore, Peter Rice. Choreography by John Heawood, Wendy Toye, Alfred Rodrigues, Beryl Kaye, Paddy Stone, Irving Davies. Additional arrangements by George Bauer. Additional orchestrations by Clare Grundman. Produced by Producers Theatre (Lyn Austin and Thomas Noyes). Opened 10 October 1955 at the Bijou Theatre and closed 3 December 1955 after 64 performances.

CAST: JOYCE GRENFELL, BERYL KAYE, PADDY STONE, IRVING DAVIES.

ACT 1[8]
Scene 1
   "Welcome"
      (*by* Joyce Grenfell) J. Grenfell
         Proscenium by Joan and David de Bethel. *Decor by* Peter Rice. *Dress by* Victor Stiebel.
Scene 2
   "Three's Company"
      B. Kaye, P. Stone, I. Davies
      (*Music by* George Bauer. *Costumes by* Joan and David de Bethel. *Dance arranged by* John Heawood.)
Scene 3
   "The Music's Message"
      J. Grenfell
      (*Music by* Richard Addinsell. *Lyrics by* Joyce Grenfell.)
Scene 4
   "Edinburgh Rock"
      B. Kaye, P. Stone, I. Davies
      (*Music by* Richard Addinsell. *Decor by* Jack Notman. *Dance arranged by* Alfred Rodrigues.)

---

[2]First presented in New York 17 October 1888 at the Casino Theatre for 100 performances. For Synopsis of Scenes and Musical Numbers, see original 1888 production.
[3]First presented in New York 31 December 1879 at the Fifth Avenue Theatre for a total of 91 performances in two engagements. For Synopsis of Scenes and Musical Numbers, see original 1879 production.
[4]Scenery uncredited.
[5]First English language production presented in New York 16 March 1885 at the Casino Theatre for 42 performances. First New York production of this adaptation 20 December 1950 at the Metropolitan Opera House. For Synopsis of Scenes and Musical Numbers, see May 1954 revival.
[6]Settings uncredited; settings and costumes were assembled from various sources, a previous Sol Hurok tour of DIE FLEDERMAUS and the Broadway production of MY DARLIN' AIDA.

[7]First presented in New York 20 July, 10-29 August 1885 at the Union Square and People's Theatres for 22 performances. First authorized production presented 19 August 1885 at the Fifth Avenue Theatre by Richard D'Oyly Carte for 250 performances. For Synopsis of Scenes and Musical Numbers, see 19 August 1885 D'Oyly Carte production.
[8]The following songs were also included:
   "Just the Way You Are"
      (Walt Disney music)
   "I'll Lend You Everything I've Got Except My Wife" (from ZIEGFELD FOLLIES OF 1910)
      (*Music by* Harry Von Tilzer. *Lyrics by* Jean C. Havez.)
   "My Little Home in Tennessee"
      (*Music by* Carson J. Robison.)

Scene 5

Women at Work: 1. Curiosity Shop, 2. Nursery School
J. Grenfell
(*Written by* Joyce Grenfell. *Dress by* Victor Stiebel.)

Scene 6

"Two Loves"
B. Kaye, P. Stone, I. Davies
(*Music by* Joan Chorlton and Douglas Gamlin. *Dance arranged by* Kaye, Stone and Davies.)

Scene 7

"Basquette"
B. Kaye, P. Stone, I. Davies
(*Music by* William Blezard. *Dance arranged by* Wendy Toye.)

Scene 8

"Period Piece"
J. Grenfell
(*Music by* Richard Addinsell. *Lyrics by* Joyce Grenfell. *Decor by* Joan and David de Bethel. *Dress by* Victor Stiebel.)

Scene 9

"Heart Ride"
I. Davies
(*Music by* Terry Stanford. *Lyrics by* Oliver Bernard. *Dance arranged by* John Heawood. *Decor by* Paul Morrison.)

Scene 10

The Understanding Mother
(*by* Joyce Grenfell) J. Grenfell

Scene 11

"Nothing to Do"
B. Kaye
(*Music by* A. Reif. *Dance arranged by* Peter Hamilton.)

Scene 12

Thought for Today
(*by* Joyce Grenfell) J. Grenfell
(*Decor by* Peter Rice. *Dress by* Victor Stiebel.)

Scene 13

"Favour"
B. Kaye, P. Stone
(*Music by* Donald Swann. *Decor by* Joan and David de Bethel. *Dance arranged by* Wendy Toye.)

Scene 14

"Three Brothers"
J. Grenfell
(*Music by* Richard Addinsell. *Lyrics by* Joyce Grenfell.)

Scene 15

"Palais Dancers"
J. Grenfell, B. Kaye, P. Stone, I. Davies
(*Music by* Richard Addinsell. *Lyrics by* Joyce Grenfell. *Decor by* Stanley Moore. *Dance arranged by* Alfred Rodrigues.)

ACT 2

Scene 1

"Slap Happy"
B. Kaye, P. Stone, I. Davies
("Begin the Beguine" *composed by* Cole Porter. *Dress by* Joan David de Bethel. *Dance arranged by* Wendy Toye.)

Scene 2

Two Young People and a Visitor:
(*by* Joyce Grenfell) J. Grenfell
1. Travel Talk, 2. Musician, 3. Visitor.
(*Dress by* Victor Stiebel.)

Scene 3

"Manana"
P. Stone, I. Davies
(*Music by* William Blezard. *Decor by* Stanley Moore. *Dance arranged by* Alfred Rodrigues.)

Scene 4

"Running Commentary"
J. Grenfell
(*Music by* Richard Addinsell. *Lyrics by* Joyce Grenfell.)

Scene 5

"Ordinary Morning"
B. Kaye, I. Davies
(*Music by* Richard Addinsell. *Lyrics by* Joyce Grenfell. *Decor by* Joan and David de Bethel. *Dance arranged by* John Heawood.)

Scene 6

"Paddy's Nightmare"
P. Stone
(*Music by* Malcolm Arnold. *Costume designed by* Joan and David de Bethel. *Dance devised and arranged by* Paddy Stone.)

Scene 7

"Songs My Mother Taught Me"
J. Grenfell
(*Music arranged by* Viola Tunnard. *Decor by* Paul Morrison. *Dress by* Joan and David de Bethel.)

Scene 8

Life and Literature
(*by* Joyce Grenfell) J. Grenfell

Scene 9

"Three in Time"
B. Kaye, P. Stone, I. Davies
(*Music by* Dennis Holloway. *Dance arranged by* Wendy Toye.)

Scene 10

"Envoi"
B. Kaye, P. Stone, I. Davies
(*Music by* Ralph Freed. *Dance arranged by* Wendy Toye.)

Scene 11

"Farewell"
(*by* Joyce Grenfell. *Dress by* Victor Stiebel.) J. Grenfell

PRINCESS IDA,
or Castle Adamant

1955.20

A Revival of the Comic Operetta in Three Acts[9]. Libretto by William S. Gilbert. Music by Arthur Sullivan. Directed by Robert A. Gibson. Scenery and costumes by James Wade. Orchestra directed by Isidore Godfrey. Produced by the D'Oyly Carte Opera Company. Opened 13 October 1955 at the Sam S. Shubert Theatre, closing 15 October 1955; re-opened 7 November 1955 and closed 9 November 1955 after 8 performances in repertory.

<u>CAST</u>: *King Hildebrand:* FISHER MORGAN. *Hilarion:* JOHN FRYATT. *Hilarion's Two Friends: Cyril:* LEONARD OSBORN. *Florian:* JEFFREY SKITCH. *King Gama:* PETER PRATT. *His Sons: Arac:* DONALD ADAMS. *Guron:* JOHN BANKS. *Scythius:* Trevor Hills. *Princess Ida, Gama's Daughter:* MURIEL HARDING. *Lady Blanche, Professor of Abstract Science:* ANN DRUMMOND-GRANT. *Lady Psyche, Professor of Humanities:* CYNTHIA MOREY. *Melissa, Lady Blanche's Daughter:* BERYL DIXON. *Sacharissa:* MAUREEN MELVIN. *Chloe:* Margaret Dobson. *Ada:* Jennifer Toye. *Soldiers, Courtiers, Girl Graduates, Daughters of the Plough, etc.*

TRIAL BY JURY

1955.21

A Revival of the Comic Opera in One Act[10]. Libretto by William S. Gilbert. Music by Arthur Sullivan. Ladies costumes designed by George Sheringham. Scenery by Joseph and Phil Harker. Directed by Robert A. Gibson. Musical director, Isidore Godfrey. Produced by the D'Oyly Carte Opera Company. Opened 17 October 1955 at the Sam S. Shubert Theatre, closing 19 October 1955; re-opened 10-12 November 1955; re-opened 21 November 1955, and closed 24 November 1955 after 13 performances in repertory.

<u>CAST</u>: *The Learned Judge:* JOHN REED. *Counsel for the Defendant:* ALAN STYLER. *The Defendant:* JOHN FRYATT. *Foreman of the Jury:* John Banks. *Usher:* TREVOR HILLS. *Associate:* GEORGE COOK. *The Plaintiff:* KATHLEEN WEST. *First Bridesmaid:* Margaret Dobson. *Chorus of Jurymen, Bridesmaids and Public.*

---

[9]Originally presented in New York City 11 February 1884 at the Fifth Avenue Theatre for 42 performances. For Synopsis of Scenes and Musical Numbers, see original 1884 production.

[10]First presented in New York 15 November 1875 at the Eagle Theatre for 8 performances. For Synopsis of Scenes and Musical Numbers, see original 1875 production.

H.M.S. PINAFORE,
1955.22   or The Lass That Loved a Sailor

A Revival of the Comic Opera in Two Acts[11]. Libretto by William S. Gilbert. Music by Arthur Sullivan. Directed by Robert A. Gibson. Designed and painted by Joseph and Paul Harker. Ladies' costumes designed by George Sheringham. Musical director, Isidore Godfrey. Presented by the D'Oyly Carte Opera Company. Opened 17 October 1955 at the Sam S. Shubert Theatre, closing 19 October 1955; re-opened 10-12 November 1955; re-opened 21 November 1955, and closed 24 November 1955 after 13 performances in repertory.

CAST: *The Rt. Hon. Sir Joseph Porter, K.C.B., First Lord of the Admiralty*: PETER PRATT. *Captain Corcoran, Commanding the H.M.S. Pinafore*: JEFFREY SKITCH. *Ralph Rackstraw*, Able Seaman: NEVILLE GRIFFITHS. *Dick Deadeye*, Able Seaman: DONALD ADAMS. *Bill Bobstay*, Bo'sun's Mate: Trevor Hills. *Bob Beckett*, Carpenter's Mate: George Cook. *Josephine*, the Captain's Daughter: MURIEL HARDING. *Hebe*, Sir Joseph's First Cousin: Joyce Wright. *Little Buttercup*, a Portsmouth Bumboat Woman: ANN DRUMMOND-GRANT. *First Lord's Sisters, his Cousins, his Aunts, Sailors, Marines.*

RUDDIGORE,
1955.23   or The Witch's Curse

A Revival of the Comic Opera in Two Acts[12]. Libretto by William S. Gilbert. Music by Arthur Sullivan. Directed by Robert A. Gibson. Costumes and settings by Peter Goffin. Orchestra directed by Isidore Godfrey. Produced by the D'Oyly Carte Opera Company. Opened 20 October 1955 at the Sam S. Shubert Theatre, closing 22 October 1955; re-opened 14 November 1955 and closed 16 November 1955 after 8 performances in repertory.

CAST: *Sir Ruthven Murgatroyd*: PETER PRATT. *Richard Dauntless*: LEONARD OSBORN. *Sir Despard Murgatroyd*: FISHER MORGAN. *Old Adam Goodheart*: John Banks. *Sir Roderic Murgatroyd*: DONALD ADAMS. *Rose Maybud*: CYNTHIA MOREY. *Mad Margaret*: JOYCE WRIGHT. *Dame Hannah*: ANN DRUMMOND-GRANT. *Zorah*: May Sanderson. *Ruth*: Joyce Farrer. *Chorus of Officers, Ancestors, Professional Bridesmaids, etc.*

IOLANTHE,
1955.24   or The Peer and the Peri

A Revival of the Comic Opera in Two Acts[13]. Libretto by William S. Gilbert. Music by Arthur Sullivan. Costumes designed by Pat Freeborn. Directed by Robert A. Gibson. Musical director, Isidore Godfrey. Produced by the D'Oyly Carte Opera Company. Opened 24 October 1955 at the Sam S. Shubert Theatre, closing 26 October 1955; re-opened 25 November 1955 and closed 26 November 1955 after 7 performances.[14]

CAST: *The Lord Chancellor*: PETER PRATT. *Earl of Mountararat*: DONALD ADAMS. *Earl Tolloller*: LEONARD OSBORN. *Private Willis* of the Grenadier Guards: FISHER MORGAN. *Strephon*, an Arcadian Shepherd: ALAN STYLER. *Queen of the Fairies*: ANN DRUMMOND-GRANT. *Iolanthe*, a Fairy, Strephon's Mother: JOYCE WRIGHT. *Celia, Leila, Fleta*, Fairies: Maureen Melvin, Beryl Dixon, Margaret Dobson. *Phyllis*, an Arcadian Shepherdess and Ward in Chancery: CYNTHIA MOREY. *Chorus of Dukes, Marquises, Earls, Viscounts, Barons and Fairies.*

1955.25   ## THE VAMP

A Musical Comedy in Two Acts, 10 Scenes. Book by John Latouche and Sam Locke. Music by James Mundy. Based on a story by John Latouche. Choreography by Robert Alton. Sets and costumes by Raoul Pene du Bois. Musical direction and vocal arrangements by Milton Rosenstock. Incidental music by Jack Pfeiffer. Orchestrations by James Mundy. Directed by David

Alexander. Entire production supervised by Robert Alton. Associate producer, Manuel D. Herbert. Produced by Oscar Lerman, Martin Cohen and Alexander Carson. Opened 10 November 1955 at the Winter Garden and closed 31 December 1955 after 60 performances.

CAST (in order of appearance): *Myron H. Hubbard*: JACK WALDRON. *Bessie Bisco*: BIBI OSTERWALD. *Muscle Man*: Steve Reeves. *Barney Ostertag*: Paul Lipson. *Oliver J. Oxheart*: DAVID ATKINSON. *Ticket Girl*: Phyllis Dorne. *Stanley Hubermyer*: ROBERT RIPPY. *Stark Clayton*: MALCOLM LEE BEGGS. *Elsie Chelsea*: PATRICIA HAMMERLEE. *Bluestone*: Jack Harrold. *Flora Weems*: CAROL CHANNING. *Uncle Garvey*: WILL GEER. *Aunt Hester*: Sandyl Cordell. *Fire Commissioner*: Roger Franklin. *Snake Charmer*: David Neuman. *Samson*: STEVE REEVES. *Whip Man*: David Kashner. *High Priest*: David Neuman. *Charlie*: MATT MATTOX. *Second Cameraman*: Dick Eskeli. *Tyrolean Couples*: Cathryn Damon, Hugh Lambert, Helen Silver, Ron Cecill.

Dancers: Cathryn Damon, Mary Jane Doerr, Phyllis Dorne, Susan Hartman, Barbara Heath, Betty Koerber, Lucia Lambert, Barbara Leigh, Lila Popper, Helen Silver, Pat Wharton, Mark Aldon, Chad Block, Ron Cecill, Robert Daley, Pepe de Chazza, Burnell Dietsch, Rudy Del Campo, Hugh Lambert, Robert Norris, Dom Salinaro, Mike Stevens. *Singers*: Charleen Clark, Joyce Gladmond, Bernice Massi, Donna Sanders, Kelley Stephens, Kay Turner, Dick Eskeli, Roger Franklin, Stokely Gray, William Krach, Vincent McMahon, Ralph Wayne.

Act 1, Scene 1: Hubbard's Coliseum, Fourteenth Street (New York City, 1913). *Scene 2*: A farm in the Bronx. The following morning. *Scene 3*: Hubbard's Movie House. A few weeks later. *Scene 4*: Grand Central Station. Three months later. *Scene 5*: A rooftop in Manhattan. Sometime later.

Act 2, Scene 1: a. The northeast corner of Hollywood and Vine. b. OHO Film Company. One year later. *Scene 2*: Interior of OHO Studios. *Scene 3*: Flora's Dressing Room. *Scene 4*: Executive office, OHO Film Company. The next day. *Scene 5*: Hubbard's Movie Cathedral, Hollywood.

ACT 1
Scene 1
    "The Spiel"
        J. Waldron, B. Osterwald, Patrons of the Coliseum
    "The Flickers"
        P. Dorne, Patrons
Scene 2
    "Keep Your Nose to the Grindstone"
        C. Channing, W. Geer, S. Cordell
    "That's Where a Man Fits In"
        C. Channing
    "I've Always Loved You"[15]
        C. Channing, Farm Folk
Scene 3
    "You're Colossal"
        P. Hammerlee, R. Rippy
    "Fan Club Chant"
        Movie Fans
Scene 4
    "Have You Met Delilah?"
        D. Atkinson
    "Yeemy Yeemy"
        C. Channing, Oriental Entourage
    "The Vamps"
        M. Mattox, B. Heath, C. Damon, Fans
Scene 5
    "Delilah's Dilemma"
        C. Channing, Movie Fans
ACT 2
Scene 1
    "Four Little Misfits"
        P. Hammerlee, B. Osterwald, R. Rippy, M. Mattox
Scene 2
    "Samson and Delilah"
        C. Channing,
        M. Mattox, S. Reevs, D. Kashner, D. Neuman, C. Damon, Movie Company
    "Why Does It Have To be You?"
        D. Atkinson

---

[11]Originally presented in New York 15 January 1879 at the Standard Theatre for 175 performances. For Synopsis of Scenes and Musical Numbers, see original 1879 production.
[12]First presented in New York 21 February 1887 at the Standard Theatre for 53 performances. For Synopsis of Scenes and Musical Numbers, see original 1887 production.
[13]First presented in New York 25 November 1882 at the Standard Theatre for 105 performances. For Synopsis of Scenes and Musical Numbers, see original 1882 production.
[14]Scenery uncredited.

---

[15]Dropped during the run.

"Ragtime Romeo"
    B. Osterwald, M. Mattox, Boys
Scene 3
    "I'm Everybody's Baby"
        C. Channing
Scene 4
    "I'm Everybody's Baby" (reprise)
        C. Channing, P. Lipson, R. Rippy, J. Waldron, M. L. Beggs
    "The Impossible She"[16]
        D. Atkinson, OHO Boys
Scene 5
    Finale
        Company

KATHERINE DUNHAM AND HER COMPANY

1955.26

A Dance Revue in Three Acts, 12 Scenes[17]. Costumes and scenery by John Pratt. Orchestra directed by Gilberto Valdes. Choreography and direction by Katherine Dunham. Produced by Sol Hurok. Opened 22 November 1955 at the Broadway Theatre and closed 17 December 1955 after 32 performances.

CAST: KATHERINE DUNHAM.
Dancers: VANOYE AIKENS, RICARDO AVALOS, Walter Davis, LUCILLE ELLIS, Kupi Fraker, LAVINIA HAMILTON, John Lewis, Marvel Martin, Jewell André, LENWOOD MORRIS, Raimonda Orselli, Madeline Preston, Antonio Rodrigues, Jorge Saenz, Eleanor St. Ann, URAL WILSON, Camille Yarborough.

Singers: ROSALIE KING, Dorothy Speights, Gordon Simpson, URAL WILSON, Robert Wise. *Drummers*: Julito Collazo, Albert Longuerre, Francisco Urrutia, RICARDO AVALOS, Antonio Rodrigues.

ACT 1
Scene 1

Brazilian Suite:

a. Hommage to Dorival Caymmi
    (*Music by* Caymmi, arr. Noriega.)
        R. King, D. Thompson, G. Simpson, U. Wilson, R. Wise, Company
Dorival Caymmi, Brazilian poet, sings the beauties of his native Bahia. His songs of the sea are full of haunting mystery, his poems of the people are moving and charming. No other Brazilian folkloric writer nor composer has achieved such simplicity of expression.

b. A Preta Do Acaraje
    (*Music by* Caymmi, arr. Noriega.)K. Dunham, Company
Late at night, in the deserted streets of Bahia, a street vendor offers her wares to the late passers-by. A few of them stop for a moment and dance.

c. Choros 1 and 4
    (*Music by* Vadico Gogliano, Noriega.)
        L. Hamilton, R. Orselli, L. Morris, J. Saenz
Variation on a Brazilian Quadrille of the early nineteenth century.

d. Carnevao!
The spirit of Brazil is in its carnivals. From Pernambuco to Rio Grande do Sul excitement and gaiety take over and Carnival is King.

(i) Xaxaado (from the North)
    (*Music by* Rodriguez.)
        K. Dunham, V. Aikens, Company
(ii) Samba (in Rio the Samba)
    (*Music by* Dunham, Rodriguez.)
        A. Rodrigues, L. Ellis, L. Hamilton, M. Martin, E. St. Ann
(iii) Frevo (from Recife O Frevo)
    (arr. Noreiga)
        L. Morris, R. Orselli, M. Martin, C. Yarborough, R. Avalos, J. Lewis
e. Los Indios (Native Air)
    W. Davis, K. Fraker, E. St. Ann
In the west of Brazil in the High Andes, two women stop to flirt with a flute player.

Scene 2
Tango (in memory of Pepita Cano)
    (*Music by* Osvaldo Pugliese.)
        K. Dunham, V. Aikens, L. Ellis, R. Avalos, U. Wilson
In the Argentine there have been many changes in recent years, but the vast city of Buenos Aires still covers the underbeat of the tango. In the cantinas of the street people Katherine Dunham felt the nostalgia of the tango and the restlessness of the times.

Scene 3
Veracruzana
    (*Music by* Dorothea Freitag and Foster, adapted by Gogliano-Nardini.)
        The Mariachis: R. Orselli, J. Collazo, J. Saenz, F. Urrutia. *The family from Yucatan*: R. King, G. Simpson, K. Fraker. *A 'Tacos' Vendor*: D. Speights. *El Raton*: R. Avalos. *The cuckold*: L. Morris. *The Veracruzana*: K. Dunham. *The favored one*: V. Aikens. *The strong man*: A. Rodrigues. *Bamba dancers of the village*: L. Ellis, L. Hamilton, M. Martin.

ACT 2
Rituals: These rites encompass the transition of an individual or a group of individuals from one important stage of life to another. These rites at the same time sacred and dangerous occur under the supervision of the elders of those already initiated in the community. Their presence is necessary at this critical transition by which the individual who has heretofore occupied a position on a different level in the community should become integrated into complete union with his new level. These rites herein represented do not refer to any one particular society, neither do they pretend to represent the enaction of a realistic ceremony. They have been created in an effort to present, at least partially, the deep emotional interest which every primitive community feels in the individual and to expose the intense personal experience which accompanies every profound change. The primitive community finds itself sensitive to these personal reactions and protective of the individual.

Scene 1
Puberty Ritual
    (*Music by* Anderson.)
        The Boy: L. Morris. *The Warrior*: V. Aikens.
The ceremony of initiation by which a boy passes from the age of puberty and into manhood. In the first part the boy is isolated and the warrior which he is to become approaches him in a semi-dream state. In the second part the men of his tribe, masked for their own secret society and led by the warrior enter to take the boy, who is filled with both terror and anticipation, to the finalization of his rites of masculinity.

Scene 2
Fertility Ritual
    (*Music by* Paquita Anderson.)
        The Woman: L. Ellis. *The Man*: W. Davis.
The ceremony of the fertility ritual here concerned with marriage or mating in a primitive society.

Scene 3
Death
    (*Music by* Dorothea Freitag, arr. Auric.)
        Gede: U. Wilson. *The Queen Widow*: K. Dunham. *The consort*: V. Aikens. *Other widows and warriors*: The Company.
Death is vanquished by life and the newly born takes the place of the dead. In a primitive society orgiastic ceremonies often replace the funeral rites which are the custom in modern societies. In the cult of Rada Dahomey, it is Gede who presides over the ceremony of the dead. God of Death, he struts pompously and by the vulgarity of his gestures he attempts to overcome sorrow, by his obscenity he shows the need to conquer death in order to assure the continuity of life. The community awaits the death of the King, the passage of the royal robe, the widows mourn, the queen accepts the command of Gede and selects a mate to replace her deceased husband.

Scene 4
Shango
    (*Music by* [Baldwin] Bergersen.)
        Shango priest: J. Collazo. *Shango priestess*: H. Alvarez. *The boy possessed by the snake*: U. Wilson.
The scarifice of the white cock to the Yoruba God Shango takes place in Trinidad, but is known throughout the West Indies.

---

[16]Dropped during the run.
[17]KATHERINE DUNHAM AND HER COMPANY previously appeared on Broadway 19 April 1950 at the Broadway Theatre for 37 performances.

ACT 3

Americana: Out of the sufferings of slavery came a music rich in rhythms and dances evolved from African origins and overlaid with American forms. The Negroes adopted, interpreted and modified many creative expressions of their masters, and developed dances of strange and extravagant gaiety. In the 'Spirituals,' however, there is the awareness of tragedy but with evidences of hope, one of the most pronounced characteristics of Negro peoples.

Scene 1

Spirituals (Traditional)
R. King, D. Speights, M. Preston, U. Wilson, R. Wise
Dancer: L. Hamilton.

Deepest expression of despair and hope following a direct line from the plaints of the days of slavery.

Scene 2

Barrelhouse: Florida Swamp Shimmy (*Music by* Stacy.)
K. Dunham, Company

A Saturday night encounter during the 1920s.

Scene 3

Flaming Youth
R. King
Kansas City Woman: L. Ellis.

The Charles, the Black Bottom, the Mooch, the Fishtail, Snakehips (Dances)
L. Hamilton, W. Davis, L. Morris, Company

Scene 4

Strutters' Ball
R. King, D. Speights, G. Simpson, U. Wilson, R. Wise

Songs of the turn of the century.

Scene 5

Cakewalk
K. Dunham, V. Aikens, Company

Before the turn of the century the Cakewalk became a dance mania that spread to Europe. Couples competed with exhibitionistic and athletic variations for prizes of elaborately trimmed cakes.

1955.27

PIPE DREAM

A Musical in Two Acts, 18 Scenes. Book and lyrics by Oscar Hammerstein II. Based on the novel "Sweet Thursday" by John Steinbeck. Music by Richard Rodgers. Directed by Harold Clurman. Scenery and lighting by Jo Mielziner. Costumes by Alvin Colt. Orchestrations by Robert Russell Bennett. Musical director, Salvatore Dell'Isola. Dances and musical numbers staged by Boris Runanin. Dance arrangements by John Morris. Produced by Richard Rodgers and Oscar Hammerstein II. Opened 30 November 1955 at the Sam S. Shubert Theatre and closed 30 June 1956 after 246 performances.

CAST (in order of appearance): *Doc:* WILLIAM JOHNSON. *Hazel:* MIKE KELLIN. *Millicent Henderson:* Jayne Heller. *Mac:* G. D. WALLACE. *Suzy:* JUDY TYLER. *Fauna:* HELEN TRAUBEL. *Jim Blaikey:* Rufus Smith. *Ray Busch:* John Call. *George Herman:* Gus Raymond. *Bill:* Steve Roland. *Red:* Keith Kaldenberg. *Whitey:* Hobe Streiford. *Dizzy:* Nicolas Orloff. *Eddie:* Warren Kemmerling. *Alec:* Warren Brown. *Joe, the Mexican:* Kenneth Harvey. *Pancho, a Wetback:* Ruby Braff. *Agnes:* Temple Texas. *Mable:* Jackie McElroy. *Emma:* Marilyn Bradley. *Beulah:* Mildred Slavin. *Marjorie:* Louise Troy. *Cho Cho Sen:* Pat Creighton. *Sumi:* Sandra Devlin. *Sonny Boy:* Joseph Leon. *Esteban, a Wetback:* Jerry LaZarre. *Harriet:* Patricia Wilson. *A Waiter:* Kazimir Kokich. *Hilda:* Ruth Kobart. *Fred:* Marvin Krauter. *Slick:* Gene Kevin. *Slim:* Don Weissmuller. *Basha:* Sigyn. *Bubbles:* Marsha Reynolds. *Sonya:* Annabelle Gold. *Kitty:* Jenny Workman. *Weirde:* Patti Karkalits. *Johnny Carriagra:* Scotty Engel. *Pedro:* Rudolfo Cornejo. *Dr. Ormondy:* Calvin Thomas.

The action takes place in Cannery Row, Monterey County, California at the present time.

Act 1, Scene 1: The Western Biological Laboratory. *Scene 2:* Cannery Row, a few weeks later. *Scene 3:* The Palace Flophouse, immediately following. *Scene 4:* Cannery Row, a few days later, on a Sweet Thursday. *Scene 5:* The Western Biological Laboratory. *Scene 6:* Cannery Row. *Scene 7:* A room in the Bear Flag Cafe. *Scene 8:* Cannery Row. *Scene 9:* Sonny Boy's Pier Restaurant.

Act 2, Scene 1: A room in the Bear Flag Cafe, the following morning. *Scene 2:* Cannery Row, the following night. *Scene 3:* The Palace Flophouse, the following night. *Scene 4:* Cannery Row, the next night. *Scene 5:* The Bear Flag Cafe, a few weeks later. *Scene 6:* Cannery Row, the next morning. *Scene 7:* Inside 'The Pipe.' *Scene 8:* Cannery Row, the next morning. *Scene 9:* The Western Biological Laboratory.

ACT 1
Scene 1

"All Kinds of People"
W. Johnson, M. Kellin

"The Tide Pool"
W. Johnson, M. Kellin, G. D. Wallace, J. Tyler

"All Kinds of People" (reprise)
R. Smith

"Everybody's Got a Home But Me"
J. Tyler

Scene 3

"A Lopsided Bus"
G. D. Wallace, M. Kellin, J. Workman, A. Gold, Flophouse Gang

"Bum's Opera"
H. Traubel, K. Harvey, R. Braff, Flophouse Gang

Scene 5

"The Man I Used To Be"
W. Johnson
Danced by D. Weissmuller.

"Sweet Thursday"
H. Traubel

Scene 7

"Suzy Is a Good Thing"
H. Traubel, J. Tyler

Scene 9

"All at Once You Love Her"
W. Johnson, J. Tyler, J. LaZarre

ACT 2
Scene 1

"The Happiest House on the Block"
H. Traubel, Girls

Scene 2

"The Party That We're Gonna Have Tomorrow Night"
G. D. Wallace, Ensemble

Scene 3

Masquerade Brawl at the Flophouse

a) The Party Gets Going
(Company)

b) "I Am a Witch"
H. Traubel, T. Texas, L. Troy, M. Slavin, J. McElroy

c) "Will You Marry Me?"
J. Tyler, H. Traubel, W. Johnson

Scene 4

"Thinkin'"
M. Kellin

Scene 5

"All at Once You Love Her" (reprise)
H. Traubel

Scene 6

"How Long?"
H. Traubel, W. Johnson, Flophouse Boys, Bear Flag Girls

Scene 7

"The Next Time It Happens"
J. Tyler, W. Johnson

Scene 9

"Sweet Thursday" (reprise)
Entire Company

Finale
Entire Company

1956.01

MY FAIR LADY

A Musical in Two Acts, 18 Scenes. Book and lyrics by Alan Jay Lerner. Based on the play "Pygmalion" by George Bernard Shaw, produced on the screen by Gabriel Pascal. Music by Frederick Loewe. Staged by Moss Hart. Choreography and musical numbers staged by Hanya Holm. Production (settings) designed by Oliver Smith. Costumes by Cecil Beaton. Musical arrangements by Robert Russell Bennett and Philip J. Lang. Lighting by (Abe) Feder. Dance music arranged by Trude Rittman. Musical director, Franz Allers. Produced by Herman Levin. Opened 15 March 1956 at the Mark Hellinger Theatre, moved 28 February 1962 to the Broadhurst Theatre, moved 18 April 1962 to the Broadway Theatre, and closed 29 September 1962 after 2717 performances.

CAST (in order of appearance): *Buskers:* Imelda De Martin, Carl Jeffrey, Joe Rocco. *Mrs. Eynsford-Hill:* Viola Roche. *Eliza Doolittle:* JULIE ANDREWS. *Freddy Eynsford-Hill:* JOHN MICHAEL KING. *Colonel Pickering:* ROBERT COOTE. *A Bystander:* Christopher Hewett. *Henry Higgins:* REX HARRISON. *Selsey Man:* Gordon Dilworth. *Hoxton Man:* David Thomas. *Another Bystander:* Rod McLennan. *First Cockney:* Reid Shelton. *Second Cockney:* Glenn Kezer. *Third Cockney:* James Morris. *Fourth Cockney:* Herb Surface. *Bartender:* David Thomas. *Harry:* Gordon Dilworth. *Jamie:* Rod McLennan. *Alfred P. Doolittle:* STANLEY HOLLOWAY. *Mrs. Pearce:* Philippa Bevans. *Mrs. Hopkins:* Olive Reeves-Smith. *Butler:* Reid Shelton. *Servants:* Rosemary Gaines, Colleen O'Connor, Muriel Shaw, Gloria Van Dorpe, Glenn Kezer. *Mrs. Higgins:* CATHLEEN NESBITT. *Chauffeur:* Barton Mumaw. *Footmen:* Gordon Ewing, William Krach. *Lord Boxington:* Gordon Dilworth. *Lady Boxington:* Olive Reeves-Smith. *Constable:* Barton Mumaw. *Flower Girl:* Cathy Conklin. *Zoltan Karpathy:* Christopher Hewett. *Flunkey:* Paul Brown. *Queen of Transylvania:* Maribel Hammer. *Ambassador:* Rod McLennan. *Bartender:* Paul Brown. *Mrs. Higgins' Maid:* Judith Williams.

Singing Ensemble: Melisande Congdon, Lola Fisher, Rosemary Gaines, Maribel Hammer, Colleen O'Connor, Muriel Shaw, Patti Spangler, Gloria Van Dorpe, Paul Brown, Gordon Ewing, Glenn Kezer, William Krach, James Morris, Reid Shelton, Herb Surface, David Thomas. *Dancing Ensemble:* Estelle Aza, Cathy Conklin, Margaret Cuddy, Imelda De Martin, Pat Diamond, Pat Drylie, Barbara Heath, Vera Lee, Nancy Lynch, Judith Williams, Thatcher Clarke, Crandall Diehl, David Evans, Carl Jeffrey, Barton Mumaw, Gene Nettles, Paul Olson, Joe Rocco, Fernando Schaffenburg, James White.

The place is London, the time 1912.

Act 1, Scene 1: Outside the Opera House, Covent Garden. A cold March night. *Scene 2:* A tenement section—Tottenham Court Road. Immediately following. *Scene 3:* Higgins' Study. The following morning. *Scene 4:* Tenement Section—Tottenham Court Road. Three days later. *Scene 5:* Higgins' study. Later that day. *Scene 6:* Near the race meeting, Ascot. A July afternoon. *Scene 7:* Inside a club tent, Ascot. Immediately following. *Scene 8:* Outside Higgins' house, Wimpole Street. Later that afternoon. *Scene 9:* Higgins' study. Six weeks later. *Scene 10:* The Promenade of the Embassy. Later that night. *Scene 11:* The ballroom of the Embassy. Immediately following.

Act 2, Scene 1: Higgins' study. 3:00 the following morning. *Scene 2:* Outside Higgins' house, Wimpole Street. Immediately following. *Scene 3:* Flower market of Covent Garden. 5:00 that morning. *Scene 4:* Upstairs hall of Higgins' house. 11:00 that morning. *Scene 5:* The conservatory of Mrs. Higgins' house. Later that day. *Scene 6:* Outside Higgins' house, Wimpole Street. Immediately following. *Scene 7:* Higgins' study. Immediately following.

ACT 1

Scene 1

Street Entertainers
I. De Martin, C. Jeffrey, J. Rocco
"Why Can't the English?"
R. Harrison
"Wouldn't It Be Lovely"
J. Andrews, Cockneys

Scene 2

"With a Little Bit of Luck"
S. Holloway, G. Dilworth, R. McLennan

Scene 3

"I'm an Ordinary Man"
R. Harrison

Scene 4

"With a Little Bit of Luck" (reprise)
S. Holloway, Ensemble

Scene 5

"Just You Wait"
J. Andrews
"The Rain in Spain"
R. Harrison, J. Andrews, R. Coote
"I Could Have Danced All Night"
J. Andrews, P. Bevans, R. Gaines, C. O'Connor, M. Shaw, G. Van Dorpe

Scene 7

"Ascot Gavotte"
Full Ensemble

Scene 8

"On the Street Where You Live"
J. M. King

Scene 11

"The Embassy Waltz"
R. Harrison, J. Andrews, C. Hewett, Full Ensemble

ACT 2

Scene 1

"You Did It"
R. Harrison, R. Coote, P. Bevans, Servants
"Just You Wait" (reprise)
J. Andrews

Scene 2

"On the Street Where You Live" (reprise)
J. M. King
"Show Me"
J. Andrews, J. M. King

Scene 3

"Wouldn't It Be Loverly" (reprise)
J. Andrews, Cockneys
"Get Me to the Church on Time"
S. Holloway, G. Dilworth, R. McLennan, Ensemble

Scene 4

"A Hymn to Him"
R. Harrison

Scene 5

"Without You"
J. Andrews, R. Harrison

Scene 6

"I've Grown Accustomed to Her Face"
R. Harrison

1956.02 MR. WONDERFUL

A Musical Comedy in Two Acts, 10 Scenes. Book by Joseph Stein and Will Glickman. Music and lyrics by Jerry Bock, Larry Holofcener and George Weiss. Production (settings) designed by Oliver Smith. Costumes designed by Robert Mackintosh. Lighting by Peggy Clark. Musical director, Morton Stevens. Musical and vocal supervision, Oscar Kosarin. Orchestrations by Ted Royal and Morton Stevens. Entire production staged by Jack Donohue. Production conceived by Jule Styne. Produced by Jule Styne and George Gilbert in association with Lester Osterman, Jr. Opened 22 March 1956 at the Broadway Theatre and closed 23 February 1957 after 383 performances.

CAST (in order of appearance): *Unemployed Actress:* Ann Buckles. *Hal:* HAL LOMAN. *Song Plugger:* Richard Curry. *Soprano:* Rina Falcone. *Rita Romano:* CHITA RIVERA. *Two Comics:* Bob Leslie, Larry B. Leslie. *Audition Annie:* Pat Wilkes. *Johnnie:* John Pelletti. *A Singer:* Karen Shepard. *Dancers:* Tempy Fletcher, Shirley Graser, Susan Hartman, Sally Neal, Patti Ann Rita, Sylvia Shay, Patti Wharton. *Sisters:* Gail Kuhr, Barbara Leigh, Sherry McCutcheon. *Acrobat:* Dorothy D'Honau. *Hoofers:* Marvin Arnold, Bill Reilly, Jimmie Thompson. *Talent Scout:* T. J. Halligan. *Annie's Friend:* Charlotte Foley. *Bop Musicians:* Harold Gordon, Albert Popwell, Claude Thompson. *Fred Campbell:* JACK CARTER. *Lil Campbell:* PAT MARSHALL. *Counterman:* Herb Fields. *Mr. Foster:* MALCOLM LEE BEGGS. *Uncle:* WILL MASTIN. *Dad:* SAMMY DAVIS, SR. *Charlie Welch:* SAMMY DAVIS, JR. *Ethel Pearson:* OLGA JAMES. *Stage Manager:* Bob Kole. *Script Girl:* Ginny Perlowin. *Stagehands:* Frank Marti, Toni Rossi. *Cigarette Girl:* Jerri Gray. *Little Girl:* Marilyn Cooper. *Sophie's Boy:* Ronnie Lee. (THE WILL MASTIN TRIO are Sammy Davis, Jr., Will Mastin, and Sammy Davis, Sr.)

Act 1, Scene 1: 1617 Broadway, New York City, the present. *Scene 2:* The Bandbox in Union City, New Jersey. *Scene 3:* 1617 Broadway. Two weeks later. *Scene 4:* Fred and Lil's Apartment. Several days later. *Scene 5:* An audition hall.

Act 1, Scene 1: The Bandbox, after hours. Several months later. *Scene 2:* An arcade in Miami, Florida. Next day. *Scene 3:* Backstage at the Palm Club, Miami Beach. *Scene 4:* Charlie's Dressing Room. *Scene 5:* The Palm Club.

ACT 1[18]

Scene 1

"1617 Broadway"
C. Rivera, H. Loman, Ensemble
"Without You, I'm Nothing"
J. Carter, P. Marshall

Scene 2

"Jacques D'Iraq"
S. Davis, Jr., Will Mastin, S. Davis, Sr., Ensemble
"Ethel, Baby"
O. James, S. Davis, Jr.
"Mr. Wonderful"
O. James
"Charlie Welch"
J. Carter

Scene 3

"Charlie Welch" (reprise)
J. Carter, Ensemble
"Talk to Him"
P. Marshall, O. James
"Too Close for Comfort"
S. Davis, Jr.

Scene 4

"Without You, I'm Nothing" (reprise)
J. Carter, S. Davis, Jr.

Scene 5

Rita's Audition
C. Rivera
Dance Improvisation: C. Rivera, H. Loman, Ensemble.
The Audition
S. Davis, Jr., W. Mastin, S. Davis, Sr.
"Sing, You Sinners" (from HONEY film)
(*Music by* Sam Coslow. *Lyrics by* W. Frank Harling.)
"Daddy, Uncle and Me"
(*Music and Lyrics by* Sid Kuller and Lyn Murray.)
"Because of You"
(*Music by* Dudley Wilkinson. *Lyrics by* Arthur Hammerstein.)
"That Old Black Magic" (from STAR SPANGLED RHYTHM film)
(*Music by* Harold Arlen. *Lyrics by* Johnny Mercer.)
"Birth of the Blues" (from GEORGE WHITE'S SCANDALS OF 1926)
(*Music by* Ray Henderson. *Lyrics by* Buddy DeSylva and Lew Brown.)
"It's All Right With Me" (from CAN CAN)
(*Music and Lyrics by* Cole Porter.)

ACT 2

Scene 1

"There"
S. Davis, Jr.

Scene 2

"Miami"
P. Marshall, Ensemble
"I've Been Too Busy"
O. James, J. Carter, P. Marshall, S. Davis, Jr.

Scene 3

"Mr. Wonderful" (reprise)
O. James

Scene 5

The Act
S. Davis, Jr., W. Mastin, S. Davis, Sr.
"Sing, You Sinners" (from HONEY film)
(*Music by* Sam Coslow. *Lyrics by* W. Frank Harling.)

---

[18]Added after opening to the end of Act 1, Scene 2:
"Big Time"
S. Davis, Jr.

"Daddy, Uncle and Me"
(*Music and Lyrics by* Sid Kuller and Lyn Murray.)
"Because of You"
(*Music by* Dudley Wilkinson. *Lyrics by* Arthur Hammerstein.)
"That Old Black Magic" (from STAR SPANGLED RHYTHM film)
(*Music by* Harold Arlen. *Lyrics by* Johnny Mercer.)
"Birth of the Blues" (from GEORGE WHITE'S SCANDALS OF 1926)
(*Music by* Ray Henderson. *Lyrics by* Buddy DeSylva and Lew Brown.)
"It's All Right With Me" (from CAN CAN)
(*Music and Lyrics by* Cole Porter.)
"Dearest (You're the Nearest to My Heart)"
(*Music by* Harry Akst. *Lyrics by* Benny Davis.)
"Liza" (from SHOW GIRL)
(*Music by* George Gershwin. *Lyrics by* Ira Gershwin and Gus Kahn.)
Finale: "Mr. Wonderful" (reprise)
Entire Company

1956.03 # THE KING AND I

A Revival of the Musical Play in Two Acts, 17 Scenes[19]. Book and lyrics by Oscar Hammerstein II. Music by Richard Rodgers. Based on the novel "Anna and the King of Siam" by Margaret Landon. Settings by Jo Mielziner. Costumes by Irene Sharaff. Lighting by Jean Rosenthal. Choreography by Jerome Robbins, remounted by June Graham. Orchestrations by Robert Russell Bennett. Musical director, Frederick Dvonch. Directed by John Fearnley. Produced by New York City Center Light Opera Company (William Hammerstein, General director). Opened 18 April 1956 at the New York City Center and closed 6 May 1956 after 23 performances.

CAST (in order of appearance): *Captain Orton*: Leon Shaw. *Louis Leonowens*: Kevin Coughlin. *Anna Leonowens*: JAN CLAYTON. *The Interpreter*: John George. *The Kralahome*: Leonard Graves. *The King*: ZACHARY SCOTT. *Phra Alack*: Hubert Bland. *Lun Tha*: PHILIP WENTWORTH. *Tuptim*: CHRISTINE MATHEWS. *Lady Thiang*: MURIEL SMITH. *Prince Chulalongkorn*: Patrick Adiarte. *Princess Ying Yaowalak*: Lynn Kikuchi. *Sir Edward Ramsay*: Ben Lackland. *Narrator* (The Small House of Uncle Thomas): Christine Mathews. *Uncle Thomas*: Bettina Dearborn. *Little Eva*: Wonci Lui. *Topsy*: Alice Uchida. *Eliza*: Yuriko. *King Simon*: Marion Jim. *Angel*: Dusty Worrall.

Princesses and Princes: Linda Campano, Louis Hernandez, Susan Kikuchi, Barbara Norman, Antonio Obregon, Valentine Obregon, Judith Ramsay, Ronald Harvey, Toby Stevens. *The Royal Dancers*: Olga Bergstrom, Annita Beryll, Hazel Chung, Bettina Dearborn, Dorothy Etheridge, Marion Jim, Norma Kaiser, Wonci Lui, Julie Oser, Nadine Revene, Joan Sandes, Tao Strong, Alice Uchida, Dusty Worrall, Yuriko, Rosemary Zinner, Hubert Bland, John George, James McMillan. *Singers* (Wives, Priests, Amazons, Slaves): Doris Galiber, Jean Maggio, Rose Rosett, Jeanette Scovotti, Rita Shay, Yolanda Vasquez, John Keelin, Robert Reim, Sherman Sneed.

1956.04 # THE MOST HAPPY FELLA

A Musical in Three Acts, 11 Scenes. Book, music and lyrics by Frank Loesser. Based on the play "They Knew What They Wanted" by Sidney Howard. Directed by Joseph Anthony. Choreography by Dania Krupska. Scenery and lighting by Jo Mielziner. Costumes by Motley. Orchestrations by Don Walker. Orchestra and choral direction by Herbert Greene. Produced by Kermit Bloomgarden and Lynn Loesser. Opened 3 May 1956 at the Imperial Theatre, moved 21 October 1957 to the Broadway Theatre, and closed 14 December 1957 after 678 performances.

CAST (in order of appearance): *The Cashier*: LEE CASS. *Cleo*: SUSAN JOHNSON. *Rosabella*: JO SULLIVAN. *Waitresses*: Marlyn Greer, Martha Mathes, Myrna Aaron, Meri Miller, Beverly Gaines. *The Postman*: LEE CASS. *Tony*: ROBERT WEEDE, Richard Torigi (alt.). *Marie*: MONA PAULEE. *Max*: Louis Polacek. *Gladys*: Betsy Bridge. *Herman*: SHORTY LONG. *Clem*: Alan Gilbert. *Jake*: JOHN HENSON. *Al*: Roy Lazarus. *Joe*: ART LUND. *Giuseppe*: ARTHUR RUBIN. *Pasquale*: RICO FROEHLICH. *Ciccio*: JOHN HENSON. *Country Girl*: Meri Miller. *City Boy*: John Sharpe. *The Doctor*: KEITH KALDENBERG. *The Priest*: Russell Goodwin. *Tessie*: Zina Bethune. *Gussie*: Christopher Snell. *Neighbors*: Helon Blount, Myrna Aaron, Beverly Gaines, Henry Director, Hunter Ross, Bob Daley. *Neighbor Ladies*: Lillian Shelby, Lois Van Pelt, Marjorie Smith. *Brakeman*: Norris Greer. *Bus Driver*: Ralph Farnworth.

---

[19]First produced in New York 29 March 1951 at the St. James Theatre for 1246 performances. For Synopsis of Scenes and Musical Numbers, see original 1951 production.

All the Neighbors, and All the Neighbors' Neighbors: Helen Blount, Thelma Dare, Carolyn Maye, Genevieve Owens, Lillian Shelby, Marjorie Smith, Toba Sherwood, Lois Van Pelt, Betsy Bridge, Theodora Brandon, Art Arney, Ken Ayers, Lanier Davis, Henry Director, Ralph Farnworth, Alan Gilbert, Russell Goodwin, Norris Greer, Richard Hermany, Walter Kelvin, Roy Lazarus, Louis Polacek, Evans Thornton, Myrna Aaron, Patti Schmidt, Beverly Gaines, Marlyn Greer, Martha Mathes, Meri Miller, Bob Daley, Athan Karras, Jerry Kurland, Arthur Partington, Hunter Ross, John Sharpe.

Act 1, Scene 1: A Restaurant in San Francisco, January 1927. *Scene 2*: Main Street, Napa, Calaifornia. In April. *Scene 3*: Tony's Barn. A few weeks later. *Scene 4*: Tony's front yard.

Act 2, Scene 1: The Vineyards in May. *Scene 2*: Later in May. *Scene 3*: The Vineyards in June. *Scene 4*: The Barn. *Scene 5*: The Vineyards in July.

Act 3, Scene 1: The Barn an hour later. *Scene 2*: Napa Station. A little later.

ACT 1

Scene 1

"Ooh! My Feet!"
S. Johnson

"I Know How It Is"
J. Sullivan, S. Johnson

"Seven Million Crumbs"
S. Johnson

"I Don't Know" (The Letter)
J. Sullivan

"Maybe He's Kind of Crazy"
S. Johnson

"Somebody, Somewhere"
J. Sullivan

Scene 2

"The Most Happy Fella"
R. Weede, Company

"A Long Time Ago"
M. Paulee, R. Weede

"Standing on the Corner"
S. Long, J. Henson, A. Gilbert, R. Lazarus

"Joey, Joey, Joey"
A. Lund

"Soon You Gonna Leave Me, Joe"
R. Weede

"Rosabella"
R. Weede

Scene 3

"Abbondanza"
R. Froehlich, A. Rubin, J. Henson

"Plenty Bambini"
R. Weede

Scene 4

"Sposalizio"
A. Rubin, J. Henson, R. Froehlich, Ensemble

"Special Delivery!" (I Seen Her at the Station)
L. Cass

"Benvenuta"
R. Froehlich, J. Henson, A. Rubin

"Aren't You Glad?"
J. Sullivan

"No Home, No Job"
J. Sullivan

"Don't Cry"
A. Lund

ACT 2

Scene 1

"Fresno Beauties"/"Cold and Dead"
Ensemble, A. Lund, J. Sullivan

"Love and Kindness"
K. Kaldenberg

"Happy to Make Your Acquaintance"
R. Weede, J. Sullivan, S. Johnson

"I Don't Like This Dame"
M. Paulee, S. Johnson

"Big D"
S. Long, S. Johnson, Ensemble

Scene 2

"How Beautiful the Days"
R. Weede, J. Sullivan, A. Lund

Scene 3

"Young People"
M. Paulee, R. Weede, Ensemble

"Warm All Over"
J. Sullivan

"Old People Gotta"
R. Weede

Scene 4

"I Like Everybody"
S. Long, S. Johnson

Scene 5

"I Love Him"/"I Know How It Is"
J. Sullivan, S. Johnson

"Like a Woman Loves a Man"
J. Sullivan, R. Weede

"My Heart Is So Full of You"
R. Weede, J. Sullivan

"Hoedown"
R. Weede, J. Sullivan, Ensemble

"Mamma, Mamma"
R. Weede

ACT 3

Scene 1

"Abbondanza" (reprise)
R. Froehlich, A. Rubin, J. Hensen

"Goodbye, Darlin'"/"I Like Everybody" (reprise)
S. Johnson, S. Long

"Song of a Summer Night"
K. Kaldenberg, Ensemble

"Please Let Me Tell You"
J. Sullivan

Scene 2

"Tell Tony and Rosabella Goodbye for Me" (Tony's Thoughts)
A. Lund

"She Gonna Come Home Wit' Me"
R. Weede

"Nobody's Ever Gonna Love You"
M. Paulee, R. Weede, S. Johnson

"I Made a Fist"
S. Johnson, S. Long

Finale
R. Weede, J. Sullivan, Ensemble

1956.05　　　**KISS ME, KATE**

A Revival of the Musical Comedy in Two Acts, 16 Scenes[20]. Book by Sam [Samuel] and Bella Spewack. (Based on William Shakespeare's "The Taming of the Shrew.") Music and lyrics by Cole Porter. Directed by Burt Shevelove. Choreography by Ray Harrison, based on the original dances by Hanya Holm. Settings by Watson Barratt. Costumes by Alvin Colt. Lighting by Jean Rosenthal. Musical director, Frederick Dvonch. Orchestrations by Robert Russell Bennett. Incidental ballet music arranged by Genevieve Pitot. Produced by the New York City Center Light Opera Company (William Hammerstein, General director). Opened 9 May 1956 at the New York City Center and closed 27 May 1956 after 23 performances.

CAST (in order of appearance): *Fred Graham*: DAVID ATKINSON. *Harry Trevor*: HARRISON DOWD. *Lois Lane*: BARBARA RUICK. *Ralph*, Stage Manager: Vincent

---

[20]Originally produced in New York 30 December 1948 at the New Century Theatre for 1077 performances. For Synopsis of Scenes and Musical Numbers, see original 1948 production.

McMahon. *Lilli Vanessi*: KITTY CARLISLE. *Hattie*: DELORES MARTIN. *Stage Doorman*: Robert Reim. *Paul*: Bobby Short. *Bill Calhoun*: RICHARD FRANCE. *First Man*: AL NESOR. *Second Man*: TOM PEDI. *Harrison Howell*: Ben Lackland.

"*The Taming of the Shrew*" Players: *Bianca* (Lois Lane): BARBARA RUICK. *Baptista* (Harry Trevor): HARRISON DOWD. *Gremio* (First Suitor): Philip Wentworth. *Hortensio* (Second Suitor): Ray Weaver. *Lucentio* (Bill Calhoun): RICHARD FRANCE. *Katharine* (Lilli Vanessi): KITTY CARLISLE. *Petruchio* (Fred Graham): DAVID ATKINSON. *Haberdasher*: Arthur Mitchell.

Dancers: Olga Bergstrom, Patricia Birsh (Birch), Dorothy Etheridge, Kate Friedlich, Norma Kaiser, Nadine Revene, Kathleen Stanford, Rosemary Weekly, Gene Gavin, William Inglis, Donald Mahler, Gene Myers, Arthur Mitchell, Robert Norris, Baird Searles, Jon Young. *Singers*: Helen Baisley, Doris Galiber, Nina Greer, Jean Maggio, Louise Pearl, Rose Rosett, Barbara Saxby, Jack Irwin, John Keelin, Vincent McMahon, Robert Reim, Jay Stern, Ray Weaver, Philip Wentworth.

1956.06

CARMEN JONES

A Revival of the Musical Play in Two Acts, 5 Scenes[21]. Book and lyrics by Oscar Hammerstein II. Based on Henri Meilhac and Ludovic Halévy's operatic adaptation of Prosper Merimée's novel "Carmen." Music by Georges Bizet. Directed by William Hammerstein. Musical adaptation by Robert Russell Bennett. Settings and lighting designed by Howard Bay. Costumes for original production by Raoul Pene du Bois, supervised for the City Center by Stanley Simmons. Choreography by Onna White. Choral direction by Leonard Depaur. Musical director, Julius Rudel. Produced by the New York City Center Light Opera Company (William Hammerstein, General director). Opened 31 May 1956 at the New York City Center and closed 17 June 1956 after 22 performances.

CAST (in order* of appearance): *Corporal Morrell*: Sherman Sneed. *Foreman*: Stefan Lind. *Cindy Lou*: RERI GRIST. *Sergeant Brown*: WALTER P. BROWN. *Joe*: WILLIAM DuPREE. *Carmen*: MURIEL SMITH. *Sally*: Glory Van Scott. *T-Bone*: Walter Nicks. *Tough Kid*: Peter Burke. *Drummer*: COZY COLE. *Bartender*: Herbert Stubbs. *Waiter*: James Wamen. *Frankie*: DELORES MARTIN. *Myrt*: AUDREY VANTERPOOL. *Rum*: JOSEPH JAMES. *Dink*: JOHN BUIE. *Husky Miller*: JIMMY RANDOLPH. *Mr. Higgins*: CLYDE TURNER. *Miss Higgins*: Carol Joy. *Photographer*: John Greenwood. *Card Players*: Mary Louise, Carol Joy, Christine Spencer, Louise Parker. *Poncho*: Herbert Stubbs. *Dancing Boxers*: Joseph Nash, James McMillan. *Referee*: Walter Nicks.

Soldiers, Factory Workers, Socialites: Adelaide Boatner, Mareda Gaither, Doris Galiber, John Greenwood, Robert Henson, Addison Hill, Bernice Jackson, Carol Joy, John Keelin, Elzar Levister, Stefan Lind, Mary Louise, Vivan Martin, John Nielsen, Louise Parker, Annabelle Parrish, Sherman Sneed, Christine Spencer, Bill Starling, Herbert Stubbs, Fred Thomas, Rodester Timmons, Clyde Turner, Ruth Tyler, James Wamen, Leontyne Watts, Alexander Yancy. *Dancers*: Georgia Collins, Frank Glass, Lavinia Hamilton, Nathaniel A. Horne, Erona Harris, Jim McMillan, Arthur Mitchell, Joseph Nash, Walter Nicks, Charles Queenan, Kathleen Stanford, Elizabeth Taylor, Ella Thompson, Glory Van Scott, Elizabeth Williamson, Billy Wilson. *Children*: Dennis Butler, Peter Burke, Michael Gilford, Leonard Grinnage, Deborah Jones, Gregory Clinton, Charles Stewart, Jr.

---

[21]Originally produced in New York 2 December 1943 at the Broadway Theatre for 503 performances. For Synopsis of Scenes and Musical Numbers, see original 1943 production.

Judy Holliday in BELLS ARE RINGING (Photo: Friedman-Abeles)
Billy Rose Theatre Collection, New York Public Library for the Performing Arts

1956–1957 SEASON

1956.07   SHANGRI-LA

A Musical in Two Acts, 22 Scenes. Book and lyrics by James Hilton, Jerome Lawrence and Robert E. Lee. Based on the novel of the same name by James Hilton. Music by Harry Warren. Production (Settings) designed by Peter Larkin. Costumes by Irene Sharaff. Musical direction, choral arrangements and musical continuity by Lehman Engel. Musical arrangements (orchestrations) by Philip J. Lang. Ballet music composed and arranged by Genevive Pitot. Additional dance arrangements by John Morris. Dances and musical numbers staged by Donald Saddler. Directed by Albert Marre. Produced by Robert Fryer and Lawrence Carr. Opened 13 June 1956 at the Winter Garden and closed 30 June 1956 after 21 performances.

CAST (in order of appearance): *Hugh Conway*: DENNIS KING. *Chao-Li*: Kale Deei. *Robert Henderson*: HAROLD LANG. *Rita Henderson*: JOAN HOLLOWAY. *Charles Mallinson*: JACK CASSIDY. *Miss Brinklow*: ALICE GHOSTLEY. *Chang*: MARTYN GREEN. *Arana*: CAROL LAWRENCE. *Ti*: Edwin Kim Ying. *The Little One*: Leland Mayforth. *Lo-Tsen*: SHIRLEY YAMAGUCHI. *Rimshi*: Ed Kenney. *High Lama*: BARRY KROEGER. *The Dancer Perrault*: ROBERT COHAN.

   The People of Shangri-La: Singers: Edward Becker, Walter Farrell, George Lenz, Bob McClure, David McDaniel, Jack Rains, Ed Stroll, Ted Wills, Marvin Zeller, Jay Bacon, Sara Bettis, Elizabeth Burgess, Joan Cherof, Sylvia Fabry, Teresa Montes, Eileen Moran, Maggie Worth. Dancers: Ralph Beaumont, Michael DeMarco, Ray Dorian, Eddie Heim, Rico Riedl, Ed Stinnett, Dorothy Hill, Greb Lober, Ellen Matthews, Ilona Murai, Mary Ann Niles, Doris Wright.

Act 1, Scene 1: A Patrol Station on the Tibetan border. *Scene 2*: Night on the Mountain. *Scene 3*: The Mountain Pass. *Scene 4*: The Terrace of the Lamasery. *Scene 5*: A Bedchamber in the Lamasery. *Scene 6*: A Music Room. *Scene 7*: The Rope Bridge. *Scene 8*: The Terrace. *Scene 9*: A Corridor. *Scene 10*: The Terrace. *Scene 11*: Outside Conway's Room. *Scene 12*: Chamber of the High Lama.

Act 2, Scene 1: A Prison Camp. *Scene 2*: Chang's Library. *Scene 3*: A Bedchamber in the Lamasery. *Scene 4*: A Corridor. *Scene 5*: Chamber of the High Lama. *Scene 6*: A Corridor. *Scene 7*: A Terrace. *Scene 8*: A Glacier. *Scene 9*: A Prison Camp. *Scene 10*: The Terrace.

ACT 1

Scene 2

  "Om Mani Padme Hum"
    Male Singers

Scene 4

  "Lost Horizon"
    Entire Company

  Dance of Welcome
    R. Cohan, E. K. Ying
      Pole Boys: R. Dorian, E. Heim, R. Riedl. *Lotus Girl*: I. Murai.
      Tigers: E. Stinnett, M. DeMarco. *Tiger Tamer*: R. Beaumont.

  "The Man I Never Met"
    S. Yamaguchi

Scene 5

  "Every Time You Danced With Me"
    H. Lang, J. Holloway

Scene 6

  Dance of Moderate Chastity
    A. Ghostley, Dancers

Scene 7

  "The World Outside"
    S. Yamaguchi, J. Cassidy

Scene 8

  Requiem
    Singers, Dancers

Scene 9

  "I'm Just a Bit Confused"
    A. Ghostley

Scene 10

  "The Beetle Race"
    M. Green, Ensemble

Scene 11

  "Somewhere"
    J. Cassidy

Scene 12

  The Story of Shangri-La (Dance)
    R. Cohan, Dancers

ACT 2

Scene 2

  "What Every Old Girl Should Know"
    A. Ghostley, M. Green

Scene 3

  "Second Time in Love"
    H. Lang, J. Holloway

  "Talkin' With Your Feet"
    H. Lang, J. Holloway

Scene 4

  "Walk Sweet"
    S. Yamaguchi

Scene 6

  "Love Is What I Never Knew"
    S. Yamaguchi, J. Cassidy

Scene 7

  "We've Decided to Stay"
    A. Ghostley, H. Lang, J. Holloway

Scene 8

  Dance of Time
    S. Yamaguchi, Dancers

Scene 10

  "Shangri-La"
    D. King

1956.08   (LEONARD SILLMAN'S) NEW FACES OF 1956

A Musical Revue in Two Acts, 32 Scenes[1]. Music and lyrics mostly by June Carroll, Arthur Siegel, Marshall Barer, Dean Fuller, Murray Grand, Matt Dubey, Harold Karr, Irvin Graham, Ronny Graham, Paul Nassau, John Rox, Michael Brown, (Leslie Julian-Jones, Elisse Boyd, Richard Maury, Robert Stringer, Sid Silvers.) Sketches mostly by Paul Lynde, Richard Maury, Louis Botto, (Danny and Neil Simon, Terry Ryan, Barry Blitzer, Phil Green, Richard Maury.) Musical numbers staged and directed by David Tihmar, assisted by Peter Conlow. Sketches directed by Paul Lynde. Settings by Peter Larkin. Costumes by Thomas Becher. Lighting by Peggy Clark. Orchestrations by Ted Royal, Albert Sendrey, Joe Glover. Musical direction by Jay Blackton. Entire production conceived and supervised by Leonard Sillman. Produced by Leonard Sillman and John Roberts in association with Yvette Schumer. Opened 14 June 1956 at the Ethel Barrymore Theatre and closed 22 December 1956 after 221 performances.

CAST: Franca Baldwin, Suzanne Bernard, Jane Connell, Billie Hayes, Johnny Haymer, Tiger Haynes, Ann Henry, T. C. [Thomas Craig] Jones, Johnny Laverty, Virginia Martin, Bill McCutcheon, John Reardon, Amru Sani, Bob Shaver, Jimmy Sisco, Maggie Smith, Dana Sosa, Rod Strong, Inga Swenson.

ACT 1

Scene 1

  Opening
    Entire Company
    (*Music and Lyrics by* Ronny Graham.)
    Introduction: T. C. Jones.

Scene 2

  Madame Interpreter
    (*by* Danny and Neil Simon)

---

[1]The Fifth in the series of revues conceived by Leonard Sillman as a showcase for new talent. The first was produced in 1934.

France: M. Smith. *United States*: B. Shaver. *Italy*: J. Haymer.
Great Britain: B. McCutcheon. *India*: A. Sani. *Brazil*: V. Martin.
U.S.S.R.: J. Reardon. *Mme. Interpreter*: J. Connell.

Scene 3

"What Does That Dream Mean?"

(*Music by* Harold Karr. *Lyrics by* Matt Dubey.)
The Dreamer: J. Haymer. *His Dreams*: F. Baldwin, S. Bernard, D. Sosa,
J. Laverty, J. Sisco, R. Strong, J. Haymer, A. Henry, T. Haynes,
B. McCutcheon, V. Martin, B. Hayes.

Scene 4

Stars in the Rough

(*by* Paul Lynde)
Announcer: J. Reardon. *Soprano*: I. Swenson. *Helen Hunt*: T. C. Jones.
Patty Potts: D. Sosa. *Old Lady*: J. Connell. *Tony Taps*: J. Laverty.

Scene 5

"One Perfect Moment"

(M. Smith)
(*Music by* Dean Fuller. *Lyrics by* Marshall Barer, Leslie Julian-Jones.)
Woman: M. Smith. *Violinist*: J. Haymer. *Lover*: M. McCutcheon.

Scene 6

"Tell Her"

J. Reardon
(*Music by* Arthur Siegel. *Lyrics by* June Carroll.)
Danced by F. Baldwin, J. Sisco.

Scene 7

"The Washingtons Are Doin' Okay"

T. Haynes
(*Music and Lyrics by* Michael Brown.)

Scene 8

A Canful of Trash

(*by* Louis Botto)
Introduction: M. Smith. *Zelda*: V. Martin. *Manny*: B. McCutcheon.
Moe: J. Haymer. *Junk Man*: B. Shaver. *First Sanitation Man*: R. Strong.
Second Sanitation Man: J. Laverty.

Scene 9

"April in Fairbanks"

J. Connell
(*Music and Lyrics by* Murray Grand.)

Scene 10

"A Doll's House"

(I. Swenson)
(*Music by* Arthur Siegel. *Lyrics by* June Carroll.)
Nurse: M. Smith. *Tina*: I. Swenson. *Urchin*: S. Bernard.
Father Doll: J. Sisco. *Mother Doll*: V. Martin. *Girl Doll*:
D. Sosa. *Princess Doll*: F. Baldwin. *Prince Doll*: R. Strong.
Sweeper Doll: B. Hayes.

Scene 11

"And He Flipped"

A. Henry
(*Music and Lyrics by* John Rox. *Staged by* Bob Hamilton.)

Scene 12

"Girls 'n' Girls 'n' Girls"

(J. Reardon, I. Swenson)
(*Music and Lyrics by* Irvin Graham.)
Mother: I. Swenson. *Johnny*: J. Laverty. *Father*: J. Reardon.
Grace: F. Baldwin. *Ava*: S. Bernard. *Marilyn*: V. Martin.

Scene 13

"I Could Love Him"

B. Hayes
(*Music and Lyrics by* Paul Nassau.)

Scene 14

Steady Edna

(*by* Paul Lynde)
Introduction: T. C. Jones. *Eric*: J. Haymer. *Edna*: J. Connell.
Doc: B. McCutcheon. *Steffany*: M. Smith. *Father*: J. Laverty.
Native Chief: R. Strong.

Scene 15

"Hurry"

A. Sani
(*Music by* Murray Grand. *Lyrics by* Murray Grand and
Elisse Boyd.)

Scene 16

"Isn't She Lovely"

(T. C. Jones, Company)
(*Music by* Dean Fuller. *Lyrics by* Marshall Barer.)
Introduction: T. C. Jones. *Production Singer*: J. Reardon. *Ponies*: F. Baldwin,
S. Bernard, D. Sosa, B. Hayes. *Chorus Boys*: J. Laverty, B. Shaver, J. Sisco,
R. Strong. *The Boy Friend*: B. McCutcheon. *Miss Bird Cage*: V. Martin.
Miss Blue Fish: I. Swenson. *Miss Orange*: M. Smith. *Miss Hat*: J. Connell.
Moth of Desire: T. C. Jones.

ACT 2[2]

Scene 1

Entr'acte. *Introduction*: T. C. Jones.

"I Could Love Him" J. Laverty

"Girls 'n Girls"

D. Sosa

"Blues"

J. Sisco

"Don't Wait"

F. Baldwin

"Tell Her"

R. Strong

Scene 2

Twenty Years in the Blackboard Jungle

(*by* Terry Ryan and Barry Blitzer)
Introduction: T. C. Jones. *Teacher*: B. Hayes. *Mahoney*: J. Sisco. *Levine*:
T. Haynes. *Kowalski*: B. Shaver. *Roger*: J. Laverty. *Hairy Hilda*: V. Martin.
Girl Monitor: F. Baldwin. *Policeman*: R. Strong. *Principal*: B. McCutcheon.

Scene 3

"Don't Wait 'til It's Too Late to See Paris"

(J. Reardon, S. Bernard)
(*Music by* Arthur Siegel. *Lyrics by* June Carroll.)
Husband: J. Reardon. *Wife*: I. Swenson. *Gamin*: S. Bernard.
Flower Vendor: J. Sisco. *Girl*: D. Sosa. *Boy*: R. Strong.

Scene 4

"Rouge"

J. Connell
(*Music and Lyrics by* Murray Grand.)

Scene 5

Darts

(*by* Phil Green and Paul Lynde)
George: B. McCutcheon. *Harriet*: M. Smith. *Man*: J. Reardon.

Scene 6

"Scratch My Back"

A. Henry, T. Haynes
(*Music by* Dean Fuller. *Lyrics by* Marshall Barer.)

Scene 7

"Boy Most Likely to Succeed"

I. Swenson
(*Music by* Arthur Siegel. *Lyrics by* June Carroll.)
Graduating Class: F. Baldwin, S. Bernard, D. Sosa, J. Laverty, J. Sisco, R.
Strong. *Class Valedictorian*: B. Shaver. *Principal*: B. McCutcheon.

Scene 8

"Talent"

V. Martin
(*Music and Lyrics by* Paul Nassau.)

Scene 9

"The Broken Komona"

(T. C. Jones, Entire Company)
(*Sketch and Lyrics by* Richard Maury. *Music by* Robert Stringer.)
Introduction: M. Smith. *Messenger*: J. Laverty. *Bamboo Brothers*: B.
McCutcheon, J. Reardon, R. Strong. *Daughter*: T. C. Jones.
Broken Komona: J. Haymer. *Water Color*: T. Haynes. *Pura*: M. Smith.
Caller: B. Shaver. *Townspeople*: F. Baldwin, S. Bernbard, B. Hayes,
D. Sosa. *Filly*: A. Henry.

---

[2]Added to Act 2 after opening:
"The Pioneer"
J. Haymer
(*Music and Lyrics by* Bob van Scoyk and Allan Mannings.)

Scene 10

La Ronde: ("This Is Quite a Perfect Night")
(*Music by* Dean Fuller. *Lyrics by* Marshall Barer.)
Introduction: R. Strong. *Roue:* J. Haymer. *Jeune Fille:* I. Swenson.
Adolescent: B. Shaver. *Femme du Monde:* V. Martin.

Scene 11

"The White Witch of Jamaica"
(J. Reardon)
(*Music by* Arthur Siegel. *Lyrics by* June Carroll.)
Tourists: S. Bernard, M. Smith, J. Lavery, B. Shaver. *Native Man:* J. Reardon.
Native Woman: D. Sosa. *Lola:* F. Baldwin. *Overseer:* J. Sisco.

Scene 12

"The Greatest Invention"
B. Hayes, J. Haymer
(*Music and Lyrics by* Matt Dubey, Harold Karr and Sid Silvers.)

Scene 13

"Mustapha Abdullah Abu Ben Al Raajid"
(A. Sani)
(*Music by* Dean Fuller. *Lyrics by* Marshall Barer.)
Mrs. Mustapha: A. Sani. *Harem Houris:* M. Smith, I., Swenson, J. Connell,
S. Bernard, D. Sosa, F. Baldwin.

Scene 14

Powers Below[3]
(by Paul Lynde)
Introduced by T. C. Jones. *Wife:* J. Connell. *Superintendent:* J. Haymer.
Mrs. Carruthers: V. Martin.

Scene 15

"She's Got Everything"
(T. C. Jones, Company)
(*Music by* Dean Fuller. *Lyrics by* Marshall Barer.)
Four Aristiocrats: J. Laverty, J. Reardon, B. Shaver, J. Sisco. *Hope Diamond:*
T. C. Jones.

Scene 16

Finale
Entire Company

ORPHEUS IN
THE UNDERWORLD

1956.09

A Revival of the Opera Bouffe in Four Acts[4]. Original French libretto (Orphée Aux Enfers) by Hector Crémieux and Ludovic Halévy. Music by Jacques Offenbach. New English libretto by Eric Bentley. Staged and (settings) designed by Leo Kerz. Costumes designed by Leo Van Witsen. Dances by Anna Sokolow. Choral director, Margaret Hills. Conducted by Erich Leinsdorf. Produced by the New York City Opera (Erich Leinsdorf, Director). Opened 20 September 1956 at the New York City Center and closed 2 November 1956 after 7 performances in repertory.

CAST: *Eurydice:* SYLVIA STAHLMAN. *Orpheus:* JON CRAIN. *Pluto, (Aristeus):* NORMAN KELLEY. *Miss P. Opinion:* PAULA LAURENCE. *Cupid:* Jacquelynne Moody. *Mars:* Joshua Hecht. *Venus:* Mariquita Moll. *Jupiter:* HIRAM SHERMAN. *Diana:* Beverly Bower. *Juno:* Irene Kramarich. *Mercury:* Michael Pollock. *Minerva:* Mignon Dunn. *John Styx:* Richard Humphrey. *Ensemble:* New York City Opera Chorus.

ACT 1

"On the Parthenon"
Tourists' Chorus
"The House by the Olive Tree"
S. Stahlman
"High Infidelity"
J. Crain, S. Stahlman, Orpheus' Violin
Tourists' Dance
Ballet Ensemble
"Hurrah for the Great Out-of-Doors"
N. Kelley
"To Death: A Valentine"
S. Stahlman

Finale:
"The Power of Negative Thinking"
P. Laurence
Waltz of Orpheus' Music Students

ACT 2

"Goetterdaemmerung"
M. Moll, J. Moody, J. Hecht
"Jupiter's Levee"
H. Sherman, Chorus
"The Man by the Fountain"
B. Bower
"Mercurial"
M. Pollock
"Wish I Were Here, or, La Vie en Prose"
N. Shelley
"The War in Heaven"
Chorus
"The Great Lover"
B. Bower, M. Moll, M. Dunn, J. Moody
Finale: "Tactless Little Troubadour"

ACT 3

"The Underworld: An Expose"
S. Stahlman
"Erewhonia, a Jailer's Song"
R. Humphrey
"In Praise of Police"
Quartet
"Cupid's Biology Book"
J. Moody
"Father's Day"
Quartet
"Buzz, Buzz, or The Life of the Bee"
H. Sherman, S. Stahlman
Dance of the Bees
Ballet Ensemble

ACT 4

"Grand Hotel"
Chorus
"Did You Ever See Your King?"
H. Sherman, Goddesses
Finale:
"Will He Turn?"
"Please Be Good on Sunday"
"Back to the Parthenon"

DIE FLEDERMAUS

1956.10

A Revival of the Operetta in Three Acts[5]. (Original libretto by Carl Haffner and Richard Genée. Lyrics by Richard Genée. Based on the comedy "Le Réveillon" by Henri Meilhac and Ludovic Halévy.) English libretto by Ruth and Thomas Martin. Music by Johann Strauss. (Settings) Designed by Leo Kerz. Costume supervisor, Robert Fletcher. Staged by David Pressman. Choreography, John Butler. Conducted by Thomas P. Martin. Choreographed by Anna Sokolow. Conducted by Joseph Rosenstock. Produced by the New York City Opera (Erich Leinsdorf, Director). Opened 29 September 1956 at the New York City Center and closed 12 October 1956 after 2 performances in repertory.

CAST: *Rosalinda:* BEVERLY SILLS. *Eisenstein:* ERNEST McCHESNEY. *Adele:* JACQUELYNNE MOODY. *Sally:* Naomi Collier. *Alfred:* JON CRAIN. *Prince Orlofsky:* FRANCES BIBLE. *Falke:* WILLIAM WILDERMAN. *Frank:* Richad Wentworth. *Frosch:* Coley Worth. *Blind:* Michael Pollock.

---

[3]Dropped after opening.
[4]First presented in New York in English 1 December 1883 at the Bijou Theatre for 107 performances.

[5]First English language production in New York 16 March 1885 at the Casino Theatre for 42 performances. First New York production of this adaptation 20 December 1950 at the Metropolitan Opera House. For Synopsis of Scenes and Musical Numbers, see May 1954 revival.

1956.11 THAT GIRL AT THE BIJOU

A One Woman Musical Revue. Composer, pianist, etc., Harvey Brown. Staged by Gene Perlowin. Costumes and choreography by Iva Kitchell. Produced by Luben Vichey. Opened 9 November 1956 at the Bijou Theatre and closed 18 November 1956 after 11 performances.

CAST: IVA KITCHELL.

Dear Audience: Hello! You know, I've been looking forward for years to doing something on Broadway. Now that I'm here, I can't decide what to do. You see, I have accumulated about 50-odd characters and dances through these forward-looking years. Anyway, ever since the Bijou and I came to terms on these dates we have together, I've been trying to pick and choose which dozen numbers I wanted to do. (That's about as many as you or I can manage in one evening.) This didn't work out, however, because I still have 26 left on the list, as you can see by your programs. So tonight, from those remaining 26, I'm just going to pick your dozen as I go along. Must dash now—see you in a few minutes.

Fondly, Iva

P.S. I'll let you know about intermissions and such.

CAST OF CHARACTERS (not in order of their appearance—In fact, all of them won't appear at every performance, but when they do, they will be played by Iva Kitchell.):

Bacchanale (as Seen at the Opera)
  (*Music by* Camille Saint-Saëns.)
Chanteuse-Danseuse
  (*Music by* Harry Pease, Ed G. Nelson and Gilbert Dodge.)
Dance Espagnole
  (*Music by* Georges Bizet, arranged by Harvey Brown.)
Chorus Girl (Vintage 1920)
  (*Music by* [Fred] Fisher.)
Coloratura
  (*Music by* Harvey Brown.)
Dance & Encore
  (*Music by* Frederic Chopin.)
Growing Up
  (*Music by* Friedman-Gartner.)
Maisie at the "Moovies"
  (arr. by Harvey Brown)
Me-ow
  (*Music by* Alda Astori.)
Nocturne
  (*Music by* Sergei Rachmaninoff.)
Non-Objective
  (No Music)
Obsession
  (*Music by* Harvey Brown.)
Oriental Dance (by an Occidental Girl)
  (*Music by* [Lily] Strickland.)
Pseudo-Voodoo
  (*Music by* Harvey Brown.)
Romance
  (*Music by* Friedman-Gartner.)
Salesman (with apologies to the Fuller Brush Man)
  (*Music by* Peter Paul Fuchs.)
Something Classic
  (*Music by* Ludwig van Beethoven and Franz Schubert)
    Scarf Dance—Garland Dance
Fantasy for Body and Piano
  (*Music by* Harvey Brown.)
Sonatina Roccoco
  (*Music by* Harvey Brown.)
    Allegro Artificial—Andante Sentimentale—Rondo con Esprit
Soul in Search (There Isn't Any)
Tale of a Bird
  (*Music by* Harvey Brown.)
The Gentleman Friend
  (*Music by* Harvey Brown.)
The Vert Bros. (Intro & Extro)
  (*Music by* Harvey Brown.)

Valse Triste
  (*Music by* Jean Sibelius.)
When I Was Eight
  (*Music by* [Théophile] Gautier.)
Ze Ballet
  (*Music by* Amilcare Ponchielli.)

1956.12 LI'L ABNER

A Musical Comedy in Two Acts, 20 Scenes. Book by Norman Panama and Melvin Frank. Based on the characters created by Al Capp (from his comic strip of the same name). Music by Gene de Paul. Lyrics by Johnny Mercer. Direction and choreography by Michael Kidd. Scenery and lighting by William and Jean Eckart. Costumes designed by Alvin Colt. Musical direction, continuity and vocal arrangements by Lehman Engel. Orchestrations by Philip J. Lang. Ballet music arranged by Genevieve Pitot. Produced by Norman Panama, Melvin Frank and Michael Kidd. Opened 15 November 1956 at the St. James Theatre and closed 12 July 1958 after 693 performances.

CAST (in order of appearance): *Lonesome Polecat*: Anthony [Tony] Mordente. *Hairless Joe*: Chad Block. *Romeo Scragg*: Marc Breaux. *Clem Scragg*: James Hurst. *Alf Scragg*: Anthony Salverino. *Moonbeam McSwine*: Carmen Alvarez. *Marryin' Sam*: STUBBY KAYE. *Earthquake McGoon*: BERN HOFFMAN. *Daisy Mae*: EDITH ADAMS. *Pappy Yokum*: JOE E. MARKS. *Li'l Abner*: PETER PALMER. *Cronies*: Marc Breaux, Ralph Linn, Jack Matthew, Robert McClure, George Reeder. *Mayor Dawgmeat*: Oran Osburn. *Senator Jack S. Phogbound*: TED THURSTON. *Dr. Rasmussen T. Finsdale*: STANLEY SIMMONDS. *Government Man*: Richard Maitland. *Available Jones*: WILLIAM LANTEAU. *Stupefyin' Jones*: JULIE NEWMAR. *Colonel*: George Reeder. *Radio Commentators*: James Hurst, Robert McClure, Jack Matthew. *President*: Lanier Davis. *General Bullmoose*: HOWARD ST. JOHN. *Secretaries*: Lanier Davis, Robert McClure, Jack Matthew, George Reeder. *Appassionata Von Climax*: TINA LOUISE. *Evil Eye Fleagle*: AL NESOR. *Dr. Smithborn*: George Reeder. *Dr. Krogmeyer*: Ralph Linn. *Dr. Schleifitz*: Marc Breaux. *State Department Man*: Lanier Davis. *Wives*: Carmen Alvarez, Pat Creighton, Lillian D'Honau, Bonnie Evans, Hope Holiday, Deedee Wood. *Butler*: James J. Jeffries. *Colonel*: Lanier Davis.

  Singers: Margaret Baxter, Joan Cherof, Pat Creighton, Joyce Gladmond, Hope Holiday, Jane House, Louise Pearl, Jeanette Scovotti, Don Braswell, Lanier Davis, James Hurst, Jack Matthew, Robert McClure, Oran Osburn, George Ritner, Anthony Saverino. *Dancers*: Carmen Alvarez, Lillian D'Honau, Bonnie Evans, Maureen Hopkins, Barbara Klopfer, Christy Peterson, Sharon Shore, Rebecca Vorno, Deedee Wood, Chad Block, Marc Breaux, Grover Dale, Robert Karl, Ralph Linn, Richard Maitland, Anthony Mordente, Tom Panko, George Reeder. *And*: Jan Gunnar, Lucky Kargo, Mario Lamm, Reed Morgan, Aldo Ventura, Robert Wiensko.

Act 1, Scene 1: Dogpatch, U.S.A. *Scene 2*: The Yokum Cabin. *Scene 3*: The Fishing Hole. *Scene 4*: Cornpone Square. *Scene 5*: Dogpatch Road. *Scene 6*: Cornpone Square. *Scene 7*: Washington D. C. Sequence: a. Government Laboratory, b. The President's Office. *Scene 8*: General Bullmoose's Office. *Scene 9*: Dogpatch Road. *Scene 10*: Dogpatch. *Scene 11*: Dogpatch Road. *Scene 12*: Dogpatch.

Act 2, Scene 1: Government Testing Laboratory, Washington. *Scene 2*: The Yokum Cabin. *Scene 3*: General Bullmoose's Cabin. *Scene 4*: Corridor in Bullmoose Mansion. *Scene 5*: Ballroom in Bullmoose Mansion. *Scene 6*: Corridor in Bullmoose Mansion. *Scene 7*: The Government Testing Laboratory. *Scene 8*: Cornpone Square.

ACT 1[6]
"A Typical Day"
  Dogpatchers
"If I Had My Druthers"
  P. Palmer, Cronies
"If I Had My Druthers" (reprise)
  E. Adams
"Jubilation T. Cornpone"
  S. Kaye, Dogpatchers
"Rag Offen the Bush"
  Dogpatchers
"Namely You"
  E. Adams, P. Palmer
"Unnecessary Town"
  P. Palmer, E. Adams, Dogpatchers

---

[6]Added during run to Act 1 after "What Good Enough for General Bullmoose":
  "There's Room Enough for Us"
    Dogpatchers

"What's Good for General Bullmoose"
    Secretaries
"The Country's in the Very Best of Hands"
    P. Palmer, S. Kaye
"Sadie Hawkins Day" (Ballet)
    Dogpatchers
ACT 2
"Oh, Happy Day"
    S. Finsdale, G. Reeder, R. Linn, M. Breaux
"I'm Past My Prime"
    E. Adams, S. Kaye
"Love in a Home"
    P. Palmer, E. Adams
"Progress Is the Root of All Evil"
    H. St. John
"Society Party"
    Guests, Dogpatchers
"Progress Is the Root of All Evil" (reprise)
    H. St. John
"Put 'Em Back"
    Wives
"Namely You" (reprise)
    E. Adams
"The Matrimonial Stomp"
    S. Kaye, Dogpatchers
Finale
    Entire Company

1956.13   CRANKS

A Musical Revue in Two Acts, 30 Scenes. (Sketches and lyrics) Written and directed by John Cranko. Music by John Addison. Decor by John Piper. Musical direction by Anthony Bowles. Set supervision and lighting by Paul Morrison. Produced by Richard Charlton and John Krimsky. Opened 26 November 1956 at the Bijou Theatre and closed 29 December 1956 after 40 performances.

CAST: HUGH BRYANT, ANTHONY NEWLEY, ANNIE ROSS, GILBERT VERNON.

ACT 1[7]
"Who's Who"
"Adrift"
"Tra La La"
"Where Has Tom Gone?"
"Cold Comfort"
"Lullaby"
"Broadminded"
"Waiting Room"
"Bats"
"Passacaglia"
"Boo to a Goose"
"Who Is It Always There?"
"Gloves"
"This Is the Sign"
"Chiromancy"
"Valse Anglaise"
ACT 2
"Telephone Tango"
"Don't Let Him Know You"
"Sea Song"
"L'Après-Midi de Gilbert"
"Present for Gilbert"
"Elisabeth"

[7]Program insert details revised song order for opening night.

"Blue"
"I'm the Boy"
"Metamorphosis"
"Would You Let Me Know?"
"Cove in Hove"
"Dirge"
"Arthur, Son of Martha"
"Goodnight"

1956.14   BELLS ARE RINGING

A Musical Comedy in Two Acts, 22 Scenes. Book and lyrics by Betty Comden and Adolph Green. Music by Jule Styne. Entire production directed by Jerome Robbins. Sets and costumes designed by Raoul Pene du Bois. Lighting by Peggy Clark. Orchestrations by Robert Russell Bennett. Musical director, Milton Rosenstock. Vocal arrangements and direction by Herbert Greene and Buster Davis. Dance arrangements and incidental scoring by John Morris. Dances and musical numbers staged by Jerome Robbins and Bob Fosse. Produced by The Theatre Guild. Opened 29 November 1956 at the Sam S. Shubert Theatre, moved 15 December 1958 to the Alvin Theatre, and closed 7 March 1959 after 924 performances.

CAST (in order of appearance): *Sue:* JEAN STAPLETON *Gwynne:* Pat Wilkes. *Ella Peterson:* JUDY HOLLIDAY. *Carl:* PETER GENNARO. *Inspector Barnes:* Dort Clark. *Francis:* Jack Weston. *Sandor:* Eddie Lawrence. *Jeff Moss:* SYDNEY CHAPLIN. *Larry Hastings:* GEORGE S. IRVING. *Telephone Man:* Eddie Heim. *Ludwig Smiley:* Frank Milton. *Charles Bessemer:* Frank Green. *Dr. Kitchell:* Bernie West. *Blake Barton:* Frank Aletter. *Another Actor:* Frank Green. *Joey:* Tom O'Steen. *Olga:* Norma Doggett. *Man from Corvello Mob:* John Perkins. *Other Man:* Kasimir Kokich. *Carol:* Ellen Ray. *Paul Arnold:* Steve Roland. *Michelle:* Michelle Reiner. *Master of Ceremonies:* Eddie Heim. *Singer at Night Club:* Frank Green. *Waiter:* Ed Thompson. *Maitre d'Hotel:* David McDaniel. *Police Officer:* Gordon Woodburn. *Madame Grimaldi:* Donna Sanders. *Mrs. Mallet:* Jeannine Masterson.

Dancers: Norma Doggett, Phyllis Dorne, Patti Karr, Barbara Newman, Nancy Perkins, Marsha Rivers, Beryl Towbin, Anne Wallace, Doria Avila, Frank Derbas, Don Emmons, Eddie Heim, Kasimir Kokich, Tom O'Steen, Willy Sumner, Ben Vargas, Billy Wilson. *Singers:* Pam Abbott, Joanne Birks, Urylee Leonardos, Jeannine Masterson, Michelle Reiner, Donna Sanders, Frank Green, Marc Leon, David McDaniel, Paul Michael, Julian Patrick, Steve Roland, Ed Thompson, Gordon Woodburn.

Act 1, Scene 1: Office of Susanswerphone. Late afternoon. *Scene 2:* Jeff Moss' Living Room. *Scene 3:* An Alley at Night. *Scene 4:* The Office. Early morning. *Scene 5:* A Street in front of the Office. *Scene 6:* Jeff Moss' Living Room. *Scene 7:* A Street. *Scene 8:* A Subway Car. *Scene 9:* A Street. *Scene 10:* Dr. Kitchell's Office. *Scene 11:* A Street. *Scene 12:* A Drug Store. *Scene 13:* A Street. *Scene 14:* The Office. A week later. *Scene 15:* Jeff Moss' Living Room.

Act 2, Scene 1: The Office. The next night. *Scene 2:* The Park. *Scene 3:* Larry Hastings' Penthouse. *Scene 4"* The 'Crying Gypsy' Cafe. *Scene 5:* The 'Pyramid' Night Club. *Scene 6:* Bay Ridge Subway Platform. *Scene 7:* The Office.

ACT 1[8]
"Bells Are Ringing"
    Sunsanswerphone Advertisement (Chorus)
Scene 1
"It's a Perfect Relationship"
    J. Holliday
Scene 2
"On My Own"
    S. Chaplin, Ensemble
"You've Got to Do It"
    S. Chaplin
Scene 3
"It's a Simple Little System"
    E. Lawrence, Ensemble
Scene 5
"Is It a Crime?"
    J. Holliday

[8]Added to Act 1, Scene 6 for National Tour:
    "It's Better Than a Dream"
        J. Holliday, Hal Linden (Jeff)

Scene 8
"Hello, Hello There!"
J. Holliday, S. Chaplin, Ensemble
Scene 9
"I Met a Girl"
S. Chaplin, Ensemble
Scene 15
"Long Before I Knew You"
J. Holliday, S. Chaplin

ACT 2
Scene 1
"Mu-Cha-Cha"
J. Holliday, P. Gennaro
Dance
E. Ray, P. Gennaro, Dancing Ensemble
Scene 2
"Just in Time"
S. Chaplin, J. Holliday, Ensemble
Scene 3
"Drop That Name"
J. Holliday, Ensemble
"The Party's Over"
J. Holliday
Scene 4
"Salzburg"
J. Stapleton, E. Lawrence
Scene 5
"The Midas Touch"
F. Green, Boys, Girls
Scene 6
"Long Before I Knew You" (reprise)
J. Holliday
Scene 7
"I'm Goin' Back"
J. Holliday
Finale
The Company

1956.15 CANDIDE

A Comic Operetta in Two Acts, 11 Scenes. Book by Lillian Hellman. Based on the satire by Voltaire. Music by Leonard Bernstein. Lyrics by Richard Wilbur. Additional lyrics by John Latouche and Dorothy Parker. Production (settings) designed by Oliver Smith. Costumes by Irene Sharaff. Lighting by Paul Morrison. Musical director, Samuel Krachmalnick. Orchestrations by Leonard Bernstein and Hershy Kay. Directed by Tyrone Guthrie, assisted by Tom Brown. Dance supervisor, Wallace Seibert. Produced by Ethel Linder Reiner in association with Lester Osterman, Jr. Opened 1 December 1956 at the Martin Beck Theatre and closed 2 February 1957 after 73 performances.

CAST (in order of appearance): Dr. Pangloss: MAX ADRIAN. Cunegonde: BARBARA COOK. Candide: ROBERT ROUNSEVILLE. Baron: Robert Mesrobian. Maximilian: LOUIS EDMONDS. King of Hesse: Conrad Bain. Hesse's General: Norman Roland. Man: BORIS APLON. Woman: Doris Okerson. Dutch Lady: Margaret Roy. Dutch Man: Tony Drake. Atheist: Robert Rue. Arab Conjuror: Robert Barry. Infant Casmira: Maria Novotna. Lawyer: WILLIAM CHAPMAN. Very, Very Old Inquisitor: Conrad Bain. Very Old Inquisitor: Charles Aschman. Junkman: Robert Cosden. Wine-Seller: Stanley Grover. Bear: Charles Morrell. Bear Man: Robert Rue. Alchemist: Charles Aschman. Grocery Lady: Margaret Roy. Beggars: Margaret Roy, Robert Cosden, Thomas Pyle. French Lady: Maud Scheerer. Old Lady: IRRA PETINA. Marquis Milton: BORIS APLON. Sultan Milton: JOSEPH BERNARD. Pilgrim Father: Robert Rue. Pilgrim Mother: Dorothy Krebill. Captain: Conrad Bain. Martin: MAX ADRIAN. Governor of Buenos Aires: WILLIAM OLVIS. Officers: George Blackwell, Tony Drake, Thomas Pyle. Ferone: WILLIAM CHAPMAN. Madame Sofronia: IRRA PETINA. Duchess: Maud Scheerer. Prefect of Police (Bazzini): Norman Roland. Prince Ivan: Robert Mesrobian. Scrub Lady: BARBARA COOK. Sultan Milton: JOSEPH BERNARD. Marquis Milton: Boris Aplon. Duke of Naples: Charles Aschman. Croupier: Robert Barry. Lady Cutely: Dori Davis. Lady Toothly: George Blackwell. Lady Soothly: Fred Jones. Lady Richmond: Thomas Pyle. (Standby for Cunegonde: MARGOT MOSER.)
Singers: Peggyann Alderman, Charles Aschman, Robert Barry, George Blackwell, Dori Davis, Jack DeLon, Tony Drake, Naomi Farr, Stanley Grover, Fred Jones, Mollie Knight, Dorothy Krebill, Vivian Laurence, Henry Lawrence, Robert Mesrobian, Lois

Monroe, Doris Okerson, Thomas Pyle, Margaret Roy, Robert Rue, Mara Schorr, Dorothy White. Dancers: Alvin Beam, Charles Czarny, Marvin Gordon, Carmen Gutierrez, Charles Morrell, Frances Noble, Liane Plane, Gloria Stevens.

Act 1, Scene 1: Westphalia. Scene 1A: Candide Travels to Lisbon. Scene 2: Lisbon. Scene 2A: Candide Travels to Paris. Scene 3: Paris. Scene 3A: They Travel to Buenos Aires. Scene 4: Buenos Aires.

Act 2, Scene 1: Buenos Aires. Scene 1A: Candide Travels to Venice. Scene 2: Venice. Scene 3: Westphalia.

ACT 1
Scene 1
"The Best of All Possible Worlds" (Ensemble)
(Lyrics by Richard Wilbur.)M. Adrian, (B. Cook, R. Rounseville), Chorus
"Oh, Happy We" (Duet)
R. Rounseville, B. Cook
(Lyrics by Richard Wilbur.)
"It Must Be So" (Song)
R. Rounseville
(Lyrics by Richard Wilbur.)
Scene 2
Lisbon Sequence
M. Novotna, R. Barry, Chorus
(Lyrics by Leonard Bernstein.)
Scene 2A
"It Must Be Me" (Song)
R. Rounseville
Scene 3
Mazurka
(Orchestra)
"Glitter and Be Gay" (Aria)
B. Cook
(Lyrics by Richard Wilbur.)
"You Were Dead, You Know" (Duet)
R. Rounseville, B. Cook
(Lyrics by Richard Wilbur, John Latouche.)
Scene 3A
"Pilgrims' Procession"
Pilgrims (Chorus)
(Lyrics by Richard Wilbur.)
Scene 4
"My Love" (Serenade)
W. Olvis, B. Cook, I. Petina
(Lyrics by John Latouche, Richard Wilbur.)
"I Am Easily Assimilated" (Tango)
(Lyrics by Leonard Bernstein.)I. Petina, B. Cook, (G. Blackwell, T. Pyle), Chorus
Quartet Finale
B. Cook, R. Rounseville, I. Petina, W. Olvis
(Lyrics by Richard Wilbur.)

ACT 2
Scene 1
"Quiet" (Trio)
B. Cook, I. Petina, W. Olvis, (R. Rue)
(Lyrics by Richard Wilbur.)
"Eldorado" (Ballad)
R. Rounseville, (Chorus)
(Lyrics by Lillian Hellman.)
"Bon Voyage" (Schottische)
W. Olvis, Chorus
(Lyrics by Richard Wilbur.)
Scene 2
"What's the Use?" (Waltz)
I. Petina, N. Roland, W. Chapman, R. Mesrobian, Chorus
(Lyrics by Richard Wilbur.)
Gavotte
M. Adrian, I. Petina, B. Cook, R. Rounseville
(Lyrics by Dorothy Parker.)
Scene 3
Finale: "Make Our Garden Grow"
Entire Company
(Lyrics by Richard Wilbur.)

56

1956.16 HAPPY HUNTING

A Musical Comedy in Two Acts, 16 Scenes. Book by Howard Lindsay and Russel Crouse. Music by Harold Karr. Lyrics by Matt Dubey. Settings and lighting by Jo Mielziner. Costumes by Irene Sharaff. Dances and musical numbers staged by Alex Romero and Bob Herget. Musical direction by Jay Blackton. Orchestrations by Ted Royal. Additional orchestrations by Joe Glover, Don Walker, Seymour Ginzler. Dance music devised by Roger Adams. Directed by Abe Burrows. Produced by Jo Mielziner. Opened 6 December 1956 at the Majestic Theatre and closed 30 November 1957 after 413 performances.

CAST (in order of appearance): *Sanford Stewart, Jr.*: Gordon Polk. *Mrs. Sanford Stewart, Sr.*: Olive Templeton. *Joseph*: Mitchell M. Gregg. *Beth Livingstone*: VIRGINIA GIBSON. *Jack Adams, reporter*: Seth Riggs. *Harry Watson, reporter*: Gene Wesson. *Man who looks like Farouk*: Edward Becker. *Charley, photographer*: Delbert Anderson. *Liz Livingstone*: ETHEL MERMAN. *Photographers (4): Sam*: Clifford Fearl. *Joe*: John Craig. *Freddy*: George Martin. *Wes*: Jim Hutchison. *Reporters (3): Mary Mills*: Estelle Parsons. *Dick Davis*: Robert C. Held. *Bob Grayson*: Carl Nicholas. *Maud Foley*: MARY FINNEY. *Police Sergeant*: Mark Zeller. *Arturo*: Leon Belasco. *The Duke of Grenada*: FERNANDO LAMAS. *Count Carlos*: Renato Cibelli. *Waiter*: Don Weissmuller. *Ship's Officer*: John Leslie. *Barman*: Warren J. Brown. *Mrs. B.*: Florence Dunlap. *Mrs. D.*: Madeleine Clive. *Mrs. L.*: Kelley Stephens. *Terence, a groom*: Jim Hutchison. *Tom, a groom*: Eugene Louis. *Daisy*: Moe. *Mr. T.: a member of the Hunt*: John Leslie. *Mr. M.: a member of the Hunt*: Jay Velie. *Albert, a groom*: George Martin. *Margaret, a maid*: Mara Landi.
  Singers: Peggy Acheson, Marilynn Bradley, Deedy Irwin, Jane Johnston, Jean Kraemer, Mara Landi, Betty McGuire, Estelle Parsons, Noella Peloquin, Ginny Perlowin, Mary Roche, Kelley Stephens, Helene Whitney, Delbert Anderson, Edward Becker, Warren J. Brown, David Collyer, John Craig, Jack Dabdoub, Clifford Fearl, Robert C. Held, Carl Nicholas, Seth Riggs, Charles Rule, Mark Zeller. *Dancers*: Betty Carr, Alice Clift, Jane Fischer, Roberta Keith, Svetlana McLee, Patti Nestor, Wendy Nickerson, Fleur Raup, Sigyn, Bob Bakanic, John Harmon, Jim Hutchison, Dick Korthaze, Eugene Louis, George Martin, Jim Moore, Lowell Purvis, Don Weissmuller, Roy Wilson.

The time is the present, and the action occurs in Monaco, on ship board and near Philadelphia.

Act 1, Scene 1: Outside the Palace. Monaco. *Scene 2*: Liz Livingstone's Suite, Hotel Riviera. Monaco. *Scene 3*: Terrace of the Hotel. *Scene 4*: Veranda of the Duke's Suite, Hotel Riviera. *Scene 5*: Quai. *Scene 6*: In the ship's bar. *Scene 7*: Afterdeck of the ship. *Scene 8*: In the ship's bar. *Scene 9*: Afterdeck of the ship.

Act 2, Scene 1: Liz Livingstone's estate, near Philadelphia. *Scene 2*: The Livingstone stables. *Scene 3*: Summerhouse. Liz's estate. *Scene 4*: The Philadelphia Hunt Club. *Scene 5*: Another part of the forest. *Scene 6*: Liz's boudoir. *Scene 7*: The Hunt Ball.

ACT 1
Scene 1
  "Postage-Stamp Principality"
    Tourists, Monegasques
  "Don't Tell Me"
    G. Polk, V. Gibson
  "(Gee, But) It's Good To Be Here"
    E. Merman, Reporters
Scene 2
  "Mutual Admiration Society"
    E. Merman, V. Gibson
Scene 3
  "For Love or Money"
    Girls
  Bikini Dance
    V. Gibson
Scene 4
  "It's Like a Beautiful Woman"
    F. Lamas
Scene 5
  "Wedding-of-the-Year Blues"
    M. Finney, G. Wesson, S. Riggs, Reporters, Photographers
Scene 6
  "Mr. Livingstone"
    E. Merman
Scene 7
  "If'n"
    V. Gibson, G. Polk, Passengers

Scene 9
  "This Is What I Call Love"[9]
    E. Merman
ACT 2
Scene 1
  "A New-Fangled Tango"
    E. Merman, V. Gibson, L. Belasco, Guests
  "She's Just Another Girl"
    G. Polk
Scene 2
  "The Game of Love"[10]
    E. Merman
Scene 4
  "Happy Hunting"
    E. Merman, F. Lamas, Members of the Hunt
Scene 6
  "I'm a Funny Dame"
    E. Merman
  "This Much I Know"
    F. Lamas
  "Just Another Guy"
    E. Merman
Scene 7
  "Everyone Who's "Who's Who""
    S. Riggs, G. Wesson, Footmen
  "Mutual Admiration Society" (reprise)
    E. Merman, F. Lamas

1957.01 ZIEGFELD FOLLIES (OF 1957)

A Musical Revue in Two Acts, 24 Scenes. Music and lyrics by Jack Lawrence and Richard Myers, Howard Dietz and Sammy Fain, David Rogers and Colin Romoff, Dean Fuller and Marshall Barer, Carolyn Leigh and Philip Springer, (Tony Velone, Larry Spier, Ulpio Minucci.) Sketches by Arnie Rosen and Coleman Jacoby, David Rogers, Alan Jeffreys, Maxwell Grant, (Beatrice Lillie.) Sketch editor, Arnold Auerbach. Dances staged by Frank Wagner. Scenery and costumes by Raoul Pene du Bois. Lighting by Paul Morrison. Musical director, Max Meth. Orchestrations by (Robert) Russell Bennett, Bill Stegmeyer, Joe Glover, Bob Noelneter. Dance composition by Rene Weigert. Vocal arrangements by Earl Rogers. Entire production directed by John Kennedy. Produced by Mark Kroll and Charles Conaway. Opened 1 March 1957 at the Winter Garden and closed 15 June 1957 after 123 performances.

CAST: BEATRICE LILLIE, BILLY DE WOLFE, HAROLD LANG, JANE MORGAN, HELEN WOOD, MICKI MARLO, JOHN PHILIP, BOB and LARRY LESLIE, CAROL LAWRENCE, JAY MARSHALL, TONY FRANCO.
  Ziegfeldians: Billie Bensing, Bette Graham, Faith Hilton, Frances Koll, Susan Shaute, Paula Wayne, Chuck Green, Robert Feyti, Tony Franco, Ed Powell, James Stevenson, Gene Varrone. *Dancers*: Vicki Barrett, Ruth Chamberlain, Dorothy D'Honau, Mary Jane Doerr, Wisa D'Orso, Nancy Hachenberg, Marcia Hewitt, Julie Marlowe, Sylvia Shay, Gini Turner, Shirley Vincent, Bob Bernard, James Brooks, Ron Cecill, Alan Conroy, Allan Craine, Hugh Lambert, Jack Leigh, Ted Monson, Lou Richards, Rod Strong, Meritt Thompson. *Ziegfeld Girls*: Roberta Brown, Denise Collette, Ann Drake, Charlotte Foley, Pat Gaston, Nancy Westbrook, Barbara Hall, Gloria Kristy.

ACT 1
Scene 1
  "Bring on the Girls"
    The Ziegfeldians, Ensemble
    (*Music by* Richard Myers. *Lyrics by* Jack Lawrence.)

---

[9]Replaced during the run by :
  "Just a Moment Ago"
    E. Merman
    (*Music and Lyrics by* Kay Thompson.)
[10]Replaced during the run by :
"I'm Old Enough To Know Better and Young Enough Not to Care"
    E. Merman
    (*Music and Lyrics by* Kay Thompson.)

Scene 2
"Double Indemnity"
(*by* Alan Jeffreys and Maxwell Grant)
Secretary: C. Foley. *Mr. Wedgecliffe*: B. DeWolfe. *Lola La Moundsville*:
J. Morgan.
Scene 3
"If You Got Music"
H. Lang, H. Wood, Ensemble
(*Music by* Colin Romoff. *Lyrics by* David Rogers.)
Scene 4
Milady Dines Alone
(*by* Beatrice Lillie)
The Lady: B. Lillie. *Waiter*: B. Laffey.
Scene 5
"The Lover in Me"[11]
M. Marlo
(*Music by* Philip Springer. *Lyrics by* Carolyn Leigh.)
Scene 6
High and Flighty
(*by* Arnie Rosen and Coleman Jacoby)
Hostess: B. Lillie. *Passengers*: J. Philip, B. Leslie, L. Leslie, B. Graham, R.
Feyti. *Betty*: J. Doerr.
Scene 7
"I Don't Wanna Rock"
(*Music by* Colin Romoff. *Lyrics by* David Rogers.)
Juvenile Delinquent: B. DeWolfe. *Tenth Street Sheiks*: V. Barrett, J. Brooks,
W. D'Orso, C. Green, N. Hachenberg, H. Lambert, J. Marlowe, E. Powell,
L. Richards, J. Stevenson, R. Strong, G. Varrone.
Scene 8
Jay Marshall[12] (comedy, prestidigitation, ventriloquism)
Scene 9
"Music for Madame"
(*Music by* Richard Myers. *Lyrics by* Jack Lawrence.)
The Boy: H. Lang. *The Girl*: H. Wood. *Maitre D'*: J. Philip. And Ziegfeldians,
Dancers.
Scene 10
"Intoxication"
B. Lillie
(*Music by* Dean Fuller. *Lyrics by* Marshall Barer.)
The Escort: A. Conroy.
Scene 11
Dramatically Speaking
B. DeWolfe
Scene 12
"Song of India"
The Rajah: J. Philip. *His Favorite*: B. Lillie. Assisted by Dancers, The
Ziegfeldians.
ACT 2
Scene 1
"Two a Day On the Milky Way"
H. Lang, Ensemble
(*Music by* Dean Fuller. *Lyrics by* Marshall Barer.)
Agent: B. Leslie.
Scene 2
Large Talk
(*by* David Rogers)
First Girl: C. Foley. *Second Girl*: S. Shaute. *Lucille*: B. Lillie. *Harriet*: B.
DeWolfe.
Scene 3
"Salesmanship"
J. Morgan, M. Marlo, C. Lawrence, Ziegfeld Girls
(*Music by* Philip Springer. *Lyrics by* Carolyn Leigh.)
Scene 4
Kabuki Lil
(*by* Beatrice Lillie)
B. Lillie

___

[11]Replaced during the run by:
"Mangos"
M. Marlo
(*Music and Lyrics by* Dee Libbey and Sid Wayne.)
Assisted by R. Cecill, A. Craine, M. Davidson, T. Franko, C. Green, H.
Lambert, J. Leigh, E. Powell, J. Stevenson, G. Varrone.
[12]Dropped during run.

Scene 5
"Honorable Mambo"
C. Lawrence, Ensemble
(*Music by* Dean Fuller. *Lyrics by* Marshall Barer.)
Scene 6
"Miss Follies"
B. DeWolfe, C. Green, E. Powell, J. Stevenson, G. Varrone, Ziegfeld Girls
(*Music by* Colin Romoff. *Lyrics by* David Rogers.)
Scene 7
"Make Me"
J. Morgan, The Ziegfeldians
(*Music and Lyrics by* Tony Velone, Larry Spier, Uhpio Minucci.)
Scene 8
"Miss (All You Don't Catch) Follies of 192—"
B. Lillie
(*Music and Lyrics by* Herman Hupfeld.)
Page Girl: N. Hachenberg.
Scene 9
Jay Marshall[13]
Scene 10
"An Element of Doubt"[14]
H. Lang, M. Marlo
(*Music by* Sammy Fain. *Lyrics by* Howard Dietz.)
Scene 11
"My Late, Late Lady" (parody of 'My Fair Lady')
(*Music by* Dean Fuller. *Lyrics by* Marshall Barer.)
Announcer: E. Powell. *The Original Cast*: B. Lillie, B. DeWolfe, J. Philip.
Scene 12
Finale
Entire Company
(*Music by* Richard Myers. *Lyrics by* Jack Lawrence.)

1957.02　　**THE BEGGAR'S OPERA**

A Revival of the Comic Opera in Two Acts[15]. Original libretto and music by
John Gay. New adaptation by Richard Baldridge. Music adapted and arranged
by Daniel Pinkham. Musical staging by John Heawood. Setting by Watson
Barratt. Costumes by Robert Fletcher. Lighting by Jean Rosenthal. Directed
by Richard Baldridge. Musical director and conductor, Miles Morgan. Entire
production supervised by Burt Shevelove. Produced by the New York City
Center Light Opera Company (Jean Dalrymple, Director), as originally produced at the Cambridge Drama Festival. Opened 13 March 1957 at the New
York City Center and closed 24 March 1957 after 15 performances.

CAST (in order of appearance): *Beggar Poet*: PETER TURGEON. *Filch*: Charles
Bolender. *Macheath*: JACK CASSIDY. *Matt of the Mint*: Robert Burr. *Jemmy the
Twitcher*: Hal England. *Crooked Finger Jack*: Maurice Edwards. *Wat Dreary*: Francis
Barnard. *Nimming Ned*: J. C. McCord. *Slippery Sam*: Jack DeLon. *Bob Booty*: DAVID
NILLO. *Tom Tizzle*: William Inglis. *Polly Peachum*: SHIRLEY JONES. *Mr. Peachum*:
GEORGE S. IRVING. *Mrs. Peachum*: ZAMAH CUNNINGHAM. *Mr. Lockit*:
GEORGE GAYNES. *Lucy Lockit*: JEANNE BEAUVAIS. *Mrs. Coaxer*: PAULA
LAURENCE. *Jenny Diver*: CONSTANCE BRIGHAM. *Dolly Trull*: MARIA
KARNILOVA. *Mrs Vixen*: Anita Cooper. *Betty Doxy*: Jenny Lou Law. *Mrs. Slammekin*:
Adnia Rice. *Suky Tawdry*: Shirley Chester. *Molly Brazen*: Charlotte Ray.
  Prisoners, Guards and Other Ladies of the Town: William Ashley, Hal Barnet,
George Broadhurst, Willie Cooper, Joan DuBrow, Jack Emrek, James Karr, Sara
Meade, Louis Saporito, Lee Warren, Hurd Wiese. *Chorus of Prisoners*: Louis Algarra,
Jennie Andrea, Evelyn Aring, Robert Atherton, Nicola Barbusci, Don Becker, June
Bucknor, Julia Gerace, Peter Held, Maurice Kostroff, Mary Lesawyer, Maria Martell,
John Person, Thomas Powell, Robert Ruddy, Mary Thompson, Mara Yavne.

The action takes place at night in Newgate Prison, London. (1728, ca.)

ACT 1
"Let Us Take the Road"
J. Cassidy, the Gang
"My Heart Was So Free"
J. Cassidy

___

[13]Dropped during run.
[14]Dropped during run.
[15]First presented in New York 3 December 1750 at the Theatre in Nassau
Street for 2 performances.

"Were I Laid on Greenland Coast" (Duet)
J. Cassidy, S. Jones

"Virgins Are Like the Fair Flower"
S. Jones

"Our Polly Is a Sad Slut" (Trio)
G. S. Irving, Z. Cunningham, S. Jones

"The Turtle Thus With Plaintive Crying"
S. Jones

"'Tis Woman That Seduces All Mankind"
G. Gaynes

"Through All the Employments of Life" (Duet)
G. S. Irving, G. Gaynes

"Hanging Is My Only Sport"
G. S. Irving

"Were I Laid on Greenland Coast" (reprise Duet)
S. Jones, J. Cassidy

"O, What a Pain It Is to Part"
S. Jones, J. Cassidy

"No Power on Earth Can E'er Divide"
S. Jones

"Man May Escape from Rope and Gun"
Prisoners

"Why How Now Madam Flirt" (Trio)
J. Beauvais, S. Jones, J. Cassidy

"Is Then His Fate Decreed, Sir?" (Quartet)
S. Jones, J. Beauvais, G. S. Irving, G. Gaynes

ACT 2

"Fill Every Glass"
R. Burr, The Gang, Ladies of the Town
Danced by M. Karnilova, D. Nillo.

"The Ways of the World"
J. Cassidy, The Gang

"Let Us Take the Road" (reprise)
The Gang, Ladies of the Town

"If the Heart of a Man"
P. Laurence

"Youth's a Season Made for Joys"
Ladies of the Town

"When Young at the Bar"
C. Brigham

"In the Days of My Youth" (Trio)
P. Laurence, G. S. Irving, G. Gaynes

"At the Tree I Shall Suffer With Pleasure"
J. Cassidy

"When Young at the Bar" (reprise)
C. Brigham

"I'm Like a Skiff on the Ocean Toss'd"
J. Beauvais

"Come Sweet Lass" (Duet)
J. Beauvais, S. Jones

"The Charge Was Prepar'd"
J. Cassidy, Chorus

"Would I Might Be Hanged"
J. Beauvais, S. Jones, J. Cassidy

"Since Laws Were Made for Every Degree"
Entire Company

"See the Conquering Hero" (Finale)
Entire Company

1957.03 ## BRIGADOON

A Revival of the Musical Play in Two Acts, a Prologue and 11 Scenes[16]. Book and lyrics by Alan Jay Lerner. Music by Frederick Loewe. Dances and musical numbers by Agnes de Mille, re-staged by James Jamieson. Produc-

tion directed by George H. Englund. Settings by Oliver Smith. Costumes by Paul duPont. Lighting by Peggy Clark. Musical director, Julius Rudel. Associate conductor, Samuel Matlovsky. (Vocal arrangements by Frederick Loewe. Orchestrations by Ted Royal.) Produced by the New York City Center Light Opera Company (Jean Dalrymple, Director.). Opened 27 March 1957 at the New York City Center, moved 9 April 1957 to the Adelphi Theatre and closed 5 May 1957 after 47 performances.

CAST (in order of appearance): *Tommy Albright*: DAVID ATKINSON. *Jeff Douglas*: SCOTT McKAY. *Archie Beaton*: Elliott Sullivan. *Harry Beaton*: MATT MATTOX. *Angus MacGuffie*: Guy Gordon. *Sandy Dean*: John Dorrin. *Andrew MacLaren*: Russell Gaige. *Fiona MacLaren*: VIRGINIA OSWALD. *Jean MacLaren*: Virginia Bosler. *Meg Brockie*: HELEN GALLAGHER. *Charlie Dalrymple*: ROBERT ROUNSEVILLE. *Maggie Anderson*: Lidija Franklin. *Mr. Lundie*: John C. Becher. *Sword Dancers*: Glenn Olson, Keith Willis. *Frank*: Jack Emrek. *Jane Ashton*: Sloan Simpson. *Bagpiper*: Duncan MacGaskill.

Singers: Jennie Andrea, June Buckner, Marilyn Cooper, Dori Davis, Julia Gerace, Patricia Hall, Jean Maggio, Maria Martell, Sheila Mathews, Mary Thompson, Robert Atherton, Don Becker, Norris Brannstrom, Austin Colyer, Arthur Dilks, John Dorrin, Peter Held, Vincent MacMahon, William Nahr, Stanley Page. *Dancers*: Jeanna Belkin, Pat Birsh (Birch), Anne Boley, Ann Crowell, Geralyn Donald, Dorothy Etheridge, Rosemary Jourdan, Evelyn Taylor, Mona Jo Tritsch, Robert Barnett, Anthony Blum, Jim Brusock, Walter Georgov, Charles McCraw, Glenn Olson, Ray Pointer, Keith Willis, Emmanuel Winston.

1957.04 ## THE MERRY WIDOW

A Revival of the Operetta in Three Acts and a Prologue[17]. Music by Franz Lehár. (Original Viennese libretto, Die Lustige Witwe by Victor Léon and Leo Stein after "L'Attaché d'Ambassade" by Henri Meilhac. New musical version by Robert Stolz.) New book by Sidney Sheldon and Ben Roberts. New lyrics by Adrian Ross (and Robert Gilbert). Directed by Felix Brentano. Original choreography by George Balanchine. Dances by Edward Brinkman. Settings by George Jenkins. Costumes by Paul duPont. Lighting by Peggy Clark. Produced by the New York City Center Light Opera Company (Jean Dalrymple, Director.). Opened 10 April 1957 at the New York City Center and closed 21 April 1957 after 15 performances.

CAST (in order of appearance): *The King*: Jose Duval. *Popoff*: MELVILLE COOPER. *Cascada*: Alex Alexander. *Natalie*: HELENA SCOTT. *Khadja*: C. K. Alexander. *Olga Bardini*: Lucy Hillary. *General Bardini*: GEORGE LIPTON. *Novakovich*: Lewis Brooks. *Jolidon*: JIM HAWTHORNE. *Guests*: Sonja Savig, Casper Roos. *Nish*: NORMAN BUDD. *Sonia*: MARTA EGGERTH. *St. Brioche*: Warde Donovan. *Prince Danilo*: JAN KIEPURA. *Clo-Clo*: MONIQUE VAN VOOREN. *Gaston*: Jose Duval. *Premiere Danseuse*: MARY ELLEN MOYLAN. *Premier Danseur*: MICHAEL MAULE. *Ballerina*: PAULA LLOYD.

Singers: Jeanne Anderson, Josephine Annunciata, Carol O'Day, June House, Claudine Manson, Sonja Savig, Jan Speers, Barbara Saxby, Yolanda Vasquez, Charles O. Aschmann, Jr., Alan Cole, Wendell Grey, David London, Jack McMinn, Mitchell May, Casper Roos, David Smith, Marvin Solley. *Dancers*: Ann Barry, Marilyn d'Honau, Ruby Herndon, Joan Kruger, Eloise Milton, Charlotte Rae, John Grigas, Scott Hunter, William Inglis, Bill Miller, Richard Monahan, Bob St. Clair. *Lackeys*: Bruce Blaine, James Feeney, Eben Snow.

1957.05 ## SHINBONE ALLEY

A Musical in Two Acts, 20 Scenes. Book by Joe Darion and Mel Brooks. Based on the 'archy and mehitabel' stories by Don Marquis. Music by George Kleinsinger. Lyrics by Joe Darion. (Direction uncredited[18].) Dances and musical numbers staged by Rod Alexander. Music and choral direction by Maurice Levine. Production (settings) designed by Eldon Elder. Costumes by Motley. Lighting by Tharon Musser. Orchestrations by George Kleinsinger, Irwin Kostal. Additional musical routines by John Morris. Produced by Peter Lawrence. Opened 13 April 1957 at the Broadway Theatre and closed 25 May 1957 after 49 performances.

CAST (in order of appearance): *Voice of Newspaperman*: Julian Barry. *archy*: EDDIE BRACKEN. *mehitabel*: EARTHA KITT. *Phyllis*: Reri Grist. *Mother*: Lillian Hayman.

---

[16]First presented 13 March 1947 at the Ziegfeld Theatre for 581 performances. For Synopsis of Scenes and Musical Numbers, see original 1947 production.

[17]Original New York production first presented 21 October 1907 at the New Amsterdam Theatre for 416 performances; this adaptation first presented in New York 4 August 1943 at the Majestic Theatre for 322 performances. For Synopsis of Scenes and Musical Numbers, see 1943 revival.

[18]During previews, Norman Lloyd withdrew as director.

Ricky: Dorothy Aull. *Jail Cronies*: Buzz Halliday, Elmarie Wendel, Cathryn Damon, Elizabeth Taylor, Carmen Gutierrez, Nora Reho, GWEN HARMON. *'Copper'*: James Marley. *Buzz*: Howard Roberts. *Butch*: Moses LaMarr. *Rusty*: Cathryn Damon. *Big Bill*: GEORGE S. IRVING. *Broadway*: ROSS MARTIN. *Edie*: GWEN HARMON. *Blackie*: Larry Montaigne. *Gladys*: Carmen Gutierrez. *Frankie*: JACQUES D'AMBOISE. *Fighting Dogs*: Don Farnworth, Gene Gavin, Harold E. Gordon, Claude Thompson. *Tyrone T. Tattersal*: ERIK RHODES. *Shorty*: David Winters. *Harry*: Jack Eddleman. *Lady Bugs*: Dorothy Aull, GWEN HARMON, Buzz Halliday. *Bartender*: Bruce MacKay. *Penny*: ALLEGRA KENT. *Tall Cats*: Albert Popwell, James Tarbutton.

Singers: Dorothy Aull, Jack Eddleman, Reri Grist, Buzz Halliday, Gwen Harmon, Lillian Hayman, Moses LaMarr, James Marley, Bruce MacKay, Jack Rains, Howard Roberts, Elmarie Wendel. *Dancers*: Jacques D'Amboise, Cathryn Damon, Don Farnworth, Gene Gavin, Carolyn George, Harold E. Gordon, Carmen Gutierrez, Allegra Kent, Albert Popwell, Nora Reho, Dorothy Scott, James Tarbutton, Eliuzabeth Taylor, Claude Thompson, Myrna White, David Winters.

The entire action takes place in Shinbone Alley and its environs.

Act 1, Scene 1: A Newspaper Office. *Scene 2*: Shinbone Alley. *Scene 3*: The ASPCA Lock-Up. *Scene 4*: Shinbone Alley. *Scene 5*: A Street. *Scene 6*: Shinbone Alley. *Scene 7*: A Street. *Scene 8*: Tyrone's Trunk in Greenwich Village. *Scene 9*: Shinbone Alley.

Act 2, Scene 1: A Street. *Scene 2*: Shinbone Alley. *Scene 3*: A Street Corner. *Scene 4*: Shinbone Alley. *Scene 5*: Another Street. *Scene 6*: Mehitabel's New Home. *Scene 7*: A Bar Beneath the Street. *Scene 8*: A Vacant Lot. *Scene 9*: Mehitabel's New Home. *Scene 10*: A Quiet Street. *Scene 11*: Shinbone Alley.

ACT 1[19]

Scene 2
  "What Do We Care?"
    E. Kitt, Singing and Dancing Ensemble
Scene 3
  "Toujours Gai" (Cheerio My Deerio)
    E. Kitt
  "Queer Little Insect"
    E. Kitt, E. Bracken
Scene 4
  "Big Bill"
    G. S. Irving, Ladies of Dance Ensemble
  "True Romance"
    E. Kitt, G. S. Irving
    Danced by E. Kitt.
Scene 5
  "The Lightning Bug Song"
    E. Bracken
  "I gotta be"
    R. Martin, E. Bracken
Scene 6
  Dog and Cat Ballet
    Danced by J. D'Amboise, Ensemble
  "Flotsam and Jetsam"
    E. Bracken, E. Kitt
  "Come to Mee-ow"
    E. Rhodes
  "Suicide Song"
    E. Bracken
  "Shinbone Alley"
    G. S. Irving, Denizens of Shinbone Alley

---

[19]In late April, Act 1 was shortened, and Act 2 of the show was totally revised. Added credits: Additional Choreography by Arthur Mitchell. Production supervised by Sawyer Falk. Added songs in Act 2:
  "The Lullaby"
    E. Kitt, Singing Girls
  "Mehitabel's a House Cat" (then dropped)
    E. Bracken, G. S. Irving, Ensemble
  "Flotsam and Jetsam" (reprise)
    E. Bracken, E. Kitt
  "Shinbone Alley" (Finale)
    E. Bracken, E. Kitt, Ensemble

ACT 2
Scene 1
  "The Moth Song"
    E. Bracken
Scene 2
  "A Woman Wouldn't Be a Woman"
    E. Kitt, Ensemble
Scene 5
  "What the Hell"[20]
    E. Kitt
Scene 6
  "Pretty Kitty"
    Singing Girls, *Danced by* E. Kitt
  "Way Down Blues"[21]
    E. Kitt
Scene 7
  "The Lady Bug Song"
    D. Aull, G. Harmon, B. Halliday
Scene 8
  Vacant Lot Ballet
    Danced by J. D'Amboise, A. Kent, C. Damon, D. Winters, Dancing Ensemble
Scene 9
  "Be a Pussycat"
    E. Kitt, Dancing Girls
Scene 10
  "Quiet Street"[22]
    E. Bracken
Scene 11
  "Toujours Gai" (reprise)[23]
    E. Kitt, E. Bracken, Ensemble

1957.06 SOUTH PACIFIC

A Revival of the Musical Play in Two Acts, 23 Scenes[24]. Book by Oscar Hammerstein II and Joshua Logan. Adapted from James A. Michener's novel "Tales of the South Pacific." Music by Richard Rodgers. Lyrics by Oscar Hammerstein II. Directed by John Fearnley. Scenery by Jo Mielziner. Adaptation and lighting by Peggy Clark. Costumes by Motley, supervised by Florence Klotz Musical director, Frederick Dvonch. (Orchestrations by Robert Russell Bennett.) Produced by the New York City Center Light Opera Company (Jean Dalrymple, Director). Opened 24 April 1957 at the New York City Center and closed 12 May 1957 after 23 performances.

CAST (in order of appearance): *Ngana*: Lynn Kikuchi. *Jerome*: Afredo DeArco. *Henry*: Mark Satow. *Ensign Nellie Forbush*: MINDY CARSON. *Emile DeBecque*: ROBERT WRIGHT. *Bloody Mary*: JUANITA HALL. *Bloody Mary's Assistant*: Julia Gerace. *Abner*: Jim McMillan. *Stewpot*: Lou Wills, Jr. *Luther Billis*: HARVEY LEMBECK. *Professor*: Bill Mullikin. *Lt. Joseph Cable, U.S.M.C.*: ALLEN CASE. *Capt. George Brackett, U.S.N.*: MARTIN WOLFSON. *Cmdr. William Harbison, U.S.N.*: ALAN BAXTER. *Yeoman Herbert Quale*: Ray Weaver. *Sgt. Kenneth Johnson*: Van Stevens. *Marine Cpl. Richard West*: Dan Hannafin *Seabee Morton Wise*: Evans Thornton. *Sgt. Juan Cortez*: Quinto Bagioni. *Seaman Tom O'Brien*: Jack McMinn. *Radio Operator Bob McCaffrey*: Sam Kirkham. *Marine Cpl. Hamilton Steeves*: Lee Warren. *Staff Sgt. Thomas Hassinger*: Charles Aschman. *Seaman James Hayes*: Ralph Vucci. *Lt. Genevieve Marshall*: Miriam Gulager. *Ensign Dinah Murphy*: Christy Palmer. *Ensign Janet MacGregor*: Mildred Slavin. *Ensign Cora MacRae*: Pat Finch. *Ensign Bessie Noonan*: Barbara Saxby. *Ensign Pamella Whitmore*: Betty Graeber. *Ensign Sue Yaeger*: Peggy Hadley. *Ensign Lisa Minelli*: Betty McNamara. *Liat*: IMELDA DE MARTIN. *Lt. Buzz Adams*: Dick Button. *Shore Patrol Officer*: Peter Held. *Islanders*: Vie-Von Thom, Andrea Del Rosario, Claudia Satow.

---

[20]Dropped during run.
[21]Dropped during run.
[22]Dropped during run.
[23]Dropped during run.
[24]Originally presented in New York 7 April 1949 at the Majestic Theatre for 1925 performances. For Synopsis of Scenes and Musical Numbers, see original 1949 production.

1957.07 NEW GIRL IN TOWN

A Musical in Two Acts, 16 Scenes. Book by George Abbott. Based on the play "Anna Christie" by Eugene O'Neill. Music and lyrics by Bob Merrill. Dances and musical numbers staged by Bob Fosse. Production (settings, costumes) designed by Rouben Ter-Arutunian. Musical direction by Hal Hastings. Dance music devised by Roger Adams. Orchestrations by Robert Russell Bennett and Philip J. Lang. Directed by George Abbott. Produced by Frederick Brisson, Robert E. Griffith and Harold S. Prince. Opened 14 May 1957 at the 46th Street Theatre and closed 24 May 1958 after 432 performances.

CAST (in order of appearance): *Lily*: Lulu Bates. *Moll*: Pat Ferrier. *Katie*: Mara Lynn. *Alderman*: Michael Quinn. *Chris*: CAMERON PRUD'HOMME. *Johnson*: Jeff Killion. *Seaman*: H. F. Green. *Marthy*: THELMA RITTER. *Oscar*: Del Anderson. *Pete*: Eddie Phillips. *Mrs. Dowling*: Ann Willaims. *Smith*: Stokely Gray. *Mrs. Smith*: Dorothy Stinnette. *Bartender*: Mark Dawson. *Ivy*: Rita Noble. *Rose*: Ginny Perlowin. *Anna*: GWEN VERDON. *Flo*: Drusilla Davis. *Pearl*: Mara Landi. *Mat*: GEORGE WALLACE. *Mrs. Hammacher*: Jean Handzlik. *Reporter*: Herb Fields. *Masher*: John Aristedes. *Svenson*: Ray Mason. *Violet*: Deedy Irwin. *Waiter*: Louis Polacek. *Dowling*: Ripple Lewis. *Politician*: H. F. Green. *Krimp*: John Ford. *Henry*: Edgar Daniels.

Dancers: Claiborne Cary, Drusilla Davis, Dorothy Dushock, Pat Ferrier, Marie Kolin, Mara Lynn, Ethel Martin, Joan Petlak, John Aristedes, Robert Bakanic, Harvey Hohnecker, Harvey Jung, Dale Moreda, John Nola, Eddie Phillips, Alton Ruff. *Singers*: Jean Handzlik, Deedy Irwin, Mara Landi, Rita Noble, Ginny Perlowin, Dorothy Stinnette, Ann Williams, Del Anderson, Edgar Daniels, Herb Fields, John Ford, Stokely Gray, H. F. Green, Jeff Killion, Ripple Lewis, Ray Mason, Louis Polacek, Michael Quinn.

The action takes place near the Waterfront, New York City, at the turn of the century.

Act 1, Scene 1: The Waterfront. *Scene 2*: A Street with a mesh fence. *Scene 3*: Johnny-the-Priest's Saloon. *Scene 4*: A Street in the Warehouse District. *Scene 5*: Chris's Barge on a foggy night at sea, off Provincetown. *Scene 6*: A Street near the Waterfront. *Scene 7*: The Waterfront. *Scene 8*: The Street with the fence. *Scene 9*: Chris's Room. *Scene 10*: A Street Scene. *Scene 11*: The Check Apron Ball.

Act 2, Scene 1: The Check Apron Ball. *Scene 2*: In the Street, outside the Brewery. *Scene 3*: A Street in the Warehouse District. *Scene 4*: Chris's Room. *Scene 5*: The Waterfront. One year later.

ACT 1

Scene 1

"Roll Yer Socks Up"
H. F. Green, Dancers, Singers

Scene 2

"Anna Lilla"
C. Prud'Homme

Scene 3

"Sunshine Girl"
D. Anderson, E. Phillips, M. Dawson

"On the Farm"
G. Verdon

Scene 4

"Flings"
T. Ritter, L. Bates, M. Landi

Scene 5

"It's Good To Be Alive"
G. Verdon

Scene 6

"Look at 'Er"
G. Wallace

Scene 7

"It's Good To Be Alive" (reprise)
G. Wallace

Scene 8

"Yer My Friend, Aintcha?"
T. Ritter, C. Prud'Homme

Scene 9

"Did You Close Your Eyes?"
G. Verdon, G. Wallace

Scene 10

"At the Check Apron Ball"
Dancers, Singers

Scene 11

"There Ain't No Flies on Me"
G. Verdon, H. Hohnecker, H. Jung, E. Phillips, D. Moreda, Company

ACT 2

Scene 1

"Ven I Valse"
G. Verdon, C. Prud'Homme, Dancers, Singers

Scene 3

"Sunshine Girl" (reprise)
Dancers, Singers

Scene 4

"If That Was Love"
G. Verdon

Ballet
G. Verdon, J. Aristedes, Dancers

Scene 5

"Chess and Checkers"
T. Ritter, Dancers, Singers

"Look at 'Er" (reprise)
G. Wallace

1957.08 THE PAJAMA GAME

A Revival of the Musical Comedy in Two Acts, 17 Scenes[25]. Book by George Abbott and Richard Bisssell. Based on the novel "7 1/2 Cents" by Richard Bissell. Music and lyrics by Richard Adler and Jerry Ross. Original production directed by George Abbott and Jerome Robbins. Directed by Jean Barrere. Scenery and costumes by Lemuel Ayers. Costume supervisor, Ruth Morley. Dances based on original choreography by Bob Fosse as executed by Erik Kristen. Lighting by Peggy Clark. Musical director, Frederick Dvonch. Orchestrations by Don Walker. Dance music arrangements by Roger Adams. Produced by the New York City Center Light Opera Company (Jean Dalrymple, Director). Opened 15 May 1957 at the New York City Center and closed 2 June 1957 after 23 performances.

CAST (in order of appearance): *Hines*: PAUL HARTMAN. *Prez*: STANLEY PRAGER. *Joe*: Sam Kirkham. *Hasler*: Ralph W. Chambers. *Gladys*: PAT STANLEY. *Sid Sorokin*: LARRY DOUGLASS. *Mabel*: MARGUERITE SHAW. *First Helper*: Richard France. *Second Helper*: Cy Young. *Charlie*: Eugene Wood. *Babe Williams*: JANE KEAN. *Mae*: Thelma Pelish. *Brenda*: Ann Buckles. *Poopsie*: Chele Graham. *Salesman*: Jack Waldron *Pop*: William David.

Dancers: Dorothy Etheridge, Chele Graham, Mickey Gunnerson, Rosemary Jourdan, Vivian Joyce, Barbara Siman, Bonnie West, Jim Brusock, Richard Colacino, Jack Konzal, Richard Monahan, Tom Snow, Keith Willis, Emanuel Winston. *Singers*: Helen Baisley, Julia Gerace, Betty Graeber, Miriam Gulager, Peg Hadley, Sheila Mathews, Barbara Saxby, Mildred Slavin, Don Becker, Norris Branstrom, Arthur Dilks, Peter Held, Sam Kirkham, Vince McMahon, Stanley Page, Ralph Vucci.

---

[25]First presented in New York 13 May 1954 at the St. James Theatre for 1063 performances. For Synopsis of Scenes and Musical Numbers, see original 1954 production.

1957–1958 SEASON

Carol Lawrence (with mirror) in WEST SIDE STORY
Martha Swope/TimePix

1957–1958 SEASON

1957.09
SIMPLY HEAVENLY

A Musical Folk Comedy in Two Acts, 17 Scenes[1]. Book and lyrics by Langston Hughes. (Based on his novel "Simple Takes a Wife" and other "Simple" stories.) Music and orchestrations by David Martin. Directed by Joshua Shelley. Setting and lighting by Raymond Sovey. Musical director, Sticks Evans. (Produced by Vincent Cerow and Abel Enklewitz.) Opened 20 August 1957 at the Playhouse and closed 12 October 1957 after 62 performances. After Broadway run, re-opened Off-Broadway 8 November 1957 at the Renata Theatre, and closed 31 December 1957 after 63 additional performances. Total for all 3 engagements: 169 performances.

CAST[2] (in order of appearance): *Simple:* MELVIN STEWART. *Madam Butler:* Wilhelmina Gray. *Boyd:* Stanley Greene. *Mrs. Caddy:* Dagmar Craig. *Joyce Lane:* MARILYN BERRY. *Hopkins:* Duke Williams. *Bar Pianist:* Willie Pritchett. *Mamie:* CLAUDIA McNEIL. *Bodiddly:* Charles A. McRae. *Character:* Allegro Kane. *Melon:* JOHN BOUIE. *Gitfiddle:* Brownie McGhee. *Zarita:* ANNA ENGLISH. *Arcie:* Josephine Woods. *John Jasper:* Charles Harrigan. *Big Boy, Cop:* Maxwell Glanville. *Nurse, Party Guest:* Dagmar Craig.

Act 1, Scene 1: Simple's Room, Harlem, New York City. An early Spring evening. *Scene 2:* Joyce's Room. Same evening. *Scene 3:* Paddy's Bar. Just before midnight. *Scene 4:* Hospital Room. Next day. *Scene 5:* Paddy's Bar. Saturday night. *Scene 6:* Joyce's Room. Sunday evening. *Scene 7:* Simple's Room. A month later.

Act 2, Scene 1: Paddy's Bar. A week later, evening. *Scene 2:* Joyce's Room. Evening, two weeks later. *Scene 3:* Simple's Room. Evening, a week later. *Scene 4:* Paddy's Bar. Next morning. *Scene 5:* Lenox Avenue. That evening. *Scene 6:* Joyce's Room. Same evening. *Scene 7:* Simple's Room. Same evening. *Scene 8:* Paddy's Bar. A Winter evening. *Scene 9:* A Phone Booth. Christmas Eve. *Scene 10:* Simple's Room. Same evening.

ACT 1
Scene 2

"Love Is Simply Heavenly"
M. Berry
Scene 3

"Let Me Take You for a Ride"
A. English, M. Stewart
"Broken String Blues"
B. McGhee
Scene 5

"Did You Ever Hear the Blues?"
C. McNeil, J. Bouie, Bar Characters
Scene 7

"I'm Gonna Be John Henry"
M. Stewart
ACT 2
Scene 1

"When I'm in a Quiet Mood"
C. McNeil, J. Bouie
"Look For the Morning Star"[3]
A. English
Scene 3

"Let's Ball Awhile"
A. English, Ensemble
Scene 4

"The Men in My Life"
A. English

---

[1]First produced in New York Off-Broadway 21 May 1957 at the 85th Street Playhouse for 44 performances.
[2]Those actors who originated their roles Off-Broadway but did not transfer to Broadway were as follows: *Madam Butler:* Alma Hubbard. *Mrs. Caddy:* Javotte S. Greene. *Hopkins:* Lewison Bates. *Gitfiddle:* Ray Thompson. *Zarita:* ETHEL AYLER. *Big Boy, Cop:* Pierre Rayon. *Nurse, Party Guest:* Javotte S. Greene.
[3]Replaced "Shade and Shadows" (from Off-Broadway run)(E. Ayler).

Scene 8

"I'm a Good Old Girl"
C. McNeil
Scene 10

"Look for the Morning Star" (reprise)
Ensemble

1957.10
MASK AND GOWN

A Musical Revue in Two Acts, 17 Scenes. Continuity (dialogue) by Ronny Graham and Sidney Carroll. Musical numbers staged and choreographed by Jim Russell. New music and lyrics by Ronny Graham, June Carroll, Arthur Siegel, Dorothea Freitag. Musical direction and arrangements by Dorothea Freitag. Lighting supervision by Lee Watson. Entire production conceived and directed by Leonard Sillman. Produced by Leonard Sillman and Bryant Haliday. Opened 10 September 1957 at the John Golden Theatre and closed 12 October 1957 after 39 performances.

CAST: MR. T. C. [Thomas Craig] JONES , BETTY CARR, GABY MONET, JOHN SMOLKO, ROD STRONG.

ACT 1
Scene 1

"The Circus Is Over"
J. Smolko
(*Music by* Arthur Siegel. *Lyrics by* June Carroll.)
With T. C. Jones, B. Carr, G. Monet, R. Strong.
Scene 2

T. C. on T. C.
(*by* Sidney Carroll) T. C. Jones
Scene 3

T. C. on T. V.
(*by* Ronny Graham) T. C. Jones
With B. Carr, G. Monet, J. Smolko, R. Strong.
Scene 4

"Make Friends"
B. Carr, G. Monet, J. Smolko, R. Strong
(*Music by* Arthur Siegel.)
Scene 5

Catch
T. C. Jones, B. Carr, G. Monet, J. Smolko, R. Strong
Scene 6

"Hesitation Waltz"
B. Carr, R. Strong
(*Music by* Emile Waldteufel.)
Scene 7

"T. C. A. Dance" (from SIMPLE SIMON)
T. C. Jones
(*Music by* Richard Rodgers. *Lyrics by* Lorenz Hart.)
Scene 8

Bolero
(*Music by* Dorothea Freitag.) G. Monet, J. Smolko
Scene 9

T. C. on Hollywood
(*by* Leonard Sillman and Everett Marcy) T. C. Jones, J. Smolko
Scene 10

T. C. on Taps Topside:
"Don't Give Up the Ship" (from film SHIPMATES FOREVER)
T. C. Jones, B. Carr, G. Monet, J. Smolko, R. Strong
(*Music by* Harry Warren. *Lyrics by* Al Dubin.)
Scene 11

On Their Own:
House of Blue Lights
G. Monet
Shangri-La
J. Smolko
"Speedy Gonzales"
B. Carr
(*Music and Lyrics by* Ronny Graham.)

Chopin Waltz in E Minor
R. Strong
Scene 12
T. C. on Certain Singers
T. C. Jones
With B. Carr, G. Monet, J. Smolko, R. Strong.
"Remind Me" (from film ONE NIGHT IN THE TROPICS)
(*Music by* Jerome Kern. *Lyrics by* Dorothy Fields.)
"I Cover the Waterfront" (from film I COVER THE WATERFRONT)
(*Music by* Johnny Green. *Lyrics by* Edward Heyman.)
"How Did he Look?"
(*Music by* Abner Silver. *Lyrics by* Gladys Shelley.)
"New Sounds"
(*Music and Lyrics by* Ronny Graham.)
ACT 2
Scene 1
Setting the Stage
(*Music by* Scarlatti.) R. Strong
Scene 2
T. C. on Avon
(*Idea Conceived by* Mr. Jones.) T. C. Jones
With B. Carr, G. Monet, J. Smolko, R. Strong.
Ethel Merman as Juliet
Marilyn Monroe as Ophelia
Tallulah as Cleopatra
Mae West, Claudette Colbert or Ethel Barrymore as Kate
Bette Davis as Lady Macbeth
Judy Holliday as Portia
Katharine Hepburn as Rosalind
Scene 3
"You Better Go Now" (from NEW FACES OF 1936)
T. C. Jones
With B. Carr, G. Monet, J. Smolko, R. Strong.
(*Music by* Irvin Graham. *Lyrics by* Bickley Reichner.)
Scene 4
"I'll Be Seeing You" (from RIGHT THIS WAY)
T. C. Jones
(*Music by* Sammy Fain. *Lyrics by* Irving Kahal.)
Scene 5
T. C.
Himself

1957.11   CAROUSEL

A Revival of the Musical Play in Two Acts, Prelude and 9 Scenes[4]. Book and lyrics by Oscar Hammerstein II. Based on Ferenc Molnar's "Liliom" as adapted by Benjamin F. Glazer. Music by Richard Rodgers. Directed by John Fearnley. Choreography by Agnes de Mille, restaged by Robert Pagent. Ensemble staging by John Fearnley and Robert Pagent. Scenery by Oliver Smith. Costume supervisor, Florence Klotz. Lighting by Peggy Clark. Musical director, Julius Rudel. Choral director, Charles Smith. (Orchestrations by Don Walker.) Produced by the New York City Center Light Opera Company (Jean Dalrymple, Director). Opened 11 September 1957 at the New York City Center and closed 29 September 1957 after 24 performances.

CAST (in order of appearance): *Carrie Pipperidge:* PAT STANLEY. *Julie Jordan:* BARBARA COOK. *Mrs. Mullin:* KAY MEDFORD. *Billy Bigelow:* HOWARD KEEL. *First Policeman:* Evans Thornton. *David Bascombe:* Robert Eckles. *Girl With Bear:* Elisa Monte. *Nettie Fowler:* MARIE POWERS. *June Girl:* Evelyn Taylor. *Enoch Snow:* RUSSELL NYPE. *Jigger Craigin:* JAMES MITCHELL. *Hannah:* Joan Eheman. *Boatswain:* ROBERT PAGENT. *Second Policeman:* James Gannon. *Captain:* Sam Kirkham. *Heavenly Friend (Brother Joshua):* Leo Lucker. *Starkeeper:* VICTOR MOORE. *Louise:* BAMBI LINN. *Carnival Boy:* ROBERT PAGENT. *Enoch Snow, Jr.:* Larry Fuller. *Principal:* Bruce Baggett.

Townspeople: Jane Burke, Shirley Chester, Faith Compo, Charry Davis, Elizabeth Edwards, Lindsay McGregor, Beth Parks, Basha Regis, Jeanne Shea, Joy Lynne Sica, Bruce Baggett, Don Becker, Jack Eddleman, James E. Gannon, Sam Kirkham, David London, Vincent B. McMahon, Bob Newkum, Ted Otis, Robert B. Reim. *Dancers:* Patricia Birsh (Birch), Verna Cain, Dorothy Etheridge, Mickey Gunnerson, Sally Gura, Ruby Herndon, Catherine Horn, Reba Howells, Rosemary Jourdan, Eloise Milton, Kiki Minor, Evelyn Taylor, Jim Albright, Charles J. Carow, Gerald Fries, Larry Fuller William T. Inglis, Donald Martin, Glenn Olson, Robert St. Clair, Gerald M. Teijolo, Jr.

1957.12   WEST SIDE STORY

A Musical in Two Acts, 15 Scenes. Book by Arthur Laurents. Based on a conception of Jerome Robbins. Music by Leonard Bernstein. Lyrics by Stephen Sondheim. Entire production directed and choreographed by Jerome Robbins. Scenic production by Oliver Smith. Costumes by Irene Sharaff. Lighting by Jean Rosenthal. Co-choreographer, Peter Gennaro. Musical direction by Max Goberman. Orchestrations by Leonard Bernstein, with Sid Ramin, Irwin Kostal. Produced by Robert E. Griffith and Harold S. Prince by arrangement with Roger L. Stevens. Opened 26 September 1957 at the Winter Garden, moved 2 March 1959 to the Broadway Theatre, and closed 27 June 1959 after 732 performances.[5]

CAST: *THE JETS: Riff,* the Leader: MICKEY CALIN. *Tony,* his friend: LARRY KERT. *Action:* Eddie Roll. *A-Rab:* Tony Mordente. *Baby John:* David Winters. *Snowboy:* Grover Dale. *Big Deal:* Martin Charnin. *Diesel:* Hank Brunjes. *Gee-Tar:* Tommy Abbott. *Mouth Piece:* Frank Green. *Tiger:* Lowell Harris. *Their Girls: Graziella:* Wilma Curley. *Velma:* Carole D'Andrea. *Minnie:* Nanette Rosen. *Clarice:* Marilyn D'Honau. *Pauline:* Julie Oser. *Anybodys:* Lee Becker.
THE SHARKS: Bernardo, the Leader: KEN LeROY. *Maria,* his Sister: CAROL LAWRENCE. *Anita,* his Girl: CHITA RIVERA. *Chino,* his Friend: Jamie Sanchez. *Pepe:* George Marcy. *Indio:* Noel Schwartz. *Luis:* Al De Sio. *Anxious:* Gene Gavin. *Nibbles:* Ronnie Lee. *Juano:* Jay Norman. *Toro:* Erne Castaldo. *Moose:* Jack Murray. *Their Girls: Rosalia:* Marilyn Cooper. *Consuelo:* Reri Grist. *Teresita:* Carmen Guiterrez. *Francisca:* Elizabeth Taylor. *Estella:* Lynn Ross. *Marguerita:* Liane Plane.
THE ADULTS: Doc: ART SMITH. *Schrank:* Arch Johnson. *Krupke:* William Bramley. *Gladhand:* John Harkins.

The action takes place on the West Side of New York City during the last days of Summer.

Act 1, Scene 1: Prologue: The months before. The Street. 5:00 P.M. *Scene 2:* A Back Yard 5:30 P.M. *Scene 3:* The Bridal Shop. 6:00 P.M. *Scene 4:* The Gym. 10:00 P.M. *Scene 5:* A Back Alley. 11:00 P.M. *Scene 6:* The Drugstore. Midnight. *Scene 7:* The Bridal Shop. The next day, 5:30 P.M. *Scene 8:* The Neighborhood. 6:00 to 9:00 P.M. *Scene 9:* Under the Highway. 9:00 P.M.

Act 2, Scene 1: The Bedroom. 9:15 P.M. *Scene 2:* Another Alley. 10:00 P.M. *Scene 3:* The Bedroom. 11:30 P.M. *Scene 4:* The Drugstore. 11:40 P.M. *Scene 5:* The Cellar. 11:50 P.M. *Scene 6:* The Street. Midnight.

ACT 1
Scene 1
Prologue
Danced by Jets and Sharks
"Jet Song"
M. Calin, D. Winters, G. Dale, Jets
Scene 2
"Something's Coming"
L. Kert
Scene 4
The Dance at the Gym
Jets and Sharks
"Maria"
L. Kert
Scene 5
"Tonight"
L. Kert, C. Lawrence
"America"
C. Rivera, M. Cooper, Shark Girls
Scene 6
"Cool"
M. Calin, Jets

---

[4]Originally produced in New York 19 April 1945 at the Majestic Theatre for 890 performances. For Synopsis of Scenes and Musical Numbers, see original 1945 production.

[5]Re-opened a return engagement 27 April 1960 at the Winter Garden; see separate entry below.

Scene 7

"One Hand, One Heart"
L. Kert, C. Lawrence

Scene 8

"Tonight" (Quintet and Chorus)
Company

Scene 9

The Rumble
Danced by M. Calin, K. LeRoy, Jets and Sharks

ACT 2

Scene 1

"I Feel Pretty"
C. Lawrence, M. Cooper, C. Guiterrez, E. Taylor

"Somewhere"
R. Grist
Danced by the Company.

Scene 2

"Gee, Officer Krupke"
E. Roll, G. Dale, Jets

Scene 3

"A Boy Like That"
C. Rivera, C. Lawrence

"I Have a Love"
C. Rivera, C. Lawrence

Scene 4

Taunting
C. Rivera, Jets

Scene 6

Finale
The Company

1957.13   DIE FLEDERMAUS

A Revival of the Operetta in Three Acts[6]. (Original Viennese libretto by Carl Haffner and Richard Genée. Lyrics by Richard Genée. Based on the comedy "Le Réveillon" by Henri Meilhac and Ludovic Halévy.) English libretto by Ruth and Thomas Martin. Music by Johann Strauss. Staged by Michael Pollock. Choreographed by Robert Joffrey. (Settings) Designed by Leo Kerz. Conducted by Franz Allers. Produced by the New York City Opera. Opened 13 October 1957 at the New York City Center and closed 17 November 1957 after 3 performances in repertory.

CAST: Rosalinda: PHYLLIS CURTIN. Eisenstein: ERNEST McCHESNEY. Adele: JACQUELYNNE MOODY. Sally: Naomi Collier. Alfred: DAVID LLOYD. Prince Orlofsky: LOREN DRISCOLL. Falke: CHESTER LUDGIN. Frank: Richard Wentworth. Frosch: Coley Worth. Blind: David Williams. Solo Dancers: Dianne Consoer, Jonathan Watts.

1957.14   COPPER AND BRASS

A Musical Comedy in Two Acts. Book by Ellen Violett and David Craig. Music by David Baker. Lyrics by David Craig. Directed by Marc Daniels. Choreography by Anna Sokolow. Settings and lighting by William and Jean Eckart. Costumes by Alvin Colt. Musical direction and vocal arrangements by Maurice Levine. Orchestrations by Ralph Burns. Dance arrangements by John Morris. Produced by Lyn Austin and Thomas Noyes in association with Anderson Lawlor. Opened 17 October 1957 at the Martin Beck Theatre and closed 16 November 1957 after 36 performances.

CAST (in order of appearance): First Expert: Byron Mitchell. Second Expert: David Gold. Third Expert: Stanley Papich. Fourth Expert: Jeff Duncan. Fifth Expert: John Dorrin. Sixth Expert: Kevin Carlisle. Seventh Expert: Bob Roman. Eighth Expert: Sam Greene. Katey O'Shea: NANCY WALKER. Commissioner: Beau Tilden. Captain: ALAN BUNCE. Sergeant: Bruce Mackay. Ethel Potts: Michele Burke. Mary Potts: Evelyn Russell. Estelle O'Shea: BENAY VENUTA. Mrs. Zimmer: Alice Nunn. Mr. Morphky: Michael Roberts. Mrs. Morphky: Doreen McLean. Piggy: Byron Mitchell.

Brawn: Norma Douglas. Brains: Peter Conlow. Boy: Stanley Papich. Principal: ALICE PEARCE. Instructor: Clyde Turner. George: DICK WILLIAMS. Limey: Hank Jones. Slam: Doug Rogers. Professor: Ernie Furtado. Traintime: Frank Rehak. Slam's Girl: Elmarie Wendel. Limey's Wife: Elton Warren. Professor's Girl: Bette Graham. Rookie Cops: Sam Greene, Michael Roberts, John Dorrin, Bob Roman, Nat Wright, Larry Mitchell, Jack Moore. Roderick: David Gold. Policewomen: Dorothy Aull, Joy Lane, Bette Graham. Woman in the Window: Joy Lane. Guard: Michael Roberts.

Dancers: Shawneequa Baker, Eve Beck, Judith Coy, Anita Dencks, Kate Friedlich, Ellen Hubel, Coco Ramirez, Tina Ramirez, Ella Thompson, Kevin Carlisle, Jeff Duncan, David Gold, Donald MacKayle, Jack Moore, Stanley Papich, Harold Pierson, Willard Nagel. Singers: Dorothy Aull, Laurie Franks, Bette Graham, Buzz Halliday, Joy Lane, Elton Warren, Elmarie Wendel, John Dorrin, Sam Greene, Bruce Mackay, Byron Mitchell, Larry Mitchell, Michael Roberts, Bob Roman, Clyde Turner, Nat Wright.

The action takes place in and around the island of Manhattan.

ACT 1

"Career Guidance"
N. Walker, Eight Experts

"Wearing of the Blue"
N. Walker, Company

"I Need All the Help I Can Get"
N. Walker

"Cool Combo Mambo"
The Kids

"You Walked Out"
D. Williams

"Cool Credo"
D. Williams, N. Walker, Combo, Bandannies, Kids

"Bringing Up Daughter"
B. Venuta

"Don't Look Now"
N. Walker, D. Williams, Dancers

"Baby's Baby"
N. Douglas, P. Conlow, S. Baker, C. Ramirez, T. Ramirez
(Dance choreographed by Bob Fosse.)

"You Walked Out" (reprise)
N. Walker

ACT 2

"Call the Police"
N. Walker, Policewomen

"Unmistakable Sign"
N. Walker, B. Venuta

"Why Her?"
D. Williams

"Me and Love"
N. Walker

"Remember the Dancing"
B. Venuta, A. Pearce, A. Bunce,
D. McLean, M. Roberts, A. Nunn, P. Conlow, N. Douglas, Company

"Honk Kong"
B. Venuta, Company

"Argentine Tango"
A. Pearce, A. Bunce

"Sweet William"
B. Venuta, Company

"Don't Look Now" (reprise)
D. Williams

"Little Woman"
N. Walker

"Call the Police" (Finale)
Entire Company

1957.15   THE MERRY WIDOW

A Revival of the Operetta in Three Acts[7]. Music by Franz Lehár. Original Viennese libretto (Die Lustige Witwe) by Victor Léon and Leo Stein after "L'Attaché d'Ambassade." English libretto by Adrian Ross. Staged by Glenn

---

[6]First English language production in New York 16 March 1885 at the Casino Theatre for 42 performances. First New York production of this adaptation 20 December 1950 at the Metropolitan Opera House. For Synopsis of Scenes and Musical Numbers, see May 1954 revival.

[7]Originally produced in New York 21 October 1907 at the New Amsterdam Theatre for 416 performances. For Synopsis of Scenes and Musical Numbers, see original 1907 production.

Jordan. Choreographed by Robert Joffrey. Scenic design by George Jenkins. Conducted by Franz Allers. Produced by the New York City Opera. Opened 27 October 1957 at the New York City Center and closed 10 November 1957 after 3 performances in repertory.

CAST: *Sonia*: BEVERLY SILLS. *Prince Danilo*: ROBERT ROUNSEVILLE. *Baron Popoff*: HIRAM SHERMAN. *Natalie*: Peggy Bonini. *De Jolidon*: WILLIAM LEWIS. *Marquis de Cascada*: Herbert Beattie. *St. Brioche*: JOHN REARDON. *Admiral Khadja*: Arthur Newman. *Mme. Khadja*: Helen Baisley. *General Novikovich*: Richard Wentworth. *Mme. Novikovich*: Lu Leonard. *Nish*: Coley Worth. *King*: George Del Monte. *Lo-Lo*: Naomi Collier. *Solo Dancers*: Dianne Consoer, Beatrice Tompkins, Gerald Arpino. *Ensemble*: New York City Opera Chorus.

1957.16   # JAMAICA

A Musical Comedy in Two Acts, 17 Scenes. Book by E. Y. Harburg and Fred Saidy. Music by Harold Arlen. Lyrics by E. Y. Harburg. Entire production directed by Robert Lewis. Production (Settings) designed by Oliver Smith. Costumes designed by Miles White. Lighting by Jean Rosenthal. Orchestrations by Philip J. Lang. Musical direction, continuity and vocal arrangements by Lehman Engel. Dance music and additional vocal arrangements by Peter Matz. Choreography by Jack Cole. Produced by David Merrick. Opened 31 October 1957 at the Imperial Theatre, closing for vacation 28 June 1958; reopened 11 August 1958 at the Imperial Theatre and closed 11 April 1959 after 558 performances.

CAST (in order of appearance): *Koli*: RICARDO MONTALBAN. *Quico*: Augustine Rios. *Savannah*: LENA HORNE. *Grandma Obeah*: ADELAIDE HALL. *Ginger*: JOSEPHINE PREMICE. *Snodgrass*: Roy Thompson. *Huckabuck*: Hugh Dilworth. *Island Women*: Ethel Ayler, Adelaide Boatner. *The Governor*: ERIK RHODES. *Cicero*: OSSIE DAVIS. *Lancaster*: James E. Wall. *First Ship's Officer*: Tony Martinez. *Second Ship's Officer*: Michael Wright. *Joe Nashua*: JOE ADAMS. *Dock Worker*: Allen Richards. *Radio Announcer*: Alan Shayne. *Lead Dancers*: Alvin Ailey, Christyne Lawson.

Islanders: Ethel Ayler, Adelaide Boatner, Jayne Craddock, Norma Donaldson, Patricia Dunn, Doris Galiber, Lavinia Hamilton, Sandra Hinton, Chailendra Jones, Audrey Mason, Sally Neal, Pearl Reynolds, Christine Spencer, Carolyn Stanford, Jacqueline Walcott, Barbara Wright, George Boreland, Hugh Bryant, Herb Coleman, Hugh Dilworth, Frank Glass, Harold Gordon, Nat Horne, Albert Johnson, Tony Martinez, Jim McMillan, Charles Moore, Allen Richards, Claude Thompson, Roy Thompson, Billy Wilson, Michael Wright, Ben Vargas.

The action takes place on Pigeon Island, a mythical island off Jamaica at the present time.

Act 1, Scene 1: Grandma Obeah's shack. A day in spring. *Scene 2*: The knoll near Grandma's shack. Next day. *Scene 3*: Ginger's hut. That evening. *Scene 4*: Grandma's shack. Later that evening. *Scene 5*: Koli's boat. the same night. *Scene 6*: Dockside. The next morning. *Scene 7*: The Governor's mansion. A few days later. *Scene 8*: A night club. *Scene 9*: The beach at night. *Scene 10*: Grandma's shack. Early evening. *Scene 11*: Dockside. Next morning.

Act 2, Scene 1: A bluff on the coast. Three days later. *Scene 2*: The Governor's mansion. Next afternoon. *Scene 3*: A room in the Governor's mansion. A few days later. *Scene 4*: Koli's fish market. Next day. *Scene 5*: The Governor's mansion. The same day. *Scene 6*: The knoll. Later afternoon of the same day.

ACT 1[8]
Scene 1
  "Savannah"
    (R. Montalban, Men)
Scene 2
  "Savannah's Wedding Day"
    (A. Hall, R. Thompson, H. Dilworth, A. Rios, Chorus)
  "Pretty to Walk With"
    (L. Horne, Chorus)
  "Push the Button"
    (L. Horne, Chorus)
  "Incompatibility"
    (R. Montalban, Men)
Scene 3
  "Little Biscuit"
    (O. Davis, J. Premice)

---

[8]Vocalists not identified in the program. List below prepared from production typescript and cast recording.

Scene 4
  "Cocoanut Sweet"
    (L. Horne)
Scene 5
  "Pity the Sunset"
    (R. Montalban, L. Horne)
Scene 6
  "(Hooray for De) Yankee Dollar"
    (J. Premice, Chorus)
  "What Good Does It Do?"
    (J. Premice, O. Davis, R. Montalban, A. Rios)
Scene 7
  "Monkey in the Mango Tree"
    (R. Montalban, Men)
Scene 8
  "Take It Slow, Joe"
    (L. Horne)
Scene 9
  Beach at Night—Dance
Scene 10
  "Ain't It the Truth"
    (L. Horne)
ACT 2
Scene 1
  "Leave the Atom Alone"
    (J. Premice, Chorus)
  "Cocoanut Sweet" (reprise)
    (L. Horne)
Scene 2
  "For Every Fish (There's a Little Bigger Fish)"
    (A. Hall, Men)
  "I Don't Think I'll End It All Today"
    (L. Horne, R. Montalban, Chorus)
Scene 3
  "Napoleon"
    (L. Horne)
Scene 4
  "Ain't It the Truth" (reprise)
    (L. Horne, Chorus)
Scene 5
  "Savannah" (reprise)
    (L. Horne, R. Montalban, Chorus)

1957.17   # RUMPLE

A Musical Comedy in Two Acts, a Prologue and 10 Scenes. Book by Irving Phillips. Music by Ernest G. Schweikert. Lyrics by Frank Reardon. Directed by Jack Donohue. Choreography by Bob Hamilton. Settings and Lighting by George Jenkins. Costumes by Alvin Colt. Orchestrations by Ted Royal. Musical director, Frederick Dvonch. Dance music arranged by Robert Atwood. Original caricatures of Rumple by Mort Drucker. Produced by Paula Stone and Mike Sloan. Opened 6 November 1957 at the Alvin Theatre and closed 14 December 1957 after 45 performances.

CAST (in order of appearance): *The Chief of Oblivia*: Clayton Coots. *Judy Marlowe*: LOIS O'BRIEN. *Ginny*: Ginny Perlowin. *Judy's Friends*: Bonnie West, Janice Wagner, Sally Wile, Sari Clymas. *Nelson Crandal*: STEPHEN DOUGLASS. *Kate Drew*: GRETCHEN WYLER. *Rumple*: EDDIE FOY. *Anna*: BARBARA PERRY. *J. B. Conway*: MILO BOULTON. *The Photographers*: Elliott Gould, Larry Stevens. *Brannigan*: Ken Harvey. *Barney*: Jackie Warner. *Dr. Wellington Winslow*: JEROME COWAN. *Nurse*: Sari Clymas. *The Weird Ones*: Elliott Gould, Doris Lorenz, Pat White, Lila Popper, Gail Kuhr, William Milié. *The Dissenter*: George Martin. *The Match Box*: Claire Gunderman. *He Who Gets Slapped*: Elliott Gould. *Reporter*: Eddie Weston. *The Powder Room*: Pat White. *The Unravelled*: Bonnie West. *Girls on a Bench*: Doris Lorenz, Lila Popper. *Lieutenant Mallory*: Ken Harvey. *The Voice of Oblivia*: Ken Harvey.

Ensemble: Sari Clymas, Claire Gunderman, Gail Kuhr, Doris Lorenz, Lila Popper, Janice Wagner, Bonnie West, Pat White, Sally Wile, Bill Carter, Elliott Gould, Larry Howard, George Martin, William Milié, Roy Palmer, Larry Stevens, Eddie Weston.

Prologue: Somewhere in Oblivia.

Act 1, Scene 1: Nelson Crandal's New York Studio Apartment. Evening. *Scene 2*: Barney's Bar. Later that night. *Scene 3*: Nelson's Apartment. Next morning. *Scene 4*: Central Park. Later that morning. *Scene 5*: Nelson's Apartment. That night.

Act 2, Scene 1: Office of Dr. Winslow, Psychiatrist. Afternoon. *Scene 2*: Barney's Bar. Later that afternoon. *Scene 3*: Nelson's Apartment. *Scene 4*: Central Park. That night. *Scene 5*: Nelson's Apartment. Later that night.

ACT 1

Scene 1

"It's You for Me"
S. Douglass, L. O'Brien

"In Times Like These"
E. Foy, B. Perry

Scene 2

"Red Letter Day"
G. Wyler, Ensemble, J. Warner

"The First Time I Spoke of You"
S. Douglass, L. O'Brien

Scene 3

"Oblivia"
E. Foy, B. Perry, Cartoon Characters, Holiday Girls

"Peculiar State of Affairs"
E. Foy, G. Wyler

Scene 4

"How Do You Say Goodbye"
L. O'Brien

Scene 5

"Gentlemen of the Press"
S. Douglass, Cartoon Characters, Holiday Girls

ACT 2

Scene 1

"To Adjust Is a Must"
J. Cowan, Weird Ones

"Coax Me"
G. Wyler

Scene 2

"How Do You Say Goodbye" (reprise)
S. Douglass

"All Dressed Up (and No Place to Go)"
G. Wyler, Ensemble

Scene 3

"In Times Like These" (reprise)
G. Wyler, J. Cowan

"Peculiar State of Affairs" (reprise)
B. Perry

Scene 4

"Wish"
E. Foy

Scene 5

Finale
Entire Company

1957.18 THE MUSIC MAN

A Musical Comedy in Two Acts, 16 Scenes. Book, music and lyrics by Meredith Willson. Story by Meredith Willson and Franklin Lacey. Entire production staged by Morton Da Costa. Choreography by Onna White. Settings and lighting by Howard Bay. Costumes by Raoul Pene du Bois. Orchestrations by Don Walker. Dance arrangements by Laurence Rosenthal. Musical direction and vocal arrangements by Herbert Greene. Produced by Kermit Bloomgarden with Herbert Greene in association with Frank Productions. Inc. Opened 19 December 1957 at the Majestic Theatre, moved 24 October 1960 to the Broadway Theatre, and closed 15 April 1961 after 1375 performances.

CAST (in order of appearance): *Travelling Salesmen*: Russell Goodwin, Hal Norman, Robert Howard, James Gannon, Robert Lenn, Vernon Lusby, Robert Evans. *Charlie Cowell*: PAUL REED. *Conductor*: Carl Nicholas. *Harold Hill*: ROBERT PRESTON. *Mayor Shinn*: DAVID BURNS. THE BUFFALO BILLS (4): *Ewart Dunlop*: Al Shea.

Oliver Hix: Wayne Ward. *Jacey Squires*: Vern Reed. *Olin Britt*: Bill Spangenberg. *Marcellus Washburn*: IGGIE WOLFINGTON. *Tommy Djilas*: DANNY CARROLL. *Marian Paroo*: BARBARA COOK. *Mrs. Paroo*: PERT KELTON. *Amaryllis*: Marilyn Siegel. *Winthrop Paroo*: EDDIE HODGES. *Eulalie Mackecknie Shinn*: HELEN RAYMOND. *Zaneeta Shinn*: DUSTY WORRALL. *Gracie Shinn*: Barbara Travis. *Alma Hix*: Adnia Rice. *Maud Dunlop*: Elaine Swann. *Ethel Toffelmier*: Peggy Mondo. *Mrs. Squires*: Martha Flynn. *Constable Locke*: Carl Nicholas.

River City Townspeople and Kids: Pamela Abbott, Babs Delmore, Martha Flynn, Janet Hayes, Peggy Mondo, Barbara Williams, Elaine Swann, Marie Santella, Marlys Watters, James Gannon, Russell Goodwin, Robert Howard, Peter Leeds, Robert Lenn, Hal Norman, Carl Nicholas, Joan Bowman, Alice Clift, Nancy Davis, Penny Ann Green, Lynda Lynch, Jacqueline Maria, Marilyn Poudrier, Pat Mariano, Elisabeth Buda, Babs Warden, Tom Panko, Ronn Cummins, Robert Evans, Vernon Lusby, Gary Menteer, John Sharpe, Roy Wilson, Gerald Teijelo, Bob Mariano, Vernon Wendorf.

Act 1, Scene 1: A Railway Coach. Morning, July 4, 1912. *Scene 2*: River City, Iowa. Center of Town. Immediately following. *Scene 3*: The Paroo's House. That evening. *Scene 4*: Madison Gymnasium. Thirty minutes later. *Scene 5*: Exterior of Madison Library. Immediately following. *Scene 6*: Interior of Madison Library. Immediately following. *Scene 7*: A Street. The following Saturday noon. *Scene 8*: The Paroos' Porch. That evening. *Scene 9*: Center of Town. Noon, the following Saturday.

Act 2, Scene 1: Madison Gymnasium. The following Tuesday evening. *Scene 2*: The Hotel Porch. The following Wednesday evening. *Scene 3*: The Paroos' Porch. Immediately following. *Scene 4*: The Footbridge. Fifteen minutes later. *Scene 5*: A Street. Immediately following. *Scene 6*: Madison Park. A few minutes later. *Scene 7*: River City High School Assembly Room. Immediately following.

ACT 1

Scene 1

"Rock Island"
P. Reed, Travelling Salesmen

Scene 2

"Iowa Stubborn"
Townspeople of River City

"(Ya Got) Trouble"
R. Preston, Townspeople

Scene 3

"Piano Lesson"
B. Cook, P. Kelton, M. Siegel

"Goodnight, My Someone"
B. Cook

Scene 4

"Seventy Six Trombones"
R. Preston, Boys, Girls

"Sincere"
The Buffalo Bills

Scene 5

"The Sadder-But-Wiser Girl"
R. Preston, I. Wolfington

"Pickalittle (Talkalittle)"
H. Raymond, E. Swann, P. Mondo,
A. Rice, M. Flynn, Ladies of River City

"Goodnight Ladies"
The Buffalo Bills

Scene 6

"Marian the Librarian"
R. Preston, Boys, Girls

Scene 8

"My White Knight"
B. Cook

Scene 9

"Wells Fargo Wagon"
E. Hodges, Townspeople

ACT 2

Scene 1

"It's You"
The Buffalo Bills, H. Raymond, E. Swann, P. Mondo, A. Rice,
M. Flynn

"Shipoopi"
I. Wolfington, R. Preston, B. Cook, D. Carroll, D. Worrall, Kids

"Pickalittle" (reprise)
H. Raymond, E. Swann, P. Mondo, A. Rice, M. Flynn, Ladies of River City

Scene 2
  "Lida Rose"
    The Buffalo Bills
  "Will I Ever Tell You"
    B. Cook
Scene 3
  "Gary, Indiana"
    E. Hodges
Scene 4
  "It's You" (reprise)
    Townspeople, Boys, Girls
  "Till There Was You"
    B. Cook, R. Preston
Scene 5
  "Seventy Six Trombones"/"Goodnight, My Someone" (reprise)
    R. Preston, B. Cook
Scene 6
  "Till There Was You" (reprise)
    R. Preston
Scene 7
  Finale
    Entire Company

THE BODY BEAUTIFUL

1958.01

A Musical Comedy in Two Acts, 18 Scenes. Book by Joseph Stein and Will Glickman. Music by Jerry Bock. Lyrics by Sheldon Harnick. Musical direction and vocal arrangements by Milton Greene. Ballet music by Genevieve Pitot. Orchestrations by Ted Royal. Costumes by Noel Taylor. Settings and lighting by William and Jean Eckart. Dances and musical numbers by Herbert Ross. Production Staged by George Schaefer. Produced by Richard Kollmar and Albert Selden. Opened 23 January 1958 at the Broadway Theatre and closed 15 March 1958 after 60 performances.

CAST (in order of appearance): *Dave*: JACK WARDEN. *Albert*: William Hickey. *Harry*: LONNIE SATTIN. *Bob*: STEVE FORREST. *Ann*: MINDY CARSON. *Dominic*: Edward Becker. *Eddie*: Tom Raskin. *Richie*: Bob Wiensko. *Florence*: Jane Romano. *Boxer*: Bill Richards. *Handler*: Knute Sullivan. *Frank*: Richard Chitos. *Nicky*: Tony Atkins. *Trainer*: Albert Popwell. *Boxer*: Bob Wiensko. *Marge*: BARBARA McNAIR. *Jane*: Helen Silver. *Kathy*: Kathie Forman. *Danny*: Tommy Halloran. *George*: Armand Bonay. *Artie*: Jeff Roberts. *Josh*: Alan Weeks. *Pete*: Richard DeBella. *Phil*: Edmund Gaynes. *Announcer*: Jack DeLon. *Referee*: Bill Richards. *Reporters*: Mace Barrett, Harry Lee Rogers, Mitchell Nutick, Stanley Papich. *Gloria*: MARA LYNN. *Campbell*: Mark Allen. *Two Men*: Knute Sullivan, Jack DeLon. *Ben*: Joe Ross.

  Singers: Dorothy Aull, Mace Barrett, Edward Becker, Jack DeLon, Bette Graham, Buzz Halliday, Mary Louise, Broc Peters, Tom Raskin, Joe Ross, Knute Sullivan, Bob Wiensko. *Dancers*: Bob Daley, Ethelyne Dunfee, Shellie Farrell, Jeanna Belkin, Patti Karr, Patsi King, Louis Kosman, Ralph McWilliams, Mitchell Nutick, Stanley Papich, Albert Popwell, Nora Reho, Bill Richards, Harry Lee Rogers, Yvonne Othon, James McAnany.

The action takes place in and around New York City at the present time.

Act 1, Scene 1: Dave Coleman's Office and the Gym. *Scene 2*: Corridor of the Jersey City Arena. Next night. *Scene 3*: The Gym. The following day. *Scene 4*: The office. *Scene 5*: Community Center Playground and nearby street. *Scene 6*: Several Stadiums. *Scene 7*: Another section of the Gym. A few weeks later. *Scene 8*: The office. *Scene 9*: Dressing rooms in the Hartford Arena. *Scene 10*: The Arena.

Act 2, Scene 1: Summer Training Camp. *Scene 2*: Several Stadiums. *Scene 3*: The office. Three months later. *Scene 4*: A steam bath. *Scene 5*: The street. *Scene 6*: Terrace and Ball Room of the Stockton home. *Scene 7*: Dressing rooms. *Scene 8*: A Stadium corner.

ACT 1
  "Where Are They?"
    J. Warden, Boy Dancers and Singers
  "The Body Beautiful"
    M. Carson, B. Daley, L. Kosman, M. Nutick, B. Richards, H. L. Rogers
  "Pffft!"[9]
    S. Forrest, W. Hickey

[9]Dropped during the run.

  "Fair Warning"
    B. McNair, L. Sattin, D. Aull, B. Graham,
    B. Halliday, M. Louise, M. Barrett, J. DeLon, T. Raskin, K. Sullivan
  "Leave Well Enough Alone"[10]
    M. Carson
  "Blonde Blues"
    J. Warden
  Dance
    M. Lynn, J. Warden
  "Uh-Huh, Oh-Yeah!"
    T. Atkins, A. Bonay, R. Chitos, R. DeBella,
    E. Gaynes, T. Halloran, J. Roberts, A. Weeks
  "All of These and More"
    M. Carson, S. Forrest, Ensemble
  "Nobility"
    E. Becker, B. Daley, J. DeLon, B. Peters,
    A. Popwell, T. Raskin, K. Sullivan, B. Wiensko
  "The Body Beautiful" (reprise)
    M. Carson
ACT 2
  "Summer Is"
    Singers, Dancers, K. Forman
  "The Honeymoon Is Over"
    M. Lynn, J. Romano, H. Silver
  "Just My Luck"
    M. Carson, Kids
  "All of These and More" (reprise)
    B. McNair, L. Sattin
  "Art of Conversation"
    W. Hickey, Singers, Dancers
  "Gloria"
    J. Warden, M. Lynn, Dancers
  "A Relatively Simple Affair"
    M. Carson, B. McNair
  Finale
    Entire Company
    M. Carson, B. McNair

OH CAPTAIN!

1958.02

A Musical Comedy in Two Acts. Book by Al Morgan and Jose Ferrer. Based on an original screenplay ("The Captain's Paradise") by Alec Coppel. Music and lyrics by Jay Livingston and Ray Evans. Scenery and lighting by Jo Mielziner. Costumes by Miles White. Dances and musical numbers created by James Starbuck. Musical direction, vocal and ballet arrangements by Jay Blackton. Orchestrations by Robert Ginzler, Joe Glover, Ray Jaimes, Philip J. Lang, Walter Eiger, Sy Oliver, Cornel Tanassy, Oscar Kosarin. Directed by Jose Ferrer. Produced by Howard Merrill and Theatre Corporation of America. Opened 4 February 1958 at the Alvin Theatre and closed 19 July 1958 after 192 performances.

CAST (in order of appearance): *Captain Henry St. James*: TONY RANDALL. *Mrs. Maud St. James*: JACQUELYN McKEEVER. *Enrico Manzoni*: EDWARD PLATT. *The Crew, S.S. Paradise*: George Ritner, Bruce MacKay, Louis Polacek, Nolan Van Way. *A Clerk*: Jack Eddleman. *The Neighbors*: Betty McGuire, Dee Harless, Jean Sincere. *Lisa*: ALEXANDRA DANILOVA. *Bobo*: ABBE LANE. *The Guide*: STANLEY CARLSON. *A Spaniard*: PAUL VALENTINE. *Mae*: SUSAN JOHNSON.

  English Townspeople, Dockworkers, Tourists, Parisians: Cherie Burgess, Shirley De Burgh, Sally Gura, Birgitta Kiviniemi, Asia Mercoolova, Kiki Minor, Adriane Rogers, Mona Pivar, Sybil Scotford, Mona Tritsch, Joyce Carroll, Dee Harless, Sheila Matthews, Betty McGuire, Alice Nunn, Jean Sincere, Helene Whitney, Bill Atkinson, Alvin Beam, Kevin Carlisle, Allen Conroy, David Lober, Gordon Marsh, Doug Springler, Ken Urmston, Eddie Verso, Jack Eddleman, Bruce MacKay, Louis Polacek, George Ritner, Tony Rossi, Charles Rule, James Stevenson, Nolan Van Way.

The action takes place in suburban London, on board the S.S. *Paradise*, and in Paris.

[10]Replaced during the run by:
  "A Relatively Simple Affair"
This song also retained its Act 2 position as a reprise.

ACT 1

"A Very Proper Town"
T. Randall, Company
"Life Does a Man a Favor (When It Gives Him Simple Joys)"
J. McKeever, T. Randall
"A Very Proper Week"
English Townspeople
"Life Does a Man a Favor (When It Leads Him Down to the Sea)"
T. Randall, E. Platt, the Crew
"Captain Henry St. James"
Crew of the S.S. Paradise
The Dock Dance
Dockworkers
"Three Paradises"
T. Randall
"Surprise"
J. McKeever, Neighbors
"Life Does a Man a Favor (When It Puts Him in Paree)"
T. Randall
"Hey Madame"
T. Randall, A. Danilova
"Femininity"
A. Lane
"It's Never Quite the Same"
E. Platt, Crew
"It's Never Quite the Same" (reprise)
J. McKeever, E. Platt, Crew
"We're Not Children"
J. McKeever, P. Valentine
"Give It All You Got"
S. Johnson, Tourists
"Love Is Hell"
S. Johnson, Ladies of the Ensemble
"Keep It Simple"
A. Lane, Dancing Companions

ACT 2

"The Morning Music of Montmartre"
S. Johnson, People of Montmartre
"You Don't Know Him"
A. Lane, J. McKeever
"I've Been There and I'm Back"
E. Platt, T. Randall
"Double Standard"
A. Lane, J. McKeever
"All the Time"
T. Randall
"You're So Right for Me"
E. Platt, A. Lane
"All the Time" (reprise)
J. McKeever
Finale
Entire Company

1958.03 ANNIE GET YOUR GUN

A Revival of the Musical in Two Acts, 10 Scenes[11]. Book by Herbert and Dorothy Fields. Music and lyrics by Irving Berlin. Production directed by Donald Burr. Scenery by George Jenkins. Lighting by Peggy Clark. Costume supervisor, Florence Klotz. Dances and musical numbers staged by Helen Tamiris. Musical director, Frederick Dvonch. Orchestrations by Philip J. Lang, (Robert) Russell Bennett, Ted Royal. Produced by the New York City Center Light Opera Company (Jean Dalrymple, Director). Opened 19 February 1958 at the New York City Center and closed 2 March 1958 after 15 performances.

---

[11]First produced in New York 16 May 1946 at the Imperial Theatre for 1147 performances. For Synopsis of Scenes and Musical numbers, see original 1946 production.

CAST (in order of appearance): *Little Boy*: Christopher Shea Trenkle. *Little Girl*: Diane Ramey. *Charlie Davenport*: JACK WHITING. *Iron Tail*: STUART HODES. *Yellow Foot*: Edward Villela. *Mac* (Property Man): Jack Emrek. *Foster Wilson*: Leo Lucker. *Coolie*: Bert Wood. *Dolly Tate*: MARGARET HAMILTON. *Winnie Tate*: RAIN WINSLOW. *Tommy Keeler*: RICHARD FRANCE. *Frank Butler*: DAVID ATKINSON. *Annie Oakley*: BETTY JANE WATSON. *Minnie*, Annie's Sister: Dorleen Thomas. *Jessie*, Another Sister: Elaine Lynn. *Nellie*, Another Sister: Penny Grayam. *Little Jake*, Her Brother: Flip Mark. *Col. Wm.F. Cody (Buffalo Bill)*: JAMES RENNIE. *Mrs. Little Horse*: Hertha Shea. *Mrs. Black Tooth*: Jan Canada. *Trainman*: Laurence Watson. *Porter*: John Buie. *Second Porter*: Walter P. Brown. *Riding Mistress*: RUTHANNA BORIS. *Major Gordon Lillie*, Pawnee Bill: WILLIAM LeMASSENA. *Chief Sitting Bull*: HARRY BELAVER. *The Wild Horse*, Ceremonial Dancer: STUART HODES. *Pawnee's Messenger*: Jack Irwin. *Major Domo*: John Bouie. *First Waiter*: Walter P. Brown. *SecondWaiter*: Laurence Watson. *Mr. Schuyler Adams*: Jack Rains. *Mrs. Schuyler Adams*: Basha Regis. *Dr. Percy Ferguson*: Jack Irwin. *Mrs. Percy Ferguson*: Barbara Saxby. *Sylvia Potter-Porter*: Clare Waring.
Singers: Jane Burke, Janet Canada, Naomi Collier, Patricia Finch, Bonnie Lawrence, Nancy Radcliffe, Basha Regis, Barbara Saxby, Kenneth Ayers, Ralph W. Farnworth, Jack Irwin, Sam Kirkham, Stanley Page, Edgar Powell, Jack Rains, Casper Roos, Van Stevens, Ralph Vucci, Wendell Lynn. *Dancers*: Joan Dubrow, Beverly Gains, Lida Gaschke, Dorothy Hill, Iva March, Miriam Pandor, Fleur Raup, Renee Slade, Carolee Winchester, Doris Wright, Allan Byrns, Marvin Gordon, Charles Jackson, Daniel Jogalsky, Edward Monson, James Moore, Harold Pittard, Parker Wilson, Vic Vallaro.

1958.04 PORTOFINO

A Musical Comedy in Two Acts, a Prologue and 3 Scenes. Book and lyrics by Richard Ney. Music by Louis Bellson and Will Irwin. Additional lyrics by Sheldon Harnick. Choreography by Charles Weidman and Ray Harrison. Scenery by Wolfgang Roth. Costumes by Michael Travis. Lighting by Lee Watson. Orchestrations by Philip J. Lang. Vocal arrangements by Joseph Moon. Musical director, Will Irwin. Underscoring, Will Irwin. Entire production staged by Karl Genus. Produced by Richard Ney. Opened 21 February 1958 at the Adelphi Theatre and closed 22 February 1958 after 3 performances.

CAST: *Nicky*: GEORGES GUETARY. *Kitty*: HELEN GALLAGHER. *Padre, Guido*: ROBERT STRAUSS. *Angela*: Jan Chaney. *Sandro*: Wallace Eley. *Tullio*: Darryl Richard. *Tavern Keeper*: Webb Tilton.
Singers: Patricia Greenwood, Louise Pearl, Joy Marlene, Joy Lynne Sica, Lynne Stuart, Marvin Goodis, Mitchell May, Charles Aschmann, Bill Ryan, Pat Tolson, Jim Fullerton. *Dancers*: Kenley Hammond, Leslie Snow, Sally Wile, Barbara Richman, Gerrie Still, Sari Clymas, Patricia Ann White, Karen Sargent, Roy Palmer, Diki Lerner, Harvey Jung, Jimmy Kirby, Stuart Fleming, John Foster, Hilbert Rapp, Tom Hester.

Act 1: A Piazza in Portofino, a lovely Italian resort town. Early evening, today.

Act 2, Scene 1: Immediately following. *Scene 2*: The next morning.

Prologue
R. Strauss
(*Music by* Will Irwin. *Lyrics by* Sheldon Harnick.)

ACT 1

Opening—"Come Along"
Company
(*Music by* Will Irwin. *Lyrics by* Sheldon Harnick.)
"No Wedding Bells For Me"
G. Guetary
(*Music by* Will Irwin. *Lyrics by* Richard Ney.)
Festa—"Come Along" (reprise)
Company
"Red Collar Job"
R. Strauss
(*Music by* Louis Bellson and Will Irwin. *Lyrics by* Sheldon Harnick.)
"Here I Come"
H. Gallagher
(*Music by* Louis Bellson and Will Irwin. *Lyrics by* Sheldon Harnick.)
"New Dreams for Old"
G. Guetary
(*Music by* Louis Bellson. *Lyrics by* Richard Ney.)
"A Dream for Angela"
J. Chaney
(*Music by* Louis Bellson. *Lyrics by* Richard Ney.)
"Isn't It Wonderful?"
H. Gallagher, G. Guetary, Company
(*Music by* Louis Bellson. *Lyrics by* Richard Ney.)

"Dance of the Whirling Wimpus"
    J. Chaney
"Under a Spell"
    R. Guetary, Girls
    (*Music by* Louis Bellson. *Lyrics by* Richard Ney and Sheldon Harnick.)

ACT 2
Scene 1
    "Under a Spell" (reprise)
        G. Guetary, Girls
    "That's Love"
        G. Guetary, Company
        (*Music and Lyrics by* Richard Ney.)
    "Too Little Time for Love"
        W. Tilton
        (*Music by* Will Irwin. *Lyrics by* Richard Ney.)
    "Guido's Tango"
        R. Strauss, H. Gallagher
    "It Might Be Love"
        G. Guetary
        (*Music by* Louis Bellson. *Lyrics by* Richard Ney.)
    "Here I Come" (reprise)
        H. Gallagher
    "Bacchanale"
        Company
Scene 2
    "Morning Prayer"
        Company
        (*Music by* Will Irwin. *Lyrics by* Richard Ney.)
    "Kitty Car Ballet"
        H. Gallagher, Boys
    "The Grand Prix of Portofino"
        Company
        (*Music by* Will Irwin. *Lyrics by* Richard Ney.)
    "Portofino"
        G. Guetary
        (*Music by* Louis Bellson. *Lyrics by* Richard Ney.)
    "I'm in League With the Devil"
        H. Gallagher
        (*Music by* Will Irwin. *Lyrics by* Richard Ney.)
    "Why Not For Marriage?"
        G. Guetary
        (*Music by* Louis Bellson. *Lyrics by* Richard Ney.)
    "Portofino" (reprise)
        Company

1958.05   WONDERFUL TOWN

A Revival of the Musical Comedy in Two Acts, 13 Scenes[12]. Book by Joseph Fields and Jerome Chodorov. Based on the play "My Sister Eileen" by Joseph Fields and Jerome Chodorov and the stories by Ruth McKinney. Music by Leonard Bernstein. Lyrics by Betty Comden and Adolph Green. Directed by Jerome Chodorov. Choreography by Ralph Beaumont. Entire production supervised by Herbert Ross. Sets and costumes by Raoul Pene du Bois. Costume supervision by Ruth Morley. Lighting by Peggy Clark. Musical direction and vocal arrangements by Lehman Engel. Associate conductor, Gino Smart. Orchestrations by Don Walker. Produced by the New York City Center Light Opera Company (Jean Dalrymple, Director). Opened 5 March 1958 at the New York City Center and closed 16 March 1958 after 15 performances.

CAST (in order of appearance): *Guide*: Wayne Sherwood. *Appopoulos*: GEORGE GIVOT. *Lonigan*: Jack Rains. *Helen*: BETSY VON FURSTENBERG. *Wreck*: JORDAN BENTLEY. *Violet*: Paula Wayne. *Valenti*: Ted Beniades. *Eileen*: JO SULLIVAN. *Ruth*: NANCY WALKER. *A Strange Man*: Don Grusso. *Drunks*: Daniel P. Hannafin, Jack Fletcher. *Robert Baker*: PETER COOKSON. *Associate Editors*: Bill

---

[12]Originally produced in New York 25 February 1953 at the Winter Garden for 559 performances. For Synopsis of Scenes and Musical Numbers, see original 1953 production.

Walker, Mark Zeller. *Mrs. Wade*: Isabella Hoopes. *Frank Lippencott*: CRIS ALEXANDER. *Chef*: Mark Zeller. *Waiter*: Robert Grant. *Delivery Boy*: Alan Johnson. *Chick Clark*: Frank Maxwell. *Shore Patrolman*: Bill Walker. *First Cadet*: Rudy del Campo. *Second Cadet*: Gerald Fries. *Policeman*: Daniel P. Hannafin. *Ruth's Escort*: Jack Fletcher.
    Greenwich Villagers: Singers: Joan Fagan, Pat Hall, Jane A. Johnston, Barbara A. Lockard, Sadie McCollum, Genevieve Owens, Laine Roberts, Susan Terry, Paula Wayne, Elmarie Wendel, Robert Atherton, Robert Grant, Daniel P. Hannafin, Bob Maxwell, Jack Rains, Wayne Sherwood, Bill Walker, Millard Williams, Mark Zeller. *Dancers*: Nora Bristow, Barbara Giné, Bettye Jenkins, Jeannie Jones, Svetlana McLee, Odette Phillips, Carol-Sue Shaer, Gina Trichonis, Rudy del Campo, Ted Forlow, Jerry Fries, Alan Johnson, John Ira Moore, Eddie Pfeiffer, Marc Scott, Larry Stevens.

1958.06   INTERNATIONAL SOIRÉE

A Musical Revue in Two Acts, 4 Scenes. English Commentary by Arthur Lesser. Orchestra conducted by Jo Basile. Produced by Arthur Lesser. Opened 12 March 1958 at the Bijou Theatre and closed 29 March 1958 after 21 performances.

CAST: PATACHOU, HIRAM SHERMAN, MARCEL CORNELIS, GEORGE LA FAYE and COMPANY (Michele La Faye, Françoise Houlle, René Coquerelle, Loly Pinel), CARACOLILLO and MARIA ROSA, Rogelio Reguera.

ACT 1
Hiram Sherman presents:
Scene 1
    Marcel Cornelis (Comic impressionist from Brussels, Belgium)
Scene 2
    Georges La Faye and Company (Theatre of Animation from France)
Scene 3
    Caracolillo and Maria Rosa (Spanish Dancers), assisted by Rogelio Reguera (Guitarist):
    1. "Mezquita", a dance of Andalucia
    2. "Soleares de Triana", a flamenco guitar solo
    3. "Jota de la Dolores", a peasant dance of Aragon
    4. "Allegrias", a flamenco of Cadiz
    5. "Farruca con Zapateado", a flamenco of Andalucia
    6. "Seguirillas Gitanas"

ACT 2
Hiram Sherman presents Patachou (French singer) whose repertoire was chosen from among the following:
    "Ah!"
    "Allume Tes Lampions"
    "A Paris" (Lemarque)
    "Brave Margot"
        (*Music and Lyrics by* Georges Brassens.)
    "Eh! Bien"
    "La Complainte de la Butte" (from the film FRENCH CANCAN)
        (*Music and Lyrics by* Jean Renoir, G. Van Parys.)
    "La Goualante du Pauvre Jean"
        (*Music and Lyrics by* Marguerite Monnot.)
    "La Musique"
    "Le Piano du Pauvre"
        (*Music and Lyrics by* Leo Ferré.)
    "Les Jambes Roses"
        (*Music and Lyrics by* F. Véran, R. Thoreau.)
    "Mon Homme"
        (*Music by* Maurice Yvain. *Lyrics by* Albert Willemetz, Jacques Charles.)
    "Parce Que"
        (*Music and Lyrics by* G. Wagenheim, Charles Aznavour.)
    "Paris Se Regarde"
    "Pot-Pourri"
    "Rue Lepic" (Emer)
    "Un Jour Tu Verras"
    "Va-Pas T'Imaginer"

1958.07 OKLAHOMA!

A Revival of the Musical Comedy in Two Acts, 6 Scenes[13]. Book and lyrics by Oscar Hammerstein II. Music by Richard Rodgers. Based on the play "Green Grow the Lilacs" by Lynn Riggs. Directed by John Fearnley. (Originally directed by Rouben Mamoulian.) Dances by Agnes de Mille, restaged by Gemze de Lappe. Musical direction by Frederick Dvonch. Settings by Lemuel Ayers. Costume supervision by Florence Klotz. Lighting by Peggy Clark. Produced by The New York City Center Light Opera Company (Jean Dalrymple, Director). Opened 19 March 1958 at the New York City Center and closed 30 March 1958 after 15 performances.

CAST (in order of appearance): *Aunt Eller*: BETTY GARDE. *Curly*: HERBERT BANKE. *Laurey*: LOIS O'BRIEN. *Will Parker*: GENE NELSON. *Jud Fry*: DOUGLAS FLETCHER RODGERS. *Ado Annie Carnes*: HELEN GALLAGHER. *Ali Hakim*: HARVEY LEMBECK. *Gertie Cummings*: Patricia Finch. *Sylvie*: GENZE DE LAPPE. *Curly* (in ballet): MICHAEL MAULE. *Laurey* (in ballet): GEMZE DE LAPPE. *Jud* (in ballet): GEORGE CHURCH. *The Girl Who Falls Down*: Evelyn Taylor. *Andrew Carnes*: OWEN MARTIN. *Cord Elam*: SHEPPARD KERMAN.

Singers: Jane Burke, Jan Canada, Naomi S. Collier, Patricia Finch, Bonnie Lawrence, Wendy Martin, Nancy Radcliffe, Barbara Saxby, Lois Van Pelt, Lynn Wendell, Kenneth Ayers, Ralph Farnworth, Jack Irwin, Barney Johnston, Sam Kirkham, Stanley Page, Edgar Powell, Casper Roos, Van Stevens, Ralph Vucci. *Dancers*: Patricia Birsh (Birch), Isabelle Farrell, Ruby Herndon, Marilyn Kessler, Naomi Marritt, Ellen Matthews, Elicia Miller, Ilona Murai, Nana Predente, Evelyn Taylor, Toodie Wittmer, Jenny Workman, Richard Colacino, Marvin Gordon, Thomas W. Hasson, James Maher, Gene Neal, David Neuman, William Ross, Eddie Weston.

1958.08 SAY, DARLING

A Comedy about a Musical in Three Acts, 14 Scenes. Book by Richard and Marian Bissell and Abe Burrows. Based on the novel of the same name by Richard Bissell. Music by Jule Styne. Lyrics by Betty Comden and Adolph Green. (Scenery) Designed by Oliver Smith. Costumes by Alvin Colt. Lighting by Peggy Clark. Directed by Abe Burrows. Dances by Matt Mattox. At the pianos, Colin Romoff and Peter Howard. Associate producer, George Gilbert. Produced by Jule Styne and Lester Osterman. Opened 3 April 1958 at the ANTA Theatre, moved 8 December 1958 to the Martin Beck Theatre, and closed 17 January 1959 after 332 performances.

CAST (in order of appearance): *Mr. Schneider*: Gordon B. Clarke. *Frankie Jordan*: CONSTANCE FORD. *Jack Jordan*: DAVID WAYNE. *Photographer*: Jack Naughton. *Pilot Roy Peters*: Jack Manning. *Ted Snow*: ROBERT MORSE. *June, the Secretary*: Eileen Letchworth. *Schatzie Harris*: HORACE McMAHON. *Richard Hackett*: JEROME COWAN. *Irene Lovelle*: VIVIAN BLAINE. *Rudy Lorraine*: JOHNNY DESMOND. *Sidemen*: Wendell Marshall, Peter Howard. *Charlie Williams*: Robert Downing. *Maurice, a Pianist*: Colin Romoff. *Arlene McKee*: Wana Allison. *Jennifer Stevenson*: Jean Mattox. *Earl Jorgeson*: Elliott Gould. *Cheryl Merrill*: Virginia Martin. *Accompanist*: Peter Howard. *Sammy Miles*: Steve Condos. *Rex Dexter*: MITCHELL GREGG. *Boris Reshevsky*: MATT MATTOX. *Waiter*: Jack Naughton. *Morty Krebs*: WALTER KLAVUN. *Tatiana*: Jean Mattox. *Joyce*: Kelly Leigh.

Kids in the Show: Wana Allison, Marcella Dodge, Barbara Hoyt, Kelly Leigh, Julia Marlowe, Jean Mattox, Carolyn Morris, Elliott Gould, Charles Morrell, Richard Tone, Calvin von Reinhold.

Act 1, Scene 1: An Airport in the Corn Country. Time is the present. *Scene 2*: Hackett & Snow's Office in the Big City. *Scene 3*: Stamford … The House That Jack Took. *Scene 4*: The Office.

Act 2, Scene 1: The Auditions. *Scene 2*: Stamford. *Scene 3*: Rehearsals. *Scene 4*: Stamford. *Scene 5*: Irene Lovelle's Apartment! *Scene 6*: Stamford[14].

Act 3, Scene 1: That Hotel Room in New Haven. *Scene 2*: Stamford. *Scene 3*: Back to That Hotel Room in New Haven. *Scene 4*: Idlewild Airport in New York.

ACT 1[15]
Scene 2
 "Chief of Love"
  (recording)
Scene 4
 "Try to Love Me"
  (V. Blaine)

"It's Doom"
 (J. Desmond)
"The Husking Bee"
 (J. Desmond, D. Wayne)
ACT 2
Scene 1
 "It's the Second Time You Meet That Matters"
  (J. Desmond)
 ("Let the Lower Lights Be Burning")
  (D. Wayne, J. Cowan)
 "Chief of Love"
  (V. Blaine)
Scene 3
 "Say, Darling"
  (J. Desmond)
 "The Carnival Song"
  (D. Wayne, V. Blaine, S. Condos)
 (Boris' Dance)
  (M. Mattox)
ACT 3
Scene 3
 "Try to Love Me" (reprise)
  (J. Desmond)
 "Dance Only With Me"
  (V. Blaine, M. Gregg)
 "Something's Always Happening on the River"
  (D. Wayne, J. Desmond, V. Blaine, M. Gregg, others)

1958.09 TROUBLE IN TAHITI

A Revival of the One Act Opera in 7 Scenes[16]. Libretto and music by Leonard Bernstein. (Presented on a double-bill with the opera "Tale For A Deaf Ear" by Mark Bucci) (Staged by Michael Pollock. Designed by Andreas Nomikos. Conducted by Leonard Bernstein. Produced by the New York City Opera. Opened 6 April 1958 at the New York City Center and closed 18 April 1958 after 3 performances in repertory.

CAST: *Dinah*: BEVERLY WOLFF. *Sam*: DAVID ATKINSON. *Trio*: Naomi Collier, William Metcalf, Stanley Kolk.

JOYCE GRENFELL:
1958.10 MONOLOGUES AND SONGS

A Musical Revue[17] in Two Acts, 20 Scenes. (Sketches and lyrics) Written by Joyce Grenfell. Music by Richard Addinsell. Miss Grenfell's Dresses by Victor Stiebel. At the piano, George Bauer. Produced by Roger L. Stevens and Laurier Lister. Opened 7 April 1958 at the Lyceum Theatre and closed 26 April 1958 after 24 performances.

CAST: JOYCE GRENFELL.

ACT 1
Scene 1
 "Opening Numbers"
Scene 2
 Wibberly
Scene 3
 Songs of Many Lands
Scene 4
 Writers of Children's Books

---

[13]Originally produced in New York 31 March 1943 at the St. James Theatre for 2212 performances. For Synopsis of Scenes and Musical Numbers, see original 1943 production.
[14]Act 2, Scene 6 dropped after opening.
[15]Vocalists not identified in program. List below prepared from production typescript and cast recording.

[16]Originally produced in New York as part of a triple bill ALL IN ONE 19 April 1955 at the Playhouse for 49 performances. For Synopsis of Scenes, see original 1955 production.
[17]Billed as an All New Program. Miss Grenfell appeared previously on Broadway in the revue JOYCE GRENFELL REQUESTS THE PLEASURE 10 October 1955 at the Bijou Theatre for 65 performances.

Scene 5

Piano Interlude: "Bess, You Is My Woman Now," and "There's a Boat Dat's Leavin' Soon for New York" (from PORGY AND BESS)
G. Bauer
(*Music by* George Gershwin.)

Scene 6

Artist's Room

Scene 7

"Picture Postcard"

Scene 8

Boat Train

Scene 9

"Joyful Noise"
(*Music by* Donald Swann.)

ACT 2

Scene 1

"The Woman on the Bus"

Scene 2

Friend to Tea

Scene 3

Songs My Mother Taught Me
(*Arranged by* Viola Tunnard) selected from the following: "Hand Me Down My Bonnet," "The Yellow Rose of Texas," "Since Bacon Has Gone Up," "All Night," "Sit Down Sister," "I'll Lend You My Horse," "I'm Gwine Away," "Old Joe Clark," "Step Light Lady," "All the Pretty Little Horses"

Scene 4

"Committee"

Scene 5

"Three Brothers"

Scene 6

Shirl's Girl Friend: The Giant Wheel

Scene 7

Piano Interlude: "Do It Again" and "I've Got Rhythm"
G. Bauer
(*Music by* George Gershwin.)

Scene 8

A Thought for Today

Scene 9

"Time"

Scene 10

Nursery School: Free Activity Period

Scene 11

"It's Almost Tomorrow"

1958.11   LOST IN THE STARS

A Revival of the Musical Tragedy in Two Acts, 20 Scenes[18]. Words (book, lyrics) by Maxwell Anderson. Based on the novel "Cry, the Beloved Country" by Alan Paton. Music by Kurt Weill. Entire production conceived and staged by Jose Quintero. Scenery and costumes by Andreas Nomikos. Lighting by Lee Watson. Conductor, Julius Rudel. Chorus master, Gino Smart. (Musical arrangements and orchestrations by Kurt Weill.) Produced by the New York City Opera Company. Opened 9 April 1958 at the New York City Center and closed 11 May 1958 after 14 performances in repertory.

CAST (in order of appearance): *Leader:* LEE CHARLES. *Answerer:* Robert Atherton. *Nita:* Patti Austin. *Grace Kumalo:* Rosetta LeNoire. *Stephen Kumalo:* LAWRENCE WINTERS. *Station Master:* Robert Ruddy. *The Young Man:* Alexander Yancy, Jr. *The Young Woman:* Mary Louise. *James Jarvis:* NICHOLAS JOY. *Edward Jarvis:* Chris Snell. *Arthur Jarvis:* John Irving. *John Kumalo:* FREDERICK O'NEIL. *Paulus:* Emory

---

[18]Originally produced in New York 30 October 1949 at the Music Box Theatre for 281 performances. For Synopsis of Scenes and Musical Numbers, see original 1949 production.

Richardson. *William:* Lawson Bates. *Alex:* Frank Riley, Jr. *Foreman:* John Dennison. *Mrs. M'Kize:* Eva Jessye. *Hlabeni:* Garwood Perkins. *Eland:* Conrad Bain. *Linda:* OLGA JAMES. *Johannes Pafuri:* Godfrey Cambridge. *Matthew Kumalo:* DOUGLAS TURNER. *Absalom Kumalo:* LOUIS GOSSETT. *Rose:* Alyce Webb. *The Other Girl:* Claretta Fabray. *Irina:* SHIRLEY CARTER. *Servant:* Laurence Watson. *Policeman:* William Zakariasen. *White Woman:* Naomi Collier. *White Man:* John Dennison. *Burton:* Richard Bowler. *The Judge:* Neil Fitzgerald. *Ensemble:* New York City Opera Chorus.

1958.12   THE NEXT PRESIDENT

A Musical Salmagundi (Revue) in Two Acts, 13 Scenes. Staged by Frank B. Nichols. Entire production designed by Lee Watson. Produced by Frank B. Nichols. Opened 9 April 1958 at the Bijou Theater and closed 19 April 1958 after 13 performances.

CAST: MORT SAHL (Monologuist, Political Satirist), THE JIMMY GIUFFRE 3 (Jimmy Giuffre, Bob Brookmeyer, Jim Hall), THE FOLK SINGERS (David Allen, Erik Darling, Robin Howard, Dylan Todd, Mary Allin Travers, Donald Vogel, Stan Watt, Caroly Wilcox), ANNELIESE WIDMAN.

ACT 1

THE STATUS QUO

Scene 1

"The Chorus of Collective Conscience"
The Folk Singers

Scene 2

"Cry Holy"
The Folk Singers

Scene 3

A Night-to-Night Report of the News with Complete Flexibility as to Foreign Policy
M. Sahl

Scene 4

"The Train and the River"
The Jimmy Giuffre 3
(*Music by* Jimmy Giuffre.)

Scene 5

"Gotta Dance"
A. Widman
(*Music by* Jimmy Giuffre.)

Scene 6

"Deep Blue Sea"
The Folk Singers

Scene 7

Mort Sahl

ACT 2

A BRAND NEW ATTITUDE WITH THE SAME OLD PREJUDICES

Scene 1

"He's Gone Away"
The Folk Singers, featuring R. Howard, D. Todd

Scene 2

"The Green Country"
The Jimmy Giuffre 3
(*Music by* Jimmy Giuffre.)

Scene 3

"Animation"
A. Widman
(*Music by* Marvin Fisher. *Lyrics by* Joe McCarthy, Jr.)

Scene 4

Mort Sahl

Scene 5

"Cloudy Morning"
D. Allen

Scene 6

Press Conference
M. Sahl, The Folk Singers

1958.13

REGINA

A Revival of the Musical Drama (Opera) in Three Acts, Prologue and 4 Scenes[19]. Written and composed by Marc Blitzstein. Based on the play "The Little Foxes" by Lillian Hellman. Staged by Herman Shumlin. Conducted by Samuel Krachmalnick. Scenery by Howard Bay. Costumes designed by Aline Bernstein. Choreography by Robert Joffrey. (Orchestrations by Marc Blitzstein.) Produced by the New York City Opera Company. Opened 17 April 1958 at the New York City Center and closed 2 May 1958 after 3 performances in repertory.

CAST (in order of appearance): *Addie*, Cook: CAROL BRICE. *Cal*, Butler: ANDREW FRIERSON. *Alexandra Giddens*, Regina's Daughter: HELEN STRINE. *Birdie Hubbard*, Oscar's Wife: ELISABETH CARRON. *Oscar Hubbard*, Regina's Brother: EMILE RENAN. *Leo Hubbard*, Oscar's Son: LOREN DRISCOLL. *Regina Giddens*: BRENDA LEWIS. *William Marshall*: ERNEST McCHESNEY. *Benjamin Hubbard*, Regina's Brother: GEORGE S. IRVING. *Horace Giddens*, Regina's Husband: JOSHUA HECHT. *Manders*: Robert Ruddy. *Dancers*: Gloria Gustafson, Marie Paquet, Francoise Martinet, Gerald Arpino, Nels Jorgensen, Vicente Nebreda. *Servants, Townspeople, Field Workers*: New York City Opera Chorus.

---

[19]Originally produced in New York 31 October 1949 at the 46th Street Theatre for 56 performances. For Synopsis of Scenes and Musical Numbers, see original 1949 production. For this revival, an intermission was added between Act 1, Scenes 1 and 2. The Jazz Band was totally eliminated.

1958–1959 SEASON

Gwen Verdon and Richard Kiley in REDHEAD (Photo: Vandamm Studio)
Billy Rose Theatre Collection, New York Public Library for the Performing Arts

1958–1959 SEASON

GOLDILOCKS

1958.14

A Musical Comedy in Two Acts, 11 Scenes. Book by Walter and Jean Kerr. Music by Leroy Anderson. Lyrics by Jean Ford, Walter and Jean Kerr. Dances and musical numbers staged by Agnes de Mille. Directed by Walter Kerr. Settings by Peter Larkin. Costumes by Castillo. Lighting by Feder. Musical director, Lehman Engel. Orchestrations by Leroy Anderson and Philip J. Lang. Dance music arranged by Laurence Rosenthal. Production associate, Joseph I. Levine. Produced by The Producers Theatre and Robert Whitehead. Opened 11 October 1958 at the Lunt-Fontanne Theatre and closed 28 February 1959 after 161 performances.

CAST (in order of appearance): *Maggie Harris*: ELAINE STRITCH. *Clown*: Del Anderson. *George Randolph Brown*: RUSSEL NYPE. *Max Grady*: DON AMECHE. *Lois Lee*: PAT STANLEY. *Pete*: NATHANIEL FREY. *Andy*: Richard Armbruster. *Max's Assistants*: Gene Varrone, Sam Greene. *J.C.*: Martin Wolfson. *Bessie*: MARGARET HAMILTON. *Deputies*: Del Anderson, Beau Tilden. *Chauffeur*: Samye Van.

Singers: Jane Carlyle, Jeanne Grant, Joanne Lavalle, Sadie McCollum, Rita Noble, Suzanne Stahl, Richard Armsbruster, Del Anderson, John Carter, Sam Greene, Ben Parrish, Rufus Smith, Gene Varrone. *Dancers*: Patricia Birsh (Birch), Lynne Broadbent, Judith Chazin, Bunty Kelley, Margaret Lithander, Imelda de Martin, Carolyn Morris, Ilona Murai, Patti Nestor, Evelyn Taylor, Diana Turner, Kelly Brown, Donald Barton, Michael Fesco, Loren Hightower, George Jack, Ronnie Landry, David Nillo, Paul Olson, Peter Saul, Ron Stratton.

Act 1, Scene 1: Onstage, New York City, 1913. (Finale of "Lazy Moon.") *Scene 2*: Maggie's Dressing Room. Immediately following. *Scene 3*: Max's Lot. Next morning. *Scene 4*: Outside Max's Lot. That evening. *Scene 5*: Max's Lot. Four days later. *Scene 6*: The Fat Cat Roof Garden. Later that night. *Scene 7*: Huckleberry Island. Several days later.

Act 2, Scene 1: A Rest Home on the Mainland. Two days later. *Scene 2*: Bessie's Barn, up the Hudson. That afternoon. *Scene 3*: Ballroom, George's Town House. *Scene 4*: Egypt on the Hudson. Next morning.

ACT 1
Scene 1
  "Lazy Moon"
    Company
Scene 2
  "Give the Little Lady"
    E. Stritch, Company
  "Save a Kiss"
    R. Nype, E. Stritch
Scene 4
  "No One'll Ever Love You"
    E. Stritch, D. Ameche
Scene 5
  "Who's Been Sitting in My Chair?"
    E. Stritch
  Dance
    D. Barton, E. Stritch
  "There Never Was a Woman"
    D. Ameche
Scene 6
  "The Pussy Foot"
    P. Stanley, Company
    Tom Cat: K. Brown. *Brunette*: I. Murai. *Blonde*: L. Broadbent.
Scene 7
  Pirate Orgy[1]
    Company
ACT 2
Scene 1
  "Lady in Waiting"
    P. Stanley, R. Nype
  Dance
    P. Stanley, K. Brown, E. Taylor, Company
  "The Beast in You"
    E. Stritch

---

[1] Programs from the first week of the Broadway run list "Huckleberry Island Ballet" in lieu of Pirate Orgy.

  "Shall I Take My Heart and Go?"
    R. Nype
Scene 2
  "Bad Companions"
    N. Frey, M. Hamilton, R. Armbruster, G. Varrone
  "I Can't Be in Love"
    D. Ameche
Scene 3
  "I Never Know When to Say When"
    E. Stritch
  "The Town House Maxixe" Dance
    P. Stanley, D. Nillo, Company
  "Two Years in the Making"
    N. Frey, M. Hamilton, Singers
Scene 4
  "Heart of Stone" (Pyramid Dance)
    I. Murai, Company

DIE FLEDERMAUS

1958.15

A Revival of the Operetta in Three Acts[2]. (Original Libretto by Carl Haffner and Richard Genée. Lyrics by Richard Genée. Based on the comedy "Le Réveillon" by Henri Meilhac and Ludovic Halévy). English libretto by Ruth and Thomas Martin. Music by Johann Strauss. Stage director, Barbara Owens. Conducted by Seymour Lipkin. Produced by the New York City Opera. Opened 19 October 1958 at the New York City Center and closed 9 November 1958 after 3 performances in repertory.

CAST: *Rosalinda*: BEVERLY BOWER. *Eisenstein*: ERNEST McCHESNEY. *Adele*: MONTE AMUNDSEN. *Sally*: Jennie Andrea. *Alfred*: JON CRAIN. *Prince Orlofsky*: LOREN DRISCOLL. *Falke*: CHESTER LUDGIN. *Frank*: Paul Ukena. *Frosch*: Coley Worth. *Blind*: Grant Williams. *Solo Dancers*: Dianne Consoer, Jonathan Watts. *Ensemble*: New York City Opera Chorus.

THE MERRY WIDOW

1958.16

A Revival of the Operetta in Three Acts[3]. Music by Franz Lehár. Original German libretto (Die Lustige Witwe) by Victor Léon and Leo Stein after "L'Attaché d'Ambassade." English libretto by Adrian Ross. Staged by Michael Pollock. Conducted by Julius Rudel. Produced by the New York City Opera. Opened 31 October 1958 at the New York City Center and closed 16 November 1958 after 3 performances in repertory.

CAST: *Sonia*: BEVERLY SILLS. *Prince Danilo*: JOHN REARDON. *Baron Popoff*: JACK HARROLD. *Natalie*: Helena Scott. *De Jolidon*: John Alexander. *Marquis de Cascada*: Arnold Voketaitis. *St. Brioche*: Chester Ludgin. *Admiral Khadja*: Arthur Newman. *Mme. Khadja*: Helen Baisley. *General Novikovich*: Keith Kaldenberg. *Mme. Novikovich*: Barbara Lockard. *Nish*: Coley Worth. *Lo-Lo*: Helen Baisley. *Solo Dancers*: Françoise Martinet, Beatrice Tompkins, Gerald Arpino. *Ensemble*: New York City Opera Chorus.

MARIA GOLOVIN

1958.17

A Musical Drama (Opera) in Three Acts, 7 Scenes[4]. Libretto and music by Gian Carlo Menotti. Staged by Gian Carlo Menotti. Supervised by Samuel Chotzinoff. Orchestra conducted by Herbert Grossman. Production co-ordinator, Louis B. Ames. Scenery by Rouben Ter-Arutunian. Lighting by Charles Elson. Costumes supervised by Helene Pons. Produced by David Merrick and the National Broadcasting Company in association with Byron Goldman. Opened 5 November 1958 at the Martin Beck Theatre and closed 8 November 1958 after 5 performances.

CAST: *Donato*: RICHARD CROSS. *Agata*: RUTH KOBART. *The Mother*: PATRICIA NEWAY. *Dr. Zuckertanz*: NORMAN KELLEY. *Maria Golovin*: FRANCA DUVAL. *Trottolo*: Lorenzo Muti. *The Prisoner*: WILLIAM CHAPMAN. *Servant*: John Kuhn.

---

[2] First English language production in New York 16 March 1885 at the Casino Theatre for 42 performances. First New York production of this adaptation 20 December 1950 at the Metropolitan Opera House. For Synopsis of Scenes and Musical Numbers, see May 1954 revival.
[3] Originally produced in New York 21 October 1907 at the New Amsterdam Theatre for 416 performances. For Synopsis of Scenes and Musical Numbers, see original 1907 production.
[4] Produced as an opera; no individual musical numbers listed in program.

The entirze action takes place at Donato's villa near a frontier in a European country. A few years after a recent war.

Act 1, Scene 1: A Living Room in the Villa. Early spring. *Scene 2*: The same. A month later.

Act 2, Scene 1: The Terrace of the Villa. Late afternoon, midsummer. *Scene 2*: The same. That night.

Act 3, Scene 1: The Living Room. Afternoon, early fall. *Scene 2*: The same. In the evening, a week later. *Scene 3*: The same. A few hours later.

1958.18   # LA PLUME DE MA TANTE

A Musical (Revue) in Two Acts, 32 Scenes. Written, devised and directed by Robert Dhery. Music and arrangements by Gerard Calvi. English lyrics by Ross Parker. French lyrics by Francis Blanche. Choreography by Colette Brosset. Staged by Alec Shanks. Musical direction by Gershon Kingsley. Scenery supervised and lighted by Charles Elson. Orchestration by Gerard Calvi, Billy Ternent and Ronnie Monro. Overture curtain by Vertes. Produced by David Merrick and Joseph Kipness, by arrangement with Jack Hylton. Opened 11 November 1958 at the Royale Theatre and closed 17 December 1960 1960 after 835 performances.

CAST: ROBERT DHERY, COLETTE BROSSET, PIERRE OLAF, JACQUES LEGRAS, ROGER CACCIA, JEAN LEFEVRE, ROSS PARKER, NICOLE PARENT, PAMELA AUSTIN, HENRI PENNEC, YVONNE CONSTANT, MICHAEL KENT, MICHEL MODO, GENEVIEVE COULOMBEL, Coka Brossecola, Genevieve Zanetti, Francoise Dally, Brigitte Peynaud, Anna Stroppini, Claude Perrin, Mary Reynolds, Jill Hougham, Nadine Gorbatcheff. *Musicians*: Stan Krell (drums), Ernie Mauro (clarinet), Milt Kraus (piano), Aaron Juvelier (bass).

ACT 1

Scene 1
The Company is introduced by Robert Dhery.

Scene 2
Speakerine
C. Brosset

Scene 3
Amsterdam
J. Lefevre

Scene 4
Mobile Squad (Bicycles)
The Pride of the Force: J. Legras, P. Olaf, M. Modo, H. Pennec.

Scene 5
"Rider to the Sea"
M. Kent

Scene 6
"Le Bal Chez Madame Mortemouille"
(*Designed by* Dignimont)
Madame de Mortemouille: P. Austin. *The Major Domo*: M. Kent. *Général Grosfut*: R. Parker. *The Attaché*: H. Pennec. *The Maitre d'Hotel*: R. Caccia. *The Spahi*:. M. Modo. *Johnny Walker*: J. Lefevre. *Master Percy Smith*: P. Olaf. *Mr. Spratts*: J. Legras. *Miss Innocent*: M. Reynolds. *Mademoiselle Colette*: C. Brosset. *Monsieur Robert*: R. Dhery.

Scene 7
Husbands Beware! (includes "Dance of the Wardrobes")
The Wife: Y. Constant. *The Lover*: P. Olaf. *The Elevator Attendant*: H. Pennec. *The Husband*: R. Parker.

Scene 8
Light Soprano ("The Song of the Balloon")
(*Designed by* Erté)P. Austin

Scene 9
In a Small Cafe
(*Designed by* Lilla De Nobili)
The Waiter: R. Dhery. *The Late Diner*: R. Parker.

Scene 10
"Ballet Classique"
(*Designed by* Erté)
The Spirit of the Night: C. Brossecola. *The Prince*: P. Olaf. *The Princess*: G. Coulombel. *The Witch Girl*: N. Parent. With the Entire Corps de Ballet.

Scene 12
"Song of the Swing"
(*Designed by* Alec Shanks.)
Véronique: P. Austin. *Florestan*: M. Kent.

Scene 13
"Precision" (Kickline routine)
The Royal Croquettes

Scene 14
Courting Time
(*Designed by* Erté)
The Father: R. Parker. *The Mother*: R. Caccia. *Their Daughter*: B. Peynaud. *Her Lover*: P. Olaf. *The Explorer*: M. Modo. *The Gendarme*: J. Legras.

Scene 15
"Femmes Fatales" (Dance)
(*Dresses designed by* Jacques Estérel)
Les Femmes: N. Parent, J. Hougham, Y. Constant, M. Reynolds, B. Peynaud, C. Brosset.

Scene 16
On the Beach
R. Caccia, J. Legras, J. Lefevre, R. Parker, G. Zanetti, A. Stroppini

Scene 17
Queen of the Strip-Tease ("Ne Comptez Pas Sur Moi. .Pour Me Montrer Toute Nue")
C. Brosset
("La Plume de Ma Tante")
Girls

Scene 18
Freres Jacques (Bell-ringing Monks)
P. Olaf, J. Legras, R. Caccia, M. Modo, R. Parker

ACT 2

Scene 1
"Hommage Musical"
(*Designed by* Henri Pennec.)R. Dhery, His Festival Ensemble
Guest Artistes: The Ladies Athenian Choir.

Scene 2
Domingo Blazes and his Latin-American Orchestra

Scene 3
In an Indian Temple (Dance)
Temple Girls: The Dugudu Dancers. *The High Priestess*: Y. Constant.

Scene 4
This Other Eden (includes "Like a Little Pussy Cat")
Eve: C. Brosset. *Adam*: R. Dhery. *The Serpent*: J. Legras.

Scene 5
Men at Work
The Workmen: J. Lefevre, H. Pennec.

Scene 6
"Administration"
(*Designed by* Lilla De Nobili.)
Filing Clerks: R. Caccia, J. Legras. *The Secretary*: Y. Constant. *The Boss*: R. Parker.

Scene 7
In the Tuileries Gardens
(*Designed by* Dignimont.)
The Tie Vendor: J. Lefevre. *The Curé*: H. Pennec. *The Bystander*: M. Modo. *The Lovers*: N. Gorbatcheff, Y. Constant. *The Bird Lover*: M. Reynolds. *Agent de Police*: M. Kent. *The Schoolmistress*: P. Austin. *Her Pupils*: G. Coulombel, A. Stroippini, F. Dally, J. Hougham, B. Peynaud, C. Perrin. *Pickpockets*: R. Caccia, J. Legras. *Clowns*: P. Olaf, C. Brosset.

Scene 8
Take-Off
Air Hostess: Y. Constant. *The Passenger*: R. Caccia.

Scene 9
"Ballet Moderne"
The Dancers: G. Coulombel, F. Dally, N. Parent, M. Reynolds. *The Musicians*: S. Krell, E. Mauro, M. Kraus, A. Juvelier.

Scene 10
The Ventriloquist
J. Lefevre

Scene 12
Trapped (Pissotiere)
(*Designed by* Dignimont.)
The Victims: J. Legras, R. Dhery. *A Butcher*: R. Parker. *A Policeman*: H. Pennec. *A Passer-by*: M. Reynolds.

Scene 13
Acrobatie
C. Brosset

Scene 14
Le Finale de Paris
(*Designed by* Erté.)
Entire Company, Entire Corps de Ballet
(Paris is the End!)
("La Plume de Ma Tante"/Striptease/Monks reprise)

1958.19 FLOWER DRUM SONG

A Musical in Two Acts, 14 Scenes. Book by Oscar Hammerstein II and Joseph Fields. Based on the novel "The Flower Drum Song" by C. Y. Lee. Music by Richard Rodgers. Lyrics by Oscar Hammerstein II. Directed by Gene Kelly. Choreography by Carol Haney. Scenic production by Oliver Smith. Costumes by Irene Sharaff. Lighting by Peggy Clark. Orchestrations by Robert Russell Bennett. Musical director, Salvatore Dell'Isola. Dance arrangements by Luther Henderson, Jr. Produced by Richard Rodgers and Oscar Hammerstein II in association with Joseph Fields. Opened 1 December 1958 at the St. James Theatre and closed 7 May 1960 after 600 performances.

CAST (in order of appearance): *Madam Liang*: JUANITA HALL. *Liu Ma*: Rose Quong. *Wang San*: PATRICK ADIARTE. *Wang Ta*: ED KENNEY. *Wang Chi Yang*: KEYE LUKE. *Sammy Fong*: LARRY BLYDEN. *Dr. Li*: Conrad Yama. *Mei Li*: MIYOSHI UMEKI. *Linda Low*: PAT SUZUKI. *Mr. Lung*: Harry Shaw Lowe. *Mr. Huan*: Jon Lee. *Helen Chao*: ARABELLA HONG. *Professor Cheng*: Peter Chan. *Frankie Wing*: Jack Soo. *Head Waiter*: George Yuong. *Night Club Singer*: ANITA ELLIS. *Dr. Lu Fong*: Chao Li. *Madam Fong*: Eileen Nakamura.
Children: Linda Ribuca, Yvonne Ribuca, Susan Lynn Kikuchi, Luis Robert Hernandez. *Dancing Ensemble*: Fumi Akimoto, Paula Chin, Helen Funai, Pat Griffith, Mary Huie, Marion Jim, Betty Kawamura, Baayork Lee, Wonci Lui, Jo Anne Miya, Denise Quan, Vicki Racimo, Shawnee Smith, Maureen Tiongco, Mabel Wing, Yuriko, Jose Ahumada, Victor Duntiere, George Li, David Lober, Robert Lorca, George Minami, David Toguri, George Young.

The action takes place in San Francisco's Chinatown at the present time.

Act 1, Scene 1: The Living Room in the House of Master Wang Chi Yang. *Scene 2*: A Hill overlooking San Francisco Bay. *Scene 3*: The Wang Living Room. *Scene 4*: Wang Chi Yang's Bedroom. *Scene 5*: The Garden of the Wang House. *Scene 6*: Linda's Dressing Room in the Celestial Bar. *Scene 7*: The Celestial Bar.

Act 2, Scene 1: Helen Chao's Room. *Scene 2*: The Wang Living Room. *Scene 3*: Sammy Fong's Penthouse Apartment. *Scene 4*: The Three Family Association. *Scene 5*: Sammy Fong's Penthouse Apartment. *Scene 6*: Grant Avenue, San Francisco's Chinatown. *Scene 7*: The Three Family Association.

ACT 1
Scene 1
"You Are Beautiful"
E. Kenney, J. Hall
"A Hundred Million Miracles"
M. Umeki, C. Yama, K. Luke, J. Hall, R. Quong
Scene 2
"I Enjoy Being a Girl"
P. Suzuki, Dancers
Scene 3
"I Am Going to Like It Here"
M. Umeki
Scene 4
"Like a God"
E. Kenney
Scene 5
"Chop Suey"
J. Hall, P. Adiarte, Ensemble
"Don't Marry Me"
L. Blyden, M. Umeki
"Grant Avenue"
P. Suzuki, Ensemble
Scene 6
"Love Look Away"
A. Hong
Scene 7
"Fan Tan Fannie"
A. Ellis, Girls
"Gliding Through My Memoree"
J. Soo, Girls

Finale: "Grant Avenue" (reprise)
Company
ACT 2
Scene 1
Ballet
Wang Ta: E. Kenney. *Mei Li*: Yuriko. *Linda Low*: J. A. Miya. And Dancers.
"Love Look Away" (reprise)
A. Hong
Scene 2
"The Other Generation"
J. Hall, K. Luke
Scene 3
"Sunday"
P. Suzuki, L. Blyden
Scene 4
"The Other Generation" (reprise)
P. Adiarte, Children
Scene 6
"Wedding Parade"
M. Umeki, Dancers
Scene 7
Finale
Entire Company

1958.20 WHOOP-UP

A Musical Comedy in Two Acts. Book by Cy Feuer, Ernest H. Martin and Dan Cushman. Based on the novel "Stay Away, Joe" by Dan Cushman. Music by Moose Charlap. Lyrics by Norman Gimbel. Settings and lighting by Jo Mielziner. Costumes by Anna Hill Johnstone. Choreography by Onna White. Musical And vocal direction, Stanley Lebowsky. Orchestrations by Philip J. Lang. Dance music arranged by Peter Matz. Directed by Cy Feuer. Produced by Cy Feuer and Ernest H. Martin. Opened 22 December 1958 at the Sam S. Shubert Theatre and closed 7 February 1959 after 56 performances.

CAST (in order of appearance): *Glenda Swenson*: SUSAN JOHNSON. *Jiggs Rock Medicine*: Michael Kermoyan. *Walt Stephenpierre*: Tom Rasking. *Dub Winter Owl*: Jackie Warner. *Bix Winter Owl*: Bobby Shields. *Louis Champlain*: ROMO VINCENT. *Annie Champlain*: SYLVIA SYMS. *Mary Champlain*: JULIENNE MARIE. *Matthew Bearchaser*: Tony Gardell. *Karl Kellenbach*: PAUL FORD. *Clyde Walschmidt*: Wallace Rooney. *George Potter*: DANNY MEEHAN. *Medicine Man*: Tony Gardell. *Joe Champlain*: RALPH YOUNG. *Marlene Standing Rattle*: Ann Barry. *Gran'pere*: P. J. KELLY. *Billie Mae Littlehorse*: ASIA (MERCOOLOVA). *Juke Box Voice*: Bobby Shields. *Mrs. Kellenbach*: Vera Walton. *Baptiste Three Bird*: Paul Michael. *Hotel Proprietor*: Robert Lenn. *Teenager*: Robert Karl. *State Trooper*: Steve Wiland. *Justice of the Peace*: Earl Lippy. *First Stranger*: Edward Becker. *Second Stranger*: Socrates Birsky.
Reservation Residents: Mari Arnell, Ann Barry, Edward Becker, Jeanna Belkin, Socrates Birsky, Tim Brown, Sandra Devlin, Eleanor Dian, Tina Faye, Tony Gardell, Martha Granese, H. F. Green, Salvador Juarez, Robert Karl, Robert Lenn, Earl Lippy, Rae McLean, Michelle Newton, Estelle Parsons, Yolanda Poropat, Tom Raskin, Tony Rosa, Marla Stevens, Ben Vargas, Barbara Webb, Steve Wiland.

The action takes place on or near a United States Indian reservation in northern Montana at the present time.
ACT 1
"Glenda's Place"
S. Johnson, Indinas
"When the Tall Man Talks"
S. Johnson
"Nobody Throw Those Bull"
R. Vincent, Indians
"Rocky Boy Ceremonial" (Chief Rocky Boy)
T. Gardell, Members of the Tribe
"Love Eyes"
R. Young
"Men"
S. Johnson
"Never Before"
J. Marie
"Caress Me, Possess Me Perfume"
B. Shields
"Flattery"
R. Young, S. Johnson

"The Girl in His Arms"
 B. Shields
"The Best of What This Country's Got"
 D. Meehan

ACT 2
 "I Wash My Hands"
 R. Young, J. Marie, M. Kermoyan, T. Raskin
"Quarrel-tet"
 S. Johnson, R. Young, R. Lenn, T. Raskin
"Sorry for Myself"
 S. Syms
"'Til the Big Fat Moon Falls Down"
 J. Marie, Asia, Friends
"What I Mean to Say"
 D. Meehan
"Montana"
 S. Johnson
"She or Her"
 R. Young

A PARTY WITH BETTY COMDEN AND ADOLPH GREEN

1958.21

An Intimate Revue in Three Acts, 11 Scenes[5]. Sketches and lyrics by Betty Comden and Adolph Green. (Music by Leonard Bernstein, Morton Gould, Jule Styne, Roger Edens, Andre Previn, Saul Chaplin.) At the Piano, Peter Howard. Decor and lighting by Marvin Ross. Associate producer, Frank Perry. Produced by the Theatre Guild by special arrangement and in association with Town Productions, Inc. as originally presented by JJG Productions under the supervision of Gus Schirmer, Jr. Opened 23 December 1958 at the John Golden Theatre, closing 24 January 1959 after 38 performances; re-opened 16 April 1959 at the John Golden Theatre and closed 23 May 1959 after 44 additional performances. Total performances: 82.

CAST: BETTY COMDEN, ADOLPH GREEN.

ACT 1
THE PERFORMERS
Scene 1
 Opening ("I Said Good Morning" from the film IT'S ALWAYS FAIR WEATHER)
  (*Music by* Andre Previn.)
Scene 2
 The Revuers—Night Club Act
  (*Sketches, Music and Lyrics by* The Revuers {Betty Comden, Adolph Green, Judy Holliday, Alvin Hammer, John Frank}.)
 1. Movie Ads
 2. The Reader's Digest
 3. The Screen Writers
 4. The Banshee Sisters
 5. "The Baroness Bazooka"

ACT 2
THE PERFORMER-WRITERS
Scene 1
 ON THE TOWN
  (*Music by* Leonard Bernstein.)
 1. "New York, New York"
 2. "Lonely Town"
 3. "Lucky to be Me"
 4. "Come Up to My Place"
 5. "I Get Carried Away"
Scene 2
 BILLION DOLLAR BABY
  (*Music by* Morton Gould.)
 1. "Bad Timing"
 2. "Broadway Blossoms"

Scene 3
 GOOD NEWS (Film)
  (*Music by* Roger Edens.)
 1. "French Lesson"
Scene 4
 TWO ON THE AISLE
  (*Music by* Jule Styne.)
 1. "If You Hadn't But You Did"
 2. "Catch Our Act at the Met"
 3. "He'll Never Know"

ACT 3
THE WRITER-PERFORMERS
Scene 1
 WONDERFUL TOWN
  (*Music by* Leonard Bernstein.)
 1. "A Hundred Easy Ways to Lose a Man"
 2. "Ohio"
 3. "Wrong Note Rag"
 4. "A Quiet Girl"
 5. "It's Love"
Scene 2
 PETER PAN
  (*Music by* Jule Styne.)
 1. "Oh, My Mysterious Lady"
 2. "Captain Hook's Waltz"
 3. "Never Never Land"
 4. "Once Upon a Time and Long Ago"
Scene 3
 A Show [BONANZA BOUND]
  (*Music by* Saul Chaplin.)
 1. "Inspiration"
Scene 4
 SAY, DARLING
  (*Music by* Jule Styne.)
 1. Medley
Scene 5
 BELLS ARE RINGING
  (*Music by* Jule Styne.)
 1. "Just in Time"
 2. "The Party's Over"

REDHEAD

1959.01

A Musical Comedy in Two Acts, a Prologue and 16 Scenes. Book by Herbert and Dorothy Fields, Sidney Sheldon and David Shaw. Music by Albert Hague. Lyrics by Dorothy Fields. Production (sets, costumes) designed by Rouben Ter-Arutunian. Lighting by Jean Rosenthal. Orchestrations by Philip J. Lang and Robert Russell Bennett. Musical direction and vocal arrangements by Jay Blackton. Dance music arranged by Roger Adams. Associate choreographer, Donald MacKayle. Directed and choreographed by Bob Fosse. Produced by Robert Fryer and Lawrence Carr. Opened 5 February 1959 at the 46th Street Theatre and closed 19 March 1960 after 455 performances.

CAST (in order of appearance): *Ruth LaRue*: Pat Ferrier. *Maude Simpson*: CYNTHIA LATHAM. *Sarah Simpson*: DORIS RICH. *May*: Joy Nichols. *Tilly*: Pat Ferrier. *Essie Whimple*: GWEN VERDON. *Inspector White*: Ralph Sumpter. *Howard Cavanaugh*: WILLIAM LE MASSENA. *George Poppett*: LEONARD STONE. *Tom Baxter*: RICHARD KILEY. *Alfy, Stage Doorman*: Lee Krieger. *Sir Charles Willingham*: Patrick Horgan. *Tenor*: Bob Dixon. *Inez, the Blonde*: Bette Graham. *Jailer*: Buzz Miller.
 Singers: Mame Dennis, Joan Fagan, Lydia Fredericks, Bette Graham, Dee Harless, Janie Janviar, Kelley Stephens, Bob Dixon, Clifford Fearl, John Lankston, Larry Mitchell, Stan Page, Shev Rodgers. *Dancers*: Margery Beddow, Shirley de Burgh, Pat Ferrier, Reby Howells, Patti Karr, Liane Plane, Elaine King, Dean Taliferro, John Aristides, Kevin Carlisle, David Gold, Harvey Hohnecker, Kazimir Kokich, Dale Moreda, Noel Parenti, Alton Ruff.

Prologue: A Theatre Dressing Room.

Act 1, Scene 1: Outside the Simpson Sisters' Waxworks. *Scene 2*: The Interior of the Waxworks. *Scene 3*: Essie's Workshop. *Scene 4*: A Street. *Scene 5*: Stage of the Odeon Theatre. *Scene 6*: Corridor, Backstage. *Scene 7*: Tom's Apartment. *Scene 8*: Outside the

---

[5]First produced in New York Off-Broadway for a series of Monday night performances 10 November 1958 at the Cherry Lane Theatre.

Museum. *Scene 9*: Backstage of the Odeon Theatre. *Scene 10*: Stage of the Odeon Theatre.

Act 2, Scene 1: Tom's Apartment. *Scene 2*: A Street. *Scene 3*: The Green Dragon Pub. *Scene 4*: The Jail Cell. *Scene 5*: Corridor, Backstage. *Scene 6*: The Museum.

ACT 1

Scene 1

"The Simpson Sisters"
  Singers, Dancers

Scene 2

"The Right Finger of My Left Hand"
  G. Verdon

Scene 3

"Just For Once"
  G. Verdon, R. Kiley, L. Stone

"(I Feel) Merely Marvelous"
  G. Verdon

Scene 5

"The Uncle Sam Rag"
  L. Stone, Singers, Dancers

"Erbie Fitch's Twitch"
  G. Verdon

Scene 6

"Behave Yourself"
  G. Verdon, C. Latham, D. Rich, R. Kiley

Scene 7

"Look Who's in Love"
  G. Verdon, R. Kiley

Scene 8

"My Girl Is Just Enough Woman for Me"
  R. Kiley, Passersby

Scene 9

"Essie's Vision"
  G. Verdon, Her Dream People

Scene 10

"Two Faces in the Dark"
  G. Verdon, B. Dixon, Singers, Dancers

ACT 2

Scene 1

"I'm Back in Circulation"
  R. Kiley

Scene 3

"We Loves Ya, Jimey"
  G. Verdon, J. Nichols, P. Ferrier, Ensemble

Scene 4

"Pick-Pocket Tango"
  G. Verdon, B. Miller

Scene 5

"Look Who's in Love" (reprise)
  R. Kiley

Scene 6

"I'll Try"[6]
  G. Verdon, R. Kiley

(The Chase)/Finale
  G. Verdon, R. Kiley, Company

1959.02

THE MOST HAPPY FELLA

A Revival of the Musical in Three Acts, 11 Scenes[7]. Book, music and lyrics by Frank Loesser. Based on the play "They Knew What They Wanted" by Sidney Howard. Entire Production directed and supervised by Dania Krupska. Choreography by Dania Krupska, restaged by Arthur Partington. Scenery and lighting by Jo Mielziner. Costumes by Ruth Morley. Art director, Watson Barratt. (Orchestrations by Don Walker.) Musical direction, Abba Bogin. Produced by the New York City Center Light Opera Company

(Jean Dalrymple, Director). Opened 10 February 1959 at the New York City Center and closed 22 February 1959 after 16 performances.

CAST (in order of appearance): *The Cashier*: Lee Cass. *Cleo*: LIBI STAIGER. *Rosabella*: PAULA STEWART. *Waitresses*: Jessica Albright, Betty Jenkins, Gloria Kaye, Kitty Malone, Sherry McCutcheon, Sybil Scotford. *The Postman*: Lee Cass. *Tony*: NORMAN ATKINS. *Marie*: MURIEL BIRKHEAD. *Max*: Win Mayo. *Herman*: JACK DE LON. *Clem*: James Schlader. *Jake*: Ken Adams. *Al*: Roy Lazarus. *Joe*: ART LUND. *Giuseppe*: Kenneth Lane. *Pasquale*: Bruce MacKay. *Ciccio*: Michael Davis. *Country Girl*: Jessica Albright. *Country Boy*: Garold Gardner. *Doctor*: Keith Kaldenberg. *Priest*: Fred Conway. *Tessie*: Bernadette Peters. *Gussie*: Johnny Borden. *Train Conductor*: Win Mayo. *Neighbors*: Mary Sue Berry, Gloria Kaye, Barbara Saxby, John Dorrin, Roy Lazarus, George Zima. *Neighbor Ladies*: Thea Bradon, Terry DeLiva, Maggie Task. *Brakeman*: Sheldon Ossosky. *Bus Driver*: Jordan Howard.

All the Neighbors, and All the Neighbors' Neighbors: Lorrie Bentley, Mary Sue Berry, Jan Canada, Terry Deliva, Mary Ann Heitzig, Barbara Saxby, Jeanne Schlegel, Sheila Swenson, Maggie Task, Ken Adams, Fred Conway, Michael Davis, John Dorrin, Jordan Howard, Del Horstmann, Robert Ethridge, Roy Lazarus, Jack McMinn, Win Mayo, Jack McCann, James Schlader, Jessica Albright, Betty Jenkins, Gloria Kaye, Kitty Malone, Sherry McCutcheon, Sybil Scotford, Garold Gardner, Bob LaCrosse, Sheldon Ossosky, Michael Scrittorale, James Senn, George Zima.

1959.03

SAY, DARLING

A Revival of the Comedy about a Musical in Three Acts, 11 Scenes[8]. Book by Richard and Marian Bissell and Abe Burrows. Music by Jule Styne. Lyrics by Betty Comden and Adolph Green. (Scenery) Designed by Oliver Smith. Costumes by Alvin Colt. Lighting by Peggy Clark. Dances by Matt Mattox. Musical director, Colin Romoff. Directed by David Clive. Produced by the New York City Center Light Opera Company (Jean Dalrymple, Director). Opened 25 February 1959 at the New York City Center and closed 8 March 1959 after 16 performances.

CAST (in order of appearance): *Mr. Schneider*: Gordon B. Clarke. *Frankie Jordan*: BETSY VON FURSTENBERG. *Jack Jordan*: ORSON BEAN. *Photographer*: Stephen Franken. *Pilot Roy Peters*: Rober Herrman. *Ted Snow*: ROBERT MORSE. *June, the Secretary*: Kelly Leigh. *Schatzie Harris*: Jack Waldron. *Richard Hackett*: Alexander Clark. *Irene Lovelle*: MINDY CARSON. *Rudy Lorraine*: DAVID ATKINSON. *Charlie Williams*: James Karr. *Maurice*: Brooks Morton. *Arlene McKee*: Janyce Wagner. *Jennifer Stevenson*: Jean Mattox. *Earl Jorgeson*: Elliott Gould. *Cheryl Merrill*: Paula Wayne. *Accompanist*: Joe Richter. *Sammy Miles*: Buddy Ferrard. *Rex Dexter*: Mitchell Gregg. *Boris Reshevsky*: Matt Mattox. *Waiter*: Stephen Franken. *Morty Krebs*: Edward Hunt.

Kids in the Show: Marcella Dodge, Kelly Leigh, Paula Lloyd, Jean Mattox, Janyce Wagner, Elliott Gould, George Martin, Calvin von Reinhold, Eddie Weston. *Sidemen*: Andrew Bagni, Joseph Castka, Tommy Lucas, Ted Flowerman.

1959.04

JUNO

A Musical in Two Acts, a Prologue and 16 Scenes. Book by Joseph Stein. Based on the play "Juno and the Paycock" by Sean O'Casey. Music and lyrics by Marc Blitzstein. Dances and musical numbers staged by Agnes de Mille. Scenery designed by Oliver Smith. Costumes by Irene Sharaff. Lighting by Peggy Clark. Music direction, Robert Emmett Dolan. Orchestrations by Robert Russell Bennett, Marc Blitzstein, Hershy Kay. Associate producer, Lyn Austin. Directed by José Ferrer. Produced by The Playwrights' Company, Oliver Smith and Oliver Rea. Opened 9 March 1959 at the Winter Garden and closed 21 March 1959 after 16 performances.

CAST (in order of appearance): *Mary Boyle*: MONTE AMUNDSEN. *Johnny Boyle*: TOMMY RALL. *Juno Boyle*: SHIRLEY BOOTH. *Jerry Devine*: Loren Driscoll. *Mrs. Madigan*: Jean Stapleton. *Mrs. Brady*: Nancy Andrews. *Mrs. Coyne*: Sada Thompson. *Miss Quinn*: Beulah Garrick. *Charlie Bentham*: Earl Hammond. *Foley*: Arthur Rubin. *Sullivan*: Rico Froehlich. *Michael Brady*: Robert Rue. *Paddy Coyne*: Julian Patrick. *"Captain" Jack Boyle*: MELVYN DOUGLAS. *"Joxer" Daly*: JACK MacGOWRAN. *Molly*: Gemze de Lappe. *"Needle" Nugent*: Liam Lenihan. *I.R.A. Men*: Tom Clancy, Jack Murray. *Mrs. Tancred*: Clarice Blackburn. *Mrs. Dwyer*: Betty Low. *I.R.A. Singer*: Robert Hoyem. *Furniture Removal Men*: George Ritner, Frank Carroll. *Policeman*: Rico Froehlich.

Singers: Anne Fielding, Cleo Fry, Pat Huddleston, Gail Johnston, Barbara Lockard, Pat Ruhl, Diana Sennett, Joanne Spiller, Frank Carroll, Rico Froehlich, Robert Hoyem, Jack Murray, Julian Patrick, George Ritner, Robert Rue, James Tushar. *Dancers*: Sharon Enoch, Mickey Gunnersen, Pat Heyes, Rosemary Jourdan, Annabelle Lyon, Marjorie Wittmer, Jenny Workman, Chuck Bennett, Ted Forlow, Curtis Hood, Scott Hunter, Eugene Kelton, James Maher, Enrique Martinez, Howard Parker, Jim Ryan, Glen Tetley.

---

[6]Dropped during run and for tour.
[7]Originally produced 3 May 1956 at the Imperial Theatre for 678 performances. For Synopsis of Scenes and Musical Numbers, see original 1956 production.

[8]Originally produced 3 April 1958 at the ANTA Theatre for 332 performances. For Synopsis of Scenes and Musical Numbers, see original 1958 production. "My Little Yellow Dress" added to the end of Act 2. Act 3 (formerly 4 Scenes) re-set as one scene in That Hotel Room in New Haven.

The action takes place in Dublin, 1921.

Prologue: The street in front of the Boyle home. Early evening in summer.

Act 1, Scene 1: The Boyle home. *Scene 2:* Another street. *Scene 3:* The street and Foley's bar. *Scene 4:* A park square. *Scene 5:* The Boyle home. *Scene 6:* Another street. *Scene 7:* A square in the city. *Scene 8:* A park square. Evening, a few days later. *Scene 9:* The street.

Act 2, Scene 1: The Boyle home. Evening, a few days later. *Scene 2:* The yard behind the house. *Scene 3:* A street. *Scene 4:* The Boyle home. *Scene 5:* A park square. *Scene 6:* The Boyle home. *Scene 7:* The street and Foley's bar.

ACT 1
Prologue
"We're Alive"
Ensemble
Scene 1
"I Wish It So"
M. Amundsen
"Song of the Ma"
S. Booth
Scene 3
"We Can Be Proud"
A. Rubin, R. Froehlich, R. Rue, J. Patrick
"Daarlin' Man"
M. Douglas, J. MacGowran, Ensemble
Scene 4
"One Kind Word"
L. Driscoll
Scene 5
"Old Sayin's"
S. Booth, M. Douglas
"What Is the Stars?"
M. Douglas, J. MacGowran
"Old Sayin's" (reprise)
S. Booth, M. Douglas
Scene 6
"You Poor Thing"
J. Stapleton, N. Andrews, S. Thompson, B. Garrick
Scene 7
"Dublin Night" (Ballet)
T. Rall, G. de Lappe, Ensemble
(*Ballet Music by* Trude Rittman and Marc Blitzstein.)
Scene 8
"My True Heart"
M. Amundsen, E. Hammond
Scene 9
"On a Day Like This" (Finale Act 1)
S. Booth, M. Douglas, Ensemble
Jig
H. Parker, E. Kelton
Slip Jig
G. Tetley
Shillelagh Dance
C. Hood, E. Martinez, C. Bennett, S. Hunter
Jig
S. Booth, M. Douglas, Ensemble
ACT 2
Scene 1
"Bird Upon the Tree"
S. Booth, M. Amundsen
Scene 2
The Party
(a) "Music in the House"
M. Douglas, Ensemble
(b) "It's Not Irish" (Gramophone)
A. Rubin
(c) "It's Not Irish" (Quartet)
A. Rubin, R. Froehlich, R. Rue, M. Douglas
(d) "The Liffey Waltz"
Ensemble

"Hymn"
R. Hoyem
"Johnny" (Ballet)
T. Rall, G. de Lappe
(*Ballet Music by* Marc Blitzstein.)
Scene 3
"You Poor Thing" (reprise)
J. Stapleton, N. Andrews, S. Thompson, B. Garrick
Scene 5
"For Love"
M. Amundsen
"One Kind Word" (reprise)
L. Driscoll
Scene 6
"Where?"
S. Booth
Scene 7
Finale Act 2
S. Booth, M. Amundsen, M. Douglas, J. MacGowran

1959.05

LUTE SONG

A Revival of the Love Story With Music in Two Acts, 16 Scenes[9]. Book by Sidney Howard and Will Irwin from the famous Chinese play "Pi-Pa-Ki." Music by Raymond Scott. Lyrics by Bernard Hanighen. Directed by John Paul. Choreography by Yeichi Nimura. Musical director, Sylvan Levin. (Orchestrations by Raymond Scott.) Scenery, Costumes and lighting by Robert Edmond Jones. Art director, Watson Barratt. Costume supervisor, Ruth Morley. Produced by the New York City Center Light Opera Company (Jean Dalrymple, Director). Opened 12 March 1959 at the New York City Center and closed 22 March 1959 after 14 performances.

CAST (in order of their appearance): *The Manager, The Honorable Tschang:* CLARENCE DERWENT. *First Propertyman:* Andre Gregory. *Second Propertyman:* Epy Baca. *Tsai-Yong,* the Husband: SHAI-K-OPHIR. *Tsai,* the father: TONIO SELWART. *Madame Tsai,* the Mother: ESTELLE WINWOOD. *Tchao-ou-Niang,* the Wife: DOLLY HAAS. *Prince Nieou,* the Imperial Preceptor: PHILIP BOURNEUF. *Princess Nieou-Chi,* his daughter: LEUEEN MacGRATH. *Si-Tchun,* a Lady in Waiting: Rain Winslow. *Waiting Women:* Maxine Taylor, Margaret Sheehan. *Hand Maiden:* Shizu Moriya. *Chi-Mao-Chiu Players:* Isabel Farrell, Trudi Gasparinetti, Sigrid Geiger, Barbara Monte. *Youen-Kong,* the Steward: JOSEPH DAUBENAS. *Marriage Broker:* Diane De Brett. *A Sweeper of Heaven and Earth:* ASIA. *Imperial Chamberlain:* DONALD SYMINGTON. *Food Commissioner:* Gene Galvin. *First Clerk:* Anthony Edwards. *Second Clerk:* Epy Baca. *First Applicant:* John Darren. *Second Applicant:* Donald Hotton. *Street Beggar:* Mark Fleischman. *Crippled Beggar:* Michael De Marco. *Blind Beggar:* Alan Kirk. *Imperial Guards:* Anthony Edwards, Carl Clark. *Imperial Attendants:* Bob Daley, Michael Fesco, Arnott Mader, Sheldon Ossosky. *The Genie:* DONALD SYMINGTON. *The White Tiger:* ASIA. *The Ape:* Dean Crane. *Phoenix Birds:* Asia, Dean Crane. *Li-Wang:* Ted Van Griethuysen. *Priest of Amida Buddha:* Tom Emlyn Williams. *A Bonze:* Gene Galvin. *Two Lesser Bonzes:* Andre Gregory, Epy Baca. *A Rich Man:* Wesley Owen. *The Lion:* Dean Crane, Dick Colacino. *Ribbon Spinner:* Asia. *Children:* Olivia Johnson, Gloria Kaye, Coco Ramirez, Tina Ramirez. *Palace Guards:* Walter Adams, Peter Deign, Paul Eden, John Pero, Vic Vallaro. *A Secretary:* Epy Baca.
Travellers on the North Road, Beggars, Guards, Attendants, Gods and Othgers: Isabel Farrell, Trudi Gasparinetti, Sigrid Geiger, Olivia Johnson, Gloria Kaye, Barbara Monte, Shizu Moriya, Coco Ramirez, Tina Ramirez, Margaret Sheehan, Maxine Taylor, Walter Adams, Carl Clark, Dick Colacino, Bob Daley, Peter Deign, Michael de Marco, John Darren, Paul Eden, Anthony Edwards, Michael Fesco, Mark Fleischman, Andre Gregory, Donald Hotton, Alan Kirk, Arnott Mader, Sheldon Ossosky, Wesley Owen, John Pero, Vic Vallaro, Ted Van Griethuysen.

1959.06

FIRST IMPRESSIONS

A Musical Comedy in Two Acts, 15 Scenes. Book by Abe Burrows. Based on the novel "Pride and Prejudice" by Jane Austen and the play of the same name by Helen Jerome. Music and lyrics by Robert Goldman, Glenn Paxton and George Weiss. Directed by Abe Burrows. Choreography by Jonathan Lucas. Production (Settings) designed by Peter Larkin. Costumes

---

[9]Originally produced in New York 6 February 1946 at the Plymouth Theatre for 142 performances. For Synopsis of Scenes and Musical Numbers, see original 1946 production. For this production, the intermission between Acts 1 and 2 has been eliminated; Act 1, Scene 6 and Act 2, Scene 1 have been combined as one scene.

by Alvin Colt. Lighting by Charles Elson. Musical direction by Frederick Dvonch. Orchestrations by Don Walker. Dance arrangements by John Morris. Vocal arrangements and direction by Buster Davis. Produced by George Gilbert and Edward Spector Productions, Inc. (with the assistance of) The Jule Styne Organization. Opened 19 March 1959 at the Alvin Theatre and closed 30 May 1959 after 84 performances.

CAST (in order of appearance): *Mr. Bennet*: Laurie Main. *Mary Bennet*: Lois Bewley. *Mrs. Bennet*: HERMIONE GINGOLD. *Lydia Bennet*: Lynn Ross. *Kitty Bennet*: Lauri Peters. *Jane Bennet*: PHYLLIS NEWMAN. *Maid*: Beverley Jane Welch. *Elizabeth Bennet*: POLLY BERGEN. *Lady Lucas*: Sibyl Bowan. *Charlotte Lucas*: ELLEN HANLEY. *Caroline Bingley*: Marti Stevens. *Charles Bingley*: DONALD MADDEN. *Fitzwilliam Darcy*: FARLEY GRANGER. *Coachmen*: Garrett Lewis, John Starkweather. *Captain Wickham*: JAMES MITCHELL. *Lieutenant Denny*: Bill Carter. *Lieutenant Rockingham*: Stuart Hodes. *Sir William Lucas*: Richard Bengal. *Butler*: Norman Fredericks. *Mr. Stubbs*: Casper Roos. *Williams*: Jay Stern. *Collins*: CHRISTOPHER HEWETT. *Butler at Rosings*: John Starkweather. *Lady Catherine de Bourgh*: MARY FINNEY. *Lady Anne*: Martha Mathes.

Dancers: Arlene Avril, Janise Gardner, Sally Gura, Harriet Leigh, Martha Mathes, Dorothy Jeanne Mattis, Wendy Nickerson, Alvin Beam, Jim Corbett, Stuart Fleming, Richard Gain, Stuart Hodes, Garrett Lewis, John Starkweather. *Singers*: Adrienne Angel, Suzie Baker, Marian Haraldson, Jeannine Masterson, Louise Pearl, Beverley Jane Welch, Stuart Damon, Norman Fredericks, Warren Hays, Casper Roos, Tony Rossi, Jay Stern.

Act 1, Scene 1: Longbourn. Home of the Bennets in Hertfordshire, England, 1813. *Scene 2*: A Road in Meryton. *Scene 3*: The Assembly at Meryton. *Scene 4*: Longbourn. *Scene 5*: Netherfield Hall. *Scene 6*: Longbourn. *Scene 7*: The Garden at Netherfield Hall. *Scene 8*: The Lawn at Netherfield Hall. *Scene 9*: Longbourn.

Act 2, Scene 1: A Church in Kent. *Scene 2*: Rosings. Home of Lady Catherine de Bourgh in Kent. *Scene 3*: A Street in Meryton. *Scene 4*: Longbourn. *Scene 5*: Longbourn. *Scene 6*: Netherfield Hall.

ACT 1[10]

Scene 1
 "Five Daughters"
  H. Gingold
 "I'm Me"
  P. Bergen, L. Bewley, L. Ross, L. Peters, P. Newman
Scene 2
 "Have You Heard the News?"
  H. Gingold, Townspeople
Scene 3
 The Assembly Dance
  Townspeople, Officers
 "A Perfect Evening"
  F. Granger, P. Bergen
Scene 4
 "As Long as There's a Mother"
  H. Gingold, M. Benentt, L. Ross, L. Peters, P. Newman
Scene 5
 "Love Will Find Out the Way"
  P. Bergen
 "Gentlemen Don't Fall Wildly in Love"
  F. Granger
Scene 6
 "Fragrant Flower"
  C. Hewett, P. Bergen
Scene 7
 "I Feel Sorry for the Girl"
  P. Newman, D. Madden, Ensemble
 Dance
  L. Bewley, B. Carter, L. Ross, J. Mitchell, L. Peters, S. Hodes
Scene 8
 "I Suddenly Find It Agreeable"
  P. Bergen, F. Granger
 "This Really Isn't Me"
  P. Bergen
Scene 9
 Finaletto
  H. Gingold, L. Bewley, L. Ross, L. Peters, P. Newman

---

[10]Added during run to the beginning of Act 1, Scene 5:
 "Jane"
  D. Madden, F. Granger

ACT 2
Scene 1
 "Wasn't It a Simply Lovely Wedding?"
  P. Bergen, H. Gingold, E. Hanley, C. Hewett, Ensemble
Scene 2
 "A House in Town"
  H. Gingold
 "The Heart Has Won the Game"
  F. Granger
 "I'm Me" (reprise)
  P. Bergen
Scene 3
 Dance
  J. Mitchell, L. Ross, Officers
Scene 5
 "Let's Fetch the Carriage"
  P. Bergen, H. Gingold
Scene 6
 "The Heart Has Won the Game" (reprise)
  F. Granger, P. Bergen

1959.07 MARIA GOLOVIN

A Revival of the Musical Drama (Opera) in Three Acts, 7 Scenes[11]. Libretto and music by Gian Carlo Menotti. Staged by Kirk Browning. Conducted by Herbert Grossman. Chorus master, Gino Smart. Scenery by Rouben Ter-Arutunian. Lighting by Lee Watson. Costumes by Ruth Morley. Produced by the New York City Opera Company. Opened 30 March 1959 at the New York City Center and closed 23 April 1959 after 2 performances in repertory.

CAST (in order of appearance): *Donato*: RICHARD CROSS. *Agata*: REGINA SARFATY. *The Mother*: PATRICIA NEWAY. *Dr. Zuckertanz*: NORMAN KELLEY. *Maria Golovin*: ILONA KOMBRINK. *Trottolo*: Craig Sechler. *The Prisoner*: CHESTER LUDGIN.

1959.08 STREET SCENE

A Revival of the American Opera (Dramatic Musical) in Two Acts, 3 Scenes[12]. Book by Elmer Rice from his play of the same name. Music by Kurt Weill. Lyrics by Langston Hughes. Staged by Herbert Machiz. Conducted by Samuel Krachmalnick. Scenery and costumes by Paul Sylbert. Children's number supervised by Robert Joffrey. Chorus master, Gino Smart. (Orchestrations by Kurt Weill.) Produced by the New York City Opera Company. Opened 2 April 1959 at the New York City Center and closed 29 April 1959 after 7 performances in repertory.

CAST (in order of appearance): *Abraham Kaplan*: Howard Fried. *Greta Fiorentino*: Dolores Mari, Jacquelynne Moody (alt.). *Carl Olsen*: Arnold Voketaitis. *Emma Jones*: RUTH KOBART. *Olga Olsen*: Beatrice Krebs. *Shirley Kaplan*: Florence Anglin. *Mrs. Davis*: Marie Louise. *Henry Davis*: Andrew Frierson. *Willie Maurrant*: Michael Mann. *Anna Maurrant*: WILMA SPENCE, Elisabeth Carron (alt.). *Sam Kaplan*: DAVID POLERI, Frank Poretta (alt.). *Daniel Buchanan*: Keith Kaldenberg. *Frank Maurrant*: WILLIAM CHAPMAN. *George Jones*: Arthur Newman. *Steve Sankey*: Arthur Storch, David Frank (alt.). *Lippo Fiorentino*: JACK DE LON. *Jennie Hildebrand*: Nancy Dussault. *Second Graduate*: Fiddle Viracola. *Third Graduate*: Jennie Andrea. *Mrs. Hildebrand*: Elizabeth Mannion. *Charlie Hildebrand*: Richard Clemence. *Mary Hildebrand*: Lynn Taussig. *Grace Davis*: Sharon Williams. *Rose Maurrant*: HELENA SCOTT, Joy Clements (alt.). *Harry Easter*: Scott Merrill. *Mae Jones*: Sondra Lee. *Dick McGann*: Richard Tone. *Vincent Jones*: Albert Lewis. *Dr. John Wilson*: John Macurdy. *Officer Harry Murphy*: Dan Merriman. *City Marshall James Henry*: George Del Monte. *Fred Cullen*: William Zachariasen, William Saxon (alt.). *First Nursemaid*: Mary LeSawyer. *Second Nursemaid*: Greta Wolff.

Policemen, Milkman, Old Clothes Man, Music Pupil, Interne, Ambulance Driver, Married Couple, Passersby, Neighbors, Children, etc.: New York City Opera Chorus.

---

[11]Originally produced in New York 5 November 1958 at the Martin Beck Theatre for 5 performances. For Synopsis of Scenes, see original 1958 production. Performed as an opera; no individual musical numbers listed in program.
[12]Originally produced in New York 9 January 1947 at the Adelphi Theatre for 148 performances. For Synopsis of Scenes and Musical Numbers, see original 1947 production.

THE DEVIL AND DANIEL WEBSTER

1959.09

A Revival of the Musical Folk Play (Opera) in One Act[13]. Book and lyrics by Stephen Vincent Benét. Adapted from his own short story of the Faust legend. Music by Douglas Moore. Staged by John Houseman. Conductor, Max Goberman. Scenery and costumes by Rouben Ter-Arutunian. Choreography by Robert Joffrey. Produced by the New York City Opera. Opened 5 April 1959 at the New York City Center amd closed 26 (matinee) April 1959 after 3 performances in repertory. (Preceded by the opera "The Scarf," Music by Lee Hoiby, Libretto by Harry Duncan.)

CAST (in order of appearance): *Jabez Stone*: Joshua Hecht. *Mary Stone*: ADELAIDE BISHOP. *Daniel Webster*: WALTER CASSEL. *A Fiddler*: Keith Kaldenberg. *Mr. Scratch*: NORMAN KELLEY. *Justice Hathorne*: Emile Renan. *Clerk of the Court*: Arthur Newman.

Jury of the Dead: Walter Butler: Chester Ludgin. *Blackbeard Teach*: George Del Monte. *King Philip*: Arnold Voketaitis. *Simon Girty*: Grant Williams. *Others*: Jack De Lon, Howard Fried, Andrew Frierson, Paul Huddleston, John Macurdy, Dan Merriman, William Nahr, Harry Theard.

REGINA

1959.10

A Revival of the Musical Drama (Opera) in Three Acts, Prologue and 4 Scenes[14]. Written and composed by Marc Blitzstein. Based on the play "The Little Foxes" by Lillian Hellman. Staged by Herman Shumlin. Conducted by Samuel Krachmalnick. Scenery by Howard Bay. Costumes designed by Aline Bernstein. Choreography by Robert Joffrey. (Orchestrations by Marc Blitzstein.) Produced by the New York City Opera Company. Opened 19 April 1959 at the New York City Center and closed 1 May 1959 after 2 performances in repertory.

CAST (in order of appearance): *Addie*, Cook: CAROL BRICE. *Cal*, Butler: ANDREW FRIERSON. *Alexandra Giddens*, Regina's Daughter: MARGOT MOSER. *Birdie Hubbard*, Oscar's Wife: ELISABETH CARRON. *Oscar Hubbard*, Regina's Brother: EMILE RENAN. *Leo Hubbard*, Oscar's Son: LOREN DRISCOLL. *Regina Giddens*: BRENDA LEWIS. *William Marshall*: ERNEST McCHESNEY. *Benjamin Hubbard*, Regina's Brother: GEORGE IRVING. *Horace Giddens*, Regina's Husband: JOSHUA HECHT. *Manders*: Edson Hoel. *Servants, Townspeople, Field Workers*: New York City Opera Chorus.

DESTRY RIDES AGAIN

1959.11

A Musical in Two Acts, 12 Scenes. Book by Leonard Gershe. Based on the story (novel of the same name) by Max Brand. Music and lyrics by Harold Rome. (Settings) Designed by Oliver Smith. Costumes by Alvin Colt. Lighting by Jean Rosenthal. Musical direction and vocal arrangements by Lehman Engel. Orchestrations by Philip J. Lang. Dance music arranged by Genevieve Pitot. Entire production directed and choreographed by Michael Kidd. Produced by David Merrick in association with Max Brown. Opened 23 April 1959 at the Imperial Theatre and closed 18 June 1960 after 473 performances.

CAST (in order of appearance): *Prologue*: Don Crabtree, David London, Lanier Davis, Nolan Van Way. *Bartender*: Ray Mason. *Frenchy*: DOLORES GRAY. *Wash*: JACK PRINCE. *Sheriff Keogh*: Oran Osburn. *Kent's Gang (3)*: *Gyp Watson*: MARC BREAUX. *Bugs Watson*: SWEN SWENSON. *Rockwell*: GEORGE REEDER. *Mayor Slade*: DON McHENRY. *Claggett*: Don Crabtree. *Kent*: SCOTT BRADY. *Chloe*: LIBI STAIGER. *Rose Lovejoy*: Elizabeth Watts. *Jack Tyndall*: Nolan Van Way. *Destry*: ANDY GRIFFITH. *Stage Driver*: Chad Block. *Ming Li*: Reiko Sato. *Mrs. Claggett*: May Muth. *Bailey*: Ray Mason. *Clara*: ROSETTA LE NOIRE. *Dimples*: Sharon Shore.

Rose Lovejoy Girls: Lynne Broadbent, Joan Broderick, Shelah Hackett, Reiko Sato, Sharon Shore, Carol Stevens. *Frenchy's Girls*: Shelley Chaplan, Lillian D'Honau, Maureen Hopkins, Betty Jenkins, Jillana, Andrina Miller, Shirley Nelson, Adriane Rogers, Carol Warner. *Cowboys*: Jack Beaber, Chad Block, Mel Davidson, Al Lanti, Ken Malone, Frank Pietri, John Ray, Larry Roquemore, Merritt Thompson. *Townspeople*: Maria Graziano, Betty Kent, Sheila Mathews, May Muth, Don Crabtree, Lanier Davis, Ralph Farnworth, David London, Ray Mason, Oran Osburn, Nolan Van Way.

Act 1, Scene 1: The Last Chance Saloon in the western town of Bottleneck, just before the turn of the century. *Scene 2*: The Last Chance Saloon. *Scene 3*: A Street. *Scene 4*: A

Corral. *Scene 5*: French's House. *Scene 6*: Paradise Alley. *Scene 7*: A Road in Bottleneck. *Scene 8*: The Last Chance Saloon.

Act 2, Scene 1: Outside the Jailhouse. *Scene 2*: Frenchy's House. *Scene 3*: The Sheriff's Office. *Scene 4*: The Last Chance Saloon.

ACT 1
Scene 1
"Bottleneck"
Patrons of the Last Chance Saloon
"Ladies"
D. Gray, Girls
"Hoop-de-Dingle"
J. Prince, Patrons of the Saloon
Scene 2
"Tomorrow Morning"
A. Griffith
Scene 3
"Ballad of the Gun"
A. Griffith, J. Prince
Scene 4
"The Social"
Townspeople of Bottleneck, S. Swenson, G. Reeder
Scene 5
"I Know Your Kind"
D. Gray
"I Hate Him"
D. Gray
Scene 6
"(Rose Lovejoy of) Paradise Alley"
Cowboys, Rose Lovejoy Girls
"Anyone Would Love You"
A. Griifth, D. Gray
Scene 7
"Once Knew a Fella"
A. Griffith, J. Prince, Friends
Scene 8
"Every Once in a While"
M. Breaux, S. Swenson, G. Reeder, Cowboys, Saloon Girls
"Fair Warning"
D. Gray
ACT 2
Scene 1
"Are You Ready, Gyp Watson?"
(D. Gray,) Friends of Gyp Watson (Ensemble)
"Not Guilty"
The Jury (Male Ensemble)
"Only Time Will Tell"
A. Griffith
"Respectability"[15]
E. Watts, Girls
Scene 2
"That Ring on the Finger"
D. Gray, Girls
"Once Knew a Fella" (reprise)
A. Griffith, D. Gray
"I Say Hello"
D. Gray
Scene 4
(Finale: "Ballad of the Gun" reprise)
(Chorus)

THE NERVOUS SET

1959.12

A Musical in Two Acts, 10 Scenes. Book by Jay Landesman and Theodore J. Flicker. Based on the novel of the same name by Jay Landesman. Music by Tommy Wolf. Lyrics by Fran Landesman. Directed by Theodore J. Flicker. Settings and lighting by Paul Morrison. Costumes by Theoni Vachlioti Aldredge. Music arrangements and direction by Tommy Wolf. Produced by Robert Lantz. Opened 12 May 1959 at the Henry Miller's Theatre and closed 30 May 1959 after 23 performances.

---

[13]Originally produced in New York 18 May 1939 at the Martin Beck Theatre for 6 performances. For Synopsis of Scene, see original 1939 production; no individual musical numbers listed.

[14]Originally produced in New York 31 October 1949 at the 46th Street Theatre for 56 performances. For Synopsis of Scenes and Musical Numbers, see original 1949 production. For this revival, an intermission was added between Act 1, Scenes 1 and 2. The Jazz Band was totally eliminated.

[15]Dropped for national tour.

CAST (in order of appearance): *Bunny Carwell:* LARRY HAGMAN. *Brad:* RICHARD HAYES, Don Heller (alt.). *Danny:* THOMAS ALDREDGE. *Jan:* TANI SEITZ. *Yogi:* DEL CLOSE. *A Customer:* Barry Primus. *Landlady:* Florence Gassner. *Joan:* Arlene Corwin. *Sari Shaw:* Janice Meshkoff. *Danny's Girl:* Elvira Pallas. *Max the Millionaire:* GERALD HIKEN. *Henry Calhoun:* David Sallade. *Katherine Sloan-Wittiker:* Florence Gassner. *Irving:* Don Heller. *Tony:* Lee Lindsey. *Rejected Boy:* Zale Kessler.

Act 1, Scene 1: Sunday Afternoon, late summer. Washington Square Park, New York City. Now. *Scene 2:* The following spring, Brad and Jan's apartment on Perry Street. *Scene 3:* That weekend. *Scene 4:* Jan's parents' home, Fairfield County, Connecticut. *Scene 5:* Later. The bottom of an unfilled pool. *Scene 5:* Later. Inside the house again. *Scene 6:* The next weekend. Bummy Carwell's apartment on Avenue A.

Act 2, Scene 1: A few days later. Brad and Jan's apartment. *Scene 2:* Later the same day. The Melancholy Pigeon. *Scene 3:* That evening. Katherine Sloan Wittiker's apartment on Sutton Place. *Scene 4:* Later at Brad and Jan's apartment.

ACT 1

"Man, We're Beat"
(The Company)
"New York"
(R. Hayes, T. Aldredge, T. Seitz)
"What's to Lose"
(T. Seitz, R. Hayes)
"Stars Have Blown My Way"
(T. Seitz, R. Hayes)
"Fun Life"
(R. Hayes)
"How Do You Like Your Love?"
(D. Close)
"Party Song"
(The Company)
"If I Could Put You in a Song"
"Night People"
(R. Hayes, T. Seitz)
"I've Got a Lot to Learn About Life"
(T. Seitz)
"Rejection"
(T. Aldredge, Company)
"The Ballad of the Sad Young Men"
(T. Seitz)

ACT 2

"A Country Gentleman"
(R. Hayes, T. Seitz)
"Max the Millionaire"
(G. Hiken, R. Hayes, D. Close, T. Aldredge)
"Laugh, I Thought I'd Die"
(R. Hayes)
"Travel the Road of Love"
(L. Hagman, Company)
("Fun Life" reprise)
(The Company)

1959.13 GYPSY

A Musical in Two Acts, 17 Scenes. Book by Arthur Laurents. Suggested by the memoirs (of the same name) by Gypsy Rose Lee. Music by Jule Styne. Lyrics by Stephen Sondheim. Settings and lighting by Jo Mielziner. Costumes designed by Raoul Pène du Bois. Entire production directed and choreographed by Jerome Robbins. Musical direction by Milton Rosenstock. Orchestrations by Sid Ramin with Robert Ginzler. Dance music arranged by John Kander. Additional dance music by Betty Walberg. Produced by David Merrick and Leland Hayward. Opened 21 May 1959 at the Broadway Theatre, vacationed from 11 July 1960 and resumed 13 August 1960 at the Imperial Theatre, and closed 25 March 1961 after 702 performances.

CAST (in order of appearance): *Uncle Jocko:* Mort Marshall. *George:* Willy Sumner. *Arnold and His Guitar:* John Borden. *Balloon Girl:* Jody Lane. *Baby Louise:* Karen Moore. *Baby June:* JACQUELINE MAYRO. *Rose:* ETHEL MERMAN. *Pop:* Erv Harmon. *Newsboys:* Bobby Brownell, Gene Castle, Steve Curry, Billy Harris. *Weber:* Joe Silver. *Herbie:* JACK KLUGMAN. *Louise:* SANDRA CHURCH. *June:* Lane Bradbury. *Tulsa:* PAUL WALLACE. *Yonkers:* David Winters. *Angie:* Ian Tucker. *L.A.:* Michael Parks. *Kringelein:* Loney Lewis. *Mr. Goldstone:* Mort Marshall. *Farm Boys:* Marvin Arnold, Ricky Coll, Don Emmons, Michael Parks, Ian Tucker, Paul Wallace, David Winters. *Miss Cratchitt:* Peg Murray. *Hollywood Blondes (6): Agnes:* Marilyn Cooper. *Marjorie May:* Patsy Bruder. *Dolores:* Marilyn D'Honau. *Thelma:* Marle Letowt. *Edna:*

Joan Petlak. *Gail:* Imelda de Martin. *Pastey:* Richard Porter. *Tessie Tura:* MARIA KARNILOVA. *Mazeppa:* FAITH DANE. *Cigar:* Loney Lewis. *Electra:* CHOTZI FOLEY. *Showgirls:* Kathryn Albertson, Gloria Kristy, Denise McLaglen, Barbara London, Theda Nelson, Carroll Jo Towers, Marie Wallace. *Maid:* Marsha Rivers. *Phil:* Joe Silver. *Bougeron-Cochon:* George Zima. *Cow* Willy Sumner, George Zima.

Act 1, Scene 1: The Stage of a Vaudeville Theatre in Seattle, early 1920s. *Scene 2:* The Kitchen of a frame house, shortly afterward. *Scene 3:* A car enroute from Seattle to Los Angeles. *Scene 4:* Backstage of a Vaudeville Theatre in Los Angeles. *Scene 5:* The Stage of the Vaudeville Theatre in Los Angeles, then Akron, Ohio. *Scene 6:* Two plaster-cracked hotel rooms in Akron, Ohio. *Scene 7:* A Chinese Restaurant in New York City. *Scene 8:* The Stage of Grantziger's Palace Theatre, New York City. *Scene 9:* Grantziger's Office. *Scene 10:* A theatre alley outside the stage door of a vaudeville theatre in Buffalo. *Scene 11:* A railroad platform in Omaha, Nebraska.

Act 2, Scene 1: In the Texas desert. Late afternoon. *Scene 2:* Backstage of a Burlesque Theatre in Wichita, Kansas. *Scene 3:* A backstage corridor. *Scene 4:* The dressing room and corridor. Wichita, then Detroit, Philadelphia, New York City. *Scene 5:* A dressing room backstage at Minsky's Burlesque, New York City. *Scene 6:* An empty stage.

ACT 1

Scene 1
"May We Entertain You"
J. Mayro, K. Moore
Scene 2
"Some People"
E. Merman
Scene 3
Traveling
Scene 4
"Small World"
E. Merman, J. Klugman
Scene 5
Baby June and her Newsboys
(J. Mayro, B. Brownell, G. Castle, S. Curry, B. Harris)
Scene 6
"Mr. Goldstone, I Love You"
E. Merman, (Boys)
"Little Lamb"
S. Church
Scene 7
"You'll Never Get Away from Me"
E. Merman, J. Klugman
Scene 8
Dainty June and her Farmboys
(L. Bradbury, S. Church, M. Arnold,
R. Coll, D. Emmons, M. Parks, I. Tucker, P. Wallace, D. Winters)
Scene 9
"If Momma Was Married"
S. Church, L. Bradbury
Scene 10
"All I Need Is the Girl"
P. Wallace, S. Church
Scene 11
"Everything's Coming Up Roses"
E. Merman

ACT 2

Scene 1
"Madame Rose's Toreadorables"
S. Church, Toreadorables
"Together, Wherever We Go"
E. Merman, S. Church, J. Klugman
Scene 2
"You Gotta Have a Gimmick"
M. Karnilova, F. Dane, C. Foley
Scene 4
"Small World" (reprise)
E. Merman
"Let Me Entertain You"
S. Church, Company
Scene 6
"Rose's Turn"
E. Merman

1959–1960 SEASON

Chita Rivera in BYE BYE BIRDIE (Photo: Friedman-Abeles)
Billy Rose Theatre Collection, New York Public Library for the Performing Arts

1959–1960 SEASON

1959.14   BILLY BARNES REVUE

A Musical Revue in Two Acts, 28 Scenes[1]. Music and lyrics by Billy Barnes. Sketches and dialogue by Bob Rodgers. (Settings) Designed by Glenn Holse. Musical director, Billy Barnes. Lighting by Peggy Clark. Costumes supervised by Berman Costume Company. Associate musical director, Armin Hoffman. New York costume supervsion by Peggy Morrison. At the Pianos, Billy Barnes and Armin Hoffman. Produced by George Eckstein in association with Bob Reese. Opened 4 August 1959 at the John Golden Theatre, moved 28 September 1959 to the Lyceum Theatre and closed 17 October 1959 after 87 performances. Transferred Off-Broadway 20 October 1959 to the Carnegie Hall Playhouse and closed 29 November 1959 after 48 additional performances. Total performances : 199.

CAST: JOYCE JAMESON, BERT CONVY, PATTI REGAN, KEN BERRY, ANN GUILBERT, BOB RODGERS, JACKIE JOSEPH, LEN WEINRIB.

ACT 1

Scene 1

"Do a Revue!"
> The Company

Scene 2

"Where Are Your Children?"
> K. Berry, B. Convy, J. Joseph, A. Guilbert, P. Regan, L. Weinrib

Scene 3

"Las Vegas"
> *Herman*: B. Rodgers. *Girl with Hat*: A. Guilbert. *Tanya*: J. Jameson. *Her Fellas*: B. Convy, K. Berry.

Scene 4

Medic
> *Surgeon*: L. Weinrib. *Staff*: A. Guilbert, P. Regan.

Scene 5

"Foolin' Ourselves"
> B. Convy, K. Berry

Scene 6

Safari a la Marilyn
> *Papa*: L. Weinrib. *Arthur*: B. Rodgers. *Marilyn*: J. Jameson.

Scene 7

The Pembrooke Story
> *Arthur*: K. Berry. *Edythe*: A. Guilbert. *Miss O'Brien*: J. Joseph. *John*: B. Convy. *Peter*: L. Weinrib.

Scene 8

"Whatever" (Whatever Happened? No. 1)
> P. Regan

Scene 9

"City of the Angels"
> *Lilly*: J. Jameson. *Lolly*: A. Guilbert. *Dolly*: J. Joseph.

Scene 10

"Listen to the Beat!"
> *Host*: L. Weinrib. *Jack*: K. Berry. *Mary Lou*: A. Guilbert. *Dean*: B. Convy. *Sarah*: J. Jameson. *The Prophet*: L. Weinrib. *Beatniks*: B. Rodgers, P. Regan, J. Joseph.

Scene 11

Home in Mississippi (Parody of "Cat on a Hot Tin Roof")
> *Maggie*: P. Regan. *Big Daddy*: L. Weinrib. *Big Mama*: A. Guilbert. *Brick*: B. Rodgers. *No-neck Monsters*: Themselves.

Scene 12

"Tyler My Boy"
> B. Convy

Scene 13

"Whatever Happened?" (No. 2)
> P. Regan

---

[1]Originally produced Off-Broadway 9 June 1959 at the York Playhouse for 64 performances.

Scene 14

The Thirties
> *Narrator*: B. Rodgers. *Peddler*: P. Regan. *Fred*: K. Berry. *Ginger*: J. Jameson. *Forgotten Woman*: A. Guilbert. *Forgotten Man*: L. Weinrib. *Shirley*: J. Jameson. *Daddy*: B. Convy. *Step-Mommy*: P. Regan. *Gold Digger*: J. Joseph. *J. N.*: L. Weinrib. *Sam*: K. Berry. *Ruby*: A. Guilbert. *Dick*: B. Convy. *Jeanette*: J. Jameson. *Nelson*: B. Rodgers.

ACT 2

Scene 1

A Dissertation on Transportation, or, It All Started With the Wheel
> *Principal*: B. Rodgers. *P. T. A. President*: J. Jameson. *Teacher*: P. Regan. *Sweet Little Girl*: J. Joseph. *Sour Little Girl*: A. Guilbert. *Teacher's Pet*: K. Berry. *Bully*: L. Weinrib. *Bert Convy*: B. Convy.

Scene 2

"The Fights"
> *Introduced by* A. Guilbert. *Shirley*: J. Jameson. *Harry*: B. Rodgers.

Scene 3

The Vamp and Friends
> *Vamp*: A. Guilbert. *Champ*: K. Berry. *Tramp*: P. Regan. *Camp*: L Weinrib.

Scene 4

"Blocks"
> *Husband*: B. Rodgers. *Wife*: J. Joseph.

Scene 5

Hellahahana
> *Natives*: B. Convy, K. Berry, J. Jameson, L. Weinrib, J. Joseph. *Turista*: A. Guilbert.

Scene 6

"Whatever Happened to" (No. 3)
> P. Regan

Scene 7

World at Large
> *Moderator*: B. Convy.

Scene 8

World at Large No. 1
> *Rosabelle Haley*: J. Jameson. *Warden*: L. Weinrib. *Matron*: A. Guilbert.

Scene 9

Station Break
> *Fire Prevention Queen*: P. Regan.

Scene 10

World at Large No.2
> *Mr. Lernstein*: B. Rodgers. *Choral Group*: Choral Group (The Company).

Scene 11

World at Large Preview
> *Oed*: K. Berry. *Jo*: P. Regan.

Scene 12

"(Have I Stayed) Too Long at the Fair"
> J. Jameson

Scene 13

"One of Those Days"
> *Poor Soul*: L. Weinrib. *Ads*: B. Convy, J. Joseph, K. Berry.

Scene 14

Finale
> The Company

1959.15   AN EVENING WITH YVES MONTAND

A Solo Performance in Two Acts. Staged and lighted by Yves Montand. Produced by Norman Granz in association with Jacques Canetti. Opened 22 September 1959 at the Henry Miller's Theatre, moved 12 October 1959 to the Longacre Theatre and closed 31 October 1959 after 42 performances.

CAST: YVES MONTAND. *Piano*: Bob Castella. *Accordionist*: Nick Perito. *Guitar*: Jim Hall. *Clarinet*: Jimmy Guiffre. *Bass*: Al Hall. *Drums*: Charles Persip. *Trombone*: Billy Byers.

ACT 1

"Les Amis" (The Friends)
> (Music by Bob Castella. Lyrics by Francis Lemarque.)

"La Fete A Loulou" (The Birthday of Loulou)
   (*Music by* Bob Castella. *Lyrics by* Rene Rouzaud.)
"Une Demoiselle Sur Une Balancoire" (A Young Lady in a Swing)
   (*Music by* Mireille. *Lyrics by* Jean Nohain.)
"Ma Mome, Ma P'tite Mome"
   (*Music by* Marguerite Monnot. *Lyrics by* Henri Contet.)
"Sir Godfrey"
   (*Music by* Georges Liferman. *Lyrics by* Jacques Mareuil.)
"Le Carosse" (The Golden Chariot)
   (*Music by* Mireille. *Lyrics by* Henri Contet.)
"Luna-Park"
   (*Music by* Loulou Gaste. *Lyrics by* Jean Guigo.)
"Les Feuilles Mortes" (Autumn Leaves)
   (*Music by* Joseph Cosma. *Lyrics by* Jacques Prevert.)
"Les Grands Boulevards"
   (*Music by* Norbert Glanzberg. *Lyrics by* Jacques Plante.)
"Flamenco De Paris"
   (*Music and Lyrics by* Leo Ferré.)
"Un Garcon Dansait" (A Boy Was Dancing)
   (*Music by* Georges Liferman. *Lyrics by* Jacques Mareuil.)

ACT 2
"Les Petits Riens" (The Little Daily Nothings)
   (*Music and Lyrics by* Francis Lemarque.)
"Simple Comme Bonjour" (Simple as Bonjour)
   (*Music by* Henri Crolla. *Lyrics by* Jacques Prevert.)
"Mais Qu'est-ce que J'ai?" (What's Wrong With Me?)
   (*Music by* Henri Betti. *Lyrics by* Edith Piaf.)
"La Marie-Vision" (Marie's Mink Coat)
   (*Music by* Marc Henyral. *Lyrics by* Roger Varanay.)
"Planter Cafe"
   (*Music by* Emil Stern. *Lyrics by* Eddy Marnay.)
"Le Chef D'Orchestre Est Amoureux" (The Conductor Is in Love)
   (*Music by* Georges Liferman. *Lyrics by* Jacques Mareuil.)
"A Paris"
   (*Music and Lyrics by* Francis Lemarque.)
"Il Fait Des . . . " (Le Fanatique de Jazz)
   (*Music by* Edouard Chekle. *Lyrics by* Edith Piaf.)
"Mon Menage a Moi"
   (*Music by* Norbert Glanzberg. *Lyrics by* Jean Constantin.)

1959.16   DIE FLEDERMAUS

A Revival of the Operetta in Three Acts[2]. (Original Libretto by Carl Haffner and Richard Genée. Lyrics by Richard Genée. Based on the comedy "Le Réveillon" by Henri Meilhac and Ludovic Halévy.) English libretto by Ruth and Thomas Martin. Music by Johann Strauss. Staged by Michael Pollock. Conducted by Julius Rudel. Produced by the New York City Opera. Opened 26 September 1959 at the New York City Center and closed 24 October 1959 after 3 performances in repertory.

CAST: *Rosalinda:* BEVERLY BOWER. *Eisenstein:* ERNEST McCHESNEY. *Adele:* JACQUELYNNE MOODY. *Sally:* Jennie Andrea. *Alfred:* Thomas Hayward. *Prince Orlofsky:* JACK HARROLD. *Falke:* CHESTER LUDGIN. *Frank:* PAUL UKENA. *Frosch:* Philip Bruns. *Blind:* Grant Williams. *Solo Dancers:* Diane Consoer, Jonathan Watts. *Ensemble:* New York City Opera Chorus.

1959.17   STREET SCENE

A Revival of the American Opera (Dramatic Musical) in Two Acts, 3 Scenes[3]. Book by Elmer Rice from his play of the same name. Music by Kurt Weill. Lyrics by Langston Hughes. Staged by Herbert Machiz. Conducted by Samuel Krachmalnick. Scenery and Costumes by Paul

Sylbert. Children's Number supervised by Robert Joffrey. Chorus Master, Gino Smart. (Orchestrations by Kurt Weill.) Produced by the New York City Opera Company. Opened 27 September 1959 at the New York City Center and closed 15 October 1959 after 2 performances in repertory Reopened 13 February 1960 at the New York City Center and closed 19 February 1960 after 3 additional performances. Total this season: 5 performances.

CAST (in order of appearance): *Abraham Kaplan:* Grant Williams. *Greta Fiorentino:* Dolores Mari. *Carl Olsen:* Arnold Voketaitis. *Emma Jones:* RUTH KOBART. *Olga Olsen:* Beatrice Krebs. *Shirley Kaplan:* Florence Anglin. *Mrs. Davis:* Marie Louise. *Henry Davis:* Andrew Frierson. *Willie Maurrant:* Michael Mann. *Anna Maurrant:* ELISABETH CARRON. *Sam Kaplan:* FRANK PORETTA. *Daniel Buchanan:* Keith Kaldenberg. *Frank Maurrant:* WILLIAM CHAPMAN. *George Jones:* Chester Ludgin. *Steve Sankey:* Arthur Storch. *Lippo Fiorentino:* JACK HARROLD. *Jennie Hildebrand:* Nancy Dussault. *Second Graduate:* Sylvia De Van. *Third Graduate:* Jennie Andrea. *Mrs. Hildebrand:* Sophia Steffan. *Charlie Hildebrand:* Richard Clemence. *Mary Hildebrand:* Lynn Taussig. *Grace Davis:* Sharon Williams. *Rose Maurrant:* HELENA SCOTT, Joy Clements (alt.). *Harry Easter:* Seth Riggs. *Mae Jones:* Sondra Lee. *Dick McGann:* Richard Tone. *Vincent Jones:* Albert Lewis. *Dr. John Wilson:* John Macurdy. *Officer Harry Murphy:* Dan Merriman. *City Marshall James Henry:* George Del Monte. *Fred Cullen:* William Zakariasen. *First Nursemaid:* Mary LeSawyer. *Second Nursemaid:* Rita Metzger.
   Policemen, Milkman, Old Clothes Man, Music Pupil, Interne, Ambulance Driver, Married Couple, Passersby, Neighbors, Children, etc.: New York City Opera Chorus.

1959.18   THE MIKADO, or The Town of Titipu

A Revival of the Comic Opera in Two Acts[4]. Libretto by William S. Gilbert. Music by Arthur Sullivan. Staged by Dorothy Raedler. Scenic and lighting design by Donald Oenslager. Costume design by Patton Campbell. Conducted by Robert Irving. Produced by the New York City Opera. Opened 1 October 1959 at the New York City Center and closed 1 November 1959 after 4 performances in repertory.

CAST: *The Mikado of Japan:* GEORGE GAYNES. *Nanki-Poo,* his son, disguised as a wandering minstrel in love with Yum-Yum: FRANK PORETTA. *Ko-Ko,* Lord High Executioner of Titipu: NORMAN KELLEY. *Pooh-Bah,* Lord High Everything Else: HERBERT BEATTIE. *Pish-Tush,* a Noble Lord: Robert Kerns. *Yum-Yum, Pitti-Sing, Peep-Bo,* three sisters, wards of Ko-Ko: BARBARA MEISTER, NANCY DUSSAULT, SOPHIA STEFFAN. *Katisha:* CLARAMAE TURNER. *Chorus of School Girls, Nobles, Guards and Coolies:* New York City Opera Chorus.

1959.19   HAPPY TOWN

A Musical Comedy in Two Acts, 23 Scenes. Book adapted (from an original by Harry M. Haldane) by Max Hampton. Music by Gordon Duffy. Lyrics by Harry M. Haldane. Additional Music and lyrics by Paul Nassau. Directed by Allan A. Buckhantz. Choreography by Lee Scott. Settings By Curt Nations. Costumes by J. Michael Travis. Lighting by Paul Morrison. Musical direction and vocal arrangements by Samuel Krachmalnick. Orchestrations by Nicholas Carras. Associate director, Ernest Sarracino. Produced by b & m Productions. Opened 7 October 1959 at the 54th Street Theatre and closed 10 October 1959 after 5 performances.

CAST (in order of appearance): *Lint Richards:* George Blackwell. *Bub Richards:* Bruce MacKay. *Sib Richards:* George Ives. *Glenn Richards:* Michael Kermoyan. *Janice Dawson:* CINDY ROBBINS. *Craig Richards:* BIFF McGUIRE. *Clint Yoder:* TOM WILLIAMS. *Bobbie Jo Hartman:* Alice Clift. *Molly Bixby:* LEE VENORA. *Judge Ed Bixby:* DICK ELLIOTT. *Jim Jo Jamieson:* Frederic Tozere. *A Reporter:* Rico Froehlich. *Pert Hawkins:* RALPH DUNN. *Claney:* Charles May. *Doc Spooner:* WILL WRIGHT. *Mrs. Hawkins:* Liz Pritchett. *Reverend Hornblow:* EDWIN STEFFE. *Mult:* Roy Wilson. *Luke Granger:* Chester Watson. (*Susan Grey:* Leigh Evans.)
   Townswomen of Back-A-Heap: Diana Baron, Lillian Bozinoff, Alice Clift, Colleen Corkrey, Dori Davis, Isabelle Farrell, Laurie Franks, Rita Golden, Connie Greco, Marian Haraldson, Marilyn Harris, Judy Keirn, Maxine Kent, Patricia Mount, Robbi Palmer. *Townsmen of Back-A-Heap:* John Buwen, Bob Daley, Rico Froehlich, James Gannon, George Jack, Danny Joel, Charles May, Jim McAnany, Nixon Miller, Howard Parker, Tom Pocoroba, Stewart Rose, Roy Wilson.

---

[2]First English Language Production in New York 16 March 1885 at the Casino Theatre for 42 performances. First New York production of this adaptation 20 December 1950 at the Metropolitan Opera House. For Synopsis of Scenes and Musical Numbers, see May 1954 revival.
[3]Originally produced in New York 9 January 1947 at the Adelphi Theatre for 148 performances. For Synopsis of Scenes and Musical Numbers, see original 1947 production.

---

[4]First presented in New York 20 July, 10-29 August 1885 at the Union Square and People's Theatres for 22 performances. First authorized production presented 19 August 1885 at the Fifth Avenue Theatre by Richard D'Oyly Carte for 250 performances. For Synopsis of Scenes and Musical Numbers, see 19 August 1885 D'Oyly Carte production.

Act 1, Scene 1: A Private Office in the T.B.A. Exchange. *Scene 2*: Back-A-Heap, Texas. The Main Street. A few hours later. *Scene 3*: Bixby's Super Market. A little later. *Scene 4*: The Main Street. Immediately following. *Scene 5*: Bixby's Super Market. Immediately following. *Scene 6*: The T.B.A. Office. A little later. *Scene 7*: The Main Street. That evening. *Scene 8*: Back-A-Heap Town Hall. Immediately following. *Scene 9*: The Main Street. Immediately following. *Scene 10*: Fairgrounds. Next morning. *Scene 11*: The T.B.A. Office. *Scene 12*: The Prairie.

Act 2, Scene 1: The Main Street. Late the next day. *Scene 2*: E. Street. Immediately following. *Scene 3*: The T.B.A. Office. At about the same time. *Scene 4*: Fairgrounds. Two weeks later. *Scene 5*: A Street. Immediately following. *Scene 6*: The Main Street. *Scene 7*: T.B.A. Office. *Scene 8*: Main Street, Later. *Scene 9*: Bixby's Super Market. *Scene 10*: A Street, Immediately following. *Scene 11*: Town Hall, later.

ACT 1

Scene 1

"It Isn't Easy"
C. Robbins, M. Kermoyan, B. MacKay, G. Blackwell, G. Ives

Scene 2

"Celebration!"
Townspeople

"Something Special"
B. McGuire

Scene 4

"The Legend of Black-Eyed Susan Grey" (Dance)
L. Evans, Townspeople

"Opportunity!"
B. McGuire, E. Steffe, L. Pritchett, Townspeople

"As Busy As Anyone Can Be"
T. Williams, Girls

"Heaven Protect Me!"
C. Robbins, Girls

Scene 7

"I Feel Like a Brother to You"
B. McGuire, L. Venora

Scene 8

"Hoedown!"
Townspeople

Scene 9

"I Am What I Am!"
B. McGuire, L. Venora

"The Beat of a Heart"
L. Venora

"Mean"
C. Robbins

Scene 11

"It Isn't Easy" (reprise)
M. Kermoyan, B. MacKay, G. Blackwell, G. Ives

Scene 12

"When the Time Is Right"
E. Steffe

ACT 2

Scene 1

"Pick-Me-Up!"
Townspeople

Scene 2

"I'm Stuck With Love"
L. Venora

Scene 3

"It Isn't Easy" (reprise)
M. Kermoyan, B. MacKay, G. Blackwell, G. Ives

Scene 4

"Nothing in Common"
C. Robbins, L. Venora

"Talkin' 'Bout You"
C. Robbins, T. Williams, Townspeople

"Something Special" (reprise)
B. McGuire, L. Venora

Scene 8

"Y' Can't Win"
C. Robbins

Scene 11

"Opportunity" (reprise)
Entire Company

AT THE DROP OF A HAT

1959.20

An After Dinner Farrago (Intimate Revue) in Two Acts. Music by Donald Swann. Words by Michael Flanders. Produced by Alexander H. Cohen in association with Joseph I. Levine. Lighting by Ralph Alswang. Frontcloth by Al Hirschfeld. Opened 8 October 1959 at the John Golden Theatre and closed 14 May 1960 after 216 performances.

CAST: MICHAEL FLANDERS, DONALD SWANN.

ACT 1

"Song of Reproduction"

"The Hog Beneath the Skin" (The Warthog)

"A Transport of Delight"

"The Youth of the Heart"
Lyrics by Sydney Carter.)

"Greensleeves"

"The Wompom"

"Sea Fever"

"A Gnu"

"Judgement of Paris"

Songs for Our Time: ("Philological Waltz," "Satellite Moon," "A Happy Song")

ACT 2

"A Song of the Weather"

"The Reluctant Cannibal"

"In the Bath"

"Design for Living"

"Tried by the Centre Court"

"Misalliance"

"Kokoraki" (A Greek Song)

"Madeira, M' Dear?"

"The Hippopotamus"

THE MERRY WIDOW

1959.21

A Revival of the Operetta in Three Acts[5]. Music by Franz Lehár. Original German libretto (Die Lustige Witwe) by Victor Léon and Leo Stein after "L'Attaché d'Ambassade." English libretto by Adrian Ross. Staged by Michael Pollock. Conducted by Julius Rudel. Produced by the New York City Opera. Opened 10 October 1959 at the New York City Center and closed 24 October 1958 after 4 performances in repertory.

CAST: *Sonia*: BEVERLY BOWER. *Prince Danillo*: JOHN REARDON. *Baron Popoff*: JACK HARROLD. *Natalie*: Helena Scott. *De Jolidon*: Frank Poretta. *Marquis de Cascada*: Arnold Voketaitis. *St. Brioche*: Chester Ludgin. *Admiral Khadja*: Dan Merriman. *Mme. Khadja*: Dorothy White. *General Novikovich*: Grant Williams. *Mme. Novikovich*: Lynda Jordan. *Nish*: Roy Stuart. *Lo-Lo*: Lynn Starling. *Solo Dancers*: Dianne Consoer, Jonathan Watts. *Ensemble*: New York City Opera Chorus.

TAKE ME ALONG

1959.22

A Musical in Two Acts, 13 Scenes. Book by Joseph Stein and Robert Russell. Based on the play "Ah, Wilderness!" by Eugene O'Neill. Music and lyrics by Bob Merrill. Dances and musical numbers Staged by Onna White. Production (Settings) sesigned by Oliver Smith. Costumes by Miles White. Lighting by Jean Rosenthal. Musical direction and vocal arrangements by Lehman Engel. Ballet and incidental music by Laurence Rosenthal.

[5]Originally produced in New York 21 October 1907 at the New Amsterdam Theatre for 416 performances. For Synopsis of Scenes and Musical Numbers, see original 1907 production.

Orchestrations by Philip J. Lang. Directed by Peter Glenville. Produced by David Merrick. Opened 22 October 1959 at the Sam S. Shubert Theatre and closed 17 December 1960 after 448 performances.

CAST (in order of appearance): *Nat Miller*: WALTER PIDGEON. *Mildred Miller*: Zeme North. *Art Miller*: James Cresson. *Tommy Miller*: Luke Halpin. *Essie Miller*: UNA MERKEL. *Lily*: EILEEN HERLIE. *Richard Miller*: ROBERT MORSE. *Muriel Macomber*: Susan Luckey. *Dave Macomber*: Fred Miller. *Sid*: JACKIE GLEASON. *Wint*: Peter Conlow. *Lady Entertainers*: Valerie Harper, Diana Hunter, Rae McLean. *Bartender*: Jack Collins. *Belle*: Arlene Golonka. *The Drunk*: Gene Varrone. *Bar Patrons*: Elna Laun, Paula Lloyd, Janice Painchaud, Jack Konzal, Pat Tolson, Lee Howard. *Salesman*: Bill McDonald. *Beardsley Dwarf*: Charles Bolender. *Salome*: Rae McLean.
  Townswomen: Nicole Barth, Renee Byrns, Lyn Connorty, Barbara Doherty, Katia Geleznova, Valerie Harper, Diana Hunter, Elna Laun, Paula Lloyd, Nancy Lynch, Rae McLean, Janice Painchaud. *Townsmen*: Alvin Beam, Frank Borgman, John Carter, Lee Howard, Jack Konzal, Bill McDonald, Henry Michel, Jack Murray, John Nola, Bill Richards, Harry Lee Rogers, Walter Strauss, Jimmy Tarbutton, Gene Varrone, Marc West, Pat Tolson, Rusty Parker, Chad Block, Bill Starr.

Act 1, Scene 1: The Miller Home in Centerville, Connecticut, 1910. Early the morning of July 4th. *Scene 2*: The Macomber Home. The same morning. *Scene 3*: The Car Barn. Later that morning. *Scene 4*: The Miller Home. A little later. *Scene 5*: A Street. *Scene 6*: The Picnic Grounds. That afternoon. *Scene 7*: The Miller Home. That evening.

Act 2, Scene 1: Bar Room of the Pleasant Beach House. The same night. *Scene 2*: The Miller Home. Later that night. *Scene 3*: Richard's Bedroom. Afternoon of the following day. *Scene 4*: The Beach. That evening. *Scene 5*: The Miller Home. A little later. *Scene 6*: The Car Barn. Later that evening.

ACT 1
Scene 1
  "The Parade" (Marvelous Fire Machine)
    W. Pidgeon, Townspeople
  "Oh, Please"
    W. Pidgeon, U. Merkel, E. Herlie, Family
Scene 2
  "I Would Die"
    S. Luckey, R. Morse
Scene 3
  "Sid, Ol' Kid"
    J. Gleason, Townspeople
Scene 4
  "Staying Young"
    W. Pidgeon
  "I Get Embarassed"
    J. Gleason, E. Herlie
  "We're Home"
    E. Herlie
Scene 5
  "Take Me Along"
    J. Gleason, W. Pidgeon
Scene 6
  "For Sweet Charity" (Volunteer Firemen Picnic)
    J. Gleason, W. Pidgeon, V. Harper, D. Hunter, R. McLean, Townsmen
Scene 7
  "Pleasant Beach House" (Wint's Song)
    P. Conlow
  "That's How It Starts"
    R. Morse
ACT 2
Scene 1
  "The Beardsley Ballet"
    R. Morse, S. Luckey, C. Bolender, R. McLean, Ensemble
Scene 2
  "Oh, Please" (reprise)
    W. Pidgeon, U. Merkel
  "Promise Me a Rose" (A Slight Detail)
    E. Herlie, J. Gleason
  "Staying Young" (reprise)
    W. Pidgeon
Scene 3
  "Little Green Snake"
    J. Gleason

Scene 4
  "Nine O'Clock"
    R. Morse
Scene 5
  "But Yours"
    J. Gleason, E. Herlie
Scene 6
  "Take Me Along" (reprise)
    E. Herlie, J. Gleason, Townspeople

1959.23 THE GIRLS AGAINST THE BOYS

A Musical Revue in Two Acts, 20 Scenes. Sketches and lyrics by Arnold B. Horwitt. Music by Richard Lewine. Additional music by Albert Hague. Sketches directed by Aaron Ruben. Dances and musical numbers staged by Boris Runanin. Scenery and lighting by Ralph Alswang. Costumes by Sal Anthony. Dance music arranged by John Morris. Musical director, Irving Actman. Orchestrations by Sid Ramin and Robert Ginzler. Produced by Albert Selden. Opened 2 November 1959 at the Alvin Theatre and closed 14 November 1959 after 16 performances.

CAST: BERT LAHR, NANCY WALKER, SHELLEY BERMAN, DICK VAN DYKE, Joy Nichols, Imelda De Martin, Richard France, June L. Walker, Maureen Bailey, Buzz Halliday, Mace Barrett.
  Ensemble: Caroljane Abney, Sandra Devlin, Ray Pointer, Noel Schwartz, Martin Charnin, Bob Roman, Cy Young, Jo Ann Tenney, Roger LePage, Mal Throne, Mona Pivar, Al Fiorella, Margaret Gathright, Mitchell Nutick, Beatrice Salten, Jim Sisco, Ellen Graff.

ACT 1
Scene 1
  "The Girls Against the Boys"
    D. Van Dyke, M. Barrett, B. Halliday, Ensemble
Scene 2
  "Rich Butterfly"
    Husband: S. Berman. *Wife*: N. Walker.
Scene 3
  Can We Save Our Marriage?
    Counselor: D. Van Dyke. *Stella*: J. L. Walker. *Harry*: B. Lahr.
Scene 4
  "I Gotta Have You"
    I. DeMartin, R. France, C. Abney, S. Devlin, R. Pointer, N. Schwartz
Scene 5
  Home Late (based on an idea by Robert Mott)
    Husband: D. Van Dyke. *Wife*: B. Halliday.
Scene 6
  I Remember
    B. Lahr
    Butler: M. Barrett.
Scene 7
  Assignation
    Jock: D. Van Dyke. *Cynthia*: J. Nichols. *Essie*: N. Walker. *Waiter*: M. Charnin. *Counterman*: R. Pointer. *Man at Center Table*: B. Roman. *Max*: N. Schwartz. *Other Patrons*: C. Young, J. A. Tenny, R. LePage, M. Throne, M. Pivar, A. Fiorella.
Scene 8
  Comic Monologue (Phone Call With Jewish Father)
    (*by* Shelley Berman) S. Berman
Scene 9
  "Where Did We Go? Out"
    M. Barrett, M. Bailey, R. France, I. DeMartin
    (by permission of Robert Paul Smith)
Scene 10
  "Too Young to Live"
    B. Lahr, N. Walker
Scene 11
  "Overspend"
    S. Berman, J. Nichols, Ensemble

ACT 2

Scene 1

"Girls and Boys"

Observer: M. Barrett. *Mother*: J. Nichols. *Groom*: D. Van Dyke. *Bride*: I. DeMartin. *Best Man*: R. France. *Father*: B. Roman. *Maid of Honor*: M. Bailey. *Bridesmaids*: M. Pivar, M. Gathright, S. Devlin, B. Halliday. *Guests*: Ensemble.

Scene 2

Nightflight

(*by* Arnold Horwitt and Aaron Ruben)

Passenger: B. Lahr. *Girl*: J. Nichols. *Man*: M. Throne. *Hostess*: J. L. Walker. *Mother*: B. Halliday. *Four People*: M. Barrett, C. Young, B. Roman, N. Popova.

Scene 3

"Light Travelin' Man"

(*Music by* Albert Hague.)S. Berman, R. France

Girls: S. Devlin, C. Abney, M. Gathright.

Scene 4

He and She

Introduction: S. Berman. *He*: D. Van Dyke. *Goat*: N. Schwartz. *Skunks*: C. Abney, R. LePage. *Rabbits*: M. Nutick, B. Salten. *Ducks*: R. Pointer, M. Pivar. *Wolf*: A. Fiorella. *Lamb*: J. A. Tenney. *She*: N. Walker. *Snake*: S. Devlin. *It*: J. Sisco.

Scene 5

"Old-Fashioned Girl"

Doorman: M. Throne. *Monroe Fuller*: B. Lahr. *Tawny*: J. L. Walker. *Usher*: B. Salten. *Treasurer*: S. Devlin. *Male Dancer*: R. LePage. *Show Girls*: B. Halliday, M. Gathright, C. Abney, J. A. Tenney, E. Graff, M. Pivar.

Scene 6

Comic Monologue: (Phone Call to Girl Friend After a Date)

(*by* Shelley Berman)

S. Berman

Scene 7

Hostility

(*by* Arnold Horwitt and Aaron Ruben)

Husband: B. Lahr. *Wife*: N. Walker.

Scene 8

"Nobody Else But You"

(*Music by* Albert Hague.)B. Lahr, N. Walker

Scene 9

Finale

Entire Company

1959.24 THE SOUND OF MUSIC

A Musical Play in Two Acts, 19 Scenes. Book by Howard Lindsay and Russel Crouse. Suggested by the book "The Trapp Family Singers" by Maria Augusta Trapp. Music by Richard Rodgers. Lyrics by Oscar Hammerstein II. Entire production directed by Vincent J. Donahue. Musical numbers staged by Joe Layton. Scenic production by Oliver Smith. Costumes by Lucinda Ballard; Mary Martin's clothes[6] by Mainbocher. Lighting by Jean Rosenthal. Musical director, Frederick Dvonch. Choral arrangements by Trude Rittman. Orchestrations by Robert Russell Bennett. Produced by Leland Hayward, Richard Halliday, Richard Rodgers and Oscar Hammerstein II. Opened 16 November 1959 at the Lunt-Fontanne Theatre, vacationed 2-16 July 1961, moved 6 November 1962 to the Mark Hellinger Theatre, and closed 15 June 1963 after 1443 performances.

CAST (in order of appearance): *Maria Rainer*, a Postulant at Nonnberg Abbey: MARY MARTIN. *Sister Berthe*, Mistress of Novices: Elizabeth Howell. *Sister Margaretta*, Mistress of Postulants: Muriel O'Malley. *The Mother Abbess*: PATRICIA NEWAY. *Sister Sophia*: Karen Shepard. *Captain Georg von Trapp*: THEODORE BIKEL. *Franz*: John Randolph. *Frau Schmidt*, the Housekeeper: Nan McFarland. *Children of Captain von Trapp* (7): *Liesl*: Lauri Peters. *Friedrich*: William Snowden. *Louisa*: Kathy Dunn. *Kurt*: Joseph Stewart. *Brigitta*: Marilyn Rogers. *Marta*: Mary Susan Locke. *Gretl*: Evanna Lien. *Rolf Gruber*: Brian Davies. *Elsa Schraeder*: MARION MARLOWE. *Ursula*: Luce Ennis. *Max Detweiler*: KURT KASZNAR. *Herr Zeller*: Stefan Gierasch. *Baron Elberfeld*: Kirby Smith. *A Postulant*: Sue Yaeger. *Admiral Von Schreiber*: Michael Gorrin.

Neighbors of Captain von Trapp, Nuns, Novices, Postulants, Contestants in the Festival Concert: Joanne Birks, Patricia Brooks, June Card, Dorothy Dallas, Ceil Delli,

Luce Ennis, Cleo Fry, Barbara George, Joey Heatherton, Lucas Hoving, Patricia Kelly, Maria Kova, Shirley Mendonca, Kathy Miller, Lorna Nash, Keith Prentice, Nancy Reeves, Bernice Saunders, Connie Sharman, Gloria Stevens, Tatiana Troyanos, Mimi Vondra.

Act 1, Scene 1: Nonnberg Abbey in Austria early in 1938. *Scene 2*: Mountainside near the Abbey. *Scene 3*: The office of the Mother Abbess, the next morning. *Scene 4*: A corridor in the Abbey. *Scene 5*: The living room of the Trapp Villa, that afternoon. *Scene 6*: Outside the Trapp Villa, that evening. *Scene 7*: Maria's bedroom, late that evening. (*Scene 7a*: A Hallway in the Trapp Villa.) *Scene 8*: The terrace of the Trapp Villa, one week later. *Scene 9*: A hallway in the Trapp Villa, one week later. *Scene 10*: The living room, the same evening. *Scene 11*: A corridor in the Abbey. *Scene 12*: The office of the Mother Abbess, three days later.

Act 2, Scene 1: The terrace, the same day. *Scene 2*: A corridor in the Abbey, two weeks later. *Scene 3*: The office of the Mother Abbess, immediately following. *Scene 4*: A cloister overlooking the chapel. *Scene 5*: The living room, one month later. *Scene 6*: The concert hall, three days later. *Scene 7*: The garden of Nonnberg Abbey, that night.

ACT 1

Scene 1

Preludium

Nuns

Scene 2

"The Sound of Music"

M. Martin

Scene 3

"Maria"

P. Neway, M. O'Malley, E. Howell, K. Shepard

"My Favorite Things"

M. Martin, P. Neway

Scene 5

"Do-Re-Mi"

M. Martin, Children

Scene 6

"You Are Sixteen" (Sixteen Going on Seventeen)

L. Peters, B. Davies

Scene 7

"The Lonely Goatherd"

M. Martin, Children

Scene 8

"How Can Love Survive?"

M. Marlowe, K. Kasznar, T. Bikel

"The Sound of Music" (reprise)

M. Martin, T. Bikel, Children

Scene 10

("Laendler" Dance)

(M. Martin, T. Bikel)

"So Long, Farewell"

Children

Scene 12

"Climb Every Mountain"

P. Neway

ACT 2

Scene 1

"No Way to Stop It"

T. Bikel, K. Kasznar, M. Marlowe

"(An) Ordinary Couple"

M. Martin, T. Bikel

Scene 4

Processional

Ensemble

("Maria" reprise)

(Ensemble)

Scene 5

"You Are Sixteen" (reprise)

M. Martin, L. Peters

"Do-Re-Mi" (reprise)

M. Martin, T. Bikel, Children

[6]Miss Martin's postulant costume and last two costumes designed by Lucinda Ballard.

Scene 6

"Edelweiss"
  T. Bikel, M. Martin, Children
"So Long, Farewell" (reprise)
  M. Martin, T. Bikel, Children
Scene 7

"Climb Every Mountain" (reprise)
  Company

1959.25 FIORELLO!

A Musical in Two Acts, a Prologue and 19 Scenes. Book by Jerome Weidman and George Abbott. Music by Jerry Bock. Lyrics by Sheldon Harnick. Choeography by Peter Gennaro. Scenery, costumes and lighting by William and Jean Eckart. Musical direction, Hal Hastings. Orchestrations by Irwin Kostal. Dance music arranged by Jack Elliott. Production directed by George Abbott. Produced by Robert E. Griffith and Harold S. Prince. Opened 23 November 1959 at the Broadhurst Theatre, moved 9 May 1960 to the Broadway Theatre and closed 28 October 1961 after 795 performances.

CAST (in order of appearance): Announcer: Del Hortsmann. Fiorello: TOM BOSLEY. Neil: Bob Holiday. Morris: NATHANIEL FREY. Mrs. Pomerantz: Helen Verbit. Mr. Lopez: H. F. Green. Mr. Zappatella: David Collyer. Dora: PAT STANLEY. Marie: PATRICIA WILSON. Ben: HOWARD DA SILVA. Ed Peterson: Del Hortsmann. Second Player: Stanley Simmonds. Third Player: Michael Quinn. Fourth Player: Ron Husmann. Fifth Player: David London. Sixth Player: Julian Patrick. Seedy Man: Joseph Toner. First Heckler: Bob Bernard. Second Heckler: Michael Scrittorale. Third Heckler: Jim Maher. Fourth Heckler: Joseph Toner. Nina: Pat Turner. Floyd: MARK DAWSON. Sophie: Lynn Ross. Thea: ELLEN HANLEY. Secretary: Mara Landi. Commissioner: Frederic Downs. Politician: H. F. Green. Frankie Scarpini: Michael Scrittorale. Mitzi: EILEEN RODGERS. Florence: Deedy Irwin. Reporter: Julian Patrick. First Man: Scott Hunter. Second Man: Michael Scrittorale. Tough Man: David London. Derby: Bob Bernard. Frantic: Stanley Simmonds. Judge Carter: Joseph Toner.

Singers: David Collyer, Barbara Gilbert, Del Hortsmann, Deedy Irwin, Mara Landi, David London, Julian Patrick, Ginny Perlowin, Patsy Peterson, Silver Saundors, Ron Husmann. Dancers: Charlene Carter, Bob Bernard, Elaine Cancilla, Ellen Harris, Patricia Harty, Scott Hunter, Bob La Crosse, Lynda Lynch, James Maher, Gregg Owen, Lowell Purvis, Dellas Rennie, Lynn Ross, Dan Siretta, Michael Scrittorale, Pat Turner.

Prologue: WNYC Radio Station Studios, New York City. 1914.

Act 1, Scene 1: Law Offices of Fiorello H. LaGuardia in Greenwich Village. Scene 2: Main Room of the Ben Marino Association. Scene 3: A Street outside strike headquarters. Scene 4: Fiorello's Office immediately following. Scene 5: A Street Corner. Scene 6: The same, after Fiorello's election. Scene 7: The Roof of a Greenwich Village Tenement House. Scene 8: Fiorello's office in the Congressional Office Building in Washington. Scene 9: A Street. Scene 10: The Main Room of the Ben Marino Association. Scene 11: A Pathé News Screening; a ship's gangplank.

Act 2, Scene 1: The LaGuardia Home. Ten years later. Scene 2: The Terrace of Floyd and Dora McDuff's Penthouse Home. Scene 3: Fiorello's Law Office. Scene 4: Madison Avenue and 105th Street. Scene 5: Fiorello's Law Office. Scene 6: Radio Announcement Scene 7: The Main Room of the Ben Marino Association. Scene 8: Fiorello's Office.

ACT 1
Scene 1

"On the Side of the Angels"
  B. Holiday, N. Frey, P. Wilson
Scene 2

"Politics and Poker"
  H. DaSilva, Politicians
Scene 3

"Unfair"
  T. Bosley, P. Stanley, Girls
Scene 4

"Marie's Law"
  P. Wilson, N. Frey
Scene 5

"The Name's LaGuardia"
  T. Bosley, Company

Scene 6

"The Bum Won"
  H. DaSilva, Politicians
Scene 7

"I Love a Cop"
  P. Stanley
Scene 9

"I Love a Cop" (reprise)
  P. Stanley, M. Dawson
Scene 10

"Till Tomorrow"
  E. Hanley, Company
Scene 11

"Home Again"
  Company

ACT 2
Scene 1

"When Did I Fall in Love"
  E. Hanley
Scene 2

"Gentleman Jimmy"
  E. Rodgers, Dancing Girls
Scene 6

"Gentleman Jimmy" (reprise)
  Company
Scene 7

"Little Tin Box"
  H. DaSilva, Politicians
"The Very Next Man"
  P. Wilson
("Politics and Poker" reprise)
  (H. DaSilva, Politicians)
Scene 8

"The Very Next Man" (reprise)
  P. Wilson
Finale ("The Name's LaGuardia" reprise)
  Politicians

1959.26 ONCE UPON A MATTRESS

A Musical (Comedy) in Two Acts, a Prologue and 17 Scenes[7]. Book by Jay Thompson, Marshall Barer and Dean Fuller. (Based on the story "The Princess and the Pea" by Hans Christian Andersen.) Music by Mary Rodgers. Lyrics by Marshall Barer. Directed by George Abbott. Dances and musical numbers staged by Joe Layton. Scenery and costumes by William and Jean Eckart. Lighting by Tharon Musser. Musical direction, Hal Hastings. Orchestrations by Hershy Kay, Arthur Beck and Carroll Huxley. Dance music arranged by Roger Adams. Orchestra conducted by Clay Warnick. Produced by T. Edward Hambleton, Norris Houghton, William and Jean Eckart. Opened 25 November 1959 at the Alvin Theatre, moved 24 February 1960 to the Winter Garden, moved 25 April 1960 to the Cort Theatre, moved 9 May 1960 to the St. James Theatre and closed 2 July 1960 after 244 performances. Total: 460 performances.

---

[7]Originally produced Off-Broadway 11 May 1959-15 November 1959 at the Phoenix Theatre for 216 performances. Those actors who originated their roles Off-Broadway but did not transfer to Broadway are listed below: Prince: Jim Maher. Queen: Gloria Stevens. Lady Rowena: Dorothy Aull. Lady Merrill: Patsi King. Lady Lucille: Luce Ennis. Sir Studley: Jerry Newby. The King: JACK GILFORD. Jester: MATT MATTOX. Lady Beatrice: Gloria Stevens. Sir Luce: Tom Mixon. Lady Mabelle: Chris Karner. Nightingale of Samarkand: Ginny Perlowin. Lord Howard: Howard Parker. Sir Steven: Jim Stevenson. Several minor Lords and Ladies from the Ensemble roles also changed character names.

CAST (in order of appearance): *Minstrel*: HARRY SNOW. *Prince*: Gene Kelton. *Princess*: Chris Karner. *Queen*: Dorothy Frank. *Wizard*: Robert Weil. *Princess Number Twelve*: Mary Stanton. *Lady Rowena*: Patti Karr. *Lady Merrill*: Cheryl Kilgren. *Prince Dauntless*: JOE BOVA. *The Queen*: JANE WHITE. *Lady Larken*: ANNE JONES. *Sir Studley*: Tom Mixon. *The King*: WILL LEE. *Jester*: JERRY NEWBY. *Sir Harry*: DAN RESIN. *Princess Winnifred*: CAROL BURNETT. *Sir Harold*: David Neuman. *Lady Beatrice*: Dorothy Frank. *Sir Luce*: Stuart Hodes. *Lady Mabelle*: Marjorie Pragon. *Nightingale of Samarkand*: Gina Viglione. *Lady Dorothy*: Dorothy D'Honau. *Sir Nicholas*: Peter Holmes. *Sir Joseph*: Joseph Carow. *Lord Howard*: Gene Kelton. *Lady Jerane*: Jerane Michel. *Lord Casper*: Casper Roos. *Sir Steven*: Jack Schwartz. *Sir Paul*: Paul Richards.

The action takes place in a small kingdom in medieval times.

Act 1, Scene 1: Throne Room. *Scene 2*: The Yellow Gallery. *Scene 3*: Courtyard. *Scene 4*: A Corridor. *Scene 5*: Winnifred's Dressing Chamber. *Scene 6*: The Grey Gallery. *Scene 7*: On the Greensward. *Scene 8*: The Yellow Gallery. *Scene 9*: Great Hall.

Act 2, Scene 1: Castle. *Scene 2*: Winnifred's Dressing Chamber. *Scene 3*: A Corrdior. *Scene 4*: Wizard's Chamber. *Scene 5*: The Grey Gallery. *Scene 6*: The Bed Chamber. *Scene 7*: A Corridor. *Scene 8*: Breakfast Hall.

ACT 1

Prologue
"Many Moons Ago"
H. Snow, Court

Scene 1
"An Opening for a Princess"
J. Bova, A. Jones, Knights and Ladies
"In a Little While"
A. Jones, D. Resin

Scene 2
"In a Little While" (reprise)
A. Jones, D. Resin

Scene 3
"Shy"
C. Burnett, T. Mixon, Knights and Ladies
"The Minstrel, the Jester and I"
W. Lee, H. Snow, J. Newby

Scene 4
"Sensitivity"
J. White, R. Weil

Scene 5
"(The) Swamps of Home"
C. Burnett, J. Bova, Ladies

Scene 7
"Normandy"
H. Snow, J. Newby, W. Lee, A. Jones

Scene 9
"Spanish Panic"
H. Snow, J. Michel, D. Frank, J. White, C. Burnett, J. Bova, Knights and Ladies
"Song of Love"
J. Bova, C. Burnett, Knights and Ladies

ACT 2
Scene 1
"Quiet"
J. Newby, (J. White), Knights and Ladies
Scene 2
"Happily Ever After"
C. Burnett
Scene 3
"Man to Man Talk"
W. Lee, J. Bova
Scene 5
"Very Soft Shoes"
J. Newby, Knights and Ladies
Scene 6
"Yesterday I Loved You"
D. Resin, A. Jones
Scene 7
"Lullaby"
G. Viglione

Scene 9
Finale
Entire Court

1959.27 # SARATOGA

A Musical Comedy in Two Acts, 17 Scenes. (Book) Dramatized and directed by Morton DaCosta. Based on the novel "Saratoga Trunk" by Edna Ferber. Music by Harold Arlen. Lyrics (and additional music) by Johnny Mercer. Settings and costumes by Cecil Beaton. Choreography by Ralph Beaumont. Lighting by Jean Rosenthal. Musical direction by Jerry Arlen. Vocal arrangements by Herbert Greene. Orchestrations by Philip J. Lang. Music for dances by Genevieve Pitot. Produced by Robert Fryer. Opened 7 December 1959 at the Winter Garden and closed 13 February 1960 after 80 performances.

CAST (in order of appearance): *Cupide*: TUN TUN. *Clio Dulaine*: CAROL LAWRENCE. *Kakou*: CAROL BRICE. *Belle Piquery*: ODETTE MYRTIL. *The Drapery Man*: Mark Zeller. *The Carpenter*: Albert Popwell. *Shorty*: Augie Rios. *Maudey*: Brenda Long. *The Charwoman*: Virginia Capers. *Mrs. LeClerc*: Martha King. *M. Augustin Haussy*: Richard Graham. *Clint Maroon*: HOWARD KEEL. *M. Begué*: Truman Gaige. *Grandmother Dulaine*: Natalie Core. *Madame Dulaine*: Beatrice Bushkin. *Charlotte Thérèse*: Jeannine Masterson. *Léon, a Waiter*: Mark Zeller. *Editor*: Truman Gaige. *Haberdashery Clerk*: Frank Green. *Fabric Salesman*: Barney Johnston. *M. LaFosse*: Lanier Davis. *Mrs. Sophie Bellop*: EDITH KING. *Mrs. Porcelain*: Natalie Core. *Mr. Gould*: Truman Gaige. *Bart Van Steed*: WARDE DONOVAN. *Mr. Bean*: James Millhollin. *Daisy Porcelain*: Gerrianne Raphael. *Clarissa Van Steed*: Isabella Hoopes. *Miss Diggs*: Janyce Wagner.

Children: Brenda Long, Linda Wright, Augie Rios, Wayne Robertson. *Townspeople, Guests, etc.*: Betsy Bridge, Beatrice Bushkin, Virginia Capers, Martha King, Ina Kurland, Jeannine Masterson, Carol Taylor, Gerrianne Raphael, Lois Van Pelt, Janyce Wagner, Beverley Jane Welch, Socrates Birsky, John Blanchard, Joseph Crawford, Lanier Davis, Paul Dixon, Vito Durante, José Falcion, Julius Fields, John Ford, Jerry Fries, Gene Gavin, Frank Green, Nathaniel Horne, Barney Johnston, Louis Kosman, Jack Matthew, Oran Osburn, John Pero, Harold Pierson, Albert Popwell, Charles Queenan, Mark Zeller, Merritt Thompson.

Act 1, Scene 1: The Rampart Street House, New Orleans, 1880. *Scene 2*: Exterior of the Rampart Street House. *Scene 3*: The Waterfront Market. *Scene 4*: The Museum. *Scene 5*: Begué's Restaurant. *Scene 6*: The Garden of the Rampart Street House. *Scene 7*: The Casino. *Scene 8*: The United States Hotel, Saratoga. *Scene 9*: Clint and Clio's Rooms in the United States Hotel.

Act 2, Scene 1: The Springs, Saratoga. *Scene 2*: Corridor of the United States Hotel. *Scene 3*: Clint's and Clio's Rooms. *Scene 4*: The Verandah. *Scene 5*: The Corridor. *Scene 6*: On a Flatcar and at the Railroad Station, Binghamton, New York. *Scene 7*: The Corridor. *Scene 8*: The Ballroom of the United States Hotel.

ACT 1
Scene 1
"I'll Be Respectable"
C. Lawrence
"One Step—Two Step"
C. Lawrence, A. Rios, B. Long, Ensemble
"Gettin' a Man"
O. Myrtil, C. Brice
(*Music by* Johnny Mercer.)
Scene 3
"Petticoat High"
V. Capers, C. Lawrence, O. Myrtil, Tun Tun, Ensemble
Scene 5
"Why Fight This?"
C. Lawrence, H. Keel
(*Music by* Johnny Mercer.)
"(A) Game of Poker"
H. Keel, C. Lawrence
Scene 6
"Love Held Lightly"
O. Myrtil
"(A) Game of Poker" (reprise)
C. Lawrence, H. Keel, O. Myrtil
Scene 7
"The Gamblers" (dance)
C. Lawrence, Gamblers, Croupiers
"Saratoga"
H. Keel, C. Lawrence

Scene 8
  "Saratoga" (reprise)
    Ensemble
  "The Gossip Song"
    E. King, Ensemble
Scene 9
  "Countin' Our Chickens"
    C. Lawrence, H. Keel
  "You or No One"
    H. Keel

ACT 2
Scene 1
  "The Cure"
    Ensemble
  "The Men Who Run the Country"
    The Robber Barons
    (*Music by* Johnny Mercer.)
Scene 3
  "The Man in My Life"
    C. Lawrence, H. Keel
Scene 4
  "The Polka" (dance)
    C. Lawrence, W. Donovan, Ensemble
  "Love Held Lightly" (reprise)
    C. Lawrence
Scene 5
  "Goose Never Be a Peacock"
    C. Brice
Scene 6
  "Dog Eat Dog"
    H. Keel, His Men
  "The Railroad Fight" (dance)
    H. Keel, Tun Tun, the Men
Scene 8
  "Petticoat High" (reprise)
    C. Lawrence, Ensemble

1960.01 BEG, BORROW OR STEAL

A Musical Comedy in Two Acts, 21 Scenes. Book and lyrics by Bud Freeman, from an (unpublished) story ("Steal—A Disc Jockey's Handbook") by Marvin Seiger and Bud Freeman. Music by Leon Pober. Staged by Billy Matthews. Dances and musical mumbers by Peter Hamilton. Directed by David Doyle. Scenery, costumes and lighting by Carter Morningstar. Musical direction by Hal Hidey. Orchestrations by Peter Matz and Hal Hidey. Produced by Eddie Bracken, with Carroll and Harris Masterson. Opened 10 February 1960 at the Martin Beck Theatre and closed 13 February 1960 after 5 performances.

CAST (in order of appearance): *Mrs. Plonsky:* Jean Bruno. *Junior:* BIFF McGUIRE. *Ollie:* Estelle Parsons. *Phil:* Betty Rhodes. *Judy:* Karen Sargent. *Clara:* BETTY GARRETT. *Pistol:* EDDIE BRACKEN. *Rafe:* LARRY PARKS. *Jason:* Roy Stuart. *Ethel:* Bernice Massi. *Lovers:* Mary Sullivan, Del Hanley. *Modern Dance Leader:* Sally Lee. *Dance Class:* Carmen Morales, Garold Gardner Ellen Halpin, Willard Nagel. *Rug Hooker:* Michael Davis. *Pottery Girl:* Colleen Corkrey. *Bar Girl:* Esther Horrocks. *Knitters:* Fran Leone, Keith Willis. *Painter:* Tom Hester. *Chess Players:* Michael Stuart, Arthur Whitfield. *Flamenco Dancers:* Adriana Keathley, Harold DaSilva. *Guitarist:* Fred Kimbrough. *Kibitzer:* Mara Wirt. *Poet:* John Tormey. *Poetry Lovers:* Shelia Dee, Georgia Kennedy, Virginia Barnes. *Sculptor:* Chuck Arnett. *Model:* Beti Seay. *Mobile Artist:* Lucinda Stevens. *Frieda:* Claiborne Carey. *Patriot:* Jack Drummond. *Sam Lee Howard:* Richard Armbruster. *Muscle:* Bill Linton. *Koppisch:* Richard Woods. *Blanding:* David Doyle.

Act 1, Scene 1: The Street. A run-down section of a monster American city in the 1950s. *Scene 2:* The Store. *Scene 3:* The Street. *Scene 4:* The Pit. *Scene 5:* The Park. *Scene 6:* The Street. *Scene 7:* The Pit. *Scene 8:* Rafe's Attic. *Scene 9:* The Store. *Scene 10:* The Street. *Scene 11:* The Pad. *Scene 12:* The Pit.

Act 2, Scene 1: The Office. Six months later. *Scene 2:* The Street. *Scene 3:* Chez Pit. *Scene 4:* The Office. *Scene 5:* The Street. *Scene 6:* The Pad. *Scene 7:* Chez Pit. *Scene 8:* The Street. *Scene 9:* The Store.

ACT 1
  "Some Little People"
    Ensemble
  "Rootless"
    B. McGuire
  "What Are We Gonna Do Tonight?"
    E. Parsons, B. Rhodes, K. Sargent
  "Poetry and All That Jazz"
    C. Cary, Ensemble
  "Don't Stand Too Close to the Picture"
    L. Parks, B. Garrett, Ensemble
  "Beg, Borrow or Steal," Recitative
    L. Parks
  "Beg, Borrow or Steal"
    L. Parks
  "No One Knows Me"
    B. Garrett
  "Zen Is When"
    E. Bracken, B. McGuire, B. Massi, R. Stuart
  Ballet
    Ensemble
      Soloist: C. Corkrey. *The Lovers:* C. Morales, A. Whitfield.
  "Clara"
    B. McGuire
  "You've Got Something to Say"
    L. Parks, B. Garrett
  "You've Got Something to Say" (reprise)
    L. Parks, B. Garrett, E. Bracken, B. McGuire, Company
ACT 2
  "Presenting Clara Spencer"
    B. Garrett, assisted by K. Willis, M. Stuart,
    C. Arnett, H. DaSilva, W. Nagel, G. Gardner, A. Whitfield
  "I Can't Stop Talking"
    B. Garrett, B. McGuire
  "It's All in Your Mind"
    L. Parks, B. Garrett
  "In Time"
    B. McGuire
  "Think"
    B. Garrett
  "Little People"
    E. Bracken, Company
      Danced by K. Willis, S. Lee, M. Stuart.
  "Rafesville, U.S.A."
    B. Massi, R. Stuart
  "Beg, Borrow or Steal"
    L. Parks, Ensemble
  "Let's Be Strangers Again"
    B. Garrett, B. McGuire
  "Little People" (reprise)
    Entire Company

1960.02 THE CRADLE WILL ROCK

A Revival of the Play in Music in One Act[8], 10 Scenes. Play, music and lyrics by Marc Blitzstein. Staged by Howard DaSilva. Scenic design by David Hays. Costume design by Ruth Morley. Choreographed by Billy Parsons. Conducted by Lehman Engel. Produced by the New York City Opera. Opened 11 February 1960 at the New York City Center and closed 21 February 1960 after 4 performances in repertory.

CAST: *Moll:* TAMMY GRIMES. *Gent:* Seth Riggs. *Dick:* Arnold Voketaitis. *Cop:* Dan Merriman. *Reverend Salvation:* Kenneth Smith. *Editor Daily:* Jack Harrold. *Yasha:* Michael Wager. *Dauber:* Chandler Cowles. *President Prexy:* John Macurdy.

---

[8]First presented in New York 16 June 1937 at the Venice Theatre for 19 performances, subsequently at the Mercury and Windsor Theatres for 112 performances. For Synopsis of Scenes and Musical Numbers, see original 1937 production.

Professor Trixie: Philip Bruns. *Professor Mamie*: Maurice Stern. *Professor Scoot*: Howard Fried. *Doctor Specialist*: Joshua Hecht. *Harry Druggist*: WILLIAM GRIFFIS. *Clerk*: Lehman Engel. *Mr. Mister*: CRAIG TIMBERLAKE. *Mrs. Mister*: RUTH KOBART. *Junior Mister*: Keith Kaldenberg. *Sister Mister*: Nancy Dussault. *Steve*: Frank Poretta. *Sadie Polock*: Sophie Ginn. *Gus Polock*: Robert Kerns. *Bugs*: George Del Monte. *Larry Foreman*: DAVID ATKINSON. *Ella Hammer*: JANE JOHNSTON. *Reporters*: Seth Riggs, William Zachariesen. *Ensemble*: New York City Opera Chorus.

1960.03

THE CONSUL

A Revival of the Opera (Musical Drama) in Three Acts, 6 Scenes[9]. Libretto and music by Gian-Carlo Menotti. Conductor, Werner Torkanowsky. Settings and costumes by Horace Armistead. Lighting by Jean Rosenthal. Magic sequences created and staged by Fred Keating. Staged by Gian-Carlo Menotti. Produced by the New York City Opera Company. Opened 14 February 1960 at the New York City Center and closed 21 February 1960 after 2 performances in repertory.

CAST: (in order of appearance): *John Sorel*: CHESTER LUDGIN. *Magda Sorel*: PATRICIA NEWAY. *The Mother*: EVELYN SACHS. *Secret Police Agent*: JOSHUA HECHT. *First Plainclothesman*: William Zachariasen. *Second Plainclothesman*: Sam Kirkham. *The Secretary*: REGINA SARFATY. *Mr. Kofner*: ARNOLD VOKETAITIS. *The Foreign Woman*: MARIA MARLO. *Anna Gomez*: Maria Di Gerlando. *Vera Boronel*: Ruth Kobart. *Nika Magadoff* (The Magician): JACK HARROLD. *Assan*: Dan Merriman. *Voice on the Record*: Mabel Mercer.

1960.04

A THURBER CARNIVAL

A Revue in Two Acts, 15 Scenes. Play (sketches, lyrics) by James Thurber. Conceived and directed by Burgess Meredith. Music composed and performed by Don Elliott. Scenery by Marvin Reiss. Associate director, James Starbuck. Men's costumes by Ramsé Stevens. Women's clothes from Jenkins Gowns. Lighting by Paul Morrison. Produced by Michael Davis, Helen Bonfils and Haila Stoddard. Opened 26 February 1960 at the ANTA Theatre, closing 25 June 1960 after 127 performances; re-opened a return engagement 5 September 1960 at the ANTA Theatre and closed 26 November 1960 after 96 performances. Total: 223 performances.

CAST: TOM EWELL, PEGGY CASS, PAUL FORD, ALICE GHOSTLEY, JOHN McGIVER, WYNNE MILLER, PETER TURGEON, Charles Braswell, Margo Lundgreen, Don Elliott Quartet (Don Elliott, Jack Six, Jim Raney, Ronnie Bedford).

ACT 1

Scene 1

"Word Dance (Part 1)"
  (*Staged by* James Starbuck.)P. Cass, P. Turgeon, P. Ford,
    W. Miller, J. McGiver, M. Lungreen, A. Ghostley, C. Braswell, (Don Elliott Quartet)

Scene 2

The Night the Bed Fell
  T. Ewell

Scene 3

Fables (Part 1):
  (*Staged by* James Starbuck.)
  A. The Wolf at the Door
    Narrator: A. Ghostley. *Daughter*: W. Miller. *Mother*: P. Cass. *Father*: P. Ford. *Wolf*: C. Braswell.
  B. The Unicorn in the Garden
    Narrator: P. Turgeon. *Man*: P. Ford. *She*: A. Ghostley. *Psychiatrist*: J. McGiver. *Policeman*: C. Braswell.
  C. The Little Girl and the Wolf
    Narrator: P. Cass. *Wolf*: P. Ford. *Little Girl*: W. Miller.

Scene 4

If Grant Had Been Drinking at Appomattox
  Narrator: P. Turgeon. *Shultz*: C. Braswell. *Grant*: T. Ewell. *Lee*: P. Ford. *Lee's Staff Man*: J. McGiver. *Officer*: P. Turgeon.

Scene 5

Casuals of the Keys
  Visitor: J. McGiver. *Darrel Darke*: P. Ford.

Scene 6

The Macbeth Murder Mystery
  He: T. Ewell. *She*: P. Cass.

Scene 7

"Gentlemen Shoppers"
  Narrator: P. Turgeon. *Salesgirl*: A. Ghostley. *Westwater*: J. McGiver. *Bargirl*: W. Miller. *Anderson*: T. Ewell. *Bailey*: P. Ford.

Scene 8

The Last Flower
  T. Ewell

ACT 2

Scene 1

(The) Pet Department
  Announcer: P. Turgeon. *The Pet Counsellor*: T. Ewell. *Miss Whittaker*: A. Ghostley. *A Girl*: W. Miller.

Scene 2

Mr. Preble Gets Rid of His Wife
  Preble: P. Ford. *Miss Daley*: W. Miller. *Mrs. Preble*: P. Cass.

Scene 3

File and Forget
  James Thurber: T. Ewell. *Miss Bagley*: M. Lungreen. *Miss Alma Winege*: P. Cass. *Miss Wynne*: W. Miller. *Jeannette Gaines*: A. Ghostley. *Clint Jordan*: P. Ford. *H. F. Cluffman*: J. McGiver.

Scene 4

Take Her Up Tenderly
  John: P. Ford. *Nellie*: A. Ghostley. *Lou*: P. Cass.

Scene 5

Fables (Part 2)
  (*Staged by* James Starbuck.)
  A. The Owl Who Was God
    Narrator: A. Ghotsley. *Owl*: J. McGiver.*Moles*: P. Tugeon, C. Braswell. *Secretary Bird*: P. Ford. *Red Fox*: M. Lungreen.
  B. The Clothes Moth and the Luna Moth
    Narrator: T. Ewell. *Luna Moth*: W. Miller. *Clothes Moth*: C. Braswell.

Scene 6

The Secret Life of Walter Mitty
  Narrator: P. Turgeon. *Walter Mitty*: T. Ewell. *Mrs. Mitty*: P. Cass. *First Voice*: C. Braswell. *Lieut. Berg*: P. Turgeon. *Nurse*: W. Miller. *Dr. Renshaw*: J. McGiver. *Dr. Benbow*: C. Braswell. *Dr. Remington*: P. Turgeon. *Mr. Pritchard-Mitford*: P. Ford. *The Leader*: P. Ford.

Scene 7

"Word Dance (Part 2)"
  (*Staged by* James Starbuck.)
    T. Ewell, J. McGiver, W. Miller, P. Cass, A. Ghostley, M. Lundgreen, P. Ford, P. Turgeon, C. Braswell, Don Elliott Quartet

1960.05

GREENWILLOW

A Musical Comedy in Two Acts, 15 Scenes. Book by Lesser Samuels and Frank Loesser. Based on the novel of the same name by B. J. Chute. Music and lyrics by Frank Loesser. Directed by George Roy Hill. Choreography by Joe Layton. Settings by Peter Larkin. Costumes by Alvin Colt. Lighting by Feder. Orchestrations by Don Walker. Musical direction by Abba Bogin. Produced by Robert A. Willey in association with Frank Productions, Inc. Opened 8 March 1960 at the Alvin Theatre and closed 28 May 1960 after 95 performances.

CAST (in order of appearance): *Jabez Briggs*: John Megna. *Clara Clegg*: Dortha Duckworth. *Mrs. Hasty*: Maggie Task. *Mr. Preebs*: Jordon Howard. *Mrs. Lunny*: Marie Foster. *Reverend Lapp*: WILLIAM CHAPMAN. *Gramma Briggs*: PERT KELTON. *Maidy*: Elaine Swann. *Emma*: Saralou Cooper. *Gideon Briggs*: ANTHONY PERKINS. *Dorrie Whitbred*: ELLEN McCOWN. *Amos Briggs*: Bruce MacKay. *Micah Briggs*: Ian Tucker. *Martha Briggs*: Lynn Brinker. *Sheby Briggs*: Brenda Harris. *Thomas Clegg*: Lee Cass. *Reverend Birdsong*: CECIL KELLAWAY. *Young Churchgoer*: Thomas Norden. *Will*: David Gold. *Nell*: Margery Gray. *Andrew*: Grover Dale.
  Singers: Kenny Adams, Betsy Bridge, Marie Foster, Rico Froehlich, Russell Goodwin, Jordon Howard, Marion Mercer, Carl Nicholas, Virginia Oswald, Bob

---

[9]Originally produced in New York 15 March 1950 at the Ethel Barrymore Theatre for 269 performances. For Synopsis of Scenes and Musical Numbers, see original 1950 production.

Roman, Shelia Swenson, Maggie Task, Karen Thorsell. *Dancers:* Jere Admire, Don Atkinson, Estelle Aza, Joan Coddington, Ethelyne Dunfee, Richard Englund, David Gold, Margery Gray, Mickey Gunnerson, Patsi King, Jack Leigh, Nancy Van Rhein, Jimmy White.

The action takes place during four seasons in and about the (New England) village of Greenwillow.

Act 1, Scene 1: The Square. *Scene 2:* Briggs Farm. *Scene 3:* The Mill. *Scene 4:* The Willow. *Scene 5:* The Square. *Scene 6:* Cleggs Farm. *Scene 7:* The Mill. *Scene 8:* Briggs Farm. *Scene 9:* The Church. *Scene 10:* The Square.

Act 2, Scene 1: The Square. *Scene 2:* Briggs Farm. *Scene 3:* Cleggs House. *Scene 4:* The Square. *Scene 5:* Briggs Farm.

ACT 1
"A Day Borrowed from Heaven"
   The Villagers
"A Day Borrowed from Heaven" (reprise)
   A. Perkins
"Dorrie's Wish"
   E. McCown
"The Music of Home"
   B. MacKay, A. Perkins, the Villagers
"Gideon Briggs, I Love You"
   A. Perkins, E. McCown
"The Autumn Courting" (dance)
   All the Villagers
"The Call to Wander"
   B. MacKay
"Summertime Love"
   A. Perkins, the Villagers
"Walking Away Whistling"
   E. McCown
"The Sermon"
   W. Chapman, C. Kellaway
"Could've Been a Ring"
   L. Cass, P. Kelton
"Gideon Briggs, I Love You" (reprise)
   E. McCown
"Halloweve" (dance)
   The Young Villagers
"Never Will I Marry"
   A. Perkins
"Greenwillow Christmas" (Carol)
   L. Brinker, Villagers
ACT 2
"The Music of Home" (reprise)
   The Villagers
"Faraway Boy"
   E. McCown
"Clang Dang the Bell"
   A. Perkins, P. Kelton, L. Brinker, I. Tucker, B. Harris, J. Megna
"What a Blessing"
   C. Kellaway
"He Died Good"
   The Villagers
"The Spring Courting" (dance)
   G. Dale, E. McCown, the Young Villagers
"Summertime Love" (reprise)
   A. Perkins
"What a Blessing" (reprise)
   C. Kellaway
"The Call"
   A. Perkins
The Music of Home" (reprise)
   All of Greenwillow

1960.06   BYE BYE BIRDIE

A Musical (Comedy) in Two Acts, 18 Scenes. Book by Michael Stewart. Music by Charles Strouse. Lyrics by Lee Adams. Scenery by Robert Randolph. Costumes by Miles White. Lighting by Peggy Clark. Musical

director, Elliott Lawrence. Orchestrations by Robert Ginzler. Dance arrangements by John Morris. Additional scoring by Elliott Lawrence. Directed and choreographed by Gower Champion. Associate choreographer, Gene Bayliss. Film sequences by Robert J. McCarty in association with Robert Gaffney. Produced by Edward Padula in association with L. Slade Brown. Opened 14 April 1960 at the Martin Beck Theatre, moved 24 October 1960 to the 54th Street Theatre, moved 16 January 1961 to the Sam S. Shubert Theatre, and closed 7 October 1961 after 607 performances.

CAST (in order of appearance): *Albert Peterson:* DICK VAN DYKE. *Rose Grant:* CHITA RIVERA. *Teenagers (17): Helen:* Karin Wolfe. *Nancy:* Marissa Mason. *Alice:* Sharon Lerit. *Margie Ann:* Louise Quick. *Penelope Ann:* Lada Edmund. *Deborah Sue:* Jessica Albright. *Suzie:* Lynn Bowin. *Linda:* Judy Keirn. *Carol:* Penny Ann Green. *Martha Louise:* Vicki Belmonte. *Harold:* Michael Vita. *Karl:* Jerry Dodge. *Harvey:* Dean Stolber. *Henry:* Ed Kresley. *Arthur:* Bob Spencer. *Freddie:* Tracy Everitt. *Peyton:* Gary Howe. *Ursula Merkle:* BARBARA DOHERTY. *Kim MacAfee:* SUSAN WATSON. *Mrs. MacAfee:* MARIJANE MARICLE. *Mr. MacAfee:* PAUL LYNDE. *Teen Trio:* Louise Quick, Jessica Albright, Vicki Belmonte. *Sad Girl:* Sharon Lerit. *Another Sad Girl:* Karin Wolfe. *Mae Peterson:* KAY MEDFORD. *Reporters:* Lee Howard, Jim Sisco, Don Farnworth, John Coyle. *Conrad Birdie:* DICK GAUTIER. *Guitar Man:* Kenny Burrell. *Conductor:* Kasimir Kokich. *Cheerleaders:* Judy Keirn, Lynn Bowin. *Mayor:* Allen Knowles. *Mayor's Wife:* Amelia Haas. *Hugo Peabody:* MICHAEL J. POLLARD. *Randolph MacAfee:* JOHNNY BORDEN. *Mrs. Merkle:* Pat McEnnis. *Old Woman:* Dori Davis. *Neighbors:* Amelia Haas, Jeannine Masterson, Ed Becker, Oran Osburn, George Blackwell, Lee Howard. *Mr. Henkel:* Charles Nelson Reilly. *Gloria Rasputin:* NORMA RICHARDSON. *Ed Sullivan's Voice:* Will Jordan. *TV Stage Manager:* Tony Mordente. *Charles F. Maude:* George Blackwell. *Shriners:* Allen Knowles, John Coyle, Dick Crowley, Don Farnworth, Bud Fleming, Kasimir Kokich, Jim Sisco.

Act 1, Scene 1: Office of Almaelou Music, New York. *Scene 2:* Sweet Apple, Ohio. *Scene 3:* MacAfee Home, Sweet Apple. *Scene 4:* Pennsylvania Station, New York. *Scene 5:* Railroad Station, Sweet Apple. *Scene 6:* Courthouse Steps, Sweet Apple. *Scene 7:* MacAfee Home, Sweet Apple. *Scene 8:* Stage, Central Movie Theatre, Sweet Apple. *Scene 9:* Backstage Office, Central Movie Theatre, Sweet Apple. *Scene 10:* Stage, Central Movie Theatre, Sweet Apple.

Act 2, Scene 1: MacAfee Home, Sweet Apple. *Scene 2:* Street Outside MacAfee Home. *Scene 3:* MacAfee's Back Door. *Scene 4:* Maude's Roadside Retreat. *Scene 5:* Private Dining Room, Maude's Roadside Retreat. *Scene 6:* Back Door, Maude's Roadside Retreat. *Scene 7:* The Ice House. *Scene 8:* Railroad Station, Sweet Apple.

ACT 1
Scene 1
   "An English Teacher"
      C. Rivera, D. Van Dyke
Scene 2
   "The Telephone Hour"
      Sweet Apple Kids (Teenagers)
Scene 3
   "How Lovely to Be a Woman"
      S. Watson
Scene 4
   "We Love You, Conrad!"
      L. Quick, J. Albright, V. Belmonte
   "Put on a Happy Face"
      D. Van Dyke, S. Lerit, K. Wolfe
   "Normal American Boy"
      C. Rivera, D. Van Dyke, Chorus
Scene 5
   "One Boy"
      S. Watson, J. Albright, S. Lerit
   "One Boy" (reprise)
      C. Rivera
Scene 6
   "Honestly Sincere"
      D. Gautier, Townspeople
Scene 7
   "Hymn for a Sunday Evening"
      P. Lynde, M. Maricle, S. Watson, J. Borden, Neighbors
Scene 9
   "How to Kill a Man" (ballet)
      C. Rivera, D. Van Dyke, Company
Scene 10
   "One Last Kiss"
      D. Gautier, Company

ACT 2

Scene 1

"What Did I Ever See in Him?"
C. Rivera, S. Watson

Scene 2

"A Lot of Livin' to Do"
D. Gautier, S. Watson, Teenagers

Scene 3

"Kids"
P. Lynde, M. Maricle

Scene 4

"Baby, Talk to Me"
D. Van Dyke, Quartet

Scene 5

"Shriners' Ballet"
C. Rivera, Shriners

Scene 6

"Kids" (reprise)
P. Lynde, M. Maricle, J. Borden, Townspeople

Scene 7

"Spanish Rose"
C. Rivera

Scene 8

"Rosie"
D. Van Dyke, C. Rivera

1960.07 FROM A TO Z

A Musical Revue in Two Acts, 27 Scenes. (Sketches by Woody Allen, Herbert Farjeon, Don Parks, Nina Warner Hook. Music and lyrics by Jay Thompson, Dickson Hughes, Everett Sloane, Jack Holmes, Mary Rodgers, Marshall Barer, Paul Klein, Fred Ebb, Norman Martin, Don Parks, William Dyer, Lee Goldsmith, Charles Zwar, Alan Melville.) Directed by Christopher Hewett. Choreography by Ray Harrison. Sets, lighting and costumes by Fred Voelpel. Miss Gingold's gowns by Scaasi. Musical direction and vocal arrangements by Milton Greene. Orchestrations by Jay Brower and Jonathan Tunick. Dance arrangements by Jack Holmes. Produced by Carroll and Harris Masterson. Opened 20 April 1960 at the Plymouth Theatre and closed 7 May 1960 after 21 performances.

CAST: HERMIONE GINGOLD, ELLIOTT REID, ALVIN EPSTEIN, LOUISE HOFF, NORA KOVACH, KELLY BROWN, PAULA STEWART, Stuart Damon, Bob Dishy, Isabelle Farrell, Beryl Towbin, Michael Fesco, Larry Hovis, Virginia Vestoff, Doug Spingler.

ACT 1

Scene 1 (A)

"Best Gold"
H. Gingold, N. Kovach,
K. Brown, M. Fesco, D. Spingler, B. Towbin, V. Vestoff, S. Damon, P. Stewart
(*Music and Lyrics by* Jerry Herman.)

Scene 2 (B)

Bardolatry
L. Hoff, E. Reid

Scene 3 (C)

"Pill Parade"
(*Music and Lyrics by* Jay Thompson.)
Narrator: A. Epstein. *Average Man*: K. Brown. *Vitamins*: M. Fesco, D. Spingler. *Benzabang*: B. Towbin. *Pilltown*: V. Vestoff. *Sexaphine*: N. Kovach. *One More Pill*: I. Farrell.

Scene 4 (D)

"Togetherness"
(*Music and Lyrics by* Dickson Hughes and Everett Sloane.)
Grandmother: H. Gingold. *Father*: E. Reid. *Mother*: L. Hoff. *Daughter*: P. Stewart. *Son*: S. Damon.

Scene 5 (E)

Pschological Warfare
(*by* Woody Allen)
Sergeant: A. Epstein. *Privates*: L. Hovis, D. Spingler. *Enemy*: B. Dishy. *Medics*: S. Damon, M. Fesco.

Scene 6 (F)

"Balloons"
N. Kovach, K. Brown, M. Fesco, D. Spingler, B. Towbin, V. Vestoff
(*Music and Lyrics by* Jack Holmes.)

Scene 7 (G)

Music Talk
H. Gingold

Scene 8 (H)

"Hire a Guy"
(*Music by* Mary Rodgers. *Lyrics by* Marshall Barer.)
The Star: L. Hoff. *The Director*: E. Reid. *The Writer*: S. Damon. *Patsy*: B. Dishy.

Scene 9 (I)

"Interlude"
(*Music by* Jack Holmes.)
Ladies: B. Towbin, V. Vestoff, I. Farrell. *Gentlemen*: K. Brown, M. Fesco, D. Spingler. *A Stranger*: N. Kovach. *A Man*: S. Damon.

Scene 10 (J)

Hit Parade
(*by* Woody Allen)
Girl: H. Gingold. *Boy*: A. Epstein.

Scene 11 (K)

Coventional Behavior
E. Reid

Scene 12 (L)

"I Said to Love"
L. Hoff
(*Music by* Paul Klein. *Lyrics by* Fred Ebb.)

Scene 13 (M)

Winter in Palm Springs
(*by* Herbert Farjeon)
Colonel Spicer: A. Epstein. *Mrs. Twiceover*: H. Gingold. *Alice*: B. Towbin.

Scene 14 (N)

"Charlie"
P. Stewart
(*Music by* Norman Martin. *Lyrics by* Fred Ebb.)

Scene 15 (O)

"The Sound of Schmaltz" (Parody of "the Sound of Music")
(*Words by* Don Parks. *Music by* William Dyer.)
Head Nanny: L. Hoff. *Nannies*: N. Kovach, B. Towbin, V. Vestoff, I. Farrell. *Alicia Cadwallader-Smith*: H. Gingold. *Baron von Klaptrap*: E. Reid. *Children*: K. Brown, A. Epstein, M. Fesco, D. Spingler, S. Damon, B. Dishy, P. Stewart.
Scene 1: The Offices of "International Nannies, Ltd." (with an interlude in Central Park). *Scene 2*: The von Klaptrap Nursery. *Scene 3*: Baron von Klaptrap's Apartment. *Scene 4*: The von Klaptrap Living Room.

ACT 2

Scene 1 (P)

"Grand Jury Jump"
N. Kovach, P. Stewart, B. Towbin, V. Vestoff, I. Farrell, K. Brown, S. Damon, M. Fesco, D. Spingler, L. Hovis
(*Music by* Paul Klein. *Lyrics by* Fred Ebb.)

Scene 2 (Q)

"South American Way"
A. Epstein, B. Dishy
(*Music by* Norman Martin. *Lyrics by* Noman Martin and Fred Ebb.)

Scene 3 (R)

Snapshots
(*by* Herbert Farjeon)
She: H. Gingold. *He*: E. Reid.

Scene 4 (S)

"Time Step"
K. Brown
(*Music by* Paul Klein. *Lyrics by* Fred Ebb.)

Scene 5 (T)

Bobo
E. Reid

Scene 6 (U)

"Queen of Song"
H. Gingold
(*Music and Lyrics by* Eric Maschwitz and Jack Strachey.)

Scene 7 (V)

Surprise Party

(*by* Woody Allen)

Fred: B. Dishy. *Harry:* K. Brown. *Myrna:* L. Hoff. *Linda:* B. Towbin. *Ruthie:* N. Kovach. *Rita:* I. Farrell. *Virginia:* V. Vestoff. *Blonde:* P. Stewart.

Scene 8 (W)

"Countermelody"

P. Stewart, S. Damon

(*Music by* Mary Rodgers and Jay Thompson. *Lyrics by* Marshall Barer.)

Scene 9 (X)

Park Meeting

(*by* Nina Warner Hook)

Governess: H. Gingold. *Woman:* L. Hoff.

Scene 10 (Y)

"Red Shoes"

(*Music by* Jack Holmes.)

Introduced by B. Dishy. *Danced by* I. Farrell, M. Fesco, L. Hovis, D. Spingler, B. Towbin, V. Vestoff.

Scene 11 (Z)

"Four for the Road"

H. Gingold

(*Music by* Paul Klein. *Lyrics by* Lee Goldsmith and Fred Ebb.)

Scene 12 (&)

"What Next?"

The Company

(*Music by* Charles Zwar. *Lyrics by* Alan Melville.)

1960.08 WEST SIDE STORY

A Return Engagement of the Musical in Two Acts, 15 Scenes[10]. Book by Arthur Laurents. Based on a conception of Jerome Robbins. Music by Leonard Bernstein. Lyrics by Stephen Sondheim. Entire production directed and choreographed by Jerome Robbins. Scenic production by Oliver Smith. Costumes by Irene Sharaff. Lighting by Jean Rosenthal. Co-choreographer, Peter Gennaro. Assistant dance director, Howard Jeffrey. Musical direction, Joseph Lewis. Orchestrations by Leonard Bernstein, with Sid Ramin, Irwin Kostal. Produced by Robert E. Griffith and Harold S. Prince by arrangement with Roger L. Stevens. Opened 27 April 1960 at the Winter Garden and closed 10 December 1960 after 249 performances. Total performances, including original run: 981.

CAST: THE JETS: *Riff*, the Leader: THOMAS HASSON. *Tony*, his friend: LARRY KERT. *Action:* George Liker. *A-Rab:* Alan Johnson. *Baby John:* Barry Burns. *Big Deal:* Martin Charnin. *Diesel:* Donald Corby. *Snowboy:* Eddie Gaspar. *Mouth Piece:* Eddie Miller. *Tiger:* Richard Corrigan. *Gee-Tar:* Glenn Gibson. *Their Girls: Graziella:* Sandy Leeds. *Velma:* Audrey Hays. *Clarice:* Lee Lewis. *Pauline:* Judy Aldene. *Anybodys:* Pat Birch. *Minnie:* Barbara Monte.

THE SHARKS: *Bernardo*, the Leader: GEORGE MARCY. *Maria*, his Sister: CAROL LAWRENCE. *Anita*, his Girl: ALLYN ANN McLERIE. *Chino*, his Friend: Miguel De Vega. *Pepe:* Ben Vargas. *Indio:* Robert Avian. *Luis:* Sterling Clark. *Estella:* Danii Prior. *Burro:* Vince Baggetta. *Nibbles:* Ed Dutton. *Toro:* Kent Thomas. *Moose:* Marc Scott. *Their Girls: Rosalia:* Gloria Lambert. *Teresita:* Hope Clarke. *Francisca:* Anna Marie Moylan. *Marguerita:* Poligena Rogers. *Consuelo:* Genii Prior.

THE ADULTS: *Doc:* ALBERT M. OTTENHEIMER. *Schrank:* Ted Gunther. *Krupke:* Roger Franklin. *Gladhand:* Ross Hertz.

1960.09 FINIAN'S RAINBOW

A Revival of the Musical in Two Acts, 10 Scenes[11]. Book by E. Y. Harburg and Fred Saidy. Lyrics by E. Y. Harburg. Music by Burton Lane. Directed and choreographed by Herbert Ross. Scenery and lighting by Howard Bay. Costumes by Stanley Simmons. Orchestrations by Robert Russell Bennett and Don Walker. Musical director, Max Meth. Produced by the New York City Center Light Opera Company (Jean Dalrymple, Director.) Opened 27

April 1960 at the New York City Center, closing 8 May 1960 after 15 performances; re-opened 23 May 1960 at the 46th Street Theatre under the auspices of Robert Fryer and Lawrence Carr with John F. Herman and Theatrical Interests Plan, Inc. and closed 1 June 1960 after 12 additional performances. Total: 27 performances.

CAST[12] (in order of appearance): *Buzz Collins:* Eddie Bruce. *Sheriff:* Tom McElhany, (Tom McElhany). *First Sharecropper:* John McCurry. *Second Sharecropper:* Knute Sullivan. *Susan Mahoney:* ANITA ALVAREZ. *Henry:* Michael Darden. *Finian McLonergan:* BOBBY HOWES. *Sharon McLonergan:* JEANNIE CARSON. *Sam:* Arthur Garrison. *Woody Mahoney:* BIFF McGUIRE. *Og*, a Leprechaun: HOWARD MORRIS. *Senator Billboard Rawkins:* SORRELL BOOKE. *First Geologist:* Barney Johnston. *Second Geologist:* Robert Guillaume. *Howard:* Jim McGillan. *Diane:* Patty Austin. *Mr. Robust:* Edgar Daniels. *Mr. Shears:* Joe Ross. *First Passion Pilgrim Gospeller:* Jerry Laws. *Second Passion Pilgrim Gospeller:* Bill Glover. *Third Passion Pilgrim Gospeller:* Tiger Haynes. *First Deputy:* Don Gray. *Second Deputy:* Larry Mitchell.

Singers: Issa Arnal, Nan Courtney, Marnell Higley, Mary Louise, Lispet Nelson, Stephanie Reynolds, Alice Elizabeth Webb, Beverly Jane Welch, John Boni, Hugh Dilworth, Bill Glover, Don Gray, Robert Guillaume, Tiger Haynes, Barney Johnston, Jerry Laws, John McCurry, Larry Mitchell, Knute Sullivan. *Dancers:* Marilynn Allwyn, Ellen Halpin, Sally Lee, Diane McDaniel, Carmen Morales, Mavis Ray, Sandra Roveta, Jacqueline Walcott, Myrna White, Julius C. Fields, Jerry Fries, Gene Gavin, Loren Hightower, Nat Horne, Ronald Lee, Paul Olsen, Wakefield Poole, Jaime Juan Rogers, Ron Schwinn.

1960.10 CHRISTINE

A Musical in Two Acts, 18 Scenes. Book by Pearl S. Buck and Charles K. Peck, Jr. Based on the book "My Indian Family" by Hilda Wernher. Music by Sammy Fain. Lyrics by Paul Francis Webster. (Direction uncredited[13].) Choreography and musical numbers by Hanya Holm. Consultant on Indian customs, Bhaskar. Settings and lighting by Jo Mielziner. Costumes by Alvin Colt. Vocal and dance arrangements by Trude Rittman. Orchestrations by Philip J. Lang. Associate producer, Ben Frye. Produced by Oscar S. Lerman and Martin B. Cohen in association with Walter Cohen. Opened 28 April 1960 at the 46th Street Theatre and closed 7 May 1960 after 12 performances.

CAST (in order of appearance): *Beggar:* Joseph Crawford. *Servants to Dr. Singh:* Arthur Tookoyan, Tony Gardell, John Anania. *Auntie:* NANCY ANDREWS. *Uncle:* PHIL LEEDS. *Rainath:* BHASKAR. *Jaya:* Leslye Hunter. *Rajendra:* Augie Rios. *Krishna:* Steve Curry. *Mohan Roy:* Jonathan Morris. *Servant to Mohan Roy:* Nicholas Bianchi. *Station Master:* Louis Polacek. *Sita Roy:* JANET PAVEK. *Lady Christine FitzSimons:* MAUREEN O'HARA. *Dr. Rashil Singh:* MORLEY MEREDITH. *Dr. MacGowan:* Daniel Keyes. *The Matchmaker:* Barbara Webb. *The Prospective Brides (5): Tara:* Mai-Lan. *Lakshmi:* Jinja. *Amora:* Laurie Archer. *Twins:* Anjali Devi, Sasha. *Children of the Town:* Donna Lyn, Jan Rhodes, Louis Hernandez. *Priest:* John Anania.

Townspeople, Hindus, Muslims, Vendors, Beggars: Dancers: Laurie Archer, Sandra Bowman, Anjali Devi, Jinja, Mai-Lan, Jonalee Sanford, Sasha, Vito Durante, Dino Laudicino, Joseph Nelson, Alan Peterson, Joe Rocco, Gil Schwartz. *Singers:* Bea Barrett, Diana Corto, Marceline Dacker, Josephine Lang, Jen Nelson, Barbara Webb, John Anania, Nicholas Bianchi, Joseph Crawford, Tony Gardell, Louis Polacek, Arthur Tookoyan.

The story is laid in the little town of Akbarabad, India, at the present time.

Act 1, Scene 1: The Railroad Station in Akbarabad. *Scene 2:* The Study in Dr. Rashil Singh's home. *Scene 3:* Outside the Clinic. *Scene 4:* The Living Room, six days later. *Scene 5:* The Veranda, two months later. *Scene 6:* The Living Room. *Scene 7:* The Veranda. *Scene 8:* The Drawing Room. *Scene 9:* The Clinic. *Scene 10:* The City Square.

Act 2, Scene 1: The Veranda at Rashil's house. *Scene 2:* An open plain. *Scene 3:* A Shrine. *Scene 4:* The Living Room. *Scene 5:* The Veranda. *Scene 6:* The Drawing Room. *Scene 7:* The Veranda. *Scene 8:* Mohan Roy's Home.

ACT 1

"Welcome Song"

N. Andrews, P. Leeds, Bhaskar, Children, Chorus

"My Indian Family"

M. O'Hara

---

[10]Originally produced in New York 26 September 1957 at the Winter Garden for 732 performances. For Synopsis of Scenes and Musical Numbers, see original 1957 production.

[11]Originally produced in New York 10 January 1947 at the 46th Street Theatre for 725 performances. For Synopsis of Scenes and Musical Numbers, see original 1947 production. Michael Kidd's original choreography credited in "Dance of the Golden Crock."

[12]Cast changes for the transfer were as follows: *Sheriff:* Judson Morgan. *Susan Mahoney:* CARMEN GUTIERREZ. *Mr. Shears:* Cris Alexander. Withdrawn from the ensemble were *Singers:* Marnell Higley, John Boni, Hugh Dilworth, Don Gray. *Dancers:* Marilynn Allwyn, Ellen Halpin, Mavis Ray, Gene Gavin, Jaime Juan Rogers. Added to singing ensemble was Don Grilley.

[13]Direction credited to Edward Chodorov prior to New York opening.

"A Doctor's Soliloquy"
  M. Meredith
"UNICEF Song"
  Children
"My Little Lost Girl"
  M. O'Hara, M. Meredith
"I'm Just a Little Sparrow"
  L. Hunter, N. Andrews, Bhaskar, Servants, Children
"We're Just a Pair of Sparrows"
  M. O'Hara, L. Hunter
Cobra Ritual Dance
  Bhaskar, Dancers
"How to Pick a Man a Wife"
  N. Andrews, P. Leeds
"The Lovely Girls of Akbarabad"
  B. Weeb, Chorus
"Room in My Heart"
  M. O'Hara
"The Divali Festival"
  Bhaskar, Dancers, Singers
"I Never Meant to Fall in Love"
  M. Meredith, M. O'Hara

ACT 2

"Freedom Can Be a Most Uncomfortable Thing"
  N. Andrews, Friends
"Ireland Was Never Like This"
  M. O'Hara, Dancers
"He Loves Her"
  J. Pavek
"Christine"
  M. Meredith
"Room in My Heart" (reprise)
  M. O'Hara
"Freedom Can Be a Most Uncomfortable Thing" (reprise)
  N. Andrews, P. Leeds
a. Kathak (Plate Dance)
  Bhaskar, Girls

b. Kathakali
  Dancing Boys
c. Bharatha Natyan
  Bhaskar, Dancing Girls and Boys
"The Woman I Was Before"
  M. O'Hara
"A Doctor's Soliloquy" (reprise)
  M. O'Hara, M. Meredith
"I Never Meant to Fall in Love" (reprise)
  M. O'Hara, M. Meredith

1960.11 # THE KING AND I

A Revival of the Musical Play in Two Acts, 17 Scenes[14]. Book and lyrics by Oscar Hammerstein II. Music by Richard Rodgers. Based on the novel "Anna and the King of Siam" by Margaret Landon. Settings by Jo Mielziner. Costumes by Irene Sharaff, supervised by Stanley Simmons. Lighting by Klaus Holm. Choreography by Jerome Robbins, reproduced by Yuriko. Orchestrations by Robert Russell Bennett. Musical director, Pembroke Davenport. Directed by John Fearnley. Produced by the New York City Center Light Opera Company (Jean Dalrymple, Director). Opened 11 May 1960 at the New York City Center and closed 29 May 1960 after 15 performances.

CAST (in order of appearance): *Captain Orton*: Sam Kirkham. *Louis Leonowens*: Richard Mills. *Anna Leonowens*: BARBARA COOK. *The Interpreter*: Murray Gitlin. *The Kralahome*: Ted Beniades. *The King*: FARLEY GRANGER. *Phra Alack*: Mark Satow. *Lun Tha*: SETH RIGGS. *Tuptim*: JOY CLEMENTS. *Lady Thiang*: ANITA DARIAN. *Prince Chulalongkorn*: Miki Lamont. *Princess Ying Yaowalak*: Susan Lynn Kikuchi. *Sir Edward Ramsay*: Claude Horton.
  The Small House of Uncle Thomas: *Narrator*: JOY CLEMENTS. *Uncle Thomas*: Bettina Dearborn. *Little Eva*: Wonci Lui. *Topsy*: Julie Oser. *Eliza*: YURIKO. *King Simon*: GEMZE DE LAPPE. *Angel*: MARION JIM. *Drummer*: Murray Gitlin.
  Princes and Princesses: Alfred De Arco, Delfino De Arco, Evelyn Eng, Vivian Hernandez, Lauretta Lee, Roger Mahabirishingh, Richard Mills, Paul Petrillo, Ado Sato, Claudia Satow. *The Royal Dancers*: Diane Adler, Fumi Akimoto, Ted August, Ethel Bell, Paula Chin, Barbara Creed, Bettina Dearborn, Barrie Duffus, Victor Duntiere, Jan Goldin, Marion Jim, Wonci Lui, Julie Oser, Wintress Perkins, Joysanne Sidimus, Nancy Stevens, Roland Vasquez. *Singers (Wives, Priests, Amazons, Slaves)*: Jyll Alexander, Jennie Andrea, Irving Barnes, Ellen Berse, Jim Connor, Marvin Goodis, Ann Marisse, Claire Richard, Beatrice Ruth.

[14]Originally produced in New York 29 March 1951 at the St. James Theatre for 1246 performances. For Synopsis of Scenes and Musical Numbers, see original 1951 production.

Richard Burton in CAMELOT (Photo: Friedman-Abeles)
Billy Rose Theatre Collection, New York Public Library for the Performing Arts

1960–1961 SEASON

1960.12 ## VINTAGE '60

A Musical Revue in Two Acts, 31 Scenes. Written by Jack Wilson, Alan Jeffreys, Maxwell Grant. Choreography and staging by Jonathan Lucas. Comedy direction by Michael Ross. Set design by Fred Voelpel. Costumes by Raymond Aghayan. Original men's costumes by Ret Turner. Costumes for New York production supervised by Fred Voelpel. Musical arrangements by Allyn Ferguson. Musical direction by Gershon Kingsley. Entire production supervised by Michael Ross. Produced by David Merrick, with Zev Bufman, George Skaff, Max Perkins. Opened 12 September 1960 at the Brooks Atkinson Theatre and closed 17 September 1960 after 8 performances.

CAST: BARBARA HELLER, FAY DeWITT, DICK PATTERSON, MICKEY DEEMS, EMMALINE HENRY, BERT CONVY, Sylvia Lewis, Marc Wilder, Garrett Lewis, Bob Trevis, Bonnie Scott, Michele Lee, Larry Billman, Vilma Auld, Harvey Church, Sue Sellors, Robert Lone.

ACT 1

Scene 1

"The Time Is Now"
The Company
(*Music by* Mark Bucci. *Lyrics by* David Rogers.)

Scene 2

Well Dressed Man
(*by* Mickey Deems)
Announcer: D. Patterson. *Well Dressed Man*: M. Deems.

Scene 3

"More"
(*Music and Lyrics by* Jack Wilson and Alan Jeffreys.)
Girl: B. Heller. *Dancers*: M. Wilder, G. Lewis, L. Billman.

Scene 4

"All American"
(*Music by* Mark Bucci. *Lyrics by* David Rogers.)
First Scientist: G. Lewis. *Second Scientist*: M. Deems. *Third Scientist*: D. Patterson. *Officer*: B. Lone.

Scene 5

Conversation Piece
(*by* Mickey Deems)
Wife: F. DeWitt. *Husband*: M. Deems.

Scene 6

"Isms"
B. Heller
(*Music by* David Baker. *Lyrics by* Sheldon Harnick.)

Scene 7

"Five Piece Band"
(*Music and Lyrics by* Jack Wilson, Alan Jeffreys, Maxwell Grant.)
Singer: M. Lee. *Band*: M. Wilder, G. Lewis, L. Billman, H. Church, B. Lone.

Scene 8

Two Piece Band
(*by* Barbara Heller and Fay DeWitt)
Band: B. Heller, F. DeWitt.

Scene 9

Here I Am
(*by* Jack Wilson and Alan Jeffreys)
Man: M. Deems. *Secretary*: L. Billman.

Scene 10

Moral Climate
(*by* Maxwell Grant and Alan Jeffreys)
First Couple: B. Heller, L. Billman. *Second Couple*: F. DeWitt, D. Patterson.

Scene 11

Cat
(*by* Jack Wilson and Alan Jeffreys)
Cat: G. Lewis. *First Girl*: B. Scott. *Second Girl*: S. Lewis. *Third Girl*: S. Sellors.

Scene 12

Dueling
(*by* Maxwell Grant, Alan Jeffreys and Phil Green)
D. Patterson

Scene 13

"Down in the Streets"
F. DeWitt
(*Music and Lyrics by* Tommy Garlock and Alan Jeffreys.)
Chorus: M. Wilder, G. Lewis, H. Church, L. Billman, B. Lone.

Scene 14

Raven
(*by* Jack Wilson and Alan Jeffreys)
Man: D. Patterson. *Raven*: S. Lewis.

Scene 15

Our Town
(*by* William Lanteau)
Narrator: M. Deems. *Lucy Platz*: B. Heller. *Loretta Crawford*: E. Henry. *Villain*: B. Trevis. *Dancer*: L. Billman. *Pilot*: D. Patterson. *Nurse*: V. Auld.

Scene 16

"Convention"
(*Sketch, Music and Lyrics by* Jack Wilson, Alan Jeffreys, Maxwell Grant.)
Announcer: B. Trevis. *M.C.*: M. Deems. *Barbara Bitton*: B. Heller. *Representative from New York*: L. Billman. *First Stripper*: E. Henry. *Second Stripper*: S. Lewis. *Richard Nixon*: D. Patterson. *Representative from Arkansas*: M. Wilder. *Representative from California*: G. Lewis. *Pat Nixon*: F. DeWitt. *G.O.P. Chorus and Dancers*: B. Scott, M. Lee, V. Auld, S. Sellors, H. Church, B. Lone.

ACT 2

Scene 1

"Do It in Two"
B. Scott
(*Music and Lyrics by* Jack Wilson and Alan Jeffreys.)
Lead Dancers: M. Wilder, S. Lewis. *Dancers*: G. Lewis, M. Lee, L. Billman, V. Auld, S. Sellors, H. Church, B. Lone.

Scene 2

"Dublin Town"
F. DeWitt
(*Music by* Paul Klein. *Lyrics by* Fred Ebb and Lee Goldsmith.)

Scene 3

Strained Relations
(*by* Alan Jeffreys and Maxwell Grant)
Announcer: E. Henry. *The Group*: L. Billman, M. Deems, F. DeWitt, B. Heller, M. Wilder, E. Henry, D. Patterson, B. Scott, G. Lewis, S. Lewis.

Scene 4

Treat 'Em Rough
(*by* Ronald Axe, William Link, Richard Levinson)
Friend: M. Deems. *Boy*: D. Patterson. *Girl*: F. DeWitt.

Scene 5

Angry Young Girl
(*by* Jack Wilson)B. Heller
(*Background Music by* Armin Hoffman.)

Scene 6

"No Words" (dance)
(*by* Jack Wilson, Alan Jeffreys, Maxwell Grant)
Lead Dancer: M. Wilder. *Dancers*: S. Lewis, V. Auld, S. Sellors, L. Billman, G. Lewis, H. Church, B. Lone.

Scene 7

"Forget Me"
(*Music by* David Baker. *Lyrics by* Sheldon Harnick.)
Girl: B. Heller. *Boy*: G. Lewis.

Scene 8

Mother and Son
(*by* Maxwell Grant and Alan Jeffreys)
Mother: E. Henry. *Son*: M. Deems.

Scene 9

The Man
(*by* Jack Wilson, Alan Jeffreys and Maxwell Grant)
Dino: B. Convy. *Shirley*: B. Scott. *Peter*: L. Billman. *Franky*: D. Patterson.

Scene 10

"Tranquilizers"
(*Music and Lyrics by* Bud McCreery.)
F. DeWitt

Scene 11

Vanityades
(*by* David Rogers)
Husband: M. Deems. *Wife*: B. Heller.

Scene 12

   The Lobster and the Crab
      (*by* Mickey Deems) M. Deems

Scene 13

   "Afraid of Love"
      (*Sketch by* Michael Ross. *Music and Lyrics by* Alice Clark and
      David Morton.)
         Woman: B. Heller. *Waiters*: M. Wilder, L. Billman.

Scene 14

   The Kinney System Parking Lot Plot
      The Company
      (*by* Jack Wilson, Alan Jeffreys, Maxwell Grant)

Scene 15

   Finale
      The Company

IRMA LA DOUCE

1960.13

A Musical Comedy in Two Acts, 20 Scenes. Original (French) book and
lyrics by Alexandre Breffort. Music by Marguerite Monnot. English book
and lyrics by Julian More. Directed by Peter Brook. Choreography by Onna
White. Settings and costumes by Rolf Gerard. Lighting by Joe Davis.
Orchestrations by Andre Popp. Additional orchestrations by Robert Ginzler.
Dance music by John Kander. Vocal arrangements by Bert Waller and
Stanley Lebowsky. Musical director, Stanley Lebowsky. Produced by David
Merrick in association with Donald Albery and H. M. Tennent, Ltd. and by
arrangement with Henry Hall. Opened 29 September 1960 at the Plymouth
Theatre, moved 30 October 1961 to the Alvin Theatre, and closed 31
December 1961 after 527 performances.

CAST (in order of appearance): *Bob-Le-Hotu*, Proprietor of the Bar-des-Inquiets:
CLIVE REVILL. *Irma-La-Douce*, a Poule: ELIZABETH SEAL. *A Client*: Eddie
Gasper. *Jojo-Les-Yeux-Sales*, a Mec: ZACK MATALON. *Roberto-Les-Diams*, a Mec:
Aric Lavie. *Persil-Le-Noir*, a Mec: Osborne Smith. *Frangipane*: Stuart Damon. *Polyte-
Le-Mou*, a Mec: Fred Gwynne. *Police Inspector*: George S. Irving. *Nestor-Le-Fripe*, a
Law Student: KEITH MICHELL. *M. Bougne*, a Ballroom Owner: George Del Monte.
Counsel for the Prosecution: Rico Froehlich. *Counsel for the Defense*: Rudy Tronto. *An
Usher*: Elliott Gould. *An Honest Man*: Joe Rocco. *Court Gendarme*: Byron Mitchell.
First Warder: Elliott Gould. *Second Warder*: George Del Monte. *Third Warder*: Rico
Froehlich. *A Priest*: Elliott Gould. *A Tax Inspector*: Rudy Tronto.
   Gendarmes, Prisoners, Irma's Admirers: George Del Monte, Michael Fesco, Rico
Froehlich, Eddie Gasper, Elliott Gould, Byron Mitchell, Rudy Tronto.

Act 1, Scene 1: Outside the Bar-des-Inquiets, Pigalle, Paris, France. *Scene 2*: Inside the
Bar. *Scene 3*: Irma's Room. *Scene 4*: The Bridge Caulaincourt. *Scene 5*: Hotel Rapid—
Bedroom. *Scene 6*: The Bar. *Scene 7*: Hotel Rapid. *Scene 8*: Nestor and Irma's Room.
Scene 9: Narrow Street. *Scene 10*: The Banks of the Seine. *Scene 11*: The Bar.

Act 2, Scene 1: A Low Court. *Scene 2*: Prison Ship. *Scene 3*: The Street outside Irma's
House. *Scene 4*: Devil's Island. *Scene 5*: The Raft. *Scene 6*: A Paris Street. *Scene 7*: The
Police Station. *Scene 8*: The Street. *Scene 9*: Irma's Room.

ACT 1

Scene 1

   "Valse Milieu"
      C. Revill

Scene 2

   "Sons of France"
      Z. Matalon, A. Lavie, O. Smith, F. Gwynne, G. S. Irving

   "The Bridge of Caulaincourt"
      E. Seal, K. Michell

Scene 3

   "Our Language of Love"
      E. Seal, K. Michell

Scene 4

   "She's Got the Lot"
      G. S. Irving, Irma's Admirers

Scene 5

   "Our Language of Love" (reprise)
      E. Seal

Scene 6

   "Dis-Donc"
      E. Seal

   "Le Grisbi is le Root of le Evil in Man"
      C. Revill, K. Michell, Z. Matalon, A. Lavie, O. Smith

Scene 8

   "Wreck of a Mec"
      K. Michell

Scene 9

   "That's a Crime"
      C. Revill, K. Michell, Z. Matalon, A. Lavie, O. Smith

ACT 2

Scene 1

   "The Bridge of Caulaincourt" (reprise)
      E. Seal, K. Michell

Scene 2

   "From a Prison Cell"
      K. Michell, Z. Matalon, A. Lavie, O. Smith

Scene 3

   "Irma-la-Douce"
      E. Seal

Scene 4

   "There Is Only One Paris for That"
      K. Michell, Z. Matalon, A. Lavie, O. Smith, Prisoners

Scene 5

   "The Freedom of the Seas"
      K. Michell, Z. Matalon, A. Lavie, O. Smith

   Storm Ballet (Arctic Ballet)
      E. Seal, Company

Scene 6

   "There Is Only One Paris for That" (reprise)
      K. Michell, Z. Matalon, A. Lavie, O. Smith

   "Our Language of Love" (reprise)
      E. Seal

Scene 7

   "But"
      K. Michell, G. S. Irving, R. Tronto, G. Del Monte, F. Gwynne

Scene 9

   "Christmas Child" (Finale)
      Company

THE MIKADO,
   or The Town of Titipu

1960.14

A Revival of the Comic Opera in Two Acts[1]. Libretto by William S. Gilbert.
Music by Arthur Sullivan. Staged by Dorothy Raedler. Scenic and lighting
design by Donald Oenslager. Costume design by Patton Campbell.
Conducted by Robert Irving. Produced by the New York City Opera.
Opened 30 September 1960 at the New York City Center and closed 29
October 1960 after 4 performances in repertory.

CAST: *The Mikado of Japan*: JAMES PEASE. *Nanki-Poo*, his son, disguised as a
wandering minstrel in love with Yum-Yum: FRANK PORETTA. *Ko-Ko*, Lord High
Executioner of Titipu: NORMAN KELLEY. *Pooh-Bah*, Lord High Everything Else:
HERBERT BEATTIE. *Pish-Tush*, a Noble Lord: William Metcalf. *Yum-Yum, Pitti-
Sing, Peep-Bo*, three sisters, wards of Ko-Ko: BARBARA MEISTER, NANCY
DUSSAULT, SOPHIA STEFFAN. *Katisha*: RUTH KOBART. *Chorus of School Girls,
Nobles, Guards and Coolies*: New York City Opera Chorus.

THE PIRATES OF PENZANCE,
   or The Slave of Duty

1960.15

A Revival of the Comic Opera in Two Acts[2]. Libretto by William S. Gilbert.
Music by Arthur Sullivan. Staged by Dorothy Raedler. Costume design by
Patton Campbell. Conducted by Robert Irving. Produced by the New York

---

[1]First presented in New York 20 July, 10-29 August 1885 at the Union
Square and People's Theatres for 22 performances. First authorized pro-
duction presented 19 August 1885 at the Fifth Avenue Theatre by Richard
D'Oyly Carte for 250 performances. For Synopsis of Scenes and Musical
Numbers, see 19 August 1885 D'Oyly Carte production.
[2]First presented in New York 31 December 1879 at the Fifth Avenue
Theatre for a total of 91 performances in two engagements. For Synopsis of
Scenes and Musical Numbers, see original 1879 production.

City Opera. Opened 6 October 1960 at the New York City Center and closed 4 November 1960 after 4 performances in repertory.

CAST: *Major General Stanley:* WILLIAM CHAPMAN. *The Pirate King:* ARNOLD VOKETAITIS. *Samuel,* his Lieutenant: William Metcalf. *Frederic,* the Pirate Apprentice: FRANK PORETTA. *Sergeant of Police:* HERBERT BEATTIE. *Mabel, Edith Kate, Isabel,* General Stanley's Daughters: BARBARA MEISTER, JOY CLEMENS, SOPHIA STEFFAN, Ritz Metzger. *Ruth,* Pirate Maid-of-all-work: RUTH KOBART. *Chorus of Pirates, Police and General Stanley's Daughters:* New York City Opera Chorus.

AN EVENING WITH MIKE NICHOLS AND ELAINE MAY
1960.16

A Comedy Revue in Two Acts. (Conceived and written by Mike Nichols and Elaine May.) Directed by Arthur Penn. Designed by Marvin Reiss. Music composed by William Goldenberg. Costumes by Hazel Roy. Associate producer, Peter S. Katz. Produced by Alexander H. Cohen (A Nine O'Clock Theatre Production). Opened 8 October 1960 at the John Golden Theatre and closed 1 July 1961 after 306 performances.

CAST: MIKE NICHOLS, ELAINE MAY.

The program will be announced by the performers. Sketches performed by Nichols and May were drawn from the following:

Adultery

Telephone

Mother and Son

Disc Jockey

The Dawn of Love, or The Sun Also Rises in an Automobile

P.T.A.Chairman

Boss and Secretary (Cocktail Piano)

Spy Sketch (Mysterioso)

Dentist (Second Piano Concerto)

"Everybody's Doin' It"
(Music and Lyrics by Irving Berlin.)

Bach to Bach

Tango

Psychiatrist (Sonata for Piano and Celeste)

Father and Daughter (Chopin)

Pirandello sketch

Interview of Screen Star as Gertrude Stein

1960.17 LAUGHS AND OTHER EVENTS

A One Man Musical Revue in Two Acts. Staged by Tony Charmoli. (Settings) Designed and lighted by John Robert Lloyd. Produced by Martin Tahse. Opened 10 October 1960 at the Ethel Barrymore Theatre and closed 15 October 1960 after 8 performances.

CAST: STANLEY HOLLOWAY.
Musicians: Richmond Gale and Arthur Siegel (Pianos), Jerry Silverman (Banjo), Allan Atlas (Concertina).

ACT 1

"A Cup O' Tea"

"I Knew a Private"

Gunner Joe
(Monologue by George Edgar.)

"You Gotta Get Aut"

"My Word, You Do Look Queer"
(Music and Lyrics by R. P. Weston and Bert Lee.)

"Poppies"

The 'Ole in the Ark
(Monologue by Stanley Holloway.)

"Je Sais Que Vous Etes Jolie"

"The Christening"

"The Little Shirt My Mother Made for Me"
(Music and Lyrics by H. Wincott.)

"And Yet I Don't Know" (Buying a Wedding Present)
(Music and Lyrics by R. P. Weston.)

"Signalman Dan"

The Lion and Albert
(Monologue by Marriott Edgar.)

Old Tavern Songs:

"Champagne Charlie"

"So We Will Sing"

"(Shelling) Green Peas"

"Going to the Derby"

ACT 2

"Sentry Song"

On Strike
(Monologue by Charles Pond.)

"I Love Mary"

Three Ha' Pence a Foot
(Monologue by Marriott Edgar.)

"(Oh,) I Must Go Home Tonight"
(Music and Lyrics by William Hargreaves.)

"Old Sam" (Sam, pick oop tha' Musket)
(Monologue by Stanley Holloway. Music by Wolseley Charles.)

"Brahn Boots"
(Music and Lyrics by R. P. Weston and Bert Lee.)

"The Gay Young Farmer"

Return of Albert
(Monologue by Marriott Edgar.)

"Two Lovely Black Eyes"
(Music and Lyrics by Charles Coburn.)

"Wotcher" (Knock'd 'Em in the Old Kent Road)
(Music and Lyrics by Charles Ingle.)

"A Little Bit of Cucumber"
(Music and Lyrics by T. W. Connor.)

"I'm 'Enery the VIII, (I Am)"
(Music and Lyrics by Fred Murray and R. P. Weston.)

"Any Old Iron"
(Music and Lyrics by Charles Collins, E. A. Sheppard, Fred Terry.)

"It'll All Be the Same (A Hundred Years from Now)"
(Music and Lyrics by Arthur Anderson and Melville Gideon.)

1960.18 THE WALL

A Drama (with music) in Two Acts by Millard Lampell. Based on the novel of the same name by John Hersey. Songs adapted from the Yiddish by Robert DeCormier and Millard Lampell. Directed by Morton DaCosta. Settings and lighting by Howard Bay. Costumes by Noel Taylor. Produced by Kermit Bloomgarden and Billy Rose. Opened 11 October 1960 at the Billy Rose Theater and closed 4 March 1961 after 162 performances.

CAST (in order of appearance): *Pavel Menkes:* Vincent Gardenia. *Fishel Shpunt:* Joseph Buloff. *Dolek Berson:* GEORGE C. SCOTT. *German Private:* James Nielsen. *Katz:* James Ray. *Reb Mazur:* Muni Seroff. *Halinka Apt:* Claudette Nevins. *Clerk:* Joseph Bernard. *Rachel Apt:* Yvonne Mitchell. *Symka Berson:* Marian Seldes. *Mordecai Apt:* Michael Ebert. *Pan Apt:* David Opatoshu. *David Apt:* Paul Mace. *Stefan Mazur:* Robert Drivas. *Rutka Mazur:* Leila Martin. *Pan Kogan:* Truman Gaige. *Pani Kogan:* Marketa Kimbrell. *Regina Kogan:* Lorraine Abate. *German Sergeant:* Robert Burr. *Man and Wife:* James Stevenson, Alberta Nelson. *Woman in Babushka:* Rita Karin. *Rappaport:* Leon B. Stevens. *Beggar Man:* Don Doherty. *Beggar Children:* Rochelle Horowitz, Richard Carafa. *German Oficer:* Norbert Horowitz. *Woman in Selection:* Honey MacKenzie. *Slonim:* Sol Frieder.
Men and Women of the Ghetto: Joe Alfasa, Alice Beardsley, Al Verb, Kenneth Reid.

The action covers the period from the spring of 1940 to the spring of 1943 on a street in Warsaw.

MUSICAL NUMBERS

"Oy, a nacht a sheyne" (Oh, What a Lovely Night)

"Sheyn bin ich, sheyn" (Pretty am I, So Pretty)

"Tsipele" (Little Tsipele)
(Music by I. Glatstein. Yiddish Lyrics by M. Broderson.)

"Van der ershter vet lachn" (Who will be the first to laugh)
(Music and Yiddish Lyrics by M. Gebirtig.)

"Shtil, di nacht iz oysgeshternt" (Silent, the starry night)
(Words by Hirsch Glick.)

"Yisrolik" (My name is Yisrolik)
  (*Music by* M. Weksler. *Yiddish Lyrics by* L. Rosenthal.)
"Farvos iz der himl geven nechtn loyter?" (Why was the sky so bright yesterday?)
  (*Words by* L. Opeskin.)
"Oyf dem zamd fun negev" (On the sands of the Negev)
  (*Music:* Anonymous. *Yiddish Lyrics by* M. L. Gisser, based on Israeli Hebrew text by R. Klatchkin.)
"A mame's nign" (A mother's melody)
  (*Words by* R. Lifshitz.)
"Findjan" (arabic term for the steaming kettle)
  (*Music:* Anonymous. *Yiddish Lyrics by* R. Karpinovitch, based on an Israeli Hebrew text by H. Feiner.)
"Oy, dortn, dortn ibern vaserl" (Oh, there across the water)
"Frunze verde" (Green leaves)
  (*Music from* a Roumanian doina. *Lyrics by* I. Horowitz.)
"Noch a glezele tey" (Another little cup of tea)
  (*Music and Lyrics by* M. Gebirtig.)
"Idish" (Yiddish)
  (*Music from* a popular tango. *Yiddish Lyrics by* I. Kotliar.)
"Motele"
  (*Music and Lyrics by* M. Gebirtig.)

TENDERLOIN

1960.19

A Musical Comedy in Two Acts, 23 Scenes and an Epilogue. Book by George Abbott and Jerome Weidman. Based on the novel of the same name by Samuel Hopkins Adams. Music by Jerry Bock. Lyrics by Sheldon Harnick. Directed by George Abbott. Dances and musical numbers staged by Joe Layton. Sets and costumes by Cecil Beaton. (Lighting uncredited.) Musical direction by Hal Hastings. Orchestrations by Irwin Kostal. Dance music arranged by Jack Elliott. Produced by Robert E. Griffith and Harold S. Prince. Opened 17 October 1960 at the 46th Street Theatre and closed 23 April 1961 after 216 performances.

CAST (in order of appearance): *Tommy:* RON HUSMANN. *Nita:* EILEEN RODGERS. *Lieut. Schmidt* (The Pantata): RALPH DUNN. *Reverend Brock:* MAURICE EVANS. *Gertie:* LEE BECKER (Theodore). *Margie:* Margery Gray. *Dorothy:* Dorothy Frank. *Girl:* Patsy Peterson. *Young Man:* Dargan Motgomery. *Jessica:* IRENE KANE. *Laura:* WYNNE MILLER. *Ellington:* Gordon Cook. *Joe:* REX EVERHART. *Purdy:* RAYMOND BRAMLEY. *Martin:* Lanier Davis. *Deacon:* ROY FANT. *Frye:* EDDIE PHILLIPS. *Rooney:* Jordan Howard. *Nellie:* Marguerite Shaw. *Becker:* Michael Roberts. *Callahan:* Jack McCann. *Prostitutes:* Erin Martin, Margery Gray. *Drunk:* Bob Fitch. *Maggie:* Pat Turner. *Liz:* Christine Norden. *Mrs. Barker:* Elaine Rogers. *Chairman:* Joe Hill.
  Dancers: Jere Admire, David Evans, Bob Fitch, Dorothy Frank, Margery Gray, Mickey Gunnersen, Sandy Leeds, Jack Leigh, Erin Martin, Marjorie Pragon, Wakefield Poole, Ronald B. Stratton, Jayne Turner, Pat Turner. *Singers:* Charles Aschmann, Carvel Carter, Nancy Emes, John Ford, Stokeley Gray, Maria Graziano, Joe Hill, Jordan Howard, Gail Johnston, Jack McCann, Dargan Montgomery, Patsy Peterson, Claire Richard, Michael Roberts, Elaine Rogers.

Act 1, Scene 1: Limbo; Reverend Brock's Church. New York City, 1890s. *Scene 2:* A Street outside the Church. *Scene 3:* Parish House. *Scene 4:* A Street in front of the Nineteenth Precinct. *Scene 5:* The Nineteenth Precinct Police Station. *Scene 6:* Precinct street. *Scene 7:* The Living Room of Laura Crosbie's Fifth Avenue House. *Scene 8:* A Street in front of Clark's. *Scene 9:* Clark's, a popular Tenderloin haunt. *Scene 10:* Street in front of Clark's. *Scene 11:* A Beach. *Scene 12:* A Street in front of Clark's. *Scene 13:* Clark's, 11:00PM.

Act 2, Scene 1: Central Park. *Scene 2:* A Street. *Scene 3:* Clark's. *Scene 4:* The Trial. *Scene 5:* Clark's. *Scene 6:* The Parish House at night. *Scene 7:* Precinct street. *Scene 8:* The Courtroom. *Scene 9:* A Street. *Scene 10:* Parish House. *Epilogue:* Detroit.

ACT 1

Scene 1
  "Bless This Land"
    The Choir
  "Little Old New York"
    E. Rodgers, L. Becker, Company
Scene 3
  "Dr. Brock"
    M. Evans
  "Artificial Flowers"
    R. Husmann
  "What's In It for You?"
    M. Evans, R. Husmann

Scene 6
  "Reform"
    L. Becker, N. Emes, C. Carter
Scene 7
  "Tommy, Tommy"
    W. Miller
Scene 9
  "Artificial Flowers" (Reprise)
    M. Gray
  "The Picture of Happiness"
    R. Husmann
  Dance
    L. Becker, E. Phillips, Company
Scene 11
  "Dear Friend"
    M. Evans, W. Miller, I. Kane, J. Turner
  "The Army of the Just"
    M. Evans, L. Davis, J. Leigh, C. Aschmann, S. Gray
Scene 13
  "How the Money Changes Hands"
    M. Evans, E. Rodgers, C. Norden, E. Phillips, L. Becker, Company

ACT 2
Scene 1
  "Good Clean Fun"
    M. Evans, Company
  "My Miss Mary"
    R. Husmann, W. Miller, Singers
Scene 3
  "My Gentle Young Johnny"
    E. Rodgers
Scene 4
  "The Trial"
    Company
Scene 5
  "The Tenderloin Celebration"
    E. Phillips, L. Becker, Company
Scene 9
  "Reform" (reprise)
    L. Becker, M. Gray, C. Norden, Company
Scene 10
  "Tommy, Tommy" (reprise)
    W. Miller
  Epilogue
  "Little Old New York" (Detroit reprise)
    Company

THE UNSINKABLE MOLLY BROWN

1960.20

A Musical Comedy in Two Acts, 20 Scenes. Book by Richard Morris. Music and lyrics by Meredith Willson. Directed by Dore Schary. Musical numbers staged by Peter Gennaro. Costumes by Miles White. Sets by Oliver Smith. Lighting by Peggy Clark. Orchestrations by Don Walker. Vocal arrangements and musical direction by Herbert Greene. Ballet music arranged by Sol Berkowitz. Associate producer, Walter Reilly. Produced by the Theatre Guild and Dore Schary. Opened 3 November 1960 at the Winter Garden and closed 10 February 1962 after 532 performances.

CAST (in order of appearance): *Molly Tobin:* TAMMY GRIMES. *Michael Tobin:* Sterling Clark. *Aloysius Tobin:* Bill Starr. *Patrick Tobin:* Bob Daley. *Father Flynn:* Norman Fredericks. *Shamus Tobin:* CAMERON PRUD'HOMME. *Brawling Miners:* Alex Stevens, Joe Pronto. *Charlie:* Woody Hurst. *Christmas Morgan:* Joseph Sirola. *Burt:* Tom Larson. *Banjo:* Billy Faier. *Prostitutes:* Rae McLean, Lynn Gay Lorino. *Johnny 'Leadville' Brown:* HARVE PRESNELL, (James Hurst, alt.). *Gitter:* Joe Pronto. *A Boy:* Paul Floyd. *Sheriff:* Terry Violino. *Mrs. McGlone:* EDITH MEISER. *Monsignor Ryan:* Jack Harrold. *Roberts:* Christopher Hewett. *Professor Gardella:* Dale Malone. *Germaine:* June Card. *Princess DeLong:* Anna Maria Moylan, Mony Dalmes. *Prince DeLong:* Mitchell Gregg. *Countess Ethanotous:* Wanda Saxon. *Jenab-ashros:* Marvin Goodis. *Grand Duchess Marie Nicholaiovna:* Patricia Kelly. *Count Feranti:* Michael Davis. *Duchess of Burlingame:* Barbara Newman. *Duke of Burlingame:* Ted Adkins. *Baron of Auld:* Bob Daley. *Malcolm Broderick:* Barney Johnston. *Mrs. Wadlington:*

Lynne Osborne. *Mr. Wadlington:* Norman Fredericks. *Young Waiter:* Michael Davis. *Maitre D':* Dale Malone. *Page:* Bobby Brownell. *Male Passenger:* Marvin Goodis. *Mother:* Nada Rowand. *Wounded Sailor:* Bill Starr.

Singers: June Card, Ceil Delli, Pat Finch, Marian Heraldson, Patricia Kelly, Lynne Osborne, Nada Rowland, Wanda Saxon, Michael Davis, Norman Fredericks, Marvin Goodis, Woody Hurst, Barney Johnson, Tom Larson, Dale Malone, Louis Polacek. *Dancers:* Barbara Gine, Diana Hunter, Lynn Gay Lorino, Susan May, Anna Marie Moylan, Rae McLean, Barbara Newman, Nanette Rosen, Ted Adkins, Sterling Clark, Bob Daley, Vito Durante, Don Emmons, Joe Pronto, Mark Ross, Bill Starr, Alex Stevens, Terry Violino.

Act 1, Scene 1: Exterior of the Tobin Shack, Hannibal, Missouri. The turn of the century. *Scene 2:* The road by the Tobin shack. Sun-up the next morning. *Scene 3:* The Saddle Rock Saloon. Leadville, Colorado. Weeks later. *Scene 4:* The street in front of the Saddle Rock. Sunday night, three weeks later. *Scene 5:* Johnny's log cabin. A month later. *Scene 6:* The same, three weeks later. *Scene 7:* Pennsylvania Avenue, Denver, Colorado. Six months later. *Scene 8:* The Terrace of Mrs. McGlone's Denver Mansion. Later that evening. *Scene 9:* Pennsylvania Avenue. Immediately following. *Scene 10:* The Red Parlor of the Browns' Denver Mansion. The evening of their house-warming.

Act 2, Scene 1: The Browns' Paris Salon. A spring afternoon, years later. *Scene 2:* Upper hallway of the Brwons' Denver Mansion. An evening months later. *Scene 3:* The Red Parlor, 8 P.M. that evening. *Scene 4:* The Red Parlor. Next morning. *Scene 5:* The street in front of the Saddle Rock. Months later. *Scene 6:* Monte Carlo. A club off the Casino. Early spring, 1912. *Scene 7:* Outside the club. A moment later. *Scene 8:* The mid-Atlantic. Shortly after 2:30 A.M. April 15, 1912. *Scene 9:* Upper hallway, Brown home. Two weeks later. *Scene 10:* The Rockies.

ACT 1
Scene 1
 "I Ain't Down Yet"
  T. Grimes, S. Clark, B. Starr, B. Daley
Scene 3
 "Belly Up to the Bar, Boys"
  T. Grimes, J. Sirola, Miners
Scene 4
 "I've A'ready Started In"
  H. Presnell, J. Sirola, W. Hurst, T. Larson, J. Pronto
Scene 5
 "I'll Never Say No"
  H. Presnell
 "My Own Brass Bed"
  T. Grimes
Scene 7
 "The Denver Police"
  M. Ross, T. Violino, D. Emmons
Scene 8
 "Beautiful People of Denver"
  T. Grimes
 "Are You Sure?"
  T. Grimes, Guests
Scene 10
 "I Ain't Down Yet" (reprise)
  T. Grimes, H. Presnell

ACT 2
Scene 1
 "Happy Birthday, Mrs. J. J. Brown"
  M. Dalmes, M. Gregg, International Set
 "Bon Jour" (The Language Song)
  T. Grimes, M. Gregg, International Set
 "If I Knew"
  H. Presnell
Scene 2
 "Chick-a-Pen"
  T. Grimes, H. Presnell
Scene 5
 "Keep-a-Hoppin'"
  H. Presnell, His Leadville Friends
 "Leadville Johnny Brown" (Soliloquy)
  H. Presnell
Scene 6
 "Up Where the People Are" (dance)
  Monte Carlo Guests

 "Dolce Far Niente"/("I May Never Fall in Love With You")
  M. Gregg, T. Grimes
Scene 10
 "I Ain't Down Yet" (reprise)
  H. Presnell, T. Grimes, Leadville Friends

1960.21

CAMELOT

A Musical in Two Acts, 20 Scenes. Book and lyrics by Alan Jay Lerner. Based on the novel "The Once and Future King" by T. H. White. Music by Frederick Loewe. Staged by Moss Hart. Choreography and musical numbers by Hanya Holm. Scenic production by Oliver Smith. Costumes designed by Adrian and Tony Duquette. Lighting by Feder. Musical director, Franz Allers. Orchestrations by Robert Russell Bennett and Philip J. Lang. Dance and choral arrangements, Trude Rittman. Produced by Alan Jay Lerner, Frederick Loewe and Moss Hart. Opened 3 December 1960 at the Majestic Theatre and closed 5 January 1963 after 873 performances.

CAST (in order of appearance): *Sir Dinadan:* JOHN CULLUM. *Sir Lionel:* Bruce Yarnell. *Merlyn:* David Hurst. *Arthur:* RICHARD BURTON. *Guenevere:* JULIE ANDREWS. *Nimue:* Marjorie Smith. *A Page:* Leland Mayforth. *Lancelot:* ROBERT GOULET. *Dap:* Michael Clarke-Laurence. *Pelinore:* ROBERT COOTE. *Clarius:* Richard Kuch. *Lady Anne:* Christina Gillespie. *A Lady:* Leesa Troy. *Sir Sagramore:* James Gannon. *A Page:* Peter De Vise. *Herald:* John Starkweather. *Lady Catherine:* Virginia Allen. *Mordred:* RODDY McDOWALL. *Sir Ozanna:* Michael Kermoyan. *Sir Gwilliam:* Jack Dabdoub. *Morgan Le Fey:* M'EL DOWD. *Tom:* Robin Stewart.

Singers: Joan August, Mary Sue Berry, Marnell Bruce, Judy Hastings, Benita James, Marjorie Smith, Shelia Swenson, Leesa Troy, Dorothy White, Frank Bouley, Jack Dabdoub, James Gannon, Murray Goldkind, Warren Hays, Paul Huddleston, Michael Kermoyan, Donald Maloof, Larry Mitchell, Paul Richards, John Taliaferro. *Dancers:* Virginia Allen, Judi Allinson, Laurie Archer, Carlene Carroll, Joan Coddington, Katia Geleznova, Adriana Keathley, Dawn Mitchell, Claudia Schroeder, Beti Seay, Jerry Bowers, Peter Deign, Randy Doney, Richard Englund, Richard Gain, Gene GeBauer, James Kirby, Richard Kuch, Joe Nelson, John Starkweather, Jimmy Tarbutton.

Act 1, Scene 1: A hilltop near Camelot—a long time ago. *Scene 2:* Near Camelot—immediately following. *Scene 3:* Arthur's Study—Five years later. *Scene 4:* A Roadside near Camelot—A few months later. *Scene 5:* A Park near the Castle—Immediately following. *Scene 6:* A Terrace of the Castle—A few weeks later. *Scene 7:* The Tents outside the Jousting Field—A few days later. *Scene 8:* The Grandstand of the Field. *Scene 9:* The Tents Outside the Jousting Field—Immediately following. *Scene 10:* The Terrace—Two years later. *Scene 11:* The Corridor leading to the Great Hall—Immediately following. *Scene 12:* The Great Hall—Immediately following.

Act 2, Scene 1: The Castle Garden—A few years later. *Scene 2:* The Terrace—A few weeks later. *Scene 3:* Near the Forest of Morgan Le Fey—A few days later. *Scene 4:* The Forest of Morgan Le Fey—Immediately following. *Scene 5:* Corridor—That night. *Scene 6:* The Queen's Bedchamber—Immediately following. *Scene 7:* Camelot—Several days later. *Scene 8:* A Battlefield near Joyous Gard—A few weeks later.

ACT 1[3]
Scene 1
 "I Wonder What the King is Doing Tonight?"
  R. Burton
 "The Simple Joys of Maidenhood"
  J. Andrews
 "Camelot"
  R. Burton, J. Andrews
Scene 2
 "Follow Me"
  M. Smith
Scene 4
 "C'est Moi"
  R. Goulet
Scene 5
 "The Lusty Month of May"
  J. Andrews, Ensemble
 "Then You May Take Me to the Fair"[4]
  J. Andrews, J. Cullum, J. Gannon, B. Yarnell

---

[3]After opening, the following changes were made to Act 1:
 "Camelot" (reprise)(Added to Scene 3)
  R. Burton, J. Andrews
Scene 9 revised as The Terrace—Immediately following.
Scene 10 dropped.
[4]Dropped after opening.

Scene 6
　"How to Handle a Woman"
　　R. Burton
Scene 8
　"The Jousts"
　　R. Burton, J. Andrews, Ensemble
Scene 9
　"Before I Gaze at You Again"
　　J. Andrews

ACT 2
Scene 1
　"If Ever I Would Leave You"
　　R. Goulet
　"The Seven Deadly Virtues"
　　R. McDowall
Scene 2
　"What Do the Simple Folk Do?"
　　J. Andrews, R. Burton
Scene 4
　"The Persuasion"
　　R. McDowall, M. Dowd
Scene 5
　"Fie on Goodness!"
　　Knights
Scene 6
　"I Loved You Once in Silence"
　　J. Andrews
Scene 7
　"Guenevere"
　　Ensemble
Scene 8
　"Camelot" (reprise)
　　R. Burton

WILDCAT

1960.22

A Musical Comedy in Two Acts, 19 Scenes. Book by N. Richard Nash. Music by Cy Coleman. Lyrics by Carolyn Leigh. Settings by Peter Larkin. Costumes by Alvin Colt. Lighting by Charles Elson. Musical direction, dance and vocal arrangements by John Morris. (Musical) arrangements and orchestrations by Robert Ginzler and Sid Ramin. Directed and choreographed by Michael Kidd. Produced by Michael Kidd and N. Richard Nash. Opened 16 December 1960 at the Alvin Theatre and closed 3 June 1961 after 171 performances.

CAST (in order of appearance): *Jane Jackson:* PAULA STEWART. *Wildcat Jackson (Wildy):* LUCILLE BALL. *Sheriff Sam Gore:* HOWARD FISCHER. *Barney:* Ken Ayers. *Luke:* Anthony Saverino. *Countess Emily O'Brien:* EDITH KING. *Joe Dynamite:* KEITH ANDES. *Hank:* CLIFFORD DAVID. *Miguel:* H. F. Green. *Sookie:* DON TOMKINS. *Matt:* CHARLES BRASWELL. *Corky:* Bill Linton. *Oney:* SWEN SWENSON. *Sandy:* Ray Mason. *Tattoo:* Bill Walker. *Cisco:* Al Lanti. *Postman:* Bill Richards. *Inez:* Marsha Wagner. *Blonde:* Wendy Nickerson.
Singers: Ken Ayers, Lee Green, Jan Leighton, Urylee Leonardos, Virginia Oswald, Anthony Saverino, Jeanne Steel, Gene Varrone. *Dancers:* Robert Bakanic, Barbara Beck, Mel Davidson, Penny Ann Green, Valarie Harper, Lucia Lambert, Ronald Lee, Jacqueline Maria, Wendy Nickerson, Frank Pietri, Bill Richards, Adriane Rogers, John Sharpe, Gerald Teijelo, Marsha Wagner.

Act 1, Scene 1: A Street in Centavo City, a border town, in 1912. *Scene 2:* A Prairie. Sunset, a few days later. *Scene 3:* The Street. The following morning. *Scene 4:* The Plaza in the Mexican part of town. Sunset, the same day. *Scene 5:* The Countess' Sitting Room. The following morning. *Scene 6:* Sookie's House. An hour later. *Scene 7:* Prairie. The same evening. *Scene 8:* The Street. An hour later. *Scene 9:* Plaza. Late afternoon, the following day. *Scene 10:* The Jail. A half hour later. *Scene 11:* Sookie's Hill. Early evening, the same day.

Act 2, Scene 1: The Countess' Sitting Room. Two days later. *Scene 2:* On the way tot he Fiesta. The following afternoon. *Scene 3:* The Plaza. Immediately following. *Scene 4:* The Street. A few days later. *Scene 5:* Sookie's House. Derrick Day, the following day. *Scene 6:* Sookie's Hill. Immediately following. *Scene 7:* Outside Miguel's Cantina. Evening, two days later. *Scene 8:* Sookie's Hill. The following day.

ACT 1
Scene 1
　"I Hear"
　　People of Centavo City
Scene 2
　"Hey Look Me Over"
　　L. Ball, P. Stewart
Scene 3
　"Wildcat"
　　L. Ball, Townspeople
Scene 4
　"You've Come Home"
　　K. Andes
Scene 6
　"What Takes My Fancy"
　　L. Ball, D. Tomkins
Scene 7
　"You're a Liar"
　　L. Ball, K. Andes
Scene 8
　"One Day We Dance"
　　C. David, P. Stewart
Scene 9
　"Give a Little Whistle and I'll Be There"
　　L. Ball, K. Andes, Crew, Townspeople
Scene 11
　"Tall Hope"
　　B. Walker, S. Swenson, R. Mason, C. Braswell, Crew

ACT 2
Scene 1
　"Tippy Tippy Toes"
　　L. Ball, E. King
Scene 3
　"El Sombrero"
　　L. Ball, A. Lanti, S. Swenson, Crew, Townspeople
Scene 6
　"Corduroy Road"
　　K. Andes, Crew, Townspeople
Scene 7
　"You've Come Home" (reprise)
　　K. Andes
Scene 8
　Finale
　　Entire Company

DO RE MI

1960.23

A Musical in Two Acts, 16 Scenes. Book by Garson Kanin. (Based on his novel of the same name.) Music by Jule Styne. Lyrics by Betty Comden and Adolph Green. Scenery by Boris Aronson. Costumes by Irene Sharaff. Musical direction by Lehman Engel. Choreography by Marc Breaux and Deedee Wood. Lighting by Al Alloy. Associate director, William Hammerstein. Orchestrations, Luther Henderson. Vocal arrangements and Vocal direction, Buster Davis. Dance arrangements by David Baker. Directed by Garson Kanin. Associate producer, Jones Harris. Produced by David Merrick. Opened 26 December 1960 at the St. James Theatre, closing 24 July-19 August 1961 for a 1 month vacation, moved 25 December 1961 to the 54th Street Theatre, and closed 13 January 1962 after 400 performances.

CAST (in order of appearance): *The Casa Girls:* Marilyn Allwyn, Diane Ball, Sandra Devlin, Regina Groves, Nancy Van Rhein, Carol Stevens, Dean Taliaferro. *The Dance Team:* Patti Karr, Ray Kirchner. *Kay Cram:* NANCY WALKER. *Hubert Cram (Hubie):* PHIL SILVERS. *Waiter:* Frank Derbas. *John Henry Wheeler:* JOHN REARDON. *The Swingers:* Betty Kent, Donna Sanders, Suzanne Shaw. *Headwaiter:* Marc Jordan. *Fatso O'Rear:* GEORGE MATHEWS. *Skin Demopoulos:* GEORGE GIVOT. *Brains Berman:* DAVID BURNS. *Thelma Berman:* Marilyn Child. *Interviewer:* David Gold. *Photographer:* Stuart Hodes. *Wheeler's Secretaries:* Carol Stevens, Dean Taliaferro. *James Russell Lowell IV:* Chad Block. *Sumo Student:* Ray Kirchner. *Tilda Mullen:*

NANCY DUSSAULT. *Wolfie*: Al Nesor. *Marsha*: Carolyn Ragaini. *Lou*: Steve Roland. *Gretchen*: Betty Kent. *Recording Engineer*: Albert Linville. *Maitre D'*: Bob McClure. *Animal Girls*: Marilyn Allwyn, Diane Ball, Sandra Devlin, Regina Groves, Patti Karr, Nancy Van Rhein, Carol Stevens, Dean Taliaferro. *Moe Shtarker*: Al Lewis. *Commentators*: Bob McClure, Allan Stevenson. *Senator Rogers*: Albert Linville. *Senator Redfield*: Edward Grace. *Chief Counsel*: Steve Roland. *Fatso's Lawyer*: Marc Jordan. *Brain's Lawyer*: Pat Tolson.

The Public: Marilyn Allwyn, Doria Avila, Diane Ball, Frank Derbas, Sandra Devlin, David Gold, Edward Grace, Regina Groves, Stuart Hodes, Curtis Hood, Daniel Jasinski, Marc Jordan, Patti Karr, Betty Kent, Ray Kirchner, Barbara Lang, Josephine Lang, Bob McClure, Ken Malone, Jim Marley, James Moore, Dawn Nickerson, Ed Pfeiffer, Carolyn Ragaini, Steve Roland, Donna Sanders, Suzanne Shaw, Carol Stevens, Liza Stuart, Dean Taliaferro, Pat Tolson, Nancy Van Rhein, Richard Young.

Act 1, Scene 1: The Casacabana. New York City, now. *Scene 2*: Hubie and Kay's Bedroom. *Scene 3*: Fatso's Ice Cream Parlor. *Scene 4*: Brains' Chicken Farm. A Box at Hialeah. A Street. *Scene 5*: John Henry Wheeler's Office. *Scene 6*: The Zen Pancake Parlor. *Scene 7*: The Music Enterprise Associates, Inc. *Scene 8*: The Zen Pancake Parlor. *Scene 9*: All Over Town. *Scene 10*: A Recording Studio. *Scene 11*: The Imperial Room.

Act 2, Scene 1: Hubie and Kay's Bedroom. *Scene 2*: John Henry Wheeler's Office. *Scene 3*: The Music Enterprise Associates, Inc. *Scene 4*: The City. *Scene 5*: A Hearing Room in the Senate Office Building, Washington, D.C.

ACT 1
Scene 1
"Waiting, Waiting"
N. Walker
"All You Need Is a Quarter"
B. Kent, D. Sanders, S. Shaw
Scene 2
"Take a Job"
P. Silvers, N. Walker
Scene 3
The Juke Box Hop (dance)[5]
Fatso's Customers
Scene 4
"It's Legitimate"
P. Silvers, G. Mathews, D. Burns, G. Givot, The Loaders
Scene 5
"I Know About Love"
J. Reardon
Scene 7
The Auditions
C. Ragaini, S. Roland, B. Kent
Scene 8
"Cry Like the Wind"
N. Dussault
"Ambition"
P. Silvers, N. Dussault
Scene 9
Success
Tilda Mullen Fans, N. Dussault, P. Silvers, G. Mathews, D. Burns, G. Givot
Scene 10
"Fireworks"
N. Dussault, J. Reardon
Scene 11
"What's New at the Zoo"
N. Dussault, the Animal Girls
"Asking for You"
J. Reardon
"The Late, Late Show"
P. Silvers

ACT 2
Scene 1
"Adventure"
P. Silvers, N. Walker
Scene 2
"Make Someone Happy"
J. Reardon, N. Dussault

Scene 3
"Don't Be Afraid of a Teardrop"[6]
P. Silvers, G. Mathews, D. Burns, G. Givot
Scene 4
The Juke Box Trouble (dance)
A. Lewis, Cohorts, Company
Scene 5
"V.I.P."
The Public, P. Silvers
"All of My Life"
P. Silvers
Finale
P. Silvers, N. Walker, Company

1961.01 # SHOW GIRL

A Small (Musical) Revue in Two Acts, 16 Scenes. Sketches, music and lyrics by Charles Gaynor. Additional sketches by Ernest Chambers. Settings by Oliver Smith. Costumes by Miles White. Lighting by Peggy Clark. Musical direction and orchestrations, Robert Hunter. Additional orchestrations, Clare Grundman. Sketches staged by Charles Gaynor. Musical numbers staged by Richard D'Arcy. Entire production supervised by Oliver Smith. Miss Channing's gowns by Orry-Kelly. Produced by Oliver Smith, James A. Doolittle and Charles Lowe. Opened 12 January 1961 at the Eugene O'Neill Theatre and closed 8 April 1961 after 100 performances.

CAST: CAROL CHANNING, JULES MUNSHIN, LES QUAT' JEUDIS (Raoul Curet, George Denis, André Fuma, Roger Lagier).

ACT 1
Scene 1
Opening—"The Girl in the Show"
C. Channing
Scene 2
Report from Las Vegas
C. Channing
Scene 3
Theatre Piece
Lynn: C. Channing. *Alfred*: J. Munshin.
Scene 4
"Calypso Pete"
C. Channing
Scene 5
Report from Paris: ("Mamba-Java")
Les Quat' Jeudis
(*Music and Lyrics by* Noel Guyves.)
Scene 6
Keeping Up with the Noahs
(*by* Ernest Chambers)
Naomi: C. Channing. *Elijah*: J. Munshin.
Scene 7
"The Girl Who Lived in Montparnasse"
J. Munshin, Les Quat' Jeudis
Scene 8
Carol's Musical Theatre:
C. Channing
a. The Opening Choruses:
"Join Us in a Little Cup of Tea" (from LEND AN EAR)
"This is a Darned Fine Funeral"
b. The Love Songs
"In Our Teeny Little Weeny Nest for Two" (from LEND AN EAR)
"Love Is a Sickness"
c. The Dance Numbers
"The Yahoo Step" (from LEND AN EAR)
"Switchblade Bess"

---

[5]Added after opening: The Juke Box Twist.

[6]Dropped after opening.

105

ACT 2
Scene 1
  "The Story of Marie"
    C. Channing, Les Quat' Jeudis
Scene 2
  S. Eureka Presents
    (*by* Ernest Chambers. *Music by* Charles Gaynor.)
    J. Munshin
Scene 3
  "My Kind of Love"
    C. Channing, J. Munshin
Scene 4
  The Inside Story (Cecilia Sisson sketch)
Scene 5
  The Foreign Star (Marlene Dietrich sketch)
Scene 6
  Les Quat' Jeudis
Scene 7
  The Palace Theatre:
  ("You Haven't Lived Until You've Played the Palace"/
  "Somewhere There's a Little Bluebird")
    C. Channing
Scene 8
  Finale
    C. Channing, Company

1961.02 ## THE CONQUERING HERO

A Musical Comedy in Two Acts, 16 Scenes. Book by Larry Gelbart. Based on the screenplay "Hail, the Conquering Hero" by Preston Sturges. Music by Moose Charlap. Lyrics by Norman Gimbel. Settings by Jean Rosenthal and William Pitkin. Costumes designed by Patton Campbell. Lighting by Jean Rosenthal. (Musical) arrangements and orchestrations by Robert Ginzler and Sid Ramin. Dance music arranged by Fred Werner. Musical direction and choral arrangements by Sherman Frank. (Direction and choreography uncredited, by Bob Fosse prior to opening.) Produced by Robert Whitehead and Roger L. Stevens by special arrangement with Emka Ltd. Opened 16 January 1961 at the ANTA Theatre and closed 21 January 1961 after 8 performances.

CAST (in order of appearance): *Doorman:* Lee Barry. *Pfc. Doyle:* Walter Farrell. *Pfc. O'Dell:* Bob Dixon. *Cpl. Ganz:* Bill McDonald. *Pfc. Pasco:* Bernie Meyer. *Sgt. Murdock:* LIONEL STANDER. *Nightclub Performer:* Marilyn Stark. *Master of Ceremonies:* Bob Kaliban. *Waiter:* Erik Kristen. *Nightclub Manager:* William LeMassena. *Woodrow Truesmith:* TOM POSTON. *MP:* Burt Bier. *Bartender:* Samye Van. *A General:* T. J. Halligan. *Conductor:* Don Morgan. *Mayor Noble:* FRED STEWART. *Judge Callan:* William LeMassena. *Forrest Noble:* John McMartin. *Whiteman:* Bob Kaliban. *Mrs. Noble:* Edith Gresham. *Rev. Cox:* Geoffrey Bryan. *Sue Anne Barnes:* JANE MASON. *Ronnie:* Richard Buckley. *Mrs. Truesmith:* Elizabeth Kerr. *Libby Callan:* KAY BROWN. *Gene:* Kenny Kealy. *Doc Johnson:* T. J. Halligan. *The Enemy Captain:* John Aristides. *Effie:* Brina Dexter.

Dancers: Margery Beddow, Pat Ferrier, Reby Howells, Shellie Farrell, Marlene Dell, Betty Hyatt Linton, Kathe Howard, William Guske, John Aristides, Dale Moreda, Erik Kristen, Dick Korthaze, Michel Stuart, James Senn. *Singers:* Georgia Creighton, Brina Dexter, Marianne Gale, Charlotte Frazier, Marilyn Stark, Shirley Chester, Burt Bier, Lee Barry, Ed Mastin, Don Morgan, Tony Craig, Charles Rule.

Act 1, Scene 1: The 'Chez Victory' Club. *Scene 2:* The Train. *Scene 3:* The Station at Hillsdale. *Scene 4:* The Truesmith Porch. *Scene 5:* The Church. *Scene 6:* The Truesmith House. *Scene 7:* The River Bank. *Scene 8:* Woodrow's Room. *Scene 9:* The Campaign.

Act 2, Scene 1: The Election. *Scene 2:* The Town Hall. *Scene 3:* The House. *Scene 4:* The Railroad Station. *Scene 5:* The Mayor's Office. *Scene 6:* The Town Hall. *Scene 7:* The Station.

ACT 1
Scene 1
  "Girls! Girls!"
    L. Barry, Marines
  "Five Shots of Whiskey"
    L. Stander, B. Dixon, W. Farrell, B. McDonald, B. Meyer

Scene 3
  "Hail, the Conquering Hero!"
    T. Poston, Company
  "Must Be Given to You"
    Company
Scene 4
  "Wonderful, Marvelous You"
    T. Poston, K. Brown, K. Kealey
Scene 5
  "Truth"
    Entire Company
  "Won't You Marry Me?"
    K. Brown
Scene 7
  The River Bank
    J. Mason, T. Poston
Scene 8
  "Only Rainbows"
    T. Poston, B. Dixon, W. Farrell, B. McDonald
Scene 9
  The Campaign
    T. Poston, Ensemble
ACT 2
Scene 2
  "One Mother Each"
    L. Stander, B. Dixon, W. Farrell, B. McDonald, B. Meyer
  "Must Be Given to You" (reprise)
    Entire Company
Scene 3
  "I'm Beautiful"
    K. Brown, Marines
Scene 4
  "Rough Times"
    K. Brown, K. Kealey
Scene 5
  "Yours, All Yours"
    T. Poston, J. Mason, Ensemble
Scene 7
  "Won't You Marry Me?" (reprise)
    T. Poston
  "Hail, the Conquering Hero"/"Only Rainbows" (reprise)
    Entire Company

THE MIKADO,
1961.03 or The Town of Titipu

A Revival of the Comic Opera in Two Acts[7]. Libretto by William S. Gilbert. Music by Arthur Sullivan. Staged by Dorothy Raedler. Scenery and lighting by Donald Oenslager. Costumes by Patton Campbell. Conductors, Robert Irving, Felix Popper. Chorus master, William Jonson. Produced by the New York City Center Gilbert and Sullivan Company (Julius Rudel, General Director). Opened 17 January 1961 at the New York City Center and closed 5 February 1961 after 8 performances in repertory.

CAST: *The Mikado of Japan:* GEORGE GAYNES, ARNOLD VOKETAITIS. *Nanki-Poo:* FRANK PORETTA, CARL OLSEN. *Ko-Ko:* NORMAN KELLEY, RAYMOND ALLEN. *Pooh-Bah:* HERBERT BEATTIE, SPIRO MALAS. *Pish-Tush:* WILLIAM METCALF. *Three Sisters, Wards of Ko-Ko: Yum-Yum:* BARBARA MEISTER. *Pitti-Sing:* JANET PAVEK. *Peep-Bo:* SOPHIA STEFFAN. *Katisha:* RUTH KOBART, EVELYN SACHS.

---

[7]First presented in New York 20 July, 10-29 August 1885 at the Union Square and People's Theatres for 22 performances. First authorized production presented 19 August 1885 at the Fifth Avenue Theatre by Richard D'Oyly Carte for 250 performances. For Synopsis of Scenes and Musical Numbers, see 19 August 1885 D'Oyly Carte production.

Chorus of School Girls, Nobles, Guards and Coolies: Paula Coonen, Donna Curtis, Harris Davis, Marceline Decker, David Dodds, Glenn Dowlen, Beverly Evans, Margaret Goz, Norman Grogan, Helen Guile, Edson Hoel, Alan Keene, Carmen Lindsay, Dean Linton, George McWhorter, Kellis Miller, John Minto, Hanna Owen, Charlotte Povia, Betty Jane Schwering, John Smith, Stephanie Reynolds, Mara Yaven, Don Yule, Mariano Parra.

THE PIRATES OF PENZANCE,
1961.04   or The Slave of Duty

A Revival of the Comic Opera in Two Acts[8]. Libretto by William S. Gilbert. Music by Arthur Sullivan. Staged by Dorothy Raedler. Scenery by H. A. Condell. Costumes by Patton Campbell. Conductors, Julius Rudel, Kurt Safir. Chorus master, William Jonson. Produced by the New York City Center Gilbert and Sullivan Company (Julius Rudel, General director). Opened 19 January 1961 at the New York City Center and closed 29 January 1961 after 6 performances in repertory.

CAST: *Major-General Stanley:* COLEY WORTH. *The Pirate King:* WILLIAM CHAPMAN. *Samuel:* MAURICE STERN. *Frederic:* FRANK PORETTA, WILLIAM DIARD. *Sergeant of Police:* HERBERT BEATTIE, SPIRO MALAS. *General Stanley's Daughters (4): Mabel:* JACQUELYNNE MOODY. *Edith:* JOY CLEMENTS. *Kate:* SOPHIA STEFFAN. *Isabel:* Stephanie Reynolds. *Ruth:* BEATRICE KREBS. *Chorus of Pirates, Police and General Stanley's Wards:* same as THE MIKADO above.

THE GONDOLIERS,
1961.05   or The King of Barataria

A Revival of the Comic Opera in Two Acts[9]. Libretto by William S. Gilbert. Music by Arthur Sullivan. Staged by Dorothy Raedler. Scenery and costumes by Ed Wittstein. Conductor, Julius Rudel. Chorus master, William Jonson. Produced by the New York City Center Gilbert and Sullivan Company (Julius Rudel, General director). Opened 25 January 1961 at the New York City Center and closed 2 February 1961 after 4 performances in repertory.

CAST: *The Duke of Plaza-Toro:* NORMAN KELLEY. *Luiz:* WILLIAM DIARD. *Don Alhambra Del Bolero:* GEORGE GAYNES. *Marco Palmieri:* JOHN ALEXANDER, FRANK PORETTA. *Giuseppe Palmieri:* RICHARD FREDERICKS. *Antonio:* William Metcalf. *Francesco:* Maurice Stern. *Giorgio:* Norman Grogan. *The Duchess of Plaza-Toro:* EVELYN SACHS. *Casilda:* BARBARA MEISTER. *Gianetta:* JANET PAVEK, JOY CLEMENTS. *Tessa:* CECILIA WARD. *Fiametta:* Doris Yarick. *Vittoria:* Sophia Steffan. *Giulia:* Beverly Evans. *Inez:* Gladys Kriese. *Solo Cachucha Dancers:* Adele Valle, Mariano Parra. *Chorus of Gondoliers, Contadine, Men-at-Arms, Heralds and Pages:* same as THE MIKADO above.

H.M.S. PINAFORE,
1961.06   or The Lass That Loved a Sailor

A Revival of the Comic Opera in Two Acts[10]. Libretto by William S. Gilbert. Music by Arthur Sullivan. Staged by Allen Fletcher. Scenery and costumes by Patton Campbell. Conductors, Robert Irving, Felix Popper. Chorus master, William Jonson. Produced by the New York City Center Gilbert and Sullivan Company (Julius Rudel, General director). Opened 1 February 1961 at the New York City Center and closed 4 February 1961 after 4 performances in repertory.

CAST: *The Rt. Hon. Sir Joseph Porter, K.C.B., First Lord of the Admiralty:* COLEY WORTH. *Captain Corcoran, Commander of the H.M.S. Pinafore:* WILLIAM CHAPMAN. *Ralph Rackstraw, Able Seaman:* FRANK PORETTA, CARL OLSEN. *Dick Deadeye, Able Seaman:* PAUL UKENA, HERBERT BEATTIE. *Bill Bobstay, Boatswain:* Richard Fredericks. *Bob Becket:* John Macurdy. *Josephine, the Captain's Daughter:* DORIS YARICK, JOY CLEMENTS. *Hebe, Sir Joseph's First Cousin:*

Cecilia Ward. *Little Buttercup,* Mrs. Cripps, a Portsmouth bum-boat woman: BEATRICE KREBS, GLADYS KRIESE. *First Lord's Sisters, His Cousins, His Aunts, Sailors, Marines, etc.:* same as THE MIKADO above.

1961.07   # 13 DAUGHTERS

A Musical in Two Acts, a Prologue and 14 Scenes. Book, music and lyrics by Eaton Magoon, Jr. Additional book material by Leon Tokatyan. Choreography by Rod Alexander. Staged by Billy Matthews. Scenery designed and lighted by George Jenkins. Costumes by Alvin Colt. Musical direction and vocal arrangements by Pembroke Davenport. Orchestrations by Joe Glover. Additional orchestrations by Robert Russell Bennett. Assistant to the choreographer and Hawaiian consultant, Nona Beamer. Dance arrangements by Bob Atwood. Produced by Jack H. Silverman. Opened 2 March 1961 at the 54th Street Theatre and closed 25 March 1961 after 28 performances.

CAST (in order of appearance): *Kahuna:* Paul Michael. *Young Kahuna and Chanter:* Keola Beamer. *Boys:* Miki Lamont, Augie Rios, Delphino De Arco, Ado Sato, Steve Curry. *Kinau:* SYLVIA SYMS. *Chun:* DON AMECHE. *Emmaloa:* MONICA BOYAR. *Mana,* Prince of Hawaii: ED KENNEY. *Malia:* DIANA CORTO. *Kamakia:* Honey Sanders. *William:* JOHN BATTLES. *Jacques:* RICHARD TONE. *Isabel:* GINA VIGLIONE. *Susie:* Constance Di Giovanni. *Sally:* Vivian Hernandez. *Willoughby:* STANLEY GROVER. *Jane:* Diana Baffa. *Maude:* Karen Lynn Reed. *Desdemona:* Shirley De Burgh. *Cora:* Jo Anne Leeds. *Mary:* Nikki Sowinski. *May:* Connie Burnett. *Millie Lee:* Gloria Gabriel. *Minnie Lou:* Jeanne Armin. *Cecilia:* ISABELLE FARRELL. *Governors:* Paul Michael, Jack Murray, Jack Mathers, Irving Barnes. *Prime Minister:* George Hirose. *Keoki, King of Hawaii:* GEORGE LIPTON. *David Scott, Attorney General:* Konrad Matthaei. *Guards:* Bill Jason, Jose Ahumada. *Governor's Wives:* Kelli Scott, Doris Galiber, Lynn Barret, Veronica McCormick. *Sir Cyril:* Peter Pagan. *Assistant Consul:* Nathaniel White.
Singers: Irving Barnes, Lynn Barret, Doris Galiber, Jack Mathers, Paul Michael, Jack Murray, Veronica McCormick, Kelli Scott. *Dancers:* Jeanne Armin, Diana Baffa, Carlos Bas, Keola Beamer, Connie Burnett, Shirley De Burgh, Humberto D'Elia, Antony De Vecchi, Gloria Gabriel, Blair Hammond, Jo Anne Leeds, Roger LePage, Carlos Macri, Michael Maurer, Jerome Michael, Mitchel Nutick, Candy Recla, Nikki Sowinski, Mary Zahn. *Children:* Steve Curry, Delfino De Arco, Constance Di Giovanni, Vivian Hernandez, Miki Lamont, Karen Lynn Reed, Augie Ross, Ado Sato. *Servants:* Jose Ahumada, Kalani Cockett, Bill Jason.
The action takes place in Hawaii in the late nineteenth century.

Prologue: The Valley.

Act 1, Scene 1: Chun's House. 26 years later. *Scene 2:* King's Pavilion. *Scene 3:* By a Stream. *Scene 4:* Mission School. *Scene 5:* By a Stream. *Scene 6:* The Valley. *Scene 7:* Emmaloa's Bedroom. *Scene 8:* The Gold Pavillion of the Waikiki Hotel.

Act 2, Scene 1: Chun's House. *Scene 2:* Chun's Shop. *Scene 3:* Chun's House. *Scene 4:* A Beach near Honolulu Harbor. *Scene 5:* King's Pavilion. *Scene 6:* The Valley.

ACT 1
Prologue
"Kuli Kuli"
  S. Syms, Company
"House on the Hill"
  D. Ameche
Scene 1
"13 Daughters"
  D. Ameche, the Daughters
"Paper of Gold" (dance)
  R. Tone, the Daughters
Scene 3
"Let-A-Go Your Heart"
  E. Kenney, D. Corto
Scene 4
"Alphabet Song" (*Music by* Nona Beamer.)
  The Children
Scene 5
"Throw a Petal"
  D. Corto
"When You Hear the Wind"
  E. Kenney
Scene 6
"Ka Wahine Akamai" (Smart Woman)
  S. Syms, H. Sanders, M. Boyar, Daughters, Suitors

[8]First presented in New York 31 December 1879 at the Fifth Avenue Theatre for a total of 91 performances in two engagements. For Synopsis of Scenes and Musical Numbers, see original 1879 production.
[9]Originally presented in New York 7 January 1890 at Park Theatre for 103 performances. For Synopsis of Scenes and Musical Numbers, see original 1890 production.
[10]Originally presented in New York 15 January 1879 at the Standard Theatre for 175 performances. For Synopsis of Scenes and Musical Numbers, see original 1879 production.

Scene 7

"You Set My Heart To Music"
M. Boyar, D. Ameche, G. Viglione

Scene 8

"13 Daughters" (reprise)
D. Ameche, Daughters, Suitors

"The Cotillion"
Company

ACT 2

Scene 1

"Old Maids"
Daughters

Scene 2

"Oriental Plan"[11]
D. Ameche
(*Music and Lyrics by* Sherman Edwards and Sid Wayne.)

Scene 3

"Hoomalimali" (Baiting the Hook)
S. Syms

"My Pleasure"
S. Grover, G. Viglione

"Puka Puka Pants"
I. Farrell, R. Tone

Scene 4

"My Hawaii"
E. Kenney

Scene 6

Hiiaka Ritual Dance
Dancers

"Hiiaka"
M. Boyar

"House on the Hill" (reprise)
D. Ameche

"My Hawaii" (reprise)
Company

THE HAPPIEST GIRL
IN THE WORLD

1961.08

A Musical Comedy in Two Acts, 14 Scenes. Book by Fred Saidy and Henry Myers. Story by E. Y. Harburg (with a bow to Aristophanes "Lysistrata" and Bulfinch). Music by Jacques Offenbach. Lyrics by E. Y. Harburg. Settings and lighting by William and Jean Eckart. Costumes by Robert Fletcher. Choreography by Dania Krupska. Musical direction and vocal arrangements by Robert DeCormier. Orchestrations by Robert Russell Bennett and Hershy Kay. Dance arrangements by Gerald Alters. Musical research by Jay Gorney. Directed by Cyril Ritchard. Electronic tonalities by Louis and Bebe Barron. Produced by Lee Guber. Opened 3 April 1961 at the Martin Beck Theatre and closed 24 June 1961 after 97 performances.

CAST (in order of appearance): *First Courier*: Alton Ruff. *Second Courier*: Ronald B. Stratton. *First Minister*: TED THURSTON. *Second Minister*: DON CRABTREE. *Third Minister*: RICHARD WINTER. *Chief of State*: CYRIL RITCHARD. *A Herald*: Don Atkinson. *General Kinesias*: BRUCE YARNELL. *Phoebe*: Rita Metzger. *Lysistrata*: DRAN SEITZ. *Captain Crito*: JOHN NAPIER. *Jupiter*: MICHAEL KERMOYAN. *Juno*: LU LEONARD. *Bacchus*: TED THURSTON. *Mercury*: Don Atkinson. *Apollo*: JOHN NAPIER. *Neptune*: RICHARD WINTER. *Aphrodite*: JOY CLAUSSEN. *Pluto*: CYRIL RITCHARD. *Diana*: JANICE RULE. *Amaryllis*: JOY CLAUSSEN. *Myrrhina*: LU LEONARD. *A Heckler*: CYRIL RITCHARD. *Daphne*: Norma Donaldson. *Hector*: David Canary. *Ataraxohymonides*: John Wheeler. *Ulysses*: RICHARD WINTER. *Sergeant*: DON CRABTREE. *A Gay Blade*: CYRIL RITCHARD. *A Wine Smuggler*: CYRIL RITCHARD. *Sentinel*: Nancy Windsor. *The Pied Piper of Hamelin*: CYRIL RITCHARD. *Theodora*: Lainie Kazan. *Spartan Woman*: Maura K. Wedge. *A Playwright*: CYRIL RITCHARD. *Rhodope*: Janice Painchaud. *An Ambassador*: CYRIL RITCHARD.
Singers: Ellen Berse, Joy Claussen, Norma Donaldson, Lainie Kazan, Leonora Lanzillotti, Rita Metzger, Elaine Spaulding, Maura K. Wedge, Nancy Windsor, David

---

[11]Replaced during run by:

"Nothing Man Cannot Do"
D. Ameche

Canary, Jeff Killian, Paul Merrill, Theodore Morill, Arthur Tookoyan, Mark Tully, John Wheeler, Richard Winter. *Dancers*: Bonnie Brandon, Candace Caldwell, Natasha Crishin, Judith Haskell, Lisa James, Gloria Kaye, Susan May, Carmen Morales, Janice Painchaud, Bill Atkinson, Don Atkinson, Grant Delaney, Victor Duntiere, Louis Kosman, Alton Ruff, Kenneth Scott, Ron Sequoio, Ronald B. Stratton.

Act 1, Scene 1: Office of the Chief of State of Athens. 400 B.C. *Scene 2*: The Rotunda. *Scene 3*: The Agora. *Scene 4*: Patio of the General's Home. *Scene 5*: Atop Mount Olympus. *Scene 6*: Garden of the General's Home. *Scene 7*: The Agora. *Scene 8*: The Patio. *Scene 9*: Lysistrata's Boudoir.

Act 2, Scene 1: The Public Baths. *Scene 2*: Outside the Citadel. *Scene 3*: The Patio. *Scene 4*: Steps leading to the Temple of Diana. *Scene 5*: The Agora.

ACT 1

"The Olympics" (ballet)
(Dance Ensemble)

"Cheers for the Hero"
Ensemble

"The Glory That Is Greece"
C. Ritchard, B. Yarnell, Ensemble

"The Happiest Girl in the World"
D. Seitz, B. Yarnell

"The Greek Marine"
C. Ritchard, T. Thurston, D. Crabtree, R. Winter, Soldiers

"Shall We Say Farewell"
D. Seitz

"Never Be-Devil the Devil"
C. Ritchard

"Whatever That May Be"
J. Rule, the Gods

"Eureka"
M. Kermoyan, the Gods

Diana's Arrival in Athens (dance)
J. Rule

"The Oath"
D. Seitz, Women

"Diana's Transformation"
C. Ritchard, J. Rule, Two Suitors

"Vive la Virtue!"
C. Ritchard, J. Rule

"Adrift on a Star"
D. Seitz, B. Yarnell

"The Happiest Girl in the World" (reprise)
D. Seitz, B. Yarnell

Finale (Act 1)
D. Seitz, B. Yarnell, Ensemble

ACT 2

"That'll Be the Day"
Men

"How Soon, Oh Moon?"
D. Seitz, N. Windsor, Women

"Love-Sick Serenade"
C. Ritchard, L. Leonard

"Five Minutes of Spring"
B. Yarnell, D. Seitz, J. Rule

"The Greek Marine" (reprise)
Soldiers

"Five Minutes of Spring" (reprise)
Soldiers

"Never Trust a Virgin"
C. Ritchard, Women

"Entrance of the Courtesans"
Women

"The Pied Piper's Can-Can"
C. Ritchard, Dancers

"Vive la Virtue!" (reprise)
C. Ritchard, J. Rule

Finale (Act 2)
Entire Company

SHOW BOAT

1961.09

A Revival of the Musical Play in Two Acts, 15 Scenes[12]. Music by Jerome Kern. Book and Lyrics by Oscar Hammerstein II. Based on the novel of the same name by Edna Ferber. Staged by Dania Krupska. Choreography by Arthur Partington. Scenery and lighting by Howard Bay. Costumes by Stanley Simmons. Musical director and conductor, Julius Rudel. Assistant conductor and choral director, William Jonson. (Orchestrations by Robert Russell Bennett.) Produced by the New York City Center Light Opera Company (Jean Dalrymple, Director). Opened 12 April 1961 at the New York City Center and closed 23 April 1961 after 14 performances.

CAST (in order of their appearance): Pete: William Coppola. Windy McLain: Scott Moore. Queenie: CAROL BRICE. Captain Andy: JOE E. BROWN. Parthy Ann Hawkes: ISABELLA HOOPES. Ellie: JANE KEAN. Frank: RICHARD FRANCE. Julie: ANITA DARIAN. Steve: HERBERT FIELDS. Gaylord Ravenal: ROBERT ROUNSEVILLE. Sheriff Ike Vallon: John Martin. Magnolia: JO SULLIVAN. Joe: ANDREW FRIERSON. Rubberface: J. Patrick Carter. Backwoodsman: Norman A. Grogan. Jeb: Feodore Tedick. Miss Parkington: Carmen Lindsay. Barker: Henry Lawrence. Old Sport: Jack Rains. Ethel: Alyce Webb. Landlady: Claire Waring. Al: John Smith. Mazie: Sherry McCutcheon. Jim: Henry Lawrence. Jake: William Coppola. Pianist: John Cooke. Charley: Ned Wright. Man With Guitar: J. Patrick Carter. Mother Superior: Miriam Lawrence. Kim, as a child: Bridget Knapp. Dottie: Helen Guile. Dolly: Mara Wirt. Headwaiter: Feodore Tedick. Old Lady on Levee: Sarah Floyd. Kim, in her Twenties: Jo Sullivan.

Singers: Beverly Evans, Helen Guile, Miriam Lawrence, Carmen Lindsay, Hanna Owen, Betty Jane Schwering, Mara Wirt, Maggie Worth. John Bessinger, Lawrence Bogue, William Coppola, J. Patrick Carter, Norman A. Grogan, Henry Lawrence, Kellis Miller, Jack Rains, John J. Smith, Feodore Tedick. Dancers: Mimi Alexander, Margery Beddow, Geralyn Donald, Ellen Halpin, Linda Howe, Bettye Jenkins, Sherry McCutcheon, Barbara Monte. Todd Butler, Garold Gardner, Eric Kristen, Ronnie Snook. Jubilee Singers: Issa Arnal, Ruby Green Aspinall, Kay Barnes, Claretta Freeman, H. Scott Gibson, Joli Gonsalves, Robert Henson, Wanza King, Mary Louise, Rosalie Maxwell, Caryl Paige, Charles Scott, Alyce E. Webb, Arthur Williams, Ned Wright. Jubilee Dancers: Leu Comacho, Julius Fields, LaVinnia Hamilton, Nathaniel Horne, Bernard Johnson, Jan Aubrey Mickens, Joan Peters, Harold Pierson, Ronald Platts, Ella Thompson, Glory Van Scott, Myrna White.

CARNIVAL

1961.10

A Musical Comedy in Two Acts, 24 Scenes. Book by Michael Stewart. (Based on the novela "The Love of Seven Dolls" by Paul Gallico and its film adaptation "Lili" by Helen Deutsch.) Music and lyrics by Bob Merrill. Directed and choreographed by Gower Champion. Settings and lighting by Will Steven Armstrong. Costumes by Freddy Wittop. Musical direction and vocal arrangements by Saul Schechtman. Orchestrations by Philip J. Lang. Dance arrangements by Peter Howard. Associate choreographer, Gene Bayliss. Puppets created and supervised by Tom Tichenor. Designer and supervisor of magic and illusion, Roy Benson. Produced by David Merrick. Opened 13 April 1961 at the Imperial Theatre, moved 21 December 1962 to the Winter Garden, and closed 5 January 1963 after 719 performances.

CAST (in order of appearance): Jacquot: PIERRE OLAF. Mr. Schlegel: HENRY LASCOE. Grobert: Will Lee. Roustabouts: George Marcy, Tony Gomez, John Nola, Buff Shurr. Cyclist: Bob Murray. Miguelito: George Marcy. Dog Trainer: Paul Sydell. Wardrobe Mistress: Carvel Carter. Harem Girls: Nicole Barth, Iva March, Beti Seay. Bear Girl: Jennifer Billingsley. Princess Olga: Luba Lisa. Band: C. B. Bernard, Peter Lombard. Stilt-Walker: Dean Crane. Jugglers: Martin Brothers. Clowns: Bob Dixon, Harry Lee Rogers. Strongman: Pat Tolson. Gladys Zuwicki: Mary Ann Niles. Gloria Zuwicki: Christine Bartel. Gypsy: Anita Gillette. Marco the Magnificent: JAMES MITCHELL. The Incomparable Rosalie: KAYE BALLARD. Greta Schlegel: June Meshonek. Lili: ANNA MARIA ALBERGHETTI. Paul Berthalet: JERRY ORBACH. Blue Birds: Nicole Barth, Jennifer Billingsley, Iva March, Beti Seay. Aerialist: Dean Crane. Dr. Glass: Igors Gavon.

Act 1, Scene 1: The Carnival Area on the outskirts of a town in Southern Europe. Scene 2: The Puppet Booth. Scene 3: Inside Schlegel's Office. Scene 4: The Carnival Area. Scene 5: The Carnival Area. Scene 6: Interior of Main Tent. Scene 7: Carnival Area at Night.

Act 2, Scene 1: The Midway. Scene 2: Trailer Camp. Scene 3: Outside Main Tent.

ACT 1

Scene 1

"Direct from Vienna"
K. Ballard, J. Meshonek, Carnival People

"A Very Nice Man"
A. M. Alberghetti

Scene 2

"Fairyland"
Puppets

"I've Got to Find a Reason"
J. Orbach

"Mira" (Can You Imagine That?)
A. M. Alberghetti

"Sword, Rose and Cape"
J. Mitchell, G. Marcy, T. Gomez, J. Nola, B. Shurr

Scene 3

"Humming"
K. Ballard, J. Meshonek

Scene 4

"Yes, My Heart"
A. M. Alberghetti

Scene 5

"Everybody Likes You"
J. Orbach

Scene 6

"Magic, Magic"
J. Mitchell, K. Ballard, A. M. Alberghetti

"Tanz Mit Mir" (Dance With Me)
N. Barth, J. Billingsley, I. March, B. Seay

"Carnival Ballet"
A. M. Alberghetti, Carnival People, Townspeople

Scene 7

"Mira" (reprise)
A. M. Alberghetti

Theme from 'Carnival'("Love Makes the World Go Round")
A. M. Alberghetti, Puppets

ACT 2

Scene 1

"Yum Ticky" (Ticky Tum Tum)
A. M. Alberghetti, Puppets

"The Rich"
A. M. Alberghetti, Puppets

Theme from 'Carnival' (reprise)
A. M. Alberghetti, Puppets

"Beautiful Candy"
A. M. Alberghetti, Puppets, Vendors

"Her Face"
J. Orbach

"Grand Imperial Cirque de Paris"
P. Olaf, Carnival People

Scene 2

"I Hate Him"/"Her Face" (reprise)
A. M. Alberghetti/J. Orbach

Scene 3

"Grand Imperial Cirque de Paris" (reprise)
Carnival People

"Always, Always You"
J. Mitchell, K. Ballard

"She's My Love"
J. Orbach

YOUNG ABE LINCOLN

1961.11

A Musical in Two Acts, 7 Scenes[13]. Book by Richard N. Bernstein and John Allen. Music by Victor Ziskin. Lyrics by Joan Javits. Special dialogue and lyrics by Arnold Sundgaard. Musical director, Victor Ziskin. Musical numbers Staged by Rhoda Levine. Sets, costumes and lighting by Fred Voelpel.

[12]First presented December 27, 1927 at the Ziegfeld Theatre for 572 performances. This revised version first presented 5 January 1946 at the Ziegfeld Theatre for 418 performances. For Synopsis of Scenes and Musical Numbers, see 1946 revival. Act 2, Scene 8 reset on the Levee at Natches.

[13]First produced in New York Off-Broadway 3-8 April 1961 at the York Theatre for 18 performances. This show played 3 matinees daily in its first engagement at the York, 12 matinees weekly at the Eugene O'Neill, and a split schedule of tour dates and regular matinees in its return to the York.

Directed by Jay Harnick. Produced by Arthur Shimkin. Opened 25 April 1961 at the Eugene O'Neill Theatre and closed 7 May 1961 after 27 performances. Re-opened Off-Broadway 10 May 1961 at the York Playhouse and closed 24 June 1961 after 48 additional performances, and 34 performances touring in New York City area schools. Total at the York and O'Neill Theatres: 93 performances.

CAST: *Abe Lincoln*: DARRELL SANDEEN. *William Berry*: Lou Cutell. *Minnie*: Joan Kibrig, (Travis Hudson). *Ann Rutledge*: Judy Foster. *John McNeil*: Ray Hyson. *Bowling Green*: Tom Noel. *Ninian Edwards*: Dan Resin. *Josh*: Ken Kercheval, (Jack Kauflin). *Jack Armstrong*: Robert Darnell. *Seth*: Ralston Hill. *Hannah*: Barbara Cornett. (Actors who originated roles but did not come to Broadway are listed in parentheses; the roles of Hannah and Seth were added for the Broadway run.)

Act 1, Scene 1: The Town Square of New Salem, Illinois in 1833. *Scene 2*: A Drill Field.

Act 2, Scene 1: A Grove in New Salem, Illinois. *Scene 2*: Ann's Room. *Scene 3*: A Clearing in the Woods. *Scene 4*: The Election Site. *Scene 5*: The Election Site.

ACT 1
Scene 1
  "The Same Old Me"
    Company
  "Cheer Up!"
    J. Kibrig, L. Cutell
  "You Can Dance"
    J. Foster, D. Sandeen
  "Someone You Know"
    D. Sandeen, J. Foster
  "I Want to be a Little Frog in a Little Pond"
    D. Sandeen, J. Kibrig, L. Cutell, T. Noel, D. Resin, J. Foster
  "Clarey Grove Song"
    R. Darnell, R. Hyson, K. Kercheval
  "Don't P-P-Point Them Guns at Me"
    R. Darnell, R. Hyson, K. Kercheval
Scene 2
  "The Captain Lincoln March" (Drill Song)
    L. Cutell, K. Kercheval, R. Hyson, R. Hill, T. Noel, D. Sandeen
  "Run, Indian, Run" (Run Injuns)
    R. Darnell, R. Hyson, K. Kercheval, L. Cutell, R. Hill, D. Sandeen

ACT 2
Scene 1
  "Welcome Home March"
    Company
  "Vote for Lincoln"
    D. Resin, T. Noel, R. Darnell, R. Hyson, K. Kercheval, L. Cutell, R. Hill
  "I Want to Be a Little Frog in a Little Pond" (reprise)
    D. Sandeen, Men
Scene 3
  "Cheer Up" (reprise)
    J. Kibrig, L. Cutell
Scene 4
  "Frontier Politics"
    D. Resin, R. Darnell, R. Hyson, K. Kercheval, R. Hill, T. Noel, L. Cutell
Scene 5
  Finale ("The Same Old Me" reprise)
    Company

1961.12 SOUTH PACIFIC

A Revival of the Musical Play in Two Acts, 23 Scenes[14]. Music by Richard Rodgers. Lyrics by Oscar Hammerstein II. Book by Oscar Hammerstein II and Joshua Logan. Adapted from James A. Michener's novel "Tales of the South Pacific." Directed by John Fearnley. Scenery by Jo Mielziner, adapted by Paul Morrison. Original costumes by Motley. Costumes by Stanley Simmons. Musical director, Julius Rudel. (Orchestrations by Robert Russell Bennett.) Produced by the New York City Center Light Opera Company

(Jean Dalrymple, Director). Opened 26 April 1961 at the New York City Center and closed 14 May 1961 after 23 performances.

CAST (in order of appearance): *Ngana*: Vivian Hernandez. *Jerome*: Delfino De Arco. *Henry*: Viraj Amonsin. *Ensign Nellie Forbush*: ALLYN ANN McLERIE. *Emile DeBecque*: WILLIAM CHAPMAN. *Bloody Mary*: ROSETTA LeNOIRE. *Bloody Mary's Assistant*: Musa Williams. *Abner*: Jim McMillan. *Stewpot*: JEFF HARRIS. *Luther Billis*: DORT CLARK. *Professor*: Art Ostrin. *Lt. Joseph Cable, U.S.M.C.*: STANLEY GROVER. *Capt. George Brackett, U.S.N.*: EDMUND BAYLIES. *Cmdr. William Harbison, U.S.N.*: WESLEY ADDY. *Yeoman Herbert Quale*: Kenny Adams. *Sgt. Kenneth Johnson*: Daniel P. Hannafin. *Cpl. Richard West*: Don Becker. *Seabee Morton Wise*: Jim Conner. *Sgt. Juan Cortez*: Saran Wallach. *Seaman Tom O'Brien*: Robert Lenn. *Radio Operator Bob McCaffery*: John Aman. *Cpl. Hamilton Steeves*: Thomas Edwards. *Staff Sgt. Guilio Fascinato*: Richard Nieves. *Seaman James Hayes*: Ralph Vucci. *Lt. Genevieve Marshall*: Barbara Saxby. *Ensign Dinah Murphy*: Maggie Worth. *Ensign Janet MacGregor*: Betty Jane Schwering. *Ensign Cora MacRae*: Penny Fuller. *Ensign Bessie Noonan*: Francesca Bell. *Ensign Pamela Whitmore*: Miriam Lawrence. *Ensign Sue Yaeger*: Sybil Scotford. *Ensign Lisa Minelli*: Karen Styne. *Liat*: COCO RAMIREZ. *Lt. Buzz Adams*: Don Corby. *Shore Patrol Officer*: Casper Roos. *Islanders*: Mark Richard Satow, Ado Sato, Eigel Silju.

1961.13 PORGY AND BESS

A Revival of the Folk Opera in Two Acts, 9 Scenes[15]. Book by DuBose Heyward adapted from the play "Porgy" by DuBose and Dorothy Heyward. Music by George Gershwin. Lyrics by DuBose Heyward and Ira Gershwin. Directed by William Ball. Choral director and associate conductor, William Jonson. Settings by Stephen O. Saxe. Costumes by Stanley Simmons. Musical director, Julius Rudel. Lighting by Paul Morrison. Produced by the New York City Center Light Opera Company (Jean Dalrymple, Director). Opened 17 May 1961 at the New York City Center and closed 28 May 1961 after 16 performances.

CAST (in order of appearance): *Clara*: BILLIE LYNN DANIEL. *Mingo*: Jerry Laws. *Sportin' Life*: RAWN SPEARMAN, LEONARD PARKER (alt.). *Jake*: IRVING BARNES. *Serena*: BARBARA WEBB. *Robbins*: Ned Wright. *Jim*: Scott Gibson. *Peter, the Honey Man*: Joseph Crawford. *Lily, the Strawberry Woman*: Edna Ricks. *Maria*: CAROL BRICE. *Porgy*: WILLIAM WARFIELD, IRVING BARNES (alt.). *Crown*: JAMES RANDOLPH. *Bess*: LEESA FOSTER, MARTHA FLOWERS (alt.). *Policemen*: Harry Bessinger, Howard Poyro. *Detective*: William Coppola. *Police Sergeant*: Norman Grogan. *Undertaker*: Wanza King. *Annie*: Alyce Webb. *Frazier*: Eugene Brice. *Nelson*: Arthur Williams. *Strawberry Woman*: Doreese Duquan. *Crabman*: Clyde Turner. *Coroner*: Eugene Wood.
  Residents of Catfish Row: Ruby Green Aspinall, Kay Barnes, Phyllis Bash, Catherine Eason, Claretta Freeman, Victoria Harrison, Lillian Hayman, Joan Montgomery, Janet Moodyors, Caryl Paige, Joyce Phipps, Eloise C. Uggams, Catherine Van Buren, Glory Van Scott, Catherine Wallace, William H. Eaton, Jr., Cortez Franklin, Joli Gonsalves, Robert Guillaume, Elijah Hodges, Cullen Maiden, Tony L. Martinez, Garrett Morris, Garwood Perkins, Harold Pierson, John Richardson, Mal Scott, James Wamen, Laurence Watson. *Children*: Joey Lewis, Donna Mills, Cederic Rose, Lisa Scott, Alan Weeks, Jerry Wimberly.

1961.14 DONNYBROOK!

A Musical Comedy in Two Acts, 22 Scenes. Book by Robert E. McEnroe. Based on the film "The Quiet Man," (screenplay by Frank S. Nugent based on the short story of same name published in collection "Green Rushes") by Maurice Walsh. Music and lyrics by Johnny Burke. Directed and choreographed by Jack Cole. (Settings and costumes) Designed by Rouben Ter-Arutunian. Lighting by Klaus Holm. Musical direction and vocal arrangements by Clay Warnick. (Musical) arrangements and orchestrations by Robert Ginzler. Ballet music arranged and orchestrated by Laurence Rosenthal. Produced by Fred Hebert and David Kapp. Opened 18 May 1961 at the 46th Street Theatre and closed 15 July 1961 after 68 performances.

CAST (in order of appearance): *Willie O'Bantie*: Bruce MacKay. *Matthew Gilbane*: James Gannon. *Gavin Collins*: Alfred DeSio. *Old Man Toomey*: CLARENCE NORDSTROM. *Tim O'Connell*: Darrell J. Askey. *Will Danaher*: PHILIP BOSCO. *Ellen Roe Danaher*: JOAN FAGAN. *Esme Gillie*: Marissa Mason. *Sadie McInty*: SIBYL BOWAN. *Birdy Monyhan*: GRACE CARNEY. *Mikeen Flynn*: EDDIE FOY (JR.) *John Enright*: ART LUND. *Father Finucane*: Charles Welch. *An Irish Boy*: Eddie Ericksen.

---

[14]First produced in New York 7 April 1949 at the Majestic Theatre for 1925 performances. For Synopsis of Scenes and Musical Numbers, see original 1949 production.

[15]First produced in New York 10 October 1935 at the Alvin Theatre for 124 performances. For Synopsis of Scenes and Musical Numbers, see original 1935 production.

Jamie, a Bartender: George Harwell. *Kathy Carey*: SUSAN JOHNSON. *Principal Dancer*: Norman Maen.

Singing Ensemble: Georgia Creighton, Charlote Frazer, Nancy Foster, Dee Harless, Georgia Kennedy, Maudeen Sullivan, Darrell J. Askey, Eddie Ericksen, John Ford, George Harwell, Charles Rule, Bob Murdock. *Dancing Ensemble*: Gloria Ann Bowen, Judy Dunford, Mickey Gunnersen, Marissa Mason, Carol Sherman, Suanne Shirley, Pamela Wood, John Aristides, Robert Evans, Larry Fuller, William Guske, David Lober, George Martin, Keith Stewart.

Act 1, Scene 1: Overture. *Scene 2*: Kitchen of Will Danaher's house. *Scene 3*: The Countryside *Scene 4*: Outside "White O'Morn" Cottage. *Scene 5*: Carey's Pub. *Scene 6*: The Countryside. *Scene 7*: The Interior of Enright's Cottage. *Scene 8*: The Church. *Scene 9*: Kathy's Sitting Room; the Irish Countryside. *Scene 10*: Kitchen of Will Danaher's house. *Scene 11*: Danaher's Backyard. *Scene 12*: The Danaher Parlor.

Act 2, Scene 1: The Low Road. *Scene 2*: The Interior of "White O'Morn" Cottage. *Scene 3*: The High Road. *Scene 4*: The Interior of "White O'Morn" Cottage. *Scene 5*: Carey's Pub. *Scene 6*: The (Gravestone in the Ruins of the) Church Yard. *Scene 7*: The Interior of "White O'Morn" Cottage. *Scene 8*: Railway Station. *Scene 9*: (A Rock Wall in) Danaher's Field. *Scene 10*: The Interior of "White O'Morn" Cottage.

ACT 1

Scene 1

Overture
E. Ericksen, S. Bowan, G. Carney, C. C. Welch, J. Fagan,
Dancing Ensemble

Scenes 2 and 3

"Sez I"
J. Fagan, C. Nordstrom, B. Mackay, J. Gannon, A. Desio,
D. J. Askey

Scene 5

"The Day the Snow Is Meltin'"
E. Ericksen

"Sad Was the Day"
S. Johnson, Ensemble

"Donnybrook"
Ensemble

Scene 6

"The Day the Snow Is Meltin'" (reprise)
E. Ericksen, A. DeSio, D. J. Askey, A. Lund

Scene 7

"Ellen Roe"
A. Lund

Scene 8

"Sunday Morning"
Ensemble

"The Loveable Irish"
A. Lund, C. C. Welch

Scene 9

"I Wouldn't Bet One Penny"
S. Johnson, E. Foy

Scene 10

"He Makes Me Feel I'm Lovely"
J. Fagan

Scene 11

"The Courting"
Ensemble

"I Have My Own Way"
A. Lund, J. Fagan

Scene 12

"A Toast to the Bride"
C. Nordstrom, Ensemble

ACT 2

Scene 1

"Wisha Wurra"
E. Foy, C. Nordstrom, B. MacKay, J. Gannon, A. DeSio

Scene 3

("Wisha Wurra" reprise)
E. Foy, C. Nordstrom, B. MacKay, J. Gannon, A. DeSio

"He Makes Me Feel I'm Lovely" (reprise)
J. Fagan

Scene 4

"A Quiet Life"
A. Lund

Scene 5

"Mr. Flynn"
S. Johnson, S. Bowan, G. Carney

"Hornpipe Dance"[16]

"Dee-lightful is the Word"
E. Foy, S. Johnson

Scene 6

"For My Own"
J. Fagan, A. Lund

Scene 10

(Finale "Sez I" reprise)
P. Bosco, A. Lund, Ensemble

1961.15

PAL JOEY

A Revival of the Musical Play in Two Acts, 12 Scenes[17]. Book by John O'Hara based on his collected short stories of the same name. Music by Richard Rodgers. Lyrics by Lorenz Hart. Settings and lighting by Howard Bay. Costumes by Frank Thompson. Musical director, Jay Blackton. (Orchestrations by Don Walker, Hans Spialek.) Choreography by Ralph Beaumont. Directed by Gus Schirmer. Produced by the New York City Center Light Opera Company (Jean Dalrymple, Director). Opened 31 May 1961 at the New York City Center and closed 25 June 1961 after 31 performances.

CAST (in order of appearance): *Mike*: JACK WALDRON. *Joey Evans*: BOB FOSSE. *Kid*: Marjorie Graner. *Gladys*: SHEILA BOND. *Iris*: Lillian D'Honau. *Mickey*: Aura Vainio. *Diane*: Dorothy Dushock. *Dottie*: Billie Mahoney. *Sandra*: Pat Turner. *Adele*: Barbara Monte. *Francine*: Ellen Halpin. *Linda English*: CHRISTINE MATHEWS. *Vera Simpson*: CAROL BRUCE. *Valerie*: Betty Hyatt Linton. *Ernest*: Emory Bass. *Vera's Escort*: Philip Salem. *Victor*: Joe Milan. *Scholtz*: Gene Gavin. *Louis*, (The Tenor): John Lankston. *Melba Snyder*: EILEEN HECKART. *Ludlow Lowell*: HARVEY STONE. *O'Brien*: Charles Reynolds. *Mr. Hoople*: Alexander Clark.

Dancers: Lillian D'Honau, Marilyn D'Honau, Dorothy Dushock, Tina Faye, Ellen Fluhr, Marjorie Graner, Ellen Halpin, Carol Ann Kroon, Sara Letton, Betty Hyatt Linton, Billie Mahoney, Barbara Monte, Mona Pivar, Eleanor Rogers, Marla Stevens, Pat Turner, Aura Vainio, Judith West, Gene Gavin, Tod Jackson, Richard E. Korthaze, Vernon Lusby, Mitchell Nutick, Frank Paige, Alan Peterson, Tom Roba, Philip Salem, Bud Spencer, Vernon Wendorf.

---

[16]Dropped during run.

[17]Originally produced in New York 25 December 1940 at the Ethel Barrymore Theatre for 374 performances. For Synopsis of Scenes and Musical Numbers, see original 1940 production. For this production, "What Is a Man" replaced "Love Is My Friend" in Act 1, Scene 4; "Joey's Tango" (danced by B. Fosse) added to Act 2, Scene 4 between "Take Him" and the reprise of "Bewitched."

Barbara Cook in THE GAY LIFE (Photo: Friedman-Abeles)
Billy Rose Theatre Collection, New York Public Library for the Performing Arts

1961–1962 SEASON

1961.16   ## THE BILLY BARNES PEOPLE

A Musical Revue in Two Acts, 26 Scenes. Music and lyrics by Billy Barnes. Sketches and direction by Bob Rodgers. Production (settings) designed by Spencer Davies. Costumes by Grady Hunt. Musical arrangements and supervision, Ray Henderson. Cartoons, William Box. Produced by John Pool. Opened 13 June 1961 at the Royale Theatre and closed 17 June 1961 after 7 performances.

CAST: JOYCE JAMESON, DICK PATTERSON, PATTI REGAN, DAVE KETCHUM, KEN BERRY, JACKIE JOSEPH, JACK GRINNAGE, JO ANNE WORLEY.

ACT 1

Scene 1

"If It Wasn't for People"
Entire Cast

Scene 2

"There's Nothing Wrong With Our Values"
J. Jameson, D. Ketchum, P. Regan, D. Patterson

Scene 3

Vegas Revisited
Barker: J. Grinnage. *Statue*: J. Joseph. *Chorus Girl*: P. Regan. *Herman Hepplewhite*: D. Ketchum. *Fellas*: J. Grinnage, D. Patterson. *Opera Diva*: J. A. Worley.

Scene 4

"Don't Bother"
J. Joseph, K. Berry

Scene 5

I Wrote a Book
Authoress: J. Jameson. *Fans*: J. A. Worley, D. Patterson.

Scene 6

"If It Makes You Happy" (The Syndicate Song)
The Boss: D. Ketchum. *His Girl*: J. Joseph. *The Boys*: J. Grinnage, K. Berry.

Scene 7

"Damn-ALot" (Parody of "Camelot" in the style of Brendan Behan)
Introduced by J. Grinnage. *Guenevere*: P. Regan. *Morgan O'Fey*: J. Jameson. *King Arthur*: D. Ketchum. *Lancelot*: D. Patterson.

Scene 8

"What Do Have To Hold On To?"
J. A. Worley

Scene 9

"I Like You"
Romantic Couple: J. Joseph, K. Berry. *Neurotic Couple*: J. A. Worley, J. Grinnage. *Sophisticated Couple*: J. Jameson, D. Patterson.

Scene 10

"Before and After"
D. Ketchum, D. Patterson

Scene 11

"Let's Get Drunk"
K. Berry

Scene 12

"It's Not Easy"
Ethel: P. Regan. *Janet*: J. Jameson. *Adele*: J. A. Worley.

Scene 13

The Speech Teacher
Teacher: D. Patterson. *Client*: J. Grinnage.

Scene 14

"The Matinee"
Entire Cast

ACT 2

Scene 1

"If It Wasn't For People" (reprise)
J. Grinnage

The Couch: J. Joseph, D. Patterson. *The Balcony*: J. A. Worley, D. Ketchum. *Bus Stop*: P. Regan, K. Berry.

Scene 2

Liberated Woman
Sally O'Toole: J. Jameson. *Johnny, her boy friend*: J. Grinnage. *Narrator*: D. Patterson.

Scene 3

"What Do We Have to Hold On To?" (reprise)
J. A. Worley

Scene 4

"The End?"
D. Patterson, K. Berry, D. Ketchum

Scene 5

Alice
Alice: J. Joseph. *Felicia Fashion*: P. Regan. *Marty Market*: D. Patterson. *Housewife*: J. A. Worley. *Mrs. Karr*: J. Jameson. *Mr. Karr*: K. Berry. *Mr. Big Business, Sr.*: D. Ketchum. *Mr. Big Business, Jr.*: J. Grinnage.

Scene 6

Grauman's Chinese
D. Patterson, P. Regan, K. Berry

Scene 7

"Second Best"
J. Jameson

Scene 8

"What Do We Have to Hold On To?" (reprise)
J. A. Worley

Scene 9

"Dolls"
D. Ketchum, D. Patterson, P. Regan

Scene 10

"Where Is the Clown?"
J. Jameson, K. Berry

Scene 11

"Marital Infidelity"
Entire Cast

Scene 12

"I Like You" (reprise)
Entire Cast

1961.17   ## FROM THE SECOND CITY

A Comedy Revue in Two Acts, 24 Scenes[1]. Scenes and dialogues created by the Company. Director, Paul Sills. Music by William Mathieu. Settings and lighting designed by Frederick Fox. Produced by Max Liebman, Bernard Sahlins, Howard Alk, Paul Sills. Opened 26 September 1961 at the Royale Theatre and closed 9 December 1961 after 87 performances.

CAST: HOWARD ALK, ALAN ARKIN, SEVERN DARDEN, ANDREW DUNCAN, BARBARA HARRIS, MINA KOLB, PAUL SAND, EUGENE TROOBNICK. *At the piano*: Garry Sherman.

ACT 1

Scene 1

Max and Mortiz
S. Darden, H. Alk, B. Harris

Scene 2

Great Books
E. Troobnick, B. Harris, A. Duncan, M. Kolb, S. Darden

---

[1]Unlike all previous and subsequent Second City productions in Chicago, Off-Broadway and elsewhere, this edition was fully scripted and featured little of the improvisation for which the Second City was known. Following the Broadway run, the Second City re-opened Off-Broadway at the Square East in a series of revues in their traditional format: SEACOAST OF BOHEMIA, ALARUMS AND EXCURSIONS, TO THE WATER TOWER, WHEN THE OWL SCREAMS, OPEN SEASON AT SECOND CITY, and THE WRECKING BALL.

Scene 3

   Hollywood Ten

      A. Arkin, M. Kolb, S. Darden

Scene 4

   Phono Pal

      P. Sand, E. Troobnick

Scene 5

   The Hoboken Story (Parody of West Side Story)

      P. Sand, B. Harris, A. Duncan, A. Arkin, H. Alk, S. Darden

Scene 6

   The Silent Film

      S. Darden, E. Troobnick, P. Sand

Scene 7

   The Bergman Film

      S. Darden, P. Sand, B. Harris

Scene 8

   Interview: West Germany

      E. Troobnick, A. Arkin

Scene 9

   Interview: Louisiana

      A. Duncan, S. Darden

Scene 10

   A Short Message

      M. Kolb, E. Troobnick

Scene 11

   Football Comes to the U. of C.

      A. Duncan, H. Alk, E. Troobnick, S. Darden

Scene 12

   Museum Piece

      B. Harris, A. Arkin

Scene 13

   "Second City Symphony"

ACT 2

Scene 1

   "Tempo"

      The Company

Scene 2

   Laos

      P. Sand, A. Duncan

Scene 3

   "I Got Blues"

      B. Harris, S. Darden, H. Alk

Scene 4

   "Minstrel Show"

      E. Troobnick, A. Duncan, P. Sand, H. Alk

Scene 5

   A Piece of String

      S. Darden, P. Sand

Scene 6

   No George Don't

      A. Arkin, M. Kolb

Scene 7

   News Broadcast — 1965

      E. Troobnick

Scene 8

   First Affair

      B. Harris, S. Darden

Scene 9

   Mountain Climbing

      H. Alk, A. Arkin, P. Sand, A. Duncan, E. Troobnick

Scene 10

   Caesar's Wife

      M. Kolb, B. Harris, H. Alk

Scene 11

   Noah

      The Company

1961.18   # SAIL AWAY

A Musical Comedy in Two Acts, 18 Scenes. Book, music, lyrics and direction by Nöel Coward. (Settings) designed by Oliver Smith. Costumes by Helene Pons and Oliver Smith. Lighting by Peggy Clark. Musical numbers and dances staged by Joe Layton. Orchestrations by Irwin Kostal. Musical direction and dance arrangements by Peter Matz. Vocal arrangements, Fred Werner. Associate choreographer, Buddy Schwab. Produced by Bonard Productions (Helen G. Bonfils, Haila Stoddard, Donald R. Seawell) in association with Charles Russell. Opened 3 October 1961 at the Broadhurst Theatre and closed 24 February 1962 after 167 performances.

<u>CAST</u> (in order of appearance): *Joe*, the ship's purser: CHARLES BRASWELL. *Shuttleworth*, a steward: Keith Prentice. *Rawlings*, a passenger who drinks: James Pritchett. *Sir Gerald Nutfield*: C. Stafford Dickens. *Lady Nutfield*: Margaret Mower. *Barnaby Slade*: GROVER DALE. *Elmer Candijack*: Henry Lawrence. *Maimie Candijack*, his wife: BETTY JANE WATSON. *Glen Candijack*, their son: Alan Helms. *Shirley Candijack*, their daughter: Patti Mariano. *Mr. Sweeney*: Jon Richards. *Mrs. Sweeney*: PAULA BAUERSMITH. *Elinor Spencer-Bollard*: ALICE PEARCE. *Nancy Foyle*, her neice: PATRICIA HARTY. *Alvin Lush*: PAUL O'KEEFE. *Mrs. Lush*, his mother: EVELYN RUSSELL. *John Van Mier*: JAMES HURST. *Mrs. Van Mier*, his mother: MARGALO GILLMORE. *Mimi Paragon*: ELAINE STRITCH. *Ali*, an Arab guide: CHARLES BRASWELL. *Man from American Express*: Richard Woods.

   Passengers, Stewards, Arabs, Italians, Children: Jere Admire, Bobby Allen, Don Atkinson, Gary Crabbe, David Evans, Pat Ferrier, Dorothy Frank, Ann Fraser, James Frasher, Gene Gavin, Paul Gross, S. Curtis Hood, Wish Mary Hunt, Cheryl Kilgren, Bridget Knapp, Nancy Lynch, Patti Mariano, Mary Ellen O'Keefe, Alan Peterson, Dennis Scott, Alice Shanahan, Dan Siretta, Gloria Stevens, Christopher Votos.

Act 1, Scene 1: The Main Hall of the Cunard Steam-Ship, *Coronia* .*Scene 2*: John Van Mier's Cabin. *Scene 3*: The Sun Deck, New York Harbor. *Scene 4*: Elinor Spencer-Bollard's Cabin. *Scene 5*: The Sun-Deck, at sea several days later. *Scene 6*: Mimi Paragon's Cabin. *Scene 7*: The Sun Deck. Moonlight. *Scene 8*: The Promenade Deck. Later that night. *Scene 9*: The Sun Deck. Gibraltar.

Act 2, Scene 1: Tangier. *Scene 2*: Italian Interlude. *Scene 3*: The Ship's Nursery. *Scene 4*: The Sun Deck. The Bay of Naples. *Scene 5*: The Boat Deck. Villefranche. *Scene 6*: The Parthenon. *Scene 7*: The Sun Deck. *Scene 8*: The Promenade Deck. *Scene 9*: The Main Hall.

ACT 1

Scene 1

   "Come To Me"

      E. Stritch, Stewards

Scene 2

   "Sail Away"[2]

      J. Hurst

Scene 3

   "Come To Me" (reprise)

      E. Stritch

   "Sail Away" (reprise)

      J. Hurst, Company

Scene 4

   "Where Shall I Find Him?"

      P. Harty

Scene 5

   "Beatnik Love Affair"

      G. Dale, P. Harty, Passengers

   "Later Than Spring"

      J. Hurst

   "The Passenger's Always Right"

      C. Braswell, Stewards

Scene 6

   "Useful Phrases"

      E. Stritch

Scene 7

   "Where Shall I Find Her?" (reprise)

      G. Dale

Scene 8

   "Go Slow, Johnny"

      J. Hurst

---

[2]Previously used in ACE OF CLUBS, London, 1950.

Scene 9

"You're a Long, Long Way from America"
E. Stritch, Company

ACT 2

Scene 1

"The Customer's Always Right"
C. Braswell, Arabs

"Something Very Strange"
E. Stritch

Scene 2

Italian Interlude
The Company

Scene 3

"The Little Ones' ABC"
E. Stritch, P. O'Keffe, Children

Scene 4

"Don't Turn Away from Love"
J. Hurst

Scene 6

"When You Want Me"
G. Dale, P. Harty

Scene 7

"Later Than Spring" (reprise)
E. Stritch

Scene 8

"Why Do the Wrong People Travel?"
E. Stritch

Scene 9

"When You Want Me" (reprise)
The Company
Finale

THE MIKADO,
or The Town of Titipu

1961.19

A Revival of the Comic Opera in Two Acts[3]. Libretto by William S. Gilbert. Music by Arthur Sullivan. Staged by Dorothy Raedler. Scenic design by Donald Oenslager. Costume design by Patton Campbell. Conducted by Emerson Buckley. Produced by the New York City Opera. Opened 8 October 1961 at the New York City Center and closed 4 November 1961 after 3 performances in repertory.

CAST: *The Mikado of Japan*: GEORGE GAYNES. *Nanki-Poo*, his son, disguised as a wandering minstrel in love with Yum-Yum: FRANK PORETTA. *Ko-Ko*, Lord High Executioner of Titipu: NORMAN KELLEY. *Pooh-Bah*, Lord High Everything Else: HERBERT BEATTIE. *Pish-Tush*, a Noble Lord: William Metcalf. *Yum-Yum, Pitti-Sing, Peep-Bo*, three sisters, wards of Ko-Ko: JOY CLEMENTS, JANET BROADHURST, SOPHIA STEFFAN. *Katisha*: GLADYS KRIESE. *Chorus of School Girls, Nobles, Guards and Coolies*: New York City Opera Chorus.

1961.20 ## MILK AND HONEY

A Musical in Two Acts, 12 Scenes. Book by Don Appell. Music and lyrics by Jerry Herman. Production staged by Albert Marre. Choreography, Donald Saddler. Settings and lighting by Howard Bay. Costumes by Miles White. Orchestrations by Hershy Kay and Eddie Sauter. Choral arrangements, Robert de Cormier. Musical director, Max Goberman. Dance arrangements, Genevieve Pitot. Produced by Gerard Oestreicher. Opened 10 October 1961 at the Martin Beck Theatre and closed 26 January 1963 after 543 performances.

[3]First presented in New York 20 July, 10-29 August 1885 at the Union Square and People's Theatres for 22 performances. First authorized production presented 19 August 1885 at the Fifth Avenue Theatre by Richard D'Oyly Carte for 250 performances. For Synopsis of Scenes and Musical Numbers, see 19 August 1885 D'Oyly Carte production.

CAST (in order of appearance): *Porter*: Burt Bier. *Shepherd Boy*: Johnny Borden. *Policeman*: Ronald Holgate. *Ruth*: MIMI BENZELL. *Phil*: ROBERT WEEDE. *Clara Weiss*: MOLLY PICON. *The Guide*: Ellen Berse. *Mrs. Weinstein*: Addi Negri. *Mrs. Strauss*: Dorothy Richardson. *Mrs. Breslin*: Rose Lischner. *Mrs. Segal*: Diane [Diana] Goldberg. *Mrs. Kessler*: Ceil Delli. *Mrs. Perlman*: Thelma Pelish. *Barbara, Phil's Daughter*: LANNA SAUNDERS. *David, Barbara's Husband*: TOMMY RALL. *Adi*: JUKI ARKIN. *Zipporah*; Ellen Madison. *The Cantors*: Lou Polacek, David London. *Maid of Honor*: Matt Turney. *Wedding Couples*: Jose Gutierrez, Linda Howe, Michael Nestor, Jane Zachary. *Cafe Arab*: Renato Cibelli. *Man of the Moshav*: Art Tookoyan. *Mr. Horowitz*: Reuben Singer.

Soldiers, Hassidim, Arabs, Tourists, etc.: Marceline Decker, Urylee Leonardos, Terry Marone, Sandra Stahl, Marilyn Stark, Patti Winston, Myrna Aaron, Nina Feinberg, Penny Ann Green, Judith Haskell, Linda Howe, Susan May, Matt Turney, Jane Zachary, Burt Bier, Gerald Cardoni, Renato Cibelli, Murray Goldkind, David London, Ed Mastin, Lou Poalcek, Robert Rue, Art Tookoyan, Anthony De Vecchi, Louis Gasparinetti, Jose Gutierrez, Stuart Hodes, Alex Kotimski, Carlos Macri, John Mandia, Michael Nestor, Dom Salinaro, Walter Stratton, Eddie Roll, Ronald Holgate.

Act 1, Scene 1: A Street in Jerusalem. (Present time.) *Scene 2*: Another Street. That night. *Scene 3*: A Moshav in the Desert. A few days later. *Scene 4*: David's House. A week later. *Scene 5*: The Barn. *Scene 6*: A Hill overlooking the Valley. *Scene 7*: The Wedding.

Act 2, Scene 1: Another Part of the Moshav. Next morning. *Scene 2*: The Cafe Hotok, Tel Aviv, the same day. *Scene 3*: A Street in Jerusalem, that night. *Scene 4*: Outside Adi's House. A day later. *Scene 5*: The Airport, Tel Aviv.

ACT 1

Scene 1

"Shepherd's Song"
J. Borden, R. Weede

"Shalom"
R. Weede, M. Benzell

Scene 2

"Independence Day Hora"
Company

Scene 3

"Milk and Honey"
T. Rall, J. Arkin, Company

Scene 4

"There's No Reason in the World"
R. Weede

"Chin Up, Ladies"
M. Picon, Widows

Scene 5

"That Was Yesterday"
M. Benzell, R. Weede, T. Rall, K. Arkin, Company

Scene 6

"Let's Not Waste a Moment"
R. Weede

Scene 7

"The Wedding"
M. Benzell, R. Weede, Company

ACT 2

Scene 1

"Like a Young Man"
R. Weede

"I Will Follow You"
T. Rall

Scene 2

"Hymn to Hymie"
M. Picon

Scene 3

"There's No Reason in the World" (reprise)
M. Benzell

Scene 4

"Milk and Honey" (reprise)
J. Arkin, Company

"As Simple As That"
M. Benzell, R. Weede

Scene 5

"Shalom" (reprise)
M. Benzell, R. Weede, Company

1961.21 LET IT RIDE!

A Musical Comedy in Two Acts, 18 Scenes. Book by Abram S. Ginnes. Based on the play "Three Men on a Horse" by John Cecil Holm and George Abbott. Music and lyrics by Jay Livingston and Ray Evans. Additional material by Ronny Graham. Directed by Stanley Prager. Dances and musical numbers Staged by Onna White. Settings and lighting by William and Jean Eckart. Costumes by Guy Kent. Musical director, Jay Blackton. Vocal director, Jerry Packer. Orchestrations, Raymond Jaimes. Dance music arranged by Billy Goldenberg. Produced by Joel Spector. Opened 12 October 1961 at the Eugene O'Neill Theatre and closed 9 December 1961 after 68 performances.

CAST (in order of appearance): *Erwin:* GEORGE GOBEL. *Audrey:* PAULA STEWART. *Carver:* STANLEY GROVER. *Harry:* HAROLD GARY. *Charlie:* ALBERT LINVILLE. *Frankie:* LARRY ALPERT. *Mabel:* BARBARA NICHOLS. *Patsy:* SAM LEVENE. *Birthday Girls:* Pat Turner, Sandra Devlin, Ann Johnson, Sandy Walsh, Rae McLean, Carol Glade, Sally Lee, Sally Kirk, Barbara Marcon. *Nice Nose Brophy:* DORT CLARK. *Mother:* Maggie Worth. *Chief Schermerhorn:* TED THURSTON. *Repulski:* STANLEY SIMMONDS. *First Cop:* John Ford. *Announcer's Voice:* TED THURSTON.

Dancers: Ted Adkins, Robert Bakanic, Rhett Dennis, Sandra Devlin, Bob Evans, Dick Gingrich, Ann Johnson, Sally Kirk, Sally Lee, Jack Leigh, Vernon Lusby, Rae McLean, Barbara Marcon, Pat Turner, Sandra Walsh, Marty Allen, Marc West. *Singers:* Helen Baisley, Francine Bond, Austin Colyer, Clifford Fearl, John Ford, Carol Glade, Robert Lenn, Virginia Perlowin, Michael Roberts, Maggie Worth.

Act 1, Scene 1: Bus. *Scene 2:* Main Office of Modern Greeting Card Company. *Scene 3:* Street outside Hotel Lavillere. *Scene 4:* Bar, Hotel Lavillere. *Scene 5:* Corridor, Modern Greeting Card Company. *Scene 6:* Patsy's Party. *Scene 7:* Audrey's Porch. *Scene 8:* Mabel's Room.

Act 2, Scene 1: Opening. *Scene 2:* Bar. *Scene 3:* Audrey's Porch. *Scene 4:* Mabel's Room. *Scene 5:* Rogues Gallery. *Scene 6:* Lineup. *Scene 7:* Outside Police Station. *Scene 8:* Erwin's Island. *Scene 9:* Bar. *Scene 10:* Finale.

ACT 1
"Run Run Runn"
   Singers, Dancers
"The Nicest Thing"
   P. Stewart
"Hey, Jimmy, Joe, John, Jim, Jack"
   G. Gobel
"Broads Ain't People"
   G. Gobel, H. Gary, L. Alpert, A. Linville
"Let It Ride"
   S. Levene, Singers, Dancers
"I'll Learn Ya"
   G. Gobel, S. Levene
"Love Let Me Know"
   P. Stewart, S. Grover
"Happy Birthday"
   Birthday Girls
"Everything Beautiful"
   G. Gobel, Birthday Girls
"Who's Doing What to Erwin"
   P. Stewart, T. Thurston, S. Grover, M. Worth
"I Wouldn't Have Had To"
   B. Nichols

ACT 2
"There's Something About a Horse"
   Singers, Dancers
"He Needs You"
   G. Gobel, L. Alpert, A. Linville
"Just an Honest Mistake"
   T. Thurston, S. Simmonds, Cops
"His Own Little Island"
   G. Gobel
"If Flutterby Wins"
   G. Gobel, S. Leve, L. Alpert, A. Linville, H. Gary, Hoods
Finale
   (Entire Company)

HOW TO SUCCEED IN BUSINESS
1961.22 WITHOUT REALLY TRYING

A Musical (Comedy) in Two Acts, 24 Scenes. Book by Abe Burrows, Jack Weinstock and Willie Gilbert. Based on the novel of the same name by Shepherd Mead. Music and lyrics by Frank Loesser. Scenery and lighting by Robert Randolph. Costumes by Robert Fletcher. Choreography by Hugh Lambert. Musical staging by Bob Fosse. Musical direction, Elliot Lawrence. Orchestrations by Robert Ginzler. Directed by Abe Burrows. Produced by Cy Feuer and Ernest H. Martin in association with Frank Productions, Inc. Opened 14 October 1961 at the 46th Street Theatre and closed 6 March 1965 after 1417 performances.

CAST (in order of appearance): *Finch:* ROBERT MORSE. *Gatch:* RAY MASON. *Jenkins:* Bob Kaliban. *Tackaberry:* David Collyer. *Peterson:* Casper Roos. *J. B. Biggley:* RUDY VALLEE. *Rosemary:* BONNIE SCOTT. *Bratt:* PAUL REED. *Smitty:* CLAUDETTE SUTHERLAND. *Frump:* CHARLES NELSON REILLY. *Miss Jones:* RUTH KOBART. *Mr. Twimble:* SAMMY SMITH. *Hedy:* VIRGINIA MARTIN. *Scrubwomen:* Mara Landi, Silver Saundors. *Miss Krumholtz:* Mara Landi. *Toynbee:* RAY MASON. *Ovington:* Lanier Davis. *Policeman:* Bob Murdock. *Womper:* SAMMY SMITH.

Singers: David Collyer, Lanier Davis, Bob Kaliban, Bob Murdock, Casper Roos, Charlotte Frazier, Mara Land, Fairfax Mason, Silver Saundors, Maudeen Sullivan. *Dancers:* Nick Andrews, Tracy Everitt, Stuart Fleming, Richard Korthaze, Dale Moreda, Darrell Notara, Merritt Thompson, Carol Jane Abney, Madilyn Clark, Elaine Cancilla, Suzanne France, Donna McKechnie, Ellie Somers, Rosemarie Yellen.

Act 1, Scene 1: Exterior of the World Wide Wicket Company, Park Avenue, New York City. (Present time.) *Scene 2:* Corridor of the World Wide Wicket Company. *Scene 3:* Outer Office of the World Wide Wicket Company. *Scene 4:* The Mail Room. *Scene 5:* J. B. Biggley's Desk. *Scene 6:* Corridor of the World Wide Wicket Company. *Scene 7:* The Elevator Landing. *Scene 8:* The Outer Office. *Scene 9:* Finch's First Office. *Scene 10:* Plans and Systems Office. *Scene 11:* Corridor. *Scene 12:* The Roof. *Scene 13:* Elevator Landing. *Scene 14:* J. B. Biggley's Office.

Act 2, Scene 1: The Outer Office. *Scene 2:* Finch's New Advertising Office. *Scene 3:* J. B. Biggley's Office. *Scene 4:* Men's Washroom. *Scene 5:* Boardroom. *Scene 6:* Television Show. *Scene 7:* Wrecked Outer Office. *Scene 8:* Elevator Landing. *Scene 9:* J. B. Biggley's Office. *Scene 10:* The Outer Office.

ACT 1
Scene 1
"How To (Succeed)"
   R. Morse
Scene 2
"Happy To Keep His Dinner Warm"
   B. Scott
Scene 3
"Coffee Break"
   C. N. Reilly, C. Sutherland, Office Staff
Scene 4
"The Company Way"
   R. Morse, S. Smith
"The Company Way" (reprise)
   C. N. Reilly, S. Smith, Office Staff
Scene 6
"A Secretary Is Not a Toy"
   P. Reed, C. Nelson Reilly, Office Staff
Scene 7
"Been a Long Day"
   R. Morse, B. Scott, C. Sutherland
"Been a Long Day" (reprise)
   R. Vallee, V. Martin, C. N. Reilly
Scene 8
"Grand Old Ivy"
   R. Morse, R. Vallee
Scenes 11 and 12
"Paris Original"
   B. Scott, C. Sutherland, R. Kobart, Secretaries
Scene 14
"Rosemary"
   R. Morse, B. Scott
Finaletto
   R. Morse, B. Scott, C. N. Reilly

ACT 2

Scene 1

"Cinderella Darling"
B. Scott, C. Sutherland, Secretaries

Scene 2

"Happy To Keep His Dinner Warm" (reprise)
B. Scott

Scene 3

"Love From a Heart of Gold"
R. Vallee, V. Martin

Scene 4

"I Believe in You"
R. Morse, C. N. Reilly, P. Reed, Executives

Scene 6

"The Yo Ho Ho" (Pirate Dance)
The Jolly Wickets and Wickettes

Scene 7

"I Believe in You" (reprise)
B. Scott

Scene 9

"Brotherhood of Man"
R. Morse, R. Vallee, C. N. Reilly, P. Reed, S. Smith, R. Kobart,
Office Staff

Scene 10

Finale
Company

H.M.S. PINAFORE,
1961.23   or The Lass That Loved a Sailor

A Revival of the Comic Opera in Two Acts[4]. Libretto by William S. Gilbert. Music by Arthur Sullivan. Staged by Allen Fletcher. (Costumes and settings) designed by Patton Campbell. Conducted by Felix Popper. Produced by the New York City Opera. Opened 15 October 1961 at the New York City Center and closed 11 November 1961 after 4 performances in repertory.

CAST: *The Rt. Hon. Sir Joseph Porter, K.C.B.*, First Lord of the Admiralty: NORMAN KELLEY. *Captain Corcoran*, Commanding *H.M.S. Pinafore*: WILLIAM CHAPMAN. *Ralph Rackstraw*, Able Seaman: FRANK PORETTA. *Dick Deadeye*, Able Seaman: PAUL UKENA. *Bill Bobstay*, Bo'sun's Mate: Richard Fredericks. *Bob Beckett*, Carpenter's Mate: John Macurdy. *Josephine*, the Captain's Daughter: DORIS YARICK. *Hebe*, Sir Joseph's First Cousin: Sophia Steffan. *Little Buttercup*, a Portsmouth Bumboat Woman: GLADYS KRIESE. *First Lord's Sisters, his Cousins, his Aunts, Sailors, Marines*: New York City Opera Chorus.

1961.24   KWAMINA

A Musical in Two Acts, 15 Scenes. Book by Robert Alan Arthur. Music and lyrics by Richard Adler. Dances and musical numbers Staged by Agnes de Mille. Settings and lighting designed by Will Steven Armstrong. Costumes designed by Motley. Musical and choral direction, Colin Romoff. Dance arrangements, John Morris. Orchestrations by Sid Ramin, Irwin Kostal. Technical consultant, Albert Opoku. Directed by Robert Lewis. Produced by Alfred de Liagre, Jr. Opened 23 October 1961 at the 54th Street Theatre and closed 18 November 1961 after 32 performances.

CAST (in order of appearance): *Obitsebi*: BROCK PETERS. *Blair*: NORMAN BARRS. *Ako*: Robert Guillaume. *Eve*: SALLY ANN HOWES. *Naii*: ETHEL AYLER. *Akufo*: Joseph Attles. *Kwamina (Peter)*: TERRY CARTER. *Kojo*: Ainsley Sigmond. *Children*: Vaughn Fubler, Renaye Fubler. *Nana Mwalla*: REX INGRAM. *Alla*: Rosalie Maxwell. *Mammy Trader*: Lillian Hayman. *Policemen*: Ronald Platts, Edward Thomas. *Drummers*: Montego Joe, Robert Crowder.
  Singers: Issa Arnal, Doresse DuQuan, Victoria Harrison, Lillian Hayman, Lee Hooper, Mary Louise, Rosalie Maxwell, Helen Phillips, Joseph Crawford, Scott

Gibson, Wanza King, James Lowe, John Miles, Clark Morgan, Mal Scott, Rawn Spearman, George Tipton, Gordon Watkins, Arthur Wright. *Dancers*: Hope Clark, Doris deMendez, Altovise Gore, Minnie Marshall, Joan Peters, Lucinda Ransom, Joan Seabrook, Barbara Teer, Glory Van Scott, Myrna White, Camille Yarborough, Pepsi Bethel, Zebedee Collins, Julius Fields, Frank Glass, Louis Johnson, Charles Moore, Ronald Platts, Mike Quashie, Charles Queenan, Philip Stamps, Edward Thomas.

The action takes place in a village in West Africa at the present time.

ACT 1

Scene 2

"The Cocoa Bean Song"
R. Guillaume, S. Gibson, G. Watkins, Company

Scene 3

"Welcome Home"
S. Hibson, M. Scott, L. Hooper, M. Quashie, Company
Spear Dancers: C. Moore, C. Queenan. *Fonga*: J. Seabrook, B. Teer, G. Van Scott, M. White.

"The Sun Is Beginning to Crow"
Company

Scene 4

"Did You Hear That?"
S. A. Howes, T. Carter

"You're As English As"
S. A. Howes

Scene 5

"Seven Sheep, Four Red Shirts and a Bottle of Gin"
J. Attles, S. Gibson, C. Queenan, G. Tipton, Company

Scene 6

"Nothing More to Look Forward To"
R. Guillaume, E. Ayler

"What's Wrong WIth Me?"
S. A. Howes

Scene 7

"Something Big"
T. Carter, Company

"Ordinary People"
S. A. Howes, T. Carter

Scene 8

Mammy Traders (dance)
Girl With Parasol: G. Van Scott. *Admirers*: C. Moore, Z. Collins, Dance Company.

Scene 9

"A Man Can Have No Choice"
B. Peters

Scene 10

"What Happened to Me Tonight?"
S. A. Howes

ACT 2

Scene 1

Naii's Nuptial Dance
E. Ayler, H. Clarke, Company

"One Wife"
L. Hayman, R. Maxwell, I. Arnal,
V. Harrison, L. Hooper, M. Louise, H. Phillips, Dancers

"Nothing More To Look Forward To" (reprise)
E. Ayler

Scene 2

"Something Big" (reprise)
Company

"Another Time, Another Place"
S. A. Howes

Scene 5

Fetish (dance)
B. Peters
Priests: Z. Collins, F. Glass, C. Moore, M. Quashie, C. Queenan, P. Stamps.

---

[4]Originally presented in New York 15 January 1879 at the Standard Theatre for 175 performances. For Synopsis of Scenes and Musical Numbers, see original 1879 production.

1961.25

AN EVENING WITH
YVES MONTAND

A One Man Show in Two Acts. Staged and lighted by Yves Montand. Conductor, Bob Castella. Produced by Salle Productions, Inc. Presented by Norman Granz in association with Jacques Canetti and Alexander H. Cohen. Opened 24 October 1961 at the John Golden Theatre and closed 16 December 1961 after 55 performances.

CAST: YVES MONTAND.

Accordion: Bob Creash. *Clarinet:* Edmund Hall. *Trombone:* Morty Trautman. *Drums:* Charles Persip. *Bass:* Al Hall. *Guitar:* Jim Hall.

ACT 1
  "Je suis venu á pieds"
    (*Music and Lyrics by* Francis Lemarque.)
  "Battling Joe"
    (*Music by* Louis Gaste. *Lyrics by* Jean Guigo.)
  "La tête á l'ombre"
    (*Music and Lyrics by* Paul Misraki.)
  "Une demoiselle sur une balancoire" (A Young Lady in a Swing)
    (*Music by* Mireille. *Lyrics by* Jean Nohain.)
  "Just in Time" (From BELLS ARE RINGING)
    (*Music by* Jule Styne. *Lyrics by* Betty Comden and Adolph Green.)
  "Gilet Raye" (The Night Porter)
    (*Music by* Louiguy. *Lyrics by* Henri Contet.)
  "Sous le ciel de Paris"
    (*Music by* Hubert Giraud. *Lyrics by* Jean Drejac.)
  "Le carosse" (The Golden Chariot)
    (*Music by* Mireille. *Lyrics by* Henri Contet.)
  "Les grands boulevards"
    (*Music by* Norman Glanzberg. *Lyrics by* Jacques Plante.)
  "Flamenco of Paris"
    (*Music and Lyrics by* Leo Ferre.)
  "Un garçon dansait"
    (*Music by* Georges Liferman. *Lyrics by* Jacques Mareuil.)
ACT 2
  "Mais qu'est-ce que j'ai?" (What's Wrong With Me?)
    (*Music by* Henri Betti. *Lyrics by* Edith Piaf.)
  "I've Grown Accustomed to Her Face" (from MY FAIR LADY)
    (*Music by* Frederick Loewe. *Lyrics by* Alan Jay Lerner.)
  "Dis-moi jo" (Tell Me Jo)
    (*Music by* Henri Crolla. *Lyrics by* Jean Cosmos.)
  "La Marie vision" (Marie's Mink Coat)
    (*Music by* Marc Heyrai. *Lyrics by* Roger Varnay.)
  "Planter cafe"
    (*Music by* Emil Stern. *Lyrics by* Eddy Marnay.)
  "Le chef d'orchestre est amoureux" (The Conductor Is in Love)
    (*Music by* Georges Liferman. *Lyrics by* Jacques Mareuil.)
  "C'est á l'aube" (Dawn)
    (*Music by* Philippe Gerard. *Lyrics by* Flavien Monod.)
  "Barbara"
    (*Poem by* Jacques Prévert.)
  "Á Paris"
    (*Music and Lyrics by* Francis Lemarque.)
  "Il fait des … le fanatique du jazz"
    (*Music by* Edouard Chekle. *Lyrics by* Edith Piaf.)
  "Mon manege á moi"
    (*Music by* Norbert Glanzberg. *Lyrics by* Jean Constantin.)

1961.26

KEAN

A Musical Comedy in Two Acts, a Prologue and 12 Scenes. Book by Peter Stone from the comedy of the same name by Jean-Paul Sartre, based on a play by Alexandre Dumas. Music and lyrics by Robert Wright and George Forrest. Production (settings and costumes) designed by Ed Wittstein. Lighting by John Harvey. Musical direction and vocal arrangements, Pembroke Davenport. Ballet and incidental music, Elie Siegmeister. Staged and choreographed by Jack Cole. Produced by Robert Lantz. Opened 2 November 1961 at the Broadway Theatre and closed 20 January 1962 after 92 performances.

CAST (in order of appearance): *Christie:* Alfred DeSio. *Barnaby:* Christopher Hewett. *Edmund Kean:* ALFRED DRAKE. *Stage Manager:* Alfred Toigo. *Ben:* ROBERT PENN. *Francis:* Arthur Rubin. *Solomon:* TRUMAN SMITH. *Lord Neville:* RODERICK COOK. *Countess Elena De Koeberg:* JOAN WELDON. *Lady Amy Goswell:* PATRICIA CUTTS. *Count De Koeberg:* PATRICK WADDINGTON. *Lord Delmore:* John Lankston. *Major-Domo:* Martin Ambrose. *Prince of Wales:* OLIVER GRAY. *Anna Danby:* LEE VENORA. *Prop Boy:* Eddie Ericksen. *Secretary:* Joseph McGrath. *Maxwell:* Larry Shadur. *Henchman:* Martin Ambrose. *Pott:* George Harwell. *St. Albands:* Rene Jarmon. *Sparrow:* Margaret Gathright. *Bolt:* Gloria Warner. *Tim:* Randy Doney. *David:* John Jordan. *Pip:* Paul Jordan. *Patrick:* Charles Dunn. *Guards:* Larry Shadur, John Wheeler.

Dancers: John Aristides, Barbara Beck, Johanna Carothers, Lois Castle, Charles Corbett, Kenneth Creel, Randy Doney, Judy Dunford, Larry Fuller, Mickey Gunnersen, Pamela Hayford, Jim Hutchison, Lisa James, Rene Jarmon, Richard Lyle, George Martin, Roger Puckett, Suanne Shirley. *Singers:* Martin Ambrose, Charise Amidon, Charles Dunn, Eddie Ericksen, Nancy Foster, Margaret Gathright, Maggie Goz, George Harwell, John Lankston, Joseph McGrath, Lispet Nelson, Mary Nettum, Larry Shadur, Susan Terry, Alfred Toigo, Gloria Warner, John Wheeler.

The action takes place in London in the early nineteenth century.

Prologue: Drury Lane Theatre. The Stage.

Act 1, Scene 1: The Danish Embassy. A Ballroom. *Scene 2:* The Street. Drury Lane. *Scene 3:* Drury Lane Theatre. Kean's Dressing Room. *Scene 4:* The Danish Embassy. A private room. And Carlton House. A private room. *Scene 5:* A Street in front of a Thames-side tavern. *Scene 6:* The Green Frog," a tavern.

Act 2, Scene 1: Drury Lane Theatre. Kean's dressing room. *Scene 2:* Drury Lane Theatre. The stage boxes. *Scene 3:* The Street. Drury Lane. *Scene 4:* Kean's House. A drawing room. *Scene 5:* The Street. Drury Lane. *Scene 6:* Drury Lane Theatre. The Stage.

ACT 1
  Prologue
    "Penny Plain, Twopence Colored"
      A. DeSio
    "Man and Shadow"
      A. Drake
  Scene 1
    "Mayfair Affair"
      J. Weldon, P. Cutts, Dancing and Singing Ensemble
    "Sweet Danger"
      J. Weldon, A. Drake
  Scene 2
    "Queue at Drury Lane"
      C. Hewett, R. Penn, A. Rubin, Ensemble
    "King of London"
      C. Hewett, R. Penn, A. Rubin, Ensemble
  Scene 3
    "To Look Upon My Love"
      A. Drake, T. Smith
    "Let's Improvise"
      A. Drake, L. Venora
    "Elena"
      A. Drake, A. Rubin, Ensemble
  Scene 4
    "Social Whirl"
      J. Weldon, P. Cutts, O. Gray, P. Waddington
  Scene 5
    "The Fog and the Grog"
      C. Hewett, R. Penn, A. Rubin, A. Drake, Ensemble
  Scene 6
    Finale (Act 1)
      A. Drake, Ensemble

ACT 2
  Scene 1
    "Civilized People"
      A. Drake, L. Venora, J. Weldon
    "Service for Service"
      J. Weldon, A. Drake
    "Willow, Willow, Willow"
      L. Venora
  Scene 3
    "Fracas at Old Drury"
      C. Hewett, R. Penn, A. Rubin, A. DeSio, Ensemble

"Chime In!"
A. DeSio, C. Hewett, R. Penn, A. Rubin, Ensemble
Scene 4
"Swept Away"
J. Weldon, A. Drake
"Domesticity"
L. Venora, A. Drake
Scene 5
"Clown of London"
Ensemble
Scene 6
"Apology?"
A. Drake

1961.27 THE GAY LIFE

A Musical Comedy in Two Acts, 15 Scenes. Book by Fay and Michael Kanin. Suggested by the play "Anatol" by Arthur Schnitzler. Music by Arthur Schwartz. Lyrics by Howard Dietz. Directed by Gerald Freedman. Dances and musical numbers staged by Herbert Ross. Scenic production by Oliver Smith. Costumes by Lucinda Ballard. Lighting by Jean Rosenthal. Orchestrations by Don Walker. Vocal arrangements and musical direction, Herbert Greene. Dance arrangements, Robert Starer. Magical illusions created and designed by Jack Adams. Produced by Kermit Bloomgarden. Opened 18 November 1961 at the Sam S. Shubert Theatre and closed 24 February 1962 after 113 performances.

CAST (in order of appearance): *Max*: JULES MUNSHIN. *Usher*: Sterling Clark. *Anatol*: WALTER CHIARI. *Franz*: LEONARD ELLIOTT. *Helene*: JEANNE BAL. *Liesl Brandel*: BARBARA COOK. *Herr Brandel*: LORING SMITH. *Frau Brandel*: LU LEONARD. *Mimi*: YVONNE CONSTANT. *Proprietor*: Michael Quinn. *The Great Gaston*: Jack Adams. *Otto*: Rico Froehlich. *Waiters*: Ted Lambrinos, Russell Goodwin. *Anna*: Joanne Spiller. *Grandmother*: Aura Vainio. *Photographer*: Gerald Teijelo. *Doorman*: Rico Froehlich. *Headwaiter*: Carl Nicholas. *Waiters*: Hal Norman, Ted Lambrinos. *Magda*: ELIZABETH ALLEN.
Singers: Ken Ayers, Russell Goodwin, Tony LaRusso, Ted Lambrinos, Carl Nicholas, Hal Norman, Michael Quinn, Loyce Baker, Joan Bishop, June Card, Luce Ennis, Jeanne Grant, Carole O'Hara, Nancy Radcliffe, Joanne Spiller. *Dancers*: Kip Andrews, Karoly Barta, Sterling Clark, Thatcher Clarke, Ray Kirchner Louis Kosman, Michel Stuart, Gerald Teijelo, Patrick King, Bonnie Brandon, Carolyn Clark, Marion Fels, Carol Flemming, Leslie Franzos, Bettye Jenkins, Doris Ortiz, Eleonore Treiber, Aura Vainio, Jenny Workman.

Act 1, Scene 1: Vienna, 1904. A church. *Scene 2*: Anatol's Apartment. *Scene 3*: Carlsbad. A pavilion. *Scene 4*: Terrace of the Brandel suite in Carlsbad. *Scene 5*: The casino in Carlsbad. A gala. *Scene 6*: A street in Vienna. Christmas Eve. *Scene 7*: A private room at Scaher's Restaurant. *Scene 8*: The Brandel living room.

Act 2, Scene 1: Sacher's Restaurant. Anatol's bachelor party. *Scene 2*: Anatol's Apartment. *Scene 3*: The Brandel living room. *Scene 4*: A street. Liesl's bedroom. *Scene 5*: Outside the Paprikás Cafe. *Scene 6*: The Paprikás Cafe. *Scene 7*: Anatol's Apartment.

ACT 1
Scene 1
"What a Charming Couple"[5]
Ensemble
Scene 2
"Why Go Anywhere at All?"[6]
J. Bal
Scene 3
"Bring Your Darling Daughter"
J. Munshin, Ensemble
"Now I'm Ready for a Frau"
W. Chiari, J. Munshin
Scene 4
"Magic Moment"
B. Cook
"Who Can? You Can?"
W. Chiari, B. Cook

Scene 5
"Oh Mein, Liebchen"
Ensemble
Liebchen Waltz
J. Workman, L. Franzos, T. Clarke, A. Vainio, L. Kosman, S. Clarke, Ensemble
"The Label on the Bottle"
B. Cook
Danced by L. Kosman, R. Kirchner, M. Stuart.
Scene 6
"This Kind of a Girl"
W. Chiari, B. Cook
Scene 7
"The Bloom Is Off the Rose"
J. Munshin, Male Ensemble
Scene 8
"Who Can? You Can" (reprise)
Ensemble
"Now I'm Ready for a Frau" (reprise)
W. Chiari
"Magic Moment" (reprise)
B. Cook
ACT 2[7]
Scene 1
"I'm Glad I'm Single"
Male Ensemble
Nursemaid: L. Franzos. *Anatol, the Boy*: S. Clark. *Strong Man*: L. Kosman. *Celestina*: M. Fels. *Magda*: J. Workman. *Anatol, the Man*: R. Kirchner. *Third Swan from the Left*: E. Treiber. *Helene*: A. Vainio. *Mimi*: B. Brandon.
"I'm Glad I'm Single" (reprise)
Male Ensemble
"Now I'm Ready for a Frau" (reprise)
W. Chiari, J. Munshin
Scene 2
"Something You Never Had Before"
B. Cook
Scene 3
"You Will Never Be Lonely"
L. Leonard, L. Smith, Ensemble
Scene 4
"You're Not the Type"
W. Chiari, B. Cook
Scene 6
"Come A-Wandering With Me"
E. Allen, Male Dancers
Scene 7
"I Never Had a Chance"
W. Chiari
"I Wouldn't Marry You"
B. Cook
"For the First Time"
W. Chiari

1961.28 SUBWAYS ARE FOR SLEEPING

A Musical Comedy in Two Acts, 18 Scenes. Book and lyrics by Betty Comden and Adolph Green. Suggested by the novel of the same name by Edmund G. Love. Music by Jule Styne. Directed and choreographed by Michael Kidd. Settings and lighting by Will Steven Armstrong. Costumes by Freddy Wittop. Musical direction, Milton Rosenstock. Orchestrations, Philip J. Lang. Associate choreographer, Marc Breaux. Dance music arrangements by Peter Howard. Produced by David Merrick. Opened 27 December 1961 at the St. James Theatre and closed 23 June 1962 after 205 performances.

---

[5]Dropped during the run.
[6]Dropped during the run.

[7]Added during run to Act 2, beginning Scene 7:
"Magic Moment" (reprise)
B. Cook

CAST (in order of appearance): *Sleepers*: Gene Varrone, CY YOUNG, Robert Gorman, JOHN SHARPE. *Myra Blake*: GRAYSON HALL. *Angela McKay*: CAROL LAWRENCE. *Tom Bailey*: SYDNEY CHAPLIN. *Station Guard*: Robert Howard. *J. Edward Sykes*: Joe Hill. *Bill*: Anthony Saverino. *Harry Shelby*: Eugene R. Wood. *Gus Holt*: CY YOUNG. *Charlie Smith*: ORSON BEAN. *Jack*: Gene Varrone. *A Drunk*: Jim Weiss. *Max Hillman*: Gene Varrone. *Martha Vail*: PHYLLIS NEWMAN. *Mr. Pitman*: GORDON CONNELL. *Delivery Boy*: Michael Bennett. *Lancelot Zuckerman*: Horase. *Freddie*: Robert Gorman. *Mac, a Caretaker*: JOHN SHARPE. *Social Worker*: Joe Hill. *Photographer*: JOHN SHARPE. *Models*: Sari Clymas, Diane Ball. *Teenagers*: JOHN SHARPE, Michael Bennett. *Zack Flint*: Lawrence Pool. *Lieut. Pilsudski*: Robert Howard. *Mary Tompkins*: Dean Taliaferro. *Joe, the Museum Guard*: Anthony Saverino. *Relief Doorman*: Robert Howard. *Mr. Barney*: Joe Hill.

Singers: Helen Baisley, Vicki Belmonte, Robert Gorman, Stokely Gray, Joe Hill, Robert Howard, Jeannine Michael, Bruce Payton, Anthony Saverino, Joan Sheller, Ruth Shepard. *Dancers*: Diane Ball, Carlos Bas, Michael Bennett, Pepe de Chazza, Sari Clymas, Joel Craig, Robert Evans, Ted Forlow, Valerie Harper, Reby Howells, Gene Kelton, Victoria Mansfield, Wendy Nickerson, Larry Roquemore, Sandra Roveta, Ron Stratton, Dean Taliaferro, Jim Weiss.

Act 1, Scene 1: A Street in New York at the present time. *Scene 2*: Executive Office of Madame Magazine. *Scene 3*: Grand Central Station. *Scene 4*: A Subway Platform. *Scene 5*: A Corridor in the Brunswick Arms. *Scene 6*: Martha's Room. *Scene 7*: A Street. *Scene 8*: The Egyptian Wing of the Metropolitan Museum. *Scene 9*: A Telephone Booth. *Scene 10*: A Street near Madison Square Park. *Scene 11*: Times Square. *Scene 12*: Rockefeller Plaza.

Act 2, Scene 1: The Subway. *Scene 2*: A Street. *Scene 3*: Martha's Room. *Scene 4*: The French Wing of the Metropolitan Museum. *Scene 5*: A Street. *Scene 6*: A Parking Lot.

ACT 1
Scene 1
"Subways Are For Sleeping"
G. Varrone, C. Young, B. Gorman, J. Sharpe
Scene 2
"Girls Like Me"
C. Lawrence
Scene 3
"Station Rush"
People Who Are Going Places (Ensemble)
"I'm Just Taking My Time"
S. Chaplin
Scene 4
"Subways Directions"
S. Chaplin, C. Lawrence, Subway Riders
"Ride Through the Night"
S. Chaplin, C. Lawrence, Subway Riders
Scene 6
"I Was a Shoo-In"
P. Newman
Scene 7
"Who Knows What Might Have Been"
C. Lawrence, S. Chaplin
Scene 8
"Swing Your Projects"
S. Chaplin
Scene 9
"Strange Duet"
P. Newman, O. Bean
Scene 10
"I Said It and I'm Glad"[8]
C. Lawrence
Scene 11
"Be a Santa"
S. Chaplin, C. Lawrence, Santas, Shoppers

ACT 2
Scene 1
"Subway Incident"
C. Lawrence, Teenagers

Scene 2
"How Can You Describe a Face?"[9]
S. Chaplin
Scene 3
"I Just Can't Wait"
O. Bean
Scene 4
"Comes Once in a Lifetime"
C. Lawrence, S. Chaplin
Scene 6
"What Is This Feeling in the Air?"
S. Chaplin, C. Lawrence, O. Bean, Entire Company

A FAMILY AFFAIR

1962.01

A Musical Comedy in Two Acts. Book and lyrics by James Goldman and William Goldman. Music by John Kander. Directed by Harold Prince. Choreography by John Butler. Musical numbers staged by Bob Herget. Settings and lighting by David Hays. Costumes by Robert Fletcher. Musical and vocal direction, Stanley Lebowsky. Orchestrations by Robert Ginzler. Dance music arranged by Gerald Alters. Produced by Andrew Siff. Opened 27 January 1962 at the Billy Rose Theatre and closed 25 March 1962 after 65 performances.

CAST (in order of appearance): *Sally Nathan*: RITA GARDNER. *Gerry Siegal*: LARRY KERT. *Alfie Nathan*: SHELLEY BERMAN. *Morris Siegal*: MORRIS CARNOVSKY. *Tilly Siegal*: EILEEN HECKART. *Mrs. Forsythe*: PAULA TRUEMAN. *Mother Lederer*: LULU BATES. *Babs Sanditz*: Beryl Towbin. *Selma Siegal*: Barbara Ann Walters. *Cindy*: Joan Lowe. *Jenny Stone*: CATHRYN DAMON. *Irma*: Kelli Scott. *Wilma*: Linda Lavin. *Betty Jane*: Carolsue Shaer. *Marie Rose*: Judi West. *Crying Daughter*: Linda Lavin. *Mother*: Alice Nunn. *Christopher Davis*: Randy Garfield. *Mr. Weaver*: JACK DeLON. *Wolfgang Demott*: Sam Greene. *Kenwood Sanditz*: Bill McDonald. *Morton Lederer*: Ferdinand Hilt. *Bernice Lederer*: Lynne Charnay. *Milton Lederer*: Bill Linton. *Helen Lederer*: Yettanda Enelow. *Simon Lederer*: Don Crabtree. *Emil Lederer*: Ed Becker. *Big Sadie Lederer*: Jean Bruno. *Little Sadie Lederer*: Maggie Task. *Sports Announcer*: Sam Greene. *Miss Lumpe*: BIBI OSTERWALD. *Harry Latz*: Gino Conforti. *Fifi of Paris*: Linda Lavin. *Brash Girl*: Charlene Carter. *Quiet Girl*: Linda Lavin. *Stop and Shop Answering Service*: Alice Nunn.

Singers: Ed Becker, Theodora Brandon, Jean Bruno, Yettanda Enelow, Sam, Greene, Linda Lavin, Gary Leatherman, Ripple Lewis, Alice Nunn, Kelli Scott, Maggie Task, Barbara Ann Walters. *Dancers*: Tom Abbott, Robert Bishop, Charlene Carter, Jeremy Ives, Bob LaCrosse, Carolsue Shaer, Judi West.

The action takes place in Chicago and its suburbs at the present time.

ACT 1
"Anything For You"
L. Kert, R. Gardner
"Beautiful"
S. Berman
"Beautiful" (reprise)
E. Heckart
"My Son, the Lawyer"
E. Heckart, L. Bates, B. Towbin, Ladies
"Every Girl Wants to Get Married"
R. Gardner, B. Towbin
"Right Girls"
(*Staged by* John Butler.)
S. Berman, J. DeLon, Gentlemen of the Gym
"Kalua Bay"
(*Staged by* John Butler.)
E. Heckart, M. Carnovsky
"There's a Room in My House"
L. Kert, R. Gardner
"Siegal Marching Song" (Football Game)
B. Towbin, R. Garfield, B. McDonald
"Nathan Marching Song" (Football Game)
S. Berman, Ensemble
"Harmony"
B. Osterwald, J. DeLon, G. Conforti, L. Lavin

---

[8]Dropped during run.

[9]Dropped during run.

ACT 2

"Now, Morris"
  M. Carnovsky
"Wonderful Party"
  L. Kert, B. McDonald
"Revenge"
  (*Staged by* John Butler.)
  S. Berman, (A. Nunn), Voices
"Summer Is Over"
  E. Heckart
"Harmony" (reprise)
  S. Berman, E. Heckart, B. Osterwald, Ensemble
"I'm Worse Than Anybody"
  E. Heckart, M. Carnovsky, S. Berman
"What I Say Goes"
  L. Kert
"The Wedding"
  Entire Company

(LEONARD SILLMAN'S)
1962.02   NEW FACES OF 1962

A Musical Revue in Two Acts, 34 Scenes[10]. Sketches by Ronny Graham, Paul Lynde, Jean Shepherd, Richard Maury, Joey Carter, R. G. Brown. Music and lyrics by June Carroll, Arthur Siegel, David Rogers, Mark Bucci, Jack Holmes, Ronny Graham. Choreography, James Moore. Sketches co-staged by Richard Maury. Settings and lighting by Marvin Reiss. Costumes by Thomas Becher. Orchestrations by Jay Bower, Ted Royal, Mark Bucci, Sy Oliver, David Terry. Dance arrangements by Jack Holmes. Musical director, Abba Bogin. Conceived and directed by Leonard Sillman. Produced by Carroll and Harris Masterson. Opened 1 February 1962 at the Alvin Theatre and closed 24 February 1962 after 28 performances.

CAST: Tom Arthur, Charles Barlow, R. G. Brown, Joey Carter, Jim Corbettt, Juan Carlos Copes, Michael Fesco, Travis Hudson, Helen Kardon, Patti Karr, Sylvia Lord, Erin Martin, Marian Mercer, James Moore, Maria Nieves, Sylvia, Joan Thornton, Mickey Wayland.

ACT 1

Scene 1
  "Opening"
    Entire Company
    (*Music and Lyrics by* Ronny Graham.)
      Dialogue: J. Carter. *Introduction*: J. Corbett. *Gowns from the Collection of* Luis Estevéz. *Choreography by* James Moore.
Scene 2
  Quickies
Scene 3
  The Reds Visit Mount Vernon
    (*by* Paul Lynde)
      Introduced by P. Karr. *Father*: R. G. Brown. *Mother*: M. Mercer. *George*: J. Carter.
Scene 4
  "Moral Rearmament"
    T. Hudson, J. Moore, T. Arthur
    (*Music and Lyrics by* Jack Holmes.)
Scene 5
  "Pi in the Sky"
    (*by* Jean Shepherd. *Music by* Mark Bucci.)
      Pilot: M. Fesco. *Stewardesses*: M. Nieves, M. Wayland.
      Passengers: P. Karr, J. Moore, E. Martin, C. Barlow, J. Thornton, R. C. Brown, M. Mercer, M. Fesco, H. Kardon, J. Corbett.
Scene 6
  "In the Morning"
    S. Lord
    (*Music and Lyrics by* Ronny Graham.)

Scene 7
  "Happiness"
    (*Music by* Marie Gordon. *Lyrics by* David Rogers.)
      Man: R. G. Brown. *Happiness Girls*: J. Thornton, H. Kardon, Sylvia, M. Mercer, T. Hudson, M. Wayland.
Scene 8
  "Impressions and Folk Songs"
    J. Carter
    (*Written by* Joey Carter.)
Scene 9
  "Togetherness"[11]
    (*Music and Lyrics by* Mavor Moore.)
      Cardinal: R. G. Brown. *Bishop*: C. Barlow. *Patriarch*: M. Fesco. *Moderator*: J. Moore.
Scene 10
  "Moment of Truth"
    P. Karr
    (*Music and Lyrics by* Jack Holmes. Suggested by Ronny Graham.)
Scene 11
  "I Want You To Be the First To Know"
    M. Wayland, .C. Barlow, M. Fesco
    (*Music by* Arthur Siegel. *Lyrics by* June Carroll.)
      First Couple: J. Moore, E. Martin. *Second Couple*: J. C. Copes, M. Nieves. *Third Couple*: J. Corbett, P. Karr. *Young Man*: T. Arthur.
Scene 12
  Lemon Coke[12]
    (*by* R. G. Brown)
      Boy: R. G. Brown. *Girl*: M. Mercer.
Scene 13
  "ABCs"
    (*Music by* Mark Bucci. *Lyrics by* David Rogers.)
      Girl: H. Kardon. *Children*: E. Martin, M. Nieves, J. Corbett, J. C. Copes, J. Moore.
Scene 14
  "It Depends on How You Look at Things"
    (*Music by* Arthur Siegel. *Lyrics by* June Carroll.)
      Husband: R. G. Brown. *Wife*: T. Hudson. *Things*: H. Kardon, J. Thornton, M. Wayland, E. Martin, P. Karr, M. Nieves, Sylvia.
Scene 15
  It Takes a Heap
    (*by* Tony Geiss and Paul Lynde)
      Introduced by P. Karr. *Foreman*: J. Carter. And M. Fesco, H. Kardon, J. Corbett, M. Wayland, M. Nieves, E. Martin.
Scene 16
  "Freedomland"
    M. Mercer
    (*Music and Lyrics by* Jack Holmes.)
Scene 17
  "Over the River and Into the Woods"
    S. Lord
    (*Music and Lyrics by* Jack Holmes. Gown from the collection of Luis Estevéz.)
Scene 18
  Nose Cone
    (*by* R. G. Brown)
      Reporter: M. Fesco. *Mr. and Mrs. Thurman*: R. G. Brown, M. Mercer.
Scene 19
  "Johnny Mishuga"
    (*Sketch by* David Rogers. *Music by* Mark Bucci. *Lyrics by* David Rogers and Mark Bucci.)
      Introduced by T. Arthur. *Momma*: T. Hudson. *Hymie*: J. Carter. *Waiter*: J. Corbett. *Gringo*: C. Barlow. *Johnny*: R. G. Brown. *Yasmin*: M. Mercer. *Deputy*: J. Moore. *Customers*: E. Martin, P. Karr, Sylvia, M. Nieves, H. Kardon, M. Fesco.

ACT 2
Scene 1
  Entr'acte
    (*Choreography by* James Moore.)
    Introduced by J. Thornton, Sylvia

---

[10]The Sixth in the series of revues conceived by Leonard Sillman as a showcase for new talent. The first was produced in 1934.

[11]Dropped during run.
[12]Dropped during run.

Dancers: J. Corbett, J. C. Copes, M. Fesco, P. Karr, E. Martin, J. Moore, M. Nieves. *Choreography of Argentinian Section by* Juan Carlos Copes. *Danced by* M. Nieves.

Scene 2

Quickies

Scene 3

The Scarsdale Sentence
(*by* David Rogers)
Introduced by P. Karr. *Bettina*: M. Mercer. *Warren*: R. G. Brown.

Scene 4

Madison Avenue Executive
(*by* Ronny Graham)
Executive: J. Moore.

Scene 5

"Collective Beauty"
(*Music by* William Roy. *Lyrics by* Michael McWhinney.)
Lady: T. Hudson. *Revlonites*: H. Kardon, M. Wayland, C. Barlow, J. Corbett, M. Nieves, P. Karr. *Customers*: E. Martin, Sylvia, J. Thornton.

Scene 6

Happy Person
(*by* Herbert Hartig)
Girl: M. Mercer. *Boy*: R. G. Brown.

Scene 7

Untouchables
(*by* Joey Carter)
E. Martin, C. Barlow

Scene 8

"The Other One"
(*Music by* Arthur Siegel. *Lyrics by* June Carroll.)
Woman: M. Mercer. *Man*: J. Corbett. *Dancers*: P. Karr, Sylvia, J. Thornton, M. Wayland, T. Arthur, C. Barlow, M. Fesco, J. C. Copes. (Gowns by Baba Originals.)

Scene 9

Our Models
J. Thornton, Sylvia

Scene 10

"The Untalented Relative"
(*Music by* Arthur Siegel. *Lyrics by* Joey Carter and Richard Maury.)
Introduced by P. Karr. *Folk Singer*: J. Carter. *Folk*: P. Karr, J. C. Copes, M. Mercer, M. Wayland, J. Moore, M. Fesco, C. Barlow, H. Kardon, E. Martin, J. Corbett.

Scene 11

It's All in a Day's Work
(*by* Joey Carter)
Girl: J. Thornton.

Scene 12

"Love Is Good for You"
S. Lord
(*Music by* Arthur Siegel. *Lyrics by* June Carroll.)

Scene 13

Where Are Our Parents
(*by* Ronny Graham, Arnie Sultan and Marvin Worth)
Father: J. Carter. *Mother*: M. Mercer. *Roger*: R. G. Brown. *Mary*: M. Wayland. *Cop*: J. Corbett.

Scene 14

"Wall Street Reel"
Entire Company
(*Music by* Arthur Siegel. *Lyrics by* Jim Fuerst. *Introduction written by* Richard Maury.) *Introduced by* P. Karr.

Scene 15

Finale
(Entire Company)

1962.03

NO STRINGS

A Musical in Two Acts. Book by Samuel Taylor. Music and lyrics by Richard Rodgers. Directed and choreograhped by Joe Layton. Settings and lighting by David Hays. Costumes by Fred Voelpel and Donald Brooks. Musical direction and dance arrangements, Peter Matz. Orchestrations by Ralph Burns. Associate choreographer, Buddy Schwab. Production supervisor, Jerome Whyte. Assistant conductor, Milton Greene. Produced by Richard Rodgers in association with Samuel Taylor. Opened 15 March 1962 at the 54th Street Theatre, moved 1 October 1962 to the Broadhurst Theatre and closed 3 August 1963 after 580 performances.

CAST (in order of appearance): *Barbara Woodruff*: DIAHANN CARROLL. *David Jordan*: RICHARD KILEY. *Jeanette Valmy*: NOELLE ADAM. *Luc Delbert*: ALVIN EPSTEIN. *Mollie Plummer*: POLLY ROWLES. *Mike Robinson*: DON CHASTAIN. *Louis dePourtal*: MITCHELL GREGG. *Comfort O'Connell*: BERNICE MASSI. *Gabrielle Bertin*: Ann Hodges. *Marcello Agnolotti*: Paul Cambeilh.

Dancers: Alan Johnson, Susanne Cansino, Julie Drake, Jean Eliot, Ginny Gan, Ellen Graff, Kay Hudson, Ann Hodges, Diana Hrubetz, Sandy Leeds, Anna Marie Moylan, Patti Pappathatos, Janet Paxton, Dellas Rennie, Bea Salten, Carol Sherman, Mary Zahn, Gene Gebauer, Scott Hunter, Larry Merritt, Michael Maurer, David Neuman, Wakefield Poole, Calvin von Reinhold. *Instrumental Characters*: *Flute*: Walter Wegner. *Clarinet*: Aaron Sachs. *Oboe*: Ernest Mauro. *Trumpet*: James Sedler. *Trombone*: James Dahl. *Drums*: Ronnie Bedford. *Bassoon*: Walter Dane.

The action of the play takes place in Paris, Monte Carlo, Honfleur, Deauville and St. Tropez.

ACT 1

"The Sweetest Sounds"
D. Carroll, R. Kiley

"How Sad"
R. Kiley

"Loads of Love"
D. Carroll

"The Man Who Has Everything"
M. Gregg

"Be My Host"
R. Kiley, B. Massi, D. Chastain, A. Epstein, A. Hodges, Dancers

"La La La"
N. Adam, A. Epstein

"You Don't Tell Me"
D. Carroll

"Love Makes the World Go"
P. Rowles, B. Massi, Dancers

"Nobody Told Me"
R. Kiley, D. Carroll

ACT 2

"Look No Further"
R. Kiley, D. Carroll

"Maine"
R. Kiley, D. Carroll

"An Orthodox Fool"
D. Carroll

"Eager Beaver"
B. Massi, D. Chastain, Dancers

"No Strings"
R. Kiley, D. Carroll

"Maine" (reprise)
D. Carroll, R. Kiley

"The Sweetest Sounds" (reprise)
R. Kiley, D. Carroll

1962.04

ALL AMERICAN

A Musical Comedy in Two Acts, 22 Scenes. Book by Mel Brooks. Based on the novel ("Professor Fodorski") by Robert Lewis Taylor. Music by Charles Strouse. Lyrics by Lee Adams. Entire production directed by Joshua Logan. Scenery and lighting by Jo Mielziner. Costumes by Patton Campbell. Choreography by Danny Daniels. Dance arrangements and musical direction, John Morris. Orchestrations by Robert Ginzler. Musical continuity by Trude Rittman. Produced by Edward Padula in association with L. Slade Brown. Opened 19 March 1962 at the Winter Garden and closed 26 May 1962 after 80 performances.

CAST (in order of appearance): *Airline Stewardess*: Lori Rogers. *Flight Attendant*: Robert Lone. *Head Immigration Officer*: Barney Martin. *Immigration Officer*: Michael Gentry. *Fleisser*: Mort Marshall. *Shindler*: David Thomas. *Feinschveiger*: Bernie West. *Katrinka*: Betty Oakes. *Immigrants*: Will B. Able, Jed Allan, Don Atkinson, Vicki Belmonte, Bonnie Brody, Bill Burns, Trudy Carole, John Drew, Anthony Falco, Mary Jane Ferguson, Catherine Gale, Joseph Gentry, Linda Rae Hager, Warren Hays, Jerry

Howard, Bill Landrum, George Lindsey, Selma Malinou, Joe McWherter, Norman Riggins, Bill Starr, Sharon Vaughn. *Professor Fodorski*: RAY BOLGER. *Taxis*: Michael Gentry, Barney Martin, Fred Randall, Norman Riggins, Will B. Able. *Policeman*: Jed Allan. *Gorilla*: Bob Bakanic. *Bride*: Bonnie Brody. *Mannikin*: Mary Jane Ferguson. *Peddler*: Will B. Able. *Chewing Gum Girl*: Bonnie Brody. *Drunk*: Mort Marshall. *Con Ed Worker*: Joseph Gentry. *Cowboys*: Bill Burns, Robert Lone. *Park Avenue Couple*: Betty Oakes, David Thomas. *Sightseeing Tour Guide*: Bernie West. *Second Sightseeing Tour Guide*: George Lindsey. *Elizabeth Hawkes-Bullock*: EILEEN HERLIE. *Susan*: ANITA GILLETTE. *Edwin Bricker*: RON HUSMANN. *Dr. Snopes*: Bernie West. *Coach Hylkington Stockworth (Hulk)*: Mort Marshall. *Assistant Coach*: Barney Martin. *Moose*: George Lindsey. *Football Players*: Jed Allan, Bill Burns, John Drew, Joseph Gentry, Michael Gentry, Jerry Howard, Bill Landrum, Joseph McWherter, Fred Randall, Bill Starr. *President Piedmont*: Will B. Able. *Professor Dawson*: David Thomas. *Professor White*: Warren Hays. *First Boy*: Robert Lone. *First Girl*: Trudy Carole. *Second Girl*: Karen Sargent. *Second Boy*: Ed Kresley. *House Mother*: Betty Oakes. *Baton Twirler*: Karen Sargent. *Red Stern*: Barney Martin. *Henderson*: FRITZ WEAVER. *Whistler's Mother*: Betty Oakes. *Craven*: Jed Allan. *Phillips*: Anthony Falco. *Wyler*: Bill Burns. *Homecoming Queen*: Sharon Vaughn. *Secretary*: Betty Oakes. *Farquar*: Bill Starr. *Fountainhead*: Bob Bakanic.

Singers: Vicki Belmonte, Bonnie Brody, Catherine Gale, Selma Malinou, Lori Rogers, Sharon Vaughn, Jed Allan, Bill Burns, John Drew, Anthony Falco, Warren Hays, Norman Riggins. *Dancers*: Trudy Carole, Cathy Conklin, Mary Jane Ferguson, Linda Rae Hager, Charlene Mehl, Karen Sargent, Don Atkinson, Bob Bakanic, Ed Kresley, Bill Landrum, Robert Lone, Kip Watson. *Swing Boy*: Frank Virgulto.

Act 1, Scene 1: Idlewild Airport, (New York). Today. *Scene 2*: New York and Panorama of America. *Scene 3*: Dean's Office, S.B.I.T. (Southern Baptist Institute of Technology) *Scene 4*: Football Field. *Scene 5*: Classroom, S.B.I.T. *Scene 6*: On the Campus. *Scene 7*: Classroom, S.B.I.T. *Scene 8*: Front Porch of Elizabeth's House. *Scene 9*: Front Porch of Girls' Dormitory. *Scene 10*: Susan's Room in Girls' Dormitory. *Scene 11*: On the Window of Susan's Room. *Scene 12*: Locker Room. *Scene 13*: Football Field and Stadium.

Act 2, Scene 1: Office of Exploiters Unlimited. *Scene 2*: Exterior and Interior of Union Building, S.B.I.T. *Scene 3*: Fodorski's Seduction. *Scene 4*: On the Campus. *Scene 5*: Office of Fodorski Foundation. *Scene 6*: Bricker's Room in Boys' Dormitory. *Scene 7*: On the Campus. *Scene 8*: The Cotton Bowl. *Scene 9*: Classroom, S.B.I.T.

ACT 1[13]

Scene 1

"Melt Us"
  R. Bolger, Immigrants

Scene 2

"What a Country!"
  R. Bolger, Company

Scene 3

"Our Children"
  R. Bolger, E. Herlie
"Animal Attraction"
  A. Gillette, R. Husmann
"Our Children" (reprise)
  R. Bolger, E. Herlie

Scene 5

"We Speak the Same Language"
  R. Bolger, R. Husmann

Scene 6

"I Can Teach Them!"
  R. Bolger, E. Herlie, R. Husmann, D. Thomas

Scene 7

"It's Fun to Think"
  R. Bolger, Professors, Students

Scene 8

"Once Upon a Time"
  R. Bolger, E. Herlie

Scene 10

"Nightlife"
  A. Gillette, Girls

Scene 11

"I've Just Seen Her"
  R. Husmann

"Once Upon a Time"[14] (reprise)
  A. Gillette

Scene 12

"Physical Fitness"
  The Football Team
"The Fight Song"
  R. Bolger, the Football Team

Scene 13

"What A Country!" (reprise)
  R. Bolger, Company

ACT 2

Scene 2

"I Couldn't Have Done It Alone"
  R. Husmann, A. Gillette
"If I Were You"
  R. Bolger, E. Herlie

Scene 3

"Have a Dream"
  R. Bolger, F. Weaver, Company

Scene 4

"I've Just Seen Him" (reprise)
  A. Gillette

Scene 5

"I'm Fascinating"
  R. Bolger
"Once Upon a Time" (reprise)
  E. Herlie

Scene 6

"The Real Me"
  E. Herlie

Scene 7

"It's Up to Me"
  R. Bolger

Scene 8

"The Fight Song" (reprise)
  R. Bolger, Company

Scene 9

"It's Fun to Think" (reprise)
  Company

I CAN GET IT FOR YOU WHOLESALE

1962.05

A Musical Play in Two Acts, a Prologue and 17 Scenes. Book by Jerome Weidman based on his novel of the same name. Music and lyrics by Harold Rome. Musical staging by Herbert Ross. Settings and lighting by Will Steven Armstrong. Costumes by Theoni V. Aldredge. Musical direction and vocal arrangements by Lehman Engel. Orchestrations by Sid Ramin. Dance and incidental music arranged by Peter Howard. Directed by Arthur Laurents. Produced by David Merrick. Opened 22 March 1962 at the Sam S. Shubert Theatre and closed 8 December 1962 after 300 performances.

CAST (in order of appearance): *Miss Marmelstein*: BARBRA STREISAND. *Maurice Pulvermacher*: JACK KRUSCHEN. *Meyer Bushkin*: KEN LeROY. *Harry Bogen*: ELLIOTT GOULD. *Tootsie Maltz*: James Hickman. *Ruthie Rivkin*: MARILYN COOPER. *Mrs. Bogen*: LILLIAN ROTH. *Martha Mills*: SHEREE NORTH. *Mario*: William Reilly. *Mitzi*: Barbara Monte. *Eddie*: Edward Verso. *Blanche Bushkin*: BAMBI LINN. *Teddy Asch*: HAROLD LANG. *Buggo*: Kelly Brown. *Miss Springer*: Pat Turner. *Velma*: Francine Bond. *Lenny*: William Sumner. *Norman*: Stanley Simmonds. *Manette*: Luba Lisa. *Gail*: Wilma Curley. *Rosaline*: Marion Fels. *Noodle*: Jack Murray. *Sam*: Don Grilley. *Moxie*: Ed Collins. *Sheldon Bushkin*: Steve Curry. *Edith*: Margaret Gathright.

Prologue: Seventh Avenue, New York City, 1937.

---

[13]During run, the following song was added:
  "Back to School Again" (Act 1, beginning Scene 5)
  Students

---

[14]Dropped during run.
[15]Apex Modes changed early in the run to Acme Modes.

Act 1, Scene 1: Office of Maurice Pulvermacher, Inc. *Scene 2*: Seventh Avenue. *Scene 3*: A Bronx Stoop. *Scene 4*: Mrs. Bogen's Kitchen in the Bronx. *Scene 5*: Club Rio Rhumba. *Scene 6*: Mrs. Bogen's Kitchen. *Scene 7*: A Bronx Stoop. *Scene 8*: Apex¹⁵ Modes, Inc. *Scene 9*: Apex Modes Showroom.

Act 2, Scene 1: Harry Bogen's Penthouse. *Scene 2*: Apex Modes Inc. *Scene 3*: Apex Modes Inc. *Scene 4*: The Club Rio Rhumba. *Scene 5*: Apex Modes Showroom. *Scene 6*: Mrs. Bogen's Kitchen. *Scene 7*: Office of Maurice Pulvermacher, Inc. *Scene 8*: Seventh Avenue.

ACT 1
Scene 1
"(He's Not a) Well Man"
B. Streisand, J. Kruschen
Scene 2
"The Way Things Are"
E. Gould
Scene 3
"When Gemini Meets Capricorn"
M. Cooper, E. Gould
Scene 4
"Momma, Momma"
E. Gould, L. Roth
Scene 5
"The Sound of Money"
E. Gould, S. North, B. Monte, W. Reilly, E. Verso
Scene 6
"(The) Family Way"
L. Roth, E. Gould, M. Cooper, H. Lang, B. Linn, K. LeRoy
"Too Soon"
L. Roth
Scene 7
"Who Knows?"
M. Cooper
Scene 8
"Have I Told You Lately?"
B. Linn, K. LeRoy
Scene 9
"Ballad of the Garment Trade"
B. Streisand, M. Cooper, B. Linn, E. Gould, H. Lang, K. LeRoy, Company

ACT 2
Scene 1
"A Gift Today"
S. Curry, E. Gould, L. Roth, B. Linn, K. LeRoy, M. Cooper
Dance
B. Linn, K. LeRoy, S. Curry
Scene 2
"Miss Marmelstein"
B. Streisand
"The Sound of Money" (reprise)
E. Gould
Scene 3
"A Funny Thing Happened" (On My Way to Love)
M. Cooper, E. Gould
Scene 4
"What's In It for Me?"
H. Lang, S. North
Scene 5
"What Are They Doing to Us Now?"
B. Streisand, K. Brown, J. Hickman, L. Lisa, W. Curley, P. Turenr, Creditors
Scene 6
"Eat a Little Something"
L. Roth, E. Gould
Scene 7
Epilogue
The Company

THE CONSUL

1962.06

A Revival of the Opera (Musical Drama) in Three Acts, 6 Scenes¹⁶. Libretto and music by Gian-Carlo Menotti. Conductor, Werner Torkanowsky. Settings and costumes by Horace Armistead. Staged by Roger Englander Produced by the New York City Opera. Opened 28 March 1962 at the New York City Center and closed 8 April 1962 after 4 performances in repertory.

CAST: (in order of appearance): *John Sorel*: RICHARD FREDERICKS. *Magda Sorel*: PATRICIA NEWAY. *The Mother*: EVELYN SACHS. *Secret Police Agent*: WILLIAM CHAPMAN. *First Plainclothesman*: Glenn Dowlen. *Second Plainclothesman*: Norman Grogan. *The Secretary*: MARIJA KOVA. *Mr. Kofner*: GEORGE GAYNES. *The Foreign Woman*: MARIA MARLO. *Anna Gomez*: Mary LeSawyer. *Vera Boronel*: Teresa Racz *Nika Magadoff* (The Magician): NORMAN KELLEY. *Assan*: Fredric Milstein. *Voice on the Record*: Mabel Mercer.

PORGY AND BESS

1962.07

A Revival of the Folk Opera in Two Acts, 3 Scenes¹⁷. Book by DuBose Heyward adapted from the play "Porgy" by DuBose and Dorothy Heyward. Music by George Gershwin. Lyrics by DuBose Heyward and Ira Gershwin. Directed by William Ball. Scenic design by Stephen O. Saxe. Costume design by Stanley Simmons. Conducted by Julius Rudel. Produced by the New York City Opera. Opened 31 March 1962 at the New York City Center and closed 7 April 1962 after 6 performances in repertory.

CAST (in order of appearance): *Clara*: GWENDOLYN WALTERS. *Mingo*: Harold Pierson. *Sportin' Life*: RAWN SPEARMAN. *Jake*: IRVING BARNES. *Serena*: BARBARA WEBB. *Robbins*: Ned Wright. *Jim*: Scott Gibson. *Peter, the Honey Man*: Jerry Crawford. *Lily, the Strawberry Woman*: Edna Ricks. *Maria*: CAROL BRICE. *Porgy*: LAWRENCE WINTERS. *Crown*: JAMES RANDOLPH. *Bess*: LEESA FOSTER. *Policemen*: Glenn Dowlen, James Fels. Walter Riemer. *Undertaker*: Wanza King. *Annie*: Alyce Webb. *Frazier*: Eugene Brice. *Strawberry Girl*: Doreese Duquan. *Detective*: Richard Fredericks. *Nelson*: Arthur Williams. *Crab Man*: Clyde Turner. *Coroner*: Richard Krause. *Police Sergeant*: Norman Grogan. *Residents of Catfish Row*: New York City Opera Chorus.

IOLANTHE,
1962.08 or The Peer and the Peri

A Revival of the Comic Opera in Two Acts¹⁸. Libretto by William S. Gilbert. Music by Arthur Sullivan. Staged by Dorothy Raedler. Scenery and costumes by Gordon Micunis. Choreography, Helen Andreau. Conductor, Julius Rudel. Chorus master, William Jonson. Produced by the New York City Center Gilbert and Sullivan Company. Opened 11 April 1962 at the New York City Center and closed 22 April 1962 after 3 performances in repertory.

CAST: *The Lord Chancellor*: NORMAN KELLY. *Lord Mountararat*: ROBERT TREHY. *Lord Tolloller*: RICHARD KRAUSE. *Private Willis* of the Grenadier Guards: GEORGE GAYNES, SPIRO MALAS. *Strephon*, an Arcadian Shepherd: RICHARD FREDRICKS. *Queen of the Fairies*: CLARAMAE TURNER. *Iolanthe*, a Fairy, Strephon's Mother: MARLENA KLEINMAN. *Celia, Leila, Fleta*, Fairies: Shirley Chester, Teresa Racz, Betty Jane Schwering. *The Bee*: Helene Andreu. *The Dragonfly*: Beverly Evans. *The Butterfly*: Helen Guile. *Phyllis*, an Arcadian Shepherdess and Ward in Chancery: DORIS YARICK.
Chorus of Dukes, Marquises, Earls, Viscounts, Barons and Fairies: Helene Andreu, Jon Berberian, Joyce Castle, Micahel Cavallaro, Jerry Crawford, Harris Davis, Glenn Dowlen, Beverly Evans, James Fels, Norman Grogan, Helen Guile, Betsy Hepburn,

¹⁶Originally produced in New York 15 March 1950 at the Ethel Barrymore Theatre for 269 performances. For Synopsis of Scenes and Musical Numbers, see original 1950 production.
¹⁷First produced in New York 10 October 1935 at the Alvin Theatre for 124 performances. Originally produced in Three Acts, 9 Scenes. This production dispensed with the scene breaks and second intermission. For Synopsis of Scenes and Musical Numbers, see original 1935 production.
¹⁸First presented in New York 25 November 1882 at the Standard Theatre for 105 performances. For Synopsis of Scenes and Musical Numbers, see original 1882 production.

Edson Hoel, Leonore Lanzillotti, George McWhorter, Joyce Miko, Kellis Miller, Donald Morgan, Hanna Owen, Mariano Parra, Lorraine Phillips, Charlotte Povia, Lourette Raymon, Betty jane Schwering, John Smith, Maggie Worth.

H.M.S. PINAFORE,
1962.09 or The Lass That Loved a Sailor

A Revival of the Comic Opera in Two Acts[19]. Libretto by William S. Gilbert. Music by Arthur Sullivan. Staged by Allen Fletcher. Scenery and costumes by Patton Campbell. Conductor, Felix Popper. Chorus master, William Jonson. Produced by the New York City Center Gilbert and Sullivan Company. Opened 12 April 1962 at the New York City Center and closed 21 April 1962 after 4 performances in repertory.

CAST: *The Rt. Hon. Sir Joseph Porter, K.C.B.,* First Lord of the Admiralty: RAYMOND ALLEN. *Captain Corcoran,* Commander of the *H.M.S. Pinafore:* WILLIAM CHAPMAN. *Ralph Rackstraw,* Able Seaman: CARL OLSEN. *Dick Deadeye,* Able Seaman: ROBERT TREHY. *Bill Bobstay,* Boatswain: David Smith. *Bob Becket:* Spiro Malas. *Josephine,* the Captain's Daughter: DORIS YARICK. *Hebe,* Sir Joseph's First Cousin: Marlena Kleinman. *Little Buttercup,* Mrs. Cripps, a Portsmouth bum-boat woman: GLADYS KRIESE. *First Lord's Sisters, His Cousins, His Aunts, Sailors, Marines, etc.:* same as IOLANTHE above.

THE MIKADO,
1962.10 or The Town of Titipu

A Revival of the Comic Opera in Two Acts[20]. Libretto by William S. Gilbert. Music by Arthur Sullivan. Staged by Dorothy Raedler. Scenery and lighting by Donald Oenslager. Costumes by Patton Campbell. Conductors, Dean Ryan, Charles Wilson. Chorus master, William Jonson. Produced by the New York City Center Gilbert and Sullivan Company. Opened 14 April 1962 at the New York City Center and closed 21 April 1962 after 5 performances in repertory.

CAST: *The Mikado of Japan:* GEORGE GAYNES, WILLIAM CHAPMAN. *Nanki-Poo:* WILLIAM DIARD. *Ko-Ko:* KEITH KALDENBERG. *Pooh-Bah:* SPIRO MALAS. *Pish-Tush:* DAVID SMITH. *Three Sisters, Wards of Ko-Ko: Yum-Yum:* JOY CLEMENTS. *Pitti-Sing:* BEVERLY EVANS. *Peep-Bo:* SHIRLEY CHESTER. *Katisha:* GLADYS KRIESE. *Chorus of School Girls, Nobles, Guards and Coolies:* same as IOLANTHE above.

THE GONDOLIERS,
1962.11 or The King of Barataria

A Revival of the Comic Opera in Two Acts[21]. Music by Arthur Sullivan. Staged by Dorothy Raedler. Scenery and costumes by Ed Wittstein. Conductors, Julius Rudel, Felix Popper. Chorus master, William Jonson. Produced by the New York City Center Gilbert and Sullivan Company. Opened 18 April 1962 at the New York City Center and closed 22 April 1962 after 3 performances in repertory.

CAST: *The Duke of Plaza-Toro:* NORMAN KELLEY. *Luiz:* WILLIAM DIARD. *Don Alhambra Del Bolero:* GEORGE GAYNES. *Marco Palmieri:* JON CRAIN. *Giuseppe Palmieri:* WILLIAM METCALF. *Antonio:* David Smith. *Francesco:* Richard Krause. *Giorgio:* Norman Grogan. *The Duchess of Plaza-Toro:* CLARAMAE TURNER. *Casilda:* EILEEN SCHAULER. *Gianetta:* JOY CLEMENTS. *Tessa:* MARLENA KLEINMAN. *Fiametta:* Shirley Chester *Vittoria:* Teresa Racz. *Giulia:* Beverly Evans. *Inez:* Gladys Kriese. *Solo Cachucha Dancers:* Helene Andreu, Mariano Parra. *Chorus of Gondoliers, Contadine, Men-at-Arms, Heralds and Pages:* same as IOLANTHE above.

---

[19]Originally presented in New York 15 January 1879 at the Standard Theatre for 175 performances. For Synopsis of Scenes and Musical Numbers, see original 1879 production.
[20]First presented in New York 20 July, 10-29 August 1885 at the Union Square and People's Theatres for 22 performances. First authorized production presented 19 August 1885 at the Fifth Avenue Theatre by Richard D'Oyly Carte for 250 performances. For Synopsis of Scenes and Musical Numbers, see 19 August 1885 D'Oyly Carte production.
[21]Originally presented in New York 7 January 1890 at Park Theatre for 103 performances. For Synopsis of Scenes and Musical Numbers, see original 1890 production.

A FUNNY THING HAPPENED
1962.12 ON THE WAY TO THE FORUM

A Musical Comedy in Two Acts. Book by Burt Shevelove and Larry Gelbart. Based on the plays ("The Haunted House," "Mostellaria," etc.) of Plautus. Music and lyrics by Stephen Sondheim. Directed by George Abbott. Choreography and musical staging by Jack Cole. Settings and costumes by Tony Walton. Lighting by Jean Rosenthal. Musical direction, Harold Hastings. Orchestrations by Irwin Kostal and Sid Ramin. Dance music arranged by Hal Schaefer. Additional dance music by Betty Walberg. Produced by Harold Prince. Opened 8 May 1962 at the Alvin Theatre, moved 9 March 1964 to the Mark Hellinger Theatre, moved 12 May 1964 to the Majestic Theatre, and closed 29 August 1964 after 964 performances.

CAST (in order of appearance): *Prologus:* ZERO MOSTEL. *The Proteans:* Eddie Phillips, George Reeder, David Evans. *Senex,* a citizen of Rome: DAVID BURNS. *Domina,* his wife: RUTH KOBART. *Hero,* his son: BRIAN DAVIES. *Hysterium,* slave to Senex and Domina: JACK GILFORD. *Lycus,* a dealer in courtesans: JOHN CARRADINE. *Pseudolus,* slave to Hero: ZERO MOSTEL. *Tintabula,* a courtesan: Roberta Keith. *Panacea,* a courtesan: Lucienne Bridou. *The Geminae,* courtesans: Lisa James, Judy Alexander. *Vibrata,* a courtesan: Myrna White. *Gymnasia,* a courtesan: Gloria Kristy. *Philia,* a virgin: PRESHY MARKER. *Erronius,* a citizen of Rome: RAYMOND WALBURN. *Miles Gloriosus,* a warrior: RONALD HOLGATE.

The time is two hundred years before the Christian era, a day in spring. The place is a street in Rome in front of houses of Erronius, Senex and Lycus.

ACT 1
"Comedy, Tonight"
  Z. Mostel, the Proteans, Company
"Love, I Hear"
  B. Davies
"Free"
  Z. Mostel, B. Davies
"The House of Marcus Lycus"
  J. Carradine, Z. Mostel, Courtesans
"Lovely"
  B. Davies, P. Marker
"Pretty Little Picture"
  Z. Mostel, B. Davies, P. Marker
"Everybody Ought To Have a Maid"
  D. Burns, Z. Mostel, J. Gilford, J. Carradine
"I'm Calm"
  J. Gilford
"Impossible"
  D. Burns, B. Davies
"Bring Me My Bride"
  R. Holgate, Z. Mostel, Courtesans, Proteans
ACT 2
"That Dirty Old Man"
  R. Kobart
"That'll Show Him"
  P. Marker
"Lovely" (reprise)
  Z. Mostel, J. Gilford
Funeral Sequence and Dance (Dirge)
  Z. Mostel, R. Holgate, Courtesans, Proteans
"Comedy Tonight" (reprise)
  The Company

CAN-CAN
1962.13

A Revival of the Musical Comedy in Two Acts, 17 Scenes[22]. Book by Abe Burrows. Music and lyrics by Cole Porter. Directed by Gus Schirmer. Lighting and scenic adaptation of Jo Mielziner's original designs by Helen Pond. Costumes by Stanley Simmons. Choreography by Ellen Ray. Musical

---

[22]Originally produced in New York 7 May 1953 at the Sam S. Shubert Theatre for 892 performances. For Synopsis of Scenes and Musical Numbers, see original 1953 production. "Every Man Is a Stupid Man" was dropped for this production.

direction by James Leon. (Orchestrations by Philip J. Lang. Dance music arranged by Genevieve Pitot.) Produced by the New York City Center Light Opera Company (Jean Dalrymple, Director). Opened 16 May 1962 at the New York City Center and closed 27 May 1962 after 16 performances.

CAST (in order of appearance): *Bailiff:* Phil Roth. *Registrar:* Peter Saul. *Policemen:* George Del Monte, Darrell Sandeen. *Judge Paul Barriere:* Warner Schreiner. *Court President,* Henri Marceaux: Charles Reynolds. *Judge Aristede Forestier:* GEORGE GAYNES. *Claudine:* MARA LYNN. *Gabrielle:* Maggie Worth. *Marie:* Lillian D'Honau. *Celestine:* Marilyn D'Honau. *Hilaire Jussac:* FERDINAND HILT. *Boris Adzinidzinadze:* GABRIEL DELL. *Hercule:* IGGIE WOLFINGTON. *Theophile:* BOB DISHY. *Etienne:* JACK FLETCHER. *Waiter:* Michael Cavallaro. *La Mome Pistache:* GENEVIEVE. *Second Waiter:* Darrell Sandeen. *Cafe Waiter:* Phil Roth. *Nun:* Nora Bristow. *Model:* Betty Hyatt Linton. *Mimi:* Dorothy D'Honau. *Customers:* Nora Bristow, Darell Sandeen. *Doctor:* Charles Reynolds. *Second:* Darrell Sandeen. *Rainbow:* Victor Duntiere. *Prosecutor:* Jack Davison. (*Principal Dancer:* PETER GLADKE.)

Dancers: Joseph Ahumada, Marilyn Charles, Sterling Clark, Victor Duntiere, Gloria Danyl, Dorothy D'Honau, Lillian D'Honau, Marilyn D'Honau, Don Emmons, Natasha Grishin, Janan Hart, Douglas Hinshaw, Robert Holloway, Betty Hyatt Linton, Sally Lou Lee, David Lober, Jami Landi, Mary Jane Moncrieff, Louise Quick, Peter Saul, Fabian Stuart, Alice Shanahan.

BRAVO, GIOVANNI

1962.14

A Musical Comedy in Two Acts, 22 Scenes. Book by A. J. Russell. Based on the novel ("The Crime of Giovanni Venturi") by Howard Shaw. Music by Milton Schafer. Lyrics by Ronny Graham. Scenery and lighting by Robert Randolph. Costumes by Ed Wittstein. Choreography by Carol Haney. Assistant choreograher, Buzz Miller. Musical direction, Continuity and vocal arrangements by Anton Coppola. (Musical) arrangements and orchestrations by Robert Ginzler. Dance music arranged and orchestrated by Luther Henderson. Directed by Stanley Prager. Produced by Philip Rose. Opened 19 May 1962 at the Broadhurst Theatre, closing for vacation 14 July 1962; re-opened 7 September 1962, and closed 15 September 1962 after 76 performances.

CAST (in order of appearance): *Giovanni Venturi:* CESARE SIEPI. *Signor Bellardi:* GEORGE S. IRVING. *Uriti Waiters:* RICO FROEHLICH, Joe McGrath, Ed Dumont, Barney Johnston. *Amedeo:* DAVID OPATOSHU. *Furniture Dealer:* Harry Davis. *Nino:* Al Sambogna. *Gino:* Thatcher Clarke. *Dino:* Buzz Miller. *Miranda:* MICHELE LEE. *Moscolito:* ARNOLD SOBOLOFF. *Carlo:* AL LANTI. *Signora Pandolfi:* MARIA KARNILOVA. *Musicians:* GENE VARRONE, Nino Banome, RICO FROEHLICH. *Night Club Manager:* BUZZ MILLER. *Professor Panfredoni:* HARRY DAVIS. *Troubador:* GENE VARRONE. *Celestina:* LU LEONARD. *Head Chef:* BUZZ MILLER. *Pizza Maker:* GENE VARRONE. *Salad Chef:* Gene Gavin. *Bakers:* Nino Banome, Larry Fuller. *Soup Cook:* Thatcher Clarke. *Helpers:* Alan Peterson, Alvin Beam, Al Sambogna. *Signora Elli:* Penny Gaston. *La Contessa:* Lainie Kazan. *Signor Brancusi:* John Taliaferro. *Professor Musa:* RICO FROEHLICH. *Brigadiere:* GENE VARRONE. *Policeman:* Barney Johnston.

Singing Ensemble: Jyll Alexander, Norma Donaldson, Penny Gaston, Marcia Gilford, Maria Graziano, Lainie Kazan, Betty Kent, Rita Metzger, Ed Dumont, Tom Head, Barney Johnston, Ronald Knight, Joe McGrath, Richard Park, John Taliaferro. *Dancing Ensemble:* Ann Barry, Ellen Halpin, Shellie Farrell, Michele Franchi, Herad Gruh, Baayork Lee, Barbara Richman, Nikki Sowinski, Nino Banome, Alvin Beam, Thatcher Clarke, Larry Fuller, Gene Gavin, Alan Peterson, Al Sambogna, Claude Thompson.

Act 1, Scene 1: A Piazza in Trastavere, Rome, Italy. Dawn of a spring day, at the present time. *Scene 2:* Giovanni's Restaurant. Three weeks later. *Scene 3:* The Piazza. The following afternoon. *Scene 4:* A Fountain in Rome. The following afternoon. *Scene 5:* The Tunnel. A few nights later. *Scene 6:* A Nightclub in Rome. The following morning. *Scene 7:* The Tunnel. The following night. *Scene 8:* The Etruscan Room in the Villa Guilia Museum. A few days later. *Scene 9:* The Tunnel. A few days later. *Scene 10:* Giovanni's Room. Immediately following. *Scene 11:* The Piazza. Late the following Saturday night.

Act 2, Scene 1: The Tunnel. Noon the following Monday. *Scene 2:* A Street in Rome. A month later. *Scene 3:* The Uriti Kitchen. Immediately following. *Scene 4:* The Street. Immediately following. *Scene 5:* Giovanni's Kitchen. A few days later. *Scene 6:* The Etruscan Restaurant. Six months later. *Scene 7:* Giovanni's Room. A few nightds later. *Scene 8:* The Tunnel. Lunchtime, the following day. *Scene 9:* The Etruscan Restauarnt. Immediately following. *Scene 10:* The Tunnel. Immediately following. *Scene 11:* The Piazza. Immediately following.

ACT 1
Scene 1
  "Rome"
    C. Siepi
  "Uriti"
    G. S. Irving, Full Ensemble

Scene 2
  "Breachy's Law"
    C. Siepi, D. Opatoshu
Scene 3
  "I'm All I've Got"
    M. Lee
Scene 4
  "The Argument"
    C. Siepi, G. S. Irving
Scene 6
  "Signora Pandolfi"
    D. Opatoshu, M. Karnilova, B. Miller, Musicians
  "The Kangaroo"
    M. Karnilova, B. Miller, Waiters, Musicians, Kitchen Help
Scene 8
  "If I Were the Man"
    C. Siepi
  "Steady, Steady"
    M. Lee
Scene 9
  "We Won't Discuss It"
    C. Siepi, D. Opatoshu
Scene 11
  "Ah! Camminare"
    G. Varrone, C. Siepi, Entire Company

ACT 2
Scene 1
  "Breachy's Law" (reprise)
    C. Siepi, D. Opatoshu, M. Karnilova, M. Lee
Scene 3
  "Uriti Kitchen"
    G. S. Irving, A. Soboloff, A. Lanti, B. Miller,
    G. Varrone, G. Gavin, N. Banome, L. Fuller, T. Clarke, Helpers
Scene 4
  "Virtue Arrivederci"
    G. S. Irving
Scene 6
  "Bravo, Giovanni"
    C. Siepi, G. S. Irving, Singing Ensemble
  "One Little World Apart"
    M. Lee
Scene 8
  "Connubiality"[23]
    M. Karnilova, D. Opatoshu
Scene 10
  "Miranda"
    C. Siepi

BRIGADOON

1962.15

A Revival of the Musical Play in Two Acts, a Prologue and 11 Scenes[24]. Book and lyrics by Alan Jay Lerner. Music by Frederick Loewe. Dance and musical numbers by Agnes de Mille, assisted by James Jamieson. Directed by John Fearnley. Settings by Oliver Smith. Art director, Watson Barratt. Costumes designed by Stanley Simmons. Musical director, Julius Rudel. Conductor, Don Smith. Produced by the New York City Center Light

---

[23]During run, replaced by:
  "Jump In"
  M. Karnilova, D. Opatoshu
[24]Originally produced in New York 13 March 1947 at the Ziegfeld Theatre for 581 performances. For Synopsis of Scenes and Musical Numbers, see original 1947 production.

Opera Company (Jean Dalrymple, Director). Opened 30 May 1962 at the New York City Center and closed 10 June 1962 after 16 performances[25].

CAST (in order of appearance): *Tommy Albright*: PETER PALMER. *Jeff Douglas*: FARLEY GRANGER. *Sandy Dean*: Kenny Adams. *Meg Brockie*: ANN FRASER. *Archie Beaton*: Moultrie Patten. *Harry Beaton*: EDWARD VILLELLA. *Andrew MacLaren*: Alexander Clark. *Fiona MacLaren*: SALLY ANN HOWES. *Jean MacLaren*: Jenny Workman. *Angus MacGuffie*: Walter Blocher. *Charlie Dalrymple*: HARRY SNOW. *Maggie Anderson*: Gemze de Lappe. *Sword Dancers*: Richard Rutherford, James Clouser, James McArdle, David Shields, Frank Andre. *Mr. Lundie*: John C. Becher. *Bagpiper*: Maurice Eisenstadt. *Frank*: Felice Orlandi. *Jane Ashton*: Susan Fellows.

Townsfolk of Brigadoon: Singers: Faith Daltry, Beverly G. Evans, Susan Fellows, Helen Guile, Marilyn Mason, Hanna Owen, Betty Jane Schwering, Kelli Scott, Lynn Wendell, Kenny Adams, John Aman, Ken Ayers, Donald E. Becker, Jerry Crawford, Harris W. Davis, Marvin Goodis, Robert Lenn, George T. McWhorter, John Sarkis. *Dancers*: Barbara Beck, Lynn Broadbent, Mickey Gunnerson, Michele D. Hardy, Rosalie Kurowska, Lucia Lambert, Loi Leabo, Anna-Marie, Jane Meserve, Esther Villavicencio, Frank André, Robert Bishop, James Clouser, Ben Gillespie, Art Hutchinson, Vernon Lusby, Jim McArdle, Charles B. McCraw, Richard Rutherford, David Shields.

---

[25]Vocal arrangements by Frederick Loewe. Orchestrations by Ted Royal. Lighting uncredited.

1962–1963 SEASON

Nancy Andrews (center) in LITTLE ME (Photo: Friedman-Abeles, 1962)
Museum of the City of New York, Gift of Annette Trubowitsch, 88.86.49.4

1962–1963 SEASON

1962.16 ## FIORELLO!

A Revival of the Musical in Two Acts, a Prologue and 19 Scenes[1]. Book by Jerome Weidman and George Abbott. Music by Jerry Bock. Lyrics by Sheldon Harnick. Scenery and lighting by William and Jean Eckart. Costume supervision by Joseph Codori. Musical direction, Jay Blackton. (Orchestrations by Irwin Kostal. Dance music arranged by Jack Elliott.) Entire production staged and directed by Dania Krupska. Choreography by Kevin Carlisle. Produced by the New York City Center Light Opera Company (Jean Dalrymple, Director). Opened 13 June 1962 at the New York City Center and closed 24 June 1962 after 16 performances.

CAST (in order of appearance): Announcer: Del Hortsmann. Fiorello: SORRELL BOOKE. Neil: Richard France. Morris: PAUL LIPSON. Mrs. Pomerantz: Helen Verbit. Mr. Lopez: Tony Gardell. Mr. Crawford: Joseph Crawford. Dora: DODY GOODMAN. Marie: BARBARA WILLIAMS. Ben Marino: ART LUND. Dealer (Ed Peterson): Del Horstman. Seedy Man: Terry Violino. Third Player: Michael Quinn. Fifth Player: Ned Wright. Second Player: Feodore Tedick. Fourth Player: Walter P. Brown. Kibitzer: Will Roy. First Heckler: Mike Scrittorale. Second Heckler: Bobby Barry. Third Heckler: Louis Kosman. Fourth Heckler: Ed Pfeiffer. Fifth Heckler: Paul Eden. Nina: Jeanna Belkin. Sophie: Jami Landi. Floyd: DORT CLARK. Thea: LOLA FISHER. Washington Secretary: Mary Louise. Senator: Feodore Tedick. Drunk: Louis Kosman. Butler: Norman Grogan. Judge: Bobby Barry. Politicians: Jack Rains, Ned Wright. Commissioner: John Martin. Mitzi: SHEILA SMITH. Frank Scarpini: Mike Scrittorale. Reporter: Robert Kya-Hill. Florence: Maggie Worth. Tough Man: Jack Rains. Frantic: Louis Kosman.

Singers: Rosalind Cash, Doreese Du Quan, Joanne Hill, Mary Louise Jones, Bobbi Lange, Estelle Moss, Maura Wedge, Betty Weston, Maggie Worth, Bobby Barry, Walter P. Brown, Joseph Crawford, Tony Gardell, H. Scott Gibson, Norman Grogan, (Edward) Del Horstman, Robert Kya-Hill, Michael Quinn, Jack K. Rains, Will Roy, Feodore Tedick, Ned Wright. Dancers: Chele Abel, Nancy Baron, Margery J. Beddow, Jeanna Belkin, Louise Ferrand, Lois Grandi, Carole Kroon, Jami Landi, Lynn G. Lorino, Carol Sue Shafer, Jere Admire, Jean L. Blanchard, Sterling Clark, Paul Eden, Bob Holloway, Bernard Johnson, Louis Kosman, Ed A. Pfeiffer, Paul R. Roman, Miek Scrittorale, Terry Violino.

1962.17 ## EDDIE FISHER AT THE WINTER GARDEN

A Variety Show in Two Acts, 4 Scenes. Special material by Gordon Jenkins. Directed by John Fearnley. Settings by Oliver Smith. Lighting by Peggy Clark. Orchestrations by Jerry Fielding. Conducted by Pembroke Davenport. Miss Prowse's numbers staged and choreographed by Tony Charmoli. Miss Prowse's costumes by Ray Aghayan. Associate producer, Bernie Rich. A Ramrod Production. Produced by Monte Proser and Milton Blackstone. Opened 2 October 1962 at the Winter Garden and closed 3 November 1962 after 48 performances.

CAST: EDDIE FISHER, JULIET PROWSE, DICK GREGORY, Nicholas Couacevich, Brad Craig, Norman Edwards, Lance Avant, John Frayer, Burnell Deitch.

ACT 1[2]

Scene 1

"The Broadway Zoo"

(Chorus)

(Music and Lyrics by Gordon Jenkins. Projection Designed by Glenn Holse.)

Scene 2

Dick Gregory (Comedian)

---

[1]Originally produced in New York 23 November 1959 at the Broadhurst Theatre for 795 performances. For Synopsis and Scenes and Musical Numbers, see original 1959 production. For this production, the following revisions were made:

Act 1, Scene 11 (Gangplank for Returning Soldiers from Overseas: "Home Again") became Act 2, Scene 1. Added to this production (Act 2, Scene 6) was the previously cut song:

"Where Do I Go From Here?"

B. Williams (Marie)

[2]No song list appeared in the program. The following was prepared from reviews and recordings.

Scene 3

Miss Juliet Prowse (Song and Dance):

"Bewitched" (from PAL JOEY)

(Music by Richard Rodgers. Lyrics by Lorenz Hart.)

"Smoke Gets in Your Eyes" (from ROBERTA)

(Music by Jerome Kern. Lyrics by Otto Harbach.)

Great Heroines of Literature in a Broadway Musical Style:

Joan of Arc, Cleopatra, Camille

(Music and Lyrics by Jimmy Van Heusen and Sammy Cahn.)

The Boys: N. Couacevich, L. Avant, B. Craig, J. Frayer, N. Edwards, B. Deitch.

ACT 2

Eddie Fisher (Orchestra conducted by Eddy Samuels.):

"Don't Let It Get You Down" (from HOLD ONTO YOUR HATS)

(Music by Burton Lane. Lyrics by E. Y. Harburg.)

"Back in Your Own Back Yard" (from the film SAY IT WITH SONGS)

(Music and Lyrics by Al Jolson, Billy Rose and Dave Dreyer.)

WEST SIDE STORY Medley: "Tonight", "Maria", "Something's Coming"

(Music by Leonard Bernstein. Lyrics by Stephen Sondheim.)

"You Made Me Love You" (from THE PASSING SHOW OF 1913, THE HONEYMOON EXPRESS)

(Music by James V. Monaco. Lyrics by Joseph McCarthy.)

"Never on Sunday" (from the film NEVER ON SUNDAY)

(Music by Manos Hadjidakis. English Lyrics by Billy Towne.)

"This Nearly Was Mine" (from SOUTH PACIFIC)

(Music by Richard Rodgers. Lyrics by Oscar Hammerstein II.)

"Mack the Knife" (from THE THREEPENNY OPERA)

(Music by Kurt Weill. Lyrics by Bertolt Brecht and Marc Blitzstein.)

"Hava Naguila" (Music and Lyrics adapted by Sid Danoff.)

"Moon River" (from film BREAK FAST AT TIFFANY'S)

(Music by Henry Mancini. Lyrics by Johnny Mercer.)

AL JOLSON Medley:

"Swanee" (from SINBAD)

(Music by George Gershwin. Lyrics by Irving Caesar.)

"About a Quarter to Nine" (from film GO INTO YOUR DANCE)

(Music by Harry Warren. Lyrics by Al Dubin.)

"Liza" (All the Clouds'll Roll Away) (from SHOW GIRL)

(Music by George Gershwin. Lyrics by Ira Gershwin and Gus Kahn.)

"I'm Sitting on Top of the World" (from film THE SINGING FOOL)

(Music by Ray Henderson. Lyrics by Sam M. Lewis and Joe Young.)

"Toot Toot Tootsie, Goodbye" (from BOMBO)

(Music and Lyrics by Ted Fio Rito, Robert A. King, Gus Kahn, Ernie Erdman.)

"April Showers" (from BOMBO)

(Music by Louis Silvers. Lyrics by Buddy G. DeSylva.)

"Waiting for the Robert E. Lee"

(Music by Lewis F. Muir. Lyrics by L. Wolfe Gilbert.)

"Rock-A-Bye Your Baby With a Dixie Melody" (from SINBAD)

(Music by Jean Schwartz. Lyrics by Sam M. Lewis and Joe Young)

"Sonny Boy" (from film THE SINGING FOOL)

(Music by Ray Henderson. Lyrics by Buddy G. DeSylva and Lew Brown.)

"Makin' Whoopee" (from WHOOPEE)

(Music by Walter Donaldson. Lyrics by Gus Kahn.)

Medley: "Anytime" (Music and Lyrics by Herbert Happy Lawson), "I Need You Now" (Music and Lyrics by Jimmy Crane and Al Jacobs), "Wish You Were Here" (from WISH YOU WERE HERE, Music and Lyrics by Harold Rome.), "Heart" (from DAMN YANKEES, Music and Lyrics by Richard Adler and Jerry Ross.), "Oh Mein Papa" (from the Swiss/English musical OH MY PAPA!, Music by Paul Burkhard. English Lyrics by Geoffrey Parsons and John Turner.)

"What Kind of Fool Am I?" (from STOP THE WORLD—I WANT TO GET OFF)

(Music and Lyrics by Leslie Bricusse and Anthony Newley.)

"Mein Shtetele Belz" (That Wonderful Girl of Mine)

(Music and Lyrics by Bregman, Vocco, Chester Conn and J. J. Kamen.)

"The Sweetest Sounds" (from NO STRINGS)

(Music and Lyrics by Richard Rodgers.)

STOP THE WORLD — I WANT TO GET OFF

1962.18

A New-Style Musical in Two Acts. Book, Music and lyrics by Leslie Bricusse and Anthony Newley. Setting and lighting by Sean Kenny. Musical supervision, Ian Fraser. Musical director, Milton Rosenstock. Orchestrations by Ian Fraser with David Lindup. Burt Rhodes, Gordon Langford. John Broome's choreography restaged by Virginia Mason. Directed by Anthony Newley. Produced by David Merrick in association with Bernard Delfont. Opened 3 October 1962 at the Sam S. Shubert Theatre, moved 9 September 1963 to the Ambassador Theatre, and closed 1 February 1964 after 556 performances.

CAST: *Littlechap*: ANTHONY NEWLEY. *Evie, Anya, Ilse, Ginnie*: ANNA QUAYLE. *Jane*: Jennifer Baker. *Susan*: Susan Baker. *Chorus (and All Other Roles)*: Rawley Bates, Bonnie Brody, Diana Corto, Jo Anne Leeds, Karen Lynn Reed, Sylvia Tysick, Stephanie Winters, Mark Hunter, Paul Rufo.

ACT 1

"The A.B.C. Song"
(Chorus)
"I Want To Be Rich"
(A. Newley, Chorus)
"Typically English"
(A. Quayle)
"A Special Announcement"
(Chorus)
"Lumbered"
(A. Newley)
"Welcome to Sludgepool"
(Chorus)
"Gonna Build a Mountain"
(A. Newley, Chorus)
"Glorious Russian"
(A. Quayle)
"Meilinki Meilchick"
(A. Newley, A. Quayle)
"Family Fugue"
(A. Newley, A. Quayle, J. Baker, S. Baker)
"Typische Deutsche"
(A. Quayle, Chorus)
"Nag! Nag! Nag!"
(A. Newley, A. Quayle, J. Baker, S. Baker, Chorus)

ACT 2

"All American"
(A. Quayle)
"Once in a Lifetime"
(A. Newley)
"Mumbo Jumbo"
(A. Newley)
"Welcome to Sunvale"
(Chorus)
"Someone Nice Like You"
(A. Newley, A. Quayle)
"What Kind of Fool Am I?"
(A. Newley)

THE MIKADO, or The Town of Titipu

1962.19

A Revival of the Comic Opera in Two Acts[3]. Libretto by William S. Gilbert. Music by Arthur Sullivan. Staged by Dorothy Raedler. Scenic design by Donald Oenslager. Costume design by Patton Campbell. Conducted by William Jonson. Produced by the New York City Opera. Opened 13 October 1962 (matinee) at the New York City Center and closed 4 November 1961 after 2 performances in repertory.

[3] First presented in New York 20 July, 10-29 August 1885 at the Union Square and People's Theatres for 22 performances. First authorized production presented 19 August 1885 at the Fifth Avenue Theatre by Richard D'Oyly Carte for 250 performances. For Synopsis of Scenes and Musical Numbers, see 19 August 1885 D'Oyly Carte production.

CAST: *The Mikado of Japan*: PAUL UKENA. *Nanki-Poo*, his son, disguised as a wandering minstrel in love with Yum-Yum: WILLIAM DIARD. *Ko-Ko*, Lord High Executioner of Titipu: NORMAN KELLEY. *Pooh-Bah*, Lord High Everything Else: SPIRO MALAS. *Pish-Tush*, a Noble Lord: David Smith. *Yum-Yum, Pitti-Sing, Peep-Bo*, three sisters, wards of Ko-Ko: JOY CLEMENTS, BEVERLY EVANS, MARIJA KOVA. *Katisha*: EVELYN SACHS. *Chorus of School Girls, Nobles, Guards and Coolies*: New York City Opera Chorus.

MR. PRESIDENT

1962.20

A Musical Comedy in Two Acts, 22 Scenes. Book by Howard Lindsay and Russel Crouse. Music and lyrics by Irving Berlin. Directed by Joshua Logan. Choreography by Peter Gennaro. Settings and lighting by Jo Mielziner. Costumes by Theoni V. Aldredge. Musical direction, Jay Blackton. Dance arrangements, Jack Elliott. Orchestrations, Philip J. Lang. Produced by Leland Hayward. Opened 20 October 1962 at the St. James Theatre and closed 8 June 1963 after 265 performances.

CAST (in order of appearance): *Manager*: DAVID BROOKS. *President Stephen Decatur Henderson*: ROBERT RYAN. *Nell Henderson*: NANETTE FABRAY. *Walter O'Connor*, a Secretary: Jack Rains. *David Caldwell*: Warren J. Brown. *Leslie Henderson*: ANITA GILLETTE. *Larry Henderson*: JERRY STRICKLER. *Youssein Davair*: JACK WASHBURN. *Tippy Taylor*, a Secretary: Charlotte Fairchild. *Pat Gregory*, of the Secret Service: JACK HASKELL. *Charley Wayne*, of the Secret Service: STANLEY GROVER. *Princess Kyra*: WISA D'ORSO. *Russian Soldier*: Jack Mette. *Colonel Wilson*: Van Stevens. *Mrs. Lotta Pendleton*: Marian Haraldson. *George Perkins*: Beau Tilden. *Mr. Thomas*: Carl Nicholas. *Deborah Chakronin*: Baayork Lee. *Arthur Blanchard*: Jack McMinn. *Radio Operator*: John Aman. *Ali Hassoud*: Anthony Falco. *Abou*: Carlos Bas. *Commentators*: Louis Kosman, Jack McMinn. *A Workman*: Dan Siretta. *Miss Barnes*: Lipset Nelson. *The Deacon*: Carl Nicholas. *Sergeant Stone*, of the Secret Service: Beau Tilden. *Chester Kincaid*: John Cecil Holm. *Betty Chandler*: Carol Lee Jensen. *Spieler*: Jack Rains. *Governor Harmon Bardahl*: DAVID BROOKS.

Singing Ensemble: Kellie Brytt, Marian Haraldson, Carol Lee Jensen, Mary Louise, Donna Monroe, Lispet Nelson, Ruth Shepard, Maggie Worth, John Aman, Anthony Falco, Jack McMinn, Jack Mette, Carl Nicholas, Jack Rains, Van Stevens. *Dancing Ensemble*: Lynn Bernay, Connie Burnett, Baayork Lee, Lynn Gay Lorino, Anna Marie Moylan, Barbara Newman, Lynn Ross, Mari Shelton, Arline Woods, Don Atkinson, Bob Bakanic, Carlos Bas, Sterling Clark, Laverne French, Louis Kosman, Bob LaCrosse, Lowell Purvis, Dan Siretta. *Tahitians*: Louis Kosman, Carlos Bas, Lynn Gay Lorino. *Butterflies*: Anna Marie Moylan, Barbara Newman, Mari Shelton. *Kabuki Spider*: Lowell Purvis. *Japanese Beatniks*: Lynn Ross, Bob Bakanic. *Kabuki Lion*: Anthony Falco. *South Sea Warrior*: Laverne French. *Elephant*: Carlos Bas, Louis Kosman. *Lord Krishna*: Connie Burnett. *East Indian Marching Team*: Lynn Bernay, Anna Marie Moylan, Barbara Newman, Mari Shelton, Arline Woods, Don Atkinson, Sterling Clark, Dan Siretta. *Leader*: Baayork Lee.

Act 1, Scene 1: Oval Room at the White House. Scene 2: Private Sitting Room in the White House. Scene 3: A Lawn Party in Chevy Chase. Scene 4: The President's Bedroom. Scene 5: The President's Office. Scene 6: The Trip. Scene 7: The President's Plane. Scene 8: A Street in the Middle East. Scene 9: Youssein's Apartment. Scene 10: The President's Plane. Scene 11: Airfield. Scene 12: Television Studios. Scene 13: The Private Sitting Room in the White House. Scene 14: An Office in the White House. Scene 15: The President's Office.

Act 2, Scene 1: A Street in Mansfield. Scene 2: The Living Room of the Henderson Home. Scene 3: An Anteroom in the White House. Scene 4: The Judging Pavilion of the Tioga County Fair. Scene 5: The Midway of the Fair. Scene 6: Another Part of the Fair. Scene 7: The Living Room of the Henderson Home.

ACT 1
Scene 1
"Let's Go Back to the Waltz"
N. Fabray, Ensemble
Scene 2
"In Our Hide-Away"
N. Fabray, R. Ryan
"The First Lady"
N. Fabray
Scene 3
"Meat and Potatoes"
J. Haskell, S. Grover
"I've Got To Be Around"
J. Haskell
"The Secret Service"
A. Gillette
Scene 4
"It Gets Lonely in the White House"
R. Ryan

Scene 5

"Is He the Only Man in the World"
N. Fabray, A. Gillette

Scene 6

"They Love Me"
N. Fabray

Scene 7

"Pigtails and Freckles"
J. Haskell, A. Gillette

Scene 9

"Don't Be Afraid of Romance"
J. Washburn

Scene 13

"Laugh It Up"
N. Fabray, R. Ryan, A. Gillette, J. Strickler

Scene 14

"Empty Pockets Filled With Love"
J. Haskell, A. Gillette

Scene 15

"In Our Hide-Away" (reprise)
N. Fabray, R. Ryan

ACT 2

Scene 1

"Glad To Be Home"
N. Fabray, Ensemble

Scene 2

"Laugh It Up" (reprise)
N. Fabray, R. Ryan

"You Need a Hobby"
N. Fabray, R. Ryan

Scene 3

"Don't Be Afraid of Romance" (reprise)
J. Washburn

"The Washington Twist"
A. Gillette, Dancers

Scene 4

"Pigtails and Freckles" (reprise)
J. Haskell

Scene 5

"The Only Dance I Know"
W. D'Orso

Scene 6

"Meat and Potatoes" (reprise)
J. Haskell

"Is He the Only Man in the World" (reprise)
A. Gillette

"I'm Gonna Get Him"
N. Fabray, A. Gillette

Scene 7

"This Is a Great Country"
R. Ryan

Finale

Entire Company

1962.21   THE MERRY WIDOW

A Revival of the Operetta in Three Acts[4]. Music by Franz Lehár. Original German book ("Die Lustige Witwe") and lyrics by Victor Léon and Leo Stein after "L'Attaché d'Ambassade" by Henri Meilhac. English libretto by Adrian Ross. Staged by Michael Pollock. Scenic design by George Jenkins. Choreographed by Thomas Andrew. Conducted by Carl Bamberger. Produced by the New York City Opera. Opened 21 October 1962 at the

---

[4]Originally produced in New York 21 October 1907 at the New Amsterdam Theatre for 416 performances. For Synopsis of Scenes and Musical Numbers, see original 1907 production.

New York City Center and closed 11 November 1962 after 3 performances in repertory.

CAST: *Sonia*: ARLENE SAUNDERS. *Prince Danilo*: JOHN REARDON. *Baron Popoff*: JACK HARROLD. *Natalie*: Nancy Foster. *De Jolidon*: JON CRAIN. *Marquis de Cascada*: David Smith. *St. Brioche*: Richard Krause. *Admiral Khadja*: Thomas Paul. *Mme. Khadja*: Lynda Jordan. *General Novikovich*: Spiro Malas. *Mme. Novikovich*: Charlotte Povia. *Nish*: Roy Stuart. *Head Waiter*: George John Smith. *Lo-Lo*: Helen Guile. *Solo Dancers*: Irene Apinée, Jury Gotshalks. *Ensemble*: New York City Opera Chorus.

1962.22   BAMBOCHE!

A Dance Revue in Three Acts, 13 Scenes. Production created and directed by Katherine Dunham. Settings and costumes by John Pratt. Orchestra under the direction of Leslie Harnley. Produced by Stephen Papich in association with Dorothy Gray and Ludwig Gerber. Opened 22 October 1962 at the 54th Street Theatre and closed 28 October 1962 after 8 performances.

CAST: KATHERINE DUNHAM, BESSIE GRIFFIN.
Katherine Dunham Dancers: VANOYE AIKENS, LUCILLE ELLIS, URAL WILSON, RICARDO AVALOS, Hope Clarke, Joan Seabrook, Odile Reifsteck, Lois Rollins, Maria Costoso, Candy Alexander, Carlton Johnson, Clifford Fears, Glenn Standifer, Wesley Gale, Monique LaSalle, David Henderson, Zach Thompson, Pearl Reynolds. *Singers*: ROBERT GUILLAUME, DOROTHY SPEIGHTS, Rosalie Maxwell, Clark Morgan, Gordon Watkins. *Drummers*: Camara Ladji, Julio Mendez, La Rosa Estrada. *Pianist*: Charles Barnett. *Bass Saxophone*: Jerome Richardson.
The Royal Troupe of Morocco: Che Dad Salem, Messaoud Ben Othman, Abderkader Ben Ahmed, El Kaaoui Allal, Marir Boujema, Driss Beid Mohammed, Hayat Khaddouj, Anouar Rabha, Heto Said Ben Brahim, Abderaham Ali Abderahaman, El Serife Buker, Ahmed Abselam, El Serife Takrchtba, Fatima Lahoucine, Tibikcht Fatima Brahim.

ACT 1

Scene 1

Marrakech!

(Music adapted from original themes by Leslie Harnley.)

The dances of Morocco are as varied as its tribal groups. In the courtyard of the Caliph in Marrakech, dancers gather from the Blue people of Goulimine in the South; from the Gnauwa, the tall dark men of Marrakech; from the Berbers of Khenifra, famous for their beautiful women. The musicians play the violins and the Gaitero, a reed instrument as old as the Sahara. The Koraish are proud of their descendency from tribes older than the Prophet Himself and proud of the many generations of artistry and the special favors they have received from the royal families for generations.

Guitera: E. K. Allal. *Acrobat*: A. B. Ahmed. *Dancing Girls*: H. Clarke, L. Rollins. *Wives of the Sultan*: O. Reifsteck, M. Costoso, C. Alexander, L. Ellis. *Berber Girls of the Khenifra* (in the Dance of the Tasadbat): H. Khaddouj, A. Rabha.

The blue Arab women of Goulimine, near the border of Mauritania, are called "blue" because of the Indigo in the garments which rubs off on the faces of the men and the women. The dance is the mysterious Guedra, believed by some to have been evolved from the Oriental people of the Pacific area.

Guedra Dancers: B. B. Mohammed, E. S. Takrchtba, F. Lahouchine, T. F. Brahim. *Gamni Dancers*: M. B. Othman, M. Boujema.

The chief drummers and dancers of the Gnauwa tribes perform the vigorous Gamni, a men's dance in preparation for war.

The Tjballa Dancer: A. A. Abderahaman.

A young boy from the Tjballa Tribes, dressed and veiled as a woman. He is accompanied by a violin player from their native village of Zahyouka, where the Tjballa has for many generations been popular among the young men.

The Desert Scene (Danse du Ventre)
K. Dunham, V. Aikens, Singers, Dancers, Musicians

Guedra (The Mystic Dance by the blue women of Goulimine)
B. B. Mohammed, E. S. Takrchtba, F. Lahoumine, T. F. Brahim

Scene 2

Brazilian Suite

Choros
H. Clarke, O. Reifsteck, C. Fears, C. Johnson

Variations of a Brazilian Quadrille from the nineteenth century.

Batucada
K. Dunham, V. Aikens, Company

A group of fisherwomen from bahia flirt with a woman from their own district.

Los Indios

M. Costoso, J. Seabrook, C. Johnson

High in the Andes, two Indian girls break their journey and meet a flute player.

Scene 3

Haitian Suite

"Yanvalou"

D. Speights, R. Guillaume, Gentlemen of the Company
La Place: U. Wilson.

For many years, Katherine Dunham has studied and participated in the deep mysteries of the Vaudun Cult. More recently, the pleasure-loving side of the Haitian people has attracted her. The Yanvalou is the fluid, hypnotic dance of veneration to Damballa, the Serpent God of the Dahomey.

"Bamboche!"

K. Dunham, V. Aikens, Company
(*Music and Lyrics by* Katherine Dunham.)

Bamboche is Haitian Creole for a "get-together to have a good time."

ACT 2

"The Diamond Thief"

(*Music by* Richard Markowitz. *Lyrics by* Le Clerc.)
Zulu Warrior: V. Aikens. *The Overseer*: A. Cooke. *Leader*: R. Guillaume. *The Diamond Thief*: R. Avalos. *Matriarch*: B. Graham. *Witch Doctor*: U. Wilson. *Lady in the Gold Dress*: K. Dunham. *Waiter*: D. Henderson. *Drummer*: C. Ladji. And Villagers, Patrons of the club, and the miners.
Place: Somewhere in the South of Africa. *Scene 1*: The Diamond Mine. *Scene 2*: Street of the Money Lender. *Scene 3*: The Happy Village. *Scene 4*: "De Highlife Bar" *Scene 5*: The Diamond Mine.

Africa is still full of mysteries and witchdoctors and villages within city squalor which revert to their ancient tribal exhibitions. In our locale, the only place to spend money is where the West filters in — in the native bars and cafes. The mines must be full of dreamers. Although the author has obviously not acquired information firsthand, there must be water girls passing at the end of the day, perhaps even one who would flirt with the overseer to ease the situation of the Diamond Thief. There must be an old, disillusioned Matriarch who has taken to Palm Wine and a Zulu Man still fine and handsome, who helps keep the spirit of Old Africa alive. Undoubtedly, to have money on hand from the sale of the diamond to the money lender would turn the Highlife Bar into a real "Gone" spot. There would be flirtatious girls and even a lady who worked her way up to a gold dress. It would be hard for the diamond thief to decide whether it all happened or not but the villagers are happy because in any event it was a great find.

ACT 3

Scene 1

Interior of The Mission House

Piano Player: C. Barnett. *Preacher*: U. Wilson. *A Worshipper*: R. Guillaume. *The Visiting Evangelist*: B. Griffin. And Congregation Members.

Scene 2

Barrelhouse: Florida Swamp Shimmy, Saturday Afternoon: Jacksonville.

K. Dunham, V. Aikens, Ensemble

Scene 3

Flaming Youth: Charleston, Black Bottom, Mooch, Fishtale, Snakehips

A Memory from the Twenties

Kansas City Woman: B. Griffin. *A Woman from Kansas City*: L. Ellis. *Snakehips*: C. Fears. *Drunken Woman*: L. Rollins.

Scene 4

Nostalgia: Songs from the Turn of the Century

D. Speights, R. Guillaume, R. Maxwell, C. Morgan, G. Watkins

Scene 5

Cakewalk

K. Dunham, V. Aikens, L. Ellis, U. Wilson

From the beginning of the century this dance mania of the athletic and exhibitionistic variation spread to Europe (and) completely conquered any existing dance style.

1962.23 # BEYOND THE FRINGE

A (Comedy) Revue in Two Acts. Written by Alan Bennett, Peter Cook, Joanthan Miller and Dudley Moore[5]. Staged by Alexander H. Cohen. Original London production directed by Eleanor Fazan. Setting by John Wyckham. Lighting by Ralph Alswang. Production associates, Andre Goulston, Gabriel Katzka. Originally conceived and produced for the Edinburgh Festival by Jonathan Bassett. A Nine O'Clock Theatre Production. Produced by Alexander H. Cohen by arrangement with William Donaldson and Donald Albery. Opened 27 October 1962 at the John Golden Theatre and closed 30 May 1964 after 673 performances. On 8 January 1964 title changed to BEYOND THE FRINGE '64[6]; see entry immediately below.

CAST: ALAN BENNETT, PETER COOK, JONATHAN MILLER, DUDLEY MOORE.

ACT 1

Steppes in the Right Direction[7]

A. Bennett, P. Cook, J. Miller, D. Moore

Royal Box

(*by* Alan Bennett)
P. Cook, D. Moore

"Man Bites God"

J. Miller, D. Moore

Fruits of Experience (Let's Face It)

(*by* Alan Bennett)
A. Bennett

Bollard

(*by* Peter Cook)
A. Bennett, P. Cook, J. Miller, D. Moore

A Piece of My Mind (The Heat Death of the Universe)

(*by* Jonathan Miller)
J. Miller

"Deutscher Chansons" (Chanson; Die Flabbergast)

(*by* Dudley Moore)
J. Miller, D. Moore

The Sadder and Wiser Beaver

(*by* Peter Cook)
A. Bennett, P. Cook

Groves of Academe (Words . . . and Things)

(*by* Alan Bennett and Peter Cook)
A. Bennett, J. Miller

The Prime Minister Speaks (T.V.P.M.)

(*by* Peter Cook)[8]
P. Cook

"And the Same to You" (piano solo)

(*by* Dudley Moore)
D. Moore

Aftermyth of War

A. Bennett, P. Cook, J. Miller, D. Moore

ACT 2

Civil War

A. Bennett, P. Cook, J. Miller, D. Moore

Real Class

A. Bennett, P. Cook, J. Miller, D. Moore

"Little Miss Britten"

(*by* Dudley Moore)
J. Miller, D. Moore

The Suspense Is Killing Me

(*by* Alan Bennett, Jonathan Miller)
A. Bennett, P. Cook, J. Miller, D. Moore

Purn Shooting

(*by* Jonathan Miller)
J. Miller

---

[5]Unless otherwise indicated below, all material written by all four performers.
[6]Return engagement opened 15 December 1964 at the Ethel Barrymore Theatre for 30 performances; see separate entry in 1964-1965 season.
[7]Dropped during run.
[8]Replaced during the run by:
The Great Train Robbery
(*by* Peter Cook)
A. Bennett, P. Cook

Studio 5 (Interviews)
    (*by* Peter Cook, Jonathan Miller)
        A. Bennett, P. Cook, J. Miller
Sitting on the Bench
    (*by* Peter Cook)
        P. Cook
Men Only (Bread Alone)
    A. Bennett, P. Cook, J. Miller, D. Moore
Take a Pew
    (*by* Alan Bennett)
        A. Bennett
"So That's the Way You Like It"
    A. Bennett, P. Cook, J. Miller, D. Moore
The End of the World
    (*by* Peter Cook)
        A. Bennett, P. Cook, J. Miller, D. Moore

1962.23 BEYOND THE FRINGE '64

This revised edition opened 8 January 1964 as part of the show's continuous run. Jonathan Miller was succeeded by Paxton Whitehead.

ACT 1
Home Thoughts from Abroad
    A. Bennett, P. Cook, P. Whitehead D. Moore
Royal Box
    (*by* Peter Cook)
        P. Cook, D. Moore, A. Bennett
"Man Bites God"
    P. Whitehead, D. Moore
The English Way of Death
    (*by* Alan Bennett)
        A. Bennett
Bollard
    (*by* Peter Cook)
        A. Bennett, P. Cook, P. Whitehead D. Moore
A Piece of My Mind (The Heat Death of the Universe)
    (*by* Jonathan Miller)
        P. Whitehead
Song ("Little Miss Britten"/"Old Meg She Was a Gypsy"
by Dudley Moore)
    D. Moore
The Philosophers
The Great Train Robbery
    (*by* Peter Cook)
        A. Bennett, P. Cook
Colonel Bogey
The Aftermyth of War
    A. Bennett, P. Cook, P. Whitehead D. Moore
ACT 2
Civil War
    A. Bennett, P. Cook, P. Whitehead D. Moore
Real Class
    A. Bennett, P. Cook, P. Whitehead D. Moore
"Weill Song" (Ballad of Gangster Joe)
    (*by* Dudley Moore and Peter Cook)
        D. Moore, P. Whitehead
One Leg Too Few
    (*by* Peter Cook)
        P. Cook, D. Moore
Portraits from Memory
    (*by* Jonathan Miller)P. Whitehead
The Death of (Lord) Nelson
    (*by* Jonathan Miller)
        P. Whitehead
The Scientist (Studio Five Interviews)
    P. Cook, A. Bennett
The Doctor
The Duke/Lord Cobbold (Studio Five Interviews)
    (*by* Peter Cook, A. Bennett, Jonathan Miller)
        P. Cook, A. Bennett, P. Whitehead

The Miner (Sitting on the Bench revised)
    (*by* Peter Cook)
        P. Cook
The Restaurant
The Sermon (Take a Pew revised)
    (*by* Alan Bennett)
So That's the Way You Like It
The End of the World
    (*by* Peter Cook)
        A. Bennett, P. Cook, P. Whitehead D. Moore

1962.24 NOWHERE TO GO BUT UP

A Musical Comedy in Two Acts, 19 Scenes. Book and lyrics by James Lipton. Music by Sol Berkowitz. Directed by Sidney Lumet. Settings by Peter Larkin. Costumes by Robert Fletcher. Choreography by Ronald [Ron] Field. Lighting by Tharon Musser. (Musical) Arrangements and orchestrations by Robert Ginzler. Vocal arrangements and musical direction by Herbert Greene. Produced by Kermit Bloomgarden and Herbert Greene with Steven H. Scheuer. Opened 10 November 1962 at the Winter Garden and closed 17 November 1962 after 9 performances.

CAST (in order of appearance):*Izzy Einstein*: TOM BOSLEY. *Moe Smith*: MARTIN BALSAM. *Anthony Baiello*: BRUCE GORDON. *Wilma Risque*: DOROTHY LOUDON. *Tommy Dee*: BERT CONVY. *Jean Morgan*: MARY ANN MOBLEY. *Hymie*: PHIL LEEDS. *Beggar*: Bob Avian. *Lady with Laundry*: Sally Ann Carlson. *Hop Wong*: PHIL LEEDS. *Hop Family*: Sally Lee, Jodi Kim Long, Bill Star, Eleanore Treiber. *Policeman*: Rico Froehlich. *Reporters*: H. F. Green, Val Avery, Art Wallace. *Woman with Poodle*: Eleonore Treiber. *Lupo*: FRANK CAMPANELLA. *The Gang*: Marty Allen, Bob Avian, Tod Jackson, Larry Merritt, Frank Pietri, Bill Starr, Gerald Teijelo, James Weiss, Blair Hammond, Michael Maurer. *Stage Manager*: Joel Craig. *La Vie Girls*: Nicole Barth, Sally Ann Carlson, Diane Coupé, Dorothy D'Honau, Lillian D'Honau, Maureen Hopkins, Jami Landi, Sally Lee, Sandra Roveta, Dean Taliaferro, Barbara Marcon, Eleanore Treiber. *Sally*: Sally Lee. *Policeman*: Val Avery. *Guard*: Don Rehg.

Act 1, Scene 1: A Cartoon. *Scene 2*: A Street. *Scene 3*: Hop Wong Laundry. *Scene 4*: A Speakeasy. *Scene 5*: A Street. *Scene 6*: Baiello's Office. *Scene 7*: Backstage Corridor, Club La Vie Est Gaie. *Scene 8*: La Vie Est Gaie. *Scene 9*: Exterior, La Vie Est gaie. *Scene 10*: Baiello's Office. *Scene 11*: Backstage Corridor. *Scene 12*: La Vie Est Gaie.

Act 2, Scene 1: La Vie Est Gaie. *Scene 2*: The La Vie Girls' Dressing Room. *Scene 3*: The Backstage Corridor. *Scene 4*: Exterior, La Vie Est Gaie. *Scene 5*: Baiello's Office. *Scene 6*: The Backstage Corridor, then the City. *Scene 7*: The Distillery.

ACT 1
Scene 2
    "Ain't You Ashamed"
        T. Bosley, M. Balsam
Scene 3
    "The 'We Makin' Cash with Sour Mash, No Rickie-Tickie No Licq-ie' Rag"
        P. Leeds
    "The 'We Makin' Cash with Sour Mash, No Rickie-Tickie No Licq-ie' Rag" (reprise)
        P. Leeds, S. Lee, J. K. Long, B. Starr, E. Treiber, T. Bosley, M. Balsam
Scene 4
    "Live a Little"
        D. Loudon, T. Bosley, M. Balsam, Company
Scene 6
    "Yes, Mr. Baiello"
        B. Gordon, The Gang
    Dance
        The Gang
Scene 7
    "When a Fella Needs a Friend"
        T. Bosley, M. Balsam, B. Convy, M. A. Mobley
    Dance
        T. Bosley, M. Balsam, B. Convy, M. A. Mobley
Scene 8
    "The Odds and Ends of Love"
        D. Loudon
    "Nowhere To Go But Up"
        D. Loudon, The La Vie Girls

Scene 10

"Take Me Back"
B. Gordon, M. A. Mobley

"Yes, Mr. Baiello" (reprise)
B. Gordon, The Gang

Scene 11

"I Love You for That"
D. Loudon, M. Balsam

Scene 12

"Nowhere To Go But Up" (reprise)
The La Vie Girls

ACT 2

Scene 1

"Baby, Baby"
M. Balsam, D. Loudon

Scene 2

"Natural Allies"
T. Bosley, The La Vie Girls

Scene 4

"Out of Sight, Out of Mind"
B. Convy

Scene 5

"Follow the Leader" Septet
B. Gordon, T. Bosley, M. Balsam, D. Loudon,
M. A. Mobley, B. Convy, P. Leeds

Scene 6

"Dear Mom"
T. Bosley, M. Balsam

Responses
B. Gordon, F. Campanella, The Gang

Scene 7

"Nowhere to Go But Up" (reprise/Finale)
T. Bosley, M. Balsam, Company

THE MIKADO,
or The Town of Titipu

1962.25

A Revival of the Comic Opera in Two Acts[9]. Libretto by William S. Gilbert. Music by Arthur Sullivan. Costumes designed by Charles Ricketts. Basic unit set for the full repertory designed by Peter Goffin. Director of productions, Herbert Newby. Dances arranged by John Reed. Musical director, Isidore Godfrey. Produced by the D'Oyly Carte Opera Company under the management of Sol Hurok. Opened 13 November 1962 at the New York City Center and closed 9 December 1962 after 10 performances in repertory.

CAST: *The Mikado of Japan*: DONALD ADAMS. *Nanki-Poo*, his son, disguised as a wandering minstrel in love with Yum-Yum: THOMAS ROUND. *Ko-Ko*, Lord High Executioner of Titipu: JOHN REED. *Pooh-Bah*, Lord High Everything Else: KENNETH SANDFORD. *Pish-Tush*, *Go-To*, Noble Lords: Jeffrey Skitch, George Cook. *Yum-Yum*, *Pitti-Sing*, *Peep-Bo*, three sisters, wards of Ko-Ko: JENNIFER TOYE, JOANNE MOORE, PEGGY ANN JONES. *Katisha*: GILLIAN KNIGHT. *Chorus of School Girls, Nobles, Guards and Coolies*: (uncredited).

THE GONDOLIERS,
or The King of Barataria

1962.26

A Revival of the Comic Opera in Two Acts[10]. Libretto by William S. Gilbert. Music by Arthur Sullivan. Costumes designed by Charles Ricketts. Basic unit set for the full repertory designed by Peter Goffin. Director of productions, Herbert Newby. Dances arranged by John Reed. Musical director,

Isidore Godfrey. Produced by the D'Oyly Carte Opera Company under the management of Sol Hurok. Opened 15 November 1962 at the New York City Center and closed 9 December 1962 after 5 performances in repertory.

CAST: *The Duke of Plaza-Toro*, a Grandee of Spain: JOHN REED. *Luiz*, his attendant: PHILIP POTTER. *Don Alhambra Del Bolero*, The Grand Inquisitor: KENNETH SANDFORD. *Marco Palmieri, Giuseppe Palmieri, Antonio, Francesco, Giorgio*, Venetian Gondoliers: THOMAS ROUND, ALAN STYLER, John Cartier, Joseph Riordan, Anthony Raffell. *Annibale*: John Cartier. *The Duchess of Plaza Del Toro*: GILLIAN KNIGHT. *Casilda*, Her Daughter: JENNIFER TOYE. *Gianetta, Tessa, Fiametta, Vittoria, Giulia*, Contadine: JEAN HINDMARSH, PEGGY ANN JONES, Mary Sansom, Joanne Moore, Anne Sessions. *Inez*, The King's Foster-Mother: Jeanette Roach. *Chorus of Gondoliers, Contadine, Men-at-Arms, Heralds and Pages*: (uncredited).

1962.27

LITTLE ME

A Musical Comedy in Two Acts, 35 Scenes. Book by Neil Simon. Based on the novel of the same name by Patrick Dennis. Music by Cy Coleman. Lyrics by Carolyn Leigh. Musical numbers and dances staged by Bob Fosse. Directed by Cy Feuer and Bob Fosse. Scenery and lighting by Robert Randolph. Costumes by Robert Fletcher. Orchestrations by Ralph Burns. Dance music arranged by Fred Werner. Vocal arrangements by Clay Warnick. Musical direction, Charles Sanford. Produced by Cy Feuer and Ernest H. Martin. Opened 17 November 1962 at the Lunt-Fontanne Theatre and closed 29 June 1963 after 257 performances.

CAST (in order of appearance): *Butler*: John Anania. *Patrick Dennis*: PETER TURGEON. *Miss Poitrine, today*: NANCY ANDREWS. *Momma*: ADNIA RICE. *Belle*: VIRGINIA MARTIN. *George Musgrove as a boy*: John Sharpe. *Brucey*: James Senn. *Ramona*: Else Olufsen. *Noble Eggleston*: SID CAESAR. *Mrs. Eggleston*: NANCY CUSHMAN. *Miss Kepplewhite*: Gretchen Cryer. *Pinchley, Junior*: MICKEY DEEMS. *Nurse*: Margery Beddow. *Mr. Pinchley*: SID CAESAR. *Kleeg*: Burt Bier. *Newsboy*: Michael Smuin. *Bernie Buchsbaum*: JOEY FAYE. *Bennie Buchsbaum*: MORT MARSHALL. *Defense Lawyer*: MICKEY DEEMS. *Val Du Val*: SID CAESAR. *George Musgrove*: SWEN SWENSON. *Fred Poitrine*: SID CAESAR. *Preacher*: Ken Ayers. *German Officer*: MICKEY DEEMS. *General*: Michael Quinn. *Courier*: Eddie Gasper. *Red Cross Nurse*: Sandra Stahl. *Steward*: David Gold. *Otto Schnitzler*: SID CAESAR. *Secretary*: Marcia Gilford. *Production Assistant*: MICKEY DEEMS. *Victor*: Marc Jordan. *Prince Cherney*: SID CAESAR. *Yulnick*: MICKEY DEEMS. *Baby*: VIRGINIA MARTIN. *Noble, Junior*: SID CAESAR.

Singers: Gretchen Cryer, Marcia Gilford, Else Olufsen, Sandra Stahl, Lory Stark, John Anania, Ken Ayers, Burt Bier, Harris Hawkins, Marc Jordan, Michael Quinn. *Dancers*: Barbara Beck, Margery Beddow, Reby Howells, Odette Phillips, Dounia Rathbone, Barbara Sharma, Renata Vaselle, Eddie Gasper, Gene Gavin, David Gold, James Kirby, John Sharpe, Michael Smuin, James Senn, Michel Stuart.

Act 1, Scene 1: Belle's estate in Southampton, Long Island. The present. *Scene 2*: The past. A tumbledown shack in Drifters' Row, Venezuela, Illinois. *Scene 3*: The Eggleston's elegant living room. *Scene 4*: Exterior of the Eggleston home. *Scene 5*: Belle's estate. (The present.) *Scene 6*: Interior of a small-town bank. (The past.) *Scene 7*: A golf course. (The present.) *Scene 8*: A hotel room in Peoria. (The past.) *Scene 9*: A prison. *Scene 10*: A courtroom in Chicago. *Scene 11*: (A Chicago stage.) *Scene 12*: The present. *Scene 13*: The Skylight Roof. Chicago. (The past.) *Scene 14*: The present. *Scene 15*: A small, gaily decorated apartment. (Chicago. The past.) *Scene 16*: (At the front and in Chicago.) *Scene 17*: A base hospital, somewhere in France.

Act 2, Scene 1: Belle's Estate. The present. *Scene 2*: On board the S.S. *Gigantic*, on the North Atlantic. (The past.) *Scene 3*: Belle's Estate. (The present.) *Scene 4*: Hollywood. (The past.) *Scene 5*: Belle in Hollywood. *Scene 6*: The office of the Buchsbaum Brothers. Hollywood. *Scene 7*: A biblical movie set. *Scene 8*: Belle's Estate. (The present.) *Scene 9*: The Casino in Monte Carlo. (The past.) *Scene 10*: (The present.) *Scene 11*: The royal bedchamber of Prince Cherny of Rosenzweig. (The past.) *Scene 12*: The Rumpus Room in Belle's Estate. The present. *Scene 13*: The Dakotas. (The past.) *Scene 14*: The Rumpus Room in Belle's Estate. (The present.) *Scene 15*: The exterior of the house, Belle's Estate. (The past.) *Scene 16*: Belle's Estate. (The present.) *Scene 17*: Belle's Estate. The present.

ACT 1[11]

Scene 1

"The Truth"
N. Andrews, P. Turgeon, Servants

Scene 2

"The Other Side of the Tracks"
V. Martin

"Birthday Party" (The Rich Kids' Rag)
Boys, Girls

---

[9]First presented in New York 20 July, 10-29 August 1885 at the Union Square and People's Theatres for 22 performances. First authorized production presented 19 August 1885 at the Fifth Avenue Theatre by Richard D'Oyly Carte for 250 performances. For Synopsis of Scenes and Musical Numbers, see 19 August 1885 D'Oyly Carte production.

[10]Originally presented in New York 7 January 1890 at Park Theatre for 103 performances. For Synopsis of Scenes and Musical Numbers, see original 1890 production.

---

[11]Description of scenes does not appear in programs; list prepared from published script.

Scene 3
"I Love You"
    S. Caesar, V. Martin
Scene 4
"The Other Side of the Tracks" (reprise)
    V. Martin
Scene 6
"Deep Down Inside"
    S. Caesar, V. Martin, M. Deems, Poor People
Scene 9
"Be a Performer!"
    M. Marshall, J. Faye
Scene 11
"(Oh! Dem Doggone) Dimples"
    V. Martin, Police Escort (Chorus)
Scene 13
"Boom-Boom"
    S. Caesar, Girls
"I've Got Your Number"
    S. Swenson, V. Martin
Scene 15
"Real Live Girl"
    S. Caesar
Scene 17
"Real Live Girl" (reprise)
    The Doughboys (Men's Chorus)
"Boom-Boom" (reprise)
    V. Martin, Howitzers
ACT 2
Scene 5
"Poor Little Hollywood Star"
    V. Martin
Scene 6
("To Be a Performer" reprise)
    (M. Marshall, J. Faye)
Scene 8
"Little Me"
    N. Andrews, V. Martin
Scene 11
"The Prince's Farewell" (Goodbye)
    S. Caesar, M. Deems, Loyal Subjects (Chorus)
Scene 14
"Here's To Us"
    N. Andrews, Guests
Scene 17
Finale
    S. Caesar, V. Martin

THE PIRATES OF PENZANCE,
1962.28   or The Slave of Duty

A Revival of the Comic Opera in Two Acts[12]. Libretto by William S. Gilbert. Music by Arthur Sullivan. Costumes designed by Charles Ricketts. Basic unit set for the full repertory designed by Peter Goffin. Director of productions, Herbert Newby. Dances arranged by John Reed. Musical director, Isidore Godfrey. Produced by the D'Oyly Carte Opera Company under the management of Sol Hurok. Opened 20 November 1962 at the New York City Center and closed 9 December 1962 after 6 performances in repertory.

CAST: *Major General Stanley*: JOHN REED. *The Pirate King*: DONALD ADAMS. *Samuel*, his Lieutenant: Alan Styler. *Frederic*, the Pirate Apprentice: PHILIP

POTTER. *Sergeant of Police*: GEORGE COOK. *Mabel, Edith, Kate, Isabel*, General Stanley's Daughters: JEAN HINDMARSH, MARY SANSOM, PEGGY ANN JONES, Pauline Wales. *Ruth*, Pirate Maid-of-all-work: GILLIAN KNIGHT. *Chorus of Pirates, Police and General Stanley's Daughters.*

1962.29   TRIAL BY JURY

A Revival of the Comic Opera in One Act[13]. Libretto by William S. Gilbert. Music by Arthur Sullivan. Costumes designed by George Sheringham. Basic unit set for the full repertory designed by Peter Goffin. Director of productions, Herbert Newby. Dances arranged by John Reed. Musical director, Isidore Godfrey. Produced by the D'Oyly Carte Opera Company under the management of Sol Hurok. Opened 22 November 1962 at the New York City Center and closed 9 December 1962 after 7 performances in repertory.

CAST: *The Learned Judge*: JEFFREY SKITCH. *Counsel for the Plaintiff*: ALAN STYLER. *The Defendant*: PHILIP POTTER. *Foreman of the Jury*: Peter Sugden *Usher*: GEORGE COOK. *Associate*: ALAN BARRETT. *The Plaintiff*: MARY SANSOM. *First Bridesmaid*: Dawn Bradshaw. *Chorus of Jurymen, Bridesmaids and Public*: (uncredited).

H.M.S. PINAFORE,
1962.30   or The Lass That Loved a Sailor

A Revival of the Comic Opera in Two Acts[14]. Libretto by William S. Gilbert. Music by Arthur Sullivan. Costumes designed by Peter Goffin. Basic unit set for the full repertory designed by Peter Goffin. Director of productions, Herbert Newby. Dances arranged by John Reed. Musical director, Isidore Godfrey. Produced by the D'Oyly Carte Opera Company under the management of Sol Hurok. Opened 22 November 1962 at the New York City Center and closed 9 December 1962 after 7 performances in repertory.

CAST: *The Rt. Hon. Sir Joseph Porter, K.C.B.*, First Lord of the Admiralty: JOHN REED. *Captain Corcoran*, Commanding the *H.M.S. Pinafore*: JEFFREY SKITCH. *Ralph Rackstraw*, Able Seaman: THOMAS ROUND. *Dick Deadeye*, Able Seaman: DONALD ADAMS. *Bill Bobstay*, Bo'sun's Mate: George Cook. *Bob Beckett*, Carpenter's Mate: Anthony Raffell. *Josephine*, the Captain's Daughter: JEAN HINDMARSH. *Hebe*, Sir Joseph's First Cousin: Joanne Moore. *Little Buttercup*, a Portsmouth Bumboat Woman: GILLIAN KNIGHT. *First Lord's Sisters, his Cousins, his Aunts, Sailors, Marines*: (uncredited).

IOLANTHE,
1962.31   or The Peer and the Peri

A Revival of the Comic Opera in Two Acts[15]. Libretto by William S. Gilbert. Music by Arthur Sullivan. (Costumes uncredited.) Basic unit set for the full repertory designed by Peter Goffin. Director of productions, Herbert Newby. Dances arranged by John Reed. Musical director, Isidore Godfrey. Produced by the D'Oyly Carte Opera Company under the management of Sol Hurok. Opened 27 November 1962 at the New York City Center and closed 9 December 1962 after 4 performances in repertory.

CAST: *The Lord Chancellor*: JOHN REED. *Earl of Mountararat*: DONALD ADAMS. *Earl Tolloller*: PHILIP POTTER. *Private Willis* of the Grenadier Guards: KENNETH SANDFORD. *Strephon*, an Arcadian Shepherd: JEFFREY SKITCH. *Queen of the Fairies*: GILLIAN KNIGHT. *Iolanthe*, a Fairy, Strephon's Mother: JOANNE MOORE. *Celia, Leila, Fleta*, Fairies: Jennifer Toye, Pauline Wales, Jacqueline Mitchell. *Phyllis*, an Arcadian Shepherdess and Ward in Chancery: MARY SANSOM. *Chorus of Dukes, Marquises, Earls, Viscounts, Barons and Fairies*: (uncredited).

---

[12]First presented in New York 31 December 1879 at the Fifth Avenue Theatre for a total of 91 performances in two engagements. For Synopsis of Scenes and Musical Numbers, see original 1879 production.

[13]First presented in New York 15 November 1875 at the Eagle Theatre for 8 performances. For Synopsis of Scenes and Musical Numbers, see original 1875 production.

[14]Originally presented in New York 15 January 1879 at the Standard Theatre for 175 performances For Synopsis of Scenes and Musical Numbers, see original 1879 production.

[15]First presented in New York 25 November 1882 at the Standard Theatre for 105 performances. For Synopsis of Scenes and Musical Numbers, see original 1882 production.

1963.01 # OLIVER!

A Musical in Two Acts, 12 Scenes. Book, music and lyrics by Lionel Bart. Freely adapted from the novel "Oliver Twist" by Charles Dickens. Directed by Peter Coe. (Scenery) Designed by Sean Kenny. Costumes by M. Berman Ltd. Lighting by John Wyckham. Orchestrations by Eric Rogers. Musical director, Don Pippin. Technical supervisor, Ian Albery. Produced by David Merrick and Donald Albery. Opened 6 January 1963 at the Imperial Theatre, moved 14 September 1964 to the Sam S. Shubert Theatre, and closed 14 November 1964 after 774 performances[16].

CAST: *Oliver Twist*: BRUCE PROCHNIK. *At the Workhouse*: *Mr. Bumble*, the Beadle: WILLOUGHBY GODDARD. *Mrs. Corney*, the Matron: HOPE JACKMAN. *Old Sally*, a pauper: Ruth Maynard. *At the Undertaker's*: *Mr. Sowerberry*, the Undertaker: BARRY HUMPHRIES. *Mrs. Sowerberry*, his wife: HELENA CARROLL. *Charlotte*, their daughter: Cherry Davis. *Noah Claypole*, their apprentice: Terry Lomax. *At the Thieves' Kitchen*: *Fagin*: CLIVE REVILL. *The Artful Dodger*: DAVID JONES. *Nancy*: GEORGIA BROWN. *Bet*: Alice Playten. *Bill Sykes*: DANNY SEWELL. *At the Brownlow's*: *Mr. Brownlow*: GEOFFREY LUMB. *Dr. Grimwig*: JOHN CALL. *Mrs. Bedwin*: Dortha Duckworth.

Workhouse Boys and Fagin's Gang: Johnny Borden, Eugene Endon, Bryant Fraser, Randy Gaynes, Bobby Gold, Sal Lombardo, Christopher Month, Patrick O'Shaughnessy, Alan Paul, Barry Pearl, George Priolo, Robbie Reed, Christopher Votos. *Londoners*: Jed Allan, Barbara Bossert, Jack Davison, James Glenn, Lesley Hunt, John M. Kimbro, Michael Lamont, Allan Lokos, Dodie Marshall, Richard Miller, Moose Peting, Ruth Ramsey, Nita Reiter, Ray Tudor, Maura K. Wedge.

The action takes place about 1850, in the North of England and London.

Act 1, Scene 1: The Workhouse. *Scene 2*: The Workhouse Parlor. *Scene 3*: The Undertaker's. *Scene 4*: Paddington Green. *Scene 5*: The Thieves' Kitchen. *Scene 6*: Streets of London.

Act 2, Scene 1: The "Three Cripples." *Scene 2*: The Brownlow's. *Scene 3*: The Thieves' Kitchen. *Scene 4*: The Workhouse. *Scene 5*: The Brownlow's. *Scene 6*: London Bridge.

ACT 1
"Food, Glorious Food"
   The Boys
"Oliver!"
   W. Goddard, H. Jackman, B. Prochnik, Boys
"I Shall Scream"
   H. Jackman, W. Goddard
"Boy For Sale"
   W. Goddard
"That's Your Funeral"
   B. Humphries, W. Goddard, H. Carroll
"Where Is Love?"
   B. Prochnik
"Consider Yourself"
   D. Jones, B. Prochnik, Crowd
"You've Got To Pick a Pocket or Two"
   C. Revill, B. Prochnik, Boys
"It's a Fine Life"
   G. Brown, A. Playten
"I'd Do Anything"
   D. Jones, G. Brown, B. Prochnik, A. Playten, C. Revill
"Be Back Soon"
   C. Revill, D. Jones, B. Prochnik, Boys

ACT 2
"Oom-Pah-Pah"
   G. Brown, Company
"My Name"
   D. Sewell
"As Long as He Needs Me"
   G. Brown
"Where Is Love?" (reprise)
   D. Duckworth
"Who Will Buy?"
   B. Prochnik, Chorus
"It's a Fine Life" (reprise)
   D. Sewell, G. Brown, C. Revill, Boys

"Reviewing the Situation"
   C. Revill
"Oliver!" (reprise)
   W. Goddard, H. Jackman
"As Long As He Needs Me" (reprise)
   G. Brown
"Reviewing the Situation" (reprise)
   C. Revill
Finale: "Food, Glorious Food"/"Consider Yourself"/"I'd Do Anything"
   Full Company

1963.02 # MAURICE CHEVALIER

A One Man Show in Two Acts. (Sketches by Maurice Chevalier.) Decor and lighting by Raoul Pene Du Bois. Mr. Chevalier's clothes by Larsen in Paris. Produced by Alexander H. Cohen. Opened 28 January 1963 at the Ziegfeld Theatre and closed 23 February 1963 after 28 performances.

CAST: MAURICE CHEVALIER. *At the piano*: Fred Stamper.

MUSICAL NUMBERS AND SKETCHES[17]
"Thank Heaven for Little Girls" (from the film GIGI)
   (*Music by* Frederick Loewe. *Lyrics by* Alan Jay Lerner.)
"Quai de Bercy"
   (*Music and Lyrics by* Maurice Chevalier and Louis Poterat Alstone.)
"Le twist Canotier"
   (*Music and Lyrics by* Noel Roux and Georges Garvarentz.)
"I Still See Elisa" (from PAINT YOUR WAGON)
   (*Music by* Frederick Loewe. *Lyrics by* Alan Jay Lerner.)
"Place Pigalle"
   (*Music and Lyrics by* Maurice Chevalier and Louis Poterat Alstone.)
George Gershwin Medley
Spectators
   (*by* Maurice Chevalier)
"You Must Have Been a Beautiful Baby" (from film HARD TO GET)
   (*Music by* Harry Warren. *Lyrics by* Johnny Mercer.)
"Some of These Days"
   (*Music and Lyrics by* Shelton Brooks.)
"Contre l'amour y'a rien à faire"
   (*Music and Lyrics by* Michel Rivgauche and Ma. Eva Wallis.)
"How to Handle a Woman" (from CAMELOT)
   (*Music by* Frederick Loewe. *Lyrics by* Alan Jay Lerner.)
"Les chapeaux"
   (*Music and Lyrics by* Jacques Mareuil and Fred Freed.)
"You Made Me Love You"
   (*Music by* James V. Monaco. *Lyrics by* Joseph McCarthy.)
From Rag to Twist
   (*by* Maurice Chevalier)
"Yankee Doodle Parisien"
   (*Music and Lyrics by* George M. Cohan.)
"There's a Rainbow Round My Shoulder" (from the film THE SINGING FOOL)
   (*Music and Lyrics by* Billy Rose, Dave Dreyer and Al Jolson.)
"Ah donnez m'en de la chanson"
   (*Music and Lyrics by* Rene Rouzaud and Marguerite Monnot.)
"Louise" (from the film INNOCENTS OF PARIS)
   (*Music by* Richard A. Whiting. *Lyrics by* Leo Robin.)
"I'm Glad I'm Not Young Anymore" (from the film GIGI)
   (*Music by* Frederick Loewe. *Lyrics by* Alan Jay Lerner.)
"À Las Vegas"
   (*Music and Lyrics by* Albert Willemetz and Louiguy)
Accents Melodiques
   (*by* Maurice Chevalier)
CAN-CAN Medley
   (*Music and Lyrics by* Cole Porter.)

---

[16]Reopened a return engagement 2 August 1965 at the Martin Beck Theatre for 64 performances; see separate entry in 1964-65 season.

[17]Program Note: These are the songs associated with Chevalier, most of which he will sing in the order that fits the mood and the music with one intermission.

"Mimi" (from the film LOVE ME TONIGHT)
(*Music by* Richard Rodgers. *Lyrics by* Lorenz Hart.)
"Valentine"
(*Music and Lyrics by* Albert Willemetz and Henri Christiné)
Stations of Life
(*by* Maurice Chevalier)
"La tête de roi"
(*Music and Lyrics by* Jean-Pierre Moulin.)

1963.03 THE HOLLOW CROWN

A Royal Revue in Two Acts, 32 Scenes. An entertainment by and about the Kings and Queens of England. Devised and staged by John Barton. Musical director, Brian Priestman. Produced by Bonard Productions (Helen G. Bonfils, Haila Stoddard, Donald R. Seawell) by arrangement with the Governors of the Royal Shakespeare Theatre, Stratford-on-Avon. Opened 29 January 1963 at Henry Miller's Theatre and closed 9 March 1963 after 46 performances.

CAST: MAX ADRIAN, DOROTHY TUTIN, JOHN BARTON, PAUL HARDWICK. *Musicians:* Richard Golding (bass), Stephen Manton (tenor), John Lawrenson (baritone), James Walker (piano and harpsichord).

ACT 1

KINGS ACCORDING TO LEGEND AND THE CHRONICLERS

Scene 1

Prologue: The Hollow Crown
(*by* William Shakespeare)M. Adrian

Scene 2

The Death of Kings (from Stow and the Anglo-Saxon Chronicles)
J. Barton
William I (1066-1087), William II (1087-1100), Henry I (1100-1135), Stephen (1135-1154).

Scene 3

An Anonymous Ballad Concerning Henry II and Queen Elinor (1154-1189)
M. Adrian

Scene 4

Sixteenth and Seventeenth Century Chroniclers (Holinshed, Hall, Baker and Churchill) on Henry II (1154-1189), Richard I (1189-1199), John (1199-1216), Henry III (1216-1272), Edward I (1272-1307), Edward II (1307-1327)
P. Hardwick

Scene 5

Ballade by Richard I made during his captivity in the Castle of Durrenstein
J. Lawrenson

Scene 6

From Froissart's Chronicles (Lord Berners):
Richard II (1377-1399) surrenders at Flint Castle to Henry IV (1399-1413) at that time Duke of Lancaster
J. Barton

Scene 7

'A Partial, Prejudiced and Ignorant Historian' (Jane Austen, aged fifteen) on:
Henry IV (1399-1413), Henry V (1413-1422), Henry VI (1422-1461), Edward IV (1461-1483), Edward V (1483), Richard III (1483-1485), Henry VII (1485-1509), Henry VIII (1509-1547), Edward VI (1547-1553), Mary I (1553-1558), Elizabeth I (1558-1603), James (1603-1625), Charles I (1625-1649).
D. Tutin

Scene 8

Henry V—"Agincourt Song"
S. Manton, J. Lawrenson, R. Golding

THE MONARCHS SPEAK FOR THEMSELVES

Scene 9

Diplomacy: Henry VII sends a secret memorandum to his Ambassadors

concerning a proposed marriage between himself and the Queen of Naples, and they reply to it.
M. Adrian, J. Barton

Scene 10

The Queene's Command—
(*Music by* Orlando Gibbons)
J. Walker (harpsichord)

Scene 11

A Speech: Mary I denounces the rebellion of Sir Thomas Wyatt, raised in protest against her proposed marriage to Philip of Spain.
D. Tutin

Scene 12

Henry VIII—"The King's Hunt"
S. Manton, J. Lawrenson, R. Golding

Scene 13

Letters:
Henry VIII proposes to Anne Boleyn, a lady in waiting at his court.
P. Hardwick
Anne Boleyn writes to Henry from the Tower before her execution.
D. Tutin

Scene 14

Poems:
Henry VI: 'Kingdoms are but cares'
J. Barton
Henry VIII: 'As the Holly groweth green'
P. Hardwick
Elizabeth I complains of being importuned with love
D. Tutin
Charles II: 'I pass all my hours in a shady old grove'
M. Adrian

Scene 15

Charles II—"Here's a health unto His Majesty"
S. Manton, J. Lawrenson, R. Golding

ACT 2

THE STUARTS

Scene 1

A Reel by James I
(J. Walker)

Scene 2

James I (1603-1625) blows a 'Counterblast to Tobacco'
M. Adrian

Scene 3

Charles I (1625-1649) confronts John Bradshaw, President of the Court, at his trial for high treason and is condemned to death.
P. Hardwick, J. Barton

Scene 4

Ayre by Charles I
S. Manton

Scene 5

Charles II marries Catharine of Braganza—from a speech to Parliament and a letter to the Lord Chancellor.
M. Adrian, J. Barton

Scene 6

Charles II is anatomised by the Marquis of Halifax, one of his ministers.
J. Barton

Scene 7

"The Vicar of Bray" upholds the Protestant Succession: Charles II (1649-1685), James II (1685-1688), William and Mary (1689-1702), Anne (1702-1714), George I (1714-1727).
R. Golding, J. Lawrenson, S. Manton

THE ILLUSTRIOUS HOUSE OF WINDSOR

Scene 8

Queen Caroline: The death of George II's wife
(*by* Lord Hervey)
P. Hardwick

Scene 9

George II (1727-1760) is buried in Westminster Abbey
(*by* Horace Walpole)
M. Adrian

Scene 10

George III (1760-1820) discusses the Arts with the novelist and diarist Fanny Burney.
D. Tutin

Scene 11

Eulogy on George III and the House of Hanover (Dedicated to Her Majesty Queen Charlotte)

Scene 12

The Regency (1811-1820): The Madness of George III (Marianne Thornton to E. M. Forster)
D. Tutin

Scene 13

William IV (1830-1837) makes a good start. (The Greville Memoirs)
P. Hardwick

THE VICTORIAN AGE

Scene 14

"Ballad to an Absent Friend"
R. Golding or J. Lawrenson
(*Music by* Albert, Prince Consort, with words by his brother, Ernest)

Scene 15

Victoria (1837-1901) describes her Coronation at the age of nineteen (from her private journal).
D. Tutin

Scene 16

Variations on "God Save the King"
(*Music by* Beethoven)
J. Walker (piano)

Scene 17

Epilogue: from the 'Morte D'Arthur'
(*by* Sir Thomas Malory)
M. Adrian, P. Hardwick, J. Barton

BRIGADOON

1963.04

A Revival of the Musical Play in Two Acts, a Prologue and 11 Scenes[18]. Book and lyrics by Alan Jay Lerner. Music by Frederick Loewe. Dance and musical numbers by Agnes de Mille, assisted by James Jamieson. Directed by John Fearnley. Settings by Oliver Smith. Costumes by Stanley Simmons. Lighting by Peggy Clark. Conductor, Julius Rudel. Assistant conductor, Rene Wiegert (Vocal arrangements by Frederick Loewe. Orchestrations by Ted Royal.) Produced by the New York City Center Light Opera Company (Jean Dalrymple, Director). Opened 30 January 1963 at the New York City Center and closed 10 February 1963 after 15 performances.

CAST (in order of appearance): *Tommy Albright*: PETER PALMER. *Jeff Douglas*: RUSSELL NYPE. *Sandy Dean*: William Kennedy. *Meg Brockie*: ANN FRASER. *Archie Beaton*: John Carver. *Harry Beaton*: EDWARD VILLELLA. *Andrew MacLaren*: Frank Milan. *Fiona MacLaren*: SALLY ANN HOWES. *Jean MacLaren*: Virginia Bosler. *Angus MacGuffie*: Daniel Hannafin. *Charlie Dalrymple*: HARRY DAVID SNOW. *Maggie Anderson*: Jenny Workman. *Sword Dancers*: Frank Andre, Ben Gillespie, Loren Hightower, Art Hutchinson, Vernon Lusby, Charles McGraw, Paul Olson. *Mr. Lundie*: John C. Becher. *Bagpiper*: Maurice Eisenstadt. *Frank*: Felice Orlandi. *Jane Ashton*: Kelly Stevens.

Townsfolk of Brigadoon: Singers: Penny Gaston, Helen Guile, Betsy Hepburn, Marilyne Mason, Hanna Owen, Julie Sargent, Betty Jane Schwering, Jamie Thomas, Lynn Wendall, Robert Carle, Jerry Crawford, Harry W. Davis, James Fels, Marvin Goodis, William Kennedy, Robert Lenn, Herbert Surface, Ralph Vucci. Dancers: Virginia Allen, Lucia Lambert, Loi Leabo, Diana Lee Nielson, Mavis Ray, Dorothy Scott, Evelyn Taylor, Mona Jo Tritsch, Esther Villavicencio, Toodie Wittmer, Frank Andre, Robert Charles Bishop, Dennis Cole, Ben Gillespie, José Gutierrez, Loren Hightower, Art Hutchinson, Vernon Lusby, Charles McCraw, Paul Olson.

WONDERFUL TOWN

1963.05

A Revival of the Musical Comedy in Two Acts, 13 Scenes[19]. Book by Joseph Fields and Jerome Chodorov. Based on the play "My Sister Eileen" by Joseph Fields and Jerome Chodorov and the stories by Ruth McKinney. Music by Leonard Bernstein. Lyrics by Betty Comden and Adolph Green. Directed by Gus Schirmer. Musical numbers and dances staged by Ralph Beaumont. Sets by Raoul Pene du Bois. Costumes by Ruth Morley. Lighting by Peggy Clark. Musical conductor, Lehman Engel. Associate conductor, James Leon. (Orchestrations by Don Walker.) Produced by the New York City Center Light Opera Company (Jean Dalrymple, Director). Opened 13 February 1963 at the New York City Center and closed 24 February 1963 after 15 performances.

CAST (in order of appearance): *Guide*: Warren Galjour. *Appopoulos*: PHIL LEEDS. *Lonigan*: Walter Kelvin. *Helen*: PAT TURNER. *Wreck*: STEWART ROSE. *Violet*: Betty Hyatt Linton. *Valenti*: Ted Beniades. *Eileen*: JACQUELYN McKEEVER. *Ruth*: KAYE BALLARD. *A Strange Man*: Eric Barnes. *Drunks*: Steve Elmore, Eric Barnes. *Robert Baker*: ROBERT KAYE. *Associate Editors*: Reid Shelton, Warren Galjour. *Mrs. Wade*: Paula Trueman. *Frank Lippencott*: JIM KIRKWOOD. *Chef*: Taylor Reed. *Waiter*: Vito Durante. *Delivery Boy*: Will Mackenzie. *Chick Clark*: Gabriel Dell. *Shore Patrolman*: Stephen Elmore. *First Cadet*: Dom Salinaro. *Second Cadet*: Jose Ahumada. *Policemen*: Warren Galjour, Reid Shelton. *Ruth's Escort*: Reid Shelton.

Greenwich Villagers: Singers: Darrell Jay Askey, Eric Barnes, James E. Carville, Norma Donaldson, Steve Elmore, Lynne Ephron, Maria Graziano, Ginger L. McFadden, Will Mackenzie, Larry Mitchell, Judy Rawlings, Taylor Reed, Will Roy, Patricia Sigris, Elise Warner. Dancers: Jose Ahumada, Guy Allen, Gerard Brentte, Vito Durante, Mercedes Ellington, Shellie Farrell, Barbara Heath, Sally Kirk, Svetlana McLee, Eleanor Rogers, Nanette Rosen, Dom Salinaro, Marc Scott, Mark Taylor, Pat Trott, Aura Vainio, Doug Weese, James E. M. Weiss.

OKLAHOMA!

1963.06

A Revival of the Musical Comedy in Two Acts, 6 Scenes[20]. Book and lyrics by Oscar Hammerstein II. Music by Richard Rodgers. Based on the play "Green Grow the Lilacs" by Lynn Riggs. Directed by John Fearnley. (Originally directed by Rouben Mamoulian.) Dances by Agnes de Mille, assisted by Mavis Ray. Conducted by Julius Rudel. Assistant conductor, Rudolph Bennett. Settings by Lemuel Ayers. Costumes by Stanley Simmons. Lighting by Peggy Clark. Produced by the New York City Center Light Opera Company (Jean Dalrymple, Director). Opened 27 February 1963 at the New York City Center and closed 10 March 1963 after 15 performances; re-opened a return engagement 15-26 May 1963 at the New York City Center for 15 additional performances. Total: 30 performances.

CAST (in order of appearance): *Aunt Eller*: BETTY GARDE. *Curly*: PETER PALMER. *Laurey*: LOUISE O'BRIEN. *Will Parker*: RICHARD FRANCE. *Jud Fry*: DANIEL P. HANNAFIN. *Ado Annie Carnes*: FAY DE WITT. *Ali Hakim*: BARRY NEWMAN *Gertie Cummings*: Marilyne Mason. *Curly* (in ballet): GROVER DALE. *Laurey* (in ballet): EVELYN TAYLOR. *Jud* (in ballet): GEORGE CHURCH. *The Child* (in ballet): Judy Thelen. *The Girl Who Falls Down*: Mavis Ray. *Andrew Carnes*: WILLIAM TIERNEY. *Cord Elam*: KERMIT KEGLEY.

Dancers: Virginia Bosler, Lucia Lambert, Loi Leabo, Beatrice Lismore, Marlene Messavage, Susana Aschieri, Judy Thelen, Mona Jo Tritsch, Esther Villavicencio, Toodie Wittmer, Frank Andre, Paul Berne, Dennis Cole, Ben Gillespie, Loren Hightower, Vernon Lusby, Charles McGraw, Paul Olson. Singers: Faith Daltry, Penny Gaston, Helen Guile, Marilyne Mason, Hanna Owen, Julie Sargent, Sharon J. Vaughn, Christine Watson, Lynn Wendell, Robert Carle, Jerry Crawford, Harris W. Davis, James Fels, Marvin Goodis, William Kennedy, Robert Lenn, Herbert Surface, Ralph Vucci.

JACK BENNY

1963.07

A Variety Revue in Two Acts, 10 Scenes. Design and lighting by Sam Leve. Musical director, Mahlon Merrick. Producer (for Jack Benny), Irving Fein. Presented by Theatre Guild Productions, Inc. (Don Herbert). Opened 27 February 1963 at the Ziegfeld Theatre and closed 6 April 1963 after 52 performances.

---

[18]Originally produced in New York 13 March 1947 at the Ziegfeld Theatre for 581 performances. For Synopsis of Scenes and Musical Numbers, see original 1947 production.

[19]Originally produced in New York 25 February 1953 at the Winter Garden for 559 performances. For Synopsis of Scenes and Musical Numbers, see original 1953 production.

[20]Originally produced in New York 31 March 1943 at the St. James Theatre for 2212 performances. For Synopsis of Scenes and Musical Numbers, see original 1943 production.

CAST: JACK BENNY, JANE MORGAN, Toni Marcus, Clara Ward and the Ward Singers[21], the Half Brothers (Roberto and Al Halfss).

ACT 1

Scene 1

The Half Brothers (Juggling Act)

Scene 2

A Few Minutes With Jack Benny (Comedy)

Scene 3

A Few Songs with Jane Morgan ("Fascination," etc.)

Scene 4

Jane Morgan and Jack Benny

Scene 5

Clara Ward and the Ward Singers

ACT 2

Scene 1

Jack Benny Again

Scene 2

Jane Morgan Again

Scene 3

Buck Benny and the Waukegan Hillbillies with Toni Marcus

Scene 4

Jack Benny and Toni Marcus (Violinist)("Getting to Know You")

Scene 5

Jack Benny

1963.08 ## TOVARICH

A Musical Comedy in Two Acts, a Prologue and 14 Scenes. Book by David Shaw. Based on the play of the same name by Jacques Deval and its English adaptation by Robert E. Sherwood. Music by Lee Pockriss. Lyrics by Anne Croswell. Directed by Peter Glenville. Dances and musical numbers staged by Herbert Ross. Production designed by Rolf Gerard. Costumes by Motley. Lighting by John Harvey. Vocal arrangements and musical direction by Stanley Lebowsky. Orchestrations by Philip J. Lang. Dance music by Lee Pockriss. Additional dance music, Dorothea Freitag. Associate producer, Monty Shaff. Produced by Abel Farbman and Sylvia Harris in association with Joseph P. Harris. Opened 18 March 1963 at the Broadway Theatre, moved 10 June 1963 to the Majestic Theatre, moved 7 October 1963 to the Winter Garden, and closed 9 November 1963 after 264 performances.

CAST (in order of appearance): *Gorotchenko*: ALEXANDER SCOURBY. *Vassily*: Paul Michael. *Mikail*: JEAN PIERRE AUMONT. *Admiral Boris Soukhomine*: Michael Kermoyan. *Count Ivan Shamforoff*: Gene Varrone. *Baroness Roumel*: Katia Geleznova. *Marina*: Rita Metzger. *M. Chauffourier-Dubieff*: Don McHenry. *Tatiana*: VIVIEN LEIGH. *Natalia Mayovskaya*: LOUISE TROY. *Helen Davis*: MARGERY GRAY. *George Davis*: BYRON MITCHELL. *Charles Davis*: GEORGE S. IRVING. *Grace Davis*: LOUISE KIRTLAND. *Louise*: Maggie Task. *Ballet Master*: Tom Abbott. *Nadia*: Barbara Monte. *Mme. Van Hemert*: Pat [Patricia] Kelly. *Mme. Van Steuben*: Eleonore Treiber. *The Footman at the Davis Home*: Harald Horn. *Night Club Singer*: Dale Malone. *Kukla Katusha*: Bette Jenkins. *Ivan*: William Reilly. *Sergei*: Larry Roquemore. *Kukla's Friends*: Lorenzo Bianco, Antony De Vecchi, William Glassman. *A Footman at the Grand Ball*: Elliott Savage. *Baron General Rasumov*: Harald Horn. *Baroness Rasumov*: Michele Franchi. *Prince Dobrynin*: Antony De Vecchi. *Princess Dobrynin*: Marion Fels. *General Boruvsky*: Dale Malone. *Madame Boruvsky*: Eleonore Treiber. *Count Yuriev Neglinsky*: Tom Abbott. *Lady Soukhomine*: Joan Trona. *Maria Soukhomine*: Bettye Jenkins. *Count Rostoff*: Will Parkins. *Madame Muratova*: Carol Flemming. *Essaul of Cossacks Volinin*: Lorenzo Bianco. *Katrina Volinin*: Barbara Monte. *Elena Volinin*: Charlene Mehl. *Princess Mondrovska*: Pat Kelly. *Igor Mondovsky of the Imperial Corps of Cadets*: William Glassman. *Prince Ossipovsky*: Larry Roquemore. *Colonel Yarov*: William Reilly.

Singing Ensemble: Alice Evans, Pat Kelly, Rita Metzger, Maggie Task, Joan Trona, Del Horstmann, Barney Johnston, Jeff Killion, Dale Malone, Elliott Savage. *Dancing Ensemble*: Marion Fels, Carol Flemming, Michele Franchi, Katia Geleznova, Bette Jenkins, Charlene Mehl, Barbara Monte, Barbara Richman, Eleonore Treiber, Tom Abbott, Lorenzo Bianco, Antony De Vecchi, Harald Horn, William Glassman, Will Parkins, William Reilly, Larry Roquemore.

---

[21]Withdrew from production during the run.

Prologue: Russia.

Act 1, Scene 1: Tsar Nicholas II's Room at the Palace of Tsarskoe Selo. *Scene 2*: A Garret in Paris, the late 1920s. *Scene 3*: A Corridor in the House of Mr. and Mrs. Davis, Paris. *Scene 4*: The Drawing Room of the Davis House. *Scene 5*: The Rehearsal Room in the Basement of the Kasbek Cafe, Paris. *Scene 6*: The Wintergarden in the Davis House. *Scene 7*: The Drawing Room.

Act 2, Scene 1: A Street Outside the Kasbek Cafe. *Scene 2*: The Club Room of the Kasbek Cafe. *Scene 3*: A Street Outside the Kasbek Cafe. *Scene 4*: The Drawing Room of the Davis House. *Scene 5*: A Street in Paris. *Scene 6*: The Kitchen of the Davis House. *Scene 7*: A Ballroom.

ACT 1

"Nitchevo"

J. P. Aumont, M. Kermoyan, G. Varrone, R. Metzger, Singing and Dancing Ensembles

"I Go To Bed"

J. P. Aumont

"You'll Make an Elegant Butler (And I'll Make an Elegant Maid)"

V. Leigh

(*Music and Lyrics by* Joan Javits and Phillip Springer.)

"Stuck With Each Other"

M. Gray, B. Mitchell

"Say You'll Stay"

L. Kirtland, G. S. Irving

"You Love Me"

V. Leigh, J. P. Aumont

"Introduction Tango"

V. Leigh, M. Gray, J. P. Aumont, B. Mitchell

"That Face"

L. Troy

"Wilkes-Barre, P.A."

V. Leigh, B. Mitchell

"No! No! No!"

M. Gray, J. P. Aumont

"A Small Cartel"

L. Kirtland, G. S. Irving, Singing Ensemble

ACT 2

"It Used To Be"

M. Kermoyan, G. Varrone, L. Troy, P. Michael

"Kukla Katusha"

Dancing Ensemble

"Make a Friend"

V. Leigh, M. Gray, L. Troy, J. P. Aumont, B. Mitchell, M. Kermoyan, G. Varrone, L. Roquemore, W. Reilly

"The Only One"

V. Leigh

"Uh-Oh!"

M. Gray, B. Mitchell

"Managed"

J. P. Aumont

"I Know the Feeling"

V. Leigh

"All for You"

V. Leigh, J. P. Aumont

"Grand Polonaise"

M. Gray, L. Kirtlnad, B. Mitchell, G. S. Irving, Dancing Ensemble

MOTHER COURAGE AND HER CHILDREN

1963.09

A Chronicle of the Thirty Years War (A Play with Songs) in Two Acts, a Prologue and 12 Scenes. Original (German) Play by Bertolt Brecht, adapted (into English) by Eric Bentley. Music by Paul Dessau. Directed by Jerome Robbins. Settings by Ming Cho Lee. Costumes designed by Motley. Lighting by Tharon Musser. Musical direction by Samuel Matlovsky. Produced by Cheryl Crawford and Jerome Robbins. Opened 28 March 1963 at the Martin Beck Theatre and closed 11 May 1963 after 52 performances.

CAST (in order of appearance): *Prologue*: *Mother Courage*: ANNE BANCROFT. *Kattrin*: ZOHRA LAMPERT. *Eilif*: Conrad Bromberg. *Swiss Cheese*: James Catusi. *Scene 1*: *Recruiting Officer*: John Randolph. *Protestant Sergeant*: Louis Guss. *Scene 2*: *Cook*: MIKE KELLIN. *Swedish Commander*: Eugene Roche. *Chaplain*: GENE

139

WILDER. *Scene 3: Ordnance Officer:* Benjamin Hammer. *Yvette Pottier:* BARBARA HARRIS. *One Eye:* John Harkins. *Catholic Sergeant:* Bruce Glover. *Old Colonel:* Donald Hotton. *Scene 4: Regimental Clerk:* Harry Eno. *Older Soldier:* Benjamin Hammer. *Young Soldier:* Bruce Glover. *Scene 5: First Soldier:* Donald Hotton. *Second Soldier:* Eugene Roche. *Peasant:* John Randolph. *Peasant Woman:* Jane Hoffman. *Act 2, Scene 1: Old Woman:* Jane Hoffman. *Young Man:* Richard Morse. *First Soldier:* John Randolph. *Second Soldier:* Eugene Roche. *Scene 3: Girl Singer:* BARBARA HARRIS. *Scene 4: Lieutenant:* John Harkins. *First Soldier:* Bruce Glover. *Second Soldier:* Donald Hotton. *Third Soldier:* Dick Bradford. *Peasant Woman:* Jane Hoffman. *Peasant:* Louis Guss. *Young Peasant:* Harry Eno.

Act 1, Scene 1: Sweden, 1624. A Highway. *Scene 2:* Poland, 1626. An Officer's Tent. *Scene 3:* Poland, 1626. A Camp. *Scene 4:* Poland, 1629. An Officer's Tent. *Scene 5:* Saxony, 1631. A War-Ravaged Village. *Scene 6:* Bavaraia, 1632. Inside a Tent. *Scene 7:* The same.

Act 2, Scene 1: Alsace, 1632. A Camp. *Scene 2:* Fichtelgebirge, 1634. A Village. *Scene 3:* Fichtelgebirge, 1635. A Highway. *Scene 4:* Saxony, 1636. A Farm. *Scene 5:* Saxony, 1636. The Same Farm.

ACT 1

Scene 1

"Song of Mother Courage"
A. Bancroft

Scene 2

"Song of the Wise Woman and the Soldier"
C. Bromberg

Scene 3

"The Fraternization Song"
B. Harris

"The Song of the Hours"
G. Wilder

Scene 4

"Song of the Great Capitulation"
A. Bancroft

Scene 6

("Emperor Song"/Ballad of the Soldier)
(D. Hotton)

Scene 7

"Song of Mother Courage" (reprise)
A. Bancroft

ACT 2

Scene 1

("Song of Mother Courage" reprise)
(A. Bancroft)

Scene 2

"The Song of the Great Souls of the Earth"
M. Kellin

Scene 3

(Farm Song)
B. Harris

Scene 5

"Lullaby, Baby"
A. Bancroft

"Song of Mother Courage" (reprise)
A. Bancroft

1963.10 DANNY KAYE

A Variety Revue in Two Acts, 4 Scenes. Lighting by David Bines. Choral arrangements and musical direction by Johnny Mann. Girls' fashions by Mr. Mort. (Producer uncredited.) Opened 10 April 1963 at the Ziegfeld Theatre and closed 11 May 1963 after 39 performances.

CAST: DANNY KAYE, SENOR WENCES, THE DUNHILLS (Art Stanley, John Buwen, Jerry Kurland), THE MARQUIS FAMILY, THE JOHNNY MANN SINGERS (Gloria Gilbert, Pat Morling, Karen Wessler, Kelly Wood, Bill DeBell, John Guarnieri, David McDaniel, Tom Traynor, Dick Wessler, Ted Wills). At the piano, Sammy Prager. *At the drums:* Sidney Kaye.

ACT 1

Scene 1

The Dunhills (Dance Trio)

Scene 2

The Marquis Family (Monkey Act; Trainer, Gene Detroy)

Scene 3

Senor Wences (Ventriloquist)

ACT 2[22]

Danny Kaye (with the Johnny Mann Singers):

"Glory Hallelujah Twist"

"Minnie the Moocher"
(*Music and Lyrics by* Cab Calloway, Clarence Gaskill, Irving Mills.)

"I Took My Love to See 'Who's Afraid of Virginia Woolf?'" (Madrigal)

"Tschaikowsky" (from LADY IN THE DARK)
(*Music by* Kurt Weill. *Lyrics by* Ira Gershwin.)

"Dry Bones"

Yoga sketch

Maurice Chevalier impression

"Begin the Beguine" (from JUBILEE)
(*Music and Lyrics by* Cole Porter.)

Harry Lauder impression

Japanese Television Western

"Zoom"

Ludvig von Schtickfritz (Psychiatrist from Dusseldorf)

1963.11 MAN IN THE MOON

A Puppet Musical Entertainment in Two Acts, by Bil and Cora Baird's Marionette Theatre. Book by Arthur Burns. Based on a story by Bil Baird. Music by Jerry Bock. Lyrics by Sheldon Harnick. Directed by Gerald Freedman. (Musical) Arrangements by Alvy West. Produced by Arthur Cantor and Joseph P. Harris. Opened 11 April 1963 at the Biltmore Theatre and closed 21 April 1963 after 7 performances.

CAST: *Act 1: Prologue:* Frank Sullivan. *Jerry:* Franz Fazakas. *Flicker Martin:* Bil Baird. *Sleeves:* Michael King. *Skin:* Bob Brown. *Happy:* Faz Korabel. *Nose Nolan:* Frank Sullivan. *Fluffy:* Franz Fazakas. *Mondo:* Bil Baird. *Chandra:* Cora Baird. *The Man in the Moon:* Frank Sullivan. *Buz:* Waxey Gibbons. *The Giant:* Emil Maurer. *Assosrted Moonbirds, Hi-Behinds, Gollywhoppers:* Carl Harms, George Baird, Bob Brown, Mike King.

ACT 1

MAN IN THE MOON

"Look Where I Am"

"Itch to Be Rich"

"Worlds Apart"

"You Treacherous Men"

"Ain't You Never Been Afraid?"

ACT 2

A pageant of puppetry which will include various characters from Asia, Africa, Europe, and both Americas, to be accompanied by classical, folk, and popular music and during which the puppeteers will disclose some of the secrets of the world of marionettes.

1963.12 SOPHIE

A Musical in Two Acts, 20 Scenes. Book by Phillip Bruneau. Based on the life of Sophie Tucker. Music and Lyrics by Steve Allen. Directed by Jack Sydow. Dances and musical numbers staged by Donald Saddler. Settings and lighting by Robert Randolph. Costumes by Fred Voelpel. Musical direction and vocal arrangements by Liza Redfield. (Musical) Arrangements and orchestrations by Sid Ramin and Arthur Beck. Dance music arrangements by Genevieve Pitot. Produced by Len Bedsow and Hal Grossman in association with Michael Pollock and Max Fialkov. Opened 15 April 1963 at the Winter Garden and closed 20 April 1963 after 8 performances.

---

[22]Inasmuch as Danny Kaye's material was not listed in the program, the above list is not in performance order and was prepared from reviews.

CAST (in order of appearance): *Sophie Tucker*: LIBI STAIGER. *Moe*: Douglas Clarke. *Mama*: BERTA GERSTEN. *William Morris*: PHIL LEEDS. *Theona*: Diana Hunter. *Mrs. Quive*: Urylee Leonardos. *Schmidt*: Don Crabtree. *Policemen*: Nat Horne, Ralph McWilliams. *Chris Brown*: TED THURSTON. *Stage Manager*: John Drew. *Girl*: Bella Shalom. *Mother*: Janet Gaylord. *Acrobat*: Tim Harum. *Sylvain Krouse*: PATSI KING. *Stagehand*: Jordan Bowers. *Juggler*: Stuart Hodes. *Mollie*: ROSETTA LeNOIRE. *Marcus Loew*: DAVID THOMAS. *Mickey Muldoon*: EDDIE ROLL. *Harry Emerson*: DAVID THOMAS. *Frank Westphal*: ART LUND. *Queenie*: Maralyn Thoma. *Julian Mitchell*: TED THURSTON. *Sandy*: Richard Hermany. *Nora Bayes*: Betty Colby. *Stella*: Diana Hunter. *Mr. Kilby*: DAVID THOMAS. *Reporters*: Don Crabtree, John Drew, Richard Hermany. *Theatre Manager*: TED THURSTON. *Ted*: Michael Nestor. *Metropole Manager*: DAVID THOMAS.

Ensemble: Jordan Bowers, Carol Carlin, Douglas Clarke, Betty Colby, John Drew, Louise Ferrand, Janet Gaylord, Ellen Graff, Tim Harum, Florence Hayle, Richard Hermany, Stuart Hodes, Nat Horne, Diana Hunter, Urylee Leonardos, Ralph McWilliams, Michael Nestor, Kelli Scott, Beti Seay, Bella Shalom, Maralyn Thoma, Elizabeth Wullen.

The action of the play covers the early years of Sophie Tucker's preofessional life.

Act 1, Scene 1: Sophie Tucker Tonight. *Scene 2*: The Family Restaurant in Hartford. *Scene 3*: Sophie in New York. *Scene 4*: Backstage 125th Street Theatre. *Scene 5*: Theatre Alley. *Scene 6*: Third Avenue "El." *Scene 7*: A Street. *Scene 8*: Gaiety Burlesque Theatre. *Scene 9*: Sophie Trouping. *Scene 10*: Backstage Ziegfeld Follies.

Act 2, Scene 1: Roof of a Theatrical Hotel. *Scene 2*: Frank's Dressing Room. *Scene 3*: Sophie's Dressing Room. *Scene 4*: Freeport Variety Club. *Scene 5*: Hartford Railroad Station. *Scene 6*: Dressing Rooms and On Stage. *Scene 7*: Freeport Variety Club. *Scene 8*: Dockside. *Scene 9*: Dressing Room in London. *Scene 10*: Cafe Metropole, London.

ACT 1
"Red Hot Mama"
 L. Staiger
"Sunshine Face"
 L. Staiger
"Mr. Henry Jones"
 L. Staiger
"Sophie in New York"
 L. Staiger, Company
"Patsy"
 R. LeNoire
"I'll Show Them All"
 L. Staiger
"I'll Show Them All" (reprise)
 L. Staiger
"Hold Onto Your Hats"
 P. Leeds, R. LeNoire
"Fast Cars and Fightin' Women"
 A. Lund
"Queen of the Burlesque Wheel"
 P. King, Ensemble
"When You Carry Your Own Suitcase"
 L. Staiger, E. Roll, Ensemble
"When You Carry Your Own Suitcase" (reprise)
 A. Lund
"When I'm in Love"
 L. Staiger, R. LeNoire
"Sailors of the Sea"
 Ensemble
"I Want the Kind of a Fella"
 L. Staiger
"I'll Show Them All" (reprise)
 L. Staiger

ACT 2
"Who Are We Kidding"
 E. Roll, P. King
"Don't Look Back"
 Entire Company
"I'd Know It"
 A. Lund
"You've Got to Be a Lady"
 R. LeNoire
"Ragtime"
 Ensemble

"Waltz"
 L. Staiger, A. Lund, Ensemble
"When I'm in Love" (reprise)
 A. Lund
"I Love You Today"
 L. Staiger, A. Lund
"With You"
 L. Staiger
"Red Hot Mama" (reprise)
 L. Staiger
"I've Got 'Em Standin' in Line"
 L. Staiger
"They've Got a Lot to Learn"
 A. Lund
"Red Hot Mama" (reprise)
 L. Staiger

1963.13

HOT SPOT

A Musical Comedy in Two Acts, 24 Scenes. Book by Jack Weinstock and Willie Gilbert. Music by Mary Rodgers. Lyrics by Martin Charnin. Scenery and costumes by Rouben Ter-Arutunian. Lighting by John Harvey. Musical director, Milton Rosenstock. Dance music and vocal arrangements by Trude Rittman and John Morris. (Musical) Arrangements and orchestrations by Luther Henderson and Ralph Burns. Produced by Robert Fryer and Lawrence Carr with John Herman. Opened 19 April 1963 at the Majestic Theatre and closed 25 May 1963 after 43 performances[23].

CAST (in order of appearance): *Anderson*: James Cresson. *Henderson*: Charles Braswell. *Sally Hopwinder*: JUDY HOLLIDAY. *George Higgins*: Conrad Bain. *The Peace Corps* (3): *Sue Ann*: MARY LOUISE WILSON. *Howard Mason*: Bob McClure. *Vernon Breen*: James Moore. *Harley, the pilot*: George Furth. *Duke, the co-pilot*: James Cresson. *The D'humians* (4): *Nadir of D'hum*: ARNY FREEMAN. *Shim*: JOSEPH BOVA. *Ministers of State*: Jack Dabdoub, Howard Kahl. *Deva*: Jack Eddleman. *Iram and Rami*: Carmen DeLavallade, Buzz Miller. *Gabriel Snapper*: JOSEPH CAMPANELLA. *Sumner Tubb, Sr.*: HOWARD FREEMAN. *Mrs. Sumner Tubb*: Virginia Craig. *Sumner Tubb, Jr.*: George Furth. *Allison Kent*: Sheila Smith. *Grobanykov*: Gerald Teijelo. *Pulski*: Buzz Miller.

Singers and Dancers: Sandra Devlin, Jill Bartholomew, Virginia Craig, Audre Johnston, Virginia Oswald, John Herbert, Diane Ede, Gloria Mills, Diane Coupe, Dean Taliaferro, Gildo DiNunzio, Marty Allen, Rhett Dennis, David Bean, Jim McArdle, Doria Avila, Bill Richards, Alvin Beam, Jamie Landi, Lee Hopper, Mary Sue Berry, Marnell Bruce, John Cunningham, Frank Bouley.

Act 1, Scene 1: The 6:45 Report. *Scene 2*: Peace Corps Headquarters. *Scene 3*: national Airport. *Scene 4*: In the air over D'hum. *Scene 5*: The D'hum Airstrip. *Scene 6*: The American Consulate in D'hum. *Scene 7*: The Market Place. *Scene 8*: The Clinic. *Scene 9*: The D'hum Airstrip. *Scene 10*: The Palace. *Scene 11*: The 6:45 Report. *Scene 12*: A Beauty Salon in Washington. *Scene 13*: All of D'hum.

Act 2, Scene 1: Exterior of Yakacabana. *Scene 2*: Interior of Yakacabana. *Scene 3*: Moscow. *Scene 4*: A Street in D'hum. *Scene 5*: The back room of the Clinic. *Scene 6*: Snapper's Apartment at the Consulate. *Scene 7*: Outside the Yakacabana. *Scene 8*: The Yakacabana. *Scene 9*: The 6:45 Report. *Scene 10*: The Consulate Yard. *Scene 11*: Peace Corps Headquarters.

ACT 1
"Don't Laugh"
 J. Holliday
 (Music by Mary Rodgers and Stephen Sondheim. Lyrics by Martin Charnin and Stephen Sondheim.)
"Don't Laugh" (reprise)
 J. Holliday, Peace Corps
"Welcome"
 D'humians
Welcome Dance
 C. DeLavallade, J. Moore, B. Miller
"This Little Yankee"
 J. Campanella

---

[23]Direction and choreography uncredited at time of the opening; Morton DaCosta and Onna White withdrew as director and choreographer prior to opening.

"Smiles"
  J. Holliday, J. Eddleman, J. Cunningham, H. Kahl,
  B. McClure, J. Herbert, D. Bean, A. Beam, B. Miller
"A Little Trouble"
  J. Holliday, J. Bova, A. Freeman, D'humians
"You'd Like Nebraska"
  J. Moore, C. DeLavallade
"Hey, Love"
  J. Holliday
"I Had Two Dregs"
  J. Holliday, J. Bova, H. Freeman, D'humians
"Rich, Rich, Rich"
  J. Bova, M. L. Wilson, Peace Corps, D'humians

ACT 2
"That's Good—That's Bad"
  J. Holliday
Iram and the Royal D'humian Dancers
  C. DeLavallade, (Dancers)
"I Think the World of You"
  M. L. Wilson, J. Bova
"Gabie"
  J. Holliday
"A Matter of Time"
  J. Campanella, J. Holliday
"Gabie" (reprise)
  J. Campanella
"Big Meeting Tonight"
  B. Miller, G. Teijelo, Ensemble
Russian Dance at the Yakacabana
  J. Holliday, B. Miller, G. Teijelo
"A Far, Far Better Way"
  J. Holliday
"Don't Laugh" (reprise)
  J. Holliday, J. Campanella, Ensemble

SHE LOVES ME

1963.14

A Musical Comedy in Two Acts. Book by Joe Masteroff. Based on the play "Parfumerie" by Miklos Laszlo[24]. Music by Jerry Bock. Lyrics by Sheldon Harnick. Musical numbers Staged by Carol Haney. Directed by Harold Prince. Settings and lighting by William and Jean Eckart. Costumes by Patricia Zipprodt. Musical direction by Harold Hastings. Orchestrations by Don Walker. Incidental music arranged by Jack Elliott. Produced by Harold Prince in association with Lawrence Kasha and Philip C. McKenna. Opened 23 April 1963 at the Eugene O'Neill Theatre and closed 11 January 1964 after 301 performances.

CAST (in order of appearance): *Arpad:* RALPH WILLIAMS. *Mr. Sipos:* NATHANIEL FREY. *Miss Ritter:* BARBARA BAXLEY. *Mr. Kodaly:* JACK CASSIDY. *Georg Nowack:* DANIEL MASSEY. *Mr. Maraczek:* LUDWIG DONATH. *Window Shoppers:* Jety Herlick, Judy West. *First Customer:* Marion Delano. *Second Customer:* Peg Murray. *Third Customer:* Trude Adams. *Amalia Balash:* BARBARA COOK. *Fourth Customer:* Judy West. *Fifth Customer:* Jety Herlick. *Sixth Customer:* Vicki Mansfield. *Mr. Keller:* Gino Conforti. *Waiter:* Wood Romoff. *Busboy:* Al De Sio. *Violinist:* Gino Conforti. *Viktor:* Pepe De Chazza. *Stefanie:* Vicki Mansfield. *Magda:* Judy West. *Ferencz:* Bob Bishop. *Couple:* Peg Murray, Joe Ross. *Nurse:* Jety Herlick. *Carolers:* Jo Wilder, Joe Ross, Gino Conforti. *Paul:* Les Martin.

The action takes place in a city in Europe in the 1930s (inside and outside Maraczek's Parfumerie, the Cafe Imperiale, a hospital room and Miss Balash's apartment).

ACT 1
"Good Morning, Good Day"
  R. Williams, N. Frey, B. Baxley, J. Cassidy, D. Massey
"Sounds While Selling"
  D. Massey, N. Frey, J. Cassidy, M. Delano, P. Murray, T. Adams
"Thank You, Madam"
  N. Frey, D. Massey, J. Cassidy, B. Baxley, M. Delano, P. Murray
"Days Gone By"
  L. Donath

"No More Candy"
  B. Cook
"Three Letters"
  B. Cook, D. Massey
"Tonight at Eight"
  D. Massey
"I Don't Know His Name"
  B. Cook, B. Baxley
"Perspective"
  N. Frey
"Goodbye Georg"
  D. Massey, B. Baxley, N. Frey, J. Cassidy, R. Williams, Customers
"Will He Like Me?"
  B. Cook
"Ilona"
  J. Cassidy
"I Resolve"
  B. Baxley
"A Romantic Atmosphere"
  W. Romoff, A. DeSio, G. Conforti, P. Murray,
  J. Ross, V. Mansfield, P. DeChazza, J. West, B. Bishop
"Tango Tragique"
  D. Massey
"Dear Friend"
  B. Cook

ACT 2
"Try Me"
  R. Williams
"Days Gone By" (reprise)
  L. Donath
"Where's My Shoe?"
  B. Cook, D. Massey
"(Vanilla) Ice Cream"
  B. Cook
"She Loves Me"
  D. Massey
"A Trip to the Library"
  B. Baxley
"Grand Knowing You"
  J. Cassidy
"Twelve Days to Christmas"
  J. West, G. Conforti, J. Ross, Company
"Ice Cream" (reprise){Finale}
  B. Cook, D. Massey

STREET SCENE

1963.15

A Revival of the American Opera (Dramatic Musical) in Two Acts, 3 Scenes[25]. Book by Elmer Rice from his play of the same name. Music by Kurt Weill. Lyrics by Langston Hughes. Staged by Herbert Machiz. Conducted by Skitch Henderson. Scenery and costumes by Paul Sylbert. Choreographed by Sondra Lee and Richard Tone. Chorus master, William Jonson. (Orchestrations by Kurt Weill.) Produced by the New York City Opera. Opened 26 April 1963 at the New York City Center and closed 10 May 1963 after 3 performances in repertory.

CAST (in order of appearance): *Abraham Kaplan:* Howard Fried. *Greta Fiorentino:* Dolores Mari. *Carl Olsen:* Arnold Voketaitis. *Emma Jones:* RUTH KOBART. *Olga Olsen:* Muriel Greenspon. *Shirley Kaplan:* Florence Anglin. *Henry Davis:* Andrew Frierson. *Willie Maurrant:* Robert Buckley. *Anna Maurrant:* ELISABETH CARRON. *Sam Kaplan:* William DuPree. *Daniel Buchanan:* L. D. Clements. *Frank Maurrant:* ROBERT TREHY. *George Jones:* Richard Wentworth. *Steve Sankey:* Richard Armbruster. *Lippo Fiorentino:* JACK HARROLD. *Jennie Hildebrand:* Barbara Maier. *Second Graduate:* Anthea DeForest. *Third Graduate:* Marilyn Mason. *Mrs. Hildebrand:* Anita Lynch. *Charlie Hildebrand:* Charles Cash. *Mary Hildebrand:* Neva Small. *Grace Davis:* Andrea Frierson. *Rose Maurrant:* JOY CLEMENTS. *Harry Easter:* John Reardon. *Mae Jones:* Sondra Lee. *Dick McGann:* Richard Tone. *Vincent Jones:* Albert

---

[24]Elsewhere known as "The Honest Finder" by Aladar Laszlo.

[25]Originally produced in New York 9 January 1947 at the Adelphi Theatre for 148 performances. For Synopsis of Scenes and Musical Numbers, see original 1947 production.

Lewis. *Dr. John Wilson*: Glenn Dowlen. *Officer Harry Murphy*: David Smith. *City Marshall James Henry*: Arthur Graham. *Fred Cullen*: Don Yule. *First Nursemaid*: Helen Guile. *Second Nursemaid*: Lou Ann Wyckoff. *Policemen, Milkman, Old Clothes Man, Music Pupil, Interne, Ambulance Driver, Married Couple, Passersby, Neighbors, Children, etc.*: New York City Opera Chorus.

1963.16 THE BEAST IN ME

A Musical Revue in Two Acts, 11 Scenes. Book and lyrics by James Costigan. Based on the book "Fables for Our Time" by James Thurber. Music by Don Elliott. Conceived by Haila Stoddard. Directed by John Lehne. Musical staging by John Butler. Settings and lighting by Jean Rosenthal. Costumes by Leo Van Witsen. Orchestrations by Bill Byers. Dance arrangements by Judd Woldin. Musical director, Don Elliott. Conductor, Lehman Engel. Produced by Bonard Productions (Helen G. Bonfils, Haila Stoddard, Donald R. Seawell). Opened 16 May 1963 at the Plymouth Theatre and closed 18 May 1963 after 4 performances.

CAST: KAYE BALLARD, ALLYN ANN McLERIE, RICHARD HAYES, BERT CONVY, NANCY HAYWOOD, JAMES COSTIGAN, DON ELLIOTT and His Orchestra.

ACT 1
Scene 1

There's a Beast in Everybody
Entire Company
Scene 2

The Sea and the Shore
Gibbous Female: K. Ballard. *Gibbous Male*: R. Hayes.
Scene 3

The Lover and His Lass
Mrs. Hippo: K. Ballard. *Hippo*: R. Hayes. *Mrs. Parrot*: A. A. McLerie. *Parrot*: B. Convy. *Girl*: N. Haywood.
Scene 4

The Lady of the Legs
Tourist: R. Hayes. *Frog*: A. A. McLerie. *Restauranteur*: J. Costigan.
Scene 5

Tea for One
Bride: K. Ballard. *Groom*: R. Hayes.
Scene 6

The Wolf Who Went Places
Professor: R. Hayes. *Wolf*: B. Convy. *Wolfess*: A. A. McLerie.
Scene 7

The Unicorn in the Garden
Man: J. Costigan. *Wife*: K. Ballard. *Dr. Clisbie*: R. Hayes. *Policeman*: B. Convy. *Nymphs*: A. A. McLerie, N. Haywood.
ACT 2
Scene 1

The Foolhardy Mouse and the Cautious Cat
Pouncetta: A. A. McLerie. *Mervyn*: J. Costigan. *Ring Leader*: R. Hayes. *The Gang*: K. Ballard, N. Haywood, B. Convy.
Scene 2

A Moment With Mandy
Mandy: K. Ballard. *Daddy*: B. Convy.
Scene 3

The Moth and the Star
Old Moth: J. Costigan. *Mother Moth*: A. A. McLerie. *Father Moth*: R. Hayes.

Scene 4

The Stork Who Married a Dumb Wife
Cigarette Girl: A. A. McLerie. *Spouse*: K. Ballard. *Stork*: R. Hayes. *The Girl*: N. Haywood. *Mysterious Stranger*: B. Convy. *Waiter*: J. Costigan.
Scene 5

The Shore and the Sea
Evangelist: K. Ballard. *Scholarly Lemming*: J. Costigan. *Congregation*: A. A. McLerie, N. Haywood, R. Hayes, B. Convy.
ACT 1
"Percussion"
"So Beautiful"
"You're Delicious"
"J'Ai"
"I Owe Ohio"
"Go, Go, Go!"
"Breakfast"
"Eat Your Nice Lily, Unicorn"
"Bacchanale"
ACT 2
"Calypso Kitty"
"Glorious Cheese"
"Why?"
"What Do You Say"
"When I'm Alone"
"Hallelujah"

1963.17 PAL JOEY

A Revival of the Musical Play in Two Acts, 12 Scenes[26]. Book by John O'Hara based on his collected short stories of the same name. Music by Richard Rodgers. Lyrics by Lorenz Hart. Settings by Howard Bay. Costumes by Frank Thompson. Lighting by Peggy Clark. Musical director and conductor, Pembroke Davenport. (Orchestrations by Don Walker, Hans Spialek.) Choreography by George and Ethel Martin. Directed by Gus Schirmer. Produced by the New York City Center Light Opera Company (Jean Dalrymple, Director). Opened 29 May 1963 at the New York City Center and closed 9 June 1963 after 15 performances.

CAST (in order of appearance): *Mike*: ART BARNETT. *Joey Evans*: BOB FOSSE. *Kid*: Pat Turner. *Gladys*: ELAINE DUNN. *Iris*: Dorothy D'Honau. *Mickey*: Carol Kroon. *Diane*: Dorothy Dushock. *Dottie*: Shellie Farrell. *Sandra*: Mercedes Ellington. *Adele*: Jan LaPrade. *Francine*: Marilyn D'Honau. *Linda English*: RITA GARDNER. *Vera Simpson*: VIVECA LINDFORS. *Valerie*: Betty Hyatt Linton. *Ernest*: Emory Bass. *Vera's Escort*: John Coyle. *Victor*: Charles Basile. *Scholtz*: George Zima. *Louis, the Tenor*: John Lankston. *Melba Snyder*: KAY MEDFORD. *Ludlow Lowell*: JACK DURANT. *Lester*: Lester Wilson. *O'Brien*: George Church. *Mr. Hoople*: John D. Seymour.

Dancers: Nancy Baron, Carol Carlin, Sheila Cass, Dorothy D'Honau, Marilyn D'Honau, Dorothy Dushock, Mercedes Ellington, Shellie Farrell, Judith Haskell, Carole Kroon, Jan LaPrade, Sigyn Lund, Carmen Morales, Barbara Richman, Patricia Sigris, Babs Warden. Alan Castner, Gerard Brentte, John Coyle, Larry Davids, Hamp Dickens, Jim Hovis, Danny Jasinski, David M. Lober, Paul Reid Roman, Bentley Roton, Roy Smith, George Zima.

---

[26]Originally produced in New York 25 December 1940 at the Ethel Barrymore Theatre for 374 performances. For Synopsis of Scenes and Musical Numbers, see original 1940 production. "What Is a Man" succeeded "Love Is My Friend" in Act 1, Scene 4; "Pal Joey" ("What Do I Care for a Dame?" sung by B. Fosse as Joey) added to Scene 6 after "Bewitched." "Joey's Class Act" (danced by B. Fosse and L. Wilson) added to Act 2, Scene 4 between "Take Him" and the reprise of "Bewitched."

1963–1964 SEASON

Robert Horton and Inge Swenson in 110 IN THE SHADE (Photo: Friedman-Abeles)
Billy Rose Theatre Collection, New York Public Library for the Performing Arts

1963–1964 SEASON

1963.18 ## THE KING AND I

A Revival of the Musical Play in Two Acts, 17 Scenes[1]. Book and lyrics by Oscar Hammerstein II. Music by Richard Rodgers. Based on the novel "Anna and the King of Siam" by Margaret Landon. Settings by Jo Mielziner. Costumes by Irene Sharaff, supervised by Stanley Simmons. Lighting by Peggy Clark. Choreography by Jerome Robbins, reproduced by Yuriko. Orchestrations by Robert Russell Bennett. Musical director and conductor, Pembroke Davenport. Directed by John Fearnley. Produced by the New York City Center Light Opera Company (Jean Dalrymple, Director). Opened 12 June 1963 at the New York City Center and closed 23 June 1963 after 15 performances.

CAST (in order of appearance): *Captain Orton*: Sam Kirkham. *Louis Leonowens*: Tommy Leap. *Anna Leonowens*: EILEEN BRENNAN. *The Interpreter*: Paul Flores. *The Kralahome*: Ken LeRoy. *The King*: MANOLO FABREGAS. *Phra Alack*: John Garces. *Lun Tha*: L. D. CLEMENTS. *Tuptim*: JOY CLEMENTS. *Lady Thiang*: ANITA DARIAN. *Prince Chulalongkorn*: Ramon Caballero. *Princess Ying Yaowalak*: Lisa Jo Abe. *Sir Edward Ramsay*: John D. Seymour.

The Small House of Uncle Thomas: *Narrator*: JOY CLEMENTS. *Uncle Thomas*: Bettina Dearborn. *Little Eva*: Susan L. Kikuchi. *Topsy*: Paula Chin. *Eliza*: YURIKO. *King Simon*: Linda Hodes. *Angel*: Marion Jim. *Drummer*: Jim E. McMillan. *Buddha*: Lisa Jo Abe.

Princes and Princesses: David Aguilar, Paul Chin, Delfino DeArco, Capri Hermany, Roma Hermany, Vivian Hernandez, Lawrence Kikuchi, Susan I. Kikuchio, Peter Martinez, Ado Sato, Ramon Torres. *The Royal Dancers*: Susan Ascheri, Hadassah Badoch, Mavis Ray Booth, Noemi Chiesa, Miriam Cole, Barbara Creed, Victor Duntiere, Carol Fried, Phyllis A. Gutelius, Edith Jerell, Marion Jim, Loi Leabo, Paul E. Olson, Clive Thompson. *Singers (Wives, Priests, Amazons, Slaves)*: Faith Daltry Compo, Harris W. Davis, James Fels, Helene Guile, Janet Hayes, Bill Kennedy, Joy Lynne Sica, Sharon Vaughn, Lynn Wendell.

1963.19 ## SPOON RIVER ANTHOLOGY

A Theatrical Adaptation (Musical Revue) of the Collected Poems of Edgar Lee Masters of the same title in Two Acts. Conceived and directed by Charles Aidman. Original songs, music by Naomi Caryl Hirshhorn, lyrics by Charles Aidman. Lighting by Jules Fisher. (Setting and costumes uncredited.) Originally produced by the Theatre Group, University Extension, UCLA. Production supervised by Robert Weiner. Produced by Joseph Cates. Opened 29 September 1963 at the Booth Theatre, moved 19 November 1963 to the Belasco Theatre and closed 4 January 1964 after 111 performances.

CAST: BETTY GARRETT, ROBERT ELSTON, JOYCE VAN PATTEN, CHARLES AIDMAN. *Singers*: Naomi Caryl Hirshhorn, Hal Lynch.

ACT 1

"He's Gone Away"
  N. C. Hirshhorn
The Hill
  C. Aidman
Tom Beatty
  C. Aidman
"Illinois"
  N. C. Hirshhorn, H. Lynch
Mrs. Williams
  J. V. Patten
Dora Williams
  B. Garrett
Archibald Higbie
  R. Elston
Walter Simmons
  C. Aidman
Deacon Taylor
  R. Elston
Emily Sparks
  B. Garrett

Benjamin Pantier
  C. Aidman
Mrs. Banjamin Pantier
  J. V. Patten
Emily Sparks
  B. Garrett
Reuben Pantier
  R. Elston
Emily Sparks
  B. Garrett
Margaret Fuller Slack
  J. V. Patten
"Soldier, Oh Soldier"
  H. Lynch
Knowlt Hoheimer
  C. Aidman
Lydia Puckett
  B. Garrett
Fiddler Jones
  R. Elston
Ollie McGee
  B. Garrett
Fletcher McGee
  C. Aidman
Hamilton Greene, Elsa Wertman
  R. Elston, J. V. Patten
Rosie Roberts
  B. Garrett
Russian Sonia
  J. V. Patten
Lucius Atherton
  R. Elston
"Times Are Gettin' Hard, Boys"
  N. C. Hirshhorn
Eugene Carman
  C. Aidman
"The Water Is Wide"
  N. C. Hirshhorn, H. Lynch
William and Emily
  R. Elston, J. V. Patton
"The Water Is Wide" (reprise)
  N. C. Hirshhorn, H. Lynch
Yee Bow
  B. Garrett
Enoch Dunlap
  C. Aidman
Mrs. Kessler
  J. V. Patten
Nancy Knapp
  B. Garrett
George Gray
  C. Aidman
Harry Wilmans
  R. Elston
Nellie Clark
  J. V. Patten
"Paper of Pins"
  N. C. Hirshhorn, H. Lynch
Roscoe Purkapile
  C. Aidman
Mrs. Purkapile
  B. Garrett
A. D. Blood
  R. Elston
Shack Dye
  C. Aidman
"Freedom"
  H. Lynch

---

[1]Originally produced in New York 29 March 1951 at the St. James Theatre for 1246 performances. For Synopsis of Scenes and Musical Numbers, see original 1951 production.

Hannah Armstrong
B. Garrett
Faith Matheny
J. V. Patten

ACT 2

"Three Nights Drunk"
N. C. Hirshhorn, H. Lynch
Judge Selah Lively
C. Aidman
Zilpha Marsh
B. Garrett
Searcy Foote
R. Elston
Mrs. Charles Bliss
J. V. Patten
"Far Away from Home"
H. Lynch
Pauline Barrett
B. Garrett
The Village Atheist
R. Elston
Mabel Osborne
J. V. Patten
Franklin Jones
C. Aidman
"In the Night"
N. C. Hirshhorn
Dippold the Optician
C. Aidman, Company
"In the Night" (reprise)
N. C. Hirshhorn
Elijah Browning
R. Elston
"Mornin's Come"
N. C. Hirshhorn, H. Lynch
Alexander Throckmorton
C. Aidman
Amanda Barker
B. Garrett
Willard Fluke
R. Elston
Lois Spears
J. V. Patten
"God Bless the Moon"
N. C. Hirshhorn
"Sow Took the Measles"
H. Lynch
Abel Melveney
R. Elston
Hod Putt
C. Aidman
Ida Frickey
B. Garrett
Silas Dement
C. Aidman
Aner Clute, Daily Fraser
J. V. Patten, B. Garrett
'Indignation' Jones
R. Elston
Minerva Jones
J. V. Patten
Doctor Meyers
C. Aidman
Mrs. Meyers
B. Garrett

"Who Knows Where I'm Goin'?"
H. Lynch
Reverend and Mrs. Sibley
R. Elston, J. V. Patten
"My Rooster"
N. C. Hirshhorn
Willie Metcalf
C. Aidman
"I Am, I Am"
N. C. Hirshhorn
"A Horse Named Bill"
H. Lynch
Batterton Dobyns
R. Elston
Flossie Cabanis
B. Garrett
Hortense Robbins
J. V. Patten
Frank Drummer
R. Elston
Barney Hainsfeather
C. Aidman
"Spoon River"
N. C. Hirshhorn, H. Lynch
Lucinda Matlock
B. Garrett
Petit, the Poet
R. Elston
Anne Rutledge
J. V. Patten
"Spoon River"
N. C. Hirshhorn, H. Lynch
Last Poem (Epilogue)
C. Aidman

THE STUDENT GYPSY,
or The Prince of Liederkranz

1963.20

A Musical Comedy in Two Acts, 14 Scenes. Book, music, lyrics and direction by Rick Besoyan. Musical numbers staged by Ray Harrison. Sets and costumes by Raoul Pene Du Bois. Lighting by Paul Morrison. Musical direction by Shepard Coleman. Orchestrations and (musical) arrangements by Arnold Goland. Produced by Sandy Farber. Opened 30 September 1963 at the 54th Street Theatre and closed 12 October 1963 after 16 performances.

CAST (in order of appearance): 'Papa' Johann Sebastian Glockenspiel, Proprietor of the Round Robin Tavern: ALLEN SWIFT. Ginger Glockenspiel, Papa Johann's adopted daughter: MITZIE WELCH. Edelweiss Glockenspiel, another adopted daughter: JOLEEN FODOR. Merry May Glockenspiel, another adopted daughter: EILEEN BRENNAN. Rudolph von Schlump, a Grenadier: DON STEWART. Muffin T. Ragamuffin D D., Ret., a Vagabond: DOM DE LUISE. Gryphon Allescu, the Gypsy Prince: BILL FLETCHER. Zampa Allescu, the Gypsy Queen: SHANNON BOLIN. Colonel Helmet Blunderbuss, another Grenadier: DICK HOH. Pfc. Wolfgang Humperdinck, another Grenadier: EDWARD MILLER. Osgood the Good, King of Liederkranz: Donald Babcock. Elsie Umlaut, his Ward: Linda Segal.
The Glockenspiel Girls: Brunhilde: Rosemary McNamara. Puppchen: Mary Jay. Dresden: Jean Palmerton. Ermintrout: Maria Garziano. Shoenheit: Jacque Dean. Rosalinde: Ann Collins. Zucker: Jean Middlebrooks. Schmetterling: Katherine Sutter. Pampelmuse: Jamie Simmons. Privates in the Royal Grenadiers: Offenbach: Ralph Vucci. Romberg: Doug Robinson. Korngold: Robert Edsel. Straus II: Marc Destin. Von Weber: Richard Marshall. Mozart: William Wheless. Lehar: Nino Galanti. Von Flotow: Tony Marlowe. Sullivan: Arnold Whyler.

The action takes place late in the nineteenth century in the Kingdom of Singspielia.

Act 1, Scene 1: The Border of Singspielia. A summer afternoon. Scene 2: In front of the Round Robin Tavern. Scene 3: A Forest Path. Scene 4: In front of Muffin's Wagon. Scene 5: In front of the Tavern. Scene 6: Inside the Tavern. Scene 7: Muffin's Wagon. Scene 8: In front of the Tavern.

Act 2, Scene 1: The Grenadier's Campsite. That evening. Scene 2: The Wine Cellar. Scene 3: The Path. Scene 4: Muffin's Wagon. Scene 5: In front of the Tavern. Scene 6: The Border of Singspielia.

ACT 1

"Welcome Home Anthem"
Glockenspiel Girls

"Singspielia"
Glockenspiel Girls

"Romance"
E. Brennan, Glockenspiel Girls

"Somewhere"
D. Stewart

"It's a Wonderful Day to Do Nothing"
D. DeLuise

"The Gypsy Life"
S. Bolin, D. DeLuise, E. Brennan

"The Grenadiers' Marching Song"
D. Hoh, Grenadiers

"Welcome Home Anthem" (reprise)
Glockenspiel Girls

"Greetings"
Grenadiers

"Kiss Me"
Glockenspiel Girls, Grenadiers

"Ting-A-Ling Dearie"
M. Welch, D. Hoh

"Merry May"
D. DeLuise, E. Brennan

"Seventh Heaven Waltz"
E. Brenna, D. Stewart

"A Gypsy Dance"
S. Bolin, D. DeLuise, B. Fletcher

"Walk-On"
S. Bolin

"You're a Man" (Finale Act 1)
Tutti (Entire Company)

ACT 2

"A Whistle Works"
E. Miller

"Gypsy of Love"
D. Stewart

"Our Love Has Flown Away"
E. Brennan

"A Woman Is a Woman Is a Woman"
D. Hoh, D. Stewart, D. DeLuise

"Romance" (reprise)
Glockenspiel Girls

"Very Much in Love"
M. Welch, Glockenspiel Girls

"My Love Is Yours"
D. Stewart, E. Brennan

"There's Life in the Old Folks Yet"
A. Swift, S. Bolin, D. Babcock

"The Drinking Song"
E. Brennan, D. DeLuise, M. Welch, D. Hoh

Finale Act 2
Tutti (Entire Company)

1963.21   HERE'S LOVE

A Musical in Two Acts, 23 Scenes. Book, music and lyrics by Meredith Willson. Based on "Miracle on 34th Street," story by Valentine Davies, screenplay by George Seaton. Directed by Stuart Ostrow. Settings by William and Jean Eckart. Costumes by Alvin Colt. Lighting by Tharon Musser. Musical direction, vocal arrangements and additional scoring by Elliot Lawrence. Orchestrations by Don Walker. Dance music arranged by Peter Howard. Dance and musical numbers staged by Michael Kidd. Produced by Stuart Ostrow. Opened 3 October 1963 at the Sam S. Shubert Theatre and closed 25 July 1964 after 338 performances.

CAST (in order of appearance): *Mr. Kris Kringle*: LAURENCE NAISMITH. *Fred Gaily*: CRAIG STEVENS. *Susan Walker*: VALERIE LEE. *Marvin Shellhammer*: FRED GWYNNE. *Doris Walker*: JANIS PAIGE. *Clerks*: Michael Bennett, Gene Kelton, Bill Stanton, Patrick Cummings, Diane Ball, Sandra Roveta, Patti Pappathatos, Elaine Cancilla. *R. H. Macy*: PAUL REED. *Harry Finfer*: Sal Lombardo. *Mrs. Finfer*: Mara Landi. *Hendrika*: Kathy Cody. *Hendrika's New Mother*: Suzanne France. *Miss Crookshank*: Reby Howells. *Mr. Psawyer*: DAVID DOYLE. *Governor*: Darrell Sandeen. *Mayor*: Hal Norman. *Mr. Gimbel*: William Griffis. *Policeman*: Bob McClure. *Clara*: Mary Louise. *Judge Martin Group*: CLIFF HALL. *District Attorney Thomas Mara*: Larry Douglas. *Tammany O'Halloran*: Arthur Rubin. *Nurse*: Leesa Troy. *Marines*: John Sharpe, Bob McClure, Darrell Sandeen. *Girl Scout Leader*: Mara Landi. *Bailiff*: Del Horstmann. *Mailman*: Hal Norman. *Thomas Mara, Jr.*: Ronnie Kroll. *Murphy*: William Griffis.

Children: Debbie Breen, Kathy Cody, Sal Lombardo, Ronnie Kroll, Terrin Miles. *Dancers*: Diane Ball, Michael Bennett, Duane Bodin, Elaine Cancilla, Patrick Cummings, Suzanne France, Reby Howells, Gene Kelton, Baayork Lee, David Lober, Bill Louther, Patti Pappathatos, Sandra Roveta, John Sharpe, Bill Stanton, Carolsue Shaer. *Singers*: Ceil Delli, Penny Gaston, Del Horstmann, Mara Landi, Mary Louise, Bob McClure, Hal Norman, Darrell Sandeen, Leesa Troy.

Act 1, Scene 1: West 73rd Street, New York City. Thursday morning, Thanksgiving Day. *Scene 2*: Assembly Parade Area. Immediately following. *Scene 3*: Along Central park West. Immediately following. *Scene 4*: 34th Street Roof. Immediately following. *Scene 5*: Doris Walker's Apartment. That evening. *Scene 6*: Briefing Room at Macy's. 3 P.M., the next afternoon. *Scene 7*: Macy's Toy Department, Elevators, Escalator, and into Herald Square. Immediately following. *Scene 8*: Playground in Central Park. Later that afternoon. *Scene 9*: Doris Walker's Office. In the meantime. *Scene 10*: Fred Gaily's Apartment. After work that day. *Scene 11*: On the way to Doris' Apartment. Immediately following. *Scene 12*: Store Psychologist's Office at Macy's. The following Monday morning. *Scene 13*: Macy's Toy Department. That evening. *Scene 14*: The Party. *Scene 15*: Macy's Toy Department.

Act 2, Scene 1: Judge Martin Group's Chambers. Several Weeks later, December 19th, morning. *Scene 2*: In Isolation. Later that day. *Scene 3*: Fred's Apartment. That evening. *Scene 4*: A Corridor in the New York Supreme Court. 10 A.M. the next day. *Scene 5*: The Courtroom. Immediately following. *Scene 6*: The Courthouse Corridor. 3 P.M. the following Tuesday afternoon, December 24th. *Scene 7*: The Courtroom. Immediately following. *Scene 8*: Macy's Living Room Display. Christmas Eve, immediately following.

ACT 1

Scene 3

"The Big Clown Balloons"
Paradesters

Scene 5

"Arm in Arm"
J. Paige, V. Lee

"You Don't Know"
J. Paige

Scene 6

"The Plastic Alligator"
F. Gwynne, Clerks

Scene 7

"The Bugle"
L. Naismith, K. Cody

"Here's Love"
L. Naismith, C. Stevens, V. Lee, Ensemble

Scene 8

"My Wish"
C. Stevens, V. Lee

Scene 9

"Pine Cones and Holly Berries"
L. Naismith, J. Paige, F. Gwynne

Scene 10

"Look Little Girl"
C. Stevens

Scene 11

"Look Little Girl" (reprise)
J. Paige

Scene 13

"Expect Things To Happen"
L. Naismith

Scene 14

"Love Come Take Me Again" (Waltz)
Ballet Corps

ACT 2[2]

Scene 2

"Pine Cones and Holly Berries" (reprise)
L. Naismith, V. Lee

Scene 3

"She Hadda Go Back"
C. Stevens, Marines

Scene 5

"That Man Over There"
P. Reed

"My State"
J. Paige, P. Reed, F. Gwynne, A. Rubin, C. Hall

Scene 6

"Nothin' in Common"
J. Paige

Scene 7

"That Man Over There" (reprise)
Court Personnel, Spectators

1963.22 GENTLEMEN, BE SEATED!

A Musical Entertainment in Two Acts, 22 Scenes. Book by Jerome Moross and Edward Eager. Music by Jerome Moross. Lyrics by Edward Eager. Directed by Robert Turoff. Scenic design by William Pitkin. Costume design by Henry Heymann. Lighting by Jules Fisher. Choreographed by Paul Draper, assisted by Bob Bernard. Conducted by Emerson Buckley. Produced by the New York City Opera. Opened 10 October 1963 at the New York City Center and closed 10 November 1963 after 3 performances in repertory.

CAST (in order of appearance): *Interlocutor, (Mr. Brady):* DICK SHAWN. *Mr. Tambo:* Avon Long. *Mr. Bones:* Charles Atkins. *The Comedienne, (Dowager, Belle Boyd, Dorothea Dix):* ALICE GHOSTLEY. *The Contralto, (Harriet Tubman, Amanda):* Carol Brice. *Johnny Reb:* William McDonald. *Billy Yank:* Richard Fredricks. *Southern Girl:* June Card. *Northern Girl:* Mary Burgess. *Mr. Banjo:* Bernard Addison. *The Character Actor, (The Senator, The General, The Pinkerton Man. Mr. Brady's Assistant):* RICHARD KRAUSE. *Mr. Taps:* PAUL DRAPER. *Ermyntrude:* Charlotte Povia. *Farmer McLean:* David Smith. *Miss Florida Cotton:* Michele Hardy. *Two Soldiers:* Kellis Miller, Don Henderson. *Drill Team:* Bob Bernard, John Tormey, Rec Russell, Bob Ellis. *Horse:* Bob Bernard, Bob Ellis. *Two Other Soldiers:* Kellis Miller, Don Yule. *Two Girls:* Joyce Miko, Beverly Evans. *Four Nurses:* Joyce Miko, Candida Pilla, Beverly Evans, Charlotte Povia. *Minstrels, Waltzers, Soldiers, Nurses, Spectators, Slaves, etc.:* New York City Opera Chorus.

ACT 1[3]

Scene 1

"Grand March"
A. Long, C. Atkins, Chorus, W. McDonald, R. Fredricks, J. Card, M. Burgess

Scene 2

"In the Sunny Old South"
D. Shawn, A. Long, C. Atkins, Chorus

Scene 3

"The Freedom Train"
C. Brice

Scene 4

"Waltzing in the Shadow"
D. Shawn, W. McDonald, R. Fredricks, Chorus

Scene 5

"Fare You Well"
J. Card, W. McDonald, M. Burgess, R. Fredricks

Scene 6

"Why Ain't We Got a Dome?"
A. Long, C. Atkins, D. Shawn

"Tap Dance Drill"
P. Draper, Men's Dance Ensemble

Scene 7

"O, the Picnic in Manassas"
A. Ghostley, R. Krause, C. Povia

Scene 8

"Mocking Bird"
J. Card

Scene 9

"Shiloh"
W. McDonald, Men's Chorus

Scene 10

"The Ballad of Belle Boyd" (Belle Boyd's Back in Town)
Ladies' Chorus

"I Spy"
A. Ghostley

"It's the Witching Hour by the Old Water Tower"
Men's Chorus, A. Ghostley

"I'm a Pinkerton Man"
R. Krause

"Belle Boyd, Where Have You Been?"
Ladies' Chorus

Scene 11

"'Mancipation"
A. Long, C. Atkins, C. Brice

"Pardon, Ma'am"?

"Look Who I Am, Surprise! Surprise!"?

Scene 12

"This Isn't a Gentleman's War Anymore"
D. Shawn

Scene 13

"The Contraband Ball"
A. Ghostley, J. Card, C. Atkins, A. Long, R. Fredricks, Chorus

"O, Miss Walkaround, Come Walking Out With Me"
D. Shawn, A. Ghostley, R. Fredricks, A. Long, C. Atkins, J. Card, Entire Company

ACT 2

Scene 1

"Gentlemen, Be Seated"
D. Shawn

Scene 2

"It's Quiet on the Potomac Tonight"
A. Long, C. Atkins

Scene 3

"The Ballad of Stonewall Jackson"
W. McDonald, Men's Chorus

Scene 4

"I'm Mathew P. Brady, the Camera Man"
D. Shawn,. R. Krause

"Miss Dorothea Dix"
A. Ghostley, Nurses, D. Shawn

Scene 5

"I Can't Remember"
M. Burgess

Scene 6

"From Atlanta to the Sea"
R. Fredricks, C. Brice, Chorus

Scene 7

"What Has Become of Beauty?"
D. Shawn

Scene 8

"Have You Seen Him, Did He Pass This Way?"
C. Brice

---

[2]Added to Act 2, Scene 7 after "That Man Over There" for tour:

"Love Come Take Me Again" (vocal)
Lisa Kirk (Doris)

[3]Scenes and Musical Numbers not in program. List prepared from production manuscript, score and recording.

Scene 9

"This Was the War, What Did It Do for Me and You?"
Entire Company

1963.23

THE MIKADO,
or The Town of Titipu

A Revival of the Comic Opera in Two Acts[4]. Libretto by William S. Gilbert. Music by Arthur Sullivan. Staged by Dorothy Raedler. Scenic design by Donald Oenslager. Costume design by Patton Campbell. Lighting by Jules Fisher. Conducted by William Jonson. Produced by the New York City Opera. Opened 12 October 1963 at the New York City Center and closed 9 November 1963 after 3 performances in repertory.

CAST: *The Mikado of Japan*: PAUL UKENA. *Nanki-Poo*, his son, disguised as a wandering minstrel in love with Yum-Yum: WILLIAM DIARD. *Ko-Ko*, Lord High Executioner of Titipu: NORMAN KELLEY. *Pooh-Bah*, Lord High Everything Else: SPIRO MALAS. *Pish-Tush*, a Noble Lord: David Smith. *Yum-Yum, Pitti-Sing, Peep-Bo*, three sisters, wards of Ko-Ko: CAROL BERGEY, MARY BURGESS, MARLENA KLEINMAN. *Katisha*: MURIEL GREENSPON. *Chorus of School Girls, Nobles, Guards and Coolies*: New York City Opera Chorus.

1963.24

THE MERRY WIDOW

A Revival of the Operetta in Three Acts[5]. Music by Franz Lehár. Original German book (Die Lustige Witwe) and lyrics by Victor Léon and Leo Stein after "L'Attaché d'Ambassade." English libretto by Adrian Ross. Staged by Michael Pollock. Scenic design by George Jenkins. Lighting by Jules Fisher. Choreographed by Thomas Andrew. Conducted by Carl Bamberger. Produced by the New York City Opera. Opened 13 October 1963 (matinee) at the New York City Center and closed 10 November 1963 after 4 performances in repertory.[6]

CAST: *Sonia*: ARLENE SAUNDERS. *Prince Danilo*: JOHN REARDON. *Baron Popoff*: JACK HARROLD. *Natalie*: Gillian Grey. *De Jolidon*: FRANK PORETTA. *Marquis de Cascada*: David Smith. *St. Brioche*: Richard Krause. *Admiral Khadja*: Thomas Paul. *Mme. Khadja*: Charlotte Povia. *General Novikovich*: R. G. Webb. *Mme. Novikovich*: Lynda Jordan. *Nish*: Coley Worth. *Head waiter*: Harris Davis. *Clo-Clo*: Helen Guile. *Solo Dancers*: Rochelle Zide, Ron Sequoio. *Ensemble*: New York Citry Opera.

1963.25

JENNIE

A Musical in Two Acts, 14 Scenes. Book by Arnold Schulman. Suggested by "Laurette"[7] by Marguerite Courtney by arrangement with Alan J. Pakula. Music by Arthur Schwartz. Lyrics by Howard Dietz. Directed by Vincent J. Donahue. Choreography by Matt Mattox. Settings by George Jenkins. Costumes by Irene Sharaff. Lighting by Jean Rosenthal. Musical director, John Lesko. Orchestrations by Philip J. Lang and Robert Russell Bennett. Dance music, vocal arrangements and incidental music by Trude Rittman. Produced by Cheryl Crawford and Richard Halliday. Opened 17 October 1963 at the Majestic Theatre and closed 28 December 1963 after 82 performances.

CAST (in order of appearance): THE MOUNTIE GETS HIS MAN, or, CHANG LU, KING OF THE WHITE SLAVES: *The Evil Chang Lu*: Kirby Smith. *Randolph of the Royal Mounted*: GEORGE WALLACE. *Misguided Coolies (2): Lu Wong*: Gerald Teijelo. *Dong Foo*: Robert Murray. *Our Melissa*: MARY MARTIN. *The Bear*: Jeremiah

---

[4]First presented in New York 20 July, 10-29 August 1885 at the Union Square and People's Theatres for 22 performances. First authorized production presented 19 August 1885 at the Fifth Avenue Theatre by Richard D'Oyly Carte for 250 performances. For Synopsis of Scenes and Musical Numbers, see 19 August 1885 D'Oyly Carte production.
[5]Originally produced in New York 21 October 1907 at the New Amsterdam Theatre for 416 performances. For Synopsis of Scenes and Musical Numbers, see original 1907 production.
[6]Costumes uncredited; one reviewer noted the costumes were acquired from a production from Casa Manana Musicals, Inc. Texas.
[7]Biography of Laurette Taylor.

Morris. *Wicked Owner of a House of Ill Repute*: Elaine Swann. *A Tragic Virgin Sold into White Slavery*: Linda Donovan. *A Sinful Woman of Ill Repute*: Sharon Vaughn. *A Croupier*: Steve Elmore. *A Woodsman*: Rico Froehlich. *A Pioneer Woman*: Julie Sargant.
Jennie Malone: MARY MARTIN. *James O'Connor*: GEORGE WALLACE. *Bessie Mae Sue*: Elaine Swann. *Stella*: Linda Donovan. *Sydney Harris*: JEREMIAH MORRIS. *Frank Granada*: Rico Froehlich. *Casey O'Harrison*: Steve Elmore. *Gregory Hyman*: Kirby Smith. *Sheriff Pugsley*: Jay Velie. *Abe O'Shaughnessy*: JACK DE LON. *Kevin O'Conner*: Brian Chapin. *Lois Houser*: IMELDA DeMARTIN. *O'Conner's Wardrobe Mistress*: Bernice Saunders. *Deputies*: Martin Ambrose, Oran Osburn. *Linda O'Conner*: CONNIE SCOTT. *Nellie Malone*: ETHEL SHUTTA. *Delivery Man*: Stephen Elmore. *Charlie the Juiceman*: Stan Watt. *Flower Girl*: Debbie Scott. *Rita Bradley*: Diane Coupe. *Christopher Lawrence Cromwell*: ROBIN BAILEY. *Shine Boy*: Robert Murray. *Teddy*: Sean Peters. *Gentleman*: Jay Velie. *Stage Manger*: Stan Watt. *Piano Player*: Woody Kessler. *The Pony*: Misty. *Fire Chief*: Jay Velie.
THE SULTAN'S FIFTIETH BRIDE: *Sultan*: Kirby Smith. *Harem Girls*: Diane Coupe, Sally Ackerman, Linda Donovan. *Guardians*: Gerald Teijelo, Robert Murray, Al Sambogna. *Eunuchs*: Blair Hammond, Martin Ambrose. *Indian Fakir*: Jeremiah Morris. *Shalamar*: MARY MARTIN. *Omar*: GEORGE WALLACE.
Dancing Ensemble: Sally Ackerman, Diane Coupe, Mollie Sterns, Blair Hammond, Robert Murray, Al Sambogna, Gerald Teijelo. *Singing Ensemble*: Lispet Nelson, Julie Sargant, Sharon Vaughn, Martin Ambrose, Steve Elmore, Rico Froehlich, Oran Osburn.

Act 1, Scene 1: The Stage of a Theatre in a small town in South Dakota. Early Spring 1906. Melodrama: 'The Mountie Gets His Man." Scene 2: Backstage immediately after. Scene 3: The town square, a few minutes later. Scene 4: Living room of Nellie Malone's Brownstone. New York City, two months later. Scene 5: Stage door alley, New York City. The next morning. Scene 6: Exterior Nellie Malone's Brownstone, a few hours later. Scene 7: Christopher Lawrence Cromwell's New York Town House. Eight weeks later. Scene 8: The living room of Nellie Malone's Brownstone. The following Sunday afternoon.

Act 2, Scene 1: Seattle, Washington. Several weeks later. Scene 2: O'Conner's Crystal Palace, backstage. Three weeks later. Scene 3: Several hours later. Scene 4: On stage. Imemdiately after. Scene 5: Several hours later. Melodrama: 'The Sultan's Fiftieth Bride." Scene 6: Seattle Railroad Station.

ACT 1
Scene 2
    "Waitin' For the Evening Train"
        M. Martin, G. Wallace
Scene 3
    "When You're Far Away From New York Town"
        J. De Lon, Company
    "I Still Look at You That Way"
        M. Martin
Scene 4
    "When You're Far Away from New York Town" (reprise)
        B. Chapin, Sewing Girls
    "For Better or Worse"
        E. Shutta
Scene 5
    "Born Again"
        M. Martin, J. De Lon, Company
    "Over Here"
        R. Bailey, M. Martin
Scene 6
    "Before I Kiss the World Goodbye"
        M. Martin
Scene 7
    "Sauce Diable" (dance)
        Dance Company
    "Where You Are"
        R. Bailey, M. Martin
    "The Jig"
        R. Bailey, M. Martin, Company
Scene 8
    "See Seattle"
        G. Wallace

ACT 2
Scene 1
    "High Is Better Than Low"
        G. Wallace, M. Martin, Company

"The Night May Be Dark"
M. Martin, E. Shutta
Scene 2
Dance Rehearsal
Harem Girls
"I Believe in Takin' a Chance"
G. Wallace, J. De Lon
Scene 4
"Welcome"
Harem Girls
"Lonely Nights"
M. Martin
Scene 6
"Before I Kiss the World Goodbye" (reprise)
M. Martin

1963.26   110 IN THE SHADE

A Musical Play in Two Acts, 11 Scenes. Book by N. Richard Nash. Based on his play "The Rainmaker." Music by Harvey Schmidt. Lyrics by Tom Jones. Directed by Joseph Anthony. Musical numbers staged by Agnes de Mille. Settings by Oliver Smith. Costumes by Motley. Lighting by John Harvey. Musical director, Don Pippin. Orchestrations by Hershy Kay. Dance music by Billy Goldenberg. Vocal arranger, Robert De Cormier. Produced by David Merrick. Opened 24 October 1963 at the Broadhurst Theatre and closed 8 August 1964 after 330 performances.

CAST (in order of appearance): *Toby*: GEORGE CHURCH. *File*: STEPHEN DOUGLASS. *H.C. Curry*: WILL GEER. *Noah Curry*: STEVE ROLAND. *Jimmy Curry*: SCOOTER TEAGUE. *Lizzie Curry*: INGA SWENSON. *Snookie*: LESLEY WARREN. *Mrs. Jensen*: Diane Deering. *Phil Mackey*: Seth Riggs. *Tommy*: Christopher Votos. *Belinda*: Renee Dudley. *Gershy Toops*: Don Crabtree. *Gil Demby*: Jerry Dodge. *Olive Barrow*: Leslie Franzos. *Wally Skacks, III*: Loren Hightower. *Maurine Toops*: Evelyn Toops. *Bo Dollivon*: Vernon Lusby. *Mr. Curtis*: Robert Shepard. *Bill Starbuck*: ROBERT HORTON. *Wally Skacks*: Carl Nicholas.

Townspeople: Lynne Broadbent, Leslie Franzos, Lucia Lambert, Paula Lloyd, Evelyn Taylor, Esther Villavicencio, Florence Willson, Don Atkinson, Frank Derbas, Jerry Dodge, Ben Gillespie, Loren Hightower, Vernon Lusby, Arthur Whitfield, Barbara Bossert, Gretchen Cryer, Dori Davis, Diane Deering, Corlyn Kemp, Urylee Leonardos, Donna Sanders, Clifford Fearl, David London, Carl Nicholas, Stan Page.

The play takes place in a western state from dawn to midnight of a summer day in a time of drought.

Act 1, Scene 1: The Depot. *Scene 2*: File's Office. Main Street. *Scene 3*: A Picnic Area, near the Bandstand. *Scene 4*: The Rainwagon. *Scene 5*: Another Picnic Area. *Scene 6*: The Edge of the Woods.

Act 2, Scene 1: The Pavilion. *Scene 2*: The Rainwagon. *Scene 3*: A Picnic Area. *Scene 4*: The Rainwagon. *Scene 5*: Near the Bandstand.

ACT 1
"(Gonna Be) Another Hot Day"
S. Douglass, Townspeople
"Lizzie's Coming Home"
W. Geer, S. Roland, S. Teague
"Love, Don't Turn Away"
I. Swenson
"Poker Polka"
S. Douglass, W. Geer, S. Roland
"Hungry Men"
Townspeople
"The Rain Song"
R. Horton, Townspeople
"You're Not Foolin' Me"
I. Swenson, R. Horton
"Raunchy"
I. Swenson, W. Geer
"A Man and a Woman"
I. Swenson, S. Douglass
"Old Maid"
I. Swenson
ACT 2
"Everything Beautiful Happens at Night"
G. Church, S. Teague, L. Warren, Townspeople

"Melisande"
R. Horton
"Simple Little Things"
I. Swenson
"Little Red Hat"
L. Warren, S. Teague
"Is It Really Me?"
I. Swenson, R. Horton
"Wonderful Music"
S. Douglass, R. Horton, I. Swenson
Finale ("The Rain Song")
Full Company

1963.27   TAMBOURINES TO GLORY

A Gospel Singing Play in Two Acts, 10 Scenes. Play (book and lyrics) by Langston Hughes. Based on his novel of the same name Music by Jobe Huntley. Directed by Nikos Psacharopoulos. Settings and costumes by John Conklin. Lighting by Peter Hunt. Choral director, Clara Ward. Dance assistant, Judd Jones. Musical consultant, Abba Bogin. Produced by S. & H. Venture (Joel Schenker and Hexter Productions, Inc.) in association with Sydney S. Baron. Opened 2 November 1963 at the Little Theatre and closed 23 November 1963 after 24 performances.

CAST (in order of appearance): *C. J. Moore*: ROBERT GUILLAUME. *Marshalls*: Rudy Challenger, Garwood Perkins. *Essie Belle Johnson*: ROSETTA LE NOIRE. *Youth*: Clyde Williams. *Mattie Morningside*: Rosalie King. *Laura Wright Reed*: HILDA SIMMS. *Policeman*: Rudy Challenger. *Big-Eyed Buddy Lomax*: LOUIS [Lou] GOSSETT. *Birdie Lee*: CLARA WARD. *Gloria Dawn*: ANNA ENGLISH. *The Gloriettas*: Helen Ferguson, Tina Sattin. *Bartender*: Garwood Perkins. *Brother Bud*: BROTHER JOHN SELLERS. *Brother Clyde*: Clyde Williams. *Marietta Johnson*: MICKI GRANT. *Deacons*: Clark Morgan, Garwood Perkins, BROTHER JOHN SELLERS, Laurence Watson. *Deaconess Lucy Mae Hobbs*: Lynn Hamilton. *Chicken-Crow-For-Day*: JOSEPH ATTLES. *Ministers of Music*: Clyde Williams, Alton Williams. *Windus*: Rudy Challenger. *Prison Warden*: Garwood Perkins.

Tambourine Temple Choir, Passersby, Cabarte Patrons, Neighborhood Folk: Rudy Challenger, Voyla Crowley, Dorothy Drake, Helen Ferguson, Claretta Freemon, Carl Hall, Alma Hubbard, Judd Jones, Rosalie King, Julie Merrell, Theresa Merritt, Clark Morgan, Garwood Perkins, Tina Sattin, Adele Schofield, Laurence Watson.

The action of the play takes place in Harlem, New York City, some time in the past.

Act 1, Scene 1: A Sidewalk in Harlem. Early spring. *Scene 2*: A street corner. A week later. *Scene 3*: A Night Club. Immediately following. *Scene 4*: A Store Front Church. Autumn. *Scene 5*: Laura's Living Room. A few months later. *Scene 6*: Tambourine Temple.

Act 2, Scene 1: The Living Room, again. Summer night. *Scene 2*: The Robing Room of Tambourine Temple. Late Summer. *Scene 3*: A Jail. The next day. *Scene 4*: Tambourine Temple. A few days later.

MUSICAL NUMBERS
"Nobody Knows the Trouble I've Seen"
"O, What Blessings to Receive"
"Travelling Show"
"The New York Blues"
"Scat With Me"
"Moon Outside My Window"
"As I Go"
"Just To Be a Flower in the Garden of the Lord"
"I've Come Back to the Fold"
"I'm Goin to Testify"
"Away from Temptation"
"Devil, Devil, Take Yourself Away"
"Yes, Ma'am"
"Fix Me"
"Just Trust in Him"
"God's Got a Way"
"Let the Church Say Amen"
"God's Love Can Save"
"If You've Got a Tambourine Shake It for the Glory of God"
(Tambourines to Glory)

1963.28   # THE GOLDEN AGE

An Entertainment (Revue) in the Words and Music of the Elizabethan Age, in Two Acts. Devised by Richard Johnson. Directed by Douglas Campbell. Music devised and directed by Sydney Beck. Men's evening wear by After Six. Gowns by Domingo A. Rodriguez. Produced by Santa Fe Productions, Inc. Presented by Arthur Cantor and E. E. Fogelson. Opened 18 November 1963 at the Lyceum Theatre and closed 23 November 1963 after 7 performances.

CAST: DOUGLAS CAMPBELL, NANCY WICKWIRE, DOUGLAS RAIN, LESTER RAWLINS. *Singers:* Betty Wilson (soprano), James Stover (tenor), Gordon Myers (baritone). *Consort of Instruments:* Blanche Winogrom (virginals, cittern), James Tyler (lute, tenor viol and recorders), Leonid Bolotine (pandora and violin), Robert Kuehn (bass viol).

ACT 1

SPRING AND SUMMER

Elizabeth Regina
(Sir John Davies)
D. Rain, D. Campbell, L. Rawlins

"Blow, Shepherds, Blow!"
(Thomas Morley)
B. Wilson, J. Stover, G. Myers

See Where She Sits
(Edmund Spenser)
The Company

"The Shepherd's Delight"
(Anonymous)
Consort, B. Wilson, J. Stover, G. Myers

The Fair Milkmaid
(Sir Thomas Overbury)
L. Rawlins

I Would I Had Some Flowers
(Shakespeare)
N. Wickwire

The Countryman's Letter
(Nicholas Breton)D. Campbell

Ah, What Is Love?
(Robert Greene)
N. Wickwire

"It Was a Lover and His Lass"
(Morley)
B. Wilson, J. Stover, Virginals

Shakespeare: 'As You Like It'

Phillidah Flouts Me
(Anonymous)
D. Rain

The Shepherd To His Love
(Christopher Marlowe)
D. Campbell

The Shepherdess Replies
(Sir Walter Raleigh)
N. Wickwire

"I Care Not for These Ladies"
(Thomas Campion)
G. Myers, Lute, Bass Viol

The Country Life
(Thomas Dekker)
L. Rawlins

Shepherd and Courtier
(Shakespeare: 'As You Like It')
D. Campbell, D. Rain

"Lord Souche's Masque"
(Anonymous)
Consort

Royal Progress
(Edited from various sourecs)
The Company

"Michells Galliard"
(Anonymous)The Consort

"Now Is the Month of Maying"
(Morley)
B. Wilson, J. Stover, G. Myers, Consort

An English Housewife
(Gervase Markham)
D. Rain

Oh, These Men
(Shakespeare: 'Othello'
N. Wickwire

"Sigh No More Ladies"
(Shakespeare: 'Much Ado About Nothing')
(Music: Sixteenth Century Manuscript)
B. Wilson, J. Stover, Bass Viol

Doctors—Good and Bad
(Nicholas Breton)
L. Rawlins

What Is't You Lack?
(Anonymous Masque)
B. Wilson, J. Stover, G. Myers, Virginals

Neurosis
(Reginald Scot)
D. Rain

To Bed With Mirth
(Andrew Boorde)
N. Wickwire

"Lullaby"
(Thomas Dekker, *Music by* Sydney Beck)
B. Wilson, Pandora

"The Hunt Is Up"
(Anonymous, *Music by* Sydney Beck)
B. Wilson, J. Stover, G. Myers

Hunting
(Gervase Markham)
D. Campbell

"The King's Hunt"
(John Bull)
Virginals

Football
(Philip Stubbes)
D. Rain

The Road to London
(Thomas Deloney)
The Company

"To Portsmouth"
(Melville Collection)
B. Wilson, J. Stover, G. Myers

A Good Sherris-Sack
(Shakespeare)
D. Campbell

The Nut Brown Ale
D. Rain, L. Rawlins

Troll the Bowl
(Thomas Dekker)
L. Rawlins

A Drinking Song
The Company

ACT 2

FALL AND WINTER

Barafostus Dreame
(Anonymous, *Music by* Sydney Beck)
The Consort

It Is Now the Seventh Hour
(Nicholas Breton)
N. Wickwire

"The Cries of London"
(Anonymous, Sixteenth Century Manuscript)
B. Wilson, J. Stover, G. Myers, Consort

Where Be These Boys
(Thomas Dekker: 'A Shoemaker's Holiday')
The Company

London
(Thomas Dekker)
D. Rain

London: A Foreigner's View
(Edited from various sources)
D. Campbell, N. Wickwire, D. Rain

The Theatre
(Thoams Platter) The Company
"Irish Jig"
(Anonymous) Virginals
Sermon
(Edited from various sources) D. Rain
How to Behave at the Theatre
(Thomas Dekker) D. Campbell
"Oxenford's March"
(Anonymous) The Consort
Prologue: The Armada
(Shakespeare) L. Rawlins
The Queen Speaks
(Queen Elizabeth) N. Wickwire
"Joyne Hands"
(Thomas Morley) The Consort
Happy and Glorious
(Sir John Hayward) L. Rawlins
The Queen in Her Good Court
(Paul Hentzner) D. Campbell, D. Rain, L. Rawlins
The Golden Speech
(Queen Elizabeth) N. Wickwire
"The Queen's Galliard"
(John Dowland) Lute, Pandora
To Ride Comely
D. Campbell
A Courtier To All Men's Thinking
(Charles Ascham) D. Rain
Why Do You Stand Bare Headed?
D. Campbell, D. Rain
"Winter Song"
(Music by Sydney Beck) J. Stover, Virginals
Shakespeare: 'As You Like It'
Storm At Sea
(John Jane) L. Rawlins
The Peril of Waters
(The Bible, Psalm 107) The Company
"In Darkness Let Me Dwell"
(John Dowland) G. Myers, Virginals, Bass Viol
Tichborne's Elegy
(Chidlock Tichborne) D. Campbell
The Queen Repents
(Queen Elizabeth) N. Wickwire
That Time of Year
(Shakespeare) D. Rain
His Pilgrimage
(Sir Walter Raleigh) L. Rawlins
"A Carol for New Year's Day"
B. Wilson, J. Stover, G. Myers, Consort
(William Byrd, Music by Sydney Beck)
Epilogue
(Richard Breton) D. Campbell

THE GIRL WHO CAME TO SUPPER

1963.29

A Musical Comedy in Two Acts, 16 Scenes. Book by Harry Kurnitz. Based on the play "The Sleeping Prince" by Terence Rattigan. Music and lyrics by Nöel Coward. Entire production staged by Joe Layton. Scenery by Oliver Smith. Costumes by Irene Sharaff. Lighting by Peggy Clark. Musical direction and vocal arrangements by Jay Blackton. Orchestrations by Robert Russell Bennett. Dance music arranged by Genevieve Pitot. Produced by Herman Levin. Opened 8 December 1963 at the Broadway Theatre and closed 14 March 1964 after 112 performances.

CAST (in order of appearance): *Jessie Maynard*: Marian Haraldson. *Mary Morgan*: FLORENCE HENDERSON. *Tony Morelli*: Jack Eddleman. *Mr. Grimes*: Peter Pagan. *Violetta Vines*: Maggie Worth. *Peter Northbrook*: RODERICK COOK. *Colonel Hofmann*: Chris Gampel. *Grand Duke Charles, Prince Regent of Carpathia*: JOSE FERRER. *First Girl*: Donna Monroe. *Second Girl*: Ruth Shepard. *Major-Domo*: Carey Nairnes. *King Nicholas III of Carpathia*: SEAN SCULLY. *Simka*: Murray Adler. *Queen Mother*: IRENE BROWNE. *Ada Cockle*: TESSIE O'SHEA. *Baroness Brunheim*: Lucie Lancaster. *Lady Sunningdale*: Ilona Murai.

Dancers: Nancy Lynch, Julie Drake, Sheila Forbes, Jami Landi, Sandy Leeds, Carmen Morales, Ilona Murai, Mari Shelton, Gloria Smith, Mary Zahn, Ivan Allen, Robert [Bob] Fitch, Jose Gutierrez, Peter Holmes, Scott Ray, Paul Reid Roman, Dan Siretta, Mike Toles. *Singers*: Jermey Brown, Kellie Brytt, Carol Glade, Marian Haraldson, Elaine Labour, Donna Monroe, Ruth Shepard, Maggie Worth, Jack Eddleman, John Felton, Dell Hanley, Barney Johnston, Art Matthews, Bruce Peyton, Jack Rains, Mitchell Taylor.

The play takes place in London, just prior to and during the Coronation of His Majesty George V.

Act 1, Scene 1: Backstage at the Majestic Theatre. *Scene 2*: A Dressing Room Backstage. *Scene 3*: Backstage. *Scene 4*: The Regent's Apartment, Carpathian Embassy, Belgrave Square. *Scene 5*: St. Martin's Lane. *Scene 6*: Trafalgar Square. *Scene 7*: St. Martin's Lane. *Scene 8*: The Regent's Apartment. The next morning. *Scene 9*: The Great Hall of the Embassy.

Act 2, Scene 1: Westminster Abbey. *Scene 2*: The Regent's Apartment. *Scene 3*: A Drawing Room, Carpathian Embassy. *Scene 4*: The Foreign Office Ball. *Scene 5*: St. Martin's Lane. *Scene 6*: The Regent's Apartment, after the Ball. *Scene 7*: The Regent's Apartment. The next morning.

ACT 1
Scene 1
"Swing Song"
M. Haraldson, J. Eddleman, Ensemble
"Yasni Kozkolai" (Carpathian National Anthem)
Ensemble
"My Family Tree"
J. Ferrer, R. Cook, Regent's Aides
Scene 2
"I've Been Invited to a Party"
F. Henderson
Scene 3
Waltz
Ensemble
"I've Been Invited to a Party" (reprise)
F. Henderson
Scene 4
"When Foreign Princes Come to Visit Us"
C. Nairnes, Footmen
"Sir or Ma'am"
R. Cook
"Soliloquies"
J. Ferrer, F. Henderson
"Lonely"
J. Ferrer
Scene 6
"London Is a Little Bit of All Right"
"What Ho, Mrs. Brisket"
"Don't Take Our Charlie for the Army"
"Saturday Night at the Rose and Crown"
T. O'Shea, S. Scully, Ensemble
Scene 7
"London Is a Little Bit of All Right" (reprise)
T. O'Shea
Scene 8
"Here and Now"
F. Henderson
"I've Been Invited to a Party" (reprise)
F. Henderson
Scene 9
"Soliloquies" (reprise)
J. Ferrer, F. Henderson
ACT 2
Scene 1
"Coronation Chorale"
F. Henderson, J. Ferrer, Principals, Ensemble
Scene 2
"How Do You Do, Middle Age?"
J. Ferrer
Scene 3
"Here and Now" (reprise)
F. Henderson

Scene 4

"The Stingaree"
J. Ferrer, I. Murai, Ensemble

"Curt, Clear and Concise"
J. Ferrer, R. Cook

"Tango"
J. Ferrer, F. Henderson, Dancing Ensemble

Scene 5

"The Cocoanut Girl":

"Welcome to Pootzie Van Doyle"/"Paddy MacNeil and His
Automobile"/"Swing Song"/"Six Lillies of the Valley"/"The Walla Walla
Boola"
F. Henderson

Scene 6

"This Time It's True Love"
F. Henderson

Scene 7

"This Time It's True Love" (reprise)
J. Ferrer

"I'll Remember Her"
J. Ferrer

1963.30 DOUBLE DUBLIN

An Entertainment (Revue) in Two Acts. Supervised by Gus Schirmer.
Musical direction by Baldwin Bergersen. Setting and lighting by Helen
Pond and Herbert Senn. Musical numbers edited by David Nillo. Music
arranged and played by Baldwin Bergersen. Produced by Josephine
Forrestal Productions, Inc. Opened 26 December 1963 at the Little Theatre
and closed 28 December 1963 after 4 performances.

CAST: JOHN MOLLOY, NOEL SHERIDAN, DEIRDRE O'CALLAGHAN,
PATRICIA BROGAN.

ACT 1

Audience Reflections
J. Molloy, N. Sheridan

Window Dressing
J. Molloy

100, 000 Welcomes
N. Sheridan

Darts
J. Molloy

Rural Character
J. Molloy

"Gaelic Air"
D. O'Callaghan

The Importance of Behan
N. Sheridan

Amateur Theatricals
J. Molloy, N. Sheridan, P. Brogan, D. O'Callaghan

Joyce's Dublin
J. Molloy, N. Sheridan, P. Brogan, D. O'Callaghan

"Dublin Saunter"
D. O'Callaghan

"Irish Jig"
P. Brogan

ACT 2

Irish Station Break

Four Portraits
J. Molloy

Bonnet Trimmed With the Blue
D. O'Callaghan, N. Sheridan

Folk Singer
J. Molloy, N. Sheridan

Keeping Up With the Jones
N. Sheridan

The Fish Gutter
J. Molloy

"I Was Strolling"
D. O'Callaghan

Portrait in Oils
N. Sheridan

"The Green Bushes"
D. O'Callaghan

Matchmaker
J. Molloy, N. Sheridan

Finale
The Company

1964.01 HELLO, DOLLY!

A Musical Comedy in Two Acts, 15 Scenes. Book by Michael Stewart.
Based on the play "The Matchmaker" by Thornton Wilder. Music and lyrics
by Jerry Herman. Directed and choreographed by Gower Champion.
Settings by Oliver Smith. Costumes by Freddy Wittop. Lighting by Jean
Rosenthal. Musical direction and vocal arrangements by Shepard Coleman.
Orchestrations by Philip J. Lang. Dance and incidental music arranged by
Peter Howard. Assistant to the director, Lucia Victor. A David Merrick-
Champion Five Inc. Production. Produced by David Merrick. Opened 16
January 1964 at the St. James Theatre and closed 27 December 1970 after
2844 performances[8].

CAST (in the order of appearance): *Mrs. Dolly Gallagher Levi*: CAROL CHANNING.
Ernestina: Mary Jo Catlett. *Ambrose Kemper*: Igors Gavon. *Horse*: Jan LaPrade, Bonnie
Mathis. *Horace Vandergelder*: DAVID BURNS. *Ermengarde*: Alice Playten. *Cornelius
Hackl*: CHARLES NELSON REILLY. *Barnaby Tucker*: JERRY DODGE. *Irene Molloy*:
EILEEN BRENNAN. *Minnie Fay*: SONDRA LEE. *Mrs. Rose*: Amelia Haas. *Rudolph*:
David Hartman. *Judge*: Gordon Connell. *Court Clerk*: Ken Ayers.

Townspeople, Waiters, Etc.: Nicole Barth, Monica Carter, Carvel Carter, Amelia
Haas, Jan LaPrade, Joan Buttons Leonard, Marilyne Mason, Bonnie Mathis, Else
Olufsen, Yolanda Poropat, Bonnie Schon, Barbara Sharma, Mary Ann Snow, Jamie
Thomas, Pat Trott, Ken Ayers, Alvin Beam, Joel Craig, Dick Crowley, Gene Gebauer,
Joe Helms, Richard Hermany, Neil Jones, Charles Karel, Paul Kastl, Jim Maher, Joe
McWherter, John Mineo, Randy Phillips, Lowell Purvis, Michael Quinn, Will Roy,
Paul Solen, Ronnie Young.

The action takes place in Yonkers and New York City in the 1890s.

Act 1, Scene 1: Along Fourth Avenue, New York City. *Scene 2*: Grand Central Station.
Scene 3: A Street in Yonkers. *Scene 4*: Vandergelder's Hay and Feed Store, Yonkers.
Scene 5: The Yonkers Depot. *Scene 6*: Outside Mrs, Malloy's Hat Shop. Water Street,
New York City. *Scene 7*: Inside the Hat Shop. *Scene 8*: A Quiet Street. *Scene 9*:
Fourteenth Street.

Act 2, Scene 1: In front of the Hoffman House Hotel on Fifth Avenue. *Scene 2*: Outside
the Harmonia Gardens Restaurant on the Battery. *Scene 3*: Inside the Harmonia
Gardens Restaurant. *Scene 4*: Tableaux Vivantes. *Scene 5*: A Courtroom on Centre
Street. *Scene 6*: The Hay and Feed Store, Yonkers.

ACT 1[9]

Scene 2

"I Put My Hand In"
C. Channing, Company

Scene 4

"It Takes a Woman"
D. Burns, Instant Glee Club

"Put on Your Sunday Clothes"
C. N. Reilly, J. Dodge, C. Channing, I. Gavon, A. Playten

Scene 5

"Put on Your Sunday Clothes" (reprise)
The People of Yonkers

Scene 7

"Ribbons Down My Back"
E. Brennan

---

[8]Pearl Bailey and Cab Calloway headed an all-black cast which performed
two years of the show's continuous run (889 performances) 12 November
1967-20 December 1969; see separate entry in 1967-1968 season.
[9]When Ethel Merman assumed the role of Dolly Levi in March 1970,
added were:

"World, Take Me Back"
E. Merman

(added to Act 1, Scene 4 between "It Takes a Woman" and "Sunday
Clothes")

"Love, Look in My Window" (Act 1, Scene 8)
E. Merman

"Motherhood"
C. Channing, D. Burns, E. Brennan, S. Lee, C. N. Reilly, J. Dodge
"Dancing"
C. Channing, C. N. Reilly, J. Dodge, S. Lee, E. Brennan, Dancers
Scene 9
"Before the Parade Passes By"
C. Channing, D. Burns, Company

ACT 2
Scene 1
"Elegance"
E. Brennan, C. N. Reilly, S. Lee, J. Dodge
Scene 3
"The Waiter's Gallop"
D. Hartman, Waiters
"Hello, Dolly!"
C. Channing, D. Hartman, Waiters, Cooks
Scene 4
"Come and Be My Butterfly"[10]
I. Gavon, Muses, Nymphs, Flowers, Butterflies
Scene 5
"It Only Takes a Moment"
C. N. Reilly, E. Brennan, Prisoners, Policemen
"So Long Dearie"
C. Channing, D. Burns
Scene 6
"Hello, Dolly!" (reprise)
C. Channing, D. Burns
Finale
Company

JOSEPHINE BAKER
AND HER COMPANY

1964.02

A Musical Revue in Two Acts, 12 Scenes. Production consultant and staging by Felix G. Gerstman. Miss Baker's costumes by Christian Dior, Pierre Balmain, House of Lanvin, and Balenciaga. Scenery by Joseph Hansen. Musical director, Gershon Kingsley. Lighting by Michael Price. Produced by Sherman S. Krellberg. Opened 4 February 1964 at the Brooks Atkinson Theatre and closed 16 February 1964 after 16 performances; reopened 31 March 1964 at the Henry Miller's Theatre and closed 19 April 1964 after 24 additional performances. Total: 40 performances.

CAST: JOSEPHINE BAKER, GEOFFREY HOLDER, AVIV DANCERS (Frances Alenikoff, Larry Bianco, Mary Ann Bruning, Carol Flemming, Jerry Scott), Eliezer Adoram (Singer, Accordionist, Music director for the Aviv Dancers), LARL BECHAM TRIO (Primitive and Modern Dance Group).

ACT 1
Scene 1
"Avec" (from the French revue PARIS MES AMOURS)
(*Music and Lyrics by* Henri Betti, Bruno Coquatrix and Andre Hornez.)
"Quand tu m'embrasse"
(*Music and Lyrics by* Charles Aznavour and Eddie Barclay.)
"Make Believe" (from SHOWBOAT)
(*Music by* Jerome Kern. *Lyrics by* Oscar Hammerstein II.)
"Quando, Quando"
(*Music by* Tony Renis. *Italian Lyrics by* A. Testa.)
J. Baker
Scene 2
Geoffrey Holder
Scene 3
"Don't Touch My Tomatoes" (from the French revue PARIS MES AMOURS)
(*Music and Lyrics by* Henry Lemarchand and Jo Bouillon.)
J. Baker

Scene 4
Larl Becham Trio
Scene 5
"La Seine"
(*Music and Lyrics by* Guy Lafarge and Flavien Monod. *English Lyrics by* Geoffrey Parsons.)
"Hello, Young Lovers" (from THE KING AND I)
(*Music by* Richard Rodgers. *Lyrics by* Oscar Hammerstein II.)
"Mon bateau blanc"
(*Music and Lyrics by* Gilbert Becaud and Maurice Vidalin.)
"Felicida" (Esto es Felicidad)
J. Baker
(*Music and Lyrcis by* Oscar de la Rosa, Bobby Collazo, Carlos Menendez.)
Scene 6
Israeli Festival (Variations and Debka)
Polynka (A Russian Peasant Dance)
The Aviv Dancers
Scene 7
"(En) Avril à Paris"
(*Music and Lyrics by* Charles Trenet.)/
"April in Paris" (from WALK A LITTLE FASTER)
(*Music by* Vernon Duke. *Lyrics by* E. Y. Harburg. *French Lyrics by* Duck.)
"Addios, Addios"
"Bill" (from SHOWBOAT)
(*Music by* Jerome Kern. *Lyrics by* P. G. Wodehouse.)
"Je pars"
(*Music and Lyrics by* Morton and Selma Craft.)
J. Baker

ACT 2
Scene 1
"Melodie perdue"
(*Music and Lyrics by* Hubert Giraud and Jean Broussolle.)
"(You Are My) Lucky Star" (from film BROADWAY MELODY OF 1936)
(*Music by* Nacio Herb Brown. *Lyrics by* Arthur Freed.)
"Enamorada"
(*Music and Lyrics by* Augusto Alguerro and Leon Arias Rafael.)
"J'ai deux amours"
(*Music and Lyrics by* Georges Koger, Henri Varna, and Vincent Scotto.)
J. Baker
Scene 2
The Aviv Dancers
Scene 3
"Hava Naguila"
(*Arranged by* Harry Belafonte and Lorin.)
J. Baker
Scene 4
Geoffrey Holder
Scene 5
"Fan, Fan"
"La Novia"
(*Music and Lyrics by* J. Prieto.)
"Et pourtant"
(*Music by* Georges Garvarentz. *Lyrics by* Charles Aznavour.)
"Dans mon village"
(*Music and Lyrics by* Henry Lemarchand and Francis Lopez.)
"J'attendrai"
(*Music and Lyrics by* Rastelli, Dino Olivieri and Louis Poterat.)
J. Baker

RUGANTINO

1964.03

A Roman Musical Spectacle (Musical Comedy) in Two Acts, 24 Scenes, in Italian[11]. Book, lyrics and direction by (Pietro) Garinei and (Sandro) Giovannini. Book in collaboration with Festa Campanile and Massimo

---

[10]Dropped early in the run and replaced by:
"The Polka Contest"
I. Gavon, A. Playten, E. Brennan, C. N. Reilly, S. Lee, J. Dodge, Ensemble

---

[11]Presented with English subtitles projected on a screen. Title consultant was Herman G. Weinberg with title coordination by Jack Harrold and projection by Bob Swanson, Telesync.

Franciosa. Music by Armando Trovaioli. English version [supertitles] by Alfred Drake. Lyric translation by Edward Eager. Scenery and costumes by Giulio Coltellacci. Musical numbers staged by Dania Krupska. Musical director, Anton Coppola. Scenic supervision, Eldon Elder. Lighting by Vannio Vanni. Technical direction by Ralph Alswang. Production associate, Andre Goulston. Produced by Alexander H. Cohen and Jack Hylton. Opened 6 February 1964 at the Mark Hellinger Theatre and closed 29 February 1964 after 28 performances.

CAST (in order of appearance): *Rugantino*: NINO MANFREDI. *Mariotto*: Goffredo Spinedi. *Rubastracci*: Giuseppe Pennese. *Strappalenzola*: Fernando Martino. *Brother Tappeto*: Lino Benedetti. *Bellachioma*: Toni Ventura. *The Brigadier*: Willy Colombini. *Chief Bandit*: Armando Silverini. *Rosetta*: ORNELLA VANONI. *Gnecco*, Rosetta's husband: RENZO PALMER. *Mastro Titta*: ALDO FABRIZI. *Bojetto*, Mastro Titta's son: CARLO DELLE PIANE. *Donna Marta Paritelli*: FRANCA TAMANTINI. *Don Nicoló Paritelli*: Toni Ucci. *Eusebia*: BICE VALORI. *The Barber*: Giorgio Zaffaroni. *Thorwaldsen*, the sculptor: Cesare Gelli. *Don Fulgenzio*: Giorgio Fabretti. *The Troubador* (Calascione): LANDO FIORINI. *The Lover*: Marcello Serrallonga. *The Goat Keeper*: Luciano Bonanni. *Old Lady of the Cats*: Simona Sorlisi. *Cardinal Severini*: Gino Mucci. *Gentleman*: Angelo Pericet. *Gendarmes*: Renato Ghigi, Angelo Michelotti.

Dancers and Singers: Goffredo Spinedi, Toni Ventura, Willy Colombini, Giorgio Zaffaroni, Marcello Serrallonga, Angelo Infanti, Luciano Bernardi, Fernando Martino, Franco Di Toro, Gabriele Villa, Giuseppe Pennese, Lino Benedetti, Josephine Spinedi, Gianna Zorini, Lettie Zaffaroni, Gina Sampieri, Lida Vianello, Renata Zamengo, Brigitte Kirfel, Gabriella Panenti, Carla Russo, Barbara Schaub, Yvonne De Vintar, Maurizia Camilli. *Chorus of Nora Orlandi*: Armando Silverini, Ercole Vulpiani, Margherita Brancucci, Raffaella Caratelli.

The action takes place in Rome in the year 1830 during the reign of Pope Pius VIII.

Act 1, Scene 1: The Square before Mastro Titta's Tavern. *Scene 2*: Rosetta's Bedroom. *Scene 3*: A Room in the Paritelli Palace. *Scene 4*: The Square. *Scene 5*: Rosetta's Bedroom. *Scene 6*: The Square. *Scene 7*: Outside the Paritelli Palace. *Scene 8*: The Docks. *Scene 9*: The Dining Hall of Paritelli Palace. *Scene 10*: The Street-Barber's. *Scene 11*: The Studio of the Sculptor, Thorwaldsen. *Scene 12*: The Parish Church. *Scene 13*: The Square. *Scene 14*: San Michele Prison. *Scene 15*: The Square on Lantern Night. *Scene 16*: Rosetta's Bedroom.

Act 2, Scene 1: A Corner of Campo Vaccino. *Scene 2*: The Square before the Church of San Pasquale. *Scene 3*: A Corner of the Forum frequented by the hungry stray cats of Rome. *Scene 4*: The Square. *Scene 5*: The Churchyard. *Scene 6*: Mastro Titta's Cellar. *Scene 7*: San Michele Prison. *Scene 8*: A Square in Rome at dawn.

ACT 1

"The Game of Morra" (La Morra)
  The Men

"Rugantino in the Stocks" (La Berlina)
  Rugantino's 'Friends'

"A House Is Not the Same Without a Woman" (E Bello Avè 'na Donna Dentro Casa)
  A. Fabrizi

"Nothing to Do" (Ballata Di Rugantino)
  N. Manfredi, the Romans

"Just Look!" (Anvedi Sì Che Paciocca)
  O. Vanoni, L. Fiorini, Boys

"The Saltarello"
  B. Valori, A. Fabrizi, Ensemble

"Tirrallallera" (Tirollallero)
  L. Fiorini

"The Headsman and I"
  B. Valori

"Nothing To Do" (reprise)
  N. Manfredi

"Ciumachella" (Ciumachella De Trastevere)
  L. Fiorini

"Lantern Night"
  Ensemble

"Roma" (Roma Nun Fa La Stupida Stasera)
  N. Manfredi, O. Vanoni, B. Valori, A. Fabrizi, Ensemble

ACT 2

"Ciumachella" (reprise)
  Ensemble

"I'm Happy" (Tira a Campà)
  N. Manfredi

"Just Stay Alive" (Sempre Boia È)
  A. Fabrizi, Ensemble

"San Pasquale"
  B. Valori, Spinsters

"Passatella" (The Drinking Game)
  L. Fiorini, G. Spinedi, N. Manfredi, Boys

"It's Quick and Easy" ('Na Botta E Via)
  O. Vanoni, Boys

"Dance of the Candle Killers"
  Ensemble

"Boy and Man" (È L'Omo Mio)
  O. Vanoni

Finale
  B. Valori, O. Vanoni, A. Fabrizi, N. Manfredi

1964.04   FOXY

A Musical Comedy in Two Acts, 14 Scenes. Book by Ian McLellan Hunter and Ring Lardner, Jr. Suggested by Ben Jonson's play "Volpone." Music by Robert Emmett Dolan. Lyrics by Johnny Mercer. Directed by Robert Lewis. Choreography and musical numbers staged by Jack Cole. Scenery and lighting by Robert Randolph. Costumes by Robert Fletcher. Musical direction and vocal arrangements by Don Pippin. Orchestrations by Eddie Sauter and Hal Schaefer. Dance music arranged by Hal Schaefer. Produced by David Merrick. Opened 16 February 1964 at the Ziegfeld Theatre and closed 18 April 1964 after 72 performances.

CAST (in order of appearance): *Doc*: LARRY BLYDEN. *Foxy*: BERT LAHR. *Bedrock*: ROBERT H. HARRIS. *Buzzard*: EDWARD GREENHALGH. *Shortcut*: GERALD HIKEN. *Drunk*: Tony Kraber. *Mountie*: John Hallow. *Brandy*: CATHRYN DAMON. *Oliver*: Will Parkins. *Celia*: JULIENNE MARIE. *First Prospector*: Newt Sullivan. *Second Prospector*: Eddie James. *Third Prospector*: Herb Fields. *Stirling*: David Rounds. *First Eskimo*: John Waller. *Second Eskimo*: John Aristides. *Lord Rottingham*: ANTHONY KEMBLE COOPER. *Clergyman*: John Taliaferro. *Ben*: JOHN DAVIDSON. *Laurette*: Mary Ann Corrigan. *Marie*: Constance Meng. *Bellboy*: John Taliferro.

Prospectors: John Aristides, Carlos Bas, Charles Cagle, George Del Monte, Lang Des Jardins, Herbert Fields, Tim Harum, Lee Howard, Eddie James, John Keatts, Robert LaCrosse, Will Parkins, Newt Sullivan, John Taliaferro, John Waller. *Saloon Girls*: Helen Baisley, Mary Ann Corrigan, Virginia Craig, Judith Dunford, Alice Glenn, Marlena Lustik, Ethel Martin, Constance Meng, Nancy Myers, Shelly Rann, Sueanne Shirley, June Eve Story, Susan Terry.

Act 1, Scene 1: Trading Post, Alaska. *Scene 2*: Brandy's Saloon. *Scene 3*: Buzzard's Cabin. *Scene 4*: Buzzard's Cabin. *Scene 5*: Steamboat Landing. *Scene 6*: Buzzard's Cabin. *Scene 7*: Brandy's Saloon.

Act 2, Scene 1: Outside Hotel. *Scene 2*: Hotel Room. *Scene 3*: Outside Hotel. *Scene 4*: Buzzard's Cabin. *Scene 5*: Front Street—Saloon. *Scene 6*: Brandy's Office. *Scene 7*: Brandy's Saloon.

ACT 1

Prologue
  L. Blyden

"Many Ways to Skin a Cat"
  B. Lahr, L. Blyden

"Rollin' in Gold"
  C. Damon, Ensemble

"My Weight in Gold"
  J. Marie

"Money Isn't Everything"
  B. Lahr, L. Blyden, R. H. Harris, G. Hiken, E. Greenhalgh, Ensemble

"Larceny and Love"
  C. Damon, L. Blyden

"Ebeneezer McAfee III"
  Ensemble

"Talk to Me, Baby"
  J. Marie, J. Davidson

"This Is My Night to Howl"
  G. Hiken, J. Davidson, Ensemble

"Bon Vivant"
  B. Lahr, Ensemble

Finale Act 1
  Ensemble

ACT 2

Entr'acte
  Ensemble

"It's Easy When You Know How"
  L. Blyden

"Run, Run, Run Cinderella"
  J. Marie
"Talk To Me, Baby" (reprise)
  J. Davidson
"I'm Way Ahead of the Game"
  C. Damon, L. Blyden
"A Case of Rape"
  J. Marie, J. Davidson, Ensemble
"In Loving Memory"
  B. Lahr, L. Blyden, R. H. Harris, G. Hiken, E. Greenhalgh, Ensemble
Finale
  B. Lahr, L. Blyden, Ensemble

1964.05 WHAT MAKES SAMMY RUN?

A Musical Comedy in Two Acts, 16 Scenes. Book by Budd and Stuart Schulberg. Based on the novel of the same name by Budd Schulberg. Music and lyrics by Ervin Drake. Directed by Abe Burrows. Musical staging by Matt Mattox. Settings and lighting by Herbert Senn and Helen Pond. Costumes by Noel Taylor. Vocal arrangements and musical direction by Lehman Engel. Orchestrations by Don Walker. Dance arrangements by Arnold Goland. Orchestrations by Don Walker. Production supervised by Robert Weiner. A Cates Brothers Production in association with Beresford Productions Ltd. Produced by Joseph Cates. Opened 27 February 1964 at the 54th Street Theatre and closed 12 June 1965 after 540 performances.

CAST (in order of appearance): *Al Manheim:* ROBERT ALDA. *Sammy Glick:* STEVE LAWRENCE. *O'Brien:* RALPH STANTLEY. *Osborn:* John Dorrin. *Bartender:* Ralph Vucci. *Julian Blumberg:* George Coe. *Rita Rio:* GRACIELA DANIELE. *Tracy Clark:* RICHARD FRANCE. *Lucky Dugan:* Edward McNally. *Shiek Orsini:* BARRY NEWMAN. *Technical Advisor:* Bob Maxwell. *Sidney Fineman:* ARNY FREEMAN. *Kit Sargent:* SALLY ANN HOWES. *H. L. Harrington:* WALTER KLAVUN. *Laurette Harrington:* BERNICE MASSI. *Seymour Glick:* MACE BARRETT.
  Singing Ensemble: Lillian Bozinoff, Natalie Costa, Judith Hastings, Jamie Simmons, Darrell J. Askey, John Dorrin, Richard Terry, Ralph Vucci. *Dancing Ensemble:* Diaan Ainslee, Nancy Carnegie, Barbara Gine, Lavina Hamilton, Bella Shalom, Maralyn Thoma, Jean Blanchard, Marco Gomez, Buck Heller, Nat Horne, Jack Kresy. *Swing Couple:* Lynn Gremmler, Doug Spingler.

The action takes place in New York and Hollywood a generation ago.

Act 1, Scene 1: The City Room of the *New York Record. Scene 2:* Joe's Bar. *Scene 3:* The *New York Record. Scene 4:* World-Wide Pictures Sound Stage. *Scene 5:* The Studio Street. *Scene 6:* The Sound Stage. *Scene 7:* The Patio of Fineman's Mansion. *Scene 8:* Kit's House.

Act 2, Scene 1: The Court of Grauman's Chinese Theatre. *Scene 2:* Joe's Bar. *Scene 3:* Kit's Terrace. *Scene 4:* The World-Wide Penthouse in New York. *Scene 5:* Kit's Terrace. *Scene 6:* Sammy's Office. *Scene 7:* Sammy's Mansion. *Scene 8:* Sammy's Mansion.

ACT 1
Scene 1
  "A New Pair of Shoes"
    S. Lawrence, R. Alda, Ensemble
Scene 2
  "You Help Me"
    S. Lawrence, R. Alda
Scene 4
  "A Tender Spot"
    S. A. Howes
Scene 5
  "Lites-Camera-Platitude"
    S. Lawrence, S. A. Howes, R. Alda
Scene 6
  "My Hometown"
    S. Lawrence
  "Monsoon" (Ballet)
    G. Daniele, R. France, Ensemble
Scene 7
  "I See Something"
    B. Massi, S. Lawrence
Scene 8
  "Maybe Some Other Time"
    S. A. Howes, R. Alda

"You Can Trust Me"
  S. Lawrence
"A Room Without Windows"
  S. A. Howes, S. Lawrence
"Kiss Me No Kisses"
  S. A. Howes, S. Lawrence
ACT 2
Scene 1
  "I Feel Humble"
    S. Lawrence, B. Newman, Ensemble
Scene 3
  "Something to Live For"
    S. A. Howes
Scene 4
  "Paint a Rainbow"
    G. Daniele, R. France, Ensemble
  "You're No Good"
    B. Massi, S. Lawrence
Scene 5
  "Something To Live For" (reprise)
    R. Alda
Scene 6
  "My Hometown" (reprise)[12]
    S. Lawrence
  "The Friendliest Thing"
    B. Massi
Scene 7
  "Wedding of the Year"
    Ensemble
Scene 8
  "Some Days Everything Goes Wrong"
    S. Lawrence

1964.06 LA VIE PARISIENNE

A Revival of the Opéra-Bouffe in Four Acts, in French[13]. Libretto by Henri Meilhac and Ludovic Halévy. Music by Jacques Offenbach. Decor and costumes by Jean-Denis Malcles. Directed by Jean-Louis Barrault. Dances arranged by Roger Stefani. Orchestra conducted by Andre Girard. The Theatre De France Company produced by Sol Hurok, by arrangement with the Government of the French Republic. Opened 10 March 1964 at the New York City Center and closed 15 March 1964 after 8 performances.

CAST: *Bobinet:* Jean-Pierre Granval. *Gardefeu:* Jean Desailly. *The Baron:* Pierre Bertin. *The Brazilian:* JEAN-LOUIS BARRAULT. *Frick, Prosper, Alfred:* JEAN PAREDES. *Gontran, Urbain:* Dominique Santarelli. *Joseph:* Robert Lombardi. *Alphonse:* Regis Outin. *The Man Who Waits:* Michel Bertay. *Metella:* SUZY DELAIR. *The Baroness:* Sarah Sanders. *Gabrielle:* Simone Valère. *Pauline:* Denise Benoît. *The Sweeper:* Marie-Helene Daste.
  Chorus and French Can-Can: Judith Alexandre, Dominique Arden, Paulette Attie, Christine Bottai, Claudie Bourlon, Josette Grisy, Sabine Lods, Jane Martel, Nicole Levat, Celine Salles, Andre Batiste, Georges Coste, Henri Gilabert, Jean-Guy Henneveux, Bernard Laik, Gilbert Lefevre, Luis Masson, Gerard Quenez, Stanislas Staskewitsch, Jean Winkler.

THE YEOMEN OF THE GUARD,
1964.07 or The Merryman and His Maid

A Revival of the Comic Opera in Two Acts[14]. Libretto by William S. Gilbert. Music by Arthur Sullivan. Staged by Allen Fletcher. Scenery by Stephen O. Saxe. Costumes by Alvin Colt. Conducted by Julius Rudel. Produced by the New York City Center Gilbert and Sullivan Company. Opened 18 March 1964 at the New York City Center and closed 29 March 1964 after 3 performances in repertory.

---

[12]Dropped from programs during run.
[13]First produced in New York 29 March 1869 at the Theatre Francais. For Synopsis of Scenes and Musical Numbers, see original 1869 production.
[14]First presented in New York 17 October 1888 at the Casino Theatre for 100 performances. For Synopsis of Scenes and Musical Numbers, see original 1888 production.

CAST: *Sir Richard Cholmondeley*, Lieutenant. of the Tower: PAUL UKENA. *Colonel Fairfax* under sentence of death: ROBERT ROUNSEVILLE. *Sergeant Meryll* of the Yeomen of the Guard: GEORGE GAYNES. *Leonard Meryll*, his Son: RICHARD KRAUSE. *Jack Point*, a Strolling Jester: NORMAN KELLEY. *Wilfred Shadbolt*, Head Jailor and Assistant Tormentor: HERBERT BEATTIE. *The Headsman*: Thomas Andrew. *First Yeoman*: Herbert Pordum. *Second Yeoman*: Sean Barker. *First Citizen*: Harris Davis. *Second Citizen*: Glenn Dowlen. *Elsie Maynard*, a Strolling Player: MARY JENNINGS. *Phoebe Meryll*, Sergeant Meryll's Daughter: MARY BURGESS. *Dame Carruthers*, Housekeeper to the Tower: EVELYN SACHS. *Kate*, her Niece: VIRGINIA BITAR.

Chorus of Yeomen of the Guard, Gentlemen, Citizens, etc.: Barbara Beaman, Paul Corder, Harris Davis, Marceline Decker, Anthea de Forest, Glen Dowlen, Roebrt Edwards, Beverly Evans, Frederic Griesinger, Helen Guile, Don Henderson, Lila Herbert, David Hicks, Lynda Jordan, Robert Lee Kelly, Kellis Miller, Hanna Owen, Richard G. Park, Charlotte Povia, Lourette Raymon, Anthony Safina, Alexander Savchuck, John Smith, Dale Westerman, Lou Ann Wyckoff, Marie Young.

H.M.S. PINAFORE,
1964.08   or The Lass That Loved a Sailor

A Revival of the Comic Opera in Two Acts[15]. Libretto by William S. Gilbert. Music by Arthur Sullivan. Staged by Allen Fletcher. Scenery and costumes by Patton Campbell. Conductors, Felix Popper and Charles Wilson. Produced by the New York City Center Gilbert and Sullivan Company. Opened 20 March 1964 at the New York City Center and closed 2 April 1964 after 5 performances in repertory.

CAST: *The Rt. Hon. Sir Joseph Porter, K.C.B.*, First Lord of the Admiralty: RAYMOND ALLEN. *Captain Corcoran*, Commander of the *H.M.S. Pinafore*: WILLIAM CHAPMAN. *Ralph Rackstraw*, Able Seaman: ROBERT ROUNSEVILLE. *Dick Deadeye*, Able Seaman: PAUL UKENA. *Bill Bobstay*, Boatswain: Sean Barker. *Bob Becket*: Lee Cass. *Josephine*, the Captain's Daughter: CAROL BERGEY. *Hebe*, Sir Joseph's First Cousin: Marlena Kleinman. *Little Buttercup*, Mrs. Cripps, a Portsmouth bum-boat woman: EVELYN SACHS. *First Lord's Sisters, His Cousins, His Aunts, Sailors, Marines, etc.*: same as THE YEOMEN OF THE GUARD above.

THE MIKADO,
1964.09   or The Town of Titipu

A Revival of the Comic Opera in Two Acts[16]. Libretto by William S. Gilbert. Music by Arthur Sullivan. Staged by Dorothy Raedler. Scenery by Donald Oenslager. Costumes by Patton Campbell. Conductor, Dean Ryan. Produced by the New York City Center Gilbert and Sullivan Company. Opened 22 March 1964 at the New York City Center and closed 5 April 1964 after 6 performances in repertory.

CAST: *The Mikado of Japan*: GEORGE GAYNES. *Nanki-Poo*: WILLIAM DIARD. *Ko-Ko*: NORMAN KELLEY. *Pooh-Bah*: HERBERT BEATTIE. *Pish-Tush*: DAVID SMITH. *Three Sisters, Wards of Ko-Ko: Yum-Yum*: CAROL BERGEY. *Pitti-Sing*: MARY BURGESS. *Peep-Bo*: MARLENA KLEINMAN. *Katisha*: EVELYN SACHS. *Chorus of School Girls, Nobles, Guards and Coolies*: same as THE YEOMEN OF THE GUARD above.

PATIENCE,
1964.10   or Bunthorne's Bride

A Revival of the Comic Opera in Two Acts[17]. Libretto by William S. Gilbert. Music by Arthur Sullivan. Scenery and costumes designed by Motley. Staged by Dorothy Raedler. Solo dance choreography by Thomas Andrew. Conductor, Julius Rudel. Produced by the New York City Center Gilbert and Sullivan Company. Opened 25 March 1964 at the New York City Center and closed 5 April 1964 after 4 performances in repertory.

CAST: *Colonel Calverley*: WILLIAM CHAPMAN. *Major Murgatroyd*: James Wilson. *Lieut. the Duke of Dunstable*: RICHARD KRAUSE. *Reginald Bunthorne*, a Fleshly

---

[15]Originally presented in New York 15 January 1879 at the Standard Theatre for 175 performances. For Synopsis of Scenes and Musical Numbers, see original 1879 production.

[16]First presented in New York 20 July, 10-29 August 1885 at the Union Square and People's Theatres for 22 performances. First authorized production presented 19 August 1885 at the Fifth Avenue Theatre by Richard D'Oyly Carte for 250 performances. For Synopsis of Scenes and Musical Numbers, see 19 August 1885 D'Oyly Carte production.

[17]First presented in New York 22 September 1881 at the Standard Theatre for 177 performances. For Synopsis of Scenes and Musical Numbers, see original 1881 production.

Poet: EMILE RENAN. *Archibald Grosvenor*, an Idyllic Poet: DAVID SMITH. *Mr. Bunsthorne's Solicitor*: Thomas Andrew. *The Lady Angela, The Lady Saphir, The Lady Ella, The Lady Jane*, Rapturous Maidens: MARLENA KLEINMAN, HELEN GUILE, Virginia Bitar, CLARAMAE TURNER. *Patience*, a Dairy Maid: LEE VENORA. *Chorus of Rapturous Maidens and Officers of the Dragoon Guards*: same as THE YEOMEN OF THE GUARD above.

1964.11   ## FUNNY GIRL

A Musical in Two Acts, 22 Scenes. Book and story[18] by Isobel Lennart. Music by Jule Styne. Lyrics by Bob Merrill. Directed by Garson Kanin. Musical numbers staged by Carol Haney. Scenery and lighting by Robert Randolph. Costumes by Irene Sharaff. Musical director, Milton Rosenstock. Orchestrations by Ralph Burns. Vocal arrangements by Buster Davis. Dance orchestrations by Luther Henderson. Associate producer, Al Goldin. Associate director, Lawrence Kasha. Produced by Ray Stark in association with Seven Arts Productions. Opened 26 March 1964 at the Winter Garden, moved 14 March 1966 to the Majestic Theatre, moved 28 November 1966 to the Broadway Theatre, and closed 1 July 1967 after 1348 performances.

CAST (in order of appearance): *Fanny Brice*: BARBRA STREISAND. *John*: Robert Howard. *Emma*: Royce Wallace. *Mrs. Brice*: KAY MEDFORD. *Mrs. Strakosh*: JEAN STAPLETON. *Mrs. Meeker*: Lydia S. Fredricks. *Mrs. O'Malley*: Joyce O'Neil. *Tom Keeney*: JOSEPH MACAULAY. *Eddie Ryan*: DANNY MEEHAN. *Heckie*: Victor R. Helou. *Workmen*: Robert Howard, Robert Henson. *Snub Taylor*: Buzz Miller. *Trombone Smitty*: Blair Hammond. *Five Finger Finney*: Alan (E.) Weeks. *Trumpet Soloist*: Dick Perry. *Bubbles*: Shellie Farrell. *Polly*: Joan Lowe. *Maude*: Ellen Halpin. *Nick Arnstein*: SYDNEY CHAPLIN. *Showgirls*: Sharon Vaughn, Diana Lee Nielsen. *Stage Director*: Marc Jordan. *Florenz Ziegfeld, Jr.*: ROGER DeKOVEN. *Mimsey*: Sharon Vaughn. *Ziegfeld Tenor*: John Lankston. *Ziegfeld Lead Dancer*: George Reeder. *Adolph*: John Lankston. *Mrs. Nadler*: Rose Randoff. *Paul*: Larry Fuller. *Cathy*: Joan Cory. *Vera*: Lainie Kazan. *Jenny*: Diane Coupe. *Ben*: Buzz Miller. *Mr. Renaldi*: Marc Jordan. *Mike Halsey*: Robert Howard.

Showgirls: Prudence Adams, Joan Cory, Diane Coupe, Lainie Kazan, Diana Lee Nielsen, Sharon Vaughn, Rosmarie Yellen. *Singers*: Lydia S. Fredricks, Mary Louise, Jeanne McLaren, Joyce O'Neil, Rose Randolf, Stephanie Reynolds, Victor R. Helou, Robert Henson, Robert Howard, Marc Jordan, John Lankston, Albert Zimmerman. *Dancers*: Edie Cowan, Christine Dalsey, Shellie Farrell, Ellen Halpin, Rosemary Jelinic, Karen Kristin, Joan Lowe, Jose Ahumada, Bud Fleming, Larry Fuller, Blair Hammond, John Nola, Alan Peterson, Alan E. Weeks.

The action takes place in various theatres, onstage and backstage, on New York's Lower East Side, in Baltimore, and on Long Island shortly before and after World War I.

Act 1, Scene 1: Backstage, Fanny's Dressing Room, about 1910. *Scene 2*: Kenney's Music Hall, backstage. *Scene 3*: In front of Kenney's Music Hall. *Scene 4*: A backyard in Fanny's neighborhood, 6 A.M. *Scene 5*: Kenney's Music Hall—on stage. *Scene 6*: Keeney's Music Hall, backstage and the Chorus Dressing Room, immediately following. *Scene 7*: Mrs. Brice's Kitchen. Months later. *Scene 8*: The New York Theatre—backstage. *Scene 9*: On the Stage of the New York Theatre, the grand finale of the Ziegfeld Follies. *Scene 10*: In front of the Follies curtain, immediately following. *Scene 11*: Outside the house at 24 Henry Street. *Scene 12*: The interior of Mrs. Brice's saloon. *Scene 13*: A private dining room in Baltimore. *Scene 14*: The Baltimore Railroad Terminal.

Act 2, Scene 1: The Arnstein Long Island Mansion, unfurnished and at night. *Scene 2*: Mrs. Brice's saloon. *Scene 3*: The New Amsterdam Theatre—backstage, around 1920. *Scene 4*: The New Amsterdam Theatre—on stage. *Scene 5*: Fanny's dressing room—immediately following. *Scene 6*: The study of the Arnstein house. *Scene 7*: The New Amsterdam Theatre—a bare stage rehearsal. *Scene 8*: The New Amsterdam Theatre—backstage, Fanny's dressing room.

ACT 1[19]

Scenes 1 and 2

"If A Girl Isn't Pretty"
    J. Stapleton, K. Medford, D. Meehan, Chorus

Scene 3

"I'm the Greatest Star"
    B. Streisand

Scene 5

"Cornet Man"
    B. Streisand, B. Miller, Chorus

Scene 7

"Who Taught Her Everything"

---

[18]The life of Fanny Brice.

[19]Added to programs for National Tour, Act 1, Scene 7 (beginning):
    Rehearsal (Downtown Rag)
        Ziegfeld Company

K. Medford, D. Meehan

Scene 9

"His Love Makes Me Beautiful"

J. Lankston, Ziegfeld Girls, B. Streisand

Scene 10

"I Want To Be Seen With You Tonight"

S. Chaplin, B. Streisand

Scene 11

"Henry Street"

Chorus

"People"

B. Streisand

Scene 13

"You Are Woman"

S. Chaplin, B. Streisand

Scene 14

"Don't Rain on My Parade"

B. Streisand

ACT 2

Scene 1

"Sadie, Sadie"

B. Streisand, Friends

Scene 2

"Find Yourself a Man"

J. Stapleton, K. Medford, D. Meehan

Scenes 3 and 4

"Rat-Tat-Tat-Tat"

Ziegfeld Company, B. Streisand

Scene 5

"Who Are You Now?"

B. Streisand

Scene 7

"The Music That Makes Me Dance"

B. Streisand

Scene 8

"Don't Rain on My Parade" (reprise)

B. Streisand

THE GONDOLIERS,
or The King of Barataria

1964.12

A Revival of the Comic Opera in Two Acts[20]. Libretto by William S. Gilbert. Music by Arthur Sullivan. Staged by Dorothy Raedler. Scenery and costumes by Ed Wittstein. Conductor, Felix Popper. Cachucha dance choreography by Thomas Andrew. Produced by the New York City Center Gilbert and Sullivan Company. Opened 27 March 1964 (matinee) at the New York City Center and closed 27 March 1964 (evening) after 2 performances in repertory.

CAST: *The Duke of Plaza-Toro*: NORMAN KELLEY. *Luiz*: THEODORE MORILL. *Don Alhambra Del Bolero*: GEORGE GAYNES. *Marco Palmieri*: CHARLES HINDSLEY. *Giuseppe Palmieri*: SEAN BARKER. *Antonio*: David Smith. *Francesco*: Herbert Pordum. *Giorgio*: John Smith. *The Duchess of Plaza-Toro*: CLARAMAE TURNER. *Casilda*: DONNA PRECHT. *Gianetta*: MARY JENNINGS. *Tessa*: MARLENA KLEINMAN. *Fiametta*: Virginia Bitar *Vittoria*: Mary Burgess. *Giulia*: Beverly Evans. *Inez*: Charlotte Povia. *Solo Cachucha Dancers*: Rochelle Zide, Thomas Andrew. *Chorus of Gondoliers, Contadine, Men-at-Arms, Heralds and Pages*: same as THE YEOMEN OF THE GUARD above.

THE PIRATES OF PENZANCE,
or The Slave of Duty

1964.13

A Revival of the Comic Opera in Two Acts[21]. Libretto by William S. Gilbert. Music by Arthur Sullivan. Staged by Dorothy Raedler. Scenery by H. A. Condell. Conductor, Herbert Grossman. Produced by the New York City

Center Gilbert and Sullivan Company. Opened 28 March 1964 at the New York City Center and closed 31 March 1964 after 4 performances in repertory.

CAST: *Major General Stanley*: EMILE RENAN. *The Pirate King*: WILLIAM CHAPMAN *Samuel, his Lieutenant*: William Ledbetter. *Frederic, the Pirate Apprentice*: CHARLES HINDSLEY. *Sergeant of Police*: HERBERT BEATTIE. *Mabel, Edith Kate, Isabel, General Stanley's Daughters*: ANNE ELGAR, VIRGINIA BITAR, MARY BURGESS, Helen Guile. *Ruth, Pirate Maid-of-all-work*: MURIEL GREENSPON. *Chorus of Pirates, Police and General Stanley's Daughters*: Same as THE YEOMEN OF THE GUARD above.

IOLANTHE,
or The Peer and the Peri

1964.14

A Revival of the Comic Opera in Two Acts[22]. Libretto by William S. Gilbert. Music by Arthur Sullivan. Staged by Dorothy Raedler. Scenery and costumes by Gordon Micunis. Choreography, Thomas Andrew. Conductor, William Jonson. Produced by the New York City Center Gilbert and Sullivan Company. Opened 3 April 1964 at the New York City Center and closed 4 April 1964 after 3 performances in repertory.

CAST: *The Lord Chancellor*: NORMAN KELLY. *Lord Mountararat*: DAVID SMITH. *Lord Tolloller*: RICHARD KRAUSE. *Private Willis of the Grenadier Guards*: GEORGE GAYNES. *Strephon, an Arcadian Shepherd*: WILLIAM LEDBETTER. *Queen of the Fairies*: CLARAMAE TURNER. *Iolanthe, a Fairy, Strephon's Mother*: MARLENA KLEINMAN. *Celia, Leila, Fleta, Fairies*: Virginia Bitar, Mary Burgess, Beverly Evans. *The Bee*: Rochelle Zide. *The Dragonfly*: Hanna Owen. *The Butterfly*: Helen Guile. *Phyllis, an Arcadian Shepherdess and Ward in Chancery*: CAROL BERGEY. *Chorus of Dukes, Marquises, Earls, Viscounts, Barons and Fairies*: Same as THE YEOMEN OF THE GUARD above.

ANYONE CAN WHISTLE

1964.15

A Musical (Fable) in Two Acts, 12 Scenes. Book by Arthur Laurents. Music and Lyrics by Stephen Sondheim. Scenery by William and Jean Eckart. Costumes by Theoni V. Aldredge. Lighting by Jules Fisher. Dances and musical numbers staged by Herbert Ross. Entire Production directed by Arthur Laurents. Orchestrations by Don Walker. Vocal arrangements and musical direction by Herbert Greene. Dance arrangements by Betty Walberg. Associate producer, Arlene Sellers. Produced by Kermit Bloomgarden and Diana Krasny. Opened 4 April 1964 at the Majestic Theatre and closed 11 April 1964 after 9 performances.

CAST (in order of appearance): *Sandwich Man*: Jeff Killion. *Baby Joan*: Jeanne Tanzy. *Mrs. Schroeder*: Peg Murray. *Treasurer Cooley*: Arnold Soboloff. *Chief Magruder*: James Frawley. *Comptroller Schub*: GABRIEL DELL. *Cora Hoover Hooper*: ANGELA LANSBURY. *The Boys*: Sterling Clark, Harvey Evans, Larry Roquemore, Tucker Smith. *Fay Apple*: LEE REMICK. *J. Bowden Hapgood*: HARRY GUARDINO. *Dr. Detmold*: Don Doherty. *George*: Larry Roquemore. *June*: Janet Hayes. *John*: Harvey Evans. *Martin*: Lester Wilson. *Old Lady*: Eleonore Treiber. *Telegraph Boy*: Alan Johnson. *Osgood*: Georgia Creighton.

Cookies, Townspeople, Tourists: Susan Borree, Georgia Creighton, Janet Hayes, Bettye Jenkins, Patricia Kelly, Barbara Lang, Paula Lloyd, Barbara Monte, Odette Phillips, Hanne-Marie Reiner, Eleonore Treiber, Sterling Clark, Eugene Edwards, Harvey Evans, Dick Ensslen, Loren Hightower, Alan Johnson, Jeff Killion, Jack Murray, William Reilly, Larry Roquemore, Tucker Smith, Don Stewart, Lester Wilson.

The action takes place in a not too distant town. The time is now.

Act 1, Scene 1: The Town. *Scene 2*: The Miracle. *Scene 3*: The Interrogation. *Scene 4*: The Celebration. *Scene 5*: The Romance. *Scene 6*: The Parade. *Scene 7*: The Release.

Act 2, Scene 1: The Conspiracy. *Scene 2*: The Confrontation. *Scene 3*: The Cookie Chase. *Scene 4*: The Farewell. *Scene 5*: The End.

ACT 1

Scene 1

"I'm Like the Bluebird"

Company

"Me and My Town"

A. Lansbury, Boys

Scene 2

"Miracle Song"

A. Lansbury, A. Soboloff, Company

---

[20]Originally presented in New York 7 January 1890 at Park Theatre for 103 performances. For Synopsis of Scenes and Musical Numbers, see original 1890 production.

[21]First presented in New York 31 December 1879 at the Fifth Avenue Theatre for a total of 91 performances in two engagements. For Synopsis of Scenes and Musical Numbers, see original 1879 production.

[22]First presented in New York 25 November 1882 at the Standard Theatre for 105 performances. For Synopsis of Scenes and Musical Numbers, see original 1882 production.

Scene 3

"Simple"

H. Guardino, Company

Scene 4

"A-1 March"

Company

Scene 5

"Come Play Wiz Me"

L. Remick, H. Guardino, Boys

"Anyone Can Whistle"

L. Remick

Scene 6

"A Parade in Town"

A. Lansbury

Scene 7

"Everybody Says Don't"

H. Guardino

Ballet

L. Remick, H. Guradino, Cookies

Variation 1: L. Hightower, O. Phillips, E. Treiber. *Variation 2*: B. Monte. *Variation 3*: A. Johnson, P. Lloyd. *Variation 4*: T. Smith. *Variaton 5*: L. Wilson, H. Reiner. *Variation 6*: W. Reilly, S. Clark, E. Ttreiber, L. Roquemore, H. Evans, B. Jenkins.

ACT 2

Scene 1

"I've Got You to Lean On"

A. Lansbury, G. Dell, A. Soboloff, J. Frawley, Boys

Scene 2

"See What It Gets You"

L. Remick

Scene 3

"The Cookie Chase" (Waltzes)

A. Lansbury, L. Remick, G. Dell, Company

Dancing Deputies: L. Roquemore, T. Smith, H. Evans. *Old Lady*: E. Treiber. *Waltz 1*: O. Phillips. *Waltz 2*: B. Monte. *Waltz 3*: B. Jenkins, A. Johnson. *Waltz 4*: G. Dell, P. Lloyd, H. Reiner, S. Borree, P. Kelly. *Waltz 5*: S. Clark. *Waltz 6*: B. Jenkins. *Pas De Deux*: H. Reiner, W. Reilly. *Gallop*: L. Hightower. *Finale*: Company.

Scene 4

"With So Little to Be Sure Of"

L. Remick, H. Guardino

Scene 5

Finale

Company

1964.16 # HIGH SPIRITS

An Improbable Musical Comedy in Two Acts, 12 Scenes. Book, music and lyrics by Hugh Martin and Timothy Gray. based on the play "Blithe Spirit" by Nöel Coward. Directed by Nöel Coward[23]. Settings and costumes by Robert Fletcher. Miss Grimes' costume by Valentina. Lighting by Jules Fisher. Musical direction, Fred Werner. Vocal direction and arrangements by Hugh Martin and Timothy Gray. Orchestrations by Harry Zimmerman. Dance music by Billy Goldenberg. Dances and musical numbers staged by Danny Daniels. Produced by Lester Osterman, Robert Fletcher and Richard Horner. Opened 7 April 1964 at the Alvin Theatre and closed 27 February 1965 after 375 performances.

CAST (in order of appearance): *Charles Condomine*: EDWARD WOODWARD. *Edith*: Carol Arthur. *Ruth Condomine*: LOUISE TROY. *Mrs. Bradman*: Margaret Hall. *Dr. Bradman*: Lawrence Keith. *Madame Arcati*: BEATRICE LILLIE. *Elvira*: TAMMY GRIMES. *Bob*: Robert Lenn. *Beth*: Beth Howland. *Rupert*: Gene Castle.

Singing and Dancing Ensemble: Adrienne Angel, Syndee Balaber, Gene Castle, Jerry Craig, Jackie Cronin, Altovise Gore, Judith Haskell, Beth Howland, Jack Kauflin, Bill Kennedy, Al Lanti, Miriam Lawrence, Renee Lee, Robert Lenn, Alex MacKay, Jacqueline Maria, Stan Mazin, Joe McGrath, Don Percassi, Kathy Preston, Sybil Scotford, Tom Thornton, Ronnie Walken, Anne Wallace.

Act 1, Scene 1: The Condomines' living room. *Scene 2*: A road on the Heath; immediately following. *Scene 3*: The Condomines' living room, after dinner. *Scene 4*:

The Condomines' terrace, the next morning. *Scene 5*: The Inner Circle, early that evening. *Scene 6*: The Condomines' living room, immediately following. *Scene 7*: The Roof Garden of the Grovechester Hotel, immediately following.

Act 2, Scene 1: The Condomines' living room, immediately following. *Scene 2*: Madame Arcati's Bedroom, the following morning. *Scene 3*: The Condomines' living room, that afternoon. *Scene 4*: The Inner Circle, that evening. *Scene 5*: The Condomines' living room, several hours later.

ACT 1

"Was She Pettier Than I?"

L. Troy

"The Bicycle Song"

B. Lillie, Ensemble

"You'd Better Love Me"

T. Grimes

"Where Is the Man I Married?"

E. Woodward, L. Troy

"The Sandwich Man"

R. Lenn, B. Howland

"Go Into Your Trance"

B. Lillie, Ensemble

"Where Is the Man I Married?" (reprise)

L. Troy

"Forever and a Day"

E. Woodward, T. Grimes

"Something Tells Me"

T. Grimes, Ensemble

"I Know Your Heart"

E. Woodward, T. Grimes

"Faster Than Sound"

T. Grimes, Ensemble

ACT 2

"If I Gave You"

E. Woodward, L. Troy

"Talking to You"

B. Lillie

"Home Sweet Heaven"

T. Grimes

"Something Is Coming to Tea" (Madame Arcati's Tea Party)

B. Lillie, Ensemble

"The Exorcism"

B. Lillie, Ensemble

"What in the World Did You Want?"

E. Woodward, T. Grimes, L. Troy

"Faster Than Sound" (reprise)

Entire Company

1964.17 # WEST SIDE STORY

A Revival of the Musical in Two Acts, 15 Scenes[24]. Book by Arthur Laurents. Based on a conception of Jerome Robbins. Music by Leonard Bernstein. Lyrics by Stephen Sondheim. Original production directed and choreographed by Jerome Robbins. This production staged by Gerald Freedman. Choreography re-mounted by Tom Abbott. Original scenic production by Oliver Smith. This production designed by Peter Wolf. Costumes by Irene Sharaff, supervised by Stanley Simmons. Lighting by Jean Rosenthal. Original co-choreographer, Peter Gennaro. Musical direction, Charles Jaffe. (Orchestrations by Leonard Bernstein, with Sid Ramin, Irwin Kostal.) Produced by the New York City Center Light Opera Company (Jean Dalrymple, Director). Opened 8 April 1964 at the New York City Center and closed 3 May 1964 after 31 performances.

CAST: THE JETS: *Riff, the Leader*: JAMES MOORE. *Tony, his friend*: DON McKAY. *Action*: JOE BENNETT. *A-Rab*: Mark Jude Sheil. *Baby John*: Steve Curry. *Snowboy*: Barry Burns. *Big Deal*: Larry Moss. *Diesel*: Hamp Dickens. *Gee-Tar*: Danny Lockin. *Mouth Piece*: Joseph Corby. *Tiger*: John McCook. *Their Girls*: *Graziella*: Wilma Curley. *Velma*: Tobie Lynn. *Minnie*: Barbara Rogers. *Clarice*: Gloria Kaye. *Pauline*: Eileen Casey. *Anybodys*: Erin Martin.

---

[23]Additional direction by Gower Champion uncredited.

[24]Originally produced in New York 26 September 1957 at the Winter Garden for 732 performances and a return engagement of 249 performances. For Synopsis of Scenes and Musical Numbers, see original 1957 production.

THE SHARKS: *Bernardo*, the Leader: JAY NORMAN. *Maria*, his Sister: JULIA MIGENES. *Chino*, his Friend: B. J. DiSimone. *Pepe*: Noel Schwartz. *Indio*: Tim Ramirez. *Luis*: Jo Jo Smith. *Anxious*: Kent Thomas. *Nibbles*: Carlos Gorbea. *Juano*: Richard Balin. *Toro*: Carmine Terra. *Moose*: Eliot Feld. *Their Girls*: Anita, his Girl: LUBA LISA. *Rosalia*: Marilyn Cooper. *Consuelo*: Carmen Morales. *Teresita*: Ella Thompson. *Francisca*: Diana Corto. *Estella*: Lolli Hinton. *Marguerita*: Tina Faye.

THE ADULTS: *Doc*: HARRY DAVIS. *Schrank*: Ted Gunther. *Krupke*: Frank Downing. *Gladhand*: Brooks Morton.

1964.18 CAFE CROWN

A Musical Comedy in Two Acts, 12 Scenes. Book by Hy Kraft. Based on his play of the same name. Music by Albert Hague. Lyrics by Marty Brill. Scenery and lighting by Sam Leve. Costumes by Ruth Morley. Directed by Jerome Eskow. Choreography by Ronald [Ron] Field. Dance music by Albert Hague. Orchestrations by Hershy Kay. Vocal arrangements and musical direction by Gershon Kingsley. Additional orchestrations by Bill Stegmeier, Jack Andrews, Jay Brower. Produced by Philip Rose and Swanlee. Opened 17 April 1964 at the Martin Beck Theatre and closed 18 April 1964 after 3 performances.

CAST (in order of appearance): *Dr. Irving Gilbert*: ALAN ALDA. *Mr. Morris*: Ted Thurston. *Nathan the Waiter*: Norman Shelly. *Mme. Cole*: BRENDA LEWIS. *Bloom the Fiddler*: Joe Ross. *First Woman*: Shirley Leinwand. *Second Woman*: Fay Reed. *Mr. Edelman*: Keith Kaldenberg. *Mrs. Edelman*: Ann Marisse. *Beck*: Roy Stuart. *Rubin*: Robert Penn. *Kaplan*: Val Avery. *Mrs. Perlman*: Francine Beers. *Mr. Toplitz*: MARTIN WOLFSON. *Mendel Polan*: Wood Romoff. *Ida Polan*: Renee Orin. *Hymie the Busboy*: SAM LEVENE. *Norma Roberts*: MONTE AMUNDSEN. *David Cole*: TOMMY RALL. *Lipsky*: Michael Vale. *Petty Officer*: Val Avery. *Ship's Captain*: John Anania. *Sarah*: Betty Aberlin. *Samuel Cole*: THEODORE BIKEL. *Burton*: Edwin Bruce.

Singers: Marilyn Murphy, Bonnie Brody, Betty Aberlin, Fay Reed, Ann Marisse, Shirley Leinwand, Stephanie Winters, John Wheeler, Ken Richards. *Dancers*: Geri Spinner, Betty Rosebrock, Bonnie Walker, Cheryl Kilgren, Patsi King, Luigi Gasparanetti, Ean Benjamin, Robert Avian, Keith Stewart, Terry Violino.

The action takes place in and arouynd the Cafe Crown at the corner of Second Avenue and 12th Street in New York City in the early 1930s.

Act 1, Scene 1: The Street. Scene 2: Cafe Crown. Scene 3: The Stage of Lipsky's Theatre—Act 1. Scene 4: Mme. Cole's dressing room. Scene 5: Cafe Crown. Scene 6: The Street. Scene 7: The Stage of Lipsky's Theatre—Act 2.

Act 2, Scene 1: The Street. Scene 2: Cafe Crown. Scene 3: The Stage of Lipsky's Theatre. Scene 4: Cafe Crown. Scene 5: The Street.

ACT 1
Scene 1
"You're a Stranger in This Neighborhood"
A. Alda, Company
Scene 2
"What's the Matter With Buffalo?"
S. Levene, A. Alda, Ensemble
"All Those Years"
T. Rall, M. Amundsen
Scene 3
"Au Revoir Poland-Hello New York!"
B. Lewis, Lipsky Theatre Ensemble
Scene 4
"Make the Most of Spring"
B. Lewis
Scene 5
"So Long As It Isn't Shakespeare"
S. Levene, T. Bikel
"A Lifetime Love"
T. Bikel, B. Lewis
Scene 6
"I'm Gonna Move"
T. Rall
Scene 7
"A Mother's Heart"
B. Lewis, B. Aberlin, Lipsky Theatre Ensemble
"On This Wedding Day"
B. Lewis, Wedding Guests
ACT 2
Scene 1
"What's Gonna Be Tomorrow"
Company

Scene 2
"A Man Must Have Something to Live For"
T. Bikel, Ensemble
"That's the Life For Me"
S. Levene, T. Bikel, B. Lewis, Company
"A Lifetime Love" (reprise)
T. Rall, M. Amundsen
Scene 3
"King Lear Ballet"
T. Bikel, T. Rall, Ensemble
Scene 4
"Magical Things In Life"
S. Levene, T. Bikel, Ensemble
"That's the Life For Me" (reprise)
S. Levene, T. Bikel, B. Lewis, A. Alda, Ensemble
Scene 5
"A Man Must Have Something To Live For" (reprise)
Company

1964.19 PORGY AND BESS

A Revival of the Folk Opera in Two Acts, 9 Scenes[25]. Book by DuBose Heyward adapted from the play "Porgy" by DuBose and Dorothy Heyward. Music by George Gershwin. Lyrics by DuBose Heyward and Ira Gershwin. Directed by John Fearnley. Settings by Stephen O. Saxe. Costumes by Stanley Simmons. Lighting by Nananne Porcher. Musical director, Julius Rudel. Choral director and associate conductor, William Jonson. Produced by the New York City Center Light Opera Company (Jean Dalrymple, Director). Opened 6 May 1964 at the New York City Center and closed 17 May 1964 after 15 performances.

CAST (in order of appearance): *Clara*: MARIE YOUNG. *Mingo*: Tony Middleton. *Sportin' Life*: ROBERT GUILLAUME. *Jake*: IRVING BARNES. *Serena*: GWENDOLYN WALTERS. *Robbins*: Eugene Edwards. *Jim*: Garwood Perkins. *Peter, the Honey Man*: Garrett Morris. *Lily*: Frances Haywood. *Maria*: CAROL BRICE. *Porgy*: WILLIAM WARFIELD or IRVING BARNES. *Crown*: WILLIAM DILLARD. *Bess*: VERONICA TYLER or BARBARA SMITH CONRAD. *Policemen*: David Hicks, John Smith. *Detective*: Walter Riemer. *Undertaker*: Wanza King. *Annie*: Alyce Webb. *Frazier*: Al Fann. *Strawberry Woman*: Kay Barnes. *Crab Man*: Clyde Turner. *Scipio*: William Harris. *Pearl*: Lillian Hayman.

Residents of Catfish Row: Ruby Green Aspinall, Kaye Barnes, Phyllis Bash, Elijah Bennett, Joseph Bryant, Paul Corder, Marceline Decker, Beverly Evans, Don Forrest, Beno Foster, Claretta Freemon, Carol Joy George, Carrie Glover, Helen Guile, William G. Harris, Afrika Hayes, Lillian Hayman, Frances W. Haywood, Annette B. Jackson, Martin Jewell, Marva Josie, Wanza King, Thomas Laidman, Dorothy Lane, Garrett Morris, Caryl Paige, Garwood Perkins, Lucinda Ransom, John Richardson, Edna Ricks, Anthony Safina, Clyde Turner, Eloise C. Uggams, James Wamen, Laurence Watson, Alyce Webb, Pauline Weekes, James Wilson, James Wilson, William Wright, Lou Ann Wyckoff. *Children*: Deborah Hall, Benjamin Hines, Norman Hines, Antonell Jones.

1964.20 MY FAIR LADY

A Revival of the Musical (Comedy) in Two Acts, 18 Scenes[26]. Book and lyrics by Alan Jay Lerner. Based on the play "Pygmalion" by George Bernard Shaw, produced on the screen by Gabriel Pascal. Music by Frederick Loewe. Originally staged by Moss Hart. This production directed by Samuel Liff. Choreography and musical numbers staged by Hanya Holm. Production (settings) designed by Oliver Smith. Costumes by Cecil Beaton, supervised by Stanley Simmons. Musical arrangements (Orchestrations) by Robert Russell Bennett and Philip J. Lang. Lighting by Feder. Dance music

---

[25]First produced in New York 10 October 1935 at the Alvin Theatre for 124 performances. For Synopsis of Scenes and Musical Numbers, see original 1935 production. This production was performed in Two Acts, with the interval after "Oh, I Can't Sit Down" (Act 2, Scene 1 in the original). Note the following program changes for this production:
("Ha da da" and) "Leavin' for de Promis' Land" moved to the opening of Act 2, Scene 1 before "It Ain't Necessarily So." "Buzzard Song" reinstated to Act 1, after "I Got Plenty of Nuttin'." "Occupational Humoresque" (Ensemble) added to Act 2, Scene 5 before "Where's My Bess?"
[26]Originally produced in New York 15 March 1956 at the Mark Hellinger Theatre for 2717 peformances. For Synopsis of Scenes and Musical Numbers, see original 1956 production.

arranged by Trude Rittman. Musical director, Anton Coppola. Produced by the New York City Center Light Opera Company (Jean Dalrymple, Director). Opened 20 May 1964 at the New York City Center and closed 28 June 1964 after 47 performances.

CAST (in order of appearance): *Buskers*: Jerry Trent, Myron Curtis, Kiki Minor. *Mrs. Eynsford-Hill*: Claire Waring. *Eliza Doolittle*: MARNI NIXON. *Freddy Eynsford-Hill*: RUSSELL NYPE. *Colonel Pickering*: BYRON WEBSTER. *A Bystander*: Raymond Allen. *Henry Higgins*: MYLES EASON. *Selsey Man*: Charles Penman. *Hoxton Man*: Henry Lawrence. *Another Bystander*: Robert [Bob] Fitch. *First Cockney*: William Krach. *Second Cockney*: Stokely Gray. *Third Cockney*: Richard H. Goodlake. *Fourth Cockney*: Barney Johnston. *Bartender*: Jack Eddleman. *Harry*: Charles Penman. *Jamie*: Raymond Allen. *Alfred P. Doolittle*: REGINALD GARDINER. *Mrs. Pearce*: DOROTHY SANDS. *Mrs. Hopkins*: Olive Reeves-Smith. *Butler*: Stokely Gray. *Servants*: Jeremy Broun, Margaret Broderson, Joyce Dahl, Ruth Shepard, Art Martinson, Stokely Gray. *Mrs. Higgins*: MARGERY MAUDE. *Chauffeur*: Harry Woolever. *Footmen*: William Krach, Richard Park. *Lord Boxington*: Charles Penman. *Lady Boxington*: Olive Reeves-Smith. *Constable*: Harry Woolever. *Flower Girl*: Kiki Minor. *Zoltan Karpathy*: SANDOR SZABO. *Flunkey*: Richard Park. *Queen of Transylvania*: Terry Marone. *Ambassador*: Raymond Allen. *Bartender*: Barney Johnston. *Mrs. Higgins' Maid*: Margaret Cuddy.

Singing Ensemble: Jeremy Broun, Margaret Broderson, Diane Chase, Joyce Dahl, Elaine Labour, Terry Marone, Donna Monroe, Ruth Shepard, Jack Eddleman, Richard H. Goodlake, Stokely Gray, Barney Johnston, William Krach, Henry Lawrence, Art Martinson, Richard Park. *Dancing Ensemble*: Judi Allison, Emily Byrne, Margaret Cuddy, Katia Geleznova, Audrey Hays, Adriana Keathley, Kiki Minor, Molly Molloy, Mari Shelton, Esther Villavicencio, Dick Colacino, Myron Curtis, Robert [Bob] Fitch, Ronn Forella, Dennis Lynch, Joe Nelson, Jerry Trent, R. Michael Steele, Mark West, Harry Woolever.

1964.21   FADE OUT—FADE IN

A Musical Comedy in Two Acts, 19 Scenes. Book and lyrics by Betty Comden and Adolph Green. Music by Jule Styne. Directed by George Abbott. Dances and musical numbers staged by Ernest Flatt. Settings and lighting by William and Jean Eckart. Costumes by Donald Brooks. Musical direction and orchestrations by Ralph Burns and Ray Ellis. Vocal arrangements by Buster Davis. Dance music arranged by Richard De Benedictis. Produced by Lester Osterman and Jule Styne. Opened 26 May 1964 at the Mark Hellinger Theatre and closed 14 November 1964 after 199 performances; re-opened 15 February 1965 at the Mark Hellinger Theatre and closed 17 April 1965 after 72 additional performances. Total: 271 performances.

CAST[27] (in order of appearance): *Byron Prong*: JACK CASSIDY. *Teenagers*: Jodi Perselle, Judy Newman. *Woman*: Diana Ede. *Man*: Darrell J. Askey. *Autograph Kids*: Roger Allan Raby, Charlene Mehl. *Helga Sixtrees*: Judy Cassmore. *Pops*: Frank Tweddell. *Rosco*: Bob Neukum. *Billy Vespers*: Glenn Kezer, (Paul Michael). *Lyman*: John Dorrin. *Hope Springfield*: CAROL BURNETT. *Rex*: Darrell J. Askey. *Chauffeur*: William Louther. *First Girl*: Wendy Taylor. *First Cowboy Extra*: Steve Elmore. *Second Cowboy Extra*: Fred Cline. *Gangster Extra*: Gene Varrone. *Ralph Governor*: MITCHELL JASON. *Rudolf Governor*: DICK PATTERSON. *Nephews (4)*: George Governor: Howard Kahl. *Frank Governor*: John Dorrin. *Harold Governor*: Gene Varrone. *Arnold Governor*: Steve Elmore. *Waiters*: Fred Cline, Richard Frisch, Roger Allan Raby. *Publicity Men*: Sean Allan, Darrell J. Askey. *Convicts*: Gene Kelton; William Louther, Ed Pfeiffer, James Von Weiss. *Myra May Melrose*: Virginia Payne. *Seamstress*: Diane Arnold. *Miss Mallory*: Jo Tract. *Custer Corkley*: Dan Resin. *Approval*: Smaxie. *Photographer*: Sean Allan. *Max Welch*: Richard Frisch. *Lou Williams*: TIGER HAYNES. *Dora Dailey*: Aileen Poe. *Lionel Z. Governor*: LOU JACOBI. *Dr. Anton Taurig*: Reuben Singer. *Gloria Currie*: TINA LOUISE. *Madame Barrymore*: Penny Egelston.

Singing Ensemble: Sean Allan, Jackie Alloway, Darrell J. Askey, Fred Cline, John Dorrin, Trish Dwelley, Steve Elmore, Richard Frisch, Howard Kahl, Carolyn Kemp, Betty Kent, Glenn Kezer, Mari Nettum, Bob Neukum, Roger Allan Raby, Jo Tract, Gene Varrone. *Dancing Ensemble*: Virginia Allen, Diane Arnold, Judy Cassmore, Diana Ede, Ernie Horvath, Gene Kelton, William Louther, Charlene Mehl, Judy Newman, Jodi Perselle, Ed Pfeiffer, Carolsue Shaer, Patricia Sigris, Roy Smith, Bill Stanton, Wendy Taylor, James Von Weiss. *Lead Dancer*: Don Crichton.

The action takes place in New York and Hollywood in the mid-1930s.

Act 1, Scene 1: In front of Grauman's Chinese Theatre. *Scene 2*: Gate—F.F.F. Studio. *Scene 3*: On the Lot. *Scene 4*: Executive Dining Room. *Scene 5*: Wardrobe

Department. *Scene 6*: On the Set. *Scene 7*: Dora Dailey. *Scene 8*: Dr. Taurig's Office—Vienna. *Scene 9*: On the Set. *Scene 10*: Executive Dining Room. *Scene 11*: The Bungalow.

Act 2, Scene 1: Gate—F.F.F. Studio. *Scene 2*: Dora Dailey. *Scene 3*: Wardrobe Department. *Scene 4*: A Street. *Scene 5*: L. Z.'s Office. *Scene 6*: On the Set. *Scene 7*: In front of Grauman's Chinese Theatre. *Scene 8*: In front of Grauman's Chinese Theatre.

ACT 1[28]
Scene 1[29]
   "The Thirties"[30]
      J. Cassidy
Scene 2
   "It's Good To Be Back Home"
      C. Burnett, Ensemble
Scene 4
   "Fear"
      D. Patterson, M. Jason, Nephews
   "Fear" (reprise)
      J. Cassidy, Nephews
Scene 5
   "Call Me Savage"
      C. Burnett, D. Patterson
   "The Usher From the Mezzanine"
      C. Burnett
Scene 9
   "I'm With You"
      C. Burnett, J. Cassidy, D. Crichton, Violin Girls, Bow Boys
   "The Usher From the Mezzanine"[31] (reprise)
      C. Burnett, Ensemble
Scene 10
   "My Fortune Is My Face"
      J. Cassidy
Scene 11
   "Lila Tremaine"
      C. Burnett

ACT 2
Scene 1[32]
   "Go Home Train"[33]
      C. Burnett
Scene 3
   "Close Harmony"
      L. Jacobi, J. Cassidy, T. Louise, Nephews
Scene 4
   "You Musn't Be Discouraged"
      C. Burnett, T. Haynes
Scene 5
   "The Dangerous Age"
      L. Jacobi
   "L.Z. in Quest of His Youth" (Ballet)
      L. Jacobi, T. Louise, D. Crichton, Ensemble
Scene 6
   "The Fiddler and the Fighter"
      J. Cassidy, Ensemble
   "Fade Out—Fade In"
      C. Burnett, J. Cassidy

---

[27]Cast changes for return engagement: *Byron Prong*: DICK SHAWN. *Helga Sixtrees*: Alice Glenn. *Billy Vespers*: Paul Michael. *Rex*: Barney Johnston. *Chauffeur*: John Richardson. *First Girl*: Trish Dwelley. *First Cowboy Extra*: David Cryer. *George Governor*: Paul Eichel. *Arnold Governor*: David Cryer. *Waiters*: Stephen Elmore. *Publicity Men*: Dean Doss, Barney Johnston. *Convicts*: John Richardson, Bill Starr, Jerry Gotham. *Gloria Currie*: JUDY CASSMORE.

---

[28]For return engagement, added to Act 1, Scene 6:
   "My Heart Is Like a Violin"
      D. Shawn (Byron Prong)
For return engagement, added to Act 1, Scene 11(now Scene 10) after "Lila Tremaine":
   "A Girl To Remember"
      C. Burnett
[29]Dropped for the return engagement.
[30]Dropped for the return engagement.
[31]For return engagement, replaced by:
   "Notice Me"
      D. Patterson
[32]Dropped for the return engagement.
[33]Dropped for the return engagement.

1964–1965 SEASON

Liza Minelli in FLORA, THE RED MENACE (Photo: Friedman-Abeles, 1965)
Museum of the City of New York, The Mary Bryant Collection, 92.52.5.4

1964–1965 SEASON

1964.22 ## FOLIES BERGÈRE

A Musical Revue in Two Acts, 20 Scenes, in French. Conceived and directed by Michel Gyarmathy. Music by Henri Betti. Additional music by Philippe Gerard. Sets and costumes by Michel Gyarmathy. Choreography by George Reich. Musical director, Joe Basile. Associate producers, Nicholas A. Strater, Alvin Bojar. Produced by Stephen W. Sharmat in association with J. Robert Purdom. An Arthur Lesser Production of Paul Derval's original revue. Opened 2 June 1964 at the Broadway Theatre and closed 14 November 1964 after 191 performances.

CAST: PATACHOU, GEORGES ULMER, LILIANE MONTEVECCHI, LES HOGANAS (Gert Karlsson, Bende Hoganas, Egon Hoganas), THE TROTTER BROTHERS, PAUL SYDELL & SUZY, NICOLE CROISILLE, VASSILI SULIC, MARION CONRAD, EDMÉE REDOUIN, FRANCOISE GRÈS, The Company of Les Folies Bergère.

Dancers: Marisa Barbaria, Sarah Lee Berber, Anik David, Dorothy D'Honau, Claude Duvernoy, Diane Fox, Francoise Grès, Nancy Herselin, Marcella Hude, Yvonne Neisyter, Gordana Pechitch, Pamela Wellman, Diana West, Gerry Atkins, Flavio Bennati, Francis Ciampi, Ralf Harmer, Don Wallwork. *Les Demoiselles des Folies:* Dominique Chevallier, Nicole Gille, Margo Hamilton, Andrée Hechner, Margareta Lindblum, Mary Luger, Mikki Maher, Anna Page, Irene Peterson, Judy Tickner, Isabel Wardrop, Elizabeth West. *Mannequins:* Marion Barker, Monique Carraz, Charlotte DiSica, Francesca Fontaine, Lyn Hobart, Dale Humphries, Dany Latour, Simone Massix, André Penny, Veronica Pierce, Nancy Walker, Sara Brocket.

ACT 1[1]
Scene 1

Bonjour de Paris

"Foll' de Broadway"
N. Croisille, Dancers, Les Demoiselles des Folies, Mannequins

"Ta Ra Ra"
M. Conrad

"Bonjour Folies"
L. Montevecchi

Scene 2

"Can-Can"
G. Atkins, Dancers

Scene 3

Georges Ulmer (songs and impressions including "Pigalle," {*Music and Lyrics by* Georges Ulmer, Konyn, Newman}, and parody of a Flamenco song)

Scene 4

Souper Fin
M. Carraz, D. Chevallier, A. Hechner, J. Moussy, D. Wallwork

Scene 5

Chopin
F. Castel, Les Demoiselles des Folies

Scene 6

Paul Sydell & Suzy (acrobatic dog act)

Scene 7

Varieté de Danses:

Charleston
N. Croisille, Dancers

"C'est toi l'plus beau" (Tango)
L. Montevecchi, V. Sulic

Paris Panam
Les Demoiselles des Folies

Paris Swing: "Ca c'est Panam"
L. Montevecchi
(*Music and Lyrics by* J. Ledru.)

Les mains
F. Grès, Dancers

---

[1]Added during the run:
Cyprés
M. Hardy, M. Conrad, F. Bennati, Les Demoiselles des Folies

Scene 8

Georges Ulmer (songs and impressions)

Scene 9

Cleopatra (dance)
L. Montevecchi, V. Sulic, Dancers, Les Demoiselles des Folies, Mannequins

Scene 10

Les Hoganas (Slackwire trio)

Scene 11

"A toute à l'heure"
The Company

ACT 2
Scene 1

Texas de France
F. Grès, Dancers

Scene 2

Georges Ulmer (songs):

"Darling Be Careful" (La Trapeziste)
(*Music and Lyrics by* Georges Ulmer.)

Scene 3

"Mariage"
F. Castel, Singers

"Hymne à l'amour"
Dancers, Les Demoiselles des Folies, Mannequins

Scene 4

The Trotter Brothers (Puppetry)

Scene 5

"Gondole à Venise"
D. Latour

Scene 6

Georges Ulmer (songs)

Scene 7

"Neige"
M. Conrad, V. Sulic, Dancers

Scene 8

Patachou:

"Paris boheme"
(*Music and Lyrics by* P. Gerard.)

"Mon manege à moi"
(*Music and Lyrics by* Constantin Glanzburg.)

"Pigalle"
(*Music and Lyrics by* Georges Ulmer, Konyn, Newman.)

"What Now My Love?" (Eh Maintenant?)
(*Music and Lyrics by* Gilbert Becaud.)

"I Wish You Love" (Que Reste-til de Nos Amours)
(*Music and Lyrics by* Charles Trenet. *English Lyrics by* Albert Beach.)

"My Man" (Mon Homme)
(*English Lyrics by* Channing Pollock. *Music by* Maurice Yvain. *French Lyrics by* Albert Willemetz and Jacques Charles.)

Scene 9

Finale: "La Musique"
Entire Company
(*Music and Lyrics by* Drejac and Gerard.)

1964.23 ## THE KING AND I

A Revival of the Musical Play in Two Acts, 17 Scenes[2]. Book and lyrics by Oscar Hammerstein II. Music by Richard Rodgers. Based on the novel "Anna and the King of Siam" by Margaret Landon. Settings by Paul C. McGuire. Costumes by Irene Sharaff. (Lighting uncredited.) Original choreography by Jerome Robbins, reproduced by Yuriko. Orchestrations by Robert Russell Bennett. Musical director, Franz Allers. Directed by Edward Greenberg. Produced by the Music Theatre of Lincoln Center (Richard

---

[2]Originally produced in New York 29 March 1951 at the St. James Theatre for 1246 performances. For Synopsis of Scenes and Musical Numbers, see original 1951 production.

Rodgers, President and Producing Director). Opened 6 July 1964 at the New York State Theatre and closed 8 August 1964 after 40 performances.

CAST (in order of appearance): *Captain Orton*: Fred Miller. *Louis Leonowens*: James Harvey. *Anna Leonowens*: RISË STEVENS. *The Interpreter*: Rudy Vejar. *The Kralahome*: MICHAEL KERMOYAN. *The King*: DARREN McGAVIN. *Phra Alack*: Stuart Mann. *Tuptim*: LEE VENORA. *Lady Thiang*: PATRICIA NEWAY. *Prince Chulalongkorn*: Barry Rubins. *Princess Ying Yaowalak*: Gina Kaye. *Lun Tha*: FRANK PORETTA. *Sir Edward Ramsay*: ERIC BROTHERSON.

The Small House of Uncle Thomas: *Narrator*: LEE VENORA. *Uncle Thomas*: Bettina Dearborne. *Little Eva*: Susan Kikuchi. *Topsy*: Paula Chin. *Eliza*: Takako. *King Simon*: Linda Hodes. *Angel*: Connie Sanchez. *Drummer*: Jim McMillan.

Princes and Princesses: Kathleen Din, Gina Kaye, Lorrie Kochiyama, Debbie Kogan, May Yee Mark, Annette Misa, Robert Ader, David Aguilar, Delfino DeArco, Lawrence Kikuchi, Eddie Kochiyama, Frank Orlando, Vito Orlando. *The Royal Dancers*: Takako Asakawa, Hadassah Badock, Joan Bates, Lisa Berg, Noemi Chiesa, Paula Chin, Miriam Cole, Bettina Dearborne, Carol Drisin, Carol Fried, Phyllis Gutelius, Linda Hodes, Susan Kikuchi, Jeanne Nichtern, Connie Sanchez, Katherine Wilson. *Wives*: Anita Alpert, Theodora Brandon, Dixie Carter, Sharon Dierking, Mona Elson, Carole O'Hara, Hanna Owen, Jean Palmerton. *Amazons*: Leisha Caryle, Beverly Morrison, Joanna Owens, Jeanne Rodriguez. *Priests, Slaves*: Walter Adams, Henry Baker, Lazar Dano, Victor Duntiere, William Duvall, Julius Fields, Fred Hamilton, Stuart Mann, Jim McMillan, Ken Richards, Anthony Saverino.

1964.24   THE MERRY WIDOW

A Revival of the Operetta in Three Acts, 4 Scenes[3]. Music by Franz Lehár. Original German book (Die Lustige Witwe) and lyrics by Victor Léon and Leo Stein (after "L'Attaché d'Ambassade.") New book by by Milton Lazarus, based on a version by Edwin Lester and the London version by Christopher Hassall. New lyrics by Forman Brown. Directed by Edward Greenberg. Choreography by Zachary Solov. Settings by Rouben Ter-Arutunian. Costumes by Rene Hubert. (Lighting uncredited, by Michael Paul Price for subsequent tour.) Musical director, Franz Allers. Produced by the Music Theatre of Lincoln Center (Richard Rodgers, President and Producing Director). Opened 17 August 1964 at the New York State Theatre and closed 19 September 1964 after 40 performances.

CAST (in order of appearance): *Major Domo*: George Quick. *Nish*: SIG ARNO. *Baron Popoff*: MISCHA AUER. *Natalie, Baroness Popoff*: JOAN WELDON. *Chevalier St. Brioche*: ROBERT GOSS. *Marquis Cascada*: Rudy Vejar. *General Novikovich*: JOSEPH LEON. *Counselor Khadja*: WOOD ROMOFF. *Mme. Sylvanie Khadja*: Luce Ennis. *Mme. Novikovich*: Marian Haraldson. *Captain Pierre Jolidon*: FRANK PORETTA. *Sonia, the Widow*: PATRICE MUNSEL. *Prince Danilo*: BOB WRIGHT. *Girls from Maxim's (6)*: *Lolo*: Carol Flemming. *Clo Clo*: Jean Lee Schoch. *Dodo*: Annette Bachich. *Margot*: Kathy Wilson. *Joujou*: Skiles Ricketts. *Froufrou*: Birgitta Kiviniemi. *Michel*: William Duvall. *Zozo*: Dixie Carter. *Principal Dancers*: Birgitta Kiviniemi, Dmitry Cheremeteff. *Guests, Lackeys, Maids and Musicians.*

Singing Ladies: Theodora Brandon, Dixie Carter, Kenna Christi, Sharon Dierking, Elaine Johnson, Beverly Morrison, Hanna Owen, Jean Palmerton, Dixie Stewart, Peggy Wathen. *Singing Men*: Bruce Carrithers, Ken Corday, Gene Davis, William Duvall, Harrison Fisher, Norman Grogan, Vincent Henry, Stuart Mann, Philip Rash, Ken Richards, Carl Sloat, Stafford Wing. *Dancing Girls*: Annette Bachich, Bonnie Gene Card, Carol Flemming, Debra Lyman, Skiles Ricketts, Jean Lee Schoch, Kathy Wilson. *Dancing Men*: Ian Bruce, Richard Cousins, Jeremy Wilson, Ian Bruce, Richard Cousins, Jeremy Knight-Ives, Richard Maxon, Malcolm McCormick, Bob Remick, George Tregre.

Act 1, Scene 1: A Corridor at the Marsovian Embassy in Paris, 1905. *Scene 2*: The Reception Hall.

Act 2: The Garden Party at Sonia's Villa just outside Paris, a week later.

Act 3: At Maxim's, later that night.

ACT 1

  "When in France"
    R. Goss, R. Vejar, J. Weldon,
    M. Haraldson, L. Ennis, M. Auer, Guests
  "A Respectable Wife"
    J. Weldon, F. Poretta
  "Who Knows the Way to My Heart?"
    P. Munsel, R. Goss, R. Vejar, Bachelors
  "Maxim's"
    B. Wright, Girls from Maxim's
  "Riding on a Carousel"
    P. Munsel, R. Wright

  Finale (Act 1)
    P. Munsel, R. Wright, Ensemble

ACT 2
  Marsovian Dance
    Dancing Ensemble
  "Vilia"
    P. Munsel
  "Women"
    M. Auer, S. Arno, J. Leon, W. Romoff, R. Goss, R. Vejar
  Czardas and Waltz
    P. Munsel, B. Wright, Dancing Ensemble
  "Romance"
    F. Poretta, J. Weldon
  Finale (Act 2)
    P. Munsel, B. Wright, F. Poretta, J. Weldon, Ensemble

ACT 3
  "Girls at Maxim's"
    Maxim Girls, Waiters, P. Munsel
  "I Love You So" (The Merry Widow Waltz)
    B. Wright, P. Munsel
  Finale (Act 3)
    Entire Company

1964.25   WIENER BLUT

A Revival of the Operette in Three Acts, in German[4]. Original Viennese libretto [Vienna Life] by Victor Léon and Leo Stein. Music by Johann Strauss. New adaptation by Tony Niessner. Music arranged by Hans Hagen. Staged by Tony Niessner. Choreography by Fred Meister. Musical director, Oswald Unterhauser. Production designed by Ferry Windberger. Costumes by Hill Rheis-Gromes. Production supervised and lighting by Thomas Skelton. Produced by Harald A. Hoeller. Presented by the Greek Theatre Association—James A. Doolittle and Felix S. Gerstman. Opened 11 September 1964 at the Lunt-Fontanne Theatre and closed 3 October 1964 after 27 performances.

CAST (in order of appearance): *Mistress of Ceremonies*: GITA RENA. *Policeman*: ANDREIJ HALASZ. *Count Balduin Zedlau*, Ambassador from Reuss-Schleiz-Greiz: ERWIN VON GROSS. *Countess Zedlau*, his wife: MARIA KOWA. *Franziska Cagliari*, dancer at the Karntnertor Theatre: CLEMENTINE MAYER. *Pepi Pleininger*, a model: DAGMAR KOLLER. *Josef*, Count Zedlau's valet: HELMUT WALLNER. *Prince Ypsheim-Gindelbach*, Prime Minsiter of Reuss-Schleiz-Greiz: WILHELM POPP. *Kagler*, Cagliari's father: HUGO LINDINGER. *Anna*, Cagliari's maid: Friedericke Mann. *A Coachman*: WERNER KARMAN. *Count Bitowski*: EMMERICH GODIN. *Countess Bitowski*: ELSE PETRY. *French Ambassador*: Eric Herg. *Italian Ambassador*: Martino Stamos. *English Ambassador*: Wolfgang Hackenberg. *Prussian Ambassador*: Gerhard Kurz. *Russian Ambassador*: WERNER KARMAN. *Lisi*, laundrymaid: Friederike Mann. *Lori*, laundrymaid: Silvia Holzmayer. *A Grenadier*: Erich Herg. *A Watchman* (Deutschmeister): Wolfgang Hackenberg. *A Boy Waiter*: Eveline Kollhammer. *Proprietor of Heitzing Casino*: WERNER KARMAN.

Singing Ensemble: Maria Holoubeck, Silvia Holzmayer, Elfriede Knapp, Angelika Lignu, Friederike Mann, Katherine Stellaki, Wolfgang Hackenberg, Erich Herg, Werner Karman, Gerhard Kurz, Martino Stamos, Achilles Talos. *Dancing Soloists*: IWA SLATEWA, FLORA LOJEKOVA, ANDREJ HALASZ, KURT SCHENKER. *Dancing Ensemble*: Hulda Kuchs, Katja Doreen, Eveline Kohlhammer, Edda Green, Katja Pogacnik, Nora Zechner, Ingrid Nedbal.

The action takes place during the Congress of Vienna in 1815.

Act 1: A Street in Vienna on a summer morning. Cagliari's Villa, the same morning.

Act 2: The Palace of Count Bitowski.

Act 3: The garden of the Casino at Hietzing.

ACT 1
  Introduction
    G. Rena, Ensemble
  "Ich such' jetzt da, ich such' jetzt dort"
    H. Wallner

---

[3]Originally produced in New York 21 October 1907 at the New Amsterdam Theatre for 416 performances.

[4]Originally produced in New York in English 23 January 1901 at the Broadway Theatre for 35 performances. This is the German language Broadway premiere.

(I Am Looking Here Now, I Am Looking There Now)

"Pepi! Er?" (Pepi, He?)

    C. Mayer, H. Wallner

"Na also schreib' und tu' nicht schmieren"

    E. Von Gross, H. Wallner

(Go on, Write and Do Not Scribble)

Polka

    D. Koller, Mannequins

"Wunsch' guten Morgen, Herr von Pepi"

    D. Koller, H. Wallner

(Good Morning, Mr. van Pepi)

Finale Act 1

    C. Mayer, H. Wallner, H. Lindinger, W. Popp, E. Von Gross

ACT 2

"Polonaise"

    G. Rena, Ensemble

Pas de Deux

    F. Lojekova, A. Halasz

"Wiener Blut" (Vienna Life)

    M. Kowa, E. Von Gross

"Wiener Frauen singen gern"

    C. Mayer, E. Von Gross

(Viennese Women Love to Sing)

"So nimm, mein susser Schatz"

    E. Von Gross, D. Koller, H. Wallner

(Take It, My Sweet Darling)

Mazurka

    Solo Dancers

"Bohmische Polka" (Bohemian Polka)

    D. Koller, H. Lindinger

Czardas

    Solo Dancers

"Lagunenwalzer" (Lagoon Waltz)

    M. Stamos, Ensemble

Finale Act 2

    Ensemble

"An der schonen blauen Donau"[5]

    I. Slatewa, K. Schenker, Dancing Ensemble

(The Blue Danube Waltz)

ACT 3

"Geht's und verkauft's mei G'wand"

    F. Mann, S. Holzmayer

(Go On and Sell My Suit)

"A'Walzer von Strauss"

    H. Lindinger, W. Hackenberg, Singing Ensemble

(A Waltz by Strauss)

Polka

    Soloists, Dancing Ensemble

"Accelerationenwalzer"[6] (Acceleration Waltz)

    Ensemble

Finale Act 3

    G. Rena, Ensemble

1964.26　　　THE COMMITTEE

A (Comedy) Revue in Two Acts, 20 Scenes. Written and created by the Company. Material subject to change nightly. Incidental music composed by Ellsworth Milburn. Directed by Alan Myerson. Setting and lighting by Ralph Alswang. Produced by Arthur Cantor in association with Committee Productions. Opened 16 September 1964 at the Henry Miller's Theatre and closed 7 November 1964 after 61 performances.

CAST: SCOTT BEACH, HAMILTON CAMP, GARRY GOODROW, LARRY HANKIN, KATHRYN ISH, ELLSWORTH MILBURN, IRENE RIORDAN, DICK STAHL.

ACT 1[7]

Scene 1

  The Party

    Host: H. Camp. *Hostess:* K. Ish. *Scotty Pritikin:* S. Beach. *Roger:* L. Hankin. *Billie:* I. Riordan. *Jerry:* D. Stahl. *L. R. Truehart:* E. Milburn. *George Phillips:* G. Goodrow.

Scene 2

  Introduction

    D. Stahl

Scene 3

  Sex on the Campus

    Sy: L. Hankin. *Sharon:* K. Ish. *Room-mate:* H. Camp.

Scene 4

  The Spies

    I. Riordan, D. Stahl, H. Camp, L. Hankin, K. Ish, G. Goodrow

Scene 5

  Failure 101 (Oral Exam)

    Dr. Benway: S. Beach. *Lyman Engel:* G. Goodrow.

Scene 6

  Pregnant

    D. Stahl, K. Ish

Scene 7

  Mechanical Man

    The Mechanical Man: H. Camp. *The Bum:* L. Hankin.

Scene 8

  Stick To the Point (Interview)

    Ron Wunder: S. Beach. *Elizabeth Mainstream Rockwell:* I. Riordan.

Scene 9

  Bar Scene

    Pianist: E. Milburn. *Waiter:* D. Stahl. *Larry Number 1:* G. Goodrow. *Larry Number 2:* L. Hankin.

Scene 10

  Folk Song ("I'm Gonna Ride a Hundred, Hundred, Hundred Miles")

    (*Music and Lyrics by* Irene Riordan and Ellsworth Milburn.)

    Entire Company

ACT 2

Scene 1

  Blue Valley (California) PTA

    Moderator: I. Riordan. *Dr. Ernest:* S. Beach. *Dr. Luce:* H. Camp.

Scene 2

  Shoe Store

    Customer: G. Goodrow. *Salesman:* H. Camp.

Scene 3

  Summer Vacation

    Pat: K. Ish. *Nikki:* I. Riordan.

Scene 4

  Piano Roll (The Virtuoso)

    D. Stahl

Scene 5

  Electric Chair (Prison Scene)

    Warden: H. Camp. *Chaplain:* G. Goodrow. *Prisoner:* L. Hankin. *Governor:* S. Beach.

Scene 6

  Public Opinion

    I. Riordan, D. Stahl

Scene 7

  Liebowitz

    H. Camp, K. Ish, S. Beach

Scene 8

  Psychiatrist (The Hour)

    Patient: D. Stahl. *Doctor:* G. Goodrow.

---

[5]Added to "Wiener Blut" for this production.
[6]Added to "Wiener Blut" for this production.

---

[7]The above program running order was for the opening night performance. Also performed during run:

  Pavlov

    Dr. Pavlov: G. Goodrow. *Visitor:* S. Beach.

Scene 9

Superman
Superman: L. Hankin. *Babs' Husband*: S. Beach.

Scene 10

The Orchestra
Conductor: E. Milburn. *Violin*: I. Riordan. *Cello*: S. Beach. *Horn*: H. Camp. *Bassoon*: G. Goodrow. *Oboe*: K. Ish. *Triangle and Cymbals*: D. Stahl. *Tympany and Wood Block*: L. Hankin.

1964.27 FIDDLER ON THE ROOF

A Musical in Two Acts, a Prologue and 18 Scenes. Book by Joseph Stein. Based on stories by Sholom Aleichem's stories ("Tevye's Daughters") by special permission of Arnold Perl. Music by Jerry Bock. Lyrics by Sheldon Harnick. Entire production directed and choreographed by Jerome Robbins. Settings by Boris Aronson. Costumes by Patricia Zipprodt. Lighting by Jean Rosenthal. Orchestrations by Don Walker. Musical direction and vocal arrangements by Milton Greene. Dance music arranged by Betty Walberg. Produced by Harold Prince. Opened 22 September 1964 at the Imperial Theatre, moved 27 February 1967 to the Majestic Theatre, moved 14 December 1970 to the Broadway Theatre, and closed 2 July 1972 after 3242 performances.

CAST (in order of appearance): *Tevye, the Dairyman*: ZERO MOSTEL. *Golde, his wife*: MARIA KARNILOVA. *Their Three Daughters: Tzeitel*: JOANNA MERLIN. *Hodel*: JULIA MIGENES. *Chava*: Tanya Everett. *Shprintze*: Marilyn Rogers. *Beilke*: Linda Ross. *Yente, the Matchmaker*: BEATRICE ARTHUR. *Motel, the Tailor*: AUSTIN PENDLETON. *Perchik, the Student*: BERT CONVY. *Lazar Wolf, the Butcher*: Michael Granger. *Mordcha, the Innkeeper*: Zvee Scooler. *Rabbi*: Gluck Sandor. *Mendel, his son*: Leonard Frey. *Avram, the Bookseller*: Paul Lipson. *Nachum, the Beggar*: Maurice Edwards. *Grandma Tzeitel*: Sue Babel. *Fruma-Sarah*: Carol Sawyer. *Constable*: Joseph Sullivan. *Fyedka*: Joe Ponazecki. *Shandel*: Helen Verbit. *The Fiddler*: Gino Conforti.

Villagers: Tom Abbott, John C. Attle, Sue Babel, Sammy Bayes, Robert Berdeen, Lorenzo Bianco, Duane Bodin, Robert Currie, Sarah Felcher, Tony Gardell, Louis Genevrino, Ross Gifford, Dan Jasin, Sandra Kazan, Thom Koutsoukos, Sharon Lerit, Sylvia Mann, Peff Modelski, Irene Paris, Charles Rule, Carol Sawyer, Roberta Senn, Mitch Thomas, Helen Verbit.

The action takes place in Anatevka, a village in Russia in 1905 on the eve of the revolutionary period.

Prologue: The exterior of Tevye's house.

Act 1, Scene 1: The kitchen of Tevye's house. *Scene 2*: The exterior of Tevye's house. *Scene 3* The interior of Tevye's house. *Scene 4*: The Inn, the following evening. *Scene 5*: The street outside the Inn. *Scene 6*: The exterior of Tevye's house. *Scene 7*: Tevye's Bedroom. *Scene 8*: The village street and the interior of Motel's tailor shop. *Scene 9*: Part of Tevye's Yard. Night. *Scene 10*: The entire yard of Tevye's house.

Act 2, Scene 1: The exterior of Tevye's house. *Scene 2*: The village street. *Scene 3*: The exterior of the railroad station. *Scene 4*: The village street, some months later. *Scene 5*: Motel's tailor shop. *Scene 6*: A road. Late afternoon. *Scene 7*: Tevye's barn. *Scene 8*: Outside Tevye's house.

ACT 1

Prologue

"Tradition"
Z. Mostel, Villagers

Scene 1

"Matchmaker, Matchmaker"
J. Merlin, J. Migenes, T. Everett

Scene 2

"If I Were a Rich Man"
Z. Mostel

Scene 3

"Sabbath Prayer"
Z. Mostel, M. Karnilova, Villagers

Scene 4

"To Life"
Z. Mostel, M. Granger, Men

Scene 6

("Tradition" reprise)
(Z. Mostel)

"Miracle of Miracles"
A. Pendleton

Scene 7

"The Tailor Motel Kamzoil"
Z. Mostel, M. Karnilova, S. Babel, C. Sawyer, Villagers

Scene 9

"Sunrise, Sunset"
Z. Mostel, M. Karnilova, Villagers

Scene 10

"Wedding Dance"
Villagers

ACT 2

Scene 1

"Now I Have Everything"
B. Convy, J. Migenes

("Tradition" reprise)
(Z. Mostel)

"Do You Love Me?"
Z. Mostel, M. Karnilova

Scene 2

"I Just Heard"
B. Arthur, Villagers

Scene 3

"Far From the Home I Love"
J. Migenes

Scene 6

("Chavaleh")
(Z. Mostel)

Scene 7

"Anatevka"
Z. Mostel, M. Karnilova, B. Arthur, M. Granger, L. Frey, P. Lipson

Scene 8

Epilogue
Entire Company

1964.28 OH WHAT A LOVELY WAR

A Musical Entertainment (Revue) in Two Acts. Written by Theatre Workshop, Charles Chilton and members of the (original British) cast after a treatment by Ted Allan. Directed by Joan Littlewood. Military advisor, Raymond Fletcher. Setting and lighting by John Bury. Costumes by Una Collins. Choreography by Bob Stevenson. Musical direction by Shepard Coleman. Musical arrangements by Alfred Ralston. Design supervision by Klaus Holm. A Theatre Workshop Group Production. Produced by David Merrick and Gerry Raffles. Opened 30 September 1964 at the Broadhurst Theatre and closed 16 January 1965 after 125 performances.

THE PIERROTS (CAST): *Master of Ceremonies, General Lanrezac, Drill Sergeant*: VICTOR SPINETTI. *France, Belgium*: MURRAY MELVIN. *England, Sir John French, The Padre*: BRIAN MURPHY. *Russia, English Signaller*: Frank Coda. *French Captain, Assassin*: Richard Curnock. *Gendarme*: Peter Dalton. *Russia, Luxembourg Signaller*: Larry Dann. *Moltke, Belgium*: Colin Kemball. *Sir Henry Wilson, German Officer*: Ian Paterson. *Kaiser, Sir Douglas Haig*: George Sewell. *Swimmer, Irish Standard Bearer*: Bob Stevenson.

BARBARA WINDSOR, Fanny Carby, Jack Eddleman, Myvanwy Jenn, Linda Loftis, Reid Shelton, Valerie Walsh.

ACT 1

"Row, Row, Row" (from ZIEGFELD FOLLIES OF 1912)
Ensemble
(*Music by* James V. Monaco. *Lyrics by* William Jerome.)

"We Don't Want to Lose You (Your King and Country Want You)"
The Ladies
(*Music and Lyrics by* Paul Rubens.)

"Belgium Put the Kibosh on the Kaiser"
V. Walsh
(*Music and Lyrics by* Ellerton.)

Medley:

"Are We Downhearted, (No)"
(*Music and Lyrics by* W. David, L. Wright.)

"It's a Long Way to Tipperary"
(*Music and Lyrics by* Jack Judge and Harry H. Williams.)

"Hold Your Hand Out Naughty Boy"
    The Men
    (*Music and Lyrics by* Murphy and David.)
"I'll Make a Man of You" (from THE PASSING SHOW OF 1914, London)
    B. Windsor
    (*Music and Lyrics by* Arthur Wimperis and Herman Finck.)
"Pack Up Your Troubles (in Your Old Kit Bag)"
    The Men
    (*Music by* George Powell. *Lyrics by* George Asaf.)
"Hitchykoo"
    F. Carby
    (*Music by* Lewis F. Muir and Maurice Abrahams. *Lyrics by* L. Wolfe Gilbert.)
"Heilige Nacht" (Silent Night)
    C. Kemball
"Christmas Day in the Cookhouse"
    B. Murphy
"Goodbye . . . ee"
    V. Spinetti
    (*Music by* Bert Lee. *Lyrics by* R. P. Weston.)

ACT 2
"Oh What a Lovely War" (Oh It's a Lovely War)
    Ensemble
    (*Music and Lyrics by* J. P. Long, M. Scott, revised by B. Kelsey.)
"Gassed Last Night"
    The Men
"Roses of Picardy"
    L. Loftis, I. Paterson
    (*Music by* Haydn Wood. *Lyrics by* Frederick E. Weatherley.)
"Hush Here Comes a Whizzbang"
    The Men
    (Soldiers' parody of 'Hush, Here Comes the Dream Man')
    (*Music and Lyrics by* R. P. Weston, Barnes and Scott.)
"There's a Long Long Trail"
    I. Paterson
    (*Music by* Zo Elliott. *Lyrics by* Stoddard King.)
"I Don't Want to Be a Soldier"
    The Men
    (Soldiers' parody of 'I'll Make a Man of You" above)
"Kaiser Bill"
    The Men
"They Were Only Playing Leapfrog"
    (*Music arr. by* Alfred Ralston.)The Men
"Old Soldiers Never Die"
    M. Melvin
"If You Want the Old Batallion"
    The Men
"Far Far from Wipers"
    (*Music and Lyrics by* Bingham and Greene.)C. Kemball
"If the Sergeant Steals Your Rum"
    The Men
"I Wore a Tunic (When You Wore a Tulip)"
    I. Paterson
(Soldiers' parody of 'When You Wore a Tulip and I Wore a Big Red Rose')
    (*Music by* Percy Wenrich. *Lyrics by* Jack Mahoney.)
"Forward Joe Soap's Army"
    The Men
"Fred Karno's Army"
    The Men
"When This Lousy War Is Over"
    C. Kemball
(Parody of "When This Cruel War Is Over" {Weeping, Sad and Lonely})
    (*Music by* Henry Tucker. *Lyrics by* Charles Carroll Sawyer.)
"Wash Me in the Water"
    The Men
"I Want To Go Home"
    (*Music arr. by* Alfred Ralston.)
    The Men
"The Bells of Hell"
    (*Music arr. by* Alfred Ralston.)
    The Men

"Keep the Home Fires Burning"
    M. Jenn
    (*Music by* Ivor Novello. *Lyrics by* Lena Guilbert Ford.)
"Sister Susie's Sewing Shirts (for Soldiers)"
    B. Windsor
    (*Music by* Herman Darewski. *Lyrics by* R. P. Weston.)
Finale:
"Chanson de Craonne"
    (*Music and Lyrics by* Vaillant and Couturier.)
"I Don't Want to be A Soldier" (reprise)
"And When They Asked Us"
    (*Music by* Jerome Kern.)
    Ensemble
(Parody to melody of "They Didn't Believe Me" from THE GIRL FROM UTAH)

1964.29 # CAMBRIDGE CIRCUS

A Revue in Two Acts, 25 Scenes. Written by the company. Music by Bill Oddie, Hugh MacDonald, David Palmer. Directed by Humphrey Barclay. (Setting) designed by Stephen Mullin. Costumes by Judy Birdwood. Lighting by Robert Darling. Musical arrangements by David Palmer. Produced by Sol Hurok and David Black in association with Jay Julien and Andre Goulston. Opened 6 October 1964 at the Plymouth Theatre and closed 24 October 1964 after 23 performances[8].

CAST: TIM-BROOKE TAYLOR, GRAHAM CHAPMAN, JOHN CLEESE, DAVID HATCH, JO KENDALL, JONATHAN LYNN, BILL ODDIE.

ACT 1
Scene 1
    Bring Out the Beast
        (*by* Cardinal Richelieu)
        Cast
Scene 2
    Cloak and Dagger
        (*by* John Cleese and David Hatch)
        J. Cleese, D. Hatch, J. Lynn
Scene 3
    "London Bus"
        J. Lynn, T. Brooke-Taylor, D. Hatch, B. Oddie
        (*Music by* Bill Oddie. *Lyrics by* Tim Brooke-Taylor.)
Scene 4
    Stage Coach
        (*by* Graham Chapman and David Lipscomb)
        G. Chapman
Scene 5
    Final Episode
        (*by* John Cleese and Graham Chapman)
        Cast
Scene 6
    "Traffic Island"
        B. Oddie, J. Kendall, J. Cleese, G. Chapman
        (*Music and Lyrics by* Bill Oddie.)
Scene 7
    "Patients, For the Use of"
        T. Brooke-Taylor, B. Oddie, J. Kendall, J. Lynn
        (*Music and Lyrics by* Bill Oddie, Tim Brooke-Taylor, and Chris Stuart-Clark.)
Scene 8
    "Scatty"
        J. Kendall
        (*Music and Lyrics by* Bill Oddie and Hugh MacDonald.)

---

[8]Transferred Off-Broadway 28 October 1964 to Square East, closing 13 January 1965 after 90 performances; re-opened as NEW CAMBRIDGE CIRCUS 14 January 1965 at the Square East and closed 21 March 1965 after 78 performances.

Scene 9

How Black Was My Valley

J. Lynn
(*by* David Lewis, John Cassels, Jonathan Lynn.)

Scene 10

"Boring Straight Song"

B. Oddie
(*Music and Lyrics by* Bill Oddie.)

Scene 11

"BBCBC"

D. Hatch, J. Cleese
(*Music by* Bill Oddie. *Lyrics by* John Cleese et. al.)

Scene 12

"Sing, Sing"

B. Oddie, T. Brooke-Taylor, J. Kendall, J. Cleese,
G. Chapman
(*Music and Lyrics by* Bill Oddie.)

Scene 13

Humour Without Tears

(*by* Terry Jones)
D. Hatch, T. Brooke-Taylor, B. Oddie, J. Lynn, J. Kendall

ACT 2

Scene 1

"I Wanna Hold Your Handel"

B. Oddie, T. Brooke-Taylor, D. Hatch, J. Lynn
(*Music and Lyrics by* John Cameron.)
(Beatles parody à la Handel)

Scene 2

Prophet

(*by* Graham Chapman)G. Chapman

Scene 3

"West End Saga"

(*by* Cardinal Richelieu)Cast

Scene 4

"Music-Hall 1600"

J. Lynn, T. Brooke-Taylor
(*Music by* Bill Oddie. *Lyrics by* Tim Brooke-Taylor, Chris Stuart-Clark.)

Scene 5

"Those Were the Days"

B. Oddie
(*Music and Lyrics by* Bill Oddie.)

Scene 6

"Pride and Joy"

D. Hatch, J. Kendall
(*Music and Lyrics by* Bill Oddie.)

Scene 7

To Bury Caesar

(*by* Tony Hendra)G. Chapman, D. Hatch

Scene 8

"On Her Majesty's Service" (O.H.M.S.)

B. Oddie, T. Brooke-Taylor, D. Hatch, J. Kendall
(*Music and Lyrics by* Bill Oddie.)

Scene 9

Banana

(*by* Anthony Buffery and Richard Eyre)
J. Lynn, G. Chapman

Scene 10

"Bigger Than Both of Us"

J. Kendall, J. Cleese
(*Music by* Bill Oddie. *Lyrics by* John Cleese.)

Scene 11

Judge Not

(*by* John Cleese)
J. Cleese, B. Oddie, D. Hatch, J. Lynn, T. Brooke-Taylor,
G. Chapman

Scene 12

Foot Note

(*by* Cardinal Richelieu)
Cast

1964.30

THE MERRY WIDOW

A Revival of the Operetta in Three Acts[9]. Music by Franz Lehár. Original Viennese libretto ('Die Lustige Witwe') by Victor Léon and Leo Stein after "L'Attaché d'Ambassade" by Henri Meilhac. English libretto by Adrian Ross. Staged by Michael Pollock. Choreographed by Thomas Andrew. Scenic design by George Jenkins. Lighting by Jules Fisher. Conducted by Carl Bamberger. Produced by the New York City Opera. Opened 10 October 1964 at the New York City Center and closed 1 November 1964 after 3 performances in repertory.

CAST: *Sonia*: NADJA WITKOWSKA. *Prince Danilo*: JOHN REARDON. *Baron Popoff*: JACK HARROLD. *Natalie*: Patricia Welting. *De Jolidon*: MICHELE MOLESE. *Marquis de Cascada*: David Smith. *St. Brioche*: Richard Krause. *Admiral Khadja*: William Ledbetter. *Mme. Khadja*: Charlotte Povia. *General Novikovich*: Spiro Malas. *Mme. Novikovich*: Beverly Evans. *Nish*: Coley Worth. *Clo-Clo*: Helen Guile. *Solo Dancers*: Rochelle Zide, Michael Maule. *Ensemble*: New York City Opera Chorus.

1964.31

DIE FLEDERMAUS

A Revival of the Operetta in Three Acts[10]. Original Libretto by Carl Haffner and Richard Genée. Lyrics by Richard Genée. Based on the comedy "Le Réveillon" by Henri Meilhac and Ludovic Halévy. English libretto by Ruth and Thomas Martin. Music by Johann Strauss. Staged by Julius Rudel. Scenic design by William Pitkin. Costume design by Henry Heymann. Choreography by Thomas Andrew. Conducted by Julius Rudel. Opened 11 October 1964 at the New York City Center and closed 7 November 1964 after 4 performances in repertory.

CAST: *Eisenstein*: JOHN REARDON. *Rosalinda*: BEVERLY SILLS. *Adele*: ANNE ELGAR. *Alfred*: Jon Crain. *Falke*: RICHARD FREDERICKS. *Frank*: LEE CASS. *Blind*: Kellis Miller. *Prince Orlofsky*: DAVID SMITH. *Sally*: Beverly Evans. *Frosch*: Coley Worth. *Ivan*: Glenn Dowlen. *Solo Dancers*: Rochelle Zide, Michael Maule. *Ensemble*: New York City Opera Chorus.

1964.32

GOLDEN BOY

A Musical in Two Acts, 20 Scenes. Book by Clifford Odets and William Gibson. Based on Clifford Odets' play of the same name. Music by Charles Strouse. Lyrics by Lee Adams. Directed by Arthur Penn. Sets, costumes and projections designed by Tony Walton. Choreography by Donald McKayle. Assistant choreographer, Jaime Rogers. Lighting by Tharon Musser. Projections devised by Richard Pilbrow. Musical direction and additional musical scoring by Elliott Lawrence. Orchestrations by Ralph Burns. Musical coordinator for Mr. Davis, George Rhodes. Associate producer, George Platt. An Epic Production. Produced by Hillard Elkins. Opened 20 October 1964 at the Majestic Theatre and closed 5 March 1966 after 569 performances.

CAST (in order of appearance): *Tom Moody*: KENNETH TOBEY. *Roxy Gottlieb*: Ted Beniades. *Tokio*: Charles Welch. *Joe Wellington*: SAMMY DAVIS. *Lorna Moon*: PAULA WAYNE. *Mr. Wellington*: Roy Glenn. *Anna*: Jeannette DuBois. *Ronnie*: Johnny Brown. *Frank*: Lou Gossett. *Terry*: Terrin Miles. *Hoodlum*: Buck Heller. *Eddie Satin*: BILLY DANIELS. *Benny*: Benny Payne. *Al*: Albert Popwell. *Lola*: Lola Falana. *Lopez*: Jaime Rogers. *Mabel*: Mabel Robinson. *Les*: Lester Wilson. *Drake*: Don Crabtree. *Fight Announcer*: Maxwell Glanville. *Reporter*: Bob Daley. *Driscoll*: Ralph Vucci.

Ensemble: Marguerite Delaine, Lola Falana, Baayork Lee, Theresa Merritt, Robin Miller, Sally Neal, Louise Quick, Mabel Robinson, Amy Rouselle, Bob Daley, Maxwell Glanville, Buck Heller, Benny Payne, Harold Pierson, Albert Popwell, Kenneth Scott, Stephen Taylor, Ralph Vucci, Lamont Washington, Lester Wilson.

(The action takes place in New York City 1960-1964.)

Act 1, Scene 1: A Boxers' Gymnasium. *Scene 2*: The Wellington kitchen in Harlem. *Scene 3*: Rooftop of the tenement. *Scene 4*: Tom Moody's Office. *Scene 5*: A Schoolyard playground. *Scene 6*: A Harlem street. *Scene 7*: The Wellington kitchen. *Scene 8*: A Railroad depot. *Scene 9*: The road tour. *Scene 10*: Joe's dressing-room in Madison Square Garden.

---

[9]Originally produced in New York 21 October 1907 at the New Amsterdam Theatre for 416 performances. For Synopsis of Scenes and Musical Numbers, see original 1907 production.
[10]First English language production in New York 16 March 1885 at the Casino Theatre for 42 performances. First New York production of this adaptation 20 December 1950 at the Metropolitan Opera House. For Synopsis of Scenes and Musical Numbers, see May 1954 revival.

Act 2, Scene 1: A bar. *Scene 2*: A party at Eddie's penthouse apartment. *Scene 3*: Along the river. *Scene 4*: Dawn in the park. *Scene 5*: Tom's office. *Scene 6*: 127th Street at night. *Scene 7*: The dressing room. *Scene 8*: The boxing ring. *Scene 9*: The dressing room. *Scene 10*: A Harlem street at night.

ACT 1[11]

Scene 1

"Workout"
Boxers

Scene 3

"Night Song"
S. Davis

Scene 4

"Everything's Great"
K. Tobey, P. Wayne

Scene 5

"Gimme Some"
S. Davis, T. Miles

"Stick Around"
S. Davis

Scene 6

"Don't Forget 127th Street"
S. Davis, J. Brown, Company

Scene 8

"Lorna's Here"
P. Wayne

Scene 9

The Road Tour
S. Davis, P. Wayne, K. Tobey, T. Beniades, B. Daniels, C. Welch, Company

"This Is the Life"
B. Daniels, S. Davis, L. Falana, Company

ACT 2

Scene 1

"Golden Boy"
P. Wayne

Scene 2

"While the City Sleeps"
B. Daniels

"While the City Sleeps" (dance)
M. Robinson, J. Rogers, L. Wilson

"Colorful"
S. Davis

Scene 3

"I Want To Be With You"
S. Davis, P. Wayne

Scene 4

"Can't You See It?"
S. Davis

---

[11]For subsequent American road tour prior to London, the script and song order were revised, including the following changes:

"Colorful" (moved to Act 1 Scene 1 after "The Workout")

"Stick Around" and The Road Tour were dropped.

"Yes, I Can!" (added to close Act 1)
S. Davis

"No More" (moved to opening of Act 2)

"Golden Boy" (moved to Act 2, Scene 6, now Lorna's Bedroom)

"You're No Brother of Mine" (added to Act 2, Scene 2, now Scene 3)
S. Davis, Al Kirk (Frank)

"The Riot" (added to Act 2, Scene 8, now Harlem Street)
The Company

"Can't You See It?" dropped.

"What Became of Me" (added to Act 2, Scene 11, now Madison Square Garden)
S. Davis

Scene 6

"No More"
S. Davis, Company

Scene 8

The Fight
S. Davis, J. Rogers

1964.33   BEN FRANKLIN IN PARIS

A Musical in Two Acts, a Prologue and 14 Scenes. Play and lyrics by Sidney Michaels. Music by Mark Sandrich, Jr. Direction and choreography by Michael Kidd. Costumes by Motley. Production designed by Oliver Smith. Lighting by Jack Brown. Musical direction and vocal arrangements by Don Pippin. Orchestrations by Philip J. Lang. Dance and incidental music by Roger Adams. Produced by George W. George and Frank Granat. Opened 27 October 1964 at the Lunt-Fontanne Theatre and closed 1 May 1965 after 215 performances.

CAST (in order of appearance): *Captain Wickes*: SAM GREENE. *Benjamin Franklin*: ROBERT PRESTON. *Temple Franklin*: FRANKLIN KISER. *Benjamin Franklin Bache*: JERRY SCHAEFER. *Footman*: Anthony Falco. *Louis XVI*: OLIVER CLARK. *Vergennes*: Art Bartow. *Turgot*: Clifford Fearl. *Madame La Comtesse Diane de Vobrillac*: ULLA SALLERT. *British Grenadier*: Roger LaPage. *David Lord Stormont*: BYRON WEBSTER. *French Soldier*: Ron Schwinn. *Pierre Caron de Beaumarchais*: BOB KALIBAN. *Jacques Fincque*: John Taliaferro. *Little Boy*: Stuart Getz. *Pedro Count de Aranda*: JACK FLETCHER. *Bookseller*: Herb Mazzini. *Janine Nicolet*: SUSAN WATSON. *Abbe de Morellet*: Herb Mazzini. *Spanish Aide-de-Camp*: Kip Andrews. *Spanish Soldier*: Art Matthews. *Spanish Ambassador's Daughter*: Suzanne France. *Yvonne*: Lauren Jones.

Singers and Dancers: Barbara Bossert, Mona Crawford, Hilda Harris, Anita Maye, Caroline Parks, Art Bartow, Anthony Falco, Clifford Fearl, John Keatts, Art Matthews, Herb Mazzini, John Taliaferro, Diane Ball, Marilyn Charles, Jean Eliot, Suzanne France, Ellen Graff, Lauren Jones, Sandy Roveta, Kip Andrews, Roger LePage, George Ramos, Eddie Roll, Rec Russel, Ron Schwinn, Lou Zeldis.

The action takes place in France during 1776-1777.

Prologue: At sea aboard the *S. S. Reprisal*.

Act 1, Scene 1: The Docks. *Scene 2*: Versailles. *Scene 3*: Ben's House. *Scene 4*: The Park. *Scene 5*: Sky over Paris. *Scene 6*: The Pont Neuf. *Scene 7*: Paristown. *Scene 8*: ben's House. *Scene 9*: The Vineyards.

Act 2, Scene 1: The Spanish Embassy. *Scene 2*: Versailles. *Scene 3*: Diane's House. *Scene 4*: Ben's House. *Scene 5*: Versailles.

Prologue

"We Sail the Seas"
American Sailors

ACT 1

Scene 1

"I Invented Myself"
R. Preston, Company

Scene 2

"Too Charming"
R. Preston, U. Sallert

Scene 3

"Whatever Became of Old Temple"
F. Kiser

"Half the Battle"
R. Preston, J. Schaefer, J.F. Kiser, B. Kaliban

Scene 4

"A Balloon Is Ascending"[12]
Company

Scene 5

"To Be Alone With You"
R. Preston, U. Sallert, Company

Scene 6

"You're in Paris"
S. Watson, F. Kiser

Scene 8

"How Laughable It Is"
U. Sallert

---

[12]Dropped during the run.

Scene 9

"Hic Haec Hoc"
Monks

"God Bless the Human Elbow"
R. Preston, J. Fletcher, B. Kaliban, Monks

ACT 2

Scene 1

"When I Dance With the Person I Love"
S. Watson

Scene 3

"Diane Is"
R. Preston

"Look For Small Pleasures"
R. Preston, U. Sallert

Scene 4

"I Love the Ladies"
R. Preston, S. Greene, B. Kaliban, F. Kiser, Sailors

Scene 5

"To Be Alone With You" (reprise)
R. Preston

COMEDY IN MUSIC
Opus 2

1964.34

A New Edition of the Solo Performance in Two Acts[13]. Designed and lighted by Ralph Alswang. A Nine O'Clock Theatre Production. Produced by Alexander H. Cohen. Opened 9 November 1964 at the John Golden Theatre and closed 24 April 1965 after 192 performances.

CAST: VICTOR BORGE, LEONID HAMBRO.

The order of the program will be announced by Mr. Borge.

ACT 1

Steinway

Mike

Mr. Borge

Latecomers

Curtain

ACT 2

Steinway

Mike

Mr. Borge

Mr. Hambro

Steinway Senior

Steinway Junior

Entire Cast

Mr. Borge Entirely Alone

Curtain

SOMETHING MORE!

1964.35

A Musical Comedy in Two Acts, 17 Scenes. Book by Nate Monaster. Based on the novel "Portofino P.T.A." by Gerald Green. Music by Sammy Fain. Lyrics by Marilyn and Alan Bergman. Directed by Jule Styne[14]. Scenery and lighting by Robert Randolph. Costumes by Alvin Colt. Musical direction by Oscar Kosarin. Orchestrations by Ralph Burns. Vocal arrangements by Buster Davis. Dance arrangements and orchestrations by Robert Prince. Dances and musical numbers staged by Bob Herget. Produced by Lester Osterman. Opened 10 November 1964 at the Eugene O'Neill Theatre and closed 21 November 1964 after 15 performances.

CAST (in order of appearance): *Bill Deems:* ARTHUR HILL. *Carol Deems:* BARBARA COOK. *Suzy Deems:* Neva Small. *Freddy Deems:* Kenny Kealy. *Adam Deems:* Eric White. *Julie:* Katey O'Brady. *Dick:* Hal Linden. *Gladys:* Marilyn Murphy. *Joe Santini:* Rico Froehlich. *Tony Santini:* VICTOR R. HELOU. *Policeman:* RICO

FROEHLICH. *Mrs. Ferenzi:* PEG MURRAY. *Monte Checkovitch:* RONNY GRAHAM. *Luigi:* VICTOR R. HELOU. *Lepescu:* MICHAEL KERMOYAN. *Marchesa Valentina Crespi:* JOAN COPELAND. *Tony:* Christopher Man. *Maria:* Katey O'Brady. *The King:* Taylor Reed. *The King's Companion:* Connie Sanchez. *Mr. Veloz:* JO JO SMITH. *Mrs. Veloz:* PAULA KELLY. *Commandatorre Vermelli:* James Lavery. *Clubwoman:* Laurie Franks.

Dancers: Joan Bell, Shari Greene, Lynn Kollenberg, Connie Sanchez, Mimi Wallace, Bob Bishop, Steve Jacobs, Richard Lyle, Barry Preston, Bill Starr. *Singers:* Natalie di Silvio, Laurie Franks, Bobbi Lange, Marilyn Muphy, James Lavery, Taylor Reed, Ed Varrato.

Act 1, Scene 1: The Deems' living room, Mineola, New York. *Scene 2:* Same, a few days later. *Scene 3:* Mineola, New York, to Portofino, Italy. *Scene 4:* The Villa, Portofino. *Scene 5:* Portofino Square. *Scene 6:* The road to the Monastery. *Scene 7:* The old Monastery. *Scene 8:* The Villa.

Act 2, Scene 1: 'Bill Remembers'—Later that night. *Scene 2:* In front of the Marchesa's studio. *Scene 3:* The Marchesa's studio. *Scene 4:* In front of the Marchesa's studio. *Scene 5:* The Villa. *Scene 6:* The road to the beach. *Scene 7:* The beach. Dawn. *Scene 8:* The road to the Villa. *Scene 9:* The Villa.

ACT 1

"Something More"
A. Hill

"Who Fills the Bill"
B. Cook, N. Small, K. Nealy, E. White, H. Linden, CommitteeMemebers

"The Straw That Broke the Camel's Back"
A. Hill

"Better All the Time"
B. Cook

"Don't Make a Move"
J. Lavery, V. R. Helou

"Don't Make a Move" (reprise)
J. Lavery, V. R. Helou (Portofini Branch)

"No Questions"
B. Cook

"Church of My Choice"
R. Graham

"Jaded, Degraded Am I!"
R. Graham

"I've Got Nothin' to Do"
B. Cook, P. Murray, N. Small, K. Nealy, E. White

"I've Got Nothin' to Do" (reprise)
P. Murray

"Party Talk"
Guests

"In No Time At All"
J. Copeland

"The Master of the Greatest Art of All"
M. Kermoyan

"Grazie Par Niente"
R. Graham, B. Cook, J. J. Smith, P. Kelly, Guests

"I Feel Like New Year's Eve"
B. Cook

"One Long Last Look"
B. Cook

ACT 2

"Ode to a Key"
A. Hill

"Bravo, Bravo, Novelisto"
A. Hill, R. Froehlich

"Life Is Too Short"
R. Graham, P. Murray

"Il Lago de Innamoratti"
J. J. Smith, P. Kelly, Ensemble
(*Beach Dance composed and arranged by* Robert Prince.)

"Mineola"
B. Cook

"Come Sta"
P. Murray, N. Small, K. Kealy, E. White, K. O'Brady, C. Mann

Finale
A. Hill, B. Cook

---

[13]An earlier version of "Comedy In Music" was first produced in New York 2 October 1953 at the John Golden Theatre for 849 performances.

[14]Additional direction by Joe Layton unbilled.

IOLANTHE,

1964.36 or The Peer and the Peri

A Revival of the Comic Opera in Two Acts[15]. Libretto by William S. Gilbert. Music by Arthur Sullivan. (Costumes uncredited.) Settings designed by Peter Goffin. Director of productions, Herbert Newby. Musical director, Isidore Godfrey. Associate conductor, James Walker. Produced by the D'Oyly Carte Opera Trust, Ltd. under the management of Sol Hurok. Opened 17 November 1964 at the New York City Center and closed 17 December 1964 after 7 performances in repertory.

CAST: *The Lord Chancellor:* JOHN REED. *Earl of Mountararat:* DONALD ADAMS. *Earl Tolloller:* DAVID PALMER. *Private Willis* of the Grenadier Guards: KENNETH SANDFORD. *Strephon,* an Arcadian Shepherd: JEFFREY SKITCH. *Queen of the Fairies:* GILLIAN KNIGHT. *Iolanthe,* a Fairy, Strephon's Mother: GILLIAN HUMPHREYS. *Celia, Leila, Fleta,* Fairies: Margaret Eales, Pauline Wales, Jennifer Marks. *Phyllis,* an Arcadian Shepherdess and Ward in Chancery: VALERIE MASTERSON.
Chorus of Dukes, Marquises, Earls, Viscounts, Barons and Fairies: Glyn Adams, Keith Bonnington, Liam Cummings, Jon Ellison, Eric Greenall, John Hugill, Thomas Lawlor, James Lewington, Gordon Mackenzie, John Maguire, James Marsland, Alfred Oldridge, Derek Peatfield, Vivien Carman, Dawn Davies, Margaret Eales, Gloria Farndell, Abby Hadfield, Susan Maisey, Jennifer Marks, Marian Martin, Joy Mornay, Elizabeth Mynett, Sylvia Vale, Anna Vincent.

TRIAL BY JURY

1964.37

A Revival of the Comic Opera in One Act[16]. Libretto by William S. Gilbert. Music by Arthur Sullivan. Costumes designed by George Sheringham. Setting designed by Peter Goffin. Director of productions, Herbert Newby. Musical directors, Isidore Godfrey, James Walker. Produced by the D'Oyly Carte Trust, Ltd. under the management of Sol Hurok. Opened 19 November 1964 at the New York City Center and closed 19 December 1964 after 10 performances in repertory.

CAST: *The Learned Judge:* JEFFREY SKITCH. *Counsel for the Plaintiff* ALAN STYLER. *The Defendant:* PHILIP POTTER. *Foreman of the Jury:* Anthony Raffell. *Usher:* GEORGE COOK. *Associate:* KEITH BONNINGTON. *The Plaintiff:* JENNIFER TOYE. *First Bridesmaid:* Joy Mornay. *Chorus of Jurymen, Bridesmaids and Public:* same as IOLANTHE above.

H.M.S. PINAFORE,

1964.38 or The Lass That Loved a Sailor

A Revival of the Comic Opera in Two Acts[17]. Libretto by William S. Gilbert. Music by Arthur Sullivan. Settings and costumes designed by Peter Goffin. Back cloth, Joseph and Phil Harker. Director of productions, Herbert Newby. Musical directors, Isidore Godfrey, James Walker. Produced by the D'Oyly Carte Opera Trust, Ltd. under the management of Sol Hurok. Opened 19 November 1964 at the New York City Center and closed 19 December 1964 after 10 performances in repertory.

CAST: *The Rt. Hon. Sir Joseph Porter, K.C.B.,* First Lord of the Admiralty: JOHN REED. *Captain Corcoran,* Commanding the *H.M.S. Pinafore:* JEFFREY SKITCH. *Ralph Rackstraw,* Able Seaman: DAVID PALMER. *Dick Deadeye,* Able Seaman: DONALD ADAMS. *Bill Bobstay,* Bo'sun's Mate: George Cook. *Bob Beckett,* Carpenter's Mate: Anthony Raffell. *Josephine,* the Captain's Daughter: ANN HOOD. *Hebe,* Sir Joseph's First Cousin: Pauline Wales. *Little Buttercup,* a Portsmouth Bumboat Woman: GILLIAN KNIGHT. *First Lord's Sisters, his Cousins, his Aunts, Sailors, Marines:* same as IOLANTHE above.

---

[15]First presented in New York 25 November 1882 at the Standard Theatre for 105 performances. For Synopsis of Scenes and Musical Numbers, see original 1882 production.
[16]First presented in New York 15 November 1875 at the Eagle Theatre for 8 performances. For Synopsis of Scenes and Musical Numbers, see original 1875 production.
[17]Originally presented in New York 15 January 1879 at the Standard Theatre for 175 performances. For Synopsis of Scenes and Musical Numbers, see original 1879 production.

1964.39 ZIZI

A Musical Extravaganza in Two Acts, 8 Scenes, in French. Scenes. Entire production conceived and staged by Roland Petit. Costumes by Yves Saint-Laurent. Musical director and conductor, Michel Mention. Associate conductor, Don Plumby. Produced by Columbia Theatrical Enterprises, Inc. and Claude Giraud Productions under the auspices of the Association Française d'Action Artistique. Opened 21 November 1964 at the Broadway Theatre and closed 2 January 1965 after 49 performances.

CAST: ZIZI JEANMAIRE, FÉLIX BLASZKA.
Roland Petit Corps de Ballet: Thérèsè Thoreux, Jacqueline de min, Panchita de Peri, Nicole Dieu, Vladanka Langhofer, Marie Lys Blanc, Jacques Dombrowski, Ben de Rochemont, Daini Kudo, Hans Kroonder, Robert Richemont, Lucien Mars, Peter Smink. *Off-Stage Male Quartet:* The Revelers. *Percussionist:* Gus Wallez. *Accordionist:* Jean Cardon.

ACT 1
Scene 1
  Prologue
    (*Music by* Ward Swingle.)
    Dancers
Scene 2
  "La cervelle"
    Z. Jeamaire
    (*Music by* Jean Ferrat. *Lyrics by* Bernard Dimey.)
  I do pretty well without racking my brains, I have all I need. What makes a woman stupid is to have too much brains. Brains, brains, they're no use to me!
  "Les bras d'Antoine"
    Z. Jeanmaire, F. Blaszka
    (*Music and Lyrics by* Guy Béart.)
  These are wonderful and exciting things that I feel when I am in the arms of my beloved Antoine.
Scene 3
  Pastiches (Ballet Sketches)
    Dancers
  Scaramouche
    (*Music by* Darius Milhaud.)
  Tarantelle
    (*Music by* Gioacchino Rossini.)
  Espana
    (*Music by* Emmanuel Chabrier.)
    Introductory Duets by J. Dombrowski (dancer), G. Wallez (percussionist).
Scene 4
  La chambre
    Z. Jeanmaire, F. Blaszka, Company
    (*Ballet by* Georges Simenon. *Music by* Georges Auric.)
  A police inspector reconstructs a crime, only to find that history repeats itself. A rectangular light, orange colored, in a piece of the night, it is a window, a window is a room, a room is a man's burrow where one is born, one loves, one hates, one dies ... And sometimes one kills. In a room, once upon a time ...
Scene 5
  "Bacorope"
    (*Music by* Michel Mention.)
    N. Dieu, L. Mars, Dancers
Scene 6
  La chaloupée
    Z. Jeanmaire, B. de Rochemont or J. Dombrowski, Company
    (*Story by* Marcel Aymé. *Music by* Maurice Thiriet.)
  This dance story about a wedding party was written especially for Zizi Jeanmaire and Roland Petit. The theme of the music is adapted from "Valse Chaloupée" by Jacques Offenbach, who in turn took an old French seafarers' dance form as the basis for his lively and rollicking score.
Scene 7
  "Quail On Toast With Pink Champagne"
    (*Music by* Michel Mention.)
    Z. Jeanmaire, Company. Introduction by Félix Blaska.
  In this dance sketch (from the ballet "A La Carte" devised by Roland Petit), Roland Petit and Yves Saint-Laurent depict a gourmet delicacy of

the French cuisine: Les Cailles sur Canape, topped off with a glass of bubbling pink champagne, as portrayed by Zizi Jeanmaire.

ACT 2

Zizi sings:

"Les yeux brilliants" (Sparkling Eyes)

Z. Jeanmaire
(*Music by* Francis Lai. *Lyrics by* Bernard Dimey.)

With my sparkling eyes, my smile and the way I talk, you know where I come from.

"Les tatouages" (The Tattoos)

Z. Jeanmaire, F. Blaszka
(*Music by* Michel Legrand. *Lyrics by* Jean Drejac.)

A play on words. T'as tout is also pronounced "tattoo," and means "you have everything."

"Charleston"

Z. Jeanmaire, A. Brigoni, P. Smink, H. Kroonder

"Drole de musique"

Z. Jeanmaire
(*Music and Lyrics by* Christian Guitreau.)

The sound of the accordion reminds me of the little dance halls and bistros where I've left something of myself.

"Frankie et Johnny"

Z. Jeanmaire, J. Dombrowski, F. Blaszka, Company
(*Lyrics by* Boris Vian, from an American folk song)

A French version of the American hit which makes no pretense whatsoever of portraying our authentic Western life.

"Mon truc en plumes"

Z. Jeanmaire, Entire Company
(*Music by* Jean Constantin. *Lyrics by* Bernard Dimey.)

Although the literal translation of this production number is "My Skill With Feathers," the word "truc" as used in French slang is, with its double entendre, untranslatable.

"Mon bonhomme" (My Guy)

Z. Jeanmaire
(*Music and Lyrics by* Jean Ferrat.)

If I call him just my man, or even my master, that wouldn't give you the correct impression of how really sweet he is. Mon Bonhomme, Mon Bonhomme.

"Je te tuerai d'amour" (I Shall Kill You With Love)

Z. Jeanmaire, Rock 'n' Roll Quartet
(*Music by* Johnny Halliday. *Lyrics by* Raymond Queneau.)

This is France's eloquent answer to our rock 'n' roll. Johnny Halliday, who wrote this music, is not only the continental Elvis Presley, but also writes most of his popular material himself.

"Eh l'amour" (Ah, love!)

Z. Jeanmaire, Entire Company
(*Music and Lyrics by* Jean Ferrat.)

This Gallic hymn to l'amour invokes love in all its facets: young innocence, youthful passion, the cheap and transitory varieties as well as loftier emotions. The song is climaxed by a promise of 'seventh heaven'—or even more!

1964.40   # BAJOUR

A Musical Comedy in Two Acts, 22 Scenes. Book by Ernest Kinoy. Based on the short stories ("The Gypsy Women," "The King of the Gypsies") by Joseph Mitchell published in *The New Yorker*[18]. Music and lyrics by Walter Marks. Directed by Lawrence Kasha. Musical numbers staged by Peter Gennaro. Scenery by Oliver Smith. Costumes by Freddy Wittop. Lighting by Peggy Clark. Vocal arrangements and musical direction by Lehman Engel. Orchestrations by Mort Lindsey. Dance music arranged by Richard DeBenedictis. Assistant choreographer, Wally Seibert. Produced by Edward Padula, Carroll and Harris Masterson, Norman Twain. Opened 23 November 1964 at the Sam S. Shubert Theatre, moved 10 May 1965 to the Lunt-Fontanne Theatre and closed 12 June 1965 after 232 performances.

---

[18]Later published in book form under the collective title "Up in the Old Hotel."

CAST (in order of appearance): *Renting Agent:* Dick Ensslen. *Cockeye Johnny Dembo:* HERSCHEL BERNARDI. *Vanno:* Sal Lombardo. *Loopa:* ANTONIA REY. *First Patrolman:* Harry Danner. *Plainclothesman:* Harry Goz. *Second Patrolman:* Paul Sorvino. *Third Patrolman:* Robert Kristen. *Lou MacNiall:* ROBERT BURR. *Emily Kirsten:* NANCY DUSSAULT. *Mrs. Helene Kirsten:* MAE QUESTEL. *Rosa:* Asya. *Mitya:* Vito Durante. *Frankie:* Terry Violino. *Steve:* GUS TRIKONIS. *The King of Newark:* HERBERT EDELMAN. *Anyanka:* CHITA RIVERA. *Marfa:* Jeanne Tanzy. *Olga:* Carmen Morales. *Chairlady:* LUCIE LANCASTER. *Waiter:* Harry Danner. *J. Arnold Foster:* Ralph Farnworth.

Dancers: Asya, Eileen Barbaris, Michael Bennett, Connie Burnett, John Cashman, Betsy Dickerson, Vito Durante, Gene Foote, Bick Goss, Fernando Grahal, Kazimir Kokich, Marc Maskin, Stan Mazin, Carmen Morales, Carolyn Morris, Leland Palmer, Don Rehg, Geri Seignious, Terry Violino, Billi Vitali. *Singers:* Anita Alpert, Harry Danner, Mariana Doro, Dick Ensslen, Peter Falzone, Ralph Farnworth, Harry Goz, Liza Howell, Robert Kirsten, Urylee Leonardos, Evy Love, Madeline Miller, Eugene Morgan, Jeanne Repp, Jessica Quinn, Paul Sorvino.

(The action takes place at the present time in New York City.)

Act 1, Scene 1: The Empty Store. *Scene 2:* The City. *Scene 3:* The Pickpocket and Confidence Squad. *Scene 4:* Emily's Bedroom. *Scene 5:* The Backyard. *Scene 6:* In front of the Store. *Scene 7:* The Store (now the Ofisa). *Scene 8:* In front of the Store. *Scene 9:* The Ofisa. *Scene 10:* An Urban Renewal Site. *Scene 11:* The Ofisa.

Act 2, Scene 1: The Backyard. *Scene 2:* Momma's Kitchen. *Scene 3:* The Backyard. *Scene 4:* The Pickpocket and Confidence Squad. *Scene 5:* The Guggenheim Museum. *Scene 6:* Central Park. *Scene 7:* Momma's Kitchen. *Scene 8:* The Ofisa. *Scene 9:* An Urban Renewal Site. *Scene 10:* The Empty Store. *Scene 11:* The New Jersey Flats.

ACT 1

Scene 1

"Move Over, New York"
H. Bernardi, Ensemble

Scene 3

"Where Is the Tribe For Me?"
N. Dussault

Scene 5

"The Haggle"
C. Rivera, G. Trikonis, Ensemble

"Love-Line"
C. Rivera

Scene 7

"Words, Words, Words"
N. Dussault, H. Bernardi

Scene 9

"Mean"
C. Rivera

Scene 10

"Must It Be Love?"
N. Dussault

Scene 11

"Bajour"
C. Rivera, N. Dussault, H. Bernardi, Ensemble

ACT 2

Scene 1

"Soon"
C. Rivera, G. Trikonis

Scene 3

"I Can"
C. Rivera, N. Dussault

Scene 4

"Living Simply"
R. Burr, N. Dussault, Patrolmen

Scene 6

"Honest Man"
H. Bernardi, H. Edelman

Scene 7

"Guarantees"
M. Questel

"Love Is a Chance"
N. Dussault

Scene 8

"The Sew-Up"
C. Rivera, M. Questel, Ensemble Women

Scene 11
Finale: "Move Over, America"
Ensemble

THE PIRATES OF PENZANCE,
1964.41   or The Slave of Duty

A Revival of the Comic Opera in Two Acts[19]. Libretto by William S. Gilbert. Music by Arthur Sullivan. Settings designed by Peter Goffin. (Costumes uncredited) Director of productions, Herbert Newby. Musical directors, Isidore Godfrey, James Walker. Produced by the D'Oyly Carte Opera Trust, Ltd. under the management of Sol Hurok. Opened 24 November 1964 at the New York City Center and closed 20 December 1964 after 8 performances in repertory.

CAST: *Major General Stanley*: JOHN REED. *The Pirate King*: DONALD ADAMS. *Samuel, his Lieutenant*: Anthony Raffell. *Frederic, the Pirate Apprentice*: PHILIP POTTER. *Sergeant of Police*: GEORGE COOK. *Mabel, Edith Kate, Isabel*, General Stanley's Daughters: VALERIE MASTERSON, GILLIAN HUMPHREYS, PEGGY ANN JONES, Pauline Wales. *Ruth, Pirate Maid-of-all-work*: GILLIAN KNIGHT. *Chorus of Pirates, Police and General Stanley's Daughters*: same as IOLANTHE above.

THE MIKADO,
1964.42   or The Town of Titipu

A Revival of the Comic Opera in Two Acts[20]. Libretto by William S. Gilbert. Music by Arthur Sullivan. Production directed by Anthony Besch. Costumes designed by Disley Jones and Charles Ricketts. Settings designed by Disley Jones. Director of productions, Herbert Newby. Musical director, Isidore Godfrey, James Walker. Produced by the D'Oyly Carte Opera Trust, Ltd. under the management of Sol Hurok. Opened 26 November 1964 at the New York City Center and closed 16 December 1964 after 10 performances in repertory.

CAST: *The Mikado of Japan*: DONALD ADAMS. *Nanki-Poo, his son, disguised as a wandering minstrel in love with Yum-Yum*: PHILIP POTTER. *Ko-Ko, Lord High Executioner of Titipu*: JOHN REED. *Pooh-Bah, Lord High Everything Else*: KENNETH SANDFORD. *Pish-Tush, Go-To, Noble Lords*: Alan Styler, George Cook. *Yum-Yum, Pitti-Sing, Peep-Bo, three sisters, wards of Ko-Ko*: JENNIFER TOYE, PEGGY ANN JONES, GILLIAN HUMPHREYS. *Katisha*: GILLIAN KNIGHT. *Chorus of School Girls, Nobles, Guards and Coolies*: same as IOLANTHE above.

RUDDIGORE,
1964.43   or The Witch's Curse

A Revival of the Comic Opera in Two Acts[21]. Libretto by William S. Gilbert. Music by Arthur Sullivan. Costumes and settings by Peter Goffin. Director of productions, Herbert Newby. Musical directors, Isidore Godfrey, James Walker. Produced by the D'Oyly Carte Opera Trust, Ltd. under the management of Sol Hurok. Opened 3 December 1964 at the New York City Center and closed 18 December 1964 after 5 performances in repertory.

CAST: *Sir Ruthven Murgatroyd*: JOHN REED. *Richard Dauntless*: DAVID PALMER. *Sir Despard Murgatroyd*: KENNETH SANDFORD. *Old Adam Goodheart*: George Cook. *Sir Roderic Murgatroyd*: DONALD ADAMS. *Rose Maybud*: ANN HOOD. *Mad Margaret*: PEGGY ANN JONES. *Dame Hannah*: GILLIAN KNIGHT. *Zorah*: Jennifer Toye. *Ruth*: Jennifer Marks. *Chorus of Officers, Ancestors, Professional Bridesmaids, etc.*: same as IOLANTHE above.

----
[19]First presented in New York 31 December 1879 at the Fifth Avenue Theatre for a total of 91 performances in two engagements. For Synopsis of Scenes and Musical Numbers, see original 1879 production.
[20]First presented in New York 20 July, 10-29 August 1885 at the Union Square and People's Theatres for 22 performances. First authorized production presented 19 August 1885 at the Fifth Avenue Theatre by Richard D'Oyly Carte for 250 performances. For Synopsis of Scenes and Musical Numbers, see 19 August 1885 D'Oyly Carte production.
[21]First presented in New York 21 February 1887 at the Standard Theatre for 53 performances. For Synopsis of Scenes and Musical Numbers, see original 1887 production.

1964.44   # I HAD A BALL

A Musical Comedy in Two Acts. Book by Jerome Chodorov. Music and lyrics by Jack Lawrence and Stan Freeman. Directed by Lloyd Richards. Settings and lighting by Will Steven Armstrong. Costumes by Ann Roth. Musical direction and vocal arrangements by Pembroke Davenport. Dances and musical numbers staged by Onna White. Orchestrations by Philip J. Lang. Dance music arranged by Luther Henderson. Produced by Joseph Kipness. Opened 15 December 1964 at the Martin Beck Theatre and closed 12 June 1965 after 199 performances.

CAST (in order of appearance): *Garside*: BUDDY HACKETT. *Stan the Shpieler*: RICHARD KILEY. *Jeannie*: KAREN MORROW. *The Alley Gang (4): Gimlet*: Al Nesor. *Joe the Muzzler*: Jack Wakefield. *Ma Maloney*: ROSETTA LeNOIRE. *George Osaka*: Conrad Yama. *Morocco*: Morocco. *Lifeguard*: Marty Allen. *Jimmy*: Nathaniel Jones. *Officer Millhauser*: Ted Thurston. *Brooks*: STEVE ROLAND. *Addie*: LUBA LISA. *Children*: Sheldon Golomb, Gina Kaye.
Singers: Miriamne Burton, Jacqueline Carol, Jacque Dean, Marilyn Feder, Shirley Leinwand, Lispet Nelson, Eugene Edwards, Herbert Fields, Murray Goldkind, Marvin Goodis, Herb Surface, John Wheeler. *Dancers*: Mary Ehara, Sandra Lein, Nancy Lynch, Patti Mariano, Alice Shanahan, June Eve Story, Patti Ann Watson, Marty Allen, Doria Avila, Bob Bernard, Ray Gilbert, Edward J. Heim, Gary Hubler, Scott Hunter, John Sharpe.

Act 1: In and around Coney Island on the Fourth of July. The time is the present.

Act 2: Sixty days later.

ACT 1
"Coney Island, U.S.A."
   J. Wakefield, R. LeNoire, C. Yama, A. Nesor, Children, Ensemble
"The Other Half of Me"
   R. Kiley
"Red-Blooded American Boy"
   S. Roland, A. Nesor, J. Wakefield, R. LeNoire, C. Yama
"I Got Everything I Want"
   K. Morrow
"Freud"
   B. Hackett
"Think Beautiful"
   R. LeNoire, K. Morrow, J. Wakefield, C. Yama, A. Nesor, Ensemble
"Addie's at It Again"
   L. Lisa, J. Wakefield, C. Yama, A. Nesor
"Faith"
   R. Kiley, A. Nesor, J. Wakefield, R. LeNoire, C. Yama, Children, Ensemble
"Can It Be Possible?"
   R. Kiley, K. Morrow, S. Roland, L. Lisa, B. Hackett
ACT 2
"The Neighborhood Song"
   A. Nesor, J. Wakefield, R. LeNoire, C. Yama, Ensemble
"The Affluent Society"
   R. Kiley, S. Roland
"Boys, Boys, Boys"
   L. Lisa, Lifeguards
"Fickle Finger of Fate"
   R. Kiley
"I Had a Ball"
   K. Morrow, A. Nesor, J. Wakefield, R. LeNoire, C. Yama, Morocco, Ensemble
"Almost"[22]
   K. Morrow
"You Deserve Me"
   B. Hackett, S. Roland, L. Lisa
"You Deserve Me" (reprise)
   B. Hackett
"Tunnel of Love Chase"
   B. Hackett, R. Kiley, K. Morrow, T. Thurston, Ensemble

----
[22]Dropped during the run.

1964.45 # BEYOND THE FRINGE '65

A Return Engagement of the Revue in Two Acts[23]. Written by Alan Bennett, Peter Cook, Jonathan Miller, Dudley Moore. Staged by Alexander H. Cohen. Original London production staged by Eleanor Fazan. Setting by John Wyckham. Lighting by Ralph Alswang. Production associates, Andre Goulston, Gabriel Katzka. A Nine O'Clock Theatre Production. Produced by Alexander H. Cohen by arrangement with William Donaldson and Donald Albery. Opened 15 December 1964 at the Ethel Barrymore Theatre and closed 9 January 1965 after 30 performances.

CAST: ROBERT CESSNA, DONALD CULLEN, JOEL FABIANI, JAMES VALENTINE.

ACT 1[24]

Home Thoughts from Abroad

Royal Box

The Following Paid Political Broadcast[25]

Bollard

Blue Trousers[26]

Weill Song

The Philosophers

The Great Train Robbery

Colonel Bogey

The Aftermyth of War

ACT 2

Civil War

Real Class

Die Flabbergast[27]

Portraits from Memory

One Leg Too Few

The Death of (Lord) Nelson

The Scientist

The Doctor

The Duke (Studio Five Interviews)

The Miner (Sitting on the Bench revised)

The Restaurant

The Sermon (Take a Pew revised)

So That's the Way You Like It

The End of the World

1964.46 # BRIGADOON

A Revival of the Musical Play in Two Acts, a Prologue and 11 Scenes[28]. Book and lyrics by Alan Jay Lerner. Music by Frederick Loewe. Dance and musical Numbers by Agnes de Mille, assisted by James Jamieson. Directed by John Fearnley. Settings by Oliver Smith. Lighting by Peggy Clark. Costumes by Stanley Simmons. Conductor, William Jonson. (Vocal arrangements by Frederick Loewe. Orchestrations by Ted Royal.) Produced by New York City Center Light Opera Company (Jean Dalrymple, Director). Opened 23 December 1964 at the New York City Center and closed 3 January 1965 after 17 performances.

CAST (in order of appearance): *Tommy Albright*: PETER PALMER. *Jeff Douglas*: SCOTT McKAY. *Sandy Dean*: William [Will] Mackenzie. *Meg Brockie*: LOUISE O'BRIEN. *Archie Beaton*: Earl MacDonald. *Harry Beaton*: EDWARD VILLELLA. *Andrew MacLaren*: Alexander Clark. *Jean MacLaren*: Imelda De Martin. *Fiona MacLaren*: LINDA BENNETT. *Angus MacGuffie*: Daniel Hannafin. *Charlie*

Dalrymple: HARRY DAVID SNOW. *Maggie Anderson*: Gemze de Lappe. *Sword Dancers*: Ben Gillespie, Paul Olson, Wayne Boyd, Dennis Cole, Charles McCraw, Ron Tassone. *Mr. Lundie*: CLARENCE NORDSTROM. *Bagpiper*: Maurice Eisenstadt. *Frank*: Si Vario. *Jane Ashton*: Sharon Ritchie.

Townsfolk of Brigadoon: Singers: Diana Chase, Maria Hero, Linda Johnson, Virginia Kerr, Bobbi Lange, Leonore Lanzillotti, Joyce Olson, Jeanne Shea, Abbie Todd, Sallie Valante, Lynn Wendell, Brown Bradley, Peter Clark, William J. Coppola, Rex Downey, Glenn Kezer, Henry Lawrence, Jim Lynn, Bob Neukum, Stan Page, Stephen Rydell. *Dancers*: Virginia Allen, Lynne Broadbent, Joanna Crosson, Diana Ede, Lucia Lambert, Loi Leabo, Gracia Littauer, Mavis Ray, Judy Thelen, Mona Tritsch, Esther Villavicencio, Toodie Wittner, Paul Berné, Wayne Boyd, Allan Byrns, Dennis Cole, Joseph Fioretti, Ben Gillespie, Charles McCraw, Paul Olson, Victor Pierantozzi, Ron Tassone, Michael Toles.

1965.01 # KELLY

A Musical in Two Acts, a Prologue and 13 Scenes. Book and lyrics by Eddie Lawrence. Music by Moose Charlap. Directed and choreographed by Herbert Ross. Scenic production by Oliver Smith. Costumes by Freddy Wittop. Lighting by Tharon Musser. Orchestrations by Hershy Kay. Dance music by Betty Walberg. Associate producer, Robert L. Livingston. Produced by David Susskind and Daniel Melnick in asssociation with Joseph E. Levine. Opened and closed 6 February 1965 at the Broadhurst Theatre after 1 performance.

CAST (in order of appearance): *Hop Kelly*: DON FRANCKS. *Dan Kelly*: WILFRID BRAMBELL. *Jack Mulligan*: MICKEY SHAUGHNESSY. *Augie Masters*: LEON JANNEY. *Stickpin Sidney Crane*: JESSE WHITE. *James*: Steve Elmore. *Carruthers*: Brandon Maggart. *Fay Cherry*: EILEEN RODGERS. *Charlie*: Josip Elic. *Sparkenbroke, the butler*: Bill Richards. *Mayor Tully*: Hamilton Camp. *Englishman*: Thomas Rezarf. *Angela Crane*: ANITA GILLETTE. *Tough Kid*: Barbara Monte. *Three Tough Guys*: Louis Kosman, Anthony De Vecchi, Michael Nestor. *Sailor*: James Moore. *The Redhead*: Lynn Fields. *The Rube*: Sterling Clark. *Young Girl*: Hanne-Marie Reiner. *First Young Man*: Larry Roquemore. *Second Young Man*: Paul Charles. *The Drunk*: Ronald B. Stratton. *Three Ladies*: Leslie Franzos, Eleanore Treiber, Kathleen Doherty. *Lollypop Girl*: Bette Jenkins. *Beggar*: Bill Richards. *Bums*: James Moore, Larry Roquemore, Bill Richards. *Police Chief*: J. Vernon Oaks. *Policeman*: Robert L. Hultman. *Chief Dignitary*: Stanley Simmonds.

Dancing Ensemble: Kathleen Doherty, Lynn Fields, Leslie Franzos, Bette Jenkins, Barbara Monte, Hanne-Marie Reiner, Eleanore Treiber, Sterling Clark, Paul Charles, Antony De Vecchi, Michael Nestor, Bill Richards, Larry Roquemore, Ronald B. Stratton. *Singing Ensemble*: Georgia Creighton, Ceil Delli, Carol Joplin, Lorene Latine, Donna Monroe, Maggie Task, Walter P. Brown, Steve Elmore, Howard Hartman, Robert L. Hultman, J. Vernon Oaks, William Wendt.

Prologue: Under the Bridge.

Act 1, Scene 1: Along the Bowery. *Scene 2*: The Backroom at Augie Masters' Cabaret on the Bowery. *Scene 3*: The Kelly Shack under the Brooklyn Bridge. *Scene 4*: Sid Crane's Mansion. The Oval Room. *Scene 5*: Red Hook, Brooklyn.

Act 2, Scene 1: The Kelly Shack. *Scene 2*: Augie Masters' Cabaret. *Scene 3*: "Me and the Elements." *Scene 4*: At the foot of the Brooklyn Bridge. *Scene 5*: Below the Bridge. *Scene 6*: Atop the Brooklyn Bridge. *Scene 7*: Along the Bowery. *Scene 8*: Augie Masters' Cabaret.

PROLOGUE

"Ode to the Bridge"
   D. Francks

ACT 1

Scene 1

"Six Blocks From the Bridge"
   J. White, M. Shaughnessy, L. Janney, Company

Scene 2

"That Old Time Crowd"
   E. Rodgers, Boys

"Simple Ain't Easy"
   D. Francks, E. Rodgers

Scene 3

"I'm Gonna Walk Right Up to Her"
   D. Franks, M. Shaughnessy

Scene 4

"A Moment Ago"
   A. Gillette, D. Francks

Scene 5

"This Is a Tough Neighborhood"
   Entire Company

[23]Originally produced in New York 27 October 1962 at the John Golden Theatre for 673 performances. See original production for authors of individual sketches.

[24]For individual authors of sketches, see original 1962 production.

[25]Not in previous editions of BEYOND THE FRINGE.

[26]Not in previous editions of BEYOND THE FRINGE.

[27]Not in previous editions of BEYOND THE FRINGE.

[28]Originally produced in New York 13 March 1947 at the Ziegfeld Theatre for 581 performances. For Synopsis of Scenes and Musical Numbers, see original 1947 production.

"(I'll) Never Go There Anymore"
A. Gillette, D. Francks

ACT 2
Scene 1

"Life Can Be Beautiful"
E. Rodgers, W. Brambell, Bums

"Everyone Here Loves Kelly"
E. Rodgers

"Ballad to a Brute"
A. Gillette, D. Francks

Scene 2

"Heavyweight Champ of the World"
M. Shaughnessy, Company

Scene 3

"Me and the Elements"
D. Francks, W. Brambell

Scene 4

"Everyone Here Loves Kelly" (reprise)
E. Rodgers, Company

Scene 7

"Never Go There Anymore" (reprise)
A. Gillette

Scene 8

"Everyone Here Loves Kelly" (reprise)
Entire Company

1965.02   BAKER STREET

A Musical Adventure of Sherlock Holmes in Two Acts, a Prologue and 16 Scenes. Book by Jerome Coopersmith. Adapted from the stories ('The Adventure of the Empty House,' 'A Scandal in Bohemia' and 'The Final Problem') by Sir Arthur Conan Doyle. Music and lyrics by Marian Grudeff and Raymond Jessel. Production designed by Oliver Smith. Costumes by Motley. Lighting by Jean Rosenthal. Directed by Harold Prince. Choreography by Lee Becker Theodore. Musical direction by Harold Hastings. Orchestrations by Don Walker. Dance arrangements by John Morris. Production associate, Hildy Parks. Diamond Jubilee Parade by Bil Baird's Marionettes. Produced by Alexander H. Cohen in association with Gabriel Katzka. Opened 16 February 1965 at the Broadway Theatre, moved 3 November 1965 to the Martin Beck Theatre and closed 14 November 1965 after 313 performances.

CAST (in order of appearance): *Captain Gregg*: PATRICK HORGAN. *Dr. Watson*: PETER SALLIS. *Mrs. Hudson*: Paddy Edwards. *Sherlock Holmes*: FRITZ WEAVER. *Inspector Lestrade*: Daniel Keyes. *Irene Adler*: INGA SWENSON. *Daisy*: Virginia Vestoff. *Baxter*: Martin Wolfson. *Wiggins*: TEDDY GREEN. *Duckbellows*: Bert Michaels. *Nipper*: Sal Pernice. *Perkins*: George Lee. *Macipper*: Mark Jude Sheil. *Murillo*: Jay Norman. *The Three Killers*: Avind Harum, Christopher Walken, Tommy Tune. *Tavern Singer*: Gwenn Lewis. *Professor Moriarty*: MARTIN GABEL.

Dancers: Sara Lee Barber, Barbara Blair, Lois Castle, John Grigas, Gwenn Lewis, Diana Saunders. *Singers*: Martin Ambrose, Frank Bouley, Jack Dabdoub, Gay Edmond, Judie Elkins, Maria Graziano, Horace Guittard, Peter Johl, Mara Landi, Hal Norman, Vera Walton.

The action takes place in and around London in 1897, the year in which England celebrated the Diamond Jubilee of the reign of Queen Victoria.

Prologue: Baker Street, London.

Act 1, Scene 1: The Baker Street flat. *Scene 2*: The stage of the Theatre Royal. *Scene 3*: Backstage at the Theatre Royal. *Scene 4*: An alley in Baker Street. *Scene 5*: Irene's flat. *Scene 6*: The Baker Street flat. *Scene 7*: The London underworld. *Scene 8*: Moriarty's ship.

Act 2, Scene 1: A street in London. *Scene 2*: Moriarty's ship. *Scene 3*: Interior of a carriage. *Scene 4*: The cliffs of Dover. *Scene 5*: A part of London. *Scene 6*: The Baker Street flat. *Scene 7*: A hall in London. *Scene 8*: Baker Street.

ACT 1
Scene 1

"It's So Simple"
F. Weaver, P. Sallis, P. Horgan, D. Keyes

Scene 2

"I'm in London Again"
I. Swenson

Scene 4

"Leave It to Us, Guv"
T. Green, the Irregulars (Male Dancers)

Scene 5

"Letters"
I. Swenson

Scene 6

"Cold Clear World"
F. Weaver

"Finding Words for Spring"
I. Swenson

"What a Night This Is Going to Be"
F. Weaver, I. Swenson, P. Sallis, V. Vestoff

Scene 7

"London Underworld" (Ballet)
Company

Scene 8

"I Shall Miss You"
M. Gabel

ACT 2
Scene 1

"Roof Space"
T. Green, the Irregulars (Male Dancers)

Scene 2

"A Married Man"
P. Sallis

"I'd Do It Again"
I. Swenson

Scene 3

"Pursuit"
F. Weaver

Scene 7

"Jewelry"
M. Wolfson, Criminals (Ensemble)

1965.03   PORGY AND BESS

A Revival of the Folk Opera in Two Acts, 3 Scenes[29]. Book by DuBose Heyward adapted from the play "Porgy" by DuBose and Dorothy Heyward. Music by George Gershwin. Lyrics by DuBose Heyward and Ira Gershwin. Directed by Ella Gerber. Scenic design by Roger Sullivan. Costume design by Stanley Simmons. Conducted by Dean Ryan. Produced by the New York City Opera. Opened 5 March 1965 at the New York City Center and closed 14 March 1965 after 6 performances in repertory.

CAST (in order of appearance): *Clara*: CLAUDIA LINDSAY. *Mingo*: Jerry Laws. *Sportin' Life*: AVON LONG. *Jake*: EDWARD PIERSON. *Serena*: SERENA BASH. *Robbins*: Gordon Watkins. *Jim*: Garwood Perkins. *Peter, the Honey Man*: Carrington Lewis. *Lily, the Strawberry Woman*: Helen Dowdy. *Maria*: CAROL BRICE. *Porgy*: ANDREW FRIERSON. *Crown*: JAMES RANDOLPH. *Bess*: JOYCE BRYANT. *Policeman*: Bill Grier. *Undertaker*: Joseph James. *Annie*: Alyce Webb. *Frazier*: Eugene Brice. *Detective*: Jack Bittner. *Crab Man*: Joseph Attles. *Coroner*: Kellis Miller. *Scipio*: Oscar Sylvan. *Dancer*: Glory Van Scott. *Residents of Catfish Row*: New York City Opera Chorus.

1965.04   DIE DREIGROSCHENOPER

A Revival of the Musical [The Threepenny Opera] in Three Acts, 10 Scenes, in German[30]. Music by Kurt Weill. Original German libretto by Bertolt Brecht (and Elisabeth Hauptmann). (Adapted from "The Beggar's

---

[29]First produced in New York 10 October 1935 at the Alvin Theatre for 124 performances. For Synopsis of Scenes and Musical Numbers, see original 1935 production. Originally produced in Three Acts, 9 Scenes. This production dispensed with the scene breaks and second intermission.
[30]Previously produced in New York in English only: 13 April 1933 at the Empire Theatre for 12 performances as The 3-Penny Opera. 10 March 1954 at the Theatre de Lys (Off-Broadway) for 96 performances; reopened 30 September 1955 at the Theatre de Lys for an additional 2611 performances.

Opera" by John Gay.) Directed by Adolph Rott. Scenic design by Wolfgang Roth. Costume design by Ruth Morley. Conducted by Julius Rudel. Produced by the New York City Opera. Opened 11 March 1965 at the New York City Center and closed 27 March 1965 after 6 performances in repertory.

CAST: *Ansager (Narrator):* GEORGE S. IRVING. *Jonathan Jeremiah Peachum:* STEFAN SCHNABEL. *Mrs. Peachum:* LILIA SKALA. *Polly Peachum:* ANITA HOEFER. *Macheath:* KURT KASZNAR. *Brown:* Ralph Herbert. *Lucy:* MARION BRASH. *Filch:* Mathew Anden. *Die Platte (the Gang)(6): Hakenfingerjakob:* Sol Frieder. *Münzmatthias:* John Garson. *Trauerweidenwalter:* Paul Andor. *Ede:* Michael Haeusserman. *Sägerobert:* Claus Jurgens. *Jimmy:* Curt Lowens. *Die Spelunken-Jenny:* MARTHA SCHLAMME. *Huren* (Ladies of Ill-Repute): Constance Conrad, Carla Huston, Erna Rossman, Ruth Sobotka, Ludmilla Tchor. *Smith:* David Smith. *Pastor Kimball:* Henry Cordy. *Ensemble:* New York City Opera Chorus.

The action takes place in Soho, London, just before the coronation of Queen Victoria.

Act 1, Scene 1: A Fair in Soho. *Scene 2:* The Shop of Jonathan Jeremiah Peachum, outfitter of beggars. *Scene 3:* The Stable. *Scene 4:* Peachum's Shop.

Act 2, Scene 1: The Stable. *Scene 2:* A Bordello in Turnbridge. *Scene 3:* A Cell in the Old Bailey Prison.

Act 3, Scene 1: The Street Outside Peachum's Shop. *Scene 2:* The Death Cell in the Old Bailey Prison. *Scene 3:* The Gallows.

ACT 1
Scene 1
"Die Moritat von Mackie Messer" (The Ballad of Mack the Knife)
G. S. Irving
Scene 2
"Der Morgenchoral des Peachum" (Mr. Peachum's Morning Hymn)
S. Schnabel
"Der Anstatt-Dass-Song" (Instead-of Song)
L. Skala, S. Schnabel
Scene 3
"Das Hochzeitslied für ärmere Leute" (Wedding Song for Poor People)
Ensemble
"Die Seeräuber-Jenny" (Pirate Jenny)
A. Hoefer
"Der Kanonen-Song" (Cannon Song)
K. Kasznar
"Siehst du den Mond über Soho" (Liebeslied/Love Song)
A. Hoefer, K. Kasznar
Scene 4
"Der Song vom Nein und Ja" (Barbara-Song)
(Einst glaubte ich, als ich noch unschuldig war)
A. Hoefer
"Erstes Dreigroschen-Finale" (Über die Unsicherheit menschlicher Verhältnisse)
(The Uncertainty of Human Conditions)
A. Hoefer, S. Schnabel, L. Skala
ACT 2
Scene 1
"Der Ballade von der sexuellen Hörigkeit" (The Ballad of Sexual Dependency)
L. Skala
Scene 2
"Die Zuhälterballade" (The Procurer's Ballad)
K. Kasznar, M. Schlamme
Scene 3
"Die Ballade vom Angenehmen Leben" (The Ballad of Pleasant Living)
K. Kasznar
"Das Eifersuchtsduett" (The Jealousy Duet)
M. Brash, A. Hoefer
"Zweies Dreigroschen-Finale" (Denn Wovon Lebt Der Mensch?)
(What Keeps a Man Alive?)
K. Kasznar, M. Schlamme, Ensemble
ACT 3
Scene 1
"Die Ballade von der sexuellen Hörigkeit" (reprise)
L. Skala
"Das Lied von der Unzulänglichkeit menschlichen Strebens"
(The Song About Inadequacy)
S. Schnabel

"Salomon-Song" (Song of Solomon)
M. Schlamme
Scene 3
"Ballade, in der Macheath jedermann Abbitte leistet"
(Ballad in which Macheath Asks Everyone for Forgiveness)
K. Kasznar
"Drittes Dreigroschen-Finale" (Auftauchen des Reitenden Boten)
(Act 3 Finale-The Riding Messenger)
A. Hoefer, L. Skala, M. Schlamme, K. Kasznar, R. Herbert, S. Schnabel, Ensemble
"Die Schluss-Strophen der Moritat" (Moritat reprise)
G. S. Irving

1965.05 ## THIS WAS BURLESQUE

A Musical Satire (Revue) in Two Acts, 24 Scenes[31]. Entire Production supervised and directed by Ann Corio, based on her recollections. (Music, lyrics and special material mostly by Sonny Lester and Bill Grundy.) Musical conductor, Nick Francis. Choreography by Paul Morokoff. Costumes by Rex Huntington. Miss Corio's gowns by Jacks of Hollywood, Martier-Raymond, and Rex Huntington. Produced by Michael P. Iannucci. Opened 16 March 1965 at the Hudson Theatre and closed 6 June 1965 after 124 performances. Total, including previous Off-Broadway run: 1633 performances.

CAST: ANN CORIO, STEVE MILLS, Harry Conley, Dick Bernie, Paul West, Mac Dennison, Dexter Maitland, Kitty Lynne, Marilyn Marshall, Tina Kaye.
The Burley Cuties: Nicole Jaffee, Linda Donovan, Maria Bradley, Barbara Rhodes, Sharon Taylor, Jerry Beth Shotwell, Mary Alagia, Geraldine Barron, Betsy Haug, Rita O'Connor.

ACT 1
Scene 1
Prologue
S. Mills, D. Maitland, M. Dennison, R. O'Connor, B. Haug
Scene 2
"Hello, Everybody"
The Burley Cuties
Scene 3
Flirtation
S. Mills, P. West, A. Corio
Scene 4
"Bill Bailey"
M. Dennison, the Burley Cuties
(Music and Lyrics by Hughie Cannon.)
Scene 5
Hee Haw
D. Bernie, D. Maitland, L. Donovan, S. Taylor
Scene 6
Ecdysiast
M. Bradley
Scene 7
Hotel de France
H. Conley, P. West, N. Jaffee
Scene 8
Dance L'Orient (Seduction of the Virgin Princess)
The Burley Cuties
(Music and Lyrics by Sonny Lester and Bill Grundy.)
Scene 9
"St. James Infirmary"
M. Dennison, D. Maitland, A. Corio
Scene 10
Exotic
K. Lynne
Scene 11
Schoolroom
D. Bernie, D. Maitland, B. Rhodes, N. Jaffee, M. Bradley

---

[31]First produced in New York Off-Broadway 6 March 1962 at the Casino East Theatre for 1509 performances.

Scene 12
  "Les Poules"
    The Burley Cuties, 'La Madame' S. Taylor
Scene 13
  Mills and West (comedy)
Scene 14
  Marilyn Marshall (tassel routine)
Scene 15
  Finale—Candy Butcher
ACT 2
Scene 1
  "Powder My Back"
    L. Donovan, the Burley Cuties
Scene 2
  Sutton Place
    H. Conley, A. Corio, T. Kay
Scene 3
  Tina Kay
Scene 4
  White Cargo
    S. Mills, P. West, A. Corio, M. Dennison
Scene 5
  "Evolution of Dance"
    The Burley Cuties
Scene 6
  Hall of Fame
    A. Corio, L. Donovan
Scene 7
  Crazy House
    Entire Cast
Scene 8
  Ann Corio (Specialty):
  ["Would You Like to Lay Your Head Upon My Pillow?"]
  ["A Pretty Girl Is Like a Melody"]
    (*Music and Lyrics by* Irving Berlin.)
Scene 9
  Finale
    (Entire Company)

1965.06 ## DO I HEAR A WALTZ?

A Musical in Two Acts, 11 Scenes. Book by Arthur Laurents. Based on his play "The Time of the Cuckoo." Music by Richard Rodgers. Lyrics by Stephen Sondheim. Directed by John Dexter. Choreography by Herbert Ross. Scenery and costumes by Beni Montresor. Lighting by Jules Fisher. Orchestrations by Ralph Burns. Musical director, Frederick Dvonch. Dance music arranged by Richard DeBenedictis. Choreographic associate, Wakefield Poole. Production supervisor, Jerome Whyte. Produced by Richard Rodgers. Opened 18 March 1965 at the 46th Street Theatre and closed 25 September 1965 after 220 performances.

CAST (in order of appearance): *Leona Samish*: ELIZABETH ALLEN. *Mauro*: Christopher Votos. *Signora Fioria*: CAROL BRUCE. *Eddie Yaeger*: STUART DAMON. *Jennifer Yaeger*: JULIENNE MARIE. *Mrs. McIlhenny*: MADELEINE SHERWOOD. *Mr. McIlhenny*: JACK MANNING. *Giovanna*: FLEURY D'ANTONAKIS. *Vito*: James Dybas. *Renato Di Rossi*: SERGIO FRANCHI. *Man on Bridge*: Michael Lamont. *Mrs. Victoria Haslam*: Helon Blount.
  Singers: Darrell Askey, Syndee Balaber, Bill Berrian, Helon Blount, Rudy Challenger, Pat Kelly, Liz Lamkin, Michael Lamont, James Luisi, Jack Murray, Carl Nicholas, Candida Pilla, Casper Roos, Bernice Saunders, Liza Stuart. *Dancers*: Jere Admire, Bob Bishop, Wayne De Rammelaere, Steve Jacobs, Sandy Leeds, Joe Nelson, Janice Peta, Walter Stratton, Nancy Van Rijn, Mary Zahn.

Act 1, Scene 1: Venice. *Scene 2*: Garden of Pensione Fioria. Evening. *Scene 3*: Di Rossi's Shop. The next day. *Scene 4*: Piazza San Marco. The same evening. *Scene 5*: Interior of Pensione Fioria. The following day. *Scene 6*: Garden of Pensione Fioria. Immediately afterwards.

Act 2, Scene 1: Facade of Pensione Fioria. The same night. *Scene 2*: Outside the Garden of Pensione Flioria. The enxt evening. *Scene 3*: The Piazza. The following

morning. *Scene 4*: Garden of Pensione Fioria. That night. *Scene 5*: Same. The next morning.
ACT 1
Scene 1
  "Someone Woke Up"
    E. Allen
Scene 2
  "This Week Americans"
    C. Bruce
  "What Do We Do? We Fly!"
    E. Allen, M. Sherwood, J. Manning, S. Damon, J. Marie
Scene 3
  "Someone Like You"
    S. Franchi
  "Bargaining"
    S. Franchi
Scene 4
  "Here We Are Again"
    E. Allen, J. Dybas, S. Jacobs, S. Leeds, J. Nelson, N Van Rijn, M. Zahn
Scene 5
  "Thinking"
    S. Franchi, E. Allen
Scene 6
  "No Understand"
    C. Bruce, S. Damon, F. D'Antonakis
  "Take the Moment"
    S. Franchi
ACT 2
Scene 1
  "Moon in My Window"
    J. Marie, C. Bruce, E. Allen
Scene 2
  "We're Gonna Be All Right"
    S. Damon, J. Marie
  "Do I Hear a Waltz?"
    E. Allen, Company
Scene 3
  "Stay"
    S. Franchi
Scene 4
  "Perfectly Lovely Couple"
    E. Allen, S. Franchi,
    J. Manning, M. Sherwood, J. Marie, S. Damon, F. D'Antonakis, C. Bruce
Scene 5
  "Thank You So Much"
    S. Franchi, E. Allen

THE SAINT OF
1965.07 ## BLEECKER STREET

A Revival of the Opera (Musical Drama) in Three Acts, 5 Scenes[32]. Music and libretto by Gian-Carlo Menotti. Staged by Gian-Carlo Menotti. Production designed by Robert Randolph. Conducted by Vincent La Selva. Produced by the New York City Opera. Opened 18 March 1965 at the New York City Center and closed 28 March 1965 after 2 performances in repertory.

CAST (in order of appearance): *Assunta*: Muriel Greenspon. *Carmela*: Mary Jennings. *Maria Corona*: Anita Darian. *Her Son*: Clyde Ventura. *Don Marco*: Thomas Paul. *Annina*: JOAN SENA. *Michele*: ENRICO DI GIUSEPPE. *Desideria*: BEVERLY WOLFF. *Salvatore*: David Smith. *Concettina*: Wendy Morris. *A Young Man*: Anthony Safina. *A Young Woman*: Charlotte Povia. *Woman*: Anthea De Forest. *Bartender*: Don Henderson. *First Guest*: Richard Krause. *Second Guest*: Wiliiam Ledbetter.
  Neighbors, Friends, Policemen, etc.: New York City Opera Chorus.

---

[32]Originally produced in New York 27 December 1954 at the Broadway Theatre for 92 performances. For Synopsis of Scenes, see original 1954 production.

1965.08 ## MAURICE CHEVALIER AT 77

A One Man Show in Two Acts. Lighting by Jean Rosenthal. At the piano, Fred Stamer. Produced by Alexander H. Cohen. Opened 1 April 1965 at the Alvin Theatre and closed 1 May 1965 after 35 performances.

CAST: MAURICE CHEVALIER.

PROGRAM
"Thank Heaven for Little Girls" (from film GIGI)
    (*Music by* Frederick Loewe. *Lyrics by* Alan Jay Lerner.)
Stations of Life (*by* Mauruce Chevalier)
"Place Pigalle"
    (*Music and Lyrics by* Maurice Chevalier and Alstone.)
Cole Porter Medley
"Valentine"
    (*Music and Lyrics by* Albert Willemetz and
    Henri Christiné.)
"Some People" (from GYPSY)
    (*Music by* Jule Styne. *Lyrics by* Stephen Sondheim.)
"Un p'tit air"
    (*Music and Lyrics by* Albert Willemetz and Mireille.)
"I Remember It Well" (from film GIGI)
    (*Music by* Frederick Loewe. *Lyrics by* Alan Jay Lerner.)
"Un clochard m'a dit"
    (*Music and Lyrics by* Noel Roux and
    Georges Garvarentz.)
"You Brought a New Kind of Love to Me"
(from film THE BIG POND)
    (*Music and Lyrics by* Sammy Fain, Irving Kahal and
    Pierre Norman.)
"When You're Smiling (the Whole World Smiles
With You)"
    (*Music and Lyrics by* Mark Fisher, Joe Goodwin and
    Larry Shay.)
"Hello, Dolly" (from HELLO, DOLLY!)
    (*Music and Lyrics by* Jerry Herman.)
"You Must Have Been a Beautiful Baby"
(from film HARD TO GET)
    (*Music by* Harry Warren. *Lyrics by* Johnny Merrcer.)
"La leçon de piano"
    (*Music and Lyrics by* Maurice Vandair and Henri Betti.)
"Paris tu rajeunis"
    (*Music and Lyrics by* Noel Roux and André Popp.)
"Louise" (from film INNOCENTS OF PARIS)
    (*Music by* Richard A. Whiting. *Lyrics by* Leo Robin.)
"A Las Vegas"
    (*Music and Lyrics by* Albert Willemetz and Louiguy.)
"Hello, Beautiful"
    (*Music and Lyrics by* Walter Donaldson.)
"Mimi La Blonde"
    (*Music and Lyrics by* Jean Drejac and Heino Gaze.)
Accents melodiques
    (*by* Maurice Chevalier)
"I'm Glad I'm Not Young Anymore" (from film GIGI)
    (*Music by* Frederick Loewe. *Lyrics by* Alan Jay Lerner.)
"Au revoir"
    (*Music and Lyrics by* Jean Drejac and Fred Freed.)
"Mimi" (from film LOVE ME TONIGHT)
    (*Music by* Richard Rodgers. *Lyrics by* Lorenz Hart.)
"Ah donnez m'en de la chanson"
    (*Music and Lyrics by* Rene Rouzaud and Marguerite Monnot.)
George Gershwin Medley
Spectateurs spectaculaires
    (*by* Maurice Chevalier)
"La tendresse"
    (*Music and Lyrics by* Noel Roux and Hubert Giraud.)
"Paris je t'aime"
    (*Music and Lyrics by* Battaille-Henri and
    Victor Schertzinger.)
"La miss"
    (*Music and Lyrics by* Henri Salvador.)

1965.09 ## H.M.S. PINAFORE,
or The Lass That Loved a Sailor

A Revival of the Comic Opera in Two Acts[33]. Libretto by William S. Gilbert. Music by Arthur Sullivan. Directed by John Bishop. Scenery and costumes by Patton Campbell. Conductor, Felix Popper. Produced by the New York City Center Gilbert and Sullivan Company. Opened 14 April 1965 at the New York City Center and closed 22 April 1965 after 5 performances in repertory.

CAST: *The Rt. Hon. Sir Joseph Porter, K.C.B.,* First Lord of the Admiralty: NORMAN KELLEY. *Captain Corcoran,* Commander of the *H.M.S. Pinafore:* WILLIAM CHAPMAN, RICHARD FREDERICKS. *Ralph Rackstraw,* Able Seaman: JOHN STAMFORD, WILLIAM GREENE. *Dick Deadeye,* Able Seaman: PAUL UKENA. *Bill Bobstay,* Boatswain: William Ledbetter. *Bob Becket:* Lee Cass. *Josephine,* the Captain's Daughter: ANNE ELGAR, CAROL BAYARD. *Hebe,* Sir Joseph's First Cousin: Marlena Kleinman. *Little Buttercup,* Mrs. Cripps, a Portsmouth bum-boat woman: MURIEL GREENSPON.
    First Lord's Sisters, His Cousins, His Aunts, Sailors, Marines, etc.: Joan August, Barbara Beaman, Paul Corder, Harris Davis, Marceline Decker, Anthea de Forest, Glenn Dowlen, Joyce Gerber, Margaret Goodman, Helen Guile, Don Henderson, Lila Herbert, David Hicks, Robert Lee Kelly, Jodell Kenting, Hanna Owen, Richard G. Park, Charlotte Povia, Frank Redfield, Anthony Safina, Alexander Savchuck, John Smith, Marie Young, Don Yule. *Solo Dancer:* Rochelle Zide.

1965.10 ## PATIENCE,
or Bunthorne's Bride

A Revival of the Comic Opera in Two Acts[34]. Libretto by William S. Gilbert. Music by Arthur Sullivan. Scenery and costumes designed by Motley. Staged by Dorothy Raedler. Choreography by Thomas Andrew. Conductor, Julius Rudel. Produced by the New York City Center Gilbert and Sullivan Company. Opened 15 April 1965 at the New York City Center and closed 23 April 1965 after 3 peformances in repertory.

CAST: *Colonel Calverley:* WILLIAM CHAPMAN. *Major Murgatroyd:* James Wilson. *Lieut. the Duke of Dunstable:* RICHARD KRAUSE. *Reginald Bunthorne,* a Fleshly Poet: EMILE RENAN. *Archibald Grosvenor,* an Idyllic Poet: DAVID SMITH. *Mr. Bunsthorne's Solicitor:* Thomas Andrew. *The Lady Angela, The Lady Saphir, The Lady Ella, The Lady Jane,* Rapturous Maidens: MARLENA KLEINMAN, HELEN GUILE, Virginia Bitar, CLARAMAE TURNER. *Patience,* a Dairy Maid: PATRICIA WELTING, ANNE ELGAR. *Chorus of Rapturous Maidens and Officers of the Dragoon Guards:* same as H.M.S. PINAFORE above.

1965.11 ## THE MIKADO,
or The Town of Titipu

A Revival of the Comic Opera in Two Acts[35]. Libretto by William S. Gilbert. Music by Arthur Sullivan. Staged by Dorothy Raedler. Scenery by Donald Oenslager. Costumes by Patton Campbell. Conductor, Charles Wilson. Produced by the New York City Center Gilbert and Sullivan Company. Opened 16 April 1965 at the New York City Center and closed 25 April 1965 after 6 performances in repertory.

CAST: *The Mikado of Japan:* GEORGE GAYNES, PAUL UKENA. *Nanki-Poo:* WILLIAM DIARD, RICHARD KRAUSE. *Ko-Ko:* NORMAN KELLEY, JAMES WILSON, HERBERT BEATTIE. *Pooh-Bah:* HERBERT BEATTIE, LEE CASS, NORMAN KELLEY. *Pish-Tush:* DAVID SMITH. *Three Sisters, Wards of Ko-Ko:* Yum-Yum: MARY JENNINGS, VIRGINIA BITAR, PATRICIA WELTING. *Pitti-Sing:* MARY BURGESS. *Peep-Bo:* MARLENA KLEINMAN, HELEN GUILE. *Katisha:* CLARAMAE TURNER, ELAINE BONAZZI, MURIEL GREENSPON. *Chorus of School Girls, Nobles, Guards and Coolies:* same as H.M.S. PINAFORE above.

---

[33]Originally presented in New York 15 January 1879 at the Standard Theatre for 175 performances. For Synopsis of Scenes and Musical Numbers, see original 1879 production.
[34]First presented in New York 22 September 1881 at the Standard Theatre for 177 performances. For Synopsis of Scenes and Musical Numbers, see original 1881 production.
[35]First presented in New York 20 July, 10-29 August 1885 at the Union Square and People's Theatres for 22 performances. First authorized production presented 19 August 1885 at the Fifth Avenue Theatre by Richard D'Oyly Carte for 250 performances. For Synopsis of Scenes and Musical Numbers, see 19 August 1885 D'Oyly Carte production.

THE PIRATES OF PENZANCE,

1965.12   or The Slave of Duty

A Revival of the Comic Opera in Two Acts[36]. Libretto by William S. Gilbert. Music by Arthur Sullivan. Staged by Dorothy Raedler. Scenery by H. A. Condell. Conductor, Dean Ryan. Produced by the New York City Center Gilbert and Sullivan Company. Opened 20 April 1965 at the New York City Center and closed 24 April 1965 after 4 performances in repertory.

CAST: *Major General Stanley:* EMILE RENAN. *The Pirate King:* PAUL UKENA, WILLIAM CHAPMAN. *Samuel,* his Lieutenant: William Ledbetter. *Frederic,* the Pirate Apprentice: WILLIAM DIARD, WILLIAM GREENE. *Sergeant of Police:* HERBERT BEATTIE, LEE CASS. *Mabel, Edith Kate, Isabel,* General Stanley's Daughters: ANNE ELGAR, VIRGINIA BITAR, MARY BURGESS, Helen Guile. *Ruth,* Pirate Maid-of-all-work: MURIEL GREENSPON. *Chorus of Pirates, Police and General Stanley's Daughters:* Same as H.M.S. PINAFORE above.

THE YEOMEN OF THE GUARD,

1965.13   or The Merryman and His Maid

A Revival of the Comic Opera in Two Acts[37]. Libretto by William S. Gilbert. Music by Arthur Sullivan. Staged by Allen Fletcher. Stage director, Ruth M. Hider. Scenery by Stephen O. Saxe. Costumes by Alvin Colt. Conducted by Julius Rudel. Produced by the New York City Center Gilbert and Sullivan Company. Opened 21 April 1965 at the New York City Center and closed 25 April 1965 after 2 performances in repertory.

CAST: *Sir Richard Cholmondeley,* Lieutenant of the Tower: PAUL UKENA. *Colonel Fairfax* under sentence of death): JOHN STAMFORD. *Sergeant Meryll* of the Yeomen of the Guard: GEORGE GAYNES. *Leonard Meryl,* his Son: RICHARD KRAUSE. *Jack Point,* a Strolling Jester: NORMAN KELLEY. *Wilfred Shadbolt,* Head Jailor and Assistant Tormentor: HERBERT BEATTIE. *The Headsman:* Thomas Andrew. *First Yeoman:* William Greene. *Second Yeoman:* William Ledbetter. *First Citizen:* Harris Davis. *Second Citizen:* Glenn Dowlen. *Elsie Maynard,* a Strolling Player: MARY JENNINGS. *Phoebe Meryll,* Sergeant Meryll's Daughter: MARY BURGESS. *Dame Carruthers,* Housekeeper to the Tower: ELAINE BONAZZI. *Kate,* her Niece: VIRGINIA BITAR. *Chorus of Yeomen of the Guard, Gentlemen, Citizens, etc.:* same as H.M.S. PINAFORE above.

HALF A SIXPENCE

1965.14

A Musical Comedy in Two Acts, 18 Scenes. Book by Beverley Cross. Based on the novel "Kipps" by H. G. Wells. Music and Lyrics by David Heneker. Directed by Gene Saks. Dances and musical numbers staged by Onna White. Scenery and costumes by Loudon Sainthill. Lighting by Jules Fisher. Musical direction by Stanley Lebowsky. Costume supervision by Jane Greenwood. Original ballet music by Robert Prince. Assistant choreographer, Tom Panko. Vocal arrangements by Buster Davis. Orchestrations by Jim Tyler. Dance arrangements and orchestrations by Robert Prince. Associate producer, Jane C. Nusbaum. Produced by Allen-Hodgdon (Lewis Allen, Dana Hodgdon), Stevens Productions and Harold Fielding. Opened 25 April 1965 at the Broadhurst Theatre and closed 16 July 1966 after 512 performances.

CAST (in order of appearance): *Arthur Kipps:* TOMMY STEELE. *Sid Pornick:* WILL MACKENZIE. *Buggins:* NORMAN ALLEN. *Pearce:* GROVER DALE. *Carshot:* William Larsen. *Flo:* Michele Hardy. *Emma:* Reby Howells. *Kate:* Louise Quick. *Victoria:* Sally Lee. *Mr. Shalford:* Mercer McLeod. *Mrs. Walsingham:* Ann Shoemaker. *Mrs. Botting:* Trescott Ripley. *Ann Pornick:* POLLY JAMES. *Young Walsingham:* JOHN CLEESE. *Helen Walsingham:* CARRIE NYE. *Chitterlow:* JAMES GROUT. *Laura:* Eleonore Treiber. *Girl Student:* Rosanna Huffman. *Boy Student:* Sterling Clark. *Photographer:* Sean Allan. *Photographer's Assistant:* Robert Gorman. *First Reporter:* Reid Kline. *Second Reporter:* Fred Cline. *Gwendolin:* Ann Rachel.

Dancers: Diane Blair, Lynn Fields, Sally Ransone, Sterling Clark, Robert Karl, Alan Peterson, Bill Stanton, Ron Schwinn. *Singers:* Sean Allan, Fred Cline, Robert Gorman, Glenn Kezer, Reid Kline, John Knapp, Max Norman, Carol Richards, Ann Rachel, Constance Moffit, Rosanna Huffman.

Act 1, Scene 1: The Emporium. Folkestone, England, 1900. *Scene 2:* The Promenade. *Scene 3:* The Emporium. *Scene 4:* The 'Hope and Anchor' Bar. *Scene 5:* The street.

Scene 6: The classroom. *Scene 7:* The Emporium. *Scene 8:* The Promenade. *Scene 9:* The old lighthouse. *Scene 10:* The Military Canal Regatta.

Act 2, Scene 1: Mrs. Botting's solarium. *Scene 2:* Kitchen. *Scene 3:* Photographer's Studio. *Scene 4:* Parlor of rented house. *Scene 5:* The Pier. *Scene 6:* The building site. *Scene 7:* The Promenade. *Scene 8:* The bookshop.

ACT 1

Scene 2

  "All in the Cause of Economy"
    T. Steele, W. Mackenzie, N. Allen, G. Dale

  "Half a Sixpence"
    T. Steele, P. James

Scene 4

  "Money To Burn"
    T. Steele, E. Treiber, Men

Scene 8

  "A Proper Gentlemen"
    T. Steele, W. Mackenzie, N. Allen, G. Dale, Shopgirls

  "She's Too Far Above Me"
    T. Steele

Scene 9

  "If the Rain's Got to Fall"
    T. Steele, G. Dale, W. Mackenzie, N. Allen, Shopgirls, Singers, Dancers

Scene 10

  "The Old Military Canal"
    Singers

  ("If the Rain's Got to Fall" reprise)
    (Singers)

ACT 2

Scene 1

  "A Proper Gentleman" (reprise)
    T. Steele, A. Shoemaker, C. Nye, T. Ripley, J. Cleese, Party Guests

Scene 2

  "Long Ago"
    T. Steele, P. James

Scene 3

  "Flash Bang Wallop"
    T. Steele, P. James,
    J. Grout, M. McLeod, G. Dale, W. Mackenzie, N. Allen, Shopgirls, Singers

Scene 4

  "I Know What I Am"
    P. James

Scene 6

  "The Party's on the House"
    T. Steele, G. Dale, W. Mackenzie, N. Allen, Shopgirls, Singers, Dancers

  "Half a Sixpence" (reprise)
    T. Steele, P. James

Scene 7

  "All in the Cause of Economy" (reprise)
    M. Hardy, G. Dale, W. Mackenzie, N. Allen

Scene 8

Finale
    Entire Company

GUYS AND DOLLS

1965.15

A Revival of the Musical Fable (Comedy) in Two Acts, 17 Scenes[38]. Book by Jo Swerling and Abe Burrows. Based on a story and characters by Damon Runyon. Music and lyrics by Frank Loesser. Choreography by Ralph Beaumont. Adaptation of Jo Mielziner's original (scenic) designs by Peter Wolf. Costumes by Frank Thompson. Lighting by Peggy Clark. (Orchestral arrangements by George Bassman and Ted Royal.) Conductor, Irving Actman. Directed by Gus Schirmer. Produced by the New York City Center

---

[36]First presented in New York 31 December 1879 at the Fifth Avenue Theatre for a total of 91 performances in two engagements. For Synopsis of Scenes and Musical Numbers, see original 1879 production.

[37]First presented in New York 17 October 1888 at the Casino Theatre for 100 performances. For Synopsis of Scenes and Musical Numbers, see original 1888 production.

[38]First presented in New York 24 November 1950 at the 46th Street Theatre for 1200 performances. For Synopsis of Scenes and Musical Numbers, see original 1950 production. "Havana" now retitled "San Juan."

Light Opera Company (Jean Dalrymple, General director). Opened 28 April 1965 at the New York City Center and closed 9 May 1965 after 15 performances.

CAST (in order of appearance): *Nicely-Nicely Johnson:* JACK DE LON. *Benny Southstreet:* JOEY FAYE. *Rusty Charlie:* Ed Becker. *Sarah Brown:* ANITA GILLETTE. *Arvide Abernathy:* CLARENCE NORDSTROM. *Mission Band:* Jeanne Schlegel, CLARENCE NORDSTROM, Maria Hero, CLAIRE WARING, Arthur Santry, Joy Franz. *Harry the Horse:* TOM PEDI. *Lieut. Brannigan:* FRANK CAMPANELLA. *Nathan Detroit:* ALAN KING. *Angie the Ox:* Vern Shinnal. *Miss Adelaide:* SHEILA MacRAE. *Sky Masterson:* JERRY ORBACH. *Joey Biltmore:* Ed Becker. *Mimi:* Ginna Carr. *General Matilda B. Cartwright:* CLAIRE WARING. *Big Jule:* JAKE LaMOTTA. *Drunk:* Stuart Mann. *Waiter:* Philip Lucas.

Dancers: Rita Agnese, Suzanne Channel, Dorothy D'Honau, Tina Faye, Shelley Frankel, Leslie Franzos, Ginny Gan, Altouise Gore, Shari Greene, Maureen Hopkins, Joan Kruger, Violetta Landek, Maria Strattin, Frank Coppola, Luigi Gasparinetti, Fernando Grahal, Mark J. Holliday, Daniel Joel, Carlos Macri, Mitchell Nutick, Paul Owsley, Charles Reeder, Marc Scott, Ronald Stratton. *Singers:* Joy Franz, Maria Hero, Jeanne Schlegel, Ken Ayres, Edward Becker, Walter P. Brown, Victor P. Helou, Henry Lawrence, Philip Lucas, Jim Lynn, Stuart Mann, John Peck, Michael Quinn, Darrell Sandeen, Arthur Santry.

1965.16   KEN MURRAY'S HOLLYWOOD

A Revue (Commentary and Film) in Two Acts, 6 Scenes. (Conceived by Ken Murray.) Designed and lighted by Ralph Alswang. Music arranged and played by Armin Hoffman. A Nine O'Clock Theatre Production. Produced by Alexander H. Cohen in association with Arthur Whitelaw. Opened 10 May 1965 and closed 22 May 1965 after 16 performances.

CAST: KEN MURRAY.

ACT 1

Scene 1

Prelude by Armin Hoffman

Scene 2

Hollywood's Number One Movie Fan Ken Murray

Scene 3

Hollywood Family Album:

A period of retrospection for one generation and a glimpse into an unfamiliar world for the younger set.

Scene 4

San Simeon

The fabulous castle and estate of the late William Randolph Hearst: first showing of films taken some thirty years ago, giving an intimate portrait of this showplace, its owner, and the glamorous people invited there.

ACT 2

Scene 1

Backstage with Bill and Coo
    K. Murray

A visit on the set of Ken Murray's Academy Award-winning feature length motion picture, made with three hundred parakeets. 'Bill and Coo' will be re-released soon in your favorite motion picture theatre.

Scene 2

Hollywood Thirty Years Later

Dedicated to all those who cherish the movies as the living historical record of our changing styles, manners and customs.

1965.17   FLORA, THE RED MENACE

A Musical Comedy in Two Acts, 14 Scenes. Book by George Abbott and Robert Russell. Based on the novel "Love Is Just Around the Corner" by Lester Atwell. Music by John Kander. Lyrics by Fred Ebb. Dance and musical numbers staged by Lee Theodore. Settings by William and Jean Eckart. Costumes by Donald Brooks. Lighting by Tharon Musser. Musical direction by Harold Hastings. Orchestrations by Don Walker. Dance arrangements by David Baker. Production supervisor, Ruth Mitchell. Production directed by George Abbott. Produced by Harold Prince. Opened 11 May 1965 at the Alvin Theatre and closed 24 July 1965 after 87 performances.

CAST (in order of appearance): *F.D.R.'s Voice:* Art Carney. *Apple Seller:* J. Vernon Oaks. *Pencil Seller:* Clark Morgan. *Policeman:* Daniel P. Hannafin. *Broker:* Henry

LeClair. *Fourth Man:* John Taliaferro. *Woman:* Anne C. Russell. *Fifth Man:* Anthony Falco. *Sixth Man:* Les Freed. *Seventh Man:* Robert [Bob] Fitch. *School Principal:* Abbie Todd. *Flora (Meszaros):* LIZA MINNELLI. *Harry Toukarian:* BOB DISHY. *Lilly:* Anne C. Russell. *Artists:* Les Freed, John Taliaferro, J. Vernon Oaks, Diane McAfee, Anthony Falco, Marie Santell. *Comrade Galka:* Louis Guss. *Comrade Ada:* MARY LOUISE WILSON. *Comrade Jackson:* Clark Morgan. *Comrade Charlotte:* CATHRYN DAMON. *Elsa:* Stephanie Hill. *The Lady:* DORTHA DUCKWORTH. *Mr. Weiss:* Joe E. Marks. *Bronco Smallwood:* JAMES CRESSON. *Joe:* Danny Carroll. *Katie:* Marie Santell. *Mr. Rearson:* Gordon Dilworth. *Mr. Stanley:* Robert Kaye. *Lulu:* Jamie Donnelly. *Maggie:* Elaine Cancilla.

Dancers: Elaine Cancilla, Ciya Challis, Barbara Doherty, Judith Doren, Ellen Graff, Mary Ann Niles, Phyllis Wallach, Harry Bell, Robert [Bob] Fitch, Marcello Gamboa, Charles Kalan, James McArdle, Neil J. Schwartz. *Singers:* Jamie Donnelly, Barbara Christopher, Diane McAfee, Abbie Todd, Anthony Falco, Les Freed, Daniel P. Hannafin, Henry LeClair, J. Vernon Oaks, John Taliaferro.

Act 1, Scene 1: A street in New York and the High School of Commercial Art. New York City, 1933. *Scene 2:* The advertising office at Garrett and Mellick's Department Store. *Scene 3:* The Park. *Scene 4:* Flora's Studio. *Scene 5:* The Party Meeting. *Scene 6:* Flora's Studio. *Scene 7:* Mr. Stanley's Office at Garrett and Mellick's Department Store. *Scene 8:* Flora's Studio. *Scene 9:* Union Square and the street in front of Harry's house.

Act 2, Scene 1: Harry's apartment. *Scene 2:* The Park. *Scene 3:* Flora's Studio. *Scene 4:* Mr. Stanley's office at Garrett and Mellick's Department Store. *Scene 5:* Flora's Studio.

ACT 1

Scene 1

Prologue
    Ensemble
"Unafraid"
    L. Minnelli, Students, Ensemble

Scene 2

"All I Need Is One Good Break"
    L. Minnelli, B. Dishy, Artists

Scene 3

"Not Every Day of the Week"
    L. Minnelli, B. Dishy

Scene 4

"All I Need Is One Good Break" (reprise)
    L. Minnelli, S. Hill, D. Duckworth
"Sign Here"
    B. Dishy

Scene 5

"The Flame"
    M. L. Wilson, B. Dishy, Comrades

Scene 6

"Palomino Pal"
    D. Duckworth, J. Cresson

Scene 7

"A Quiet Thing"
    L. Minnelli

Scene 8

"Hello Waves"
    B. Dishy, L. Minnelli

Scene 9

"Dear Love"
    L. Minnelli, Ensemble

ACT 2

Scene 1

"Express Yourself"
    C. Damon, B. Dishy

Scene 2

"Knock, Knock"
    M. L. Wilson, J. Cresson

Scene 3

Comrade Charlotte's Ballet—"The Tree of Life"
    C. Damon, M. L. Wilson, B. Dishy, Ensemble
    Trunk: N. J. Schwartz. *Vine:* R. Fitch. *Spirit of Revolution:*
    M. A. Niles.

Scene 4

"Sing Happy"
    L. Minnelli

Scene 5
"You Are You"
J. E. Marks, S. Hill, L. Minnelli, R. Kaye, J. Donnelly, M. Santell, D. Carroll
Finale
Entire Company

1965.18 KISS ME, KATE

A Revival of the Musical Comedy in Two Acts, 17 Scenes[39]. Book by Sam (Samuel) and Bella Spewack. (Based on William Shakespeare's "The Taming of the Shrew.") Music and lyrics by Cole Porter. Directed by John Fearnley and Billy Matthews. Dances and musical numbers staged by Hanya Holm. Scenery by Robert O'Hearn. Costumes by Stanley Simmons after originals by Lemuel Ayers. Lighting by Peggy Clark. Musical director, Pembroke Davenport. (Orchestrations by Robert Russell Bennett.) Dance music arranged by Genevieve Pitot. Produced by the New York City Center Light Opera Company (Jean Dalrymple, Director). Opened 12 May 1965 at the New York City Center and closed 30 May 1965 after 23 performances.

CAST (in order of appearance): *Fred Graham*: BOB [Robert] WRIGHT. *Harry Trevor*: ALEXANDER CLARK. *Lois Lane*: NANCY AMES. *Ralph* (Stage Manager): William H. Batchelder. *Lilli Vanessi*: PATRICIA MORISON. *Paul*: TIGER HAYNES. *Hattie*: ALYCE ELIZABETH WEBB. *Stage Doorman*: Eugene R. Wood. *Bill Calhoun*: KELLY BROWN. *Cab Driver*: Bill [William] Kennedy. *First Man*: JESSE WHITE. *Second Man*: VICTOR HELOU. *Harrison Howell*: Royal Beal. *Specialty Dancers*: Charles Cook, Ernest Brown. *Doctor*: Don Henderson. *Nurses*: Patricia Finch, Lynn Wendell. *Messengers*: Anthony Santiago, Michael Whaley, Loren Hightower. *Banker*: Richard Lyle. *Truck Driver*: Ben Gillespie.
"*Taming of the Shrew*" Players: *Bianca* (Lois Lane): NANCY AMES. *Baptista* (Harry Trevor): ALEXANDER CLARK. *Gremio* (First Suitor): William Wendt. *Hortensio* (Second Suitor): Stephen John Rydell. *Lucentio* (Bill Calhoun): KELLY BROWN. *Katharine* (Lilli Vanessi): PATRICIA MORISON. *Servants* (3): *Nathaniel*: Ben Gillespie. *Gregory*: Richard Lyle. *Philip*: Anthony Santiago. *Petruchio* (Fred Graham): BOB [Robert] WRIGHT. *Haberdasher*: Loren Hightower. *Innkeeper*: Philip Rash. *Waiter*: Brown Bradley.
Dancers: Myrna Aaron, Joanna Crosson, Kiki Minor, Rande Rayburn, Joy Serio, Lucia Lambert, Esther Villavicencio, Ben Gillespie, Loren Hightower, Richard Lyle, Paul Plson, Don Redlich, Anthony Santiago, Michael Whaley. *Singers*: Patricia Finch, Margaret Goz, Madeline Kahn, Jeanne Shea, Mauren Smith, Elise Warner, Lynn Wendell, Maggie Worth, Brown Bradley, Jack L. Fletcher, Don Henderson, Bill Kennedy, Philip Rash, Stephen John Rydell, William Wendt.

1965.19 THE ROAR OF THE GREASEPAINT – THE SMELL OF THE CROWD

A Musical Entertainment in Two Acts. Book, music and lyrics by Leslie Bricusse and Anthony Newley. Directed by Anthony Newley. Musical numbers staged by Gillian Lynne. (Production) Designed and lighted by Sean Kenny. Costumes by Freddy Wittop. Musical director, Herbert Grossman. Orchestrations, Philip J. Lang. Vocal and dance music arrangements by Peter Howard. Assistant choreographer, Buff Shurr. Associate producer, Samuel Liff. Produced by David Merrick. Opened 16 May 1965 at the Sam S. Shubert Theatre and closed 4 December 1965 after 232 performances.

CAST (in order of appearance): *Cocky*: ANTHONY NEWLEY. *Sir*: CYRIL RITCHARD. *The Kid*: SALLY SMITH. *The Girl*: JOYCE JILLSON. *The Negro*: GILBERT PRICE. *The Bully*: Murray Tannenbaum.
The Urchins: Rawley Bates, Lori Browne, Lori Cesar, Jill Choder, Gloria Chu, Kay Cole, Marlene Dell, Boni Enten, Mitzi Feinn, Pamela Gruen, Linda Rae Hager, Cyndi Howard, Laura Michaels, Debbie Palmer, Heather Taylor.

The action takes place on a rocky place.

ACT 1
"The Beautiful Land"
The Urchins
"A Wonderful Day Like Today"
C. Ritchard, A. Newley, The Urchins
"It Isn't Enough"
A. Newley, The Urchins
"Things to Remember"
C. Ritchard, S. Smith, The Urchins
"Put It in the Book"
S. Smith, The Urchins
"This Dream"
A. Newley
"Where Would You Be Without Me?"
C. Ritchard, A. Newley, S. Smith
"Look At That Face"
C. Ritchard, S. Smith, The Urchins
"My First Love Song"
A. Newley, J. Jillson
"The Joker"
A. Newley
"Who Can I Turn To (When Nobody Needs Me)?"
A. Newley
ACT 2
"A Funny Funeral"
"That's What It Is To Be Young"
The Urchins
"What a Man!"
A. Newley, C. Ritchard, S. Smith, The Urchins
"Feeling Good"
G. Price, The Urchins
"Nothing Can Stop Me Now!"
A. Newley, The Urchins
"Things to Remember" (reprise)
C. Ritchard
"My Way"
A. Newley, C. Ritchard
"Who Can I Turn To?" (reprise)
C. Ritchard
"The Beautiful Land" (reprise)
The Urchins
"Sweet Beginning"
A. Newley, C. Ritchard

[39]First produced in New York 30 December 1948 at the New Century Theatre for 1077 performances. For Synopsis of Scenes and Musical Numbers, see original 1948 production. For this production, former Scene 8 (The Church) was divided into 2 Scenes. "Pavane" for Dancing Ensemble added to Act 2, Scene 8 before "I Am Ashamed That Women Are So Simple."

Barbara Harris in ON A CLEAR DAY YOU CAN SEE FOREVER (Photo: Friedman-Abeles)
Billy Rose Theatre Collection, New York Public Library for the Performing Arts

1965–1966 SEASON

1965.20 SOUTH PACIFIC

A Revival of the Musical Play in Two Acts, 23 Scenes[1]. Music by Richard Rodgers. Lyrics by Oscar Hammerstein II. Book by Oscar Hammerstein II and Joshua Logan. Adapted from James A. Michener's novel "Tales of the South Pacific." Directed by James Hammerstein. Dances by Albert Popwell. Scenery by Jo Mielziner. Costumes by Stanley Simmons. Lighting by Peggy Clark. Musical director, Anton Coppola. Orchestrations by Robert Russell Bennett. Produced by the New York City Center Light Opera Company (Jean Dalrymple, Director). Opened 2 June 1965 at the New York City Center and closed 13 June 1965 after 15 performances.

CAST (in order of appearance): *Ngana*: Dana Shimizu. *Jerome*: Keenan Shimizu. *Henry*: Sab Shimono. *Ensign Nellie Forbush*: BETSY PALMER. *Emile DeBecque*: RAY MIDDLETON. *Bloody Mary*: HONEY SAUNDERS. *Bloody Mary's Assistant*: Maureen Tionco. *Abner*: Victor Duntiere. *Stewpot*: TOM PEDI. *Luther Billis*: ALAN NORTH. *Professor*: Mickey [Michael] Karm. *Lt. Joseph Cable, U.S.M.C.*: RICHARD ARMBRUSTER. *Capt. George Brackett, U.S.N.*: MURVYN VYE. *Cmdr. William Harbison, U.S.N.*: SAM KIRKHAM. *Yeoman Herbert Quayle*: Walter P. Brown. *Marine Sgt. Kenneth Johnson*: William Wendt. *Seaman Richard West*: Ken Ayers. *Seabee Morton Wise*: Scott Blanchard. *Seaman Tom O'Brien*: Mel Gordan. *Radio Operator Bob McCaffrey*: Gregg Nickerson. *Staff Sgt. Thomas Hassinger*: Philip Lucas. *Lt. Genevieve Marshall*: Carol Joplin. *Ensign Dinah Murphy*: Terri Baker. *Ensign Janet MacGregor*: Nancy McGeorge. *Ensign Cora MacRae*: Renee Gorsey. *Ensign Bessie Noonan*: Patricia O'Riordan. *Ensign Connie Walewska*: Marlene Kay. *Ensign Pamela Whitmore*: Dorothy Hanning. *Ensign Sue Yaeger*: Jody Lane. *Ensign Teya Ryan*: Mary E. Small. *Ensign Lisa Minelli*: Maria Hero. *Marine Cpl. Hamilton Steeves*: Michael Quinn. *Seaman John Clark*: Don Yule. *Liat*: ELEANOR CALBES. *Lt. Buzz Adams*: Stan Page. *Shore Patrol Officer*: Joe Bellomo.

1965.21 THE MUSIC MAN

A Revival of the Musical Comedy in Two Acts, 16 Scenes[2]. Book, music and lyrics by Meredith Willson. Story by Meredith Willson and Franklin Lacey. Production directed by Gus Schirmer. Choreography by Vernon Lusby based on the original by Onna White. Settings and lighting by Howard Bay. Costumes by Raoul Pene du Bois. Orchestrations by Don Walker. Dance arrangements by Laurence Rosenthal. Musical direction by Liza Redfield. Vocal arrangements by Herbert Greene. Produced by the New York City Center Light Opera Company (Jean Dalrymple, Director). Opened 16 June 1965 at the New York City Center and closed 27 June 1965 after 15 performances.

CAST (in order of appearance): *Travelling Salesmen*: Russell Goodwin, John Herbert, Jack Davison, Ronald B. Stratton, Howard Kahl, Joseph Carow, Ronn Forella. *Charlie Cowell*: ALAN DEXTER. *Conductor*: Van Stevens. *Harold Hill*: BERT PARKS. *Mayor Shinn*: MILO BOULTON. THE BUFFALO BILLS (4): *Ewart Dunlop*: Al Shea. *Oliver Hix*: Wayne Ward. *Jacey Squires*: Vern Reed. *Olin Britt*: Dale Jones. *Marcellus Washburn*: ART WALLACE. *Tommy Djilas*: WILLIAM GLASSMAN. *Marian Paroo*: GAYLEA BYRNE. *Mrs. Paroo*: SIBYL BOWAN. *Amaryllis*: Garda Hermany. *Winthrop Paroo*: DENNIS SCOTT. *Eulalie Mackecknie Shinn*: DORO MERANDE. *Zaneeta Shinn*: SANDY DUNCAN. *Gracie Shinn*: Roma Hermany. *Alma Hix*: Adnia Rice. *Maud Dunlop*: Jeanne Schlegel. *Ethel Toffelmier*: Amelia Varney. *Mrs. Squires*: Paula Trueman. *Constable Locke*: Van Stevens.

River City Townspeople and Kids: Robin Adair, Rita Agnese, Barbara Beck, Carol B. Bostick, Bonnie Gene Card, Joanne Crosson, Suzanne Crumpler, Joan Lindsay, Sandra Ray, Alice Mary Riley, Joy Serio, Betty Chretien, Peggy Cooper, Laurie Franks, Jodell Ann Kenting, Ora McBride, Addi Negri, Jeannette Seibert, Peggy Wathen, Lynn Wendell, Joseph Carow, Ronn Forella, Carlos Macri, David Moffat, Eric Paynter, Michael Scotlin, Ronald B. Stratton, George Tregre, Gary Wales, Arthur Whitfield, Austin Colyer, Jack Davison, Russell Goodwin, John Herbert, Howard Kahl, Ben Laney, Ripple Lewis, Dan Resin, Van Stevens.

1965.22 KISMET

A Revival of the Musical Arabian Night (Musical Play) in Two Acts, 14 Scenes, a Prologue and an Epilogue[3]. Book by Charles Lederer and Luther Davis. Based on the play of the same name by Edward Knoblock. Music based on themes by Alexander Borodin. Musical adaptation and lyrics by Robert Wright and George Forrest. Production (settings) designed by Lemuel Ayers. Costumes by Frank Thompson. Lighting by Peter Hunt. Orchestral and choral arrangements by Arthur Kay. Musical direction by Franz Allers. Choreography and musical staging by Jack Cole. Production directed by Edward Greenberg. Produced by the Music Theatre of Lincoln Center (Richard Rodgers, Producing Director). Opened 22 June 1965 at the New York State Theatre and closed 31 July 1965 after 39 performances.

CAST (in order of appearance): *Imam of The Mosque*: Rudy Vejar. *Muezzins*: Grant Spradling, Paul Veglia, Vincent Henry, Martin Jewell. *Mullah*: Julius Fields. *First Beggar*: Earle MacVeigh. *Second Beggar*: Robert Lamont. *Third Beggar*: Andre St. Jean. *Dervishes*: Buddy Bryan, Eddie James. *Omar*: DON BEDDOE. *A Public Poet, later called Hajj*: ALFRED DRAKE. *Marsinah, His Daughter*: LEE VENORA. *A Merchant*: Neil McNelis. *Hassan-Ben*: Frank Coleman. *Jawan*: TRUMAN GAIGE. *The Bangle Man*: Rudy Vejar. *Street Dancer*: Sally Neal. *Akbar*: Buddy Bryan. *Assiz*: Eddie James. *Chief Policeman*: Alfred Toigo. *Second Policeman*: Allen Peck. *The Wazir of Police*: HENRY CALVIN. *Wazir's Guards*: Nick Littlefield, Jerry Meyers. *Lalume*: ANNE JEFFREYS. *Attendants*: Henry Baker, James Warnen. *Princesses of Ababu*: Reiko Sato, Diana Banks, Nancy Roth. *The Caliph*: RICHARD BANKE. *Slave Girls*: Michele Evans, Carol Hallock, Eleanore Kingsley, Ingeborg Kjeldsen. *Servant*: Paul Veglia. *Princess Zubbediya of Damascus*: Sally Neal. *Ayah to Zubbediya*: Anita Alpert. *Princess Samaris of Bangalore*: BEATRICE KRAFT. *Prosecutor*: Earle MacVeigh. *Widow Yussef*: Anita Alpert.

Singers: Bonnie Glasgow, Bobbi Lange, Joyce McDonald, Lucille Perret, Susan Sanders, Wanda Saxon, Bonnie Ellen Spark, Henry Baker, Frank Coleman, Vincent Henry, Martin Jewell, Richard Khan, Nick Littlefield, Neil McNelis, Bob Neukum, Allen Peck, Grant Spradling, Paul Veglia. *Dancers*: Joanne DiVito, Marti Hespen, Shai Holsaert, Indra-nila, Bette Scott, Susan Sigrist, Jenny Workman, Julius Fields, Andre St. Jean.

1965.23 OLIVER!

A Return Engagement of the Musical in Two Acts, 12 Scenes[4]. Book, music and lyrics by Lionel Bart. Based on the novel "Oliver Twist" by Charles Dickens. Directed by Peter Coe. (Scenery) Designed by Sean Kenny. Costumes by M. Berman Ltd. Lighting by John Wyckham. Orchestrations by Eric Rogers. Musical director, Robert McNamee. Technical supervisor, Ian Albery. Produced by David Merrick and Donald Albery. Opened 2 August 1965 at the Martin Beck Theatre and closed 25 September 1965 after 64 performances. Total, including original run: 838 performances.

CAST: *Oliver Twist*: VICTOR STILES. *Mr. Bumble*, the Beadle: ALAN CROFOOT. *Mrs. Corney*, the Matron: DAWNA SHOVE. *Old Sally*, a pauper: SHERILL PRICE. *Mr. Sowerberry*, the Undertaker: JOHN MIRANDA. *Mrs. Sowerberry*, his wife: SHERILL PRICE. *Charlotte*, their daughter: Lynda Sturner. *Noah Claypole*, their apprentice: Billy Brandon. *Fagin*: ROBIN RAMSAY. *The Artful Dodger*: JOEY BAIO. *Nancy*: MAURA K. WEDGE. *Bet*: Donnie Smiley. *Bill Sykes*: DANNY SEWELL. *Mr. Brownlow*: BRAM NOSSEN. *Dr. Grimwig*: FRED MILLER. *Mrs. Bedwin*: Dodi Protero.

Workhouse Boys and Fagin's Gang: Tommy Battreall, Ronnie K. Douglas, Paul Dwyer, Anthony Endon, Eugene Endon, Harry Gold, Lee Koenig, Bart Larsen, Christopher Month, Jackie Perkuhn, Sonny Rocco, Ricky Rosenthal, Brett Smiley. *Londoners*: Walter Blocher, Ted Bloecher, Reese Burns, Dominic Chianese, Sally Cooke, Marise Counsell, Georgia Dell, Walter Hook, Lesley Hunt, Michael McCormick, Richard Miller, Moose Peting, Terry Robinson, Virginia Sandifur, Gretchen Van Aken, Richard Wulf.

1965.24 CAROUSEL

A Revival of the Musical Play in Two Acts, 9 Scenes[5]. Based on Ferenc Molnar's play "Liliom" as adapted by Benjamin F. Glazer. Music by Richard Rodgers. Book and lyrics by Oscar Hammerstein II. Directed by Edward

---

[1]First produced in New York 7 April 1949 at the Majestic Theatre for 1925 performances. For Synopsis of Scenes and Musical Numbers, see original 1949 production.

[2]Originally produced in New York 19 December 1957 at the Majestic Theatre for 1375 performances. For Synopsis of Scenes and Musical Numbers, see original 1957 production.

[3]Originally produced in New York 3 December 1953 at the Ziegfeld Theatre for 583 performances. For Synopsis of Scenes and Musical Numbers, see original 1953 production.

[4]Originally produced in New York 6 January 1963 at the Imperial Theatre for 774 performances. For Synopsis of Scenes and Musical Numbers, see original 1963 production.

[5]First produced in New York 19 April 1945 at the Majestic Theatre for 890 performances. For Synopsis of Scenes and Musical Numbers, see original 1945 production.

Greenberg. Choreography by Agnes de Mille, restaged by Gemze deLappe. Settings by Paul C. McGuire. Costumes by Stanley Simmons. Lighting by Peter Hunt. Musical director, Franz Allers. Orchestrations by Don Walker. Produced by the Music Theatre of Lincoln Center (Richard Rodgers, Producing Director). Opened 10 August 1965 at the New York State Theater and closed 18 September 1965 after 47 performances.

CAST (in order of appearance): *Carrie Pipperidge*: SUSAN WATSON. *Julie Jordan*: EILEEN CHRISTY. *Mrs. Mullin*: BENAY VENUTA. *Billy Bigelow*: JOHN RAITT. *Policeman*: Thomas Barry. *Mr. Bascombe*: Ralston Hill. *Nettie Fowler*: KATHERINE HILGENBERG. *Enoch Snow*: REID SHELTON. *Jigger Craigin*: JERRY ORBACH. *Hannah*: Jenny Workman. *Boatswain*: Birl Jonns. *Arminy*: Dixie Carter. *Captain*: John Dorrin. *Heavenly Friend* (Brother Joshua): Gwyllum Evans. *Starkeeper*: EDWARD EVERETT HORTON. *Louise*: Linda Howe. *Carnival Boy*: Birl Jonns. *Enoch Snow, Jr.*: Alan Johnson. *Principal*: John Dorrin.

Singers: Lynn Carroll, Ronn Carroll, Dixie Carter, Cathy Corkill, Gene Davis, Audrey Dearden, John Dorrin, Dorothy Emmerson, Cleo Fry, Ben Laney, Terry Marone, Laried Montgomery, Bob Neukum, Lucille Perret, Joseph Pichette, Philip Rash, Sean Walsh, Peggy Wathen. *Dancers*: Bonnie Gene Card, Dennis Cole, Richard Cousins, Victor Duntiere, Lois Etelman, Frank Hoopman, Anita Jones, Linda Keeler, Lucia Lambert, Arnott Mader, Richard Oliver, Carol Perea, J. Hunter Ross, Terry Ryland, Eva Marie Sage, Melissa Stoneburn, Kathy Wilson, Toodie Wittmer.

1965.25
DIE FLEDERMAUS

A Revival of the Operetta in Three Acts[6]. Original Viennese libretto by Carl Haffner and Richard Genée. Lyrics by Richard Genée. (Based on the comedy "Le Réveillon" by Henri Meilhac and Ludovic Halévy.) English libretto by Ruth and Thomas Martin. Scenic design by William Pitkin. Costume design by Henry Heymann. Conducted by Julius Rudel. Produced by the New York City Opera. Opened 25 September 1965 at the New York City Center and closed 7 November 1965 after 4 performances in repertory.

CAST: *Eisenstein*: JOHN STAMFORD. *Rosalinda*: BEVERLY SILLS. *Frank*: RICHARD WENTWORTH. *Prince Orlofsky*: DAVID SMITH. *Alfred*: Jon Crain. *Falke*: WILLIAM LEDBETTER. *Blind*: Kellis Miller. *Adele*: ANNE ELGAR. *Frosch*: Coley Worth. *Sally*: Beverly Evans. *Ivan*: Don Yule. *Solo Dancers*: Nora Kovach, Istvan Rabovsky, Joan Peterson, Betty Ann Terrell. *Ensemble*: New York City Opera Chorus.

1965.26
THE SAINT OF BLEECKER STREET

A Revival of the Opera (Musical Drama) in Three Acts, 5 Scenes[7]. Music and libretto by Gian-Carlo Menotti. Staged by Francis Rizzo. Production designed by Robert Randolph. Produced by the New York City Opera. Opened 29 September 1965 at the New York City Center and closed 9 October 1965 after 2 performances in repertory.

CAST (in order of appearance): *Assunta*: Muriel Greenspon. *Carmela*: Mary Jennings. *Maria Corona*: Anita Darian. *Her Son*: Clyde Ventura. *Don Marco*: Malcolm Smith. *Annina*: JULIA MIGENES. *Michele*: HARRY THEYARD. *Desideria*: BEVERLY WOLFF. *Salvatore*: William Beck. *Concettina*: Wendy Morris. *A Young Man*: Anthony Safina. *A Young Woman*: Jodell Kenting. *Bartender*: Don Henderson. *First Guest*: Richard Krause. *Second Guest*: Wiliiam Ledbetter. *Neighbors, Friends, Policemen, etc.*: New York City Opera Chorus.

1965.27
THE MERRY WIDOW

A Revival of the Operetta in Three Acts[8]. Music by Franz Lehár. Original Viennese libretto ('Die lustige witwe') by Victor Léon and Leo Stein. (Based on the comedy "L'Attaché d'Ambassade" by Henri Meilhac.) English libretto by Adrian Ross. Staged by Jack Harrold. Scenic design by George Jenkins. Lighting by Jules Fisher. Choreographed by Thomas Andrew.

Conducted by Charles Wilson. Produced by the New York City Opera. Opened 2 October 1965 at the New York City Center and closed 14 November 1965 after 4 performances in repertory.

CAST: *Sonia*: EILEEN SCHAULER. *Prince Danilo*: DAVID SMITH. *Nish*: Coley Worth. *Baron Popoff*: JACK HARROLD. *Natalie*: Anne Elgar. *De Jolidon*: JOHN CRAIG. *Marquis de Cascada*: William Beck. *St. Brioche*: Richard Krause. *Admiral Khadja*: William Ledbetter. *Mme. Khadja*: Beverly Evans. *General Novikovich*: Jack Bittner. *Mme. Novikovich*: Charlotte Povia. *Clo-Clo*: Helen Guile. *Solo Dancers*: Nora Kovach, Istvan Rabovsky. *Ensemble*: New York City Opera Chorus.

1965.28
PICKWICK

A Musical ('Designed for the Introduction of Diverting Characters and Incidents Attempting No Ingenuity of Plot'[9]) in Two Acts, 12 Scenes. Book by Wolf Mankowitz. Based on the novel "The Pickwick Papers" by Charles Dickens. Music by Cyril Ornadel. Lyrics by Leslie Bricusse. Directed by Peter Coe. Settings by Sean Kenny. Costumes by Roger Furse and Peter Rice. Lighting by Jules Fisher. Choreography by Gillian Lynne. Musical direction and vocal arrangements by Ian Fraser. Orchestrations by Eric Rogers. Produced by David Merrick in association with Bernard Delfont. Opened 4 October 1965 at the 46th Street Theatre and closed 20 November 1965 after 56 performances.

CAST (in order of appearance): *Hot Toddy Seller*: Jim Connor. *Cold Drinks Seller*: Edmond Varrato. *Bird Seller*: Roger LePage. *Hot Potato Man*: Gerrit de Beer. *Turnkey*: Allan Lokos. *Roker*: Peter Costanza. *Pickwick*: HARRY SECOMBE. *Augustus Snodgrass*: JULIAN ORCHARD. *Tracy Tupman*: John Call. *Nathaniel Winkle*: OSCAR QUITAK. *Sam Weller*: ROY CASTLE. *Mr. Wardle*: MICHAEL LOGAN. *Rachel*: HELENA CARROLL. *Isabella*: Nancy Haywood. *Emily*: Sybil Scotford. *Fat Boy*: Joe Richards. *Mrs. Bardell*: CHARLOTTE RAE. *Bardell, Jr.*: Brian Chapin. *Mary*: Nancy Barrett. *Mr. Jingle*: ANTON RODGERS. *Major Domo*: Jim Connor. *Dr. Slammer*: Peter Costanza. *First Officer*: Richard Neilson. *Second Officer*: Haydon Smith. *Landlord*: Edmond Varrato. *Mrs. Leo Hunter*: Elizabeth Parrish. *Mr. Leo Hunter*: Gerrit de Beer. *Dodson*: MICHAEL DARBYSHIRE. *Fogg*: Tony Sympson. *Wicks*: Haydon Smith. *Jackson*: Keith Perry. *Usher*: Taylor Reed. *Bailiff*: Stanley Simmonds. *Sergeant Buzfuz*: PETER BULL. *Judge*: Richard Neilson. *Sergeant Snubbins*: Allan Lokos. *Jury Foreman*: Roger LePage.

Passersby, Ostlers, Debtors, Maids, Drinkers and Pot Boys: Jill Alexander, Michael Amber, Bill Black, William Coppola, Ann Davies, Selma Marcus, Ann Tell, Bill Nuss, Edmond Varrato, Larry Whiteley, Gerrit de Beer, Clyde Laurents, Keith Perry, Taylor Reed, Bruce Becker, Susan Cartt, Jo Freilich, Mary Keller, Don Lawrence, Ginia Mason, Lani Michaels, Ross Miles, Nancy Stevens, Don Strong, Haydon Smith, Roger LePage. *Children*: Michael Easton, Richard Easton, Tracy Evans, Leslie Ann Mapes, Bonnie Turner.

The action takes place in and around London and Rochester in 1827.

Act 1, Scene 1: The Pickwickians. *Scene 2*: Introduces Mr. Pickwick to a new and not uninteresting scene in the great drama of life. *Scene 3*: The first day's adventures. *Scene 4*: Strongly illustrative of the position, that the course of true love is not a railway. *Scene 5*: Descriptive of a very important proceeding on the part of Mr. Pickwick; no less an epoch in his life, then in his history. *Scene 6*: Too full of adventure to be briefly described.

Act 2, Scene 1: Some account of Eatanswill; the state of parties therein; and of the election of a member to serve in Parliament for that ancient, loyal and patriotic borough. *Scene 2*: How the Pickwickians, when Mr. Pickwick stepped out of the frying pan, walked gently and comfortably into the fire. *Scene 3*: Showing how Dodson and Fogg were men of Business; and how an affecting interview took place between Mr. Weller and his employer. *Scene 4*: Is wholly devoted to a full and faithful report of the memorable trial of Bardell against Pickwick. *Scene 5*: What befell Mr. Pickwick when he got into the Fleet; what prisoners he saw there; and how he passed the night. *Scene 6*: In which the Pickwick Club is finally dissolved and everything concluded to the satisfaction of everybody.

ACT 1

"I Like the Company of Men"
   H. Secombe, J. Orchard, J. Call, O. Quitak
"That's What I'd Like for Christmas"
   H. Secombe, Company
"The Pickwickians"
   H. Secombe, J. Orchard, J. Call, O. Quitak
"A Bit of a Character"
   A. Rodgers, J. Orchard, O. Quitak, J. Call
"There's Something About You"
   A. Rodgers, H. Carroll, Company

---

[6]First English language production in New York 16 March 1885 at the Casino Theatre for 42 performances. First New York production of this adaptation 20 December 1950 at the Metropolitan Opera House. For Synopsis of Scenes and Musical Numbers, see May 1954 revival.
[7]Originally produced in New York 27 December 1954 at the Broadway Theatre for 92 performances. For Synopsis of Scenes, see original 1954 production.
[8]Originally produced in New York 21 October 1907 at the New Amsterdam Theatre for 416 performances. For Synopsis of Scenes and Musical Numbers, see original 1907 production.

[9]Charles Dickens' preface to "Pickwick Papers."

"A Gentleman's Gentleman"
R. Castle, N. Barrett
"You Never Met a Feller Like Me"
H. Secombe, R. Castle
"I'll Never Be Lonely Again"
H. Secombe, C. Rae
ACT 2
"Fizkin and Pickwick"
The Company
"Very"
A. Rodgers, H. Secombe, M. Logan
"If I Ruled the World"
H. Secombe, Company
"I'll Never be Lonely Again" (reprise)
The Pickwickians
"Talk"
R. Castle, Company
"That's the Law"
H. Secombe, M. Darbyshire, T. Sympson, Company
"Damages"
H. Secombe, C. Rae
Finale
H. Secombe, Company

1965.29 DRAT! THE CAT!

A Musical Spoof in Two Acts, 16 Scenes. Book and lyrics by Ira Levin. Music by Milton Schafer. Directed and choreographed by Joe Layton. Scenery and lighting by David Hays. Costumes by Fred Voelpel. Musical direction and vocal arrangements by Herbert Grossman. Orchestrations by Hershy Kay and Clare Grundman. Dance music by Genevieve Pitot. Produced by Jerry Adler and Norman Rosemont. Opened 10 October 1965 at the Martin Beck Theatre and closed 16 October 1965 after 8 performances.

CAST (in order of appearance): *The Mayor*: Alfred Spindelman. *Pincer*, Superintendent of Police: CHARLES DURNING. *Mallet*, Chief of Detectives : GENE VARRONE. *Roger "Bulldog" Purefoy*, Former Chief of Detectives: David Gold. *Kate Purefoy, his wife*: LU LEONARD. *Emma*, a Patrolwoman: Sandy Ellen. *Bob Purefoy*, the Purefoy's Son, a Patrolman: ELLIOTT GOULD. *The Van Guilder's Butler*: Harry Naughton. *Matilda Van Guilder*, a Socialite: JANE CONNELL. *Lucius Van Guilder*, Her Husband, a Millionaire: JACK FLETCHER. *Alice Van Guilder*, their Daughter: LESLEY ANN WARREN. *The Maid*: Jacque Dean. *The Minister*: Al Lanti. *The Mayor's Wife*: Marian Haraldson. *Julietta Onderdonck*, a Dowager from Boston: Mariana Doro. *The Judge*: David Gold. *The Prosecutor*: Leo Bloom.
Patrolmen: Leo Bloom, Ralph Farnworth, Ian Garry, David Gold, Barney Johnston, Al Lanti, William Lutz, George Marcy, Larry Moss, Harry Naughton, Ronald Paré, James Powers, Dan Siretta, Bill Starr. *Ensemble*: Jeri Barto, Nancy Lynch, Carmen Morales, Mary Zahn, Lillian Bozinoff, Beth Howland, Meg Walter, Margery Gray.

The action takes place in New York City and environs. The time is spring in the latter part of the nineteenth century.

Act 1, Scene 1: Various places in New York City. *Scene 2*: A Bedroom in the Purefoy's Flat. *Scene 3*: Lucius Van Guilder's Study and Counting Room. *Scene 4*: Alice Van Guilder's Boudoir and a Secret Chamber. *Scene 5*: The Purefoy's Kitchen. *Scene 6*: Pier Fourteen. *Scene 7*: Van Guilder's Study and the Garden. *Scene 8*: The Van Guilders' Cellar.

Act 2, Scene 1: Police Headquarters. *Scene 2*: The Cellar. *Scene 3*: Van Guilder's Study. *Scene 4*: The Woods North of the City. *Scene 5*: Various Places in the City. *Scene 6*: The Woods and the City. *Scene 7*: Van Guilder's Study. *Scene 8*: A Courtroom.

ACT 1
Scene 1
"Drat! The Cat!"
Citizens, Patrolmen, A. Spindelman, C. Durning, G. Varrone
Scene 2
"My Son, Uphold the Law"
D. Gold, Patrolmen
Scene 3
"Holmes and Watson"
L. A. Warren, E. Gould
"She Touched Me"
E. Gould

Scene 4
"Wild and Reckless"
L. A. Warrne
Scene 5
"She's Roses"
E. Gould, L. Leonard
Scene 6
"Ignoble Theft of the Idol's Eyes" (ballet)
L. A. Warren, Patrolmen, Attendants of the Idol
Property Men: J. Barto, W. Lutz, L. Moss. *Warriors*: I. Garry, G. Marcy, H. Naughton, R. Paré. *Geishas*: N. Lynch, C. Morales, M. Zahn. *Lion*: B. Starr. *High Priest*: D. Gold. *Cantor*: G. Varrone.
Scene 7
"Dancing With Alice"
E. Gould, L. A. Warren, J. Fletcher, J. Connell, Guests
"Drat! The Cat!" (reprise)
J. Fletcher, J. Connell, Guests
Scene 8
"Purefoy's Lament"
E. Gould
ACT 2
Scene 1
"A Pox Upon the Traitor's Brow"
C. Durning, G. Varrone, S. Ellen, Patrolmen
Scene 2
"Deep in Your Heart"
E. Gould
Scene 3
"Let's Go"
L. A. Warren, E. Gould
"It's Your Fault"
J. Fletcher, J. Connell
Scene 4
"Wild and Reckless" (reprise)
E. Gould
Scene 5
"The Upside-Down Thief" (ballet)
E. Gould, Citizens, Patrolmen, L. Leonard
Tenors: R. Farnworth, G. Varrone. *Concert-Goers*: L. Bozinoff, D. Gold, M. Haraldson, J. Powers, M. Walter. *Soprano*: M. Doro. *Mayor's Companion*: M. Gray. *Patrolmen*: I. Garry, A. Lanti, R. Paré, D. Siretta, B. Starr.
Scene 6
"Today Is a Day for a Band to Play"
C. Durning, G. Varrone, S. Ellen, Patrolmen, Citizens
"She Touched Me" (reprise)
E. Gould, L. A. Warren
Scene 7
"I Like Him"
L. A. Warren
Scene 8
"Justice Triumphant"
Entire Company
"Today Is a Day for a Band to Play" (reprise)
Entire Company

1965.30 THE WORLD OF CHARLES AZNAVOUR

Songs of Love and Other Sorrows (A One-Man Show) in Two Acts. All music by Charles Aznavour. Scenery and lighting by Ralph Alswang. Musical director, Henry Byrs. Produced by Norman Twain and Sid Bernstein in association with Henri Goldgram. Opened 14 October 1965 at the Ambassador Theatre and closed 6 November 1965 after 28 performances.

CAST: CHARLES AZNAVOUR.

ACT 1
"Le temps" (There Is a Time)
(*Lyrics by* Davis.)

"Avec"

"For Me Formidable"
(*Lyrics by* Jacques Plante and Gene Lees.)

"Je Te Rechaufferais"

"Who (Will Take My Place?)" (Qui?)
(*Lyrics by* Herbert Kretzmer.)

"J'ai perdu la tête"
(*Lyrics by* Charles Aznavour.)

"Never Again" (A tout jamais)
(*Lyrics by* Falcone.)

"Parceque"

"Isabelle"
(*Lyrics by* Charles Aznavour.)

"The Boss Is Dead"

"Reste" (Stay)
(*Lyrics by* Bachelor.)

"Two Guitars"

"Que c'est triste Venice"(Venice Blue)
(*Lyrics by* F. Dorin.)

"You've Let Yourself Go"(Tu te laisses aller)
(*Lyrics by* Marcel Stellman.)

ACT 2

"I Dig You That Way" (Je T'Aime Comme Ca)
(*Lyrics by* Davis and Falcone.)

"C'est fini"

"The Time Is Now"

"Quant tu viens chez moi"

"L'amour c'est comme un jour"

"I'm Wrong"

"Et pourtant"
(*Lyrics by* Georges Garvarentz.)

"Les comediens"
(*Lyrics by* Jacques Plante.)

"Love At Last You Have Found Me" (J'en deduis que je t'aime)
(*Lyrics by* Worth.)

"Paris Is at Her Best in May" (J'aime Paris au mois de Mai)
(*Lyrics by* Gene Lees and Roche.)

"La Boheme"

"You've Got to Learn" (Il faut savoir)
(*Lyrics by* Marcel Stellman.)

"La Mamma" (For Mama)
(*Lyrics by* Robert Gall.)

ON A CLEAR DAY YOU CAN SEE FOREVER

1965.31

A Musical in Two Acts, 11 Scenes. Book and lyrics by Alan Jay Lerner. Music by Burton Lane. Directed by Robert Lewis. Dances and musical numbers staged by Herbert Ross. Scenery designed by Oliver Smith. Costumes by Freddy Wittop. Lighting by Feder. Orchestrations by Robert Russell Bennett. Music continuity and vocal (arrangements) by Trude Rittman. Dance music by Betty Walberg. Musical direction by Theodore Saidenberg. Miss Harris' modern clothes by Donald Brooks. Production supervisor, Stone Widney. Produced by Alan Jay Lerner in association with Rogo Productions. Opened 17 October 1965 at the Mark Hellinger Theatre and closed 11 June 1966 after 280 performances.

CAST (in order of appearance): *Dr. Mark Bruckner:* JOHN CULLUM. *Mrs. Hatch:* Rae Allen. *Student:* Gerald Teijelo. *Daisy Gamble:* BARBARA HARRIS. *Muriel Bunson:* Barbara Monte. *James Preston:* William Reilly. *Samuel Welles:* Gordon Dilworth. *Mrs. Welles:* Blanche Collins. *Sir Hubert Insdale:* Byron Webster. *Dolly Wainwhistle:* Hanne Marie Reiner. *Blackamoor:* Bernard Johnson. *Bob Brody:* Dan Resin. *Jimmy Dern:* Ken Richards. *Millard Cross:* Gerald M. Teijolo, Jr. *Warren Smith:* WILLIAM DANIELS. *Prudence Cumming:* Barbara Remington. *Edward Moncrief:* CLIFFORD DAVID. *Flora:* Carol Flemming. *Dr. Paul Bruckner:* Gerry Matthews. *Dr. Conrad Bruckner:* Michael Lewis. *Evans Bolagard:* Hamilton Camp. *Themistocles Kriakos:* TITOS VANDIS. *T.A.A. Official:* David Thomas. *Melinda:* BARBARA HARRIS.

Singing Ensemble: Rudy Challenger, Paul Eichel, Eddie Erickson, Stokely Gray, Bennett Hill, Art Matthews, Dan Resin, Ken Richards, Rita Golden, Joy Holly, Zona Kennedy, Pat Lysinger, Caroline Parks, Nancy Reeves, Jeannette Seibert, Dixie Stewart. *Dancing Ensemble:* Sterling Clarke, Luigi Gasparinetti, Bernard Johnson, Louis Kosman, Kazimir Kokich, Marco Pogacar, Ronald B. Stratton, Gerald Teijolo, William Reilly, Rita Agnese, Carol Flemming, Marion Fels, Leslie Franzos, Bettye Jenkins, Charlene Mehl, Barbara Monte, Hanne Marie Reiner, Barbara Remington.

The action takes place in New York City at the present time.

Act 1, Scene 1: A Lecture Room at the Bruckner Clinic. Afternoon, late spring. *Scene 2:* The Solarium of the Bruckner Clinic, several days later. *Scene 3:* Dr. Mark Bruckner's Office, immediately following. *Scene 4:* The Rooftop of Daisy's Apartment. Later that night. *Scene 5:* Dr. Mark Bruckner's Office. The following afternoon. *Scene 6:* Dr. Mark Bruckner's Office. Early evening, a week later.

Act 2, Scene 1: The Solarium of the Bruckner Clinic. A week later. *Scene 2:* Dr. Mark Bruckner's Office. Immediately following. *Scene 3:* The Rooftop of Daisy's Apartment. Late that night. *Scene 4:* Dr. Mark Bruckner's Office. Afternoon, one week later. *Scene 5:* The Municipal Airport. Later that day.

ACT 1[10]

Scene 3

"Hurry! It's Lovely Up Here"
B. Harris

"Ring Out the Bells"[11]
Servants (Ensemble)

"I'll Not Marry"[12]
B. Harris

"On a Clear Day You Can See Forever"
J. Cullum

Scene 4

"On the S.S. *Bernard Cohn*"
B. Harris, B. Monte, W. Reilly, G. M. Teijolo, Jr.

Scene 5

"At the Hellrakers'"[13] (dance)
Dance Ensemble

"Don't Tamper With My Sister"
C. David, Ensemble

"She Wasn't You"
C. David

Scene 6

"Melinda"
J. Cullum

ACT 2

Scene 1

"When I'm Being Born Again"[14]
T. Vandis

---

[10]Added for the 1966 tour was the following:
"Marriage a la Mode"
Solicitor (Fred Bennett), Sir Hubert (Don Wofford),
Mr. Welles (Sean Walsh), Mrs. Welles (Elaine Johnson), Ensemble
Added for 1967 tour were the following: "Marriage a La Mode" dropped.
"First Regression"
Melinda (Linda Lavin), Edward (Lester James)
"Solicitor's Song"
Solicitor (George Comtois),Sir Hubert (William J. Coppola),
Hubert Insdale (Joseph Pichette), Samuel Welles (Leon Benedict)
"The Spasm"
Muriel (Jodi Perselle), Company
Added for 1968 tour: "First Regression" and "The Spasm" dropped.
"The Gout"
Daisy (Tammy Grimes), Muriel (Sandra Nitz), Chorus
"Trelawney No. 1"
Chorus
[11]Dropped for subsequent 1966 tour.
[12]Replaced immediately after opening with:
"Tosy and Cosh"
B. Harris
Also, the three opening scenes were condensed into one.
[13]Dropped for subsequent 1966 tour.
[14]Retitled for subsequent tours:
"When I Come Around Again"
James Preston (Walter Willison), Students

Scene 2

"What Did I Have That I Don't Have"
B. Harris

Scene 3

"Wait 'Til We're Sixty-Five"
W. Daniels, Rooftoppers (Ensemble)

Scene 4

"Come Back to Me"
J. Cullum

Scene 5

"Come Back to Me" (reprise)
Ensemble

"On a Clear Day You Can See Forever" (reprise)
J. Cullum, (Ensemble)

1965.32   THE ZULU AND THE ZAYDA

A Comedy With Music in Two Acts, 18 Scenes. Play by Howard Da Silva and Feliz Leon. Music and lyrics by Harold Rome. Based on the (short) story "The Zulu and the Zeide" by Dan Jacobson. Directed by Dore Schary. Settings and lighting by William and Jean Eckart. Costumes by Frank Thompson. Musical supervision and orchestrations by Meyer Kupferman. Conductor, Michael Spivakowsky. Language coach, Barbara Masekela. Produced by Theodore Mann and Dore Schary. Opened 10 November 1965 at the Cort Theatre and closed 16 April 1966 after 179 performances.

CAST (in order of appearance): *Johannes*: OSSIE DAVIS. *Koofer*: James Higgins. *Harry Grossman*: Joe Silver. *Helen Grossman*: Sarah Cunningham. *Arthur Grossman*: Philip Vandervort. *David Grossman*: John Pleshette. *Eric*: John Randolph Jones. *Zayda*: MENASHA SKULNICK. *Tommy Layton*: Norman Barrs. *Paulus*: LOUIS [Lou] GOSSETT. *Woman with Baby Carriage*: Sandra Kent. *Policeman*: David Mogck. *Peter*: Peter DeAnda. *John*: Yaphet Kotto. *Joan*: Christine Spencer. *William*: Ed Hall. *Mr. Lamene*: Charles Moore. *Mrs. Lamene*: Ella Thompson. *Groenwald*: Robert Hewitt. *Dyckboom*: Max Jacobs. *Mourner*: Sholom Ludvinsky. *Nurse*: Sandra Kent.

The action takes place in Johannesburg, Republic of South Africa, at the present time.

Act 1, Scene 1: Botanical Gardens. *Scene 2*: Grossman Terrace. *Scene 3*: L&G Hardware Store. *Scene 4*: Grossman Dining Room. *Scene 5*: Grossman Garden. *Scene 6*: Botanical Gardens. *Scene 7*: Grossman Terrace. *Scene 8*: Grossman Dining Room. *Scene 9*: Grossman Garden. *Scene 10*: A Hill. *Scene 11*: Green Meadows.

Act 2, Scene 1: A Jail. *Scene 2*: The Cemetary. *Scene 3*: Grossman Terrace. *Scene 4*: Grossman Dining Room. *Scene 5*: Hospital Corridor. *Scene 6*: Alley. *Scene 7*: Hospital Garden.

ACT 1
Scene 1

"Tkambuza"
O. Davis

Scene 5

"Crocodile Wife"
O. Davis

Scene 8

"It's Good To Be Alive" (Lebe Is Gut)
M. Skulnick, L. Gossett

Scene 9

"The Water Wears Down the Stone"
O. Davis

Scene 10

"Rivers of Tears"
M. Skulnick

Scene 11

"Like the Breeze Blows"
P. DeAnda, C. Spencer, Ensemble

"Oisgetzaichnet" (Out of This World)
M. Skulnick, Ensemble

ACT 2
Scene 1

"Some Things"
Ensemble

Scene 2

"Zulu Love Song"
L. Gossett

Scene 4

"L'Chayim!" (May Your Heart Stay Young)
M. Skulnick

Scene 5

"How Cold, Cold, Cold, an Empty Room"
O. Davis

Scene 6

Eagle Soliloquy
L. Gossett

Scene 7

"It's Good To Be Alive" (reprise)(Finale)
L. Gossett, M. Skulnick

1965.33   SKYSCRAPER

A Musical Comedy in Two Acts, 25 Scenes. Book by Peter Stone. Based on the play "Dream Girl" by Elmer Rice. Music by James Van Heusen. Lyrics by Sammy Cahn. Directed by Cy Feuer. Dances and musical numbers staged by Michael Kidd. Scenery and lighting by Robert Randolph. Costumes by Theoni V. Aldredge. Musical director, John Lesko. Dance music arranged by Marvin Laird. Associate conductor, Fred Manzella. Produced by Cy Feuer and Ernest H. Martin. Opened 13 November 1965 at the Lunt-Fontanne Theatre and closed 11 June 1966 after 248 performances.

CAST (in order of appearance): *Georgina (Allerton)*: JULIE HARRIS. *Mrs. Allerton*: NANCY CUSHMAN. *Mr. Allerton*: DONALD BURR. *Charlotte*: LESLEY STEWART. *Mayor*: Burt Bier. *Doctor*: Richard Korthaze. *Herbert Bushman*: DICK O'NEILL. *Stanley*: REX EVERHART. *Timothy Bushman*: PETER L. MARSHALL. *Roger Summerhill*: CHARLES NELSON REILLY. *Woman Customer*: Georgia Creighton. *Auctioneer*: Burt Bier. *Harry the Waiter*: John Anania. *Cab Driver*: Ken Ayers. *Jazz Musician*: Walter P. Brown. *Photographer*: Christian Gray.

In film sequence: *Paola*: Pola Chapelle. *Francesco*: Paul Sorvino.

Singers: John Anania, Ken Ayers, Burt Bier, Walter P. Brown, Christian Gray, Randy Phillips, Casper Roos, Eleanor Bergquist, Georgia Creighton, Ceil Delli, Maryann Kerrick. Dancers: Ray Chabeau, Gene Gavin, Curtis Hood, Gene Kelton, Ray Kirchner, Richard Korthaze, Darrell Notara, Bill Starr, Kent Thomas, Barbara Beck, Trudy Carson, Marilyn Charles, Suzanne France, Ellen Graff, Lauren Jones, Renata Powers.

The action took place yesterday in New York City in and around a large skyscraper and a very small brownstone.

Act 1, Scene 1: Georgina's Bedroom. *Scene 2*: The Construction Site. *Scene 3*: The Bushman Building; Construction Shack. *Scene 4*: The Construction Site. *Scene 5*: Skyscraper—Ground Level. *Scene 6*: The Construction Site. *Scene 7*: The Construction Shack. *Scene 8*: The Construction Site. *Scene 9*: The Litter Bug (Antique Shop). *Scene 10*: The Construction Site. *Scene 11*: The Litter Bug. *Scene 12*: The Construction Site. *Scene 13*: Two Phones. *Scene 14*: Knickerbocker Auction Galleries. *Scene 15*: Two Phones. *Scene 16*: Georgina's Bedroom at night.

Act 2, Scene 1: The Gaiety Delicatessen. *Scene 2*: Limbo. *Scene 3*: The Film Festival. *Scene 4*: The Construction Site. *Scene 5*: Atop the unfinished skyscraper. *Scene 6*: The Construction Site. *Scene 7*: The Litter Bug. *Scene 8*: The Skyscraper—A Dream. *Scene 9*: The Allerton Bedroom.

ACT 1
Scene 1

"Occasional Flight of Fancy"
J. Harris, Officials

Scene 3

"Run For Your Life"
P. L. Marshall, D. O'Neill

Scene 4

"Local 403" (Socially Conscious Iron Workers)
R. Everhart, Construction Workers, Girls

Scene 7

"Opposites"
J. Harris, P. L. Marshall

"Run For Your Life" (reprise)
P. L. Marshall

Scene 10
  "Just the Crust"
    C. N. Reilly, R. Everhart
Scene 11
  "Everybody Has the Right to Be Wrong"
    J. Harris, P. L. Marshall
  "Everybody Has the Right to Be Wrong" (reprise)
    J. Harris
  "Wrong!"
    J. Harris, N. Cushman, L. Stewart, Customers
Scene 14
  "The Auction" (Ballet)
    Customers
Scene 16
  "Occasional Flight of Fancy" (reprise)
    J. Harris

ACT 2
Scene 1
  "The Gaiety"
    Customers
Scene 5
  "More Than One Way"
    P. L. Marshall
Scene 6
  "Haute Couture"
    R. Everhart, Models, Workers
Scene 7
  "Don't Worry"
    C. N. Reilly, D. O'Neill
  "Don't Worry" (reprise)
    J. Harris, C. N. Reilly
  "I'll Only Miss Her When I Think of Her"
    P. L.Marshall
Scene 8
  "Spare That Building"
    J. Harris, P. L. Marshall, C. N. Reilly, Company

1965.34 ## MAN OF LA MANCHA

A Musical Play in One Act. Book by Dale Wasserman. [Based on his tele-play "I, Don Quixote."] Suggested by the life and work ("Don Quixote") of Miguel de Cervantes y Saavedra. Music by Mitch Leigh. Lyrics by Joe Darion. Book and musical staging by Albert Marre. Choreography by Jack Cole. Settings and lighting by Howard Bay. Costumes by Howard Bay and Patton Campbell. Musical direction and dance arrangements by Neil Warner. Musical arrangements by Music Makers Inc. An ANTA-Goodspeed Production. Produced by Albert W. Selden and Hal James. Opened 22 November 1965 at the ANTA Washington Square Theatre, moved 19 March 1968 to the Martin Beck Theatre, moved 2 March 1971 to the Eden Theatre (Off-Broadway), moved 25 May 1971 to the Mark Hellinger Theatre and closed 26 June 1971 after 2328 performances.

CAST (in order of appearance): *Don Quixote (Cervantes)*: RICHARD KILEY. *Sancho*: IRVING JACOBSON. *Captain of the Inquisition*: Renato Cibelli. *Aldonza*: JOAN DIENER. *The Innkeeper*: RAY MIDDLETON. *Dr. Carrasco*: JON CYPHER. *The Padre*: ROBERT ROUNSEVILLE. *Antonia*: Mimi Turque. *The Housekeeper*: Eleanore Knapp. *The Barber*: Gino Conforti. *Pedro*, Head Muleteer: Shev Rodgers. *Anselmo*, a Muleteer: Harry Theyard. *Jose*, a Muleteer: Eddie Roll. *Juan*, a Muleteer: John Aristides. *Paco*, a Muleteer: Anthony De Vecchi. *Tenorio*, a Muleteer: Fernando Grahal. *Maria*, the Innkeeper's Wife: Marceline Decker. *Fermina*, a Servant Girl: Gerrianne Raphael. *The Guitarist*: David Serva.

Guards, Men of the Inquisition: Ray Dash, Jonathan Fox, John Fields, Samye Van, David Matson.

The action takes place in a dungeon in Seville at the end of the sixteenth century and in the imagination of Miguel de Cervantes.

MUSICAL NUMBERS
  "Man of La Mancha" (I, Don Quixote)
    R. Kiley, I. Jacobson, Horses
  "It's All the Same"
    J. Diener, Muleteers

"Dulcinea"
  R. Kiley, Muleteers
"I'm Only Thinking of Him"
  R. Rounseville, M. Turque, E. Knapp, J. Cypher
"I Really Like Him"
  I. Jacobson
"What Does He Want of Me?"
  J. Diener
"Little Bird, (Little Bird)"
  S. Rodgers, Muleteers
"Barber's Song"
  G. Conforti
"Golden Helmet of Mambrino"
  R. Kiley, I. Jacobson, G. Conforti, Muleteers
"To Each His Dulcinea (To Every Man His Dream)"
  R. Rounseville
"The Quest" (The Impossible Dream)
  R. Kiley
"The Combat"
  R. Kiley, J. Diener, I. Jacobson, Muleteers
"The Dubbing" (Knight of the Woeful Countenance)
  R. Middleton, J. Diener, I. Jacobson
"The Abduction"
  J. Diener, Muleteers
Moorish Dance
  Ensemble
"Aldonza"
  J. Diener
"The Knight of the Mirrors" (dance)
  R. Kiley, J. Cypher, Ensemble
"A Little Gossip"
  I. Jacobson
"Dulcinea" (reprise)
  J. Diener
"Man of LaMancha" (reprise)
  R. Kiley, J. Diener, I. Jacobson
"The Psalm"
  R. Rounseville
"The Quest" (reprise)
  Company

1965.35 ## ANYA

A Musical in Two Acts, a Prelude and 12 Scenes. Book by George Abbott and Guy Bolton. Based on the play "Anastasia" by Marcelle Maurette and Guy Bolton. Music and lyrics by Robert Wright and George Forrest. Based on themes by Sergei Rachmaninoff. Directed by George Abbott. Choreography and musical numbers by Hanya Holm. Scenery by Robert Randolph. Costumes by Patricia Zipprodt. Lighting by Richard Casler. Musical direction by Harold Hastings. Orchestrations by Don Walker. Produced by Fred R. Fehlhaber. Opened 29 November 1965 at the Ziegfeld Theatre and closed 11 December 1965 after 16 performances.

CAST (in order of appearance): *Anya*: CONSTANCE TOWERS. *Nurse*: Patricia Hoffman. *Bounine*: MICHAEL KERMOYAN. *Josef*: BORIS APLON. *Count Drivinitz*: Lawrence Brooks. *Count Dorn*: Adair McGowan. *Sergei*: Jack Dabdoub. *Yegor*: Walter Hook. *Katrina*: IRRA PETINA. *Petrovin*: EDWIN STEFFE. *Balalika Player*: Konstantin Pio-Ulsky. *Genia, the Countess Hohenstadt*: KAREN SHEPARD. *Chernov*: GEORGE S. IRVING. *Olga*: Laurie Franks. *Masha*: Rita Metzger. *Sleigh Driver*: Lawrence Boyll. *Anouchka*: Elizabeth Howell. *Tinka*: Barbara Alexander. *Mother*: Maggie Task. *Father*: Michael Quinn. *Dowager Empress*: LILLIAN GISH. *Prince Paul*: JOHN MICHAEL KING. *Countess Drivinitz*: Elizabeth Howell. *First Policeman*: Lawrence Boyll. *Second Policeman*: Bernard Frank. *Police Sergeant*: Howard Kahl. *Baroness Livenbaum*: MARGARET MULLEN.

Dancers: Barbara Alexander, Ciya Challis, Patricia Drylie, Juliette Durand, Kip Andrews, Steven Boockvor, Randy Doney, Joseph Nelson. *Singers*: Laurie Franks, Patricia Hoffman, Rita Metzger, Mia Powers, Lourette Raymon, Diane Tartleton, Maggie Task, Darrel Askey, Lawrence Boyll, Les Freed, Horace Guittard, Walter Hook, Howard Kahl, Adair McGowan, Richard Nieves, J. Vernon Oaks, Robert Sharp, John Taliaferro, Bernard Frank.

Act 1, Scene 1: The Sanitorium. Berlin, 1925. *Scene 2*: The Cafe Czarina. *Scene 3*: The Chateau. *Scene 4*: The Library. *Scene 5*: The Courtyard. *Scene 6*: The Library. *Scene 7*: The Chateau.

Act 2, Scene 1: The Chateau. *Scene 2*: The Empress' Drawing Room in Copenhagen. *Scene 3*: The Courtyard. *Scene 4*: The Library. *Scene 5*: The Chateau.

ACT 1

Choral Prelude (from Piano Concerto No. 1, Op. 1; Etudes Tableaux, Op. 33, No. 2)
　　Chorus

Scene 1

"A Song from Somewhere" (from Trio Elegiaque, Op. 9; Symphony No. 2, Op. 27; Melodie, Op. 3, No. 5)
　　C. Towers

Scene 2

"Vodka, Vodka!" (from Polka Italienne)
　　I. Petina, B. Aplon, Emigres

"So Proud" (from Symphony No. 1, Op. 13; Piano Concerto No. 3, Op. 30)
　　M. Kermoyan, G. S. Irving, E. Steffe, B. Aplon

"Homeward" (from Prelude, Op. 23, No. 5)
　　I. Petina, Emigres

Scene 3

"Snowflakes and Sweethearts" (The Snowbird Song) (from Polka on a Theme de W. R.; Valse, Suite for 2 Pianos, Op. 17, No. 2; "Thou, My Beloved Harvest Field," Op. 4, No. 5)
　　B. Alexander, C. Towers, M. Quinn, M. Task, Peasants

"On That Day" (from String Quartet in G Minor; "A Dream," Op. 38, No. 5)
　　G. S. Irving, E. Steffe, B. Aplon, I. Petina

Scene 4

"Anya" (reprise)
　　M. Kermoyan

"Six Palaces" (from Etudes Tableaux, Op. 33, No. 7; Barcarolle, Suite for 2 Pianos, Op. 5, No. 1; Polichinelle, Op. 3, No. 4; Mazurka, Op.10, No. 7)
　　C. Towers, M. Kermoyan, G. S. Irving, E. Steffe
　　Livadia, on the Black Sea: *Young Prince Paul*: R. Doney. *Young Anya*: B. Alexander.
　　The Palace of Peterhof
　　The Winter Palace: *Dowager Empress*: L. Gish.

Scene 5

"Hand in Hand" (from Romance, Suite for 2 Pianos, Op. 17, No. 3)
　　C. Towers, J. M. King

"This Is My Kind of Love" (from Piano Concerto No. 2, Op. 18)
　　C. Towers, M. Kermoyan

Scene 7

"On That Day" (reprise)
　　J. M. King, Investors

ACT 2

Scene 1

"That Prelude!" (from prelude in C Sharp Minor, Op. 3, No. 2)
　　M. Kermoyan, I. Petina, E. Steffe, B. Aplon, G. S. Irving, J. Dabdoub, W. Hook, R. Metzger, L. Franks, Policemen

Scene 2

"A Quiet Land" (from Symphony No. 2, Op. 27)
　　C. Towers

Scene 3

"Here Tonight, Tomorrow Where?" (from Danse Hongroise, Op. 5, No. 2; "So Many Hours," Op. 4, No. 6)
　　G. S. Irving, E. Steffe, B. Aplon

"Leben Sie Wohl" (from Prelude, Op. 23, No. 5; Polichinelle, Op. 3, No. 4)
　　I. Petina, Policemen

"If This Is Goodbye" (from Piano Concerto, No. 2, Op. 18)
　　C. Towers, M. Kermoyan

Scene 4

"Little Hands" (from Vocalise, Op. 34, No. 14)
　　L. Gish, C. Towers

Scene 5

"All Hail the Empress" (from Symphony No. 1, Op. 13)
　　Emigres

1965.36

THE YEARLING

A Musical in Two Acts, 16 Scenes. Book by Herbert Martin and Lore Noto. Based on the novel of the same name by Marjorie Kinnan Rawlings. Music by Michael Leonard. Lyrics by Herbert Martin. Directed by Lloyd Richards. Sets and costumes by Ed Wittstein. Lighting by Jules Fisher. Music direction and vocal arrangements by Julian Stein. Orchestrations by Larry Wilcox. Dance music by David Baker. Choreography by Ralph Beaumont. Associate producer, Michael Balistreri. Produced by Lore Noto. Opened 10 December 1965 at the Alvin Theatre and closed 11 December 1965 after 3 performances.

CAST (in order of appearance): *Jody Baxter*: STEVE SANDERS. *Ezra (Penny) Baxter*: DAVID WAYNE. *Ora Baxter*: DOLORES WILSON. *Fodder-Wing*: PETER FALZONE. *Ma Forrester*: Fay Sappington. *Buck Forrester*: Allan Louw. *Arch Forrester*: Rod Barry. *Pack Forrester*: Roy Barry. *Gabby Forrester*: Bob LaCrosse. *Millwheel Forrester*: Tom Fleetwood. *Lem Forrester*: Robert Goss. *Mrs. Hutto*: CARMEN MATHEWS. *Oliver Hutto*: David Hartman. *Eulalie*: Janet Campano. *Twink*: Carmen Alvarez. *Dock Wilson*: Gordon B. Clarke. *Preacher*: Frank Bouley. *Captain*: David Sabin. *Townspeople*: Loyce Baker, Lynette Bennett, Lois Grandi, Bobbi Lange, Ruth Lawrence, Barbara Miller, Bella Shalom, Myrna Strom, Mimi Wallace, Trudy Wallace, Vito Durante, Anthony Endon, Harrison Fisher, Scott Hunter, Martin Ross, Herbert Sanders, Ted Sprague.

Act 1, Scene 1: The Baxter Clearing. *Scene 2*: The Forrester Clearing. *Scene 3*: The Woods. *Scene 4*: The Hutto House. *Scene 5*: The Town of Volusia. *Scene 6*: The Glen. *Scene 7*: The Woods. *Scene 8*: The Forrester Clearing. *Scene 9*: The Baxter Cabin.

Act 2, Scene 1: The Baxter Cabin. The week before Christmas. *Scene 2*: Volusia. *Scene 3*: Wharf. *Scene 4*: The Baxter Cabin. *Scene 5*: The Baxter Cabin. *Scene 6*: The Runaway. *Scene 7*: The Baxter Clearing.

ACT 1

Scene 1

"Let Him Kick Up His Heels"
　　D. Wayne, D. Wilson

Scene 2

"Boy Talk"
　　S. Sanders, P. Falzone

"Bear Hunt"
　　D. Wayne, S. Sanders, Forresters

"Some Day I'm Gonna Fly"
　　S. Sanders, P. Falzone, Forresters

Scene 3

"Lonely Clearing"
　　D. Wayne

Scene 4

"Everything in the World I Love"
　　S. Sanders, C. Mathews

Scene 5

"I'm All Smiles"
　　C. Alvarez

Scene 9

"The Kind of Man a Woman Needs"
　　D. Wilson

"What a Happy Day"
　　D. Wilson, S. Sanders, G. B. Clarke, A. Louw, T. Fleetwood

"What a Happy Day" (reprise)
　　S. Sanders, A. Louw, G. B. Clarke, T. Fleetwood

ACT 2

Scene 1

"Ain't He a Joy?"
　　D. Wayne, S. Sanders

"Why Did I Choose You?"
　　D. Wayne, D. Wilson

"One Promise"
　　D. Wilson

Scene 2

"One Promise" (reprise)
　　D. Wilson, Townspeople

"Bear Hunt" (reprise)
　　Entire Company

Scene 3

"Eveything in the World I Love" (reprise)
D. Wayne, S. Sanders, C. Mathews, D. Hartman, C. Alvarez, Townspeople

Scene 4

"What a Happy Day" (reprise)
S. Sanders

Scene 5

"Nothing More"
D. Wayne, S. Sanders

Scene 7

"Everything Beautiful"
D. Wilson

1965.37   LA GROSSE VALISE

A Musical in Two Acts. Book by Robert Dhery. (Based on the French revue "La Grosse Valise.") Music and orchestrations by Gerard Calvi. Lyrics by Harold Rome. Directed by Robert Dhery. Choreography by Colette Brosset. Associate choreographer, Tom Panko. Musical director, Lehman Engel. Scenery and costumes by Jacques Dupont. Scenery and costumes supervised by Frederick Fox. Lighting by John Gleason. Assistant conductor, Karen Gustafson. Associate producer, Arthur Cantor. Produced by Joseph Kipness and Arthur Lesser. Opened 14 December 1965 at the 54th Street Theatre and closed 18 December 1965 after 7 performances.

CAST (in order of appearance): *Traveler to Bordeaux*: Jacques Ebner. *Antoine, Customs inspector*: MICHEL MODO. *Spanish Tourists*: Marcello Gamboa, Diane Coupe. *Pepito, a customs inspector*: GUY GROSSO. *Jean-Loup Roussel: assistant chief of customs*: RONALD FRASER. *La Fouillette*, an airport police ofcier: Tony Doonan. *La Nana*: FRANCE ARNELL. *Photographers*: Max Vialle, Bernard Gauthron. *Nicolas*: Brigitte Valadin. *Svatsou, the clown (M. Cheri)*: VICTOR SPINETTI. *Vlaminsky*: Guy Bertil. *Raoul*: Barry L. Martin. *Chief of Customs*: John Maxim. *The Little Porter*: Bert Michaels. *DeWalleyne*: Sybil Bartrop. *Baby's Maid*: Maureen Byrnes. *Chef d'Etat, a diplomatic official*: Max Vialle. *Old Lady*: Rita Charisse. *Andre*: Jean-Michel Mole. *Baby*: Joyce Jillson. *Mireille*: Mireille Chazal. *Pedralini, head scout*: John Maxim. *First Scout*: George Tregre. *Bald Man*: Bernard Gauthron. *Berthozeau*: Tony Doonan.

Ensemble: Diane Baffa, Maureen Byrnes, Diane Coupe, Ronn Forella, Marcello Gamboa, Pat Gosling, Carolyn Kirsch, Alex Mackay, Bert Michaels, Donna Sanders, George Tregre, Mary Zahn.

The action takes place in Customs, Orly Airport, Paris, France, at the present time.

ACT 1

"La Grosse Valise"
R. Fraser, V. Spinetti, B. Valadin, Company

"A Big One"
R. Fraser, M. Modo, G. Grosso, V. Spinetti, B. Valadin, Company

"C'est Defendu"
R. Fraser, F. Arnell, G. Groso, M. Modo

"Hamburg Waltz"
All Principals, Dancing Girls and Boys

"Happy Song"
R. Fraser, G. Grosso, M. Modo, J. Maxim

"For You"
J. Jillson

"Sandwich for Two"
V. Spinetti, B. Valadin

"'La Java"
F. Arnell, J. Maxim, J. Jillson, Dancing Girls and Boys

"Xanadu"
F. Arnell, V. Spinetti, R. Fraser

ACT 2

"Slippy Sloppy Shoes"
V. Spinetti, R. Fraser, Dancing Girls and Boys

"Spanish Dance"
R. Fraser, M. Chazal

"For You" (reprise)
R. Fraser, J. Jillson

"Delilah Done Me Wrong"
V. Spinetti, F. Arnell, and the Slaves

"Hawaii"
F. Arnell, J. Jillson, Dancing Girls

1965.38   OKLAHOMA!

A Revival of the Musical Play in Two Acts, 6 Scenes[15]. Book and lyrics by Oscar Hammerstein II. Music by Richard Rodgers. Based on the play "Green Grow the Lilacs" by Lynn Riggs. Entire production directed by John Fearnley. (Originally directed by Rouben Mamoulian.) Original dances by Agnes de Mille, restaged by Gemze de Lappe. Music director, Pembroke Davenport. Assistant conductor, Abba Bogin. Settings by Lemuel Ayers. Costumes by Stanley Simmons. Lighting by Peggy Clark. Produced by the New York City Center Light Opera Company (Jean Dalrymple, Director). Opened 15 December 1965 at the New York City Center and closed 2 January 1966 after 24 performances.

CAST (in order of appearance): *Aunt Eller*: RUTH KOBART. *Curly*: JOHN DAVIDSON. *Laurey*: SUSAN WATSON. *Will Parker*: RICHARD FRANCE. *Jud Fry*: DANIEL P. HANNAFIN. *Ado Annie Carnes*: KAREN MORROW. *Ali Hakim*: JULES MUNSHIN. *Gertie Cummings*: Loi Leabo. *Curly in ballet*: DEAN CRANE. *Laurey in ballet*: SUSAN WATSON. *Jud in ballet*: James Albright. *The Child in ballet*: Jane Levin. *The Girl Who Falls Down*: Loi Leabo. *Andrew Carnes*: SAMMY SMITH. *Cord Elam*: Herbert Surface.

Dancers: *Girls*: Cathy Conklin, Joanne Crosson, Carolyn Dyer, Carol Estey, Sharon Herr, Loi Leabo, Jane Levin, Marie Patrice, Betty Ann Rapine, Rande Rayburn, Julie Theobald, Toodie Wittmer. *Boys*: Don Angelo, Gerry Dalton, Jeremy Ives, Brynnar Mehl, Philip Rice, Bud Spencer, Fabian Suart. *Singers*: *Girls*: Vicki Belmonte, Maria Bradley, Judie Elkins, Jeanne Frey, Marie Hero, Joyce Olson, Susan Sidney, Maggie Worth. *Boys*: Kenny Adams, Brown Bradley, Roger Alan Brown, Joseph Corby, Peter Clark, Lang Des Jardins, Konstantin Moskalenko, Stephen John Rydell, Herbert Surface, Victor Helou.

THE PERSECUTION AND ASSASSINATION OF MARAT AS PERFORMED BY THE INMATES OF THE ASYLUM OF CHARENTON UNDER THE DIRECTION OF THE MARQUIS DE SADE
1965.39   (MARAT/SADE)

A Drama with Music in Two Acts, 33 Scenes[16]. (Original German) Play by Peter Weiss. English version by Geoffrey Skelton. Verse adaptation by Adrian Mitchell. Music by Richard Peaslee. Directed by Peter Brook. Settings and properties by Sally Jacobs. Costumes by Gunilla Palmstierna-Weiss. Choreograhy by Malcolm Goddard. Original Lighting by David Read. Lighting and design supervision by Lloyd Burlingame. Assistant to the director, Ian Richardson. Production supervisor, Samuel Liff. (A Royal Shakespeare Company Production.) Produced by the David Merrick Arts Foundation by arrangement with the Governors of the Royal Shakespeare Theatre. Opened 27 December 1965 at the Martin Beck Theatre and closed 30 April 1966 after 145 performances.

CAST (in order of appearance): *M. Coulmier*: CLIFFORD ROSE. *Mme. Coulmier*: Brenda Kempner. *Mlle. Coulmier*: Ruth Baker. *Herald*: MICHAEL WILLIAMS. *Cucururu*: Freddie Jones. *Kokol*: Hugh Sullivan. *Polpoch*: Jonathan Burn. *Rossignol*: Jeanette Landis. *Jacques Roux*: Robert Lloyd. *Charlotte Corday*: GLENDA JACKSON. *Jean-Paul Marat*: IAN RICHARDSON. *Simonne Evrard*: SUSAN WILLIAMSON. *Marquis de Sade*: PATRICK MAGEE. *Duperret*: JOHN STEINER. *Abbot*: Mark Jones. *A Mad Animal*: Morgan Sheppard. *Schoolmaster*: James Mellor. *The Military Representative*: Ian Hogg. *Mother*: Mark Jones. *Father*: Henry Woolf. *A Newly-Rich Lady*: John Hussey. *Voltaire*: John Harwood. *Lavoisier*: Leon Lissek. *Nuns*: Heather Canning, Jennifer Tudor. *Guards*: Timothy Hardy, Stanford Trowell.

Patients: Mary Allen, Michael Farnsworth, Maroussia Frank, Tamara Fuerst, Guy Gordon, Sheila Grant, Michael Percival, Lyn Pinkney, Carol Raymont. *Musicians*: Patrick Gowers (Music director/harmonium/tuba), Richard Callinan (percussion), Michael Gould (trumpet), Nicholas Moes (guitar/harmonium), Rainer Schuelein (flute/piccolo/alto flute).

The action takes place in the Charenton Asylum in France sometime between 1803 and 1814.

Act 1, Scene 1: Assembly. *Scene 2*: Prologue. *Scene 3*: Preparation. *Scene 4*: Presentation. *Scene 5*: Homage to Marat. *Scene 6*: Stifled Unrest. *Scene 7*: Corday Is Introduced. *Scene 8*: I Am the Revolution. *Scene 9*: Corday's First Visit. *Scene 10*: Song

---

[15]Originally produced in New York 31 March 1943 at the St. James Theatre for 2212 performances. For Synopsis of Scenes and Musical Numbers, see original 1943 production.

[16]Scenes and Song Titles do not appear in the program, but have been prepared from the production typescript, published text, musical score and recordings.

and Mime of Corday's Arrival in Paris. *Scene 11*: Death's Triumph. *Scene 12*: Conversation Concerning Life and Death. *Scene 13*: Marat's Liturgy. *Scene 14*: A Regrettable Intervention. *Scene 15*: Continuation of the Conversation Between Marat and Sade. *Scene 16*: The People's Reaction. *Scene 17*: First Conversation between Corday and Duperret. *Scene 18*: Sade Turns His Back on All the Nations. *Scene 19*: First Rabble-Rousing of Jacques Roux. *Scene 20*: Monsieur de Sade Is Whipped. *Scene 21*: Poor Old Marat. *Scene 22*: Second Conversation Between Corday and Duperret. *Scene 23*: These Lies They Tell. *Scene 24*: Song and Mime of the Glorification of the Beneficiary. *Scene 25*: Corday's Second Visit. *Scene 26*: The Faces of Marat.

Act 2, Scene 1: The National Assembly. *Scene 2*: Poor Marat in Your Bathtub Seat. *Scene 3*: Preparations for the Third Visit. *Scene 4*: Corday's Third and Last Visit. *Scene 5*: Interruptus. *Scene 6*: The Murder. *Scene 7*: Epilogue.

ACT 1
Scene 5

"Homage to Marat"
    H. Sullivam, J. Burn, F. Jones, J. Landis, Chorus
Scene 7

"The Corday Waltz"
    G. Jackson
Scene 10

"Song and Mime of Corday's Arrival in Paris"
    H. Sullivam, J. Burn, F. Jones, J. Landis
"The Tumbrel Song"
    H. Sullivam, J. Burn, F. Jones, J. Landis
Scene 16

"The People's Reaction"
    H. Sullivam, J. Burn, F. Jones, J. Landis, Chorus
Scene 18

"Those Fat Monkeys"
    H. Sullivam, J. Burn, F. Jones, J. Landis
Scene 21

"Poor Old Marat"
    H. Sullivam, J. Burn, F. Jones, J. Landis
Scene 22

"One Day It Will Come to Pass"
    G. Jackson, J. Steiner
Scene 24

"Song and Mime of the Glorification of the Beneficiary"
    P. Magee, I. Richardson, H. Sullivam, J. Burn, F. Jones, J. Landis,

ACT 2
Scene 2

"Poor Marat in Your Bathtub Seat"
    H. Sullivam, J. Burn, F. Jones, J. Landis
"Poor Old Marat" (reprise)
    H. Sullivam, J. Burn, F. Jones, J. Landis
Scene 4

"Copulation Round"
    Chorus
Scene 5

"Fifteen Glorious Years"
    H. Sullivam, J. Burn, F. Jones, J. Landis, Company
Scene 7

Finale (Epilogue)
    Entire Company

1966.01   SWEET CHARITY

A Musical in Two Acts, a Prologue and 18 Scenes. Book by Neil Simon. Based on the film "Le Notte di Cabiria" [Nights of Cabiria] by Federico Fellini, Tullio Pinelli, Ennio Flaiano. Music by Cy Coleman. Lyrics by Dorothy Fields. Conceived, staged and choreographed by Bob Fosse. Scenery and lighting by Robert Randolph. Costumes by Irene Sharaff. Musical direction and dance music arranged by Fred Werner. Orchestrations by Ralph Burns. Production manager, Robert Linden. Associate producer, John Bowab. Assistant conductor, Oscar Kosarin. Produced by Robert Fryer, Lawrence Carr, Joseph P. and Sylvia Harris. Opened 29 January 1966 at the Palace Theatre and closed 15 July 1967 after 608 performances.

CAST (in order of appearance): *Charity*: GWEN VERDON. *Dark Glasses*: Michael Davis. *Bystander*: John Stratton. *Married Couple*: Bud Vest, Elaine Cancilla. *Woman with hat*: Ruth Buzzi. *Football Player*: John Sharpe. *Ice Cream Vendor*: Gene Foote. *Ballplayers*: Harold Pierson, Eddie Gasper. *Career Carl*: Barbara Sharma. *Young Spanish Man*: Lee Roy Reams. *First Cop*: John Wheeler. *Second Cop*: David Gold. *Helene*: THELMA OLIVER. *Carmen*: Carmen Morales. *Nickie*: HELEN GALLAGHER. *Herman*: John Wheeler. *Doorman*: I. W. Klein. *Ursula*: Sharon Ritchie. *Vittorio Vidal*: JAMES LUISI. *Waiter*: John Stratton. *Manfred*: Bud Vest. *Receptionist*: Ruth Buzzi. *Old Maid*: Elaine Cancilla. *Oscar*: JOHN McMARTIN. *Daddy Johann Sebastian Brubeck*: Arnold Soboloff. *Brother Harold*: Harold Pierson. *Brother Eddie*: Eddie Gasper. *Policeman*: Harold Pierson. *Rosie*: Barbara Sharma. *Barney*: David Gold. *Mike*: Michael Davis. *Good Fairy*: Ruth Buzzi.

Singers and Dancers of Times Square: I. W. Klein, Mary Louise, Alice Evans, Betsy Dickerson, Kathryn Doby, Suzanne Charny, Elaine Cancilla, Carmen Morales, Christine Stewart, Charlene Ryan, David Gold, Gene Foote, Harold Pierson, Bud Vest, Darrell Notara, John Sharpe, Eddie Gasper, Michael Davis, Patrick Heim.

The action takes place in and around New York City at the present time.

Act 1, Scene 1: The Park. *Scene 2*: The Hostess Room (of the Fan-Dango Ballroom). *Scene 3*: Fan-Dango Ballroom. *Scene 4*: A New York Street (outside the Pompeii Club). *Scene 5*: (The Interior of the) Pompeii Club. *Scene 6*: Vittorio Vidal's Apartment. *Scene 7*: The Hostess Room. *Scene 8*: YMHA—92nd Street "Y."

Act 2, Scene 1: YMHA—92nd Street "Y." *Scene 2*: The Rhythm of Life Church. *Scene 3*: (On a New York Street) Going Cross-town. *Scene 4*: Charity's Apartment. *Scene 5*: Coney Island. *Scene 6*: The Fan-Dango Ballroom. *Scene 7*: Times Square. *Scene 8*: Barney's Chile Hacienda. *Scene 9*: The Fan-Dango Ballroom. *Scene 10*: The Park.

ACT 1
Prologue

"Charity's Wish" (Charity's Theme)(dance)
    G. Verdon
Scene 1

"You Should See Yourself"[17]
    G. Verdon
"The Rescue"
    The Passers-by
Scene 3

"Big Spender"
    H. Gallgher, T. Oliver, the Fan-Dango Girls
"Charity's Soliloquy"
    G. Verdon
Scene 5

"Rich Man's Frug"
    B. Sharma, E. Gasper, J. Sharpe, Patrons
Scene 6

"If My Friends Could See Me Now"
    G. Verdon
"Too Many Tomorrows"
    J. Luisi
Scene 7

"There's Gotta Be Something Better Than This"
    G. Verdon, H. Gallagher, T. Oliver
Scene 8

"I'm the Bravest Individual"
    G. Verdon, J. McMartin
ACT 2
Scene 2

"Rhythm of Life"
    A. Soboloff, H. Pierson, E. Gasper, Worshippers
Scene 4

"Baby Dream Your Dream"
    H. Gallagher, T. Oliver
Scene 5

"Sweet Charity"
    J. McMartin
Scene 6

"Where Am I Going?"[18]
    G. Verdon

-----

[17]Dropped shortly after opening.
[18]Dropped shortly after opening.

Scene 9

"I'm a Brass Band"
G. Verdon

Scene 10

"I Love to Cry at Weddings"
J. Wheeler, M. Davis, H. Gallagher, T. Oliver, Girls, Patrons

1966.02 STREET SCENE

A Revival of the American Opera (Musical) in Two Acts, 3 Scenes[19]. Book by Elmer Rice from his play of the same name. Music by Kurt Weill. Lyrics by Langston Hughes. Staged by Herbert Machiz. Choreographed by Richard Tone. Conducted by Charles Wilson. Scenery and costumes by Paul Sylbert. (Orchestrations by Kurt Weill.) Produced by the New York City Opera. Opened 24 February 1966 at the New York State Theatre and closed 19 March 1966 after 6 performances in repertory.

CAST (in order of appearance): *Abraham Kaplan*: Nico Castel. *Greta Fiorentino*: Dolores Mari. *Carl Olsen*: George S. Irving. *Emma Jones*: RUTH KOBART. *Olga Olsen*: Muriel Greenspon. *Shirley Kaplan*: Florence Anglin. *Henry Davis*: Edward Pierson. *Willie Maurrant*: Bruce Papa. *Anna Maurrant*: EILEEN SCHAULER. *Sam Kaplan*: William DuPree. *Daniel Buchanan*: L. D. Clements. *Frank Maurrant*: WILLIAM CHAPMAN. *George Jones*: Jack Bittner. *Steve Sankey*: Richard Armbruster. *Lippo Fiorentino*: JACK DeLON. *Jennie Hildebrand*: Betsy Hepburn. *Second Graduate*: Janet Morris. *Third Graduate*: Lila Herbert. *Mrs. Hildebrand*: Beverly Evans. *Charlie Hildebrand*: Tom Brooke. *Mary Hildebrand*: Jeanne Tanzy. *Grace Davis*: Donna Babbs. *Rose Maurrant*: ANNE ELGAR. *Harry Easter*: Seth Riggs. *Mae Jones*: Sondra Lee. *Dick McGann*: Alan Peterson. *Vincent Jones*: Barney Martin. *Dr. John Wilson*: Don Carlo. *Officer Harry Murphy*: David Smith. *City Marshall James Henry*: Don Yule. *Fred Cullen*: Paul Corder. *First Nursemaid*: Charlotte Povia. *Second Nursemaid*: Marie Wyckoff.

Policemen, Milkman, Old Clothes Man, Music Pupil, Interne, Ambulance Driver, Married Couple, Passersby, Neighbors, Children, etc.: New York City Opera Chorus.

1966.03 WAIT A MINIM!

A Musical Entertainment (Revue from South Africa) in Two Acts, 24 Scenes. Devised and directed by Leon Gluckman. Musical arrangements[20] and direction by Andrew Tracey. Decor and lighting by Frank Rembach and Leon Gluckman. Decor executed by Frank Rembach. Costumes by Heather Macdonald-Rouse. Choreography by Frank Staff and Kendrew Lascelles. Lighting and design supervision by Klaus Holm. Costume supervision by Patton Campbell. Production supervisior, Lanier Davis. Produced by Frank Productions, Inc. (Allen B. Whitehead, President). Opened 7 March 1966 at the John Golden Theatre and closed 15 April 1967 after 457 performances.

CAST: ANDREW TRACEY, PAUL TRACEY, KENDREW LASCELLES, MICHEL MARTEL, NIGEL PEGRAM, APRIL OLRICH, DANA VALERY, SARAH ATKINSON.

ACT 1[21]
Scene 1

This Is the Land:

"Ndinosara Nani?" (Karanga Folk Song, Southern Rhodesia)
A. Tracey, N. Pegram, M. Martel, D. Valery, P. Tracey

"Hoe Ry Die Boere" (Afrikaans Folk Song)
N. Pegram, P. Tracey, A. Tracey

"This Is Worth Fighting For"[22]
S. Atkinson

"Subuhi Sana" (Swahili)
A. Tracey

"Jikel' Emaweni"[23] (Xhosa Fighting Song, Tanskei)
(arr. by Makeba)
D. Valery

Scene 2

Dingere Dingale:

"Ajade Papa" (Tamil Lullaby)
M. Martel

Dingere Dingale" (Tamil Song)
The Company

"Tuba Man"
K. Lascelles

Scene 3

Over the Hills:

"I Know Where I'm Going" (Irish Folk Song)
P. Tracey, S. Atkinson, A. Tracey

"Over the Hills"
A. Olrich, A. Tracey

"I Gave My Love a Cherry" (English Folk Song)
P. Tracey, D. Valery, M. Martel, N. Pegram, A. Tracey

Scene 4

"Black-White Calypso"
N. Pegram
(*Music and Lyrics by* Jeremy Taylor.)

Scene 5

Die Meistertrinker

"Deutches Weinlied"
The Company

"Gretl's Cow"
A. Olrich

"Eine kleine bombardonmusik" (Mozart)
N. Pegram, A. Tracey, P. Tracey, K. Lascelles

"Watschplattlanz"
The Company

Scene 6

"Buttermilk Hill"[24] (Irish-American)
D. Valery

Scene 7

"Aria"
P. Tracey

Scene 8

"Out of Focus"
The Company

Snap Happy
A. Olrich, K. Lascelles

"Hoshoryu" (Japanese Folk Song)
M. Martel, S. Atkinson

The Gentle Art
K. Lascelles, M. Martel, P. Tracey

Scene 9

"Dirty Old Town"
A. Tracey, P. Tracey, D. Valery, N. Pegram
(*Music and Lyrics by* Ewan MacColl.)

Scene 10

"Last Summer"
A. Tracey, P. Tracey, N. Pegram, K. Lascelles

Scene 11

Vive La Difference:

---

[19]Originally produced in New York 9 January 1947 at the Adelphi Theatre for 148 performances. For Synopsis of Scenes and Musical Numbers, see original 1947 production.

[20]All musical arrangements for WAIT A MINIM! are played by:
Andrew Tracey: Guitar, guitar-lute, bamboo pipe, Portuguese guitar, mandolin, treble and soprano recorder, Rhodesian mbira, Chopi timbila, Lozi drums, tuba, bagpipes, Indian tabla drums, clarient, Trinidadian steel drum, sousaphone, Indian gong.
Paul Tracey: Guitar, H. M. Bull Fiddle, flute, Chopi timbila, Lozi drums, piccolo, melodica, squeezebox, bagpipes, kalimba, tuba, sousaphone, Indian gong.
Nigel Pegram: Guitar, H.M. Bull Fiddle, double respiratory linguaphone, Lozi drums, bagpipes, Japanese koto zither, trombone, Chopi timbila, penny whistle, Indian tanpura drone. Kendrew Lascelles: Trumpet. Other percussion instruments by the Company.

[21]The following song was added during the course of the run and subsequent tour:
"Home Sweet Home" (Act 1, Scene 1)

[22]Dropped during run and tour.
[23]Dropped during tour.
[24]Replaced after opening with:
"Johnny Soldier" (Irish-American)
D. Valery

"Lalirette"
P. Tracey, A. Tracey, M. Martel, N. Pegram
"Le Roi A Fait Battre Tambour" (Medieval ballade)
M. Martel, N. Pegram, P. Tracey, A. Tracey
Tour de France
K. Lascelles, A. Olrich, A. Tracey, P. Tracey, M. Martel
Scene 12
"A Piece of Ground"
N. Pegram
(*Music and Lyrics by* Jeremy Taylor.)
Scene 13
"Ayama"
A. Tracey, P. Tracey, M. Martel
Scene 14
North of the 'Popo:
Professor Piercing
P. Tracey
The Chairwoman
N. Pegram
"Mgeniso waMgodo waShambini" (Chopi Timbila)
A. Tracey, P. Tracey, N. Pegram
"Kupura Kupika" (Pounding Song, Nyasaland)
S. Atkinson, D. Valery, A. Olrich
"The Izicatulo Gumboot Dance"
The Company

ACT 2
Scene 1
Tunes of Glory
"The Wee Cooper o' Fife" (Doric Diddling)
P. Tracey, A. Tracey, N. Pegram
"Red Red Rose" (Robert Burns)
P. Tracey
Scene 2
"Hammer Song" (If I Had a Hammer)
A. Tracey, N. Pegram, M. Martel, P. Tracey
(*Music and Lyrics by* Pete Seeger and Lee Hays.)
Scene 3
"London Talking Blues"
N. Pegram
(*Music and Lyrics by* Jeremy Taylor.)
Scene 4
The Love Life of a Gondolier"
K. Lascelles, M. Martel, A. Olrich
Scene 5
"Foyo" (Haitian Patois Lullaby)
P. Tracey, A. Tracey, N. Pegram
Scene 6
"Cool"
D. Valery, P. Tracey, N. Pegram, A. Tracey
(*Music and Lyrics by* Andrew and Paul Tracey.)
Scene 7
On Guard
K. Lascelles, A. Olrich
Scene 8
Sir Oswald Sodde:
Opening Knight
The Company
"Sir Oswald Sodde"
A. Tracey, S. Atkinson, N. Pegram, P. Tracey, M. Martel
(*Music and Lyrics by* Jeffrey Smith.)
Scene 9
"Table Bay"
D. Valery
(Cape Malay, *arranged and adapted by* Stanley Glasser and Adolf Wood.)
Scene 10
This Is South Africa:
"Chuzi Mama Gwabi Gwabi" (Marabi Dance Song)
D. Valery, M. Martel

"Celeste Aida"*
M. Martel
"Cingoma Chakabaruka" (Tumbuka/Henga party song, Nyasaland)
The Company
"Skalo-Zwi"
(*Music by* Stanley Glasser. *Lyrics by* Gwigwi Mrwebe. Pedi Pipe Dance specially arranged by Andrew Tracey.)
D. Valery, Company
"Samandoza-we!" (Ndau, Southern Rhodesia)
The Company
"Amasalela" (Baca Fighting Song, Transkei)
The Company

1966.04   # THE CONSUL

A Revival of the Opera (Musical Drama) in Three Acts, 6 Scenes[25]. Libretto and music by Gian-Carlo Menotti. Staged by Gian-Carlo Menotti. Conductor, Vincent La Selva. Settings and costumes by Horace Armistead. Produced by the New York City Opera. Opened 17 March 1966 at the New York State Theatre and closed 23 March 1966 after 3 performances in repertory.

CAST: (in order of appearance): *John Sorel:* SHERRILL MILNES. *Magda Sorel:* PATRICIA NEWAY. *The Mother:* EVELYN SACHS. *Secret Police Agent:* HERBERT BEATTIE. *First Plainclothesman:* Philip Erickson. *Second Plainclothesman:* Richard Park. *The Secretary:* BEVERLY EVANS. *Mr. Kofner:* DAVID SMITH. *The Foreign Woman:* ELISABETH CARRON. *Anna Gomez:* Ludmilla Azova. *Vera Boronel:* Elisabeth Farmer. *Nika Magadoff*, The Magician: GENE BULLARD. *Assan:* Jack Bittner. *Voice on the Record:* Mabel Mercer.

1966.05   # POUSSE-CAFÉ

A Musical in Two Acts, a Prologue and 17 Scenes. Book by Jerome Weidman[26]. Music by Duke Ellington. Lyrics by Marshall Barer and Fred Tobias. Entire production directed by José Quintero. Scenery by Will Steven Armstrong. Costumes by Patricia Zipprodt, Albert Wolsky. Lighting by J. C. Fuqua. Musical direction, Sherman Frank. Production consultant, Charles Conaway. Orchestrations by Larry Wilcox. Choreography, Valerie Bettis. Musical numbers and dances staged by Marvin Gordon. Associate producer, Monty Shaff. Produced by Guy de La Passardiere. Opened 18 March 1966 at the 46th Street Theatre and closed 19 March 1966 after 3 performances.

CAST (in order of appearance): *Ellis:* Ellis Larkins. *Havana:* TRAVIS HUDSON. *Duchess:* Madge Cameron. *Monty:* Al Nesor. *Harry:* Tommy Karaty. *Sourball:* Robert Rovin. *Bill:* Ben Bryant. *Arthur Owen, Jr.:* Jeff Siggins. *John Harmon:* GARY KRAWFORD. *Professor George Ritter:* THEODORE BIKEL. *Solange:* LILO. *Sailor:* Dom Angelo. *Policeman:* Hal Norman. *Paul:* Don Crabtree. *Maurice:* Charles Durning. *Artie:* Coley Worth. *Tourist Lady:* Fran Stevens. *Louise:* Marlena Lustik. *Dean Stewart:* Charles Durning. *Danny:* RICHARD TONE.
Ensemble: Dom Angelo, Kay Cole, Joel Conrad, Mervin Crook, Elaine Giftos, Altovise Gore, Peter Hamparian, Jo Ann Lehmann, Marlena Lustik, Iva March, Simon McQueen, Rita O'Connor, Martin Ross, Barbara Saatan, Scotty Salmon.

The action takes place in New Orleans during the early 1920s.

Act 1, Scene 1: Schoolroom. *Scene 2:* Cafe and Bar. *Scene 3:* Solange's Dressing Room. *Scene 4:* Cafe and Bar. *Scene 5:* Dormitory. *Scene 6:* Solange's Dressing Room. *Scene 7:* Same, the next morning. *Scene 8:* Professor's Quarters. *Scene 9:* Professor's Quarters and Solange's Dressing Room. *Scene 10:* Cafe and Bar.

Act 2, Scene 1: Cafe and Bar. *Scene 2:* Solange's Dressing Room. *Scene 3:* Cafe and Bar. *Scene 4:* Professor's Quarters. *Scene 5:* Cafe and Bar. *Scene 6:* Solange's Dressing Room. *Scene 7:* Schoolroom.

ACT 1
"The Spider and the Fly"
T. Hudson, Dance Ensemble
"Rules and Regulations"
T. Bikel, G. Krawford, R. Rovin, B. Bryant, J. Siggins, T. Karaty
"Follow Me Up the Stairs"
Lilo

---

[25]Originally produced in New York 15 March 1950 at the Ethel Barrymore Theatre for 269 performances. For Synopsis of Scenes and Musical Numbers, see original 1950 production.
[26]Source credit dropped prior to New York opening. Based on the novel "Professor Unrath" by Heinrich Mann. The film "The Blue Angel" by Karl Zuckmayer was adapted from the same source.

"Goodby Charlie"
    T. Hudson, Ensemble
"C'est Comme Ça"
    Lilo
"Thank You, Ma'am"
    T. Bikel, Lilo
"The Eleventh Commandment"
    R. Rovin, J. Siggins, B. Bryant, T. Karaty
"Someone to Care For"
    T. Bikel
"The Wedding"
    Ensemble

ACT 2
"Let's" (Rehearsal Scene)
    R. Tone, M. Lustik, Dancers
"The Good Old Days"
    T. Hudson, D. Crabtree, A. Nesor, C. Worth, C. Durning
"Easy To Take"
    R. Tone, Lilo
"C'est Comme Ça" (reprise)
    T. Bikel
"C'est Comme Ça" (reprise)
    Lilo
"Let's" (reprise)
    Lilo, Dancers
"Old World Charm"
    T. Bikel
"The Spider and the Fly" (reprise)
    T. Hudson

IT'S A BIRD ... IT'S A PLANE ... IT'S SUPERMAN

1966.06

A Musical Comedy in Two Acts, 18 Scenes. Book by David Newman and Robert Benton. Based on the comic strip "Superman.[27]" Music by Charles Strouse. Lyrics by Lee Adams. Directed by Harold Prince. Dances and musical numbers staged by Ernest Flatt. Scenery and lighting by Robert Randolph. Costumes by Florence Klotz. Musical direction, Harold Hastings, Orchestrations by Eddie Sauter. Dance arrangements by Betty Walberg. Filmed sequences by MPO Pictures, Inc. Produced by Harold Prince in association with Ruth Mitchell. Opened 29 March 1966 at the Alvin Theatre and closed 17 July 1966 after 129 performances.

CAST (in order of appearance): *Superman/Clark Kent*: BOB HOLIDAY. *Max Mencken*: JACK CASSIDY. *Lois Lane*: PATRICIA MARAND. *Perry White*: Eric Mason. *Sydney*: LINDA LAVIN. *Dr. Abner Sedgewick*: MICHAEL O'SULLIVAN. *Jim Morgan*: DON CHASTAIN. *Father Ling*: Jerry Fujikawa. *Dong Ling*: Bill Starr. *Tai Ling*: Murphy James. *Fan Po Ling*: Juleste Salve. *Ming Foo Ling*: Michael Gentry. *Joe Ling*: Joseph Gentry. *Suspects (5)*: *One*: Les Freed. *Two*: Dick Miller. *Three*: Dal Richards. *Four*: John Grigas. *Five*: John Smolko.
    Citizens of Metropolis: *Byron*, the Bank Guard: Eugene Edwards. *Harvey*, the Tour Guide: Bob Scherkenbach. *Bonnie*, the Moll: April Nevins. *Sue-Ellen*, the Teenager: Tina Faye. *Marnie*, the Model: Judy Newman. *Gordon*, the Student: Bick Goss. *Annette*, the Secretary: Michelle Barry. *Wanda*, the Waitress: Gay Edmond. *Rosalie*, the High School Girl: Marilyne Mason. *Leslie*, the Shopper: Jayme Mylroie. *Cathy*, the Child: Lori Browne. *Barbie*, the Receptionist: Mara Landi. *Al*, the Bank Robber: George Bunt. *Milton*, the Hood: Dallas Edmunds. *Kevin*, the College Boy: Roy Smith. *William*, the Exchange Student: Haruki Fujimoto.

The action takes place in and around the city of Metropolis, U.S.A. at the present time.

Act 1, Scene 1: Outside the Chase-Metropolis Bank. *Scene 2*: The Office of *The Daily Planet*. *Scene 3*: A Telephone Booth. *Scene 4*: The Nuclear Ractor at M.I.T. *Scene 5*: The Offices of *The Daily Planet*. *Scene 6*: Dr. Sedgewick's Study. *Scene 7*: The Screening Room. *Scene 8*: Dr. Sedgewick's Home. *Scene 9*: The Offices of *The Daily Planet*. *Scene 10*: Atop City Hall Tower. *Scene 11*: The M.I.T. Dedication Grounds.

Act 2, Scene 1: The Front Page, one week later. *Scene 2*: Clark Kent's Apartment. *Scene 3*: A Street in Metropolis. *Scene 4*: Dr. Sedgewick's Laboratory. *Scene 5*: Meanwhile. *Scene 6*: An Abandoned Power Station outside Metropolis. *Scene 7*: The Power Station, next morning.

---

[27]The Superman comic strip first appeared in 1938 from author-illustrators Jerry Siegel and Joe Shuster, published by Detective Comics.

ACT 1
Scene 1
    "Doing Good"
        B. Holiday
    "We Need Him"
        J. Cassidy, P. Marand, B. Holiday, Company
Scene 2
    "It's Superman"
        P. Marand
Scene 4
    "We Don't Matter At All"
        D. Chastain, P. Marand
    "Revenge"
        M. O'Sullivan
Scene 5
    "The Woman For the Man"
        J. Cassidy
    "You've Got Possibilities"
        L. Lavin
Scene 7
    "What I've Always Wanted"
        P. Marand
    "Revenge" (reprise)
        M. O'Sullivan
Scene 8
    "Everything's Easy When You Know How"
        The Flying Lings
Scene 11
    "It's Super Nice"
        The Company

ACT 2
Scene 1
    "So Long, Big Guy"
        J. Cassidy
Scene 2
    "The Strongest Man in the World"
        B. Holiday
Scene 3
    "Ooh, Do You Love You!"
        L. Lavin
Scene 4
    "You've Got What I Need"
        J. Cassidy, M. O'Sullivan
Scene 5
    "It's Superman" (reprise)
        The Company
Scene 7
    "I'm Not Finished Yet"
        P. Marand
    "Pow! Bam! Zonk!"
        B. Holiday, the Flying Lings

HOW TO SUCCEED IN BUSINESS WITHOUT REALLY TRYING

1966.07

A Revival of the Musical (Comedy) in Two Acts, 24 Scenes[28]. Book by Abe Burrows, Jack Weinstock and Willie Gilbert. Based on the novel of the same name by Shepherd Mead. Music and lyrics by Frank Loesser. Scenery by Robert Randolph. Costumes by Stanley Simmons. Lighting by Peggy Clark. Production directed by Gus Schirmer. Original choreography for "The Yo Ho Ho" by Hugh Lambert. Original musical staging by Bob Fosse. Musical direction, Anton Coppola. (Orchestrations by Robert Ginzler.) Original production directed by Abe Burrows. Produced by the New York City Center

---

[28]Originally opened in New York 14 October 1961 at the 46th Street Theatre for 1417 performances. For Synopsis of Scenes and Musical Numbers, see original 1961 production.

Light Opera Company (Jean Dalrymple, Director). Opened 20 April 1966 at the New York City Center and closed 8 May 1966 after 23 performances.

CAST (in order of appearance): *Finch*: LEN GOCHMAN. *Gatch*: Lang des Jardins. *Jenkins*: Austin Colyer. *Peterson*: Reese Burns. *Tackaberry*: Henry Lawrence. *J. B. Biggley*: BILLY DE WOLFE. *Rosemary*: SHEILA SULLIVAN. *Bratt*: ART BARNETT. *Smitty*: PAT McENNIS. *Frump*: LEE GOODMAN. *Miss Jones*: JUSTINE JOHNSTON. *Mr. Twimble*: LOU CUTELL. *Hedy*: BETTY LINTON. *Scrubwomen*: Natasha Grishin, Renee Gorsey. *Miss Krumholtz*: Del Green. *Ovington*: Richard Davis. *Policeman*: Paul Adams. *Womper*: LOU CUTELL.

Singers: Paul Adams, Reese Burns, Austin Colyer, Lang des Jardins, Walter E. Hook, Mickey Karm, Henry Lawrence, Richard Marr, Marie Bradley, Jane Coleman, Jacque Dean, Renee Gorsey, Del Green, Maria Hero, Judy McMurdo. *Dancers*: Doria Avila, Richard Denny, Garold Gardner, Jerry Kent, Stan Mazin, Leo J. Muller, Terry Nicholson, Roger Allan Raby, Nephele Buecher, Patricia Cope, Mickey Gunnersen, Natasha Grishin, Rosie Holotik, Beth Howland, Joan Lindsay, Sharron Miller.

1966.08   THE MOST HAPPY FELLA

A Revival of the Musical in Three Acts, 11 Scenes[29]. Book, music and lyrics by Frank Loesser. Based on the play "They Knew What They Wanted" by Sidney Howard. Stage direction and choreography by Ralph Beaumont. Settings by Jo Mielziner. Costumes by Frank Thompson. Lighting by Peggy Clark (Orchestrations by Don Walker.) Musical direction, Abba Bogin. Produced by the New York City Center Light Opera Company (Jean Dalrymple, Director). Opened 11 May 1966 at the New York City Center and closed 22 May 1966 after 15 performances.

CAST (in order of appearance): *The Cashier*: Lee Cass. *Cleo*: KAREN MORROW. *Rosabella*: BARBARA MEISTER. *Waitresses*: Joanna Crosson, Rita O'Connor, Joy Serio, Susan Sigrist. *The Postman*: Lee Cass. *Tony*: NORMAN ATKINS. *Marie*: FRAN STEVENS. *Max*: Joe McGrath. *Herman*: JACK DE LON. *Clem*: James Hobson. *Jake*: Robert E. Maxwell, Jr. *Al*: John A. Boni. *Joe*: ART LUND. *Giuseppe*: Montes de Oca. *Pasquale*: Will Roy. *Ciccio*: Ed Becker. *The Doctor*: Carl Nicholas. *The Priest*: Dick Ensslen. *Tessie*: Karen Grant. *Gussie*: Jody La Rocco. *Sissy*: Marci Phillips. *Neighbor Ladies*: Joyce Olson, Rosemary McNamara, Rita Metzger. *Brakeman*: Dale Westerman. *Bus Driver*: Doug Hunt.

All the Neighbors, and All the Neighbors' Neighbors: Lillian Bozinoff, Susan Cogan, Jeanne Frey, Marlene Kay, Evelyn Kingsley, Rosemary McNamara, Rita Metzger, Barbara Miller, LaVergne Monette, Joyce Olson, Patti Winston, Gene Albano, John A. Boni, Marvin Goodis, James Hobson, Doug Hunt, Philip Lucas, Stuart Mann, Robert E. Maxwell, Jr., Joe McGrath, George T. McWhorter, Dale Westerman, Wilson Robey, Diane Arnold, Linda Bonem, Connie Burnett, Kay Cole, Joanna Crosson, Judith Dunford, Ina Kurland, Rita O'Connor, Joy Serio, Susan Sigrist, Myrna Strom, Dom Angelo, Frank Coppola, Vito Durante, Jerry Fries, Bob LaCrosse, Teak Lewis, Carlos Macri, Donald Mark, Victor Pieran, Dom Salinar, Marc Scott.

1966.09   A TIME FOR SINGING

A Musical in Two Acts. Book and lyrics by Gerald Freedman and John Morris. Based on the novel "How Green Was My Valley" by Richard Llewellyn. Music by John Morris. Directed by Gerald Freedman. Choreography by Donald McKayle. Production (settings) designed by Ming Cho Lee. Costumes by Theoni V. Aldredge. Lighting by Jean Rosenthal. Musical direction, Jay Blackton. Orchestrations by Don Walker. Production associate, Hildy Parks. Production supervisor, Jerry Adler. Produced by Alexander H. Cohen in association with Joe Wishy. Opened 21 May 1966 at the Broadway Theatre and closed 25 June 1966 after 41 performances.

CAST (in order of appearance): *David Griffith*: IVOR EMMANUEL. *Paymaster*: Jay Gregory. *Dai Bando*: John Call. *Cyfartha Lewis*: George Mathews. *Gwillym Morgan (Dada)*: LAURENCE NAISMITH. *Davey Morgan*: Gene Rupert. *Ivor Morgan*: Brian Aver. *Ianto Morgan*: George Hearn. *Owen Morgan*: Harry Theyard. *Evan Morgan*: Philip Proctor. *Huw Morgan*: Frank Griso. *Beth Morgan*: TESSIE O'SHEA. *Angharad Morgan*: SHANI WALLIS. *Bronwen Jenkins*: Elizabeth Hubbard. *Mr. Evans*: John Malcolm. *Iestyn Evans*: David O'Brien. *School Teacher*: David Thomas.

Singers: Robert Carle, Ed Ericksen, Jay Gregory, Marian Haraldson, Zona Kennedy, Reid Klein, Henry LeClair, Constance Moffit, Jack Murray, Mari Nettum, Joyce O'Neil, Michael Quinn, Maggie Task, Ann Tell, David Thomas, Maggie Worth. *Dancers*: Bruce Becker, Steven Boockvor, Sandra Brewer, Roger Briant, Sterling Clark, Carolyn Dyer, Mary Ehara, Rodney Griffin, Patty Mount, Mimi Wallace. *Children*: Paul Dwyer, Peter Falzone, Dewey Golkin, Laura Michaels, Janice Notaro.

The action takes place in the memory of David Griffith, flowing freely in time in the Valley, the Town and the Morgan Home in South Wales in 1900.

---

[29]Originally produced in New York 3 May 1956 at the Imperial Theatre for 678 performances. For Synopsis of Scenes and Musical Numbers, see original 1956 production.

ACT 1
"Come You Men"
  Male Singing Chorus
"How Green Was My Valley"
  I. Emmanuel, Chorus
"Old Long John"
  Male Singing Chorus
"Here Come Your Men"
  Male Singing Chorus
"What a Good Day Is Saturday"
  T. O'Shea, L. Naismith, S. Wallis, Brothers, Company
"Peace Come to Every Heart"
  Company
"Someone Must Try"
  I. Emmanuel
"Oh, How I Adore Your Name"
  S. Wallis
"That's What Young Ladies Do"
  I. Emmanuel
"When He Looks at Me"
  S. Wallis
"Far From Home"
  T. O'Shea, S. Wallis, L. Naismith, Brothers
"I Wonder If"
  Brothers
"What a Party"
  L. Naismith, I. Emmanuel, G. Mathews, J. Call, Brothers
"Let Me Love You"
  S. Wallis
"Why Would Anyone Want to Get Married?"
  F. Griso, Brothers, T. O'Shea, L. Naismith
"A Time for Singing"
  T. O'Shea, Company

ACT 2
"When the Baby Comes"
  Company
"I'm Always Wrong"
  S. Wallis
"There Is Beautiful You Are"
  I. Emmanuel
"Three Ships"
  T. O'Shea, E. Hubbard, B. Avery, Company
"Tell Her"
  F. Griso, L. Naismith
"There Is Beautiful You Are" (reprise)
  I. Emmanuel
"Let Me Love You" (reprise)
  S. Wallis, I. Emmanuel
"And the Mountains Sing Back"
  I. Emmanuel
"Gone in Sorrow"
  Company
"How Green Was My Valley" (reprise)
  Company

1966.10   MAME

A Musical in Two Acts, 16 Scenes. Book by Jerome Lawrence and Robert E. Lee. Based on the novel "Auntie Mame" by Patrick Dennis and the play of the same name by Lawrence and Lee. Music and lyrics by Jerry Herman. Directed by Gene Saks. Dances and musical numbers staged by Onna White. Settings by William and Jean Eckart. Costumes by Robert Mackintosh. Lighting by Tharon Musser. Musical direction and vocal arrangements by Don Pippin. Orchestrations by Philip J. Lang. Dance music arranged by Roger Adams. Associate producer, John Bowab. Produced by Robert Fryer, Lawrence Carr, Sylvia and Joseph P. Harris. Opened 24 May 1966 at the Winter Garden, moved 7 October 1969 to the Broadway Theatre, and closed 3 January 1970 after 1508 performances.

CAST (in order of appearance): *Patrick Dennis, age 10:* FRANKIE MICHAELS. *Agnes Gooch:* JANE CONNELL. *Vera Charles:* BEATRICE ARTHUR. *Mame Dennis:* ANGELA LANSBURY. *Ralph Devine:* Ronald Young. *Bishop:* Jack Davison. *M. Lindsay Woolsey:* George Coe. *Ito:* Sab Shimono. *Doorman:* Art Matthews. *Elevator Boy:* Stan Page. *Messenger:* Bill Stanton. *Dwight Babcock:* WILLARD WATERMAN. *Art Model:* Jo Tract. *Dance Teacher:* Johanna Douglas. *Leading Man:* Jack Davison. *Stage Manager:* Art Matthews. *Madame Branislowski:* Charlotte Jones. *Gregor:* John Taliaferro. *Beauregard Jackson Pickett Burnside:* CHARLES BRASWELL. *Uncle Jeff:* Clifford Fearl. *Cousin Fan:* Ruth Ramsey. *Sally Cato:* MARGARET HALL. *Mother Burnside:* Charlotte Jones. *Patrick Dennis, age 19-29:* JERRY LANNING. *Junior Babcock:* Tommy Karaty. *Mrs. Upson:* Johanna Douglas. *Mr. Upson:* John C. Becher. *Gloria Upson:* Diana Walker. *Pegeen Ryan:* Diane Coupe. *Peter Dennis:* Michael Maitland.

Mame's Friends: Diana Baffa, Jack Blackton, David Chaney, Pat Cummings, Jack Davison, Hilda Harris, Tommy Karaty, Nicole Karol, Gene Kelton, Nancy Lynch, Art Matthews, Ross Miles, Stan Page, Ruth Ramsey, Betty Rosebrock, Scott Salmon, Bella Shalom, Bill Stanton, John Taliaferro, Jo Tract, Jodi Williams, Kathy Wilson.

Act 1, Scene 1: Somewhere in New York, 1928. *Scene 2:* Mame's Apartment. *Scene 3:* Hallway of Mame's Apartment. *Scene 4:* Mame's Bedroom. *Scene 5:* Mame's Living Room (and all around New York). *Scene 6:* Mame's Apartment. *Scene 7:* Shubert Theatre, New Haven. *Scene 8:* Salon Pour Messieurs. *Scene 9:* Mame's Apartment. *Scene 10:* Peckerwood.

Act 2, Scene 1: Prep School and College (and Singapore). *Scene 2:* Mame's Apartment. *Scene 3:* Mame's Apartment, six months later. *Scene 4:* Upson Farm. *Scene 5:* Mame's Apartment. *Scene 6:* Mame's Apartment, 1946.

ACT 1

Scene 1

"St. Bridget"
F. Michaels, J. Connell

Scene 2

"It's Today"
A. Lansbury, All

Scene 5

"Open a New Window"
A. Lansbury, All

Scene 7

"The Man in the Moon"
B. Arthur, A. Lansbury, All

"My Best Girl"
F. Michaels, A. Lansbury

Scene 9

"We Need a Little Christmas"
A. Lansbury, F. Michaels, J. Connell, S. Shimono, C. Braswell

Scene 10

"The Fox Hunt"
C. Fearl, F. Michaels, R. Ramsey, C. Jones, Cousins

"Mame"
C. Braswell, All

ACT 2

Scene 1

"Mame" (reprise)(The Letter)
F. Michaels, J. Lanning

"My Best Girl" (reprise)
J. Lanning

Scene 2

"Bosom Buddies"
A. Lansbury, B. Arthur

Scene 3

"Gooch's Song"
J. Connell

Scene 4

"That's How Young I Feel"
A. Lansbury, All

"If He Walked into My Life"
A. Lansbury

Scene 5

"It's Today" (reprise)
A. Lansbury, All

"My Best Girl" (reprise)
J. Lanning

Scene 6

"Open a New Window" (reprise)/(Finale)
A. Lansbury, Company

WHERE'S CHARLEY?

1966.11

A Musical Comedy in Two Acts, 9 Scenes[30]. Book by George Abbott. Based on the play "Charley's Aunt" by Brandon Thomas. Music and lyrics by Frank Loesser. Production directed by Christopher Hewett. Choreography by John Sharpe. (Sets uncredited.) Costumes by Frank Thompson. Lighting and additional settings designed by Peggy Clark. Ballet music adapted by Marvin Laird (Orchestrations by Ted Royal, Hans Spialek, Philip J. Lang.) Musical direction by Pembroke Davenport. Produced by the New York City Center Light Opera Company (Jean Dalrymple, Artistic director). Opened 25 May 1966 at the New York City Center and closed 5 June 1966 after 15 performances.

CAST (in order of appearance): *Brassett:* Tom Bate *Professor Fortesque:* Donald Barton. *Jack Chesney:* DAVID SMITH. *Charley Wykeham:* DARRYL HICKMAN. *Kitty Verdun:* KAREN SHEPARD. *Amy Spettigue:* SUSAN WATSON. *Wilkinson:* Emory Bass. *Sir Francis Chesney:* FERDINAND HILT. *Mr. Spettingue:* MORT MARSHALL. *Donna Lucia D'Alvadorez:* ELEANOR STEBER. *Photographer:* Stan Mazin. *Patricia:* Maria Hero. *Reggie:* Austin Colyer. *Photographer's Assistants:* Violetta Landek, Zebra Nevins.

Band Members: Rodd Barry, Dennis Cole, Gordon Cook, Jack Fletcher, Mario Maroze, Doug Spingler. *Dancers:* Rodd Barry, Dennis Cole, Myron Curtis, Richard Denny, Jerry Kent, Don Lawrence, Mario Maroze, Richard Maxon, Stan Mazin, Doug Spingler, Clive Thompson, Cathy Conklin, Mickey Gunnerson, Beth Howland, Violetta Landek, Sara Letton, Sharron Miller, Zebra Nevins, Rande Rayburn, Alice Mary Riley, Skiles Ricketts, Toodie Wittmer. *Singers:* Paul Adams, Austin Colyer, Gordon Cook, Stephen Everett, Jack Fletcher, William James, Konstantin Moskalenko, Hal Norman, Fred Osin, David Wilder, Laverne Burden, Jane Coleman, Renee Gorsey, Maria Hero, Nina Hirschfeld, Miriam Lawrence, Joyce McDonald, Betsy Norden, Mary Ann Rydzeski, Susan Stockwell, Elise Warner.

ANNIE GET YOUR GUN

1966.12

A Revival of the Musical in Two Acts, 8 Scenes[31]. Music and lyrics by Irving Berlin. Book by Herbert and Dorothy Fields. (Book revisions by Dorothy Fields.) Directed by Jack Sydow. Scenery by Paul C. McGuire. Costumes by Frank Thompson. Lighting by Peter Hunt. Dances and production numbers staged by Danny Daniels. Musical director, Franz Alllers. Orchestrations by Robert Russell Bennett. Dance arrangements by Richard De Benedictis. Produced by The Music Theatre of Lincoln Center (Richard Rodgers, President and Producing Director). Opened 31 May 1966 at the New York City Center and closed 9 July 1966 after 47 performances; re-opened 21 September 1966 at the Broadway Theatre and closed 26 November 1966 after 77 additional performances. Total: 124 performances.

CAST (in order of appearance): *Little Boy:* Jeffrey Scott. *Little Girl:* Deanna Melody. *Charlie Davenport:* JERRY ORBACH. *Dolly Tate:* BENAY VENUTA. *Iron Tail:* Brynar Mehl. *Yellow Foot:* Gary Jendell. *Mac (Property Man):* John Dorrin. *Foster Wilson:* Ronn Carroll. *Frank Butler:* BRUCE YARNELL. *Annie Oakley:* ETHEL MERMAN. *Little Jake, Her Brother:* David Manning. *Her Sisters (3): Nellie:* Donna Conforti. *Jessie:* Jeanne Tanzy. *Minnie:* Holly Sherwood. *Col. William F. Cody (Buffalo Bill):* RUFUS SMITH. *Mrs. Little Horse:* Mary Falconer. *Mrs. Black Tooth:* Jaclynn Villamil. *Mrs. Yellow Foot:* Kuniko Narai. *Indian Boy:* Jeffrey Scott. *Conductor:* Jim Lynn. *Porter:* Beno Foster. *Waiter:* David Forssen. *Major Gordon Lillie, Pawnee Bill:* JACK DABDOUB. *Chief Sitting Bull:* HARRY BELAVER. *The Wild Horse, Ceremonial Dancer:* JAIME ROGERS. *Pawnee's Messenger:* Walt Hunter. *Major Domo:* Ben Laney. *Mr. Schuyler Adams:* Ronn Carroll. *Mrs. Schuyler Adams:* Patricia Hall. *Dr. (Percy) Ferguson:* Marc Rowan. *Mrs. (Percy) Ferguson:* Bobbi Baird. *Mr. T. L. C. Keefer:* Walt Hunter. *Mr. Ernest Henderson:* Grant Spradling. *Mrs. Ernest Henderson:* Lynn Carroll. *Mrs. Sylvia Potter-Porter:* Mary Falconer. *Mr. Clay:* John Dorrin.

Singers: Bobbi Baird, Vicki Belmonte, Chrysten Caroll, Lynn Carroll, Audrey Dearden, Lynn Dovel, Mary Falconer, Patricia Hall, Florence Mercer, Susan Terry, Kenny Adams, Ronn Carroll, John Dorrin, David Forssen, Beno Foster, Walt Hunter, Ben Laney, Jim Lynn, Marc Rowan, Grant Spradling. *Dancers:* Diane Banks, Joanne

---

[30]Originally produced in New York 11 October 1948 at the St. James Theatre for 792 performances. For Synopsis of Scenes and Musical Numbers, see original 1948 production.

[31]First produced in New York 16 May 1946 at the Imperial Theatre for 1147 performances. For this revival, "Why Do You Love I Hope" and "I'd Share It All with You" were dropped. For return engagement detail, see entry in the following season.

DiVito, Rozann Ford, Barbara Hancock, Ruth Lawrence, Kuniko Narai, Eva Marie Sage, Evelyn Taylor, Jaclynn Villamil, Anne Wallace, Bjarne Buchtrup, Tony Catanzaro, Frank Derbas, Ronn Forella, Marcelo Gamboa, Jeremy Ives, Gary Jendell, Daniel Joel, Brynar Mehl, Gene Myers.

Act 1, Scene 1: The Wilson House, a summer hotel on the outskirts of Cincinnati, Ohio. July. *Scene 2:* A Pullman Parlor in an Overland Steam train. Six weeks later. *Scene 3:* The Fair Grounds at Minneapolis, Minnesota. A few days later. *Scene 4:* The Arena of the Big Tent. Later that night.

Act 2, Scene 1: The deck of a cattle boat. Eight months later. *Scene 2:* The ballroom of the Hotel Brevoort, (New York City). The next night. *Scene 3:* Aboard a ferry, en route to Governor's Island. Next morning. *Scene 4:* Governor's Island, near the Fort. Immediately following.

ACT 1

Scene 1

"Colonel Buffalo Bill"
J. Orbach, B. Venuta, Ensemble

"I'm a Bad, Bad Man"
B. Yarnell, Girls

"Doin' What Comes Naturally'
E. Merman, Children, R. Carroll

"The Girl That I Marry"
B. Yarnell

"You Can't Get a Man With a Gun"
E. Merman

"There's No Business Like Show Business"
E. Merman, B. Yarnell, R. Smith, J. Orbach

Scene 2

"They Say It's Wonderful"
E. Merman, B. Yarnell

"Moonshine Lullaby"
E. Merman, Trio, Children

Scene 3

"Wild West Pitch Dance"
J. Rogers, Dancers

"There's No Business Like Show Business" (reprise)
E. Merman

"My Defenses Are Down"
B. Yarnell, Boys

Scene 4

"Wild Horse Ceremonial Dance"
J. Rogers, Braves

"I'm an Indian Too"
E. Merman

"Adoption Dance"
E. Merman, J. Rogers, Braves

"You Can't Get a Man With a Gun" (reprise)
E. Merman

ACT 2

Scene 1

"(I Got) Lost in His Arms"
E. Merman, Singers

Scene 2

"There's No Business Like Show Business" (reprise)
B. Yarnell, B. Venuta, J. Dabdoub, R. Carroll, P. Hall

"I Got the Sun in the Morning"
E. Merman, Company

"Old Fashioned Wedding"[32]
E. Merman, B. Yarnell

"The Girl That I Marry" (reprise)
B. Yarnell

Scene 4

"Anything You Can Do"
E. Merman, B. Yarnell

"There's No Business Like Show Business" (reprise)
Ensemble

Finale: "They Say It's Wonderful" (reprise)
Entire Company

---

[32]Newly written for this production.

1966–1967 SEASON

Leslie Uggams in HALLELUJAH, BABY!
Billy Rose Theatre Collection, New York Public Library for the Performing Arts

1966–1967 SEASON

1966.13 GUYS AND DOLLS

A Revival of the Musical Fable (Comedy) in Two Acts, 17 Scenes[1]. Book by Jo Swerling and Abe Burrows. Based on a story and characters by Damon Runyon. Music and lyrics by Frank Loesser. Production directed by Gus Schirmer. Choreography by Ralph Beaumont. Adaptation of Jo Mielziner's original designs by Peter Wolf. Costumes by Frank Thompson. (Orchestral arrangements by George Bassman and Ted Royal.) Musical director, Irving Actman. Associate conductor, Abba Bogin. Produced by the New York City Center Light Opera Company (Jean Dalrymple, Director). Opened 8 June 1966 at the New York City Center and closed 26 June 1966 after 23 performances.

CAST (in order of appearance): *Nicely-Nicely Johnson*: DALE MALONE. *Benny Southstreet*: JOE ROSS. *Rusty Charlie*: Ed Becker. *Sarah Brown*: BARBARA MEISTER. *Arvide Abernathy*: CLARENCE NORDSTROM. *Mission Band*: Jeanne Schlegel, Clarence Nordstrom, Carl Nicholas, Susan Cogan, Jeanne Frey. *Harry the Horse*: TOM PEDI. *Lieut. Brannigan*: FRANK CAMPANELLA. *Nathan Detroit*: JAN MURRAY. *Angie the Ox*: Roger Brown. *Miss Adelaide*: VIVIAN BLAINE. *Sky Masterson*: HUGH O'BRIAN. *Mimi*: Rita O'Connor. *General Matilda B. Cartwright*: CLAIRE WARING. *Big Jule*: B. S. PULLY. *Drunk*: Eddie Phillips. *Waiter*: Marvin Goodis.

Dancers: Diane Arnold, Nephele Buecher, Marilyn D'Honau, Judy Dunford, Mercedes Ellington, Shelly Frankel, Altovise Gore, Rose Holotik, Joan Lindsay, Rita O'Connor, Melissa Stoneburn, Maria Strattin, Gerard Brentte, Frank Coppola, Vito Durante, Philip Filiato, Mark Holliday, Robert La Crosse, Teak Lewis, Carlos Macri, Mitchell Nutick, Paul Owsley, Dom Salinaro, Marc Scott. *Singers*: Susan Cogan, Edward Becker, Roger Brown, Joe Bellomo, Reese Burns, Richard Ensslen, Paul Flores, Marvin Goodis, Joseph Gustern, Mark Howard, Doug Hunt, Robert Maxwell, Sean Walsh.

1966.14 SHOWBOAT

A Revival of the Musical Play in Two Acts, 14 Scenes[2]. Music by Jerome Kern. Book and lyrics by Oscar Hammerstein II. Based on the novel of the same name by Edna Ferber. Directed by Lawrence Kasha. Choreography by Ronald [Ron] Field. Scenic production by Oliver Smith. Costumes by Stanley Simmons. Lighting by Jean Rosenthal. Musical director, Franz Allers. Associate conductor, William [Bill] Brohn. Dance arrangements by Richard De Benedictis. New orchestrations by Robert Russell Bennett. Produced by the Music Theater of Lincoln Center (Richard Rodgers, Producing Director). Opened 19 July 1966 at the New York State Theatre and closed 10 September 1966 after 64 performances.

CAST (in order of their appearance): *Rubberface*: Bob La Crosse. *Captain Andy*: DAVID WAYNE. *Windy (McLain)*: David Thomas. *Joe*: WILLIAM WARFIELD. *Queenie*: ROSETTA LeNOIRE. *Ellie*: ALLYN ANN McLERIE. *Frank*: EDDIE PHILLIPS. *Parthy Ann Hawkes*: MARGARET HAMILTON. *Pete*: Bob Monroe. *Julie*: CONSTANCE TOWERS. *Steve*: WILLIAM TRAYLOR. *Gaylord Ravenal*: STEPHEN DOUGLASS. *(Sheriff Ike) Vallon*: Barton Stone. *Magnolia*: BARBARA COOK. *Backwoodsman*: Neil McNelis. *Jeb*: Jess Green. *First Barker*: George McWhorter. *Strong Woman*: D. Spingler. *Second Barker*: Garrett Morris. *Congress of Beauties*: Emilina Escariz, Rita O'Connor, Nancy Van Rijn, Carol Hanzel. *Third Barker*: Neil McNelis. *Fatima*: Sally Neil. *Landlady*: Helen Noyes. *Ethel*: Joyce McDonald. *Sister*: Frances Haywood. *Mother Superior*: Mary Manchester. *Kim*: Maureen McNabb. *Man With Guitar*: Paul Adams. *Doorman at Trocadero*: Edward Taylor. *Drunk*: John Roberson. *Lottie*: Martha Danielle. *Dolly*: Trudy Wallace. *Sally*: Frances Buffalino. *Maisie*: Judith Keller. *A Girl*: Barbara Lindner. *A Man*: Dale Westerman. *Old Lady on Levee*: Helen Noyes.

Female Dancers: Emilina Escariz, Lois Etelman, Carol Hanzel, Vivian Houston, Eileen Lawlor, Sally Neal, Rita O'Connor, Carol Perea, Nancy Van Rijn. *Male Dancers*: Bryant Baker, Allan Byrns, Peter DeNicola, Ronald Dennis, Bob Hall, Bob

LaCrosse, Donald Mark, Robert St. John, Doug Spingler. *Female Singers*: Phyllis Bash, Frances Buffalino, Jane Coleman, Martha Danielle, Dolores Godwin, Frances Haywood, Ernestine Jackson, Judith Keller, Mary Manchester, Barbara Lindner, Joyce McDonald, Estella Munson, Geraldine Overstreet, Lorice Stevens, Trudy Wallace. *Male Singers*: Paul Adams, Donald Coleman, Ray Duval, Scott Gibson, Jess Green, Vincent Henry, Richard Kahn, James Kelley, James Kennon-Wilson, George McWhorter, Laried Montgomery, Garrett Morris, Garwood Perkisn, John Roberson, Alan Sanderson, Richard Sparks, Edward Taylor, Clyde Walker, Dale Westerman, Joe Williams, Lee Winston. *Children*: Paul Dwyer, Michael Grady, Lisa Huggins, Jeanne Ladomirak, William Sims.

Act 1, Scene 1: The Levee on the Natchez on the Mississippi, in the 1880s. *Scene 2*: Kitchen pantry of the *Cotton Blossom*. Five minutes later. *Scene 3*: Auditorium and Stage of the *Cotton Blossom*. One hour later. *Scene 4*: Box office, on foredeck. Three weeks later. *Scene 5*: Auditorium and stage during the Third Act of "The Parson's Bride," that night. *Scene 6*: Stage door. *Scene 7*: The top deck. Later that night. *Scene 8*: The Levee at Greenville. Next morning.

Act 2, Scene 1: The Midway Plaisance, Chicago World's Fair, 1893. *Scene 2*: A room on Ontario Street, 1904. *Scene 3*: Trocadero Music Hall. A few days later. *Scene 4*: St. Agatha's Convent. About the same time. *Scene 5*: Trocadero Music Hall. Just before midnight, New Year's Eve, 1905. *Scene 6*: The *Cotton Blossom* at the Greenville levee, 1927.

ACT 1[3]

"Cotton Blossom"
  Entire Ensemble
"Show Boat Ballyhoo"
  D. Wayne, Showboat Troupe and Ensemble
"Only Make Believe"
  S. Douglass, B. Cook
"Ol' Man River"
  W. Warfield, Stevedores
"Can't Help Lovin' Dat Man"
  C. Towers, R. LeNoire, B. Cook, W. Warfield, Quartette
"Queenie's Ballyhoo"
  R. Le Noire, D. Wayne, Ensemble
"Life Upon the Wicked Stage"
  A. A. McLerie, Ensemble
"You Are Love"
  B. Cook, S. Douglass
Cakewalk and Finale
  Entire Company

ACT 2

"At the Fair"
  Sightseers, Barkers, Ushers
"Why Do I Love You?"
  B. Cook, S. Douglass, Ensemble
"Bill"
  C. Towers
  (*Lyrics by* P. G. Wodehouse.)
"Can't Help Lovin' Dat Man" (reprise)
  B. Cook
Service and Scene Music-St. Agnes Convent
"Only Make Believe" (reprise)
  S. Douglass
"Goodbye, My Lady Love"—Cakewalk
  E. Phillips, A. A. McLerie
"After the Ball"
  B. Cook
"You Are Love" (reprise)
  S. Douglass
"Ol' Man River" (reprise)
  W. Warfield, Company
  A. A. McLerie, E. Phillips
Finale (Act 2)
  Entire Company

---

[1]First presented in New York 24 November 1950 at the 46th Street Theatre for 1200 performances. For Synopsis of Scenes and Musical Numbers, see original 1950 production. Act 1, Scene 8, now set in San Juan, Puerto Rico, and the accompanying dance now named "San Juan."
[2]First presented December 27, 1927 at the Ziegfeld Theatre for 572 performances.

[3]Added to program for subsequent tour:
  "I Might Fall Back on You" (Act 1 before "Queenie's Ballyhoo")

1966.15   A HAND IS ON THE GATE

A Evening (Revue) of Poetry and Folk Music by American Negroes in Two Acts[4]. Arranged and directed by Roscoe Lee Browne. Music arranged by Bill Lee and Stuart Scharf. Lighting consultant, Jules Fisher. Associate producer, Stephen Aaron. Produced by Ivor David Balding for The Establishment Theatre Company, Inc. (Ivor David Balding, Peter Cook, Joseph E. Levine, with Rita Fredericks). Opened 21 September 1966 at the Longacre Theatre and closed 8 October 1966 after 20 performances.

CAST: LEON BIBB, ROSCOE LEE BROWNE, GLORIA FOSTER, MOSES GUNN, ELLEN HOLLY, JAMES EARL JONES, JOSEPHINE PREMICE, CICELY TYSON. *Musicians:* Stuart Scharf (guitar), Bill Lee (bass), Floyd Williams (percussionist), Sheldon Powell (flutist).

ACT 1

On Liberty and Slavery
(*by* George Moses Horton)
J. E. Jones

The Negro Speaks of Rivers
(*by* Langston Hughes)
E. Holly

Frederick Douglass
(*by* Robert Hayden)
M. Gunn

We Wear the Mask
(*by* Paul Laurence Dunbar)
C. Tyson

Southern Mansion
(*by* Arna Bontemps)
L. Bibb

from The Dark Symphony: Lento Grave
(*by* Melvin Tolson)
J. Premice

from O Black and Unknown Bards
(*by* James Weldon Johnson)
J. E. Jones, G. Foster, R. L. Browne

"'Buked and Scorned" (Traditional)
L. Bibb

From the Dark Tower
(*by* Countee Cullen)
J. E. Jones

An Old Woman Remembers
(*by* Sterling Brown)
G. Foster

My City
(*by* James Weldon Johnson)
M. Gunn

Sonnet to a Negro in Harlem
(*by* Helene Johnson)
J. Premice

Precocious Curiosity
(*by* Gwendolyn Brooks)
C. Tyson

Mother to Son
(*by* Langston Hughes)
E. Holly

Sence You Went Away
(*by* James Weldon Johnson)
G. Foster

Miss Meleree
(*by* John Holloway)
L. Bibb

When Malindy Sings
(*by* Paul Laurence Dunbar)
C. Tyson

"A Negro Love Song"
(*by* Paul Laurence Dunbar)
R. L. Browne

"Jane Jane" (A Children's Playgame)(Traditional)
Ensemble

Ol' Lem
(*by* Sterling Brown)
J. E. Jones, M. Gunn

Runagate Runagate
(*by* Robert Hayden)
G. Foster, J. E. Jones, M. Gunn

Letter from the South
(*by* Robert Hayden)
R. L. Browne

"'Buked and Scorned " (reprise)
L. Bibb

On Neglect
(*by* Roscoe Lee Browne)
E. Holly

After Winter
(*by* Sterling Brown)
M. Gunn

"All Hid" (A Children's Playgame) (Traditional)
Ensemble

"Little Boy, Little Boy" (Traditional)
J. Premice, L. Bibb

For a Lady I Know
(*by* Countee Cullen)
C. Tyson

No Images
(*by* Waring Cuney)
J. E. Jones

Why Try
(*by* Ted Joans)
R. E. Browne

Robert Whitmore
(*by* Frank Marshall Davis)
E. Holly

Epigram
(*by* Armand Lanusse)
J. Premice

Conception
(*by* Waring Cuney)
C. Tyson

Preface to a 20-Volume Suicide Note
(*by* LeRoi Jones)
L. Bibb

"Careless Love"
(*by* W. C. Handy)
J. Premice

Appoggiatura
(*by* Donald Hayes)
M. Gunn

Witch Doctor
(*by* Robert Hayden)
R. L. Browne

You Are a Part of Me
(*by* Frank Yerby)
G. Foster

At Early Morn
(*by* Binga Dismond)
J. E. Jones

"Dink's Song" (Traditional)
J. Premice

ACT 2

Notes for a Movie Script
(*by* M. Carl Holman)
J. E. Jones

"The Ballad of Rudolph Reed"
(*by* Gwendolyn Brooks)
C. Tyson

Four Questions Addressed to His Excellency, The Prime Minister
(*by* James Vaughn)
R. L. Browne

La Vie C'est La Vie
(*by* Jessie Fauset)
E. Holly

---

[4]First presented in New York Off-Broadway 15 August 1966 at the New York Shakespeare Festival in Central Park for 1 performance.

Journey to a Parallel
(*by* Bruce Wright)
M. Gunn
The Elevator Man Adheres to His Form
(*by* Margaret Danner)
J. Premice
Ontogeny Recapitulates
(*by* Roscoe Lee Browne)
J. E. Jones
To a Young Poet
(*by* Myron O'Higgins)
G. Foster
Counterpoint
(*by* Owen Dodson)
L. Bibb
... Meanwhile a Mississippi Mother Burns Bacon and
the Last Quatrain of the Ballad of Emmett Till
(*by* Gwendolyn Brooks)
E. Holly, R. L. Browne
Bound No'th Blues
(*by* Langston Hughes)
G. Foster
Ma Rainey
(*by* Sterling Brown)
J. Premice
Get Up, Blues
(*by* James Emanuel)
C. Tyson
The Rebel
(*by* Mari Evans)
C. Tyson
"Harlem Sweeties"
(*by* Langston Hughes)
L. Bibb, M. Gunn, J. E. Jones, R. L. Browne
from A Street in Bronzeville: Kitchenette
(*by* Gwendolyn Brooks)
J. Premice
Rag Doll and Summer Birds
(*by* Owen Dodson)
E. Holly
Between the World and Me
(*by* Richard Wright)
J. E. Jones
My Angel
(by Jonathan Brooks)
L. Bibb
Look at That Gal
(*by* Julian Bond)
R. L. Browne
"Glory, Glory"
(Traditional)
Ensemble
The Progress
(*by* Gwendolyn Brooks)
M. Gunn
The End of Man Is His Beauty
(*by* LeRoi Jones)
E. Holly
A Moment Please
(*by* Samuel Allen)
J. E. Jones, R. L. Browne
The Distant Drum
(*by* Calvin Hernton)
R. L. Browne
We Have Been Believers
(*by* Margaret Walker)
G. Foster
"Oh Shenandoah"
(Traditional)
L. Bibb
When in Rome
(*by* Mari Evans)
C. Tyson

My Lord, What a Morning
(*by* Waring Cuney)
G. Foster
American Gothic: To Snatch
(*by* Samuel Allen)
J. E. Jones
The Preacher Ruminates
(*by* Gwendolyn Brooks)
J. Premice
Personal
(*by* Gwendolyn Brooks)
R. L. Browne
Alien
(*by* Donald Hayes)
M. Gunn
The Crazy Woman
(*by* Gwendolyn Brooks)
C. Tyson
"If the Birds (Song)"
(*by* Roscoe Lee Browne)
R. L. Browne
"Rocks and Gravel" (Collected by Allan Lomax, arr. by Leon Bibb)
L. Bibb

1966.16

ANNIE GET YOUR GUN

A Return Engagement of the Revival of the Musical in Two Acts, 8 Scenes[5]. Music and lyrics by Irving Berlin. Book by Herbert and Dorothy Fields. (Book revisions by Dorothy Fields.) Directed by Jack Sydow. Scenery by Paul C. McGuire. Costumes by Frank Thompson. Lighting by Peter Hunt. Dances and production numbers staged by Danny Daniels. Musical director, Jonathan Anderson. Orchestrations by Robert Russell Bennett. Dance arrangements by Richard DeBenedictis. Produced by the Music Theatre of Lincoln Center (Richard Rodgers, President and Producing Director). Opened 21 September 1966 at the Broadway Theatre and closed 26 November 1966 after 77 additional performances. Total including first engagement: 124 performances.

CAST (in order of appearance): *Little Boy*: Jeffrey Scott. *Little Girl*: Deanna Melody. *Charlie Davenport*: JIM LYNN. *Dolly Tate*: BENAY VENUTA. *Iron Tail*: Brynar Mehl. *Yellow Foot*: Gary Jendell. *Mac*, Property Man: John Dorrin. *Foster Wilson*: Ronn Carroll. *Frank Butler*: BRUCE YARNELL. *Annie Oakley*: ETHEL MERMAN. *Little Jake*, Her Brother: David Manning. *Her Sisters (3)*: *Nellie*: Donna Conforti. *Jessie*: Jeanne Tanzy. *Minnie*: Holly Sherwood. *Col. William F. Cody (Buffalo Bill)*: RUFUS SMITH. *Mrs. Little Horse*: Mary Falconer. *Mrs. Black Tooth*: Eva Marie Sage. *Mrs. Yellow Foot*: Kuniko Narai. *Indian Boy*: Jeffrey Scott. *Conductor*: Ben Laney. *Porter*: Beno Foster. *Waiter*: David Forssen. *Major Gordon Lillie* (Pawnee Bill): JACK DABDOUB. *Chief Sitting Bull*: HARRY BELAVER. *The Wild Horse* (Ceremonial Dancer): TONY CATANZARO. *Pawnee's Messenger*: Walt Hunter. *Major Domo*: Ben Laney. *Mr. Schuyler Adams*: Ronn Carroll. *Mrs. Schuyler Adams*: Patricia Hall. *Dr. (Percy) Ferguson*: Marc Rowan. *Mrs. (Percy) Ferguson*: Bobbi Baird. *Mr. T. L. C. Keefer*: Walt Hunter. *Mr. Ernest Henderson*: Grant Spradling. *Mrs. Ernest Henderson*: Lynn Carroll. *Mrs. Sylvia Potter-Porter*: Mary Falconer. *Mr. Clay*: John Dorrin. *The Shy Girl*: Diana Banks.

Singers: Bobbi Baird, Chrysten Caroll, Lynn Carroll, Audrey Dearden, Lynn Dovel, Mary Falconer, Patricia Hall, Florence Mercer, Susan Terry, Kenny Adams, Ronn Carroll, John Dorrin, David Forssen, Beno Foster, Walt Hunter, Ben Laney, Jim Lynn, Marc Rowan, Grant Spradling. *Dancers*: Diane Banks, Joanne DiVito, Carolyn Dyer, Rozann Ford, Barbara Hancock, Ruth Lawrence, Kuniko Narai, Eva Marie Sage, Evelyn Taylor, Bjarne Buchtrup, Tony Catanzaro, Frank Derbas, Ronn Forella, Marcelo Gamboa, Jeremy Ives, Gary Jendell, Daniel Joel, Brynar Mehl, Gene Myers.

1966.17

THE CONSUL

A Revival of the Opera (Musical Drama) in Three Acts, 6 Scenes[6]. Libretto and music by Gian-Carlo Menotti. Conductor, Charles Wilson. Settings by Horace Armistead. Staged by Gian-Carlo Menotti. Produced by the New

---

[5]First produced in New York 16 May 1946 at the Imperial Theatre for 1147 performances. This revival previously presented 31 May 1966 at the New York State Theatre for 47 performances. For Synopsis of Scenes and Musical Numbers, see 1966 revival from previous season.
[6]Originally produced in New York 15 March 1950 at the Ethel Barrymore Theatre for 269 performances. For Synopsis of Scenes and Musical Numbers, see original 1950 production.

York City Opera. Opened 6 October 1966 at the New York State Theatre and closed 30 October 1966 after 2 performances in repertory.

CAST: (in order of appearance): *John Sorel*: DAVID CLATWORTHY *Magda Sorel*: PATRICIA NEWAY. *The Mother*: EVELYN SACHS. *Secret Police Agent*: JOSEPH FAIR. *First Plainclothesman*: Philip Erickson. *Second Plainclothesman*: Richard Park. *The Secretary*: BEVERLY EVANS. *Mr. Kofner*: DAVID SMITH. *The Foreign Woman*: JULIA MIGENES. *Anna Gomez*: LaVergne Monette. *Vera Boronel*: Charlotte Povia. *Nika Magadoff* (The Magician): GENE BULLARD. *Assan*: Jack Bittner. *Voice on the Record*: Mabel Mercer.

1966.18 THE APPLE TREE

A Musical in Three Acts. (3 One Act Musicals.) Book by Jerry Bock and Sheldon Harnick. Based on stories by Mark Twain, Frank R. Stockton and Jules Feiffer. Additional book material by Jerome Coopersmith. Music by Jerry Bock. Lyrics by Sheldon Harnick. Entire production directed by Mike Nichols. Additional musical staging by Herbert Ross. Choreography by Lee Theodore. Production (Settings) and costume design by Tony Walton. Lighting by Jean Rosenthal. Orchestrations by Eddie Sauter. Musical direction and vocal arrangements by Elliot Lawrence. Animation film sequence by Richard Williams. Produced by Stuart Ostrow. Opened 18 October 1966 at the Sam S. Shubert Theatre and closed 25 November 1967 after 463 performances.

ACT 1: "The Diary of Adam and Eve"

Based on the short story "The Diary of Adam and Eve" by Mark Twain. The action takes place on Saturday, 1 June in Eden.

CAST: *Adam*: ALAN ALDA. *Eve*: BARBARA HARRIS. *Snake*: LARRY BLYDEN.

MUSICAL NUMBERS
"Here in Eden"
    B. Harris
"Feelings"
    B. Harris
"Eve"
    A. Alda
"Friends"
    B. Harris
"The Apple Tree" (Forbidden Fruit)
    L. Blyden
"Beautiful, Beautiful World"
    A. Alda
"It's a Fish"
    A. Alda
"Go to Sleep, Whatever You Are"
    B. Harris
"What Makes Me Love Him"
    B. Harris

ACT 2: "The Lady or the Tiger?"

Based on the short story "The Lady or the Tiger?" by Frank R. Stockton. The action takes place a long time ago in a semi-barbaric kingdom.

CAST: *Balladeer*: LARRY BLYDEN. *King Arik*: Marc Jordan. *Princess Barbara*: BARBARA HARRIS. *Prisoner*: Jay Norman. *Prisoner's Bride*: Jaclynn Villamil. *Nadjira*: Carmen Alvarez. *Captain Sanjar*: ALAN ALDA. *Guard*: Robert Klein. *King Arik's Court*: Jackie Cronin, Barbara Lang, Mary Louise, Michael Davis, Neil F. Jones.

MUSICAL NUMBERS
"I'll Tell You a Truth"
    L. Blyden
"Make Way"
    King's Court, M. Jordan
"Forbidden Love" (In Gaul)
    B. Harris, A. Alda
"The Apple Tree" (reprise)
    L. Blyden
"I've Got What You Want"
    B. Harris
"Tiger, Tiger"
    B. Harris
"Make Way" (reprise)
    King's Court

"Which Door?"
    A. Alda, B. Harris, M. Jordan, King's Court
"I'll Tell You a Truth" (reprise)
    L. Blyden

ACT 3: "Passionella"

Based on the novella "Passionella" by Jules Feiffer. The action takes place now and here.

CAST: *Narrator*: LARRY BLYDEN. *Ella and Passionella*: BARBARA HARRIS. *Mr. Fallible*: Robert Klein. *Producer*: Marc Jordan. *Flip, the Prince, Charming*: ALAN ALDA. *Subways Riders, El Morocco Patrons, Fans, Flip's Following Movie Set Crew, etc.*: Carmen Alvarez, Jackie Cronin, Michael Davis, Neil F. Jones, Marc Jordan, Robert Klein, Barbara Lang, Mary Louise, Jay Norman, Jaclynn Villamil.

MUSICAL NUMBERS[7]
"Oh, To Be a Movie Star"
    B. Harris
"Gorgeous"
    B. Harris
"(Who, Who, Who, Who) Who Is She?"
    The Company
"Wealth"
    B. Harris
"You Are Not Real"
    A. Alda, Company
"George L."
    B. Harris, A. Alda

1966.19 THE THREEPENNY OPERA

The Stockholm Marionette Theatre of Fantasy Production of the Musical Play in Two Acts[8]. Text and lyrics by Bert Brecht. Music by Kurt Weill. English adaptation by Marc Blitzstein. Directed by Michael Meschke. Puppets, masques and settings by Franciszka Themerson. Lighting design by Jules Fisher. Choreography by Holger Rosenquist. Produced by Jay K. Hoffman. Opened 27 October 1966 at the Billy Rose Theatre and closed 6 November 1966 after 13 performances.

CAST (in order of *character, puppet player, spoken voice, singing voice*): *A Street Singer, Filch*: Arne Hogsander, Hakan Serner, Gerald Price. *Mr. J. J. Peachum*: Ulf Hakan Jansson, Ingvar Kjellson, Martin Wolfson. *Mrs. Peachum*: Zanza Lidurns, Ulla Sjoblom, Charlotte Rae. *Polly Peachum*: Ellika Linden, Helena Brodin, Jo Sullivan. *Macheath (Mack the Knife)*: Per Nielsen, Goran Graffman, Scott Merrill. *Jenny*: Ellika Linden, Ulla Sjoblom, Lotte Lenya. *Tiger Brown, Commissioner of Police*: Arne Hogsander, Jan Blomberg, George Tyne. *Lucy Brown*: Lydia de Lind van Wijngaarden, Meta Velander, Beatrice Arthur. *Mack's Gang (Matt, Jake, Boba, Walt)*: Jan Blomberg/Heinz Spira/Folke Tragardh/Michael Meschke. *Reverend Kimball, Constable Smith, Whores, Beggars, A Crowd, A Horse*: The Company. (*Additional Voices on Recording*): John Astin, Joseph Beruh, Bernard Bogin, Paul Dooley, William Duell.)

MUSICAL NUMBERS (from recording[9])
Prologue
    G. Price
"The Ballad of Mack the Knife"
    G. Price
"Morning Anthem"
    M. Wolfson
"Instead-Of Song"
    M. Wolfson, C. Rae
"Army Song"
    S. Merrill, G. Tyne, P. Astin, J. Beruh, B. Bogin, P. Dooley

---

[7]Added shortly after opening:
    "I Know" (Act 3 before "Wealth")
        B. Harris, Company
[8]The performance was accompanied by the MGM recording of the 1954 Theatre de Lys production for musical numbers. This version previously staged in New York with live actors Off-Broadway 10 March 1954 at the Theatre de Lys for 96 performances; returned 30 September 1955 to the Theater de Lys for an additional 2611 performances.
[9]Reviewers remarked that some musical numbers were truncated, edited or dropped.

"Wedding Song"
J. Astin, J. Beruh, B. Bogin, P. Dooley
"Love Song"
S. Merrill, J. Sullivan
"Ballad of Dependency"
C. Rae
First Threepenny Finale: "The World Is Mean"
J. Sullivan, M. Wolfson, C. Rae
Melodrama and "Polly's Song"
S. Merrill, J. Sullivan
"Pirate Jenny"
L. Lenya
"Tango-Ballad"
L. Lenya, S. Merrill
"Ballad of the Easy Life"
S. Merrill
"Barbara Song"
B. Arthur
"Jealousy Duet"
J. Sullivan, B. Arthur
Second Threepenny Finale: "How to Survive"
S. Merrill, C. Rae, Ensemble
"Useless Song"
M. Wolfson
"Solomon Song"
L. Lenya
"Call from the Grave"
S. Merrill
"Death Message"
S. Merrill
Third Threepenny Finale: "The Mounted Messenger"
W. Duell, Ensemble

1966.20 GILBERT BECAUD ON BROADWAY

A One-Man Show in Two Acts. All music composed by Gilbert Becaud. Scenery and lighting by Ralph Alswang. Musical director, Raymond Bernard. Production coordinator, Jean Silly. Produced by Norman Twain. Opened 31 October 1966 at the Longacre Theatre and closed 20 November 1966 after 19 performances.

CAST: GILBERT BECAUD.

ACT 1
"Je t'attends"
"Viens dans la lumière"
"Les jours meilleurs"
"C'était mon copain"
"Age tendre et têtes de bois"
"Le bateau blanc"
"Rosy and John"
"Forever"
"Quand il est mort le poete"
"T'es venu de loin"
"Le pianiste de varsowie"
"La corrida"

ACT 2
"Alors raconte"
"Mon arbre"
"Mademoiselle Lise"
"Sand and Sea"
"L'oiseau de toutes les couleurs"
"The Other Tree"
"L'orange"
"Nathalie"
"Le jour ou la pluie viendra"

"Et maintenant"
"La ballade des baladins"

1966.21 LET'S SING YIDDISH

A Musical Show in Two Acts, in Yiddish. Based on Yiddish folklore, humor and art songs by Itzik Manger, Mordecai Gebirtig, Moris Rosenfeld, M. Nudelman, and Wolf Younin. Directed by Mina Bern. Assistant director and choreographer, Felix Fibich. Music arranged and conducted by Renee Solomon. Literary supervision by Wolf Younin. Production supervisor, Bernard Sauer. "Once Upon a Shtetl" envisioned by Sylvia Younin and Naomi Hoffman. Produced by Ben Bonus. Opened 9 November 1966 at the Brooks Atkinson Theatre and closed 29 January 1967 after 107 performances.

CAST (in order of appearance): Girl: SUSAN WALTERS. Shadchen: MAX BOZYK. Neighbor: ROSE BOZYK. Minstrel: MINA BERN. Organ Grinder: SMULIK GOLDSTEIN. Drummer: BERNARD SAUER. Yosi-Ber: BEN BONUS. Dancers: Donna Shadden, James May, Martha Pollak, Tamara Woshak, Tony Masullo, Dan Taylor. Shaindele: SUSAN WALTERS. Mother: ROSE BOZYK. Boarders (3): Baile: MINA BERN. Berl: MAX BOZYK. Actor: BEN BONUS.

Act 1: A European shtetl (little town) before the two World Wars.

Act 2: In America.

ACT 1: "Once Upon a Shtetl"
Shadchen Dance and Wedding Dance
Dance Ensemble
Let's Sing Yiddish (Hassidic Melodies)
B. Bonus, Entire Ensemble
("Amul in a Shtetl;" "Oifn Gonickle;" "Hoifzinger;" "Yussel Baer;" "Odesser Motiven;" "Shaindeleh;" "Nigun.")
ACT 2
"Castle Garden" (Leben Zul Colombus)
S. Walters, B. Sauer, M. Bern, S. Goldstein
"Life in the Shop" (Machinen)
B. Bonus, F. Dancers, M. Bern, S. Walters, B. Sauer, S. Goldstein, H. Rosen
"On the Subway" (Klain Yingeleh)
M. Bozyk, R. Bozyk
"Encounter in the Park"
M. Bozyk, R. Bozyk
"Wishful Thinking" (Shnyderisher Gezong)
M. Bern, B. Bonus
"American in Israel"
M. Bern, B. Sauer, Entire Ensemble
"Let's Sing Yiddish" (Lo'Mir Zingen Yiddish)
B. Bonus, Entire Ensemble
(Ami Gilad, accordianist)

1966.22 THE PIRATES OF PENZANCE, or The Slave of Duty

A Revival of the Comic Opera in Two Acts[10]. Libretto by William S. Gilbert. Music by Arthur Sullivan. Settings designed by Peter Goffin. Director of productions, Herbert Newby. Musical director, Isidore Godfrey. Associate conductor and chorus master, James Walker. Produced by the D'Oyly Carte Opera Trust, Ltd. under the personal supervision of Bridget D'Oyly Carte and under the management of Sol Hurok. Opened 15 November 1966 at the New York City Center and closed 11 December 1966 after 7 performances in repertory.[11]

CAST: Major General Stanley: JOHN REED. The Pirate King: DONALD ADAMS. Samuel, his Lieutenant: Anthony Raffell. Frederic, the Pirate Apprentice: PHILIP POTTER. Sergeant of Police: GEORGE COOK. Mabel, Edith Kate, Isabel, General Stanley's Daughters: VALERIE MASTERSON, PEGGY ANN JONES, PAULINE WALES, Jennifer Marks. Ruth, Pirate Maid-of-all-work: CHRISTENE PALMER.
Chorus of Pirates, Police and General Stanley's Daughters: Glyn Adams, John Banks, George Cook, Neville Grave, John Hugill, Thomas Lawlor, Peter Lodwick, Gordon Mackenzie, Ralph Mason, Alfred Oldridge, Clifford Parkes, Anthony Raffell, David Rayson, John Webley, Howard Williamson, Adrienne de Winters, Katherine Dyson,

---

[10]First presented in New York 31 December 1879 at the Fifth Avenue Theatre for a total of 91 performances in two engagements. For Synopsis of Scenes and Musical Numbers, see original 1879 production.
[11]Costumes uncredited.

Mercia Glossop, Abby Hadfield, Beti Lloyd-Jones, Susan Maisey, Jennifer Marks, Marian Martin, Norma Millar, Alison Parker, Abigail Ryan, Vera Ryan, Anne Sessions, Anna Vincent, Pauline Wales.

THE MIKADO,
1966.23   or The Town of Titipu

A Revival of the Comic Opera in Two Acts[12]. Libretto by William S. Gilbert. Music by Arthur Sullivan. Production directed by Anthony Besch. Costumes designed by Charles Ricketts; Nanki-Poo Act 1 Costume designed by Disley Jones. Settings designed by Peter Goffin. Director of productions, Herbert Newby. Musical director, Isidore Godfrey. Associate conductor and chorus master, James Walker. Produced by the D'Oyly Carte Opera Trust, Ltd. under the personal supervision of Bridget D'Oyly Carte and under the management of Sol Hurok. Opened 17 November 1966 at the New York City Center and closed 7 December 1966 after 9 performances in repertory.

CAST: *The Mikado of Japan*: DONALD ADAMS. *Nanki-Poo*, his son, disguised as a wandering minstrel in love with Yum-Yum: PHILIP POTTER. *Ko-Ko*, Lord High Executioner of Titipu: JOHN REED. *Pooh-Bah*, Lord High Everything Else: KENNETH SANDFORD. *Pish-Tush, Go-To, Noble Lords*: Thomas Lawlor, George Cook. *Yum-Yum, Pitti-Sing, Peep-Bo*, three sisters, wards of Ko-Ko: VALERIE MASTERSON, PEGGY ANN JONES, PAULINE WALES. *Katisha*: CHRISTENE PALMER. *Chorus of School Girls, Nobles, Guards and Coolies*: same as THE PIRATES OF PENZANCE above.

CABARET
1966.24

A Musical in Two Acts, 19 Scenes. Book by Joe Masteroff. Based on the play ("I Am a Camera") by John Van Druten and stories ("The Berlin Stories") by Christopher Isherwood. Music by John Kander. Lyrics by Fred Ebb. Directed by Harold Prince. Dances and cabaret numbers by Ronald [Ron] Field. Scenery by Boris Aronson. Costumes by Patricia Zipprodt. Lighting by Boris Aronson. Musical direction by Harold Hastings. Orchestrations by Don Walker. Dance arrangements by David Baker. Produced by Harold Prince in association with Ruth Mitchell. Opened 20 November 1966 at the Broadhurst Theatre, moved 7 March 1967 to the Imperial Theatre, moved 7 October 1968 to the Broadway Theatre, and closed 6 September 1969 after 1166 performances.

CAST (in order of appearance): *Master of Ceremonies*: JOEL GREY. *Clifford Bradshaw*: BERT CONVY. *Ernst Ludwig*: EDWARD WINTER. *Custom Official*: Howard Kahl. *Fraulein Schneider*: LOTTE LENYA. *Herr Schultz*: JACK GILFORD. *Fraulein Kost*: PEG MURRAY. *Telephone Girl*: Tresha Kelly. *Kit Kat Club Kittens*: Maryann Burns, Janice Mink, Nancy Powers, Viola Smith. *Maitre D'*: Frank Bouley. *Max*: John Herbert. *Bartender*: Ray Baron. *Sally Bowles*: JILL HAWORTH. *Two Ladies*: Mary Ehara, Rita O'Connor. *German Sailors*: Bruce Becker, Steven Boockvor, Roger Briant, Edward Nolfi. *Frau Wendel*: Mara Landi. *Herr Wendel*: Eugene Morgan. *Frau Kruger*: Miriam Lehmann-Haupt. *Herr Erdmann*: Sol Frieder. *Kit Kat Girls (6)*: *Maria*: Pat Gosling. *Lulu*: Lynn Winn. *Rosie*: Bonnie Walker. *Fritzie*: Marianne Selbert. *Texas*: Kathie Dalton. *Frenchie*: Barbara Alston. *Bobby*: Jere Admire. *Victor*: Bert Michaels. *Greta*: Jayme Mylroie. *Felix*: Robert Sharp.

The action takes place in Berlin, Germany in 1929-1930 before the start of the Third Reich.

Act 1, Scene 1: The Kit Kat Klub. *Scene 2*: Aboard a European railway train. *Scene 3*: Fraulein Schneider's flat. *Scene 4*: The Kit Kat Klub. New Year's Eve, 1930. *Scene 5*: Cliff's room. *Scene 6*: The Kit Kat Klub. *Scene 7*: Fraulein Schneider's living room. *Scene 8*: The Kit Kat Klub. *Scene 9*: Cliff's room. *Scene 10*: The Kit Kat Klub. *Scene 11*: Fraulein Schneider's living room and Kraulein Kost's room. *Scene 12*: Herr Schultz's fruit shop.

Act 2, Scene 1: The Kit Kat Klub. *Scene 2*: Herr Schultz's shop. *Scene 3*: The Kit Kat Klub. *Scene 4*: Cliff's room. *Scene 5*: The Kit Kat Klub. *Scene 6*: Cliff's room. *Scene 7*: A Railroad compartment, then The Kit Kat Klub.

ACT 1
Scene 1
   "Wilkommen"
      J. Grey, Company

Scene 3
   "So What?"
      L. Lenya
Scene 4
   "Don't Tell Mama"
      J. Haworth, Girls
   "Telephone Song"
      Company
Scene 5
   "Perfectly Marvelous"
      B. Convy, J. Haworth
Scene 6
   "Two Ladies"
      J. Grey, M. Ehara, R. O'Connor
Scene 7
   "It Couldn't Please Me More"
      L. Lenya, J. Gilford
Scene 8
   "Tomorrow Belongs to Me"
      J. Grey, Waiters
Scene 9
   "Why Should I Wake Up?"
      B. Convy, J. Haworth
Scene 10
   "The Money Song" (Money)
      J. Grey, Cabaret Girls
Scene 11
   "Married"
      L. Lenya, J. Gilford
Scene 12
   "Meeskite"
      J. Gilford
   "Tomorrow Belongs to Me" (reprise)
      P. Murray, E. Winter, Guests

ACT 2
Scene 1
   "If You Could See Her"
      J. Grey, Girls
Scene 2
   "Married" (reprise)
      L. Lenya, J. Gilford
Scene 3
   "If You Could See Her" (reprise)
      J. Grey, J. Admire
Scene 4
   "What Would You Do?"
      L. Lenya
Scene 5
   "Cabaret"
      J. Haworth
Scene 7
   Finale
      B. Convy, J. Haworth, L. Lenya, J. Gilford, J. Grey, Company

RUDDIGORE,
1966.25   or The Witch's Curse

A Revival of the Comic Opera in Two Acts[13]. Libretto by William S. Gilbert. Music by Arthur Sullivan. Costumes and settings by Peter Goffin. Musical director, Isidore Godfrey. Associate conductor and chorus master, James Walker. Produced by the D'Oyly Carte Opera Trust, Ltd. under the personal supervision of Bridget D'Oyly Carte and under the management of Sol

---

[12]First presented in New York 20 July, 10-29 August 1885 at the Union Square and People's Theatres for 22 performances. First authorized production presented 19 August 1885 at the Fifth Avenue Theatre by Richard D'Oyly Carte for 250 performances. For Synopsis of Scenes and Musical Numbers, see 19 August 1885 D'Oyly Carte production.

[13]First presented in New York 21 February 1887 at the Standard Theatre for 53 performances. For Synopsis of Scenes and Musical Numbers, see original 1887 production.

Hurok. Opened 22 November 1966 at the New York City Center and closed 9 December 1966 after 4 performances.

CAST: *Sir Ruthven Murgatroyd*: JOHN REED. *Richard Dauntless*: DAVID PALMER. *Sir Despard Murgatroyd*: KENNETH SANDFORD. *Old Adam Goodheart*: George Cook. *Sir Roderic Murgatroyd*: DONALD ADAMS. *Rose Maybud*: ANN HOOD. *Mad Margaret*: PEGGY ANN JONES. *Dame Hannah*: CHRISTENE PALMER. *Zorah*: Jennifer Marks. *Ruth*: Pauline Wales. *Chorus of Officers, Ancestors, Professional Bridesmaids, etc.*: same as THE PIRATES OF PENZANCE above.

H.M.S. PINAFORE,
1966.26   or The Lass That Loved a Sailor

A Revival of the Comic Opera in Two Acts[14]. Libretto by William S. Gilbert. Music by Arthur Sullivan. Settings designed by Peter Goffin. Little Buttercup costume designed by Anne and Janet Grahame-Johnstone. Director of productions, Herbert Newby. Musical director, Isidore Godfrey. Associate conductor and chorus master, James Walker. Produced by the D'Oyly Carte Opera Trust, Ltd. under the personal supervision of Bridget D'Oyly Carte and under the management of Sol Hurok. Opened 23 November 1966 at the New York City Center and closed 10 December 1966 after 8 performances in repertory.

CAST: *The Rt. Hon. Sir Joseph Porter, K.C.B., First Lord of the Admiralty*: JOHN REED. *Captain Corcoran, Commanding the H.M.S. Pinafore*: THOMAS LAWLOR. *Ralph Rackstraw, Able Seaman*: DAVID PALMER. *Dick Deadeye, Able Seaman*: DONALD ADAMS. *Bill Bobstay, Bo'sun's Mate*: George Cook. *Bob Beckett, Carpenter's Mate*: Anthony Raffell. *Josephine, the Captain's Daughter*: ANN HOOD. *Hebe, Sir Joseph's First Cousin*: Pauline Wales. *Little Buttercup, a Portsmouth Bumboat Woman*: CHRISTENE PALMER. *First Lord's Sisters, his Cousins, his Aunts, Sailors, Marines*: same as THE PIRATES OF PENZANCE above.

WALKING HAPPY
1966.27

A Musical in Two Acts, 17 Scenes. Book by Roger O. Hirson and Ketti Frings. Based on the play "Hobson's Choice" by Harold Brighouse. Music by James Van Heusen. Lyrics by Sammy Cahn. Scenery and lighting by Robert Randolph. Costumes by Robert Fletcher. Musical direction and vocal arrangements by Herbert Grossman. Orchestrations by Larry Wilcox. Dance music arranged by Ed Scott. Dances and musical numbers staged by Danny Daniels. Directed by Cy Feuer. Produced by Cy Feuer and Ernest H. Martin by arrangement with Lester Linsk. Opened 26 November 1966 at the Lunt-Fontanne Theatre and closed 16 April 1967 after 161 performances.

CAST (in order of appearance): *Henry Horatio Hobson*: GEORGE ROSE. *George Beenstock*: Ed Bakey. *Minns*: Thomas Boyd. *Denton*: Casper Roos. *Tudsbury*: Carl Nicholas. *Heeler*: Michael Quinn. *Maggie Hobson*: LOUISE TROY. *Alice Hobson*: Sharon Dierking. *Vickie Hobson*: Gretchen Van Aken. *Albert Beenstock*: James B. Spann. *Freddie Beenstock*: Michael Berkson. *Mrs. Hepworth*: Emma Trekman. *Footman*: Steven Jacobs. *Tubby Wadlow*: Gordon Dilworth. *Will Mossop*: NORMAN WISDOM. *Ada Figgins*: Jane Laughlin. *Mrs. Figgins*: Lucille Benson. *The Figgins Brothers*: Ian Garry, Al Lanti. *Customer*: Eleanor Bergquist. *Handbill Boy*: Richard Sederholm. *Thief*: Burt Bier. *Policeman*: Chad Block. *Beggar*: Richard Korthaze.

Townsmen: Burt Bier, Chad Block, Thomas Boyd, Ian Garry, Gene Gavin, Steven Jacobs, Richard Korthaze, Al Lanti, Carl Nicholas, Don Percassi, Michael Quinn, Casper Roos, Richard Sederholm, Dan Siretta. Townswomen: Eleanor Bergquist, Diane L. Blair, Sandra Brewer, Ellen Graff, Marian Haraldson, Jane Laughlin, Marie Patrice O'Neill, Nada Rowland, Anne Wallace.

The action takes place in Salford, an industrial town in Lancashire, England, in 1880.

Act 1, Scene 1: The Moonrakers Pub. Night. *Scene 2*: Hobson's Bootery. *Scene 3*: The Cellar of the Bootery. *Scene 4*: The Moonrakers Pub. *Scene 5*: The Park. *Scene 6*: A Street in the poor section of Salford. *Scene 7*: An Alley lit by gaslight. Evening of the same day. *Scene 8*: The Bootery.

Act 2, Scene 1: Mrs. Hepworth's Sitting Room. *Scene 2*: A Cellar. *Scene 3*: Flat Iron Market. *Scene 4*: Will and Maggie's Cellar. *Scene 5*: Outside Moonrakers Pub. Three weeks later. *Scene 6*: Outside Beenstock's Corn Warehouse. *Scene 7*: Hobson's Bootery. *Scene 8*: Inside Beenstock's Corn Warehouse. *Scene 9*: The Mossop Bootery.

ACT 1
Scene 1
  "Think of Something Else"
    G. Rose, E. Bakey, Townsmen
Scene 2
  "Where Was I?"
    L. Troy
Scene 3
  "How D'ya Talk to a Girl?"
    N. Wisdom, G. Dilworth
Scene 4
  "Clog and Grog" (dance)
    Townsmen
Scene 5
  "If I Be Your Best Chance"
    N. Wisdom
Scene 6
  "A Joyful Thing" (dance)
    N. Wisdom, L. Benson, J. Laughlin, Townspeople
Scene 7
  "What Makes It Happen?"
    N. Wisdom
Scene 8
  "Use Your Noggin"
    L. Troy, G. Van Aken, S. Dierking
ACT 2
Scene 1
  "You're Right, You're Right"[15]
    L. Troy
  "I'll Make a Man of the Man"
    L. Troy
Scenes 2 and 3
  "Walking Happy"
    N. Wisdom, L. Troy, Townspeople
Scene 4
  "I Don't Think I'm in Love"
    N. Wisdom, L. Troy
Scenes 5 and 6
  "Such a Sociable Sort"
    G. Rose, Friends
Scene 7
  "It Might As Well Be Her"
    N. Wsdom, G. Dilworth
Scene 8
  "People Who Are Nice"[16]
    G. Rose
Scene 9
  "You're Right, You're Right" (reprise)
    N. Wisdom, L. Troy, G. Rose
  "I Don't Think I'm in Love" (reprise)
    N. Wisdom

PATIENCE,
1966.28   or Bunthorne's Bride

A Revival of the Comic Opera in Two Acts[17]. Libretto by William S. Gilbert. Music by Arthur Sullivan. Directed and designed by Peter Goffin. Director of productions, Herbert Newby. Musical director, Isidore Godfrey. Associate conductor and chorus master, James Walker. Produced by the D'Oyly Carte

[14]Originally presented in New York 15 January 1879 at the Standard Theatre for 175 performances. For Synopsis of Scenes and Musical Numbers, see original 1879 production.

[15]Dropped during the run.
[16]Dropped during the run.
[17]First presented in New York 22 September 1881 at the Standard Theatre for 177 performances. For Synopsis of Scenes and Musical Numbers, see original 1881 production.

Opera Trust, Ltd. under the personal supervision of Bridget D'Oyly Carte and under the management of Sol Hurok. Opened 29 November 1966 at the New York City Center and closed 11 December 1966 after 4 performances.

CAST: *Colonel Calverley*: DONALD ADAMS. *Major Murgatroyd*: Alfred Oldridge. *Lieut. the Duke of Dunstable*: PHILIP POTTER. *Reginald Bunthorne, a Fleshly Poet*: JOHN REED. *Archibald Grosvenor, an Idyllic Poet*: KENNETH SANDFORD. *Mr. Bunsthorne's Solicitor*: James Marsland. *The Lady Angela, The Lady Saphir, The Lady Ella, The Lady Jane, Rapturous Maidens*: PEGGY ANN JONES, PAULINE WALES, Jennifer Marks, CHRISTENE PALMER. *Patience, a Dairy Maid*: ANN HOOD. *Chorus of Rapturous Maifdens and Officers of the Dragoon Guards*: same as THE PIRATES OF PENZANCE above.

1966.29 I DO! I DO!

A Musical in Two Acts. Book and lyrics by Tom Jones. Based on the play "The Fourposter" by Jan de Hartog. Music by Harvey Schmidt. Directed by Gower Champion. Scenic production by Oliver Smith. Costumes by Freddy Wittop. Lighting by Jean Rosenthal. Musical direction, John Lesko. Orchestrations by Philip J. Lang. Assistant to the director (Production supervisor), Lucia Victor. A David Merrick and Champion-Six Inc. Production. Produced by David Merrick. Opened 5 December 1966 at the 46th Street Theatre and closed 15 June 1968 after 561 performances.

CAST: *She (Agnes)*: MARY MARTIN. *He (Michael)*: ROBERT PRESTON.
At the two pianos: Woody Kessler, Albert Mello.

The action takes place in a bedroom, and covers fifty years of a marriage, beginning just before the turn of the century.

ACT 1
Prologue:
"All the Dearly Beloved"
"Together Forever"
"I Do! I Do!"
 M. Martin, R. Preston
"Good Night"
 M. Martin, R. Preston
"I Love My Wife"
 R. Preston
"Something Has Happened"
 M. Martin
"My Cup Runneth Over"
 M. Martin, R. Preston
"Love Isn't Everything"
 M. Martin, R. Preston
"Nobody's Perfect"
 M. Martin, R. Preston
"A Well Known Fact"
 R. Preston
"Flaming Agnes"
 M. Martin
"The Honeymoon Is Over"
 M. Martin, R. Preston

ACT 2
"Where Are the Snows?"
 M. Martin, R. Preston
"When the Kids Get Married"
 M. Martin, R. Preston
Another Wedding:
"The Father of the Bride"
 R. Preston
"What Is a Woman?"
 M. Martin
"Someone Needs Me"
 M. Martin
"Roll Up the Ribbons"
 M. Martin, R. Preston
"This House"
 M. Martin, R. Preston

1966.30 A JOYFUL NOISE

A Musical in Two Acts, 12 Scenes. Book by Edward Padula. Based on the novel "The Insolent Breed" by Borden Deal. Music and lyrics by Oscar Brand and Paul Nassau. Directed by Edward Padula. Settings and lighting by Peter Wexler. Costumes by Peter Joseph. Musical direction by Rene Weigert. Orchestrations and vocal arrangements by William Stegmeyer. Dance music by Lee Holdridge. Dances and musical numbers staged by Michael Bennett. Assistant choreographers, Leland Palmer, Jo Jo Smith. Production supervisor, Jeb Schary. Produced by Edward Padula and Slade Brown in association with Sid Bernstein. Opened 15 December 1966 at the Mark Hellinger Theatre and closed 24 December 1966 after 12 performances.

CAST (in order of appearance): *Shade Motley*: JOHN RAITT. *Brother Locke*: CLIFFORD DAVID. *Walter Wishenant*: GEORGE MATHEWS. *Jenny Lee*: SUSAN WATSON. *Sam Fredrickson*: ART WALLACE. *Miss Jimmie*: LELAND PALMER. *Saw Mill Boys and THE MOTLEY CREW (5)*: *DeWitt*: Eric Weissberg. *Freddy*: Martin Ambrose. *Jaybird*: Charles Morley. *Oscar*: Oatis Stephens. *Tommy*: Tommy Tune. *Bliss Stanley*: SWEN SWENSON. *Stage Manager*: Jack Fletcher. *Director*: Ken Ayers. *Mary Texas*: KAREN MORROW. *Boys*: Paul Charles, Scott Pearson, Alan Peterson, Barry Preston. *Announcer*: Jack Metté. *Bailey*: Jo Jo Smith. *John Tom*: Shawn Campbell.
 Townspeople and City People: *Singers*: Veronica McCormick, Jessica Quinn, Diane Tarleton, Linda Theil, Jamie Thomas, Ken Ayers, Jack Fletcher, Stuart Mann, Eric Mason, Jack Metté, Darrell Sandeen. *Dancers*: Christine Bocchino, Susan Donovan, Baayork Lee, April Nevins, Diane Phillips, Joy Serio, Melissa Stoneburn, Carol Lynn Vazquez, Bonnie Ano, Paul Charles, Winston DeWitt Hemsley, Scott Pearson, Alan Peterson, Barry Preston, Steven Ross, Jo Jo Smith, Tommy Tune.

The action takes place yesterday and today in Macedonia and Nashville, Tennessee.

Act 1, Scene 1: A Clearing in the Hills. *Scene 2*: The Town Square. *Scene 3*: A Clearing. *Scene 4*: The Saw Mill. *Scene 5*: The Field. *Scene 6*: The Top of the Valley.

Act 2, Scene 1: Backstage, Nashville. *Scene 2*: A Clearing in Macedonia. *Scene 3*: The Grand Ole Opry. *Scene 4*: The Recording Studio. *Scene 5*: The State Fair. *Scene 6*: The Town Square.

ACT 1
"Long Time Travelin'"
 J. Raitt
"A Joyful Noise"
 J. Raitt, Townspeople
"I'm Ready"
 S. Watson, L. Palmer, Girls
"Spring Time of the Year"
 J. Raitt
"I Like to Look My Best"
 J. Raitt, A. Wallace, The Saw Mill Boys
"No Talent"
 S. Swenson
"Not Me"
 S. Watson, L. Palmer
"Until Today"
 J. Raitt, S. Watson
"Swinging a Dance"
 J. Raitt, Company
"To the Top"
 S. Swenson, J. Raitt

ACT 2
"I Love Nashville"
 K. Morrow, Boys
"Whither Thou Goest"
 C. David
"We Won't Forget to Write"
 L. Palmer, A. Wallace, The Saw Mill Boys
Grand Ole Opry:
"Ballad Maker"
 J. Raitt, K. Morrow, The Motley Crew, Ensemble
"Barefoot Gal"
 K. Morrow
"Clog Dance"
 Dance Ensemble
"Fool's Gold"
 J. Raitt, K. Morrow, The Motley Crew, Ensemble

"The Big Guitar"
S. Swenson
"Love Was"
S. Watson
"I Say Yes"
J. Raitt, The Motley Crew, Ensemble
"Lord, You Sure Knew How to Make a New Day"
J. Raitt
"A Joyful Noise" (reprise)
J. Raitt, Townspeople

1966.31 CAROUSEL

A Revival of the Musical Play in Two Acts, 9 Scenes[18]. Based on Ferenc Molnar's play "Liliom" as adapted by Benjamin F. Glazer. Music by Richard Rodgers. Book and lyrics by Oscar Hammerstein II. Original production directed by Rouben Mamoulian. Directed by Gus Schirmer. Choreography by Agnes de Mille, restaged by Gemze deLappe. Settings by Paul C. McGuire. Costumes by Stanley Simmons. Lighting by Feder. Musical director, Jonathan Anderson. (Orchestrations by Don Walker.) Produced by the New York City Center Light Opera Company (Jean Dalrymple, Director). Opened 15 December 1966 at the New York City Center and closed 1 January 1967 after 22 performances.

CAST (in order of appearance): *Carrie Pipperidge*: NANCY DUSSAULT. *Julie Jordan*: CONSTANCE TOWERS. *Mrs. Mullin*: Louise Larabee. *Billy Bigelow*: BRUCE YARNELL. *First Policeman*: Paul Adams. *David Bascombe*: Alexander Clark. *Nettie Fowler*: PATRICIA NEWAY. *Enoch Snow*: JACK DE LON. *Jigger Craigin*: MICHAEL KERMOYAN. *Hannah*: Jenny Workman. *Boatswain*: Darrell Notara. *Second Policeman*: Gene Albano. *Captain*: William R. Miller. *Heavenly Friend* (Joshua): Jay Velie. *Starkeeper*: PARKER FENNELLY. *Louise*: Sandy Duncan. *Carnival Boy*: Darrell Notara. *Enoch Snow, Jr.*: Dennis Cole. *Principal*: Philip Ewart.

Townspeople (Singers): Phyllis Bash, Jane Coleman, Mona Elson, Maria Hero, Joyce McDonald, Estella Munson, Marie O'Kelley, Joyce Olson, Eleanor Shaw, Maggie Task, Paul Adams, Gene Albano, Darrell Askey, Bob Barbieri, Austin Colyer, Gordon Cook, Philip Ewart, Marvin Goodis, William Miller, Laried Montgomery, Joe R. Rhyne, Joseph Williams, Jerry Wyatt. *Dancers*: Karen Brock, Linda Caputi, Alice Condodina, Joanna Crosson, Lois Eteleman, Carol Flemming, Joanne Geahry, Mickey Gunnersen, Lucia Lambert, Gilda Mullett, Toddie Wittmer, Roy Barry, Joseph Carow, D. R. Haworth, Curtis Hood, Paul Olson, Vernon Wendorf.

1966.32 AT THE DROP OF ANOTHER HAT

More of their own words and music[19]. (A Musical Revue in Two Acts.) Music by Donald Swann. Lyrics by Michael Flanders. Designed by Ralph Alswang. Associate producer, Sidney Lanier. Production supervisor, Jerry Adler. Production associate, Hildy Parks. A Nine O'Clock Theatre Production. Produced by Alexander H. Cohen. Opened 27 December 1966 at the Booth Theatre and closed 9 April 1967 after 105 performances.

CAST: MICHAEL FLANDERS, DONALD SWANN.

ACT 1
"The Gasman Cometh"
"From Our Bestiary"
'"P** P* B**** B** D*****"
"Bilbo's Song"
(*Lyrics by* J. R. R. Tolkien)
"Slow Train"
"Thermodynamic Duo"
"Sloth"

"More Songs for Our Time"
"In the Desert"
"Los Olividados"
"Motor Perpetuo"
"A Song of Patriotic Prejudice"

ACT 2
"All Gall"
"Horoscope"
"Armadillo Idyll"
"Twenty Tons of T.N.T."
"Ill Wind"
(*Music by* Wolfgang Amadeus Mozart.)
"Food For Thought"
"Prehistoric Complaint"
"Twice Shy"

1967.01 THE PERSECUTION AND ASSASSINATION OF MARAT AS PERFORMED BY THE INMATES OF THE ASYLUM OF CHARENTON UNDER THE DIRECTION OF THE MARQUIS DE SADE

A Revival of the Drama in Two Acts with Music[20]. Play by Peter Weiss. English version by Geoffrey Skelton. Verse adaptation by Adrian Mitchell. Music by Richard Peaslee. Entire production directed by Donald Driver. Scenery by Edward Burbridge. Costumes by Lewis Brown. Lighting by Martin Aronstein. Musical director, Rod Derefinko. Produced by Zev Bufman (The National Players Company Production). Opened 3 January 1967 at the Majestic Theatre and closed 18 February 1967 after 55 performances.

CAST (in order of appearance): *M. Coulmier*: Stephen Elliott. *Mme. Coulmier*: Barbara Cason. *Mlle. Coulmier*: Cynthia Towne. *Marquis de Sade*: WILLIAM ROERICK. *Herald*: Douglas Watson. *Jean-Paul Marat*: DENNIS PATRICK. *Simonne Evrard*: SHELLIE FELDMAN. *Charlotte Corday*: VERNA BLOOM. *Duperret*: Jered Barclay. *Jacques Roux*: Robert Fields. *Cucuru*: Leonard Drum. *Polpoch*: Igors Gavon. *Kokol*: Gerard Russak. *Rossignol*: Christine Norden. *Mad Animal*: Abe Vigoda. *Schoolmaster*: James Cahill. *Mother*: Fay Chaiken. *Father*: Peter Blaxill. *Voltaire*: John Tormey. *Lavoisier*: Allan Louw. *Patients*: Fayne Blackburn, Imogene Bliss, Beatrice Brooks, Madlyn Cates, Lousie Clay, Zola Long, Helen F. Ross, Carol Teitel, Geri Wolcott. *Nuns*: John Toland, Edmond Varrato. *Guards*: Sam Kirkham, Robert Keegan, Richard Kinter. *Musicians*: Bernie Moore (guitar), Roberta Russell (flute-piccolo), Patrick Harrison (percussion), Frank Emerson (trumpet).

1967.02 SHERRY!

A Musical Comedy in Two Acts, 12 Scenes. Book and lyrics by James Lipton. Based on the play "The Man Who Came to Dinner" by George S. Kaufman and Moss Hart. Music by Laurence Rosenthal. Scenery and lighting by Robert Randolph. Costumes by Robert Mackintosh. Musical direction and vocal arrangements by Jay Blackton. Orchestrations by Philip J. Lang. Dance arrangements by John Morris. Staging and direction supervised by Joe Layton. Associate producer, Marvin A. Krauss. Produced by Lee Guber, Frank Ford and Shelly Gross. Opened 28 March 1967 at the Alvin Theatre and closed 27 May 1967 after 72 performances.

CAST (in order of appearance): *Daisy Stanley*: MARY LOANE. *Miss Preen*: Janet Fox. *John*: Merritt Smith. *Sarah*: Barbara Webb. *Maggie Cutler*: ELIZABETH ALLEN. *Ernest W. Stanley*: DONALD BURR. *Dr. Bradley*: CLIFF HALL. *Sheridan Whiteside*: CLIVE REVILL. *Harriet Stanley*: PAULA TRUEMAN. *Bert Jefferson*: JON CYPHER. *Lorraine Sheldon*: DOLORES GRAY. *Cosette*: June Lynn Compton. *Beverly Carlton*: BYRON WEBSTER. *Westcott*: Haydon Smith. *Billy*: Del Hinkley. *Banjo*: EDDIE LAWRENCE. *Ginger*: Leslie Franzos.

---

[18]First produced in New York 19 April 1945 at the Majestic Theatre for 890 performances. For Synopsis of Scenes and Musical Numbers, see original 1945 production.
[19]A sequel to the authors' previous British revue success, AT THE DROP OF A HAT, which opened 8 October 1959 at the John Golden Theatre for 215 performances.
[20]Originally produced in New York 27 December 1965 at the Martin Beck Theatre for 145 performances. For Synopsis of Scenes and Musical Numbers, see original 1965 production.

Ensemble (Mesalians): Diane Arnold, Edie Cowan, Carol Estey, Leslie Franzos, Altovise Gore, Carol Hanzel, Carol Perea, Peter De Nicola, Frank De Sal, Luigi Gasparinetti, Roger Allan Raby, Haydon Smith, Doug Spingler, Ted Sprague, Lucille Blackton, June Lynn Compton, Rita Metzger, Jeannette Seibert, Trudy Wallace, Herb Fields, Del Hinkley, Joe Kirkland, Duane Morris, Clyde Williams, Denise Nickerson, Glenn Dufford, Robert Fitch.

The action takes place between December 10th and Christmas Day, 1938, in Mesalia, Ohio.

Act 1, Scene 1: The Stanley Living Room. *Scene 2:* Township of Mesalia. *Scene 3:* Exterior of Stanley Residence. *Scene 4:* The Stanley Residence. *Scene 5:* A Jewelry Shop. *Scene 6:* The Stanley Living Room. *Scene 7:* Mansion House Hotel in Mesalia. *Scene 8:* The Stanley Living Room.

Act 2, Scene 1: Billy's Tavern. *Scene 2:* The Stanley Solarium. *Scene 3:* The Stanley Library. *Scene 4:* The Stanley Living Room.

ACT 1

Scene 1

"Turn on Your Radio"
B. Webb, E. Allen, M. Loane, Ensemble

"Why Does the Whole Damn World Adore Me?"
C. Revill

Scene 2

"Meet Mesalia"
E. Allen, J. Cypher, Ensemble

Scene 3

"Maybe It's Time for Me"
E. Allen

Scene 4

"How Can You Kiss Those Good Times Goodbye?"
C. Revill, E. Allen

Scene 5

"With This Ring"
E. Allen, J. Cypher, C. Revill, C. Hall

Scene 6

"Sherry"
D. Gray, C. Revill

"Alas, Lorraine"
B. Webster

"Au Revoir"
B. Webster

Scene 7

"Proposal Duet"
D. Gray, B. Webster

"Listen Cosette"
D. Gray, J. L. Compton

Scene 8

"Christmas Eve Broadcast"
C. Revill, D. Gray, Ensemble

ACT 2

Scene 1

"Putty in Your Hands"
D. Gray, Ensemble

Scene 2

"Harriet's Pavan"
P. Trueman

"Imagine That"
E. Allen, C. Revill

Scene 3

"Marry the Girl Myself"
C. Revill, E. Lawrence

"The Fred Astaire Affair"
C. Revill, E. Lawrence, L. Franzos, Ensemble

"How Can You Kiss Those Good Times Goodbye?" (reprise)
E. Allen

Scene 4

"Putty in Your Hands" (reprise)
D. Gray, C. Revill, E. Lawrence

"Harriet Sedley"
C. Revill, E. Lawrence, D. Burr

1967.03

HELLO, SOLLY!

An American Yiddish Musical Revue in Two Acts, 6 Scenes[21]. (Costumes, settings, lighting, direction uncredited.) Produced by Hal Zeiger. Opened 4 April 1967 at Henry Miller's Theatre and closed 28 May 1967 after 68 performances.

CAST: MICKEY KATZ, LARRY BEST, MICHAEL (GETZEL) ROSENBERG, STAN PORTER, LITTLE TANYA.

ACT 1[22]

Scene 1

Songs, Stories, Instrumentals:
M. Katz
"Darktown Strutter's Ball"
(*Music and Lyrics by* Shelton Brooks.)
"Sunrise, Sunset" (from FIDDLER ON THE ROOF)
(*Music by* Jerry Bock. *Lyrics by* Sheldon Harnick.)
Yiddish Folk Song (Traditional)
Stories, Sing-along, Bepop:
"Die Greene Koseene"
(*Music and Lyrics by* Abe Schwartz and Hyman Prizant.)
"The Wedding Dance"
(*Music by* Mickey Katz.)

Scene 2

Little Tanya
[Old-country ballad; cantorial tune; "People" from FUNNY GIRL.
(*Music by* Jule Styne. *Lyrics by* Bob Merrill.)]

Scene 3

Jokes and Stories
L. Best

ACT 2

Scene 1

Songs of Childhood and Israel:
S. Porter, V. Lloyd
Childhood Medley:
"Seise Kinder Yohren"
(*Music and Lyrics by* David Meyerowitz.)
"Zing, Faigele, Zing"
(*Music and Lyrics by* Max Kletter.)
Chassidic Nigun :
"A Zemmer"
(*Music and Lyrics by* Samuel Bugatch.)
"Sheyibone Beis Hamikdosh"
(*Music and Lyrics by* Yisroll Shorr.)

Scene 2

Michael Rosenberg (Comic sketches)

Scene 3

Finale

1967.04

FINIAN'S RAINBOW

A Revival of the Musical in Two Acts, 10 Scenes[23]. Book by E. Y. Harburg and Fred Saidy. Lyrics by E. Y. Harburg. Music by Burton Lane. Directed by Gus Schirmer. Choreographed by Betty Hyatt Linton. Scenery by Howard Bay. Costumes by Frank Thompson. Lighting by Peggy Clark. (Orchestrations by Robert Russell Bennett and Don Walker.) Musical director, Jonathan Anderson. Produced by the New York City Center Light Opera Company (Jean Dalrymple, Director.) Opened 5 April 1967 at the New York City Center and closed 23 April 1967 after 23 performances.

---

[21]Previously produced in New York 10-11 September 1966 at Carnegie Hall for 3 performances, with the same cast, Little Tanya excepted. Dina Claire appeared on the program.
[22]Neither songs nor sketches were listed in the program. The above list was prepared from reviews, press representative materials and recordings.
[23]Originally produced in New York 10 January 1947 at the 46th Street Theatre for 725 performances. For Synopsis of Scenes and Musical Numbers, see original 1947 production.

CAST (in order of appearance): *Sunny* (Harmonica Player): Elliot Levine. *Buzz Collins*: Ronn Carroll. *Sheriff*: Howard Fischer. *First Sharecropper*: John Dorrin *Second Sharecropper*: Laried Montgomery. *Susan Mahoney*: SANDY DUNCAN. *Henry*: Kevin Featherstone. *Maude*: CAROL BRICE. *Finian McLonergan*: FRANK McHUGH. *Sharon McLonergan*: NANCY DUSSAULT. *Woody Mahoney*: STANLEY GROVER. *Og* (A Leprechaun): LEN GOCHMAN. *Senator Billboard Rawkins*: HOWARD I. SMITH. *First Geologist*: Ronald B. Stratton. *Second Geologist*: Clark Salonis. *Howard*: Jim McMillan. *Diane*: Ellen Hansen. *Mr. Robust*: Austin Colyer. *Mr. Shears*: Paul Adams. *First Passion Pilgrim Gospeller*: Jerry Laws. *Second Passion Pilgrim Gospeller*: Tiger Haynes. *Third Passion Pilgrim Gospeller*: John McCurry. *First Deputy*: Paul Eichel. *Second Deputy*: Joey Carow. *John the Preacher*: Garwood Perkins.

Singers: Barbara Christopher, Jane Coleman, Mary Falconer, Ellen Harris, Ernestine Jackson, Mina Jo King, Joyce McDonald, Dixie Stewart, Alyce Webb. Paul Adams, Austin Colyer, John Dorrin, Paul Eichel, Doug Hunt, Elliot Levine, Laried Montgomery, Garrett Morris, Garwood Perkins, Clark Salonis, Grant Spradling. *Dancers*: Mary Barnett, Josetta Cherry, Joanna Crosson, Joanne De Vito, Ruth Lawrence, Sally Lou Lee, Joy Serio, Toodie Wittmer, Mary Zahn. Guy Allen, Bjarne Buchtrup, Joey Carow, Dennis Edenfield, Jerry Fries, Garold Gardner, Ted Goodridge, Mark Holliday, Bob La Crosse, Ronald B. Stratton, Mark Scott. *Children*: Ellen Hansen, Lisa Huggins, Tom Brooke, Kevin Featherstone, William Sims.

1967.05 ILLYA, DARLING

A Musical in Two Acts, 18 Scenes. Book and direction by Jules Dassin. Based on the film "Never on Sunday" (by Jules Dassin.) Music by Manos Hadjidakis. Lyrics by Joe Darion. Scenery by Oliver Smith. Costumes by Theoni V. Aldredge. Lighting by Jean Rosenthal. Musical direction by Karen Gustafson. Dance and musical numbers staged by Onna White. Orchestrations by Ralph Burns. Dance music arranged by Roger Adams. Assistant choreographer, Tom Panko. Produced by Kermit Bloomgarden in association with United Artists. Opened 11 April 1967 at the Mark Hellinger Theatre and closed 13 January 1968 after 320 performances.

CAST (in order of appearance): *Yorgo*: TITOS VANDIS. *Costa*: Thomas Raskin. *Workman*: Dom Angelo. *Tonio*: NIKOS KOURKOULOS. *Captain*: RUDY BOND. *Illya*: MELINA MERCOURI. *Homer Thrace*: ORSON BEAN. *Waiter*: HAROLD GARY. *Garbage*: WILLIAM DUELL. *Despo*: DESPO. *Musician*: Joseph Alfasa. *Little Man*: Gerrit de Beer. *Forward Sailor*: Joseph Corby. *Timid Sailor*: Robert La Tourneaux. *Vassily*: JOE E. MARKS. *Voula*: Lou Rodgers. *Kiki*: Sandy Ellen. *Cassandra*: Gloria Lambert. *Playgoer*: Nick Athas. *Drama Critic*: Fred Burrell. *Wife*: Del Green. *No Face*: HAL LINDEN. *Bodyguards*: Gerrit de Beer, Harry Kalkanis. *The Other Girl*: Ann Barry. *Bouzouki Soloist*: Harry Lemonopoulos.

Ensemble: Ann Barry, Sandy Ellen, Del Green, Eileen Joy Haber, Suzanne Horn, Robert La Tourneaux, Urylee Leonardos, Lou Rodgers, Arthur Shaffer, Maria Strattin, Martin Allen, Dom Angelo, Lonnie Davis, Marcelo Gamboa, Louis Genevrino, Nat Horne, Harry Kalkanis, Robert Karl, Juleste Salve, Bill Starr, Mitch Thomas, Terry Violino, Nick Athas, Edward Becker, Alvin Cohen, Joseph Corby, Gerrit de Beer, Johnny LaMotta, Stephen Lardas, Thomas Raskin, Loukas Skipitaris.

The action takes place in the Port of Piraeus, Greece at the present time.

Act 1, Scene 1: A Shipyard in Piraeus. *Scene 2*: A Bouzouki Place. *Scene 3*: Illya's Bedroom. *Scene 4*: Outside Illya's House. *Scene 5*: Seaside. *Scene 6*: Shipyard. *Scene 7*: Illya's Apartment. *Scene 8*: The Acropolis. *Scene 9*: The Bouzouki Place. *Scene 10*: Illya's Bedroom.

Act 2, Scene 1: Illya's Apartment. *Scene 2*: Outside Illya's House. *Scene 3*: Illya's Bedroom. *Scene 4*: A Street in Piraeus. *Scene 5*: Illya's Apartment. *Scene 6*: Street of the Girls. *Scene 7*: The Bouzouki Place. *Scene 8*: The Port.

ACT 1[24]

"Po, Po, Po"
    O. Bean, N. Kourkoulos
Dance
    Ensemble
"Zebekiko"
    T. Vandis
"Piraeus, My Love"
    M. Mercouri, Men
"Golden Land"
    O. Bean, Ensemble
"Zebikiko" (reprise)
    T. Vandis
"Love, Love, Love"[25]
    M. Mercouri

"I Think She Needs Me"
    O. Bean
"I'll Never Lay Down Anymore"
    Despo
"After Love"[26]
    N. Kourkoulos
"Birthday Song"
    N. Kourkoulos, R. Bond, Men
"Medea Tango"
    M. Mercouri, Men
"Illya, Darling"
    M. Mercouri, T. Vandis, Ensemble
ACT 2
"Dear Mr. Schubert"
    M. Mercouri
"The Lesson"
    M. Mercouri, O. Bean
"Never on Sunday"
    M. Mercouri, Ensemble
"Piraeus, My Love" (reprise)
    M. Mercouri
"Medea Tango" (reprise)
    N. Kourkoulos
"Heaven Help the Sailors on a Night Like This"
    Ensemble
Dance
    M. Mercouri, O. Bean, T. Vandis, N. Kourkoulos,
    R. Bond, J. E. Marks, H. Gary, Ensemble
"Ya Chara"
    Company

1967.06 HALLELUJAH, BABY!

A Musical in Two Acts, a Prologue and 6 Scenes. Book by Arthur Laurents. Music by Jule Styne. Lyrics by Betty Comden and Adolph Green. Directed by Burt Shevelove. Dances and musical numbers staged by Kevin Carlisle. Settings designed by William and Jean Eckart. Costumes by Irene Sharaff. Lighting by Tharon Musser. Musical direction and vocal arrangements by Buster Davis. Orchestrations by Peter Matz. Dance orchestrations by Luther Henderson. Assistant choreographers, William Guske, Marie Lake. Associate producer, Joe Linhart. Produced by Albert W. Selden and Hal James, Jane C. Nusbaum and Harry Rigby. Opened 26 April 1967 at the Martin Beck Theatre and closed 13 January 1968 after 293 performances.

CAST (in order of appearance): *Georgina*: LESLIE UGGAMS. *Momma*: LILLIAN HAYMAN. *Clem*: ROBERT HOOKS. *Provers*: Clifford Allen, Garrett Morris, Kenneth Scott, Alan Weeks. *Harvey*: ALLEN CASE. *Captain Yankee*: Justin McDonough. *Calhoun*: Lou Angel. *Mary*: BARBARA SHARMA. *Mister Charles*: Frank Hamilton. *Mrs. Charles*: Marilyn Cooper. *Tip and Tap*: Winston DeWitt Hemsley, Alan Weeks. *Cuties*: Hope Clarke, Sandra Lein, Saundra McPherson. *Prince*: Bud Vest. *Princess*: Carol Flemming. *Sugar Daddy*: Darrell Notara. *Bouncer*: Chad Block. *Mistress*: Marilyn Cooper. *Master*: Darrell Notara. *Director*: Alan Peterson. *Ethel*: Marilyn Cooper. *Official*: Chad Block. *Brenda*: Ann Rachel. *Timmy*: Frank Hamilton. *G.I.s*: Winston DeWitt Hemsley, Kenneth Scott, Alan Weeks, Clifford Allen. *Bus Driver*: Lou Angel. *Dorothy*: Marilyn Cooper. *Maid*: Hope Clarke.

Ensemble: Clifford Allen, Barbara Andrews, Lou Angel, Chad Block, Hope Clarke, Norma Donaldson, Carol Flemming, Nat Gales, Maria Hero, Lee Hooper, Alan Johnson, Sandra Lein, Justin McDonough, Saundra McPherson, Garrett Morris, Darrell Notara, Paul Reid Roman, Suzanne Rogers, Kenneth Scott, Ella Thompson, Bud Vest.

The action takes place in this country from the turn of the century until now.

Act 1, Scene 1: 1900s. The kitchen. *Scene 2*: 1920s. A cabaret. *Scene 3*: 1930s. The bread line.

Act 2, Scene 1: 1940s. An Army camp, outside a night club. *Scene 2*: 1950s. A night club. *Scene 3*: 1960s. An apartment.

ACT 1[27]

---

[24]After opening, Act 1 revised and shortened.
[25]Dropped after opening

[26]Dropped after opening
[27]Added during the run:
    "You Ain't Gonna Shake Them Feathers No More"
    (added to Act 1, Scene 2, after "Feet Do Yo' Stuff")
    R. Hooks

Introduction
Prologue
  L. Uggams
Scene 1
  "Back in the Kitchen"
    L. Hayman
  "My Own Morning"
    L. Uggams
  "The Slice"
    R. Hooks, C. Allen, G. Morris, K. Scott, A. Weeks
  "Farewell, Farewell"
    L. Angel, J. McDonough, L. Uggams, A. Case
Scene 2
  "Feet Do Yo' Stuff"
    L. Uggams, Chorines, W. D. Hemsley, A. Weeks
  "Watch My Dust"[28]
    R. Hooks
  "Smile, Smile"
    R. Hooks, L. Uggams, L. Hayman
Scene 3
  "Witches' Brew" (Double, Double)
    L. Uggams, B. Sharma, M. Cooper, Company
  Breadline Dance
    Bums (Ensemble)
  "Another Day"
    A. Case, R. Hooks, B. Sharma, L. Uggams
  "I Wanted to Change Him"[29]
    L. Uggams
  "Being Good Isn't Good Enough"
    L. Uggams

ACT 2
Scene 1
  Dance Drill (Clem's Drill)
    W. D. Hemsley, A. Weeks, K. Scott, C. Allen
  "Talking to Yourself"
    L. Uggams, R. Hooks, A. Case
  Limbo Dance
    Night Club Patrons (Ensemble)
Scene 2
  "Hallelujah, Baby!"
    L. Uggams, W. D. Hemsley, A. Weeks
  "Not Mine"
    A. Case

"Hey!" (added to Act 1, Scene 2, after "You Ain't Gonna Shake. .")
  L. Uggams
Added for subsequent National Tour:
"When the Weather's Better"
  Adam Wade (Clem), Kim Weston (Georgina)
(added to Act 1, Scene 1, after "The Slice;" also reprised in Act 1, Scene 3 before "Another Day." for Julius La Rosa (Harvey), Bobbi Baird (Mary).)
"You're Welcome" (added to Act 1, Scene 2, after "Watch My Dust")
  K. Weston
"Under the Ropes" (added to Act 2, Scene 2 before "Hallelujah, Baby!")
  Dancers
"Freedom March" (added to Act 2, Scene 3, before "Now's the Time" reprise)
  Dancers
Dropped for National Tour:
  Breadline Dance, "I Wanted to Change Him," Limbo Dance, "Hey!," "You Ain't Gonna Shake Them Feathers No More."
[28] Dropped during the New York run.
[29] Dropped during the New York run.

"I Don't Know Where She Got It"
  L. Hayman
"Now's the Time"
  L. Uggams
Scene 3
  "Now's the Time" (Reprise)
    Entire Company

1967.07 THE SOUND OF MUSIC

A Revival of the Musical Play in Two Acts, 19 Scenes[30]. Book by Howard Lindsay and Russel Crouse. Suggested by the book "The Trapp Family Singers" by Maria Augusta Trapp. Music by Richard Rodgers. Lyrics by Oscar Hammerstein II. Directed by John Fearnley. Musical numbers staged by Reid Klein. Scenery by Oliver Smith. Costumes by Stanley Simmons. Lighting by Peggy Clark. Musical director, Frederick Dvonch. Choral arrangements by Trude Rittman. Orchestrations by Robert Russell Bennett. Produced by the New York City Center Light Opera Company (Jean Dalrymple, Director). Opened 26 April 1967 at the New York City Center and closed 14 May 1967 after 23 performances.

CAST (in order of appearance): *Maria Rainer*, a Postulant at Nonnberg Abbey: CONSTANCE TOWERS. *Sister Berthe*, Mistress of Novices: Jessica Quinn. *Sister Margaretta*, Mistress of Postulants: Nadine Lewis. *The Mother Abbess*: ELEANOR STEBER. *Sister Sophia*: Bernice Saunders. *Captain Georg von Trapp*: BOB WRIGHT. *Franz*, the Butler: Jim Oyster. *Frau Schmidt*, the Housekeeper: Helen Noyes. *Children of Captain Von Trapp* (7): SHERWOOD SISTERS, HAMILTON BROTHERS: *Liesl*: SANDY DUNCAN. *Friedrich*: Gary Hamilton. *Louisa*: Holly Sherwood. *Kurt*: Eric Hamilton. *Brigitta*: Dawn Sherwood. *Marta*: Maindy Sherwood. *Gretl*: Robin Sherwood. *Rolf Gruber*: REID KLEIN. *Elsa Schraeder*: M'EL DOWD. *Ursula*: Alison Sherwood. *Max Detweiler*: CHRISTOPHER HEWETT. *Herr Zeller*: Larry Swanson. *Baron Elberfeld*: Grant Gordon. *A Postulant*: Kyle Sherwood. *Admiral von Schreiber*: Jay Velie.
  Neighbors of Captain Von Trapp, Nuns, Novices, Postulants, Contestants in the Festival Concert, and Storm Troopers: Mona Elson, Susan Feldon, Barbara Gregory, Joy Ellyn Holly, Oksana Iwaszczenko, Patti Kogin, Estella Munson, Marilyn Murphy, Joyce Olson, Candida Pilla, Mary Ann Rydzeski, Ellen Shade, Ann Tell, Beverly Jane Welch, Maggie Worth, Bill Galarno, Garold Gardner.

1967.08 SING, ISRAEL, SING

A Musical Offering (Revue) of Yiddish and Israeli Folklore, Humor and Art Songs in Two Acts. Based on texts and music by Asaf Halevi, Moishe Broderson, Z. Berdi Tswever, M. M. Warshavsky, Itzik Manger, L. Neidus, M. Noy (Neu), Shlomo Weisfisch, Joel Chayes, E. Kishon, H. Kon, Ami Gilad. Special material by M. Nudelman. Directed by Mina Bern. Assistant director and choreographer, Felix Fibich. Music arranged and conducted by Ami Gilad. Assistant conductor, Renee Solomon. Libretto by Wolf Younin. Costumes by Judith. Kibbutz envisioned by Sylvia Younin. Production supervisor, Bernard Sauer. Produced by Ben Bonus. Opend 11 May 1967 at the Brooks Atkinson Theatre and closed 21 May 1967 after 14 performances. Re-opened in an English language adaptation 7 June 1967 at the Brooks Atkinson Theatre and closed 11 June 1967 after 8 performances. Total: 22 performances.

CAST (in order of appearance): *Guards*: ITAMAR, BEN BONUS. *Kibbutz Girls*: MINA BERN, SUSAN WALTERS. *Kibbutz Men*: DANIEL FRANKLIN, BERNARD SAUER. *Oldtimers*: MAX BOZYK, ROSE ROZYK. *Kibbutzniks*: Dance Ensemble. *Dora*: ROSE BOZYK. *David*: DANIEL FRANKLIN.
  Dance Ensemble: HADASSAH BODOCH, Melita Ross, Donna Shadden, Marsha Wolfson, Edward Effron, Tony Masullo, Ralph Nelson.

Act 1: In the Kibbutz.

---

[30] Originally produced in New York 16 November 1959 at the Lunt-Fontanne Theatre for 1443 performances. For Synopsis of Scenes and Musical Numbers, see original 1959 production. Dropped for this production: "An Ordinary Couple."
  Added for this production:
  "My Favorite Things" (reprise)(added to Act 2, Scene 1 opening)
  "Something Good" (added to Act 2, before "Processional")
    C. Towers
    (*Music and Lyrics* by Richard Rodgers, from the film adaptation.)

Act 2: Kumzits (A Joyful Get-Together) in the Kibbutz.

ACT 1

"The Dream"
Itamar, H. Badoch
Mazal, The Bride: S. Walters. *Companions of the Bride:* Dance Ensemble.

"Only I and You"
S. Walters, D. Franklin

Encounter No. 1
S. Goldstein, M. Bern

Bus Station
B. Sauer, M. Bern

Dance of the Rain
Dance Ensemble

"Song of the Rain"
B. Bonus

Encounter No. 2
S. Goldstein, R. Rozyk

The Law Is the Law
(*by* M. Nudelman)
Policewoman: R. Bozyk. *Kibbutznik:* M. Bozyk.

"Meeting"
Entire Ensemble

"Sing Israel Sing"
B. Bonus

ACT 2

Accordionist
A. Gilad

"We the Sheppards"
Itamar, Dance Ensemble

Boy's Dance (Debka)
Itamar, Dance Ensemble, D. Franklin, B. Sauer

"The Bride Sings"
S. Walters

Economics
(*by* M. Nudelman)
M. Bozyk, S. Goldstein

Reminiscing
B. Bonus

Dances of Many Lands
Dance Ensemble

Two American Business Women
(*by* M. Nudelman)
M. Bern, R. Bozyk
Bride's Side: H. Badoch, Itamar, Dance Ensemble, T. Masullo, M. Ross, D. Shadden, M. Wolfson, E. Effron, R. Nelson. *Groom's Side: Musicians:* R. Bozyk, M. Bern, S. Walters, S. Goldstein. *Fathers-in-law:* M. Bozyk, M. Bern. *Bride and Groom:* S. Walters, D. Franklin. *Mothers-in-law:* M. Bern, R. Bozyk.

"Wedding Dance"
Entire Ensemble

"Guard of Israel"
B. Bonus

1967.09   WONDERFUL TOWN

A Revival of the Musical Comedy in Two Acts, 13 Scenes[31]. Book by Joseph Fields and Jerome Chodorov. Based on the play "My Sister Eileen" by Joseph Fields and Jerome Chodorov and the stories of the same name by Ruth McKinney. Music by Leonard Bernstein. Lyrics by Betty Comden and Adolph Green. Directed by Gus Schirmer. Musical numbers and dances staged by Ralph Beaumont. Scenery by Raoul Pene du Bois. Costumes by Frank Thompson. Lighting by Peggy Clark. Musical director, Irving Actman. (Orchestrations by Don Walker.) Produced by the New York City Center Light Opera Company (Jean Dalrymple, Director). Opened 17 May 1967 at the New York City Center and closed 4 June 1967 after 23 performances.

CAST (in order of appearance): *Guide:* Austin Colyer. *Appopoulos:* TED THURSTON. *Lonigan:* Ronn Carroll. *Helen:* BETSY VON FURSTENBERG. *Wreck:* JACK KNIGHT. *Violet:* Betty Hyatt Linton. *Speedy Valenti:* George Marcy. *Eileen:* LINDA BENNETT. *Ruth:* ELAINE STRITCH. *A Strange Man:* Richard Miller. *Drunks:* Ben Laney, Henry Lawrence. *Robert Baker:* NOLAN VAN WAY. *Associate Editors:* Paul Adams, Michael Harrison. *Mrs. Wade:* Claire Waring. *Frank Lippencott:* JACK FLETCHER. *Chef:* Marvin Goodis. *Waiter:* Henry LeClair. *Delivery Boy:* Ronny Hedrick. *Chick Clark:* RICHARD FRANCE. *Shore Patrolman:* Edward Taylor. *First Cadet:* Tim Ramirez. *Second Cadet:* Vito Durante. *Ruth's Escort:* Stokely Gray.

Greenwich Villagers: Singers: Maria Bradley, Jacqueline Dean, Mona Elson, Joan Nelson, Barbara Miller, Susan Stockwell, Peggy Walthen, Alyce Elizabeth Webb, Maggie Worth. Paul Adams, Austin Colyer, Marvin Goodis, Stokely Gray, Michael Harrison, Ben Laney, Henry Lawrence, Henry LeClair, Richard Miller, Edward Taylor. *Dancers:* Bonnie Ano, Patty Cope, Judith Danford, Shelley Frankel, Judith Haskell, Ellie Knowles, Ina Kurland, Kuniko Narai, Mary Ann Niles. Guy Allen, Rodd Barry, George Bunt, Vito Durante, Raphael Gilbert, Ronnie Headrick, Dan Joel, Tim Ramirez, Tony Stevens.

---

[31]Originally produced in New York 25 February 1953 at the Winter Garden for 559 performances. For Synopsis of Scenes and Musical Numbers, see original 1953 production.

1967–1968 SEASON

Neva Small and Robin Wilson in HENRY, SWEET HENRY (Photo: Friedman-Abeles)
Billy Rose Theatre Collection, New York Public Library for the Performing Arts

1967-1968 SEASON

1967.10

SOUTH PACIFIC

A Revival of the Musical Play in Two Acts, 23 Scenes[1]. Music by Richard Rodgers. Lyrics by Oscar Hammerstein II. Book by Oscar Hammerstein II and Joshua Logan. Adapted from James A. Michener's novel "Tales of the South Pacific." Directed by Joe Layton. Scenery and costumes by Fred Voelpel. Lighting by Jules Fisher. Musical director, Jonathan Anderson. Orchestrations by Robert Russell Bennett. Produced by the Music Theater of Lincoln Center (Richard Rodgers, Producing director). Opened 12 June 1967 at the New York State Theatre and closed 9 September 1967 after 104 performances.

CAST (in order of appearance): *Ngana*: Dana Shimizu. *Jerome*: Keenan Shimizu. *Henry*: Robert Ito. *Ensign Nellie Forbush*: FLORENCE HENDERSON. *Emile DeBecque*: GIORGIO TOZZI. *Bloody Mary*: IRENE BYATT. *Abner*: Judd Jones. *Stewpot*: Brad Sullivan. *Luther Billis*: DAVID DOYLE. *Professor*: Mickey [Michael] Karm. *Lt. Joseph Cable, U.S.M.C.*: JUSTIN McDONOUGH. *Capt. George Brackett, U.S.N.*: LYLE TALBOT. *Cmdr. William Harbison, U.S.N.*: Bob Monroe. *Yeoman Herbert Quale*: Ted Story. *Sgt. Kenneth Johnson*: William Lutz. *Seaman Richard West*: Mark East. *Seaman Morton Wise*: Gordon Cook. *Seaman Tom O'Brien*: James O'Sullivan. *Radio Operator Bob McCaffrey*: Roger Brown. *Marine Cpl. Hamilton Steves*: Dick Ensslen. *Seabee Thomas Hassinger*: Philip Lucas. *Seabee James Jerome*: Joseph della Sorte. *Pvt. Sven Larsen*: Don Dolan. *Pvt. Jack Walters*: Bob Barbieri. *Pvt. Dick Sederholm*: Jess. Richards. *Seabee Roger Pitt*: Marvin Camillo. *Seabee John Nathan*: David Jarrett. *Seabee Keith Moore*: Dale Westerman. *Lt. Genevieve Marshall*: Jane Coleman. *Ensign Lisa Manelli*: Lisa Damon. *Ensign Connie Walewska*: Martha Danielle. *Ensign Janet MacGregor*: Susan Campbell. *Ensign Bessie Noonan*: JOYCE MARET. *Ensign Rita Adams*: Ann Nathan. *Ensign Sue Yaeger*: Joyce McDonald. *Ensign Cora MacRae*: Lynn Dovel. *Ensign Dinah Murphy*: Bobbi Baird. *Liat*: JOYCE MARET. *Lt. Buzz Adams*: Jack Knight.

1967.11

JUDY GARLAND AT HOME AT THE PALACE

A Variety Revue in Two Acts[2]. Staged by Richard Barstow. Costumes by Bill Smith, Travilla. Lighting by Ralph Alswang. Musical director, Bobby Cole. A Group V Ltd. Production. Produced by Sid Luft. Opened 31 July 1967 at the Palace Theatre and closed 26 August 1967 after 24 performances; reopened a return engagement 25-27 December 1967 at the Felt Forum, Madison Square Garden for 3 additional peformances. Total: 27 performances.

CAST: JUDY GARLAND, John Bubbles, Jackie Vernon, Francis Brunn, Lorna Luft, Joey Luft.

ACT 1

Scene 1

  Francis Brunn

Scene 2

  John Bubbles (song and dance)

Scene 3

  Jackie Vernon (comedy)

ACT 2[3]

Judy Garland:

"I Feel a Song Coming On" (from film EVERY NIGHT AT EIGHT)
  (*Music by* Jimmy McHugh. *Lyrics by* Dorothy Fields and George Oppenheimer.)

---

[1]First produced in New York 7 April 1949 at the Majestic Theatre for 1925 performances. For Synopsis of Scenes and Musical Numbers, see original 1949 production.
[2]Miss Garland appeared before at the Palace Theatre 16 October 1951 for 266 performances, and returned again 26 September 1956 to the Palace, and later to the Metropolitan Opera House (1959) and Carnegie Hall (1961). Details of these performances are beyond the scope of this book.
[3]Not in performance order.

"Almost Like Being in Love" (from BRIGADOON)
  (*Music by* Frederick Loewe. *Lyrics by* Alan Jay Lerner.)
"This Can't Be Love" (from THE BOYS FROM SYRACUSE)
  (*Music by* Richard Rodgers. *Lyrics by* Lorenz Hart.)

Medley (of her film hits):

"You Made Me Love You" (from film THE BROADWAY MELODY OF 1938)
  (*Music by* James V. Monaco. *Lyrics by* Joseph McCarthy.)
"For Me and My Gal" (from film FOR ME AND MY GAL)
  (*Music by* George W. Meyer. *Lyrics by* Edgar Leslie and Ray Goetz.)
"The Trolley Song" (from film MEET ME IN ST. LOUIS)
  (*Music and Lyrics by* Hugh Martin and Ralph Blane.)
"What Now My Love"
  (*Music by* Gilbert Becaud. *Lyrics by* Carl Sigman.)

(Medley with family):

"Bob White"
  J. Garland, L. Luft
  (*Music and Lyrics by* Johnny Mercer and Bernard Hanighen.)
"Jamboree Jones"
  J. Garland, L. Luft
  (*Music and Lyrics by* Johnny Mercer.)
"Together" (from GYPSY)
  J. Garland, L. Luft, J. Luft
  (*Music by* Jule Styne. *Lyrics by* Stephen Sondheim.)
"Ol' Man River" (from SHOWBOAT)
  (*Music by* Jerome Kern. *Lyrics by* Oscar Hammerstein II.)
"That's Entertainment" (from film THE BANDWAGON)
  (*Music by* Arthur Schwartz. *Lyrics by* Howard Dietz.)
"I Loved Him, But He Didn't Love Me" (from WAKE UP AND DREAM, London)
  (*Music and Lyrics by* Cole Porter.)
"Rock-a-Bye Your Baby With a Dixie Melody" (from SINBAD)
  (*Music by* Jean Schwartz. *Lyrics by* Sam M. Lewis and Joe Young)
"Me and My Shadow"
  (*Music by* Al Jolson and Dave Dreyer. *Lyrics by* Billy Rose.)
"Over the Rainbow" (from film THE WIZARD OF OZ)
  (*Music by* Harold Arlen. *Lyrics by* E. Y. Harburg.)

1967.12

BUDDY HACKETT AND EDDIE FISHER

A Two-Man Revue in Two Acts. Musical director, Colin Romoff. (Produced by Hackett Productions and Fisher Productions.) Opened 28 August 1967 at the Palace Theatre and closed 7 October 1967 after 42 performances.

CAST: BUDDY HACKETT (Comedy monologues), EDDIE FISHER. (Songs). (Opening Act alternates nightly.)

Eddie Fisher's repertoire[4]:

"Let Me Entertain You" (from GYPSY)
  (*Music by* Jule Styne. *Lyrics by* Stephen Sondheim.)
"The Impossible Dream" (from MAN OF LA MANCHA)
  (*Music by* Mitch Leigh. *Lyrics by* Joe Darion.)
"If She Walked Into My Life" (from MAME)
  (*Music and Lyrics by* Jerry Herman.)
"Mame" (from MAME)
  (*Music and Lyrics by* Jerry Herman.)
"People Like You"
  (*Music and Lyrics by* Larry Kusik and Eddie Snyder.)
"Do-Re-Mi" (from THE SOUND OF MUSIC)
  (*Music by* Richard Rodgers. *Lyrics by* Oscar Hammerstein II.)
Finale (Duet with Buddy Hackett)

---

[4]Not in performance order.

1967.13 MARLENE DIETRICH

A One-Woman Show in One Act. Musical arrangements and orchestra conducted by Burt Bacharach. Lighting by Joe Davis. Production supervisor, Jerry Adler. A Nine O'Clock Theatre Production. Produced by Alexander H. Cohen. Opened 9 October 1967 at the Lunt-Fontanne Theatre and closed 18 November 1967 after 48 performances.

CAST: MARLENE DIETRICH.

REPERTOIRE[5]

"I Can't Give You Anything But Love, Baby" (from BLACKBIRDS OF 1928)
(*Music by* Jimmy McHugh. *Lyrics by* Dorothy Fields.)

"You're the Cream in My Coffee" (from HOLD EVERYTHING)
(*Music by* Ray Henderson. *Lyrics by* Buddy G. DeSylva and Lew Brown.)

"My Blue Heaven" (from ZIEGFELD FOLLIES OF 1927)
(*Music by* Walter Donaldson. *Lyrics by* George Whiting.)

"(See What) The Boys in the Back Room (Will Have)" (from film DESTRY RIDES AGAIN)
(*Music by* Frederick Holl' ander. *Lyrics by* Frank Loesser.)

"The Laziest Gal in Town" (from film STAGE FRIGHT)
(*Music and Lyrics by* Cole Porter.)

"When the World Was Young" (*Original French Lyrics by* Angela Vannier.)
(*Music by* M. Philippe-Gerard. *Lyrics by* Johnny Mercer.)

"Jonny" (from film SONG OF SONGS)
(*Music by* Frederick Holl' ander. *Lyrics by* Edward Heyman.)

"Go Away from My Window"
(*arr. by* J. J. Niles.)

"I Wish You Love"
(*Music by* Charles Trenet. *Lyrics by* Albert Beach.)

"The War's Over, Seems We Won, Hooray"

"Boomerang Baby"

"(Naughty) Lola" (from film THE BLUE ANGEL)
(*Music and Lyrics by* Frederick Holl' ander.)

"Don't Ask Me Why"

"Everyone's Gone to the Moon"
(*Music and Lyrics by* Kenneth King.)

"Marie, Marie"
(*Music by* Gilbert Becaud. *Lyrics by* Pierre Delanoe and Kolpe.)

"Lili Marlene"
(*Music by* Norbert Schultze. *Lyrics by* Hans Leip and Tommie Connor.)

"Where Have All the Flowers Gone?"
(*Music and Lyrics by* Pete Seeger.)

"Honeysuckle Rose" (from HOT CHOCOLATES)
(*Music by* Fats Waller. *Lyrics by* Andy Razaf.)

"Falling in Love Again" (from film THE BLUE ANGEL)
(*Music and Lyrics by* Frederick Holl' ander.)

"La Vie en Rose"
(*Music by* Louiguy. *Lyrics by* Edith Piaf.)

"Shir Hatan"
(*Music and Lyrics by* Z. Sahar.)

1967.14 HENRY, SWEET HENRY

A Musical in Two Acts, 20 Scenes. Book by Nunnally Johnson. Based on the novel "The World of Henry Orient" by Nora Johnson. Music and lyrics by Bob Merrill. Entire Production directed by George Roy Hill. Choreography by Michael Bennett. Scenery and lighting by Robert Randolph. Costumes by Alvin Colt. Musical direction and vocal arrangements by Shepard Coleman. Orchestrations by Eddie Sauter. Dance music by William Goldenberg and Marvin Hamlisch. Associate producer, Joseph H. Shoctor. Produced by Edward Spector Productions and Norman Twain. Opened 23 October 1967 at the Palace Theatre and closed 31 December 1967 after 80 performances.

CAST (in order of appearance): *Kafritz:* ALICE PLAYTEN. *Valerie Boyd:* ROBIN WILSON. *Miss Cooney:* Barbara Beck. *Marian Gilbert:* NEVA SMALL. *Henry Orient:* DON AMECHE. *Stella:* LOUISE LASSER. *Mrs. Gilbert:* Trudy Wallace. *Usherette:* Julie Sargant. *Mrs. Boyd:* CAROL BRUCE. *Russ:* John Mineo. *Captain Kenneth:* George NeJame. *Hal:* Robert Iscove. *Policeman:* Gerard Brentte. *Mr. Boyd:* MILO BOULTON. *Policeman:* Charles Rule. *Big Val:* K. C. TOWNSHEND.

Norton School Students: Chris Bocchino, Lori Cesar, Terry Forman, Joyce James, Baayork Lee, Gina Page, Ilene Schatz, Joy Stark, Rebecca Urich, Pia Zadora. *Knickerbocker Greys:* Paul Charles, Robert Iscove, Joe Mazzello, Kim Milford, John Mineo, George NeJame, Craig Wineline. *Adult Ensemble:* Robert Avian, Barbara Beck, Gerard Brentte, Gene Castle, Robert Fitch, Marvin Goodis, Neil Jones, Mary Ann Kerrick, Priscilla Lopez, Lee Lund, Laried Montgomery, Charles Rule, Julie Sargant, Mary Ann Snow, Trudy Wallace.

The action takes place in present day New York City.

Act 1, Scene 1: A Street in New York City. *Scene 2:* Locker Room. *Scene 3:* Central Park Zoo. *Scene 4:* Two Bedrooms. *Scene 5:* Concert Hall. *Scene 6:* Val's Bedroom. *Scene 7:* Telephone Booths. *Scene 8:* Luncheonette. *Scene 9:* Street Telephone Booth. *Scene 10:* Orient's Apartment—Exterior and Interior.

Act 2, Scene 1: Boyd's Living Room. *Scene 2:* Washington Square. *Scene 3:* Orient's Apartment. *Scene 4:* Boyd's Living Room. *Scene 5:* Exterior School and Locker Room. *Scene 6:* Cocktail Bar. *Scene 7:* Exterior Orient's Apartment. *Scene 8:* Boyd's Living Room. *Scene 9:* Orient's Bedroom. *Scene 10:* Val's Bedroom; Knickerbocker Grey Happening.

ACT 1
Scene 1
"Academic Fugue"
Company
Scene 2
"In Some Little World"
R. Wilson
Scene 3
"Pillar to Post"
D. Ameche, L. Lasser
Scene 4
"Here I Am"
R. Wilson
Scene 6
"Whereas"[6]
R. Wilson, N. Small
Scene 8
"I Wonder How It Is to Dance With a Boy"
N. Small, Girls
Scene 9
"Nobody Steps on Kafritz"
A. Playten
Scene 10
"Henry, Sweet Henry"
R. Wilson, N. Small
"Woman in Love"
R. Wilson, N. Small
"The People Watchers"
Company

ACT 2
Scene 2
"Weary Near to Dyin'"
R. Wilson, Hippies
Scene 5
"Poor Little Person"
A. Playten, Girls, Knickerbocker Greys
"I'm Blue Too"
R. Wilson, N. Small
Scene 6
"To Be Artistic"
D. Ameche, C. Bruce

---

[5]Not in performance order.

[6]Dropped after opening.

Scene 9

"Forever"

    D. Ameche

Scene 10

"Do You Ever Go to Boston"

    R. Wilson

Finale: "Here I Am" (reprise)

    R. Wilson

1967.15   HELLO, DOLLY!

(All All-Black Cast takes over the) Musical Comedy in Two Acts, 15 Scenes[7]. Book by Michael Stewart. Based on the play "The Matchmaker" by Thornton Wilder. Music and lyrics by Jerry Herman. Directed and choreographed by Gower Champion. Re-staged by Lucia Victor. Settings by Oliver Smith. Costumes by Freddy Wittop. Lighting by Jean Rosenthal. Musical direction, Saul Schechtman. Orchestrations by Philip J. Lang. Dance and incidental music arranged by Peter Howard. Assistant to the director, Lucia Victor. A David Merrick-Champion Five Inc. Production. Produced by David Merrick. Opened 12 November 1967 (as part of the show's continuous run) at the St. James Theatre and closed 20 December 1969 after 889 performances[8].

CAST (in the order of appearance): *Mrs. Dolly Gallagher Levi*: PEARL BAILEY. *Ernestina*: Mary Mable King. *Ambrose Kemper*: Roger Lawson. *Horse*: Diane Conway, Barbara Harper. *Horace Vandergelder*: CAB CALLOWAY. *Ermengarde*: Sherri 'Peaches' Brewer. *Cornelius Hackl*: JACK CROWDER. *Barnaby Tucker*: WINSTON DeWITT HEMSLEY. *Irene Molloy*: EMILY YANCY. *Minnie Fay*: CHRIS CALLOWAY. *Mrs. Rose*: Marie Bryant. *Rudolph*: Morgan Freeman. *Judge*: Walter P. Brown. *Court Clerk*: James Kennon-Wilson.

Townspeople, Waiters, Etc.: Marki Bey, Edloe R. Brown, Dianne Conway, Merle Derby, Dolores Easty, Demarest Gray, Lavinia Hamilton, Barbara Harper, Pattie Harris, Lolli Hinton, Ernestine Jackson, Laverne Ligon, Joni Palmer, Saundra Sharp, Freda Turner, Guy Allen, Bryant Baker, Fred Benjamin, Walter P. Brown, Donald Coleman, Peter Colly, Dowlin Davis, Clifton Davis, Sargent Faulkner, Larry Ferrell, Julius Fields, Ray Gilbert, Olon Godare, Reginald Jackson, Don Jay, Bob Johnson, James Kennon-Wilson, Peter Norman, E. B. Smith, Joe Williams.

1967.16   HOW NOW, DOW JONES

A Musical Comedy in Two Acts, 18 Scenes. Book by Max Shulman. Based on an original idea by Carolyn Leigh. Music by Elmer Bernstein. Lyrics by Carolyn Leigh. Production directed by George Abbott. Scenic production by Oliver Smith. Costumes by Robert Mackintosh. Lighting by Martin Aronstein. Musical direction, dance and vocal arrangements by Peter Howard. Orchestrations by Philip J. Lang. Dances and musical numbers staged by Gillian Lynne. Associate producer, Samuel Liff. Produced by David Merrick by arrangement with Edwin H. Morris and Company. Opened 7 December 1967 at the Lunt-Fontanne Theatre and closed 15 June 1968 after 220 performances.

CAST (in order of appearance): *Cynthia*: BRENDA VACCARO. *Herbert*: JAMES CONGDON. *Broker*: Joe McGrath. *Kate*: MARLYN MASON. *Wingate*: HIRAM SHERMAN. *Nichols*: Bob Gorman. *Judy Evans*: Patti Davis. *Wally*: Alexander Orfaly. *Charley*: ANTHONY [Tony] ROBERTS. *Sue Ellen*: JENNIFER DARLING. *Bradbury*: REX EVERHART. *Waiter*: Tommy Tune. *Senator McFetridge*: BARNARD HUGHES. *Dow*: Stanley Simmonds. *Jones*: Martin Ambrose. *Tycoons*: Frank DeSal, Bob Gorman, John Joy, Alexander Orfaly. *Lion*: Ron Schwinn. *Customers' Men*: Bob Gorman, Frank DeSal, John Joy, Doug Spungler. *Dr. Gilman*: SAMMY SMITH. *Widows: (4): Mrs. Ragosa*: Francesca Smith. *Mrs. Klein*: Fran Stevens. *Mrs. Harris*: Sally DeMay. *Mrs. Callahan*: Lucie Lancaster. *Mrs. Millhauser*: CHARLOTTE JONES. *A.K.*: ARTHUR HUGHES.

Dancers: Oscar Anthony, Linnea Chandler, Joel Conrad, Patricia Cope, Frank DeSal, Lois Etelman, Cyndi Howard, Yanco Inone, Eileen Lawlor, Debra Lyman, Diana Quijano, Sally Ransone, George Ramos, Ron Schwinn, Doug Spingler, Ron L.

Steinbeck, Pat Trott. *Singers*: Martin Ambrose, Leigh Curran, Patti Davis, Bill Gibbens, Bob Gorman, Maria Hero, John Joy, Joe McGrath, Jack Murray, Alexander Orfaly, Anna Pagan, Dixie Stewart, Mara Worth.

The action takes place in present day New York City.

Act 1, Scene 1: Financial District. *Scene 2*: Child's Restaurant. *Scene 3*: Wingate's Private Office. *Scene 4*: Kate's Apartment. *Scene 5*: Wall Street—Early A.M. *Scene 6*: Wingate & Co., Brokers. *Scene 7*: Mrs. Millhauser's Living Room. *Scene 8*: Kate's Apartment. *Scene 9*: Wingate's Private Office. *Scene 10*: Wall Street. *Scene 11*: Dow Jones Office.

Act 2, Scene 1: New York City. *Scene 2*: Wingate's Private Office. *Scene 3*: Mrs. Millhauser's Living Room. *Scene 4*: Cynthia's Apartment. *Scene 5*: Financial District. *Scene 6*: Kate's Apartment. *Scene 7*: Wingate & Co., Brokers.

ACT 1

Scene 1

"A-B-C"

    B. Vaccaro, Tourists, Wall Streeters

Scene 2

"They Don't Make 'Em Like That Anymore"

    M. Mason, B. Vaccaro

"Live a Little"

    A. Roberts, M. Mason, New Yorkers

Crazy Night Ballet

"The Pleasure's About to Be Mine"

    A. Roberts, M. Mason

Scene 3

"A Little Investigation"

    H. Sherman, B. Hughes, S. Simmonds, M. Ambrose, Tycoons

Scene 4

"Walk Away"

    M. Mason

Scene 6

"Goodbye, Failure, Goodbye"

    A. Roberts, Customers' Men, Brokers

Scene 7

"Step to the Rear"

    A. Roberts, C. Jones, Widows, Ensemble

Scene 8

"Shakespeare Lied"

    M. Mason, B. Vaccaro, S. Smith

Scene 11

"Big Trouble"

    M. Mason

ACT 2

Scene 1

"Credo"

    S. Smith, F. Stevens, Widows, New Yorkers

"One of Those Moments"

    M. Mason

Scene 2

"Big Trouble" (reprise)

    H. Sherman, Tycoons

Scene 4

"He's Here!"

    B. Vaccaro

Scene 5

"Panic"

    Entire Cast

Scene 6

"Touch and Go"

    A. Roberts, M. Mason

Scene 7

"That's Good Enough For Me"

    Entire Cast

---

[7]Originally produced 16 January 1964 at the St. James Theatre. For Synopsis of Scenes and Musical Numbers, see original 1964 production.

[8]Production resumed with white principals 26 December 1969.

1967.17

BRIGADOON

A Revival of the Musical Play in Two Acts, a Prologue and 11 Scenes[9]. Book and lyrics by Alan Jay Lerner. Music by Frederick Loewe. Original dances and musical numbers staged by Agnes de Mille, restaged by Gemze de Lappe and Dennis Cole. Directed by Gus Schirmer. Settings by Oliver Smith. Lighting by Peggy Clark. Costumes by Stanley Simmons. Musical director, Jonathan Anderson. (Vocal arrangements by Frederick Loewe. Orchestrations by Ted Royal.) Produced by the New York City Center Light Opera Company (Jean Dalrymple, Director). Opened 13 December 1967 at the New York City Center and closed 31 December 1967 after 23 performances.

CAST (in order of appearance): *Tommy Albright:* BILL HAYES. *Jeff Douglas:* RUSSELL NYPE. *Sandy Dean:* Henry Lawrence. *Meg Brockie:* KAREN MORROW. *Archie Beaton:* Earl McDonald. *Harry Beaton:* EDWARD VILLELLA. *Andrew MacLaren:* Alexander Clark. *Jean MacLaren:* Sarah Jane Smith. *Fiona MacLaren:* MARGOT MOSER. *Angus MacGuffie:* Gordon Cook. *Charlie Dalrymple:* EVAN THOMAS. *Maggie Anderson:* Leslie Franzos. *Sword Dancers:* Dennis Cole, Wilfred Schuman. *Mr. Lundi:* William LeMassena. *Bagpiper:* Maurice Eisenstadt. *Frank:* Paul Adams. *Jane Ashton:* Jeanne Murray Vanderbilt.

Townsfolk of Brigadoon: Singers: Chris Callen, Phyllis Bash, Jane Coleman, Peggy Cooper, Mona Elson, Marta Heflin, Oksana Iweszczenko, Mina Jo King, Barbara Miller, Roberta Vatske, Paul Adams, Donald Brassington, Edward Becker, Peter Clark, Gordon Cook, Henry Lawrence, Ken Richards, Robert Monteil, Don Wonder. *Dancers:* Anita Arnell, Joanna Crosson, Chele Graham, Jane Jaffe, Nicole Karol, Karen Kristin, Lucia Lambert, Toodie Wittmer, Marget Wyeth, Paul Berne, Scott Hunter, J. David Kirby, William Koch, Dick Korthaze, Wilfred Schuman, Bud Spencer, Ron Tassone, Duane Taylor.

1967.18

HOW TO BE A JEWISH MOTHER

A Comedy with Music in Two Acts. Conceived by Seymour Vall. Based on the book of the same name by Dan Greenburg. Music by Michael Leonard. Lyrics by Herbert Marshall. Directed by Avery Schreiber. Scenery by Robert Randolph. Costumes by Michael Travis. Lighting by John J. Moore. Musical staging by Doug Rogers. Musical direction and arrangements by Julian Stein. Associate producers, Rick Mandell, Margaret Aldrich. Produced by Jon-Lee and Seymour Vall. Opened 28 December 1967 at the Hudson theatre and closed 13 January 1968 after 21 performances.

CAST: MOLLY PICON, GODFREY CAMBRIDGE.

ACT 1
"Once the Man You Laughed At"
"Laugh a Little"

ACT 2
"Since the Time We Met"
"The Wedding Song"
"Child You Are"

1968.01

THE HAPPY TIME

A Musical in Two Acts, 15 Scenes. Book by N. Richard Nash. Based on the novel by Robert L. Fontaine and the play of the same name by Samuel Taylor. Music by John Kander. Lyrics by Fred Ebb. Directed, filmed and choreographed by Gower Champion. Settings by Peter Wexler. Costumes by Freddy Wittop. Lighting by Jean Rosenthal. Film sequences created by Christopher Chapman. Film technical direction by Barry O. Gordon. Orchestrations by Don Walker. Musical direction and vocal arrangements by Oscar Kosarin. Associate choreographer, Kevin Carlisle. Dance and incidental music arrangements by Marvin Laird. Associate producer, Samuel Liff. Produced by David Merrick. Opened 18 January 1968 at the Broadway Theatre and closed 28 September 1968 after 286 performances.

CAST (in order of appearance): *Jacques Bonnard:* ROBERT GOULET. *Suzanne Bonnard:* Jeanne Arnold. *Philippe Bonnard:* GEORGE S. IRVING. *Bibi Bonnard:* MIKE [Michael] RUPERT. *Louis Bonnard:* CHARLES DURNING. *Annabelle Bonnard:* Kim Freund. *Gillie Bonnard:* Julane Stites. *Nanette Bonnard:* Connie Simmons. *Felice Bonnard:* JUNE SQUIBB. *Grandpere Bonnard:* DAVID WAYNE. *The Six Angels: Lizette:* Jacki Garland. *Dorine:* Mary Gail Laverenz. *Sylvie:* Tammie Fillhart. *Monique:* Mary Ann O'Reilly. *Bella:* Vicki Powers. *Grace:* Susan Sigrist. *Laurie Mannon:* JULIE GREGG. *Foufie:* Jeffrey Golkin. *Ganache:* Dallas Johann. *Swing Dancer:* Sammy Williams.

Dancers: Ron Abshire, Jovanni Anthony, Quinn Baird, Andy Bew, Blake Brown, Leonard Crofoot, Ron Crofoot, Wayne Dugger, Joe Giamalva, Dallas Johann, Gene Law, Steve Reinhart, Jon Simonson, Michael Stearns. *Singers:* Marc Anthony, Alan Blight, George Connolly, Tom De Mastri, Paul Dwyer, Scott Gandert, Eric Hamilton, Gary Hamilton, Jeffrey Hamilton, Kevin Hamilton, Mark Lonergan, Brian Shyer, Brandy Wayne, Teddy Williams, Marc Winters.

The action takes place in the past in Jacques Bonnard's studio; and earlier still, in his home in a small town in Canada.

Act 1, Scene 1: Jacques' Studio. *Scene 2:* The Bonnard Home. *Scene 3:* The theatre. *Scene 4:* Bibi's bedroom. *Scene 5:* The Classroom. *Scene 6:* The Schoolyard. *Scene 7:* The Bonnard garden.

Act 2, Scene 1: Jacques' studio. *Scene 2:* A street in St. Pierre. *Scene 3:* The gymnasium. *Scene 4:* After the party. *Scene 5:* The Schoolyard. *Scene 6:* Grandpere's room. *Scene 7:* Jacques' studio. *Scene 8:* The School, Bibi's graduation.

ACT 1
Scene 1
    "The Happy Time"
        R. Goulet, Family
Scene 2
    "He's Back"
        The Family
Scene 3
    "Catch My Garter"
        The Six Angels
    "Tomorrow Morning"
        R. Goulet, D. Wayne, M. Rupert, The Six Angels
Scene 4
    "Please Stay"
        M. Rupert, R. Goulet
    "I Don't Remember You"
        R. Goulet
Scene 5
    "St. Pierre"
        The Glee Club
    "I Don't Remember You" (reprise)
        J. Gregg, R. Goulet
Scene 6
    "Without Me"
        M. Rupert, Schoolmates
Scene 7
    "The Happy Time" (reprise)
        R. Goulet

ACT 2
Scene 1
    "(Walking) Among My Yesterdays"
        R. Goulet
Scene 2
    ("Please Stay" reprise)
        (J. Gregg)
Scene 3
    "The Life of the Party"
        D. Wayne, The Six Angels, Schoolboys
Scene 4
    "Seeing Things"
        R. Goulet, J. Gregg
Scene 5
    Ballet
        M. Rupert, J. Stites, K. Freund, C. Simmons, Schoolboys

[9]Originally produced in New York 13 March 1947 at the Ziegfeld Theatre for 581 performances. For Synopsis of Scenes and Musical Numbers, see original 1947 production.

Scene 6

   "A Certain Girl"

      D. Wayne, R. Goulet, M. Rupert

Scene 7

   "Being Alive"[10]

      R. Goulet

Scene 8

   ("St. Pierre" reprise)

   (Schoolboys)

   "The Happy Time" (reprise)

      R. Goulet, Entire Company

1968.02   DARLING OF THE DAY

A Musical Comedy in Two Acts, 14 Scenes. Based on the novel "Buried Alive" by Arnold Bennett. Music by Jule Styne. Lyrics by E. Y. Harburg. Directed by Noel Willman. Choreography by Lee Theodore. Scenery by Oliver Smith. Costumes by Raoul Pene du Bois. Lighting by Peggy Clark. Musical direction and vocal arrangements by Buster Davis. Dance music by Trude Rittman. Orchestrations by Ralph Burns. Produced by The Theatre Guild and Joel Schenker. Opened 27 January 1968 at the George Abbott Theatre and closed 24 February 1968 after 33 performances[11].

CAST (in order of appearances): *Oxford*: PETER WOODTHORPE. *Priam Farll*: VINCENT PRICE. *Henry Leek*: Charles Welch. *Old Gentleman*: Carl Nicholas. *Lady Vale*: BRENDA FORBES. *Cabby*: Ross Miles. *Doctor*: Leo Leyden. *Alice Challice*: PATRICIA ROUTLEDGE. *Daphne*: Joy Nichols. *Alf*: TEDDY GREEN. *Bert*: Marc Jordan. *Rosalind*: Beth Howland. *Sydney*: Reid Klein. *Attendant*: Larry Brucker. *Frame Maker*: Paul Eichel. *Duncan*: Mitchell Jason. *Equerry*: John Aman. *The King*: Charles Gerald. *Constable*: John Aman. *Mrs. Leek*: Camila Ashland. *Curates*: Herb Wilson, Fred Siretta. *Pennington*: Micahel Lewis. *Judge*: Leo Leyden.

   Singers: Marian Haraldson, Kay Oslin, Jeannette Seibert, Maggie Task, Maggie Worth, John Aman, Larry Brucker, Paul Eichel, Reid Klein, Carl Nicholas, Albert Zimmerman. *Dancers*: Bonnie Ano, Reby Howells, Beth Howland, Georgianne Thon, Phyllis Wallach, Denise Winston, Christopher Chadman, George Lee, Jim May, Ross Miles, Fred Siretta, Herb Wilson.

The action takes place in London and Putney in 1905.

Act 1, Scene 1: Oxford's Art Gallery—London. *Scene 2*: Farll's London House. *Scene 3*: The Pub in Putney. *Scene 4*: Farll's London House. *Scene 5*: London Street. *Scene 6*: Paradise Villa, Putney. *Scene 7*: Oxford's Salon. *Scene 8*: The Thames River Bank. *Scene 9*: Paradise Villa.

Act 2, Scene 1: Oxford's Salon. *Scene 2*: Paradise Villa Garden. *Scene 3*: Putney High Street. *Scene 4*: The Pub. *Scene 5*: The Courtroom.

ACT 1

Scene 1

   "Mad For Art"

      Art Lovers (Ensemble)

   "He's a Genius"

      P. Woodthorpe, V. Price, C. Welch

Scene 2

   "To Get Out of This World Alive"

      V. Price

Scene 3

   "It's Enough To Make a Lady Fall in Love"

      P. Routledge, T. Green, M. Jordan, Putney Friends
      (Ensemble)

Scene 5

   "A Gentleman's Gentleman"

      P. Routledge, T. Green, M. Jordan, V. Price, M. Jason, Bystanders
      (Ensemble)

Scene 6

   "Double Soliloquy"

      V. Price, P. Routledge

---

[10]Dropped after opening.

[11]Book uncredited; bookwriter Nunnally Johnson withdrew his name from credits during tryout.

   "Let's See What Happens"

      P. Routledge, V. Price

Scene 7

   "Panache"

      P. Woodthorpe, B. Forbes

Scene 8

   "I've Got a Rainbow Working for Me"

      V. Price, Putney Friends (Ensemble)

Scene 9

   "Money, Money, Money"

      T. Green, M. Jordan, R. Klein

   "That Something Extra Special"

      P. Routledge

   "Money, Money, Money" (reprise)

      T. Green, M. Jordan, R. Klein

ACT 2

Scene 2

   "What Makes a Marriage Merry"

      P. Routledge, V. Price, T. Green, M. Jordan, J. Nichols,
      B. Howland

   "He's a Genius" (reprise)

      P. Woodthorpe, Assistants

Scene 4

   "Not on Your Nellie"

      P. Routledge, T. Green, M. Jordan, Putney Friends
      (Ensemble)

   "Sunset Tree"

      V. Price, P. Routledge

Scene 5

   "Butler in the Abbey"

      V. Price, Courtroom (Ensemble)

   "Not on Your Nellie" (reprise)

      Entire Company

1968.03   GOLDEN RAINBOW

A Musical (Comedy) in Two Acts, 13 Scenes. Book by Ernest Kinoy. Based on a play ("A Hole in the Head") by Arnold Schulman. Music and lyrics by Walter Marks. Directed by Arthur Storch. Choreography by Tom Panko. Scenery and lighting by Robert Randolph. Costumes by Alvin Colt. Musical direction and vocal arrangements by Elliot Lawrence. Orchestrations by Pat Williams and Jack Andrews. Dance music arranged by Marvin Hamlisch and Luther Henderson. Associate choreographer, Martin Allen. Additional scoring by Elliot Lawrence. A Diplomat Production. Produced by Joseph P. Harris and Ira Bernstein. Opened 4 February 1968 at the Sam S. Shubert Theatre and closed 12 January 1969 after 385 performances.

CAST (in order of appearance): *Mr. Novotny*: Alan Kass. *Ally*: SCOTT JACOBY. *Mr. Hausknecht*: Howard Mann. *Eloise*: Linda Jorgens. *Laundryman*: Charles Karel. *Henry*: Will Hussung. *Mr. Diamond*: Sid Raymond. *Larry Davis*: STEVE LAWRENCE. *Mrs. Magruder*: Fay Sappington. *Lou Garrity*: JOSEPH SIROLA. *Jerome Stone*: Gene Foote. *Rosemary Garrity*: Marilyn Cooper. *Gordon*: John Anania. *Mr. Korngold*: Sam Kressen. *First Reporter*: Charles Karel. *Second Reporter*: Lanier Davis. *Lead Dancer*: Diana Saunders. *Judy Harris*: EYDIE GORME. *Georgia*: Carol Conte. *Stripper*: Thelma Sherr. *Sam*: Frank Pietri. *Umbawa*: Larry Merritt. *Persian Girl*: Linda Jorgens. *Cat Girl*: Carole Bishop. *Nebuchadnezzar*: John Anania. *Virgin*: Diana Saunders. *Hero*: Antony DeVecchi. *Stage Manager*: Charles Karel. *Victor*: Lanier Davis. *Gambler*: Michael Vita.

   Dancers: Carole Bishop, Carol Conte, Susan Donovan, Antony DeVecchi, Tina Faye, Alice Glenn, Linda Jorgens, Maralyn Miles, Jean Preece, Wayne Boyd, Gene Foote, Blair Hammond, Larry Merritt, Frank Pietri, Tom Rolla, Michael Shawn, Michael Vita. *Showgirls*: Betty Jo Alvies, Bernadette Brookes, Rae Samuels, Thelma Sherr.

The action takes place in Las Vegas—Today.

Act 1, Scene 1: The Strip—Las Vegas. *Scene 2*: Golden Rainbow Lobby. *Scene 3*: The Airport. *Scene 4*: Golden Rainbow Lobby. *Scene 5*: The Algeria Patio Restaurant. *Scene 6*: Golden Rainbow Pantry. *Scene 7*: Golden Rainbow Lobby.

Act 2, Scene 1: Babylon Nightclub. *Scene 2*: Backstage. *Scene 3*: The Desert. *Scene 4*: Golden Rainbow Lobby. *Scene 5*: Babylon Casino. *Scene 6*: The Golden Rainbow.

ACT 1
Scene 1
  "Golden Rainbow"[12]
    Las Vegans (Ensemble)
Scene 2
  "We Got Us"
    S. Lawrence, S. Jacoby
Scene 3
  "He Needs Me Now"
    E. Gorme
Scene 4
  "Kid"
    S. Lawrence
Scene 5
  "For Once in Your Life"
    E. Gorme, S. Lawrence, Boys
Scene 6
  "Taking Care of You"
    E. Gorme, S. Jacoby, Friends (Ensemble)
Scene 7
  "I've Got To Be Me"
    S. Lawrence
ACT 2
Scene 1
  "The Fall of Babylon"
    Babylonians (Ensemble)
Scene 2
  "Taste"
    J. Sirola, Friends (Ensemble)
Scene 3
  "Desert Moon"
    S. Lawrence, E. Gorme
  "All in Fun"
    S. Lawrence, E. Gorme
Scene 4
  "It's You Again"
    E. Gorme
Scene 5
  "I've Got To Be Me" (reprise)
    S. Lawrence
Scene 6
  "How Could I Be So Wrong"
    E. Gorme
  "We Got Us" (reprise)
    S. Lawrence, E. Gorme, S. Jacoby
  Finale
    Entire Company

THE GRAND MUSIC HALL
OF ISRAEL

1968.04

A Musical Revue (from Israel) in Two Acts, 13 Scenes, in Hebrew. Staged and choreographed by Jonathan Karmon. Musical direction and arrangements by Itzchak Graziani. Assistant director, Gavri Levi. Costumes designed by Hovav Kruvi; costumes executed by Bertha Kwartz. Lighting by Jules Fisher. Assistant conductor, Ami Gilad. Produced by Lee Guber and Shelly Gross by arrangement with Bruno Coquatrix. Opened 6 February 1968 at the Palace Theatre and closed 31 March 1968 after 64 performances.

CAST: HELENA HENDEL, GEULA GILL and THE HIGH WILLOWS (David Tal, Ygal Hared, Hedva Amrani), ILAN and ILANIT, THE CARMELIM (Ruty, David, Shima, Michal, Hannan), NISHRI, BOAZ and NECHEMIA, ALICE (Abou Samra) and HANNAN (Goldblatt), THE KARMON HISTADRUTH BALLET.

[12]Replaced shortly after opening:
  "24 Hours a Day"
    Las Vegans (Ensemble)

ACT 1[13]
Scene 1
  "Israeli Rhapsody"
    Karmon Histadruth Ballet
Scene 2
  Songs of Youth:
    Ilan and Ilanit
  "Lavriada"
    (*Music and Lyrics by* M. Lavry- Itzchak Graziani.)
  "Bekol Makom"
    (*Music and Lyrics by* Gilad Ben Shachar.)
  "Nagnu Bekol"
    (*Music and Lyrics by* Fred-Nil-Drora Chafkin.)
  "Shav Ani Eleich"
    (*Music and Lyrics by* Gilad Ben Shachar.)
Scene 3
  "Dance of the Fisherman"
    Karmon Histadruth Ballet
Scene 4
  Oriental Rhythms
    Boaz and Nechema
Scene 5
  The New Sound of Isarel's Hit Parade:
    The Carmelim
  "Keren Yar"
    (*Music and Lyrics by* Naomi Shemer.)
  "Shilgia"
    (*Music and Lyrics by* Naomi Shemer and Guy Béart.)
  "Machar"
    (*Music and Lyrics by* Naomi Shemer and Itzchak Graziani.)
Scene 6
  "Hassidic"
    (*Music by* Gill Aldena.)
    Karmon Histadruth Ballet

ACT 2
Scene 1
  Desert Rhythms (On the Seaside of the Mediterranean)
    Karmon Histadruth Ballet
Scene 2
  The Story of Her People in Song
    H. Hendel
Scene 3
  A day like everyday in a Kibbutz on the Border
    Yona, Karmon Histadruth Ballet
Scene 4
  Music in a Novel Manner:
  "Sabre Dance"
    (*Music by* Aram Katchaturian.)
    Nishri (xylophone virtuoso)
Scene 5
  The New Spirit of a people in their singing style
    The High Willows, G. Gill
Scene 6
  "The Feasts of the Kibbutz"
    Karmon Histadruth Ballet
Scene 7
  Shalom from the Grand Music Hall of Israel
    Entire Company

[13]The songs and dances performed were not specifically identified in the program. Above list was prepared from reviews, press releases and cast recording. The latter was made prior to the Broadway run with a somewhat different cast, and the show continued to tour with revised cast, songs and dances subsequent to New York.

HERE'S WHERE I BELONG

1968.05

A Musical in Two Acts, 17 Scenes. Book by Alex Gordon[14]. Based on the novel "East of Eden" by John Steinbeck. Music by Robert Waldman. Lyrics by Alfred Uhry. Entire production directed by Michael Kahn. Dances and musical staging by Tony Mordente. Scenery by Ming Cho Lee. Costumes by Ruth Morley. Lighting by Jules Fisher. Musical direction and vocal arrangements by Theodore Saidenberg. Dance music by Arnold Goland. Orchestrations by Glenn Osser, Norman Leyden and Jonathan Tunick. Produced by Mitch Miller in association with United Artists. Opened and closed 3 March 1968 after 1 performance.

CAST (in order of appearance): *Adam Trask*: PAUL ROGERS. *Caleb Trask (Cal)*: WALTER McGINN. *Aron Trask*: KEN KERCHEVAL. *Lee*: JAMES COCO. *Will Hamilton*: Casper Roos. *Mrs. Bacon*: Bette Henritze. *Mrs. Tripp*: Dena Dietrich. *Mrs. Heink*: Patricia Kelly. *Abra Bacon*: HEATHER MacRAE. *School Children*: Lee Wilson, Tod Miller. *Miss Ida*: Barbara Webb. *Rabbit Holman*: Scott Jarvis. *Faith*: Graciela Daniele. *Eva*: Aniko Morgan. *Della*: Dorothy Lister. *Kate*: NANCY WICKWIRE. *Joe*: Joseph Nelson. *Juana*: Joetta Cherry. *Newspaper Man*: Taylor Reed. *British Purchasing Agent*: Darrell J. Askey.

Townspeople, Field Workers, Denizens of Castroville Street: Darrell J. Askey, Joetta Cherry, Graciela Daniele, Elisa DeMarko, Larry Devon, John Dickerson, Bud Fleming, John William Gardner, Gene Gavin, John Johann, Ray Kirchner, Jane Laughlin, Dorothy Lister, Andy Love, Richard Marr, David McCorkle, Joyce McDonald, Tod Miller, Aniko Morgan, Joan Nelson, Joseph Nelson, Donald Norris, Taylor Reed, Clifford Scott, Joy Serio, Michele Simmons, David Thomas, Barbara Webb, Lee Wilson.

Prologue: The Trask house in Salinas, California, 1915.

Act 1, Scene 1: Castroville, two years later. *Scene 2*: The Trask house, later that day. *Scene 3*: Kate's place, immediately following. *Scene 4*: The streets of Salinas, immediately following. *Scene 5*: The ice house, several weeks later. *Scene 6*: The lettuce fields, six weeks later. *Scene 7*: Near the depot, the same day. *Scene 8*: The train depot, immediately following. *Scene 9*: The Trask house, three days later. *Scene 10*: The willow tree, early the next morning.

Act 2, Scene 1: Salinas, downtown. Two months later. *Scene 2*: The Salinas bank, two weeks later. *Scene 3*: Kate's place, the same day. *Scene 4*: The willow tree, the next day. *Scene 5*: The Trask house, Thanksgiving dinner. *Scene 6*: Outside Kate's, immediately following. *Scene 7*: The Trask house, a few hours later.

ACT 1

Prologue

"We Are What We Are"
P. Rogers, W. McGinn, J. Coco, K. Kercheval

"Cal Gets By"
W. McGinn

Scene 1

"Raising Cain"
W. McGinn, Ensemble

Scene 2

"Soft Is the Sparrow"
K. Kercheval

Scene 4

"Where Have I Been"
P. Rogers, J. Coco, Townspeople (Ensemble)

Scene 5

"No Time"
W. McGinn, K. Kercheval

"Progress"
Male Ensemble

"Good Boy"

Scene 6

Ballet
W. McGinn, J. Cherry, H. MacRae, Dancing Ensemble

Scene 7

"Act Like a Lady"
H. MacRae

Scene 8

"The Send-Off"
Townspeople

[14]Book credited to Terrence McNally during tryout and previews. There is no such person as "Alex Gordon."

Scene 9

"Top of the Train"
P. Rogers, W. McGinn

Scene 10

"Waking Up Sun"
H. MacRae, W. McGinn

ACT 2

Scene 1

"Pulverize the Kaiser"
B. Henritze, D. Dietrich, P. Kelly, Townspeople

"Where Have I Been" (reprise)
P. Rogers

Scene 3

"You're Mama's"
N. Wickwire

Scene 4

"Here's Where I Belong"
W. McGinn, H. MacRae

Scene 5

"We're a Home"
P. Rogers, J. Coco, K. Kercheval, H. MacRae, W. McGinn

THE EDUCATION OF H*Y*M*A*N K*A*P*L*A*N

1968.06

A Musical in Two Acts, 13 Scenes. Book by Benjamin Bernard Zavin. Based on the collected stories (of the same name) by Leo Rosten. Music and lyrics by Paul Nassau and Oscar Brand. Production directed by George Abbott. Settings by William and Jean Eckart. Costumes by Winn Morton. Lighting by Martin Aronstein. Musical direction and vocal arrangements by Julian Stein. Orchestrations by Larry Wilcox. Dance music arranged by Lee Holdridge. Dances and musical numbers staged by Jaime Rogers. Associate producer, David W. Sampliner. Produced by Andre Goulston/Jack Farren and Stephen Mellow. Opened 4 April 1968 at the Alvin Theatre and closed 27 April 1968 after 28 performances.

CAST (in order of appearance): *Jimmy*: Stephen Bolster. *Pushcart Vendor*: Dick Ensslen. *Old Clothes Man*: Cyril Murkin. *Kathy McKenna*: Donna McKechnie. *Sam Pinsky*: NATHANIEL FREY. *Reuben Plonsky*: David Gold. *Giovanni Pastora*: Dick Latessa. *Mrs. Moskowitz*: Honey Sanders. *Sarah Moskowitz*: Susan Camber. *Mr. Parkhill*: GARY KRAWFORD. *Fanny Gidwitz*: Maggie Task. *Rose Mitnick*: BARBARA MINKUS. *Hyman Kaplan*: TOM BOSLEY. *Eileen Higby*: Dorothy Emmerson. *Marie Vitale*: Beryl Towbin. *Mrs. Mitnick*: Mimi Sloan. *Officer Callahan*: Wally Engelhardt. *Yissel Fishbein*: HAL LINDEN. *Guard*: David Ellin. *Judge Mahon*: Rufus Smith.

Dancers: Pamlea Barlow, Mickie Bier, Susan Camber, Joanne DiVito, Andrea Duda, Lee Lund, Kuniko Narai, Eileen Woliner, Takeshi Hamagaki, Yanco Inone, Pat Matera, Barry Preston, George Ramos, Steven Ross. *Singers*: Alice Cannon, Martha Danielle, Trudy Wallace, Edward Becker, David Ellin, Jack Fletcher.

The action takes place in New York City, the Lower East Side, from 1919-1920.

Act 1, Scene 1: A Street on the Lower East Side. *Scene 2*: Mr. Parkhill's Classroom. *Scene 3*: Teachers' Room. *Scene 4*: Mr. Parkhill's Classroom. *Scene 5*: Rose Mitnick's Apartment. *Scene 6*: A Street. *Scene 7*: Mr. Parkhill's Classroom. *Scene 8*: A Street.

Act 2, Scene 1: Kaplan's Flat. *Scene 2*: Mr. Parkhill's Classroom. *Scene 3*: Ellis Island Deportation Room. *Scene 4*: Judge Mahon's Chambers. *Scene 5*: Hyman Kaplan's Shop. *Scene 6*: Street in front of the School. *Scene 7*: A U.S. Courtroom.

ACT 1

Scene 1

"Strange New World"
G. Krawford

Scene 2

"OOOO-EEEE"
T. Bosley, B. Minkus, G. Krawford, Students

Scene 3

"A Dedicated Teacher" ("Teachers on Parade")
D. Emmerson, B. Towbin, G. Krawford

Scene 4

"Lieben Dich"
T. Bosley

"Loving You"
  B. Minkus
Scene 5
  "The Day I Met Your Father"
    M. Sloan
Scene 6
  "Anything Is Possible"
    T. Bosley, Students, Dancers, Singers
Scene 8
  "Spring in the City"
    D. McKechnie, D. Latessa, D. Gold, N. Frey,
    H. Sanders, M. Task, Dancers, Singers
ACT 2
Scene 1
  "Old Fashioned Husband"
    H. Linden
Scene 2
  "Julius Caesar" ("Shakespeare")
    T. Bosley
Scene 3
  "I Never Felt Better in My Life"
    T. Bosley, Dancers, Singers
Scene 5
  "When Will I Learn"
    B. Minkus
Scene 6
  "All American"
    N. Frey, Students

1968.07   GEORGE M!

A Musical in Two Acts, a Prologue, Epilogue and 16 Scenes. Book by
Michael Stewart, John and Fran Pascal. (Suggested by the life of George M.
Cohan.) Music and lyrics by George M. Cohan. Lyric and musical revisions
by Mary Cohan. Entire production directed and choreographed by Joe
Layton. Musical supervision by Laurence Rosenthal. Scenery by Tom John.
Costumes by Freddy Wittop. Lighting by Martin Aronstein. Musical direc-
tion and vocal arrangements by Jay Blackton. Orchestrations by Philip J.
Lang. Production supervisor, Jose Vega. Produced by David Black, Konrad
Matthaei and Lorin E. Price. Opened 10 April 1968 at the Palace Theatre
and closed 26 April 1969 after 435 performances.

CAST (in alphabetical order): *Dog Trainer, Second Pianist, Fay Templeton's maid
Rose*: Loni Ackerman. *Living Statue, Secretary in Cohan & Harris office*: Jonelle Allen.
Fay Templeton, Draper's Assistant, Wardrobe Lady: JACQUELINE ALLOWAY. *Living
Statue, Pushcart Girl*: Karin Baker. *First Little Girl, Mrs. Red Deer, Sharpshooter's
Assistant, Little Girl with Fay Templeton*: Susan Batson. *Acrobat, Boy in Pushcart*: Billy
Brandon. *Dr. Webb, E. F. Albee, Living Statue, Ben, Mayor*: Roger Braun. *Louis
Behman, Bell Ringer, Vendor, Fay Templeton's Manager (Freddie)*: DANNY
CARROLL. *Willie in 'Popularity,' Sharpshooter, Walt (Stage Manager of 'I'd Rather Be
Right')*: GENE CASTLE. *Jerry Cohan*: JERRY DODGE. *Ethel Levey*: JAMIE
DONNELLY. *Stagehand, Dog Trainer, Louie, Congressman Burkhardt, Actor in Strike
Scene*: James Dybas. *Sam Harris, Violinist, Bell Ringer*: Harvey Evans. *George M.
Cohan*: JOEL GREY. *Nellie Cohan*: BETTY ANN GROVE. *Second Little, Girl,
Acrobat*: Patti Mariano. *Ventriloquist, Ma Templeton*: Angela Martin. *Archie, Draper,
Dockhand, Judge Anspacher, First Policeman in "Nellie Kelly," Man on Street*: John
Mineo. *Agnes Nolan*: JILL O'HARA. *Josie Cohan*: BERNADETTE PETERS. *First
Pianist, Acrobat, Bell Ringer, Piano Player in Cohan & Harris Office*: Scott Salmon.
Living Statue, Pushcart Girl: Kathie Savage. *Madame Grimaldi, Mrs. Baker, Flame-
thrower's Assistant*: JANIE SELL. *Buck and Winger, Designer's Assistant, Sailor,
Frankie*: Alan Weeks. *Saxophonist, Flamehrower, Bell Ringer, Ship's Captain, Alderman
Hailey, Accordionist in 'Harrigan,' Director of 'I'd Rather Be Right'*: Ronald Young.

Prologue. Act 1, Scene 1: Providence, Rhode Island, 1878. *Scene 2*: Onstage, Columbia
Theatre, Cedar Rapids. *Scene 3*: Street in Cedar Rapids. *Scene 4*: Madame Grimaldi's
Boarding House. *Scene 5*: En route to New York. *Scene 6*: Adams Street Theatre,
various other theatres, New York, 1901-1903. *Scene 7*: General Area, New York, then in
front of Savoy Theatre. *Scene 8*: Stage of Liberty Theatre, New York.

Act 2, Scene 1: Office of Cohan & Harris; Fay Templeton's Apartment. *Scene 2*:
Onstage, New Amsterdam Theatre. *Scene 3*: Rector's Restaurant, January 1, 1907.
Scene 4: Street Outside Rector's, next morning. *Scene 5*: The Years till 1919. *Scene 6*:
The years till 1937. *Scene 7*: Midtown New York, February 1937. *Scene 8*: Stage of the
Alvin Theatre. *Epilogue.*

ACT 1
Scene 2
  "Musical Moon" (from THE LITTLE MILLIONAIRE)
    J. Dodge, B. A. Grove
  "Oh, You Wonderful Boy" (revised, from THE LITTLE
  MILLIONAIRE)
    B. Peters
  "All Aboard for Broadway" (from GEORGE WASHINGTON, JR.)
    J. Grey, J. Dodge, B. A. Grove, B. Peters
Scene 3
  "Musical Comedy Man"[15] (revised, from THE HONEYMOONERS)
    J. Grey, J. Dodge, B. A. Grove, B. Peters, Full Company
Scene 5
  "All Aboard for Broadway" (reprise)
    J. Grey, J. Dodge, B. A. Grove, B. Peters, Full Company
Scene 6
  "I Was Born in Virginia" (from GEORGE WASHINGTON, JR.)
    J. Donnelly
  "Twentieth Century Love" (from THE MERRY MALONES)
    J. Grey, J. Dodge, B. A. Grove, B. Peters, J. Donnelly
Scene 7
  "My Town"
    J. Grey
Scene 8
  "Billie" (from BILLIE)
    J. O'Hara
  "Push Me Along in My Pushcart" (from THE GOVERNOR'S SON,
  1906 revival)
    J. Donnelly, Pushcart Girls
  "Ring to the Name of Rose" (from THE RISE OF ROSIE O'REILLY)
    B. Peters, Bell Ringers
  "Popularity"
    G. Castle, Full Company
  "Give My Regards to Broadway" (from LITTLE JOHNNY JONES)
    J. Grey, Full Company

ACT 2
Scene 1
  "Forty Five Minutes from Broadway"
  (from FORTY FIVE MINUTES FROM BROADWAY)
    J. Grey, L. Ackerman
  "So Long Mary" (from FORTY FIVE MINUTES
  FROM BROADWAY)
    J. Grey, H. Evans, L. Ackerman, D. Carroll, A. Martin
  "Down by the Erie (Canal)" (from HELLO, BROADWAY!)
    J. Allen, Politicians, S. Batson, Full Company
Scene 2
  "Mary" (as "Mary's a Grand Old Name" from FORTY FIVE
  MINUTES FROM BROADWAY)
    J. Alloway
Scene 3
  "All Our Friends" (revised, "They're All My Boys" from LITTLE
  NELLIE KELLY)
    H. Evans, Full Company
Scene 5
  "Yankee Doodle Dandy"(as "Yankee Doodle Boy" from LITTLE
  JOHNNY JONES)
  "Harrigan" (from FIFTY MILES FROM BOSTON)
  "Nellie Kelly, I Love You" (from LITTLE NELLIE KELLY)
  "Over There"
  "You're a Grand Old Flag" (from GEORGE WASHINGTON, JR.)
    J. Grey, Full Company

---

[15]Replaced for subsequent national tour by:
  "The Four of Us" (revised "The Two of Us," from BILLIE)

Scene 6

"The City" (Montage of "The Man Who Owns Broadway" from THE MAN WHO OWNS BROADWAY)
Full Company

Scene 8

"I'd Rather Be Right" (from I'D RATHER BE RIGHT)
J. Grey, Company
(*Music by* Richard Rodgers. *Lyrics by* Lorenz Hart.)

"Give My Regards to Broadway" (reprise)
J. Grey

Epilogue[16]

"Dancing Our Worries Away" (revised, from LITTLE NELLIE KELLY)

"The Great Easter Sunday Parade"

"Hannah's a Hummer" (from THE WISE GUY)

"Barnum and Bailey Rag" (from HELLO, BROADWAY!)

"The Belle of the Barber's Ball" (from COHAN AND HARRIS MINSTRELS)

"The American Ragtime" (from THE AMERICAN IDEA)

"All in the Wearing" (from LITTLE NELLIE KELLY)

"I Want to Hear a Yankee Doodle Tune" (from MOTHER GOOSE)
Full Company

(Recording at end of epilogue by George M. Cohan.)

Four Cohans (Edie Cowan, Darryl Hickman, Linda Larson, Ted Pritchard)

I'M SOLOMON

1968.08

A Musical Fable in Two Acts. Book by Anne Croswell and Dan Almagor. Based on the (Israeli) drama "King Solomon and the Cobbler" by Sammy Gronemann. American adaptation in collaboration with Zvi Kolitz. Music by Ernest Gold. Lyrics by Anne Croswell. Entire production directed and supervised by Michael Benthall. Settings by Rouben Ter-Arutunian. Costumes by Jane Greenwood. Lighting by Martin Aronstein. Musical direction and vocal arrangements by Gershon Kingsley. Orchestrations by Hershy Kay. Special material by David Finkle and Bill Weeden. Dance arrangements by Dorothea Freitag. Dances and musical numbers staged by Donald McKayle. Associate producers, Philip Turk and Kalman Ginzburg. Produced by Zvi Kolitz, Solomon Sagall, and Abe Margolies. Opened 23 April 1968 at the Mark Hellinger Theatre and closed 27 April 1968 after 7 performances.

CAST (in order of appearance): *Meir*, the Drummer: Meir Alon. *Ali*, the Flute Player: Al DeSio. *Isaac*, a Tavern Keeper: John Dorrin. *Tavern Dancer*: Sally Neal. *Yoni*, a Cobbler: DICK SHAWN. *Na'Ama*, his wife: KAREN MORROW. *Yoel*, Temple Building Supervisor: Kenneth Scott. *Mago*, Architect of the Temple: John LaMotta. *Lemech*, a Dyer: Eddie Ericksen. *Aviva*, a Harlot: Alice Evans. *Bruria*, a Harlot: Lynn Archer. *An Officer of the Royal Guard*: Gordon Cook. *Ben Hesed*, Commander of the Royal Guard: PAUL REED. *Princess Nofrit*, Solomon's Favorite Wife: Barbara Webb. *F'htar*, her Slave: Mary Barnett. *Solomon*: DICK SHAWN. *Bathsheba*, Solomon's Mother: CARMEN MATHEWS. *An Ambassador*: Nat Horne. *Ranor*, Ambassador of the Queen of Sheba: Fred Pinkard. *Aide to Ranor*: Garrett Morris. *Rachel*, one of Solomon's wives: Caryl Tenney. *Makedah*, a Member of the Queen of Sheba's Party: SALOME JENS.

Solomon's Concubines: Jeri Barto, Connie Burnett, Miriam Ehrenberg, Carol Flemming, Mary Jane Houdina, Nina Janik, Carol Manning, Sally Neal, Martha Pollak, Renee Rose, Joan Tannen, Nina Trasoff, Myrna White. *Other Wives*: Lynn Archer, Chris Callan, Jacque Dean, Alice Evans, Carol Flemming, Marsha Hastings, Mary Jane Houdina, Sherry Lambert, Carol Manning, Sally Neal, Joan Tannen. *People of Jerusalem, Guards, Slaves, etc.*: Clifford Allen, Meir Alon, Jari Barto, Connie Burnett, Chris Callan, Al Cohen, Gordon Clark, Nikolas Dante, Jacque Dean, Esteban DeLeon, Al DeSio, John Dorrin, Miriam Ehrenberg, Eddie Ericksen, Carol Flemming, Stokely Gray, Rodney Griffin, Jerry Grimes, Marsha Hastings, Nat Horne, Mary Jane Houdina, Jason Howard, Nina Janik, Sherry Lambert, John LaMotta, Carol Manning, Garrett Morris, Sally Neal, Keith Perry, Martha Pollak, Ken Richards, Renee Rose, Jeffrey Shawn, Clay Taliaferro, Joan Tannen, Caryl Tenney, Nina Trasoff, Kyle Weaver, Bruce Wells, Myrna White.

The action takes place from the morning of one day to noon of the next, in and around Jerusalem, about 100 B.C.

---

[16]Epilogue (excepting the Cohan recording) dropped from programs during the New York run.

ACT 1

"David and Bathsheba"
D. Shawn, People of Jesusalem

"Hail the Son of David!"
D. Shawn, Courtiers, Solomon's Wives

"Preposterous"
D. Shawn

"Have You Heard?"
People of Jerusalem

"The Citation"
P. Reed

"In Love With a Fool"
K. Morrow

"Someone Like Me"
D. Shawn

"In Someone Else's Sandals"
D. Shawn, C. Mathews, Slaves, Concubines

"The Three Riddles"
(*Lyrics by* Erich Segal.)
F. Pinkard, P. Reed, D. Shawn, People of Jerusalem

ACT 2

"Once in 2.7 Years"
Solomon's Wives

"Have You Ever Been Alone With a King Before?"
D. Shawn, K. Morrow
(*Music by* Bill Weeden. *Lyrics by* David Finkle.)

"Lord I Am But a Little Child"
D. Shawn

"I Am What I Am"
D. Shawn

"Something in His Eyes"
K. Morrow

"That Guilty Feeling"
D. Shawn
(*Music by* Bill Weeden. *Lyrics by* David Finkle.)

"Time to Let Go"
C. Mathews

"With Your Hand in My Heart"
D. Shawn, K. Morrow, C. Mathews, People of Jerusalem

"Lord I Am But a Little Child" (reprise)
Entire Company

THE PIRATES OF PENZANCE,
1968.09   or The Slave of Duty

A Revival of the Comic Opera in Two Acts[17]. Libretto by William S. Gilbert. Music by Arthur Sullivan. Directed by Allen Fletcher. Scenery by Lloyd Evans. Costumes by Patton Campbell. Lighting by Hans Sondheimer. Conductor, Felix Popper. Produced by the New York City Center Gilbert and Sullivan Company (Felix Popper, General director). Opened 25 April 1968 at the New York City Center and closed 19 May 1968 after 7 performances in repertory.

CAST: *Major General Stanley*: DOUGLAS WATSON, EMILE RENAN. *The Pirate King*: WILLIAM CHAPMAN. *Samuel*, his Lieutenant: William Ledbetter. *Frederic*, the Pirate Apprentice: FRANK PORETTA, JOHN HARGER STEWART. *Sergeant of Police*: JACK BITTNER. *Mabel, Edith Kate, Isabel*, General Stanley's Daughters: PATRICIA WISE or MARGOT MOSER, ELLEN SHADE, JANET WINBURN, Diana Kehrig. *Ruth*, Pirate Maid-of-all-work: MURIEL GREENSPON.

Chorus of Pirates, Police and General Stanley's Daughters: Arlene Adler, Ronald Bentley, Don Carlo, Anthony Darius, Harris Davis, Joseph Galiano, Nino Garcia, Pearle Goldsmith, Marilyn Armstrong, Harriet Greene, Don Henderson, Lila Herbert, Douglas Hunnikin, Suzy Hunter, Diana Kehrig, Karl Patrick Krause, Donna Owen, Hanna Owen, Raymond Papay, Richard Park, Leo Postrel, Joaquin Romaguera, Stefanya Weicker, Maria West, Marie Young.

---

[17]First presented in New York 31 December 1879 at the Fifth Avenue Theatre for a total of 91 performances in two engagements. For Synopsis of Scenes and Musical Numbers, see original 1879 production.

H.M.S. PINAFORE,

1968.10   or The Lass That Loved a Sailor

A Revival of the Comic Opera in Two Acts[18]. Libretto by William S. Gilbert. Music by Arthur Sullivan. Directed by Allen Fletcher. Scenery and costumes by Patton Campbell. Lighting by Hans Sondheimer. Conductor, Thomas P. Martin. Produced by the New York City Center Gilbert and Sullivan Company (Felix Popper, General director). Opened 27 April 1968 at the New York City Center and closed 19 May 1968 after 8 performances in repertory.

CAST: *The Rt. Hon. Sir Joseph Porter, K.C.B.*, First Lord of the Admiralty: RAYMOND ALLEN, ROBERT TREHY. *Captain Corcoran*, Commander of the *H.M.S. Pinafore*: RICHARD FREDERICKS. *Ralph Rackstraw*, Able Seaman: ENRICO DiGIUSEPPE, EVAN THOMAS. *Dick Deadeye*, Able Seaman: PAUL UKENA, DON YULE. *Bill Bobstay*, Boatswain: Robert Hale. *Bob Becket*: Will Roy. *Josephine*, the Captain's Daughter: JOY CLEMENTS, BARBARA BLANCHARD. *Cousin Hebe*, Sir Joseph's First Cousin: Janet Winburn. *Little Buttercup*, Mrs. Cripps, a Portsmouth bum-boat woman: JOAN KAPLAN. *First Lord's Sisters, His Cousins, His Aunts, Sailors, Marines, etc.*: same as THE PIRATES OF PENZANCE above.

1968.11   # HAIR

The American Tribal Love-Rock Musical in Two Acts[19]. Book and lyrics by Gerome Ragni and James Rado. Music by Galt MacDermott. Directed by Tom O'Horgan. Dance director, Julie Arenal. Musical director, Galt MacDermott. Costumes by Nancy Potts. Scenery by Robin Wagner. Lighting by Jules Fisher. Sound by Robert Kiernan. Executive producer, Bertrand Castelli. Produced by Michael Butler. The Natoma Production. Opened 29 April 1968 at the Biltmore Theatre and closed 1 July 1972 after 1750 performances.

CAST (in order of appearance): *Claude*: JAMES RADO. *Ron*: RONALD DYSON. *Berger*: GEROME RAGNI. *Woof*: STEVE CURRY. *Hud*: LAMONT WASHINGTON. *Sheila*: LYNN KELLOGG. *Jeanie*: SALLY EATON. *Dionne*: MELBA MOORE. *Crissy*: SHELLEY PLIMPTON. *Mother*: SALLY EATON, JONATHAN KRAMER, PAUL JABARA. *Father*: Robert I. Rubinsky, Suzanne Norstrand, LAMONT WASHINGTON. *Principal*: Robert I. Rubinsky, Suzanne Norstrand, LAMONT WASHINGTON. *Tourist Couple*: JONATHAN KRAMER, Robert I. Rubinsky. *Waitress*: Diane Keaton. *Young Recruit*: JONATHAN KRAMER. *General Grant*: PAUL JABARA. *Abraham Lincoln*: Lorri Davis. *Sergeant*: Donnie Burks. *Parents*: Diane Keaton, Robert I. Rubinsky. *The Tribe*: Donnie Burks, Lorri Davis, Leata Galloway, Steve Gamet, Walter Harris, Diane Keaton, Hiram Keller, Marjorie LiPari, Emmaretta Marks, Natalie Mosco, Suzannah Norstrand, Robert I. Rubinsky.

The action takes place in New York City, mostly the East Village, at the present time.

ACT 1[20]

---

[18]Originally presented in New York 15 January 1879 at the Standard Theatre for 175 performances. For Synopsis of Scenes and Musical Numbers, see original 1879 production.
[19]First produced in New York Off-Broadway 29 October-10 December 1967 at the Anspacher Theatre for 49 performances; re-opened at the Cheetah 22 December 1967-28 January 1968 for 45 performances. Original Off-Broadway Credits (where different from Broadway): Directed by Gerald Freedman. Scenery by Ming Cho Lee. Costumes by Theoni V. Aldredge. Lighting by Martin Aronstein. Musical director, John Morris. Associate producer, Bernard Gersten. Manager, David Black. Produced by the New York Shakespeare Festival (Joseph Papp, Producer). Dropped from Off-Broadway production prior to Broadway:
"Red, Blue and White" (Act 1)
"Exanaplanetooch" (Act 2)
"(The) Climax" (Act 2)
[20]Added after Broadway opening:
"Dead End" (Act 1)
   M. Moore, L. Galloway, E. Marks, S. Norstrand, Joe Morton
Added for various touring productions:
"Kama Sutra" (Act 1)
   Company
"Hello There" (Act 1)
   Berger
"Oh Great God of Power" (Act 2)
   Berger, Company

"Aquarius"
   R. Dyson, Company
"Donna"
   G. Ragni, Company
"Hashish"
   Company
"Sodomy"
   S. Curry, Company
"Colored Spade"
   L. Washington, Company
"Manchester (England)"
   J. Rado, Company
"Ain't Got No"
   S. Curry, L. Washington, M. Moore, Company
"I Believe in Love"
   L. Kellogg
"Air"
   S. Eaton, S. Plimpton, M. Moore, Company
"Initials"
   Company
"I Got Life"
   J. Rado, Company
"Going Down"
   G. Ragni, Company
"Hair"
   J. Rado, G. Ragni, Company
"My Conviction"
   J. Kramer
"Easy To Be Hard"
   L. Kellogg
"Hung"[21]
   G. Ragni, Company
"Don't Put It Down"
   G. Ragni, S. Curry
"Frank Mills"
   S. Plimpton
"Hare Krishna" ("Be-In")
   Company
"Where Do I Go?"
   J. Rado, Company

ACT 2
"Electric Blues"
   S. Norstrand, L. Galloway, S. Gamet, P. Jabara
"Black Boys"
   D. Keaton, S. Norstrand, N. Mosco
"White Boys"
   M. Moore, L. Davis, E. Marks
"Walking in Space"
   Company
"Abie Baby"
   L. Washington, R. Dyson, D. Burks, L. Davis
"Prisoners in Niggertown" ("3-5-0-0")
   R. Dyson, W. Harris, Company
"What a Piece of Work is Man"
   R. Dyson, W. Harris
"Good Morning Starshine"
   L. Kellogg, M. Moore, Company
"The Bed"
   Company
"The Flesh Failures"
("Let the Sunshine In")
   J. Rado, L. Kellogg, M. Moore, Company

---

[21]Dropped after Broadway opening.

THE MIKADO,
1968.12   or The Town of Titipu

A Revival of the Comic Opera in Two Acts[22]. Libretto by William S. Gilbert. Music by Arthur Sullivan. Directed by Jack and Virginia Frymire. Scenery by Donald Oenslager. Costumes by Patton Campbell. Conductor, Byron Dean Ryan. Produced by the New York City Center Gilbert and Sullivan Company (Felix Popper, General director). Opened 1 May 1968 at the New York City Center and closed 14 May 1968 after 8 performances in repertory.

CAST: *The Mikado of Japan*: PAUL UKENA. *Nanki-Poo*: FRANK PORETTA. *Ko-Ko*: JOHN LANKSTON. *Pooh-Bah*: RICHARD WENTWORTH. *Pish-Tush*: WILLIAM LEDBETTER. *Three Sisters, Wards of Ko-Ko*: *Yum-Yum*: CAROL BERGEY. *Pitti-Sing*: MARY BURGESS. *Peep-Bo*: JANET WINBURN. *Katisha*: MURIEL GREENSPON. *Solo Dancer*: Miyoko Watanabe. *Chorus of School Girls, Nobles, Guards and Coolies*: same as THE PIRATES OF PENZANCE above.

(LEONARD SILLMAN'S)
1968.13   NEW FACES OF 1968

A Musical Revue in Two Acts, 32 Scenes[23]. Entire production conceived and staged by Leonard Sillman. Sketches by Ronny Graham, Peter DeVries, William F. Brown, Kenny Solms, Gail Parent, Jack Sharkey, David Axelrod, Robert Klein, Norman Kline. Continuity and additional dialogue by William F. Brown. Music and lyrics by Ronny Graham, June Carroll, Arthur Siegel, Clark Gesner, Sam Pottle, David Axelrod, Jerry Powell, David Shire, Richard Maltby, Jr., Murray Grand, Paul Nassau, Hal Hackady, Alonzo Levister, Kenny Solms, Gail Parent, Gene P. Bissell, Carl Friberg, Fred Hellerman, Frank Minkoff, Michael McWhinney, Sydney Shaw, Michael Cohen, Tony Geiss. Choreographed and directed by Frank Wagner. Settings and costumes by Winn Morton. Light design by Paul Sullivan. Production coordinator, Jacqueline Adams. Orchestrations by Lanny Meyers. Musical direction, Ted Simons. An All-Corduroy Production. Produced by Jack Rollins. Opened 2 May 1968 at the Booth Theatre and closed 15 June 1968 after 52 performances.

CAST: Michael K. Allen, Suzanne Astor, Rod Barry, Gloria Bleezarde, Trudy Carson, Marilyn Child, Dottie [Dorothy] Frank, Elaine Giftos, Madeline Kahn, Robert Klein, Joe Kyle, Robert Lone, Brandon Maggart, George Ormiston, Rod Perry, Nancie Phillips, Leonard Sillman.

ACT 1

Scene 1

   "Illustrated Overture"

Scene 2

   Definitions
     (*by* Random House)
     Girl: G. Bleezarde. *Boy*: R. Barry.

Scene 3

   Welcome
     The Producer: L. Sillman.

Scene 4

   "Opening"
     Entire Company
     (*Music and Lyrics by* Ronny Graham.)

Scene 5

   Audition
     (*by* Robert Klein)
     The Auditioner: R. Klein.

Scene 6

   "By the Sea"
     B. Maggart
     (*Music and Lyrics by* Clark Gesner.)

Scene 7

   "Where Is the Waltz?"
     M. K. Allen
     (*Music and Orchestration by* Alonzo Levister. *Lyrics by* Paul Nassau.)
     Danced by D. Frank, E. Giftos, T. Carson.

Scene 8

   "A New Waltz"
     M. Child
     (*Music by* Fred Hellerman. *Lyrics by* Frank Minkoff.)
     Danced by R. Lone, J. Kyle.

Scene 9

   Happy Landings
     (*by* Jack Sharkey)
     Airline Stewardess: M. Kahn.

Scene 10

   "The Girl in the Mirror"
     R. Parry
     (*Music by* Fred Hellerman. *Lyrics by* Fran Minkoff.)
   Isolation
     J. Kyle, G. Bleezarde

Scene 11

   The American Hamburger League[24]
     (*by* Norman Kline)
     Introduction: R. Barry. *Beth*: M. Kahn. *Helene*: M. Child. *Rex*: B. Maggart. *Dexter*: G. Ormiston. *Wayne*: R. Klein.
   Isolation
     T. Carson, R. Barry

Scene 12

   Love Songs:
   "Something Big"
     G. Ormiston, E. Giftos
     (*Music by* Sam Pottle. *Lyrics by* David Axelrod.)
   "Love in a Tempo"
     R. Klein
     (*Music and Lyrics by* Ronny Graham.)
   "Hungry"
     S. Astor, (R. Barry)
     (*Music and Lyrics by* Murray Grand.)

Scene 13

   "Luncheon Ballad"
     S. Astor, M. Child, M. Kahn, N. Phillips
     (*Music by* Jerry Powell. *Lyrics by* Michael McWhinney.)

Scene 14

   The Underachiever
     (*by* Peter De Vries)
     Introduction: G. Bleezarde. *Freshman*: R. Klein. *Freshman's Wife*: M. Kahn.

Scene 15

   "You're the One I'm For"
     B. Maggart
     (*Music and Lyrics by* Clark Gesner.)

Scene 16

   "Where Is Me?"
     M. Child
     (*Music by* Arthur Siegel. *Lyrics by* June Carroll.)
   Isolation— "Right About Here"
     M. K. Allen
     (*Music and Lyrics by* Arthur Siegel.)

Scene 17

   Gospel According to Jack
     (*by* William F. Brown)
     S. Astor, R. Barry, T. Carson,
     M. Child, D. Frank, M. Kahn, R. Klein, R. Lone, B. Maggart, R. Perry

Scene 18

   Mama Doll
     (*by* Charles Tobias and Nat Simon; *Conception by* George Ormiston and Nancie Phillips.)
     Doll: N. Phillips. *Little Boy*: G. Ormiston.

---

[22]First presented in New York 20 July, 10-29 August 1885 at the Union Square and People's Theatres for 22 performances. First authorized production presented 19 August 1885 at the Fifth Avenue Theatre by Richard D'Oyly Carte for 250 performances. For Synopsis of Scenes and Musical Numbers, see 19 August 1885 D'Oyly Carte production.

[23]The Seventh in the series of revues conceived by Leonard Sillman as a showcase for new talent. The first was produced in 1934.

[24]Dropped after opening.

Scene 19

"Toyland"

(*Dialogue, Music and Lyrics by* Gene P. Bissell.)
Production Singer: M. Kahn. *Compere*: R. Klein.

ACT 2

Introduction

L. Sillman, G. Bleezarde

Scene 1

"Hullabaloo At Thebes"

(*Music and Lyrics by* Ronny Graham.)
Introduction: L. Sillman. *Oedipus*: R. Klein. *Jocasta*: S. Astor.
Antigone: T. Carson. *Ismene*: E. Giftos.

Scene 2

"#X9RL-220"

G. Bleezarde
(*Music by* Jerry Powell. *Lyrics by* Michael McWhinney.)

Scene 3

"You Are"

B. Maggart
(*Music and Lyrics by* Clark Gesner.)

Scene 4

"Evil"

M. K. Allen
(*Music and Lyrics by* Sydney Shaw.)

Scene 5

The Refund

(by Peter De Vries)
Introduction and Clarification: G. Ormiston.
Fred Abernathy: R. Klein. *Ben Abernathy*: B. Maggart.
Sarah Cobleigh: D. Frank.

Scene 6

"Prisms"

M. Child
(*Music by* Carl Friberg. *Lyrics by* Hal Hackady.)

Scene 7

"Tango"

The Company
(*Music by* Sam Pottle. *Lyrics by* David Axelrod.)
Introduction: L. Sillman.

Isolation—Cymbals and Tambourines

G. Bleezarde, R. Lone
(*Music and Lyrics by* Arthur Siegel.)

Scene 8

"Philosophy"

R. Perry
(*Music by* Carl Friberg. *Lyrics by* Hal Hackady.)
Danced by D. Frank, J. Kyle, E. Giftos.

Scene 9

The Pile-Up

B. Maggart

Scene 10

"Das Chicago Song"

M. Kahn
(*Music by* Michael Cohen. *Lyrics by* Tony Geiss.)

Scene 11

"Missed America"

(*Dialogue, Music and Lyrics by* Kenny Solms and Gail Parent.
Additional Dialogue by Ronny Graham.)
M. C.: G. Ormiston. *Miss Alabama*: N. Phillips. *Miss Minnesota*:
D. Frank. *Miss Connecticut*: S. Astor.

Scene 12

"Die Zusammenfügung"

(*Music by* Sam Pottle. *Lyrics by* David Axelrod.)
Introduction: G. Bleezarde. *Scheiss*: B. Maggart. *Pfeiffer*: R. Klein.
Heidi: M. Kahn. *The Connection*: G. Ormiston.

Scene 13

Opening Reprise

Introduction: L. Sillman.

Scene 13

"The Girl of the Minute"

Entire Company
(*Music by* David Shire. *Lyrics by* Richard Maltby, Jr.)

THE YEOMEN OF THE GUARD,
1968.14 or The Merryman and His Maid

A Revival of the Comic Opera in Two Acts[25]. Libretto by William S. Gilbert. Music by Arthur Sullivan. Staged by Allen Fletcher. Scenery by Stephen O. Saxe. Costumes by Alvin Colt. Lighting by Hans Sondheimer. Conducted by Felix Popper. Produced by the New York City Center Gilbert and Sullivan Company (Felix Popper, General director). Opened 8 May 1968 at the New York City Center and closed 12 May 1968 after 3 performances in repertory.

CAST: *Sir Richard Cholmondeley*, Lieutenant of the Tower: ROBERT HALE. *Colonel Fairfax* under sentence of death: FRANK PORETTA. *Sergeant Meryll* of the Yeomen of the Guard: PAUL UKENA. *Leonard Meryll*, his Son: JOHN LANKSTON. *Jack Point*, a Strolling Jester: ROBERT TREHY. *Wilfred Shadbolt*, Head Jailor and Assistant Tormentor: JACK BITTNER. *First Yeoman*: Evan Thomas. *Second Yeoman*: David Hicks. *First Citizen*: Harris Davis. *Second Citizen*: Don Henderson. *Elsie Maynard*, a Strolling Player: MARGOT MOSER. *Phoebe Meryll*, Sergeant Meryll's Daughter: MARY BURGESS. *Dame Carruthers*, Housekeeper to the Tower: ELLEN ALEXANDER. *Kate*, her Niece: FREDREIKA WISEHART. *Chorus of Yeomen of the Guard, Gentlemen, Citizens, etc.*: same as THE PIRATES OF PENZANCE above.

PATIENCE,
1968.15 or Bunthorne's Bride

A Revival of the Comic Opera in Two Acts[26]. Libretto by William S. Gilbert. Music by Arthur Sullivan. Directed by Leon Major. Scenery and costumes designed by Motley. Lighting by Hans Sondheimer. Conductor, Felix Popper. Produced by the New York City Center Gilbert and Sullivan Company (Felix Popper, General director). Opened 15 May 1968 at the New York City Center and closed 17 May 1968 after 3 performances in repertory.

CAST: *Colonel Calverley*: WILLIAM CHAPMAN. *Major Murgatroyd*: Nico Castel. *Lieut. the Duke of Dunstable*: JOHN LANKSTON. *Reginald Bunthorne*, a Fleshly Poet: EMILE RENAN. *Archibald Grosvenor*, an Idyllic Poet: WILLIAM METCALF. *Mr. Bunsthorne's Solicitor*: John Henry Thomas . *The Lady Angela, The Lady Saphir, The Lady Ella, The Lady Jane*, Rapturous Maidens: MARY BURGESS, HELEN GUILF, Fredreika Wisehart, CLARAMAE TURNER. *Patience*, a Dairy Maid: JOY CLEMENTS. *Chorus of Rapturous Maidens and Officers of the Dragoon Guards*: same as THE PIRATES OF PENZANCE above.

THE KING AND I
1968.16

A Revival of the Musical Play in Two Acts, 17 Scenes[27]. Book and lyrics by Oscar Hammerstein II. Music by Richard Rodgers. Based on the novel "Anna and the King of Siam" by Margaret Landon. Directed by John Fearnley. Settings by Paul C. McGuire. Costumes by Irene Sharaff, supervised by Frank Thompson. Lighting by Feder. Original choreography by Jerome Robbins, reproduced by Yuriko. (Orchestrations by Robert Russell Bennett.) Musical director, Jonathan Anderson. Produced by the New York City Center Light Opera Company (Jean Dalrymple, Director). Opened 23 May 1968 at the New York City Center and closed 9 June 1968 after 22 performances.

CAST (in order of appearance): *Captain Orton*: Sam Kirkham. *Louis Leonowens*: Eric Hamilton. *Anna Leonowens*: CONSTANCE TOWERS. *The Interpreter*: Paul Flores.

[25]First presented in New York 17 October 1888 at the Casino Theatre for 100 performances. For Synopsis of Scenes and Musical Numbers, see original 1888 production.

[26]First presented in New York 22 September 1881 at the Standard Theatre for 177 performances. For Synopsis of Scenes and Musical Numbers, see original 1881 production.

[27]Originally produced in New York 29 March 1951 at the St. James Theatre for 1246 performances. For Synopsis of Scenes and Musical Numbers, see original 1951 production.

The Kralahome: Ted Beniades. *The King*: MICHAEL KERMOYAN. *Phra Alack*: Robert Lenn. *Lun Tha*: STANLEY GROVER. *Tuptim*: ELEANOR CALBES. *Lady Thiang*: ANITA DARIAN. *Prince Chulalongkorn*: Michael Thom. *Princess Ying Yaowalak*: Dana Shimizu. *Sir Edward Ramsay*: Christopher Hewett.

The Small House of Uncle Thomas: *Narrator*: Eleanor Calbes. *Uncle Thomas*: Diane Adler. *Little Eva*: Wonci Lui. *Topsy*: Paula Chin. *Eliza*: YURIKO. *King Simon*: Carol Fried. *Angel*: Jaclynn Villamil. *Drummer*: Lazar Dano. *Buddha*: Lawrence Kikuchi.

Princes and Princesses: Caryn Chow, Sonja Furiya, Dana Shimizu, Rachel Ticotin, Nancy Ticotin, Russell Chow, Lewis Gerardo, Lewis Gerardo, Lawrence Kikuchi, Jaime Roque, Jason Rosen, Keenan Shimizu, Marcus Ticotin. *Royal Dancers*: Diane Adler, Paula Chin, Carol Fried, Linda Gumiela, Joann Ogawa, Margot Parsons, Kathleen Pierini, Susan Platt, Juanita Londono, Wonci Lui, Stephanie Satie, Britt Swanson, Margot Travers, Jaclynn Villamil, Rebecca West, Lazar Dano, Gary Dutton, Vito Durante, Rodger Gerhardstein, Tim Ramirez. *Singers* (Wives, Priests, Amazons and Slaves): Joan diDonato, Lee Hooper, Charlotte Marcheret, Betsy Norden, Barbara Reisman, Rebecca West, Maggie Worth, Larry Devon, Beno Foster, Richard Kie Wye Khan.

1968–1969 SEASON

Angela Lansbury and Kurt Petersen in DEAR WORLD (Photo: Friedman-Abeles)
Billy Rose Theatre Collection, New York Public Library for the Performing Arts

1968–1969 SEASON

MY FAIR LADY

A Revival of the Musical (Comedy) in Two Acts, 18 Scenes[1]. Book and lyrics by Alan Jay Lerner. Based on the play "Pygmalion" by George Bernard Shaw, produced on the screen by Gabriel Pascal. Music by Frederick Loewe. Originally staged by Moss Hart. This production directed by Samuel Liff. Choreography and musical numbers staged by Hanya Holm, restaged by Harry Woolever. Production (settings) designed by Oliver Smith. Costumes by Cecil Beaton, supervised by Stanley Simmons. Musical arrangements (orchestrations) by Robert Russell Bennett and Philip J. Lang. Lighting by Feder. Dance music arranged by Trude Rittman. Musical director, Anton Coppola. Produced by the New York City Center Light Opera Company (Jean Dalrymple, Director). Opened 13 June 1968 at the New York City Center and closed 30 June 1968 after 22 performances.

CAST (in order of appearance): *Buskers*: George Bunt, John Johann, Kiki Minor. *Mrs. Eynsford-Hill*: Claire Waring. *Eliza Doolittle*: INGA SWENSON. *Freddy Eynsford-Hill*: EVAN THOMAS. *Colonel Pickering*: BYRON WEBSTER. *A Bystander*: James Beard. *Henry Higgins*: FRITZ WEAVER. *Selsey Man*: Charles Goff. *Hoxton Man*: Jack Fletcher. *First Cockney*: Laried Montgomery. *Second Cockney*: Stokely Gray. *Third Cockney*: Jack Fletcher. *Fourth Cockney*: William James. *Bartender*: Larry Devon. *Harry*: Charles Goff. *Jamie*: James Beard. *Alfred P. Doolittle*: GEORGE ROSE. *Mrs. Pearce*: Leta Bonynge. *Mrs. Hopkins*: Blanche Collins. *Butler*: William James. *Servants*: Jeanne Shea, Hanna Owen, Maggie Worth, Joyce Olson, William James, Stokely Gray. *Mrs. Higgins*: Margery Maude. *Chauffeur*: Todd Butler. *Footmen*: Darrell Sandeen, Peter Costanza. *Lord Boxington*: James Beard. *Lady Boxington*: Blanche Collins. *Constable*: Richard Maxon. *Flower Girl*: Kiki Minor. *Zoltan Karpathy*: ERIK RHODES. *Flunkey*: Darrell Sandeen. *Queen of Transylvania*: Maggie Worth. *Ambassador*: Charles Goff. *Bartender*: Darrell Sandeen. *Mrs. Higgins' Maid*: Jeanne Shea.

Singing Ensemble: Marcia Brushingham, Spring Fairbank, Maryann Kerrick, Joyce Olson, Hanna Owen, Jeanne Shea, Barbara Sorenson, Maggie Worth, Jim Connor, Peter Costanza, Larry Devon, Jack Fletcher, Stokely Gray, William James, Laried Montgomery, Darrell Sandeen. *Dancing Ensemble*: Lisa Ackerman, Judith Austin, Cindi Bulak, Joyce Maret, Mari McKinn, Kiki Minor, Skiles Ricketts, Britt Swanson, Margot Travers, Oscar Anthony, George Bunt, Todd Butler, Richard Dodd, Joe Helm, John Johann, Donald Mark, Richard Maxon, Duane Taylor, Jimmy White.

WEST SIDE STORY

A Revival of the Musical in Two Acts, 15 Scenes[2]. Book by Arthur Laurents. Based on a conception of Jerome Robbins. Music by Leonard Bernstein. Lyrics by Stephen Sondheim. Original direction and choreography by Jerome Robbins, reproduced for this production by Lee Theodore. Scenery by Oliver Smith. Costumes by Winn Morton. Lighting by Peter Hunt. Musical director, Maurice Peress. Orchestrations by Leonard Bernstein, with Sid Ramin, Irwin Kostal. A Lincoln Center Festival '68 Production. Produced by The Music Theater of Lincoln Center (Richard Rodgers, President and Producing director). Opened 24 June 1968 at the New York State Theatre and closed 7 September 1968 after 89 performances.

CAST: *THE JETS: Riff*, the Leader: AVIND HARUM. *Tony*, his friend: KURT PETERSON. *Action*: Ian Tucker. *A-Rab*: Robert LuPone. *Baby John*: Stephen Reinhardt. *Snowboy*: George Ramos. *Big Deal*: Roger Briant. *Diesel*: Victor Mohica. *Gee-Tar*: Chuck Beard. *Mouth Piece*: Joseph Pichette. *Tiger*: Kenneth Carr. *Their Girls: Graziella*: Garet De Troia. *Velma*: Nancy Dalton. *Minnie*: Rachel Lampert. *Clarice*: Sherry Lynn Diamant. *Pauline*: Carol Hanzel. *Pucky*: Jeanne Frey. *Anybodys*: Lee Lund.

THE SHARKS: Bernardo, the Leader: ALAN CASTNER. *Maria*, his Sister: VICTORIA MALLORY. *Anita*, his Girl: BARBARA LUNA. *Chino*, his Friend: Bobby Capo, Jr. *Pepe*: Edgar Coronado. *Indio*: Peter De Nicola. *Luis*: Pat Matera. *Anxious*: Steven Gelfer. *Nibbles*: Ramon Caballero. *Juano*: Pernett Robinson. *Toro*: Byron Wheeler. *Moose*: George Comtois. *Their Girls: Rosalia*: Kay Oslin. *Consuelo*: Lee Hooper. *Teresita*: Connie Burnett. *Francisca*: Eileen Barbaris. *Estella*: Judith Lerner. *Marguerita*: Carol Lynn Vasquez. *Felicia*: Diane McAfee.

---

[1]Originally produced in New York 15 March 1956 at the Mark Hellinger Theatre for 2717 peformances. For Synopsis of Scenes and Musical Numbers, see original 1956 production.
[2]Originally produced in New York 26 September 1957 at the Winter Garden for 732 performances. For Synopsis of Scenes and Musical Numbers, see original 1957 production.

THE ADULTS: Doc: MARTIN WOLFSON. *Schrank:* Joseph Mascolo. *Krupke:* Josip Elic. *Gladhand:* Bill McCutcheon.

NOËL COWARD'S SWEET POTATO

A Musical Revue in Two Acts. Words and Music by Noël Coward. From a conception by Roderick Cook. Material assembled and adapted by Roderick Cook and Lee Theodore. Directed and choreographed by Lee Theodore. Settings by Helen Pond and Herbert Senn. Costumes by David Toser. Lighting by Peter Hunt. Musical supervision and arrangements by Fred Werner. Musical direction and vocal arrangements by Charles Schneider. Co-choreographer, Robert Tucker. Production supervisor, Robert Linden. Assistant choreographer, Vito Durante. Produced by Robert L. Steele in association with The Erani Corporation. Opened 29 September 1968 at the Ethel Barrymore Theatre and closed 12 October 1968 after 17 performances; re-opened 1 November 1968 at the Booth Theatre and closed 23 November 1968 after 27 additional performances. Total: 44 performances.

CAST: GEORGE GRIZZARD, DORTHY LOUDON[3], CAROLE SHELLEY, ARTHUR MITCHELL, TOM KNEEBONE, BONNIE SCHON, Ian Tucker, Robert LuPone, Stephen Reinhardt.

ACT 1
A Beginning (dance)
  The Company
"Useful Phrases" (from SAIL AWAY)
  G. Grizzard, D. Loudon, A. Mitchell, B. Schon
"Dance, Little Lady" (from THIS YEAR OF GRACE)
  B. Schon, Boys
  (*Musical Arrangement by* Roland Hanna.)
"Mad Dogs and Englishmen" (from WORDS AND MUSIC, London; SET TO MUSIC)
  G. Grizzard, D. Loudon, C. Shelley, T. Kneebone
"World Weary" (from THIS YEAR OF GRACE)
  A. Mitchell, B. Schon, Boys
"A Bar on the Piccola Marina"
  G. Grizzard
Literature
  D. Loudon, T. Kneebone
"Why Does Love Get in the Way?" (from ACE OF CLUBS, London)
  C. Shelley
"Men About Town" (from TONIGHT AT 8:30)
  G. Grizzard, D. Loudon, T. Kneebone
"Matelot" (from SIGH NO MORE, London)
  A. Mitchell, C. Shelley, B. Schon
Eve
  T. Kneebone
"Consecutive Fifths"
  G. Grizzard
  (*Music by* Fred Werner and Roderick Cook.)
"Mad About the Boy" (from WORDS AND MUSIC, London; SET TO MUSIC)
  D. Loudon, C. Shelley, B. Schon, Boys
"I Wonder What Happened to Him?" (from SIGH NO MORE, London)
  G. Grizzard, T. Kneebone
Karate
  B. Schon
"A Room With a View" (from THIS YEAR OF GRACE)
  D. Loudon
Waltzes (dance)
  G. Grizzard, Boys
"I Like America" (from ACE OF CLUBS, London)
  The Company

ACT 2
"Let's Do It"
  The Company
  (*Music by* Cole Porter.)

---

[3]Succeeded by MARY LOUISE WILSON for return engagement.

"Three White Feathers" (from WORDS AND MUSIC, London; SET TO MUSIC)
  D. Loudon, T. Kneebone
"Don't Put Your Daughter on the Stage, Mrs. Worthington"
  G. Grizzard, Boys
"Headless Dance"
  A. Mitchell, R. Carter
  (*Music from* "Never Again.")
"Alice (Is At It Again)"
  T. Kneebone
Social Grace
  A. Mitchell, B. Schon, I. Tucker, D. Loudon, T. Kneebone
"Sweet Potato" (dance)
  C. Shelley, Boys
Party Chat/Amanda, Elyot and Friends
  C. Shelley, G. Grizzard, Company
"If Love Were All" (from BITTER SWEET)
  D. Loudon
Sex Talk
  T. Kneebone
"Sunset in Samolo"
  C. Shelley
  (*Music by* Fred Werner and Roderick Cook.)
"Teach Me to Dance Like Grandma" (from THIS YEAR OF GRACE)
  D. Loudon, A. Mitchell
(The) Boy Actor
  G. Grizzard
"World Weary" (reprise)
  The Company
An Ending
  The Company

MARLENE DIETRICH

1968.20

A Return Engagement of the One Woman Show in One Act[4]. (Musical) Arrangements by Burt Bacharch. Conductor, Stan Freeman. Production supervisor, Jerry Adler. Lighting by Joe Davis. A Nine O'Clock Theater Production. Produced by Alexander H. Cohen. Opened 3 October 1968 at the Mark Hellinger Theatre and closed 30 November 1968 after 64 performances.

CAST: MARLENE DIETRICH.

REPERTOIRE[5]
  "Look Me Over Closely"
  "You're the Cream in My Coffee" (from HOLD EVERYTHING)
    (*Music by* Ray Henderson. *Lyrics by* Buddy G. DeSylva and Lew Brown.)
  "Boomerang Baby"
  "My Blue Heaven"
    (*Music by* Walter Donaldson. *Lyrics by* George Whiting.)
  "(Naughty) Lola" (from film THE BLUE ANGEL)
    (*Music and Lyrics by* Frederick Holländer.)
  "Where Have All the Flowers Gone?"
    (*Music and Lyrics by* Pete Seeger.)
  "The Laziest Gal in Town" (from film STAGE FRIGHT)
    (*Music and Lyrics by* Cole Porter.)
  "Shir Hatan Biem"
    (*Music and Lyrics by* Z. Sahar.)
  "When the World Was Young"
    (*Original French Lyrics by* Angela Vannier.)
    (*Music by* M. Philippe-Gerard. *Lyrics by* Johnny Mercer.)
  "La Vie en Rose"
    (*Music by* Louiguy. *Lyrics by* Edith Piaf.)
  "Jonny" (from film SONG OF SONGS)
    (*Music by* Frederick Holländer. *Lyrics by* Edward Heyman.)

"Go 'Way from My Window"
  (*arr. by* J. J. Niles.)
"Lili Marlene"
  (*Music by* Norbert Schultze. *Lyrics by* Hans Leip and Tommie Connor.)
"Das Lied Ist Aus" (Frag' nicht warum ich gehe)
  (*Music and Lyrics by* Walter Reisch, A. Robinson, Robert Stoltz.)
"I Wish You Love"
  (*Music by* Charles Trenet. *Lyrics by* Albert Beach.)
"Marie, Marie"
  (*Music by* Gilbert Becaud. *Lyrics by* Pierre Delanoe and Kolpe.)
"Honeysuckle Rose" (from HOT CHOCOLATES)
  (*Music by* Fats Waller. *Lyrics by* Andy Razaf.)
"White Grass"
"Everyone's Gone to the Moon"
  (*Music and Lyrics by* Kenneth King.)
"Falling in Love Again" (from film THE BLUE ANGEL)
  (*Music and Lyrics by* Frederick Holländer.)

GILBERT BECAUD SINGS LOVE

1968.21

A One Man Show in Two Acts[6]. All music composed by Gilbert Becaud. Lyrics by Pierre Delanoe, Louis Amade, Maurice Vidalin, Charles Aznavour, Jean Broussolle, Mack David, Carl Sigman, Gilbert Becaud. Scenery and lighting by Ralph Alswang. Musical director, Raymond Bernard. Produced by Norman Twain and Marcel Akselrod by arrangement with Felix Marouani. Opened 6 October 1968 at the Cort Theatre and closed 26 October 1968 after 24 performances.

CAST: GILBERT BECAUD.

ACT 1
  "Le jour ou la pluie viendra"
  "Les jours meilleurs"
  "C'etait mon copain"
  "Le bateau blanc"
  "Rosy and John"
  "L'étoile"
  "La grande roue"
  "Je t'attends"
  "Je partirai"
  "T'es venu de loin"
  "Le pianiste de Varsovie"
  "Cornelius"
ACT 2
  "L'oiseau de toutes les couleurs"
  "The Other Three"
  "Les cerisiers sont blancs"
  "La grosse noce"
  "La riviere"
  "Les cloches"
  "Je reviens te chercher"
  "Nathalie"
  "Et maintenant"
  "L'important c'est la Rosa"

THE MEGILLA OF ITZIK MANGER

1968.22

A Yiddish-English Musical in Two Acts, a Prologue and 26 Scenes, in Yiddish. Entire production adapted and staged by Shmuel Bunim. (Based on the poems of Itzik Manger and the Book of Esther.) Music by Dov Seltzer. (Yiddish lyrics by Itzik Manger.) English commentaries by Joe

---

[4]Previously presented in New York 9 October October 1967 at the Lunt-Fontanne Theatre for 48 performances.
[5]Not in performance order.

[6]Gilbert Becaud previously presented in New York 31 October 1966 at the Longacre Theatre for 19 performances.

Darion. Lighting by Eldon Elder. Original Israeli production designed by Shlomo Vitkin. Musical conductor, Max Meth. Assistant director, Amnon Kabatchnik. Produced by Zvi Kolitz, Solomon Sagall and Alice Peerce. Opened 9 October 1968 at the John Golden Theatre and closed 15 December 1968 after 78 performances. Re-opened a return engagement 19 April 1969 at the Longacre Theatre and closed 27 April 1969 after 12 additional performances. Total: 90 performances.

CAST: *Interlocutor, Fastrigosso, Fanfosso, and other assorted characters*: MIKE BURSTEIN. *Ahasueras, Mordechai, Etc. Etc.*: PESACH BURSTEIN. *Vashti, Zeresh, Innkeeper and Various Mothers*: LILLIAN LUX. *Haman, Tailor, Fanfosso's Daughter and different Jews*: ZISHA GOLD. *Esther, Tailor's Apprentice, First Girl, Second Girl and other girls*: SUSAN WALTERS[7]. *Second Interlocutor, Vayzatha and characters of assorted sexes*: ARIEL FURMAN. *Market People, Palace attendants, street crowds, wedding guests, etc. etc.*: The Company.

(The action takes place in Biblical times.)

Act 1, Scene 1: Why Mordechai, the sage, hung around the King's Palace. *Scene 2*: Queen Vashti's boudoir. *Scene 3*: Scandal in the Palace. *Scene 4*: Vashti walks her last, long mile. *Scene 5*: Esther wants to be taken to the King. *Scene 6*: Esther's wedding. *Scene 7*: Mordechai returns home drunk from the wedding. *Scene 8*: Outside the Palace, a lover cries for his lost love. *Scene 9*: Inside the Palace, Queen Esther can't sleep. *Scene 10*: Outside the Palace, Fastrigossa does sleep. He dreams of Esther. *Scene 11*: Jews in trouble come to Mordechai for help. *Scene 12*: Politics in the bedroom. *Scene 13*: Fastrigossa sends a love song to Esther.

Act 1, Scene 1: Fastrigossa attacks the King in the Marketplace and Haman telephones the news to his son, the editor. *Scene 2*: The tailors wet their whistles. *Scene 3*: The King is glad to be alive. *Scene 4*: Mordechai visits Esther in the Palace. *Scene 5*: Now haman can't sleep. *Scene 6*: Haman, the charmer, comes to charm Esther. *Scene 7*: In the tailor shop, a party suit is being made for Haman. *Scene 8*: Fastrigossa's mother cries for her son and blames Esther and Mordechai for his death. *Scene 9*: Haman waits for his party suit. *Scene 10*: The day of the big masquerade. *Scene 11*: Caught in the act. *Scene 12*: Haman goes to the gallows. *Scene 13*: Finale.

ACT 1

Prologue

"The Tailor's Megilla"
    Full Company

Scene 1

"Theme of the Megilla" (Der Nigun Fun Der Megille)
    (Full Company)

Scene 3

"Oom Pa Pa Pa" (Drinking Song) (Dem Melech's Sudeh)
    (Full Company)

Scene 4

"Vashti's Farewell" (Vashti's Kloglid)
    (L. Lux)

Scene 5

"Song of the Walnut Tree" (Der Alter Nussenboim)
    (Full Company)
"Theme of the Megilla" (reprise)

Scene 8

"Fastrigossa's Lament" (Di Elegiye Fun Fastrigosso)
    (M. Burstein)

Scene 9

"Fastrigossa's Lament" (reprise)
"Song of the Golden Peacock" (Das Lid Fun Der Goldener Paveh)
    (Full Company)

Scene 13

"Fly Little Bird" (Flits Fegelech)
    (M. Burstein, Company)

ACT 2

Scene 1

"Gevald Aria" (Gevald)
    (Full Company)

Scene 2

"The Tailor's Drinking Song" (Come In to the Tavern)
(Kum Arain in Shenk)
    (Full Company)

Scene 3

"S'a Mechaye" (The King's Song)
(It's a Groove)
    (P. Burstein)

Scene 4

"Song of the Walnut Tree" (reprise)

Scene 7

"The Tailors' Song" (From Stopchet to Kolomay) (Dos Shneider Lid)
    (Full Company)

Various reprises

"Revolutionary Song" (Mir Velen Nisht Fasten)
    (Full Company)

Scene 8

"A Mother's Tears" (Fastrigossa's Mame)
    (L. Lux)

Scene 10

"'Cause Uncle Mordecai Is So Smart" (Der Fetter Mord'che Heist)
    (M. Burstein, L. Lux)

Scene 12

"Chiribim"
    (Full Company)

Scene 13

"Lechaim" for All (A Toast to the Players)
    (Full Company)

1968.23   # HER FIRST ROMAN

A Musical in Two Acts, a Prologue and 11 Scenes. Book, music and lyrics by Ervin Drake. Based on the play "Caesar and Cleopatra" by George Bernard Shaw. Dances and musical scenes staged by Dania Krupska. Entire production under the supervision by Derek Goldby. Sets and costumes by Michael Anania. Lighting by Martin Aronstein. Orchestrations and vocal arrangements by Don Walker. Musical direction, dance and incidental music by Peter Howard. Production supervised by Robert Weiner and George Thorn. Produced by Joseph Cates and Henry Fownes in association with Warner Brothers-7 Arts. Opened 20 October 1968 at the Lunt-Fontanne Theatre and closed 2 November 1968 after 17 performances.

CAST (in order of appearance): *Ftatateeta*: CLAUDIA McNEIL. *Rufio*: BRUCE MacKAY. *Roman Centurion*: Jack Dabdoub. *Caesar*: RICHARD KILEY. *Cleopatra*: LESLIE UGGAMS. *Iras*: BARBARA SHARMA. *Charmian*: Diana Corto. *Achillas*: Larry Douglas. *Pothinus*: Earl Montgomery. *Ptolemy*: Phillip Graves. *Britannus*: Brooks Morton. *Roman Sentry*: George Blackwell. *Apollodorous*: Cal Bellini. *Palace Official*: Marc Jordan.

Roman Soldiers: John Baylis, Paul Berné, George Blackwell, Gerry Buckhardt, Robert Carle, Gordon Cook, Bill Gibbens, Scott Hunter, Sean Nolan, Doug Spingler, Don StomsVik, Ronald Stratton. *Egyptians*: Pamela Barlow, Diana Corto, Priscilla Lopez, Sally Neal, Trina Parks, Suzanne Rogers, Renee Rose, Geri Seignious, Henry Baker, Marc Jordan, George Nestor, Alexander Orfaly, Kenneth Scott.

The action takes place in Egypt from October 48 through March 47 B.C.

ACT 1

Prologue

"What Are We Doing in Egypt?"
    B. MacKay, J. Dabdoub, Roman Soldiers

Scene 1

"Hail to the Sphinx"
    R. Kiley
"Save Me From Caesar"
    L. Uggams, R. Kiley

Scene 2

"Many Young Men from Now"
    L. Uggams

Scene 4

"Ptolemy"
    L. Uggams, Egyptian Women

Scene 5

"Old Gentleman"
    R. Kiley

---

[7]Succeeded by Evelyn Kingsley for return engagement.

Scene 6
"Her First Roman"
B. MacKay, B. Morton, Roman Soldiers
Scene 7
"Magic Carpet"
L. Uggams, C. Bellini, Egyptians
Scene 8
"Rome"
R. Kiley
"The Things We Think We Are"
R. Kiley, L. Uggams, B. Morton, B. MacKay

ACT 2
Scene 1
"I Cannot Make Him Jealous"
L. Uggams
Scene 2
"The Dangerous Age"
B. MacKay, B. Morton
"In Vino Veritas"
R. Kiley, B. MacKay, B. Morton, C. Bellini
"Caesar Is Wrong"
R. Kiley
"Just For Today"
L. Uggams

1968.24 MAGGIE FLYNN

A Musical in Two Acts, a Prologue and 17 Scenes. Book, music and lyrics by Hugo Peretti, Luigi Creatore and George David Weiss. Book in collaboration with Morton Da Costa. Based on an idea by John Flaxman. Entire production directed by Morton Da Costa. Choreography by Brian MacDonald. Settings by William and Jean Eckart. Costumes by W. Robert LaVine. Lighting by Tharon Musser. Musical direction and vocal arrangements by John Lesko. Orchestrations by Philip J. Lang. Dance music arrranged by Trude Rittman. Produced by John Bowab in association with Harris Associates, Inc.and Levin-Townshend Enterprises, Inc. Opened 23 October 1968 at the ANTA Theatre and closed 5 January 1969 after 82 performances.

CAST (in order of appearance):*Mulligan Sergeant*: David Vosburg. *Sprague Sergeant*: Larry Pool. *Garibaldi Sergeant*: James Senn. *Donnelly*: Austin Colyer. *O'Malley*: George Tregre. *First Soldier*: Roger Bigelow. *Carter*: Charles Rule. *O'Brien*: Stanley Simmonds. *Clancy*: Mario Maroze. *Timmy*: WILLIAM JAMES. *Walter*: Douglas Grant. *Maggie Flynn*: SHIRLEY JONES. *William*: Clarence Espinosa. *Andrew*: Giancarlo Esposito. *Erasmus*: Vincent Esposito. *Violet*: Sharon Brown. *Hyacinth*: Jewel Hoston. *Iris*: Irene Cara. *Pansy*: Stephanie Mills. *Chrysanthemum*: Cheri Welles. *Mary O'Cleary*: JENNIFER DARLING. *Bob Jefferson*: Bill Barrian. *Will Jefferson*: Mitch Taylor. *Fireman*: Charles Rule. *Officer O'Reilly*: Nick Malekos. *Effram*: PETER NORMAN. *Molly*: Hazel Steck. *Mick*: John Stanzel .*Bellini*: Robert Mandan. *Atlas*: Robert Roman. *Phineas*: JACK CASSIDY. *Young Girl*: Kathley Robey. *Goliath*: Roy Barry. *Lena, The Gorilla*: James Senn. *Acrobats*: George Bunt, Don Bonnell. *Colonel John Farraday*: ROBERT KAYE. *Mrs. Vanderhoff*: SIBYL BOWAN. *Mrs. Opdyke*: Jeannette Seibert. *Second Lady*: June Eve Story. *Mrs. Savage*: Sandie Fields. *Mrs. Van Stock*: Hazel Steck. *Deaf Lady*: Betty Hyatt Linton. *Captain Piedmont*: Charles Rule. *Lieutenant*: Larry Pool. *General Parkinton*: Robert Mandan. *Soldier Ed Waters*: Dallas Johann. *Tessie*: Hazel Steck. *Ladies of the Evening*: Reby Howells, Sandie Fields.

The action takes place in various streets of New York City in 1863.

Prologue: Streets of New York City, 1863.

Act 1, Scene 1: Dormitory and Facade of Meagan Orphan Home. *Scene 2*: Barlow's Saloon. *Scene 3*: Christopher Street. *Scene 4*: Dressing Tent. *Scene 5*: Parlor and Facade of Orphanage. *Scene 6*: The Kitchen of Orphanage and Street. *Scene 7*: Kitchen of Orphanage. *Scene 8*: Solarium of Vanderhoff Mansion. *Scene 9*: Union Army Headquarters and the Kitchen.

Act 2, Scene 1: Barlow's Saloon and a Street. *Scene 2*: Veranda of the Vanderhoff Mansion. *Scene 3*: The Basement of the Orphanage. *Scene 4*: The Parlour. *Scene 5*: A Jail. *Scene 6*: The Jail Office. *Scene 7*: Various New York Streets. *Scene 8*: The Kitchen and Front of the Orphanage.

ACT 1
Prologue
"(They're) Never Gonna Make Me Fight"
W. James, Men

Scene 1
"It's a Nice Cold Morning"
S. Jones, Children
Scene 2
"I Wouldn't Have You Any Other Way"
S. Jones, Saloon Boys
Scene 3
"Learn How to Laugh"
J. Cassidy, Townspeople
Scene 4
"Maggie Flynn"
J. Cassidy
Scene 5
"The Thank You Song"
S. Jones, J. Darling, Children
"Look Around Your Little World"
R. Kaye, J. Cassidy
Scene 6
"Maggie Flynn" (reprise)
J. Cassidy, S. Jones, Children, Saloon Boys
Scene 7
"I Won't Let It Happen Again"
S. Jones
Scene 8
"How About a Ball?"
J. Cassidy, S. Jones, S. Bowan, Ladies
Scene 9
"Pitter Patter"
J. Cassidy
"I Won't Let It Happen Again" (reprise)
S. Jones
ACT 2
Scene 1
"Never Gonna Make Me Fight" (reprise)
A. Colyer, S. Simmonds, W. James, Men
Scene 2
"Why Can't I Walk Away?"
J. Cassidy
Scene 3
"The Game of War"
Children
Scene 5
"Mr. Clown"
J. Cassidy, S. Jones, Children, Bums, Ladies of the Evening
"Pitter Patter" (reprise)
S. Jones
Scene 7
The Riot
Full Company
Scene 8
"Don't You Think It's Very Nice?"
S. Jones, J. Cassidy, Children
(Finale:) "Mr. Clown," "Maggie Flynn" (reprises)
S. Jones, J. Cassidy

H.M.S. PINAFORE,
1968.25 or The Lass That Loved a Sailor

A Revival of the Comic Opera in Two Acts[8]. Libretto by William S. Gilbert. Music by Arthur Sullivan. Settings and costumes designed by Peter Goffin. Back cloth, Joseph and Phil Harker. Director of productions, Herbert

---

[8]Originally presented in New York 15 January 1879 at the Standard Theatre for 175 performances. For Synopsis of Scenes and Musical Numbers, see original 1879 production.

Newby. Musical director, James Walker. Chorus master and assistant conductor, William Cowley. Produced by the D'Oyly Carte Opera Trust, Ltd. under the personal supervision of Bridget D'Oyly Carte and under the management of Sol Hurok. Opened 29 October 1968 at the New York City Center and closed 14 November 1968 after 4 performances in repertory.

CAST: *The Rt. Hon. Sir Joseph Porter, K.C.B.,* First Lord of the Admiralty: JOHN REED. *Captain Corcoran,* Commanding *H.M.S. Pinafore*: THOMAS LAWLOR. *Ralph Rackstraw,* Able Seaman: RALPH MASON. *Dick Deadeye,* Able Seaman: DONALD ADAMS. *Bill Bobstay,* Bo'sun's Mate: George Cook. *Bob Becket,* Carpenter's Mate: Clifford Parkes. *Josephine,* the Captain's Daughter: VALERIE MASTERSON, SUSAN JACKSON. *Hebe,* Sir Joseph's First Cousin: Pauline Wales. *Little Buttercup,* Mrs. Cripps, a Portsmouth Bumboat Woman: CHRISTENE PALMER.
  First Lord's Sisters, his Cousins, his Aunts, Sailors, Marines: Glyn Adams, John Ayldon, Derek Booth, Jeffrey Cresswell, George Cook, Jon Ellison, Arthur Jackson, Gordon Mackenzie, Clifford Parkes, Brian Peach, David Rayson, Brian Sharpe, Michael Tuckey, John Webley, Howard Williamson, David Young, Brenda Atherton, Susan Minshull-Browne, Christine Bull, Anne Eggleston, Julia Goss, Frances Gregory, Glenys Groves, Anne Guthrie, Abby Hadfield, Beti Lloyd-Jones, Elizabeth Lowry, Marian Martin, Beverly Mino, Elizabeth Mynett, Alison Parkor, Anne Sessions.

PATIENCE,
1968.26 or Bunthorne's Bride

A Revival of the Comic Opera in Two Acts[9]. Libretto by William S. Gilbert. Music by Arthur Sullivan. Settings and costumes designed by Peter Goffin. Director of productions, Herbert Newby. Musical director, James Walker. Chorus master and assistant conductor, William Cowley. Produced by the D'Oyly Carte Opera Trust, Ltd. under the personal supervision of Bridget D'Oyly Carte and under the management of Sol Hurok. Opened 31 October 1968 at the New York City Center and closed 13 November 1968 after 4 performances.

CAST: *Colonel Calverley*: DONALD ADAMS. *Major Murgatroyd*: Howard Williamson. *Lieut. the Duke of Dunstable*: RALPH MASON. *Reginald Bunthorne,* a Fleshly Poet: JOHN REED. *Archibald Grosvenor,* an Idyllic Poet: KENNETH SANDFORD. *Mr. Bunsthorne's Solicitor*: James Marsland. *The Lady Angela, The Lady Saphir, The Lady Ella, The Lady Jane,* Rapturous Maidens: PEGGY ANN JONES, PAULINE WALES, Anne Sessions, CHRISTENE PALMER. *Patience,* a Dairy Maid: SUSAN JACKSON. *Chorus of Rapturous Maidens and Officers of the Dragoon Guards*: same as H.M.S. PINAFORE above.

THE MIKADO,
1968.27 or The Town of Titipu

A Revival of the Comic Opera in Two Acts[10]. Libretto by William S. Gilbert. Music by Arthur Sullivan. Production directed by Anthony Besch. Costumes designed by Charles Ricketts. Nanki-Poo, Act 1 Costume designed By Disley Jones. Scenery by Peter Goffin. Director of productions, Herbert Newby. Musical director, James Walker. Chorus master and assistant conductor, William Cowley. Produced by the D'Oyly Carte Opera Trust, Ltd. under the personal supervision of Bridget D'Oyly Carte and under the management of Sol Hurok. Opened 1 November 1968 at the New York City Center and closed 16 November 1968 after 8 performances in repertory.

CAST: *The Mikado of Japan*: DONALD ADAMS. *Nanki-Poo,* his son, disguised as a wandering minstrel in love with Yum-Yum: PHILIP POTTER. *Ko-Ko,* Lord High Executioner of Titipu: JOHN REED. *Pooh-Bah,* Lord High Everything Else: KENNETH SANDFORD. *Pish-Tush, Go-To,* Noble Lords: Thomas Lawlor, George Cook. *Yum-Yum, Pitti-Sing, Peep-Bo,* three sisters, wards of Ko-Ko: VALERIE MASTERSON, PEGGY ANN JONES, PAULINE WALES. *Katisha*: CHRISTENE

PALMER, BETTI LLOYD-JONES. *Chorus of School Girls, Nobles, Guards and Coolies*: same as H.M.S. PINAFORE above.

THE PIRATES OF PENZANCE,
1968.28 or The Slave of Duty

A Revival of the Comic Opera in Two Acts[11]. Libretto by William S. Gilbert. Music by Arthur Sullivan. Settings designed by Peter Goffin. Director of productions, Herbert Newby. Musical director, James Walker. Chorus master and assistant conductor, William Cowley. Produced by the D'Oyly Carte Opera Trust, Ltd. under the personal supervision of Bridget D'Oyly Carte and under the management of Sol Hurok. Opened 6 November 1968 at the New York City Center and closed 17 November 1968 after 4 performances in repertory.[12]

CAST: *Major General Stanley*: JOHN REED, HOWARD WILLIAMSON. *The Pirate King*: DONALD ADAMS. *Samuel,* his Lieutenant: John Webley. *Frederic,* the Pirate Apprentice: PHILIP POTTER. *Sergeant of Police*: GEORGE COOK. *Mabel, Edith Kate, Isabel,* General Stanley's Daughters: VALERIE MASTERSON, PEGGY ANN JONES, PAULINE WALES, Julia Goss. *Ruth,* Pirate Maid-of-all-work: CHRISTENE PALMER. *Chorus of Pirates, Police and General Stanley's Daughters*: same as H.M.S. PINAFORE above.

IOLANTHE,
1968.29 or The Peer and the Peri

A Revival of the Comic Opera in Two Acts[13]. Libretto by William S. Gilbert. Music by Arthur Sullivan. Director of productions, Herbert Newby. Settings designed by Peter Goffin. Musical director, James Walker. Chorus master and assistant conductor, William Cowley. Produced by the D'Oyly Carte Opera Trust, Ltd. under the personal supervision of Bridget D'Oyly Carte and under the management of Sol Hurok. Opened 8 November 1968 at the New York City Center and closed 15 November 1968 after 4 performances in repertory[14].

CAST: *The Lord Chancellor*: JOHN REED. *Earl of Mountararat*: DONALD ADAMS. *Earl Tolloller*: RALPH MASON. *Private Willis* of the Grenadier Guards: KENNETH SANDFORD. *Strephon,* an Arcadian Shepherd: THOMAS LAWLOR. *Queen of the Fairies*: CHRISTENE PALMER. *Iolanthe,* a Fairy, Strephon's Mother: PEGGY ANN JONES. *Celia, Leila, Fleta,* Fairies: Anne Sessions, Pauline Wales, Alison Parker. *Phyllis,* an Arcadian Shepherdess and Ward in Chancery: SUSAN JACKSON. *Chorus of Dukes, Marquises, Earls, Viscounts, Barons and Fairies*: same as H.M.S. PINAFORE above.

ZORBA
1968.30

A Musical in Two Acts, 17 Scenes. Book by Joseph Stein. Adapted from the novel "Zorba the Greek" by Nikos Kazantzakis. Music by John Kander. Lyrics by Fred Ebb. Directed by Harold Prince. Choreographed by Ron Field. Scenic production by Boris Aronson. Costumes by Patricia Zipprodt. Lighting by Richard Pilbrow. Musical direction by Harold Hastings. Orchestrations by Don Walker. Dance music arranged by Dorothea Freitag. Production consultant, Vassili Lambrinos. Associate choreographer, Tom Rolla. Produced by Harold Prince in association with Ruth Mitchell. Opened 17 November 1968 at the Imperial Theatre and closed 9 August 1969 after 305 performances.

CAST: *Constable*: David Wilder. *Nikos*: JOHN CUNNINGHAM. *Alexis*: Alex Petrides. *Hortense*: MARIA KARNILOVA. *Manolako*: James Luisi. *Panayotis*: Nat Horne. *Widow*: CARMEN ALVAREZ. *Mimiko*: Al De Sio. *Konstandi*: Joseph Alfasa. *Sofia*: Marsha Tamaroff. *Kyriakos*: Jerry Sappir. *Leader*: LORRAINE SERABIAN. *Kanakis*: Ali Hafid. *Konstantinos*: Angelo Saridis. *Marina*: Alicia Helen Markarian. *Fivos*: Gerrit De Beer. *Efterpi*: Lee Hooper. *Zorba*: HERSCHEL

---

[9]First presented in New York 22 September 1881 at the Standard Theatre for 177 performances. For Synopsis of Scenes and Musical Numbers, see original 1881 production.
[10]First presented in New York 20 July, 10-29 August 1885 at the Union Square and People's Theatres for 22 performances. First authorized production presented 19 August 1885 at the Fifth Avenue Theatre by Richard D'Oyly Carte for 250 performances. For Synopsis of Scenes and Musical Numbers, see 19 August 1885 D'Oyly Carte production.

[11]First presented in New York 31 December 1879 at the Fifth Avenue Theatre for a total of 91 performances in two engagements. For Synopsis of Scenes and Musical Numbers, see original 1879 production.
[12]Costumes uncredited.
[13]First presented in New York 25 November 1882 at the Standard Theatre for 105 performances. For Synopsis of Scenes and Musical Numbers, see original 1882 production.
[14]Costumes uncredited.

BERNARDI. *Loukas*: Loukas Skiptaris. *Meropi*: Juliette Durand. *Aristos*: Charles Kalan. *Georgi*: John La Motta.

Antonis: Anthony Marciona. *Tasso*: Susan Marciona. *Thanos*: Lewis Gundunas. *Pavli*: Richard Dmitri. *Father Zacharia*: Gerard Russak. *Aliki*: Miriam Welch. *Mavrodani*: Paul Michael. *Chyristo*: Louis Garcia. *Zacharias*: Edward Nolfi. *Belly Dancer*: Jemela Omar. *Old Man*: Robert Bernard. *Katapolis*: Richard Nieves. *Despo*: Nina Dova. *Irini*: Connie Burnett. *Athena*: Peggy Cooper. *Grigoris*: Wayne Boyd. *Vasilis*: Martin Meyers.

Instrumental Interlude Soloists: Jerry Sappir, Ali Hafid, Angelo Saridis.

The action takes place in a Bouzouki Circle at the present time, and Piraeus, Greece and the island of Crete, in 1924.

Act 1, Scene 1: A Bouzouki Circle. *Scene 2*: A Waterfront Café in Piraeus. *Scene 3*: The Exterior of a Village Café, adjacent shops and Village Church in Crete. *Scene 4*: The Garden of Hortense's Inn. *Scene 5*: Hortense's Bedroom. *Scene 6*: The Entrance to the Mine. *Scene 7*: Exterior of Hortense's Inn, the next morning. *Scene 8*: Interior of a Café in Khania. *Scene 9*: Interior and Exterior of the Widow's Home, dusk of the next day.

Act 2, Scene 1: The Village Square. *Scene 2*: Exterior of the Cottage in Hortense's garden. *Scene 3*: A Road. *Scene 4*: The Village Square. *Scene 5*: The Entrance to the Mine. *Scene 6*: Hortense's Bedroom. *Scene 7*: The Road leading out of the Village. *Scene 8*: A Bouzouki Circle.

ACT 1

Scene 1

"Life Is"
L. Serrabian, the Company

Scene 2

"The First Time"
H. Bernardi

Scene 3

"The Top of the Hill"
L. Serrabian, Chorus

Scene 4

"No Boom Boom"
M. Karnilova, H. Bernardi, J. Cunningham, The Admirals

"Vive La Difference"
The Admirals, Dancers

Scene 6

"The Butterfly"
J. Cunningham, L. Serrabian, C. Alvarez, Chorus

Scene 7

"Goodbye, Canavaro"
M. Karnilova, H. Bernardi

Scene 8

Belly Dance
J. Omar

"Grandpapa"
H. Bernardi, L. Serrabian, Chorus

"Only Love"
M. Karnilova

"The Bend of the Road"
L. Serrabian, Chorus

"Only Love" (reprise)
L. Serrabian

ACT 2

Scene 1

Bells[15]
Dancers

Scene 2

"Y'assou"[16]
J. Cunningham, H. Bernardi, M. Karnilova, L. Serrabian, Chorus

Scene 3

"Why Can't I Speak?"[17]
C. Alvarez, L. Hooper

[15] Dropped for subsequent national tour.
[16] Replaced for subsequent national tour by:
"Bouboulina"
John Raitt (Zorba), Barbara Baxley (Hortense), Chita Rivera (Leader), Chorus
[17] Replaced for subsequent national tour by:
"That's a Beginning"
Marsha Tamaroff (Widow), Gary Krawford (Nikos), C. Rivera

Scene 5

Mine Celebration
H. Bernardi, Company

Scene 6

"The Crow"
L. Serrabian, Women

"Happy Birthday"
M. Karnilova

Scene 7

"I Am Free"
H. Bernardi

Scene 8

"Life Is" (reprise)
L. Serrabian, the Company

PROMISES, PROMISES

1968.31

A Musical in Two Acts, 14 Scenes. Book by Neil Simon. Based on the film "The Apartment" by Billy Wilder and I.A.L. Diamond. Music by Burt Bacharach. Lyrics by Hal David. Directed by Robert Moore. Musical numbers staged by Michael Bennett. Settings by Robin Wagner. Costumes by Donald Brooks. Lighting by Martin Aronstein. Musical direction and dance arrangements by Harold Wheeler. Orchestrations by Jonathan Tunick. Associate producer, Samuel Liff. Assistant choreographer, Bob Avian. Sound created by Admins, Ltd. Produced by David Merrick. Opened 1 December 1968 at the Sam S. Shubert Theatre and closed 1 January 1972 after 1281 performances.

CAST (in order of appearance): *Chuck Baxter*: JERRY ORBACH. *J. D. Sheldrake*: EDWARD WINTER. *Fran Kubelik*: JILL O'HARA. *Bartender Eddie*: Ken Howard. *Mr. Dobitch*: Paul Reed. *Sylvia Gilhooley*: Adrienne Angel. *Mr. Kirkeby*: Norman Shelly. *Mr. Eichelberger*: Vince O'Brien. *Vivien Della Hoya*: Donna McKechnie. *Dr. Dreyfuss*: A. LARRY HAINES. *Jesse Vanderhof*: Dick O'Neill. *Dentist's Nurse*: Rita O'Connor. *Company Nurse*: Carole Bishop. *Company Doctor*: Gerry O'Hara. *Peggy Olson*: Millie Slavin. *Lum Ding Hostess*: Baayork Lee. *Waiter*: Scott Pearson. *Madison Square Garden Attendant*: Michael Vita. *Dining Room Hostess*: Betsy Haug. *Miss Polansky*: Margo Sappington. *Miss Wong*: Baayork Lee. *Bartender Eugene*: Michael Vita. *Marge MacDougall*: Marian Mercer. *Clancy's Lounge Patrons*: Carole Bishop, Rita O'Connor, Julane Stites, Rod Barry, Gene Cooper, Bob Fitch, Neil F. Jones, Scott Pearson, Michael Shawn. *Clancy's Employees*: Graciela Daniele, Betsy Haug, Margo Sappington. *Helen Sheldrake*: Kay Oslin. *Karl Kubelik*: Ken Howard. *New Young Executive*: Rod Barry. *Interns and Dates*: Barbara Alston, Graciela Daniele, Gerry O'Hara, Michael Shawn.

Orchestra Voices: Kelly Britt, Margot Hanson, Bettye McCormick, Ilona Simon.

The action takes place in New York at the present time.

Act 1, Scene 1: The Offices of Consolidated Life; Second Avenue Bar. *Scene 2*: Chuck's Apartment House. *Scene 3*: Medical Office. *Scene 4*: Mr. Sheldrake's Office. *Scene 5*: Lobby. *Scene 6*: Lum Ding's Restaurant and Madison Square Garden. *Scene 7*: Lobby, Executive Dining Room; Executive Sun Deck. *Scene 8*: At the Elevator. *Scene 9*: Nineteenth Floor Christmas Party.

Act 2, Scene 1: Clancy's Lounge. *Scene 2*: Chuck's Apartment. *Scene 3*: The Offices of Consolidated Life. *Scene 4*: Lum Ding's Restaurant and Street. *Scene 5*: Chuck's Apartment.

ACT 1

Scene 1

"Half As Big As Life"
J. Orbach

("Grapes of Roth" dance)
(Dancers)

Scene 2

"Upstairs"
J. Orbach

Scene 3

"You'll Think of Someone"
J. O'Hara, J. Orbach

Scene 4

"Our Little Secret"
J. Orbach, E. Winter

Scene 5

"She Likes Basketball"
J. Orbach

Scene 6

"Knowing When to Leave"
J. O'Hara

Scene 7

"Where Can You Take a Girl?"
P. Reed, N. Shelly, V. O'Brien, D. O'Neill

"Wanting Things"
E. Winter

Scene 9

"Turkey Lurkey Time"
D. McKechnie, M. Sappington, B. Lee

ACT 2

Scene 1

"A Fact Can Be a Beautiful Thing"
J. Orbach, M. Mercer, Bar Patrons

Scene 2

"Whoever You Are"
J. O'Hara

"A Young Pretty Girl Like You"
J. Orbach, A. L. Haines

"I'll Never Fall in Love Again"
J. O'Hara, J. Orbach

Scene 4

"Promises, Promises"
J. Orbach

1968.32   CARNIVAL

A Revival of the Musical (Comedy) in Two Acts, 24 Scenes[18]. Book by Michael Stewart. Based on the story ("The Seven Souls of Clement O'Reilly" by Paul Gallico and its film adaptation "Lili" by Helen Deutsch. Music and lyrics by Bob Merrill. Directed by Gus Schirmer. Re-staging of Gower Champion's original choreography by John Nola. Production (settings) and lighting by Feder. Costumes by Harry Curtis, based on originals by Freddy Wittop. Musical and vocal arrangements by Saul Schechtman. Musical director, Peter Howard. Orchestrations by Philip J. Lang. Dance arrangements by Peter Howard. Designer and supervisor of magic and illusion, Jack Adams. Produced by the New York City Center Light Opera Company (Jean Dalrymple, Director). Opened 12 December 1968 at the New York City Center and closed 5 January 1969 after 30 performances.

CAST (in order of appearance): *Jacquot*: PIERRE OLAF. *Mr. Schlegel*: Carmine Caridi. *Grobert*: George Nestor. *Roustabouts*: Chuck Beard, Marcelo Gamboa, Fred Randall, Steven Ross, Paul Solen. *Dog Trainer*: Leonard Brook. *Wardrobe Mistress*: Maria Hero. *Harem Girls*: Nina Janik, Dottie Lester, Maralyn Miles, Linda Rankin. *Bear Girl*: Maureen Hopkins. *Princess Olga*: Dorothy D'Honau. *Band*: Art Ostrin, Nate Barnett. *Stilt-Walker*: Dean Crane. *Jugglers*: Martin Brothers. *Clowns*: Dean Crane, John Drew. *Strongman*: David Berk. *Gladys Zuwicki*: Mary Ann Niles. *Gloria Zuwicki*: Christine Bartel. *Gypsy*: Roberta Vatske. *Marco the Magnificent*: RICHARD FRANCE. *The Incomparable Rosalie*: KAREN MORROW. *Greta Schlegel*: Jennifer Rose. *Lili*: VICTORIA MALLORY. *Paul (Berthalet)*: LEON BIBB. *Blue Birds*: Nina Janik, Dottie Lester, Maralyn Miles, Linda Rankin. *Aerialist*: Dean Crane. *Dr. Glass*: Robert L. Hultman. *Puppets performed by* Richard Barclay.

1969.01   THE FIG LEAVES ARE FALLING

A Musical in Two Acts, a Prologue and 20 Scenes. Book and lyrics by Allan Sherman. Music by Albert Hague. Production directed by George Abbott. Dances and musical numbers staged by Eddie Gasper. Settings by William and Jean Eckart. Costumes by Robert Mackintosh. Lighting by Tharon Musser. Musical direction by Abba Bogin. Orchestrations by Manny Albam. Dance music arranged and orchestra conducted by Jack Lee. Produced by Joseph P. Harris, Lawrence Carr and John Bowab in association with Harris Associates, Inc., and Levin-Townshend Enterprises, Inc. Opened 2 January 1969 at the Broadhurst Theatre and closed 4 January 1969 after 4 performances.

---

[18]First produced in New York 13 April 1961 at the Imperial Theatre for 719 performances. For Synopsis of Scenes and Musical Numbers, see original 1961 production.

CAST (in order of appearance): *Harry Stone*: BARRY NELSON. *Lillian Stone*: DOROTHY LOUDON. *Pookie Chapman*: JENNY O'HARA. *Mr. Mittleman*: Jay Barney. *Hodgekins*: Joe McGrath. *Reverend Walters*: Darrell Sandeen. *Gelb*: Frank DeSal. *Mildred*: Jean Even. *Grace*: Mara Landi. *Mimsy*: Marilyne Mason. *Charley Montgomery*: KENNETH KIMMINS. *Marty*: Patrick Spohn. *Mother-in-Law*: Helon Blount. *Billy*: David Cassidy. *Cecelia*: Louise Quick. *LeRoy*: Alan Weeks. *Queen Victoria*: Frank DeSal. *Mary Queen of Scots*: Anna Pagan. *Elizabeth Marsden*: Pat Trott. *Mao-Tse*: John Joy. *Marlene*: Jean Even. *Cynthia*: Jocelyn McKay.

Dancers: Jean Even, Mary Jane Houdina, Renata Powers, Sally Ransone, Charlene Ryan, Pat Trott, Frank DeSal, John Medeiros, Michael Misita, Lathan Sanford, Tony Stevens, Patrick Spohn, Pi Douglas. *Singers*: Sherry Lambert, Mara Landi, Rosemary McNamara, Anna Pagan, Jocelyn McKay, Edmund Gaynes, John Joy, Joe McGrath, Darrell Sandeen, Alan Weeks.

(The action trakes place in New York City and Larchmont at the present time.)

Prologue: Larchmont, New York.

Act 1, Scene 1: The Stone's Living Room in Larchmont. *Scene 2*: Limbo. *Scene 3*: Harry's Office. *Scene 4*: The Park. *Scene 5*: Harry's Office. *Scene 6*: The Stone's Living Room; Off to Europe. *Scene 7*: The Stone's Living Room. *Scene 8*: Limbo. *Scene 9*: The Love-in in the Park. *Scene 10*: Limbo. *Scene 11*: The Stone's Bedroom: Nightmare.

Act 2, Scene 1: The Fig Leaves Are Falling. *Scene 2*: Limbo. *Scene 3*: The Stone's Living Room. *Scene 4*: The Theatre. *Scene 5*: Limbo. *Scene 6*: Charley's Apartment. *Scene 7*: Pookie's Pad. *Scene 8*: Limbo. *Scene 9*: The Colorful Living Room: The Ending (?).

ACT 1

Prologue

"All Is Well in Larchmont"
Choir

Scene 1

"Not Tonight"
D. Loudon

Scene 2

"Like Yours"
J. O'Hara, Wallstreeters

Scene 3

"The Fig Leaves Are Falling"
J. O'Hara, B. Nelson

Scene 4

"Give Me a Cause"
The Protestors

Scene 5

"Today I Saw a Rose"
B. Nelson

Scene 6

"We"
D. Loudon

Scene 7

"For Our Sake"
D. Cassidy, L. Quick

Scene 9

"Light One Candle"
A. Weeks, F. DeSal, A. Pagan, Hippies, Yippies, Et Al

Scene 10

"Oh, Boy"
Choir

ACT 2

Scene 1

"The Fig Leaves Are Falling"
The Boys Club

Scene 3

"For the Rest of My Life"
D. Loudon

Scene 4

"I Like It"
B. Nelson, J. O'Hara

Scene 5

"All of My Laughter"
D. Loudon

Scene 7

"Did I Ever Really Live?"
B. Nelson
"Old Fashioned Song"
K. Kimmins, Ensemble
"Lillian, Lillian, Lillian"
D. Loudon, L. Quick, D. Cassidy

1969.02 CELEBRATION

A Musical in Two Acts. Words (book and lyrics) by Tom Jones. Music by Harvey Schmidt. Directed by Tom Jones. Musical numbers staged and choreographed by Vernon Lusby. Settings, lighting and costumes designed by Ed Wittstein. Musical direction by Rod Derefinko. Orchestrations by Jim Tyler. Production coordination by Robert Alan Gold. A Portfolio Production. Produced by Cheryl Crawford and Richard Chandler. Opened 22 January 1969 at the Ambassador Theatre and closed 26 April 1969 after 110 performances.

CAST (in order of appearance): *Potemkin*: KEITH CHARLES. *Orphan*: MICHAEL GLENN-SMITH. *Angel*: SUSAN WATSON. *Rich*: TED THURSTON.
Revelers: Glenn Bastian, Cindi Bulak, Stephan de Ghelder, Leah Horen, Patricia Lens, Norman Mathews, Frank Newell, Pamela Peadon, Felix Rice, Sally Riggs, Gary Wales, Hal Watters.

The action takes place on a platform on New Year's Eve.

ACT 1

"Celebration"
K. Charles, the Revelers
"Orphan in the Storm"
M. Glenn-Smith, the Revelers
"Survive"
K. Charles, the Revelers
"Somebody"
S. Watson, the Hittites
"Bored"
T. Thurston
"My Garden"
M. Glenn-Smith, the Revelers
"Where Did It Go"
T. Thurston, the Sycophants
"Love Song"
S. Watson, K. Charles, T. Thurston, M. Glenn-Smith, the Revelers
"To the Garden"
Everyone

ACT 2

"I'm Glad To See You've Got What You Want"
S. Watson, M. Glenn-Smith
"It's You Who Makes Me Young"
T. Thurston, the Revelers
"Not My Problem"
K. Charles, the Machines
"Fifty Million Years Ago"
M. Glenn-Smith
"The Beautician Ballet"
T. Thurston, the Revelers
"Saturnalia"
K. Charles, the Revelers
"Under the Tree"
S. Watson, the Animals
"Winter and Summer"
Everyone
"Celebration" Finale
Everyone

1969.03 RED, WHITE AND MADDOX

A Thing With Music (Musical Comedy) in Two Acts. Book, music and lyrics by Don Tucker and Jay Broad. (Inspired by the political career of Governor Lester Maddox of Georgia.) Staged by Don Tucker and Jay Broad. Sets and costumes by David Chapman. Design supervision and lighting by Richard Casler. Visual materials by Bill Diehl, Jr. Associate producers, William Domnitz, Arthur Miller. A Theatre Atlanta Production. Produced by Edward Padula. Opened 26 January 1969 at the Cort Theatre and closed 1 March 1969 after 41 performances.

CAST (in alphabetical order): *Alberta*: Georgia Allen. *Student Leader*: Fran Brill. *Cynical Campaigner*: Lois Broad. *Senator*: Ronald Bush. *Air Force General*: Fred Chappell. *Governor of Indiana*: Mitchell Edmonds. *Standard Bearer*: Karl Emery. *The Interlocutor*: Clarence Felder. *General of the Armies*: Gary Gage. *Radio Commentator*: William Gammon. *Lester Maddox*: JAY GARNER. *Student Delegate*: Elaine Harris. *Buttercup Boy*: Ted Harris. *Bombardier*: Christopher Lloyd. *Rock Singer*: Bettye Malone. *Boy from the New Left*: Ted Martin. *The Redneck*: Sandy McCallum. *Virginia Maddox*: Muriel Moore. *Girl from the New Left*: Arlene Nadel. *Political Commentator*: Steve Renfroe. *Little Mary Sue*: Judy Schoen. *Protestor*: Susan Shaloub. *C.I.A. Chief*: William Troutman. *Rock Singer*: James Weston.

Act 1: One hundred years later.

Act 2: One hundred years too late.

ACT 1

"What America Means To Me"
(Entire Company)
"Givers and Getters"
(Company)
"Jubilee Joe"
(Company)
"Ballad of a Redneck"
(Men)
"First Campaign Song"
(Salvation Army Band/Company)
"Hoe Down"
(Entire Company)
"Phooey"
(J. Garner)
"Second Campaign Song"
(Salvation Army Band/Company)
"God Is an American"
(Entire Company)

ACT 2

"Hip-Hooray for Washington"
(J. Garner)
"City Life"
(Company)
"Song of the Malcontents"
(Company)
"The General's Song"
(Company)
"Little Mary Sue"
(Company)
"Billy Joe Ju"
(Company)
"The Impeachment Waltz"
(Company)
"Red, White and Maddox Kazoo March"
(Entire Company)

1969.04 CANTERBURY TALES

A Musical in Two Acts, 10 Scenes[19]. Book by Martin Starkie and Nevill Coghill. Based on Nevill Coghill's translation of Geoffrey Chaucer's

---

[19]For subsequent National Tour, The Nun's Priest's Tale was reinstated from the London production after The Miller's Tale:

CAST: *Miller*: PATRICK HINES. *Nicholas*: WALTER McGINN. *Alison*: LOUISA FLANINGAM. *The Carpenter*: RAY WALSTON. *Absalom*: Terry Eno. *Gervase*: PATRICK HINES. *Robin*: David Steele. *The Two Parishioners*: Marybeth Lahr, Leslie Bromley.

"Chanticleer"
Company (as above)

"Canterbury Tales." Music by Richard Hill and John Hawkins. Lyrics by Nevill Coghill. Directed by Martin Starkie (after the original London production[20]). Musical numbers and dances staged by Sammy Bayes. Musical direction, vocal and dance arrangements by Oscar Kosarin. Orchestrations by Richard Hill and John Hawkins. Scenery by Derek Cousins. Costumes by Loudon Sainthill. Lighting by Jules Fisher. Scenery supervised by Richard Seger. Assistant choreographer, Bert Michaels. Produced by Management Three Productions Ltd. (Jerry Weintraub, Martin Kummer) and Frank Productions Inc. (Allen B. Whitehead) by arrangement with Classic Presentations Ltd. Opened 3 February 1969 at the Eugene O'Neill Theatre and closed 18 May 1969 after 122 performances.

CAST (in order of appearance): *The Pilgrims: Chaucer:* MARTYN GREEN. *Host:* EDWIN STEFFE. *Miller:* ROY COOPER. *Wife of Bath:* HERMIONE BADDELEY. *Cook:* DAVID THOMAS. *Merchant:* LEON SHAW. *Knight:* REID SHELTON. *Steward:* GEORGE ROSE. *Prioress:* ANN GARDNER. *Nun:* EVELYN PAGE. *Priest:* GARNETT SMITH. *Clerk of Oxford:* BRUCE HYDE. *Squire:* ED EVANKO. *Friar:* DICK [Richard] ENSSLEN. *Pardoner:* GARNETT SMITH. *Summoner:* BERT MICHAELS. *The Sweetheart:* SANDY DUNCAN.
THE MILLER'S TALE: *Nicholas:* ED EVANKO. *Alison:* SANDY DUNCAN. *Carpenter:* GEORGE ROSE. *Absalom:* BRUCE HYDE. *Gervase:* ROY COOPER. *Robin:* Terry Eno. *Parishioners:* Mary Jo Catlett, Suzan Sidney.
THE STEWARD'S TALE: *Miller:* ROY COOPER. *Miller's Wife:* EVELYN PAGE. *Molly:* SANDY DUNCAN. *Alan:* ED EVANKO. *John:* BRUCE HYDE.
THE MERCHANT'S TALE: *January:* GEORGE ROSE. *Justinus:* MARTYN GREEN. *Placebo:* GARNETT SMITH. *May:* SANDY DUNCAN. *Damian:* ED EVANKO. *Pluto:* ROY COOPER. *Prosperpina:* ANN GARDNER. *Duenna:* EVELYN PAGE. *Page:* Tod Miller. *Bridesmaids:* Patricia Michaels, Marianne Selbert, Karen Kristin, Joyce Maret. *Attendants:* Terry Eno, Tod Miller, Gene Myers, Ron Schwinn, Jack Fletcher.
THE WIFE OF BATH'S TALE: *King:* REID SHELTON. *Queen:* ANN GARDNER. *Old Woman:* HERMIONE BADDELEY. *Young Knight:* BRUCE HYDE. *Executioner:* Roger Franklin. *Courtiers:* Terry Eno, Ron Schwinn, Tod Miller, Gene Myers. *Court Ladies:* Karen Kristin, Marianne Selbert, Joyce Maret, Patricia Michaels. *Housewife:* Mary Jo Catlett. *Sweetheart:* SANDY DUNCAN.
Other Pilgrims, Workmen: Terry Eno, Jack Fletcher, Tod Miller, Gene Myers, Ron Schwinn, David Thomas. *Village Girls:* Mary Jo Catlett, Betsy Dickerson, Karen Kristin, Joyce Maret, Patricia Michaels, Marianne Selbert, Suzan Sidney.

The action passes between the Tabard Inn, London and Canterbury Cathedral in the spring during the latter part of the fourteenth century.

Act 1, Scene 1: The Tabard Inn, Southwark, London, on a fine Spring day in 1387. *Scene 2:* On the Road. *Scene 3:* The Miller's Tale. *Scene 4:* On the Road. *Scene 5:* The Steward's Tale. *Scene 6:* The Road.

Act 2, Scene 1: Another Ale House en route to Canterbury. *Scene 2:* The Merchant's Tale. *Scene 3:* The Wife of Bath's Tale. *Scene 4:* Canterbury.

ACT 1
Scene 1

"Song of Welcome"
    E. Steffe, Company
"Good Night Hymn"
    Company
"Canterbury Day"
    Company
Scene 2
"Pilgrim Riding Music"
    Company
Scene 3
"I Have a Noble Cock"
    E. Evanko
"Darling, Let Me Teach You How to Kiss"
    B. Hyde
"There's the Moon"
    E. Evanko, S. Duncan
Scene 4
"It Depends on What You're At"
    H. Baddeley, E. Page, Company
"Love Will Conquer All"
    A. Gardner, S. Sidney, Company
Scene 5
"Beer Is Best"
    R. Cooper, E. Page, E. Evanko, B. Hyde, S. Duncan

Scene 6
"Canterbury Day" (reprise)
    Company
ACT 2
Scene 1
"Come On and Marry Me Honey"
    H. Baddeley, Company
Mug Dance
    Company
"Where Are the Girls of Yesterday"
    E. Steffe, Company
Scene 2
"Hymen, Hymen"
    Company
"If She Has Never Loved Before"
    G. Rose
"I'll Give My Love a Ring"
    E. Evanko, S. Duncan
"Pear Tree Quintet"
    E. Evanko, G. Rose, R. Cooper, A. Gardner, S. Duncan
Scene 3
"I Am All A-Blaze"
    E. Evanko
"Love Pas de Deux"
    M. Selbert, R. Schwinn
"What Do Women Want?"
    B. Hyde, Court Ladies
Scene 4
"April Song"
    Company
"Love Will Conquer All" (reprise)
    A. Gardner, S. Sidney, Company

1969.05 DEAR WORLD

A Musical in Two Acts, 7 Scenes. Book by Jerome Lawrence and Robert E. Lee. Based on the play "The Madwoman of Chaillot" by Jean Giraudoux as adapted by Maurice Valency. Music and lyrics by Jerry Herman. Directed and choreographed by Joe Layton. Scenic production by Oliver Smith. Costumes by Freddy Wittop. Lighting by Jean Rosenthal. Musical direction and vocal arrangements by Don Pippin. Orchestrations by Philip J. Lang. Dance and incidental (music) arrangements by Dorothea Freitag. Associate producer, Hildy Parks. Production supervisor, Jerry Adler. Produced by Alexander H. Cohen. Opened 6 February 1969 at the Mark Hellinger Theatre and closed 31 May 1969 after 132 performances.

CAST (in order of appearance): *The Chairman of the Board:* William Larsen. *Board Members:* Clifford Fearl, Charles Karel, Zale Kessler, Charles Welch. *Prospector:* Joe Masiell. *Julian:* KURT PETERSON. *Nina:* PAMELA HALL. *The Waiter:* Gene Varrone. *The Busboy:* Ty McConnell. *The Doorman:* Michael Davis. *The Juggler:* Ted Agress. *The Peddler:* John Taliaferro. *The Deaf-Mute:* MIGUEL GODREAU. *Countess Aurelia, The Madwoman of Chaillot:* ANGELA LANSBURY. *The Sewerman:* MILO O'SHEA. *Gabrielle, The Madwoman of Montmartre:* JANE CONNELL. *Constance, The Madwoman of the Flea Market:* CARMEN MATHEWS.
People of Paris: Nicole Barth, Bruce Becker, Toney Brealond, Jane Coleman, Jack Davison, Jacque Dean, Richard Dodd, John Grigas, Marian Haraldson, Tony Juliano, Gene Kelton, Carolyn Kirsch, Urylee Leonardos, Larry Merritt, Ruth Ramsey, Orrin Reiley, Patsy Sabline, Connie Simmons, Margot Travers, Mary Zahn.

The action takes place in Paris during an early spring.

Act 1, Scene 1: The luxurious batteau of the Chairman of the Board, afloat on the Seine. *Scene 2:* The Cafe Francais and a slice of surrounding Chaillot. *Scene 3:* The sewers underneath Paris.

Act 2, Scene 1: The Countess' Apartment underneath the Cafe Francais. *Scene 2:* A street in Chaillot in the rain. *Scene 3:* The Flea Market (Marché Aux Pouces) at midnight. *Scene 4:* The Countess' Apartment; the Park at Colombes.

ACT 1
Scene 1

"The Spring of Next Year"
    W. Larsen, J. Masiell, C. Fearl, C. Karel, Z. Kessler, C. Welch

---

[20]Original London production was directed by Vlado Habunek, and co-directed by Martin Starkie.

Scene 2
  "Each Tomorrow Morning"
    A. Lansbury, All
  "I Don't Want to Know"
    A. Lansbury
  "I've Never Said I Love You"
    P. Hall
Scene 3
  "Garbage"
    M. O'Shea, A. Lansbury, J. Connell, C. Mathews, All
  "I Don't Want to Know" Ballet
    Entire Company
  "Dear World"
    A. Lansbury, All

ACT 2
Scene 1
  "Kiss Her Now"
    A. Lansbury
  The Tea Party:
  "Memory"
    C. Mathews
  "Pearls"
    A. Lansbury, J. Connell
  "Dickie"
    J. Connell
  "Voices"
    C. Mathews
  "Thoughts"
    A. Lansbury
  "And I Was Beautiful"
    A. Lansbury
Scene 2
  "Each Tomorrow Morning" (reprise)
    K. Peterson
Scene 3
  "One Person"
    A. Lansbury, All
Scene 4
  Finale
    Entire Company

1969.06 1776

A Musical in One Act, 7 Scenes. Book by Peter Stone. Based on a conception of Sherman Edwards (about the making of the Declaration of Independence). Music and lyrics by Sherman Edwards. Scenery and lighting by Jo Mielziner. Costumes by Patricia Zipprodt. Musical direction by Peter Howard. Orchestrations by Eddie Sauter. Directed by Peter Hunt. Musical numbers staged by Onna White. Dance music arrangements by Peter Howard. Vocal arrangements by Elise Bretton. Produced by Stuart Ostrow. Opened 16 March 1969 at the 46th Street Theatre, moved to 26 April 1971 the Majestic Theatre, and closed 13 February 1972 after 1217 performances.

CAST: *Members of the Continental Congress: John Hancock,* President: David Ford. *Dr. Josiah Bartlett,* New Hampshire: Paul-David Richards. *John Adams,* Massachusetts: WILLIAM DANIELS. *Stephen Hopkins,* Rhode Island: ROY POOLE. *Roger Sherman,* Connecticut: David Vosburgh. *Lewis Morris,* New York: Ronald Kross. *Robert Livingston,* New York: Henry LeClair. *Reverend Jonathan Witherspoon,* New Jersey: Edmund Lyndeck. *Benjamin Franklin,* Pennsylvania: HOWARD DaSILVA. *John Dickinson,* Pennsylvania: PAUL HECHT. *James Wilson,* Pennsylvania: Emory Bass. *Caesar Rodney,* Delaware: Robert Gaus. *Colonel Thomas McKean,* Delaware: Bruce MacKay. *George Read,* Delaware: Duane Bodin. *Samuel Chase,* Maryland: Philip Polito. *Richard Henry Lee,* Virginia: Ronald Holgate. *Thomas Jefferson,* Virginia: Ken Howard. *Joseph Hewes,* North Carolina: Charles Rule. *Edward Rutledge,* South Carolina: CLIFFORD DAVID. *Dr. Lyman Hall,* Georgia: Jonathan Moore.
  Charles Thomson, Congressional Secretary: Ralston Hill. *Andrew McNair,* Congressional Custodian: William Duell. *A Leather Apron:* B. J. Slater. *Courier:* Scott Jarvis. *Abigail Adams:* Virginia Vestoff. *Martha Jefferson:* Betty Buckley.

The action takes place in a single setting representing the Chamber and an Anteroom of the Continental Congress, a Mall, High Street, and Thomas Jefferson's Room, in Philadelphia, and certain reaches of John Adams' mind, in May, June and July, 1776.

Scene 1: The Chamber of the Continental Congress. *Scene 2:* The Mall. *Scene 3:* The Chamber. *Scene 4:* Jefferson's Room above High Street. *Scene 5:* The Chamber. *Scene 6:* The Congressional Anteroom. *Scene 7:* The Chamber.

MUSICAL NUMBERS
Scene 1
  "Sit Down, John"
    W. Daniels, Congress
  "Piddle, Twiddle and Resolve"
    W. Daniels
  "Till Then"
    W. Daniels, V. Vestoff
Scene 2
  "The Lees of Old Virginia"
    R. Holgate, H. DaSilva, W. Daniels
Scene 3
  "But, Mr. Adams"
    W. Daniels, H. DaSilva, K. Howard, D. Vosburgh, H. LeClair
Scene 4
  "Yours, Yours, Yours"
    W. Daniels, V. Vestoff
  "He Plays the Violin"
    B. Buckley, H. DaSilva, W. Daniels
Scene 5
  "Cool, Cool, Considerate Men"
    P. Hecht, the Conservatives
  "Momma, Look Sharp"
    S. Jarvis, W. Duell, B. J. Slater
Scene 6
  "The Egg"
    H. DaSilva, W. Daniels, K. Howard
Scene 7
  "Molasses to Rum"
    C. David
  "Yours, Yours, Yours" (reprise)
    V. Vestoff
  "Is Anybody There?"
    W. Daniels
  (Finale)
    (The Congress)

1969.07 COME SUMMER

A Musical in Two Acts. Book and lyrics by Will Holt. Based on the novel "Rainbow on the Road" by Esther Forbes. Music by David Baker. Entire production directed and staged by Agnes de Mille. Scenic production by Oliver Smith. Costumes designed by Stanley Simmons. Lighting designed by Thomas Skelton. Musical direction by Milton Rosenstock. Dance music by David Baker and John Berkman. Orchestrations by Carlyle Hall. Vocal arrangements and musical continuity by Trude Rittman. Directoral assistant, James Mitchell. Choreographic assistant, Vernon Lusby. Produced by Albert W. Selden and Hal James. Opened 18 March 1969 at the Lunt-Fontanne Theatre and closed 22 March 1969 after 7 performances.

CAST (in order of appearance): *Phineas Sharp:* RAY BOLGER. *Nathaniel Burnap:* WILLIAM COTTRELL. *Jude Scribner:* DAVID CRYER. *Dorinda Pratt:* MARGARET HAMILTON. *Labe Pratt:* JOHN GERSTAD. *Submit Pratt* (Mitty): CATHRYN DAMON. *Mrs. Meserve:* Dorothy Sands. *Emma Faucett:* BARBARA SHARMA. *Francis Faucett:* WILLIAM LE MASSENA. *Dancing Lovers:* Evelyn Taylor, David Evans. *Head Logger:* William Glassman.
  The Populace: Marcia Brushingham, Ellen Everett, Sunny Hannum, Lucia Lambert, Mary Ann Rydzeski, Lana Sloniger, Sarah Jane Smith, Britt Swanson, Jeanette Williamson, Toodie Wittmer, Jenny Workman, James Albright, Paul Berné, Bjarne Buchtrup, Dennis Cole, Leonard John Crofoot, Harry Endicott, David Evans, William Glassman, Walter Hook, Doug Hunt, Del Horstmann, John Johann.

The action takes place in the towns and surrounding countryside along the Connecticut River in New England during the peddlers' season, early spring to late fall in the year 1840, just before the factories took over.

ACT 1

"Good Time Charlie"
R. Bolger, Peddlers

"Think Spring"
R. Bolger, D. Cryer, Populace

"Wild Birds Calling"
D. Cryer, C. Damon

"Goodbye, My Bachelor"
R. Bolger

"Fine, Thank You, Fine"
B. Sharma

"Road to Hampton"
D. Cryer

"Come Summer"
R. Bolger, D. Cryer, B. Sharma, C. Damon, E. Taylor, D. Evans

"Let Me Be"
C. Damon, D. Cyrer

"Feather in My Shoe"
R. Bolger

"The Logger's Song"
R. Bolger, D. Cryer, Loggers, Populace

ACT 2

"Jude's Holler"
D. Cryer, Populace

"Faucett Falls Fancy"
R. Bolger, Populace

"Rockin'"
B. Sharma, D. Cryer

"Skin and Bones"
R. Bolger

"Moonglade"
R. Bolger, D. Cryer, C. Damon, B. Sharma, M. Hamilton, J. Gerstad, W. LeMassena, Populace

"Women"
C. Damon

"No"
R. Bolger, Populace

"So Much World"
D. Cryer

1969.08   BILLY

A Musical in One Act. Book by Stephen Glassman. Suggested by Herman Melville's novel "Billy Budd." Music and lyrics by Ron Dante and Gene Allan. Sets by Ming Cho Lee. Costumes by Theoni V. Aldredge. Lighting by Martin Aronstein. Directed by Arthur A. Seidelman. Musical sequences staged by Grover Dale. Vocal arrangements and orchestrations by Ronald Frangipane. Dance music arranged by Coleridge Perkinson. Special arrangements and incidental music by Wally Harper. Sound by Admins. Ltd. A Vanark Enterprises Ltd. Production. Produced by Bruce W. Stark in assoiation with Joseph H. Shoctor. Opened and closed 22 March 1969 at the Billy Rose Theatre after 1 performance.

CAST: Officers: *Captain Edward Vere*: LAURENCE NAISMITH. *Lieutenant William Radcliffe*: WILLIAM COUNTRYMAN. *Lieutenant Roger Mordant*: Michael Tartel. *John Claggart, Master-at-Arms*: JOHN DEVLIN. *Corporal John Bernard*: Simm Landres. *Marine Corporals*: Laried Montgomery, Danny Villa.
Seamen: *Billy Budd*: ROBERT SALVIO. *Dansker*: JOHN BEAL. *Whiskers*: DOLPH SWEET. *Campbell*: GEORGE MARCY. *Boscombe*: ALAN WEEKS. *Boyer*: IGORS GAVON. *Gilbert*: Al Cohen. *Donald Taff*: Peter De Maio. *Rawley*: Danny Carroll. *John Thorp*: Joseph Dellasorte. *Stafford*: Bill Schustik. *Fallon*: Pascual Vaquer. *Smithy*: Howard Girven. *Stoker*: Laried Montgomery. *Rush*: Steven Boockvor. *Potter*: Christopher Chadman. *Roper*: Michael Peters. *Marsten*: Tim Ramirez. *Harker*: Ron Tassone. *Seeger*: Frank DeSal. *Grimer*: DeWayne Oliver. And *Molly*: BARBARA MONTE.

The action takes place aboard a Man-of-War in 1796.

MUSICAL NUMBERS
"Prelude"
"Molly"
R. Salvio
"Chanty"
B. Schustik, P. Vaquer, H. Girven, L. Montgomery
"Watch Out for Claggart"/"Work"
A. Weeks, J. Devlin, The Crew
"Shaking Hands With the Wind"
R. Salvio
"Whiskers' Dance"
D. Sweet, The Crew
"It Ain't Us Who Make the Wars"
G. Marcy, The Crew
"The Bridge to Nowhere"
L. Naismith
"It Ain't Us Who Make the Wars" (reprise)
The Crew
"There in the Dark"/"Afraid"
J. Devlin, R. Salvio
"In the Arms of a Stranger"
J. Beal
"The Fiddlers' Green"
R. Salvio, J. Dellasorte, I. Gavon, P. DeMaio, The Crew
"Molly" (reprise)
B. Monte
"Requiem"
R. Salvio

1969.09   BUT NEVER JAM TODAY

An Afro-American Adaptation of Lewis Carroll's "Alice's Adventures in Wonderland" and "Through the Looking Glass" in Two Acts[21]. Conceived and directed by Vinnette Carroll. Music by Gershon Kingsley. Additional music and lyrics by Robert Lorimer. Choreography by Talley Beatty. Associate choreographer, Herman Howell. Settings by Donald Padgett. Costumes by K. T. Fries. Lighting by Marshall Williams. Gospel arrangements, Alex Bradford. Drums, Danny Barrajanos. Produced by the City Center of Music and Drama (Norman Singer, General administration) as part of BLACK EXPO '69. Opened and closed 23 April 1969 at the New York City Center after 1 performance.

CAST (in order of appearance): *Alice*: MARIE THOMAS. *White Rabbit*: TOMMY PINNOCK. *Caterpillar*: MARVIN CAMILLO. *Black Queen*: JOSEPH PERRY. *Cheshire Cat*: LOLA HOLMAN. *First Cook*: Verna Gillis. *Second Cook*: Winston Savage. *Duchess*: CYNTHIA TOWNS. *Mad Hatter*: SHERMAN HEMSLEY. *March Hare*: Thelma Drayton. *Dormouse*: Wai Ching Ho. *White Queen*: CYNTHIA TOWNS. *Two of Spades*: LOLA HOLMAN. *Five of Spades*: ALEX ALEXANDER. *Seven of Spades*: SHERMAN HEMSLEY. *Queen of Hearts*: ALEX ALEXANDER. *King of Hearts*: STERLING ROBERTS. *Knave of Hearts*: Burt Rodriguez. *Gryphon*: LOLA HOLMAN. *Humpty Dumpty*: MARVIN CAMILLO. *Mock Turtle*: ALEX ALEXANDER. *Herald*: Danny Barrajanos.
Members of Jury: Dance Corps. *Citizens of Wonderland*: Angel Caballero, Johnny Harris, Ernest Holly. *Dancers*: Charles Augins, Glen Brooks, Annette Brown, Delores Brown, Matt Cameron, Hope Clarke, Jacquelynne Curry, Trina Frazier, Joan Peters, Gail Reece, Danny Sloan, Andy Torres.

Scene 1: Alice by the River. *Scene 2*: Dance of the Alices. *Scene 3*: Advice from a Caterpillar. *Scene 4*: Black Queen. *Scene 5*: The Duchess' Nursery. *Scene 6*: A Mad Tea Party. *Scene 7*: Alice and the White Queen. *Scene 8*: The Croquet Game. *Scene 9*: Humpty Dumpty. *Scene 10*: The Mock Turtle Story. *Scene 11*: Alice's Evidence. *Scene 12*: Queen Alice.

1969.10   TRUMPETS OF THE LORD

(A Program of Spoken Word, Poetry, Sermons, Spirituals and Gospel Music in One Act[22].) Adapted by Vinnette Carroll from "God's Trombones" by

[21]No song list available. A revised version was later presented on Broadway 31 July 1979 at the Longacre Theatre for 7 performances.
[22]First produced in New York Off-Broadway 29 December 1963 at the Astor Place Theatre for 160 performances.

James Weldon Johnson. Directed by Theodore Mann. Musical adaptations, arrangements and direction by Howard A. Roberts. Scenery by Marsha L. Eck. Costumes by Domingo A. Rodriguez. Lighting by Jules Fisher. Produced by Circle-in-the-Square (Theodore Mann, Artistic director; Paul Libin, Managing director; Gillian Walker, Associate director). Opened 29 April 1969 at the Brooks Atkinson Theatre and closed 3 May 1969 after 7 performances.

CAST: *Sister Henrietta Pinkston*: THERESA MERRITT. *Reverend Bradford Parham*: LEX MONSON. *Reverend Ridgely Washington*: BERNARD WARD. *Reverend Marion Alexander*: CICELY TYSON.

Female Voices: Berniece Hall, Ella Eure, Camille Yarbrough. *Male Voices*: Earl Baker, Bill Glover, Milton Grayson, William Stewart. *Musicians*: Robert Henson (piano), Percy Brice (drums).

MUSICAL NUMBERS
"So Glad I'm Here"
Company
"Call to Prayer"
Company
"Listen Lord—A Prayer"
B. Parham
"Amen Response"
Company
"In His Care"
B. Glover, B. Hall, Company
"The Creation"
B. Parham
"God Lead Us Along"
H. Pinkston
Noah Medley:
"Noah Built the Ark"
M. Alexander
"Run Sinner Run"
C. Yarbrough, Company
"Didn't It Rain"
B. Hall, Company
"The Judgement Day"
R. Washington
"In That Great Gettin' Up Morning"
R. Washington, Company
Funeral Suite:
"Soon One Morning"
B. Hall, Company
"There's a Man"
H. Pinkston, E. Baker, Company
"Go Down Death"
B. Parham
"He'll Understand"
H. Pinkston
"Were You There"
M. Alexander
"Calvary"
Male Voices
"Crucifixion"
Female Voices
Freedom Suite:
"Reap What You Sow"
M. Alexander, Company
"I Shall Not Be Moved"
Company
"We Are Soldiers"
Company
"Woke Up This Morning"
Company
"Let My People Go"
R. Washington
"We Shall Overcome"
H. Pinkston, Company
"Jacob's Ladder"
Company

"God Be With You"
Postlude

1969.11 FIESTA IN MADRID

A Zarzuela in Two Acts, 4 Scenes, in Spanish. Adapted by Tito Capobianco from "La Verbena de La Paloma" ('The Festival of the Dove' with Music) by Tomás Bretón. (Original Spanish libretto by Ricardo de la Vega.) Conceived and directed by Tito Capobianco. Conductor, Odon Alonso. Associate director, Elena Denda. Choreography by Teresa. Settings and costumes by Jose Varona. Associate set designer, David Mitchell. Choral director, Martinez Palomo. Lyric arrangement by G. Roepke and J. Varona. Lighting by Hans Sondheimer. Produced by the City Center of Music and Drama, Inc. (Norman Singer, General administrator). Opened 28 May 1969 at the New York City Center and closed 15 June 1969 after 23 performances.

CAST (in order of appearance): *Photographer*: Chavo Ximenez. *Don Hilarión*: NICO CASTEL. *Don Sebastian*: Alfonso Manosalvas. *Don Pepe*: Nino Garcia. *Seña Rita*: CLARAMAE TURNER. *Julián*: FRANCO IGLESIAS. *Susana*: ISABEL PENAGOS. *Teresa*: TERESA. *Casta*: KAY CREED. *Tia Antonia*: Antonia Rey. *First Maid*: MURIEL GREENSPON. *Three Grenadiers*: Roberto Lorca, Luis Olivares, Monolo Rivera. *Policeman*: Dan Kingman. *First Little Sailor*: MURIEL GREENSPON. *Juggler*: Harry De Dio.

Singing Ensemble: Arlene Adler, Marilyn Armstrong, Renee Herman, Suzy Hunter, Diana Kehrig, Donna Owen, Hanna Owen, Frances Pavlides, Sandra Jean Schaeffer, Henrietta Valor, Maria West, Marie Young, Ron Bentley, George Bohachevsky, Don Carlo, Tony Darius, Harris Davis, Joseph Galiano, Nino Garcia, Don Henderson, Douglas Hunnikin, Karl Krause, Raymond Papay, Dick Park. *Dancers*: Martha Calzado, Deardra Correa, Andrea Del Conte, Liliana Morales, Juana Ortega, Dini Roman.

The action takes place in Madrid in the nineteenth century.

Act 1, Scene 1: A Square in Madrid. *Scene 2*: The Cafe Cantante.

Act 2, Scene 1: The Verbena (Festival). *Scene 2*: A Park.

ACT 1
Scene 1
"Fiesta in Madrid"
Chorus, Dancers
"Times Have Changed" (Los tiempos han cambiado)
N. Castel, A. Manosalvas, N. Garcia
"I Also Have a Heart" (Tambien yo, tego mi corazoncito)
F. Iglesias, C. Turner
"The Tarantula"
I. Penagos, Friends
"Blondes and Brunettes, I Like Them All" (Las rubias y las moreans!)
N. Castel
"On a Girl's Hard Life" (Pobre chica, la que tiene que servir)
The Maids
(*Music by* Federico Chueca and Joaquin Valverde. *Lyrics by* J. Perez.)
"Patio Espanol"
(*Music by* Ruperto Chapi.)
Dancers
Scene 2
"Flamenco Song" (Canto flamenco)
K. Creed, A. Rey, I. Penagos, Chorus, Dancers
"The Grenadiers" (Los granaderos)
R. Lorca, L. Olivares, M. Rivera
"O, What a Lovely Evening" (Qué, hermosa noche me espera!)
N. Castel, K. Creed, I. Penagos, A. Rey
"Forget That Girl, Once and For All" (Olvida esa muchacha para siempre)
C. Turner, F. Iglesias
"Where Are You Going Wearing That Shawl from Manila?"
(Donde vas con mantòn de Manila)
I. Penagos, F. Iglesias
"The Fight" (La pelea)
I. Penagos, K. Creed, A. Rey, F. Iglesias,
C. Turner, N. Castel, D. Kingman, Chorus, Dancers

ACT 2
Scene 1
   "The Streets of Madrid" (Las calles de Madrid)
     Chorus
     (*Music by* Federico Chueca and Joaquin Valverde. *Lyrics by* J. Perez.)
   "Who Cares for Love?" (Que te importa que no venga)
     I. Penagos
     (*Music by* José Serrano. *Lyrics by* V. Sevilla and Carreño.)
   "The Barquilleros" (Los barquilleros)
     Chorus, Dancers
     (*Music by* Federico Chueca and Joaquin Valverde. *Lyrics by* J. Perez.)
   "Danza Espanola"
     (*Music by* Gimenez.)
     Dancers
   "Three Little Sailors" (Los marineritos)
     Soloists, Chorus
     (*Music by* Federico Chueca and Joaquin Valverde. *Lyrics by* J. Perez.)

   "Mazurka"
     Chorus, Dancers
   "The Best Women in the World" (Las mejores majeres del mundo)
     C. Turner
     (*Music by* J. Ileo. *Lyrics by* Perrin & Palacios.)
   "The Milord's Waltz" (Caballero de gracià)
     N. Castel
     (*Music by* Federico Chueca and Joaquin Valverde. *Lyrics by* J. Perez.)
   "The Second Fight" (La pelea)
     C. Turner, N. Castel, F. Iglesias,
     K. Creed, I. Penagos, A. Rey, D. Kingman, Chorus, Dancers
Scene 2
   "You Are the Only One for Me" (Tu eres ese)
     I. Penagos, F, Iglesias
     (*Music by* Ruperto Chapi. *Lyrics by* Fernández Shaw and José Lopez Silva.)
   "Fiesta in Madrid" (reprise)
     Soloists, Chorus, Dancers

Lauren Bacall in APPLAUSE (Photo: Friedman-Abeles)
Billy Rose Theatre Collection, New York Public Library for the Performing Arts

1969–1970 SEASON

1969.12

OKLAHOMA!

A Revival of the Musical Play in Two Acts, 6 Scenes[1]. Book and lyrics by Oscar Hammerstein II. Music by Richard Rodgers. Based on the play "Green Grow the Lilacs" by Lynn Riggs. Entire production directed by John Fearnley. Original direction by Rouben Mamoulian Choreography by Gemze de Lappe. Original choreography by Agnes de Mille. Music director, Jay Blackton. Scenery and lighting by Paul C. McGuire. Costumes by Miles White. Produced by the Music Theater of Lincoln Center (Richard Rodgers, President and Producing Director). Opened 23 June 1969 at the New York State Theatre and closed 6 September 1969 after 88 performances.

CAST (in order of appearance): *Aunt Eller*: MARGARET HAMILTON. *Curly*: BRUCE YARNELL. *Laurey*: LEE BEERY. *Ike Skidmore*: Sam Kirkham. *Slim*: Del Horstmann. *Joe*: Kurt Olson. *Will Parker*: LEE ROY REAMS. *Jud Fry*: SPIRO MALAS. *Ado Annie Carnes*: APRIL SHAWHAN. *Ali Hakim*: TED BENIADES. *Gertie Cummings*: June Helmers. *Curly* (in ballet): Brynar Mehl. *Laurey* (in ballet): Sandra Balesti. *Jud* (in ballet): James Albright. *The Child* (in ballet): Lee Wilson. *The Girl Who Falls Down*: Sandra Balesti. *Donna*: Donna Monroe. *Judith*: Judith McCauley. *Dixie*: Dixie Stewart. *Joyce*: Joyce Tomanec. *Andrew Carnes*: WILLIAM GRIFFIS. *Cord Elam*: John Gerstad.

Dancers: Girls: Graciela Daniele, Katherine Gallagher, Mary Lynn McRae, Gilda Mullett, Sally Ransone, Audrey Ross, Lana Sloniger, Eileen Taylor, Lee Wilson, Toodie Wittmer, Jenny Workman, Mary Zahn. *Boys:* Paul Berné, Andy G. Bew, Henry Boyer, Bjarne Buchtrup, Michael Ebbin, William Glassman, Michael Lane, Ralph Nelson. *Singers: Girls:* Bobbi Lange, Judith McCauley, Donna Monroe, Eleanor Rogers, Dixie Stewart, Maggie Task, Joyce Tomanec, Maggie Worth. *Boys:* John Almberg, John D. Anthony, Lester Clark, John Dorrin, Mark East, Del Horstmann, Robert Lenn, Joe McGrath, Kurt Olson, Alex Orfaly, Ken Richards, Tom Trelfa.

THE NEW MUSIC HALL OF ISRAEL

1969.13

A New Edition of the Musical Revue in Two Acts, 16 Scenes, in Hebrew[2]. Staged and choreographed by Jonathan Karmon. Costumes by Lydia Pinkus Ganay, executed by Bertha Kwartz. Additional dialogue by Al Fogel. Assistant director, Gavri Levi. Musical direction by Rafi Paz. Produced by Leon H. Gildin. Opened 2 October 1969 at the Lunt-Fontanne Theatre and closed 29 November 1969 after 77 performances.

CAST: GEULA GILL (singer), GERMAINE ONIKOWSKI (Mistress of ceremonies), LEAH DORLY TRIO (Leah Dorly, Ygal Kerza, Ygal Hared), YOEL DAN (singer), ALMONZNINO (shadow artist), ELISHEVA and MICHAEL (rock 'n roll), BOAS (oriental tambour, david flute), PNINA PERY, YONI and DANI (dance soloists).

THE KARMON DANCERS: *Girls:* Adina, Edna, Eva, Geula Haiuta, Iona Miriam, Nava, Ogira, Ora, Riki, Rina, Rinale, Shara, Tami, Tamar. *Boys:* Alex, Aron, Avi, Clod, Ehud, Iosi, Itamar, Moshe, Nathan, Naftali, Oshiri, Tuvia, Zev, Avulun, Zwi, Israel.

ACT 1

Scene 1

Popular Songs of Israel

Scene 2

Springtime in Israel
The Karmon Dancers

Scene 3

Elisheva and Michael

Scene 4

Dance of the Fisherman
The Karmon Dancers

Scene 5

Pnina Pery and Her Exylaphone[3]

Scene 6

The Legend of Timna
The Karmon Dancers

Scene 7

A New and Humorous Shadow World
Almoznino

Scene 8

Leah Dorly Trio (A girl, two boys and two guitars)

Scene 9

A Hassidik Marriage
The Karmon Dancers

ACT 2

Scene 1

Magic of the Negev
The Karmon Dancers

Scene 2

The Popular Music of Israel
Y. Dan

Scene 3

Rhythms and Dances of the Desert
Boaz

Scene 4

Lest We Forget
The Karmon Dancers

Scene 5

Songs
G. Gill

Scene 6

Mosaic
The Karmon Dancers

Scene 7

Israel Joy of Life
Entire Troupe

1969.14

JIMMY

A Musical Play of the Life and Times of Jimmy Walker in Two Acts, 18 Scenes. Book by Melville Shavelson. Based on the novel "Beau James" by Gene Fowler and the screenplay by Jack Rose and Melville Shavelson. Music and lyrics by Bill and Patti Jacob. Directed by Joseph Anthony. Scenic production by Oliver Smith. Costumes by W. Robert LaVine. Lighting by Peggy Clark. Projections by Charles E. Hoefler, James Hamilton. Musical direction and vocal arrangements by Milton Rosenstock. Musical arrangements by Jack Andrews. Dance arrangements by John Berkman. Musical numbers staged by Peter Gennaro. Assistant choreographer, Bill Guske. Associate producer, Harry Mayer. Produced by Jack L. Warner in association with Don Saxon. Opened 23 October 1969 at the Winter Garden and closed 3 January 1970 after 84 performances.

CAST (in order of appearance): *Jimmy Walker*: FRANK GORSHIN. *Bonnie*: Cindi Bulak. *Jim Hines*: JACK COLLINS. *Al Smith*: WILLIAM GRIFFIS. *Allie Walker*: JULIE WILSON. *Francis Xavier Aloysius O'Toole*: Ed Becker. *Lawrence Horatio Fink*: Stanley Simmonds. *Antonio Viscelli*: Paul Forrest. *Stanislaus Kazimir Wojciezkowski*: Henry Lawrence. *Mrs. Al Smith*: Peggy Hewett. *Miss Manhattan*: Sally Neal. *Miss Bronx*: Andrea Duda. *Miss Brooklyn*: Carol Conte. *Miss Richmond*: Nancy Dalton. *Miss Queens*: Cindi Bulak. *Stage Manager*: Gary Gendell. *Betty Compton*: ANITA GILLETTE. *Texas Guinan*: DOROTHY CLAIRE. *Edward Duryea Dowling*: LARRY DOUGLAS. *Warrington Brock*: Clifford Fearl. *Charley Hand*: EVAN THOMPSON. *Moe*: Del Horstmann. *Izzy*: Carl Nicholas. *Policeman*: Herb Fields. *Photographers*: Andy G. Bew, Tony Stevens. *Secretary*: Barbara Andres. *Reporter*: Frank Newell. *Tailor*: Carl Nicholas. *Politicians*: Del Hortsmann, Ben Laney, Joseph McGrath. *Girl in fur coat*: Carol Conte. *Policeman*: Ben Laney. *Passerby*: Sandi McCreadie. *Mrs. Compton*: SIBYL BOWAN. *Band Vocalist*: Joseph McGrath. *Process Server*: John D. Anthony. *Recorded Impersonations*: Dwight Weist.

---

[1]Originally produced in New York 31 March 1943 at the St. James Theatre for 2212 performances. For Synopsis of Scenes and Musical Numbers, see original 1943 production.

[2]A previous edition first produced in New York 6 February 1968 under the title GRAND MUSIC HALL OF ISRAEL at the Palace Theatre for 64 performances.

---

[3]Dropped during New York run.

Dancing Ensemble: Cindi Bulak, Carol Conte, Nancy Dalton, Andrea Duda, Saundra McPherson, Sally Neal, Eileen Shannon, Monica Tiller, Pat Trott, Andy G. Bew, Stephen Boockvor, Christopher Chadman, David Evans, Gary Gendell, Scott Hunter, Frank Newell, Harold Pierson, Tony Stevens. *Singing Ensemble*: Barbara Andres, Gini Eastwood, Barbara Gregory, Peggy Hewett, Mary Louise, Sandi McCreadie, Claire Thiess, Roberta Vatske, John D. Anthony, Ed Becker, Austin Colyer, Herb Fields, Paul Forrest, Del Horstmann, Ben Laney, Henry Lawrence, Joseph McGrath, Carl Nicholas.

The action takes place in New York City between 1925 and 1931.

Act 1, Scene 1: S.S. Conte Grande—1931. *Scene 2*: Jimmy's Apartment—1925. *Scene 3*: Tammany Hall—1925. *Scene 4*: Texas Guinan's—1925. *Scene 5*: Betty's Apartment—1925. *Scene 6*: The 1925 Victory Celebration. *Scene 7*: Allie's Bedroom—1925. *Scene 8*: City Hall—1926.

Act 2, Scene 1: Riverside Drive—1929. *Scene 2*: Betty's New Apartmnet—1929. *Scene 3*: Polling Booth—1929. *Scene 4*: Central Park Casino—1929. *Scene 5*: The Street—1930. *Scene 6*: Betty's Dressing Room—1931. *Scene 7*: Washington Square—1931. *Scene 8*: City Hall—1931. *Scene 9*: Yankee Stadium—1931. *Scene 10*: S. S. Conte Grande—1931.

ACT 1[4]

Scene 1
  "Will You Think of Me Tomorrow?"
    F. Gorshin
Scene 2
  "The Little Woman"
    W. Griffis, J. Collins, F. Gorshin, J. Wilson
Scene 3
  "The Darlin' of New York"
    J. Collins, W. Griffis, E. Thompson,
    J. Wilson, F. Gorshin, Five Lovely Ladies, Campaign Workers
Scene 4
  "Oh, Gee!"
    A. Gillette
  "The Walker Walk"
    D. Claire, A. Gillette, F. Gorshin, Guinan Girls, Patrons
Scene 5
  "That Old Familiar Ring"
    A. Gillette, F. Gorshin
Scene 6
  "The Walker Walk" (reprise)
    J. Collins, Politicians, Party Workers
Scene 7
  "I Only Wanna Laugh"
    J. Wilson
Scene 8
  "They Never Proved a Thing"
    F. Gorshin, J. Collins, P. Forrest,
    S. Simmonds, E. Becker, H. Lawrence, C. Fearl, C. Nicholas, Politicians
  "What's Out There for Me?"[5]
    F. Gorshin

ACT 2
Scene 1
  "Riverside Drive"
    F. Gorshin, Strollers
Scene 2
  "The Squabble Song"
    F. Gorshin, A. Gillette
Scene 4
  Medley
    J. McGrath
  "One in a Million"
    F. Gorshin, A. Gillette

---

[4]Added during the run:
  "Five Lovely Ladies" (Act 1, Scene 3)
    F. Gorshin
[5]Dropped during the run.

Scene 5
  "It's a Nice Place to Visit"
    P. Forrest, S. Simmonds, E. Becker, H. Lawrence, C. Fearl, C. Conte, Company
Scene 6
  "The Charmin' Son-of-a-Bitch"
    J. Wilson
  "Jimmy"
    A. Gillette
  "Five Lovely Ladies" (reprise)
    F. Gorshin
Scene 7
  "Our Jimmy"
    J. Collins, F. Gorshin, J. Wilson, E. Thompson,
    W. Griffis, D. Claire, Five Lovely Ladies, Policemen, Spectators
Scene 9
  "Life Is a One-Way Street"
    F. Gorshin
Scene 10
  Finale
    F. Gorshin, A. Gillette

BUCK WHITE

1969.15

A Musical in Two Acts. Book, music and lyrics by Oscar Brown, Jr. Adapted from the play "Big Time Buck White" by Joseph Dolan Tuotti. Staged by Ocar Brown, Jr. and Jean Pace. Musical arrangements by Mike Terry and Merl Saunders. Orchestrations by Mike Terry. Musical direction by Mel Saunders. Scenery by Edward Burbridge. Lighting by Martin Aronstein. Costumes by Jean Pace. Produced by Zev Bufman in association with High John Productions [Oscar Brown, Jr., Jean Pace, Sivuca]. Opened 2 December 1969 at the George Abbott Theatre and closed 6 December 1969 after 7 performances.

CAST: *Hunter*: HERSCHELL BURTON. *Honey Man*: DAVID MOODY. *Weasel*: TED ROSS. *Rubber Band*: CHARLES WELDON. *Jive*: RON RICH. *Buck White*: MUHAMMAD ALI [CASSIUS CLAY]. *Whitey*: EUGENE SMITH. *Black Man*: Don Sutherland.

The action takes place in the meeting hall of the Beautiful Allelujah Days organization.

ACT 1
  "Honey Man Song"
    D. Moody
  "Money, Money, Money"
    T. Ross, D. Moody
  "Nobody Does My Thing"
    H. Burton
  "Step Across That Line"
    C. Weldon
  "H.N.I.C."
    R. Rich
  "Beautiful Allelujah Days"
    R. Rich, T. Ross, H. Burton, C. Weldon, D. Moody
  "Tap the Plate"
    R. Rich, C. Weldon, D. Moody
  "Big Time Buck White Chant"
    The Company

ACT 2
  "Big Time Buck White Chant" (reprise)
    M. Ali, Company
  "Better Far"
    M. Ali
  "We Came in Chains"
    M. Ali, Company
  "Black Balloons"
    M. Ali, Company
  "Look at Them"
    E. Smith

"Mighty Whitey"
   M. Ali, Company
"Get Down"
   M. Ali, Company

1969.16   LA STRADA

A Musical in Two Acts, 14 Scenes. Book by Charles K. Peck, Jr. Based on the film of the same name by Federico Fellini, (Tullio Pinelli, Ennio Flaiano). Music and lyrics by Lionel Bart. Additional music and lyrics by Martin Charnin and Elliot Lawrence[6]. Directed by Alan Schneider. Dances and musical numbers staged by Joyce Trisler[7]. Sets by Ming Cho Lee. Costumes by Nancy Potts. Lighting by Martin Aronstein. Musical direction, Harold Hastings. Orchestrations by Eddie Sauter. Dance music arrangements by Peter Howard. Produced by Charles K. Peck, Jr. and Canyon Productions. Opened and closed 14 December 1969 at the Lunt-Fontanne Theatre after 1 performance.

CAST (in order of appearance): The Old Man: JOHN COE. Gelsomina: BERNADETTE PETERS. Mother: ANNE HEGIRA. Elsa: Lisa Belleran. Eva: Mary Ann Robbins. Sophia: Susan Goeppinger. Zampano: STEPHEN PEARLMAN. Castra: LUCILLE PATTON. Acrobats: Paul Charles, Harry Endicott. Mario, the Fool: LARRY KERT. Mama Lambrini: PEGGY COOPER. Alberti: John Coe. Sister Claudia: Susan Goeppinger.
   Company: Loretta Abbott, Glen Brooks, Henry Brunjes, Connie Burnett, Robert Carle, Paul Charles, Barbara Christopher, Peggy Cooper, Betsy Dickerson, Harry Endicott, Anna Maria Fanizzi, Jack Fletcher, Nino Galanti, Susan Goeppinger, Rodney Griffin, Mickey Gunnersen, Kenneth Kreel, Don Lopez, Joyce Maret, Stan Page, Odette Panaccione, Mary Ann Robbins, Steven Ross, Larry Small, Eileen Taylor.

The action takes place in and around the cities and villages of Southern Italy in the early 1950s.

Act 1, Scene 1: A Desolate Beach near Gelsomina's House. Scene 2: Along the Road (La Strada). Scene 3: The Outskirts of a Village. Scene 4: A Farm House Yard. Scene 5: The Farm Stable. Scene 6: Along the Road. Scene 7: The Alberti Circus Grounds. Scene 8: A Performance of the Alberti Circus.

Act 2, Scene 1: The Circus Grounds. Scene 2: A Village Square. Scene 3: A Convent. Scene 4: Along the Road. Scene 5: A Camp Site in the Mountains. Scene 6: The End of the Road.

ACT 1
Scene 1
   "Seagull, Starfish, Pebble"
      B. Peters
      (Music by Elliot Lawrence. Lyrics by Martin Charnin.)
Scene 2
   "The Great Zampano"
      B. Peters, S. Pearlman
   "What's Going on Inside?"
      S. Pearlman
      (Music by Elliot Lawrence. Lyrics by Martin Charnin.)
Scene 3
   "Belonging"
      B. Peters
Scene 4
   Wedding Dance
      (Dance Music by Elliott Lawrence.)
      Entire Company
Scene 5
   "I Don't Like You"
      B. Peters
      (Music by Elliot Lawrence. Lyrics by Martin Charnin.)
Scene 6
   Encounters
      (Dance Music by Elliot Lawrence.)
      B. Peters, Entire Company
   "There's a Circus in Town"
      L. Kert

---

[6]Per insert in opening night program.
[7]Per insert in opening night program.

Scene 7
   "You're Musical"
      L. Kert, B. Peters
      (Music by Elliot Lawrence.
      Lyrics by Martin Charnin.)
Scene 8
   "Only More!"
      B. Peters
      (Music by Elliot Lawrence.
      Lyrics by Martin Charnin.)

ACT 2
Scene 1
   "What a Man"
      B. Peters, P. Cooper
      (Music by Elliot Lawrence.
      Lyrics by Martin Charnin.)
   "Everything Needs Something"
      B. Peters
      (Music by Elliot Lawrence.
      Lyrics by Martin Charnin.)
Scene 2
   "Sooner or Later"
      L. Kert
      (Music by Elliot Lawrence.
      Lyrics by Martin Charnin.)
   "Sooner or Later" (reprise)
      B. Peters
Scene 3
   Belonging" (reprise)
      B. Peters
Scene 6
   The End of the Road
      Entire Company
      (Music by Elliot Lawrence.
      Lyrics by Martin Charnin.)

1969.17   COCO

A Musical in Two Acts, 9 Scenes. Book and lyrics by Alan Jay Lerner. (Suggested by the life and career of Coco Chanel.) Music by André Previn. Directed by Michael Benthall. Musical numbers and fashion sequences staged by Michael Bennett. Sets and costumes by Cecil Beaton. Lighting by Thomas Skelton. Orchestrations by Hershy Kay. Dance Music continuity by Harold Wheeler. Musical direction by Robert Emmett Dolan. Associate choreographer, Bob Avian. Associate producer, Fred Hebert. Production supervisor, Stone Widney. Film sequences by Milton Olshin, Fred Lemoine. Produced by Frederick Brisson for Brisson Productions, Inc., and by Montfort Productions. Opened 18 December 1969 at the Mark Hellinger Theatre and closed 3 October 1970 after 333 performances.

CAST (in order of appearance): Coco: KATHARINE HEPBURN. Louis Greff: GEORGE ROSE. Pignol: JEANNE ARNOLD. Helene: Maggie Task. Sebastian Baye: RENÉ AUBERJONOIS. Armand: Al DeSio. Albert: Jack Beaber. Docaton: Eve March. Georges: DAVID HOLLIDAY. Loublaye: Gene Varrone. Varne: Shirley Potter. Marie: Margot Travers. Jeanine: Rita O'Connor. Claire: Graciela Daniele. Juliette: Lynn Winn. Madelaine: Carolyn Kirsch. Lucille: Diane Phillips. Colette: Rosemarie Heyer. Simone: Charlene Ryan. Solange: Suzanne Rogers. Noelle: GALE DIXON. Dr. Petitjean: Richard Woods. Claude: David Thomas. The Buyers (4): Dwight Berkwit: Will B. Able. Eugene Bernstone: Robert Fitch. Ronny Ginsborn: Chad Block. Phil Rosenberry: Dan Siretta. Lapidus: Gene Varrone. Nadine: Leslie Daniel. Grand Duke Alexandrovitch: Bob Avian. Voice (of Grand Duke Alexandrovitch): Jack Dabdoub. Charles, Duke of Glenallen: Michael Allinson. Julian Lesage: Paul Dumont. Papa: Jon Cypher.
   Models, Seamstresses, Customers, and Fitters: Vicki Allen, Karin Baker, Kathy Bartosh, Kathie Dalton, Alice Glenn, Maureen Hopkins, Linda Jorgens, Tresha Kelly, Nancy Killmer, Jan Metternich, Marilyn Miles, Joann Ogawa, Jean Peerce, Ann Reinking, Skiles Ricketts, Marianne Seibert, Pamela Serpe, Bonnie Walker, Oscar Antony, Roy Barry, William James, Richard Marr, Don Percassi, Gerald Teijelo.

The action takes place in the Maison Chanel, Rue Cambon, Paris—either in the Salon, in the apartment above . . . or in the memory. It begins in the late Fall of 1953 and ends in the late Spring of 1954.

Act 1, *Scene 1*: The Salon. *Scene 2*: The Apartment. *Scene 3*: The Salon. *Scene 4*: The Dressing Room. *Scene 5*: The Apartment. *Scene 6*: The Salon.

Act 2, *Scene 1*: The Salon. *Scene 2*: The Apartment. *Scene 3*: The Salon.

ACT 1
Scene 1
  "But That's the Way You Are"[8]
    J. Dabdoub
  "The World Belongs to the Young"
    K. Hepburn, G. Rose, R. Auberjonois, J. Arnold, Company
  "Let's Go Home"
    D. Holliday
Scene 2
  "Mademoiselle Cliche de Paris"
    K. Hepburn
  "On the Corner of the Rue Cambon"
    K. Hepburn
  "The Money Rings Out Like Freedom"
    K. Hepburn, Ensemble
Scene 3
  "A Brand New Dress"
    G. Dixon
Scene 4
  "A Woman Is How She Loves"
    D. Holliday
Scene 5
  "Gabrielle"
    J. Cypher
  "Coco"
    K. Hepburn
Scene 6
  "The Preparation"
    K. Hepburn, Company

ACT 2
Scene 1
  "Fiasco"
    R. Auberjonois
  "When Your Lover Says Goodbye"
    G. Rose
Scene 2
  "Ohrbach's, Bloomingdale's, Best & Saks"
    W. B. Abel, R. Fitch, C. Block, D. Siretta
  "Ohrbach's, Bloomingdale's, Best & Saks" (reprise)
    K. Hepburn, Ensemble
Scene 3
  "Always Mademoiselle"
    K. Hepburn

1970.01   CHARLES AZNAVOUR

A One-Man Show in Two Acts[9]. All music and lyrics by Charles Aznavour, except where noted. Musical director and pianist, Henri Byers. Production supervisor, Leon Sanossian. Produced by Norman Twain in association with Albert I. Fill. Opened 4 February 1970 at the Music Box Theatre and closed 22 February 1970 after 23 performances.

CAST: CHARLES AZNAVOUR.

ACT 1
  "Le Tamos"
    (*Lyrics by* J. Davis.)
  "I Will Give to You"
    (*English Lyrics by* B. Morrison.)

---

[8]Dropped late in the run when Danielle Darrieux assumed the role of Coco.
[9]Charles Aznavour was previously presented on Broadway 14 October 1965 at the Ambassador Theatre for 28 performances.

"Happy Anniversary"
  (*English Lyrics by* Herbert Kretzmer.)
"We'll Drift Away"
  (*French Lyrics by* Georges Gavarentz. *English Lyrics by* Buddy Kaye.)
"Le Toreador"
"Sunday's Not My Day"
  (*French Lyrics by* T. Veran. *English Lyrics by* B. Morrison.)
"Apaga La Luz"
  (*English Lyrics by* R. Deleon.)
"Isabelle"
"I Will Warm Your Heart"
  (*English Lyrics by* Gene Lees.)
"To My Daughter"
  (*English Lyrics by* B. Morrison.)
"Et Pourtant"
  (*French Lyrics by* Georges Gavarentz.)
"The Wine of Youth"
  (*English Lyrics by* B. Morrison.)
"Yesterday When I Was Young"
  (*English Lyrics by* Herbert Kretzmer.)
"Emmenez-Moi"
"It Will Be My Day"
  (*English Lyrics by* B. Morrison.)

ACT 2
  "All Those Pretty Girls"
    (*English Lyrics by* Buddy Kaye.)
  "De T'Avoir Aimer"
  "My Hand Needs Your Hand"
    (*French Lyrics by* Pierre Roche. *English Lyrics by* Buddy Kaye.)
  "You've Let Yourself Go"
    (*English Lyrics by* Marcel Stellman.)
  "Desormais"
    (*French Lyrics by* Georges Gavarentz.)
  "Who"
    (*English Lyrics by* Herbert Kretzmer.)
  "Reste"
  "Venice Dressed in Blue"
    (*Music by* F. Dorin. *English Lyrics by* Buddy Kaye.)
  "La Boheme"
    (*Music by* Jacques Plante.)
  "August Days in Paree"
    (*French Lyrics by* Georges Gavarentz. *English Lyrics by* D. Newburg.)
  "Les Comediens"
    (*Music by* Jacques Plante.)
  "And I in My Chair"
    (*English Lyrics by* D. Newburg.)
  "You've Got to Learn"
    (*English Lyrics by* Marcel Stellman.)
  "Les Bons Moments"

1970.02   GANTRY

A Musical in Two Acts, 14 Scenes. Book by Peter Bellwood. Adapted from the novel of the same name by Sinclair Lewis. Music by Stanley Lebowsky. Lyrics by Fred Tobias. Directed and staged by Onna White. Scenery by Robin Wagner. Costumes by Ann Roth. Lighting by Jules Fisher. Orchestrations by Jim Tyler. Musical direction by Arthur Rubinstein. Dance arrangements by Dorothea Freitag. Vocal arrangements by Stanley Lebowsky. Assistant choreographer, Patrick Cummings. Production supervised by Robert Weiner. Associate producer, Fred Menowitz. Produced by Joseph Cates and Jerry Schlossberg. Opened and closed 14 February 1970 at the George Abbott Theatre after 1 performance.

CAST (in order of speaking): *Bill Morgan*: Tom Batten. *Sister Doretha*: Dorothea Freitag. *Adelberta Shoup*: Gloria Hodes. *Sharon Falconer*: RITA MORENO. *Elmer Gantry*: ROBERT SHAW. *Jim Lefferts*: Wayne Tippit. *George F. Babbitt*: Ted Thurston. *Reverend Garrison*: Kenneth Bridges. *Trosper*: Bob Gorman. *Gunch*: David Sabin. *Prout*: Zale Kessler. *Reverend Toomis*: David Hooks. *Architect*: Robert Donahue. *Photographer*: James N. Maher. *Deaf Man*: J. Michael Bloom. *Deaf Man's Wife*: Beth Fowler.

Townspeople, Revival Troupe, Students, Workmen.: Chuck Beard, J. Michael Bloom, Kenneth Bridges, Patrick Cummings, Robert Donahue, Sandy Ellen, Carol Estey, Beth Fowler, Gloria Hodes, Keith Kaldenberg, Clyde Laurents, Robert Lenn, James N. Maher, Kathleen Robey, Dixie Stewart, Diane Tarleton, Maralyn Thoma, Terry Violino, Mimi Wallace.

Act 1, Scene 1: Revival Tent—Shelton, Illinois. *Scene 2*: Train. *Scene 3*: Revival Tent—Fargo, North Dakota. *Scene 4*: Revival Tent—Page City, Kansas. *Scene 5*: Sister Sharon's Dressing Room. *Scene 6*: Revival Tent—McAllaster, Kansas. *Scene 7*: Sister Sharon's Hotel Suite in Chicago.

Act 2, Scene 1: Revival Tent—Chicago, Illinois. *Scene 2*: Revival Tent Grounds. *Scene 3*: A Warehouse in Georgia. *Scene 4*: Revival Tent. *Scene 5*: The Office of the Church Board. *Scene 6*: The Tabernacle Office. *Scene 7*: Outside the "Waters of Jordan" Tabernacle.

ACT 1

"Wave a Hand"
    T. Batten, the Troupe
Gantry Gets the Call:
    R. Shaw, the Troupe, Townspeople
"He Was There"
"Play Ball With the Lord"
"Katie Jonas"
    R. Moreno
"Thanks, Sweet Jesus!"
    R. Shaw, Townspeople
"Someone I've Already Found"
    R. Shaw
"He's Never Too Busy"
    R. Moreno, R. Shaw, T. batten, G. Hodes, the Troupe
"We're Sharin' Sharon"
    R. Shaw

ACT 2

"We Can All Give Love"
    R. Moreno, G. Hodes, Townspeople
"Foresight"
    T. Thurston, D. Sabin, B. Gorman, Z. Kessler
"These Four Walls"
    R. Moreno
"Show Him the Way"
    R. Shaw, Townspeople
"The Promise of What I Could Be"
    R. Shaw
"Gantry's Reaction"
    R. Shaw
"We're Sharin' Sharon" (reprise)
    R. Shaw

1970.03 GEORGY

A Musical in Two Acts, 16 Scenes. Book by Tom Mankiewicz. Based on a novel ("Georgy Girl") by Margaret Forster and the screenplay of the same name by Margaret Forster and Peter Nichols. Music by George Fischoff. Lyrics by Carole Bayer. Directed by Peter Hunt. Choreography by Howard Jeffrey. Settings and lighting by Jo Mielziner. Costumes by Patricia Zipprodt. Music direction and vocal arrangementss by Elliot Lawrence. Orchestrations by Eddie Sauter. Dance music arranged by Marvin Laird. Produced by Fred Coe in association with Joseph P. Harris and Ira Bernstein. Opened 26 February 1970 at the Winter Garden and closed 28 February 1970 after 4 performances.

CAST (in order of appearance): *Georgy*: DILYS WATLING. *James Leamington*: STEPHEN ELLIOTT. *Ted*: LOUIS BEACHNER. *Meredith*: MELISSA HART. *Peg*: HELENA CARROLL. *Jos*: JOHN CASTLE. *Peter*: Richard Quarry. *Health Officer*: CYNTHIA LATHAM.
    Party Guests, etc.: Kathryn Doby, Sherry Durham, Patricia Garland, Margot Head, Mary Jane Houdina, Jane Karel, Barbara Monte-Britton, Michon Peacock, Mary Zahn, Rick Atwell, Pi Douglass, Arthur Faria, Charlie Goeddertz, Neil Jones, Sal Pernice, Richard Quarry, Allan Sobek, Tony Stevens. *Children*: Kelly Boa, Mona Daleo, Jackie Paris, Donna Sands, Jill Streisant, Dewey Golkin, Anthony Marciona, Roger Morgan, Johnny Welch. *Singers*: Susan Goeppinger, Del Horstmann, Don Jay, Geoff Leon, Regina Lynn.

(The action takes place in present day London.)

Act 1, Scene 1: A Playground. *Scene 2*: Georgy and Meredith's Flat. *Scene 3*: A Street. *Scene 4*: The Flat. *Scene 5*: James Leamington's House. *Scene 6*: The Flat. *Scene 7*: London Streets. *Scene 8*: James Leamington's House. *Scene 9*: The Flat. *Scene 10*: A Street. *Scene 11*: Apollo Cinema, Piccadilly Circus.

Act 2, Scene 1: The Flat. *Scene 2*: A Street. *Scene 3*: James Leamington's House. *Scene 4*: The Flat. *Scene 5*: A Playground.

ACT 1

Scene 1
    "Howjadoo"
        D. Watling, Children
Scene 2
    "Make It Happen Now"
        D. Watling
Scene 3
    "Ol' Pease Puddin'"
        J. Castle, D. Watling
Scene 4
    "Just For the Ride"
        M. Hart, Men
    "So What?"
        D. Watling
Scene 5
    "Georgy"
        S. Elliott
Scene 6
    "A Baby, (Mrs. Jones)"/"Howjadoo" (reprise)
        D. Watling, J. Castle, M. Hart
Scene 9
    "That's How It Is"
        D. Watling, S. Elliott
Scene 11
    "There's a Comin' Together"
        J. Castle, D. Watling, Chorus

ACT 2

Scene 1
    "Something Special"
        D. Watling, J. Castle
    "Half of Me'"
        D. Watling
Scene 2
    "Gettin' Back to Me"
        M. Hart
Scene 3
    "Sweet Memory"
        L. Beachner, S. Elliott, Chorus
    "Georgy" (reprise)
        S. Elliott
Scene 4
    "Life's a Holiday"
        J. Castle, D. Watling
    "Make It Happen Now" (reprise)
        D. Watling
Scene 5
    Finale: "There's a Comin' Together" (reprise)
        Company

1970.04 OPERATION SIDEWINDER

A Play with Songs in Two Acts, 12 Scenes. Play by Sam Shepard. Music (songs) composed and performed by The Holy Modal Rounders (Steve Weber, John Wesley Annas, Richard Tyler, Peter Stampfel, Mike McCarty). Directed by Michael A. Schultz. Sets by Douglas W. Schmidt. Costumes by Willa Kim. Lighting by John Gleason. Musical directors, Marvin Sylvor, Jeff Cutler. Produced by The Repertory Theater of Lincoln Center (Jules Irving, Director; Robert Symonds, Associate director) by special arrangement with Alvin Ferleger Associates. Opened 12 March 1970 at the Vivian Beaumont Theatre and closed 25 April 1970 after 52 performances.

245

CAST (in order of appearance): *Dukie*: Robert Phalen. *Honey*: BARBARA EDA-YOUNG. *Mechanic*: Michael Miller. *Young Man*: ANDY ROBINSON. *Forest Ranger*: Robert Riggs. *Billy*: ROBERTS BLOSSOM. *Colonel Warner*: JOSEPH MASCOLO. *Captain*: Robert Phalen. *Cadet*: GUS FLEMING. *Mickey Free*: DON PLUMLEY. *First Cohort to Mickey Free*: Ralph Drischell. *Second Cohort to Mickey Free*: Arthur Sellers. *Carhop*: Catherine Burns. *Blood*: Garrett Morris. *Blade*: Paul Benjamin. *Dude*: Charles Pegues. *General Browser*: Paul Sparer. *Doctor Vector*: Ray Fry. *Spider Lady*: Michael Levin. *Edith*: Joan Pringle. *Captain Bovine*: Philip Bosco.

Indians: José Barrera, Paul Benjamin, Gregory Borst, Gus Fleming, Robert Keesler, Michael Levin, Clark Luis, Richard Mason, Muriel Miguel, Louis Mofsie, Santos Morales, Garrett Morris, Jean-Daniel Noland. *Desert Tactical Troop*: Robert Riggs, Robert Phalen, Michael Miller.

Act 1, Scene 1: In the desert. *Scene 2*: A garage. *Scene 3*: In the desert. *Scene 4*: The office of Air Force Colonel Warner. *Scene 5*: In the desert. *Scene 6*: A drive-in restaurant. *Scene 7*: The Air Force Laboratory at Fort George. *Scene 8*: In the desert.

Act 2, Scene 1: In the desert. *Scene 2*: The Kiva of the Spider Lady. *Scene 3*: The office of C.I.A. Captain Bovine. *Scene 4*: On a mesa in the desert.

ACT 1[10]

Scene 1

"Do It Girl"

(*Lyrics by* Peter Stampfel and Antonia.)

Scene 2

"Float Me Down Your Pipeline"

(*Lyrics by* Antonia.)

Scene 3

"Generalonely"

(*Lyrics by* Steve Weber.)

Scene 4

"Catch Me"

(*Lyrics by* Sam Shepard.)

Scene 5

"Euphoria"

(*Lyrics by* Robin Remaily.)

Scene 6

"Synergy"

(*Lyrics by* Peter Stampfel and Antonia.)

Scene 7

"Don't Leave Me Dangling in the Dust" (Dusty Fustchuns)

(*Lyrics by* Robin Remaily.)

Scene 8

"Alien Song"

(*Lyrics by* Sam Shepard.)

ACT 2

Scene 1

"Bad Karma"

(*Lyrics by* Peter Stampfel and Antonia.)

Scene 2

"I Disremember Quite Well"

(*Lyrics by* Antonia.)

Scene 3

"C.I.A. Men"

(*Lyrics by* Peter Stampfel, Tuli Tupferburg and Antonia.)

Scene 4

Hopi Chants

1970.05   PURLIE

A Musical (Comedy) in Two Acts, 6 Scenes, a Prologue and an Epilogue. Book by Ossie Davis, Philip Rose and Peter Udell. Based on the play "Purlie Victorious" by Ossie Davis. Music by Gary Geld. Lyrics by Peter Udell. Production directed by Philip Rose. Choreography by Louis Johnson. Scenery by Ben Edwards. Lighting by Thomas Skelton. Costumes by Ann Roth. Orchestrations and choral arrangements by Garry Sherman and Luther Henderson. Musical supervisor, Garry Sherman. Musical conductor, Joyce

Brown. Dance music arranged by Luther Henderson. Produced by Philip Rose. Opened 15 March 1970 at the Broadway Theatre, moved 15 December 1970 to the Winter Garden, moved 15 March 1971 to the ANTA Theatre and closed 7 November 1971 after 689 performances.

CAST (in order of appearance): *Purlie*: CLEAVON LITTLE. *Church Soloist*: LINDA HOPKINS. *Lutiebelle*: MELBA MOORE. *Missy*: NOVELLA NELSON. *Gitlow*: SHERMAN HEMSLEY. *Charlie*: C. DAVID COLSON. *Idella*: HELEN MARTIN. *Ol' Cap'n*: JOHN HEFFERNAN.

Dancers: Loretta Abbott, Hope Clark, Judy Gibson, Lavinia Hamilton, Arlene Rowlant, Ella Thompson, Myrna White, Morris Donaldson, George Faison, Al Perryman, Harold Pierson, William Taylor, Larry Vickers. *Singers*: Carolyn Bird, Denise Christopher, Denise Elliott, Synthia Jackson, Mildred Lane, Alyce Webb, Mildred Pratcher, Peter Colly, Milt Grayson, Tony Middleton, Ray Pollard.

The action takes place in South Georgia not too long ago.

Prologue: Big Bethel, a country church.

Act 1, Scene 1: A shack on the plantation, some time before that of the prologue. *Scene 2*: Outside Ol' Cap'n Commissary. *Scene 3*: Outside Ol' Cap'n Commissary. *Scene 4*: The shack.

Act 2, Scene 1: On the plantation, 4 A.M. *Scene 2*: The shack, just before dawn.

Epilogue: The time and place as in the Prologue.

ACT 1

Prologue

"Walk Him Up the Stairs"

Entire Company

Scene 1

"New Fangled Preacher Man"

C. Little

"Skinnin' a Cat"

S. Hemsley, The Field Hands

"Purlie"

M. Moore

"The Harder They Fall"

C. Little, M. Moore

Scene 2

Charlie's Songs: "The Barrels of War"/"The Unborn Love"

C. D. Colson

"Big Fish, Little Fish"

J. Heffernan, C. D. Colson

Scene 3

"I Got Love"

M. Moore

"Great White Father"

The Cotton Pickers (Ensemble)

"Skinnin' a Cat" (reprise)

S. Hemsley, C. D. Colson

Scene 4

"Down Home"

C. Little, N. Nelson

ACT 2

Scene 1

"First Thing Monday Mornin'"

The Cotton Pickers (Ensemble)

Scene 2

"He Can Do It"

N. Nelson, M. Moore

"The Harder They Fall"[11] (reprise)

S. Hemsley, M. Moore, N. Nelson

"The World Is Comin' to a Start"

C. D. Colson, Company

Epilogue

"Walk Him Up the Stairs" (reprise)

Entire Company

---

[10]Also performed: "Hathor" (*Lyrics by* Peter Stampfel.)

[11]Replaced for West Coast tour by:

"Easy Goin' Man"

Barry Smith (Gitlow)

1970.06 ## BLOOD RED ROSES

A Play With Songs in Two Acts, 9 Scenes. Book and lyrics by John Lewin. Music by Michael Valenti. Directed by Alan Schneider. Musical numbers staged by Larry Fuller. Scenery by Ed Wittstein. Costumes by Deidre Cartier. Lighting by Tharon Musser. Musical direction by Milton Setzer. Orchestrations by Julian Stein and Abba Bogin. Assistant director, Joan Thorne. Produced by Seymour Vall, Louis S. Goldman in association with Rick Mandell and Bjorn I. Swanstrom. Opened and closed 22 March 1970 at the John Golden Theatre after 1 performance.

CAST (in order of appearance): *Grenadier Guards*: William Tost, Bill Gibbens. *Fitzroy Somerset, Lord Raglan, Commander-in-Chief*: Sydney Walker. *Prince Albert*: Ronald Drake. *Queen Victoria*: JEANIE CARSON. *Private William Cockcroft*: JESS RICHARDS. *Private John Smalls*: PHILIP BRUNS. *Alice Crabbe*, a bawd: JEANIE CARSON. *Mr. W. H. Russell*, Correspondent for the London Times: Jay Gregory. *A Russian Soldier*: Charles Abbott. *Cornet Edwin May*, Fourth Light Dragoons: Lowell Harris. *Florence Nightingale*: JEANIE CARSON.

The action takes place in England and the Crimean Peninsula during the Crimean War of 1854-55.

Act 1, Scene 1: Buckingham Palace and Environs. *Scene 2*: A Nighthouse in London. *Scene 3*: The Hills of the Crimea. *Scene 4*: Another Part of the Terrain. *Scene 5*: Stinks—Detail. *Scene 6*: Windsor Castle.

Act 2, Scene 1: The Crimean Plateau. *Scene 2*: The Hospital at Scutari. *Scene 3*: England Again.

ACT 1
Scene 1
  "The Cream of English Youth"
    Entire British Army
  "A Garden in the Sun"
    J. Carson, R. Drake, S. Walker
  "Song of How Mucked Up Things Are"
    P. Bruns, J. Richards
  "The Cream of English Youth" (continued)
    P. Bruns, J. Richards
Scene 2
  "Song of Greater Britain"
    J. Carson
Scene 3
  "Black Dog Rum"
    S. Walker, The Fusiliers
Scene 4
  "In the Country Where I Come From"
    J. Richards
Scene 5
  "The English Rose"
    P. Bruns, J. Richards
Scene 6
  "Soldiers Prayer"
    The Fusiliers
ACT 2
Scene 1
  "Blood Red Roses"
    J. Richards
  "The Fourth Light Dragoons"
    L. Harris
  "The English Rose" (continued)
    P. Bruns
Scene 3
  "Song of the Fair Dissenter Lass"
    J. Carson
  Finale
    Entire Company

1970.07 ## MINNIE'S BOYS

A Musical in Two Acts, 12 Scenes. Book by Arthur Marx and Robert Fisher. (Suggested by the early lives of the Marx Brothers.) Music by Larry Grossman. Lyrics by Hal Hackady. Directed by Stanley Prager. Musical numbers staged by Marc Breaux. Production consultant, Groucho Marx. Settings by Peter Wexler. Costumes by Donald Brooks. Lighting by Jules Fisher. Musical direction and vocal arrangements by John Berkman. Orchestrations by Ralph Burns. Dance arrangements and incidental music by Marvin Hamlisch and Peter Howard. Associate producer, Peter N. Grad. Produced by Arthur Whitelaw, Max J. Brown and Byron Goldman. Opened 26 March 1970 at the Imperial Theatre and closed 30 May 1970 after 80 performances.

CAST (in order of appearance): *Julie Marx* (Groucho): LEWIS J. STADLEN. *Leonard Marx* (Chico): IRWIN PEARL. *Adolph Marx* (Harpo): DANIEL FORTUS. *Herbie Marx* (Zeppo): ALVIN KUPPERMAN. *Milton Marx* (Gummo): GARY RAUCHER. *Mrs. Flanagan*: Jean Bruno. *Mrs. Krupnik*: Jacqueline Britt. *Minnie Marx*: SHELLEY WINTERS. *Sam Marx* (Frenchie): ARNY FREEMAN. *Hochmeister*: MERWIN GOLDSMITH. *Al Shean*: MORT MARSHALL. *Cop*: Doug Spingler. *Sidebark*: Ronn Hansen. *Acrobats*: Evelyn Taylor, David Vaughan, George Bunt. *Cindy*: Marjory Edson. *Maxie*: RICHARD B. SHULL. *Telegraph Boy*: Stephen Reinhardt. *Robwell*: Casper Roos. *Harpist*: Jean Bruno. *Theatre Manager*: Gene Ross. *E. F. Albee*: ROLAND WINTERS. *Mrs. McNish*: JULIE KURNITZ. *Murdoch*: Jacqueline Britt. *Sandow, the Great*: Richard B. Shull. *Miss Taj Mahal*: Lynne Gannaway. *Miss White House*: Marjory Edson. *Miss Eiffel Tower*: Vicki Frederick.

Ensemble: Jacqueline Britt, Jean Bruno, Bjarne Buchtrup, George Bunt, Dennis Cole, Deede Darnell, Joan B. Duffin, Marjory Edson, Vicki Frederick, Marcela Gamboa, Lynne Gannaway, Ronn Hansen, Elaine Manzel, Stephen Reinhardt, Casper Roos, Gene Ross, Carole Schweid, William W. Sean, Doug Spingler, Evelyn Taylor, David Vaughan, Toodie Wittmer, Mary Zahn.

Act 1, Scene 1: The Street. *Scene 2*: The Marx Apartment. *Scene 3*: Backstage Nagadoches. *Scene 4*: Nagadoches Hotel. *Scene 5*: School Act. *Scene 6*: Onstage. *Scene 7*: Backstage Chicago.

Act 2, Scene 1: Mrs. McNish's Boarding House. *Scene 2*: Outside Palace Theatre. *Scene 3*: Albee's Office. *Scene 4*: Minnie's Long Island Home. *Scene 5*: Walnut Street Theatre.

ACT 1
Scene 1
  "Five Growing Boys"
    S. Winters, Neighbors
Scene 2
  "Rich Is"
    M. Marshall, S. Winters, A. Freeman,
    L. J. Stadlen, D. Fortus, I. Pearl, A. Kupperman, G. Raucher
  "More Precious Far"
    L. J. Stadlen, A. Kupperman, D. Fortus, S. Winters
Scene 3
  "Four Nightingales"
    L. J. Stadlen, D. Fortus, A. Kupperman
  "Underneath It All"
    R. B. Shull, Girls
Scene 4
  "Mama, a Rainbow"
    D. Fortus, S. Winters
  "You Don't Have To Do It for Me"
    S. Winters, L. J. Stadlen, D. Fortus, I. Pearl, A. Kupperman
Scene 6
  "If You Wind Me Up"
    S. Winters, L. J. Stadlen, D. Fortus, I. Pearl, A. Kupperman
Scene 7
  "Where Was I When They Passed Out the Luck?"
    L. J. Stadlen, D. Fortus, I. Pearl, A. Kupperman
ACT 2
Scene 1
  "The Smell of Christmas"
    L. J. Stadlen, D. Fortus, I. Pearl, A. Kupperman
  "You Remind Me of You"
    L. J. Stadlen, J. Kurnitz
Scene 2
  "Minnie's Boys"
    S. Winters, Company
Scene 4
  "Be Happy"
    S. Winters, D. Fortus, I. Pearl, A. Kupperman, G. Raucher

Scene 5

"The Act"
L. J. Stadlen, D. Fortus, I. Pearl, A. Kupperman, S. Winters

Finale
The Company

1970.08 ## LOOK TO THE LILIES

A Musical in Two Acts, 16 Scenes. Book by Leonard Spigelgass. Based on the novel "Lilies of the Field" by William E. Barrett. Music by Jule Styne. Lyrics by Sammy Cahn. Directed by Joshua Logan. Scenery and lighting by Jo Mielziner. Costumes by Carrie F. Robbins. Musical direction, Milton Rosenstock. Vocal arrangements and direction, Buster Davis. Orchestrations by Larry Wilcox. Dance arrangements by John Morris. Audio design (sound) by Robert I. Liftin. Production associate, Joseph Beruh. Produced by Edgar Lansbury, Max J. Brown, Richard Lewine, and Ralph Nelson. Opened 29 March 1970 at the Lunt-Fontanne Theatre and closed 19 April 1970 after 25 performances[12].

CAST (in order of appearance): *Homer Smith:* AL FREEMAN, JR. *Sister Gertrude:* Maggie Task. *Sister Elizabeth:* Virginia Craig. *Sister Agnes:* Linda Andrews. *Mother Maria:* SHIRLEY BOOTH. *Sister Albertine:* TAINA ELG. *Lady Guitarist:* Anita Sheer. *Juanita:* PATTI KARR. *Rosita:* CARMEN ALVAREZ. *Juan Archuleta:* TITOS VANDIS. *Bartender:* Marc Allen, III. *First Policeman:* Joe Benjamin. *Secomnd Policeman:* Richard Graham. *Courtroom Guards:* Paul Eichel, Michael Davis. *Judge:* Joe Benjamin. *District Attorney:* Don Prieur. *Defense Attorney:* Ben Laney. *Monsignor O'Hara:* Richard Graham. *Poker Players:* Michael Davis, Paul Eichel, Don Prieur. *Townspeople: Singers:* Marian Haraldson, Sherri Huff, Suzanne Horn, Maggie Worth, Marc Allen, III, Michael Davis, Paul Eichel, Tony Falco, Ben Laney, Don Prieur. *Dancers:* Carol Conte, Maria DiDia, Tina Faye, Ravah Malmuth, Glenn Brooks, Harry Endicott, Gary Gendell, Steven Ross. *Children:* Lisa Bellaran, Lori Bellaran, Ray Bellaran.

Act 1, Scene 1: The Farm. *Scene 2:* Farmhouse Kitchen. *Scene 3:* Juan's Cafe. *Scene 4:* Farmhouse Kitchen. *Scene 5:* The Farm—The next morning. *Scene 6:* Juan's Cafe.

Act 2, Scene 1: Farmhouse Kitchen. *Scene 2:* Courtroom. *Scene 3:* A Bus Stop. *Scene 4:* The Farm. *Scene 5:* Near Casamagordo. *Scene 6:* Juan's Cafe. *Scene 7:* The Farm. *Scene 8:* A Bus Stop. *Scene 9:* Chapel Exterior. *Scene 10:* Chapel Interior.

ACT 1

Scene 1

"Gott Is Gut"
S. Booth, T. Elg, V. Craig, M., Task, L. Andrews

"First Class Number One Bum"
A. Freeman, Jr.

Scene 2

"Himmlisher Vater"
S. Booth, T. Elg, V. Craig, M., Task, L. Andrews

"Follow the Lamb"
A. Freeman, Jr., S. Booth, T. Elg, V. Craig, M., Task, L. Andrews

Scene 3

"Meet My Seester"
P. Karr. C. Alvarez

Scene 4

"Don't Talk About God"
A. Freeman, Jr.

"When I Was Young"
S. Booth

Scene 5

"On That Day of Days"
P. Karr, C. Alvarez, Children, Townspeople

"You're a Rock"
A. Freeman, Jr.

"I Am What I Am"
S. Booth

"I'd Sure Like to Give It a Shot"
A. Freeman, Jr.

Scene 6

"I'd Sure Like to Give It a Shot" (Dance)
A. Freeman, Jr., P. Karr, C. Alvarez, Customers

ACT 2

Scene 1

"I Admire You Very Much, Mr. Schmidt"
T. Elg

Scene 3

"Look to the Lilies"
S. Booth, T. Elg, V. Craig, M., Task, L. Andrews

Scene 4

"Some Kind of Man"
A. Freeman, Jr.

Scene 5

"Homer's Pitch"
A. Freeman, Jr., Townspeople

Scene 7

"Casamagordo, New Mexico"
T. Elg, V. Craig, M., Task, L. Andrews

"One Little Brick at a Time"
A. Freeman, Jr., Townspeople

Scene 8

"I, Yes Me, That's Who"
S. Booth

Scene 9

"Prayer"
Townspeople

Scene 10

"I, Yes Me, That's Who" (reprise)
A. Freeman, Jr.

1970.09 ## APPLAUSE

A Musical in Two Acts, 16 Scenes. Book by Betty Comden and Adolph Green. Based on the film "All About Eve" (by Joseph Mankiewicz) and the original story ("The Wisdom of Eve") by Mary Orr. Music by Charles Strouse. Lyrics by Lee Adams. Directed and choreographed by Ron Field. Scenery by Robert Randolph. Costumes by Ray Aghayan. Lighting by Tharon Musser. Musical direction and vocal arrangements by Don Pippin. Orchestrations by Philip J. Lang. Dance and incidental music arranged by Mel Marvin. Production associate, Phyllis Dukore. Choreographic assistant, Tom Rolla. Produced by Joseph Kipness and Lawrence Kasha in association with Nederlander Productions and George M. Steinbrenner III. Opened 30 March 1970 at the Palace Theatre and closed 27 May 1972 after 898 performances.

CAST (in order of appearance): *Tony Announcer:* John Anania. *Tony Host:* Alan King. *Margo Channing:* LAUREN BACALL. *Eve Harrington:* PENNY FULLER. *Howard Benedict:* ROBERT MANDAN. *Bert:* Tom Urich. *Buzz Richards:* BRANDON MAGGART. *Bill Sampson:* LEN CARIOU. *Duane Fox:* LEE ROY REAMS. *Karen Richards:* ANN WILLIAMS. *Bartender:* Jerry Wyatt. *Peter:* John Anania. *Bob:* Howard Kahl. *Piano Player:* Orrin Reiley. *Stan Harding:* Ray Becker. *Danny:* Bill Allsbrook. *Bonnie:* BONNIE FRANKLIN. *Carol:* Carol Petri. *Joey:* Michael Misita. *Musicians:* Gene Kelton, Nat Horne, David Anderson. *TV Director:* Orrin Reiley. *Autograph Seeker:* Carol Petri.

Singers: Laurie Franks, Ernestine Jackson, Sheilah Rae, Jeannette Seibert, Henrietta Valor, Howard Kahl, Orrin Reiley, Jerry Wyatt. *Dancers:* Renee Baughman, Joan Bell, Debi Carpenter, Patti D'Beck, Marilyn D'Honau, Marybeth Kurdock, Carol Petri, Bill Allsbrook, David Anderson, John Cashman, Jon Daenen, Nikolas Dante, Gene Foote, Gene Kelton, Nat Horne, Michael Misita, Ed Nolfi, Sammy Williams.

The action takes place at the present time in and around New York City.

Act 1, Scene 1: The Tony Awards. *Scene 2:* Margo's Dressing Room. *Scene 3:* The Village Bar. *Scene 4:* Margo's Living Room. *Scene 5:* Margo's Dressing Room. *Scene 6:* Joe Allen's (Restaurant). *Scene 7:* Margo's Bedroom. *Scene 8:* Margo's Living Room. *Scene 9:* Backstage.

Act 2, Scene 1: Buzz and Karen's Connecticut Home. *Scene 2:* Margo's Dressing Room. *Scene 3:* Joe Allen's. *Scene 4:* Margo's Living Room. *Scene 5:* Backstage. *Scene 6:* Margo's Dressing Room. *Scene 7:* Backstage.

---

[12]Choreography uncredited at opening; credited to Joyce Trisler in previews.

ACT 1

Scene 2

"Backstage Babble"
First Nighters (Ensemble)

"Think How It's Gonna Be"
L. Cariou

"But Alive"
L. Bacall, Boys

Scene 3

"But Alive" (continued)
L. Bacall, Boys

Scene 4

"The Best Night of My Life"
P. Fuller

"Who's That Girl?"
L. Bacall

Scene 6

"Applause"
B. Franklin, the Gypsies (Ensemble)

Scene 7

"Hurry Back"
L. Bacall

Scene 8

"Fasten Your Seat Belts"
B. Maggart, A. Williams, R. Mandan, L. R. Reams, L. Cariou, Guests

Scene 9

"Welcome to the Theater"
L. Bacall

ACT 2

Scene 1

"Inner Thoughts"
A. Williams, B. Maggart, L. Bacall

"Good Friends"
L. Bacall, A. Williams, B. Maggart

Scene 2

"The Best Night of My Life" (reprise)
P. Fuller

Scene 3

"She's No Longer a Gypsy"
B. Franklin, L. R. Reams, the Gypsies (Ensemble)

Scene 4

"One of a Kind"
L. Cariou, L. Bacall

Scene 5

"One Hallow'een"
P. Fuller

Scene 6

"Something Greater"
L. Bacall

Scene 7

Finale
L. Bacall, Company

1970.10   CRY FOR US ALL

A Musical in One Act, 10 Scenes. Book by William Alfred and Albert Marre. Based on the play "Hogan's Goat" by William Alfred. Music by Mitch Leigh. Lyrics by William Alfred and Phyllis Robinson. Book and musical staging by Albert Marre. Choreography by Todd Bolender. Settings and lighting by Howard Bay. Costumes by Robert Fletcher. Musical direction by Herbert Grossman. Music supervision, Sam Pottle. Orchestrations by Carlyle Hall. Production coordinator, Dwight Fyre. Assistant choreographer, John Mandia. Produced by Mitch Leigh in association with C. Gerald Goldsmith. Opened 8 April 1970 at the Broadhurst Theatre and closed 15 April 1970 after 9 performances.

CAST: *Street-rats (3): Miggsy:* Scott Jacoby. *Flylegs:* Darel Glaser. *Cabbage:* Todd Jones. *Matt Stanton,* Leader of Brooklyn's Sixth Ward, and owner of the Court Cafe: STEVE ARLEN. *Kathleen Stanton,* his wife: JOAN DIENER. *Edward Quinn,* Mayor of Brooklyn: ROBERT WEEDE. *Peter Boyle,* a hanger-on of Quinn's: TOMMY RALL. *Bessie Legg,* a back-room girl: HELEN GALLAGHER. *Maria Haggerty,* the Stanton's Housekeeper: DOLORES WILSON. *John "Black Jack" Haggerty,* her husband and Assistant Ward Leader: PAUL UKENA. *James "Palsy" Murphy,* Boss of Brooklyn: EDWIN STEFFE. *Father Stanislaus Coyne,* Pastor of St. Mary Star of the Sea: WILLIAM GRIFFIS. *State Senator Thomas Walsh:* Jay Stuart. *Mortyeen O'Brien,* the Fire Commissioner: Charles Rule. *Peter Mulligan,* Chief Clerk of the Police Department: John Ferrante. *Father Maloney,* Priest of the Printers' Church: Elliott Savage. *The Cruelty Man:* Taylor Reed. *Mrs. Teresa Tuohy:* Fran Stevens. *Fiona Quigley,* factory girl: Elaine Cancilla. *Jack O'Banion,* a reporter for The Brooklyn Eagle: Jack Trussel. *Mrs. Mortyeen O'Brien:* Dora Rinehart. *Aloysius "Wishy" Doyle,* Bartender of the Court Cafe: Bill Dance. *Mutton Egan,* thirteen years old: Ronnie Douglas.

The action takes place in Brooklyn during a five-day period around 1 May 1890. The principal locale is the Court Cafe on the corner of Court Street and Fifth Place, Brooklyn: the street outside, the bar and the backroom of the cafe, and the Haggerty parlour which adjoins it. The action also moves to the street outside Ag Hogan's flat, to the Printers' Church in Brooklyn, and to the Boardwalk in Seagate.

Scene 1: Tuesday Evening. *Scene 2:* Wednesday Morning. *Scene 3:* Wednesday Evening. *Scene 4:* Thursday Evening. *Scene 5:* Friday Evening. *Scene 6:* Later Friday Evening. *Scene 7:* Saturday Afternoon. *Scene 8:* Saturday Night. *Scene 9:* Sunday Afternoon. *Scene 10:* Sunday Evening.

MUSICAL NUMBERS

Scene 1

"See No Evil"
S. Jacoby, D. Glaser, T. Jones

"The End of My Race"
S. Arlen

"How Are Ya Since?"
J. Diener, S. Arlen, The Constituents (Ensemble)

Scene 2

"The Mayor's Chair"
R. Weede

"The Cruelty Man"
S. Jacoby, D. Glaser, T. Jones

Scene 3

"The Verandah Waltz"
J. Diener, S. Arlen

Scene 4

"Home Free All"
S. Arlen, S. Jacoby, D. Glaser, T. Jones, The Constituents

"The Broken Heart of the Wages of Sin"
S. Jacoby, D. Glaser, T. Jones

"The Confessional"
S. Arlen, E. Savage

"Who To Love If Not a Stranger?"
J. Diener

Scene 5

"Cry For Us All"
T. Rall, The Mourners (Ensemble)

Scene 6

"Swing Your Bag'
H. Gallagher

"Call in to Her"
J. Diener, S. Arlen

"That Slavery Is Love"
J. Diener

Scene 7

"I Lost It"
S. Jacoby, D. Glaser, T. Jones

Scene 8

"Aggie, Oh Aggie"
R. Weede

Scene 9

"The Leg of the Duck"
T. Rall

"This Cornucopian Land"
S. Arlen, The Constituents
"How Are Ya Since?" (reprise)
J. Diener, R. Weede
"The Broken Heart or the Wages of Sin" (reprise)
S. Jacoby, D. Glaser, T. Jones
Scene 10
"Cry For Us All" (reprise)
The Constituents

1970.11 ## THE BOY FRIEND

A Revival of the Musical Comedy of the 1920's in Three Acts[13]. Book, music and lyrics by Sandy Wilson. Directed by Gus Schirmer. Dances and musical numbers staged by Buddy Schwab. Settings and costumes by Andrew and Margaret Brownfoot. Costume supervision, Stanley Simmons. Lighting by Tharon Musser. Musical director, Jerry Goldberg. Orchestrations by Ted Royal and Charles L. Cooke. Associate producer, Robert Saxon. Produced by John Yorke, Don Saxon and Michael Hellerman. Opened 14 April 1970 at the Ambassador Theatre and closed 18 July 1970 after 119 performances.

CAST (in order of appearance): *Hortense*: Barbara Andres. *Nancy*: Lesley Secombe. *Maisie*: SANDY DUNCAN. *Fay*: Mary Zahn. *Dulcie*: SIMON MCQUEEN. *Polly*: JUDY CARNE. *Marcel*: Marcelo Gamboa. *Alphonse*: Ken Mitchell. *Pierre*: Arthur Faria. *Madame Dubonnet*: JEANNE BEAUVAIS. *Bobby Van Husen*: HARVEY EVANS. *Percival Browne*: LEON SHAW. *Tony*: RONALD YOUNG. *Phillipe*: Tony Stevens. *Monica*: Carol Culver. *Lord Brockhurst*: DAVID VAUGHAN. *Lady Brockhurst*: Marie Paxton. *Gendarme*: Jeff Richards. *Waiter*: Tony Stevens. *Pepe*: Marcelo Gamboa. *Lolita*: Mary Zahn.

1970.12 ## PARK

A Musical in Two Acts. Book and lyrics by Paul Cherry. Music by Lance Mulcahy. Directed by John Stix. Scenery and costumes by Peter Harvey. Lighting by Martin Aronstein. Arrangements and musical direction, Oscar Kosarin. Musical staging by Lee Theodore. Produced by Edward Padula, a division of Eddie Bracken Ventures, Inc. Opened 22 April 1970 at the John Golden Theatre and closed 25 April 1970 after 5 performances.

CAST (in order of appearance): *Young Man*: DON SCARDINO. *Young Woman*: JOAN HACKETT. *Man*: DAVID BROOKS. *Woman*: JULIE WILSON.

The action takes place at the present time in Spring in a park.

ACT 1
"All the Little Things in the World Are Waiting"
D. Scardino
"Hello Is the Way Things Begin"
J. Hackett
"Bein' a Kid"
D. Scardino, J. Hackett
"Elizabeth"
D. Brooks
"He Talks To Me"
J. Wilson, D. Brooks
"Tomorrow Will Be the Same"
Quartet
"One Man"
J. Wilson
"Park"
D. Scardino

ACT 2
"I Want It Just to Happen"
J. Hackett
"I Can See"
J. Wilson

"Compromise"
D. Scardino
"Jamie"
D. Scardino, D. Brooks
"Tomorrow Will Be the Same" (reprise)
Ensemble
"I'd Marry You Again"
J. Wilson, D. Brooks
"Bein' a Kid" (reprise)
Quartet
"Park" (reprise)
Quartet

1970.13 ## COMPANY

A Musical in Two Acts, 11 Scenes. Book by George Furth. Music and lyrics by Stephen Sondheim. Directed by Harold Prince. Musical numbers staged by Michael Bennett. Sets and projections by Boris Aronson. Costumes by D. D. Ryan. Lighting by Robert Ornbo. Musical direction by Harold Hastings. Orchestrations by Jonathan Tunick. Dance music arrangements by Wally Harper. Production supervisor, Ruth Mitchell. Associate choreographer, Bob Avian. Produced by Harold Prince in association with Ruth Mitchell. Opened 26 April 1970 at the Alvin Theatre and closed 1 January 1972 after 690 performances.

CAST: *Robert*: DEAN JONES. *Sarah*: BARBARA BARRIE. *Harry*: CHARLES KIMBROUGH. *Susan*: MERLE LOUISE. *Peter*: JOHN CUNNINGHAM. *Jenny*: TERI RALSTON. *David*: GEORGE COE. *Amy*: BETH HOWLAND. *Paul*: STEVE ELMORE. *Joanne*: ELAINE STRITCH. *Larry*: CHARLES BRASWELL. *Marta*: PAMELA MYERS. *Kathy*: DONNA McKECHNIE. *April*: SUSAN BROWNING.
Vocal Minority: Cathy Corkill, Carol Gelfand, Marilyn Saunders, Dona D. Vaughan.

The action takes place in New York City at the present time.

Act 1, Scene 1: Robert's apartment. *Scene 2*: Sarah and Harry's living room. *Scene 3*: Peter and Susan's terrace. *Scene 4*: Jenny and David's den/playroom. *Scene 5*: A park bench. *Scene 6*: Amy's kitchen.

Act 2, Scene 1: Robert's apartment, as in Act 1, Scene 1. *Scene 2*: Robert's apartment, later. *Scene 3*: Peter and Susan's terrace. *Scene 4*: A private night-club. *Scene 5*: Robert's apartment.

ACT 1
Scene 1
"Company"
D. Jones, Company
Scene 2
"The Little Things You Do Together"
E. Stritch, Company
"Sorry-Grateful"
C. Kimbrough, G. Coe, C. Braswell
Scene 4
"You Could Drive a Person Crazy"
D. McKechnie, S. Browning, P. Myers
"Have I Got a Girl for You"
C. Braswell, J. Cunningham, S. Elmore, G. Coe, C. Kimbrough
"Someone Is Waiting"
D. Jones
Scene 5
"Another Hundred People"
P. Myers
Scene 6
"Getting Married Today"
B. Howland, S. Elmore, T. Ralston
ACT 2
Scene 1
"Side By Side By Side"
D. Jones, Company
"What Would We Do Without You"
D. Jones, Company

---

[13]Originally produced in New York 30 September 1954 at the Royale Theatre for 483 performances. For Synopsis of Scenes and Musical Numbers, see original 1954 production.

Scene 2
   "Poor Baby"
      B. Barrie, T. Ralston, M. Louise, B. Howland, E. Stritch
   "Tick Tock" (dance)
      D. McKechnie
      (*Dance Music Arranged by* David Shire.)

"Barcelona"
      D. Jones, S. Browning
Scene 4
   "The Ladies Who Lunch"
      E. Stritch
   "Being Alive"
      D. Jones

Mary McCarty (foreground) in FOLLIES
Martha Swope/TimePix

1970-1971 SEASON

BOB AND RAY--
1970.14
THE TWO AND ONLY

An Entertainment (Comedy revue) in Two Acts. Created and written by Bob Elliott and Ray Goulding. Directed by Joseph Hardy. Scenery by William Ritman. Lighting by Thomas Skelton. Associate producer, Ben Gerard. Produced by Joseph I. and Johanna Levine in association with Hy Saporta. Opened 24 September 1970 at the John Golden Theatre and closed 13 February 1971 after 162 performances.

CAST: BOB ELLIOTT, RAY GOULDING.

A revue of comedy sketches and interviews employing some of the following Bob-and-Ray characterizations:

CAST—IF USED: Hector Lassie, Captain Larson*, Wally Ballou, Dr. Derek Dexter, Ward Smith, Edgar G. Fanshaw, Martin LeSoeur, Good Professor Groggins***, Gabe Preston, McBeebee Twins, Charles (poet)**, Mayor Ralph Moody Thayer, Mary McGoon, John W. Norbis, Harlow P. Whitcomb, Larry Lovebreath, Maitland W. Montmorency, Leonard Bonfiglio, Barry Campbell, Clinton Snidely, Biff Burns, David Chetley, Fielding Backstayge*****, T. WIlton Messy****, Fahnstock P. Bodry, Neil A. Sturbush, T. Wilton Messy, Jr., Stuffy Hodgson, O. Leo Lahey, Thomas E. Röte, Word Carr, Wolfman*****, Gregg Marlowe, Dean Archer Armstead, Mr. Trace, Clyde L. "Hap" Whartney, Mister Science, Arthur Schermerhorn, Komodo Dragon Expert.

*** Missing Quit
*** Transplant Donor (Accidental)
**** Committed
***** Confined
****** In Pound

THE ROTHSCHILDS
1970.15

A Musical in Two Acts, a Prologue and 18 Scenes. Book by Sherman Yellen. Based on the book of the same name by Frederic Morton. Music by Jerry Bock. Lyrics by Sheldon Harnick. Directed and choreographed by Michael Kidd. Settings and costumes by John Bury. Lighting by Richard Pilbrow. Orchestrations by Don Walker. Musical direction and vocal arrangements by Milton Greene. Dance music arranged by Clay Fullum. Production supervision by Michael Thoma. Produced by Lester Osterman (Productions, Richard Horner) and Hillard Elkins (Productions International Corp., Emanuel Azenberg, Robert Malina, George Platt). Opened 19 October 1970 at the Lunt-Fontanne Theatre and closed 2 January 1972 after 505 performances.

CAST (in order of appearance): *Prince William of Hesse:* KEENE CURTIS. *Guard:* Roger Hamilton. *Mayer Rothschild:* HAL LINDEN. *First Urchin:* Michael Maitland. *Second Urchin:* Kim Michels. *Third Urchin:* Robby Benson. *Gutele (Mama) Rothschild:* LEILA MARTIN. *First Vendor:* Thomas Trelfa. *Second Vendor:* Kenneth Bridges. *Third Vendor:* Jon Peck. *General:* Paul Tracey. *Budurus:* LEO LEYDEN. *First Banker:* Elliott Savage. *Second Banker:* Carl Nicholas. *Young Amshel Rothschild:* Lee Franklin. *Young Solomon Rothschild:* Robby Benson. *Young Nathan Rothschild:* Michael Maitland. *Young Jacob Rothschild:* Mitchell Spera. *Blum:* Howard Honig. *Mrs. Kaufman:* Nina Dova. *Mrs. Segal:* Peggy Cooper. *Peasant:* Christopher Chadman. *Amshel Rothschild:* TIMOTHY JEROME. *Solomon Rothschild:* DAVID GARFIELD. *Jacob Rothschild:* CHRIS SARANDON. *Nathan Rothschild:* PAUL HECHT. *Kalman Rothschild:* ALLAN GRUET. *Joseph Fouche:* KEENE CURTIS. *Herries:* KEENE CURTIS. *Sceptic:* Paul Tracey. *Banker:* Roger Hamilton. *Hannah Cohen:* JILL CLAYBURGH. *Prince Metternich:* KEENE CURTIS.

Members of the Hessian Court, People of the Frankfort Ghetto, Members of the Austrian Court, Grenadiers, Couriers, Crowned Heads of Europe, Banker-Brokers: Rick Atwell, Steve Boockvor, Kenneth Bridges, Henry Brunjes, Christopher Chadman, Peggy Cooper, Patrick Cummings, Nina Dova, Vicki Frederick, Penny Guerard, Roger Hamilton, Ann Hodges, Howard Honig, Del Lewis, John Mineo, Carl Nicholas, Jon Peck, Ted Pejovich, Denise Pence, Jean Richards, Elliott Savage, Wilfred Schuman, Lani Sundsten, Paul Tracey, Thomas Trelfa.

The action takes place throughout Europe between 1772 and 1818.

Prologue: Hesse, 1772.

Act 1, Scene 1: The Gate of the Frankfort Ghetto, 1772. *Scene 2:* The Rothschild Shop, Frankfort Ghetto, 1772. *Scene 3:* The Frankfort Fair, 1773. *Scene 4:* The Study of Prince William of Hesse, 1773. *Scene 5:* The Rothschild Shop, 1788. *Scene 6:* The Rothschild Shop, 1788. *Scene 7:* The Rothschild Shop, 1804. *Scene 8:* Prince William's Study, 1804. *Scene 9:* The Rothschild Shop, 1804.

Act 2, Scene 1: The London Royal Stock Exchange, 1805. *Scene 2:* The London Royal Stock Exchange, 1806. *Scene 3:* The Garden of Hannah Cohen, London, 1806-1811. *Scene 4:* The Rothschild Home, 1812. *Scene 5:* The Ballroom at Aix-La-Chappelle, 1818. *Scene 6:* The Rothschild Home, 1818. *Scene 7:* Various European Capitals, 1818. *Scene 8:* The Rothschild Home, 1818. *Scene 9:* Finale.

ACT 1
Prologue
"Pleasure and Privilege"
  K. Curtis, Ensemble
Scene 2
"One Room"
  H. Linden, L. Martin
Scene 3
"He Tossed a Coin"
  H. Linden, T. Trelfa, K. Bridges, J. Peck, Ensemble
Scene 5
"Sons"
  H. Linden, L. Martin, L. Franklin, R. Benson, M. Maitland, M. Spera
Scene 7
"Everything"
  P. Hecht, L. Martin, D. Garfield, A. Gruet, T. Jerome, C. Sarandon
Scene 8
"Rothschild and Sons"
  H. Linden, P. Hecht, D. Garfield, A. Gruet, T. Jerome, C. Sarandon
Scene 9
"Allons"
  K. Curtis, Male Ensemble
"Rothschild and Sons" (reprise)
  H. Linden, P. Hecht, D. Garfield, A. Gruet, T. Jerome, C. Sarandon
"Sons" (reprise)
  L. Martin, H. Linden
ACT 2
Scene 1
Hymn: "Give England Strength"
  K. Curtis, Male Ensemble
"This Amazing London Town"
  P. Hecht
Scene 2
"They Say"
  P. Tracey, Male Ensemble
"I'm in Love! I'm in Love!"
  P. Hecht
Scene 3
"I'm in Love! I'm in Love!" (reprise)
  J. Clayburgh
Scene 4
"In My Own Lifetime"
  H. Linden
Scene 5
"Have You Ever Seen a Prettier Little Congress?"
  K. Curtis
"Stability"
  K. Curtis, Ensemble
Scene 7
"Bonds"
  P. Hecht, D. Garfield, A. Gruet, T. Jerome, C. Sarandon, K. Curtis, Ensemble
Scene 9
  (The Will—Finale)
  (H. Linden)

(PAUL SILLS') STORY THEATRE
1970.16

An Entertainment in Two Acts, 10 Scenes. Adapted and directed by Paul Sills. Setting and projections by Michael Devine. Costumes by Stephanie Kline. Lighting by H. R. Poindexter. (Songs by Bob Dylan, Country Joe McDonald, George Harrison, Hamid Hamilton Camp.) Music performed by The True Brethren (Raphael Grinage, Lauren Karapetian, Loren Pickford, Lewis Ross). Special consultant, Viola Spolin. Produced by Zev Bufman. Presented with the help and cooperation of City Center of Music and Drama, Inc. (Norman Singer, Executive director), The Shubert

Organization, and Theatre Development Fund, as originally presented at the Mark Taper Forum by Center Theatre Group of Los Angeles (Gordon Davidson, Artistic director). Opened 26 October 1970 at the Ambassador Theatre and closed 3 July 1971 after 245 performances[1].

CAST (in alphabetical order): PETER BONERZ, HAMID HAMILTON CAMP, MELINDA DILLON, MARY FRANN, VALERIE HARPER, RICHARD LIBERTINI, PAUL SAND, RICHARD SCHAAL.

ACT 1[2]

Scene 1

"A Lot Can Happen in a Day"
    H. H. Camp
    (*Music and Lyrics by* Hamid Hamilton Camp.)
The Little Peasant
    Little Peasant: H. H. Camp. *Peasant's Wife*: M. Dillon. *Cowherd*: P. Sand. *Judge*: P. Bonerz. *Farmer's Wife*: V. Harper. *Parson*: R. Libertini. *Farmer*: R. Schaal. *Rich Peasants*: M. Dillon, M. Frann, P. Sand, V. Harper.

Scene 2

The Bremen Town Musicians
    Ass: R. Schaal. *Hound*: P. Sand. *Cat*: P. Bonerz. *Cock*: R. Libertini. *Robbers*: V. Harper, H. H. Camp.

Scene 3

Is He Fat
    Man #1: H. H. Camp. *Man #2*: R. Schaal. *Sexton*: R. Libertini. *Parson*: P. Bonerz.

Scene 4

The Robber Bridegroom
    Miller: R. Schaal. *Daughter*: M. Dillon. *Robber Bridegroom*: P. Sand. *Old Woman*: V. Harper. *Maiden*: M. Frann. *Robbers*: P. Bonerz, R. Schaal, R. Libertini.
"I'll Be Your Baby Tonight"
    H. H. Camp
    (*Music and Lyrics by* Bob Dylan.)

Scene 5

Henny Penny
    Henny Penny: V. Harper. *Cocky Locky*: R. Schaal. *Ducky Daddles*: H. H. Camp. *Goosey Poosey*: M. Dillon. *Turkey Lurkey*: P. Sand. *Foxy Woxy*: R. Libertini.
"Fixin' To Die Rag"
    L. Ross
    (*Music and Lyrics by* Joe McDonald.)

ACT 2

"About Time"
    H.H. Camp
    (*Music and Lyrics by* Hamid Hamilton Camp.)

Scene 1

The Master Thief
    Old Man, Parson: R. Schaal. *Wife*: M. Dillon. *Master Thief*: P. Bonerz. *Count*: R. Libertini. *Soldiers*: H. H. Camp, R. Schaal, P. Sand. *Countess*: V. Harper. *Clerk*: P. Sand.
"Dear Landlord"
    H. H. Camp
    (*Music and Lyrics by* Bob Dylan.)

Scene 2

Venus and the Cat
    Man: R. Schaal. *Cat*: M. Frann. *Venus*: V. Harper.

Scene 3

The Fisherman and His Wife
    Narrator: H. H. Camp. *Fisherman*: R. Libertini. *Flounder*: P. Bonerz. *Wife*: M. Dillon.

Scene 4

Two Crows
    Crow #1: P. Bonerz. *Crow #2*: H. H. Camp.

Scene 5

The Golden Goose
    Mother, Eldest Daughter: V. Harper. *Simpleton*: P. Sand. *Eldest Son, Peasant*: R. Schaal. *Little Gray Man, King*: H. H. Camp. *Second Son, Parson*: R. Libertini. *Second Daughter*: M. Frann. *Sexton*: P. Bonerz. *Princess*: M. Dillon.

----

[1]Joined by *METAMORPHOSES* in repertory 22 April 1971.
[2]The order of scenes was substantially revised during the run.

"Here Comes the Sun"
    L. Ross
    (*Music and Lyrics by* George Harrison.)

LIGHT, LIVELY AND YIDDISH

1970.17

A Musical in Two Acts, 15 Scenes, in Yiddish. Adaptation by Ben Bonus. Music by Eli Rubinstein. Text and lyrics by Abram Shulman, Wolf and Sylvia Younin. Additional texts by M. Gershenson, Ch. N. Bialik, Ch. Cheffer, Mina Bern. Sets by Josef Ijaky. Costumes by Sylvia Friedlander. Musical conductor, Renee Solomon. Musical staging and choreography by Felix Fibich. Directed by Mina Bern. Produced by Sol Dickstein. Opened 27 October 1970 at the Belasco Theatre and closed 10 January 1971 after 87 performances.

CAST (in order of appearance): *English Narrator*: DAVID ELLIN. *Zelde with Her Koshik (Basket)*: MINA BERN. *Rag Seller*: LEON LIEBGOLD. *Dumpling Woman*: REIZL BOZYK. *Bagel Woman*: LILI LILIANA. *Sosye the Peacemaker*: MIRIAM KRESSYN. *Nokhem the Broker*: SEYMOUR REXITE. *Kvas Seller*: David Carey. *Gitele, the Young Girl*: Diane Cypkin. *Hershele of Ostropolie*: DEN BONUS. *Kalmen, the Rich Man*: LEON LIEBGOLD. *Innkeeper*: REIZL BOZYK.
    Dancers: Marcia Brooks, Helen Butleroff, Jack Dyville, Harry Endicott, Robyn Kessler, Tony Masullo, Maggie Masullo, Eileen McCabe, Joseph Tripolino.

Act 1: The shtetl.

Act 2: New York City and Tel Aviv, Israel.

ACT 1

"A Yarid" (A Fair)
"Yiddish" (Yiddish)
"Shver Tsu Zain A Tidene" (It's Hard To Be a Jewish Woman)
"Dus Hut Mir Kainer Nit Gezugt" (Nobody Told Me This)
"Tsen Azeyger" (Ten O'Clock)
"Tfile Tsu Got" (Prayer to God)
"Vu Iz Yoysher?" (Where Is Justice?)
"A Freilekhs" (A Joyful Song)

ACT 2

"Light, Lively and Yiddish"—(arrangement of Yiddish Folk Music)
"Khavertes" (Girl Friends)
"Tsu Mayn Dor" (The Song of My Generation)
"Israel" (Israel)
"A Shukh Putser" (Shoe Shine Boy)
"A Briv" (A Letter)
"S'vet Kumen Der Tog" (The Day Will Come)

THE PRESIDENT'S DAUGHTER

1970.18

A Yiddish-American Musical Comedy in Two Acts and a Prologue. Book by H. Kalmanov. Music by Murray Rumshinsky. Lyrics and direction by Jacob Jacobs. Dances staged by Henrietta Jacobson. Musical director, Murray Rumshinsky. Production design by Barry Arnold. Produced by Jacob Jacobs. Opened 3 November 1970 at the Billy Rose Theatre and closed 2 January 1971 after 72 performances.

CAST (in order of appearance): *Frances*: Michele Burke. *Esther*: Charlotte Gingold. *Yanek*: JACK RECHTZEIT. *Minke*: DIANA GOLDBERG. *Freidel*: CHAYELE ROSENTHAL. *Nathan*: JACOB JACOBS. *Sam Golden*: GEORGE GUIDALL. *Reb Yosel*: Jaime Lewin [Herman Levine]. *Bertha*: Thelma Mintz. *Miriam*: Rachela Relis.

The action takes place at the present time in Sam Golden's Flatbush (Brooklyn) home within a period of several weeks.

PROLOGUE

"Women's Liberation"
    D. Goldberg, T. Mintz, C. Cooper, R. Relis

ACT 1

"The President's Daughter"
    C. Rosenthal
"I Have What You Want!"
    D. Goldberg, J. Jacobs
"A Lesson in Yiddish"
    J. Rechtzeit

"Everything Is Possible in Life"
   C. Rosenthal, G. Guidall
"Welcome, Mr. Golden!"
   C. Rosenthal, J. Jacobs, D. Goldberg, C. Cooper, J. Lewin, M. Burke
ACT 2
"Stiochket"
   J. Rechtzeit
"Without a Mother"
   C. Rosenthal
"Love at Golden Years"
   R. Relis, J. Lewin
"If Only I Could Be a Kid Again"
   C. Rosenthal
"An Old Man Shouldn't Be Born"
   J. Jacobs
"We Two"
   D. Goldberg, J. Rechtzeit
"What More Do I Need?"
   G. Guidall
"What Would You Do?"
   C. Rosenthal, J. Jacobs

1970.19   TWO BY TWO

A Musical in Two Acts. Book by Peter Stone. Based on the play "The Flowering Peach" by Clifford Odets. Music by Richard Rodgers. Lyrics by Martin Charnin. Production conceived and directed by Joe Layton. Scenery by David Hays. Costumes by Fred Voelpel. Lighting by John Gleason. Musical direction by Jay Blackton. Orchestrations by Eddie Sauter. Dance and vocal arrangements by Trude Rittman. Production supervisor, Jerome Whyte. Projections designed by Cris Alexander. Produced by Richard Rodgers. Opened 10 November 1970 at the Imperial Theatre and closed 11 September 1971 after 351 performances.

CAST (in order of appearance): *Noah*: DANNY KAYE. *Esther*: JOAN COPELAND. *Japheth*: WALTER WILLISON. *Shem*: HARRY GOZ. *Leah*: MARILYN COOPER. *Ham*: MICHAEL KARM. *Rachel*: TRICIA O'NEILL. *Goldie*: MADELINE KAHN.

The action takes place before, during, and after the Flood (in biblical times).

Act 1: In and around Noah's home.

Act 2: Forty days and forty nights later. On the ark, and atop Mt. Ararat.

ACT 1
"Why Me?"
   D. Kaye
"Put Him Away"
   H. Goz, M. Karm, M. Cooper
The Gitka's Song
   The Gitka (instrumental)
"Something Somewhere"
   W. Willison, the Family
"You Have Got to Have a Rudder on the Ark" D. Kaye, H. Goz, M. Karm, W. Willison
"Something Doesn't Happen"
   T. O'Neil, J. Copeland
"An Old Man"
   J. Copeland
"Ninety Again!"
   D. Kaye
"Two By Two"
   D. Kaye, the Family
"I Do Not Know a Day I Did Not Love You"
   W. Willison
"Something Somewhere" (reprise)
   D. Kaye
ACT 2
"When It Dries"
   D. Kaye, the Family
"Two By Two" (reprise)
   D. Kaye, J. Copeland
"You"
   D. Kaye

"The Golden Ram"
   M. Kahn
"Poppa Knows Best"
   D. Kaye, W. Willison
"I Do Not Know a Day I Did Not Love You" (reprise)
   T. O'Neil, W. Willison
"As Far As I'm Concerned"
   H. Goz, M. Cooper
"Hey, Girlie"
   D. Kaye
"The Covenant"
   D. Kaye

1970.20   THE ME NOBODY KNOWS

A Musical in Two Acts[3]. (Book[4] adapted by Robert H. Livingston and Herb Schapiro.) Based on the book of the same name, edited by Stephen M. Joseph. Music by Gary William Friedman. Lyrics by Will Holt[5]. Original idea and additional lyrics by Herb Schapiro. Directed by Robert H. Livingston. Musical numbers staged by Patricia Birch. Scenery and lighting by Clarke Dunham. Costumes by Patricia Quinn Stuart. Media design and photography by Stan Goldberg and Mopsy. (Musical) Arrangements and orchestrations, Gary William Friedman. Musical director, Edward Strauss. Produced by Jeff Britton in association with Sagittarius Productions, Inc. Opened 18 December 1970 at the Helen Hayes Theatre, closing 28 August 1971; reopened 15 September 1971 at the Longacre Theatre and closed 28 November 1971 after 370 performances. Total, including Off-Broadway: 578 performances.

CAST (in order of appearance): *Rhoda*: Melanie Henderson. *Lillian*: Laura Michaels. *Carlos*: Jose Fernandez. *Millie Mae*: Irene Cara. *Benjamin*: Douglas Grant. *Catherine*: Beverly Ann Bremers. *Melba*: Gerri Dean. *Lloyd*: Northern J. Calloway. *Donald*: Paul Mace. *Clorox*: Carl Thoma. *William*: Kevin Lindsay. *Nell*: Hattie Winston.

The action takes place at the present time in New York's ghetto.

ACT 1
"Dream Babies" (*Lyrics by* Herb Shapiro.)
   G. Dean
"Light Sings" (*Lyrics by* Herb Shapiro.)
   K. Lindsay, Company
"This World" (*Lyrics by* Herb Shapiro.)
   Company
"Numbers"
   Company
"What Happens to Life"
   L. Michaels, N. J. Calloway
"Take Hold the Crutch"
   H. Winston, Company
"Flying Milk and Runaway Plates"
   D. Grant, Company
"I Love What the Girls Have"
   P. Mace
"How I Feel"
   B. A. Bremers, J. Fernandez
"If I Had a Million Dollars"
   Company
ACT 2
"Fugue for Four Girls"
   I. Cara, L. Michaels, B. A. Bremers, H. Winston
"Rejoice"
   C. Thoma

---

[3]First produced in New York Off-Broadway 18 May 1970 at the Orpheum Theatre for 208 performances.
[4]The spoken text in this production was written by children between the ages of 7 — 18 attending New York City public schools in Bedford-Stuyvesant, Harlem, Jamaica, Manhattan and the Youth House in the Bronx.
[5]The lyrics (Fugue for Four Girls; Rejoice; The Horse; War Babies) are children's poems, presented exactly as they wrote them. All other lyrics, except where noted, are by Will Holt.

"Sounds"
  H. Winston, B. A. Bremers
"The Tree"
  J. Fernandez
"Robert, Alvin, Wendell and Jo Jo"
  M. Henderson, L. Michaels, I. Cara, K. Lindsay
"Jail-Life Walk"
  P. Mace, N. J. Calloway, C. Thoma
"Something Beautiful"
  M. Henderson
"Black"
  D. Grant, C. Thoma, I. Cara, N. J. Calloway, G. Dean, H. Winston, M. Henderson, K. Lindsay
"The Horse" (The White Horse)
  N. J. Calloway
"Let Me Come In"
  Company
"War Babies"
  N. J. Calloway

LOVELY LADIES, KIND GENTLEMEN

1970.21

A Musical Comedy in Two Acts, 15 Scenes. Book by John Patrick. Based on the novel "The Teahouse of the August Moon" by Vern J. Sneider and the play of the same name by John Patrick. Music and lyrics by Stan Freeman and Franklin Underwood. Directed by Lawrence Kasha. Dances and musical numbers staged by Marc Breaux. Scenic production by Oliver Smith. Costumes by Freddy Wittop. Lighting by Thomas Skelton. Musical direction and choral arrangements by Theodore Saidenberg. Orchestrations by Philip J. Lang. Dance arrangements by Albert Mello. Associate choreographer, Gary Menteer. Associate producer, Angus Equities, Inc. Produced by Herman Levin. Opened 28 December 1970 at the Majestic Theatre and closed 9 January 1971 after 16 performances.

<u>CAST</u> (in order of appearance): *Sakini*: KENNETH NELSON. *Missionary*: David Steele. *Colonel Wainwright Purdy III*: DAVID BURNS. *Sergeant Gregovich*: LOU WILLS. *Captain Fisby*: RON HUSMANN. *Old Lady*: Sachi Shimizu. *Daughter*: Tisa Chang. *Children*: June Angela, Gene Profanato, Dana Shimizu. *Lady Astor*: Herself. *Ancient Man*: Sab Shimono. *Mr. Seiko*: Alvin Lum. *Miss Higa Jiga*: Lori Chinn. *Mr. Oshira*: David Thomas. *Mr. Hokaida*: Big Lee. *Lotus Blossom*: ELEANOR CALBES. *Mr. Keora*: Sab Shimono. *Captain McLean*: REMAK RAMSAY. *Logan*: David Steele. *Miller*: James Weston. *O'Malley*: Stephen Bolster. *Cabot*: Stuart Craig Wood. *Stock*: James B. Spann. *Lipshitz*: Kirk Norman. *Swenson*: James Hobson. *Cardone*: Dennis Roth. *Mancini*: Richard Nieves. *Colombo*: Charlie J. Rodriguez.

Okinawans and Americans: Barbara Coggin, Catherine Dando., Joan Nelson, Sumiko, Tisa Chang, Lori Chinn, Christi Curtis, Marjory Edson, Rosalie King, Sylvia Nolan, Jo Ann Ogawa, Sachi Shimizu, Susan Sigrist, Stephen Bolster, James Hobson, Alvin Lum, Richard Nieves, Kirk Norman, Charlie J. Rodriguez, Dennis Roth, Sab Shimono, James B. Spann, David Steele, James Weston, Stuart Craig Wood, Henry Boyer, Paul Charles, Charlie Goeddertz, J. J. Jepson, Tim Ramires, Steven Ross, Joe Milan, Ken Urmston.

The action takes place on the island of Okinawa during a few months in 1946.

Act 1, Scene 1: Okinawa. *Scene 2*: Purdy's Office. *Scene 3*: Outside Purdy's Office. *Scene 4*: Village Square in Tobiki. Fisby's Office. *Scene 5*: Outskirts of Tobiki. *Scene 6*: Purdy and Fisby's Office. *Scene 7*: Village Square in Tobiki; Fisby's Office; On the way to Big Koza. *Scene 8*: The Grove. *Scene 9*: Outskirts of Tobiki.

Act 2, Scene 1: The Teahouse. *Scene 2*: Village Street. *Scene 3*: Fisby's Office. *Scene 4*: Village Street. *Scene 5*: Village Shacks. *Scene 6*: The Teahouse.

ACT 1

Scene 1

  "With a Snap of My Finger"
    K. Nelson, Okinawans, G.I.s

Scene 2

  "Right Hand Man"
    D. Burns, K. Nelson, R. Husmann, G.I.s

Scene 4

  "Find Your Own Cricket"
    K. Nelson, D. Thomas, L. Chinn, Villagers
  "One Side of World"
    K. Nelson

Scene 5

  "Geisha"
    E. Calbes
  "You Say—They Say"
    K. Nelson, Villagers
  "This Time"
    R. Husmann

Scene 7

  "Simple Words"
    E. Calbes
  "Garden Guaracha"
    R. Ramsay
  ("Find Your Own Cricket" reprise)
    (K. Nelson, Villagers)

Scene 8

  ("Simple Words" reprise)
    (R. Husman, E. Calbes)
  "If It's Good Enough for Lady Astor"
    R. Husmann, R. Ramsay, K. Nelson, Villagers

Scene 9

  ("Batata")(K. Nelson, R. Husman, R. Ramsay, D. Thomas, Villagers)

ACT 2

Scene 1

  "Chaya"
    K. Nelson, Villagers
  "Call Me Back"
    R. Husmann, R. Ramsay, K. Nelson

Scene 2

  "Lovely Ladies, Kind Gentlemen"
    K. Nelson

Scene 3

  "You've Broken a Fine Woman's Heart"
    D. Burns
  ("Right Hand Man" reprise)
    (K. Nelson)

Scene 5

  "One More for the Last One"
    K. Nelson, L. Wills, G.I.s, Villagers

Scene 6

  ("With a Snap of My Finger" reprise)
    (K. Nelson)

SOON

1971.01

A Rock Opera in Two Acts, a Prologue and 10 Scenes. (Book) Adaption by Martin Duberman. Based on an original story by Joseph Martinez Kookoolis, Scott Fagan. Music by Joseph M. Kookoolis and Scott Fagan. Lyrics by Scott Fagan. Scenery by Kert Lundell. Lighting by Jules Fisher. Costumes by David Chapman. Orchestrations by Howard Wyeth, Jon Huston. Musical direction by Louis St. Louis. Vocal arrangements by Louis St. Louis and Jacqueline Penn. Choreography by Fred Benjamin. Additional staging by Gerald Freedman. Audio design by Jack Shearing. Produced by Bruce W. Stark and Sagittarius Productions, Inc. Opened 12 January 1971 at the Ritz Theatre and closed 13 January 1971 after 3 performances.

<u>CAST</u> (in order of appearance): *Kelly*: BARRY BOSTWICK. *Annie*: MARTA HEFLIN. *Wilson Wilson*: DENNIS BELLINE. *Michael*: RICHARD GERE. *Neil*: JOSEPH CAMPBELL BUTLER. *Henry*: PETER ALLEN. *Groupies (5)*: *Hope*: Marion Ramsey. *Faith*: Leata Galloway. *Charity*: Vickie Sue Robinson. *Rita*: Pamela Pentony. *Sharon*: Nell Carter. *Henry's Friends (3)*: *Jimmy*: Singer Williams. *Bobby*: Michael Jason. *Phil*: John C. Nelson. *Record Company Executives (4)*: *Mr. Par* (Corporation Head): Del Hinkley. *Elsworth Median* (Technical Advisor): Angus Cairns. *Gran Statisto* (Comptroller): Larry Spinelli. *Al Ti Telson* (Electronic Expert): Paul Eichel. *Songwriter*: Tony Middleton. *Psychedelic Necktie*: Pendleton Brown.

Act 1, Scene 1: On the Road. The Country. *Scene 2*: Coming to the City. *Scene 3*: The City. *Scene 4*: Henry's Office. *Scene 5*: The Club. *Scene 6*: Around the City. *Scene 7*: The Offices of the Music Industry.

Act 2, Scene 1: A Series of Recording Sessions. *Scene 2*: City Downs. *Scene 3*: On the Tour.

ACT 1

Prologue

"Let the World Begin Again"

Scene 1

"In Your Hands"

"I See the Light"/"Gentle Sighs"

Scene 2

"Roll Out the Morning"

Scene 3

"Everybody's Running"

Scene 4

"Henry Is Where It's At"

Scene 5

"Music, Music"

"Glad to Know Ya"

"Rita Cheeta"

Scene 6

"Henry's Dream Theme"

"To Touch the Sky"

Scene 7

The Chase:

"Everybody's Running"

"Marketing, Marketing"

"Sweet Henry Loves You"

"One More Time"

"Straight"

"Wait"

ACT 2

Scene 1

"Faces, Names, Places"

"Annie's Thing"

"Doing the High"

"Soon"

Scene 2

"Country Store Living"

"What's Gonna Happen to Me"

"On the Charts"

"Molecules"

"So Much That I Know"

"Child of Sympathy"

"Frustration"

Scene 3

"Doing the High" (reprise)

"It Won't Be Long"

1971.02 **ARI**

A Musical in Two Acts, 18 Scenes. Book and lyrics by Leon Uris. Based on his novel "Exodus." Music by Walt Smith. Production directed by Lucia Victor. Choreography by Talley Beatty. Scenery by Robert Randolph. Costumes by Sara Brook. Lighting by Nananne Porcher. Vocal arrangements and musical direction, Stanley Lebowsky. Orchestrations by Philip J. Lang. Dance and incidental music by Peter Howard. Additional music by William Fisher. Associate producers, Ronald Reckseit, Lisa Lipsky. Produced by Ken Gaston and Leonard J. Goldberg in association with Henry Stern. Opened 15 January 1971 at the Mark Hellinger Theatre and closed 30 January 1971 after 19 performances.

CAST (in order of appearance): *Joab*: JOSEPH DELLA SORTE. *Zev*: MARK ZELLER. *David*: MARTIN ROSS. *Mandria, the Greek*: C. K. ALEXANDER. *General Sutherland*: JACK GWILLIM. *Major Caldwell*: JAMIE ROSS. *Ari Ben Canaan*: DAVID CRYER. *Mark Parker*: NORWOOD SMITH. *Kitty Fremont*: CONSTANCE TOWERS. *Dov*: JOHN SAVAGE. *Karen*: JACQUELINE MAYRO. *Benjy*: Roger Morgan. *Armeteau*: Alexander Orfaly. *Friend of Armeteau*: Ed Becker. *Captain Henley*: Casper Roos.

Refugee Children: Tracey Eman, Kelley Boa, Mona Daleo, Toni Lund, Lynn Reynolds, Timmy Ousey, Todd Jones, Johnny Welch, Tony Dean. *Refugees and British*

Soldiers: Dancers: Bryant Baker, Bjarne Buchtrup, Ron Crofoot, Richard Dodd, Pi Douglass, Richard Maxon, Ronn Steinman, Carol Estey, Reggie Israel, Karen L. Jablons, Joanna Mendl, Gayle Pines, Deborah Strauss. *Singers*: Ed Becker, Ted Bloecher, Bennett Hill, Henry Lawrence, Art Mathews, Casper Roos, D. Brian Wallach, Bonnie Marcus, Patricia Noal, Susan Schevers, Suzanne Horn.

The action takes place on the island of Cyprus in 1947.

Act 1, Scene 1: Beach near Famagusta, Cyprus, at night. *Scene 2*: Mandria's House, immediately after. *Scene 3*: A Waterfront Cafe, the next night. *Scene 4*: Detention Camp, Children's Compound, the following afternoon. *Scene 5*: A Waterfront Cafe, Quayside, Larnaca, a few days later. *Scene 6*: Detention Camp, Children's Compound, the following week. *Scene 7*: A Military Camp, a week later. *Scene 8*: Detention Camp, a few days later. *Scene 9*: The Dispensary. *Scene 10*: Mandrias' House, a few days later. British H.G. the same day. Mandria's House, the following afternoon.

Act 2, Scene 1: A Hidden Cove, the next morning. *Scene 2*: General Sutherland's Quarters, noon. *Scene 3*: Detention Camp, 2:00 P.M. *Scene 4*: Military Camp, 5:00 P.M. *Scene 5*: Dockside, Kyrenia, 6:00 P.M. *Scene 6*: Parker's Hotel's Room, immediately thereafter. *Scene 7*: Aboard the *Exodus*, Kyrenia Harbor, 80th hour of the hunger strike through 120 hour. *Scene 8*: Dockside, Kyrenia, immediately thereafter.

ACT 1

"Children's Lament"

Children

Scene 1

"Yerushaliam"

D. Cryer

"The Saga of Haganah"

M. Ross, M. Zeller, J. Della Sorte, C. K. Alexander

Scene 2

"The Saga of Haganah" (reprise)

C. K. Alexander

Scene 3

"Give Me One Good Reason"

C. Towers

Scene 4

"Dov's Nightmare"

J. Savage, Victims of the Holocaust

"Karen's Lullaby"

J. Mayro

Scene 5

"Aphrodite"

C. K. Alexander, A. Orfaly

Scene 6

"My Galilee"

D. Cryer, Palestinians

Scene 7

"The Lord Helps Those Who Help Themselves"

M. Ross, Palestinians

Scene 8

"Alphabet Song"

C. Towers, Children

Tactics

Scene 9

"Give Me One Good Reason" (reprise)

C. Towers

Scene 10

"My Brother's Keeper"

D. Cryer

ACT 2

Scene 1

"The Exodus"

M. Ross, Ensemble

Scene 2

"He'll Never Be Mine"

C. Towers

Scene 3

"One Flag"

J. Mayro, Children

Scene 4

"The Lord Helps Those Who Help Themselves" (reprise)

C. K. Alexander

Scene 7

"I See What I Choose to See"
J. Mayro, J. Savage

"Hora-Galilee" (dance)
J. Mayro, J. Savage, Children, Palestinians

"Ari's Promise"
D. Cryer

Scene 8

Finale: "Ari's Promise" (reprise)
The Company

"The Exodus" (reprise)

1971.03 NO, NO, NANETTE

The New 1925 Musical (A Revival of the Musical Comedy) in Three Acts[6]. Book by Otto Harbach and Frank Mandel. (Book) Adapted and directed by Burt Shevelove. (Based on the comedy "My Lady Friends" by Frank Mandel and Emil Nyitray, based on the story "Oh, James"/"His Lady Friends" by May Edington). Music by Vincent Youmans. Lyrics by Irving Caesar and Otto Harbach. Dances and musical numbers staged by Donald Saddler. (Settings and costumes) Designed by Raoul Pene du Bois. Lighting by Jules Fisher. Musical direction and vocal arrangements by Buster Davis. Orchestrations by Ralph Burns. Dance music arranged and incidental music composed by Luther Henderson. Colston and Clements at the Twin Pianos. Sound by Jack Shearing. Assistant choreographer, Mary Ann Niles. Entire production supervised by Busby Berkeley. Produced by Pyxidium Ltd. (Cyma Rubin)[7]. Opened 19 January 1971 at the 46th Street Theatre and closed 4 February 1973 after 861 performances.

CAST (in order of appearance): Pauline: PATSY KELLY. Lucille Early: HELEN GALLAGHER. Sue Smith: RUBY KEELER. Jimmy Smith: JACK GILFORD. Billy Early: BOBBY VAN. Tom Trainor: Roger Rathburn. Nanette: SUSAN WATSON. Flora Latham: K. C. Townshend. Betty Brown: Loni Zoe Ackerman. Winnie Winslow: Pat Lysinger. THE BUSBY BERKELEY GIRLS.

Nanette's Friends: Bob Becker, John Beecher, Joretta Bohannon, Roger Braun, Marcia Brushingham, Kenneth Carr, Jennie Chandler, Kathy Conry, Christine Cox, Kevin Daly, Ed Dixon, Ellen Elias, Mercedes Ellington, Jon Engstrom, Marian Haraldson, Gregg Harlan, Jamie Haskins, Gwen Hillier, Sayra Hummel, Scott Hunter, Dottie Lester, Cheryl Locke, Joanne Lotsko, Mary Ann Niles, Kate O'Brady, Sue Ohman, Jill Owens, Ken Ploss, John Roach, Linda Rose, Ron Schwinn, Sonja Stuart, Monica Tiller, Pat Trott, Phyllis Wallach.

The action takes place on a weekend in early summer of 1925.

Act 1: The home of James Smith, New York City.

Act 2: The garden of Chickadee Cottage, Atlantic City.

Act 3: The living room at Chickadee Cottage, Atlantic City.

ACT 1

"Too Many Rings Around Rosie"
H. Gallagher, Boys, Girls

"I've Confessed to the Breeze"
S. Watson, R. Rathburn

"Call of the Sea"
B. Van, Girls

"I Want to Be Happy"
J. Gilford, S. Watson, R. Keeler, Boys, Girls

"No, No, Nanette"
S. Watson, R. Rathburn

Finaletto Act 1
S. Watson, Boys, Girls

ACT 2

"Peach on the Beach"
S. Watson, Boys, Girls

"Tea for Two"
S. Watson, R. Rathburn, Boys, Girls

"You Can Dance With Any Girl at All"
H. Gallagher, B. Van

Finaletto Act 2
Entire Company

---

[6]Originally produced in New York 16 September 1925 at the Globe Theatre for 321 performances.

[7]This revival originally conceived by Harry Rigby.

ACT 3

"Telephone Girlie"
B. Van, L. Z. Ackerman, K. C. Townshend, P. Lysinger

"Where-Has-My Hubby-Gone-Blues"
H. Gallagher, Boys

"Waiting for You"
S. Watson, R. Rathburn

"Take a Little One-Step" (from LOLLIPOP)
R. Keeler, B. Van, H. Gallagher, P. Kelly, Boys, Girls
(Lyrics by Zelda Sears.)

Finale
Entire Company

1971.04 OH! CALCUTTA!

A Musical Entertainment (Revue) in Two Acts, 13 Scenes[8]. Devised by Kenneth Tynan. Entire production conceived and directed by Jacques Levy. Contributors: Samuel Beckett, Jules Feiffer, Dan Greenburg, John Lennon, Jacques Levy, Leonard Melfi, David Newman and Robert Benton, Sam Shepard, Clovis Trouille, Kenneth Tynan, Sherman Yellen. Music and lyrics by The Open Window (Robert Dennis, Peter Schickele, Stanley Walden). Choreography by Margo Sappington. Scenery by James Tilton. Lighting by David F. Segal. Costumes by Fred Voelpel. Projected media designs by Gardner Compton and Emile Ardolino. Still photography by Michael Childers. Musical director, Norman Bergen. Production supervisor, Michael Thoma. An E.P.I.C. Production. Opened 25 February 1971 at the Belasco Theatre and closed 12 August 1972 after 606 performances. Total for Broadway and Off-Broadway runs: 1310 performances.

CAST: Mel Auston, Raina Barrett, Ray Edelstein, Samantha Harper, Patricia Hawkins, William Knight, Mitchell McGuire, Pamela Pilkenton, Gary Rethmeier, Nancy Tribush.

ACT 1

Prologue

Scene 1

Taking Off the Robe ("Oh! Calcutta!")
The Company

Scene 2

Dick & Jane
R. Barrett, G. Rethmeier

Scene 3

"Suite for Five Letters"
M. McGuire, S. Harper, P. Hawkins, W. Knight, P. Pilkenton

Scene 4

"(Will Answer All) Sincere Replies" (Song and Sketch)
C. Howard, S. Harper, G. Retheimer, J. Shearer

Scene 5

"Paintings of Clovis Trouille"
The Open Window

Scene 6

"Jack & Jill" (Song and Sketch)
P. Hawkins, M. McGuire

Scene 7

Delicious Indignities, (or The Deflowering of Helen Axminster)
S. Harper, W. Knight
(Scene: An Elegantly Appointed Study in Knightsbridge, 1896.)

Scene 8

Was It Good For You Too? ("Green Pants," "I Like the Look")
R. Barrett, C. Howard, W. Knight, P. Pilkenton, G. Retheimer, J. Shearer
(Scene: A Doctor's Office.)

ACT 2[9]

Scene 1

"Much Too Soon"
The Company, The Open Window
(Music and Lyrics by The Open Window and Jacques Levy.)

---

[8]Originally produced in New York Off-Broadway 17 June 1969 at the Eden Theatre for 704 performances.

[9]Added during run to open Act 2:
Who: Whom ("Exchanges of Information")
R. Barrett, C. Howard, D. Rosenbaum

Scene 2
  "One on One" (Clarence and Mildred)
    M. Auston, P. Pilkenton
Scene 3
  Rock Garden
    W. Knight, M. McGuire
    (*Scene*: Saturday afternoon, just after lunch before the ball game.)
Scene 4
  Four in Hand
    M. Auston, M. McGuire, G. Retheimer, J. Shearer
Scene 5
  "Coming Together, Going Together"
    The Company
    (Medley: "I Don't Have a Song to Sing," "I'm an Actor," "Ballerina," "I Want It," "Freeze Music," "I Want It" reprise)

1971.05 # FOLLIES

A Musical in One Act. Book by James Goldman. Music and lyrics by Stephen Sondheim. Directed by Harold Prince and Michael Bennett. Choreography by Michael Bennett. Scenic Production designed by Boris Aronson. Costumes by Florence Klotz. Lighting by Tharon Musser. Musical direction by Harold Hastings. Orchestrations by Jonathan Tunick. Dance music arrangements by John Berkman. Production supervisor, Ruth Mitchell. Associate choreographer, Bob Avian. Produced by Harold Prince in association with Ruth Mitchell. Opened 4 April 1971 at the Winter Garden and closed 1 July 1972 after 522 performances.

CAST (in order of appearance): *Major-Domo*: Dick Latessa. *Sally Durant Plummer*: DOROTHY COLLINS. *Young Sally*: Marti Rolph. *Christine Crane*: ETHEL BARRYMORE COLT. *Willy Wheeler*: Fred Kelly. *Stella Deems*: MARY McCARTHY. *Max Deems*: John J. Martin. *Heidi Schiller*: Justine Johnston. *Chauffeur*: John Grigas. *Meredith Lane*: SHEILA SMITH. *Chet Richards*: Peter Walker. *Roscoe*: MICHAEL BARTLETT. *Deedee West*: Helon Blount. *Sandra Donovan*: Sonja Levkova. *Hattie Walker*: ETHEL SHUTTA. *Young Hattie*: Mary Jane Houdina. *Emily Whitman*: Marcie Stringer. *Theodore Whitman*: Charles Welch. *Vincent*: Victor Griffin. *Vanessa*: Jayne Turner. *Young Vincent*: Michael Misita. *Young Vanessa*: Graciela Daniele. *Solange LaFitte*: FIFI D'ORSAY. *Carlotta Campion*: YVONNE DE CARLO. *Phyllis Rogers Stone*: ALEXIS SMITH. *Benjamin Stone*: JOHN McMARTIN. *Young Phyllis*: Virginia Sandifur. *Young Ben*: Kurt Peterson. *Buddy Plummer*: GENE NELSON. *Young Buddy*: Harvey Evans. *Dimitri Weisman*: Arnold Moss. *Kevin*: Ralph Nelson. *Young Heidi*: Victoria Mallory.
  Party Musicians: Taft Jordan, Aaron Bell, Charles Spies, Robert Curtis. *Showgirls*: Suzanne Briggs, Trudy Carson, Kathie Dalton, Ursula Maschmeyer, Linda Perkins, Margot Travers. *Singers and Dancers*: Graciela Daniele, Mary Jane Houdina, Rita O'Connor, Julie Pars, Suzanne Rogers, Roy Barry, Steve Boockvor, Michael Misita, Joseph Nelson, Ralph Nelson, Ken Urmston, Donald Weismuller.

The action takes place at the present time on the stage of the Weisman Theatre in New York.

MUSICAL NUMBERS
  "Beautiful Girls"
    M. Bartlett, Company
  "Don't Look at Me"
    D. Collins, J. McMartin
  "Waiting for the Girls Upstairs"
    G. Nelson, J. McMartin, A. Smith, D. Collins, H. Evans, K. Peterson, V. Sandifur, M. Rolph
  "Rain on the Roof"
    M. Stringer, C. Welch
  "Ah, Paris!"
    F. D'Orsay
  "Broadway Baby"
    E. Shutta
  "The Road You Didn't Take"
    J. McMartin
  "Bolero d'Amour" (dance)
    V. Griffin, J. Turner
  "In Buddy's Eyes"
    D. Collins
  "Who's That Woman?"
    M. McCarty, Company
  "I'm Still Here"
    Y. DeCarlo

  "Too Many Mornings"
    J. McMartin, D. Collins
  "The Right Girl"
    G. Nelson
  "One More Kiss"
    J. Johnston, V. Mallory
  "Could I Leave You?"
    A. Smith
  Loveland:
    1 — The Folly of Love
      "Loveland"
      Ensemble
      The Spirit of First Love: K. Dalton. *The Spirit of Young Love*: M. Travers. *The Spirit of True Love*: S. Briggs. *The Spirit of Pure Love*: T. Carson. *The Spirit of Romantic Love*: L. Perkins. *The Spirit of Eternal Love*: U. Maschmeyer.
    2 — The Folly of Youth
      Scene: A Bower in Loveland.
      "You're Gonna Love Tomorrow"
      K. Peterson, V. Sandifur
      "Love Will See Us Through"
      H. Evans, M. Rolph
    3 — Buddy's Folly
      Scene: A Thoroughfare in Loveland.
      "The God-Why-Don't You-Love-Me Blues"
      G. Nelson
      (With the assistance of S. Rogers, R. O'Connor.)
    4 — Sally's Folly
      Scene: A Boudoir in Loveland.
      "Losing My Mind"
      D. Collins
    5 — Phyllis's Folly
      Scene: A Honky-Tonk in Loveland.
      "The Story of Lucy and Jessie"
      A. Smith, Dance Ensemble
    6 — Ben's Folly
      Scene: A Supper Club in Loveland.
      "Live, Laugh, Love"
      J. McMartin, Dancing Ensemble

1971.06 # JOHNNY JOHNSON

A Revival of the Legend (Play) with Music in Two Acts, 14 Scenes[10]. Play (book and lyrics) by Paul Green. Music by Kurt Weill. Directed by José Quintero. Choreography by Bertram Ross. Scenery designed by Peter Harvey. Costumes designed by Robert Fletcher. Lighting designed by Roger Morgan. Musical direction by Joseph Klein. Orchestrations by Kurt Weill. Produced by Timothy Gray and Robert Fletcher in association with Midge La Guardia. Opened and closed 11 April 1971 at the Edison Theatre after 1 performance.

CAST (in order of appearance): *Johnny Johnson*: RALPH WILLIAMS. *Minny Belle Tompkins*: ALICE CANNON. *Villagers*: Entire Company. *His Honor The Mayor*: PAUL MICHAEL. *Miz Smith*: June Helmers. *Grandpa Joe*: JAMES BILLINGS. *Photographer*: BOB LYDIARD. *Messenger*: Christopher Klein. *Anguish Howington*: GORDON MINARD. *Aggie (Tompkins)*: CHARLOTTE JONES. *Recruiting Sergeant*: ALEXANDER ORFALY. *Captain Valentine*: NORMAN CHASE. *Dr. McBray*: WAYNE SHERWOOD. *Private Jessell*: Clay Johns. *Goddess of Liberty*: Nadine Lewis. *Wounded French Soldiers*: James Billings, Clay Johns, Paul Michael, Gordon Minard, Alexander Orfaly, Norman Riggins, Wayne Sherwood. *English Sergeant*: NORMAN RIGGINS. *Corporal George*: ALEXANDER ORFALY. *Private Fairfax*: Paul Michael. *Private Goldberger*: JAMES BILLINGS. *Private Harwood*: GORDON MINARD. *Private Svenson*: Clay Johns. *Private (Patrick) O'Day*: Wayne Sherwood. *Johann Lang, German Sniper*: BOB LYDIARD. *French Nurse*: JUNE HELMERS. *Orderly*: Clay Johns. *Doctor*: Norman Riggins. *Sister from the Organization for the Delight of Soldiers Disabled in the Lien of Duty*: Charlotte Jones. *Chief (of the Allied High Command)*: JAMES BILLINGS. *Belgian Major-General*: ALEXANDER ORFALY. *British Commander*: Clay Johns. *French Major-General*: NORMAN RIGGINS. *American Commander*: PAUL MICHAEL. *Scottish Colonel*: Wayne Sherwood. *Captain*: Alexander Orfaly. *Lieutenant*: Clay Johns. *American Priest*: Norman Riggins. *German*

---

[10]Originally produced in New York 19 November 1936 at the 44th Street Theatre for 68 performances. For Musical Numbers, see original 1936 production. The script was revised from Three Acts, 13 Scenes, to Two Acts, 14 Scenes, with the first two acts combined into one.
Added for this production:
  "The Sergeant's Chant" (Act 1, after "Farewell, Goodbye")
    A. Orfaly
Dropped from this production:
  "How Sweetly Friendship Binds"

Priest: Wayne Sherwood. *Military Policeman*: Clay Johns. *Dr. Mahodan*: JAMES BILLINGS. *Miss Newro*: Charlotte Jones. *Dr. Frewd*: ALEXANDER ORFALY. *Brother Thomas*: Paul Michael. *Brother George*: CLAY JOHNS. *Brother Theodore*: NORMAN RIGGINS. *Anguish Howington, Jr.*: Christopher Klein.

Act 1, Scene 1: A village somewhere in America, 1917. *Scene 2*: Minnie Belle's home, a few days later. *Scene 3*: A Recruiting Office, next day. *Scene 4*: The New York Harbor, sometime later. *Scene 5*: A road somewhere in France, several weeks later. *Scene 6*: A trench in the front, some days later. *Scene 7*: A shell-battered churchyard near the front line, before dawn the next day.

Act 2, Scene 1: An army hospital in France, a few days later. *Scene 2*: A French chateau behind the front lines, the next night. *Scene 3*: The edge of a great battlefield, later the same night. *Scene 4*: On the battlefield, a few minutes later. *Scene 5*: A psychiatrist's office in America, some weeks later. *Scene 6*: An insane asylum or house of balm, some years later. *Scene 7*: A street corner in an American city, much later.

1971.07 70, GIRLS, 70

A Musical in Two Acts, a Prologue and 18 Scenes. Book by Fred Ebb and Norman L. Martin. Based on the play "A Breath of Spring" by Peter Coke. Adapted by Joe Masteroff. Music by John Kander. Lyrics by Fred Ebb. Directed by Paul Aaron. Dances and musical numbers staged by Onna White. Sets and lighting by Robert Randolph. Costumes by Jane Greenwood. Musical direction and vocal arrangements by Oscar Kosarin. Orchestrations by Don Walker. Dance music by Dorothea Freitag. Associate choreographer, Martin Allen. Entire production supervised by Stanley Prager. Produced by Arthur Whitelaw in association with Seth Harrison. Opened 15 April 1971 at the Broadhurst Theatre and closed 15 May 1971 after 35 performances.

CAST (in alphabetical order): Thomas Anderson, Tommy Breslin, HANS CONRIED, Robert G. Dare, Sally DeMay, JOEY FAYE, DOROTHEA FREITAG, Ruth Gillette, Lloyd Harris, LILLIAN HAYMAN, HENRIETTA JACOBSON, GIL LAMB, LUCIE LANCASTER, Marjorie Leach, Abby Lewis, Steve Mills, MILDRED NATWICK, Naomi Price, LILLIAN ROTH, GOLDYE SHAW, Beau Tilden, Bobbi Tremain, Jay Velie, COLEY WORTH.

The action takes place at the present time in New York City.

Act 1, Scene 1: The Cornucopia Tea Room. *Scene 2*: The Broadhurst Theatre. *Scene 3*: Ida's Room. *Scene 4*: The Broadhurst Theatre. *Scene 5*: Sadie's Fur Salon. *Scene 6*: The Broadhurst Theatre. *Scene 7*: Lobby of the Sussex Arms. *Scene 8*: The Broadhurst Theatre. *Scene 9*: Bloomingdale's. *Scene 10*: Lobby of the Sussex Arms.

Act 2, Scene 1: The Broadhurst Theatre. *Scene 2*: Arctic Cold Storage Co. *Scene 3*: The Broadhurst Theatre. *Scene 4*: Lobby of the Sussex Arms. *Scene 5*: The Broadhurst Theatre. *Scene 6*: The Coliseum. *Scene 7*: The Broadhurst Theatre. *Scene 8*: A Chapel.

ACT 1
Prologue
"Old Folks"
Company
Scene 1
"Home"
M. Natwick, L. Roth, L. Lancaster, G. Lamb, H. Conried, L. Hayman, G. Shaw
Scene 2
"Broadway, My Street"
L. Hayman, G. Shaw, T. Anderson, J. Faye, L. Harris, H. Jacobson, B. Tilden, B. Tremain, J. Velie, C. Worth
Scene 4
"The Caper"
H. Conried
Scene 6
"Coffee in a Cardboard Cup"
L. Hayman, G. Shaw
Scene 7
"You and I, Love"
S. Mills, A. Lewis, T. Anderson, R. Gillette, L. Harris, B. Tremain, J. Velie, C. Worth
"Do We?"
L. Lancaster, G. Lamb
"Hit It, Lorraine"
M. Natwick, H. Conried, L. Roth, L. Lancaster, D. Freitag
Scene 9
"See the Light"
L. Roth, J. Faye, C. Worth, T. Anderson, J. Velie

ACT 2
Entr'acte
R. Gillette, J. Faye, L. Harris, J. Velie
Scene 1
"Boom Ditty Boom"
M. Natwick, H. Conried, L. Roth, G. Lamb, L. Hayman, L. Lancaster, G. Shaw
Scene 2
"Believe"
L. Hayman, M. Natwick, H. Conried, L. Roth, G. Lamb, L. Lancaster, G. Shaw
Scene 3
"Go Visit"
T. Breslin, H. Jacobson
Scene 4
"70, Girls, 70"
The Company
Scene 5
"The Elephant Song"
M. Natwick, L. Hayman, G. Shaw
Scene 8
"Yes"
M. Natwick, Company

1971.08 (OVID'S) METAMORPHOSES

An Entertainment in Two Acts, 10 Scenes. Adapted and translated with lyrics by Arnold Weinstein from Ovid's 'Metamorphoses.' Music composed and performed by The True Brethren. Directed by Paul Sills. Settings by James Trittipo. Costumes by Noel Taylor. Lighting by H. R. Poindexter. Produced by Zev Bufman. Opened 22 April 1971 at the Ambassador Theatre and closed 3 July 1971 after 35 performances[11].

CAST (in alphabetical order): Lewis Arquette, Regina Baff, Charles Bartlett, Hamid Hamilton Camp, Melinda Dillon, MacIntyre Dixon, Mary Frann, Valerie Harper, Paula Kelly, Richard Libertini, Paul Sand, Richard Schaal, Avery Schreiber, Penny White.

ACT 1
Scene 1
IO was the daughter of a priest, beloved (suddenly) of Jove, who changed her into a cow to protect her from the jealousy of his wife, Juno. Juno was not deceived, however, and tormented Io with a gadfly who drove her from continent to continent until she recovered her human form.
Scene 2
VULCAN AND VENUS AND MARS: Vulcan god of fire, artist in iron and other forged metals, was thrown from Olympus by his mother, Juno, because he was lame and ugly. In revenge Vulcan made a golden throne with magic chains and trapped Juno in it. He also trapped Venus, goddess of love (one of his several wives) and his brother Mars, god of war, in a golden net as they were making love.
Scene 3
PELEUS AND THETIS: Pelus was king of Iolchos. Thetis, a sea nymph, was a comfort to many of the gods, but when it was foretold that her son would be greater than his father, the gods decided to marry her to a mortal, and thus she was given to Peleus as his wife. She changed herself into many forms to avoid him, but he overcame her resistance in a grotto by the sea.
Scene 4
PROCRIS AND CEPHALUS: The hunter Cephalus, though loving his wife Procris, spends 60 days with Aurora. Upon his return he finds Procris in mourning and disguises himself as a merchant to test her fidelity by offering her gifts. Procris is enraged and flees to join Diana, but is eventually reunited with Cephalus, presenting him the spear of Diana. On his next hunting trip, Procris follows him and Cephalus thinking she is an animal in the bush, fires the spear. Procris dies in his arms.
Scene 5
CALLISTO was a nymph a hunting companion of Diana, goddess of chastity and the hunt. Jove fell in love with Callisto, changed himself into Diana, and raped her. When Diana found that Callisto was pregnant she banned her from the tribe. An angry Juno changes her into a bear. When Callisto's son, Orion, was at the point of killing her with his bow, Jove changed them into the constellation of the Archer and the Bear.

ACT 2
Scene 1
PICUS AND CANENS: Picus was a king and a forest god associated with Mars. He was faithful to his wife, the beautiful nymph Canens, and resisted the sorceress Circe, who consequently turned him into a predatory bird, sacred to the Romans.

---
[11]Performed in rotating repertory with *PAUL SILLS' STORY THEATRE*.

Scene 2

PYGMALION (was) revolted by the women he saw around him, (and) created a statue of the ideal woman. He fell in love with it and with this love brought it to life as Galatea.

Scene 3

EUROPA, a professor's daughter, was picking flowers with her playmates when Jove fell in love with her. He turned himself into a bull and carried her off to Crete where she became a mother and a goddess. It may be that Europa's mother was Africa.

Scene 4

PHAETHON discovered that his real father was Apollo, god of the sun, of poetry and of the bow. To prove his parentage, he demanded the privilege of driving for one day the horses who drew the chariot of the sun.

Scene 5

BAUCIS AND PHILEMON were mortals.

FRANK MERRIWELL,
1971.09 or Honor Challenged

A Musical in Two Acts, 12 Scenes. Book by Skip Redwine, Larry Frank and Heywood Gould. (Based on the novel "Frank Merriwell's School Days" by Burt L. Standish [Gilbert Patten].) Music and lyrics by Skip Redwine and Larry Frank. Directed and choreographed by Neal Kenyon. Scenery designed by Tom John. Costumes designed by Frank Thompson. Lighting designed by John Gleason. Orchestrations by Arnold Goland. Musical direction and vocal arrangements by Jack Lee. Conducted by and dance arrangements by Jack Holmes. Associate producer, Aaron Ziegelman. Assistant choreographer, Bonnie Ano. Production coordinator, Don Eckstein. Produced by Sandy Farber and Stanley Barnett in association with Nate Friedman. Opened and closed 24 April 1971 at the Longacre Theatre after 1 performance.

CAST (in order of appearance): Clyde: J. J. Jepson. Ned: Larry Ross. Hugh: WALTER BOBBIE. Belinda Belle Snodd: NEVA SMALL. Snella Jean: Lori Cesar. Una Marie: Ellie Smith. Professor Burrage: Thomas Ruisinger. Mrs. Snodd: LIZ SHERIDAN. Esther Carmichael: Jennifer Williams. Bart Hodge: Peter Shawn. Tad Jones: Gary Keith Steven. Frank Merriwell: LARRY ELLIS. Inza Burrage: LINDA DONOVAN. Manuel: BILL HINNANT.

Act 1, Scene 1: Fardale Train Station: The Blow of a Coward. Scene 2: Picnic Grounds: Death at the Picnic. Scene 3: Fardale Caves: Explosion in Tunnel G. Scene 4: Mrs. Snodd's Boarding House: War! Scene 5: Professor's Laboratory: The Spanish Spy. Scene 6: Mrs. Snodd's Boarding House: By Fair Means or Foul. Scene 7: Picnic Grounds: Terror at the Junction.

Act 2, Scene 1: Picnic Grounds: A Hatred Grows. Scene 2: On the Campus: Waterloo. Scene 3: Picnic Grounds: Into the Enemy's Hands. Scene 4: Burrage Front Porch: Frank Is Missing. Scene 5: Fardale Caves: Death By Dynamite.

ACT 1

Scene 1

"There's No School Like Our School"
Students, Local Girls
"Howdy, Mr. Sunshine"
L. Ellis, G. K. Steven

Scene 2

"Prim and Proper"
Students, Local Girls
"Inza"
L. Ellis

Scene 4

"Look for the Happiness Ahead"
L. Ellis, All

Scene 6

"I'd Be Crazy to Be Crazy Over You"
N. Small, P. Shawn

Scene 7

"Now It's Fall"
Students
"The Fallin'-Out-of-Love Rag"
N. Small, Students, Local Girls, L. Ellis

ACT 2

Scene 1

"Frank, Frank, Frank"
All

Scene 2

"In Real Life"
L. Ellis
"The Broadway of My Heart"
T. Ruisinger, L. Sheridan

Scene 3

"Winter's Here"
Students
"The Pure in Heart"
L. Ellis, All
"I Must Be Crazy" (reprise)
N. Small
"Don't Turn His Picture to the Wall"
G. K. Steven, Students, Local Girls

Scene 5

"Manuel Your Friend"
B. Hinnant
"The Pure in Heart" (reprise)
L. Ellis
"Look For the Happiness Ahead" (reprise)
All

EARL OF RUSTON
1971.10

A Country Rocker (Musical) in One Act. Book and lyrics by C. C. Courtney and Ragan Courtney. Music by Peter Link. (Music) Played by Goatleg (Leon Medica, Bootsie Normand, Chip McDonald, Bobby Thomas). Directed by C. C. Courtney. Production designed by Neil Peter Jampolis. Production manager, Martin Herzer. Produced by David Black. Opened 5 May 1971 at the Billy Rose Theatre and closed 8 May 1971 after 5 performances.

CAST: Earl: C. C. COURTNEY and RAGAN COURTNEY. Leda Pearl Crump: JEAN WALDO BECK. Herself: LEECY R. WOODS MOORE. Sheriff/Bass Guitar: Leon Medica. Mr. Turner/Lead Guitar: Bootsie Normand. Reverend Reynolds/Rhythm Guitar: Chip McDonald. The Doctor/Drums: Bobby Thomas. Ernestine: Lynda Lawley. Mary Lee Woods: Bonnie Guidry. Pianist: John Bergeron.

The action takes place in Ruston, Louisiana.

MUSICAL NUMBERS

"Just Your Old Friend"
"Earl Is Crazy"
"Guitar Song"
"Easy to Be Lonely"
"Standing"
"Der Blues" — Traditional
"Probably"
  (Music by C. C. Courtney and Ragan Courtney.)
"Mama, Earl Done Ate the Toothpaste Again"
  (Music by C. C. Courtney.)
"Silvers Theme"
"Mama, Mama, Mama"
"I've Been Sent Back to the First Grade"
  (Music by C. C. Courtney.)
"The Revival"
"My Name Is Leda Pearl"
  (Music by C. C. Courtney.)
"Insane Poontang"
  (Music by C. C. Courtney and Ragan Courtney.)
"You Still Love Me"
  (Music by C. C. Courtney.)
"Earl Was Ahead"

1971–1972 SEASON

Cyril Ritchard and Robert Morse in SUGAR
Martha Swope/TimePix

1971–1972 SEASON

YOU'RE A GOOD MAN, CHARLIE BROWN

A Musical Entertainment in Two Acts[1]. Book by John Gordon[2]. Based on the comic strip "Peanuts" by Charles M. Schulz. Music and lyrics by Clark Gesner. Directed by Joseph Hardy. Sets and costumes by Alan Kimmel. Lighting by Jules Fisher. Musical staging by Patricia Birch. Musical supervision, arrangements and additional material by Joseph Raposo. Associate producer, Warren Lockhart. Musical director, Jack Holmes. Produced by Arthur Whitelaw and Gene Persson. Opened 1 June 1971 at the John Golden Theatre and closed 27 June 1971 after 31 performances. Total, including Broadway and Off-Broadway runs: 1628 performances.

CAST (in order of speaking): *Linus*: Stephen Fenning. *Charlie Brown*: Dean Stolber. *Patty*: Lee Wilson. *Schroeder*: Carter Cole. *Snoopy*: Grant Cowan. *Lucy*: Liz O'Neal.

Scene: An average day in the life of Charlie Brown.

ACT 1

"You're a Good Man, Charlie Brown"
Entire Company
"Schroeder"
L. O'Neal, C. Cole
"Snoopy"
G. Cowan, D. Stolber
"My Blanket and Me"
S. Fenning
"Kite"
D. Stolber
"Dr. Lucy" (The Doctor Is In)
L. O'Neal, D. Stolber
"Book Report"
D. Stolber, L. O'Neal, S. Fenning, C. Cole

ACT 2

"The Red Baron"
G. Cowan
"T.E.A.M." (The Baseball Game)
Entire Company
"Glee Club Rehearsal"
Entire Company
"Little Known Facts"
L. O'Neal, S. Fenning, D. Stolber
"Suppertime"
G. Cowan
"Happiness"
Entire Company

JESUS CHRIST SUPERSTAR

A Musical in Two Acts, 11 Scenes. Music by Andrew Lloyd Webber. Lyrics by Tim Rice. Conceived for the stage and directed by Tom O'Horgan. Scenic design by Robin Wagner. Costumes designed by Randy Barcelo. Lighting designed by Jules Fisher. Sound designed by Abe Jacob. Musical direction by Marc Pressel. Orchestrations by Andrew Lloyd Webber. Production supervisor, Charles Gray. Assistant conductor, Seymour Miroff. Musical supervisor, Mel Rodnon. Associate producers, (Tyler) Gatchell and (Peter) Neufeld. Produced by Robert Stigwood in association with MCA Inc. by arrangement with David Land. Opened 12 October 1971 at the Mark Hellinger Theatre and closed 1 July 1973 after 711 performances.

CAST (in order of appearance): *Judas Iscariot*: BEN VEREEN. *Jesus of Nazareth*: JEFF FENHOLT. *Mary Magdalene*: YVONNE ELLIMAN. *First Priest*: Alan Braustein. *Second Priest*: Michael Meadows. *Caiaphas*: BOB BINGHAM. *Annas*:

---

[1]Originally produced in New York Off-Broadway 7 March 1967 at the Theater 80 St. Marks for 1,597 performances.
[2]John Gordon is a pseudonym for Clark Gesner and the collective company of the Original Off-Broadway Cast who devised the show.

PHIL JETHRO. *Third Priest*: Steven Bell. *Simon Zealotes, Merchant, Leper*: DENNIS BUCKLEY. *Pontius Pilate*: BARRY DENNEN. *Peter, Merchant, Leper*: MICHAEL JASON. *Maid By the Fire, Leper*: Linda Rios. *Soldier, Judas' Tormentor*: Tom Stovall. *Old Man, Apostle, Merchant, Leper*: Peter Schlosser. *Soldier, Judas' Tormentor*: Paul Sylvan. *King Herod, Merchant, Leper*: PAUL AINSLEY. *Cured Leper, Temple Lady*: Robin Grean. *Cured Leper, Apostle, Merchant, Tormentor (Judas' Death)*: James Sbano. *Cured Leper, Temple Lady*: Laura Michaels. *Cured Leper, Apostle, Merchant, Tormentor (Judas' Death)*: Clifford Lipson. *Cured Leper, Temple Lady, Reporter*: Bonnie Schon. *Cured Leper, Apostle, Reporter*: Pi Douglass. *Cured Leper, Apostle Woman, Temple Lady*: Celia Brin. *Cured Leper, Apostle, Tormentor (Judas' Death)*: Dennis Cooley. *Reporter, Apostle, Temple Lady, Leper*: Anita Morris. *Reporter, Leper*: Ted Neeley. *Reporter, Apostle Woman, Temple Lady, Leper*: Kay Cole. *Reporter, Leper*: Kurt Yaghjian. *Reporter, Apostle, Leper*: Margaret Warncke. *Reporter, Apostle, Leper*: Willie Windsor. *Reporter, Apostle Woman, Temple Lady, Leper*: Ferne Bork. *Reporter, Apostle, Leper*: Samuel E. Wright. *Apostle Woman, Temple Lady, Leper*: Denise Delapenha. *Apostle, Merchant, Leper, Tormentor*: Robalee Barnes. *Apostle, Leper, Reporter, Tormentor (Judas' Death)*: Doug Lucas. *Soul Girl, Leper*: Charlotte Crossley. *Soul Girl, Leper*: Cecelia Norfleet. *Soul Girl, Leper*: Janet Powell. *Judas' Tormentor, Soldier*: Edward Barton. *Judas' Tormentor, Soldier*: Tony Gardner. *And various Palm Sunday Attendants, Alabaster Monsters, the Mob, and Members of the Crowd.*

RANDALL'S ISLAND: Elliott Randall (Electric, Acoustic), Paul Fleisher (Soprano Sax, Tenor Sax, Baritone Sax, Flute, Clarinet), Pot Namanworth (Piano, Organ), Allen Herman (Drums, Percussion), Gary King (Bass Guitar), Jim Miller (Rhythm Guitar).

The action depicts the last seven days in the life of Jesus of Nazareth.

Act 1, Scene 1: Opening. *Scene 2*: Bethany, Friday Night. *Scene 3*: Jerusalem, Sunday. *Scene 4*: Pontius Pilate's house, Monday. *Scene 5*: Tuesday.

Act 1, Scene 1: Thursday night. *Scene 2*: The Garden. *Scene 3*: Pilate's Palace, Friday. *Scene 4*: House of Herod. *Scene 5*: Pilate's Palace. *Scene 6*: Golgotha.

ACT 1

Scene 1
"Heaven on their Minds"
B. Vereen
Scene 2
"What's the Buzz"
J. Fenholt, Y. Elliman, Apostles, Women
"Strange Thing Mystifying"
B. Vereen, J. Fenholt, Apostles, Women
"Everything's All Right"
Y. Elliman, B. Vereen, J. Fenholt, Apostles, Women
Scene 3
"This Jesus Must Die"
B. Bingham, P. Jethro, Priests, Company
"Hosanna"
B. Bingham, J. Fenholt, Company
"Simon Zealotes"
D. Buckley, Company
"Poor Jerusalem"
J. Fenholt
Scene 4
"Pilate's Dream"
B. Dennen
"The Temple"
J. Fenholt, Company
"I Don't Know How to Love Him"
Y. Elliman, J. Fenholt
Scene 5
"Damned For All Time"
B. Vereen, P. Jethro, B. Bingham, Priests

ACT 2

Scene 1
"The Last Supper"
J. Fenholt, B. Vereen, Apostles
Scene 2
"Gethsemane"
J. Fenholt
"The Arrest"
M. Jason, J. Fenholt, Apostles, Reporters, B. Bingham, P. Jethro
"Peter's Denial"
L. Rios, M. Jason, T. Stovall, P. Schlosser, Y. Elliman

263

Scene 3
  "Pilate and Christ"
    B. Dennen, T. Stovall, J. Fenholt, Company
Scene 4
  "King Herod's Song"
    P. Ainsley
  "Could We Start Again, Please"
    Y. Elliman, M. Jason
  "Judas' Death"
    B. Vereen, P. Jethro, B. Bingham
Scene 5
  "Trial Before Pilate"
    B. Dennen, B. Bingham, J. Fenholt, the Mob
  "Superstar"
    B. Vereen, Company
Scene 6
  "The Crucifixion"
    J. Fenholt, Company
  "John 19:41"
    Orchestra

AIN'T SUPPOSED TO DIE A NATURAL DEATH

1971.13

Tunes from Blackness (A Musical) in Two Acts. Book, words and music by Melvin Van Peebles. Directed by Gilbert Moses. Scenery by Kert Lundell. Costumes by Bernard Johnson. Lighting by Martin Aronstein. Musical direction and supervision by Harold Wheeler. Sound by Jack Shearing. Associate producer, Howard Friedman. Produced by Eugene V. Wolsk, Charles Blackwell, Emanuel Azenberg and Robert Malina. Opened 20 October 1971 at the Ethel Barrymore Theatre, moved 17 November 1971 to the Ambassador Theatre and closed 30 July 1972 after 325 performances.

CAST (in order of appearance): Gloria Edwards, Dick Williams, Ralph Wilcox, Joe Fields, Marilyn B. Coleman, Arthur French, Carl Gordon, Madge Wells, Lauren Jones, Clebert Ford, Sati Jamal, Jimmy Hayeson, Toney Brealond, Beatrice Winde, Albert Hall, Garrett Morris, Bill Duke, Minnie Gentry.

The action takes place here and now.

ACT 1
  "Just Don't Make No Sense"
    A. French
  "(The) Coolest Place in Town"
    G. Edwards
  "You Can Get Up Before Noon Without Being a Square"
    R. Wilcox
  "Mirror Mirror on the Wall"
    J. Fields
  "Come Raising Your Leg on Me"
    M. B. Coleman
  "You Gotta Be Holdin' Out Five Dollars on Me"
    C. Gordon, M. Wells
  "Sera Sera Jim"
    L. Jones
  "Catch That on the Corner"
    C. Ford
  "The Dozens"
    J. Hayeson
  "Funky Girl on Motherless Broadway"
    T. Brealond

ACT 2
  "Tenth and Greenwich"
    B. Winde
  "Heh Heh (Chuckle) Good Mornin' Sunshine"
    A. French
  "You Ain't No Astronaut"
    J. Hayeson
  "Three Boxes of Longs Please"
    A. Hall

  "Lily Done the Zampoughi Every Time I Pulled Her Coattail"
    G. Morris, B. Alston
  "I Got the Blood"
    B. Duke
  "Salamaggi's Birthday"
    D. Williams
  "Come on Feet Do Your Thing"
    S. Jamal
  "Put a Curse on You"
    M. Gentry
  (Finale: "Just Don't Make No Sense" reprise)
    (Entire Company)

TO LIVE ANOTHER SUMMER— TO PASS ANOTHER WINTER

1971.14

A Musical Entertainment (Revue from Israel[3]) in Two Acts. Written by Hayim Hefer. Music by Dov Seltzer. Additional music by David Krivoshei, Alexander Argov, Naomi Shemer. Additional lyrics by Naomi Shemer. Lyrics translated mostly by David Paulsen. Directed and choreographed by Jonathan Karmon. Production (settings, lighting) designed by Neil Peter Jampolis. Costumes by Lydia Pincus Gany. Music arranged and conducted by David Krivoshei. Musical supervisor, Gary McFarland. Sound designed by Anthony Alloy. Production supervisor, Martin Herzer. Produced by Leonard Soloway. Opened 21 October 1971 at the Helen Hayes Theatre, moved 10 January 1972 to the Lunt-Fontanne Theatre and closed 19 March 1972 after 173 performances.

CAST: RIVKA RAZ, ARIC LAVIE, YONA ATARI, ILI GORLIZKI, HANAN GOLD-BLATT.
  Singers: Abigail Atarri, Lisa Butbul, David Devon, Rafi Ginat, Sarah Golan, Ronit Goldblatt, Moses Goldstein, Lenore Grant, Mordechai Hamer, Yochai Azani, Judith Rosenberg, Tslila Steren, Hillik Zadok. Dancers: Zvulun Cohen, Claude Dolgicer, Katya Dror, David Glazer, Nava Harari, Yuval Harat, Hama Kiviti, Ruth Lerman, Joseph Maimon, Riki Oren, Adam Pasternak, Hadassa Shachar, Ofira Tishler, Tuvia Tishler, Efraim Zamir, Miriam Zamir.

ACT 1
  "Son of Man"
    R. Raz, A. Lavie, Company
    (Translated by David Axelrod.)
  "The Sacrifice"
    A. Lavie, Y. Hazani, Company
  "What Are the Basic Things?"
    I. Gorlizki, Company
    (Translated by Lillian Burstein.)
  "The Grove of Eucalyptus"
    R. Raz, Company
    (Music and Lyrics by Naomi Shemer. Translated by George Sherman.)
  "The Tradition That Was Destroyed: Hasidic Medley"
    H. Goldblatt, I. Gorlizki, R. Raz, Y. Atari, Company
    (Music by Sarah and Ehud Zweig, David Weinkranz, Rabbi Carlibach.)
  "The Boy With the Fiddle"
    A. Lavie
    (Music by Alexander Argov.)
  "Can You Hear My Voice?"
    Y. Atari, Company
    (Music by Samuel Kraus. Lyrics by Rachel. Translated by George Sherman.)
  "Mediteranee"
    Company
  "When My Man Returns"
    R. Raz
    (Music by George Moustaki.)
  "Better Days"
    Y. Atari, Company
  "Ha'am Haze"
    Company

ACT 2
  "To Live Another Summer, To Pass Another Winter"
    Y. Atari, A. Lavie, H. Goldblatt, R. Raz, Company

---

[3]The entire company of "To Live Another Summer, To Pass Another Winter" comes from Israel.

"Hora Hora"
  Company
  (*Music by* Alexander Argov.)
"Noah's Ark"[4]
  I. Gorlizki
  (*Music by* Naomi Shemer.)
"Don't Destroy the World"
  A. Lavie
  (*Lyrics in collaboration with* Hayim Guri.)
"Give Shalom and Sabbath to Jeruslaem"
  Company
"Sorry We Won"
  I. Gorlizki, Y. Atari, H. Goldblatt
  (*Music by* David Krivoshei.)
"I'm Alive"
  R. Raz, Company
  (*Music by* David Krivoshei.)
"Give Me a Star"
  R. Raz, A. Lavie, Company
  (*Music by* David Krivoshei.)
Finale
  Company

1971.15 **ON THE TOWN**

A Revival of the Musical Comedy in Two Acts, 17 Scenes[5]. Book and lyrics[6] by Betty Comden and Adolph Green. Book based on an idea by Jerome Robbins. Music by Leonard Bernstein. Directed and choreographed by Ron Field. Scenery designed by James Trittipo. Costumes designed by Ray Aghayan, Bob Mackie. Lighting designed by Tharon Musser. Musical direction by Milton Rosenstock. Orchestrations by Leonard Bernstein, Hershy Kay. Assistant choreographer, Michael Shawn. Musical co-ordinator, Dorothea Freitag. Associate producers, Rick Mandell, Allen Litke. The Ron Field Production. Produced by Jerry Schlossberg and Vista Productions. Opened 31 October 1971 at the Imperial Theatre and closed 1 January 1972 after 65 performances.

CAST (in order of appearance): *Workman:* David Wilder. *Chip:* JESS RICHARDS. *Ozzie:* REMAK RAMSAY. *Gabey:* RON HUSMANN. *Flossie:* Carol Petri. *Flossie's Friend:* Marybeth Kurdock. *Bill Poster:* Don Croll. *Little Old Lady:* Zoya Leporska. *Announcer:* Orrin Reiley. *Ivy Smith:* DONNA McKECHNIE. *Hildy:* BERNADETTE PETERS. *S. Uperman:* David Wilder. *Figment:* Orrin Reiley. *Claire:* PHYLLIS NEW-MAN. *Maude P. Dilly:* Fran Stevens. *Pitkin:* Tom Avera. *Lucy Schmeeler:* Marilyn Cooper. *Gina Henie:* Gina Paglia. *Master of Ceremonies at Diamond Eddie's:* Dennis Roth. *Diana Dream:* Sandra Dorsey. *Master of Ceremonies at Congacabana:* Don Croll. *Senorita Dolores:* Laura Kenyon. *Bimmy:* Larry Merritt. *Coney Island Zoot Suit Dancers:* John Mineo, Tony Stevens.

  Singers: Martha Danielle, Sandra Dorsey, Bobbi Franklin, Laura Kenyon, Gail Nelson, Marie Santell, Don Croll, Richard Marr, Orrin Reiley, Dennis Roth, Luke Stover, David Wilder, Craig Yates. *Dancers:* Carole Bishop, Eileen Casey, Jill Cook, Nancy Dalton, Marybeth Kurdock, Nancy Lynch, Gina Paglia, Pamela Peadon, Carol Petri, Andy G. Bew, Paul Charles, Larry Merritt, John Mineo, Jeff Phillips, Ken Scalice, Doug Spingler, Tony Stevens, Chester Walker.

The action takes place in New York City in June, 1944.

Act 1, Scene 1: Brooklyn Navy Yard. *Scene 2:* Subway Train. *Scene 3:* New York Street. *Scene 4:* Miss Turnstiles. *Scene 5:* Taxi Cab. *Scene 6:* Museum of Natural History. *Scene 7:* New York Street. *Scene 8:* Carnegie Hall. *Scene 9:* Claire's Apartment. *Scene 10:* Hildy's Apartment. *Scene 11:* Times Square.

Act 2, Scene 1: Night Clubs, (a) Diamond Eddie's Manhattan Roof, (b) Congacabana, (c) Slam-Bang. *Scene 2:* Subway Train. *Scene 3:* Imaginary Coney Island. *Scene 4:* Coney Island Express. *Scene 5:* Coney Island. *Scene 6:* Brooklyn Navy Yard.

ACT 1

  "I Feel Like I'm Not Out of Bed"
    Workmen

---

[4]Dropped during run and national tour and replaced with:
  "I Never Wanted to Be a Hero"
    H. Goldblatt, Company
    (*Music by* David Krivoshei. .)
[5]Originally produced in New York 28 December 1944 at the Adelphi Theatre for 462 performances.
[6]Additional lyrics by Leonard Bernstein.

"New York, New York"
  J. Richards, R. Ramsay, R. Husman
"Miss Turnstiles Ballet"
  Contestants, D. McKechnie, Manhatanites
"Come Up to My Place"
  B. Peters, J. Richards
"I Get Carried Away"
  P. Newman, R. Ramsay
"Lonely Town"
  R. Husmann, New Yorkers
"Do, Re, Do"
  D. McKechnie, F. Stevens, Teachers, Students
"I Can Cook Too"
  B. Peters, J. Richards
"Lucky to Be Me"
  R. Husmann, New Yorkers
"Times Square Ballet"
  Entire Company
ACT 2
  So Long Baby Ice Revue
    G. Paglia, Skaters
  Nightclub Song ("I'm Blue")
    S. Dorsey
  Nightclub Song (Spanish)
    L. Kenyon
  "You Got Me"
    P. Newman, R. Ramsay, B. Peters, J. Richards
  "I Understand"
    T. Avera, M. Cooper
  "Playground of the Rich Ballet"
    R. Husmann, D. McKechnie, High Society Dancers
  "Some Other Time"
    P. Newman, B. Peters, J. Richards, R. Ramsay
  "Coney Island Hep Cats" (dance)
    C. Petri, M. Kurdock, J. Mineo, T. Stevens
  "New York, New York" (reprise)
    Entire Company

1971.16 **THE GRASS HARP**

A Musical in One Act, 6 Scenes. Book and lyrics by Kenward Elmslie. Based on the novel and play of the same name by Truman Capote. Music by Claibe Richardson. Directed by Ellis Rabb. (Scenery) Design and lighting by James Tilton. Costumes by Nancy Potts. Musical director, Theodore Saidenberg. Musical arrangements by J. (Billy) Ver Planck. Choreography by Rhoda Levine. Additional orchestrations by Jonathan Tunick, Robert Russell Bennett. Dance and incidental music by John Berkman. Associate producer, Michael Kasdan. Technical advisor, Frank Hauser. A Production of the University of Michigan Professional Theatre Program. Produced by Theatre 1972 (Richard Barr, Charles Woodward, Michael Harvey.) Opened 2 November 1971 at the Martin Beck Theatre and closed 6 November 1971 after 7 performances.

CAST (in order of appearance): *Dolly Talbo:* BARBARA COOK. *Collin Talbo:* RUSS THACKER. *Catherine Creek:* CAROL BRICE. *Verena Talbo:* RUTH FORD. *Maude Riordan:* Christine Stabile. *Dr. Morris Ritz:* MAX SHOWALTER. *Judge Cool:* JOHN BARAGREY. *Babylove:* KAREN MORROW. *Heavenly Pride and Joys:* Kelly Boa, Trudy Bordoff, Colin Dufy, Eva Grant, David Craig Moskin. *Sheriff Amos Legrand:* Harvey Vernon.

The action takes place at the Talbo House, in Joy City and in River Woods, in the past.

Scene 1: The Talbo Backyard. *Scene 2:* The Talbo House. *Scene 3:* The Tree-house in River Woods. *Scene 4:* The Jail. *Scene 5:* Joy City. *Scene 6:* The Tree-house.

MUSICAL NUMBERS
Scene 1
  "Dropsy Cure Weather"
    B. Cook, C. Brice, R. Thacker
  "This One Day"
    R. Thacker

"This One Day" dance
R. Thacker, C. Stabile

Scene 2
"Think Big Rich"
M. Showalter
"If There's Love Enough"
C. Brice
"Yellow Drum"
B. Cook, C. Brice, R. Thacker

Scene 3
"Marry With Me"
C. Brice
"I'll Always Be in Love"
B. Cook
"Floozies"
R. Thacker
The Babylove Miracle Show:
"Call Me Babylove"
K. Morrow
"Walk into Heaven"
K. Morrow
"Hang a Little Moolah on the Washline"
K. Morrow, the Pride'n Joys
"Talkin' in Tongues"
K. Morrow
"Whooshin' Through My Flesh"
K. Morrow, C. Brice, B. Cook, R. Thacker, Company
"Walk into Heaven" (reprise)
K. Morrow
"Something For Nothing"
M. Showalter

Scene 4
"Indian Blues"
C. Brice, Company
"Take a Little Sip"
R. Thacker, B. Cook, C. Brice, C. Stabile, Company

Scene 5
"Yellow Drum" (reprise)
Company
"What Do I Do Now?"
R. Ford

Scene 6
"Pick Yourself a Flower"
K. Morrow, Company
"The Flower Fortune Dance"
Company
"Reach Out"
B. Cook, Company

1971.17   ONLY FOOLS ARE SAD

A Musical from Israel (Ish Hassid Haya[7]) in Two Acts, in Hebrew and English. Book by Dan Almagor, based on old Hassidic stories and parables. Translated by Shimon Wincelberg and Valerie Arnon. Music derived from Hassidic songs, arranged by Yohanan Zarai and Gil Aldema. Lyrics translated by Robert Friend. Directed by Yossi Yzraely. Musical instructor and advisor, Hanna Hakohen. Scenery by Dani Kanavan. Scenery supervised by Herbert Senn. Costumes supervised by Helen Pond. Lighting by Yehiel Orgal. Lighting supervised by Robert Brand. Consultant on English speech, Nora Dunfee. Produced by Yaacov Agmon under the patronage of the Prime Minister of Israel, Mrs. Golda Meir. Opened 22 November 1971 at the Edison Theatre and closed 26 March 1972 after 144 performances.

CAST: Galia Ishay, Danny Litanny, Don Maseng, Shlomo Nitzan, Michal Noy, Aviva Schwarz.

ACT 1[8]
"Once There Was a Melody ... "
Entire Company
Isaac, the Baker (The Treasure)
Narrators: D. Litanny, M. Noy. Issac: G. Ishay.
"A Merry Melody"
Entire Company
Berl, the Tailor (Opening a New Account)
Berl, the tailor: D. Maseng. Rabbi Levy Itzhak: S. Nitzan.
The Promise That Was Kept
Narrator: D. Litanny.
Don't Suck the Bones[9]
Narrator: S. Nitzan.
Eat, Lord, and Enjoy
Narrator: M. Noy.
"Tell Me What the Rain Is Saying"[10]
A. Schwarz (soloist)
Don't Sell It Cheap[11]
Narrator: S. Nitzan.
The Woman who sold her place in Paradise[12]
Narrator: M. Noy. The woman: G. Ishay.
"A Drinking Song"
D. Maseng (soloist)
The Ten Ruble Note
Narrator: S. Nitzan.
"Kol Rinah Vishu'ah"
Entire Company
Gedaliah, the tar-maker
Narrator: A. Schwarz. Rabbi Israel Ba'al Shem Tov: S. Nitzan. Gedaliah, the tar-maker: D. Litanny.

ACT 2
The Goat
Narrators: D. Maseng, M. Noy. The son: G. Ishay.
"Forest, Forest"[13]
M. Noy (soloist)
Smoking on the Sabbath
Narrator: S. Nitzan.
"Bim-Bam-Bom"
Entire Company
Waiting for the Messiah
Narrator: M. Noy. Rabbi Moshe Teitelbaum: D. Maseng.
The Passing of the Ba'al Shem Tov
Narrator: D. Litanny.
Haim, the goose-herder
G. Ishay
Getzl, the shoemaker (Aleph ... beth)
D. Litanny
The Rabbi who promised to wait
Narrator: S. Nitzan.
A Letter to the Rabbi
D. Maseng (soloist)

---

[8]Added during the run:
The Rich and the Poor (Act 1)
S. Nitzan
"Veha'er Eineinu" (Carlebach) (Act 1)
Entire Company
The Hassid's Dilemma (Act 1)
Narrator: S. Nitzan.
The Beggar and the Rabbi (Act 1)
Narrator: S. Nitzan.
"Hoshia et Amecha" (Act 2)
Entire Company
[9]Dropped during the run.
[10]Dropped during the run.
[11]Dropped during the run.
[12]Dropped during the run.
[13]Dropped during the run.

---

[7]In literal English, Once There Was a Hassid.

"Angel, Angel ... "
 G. Ishay
"Only Fools Are Sad"
 A. Schwarz (soloist)
"Avreymele Melamed"
 D. Litanny, S. Nitzan, D. Maseng (soloists)
"A Sabbath Song"
 S. Nitzan (soloist)
"And God Said unto Jacob"
 D. Litanny (soloist)

TWO GENTLEMEN OF VERONA

1971.18

A Musical in Two Acts[14]. Book by John Guare and Mel Shapiro. Based on the play of the same name by William Shakespeare. Music by Galt MacDermott. Lyrics by John Guare. Directed by Mel Shapiro. Setting by Ming Cho Lee. Costumes by Theoni V. Aldredge. Lighting by Lawrence Metzler. Choreography by Jean Erdman. Musical supervision by Harold Wheeler. Additional musical staging by Dennis Nahat. Sound by Jack Shearing. Associate producer, Bernard Gersten. Produced by the New York Shakespeare Festival (Joseph Papp, Producer). Opened 1 December 1971 at the St. James Theatre and closed 20 May 1973 after 614 performances. Total including Broadway and Off-Broadway runs: 628 performances.

CAST (in order of appearance): *Thurio*: Frank O'Brien. *Speed*: Jose Perez. *Valentine*: CLIFTON DAVIS. *Proteus*: RAUL JULIA. *Julia*: DIANA DAVILA. *Lucetta*: Alix Elias. *Launce*: JOHN BOTTOMS. *Antonio*: Frederic Warriner. *Crab*: Phineas. *Duke of Milan*: NORMAN MATLOCK. *Silvia*: JONELLE ALLEN. *Tavern Host*: Frederic Warriner. *Eglamour*: ALVIN LUM.
 Quartet: Black Passion: Sheila Gibbs, Signa Joy, Kenneth Lowry, Sakinah Mahammud. *Citizens of Verona and Milan*: Loretta Abbott, Christopher Alden, Roger Briant, Douglas Brickhouse, Stockard Channing, Paul DeJohn, Nancy Denning, Richard DeRusso, Arthur Erickson, Georgyn Geetlein, Sheila Gibbs, Jeff Goldblum, Edward Henkel, Albert Insinnia, Jane Jaffe, Signa Joy, Kenneth Lowry, Sakinah Mahammud, Otis Sallid, Madeline Swift.

The action takes place in Verona, Milan and the Forest.

ACT 1[15]
 "Summer, Summer"
 Ensemble
 "I Love My Father"
 Ensemble
 "That's a Very Interesting Question"
 R. Julia, C. Davis
 "I'd Like to be a Rose"
 R. Julia, C. Davis
 "Thou, Julia, Thou Has Metamorphosed Me"
 R. Julia
 "Symphony"
 R. Julia, Ensemble
 "I Am Not Interested in Love"
 D. Davila
 "Love, Is That You?"
 F. O'Brien, G. Geetlein
 "Thou, Proteus, Thou Has Metamorphosed Me"
 D. Davila
 "What Does a Lover Pack?"
 D. Davila, R. Julia, Ensemble
 "Pearls"
 J. Bottoms
 "I Love My Father" (reprise)
 R. Julia

[14]First produced Off-Broadway as *THE TWO GENTLEMEN OF VERONA* 27 July 1971 at the Delacorte Theatre for 14 performances, plus 23 performances on the New York Shakespeare Festival Mobile Tour throughout New York City.
[15]No song list appears in the program. Song list prepared from the production manuscript and recording.

"Two Gentlemen of Verona"
 D. Davila, A. Elias
"Follow the Rainbow"
 C. Davis, J. Perez, R. Julia, J. Bottoms, D. Davila, A. Elias
"Where's North?"
 C. Davis, J. Perez, V. Matlock, J. Allen, F. O'Brien, Ensemble
"Bring All the Boys Back Home"
 N. Matlock, F. O'Brien, Ensemble
"Love's Revenge"
 C. Davis
"To Whom It May Concern Me"
 J. Allen, C. Davis
"Night Letter"
 J. Allen, C. Davis
"Love's Revenge" (reprise)
 C. Davis, R. Julia, J. Perez, J. Bottoms
"Calla Lily Lady"
 R. Julia

ACT 2
 "Land of Betrayal"
 A. Elias
 "Thurio's Samba"
 F. O'Brien, N. Matlock, Ensemble
 "Hot Lover"
 J. Bottoms, J. Perez
 "What a Nice Idea"
 D. Davila
 "Who Is Silvia"
 R. Julia, F. Warriner, Ensemble
 "Love Me"
 J. Allen, Ensemble
 "Eglamour"
 A. Lum, J. Allen
 "Kidnapped"
 D. Davila, N. Matlock, R. Julia, F. O'Brien, Ensemble
 "Mansion"
 C. Davis
 "Eglamour" (reprise)
 J. Allen, A. Lum
 "What's a Nice Girl Like Her"
 R. Julia
 "Dragon Fight"
 Dragon, A. Lum, R. Julia, C. Davis
 "Don't Have the Baby"
 D. Davila, A. Elias,, J. Perez, C. Davis
 "Love Is That You" (reprise)
 F. O'Brien, A. Elias
 "Milkmaid"
 J. Bottoms, S. Gibbs
 Finale: "I Love My Father," "Love Has Driven Me Sane"
 Full Company

WILD AND WONDERFUL

1971.19

A "Big City" Fable (Musical) in Two Acts. Book by Phil Phillips. Based on an original work by Bob Brotherton and Bob Miller. Music and lyrics by Bob Goodman. Settings by Stephen Hendrickson. Directed by Burry Fredrik. Dances and musical numbers staged by Ronn Forella. Costumes by Frank Thompson. Lighting by Neil Peter Jampolis. Musical direction, vocal arrangements and dance music composed and arranged by Thom Janusz. Orchestrations by Luther Henderson. Associate producer, John C. O'Regan. Produced by Rick Hobard in association with Raymonde Weil. Opened and closed 7 December 1971 at the Lyceum Theatre after 1 performance.

CAST (in order of appearance): *Jenny*: LAURA McDUFFIE. *Charlie*: WALTER WILLISON. *Lionel Masters*: ROBERT BURR. *Brother John*: LARRY SMALL. *Father Desmond*: TED THURSTON.
 (Ensemble): *Yveline*: Yveline Baudez. *Pam*: Pam [Pamela] Blair . *Mary Ann*: Mary Ann Brauning. *Carol*: Carol Conte. *Bob*: Bob Daley. *Anna Maria*: Anna Maria Fanizzi. *Marcelo*: Marcelo Gamboa *Adam*: Adam Grammis. *Patti*: Patti Haine. *Ann*: Ann Reinking. *Jimmy*: Jimmy Roddy. *Steven*: Steven Vincent. *Eddie*: Eddie Wright, Jr.

The action takes place in The Big City.

ACT 1

"Wild and Wonderful" Dance
  Company
"My First Moment"
  L. McDuffie
"I Spy"
  W. Willison
"Desmond's Dilemma"
  T. Thurston, L. Small
"Moment Is Now"
  W. Willison, Ensemble
"Something Wonderful Can Happen"
  L. McDuffie
"Chances"
  L. McDuffie, R. Burr, A Reinking, M. A. Bruning, C. Conte, A. M. Fanizzi
"Jenny"
  W. Willison
"Fallen Angels"
  L. Small, Dropouts
Dance
  P. Blair, J. Roddy, Dropots

ACT 2

"Petty Crime"
  L. McDuffie, Judge, Company
"Come a Little Closer"
  L. McDuffie, W. Willison
"Is This My Town"
  L. McDuffie
"You Can Reach the Sun"
  L. Small, Dropouts
"A Different Kind of World"
  T. Thurston
"Wait For Me"
  W/ Willison
"Wild and Wonderful" (reprise)
  Company

1971.20

INNER CITY

A Street Cantata in Two Acts, 10 Scenes. Based on the book "The Inner City Mother Goose" by Eve Merriam. Music by Helen Miller. Lyrics by Eve Merriam. Conceived and directed by Tom O'Horgan. Scenery by Robin Wagner. Costumes by Joseph G. Aulisi. Lighting by John Dodd in association with Jane Reisman. Orchestrations and (musical) arrangements by Gordon (Lowry) Harrell. Musical direction by Clay Fullum. Vocal arrangements by Helen Miller. Sound by Gary Harris. Associate producers, Harvey Milk, John M. Nagel. Production co-ordinator, Charlotte Dicker. Produced by Joseph Kipness, Lawrence Kasha, Tom O'Horgan in association with RCA Records. Opened 19 December 1971 at the Ethel Barrymore Theatre and closed 11 March 1972 after 97 performances.

CAST: Joy Garrett, Carl Hall, Delores Hall, Fluffer Hirsch, LINDA HOPKINS, Paulette Ellen Jones, Larry Marshall, Allan Nicholls, Florence Tarlow.

The action takes place at the present time in New York City.

Act 1, Scene 1: Nub of the Nation. *Scene 2*: Urban Mary. *Scene 3*: Deep in the Night. *Scene 4*: Take-a-Tour, Congressman. *Scene 5*: The Spirit of Education

Act 2, Scene 1: Wisdom. *Scene 2*: Starlight. *Scene 3*: Crooked Man. *Scene 4*: Kindness. *Scene 5*: If.

ACT 1

Scene 1

"Fee Fi Fo Fum"
  L. Hopkins
"Now I Lay Me"
  C. Hall, D. Hall, A. Nicholls
"Locks"/"I Had a Little Teevee"
  F. Hirsch
"Hushabye Baby"/"My Mother Said"
  P. E. Jones
"Diddle Diddle Dumpling"/"Rub A Dub Dub"
  L. Marshall

"You'll Find Mice"
  L. Hopkins
"Ding Dong Bell"
  C. Hall, Cast
"The Brave Old City of New York"
  J. Garrett
"Urban Renewal"
  L. Hopkins
"The Nub of the Nation"
  Cast

Scene 2

"Mary, Mary"
  Cast
"City Life"
  F. Tarlow
"One Misty Moisty Morning"
  L. Marshall
"Jack Be Nimble"
  C. Hall, F. Hirsch, L. Marshall
"If Wishes Were Horses"
  D. Hall

Scene 3

"One Man"/"Deep in the Night"
  L. Hopkins

Scene 4

"Statistics"/"12 Rooftops Leaping"/"Take-A-Tour, Congressman"
  Cast
"Simple Simon"
  L. Marshall, A. Nicholls, Cast
"Poverty Program"
  Cast
"One, Two"
  C. Hall, Cast
"Tom, Tom"
  A. Nicholls
"Hickety, Pickety"
  Cast
"Half Alive"
  D. Hall

Scene 5

"This Is the Way We Go to School"
  Cast
"The Spirit of Education"
  F. Tarlow
"Little Jack Horner"
  Cast
"Subway Dream"
  L. Marshall
"Christmas Is Coming"
  F. Hirsch
"I'm Sorry Says the Machine"
  L. Marshall, Cast
"Jeremiah Obadiah"
  L. Marshall
"Riddle Song"
  Cast
"Shadow of the Sun"
  Cast

ACT 2

Scene 1

"Boys and Girls Come Out to Play"
  Cast
"Summer Nights"
  J. Garrett, D. Hall, P. E. Jones
"Lucy Locket"
  F. Hirsch
"Winter Nights"
  L. Hopkins, F. Tarlow

"Wisdom"
L. Marshall
"The Hooker" (You Make It Your Way)
J. Garrett
Scene 2
"Wino Will"/"Man in the Doorway"
P. E. Jones
"Starlight, Starbright"
D. Hall
"The Cow Jumped Over the Moon"
L. Marshall
"The Dealer" (You Push It You Way)
A. Nicholls
Scene 3
"Taffy"
C. Hall, F. Hirsch, Cast
"Numbers"
L. Marshall, Cast
"The Pickpocket"
C. Hall
"Law and Order"
D. Hall
Scene 4
"Kindness"
A. Nicholls, Cast
"As I Went Over"
A. Nicholls
"There Was a Little Man"
Cast
"Who Killed Nobody"
Cast
Scene 5
"It's My Belief"
L. Hopkins
"Street Sermon"
C. Hall
"The Great If"
C. Hall
"On This Rock"
Cast
"The Great If" (reprise)
Cast

1971.21   ANNE OF GREEN GABLES

A Musical in Two Acts, 23 Scenes. (Book) Adapted by Donald Harron. Based on the novel of the same name by Lucy M. Montgomery. Music by Norman Campbell. Lyrics by Donald Harron and Norman Campbell. Additional lyrics by Mavor Moore and Elaine Campbell. Directed and choreographed by Alan Lund. Production (scenery) designed by Murray Laufer. Costumes by Marie Day. Lighting by Ronald Montgomery. Musical director and orchestrations by John Fenwick. Associate music director, Fen Watkin. Associate lighting designer, Gary Craswell. A Canadian National Musical Theatre Production. Produced by the New York City Center of Music and Drama (Norman Singer, Executive director) in association with the Charlottetown Festival (Prince Edward Island, Canada). Opened 21 December 1971 at the New York City Center and closed 2 January 1972 after 16 performances.

CAST (in order of appearance): *Mrs. Rachel Lynde*: Maud Whitmore. *Mrs. MacPherson*: Cleone Duncan. *Mrs. Barry*: Nancy Kerr. *Mrs. Sloane*: Flora MacKenzie. *Mrs. Pye*: Kathryn Watt. *The Minister*: Lloyd Malenfant. *Reverend Smythe Hawkinson*: Jack Northmore. *Earl, the mailman*: Bill Hosie. *Cecil, the farmer*: George Merner. *Marilla Cuthbert*: ELIZABETH MAWSON. *Matthew Cuthbert, her brother*: PETER MEWS. *Anne Shirley*: GRACIE FINLEY. *Mrs. Spencer*: Flora MacKenzie. *Mrs. Blewett*: Roma Hearn. *Diana Barry*: Glenda Landry.
    Young Ladies at Avonlea School: *Prissy Andrews*: Sharlene McLean. *Josie Pye*: Barbara Barsky. *Ruby Gillis*: Patti Toms. *Tillie Boulter*: Lynn Marsh. *Gertie Pye*: Deborah Miller. *Boys at Avonlea School*: *Gilbert Blythe*: JEFF HYSLOP. *Charlie Sloane*: George Juriga. *Moody MacPherson*: Dan Costain. *Gerry Buote*: Andre Denis. *Tommy Sloane*: John Powell. *Malcolm Andrews*: Calvin MacRae.

Mr. Phillips, the schoolmaster: Jack Northmore. *Lucilla, clerk in Blair's store*: Cleone Duncan. *Miss Stacy, the schoolmistress*: Roma Hearn. *Stationmaster*: Bill Hosie.

The action takes place at the turn of the century in Avonlea, a tiny village in Prince Edward Island, Canada's smallest province.

Act 1, Scene 1: The Church Parlor, Avonlea. *Scene 2*: Bright River Railroad Station. *Scene 3*: The House at Green Gables. *Scene 4*: On the way to Mrs. Blewett's. *Scene 5*: Mrs. Blewett's House. *Scene 6*: On the way back to Green Gables. *Scene 7*: Green Gables. *Scene 8*: Green Gables. *Scene 9*: On the way to the Schoolhouse. *Scene 10*: The Schoolhouse. *Scene 11*: All over town. *Scene 12*: On the way to Green Gables. *Scene 13*: On the way to the Picnic; the Picnic.

Act 2, Scene 1: Outside the Schoolhouse. *Scene 2*: Schoolyard. *Scene 3*: Green Gables. *Scene 4*: Green Gables. *Scene 5*: The Nature Hunt. *Scene 6*: The Store at Carmody. *Scene 7*: The Schoolhouse. *Scene 8*: On the way home from School. *Scene 9*: Kitchen, Green Gables. *Scene 10*: Green Gables.

ACT 1
(Overture: "Anne of Green Gables")
(Chorus)
Scene 1
"Great Workers for the Cause"
M. Whitmore, Ladies
"Where Is Matthew Going?"
Townspeople
Scene 2
"Gee, I'm Glad I'm No One Else But Me"
G. Finley
Scene 3
"We Clearly Requested (A Boy)" (Trio)
E. Mawson, G. Finley, P. Mews
Scene 5
"The Facts"
G. Finley, F. MacKenzie, R. Hearn, E. Mawson
Scene 6
"Where'd Marilla Come From?" (reprise)
B. Hosie, G. Merner, Ladies
Scene 7
"Humble Pie"
P. Mews, G. Finley
"Oh, Mrs. Lynde!" (Apology)
G. Finley
Scene 9
"Back to School/ (School) Ballet"
Pupils
Scene 10
"Avonlea We Love Thee"
J. Northmore, Pupils
"Wondrin'"
J. Hyslop
Scene 11
"Did You Hear?"
B. Barsky, K. Watt, C. Duncan, N. Kerr, B. Hosie, G. Merner, M. Whitmore
Scene 13
"Ice Cream"
G. Landry, Company
"The Picnic"
Company
ACT 2
Scene 1
"Where Did the Summer Go To?"
The Pupils
"Kindred Spirits"
G. Finley, G. Landry
Scene 2
"Open the Window!"
R. Hearn, Pupils
Scene 3
"The Words"
P. Mews

Scene 5

"Open the Window!" (reprise)
R. Hearn, Pupils

"Nature Hunt Ballet"
Pupils

"I'll Show Him"
G. Finley, J. Hyslop

Scene 6

"General Store"
C. Duncan, P. Mews, Townspeople

Scene 7

"Pageant Song"
Pupils

"If It Hadn't Been for Me"
Company

Scene 8

"Where Did the Summer Go To?" (reprise)
G. Finley, J. Hyslop, Pupils

Scene 9

"Anne of Green Gables"
P. Mews

Scene 10

"The Words" (reprise)
E. Mawson

"Wondrin'" (reprise)
G. Finley, J. Hyslop

(Finale: "Ice Cream" reprise)
(Company)

THE SIGN IN SIDNEY BRUSTEIN'S WINDOW

1972.01

A Play With Music in Three Acts, 8 Scenes. (Original) Play by Lorraine Hansberry. Adapted by Robert Nemiroff and Charlotte Zaltzberg. Music by Gary William Friedman. Lyrics by Ray Errol Fox. Directed by Alan Schneider. Musical staging by Rhoda Levine. Scenery by William Ritman. Costumes by Theoni V. Aldredge. Lighting by Richard Nelson. Musical director, Mack Schlefer. Music orchestrated and arranged by Gary William Friedman. Associate producer, Robert Nemiroff. Produced by Robert Renfield. Opened 26 January 1972 at the Longacre Theatre and closed 29 January 1972 after 5 performances.

CAST (in order of appearance): Singers: Pendleton Brown, Richard Cox, John Lansing, Arnetia Walker. Sidney Brustein: HAL LINDEN. Alton Scales: John Danelle. Iris Parodus Brustein: ZOHRA LAMPERT. Wally O'Hara: MASON ADAMS. Max: Dolph Sweet. Mavis Parodus Bryson: FRANCES STERNHAGEN. David Ragin: WILLIAM ATHERTON. Gloria Parodus: Kelly Wood.
Singers: Pendleton Brown, Richard Cox, John Lansing, Arnetia Walker.

The action takes place in the Brustein's apartment and adjoining courtyard in Greenwich Village, New York City, in the early 1960s.

Act 1, Scene 1: Early evening, the late spring. Scene 2: Dusk. The following week.

Act 2, Scene 1: Just before daybreak. The following day. Scene 2: Evening. Late summer. Scene 3: Later that evening. Scene 4: Election Night. Early fall.

Act 3, Scene 1: Several hours later. Scene 2: Early the next morning.

MUSICAL NUMBERS

"Can a Flower Think?"

"In Another Life"

"Mountain Girl"

"To the People"

"While There's Still Time"

"Things As They Are"

"Sweet Evenin'"

THE SELLING OF THE PRESIDENT

1972.02

A Musical in Two Acts. Book by Jack O'Brien and Stuart Hample. Based on the book of the same name by Joe McGinniss. Music by Bob James. Lyrics

by Jack O'Brien. Scenery by Tom John. Costumes by Nancy Potts. Lighting by Thomas Skelton. Musical staging by Ethel Martin. Musical direction by Harold Hastings. Orchestrations by Jonathan Tunick. Multi-media designed by William Claxton, Mort Kasman, Gary Youngman, Jim Sant'Andrea. Produced by John Flaxman in association with Harold Hastings and Franklin Roberts. Opened 22 March 1972 at the Sam S. Shubert Theatre and closed 25 Marrch 1972 after 5 performances[16]).

CAST: Senator George W. Mason: PAT HINGLE. Grace Mason: BARBARA BARRIE. Senator Hiram Robinson: Richard Goode. Sydney Wales: ROBERT FITZSIMMONS. Irene Jantzen: KAREN MORROW. Ted Bacon: ROBERT DARNELL. Ward Nichols: JOHN GLOVER. Johnny Olson: JOHNNY OLSON. Arthur Hayes: John Bentley.
Television's Top Singers and Dancers: Minister: Tim Noble. Captain Terror: Steve Schochet. Timmy: Sheilah Rae. Creepy: Philip M. Thomas. Davey: Tim Noble. Ghoulie: Pi Douglass. Van Denisovich: Rick Atwell. Casey Steele: Jamie Carr. Franklin Douglass Pierce: Pi Douglass. Bonnie Sue Taylor: Suellen Estey. Gloria Miller: Delores Hall. Linda Allington: Pamela Myers. Ralph Reeder: Tim Noble. Burgundy Moore: Trina Parks. Molly Kilgallen: Sheilah Rae. Inga Brand: Deborah St. Darr. Barney Zawicki: Steve Schochet. Dr. Lloyd Blenheim: Bill Reinecke. Mrs. Pearline Gibbons: Lurlu Lindsay. Mr. Warren Stevenson: Peter Grounds. Randall Phillips: Philip M. Thomas. Fleetwing Horn: Vilma Vaccaro. Julie Milano: Pam Zarit. And George Andrew Robinson, Michael Serrecchia.

The action takes place in 1976 in a television studio.

ACT 1

"Something Holy"
D. Hall, Company

"If You Like People"
S. Estey, T. Noble

"Sunset"
P. Douglass, T. Noble, A. Robinson, S. Schochet

"Little Moon"
V. Carr, V. Vaccaro

"Come-on-a-Good-Life"
P. Douglass, T. Parks, P. Thomas, D. Hall

"I've Got to Trust You"
P. Myers

"If You Like People" (reprise)
Company

"Mason Cares"
S. Estey, S. Rae, D. St. Darr, P. Zarit

"On the Winning Side"
P. Myers

"Captain Terror"
S. Rae, S. Schochet, P. Douglass, P. Thomas

"He's a Man"
T. Parks, P. Zarit, D. Hall

ACT 2

"Stars of Glory"
T. Noble

"Terminix"
S. Schochet, D. St. Darr, S. Estey, P. Myers

"Take My Hand"
J. Carr, D. Hall, S. Schochet, V. Vaccaro

"A Passacaglia"
Company

"We're Gonna Live It Together"
Company

"America"
Company

A FUNNY THING HAPPENED ON THE WAY TO THE FORUM

1972.03

A Revival of the Musical Comedy in Two Acts[17]. Book by Burt Shevelove and Larry Gelbart. Based on the plays ("The Haunted House," "Mostellaria",

---

[16]Direction uncredited at opening; credited to Robert H. Livingston prior to opening.
[17]Originally produced in New York 8 May 1962 at the Alvin Theatre for 964 performances. For Synopsis of Scenes and Musical Numbers, see original 1962 production. Added for this production:

etc.) of Plautus. Music and lyrics by Stephen Sondheim. Directed by Burt Shevelove. A Larry Blyden Production. Choreography by Ralph Beaumont. Settings by James Trittipo. Costumes by Noel Taylor. Lighting by H. R. Poindexter. Musical and vocal direction by Milton Rosenstock. Orchestrations by Irwin Kostal and Sid Ramin. Dance music arranged by Hal Schaefer, Richard De Benedictis. Produced by David Black in association with Seymour Vall and Henry Honeckman. Opened 30 March 1972 at the Lunt-Fontanne Theatre and closed 12 August 1972 after 156 performances.

CAST (in order of appearance): *Prologus:* PHIL SILVERS. *Senex,* a Roman citizen: LEW PARKER. *Domina,* his wife: LIZABETH PRITCHETT. *Hero,* his son, in love with Philia: JOHN HANSEN. *Hysterium,* slave to Senex and Domina: LARRY BLYDEN. *Pseudolus,* slave to Hero: PHIL SILVERS. *Lycus,* a buyer and seller of courtesans: CARL BALLANTINE. *Erronius,* an old man: REGINALD OWEN. *Miles Gloriosus,* a warrior: CARL LINDSTROM. *Tintinabula,* a courtesan: Lauren Lucas. *Panacea,* a courtesan: Gloria Mills. *The Geminae,* courtesans: Trish Mahoney, Sonja Haney. *Vibrata,* a courtesan: Keita Keita. *Gymnasia,* a courtesan: Charlene Ryan. *Philia,* a virgin: PAMELA HALL. *The Proteans:* Joe Ross, Bill Starr, Chad Block.

1972.04 SUGAR

A Musical Comedy in Two Acts, 15 Scenes. Book by Peter Stone. Based on the film "Some Like It Hot" by Billy Wilder and I.A.L. Diamond, based on a story by Robert Thoeren. Music by Jule Styne. Lyrics by Bob Merrill. Directed and choreographed by Gower Champion. Settings by Robin Wagner. Costumes by Alvin Colt. Lighting by Martin Aronstein. Musical direction and vocal arrangements by Elliot Lawrence. Orchestrations by Philip J. Lang. Dance music arrangements by John Berkman. Associate choreographer, Bert Michaels. Produced by David Merrick. Opened 9 April 1972 at the Majestic Theatre and closed 23 June 1973 after 505 performances.

CAST (in order of appearance): *Sweet Sue:* SHEILA SMITH. *(Her) Society Syncopaters: Piano:* Harriett Conrad. *Drums:* Linda Gandell. *Bass:* Nicole Barth. *Trumpets:* Leslie Latham, Marylou Sirinek. *Trombones:* Terry Cullen, Kathleen Witmer. *Saxophones:* Pam Blair, Eileen Casey, Debra Lyman, Sally Neal, Mary Zahn. *Bienstock:* ALAN KASS. *Joe:* TONY ROBERTS. *Jerry:* ROBERT MORSE. *Spats Palazzo:* STEVE CONDOS. *Dude:* Gerard Brentte. *Spat's Gang:* Andy Bew, Roger Bigelow, Gene Cooper, Arthur Faria, Gene GeBauer, John Mineo, Don Percassi. *Knuckles Norton:* Dick Bonelle. *First Poker Player:* Igors Gavon. *Knuckles' Gang:* Ken Ayers, Richard Maxon, Dale Muchmore, Alexander Orfaly. *Sugar Kane:* ELAINE JOYCE. *Cabdriver:* Ken Ayers. *Olga:* Eileen Casey. *Sunbathers:* Nicole Barth, Pam Blair, Eileen Casey, Robin Hoctor, Debra Lyman, Peggy Lyman, Sally Neal, Pamela Sousa. *Train Conductor:* George Blackwell. *Bellboy:* Andy Bew. *Osgood Fielding, Jr.:* CYRIL RITCHARD. *"Chicago" Singers:* Ken Ayers, George Blackwell, Dick Bonelle, Igors Gavon, Hal Norman.

The action takes place in Chicago, Miami and in between in 1931.

Act 1, Scene 1: Chicago Theatre. *Scene 2:* Backstage Chicago Theatre. *Scene 3:* Chicago Street. *Scene 4:* Clark Street Garage. *Scene 5:* Dearborn Street Railroad Station. *Scene 6:* The Dixie Flyer. *Scene 7:* The Seminole-Ritz Hotel Veranda. *Scene 8:* Josephine and Daphne's Hotel Room.

Act 2, Scene 1: The Beach. *Scene 2:* The Hotel Veranda. *Scene 3:* The New Caledonia Yacht. *Scene 4:* Josephine and Daphne's Hotel Room. *Scene 5:* The Hotel Night Club. *Scene 6:* The Hotel Service Corridor. *Scene 7:* The New Caledonia Yacht.

ACT 1[18]

"Windy City Marmalade"
  S. Smith, Society Syncopaters

"Farewell" (Act 1, after "Comedy Tonight")
  L. Pritchett
"Echo Song" (Act 2, after "That Dirty Old Man")
  J. Hansen, P. Hall
Dropped for this production:
  "Pretty Little Picture," "That'll Show Him"
Note change:
  "The House of Marcus Lycus" (revised as solo)
    C. Ballantine
[18]For subsequent national tour, the following songs were added:
  "See You Around" (Act 1, after "The Beauty That Drives Men Mad")
    L. Palmer (Sugar)
  "Nice Ways" (Act 1, after "We Could Be Close")
    Leland Palmer
  "Don't Be Afraid" (Act 2, replacing "What Do You Give. .")
    Larry Kert (Joe), L. Palmer

"Penniless Bums"
  R. Morse, T. Roberts, Unemployed Musicians
"Tear the Town Apart" (dance)
  S. Condos, Spats' Gang
"The Beauty That Drives Men Mad"
  R. Morse, T. Roberts
"We Could Be Close"
  R. Morse, E. Joyce
"Sun on My Face"
  R. Morse, T. Roberts, E. Joyce, S. Smith, A. Kass, Ensemble
"November Song"
  C. Ritchard, Millionaires
"(Doin' It For) Sugar"
  R. Morse, T. Roberts

ACT 2
"Hey, Why Not!"
  E. Joyce, Ensemble
"Beautiful Through and Through"
  C. Ritchard, R. Morse
"What Do You Give to a Man Who's Had Everything?"
  T. Roberts, E. Joyce
"Magic Nights"
  R. Morse
"It's Always Love"
  T. Roberts
"When You Meet a Man in Chicago"
  R. Morse, T. Roberts, E. Joyce, S. Smith, All-Girl Band and Chorus Line

1972.05 THAT'S ENTERTAINMENT

A Musical (Revue) in Two Acts. Music by Arthur Schwartz. Lyrics by Howard Dietz. Orchestrations, arrangements and musical direction by Luther Henderson. Choreography by Larry Fuller. Production directed by Paul Aaron. Scenery and lighting designed by David F. Segal. Costumes by Jane Greenwood. Sound designed by Anthony Alloy. Produced by Gordon Crowe in association with J. Robert Breton. Opened 14 April 1972 at the Edison Theatre and closed 16 April 1972 after 4 performances.

CAST (in alphabetical order): *Greg:* David Chaney. *Richard:* Jered Holmes. *Carol:* Judith Knaiz. *Adele:* Michon Peacock. *Lena:* Vivian Reed. *Jack:* Scott Salmon. *Lucille:* Bonnie Schon. *Donald:* Michael Vita. *Sam:* Alan Weeks.

ACT 1
Overture
  The Company
Medley:
  "We Won't Take It Back" (from *INSIDE U.S.A.*)
  "Hammacher Schlemmer, I Love You" (from *THE LITTLE SHOW*)
  "Come, Oh, Come" (from *INSIDE U.S.A.*)
    M. Peacock, B. Schon, S. Slamon, D. Chaney
"I'm Glad I'm Single" (from *THE GAY LIFE*)J. Holmes
"You're Not the Type" (from *THE GAY LIFE*)/"Miserable with You" (*from THE BANDWAGON*)
  J. Knaiz, J. Holmes
"Something to Remember You By" (from *THREE'S A CROWD*)
  J. Knaiz
"Hottentot Potentate" (from *AT HOME ABROAD*)
  V. Reed, A. Weeks
"Day After Day" (from *FLYING COLORS*)/"Fly by Night" (from *BETWEEN THE DEVIL*)
  Company
"Everything"
  J. Holmes

"I'm Engaged" (Act 2, after "Magic Nights")
  R. Morse
"People in My Life" (Act 2, after "I'm Engaged")
  L. Kert
Dropped for tour:
  "Sun on My Face," "What Do You Give to a Man Who's Had Everything?," "It's Always Love."

"Blue Grass" (from *INSIDE U.S.A.*)
  A. Weeks
"Fatal Fascination" (from *FLYING COLORS*)/"White Heat" (from *THE BANDWAGON*)
  B. Schon
"Right at the Start of It" (from *THREE'S A CROWD*)
  A. Weeks
"Confession" (from *THE BANDWAGON*)
  J. Knaiz, M. Vita
"Smoking Reefers" (from *FLYING COLORS*)
  V. Reed
"How High Can a Little Bird Fly?"(from *THE GIBSON FAMILY*, radio; *FOLLOW THE SUN*, London)
  S. Salmon
"Keep Off the Grass"
  D. Chaney
"I See Your Face Before Me" (from *BETWEEN THE DEVIL*)
  M. Vita, M. Peacock
"Experience" (from *BETWEEN THE DEVIL*)
  D. Chaney
"Two Faced Woman" (from *FLYING COLORS*)
  A. Weeks
"Foolish Face" (from *THE SECOND LITTLE SHOW*)
  S. Salmon
"By Myself" (from *BETWEEN THE DEVIL*)
  V. Reed
"That's Entertainment" (from *THE BANDWAGON* film)
  M. Vita

ACT 2
  Dance Medley:
"You and the Night and the Music" (from *REVENGE WITH MUSIC*)/
"Louisiana Hayride" (from *FLYING COLORS*)
"Dancing in the Dark" (from *THE BANDWAGON*)
  The Company
"Triplets" (from *BETWEEN THE DEVIL*)
  B. Schon, D. Chaney, J. Holmes
"High and Low" (from *THE BANDWAGON*)
  S. Salmon
"How Low Can a Little Worm Go?"
  J. Knaiz
"Absent Minded"
  J. Holmes
"High Is Better Than Low" (from *JENNIE*)
  J. Knaiz, S. Salmon
"If There Is Someone Lovelier Than You" (from *REVENGE WITH MUSIC*)D. Chaney
"I've Made a Habit of You" (from *THE LITTLE SHOW*)
  B. Schon
"I Guess I'll Have to Change My Plan" (from *THE LITTLE SHOW*)
  A. Weeks
"New Sun in the Sky" (from *THE BANDWAGON*)
  V. Reed
"Farewell My Lovely" (from *AT HOME ABROAD*)
  M. Peacock
"Alone Together" (from *FLYING COLORS*)
  M. Vita
"(A) Shine on Your Shoes" (from *FLYING COLORS*)
  The Company

1972.06   LOST IN THE STARS

A Revival of the Musical Play in Two Acts, 18 Scenes[19]. Words (book and lyrics) by Maxwell Anderson. Music by Kurt Weill. Based on the novel "Cry, the Beloved Country" by Alan Paton. Directed by Gene Frankel. Scenery by Oliver Smith. Costumes by Patricia Quinn Stewart. Lighting by Paul

---

[19]Originally produced in New York 30 October 1949 at the Music Box Theatre for 281 performances.

Sullivan. Musical direction by Karen Gustafson. Choreography and musical staging by Louis Johnson. Musical arrangements and orchestrations by Kurt Weill. Projections by Alec Nesbitt. Produced by The John F. Kennedy Center for the Performing Arts (Roger L. Stevens, Diana Shumlin, producers). Opened 18 April 1972 at the Imperial Theatre and closed 21 May 1972 after 39 performances.

CAST (in order of appearance): *Answerer*: Lee Hooper. *Dancer*: Harold Pierson. *Leader*: ROD PERRY. *Drummer*: Babafumi Akunyun. *Stephen Kumalo*: BROCK PETERS. *Grace Kumalo*: ROSETTA LeNOIRE. *Stationmaster*: Adam Petroski. *The Young Man*: Sid Marshall. *The Woman*: Ruby Greene Aspinall. *Arthur Jarvis*: Don Fenwick. *James Jarvis*: JACK GWILLIM. *Edward Jarvis*: David Jay. *Mrs. Jarvis*: Karen Ford. *John Kumalo*: LEONARD JACKSON. *Paulus*: Leonard Hayward. *William*: Harold Pierson. *Alex*: Giancarlo Esposito. *Foreman*: Mark Dempsey. *Mrs. M'Kize*: Alyce Elizabeth Webb. *Hlabeni*: Garrett Saunders. *Eland*: Peter Bailey-Britton. *Linda*: Marki Bey. *Johannes Pafuri*: Autris Paige. *Matthew Kumalo*: DAMON EVANS. *Absalom Kumalo*: GILBERT PRICE. *Rose*: Judy Gibson. *Irina*: MARGARET COWIE. *First Policeman*: Mark Dempsey. *Second Policeman*: Roy Hausen. *Servant*: Richard Triggs. *The Guard*: Roy Hausen. *Burton*: Alexander Reed. *The Judge*: STAATS COTSWORTH. *McRae*: Leonard Hayward.

Singers: Lana Caradimas, Suzanne Cogan, Karen Ford, Aleesa Foster, Ruby Greene Aspinall, Amelia Haas, Edna Husband, Urylee Leonardos, Rona Leslie Pervil, Therman Bailey, Donald Coleman, Raymond Frith, Leonard Hayward, Autris Paige, Mandingo Shaka, Richard Triggs. *Dancers*: Michael Harrison, Wayne Stevenson Hayes, Oba-Ya, Michael Oiwake.

Time: The Present. *Opening*: Ndotsheni—a Small Village in South Africa. *Act 1, Scene 1*: Stephen Kumalo's Home. *Scene 2*: The Railroad Station. *Scene 3*: Johannesburg. John Kumalo's Tobacco Shop. *Scene 4*: The Search: (1) The Factory Office, (2) Mrs. M'Kize's House, (3) Hlabeni's House, (4) Parole Office. *Scene 5*: Stephen's Shantytown Lodging. *Scene 6*: A Dive in Shantytown. *Scene 7*: A Street in Shantytown. *Scene 8*: Irina's Hut in Shantytown. *Scene 9*: Arthur Jarvis' Home. *Scene 10*: A Street in Shantytown. *Scene 11*: Prison. *Scene 12*: A Street in Shantytown.

Act 2, Scene 1: Johannesburg. Stephen's Shantytown Lodging. *Scene 2*: Arthur Jarvis' Doorway. *Scene 3*: The Courtroom. *Scene 4*: Prison Cell. *Scene 5*: Stephen's Chapel. *Scene 6*: Stephen Kumalo's Home.

ACT 1
  Opening
    "The Hills of Ixtapo"
      R. Perry, L. Hooper, Singers
  Scene 1
    "Thousands of Miles"
      B. Peters
  Scene 2
    "Train to Johannesburg"
      R. Perry, Singers
  Scene 4
    "The Search"
      B. Peters, R. Perry, Singers
  Scene 5
    "The Little Grey House"
      B. Peters, Singers
  Scene 7
    "Stay Well"
      G. Price
  Scene 8
    "Trouble Man"
      M. Cowie
  Scene 9
    "Murder in Parkwold"
      Singers
  Scene 10
    "Fear"
      Singers
  Scene 12
    "Lost in the Stars"
      B. Peters, Singers
ACT 2
  Opening
    "The Wild Justice"
      R. Perry, Singers
  Scene 1
    "O Tixo, Tixo, Help Me"
      B. Peters

Scene 4
"Cry, the Beloved Country"
R. Perry, Singers
Scene 5
"Big Mole"
G. Esposito
Scene 6
"Thousands of Miles" (reprise)
Singers

1972.07 DIFFERENT TIMES

A Musical in Two Acts in a Prologue, 15 Scenes and Epilogue. Book, music, lyrics and direction by Michael Brown. Dances and musical numbers staged by Tod Jackson. Scenery and costumes by David Guthrie. Lighting by Martin Aronstein. Orchestrations by Norman Paris, Arthur Harris, Ted Simons. Musical direction, dance and vocal arrangements by Rene Wiegert. Audio (sound) by Jack Shearing. Produced by Bowman Productions Inc. (Arthur C. Twitchell, Jr., President) with William L. Witt and William J. Gumperz. Opened 1 May 1972 at the ANTA Theatre and closed 20 May 1972 after 24 performances.

CAST (in order of appearance): *Stephen Adams Levy*: SAM STONEBURNER. *Margaret Adams*: BARBARA WILLIAMS. *Gregory Adams*: JAMIE ROSS. *Mrs. Daniel Webster Hepplewhite*: MARY JO CATLETT. *Mrs. Hepplewhite's Mother*: PATTI KARR. *Nelle Harper*: Joyce Nolen. *Larry Lawrence Levy*: JOE MASIELL. *Angela Adams*: Candace Cook. *Doughboys*: Terry Nicholson, Ronnie DeMarco, David K. Thorne. *Officer*: Ronald Young. *Marianne*: Dorothy Frank. *Columbia*: Karin Baker. *The Kaiser*: MARY JO CATLETT. *Elsie*: MARY BRACKEN PHILLIPS. *Bobby*: Ronald Young. *Marilyn*: Dorothy Frank. *The Hazelnuts*: Candace Cook, Dorothy Frank, Karin Baker, Joyce Nolen. *Hazel Hughes*: MARY JO CATLETT. *Lady Ffenger*: MARY JO CATLETT. *Hattie, Pauline, and Mae Verne*: Dorothy Frank, Candace Cook, Karin Baker. *The Keynoters*: Terry Nicholson, Mary Bracken Phillips, David K. Thorne, Ronald Young. *Kimberley Langley*: PATTI KARR. *Abigail*: MARY BRACKEN PHILLIPS. *Mrs. Callahan*: MARY JO CATLETT. *Josie*: MARY JO CATLETT. *Frank*: RONALD YOUNG. *Joe*: Terry Nicholson. *Don*: David K. Thorne. *Mel*: Ronnie DeMarco. *Stan*: JOE MASIELL. *Linda*: Dorothy Frank. *Frank Gonzales*: RONALD YOUNG.

The action takes place between 1905 and 1970.

Prologue: 1970.

Act 1, Scene 1: The Fair in Portland, Oregon, 1905. *Scene 2*: A hotel room in Portland, 1905. *Scene 3*: A street in Boston, 1915. *Scene 4*: A hotel room in Boston, 1917. *Scene 5*: A theatre stage, 1917. *Scene 6*: A speakeasy in Boston, 1924-1929. *Scene 7*: The Gregory Adams house in Boston, 1929. *Scene 8*: The Bijou Ballroom in Bayonne, 1933.

Act 2, Scene 1: Ffenger, Hall, London, 1942. *Scene 2*: A street in London, 1942. *Scene 3*: The Gregory Adams house in Boston, 1942. *Scene 4*: The Stephen Adams house in Mt. Kisco and Stephen's office in Manhattan, 1963. *Scene 5*: Abigail's room in Manhattan, 1965. *Scene 6*: An art gallery, 1968. *Scene 7*: Central Park, 1970.

Epilogue: 1970.

ACT 1
"Different Times"
S. Stoneburner
"Seeing the Sights"
People of 1905
"The Spirit Is Moving"
B. Williams, People of 1905
"Here's Momma"
B. Williams
"Everything in the World Has a Place"
J. Ross, B. Williams
"I Wish I Didn't Love Him"
B. Williams
"Forward into Tomorrow"
M. J. Catlett, Suffragettes
"You're Perfect"
C. Cook
"Marianne"
R. Young, Doughboys, D. Frank, K. Baker, M. J. Catlett
"Daddy, Daddy"
C. Cooke, D. Frank, K. Baker, J. Nolen
"I Feel Grand"
M. J. Catlett, C. Cooke, D. Frank, K. Baker, J. Nolen

"Sock Life in the Eye"
J. Masiell
"I'm Not Through"
J. Masiell, Marathon Dancers
ACT 2
"I Miss Him"
D. Frank, C. Cooke, K. Baker
"One More Time"
P. Karr, T. Nicholson, M. B. Phillips, D. K. Thorne, R. Young
"Here's Momma" (reprise)
S. Stoneburner
"I Dreamed About Roses"
S. Stoneburner, P. Karr, U.S.O. Guests
"I Wish I Didn't Love Her" (reprise)
J. Ross
"The Words I Never Said"
S. Stoneburner, P. Karr
"The Life of a Woman"
P. Karr
"Here's Momma" (reprise)
P. Karr, Momma's Poppas
"He Smiles"
M. B. Phillips, M. J. Catlett
"Genuine Plastic"
S. Stoneburner, Gallery Guests
"Thanks a Lot"
R. Young, M. B. Phillips, Guests
"When They Start Again"
M. B. Phillips, R. Young
"Different Times" (reprise)
S. Stoneburner
"The Spirit Is Moving" (reprise)
Company

1972.08 TOMMY

Les Grands Ballets Canadiens in a ballet adaptation of the rock opera in One Act.[20] Music and Lyrics by Peter Townshend, John Entwistle and Keith Moon. Choreography by Fernand Nault. Sets by David Jenkins. Costumes by François Barbeau. Lighting by Nicholas Cernovitch. Film sequences by Luc-Michel Hannaux, Denys Morisset, PauL Vezina, Office du Film du Québec. Produced by Les Grand Ballets Canadiens (Ludmilla Chiriaeff, Founder and Director; Fernand Nault, Associate Artistic Director; Uriel G. Luft, General manager). Opened 3 May 1972 at the New York City Center and closed 28 May 1972 after 31 performances.

CAST: *Tommy*: MANNIE ROWE or ALEXANDER BELIN or VINCENT WARREN. *Mother*: REVA PINCUSOFF or LESLIE-MAY DOWNS or BARBARA WITHEY. *Father*: LASZLO TAMASIK or WILLIAM JOSEF. *Acid Queen*: Janet Snyder or Manon Larin or Sonia Taverner or Hae Shik Kim. *Pin Ball Wizard*: James Bates or Mannie Rowe or Maurice Lemay or Andris Toppe. *The Hawker*: Renald Rabu or Richard Beaty or Wiliam Josef. *Uncle Ernie*: JOHN STANZEL. *Cousin Kevin*: Andris Toppe or Maurice Lemay or Guillermo Gonzales. *The Lover*: David Drummond or James Boyd or Lorne Toumine. *Sally Simpson*: Carole Landry or Eileen Heath or Lorna Cameron.

With Richard Bouchard, Francine Boucher, Robert Dicello, Louise Dore, Gerry Gilbert, Eileen Heath, Barbara Jacobs, Melinda Lawrence, Helen McKergow, Conrad Peterson, Reva Pincusoff, Cathy Sharp, Richard Sugarman, Susan Taylor, Michael Thomas, Laeleen Winchiu, Barbara Withey.

Lead Vocalist on recording: ROGER DALTREY. *The Hawker*: Sonny Boy Williamson.

MUSICAL NUMBERS
"It's a boy"
"You didn't hear it"
"Amazing journey"
"Sparks"

---

[20]Preceded by two ballets, Ceremony and Hip and Straight. The ballet was performed to the pre-recorded score of TOMMY as released on Decca Records.

"Eyesight to the blind"
   (*Music and Lyrics by* Sonny Boy Williamson.)
"Christmas"
"Cousin Kevin"
   (*Music and Lyrics by* John Entwistle.)
"The acid queen"
"Underture"
"Do you think it's alright"
"Fiddle about"
   (*Music and Lyrics by* John Entwistle.)
"Pinball wizard"
"There's a doctor I've found"
"Go to the mirror boy"
"Tommy can you hear me"
"Smash the mirror"
"Sensation"
"Miracle cure"
"Sally Simpson"
"I'm free"
"Welcome"
"Tommy's holiday camp"
   (*Music and Lyrics by* Keith Moon.)
"We're not gonna take it"

1972.09   HARD JOB BEING GOD

A Rock Musical in One Act, 14 Scenes. Music and lyrics by Tom Martel. Directed by Bob Yde. Musical staging by Lee Theodore. Production designed by Ray Wilke. Costumes by Mary Whitehead. Lighting by Patrika Brown. Audio (sound) by Bill Sandreuter. Musical director, Roy Bittan. Produced by Bob Yde in association with Andy Wiswell. Opened 15 May 1972 at the Edison Theatre and closed 20 May 1972 after 7 performances.

CAST (in alphabetical order): *Sarah, Jacob's Wife, Slave, Pharaoh's Soldier, Moabite, Judean, Susanna*: Gini Eastwood. *Jacob's Son, Moses, Moabite, David*: Stu Freeman. *God*: Tom Martel. *Slave, Pharaoh's Soldier, Ruth, Judean, Shepherd*: Anne Sarofeen. *Abraham, Jacob, Pharaoh, Moabite, Judean, Amos*: John Twomey.

Scene 1: Anytime, anywhere. *Scene 2*: Canaan, c. 1935 B.C. *Scene 3*: Canaan, c. 1700 B.C. *Scene 4*: Slave Camp in Egypt, c. 1240 B.C. *Scene 5*: Court of Rameses II, Pharaoh of Egypt, same day, c. 1240 B.C. *Scene 6*: The foot of Mt. Sinai, three months later. *Scene 7*: The Land of Moab, 1110 B.C. *Scene 8*: Jerusalem, 1005 B.C. *Scene 9*: Israel, c. 812 B.C. *Scene 10*: Israel, c. 780 B.C. *Scene 11*: On the banks of the Jordan River, 760 B.C. *Scene 12*: A pasture in Judah, 750 B.C. *Scene 13*: Feast Day, Royal Shrine of Bethel in Israel, 749 B.C. *Scene 14*: Anytime, anywhere.

MUSICAL NUMBERS
Scene 1
   "Hard Job Being God"
      T. Martel, Company
Scene 2
   "Wherever You Go"
      G. Eastwood, J. Twomey
Scene 3
   "Famine"
      J. Twomey, G. Eastwood, S. Freeman
Scene 4
   "Buy a Slave"
      Egyptian Slave Merchants
   "Prayer"
      Hebrew Slaves
Scene 5
   "Moses' Song"
      S. Freeman, J. Twomey
   "The Ten Plagues"
      J. Twomey, Soldiers, S. Freeman
   "Passover"
      Soldiers, J. Twomey, S. Freeman, Slaves

Scene 6
   "The Eleven Commandments"
      S. Freeman, Freed Slaves
Scene 7
   "Tribes"
      Hebrew Woman, the Tribes
   "Ruth"
      S. Freeman, J. Twomey, A. Sarofeen
Scene 8
   "Festival"
      Judeans
   "Hail, David"
      Judeans, S. Freeman
   "A Very Lonely King"
      S. Freeman
Scene 9
   "Battle"
Scene 10
   "You're on Your Own"
      Hebrews, T. Martel
Scene 11
   "A Psalm of Peace"
      G. Eastwood, Hebrews
Scene 12
   "I'm Countin' on You"
      T. Martel, J. Twomey
Scene 13
   "Shalom L'chaim!"
      Hebrews
   "Amos Gonna Give You Hell"
      A. Sarofeen
Scene 14
   "What Do I Have to Do?"
      T. Martel Company

1972.10   DON'T PLAY US CHEAP

A Comedy Musical in Two Acts. Book, words, music and direction by Melvin Van Peebles. Scenery by Kert Lundell. Costumes by Bernard Johnson. Lighting by Martin Aronstein. Musical supervision by Harold Wheeler. Produced by Melvin Van Peebles. Opened 16 May 1972 at the Ethel Barrymore Theatre and closed 1 October 1972 after 164 performances.

CAST: *Mr. Percy*: Thomas Anderson. *Mrs. Washington*: Joshie Jo Armstead. *Harold Johnson, Rat*: Nate Barnett. *Mr. Johnson, Cockroach*: Frank Carey. *Mr. Bowser*: Robert Dunn. *Earnestine*: Rhetta Hughes. *Trinity*: Joe Keyes, Jr. *Mrs. Bowser*: Mabel King. *David*: Avon Long. *Mr. Washington*: George 'Ooppee' McCurn. *Miss Maybell*: Esther Rolle. *Mrs. Johnson*: Jay Vanleer.

The action takes place here (in Miss Maybell's apartment in Harlem) "a coupla days before tomorrow."

ACT 1
   "Some Days It Seems That It Just Don't Even Pay to Get Out of Bed"
      N. Barnett, F. Carey
   "Break That Party"
      A. Long, J. Keyes, Jr.
   "8 Day Week"
      T. Anderson, Company
   "Saturday Night'
      Company
   "I'm a Bad Character"
      J. Keyes, Jr., Company
   "You Cut Up the Clothes in the Closet of My Dreams"
      J. J. Armstead
   "It Makes No Difference"
      E. Rolle, Company
   "Quittin' Time"
      G. McCurn, Company

ACT 2

"Ain't Love Grand"
R. Hughes, Company
"The Book of Life"
R. Dunn, Company
Quartet:
"Ain't Love Grand" (reprise)
R. Hughes
"Know Your Business"
E. Rolle
"Big Future"
F. Carey, J. Vanleer
"Break That Party" (reprise)
A. Long, J. Keyes, Jr.
"Feast on Me"
M. King, Company
"The Phoney Game"
A. Long, Company
"(If You See a Devil) Smash Him"
Company

HEATHEN!

1972.11

A Musical in Two Acts, 21 Scenes. Book by Sir Robert Helpmann and Eaton Magoon, Jr. Music and lyrics by Eaton Magoon, Jr. Directed by Lucia Victor. Choreography by Sammy Bayes. Setting by Jack Brown. Costumes by Bruce Harrow. Lighting by Paul Sullivan. Orchestrations by Larry Fallon. Musical director, Clay Fullum. Associate choreographer, Dan Siretta. Musical supervision, vocal and dance and incidental music by Mel Marvin. Produced by Leonard J. Goldberg and Ken Gaston in association with R. Paul Woodville. Opened and closed 21 May 1972 at the Billy Rose Theatre after 1 performance.

CAST (in order of appearance): *Reverend Jonathan Beacon, Jonathan*: RUSS THACKER. *Kalialani, Kalia*: YOLANDE BAVAN. *Mano'Ula, Mano*: EDWARD RAMBEAU. *The Muggers*: Dennis Dennehy, Justis Skae, Sal Pernice. *Reverend Hiram Burnham*: Dan Merriman. *Hepsibah Burnham*: Ann Hodges. *Church Elders*: Christopher Barrett, Mary Walling, Michael Serrecchia. *Kaha Kai, The Chanter*: Dennis Dennehy. *Alika*: MOKIHANA. *Tourists*: Ann Hodges, Dan Merriman. *Hawaiian Boy*: Charles Goeddertz. *Policeman*: Christopher Barrett. *Pueo*: Honey Sanders. *Momona-Nui*: Tina Santiago. *Boys in Jail*: Charles Goeddertz, Michael Serrecchia, Quitman Fludd.

The Girls and Boys of Past and Present: Nancy Dafgek, Jaclyn Villamil, Mary Walling, Karen Kristin, Dennis Dennehy, Randy DiGrazio, Quitman Fludd, Charles Goeddertz, Sal Pernice, Michael Serrecchia, Justis Skae.

The action takes place in Hawaii in 1819 (the past) and 1972 (the present).

Act 1, Scene 1: A beach by a sea wall, Waikiki, 1972. *Scene 2*: A Church in Boston, 1819. *Scene 3*: Aboard a ship at sea, 1819. *Scene 4*: Mano'ula's Canoe at Sea, 1819. *Scene 5*: The Kona shore, 1819. *Scene 6*: The beach, Waikiki, 1972. *Scene 7*: A grove naer Jonathan's hut, 1819. *Scene 8*: A Jail in Honolulu, 1819. *Scene 9*: On the edge of the village, 1819. *Scene 10*: The Heiau, A Council Meeting, 1819. *Scene 11*: Mano'ula's Compound, 1819. *Scene 12*: Past and Present Blend.

Act 2, Scene 1: A Jail in Honolulu, 1972. *Scene 2*: The Church Grounds, Dedication Ceremony, 1819. *Scene 3*: Waikiki Beach Bar, 11972. *Scene 4*: Mano'ula's Compound, 1819. *Scene 5*: Riding the Breakers, 1819. *Scene 6*: A Corner of the Compound, 1819. *Scene 7*: Kalialani's hut, 1819. *Scene 8*: The village under the eruption of Mauna Loa, 1819. *Scene 9*: Past and Present Blend.

ACT 1

Scene 1

"Paradise"
R. Thacker, Beach People

Scene 2

"The Word of the Lord"
D. Merriman, A. Hodges, C. Barrett, M. Walling, M. Serrecchia

Scene 3

"My Sweet Tomorrow"
R. Thacker

Scene 4

"A Man Among Men"
E. Rambeau, Rowers

Scene 5

"Aloha"
Company
"Kalialani"
Y. Bavan

Scene 7

"No Way in Hell"
R. Thacker, Y. Bavan, E. Rambeau

Scene 9

"Battle Cry"
Y. Bavan

Scene 10

"This Is Someone I Could Love"
E. Rambeau

Scene 11

"House of Grass"
E. Rambeau

Scene 12

"Kava Ceremony"
Company

ACT 2

Scene 1

"For You Brother"
R. Thacker, C. Goeddertz, M. Serrecchia, Q. Fludd

Scene 2

"Spear Games"
Company
"Christianity"
Company

Scene 3

"This Is Someone I Could Love" (reprise)
Y. Bavan

Scene 4

"Heathen"
R. Thacker

Scene 5

"Heathen" (reprise)
R. Thacker, E. Rambeau

Scene 6

"More Better Go Easy"
Mokihana

Scene 9

"Eighth Day"
Company

1972–1973 SEASON

Glynis Johns in A LITTLE NIGHT MUSIC
Martha Swope/TimePix

1972–1973 SEASON

GREASE

1972.12

A New 50's Rock 'N Roll Musical (Comedy) in Two Acts, 12 Scenes[1]. Book, music and lyrics by Jim Jacobs and Warren Casey. Directed by Tom Moore. Musical numbers and dances staged by Patricia Birch. Musical supervision and orchestrations by Michael Leonard. Musical direction, vocal and dance arrangements by Louis St. Louis. Scenery by Douglas W. Schmidt. Costumes by Carrie F. Robbins. Lighting by Karl Eigsti. Sound by Jack Shearing. Produced by Kenneth Waissman and Maxine Fox in association with Anthony D'Amato. Opened 7 June 1972 at the Broadhurst Theatre, moved 21 November 1972 to the Royale Theatre, moved 11 February 1980 to the Majestic Theatre and closed 13 April 1980 after 3388 performances (including Off-Broadway run).

CAST[2] (in order of appearance): *Miss Lynch*: Dorothy Leon. *Patty Simcox*: Ilene Kristen. *Eugene Florczyk*: Tom Harris. *Jan*: Garn Stephens. *Marty*: Meg Bennett. *Betty Rizzo*: ADRIENNE BARBEAU. *Doody*: James Canning. *Roger*: Walter Bobbie. *Kenickie*: Timothy Meyers. *Sonny LaTierri*: Jim Borrelli. *Frenchy*: Marya Small. *Sandy Dumbrowski*: CAROLE DEMAS. *Danny Zuko*: BARRY BOSTWICK. *Vince Fontaine*: Gardner Hayes. *Johnny Casino*: Alan Paul. *Cha-Cha Di Gregorio*: Kathi Moss. *Teen Angel*: Alan Paul.

The action takes place in the late 1950s.

Act 1, Scene 1: (Rydell High Class of '59) Reunion. *Scene 2*: Cafeteria and School Steps. *Scene 3*: Pajama Party. *Scene 4*: Street Corner. *Scene 5*: Schoolyard. *Scene 6*: Park.

Act 2, Scene 1: Kids' Homes. *Scene 2*: School Gym. *Scene 3*: Front of Burger Palace. *Scene 4*: Drive-In Movie. *Scene 5*: Jan's Party. *Scene 6*: Burger Palace.

ACT 1
Scene 1
　"Alma Mater"
　　D. Leon, I. Kristen, T. Harris
　"Alma Mater" Parody
　　Pink Ladies, Burger Palace Boys
Scene 2
　"Summer Nights"
　　C. Demas, B. Bostwick, Pink Ladies, Burger Palace Boys
　"Those Magic Changes"
　　J. Canning, Burger Palace Boys, Pink Ladies
Scene 3
　"Freddy, My Love"
　　M. Bennett, G. Stephens, M. Small, A. Barbeau
Scene 4
　"Greased Lightnin'"
　　T. Meyers, Burger Palace Boys
Scene 6
　"Mooning"
　　W. Bobbie, G. Stephens
　"Look at Me, I'm Sandra Dee"
　　A. Barbeau
　"We Go Together"
　　Pink Ladies, Burger Palace Boys
ACT 2
Scene 1
　"Shakin' at the High School Hop"
　　Entire Company
　"It's Raining on Prom Night"
　　C. Demas
　　　Radio Voice: K. Moss.

Scene 2
　"Shakin' at the High School Hop" (reprise)
　　Entire Company
　"Born to Hand-Jive"
　　A. Paul, Company
Scene 3
　"Beauty School Dropout"
　　A. Paul, M. Small, Choir
Scene 4
　"Alone at a Drive-In Movie"
　　B. Bostwick, Burger Palace Boys
Scene 5
　"Rock 'N' Roll Party Queen"
　　J. Canning, W. Bobbie
　"There Are Worse Things I Could Do"
　　A. Barbeau
　"Look at Me, I'm Sandra Dee" (reprise)
　　C. Demas
Scene 6
　"All Choked Up"
　　C. Demas, B. Bostwick, Company
　Finale: "We Go Together" (reprise)
　　Entire Company

DON'T BOTHER ME, I CAN'T COPE

1972.13

A Musical Entertainment (Revue) in Two Acts[3]. Conceived and directed by Vinnette Carroll. (Music and Lyrics) Written by Micki Grant. Choreographer, George Faison. Scenery by Richard A. Miller, supervised by Neil Peter Jampolis. Costumes by Edna Watson, supervised by Sara Brook. Lighting by B. J. Sammler, supervised by Ken Billington. Musical direction and arrangements by Danny Holgate. Production supervisor, Sam Ellis. An Urban Arts Corps Production. Associate producer, Gordon, Gray, Jr. Produced by Edward Padula and Arch Lustberg, in association with Ford's Theater Society (Washington, D.C.). Opened 13 June 1972 at the Edison Theatre and closed 26 October 1974 after 1065 performances (including Playhouse run).

CAST (in alphabetcial order): ALEX BRADFORD, HOPE CLARKE, MICKI GRANT, BOBBY HILL, ARNOLD WILKERSON.
　Singers: Alberta Bradford, Charles Campbell, Marie Thomas. *Dancers*: Thommie Bush, Gerald G. Francis, Ben Harney, Leona Johnson.

ACT 1[4]
　"I Gotta Keep Movin'"
　　Alex Bradford, Alberta Bradford, C. Campbell, B. Hill
　　Danced by B. Harney.

---

[3]Originally produced 19 April 1972 at the Playhouse Theatre for 63 performances.
[4]Added during the run:
　"Lock Up the Doors" (Act 1)
　"Children's Rhymes" (Act 1)
　　Company
　"Ghetto Life" (Act 1)
　　Company
　"My Love's So Good" (Act 1)
　"Love Mississippi" (Act 2)
　"Storefront Church" (Act 2)
Added for National Tours:
　Billie Holliday Song (Act 1)
　　Sheila Ellis
　"Prayer" (Act 2)
　　S. Ellis, Every Hayes, Pat Estwick, Esther Williams, Alton Lathrop
　"Sermon" (Act 2)
　　E. Hayes, Company
　"Universe in Mourning" (Act 2)
　　Vivian Reed

---

[1]First produced in New York Off-Broadway 14 February 1972 at the Eden Theatre for 128 performances.
[2]Original artists who created their roles Off-Broadway but did not transfer to Broadway: *Marty*: Katie Hanley. *Vince Fontaine*: Don Billett. Note: Pink Ladies include Rizzo, Frenchy, Marty, Jan. Burger Palace Boys include Kenickie, Doody, Roger, Sonny.

"Harlem Streets"
 Dancers
"Lookin' Over from Your Side"
 B. Hill
"Don't Bother Me, I Can't Cope"
 Entire Company
"When I Feel Like Moving"
 H. Clarke, Dancers
"Help"
 H. Clarke, Dancers
"Fighting for Pharaoh"
 Alex Bradford, B. Hill, Alberta Bradford, C. Campbell
"Good Vibrations"
 A. Bradford, Company
"Love Power"
 B. Hill, H. Clarke, Company
"You Think I Got Rhythm"
 Dancers
"They Keep Coming"
 Entire Company
"My Name Is Man"
 A. Wilkerson

ACT 2
"Questions"
 M. Grant
"It Takes a Whole Lot of Human Feeling"
 M. Grant
"You Think I Got Rhythm?" (reprise)
 A. Wilkerson, M. Grant
"Time Brings About a Change"
 M. Grant, Alex Bradford, Alberta Bradford, C. Campbell, M. Thomas, A. Wilkerson
"So Little Time"
 M. Grant
"Thank Heaven for You"
 B. Hill, M. Grant
"Show Me That Special Gene"
 L. Johnson, M. Thomas, M. Grant
"So Long Sammy"
 B. Hill
  Danced by H. Clarke, Dancers
"All I Need"
 Alberta Bradford, Company
"I Gotta Keep Movin'" (reprise)
 M. Grant, Alex Bradford, Company

1972.14 MAN OF LA MANCHA

A Revival of the Musical Play in One Act[5]. Book by Dale Wasserman. Suggested by the life and work ("Don Quixote") of Miguel de Cervantes y Saavedra. Music by Mitch Leigh. Lyrics by Joe Darion. Book and musical staging by Albert Marre. Choreography by Jack Cole. Settings and lighting by Howard Bay. Costumes by Howard Bay and Patton Campbell. Dance arrangements by Neil Warner. Musical arrangements by Music Makers Inc. Musical direction by Joseph Klein. Produced by Albert W. Selden and Hal James by arrangement with Lincoln Center. Opened 22 June 1972 at the Vivian Beaumont Theatre and closed 21 October 1972 after 140 performances.

CAST (in order of appearance): *Don Quixote (Cervantes)*: RICHARD KILEY, DAVID ATKINSON (matinees). *Sancho*: IRVING JACOBSON, EDMOND VARRATO (opening and matinees). *Captain of the Inquisition*: Renato Cibelli. *Aldonza*: JOAN DIENER, GERRIANNE RAPHAEL (matinees). *The Innkeeper*: JACK DABDOUB. *Dr. Carrasco*: LEE BERGERE. *The Padre*: ROBERT ROUNSEVILLE. *Antonia*: Diane Barton. *The Housekeeper*: Eleanore Knapp. *The Barber*: Ted Forlow. *Pedro*, Head

[5]First produced in New York 22 November 1965 at the ANTA Washington Square Theatre for 2328 performances. For Synopsis of Scenes and Musical Numbers, see original 1965 production.

Muleteer: Shev Rodgers. *Anselmo*, a Muleteer: Ted Forlow. *Jose*, a Muleteer: Hector (Jaime) Mercado. *Juan*, a Muleteer: John Aristides. *Paco*, a Muleteer: Bill Stanton. *Tenorio*, a Muleteer: Fernando Grahal. *Maria*, the Innkeeper's Wife: Rita Metzger. *The Dancing Horses*: Fernando Grahal, Hector (Jaime) Mercado. *The Horses at the Well*: Jeff Killion, Shev Rodgers. *Fermina*, a slavey and Moorish Dancer: Laura Kenyon. *Guitarist*: Stephen Sahlein.
 Guards, Men of the Inquisition: Jeff Killion, David Wasson, Robert Cromwell, William Tatum.

1972.15 (LEONARD BERNSTEIN'S) MASS

A Theatre Piece for Singers, Players and Dancers in One Act, 17 Scenes. Music by Leonard Bernstein. Texts from the liturgy of the Roman Mass. English texts by Stephen Schwartz and Leonard Bernstein. Directed by Gordon Davidson. Choreography by Alvin Ailey. Settings by Oliver Smith. Costumes by Frank Thompson. Lighting by Gilbert V. Hemsley, Jr. Staged by Gordon Davidson and Alvin Ailey. Musical director, Maurice Peress. Production coordinator, Diana Shumlin. Sound by Richard Guy. Associate conductor, Thomas Pierson. Associate producer, Schuyler G. Chapin. Produced by the John F. Kennedy Center for the Performing Arts (Roger L. Stevens and Martin Feinstein, Producers) and Sol Hurok. Opened 28 June 1972 at the Metropolitan Opera House and closed 22 July 1972 after 22 performances.

CAST: *Celebrant*: ALAN TITUS or DAVID CRYER.
 Singing Ensemble: John D. Anthony, Cheryl Barnes, Jacqueline Britt, Jane Coleman, David Cryer, Magaret Cowie, Ed Dixon, Leigh Dodson, Eugene Edwards, Thom Ellis, Lowell Harris, Lee Hooper, Gary Lipps, Linda Lloyd, Linda Marks, Larry Marshall, Gina Penn, John Bennett Perry, Mary Bracken Phillips, Neva Small, David Spangler, Alan Titus. *The Alvin Ailey American Dance Theatre*: *Acolytes*: Judith Jamison, Dudley Williams, Clive Thompson, Linda Kent, Kenneth Pearl, Sylvia Waters, Estelle E. Spurlock. *Dancing Ensemble*: Kelvin Rotardier, Sara Yarborough, Mari Kajiwara, John Parks, Hector Mercado, Leland Schwantes, Clover Mathis, Lynne Dell Walker.
 The Norman Scribner Choir: *Sopranos*: Juanita Brown, Carol Gericke, Diane Higginbotham, Vicki Johnstone, Janet Kenney, Katherine Ray, Cynthia Richards, Diana Rothman, Sandra Willets. *Altos*: Barbara Boller, Catherine Bounds, Alicia Kopfstein-Penk, Patricia George, Suzanne Grant, Raina Mann, Anne Miller, Janet Sooy, Joy Wood. *Tenors*: Barry Butts, David Coon, Robert Dorsey, Michael Hume, William Jones, Robert Kimball, John Madden, Robert Stevenson, Robert Whitney. *Basses*: Earl Baker, Glenn Cunningham, Albert deRuiter, Richard Frisch, Arphelius Paul Gatling, Charles Greenwell, Walter Richardson, Ronald Roxbury, Michael Tronzo. *The Berkshire Boys' Choir*: David Abell, Ben Borsch, Timothy Brown, Chris Cole, Sammy Coleman, Peter Coulianos, Thomas Ettinghausen, Liam Fennelly, Tim Ferrell, Jonathan Gram, Bruce Haynes, Richard Michael, Michael Miller, Chris Negus, Edward Rosen, Robert Rough, Miles Smith, Richard Swan, David Voorhees.
 Antiphon: Betty Allen, Karen Altman, Dominic Cossa, Raymond deVoll. *Responsory*: Adrienne Albert, Maeretha Stewart, June Magruder, Charles Magruder, John Manno, William Elliot. *Second Introit*: Leonard Arner (oboe).

Scene 1: Devotions Before Mass: 1. Antiphon: Kyrie Eleison. 2. Hymn: A Simple Song. 3. Psalm: A New Song. 4: Responsory: Alleluia. *Scene 2*: First Introit: Rondo. 1. Prefatory Prayers (Kyrie, Asperges, Introibo, etc.). 2. Thrice-triple Canon: Dominus Vobiscum. *Scene 3*: Second Introit. 1. In Nomine Patris. 2. Prayer for the Congregation (Chorale: Almighty Father). *Scene 4*: Confession. 1. Confiteor. 2. Strophe: I Don't Know. 3. Strophe: Easy. *Scene 5*: Meditation #1. *Scene 6*: Gloria. 1. Gloria Tibi. 2. Gloria in Excelsis. 3. Strophe: Half of the People. 4. Strophe: Thank You. *Scene 7*: Meditation #2. *Scene 8*: Epistle: The Word of the Lord. *Scene 9*: Gospel-Sermon: God Said. *Scene 10*: Credo. 1. Credo in Unum Deum ... 2. Strophe: Non Credo. 3. Strophe: Hurry. 4. Strophe: World Without End. Strophe: I Believe in God. *Scene 11*: Meditation #3: De Profundis, part 1. *Scene 12*: Offertory: De Profundis, part 2. *Scene 13*: The Lord's Prayer: 1. Our Father. 2. Strophe: I Go On. *Scene 14*: Sanctus. *Scene 15*: Agnus Dei. *Scene 16*: Fraction: Things Get Broken. *Scene 17*: Pax: Communion.

MUSICAL NUMBERS
Scene 1
 "A Simple Song"
  A. Titus or D. Cryer
Scene 4
 "I Don't Know"
  G. Lipps, N. Small, E. Dixon
 "Easy"
  E. Edwards, L. Lloyd, D. Spangler
Scene 6
 "Gloria Tibi"
  A. Titus or D. Cryer

"Thank You"
  L. Hooper
Scene 8
  "The Word of the Lord"
    A. Titus or D. Cryer
Scene 9
  "God Said"
    L. Marshall
Scene 10
  "Non Credo"
    J. B. Perry or D. Cryer
  "Hurry"
    G. Penn
  "World Without End"
    M. B. Phillips
  "I Believe in God"
    T. Ellis
Scene 13
  "Our Father"
    A. Titus or D. Cryer
  "I Go On"
    A. Titus or D. Cryer
Scene 16
  "Things Get Broken"
    A. Titus or D. Cryer
Scene 17
  "Secret Songs"
    M. Cowie, G. Lipps, J. D. Anthony, L. Dodson, E. Dixon

JACQUES BREL IS ALIVE AND WELL AND LIVING IN PARIS

1972.16

A Musical Revue in Two Acts[6]. Music by Jacques Brel. Production conception, English lyrics and additional material by Eric Blau. Based on Jacques Brel's lyrics and commentary. Directed by Moni Yakim. Musical direction by Mort Shuman. Music arranged and conducted by Wolfgang Knittel. (Scenery by Les Lawrence.) Produced by Bill Levine. Opened 15 September 1972 at the Royale Theatre and closed 28 October 1972 after 51 performances. (Total including Broadway and Off-Broadway runs 1897 performances.)

CAST: ELLY STONE, JOE MASIELL, GEORGE BALL, HENRIETTA VALOR, Janet McCall (alt.), Joseph Neal (alt.).

ACT 1
  "Marathon"
    Company
  "Alone"
    G. Ball
  "Madeleine"
    Company
  "I Loved"
    E. Stone
  "Mathilde"
    J. Masiell
  "Bachelor's Dance"
    G. Ball
  "Timid Frieda"
    H. Valor
  "My Death"
    E. Stone
  "Girls & Dogs"
    J. Masiell, G. Ball
  "Jackie"
    J. Masiell

  "The Statue"
    G. Ball
  "Desperate Ones"
    Company
  "Sons Of"
    E. Stone
  "Amsterdam"
    J. Masiell
ACT 2
  "The Bulls"
    G. Ball
  "Old Folks"
    E. Stone
  "Marieka"
    E. Stone
  "Brussels"
    H. Valor
  "Fannette"
    G. Ball
  "Funeral Tango"
    J. Masiell
  "Middle Class"
    J. Masiell, G. Ball
  "You're Not Alone"
    E. Stone
  "Next"
    J. Masiell
  "Carousel"
    E. Stone
  "If We Only Have Love"
    Company

FROM ISRAEL WITH LOVE

1972.17

(A Musical Revue from Israel in Two Acts.) Director, Avi David. Musical director, Rafi Ben-Moshe. Choreography by Yakov Kalusky. Produced by Pageant Productions P.T.Y. Ltd. (Executive producers, Jerome M. Lapin, Regina A. Lapin. Executive director, David A. Toben. Producer, Colonel Saul Biber. Director International Operations, Herman E. Schner.) Opened 2 October 1972 at the Palace Theatre and closed 8 October 1972 after 10 performances.

CAST: Micha Adir, Dani Amihud, Chaya Arad, Itzik Barak, Shara Badishy, Eti Brechner, David Dardashi, Irith Esched, Tami Gall, Israel Klugman, Elis Menahemi, Malli Noy, Yacov Noy, Nathan Okev, Gadi Oron, Varda Sagy, Reuven Shenar, Yonnith Shoham, Nurit Zeevi, *Musicians:* David Rosenthal, Izhack Lichtenfeld, Juda Asher Shkolnik, Oded Pintus, Shymel Aroukh, Ilan Gilboa.

ACT 1[7]
  "Israel Israel"
    (*Music and Lyrics by* Shlomo Carlebach.)
  "From the South Good Will Come" (Midarom Tipatach Hatova)
    (*Music and Lyrics by* Avraham Zigman.)
  "Call for Freedom"
  "Three Legs"
  "We Take Whatever Comes"
  Ballet
  "Jerusalem of Gold" (Yerushalaim Shel Zahavi)
    (*Music and Lyrics by* Naomi Shemer.)
  "Natasha"
    (*Music and Lyrics by* Dan Almagor and Y. Kalusky.)
ACT 2
  "A Beach Song"
  "Night, Night, A Lullaby"

---

[6]Originally produced in New York Off-Broadway 22 January 1968 at the Village Gate for 1847 performances.

[7]Note: Neither Songs nor Dances were credited to individual performers in the program. Composer and lyricist credits taken from recording.

"From Across the River (Me'ever Lanahar)"
  (*Music and Lyrics by* S. Tschernichovsky and E. Rubinstein.)
"Coffee Song"
"The Parachutist"
"My Dear Son"
Potpourri, Israeli Style:
"Hava Nagila;" "Again the Night Falls;" Dance: Debka.
"I Am Dying"
"A Song of Peace" (Shir La Shalom)
  (*Music and Lyrics by* Yaakov Rotblit, Yair Rosenbloom.)

DUDE

1972.18

The Highway Life (A Musical) in Two Acts. Book and lyrics by Gerome Ragni. Music by Galt MacDermott. Directed and staged by Tom O'Horgan. Production (set) designed by Eugene Lee, Roger Morgan, Franne Lee. Costumes designed by Randy Barcelo. Musical arrangements and orchestrations by Horace Ott. Musical direction by Thomas Pierson. Produced by Adela and Peter Holzer. Opened 9 October 1972 at the Broadway Theatre and closed 21 October 1972 after 16 performances.

CAST: *The Theater Stars:* #33: ALLAN NICHOLLS. *Dude:* RALPH CARTER. *Mother Earth:* SALOME BEY. *Bread:* DELORES HALL.
  The Shubert Angels: Karen Maria Faatz, Katie Field, Helen Jennings, David Kruger, Cary Mark, Mark Perman, Aida Random, Lynn Reynolds.
  The Theatre Wings: Hero: Alan Braunstein. *Halo:* Sandra Loys Toder. *Echo:* Dawn Johnson. *Solo:* Michael Jason. *Reba:* RAE ALLEN. *Harold:* WILLIAM REDFIELD. *Suzie Moon:* NELL CARTER. *Zero:* James Patrick Farrell III. *Nero:* Leata Galloway. *Sissy:* David Lasley. *Electric Bill:* Jim Turner. *Shadow:* Dale Soules. *Shade:* Barbara Monte-Britton. *Esso:* Bobby Alessi. *Extra:* Billy Alessi. *Meadow:* Michael Meadows. *World War Too:* Georgianna Holmes. *Noname:* Carol Estey. *Texaco:* Dennis Simpson. *Dude:* NAT MORRIS.

ACT 1
  Overture
    A. Nicholls, Company
  "Theatre/Theatre"
    A. Nicholls, The Theater Wings, The Shubert Angels
  "A-Stage"
    A. Nicholls
  "The Mountains"
    S. Bey
  "Pears and Peaches"
    The Shubert Angels
  "Eat It"
    The Pioneers
  "Wah Wah"
    N. Carter
  "Suzie Moon"
    N. Carter
  "Y.O.U."
    N. Morris
  "I Love My Boo Boo"
    A. Nicholls, N. Carter, D. Hall, S. Bey
  "Hum Drum Life"
    S. L. Toder, A. Braunstein, D. Hall, S. Bey
  "Who's It?"
    N. Morris, The Shubert Angels, The Theatre Wings
  "Talk to Me About Love"
    N. Morris, J. P. Farrell
  "Goodbyes"
    R. Allen
  "I'm Small"
    A. Braunstein
  "You Can Do Nothing About It"
    L. Galloway
  "The Handsomest Man"
    D. Lasley
  "Electric Prophet"
    J. Turner

"No One"
  S. Bey
ACT 2
  "Who Will Be the Children"
    The Shubert Angels
  "Go Holy Ghost"
    The Shubert Angels
  "A Song to Sing"
    N. Morris, D. Hall, L. Galloway, D. Lasley, The Theatre Wings, The Shubert Angels
  "A Dawn"
    A. Braunstein, S. L. Toder, The Theatre Wings
  "The Days of This Life"
    Bobby Alessi, Billy Alessi, N. Morris, J. P. Farrell
  "I Never Knew"
    S. Bey
  "Air Male"
    The Theatre Wings
  "Undo"
    D. Hall
  "The Earth"
    W. Redfield, R. Allen
  "My Darling I Love You March"
    The Theatre Wings, The Shubert Angels
  "So Long Dude"
    The Theatre Wings
  "Dude All Dude"
    The Theatre Wings, The Shubert Angels
  "Peace Peace"
    The Shubert Angels
  "Jesus Hi"
    The Shubert Angels
  "Baby Breath"
    S. Bey, D. Hall, A. Nicholls, The Theatre Wings, The Shubert Angels
  "Sweet Dreams"
    A. Nicholls, Company

HURRY, HARRY

1972.19

A Musical Comedy in Two Acts, 19 Scenes. Book by Jeremiah Morris, Lee Kalcheim, Susan Perkis. Music by Bill Weeden. Lyrics by David Finkle. Directed by Jeremiah Morris. Choreography by Gerald Teijelo. Scenery designed by Fred Voelpel. Lighting designed by Martin Aronstein. Costumes designed by Sara Brook. Orchestrations and musical supervision, Lee Norris. Musical direction, Arthur Azener. Associate producer, Ed Lewis. Produced by Peter N. Grad. Opened 12 October 1972 at the Ritz Theatre and closed 13 October 1972 after 2 performances.

CAST (in order of appearance): *Harrison Fairchild IV:* SAMUEL D. RATCLIFFE. *Harrison Fairchild III:* PHIL LEEDS. *Patience Fairchild:* LIZ SHERIDAN. *Muffy Weathersford:* MARY BRACKEN PHILLIPS. *Nick:* Louis Criscuolo. *Marco:* Jack Landron. *Stavos:* Robert Darnell. *Helena:* Randee Heller. *Mama:* LIZ SHERIDAN. *Town Drunk:* PHIL LEEDS. *Melina:* Donna Liggitt Forbes. *Exodus:* Robert Darnell. *Genesis:* Jack Landron. *Deutronomy:* Louis Criscuolo. *Dr. Krauss:* PHIL LEEDS. *Writers:* Louis Criscuolo, Robert Darnell, Randee Heller, Jack Landron, Liz Sheridan. *Starlet:* Donna Liggitt Forbes. *Native #1:* Robert Darnell. *Native #2:* Donna Liggitt Forbes. *Native #3:* Liz Sheridan. *Native #4:* Randee Heller. *Native #5:* Jack Landron. *Witch Doctor:* Louis Criscuolo. *Chief:* PHIL LEEDS. *Star:* LIZ SHERIDAN. *Chorus Boys:* Louis Criscuolo, Robert Darnell, Jack Landron, Phil Leeds. *Not-So-Grand Lamas:* Louis Criscuolo, Donna Liggitt Forbes, Randee Heller, Jack Landron, Phil Leeds, Liz Sheridan. *Grand Lama:* Robert Darnell. *Winston:* Robert Darnell. *Gypsy:* Randee Heller. *Uncle Larry:* PHIL LEEDS. *Congregation:* Louis Criscuolo, Robert Darnell, Donna Liggitt Forbes, Randee Heller, Jack Landron, Phil Leeds, Liz Sheridan.

Act 1, Scene 1: The Wedding Day. *Scene 2*: Taverna in Greece. *Scene 3*: Airport. *Scene 4*: Psychiatrist's Office. *Scene 5*: Hollywood. *Scene 6*: Street in Hollywood. *Scene 7*: Psychiatrist's Office. *Scene 8*: Africa. *Scene 9*: Alone in the World.

Act 2, Scene 1: Psychiatrist's Office. *Scene 2*: Shubert Theatre. *Scene 3*: Psychiatrist's Office. *Scene 4*: Lamasery. *Scene 5*: Psychiatrist's Office. *Scene 6*: A Street. *Scene 7*: Gyspy's Store. *Scene 8*: Church. *Scene 9*: Alone in the World. *Scene 10*: Beach.

ACT 1

Scene 1

"I'm Gonna"

S. D. Ratcliffe

Scene 2

"When a Man Cries"

L. Criscuolo, L. Sheridan, R. Heller, J. Landron, R. Darnell, P. Leeds,
D. L. Forbes

Scene 3

"A Trip Through My Mind"

M. B. Phillips, Dead Sea Scrolls

Scene 5

"Life"

S. D. Ratcliffe, the Writers

Scene 6

"Love Can"

M. B. Phillips

Scene 8

"Africa Speaks"

Natives, L. Criscuolo

Scene 9

"Somewhere in the Past"

S. D. Ratcliffe

ACT 2

Scene 2

"Hurry, Harry"

L. Sheridan, Chorus Boys

Scene 3

"Goodbye"

M. B. Phillips

Scene 5

"You Won't Be Happy"

S. D. Ratcliffe, P. Leeds

Scene 8

"He Is My Bag"

S. D. Ratcliffe, Congregation

Scene 9

"Somewhere in the Past" (reprise)

S. D. Ratcliffe, M. B. Phillips

Scene 10

Finale

1972.20   PACIFIC PARADISE

A Maori Musical Revue from New Zealand in Two Acts, 4 Scenes. Directed by Jack Regas. Maori Cultural Director, Arapata Whaanga. Choral director, Kelly Harris. Opening narration compiled and edited by Kit Regas. Lighting by Four Star Stage Lighting. Sound by Masque Sound. Produced by Irving Sudrow. Opened 16 October 1972 at the Palace Theatre and closed 21 October 1972 after 5 performances.

CAST: THE NEW ZEALAND MAORI COMPANY: Faule Bryant, Huri Callaghan, Matekino Callaghan, Sera Chase, Tiramate Dennis, Karen Donaghy, Cecilia Eparaima, Richard Eparaima, Kuini Farthing, Joshua Gardiner, Dawn Hepari, Lena Hiha, Christine Hikuroa, Eva Hona, Te Kani Horsefall, Bernadette Huata, Paraire Huata, Hemi Huata, Ngamoni Huata, Rongo Kahu, Sonny Keepa, Rachel Kewene, Tangiwai Kingi, Karu Kukutai, Josephine Loader, Putiputi Mackey, Gabrielle Mareikura, Rose Maxwell, Terry Maxwell, Kipa Morehu, Gordon Moses, Helen Moses, Philip Munro, Betty Nathan, James Nathan, Brenda Nepe, Dianne Nukutarwhiti, Iti Paenga, Tomaurangi Paki, Thomas Ratima, Kuini Reedy, Percy Reedy, Rimupae Rennie, Derna Richardson, Keren Ricka, Barbara Ringiao, Norga Ringaio, James Robert, Pauline Ruru, Abie Scott, Roberta Smiler, Josephine Smiler, Hineawe Smith, Nagatai Stockman, Raana Tangira, Wiremu Tangira, Irirangi Tahuriorangi, Reverend Anaru Takurua, Putiputi Tonihi, Rongo Tuhura, Atareta Waerea, Royal Walker, Tom Ward, Vicky Ward, Leona Watene, Muriel Wehi, Ngapo Wehi, Tiu Yaes, ARAPATA WHAANGA.

Act 1, Scene 1: Maori Welcome Ceremony. *Scene 2:* Legend of the Great Maori Migration. *Scene 3:* Village Life in the New Land.

Act 2: Maori Festival.

ACT 1

Scene 1

Wero (Warrior's Challenge)

Karanga

Elder women of the tribes call upon the spirit of their ancestors to give them strength to welcome you.

Utaina (Chant of Assembly)

Te Urunga Tu (Traditional Welcome Dance)

"Karanga Tia" (Action song expressing their joy that you are here)

Scene 2

Poroporoaki (Entrance of the Tohunga, the High Preist)

Tohunga: A. Whaanga.

Whakaara (Calling of the people together for discussion)

Whaikorero

In the beginning, in the legendary land of Hawaiiki, the rulers have decreeed that no man may own his own property. All people are welcome to stay but all properties must be shared. Tales of a new land far to the south have created great debate among the Maori tribal chiefs. Some are opposed but many are in favor of seeking a new home far across the seas. In the end, the Tohunga makes the decision. The people agree.

"E Oho Te Whaanau" (Song of Decision. We will go together.)

Tohi Waka (Blessing of the canoes.)

"Uia Mai Koia" (Canoe song. The long hazardous voyage begins.)

Ma Tangi

Our minds are ever thoughtful of the ones we left behind.

Poi Waka

Using their poi balls as paddles, the women demonstrate their fervor in assisting the men. Time passes. The ocean is great. Supplies fade. Disheartened and near starvation, the Maories through suppplication, prayer and faith in their gods, finally sight the distant land of the long low clouds.

Kura Ti Waka

In their final vigorous efforts to reach the shore, the men dedicate themselves and their women to the perpetuation of their race.

"Ti Tiro Mai" (Song of Thanksgiving)

Scene 3

"Taku Patu" (Introductory song)

"Karu" (Song of the fisherman)

He Manuhiri

A visiting tribe approaches the village. They are challenged and in turn counter-challenge. A visiting maiden attracts the eye of a young warrior of the village. He is rebuked by her would-be suitor. A battle follows.

"Po Karekare Ana" (Love song)

With the blessing of the Tohunga, the young couple are joined in marriage.

Tu Mara Mara (A chant uniting the tribes)

Paki Kini (Dance of jubilation)

ACT 2

Poi dances

a. Short single poi. b. Short double poi. c. Long single poi. d. Long double poi. e. Combinations.

"Tangi Hia" (Action song of joy at being here.)

Pana Pana/Rua Moko (Dance to the earthquake gods.)

Tititoria (Women's stick games)

"Koroki" (Song of courtship)

Peru-Peru (A Tai Aha {Spear} Haka)

Ti Rakau (Exercise for timing and agility)

Three and Four Poi Competitions

E Te Hokowhitu and

Pa Aki Kini (Two evolutionary treatments of familiar music)

"E Pare Ra" (A song of departure)

Po Ata Ro

Without metals, using only woods, stone (including the famous New Zealand jade or greenstone), the Maori (pronounced MOW-RY) developed one of the most outstanding cultural nations of the South Pacific. From birth, the male and female child were cherished and taught the arts of oratory, song, dexterity of movement and feats of strength and endurance. Facial grimaces, protruding tongue, eyes rolling, the Maori both intimidates his enemy and intrigues his friends.

Traditional music was based on the quarter tone scale. Today, possessing a natural flair for the rich harmonies, he revels in the Western usage of the half tone scale.

The poi, made of swamp reed (raupo), rolled into a ball and fastened with varying lengths of flax fiber aided the women in attracting the men by demonstration of their grace and dexterity. It also strengthened them for battle in the event their men were overcome in war.

The haka (Men's dances) are of many variations and for many purposes. A display of aggressive manliness in war. A dance to placate the gods, to recall tribal victories, to dispel fear of the unknown. A chance to display manly energy and prowess.

The tiki is highly prized as a personal adornment worn like a pendant around the neck. fashioned from greenstone, as is implied by its foetal form, it is symbolic of the power of creativeness, the sacred attribute of Deity.

1972.21

MOTHER EARTH

A Musical (Revue) in Two Acts, 18 Scenes. Sketches and lyrics by Ron Thronson. Music by Toni Shearer. Directed by Ray Golden. Musical staging by Lynne Morris. Consultant, Kermit Bloomgarden. Scenery by Alan Kimmel. Costumes by Mary McKinley. Lighting by Paul Sullivan. Musical direction and supervision by Larry White. Orchestrations by Alf Clausen. Visuals by Kenneth Shearer. Dance arrangements by Sande Campbell. Associate producers, Howard Butcher IV, Graeme Howard. Entire production supervised by Roger Ailes. Produced by Roger Ailes. Opened 19 October 1972 at the Belasco Theatre and closed 28 October 1972 after 12 performances.

CAST (in alphabetical order): Gail Boggs, Frank T. Coombs, Kimberly Farr, Kelly Garrett, Will Jacobs, Carol Kristy, Laura Michaels, John Bennett Perry, Rick Podell, Charlie J. Rodriguez.

ACT 1
Scene 1
  Out of Space
  "Mother Earth"
    K. Garrett, Company
Scene 2
  The Client
  "The Time of Our Life"
    L. Michaels, C. J. Rodriguez
  "Corn on the Macabre"
    C. Kristy, R. Podell, G. Boggs
    (*Music and Lyrics by* Ron Thronson, Roger Ailes, Ray Golden.)
Scene 3
  The Mask Parade
  "Too Many Old Ideas"
    K. Garrett
Scene 4
  The Cheerleader
    (*by* Jerry Patch, William Black and Ray Golden)
  Uneasy Rider
  Landscape With Figures
  "Room to Be Free"
    R. Podell
Scene 5
  Model Wife
  "Rent a Robot"
    W. Jacobs
Scene 6
  A Hike in the Woods
    (*by* Jerry Patch and William Black)
  Flash Gordon
  "Plow It All Under"
    C. Kristy, Company
Scene 7
  Ewe Turn
    (*by* Ray Golden)
  The Offal Truth (Ain't It Offal)
    (*by* Jack Marlowe and Ray Golden)
  The Killathon
    (*by* Ron Thronson, Roger Ailes and Ray Golden)
  "Taking the Easy Way Out"
    J. B. Perry, F. T. Coombs, C. J. Rodriguez

Scene 8
  Joggers
  "Ozymandias"
    J. B. Perry
  "Talons of Time"
    K. Garrett
  "Corn on the Macabre" (reprise)
    L. Michaels, K. Farr, F. T. Coombs
Scene 9
  The Nursery
  "Save the World for Children"
    G. Boggs
  "Sail On Sweet Universe"
    K. Garrett, Company
ACT 2
Scene 1
  "Mater Terra"
    Company
  "Xanadu"
    C. Kristy, Company
Scene 2
  Breath-Out
  "Ecology Waltz"
    (*Lyrics by* Ray Golden.)
    K. Farr, R. Podell
Scene 3
  Chic Diners
  "Corn on the Macabre" (reprise)
    C. Kristy, C. J. Rodriguez, G. Boggs
Scene 4
  Women Shoppers
    (*by* Ron Thronson and Ray Golden)
  The Swan
  "Good Morning World"
    J. B. Perry
Scene 5
  The Last Redwoods
  The Animals
    (*by* Ray Golden)
  "Tiger! Tiger!"
    K. Garrett
Scene 6
  Concrete Proposal
  "Happy Mother's Day, Mother Earth"
    C. J. Rodriguez
Scene 7
  Radioactive Terminate
  "Pills"
    K. Garrett, G. Boggs, C. Kristy, Company
    (*Music and Lyrics by* Ray Golden.)
Scene 8
  The Billboards
    (*by* Jack Marlowe and Ray Golden)
  "Corn on the Macabre" (reprise)
    K. Garrett, R. Podell, F. T. Coombs
Scene 9
  Total Recall
    (*by* Ray Golden)
  Finale

1972.22

PIPPIN

A Musical Comedy in One Act, 8 Scenes. Book by Roger O. Hirson. Music and lyrics by Stephen Schwartz. Directed and choreographed by Bob Fosse. Scenery by Tony Walton. Costumes by Patricia Zipprodt. Lighting by Jules Fisher. Musical direction by Stanley Lebowsky. Orchestrations by Ralph

Burns. Dance arrangements by John Berkman. Sound by Abe Jacob. Produced by Stuart Ostrow. Opened 23 October 1972 at the Imperial Theatre, moved 15 March 1977 to the Minskoff Theatre, and closed 12 June 1977 after 1944 performances.

CAST (in order of appearance): *Leading Player*: BEN VEREEN. *Pippin*: JOHN RUBINSTEIN. *Charles*: ERIC BERRY. *Lewis*: Christopher Chadman. *Fastrada*: LELAND PALMER. *Musician*: John Mineo. *The Head*: Roger Hamilton. *Berthe*: IRENE RYAN. *Beggar*: Richard Korthaze. *Peasant*: Paul Solen. *Noble*: Gene Foote. *Field Marshall*: Roger Hamilton. *Catherine*: JILL CLAYBURGH. *Theo*: Shane Nickerson.
(*The Players*: Candy Brown, Kathryn Doby, Jennifer Nairn-Smith, Ann Reinking, Pamela Sousa.)

The action takes place in 780 A.D. and thereabouts, in the Holy Roman Empire and thereabouts.

Scene 1: The Opening. *Scene 2*: Home. *Scene 3*: War. *Scene 4*: The Flesh. *Scene 5*: Revolution. *Scene 6*: Encouragement. *Scene 7*: The Hearth. *Scene 8*: The Finale.

MUSICAL NUMBERS

Scene 1

"Magic to Do"
  B. Vereen, Players
"Corner of the Sky"
  J. Rubinstein

Scene 2

"Welcome Home"
  E. Berry, J. Rubinstein

Scene 3

"War Is a Science"
  E. Berry, J. Rubinstein
"Glory"
  B. Vereen

Scene 4

"Simple Joys"
  B. Vereen
"No Time at All"
  I. Ryan, The Boys
"With You"
  J. Rubinstein, The Girls

Scene 5

"Spread a Little Sunshine"
  L. Palmer
"Morning Glow"
  J. Rubinstein

Scene 6

"On the Right Track"
  B. Vereen, J. Rubinstein

Scene 7

"Kind of Woman"
  J. Clayburgh, The Girls
"Extraordinary"
  J. Rubinstein
"Love Song"
  J. Rubinstein, J. Clayburgh

Scene 8

Finale
  The Players

1972.23   LYSISTRATA

A Musical in One Act. Play by Aristophanes. Adapted (from the Greek) by Michael Cacoyannis. Music by Peter Link. Sets by Robin Wagner. Costumes by Willa Kim. Lighting by Jules Fisher. Sound by Abe Jacob. Associate producer, Ira Resnick. Musical director, [Henry] 'Bootsie' Normand. Produced by David Black and David Seltzer. Opened 13 November 1972 at the Brooks Atkinson Theatre and closed 18 November 1972 after 8 performances.

CAST (in order of appearance): *Lysistrata*: MELINA MERCOURI. *Kalonike*: EVELYN RUSSELL. *Myrrhine*: Priscilla Lopez. *Lampito*: Madeleine Le Roux.

Corinthian Woman: Lynda Sue Marks. *Theban Woman*: Andrea Levine. *Policewoman*: Marylou Perhacs. *Omicron*: JOHN BENTLEY. *Phi-Chi*: GORDON CONNELL. *Omega*: Joseph Palmieri. *Upsilon*: David Thomas. *Epsilon*: JACK FLETCHER. *Gamma*: JANE CONNELL. *Alphabeta*: Avril Gentles. *Deltazeta*: MARY JO CATLETT. *Theta*: Patti Karr. *Iota*: Gayla Osbourne. *Commissioner*: PHILIP BRUNS. *Woman A*: Cynthia Bullens. *Woman B*: Joanne Nail. *Woman C*: Joy Franz. *Kinesias*: RICHARD DMITRI. *Spartan Herald*: Stephen Macht. *Spartan Delegate*: Charles E. Siegel.

MUSICAL NUMBERS

"A Woman's Hands"
  M. Mercouri
"On, On, On"
  M. Mercouri, Women
"Many the Beasts"
  Men
"Are We Strong?"
  M. Mercouri, Women
"And We Are In"
  M. Mercouri, Women
"Lysistrata"
  M. Mercouri, Women
"I Miss My Man"
  P. Lopez
"To Touch the Sky"
  M. Mercouri, Women
"A Woman's Hands" (reprise)
  M. Mercouri
"Eels Are a Girl's Best Friend"
  Women
"Let Me Tell You a Little Story"
  Men, Women
"Kalimera"
  M. Mercouri, Company

1972.24   AMBASSADOR

A Musical in Two Acts, 19 Scenes. Book by Don Ettlinger and Anna Marie Barlow. Based on the novel "The Ambassadors" by Henry James. Music by Don Gohman. Lyrics by Hal Hackady. Directed by Stone Widney. Musical staging and choreography by Joyce Trisler. Sets and costumes by Peter Rice. American production supervised by Robert Guerra. Costumes supervised by Sara Brook. Lighting by Martin Aronstein. Musical arrangements and vocal arrangements by Herbert Grossman. Orchestrations by Philip J. Lang. Dance arrangements by Trude Rittman. Associate producer, Dan Rodden. Produced by Gene Dingenary, Miranda d'Ancona and Nancy Levering. Opened 19 November 1972 at the Lunt-Fontanne Theatre and closed 25 November 1972 after 9 performances.

CAST (in order of appearance): *Flower Girl*: Patricia Arnell. *Lewis Lambert Strether*: HOWARD KEEL. *Waymarsh*: DAVID SABIN. *Marie de Vionnet*: DANIELLE DARRIEUX. *Gloriani*: CARMEN MATHEWS. *Waiter*: Dwight Arno. *Bilham*: Michael Goodwin. *Chad*: Michael Shannon. *Jeanne de Vionnet*: ANDREA MARCOVICCI. *Dancing Master*: Larry Giroux. *Artist*: Larry Giroux. *Guide*: Jack Trussel. *Waiter*: Robert L. Hultman. *Innkeeper's Wife*: Marsha Tamaroff. *Bellboy*: Nikolas Dante. *Lady in Park*: Dixie Stewart. *Amelia Newsome*: M'el Dowd. *Germaine*: Patricia Arnell. *Cabaret Dancers*: Alex Hoff, Phillip Filiato, Suzanne Sponsler, Larry Giroux. *Headwaiter*: Robert L. Hultman. *Hotel Manager*: Jack Trussel.
People of Paris: Janis Ansley, Patricia Arnell, Dwight Arno, Marcia Brooks, Nikolas Dante, Richard Dodd, Vito Durante, Phillip Filiato, Lynn Fitzpatrick, Larry Giroux, Charlie Goeddertz, Gerald Haston, Alexis Hoff, Robert L. Hultman, Douglas E. Hunnikin, Genette Lane, Betsy Ann Leadbetter, Nancy Lynch, Linda-Lee MacArthur, Adam Petroski, Dean Russell, Salicia Saree, Ellie Smith, Suzanne Sponsler, Dixie Stewart, Marsha Tamaroff, Jack Trussel, Chester Walker.

The action takes place in Paris in 1906.

Act 1, Scene 1: The Tuileries. *Scene 2*: Chad's Apartment. *Scene 3*: Gloriani's Garden. *Scene 4*: Terrace of Lambert's Apartment. *Scene 5*: A Park. *Scene 6*: Notre Dame Cathedral. *Scene 7*: The Left Bank. *Scene 8*: Terrace of Lambert's Apartment. *Scene 9*: An Inn at St. Cloud.

Act 2, Scene 1: The Tuileries. *Scene 2*: Terrace (of) Lambert's Apartment. *Scene 3*: A Secluded Part of the Bois de Boulogne. *Scene 4*: Chad's Apartment. *Scene 5*: Marie's Garden. *Scene 6*: Le Petit Moulin Cabaret. *Scene 7*: Marie's Garden. *Scene 8*: A Bridge. *Scene 9*: The Hotel Lobby. *Scene 10*: A Bridge.

ACT 1
Scene 1
  "Lilas"
    P. Arnell
  "Lambert's Quandary"
    H. Keel
  "I Know the Man"
    D. Darrieux
Scene 3
  "The Right Time, the Right Place"
    Gloriani's Guests (Ensemble)
  "She Passed My Way"
    D. Darrieux, Guests
  "Valse"
    Gloriani's Guests (Ensemble)
Scene 4
  "Something More"
    H. Keel
Scene 5
  "Love Finds the Lonely"
    A. Marcovicci
Scene 6
  "Kyrie Eleison"
    Choir
Scene 7
  "Surprise"
    D. Darrieux, H. Keel, People of the Left Bank (Ensemble)
Scene 8
  "Happy Man"
    H. Keel

ACT 2
Scene 1
  "Lilas, What Happened to Paris"
    H. Keel, P. Arnell
Scene 2
  "Young With Him"
    D. Darrieux
  "Too Much to Forgive"
    H. Keel
Scene 3
  "Why Do Women Have to Call It Love?"
    C. Mathews, D. Sabin
Scene 5
  "Mama"
    A. Marcovicci
  "That's What I Need Tonight"
    D. Darrieux, H. Keel
Scene 6
  "Maxixe-Habanera"
    Cabaret Dancers, People of Paris
  "That's What I Need Tonight" (reprise)
    H. Keel, D. Darrieux, People of Paris
  "Gossip"
    Ladies of Paris
Scene 7
  "Not Tomorrow"
    D. Darrieux
Scene 8
  "All of My Life"
    H. Keel
Scene 9
  "Thank You, No"
    H. Keel

1972.25   VIA GALACTICA

A Musical in Two Acts, 7 Scenes. Book by Christopher Gore and Judith Ross. Music by Galt MacDermott. Lyrics by Christopher Gore. Entire pro-

duction conceived and directed by Peter Hall. Production (setting) and costumes designed by John Bury. Lighting by Lloyd Burlingame. Musical director, Thomas Pierson. Vocal arrangements by Joyce Brown. Orchestrations by Bhen Lazaroni, Horace Ott, Danny Hurd. Sound by Jack Shearing. Ensemble movement by George Faison. Produced by George W. George and Barnard S. Strauss in association with Nat Shapiro. Opened 28 November 1972 at the Uris Theatre and closed 2 December 1972 after 7 performances.

CAST: *The Storyteller*: Irene Cara. *Gabriel Finn*: RAUL JULIA. *Hels (Mikelli)*: DAMON EVANS. *April Whitney*: EDLOE. *Omacha*: VIRGINIA VESTOFF. *Dr. Isaacs*: KEENE CURTIS. *Provo*: Bill Starr.
    On Earth: *Spokesman*: James Dybas. *Old Man*: Chuck Cissel. *Blue People*: Mark Baker, Jacqueline Britt, Melanie Chartoff, Richard DeRusso, Sylvia DiGiorgio, Livia Genise, Marion Killinger, Toni Lund, Bob Spencer, Bonnie Walker.
    On Ithaca: *Diane*: Livia Genise. *Nicklas*: Peter Nissen. *The Roustabout*: Alex Ander. *The Cook*: Mark Baker. *The Mute's Friend*: Robert Blankshine. *The Gypsy*: Jacqueline Britt. *The Boy*: Ralph Carter. *The Geologist*: Melanie Chartoff. *The Student*: Chuck Cissel. *The Mute*: Lili Cockerille. *The Lady*: Lorrie Davis. *The Mechanic*: Richard DeRusso. *The Teacher*: Sylvia DiGiorgio. *The Entertainer*: James Dybas. *The Writer*: Livia Genise. *The Politician*: Marion Killinger. *The Child*: Toni Lund. *The Cripple*: Veronica Redd. *The Tailor*: James Rivers. *The Carpenter*: Richard Ryder. *The Doctor*: Stan Shaw. *The Gambler*: Leon Spelman. *The Janitor*: Bob Spencer. *The Nurse*: Bonnie Walker. *The Grandmother*: J. H. Washington.

(The action takes place a thousand years from now on Earth, on a remote asteroid called Ithaca, and in outer space.)

ACT 1
  "Via Galactica"
    I. Cara
  "We Are One"
    The Blue People
  "Helen of Troy"
    R. Julia
  "Oysters"
    D. Evans, Edloe
  "The Other Side of the Sky"
    D. Evans
  "Children of the Sun"
    V. Vestoff
  "Different"
    Edloe, Company
  "Take Your Hat Off"
    V. Vestoff, Company
  "Ilmar's Tomb"
    V. Vestoff
  "Shall We Friend?"
    R. Julia
  "The Lady Isn't Looking"
    V. Vestoff
  "Hush"
    R. Julia
  "Cross on Over"
    K. Curtis, V. Vestoff, Company
  "The Gospel of Gabriel Finn"
    R. Julia
ACT 2
  "Terre Haute High"
    Edloe
  "Life Wins"
    V. Vestoff
  "The Worm Germ"
    B. Starr
  "Isaac's Equation"
    K. Curtis
  "Dance the Dark Away"
    I. Cara, Company
  "Four Hundred Girls Ago"
    R. Julia
  "All My Good Mornings"
    V. Vestoff
  "Isaac's Equation" (reprise)
    K. Curtis

"Children of the Sun" (reprise)
V. Vestoff, R. Julia
"New Jerusalem"
Company

Holiday in the Kibbutz
Karmon Israeli Dancers
Finale
Entire Company

1972.26 PURLIE

A Return Engagement of the Musical Comedy in Two Acts, a Prologue, 6 Scenes and an Epilogue[8]. Book by Ossie Davis, Philip Rose and Peter Udell. Based on the play "Purlie Victorious" by Ossie Davis. Music by Gary Geld. Lyrics by Peter Udell. Production directed by Philip Rose. Choreography by Louis Johnson. Scenery by Ben Edwards. Lighting by Thomas Skelton. Costumes by Ann Roth. Orchestrations and choral arrangements by Garry Sherman and Luther Henderson. Musical supervisor, Garry Sherman. Musical conductor, Charles Austin. Dance music arranged by Luther Henderson. Produced by Philip Rose. Opened 27 December 1972 at the Billy Rose Theatre and closed 7 January 1973 after 14 performances.

CAST (in order of appearance): Purlie: ROBERT GUILLAUME. Church Soloist: SHIRLEY MONROE. Lutiebelle: PATTI JO. Missy: LAURA COOPER. Gitlow: SHERMAN HEMSLEY. Field Hands: Every Hayes, Lonnie McNeil, Ted Ross. Charlie: DOUGLAS NORWICK. Idella: HELEN MARTIN. Ol' Cap'n: ART WALLACE.

Dancers: Darlene Blackburn, Deborah Bridges, Raphael Gilbert, Linda Griffin, Every Hayes, Reggie Jackson, Alton Lathrop, Robert Martin, Karen E. McDonald, Lonnie McNeil, Debbie Palmer, Andre Peck, Zelda Pulliam. Singers: Demarest Grey, Barbara Joy, Ursuline Kairson, Shirley Monroe, Alfred Rage, Beverly G. Robnett, Ted Ross, Frances Salisbury, Vanessa Shaw, David Weatherspoon, Joe Williams, Jr.

1973.01 GRAND MUSIC HALL OF ISRAEL

A Return Engagement of the Israeli Revue in Two Acts[9]. Conceived, directed and choreographed by Jonathan Karmon. Assistant director, Gavri Levi. Musical director, Rafi Paz. Costumes by Lydia Pinkus Ganay. Produced by Madison Square Garden Productions and Hy Einhorn. Opened 4 January 1973 at the Felt Forum and closed 14 January 1973 after 15 performances.

CAST: SHOSHANA DAMARI, RON ELIRAN, MYRON COHEN (Special Guest Host), ARIELA, THE MARGANIOT (Zlila, Leah), THE TAL U'MATAR (Shlomo on drums, flute, voice; Yehezkel, sitar).

THE KARMON ISRAELI DANCERS AND SINGERS: Girls: Tami Tomer, Ofira Ofir, Dassy Shahar, Rima Meir, Ora Mor, Brurira Aviv, Varda Amir, Tirza Barir, Ruth Ramati. Boys: Tuvia Ofir, Itamar Gur, Arie Baror, Ephraim Zamir, Zvi Granit, Zvika Zohar, Shimon Ashkenzi, Jonathan Nahorai, Avi Zah.

ACT 1
Israeli Rhapsody (A Mosaic of Israeli Folk Dances)
Israeli Songs
    The Marganiot
The Fishermen of Kineret
    Karmon Israeli Dancers
Rhythm and Sound of the Desert
    The Tal U'Matar
A Night on the Gilboa Mountains
    Karmon Israeli Singers
Ron Eliran (songs)
A Panorama of Hassidic Life
    Karmon Israeli Dancers and Singers
ACT 2
The Mediterranean Flavor
    Karmon Israeli Dancers
Ariela (xylophone specialty)
Fire in the Mountains
    Karmon Israeli Dancers
Shoshana Damari (songs)

1973.02 TRICKS

A Musical Comedy in Two Acts, a Prologue and Epilogue. Book and direction by Jon Jory. Based on a play by Moliere ("Les Fourberies de Scapin," or "Monsieur Scapin."). Music by Jerry Blatt. Lyrics by Lonnie Burstein. Choreography by Donald Saddler. Scenery by Oliver Smith. Costumes by Miles White. Lighting by Martin Aronstein. Orchestrations by Bert de Coteau. Dance and incidental music arranged by Peter Howard. Conductor, David Frank. Sound by Jack Shearing. Associate producer, Samuel Liff. Produced by Herman Levin. Opened 8 January 1973 at the Alvin Theatre and closed 13 January 1973 after 8 performances.

CAST (in order of appearance): Property Mistress: Adale O'Brien. Octave, son of Argante, in love with Hyacinthe: Walter Bobbie. Sylvestre, Octave's servant: Christopher Murney. Scapin, Leandre's servant: RENE AUBERJONOIS. Hyacinthe, daughter of Geronte, in love with Octave: Carolyn Mignini. Argante, father of Octave: Mitchell Jason. Geronte, father of Leandre: Tom Toner. Leandre, son of Geronte, in love with Zerbinetta: Randy Herron. Zerbinetta, a Gypsy Queen, in love with Leandre: June Helmers. Pantanella: Suzanne Walker. Isabella: Jo Anne Ogawa. Carmella: Lani Sundsten. Gondolier: John Handy.

The Commedia: Arlecchino/Lead Singer: Joe Morton. Charlotta: Charlotte Crossley. Ernestina: Ernestine Jackson. Shezwae: Shezwae Powell.

The action takes place in and around Venice.

ACT 1
Prologue: "Love or Money"
    The Commedia
"Who Was I?"
    W. Bobbie, The Commedia
"Trouble's a Ruler"
    R. Auberjonois, C. Murney, W. Bobbie
"Enter Hyacinthe"
    W. Bobbie, The Commedia
"Believe Me"
    W. Bobbie, C. Mignini, The Commedia
"Tricks"
    R. Auberjonois, C. Murney
"A Man of Spirit"
    The Commedia
"Where Is Respect?"
    M. Jason, T. Toner
"Somebody's Doin' Somebody All the Time"
    R. Auberjonois, The Commedia
"A Sporting Man"
    R. Auberjonois, The Commedia
ACT 2
"Scapin"
    J. Morton
"Anything Is Possible"
    R. Auberjonois, C. Murney
"How Sweetly Simple"
    C. Mignini, J. Helmers
"Gypsy Girl"
    J. Helmers, The Commedia
Epilogue: "Life Can Be Funny"
    The Company

1973.03 SHELTER

A Musical in Two Acts. Book and lyrics by Gretchen Cryer. Music by Nancy Ford. Directed by Austin Pendleton. Musical staging by Sammy Bayes. Settings, costumes, projections designed by Tony Walton. Lighting and projections devised by Richard Pilbrow. Orchestrations and electronic arrangements by Thomas Pierson. Music direction and vocal arrangements by Kirk Nurock. Associate producer, Julie Hughes. Produced by Richard Fields and Peter Flood. Opened 6 February 1973 at the John Golden Theatre and closed 4 March 1973 after 31 performances.

---

[8]Originally produced in New York 15 March 1970 at the Broadway Theatre for 689 performances. For Synopsis of Scenes and Musical Numbers, see original 1970 production.
[9]First produced in New York 6 February 1968 at the Palace Theatre for 64 performances, and as NEW MUSIC HALL OF ISRAEL 2 October 1969 at the Lunt-Fontanne Theatre for 77 performances.

CAST: *Maud*: MARCIA RODD. *Michael*: TERRY KISER. *Wednesday November*: SUSAN BROWNING. *Gloria*: JOANNA MERLIN. *Television Crew*: Charles Collins, Britt Swanson. *Arthur* (not seen): TONY WELLS. *Voice of the Director* (not seen): Philip Kraus.

The action takes place at the present time in a television studio set.

ACT 1

Overture
　T. Wells
"Changing"
　M. Rodd, T. Wells
"Welcome to a New World"
　T. Kiser, T. Wells
"It's Hard to Care"
　T. Kiser, T. Wells, M. Rodd
"Woke Up Today"
　M. Rodd, T. Wells
"Mary Margaret's House in the Country"
　M. Rodd, T. Wells
"Woman on the Run"
　T. Wells
"Don't Tell Me It's Forever"
　M. Rodd, T. Kiser, T. Wells

ACT 2

"Sunshine"
　T. Wells
"I Bring Him Seashells"
　S. Browning
"She's My Girl"
　T. Kiser, M. Rodd, T. Wells
"Welcome to a New World" (reprise)
　M. Rodd, T. Kiser, T. Wells, S. Browning
"He's a Fool"
　S. Browning, M. Rodd
"Going Home with My Children"
　M. Rodd, T. Wells
"Sleep, My Baby, Sleep"
　T. Wells

1973.04 A LITTLE NIGHT MUSIC

A Musical in Two Acts, a Prologue and 15 Scenes. Book by Harold Wheeler. Suggested by a film ("Smiles of a Summer Night") by Ingmar Bergman. Music and lyrics by Stephen Sondheim. Directed by Harold Prince. Choreography by Patricia Birch. Scenic production designed by Boris Aronson. Costumes designed by Florence Klotz. Lighting designed by Tharon Musser. Musical director, Harold Hastings. Orchestrations by Jonathan Tunick. Production supervisor, Ruth Mitchell. Sound by Jack Mann. Produced by Harold Prince in association with Ruth Mitchell. Opened 25 February 1973 at the Sam S. Shubert Theatre, moved 18 September 1973 to the Majestic Theatre, and closed 3 August 1974 after 601 performances.

CAST (in order of appearance): *Mr. Lindquist*: Benjamin Rayson. *Mrs. Nordstrom*: Teri Ralston. *Mrs. Anderssen*: Barbara Lang. *Mr. Erlanson*: Gene Varrone. *Mrs. Segstrom*: Beth Fowler. *Frederika Armfeldt*: Judy Kahan. *Madame Armfeldt*: HERMIONE GINGOLD. *Frid, her butler*: GEORGE LEE ANDREWS. *Henrik Egerman*: MARK LAMBERT. *Anne Egerman*: VICTORIA MALLORY. *Fredrik Egerman*: LEN CARIOU. *Petra*: D. JAMIN-BARTLETT. *Desiree Armfeldt*: GLYNIS JOHNS. *Malla, her maid*: Despo. *Bertrand, a page*: Will Sharpe Marshall. *Count Carl-Magnus Malcolm*: LAURENCE GUITTARD. *Countess Charlotte Malcolm*: PATRICIA ELLIOTT. *Osa*: Sherry Mathis.

The action takes place in Sweden at the turn of the century.

Act 1, Scene 1: The Egerman Rooms. *Scene 2*: Stage of Local Theatre. *Scene 3*: The Egerman Rooms. *Scene 4*: Desiree's Digs. *Scene 5*: Breakfast Room in (the) Malcolm Country House. *Scene 6*: Egerman Rooms. *Scene 7*: Armfeldt Terrace.

Act 2, Scene 1: The Armfeldt Lawn. *Scene 2*: The Other Part of the Garden. *Scene 3*: Armfeldt Terrace. *Scene 4*: The Dining Room. *Scene 5*: Armfeldt Garden; Another Part of the Garden. *Scene 6*: Desiree's Bedroom. *Scene 7*: The Trees. *Scene 8*: Armfeldt House and Garden.

ACT 1

Overture
　B. Rayson, T. Ralston, B. Lang, G. Varrone, B. Fowler
Prologue
"Night Waltz"
　Company
Scene 1
"Now"
　L. Cariou
"Later"
　M. Lambert
"Soon"
　V. Mallory, M. Lambert, L. Cariou
"The Glamorous Life"
　J. Kahan, G. Johns, Despo, H. Gingold, T. Ralston, B. Fowler, B. Lang, B. Rayson, G. Varrone
Scene 2
"Remember?"
　B. Rayson, T. Ralston, B. Lang, G. Varrone, B. Fowler
Scene 3
"Remember?" (continued)
　B. Rayson, T. Ralston, B. Lang, G. Varrone, B. Fowler
Scene 4
"You Must Meet My Wife"
　G. Johns, L. Cariou
"Liaisons"
　H. Gingold
"In Praise of Women"
　L. Guittard
Scene 5
"In Praise of Women" (continued)
　L. Guittard
Scene 6
"Every Day a Little Death"
　P. Elliott, V. Mallory
Scene 7
"A Weekend in the Country"
　Company
ACT 2
Entr'acte, Scenes 1 and 2
"The Sun Won't Set"
　B. Lang, B. Fowler, T. Ralston, B. Rayson, G. Varrone
Scene 3
"It Would Have Been Wonderful"
　L. Cariou, L. Guittard
Scene 4
"Perpetual Anticipation"
　T. Ralston, B. Fowler, B. Lang
Scene 6
"Send in the Clowns"
　G. Johns
Scene 7
"The Miller's Son"
　D. Jamin-Bartlett
Scene 8
Finale
　Company

1973.05 IRENE

A Revival of the Musical Comedy in Two Acts, 10 Scenes[10]. (New) Book by Hugh Wheeler and Joseph Stein from an adaptation by Harry Rigby. Based

---

[10]Originally produced in New York 18 November 1919 at the Vanderbilt Theatre for 675 performances.

on the original play by James Montgomery. Music by Harry Tierney. Lyrics by Joseph McCarthy. Additional music and lyrics by Charles Gaynor and Otis Clements. Directed by Gower Champion. Musical numbers staged by Peter Gennaro. Production (settings) and costumes designed by Raoul Pene du Bois. Debbie Reynolds' costumes designed by Irene Sharaff. Lighting designed by David F. Segal. Music and vocal direction by Jack Lee. Orchestrations by Ralph Burns. Dance arrangements and incidental music by Wally Harper. Sound designed by Anthony Alloy. Music consultant and co-ordinator, Joseph A. McCarthy. Associate producer, Steven Beckler. Assistant choreographers, Mary Ann Niles and Tony Stevens. Produced by Harry Rigby, Albert W. Selden and Jerome Minskoff. Opened 13 March 1973 at the Minskoff Theatre and closed 7 September 1974 after 605 performances.

CAST (in order of appearance): *Mrs. O'Dare*: PATSY KELLY. *Jane Burke*: Janie Sell. *Helen McFudd*: Carmen Alvarez. *Jimmy O'Flaherty*: Bruce Lea. *Irene O'Dare*: DEBBIE REYNOLDS. *Emmeline Marshall*: RUTH WARRICK. *Clarkson*: Bob Freschi. *Donald Marshall*: MONTE MARKHAM. *Ozzie Babson*: Ted Pugh. *Madame Lucy*: GEORGE S. IRVING. *Arabella Thornsworthy*: Kate O'Brady.

Debutantes: Arlene Columbo, Meg Bussert, Carrie Fisher, Dorothy Wyn Gehgan, Marybeth Kurdock, Frances Ruth Lea, Jeanne Lehman, Kate O'Brady, Julie Pars, Pamela Peadon, Pat Trott, Sandra Voris, Jeanette Williamson, Penny Worth. *Ninth Avenue Fellas*: Paul Charles, Dennis Edenfield, David Evans, Bob Freschi, John Hamilton, Bruce Lea, Joe Lorden, Bryan Nicholas, Robert Rayow, Dennis Roth, Kenn Scalice, Ron Schwinn, David Steele, Albert Stephenson.

(The action takes place in New York City and on Long Island in 1919.)

Act 1, Scene 1: The Piano Store. *Scene 2*: The Music Room of the Marshall Estate. *Scene 3*: Ninth Avenue. *Scene 4*: Madame Lucy's Salon. *Scene 5*: The Front of the Piano Store. *Scene 6*: The Palais Royale.

Act 2, Scene 1: The Palais Royale. *Scene 2*: The Piano Store. *Scene 3*: Outside the Marquee Tent. *Scene 4*: The Italian Garden.

ACT 1

Scene 1

"The World Must be Bigger Than an Avenue"
    D. Reynolds
    (*Music by* Wally Harper. *Lyrics by* Jack Lloyd.)

Scene 2

"The Family Tree"[11]
    R. Warrick, Debutantes

"Alice Blue Gown"[12]
    D. Reynolds

"They Go Wild, Simply Wild, Over Me"
    G. S. Irving, Debutantes
    (*Music by* Fred Fisher. *Lyrics by* Joseph McCarthy.)

Scene 3

"An Irish Girl"
    D. Reynolds, Company
    (*Music and Lyrics by* Charles Gaynor and Otis Clements.)

Scene 4

"Stepping on Butterflies"
    G. S. Irving, D. Reynolds, C. Alvarez, J. Sell
    (*Music by* Wally Harper.)

Scene 5

"Mother Angel Darling"
    D. Reynolds, P. Kelly
    (*Music and Lyrics by* Charles Gaynor.)

Scene 6

"The Riviera Rage"
    D. Reynolds, Company
    (*Music by* Wally Harper.)

ACT 2

Scene 1

"The Last Part of Every Party"[13]
    Company

"We're Getting Away With It"[14]
    G. S. Irving, C. Alvarez, J. Sell, T. Pugh

Scene 2

"Irene"[15]
    D. Reynolds, Company

Scene 3

"The Great Lover Tango"
    M. Markham, C. Alvarez, J. Sell
    (*Music and Lyrics by* Charles Gaynor and Otis Clements.)

"You Made Me Love You" (from *THE HONEYMOON EXPRESS*)
    D. Reynolds, M. Markham
    (*Music by* James Monaco. *Lyrics by* Joseph McCarthy.)

"You Made Me Love You" (reprise)
    G. S. Irving, P. Kelly

Scene 4

Finale
    Company

1973.06

SEESAW

A Musical in Two Acts, 18 Scenes. Book by Michael Bennett. Based on the play "Two for the Seesaw" by William Gibson. Music by Cy Coleman. Lyrics by Dorothy Fields. Directed and choreographed by Michael Bennett. Co-choreographer, Grover Dale. Associate choreographers, Bob Avian, Tommy Tune. Scenery by Robin Wagner. Costumes by Ann Roth. Lighting by Jules Fisher. Musical direction and vocal arrangements by Don Pippin. Orchestrations by Larry Fallon. Dance arrangements supervised by Cy Coleman. Dance arrangemenbts by Elman Anderson, Cy Coleman, Marvin Hamlisch and David Spangler. Media art and photography by Sheppard Kerman. Sound by Dick Maitland, Bob Ring, Lou Gonzales. Produced by Joseph Kipness and Lawrence Kasha, James Nederlander, George M. Steinbrenner III, Lorin E. Price. Opened 18 March 1973 at the Uris Theatre, moved 1 August 1973 to the Mark Hellinger Theatre and closed 8 December 1973 after 296 performances.

CAST (in order of appearance): *Jerry Ryan*: KEN HOWARD. *Gittel Mosca*: MICHELE LEE. *David*: TOMMY TUNE. *Sophie*: CECELIA NORFLEET. *Julio Gonzales*: GIANCARLO ESPOSITO. *Sparkle*: LaMONTÉ PETERSON. *Nurse*: Judy [Judith] McCauley. *Ethel*: Cathy Brewer-Moore.

Citizens of New York City: John Almberg, Steve Anthony, Cathy Brewer-Moore, Eileen Casey, Wayne Cilento, Patti D'Beck, Terry Deck, Judy Gibson, Felix Greco, Mitzi Hamilton, Loida Iglesias, Bobby Johnson, Baayork Lee, Amanda McBroom, Judy McCauley, Anita Morris, Gerry O'Hara, Michon Peacock, Frank Pietri, Yolanda Raven, Michael Reed, Orrin Reiley, Don Swanson, William Swiggard, Tom Urich, Dona D. Vaughn, Clyde Walker, Thomas J. Walsh, Chris Wilzak.

The action takes place in New York City at the present time.

Act 1, Scene 1: Prologue. *Scene 2*: Times Square Area. *Scene 3*: Dance Studio on West 54th Street. *Scene 4*: Japanese Restaurant on 46th Street and Lincoln Center. *Scene 5*: Eas 116th Street. *Scene 6*: Gittel's Apartment in the East Village. *Scene 7*: Jerry's Apartment. *Scene 8*: Gittel's Apartment, then the street. *Scene 9*: The Banana Club. *Scene 10*: Gittel's Apartment.

Act 2, Scene 1: St. Vincent's Hospital. *Scene 2*: Dance Studio. *Scene 3*: Jerry's Apartment. *Scene 4*: Backstage at the Theatre. *Scene 5*: Central Park, later that night. *Scene 6*: Gittel's Apartment; phone booth at Kennedy Airport. *Scene 7*: Gittel's Apartment, 2:00A.M. *Scene 8*: Gittel's Apartment; Jerry's Apartment, a few days later.

ACT 1

Scene 1

"Seesaw"
    Full Company

Scene 2

"My City"
    K. Howard, Neighborhood Girls

Scene 3

"Nobody Does It Like Me"
    M. Lee

---

[11]From the original production of "Irene" in 1919.
[12]From the original production of "Irene" in 1919.
[13]From the original production of "Irene" in 1919.

[14]From the original production of "Irene" in 1919.
[15]From the original production of "Irene" in 1919.

Scene 4

"In Tune"
M. Lee, K. Howard

Scene 5

"Spanglish"
G. Esposito, M. Lee, K. Howard, C. Norfleet, Full Company

Scene 6

"Welcome to Holiday Inn"
M. Lee

Scene 7

"You're a Lovable Lunatic"
K. Howard

Scene 8

"He's Good for Me"
M. Lee

Scene 9

"Ride Out the Storm"[16]
L. Peterson, C. Norfleet, Full Company

ACT 2
Scene 1

"We've Got It"
K. Howard

"Poor Everybody Else"
M. Lee

Scene 2

"Chapter 54, Number 1909"
T. Tune, K. Howard, M. Lee, Dance Company

Scene 4

"The Concert"
M. Lee, Dance Company

"It's Not Where You Start"
T. Tune, Full Company

Scene 8

"I'm Way Ahead"/"Seesaw" (reprise)
M. Lee

1973.07 CYRANO

A Musical in Two Acts, 5 Scenes. Book and lyrics by Anthony Burgess. Based on his adaptation of Edmond Rostand's play "Cyrano de Bergerac." Music by Michael J. Lewis. Directed by Michael Kidd. Costumes by Desmond Heeley. Settings by John Jensen. Lighting by Gilbert V. Hemsley, Jr. Musical direction by Thomas Pierson. Orchestrations by Philip J. Lang. Sound by Abe Jacob. Incidental music Arranged by Clay Fullum. Dueling scenes staged by Patrick Crean, Erik Fredricksen. Produced by Richard Gregson and APJAC International. Opened 13 May 1973 at the Palace Theatre and closed 23 June 1973 after 49 performances.

CAST (in order of appearance): *Candle Lighters*: Paul Berget, Anthony Inneo. *Doorman*: Bob Heath. *Foodseller*: Tovah Feldshuh. *Marquis in Yellow*: Danny Villa. *Musketeer*: Michael Nolan. *Cavalryman*: Donavan Sylvest. *Pickpocket*: Geoff Garland. *Citizen*: James Richardson. *Citizen's Brother*: Tim Nissen. *The Marquis in Red*: Alexander Orfaly. *The Marquis in Beige*: Joel Craig. *Ragueneau*, a baker and poet: ARNOLD SOBOLOFF. *Christian de Neuvillette*: MARK LAMOS. *Madame Aubry*: Betty Leighton. *Ladies of the French Academy* (4): *Madame de Guemene*: Janet McCall. *Barthenoide*: Patricia Roos. *Felixerie*: Mimi Wallace. *Urimedonte*: Mary Straten. *Le Bret*, Captain of the Gascons: JAMES BLENDICK. *Roxana*: LEIGH BEERY. *Roxana's Duenna*: Anita Dangler. *Count de Guiche*, Guardian of Roxana: LOUIS TURENNE. *Viscount de Valvert*: J. Kenneth Campbell. *Actors*: Anthony Inneo, Richard Schneider. *Actresses*: Vicki Frederick, Jill Rose. *Jodelet*, a farceur: Michael Goodwin. *Montfleury*, a romantic tragedian: PATRICK HINES. *Cyrano de Bergerac*: CHRISTOPHER PLUMMER. *Lise*, Ragueneau's wife: Betty Leighton. *Boys after Pies*: Tim Nissen, Paul Berget. *Bakery Staff*: J. Kenneth Campbell, Geoff Garland, Janet McCall, Michael Nolan, James Richardson, Patricia Roos, Mary Straten. *Gascon Cadets and Soldiers*: J. Kenneth Campbell, Joel Craig, Michael Goodwin, Bob Heath, Anthony Inneo, Gale McNeeley, Michael Nolan, James Richardson, Richard Schneider, Donovan Sylvest, Danny Villa. *Theophraste*

Renaudot: George Spelvin. *Cyrano's Pages*: Paul Berget, Tim Nissen. *Capucine Monk*: Geoff Garland. *Sister Marguerite*: Betty Leighton. *Sister Marthe*: Anita Dangler. *Sister Claire*: Patricia Roos. *Nuns*: Tovah Feldshuh, Vicki Frederick, Janet McCall, Jill Rose, Mary Straten, Mimi Wallace.

The action takes place in Paris and environs in 1640, and in 1654.

Act 1, Scene 1: A theatre, Paris, 1640. *Scene 2*: Ragueneau's bakery, Paris.

Act 2, Scene 1: The balcony of Roxana's house, Paris. *Scene 2*: A battle camp near Arras. *Scene 3*: A convent, Paris, 14 years later.

ACT 1
Scene 1

"Cyrano's Nose" (Nose Song)
C. Plummer

"La France, La France"
Company

"Tell Her"
J. Blendick, C. Plummer

"From Now Till Forever"
C. Plummer, Company

Scene 2

"Bergerac"
C. Plummer, L. Beery

"Pocapdedious"
Cadets

"No, Thank You"
C. Plummer

"From Now Till Forever" (reprise)
C. Plummer, M. Lamos

ACT 2
Scene 1

"Roxana"
M. Lamos, Company

"It's She and It's Me"
M. Lamos

"You Have Made Me Love"
L. Beery

"Thither, Thother, Thide of the"
C. Plummer

"Pocapedious" (reprise)
Cadets

Scene 2

"Paris Cuisine"
C. Plummer, J. Blendick, Cadets

"Love Is Not Love"
L. Beery

Scene 3

"Autumn Carol"
L. Beery, Nuns

"I Never Loved You"
C. Plummer

1973.08 NASH AT NINE

A Wordsical (Musical Revue) in One Act structured from the works of Ogden Nash. Verses and Lyrics by Ogden Nash. Music by Milton Rosenstock. Conceived and directed by Martin Charnin. Orchestrations and musical supervision by John Morris. Musical direction, Karen Gustafson. Sets by David Chapman. Costumes by Theoni V. Aldredge. Lighting by Martin Aronstein. Produced by Les Schecter and Barbara Schwei in association with SRO Enterprises and Arnold Levy. Opened 17 May 1973 at the Helen Hayes Theatre and closed 2 June 1973 after 21 performances.

CAST: E. G. MARSHALL, VIRGINIA VESTOFF, Steve Elmore, Bill Gerber, Richie Schechtman.

MUSICAL NUMBERS[17]

Seaside Serenade; Farenheit Gesundheit; The Sniffle; Coefficients of Expansion (A Guide to the Infant Season); To a Small Boy Standing on

---

[16]Replaced for the subsequent National Tour by:

"The Party's on Me"
Lucie Arnaz (Gittel), Company

---

[17]The following are not so much song titles as they are a comprehensive list of the Ogden Nash verses as adapted and presented.

My Shoes While I Am Wearing Them; The Madcap Zoologist; The Panther, The Armadillo; The Canary; The Shrew; Experiment Degustatory; The Pig; A Bulletin Has Just Come In; The Fly; The Octopus; The Eel; The Kipper; The Clam; The Guppy; Barmaids Are Diviner Than Mermaids; But I Could Not Love Thee, Ann, So Much, Loved I Not Honoré More; The Armchair Golfer, or, Whimpers of a Shortchanged Viewer; Song of the Open Road; From an Antique Land; Any Millenniums Today, Lady?; Give-Away, Give-Away, Banker Man; I Will Arise and Go Now; Always Marry an April Girl; The Anniversary; Love Under the Republicans (or Democrats); A Word to Husbands; I'm Sure She Said Six-Thirty; To My Valentine; Reflections on Ice-Breaking; I Do, I Will, I Have; The Private Dining Room; One Third of a Calendar; Tin Wedding Whistle; What's in a Name? Here's What's in a Name, or, I Wonder What Became of John and Mary?;No Trouble at All, It's as Easy as Falling Off a Portable Bar; Grandpa Is Ashamed; A Brief Guide to New York; Requiem; The Pizza; All Quiet Along the Potomac, Except the Letter G; Shrinking Song; Suppose I Darken Your Door; You and Me and P. B. Shelley; Come, Come, Kerouac! My Generation is Beater than Yours; The Clean Platter; Coffee With the Meal; The Middle; The Return; Peekaboo, I Almost See You; Modest Meditations on the Here, The Heretofore, and the Hereafter; Birthday on the Beach; A Lady Thinks She Is Thirty; Crossing the Border; For a Good Dog.

1973–1974 SEASON

Ralph Carter in RAISIN
Martha Swope/TimePix

1973–1974 SEASON

1973.09 ## THE DESERT SONG

A Revival of the Musical in Two Acts, Eight Scenes[1]. Book and lyrics by Otto Harbach and Oscar Hammerstein II. Music by Sigmund Romberg. Directed by Henry Butler. Choreography by David Nillo. Costumes supervised by Sara Brook. Scenery and lighting by Clarke Dunham. Musical direction by Al Cavaliere. Dance arrangements by Dorothea Freitag. A Lehman Engel Production. Produced by Moe Septee in association with Jack L. Wolgin and Victor H. Potamkin. Opened 5 September 1973 at the Uris Theatre and closed 16 September 1973 after 15 performances.

CAST (in order of appearance): *Mindar:* Nicholas Scarpinati. *Sid El Kar:* JOHN RIBECCHI. *Hadji:* Dick Ensslen. *Palace Guard:* Frederick G. Sampson III. *Hassi:* MANDINGO SHAKA. *Neri:* Ruby Greene Aspinall. *Red Shadow/Pierre Birabeau:* DAVID CRYER. *Benjamin Kidd:* JERRY DODGE. *Captain Paul Fontaine:* STANLEY GROVER. *Lieutenant Davergne:* Kent Cottam. *Sergeant Boussac:* William Leyerle. *Azuri:* GLORIA ROSSI. *Azuri Dancing Girls:* Kita Bouroff, Lana Caradimas, Urylee Leonardos, Jane Lucas, Sandra Mannis, Dundi Wright. *Edith:* Osceola Davis. *Susan:* BRITT SWANSON. *General Birabeau:* SHEPPERD STRUDWICK. *Margot Bonvalet:* CHRIS CALLAN, Carol Jeanne Tenney (matinees). *Clementina:* GLORIA ZAGLOOL. *Ali Ben Ali:* MICHAEL KERMOYAN.

Ensemble: Ruby Greene Aspinall, Marsha Bagwell, Rita Oney Best, Kita Bouroff, Lana Caradimas, Jacqueline Clark, Osceola Davis, Karen Ford, Bonnie Hinson, Urylee Leonardos, Rona Leslie, Jane Lucas, Sandra Mannis, Berdeen E. Pigorsh, Brenda Schaffer, Dundi Wright, Donald Coleman, Bill Collins, Austin Colyer, Kent Cottam, Ronald De Felice, Dennis Dohman, Dick Ensslen, William Leyerle, Frederick G. Sampson III, Nicholas Scarpinati, Peter Schroeder, Arthur Shaffer, Anthony Tamburello, David Vogel, David Weatherspoon.

1973.10 ## RAISIN

A Musical in Two Acts, a Prologue and 14 Scenes. Book by Robert Nemiroff and Charlotte Zaltzberg. Based on Lorraine Hansberry's play "A Raisin in the Sun." Music by Judd Woldin. Lyrics by Robert Brittan. Directed and choreographed by Donald McKayle. Scenery by Robert U. Taylor. Costumes by Bernard Johnson. Lighting by William Mintzer. Musical director and conductor, Howard A. Roberts. Orchestrations by Al Cohn, Robert Freedman. Vocal arrangements by Joyce Brown, Howard A. Roberts. Dance arrangements by Judd Woldin. Incidental arrangements by Dorothea Freitag. Associate producers, Sydney Lewis, Jack Friel. First presented by Arena Stage in Washington, D.C. Produced by Robert Nemiroff. Opened 18 October 1973 at the 46th Street Theatre, moved 14 January 1975 to the Lunt-Fontanne Theatre and closed 8 December 1975 after 847 performances.

CAST (in order of appearance): *People of the Southside:* Chuck Thorpes, Eugene Little, Karen Burke, Zelda Pulliam, Elaine Beener, Renee Rose, Paul Carrington, Marenda Perry, Gloria Turner, Don Jay, Glenn Brooks, Marilyn Hamilton. *Pusher:* Al Perryman. *Victim:* Loretta Abbott. *Ruth Younger:* ERNESTINE JACKSON. *Travis Younger:* RALPH CARTER. *Mrs. Johnson:* HELEN MARTIN. *Walter Lee Younger:* JOE MORTON. *Beneatha Younger:* DEBORAH ALLEN. *Lena Younger (Mama):* VIRGINIA CAPERS. *Bar Girl:* Elaine Beener. *Bobo Jones:* Ted Ross. *Willie Harris:* Walter P. Brown. *Joseph Asagai:* ROBERT JACKSON. *African Drummer:* Chief Bey. *Pastor:* Herb Downer. *Pastor's Wife:* Marenda Perry. *Karl Lindner:* Richard Sanders.

The action takes place in Chicago in the 1950s.

Prologue: Night, The Block, Southside Chicago. *Act 1, Scene 1:* The Younger family living room/kitchenette. Early morning. *Scene 2:* The Southside and the Loop. Morning rush-hour. *Scene 3:* The apartment. Late afternoon. *Scene 4:* A Southside bar. That night. *Scene 5:* The apartment. Next morning. *Scene 6:* That night, the apartment.

Act 2, Scene 1: A Southside Church. Sunday morning. *Scene 2:* The bar. *Scene 3:* The Block and the apartment. That night. *Scene 4:* The apartment. Moving Day, some weeks later. *Scene 5:* The Block. Immediately following. *Scene 6:* The apartment, shortly later. *Scene 7:* The front stoop. Immediately following. *Scene 8:* The apartment. Immediately following.

---

[1]Originally produced in New York 30 November 1926 at the Casino Theatre for 471 performances. For Synopsis of Scenes and Song List, see original 1926 production. New lyrics by Edward Smith written for "Has Anyone Seen My Bennie?," It," and "One Good Boy Gone Wrong."

ACT 1
Prologue (jazz ballet)
Company
Scene 1
"Man Say"
J. Morton
"Whose Little Angry Man"
E. Jackson
Scene 2
"Runnin' to Meet the Man"
J. Mortn, Company
Scene 3
"A Whole Lotta Sunlight"
V. Capers
Scene 4
"Booze"
E. Beener, T. Ross, J. Morton, W. P. Brown, Company
Scene 5
"Alaiyo"
R. Jackson, D. Allen
Scene 6
("Same Old Color Scheme")(recorded)
(E. Beener)
"African Dance"
D. Allen, J. Morton, Company
"Sweet Time"
E. Jackson, J. Morton
"You Done Right"
J. Morton
ACT 2
Scene 1
"He Come Down This Morning"
H. Downer, M. Perry, V. Capers, H. Martin, E. Jackson, R. Carter, Company
Scene 3
"It's a Deal"
J. Morton
Scene 4
"Sweet Time" (reprise)
E. Jackson, J. Morton
Scene 5
"Sidewalk Tree"
R. Carter
Scene 6
"Not Anymore"
J. Morton, E. Jackson, D. Allen
Scene 7
"Alaiyo" (reprise)
R. Jackson
Scene 8
"It's a Deal"[2] (reprise)
J. Morton
"Measure the Valleys"
V. Capers
"He Come Down This Morning" (reprise)

1973.11 ## MOLLY

A Musical in Two Acts, 14 Scenes. Book by Louis Garfinkle and Leonard Adelson. Based on characters from (the radio series) "The Goldbergs" by Gertrude Berg. Music by Jerry Livingston. Lyrics by Leonard Adelson and Mack David. Directed by Alan Arkin. Dances by Grover Dale. Musical

---

[2]For International Tour, replaced by:
"Walter Lee Younger and Son"
Nate Barnett (Walter Lee)

direction and vocal arrangements by Jerry Goldberg. Orchestrations by Eddie Sauter. Dance arrangements by Arnold Gross. Scenery by Marsha L. Eck. Costumes by Carrie F. Robbins. Lighting by Jules Fisher. Sound by Gary Harris. Associate producers, Larry Fallon, Richard Vonella. Musical consultant, Ronald Snyder. Produced by Don Saxon/Don Kaufman/George Daley, in association with Complex IV. Opened 1 November 1973 at the Alvin Theatre and closed 29 December 1973 after 68 performances.

CAST (in order of appearance): *Angelina Frazini*: Suzanne Walker. *Mrs. Sullivan*: CAMILA ASHLAND. *Mr. Sullivan*: Eddie Phillips. *Mrs. Frazini*: Justine Johnson. *Molly (Goldberg)*: KAY BALLARD. *Mrs. Kramer*: Molly Stark. *Belle Seidenschneer*: RUTH MANNING. *Mrs. Bloom*: Hazel Weber Steck. *Mrs. Dutton*: Toni Darnay. *Rosalie (Goldberg)*: LISA ROCHELLE. *Jake (Goldberg)*: LEE WALLACE. *Uncle David*: ELI MINTZ. *Sammy (Goldberg)*: DANIEL FORTUS. *Stella Hazelcorn*: CONNIE DAY. *Michael Stone*: SWEN SWENSON. *Cousin Simon*: MITCHELL JASON. *Max*: Martin Garner.

Ensemble: *Skeeter*: Don Bonnell. *Ralph*: Rodney Griffin. *Reggie*: Bob Heath. *Harold*: Don Percassi. *Vinnie*: Sal Pernice. *Sheala*: Linda Rose. *George*: Leland Schwantes. *Walter*: Gerald Teijelo. *Ellen*: Mimi Wallace. *Sarah*: Miriam Welch.

The action takes place in the Bronx in the spring of 1933.

Act 1, Scene 1: (Opening.) *Scene 2*: The Goldberg Apartment. *Scene 3*: The Front Sidewalk. *Scene 4*: The Rooftop. *Scene 5*: The Sidewalk. *Scene 6*: Belle's Apartment. *Scene 7*: A Street. *Scene 8*: The Goldberg Apartment. *Scene 9*: The Goldberg Apartment. The following day.

Act 2, Scene 1: The Mandarin Palace. *Scene 2*: Outside the Mandarin Palace. *Scene 3*: The Goldberg Apartment. *Scene 4*: The Goldberg Kitchen. *Scene 5*: The Goldberg Apartment.

ACT 1

Scene 1

"There's a New Deal on the Way"
  S. Walker, Company
  (*Lyrics by* Mack David.)

"If Everyone Got What They Wanted"
  K. Ballard, Company
  (*Lyrics by* Mack David.)

Scene 2

"A Piece of the Rainbow"
  K. Ballard
  (*Lyrics by* Mack David.)

Scene 3

"Cahoots"
  S. Swenson, K. Ballard
  (*Lyrics by* Mack David.)

Scene 4

"Sullivan's Got a Job"
  Company
  (*Lyrics by* Leonard Adelson.)

"In Your Eyes"
  D. Fortus
  (*Lyrics by* Mack David.)

Scene 5

"Cahoots" (reprise)
  R. Manning, K. Ballard

Scene 8

"High Class Ladies and Elegant Gentlemen"
  S. Swenson, C. Day, K. Ballard, L. Wallace, D. Fortus, L. Rochelle
  (*Lyrics by* Mack David.)

"So I'll Tell Him"
  K. Ballard
  (*Lyrics by* Mack David.)

Scene 9

"Appointments"
  E. Mintz
  (*Lyrics by* Leonard Adelson.)

"There's Gold on the Trees"
  L. Wallace, K. Ballard, Company
  (*Lyrics by* Mack David.)

ACT 2

Scene 1

"The Mandarin Palace on the Grand Concourse"
  Company
  (*Lyrics by* Mack David.)

"I Want to Share It All With You"
  S. Swenson, C. Day, Company
  (*Lyrics by* Mack David.)

Scene 2

"In Your Eyes" (reprise)
  D. Fortus

Scene 3

"I Was There"
  K. Ballard, L. Wallace
  (*Lyrics by* Mack David.)

"Oak Leaf Memorial Park"
  K. Ballard
  (*Lyrics by* Leonard Adelson.)

"If Everyone Got What They Wanted" (reprise)
  E. Mintz, L. Rochelle

"I See a Man"
  K. Ballard
  (*Music and Lyrics by* Norman L. Martin.)

Scene 5

"The Tremont Avenue Cruisewear Fashion Show"
  Company
  (*Lyrics by* Leonard Adelson.)

"I've Got a Molly"
  L. Wallace
  (*Lyrics by* Leonard Adelson.)

"Go in the Best of Health"
  K. Ballard
  (*Lyrics by* Leonard Adelson.)

1973.12 GIGI

A Musical in Two Acts, 15 Scenes. Book and lyrics by Alan Jay Lerner. Based on the novel of the same name by Colette (and the film of the same name by the musical's authors.) Music by Frederick Loewe. Directed by Joseph Hardy. Dances and musical numbers staged by Onna White. Scenic production by Oliver Smith. Costumes by Oliver Messel. Lighting by Thomas Skelton. Orchestrations by Irwin Kostal. Dance arrangements by Trude Rittman. Musical associate, Harper MacKay. Associate dance director, Martin Allen. Musical direction by Ross Reimueller. Assistant music director, Bruce Ferden. Production coordinator, Herb Adams. A Los Angeles-San Francisco Civic Light Opera Production. Produced by Saint-Subber and Edwin Lester. Opened 13 November 1973 at the Uris Theatre and closed 10 February 1974 after 103 performances.

CAST (in order of speaking appearance): *Honore Lachailles*: ALFRED DRAKE. *Gaston Lachailles*: DANIEL MASSEY. *Liane d'Exelmans*: Sandahl Bergman. *Inez Alvarez (Mamita)*: MARIA KARNILOVA. *Gigi*: KARIN WOLFE. *Aunt Alicia*: AGNES MOOREHEAD. *Charles, her butler*: Gordon De Vol. *A French Head Waiter, Receptionist, Telephone Installer, Maitre d'Hotel*: Joe Ross. *Waiters*: Leonard John Crofoot, Thomas Stanton. *Liane's Dance Partner*: Thomas Anthony. *Artist*: Patrick Spohn. *A Count*: Joel Pressman. *Sandomir*: Randy Di Grazio. *Dancing Teacher*: Gregory Drotar. *Manuel*: Truman Gaige. *Maitre Du Fresne*: GEORGE GAYNES. *Maitre Duclos*: Howard Chitjian. *Law Clerks*: Leonard John Crofoot, Thomas Stanton. *Little Girls*: Patricia Daly, Jill Turnbull.

Ensemble: Thomas Anthony, Alvin Beam, Russ Beasley, Robyn Blair, Leonard John Crofoot, Gordon De Vol, Randy Di Grazio, John Dorrin, Gregory Drotar, Janis Eckhart, Margit Haut, Andy Keyser, Beverly Kopels, Diane Lauridsen, Merilee Magnuson, Kelley Maxwell, Vickie Patik, Joel Pressman, Patrick Spohn, Thomas Stanton, Cherie Suzanne, Marie Tillmanns, Sallie True.

The action takes place in Paris mostly at the turn of the century.

Act 1, Scene 1: The Pre-Catelan Restauarnt in the Bois, Paris. A September afternoon, 1900. *Scene 2*: Mamita's Apartment. Immediately following. *Scene 3*: Aunt Alicia's Apartment. Immediately following. *Scene 4*: The Restaurant of the Eiffel Tower. Evening. *Scene 5a*: Alicia's Apartment. Midday, the following day. *Scene 5b*: Apartment of Honore Lachailles. Simultaneously. *Scene 5c*: Alicia's Apartment. As before. *Scene 5d*: Honore's Dressing Room. As before. *Scene 6*: Mamita's Apartment. Two weeks later. *Scene 7a*: The Lobby of the Grand Hotel, Trouville. The following afternoon. *Scene 7b*: The Beach at Trouville.

Act 2, Scene 1: Mamita's Apartment. Early afternoon. Three weeks later. *Scene 2*: The Street outside Mamita's apartment. Immediately following. *Scene 3*: The Office of Maitre DuFresne. A day or two later. *Scene 4*: Mamita's Apartment. The following day. *Scene 5*: A Street Café. An hour later. *Scene 6*: Mamita's Apartment. Later that day. *Scene 7*: Maxim's. That night. *Scene 8*: Mamita's Apartment. Immediately following.

ACT 1
Scene 1
  "Thank Heaven for Little Girls"
    A. Drake
  "It's a Bore"
    A. Drake, D. Massey
Scene 3
  "The Earth and Other Minor Things"[3]
    K. Wolfe
Scene 4
  "Paris Is Paris Again"[4]
    A. Drake, Ensemble
  "She's Not Thinking of Me"
    D. Massey
Scene 5
  "It's a Bore" (reprise)
    A. Drake, D. Massey, T. Gaige, A. Moorehead
Scene 6
  "The Night They Invented Champagne"
    K. Wolfe, D. Massey, M. Karnilova
Scene 7a
  "I Remember It Well"
    A. Drake, M. Karnilova
Scene 7b
  "I Never Want to Go Home Again"[5]
    K. Wolfe, Ensemble
ACT 2
Scene 2
  "Gigi"
    D. Massey
Scene 3
  "The Contract"[6]
    A. Moorehead, M. Karnilova, H. Chitjian, G. Gaynes
Scene 5
  "I'm Glad I'm Not Young Anymore"
    A. Drake
Scene 6
  "In This Wide, Wide World"[7]
    K. Wolfe
Scene 8
  "Thank Heaven for Little Girls" (reprise)
    A. Drake

1973.13 ## GOOD EVENING

A Comedy (Revue) With Music in Two Acts. (Sketches, music and lyrics) Written by Peter Cook and Dudley Moore. Directed by Jerry Adler. (Set, costumes, lighting) Designed by Robert Randolph. Film sequences directed by Joe McGrath. Produced by Alexander H. Cohen and Bernard Delfont in association with Donald Langdon for Herndale, Ltd. Opened 14 November 1973 at the Plymouth Theatre and closed 30 November 1974 after 438 performances.

CAST: PETER COOK, DUDLEY MOORE.

ACT 1
  Hello

---

[3]Newly written for this stage presentation of "Gigi" and not from the original film.
[4]Newly written for this stage presentation of "Gigi" and not from the original film.
[5]Newly written for this stage presentation of "Gigi" and not from the original film.
[6]Newly written for this stage presentation of "Gigi" and not from the original film.
[7]Newly written for this stage presentation of "Gigi" and not from the original film.

On Location
"Madrigal"
Six of the Best
"Die Flabbergast" (German Lied)
Down the Mine
"One Leg Too Few"
"Chanson"
Soap Opera[8]
ACT 2
  Gospel Truth
Mini-Drama[9]
"The Kwai Sonata"
    (Variations on theme from "Bridge Over the River Kwai" in the style of Bach, Mozart, Chopin, etc.)
  The Frog and Peach
An Appeal
"Tea for Two"[10]

1973.14 ## BETTE MIDLER

A Musical Revue in Two Acts. Special material by Bill Hennessey, Bruce Vilanch. Musical director, Barry Manilow. Lighting by John Tedesco. Choreography by Andre De Shields and Michael Bennett. Set by Richard Mason. Sound by Claire Brothers. Costumes by Bob DeMora. Produced by Aaron Russo in association with Ron Delsener. Opened 3 December 1973 at the Palace Theatre and closed 23 December 1973 after 19 performances.

CAST: BETTE MIDLER. *The Harlettes*: (Charlotte Crossley, Robin Grean, Sharon Redd), 'Nick Brown's Hawaii '73' (*Vocals*: Jimmy Kaina; *Toere*: Marvin Stein; *Dancers*: Betty Kawamura, Cindy Curtin, Helen Estol). *Musicians*: Luther Rix, Frank Vento, Will Lee, Don Grolnick.

MUSICAL NUMBERS[11]
  "Friends"
    (*Music and Lyrics by* Mark Klingman and Buzzy Linhart.)
  "Delta Dawn"
    (*Music and Lyrics by* Alex Harvey and Larry Collins.)
  "Bad Sex"
    (*Music and Lyrics by* Bill Hennessey and Bruce Vilanch.)
  "Uptown"
    (*Music and Lyrics by* Thomas McKinney.)
  "Da Doo Run Run"
    (*Music and Lyrics by* Jeff Barry, Ellie Greenwich, Phil Spector.)
  "In the Mood"
    (*Music by* Joe Garland. *Lyrics by* Andy Razaf.)
  "Drinkin' Again"
    (*Music and Lyrics by* Doris Tauber and Johnny Mercer.)
  "Am I Blue?" (from *ON WITH THE SHOW*, film)
    (*Music by* Harry Akst. *Lyrics by* Grant Clarke.)
  "Do You Want to Dance?"
    (*Music and Lyrics by* Bobby Freeman.)
  "Optimistic Voices" (from *THE WIZARD OF OZ*, film)
    (*Music by* Harold Arlen and Herbert Stothart. *Lyrics by* E. Y. Harburg.)
  "Lullabye of Broadway" (from *GOLDDIGGERS OF 1935*, film)
    (*Music by* Harry Warren. *Lyrics by* Al Dubin.)
  "Boogie Woogie Bugle Boy"
    (*Music and Lyrics by* Don Raye and Hughie Price.)
  "Superstar"
    (*Music and Lyrics by* Leon Russell and Bonnie Bramlett.)
  "Hello in There"
    (*Music and Lyrics by* John Prine.)
  "(Your Love Keeps Lifting Me) Higher and Higher"
    (*Music and Lyrics by* Gary Lee Jackson, Raymond Miner, Carl W. Smith.)

---

[8]Replaced during run by "Tea for Two."
[9]Dropped for subsequent road tour.
[10]Dropped during run and replaced by "Resting."
[11]Not in performance order. Barry Manilow opened the second act with a set of his own songs.

1973.15 THE PAJAMA GAME

A Revival of the Musical Comedy in Two Acts[12]. Book by George Abbott and Richard Bisssell. Based on the novel "7 1/2 Cents" by Richard Bissell. Music and lyrics by Richard Adler and Jerry Ross. Production (scenery, costumes) designed by David Guthrie. Lighting by John Gleason. Musical numbers staged by Zoya Leporska. Original choreography by Bob Fosse. Musical director, Joyce Brown. Orchestrations by Don Walker. Production directed by George Abbott. Produced by Richard Adler and Bert Wood in association with Nelson Peltz. Opened 9 December 1973 at the Lunt-Fontanne Theatre and closed 3 February 1974 after 65 performances.

CAST (in order of appearance): *Hines*: CAB CALLOWAY. *Prez*: Marc Jordan. *Joe*: Gerrit de Beer. *Hasler*: Willard Waterman. *Gladys*: SHARON MILLER. *Sid Sorokin*: HAL LINDEN. *Mabel*: Mary Jo Catlett. *First Helper*: David Brummel. *Second Helper*: John Engstrom. *Charlie*: Tiger Haynes. *Babe Williams*: BARBARA McNAIR. *Mae*: Margret Coleman. *Brenda*: Chris Calloway. *Poopsie*: Wyetta Turner. *Salesman*: Hal Norman. *Pop*: Baron Wilson.

Dancers: Dru Alexandrine, Eileen Casey, Vicki Frederick, Mickey Gunnersen, Sally Neal, Jo Ann Ogawa, P. J. Benjamin, Hank Brunjes, Jon Engstrom, Ben Harney, Randal Harris, David Kresser, Jr., Cameron Mason, Chester Walker. *Singers*: Chalyce Brown, Susan Dyas, Rebecca Hoodwin, Patricia Moline, Marie Santell, Cynthia White, Gerrit deBeer, David Brummel, Doug Carfrae, Stan Page, Ward Smith, Teddy Williams.

1973.16 THE BEGGAR'S OPERA

A Revival of the Ballad Opera in Three Acts[13]. Book, music and lyrics by John Gay. Directed by Gene Lesser. Musical direction and arrangements by Roland Gagnon. Dance arranged by Elizabeth Keen. Settings by Robert Yodice. Costumes by Carrie F. Robbins. Lighting by Martin Aronstein. Produced by The City Center Acting Company (John Houseman, Artistic Director.) Opened 22 December 1973 at the Billy Rose Theatre and closed 31 December 1973 after 6 performances in repertory.

CAST (in order of appearance): *Filch*: Norman Snow. *Beggar*: Benjamin Hendrickson. *Peachum*: DAVID OGDEN STIERS. *Mrs. Peachum*: MARY LOU ROSATO. *Polly Peachum*: CYNTHIA HERMAN. *Macheath*: KEVIN KLINE. *Matt of the Mint*: Richard Ooms. *Jemmy Twitcher*: Peter Dvorsky. *Harry Paddington*: Joel Colodner. *Wat Dreary*: David Schramm. *Crook Finger'd Jack*: Jared Sakren. *Nimming Ned*: Gerald Shaw. *Mrs. Trapes*: Nita Angeletti. *Dolly Trull*: Leah Chandler. *Jenny Diver*: MARY-JOAN NEGRO. *Suky Tawdry*: Gisela Caldwell. *Betty Coaxer*: Mary Lou Rosato. *Lockit*: SAM TSOUTSOUVAS. *Lucy Lockit*: PATTI LuPONE

1973.17 AN EVENING WITH JOSEPHINE BAKER

A Musical Revue in Two Acts[14]. Stage director, Patrick Horrigan. Lighting consultant, Don Stern. Sound consultant, Robert F. Maybaum. Produced by Jack Jordan and Howard Sanders. Opened 31 December 1973 at the Palace Theatre and closed 6 January 1974 after 7 performances.

CAST: JOSEPHINE BAKER, Roberta Lorco and Company (Paco Juanas, Guitarist; Domingo Alverado, Singer), Michael Powell Ensemble (Michael Powell, Joey Coleman, Leeroy Cooks, Vinson Cunningham, Bernadette Doctor, Dorthea Doctor, Norman Hawkins, Ricardo Portlette, Charlene Ricks, Barbara Rolle, Calvin Van Meter, Esther Westbrook, Peggy Williams, Shirley Williams), Baby Laurence (tap percussionist), G. Keith Alexander (M.C.).

ACT 1

"People" (from *FUNNY GIRL*.)
  (*Music by* Jule Styne. *Lyrics by* Bob Merrill.)
"Sourire (a la Vie)"

"(It's) Impossible"
  (*Music and Lyrics by* Armando Manzanero and Sid Wayne.)
"Avec"
  (*Music and Lyrics by* Henri Betti, Bruno Coquatrix and Andre Hornez.)
"Love Story" (from the film *LOVE STORY*)
  (*Music by* Francis Lai. *Lyrics by* Carl Sigman.)
"Hello Young Lovers" (from *THE KING AND I*)
  (*Music by* Richard Rodgers. *Lyrics by* Oscar Hammerstein II.)
Medley

ACT 2

"Lend Your Ear"
"Si Me Faltas Tu"
  (*Music and Lyrics by* Armando Manzanero.)
My Fair Lady Medley
  (*Music by* Frederick Loewe. *Lyrics by* Alan Jay Lerner.)
"Demain"
  (*Music and Lyrics by* Donaggio, Pallavicini, Annoux and Vallade.)
"La Vie en Rose"
  Music and Lyrics by Edith Piaf and Louiguy.)
"Yesterday"
  (*Music and Lyrics by* John Lennon and Paul McCartney.)
"J'ai Deux Amours"
  (*Music and Lyrics by* Vincent Scotto, Georges Koger and Henri Varna.)
"My Sweet Lord"
  (*Music and Lyrics by* George Harrison.)

1974.01 LIZA

A Musical Revue in Two Acts. (Continuity) Written by Fred Ebb. Directed by Bob Fosse. Choreographed by Bob Fosse and Ron Lewis. Original musical material by Fred Ebb and John Kander. Musical coordinator, Marvin Hamlisch. Musical conductor, Jack French. Lighting designed by Jules Fisher. Audio design. Phil Ramone. Sound by Stan Miller. Production coordinator, Bill Liberman. Produced by the Shubert Organization in association with Ron Delsener. Opened 6 January 1974 at the Winter Garden Theatre and closed 26 January 1974 after 24 performances.

CAST: LIZA MINNELLI.
Dancers: Pam Barlow, Spencer Henderson, Jimmy Roddy, Sharon Wylie.

MUSICAL NUMBERS[15]

"If You Could Read My Mind"
  (*Music and Lyrics by* Gordon Lightfoot.)
"Come Back to Me" (from *ON A CLEAR DAY YOU CAN SEE FOREVER*)
  (*Music by* Burton Lane. *Lyrics by* Alan Jay Lerner.)
"Shine on Harvest Moon" (from *ZIEGFELD FOLLIES OF 1908*)
  (*Music and Lyrics by* Nora Bayes and Jack Norworth.)
"Exactly Like Me"
  (*Music by* John Kander. *Lyrics by* Fred Ebb.)
"The Circle"
  (*Music by* Edith Piaf. English Lyrics by Fred Ebb.)
"More Than You Know" (from *GREAT DAY*)
  (*Music by* Vincent Youmans. *Lyrics by* Billy Rose and Edward Eliscu.)
"I'm One of the Smart Ones"
  (*Music by* John Kander. *Lyrics by* Fred Ebb.)
"Natural Man"
  (*Music and Lyrics by* Bobby Hebb and Sandy Baron.)
"I Can See Clearly Now"
  (*Music and Lyrics by* Johnny Nash.)
"And I in My Chair"
  (*Music and Lyrics by* Jeff Davis, Charles Aznavour and Fred Ebb.)

---

[12]Originally produced in New York 13 May 1954 at the St. James Theatre for 1063 performances. For this production, the Act 2 "Jealousy Ballet" was dropped. "7 1/2 Cents" was staged by Jerome Robbins. Replacing the "Hey There" Act 2 reprise was a new song:
  "Watch Your Heart"
    B. McNair
    (*Music and Lyrics by* Richard Adler.)
[13]First produced in New York 3 December 1750 at the Theatre in Nassau Street for 2 performances. For Synopsis of Scenes and Musical Numbers, see original 1750 production.

[14]Josephine Baker And Her International Revue with Bricktop and the George Faison Universal Dance Experience previously produced 5-8 June 1973 at Carnegie Hall for 4 performances.
[15]Not in performance order. Program provided no song list; list prepared from recording.

"There Is a Time"
(*Music and Lyrics by* Jeff Davis, Charles Azanvour and Gene Lees.)
"A Quiet Thing" (from *FLORA, THE RED MENACE*)
(*Music by* John Kander. *Lyrics by* Fred Ebb.)
"Anywhere You Are"
(*Music by* John Kander. *Lyrics by* Fred Ebb.)
"I Believe You"
(*Music by* John Kander. *Lyrics by* Fred Ebb.)
"Cabaret" (from *CABARET*)
(*Music by* John Kander. *Lyrics by* Fred Ebb.)
"Ring Them Bells" (from television special *LIZA WITH A 'Z'*)
(*Music by* John Kander. *Lyrics by* Fred Ebb.)
"I Gotcha"
(*Music and Lyrics by* Joe Tex.)
"Bye Bye Blackbird"
(*Music by* Ray Henderson. *Lyrics by* Mort Dixon.)

LORELEI,
1974.02   or Gentlemen Still Prefer Blondes

A Musical Comedy in Two Acts, 10 Scenes, a Prologue and an Epilogue. New book by Kenny Solms and Gail Parent. Based on the musical comedy "Gentlemen Prefer Blondes"[16] with book by Anita Loos and Joseph Fields. Music by Jule Styne. Lyrics by Leo Robin. New music by Jule Styne. New lyrics by Betty Comden and Adolph Green. Directed by Robert Moore. Choreography by Ernest Flatt. Scenery by John Conklin. Costumes by Alvin Colt. Miss Channing's costumes by Ray Aghayan and Bob Mackie. Lighting by John Gleason. Musical direction by Milton Rosenstock. Orchestrations by Philip J. Lang, Don Walker. Vocal arrangements by Hugh Martin and Buster Davis. Dance music arrangements by Jay Thompson. A Music Fair Enterprises Inc. Production. Produced by Lee Guber and Shelly Gross. Opened 27 January 1974 at the Palace Theatre and closed 3 November 1974 after 320 performances.

CAST (in order of appearance): *Lorelei Lee*: CAROL CHANNING. *Henry Spofford*: LEE ROY REAMS. *Mrs. Ella Spofford*: DODY GOODMAN. *Lord Francis Beekman*: JACK FLETCHER. *Lady Phyllis Beekman*: Jean Bruno. *Josephus Gage*: BRANDON MAGGART. *Dorothy Shaw*: TAMARA LONG. *Gus Esmond*: PETER PALMER. *Bartender*: Ray Cox. *Frank*: Steve Short. *George*: Bob Daley. *Pierre*: Ray Cox. *Charles*: Robert Riker. *Robert Lemanteur*: Robert Fitch. *Louis Lemanteur*: Ian Tucker. *Lobster* (Un Delicieux Pince Rouge!): Brenda Holmes. *Caviar* (Un Bon Oeuf!): Linda McClure. *Pheasant* (Un Oiseau Dans Le Matin!): Aniko Farrell. *Salade* (A Votre Sante!): Marie Halton. *Dessert* (Vive La Glace Chaude!): CAROL CHANNING. *Maitre d'*: Willard Beckham. *Simone Duval*: Sherrill Harper. *Master of Ceremonies*: Robert Riker. *Announcer*: Ray Cox. *Engineer*: Bob Daley. *Mr. Esmond*: David Neuman. *Bridesmaids*: Aniko Farrell, Marie Halton, Sherrill Harper, Linda McClure.
Passengers, Tourists, Olympic Team, Wedding Guests: Aniko Farrell, Joela Flood, Marie Halton, Marian Haraldson, Sherrill Harper, Brenda Holmes, Linda Lee McArthur, Linda McClure, Susan Ohman, Gina Ramsel, Roxanna White, Willard Beckham, Ray Cox, Bob Daley, Bob Fitch, Gregg Harlan, Wayne Mattson, Jonathan Miele, Jeff Richards, Robert Riker, Rick Schneider, Steve Short, Don Swanson, Ian Tucker.

The action takes place aboard the *Ile de France*, in Paris and in New York.
Prologue: Dockside, New York, 1944. *Act 1, Scene 1*: The Pier of the *Ile de France*. *Scene 2*: The Deck of the *Ile de France*. *Scene 3*: Lorelei's Suite on the *Ile de France*. *Scene 4*: The Eiffel Tower. *Scene 5*: Lorelei's Suite, The Ritz Hotel, Paris.
Act 2, Scene 1: Pre-Catalin Nightclub. *Scene 2*: A Paris Street. *Scene 3*: Lorelei's Suite, The Ritz Hotel, Paris. *Scene 4*: On the Way Home. *Scene 5*: The Central Park Casino, New York. *Epilogue*: The present.

ACT 1
Prologue
"Looking Back"
C. Channing
(*Lyrics by* Betty Comden and Adolph Green.)
Scene 1
"Bye Bye Baby"
P. Palmer, C. Channing, Passengers, Tourists

---

[16]Originally produced in New York 8 December 1949 at the Ziegfeld Theatre for 740 performances.

Scene 2
"(It's) High Time"
T. Long, D. Goodman, Passengers
"(I'm Just a Little Girl from) Little Rock"
C. Channing
Scene 3
"I Love What I'm Doing"
T. Long
"It's Delightful Down in Chile"
C. Channing, J. Fletcher, Stewards
Scene 4
"I Won't Let You Get Away"
L. R. Reams, T. Long
(*Lyrics by* Betty Comden and Adolph Green.)
Scene 5
"Keeping Cool With Coolidge"
L. R. Reams, T. Long, D. Goodman, Guests
"Men"
C. Channing
(*Lyrics by* Betty Comden and Adolph Green. *Dance Supervised by* Robert Tucker.)

ACT 2
Scene 1
"Coquette"
T. Long, C. Channing, Showgirls
"Mamie Is Mimi"
C. Channing, B. Fitch, I. Tucker
Scene 2
"Diamonds Are a Girl's Best Friend"
C. Channing
"Homesick (Blues)"
C. Channing, P. Palmer
Scene 3
"Miss Lorelei Lee"
L. R. Reams, T. Long, D. Goodman, B. Maggart, B. Fitch, I. Tucker, Wedding Guests
(*Lyrics by* Betty Comden and Adolph Green.)
Scene 4
"Button Up With Esmond"
C. Channing, Bridesmaids
Scene 5
"Diamonds Area Girl's Best Friend" (reprise)
C. Channing
Epilogue
Finale—"Lorelei"
C. Channing, Company
(*Lyrics by* Betty Comden and Adolph Green.)

1974.03   # RAINBOW JONES

A Musical in Two Acts, 11 Scenes. Book, music and lyrics by Jill Williams. Directed by Gene Persson. Musical direction and vocal arrangements by Danny Holgate. Musical staging by Sammy Bayes. Set design by Richard Ferrer. Costume design by James Berton Harris. Lighting by Spencer Mosse. Orchestrations by Preston Sandiford. Produced by Rubykate Inc. (Gene Persson) in association with Phil Gillin and Gene Bambic. Opened and closed 13 February 1974 at the Music Box Theatre after 1 performance.

CAST (in order of appearance): *Rainbow Jones*: RUBY PERSSON. *Leona*: PEGGY HAGEN LAMPREY. *Bones*: ANDY ROHRER. *C. A. Fox*: GIL ROBBINS. *Cardigan*: STEPHANIE SILVER. *Joey Miller*: PETER KASTNER. *Aunt Felicity*: KAY ST. GERMAIN. *Uncle Ithaca*: DANIEL KEYES.

The action takes place at the present time in New York City and on Uncle Ithaca's farm.

Act 1, Scene 1: Noon, Central Park. *Scene 2*: Later, Aunt Felicity's Apartment. *Scene 3*: A few hours later, Joey Miller's Office. *Scene 4*: Minutes later, Central Park. *Scene 5*: That evening, Aunt Felicity's Apartment. *Scene 6*: The next day at noon, Central Park.

Act 2, Scene 1: A few minutes later, Central Park. *Scene 2*: A week later, Uncle Ithaca's Farm. *Scene 3*: A moment later, Central Park. *Scene 4*: A week later, the Parlour Car of the Ohio Express/Felicity's Apartment. *Scene 5*: A few hours later, Central Park.

ACT 1

Prologue

"A Little Bit of Me in You"
P. H. Lamprey, A. Rohrer, G. Robbins, S. Silver

Scene 1

"Free and Easy"
R. Persson

Scene 2

"Do Unto Others"
R. Persson, P. H. Lamprey, A. Rohrer, G. Robbins, S. Silver

Scene 3

"I'd Like to Know You Better"
P. Kastner

Scene 4

"Bad Breath"
P. H. Lamprey, A. Rohrer, G. Robbins, S. Silver

"I'd Like to Know You Better" (reprise)
P. Kastner, R. Persson, P. H. Lamprey, A. Rohrer, G. Robbins, S. Silver

Scene 5

"Alone, At Last, Alone"
K. St. Germain

Scene 6

"Free and Easy" (reprise)
R. Persson

"Her Name Is Leona"
R. Persson, P. H. Lamprey, A. Rohrer, G. Robbins, S. Silver

"We All Need Love"
P. H. Lamprey, A. Rohrer, G. Robbins, S. Silver

ACT 2

Scene 1

"We All Need Love" (reprise)
P. H. Lamprey, A. Rohrer, G. Robbins, S. Silver

"The Only Man for the Job"
A. Rohrer

Scene 2

"It's So Nice"
K. St. Germain, D. Keyes

Scene 3

"Wait a Little While"
P. H. Lamprey

Scene 4

"It's So Nice" (reprise)
R. Persson, K. St. Germain, D. Keyes, P. Kastner

"One Big Happy Family" P. Kastner, P. H. Lamprey, A. Rohrer, G. Robbins, S. Silver

Scene 5

"Who Needs the Love of a Woman"
P. Kastner, R. Persson

"We All Need Love"/"A Little Bit of Me in You" (reprise)
P. Kastner, R. Persson, P. H. Lamprey, A. Rohrer, G. Robbins, S. Silver

SEXTET

1974.04

A Musical in One Act. Book by Harvey Perr and Lee Goldsmith. Music by Lawrence Hurwitt. Lyrics by Lee Goldsmith. Direction and choreography by Jered Barclay. Scenery by Peter Harvey. Costumes by Zoe Brown. Lighting by Marc B. Weiss. Orchestrations and musical direction by David Frank. Sound by Gary Harris. Assistant choreographher, Mary Jane Houdina. Produced by Balemar Productions and Lawrence E. Sokol. Opened 3 March 1974 at the Bijou Theatre and closed 10 March 1974 after 9 performances.

CAST (in order of appearance): *David*: Robert Spencer. *Paul*: John Newton. *Fay*: Mary Small. *Kenneth*: Harvey Evans. *Ann*: Dixie Carter. *Leonard*: Jerry Lanning.

The action takes place at the present time in a New York City apartment.

MUSICAL NUMBERS

"Nervous"
Company

"What the Hell Am I Doing Here?"
J. Newton

"Keep on Dancing"
R. Spencer, H. Evans, M. Small, J. Newton

"Spunk"
M. Small, R. Spencer, H. Evans

"Visiting Rights"
D. Carter

"Going-Staying"
Company

"I Wonder"
D. Carter, M. Small

"Women and Men"
J. Lanning, R. Spencer, H. Evans

"I Love You All the Time"
J. Lanning

"Keep On Dancing" (reprise)
Company

"Hi"
H. Evans

"It'd Be Nice"
M. Small

"Roseland"
Company

"How Does It Start?"
R. Spencer

"Someone to Love"
Company

OVER HERE!

1974.05

A Musical in Two Acts. Book by Will Holt. Music and lyrics by Richard M. Sherman and Robert B. Sherman. Directed by Tom Moore. Musical numbers and dances staged by Patricia Birch. Musical coordination, vocal arrangements, Special dance music by Louis St. Louis. Orchestrations by Michael Gibson and Jim Tyler. Musical director, Joseph Klein. Scenery by Douglas W. Schmidt. Costumes by Carrie F. Robbins. Lighting by John Gleason. Media design by Stan J. Goldberg, Jeanne H. Livingston. Sound design by Jack Shearing. Associate producer, Lou Kramer. Produced by Kenneth Waissman and Maxine Fox. Opened 6 March 1974 at the Sam S. Shubert Theatre and closed 4 January 1975 after 341 performances.

CAST (in order of appearance): *Make-out*: Jim Weston. *Norwin Spokesman*: DOUGLASS WATSON. *Father*: MacIntyre Dixon. *Mother*: Bette Henritze. *Rankin*: William Griffis. *Donna*: Marilu Henner. *Wilma*: Phyllis Somerville. *Maggie*: Ann Reinking. *Mitzi*: JANIE SELL. *Misfit*: John Travolta. *Utah*: Treat Willaims. *Lucky*: John Mineo. *Sarge*: William Newman. *Sam*: Samuel E. Wright. *June*: APRIL SHAWHAN. *Bill*: John Driver. *Pauline de Paul*: MAXENE ANDREWS. *Paulette de Paul*: PATTY ANDREWS.

The action takes place in the 1940s.

ACT 1

"The Beat Begins" (Overture)
The Big Band, Company

"Since You're Not Around"
J. Weston, Company

"Over Here"[17]
P. Andrews, M. Andrews

"Buy a Victory Bond"
Company

"My Dream for Tomorrow"
A. Shawhan, Company

[17]Messrs. Sherman and St. Louis wish to acknowledge the creative contribution of Walter Weschler on these numbers.

"Charlie's Place"
    M. Andrews, A. Reinking, J. Mineo, The Big Band, Company
"Hey Yvette"/"The Grass Grows Green"
    D. Watson, W. Griffis, M. Dixon
"My Dream for Tomorrow" (reprise)
    A. Shawhan, J. Driver
"The Good-Time Girl"
    P. Andrews, Company
"Wait for Me Marlena"
    J. Sell, Company
"We Got It"[18]
    P. Andrews, M. Andrews, J. Sell, Company

ACT 2

"The Beat Continues" (Entre'Act)
    The Big Band, Company
"Wartime Wedding"
    P. Andrews, M. Andrews, Company
"Don't Shoot the Hooey to Me, Louie"
    S. E. Wright
"Where Did the Good Times Go?"
    P. Andrews
"Dream Drummin'"/"Soft Music"
    J. Travolta, The Big Band, Company
"The Big Beat"[19]
    P. Andrews, M. Andrews, J. Sell
"No Goodbyes"
    P. Andrews, M. Andrews, Company

1974.06

CANDIDE

A Revival of the Musical in One Act, 33 Scenes[20]. (New) Book adapted from Voltaire's satire (of the same name) by Hugh Wheeler. (Original book by Lillian Hellman.) Music by Leonard Bernstein. Lyrics by Richard Wilbur. Additional lyrics by Stephen Sondheim and John Latouche. Directed by Harold Prince. Choreography by Patricia Birch. Production (settings, costumes) designed by Eugene and Franne Lee. Lighting by Tharon Musser. Musical direction by John Mauceri. Orchestrations by Hershy Kay. Production supervisor, Ruth Mitchell. Produced by The Chelsea Theatre Center of Brooklyn (Robert Kalfin, Artistic director; Michael David, Executive director; Burl Hash, Productions director) in conjunction with Harold Prince and Ruth Mitchell. Opened 10 March 1974 at the Broadway Theatre and closed 4 January 1976 after 740 performances. (Total including Off-Broadway run 788 performances.)

CAST (in order of appearance): *Dr. Voltaire, Dr Pangloss, Governor, Host, Sage:* LEWIS J. STADLEN. *Chinese Coolie, Soldier, Priest, Spanish Don, Sailor, Lion, Guest:* Jim Corti. *Candide:* MARK BAKER. *Huntsman, First Recruiting Officer, Agent, Spanish Don, Cartagenian Sailor, Eunuch:* David Horwitz. *Paquette:* DEBORAH ST. DARR. *Baroness, Harpsichordist, Penitente, Steel Drummer, Houri:* Mary-Pat Green. *Baron, Grand Inquisitor, Slave Driver, Captain, Guest:* Joe Palmieri. *Cunegonde:* MAUREEN BRENNAN. *Maximilian:* SAM FREED. *Servant, Agent of The Inquisition, Spanish Don, Cartagenian Sailor:* Robert Hendersen. *Second Recruiting Officer, Aristocrat, Cartagenian:* Peter Vogt. *Penitente, Whore, Houri:* Gail Boggs. *Penitente, Cartagenian, Houri:* Lynne Gannaway. *Aristocrat, Cartagenian, Second Sheep:* Carolann Page. *Bulgarian Soldier, Aristocrat, Vendor, Sailor, Pygmy, Cow:* Carlos Gorbea. *Bulgarian Soldier, Penitente, Cartagenian Sailor, Cow:* Kelly Walters. *Westphalian Soldier, Agent, Governor's Aide, Pirate, Guest:* Chip Garnett. *Rich Jew, Judge, Man in Black, Cartagenian, Pirate, German, Botanist, Guest:* Jeff Keller. *Aristocrat, Cartagenian, Houri:* Becky McSpadden. *Aristocrat, Whore, Houri, Cunegonde (alternate):* Kathryn Ritter. *Lady with Knitting, Cartagenian, First Sheep:* Renee Semes. *Old Lady:* JUNE GABLE. *Swing Girl:* Rhoda Butler.

---

[18]Messrs. Sherman and St. Louis wish to acknowledge the creative contribution of Walter Weschler on these numbers.
[19]Messrs. Sherman and St. Louis wish to acknowledge the creative contribution of Walter Weschler on these numbers.
[20]This revival first produced Off-Broadway 11 December 1973 at the Chelsea Theater Center, Brooklyn Academy of Music for 48 performances; original production first produced in New York 1 December 1956 at the Martin Beck Theatre for 73 performances.

(The action takes place in Westphalia and throughout the world in the eighteenth century. Scenes overlap and are played simultaneously.)

Scene 1: Voltaire's Bedroom. *Scene 2*: A Forest Glade. *Scene 3*: The Baroness' Boudoir. *Scene 4*: The Baronial Garden. *Scene 5*: Maximilian's Bedroom. *Scene 6*: The Castle Schoolroom. *Scene 7*: The Baronial Orchard. *Scene 8*: The Baronial Banquet Hall. *Scene 9*: A Desolate Heath in Westphalia. *Scene 10*: The Baronial Chapel. *Scene 11*: A Meadow by Moonlight. *Scene 12*: The Battlefield. *Scene 13*: A Village Square. *Scene 14*: A Bedchamber in the Jew's Palace. *Scene 15*: (The Earthquake;) A Destroyed Fishing Village. *Scene 16*: The Central Square in Lisbon. *Scene 17*: A Room in a Lisbon Palace. *Scene 18*: A Room in the Inn outside Cadiz. *Scene 19*: The Central Plaza at Cadiz. *Scene 20*: The Grand Plaza at Cartagena, Colombia. *Scene 21*: The Slave Market at Cartagena. *Scene 22*: A Ship at Sea. *Scene 23*: The Cathedral of the Jesuits at Montevideo. *Scene 24*: Eldorado. *Scene 25*: The Rocky Shore. *Scene 26*: A Clearing in the Jungle. *Scene 27*: The Grand Plaza, Cartagena, Colombia. *Scene 28*: The Dock at Cartagena. *Scene 29*: A Desert Island. *Scene 30*: A Hall in a Palace in Constantinople. *Scene 31*: A Street Outside the Palace. *Scene 32*: The Cave of the Wisest Man in the World. *Scene 33*: Candide's Farm.

MUSICAL NUMBERS
    Scenes 2, 3, 4, 5
    "Life Is Happiness Indeed"
        M. Baker, M. Brennan, S. Freed, D. St. Darr
Scene 6
    ("Parade" instrumental)
    "The Best of All Possible Worlds"
        L. J. Stadlen, M. Baker, M. Brennan, S. Freed, D. St. Darr
Scene 7
    "Oh Happy We"
        M. Baker, M. Brennan
Scene 9
    "It Must Be So"
        M. Baker
Scene 10
    "O Misere"
        C. Page, L. Gannaway, G. Boggs, R. Hendersen
Scene 12
    "Oh Happy We" (reprise)
        M. Baker, M. Brennan
Scene 14
    "Glitter and Be Gay"
        M. Brennan
Scene 16
    "Auto da Fé" (What a Day)
        Company
    "This World"
        M. Baker
Scene 17
    "You Were Dead, You Know"
        M. Baker, M. Brennan
Scene 19
    "I Am Easily Assimilated"
        J. Gable, J. Corti, R. Hendersen, D. Horwitz
    "I Am Easily Assimilated" (reprise)
        J. Gable, M. Baker, M. Brennan
Scene 21
    "My Love"
        L. J. Stadlen
Scene 22
    ("Barcarolle" instrumental)
Scene 23
    "Alleluia"
        Company
Scene 24
    ("Eldorado" instrumental)
    Scenes 24, 25, 26
    "Sheep's Song"
        C. Page, R. Semes, J. Corti, D. St. Darr, M. Baker

Scene 28

"Bon Voyage" (Schottische)
   L. J. Stadlen, Company

Scene 29

"The Best of All Possible Worlds" (reprise)
   J. Gable, M. Baker, D. St. Darr, R. Semes, C. Page

Scene 30

("Constantinople" instrumental)
"You Were Dead, You Know" (reprise)
   M. Baker, M. Brennan

Scene 32

("Barcarolle" reprise instrumental)

Scene 33

"Make Our Garden Grow"
   Company

THE MIKADO,
1974.07   or The Town of Titipu

A Revival of the Comic Opera in Two Acts[21]. Libretto by William S. Gilbert. Music by Arthur Sullivan. Directed and choreographed by Jack Eddleman. Scenic design by Donald Oenslager. Costume design by Patton Campbell. Lighting by Hans Sondheimer. Conducted by Judith Somogi. Chorus master, Chris Nance. Produced by the New York City Opera. Opened 17 March 1974 at the New York State Theatre and closed 20 April 1974 after 5 performances in repertory.

CAST: *The Mikado of Japan:* EDWARD PIERSON. *Nanki-Poo, his son, disguised as a wandering minstrel in love with Yum-Yum:* GARY GLAZE. *Ko-Ko, Lord High Executioner of Titipu:* JAMES BILLINGS. *Pooh-Bah, Lord High Everything Else:* ARA BERBERIAN. *Pish-Tush, a Noble Lord:* Thomas Jamerson. *Yum-Yum, Pitti-Sing, Peep-Bo, three sisters, wards of Ko-Ko:* GLENYS FOWLES, JEANNE PILAND, PULI TORO. *Katisha:* BETTY ALLEN. *Chorus of School Girls, Nobles, Guards and Coolies:* New York City Opera Chorus.

THE CONSUL
1974.08

A Revival of the Opera (Musical Drama) in Three Acts, 6 Scenes[22]. Libretto and music by Gian-Carlo Menotti. Conductor, Christopher Keene. Settings by Horace Armistead. Staged by Gian-Carlo Menotti. Produced by the New York City Opera. Opened 27 March 1974 at the New York State Theatre and closed 28 April 1974 after 4 performances in repertory.

CAST: (in order of appearance): *John Sorel:* JOHN DARRENKAMP *Magda Sorel:* OLIVIA STAPP. *The Mother:* MURIEL COSTA-GREENSPON. *Secret Police Agent:* EDWARD PIERSON. *First Plainclothesman:* Jack Sims. *Second Plainclothesman:* Ray Van Orden. *The Secretary:* SANDRA WALKER. *Mr. Kofner:* DON YULE. *The Foreign Woman:* JUDITH DE ROSA. *Anna Gomez:* Barbara Hocher. *Nika Magadoff (The Magician):* NICO CASTEL. *Vera Boronel:* Virginia Brobyn. *Assan:* William Ledbetter. *Voice on the Record:* Mabel Mercer.

MUSIC! MUSIC!
1974.09

A Cavalcade (Revue) of American Music with footnotes by Alan Jay Lerner in Two Acts, Nineteen Scenes. Entire production staged and directed by Martin Charnin. Choreographed by Tony Stevens. Scenery by David Chapman. Costumes by Theoni V. Aldrdge. Lighting by Martin Aronstein. Vocal arrangements and musical direction by John Lesko. Orchestrations by Elliot Lawrence with Al Cohn, William Elton. Dance arrangements by Wally Harper. Associate producers, Howard Effron, Helen Haskell

and Myles Spector. Producers for the City Center: Robert P. Brannigan, Chuck Eisler. Produced by The New York City Center of Music and Drama (Norman Singer, Executive director) and Alvin Bojar. Opened 11 April 1974 at the New York City Center and closed 12 May 1974 after 37 performances.

CAST: GENE NELSON, LARRY KERT, KAREN MORROW, DONNA McKECHNIE, ROBERT GUILLAUME, WILL MacKENZIE, GAIL NELSON, TED PRITCHARD, ARNOLD SOBOLOFF, RUSS THACKER.
   Singing and Dancing Ensemble: Renée Baughman, Trish Garland, Denise Mauthé, Michon Peacock, Tom Offt, Michael Radigan, Yoalnda R. Raven, Fred Soiffer, Thomas J. Walsh.

Act 1: 1895-1941. *Scene 1:* Storyville. *Scene 2:* The Great White Way. *Scene 3:* World War I. *Scene 4:* The Princess Theatre. *Scene 5:* Those #%°$20's. *Scene 6:* Tin Pan Alley. *Scene 7:* Prohibition. *Scene 8:* The Boom. *Scene 9:* The Bust. *Scene 10:* Catfish Row. *Scene 11:* New York to Los Angeles.

Act 2: 1941-1974. *Scene 1:* World War II. *Scene 2:* The Great White Way Revisited. *Scene 3:* Rock and Roll. *Scene 4:* New Haven and Broadway. *Scene 5:* The New Frontier. *Scene 6:* The Great Society? *Scene 7:* Yesterday's Children. *Scene 8:* To Be Continued …

ACT 1

Scene 1

"Basin Street Blues"
   (*Music and Lyrics by* Spencer Williams.)
"When the Saints Go Marching In" (traditional)

Scene 2

"The Merry Widow Waltz" (from *THE MERRY WIDOW*)
   (*Music by* Franz Lehár.)
"Yankee Doodle Dandy" (from *LITTLE JOHNNY JONES*)
   (*Music and Lyrics by* George M. Cohan.)

Scene 3

"Over There"
   (*Music and Lyrics by* George M. Cohan.)
"I Didn't Raise My Boy to Be a Soldier"
   (*Music and Lyrics by* Alfred Bryan and Al Piantadosi.)
"How Ya Gonna Keep 'Em Down on the Farm?"
   (*Music by* Walter Donaldson. *Lyrics by* Sam Lewis, Joe Young.)
"Hinky Dinky Parlay Voo"
   (*Music and Lyrics by* Al Dubin, Irving Mills, Jimmy McHugh and Julian Dash.)

Scene 4

"Look for the Silver Lining" (from *SALLY*)
   (*Music by* Jerome Kern. *Lyrics by* Buddy G. DeSylva.)
"Bill" (from *SHOWBOAT*)
   (*Music by* Jerome Kern. *Lyrics by* P. G. Wodehouse.)

Scene 5

"Yes Sir, That's My Baby"
   (*Music by* Walter Donaldson. *Lyrics by* Gus Kahn.)

Scene 6

Gershwin Medley:
   "Fascinating Rhthm"
   "Somebody Loves Me"
   "The Babbitt and the Bromide"
   "Funny Face"
   "(I'll Build a) Stairway to Paradise"
   "The Man I Love"
   "Oh, Lady Be Good"
   "Someone to Watch Over Me"

Scene 7

"Manhattan" (from *THE GARRICK GAIETIES OF 1925*)
   (*Music by* Richard Rodgers. *Lyrics by* Lorenz Hart.)

Scene 8

"The Girl Friend" (from *THE GIRL FRIEND*)
   (*Music by* Richard Rodgers. *Lyrics by* Lorenz Hart.)
"Stouthearted Men" (from *THE NEW MOON*)
   (*Music by* Sigmund Romberg. *Lyrics by* Oscar Hammerstein II.)
"Lucky Lindy"
   (*Music and Lyrics by* Abel Bauer and L. Wolfe Gilbert.)

---

[21]First presented in New York 20 July, 10-29 August 1885 at the Union Square and People's Theatres for 22 performances. First authorized production presented 19 August 1885 at the Fifth Avenue Theatre by Richard D'Oyly Carte for 250 performances. For Synopsis of Scenes and Musical Numbers, see 19 August 1885 D'Oyly Carte production.
[22]Originally produced in New York 15 March 1950 at the Ethel Barrymore Theatre for 269 performances. For Synopsis of Scenes and Musical Numbers, see original 1950 production.

Scene 9

"Brother, Can You Spare a Dime?" (from *AMERICANA, 1932*)
(*Music by* Jay Gorney. *Lyrics by* E. Y. Harburg.)
"I'll See You Again" (from *BITTER SWEET*)
(*Music and Lyrics by* Noël Coward.)
"Great Day" (from *GREAT DAY*)
(*Music by* Vincent Youmans. *Lyrics by* Billy Rose and Edward Eliscu.)
"Stormy Weather"
(*Music by* Harold Arlen. *Lyrics by* Ted Koehler.)

Scene 10

"Bess You Is My Woman Now" (from *PORGY AND BESS*)
(*Music by* George Gershwin. *Lyrics by* Ira Gershwin and DuBose Heyward.)
"I Loves You Porgy" (from *PORGY AND BESS*)
(*Music by* George Gershwin. *Lyrics by* Ira Gershwin and DuBose Heyward.)

Scene 11

"Hooray for Hollywood" (from film *HOLLYWOOD HOTEL*)
(*Music by* Richard A. Whiting. *Lyrics by* Johnny Mercer.)
"Lullaby of Broadway" (from film *GOLDDIGGERS OF 1935*)
(*Music by* Harry Warren. *Lyrics by* Al Dubin.)

ACT 2

Scene 1

"In the Mood"
(*Music by* Joe Garland. *Lyrics by* Andy Razaf.)
"There Are Such Things"
(*Music and Lyrics by* George W. Meyer, Abel Baer and Stanley Adams.)
"The White Cliffs of Dover"
(*Music and Lyrics by* Walter Kent and Nat Burton.)

Scene 2

OKLAHOMA! Medley
(*Music by* Richard Rodgers. *Lyrics by* Oscar Hammerstein II.)
"Call Me Mister" (from *CALL ME MISTER*)
(*Music and Lyrics by* Harold Rome.)
"The Composers' Song" (A Recitation by Alan Jay Lerner.)

Scene 3

Rock and Roll Recitation

Scene 4

"Whiffenpoof Song" (Parody)
MY FAIR LADY Medley
(*Music by* Frederick Loewe. *Lyrics by* Alan Jay Lerner.)

Scene 5

WEST SIDE STORY Medley
(*Music by* Leonard Bernstein. *Lyrics by* Stephen Sondheim.)
Dance Segment from *THE MUSIC MAN, CAMELOT, BYE BYE BIRDIE* and *GYPSY*.

Scene 6

HELLO, DOLLY! Medley
(*Music and Lyrics by* Jerry Herman.)
FIDDLER ON THE ROOF Medley
(*Music by* Jerry Bock. *Lyrics by* Sheldon Harnick.)

Scene 7

"Abraham, Martin and John"
(*Music and Lyrics by* Dick Holler.)
"Mamam" (from *MATA HARI*)
(*Music by* Edward Thomas. *Lyrics by* Martin Charnin.)

Scene 8

"I Believe in Music"
(*Music and Lyrics by* Mac Davis.)

1974.10   ## WORDS AND MUSIC

A Musical Revue of the Lyrics of Sammy Cahn in One Act. (Music by James Van Heusen, Saul Chaplin, Jule Styne, Gene De Paul, Nicholas Brodszky, Alex Stordahl, Paul Weston, Jimmy Lunceford.) Directed by Jerry

Adler. Musical director, Richard Leonard. (Setting, costumes) Designed by Robert Randolph. Lighting by Marc B. Weiss. Produced by Alexander H. Cohen in association with Harvey Granat. Opened 16 April 1974 at the John Golden Theatre and closed 3 August 1974 after 127 performances.

CAST: SAMMY CAHN, KELLY GARRETT, SHIRLEY LEMMON, JON PECK.

MUSICAL NUMBERS

"Call Me Irresponsible" (from *PAPA'S DELICATE CONDITION*, film)
"Shake Your Head from Side to Side"
"Rhythm Is Our Business"
"Please Be Kind"
"I've Heard That Song Before" (from *YOUTH ON PARADE*, film)
"Five Minutes More" (from *SWEETHEART OF SIGMA CHI*, film)
"I'll Walk Alone" (from *FOLLOW THE BOYS*, film)
"It's Been a Long, Long Time"
"It's Magic" (from *ROMANCE ON THE HIGH SEAS*, film)
"Guess I'll Hang My Tears Out to Dry" (from *GLAD TO SEE YOU*)
"The Christmas Waltz"
"Teach Me Tonight"
"Three Coins in the Fountain" (from film of the same name)
"Be My Love" (from *THE TOAST OF NEW ORLEANS*, film)
"I'll Never Stop Loving You" (from *LOVE ME OR LEAVE ME*, film)
"Thoroughly Modern Millie" (from film of the same name)
"You'll Never Know"
"All the Way" (from *THE JOKER IS WILD*, film)
"The Tender Trap" (from film of the same name)
"Everybody Has the Right to Be Wrong" (from *SKYSCRAPER*)
"I'll Only Miss Him When I think of Him" (from *SKYSCRAPER*)
"Walking Happy" (from show of the same name)
"Papa, Won't You Dance With Me" (from *HIGH BUTTON SHOES*)
"Day By Day"
"Let It Snow! Let It Snow! Let It Snow!"
"A Touch of Class" (from film of the same name)
"You're My Girl" (from *HIGH BUTTON SHOES*)
"Saturday Night (Is the Loneliest Night of the Week)"
"I Should Care" (from *THRILL OF A ROMANCE*, film)
"Put 'Em in a Box, (Tie 'Em with a Ribbon, and Throw 'Em in the Deep Blue Sea)" (from *ROMANCE ON THE HIGH SEAS*, film)
"The Second Time Around" (from *HIGH TIME*, film)
"Pocketful of Miracles" (from film of the same name)
"I Fall in Love Too Easily" (from *ANCHORS AWEIGH*, film)
"I Wonder Why"
"Until the Real Thing Comes Along"
"Love and Marriage" (from *OUR TOWN*, TV musical)
"The Things We Did Last Summer"
"Time After Time" (from *IT HAPPENED IN BROOKLYN*, film)
"Come Fly With Me" (from film of the same name)
"High Hopes" (from *A HOLE IN THE HEAD*, film)
"My Kind of Town (Chicago Is)" (from *ROBIN AND THE SEVEN HOODS*, film)

1974.11   ## SAMMY

A Musical Revue in Two Acts. Musical conductor (for Mr. Davis), George Rhodes. Stage director, Darrell Giddens. Musical coordinator, Mel Rodnon. Produced by Nederlander in association with Sy Marsh. Opened 23 April 1974 at the Uris Theatre and closed 4 May 1974 after 14 performances.

CAST: SAMMY DAVIS, JR., FREDA PAYNE, THE NICHOLAS BROTHERS (Harold, Fayard).

MUSICAL NUMBERS[23]

Scene 1

"I've Gotta Be Me" (from *GOLDEN RAINBOW*)
(*Music and Lyrics by* Walter Marks.)

---

[23]No song list appeared in the program. List was prepared from press reviews, and is neither complete nor in performance order.

"Another Spring"

"The Impossible Dream" (from *MAN OF LAMANCHA*)
   (*Music by* Mitch Leigh. *Lyrics by* Joe Darion.)

"Goldfinger" (from film of the same name)
   (*Music by* John Barry. *Lyrics by* Leslie Bricusse and Anthony Newley.)

"What Kind of Fool Am I?" (from *STOP THE WORLD-I WANT TO GET OFF*)
   (*Music and Lyrics by* Leslie Bricusse and Anthony Newley.)

"Who Can I Turn To?" (from *THE ROAR OF THE GREASPAINT-THE SMELL OF THE CROWD*)
   (*Music and Lyrics by* Leslie Bricusse and Anthony Newley.)

"The Candy Man" (from *WILLY WONKA AND THE CHOCOLATE FACTORY*, film)
   (*Music and Lyrics by* Leslie Bricusse and Anthony Newley.)

"Gonna Build a Montain" (from *STOP THE WORLD-I WANT TO GET OFF*)

"Once in a Lifetime" (from *STOP THE WORLD-I WANT TO GET OFF*)
   S. Davis
   (*Music and Lyrics by* Leslie Bricusse and Anthony Newley.)

Scene 2

Medley of Songs from their films *DOWN ARGENTINA WAY, TIN PAN ALLEY, ZIEGFELD FOLLIES*
   The Nicholas Brothers

"Ol' Man River" (from *SHOWBOAT*)
   (*Music by* Jerome Kern. *Lyrics by* Oscar Hammerstein II.)

The Nicholas Brothers

Scene 3

"The Man I Love"
   (*Music by* George Gershwin. *Lyrics by* Ira Gershwin.)

"What a Little Moonlight Can Do" (from *ROADHOUSE NIGHTS*, film)
   (*Music and Lyrics by* Harry Woods.)

"Cool Blues"

"Band of Gold" (*Music and Lyrics by* Ronald Dunbar, Edythe Wayne.)

"Carousel" (from *JACQUES BREL IS ALIVE AND LIVING IN PARIS*)
   (*Music and Lyrics by* Jacques Brel.)
   F. Payne

Scene 4

"I'll Never Smile Again"
   (*Music and Lyrics by* Ruth Lowe.)

"Witchcraft"
   (*Music by* Cy Coleman. *Lyrics by* Carolyn Leigh.)

"Come Fly With Me" (from film of the same name)
   (*Music by* James Van Heusen. *Lyrics by* Sammy Cahn.)

"(I Did It) My Way"
   (*Music by* Caliude Revaux and Claude François. *English Lyrics by* Paul Anka.)

"Mr. Bojangles"
   (*Music and Lyrics by* Jerry Jeff Walker.)

"For Once In My Life"
   (*Music by* Orlando Murden. *Lyrics by* Ronald Millar.)

"The Lady Is a Tramp" (from *BABES IN ARMS*)
   (*Music by* Richard Rodgers. *Lyrics by* Lorenz Hart.)

"Come on, Baby"

"Ya Got Trouble" (from *THE MUSIC MAN*)
   (*Music and Lyrics by* Meredith Willson.)

"Birth of the Blues" (from *GEORGE WHITE'S SCANDALS OF 1926*)
   (*Music by* Ray Henderson. *Lyrics by* Buddy G. DeSylva, Lew Brown.)S. Davis

RIDE THE WINDS
1974.12

A Musical in Two Acts. Book, music and lyrics by John Driver. Directed by Lee D. Sankowich. Choreography by Jay Norman. Orchestrations, vocal arrangements and musical direction by Robert Brandzel. Technical advisor, Sensei Yoshiteru Otani. Sets and costumes by Samuel C. Ball. Lighting by Jeff Davis. Produced by Berta Walker and Bill Tchakirides. Opened 16 May 1974 at the Bijou Theatre and closed 18 May 1974 after 3 performances.

CAST (in order of appearance): *Musashi*: IRVING (ALLEN) LEE. *Yamada*: SAB SHIMONO. *Sensei (Honored Teacher) Takuan*: ERNESTO GONZALEZ. *Joshu*: NATE BARNETT. *Inari*: CHIP ZIEN. *Banzo*: TOM MATSUSAKA. *Ya Ta*: Fanny Cerito Assoluta. *Lan*: ELAINE PETRICOFF. *Toki*: MARION JIM. *Oda*: ALEXANDER ORFALY. *Tellers*: Laura May Lewis, John Gorrin. *Priests, Students, Soldiers*: Kenneth Frett, John Gorrin, Richard Loreto, Ken Mitchell.

Act 1: A feudal country in the Far East. The action takes place around a monastery along a mountain road.

Act 2: Four years later.

ACT 1
   "Run, Musashi, Run"
      The Company
   "The Emperor Me"
      I. Lee
   "The Gentle Buffoon"
      N. Barnett, T. Matsusaka
   "Those Who Speak"
      I. Lee, N. Barnett, T. Matsusaka
   "Flower Song"
      E. Gonzalez, E. Petricoff, N. Barnett, Ensemble
   "You're Loving Me"
      I. Lee
   "Breathing the Air"
      M. Jim
   "Remember That Day"
      E. Gonzalez, S. Shimono
   "Tengu"
      Ensemble

ACT 2
   "Ride the Winds"
      The Company
   "Are You a Man"
      E. Petricoff
   "Ride the Winds" (reprise)
      The Company
   "Every Days"
      E. Petricoff, M. Jim, Inari Priests
   "Loving You"
      E. Petricoff, I. Lee
   "Pleasures"
      A. Orfaly
   "Someday I'll Walk"
      I. Lee
   "That Touch"
      E. Petricoff
   Finale
      The Company

THE MAGIC SHOW
1974.13

A Magic Show with Songs in One Act[24]. Book by Bob Randall. Music and lyrics by Stephen Schwartz. Magic by Doug Henning. Direction and dances by Grover Dale. Setting by David Chapman. Costumes by Randy Barcelo. Lighting by Richard Nelson. Musical director, Stephen Reinhardt. Dance arrangements by David Spangler. Audio design by Phil Ramone. Associate producer, Nan Pearlman. Produced by Edgar Lansbury, Joseph Beruh, Ivan Reitman. Opened 28 May 1974 at the Cort Theatre and closed 31 December 1978 after 1859 performances.

CAST (in order of appearance): *Manny*: ROBERT LuPONE. *Feldman*: DAVID OGDEN STIERS. *Donna*: ANNIE McGREEVEY. *Dina*: CHERYL BARNES. *Cal*: DALE SOULES. *Doug*: DOUG HENNING. *Mike*: Ronald Stafford. *Steve*: Lloyd Sannes. *Charmin*: ANITA MORRIS. *Goldfarb*: Sam Schacht.

The action takes place in the Passaic Top Hat, a nite club in New Jersey.

---

[24]For subsequent tour, an intermission was added after "Doug's Act" in some cities.

MUSICAL NUMBERS
"Up to His Old Tricks"
Entire Company
"Solid Silver Platform Shoes"
C. Barnes, A. McGreevey
"Lion Tamer"
D. Soules
"Style"
D. O. Stiers, Company
"Charmin's Lament"
A. Morris
"Two's Company"
C. Barnes, A. McGreevey

"The Goldfarb Variations"
C. Barnes, D. O. Stiers, A. McGreevey, R. LuPone, A. Morris
"Doug's Act"
D. Henning
"A Bit of Villainy"
D. O. Stiers, C. Barnes, A. McGreevey
"West End Avenue"
D. Soules
"Sweet, Sweet, Sweet"
A. Morris, R. LuPone, R. Stafford, L. Sannes
"Before Your Very Eyes"
C. Barnes, A. McGreevey, D. O. Stiers

1974–1975 SEASON

Angela Lansbury in GYPSY
Martha Swope/TimePix

1974–1975 SEASON

THE MERRY WIDOW

1974.14

A Revival of the Operetta ('La Viuda Alegre') in Three Acts, in Spanish[1]. Original Viennese libretto by Victor Léon and Leo Stein. (Based on the play "L'Attaché d'ambassade" by Henri Meilhac.) Spanish translation by Miguel Padilla. Music by Franz Lehár. Directed by Miguel de Grandy. Scenery by Sormani di Milano. Costumes by Stivanello. Lighting by Lawrence Metzler. Musical director and conductor, Alfredo Munar. Chorus master, Juan Viccini. Choreographer, Armando Suez. Special consultant, Raymond R. Norat. Produced by VICMAN Productions (Victor del Corral, Manolo Alonso). Opened 4 June 1974 at the New York City Center and closed 9 June 1974 after 7 performances.

CAST (in order of appearance): *Viscount Zancada*: Hernando Chaviano. *Baron Mirko Zeta*: Miguel de Grandy. *Kromow*: Rosendo Gali Menendez. *Raul de saint Brioche*: Carlos de Leon. *Olga Kromow*: Nydia del Rivero. *Bogdanovitch*: Ruddi Fanetti. *Pritzky*: Jesus Zubizaretta. *Valencienne*: PULI TORO. *Camilo De Rosillon*: RAFAEL LE BRON. *Prascovia*: Lolina Gutierrez. *Niegus*: Manolo Alvan. *Ana De Glavari*: GEORGINA GRANADOS. *Count Danilo*: TOMAS ALVAREZ. *Silviana Bogdanovitch*: Lisette Palacio. *Waiters*: Pablo Alamo, Eddie Gonzales, Mario Santisteban, Pedro Trujillo.

Chorus: German Acosta, Frank Acosta, Jose Calazan, Nina Cruz, Frank Cruz, Isis Figueroa, Lourdes Galaya, Luis Gotay, Orika Gutierrez, Ernesto Gutierrez, Hector Lomba, Maria Mainegra, Rafael Morales, Amparo Navarro, Josefa Navarro, Soledad Navarro, Luis Pena, Juan Sabache, Flora Santana, Antonio Tarazona, Amparo Viccini, Elda Zubizarreta, Mercedes Zubizarreta. *Dancers*: Kate Antrobus, Joan Baker, Marissa Benetsky, Sandy Italiano, Barbara Klein, Henry Boyer, Marcos Dinnerstein, Daryl Gray, Gerald Moreno, Stephen Rockford.

The action takes place in Paris in the 1900s.

THE MIKADO,
or The Town of Titipu

1974.15

A Revival of the Comic Opera in Two Acts[2]. Libretto by William S. Gilbert. Music by Arthur Sullivan. Directed and choreographed by Jack Eddleman. Scenic design by Donald Oenslager. Costume design by Patton Campbell. Lighting by Hans Sondheimer. Conducted by Judith Somogi. Chorus master, George Branson Gray. Produced by the New York City Opera. Opened 1 September 1974 at the New York State Theatre and closed 9 November 1974 after 6 performances in repertory; returned to the repertory 9 March 1975 at the New York State Theatre for 3 additional performances. (Total 9 performances this season.)

CAST: *The Mikado of Japan*: EDWARD PIERSON. *Nanki-Poo*, his son, disguised as a wandering minstrel in love with Yum-Yum: GARY GLAZE. *Ko-Ko*, Lord High Executioner of Titipu: JAMES BILLINGS. *Pooh-Bah*, Lord High Everything Else: ARA BERBERIAN. *Pish-Tush*, a Noble Lord: Robert Termine. *Yum-Yum, Pitti-Sing, Peep-Bo*, three sisters, wards of Ko-Ko: GLENYS FOWLES, JEANNE PILAND, PULI TORO. *Katisha*: BETTY ALLEN.
Chorus of School Girls, Nobles, Guards and Coolies: New York City Opera Chorus.

DIE FLEDERMAUS

1974.16

A Revival of the Operetta in Three Acts[3]. Original Viennese libretto by Carl Haffner and Richard Genée. Lyrics by Richard Genée. (Based on the comedy "Le Réveillon" by Henri Meilhac and Ludovic Halévy.) English libretto by Ruth and Thomas Martin. Music by Johann Strauss. Directed by Gerald Freedman. Choreographed by Joyce Trisler. Scenic design by Lloyd Evans. Costume design by Theoni V. Aldredge. Lighting by Hans Sondheimer. Conducted by Mario Bernardi. Opened 18 September 1974 at the New York State Theatre and closed 7 November 1974 after 9 performances in repertory; returned to the repertory 18 March 1975 and closed 16 April 1975 after 4 additional performances. (Total 13 performances this season.)

CAST (in order of appearance): *Alfred*, an itinerant tenor: Gary Glaze. *Adele*, von Eisenstein's chambermaid: RUTH WELTING. *Rosalinda von Eisenstein*: JOHANNA MEIER. *Gabriel von Eisenstein*: ALAN TITUS. *Dr. Blind*, a lawyer: Howard Fried. *Dr. Falke*, a close friend of Eisenstein: DOMINIC COSSA. *Frank*, the prison warden: SPIRO MALAS. *Sally*, Adele's sister: Diana Kehrig. *Ivan*, servant to Orlofsky: Jack Sims. *Prince Orlofsky*, a wealthy, bored Russian: DAVID RAE SMITH. *Frosch*, the jailer: Coley Worth. *Solo Dancers*: Esperanza Galan, Juliu Horvath.
Ensemble: New York City Opera Chorus.

GYPSY

1974.17

A Revival of the Musical Fable in Two Acts[4]. Book by Arthur Laurents. Suggested by the memoirs (of the same name) by Gypsy Rose Lee. Music by Jule Styne. Lyrics by Stephen Sondheim. Scenery and lighting by Robert Randolph. Costumes by Raoul Pene du Bois. Directed by Arthur Laurents. Original New York production Directed and choreographed by Jerome Robbins. Choreography reproduced by Robert Tucker. Musical direction by Milton Rosenstock. Orchestrations by Sid Ramin with Robert Ginzler. Dance music arranged by John Kander. Miss Lansbury's costumes by Robert Mackintosh. Sound design by Jack Mann. Produced by Barry M. Brown, Edgar Lansbury, Fritz Holt and Joseph Beruh. Opened 23 September 1974 at the Winter Garden Theatre and closed 4 January 1975 after 120 performances.

CAST (in order of appearance): *Uncle Jocko*: John C. Becher. *George*: Don Potter. *Clarence* (and His Classic Clarinet): Craig Brown. *Balloon Girl*: Donna Elio. *Baby Louise*: Lisa Peluso. *Baby June*: BONNIE LANGFORD. *Rose*: ANGELA LANSBURY. *Chowsie*: Peewee. *Pop*: Ed Riley. *Newsboys*: Craig Brown, Anthony Marciona, Sean Rule, Mark Santoro. *Weber*: Charles Rule. *Herbie*: REX ROBBINS. *Louise*: ZAN CHARISSE. *June*: MAUREEN MOORE. *Tulsa*: JOHN SHERIDAN. *Yonkers*: Steven Gelfer. *L.A.*: David Lawson. *Little Rock*: Jay Smith. *San Diego*: Dennis Karr. *Boston*: Serhij Bohdan. *Kringelein*: John C. Becher. *Mr. Goldstone*: Don Potter. *Gigolo*: Edith Ann. *Waitress*: Patricia Richardson. *Miss Cratchitt*: Gloria Rossi. *Hollywood Blondes* (5): Pat Cody, Jinny Kordek, Jan Neuberger, Marilyn Olson, Patricia Richardson. *Agnes*: Denny Dillon. *Pastey*: Richard J. Sabellico. *Tessie Tura*: MARY LOUISE WILSON. *Mazeppa*: GLORIA ROSSI. *Cigar*: John C. Becher. *Electra*: Sally Cooke. *Maid*: Bonnie Walker. *Phil*: Ed Riley. *Bougeron-Cochon*: Serhij Bohdan.

MACK AND MABEL

1974.18

A Musical Love Story in One Act[5], 14 Scenes. Book by Michael Stewart. Based on an idea by Leonard Spiegelgass. Music and lyrics by Jerry Herman. Directed and choreographed by Gower Champion. Scenic design by Robin Wagner. Costume design by Patricia Zipprodt. Lighting design by Tharon Musser. Musical direction and vocal arrangements by Don Pippin. Orchestrations by Philip J. Lang. Incidental and dance music by John Morris. Associate choreographer, Buddy Schwab. Production supervisor, Lucia Victor. Associate producer, Jack Schlissel. Film coordinator, Andy Stein. Early comedy film from the Killiam Collection. Produced by David Merrick in association with Edwin H. Morris. Opened 6 October 1974 at the Majestic Theatre and closed 30 November 1974 after 65 performances.

CAST (in order of appearance): *Eddie*, the watchman: Stanley Simmonds. *Mack Sennett*: ROBERT PRESTON. *Lottie Ames*: LISA KIRK. *Ella*: Nancy Evers. *Freddie*: Roger Bigelow. *Charlie Muldoon*: Christopher Murney. *Wally*: Robert Fitch. *Frank Wyman*: Jerry Dodge. *Mabel Normand*: BERNADETTE PETERS. *Mr. Kleiman*: Tom Batten. *Mr. Fox*: Bert Michaels. *Iris*, the wardrobe mistress: Marie Santell. *William Desmond Taylor*: JAMES MITCHELL. *Phyllis Foster*: Cheryl Armstrong. *Serge*: Frank Root.

---

[1]Neither Synopsis of Scenes nor Musical Numbers given in program. For Synopsis of Scenes and Musical Numbers in English, see original 1907 production.
[2]First presented in New York 20 July, 10–29 August 1885 at the Union Square and People's Theatres for 22 performances. First authorized production presented 19 August 1885 at the Fifth Avenue Theatre by Richard D'Oyly Carte for 250 performances. For Synopsis of Scenes and Musical Numbers, see 19 August 1885 D'Oyly Carte production.
[3]First English language production presented in New York 16 March 1885 at the Casino Theatre for 42 performances. First New York production of this adaptation 20 December 1950 at the Metropolitan Opera House. For Synopsis of Scenes and Musical Numbers, see May 1954 revival.

---

[4]Originally produced in New York 21 May 1959 at the Broadway Theatre for 702 performances. For Synopsis of Scenes and Musical Numbers, see original 1959 production. The opening number "May We Entertain You" retitled as "Let Me Entertain You." "Mr Goldstone, I Love You" listed as "Mr. Goldstone." "Dainty June and Her Farmboys" was retitled "The Barnyard" for the national tour. "Together, Wherever We Go" listed as "Together." The Act 2 reprise of "Let Me Entertain You" retitled as "The Strip" performed by Zan Charisse (without Company).
[5]After opening, an intermission was added between Scenes 8 and 9.

The Grips: John Almberg, Roger Bigelow, George Blackwell, Frank Bouley, Gerard Brentte, Lonnie Burr, Chet D'Elia, Igors Gavon, Jonathan Miele, Don Percassi, Frank Root. *Mack Sennett Bathing Beauties*: Cheryl Armstrong, Claudia Asbury, Sandahl Bergman, Chrystal Chambers, Nancy Dafgek, Prudence Darby, Elaine Handel, Paula Lynn, Patricia Michaels, Carol Perea, L. J. Rose, Rita Rudner, Marianne Selbert, Jo Speros, Pat Trott, Geordie Withee.

Scene 1: The Sennett Studios, 1938. *Scene 2*: The Brooklyn Studio, 1911. *Scene 3*: Mack's Office, Brooklyn. *Scene 4*: En route to California. *Scene 5*: Los Angeles, 1912. *Scene 6*: On the Set. *Scene 7*: The Orchid Room of the Hollywood Hotel, 1919. *Scene 8*: On the Set. *Scene 9*: Mack's New Office, 1923. *Scene 10*: Studio Early Next Morning. *Scene 11*: A pier, New York. *Scene 12*: "Vitagraph Varieties of 1929" and the Terrace of William Desmond Taylor's Home. *Scene 13*: Mack's Office—then Mabel's Home. *Scene 14*: The Sennett Studios, 1938.

MUSICAL NUMBERS

Scene 1
"Movies Were Movies"
R. Preston
Scene 2
"Look What Happened to Mabel"
B. Peters, R. Fitch, C. Murney, J. Dodge, Grips
Scene 3
"Big Time"
L. Kirk, the Family
Scene 4
"I Won't Send Roses"
R. Preston
"I Won't Send Roses" (reprise)
B. Peters
Scene 5
"I Wanna Make the World Laugh"
R. Preston, Company
Scene 6
"I Wanna Make the World Laugh" (reprise)
R. Preston, Company
Scene 7
"Wherever He Ain't"
B. Peters, Waiters
Scene 8
"Hundreds of Girls"
R. Preston, Bathing Beauties
Scene 10
"When Mabel Comes into the Room"
Company
"My Heart Leaps Up"
R. Preston
Scene 11
"Time Heals Everything"
B. Peters
Scene 12
"Tap Your Troubles Away"
L. Kirk, Girls
Scene 13
"I Promise You a Happy Ending"
R. Preston

CHARLES AZNAVOUR ON BROADWAY

1974.19

A One-Man Show in Two Acts. Musical director, Aldo Frank. Music coordinator, Mel Rodnon. Lighting, Marc B. Weiss. Production manager, Levon Sayan. (All music by Charles Aznavour except as noted.) A Music Fair-Enterprises Inc. Production. Produced by Lee Guber, Shelly Gross and Joseph Harris. Opened 15 October 1974 at the Minskoff Theatre and closed 27 October 1974 after 16 performances.

CAST: CHARLES AZNAVOUR.

ACT 1
"Le Temps"
(*Music by* J. Davis. *English Lyrics by* Herbert Kretzmer.)

"Happy Anniversary"
(*English Lyrics by* Herbert Kretzmer.)
"I Live for You"
(*English Lyrics by* Herbert Kretzmer.)
"Un par un"
"Our Love, My Love"
(*Lyrics by* Erich Segal.)
"The Ham"
(*Music by* Georges Garvarentz. *English Lyrics by* B. Morrisson.)
"La Mamma"
(*Lyrics by* Robert Gall.)
"To Die of Love"
English Lyrics by Howard Liebling.)
"No I Could Never Forget"
(*Music by* Georges Garvarentz. *English Lyrics by* Al Kasha and Joel Hirschhorn.)
"I Have Lived"
(*English Lyrics by* Al Kasha and Joel Hirschhorn.)
"La Boheme"
(*Lyrics by* Jacques Plante.)
"What Makes a Man"
(*English Lyrics by* R. Craig.)
"Emmenez-moi"
ACT 2
"La Baraka"
(*English Lyrics by* Herbert Kretzmer.)
"Reste"
"We Can Never Know"
(*English Lyrics by* Al Kasha and Joel Hirschhorn.)
"You've Let Yourself Go"
(*English Lyrics by* Marcel Stellman.)
"Trousse chemise"
(*Lyrics by* J. Mareuil.)
"The 'I Love You' Song"
(*French Lyrics by* G. Bontempelli. *English Lyrics by* Herbert Kretzmer.)
"She"
(*English Lyrics by* Herbert Kretzmer.)
"Que c'est triste Venise"
(*Lyrics by* F. Dorin.)
"And I in My Chair"
(*English Lyrics by* D. Newburg.)
"Yesterday When I Was Young"
(*English Lyrics by* Herbert Kretzmer.)
"Isabelle"
"The Old Fashioned Way"
(*Music by* Georges Garvarentz. *English Lyrics by* Al Kasha and Joel Hirschhorn.)
"Les comediens"
(*Lyrics by* Jacques Plante.)
"You've Got to Learn"
(*English Lyrics by* Marcel Stellman.)

ANDY WILLIAMS with MICHEL LEGRAND

1974.20

A Musical Revue in Two Acts. Musical director, Jack Fierman. Set by Neil Peter Jampolis. Lighting by Jane Reisman. Associate conductor, Armand Migniani. Soloist, Eileen Duffy. Stage director, Jerry Grollnek. Sound consultant, Pat Baroo. Produced by Nederlander. Opened 16 October 1974 at the Uris Theatre and closed 27 October 1974 after 15 performances.

CAST: ANDY WILLIAMS, MICHEL LEGRAND.

ACT 1
Michel Legrand conducts his own songs, including a medley from "The Umbrellas of Cherbourg."
Soloist: E Duffy.
ACT 2
Andy Williams, with orchestra conducted by Jack Fierman
Finale: Andy Williams and Michel Legrand

TONY BENNETT AND LENA HORNE SING

1974.21

A Musical Revue in Two Acts. Music directors, Torrie Zito (for Tony Bennett), Robert M. Freedman (for Lena Horne). Production coordinator, Sherman Sneed. Wardrobe for Miss Horne, Georgio Sant'Angelo. Produced by Lee Guber, Shelly Gross and Joseph Harris. Opened 30 October 1974 at the Minskoff Theatre and closed 24 November 1974 after 37 performances.

CAST: TONY BENNETT, LENA HORNE.

ACT 1

Miss Horne will sing the songs of Arlen, Bloom, Denver, Freedman, Kristofferson, Porter Razaf, Raposo, Wonder.

ACT 2

Mr. Bennett will sing the songs of Arlen/Koehler, Bacharach, Cahn/Barrie, Cross/Cory, Ebb, Ellington, Gerhswin, Harrison, McCartney, McHugh, Miller, Newley/Bricusse, Rodgers/Hart, Styne. And a Special Tribute to the great American composer Harold Arlen.

ANTHONY NEWLEY & HENRY MANCINI

1974.22

A Musical Revue in Two Acts. Set designed by Neil Peter Jampolis. Theatre lighting by Jane Reisman. Lighting and sound by Jerry Grollnek, Pat Barso. Conductor for Mr. Newley, Ian Fraser. Produced by Nederlander. Opened 31 October 1974 at the Uris Theatre and closed 10 November 1974 after 15 performances.

CAST: ANTHONY NEWLEY, HENRY MANCINI.

ACT 1: Henry Mancini and His Orchestra

Overture from *TOMMY*
   (*Music by* Pete Townshend.)
Medley: "Baby Elephant Walk," "Mr. Lucky"
   (*Music by* Henry Mancini.)
Love Theme from *ROMEO AND JULIET* film
   (*Music by* Nino Rota.)
Overture from *THAT'S ENTERTAINMENT* film:
   "The Trolley Song," "Over the Rainbow," "Hi-Lili Hi-Lo," "It's a Most Unusual Day," "Singin' in the Rain," "San Francisco," "Love," That's Entertainment."
(Theme from) *THE PINK PANTHER* film
   (*Music by* Henry Mancini.)
Medley: "Love's Theme" (White); "T.S.O.P." (Gamble/Huff)
The Big Band Montage:
   "I'm Getting Sentimental Over You," "Blue Flame," "Let's Dance," "Ciribiribin," "Moonlight Serenade," "Artistry in Rhythm," "Nightmare," "Leapfrog," "Take the A Train."
Theme from *PETER GUNN* (Television)
   (*Music by* Henry Mancini.)
Ballads by Mancini:
   "Dear Heart," "The Sweetheart Tree," "Days of Wine and Roses," Moon River."

ACT 2: Anthony Newley

It's a Musical World Medley:
   "It's a Musical World" (from *THE GOOD OLD BAD DAYS*)
"The Good Old Bad Old Days" (from *THE GOOD OLD BAD DAYS*)
"Gonna Build a Mountain" (from *STOP THE WORLD-I WANT TO GET OFF*)
"On a Wonderful Day Like Today" (from *THE ROAR OF THE GREASEPAINT*)
"Goldfinger" (from *GOLDFINGER* film)
"The Good Things in Life" (from *THE GOOD OLD BAD DAYS*)
"The Candy Man" (from *WILLY WONKA AND THE CHOCOLATE FACTORY* film)
"Once in a Lifetime" (from *STOP THE WORLD-I WNAT TO GET OFF*)
   (All of the above *Music and Lyrics by* Leslie Bricusse and Anthony Newley.)
"Talk to the Animals" (from *DR. DOOLITTLE* film)
   (*Music and Lyrics by* Leslie Bricusse.)

"Love Has the Longest Memory of All" (from *QUILP* film)
   (*Music and Lyrics by* Anthony Newley.)
"Middle Age Rock & Roll Star"
   (*Music and Lyrics by* Anthony Newley.)
"No Such Thing as Love"
   (*Music and Lyrics by* Ian Fraser and Anthony Newley.)
"Who Can I Turn To?" (from *THE ROAR OF THE GREASEPAINT*)
"Feeling Good" (from *THE ROAR OF THE GREASEPAINT*)

A Broadway Medley:
   "Everything's Coming Up Roses" (from *GYPSY*)
   "Tonight" (from *WEST SIDE STORY*)
   "Get Me to the Church on Time" (from *MY FAIR LADY*)
   "My Favorite Things" (from *THE SOUND OF MUSIC*)
   "If I Were a Rich Man" (from *FIDDLER ON THE ROOF*)
   "People" (from *FUNNY GIRL*)
   "I'll Never Fall in Love Again" (from *PROMISES, PROMISES*)
   "Hello, Dolly!" (from *HELLO, DOLLY!*)
   "What Kind of Fool Am I?" (from *STOP THE WORLD-I WANT TO GET OFF*)

MOURNING PICTURES

1974.23

A Drama with Music in Two Acts. Play by Honor Moore. Music by Susan Ain. Directed by Kay Carney. Music supervisor, Larry Abel. Setting by John Jacobsen. Costumes by Whitney Blausen. Lighting by Spencer Mosse. A Lenox Arts Center/Music-Theatre Performing Group Production (Lyn Austin, Mary Silverman, Producers). Produced by Samuel H. Schwartz. Opened and closed 10 November 1974 at the Lyceum Theatre after 1 performance.

CAST (in order of appearance): *Margaret*: KATHRYN WALKER. *Maggie*: LEORA DANA. *Philip*: DONALD SYMINGTON. *Abigail*: Leslie Ackerman. *David*: Daniel Landon. *Doctors Rumbach, Cassidy, Berryman, Potter*: PHILIP CARLSON. *Singer*: DOROTHEA JOYCE.

The action takes place between March and September in Connecticut, New York and Washington, D.C.

Act 1: March-May.

Act 2: June-September.

ACT 1
   "What Will She Leave Me?"
      D. Joyce
   "It's Such a Beautiful Day"
      D. Joyce
   "What Are You Saying About Me Now?"
      D. Joyce
   "Sweet Clear Sun"
      D. Joyce
ACT 2
   "The Garden"
      D. Joyce
   "Wait Until the Sun"
      D. Joyce
   "I Want to Go Home"
      D. Joyce
   "Paul Arrives"
      D. Joyce
   "There Is a Birthday"
      D. Joyce

SGT. PEPPER'S LONELY HEARTS CLUB BAND ON THE ROAD

1974.24

A Rock Spectacle (Musical Revue) in Two Acts. (Based on the film of the same name by The Beatles.) Music and lyrics by John Lennon and Paul McCartney. Production conceived and adapted (for the Stage) by Robin Wagner and Tom O'Horgan. Entire production directed and staged by Tom O'Horgan. Scenic design by Robin Wagner. Costume design by Randy Barcelo. Lighting design by Jules Fisher. Sound design by Abe Jacob. (Music) Arranged and conducted by Gordon Lowry Harrell. Production supervisor, Richard Scanga. Executive producer, Peter Brown. Associate producers, (R. Tyler) Gatchell & (Peter) Neufeld. Presented at this theatre by Steven Singer, Steve Metz and Howard Dando. Produced by Robert Stigwood in association with Brian Avnet and Scarab Productions, Inc. Opened 17 November 1974 at the Beacon Theatre and closed 5 January 1975 after 66 performances.

CAST (in order of appearance): *Maxwell's Silver Hammermen* (3): *Jack*: ALLAN NICHOLLS. *Sledge*: WILLIAM PARRY. *Claw*: B. G. GIBSON. *Billy Shears*: TED NEELEY. *Lucy*: ALAINA REED. *Flattop*: Walter Rivera. *Sun Queen, Lovely Rita, Polythene Pam*: David Patrick Kelly. *Strawberry Fields*: KAY COLE. *Sgt. Pepper*: David Patrick Kelly.

Hammeroids: Blake Anderson, Edward Q. Bhartonn, Arlana Blue, Ron Capozzoli, Michael Meadow, Stoney Reece, Jason Roberts.

ACT 1

"Sgt. Pepper's Lonely Hearts Club Band"
A. Nicholls, W. Parry, B. G. Gibson
"With a Little Help from My Friends"
T. Neeley, A. Nicholls, W. Parry, B. G. Gibson
"Nowhere Man"
A. Nicholls, W. Parry, B. G. Gibson
"With a Little Help from My Friends" (reprise)
T. Neeley, A. Nicholls, W. Parry, B. G. Gibson
"Lucy in the Sky With Diamonds"
A. Reed, T. Neeley, A. Nicholls, W. Parry, B. G. Gibson
"I Want You"
T. Neeley, A. Reed, A. Nicholls, W. Parry, B. G. Gibson
"Come Together"
A. Reed, W. Rivera, Friends
"Nowhere Man" II
A. Nicholls, W. Parry, B. G. Gibson
"Sun Queen'
All
"Lovely Rita"
D. P. Kelly, T. Neeley, A. Nicholls, W. Parry, B. G. Gibson, A. Reed
"Polythene Pam"
D. P. Kelly, T. Neeley, A. Nicholls, W. Parry, B. G. Gibson, A. Reed
"She Came in Through the Bathroom Window"
A. Nicholls, W. Parry, B. G. Gibson
"You Never Give Me Your Money'
T. Neeley, D. P. Kelly, A. Nicholls, W. Parry, B. G. Gibson, A. Reed
"Lovely Rita" (reprise)
T. Neeley, D. P. Kelly, A. Nicholls, W. Parry, B. G. Gibson, A. Reed
"Her Majesty"
T. Neeley
"A Day in the Life"
T. Neeley
"She's Leaving Home"
A. Nicholls, W. Parry, B. G. Gibson
"Strawberry Fields Forever"
K. Cole, T. Neeley
"Getting Better"
T. Neeley, K. Cole, A. Nicholls, W. Parry, B. G. Gibson

ACT 2

"Because"
T. Neeley, K. Cole
"When I'm 64"
T. Neeley, K. Cole
"Because" (reprise)
T. Neeley, K. Cole
"Good Morning, Good Morning"
A. Nicholls, W. Parry, B. G. Gibson
"Being for the Benefit of Mr. Kite"
A. Nicholls, W. Parry, B. G. Gibson, A. Reed
"Oh Darling"
K. Cole
"Fixing a Hole" T. Neeley
"Oh Darling" (reprise)
K. Cole
"Being for the Benefit of Mr. Kite" II
A. Nicholls, W. Parry, B. G. Gibson

"Mean Mr. Mustard"
A. Reed
"Maxwell's Silver Hammer"
A. Nicholls, W. Parry, B. G. Gibson
"Being for the Benefit of Mr. Kite" III
A. Nicholls, W. Parry, B. G. Gibson
"Carry That Weight"
A. Nicholls, W. Parry, B. G. Gibson
"Golden Slumbers"
T. Neeley
"Carry That Weight" (reprise)
A. Nicholls, W. Parry, B. G. Gibson
"The Long and Winding Road"
T. Neeley
"Get Back"
D. P. Kelly, T. Neeley, A. Reed, A. Nicholls, W. Parry, B. G. Gibson
"Sgt. Pepper" (reprise)
All
"The End"
All

1974.25 WHERE'S CHARLEY?

A Revival of the Musical (Comedy) in Two Acts, 5 Scenes[6]. Book by George Abbott. Based on the play "Charley's Aunt" by Brandon Thomas. Music and lyrics by Frank Loesser. Directed by Theodore Mann. Scenery by Marjorie Kellogg. Costumes by Arthur Boccia. Lighting by Thomas Skelton. Choreography by Margo Sappington. Musical direction and new arrangements by Tom Pierson. Dialect coach, Marjorie Phillips. Produced by Circle in the Square, Inc. (Theodore Mann, Artistic director; Paul Libin, Managing director). Opened 19 December 1974 at the Circle-in-the Square Theatre and closed 23 February 1975 after 78 performances.

CAST (in order of appearance): *Brassett*: LOUIS BEACHNER. *Jack Chesney*: JERRY LANNING. *Charley Wykeham*: RAUL JULIA. *Kitty Verdun*: CAROL JO LUGENBEAL. *Amy Spettigue*: MARCIA McCLAIN. *Sir Francis Chesney*: PETER WALKER. *Mr. Spettingue*: TOM ALDREDGE. *Donna Lucia D'Alvadorez*: TAINA ELG. *Reggie*: Dennis Cooley.

Students and Young Ladies: Pamela Burrell, Jacqueline Clark, Dennis Cooley, Karen Jablons, Jack Neubeck, Craig Sandquist, Leland Schwantes, Miriam Welch.

The action takes place during the summer at Oxford University, 1892.

Act 1, Scene 1: A Room at Oxford University. *Scene 2*: The Garden.

Act 2, Scene 1: The Garden. *Scene 2*: Where the Ladies Go. *Scene 3*: The Ballroom.

ACT 1
Scene 1
"Where's Charley?"
L. Beachner, Students, Young Ladies
"The Years Before Us"
Students
"Better Get Out of Here"
M. McClain, C. J. Lugenbeal, R. Julia, J. Lanning
"The New Ashmolean Marching Society and Students' Conservatory Band"
P. Walker, T. Aldredge, L. Beachner, Students, Young Ladies
Scene 2
"My Darling, My Darling"
C. J. Lugenbeal, J. Lanning
"Make a Miracle"
R. Julia, M. McClain
"Serenade With Asides"
T. Aldredge
"Lovelier Than Ever"
T. Elg, P. Walker, Students, Young Ladies
"The Woman in His Room"
M. McClain

―――――――――――
[6]Originally produced in New York 11 October 1948 at the St. James Theatre for 792 performances.

"Pernambuco"
R. Julia, the Company
ACT 2
Scene 1
"Where's Charley?" (reprise)
M. McClain
"Once in Love With Amy"
R. Julia
Scene 2
"The Gossips"
Young Ladies
Scene 3
"At the Red Rose Cotillion"
Ensemble
Finale
Ensemble

1974.26   GOOD NEWS

A Revival of the Musical Comedy in Two Acts[7]. Original book by Laurence Schwab, Buddy G. DeSylva and Frank Mandel. Music and lyrics by (Buddy) G. DeSylva, (Lew) Brown and (Ray) Henderson. (Book) Adapted by Garry Marshall. Directed by Michael Kidd. Associate choreographer, Gary Menteer. Settings by Donald Oenslager. Costumes by Donald Brooks. Lighting by Tharon Musser. Orchestrations by Philip J. Lang. Musical direction by Liza Redfield. Sound by Tony Alloy. Musical supervision and vocal arrangements by Hugh Martin and Timothy Gray. Dance music and incidental music composed and arranged by Luther Henderson. Associate producers, Robert Anglund, Stan Hurwitz, Frank Montalvo. Production coordinator, Linda Mann Reed. Produced by Harry Rigby and Terry Allen Kramer. Opened 23 December 1974 at the St. James Theater and closed 4 January 1975 after 16 performances.

CAST (in order of appearance): *Bill Johnson*: GENE NELSON. *Tom Marlowe*: SCOTT STEVENSEN. *Beef Saunders*: Joseph Burke. *Bobby Randall*: WAYNE BRYAN. *Pooch Kearney*: STUBBY KAYE. *Flo*: Rebecca Urich. *Millie*: Paula Cinko. *Pat*: JANA ROBBINS. *Babe O'Day*: BARBARA LAIL. *Windy*: Terry Eno. *Slats*: James [Jimmy] Brennan. *Sylvester*: TOMMY BRESLIN. *Professor Kenyon*: ALICE FAYE. *Connie Lane*: MARTI ROLPH. *Muffin*: Margaret. *Colton Player*: Ernie Pysher. *Happy Days Quartet*: Tim Cassidy, Randall Robbins, Scott Stevensen, David Thome. *Acrobats*: Lisa Guignard, Mary Ann Lipson, Ernie Pysher, Jeff Spielman. *Baton Twirlers*: Tim Cassidy, Lynda Goodfriend, Lisa Guignard. *Tap Dancers*: Terry Eno, Jimmy Brennan.

   Coeds: Paula Cinko, Robin Gerson, Lynda Goodfriend, Lisa Guignard, Anne Kaye, Mary Ann Lipson, Sally O'Donnell, Rebecca Urich, Marcia Lynn Watkins. *Boys*: Michael Austin, James Brennan, Tim Cassidy, Ernie Pysher, Randall Robbins, Jeff Spielman, David Thome.

The action takes place in the mid-1930s on and around the campus of Tait College.

ACT 1
Overture
Company
"He's a Ladies' Man" (from *FOLLOW THRU*)
J. Robbins, P. Cinko, R. Urich, Students
"The Best Things in Life Are Free"
A. Faye, Students
"Just Imagine"
M. Rolph, J. Robbins, P. Cinko, R. Urich
"Happy Days"
S. Stevensen, J. Robbins, P. Cinko, R. Urich, T. Breslin, Boys
"Button Up Your Overcoat" (from *FOLLOW THRU*)
W. Bryan, B. Lail
"Lucky in Love"
M. Rolph, S. Stevensen, Students
"You're the Cream in My Coffee" (from *HOLD EVERYTHING*)
A. Faye, G. Nelson
"Varsity Drag"
B. Lail, Students

"Together"[8]
A. Faye
"Tait Song"
G. Nelson, S. Kaye, Students
"Lucky in Love" (reprise)
Company
ACT 2
"Today's the Day"
Girls
"Girl of the Pi Beta Phi"
J. Robbins, Girls
"Good News"
A. Faye, M. Rolph, Students
"Keep Your Sunny Side Up" (from *SUNNY SIDE UP* film)
S. Kaye, Boys
"The Best Things in Life Are Free" (reprise)
M. Rolph, S. Stevensen
"Life Is Just a Bowl of Cherries" (from *GEORGE WHITE'S SCANDALS OF 1931*)
A. Faye, M. Rolph, B. Lail
"The Professor and the Students"
A. Faye, S. Kaye, Students
Finale
Company

1975.01   THE WIZ

A Musical in Two Acts, 16 Scenes and a Prologue. Book by William F. Brown. Based on the novel "The Wizard of Oz" by L. Frank Baum. Music and lyrics by Charlie Smalls. Direction and costume design by Geoffrey Holder. Choreography and musical numbers staged by George Faison. Settings designed by Tom H. John. Lighting design by Tharon Musser. Orchestrations by Harold Wheeler. Musical direction and vocal arrangements by Charles H. Coleman. Dance arrangements by Timothy Graphenreed. Produced by Ken Harper. Opened 5 January 1975 at the Majestic Theatre, moved 25 May 1977 to the Broadway Theatre, and closed 28 January 1979 after 1672 performances.

CAST (in order of appearance): *Aunt Em*: Tasha Thomas. *Toto*: Nancy. *Dorothy*: STEPHANIE MILLS. *Uncle Henry*: Ralph Wilcox. *Tornado*: Evelyn Thomas. *Munchkins*: Phylicia Ayers-Allen, Pi Douglass, Joni Palmer, Andy Torres, Carl Weaver. *Addaperle*: CLARICE TAYLOR. *Yellow Brick Road*: Ronald Dunham, Eugene Little, John Parks, Kenneth Scott. *Scarecrow*: HINTON BATTLE. *Crows*: Wendy Edmead, Frances Morgan, Ralph Wilcox. *Tinman*: TIGER HAYNES. *Lion*: TED ROSS. *Kalidahs*: Phillip Bond, Pi Douglass, Rodney Green, Evelyn Thomas, Andy Torres. *Poppies*: Lettie Battle, Leslie Butler, Eleanor McCoy, Frances Morgan, Joni Palmer. *Field Mice*: Phylicia Ayers-Allen, Pi Douglass, Carl Weaver, Ralph Wilcox. *Gatekeeper*: Danny Beard. *Emerald City Citizens*: Lettie Battle, Leslie Butler, Wendy Edmead, Eleanor McCoy, Frances Morgan, Joni Palmer, Evelyn Thomas, Phillip Bond, Ronald Dunham, Rodney Green, Eugene Little, John Parks, Kenneth Scott, Andy Torres. *The Wiz*: ANDRE De SHIELDS. *Evillene*: MABEL KING. *Lord High Underling*: Ralph Wilcox. *Soldier Messenger*: Carl Weaver. *Winged Monkey*: Andy Torres. *Glinda*: DEE DEE BRIDGEWATER.
   Pit Singers: Frank Floyd, Sam Harkness, Jozella Reed, Tasha Thomas.

Prologue: Kansas.

Act 1, Scene 1: Munchkin Land. *Scene 2*: Oz Countryside. *Scene 3*: Woods. *Scene 4*: Jungle. *Scene 5*: Kalidah Country. *Scene 6*: Poppy Field. *Scene 7*: Emerald City. *Scene 8*: Throne Room.

Act 2, Scene 1: West Witch Castle. *Scene 2*: Forest. *Scene 3*: Courtyard. *Scene 4*: Emerald City Gate. *Scene 5*: Throne Room. *Scene 6*: Fairgrounds. *Scene 7*: Outskirts. *Scene 8*: Quadling Country.

ACT 1
Prologue
"The Feeling We Once Had"
T. Thomas
"Tornado Ballet"
Company

---

[7]Originally produced in New York 6 September 1927 at the 46th Street Theatre for 551 performances.

[8]A DeSylva, Brown and Henderson interpolation written as a popular song, neither for the stage or film.

Scene 1
"He's the Wizard"
. Taylor, Munchkins
Scene 2
"Soon as I Get Home"
S. Mills
"I Was Born on the Day Before Yesterday"
H. Battle, Crows
"Ease on Down the Road"
S. Mills, H. Battle, R. Dunham, E. Little, J. Parks, K. Scott
Scene 3
"Slide Some Oil to Me"
T. Haynes, S. Mills, H. Battle
Scene 4
"Mean Ole Lion"
T. Ross
Scene 5
"Kalidah Battle"
S. Mills, H. Battle, T. Haynes, T. Ross, Kalidahs, R. Dunham, E. Little, J. Parks, K. Scott
Scene 6
"Be a Lion"
S. Mills, T. Ross
"Lion's Dream"
T. Ross, Poppies
Scene 7
"Emerald City Ballet" (Psst)
S. Mills, H. Battle, T. Haynes, T. Ross, Company
(*Music by* Timothy Graphenreed and George Faison.)
Scene 8
"So You Wanted to Meet the Wizard"
A. De Shields
"To Be Able to Feel" (What Would I Do If I Could Feel)
T. Haynes

ACT 2
Scene 1
"No Bad News"
M. King
Scene 2
"Funky Monkeys"
Monkeys
Scene 3
"Everybody Rejoice"
S. Mills, H. Battle, T. Haynes, T. Ross, Winkies
(*Music and Lyrics by* Luther Vandross.)
Scene 5
"Who Do You Think You Are?"
S. Mills, H. Battle, T. Haynes, T. Ross
"Believe in Youself"
A. De Shields
Scene 6
"Y'All Got It!"
A. De Shields
Scene 8
"A Rested Body Is a Rested Mind"
D. D. Bridgewater
"Believe in Yourself" (reprise)
D. D. Bridgewater
"Home"
S. Mills

BLACK PICTURE SHOW

1975.02

A Play (with songs) in One Act by Bill Gunn. Music and lyrics by Sam Waymon. Scenery by Peter Harvey. Costumes by Judy Dearing. Lighting by Roger Morgan. Directed by Bill Gunn. Music conducted by Sam Waymon. Associate producer, Bernard Gersten. Produced by the New York Shakespeare Festival at Lincoln Center (Joseph Papp, Producer). Opened 6 January 1975 at the Vivian Beaumont Theater and closed 9 February 1975 after 40 performances.

CAST: *Vocalist:* Sam Waymon. *J.D., Alexander's son:* Albert Hall. *Alexander, a Black artist:* DICK ANTHONY WILLIAMS. *Norman, Alexander's companion:* Graham Brown. *Hospital Attendants:* William Leet, Marvin Beck. *Rita, Alexander's second wife:* Carol Cole. *Philippe, a movie producer:* Paul-David Richards. *Jan, Philippe's wife:* Linda Miller.

The action takes place at the present time in a hospital psychiatric unit in the Bronx, New York.

MUSICAL NUMBERS
"I'm So Glad"
"Mose Art" (Second Movement)
"Bird of Paradise"
Variation on "Chopin in E Minor"
"Memory"
"Black Picture Show"
(*Lyrics by* Bill Gunn.)
"Mose Art"
(First Movement)
"Bitch in Heat"
"Digits"
"Science Fiction"
"I Feel So Good"
(*Lyrics by* Bill Gunn.)
"Vintage '51"
"Afghanistan"
"Terminate"

SHENANDOAH

1975.03

A Musical in Two Acts, 18 Scenes and a Prologue. Book by James Lee Barrett and Peter Udell. Based on the film of the same name by James Lee Barrett. Music by Gary Geld. Lyrics by Peter Udell. Directed by Philip Rose. Choreography by Robert Tucker. Scenery by C. Murawski. Lighting by Thomas Skelton. Costumes by Pearl Somner and Winn Morton. Orchestrations by Don Walker. Musical direction by Lynn Crigler. Dance arrangements by Russell Warner. Originally presented by the Goodspeed Opera House (Michael Price, Executive producer). Produced by Philip Rose, Gloria and Louis K. Sher. Opened 7 January 1975 at the Alvin Theatre, moved 29 March 1977 to the Mark Hellinger Theatre, and closed 7 August 1977 after 1050 performances.

CAST (in order of appearance): *Charlie Anderson:* JOHN CULLUM. *Jacob:* TED AGRESS. *James:* JOEL HIGGINS. *Nathan:* Jordan Suffin. *John:* David Russell. *Jenny:* PENELOPE MILFORD. *Henry:* Robert Rosen. *Robert, the boy:* Joseph Shapiro. *Anne:* DONNA THEODORE. *Gabriel:* Chip Ford. *Reverend Byrd:* Charles Welch. *Sam:* GORDON HALLIDAY. *Sergeant Johnson:* Edward Penn. *Lieutenant:* Marshall Thomas. *Tinkham:* Charles Welch. *Carol:* Casper Roos. *Corporal:* Gary Harger. *Marauder:* Gene Masoner. *Engineer:* Ed Preble. *Confederate Sniper:* Craig Lucas.
Ensemble: Ted Carrere, Stephen Dubov, Gary Harger, Brian James, Robert Johanson, Sherry Lambert, Craig Lucas, Gene Masoner, Paul Myrvold, Dan Ormond, Casper Roos, J. Kevin Scannell, Jack Starkey, E. Allan Stevens, Marshall Thomas, Matt Gavin.

The action takes place during the Civil War in the Shenandoah Valley of Virginia.

Prologue: (Outside the Anderson House.)

Act 1, Scene 1: Inside the Anderson House on Sunday morning. *Scene 2:* A Country road. *Scene 3:* Inside the Church. *Scene 4:* A Country road. Moments later. *Scene 5:* The Anderson Farmyard. *Scene 6:* The Anderson Porch. *Scene 7:* Martha's Grave. *Scene 8:* Inside the Anderson Parlor. Evening. *Scene 9:* Anne's Bedroom. Minutes before the wedding. *Scene 10:* Sam and Jenny's Wedding in the farmyard. *Scene 11:* Inside the Anderson Parlor. Moments later. *Scene 12:* Anne's Bedroom.

Act 2, Scene 1: The Anderson Farmyard. Weeks later. *Scene 2:* A wooded area near a railroad track. Night. *Scene 3:* A clearing in the woods. Later that evening. *Scene 4:* Anne's Bedroom. *Scene 5:* Martha's Grave. *Scene 6:* Inside the Church.

ACT 1
Prologue
"Raise the Flag of Dixie"
Confederate and Union Soldiers

Scene 1

"I've Heard It All Before"
J. Cullum

Scene 3

"Pass the Cross to Me"
The Congregation

Scene 4

"Why Am I Me"
J. Shapiro, C. Ford

Scene 5

"Next to Lovin' (I Like Fightin')"
T. Agress, J. Higgins, J. Suffin, D. Russell, R. Rosen

Scene 6

"Over the Hill"
P. Milford

"The Pickers Are Comin'"
J. Cullum

"Next to Lovin'" (reprise)
T. Agress, J. Higgins, J. Suffin, D. Russell, R. Rosen, P. Milford

Scene 7

"Meditation"
J. Cullum

Scene 9

"We Make a Beautiful Pair"
D. Theodore, P. Milford

Scene 10

"Violets and Silverbells"
P. Milford, G. Halliday, Anderson Family

Scene 11

"It's a Boy"
J. Cullum

ACT 2

Scene 1

"Freedom"
D. Theodore, C. Ford

"Violets and Silverbells" (reprise)
J. Higgins, D. Theodore

Scene 2

"Papa's Gonna Make It Alright"
J. Cullum

Scene 3

"The Only Home I Know"
G. Harger, Soldiers

Scene 4

"Papa's Gonna Make It Alright" (reprise)
P. Milford

Scene 5

"Meditation" (reprise)
J. Cullum

Scene 6

"Pass the Cross to Me" (reprise)
The Congregation

1975.04 MAN ON THE MOON

A Musical in One Act, 4 Scenes. Book, music and lyrics by John Phillips. Directed by Paul Morrissey. Sets by John J. Moore. Costumes by Marsia Trinder. Lighting by Jules Fisher. Musical director, Karen Gustafson. Musical arrangements by Michael Gibson and Jim Tyler. Sound by Gary Harris. Costume design supervised by Michael Yeargan. Produced by Andy Warhol in association with Richard Turley. Opened 29 January 1975 at the Little Theatre and closed 1 February 1975 after 5 performances.

CAST: *Dr. Bomb:* HARLAN FOSS. *Ernie Hardy:* ERIC LANG. *Leroy* (Little Red Box): MARK LAWHEAD. *President, King Can:* DENNIS DOHERTY. *Angel:* GENEVIEVE WAITE. *Venus:* MONIQUE VAN VOOREN.
Celestial Choir: Mercury, Miss America: Brenda Bergman. *Mars:* John Patrick Sundine. *Neptune:* Jennifer Elder. *Pluto:* E. Lynn Nickerson. *Saturn:* Jeanette Chastonay.

Scene 1: Earth. *Scene 2*: Canis Minor. *Scene 3*: The Moon. *Scene 4*: Earth.

MUSICAL NUMBERS

Scene 1

Prologue
H. Foss

"Boys from the South"
E. Lang

"Midnight Deadline Blastoff"
E. Lang

"Mission Control"
H. Foss, E. Lang, M. Lwhead, D. Doherty, B. Bergman

"Speed of Light"
E. Lang, M. Lawhead

Scene 2

"Though I'm a Little Angel"
G. Waite

"Girls"
D. Doherty, M. Van Vooren, G. Waite

"Canis Minor Bolero Waltz"
D. Doherty, M. Van Vooren, G. Waite

"Starburst"
G. Waite

"Penthouse of Your Mind"
D. Doherty

"Champagne and Kisses"
M. Van Vooren

"Star Stepping Stranger/Convent"
E. Lang, G. Waite

"My Name Is Can"
D. Doherty

"American Man on the Moon"
M. Van Vooren

Scene 3

"Welcome to the Moon"
Company

"Sunny, Sunny Moon"
M. Van Vooren, H. Foss

"Love Is Coming Back"
E. Lang, G. Waite

"Truth Cannot Be Treason"
M. Lawhead

"Place in Space"
E. Lang, G. Waite

Scene 4

"Family of Man"
H. Foss

"Yesterday I Left the Earth"
Company

"Stepping to the Stars"
Company

1975.05 THE NIGHT THAT MADE AMERICA FAMOUS

A Musical Revue in Two Acts, a Prologue and Epilogue. Music and lyrics by Harry Chapin. Directed by Gene Frankel. Choreography by Doug Rogers. Scenery designed by Kert Lundell. Costumes designed by Randy Barcelo. Lighting designed by Imero Fiorentino. Lighting supervised by Fred Allison. Multi-media development consultants, Imero Fiorentino Associates. Multi-media executed by Jim Sant'Andrea. Multi-media under the direction of Joshua White. Musical direction by Stephen Chapin. Dance arrangements by John Morris. Audio design by Michael Solomon. Assistant choreographer, Mercedes Ellington. Musical coordinator, Joseph Stecko. Associate producer, Nan Pearlman. Produced by Edgar Lansbury and Joseph Beruh in association with the Shubert Organization. Opened 26 February 1975 at the Ethel Barrymore Theatre and closed 6 April 1975 after 47 performances.

CAST: HARRY CHAPIN, KELLY GARRETT, DELORES HALL, GILBERT PRICE, BILL STARR, Alexandra Borrie, Mercedes Ellington, Sid Marshall, Ernie Pysher, Lynne Thigpen, Tom Chapin, Stephen Chapin.

309

The action takes place during the last fifteen years.

Act 1: 1960s.

Act 2: 1970s.

ACT 1

Prologue
   Company
"Six String Orchestra"
   H. Chapin, Company
"Give Me a Road"
   Entire Company
"Sunday Morning Sunshine"
   H. Chapin, Company
"It's My Day"
   K. Garrett
"Give Me a Cause"
   Company
"Welfare Rag"
   D. Hall, B. Starr, G. Price, Company
"Better Place to Be"
   H. Chapin, Company
"Give Me a Wall"
   Company
"Peace Teachers"
   K. Garrett
"Pigeon Run"
   G. Price
"Changing of the Guard"
   G. Price
"When I Look Up"
   D. Hall
"Sniper"
   H. Chapin, Company

ACT 2

"Great Divide"
   H. Chapin
"Taxi"
   H. Chapin, K. Garrett
"Cockeyed John"
   Entire Company
"Mr. Tanner"
   H. Chapin, G. Price
"Maxie"
   K. Garrett
"Fugue:
"Love Can't"
   B. Starr
"When Maudey Wants a Man"
   D. Hall
"I'm a Wonderfully Wicked Woman"
   K. Garrett
"Battleground Bummer"
   G. Price
"Stoopid"
   B. Starr
"Cat's in the Cradle"
   H. Chapin, Company
"Cockeyed John, Give Me My Dream"
   Company
"Too Much World"
   K. Garrett, D. Hall, B. Starr, G. Price, H. Chapin, Company
"As I Grow Older"
   K. Garrett
"Beginning of the End"
   Company
Epilogue: "The Night That Made America Famous"
   H. Chapin, Company

1975.06

GOODTIME CHARLEY

A Musical in Two Acts, 17 Scenes. Book by Sidney Michaels. Music by Larry Grossman. Lyrics by Hal Hackady. Entire production directed by Peter H. Hunt. Dances and musical numbers Staged by Onna White. Scenery by Rouben Ter-Arutunian. Costumes by Willa Kim. Lighting by (Abe) Feder. Orchestrations by Jonathan Tunick. Incidental music by Arthur B. Rubinstein. Dance music by Daniel Troob. Produced by Max Brown and Byron Goldman in association with Robert Victor and Stone Widney. Opened 3 March 1975 at the Palace Theatre and closed 31 May 1975 after 104 performances.

CAST (in order of appearance): *Henry V*: Brad Tyrrell. *Charles VI*: Hal Norman. *Isabella of Bavaria*: Grace Keagy. *Queen Kate*: Rhoda Butler. *Philip of Burgundy*: Charles Rule. *Yolande*: Peggy Cooper. *Marie*: Nancy Killmer. *Pope*: Ed Becker. *Charley*: JOEL GREY. *Archbishop Regnault de Chartres*: JAY GARNER. *General George de La Tremouille*: LOUIS ZORICH. *Servants*: George Ramos, Ross Miles, Pat Swayze, Cam Lorendo. *Agnes Sorel*: SUSAN BROWNING. *Jesters*: Andy Hostettler, Gordon J. Weiss. *Joan of Arc*: ANN REINKING. *Minguet*: RICHARD B. SHULL. *First English Captain*: Charles Rule. *Second English Captain*: Hal Norman. *Third English Captain*: Kenneth Bridges. *Herald*: Hal Norman. *Citizen Trio, Soldier Trio, Peasant Trio Hostile Trio*: Kenneth Bridges, Brad Tyrrell, Ed Becker. *Louis*: Dan Joel. *Chef*: Charles Rule. *First Soldier*: Kenneth Bridges. *Second Soldier*: Brad Tyrrell. *Third Soldier*: Hal Norman. *Guard*: Charles Rule. *Estelle*: Kathe Dezina.

Singers: Rhoda Butler, Peggy Cooper, Kathe Dezina, Nancy Killmer, Jane Ann Sargia, Ed Becker, Kenneth Bridges, Hal Norman, Charles Rule, Brad Tyrrell. *Dancers*: Andy Hostettler, Cam Lorendo, Dan Joel, Glen McClaskey, Ross Miles, Tod Miller, Sal Pernice, George Ramos, Pat Swayze, Gordon Weiss, Jerry Yoder.

The action takes place in France between 1429 and 1461.

Act 1, Scene 1: Prologue; Charley's Nightmare, 6 March, 1429. *Scene 2*: Charley's Bedroom at Chinon, that morning. *Scene 3*: Great Hall, immediately after. *Scene 4*: Charley's Study, that evening. *Scene 5*: Before a Tapestry, immediately after. *Scene 6*: Councul Chamber, three weeks later, April. *Scene 7*: A nearby grove at twilight. *Scene 8*: Castles of the Loire, subsequent weeks. *Scene 9*: Reims Cathedral, late May, 1429.

Act 2, Scene 1: A Formal Garden, late summer. *Scene 2*: Chinon Courtyard, the following spring. *Scene 3*: A Bank of the Vienne River, immediately after sunset. *Scene 4*: Confession Booth, a week later. *Scene 5*: Cell in Rouen, 30 May, 1431. *Scene 6*: Cell and War Tent, that same day, simultaneously. *Scene 7*: Great Hall, three weeks later. *Scene 8*: Epilogue; 32 years later, 28 February 1461.

ACT 1

Scene 1
  "History"
   B. Tyrrell, H. Norman, G. Keagy, R. Butler, C. Rule, P. Cooper, N. Killmer, E. Becker, Ensemble
Scene 2
  "Goodtime Charley"
   J. Grey, Ensemble
Scene 3
  "Visions and Voices"
   A. Reinking
Scene 4
  "Bits and Pieces"
   J. Grey, A. Reinking
  "To Make the Boy a Man"
   A. Reinking
Scene 5
  "Why Can't We All Be Nice"
   J. Grey, S. Browning
Scene 6
  "Born Lover"
   J. Grey
Scene 7
  "I Am Going to Love (The Man You're Going to Be)"
   A. Reinking
Scene 8
  "Castles of the Loire"
   A. Reinking, Soldiers
   (*Music by* Arthur B. Rubinstein.)
Scene 9
  "Coronation"
   J. Grey, A. Reinking, Ensemble

ACT 2

Scene 1

"You Still Have a Long Way to Go"
A. Reinking, J. Grey

Scene 2

"Merci, Bon Dieu"
R. B. Shull, S. Browning

Scene 4

"Confessional"
L. Zorich, J. Garner

Scene 5

"One Little Year"
A. Reinking

Scene 8

"I Leave the World"
J. Grey

1975.07 ## THE LIEUTENANT

A Rock Opera in Two Acts. Book, music and lyrics by Gene Curty, Nitra Scharfman and Chuck Strand. Directed by William Martin. Choreography by Dennis Dennehy. Scenery and costumes designed by Frank J. Boros. Lighting designed by Ian Calderon. Musical direction by Chuck Strand. Music arranged by Chuck Strand and Gus Montero. Sound designed by Bill Merrill. Originally produced at the Queens Playhouse by Joseph S. Kutzreba. Produced by Joseph S. Kutzreba and Spofford J. Beadle. Opened 9 March 1975 at the Lyceum Theatre and closed 16 March 1975 after 9 performances.

CAST (in order of appearance): *Lieutenant*: EDDIE MEKKA. *Judge*: GENE CURTY. *Recruiting Sergeant*: Joel Powers. *First General*: CHET D'ELIA. *Second General*: EUGENE MOOSE. *Third General*: DANNY TAYLOR. *OCS Sergeant*: GENE CURTY. *Chaplain*: Don McGrath. *Captain*: WALT HUNTER. *Sergeant "C" Company*: Jim Litten. *"C" Company*: Steven Boockvor, Clark James, Jim-Patrick McMahon, Joseph Pugliese, Burt Rodriguez, Tom Tofel. *G.I.*: TOM TOFEL. *Senator*: Joel Powers. *First Congressman*: Don McGrath. *Clergyman*: Jim Litten. *Second Congressman*: Burt Rodriguez. *First Reporter*: Jim Litten. *Second Reporter*: Tom Tofel. *Third Reporter*: Jo Speros. *Prosecutor*: Burt Rodriguez. *Defense Attorney*: Gordon Grody. *New Recruit*: Alan K. Siegel. *Dance Captain*: Jim-Patrick McMahon.

The action alternates between Vietnam and the United States over a three-year period. Act Two takes place two years later.

ACT 1

"The Indictment"
E. Mekka, G. Curty

"Join the Army"
E. Mekka, J. Powers, Recruits

"Look for the Men With Potential"
C. D'Elia, E. Moose, D. Taylor

"Kill"
G. Curty

"I Don't Want to Go Over to Vietnam"
E. Mekka, "C" Company

"Eulogy"
D. McGrath

"At 0700 Tomorrow"
W. Hunter, "C" Company

"Massacre"
W. Hunter, E. Mekka, "C" Company, Vietnamese

"Something's Gone Wrong"
W. Hunter, E. Mekka

"Twenty-Eight"
C. D'Elia, E. Moose, D. Taylor, W. Hunter, E. Mekka

"Let's Believe in the Captain"
C. D'Elia, E. Moose, D. Taylor

"Final Report"
C. D'Elia

"I Will Make Things Happen"
T. Tofel

ACT 2

"He Wants to Put the Army in Jail"
J. Powers, D. McGrath, J. Litten, B. Rodriguez

"There's No Other Solution"
C. D'Elia, E. Moose, D. Taylor

"I'm Going Home"
E. Mekka, "C" Company

"We've Chosen You, Lieutenant"
C. D'Elia, E. Moose, D. Taylor

"The Star of This War"
J. Litten, T. Tofel, J. Speros, E. Mekka

"On Trial for My Life"
E. Mekka

"The Conscience of a Nation"
B. Rodriguez

"Damned No Matter How He Turned"
G. Grody

"On Trial for My Life" (reprise)
E. Mekka

"The Verdict"
G. Curty, Jurors

Finale
A. K. Siegel, J. Powers, The Company

1975.08 ## THE ROCKY HORROR SHOW

A Rock Musical in One Act, 11 Scenes, a Prologue and Epilogue. Book, music and lyrics by Richard O'Brien. Directed by Jim Sharman. Production (scenery) designed by Brian Thomson. Costumes by Sue Blane. Lighting by Chipmonck. Set supervisor, Peter Harvey. Costume supervisor, Pearl Somner. Sound design, Abe Jacob. Musical director, D'Vaughn Pershing. Assistant director, Nina Faso. (Music) Arrangements by Richard Hartley. Special effects by Robert E. McCarthy. Associate producer, John Beug. A Michael White Production. Produced by Lou Adler. Opened 10 March 1975 at the Belasco Theatre and closed 6 April 1975 after 45 performances.

CAST (in order of appearance): *The Belasco Popcorn Girl* (Trixie): Jamie Donnelly. *Janet*: ABIGALE HANESS. *Brad*: BILL MILLER. *Narrator*: Graham Jarvis. *Riff-Raff*: Ritz O'Brien. *Columbia*: BONI ENTEN. *Magenta*: Jamie Donnelly. *Frank*: TIM CURRY. *Rocky*: KIM MILFORD. *Eddie, Dr. Scott*: MEAT LOAF.

MUSICAL NUMBERS

"Science Fiction"
J. Donnelly

"Wedding Song"
B. Miller, A. Haness

"Over at the Frankenstein Place"
B. Miller, A. Haness

"Sweet Transvestite"
T. Curry

"Time Warp"
J. Donnelly, B. Enten, R. O'Brien, G. Jarvis

"The Sword of Damocles"
K. Milford

"Charles Atlas Song" (I Can Make You a Man)
T. Curry

"What Ever Happened to Saturday Night" (Hot Patootie, Bless My Soul)
M. Loaf

"Charles Atlas Song" (reprise)
T. Curry

"Eddie's Teddy"
M. Loaf, B. Enten, Company

"Once in Awhile"
B. Miller

"Planet Shmanet Janet"
T. Curry

"It Was Great When It All Began" (Floorshow/Rose Tint My World)
Company

"Super Heroes"
Company
"Science Fiction" (reprise)
J. Donnelly
"Sweet Transvestite" (reprise)
Company
"Time Warp" (reprise)
Company

1975.09   DOCTOR JAZZ

A Musical in Two Acts, 20 Scenes. Book, music and lyrics (mostly) by Buster Davis. Direction and choreography by Donald MacKayle. Scenery and costumes by Raoul Pene du Bois. Lighting by (Abe) Feder. Sound by Abe Jacob. Principal orchestrator, Luther Henderson. Associate orchestrators, Dick Hyman, Sy Oliver. Dance music arranger and Incidental music composer, Luther Henderson. Musical director and vocal arrangements by Buster Davis. Associate music director, Joyce Brown. Scenic coordinator, Mason Arvold. Costume coordinator, David Toser. Entire production supervised by John Berry. A Pyxidium Ltd. Production. Produced by Cyma Rubin. Opened 19 March 1975 at the Winter Garden and closed 22 March 1975 after 5 performances.

CAST (in order of appearance): *Steve Anderson*: BOBBY VAN. *Spasm Band*: Quitman D. Fludd III, Bruce Heath, HECTOR JAIME MERCADO, Jeff Veazey. *Jonathan Jackson, Jr.*: JACK LANDRON. *Henry*: Paul Eichel. *Harriet Lee*: PEGGY POPE. *Georgia Sheridan*: LILLIAN HAYMAN. *Edna Mae Sheridan*: LOLA FALANA. *Georgia's Girls*: Bonita Jackson, Michele Simmons, Annie Joe Edwards. *Harriet's Girls*: Gail Benedict, Sarah Coleman, Maggy Gorrill, Kitty Jones, Diana Mirras, Sally Neal, Yolanda R. Raven, Catherine Rice. *Lead Dancer*: HECTOR JAIME MERCADO. *The Group*: Bruce Heath, Bonita Jackson, Sally Neal, Yolanda R. Raven, Michele Simmons. *Rudy*: Paul Eichel. *Pete*: Eron Tabor. *Harry*: Paul Eichel.
Dancers: Gail Benedict, Quitman Fludd III, Maggy Gorrill, Bob Heath, Bruce Heath, David Hodo, Bonita Jackson, Michael Lichtefeld, Hector Jaime Mercado, Diana Mirras, Sally Neal, Yolanda R. Raven, Catherine Rice, Michele Simmons, Dan Strayhorn, Jeff Veazey. *Singers*: James Braet, Annie Joe Edwards, Paul Eichel, Marian Haraldson, Evelyn McCauley, Eron Tabor. *Showgirls*: Sarah Coleman, Kitty Jones. *Onstage Musicians*: George Davis, Jr., Dennis Drury, John Gill, Vince Giordano, Haywood Henry, Danny Moore, San Pilafian, Candy Ross, Bob Stewart, Allan Vache, Warren Vache, Jr., Earl Williams, Francis Williams.

Act 1, Scene 1: A Brothel Quarter in New Orleans, 1917. *Scene 2*: The Street. *Scene 3*: Georgia's Salon. *Scene 4*: Harriet's Boudoir. *Scene 5*: The Street. *Scene 6*: Georgia's Garden. *Scene 7*: The Palace of Pleasure. *Scene 8*: Shanghai Theatre. *Scene 9*: Harriet's Office. *Scene 10*: Shanghai Theatre Stage. *Scene 11*: Backstage. *Scene 12*: Harriet's Office.

Act 2, Scene 1: The Dressing Room—The Lenox Club. *Scene 2*: The Lenox Club. *Scene 3*: The Dressing Room. *Scene 4*: In front of a New York Theatre. *Scene 5*: Dressing Room—a New York Theatre. *Scene 6*: On Stage. *Scene 7*: Dressing Room. *Scene 8*: On Stage.

ACT 1

Scene 1

"Dr. Jazz"
B. Van, Musicians, Spasm Band
(*Music and Lyrics by* King Oliver and Howard Melrose.)
"We've Got Connections"
B. Van, L. Hayman, P. Pope

Scene 3

"Georgia Shows 'Em How"
L. Hayman, Her Girls

Scene 5

"Cleopatra Had a Jazz Band"
B. Van, Ballyhoo Band
(*Music by* J. L. Morgan. *Lyrics by* Jack Coogan.)
Juba Dance
L. Falana, Spasm Band

Scene 7

"Charleston Rag"
Jonathan's Band, Harriet's Girls
(*Music by* Eubie Blake.)
"I've Got Elgin Watch Movements in My Hips"
L. Falana

"Blues My Naughty Sweetie Gave to Me"
Ballyhoo Band

Scene 8

"Good-Time Flat Blues"
L. Hayman
(*Music and Lyrics by* Armand J. Piron.)

Scene 10

"Evolution Papa"
L. Falana, H. J. Mercado, Troupe

Scene 11

Rehearsal Tap
The Group
"Blues My Naughty Sweetie Gave to Me" (reprise)
B. Van
(*Music and Lyrics by* Charles McCarron, Carey Morgan and Arthur Swanstrom.)
"I Love It"
L. Falana
(*Music by* Harry Von Tilzer. *Lyrics by* E. Ray Goetz.)

Scene 12

"Anywhere the Wind Blows"
B. Van

ACT 2

Scene 2

"Those—'Shiek-of-Araby'—Blues"
Singers, Dancers
"Look Out for Lil"
L. Falana, Dancers

Scene 4

"Swanee Strut"
B. Van

Scene 6

"All I Want Is My Black Baby Back"
L. Falana

Scene 7

"Everybody Leaves You"
B. Van

Scene 8

"Free and Easy"
L. Falana, Company
"I Love It" (reprise)
B. Van, L. Falana

1975.10   A LETTER FOR QUEEN VICTORIA

An Opera in Four Acts. Written and directed by Robert Wilson. Music by Alan Lloyd in collaboration with Michael Galasso. Choreography by Andrew DeGroat. Scenery and costume supervision by Peter Harvey. Lighting supervision by Beverly Emmons, assisted by Carol Mullins. Musical direction by Michael Galasso. Sound supervisor, R. O. Willis. Verbal tape constructors by Christopher Knowles. Introductory letter by Stefan Brecht. The Sundance Kid speech by Christopher Knowles. Act 3 dialogue by Cynthia Lubar. First speech of Chinaman by James Neu. Slides by Francis Brooks. Produced by The Byrd Foundation, Inc. Opened 22 March 1975 at the ANTA Theatre and closed 5 April 1975 after 18 performances.

CAST: *Singers*: SHERYL SUTTON, CYNTHIA LUBAR, George Ashley, Stefan Brecht, Kathryn Cation, Alma Hamilton, Christopher Knowles, James Neu, Robert Wilson. *Dancers*: Andrew deGroat, Julia Busto. *Musicians*: Michael Galasso (First Violin), Susan Krongold (Second Violin), Kevin Byrnes (Violin), Laura Epstein (Cello), Kathryn Cation (Flute).

Introduction: *Queen Victoria*: A. Hamilton. *1*: K. Cation. *2*: S. Brecht. *3*: C. Knowles. *4*: R. Wilson.

Act 1: *1*: S. Sutton. *2*: C. Lubar. *1A*: G. Ashley. *2A*: S. Brecht. *Pilot*: S. Brecht. *Pilot*: J. Neu. *Billy*: K. Cation. *Warden*: S. Snyder. *Chris*: C. Knowles.

Act 2: 1: G. Ashley. *2:* C. Lubar. *3:* K. Cation. *4:* S. Brecht. *C.W. Soldier:* S. Sutton. *Warden:* S. Snyder. *Chris:* C. Knowles.

Entractes by Robert Wilson and Christopher Knowles.

Act 3: 1A: S. Brecht. *2A:* S. Snyder. *1B:* G. Ashley. *2B:* J. Busto. *1C:* C. Knowles. *2C:* S. Sutton. *1D:* J. Neu. *2D:* K. Cation. *1E:* A. deGroat. *2E:* C. Lubar.

Act 4: 1: J. Neu. *2:* S. Snyder. *2A:* S. Brecht. *3, 1:* S. Sutton. *4, 2:* C. Lubar. *Billy:* K. Cation. *Chris:* C. Knowles. *George:* G. Ashley. *Pilot:* J. Neu. *Pilot:* S. Brecht.

1975.11 THE CONSUL

A Revival of the Opera (Musical Drama) in Three Acts, 6 Scenes[9]. Libretto and Music by Gian-Carlo Menotti. Conductor, Christopher Keene. Settings by Horace Armistead. Staged by Francis Rizzo Produced by the New York City Opera. Opened 22 March 1975 at the New York State Theatre and closed 6 April 1975 after 2 performances in repertory.

CAST: (in order of appearance): *John Sorel:* JOHN DARRENKAMP *Magda Sorel:* OLIVIA STAPP. *The Mother:* MURIEL COSTA-GREENSPON. *Secret Police Agent:* EDWARD PIERSON. *First Plainclothesman:* Jack Sims. *Second Plainclothesman:* Tom Barrett. *The Secretary:* SANDRA WALKER. *Mr. Kofner:* DON YULE. *The Foreign Woman:* JUDITH DE ROSA. *Anna Gomez:* Barbara Hocher. *Nika Magadoff* (The Magician): JOHN LANKSTON. *Vera Boronel:* Sophia Steffan. *Assan:* William Ledbetter. *Voice on the Record:* Mabel Mercer.

1975.12 BETTE MIDLER'S CLAMS ON THE HALF SHELL

A Musical Revue in Two Acts, Special material by Bruce Vilanch, Bill Hennessy, Jerry Blatt. Additional lyrics by Jerry Blatt, Bette Midler. Directed and choreographed by Joe Layton. Settings and costumes designed by Tony Walton. Lighting design by Beverly Emmons. Sound by Stan Miller. Musical director, Don York. Associate choreographer, Andre De Shields. Orchestrations, Jimmie Haskell. Production coordinator, Fritz Holt. Produced by Aaron Russo in association with Ron Delsener. Opened 14 April 1975 at the Minskoff Theatre and closed 22 June 1975 after 80 performances.

CAST: BETTE MIDLER, LIONEL HAMPTON. *The HARLETTES:* Charlotte Crossley, Robin Grean, Sharon Redd.
THE MICHAEL POWELL ENSEMBLE: Michael Powell, Charlene Ricks, Doretha Doctor, Jeannie Paige, Clifford Jamerson, Peggy Williams, Ricardo Portlette, Joey Coleman, Vinson Cunningham, Shirley Underwood, Lee Roy Cooks, Norman P. Hawkins.

MUSICAL NUMBERS[10]
OKLAHOMA! Overture
(*Music by* Richard Rodgers.)
"Nobody Knows the Trouble I've Seen"
"(The) Moon of Manakoora" (from *THE HURRICANE* film)
(*Music by* Alfred Newman. *Lyrics by* Frank Loesser.)
"Ol' Man River" (from *SHOWBOAT*)
(*Music by* Jerome Kern. *Lyrics by* Oscar Hammerstein II.)
Medley of Bette's Hits
"The Bitch Is Back"
(*Music and Lyrics by* Elton John and Bernie Taupin.)
"Delta Dawn"
(*Music and Lyrics by* Alex Harvey and Larry Collins.)
The Toilet Medley (1950s Rock 'n Roll Medley)
"Sentimental Journey"
(*Music and Lyrics by* Bud Green, Les Brown and Ben Homer.)
"Ain't No Love'
(*Music and Lyrics by* John Gary Williams.)
Saloon Sequence:

"Back in the Bars Again"
(*Music and Lyrics by* Susan Taylor.)
"Drinking Again"
(*Music and Lyrics by* Johnny Mercer and Doris Tauber.)
"Fiesta in Rio"
(*Music and Lyrics by* Bette Midler and Jerry Blatt.)
"Strangers in the Night"
(*Music and Lyrics by* Charles Singleton, Eddie Snyder and Bert Kaempfert.)
"Do You Wanna Dance?"
(*Music and Lyrics by* Bobby Freeman.)
"Colette"
"If Love Were All" (from *BITTER SWEET*)
(*Music and Lyrics by* Noel Coward.)
"Friends'
(*Music and Lyrics by* Mark Klingman and Buzzy Linhart.)
"I'm Wishing" (from *SNOW WHITE AND THE SEVEN DWARFS* film)
(*Music by* Larry Churchill. *Lyrics by* Larry Morey.)
"A Dream Is a Wish Your Heart Makes"
(*Music and Lyrics by* Mack David, Al Hoffman and Jerry Livingston.)
"Lullaby of Broadway" (from *GOLDDIGGERS OF 1935* film)
(*Music by* Harry Warren. *Lyrics by* Al Dubin.)
"In the Mood"
(*Music by* Joe Garland. *Lyrics by* Andy Razaf. *Additional Lyrics by* Bette Midler and Barry Manilow.)
"Flying Home"
(*Music by* Lionel Hampton, Benny Goodman and Sid Ramin.)
Lionel Hampton Specialty
"We'll Be Together Again"
(*Music and Lyrics by* Carl Fischer and Frankie Laine.)
"Shiver Me Timbers"
(*Music and Lyrics by* Tom Waits.)
"I Don't Want the Night to End"
(*Music and Lyrics by* Phoebe Snow.)
Those Wonderful Sophie Tucker Jokes
"Hello in There"
(*Music and Lyrics by* John Prine.)
""Higher and Higher"
(*Music and Lyrics by* Gary Lee Jackson, Carl W., Smith and Raynard Miner.)
"Boogie Woogie Bugle Boy"
(*Music and Lyrics by* Don Raye and Hughie Prince.)
"Chapel of Love"
(*Music and Lyrics by* Jeff Barry, Ellie Greenwich and Phil Spector.)

1975.13 RODGERS & HART

A Musical Revue in Two Acts. Music by Richard Rodgers. Lyrics by Lorenz Hart. Concept by Richard Lewine and John Fearnley. Directed by Burt Shevelove. Choreography by Donald Saddler. Music direction and vocal arrangements by Buster Davis. Principal orchestrator and dance music arranger, Luther Henderson. Additional orchestrations by Jim Tyler, Bill Brohn, Robert Russell Bennett. Setting by David Jenkins. Costumes by Stanley Simmons. Lighting by Ken Billington. Assistant Choreographer,

[9]Originally produced in New York 15 March 1950 at the Ethel Barrymore Theatre for 269 performances. For Synopsis of Scenes and Musical Numbers, see original 1950 production.

[10]Added during the run:
"How High the Moon" (from *TWO FOR THE SHOW*)
(*Music by* Morgan Lewis. *Lyrics by* Nancy Hamilton.)
"Deep Purple"
(*Music by* Peter DeRose. *Lyrics by* Mitchell Parish.)
"I've Never Been to Flushing"
"You'll Never Be Lonely"
(*Music and Lyrics by* Tom Pacheco.)
"Bad Sex"
(*Music and Lyrics by* Bill Hennessey and Bruce Vilanch.)

Arthur Faria. Produced by Lester Osterman Productions (Lester Osterman-Richard Horner) in association with Worldvision Enterprises Inc. Opened 13 May 1975 at the Helen Hayes Theatre and closed 16 August 1975 after 108 performances.

CAST (in alphabetical order): Barbara Andres, James [Jimmy] Brennan, Wayne Bryan, David-James Carroll, Jamie Donnelly, Tovah Feldshuh, Mary Sue Finnerty, Laurence Guittard, Stephen Lehew, Jim Litten, Virginia Sandifur, Rebecca York.

During the performance the following songs, in part or in toto, will be performed:

"At the Roxy Music Hall"
(from I MARRIED AN ANGEL)

"Babes in Arms"
(from BABES IN ARMS)

"Bewitched, Bothered and Bewildered"
(from PAL JOEY)

"Blue Moon"

"Blue Room"
(from THE GIRL FRIEND)

"Bye and Bye"
(from DEAREST ENEMY)

"Careless Rhapsody"
(from BY JUPITER)

"Cause We Got Cake"
(from TOO MANY GIRLS)

"Come With Me"
(from THE BOYS FROM SYRACUSE)

"Dear Old Syracuse"
(from THE BOYS FROM SYRACUSE)

"Did You Ever Get Stung?"
(from I MARRIED AN ANGEL)

"Do I Hear You Saying (I Love You)?"
(from PRESENT ARMS)

"Down By the River"
(from MISSISSIPPI film)

"Easy to Remember"
(from MISSISSIPPI film)

"Ev'rybody Loves You (When You're Asleep)"
(from I'D RATHER BE RIGHT)

"Everything I've Got"
(from BY JUPITER)

"Falling in Love With Love"
(from THE BOYS FROM SYRACUSE)

"Flower Garden of My Heart, The"
(from PAL JOEY)

"From Another World"
(from HIGHER AND HIGHER)

"Gateway of the Temple of Minerva, (In) The"
(from BY JUPITER)

"Girl Friend, The"
(from THE GIRL FRIEND)

"Give It Back to the Indians"
(from TOO MANY GIRLS)

"Glad to be Unhappy"
(from ON YOUR TOES)

"Great Big Town" (Chicago)
(from PAL JOEY)

"Happy Hunting Horn"
(from PAL JOEY)

"Have You Met Miss Jones?"
(from I'D RATHER BE RIGHT)

"He and She"
(from THE BOYS FROM SYRACUSE)

"He Was Too Good To Me"
(from THE BOYS FROM SYRACUSE)

"Heart Is Quicker Than the Eye, The"
(from ON YOUR TOES)

"Here in My Arms"
(from DEAREST ENEMY)

"How About It?"
(from AMERICA'S SWEETHEART)

"How Was I To Know?"
(from SHE'S MY BABY)

"I Could Write a Book"
(from PAL JOEY)

"I Didn't Know What Time It Was"
(from TOO MANY GIRLS)

"I Married an Angel"
(from I MARRIED AN ANGEL)

"I Wish I Were in Love Again"
(from BABES IN ARMS)

"I'll Tell the Man in the Street"
(from I MARRIED AN ANGEL)

"Imagine"
(from BABES IN ARMS)

"Isn't It Romantic?"
(from LOVE ME TONIGHT film)

"It Never Entered My Mind"
(from HIGHER AND HIGHER)

"It's Got To Be Love"
(from ON YOUR TOES)

"I've Got Five Dollars"
(from AMERICA'S SWEETHEART)

"Johnny One Note"
(from BABES IN ARMS)

"Jupiter Forbid"
(from BY JUPITER)

"Lady Is a Tramp, The"
(from BABES IN ARMS)

"Love Me Tonight"
(from LOVE ME TONIGHT film)

"Love Never Went to College"
(from TOO MANY GIRLS)

"Lovely Day for a Murder, A"
(from HIGHER AND HIGHER)

"Lover"
(from LOVE ME TONIGHT film)

"Manhattan"
(from GARRICK GAIEITIES, THE 1925)

"Me for You!"
(from HEADS UP!)

"Mimi"
(from LOVE ME TONIGHT film)

"Mountain Greenery"
(from GARRICK GAIEITIES, THE 1926)

"My Funny Valentine"
(from BABES IN ARMS)

"My Heart Stood Still"
(from A CONNECTICUT YANKEE)

"My Prince"
(from TOO MANY GIRLS)

"No Place But Home"
(from EVERGREEN)

"Nobody's Heart"
(from BY JUPITER)

"Nothing But You"
(from HIGHER AND HIGHER)

"Oh, Diogenes"
(from THE BOYS FROM SYRACUSE)

"On a Desert Isle With Thee"
(from A CONNECTICUT YANKEE)

"On Your Toes"
(from ON YOUR TOES)

"Quiet Night"
(from ON YOUR TOES)

"Sentimental Me"
(from GARRICK GAIEITIES, THE 1925)

"She Could Shake the Maracas"
(ftrom TOO MANY GIRLS)

"Ship Without a Sail, A"
(from HEADS UP!)

"Shortest Day of the Year, The
(from THE BOYS FROM SYRACUSE)

"Sing for Your Supper"
(from THE BOYS FROM SYRACUSE)

"Slaughter on Tenth Avenue"
(from ON YOUR TOES)

"Soon"
(from MISSISSIPPI film)

"Spring Is Here"
(from I MARRIED AN ANGEL)

"Take Him"
(from PAL JOEY)

"Ten Cents a Dance"
(from SIMPLE SIMON)

"There's a Small Hotel"
(from ON YOUR TOES)

"This Can't Be Love"
(from THE BOYS FROM SYRACUSE)

"This Funny World"
(from BETSY)

"This Is My Night to Howl"
(from A CONNECTICUT YANKEE)

"Thou Swell"
(from A CONNECTICUT YANKEE)

"Three B's, The (Bach, Beethoven and Brahams)
(from ON YOUR TOES)

"To Keep My Love Alive"
(from A CONNECTICUT YANKEE revival)

"Two-Day For Keith"
(from ON YOUR TOES)

"Wait Till You See Her"
(from BY JUPITER)

"Where or When"
(from BABES IN ARMS)

"Where's That Rainbow?"
(from PEGGY-ANN)

"Why Can't I?"
(from SPRING IS HERE)

"With a Song in My Heart"
(from SPRING IS HERE)

"You Always Love the Same Girl"
(from A CONNECTICUT YANKEE)

"You Are Too Beautiful"
(from HALLELUJAH, I'M A BUM film)

"You Musn't Kick It Around"
(from PAL JOEY)

"You're Nearer"
(from TOO MANY GIRLS film)

"Zip"
(from PAL JOEY)

1975–1976 SEASON

Donna McKechnie in A CHORUS LINE
Martha Swope/TimePix

1975-1976 SEASON

CHICAGO
1975.14

A Musical Vaudeville in Two Acts, 22 Scenes. Book by Fred Ebb and Bob Fosse. Based on the play of the same name by Maurine Dallas Watkins. Music by John Kander. Lyrics by Fred Ebb. Directed and choreographed by Bob Fosse. Settings by Tony Walton. Costumes by Patricia Zipprodt. Lighting by Jules Fisher. Musical director, Stanley Lebowsky. Orchestrations by Ralph Burns. Dance music arranged by Peter Howard. Sound design by Abe Jacob. Assistant choreographer, Tony Stevens. Produced by Robert Fryer and James Cresson in association with Martin Richards. Opened 3 June 1975 at the 46th Street Theatre and closed 27 August 1977 after 947 performances.

CAST (in order of appearance): *Velma Kelly*: CHITA RIVERA. *Roxie Hart*: GWEN VERDON. *Fred Casely*: Christopher Chadman. *Sergeant Fogarty*: Richard Korthaze. *Amos Hart*: BARNEY MARTIN. *Liz*: Cheryl Clark. *Annie*: Michon Peacock. *June*: Candy Brown. *Hunyak*: Graciela Daniele. *Mona*: Pamela Sousa. *Martin Harrison*: Michael Vita. *Matron*: MARY McCARTY. *Billy Flynn*: JERRY ORBACH. *Mary Sunshine*: M. O'HAUGHEY. *Go-to-Hell Kitty*: Charlene Ryan. *Harry*: Paul Solen. *Aaron*: Gene Foote. *The Judge*: Ron Schwinn. *Court Clerk*: Gary Gendell.
The Band: Sy Berger, Harry Divito, Hank Freedman, Karen Gustafson, John Monaco, Anthony Pagano, Waymon Reed, James Sedlar, Charles Spies, William Stanley, Art Wagner, Frank Wess, Tony Posk.

The action takes place in the late 1920's in Chicago, Illinois.

Act 1, Scene 1: Opening; the Hart Bedroom. *Scene 2*: The bedroom. Three hours later. *Scene 3*: Limbo. *Scene 4*: Limbo. *Scene 5*: The Jail. *Scene 6*: The Visitors' Area. *Scene 7*: Limbo. *Scene 8*: Billy's Office. *Scene 9*: Limbo. *Scene 10*: In the Jail. *Scene 11*: Limbo and Roxie's Cell. *Scene 12*: Limbo and a bedroom, somewhere in Chicago. *Scene 13*: The Jail.

Act 2, Scene 1: The Jail. *Scene 2*: Limbo. *Scene 3*: The Jail. *Scene 4*: An anteroom in the courthouse. *Scene 5*: The anteroom of the courthouse, March 9th. *Scene 6*: The Courtroom. *Scene 7*: A room in the jail. *Scene 8*: The Courtroom. *Scene 9*: The Courtroom.

ACT 1
Scene 1
"All That Jazz"
C. Rivera, Company
Scene 2
"Funny Honey"
G. Verdon
Scene 3
"Cell Block Tango"
C. Rivera, the Girls
Scene 4
"When You're Good to Mama"
M. McCarty
Scene 6
Tap Dance
G. Verdon, B. Martin, Boys
Scene 7
"All I Care About (Is Love)"
J. Orbach, Girls
Scene 8
"A Little Bit of Good"
M. O'Haughey
"We Both Reached for the Gun"
J. Orbach, G. Verdon, M. O'Haughey, Company
Scene 9
"Roxie"
G. Verdon, Boys
Scene 11
"I Can't Do It Alone"
C. Rivera
"Chicago After Midnight"
The Band
Scene 13
"My Own Best Friend"
G. Verdon, C. Rivera

ACT 2
Scene 1
"I Know a Girl"
C. Rivera
"Me and My Baby"
G. Verdon, C. Chadman, G. Foote
Scene 2
"Mister Cellophane"
B. Martin
Scene 3
"When Velma Takes the Stand"
C. Rivera, Boys
Scene 5
"Razzle Dazzle"
J. Orbach, Company
Scene 7
"Class"
C. Rivera, M. McCarty
Scene 9
"Nowadays"
G. Verdon
"Nowadays" (reprise)/"R.S.V.P."/"Keep It Hot"
G. Verdon, C. Rivera

A CHORUS LINE
1975.15

A Musical in One Act[1]. Conceived, choreographed and directed by Michael Bennett. Book by James Kirkwood and Nicholas Dante. Music by Marvin Hamlisch. Lyrics by Edward Kleban. Co-choreographer, Bob Avian. Musical direction and vocal arrangements by Don Pippin. Settings by Robin Wagner. Costumes by Theoni V. Aldredge. Lighting by Tharon Musser. Sound by Abe Jacob. Music coordinator, Robert Thomas. Orchestrations by Billy Byers, Hershy Kay, Jonathan Tunick. Assistant to choreographers and dance captain, Baayork Lee. A New York Shakespeare Festival Production. Associate producer, Bernard Gersten. Produced by Joseph Papp in association with Plum Productions (Michael Bennett). Opened 25 July 1975[2] at the Sam S. Shubert Theatre and closed 28 April 1990 after 6137 performances. (Total including Off-Broadway run, 6238 performances.)

CAST (in alphabetical order): *Roy*: Scott Allen. *Kristine*: Renee Baughman. *Sheila*: Carole (Kelly) Bishop. *Val*: Pamela Blair. *Mike*: Wayne Cilento. *Butch*: Chuck Cissel. *Larry*: Clive Clerk. *Maggie*: Kay Cole. *Richie*: Ronald Dennis. *Tricia*: Donna Drake. *Tom*: Brandt Edwards. *Judy*: Patricia Garland. *Lois*: Carolyn Kirsch. *Don*: Ron Kuhlman. *Bebe*: Nancy Lane. *Connie*: Baayork Lee. *Diana*: Priscilla Lopez. *Zach*: Robert LuPone. *Mark*: Cameron Mason. *Cassie*: Donna McKechnie. *Al*: Don Percassi. *Frank*: Michael Serrecchia. *Greg*: Michel Stuart. *Bobby*: Thomas J. [Thommie] Walsh. *Paul*: Sammy Williams. *Vicki*: Crissy Wilzak.

The action takes place at an audition here and now.

MUSICAL NUMBERS
"I Hope I Get It"
Company
"I Can Do That"
W. Cilento
"And ... "
T. J. Walsh, R. Dennis, P. Blair, P. Garland
"At the Ballet"
C. Bishop, N. Lane, K. Cole
"Sing!"
R. Baughman, D. Percassi
"Hello Twelve, Hello Thirteen, Hello Love"
Company
"Nothing"
P. Lopez
"Dance: Ten; Looks: Three"
P. Blair
"The Music and the Mirror"
D. McKechnie

---

[1]Originally produced Off-Broadway 15 April 1975 at the Newman Theatre for 101 performances.
[2]In response to the demand for a Broadway opening night, the critics were re-invited on 19 October 1975.

"One"
    Company
"The Tap Combination"
    Company
"What I Did for Love"
    P. Lopez, Company
"One" (reprise)
    Company

The company of *A CHORUS LINE* has collectively appeared in eighty-eight different shows in which they have given a total of 37,095 performances. Collectively they have had 612 years of dance training with 748 teachers—counting duplications. They spend approximately $894 a month on dance lessons. While appearing in the shows mentioned they have sustained 30 back, 26 knee and 36 ankle injuries. The characters portrayed in *A CHORUS LINE* are, for the most part, based upon the lives and experiences of Broadway dancers. This show is dedicated to anyone who has ever danced in a chorus or marched in step . . . anywhere.

DIE FLEDERMAUS
1975.16

A Revival of the Operetta in Three Acts[3]. Original Viennese libretto by Carl Haffner and Richard Genée. Lyrics by Richard Genée. (Based on the comedy "Le Réveillon" by Henri Meilhac and Ludovic Halévy.) English libretto by Ruth and Thomas Martin. Music by Johann Strauss. Production devised and directed by Gerald Freedman. Stage director, Richard Getke. Choreography by Thomas Andrew. Scenery designed by Lloyd Evans. Costume design by Theoni V. Aldredge. Lighting by Hans Sondheimer. Conducted by Alexis Hauser. Chorus prepared by Judith Somogi. Produced by the New York City Opera. Opened 29 August 1975 at the New York State Theatre and closed 1 November 1975 after 5 performances in repertory; returned 29 February 1976 to the New York State Theatre for 5 additional performances. Total: 10 performances this season.

CAST (in order of appearance): *Alfred*, an itinerant tenor: Gary Glaze. *Adele*, von Eisenstein's chambermaid: ARLENE RANDAZZO. *Rosalinda von Eisenstein*: JOHANNA MEIER. *Gabriel von Eisenstein*: ALAN TITUS. *Dr. Blind*, a lawyer: Joaquin Romaguera. *Dr. Falke*, a close friend of Eisenstein: DAVID HOLLOWAY. *Frank*, the prison warden: SPIRO MALAS. *Sally*, Adele's sister: Puli Toro. *Ivan*, servant to Orlofsky: Jack Sims. *Prince Orlofsky*, a wealthy, bored Russian: DAVID RAE SMITH. *Frosch*, the jailer: Coley Worth. *Solo Dancers*: Sandra Balestracci, Esperanza Galan, Juliu Horvath.

Ensemble: New York City Opera Chorus.

H.M.S. PINAFORE,
1975.17   or The Lass That Loved a Sailor

A Revival of the Comic Opera in Two Acts[4]. Libretto by William S. Gilbert. Music by Arthur Sullivan. Directed by Jack Eddleman. Choreographed by Thomas Andrew. Scenery and costumes by Patton Campbell. Lighting by Hans Sondheimer. Conductor, David Effron. Produced by the New York City Opera. Opened 27 September 1975 at the New York State Theatre and closed 9 November 1975 after 5 performances in repertory; returned 22 February 1976 to the New York State Theatre and closed 3 April 1976 after 4 additional performances in repertory. Total: 9 performances this season.

CAST: *The Rt. Hon. Sir Joseph Porter, K.C.B.*, First Lord of the Admiralty: JAMES BILLINGS. *Captain Corcoran*, Commander of the *H.M.S. Pinafore*: CHARLES ROE. *Ralph Rackstraw*, Able Seaman: GARY GLAZE. *Dick Deadeye*, Able Seaman: PAUL UKENA. *Bill Bobstay*, Boatswain: William Ledbetter. *Bob Becket*: Irwin Densen. *Josephine*, the Captain's Daughter: DIANA SOVIERO. *Hebe*, Sir Joseph's First Cousin: Puli Toro. *Little Buttercup*, Mrs. Cripps, a Portsmouth bum-boat woman: MURIEL COSTA-GREENSPON.

First Lord's Sisters, His Cousins, His Aunts, Sailors, Marines, etc.: New York City Opera Chorus.

---

[3]First English language production in New York 16 March 1885 at the Casino Theatre for 42 performances. First New York production of this adaptation 20 December 1950 at the Metropolitan Opera House. For Synopsis of Scenes and Musical Numbers, see May 1954 revival.
[4]Originally presented in New York 15 January 1879 at the Standard Theatre for 175 performances. For Synopsis of Scenes and Musical Numbers, see original 1879 production.

THE ROBBER BRIDEGROOM
1975.18

A Country-Folk Musical in One Act. Book and lyrics by Alfred Uhry. Based on the novella of the same name by Eudora Welty. Music composed and arranged by Robert Waldman. Directed by Gerald Freedman. Choreography by Donald Saddler. Settings designed by Douglas W. Schmidt. Costumes designed by Jeanne Button. Lighting designed by David F. Segal. Music performed by The Wretched Refuse (Bob Jones, Alan Kaufman, David Markowitz, Richard Shulberg, Steve Tannenbaum). Produced by The Acting Company (John Houseman, Artistic director; Margot Harley, Producing director; Porter Van Zandt, Executive director). Opened 7 October 1975 at the Harkness Theatre and closed 18 October 1975 after 15 performances.

CAST (in order of appearance): *Jamie Lockhart*, a robber: KEVIN KLINE. *Mike Fink*, a flatboatman: Norman Snow. *Clemment Musgrove*, a rich planter: David Schramm. *Goat*, a simpleton: Robert Bacigalupi. *Little Harp*, a robber: J. W. Harper. *Big Harp*, the head of a robber: Anderson Matthews. *Neighbors (6)*: *Kyle Nunnery*: Brooks Baldwin. *Tom Playmale*: Richard Ooms. *Billy Brenner*: Nicholas Surovy. *John Oglesby*: Roy K. Stevens. *Ernie Summers*: Peter Dvorsky. *Herman McLaughlin*: Michael Tolaydo. *Salome*, Musgrove's second wife: MARY LOU ROSATO. *Rosamund*, Musgrove's daughter: PATTI LuPONE. *Goat's Mother*: Glynis Bell. *Airie*, Goat's sister: Sandra Halperin. *Raven*: Elaine Hausman. *Queenie Sue Stevens*: Cynthia Dickason. *The Fiddler*: Alan Kaufman.

The action takes place in legendary Mississippi.

MUSICAL NUMBERS
    "With Style"
        K. Kline, Company
    "The Real Mike Fink"
        K. Kline, D. Schramm, N. Snow
    "The Pricklepear Bloom"
        M. L. Rosato
    "Nothin' Up"
        P. LuPone
    "Deeper in the Woods"
        The Company
    "Riches"
        D. Schramm, K. Kline, M. L. Rosato, P. LuPone
    "Love Stolen"
        K. Kline
    "Poor Tied Up Darlin'"
        J. W. Harper, R. Bacigalupi
    "Goodbye Salome"
        The Company
    "Sleepy Man"
        P. LuPone

TREEMONISHA
1975.19

An Opera in Two Acts, 3 Scenes, (Libretto and Music) by Scott Joplin. Production conceived and directed by Frank Corsaro. Choeography by Louis Johnson. Orchestration and music supervision by Gunther Schuller. Conductors, Gunther Schuller, Jose Contreras. Sets and costumes by Franco Colavecchia. Lighting by Nananne Porcher. Artistic consultant, Vera Brodsky Lawrence. Assistant director, David Drisin. A Houston Grand Opera Association Production. Produced by Adela Holzer, James Nederlander and Victor Lurie by arrangement with the Dramatic Publishing Company. Opened 21 October 1975 at the Uris Theatre, moved 3 November 1975 to the Palace Theatre and closed 14 December 1975 after 64 performances.

CAST (in order of appearance): *Zodzetrick*: Ben Harney. *Ned*: WILLARD WHITE. *Monisha*, Ned's wife: BETTY ALLEN, Lorna Myers (matinees). *Treemonisha*, Ned's adopted daughter: CARMEN BALTHROP, Kathleen Battle (matinees). *Remus*: CURTIS RAYAM. *Andy*: Kenenth Hicks. *Lucy*: Cora Johnson. *Parson Alltalk*: EDWARD PIERSON. *Simon*: Raymond Bazemore. *Cephus*: Dwight Ransome. *Luddud*: Dorceal Duckens.

THE LOUIS JOHNSON DANCE THEATRE: *Dancers*: Clyde-Jacques Barrett, Thea Barnes, Dwight Baxter, Renee Brailsford, Karen Burke, Veda Jackson, Reggie Jackson, Julia Lema, Anita Littlemon, Rick Odums, Dwayne Phelps, Ivson Polk, Mabel Robinson, Martial Roumain, Katherine Singleton, James Thurston, Bobby Walker, Pamela Wilson. *Chorus*: Earl L. Baker, Kenneth Bates, Barbara Christopher, Steven Cole, Ella Eure, Gregory Gardner, Melvin Jordan, Patricia McDermott, Janette Moody, Marion Moore, Vera Moore, Lorna Myers, Glover Parham, Patricia Pates, William Penn, Dwight Ransom, Cornel Richie, Patricia Rogers, Christine Spencer, Walter Turnbull, Gloria Turner, Peter Whitehead, Arthur Williams, Barbara Young.

The action takes place on a plantation in Arkansas, northeast of the town of Texarcana and three or four miles from the Red River.

Act 1, Scene 1: Morning. *Scene 2:* Afternoon of the same day.

Act 2: That evening.

ACT 1

Scene 1

Overture
B. Harney, Dancers
"The Bag of Luck"
C. Balthrop, B. Allen, C. Rayam, W. White, B. Harney
"The Corn-Huskers"
C. Balthrop, Chorus
"We're Goin' Around"
C. Balthrop, B. Allen, C. Johnson, C. Rayam, W. White, Chorus, Dancers
"The Wreath"
C. Balthrop, B. Allen, C. Johnson
"The Sacred Tree"
B. Allen
"Surprise"
C. Balthrop
"Treemonisha's Bringing Up"
C. Balthrop, B. Allen
"Good Advice"
E. Pierson, Chorus
"Confusion"
B. Allen, C. Johnson, C. Rayam, W. White

Scene 2

"Superstition"
R. Bazemore, D. Ransom
"Treemonisha in Peril"
B. Harney, R. Bazemore, D. Duckens, D. Ransom
"The Frolic of the Bears"
Dancers
"The Wasp Nest"
R. Bazemore, D. Ransom
"The Rescue"
C. Balthrop, C. Rayam
"We Will Rest Awhile"
(Male) Quartet
"Going Home"
C. Balthrop, C. Rayam, the Foreman
"Aunt Dinah Has Blowed De Horn"
Chorus, Dancers

ACT 2

"I Want to See My Child"
B. Allen, W. White
"Treemonisha's Return"
C. Balthrop, B. Allen, C. Rayam, W. White, K. Hicks
"Wrong Is Never Right"
C. Rayam, Chorus
"Abuse"
C. Balthrop, K. Hicks
"When Villains Ramble Far and Near"
W. White
"Conjuror's Forgiven"
C. Balthrop, K. Hicks
"We Will Trust You as Our Leader"
C. Balthrop, B. Allen, C. Johnson, W. White, C. Rayam, K. Hicks, Chorus
"A Real Slow Drag"
Entire Company
"Aunt Dinah Has Blowed De Horn" (reprise)
Entire Company

1975.20   ME AND BESSIE

A Musical Evening (Revue) in Two Acts. Conceived and written by Will Holt and Linda Hopkins. Entire production directed by Robert Greenwald. Special dance sequences by Lester Wilson. Musical direction by Howlett Smith. Setting by Donald Harris. Costumes by Pete Menefee. Lighting by Tharon Musser. A Center Theatre Group/Mark Taper Forum Production.

Produced by Lee Apostoleris. Opened 22 October 1975 at the Ambassador Theatre, moved under the auspices of Norman Kean 3 December 1975 to the Edison Theatre and closed 5 December 1976 after 453 performances. (Note: From 24 September–5 December 1976 performances were in repertory with "Oh, Calcutta!")

CAST (in order of appearance): *Bessie Smith:* LINDA HOPKINS. *Man:* Lester Wilson. *Woman:* Gerri Dean.

ACT 1

"I Feel Good"
"God Shall Wipe All Tears Away"
"Moan You Mourners"
"New Orleans Hop Scop Blues"
"Romance in the Dark"
    (*Music and Lyrics by* Lil Green.)
"Preach Them Blues"
    (*Music and Lyrics by* Bessie Smith.)
"A Good Man Is Hard to Find"
    (*Music and Lyrics by* Eddie Green.)
"T'Ain't Nobody's Bizness If I Do"
    (*Music and Lyrics by* Porter Grainger, Clarence Williams, Graham Prince.)
"Gimme a Pigfoot"
    (*Music and Lyrics by* Wesley Wilson.)
"Put It Right Here"
    (*Music and Lyrics by* Porter Grainger.)
"You've Been a Good Ole Wagon"
    (*Music and Lyrics by* J. Henry.)
"Trombone Cholly"
"Jazzbo Brown"
"After You've Gone"
    (*Music by* Turner Layton. *Lyrics by* Henry Creamer.)

ACT 2

"There'll Be a Hot Time in the Old Town Tonight"
    (*Music and Lyrics by* Joseph Hayden and Theodore M. Metz.)
"Empty Bed Blues"
    (*Music and Lyrics by* J. C. Johnson.)
"Kitchen Man"
    (*Music by* Alex Belledna. *Lyrics by* Andy Razaf.)
"Mama Don't 'Low"
"Do Your Duty"
    (*Music and Lyrics by* Wesley Wilson.)
"Fare Thee Well"
"Nobody Knows You When You're Down and Out"
    (*Music and Lyrics by* Jimmy Cox.)
"Trouble"
    (*Music and Lyrics by* D. Akers.)
"The Man's All Right"

1975.21   HELLO, DOLLY!

A Revival of the Musical Comedy in Two Acts, 15 Scenes[5]. Book by Michael Stewart. Based on the play "The Matchmaker" by Thornton Wilder. Music and lyrics by Jerry Herman. Directed by Lucia Victor. Dances recreated by Jack Craig from original choreography by Gower Champion. Settings by Oliver Smith. Costumes supervised by Robert Pusilo. Lighting by John Gleason. Musical direction by Al Cavaliere. (Vocal arrangements, orchestrations, dance and incidental music uncredited.) Produced by Robert Cherin in association with Theatre Now Inc. Opened 6 November 1975 at the Minskoff Theatre and closed 21 December 1975 after 42 performances.

CAST (in the order of appearance): *Mrs. Dolly Gallagher Levi:* PEARL BAILEY. *Ernestina:* Bessye Ruth Scott. *Ambrose Kemper:* Howard Porter. *Horse:* Kathy Jennings, Karen Hubbard. *Horace Vandergelder:* BILLY DANIELS. *Ermengarde:* Karen Hubbard. *Cornelius Hackl:* TERRENCE EMANUEL. *Barnaby Tucker:* GRENOLDO FRA-

---

[5]Originally produced in New York 16 January 1964 at the St. James Theatre for 2844 performances. For Synopsis of Scenes and Musical Numbers, see original 1964 production. "Come and Be My Butterfly" was not performed in this revival.

ZIER. *Irene Molloy:* MARY LOUISE. *Minnie Fay:* CHIP FIELDS. *Mrs. Rose:* Birdie M. Hale. *Rudolph:* Jonathan Wynne. *Judge:* Ted Goodridge. *Court Clerk:* Ray Gilbert.

Townspeople, Waiters, Etc.: Sally Benoit, Terry Gene, Pat Gideon, Ann Givin, Birdie M. Hale, Karen Hubbard, Gwen Humble, Eulaulá Jennings, Francie Mendenhall, Bessye Ruth Scott, Sachi Shimizu, Guy Allen, Don Coleman, Richard Dodd, Ray Gilbert, Charles Goeddertz, Ted Goodridge, Clark James, James Kennon-Wilson, Richard Maxon, Charles Neal, Howard Porter, Jimmy Rivers, Ken Rogers, David Staller, Teddy Williams, Jonathan Wynne.

1975.22

A MUSICAL JUBILEE

A Musical Entertainment (Revue) in Two Acts, 10 Scenes. Written by Max Wilk. Devised by Marilyn Clark and Charles Burr. Entire production directed by Morton DaCosta. Musical supervision by Lehman Engel. Musical director, John Lesko. Dance arrangements and musical continuity by Trude Rittman. Orchestrations by Philip J. Lang, Hershy Kay, Elman Anderson. Scenery designed by Herbert Senn. Costumes designed by Donald Brooks. Lighting designed by Thomas Skelton. Choreography by Robert Tucker. Associate producer, Merle D. King. Produced by The Theatre Guild and Jonathan Conrow. Opened 13 November 1975 at the St. James Theatre and closed 1 January 1976 after 92 performances.

CAST: PATRICE MUNSEL, TAMMY GRIMES, CYRIL RITCHARD, JOHN RAITT, DICK SHAWN, LARRY KERT, LILLIAN GISH, Steven Boockvor, Eric Brotherson, Marcia Brushingham, Igors Gavon, Nana, David King, Jeanne Lehman, Bettye Malone, Estella Munson, Julie Pars, Dennis Perren, Leland Schwantes, Craig Yates.

Act 1, Scene 1: Opening. *Scene 2:* American Frontier. *Scene 3:* American Military. *Scene 4:* Old Vienna. *Scene 5:* Britain. *Scene 6:* Early Broadway.

Act 2, Scene 1: The Smart Set. *Scene 2:* Vaudeville. *Scene 3:* Jazz. *Scene 4:* Later Broadway.

ACT 1

Scene 1

"Happy Days"
Entire Company
(*Music by* Johann Strauss II. *Lyrics by* Howard Dietz.)

Scene2

"Whoa-Haw"
L. Kert

"Lorena"
J. Raitt
(*Music by* J. P. Webster. *Lyrics by* Reverend H. D. L. Webster.)

"Sweet Betsy from Pike"
T. Grimes

"Skip to My Lou"
P. Munsel, L. Kert

"Whoa-Haw" (reprise)
Entire Company

Scene 3

"Hold on Abraham"
Ensemble
(*Music and Lyrics by* William L. Bradbury.)

"Bonnie Blue Flag"
L. Kert, S. Boockvor, I. Gavon, D. King, D. Perren, L. Schwantes, C. Yates
(*Music by* Valentine Vousden. *Lyrics by* Harry Macarthy.)

"(It's a Long Way to) Tipperary"
T. Grimes, Male Ensemble
(*Music and Lyrics by* Jack Judge and Harry H. Williams.)

"I Didn't Raise My Boy to be a Soldier"
L. Gish
(*Music by* Al Piantadosi. *Lyrics by* Alfred Bryan.)

"Mademoiselle from Armentieres"
C. Ritchard, D. Shawn
(*Music and Lyrics by* Howard Ross.)

"Over There"
P. Munsel, Male Ensemble
(*Music and Lyrics by* George M. Cohan.)

"Battle Hymn of the Republic"
J. Raitt, Entire Company
(*Lyrics by* Julia Ward Howe.)

Scene 4

"Wien, Wien, You're Calling Me"
(*Music and Lyrics by* Rudolf Sieczynski and King.)

"I'm in Love With Vienna"
(*from* THE GREAT WALTZ film.)

(*Music by* Johann Strauss. *Lyrics by* Oscar Hammerstein II.)
P. Munsel, J. Raitt, Ensemble

"Der Shimmy"
T. Grimes
(*Music by* Emmerich Kálmán. *Lyrics by* King.)

"I've Got Something"
(*Music by* Franz Lehár. *Lyrics by* Harry B. Smith and Robert B. Smith.)
C. Ritchard, M. Brushingham, Nana, J. Lehman, B. Malone, J. Pars, E. Munson

"Oh, the Women"
L. Kert
(*Music by* Franz Lehár.)

"Gypsy Love"
(from GYPSY LOVE)
P. Munsel, Ensemble
(*Music by* Franz Lehár. *Lyrics by* Harry B. Smith and Robert B. Smith.)

Scene 5

"And Her Mother Came Too"
(from A TO Z, London)
C. Ritchard
(*Music by* Ivor Novello. *Lyrics by* Dion Titheradge.)

Scene 6

"Song of the Vagabonds"
(from THE VAGABOND KING)
J. Raitt, Male Ensemble
(*Music by* Rudolf Friml. *Lyrics by* Brian Hooker.)

"Totem Tom Tom"
(from ROSE MARIE)
T. Grimes, Female Ensemble
(*Music by* Rudolf Friml. *Lyrics by* Oscar Hammerstein II and Otto Harbach.)

"Serenade"
(from THE STUDENT PRINCE)
L. Kert
(*Music by* Sigmund Romberg. *Lyrics by* Dorothy Donnelly.)

Violetta
C. Ritchard, T. Grimes, L. Kert, E. Brotherson

"Moonstruck"
(from OUR MISS GIBBS)
L. Gish, Male Ensemble
(*Music by* Lionel Monckton. *Lyrics by* James T. Tanner.)

"You Are Love"
(from SHOWBOAT)
P. Munsel, J. Raitt
(*Music by* Jerome Kern. *Lyrics by* Oscar Hammerstein II.)

"I've Told Every Little Star"
(from MUSIC IN THE AIR)
D. Shawn, Female Ensemble
(*Music by* Jerome Kern. *Lyrics by* Oscar Hammerstein II.)

"Why Was I Born?"
(from SWEET ADELINE)
P. Munsel
(*Music by* Jerome Kern. *Lyrics by* Oscar Hammerstein II.)

"The Best Things in Life Are Free"
(from GOODNEWS)
L. Kert, Entire Ensemble
(*Music by* Ray Henderson. *Lyrics by* Buddy G. DeSylva and Lew Brown.)

"They Didn't Believe Me"
(from THE GIRL FROM UTAH)
T. Grimes
(*Music by* Jerome Kern. *Lyrics by* Herbert Reynolds [Michael E. Rourke].)

"The Song Is You"
(from MUSIC IN THE AIR)
J. Raitt
(*Music by* Jerome Kern. *Lyrics by* Oscar Hammerstein II.)

"Something Seems Tingle Ingleing"
(from HIGH JINKS)
(*Music by* Rudolf Friml. *Lyrics by* Otto Harbach.)
C. Ritchard, Female Ensemble

"(I Want to Hear a) Yankee Doodle Tune"
(from MOTHER GOOSE, 1903)
D. Shawn, Entire Company
(*Music and Lyrics by* George M. Cohan.)

ACT 2

Scene 1

"We're Blasé"
(from BOW BELLS, London)

P. Munsel, J. Raitt, T. Grimes, C. Ritchard
(*Music by* Ord Hamilton. *Lyrics by* Bruce Sievier.)
"Poor Little Rich Girl"
(from *CHARLOT'S REVUE*)
T. Grimes
(*Music and Lyrics by* Noël Coward.)
"You Go to My Head"
J. Raitt
(*Music by* J. Fred Coots. *Lyrics by* Haven Gillespie.)
"Find Me a Primitive Man"
(from *FIFTY MILLION FRENCHMEN*)
P. Munsel, T. Grimes
(*Music and Lyrics by* Cole Porter.)
"I Guess I'll Have to Change My Plan"
(from *THE LITTLE SHOW*)
D. Shawn
(*Music by* Arthur Schwartz. *Lyrics by* Howard Dietz.)
"Sophisticated Lady"
L. Kert
(*Music by* Duke Ellington. *Lyrics by* Mitchell Parish and Irving Mills.)
"Love Me or Leave Me"
(from *WHOOPEE*)
P. Munsel
(*Music by* Walter Donaldson. *Lyrics by* Gus Kahn.)
"Gilbert the Filbert"
(from *THE GIRL FROM UTAH, PASSING SHOW OF 1914*)
C. Ritchard
(*Music by* Herman Finck. *Lyrics by* Arthur Wimperis.)
"We're Blasé" (reprise)
P. Munsel, J. Raitt, C. Ritchard, T. Grimes, D. Shawn, L. Kert
Scene 2
"At the Moving Picture Ball"
Ensemble
(*Music by* Joseph H. Santly. *Lyrics by* Howard Johnson.)
The Green Eye of the Little Yellow God
C. Ritchard, D. Shawn, E. Brotherson
(*by* Reginald Purdell, based on the poem by Milton Hayes)
"I Wanna Be Loved by You"
(from *GOOD BOY*)
P. Munsel, T. Grimes, L. Gish
(*Music by* Harry Ruby. *Lyrics by* Bert Kalmar.)
"Miss Annabelle Lee"
D. Shawn
(*Music by* Lew Pollack. *Lyrics by* Sidney Clare, Harry Richman.)
Scene 3
"How Jazz Was Born"
L. Kert, Ensemble
(*Music by* Fats Waller. *Lyrics by* Andy Razaf and Henry Creamer.)
"Ain't Misbehavin'"
(from *HOT CHOCOLATES*)
L. Kert
(*Music by* Fats Waller and Harry Brooks. *Lyrics by* Andy Razaf.)
"I'm Just Wild About Harry"
(from *SHUFFLE ALONG*)
T. Grimes
(*Music and Lyrics by* Eubie Blake and Noble Sissle.)
"Me and My Shadow"
D. Shawn
(*Music by* Al Jolson and Dave Dreyer. *Lyrics by* Billy Rose.)
"Sometimes I'm Happy"
(from *HIT THE DECK*)
P. Munsel
(*Music by* Vincent Youmans. *Lyrics by* Irving Caesar.)
"Great Day"
(from *GREAT DAY*)
J. Raitt
(*Music by* Vincent Youmans. *Lyrics by* Billy Rose and Edward Eliscu.)
"How Jazz Was Born" (reprise)
P. Munsel, J. Raitt, T. Grimes, D. Shawn, L. Kert, Ensemble
Scene 4
"Lullaby of Broadway"
(from *GOLDDIGGERS OF 1935* film)
Ensemble
(*Music by* Harry Warren. *Lyrics by* Al Dubin.)
"(This Is My) Lucky Day"
(from *GEORGE WHITE'S SCANDALS OF 1926*)

D. Shawn
(*Music by* Ray Henderson. *Lyrics by* B. G. DeSylva and Lew Brown.)
"If You Knew Susie"
(from *BIG BOY*)
C. Ritchard
(*Music by* Joseph Meyer. *Lyrics by* B. G. DeSylva.)
"'S Wonderful"
(from *FUNNY FACE*)
L. Gish
(*Music by* George Gershwin. *Lyrics by* Ira Gershwin.)
"Fascinating Rhythm"
(from *LADY, BE GOOD!*)
L. Kert
(*Music by* George Gershwin. *Lyrics by* Ira Gershwin.)
"Liza" (All the Clouds'll Roll Away)
(from *SHOW GIRL*)
T. Grimes
(*Music by* George Gershwin. *Lyrics by* Gus Kahn and Ira Gershwin.)
"Where or When "
(from *BABES IN ARMS*)
P. Munsel
(*Music by* Richard Rodgers. *Lyrics by* Lorenz Hart.)
"Hallelujah"
(from *HIT THE DECK*)
J. Raitt, Entire Company
(*Music by* Vincent Youmans. *Lyrics by* Leo Robin and Clifford Grey.)

1975.23   # BOCCACCIO

A Musical in Two Acts, 8 Scenes. Dramatization (book) and lyrics by Kenneth Cavander. Based on stories[6] from "The Decameron" by Giovanni Boccaccio. Music by Richard Peaslee. Directed by Warren Enters. Musical staging by Julie Arenal. Setting by Robert U. Taylor. Costumes by Linda Fisher. Lighting by Patrika Brown. Musical director, Ken Bichel. Orchestrations and arrangements by Walt Levinsky, Richard Peaslee. Produced by Rita Fredericks, Theatre Now, Inc. and Norman Kean. Opened 24 November 1975 at the Edison Theatre and closed 30 November 1975 after 8 performances.

CAST: *Beltramo (Count of Rossiglione)*, *Egano*: MICHAEL ZASLOW. *Giletta (Beltramo's Wife)*, *Abbess*: VIRGINIA VESTOFF. *Masetto (Beltramo's Younger Brother)*, *Ferondo*: ARMAND ASSANTE. *Beatrice (Beltramo's Widowed Sister)*, *Sister Teresa, Ferondo's Wife*: CAROLINE McWILLIAMS. *Isabella (Masetto's Mistress)*, *Sister Angelica*: D'JAMIN BARTLETT. *Alibech (Masetto's Friend)*, *Sister Makaria*: JILL CHODER. *Rustico (A Cousin)*, *Leonetto, Brother Perdurabo*: MUNSON HICKS. *Anichino (Steward to the Family)*, *Nuto, Abbot*: RICHARD BAUER.

The action takes place at a villa outside Florence in the year 1348.

Act 1, Scene 1: Introduction. The Stories: *Scene 2*: Masetto. *Scene 3*: Anichino. *Scene 4*: Pretend You're Living. *Scene 5*: Devil in Hell.

Act 2, Scene 1: The She Doctor. *Scene 2*: Madonna Isabella. *Scene 3*: Ferondo.

ACT 1
Scene 1
Introduction
The Company
Scene 2
"Masetto's Song"
A. Assante, R. Bauer
"Nuns Song"
V. Vestoff, C. McWilliams, D. Bartlett, J. Choder
"God Is Good"
A. Assante, C. McWilliams, D. Bartlett, J. Choder
"Now My Season's Here"
The Company
Scene 3
"Only in My Song"
R. Bauer
"Egano D'Galluzzi"
R. Bauer, M. Zaslow

---

[6]The stories in "Boccaccio" are taken from The Decameron: Masetto: Day III, Story 1; Anichino: Day VII, Story 7; Devil in Hell: Day II, Story 10; Madonna Isabella: Day VII, Story 6; The Doctor's Daughter: Day III, Story 9; Ferondo: Day III, Story 8.

"The Men Who Have Loved Me"
    C. McWilliams
"In the Garden"
    R. Bauer, M. Zaslow
"Lucky Anichino"
    The Company
Scene 4
    "Pretend You're Living"
        D. Bartlett
Scene 5
    "Devil in Hell"
        J. Choder, M. Hicks, Company

ACT 2
Scene 1
    "She Doctor"
        V. Vestoff, M. Zaslow
    "Lover Like a Blind Man"
        V. Vestoff
    "If You Had Seen"
        V. Vestoff
    "Love Was Just a Game"
        M. Zaslow
Scene 2
    "Madonna Isabella"
        D. Bartlett, Company
Scene 3
    "My Holy Prayer"
        R. Bauer, Monks
    "Hold Me Gently"
        C. McWilliams

1975.24   ## VERY GOOD EDDIE

A Revival of the Musical (Comedy) in Two Acts, 3 Scenes[7]. Book by Guy Bolton. Based on a farce ("Over Night") by Philip Bartholomae. Music by Jerome Kern. Lyrics by Schuyler Greene. Production directed by Bill Gile. Dances and musical numbers staged by Dan Siretta. Musical direction and (vocal) arrangements by Russell Warner. Scenery and lighting by Fred Voelpel. Costumes by David Toser. Special consultant, Alfred Simon. A Goodspeed Opera House Producton (Michael Price, Producer). Produced by David Merrick, Max Brown and Byron Goldman. Opened 21 December 1975 at the Booth Theatre and closed 5 September 1976 after 307 performances.

CAST (in order of appearance): *Steward:* JAMES HARDER. *Mr. Dick Rivers:* DAVID CHRISTMAS. *Mme. Matroppo:* TRAVIS HUDSON. *Miss Elsie Lilly:* CYNTHIA WELLS. *M. de Rougemont:* JOEL CRAIG. *Mrs. Georgina Kettle:* SPRING FAIRBANK. *Mr. Eddie Kettle:* CHARLES REPOLE. *Mr. Percy Darling:* NICHOLAS WYMAN. *Mrs. Elsie Darling:* VIRGINIA SEIDEL. *Al Cleveland:* JAMES HARDER. *Miss Lily Pond:* Wendy Young. *Miss Chrystal Poole:* Karen Crossley. *Miss Carrie Closewell:* Gillian Scalici. *Miss Always Innit:* Robin Herbert. *Mr. Tayleurs Dumme:* Russ Beasley. *Mr. Dayr Thurst:* Jon Engstrom. *Mr. Dustin Stacks:* Larry McMillan. *Mr. Rollo Munn:* Hal Shane.

The action takes place in 1913.

Act 1: A Hudson River Dayliner.

Act 2, Scene 1: Lobby of the Honeymoon Inn in the Catskills. That evening. *Scene 2:* The next morning.

ACT 1
    "We're on Our Way"
        Ensemble
    "Some Sort of Somebody"
        C. Wells, D. Christmas
        (*Lyrics by* Elsie Janis.)
    "(When You Wear a) Thirteen Collar"
        C. Repole
    "Bungalow in Quogue"
        (from THE RIVIERA GIRL)
        V. Seidel, N. Wyman
        (*Lyrics by* P. G. Wodehouse.)

[7]Originally produced in New York 23 December 1915 at the Princess Theatre for 341 performances.

"Isn't It Great To Be Married"
    V. Seidel, S. Fairbank, C. Repole, N. Wyman
"Good Night Boat"
    (from THE NIGHT BOAT)
    Ensemble
    (*Lyrics by* Anne Caldwell and Frank Craven.)
"Left All Alone Again Blues"
    (from THE NIGHT BOAT)
    V. Seidel
    (*Lyrics by* Anne Caldwell.)
"Hot Dog!"
    (from THE BUNCH AND JUDY)
    Ensemble
    (*Lyrics by* Anne Caldwell.)
"If You're a Friend of Mine"
    (from LADY MARY, London)
    V. Seidel, C. Repole
    (*Lyrics by* Graham John.)
"Wedding Bells Are Calling Me"
    Ensemble
    (*Lyrics by* Harry B. Smith.)
ACT 2
    "Honeymoon Inn"
        (from HAVE A HEART)
        C. Wells, Ensemble
        (*Lyrics by* P. G. Wodehouse.)
    "I've Got to Dance"
        (dropped from VERY GOOD EDDIE)
        J. Craig, Ensemble
    "Moon Love"
        (from THE BEAUTY PRIZE)
        T. Hudson, Ensemble
        (*Lyrics by* Anne Caldwell.)
    "Old Boy Neutral"
        C. Wells, D. Christmas
    "Babes in the Wood"
        V. Seidel, C. Repole
    "Katy-did"
        (from OH, I SAY!)
        T. Hudson
        (*Lyrics by* Harry B. Smith.)
    "Nodding Roses"
        C. Wells, D. Christmas
        (*Lyrics by* Schuyler Greene and Herbert Reynolds.)
Finale
    Ensemble
    (*Lyrics by* John E. Hazzard and Herbert Reynolds.)

1976.01   ## HOME SWEET HOMER

A Musical Romantic Comedy in One Act. Book by Roland Kibbee and Albert Marre. (Suggested by Homer's "Odyssey.") Music by Mitch Leigh. Lyrics by Charles Burr and Forman Brown. Book and musical staging by Albert Marre. Scenery and lighting by Howard Bay. Costumes by Howard Bay and Ray Diffen. Musical direction by Ross Reimueller. Orchestrations by Buryl Red. Produced by The John F. Kennedy Center for the Performing Arts (Kennedy Center Productions Inc.) Opened and closed 4 January 1976 at the Palace Theatre after 1 performance.

CAST: *Odysseus:* YUL BRYNNER. *Penelope, his wife:* JOAN DIENER. *Telemachus, his son:* RUSS THACKER. *Penelope's Suitors (8): Antinous:* MARTIN VIDNOVIC. *Pilokrates:* Ian Sullivan. *Ktesippos:* Bill Mackey. *Eurymachus:* Daniel Brown. *Leokritos:* Brain Destazio. *Pimteus:* John Aristedes. *Melios:* Bill Nabel. *Polybos:* Les Freed. *King Alkinoos:* SHEV RODGERS. *Nausikaa, his daughter:* DIANA DAVILA. *Nausikaa's Handmaidens (3): Therapina:* Suzanne Sponsler. *Melantho:* Cecile Santos. *Hippodameia:* Christine Uchida. *Kerux:* Darel Glaser. *Dekati Evdomi, the Seventeenth:* P. J. Mann.

MUSICAL NUMBERS
    "The Sorceress"
        J. Diener, The Suitors
    "The Departure"
        Y. Brynner, P. J. Mann
    "Home Sweet Homer"
        Y. Brynner
    "The Ball"
        D. Davila, Handmaidens

"How Could I Dare to Dream?"
Y. Brynner, R. Thacker
"I Never Imagined Goodbye"
J. Diener
"Love Is the Prize"
Y. Brynner
"Penelope's Hand"
M. Vidnovic
"He Will Come Home Again"
R. Thacker
"Did He Really Think"
J. Diener
"I Was Wrong"
Y. Brynner
"The Rose"
J. Diener
"Tomorrow"
M. Vidnovic, The Suitors
"The Contest"
Y. Brynner, R. Thacker, M. Vidnovic, The Suitors

1976.02 PACIFIC OVERTURES

A Musical in Two Acts, 18 Scenes. Book by John Weidman. Music and lyrics by Stephen Sondheim. Additional (book) material by Hugh Wheeler. Directed by Harold Prince. Choreographed by Patricia Birch. Scenic production designed by Boris Aronson. Costumes designed by Florence Klotz. Lighting designed by Tharon Musser. Orchestrations by Jonathan Tunick. Musical direction by Paul Gemignani. Dance music by Daniel Troob. Kabuki consultant, Haruki Fujimoto. Masks and dolls by E. J. Taylor. Sound by Jack Mann. Martial arts sequence by Soon-Teck Oh. Produced by Harold Prince in association with Ruth Mitchell. Opened 11 January 1976 at the Winter Garden Theatre and closed 27 June 1976 after 193 performances.

CAST (in order of appearance): *Reciter:* MAKO. *Abe, First Councilor:* YUKI SHIMO-DA. *Manjiro:* SAB SHIMONO. *Second Councilor:* JAMES DYBAS. *Shogun's Mother:* Alvin Ing. *Third Councilor:* Freddy Mao. *Kayama:* ISAO SATO. *Tamate (Kayama's Wife), Samurai, Storyteller, Swordsman:* Soon-Teck Oh. *Samurai:* Ernest Aruba, Mark Hsu Syers. *Servant:* HARUKI FUJIMOTO. *Observers:* Alvin Ing, Ricardo Tobia. *Fisherman:* Jae Woo Lee. *Merchant:* Alvin Ing. *Son:* Timm Fujii. *Grandmother:* Conrad Yama. *Thief:* Mark Hsu Syers. *Adams:* Ernest Abuba. *Williams:* Larry Hama. *Commodore Matthew Galbraith Perry:* HARUKI FUJIMOTO. *Shogun's Wife:* Freda Foh Shen. *Physician:* Ernest Harada. *Priests:* Timm Fujii, Gedde Watanabe. *Soothsayer:* Mark Hsu Syers. *Sumo Wrestlers:* Conrad Yama, Jae Woo Lee. *Shogun's Companion:* Patrick Kinser-Lau. *Shogun:* MAKO. *Madam:* Ernest Harada. *Girls:* Timm Fujii, Patrick Kinser-Lau, Gedde Watanabe, Leslie Watanabe. *Old Man:* JAMES DYBAS. *Boy:* Gedde Watanabe. *Warrior:* Mark Hsu Syers. *Imperial Priest:* Tom Matsusaka. *Nobles:* Ernest Abuba, Timm Fujii. *British Admiral:* Ernest Harada. *Dutch Admiral:* Patrick Kinser-Lau. *Russian Admiral:* Mark Hsu Syers. *French Admiral:* JAMES DYBAS. *Lords of the South:* Larry Hama, Jae Woo Lee. *Jonathan Goble:* MAKO. *Japanese Merchant:* Conrad Yama. *Samurai's Daughter:* Freddy Mao. *British Sailors:* Timm Fujii, Patrick Kinser-Lau, Mark Hsu Syers. *Musicians:* Fusako Yoshida, Genji Ito.

Proscenium Servants, Sailors, Townspeople: Susan Kikuchi, Diane Lam, Kim Miyori, Freda Foh Shen, Kenneth S. Eiland, Timm Fujii, Joey Ginza, Patrick Kinser-Lau, Tony Marinyo, Kevin Maung, Dingo Secretario, Mark Hsu Syers, Ricardo Tobia, Gedde Watanabe, Leslie Watannabe. *Musicians:* Fusako Yoshida (Shamisen), Genji Ito (Percussion).

The action takes place in Japan in July of 1853, and from then on.

Act 1, Scene 1: Japan in July 1853; Shogun's Court. *Scene 2:* A small Japanese house in Uraga. *Scene 3:* The Japanese shore. *Scene 4:* The deck of the U.S.S. *Powhatan. Scene 5:* The Shogun's chamber. *Scene 6:* The Shogun's chamber; en route to Uraga; the house at Uraga. *Scene 7:* The village of Kanagawa. *Scene 8:* Exchange of gifts. *Scene 9:* Kanagawa. *Scene 10:* The Treaty House at Kanagawa. *Scene 11:* Lion Dance.

Act 2, Scene 1: The Imperial Court at Kyoto. *Scene 2:* The Admirals' Visit. *Scene 3:* The Imperial Court. *Scene 4:* The homes of Kayama and Manjiro. *Scene 5:* Ten years later. *Scene 6:* A private garden. *Scene 7:* Japan 1863-1975.

ACT 1
Scene 1
"The Advantages of Floating in the Middle of the Sea"
Mako, Company
Scene 2
"There Is No Other Way"
S. Oh, Observers

Scene 3
"Four Black Dragons"
J. W. Lee, M. H. Syers, Mako, Townspeople
Scene 5
"Chrysanthemum Tea"
Mako, A. Ing, F. F. Shen M. H. Syers, T. Fujii, G. Watanabe, P. Kinser-Lau, E. Harada, C. Yama, J. W. Lee
Scene 6
"Poems"
I. Sato, S. Shimono
Scene 7
"Welcome to Kanagawa"
E. Harada, Girls
Scene 10
"Someone in a Tree"
J. Dybas, Mako, G. Watanabe, M. H. Syers
Scene 11
"Lion Dance"
H. Fujimoto
ACT 2
Scene 2
"Please Hello"
Y. Shimoda, Mako, A. Ing, E. Harada, P. Kinser-Lau, M. H. Syers, J. Dybas
Scene 4
"A Bowler Hat"
I. Sato, S. Shimono
Scene 6
"Pretty Lady"
T. Fujii, P. Kinser-Lau, M. H. Syers
Scene 7
"Next"
Mako, Company

1976.03 ROCKABYE HAMLET

A Musical in Two Acts, a Prologue and 9 Scenes[8]. Book, music and lyrics by Cliff Jones. (Based on the play "Hamlet" by William Shakespeare.) Directed and choreographed by Gower Champion. Co-choreographer, Tony Stevens. Scenery designed by Kert Lundell. Costumes designed by Joseph G. Aulisi. Lighting designed by Jules Fisher. Sound design by Abe Jacob. Swordplay by Larry Carpenter. Musical direction and vocal arrangements by Gordon Lowry Harrell. Dance music arranged by Doug Katsaros. Special effects by Robert Joyce. Produced by Lester Osterman Productions (Lester Osterman, Richard Horner) and Joseph Kipness in association with Martin Richards and Victor D'Arc and Marilyn Strauss, by arrangement with Champlain Productions, Ltd. Opened 17 February 1976 at the Minskoff Theatre and closed 21 February 1976 after 7 performances.

CAST (in order of appearance): *Horatio:* RORY DODD. *Hamlet:* LARRY MARSHALL. *Claudius:* ALAN WEEKS. *Gertrude:* LAETA GALLOWAY. *Priest:* MEAT LOAF. *Polonius:* RANDAL WILSON. *Ophelia:* BEVERLY D'ANGELO. *Laertes:* KIM MILFORD. *Rosencrantz:* CHRISTOPHER CHADMAN. *Guildenstern:* WINSTON DeWITT HEMSLEY. *Player:* IRVING (ALLEN) LEE. *Playeress/ Honeybelle Huckster:* Judy Gibson.

Acolytes, Swordsmen, Nobles, Courtesans: Tommy Aguilar, Steve Anthony, Terry Calloway, Prudence Darby, George Giraldo, Larry Hyman, Kurt Johnson, Clinton Keen, Paula Lynn, Joann Ogawa, Sandi Orcutt, Merel Poloway, Joseph Pugliese, Yolanda Raven, Michelle Stubbs, Dennis Williams. *Singers:* James Braet, Judy DeAngelis, B. G. Gibson, Judy Gibson, Pat Gorman, Suzanne Lukather, Bruce Paine, William Parry. *Roadies:* Chet D'Elia, David Fredericks, David Lawson, Jeff Spielman.

The entire action takes place at a rock concert.

Act 1, Scene 1: Chapel. *Scene 2:* Throne Room. *Scene 3:* Queen's Bedchamber. *Scene 4:* The Disco. *Scene 5:* The Great Hall.

Act 2, Scene 1: The Chapel. *Scene 2:* Limbo. *Scene 3:* The Graveyard. *Scene 4:* The Great Hall.

---

[8]"Rockabye Hamlet" was originally commissioned by the Canadian Broadcasting Company's Radio Variety Department and performed as "Kronberg: 1582."

ACT 1
  Prologue
    "Why Did He Have to Die?"
      R. Dodd, Chorus
  Scene 1
    "The Wedding"
      L. Marshall, A. Weeks, L. Galloway, M. Loaf, Chorus
    "That It Should Come to This"
      L. Marshall
  Scene 2
    "Set It Right"
      A. Weeks, L. Marshall, L. Galloway, Chorus
    "Hello-Hello"
      B. D'Angelo, L. Marshall
    "Don't Unmask Your Beauty to the Moon"
      L. Marshall, K. Milford
    "If Not to You"
      B. D'Angelo, Chorus
    "Have I Got a Girl for You"
      C. Chadman, W. D. Hemsley, L. Marshall, Chorus
    "Tis Pity, Tis True"
      R. Wilson, A. Weeks, L. Galloway
  Scene 3
    "Shall We Dance"
      L. Marshall, L. Galloway
    "All My Life"
      L. Galloway
  Scene 4
    "Something's Rotten in Denmark"
      L. Marshall, I. Lee, J. Gibson, Chorus
    "Denmark Is Still"
      L. Marshall, B. D'Angelo, Chorus
    "Twist Her Mind"
      R. Dodd, L. Marshall, B. D'Angelo, Chorus
    "Gentle Lover"
      B. D'Angelo
    "Where Is the Reason"
      L. Marshall
  Scene 5
    "The Wart Song"
      Players, Chorus
    "He Got It in the Ear"
      J. Gibson
    "It Is Done"
      L. Marshall, R. Dodd

ACT 2
  Scene 1
    "Midnight—Hot Blood"
      L. Marshall
    "Midnight Mass"
      L. Marshall, L. Galloway, A. Weeks, M. Loaf, Choir
    "Hey . . . !"
      C. Chadman, W. D. Hemsley, A. Weeks
    "Sing Alone"
      L. Marshall
  Scene 2
    "Your Daddy's Gone Away"
      R. Dodd
    "Rockabye Hamlet"
      B. D'Angelo
    "All by Yourself"
      K. Milford
    "Rosencrantz & Guildenstern Boogie"
      A. Weeks, Chorus Girls
    "Laertes Coercion"
      A. Weeks, K. Milford, L. Galloway, Chorus Girls
    "The Last Blues"
      L. Galloway

Scene 3
  "Didn't She Do It for Love"
    M. Loaf, A. Weeks, L. Marshall, K. Milford, Chorus
  "If My Morning Begins"
    L. Marshall
Scene 4
  "Swordfight"
    A. Weeks, L. Marshall, K. Milford, L. Galloway, R. Dodd, Chorus

1976.04 BUBBLING BROWN SUGAR

A Musical Revue in Two Acts, 9 Scenes[9] . Book by Loften Mitchell. Based on a concept by Rosetta LeNoire. Additional music by Danny Holgate, Emme Kemp, Lillian Lopez. Directed by Robert M. Cooper. Choreography and musical staging by Billy Wilson. Musical direction by Danny Holgate. Sets by Clarke Dunham. Costumes by Bernard Johnson. Lighting by Barry Arnold. Projections by Lucie D. Grosvenor, Clarke Dunham. Choral arrangements by Chapman Roberts. Sound design by Joel S. Fichman. A Media House Production. Produced by J. Lloyd Grant, Richard Bell, Robert M. Cooper, Ashton Springer in association with Moe Septee, Inc. Opened 2 March 1976 at the ANTA Theatre and closed 31 December 1977 after 766 performances.

CAST (in order of appearance): *Skip*: Lonnie McNeil. *Bill*: VERNON WASHINGTON. *Ray*: Newton Winters. *Carolyn*: CAROLYN BYRD. *Norma*: Karen Grannum. *Gene*: Alton Lathrop. *Helen*: Dyann Robinson. *Laura*: Charlise Harris. *Marsha*: VIVIAN REED. *Tony*: Anthony Whitehouse. *Irene Paige*: JOSEPHINE PREMICE. *John Sage*: AVON LONG. *Checkers*: JOSEPH ATTLES. *Jim*: CHIP GARNETT. *Ella*: ETHEL BEATTY. *Time Man*: VERNON WASHINGTON. *Waiter*: Anthony Whitehouse. *Judy*: BARBARA RUBENSTEIN. *Charlie*: BARRY PRESTON. *Gospel Lady's Son*: Alton Lathrop. *Gospel Lady*: CAROLYN BYRD. *Young Irene*: VIVIAN REED. *Young Sage*: Newton Winters. *Young Checkers*: Lonnie McNeil. *Female Nightclub Singer*: CAROLYN BYRD. *The Solitunes*: Alton Lathrop, Lonnie McNeil, Newton Winters. *Male Nightclub Singer*: CHIP GARNETT. *Dusty*: JOSEPH ATTLES. *Rusty*: AVON LONG. *Bumpy*: VERNON WASHINGTON. *Count*: BARRY PRESTON. *Dutch*: Anthony Whitehouse. *Dutch's Girl*: BARBARA RUBENSTEIN. *Emcee*: VERNON WASHINGTON.

Chorus: Murphy Cross, Nedra Dixon, Emme Kemp, Stanley Ramsey.

Act 1, Scene 1: Harlem Today. The rest of the action takes place in old Harlem between 1920 and 1940. *Scene 2*: Downtown Speakeasy. *Scene 3*: 125th Street and Seventh Avenue. *Scene 4*: 135th Street and Lenox Avenue. *Scene 5*: Harlem Night Spots. *Scene 6*: At the Savoy.

Act 2, Scene 1: Lenox Avenue—A few minutes later. *Scene 2*: Another street in Harlem. *Scene 3*: Small's Paradise.

ACT 1
Scene 1
  "Harlem '70"[10]
    Company
    (*Music by* Danny Holgate. *Lyrics by* Loften Mitchell.)
  "Bubbling Brown Sugar"[11]
    Company
    (*Music by* Danny Holgate. *Lyrics by* Lillian Lopez and Emme Kemp.)
  "(That's) What Harlem Is to Me" (from CONNIE'S HOT CHOCOLATES OF 1935)
    (*Music and Lyrics by* Andy Razaf, Russell Wooding, Paul Denniker.)
    J. Premice
  Bill Robinson Specialty
    V. Washington
  "Harlem Sweet Harlem"[12]
    Company
    (*Music by* Danny Holgate. *Lyrics by* Loften Mitchell.)
  "Nobody" (interpolated into ZIEGFELD FOLLIES OF 1910)
    A. Long
    (*Music and Lyrics by* Axel Rogers and Bert Williams.)
  "Goin' Back in Time"[13]
    V. Washington
    (*Music by* Danny Holgate.)

---

[9]First produced in New York in an earlier version Off-Off Broadway 14 February 1975 at the AMAS Repertory Theatre for 12 performances.
[10]Original music written for this production.
[11]Original music written for this production.
[12]Original music written for this production.
[13]Original music written for this production.

Scene 2

"Some of These Days"
B. Rubenstein
(*Music and Lyrics by* Shelton Brooks.)

"Moving Uptown"[14]
V. Washington
(*Music by* Danny Holgate. *Lyrics by* Loften Mitchell and Emme Kemp.)

Scene 3

"Strolling"[15]
A. Lathrop, C. Harris, L. McNeil, K. Grannum, N. Winters, D. Robinson
(*Music by* Danny Holgate.)

Scene 4

"I'm Gonna Tell God All My Troubles" (traditional)
A. Lathrop

Medley: "His Eye Is on the Sparrow"/"Swing Low, Sweet Chariot" (traditional)
C. Byrd, Company

"Sweet Georgia Brown"
V. Reed, L. McNeil, N. Winters
(*Music and Lyrics by* Maceo Pinkard, Ben Bernie and Kenneth Casey.)

"Honeysuckle Rose" (from LOAD OF COAL)
J. Premice, A. Long
(*Music by* Fats Waller. *Lyrics by* Andy Razaf.)

Scene 5

"Stormy Monday Blues"
C. Byrd
(*Music and Lyrics by* Earl Hines, Billy Eckstine and Bob Crowder.)

"Rosetta"
A. Lathrop, L. McNeil, N. Winters
(*Music and Lyrics by* Earl Hines and Henri Woode.)

"Sophisticated Lady"
C. Garnett, D. Robinson, V. Washington
(*Music by* Duke Ellington. *Lyrics by* Irving Mills and Mitchell Parish.)

"In Honeysuckle Time (When Emaline Said She'd Be Mine)" (from SHUFFLE ALONG)
A. Long, J. Attles
(*Music by* Eubie Blake. *Lyrics by* Noble Sissle.)

"Solitude"
V. Reed, A. Lathrop, L. McNeil, N. Winters
(*Music by* Duke Ellington. *Lyrics by* Eddie DeLange and Irving Mills.)

Scene 6

"C'mon Up to Jive Time"[16]
V. Washington
(*Music by* Danny Holgate.)

Medley: "Stompin' at the Savoy"
(*Music by* Benny Goodman, Edgar Sampson and Chick Webb. *Lyrics by* Andy Razaf.)

"Take the "A" Train"
(*Music and Lyrics by* Duke Ellington and Billy Strayhorn.)
Company

ACT 2

Scene 1

"Harlem—Time"[17]
V. Washington
(*Music by* Danny Holgate.)

"Love Will Find a Way" (from SHUFFLE ALONG)
C. Garnett, E. Beatty
(*Music by* Eubie Blake. *Lyrics by* Noble Sissle.)

"Dutch's Song"[18]
A. Whitehouse
(*Music and Lyrics by* Emme Kemp.)

"Brown Gal"
A. Long
(*Music and Lyrics by* Avon Long and Lil Armstrong.)

"Pray for the Lights to Go Out"
J. Attles
(*Music and Lyrics by* Renton Tunnan and Will Skidmore.)

Scene 2

"I Got It Bad" (from JUMP FOR JOY)
E. Beatty
(*Music by* Duke Ellington. *Lyrics by* Paul Francis Webster.)

"Harlem Makes Me Feel!"[19]
B. Preston
(*Music and Lyrics by* Emme Kemp.)

Scene 3

"Jim, Jam, Jumpin' Jive"
V. Washington, L. McNeil, N. Winters
(*Music and Lyrics by* Cab Calloway.)

"There'll Be Some Changes Made"
J. Premice
(*Music and Lyrics by* W. Benton Overstreet and Billy Higgins.)

"God Bless the Child"
V. Reed
(*Music and Lyrics by* Arthur Herzog, Jr. and Billie Holliday.)

"It Don't Mean a Thing (If It Ain't Got That Swing)"
C. Garnett, A. Whitehouse, K. Premice, Company
(*Music by* Duke Ellington. *Lyrics by* Irving Mills.)

1976.05 ## MY FAIR LADY

A Revival of the Musical (Comedy) in Two Acts, 18 Scenes[20]. Book and lyrics by Alan Jay Lerner. Based on the play "Pygmalion" by George Bernard Shaw, produced on the screen by Gabriel Pascal. Music by Frederick Loewe. Directed by Jerry Adler based on the original by Moss Hart. Choreography and musical numbers staged by Crandall Diehl, based on the original by Hanya Holm. Production (settings) designed by Oliver Smith. Costumes designed by Cecil Beaton. Special costume assistant, W. Robert Lavine. Musical arrangements (orchestrations) by Robert Russell Bennett and Philip J. Lang. Lighting designed by John Gleason. Dance music arranged by Trude Rittman. Musical director, Theodore Saidenberg. Produced by Herman Levin. Opened 25 March 1976 at the St. James Theatre and closed 20 February 1977 after 384 performances.

CAST (in order of appearance): *Buskers*: Debra Lyman, Stan Picus, Ernie Pysher. *Mrs. Eynsford-Hill*: Eleanor Phelps. *Freddy Eynsford-Hill*: JERRY LANNING *Eliza Doolittle*: CHRISTINE ANDREAS. *Colonel Pickering*: ROBERT COOTE. *Henry Higgins*: IAN RICHARDSON. *First Cockney*: Kevin Marcum. *Second Cockney*: Jack Starkey. *Third Cockney*: William James. *Fourth Cockney*: Stan Page. *Bartender*: Kevin Lane Dearinger. *Harry*: John Clarkson. *Jamie*: Richard Neilson. *Alfred P. Doolittle*: GEORGE ROSE. *Mrs. Pearce*: Sylvia O'Brien. *Mrs. Hopkins*: Margaretta Warwick. *Butler*: Clifford Fearl. *Servants*: Sonja Anderson, Lynn Fitzpatrick, Karen Gibson, Vickie Patik, Kevin Lane Dearinger. *Mrs. Higgins*: BRENDA FORBES. *Chauffeur*: Jack Karcher. *Footmen*: Kevin Lane Dearinger Stan Page. *Lord Boxington*: John Clarkson. *Lady Boxington*: Margaretta Warwick. *Constable*: Timothy Smith. *Flower Girl*: Dru Alexandrine. *Flunkey*: William James. *Zoltan Karpathy*: JOHN CLARKSON. *Queen of Transylvania*: Karen Gibson. *Ambassador*: Richard Neilson. *Bartender*: Clifford Fearl. *Mrs. Higgins' Maid*: Sonja Stuart.

Singing Ensemble: Sonja Anderson, Alyson Bristol, Lynn Fitzpatrick, Karen Gibson, Cynthia Meryl, Vickie Patik, Kevin Lane Dearinger, Clifford Fearl, William James, Kevin Marcum, Stan Page, Jack Starkey. *Dancing Ensemble*: Dru Alexandrine, Sally Benoit, Marie Berry, Debra Lyman, Mari McMinn, Gina Ramsel, Catherine Rice, Sonja Stuart, Bonnie Walker, Richard Ammon, Jeremy Blanton, David Evans, Jack Karcher, Richard Maxon, Stan Picus, Ernie Pysher, Rick Schneider, Timothy Smith.

1976.06 ## MONTY PYTHON LIVE!

A Comedy Revue in Two Acts[21]. Conceived and written by Graham Chapman, John Cleese, Terry Gilliam, Eric Idle, Terry Jones, Michael Palin. American scenic supervision by Karl Eigsti. Sound by Abe Jacob. Lighting design by John Gleason. Wardrobe coordinator, Ann Goodson. Produced by Artists Consultants, Inc. (Allen Tinkley, Lou Robin, Tom

---

[14]Original music written for this production.

[15]Original music written for this production.

[16]Original music written for this production.

[17]Original music written for this production.

[18]Original music written for this production. Dropped for national tour. "Ain't Misbehavin'" added for tour.

[19]Original music written for this production.

[20]Originally produced in New York 15 March 1956 at the Mark Hellinger Theatre for 2717 peformances. For Synopsis of Scenes and Musical Numbers, see original 1956 production.

[21]Comedy sketches, with no other performance details given.

Robin). Opened 15 April 1976 at the New York City Center and closed 2 May 1976 after 22 performances.

CAST: GRAHAM CHAPMAN, JOHN CLEESE, TERRY GILLIAM, ERIC IDLE, TERRY JONES, MICHAEL PALIN, Carol Cleveland, Neil Innes.

1976.07   SHIRLEY MacLAINE

A Musical Revue in One Act. Written by Fred Ebb. Music arranged or composed by Cy Coleman. Additional material by Bob Wells. Directed and staged by Tony Charmoli. Musical director, Donn Trenner. Special choreography by Alan Johnson. Lighting design by Richard Winkler. Lighting consultant, Graham Large. Sound consultant, Steve Wooley. Produced by HMT Associates. Opened 19 April 1976 at the Palace Theatre and closed 1 May 1976 after 20 performances; returned 9 July 1976 to the Palace Theatre and closed 24 July 1976 after 20 additional performances. Total: 40 performances.

CAST: SHIRLEY MacLAINE.
   Gypsies: Candy Brown[22], Jo Ann Lehmann, Gary Flannery, Adam Grammis, Larry Vickers.

MUSICAL NUMBERS[23]

"If My Friends Could See Me Now" (from SWEET CHARITY)
   S. MacLaine, A. Grammis, G. Flannery
   (Lyrics by Dorothy Fields.)
"(My) Personal Property"[24]
   (from film SWEET CHARITY)
   S. MacLaine
   (Lyrics by Dorothy Fields.)
"Remember Me?"
   (from MR. DODDS TAKES THE AIR film)
   S. MacLaine
   (Music by Harry Warren. Lyrics by Al Dubin.)
"Hey, Big Spender"
   (from SWEET CHARITY)
   C. Brown, J. A. Lehmann, S. MacLaine
   (Lyrics by Dorothy Fields.)
"I'm a Person Too"
   S. MacLaine
   (Lyrics by Bob Wells.)
"Irma la Douce"[25]
   (from IRMA LA DOUCE film)
   S. MacLaine
   (Music by Andre Previn.)
"(The) Gypsy in My Soul"
   (from JOHN PAUL JONES, Mask & Wig Show)
   S. MacLaine, The Gypsies
   (Music and Lyrics by Clay Boland and Moe Jaffee.)
"It's Not Where You Start"
   (from SEESAW)
   S. MacLaine, The Gypsies
   (Lyrics by Dorothy Fields.)
"Every Little Movement Has a Meaning All Its Own"
   (from MADAME SHERRY)
   S. MacLaine, The Gypsies
   (Music by Karl Hoschna. Lyrics by Otto Harbach.)
"The Hustle" (The Donkey Serenade)
   (from THE FIREFLY film)
   S. MacLaine, The Gypsies
   (Music by Rudolf Friml and Herbert Stothart. Lyrics by Robert Wright and George Forrest.)
"(She's a) Star"
   S. MacLaine
   (Music and Lyrics by Serge Lama, A. Dona and Fred Ebb.)

---

[22]For return engagement Barbara Alston replaced Candy Brown.
[23]Added (after "Remember Me?") for the return engagement:
"Steam Heat" (from THE PAJAMA GAME)S. MacLaine, G. Flannery, L. Vickers
   (Music and Lyrics by Richard Adler and Jerry Ross. Choreography by Bob Fosse, recreated by Zoya Leporska.)
[24]Dropped for return engagement.
[25]Dropped for return engagement.

"I'm a Brass Band"
   (from SWEET CHARITY)
   S. MacLaine, The Gypsies
   (Lyrics by Dorothy Fields.)

1976.08   REX

A Musical in Two Acts, 23 Scenes. Book by Sherman Yellen. Music by Richard Rodgers. Lyrics by Sheldon Harnick. Directed by Edwin Sherin. Choreography by Dania Krupska. Orchestrations by Irwin Kostal. Musical director, Jay Blackton. Dance arrangements by David Baker. Scenery and costumes by John Conklin. Lighting by Jennifer Tipton. Produced by Richard Adler in association with Roger Berlind and Edward R. Downe, Jr. Opened 25 April 1976 at the Lunt-Fontanne Theatre and closed 5 June 1976 after 48 performances.

CAST (in order of appearance): Norfolk: Charles Rule. Cardinal Wolsey: WILLIAM GRIFFIS. Will Somers: TOM ALDREDGE. Henry VIII, King of England: NICOL WILLIAMSON. Mark Smeaton: ED EVANKO. Princess Mary: GLENN CLOSE. Queen Catherine of England: BARBARA ANDRES. Lady Jane Seymour: APRIL SHAWHAN. Francis, King of France: STEPHEN D. NEWMAN. English Herald: Danny Ruvolo. French Herald: Jeff Phillips. Queen Claude of France: MARTHA DANIELLE. Anne Boleyn; Princess Elizabeth: PENNY FULLER. Dauphin: KEITH KOPPMEIER. Comus: MERWIN GOLDSMITH. First Guard: Ken Henley. Lady Margaret: MARTHA DANIELLE. Lady in Waiting: Melanie Vaughan. Young Princess Elizabeth: Sparky Shapiro. Nurse: Lillian Shelby. Second Guard: Dennis Daniels. Thomas Cromwell: Gerald R. Teijelo. Catherine Howard: Valerie Mahaffey. Prince Edward: MICHAEL JOHN. Queen Katherine Parr of England: MARTHA DANIELLE.
   Ladies and Gentlemen of the Courts: Dennis Daniels, Harry Fawcett, Paul Forrest, Pat Gideon, Ken Henley, Dawn Herbert, Robin Hoff, Don Johanson, Jim Litten, Craig Lucas, Carol Jo Lugenbeal, Valerie Mahaffey, G. Eugene Moose, Jeff Phillips, Charles Rule, Danny Ruvolo, Lillian Shelby, Jo Speros, Gerald R. Teijelo, Jr., Candace Tovar, John Ulrickson, Melanie Vaughan. Sword and Morris Dancers: Dennis Daniels, Ken Henley, Don Johnson, Jim Litten, Jeff Phillips, Danny Ruvolo.

The action takes place during the reign of Henry VIII of England until his death.

Act 1, Scene 1: Greenwich Palace. Scene 2: Henry's Tent. Scene 3: Field of Cloth of Gold. Scene 4: French Pavilion. Scene 5: Comus' Chambers. Scene 6: Hever Castle. Scene 7: Hampton Court Palace. Scene 8: Chapel. Scene 9: The Throne Room. Scene 10: Hampton Court Corridor. Scene 11: Queen Anne's Bedroom .Scene 12: Comus' Lab. Scene 13: The Palace. Scene 14: The Tower of London. Scene 15: The Coronation. Scene 16: The City of London.

Act 1, Scene 1: Hampton Court Palace. Ten years later. Scene 2: The Great Wall at Hampton Court Palace. Scene 3: The Throne Room. Scene 4: Hampton Court Corridor. Scene 5: Comus' Laboratory. Scene 6: Henry's Bedroom. Scene 7: The Throne Room.

ACT 1
Scene 1
   "Te Deum"
      Company
Scene 2
   "No Song More Pleasing"
      E. Evanko
Scene 3
   "Where Is My Son?"

ACT 1
Scene 1
   "Te Deum"
      Company
Scene 2
   "No Song More Pleasing"
      E. Evanko
Scene 3
   "Where Is My Son?"
      N. Williamson
   "The Field of Cloth of Gold"
      Company
Scene 4
   Basse Dance
      Company
Scene 6
   "The Chase"
      M. Goldsmith, T. Aldredge, E. Evanko, Gentlemen of the Court

Scene 7
"Away From You"
 N. Williamson
Scene 8
"As Once I Loved You"
 B. Andres
Scene 11
"Elizabeth"
 E. Evanko, M. Danielle, M. Vaughan
Scene 12
"What Now?"[26]
 N. Williamson
Scene 13
"No Song More Pleasing" (reprise)
 A. Shawhan, N. Williamson
"Away from You" (reprise)
 P. Fuller
Scene 16
"Te Deum" (reprise)
 Company
ACT 2
Scene 1
"Christmas at Hampton Court"
 P. Fuller, M. John, G . Close
Scene 2
"The Wee Golden Warrior"
 T. Aldredge, M. John, P. Fuller, G. Close
Sword Dance and Morris Dance
 Sword and Morris dancers
"The Masque"
 Ladies and Gentlemen of the Court
Scene 3
"From Afar"
 N. Williamson
Scene 4
"In Time"
 P. Fuller, T. Aldredge
Scene 7
"In Time" (reprise)
 P. Fuller, M. John
"Te Deum" (reprise)
 Company

1976.09 SO LONG, 174th STREET

A Musical in One Act. Scenes. Book by Joseph Stein. Based on his play "Enter Laughing" from the novel by Carl Reiner. Music and lyrics by Stan Daniels. Directed by Burt Shevelove. Choreography by Alan Johnson. Scenery by James Riley. Costumes by Stanley Simmons. Lighting by Richard Nelson. Musical direction by John Lesko. Orchestrations by Luther Henderson. Dance music arrangements by Wally Harper. Production supervisor, Stone Widney. Produced by Frederick Brisson in asssociation with the Harkness Organization and Wyatt Dickerson. Opened 27 April 1976 at the Harkness Theatre and closed 9 May 1976 after 16 performances.

CAST (in order of appearance): *David (Kolowitz)*: ROBERT MORSE. *Stage Manager*: Joe Howard. *Girl*: Freda Soiffer. *Barrymore*: GENE VARRONE. *Pope*: ROBERT BARRY. *King*: Richard Marr. *Roosevelt*: David Berk. *Eleanor Roosevelt*: Nancy Killmer. *Mr. Foreman*: MITCHELL JASON. *Wanda*: LONI ACKERMAN. *Marvin*: LAWRENCE JOHN MOSS. *Miss B*: SYDNEY BLAKE. *Harry Hamburger*: ROBERT BARRY. *Waiter*: GENE VARRONE. *Pike*: GENE VARRONE. *Don Baxter*: Chuck Beard. *Don Darwin*: Michael Blue Aiken. *Angela*: BARBARA LANG. *Marlowe*: GEORGE S. IRVING. *Ziegfeld*: GENE VARRONE. *Papa*: LEE GOODMAN. *Soda Jerk*: James Brennan. *Butler*: GEORGE S. IRVING. *Judge*: GEORGE S. IRVING. *Peabody*: Richard Marr. *Man*: James Brennan.

---

[26]Replaced after opening with:
 "Why?"
 N. Williamson

Ensemble: Jill Cook, Nancy Killmer, Meribeth Kisner, Denise Mauthe, Rita Rudner, Freda Soiffer, Michael Blue Aiken, Chuck Beard, David Berk, Joe Howard, Richard Marr, William Swiggard.

The action takes place at the present time and the late 1930's in New York City.

MUSICAL NUMBERS
"David Kolowitz, the Actor"
 R. Morse, Ensemble
"It's Like"
 R. Morse, L. Ackerman
"Undressing Girls With My Eyes"
 R. Morse, L. J. Moss, Girls
"Bolero on Rye"
 R. Morse, S. Blake, G. Varrone
"Whoever You Are"
 R. Morse
"Say the Words"
 B. Lang
"My Son the Druggist"
 L. Goodman
"You Touched Her"
 R. Morse, L. J. Moss, Men
"Men"
 L. Ackerman, J. Brennan, Girls
"Boy Oh Boy"
 R. Morse, Company
"The Butler's Song"
 G. S. Irving
"Being With You"
 L. Ackerman, R. Morse
"If You Want to Break Your Father's Heart"
 R. Morse, L. Goodman, G. S.Irving, Jury
"So Long, 174th Street"
 R. Morse, Family, Friends, Neighbors
"David Kolowitz, the Actor" (reprise)
 Company
Finale
 Company

1976.10 THREEPENNY OPERA

A Revival of the Musical in Three Acts[27]. Libretto by Bertolt Brecht. Music by Kurt Weill. New translation by Ralph Manheim and John Willett. Directed by Richard Foreman. Scenic design by Douglas W. Schmidt. Costumes by Theoni V. Aldredge. Lighting by Pat Collins. Sound by Roger Jay (Joseph Dungan). Music direction by Stanley Silverman. Associate producer, Bernard Gersten. A New York Shakespeare Festival Production. Produced by Joseph Papp. Opened 1 May 1976 at the Vivian Beaumont Theatre and closed 23 January 1977 after 306 performances[28]

CAST (in order of appearance): *The Ballad Singer*: Roy Brocksmith. *Mack The Knife* (Macheath): RAUL JULIA. *Jenny Towler*: ELLEN GREENE. *Jonathan Peachum*: C. K. ALEXANDER. *Samuel*, Peachum's Assistant: Tony Azito. *Charles Filch*: Ed Zang. *Mrs. Peachum*: ELIZABETH WILSON. *Matt*: Ralph Driscoll. *Polly Peachum*: CAROLINE KAVA. *Jake*: William Duell. *Bob*: K. C. Wilson. *Ned*: Rik Colitti. *Jimmy*: Robert Schlee. *Walt*: Max Gulack. *Tiger Brown*: DAVID SABIN. *Smith*: Glenn Kezer. *Lucy Brown*: BLAIR BROWN. *A Constable*: John Ridge. *Messenger*: Jack Eric Williams.

Beggars and Policemen: Pendleton Brown, M. Patrick Hughes, George McGrath, Rick Petrucelli, John Ridge, Craig Rupp, Armin Shimerman, Jack Eric Williams, Ray Xifo. *Whores*: Penelope Bodry, Nancy Campbell, Gretel Cummings, Brenda Currin, Mimi Turque.

The action takes place in London at the time of Queen Victoria's Coronation, re-arranged in Brecht's imagination.

ACT 1
Prologue
"Ballad of Mack the Knife"
 R. Brocksmith, T. Azito, R. Schlee, J. E. Williams

---

[27]First produced in New York in English 13 April 1933 at the Empire Theatre for 12 performances; revived Off-Broadway in a translation by Marc Blitzstein at the Theatre de Lys 10 March 1954 for 96 performances, 20 September 1955 at the Theatre de Lys for 2,611 performances.
[28]Reopened a return engagement Off Broadway 6-24 July 1977 at the Delacorte Theatre for 20 performances.

Scene 1

"Peachum's Morning Hymn"
C. K. Alexander

"'No They Can't' Song"
C. K. Alexander, E. Wilson

Scene 2

"Wedding Song for the Less Well-Off"
Gang, Beggars

"The Cannon Song"
R. Julia, D. Sabin, Gang

"Liebeslied"
C. Kava, R. Julia

Scene 3

"Barbara Song"
C. Kava

First Threepenny Finale: "Concerning the Insecurity of the Human State"
C. Kava, C. K. Alexander, E. Wilson

ACT 2

Scene 1

"Polly's Lied"
C. Kava, R. Julia

"Ballad of Sexual Obsession"
E. Wilson

Scene 2

"Pirate Jenny"
E. Greene

"Ballad of Immoral Earnings"
E. Greene, R. Julia

Scene 3

"Ballad of Gracious Living"
R. Julia

"Jealousy Duet"
B. Brown, C. Kava

Second Threepenny Finale: "What Keeps Mankind Alive?"
R. Julia, E. Greene, Chorus

ACT 3

Scene 1

"Song of the Insufficiency of Human Endeavor"
C. K. Alexander

"Solomon Song"
E. Greene

Scene 3

"Call from the Grave"
R. Julia

"Ballad in Which Macheath Begs All Men for Forgiveness"
R. Julia

Third Threepenny Finale
D. Sabin, G. Kezer, R. Brocksmith, J. E. Williams, E. Wilson, C. K. Alexander, R. Julia, C. Kava, B. Brown, E. Greene, Chorus

"Ballad of Mack the Knife" (reprise)
R. Brocksmith

1976.11   1600 PENNSYLVANIA AVENUE

A Musical About the Problems of Housekeeping in Two Acts. Book and lyrics by Alan Jay Lerner. Music by Leonard Bernstein. Entire production co-directed, staged and choreographed by Gilbert Moses and George Faison. Scenery designed by Kert Lundell. Costumes coordinated by Whitney Blausen, Dona Granata. Lighting by Tharon Musser. Musical direction, Roland Gagnon. Orchestrations by Sid Ramin and Hershy Kay. Sound design by John McClure. Produced by Roger L. Stevens and Robert Whitehead by arrangement with Saint Subber. Opened 4 May 1976 at the Mark Hellinger Theatre and closed 8 May 1976 after 7 performances.

CAST: The President: KEN HOWARD. The President's Wife: PATRICIA ROUT-LEDGE. Lud: GILBERT PRICE. Seena: EMILY YANCY. Little Lud: Guy Costley. Stage Manager: David E. Thomas.
The Thirteen Delegates: New York: Howard Ross. Pennsylvania: Reid Shelton. New Hampshire: Ralph Farnworth. Rhode Island: J. T. Cromwell. Connecticut: Lee Winston. New Jersey: Walter Charles. Virginia: Edwin Steffe. North Carolina: John Witham. South Carolina: Richard Muenz. Delaware: Alexander Orfaly. Maryland: Raymond Cox. Georgia: Randolph Riscol.
The Staff: Henry: Raymond Bazemore. Rachel: Urylee Leonardos. Coley: Carl Hall. Joby: Janette Moody. Broom: Howard Ross. Jim: Cornel J. Richie. Sally: Louise Heath.
The British: Ordway: Walter Charles. Pimms: John Witham. Barker: Lee Winston. Glieg: Raymond Cox. Maitland: Alexander Orfaly. Ross: Edwin Steffe. Pratt: Richard Chappell. Scott: J. T. Cromwell. Budgen: Richard Muenz. Cockburn: Reid Shelton. Reverend Bushrod: Bruce A. Hubbard. Auctioneer: Lee Winston. James Hoban: Edwin Steffe. Royal Visitor: Raldolph Riscol. Secretary of the Senate: Howard Ross. Mr. Henry: Lee Winston. Senator Roscoe Conkling: Reid Shelton. Babcock: Lee Winston. Secretary of the Senate: Howard Ross.
Singers: Raymond Bazemore, Elaine Bunse, Nancy Callman, Richard Chappell, Walter Charles, Raymond Cox, J. T. Cromwell, Beth Fowler, Carl Hall, Louise Heath, Bruce A. Hubbard, Kris Karlowski, Urylee Leonardos, Joyce MacDonald, Janette Moody, Richard Muenz, Sharon Powers, Cornel J. Richie, Randolph Riscol, Martha Thigpen, Lee Winston. Dancers: Jo-Ann Baldo, Clyde-Jacques Barrett, Joella Breedlove, Allyne DeChalus, Linda Griffin, Bob Heath, Michael Lichtefeld, Diana Mirras, Hector Jaime Mercado, Cleveland Pennington, Al Perryman, Renee Rose, Juliet Seignious, Thomas J. Stanton, Clayton Strange, Mimi B. Wallace. Swings: Leah Randolph, Martial Roumain.

The action takes place at The White House in Washington, D.C.

ACT 1

"Rehearse!"
K. Howard, P. Routledge, G. Price, E. Yancy, Entire Company

"If I Was a Dove"
G. Costley

"On Ten Square Miles by the Potomac River"
K. Howard, Delegates

"Welcome Home Miz Adams"
R. Bazemore, U. Leonardos, Staff

"Take Care of This House"
K. Howard, P. Routeldge, G. Costley, Staff

"The President Jefferson Sunday Luncheon Party March"
K. Howard, G. Costley, Guests

"Seena"
G. Price

"Sonatina (The British)"
R. Shelton, Officers, Citizens

1. Allegro con brio

2. Temp di Menuetto (including an authentic harmonization of "To Anacreon in Heav'n" (1740) later known as "The Star Spangled Banner")

3. Rondo

"Lud's Wedding"/"I Love My Wife"
G. Price, E. Yancy, Staff

"Auctions"
L. Winston, Buyers

"The Little White Lie"
K. Howard, P. Routledge

"We Must Have a Ball"
K. Howard

"The Ball"
Entire Company

ACT 2

"Forty Acres and a Mule"
The Staff

"Bright and Black"
E. Yancy, Staff

"Duet for One" ("The First Lady of the Land")
P. Routledge [as Julia Grant, Lucy Hayes], Company

"The Robber-Baron Minstrel Parade"
The Minstrels

"Pity the Poor"
The Minstrels

"The Red White and Blues"
The Minstrels

"I Love This Land"
K. Howard

"Rehearse!" (reprise)
Entire Company

THE MIKADO,
1976.01   or The Town of Titipu

A Revival of the Comic Opera in Two Acts[29]. Libretto by William S. Gilbert. Music by Arthur Sullivan. Production director, Michael Heyland. Costumes designed by Charles Ricketts. Nanki-Poo, Act 1 Costume designed by Disley Jones. Scenery by Disley Jones. Musical director, Royston Nash. Chorus master and assistant conductor, Glyn Hale. Produced by James M. Nederlander by arrangement with the D'Oyly Carte Opera Trust, Ltd. and Dame Bridget D'Oyly Carte. Opened 5 May 1976 at the Uris Theatre and closed 23 May 1976 after 10 performances in repertory.

CAST: *The Mikado of Japan*: JOHN AYLDON. *Nanki-Poo*, his son, disguised as a wandering minstrel in love with Yum-Yum: GEOFFREY SHOVELTON. *Ko-Ko*, Lord High Executioner of Titipu: JOHN REED. *Pooh-Bah*, Lord High Everything Else: KENNETH SANDFORD. *Pish-Tush, Go-To*, Noble Lords: Michael Rayner, Jon Ellison. *Yum-Yum, Pitti-Sing, Peep-Bo*, three sisters, wards of Ko-Ko: JULIA GOSS, JANE METCALFE, PATRICIA LEONARD. *Katisha*: LYNDSIE HOLLAND.

Chorus of School Girls, Nobles, Guards and Coolies: Michael Buchan, Paul Burrows, Barry Clark, Malcolm Coy, Gareth Jones, Guy Matthews, William Palmerley, Edwin Rolles, Thomas Scholey, Alan Spencer, William Strachan, Paul Waite, Michael Westbury. Caroline Baker, Patricia Ann Bennett, Gillian Burrows, Lorraine Dulcie-Daniels, Anne Egglestone, Josephine Hinchley, Beti Lloyd-Jones, Elsie McDougall, Roberta Morrell, Helen Moulder, Suzanne O'Keefe, Andrea Phillips, Glynis Prendergast, Patricia Rea, Vivien Tierney.

THE PIRATES OF PENZANCE,
1976.13   or The Slave of Duty

A Revival of the Comic Opera in Two Acts[30]. Libretto by William S. Gilbert. Music by Arthur Sullivan. Setting designed by Peter Goffin. Production director, Michael Heyland. Musical director, Royston Nash. Chorus master and assistant conductor, Glyn Hale. Produced by James M. Nederlander by arrangement with the D'Oyly Carte Opera Trust, Ltd. and Dame Bridget D'Oyly Carte. Opened 6 May 1976 at the Uris Theatre and closed 12 May 1976 after 8 performances in repertory[31].

CAST: *Major General Stanley*: JAMES CONROY-WARD. *The Pirate King*: JOHN AYLDON. *Samuel*, his Lieutenant: Jon Ellison. *Frederic*, the Pirate Apprentice: MESTON REID. *Sergeant of Police*: MICHAEL RAYNER. *Mabel, Edith, Kate, Isabel*, General Stanley's Daughters: JULIA GOSS, JANE METCALFE, CAROLINE BAKER, Patricia Ann Bennett. *Ruth*, Pirate Maid-of-all-work: LYNDSIE HOLLAND. *Chorus of Pirates, Police and General Stanley's Daughters*: same as THE MIKADO above.

H.M.S. PINAFORE,
1976.14   or The Lass That Loved a Sailor

A Revival of the Comic Opera in Two Acts[32]. Libretto by William S. Gilbert. Music by Arthur Sullivan. Back cloth designed and painted by Joseph and Phil Harker. Production director, Michael Heyland. Musical director, Royston Nash. Chorus master and assistant conductor, Glyn Hale. Produced by James M. Nederlander by arranagement with the D'Oyly Carte Opera Trust, Ltd. and Dame Bridget D'Oyly Carte. Opened 16 May 1976 at the Uris Theatre and closed 19 May 1976 after 4 performances in repertory.

CAST: *The Rt. Hon. Sir Joseph Porter, K.C.B.*, First Lord of the Admiralty: JOHN REED. *Captain Corcoran*, Commanding the H.M.S. Pinafore: MICHAEL RAYNER.

Ralph Rackstraw, Able Seaman: MESTON REID. *Dick Deadeye*, Able Seaman: JOHN AYLDON. *Bill Bobstay*, Bo'sun: Jon Ellison. *Bob Becket*, Bo'sun's Mate, Carpenter's Mate: Michael Buchan. *Josephine*, the Captain's Daughter: BARBARA LILLEY. *Hebe*, Sir Joseph's First Cousin: Patricia Leonard. *Little Buttercup*, Mrs. Cripps, a Portsmouth Bumboat Woman: LYNDSIE HOLLAND. *First Lord's Sisters, his Cousins, his Aunts, Sailors, Marines*: same as THE MIKADO above.

SOMETHING'S AFOOT
1976.15

A Murder Mystery Musical in Two Acts. Book, Music and Lyrics by James McDonald, David Vos and Robert Gerlach. Additional music by Ed Linderman. Directed and choreographed by Tony Tanner. Scenery by Richard Seger. Costumes by Walter Watson, Clifford Capone. Lighting by Richard Winkler. Musical director, Buster Davis. Orchestrations by Peter M. Larson. Sound by Robert Weeden. Produced by Emanuel Azenberg, Dasha Epstein and John Mason Kirby. Originally produced by the Goodspeed Opera House (Michael Price, Producer). Opened 27 May 1976 at the Lyceum Theatre and closed 18 July 1976 after 61 performances.

CAST (in order of appearance): *Lettie*: NEVA SMALL. *Flint*: MARC JORDAN. *Clive*: SEL VITELLA. *Hope Langdon*: BARBARA HEUMAN. *Dr. Grayburn*: JACK SCHMIDT. *Nigel Rancour*: GARY BEACH. *Lady Grace Manley-Prowe*: LIZ SHERIDAN. *Colonel Gillweather*: GARY GAGE. *Miss Tweed*: TESSIE O'SHEA. *Geoffrey*: WILLARD BECKHAM.

The action takes place during the late spring of 1935 at Rancour's Retreat, a country estate in the English lake district.

Act 1: The Entrance Hall of Rancour's Retreat.

Act 2: The same, immediately following.

ACT 1[33]
"A Marvelous Weekend"
  (Entire Company [exc. W. Beckham])
"Something's Afoot"
  (Entire Company [exc. W. Beckham])
"Carry On"
  (T. O'Shea, L. Sheridan, N. Small, B. Heuman)
"I Don't Know Why I Trust You (But I Do)"
  (B. Heuman, W. Beckham)
"The Man With the Ginger Mustache"
  (L. Sheridan)
"Suspicious"
  (Entire Company)

ACT 2
"The Legal Heir"
  (G. Beach)
"You Fell Out of the Sky"
  (B. Heuman)
"Dinghy"
  (M. Jordan, N. Small)
"I Owe It All"
  (T. O'Shea, B. Heuman, W. Beckham)
"New Day"
  (W. Beckham, B. Heuman, Choir)

---

[29]First presented in New York 20 July, 10-29 August 1885 at the Union Square and People's Theatres for 22 performances. First authorized production presented 19 August 1885 at the Fifth Avenue Theatre by Richard D'Oyly Carte for 250 performances. For Synopsis of Scenes and Musical Numbers, see 19 August 1885 D'Oyly Carte production.
[30]First presented in New York 31 December 1879 at the Fifth Avenue Theatre for a total of 91 performances in two engagements. For Synopsis of Scenes and Musical Numbers, see original 1879 production.
[31]Costumes uncredited.
[32]Originally presented in New York 15 January 1879 at the Standard Theatre for 175 performances. For Synopsis of Scenes and Musical Numbers, see original 1879 production.

[33]Inasmuch as this is a murder mystery, the program omits the singers' names, which have been restored above based on the production manuscript.

1976–1977 SEASON

Dorothy Loudon, Robert Fitch, and Barbara Erwin in ANNIE
Martha Swope/TimePix

1976–1977 SEASON

1976.16
AN EVENING WITH DIANA ROSS

A Musical Revue in Two Acts. Special material by Billy Goldenberg and Bill Dyer. Additional material by Bruce Vilanch. Directed by Joe Layton. Musical director, Gil Askey. Lighting designed by John Gleason. Sound consultant, Trevor Jordan. A Danny O'Donovan/Sagittarius Entertainment Presentation. Produced by Danny O'Donovan. Opened 14 June 1976 at the Palace Theatre and closed 3 July 1976 after 18 performances.

CAST: DIANA ROSS, The Jones Girls (Shirley Yuvonne Jones, Brenda Elaine Jones, Valorie Denise Jones). *Mimes:* Hayward Coleman, Don McLeod, Stewart Fischer.

ACT 1
"Here I Am"
   (*Music by* Burt Bacharach. *Lyrics by* Hal David.)
"I Wouldn't Change a Thing"
   (*Music by* Burt Bacharach. *Lyrics by* Hal David.)
"The Lady Is a Tramp" (from *BABES IN ARMS*)
   (*Music by* Richard Rodgers. *Lyrics by* Lorenz Hart.)
"Touch Me in the Morning"
   (*Music and Lyrics by* Ron Miller and Michael Masser.)
"One Love in My Lifetime"
   (*Music and Lyrics by* Larry Brown, Theresa McFaddin, Leonard Perry.)
"Smile" (Theme from film *MODERN TIMES*)
   (*Music by* Charles Chaplin. *Lyrics by* John Turner and Geoffrey Parsons.)
"Love Hangover"
   (*Music and Lyrics by* Pam Sawyer and Marilyn McLeod.)
"Girls"
   (*Music and Lyrics by* John Phillips.)
Medley from "THE POINT" (*Music and Lyrics by* Harry Nilsson.):
"Everybody's Got 'Em"/"Me and My Arrow"/"Lifeline"
"Lady Sings the Blues" (used in film of the same name)
   (*Music and Lyrics by* Billie Holiday and Herbie Nichols.)
"'Tain't Nobody's Bizness"
   (*Music and Lyrics by* Porter Grainger, Clarence Williams and Graham Prince.)
"(Aux Iles) Hawaii"
   (*Music and Lyrics by* Pascal Bastia and Jean Bastia.)
"Stormy Weather" (from *COTTON CLUB PARADE*, 22nd edition, 1933)
   (*Music by* Harold Arlen. *Lyrics by* Ted Koehler.)
"(I Need a Little) Sugar in My Bowl"
   (*Music and Lyrics by* C. Williams, D. Small, T. Brymn.)
"My Man" (from *ZIEGFELD FOLLIES OF 1921*)
   (*Music by* Maurice Yvain. *Lyrics by* Channing Pollock.)

ACT 2
Motown History
Supremes
Medley from *A CHORUS LINE*:
   "Play Me the Music" ("The Music and the Mirror"}, "What I Did for Love," "T & A" ("Dance: Ten, Looks: Three)
   (*Music by* Marvin Hamlisch. *Lyrics by* Edward Kleban.)
Theme from "Mahagony" ("Do You Know Where You're Going To?")
   (*Music and Lyrics by* Michael Masser and Gerry Goffin.)
"Ain't No Mountain High Enough"
   (*Music and Lyrics by* Nick Ashford and Valerie Simpson.)
"Reach Out and Touch"
   (*Music and Lyrics by* Nick Ashford and Valerie Simpson.)

1976.17
GODSPELL

A Musical in Two Acts[1]. Conceived and directed by John-Michael Tebelak. Based on The Gospel According to St. Matthew. Music and new lyrics by

Stephen Schwartz. Lighting by Spencer Mosse. Costumes by Susan Tsu. Production supervision by Nina Faso. Musical director, Stephen Reinhardt. Sound by Robert Minor. Conductor, Paul Shaffer. Associate producer, Charles Haid. Produced by Edgar Lansbury, Stuart Duncan, Joseph Beruh and The Shubert Organization. Opened 22 June 1976 at the Broadhurst Theatre, moved 15 September 1976 to the Plymouth Theatre, moved 12 January 1977 to the Ambassador Theatre and closed 4 September 1977 after 527 performances. (Total including Off-Broadway run, 2645 performances.)

CAST (in alphabetical order): Lamar Alford, Laurie Faso, Lois Faraker, Robin Lamont, Elizabeth Lathram, Bobby Lee, Tom Rolfing, Don Scardino, Marley Sims, Valerie Williams.

ACT 1
   "Tower of Babble"
      Company
   "Prepare Ye the Way of the Lord"
      T. Rolfing, Company
   "Save the People"
      D. Scardino, Company
   "Day By Day"
      R. Lamont, Company
   "Learn Your Lessons Well"
      M. Sims
   "Bless the Lord"
      V. Williams, Company
   "All For the Best"
      D. Scardino, T. Rolfing
   "All Good Gifts"
      L. Alford, Company
   "Light of the World"
      L. Faso, Company
ACT 2
   "Learn Your Lessons Well" (reprise)
      L. Alford, Company
   "Turn Back, O Man"
      L. Foraker, Company
   "Alas for You"
      D. Scardino
   "By My Side"
      E. Lathram, Company
      (*Music by* Peggy Gordon. *Lyrics by* Jay Hamburger.)
   "We Beseech Thee"
      B. Lee, Company
   "On the Willows"
      Band
   Finale
      Company

1976.18
THE MERRY WIDOW

The Australian Ballet in a ballet adaptation of the operetta in Three Acts, 4 Scenes. Music by Franz Lehàr. Original book by Victor Leon and Leo Stein. English version by Christopher Hassall[2]. Scenario and staging by Robert Helpmann. Choreography by Ronald Hynd. Design (scenery, costumes) by Desmond Heeley. Musical adaptation by John Lanchbery. Lighting supervised by John Gleason. Musical director, John Lanchbery. Conductors, Alan Barker, Alan Abbott. Produced by (Sol) Hurok Concerts Inc. in association with the Australian Ballet Foundation. Opened 22 June 1976 at the New York State Theatre and closed 3 July 1976 after 15 performances.

CAST (Principals, Soloists): *Baron Mirko Zeta*, Pontevedrian Ambassador to France: Robert Olup or Colin Peasley. *Valencienne*, his wife: MARIA LANG or Ai-Gul Gainina or Lucette Aldous. *Count Danilo Danilowitsch*, First Secretary of the Pontevedrian Embassy: JOHN MEEHAN or JONATHAN KELLY. *Camille de Rosillon*, French attaché at the Embassy: WALTER BOURKE or KELVIN COE. *Njegus*, Private Secretary to the Ambassador: RAY POWELL or ALAN ALDER. *Kromow*, Under-Secretary at the Embassy: Dale Baker or Rex McNeill. *Pritschitsch*, Under-Secretary at the Embassy: Mark Brinkley or Paul de Masson. *Hanna Glawari*, a wealthy

---

[1]Originally produced Off-Broadway 17 May 1971 at the Cherry Lane Theatre for 2118 performances.

[2]Christopher Hassall's new English libretto was first produced by the Sadler's Wells Opera in London in 1958 and has not otherwise been performed in New York. *THE MERRY WIDOW* was first produced in New York 21 October 1907 at the New Amsterdam Theatre for 416 performances.

Pontevedrian widow: MARGOT FONTEYN or MARILYN ROWE. *Pontevedrian Dancer*: Paul Saliba or Danilo Radojevic. *Maitre d' at Chez Maxime*: Paul Saliba.

Guests at the Embassy, Pontevedrians, Can Can Ladies, etc. (Artists): Glenda Allen, Stephen Baynes, Paul Cini, Amanda Clerke, Allan Cross, Michael Curry, Sheree da Costa, Irena Fogerty, Carol Green, Deborah Lerine, Angus Lugsdin, William Pepper, Terese Power, Danilo Radojevic, Martin Raistrick, Lucinda Sharp, Olga Tamara, Meryl Tankard, Nina Thomson, Dennis Trinder, Abril Ward.

The action takes place in Paris in 1905.

Act 1, Scene 1: An ante-room in the Pontevedrian Embassy. *Scene 2*: The ballroom in the Pontevedrian Embassy.

Act 2: The garden of Hanna's villa.

Act 3: Chez Maxime.

1976.19   PAL JOEY

A Revival of the Musical (Play) in Two Acts, 12 Scenes[3]. Book by John O'Hara (based on his collected short stories of the same name). Music by Richard Rodgers. Lyrics by Lorenz Hart. Scenery by John J. Moore. Costumes by Arthur Boccia. Lighting by Ron Wallace. Musical director, Scott Oakley. Choreography by Margo Sappington. Directed by Theodore Mann. Produced by the Circle in the Square Theatre (Theodore Mann, Artistic director; Paul Libin, Managing director). Opened 27 June 1976 at the Circle in the Square Theatre and closed 29 August 1976 after 73 performances[4].

CAST (in order of appearance): *Mike*: HAROLD GARY. *Joey Evans*: CHRISTO-PHER CHADMAN. *Kid*: Terri Treas. *Gladys*: JANIE SELL. *Gail*: Gail Benedict. *Murphy*: Murphy Cross. *Rosamund*: Rosamund Lynn. *Marilu*: Marilu Henner. *Debbie*: Deborah Geffner. *Linda English*: BONI ENTEN. *Vera Simpson*: JOAN COPELAND. *Gent*: David Hodo. *Ernest*: Austin Colyer. *Waldo, the Waiter*: Denny Martin Flinn. *Victor*: Michael Leeds. *Delivery Boy*: Kenn Scalice. *Louis, the Tenor*: Adam Petroski. *Melba (Snyder)*: DIXIE CARTER. *Ludlow Lowell*: JOE SIROLA. *O'Brien*: Ralph Farnworth.

Boys and Girls: Gail Benedict, Murphy Cross, Deborah Geffner, Marilu Henner, Rosamund Lynn, Terri Treas, Denny Martin Flinn, David Hodo, Michael Leeds, Kenn Scalice.

1976.20   LET MY PEOPLE COME

A Sexual Musical (Revue) in Two Acts[5]. Music and lyrics by Earl Wilson, Jr. Directed by Phil Oesterman. Choreography by Charles Augins. Set and lighting by Duane F. Mazey. Set and costumes supervised by Douglas W. Schmidt. Lighting supervised by John Gleason. Musical direction and vocal arrangements by Norman Bergen. Conductor, Glen Roven. Produced by Phil Oesterman. Opened 22 July 1976 at the Morosco Theatre and closed 2 October 1976 after 106 performances. (Total including Off-Broadway run, 1273 performances.)

CAST (in alphabetical order): Brandy Alexander, Joanne Baron, Dwight Baxter, Pat Cleveland, Lorraine Davidson, Joelle Erasme, Yvette Freeman, Paul Gillespie, Gloria Goldman, Tulane Howard II, Bob Jockers, Empress Kilpatrick, Dianne Legro, Allan Lozito, Bryan Miller, Rod R. Neves, Rozaa, Don Scotti, Sterling Saint-Jacques, Bryan Spencer, Dean Tait, Lori Wagner, Charles Whiteside.

ACT 1

Opening ("Screw")
   The Company

"Mirror"
   B. Spencer, G. Goldman, P. Gillespie, E. Kilpatrick, R. Neves, L. Wagner, T. Howard, J. Erasme, D. Tait, P. Cleveland, S. St. Jacques

"Whatever Turns You On"
   The Company

"Give It to Me"
   L. Davidson, L. Wagner

"Giving Life"
   E. Kilpatrick, B. Miller, P. Gillespie, R. Neves, L. Wagner, J. Erasme, D. Tait, P. Cleveland, S. St. Jacques

"The Ad"
   C. Whiteside

"Fellatio 101"
   A. Lozito, Students

"I'm Gay"
   B. Jockers, B. Miller, R. Neves, P. Gillespie

"Linda, Georgina, Marilyn & Me"
   J. Baron

"Dirty Words"
   The Company

"I Believe My Body"
   The Company

ACT 2

"The Showbusiness Nobody Knows"
   The Company

"Take Me Home With You"
   B. Miller

"Choir Practice"
   A. Lozito, Company

"And She Loved Me"
   Rozaa, E. Kilpatrick, L. Wagner, J. Erasme

"Poontang"
   The Company

"Come in My Mouth"
   E. Kilpatrick

"The Cunnilingus Champion of Co. C"
   B. Miller, P. Cleveland, J. Baron, C. Whiteside

"Doesn't Anybody Love Anymore"
   Roza

"Let My People Come"
   The Company

1976.21   GUYS AND DOLLS

A Revival of the Musical Fable of Broadway (Comedy) in Two Acts, 18 Scenes[6]. Book by Jo Swerling and Abe Burrows. Based on a story and characters by Damon Runyon. Music and lyrics by Frank Loesser. Directed and choreographed by Billy Wilson. Scenery by Tom H. John. Costumes by Bernard Johnson. Lighting by Thomas Skelton. (Musical) Arrangements and orchestrations by Danny Holgate, Horace Ott. Musical director, choral arranger, Howard Roberts. Sound design by Sander Hacker. Associate producers, Ashton Springer, Carmen F. Zollo. Entire production under the supervision of Abe Burrows. Produced by Moe Septee in association with Victor Potamkin, and in association with Frank Enterprises and Beresford Productions, Ltd. Opened 21 July 1976 at the Broadway Theatre and closed 13 February 1977 after 239 performances.

CAST (in order of appearance): *Nicely-Nicely Johnson*: KEN PAGE. *Benny Southstreet*: CHRISTOPHE PIERRE. *Rusty Charlie*: Sterling McQueen. *Sister Sarah Brown*: ERNESTINE JACKSON. *Harry the Horse*: John Russell. *Lieut. Brannigan*: CLARK MORGAN. *Nathan Detroit*: ROBERT GUILLAUME. *Angie the Ox*: Jymie Charles. *Miss Adelaide*: NORMA DONALDSON. *Sky Masterson*: JAMES RAN-DOLPH. *Arvide Abernathy*: EMETT 'BABE' WALLACE. *Agatha*: Irene Datcher. *Calvin*: Bardell Conner. *Martha*: Marion Moore. *Joey Biltmore*: Derrick Bell. *Master of Ceremonies*: Andy Torres. *Waiter*: Derrick Bell. *Mimi*: Prudence Darby. *General (Matilda B.) Cartwright*: EDYE BYRDE. *Big Jule*: Walter White. *Drunk*: Andy Torres.

The Guys: Derrick Bell, Toney Brealond, Jymie Charles, Bardell Conner, Nathan Jennings, Jr., Bill Mackey, Sterling McQueen, Andy Torres, Eddie Wright, Jr. *The Dolls*: Prudence Darby, Jacquelyn DuBois, Anna Maria Fowlkes, Helen Gelzer, Julia Lema, Jacqueline Smith-Lee.

---

[3]Originally produced in New York 25 December 1940 at the Ethel Barrymore Theatre for 374 performances. For Synopsis of Scenes and Musical Numbers, see original 1940 production. "What Is a Man" permanently replaced "Love Is My Friend" in Act 1, Scene 4; "Pal Joey" (What Do I Care for a Dame? sung by C. Chadman as Joey) added to Act 1, Scene 6 after "Bewitched."
[4]Orchestrations uncredited.
[5]Originally produced Off-Broadway 8 January 1974 at the Village Gate for 1167 performances. After the opening, the composer/lyricist and choreographer withdrew their names from the credits, and the running order of songs was substantially rearranged.

[6]First presented in New York 24 November 1950 at the 46th Street Theatre for 1200 performances. For Synopsis of Scenes and Musical Numbers, see original 1950 production. Act 1, Scene 8, now set in San Juan, Puerto Rico, and the accompanying dance now named "El Cafe Felicidad."

H.M.S. PINAFORE,
1976.22   or The Lass That Loved a Sailor

A Revival of the Comic Opera in Two Acts[7]. Libretto by William S. Gilbert. Music by Arthur Sullivan. Directed by Jack Eddleman. Choreographed by Thomas Andrew. Scenery and costumes by Patton Campbell. Lighting by Hans Sondheimer. Conductor, John Miner. Produced by the New York City Opera. Opened 3 September 1976 at the New York State Theatre and closed 26 September 1976 after 4 performances in repertory.

CAST: *The Rt. Hon. Sir Joseph Porter, K.C.B.,* First Lord of the Admiralty: JAMES BILLINGS. *Captain Corcoran,* Commander of the *H.M.S. Pinafore:* RICHARD FREDERICKS. *Ralph Rackstraw,* Able Seaman: GARY GLAZE. *Dick Deadeye,* Able Seaman: IRWIN DENSEN. *Bill Bobstay,* Boatswain: WILLIAM LEDBETTER. *Bob Becket:* Philip Steele. *Josephine,* the Captain's Daughter: GLENYS FOWLES. *Hebe,* Sir Joseph's First Cousin: PULI TORO. *Little Buttercup* (Mrs. Cripps), a Portsmouth bum-boat woman: MURIEL COSTA-GREENSPON.
     First Lord's Sisters, His Cousins, His Aunts, Sailors, Marines, etc.: New York City Opera Chorus.

DIE FLEDERMAUS
1976.23

A Revival of the Operetta in Three Acts[8]. Original Viennese libretto by Carl Haffner and Richard Genée. Lyrics by Richard Genée. (Based on the comedy "Le Réveillon" by Henri Meilhac and Ludovic Halévy.) English libretto by Ruth and Thomas Martin. Music by Johann Strauss. Production devised and directed by Gerald Freedman. Stage director, Richard Getke. Choreography by Thomas Andrew. Scenery designed by Lloyd Evans Costumes design by Theoni V. Aldredge. Lighting by Hans Sondheimer. Conducted by Imre Pallo. Chorus prepared by Judith Somogi. Produced by the New York City Opera. Opened 11 September 1976 at the New York State Theatre and closed 7 November 1976 after 4 performances in repertory; returned 26 February 1977 to the New York State Theatre and closed 30 April 1977 after 6 performances in repertory. Total, 10 performances this season.

CAST (in order of appearance): *Alfred,* an itinerant tenor: Gary Glaze. *Adele,* von Eisenstein's chambermaid: GIANNA ROLANDI. *Rosalinda von Eisenstein:* JOHANNA MEIER. *Gabriel von Eisenstein:* CHARLES ROE. *Dr. Blind,* a lawyer: Jerold Siena. *Dr. Falke,* a close friend of Eisenstein: THOMAS JAMERSON. *Frank,* the prison warden: SPIRO MALAS. *Sally,* Adele's sister: Diana Kehrig. *Ivan,* servant to Orlofsky: Jack Sims. *Prince Orlofsky,* a wealthy, bored Russian: DAVID RAE SMITH. *Frosch,* the jailer: James Billings. *Solo Dancers:* Sandra Balestracci, Esperanza Galan, Juliu Horvath. *Ensemble:* New York City Opera Chorus.

THE DEBBIE REYNOLDS SHOW
1976.24

A Musical Revue in Two Acts. Staged and choreographed by Ron Lewis. Musical conductor, Tom Nygaard. Sets by Billy Morris. Lighting by Jerry Grollnek. Costumes and gowns by Bob Mackie. Sound by Trevor Jordan. Producer, Robert Fallon. Produced by Raymax Productions. Opened 16 September 1976 at the Minskoff Theatre and closed 26 September 1976 after 13 performances.

CAST: DEBBIE REYNOLDS, Bruce Lea, Albert Stevenson, Ray Chabeau, Joel Blum, Louis McKay, Gene Myers, George Eiferman, Penny Worth, Dani McCormack, Steven Lardas.

ACT 1

"Gee, But It's Great to Be Here" (from *HAPPY HUNTING*)
     D. Reynolds, Cast
     (*Music by* Harold Karr. *Lyrics by* Matt Dubey.)
Medley:
"Reach Out and Touch Somebody's Hand"
          (*Music and Lyrics by* Nick Ashford and Valerie Simpson.)
"He's Got the Whole World in His Hands" (traditional)
"Touch a Hand"
"Higher and Higher"
     D. Reynolds, Cast
     (*Music and Lyrics by* Gary Lee Jackson, Carl W. Smith, Raynard Miner.)

Singers' Medley
     S. Lardas, P. Worth, D. McCormick
Film Sequence and Medley
     D. Reynolds
"I Ain't Down Yet" (from *THE UNSINKABLE MOLLY BROWN*)
     D. Reynolds
     (*Music and Lyrics by* Meredith Willson.)
Debbie's Salute to Show Business
     Entire Company
("When the Midnight Choo-Choo Leaves for Alabam'"/"Sweet Georgia Brown"/"Me and My Shadow")
ACT 2
IRENE Medley:
"Irene"
     (*Music by* Harry Tierney. *Lyrics by* Joseph McCarthy.)
"I'm Always Chasing Rainbows"
     (*Music by* Harry Carroll. *Lyrics by* Joseph McCarthy.)
"Alice Blue Gown"
     (*Music by* Harry Tierney. *Lyrics by* Joseph McCarthy.)
"You Made Me Love You"
     (*Music by* James Monaco. *Lyrics by* Joseph McCarthy.)
Premier Night Impressions
     D. Reynolds
Bicentennial Salute to America
     Entire Company

GOING UP!
1976.25

A Revival of the Uplifting Musical Comedy in Two Acts, 4 Scenes[9]. Book and lyrics by Otto Harbach. Based on the comedy "The Aviator" by James Montgomery. Music by Louis A. Hirsch. Directed by Bill Gile. Choreography and production numbers by Dan Siretta. Musical direction and vocal arrangements by Lynn Crigler. Costumes by David Toser. Scenic design and lighting supervision by Edward Haynes. Lighting by Peter M. Ehrhardt. Special consultant, Alfred Simon. Musical arranger, Russell Warner. A Goodspeed Opera House Production (Michael Price, Producer). Associate producer, James L. D. Roser. Produced by Ashton Springer, William Callahan, (Norman) Stephens-(Max) Weitzenhoffer Productions in association with Stephen R. Friedman and Irwin Meyer. Opened 19 September 1976 at the John Golden Theatre and closed 30 October 1976 after 49 performances.

CAST (in order of appearance): *Miss Zonne:* PAT LYSINGER. *Alex:* Calvin McRae. *Gus:* Larry Hyman. *John Gordon:* Stephen Bray. *Grace Douglas:* KIMBERLY FARR. *F. H. Douglas:* LEE H. DOYLE. *Jules Gaillard:* MICHAEL TARTEL. *Hopkinson Brown:* WALTER BOBBIE. *Madeline Manners:* MAUREEN BRENNAN. *James Brooks:* NOEL CRAIG. *Robert Street:* BRAD BLAISDELL. *Sam Robinson:* RONN ROBINSON. *Dwayne:* James Bontempo. *Faye:* Deborah Crowe. *Howell:* Michael Gallagher. *Ennis:* Teri Gill. *Mollie:* Barbara McKinley.

Act 1, *Scene 1:* The Gordon Inn Lobby, Lenox, Massachusetts, 1919 ... afternoon. *Scene 2:* The Smoking Room ... later that evening.

Act 2, *Scene 1:* The Terrace ... the same evening. *Scene 2:* An Airfield near the Gordon Inn ... six o'clock the next afternoon.

ACT 1
Scene 1
"Paging Mr. Street"
     P. Lysinger, S. Bray, Bellboys, Ensemble
"I Want a Determined Boy"
     M. Brennan, W. Bobbie, Four Aviators
"If You Look in Her Eyes"
     K. Farr, B. Blaisdell, M. Brennan
"Going Up"
     B. Blaisdell, Company
Scene 2
"Hello Frisco"[10]
     P. Lysinger, Four Aviators

---

[7]Originally presented in New York 15 January 1879 at the Standard Theatre for 175 performances. For Synopsis of Scenes and Musical Numbers, see original 1879 production.

[8]First English language production in New York 16 March 1885 at the Casino Theatre for 42 performances. First New York production of this adaptation 20 December 1950 at the Metropolitan Opera House. For Synopsis of Scenes and Musical Numbers, see May 1954 revival.

[9]Originally produced in New York 25 December 1917 at the Liberty Theatre for 351 performances.

[10]Originally in *ZIEGFELD FOLLIES OF 1915* (*Lyrics by* Gene Buck).

"Down, Up, Left, Right"
　B. Blaisdell, W. Bobbie, N. Craig, R. Robinson
"Kiss Me"
　K. Farr, M. Tartel
"(Everybody Ought To Do) The Tickle Toe"
　K. Farr, Ensemble

ACT 2
Scene 1

"(There's a) Brand New Hero"
　Ensemble
"I'll Think of You"[11]
　K. Farr, B. Blaisdell
"I'll Think of You" (reprise)
　K. Farr, B. Blaisdell

Scene 2

"Do It for Me"
　M. Brennan, W. Bobbie
"My Sumurun Girl"[12]
　P. Lysinger, R. Robinson
"Going Up"/"Down, Up, Left, Right"/"The Tickle Toe" (reprises)
　Company

1976.26 ## LA BELLE HÉLÈNE

A Revival of the Opéra-bouffe in Three Acts[13]. Original French libretto by Henri Meilhac and Ludovic Halévy. Music by Jacques Offenbach. English libretto by Geoffrey Dunn, revised by Julius Rudel. Production devised and directed by Jack Eddleman. Scenic designer, Lloyd Evans. Costume design by Patton Campbell. Lighting design by Hans Sondheimer. Choreography by Thomas Andrew. Conducted by Julius Rudel. Produced by the New York City Opera. Opened 21 September 1976 at the New York State Theatre and closed 29 October 1976 after 5 performances in repertory; returned 27 February 1977 to the New York State Theatre and closed 20 April 1977 after 4 performances in repertory. Total: 9 performances this season.

CAST (in order of appearance): Calchas, Grand Augur of Jupiter: RICHARD McKEE. Philocomos, his servant: Joaquin Romaguera. First Young Lady: Joan Campbell. Second Young Lady: Myrna Reynolds. Euthycles, a blacksmith: Don Yule. Helen, Queen of Sparta: KARAN ARMSTRONG. Daphne, Helen's attendant: Puli Toro. Orestes, Son of Agamemnon: DAVID GRIFFITH. Daughters of Joy (4): Jocanthis: Vicki Grof. Anthea: Valeria Orlando. Phantis: Madeleine Mines. Chloe: Joyce Tomanec. Paris, son of King Priam: HENRY PRICE. Ajax I, King of Salamis: JEROLD SIENA. Ajax II, King of the Lochrians: MELVIN LOWERY. Achilles, King of Phthiotis: JOHN LANKSTON. Menelaus, King of Sparta: JAMES BILLINGS. Agamemnon, King of the Kings: DAVID HOLLOWAY. Living statues: Sandra Balestracci, Mikhail Korogodsky.

Princes and Princesses, Courtiers, Mourners of Adonis, Helen's Attendants, Guards, People, Slaves, etc.: New York City Opera Chorus.

Act 1: The Oracle . . . Sparta, the Temple of Jupiter.

Act 2: The Siege of Paris . . . Queen Helen's Boudoir.

Act 3: The Caravel of Venus . . . The Beach at Nauplia.

ACT 1

Immortal Jupiter. (Introduction and Chorus)
　Chorus
It's Considered as a Moral Duty . . .
　K. Armstrong, Girls
We've Had a Night Out . . . (Couplets)
　D. Griffith, R. McKee, Chorus
Dear Calchas . . . (Melodrama)
　R. McKee
On Mount Ida . . . (The Judgement of Paris)
　H. Price (Paris)

The five kings of Greece now enter. (March and Entry of the Kings)
　Chorus
Our form is perfectly splendid . . . (Couplets)
　J. Siena, D. Griffith, R. McKee, M. Lowery, J. Lankston, J. Billings, D. Holloway
Our Queen is divinely glorious. (March reprise)
　Chorus
Crown him! Crown him! (Finale Act 1)
　Principals, Chorus

ACT 2

Tonight you must wear . . . (Opening Chorus)
　K. Armstrong, P. Toro, Girls
We all begin by truly trying. (Invocation to Venus)
　K. Armstrong
Now the four Kings introduce . . . (The Goose March)
　All
Let us garland ourselves with roses . . . (Couplets)
　D. Griffith
It is Heaven that has sent . . . (Duo/Duet of the Dream)
　K. Armstrong, H. Price (Paris)
A husband who . . . (Couplets/Finale Act 2)
　K. Armstrong, J. Billings, D. Holloway, H. Price, All

ACT 3

What fun! (Opening Chorus)
　Chorus
My dear, you're simply being spiteful! (Couplets)
　K. Armstrong
When all of Greece has been ravaged . . . (Patriotic Trio)
　D. Holloway, R. McKee, J. Billings
Near a fair Ionian island . . . (Chorus)
　Chorus
Are you a Spartan madrigal society . . . (Tyrolienne)
　H. Price (Paris), Chorus
Do you see?. . (Finale Act 3)
　K. Armstrong, J. Billings, D. Griffith, R. McKee, H. Price (Paris), All

1976.27 ## OH, CALCUTTA!

A Revival of the Musical Entertainment (Revue) in Two Acts, 11 Scenes[14]. Devised by Kenneth Tynan. Entire production conceived and directed by Jacques Levy. Contributors: Jules Feiffer, Dan Greenburg, Lenore Kandel, John Lennon, Jacques Levy, Leonard Melfi, David Newman and Robert Benton, Sam Shepard, Clovis Trouille, Kenneth Tynan, Sherman Yellen. Music and lyrics by (The Open Window) Robert Dennis, Peter Schickele, Stanley Walden. Additional music and lyrics by Stanley Walden and Jacques Levy. Choreography by Margo Sappington. Scenery by James Tilton. Lighting by Harry Silverglat. Costumes by Kenneth M. Yount, supervised by James Tilton. Projection media design by Gardner Compton. Musical director, Stanley Walden. Produced by Hillard Elkins, Norman Kean and Robert S. Fishko. Opened 24 September 1976 at the Edison Theatre and closed 6 August 1989 after 5959 performances[15].

CAST (in alphabetical order): Haru Aki, Jean Andalman, Bill Bass, Dorothy Chansky, Cress Darwin, John Hammil, William Knight, Cy Moore, Coline Morse, Pamela Pilkenton.

ACT 1
Scene 1

Taking Off the Robe ("Oh! Calcutta!")
　The Company

Scene 2

"Will Answer All Sincere Replies" (Song and Sketch)
　Sue Ellen: D. Chansky. Dale: J. Hammil. Monte: W. Knight. Cherie: J. Andalman.

---

[11]Originally in THE RAINBOW GIRL (Lyrics by Rennold Wolf.)
[12]Originally in THE WHIRL OF SOCIETY (Lyrics by Al Jolson.)
[13]Originally produced in New York in French 26 March 1868 at the French Theatre for 5 weeks; in English 13 April 1868 as PARIS AND HELEN, OR THE GREEK ELOPEMENT at the New York Theatre. Musical numbers did not appear in the program, above list prepared from published libretto.

[14]Originally produced in New York Off-Broadway 17 June 1969 at the Eden Theatre for 710 performances; transferred to Broadway 25 February 1971 at the Belasco Theatre for an additional 606 performances.
[15]From 24 September–7 December 1976 performances alternated with ME AND BESSIE.

Scene 3

Rock Garden

Man: W. Knight. *Boy:* C. Darwin.
(*Scene:* Saturday afternoon, just after lunch before the ball game.)

Scene 4

Delicious Indignities, (or The Deflowering of Helen Axminster)

Helen: D. Chansky. *Alfred:* W. Knight.
(*Scene:* An Elegantly Appointed Study in Knightsbridge, 1896.)

Scene 5

"Paintings of Clovis Trouille"

Clovis Trouille, now in his 80's, is one of France's most distinguished living painters. He has been painting in the mainstream of surrealism for the past half century.

"Much Too Soon"

C. Darwin
(*Music and Lyrics by* The Open Window and Jacques Levy.)

"Dance for George"

Danced by P. Pilkenton
(Dedicated to the memory of the late George Welbes.)

Scene 6

"Suite for Five Letters"

J. Hammil, W. Knight, D. Chansky, J. Andalman, P. Pilkenton

Scene 7

One on One

H. Aki, B. Bass

"Clarence"

J. Andalman

ACT 2[16]

Scene 1

"Jack & Jill" (Song and Sketch)

P. Pilkenton, J. Hammil

Scene 2

"Spread Your Love Around"

J. Andalman

"Love Lust Poem"

P. Pilkenton, H. Aki

Scene 3

Was It Good For You Too? ("Green Pants," "I Like the Look")

(*Perlmutter:* C. Darwin. *Interviewer:* H. Aki. *Dr. Bronson:* J. Andalman. *Dr. Jaspers:* W. Knight. *Nurse:* P. Pilkenton. *Attendant:* B. Bass. *Woman:* D. Chansky. *Gypsies:* J. Hammil, H. Aki. *Gypsy Dog:* G. Grover Lightstone. *Scene:* A Doctor's Office.)

Scene 4

"Coming Together, Going Together"

The Company

1976.28   PORGY AND BESS

A Revival of the Folk Opera in Three Acts, 9 Scenes[17]. Book by DuBose Heyward adapted from the play "Porgy" by DuBose and Dorothy Heyward. Music by George Gershwin. Lyrics by DuBose Heyward and Ira Gershwin. Production directed by Jack O'Brien. Sets by Robert Randolph. Additional scenic elements for Kittiwah Island designed by John Rothgeb. Costumes by Nancy Potts. Lighting by Gilbert V. Hemsley, Jr. Musical director and choral director, John DeMain. Choreographer and assistant director, Mabel Robinson. Assistant director, Helaine Head. Production coordinator, M. Jane Weaver. Assistant conductor, Ross Reimueller. Associate conductor, Clay Fullum. Produced by Sherwin M. Goldman and the Houston Grand

---

[16]The running order was frequently altered during the run. Added during run to Act 2:

"Playin'"

J. Hammil

Four in Hand (Sketch restored from Off-Broadway production)

[17]First produced in New York 10 October 1935 at the Alvin Theatre for 124 performances. For Synopsis of Scenes and Musical Numbers, see original 1935 production. This production was performed in Two Acts, with the interval after "What You Want Wid Bess?" (Act 2, Scene 2 in the original). "Buzzard Song" reinstated to Act 1, after "I Got Plenty of Nuttin'."

Opera. Opened 25 September 1976 at the Uris Theatre, moved 7 December 1976 to the Mark Hellinger Theatre and closed 9 January 1977 after 122 performances.

CAST (in order of appearance): *Jasbo Brown:* Ross Reimueller. *Clara:* BETTY D. LANE. *Mingo:* Bernard Thacker. *Jake:* Curtis Dickson. *Sportin' Life:* LARRY MAR-SHALL. *Robbins:* Glover Parham. *Serena:* WILMA SHAKESNIDER or DELORES IVORY-DAVIS. *Jim:* Hartwell Mace. *Peter:* Mervin Wallace. *Lily:* Myra Merritt. *Maria:* CAROL BRICE. *Scipio:* Alex Carrington. *Porgy:* DONNIE RAY ALBERT, ABRAHAM LIND-OQUENDO or ROBERT MOSLEY. *Crown:* ANDREW SMITH or GEORGE ROBERT MERRITT. *Bess:* CLAMMA DALE, ESTHER HINDS or IRENE OLIVER. *Policeman:* William Gammon. *Detective:* Hansford Rowe. *Undertaker:* Cornel Richie. *Annie:* Shirley Baines. *Frazier:* Raymond Bazemore. *Strawberry Woman:* Phyllis Bash. *Crab Man:* Steven Alex-Cole. *Coroner:* John B. Ross.

Ensemble (Residents of Catfish Row): John D. Anthony, Shirley Baines, Earl Baker, Phyllis Bash, Kenneth Bates, Raymond Bazemore, Barbara Buck, Steven Alex-Cole, Ella Eure, Wilhelmenia Fernandez, Elizabeth Graham, Earl Grandison, Kenneth Hamilton, Betty Harris, Loretta Holkmann, Alma Johnson, Cora Johnson, Roberta Long, Hartwell Mace, Patricia McDermott, Myra Merritt, Naomi Moody, Glover Parham, William Penn, Dwight Ransom, Cornel Richie, Rodrick Ross, Alexander B. Smalls, Bernard Thacker, Mervin Wallace, Barbara Ann Webb, Wardell Woodard, Denice Woods, Barbara L. Young.

1976.29   SIAMSA

A Folk Entertainment in Two Acts by the National Folk Theatre of Ireland[18]. Devised and directed by Pat Ahern. Design consultant, Lona Moran. Choreography by Patricia Hanafin. Wardrobe supervisor, Phyllis O'Donoghue. Technical director, Bernard Brannigan. Produced by (Robert P.) Brannigan-(Charles) Eisler Performing Arts International, Inc. Opened 27 September 1976 at the Palace Theatre and closed 2 October 1976 after 8 performances.

CAST: *The Merrymaker:* Sean O'Mahony. *The Gardener:* Liam Heaslip. *The Shoemaker:* Sean Ahern. *Solo Dancers:* Patricia Hanafin, Jimmy Smith, Jerry Nolan, John McCarthy. *Solo Singers:* Mary Deady, Sean Ahern, Liam Heaslip, Sean O'Mahony. *Folk Dancers:* Philomena Daly, Susan Rohan, Catherine Hurley, Michael O'Shea, Aidan O'Carroll. *Children:* Mary Lyons, Marie O'Donoghue, Sandra O'Reilly, Catherine Spangler, Sean Heaslip, Oliver Hurley, John Fitzgerald. *Musicians:* Pat Kennington, Gerard Buckley, Nicholas McAuliffe, Timmy O'Shea, Pierce Heaslip, Audrey O'Carroll.

ACT 1

"Samhra"—Summertime

Dawn is breaking on a summer's morning over a simple Irish homestead. The people are going about their various chores. The barefoot children are off through the fields to gather wild flowers, or maybe to pick up a tune from the local merrymaker .... They might rob an orchard, that is if the gardener and his helper aren't looking, but there's always the chance of a little help from the daughter of the house ... The farmer has his calves to feed, but for his wife the hens come first ... There's a wandering shoemaker, with a song of a bird's nest in the thatch. The neighbors enjoy the beat of his hammer but soon it's milking time and the cows come home.

Darkness falls, the time for a love song and traditional bonfire revelry. In pagan times fire ceremonies were performed at "Bealtaine" on the eve of May Day. The cattle were driven between two fires to be purified by the smoke and preserved from disease. Each person brought a stick for the fire and the menfolk leaped through the flames. The final scene recalls those ancient forms of fire worship.

ACT 2

Scene 1

"Cois Teallaigh"—by the Fireside

The neighbors quietly gather for an evening's merriment by the open hearth. There are love songs and country dances. There is the traditional blessing of the butter churn and the making of the butter. In those days it was regarded as a token of bad luck if each visitor to the house did not take part in the butter-making. Everybody had to take a turn at the dash of the churn.

---

[18]SIAMSA (pronounced Shee-am-sa) is a folk entertainment which recaptures the spirit of the age in Ireland when Irish was the spoken language, the age from which Ireland inherited her great treasures of folk music and song. It aims to show something of the simple way of life of the people who gave her that heritage.

Scene 2

"Casadh an Sugain"—The Twisting of the Rope

A journeyman poet makes himself welcome at the half-door. The young girl plying the spinning wheel attracts his attention and he falls in lvoe with her. All goes well until her father and grandmother disapprove. They devise a plan to get him out. They put him twisting a new rope of hay so that he "twists" himself out of the house—never to return. Incidentally, the floors of the old houses were ususally made of caked mud. So, very often, the half-door was taken down to provide a platform for the stepdancers.

Scene 3

"Siamsa an Fomhair"—A Harvest Merrymaking

Set in the days of the singing scythe, the flying flail and the threshing floor, this scene portrays the older methods of cutting and threshing the corn. The "flail" was the instrument used to beat the corn from the sheaves. The straw was kept for the day of the thatching or the day of the "scollops." A scollop is a piece of stick about the length of a man's arm and pointed at both ends. It is used to secure the fresh straw on a thatched roof.

A day's thatching has left our thatcher tired and weary by evening time. The soft crooning of a young women's song as she tends him on the rooftop puts him to sleep. What happens next is something of a nightmare and he is very much relieved in the end to find it was all a dream. *SIAMSA* concludes with a Harvest Dance Festival.

1976.30 THE ROBBER BRIDEGROOM

A Revival of the (Country-Folk) Musical in One Act[19]. Book and lyrics by Alfred Uhry. Based on the novella of the same name by Eudora Welty. Music composed and arranged by Robert Waldman. Directed by Gerald Freedman. Choreography by Donald Saddler. Settings designed by Douglas W. Schmidt. Costumes designed by Jeanne Button. Lighting designed by David F. Segal. Associate producer, Porter Van Zandt. Produced by John Houseman, Margot Harley, Michael B. Kapon by arrangement with The Acting Company. Originally staged by the Musical Theatre Lab at St. Clement's. Opened 9 October 1976 at the Biltmore Theatre and closed 13 February 1977 after 145 performances.

CAST (in order of appearance): *Jamie Lockhart*, a gentleman robber: BARRY BOST-WICK. *Clement Musgrove*, a rich planter: STEPHEN VINOVICH. *Rosamund*, his daughter: RHONDA COULLET. *Salome*, his second wife: BARBARA LANG. *Little Harp*, a robber: LAWRENCE JOHN MOSS. *Big Harp*, the head of a robber: Ernie Sabella. *Goat*, a simpleton: Trip Plymale. *Goat's Mother*: Susan Berger. *Airie*: Jana Schneider. *A Raven*: Carolyn McCurry.

The Residents of Rodney: Kyle Nunnery: George DeLoy. *Harmon Harper*: Gary Epp. *Norman Ogelsby*: B. J. Hardin. *Queenie Brenner*: Mary Murray. *Rose Otto*: Melinda Tanner. *Gerry K. Summers*: Dennis Warning. *K. K. Pone*: Tom Westerman.

The action takes place in and around Rodney, Mississippi.

MUSICAL NUMBERS[20]

"Once Upon the Natchez Trace"
    The Company
"Suddenly the Day Looks Sunny"
    B. Bostwick
"Two Heads"
    E. Sabella, L. J. Moss
"Steal With Style"
    B. Bostwick
"Rosamund's Dream"
    R. Coullet
"The Pricklepear Bloom"
    B. Lang
"Nothin' Up"
    R. Coullet
"Deeper in the Woods"
    The Company

"Riches"
    S. Vinovich, B. Bostwick, B. Lang, R. Coullet
"Little Piece of Sugar Cane"
    B. Bostwick, Company
"Love Stolen"
    B. Bostwick
"Poor Tied Up Darlin'"
    L. J. Moss, T. Plymale
"Mean as a Snake"
    C. McCurry
"Goodbye Salome"
    The Company
"Sleepy Man"
    R. Coullet
"Where Oh Where (Is My Baby Darlin'?)"
    B. Bostwick, S. Vinovich, R. Coullet
"Pass Her Along"
    The Company
Finale
    B. Bostwick, Company

1976.31 THE SAINT OF BLEECKER STREET

A Revival of the Opera (Musical Drama) in Three Acts, 5 Scenes[21]. Music and libretto by Gian-Carlo Menotti. Conducted by Cal Stewart Kellogg. Directed by Francis Rizzo. Sets designed by Beeb Salzer. Costumes designed by Carol Luiken. Choreography by Thomas Andrew. Lighting by Hans Sondheimer. Chorus prepared by Conoley Ballard. Produced by the New York City Opera. Opened 5 November 1976 at the New York Stae Theatre and closed 10 November 1976 after 3 performances in repertory.

CAST (in order of appearance): *Assunta*: Jane Shaulis. *A Young Man*: Howard Hensel. *Maria Corona*: Judith De Rosa. *Her Son*: Ron Boucher. *Carmela*: Diana Soviero. *A Young Woman*: Diana Kehrig. *Don Marco*: Irwin Densen. *Annina*: CATHERINE MALFITANO. *Michele*: ENRICO diGIUSEPPE. *Concettina*: Danielle Brisebois. *Desideria*: JEANNE PILAND. *First Guest*: Jerold Siena. *Second Guest*: Alan Baker. *Salvatore*: William Ledbetter. *Bartender*: Don Henderson. *A Nun*: Charlott Thyssen. *A Young Priest*: Ronald Kelley. *Neighbors*: Kenn Dovel, James Sergi. *Neighbors, Friends, Policemen, etc.*: New York City Opera Chorus.

1976.32 BING CROSBY ON BROADWAY

A Musical Entertainment (Revue) in Two Acts. Staged and directed by Robert Sidney. (Settings and costumes uncredited.) Lighting by Martin Aronstein. Produced by William Loeb. Presented by Robert Paterson. Opened 7 December 1976 at the Uris Theatre and closed 19 December 1976 after 12 performances.

CAST: BING CROSBY, ROSEMARY CLOONEY, JOE BUSHKIN, JOE BUSHKIN QUARTET, Kathryn Crosby, Harry Crosby III, Mary-Frances Crosby, Nathaniel Crosby, Ted Rogers, Billy Byers Orchestra.

MUSICAL NUMBERS[22]

"Where the Blue of the Night (Meets the Gold of the Day)"
    (*Music and Lyrics by* Roy Turk, Bing Crosby and Fred E. Ahlert.)
"The Pleasure of Your Company" (from *THE GOOD COMPANIONS*, London)
    (*Music by* Andre Previn. *Lyrics by* Johnny Mercer.)
"Mary Lou"
    (*Music and Lyrics by* George Waggner, J. Russell Robinson and Abe Lyman.)
"Where the Morning Glories Grow"
    (*Music by* Richard A. Whiting. *Lyrics by* Raymond B. Egan and Gus Kahn.)
"At My Time of Life" (from *GREAT EXPECTATIONS*, London)
    (*Music by* Cyril Ornadel. *Lyrics by* Hal Shaper.)
"On a Slow Boat to China"
    B. Crosby, R. Clooney
    (*Music and Lyrics by* Frank Loesser.)

---

[19]Originally produced by the Acting Company in New York 7 October 1975 at the Harkness Theatre for 15 performances.
[20]For subsequent national tour, an intermission was added after "Love Stolen."

[21]Originally produced in New York 27 December 1954 at the Broadway Theatre for 92 performances. For Synopsis of Scenes, see original 1954 production.
[22]Not in performance order.

"By Myself" (from *BETWEEN THE DEVIL*)
  R. Clooney
  (*Music by* Arthur Schwartz. *Lyrics by* Howard Dietz.)
"Tenderly"
  R. Clooney
  (*Music and Lyrics by* Jack Lawrence and Walter Gross.)
"Fifty Ways to Leave Your Lover"
  (*Music and Lyrics by* Paul Simon.)
"Send in the Clowns" (from *A LITTLE NIGHT MUSIC*)
  (*Music and Lyrics by* Stephen Sondheim.)
"Gone Fishing"
  (*Music and Lyrics by* Nick and Charles Kenny.)
"Now You Has Jazz" (from *HIGH SOCIETY*, film)
  (*Music and Lyrics by* Cole Porter.)
"The Man That Got Away" (from *A STAR IS BORN*, film)
  (*Music by* Harold Arlen. *Lyrics by* Ira Gershwin.)
"Hallelujah!" (from *HIT THE DECK*)
  (*Music by* Vincent Youmans. *Lyrics by* Leo Robin and Clifford Grey.)
"Sing (Sing a Song)"
  (*Music and Lyrics by* Joe Raposo.)
"You've Got a Friend"
  (*Music and Lyrics by* Carole King.)
"My Cup Runneth Over" (from *I DO! I DO!*)
  (*Music by* Harvey Schmidt. *Lyrics by* Tom Jones.)
"Play a Simple Melody" (from *WATCH YOUR STEP*)
  (*Music and Lyrics by* Irving Berlin.)
Family Medley of Songs
  (arranged by Ken and Mitzie Welch.)
"The Way We Were" (from *THE WAY WE WERE*, film)
  (*Music by* Marvin Hamlisch. *Lyrics by* Marilyn and Alan Bergman.)
"Love Me With All Your Heart"
  (*Music and Lyrics by* Mario and Carlos Rigual, Carlos Martinoli and M. Vaughn.)
"Just One of Those Things" (from *JUBILEE*)
  R. Clooney
  (Music and Lyrics by Cole Porter.)
"A Song for You"
  (*Music and Lyrics by* Leon Russell.)
Crosby Medley
"That's What Life Is All About"
  (*Music and Lyrics by* Les Reed, Bing Crosby, Peter Dacre, Ken Barnes.)

1976.33   MUSIC IS

A Musical in Two Acts, 14 Scenes and a Prologue. Book by George Abbott. Based on William Shakespeare's comedy "Twelfth Night." Music by Richard Adler. Lyrics by Will Holt. Directed by George Abbott. Musical numbers and dances staged by Patricia Birch. Musical director, Paul Gemignani. Orchestrations by Hershy Kay. Dance and vocal arrangements by William Cox. Scenery designed by Eldon Elder. Costumes by Lewis D. Rampino. Lighting by H. R. Poindexter. Assistant director, Judith Abbott. Additional (musical) arrangements by Jim Tyler. Originally premiered at the Seattle Repertory Theatre. Produced by Richard Adler, Roger Berlind, Edward R. Downe, Jr. Opened 20 December 1976 at the St. James Theatre and closed 26 December 1976 after 8 performances.

CAST (in order of appearance): *William Shakespeare*: DANIEL BEN-ZALI. *Valentine*: WILLIAM McCLARY. *Duke Orsino*: DAVID HOLLIDAY. *Curio*: DAVID BRUMMEL. *Viola*: CATHERINE COX. *Captain*: PAUL MICHAEL. *Clown*: William Shakespeare. *Maria*: LAURA WATERBURY. *Sir Toby Belch*: DAVID SABIN. *Malvolio*: CHRISTOPHER HEWETT. *Olivia*: SHERRY MATHIS. *Antonio*: MARC JORDAN. *Sebastian*: JOEL HIGGINS. *Sir Andrew Aguecheek*: JOE PONAZECKI. *First Officer*: DAVID BRUMMEL. *Second Officer*: Doug Carfrae. *Cupids*: Helena Andreyko, Ann Crowley. *Court Musicians*: Donald Hettinger (reeds), Steve Uscher (guitar).

  Members of the Court: Helena Andreyko, Doug Carfrae, Jim Corti, Ann Crowley, Dennis Daniels, Dawn Herbert, Dana Kyle, Wayne Mattson, Jason McAuliffe, Carolann Page, Susan Elizabeth Scott, Denny Shearer, Melanie Vaughan, Mimi B. Wallace.

Act 1, Scene 1: Orsino's Garden. *Scene 2*: The Seacoast. *Scene 3*: Orsino's Garden. *Scene 4*: The Seacoast. *Scene 5*: Olivia's Garden. *Scene 6*: Olivia's Orchard. *Scene 7*: Orsino's Palace.

Act 2, Scene 1: Street with a Tailor Shop. *Scene 2*: A Haystack near Olivia's House. *Scene 3*: Olivia's Orchard. *Scene 4*: A Room in Olivia's House. *Scene 5*: Corridor— Malvolio's Bedroom. *Scene 6*: Olivia's Bedroom. *Scene 7*: Front of Olivia's House.

ACT 1
  Prologue
    "Music Is"
      D. Ben-Zali, Company
  Scene 1
    "When First I Saw My Lady's Face"
      D. Holliday
  Scene 2
    "Lady's Choice"
      C. Cox, P. Michael
  Scene 3
    "The Time Is Ripe for Loving"
      Company
    "Should I Speak of Loving You"
      C. Cox
    Dance for Six
      H. Andreyko, A. Crowley, M. B. Wallace, D. Shearer, D. Daniels, J. Corti
  Scene 4
    "Hate to Say Goodbye to You"
      M. Jordan, J. Higgins
  Scene 5
    "Big Bottom Betty"
      D. Ben-Zali
    "Twenty One Chateaux"
      C. Cox, S. Mathis, Company
    "Sudden Lilac"
      S. Mathis
  Scene 6
    "Sing Hi"
      D. Sabin, J. Ponazecki, D. Ben-Zali, L. Waterbury
  Scene 7
    Dance: "Blindman's Buff"
      C. Cox, D. Holliday, Company

ACT 2
  Scene 1
    "The Tennis Song"
      D. Holliday, W. McClary, Company
  Scene 2
    "I Am It"
      C. Hewett
  Scene 3
    "No Matter Where"
      S. Mathis, C. Cox
    "The Duel"
      D. Sabin, C. Cox, J. Ponazecki, D. Ben-Zali
  Scene 4
    "Please Be Human"
      S. Mathis, J. Higgins
  Scene 7
    "What You Will"
      D. Ben-Zali, Entire Company

BARRY MANILOW ON BROADWAY

1976.34

A Musical Revue in Two Acts. Special material by Bruce Sussman. Orchestrations by Gerald Alters. Choreography by Barry Manilow and Lady Flash. Lighting designer, Michael Newton-Brown, supervised by Spencer Mosse. Sound engineer, John Venable. Mr. Manilow's clothes by Patrick Elliott. Lady Flash's clothes by Arthur Boccia. Staging consultant, Jack Hofsiss. Production coordinator, Rick Gross. Produced by Lee Guber, Shelly Gross and Miles Lourie. Opened 21 December 1976 at the Uris Theatre and closed 2 January 1977 after 12 performances.

CAST: BARRY MANILOW, Lady Flash (Debra Byrd, Reparata, Monica Buruss); The City Rhythm Band (Lee Gurst, Alan Axelrod, Keith Loving, Steven Donaghey, Harold 'Ricardo' Alexander).

MUSICAL NUMBERS[23]

---

[23]Not in performance order.

"Riders to the Stars"
  (*Music and Lyrics by* Barry Manilow and Adrienne Anderson.)
"Why Don't We Live Together"
  (*Music and Lyrics by* Peter Thom and Phil Galston.)
"Looks Like We Made It"
  (*Music and Lyrics by* Richard Kerr and Will Jennings.)
"New York City Rhythm"
  (*Music and Lyrics by* Barry Manilow and Marty Panzer.)
A Very Strange Medley:
  "Kentucky Fried Chicken"
    (*Music and Lyrics by* Al Gorgioni and Rob Nolan.)
  "State Farm Insurance"
    (*Music and Lyrics by* Barry Manilow and Jerry Gavin.)
  "Stridex"
    (*Music and Lyrics by* Barry Manilow.)
  "Band-Aids"
    (*Music and Lyrics by* Barry Manilow.)
  "Bowlene"
    (*Music and Lyrics by* Barry Manilow and Lois Wise.)
  "Dr. Pepper"
    (*Music and Lyrics by* Randy Newman and Jake Holmes.)
  "Pepsi"
    (*Music and Lyrics by* Ellen Starr and Joe McNeil.)
  "McDonalds"
    (*Music and Lyrics by* Kevin Gavin and Sid Woloshin.)
Jump Shout Boogie Medley:
  "Jump Shout Boogie"
    (*Music and Lyrics by* Barry Manilow and Bruce Sussman.)
  "Avenue C"
    (*Music and Lyrics by* B. Clayton, Jon Hendricks and Dave Lambert.)
  "Jumpin' at the Woodside"
    (*Music and Lyrics by* Jon Hendricks and Count Basie.)
  "Cloudburst"
    (*Music and Lyrics by* Leroy Kirkland, Jimmy Harris and Jon Hendricks.)
  "Bandstand Boogie" (*Music and Lyrics by* C. Albertine, Bob Horn, Les Elgart,
    Larry Elgart, Barry Manilow, Bruce Sussman.)
"This One's for You"
  (*Music and Lyrics by* Barry Manilow and Marty Panzer.)
"Beautiful Music"
  (*Music and Lyrics by* Barry Manilow and Marty Panzer.)
"Daybreak"
  (*Music and Lyrics by* Barry Manilow and Adrienne Anderson.)
"Lay Me Down"
  (*Music and Lyrics by* Larry Weiss.)
"Weekend in New England"
  (*Music and Lyrics by* Randy Edelman.)
"Studio Musician"
  (*Music and Lyrics by* Rupert Holmes.)
"Could It Be Magic"
  (*Music and Lyrics by* Barry Manilow, Adrienne Anderson and F. Chopin.)
"Mandy"
  (*Music and Lyrics by* Scott English and Richard Kerr.)
"It's a Miracle"
  (*Music and Lyrics by* Barry Manilow and Marty Panzer.)
"It's Just Another New Year's Eve"
  (*Music and Lyrics by* Barry Manilow and Marty Panzer.)
"I Write the Songs"
  (*Music and Lyrics by* Bruce Johnson.)

YOUR ARMS TOO SHORT
1976.35   ## TO BOX WITH GOD

A Gospel Music in One Act. Conceived from the Book of Matthew by Vinnette Carroll. Music and lyrics by (Professor) Alex Bradford. Additional music and lyrics by Micki Grant. Directed by Vinnette Carroll. Choreography by Talley Beatty. Sets and costumes by William Schroder. Set supervisor, Michael J. Hotopp. Lighting by Gilbert V. Hemsley, Jr. Orchestrations and dance music by H. B. Barnum. Choral arrangements and direction by Chapman Roberts. Developed by the Urban Arts Corp for the Festival of Two Worlds, Spoleto, Italy, Summer 1975. A Ford's Theatre Production. Produced by Frankie Hewitt and The Shubert Organization in association with Theater Now, Inc. Opened 22 December 1976 at the Lyceum Theatre and closed 1 January 1978 after 429 performances.

CAST: SALOME BEY, CLINTON DERRICKS-CARROLL, DAVID ST. CHARLES, SHEILA ELLIS, DELORES HALL, WILLIAM HARDY, JR., HECTOR

JAIME MERCADO, MABEL ROBINSON, WILLIAM THOMAS, JR., Deborah Lynn Bridges, Sharon Brooks, Thomas Jefferson Fouse, Jr., Michael Gray, Cardell Hall, Bobby Hill, Lidell Jackson, Edna Krider, Leon Washington, Marilyn Winbush.
ACT 1
  "Beatitudes"
    Company
  "We're Gomnna Have a Good Time"
    C. Derricks-Carroll, Company
  "There's a Stranger in Town"
    C. Derricks-Carroll, B. Hill, Company
  "Do You Know Jesus?"/"He's a Wonder"
    T. J. Fouse, Jr., Company
  "Just a Little Bit of Jesus Goes a Long Way"
    D. Hall, Company
  "We Are the Priests and Elders"
    W. Hardy, Jr., C. Derricks-Carroll, B. Hill, M. Gray
  "Something Is Wrong in Jerusalem"
    S. Bey, M. Robinson, Company
  "It Was Alone"
    W. Thomas, Jr., D. St. Charles
  "I Ain't Had My Fill"
    C. Derricks-Carroll, D. St. Charles
  "Be Careful Whom You Kiss"
    S. Bey, Company
  "I Know I Have to Leave Here"
    W. Hardy, Jr., Company
  "It's Too Late"
    Company
  Judas Dance
    H. J. Mercado
  "Your Arms Too Short to Box With God"
    D. Hall, Company
  "Give Us Barrabas"
    Company
  "See How They Done My Lord"
    S. bBey, Company
  "Come On Down"
    S. Ellis, C. Derricks-Carroll, M. Gray
  "That's What the Bible Say"
    M. Gray, Company
  "Were You There When They Crucified My Lord?"
    S. Bey
  "Can't No Grave Hold My Body Down"
    B. Hill, Company
  "Beatitudes:" (reprise)
    B. Hill, Company
  "Didn't I Tell You"
    W. Hardy, Jr., Company
  "When the Power Comes"
    W. Hardy, Jr., Company
  "As Long As I Live"
    S. Bey
  "Everybody Has His Own Way"
    C. Derricks-Carroll, M. Gray, T. J. Fouse, Jr.
  "I Love You So Much Jesus"
    D. Hall
  "I Left My Sins Behind Me"
    D. Hall, Company
  "On That Day"
    C. Derricks-Carroll, T. J. Fouse, Jr., B. Hill, M. Gray
  "The Band"
    W. Hardy, Jr., Company

1976.36   ## FIDDLER ON THE ROOF

A Revival of the Musical in Two Acts, a Prologue and 18 Scenes[24]. Book by Joseph Stein. Based on stories by Sholom Aleichem's stories (Tevye's

---

[24]Originally produced in New York 22 September 1964 at the Imperial Theatre for 3242 performances. For Synopsis of Scenes and Musical Numbers, see original 1964 production.

Daughters) by special permission of Arnold Perl. Music by Jerry Bock. Lyrics by Sheldon Harnick. Entire production directed and choreographed by Jerome Robbins. Direction reproduced by Ruth Mitchell. Choreography reproduced by Tom Abbott. Settings by Boris Aronson. Costumes by Patricia Zipprodt. Lighting by Ken Billington. Orchestrations by Don Walker. Musical direction by Milton Rosenstock. Vocal arrangements by Milton Greene. Dance music arranged by Betty Walberg. Originally produced by Harold Prince. Produced by The Shubert Orgzanization and Nederlander Producing Company of America, and the John F. Kennedy Center for the Performing Arts, in association with Theatre Now, Inc. Opened 28 December 1976 at the Winter Garden and closed 21 May 1977 after 167 performances.

CAST (in order of appearance): *Tevye*, the Dairyman: ZERO MOSTEL. *Golde*, his wife: THELMA LEE. *Their Five Daughters: Tzeitel*: ELIZABETH HALE. *Hodel*: CHRISTOPHER CALLAN. *Chava*: Nancy Tompkins. *Shprintze*: Davia Sacks. *Beilke*: Tiffany Bogart. *Yente*, the Matchmaker: RUTH JAROSLOW. *Motel*, the Tailor: IRWIN PEARL. *Perchik*, the Student: JEFF KELLER. *Mordcha*, the Innkeeper: Leon Spelman. *Lazar Wolf*, the Butcher: Paul Lipson. *Rabbi*: Charles Mayer. *Mendel*, his son: Paul A. Corman. *Avram*, the Bookseller: Merrill Plaskow II. *Nachum*, the Beggar: David Masters. *Grandma Tzeitel*: Duane Bodin. *Fruma Sarah*: Joyce Martin. *Constable*: Alexander Orfaly. *Fyedka*: Rick Friesen. *Shandel*, Motel's Mother: Jeanne Grant. *Bottle Dancers*: Tog Richards, Myron Curtis, Matthew Inge, Wallace Munro. *The Fiddler*: Sammy Bayes.

Villagers: Shloime the Bagel Man: Matthew Inge. *Yitzuk* the Streetsweeper: Don Tull. *Chaim* the Fishmonger: Glen McClaskey. *Duvidel* the Seltzer Man: Wallace Munro. *Surcha*: Lynn Archer. *Label*: Tog Richards. *Schmeril*: David Horwitz. *Yakov* the Knife-seller: Patrick Quinn. *Hershel*: Myron Curtis. *Fredel*: Hope Katcher. *Bluma*: Debra Timmons. *Mirala*: Maureen Sadusk. *Sima*: Lynn Archer. *Rivka*: Joyce Martin. *Yussel*: Duane Bodin. *Vladimer*: Robert L. Hultman. *Sasha*: Wallace Munro. *Bascha*: Shelley Wolf.

IPI-TOMBI

1977.01

A Musical (Revue) of South Africa in Two Acts, 8 Scenes. Conceived, devised and produced by Bertha Egnos. Original music by Bertha Egnos. Lyrics by Gail Lakier. Choreography by Sheila Wartski. Additional choreography by Neil McKay and members of the cast. Scenery by Elizabeth MacLeish. Lighting by Timothy Heale and John Wain. American costume supervision by David Toser. Sound by Sander Hacker. American scenic supervision by Robert D. Mitchell. American lighting supervision by Jeremy Johnson. Produced by A. Deshe (Pashanel) and Topol by arrangement with Ray Cooney Productions, Ltd. and Academy Theatre and Brooke Theatre, Johannesburg. Opened 12 January 1977 at the Harkness Theatre and closed 13 February 1977 after 39 performances.

CAST: Count Wellington Judge, Daniel Pule, Jabu Mbalo, Matthew Bodibe, Gideon Bendile, Elliot Ngubane, Andrew Kau, Sam Hlatshwayo, Philip Gama, David Mthethwa, Shadrack Moyo, Martha Molefe, Dorcas Faku, Lydia Monamodi, Busi Dlamini, Zelda Funami, Thembi Mtshali, Linda Tshabalala, Betty-Boo Hlela, Dudu Nzimande, Coreen Pike, Nellie Khumalo, Junior Tshabalala (Chief Drumemr), Simon Nkosi (Drummer), Ali Lerefolo (Drummer).

Act 1, Scene 1: Village of Tsomo. *Scene 2*: The Baptism. *Scene 3*: Song of Hope. *Scene 4*: The City of Gold.

Act 2, Scene 1: Sunday on the Mines. *Scene 2*: The Township Wedding. *Scene 3*: Workday on the Mine. *Scene 4*: The Warriors.

ACT 1

Overture: "Ipi-Tombi" (Where Are the Girls?)

Scene 1

Daybreak sees the start of a day in the village. The women busy about their duties, grinding corn, preparing food and drink for the return of their menfolk from the hunt.

"Sesiyahamba" (We Are Going About Our Labors)
"Hamba Bhekile" (Let the Drinks Be Served)
"Uthando Luphelile" (Love Is Lost, Love Is Gone)
"Madiwa-Madiwa" (Calling for Rain)
"Qhobosha" (The Unfaithful One Will Die)
"Mokhibo" (The Sotho Girls Dance)
"Ntaba Zenyuka" (The Mountains Are High)
"Orgy, the Temptress"
"Moriva"
"Shamanile"
"Shangaan"

Scene 2

The witch-doctor is the most feared and the most powerful person in the village. Mission stations have labored to bring their faith to the people

and break the influence of the witch-doctors. The scene interprets the conflict.

Scene 3

"Nadia" (Song of Hope)

Scene 4

"Emdudeni" (Street Sweepers)
"Oo-Le-Le" (Men always sing about girls. His love is as High as the Snow-capped Mountain.)
"A Xhosa Proposition"
    A Xhosa girl laments visiting the town and being robbed. She is accosted by a man. The ensuing conversation is carried out in the "click" language which is the feature of the Xhosa tongue.
"The Refuse Collectors"
    It is a peculiarity of Johannesburg that each gang of refuse collectors are always the same tribe. The refuse collection is done "at the double."
"Arieni" (Let's Dance)
"Gum Boot dance"
"Ipi-Tombi" (Where Are the Girls?)

ACT 2

Scene 1

"Bayakhala" (Zulu)(The Child)
Help us, Lord, help us feed the child.

Scene 2

"Mama Tembu's Wedding"
"Baby Baby"
"Phata Phata" (Touch Touch)
Zulu Domestics bring wedding gifts.
"Wishing"
"Zimbaba"
"Baby Baby" (reprise)

Scene 3

"Shosholoza" (A work song)
"Going Home" A song of disillusion.

Scene 4

Prelude to battle. The throb of the drums, the undulating of the women spur on the warriors. The dance movements depict their mode of attack—the boasting of their prowess, the dodging and feinting with their imaginary enemies . . .

A PARTY WITH BETTY COMDEN & ADOLPH GREEN

1977.02

A Revival of the Intimate Revue in Two Acts, 12 Scenes[25]. Sketches and lyrics by Betty Comden and Adolph Green. (Music by Leonard Bernstein, Cy Coleman, Jule Styne, Roger Edens, André Previn, Saul Chaplin.) At the piano, Paul Trueblood. Miss Comden's gowns by Donald Brooks. Executed by John Fitzpatrick. Produced by Arthur Cantor and Leonard Friedman. Opened 10 February 1977 at the Morosco Theatre, moved 21 March 1977 to the Little Theatre and closed 30 April 1977 after 92 performances.

CAST: BETTY COMDEN, ADOLPH GREEN.

ACT 1

Scene 1

Opening ("I Said Good Morning" from *IT'S ALWAYS FAIR WEATHER*, film)
    (*Music by* Andre Previn.)

Scene 2

The Revuers—Night Club Act
    (*Sketches, Music and Lyrics by* The Revuers {Betty Comden, Adolph Green, Judy Holliday, Alvin Hammer, John Frank}.)
1. The Reader's Digest
2. The Screen Writers ("Beautiful Girl")

---

[25]First produced in New York Off-Broadway 10 November 1958 at the Cherry Lane Theatre, transferring 23 December 1958 to the John Golden Theatre for a total of 82 performances.

3. The Banshee Sisters
4. "The Baroness Bazooka"
Scene 3
ON THE TOWN Medley
(*Music by* Leonard Bernstein.)
1. "New York, New York"
2. "Lonely Town"
3. "Lucky to Be Me"
4. "Some Other Time"
5. "Carried Away"
Scene 4
WONDERFUL TOWN
(*Music by* Leonard Bernstein.)
1. "A Hundred Easy Ways to Lose a Man"
2. "Ohio"
3. "Wrong Note Rag"

ACT 2
Scene 1
SUBWAYS ARE FOR SLEEPING
(*Music by* Jule Styne.)
"Capital Gains"
Scene 2
TWO ON THE AISLE
(*Music by* Jule Styne.)
1. "If (You Hadn't But You Did)"
2. "Catch Our Act at the Met"
Scene 3
GOOD NEWS (Film)
(*Music by* Roger Edens.)
1. "The French Lesson"
Scene 4
STRAWS IN THE WIND
(*Music by* Cy Coleman.)
1. "The Lost Word"
Scene 5
PETER PAN
(*Music by* Jule Styne.)
1. "Captain Hook's Waltz"
2. "Never Never Land"
3. "Mysterious Lady"
Scene 6
STRAWS IN THE WIND
(*Music by* Cy Coleman.)
1. "Simplified Language"
Scene 7
BONANZA BOUND
(*Music by* Saul Chaplin.)
1. "Inspiration"
Scene 8
BELLS ARE RINGING
(*Music by* Jule Styne.)
1. "Just in Time"
2. "Make Someone Happy" (from *DO RE MI*)
(*Music by* Jule Styne.)
3. "The Party's Over"

THE PIRATES OF PENZANCE,
1977.03 or The Slave of Duty

A Revival of the Comic Opera in Two Acts[26]. Libretto by William S. Gilbert. Music by Arthur Sullivan. Production directed by Jack Eddleman. Scenic

---

[26]First presented in New York 31 December 1879 at the Fifth Avenue Theatre for a total of 91 performances in two engagements. For Synopsis of Scenes and Musical Numbers, see original 1879 production.

design by Lloyd Evans. Costume design by Patton Campbell. Lighting design by Hans Sondheimer. Conductor, Judith Somogi. Chorus master, George Branson Gary. Produced by the New York City Opera. Opened 26 March 1977 at the New York State Theatre and closed 17 April 1977 after 4 performances in repertory.

CAST: *Major General Stanley*: JAMES BILLINGS. *The Pirate King*: RICHARD McKEE. *Samuel*, his Lieutenant: William Ledbetter. *Frederic*, the Pirate Apprentice: HENRY PRICE. *Sergeant of Police*: IRWIN DENSEN. *Mabel, Edith, Kate, Isabel*, General Stanley's Daughters: GIANNA ROLANDI, DIANA KEHRIG, SANDRA WALKER, MADELEINE MINES. *Ruth*, Pirate Maid-of-all-work: MURIEL COSTA-GREENSPON. *Solo Dancer*: Mikhail Korogodsky.
Chorus of Pirates, Police and General Stanley's Daughters: New York City Opera Chorus.

1977.04 I LOVE MY WIFE

A Musical in Two Acts, 5 Scenes. Book and lyrics by Michael Stewart. Music composed and arranged by Cy Coleman. Based on a play ("Viens chez-moi, j'habite chez une copine") by Luis Rego. Directed by Gene Saks. Scenery by David Mitchell. Lighting by Gilbert V. Hemsley, Jr. Costumes by Ron Talsky. Musical direction by John Miller. Sound by Lou Gonzalez. Musical numbers staged by Onna White. Associate producer, Frank Montalvo. Produced by Terry Allen Kramer and Harry Rigby by arrangement with Joseph Kipness. Opened 17 April 1977 at the Ethel Barrymore Theatre and closed 20 May 1979 after 857 performances.

CAST (in order of appearance): *Cleo*: ILENE GRAFF. *Monica*: JOANNA GLEASON. *Wally*: JAMES NAUGHTON. *Stanley*: Michael Mark. *Quentin*: Joe Saulter. *Harvey*: John Miller. *Norman*: Ken Bichel. *Alvin*: LENNY BAKER.

The action takes place in Trenton, New Jersey, at the present time.

Act 1, Scene 1: Harvey's Diner. *Scene 2*: A Mover's Life. *Scene 3*: Alvin and Cleo's Apartment.

Act 2, Scene 1: Christmas Eve. *Scene 2*: Wally and Monica's Apartment.

ACT 1
Scene 1
"We're Still Friends"
Full Company
"Monica"
L. Baker, J. Gleason, M. Mark, J. Saulter, J. Miller, K. Bichel
"By Threes"
J. Naughton, L. Baker, J. Miller
Scene 2
"A Mover's Life"
L. Baker, M. Mark, J. Saulter, J. Miller, K. Bichel
Scene 3
"Love Revolution"
I. Graff
"Someone Wonderful I Missed"
J. Gleason, I. Graff
"Sexually Free"
L. Baker, I. Graff, J. Naughton
ACT 2
Scene 1
"Hey There, Good Times"
M. Mark, J. Saulter, J. Miller, K. Bichel
Scene 2
"Lovers on Christmas Eve"
J. Gleason, J. Naughton, K. Bichel
"Scream"
M. Mark, J. Saulter, J. Miller, K. Bichel
"Everybody Today Is Turning On"
L. Baker, J. Naughton
"Married Couple Seeks Married Couple"
L. Baker, I. Graff, J. Naughton, J. Gleason
"I Love My Wife"
L. Baker, J. Naughton

1977.05 SIDE BY SIDE BY SONDHEIM

A Musical Entertainment (Revue) in Two Acts. Music and lyrics by Stephen Sondheim. (Additional) Music by Leonard Bernstein, Mary Rodgers,

Richard Rodgers and Jule Styne. Directed by Ned Sherrin. Musical director, Ray Cook. Musical staging by Bob Howe. Continuity by Ned Sherrin. Scenery by Peter Docherty. Costumes by Florence Klotz. Lighting by Ken Billington. Scenery supervision by Jay Moore. Musical supervision by Paul Gemignani. Sound by Jack Mann. Produced by Harold Prince in association with Ruth Mitchell, by arrangement with The Incomes Company, Ltd. Presented in London by H. M. Tennent LTD and Cameron Mackintosh in association with the Mermaid Theatre. Opened 18 April 1977 at the Music Box, moved 22 February 1978 to the Morosco Theatre and closed 19 March 1978 after 390 performances.

CAST: MILLICENT MARTIN, JULIE N. McKENZIE, DAVID KERNAN, NED SHERRIN. *Pianists:* Daniel Troob, Albin Konopka.

ACT 1[27]

"Comedy Tonight" (from *A FUNNY THING HAPPENED ON THE WAY TO THE FORUM*)

"Love Is in the Air" (dropped from *A FUNNY THING HAPPENED ON THE WAY TO THE FORUM*)

"If Momma Was Married" (from *GYPSY*)
   (*Music by* Jule Styne.)

"You Must Meet My Wife" (from *A LITTLE NIGHT MUSIC*)

"The Little Things You Do Together" (from *COMPANY*)

"Getting Married Today" (from *COMPANY*)

"I Remember"[28] (from *EVENING PRIMROSE*, Television)

"Can That Boy Foxtrot" (dropped from *FOLLIES*)

"Company" (from *COMPANY*)

"Another Hundred People"[29] (from *COMPANY*)

"Barcelona" (from *COMPANY*)

"Marry Me a Little" (dropped from *COMPANY*)

"I Never Do Anything Twice" (from *THE SEVEN PERCENT SOLUTION* film)

"Bring on the Girls" (from *FOLLIES*)

"Ah, Paree!" (from *FOLLIES*)

"Buddy's Blues" (from *FOLLIES*)

"Broadway Baby" (from *FOLLIES*)

"You Could Drive a Person Crazy" (from *COMPANY*)

ACT 2

"Everybody Says Don't" (from *ANYONE CAN WHISTLE*)

"Anyone Can Whistle"[30] (from *ANYONE CAN WHISTLE*)

"Send in the Clowns" (from *A LITTLE NIGHT MUSIC*)

"We're Gonna Be All Right"

(from *DO I HEAR A WALTZ?*)
   (*Music by* Richard Rodgers.)

"A Boy Like That"/"I Have a Love"[31] (from *WEST SIDE STORY*)
   (*Music by* Leonard Bernstein.)

---

[27]The running order was revised repeatedly during the run. Added during the run:

"Waiting For the Girls Upstairs" (from *FOLLIES*)(Act 2)

"Being Alive" (from *COMPANY*)(Act 1)

"The Ladies Who Lunch" (from *COMPANY*)(Act 1)

"The Miller's Son" (from *A LITTLE NIGHT MUSIC*)(Act 2)

"Something's Coming" (from *WEST SIDE STORY*)
   (*Music by* Leonard Bernstein.)(Act 2)

"The Two of You"
   (written for The Kuklapolitan Players)(Act 1)

"Little Lamb" (from *GYPSY*)
   (*Music by* Jule Styne.)(Act 1)

"I Feel Pretty" (from *WEST SIDE STORY*)
   (*Music by* Leonard Bernstein.)(Act 2)

Added for subsequent national tour:

"Don't Laugh" (from *HOT SPOT*)
   (*Music by* Mary Rodgers.)

[28]Dropped during the run.
[29]Dropped during the run.
[30]Dropped during the run.
[31]Dropped during the run.

"The Boy From ... " (from *THE MAD SHOW*)
   (*Music by* Mary Rodgers.)

"Pretty Lady" (from *PACIFIC OVERTURES*)

"You Gotta Have A Gimmick" (from *GYPSY*)
   (*Music by* Jule Styne.)

"Losing My Mind" (from *FOLLIES*)

"Could I Leave You?"[32] (from *FOLLIES*)

"I'm Still Here" (from *FOLLIES*)

"Conversation Piece"
   (*arranged by* Caryl Brahms and Stuart Pedlar)

"Side By Side By Side" (from *COMPANY*)

1977.06 # ANNIE

A Musical in Two Acts, 13 Scenes. Book by Thomas Meehan. Based on the "Little Orphan Annie" comic strip (by Harold Gray). Music by Charles Strouse. Lyrics by Martin Charnin. Musical numbers choreographed by Peter Gennaro. Directed by Martin Charnin. Settings by David Mitchell. Costumes by Theoni V. Aldredge. Lighting by Judy Rasmuson. Musical direction and dance music arranged by Peter Howard. Orchestrations by Philip J. Lang. Produced by Mike Nichols, Irwin Meyer, Stephen R. Friedman, Lewis Allen, Alvin Nederlander Associates, Inc., Icarus Productions in association with Peter Krane. Opened 21 April 1977 at the Alvin Theatre, moved 16 September 1981 to the ANTA Theatre, moved 29 October 1981 to the Eugene O'Neill Theatre, moved 10 December 1981 to the Uris Theatre and closed 2 January 1983 after 2377 performances.

CAST (in order of appearance): *Molly:* Danielle Brisebois. *Pepper:* Robyn Finn. *Duffy:* Donna Graham. *July:* Janine Ruane. *Tessie:* Diana Barrows. *Kate:* Shelley Bruce. *Annie:* ANDREA McARDLE. *Miss Hannigan:* DOROTHY LOUDON. *Bundles McCloskey:* James Hosbein. *Dog Catchers:* Steven Boockvor, Donald Craig. *Sandy:* Himself. *Lieutenant Ward:* Richard Ensslen. *Harry:* RAYMOND THORNE. *Sophie, the Kettle:* LAURIE BEECHMAN. *Grace Farrell:* SANDY FAISON. *Drake:* Edwin Bordo. *Mrs. Pugh:* Edie Cowan. *Cecille:* LAURIE BEECHMAN. *Annette:* Penny Worth. *Oliver Warbucks:* REID SHELTON. *A Star to Be:* LAURIE BEECHMAN. *Rooster Hannigan:* ROBERT FITCH. *Lily:* BARBARA ERWIN. *Bert Healy:* Donald Craig. *Fred McCracken:* Bob Freschi. *Jimmy Johnson:* Steven Boockvor. *Sound Effects Man:* James Hosbein. *Bonnie Boylan:* LAURIE BEECHMAN. *Connie Boylan:* Edie Cowan. *Ronnie Boylan:* Penny Worth. *NBC Page:* Mari McMinn. *Kaltenborn's Voice:* Donald Craig. *FDR:* RAYMOND THORNE. *Ickes:* James Hosbein. *Howe:* Bob Freschi. *Morgenthau:* Richard Ensslen. *Hull:* Donald Craig. *Perkins:* LAURIE BEECHMAN. *Honor Guard:* Steven Boockvor. *Justice Brandeis:* Richard Ensslen.

Hooverville-ites, Policemen, Servants, New Yorkers: Laurie Beechman, Steven Boockvor, Edwin Bordo, Edie Cowan, Donald Craig, Richard Ensslen, Barbara Erwin, Bob Freschi, James Hosbein, Mari McMinn, Penny Worth.

The action takes place 11-25 December 1933 in New York City.

Act 1: 11-19 December 1933. *Scene 1:* The New York Municpal Orphanage (Girls' Annex). *Scene 2:* St. Mark's Place. *Scene 3:* A Hooverville under the 59th Street Bridge. *Scene 4:* The Orphanage. *Scene 5:* The Warbucks Mansion at Fifth Avenue and 82nd Street. *Scene 6:* New York City. *Scene 7:* The Orphanage. *Scene 8:* Warbucks' Study.

Act 2: 21-25 December 1933. *Scene 1:* The NBC Radio Studio at 30 Rockefeller Center and the Orphanage. *Scene 2:* The Orphanage. *Scene 3:* Washington: The White House. *Scene 4:* The Great Hall at the Warbucks Mansion. *Scene 5:* The East Ballroom of the Warbucks Mansion.

ACT 1

Scene 1

"Maybe"A. McArdle

"It's the Hard-Knock Life"
   A. McArdle, Orphans

"It's the Hard-Knock Life"
   (reprise)Orphans

Scene 2

"Tomorrow"
   A. McArdle

Scene 3

"We'd Like to Thank You (Herbert Hoover)"
   The Hoover-ites

Scene 4

"Little Girls"
   D. Loudon

---

[32]Dropped during the run.

Scene 5

"I Think I'm Gonna Like It Here"
S. Faison, A. McArdle, E. Bordo, L. Bechman, P. Worth, E. Cowan, Other Servants

Scene 6

"N.Y.C."
R. Shelton, S. Faison, A. McArdle, L. Beechman, New Yorkers

Scene 7

"Easy Street"
D. Loudon, B. Fitch, B. Erwin

Scene 8

"You Won't Be an Orphan For Long"
S. Faison, E. Bordo, E. Cowan, L. Beechman, P. Worth, Servants, R. Shelton

ACT 2

Scene 1

"You're Never Fully Dressed Without a Smile"
D. Craig, L. Beechman, E. Cowan, P. Worth, "The Hour of Smiles" Family

Scene 2

"You're Never Fully Dressed Without a Smile" (reprise)
Orphans
"Easy Street" (reprise)
D. Loudon, B. Fitch, B. Erwin

Scene 3

"Tomorrow" (reprise)
A. McArdle, R. Thorne, R. Shelton, The Cabinet

Scene 4

"Something Was Missing"
R. Shelton
"I Don't Need Anything But You"
R. Shelton, A. McArdle

Scene 5

"Annie"
S. Faison, E. Bordo, The Staff
"Maybe" (reprise)
A. McArdle
"A New Deal for Christmas"
A. McArdle, R. Shelton, S. Faison, R. Thorne, The Staff

1977.07 THE KING AND I

A Revival of the Musical Play in Two Acts, 17 Scenes[33]. Book and lyrics by Oscar Hammerstein II. Music by Richard Rodgers. Based on the novel "Anna and the King of Siam" by Margaret Landon. Original choreography by Jerome Robbins. Entire production directed by Yuriko. Settings by Peter Wolf. Costumes by Stanley Simmons, based on the original costumes by Irene Sharaff. Lighting by Thomas Skelton. (Orchestrations by Robert Russell Bennett.) Musical supervisor, Milton Rosenstock. Musical director, John Lesko. Sound by T. Richard Fitzgerald. Associate producer, Fred Walker. Produced by Lee Guber and Shelly Gross. Opened 2 May 1977 at the Uris Theatre and closed 30 December 1978 after 719 performances.

CAST (in order of appearance): *Captain Orton*: Larry Swansen. *Louis Leonowens*: Alan Amick. *Anna Leonowens*: CONSTANCE TOWERS. *The Interpreter*: Jae Woo Lee. *The Kralahome*: MICHAEL KERMOYAN. *The King*: YUL BRYNNER. *Tuptim*: JUNE ANGELA. *Lady Thiang*: HYE-YOUNG CHOI. *Prince Chulalongkorn*: Gene Profanato. *Princess Ying Yaowalak*: Julie Woo. *Lun Tha*: MARTIN VIDNOVIC. *Sir Edward Ramsay*: JOHN MICHAEL KING.
The Small House of Uncle Thomas (ballet): *Narrator*: JUNE ANGELA. *Uncle Thomas*: Jessicca Chao. *Topsy*: Lei-Lynne Doo. *Little Eva*: Diane Lam. *Eliza*: Susan Kikuchi. *King Simon*: Rebecca West. *Angel*: Patricia Weber. *Royal Dancers*: Dale Hairmoto, Barrett Hong, Faye Fujisaka Mar, Ric Ornellas, Libby Rhodes, Cecile Santos, Hope Sogawa, Chandra Tanna, Henry Yu. *Propmen*: Kaipo Daniels, Jae Woo Lee, Thomas J. Rees, Robert Vega.
The Royal Dancers and Wives: Su Applegate, Jessica Chao, Lei-Lynn Doo, Dale Harimoto, Pamela Kait, Susan Kikuchi, Faye Fujisaki Mar, Sumiko Murashima, Libby Rhodes, Cecile Santos, Hope Sogawa, Mary Ann Teng, Patricia K. Thomas. *Princesses and Princes*: Ivan Ho, Clark Huang, Annie Lam, Connie Lam, Jennifer Lam, Paul Siu,

Tim Waldrip, Kevan Weber, Kym Weber, Julie Woo, Mary Woo. *Nurses and Amazons*: Sidney Smith, Marianne Tatum, Patricia K. Thomas, Rebecca West. *Priests and Slaves*: Kaipo Daniels, Barrett Hong, Jae Woo Lee, Ric Ornellas, Simeon Den, Chandra Tanna, Robert Vega.

1977.08 HAPPY END

A Musical in Three Acts, 4 Scenes and a Prologue[34]. Original German play by Elisabeth Hauptmann. Music by Kurt Weill. (Original German) Lyrics by Bertolt Brecht. Book and lyrics adapted by Michael Feingold. Directed and staged by Robert Kalfin and Patricia Birch. Scenic design by Robert U. Taylor. Costumes by Carrie F. Robbins. Lighting by Jennifer Tipton. Musical direction by Roland Gagnon. Associate producer, Wilder Luke Burnap. Chelsea Theatre Center Production newly conceived by Robert Kalfin. Produced by Michael Harvey and the Chelsea Theater Center (Robert Kalfin, Artistic director; Michael David, Executive director). Opened 7 May 1977 at the Martin Beck Theatre and closed 10 July 1977 after 75 performances. Total including Off-Broadway, 131 performances.

CAST (in order of appearance): *The Gang: Bill Cracker*: CHRISTOPHER LLOYD. *Sam "Mammy" Wurlitzer*: BENJAMIN RAYSON. *Dr. Nakamura ("The Governor")*: Tony Azito. *Jimmy Dexter ("The Reverend")*: John A. Coe. *Bob Marker ("The Professor")*: Robert Weil. *Johnny Flint ("Baby Face")*: Raymond Barry. *A Lady in Gray ("The Fly")*: GRAYSON HALL. *Miriam, the Barmaid*: Donna Emmanuel.
The Army: Lieutenant Lillian Holiday ("Hallelujah Lil"): MERYL STREEP. *Major Stone*: Liz Sheridan. *Captain Hannibal Jackson*: Joe Grifasi. *Sister Mary*: Prudence Wright Holmes. *Sister Jane*: Alexandra Borrie. *Brother Ben Owens*: Christopher Cara.
The Fold: Kristin Joliff, Frank Kopyc, Tom Mardirosian, Martha Miller, Victor Pappas. *A Cop*: David Pursley.

The action takes place in Chicago in December of 1915.

Act 1: Bill's Beer Hall. 22 December.

Act 2: The Salvation Army Mission, Canal Street. 23 December.

Act 3, Scene 1: The Beer Hall. 24 December. *Scene 2*: The Mission Hall. Later that night.

Prologue

Prologue
Entire Company

ACT 1

"The Bilbao Song"
C. Lloyd, The Gang
"Lieutenants of the Lord"
M. Streep, The Army
"March Ahead"
The Army
"The Sailors' Tango"
M. Streep

ACT 2

"Brother, Give Yourself a Shove"
The Army, The Fold
"Song of the Big Shot"
T. Azito
"Don't Be Afraid"
A. Borrie, The Army, The Fold
"In Our Childhood's Bright Endeavor"
J. Grifasi
"The Liquor Dealer's Dream"
J. Grifasi, T. Azito, A. Borrie, The Army , The Fold

ACT 3

Scene 1

"The Mandalay Song"
B. Rayson, The Gang
"Surabaya Johnny"
M. Streep
"Song of the Big Shot" (reprise)
C. Lloyd
"Ballad of the Lily of Hell"
G. Hall

---

[33]Originally produced in New York 29 March 1951 at the St. James Theatre for 1246 performances. For Synopsis of Scenes and Musical Numbers, see original 1951 production.

[34]First produced in New York Off-Broadway 8 March 1977 at the Chelsea Theatre Center of Brooklyn for 56 performances.

Scene 2

"The Happy End"-Finale
Entire Company

TOLLER CRANSTON'S
1977.09 THE ICE SHOW

An Ice Skating Revue in Two Acts, 5 Scenes. Original music (and lyrics) by Al Kasha and Joel Hirschhorn[35]. Produced and directed by Myrl A. Schreibman. Set design by Anthony Sabatino, William H. Harris. Costume design by Miles White. Lighting design by D. Scott Linder. Sound Design by Jack Shirk. Choreography and staging by Brian Foley. Additional choreography by Ellen Burka. Music supervision by Bill Courtney. Skating consultant, Bill Turner. Produced by Dennis Bass and Robin Cranston. Opened 19 May 1977 at the Palace Theatre and closed 10 July 1977 after 60 performances.

CAST: TOLLER CRANSTON, JIM MILLNS and COLLEEN O'CONNOR, GORDON McKELLEN, JR., KEN SHELLEY, Wendy Burge, Candy Jones and Don Fraser, Kathy Malmberg, Barbara Berezowski and David Porter, Elizabeth Freeman, Jack Courtney and Emily Benenson, Janet and Mark Hominuke.

ACT 1

Overture & Introduction
Full Company
(*Music and Lyrics by Al Kasha and Joel Hirschhorn.*)
Scene 1: Trilogy
"Thus Spake Zarathustra"
D. Fraser, C. Jones
"Candide"
E. Freeman
"Somewhere"
D. Porter, B. Berezowski
"Captain from Castille"
D. Fraser, C. Jones, E. Freeman, D. Porter, B. Berezowski
"Son of a Gun"
K. Shelley, C. O'Connor
"Let's Hear It for Me"
W. Burge
"Free Again"
K. Malmberg
"On the Waterfront"
J. Courtney, E. Benenson
"Nicholas and Alexandra"
T. Cranston
Scene 2: Dance Medley
"Rock Around the Clock"
C. Jones, D. Fraser
"Charleston"
J. Courtney, E. Benenson
"Tango"
J. Courtney, E. Benenson
"Nola"
C. Jones, D. Fraser
"Sugar Blues"
B. Berezowski, D. Porter
"Fascination, "Varsity Drag," "Darktown Strutters Ball"
All the Couples
"My Wife the Dancer"
G. McKellen, Jr.

Scene 3: Russian Ode
"The Young and the Restless"
J. Millns, C. O'Connor
"Innocence"
J. Hominuke, M. Hominuke
"Love Duet"
T. Cranston, E. Benenson
"The Warlords"
G. McKellen, Jr., J. Courtney
"Loneliness of War"
T. Cranston
"Vision"
D. Porter, B. Berezowski
"Dream of Love"
T. Cranston, E. Benenson
"Emptiness and Longing"
T. Cranston
ACT 2
Scene 1: Toller's Ball
"Le Prophète"
Full Company
"Graduation Ball I"
T. Cranston
"Corsaire I"
D. Fraser, C. Jones
"Graduation Ball II"
T. Cranston
"Corsaire II"
J. Millns, C. O'Connor
"Graduation Ball III"
T. Cranston
"Le Prophète" (reprise)
Full Company
"Gaité Parisienen"
E. Freeman
"Raymonda"
W. Burge
"Pas de Deux"
J. Hominuke, M. Hominuke
"Black Orpheus"
K. Malmberg
"MacArthur Park"
G. McKellen, Jr.
"Tick-Tock"
D. Fraser, C. Jones
Scene 2: Latino
"Rodrigo"
J. Courtney, E. Benenson
"Habanera"
J. Millns, C. O'Connor
"La Carioca"
D. Porter, B. Berezowski
"Scheherezade"
K. Shelley
"A Fifth of Beethoven"
J. Millns, C. O'Connor
"I Pagliacci"
T. Cranston
Finale
Full Company

---

[35]Much of the musical score was comprised of popular standards from the worlds of popular and classical music; Messrs. Kasha and Hirshhorn's contributions were not individually identified.

1977–1978 SEASON

Judy Kaye and Madeline Kahn in ON THE TWENTIETH CENTURY
Martha Swope/TimePix

1977–1978 SEASON

1977.10 ## BEATLEMANIA

A Musical Entertainment in Two Acts, 9 Scenes. Songs (music and lyrics) written by John Lennon, Paul McCartney, George Harrison. Editorial content by Robert Rabinowitz, Bob Gill, Lynda Obst. Visuals director, Charles E. Hoeffler. Multi-media images by Robert Rabinowitz, Bob Gill, Shep Kerman, Kathleen Rabinowitz. Original concept by Steven Leber, David Krebs, Jules Fisher. All songs where indicated licensed by ATV Music Group. Scenery by Robert D. Mitchell. Lighting by Jules Fisher. Sound design by Abe Jacob. Musical supervision by Sandy Yaguda. Special consultant, Murray the K. Production supervised by Jules Fisher. Produced by David Krebs and Steven Leber. Opened 1 June 1977 at the Winter Garden, moved 1 March 1979 to the Lunt-Fontanne Theatre, and closed 17 October 1979 after 1006 performances.

CAST: JOE PECORINO (rhythm guitar), MITCH WEISSMAN (bass guitar), LESLIE FRADKIN (lead guitar), JUSTIN McNEIL (drums).

Act 1, Scene 1: Camelot: Pre-Beatles. *Scene 2*: The Coming. *Scene 3*: Making It. *Scene 4*: Listening. *Scene 5*: Tripping.

Act 2, Scene 1: Dropping Out. *Scene 2*: Flower Power. *Scene 3*: Bottoming Out. *Scene 4*: Moving On.

ACT 1
Scene 1
"Let's Twist Again"
    (*Music and Lyrics by* Kal Mann and Dave Appell.)
"Roll Over Beethoven"
    (*Music and Lyrics by* Chuck Berry.)
"Bye Bye Love"
    (*Music and Lyrics by* Felice Bryant and Boudleaux Bryant.)
"Hound Dog"
    (*Music and Lyrics by* Jerry Lieber and Mike Stoller.)
The early 1960's begin with an all-time optimism in America. Youthful and elegant, John F. Kennedy charms the public and press while his First Family welcomes the public into the White House. His assassination on 22 November 1963 shocks the country in a horrifying introduction to what's to become the most turbulent of decades.
Scene 2
"I Want to Hold Your Hand"
    (*Music and Lyrics by* John Lennon and Paul McCartney.)
"She Loves You"
    (*Music and Lyrics by* John Lennon and Paul McCartney.)
Television viewers watch open-mouthed as a group of four Liverpudlians explode on national television. Shortly after their debut in February 1964, the light-hearted mop-topped jesters begin to win recognition and attention never before given to rock and roll artists.
Scene 3
"Help!"
"If I Fell"
"Can't Buy Me Love"
"Day Tripper"
The "Fab Four" establish themselves as style-getters, innovators, movie stars, recording artists and fashion-makers with a contagious sense of humor, newness and excitement.
Scene 4
"Yesterday"
"Eleanor Rigby'
"We Can Work It Out"
"Nowhere Man"
As the group begins to mature musically, a sense of introspection is felt through their music. Critics begin to give them more serious consideration, while an increasing number and diversity of fans await the changing sounds of each newly released recording.

Scene 5
"A Day in the Life"
"Strawberry Fields Forever"
"Penny Lane"
"Magical Mystery Tour"
"Lucy in the Sky With Diamonds"
Becoming an accepted entity by the "establishment," the group takes on a whole new direction with musical experimentation and sensual, psychedelic perceptions. Their music is becoming a directional for the increasing "counter-culture" and anti-establishment youth movement.

ACT 2
Scene 1
"Lady Madonna"
"The Fool on the Hill"
"Got to Get You into My Life"
"Michelle"
"Get Back"
Their growing musical styles have connected with other cultures and life-styles through a multi-dimensional sound which defies categorization. The country's youth follows suit in more personal, individualized self-exploration and unconventional answers to an unresponsive and static society.
Scene 2
"Come Together"
"With a Little Help from My Friends"
"All You Need Is Love"
Holding its own, the youth movement becomes an established force and reality, influencing all phases of society, as the "hippies" and "street-people" of Haight-Ashbury and New York's Lower East Side reach far beyond their coastal boundaries into the homes of middle-America.
Scene 3
"Revolution"
"Helter Skelter"
"Hey Jude"
The assassinations of Martin Luther King, Jr. and Robert Kennedy traumatize the country. The War in Vietnam rages on, and the confusion, anger and violent confrontations in the streets of the U.S. splinter any hopeful ideals left from the early years of the decade. The group moves towards separation.
Scene 4
"I Am the Walrus"
"The Long and Winding Road"
"Let It Be"
The decade climaxes as the group itself splits apart. Their songs, now individual statements, are reflective of their own personal choices and life-styles, while the wealth of collective material remains, painting a spectrum of images ranging from the innocent to innovators, from the celebrities to the outlaws; always growing, creating and moving beyond their audiences.

1977.11 ## DIE FLEDERMAUS

A Revival of the Operetta in Three Acts[1]. Original Viennese libretto by Carl Haffner and Richard Genée. Lyrics by Richard Genée. (Based on the comedy "Le Réveillon" by Henri Meilhac and Ludovic Halévy.) English libretto by Ruth and Thomas Martin. Music by Johann Strauss. Production devised and directed by Gerald Freedman. Stage director, Richard Getke. Choreography by Thomas Andrew. Scenery designed by Lloyd Evans Costumes design by Theoni V. Aldredge. Lighting by Hans Sondheimer. Conducted by Julius Rudel. Chorus master, Lloyd Walser. Produced by the

---

[1]First English language production in New York 16 March 1885 at the Casino Theatre for 42 performances. First New York production of this adaptation 20 December 1950 at the Metropolitan Opera House. For Synopsis of Scenes and Musical Numbers, see May 1954 revival.

New York City Opera. Opened 2 September 1977 at the New York State Theatre and closed 1 November 1977 after 7 performances in repertory; returned 8 March 1978 to the New York State Theatre and closed 11 April 1978 after 3 performances in repertory. Total this season: 10 performances.

CAST (in order of appearance): *Alfred*, an itinerant tenor: Henry Price. *Adele*, von Eisenstein's chambermaid: BEVERLY SILLS. *Rosalinda von Eisenstein*: JOHANNA MEIER. *Gabriel von Eisenstein*: CHARLES ROE. *Dr. Blind*, a lawyer: Melvin Lowery. *Dr. Falke*, a close friend of Eisenstein: DAVID HOLLOWAY. *Frank*, the prison warden: RICHARD McKEE. *Sally*, Adele's sister: Puli Toro. *Ivan*, servant to Orlofsky: Jack Sims. *Prince Orlofsky*, a wealthy, bored Russian: DAVID RAE SMITH. *Frosch*, the jailer: Coley Worth. *Solo Dancers*: Sandra Balestracci, Esperanza Galan, Juliu Horvath.

Ensemble: New York City Opera Chorus.

1977.12   MAN OF LA MANCHA

A Revival of the Musical Play in One Act[2]. Book by Dale Wasserman. Suggested by the life and work ("Don Quixote") of Miguel de Cervantes y Saavedra. Music by Mitch Leigh. Lyrics by Joe Darion. Production (direction) and musical staging by Albert Marre. Setting and lighting by Howard Bay. Costumes by Howard Bay and Patton Campbell. Music arrangements by Music Makers Inc. Musical direction by Robert Brandzel. Produced by Eugene V. Wolsk. Opened 15 September 1977 at the Palace Theatre and closed 31 December 1977 after 124 performances.

CAST (in order of appearance): *Don Quixote (Cervantes)*: RICHARD KILEY. *Sancho*: TONY MARTINEZ. *The Horse*: Ben Vargas. *The Mule*: Hector Mercado. *The Innkeeper*: BOB WRIGHT. *Maria*, the Innkeeper's Wife: Marceline Decker. *Pedro*, Head Muleteer: Chev Rodgers. *Anselmo*, a Muleteer: Ted Forlow. *Juan*, a Muleteer: Mark Holliday. *Tenorio*, a Muleteer: Ben Vargas. *Paco*, a Muleteer: Anthony DeVecchi. *Jose*, a Muleteer: Hector Mercado. *Aldonza*: EMILY YANCY. *Fermina*, a slavey: Joan Susswein. *Guitarist*: Robin Polseno. *Jorge*, a Muleteer: Edmond Varrato. *Fernando*, a Muleteer: David Wasson. *Antonia*: HARRIETT CONRAD. *The Housekeeper*: MARGRET COLEMAN. *The Padre*: TAYLOR REED. *Dr. Carrasco*: IAN SULLIVAN. *The Barber*: Ted Forlow. *Moorish Dancer*: Joan Susswein. *The Captain of the Inquisition*: Renato Cibelli. *Guards*: Michael St. Paul, David Wasson.

1977.13   ESTRADA

The 1977 Music and Dance Festival (A Russian Language Variety Revue) from the Soviet Union in Two Acts. Artistic director, Nikolai Laktionov. Administrative director, Nadezhda Kazantzeva. Choreographer, Tamara Golovanova. Production supervisor, M. William Lettich. Production manager, Savely Onishchenko. Produced by United Euram. Opened 20 September 1977 at the Majestic Theatre and closed 24 September 1977 after 7 performances.

CAST: NANI BREGVADZE (Singer), GRIGORI DAVIDENKO and VLADIMIR KONONOVICH (Ukranian Comic Dance Team), NATALIA and OLEG KIRIUSHKIN (Mimes), LARISA KUDEYAROVA (Acrobat), YEFIM LEVINSON and GALINA KORZINA (Puppet Masters), ORERA (Georgian Vocal Instrumental Group){Nani Bregvadze, Zurab Yashvili, Vakhtang Kikabidze, Teimuraz Megvinet-Ukhutsesi, Alexander Mandjgaladze, Teimuraz Davitaya, Geno Nadirashvili}, PESNYARY (Pop-Rock Group), VLADIMIR SEROV (Cyclist/Aerialist), SOUVENIR ENSEMBLE (Dance Ensemble); ALLA, VYACHESLAV and VYACHESLAV RASSHIVKIN, JR. (Acrobats).

ACT 1

"Moscow Nights"

(*Music and Lyrics by* V. Soloviev-Sedoy.)
 Entire Cast

"Korobeiniki" (Russian Dance)
 Souvenir Ensemble

Four Contemporary Byelorussian Folk Songs
 Pesnyary Ensemble

"Dva Kuma" (Comic Dance)
 V. Kononovich, G. Davidenko

Northern Festive Dance
 Souvenir Ensemble

"A Friendship That Never Came to Be"
 Souvenir Ensemble

Puppet Sketches
 Y. Levinson, G. Korzina

"Barynya" (Russian Dance)
 Souvenir Ensemble

ACT 2

Sabre Dance
 Souvenir Ensemble

"Give My Regards to Broadway"
 Orera Ensemble
 (*Music and Lyrics by* George M. Cohan.)

Bicycle on the High Wire
 V. Serov

"Serdtse"
 Orera Ensemble
 (*Music and Lyrics by* I. Dunaevsky.)

"Svetlyachok" (Georgian Folk Song)
 Orera Ensemble

"Tbiliso"
 N. Bregvadze
 (*Music by* Revaz Lagidze. *Lyrics by* Peter Gruzinsky.)

"Dorogoy Dlinoyu" (Old Song)
 N. Bregvadze

Acrobatic Sketch with a Hoop
 L. Kudeyarova

Gypsy Fantasy
 Souvenir Ensemble

Acrobatic Sketch
 Alla, 2 Vyacheslav Rasshivkins

Specialty
 N. Kiriushkin, O. Kiriushkin

"Potekha" (Comic Dance)
 Souvenir Ensemble

Finale
 Entire Cast

1977.14   COMEDY WITH MUSIC

A Revival of the Musical Entertainment in Two Acts[3]. Conceived and devised by Victor Borge. Production designed by Neil Peter Jampolis. Miss Mulvey's gown by Donald Brooks. Associate producers, Dean Lenz, Allison McLeod. Produced by The Edgewood Organization (Lewis Friedman, John W. Ballard, Executive directors). Opened 3 October 1977 at the Imperial Theatre and closed 16 November 1977 after 64 performances.

CAST: VICTOR BORGE, MARYLYN MULVEY.

ACT 1

Victor Borge

ACT 2

The Concert
Marylyn Mulvey
Victor Borge
The Audience

1977.15   HAIR

A Revival of the American Tribal Love-Rock Musical in Two Acts[4]. Book and lyrics by Gerome Ragni and James Rado. Music by Galt MacDermott.

---

[2]First produced in New York 22 November 1965 at the ANTA Washington Square Theatre for 2328 performances. For Synopsis of Scenes and Musical Numbers, see original 1965 production.

[3]Originally produced in New York as *COMEDY IN MUSIC* 2 October 1953 at the John Golden Theatre for 849 performances.
[4]First produced in New York Off-Broadway 17 October 1967 at the Anspacher Theatre for 50 performances, at the Cheetah 22 December 1967 for 45 performances; transferred to Broadway 29 April 1968 to the

Directed by Tom O'Horgan. Choreography, Julie Arenal. Musical director, Denzil A. Miller, Jr. Costume design by Nancy Potts. Scenic design by Robin Wagner. Lighting design by Jules Fisher. Sound design by Abe Jacob. Vocal direction by Patrick Flynn. Associate producer, George Milman. Produced by Michael Butler in association with K. H. Nezhad. Opened 5 October 1977 at the Biltmore Theatre and closed 6 November 1977 after 43 performances.

CAST (in order of appearance): *Claude*: RANDALL EASTERBROOK. *Berger*: MICHAEL HOIT. *Woof*: SCOTT THORNTON. *Hud*: CLEAVANT DERRICKS. *Sheila*: ELLEN FOLEY. *Jeanie*: IRIS ROSENKRANTZ. *Dionne*: ALAINA REED. *Crissy*: KRISTEN VIGARD. *Shopping Cart Lady*: Michael Leslie. *Mothers*: ANNIE GOLDEN, LOUIS MATTIOLI, PERRY ARTHUR. *Fathers*: James Rich, Eva Charney, Martha Wingate. *Principals*: Carl Woerner, Michael Leslie, Linda Myers. *Tourist Couple*: Perry Arthur, Carl Woerner. *General Grant*: CARL WOERNER. *Abraham Lincoln*: Linda Myers. *Sergeant*: Byron Utley. *Parents*: Lori Wagner, James Rich.

The Tribe: Perry Arthur, Emily Bindinger, Paul Binotto, Eva Charney, Loretta Devine, Doug Katsaros, Michael Leslie, Louis Mattioli, Linda Myers, Raymond Patterson, James Rich, James Sbano, Deborah Van Valkenburgh, Lori Wagner, Doug Wall, Martha Wingate, Carl Woerner, Charlaine Woodard.

1977.16
THE ACT

A Musical in Two Acts, 16 Scenes. Book by George Furth. Music by John Kander. Lyrcis by Fred Ebb. Directed by Martin Scorsese. Choreography by Ron Lewis. Scenery designed by Tony Walton. Lighting designed by Tharon Musser. Costumes designed by Halston. Sound designed by Abe Jacob. Musical direction by Stanley Lebowsky. Orchestrations by Ralph Burns. Dance music arrangements by Ronald Melrose. Vocal and choral arrangements by Earl Brown. Produced by The Shubert Organization, Cy Feuer and Ernest H. Martin. Opened 29 October 1977 at the Majestic Theatre and closed 1 July 1978 after 233 performances.

CAST (in order of appearance): *Lenny Kanter*: Christopher Barrett. *Michelle Craig*: LIZA MINNELLI. *Nat Schreiber*: Arnold Soboloff. *Dan Connors*: BARRY NELSON. *Arthur*: Roger Minami. *Charley Price*: Mark Goddard. *Molly Connors*: Gayle Crofoot. *The Boys*: Wayne Cilento, Michael Leeds, Roger Minami, Albert Stephenson. *The Girls*: Carol Estey, Laurie Dawn Skinner. *Dance Alternates*: Claudia Asbury, Brad Witsger.

The action takes place at the Hotel Las Vegas at the present time and concerns Michelle Craig's nightclub act and her memories.

ACT 1
Scene 1
"Shine It On"
    (L. Minnelli, Chorus)
Scene 2
"It's the Strangest Thing"
    (L. Minnelli)
Scene 4
"Bobo's"
    (L. Minnelli, Dancers)
Scene 5
"Turning" (Shaker Hymn)
Scene 6
"Little Do They Know"
    (Boys, Girls)
Scene 7
"Arthur in the Afternoon"
    (L. Minnelli, R. Minami)
Scene 9
"Hollywood, California"[5]
    (L. Minnelli, Dancers)

Scene 11
"The Money Tree"
    (L. Minnelli)
ACT 2
Scene 1
"City Lights"
    (L. Minnelli, Chorus)
Scene 2
"There When I Need Him"
    (L. Minnelli)
Scene 4
"Hot Enough for You?"
    (L. Minnelli, Dancers)
"Little Do They Know" (reprise)
    (Boys, Girls)
Scene 5
Finale[6]
"My Own Space"
    (L. Minnelli)

1977.17
THE PIRATES OF PENZANCE,
or The Slave of Duty

A Revival of the Comic Opera in Two Acts[7]. Libretto by William S. Gilbert. Music by Arthur Sullivan. Production directed by Jack Eddleman. Scenic design by Lloyd Evans. Costume design by Patton Campbell. Lighting design by Hans Sondheimer. Conductor, Judith Somogi. Chorus master, Lloyd Walser. Produced by the New York City Opera. Opened 29 October 1977 at the New York State Theatre and closed 6 November 1977 after 2 performances in repertory.

CAST: *Major General Stanley*: JAMES BILLINGS. *The Pirate King*: RICHARD McKEE. *Samuel*, his Lieutenant: James Sergi. *Frederic*, the Pirate Apprentice: HOWARD HENSEL. *Sergeant of Police*: IRWIN DENSEN. *Mabel, Edith, Kate, Isabel*, General Stanley's Daughters: GIANNA ROLANDI, DIANA KEHRIG, SANDRA WALKER, LUXEMBURG. *Ruth*, Pirate Maid-of-all-work: MURIEL COSTA-GREENSPON. *Solo Dancer*: Rafael Romero. *Chorus of Pirates, Police and General Stanley's Daughters*: New York City Opera Chorus.

1977.18
JESUS CHRIST SUPERSTAR

A Revival of the Musical in Two Acts[8]. Music by Andrew Lloyd Webber. Lyrics by Tim Rice. Directed by William Daniel Grey. Choreography and movement by Kelly Carrol. Musical direction by Peter Phillips. Wardobe supervisor, Joan Lucas. Produced by Hal Zeiger. Opened 23 November 1977 at the Longacre Theatre and closed 12 February 1978 after 96 performances[9].

CAST (in order of appearance): *Judas Iscariot*: PATRICK JUDE. *Jesus of Nazareth*: WILLIAM DANIEL GREY. *Mary Magdalene*: BARBARA NILES. *First Priest, Apostle*: Doug Lucas. *Second Priest, Apostle*: Richard Tolin. *Caiaphas*: CHRISTOPHER CABLE. *Annas*: STEVE SCHOCHET. *Simon Zealotes*: BOBBY LONDON. *Peter*: RANDY MARTIN. *Pontius Pilate*: RANDY WILSON. *Soldier, Tormentor*: D. Bradley Jones. *Soldier, Tormentor*: George Bernhard. *Soul Girls*: Freida Ann Williams, Pauletta Pearson, Claudette Washington. *Maid by the Fire*: Celeste Hogan. *Apostles*: David Cahn, Ken Samuels, Lennie Del Duca. *King Herod*: MARK SYERS.

Biltmore Theatre for 1750 performances. For Synopsis of Scenes and Musical Numbers, see original 1968 production. For this production; the following changes were made:
    "Dead End" (added to Act 1 after "Ain't Got No")
    "Hung" (dropped)
    "Prisoners in Niggertown" retitled "Three-Five-Zero-Zero."
[5]Dropped during run.

---

[6]Replaced after opening with:
    "Walking Papers"
        (L. Minnelli)
[7]First presented in New York 31 December 1879 at the Fifth Avenue Theatre for a total of 91 performances in two engagements. For Synopsis of Scenes and Musical Numbers, see original 1879 production.
[8]First produced in New York 12 October 1971 at the Mark Hellinger Theatre for 711 performances. For Synopsis of Scenes and Musical Numbers, see original 1971 production.
[9]This revival was staged concert style; orchestrations, costumes, sets, lighting and sound were uncredited.

ELVIS: THE LEGEND LIVES!

1978.01

A Musical Entertainment in Two Acts, 5 Scenes. Production concept by John Finocchio, Larry Marshak, David Zaan. (Based on the life and music of Elvis Presley.) Directed by Jim Sotos and Henry Scarpelli. Musical director, Peter Dino. Special consultant, Paul Lichter. Title music by Doc Pomus and Bruce Foster. Lighting by Barry Arnold. Sound by Joe Golden. Visual concepts and design by Productions Two. Produced by DL Theatrical Productions Inc. (John Finocchio, Larry Marshak, David Zaan). Opened 31 January 1978 at the Palace Theatre and closed 30 April 1978 after 101 performances.

CAST: RICK SAUCEDO, THE JORDANAIRES (Gordon Stoker, Neal Matthews, Hoyt Hawkins), WILL JORDON, D. J. FONTANA. *Kharisma*: Bernice Frazier, Judith O'Dell, April Epps.

Act 1, Scene 1: The Music That Led to the King of Rock 'n Roll. *Scene 2*: Sun Recording Session. *Scene 3*: The Louisiana Hayride. *Scene 4*: The Ed Sullivan Show.

Act 2: International Hotel, Las Vegas.

ACT 1[10]

Scene 1

"Mood Indigo"

"Anytime"

"When the Saints Go Marching In"

"In the Mood"

"Johnny Be Good"

"C. C. Rider"

Scene 2

"Blue Moon of Kentucky"

"When My Blue Moon Turns to Gold Again"

Scene 3

"Heartbreak Hotel"

"How Great Thou Art"

Scene 4

"Reddy Teddy"/"Tutti Fruiti" medley

"Don't Be Cruel"

"One Night With You"

"Lawdy Miss Clawdy"

"A Fool Such As I"

"Hound Dog"

ACT 2

"Theme from 2001"

"Burning Love"

"Are You Lonesome Tonight?"

"I Just Can't Help Believing"

"You Lost That Lovin' Feeling"

"Polk Salad Annie"

"The Wonder of You"

"My Way"

"Moody Blue"

"Little Darlin'"

"In the Ghetto"

"Whole Lot of Shakin'"/"Hound Dog" (reprise)

"Sweet Caroline"

"Suspicious Minds"

"The Legend Lives On"

"American Trilogy"

[10]This composite score was made up of many rock 'n' roll and pop standards for which no credits were given.

ON THE TWENTIETH CENTURY

1978.02

A Musical Comedy in Two Acts, 15 Scenes. Book and lyrics by Betty Comden and Adolph Green. Based on the play ("Twentieth Century") by Ben Hecht, Charles MacArthur and Bruce Milholland. Music by Cy Coleman. Directed by Harold Prince. Musical numbers staged by Larry Fuller. Scenery designed by Robin Wagner. Costumes designed by Florence Klotz. Lighting designed by Ken Billington. Musical director, Paul Gemigani. Orchestrations by Hershy Kay. Furs by Ben Kahn. Associate producers, Sam Crothers, Andre Pastoria. Produced by The Producers Circle 2, Inc. (Robert Fryer, Mary Lea Johnson, James Cresson, Martin Richards) in association with Joseph Harris and Ira Bernstein. Opened 19 February 1978 at the St. James Theatre and closed 18 March 1979 after 460 performances.

CAST (in order of appearance): *Porters*: Keith Davis, Quitman Fludd III, Ray Stephens, Joseph Wise. *Conductor Flanagan*: TOM BATTEN. *Train Secretary Rogers*: STANLEY SIMMONDS. *Letitia Primrose*: IMOGENE COCA. *Owen O'Malley*: GEORGE COE. *Oliver Webb*: DEAN DITTMAN. *Redcap*: Mel Johnson, Jr. *Congressman Lockwood*: RUFUS SMITH. *Anita*: Carol (Jo) Lugenbeal. *Oscar Jaffee*: JOHN CULLUM. *Max Jacobs*: GEORGE LEE ANDREWS. *Imelda*: Willi Burke. *Maxwell Finch*: David Horwitz. *Mildred Plotka/Lily Garland*: MADELINE KAHN. *Otto Von Bismark*: Sal Mistretta. *Bruce Granit*: KEVIN KLINE. *Agnes*: JUDY KAYE. *Hospital Attendants*: Sal Mistretta, Carol Lurie. *Dr. Johnson*: WILLI BURKE.

Singers: Susan Cella, Maris Clement, Peggy Cooper, Karen Gibson, Carol Lugenbeal, Carol Lurie, Melanie Vaughan, Linda Poser, Ray Gill, Ken Hilliard, David Horwitz, Craig Lucas, Sal Mistretta, Hal Norman, Charles Rule, David Vogel, Gerald Teijelo.

The action takes place in the early 1930s, mainly on the 20th Century Limited (train) from Chicago to New York.

Act 1, Scene 1: Chicago, La Salle Station platform. *Scene 2*: The Observation Car and Drawing Room "A." *Scene 3*: Flashback to the bare stage of a theatre. *Scene 4*: Drawing Room "A." *Scene 5*: The Observation Car and Corridor. *Scene 6*: Drawing Room "B." *Scene 7*: The Observation Car. *Scene 8*: Triple Scene of the Observation Car, Drawing Room "A," Drawing Room "B." *Scene 9*; Drawing Rooms "A" and "B." *Scene 10*: Drawing Room "A."

Act 2, Scene 1: "Drawing Room "A." *Scene 2*: "Drawing Room "B." *Scene 3*: The Observation Car. *Scene 4*: Drawing Room "B" in the middle of the night. *Scene 5*: The Observation Car.

ACT 1[11]

Scene 1

"On the Twentieth Century"

Porters, I. Coca, T. Batten, S. Simmonds, Passengers

Scene 2

"I Rise Again"

J. Cullum, G. Coe, D. Dittman

Scene 3

"Indian Maiden's Lament"

W. Burke, M. Kahn

"Veronique"

M. Kahn, Male Singers

Scene 4

"I Have Written a Play"

T. Batten

Scene 5

"Together"

Porters, Passengers, J. Cullum

Scene 6

"Never"

M. Kahn, G. Coe, D. Dittman

"Our Private World"

M. Kahn, J. Cullum

Scene 7

"Repent"

I. Coca

[11]After opening, added as an additional scene set on stage during a play:

"Stranded Again"

C. Rule (as Bishop), Singers

Scene 8
  "Mine"
    J. Cullum, K. Kline
Scene 9
  "I've Got It All"
    M. Kahn, J. Cullum
Scene 10
  "On the Twentieth Century" (reprise)
    Company

ACT 2
  Entr'acte ("Life Is Like a Train")
    Porters
Scene 1
  "Five Zeros"
    G. Coe, D. Dittman, I. Coca, J. Cullum
Scene 2
  "Sextet"
    G. Coe, D. Dittman, J. Cullum, I. Coca, M. Kahn, K. Kline
Scene 3
  "She's a Nut"
    Company
  "Max Jacobs"
    G. L. Andrews
Scene 4
  "Babbette"
    M. Kahn
Scene 5
  "The Legacy"
    J. Cullum
  "Lily, Oscar"
    M. Kahn, J. Cullum

1978.03   TIMBUKTU!

A Musical Fable in Two Acts, 12 Scenes. Book by Luther Davis, based on the musical "Kismet"[12] by Charles Lederer and Luther Davis, from the play of the same name by Edward Knoblock. Music and lyrics by Robert Wright and George Forrest from the themes of Alexander Borodin and African Folk Music. Directed, choreographed and costumed by Geoffrey Holder. Scenery by Tony Straiges. Lighting by Ian Calderon. Sound by Abe Jacob. Musical direction and incidental music by Charles H. Coleman. Additional orchestrations by Bill Brohn. Associate producer, Alan Eichler. Produced by Luther Davis, in association with Sarnoff International Enterprises, William D. Cunningham, John F. Kennedy Center for the Performing Arts. Opened 1 March 1978 at the Mark Hellinger Theatre and closed 10 September 1978 after 243 performances.

CAST (in order of appearance): *The Chakaba*, Stiltwalker: Obba Babatunde. *Beggars*: Harold Pierson, Shezwae Powell, Lewis Tucker. *Hadji*: IRA HAWKINS. *Marsinah*, his daughter: MELBA MOORE. *Witchdoctor*: Harold Pierson. *Child*: Deborah Waller. *M'Ballah of the River*: Daniel Barton. *Najua*, Servant to Sahleem-La-Lume: Eleanor McCoy. *The Wazir*: GEORGE BELL. *Chief Policeman*: BRUCE A. HUBBARD. *Sahleem-La-Lume*: EARTHA KITT. *The Three Princesses of Baguezane*: Deborah K. Brown, Sharon Cuff, Patricia Lumpkin. *Munshi*, Bodyservant to the Mansa: MIGUEL GODREAU. *The Mansa of Mali*: GILBERT PRICE. *Orange Merchant*: Obba Babatunde. *Birds of Paradise*: Miguel Godreau, Eleanor McCoy. *Antelopes*: Obba Babatunde, Luther Fontaine. *Woman in the Garden*: Shezwae Powell. *Zubbediya*: Vanessa Shaw.

Citizens of Timbuktu: Obba Babtunde, Gregg Baker, Daniel Barton, Joella Breedlove, Deborah K. Brown, Tony Carroll, Sharon Cuff, Cheryl Cummings, Luther Fontaine, Michael F. Harrison, Dyane Harvey, Marzetta Jones, Jimmy Justice, Eugene Little, Patricia Lumpkin, Joe Lynn, Tony Ndogo, Harold Pierson, Ray Pollard, Shezwae Powell, Ronald Richardson, Vanessa Shaw, Louis Tucker, Deborah Waller, Renee Warren.

The action takes place in Timbuktu, in the ancient empire of Mali, West Africa, in the year 1361 (of Islam 752).

Act 1: From Dawn to Dusk. *Scene 1*: The City Square of Timbuktu—Dawn. *Scene 2*: The Gates of the City. *Scene 3*: The City Square at Market Time. *Scene 4*: A Garden of a House near the Palace. *Scene 5*: A Courtyard of the Palace. *Scene 6*: An Attiring Pavilion in the Palace.

Act 2: From Dusk to Dawn. *Scene 1*: Enroute to the Garden. *Scene 2*: The Garden. *Scene 3*: A Corridor in the Palace. *Scene 4*: The Wazir's Harem. *Scene 5*: Another Part of the Palace. *Scene 6*: Palace Court.

ACT 1
Scene 1
  "Rhymes Have I"
    I. Hawkins, M. Moore, Beggars
  "Fate"
    I. Hawkins
Scene 2
  "In the Beginning, Woman"[13]
    E. Kitt
Scene 3
  "Baubles, Bangles and Beads"
    M. Moore, Merchants
Scene 4
  Dance: Birds in Paradise Garden[14]
  "Stranger in Paradise"
    G. Price, M. Moore
Scene 5
  "Gesticulate"
    I. Hawkins, Council
Scene 6
  "Night of My Nights"
    G. Price, Courtiers
ACT 2
Scene 1
  Dance: Nuptual Celebration[15]
    People of Mali
Scene 2
  "My Magic Lamp"[16]/"Stranger in Paradise"
    M. Moore
Scene 4
  "Rahadlakum"
    E. Kitt, Ladies of the Harem
Scene 5
  "And This Is My Beloved"
    I. Hawkins, M. Moore, G. Price, G. Bell
Scene 6
  "Golden Land, Golden Life"[17]
    B. A. Hubbard, Nobles of the Court
  "Zubbediya" and Dances
    V. Shaw, Ensemble
  "Night of My Nights" (reprise)
    G. Price, M. Moore, I. Hawkins, Nobles of the Court
  "Sands of Time"
    I. Hawkins, E. Kitt

[12]First produced in New York 3 December 1953 at the Ziegfeld Theatre for 583 performances.

[13]Newly written for this production, and not from the original musical score of "Kismet."
[14]Newly written for this production, and not from the original musical score of "Kismet."
[15]Newly written for this production, and not from the original musical score of "Kismet."
[16]Newly written for this production, and not from the original musical score of "Kismet."
[17]Newly written for this production, and not from the original musical score of "Kismet."

1978.04

HELLO, DOLLY!

A Revival of the Musical Comedy in Two Acts, 13 Scenes[18]. Book by Michael Stewart. Based on the play "The Matchmaker" by Thornton Wilder. Music and lyrics by Jerry Herman. Directed by Lucia Victor. Choreographed by Jack Craig. Original production directed and choreographed by Gower Champion. Settings by Oliver Smith. Costumes by Freddy Wittop. Lighting by Martin Aronstein. Musical direction by John DeMain. Conducted by Jack Everly. (Orchestrations uncredited.) Dance and incidental music arranged by Peter Howard. Production supervision by Jerry Herman. Associate producer, Robert A. Buckley. Produced by James M. Nederlander and the Houston Grand Opera Opened 5 March 1978 at the Lunt-Fontanne Theatre and closed 9 July 1978 after 147 performances.

<u>CAST</u> (in the order of appearance): *Mrs. Dolly Gallagher Levi*: CAROL CHANNING. *Ernestina*: P. J. Nelson. *Ambrose Kemper*: Michael C. Booker. *Horse*: Carole Banninger, Debra Pigliavento. *Horace Vandergelder*: EDDIE BRACKEN. *Ermengarde*: K. T. Baumann. *Cornelius Hackl*: LEE ROY REAMS. *Barnaby Tucker*: ROBERT LYDIARD. *Minnie Fay*: ALEXANDRA KOREY. *Irene Molloy*: FLORENCE LACEY. *Mrs. Rose*: Marilyn Hudgins. *Rudolph*: John Anania. *Judge*: Bill Bateman. *Court Clerk*: Randolph Riscol.

Townspeople, Waiters, Etc.: Diane Abrams, Carole Banninger, JoEla Flood, Marilyn Hudgins, Deborah Moldow, Janyce Nyman, Jacqueline Payne, Debra Pigliavento, Theresa Rakov, Barbara Ann Thompson, Richard Ammon, Bill Bateman, Kyle Cittadin, Ron Crofott, Don Edward Detrick, Richard Dodd, Rob Draper, David Evans, Tom Garrett, Charlie Goeddertz, James Homan, Alex MacKay, Richard Maxon, Randy Morgan, Randolph Riscol, Mark Waldrop. *Swing Dancers*: Coby Grossbart, Bubba Rambo.

1978.05

DANCIN'

A Musical Entertainment (Revue) in Three Acts, Thirteen Scenes. (Conceived,) directed and choreographed by Bob Fosse. Scenery designed by Peter Larkin. Cotumes designed by Willa Kim. Lighting designed by Jules Fisher. Music and lyrics by Johann Sebastian Bach, Ralph Burns, George M. Cohan, Neil Diamond, Bob Haggart, Ray Bauduc, Gil Rodin and Bob Crosby, Jerry Lieber and Mike Stoller, Johnny Mercer and Harry Warren, Louis Prima, John Philip Sousa, Carole Bayer Sager and Melissa Manchester, Barry Mann and Cynthia Weil, Felix Powell and George Asaf, Sigmund Romberg and Oscar Hammerstein II, Cat Stevens, Edgard Varèse, Jerry Jeff Walker. Music arranged and conducted by Gordon Lowry Harrell. Orchestrations by Ralph Burns. Sound by Abe Jacob. Associate producer, Patti Grubman. Produced by Jules Fisher, The Shubert Organization, and Columbia Pictures. Opened 27 March 1978 at the Broadhurst Theatre, moved 4 December 1980 to the Ambassador Theatre, and closed 27 June 1982 after 1774 performances.

<u>CAST</u> (in alphabetical order):Gail Benedict, Sandahl Bergman, Karen G. Burke, Rene Ceballos, Christopher Chadman, Wayne Cilento, Jill Cook, Gregory B. Drotar, Vicki Frederick, Linda Haberman, Richard Korthaze, Edward Love, John Mineo, Ann Reinking, Blane Savage, Charles Ward. *Alternates*: Christine Colby, William Whitener, Valerie Miller.

ACT 1

Scene 1

Opening:

Prologue: "Hot August Night"
  (*Music and Lyrics by* Neil Diamond.)
"Crunchy Granola Suite"
  W. Cilento, J. Mineo
Danced by the Company
  (*Music and Lyrics by* Neil Diamond.)

Scene 2

Recollections of an Old Dancer:

"Mr. Bojangles"
  W. Cilento
    Mr. Bojangles: C. Chadman. *Mr. Bojangles' Spirit*: G. B. Drotar.
  (*Music and Lyrics by* Jerry Jeff Walker.)

Scene 3

The Dream Barre:

"Chaconne" (A transcription from Bach's Sonata for Violin Solo No. 4)
  A Boy: C. Ward. *A Girl*: A. Reinking. *Ballet Master*: R. Korthaze.

Scene 4

Percussion:

Part 1
  R. Ceballos, V. Frederick, L. Haberman
Part 2
  C. Chadman, W. Cilento, J. Mineo
Part 3
  S. Bergman, G. Benedict, K. G. Burke, J. Cook, G. B. Drotar, E. Love, A. Reinking, B. Savage
Part 4: "Ionisation"
  C. Ward
  (*Music by* Edgard Varèse.)

ACT 2

Scene 1

Dancin' Man:

"I Wanna Be a Dancin' Man" (from the film *THE BELLE OF NEW YORK*)
  The Company
  (*Music by* Harry Warren. *Lyrics by* Johnny Mercer.)

Scene 2

Three in One:

"Big Noise from Winnetka"
  K. G. Burke, W. Cilento, J. Cook
  (*Music and Lyrics by* Bob Haggart, Ray Bauduc, Gil Rodin and Bob Crosby.)

Scene 3

"If It Feels Good, Let It Ride"
  Pas de Deux: V. Frederick, C. Ward; R. Ceballos, G. B. Drotar; S. Bergman, B. Savage.
  (*Music and Lyrics by* Carole Bayer Sager and Melissa Manchester.)
"Easy"
  C. Chadman, W. Cilento, E. Love, J. Mineo
  (*Music and Lyrics by* Carole Bayer Sager and Melissa Manchester.)
  Danced by A. Reinking

Scene 4

A Manic Depressive's Lament:

"I've Got Them Feelin' Too Good Today Blues"
  E. Love
  (*Music and Lyrics by* Jerry Leiber and Mike Stoller.)

Scene 5

Fourteen Feet:

"Was Dog a Doughnut"
  S. Bergman, C. Chadman, W. Cilento, G. B. Drotar, V. Frederick, A. Reinking, B. Savage
  (*Music and Lyrics by* Cat Stevens.)

ACT 3

Scene 1

Benny's Number:

"Sing, Sing, Sing"
  (*Music by* Louis Prima.)
    Part 1: The Company.
    Part 2: *Trombone Solo*: V. Frederick, B. Savage, C. Ward. *Trumpet Solo*: A. Reinking. *Clarinet Solo*: The Company. *Piano Solo*: W. Cilento, J. Mineo.

Scene 2

The Female Star Spot:

"Here You Come Again"
  S. Bergman, K. G. Burke, R. Ceballos, V. Frederick
  (*Music and Lyrics by* Barry Mann and Cynthia Weil.)

Scene 3

America:

"(I'm a) Yankee Doodle Dandy" (from *LITTLE JOHNNY JONES*)The Company
  (*Music and Lyrics by* George M. Cohan.)
"Gary Owen"
  G. Benedict, L. Haberman, G. B. Drotar
"Stout Hearted Men" (from *THE NEW MOON*)
  S. Bergman, V. Frederick, A. Reinking
  (*Music by* Sigmund Romberg. *Lyrics by* Oscar Hammerstein II.)

---

[18]Originally produced in New York 16 January 1964 at the St. James Theatre for 2844 performances. For Synopsis of Scenes and Musical Numbers, see original 1964 production. "Come and Be My Butterfly" was not performed in this revival. Act 1, Scene 3, and Act 2, Scene 4, were eliminated from this production.

"Under the Double Eagle"
  W. Cilento, J. Mineo, B. Savage
"Dixie"
  K. G. Burke, E. Love
"When Johnny Comes Marching Home"
  A. Reinking
"Rally Round the Flag"
  R. Ceballos
"Pack Up Your Troubles in Your Old Kit Bag"
  V. Frederick, G. Benedict, J. Mineo
  (*Music by* Felix Powell. *Lyrics by* George Asaf.)
"The Stars and Stripes Forever"
  C. Ward
  (*Music by* John Philip Sousa.)
"Yankee Doodle Disco"
  The Company
  (*Choreographed by* Christopher Chadman.)

Scene 4

Improvisation:

"Dancin'"
  The Company
  (*Music by* Ralph Burns.)

A HISTORY OF THE AMERICAN FILM

1978.06

A Play with Music in Two Acts, 35 Scenes. Play (and lyrics) by Chris Durang. Music by Mel Marvin. Entire production directed by David Chambers. Musical staging by Graciela Daniele. Set designed by Tony Straiges. Costumes designed by Marjorie Slaiman. Lighting designed by William Mintzer. Sound design by Lou Shapiro. Musical direction by Clay Fullum. Orchestrations by Robert M. Freedman. Associate producers, Marc Howard, Sheila-Barbara-Dinah Productions. Produced by Judith [Judy] Gordon and Richard S. Bright. Opened 30 March 1978 at the ANTA Theatre and closed 16 April 1978 after 21 performances.

CAST (in alphabetical order): *Contract Player #8, whose roles are Blessed Virgin Mother, Speakeasy Patron, Nurse, Voice of Anna Karenina, Ma Joad, Cucumber Girl, Voice of Sonja Henie*: Maureen Anderman. *Jimmy*: Gary Bayer. *Contract Player #1, whose roles are Michael, Salad Chef*: Walter Bobbie. *Contract Player #5, whose roles are Ticket Man, Newsboy, Young Speakeasy Patron, Young Reporter, Grandma Joad, Mickey*: Jeff Brooks. *Contract Player #7, whose roles are Cop, Bartender, Judge, Edward Mortimer, Von Leffing, Navy Officer, Victor Henreid, Theatre Manager, Voices of Vronsky, John, Academy Award Announcer, F81 Narrator, God*: Bryan Clark. *Contract Player #4, whose roles are Jesus, Ferruchi, Ernie the Reporter, Abdhul, Pa Joad, Make-up Man, Harkness, Uncle Sam, Marine Officer, Robot*: David Cromwell. *Contract Player #10 whose roles are Minstrel, Clarinet Man, "Big" Hit Man, David, Fife*: David Garrison. *Contract Player #3, whose roles are Piano Man, Viola, Indian, Ito, Sailor, Stuart*: Ben Halley, Jr. *Bette*: Swoosie Kurtz. *Contract Player #6, whose roles are Orphanage Lady, Ma O'Reilly, Allison Martimer, Prison Warden, Lettuce Girl, Gold Star Mother, WAC*: Kate McGregor-Stewart. *Eve*: Joan Pape. *Loretta*: April Shawhan. *Hank*: Brent Spiner. *Contract Player #9, whose roles are God, Little Hit Man, Eric, Santa, Snare, Voice of Robot*: Eric Weitz. *Contract Player #2, whose roles are Silent Mother, Bartender's Girl, Clara Mortimer, Carrot Girl*: Mary Catherine Wright. *Pianist* (On-Stage): Robert Fisher.

The action takes place in a large movie palace with an upstage balcony.

ACT 1

Scene 1

"The Silent Years" (instrumental)

"Minstrel Song"
  D. Garrison

Scene 3

"Shanty Town Romance"
  G. Bayer, A. Shawhan

Scene 7

"They Can't Prohibit Love"
  S. Kurtz

Scene 12

"We're in a Salad"
  B. Spiner, Salad Girls, D. Garrison, E. Weitz, W. Bobbie
  Salad Girls: Bean: A. Shawhan. *Tomato*: S. Kurtz. *Celery*: J. Pape. *Cucumber*: M. Anderman. *Lettuce*: K. McGregor-Stewart. *Carrot*: M. C. Wright.

Scene 14

"Euphemism"
  A. Shawhan

Scene 18

"Ostende Nobis Tosca"
  S. Kurtz, B. Spiner, D. Garrison, E. Weitz
"The Red, the White and the Blue"
  J. Pape, Company

ACT 2

Scene 3

"Pretty Pin-Up"
  J. Pape, A. Shawhan, S. Kurtz, M. C. Wright

Scene 12

"Apple Blossom Victory"
  S. Kurtz, J. Pape, K. McGregor-Stewart

Scene 14

"Isn't It Fun to Be in the Movies"
  D. Morrison, E. Weitz

Scene 17

"Search for Wisdom"
  G. Boyer, A. Shawhan, Company

THE MERRY WIDOW

1978.07

A Revival of the Operetta in Three Acts, 4 Scenes[19]. Original Viennese libretto ('Die lustige witwe') and lyrics by Victor Léon and Leo Stein (after "L'Attaché d'Ambassade" by Henri Meilhac.) Music by Franz Lehár. New English translation and dialogue by Ursula Eggers and Joseph de Rugeris. New lyrics by Sheldon Harnick. This San Diego Opera production directed by Tito Capobianco. Stage director and choreographer, Gigi Denda. Production (settings, costumes) design by Carl Toms. Lighting design by Ken Billington. Conductor, Julius Rudel. Produced by the New York City Opera. Opened 2 April 1978 at the New York State Theatre and closed 27 April 1978 after 8 performances in repertory.

CAST: *Baron Mirko Zeta*: DAVID RAE SMITH. *Valencienne*: Glenys Fowles. *Count Danilo*: ALAN TITUS. *Anna Glawari*: BEVERLY SILLS. *Camille de Rosillon*: BRUCE REED. *Vicomte Cascada*: HARLAN FOSS. *Raoul St. Brioche*: HOWARD HENSEL. *Bogdanovitch*: JOHN LANKSTON. *Sylviane*: Jane Shaulis. *Kromov*: William Ledbetter. *Olga*: Sandra Walker. *Pritchitch*: Jonathan Green. *Praskovia*: Puli Toro. *Njegus*: JAMES BILLINGS. *(Grisettes:) Lolo*: Candace Itow. *Dodo*: Jane Shaulis. *Jou-Jou*: Sandra Walker. *Frou-Frou*: Toni-Ann Gardella. *Clo-Clo*: Puli Toro. *Margot*: Emilietta Ettlin. *Ensemble*: New York City Opera Chorus.

Act 1: At the Petrovenian Embassy in Paris, 1905.

Act 2: At the home of Hannah Glawari.

Act 3: At Maxim's.

ACT 1

"Thank you for your invitation, sir"
  H. Foss, D. R. Smith, Ensemble
"Do listen, please"
  G. Fowles, B. Reed
"Gentlemen, how kind" (Anna's entrance)
  B. Sills, H. Foss, H. Hensel, Men
"Oh Fatherland" (Maxim's)
  A. Titus
"Ladies choice!" (Act 1 Finale)
  Company

ACT 2

"If you'll indulge us" (Dances and Vilia)
  B. Sills, Ensemble
"Heia! See the horseman come"
  B. Sills, A. Titus
"Ev'ry woman ... "
  A. Titus, Men

---

[19]Originally produced in New York 21 October 1907 at the New Amsterdam Theatre for 416 performances.

"I'm often at Maxim's"
 A. Titus
"Just as a rosebud blossoms"
 G. Fowles, B. Reed
"Ha! Ha! Ha!" (Act 2 Finale)
 Company

ACT 3
"Here we are: Grisettes and Playgirls" (Grisette Song)
 G. Fowles, Grisettes
"I'm a loyal native son" (Très parisien)
 J. Billings, Ensemble
"Strings are sighing" (Waltz)
 A. Titus, B. Sills
"Oh the study of feminine ways" (Act 3 Finale)
 Company

THE SAINT OF BLEECKER STREET

1978.08

A Revival of the Opera (Musical Drama) in Three Acts, 5 Scenes[20]. Music and libretto by Gian-Carlo Menotti. Conducted by Cal Stewart Kellogg. Directed by Francis Rizzo. Sets designed by Beeb Salzer. Costumes designed by Carol Luiken. Choreography by Thomas Andrew. Lighting by Hans Sondheimer. Chorus master, Lloyd Walser. Produced by the New York City Opera. Opened 13 April 1978 at the New York State Theatre and closed 23 April 1978 after 3 performances in repertory.

CAST (in order of appearance): *Assunta*: Jane Shaulis. *A Young Man*: Alan Kays. *Maria Corona*: Judith De Rosa. *Her Son*: Bobby Scalese. *Carmela*: Diana Soviero. *A Young Woman*: Martha Thigpen. *Don Marco*: Irwin Densen. *Annina*: CATHERINE MALFITANO. *Michele*: ENRICO diGIUSEPPE. *Concettina*: Lila Herbert. *Desideria*: SANDRA WALKER. *First Guest*: Alan Kays. *Second Guest*: Alan Baker. *Salvatore*: William Ledbetter. *Bartender*: Kenn Dovel. *A Nun*: Charlott Thyssen. *A Young Priest*: Ron Boucher. *Neighbors*: Don Henderson, Harris Davis. *Neighbors, Friends, Policemen, etc.*: New York City Opera Chorus.

AIN'T MISBEHAVIN'

1978.09

A Musical Revue in Two Acts, 22 Scenes[21], based on the music of Thomas "Fats" Waller. Conceived and directed by Richard Maltby, Jr. Based on an idea by Murray Horwitz and Richard Maltby, Jr. Musical numbers staged by Arthur Faria. Music supervision by Luther Henderson. Associate director, Murray Horwitz. Orchestrations and arrangements by Luther Henderson. Vocal arrangements by William Elliott, Jeffrey Gutcheon. Sets by John Lee Beatty. Costumes by Randy Barcelo. Lighting by Pat Collins. Sound by Otts Munderloh. Originally produced (Off-Broadway) by the Manhattan Theatre Club. Produced by Emanuel Azenberg, Dasha Epstein, The Shubert Organization, Jane Gaynor and Ron Dante. Opened 9 May 1978 at the Longacre Theatre, moved 29 January 1979 to the Plymouth Theatre, moved 26 January 1981 to the Belasco Theatre and closed 21 February 1982 after 1604 performances. Total, including Off-Broadway, 1632 performances.

CAST: NELL CARTER, ANDRE DeSHIELDS, ARMELIA McQUEEN, KEN PAGE, CHARLAINE WOODARD. *Pianist*: LUTHER HENDERSON.

ACT 1[22]
Scene 1
"Ain't Misbehavin'" (1929)(from *HOT CHOCOLATES*)
 Company
 (*Music by* Thomas Waller and Harry Brooks. *Lyrics by* Andy Razaf.)
Scene 2
"Lookin' Good But Feelin' Bad" (1929)
 Company
 (*Lyrics by* Lester A. Santly. *Vocal Arrangement by* Jeffrey Gutcheon.)

[20]Originally produced in New York 27 December 1954 at the Broadway Theatre for 92 performances. For Synopsis of Scenes, see original 1954 production.
[21]First produced in New York Off-Broadway 8 February–5 March 1978 at the Manhattan Theatre Club for 28 performances.
[22]All music by Thomas "Fats" Waller alone, except where indicated. Songs not written by "Fats" Waller were recorded by him.

Scene 3
""T Aint Nobody's Biz-ness If I Do" (1922)
 A. DeShields, Company
 (*Music and Lyrics by* Porter Grainger and Everett Robbins. *Additional Lyrics by* Richard Maltby, Jr. and Murray Horwitz.)
Scene 4
"Honeysuckle Rose" (1929)(from *LOAD OF COAL*)
 K. Page, N. Carter
 (*Lyrics by* Andy Razaf.)
Scene 5
"Squeeze Me" (1925)
 A. McQueen
 (*Lyrics by* Clarence Williams.)
Scene 6
"Handful of Keys" (1933)
 Company
 (*Lyrics by* Richard Maltby, Jr. and Murray Horwitz based on an idea by Marty Grosz. *Vocal Arrangement by* William Elliott.)
Scene 7
"I've Got a Feeling I'm Falling" (1929)(from *APPLAUSE* film)
 N. Carter, Company
 (*Music by* Thomas Waller and Harry Link. *Lyrics by* Billy Rose.)
Scene 8
"How Ya Baby" (1938)
 A. DeShields, C. Woodard, Company
 (*Lyrics by* J. C. Johnson.)
Scene 9
"The Jitterbug Waltz" (1942)
 Company
 (*Lyrics by* Richard Maltby, Jr. *Vocal Arrangement by* William Elliott.)
Scene 10
"The Ladies Who Sing with the Band" (1943)(from *EARLY TO BED*)
 A. De Shields, K. Page
 (*Lyrics by* George Marion, Jr.)
"Yacht Club Swing" (1938)
 C. Woodard
 (*Music by* Thomas Waller and Herman Autry. *Lyrics by* J. C. Johnson.)
"When the Nylons Bloom Again" (1943)(from *EARLY TO BED*)
 A. McQueen, C. Woodard, N. Carter
 (*Lyrics by* George Marion, Jr.)
"Cash for Your Trash" (1942)
 N. Carter
 (*Lyrics by* Ed Kirkeby.)
"Off-Time" (1929)
 Company
 (*Music by* Thomas Waller and Harry Brooks. *Lyrics by* Andy Razaf. *Vocal Arrangement by* Jeffrey McGutcheon.)
Scene 11
"The Joint Is Jumpin'" (1938)
 Company
 (*Lyrics by* Andy Razaf and J. C. Johnson.)

ACT 2
Scene 1
"Spreadin' Rhythm Around" (1935)(from *KING OF BURLESQUE* film)
 Company
 (*Music by* Jimmy McHugh. *Lyrics by* Ted Koehler. *Additional Lyrics by* Richard Maltby, Jr.)
Scene 2
"Lounging at the Waldorf" (1936)
 A. McQueen, C. Woodard, K. Page, N. Carter
 (*Lyrics by* Richard Maltby, Jr. *Vocal Arrangement by* William Elliott.)
Scene 3
"The Viper's Drag" (1934)
 A. DeShields, Company
 (Traditional-"The Reefer Song")
Scene 4
"Mean to Me" (1929)N. Carter
 (*Music and Lyrics by* Roy Turk and Fred E. Ahlert.)

Scene 5

"Your Feet's Too Big" (1936)
K. Page
(*Music and Lyrics by* Ada Benson and Fred Fisher.)

Scene 6

"That Ain't Right" (1943)
A. DeShields, A. McQueen, Company
(*Music and Lyrics by* Nat King Cole. *Additional Lyrics by* Richard Maltby, Jr.
and Murray Horwitz.)

Scene 7

"Keepin' Out of Mischief Now" (1932)
C. Woodard
(*Lyrics by* Andy Razaf.)

Scene 8

"Find Out What They Like (and How They Like It)" (1929)
A. McQueen, N. Carter
(*Lyrics by* Andy Razaf.)

Scene 9

"Fat and Greasy" (1936)
A. DeShields, K. Page
(*Music and Lyrics by* Porter Grainger and Charlie Johnson.)

Scene 10

"Black and Blue" (1929) (from *HOT CHOCOLATES*)
Company
(*Music by* Thomas Waller and Harry Brooks. *Lyrics by* Andy Razaf. *Vocal
Arrangements by* William Elliott.)

Scene 11

Finale: songs by others which Fats Waller made hits
Company
"I'm Gonna Sit Right Down and Write Myself a Letter" (1933)
K. Page
(*Music by* Fred E. Ahlert. *Lyrics by* Joe Young.)
"Two Sleepy People" (1938) (from *THANKS FOR THE MEMORY* film)
A. McQueen, K. Page
(*Music by* Hoagy Carmichael. *Lyrics by* Frank Loesser.)
"I've Got My Fingers Crossed" (1935) (from *KING OF BURLESQUE* film)
A. McQueen, C. Woodard, K. Page
(*Music by* Jimmy McHugh. *Lyrics by* Ted Koehler.)
"I Can't Give You Anything But Love" (1928) (from *BLACKBIRDS OF 1928*)
A. DeShields, C. Woodard
(*Music by* Jimmy McHugh. *Lyrics by* Dorothy Fields.)
"It's a Sin to Tell a Lie" (1933)
N. Carter, Company
(*Music and Lyrics by* Billy Mayhew.)
"Honeysuckle Rose" (reprise) Company

1978.10 ANGEL

A Musical in Two Acts, 4 Scenes. Book by Ketti Frings and Peter Udell.
Based on the play "Look Homeward Angel" by Ketti Frings, adapted from
the novel of the same name by Thomas Wolfe. Music by Gary Geld. Lyrics
by Peter Udell. Directed by Philip Rose. Choreography by Robert Tucker.
Scenery by Ming Cho Lee. Lighting John Gleason. Costumes by Pearl
Somner. Orchestrations by Don Walker. Musical direction and dance
arrangements by William Cox. Associate producers, Karen Wald, Norman
Main. Originally produced at Northstage, Glen Cove, New York, by
Norman Main, Executive producer. Produced by Philip Rose and Ellen
Madison. Opened 10 May 1978 at the Minskoff Theater and closed 13 May
1978 after 5 performances.

CAST (in order of appearance): *Helen Gant*: Donna Davis. *Ben Gant*: JOEL HIG-
GINS. *Mrs. Fatty Pert*: PATTI ALLISON. *Mrs. Snowden*: Grace Carney. *Eugene Gant*:
DON SCARDINO. *Eliza Gant*: FRANCES STERNHAGEN. *Will Pentland*: Elek
Hartman. *Florry Mangle*: Rebecca Seay. *Mrs. Clatt*: Justine Johnston. *Jake Clatt*: Gene
Masoner. *Mr. Farrell*: Billy Beckham. *Miss Brown*: Jayne Barnett. *Laura James*:
LESLIE ANN RAY. *W. O. Grant*: FRED GWYNNE. *Dr. Maguire*: Daniel Keyes. *Joe
Tarkington*: Rex David Hays. *Reed McKinney*: Carl Nicholas. *Tim Laughran*: Norman
Stotz. *Madame Victoria*: PATRICIA ENGLUND.

The action takes place in Altamount, North Carolina, during the autumn of 1916.

Act 1: The Dixieland Boarding Home.

Act 2, Scene 1: Gant's marble yard and shop; one week later. *Scene 2*: Dixieland
Boarding House; that evening. *Scene 3*: Dixieland; two weeks later, just before dawn.

ACT 1

Angel Theme

"All the Comforts of Home"
Boarders

"Like the Eagles Fly"
J. Higgins

"Make a Little Sunshine"
F. Sternhagen, D. Scardino, J. Higgins

"Fingers and Toes"
F. Gwynne, N. Stotz, C. Nicholas, R. D. Hays

"Fatty"
J. Higgins

"Astoria Gloria"
P. Allison, Boarders

"Railbird"
D. Scardino

"If I Ever Loved Him"
L. A. Ray

"A Dime Ain't Worth a Nickel"
J. Higgins, P. Allison

"I Got a Dream to Sleep On"
D. Scardino

"Drifting"
F. Sternhagen

ACT 2

Scene 1

"I Can't Believe It's You"
F. Gwynne, P. Englund

"Feelin' Loved"
D. Scardino, L. A. Ray

Scene 2

A Medley
J. Higgins, P. Allison, F. Sternhagen, L. A. Ray

Scene 3

"Tomorrow I'm Gonna Be Old"
F. Gwynne

"Feelin' Loved" (reprise)
D. Scardino, L. A. Ray

"How Do You Say Goodbye"
L. A. Ray

"Gant's Waltz"
F. Gwynne, F. Sternhagen

"Like the Eagles Fly" (reprise)
D. Scardino

1978.11 RUNAWAYS

A Musical Theatre Piece in Two Acts[23]. Written, composed and directed by
Liz Swados. Settings by Douglas W. Schmidt, Woods Mackintosh.
Costumes by Hilary Rosenfeld. Sound by Bill Dreisbach. Lighting by
Jennifer Tipton. Production supervisor, Jay David Cohen. Associate produc-
er, Bernard Gersten. A New York Shakespeare Festival Production.
Produced by Joseph Papp. Opened 13 May 1978 at the Plymouth Theatre
and closed 31 December 1978 after 199 performances. Total, including Off-
Broadway run: 261 peformances.

CAST (in order of appearance): *Hubbell*: Bruce Hlibok. *Interpreter for Hubbell*: Lorie
Robinson. *A.J.*: Carlo Imperato. *Jackie*: Rachael Kelly. *Luis*: Ray Contreras. *Nikki Kay
Kane*: Nan-Lynn Nelson. *Lidia*: Jossie deGuzman. *Manny*: Randy Ruiz. *Eddie*: Jon
Matthews. *Sundar*: Bernie Allison. *Roby*: Venustra K. Robinson. *Lazar*: David
Schechter. *Eric*: Evan H. Miranda. *Iggy*: Jonathan Feig. *Jane*: Kate Schellenbach. *Ez*:
Leonard D. Brown. *Mex-Mongo*: Mark Anthony Butler. *Melinda*: Trini Alvarado.
Deidre: Karen Evans. *Mocha*: Sheila Gibbs.
Chorus: Paula Anderson, Kenya Brome, Jerome Dekie, Karin Dekie, Lisa Dekie,
John Gallogly, Timmy Michaels, Toby Parker. *Musicians*: *Piano and Toy Drum*: Judith
Flesiher. *String Bass*: J. Schimmel. *Congas, Timbales, Bongos, Bells Siren and Others*:

[23]First produced in New York Off-Broadway 9 March 1978 at the Public
Theatre Cabaret/Martinson Hall for 62 performances.

Lepoldo F. Fleming. *Trap Set, Triangle, Glass and Ratchet*: David Sawyer. *Saxophones and Flutes*: Patience Higgins. *Guitar*: Elizabeth Swados.

The text for "Runaways" is written by Elizabeth Swados except for the following contributions improvised and formed by the actors: "Hubbell—You Don't Understand"—Bruce Hlibok; Spanish Argument from "Footsteps"—Jossie De Guzman, Randy Ruiz; "Hubbell—Out on the Street"—Bruce Hlibok; "Lazar's Heroes"—David Schechter; "In the Sleeping Line"—"A.J.'s Dream"—Carlo Imperato; "Roby's Dream"—Venustra K. Robinson; "Jackie's Dream"—Diane Lane; "Lazar's Dream"—David Schechter; "Eddie's Dream"—Vincent Stewart; "Nightmares in Spanish"—Jossie De Guzman, Randy Ruiz, Ray Contreras. The director gratefully acknowledges the ideas and help of all the actors in the choreography. All instrumental arrangements are improvised by the team of musicians. English-Spanish translations by Jossie deGuzman.

The action takes place at the present time on a playground.

ACT 1

"You Don't Understand"
  B. Hlibok, L. Robinson
"I Had to Go"
  C. Imperato, J. Schimmel
"Parent/Kid Dance"
  Company
"Appendectomy"
  R. Kelly
"Where Do People Go"
  Company
"Footstep"
  N. Nelson, J. Schimmel, J. deGuzman, R. Ruiz
"Once Upon a Time"
  J. deGuzman, Company
"Current Events"
  J. Matthews
"Every Now and Then"
  C. Imperato, B. Allison, Company
"Out on the Street"
  B. Hlibok, L. Robinson
"Minnesota Strip"
  V. K. Robinson
"Song of a Child Prostitute"
  R. Kelly, J. deGuzman, R. Ruiz, R. Contreras
"Christmas Puppies"
  N. Nelson
"Lazar's Heroes"
  D. Schechter
"Find Me a Hero"
  D. Schechter, Company
"Scrynatchkielooaw"
  N. Nelson
"The Undiscovered Son"
  E. H. Miranda, J. Fleisher, J. Schimmel
"I Went Back Home"
  J. Feig, K. Schellenbach
"This Is What I Do When I'm Angry"
  C. Imperato, N. Nelson
"The Basketball Song"
  L. Brown, Company
    DanceR. Contreras, M. A. Butler
"Spoons"
  R. Ruiz
"Lullaby for Luis"
  J. deGuzman, R. Contreras, P. Higgins, Company
"We Are Not Strangers"
  E. H. Miranda, Company

ACT 2

"In the Sleeping Line"
  Company
"Lullaby from Baby to Baby"
  T. Alvarado, B. Hlibok
"Tra Gog Vo In Dein Whole"(I Will Not Tell a Soul)
  D. Schechter, B. Hlibok
"Revenge Song"
  Company

"Enterprise"
  K. Evans, N. Nelson, M. A. Butler, Company
"Sometimes"
  V. K. Robinson, D. Schechter
"Clothes"
  J. Feig
"Mr. Graffiti"
  M. A. Butler
"The Untrue Pigeon"
  N. Nelson
"Senoras de la Noche"
  J. deGuzman, R. Ruiz, N. Nelson
"We Have to Die?"
  K. Evans
"Where Are Those People Who Did 'Hair'?"
  D. Schechter, K. Evans, Company
"Appendectomy II"
  R. Kelly, T. Alvarado
"Let Me Be a Kid"
  Company
"To the Dead of Family Wars"
  K. Evans
"Problem After Problem"
  B. Hlibok, L. Robinson
"Lonesome of the Road"
  R. Contreras, B. Allison, Company

1978.12 # WORKING

A Musical in Two Acts. Based on the book of the same name by Studs Terkel. Adapted and directed by Stephen Schwartz. Music and lyrics by Craig Carnelia, Micki Grant, Mary Rodgers and Susan Birkenhead, Stephen Schwartz, James Taylor. Dances and musical staging by Onna White. Settings by David Mitchell. Costumes by Marjorie Slaiman. Lighting by Ken Billington. Musical direction and vocal arrangements by Stephen Reinhardt. Orchestrations by Kirk Nurock. Dance and incidental music by Michele Brourman. Associate director, Nina Faso. Sound by Jack Mann. Assistant conductor, Kenneth Bichel. Produced by Stephen R. Friedman and Irwin Meyer in association with Joseph Harris. Opened 14 May 1978 at the 46th Street Theatre and closed 4 June 1976 after 25 performances.

CAST (in order of appearance): *Act 1: Mike LeFevre*, steelworker: Brad Sullivan. *Al Calinda*, parking lot attendant: David Langston Smyrl. *Nora Watson*, editor: Patti LuPone. *John Fortune*, advertising copy chief: Steven Boockvor. *Diane Wilson*, secretary: Lynne Thigpen. *Herb Rosen*, corporate executive: Rex Everhart. *Anthony Palazzo*, stonemason: Arny Freeman. *John Rushton*, newsboy: Matthew McGrath. *Rose Hoffman*, teacher: Bobo Lewis. *Babe Secoli*, supermarket checker: Lenora Nemetz. *Brett Meyer*, boxboy: David Patrick Kelly. *Emilio Hernandez*, migrant worker: Joe Mantegna. *Conrad Swibel*, gas meter reader: Matt Landers. *Kate Rushton*, housewife: Susan Bigelow. *Barbara Herrick*, agency vice-president: Robin Lamont. *Terry Mason*, stewardess: Lenora Nemetz. *Jill Torrance*, model: Terri Treas. *Roberta Victor*, call girl: Patti LuPone. *Grace Clements*, millworker: Bobo Lewis. *Bud Jonas*, football coach: Bob Gunton. *Marco Camerone*, hockey player: Steven Boockvor. *Joe Zutty*, retired shipping clerk: Arny Freeman. *Tom Patrick*, fireman: Matt Landers.

Act 2: Benny Blue, bar pianist: David Patrick Kelly. *Delores Dante*, waitress: Lenora Nemetz. *Heather Lamb*, telephone operator: Lynne Thigpen. *Fran Swenson*, hotel switchboard operator: Bobo Lewis. *Sharon Atkins*, receptionist: Robin Lamont. *Frank Decker*, interstate trucker: Bob Gunton. *Dave McCormick*, interstate trucker: Joe Mantegna. *Booker Page*, seaman: Rex Everhart. *Lucille Page*, his wife: Bobo Lewis. *Will Robinson*, bus driver: David Langston Smyrl. *Jo Anne Robinson*, his wife: Lynne Thigpen. *Tim Devlin*, salesman: Matt Landers. *Carla Devlin*, his wife: Terri Treas. *Ralph Werner*, tie salesman: Matt Landers. *Cathleen Moran*, hospital aide: Robin Lamont. Charlie Blossom, copy boy: David Patrick Kelly. *Maggie Holmes*, cleaning woman: Lynne Thigpen. *Mike LeFevre*, steelworker: Brad Sullivan.

The action takes place at the present time in numerous places of employment. The characters in "Working" are non-fictional characters. Their names have been changed, but their words have not. Even in the case of song lyrics, the writers have tried to remain as faithful as possible to the character's original words. It is our feeling that the value of this piece stems chiefly from the fact that it is true, and we have made every effort to keep from sliding into the realm of "playwriting."

ACT 1

"All the Livelong Day"
  Company
  ("I Hear America Singing" *Lyrics by* Walt Whitman; *Music and Additional Lyrics by* Stephen Schwartz.)

"Lovin Al"
  D. L. Smyrl, Ensemble
  (*Music and Lyrics by* Micki Grant.)
"The Mason"
  D. P. Kelly
  (*Music and Lyrics by* Craig Carnelia.)
"Neat to Be a Newsboy"
  M. McGrath, Newsboys
  (*Music and Lyrics by* Stephen Schwartz.)
"Nobody Tells Me How"
  B. Lewis
  (*Music by* Mary Rodgers. *Lyrics by* Susan Birkenhead.)
"Treasure Island Trio"
  Danced by T. Treas, L. Nemetz, L. Thigpen
  (*Music by* Michele Brourman.)
"Un Mejor Dia Vendra"
  J. Mantegna, M. Landers, Migrants
  (*Music by* James Taylor. *Spanish Lyrics by* Graciela Daniele and Matt Landers.)
"Just a Housewife"
  S. Bigelow, K. Rushton, Housewives
  (*Music and Lyrics by* Craig Carnelia.)
"Millwork"
  R. Lamont, D. P. Kelly, M. Landers
  (*Music by* Michele Brourman and Stephen Schwartz.)*Danced by* T. Treas
"Nightskate"
  Danced by S. Boockvor
  (*Music by* Michele Brourman and Stephen Schwartz.)

"Joe"
  A. Freeman
  (*Music and Lyrics by* Craig Carnelia.)
"If I Could've Been"
  Company
  (*Music and Lyrics by* Micki Grant.)
ACT 2
"It's an Art"
  L. Nemetz, Customers
  (*Music and Lyrics by* Stephen Schwartz.)
"Brother Trucker"
  J. Mantegna, B. Gunton, D. P. Kelly, M. Landers
  (*Music and Lyrics by* James Taylor.)
"Husbands and Wives"
  Danced by R. Everhart, B. Lewis; D. L. Smyrl, L. Thigpen; M. Landers, T. Treas, couples
  (*Music by* Michele Brourman.)
"Fathers and Sons"
  B. Gunton
  (*Music and Lyrics by* Stephen Schwartz.)
"Cleanin' Women"
  L. Thigpen
  (*Music and Lyrics by* Micki Grant.)
"Something to Point To"
  Company
  (*Music and Lyrics by* Craig Carnelia.)

Angela Lansbury and Len Cariou in SWEENEY TODD
Martha Swope/TimePix

THE BEST LITTLE WHOREHOUSE IN TEXAS

1978.13

A Musical Comedy in Two Acts, a Prologue and 17 Scenes[1]. Book by Larry L. King and Peter Masterson. (Based on a short story by Larry L. King) Music and lyrics by Carol Hall. Directed by Peter Masterson and Tommy Tune. Musical numbers staged by Tommy Tune. Sets by Marjorie Kellogg. Costumes by Ann Roth. Lighting by Dennis Parichy. Musical supervision, direction and vocal arrangements by Robert Billig. Associate choreographer, Thommie Walsh. Produced by Universal Pictures (Stevie Phillips, Producer). Opened 19 June 1978 at the 46th Street Theatre and closed 27 March 1982 after 1584 performances. (Total, including Off-Broadway runs, 1669 performances.)

CAST (in order of appearance): *RIO GRANDE BAND*: Craig Chambers (Band Leader). *Girls*: Lisa Brown, Carol Chambers, Donna King, Susan Mansur, Louise Quick-Bowen, Debra Zalkind. *Cowboys*: Jay Bursky, Bradley Clayton King, Michael Scott, Paul Ukena, Jr. *Farmer*: CLINT ALLMON. *Shy Kid*: Gerry Burkhardt. *Miss Wulla Jean*: Edna Milton. *Travelling Salesman*: JAY GARNER. *Slick Dude*: K. C. Kelly. *Choir*: Jay Bursky, Becky Gelke, Edwina Lewis, Jan Merchant, James Rich, Marta Sanders. *Amber*: PAMELA BLAIR. *Shy*: JOAN ELLIS. *Jewel*: DELORES HALL. *Mona Stangley*: CARLIN GLYNN. *The Girls at Miss Mona's*: *Linda Lou*: Donna King. *Dawn*: Lisa Brown. *Ginger*: Louise Quick-Bowen. *Beatrice*: Jan Merchant. *Taddy Jo*: Carol Chambers. *Ruby Rae*: Becky Gelke. *Eloise*: Marta Sanders. *Durla*: Debra Zalkind.

Leroy Sliney: Bradley Clayton King. *The Dogettes*: Gerry Burkhardt, Jay Bursky, Michael Scott, Paul Ukena, Jr. *Melvin P. Thorpe*: CLINT ALLMON. *Soundman*: K. C. Kelly. *Stage Manager*: Tom Cashin. *Melvin Thorpe Singers*: Becky Gelke, Bradley Clayton King, Susan Mansur, Jan Merchant, James Rich, Marta Sanders. *Sheriff Ed Earl Dodd*: HENDERSON FORSYTHE. *Cameraman*: Tom Cashin. *Scruggs*: JAY GARNER. *Mayor Rufus Poindexter*: J. FRANK LUCAS. *Edsel Mackey*: Don Crabtree. *Doatsey Mae*: SUSAN MANSUR. *Townspeople*: Carol Chambers, Bradley Clayton King, Edna Milton, James Rich, Marta Sanders. *TV Announcer*: Larry L. King. *Angelette Imogene Charlene*: Lisa Brown. *Angelettes*: Louise Quick-Bowen, Becky Gelke, Donna King, Debra Zalkind, Jan Merchant. *TV Colorman*: JAY GARNER. *Senator Wingwoah*: J. FRANK LUCAS. *Aggie #21*: Paul Ukena, Jr. *Aggie #71*: Michael Scott. *Aggie #11*: Jay Bursky. *Ukrainian Placekicker—Aggie #1*: K. C. Kelly. *Aggie #17*: James Rich. *Aggie #7*: Gerry Burkhardt. *Aggie #12—Specialty Dancer*: Tom Cashin. *Aggie #77*: Bradley Clayton King. *Photographers*: Michael Scott, Paul Ukena, Jr. James Rich, Jay Bursky. *Reporter #1*: Susan Mansur. *Governor' Aide*: Jay Bursky. *Governor*: JAY GARNER. *Reporter #3*: Michael Scott. *Alternate Dancers*: Monica Tiller, Jerry Yoder, Gena Ramsel.

The action takes place in the state of Texas.

Act 1, Scene 1: The Chicken Ranch, 1930s. *Scene 2*: The Chicken Ranch, early 1970s. *Scene 3*: Same. *Scene 4*: Melvin P. Thorpe's TV Show. *Scene 5*: Back at the Chicken Ranch. *Scene 6*: Same. *Scene 7*: Courthouse Steps, Gilbert, Texas. *Scene 8*: Texas Twinkle Cafe. *Scene 9*: The Texas Aggie Angelettes at the Football Game. *Scene 10*: After the Game and on the way to the Chicken Ranch. *Scene 11*: The Chicken Ranch. *Scene 12*: The Chicken Ranch, later that night.

Act 2, Scene 1: Same as Act 1, Scene 12; at the State Capitol (Austin). *Scene 2*: The Chicken Ranch. *Scene 3*: Sheriff's Office. *Scene 4*: The Chicken Ranch. *Scene 5*: Same.

ACT 1
Prologue
   C. Chambers, The Rio Grande Band
Scene 1
  "20 Fans"
   C. Glynn, the Girls, the Cowboys, C. Allmon, G. Burkhardt, E. Milton, J. Garner, K. C. Kelly, Choir
Scene 2
  "A Lil Ole Bitty Pissant Country Place"
   C. Glynn, the Girls
Scene 3
  "Girl You're a Woman"
   C. Glynn, J. Ellis, D. Hall, the Girls

[1]First produced in New York Off-Broadway 17 April 1978 at the Entermedia Theatre for 85 performances.

Scene 4
  "Watch Dog Theme"
   C. Allmon, the Dogettes
  "Texas Has a Whorehouse in It"
   C. Allmon, the Thorpe Singers, the Dogettes
Scene 6
  "Twenty-Four Hours of Lovin'"
   D. Hall, the Girls
Scene 7
  "Watchdog Theme" (reprise)
   The Dogettes
  "Texas Has a Whorehouse in It" (reprise)
   C. Allmon, the Dogettes, J. F. Lucas, J. Garner, D. Crabtree, S. mansur, Townspeople
Scene 8
  "Doatsey Mae"
   S. Mansur
Scene 9
  "Angelette March"
   L. Brown, the Angelettes
Scene 10
  "The Aggie Song"
   The Aggies
Scene 11
  "Bus from Amarillo"
   C. Glynn
ACT 2[2]
Scene 1
  "The Sidestep"
   J. Garner, J. Bursky, J. F. Lucas, C. Allmon, the Dogettes, Melvin Thorpe Singers
Scene 2
  "No Lies"
   C. Glynn, D. Hall, the Girls
Scene 3
  "Good Ole Girl"
   H. Forsythe, the Aggies
Scene 4
  "Hard Candy Christmas"
   P. Blair, D. King, L. Quick-Bowen, L. Brown, B. Gelke, J. Merchant
  "Hard Candy Christmas" (reprise)
   The Girls
Scene 5
Finale
   The Company

IOLANTHE,
or The Peer and the Peri

1978.14

A Revival of the Comic Opera in Two Acts[3]. Libretto by William S. Gilbert. Music by Arthur Sullivan. Costumes and scenery designed by Bruno Santini. Lighting by Joe Davis, assisted by Howard Eaton. Choreography by Virginia Mason. Producer, Michael Heyland. Director of productions, Leonard Osborn. Musical director, Royston Nash. Chorus master and associate conductor, David Mackie. Executive producer, Lillian Libman. Technical consultant, Rouben Ter-Arutunian. Produced by James and Joseph Nederlander in association with the City Center of Music and Drama, Inc. and in association with the D'Oyly Carte Opera Trust, Ltd. and Dame Bridget D'Oyly Carte by arrangement with Barclays Bank International. Opened 17 July 1978 at the New York State Theater and closed 20 July 1978 after 2 performances in repertory.

[2]Added for the National Tour to Act 2, Scene 1 after "The Sidestep":
  "Lonely at the Top"
   Larry Hovis (Melvin P. Thrope), Jeffry George (Co-Dog)
[3]First presented in New York 25 November 1882 at the Standard Theatre for 105 performances. For Synopsis of Scenes and Musical Numbers, see original 1882 production.

CAST: *The Lord Chancellor:* JOHN REED. *Earl of Mountararat:* JOHN AYLDON. *Earl Tolloller:* GEOFFREY SHOVELTON. *Private Willis of the Grenadier Guards:* KENNETH SANDFORD. *Strephon, an Arcadian Shepherd:* GARETH JONES. *Queen of the Fairies:* PATRICIA LEONARD. *Celia, Leila, Fleta,* Fairies: Suzanne O'Keeffe, Lorraine Dulcie Daniels, Patricia Ann Bennett. *Phyllis, an Arcadian Shepherdess and Ward in Chancery:* BARBARA LILLEY.

Chorus of Dukes, Marquises, Earls, Viscounts, Barons and Fairies: Richard Brabrooke, Michael Buchan, Barry Clark, Malcolm Coy, Jon Ellison, Michael Farran-Lee, Gareth Jones, Guy Matthews, Richard Mitchell, Edwin Rolles, Thomas Scholey, Bryan Secombe, Alan Spencer, William Strachan, Kevin West, Patrick Wilkes. Susan Cochrane, Linda D'Arcy, Elizabeth Denham, Madeleine Hudson, Beti Lloyd-Jones, Roberta Morrell, Andrea Phillips, Patricia Rea, Suzanne Sloane.

THE MIKADO,
1978.15 or The Town of Titipu

A Revival of the Comic Opera in Two Acts[4]. Libretto by William S. Gilbert. Music by Arthur Sullivan. Costumes designed by Disley Jones. Sets designed by Charles Ricketts; Nanki-Poo, Act 1, designed by Disley Jones. Lighting supervision by Martin Aronstein. Production director, Leonard Osborn. Musical director, Royston Nash. Chorus master and associate conductor, David Mackie. Executive producer, Lillian Libman. Technical consultant, Rouben Ter-Arutunian. Produced by James and Joseph Nederlander in association with the City Center of Music and Drama, Inc. and in association with the D'Oyly Carte Opera Trust, Ltd. and Dame Bridget D'Oyly Carte by arrangement with Barclays Bank International. Opened 18 July 1978 at the New York State Theater and closed 19 July 1978 after 3 performances in repertory.

CAST: *The Mikado of Japan:* JOHN AYLDON. *Nanki-Poo, his son, disguised as a wandering minstrel in love with Yum-Yum:* GEOFFREY SHOVELTON. *Ko-Ko, Lord High Executioner of Titipu:* JOHN REED. *Pooh-Bah, Lord High Everything Else:* KENNETH SANDFORD. *Pish-Tush, Go-To,* Noble Lords: Michael Rayner, Jon Ellison. *Yum-Yum, Pitti-Sing, Peep-Bo,* three sisters, wards of Ko-Ko: JULIA GOSS, JANE METCALFE, ROBERTA MORRELL. *Katisha, an elderly lady in love with Nanki-Poo:* PATRICIA LEONARD. *Chorus of School Girls, Nobles, Guards and Coolies:* same as IOLANTHE above.

H.M.S. PINAFORE,
1978.16 or The Lass That Loved a Sailor

A Revival of the Comic Opera in Two Acts[5]. Libretto by William S. Gilbert. Music by Arthur Sullivan. Back cloth designed and painted by Joseph and Phil Harker. Director of productions, Leonard Osborn. Musical director, Royston Nash. Chorus master and associate conductor, David Mackie. Executive producer, Lillian Libman. Technical consultant, Rouben Ter-Arutunian. Produced by James and Joseph Nederlander in association with the City Center of Music and Drama, Inc. and in association with the D'Oyly Carte Opera Trust, Ltd. and Dame Bridget D'Oyly Carte by arrangement with Barclays Bank International. Opened 21 July 1978 at the New York State Theater and closed 22 July 1978 after 3 performances in repertory[6].

CAST: *The Rt. Hon. Sir Joseph Porter, K.C.B.,* First Lord of the Admiralty: JOHN REED. *Captain Corcoran,* Commanding the *H.M.S. Pinafore:* MICHAEL RAYNER. *Ralph Rackstraw,* Able Seaman: MESTON REID. *Dick Deadeye,* Able Seaman: JOHN AYLDON. *Bill Bobstay,* Boatswain: Jon Ellison. *Bob Becket,* Boatswain's Mate: Michael Buchan. *Josephine,* the Captain's Daughter: BARBARA LILLEY. *Hebe,* Sir Joseph's First Cousin: Roberta Morrell. *Little Buttercup,* Mrs. Cripps, a Portsmouth Bumboat Woman: PATRICIA LEONARD. *First Lord's Sisters, his Cousins, his Aunts, Sailors, Marines:* same as IOLANTHE above.

THE PIRATES OF PENZANCE,
1978.17 or The Slave of Duty

A Revival of the Comic Opera in Two Acts[7]. Libretto by William S. Gilbert. Music by Arthur Sullivan. Scenery by Peter Goffin. Director of productions, Leonard Osborn. Musical director, Royston Nash. Chorus master and associate conductor, David Mackie. Executive producer, Lillian Libman. Technical consultant, Rouben Ter-Arutunian. Produced by James and Joseph Nederlander in association with the City Center of Music and Drama, Inc. and in association with the D'Oyly Carte Opera Trust, Ltd. and Dame Bridget D'Oyly Carte by arrangement with Barclays Bank International. Opened 24 July 1978 at the New York State Theater and closed 25 July 1978 after 2 performances in repertory.

CAST: *Major General Stanley:* JAMES CONROY-WARD. *The Pirate King:* JOHN AYLDON. *Samuel,* his Lieutenant: Jon Ellison. *Frederic,* the Pirate Apprentice: MESTON REID. *Sergeant of Police:* MICHAEL RAYNER. *Mabel, Edith, Kate, Isabel,* General Stanley's Daughters: JULIA GOSS, LORRAINE DULCIE DANIELS, ROBERTA MORRELL, Patricia Ann Bennett. *Ruth,* Pirate Maid-of-all-work: PATRICIA LEONARD. *Chorus of Pirates, Police and General Stanley's Daughters:* same as IOLANTHE above.

STOP THE WORLD-
1978.18 I WANT TO GET OFF

A Revival of the Musical in Two Acts[8]. Book, music and lyrics by Leslie Bricusse and Anthony Newley. Sets and costumes by Santo Loquasto. Lighting by Pat Collins. Music supervised and arranged by Ian Fraser. Musical director, George Rhodes. Orchestrations by Billy Byers, Joseph Lipman. Choreography and musical staging by Billy Wilson. Entire production directed by Mel Shapiro. A Hillard Elkins Production. Associate producers, Barbara Platoff, William Ross. Produced by James and Joseph Nederlander in association with City Center of Music and Drama Inc. Opened 3 August 1978 at the New York State Theatre and closed 27 August 1978 after 29 performances.

CAST (in order of appearance): *Littlechap:* SAMMY DAVIS, JR. *Baton Twirler, Death:* Dennis Daniels. *Schoolgirl:* Donna Lowe. *Evie:* MARIAN MERCER. *First Girl in Crow's Nest:* Debora Masterson. *Second Girl in Crow's Nest:* Joyce Nolen. *Susan:* Wendy Edmead. *Guitar Player:* Patrick Kinser-Lau. *Jane:* MARIAN MERCER. *The Boy:* Charles Willis, Jr. *Ilse:* MARIAN MERCER. *Lorene:* MARIAN MERCER. *M.C., Snobbs Country Club:* Dennis Daniels. *M.C., Black Organization:* Edwetta Little. *M.C., Spanish Group:* Patrick Kinser-Lau. *M. C., Hadassah:* Joyce Nolen. *Speaker of the House:* Edwetta Little. *Newscaster:* Donna Lowe. *Solo Singer in Sunvale:* Joyce Nolen.

Ensemble: Marcus B. F. Brown, Dennis Daniels, Karen Giombetti, Linda Griffin, Patrick Kinser-Lau, Edwetta Little, Donna Lowe, Debora Masterson, Billy Newton-Davis, Joyce Nolen, Robert Yori-Tanna.

ACT 1
"I Want To Be Rich"
  S. Davis
"Typically English"
  M. Mercer
"Lumbered"
  S. Davis
"Welcome to Sludgeville"
  Chorus
"Gonna Build a Mountain"
  S. Davis
"Glorious Russian"
  M. Mercer
"Meilinki Meilchick"
  S. Davis, M. Mercer

---

[4]First presented in New York 20 July, 10-29 August 1885 at the Union Square and People's Theatres for 22 performances. First authorized production presented 19 August 1885 at the Fifth Avenue Theatre by Richard D'Oyly Carte for 250 performances. For Synopsis of Scenes and Musical Numbers, see 19 August 1885 D'Oyly Carte production.
[5]Originally presented in New York 15 January 1879 at the Standard Theatre for 175 performances. For Synopsis of Scenes and Musical Numbers, see original 1879 production. No program found for this revival.
[6]Costumes uncredited.

[7]First presented in New York 31 December 1879 at the Fifth Avenue Theatre for a total of 91 performances in two engagements. For Synopsis of Scenes and Musical Numbers, see original 1879 production.
[8]Originally produced in New York 3 October 1962 at the Sam S. Shubert Theatre for 556 performances. Dropped from this production: "The A.B.C. Song," "A Special Announcement," "Nag! Nag! Nag!" (replaced by "Life Is a Woman"). "Welcome to Sludgepool" retitled "Welcome to Sludgeville."

"Family Fugue"
S. Davis, M. Mercer, W. Edmead, S. Burch
"Typische Deutsche"
M. Mercer
"Life Is a Woman"
S. Davis

ACT 2
"All American"
M. Mercer
"Once in a Lifetime"
S. Davis
"Mumbo Jumbo"
S. Davis
"Welcome to Sunvale"

Chorus
"Someone Nice Like You"
S. Davis, M. Mercer
"What Kind of Fool Am I?"
S. Davis

1978.19 NAUGHTY MARIETTA

A Revival of the Musical Comedy in Two Acts, 4 Scenes[9]. Music by Victor Herbert. New book and Additional lyrics by Frederick S. Roffman based on the original by Rida Johnson Young. Directed by Gerald Freedman. Musical numbers staged by Graciela Daniele. Costumes designed by Patricia Zipprodt. Sets designed by Oliver Smith. Lighting designed by Ken Billington. Musical director and conductor, John Mauceri. Chorus master, Lloyd Walser. Production conceived by Frederick S. Roffman. Produced by the New York City Opera. Opened 31 August 1978 at the New York State Theatre and closed 10 September 1978 after 14 performances.

CAST: *Marietta d'Altena*: GIANNA ROLANDI. *Captain Richard Warrington* of Kentucky: JACQUE TRUSSEL. *Etienne Grandet*: ALAN TITUS. *Adah Le Clercq, his Quadroon Mistress*: JOANNA SIMON. *Private Silas Slick of the Rangers*: RUSS THACKER. *Acting Governor Grandet, Etienne's Father*: JAMES BILLINGS. *Florenze, His Secretary*: BROOKS MORTON. *Sergeant Harry Blake of the Rangers*: DON YULE. *Rudolfo*: HARLAN FOSS. *Pierre LaFarge, Envoy from Napoleon*: Richard McKee. *Pirates*: Dan Kingman, James Sergi. *Sister Domenique*: Rita Metzger. *Casquette Girls*: Patricia Price, Sally Lambert, Lee Bellaver. *Ranger*: Herbert Hunsberger. *Town Crier*: Edward Vaughan. *Thomas Bailey*: James Sergi. *Flower Girls*: Susan Delery-Whedon, Sally Lambert. *Flower Vendor*: George Bohachevsky. *Bird Vendor*: Louis Perry. *Fruit Vendor*: Robert Brubaker. *Sugar Cane Vendor*: Harris Davis. *Citizens*: Leslie Luxemburg, Lila Herbert, Marie Young. *Vendor*: Robert Brubaker. *Men*: James Brewer, Louis Perry, Herbert Hunsberger, Edward Caughan. *Giovanni*: Jose Bourbon. *Gambler*: Don Carlo. *Pierre*: Kenn Dovel. *Robillard*: Herbert Hunsberger. *Plauche*: James Brewer. *Beaurivage*: Harris Davis. *Major-Domo*: Glenn Rowen. *Spanish Dancer*: Esperanza Galan. *Quadroons*: Sharon Claveau, Rosalie Tisch, Rita Metzger, Marie Young, Madeleine Soyka, Lila Herbert. *French Girls*: Susan Delery-Whedon, Sally Lambert, Jean Rawn, Myrna Reynolds. *Bordenave*: James Sergi. *Durand*: Louis Perry. *La Fourche*: Dan Kingman. *San Domingo Ladies*: Toni-Ann Gardella, Candace Itow, Rebeka Pradera.
Ensemble: New York City Opera Chorus.

The action takes place in Louisiana in 1803.

Act 1, Scene 1: Barataria, the island hideout of privateers, at the mouth of the Mississippi River. *Scene 2*: The Main Square in New Orleans. *Scene 3*: Rudolfo's Theatre. A week or two later.

Act 2: The Jeunesse Dorée Club in New Orleans.

ACT 1
Prologue
G. Rolandi
"It Never, Never Can Be Love"
G. Rolandi, J. Trussel
Opening Chorus
Ensemble

"This Brave New Land" (from THE PRINCE ANANAIS)
J. Simon, A. Titus
(Orchestration by Hershy Kay.)
"Tramp, Tramp, Tramp"
J. Trussel, Rangers
"Taisez-Vous"
Ensemble
"All I Crave Is More of Life"
G. Rolandi
"Italian Street Song"
G. Rolandi, Ensemble
Intermezzo
Orchestra
Opening Music
G. Rolandi, H. Foss
"Naughty Marietta"
G. Rolandi
"If I Were Anyone Else But Me"
R. Thacker, G. Rolandi
Dance
Orchestra
Finale
Principals, Ensemble

ACT 2
"New Orleans Jeunesse Dorée"
Male Ensemble
"You Marry a Marionette"
A. Titus, Men
"'Neath the Southern Moon"
J. Simon
"Loves of New Orleans"
Ensemble
"It's Pretty Soft for Silas"
R. Thacker
"Live for Today"
G. Rolandi, J. Simon, J. Trussel, A. Titus, Ensemble
"The Sweet By and By"
J. Billings
"I'm Falling in Love With Someone"
J. Trussel
"Ah, Sweet Mystery of Life"
G. Rolandi, J. Trussel, Company

1978.20 THE MERRY WIDOW

A Revival of the Operetta in Three Acts, 4 Scenes[10]. Music by Franz Lehár. Original German libretto (Die lustige witwe) and lyrics by Victor Léon and Leo Stein (after "L'Attaché d'Ambassade" by Henri Meilhac.) New English translation and dialogue by Ursula Eggers and Joseph de Rugeris. New lyrics by Sheldon Harnick. This San Diego Opera production directed by Tito Capobianco. Stage director, Antoni Jaworski. Choreographer, Jessica Redel. Production (settings, costumes) design by Carl Toms. Lighting design by Ken Billington. Conductor, Imre Pallo. Produced by the New York City Opera. Opened 17 September 1978 at the New York State Theatre and closed 11 November 1978 after 6 performances in repertory.

CAST: *Baron Mirko Zeta*: DAVID RAE SMITH. *Valencienne*: Diana Soviero. *Count Danilo*: HOWARD HENSEL. *Anna Glawari*: JOHANNA MEIER. *Camille de Rosillon*: BRUCE REED. *Vicomte Cascada*: HARLAN FOSS. *Raoul St. Brioche*: ALAN KAYS. *Bogdanovitch*: Herbert Hunsberger. *Sylviane*: Kathleen Murphy. *Kromov*: William Ledbetter. *Olga*: Myrna Reynolds. *Pritchitch*: Louis Perry. *Praskovia*: Susan Delery-Whedon. *Njegus*: JAMES BILLINGS. *Lolo*: Candace Itow. *Dodo*: Kathleen Murphy. *Jou-Jou*: Myrna Reynolds. *Frou-Frou*: Toni-Ann Gardella. *Clo-Clo*: Susan Delery-Whedon. *Margot*: Raven Wilkinson.
Ensemble: New York City Opera Chorus.

---

[9]Originally produced in New York 7 November 1910 at the New York Theatre for 136 performances. This production has been made possible by deeply appreciated gifts from the Fan Fox and Leslie R. Samuels Foundation, Inc., and by the Victor Herbert Foundation.

[10]Originally produced in New York 21 October 1907 at the New Amsterdam Theatre for 416 performances; this adaptation first produced in New York 2 April 1978 at the New York State Theatre for 8 performances. For Synopsis of Scenes and Musical Numbers, see 1978 revival.

EUBIE!

1978.21

A Musical Revue in Two Acts[11]. Music by Eubie Blake. Conceived and directed by Julianne Boyd. Co-choreographer and musical staging by Billy Wilson. Co-choreography and tap choreography by Henry LeTang. Musical supervision and arangements by Danny Holgate. Set design by Karl Eigsti. Costume design by Bernard Johnson. Lighting design by William Mintzer. Sound design by Lou Gonzalez. Choral arrangements by Chapman Roberts. Musical direction by Vicki Carter. Production supervisor, Ron Abbott. Orchestrations by Neal Tate. Associate producer, John N. Hart, Jr. Produced by Ashton Springer in association with Frank C. Pierson and Jay J. Cohen. Opened 20 September 1978 at the Ambassador Theatre and closed 7 October 1979 after 439 performances.

CAST (in alphabetical order): Ethel Beatty, Terry Burrell, Leslie Dockery, Lynnie Godfrey, Gregory Hines, Maurice Hines, Mel Johnson, Jr., Lonnie McNeil, Janet Powell, Marion Ramsey, Alaina Reed, Jeffery V. Thompson.

ACT 1

Prologue: "Goodnight Angeline" (1919); "Charleston Rag" (1899)

"Shuffle Along" (from *SHUFFLE ALONG*)(1921)
The Company
(*Lyrics by* Noble Sissle.)

"In Honeysuckle Time" (from *SHUFFLE ALONG*)(1921)
L. McNeil, J. Powell, Company
(*Lyrics by* Noble Sissle.)

"I'm Just Wild About Harry" (from *SHUFFLE ALONG*)(1921)
M. Hines, J. Powell, L. Godfrey, M. Ramsey, E. Beatty
(*Lyrics by* Noble Sissle.)

"Baltimore Buzz" (from *SHUFFLE ALONG*)(1921)
L. McNeil, J. V. Thompson, M. Johnson, Jr., J. Powell, G. Hines, L. Dockery
(*Mime Staged by* Dana Manno.)

"Daddy (Won't You Please Come Home)" (from *SHUFFLE ALONG*)(1921)
L. Godfrey
(*Lyrics by* Noble Sissle. *Musical Staging by* Julianne Boyd.)

"There's a Million Little Cupids in the Sky" (1924)
M. Hines, L. McNeil, G. Hines, E. Beatty, M. Johnson, Jr., J. V. Thompson, M. Ramsey, J. Powell, L. Dockery, A. Reed
(*Lyrics by* Noble Sissle.)
(dropped from *THE CHOCOLATE DANDIES*)

"I'm a Great Big Baby" (from *TAN MANHATTAN*)(1940)
J. V. Thompson
(*Lyrics by* Andy Razaf.)

"My Handyman Ain't Handy Anymore" (from *BLACKBIRDS OF 1930*)
A. Reed, M. Johnson, Jr.
(*Lyrics by* Andy Razaf.)

"Low Down Blues" (from *SHUFFLE ALONG*)(1921)
G. Hines
(*Lyrics by* Noble Sissle.)

"Gee, I Wish I Had Someone to Rock Me in the Cradle of Love" (1919)
E. Beatty
(*Lyrics by* Noble Sissle. *Duet arrangement by* Vicki Carter.)

"I'm Just Simply Full of Jazz" (from *SHUFFLE ALONG*)(1919)
The Company
(*Lyrics by* Noble Sissle.)

ACT 2

"High Steppin' Days" (1921)
The Company
(*Lyrics by* Johnny Brandon. 1978)

"Dixie Moon" (from *THE CHOCOLATE DANDIES*)(1924)
M. Johnson, Jr., G. Hines, M. Hines, Company
(*Lyrics by* Noble Sissle.)

"Weary" (from *TAN MANHATTAN*)(1940)
T. Burrell, Company
(*Lyrics by* Andy Razaf.)

"Roll Jordan" (from *BLACKBIRDS OF 1930*)
A. Reed, T. Burrell, J. Powell, Company
(*Lyrics by* Andy Razaf.)

"Memories of You" (from *BLACKBIRDS OF 1930*)
E. Beatty
(*Lyrics by* Andy Razaf.)

"If You've Never Been Vamped by a Brownskin, You've Never Been Vamped at All" (from *SHUFFLE ALONG*)(1921)
M. Ramsey, M. Johnson, Jr., L. Godfrey, G. Hines, J. V. Thompson, L. Dockery, J. Powell, M. Hines, L. McNeil
(*Lyrics by* Noble Sissle.)

"You Got to Git the Gittin While the Gittin's Good" (1956)
M. Hines
(*Lyrics by* F. E. Miller.)

"Oriental Blues"[12] (from *SHUFFLE ALONG*)(1921)
J. V. Thompson, E. Beatty, L. Godfrey, J. Powell, M. Ramsey
(*Lyrics by* Noble Sissle.)

"I'm Craving for That Kind of Love" (from *SHUFFLE ALONG*)(1921)
L. Godfrey
(*Lyrics by* Noble Sissle. *Musical Staging by* Julianne Boyd.)

"Hot Feet" (1958)
G. Hines
(*Lyrics by* Noble Sissle.)

"Goodnight Angeline" (from *SHUFFLE ALONG*)(1919)
E. Beatty, M. Johnson, Jr., L. McNeil, J. Powell
(*Lyrics by* Noble Sissle, James Reese Europe)

Finale
The Company

KING OF HEARTS

1978.22

A Musical in Two Acts, 14 Scenes. Book by Joseph Stein. Based on a screenplay by Philippe de Broca, Maurice Bessy and Daniel Boulanger. Music by Peter Link. Lyrics by Jacob Brackman. Directed and choreographed by Ron Field. Settings by Santo Loquasto. Costumes by Patricia Zipprodt. Lighting by Pat Collins. Musical director, Karen Gustafson. Dance arangements by Dorothea Freitag. Orchestrations by Bill Brohn. Sound design by Jack Shearing. Production associate, Nan Pearlman. Associate producers, Lee Minskoff, Charlotte Dicker. Produced by Joseph Kipness and Patty Grubman in association with Jerome Minskoff. Opened 22 October 1978 at the Minskoff Theatre and closed 3 December 1978 after 48 performances.

CAST: *Inmates: Demosthenes* (Le Muet): GARY MORGAN. *Madeleine* (La Madame): MILLICENT MARTIN. *Genevieve* (La Courtisane): Mitzi Hamilton. *Simone* (La Ballerine): Marilyn D'Honau. *Dahlia* (La Servante): Isabelle Farrell. *Raoul* (Le Patron du Cirque): BOB GUNTON. *Jeunefille* (La Jeune Fille): PAMELA BLAIR. *Valerie* (La Flutiste): Neva Rae Powers. *Jacques* (Le Fermier): Rex David Hays. *DuBac* (Le Monseigneur): Michael McCarty. *Therese* (La Maman): Maria Guida. *Isolde* (La Chanteuse d'Opéra): Gerianne Raphael. *Claude* (Le Coiffeur): GORDON J. WEISS. *Guy-Louis* (Le Petit Garcon): Timothy Scott. *M. Clichy* (Le Photographe): David E. Thomas. *Philippe* (Le Maitre d'Hotel): Bryan Nicholas. *Marie-Claire* (La Duchesse): Julia Shelley. *Henri* (Le Duc): Will Roy. *Monsieur Cochon* (Le Porc): Wilbur.

American Soldiers: Private Johnny Perkins: DON SCARDINO. *Lieutenant McNeill:* Jay Devlin. *Frank:* Robert Brubach. *Steve:* Harry Fawcett. *Joe:* John Scoullar. *Tom:* Jamie Haskins. *Phillip:* Richard Christopher.

German Soldiers: Hans: Scott Allen. *Kapitan Kost:* Alexander Orfaly. *Siegfried:* Scott Barnes. *Fritz:* Roger Berdahl. *Karl:* Timothy Wallace. *Willie:* Karl Heist.

The action takes place during one day in September, 1918, toward the end of World War I in the French town of DuTemps, and the trenches that surround it.

Act 1, Scene 1: DuTemps and the American and German Trenches. *Scene 2:* Asylum of Ste. Anne. *Scene 3:* Outside the Asylum Gate. *Scene 4:* The Main Square of DuTemps. *Scene 5:* Madeleine's Establishment. *Scene 6:* Chamber of Love. *Scene 7:* DuTemps. *Scene 8:* American and German Trenches. *Scene 9:* Roof of Cathedral.

Act 2, Scene 1: An Abandoned Circus. *Scene 2:* Outskirts of DuTemps. *Scene 3:* German and American Trenches. *Scene 4:* The Terrace. *Scene 5:* DuTemps and No Man's Land.

ACT 1

Scene 2

"A Stain on the Name"
Inmates

Scene 4

"Deja Vu"
M. Martin

"Promenade" (The Transformation)
Inmates

---

[11]Originally presented 2 February 1979 at Theatre-Off-Park for 12 performances in substantially different form as a revival of *SHUFFLE ALONG*.

[12]Replaced for National Tour by:
"Baltimo' Joe" (1935)
(*Revised Lyrics by* Cheryl Hardwick, 1978.)

Scene 5
  "Turn Around"
    M. Martrin, Inmates
Scene 6
  "Nothing, Only Love"
    P. Blair, D. Scardino, M. Martin
Scene 7
  "King of Hearts"
    G. Morgan, P. Blair, B. Gunton, M. Martin, Inmates
  "Close Upon the Hour"
    D. Scardino
Scene 9
  "A Brand New Day"
    M. McCarty, D. Scardino, Inmates
ACT 2
Scene 1
  "Le Grand Cirque de Provence"
    B. Gunton, Inmates
  "Hey, Look at Me, Mrs. Draba"
    D. Scardino
Scene 3
  "Going Home Tomorrow"
    Soldiers
Scene 4
  "Somewhere Is Here"
    M. Martin
  "Nothing, Only Love" (reprise)
    B. Gunton, M. Martin, P. Blair, D. Scardino
Scene 5
  "March, March, March"
    D. Scardino, Inmates
  "The Battle"
    Soldiers

1978.23 STREET SCENE

A Revival of the American Opera (Dramatic Musical) in Two Acts, 3 Scenes[13]. Book by Elmer Rice from his play of the same name. Music by Kurt Weill. Lyrics by Langston Hughes. Directed by Jack O'Brien. Conducted by John Mauceri. Scenery designed by Paul Sylbert. Costumes designed by Nancy Potts. Lighting by Gilbert V. Hemsley, Jr. Choreography by Patricia Birch. Chorus master, Lloyd Walser. Chorus prepared by Leann Hillmer. (Orchestrations by Kurt Weill.) Produced by the New York City Opera. Opened 28 October 1978 at the New York State Theatre and closed 12 November 1978 after 4 performances in repertory.

CAST (in order of appearance): *Greta Fiorentino*: Martha Thigpen. *Emma Jones*: DIANE CURRY. *Olga Olsen*: Rosemarie Freni. *Carl Olsen*: Ralph Bassett. *Neighborhood Woman*: Marie Young. *Shirley Kaplan*: Lynn Cohen. *Abraham Kaplan*: Nico Castel. *Salvation Army Girls*: Myrna Reynolds, Kay Schoenfeld. *Henry Davis*: Andrew Smith. *Willie Maurrant*: Robert Sapolsky. *Anna Maurrant*: EILEEN SCHAULER. *Sam Kaplan*: ALAN KAYS. *Daniel Buchanan*: James Clark. *Mrs. Buchanan*: Lila Herbert. *Frank Maurrant*: WILLIAM CHAPMAN. *George Jones*: Robert Paul. *Steve Sankey*: William Ledbetter. *Lippo Fiorentino*: JONATHAN GREEN. *Mrs. Hildebrand*: Sally Lambert. *Jenny Hildebrand*: Kathleen Hegierski. *Graduates*: Denise Adoff, Vanessa Williams. *Charlie Hildebrand*: Timothy Eaton. *Mary Hildebrand*: Dela Bartolini. *Grace Davis*: Kimara Love. *Rose Maurrant*: CATHERINE MALFITANO. *Harry Easter*: ALAN TITUS. *Mae Jones*: Bronwyn Thomas. *Dick McGann*: Daniel Levans. *Vincent Jones*: Bill Herndon. *Dr. John Wilson*: Don Carlo. *Officer Murphy*: Ken Dovel. *Milkman*: Robert Brubaker. *Joan*: Ann Cawlo. *Myrtle*: Alexandra Sabin. *Workman*: Harris Davis. *Eddie*: John Henry Thomas. *Sally*: Brigitte Stocker. *Joe*: Billy Ross. *Strawberry Seller*: Richard Nelson. *Corn Seller*: Susan Delery-Whedon. *James Henry*: Don Yule. *Fred Cullen*: Alan Baker. *Old Clothes Man*: Dan Kingman. *Men*: Frank Tippie, James Brewer, Herbert Hunsberger. *Grocery Boy*: Ken Rubenfeld. *Ambulance Driver*: Edward Vaughan. *Music Student*: Patricia Charbonneau. *Intern*: James Sergi. *Furniture Mover*: Frank Tippie. *Nursemaids*: Marie Young, Rita Metzger. *Middle-Aged Couple*: Dan Kingman, Harriet Greene. *Off Stage Voices*: Vanessa Williams, Timothy Eaton, Lila Herbert.

---

[13]Originally produced in New York 9 January 1947 at the Adelphi Theatre for 148 performances. For Synopsis of Scenes and Musical Numbers, see original 1947 production.

1978.24 GOREY STORIES

An Entertainment (Revue) with Music in Two Acts[14]. Written and designed by Edward Gorey. Adaptation by Stephen Currens. Music composed and orchestrated by David Aldrich. Directed by Tony Tanner. Scenery supervised by Lynn Pecktal. Costumes supervised by David Murin. Lighting designed by Roger Morgan. Musical director, Martin Silvestri. Furs by Ben Kahn. Produced by Terry Allen Kramer, Harry Rigby, Hale Matthews and John Wulp. Opened and closed 30 October 1978 at the Booth Theatre after 1 performance.

CAST (in order of appearance): *Mona*, a maid: Gemze de Lappe. *Harold*, a butler: Sel Vitella. *Lady Celia*, the hostess: Julie Kurnitz. *Mary Rosemarch*, a spinster: June Squibb. *Ortenzia Caviglia*, a singer: Susan Marchand. *Little Henry*, a child: Tobias Haller. *Jasper Ankle*, an opera freak: Dennis McGovern. *C. F. Earbrass*, an author: Leon Shaw. *Hamish*, a beautiful young man: John Michalski.

Act 1: Lady Celia's Drawing Room.

Act 2: The summer house.

THE STORIES (in order of appearance)

ACT 1
  Assembly
  Limericks from The Listing Attic
    (Company)
  The Hapless Child
    (S. Vitella, J. Squibb, L. Shaw, G. deLappe, D. McGovern, J. Michalski, J. Kurnitz, S. Marchand)
  "The Wuggly Ump"
    (Company)
  The Curious Sofa
    (Company)
  The Sinking Spell
    (Company)
  The Gilded Bat
    (Company)
  "The Insect God"
    (Company)
  The Willowdale Handcar
    (Company)
  The Doubtful Guest
    (Company)
  "The Blue Aspic" (an opera)
    (Company)
    (*Lyrics by* Stephen Currens.)
ACT 2
  The Unstrung Harp, or Mr. Earbrass Writes a Novel:
    (J. Kurnitz, L. Shaw)
  The Pious Infant
    (Company)
  "The Osbick Bird"
    (S. Vitella, T. Haller)
  The Deranged Cousins
    (L. Shaw, D. McGovern, S. Marchand, J. Squibb)
  "The Eleventh Episode"
    (J. Squibb, S. Marchand)
  The Lost Lions
    (J. Michalski, L. Shaw, J. Kurnitz)
  The Loathsome Couple
    (Company)
  "The Gashlycrumb Tinies"
    (Company)

1978.25 PLATINUM

A Musical with a Flip Side in Two Acts. Book by Will Holt and Bruce Vilanch based on an original idea by Will Holt. Music by Gary William

---

[14]First produced in New York Off Broadway 8 December 1977 at the WPA Theatre for 12 performances.

Friedman. Lyrics by Will Holt. Directed and choreographed by Joe Layton. Scenery designed by David Hays. Lighting designed by John Gleason. Costumes designed by Bob Mackie. Orchestrations by Fred Thaler, Jimmie Haskell. (Musical) Arrangements by Fred Thaler, Jimmie Haskell, Gary William Friedman. Musical director, Fred Thaler. Sound by Paramount Sound, Steve Wooley. Multi-media designed by Sheppard Kerman. Produced by Gladys Rackmil, Fritz Holt and Barry M. Brown. Opened 12 November 1978 at the Mark Hellinger Theatre and closed 10 December 1978 after 33 performanes.

CAST (in order of appearance): Shultz: Tony Shultz. Lila Halliday: ALEXIS SMITH. Snake: Ronnie B. Baker. Minky: Jonathan Freeman. Boris: John Hammil. Damita: Damita Jo Freeman. Robin: Robin Frean. Avery: Avery Sommers. Jeff Leff: Stanley Kamel. Crystal Mason: LISA MORDENTE. Dan Danger: RICHARD COX. Christine: Christine Faith. Wenndy: Wenndy Leigh MacKenzie. Alan Fairmont: Jonathan Freeman. The Sidemen: Fred Thaler (Conductor/Piano), Gregory Block (Violon), Dick Frank (Guitar), Steve Mack (Bass), Roy Markowitz (Drums).

"Wings of Destiny" Film Sequence Cast: War Bride: Lila Halliday (ALEXIS SMITH). Mack: Alan Fairmont. (Jonathan Freeman). "Wings of Destiny" conceived and directed by Joe Layton.

Act 1: The newest environmental recording studio in Hollywood.

Act 2,: Six weeks later.

ACT 1
"Back With a Beat"/"Nothing But"
    A. Smith
"Sunset"
    L. Mordente, A. Sommers, D. J. Freeman, R. Frean
"Ride, Baby, Ride"
    R. Cox, D. J. Freeman, R. Frean, A. Sommers
"Destiny"
    A. Smith
"Disco Destiny"[15]
    L. Mordente, A. Sommers, D. J. Freeman, R. Frean
"I Am the Light"
    R. Cox
"Movie Star Mansions"
    R. Cox, A. Smith

ACT 2
"Platinum Dreams"
    A. Sommers, D. J. Freeman, R. Frean
"Trials and Tribulations"/"I Like You"
    L. Mordente, A. Smith
"1945"
    R. Cox, A. Smith
"Too Many Mirrors"
    A. Smith
"Old Times, Good Times"[16]
    A. Smith, Company

(JOHN CURRY'S)
ICE DANCING

1978.26

An Ice-Skating Revue in Two Acts, 10 Scenes. Choreographed by (in alphabetical order) Jean-Pierre Bonnefous, Robert Cohan, John Curry, Norman Maen, Kenneth MacMillan, Peter Martins, Douglas Norwick, Donald Saddler, Twyla Tharp. Settings by Tony Straiges. Costumes supervised by Florence Klotz. Lighting by Marilyn Rennagel. Costumes designed by (in alphabetical order) Nadine Baylis., Sara Brook, Norberto Chiesa, Joe Eula, Florence Klotz, Santo Loquasto, D. D. Ryan. Sound design by Jack Mann. Entire production supervised by Ruth Mitchell. Produced by Charlotte Kirk, David Singer and Cubby Downe in association with Peter Wiese. Opened 21 November 1978 at the Felt Forum, closing 3 December 1978; re-opened 19 December 1978 at the Minskoff Theatre[17] and closed 31 December 1978 after 37 performances.

CAST: JOHN CURRY, JOJO STARBUCK, Ron Alexander, Yvonne Brink, Lorna Brown, Jack Courtney, Patricia Dodd, Cathy Foulkes, Brian Grant, Muki Held, Deborah Page, Paul Toomey.

---

[15]Orchestrated by Harold Wheeler.
[16]Orchestrated by Harold Wheeler.
[17]For the Broadway transfer the running order was revised; Angela Adney joined the cast, and Muki Held departed the cast.

ACT 1
Scene 1
"Palais de Glace" (World Premiere)
    (Music by Giacomo Myerbeer. Costumes Designed by Florence Klotz. Choreography by Donald Saddler.)

Paris 1912: Skating in the afternoon was de rigueur, for where else would you find royalty, Ladies of Paris in all their glamour, famous artists of the day, and rich Americans all cavorting?
    Major domo: R. Alexander. Lovers: C. Foulkes, J. Courtney. Famous poet: P. Toomey. Famous dancer: P. Dodd. American: L. Brown. Young Count: B. Grant. A darling of Paris, well protected: M. Held. Another darling of Paris, very well protected: J. Starbuck. Prince: J. Curry.

Scene 2
"Scoop"
    P. Toomey, D. Page, Y. Brink
    (Stage premiere: March 1976)(Ice Premiere)
    (Music composed and played by Donald Ashwander. Costumes designed by Sara Brook. Choreography by Douglas Norwick. "Scoop" by special permission from The Paper Bag Players.)

Scene 3
"After All" (in Three Movements)
    J. Curry
    (Music by Tomasso Albinoni. Costume designed by Santo Loquasto. Choreography by Twyla Tharp.)

This work was commissioned by John Curry and the U.S. Olympic Committee especially for Mr. Curry's appearance in "Superskates III" at Madison Square Garden, November 1976.

Scene 4
"Moon Dances" (World Premiere)
    M. Held, L. Brown, P. Dodd, R. Alexander, B. Grant, P. Toomey
    (Music by Camille St-Saens. Choreography by John Curry.)

This work made possible by a generous grant from Chanel, Inc.

Scene 5
"Tango-Tango" (World Premiere)
    J. Curry, J. Starbuck
    ("Tango" by Igor Stravinsky. "Jalousie" by Niels Gade. Choreography by Peter Martins. Costumes designed by D. D. Ryan.)

This work supported by a generous grant from the Doll Foundation.

ACT 2
Scene 1
"Icemoves" (World Premiere)
    J. Curry, C. Foulkes, M. Held, P. Dodd, Y. Brink, L. Brown, D. Page, R. Alexander, J. Courtney
    (Music by Hector Berlioz. Costumes designed by Joe Eula. Choreography by Jean-Pierre Bonnefous.)

Scene 2
"Night and Day" pas de deux from MYTH
    Night: J. Starbuck. Day: J. Courtney.
    (Mask of Separation composed by Burt Alcantara. Costumes designed by Norberto Chiesa. Choreography by Robert Cohan. Costumes executed by Suzanne Joelson.)

Scene 3
"Feux Follets"
    J. Curry
    (Music by Franz Liszt. Costume designed by Harry Lines. Choreography by Kenneth MacMillan.)

Scene 4
"Anything Goes" (World Premiere)
    J. Starbuck, J. Courtney, L. Brown, D. Page, D. Barker
    (Music by Leonard Bernstein. Choreography by John Curry.)

Scene 5
"Afternoon of a Faun"
    J. Curry, C. Foulkes
    (Music by Claude Debussy. Costumes designed by Nadine Baylis. Choreography by Norman Maen.)

BALLROOM

1978.27

A Musical in One Act, 13 Scenes. . Book by Jerome Kass. (Based on his teleplay "Queen of the Stardust Ballroom.") Music by Billy Goldenberg.

Lyrics by Marilyn and Alan Bergman. Directed and choreographed by Michael Bennett. Co-choreographer, Bob Avian. Scenic design by Robin Wagner. Costume design by Theoni V. Aldredge. Lighting design by Tharon Musser. Orchestrations by Jonathan Tunick. Sound by Otts Munderloh. Musical direction by Don Jennings. Co-producers, Bob Avian, Bernard Gersten, Susan MacNair. Produced by Michael Bennett. Opened 14 December 1978 at the Majestic Theatre and closed 24 March 1979 after 116 performances.

CAST: *The Family: Bea Asher:* DOROTHY LOUDON. *Helen,* her sister-in-law: Sally-Jane Heit. *Jack,* her brother-in-law: John Hallow. *Diane,* her daughter: Dorothy Danner. *David,* her son: Pater Alzado.

At the Stardust Ballroom: Alfred Rossi: VINCENT GARDENIA. *Marlene:* Lynn Roberts. *Nathan Bricker:* Bernie Knee. *Angie:* Patricia Drylie. *Johnny "Lightfeet":* Howard Parker. *Martha:* Barbara Erwin. *Petey:* Gene Kelton. *Shirley:* Liz Sheridan. *Paul:* Michael Vita. *"Scooter":* Danny Carroll. *Eleanor:* Jayne Turner. *Pauline Krim:* Janet Stewart White. *Faye:* Roberta Haze. *Harry "the Noodle":* Victor Griffin. *Marie:* Adriana Keathley. *Emily:* Mary Ann Niles. *Mario:* Terry Violino. *Anitra:* Svetlana McLee Grody. *Carl:* David Evans. *Margaret:* Mavis Ray. *Thomas:* Peter Gladke. *Bill:* Rudy Tronto. And Marilyn Cooper, Dick Corrigan, Bud Fleming, Carol Flemming, Mickey Gunnersen, Alferd Karl, Dorothy D. Lister, John J. Martin, Joe Milan, Frank Pietri.

Customer's at Bea's Store: Natalie: Marilyn Cooper. *Estelle:* Roberta Haze. *Kathy:* Carol Flemming.

The action takes place in the Bronx at the present time.

Scene 1: Bea's Junk Shop. *Scene 2:* Outside the Stardust Ballroom. *Scene 3:* Stardust Ballroom. *Scene 4:* Bea's Living Room. *Scene 5:* Stardust Ballroom. *Scene 6:* Bea's Living Room. *Scene 7:* Bea's Junk Store. *Scene 8:* Stardust Ballroom. *Scene 9:* Bea's Living Room. *Scene 10:* Stardust Ballroom. *Scene 11:* Outside the Ballroom. *Scene 12:* Bea's Living Room. *Scene 13:* Stardust Ballroom.

MUSICAL NUMBERS
Scene 2
 "A Terrific Band and a Real Nice Crowd"
  D. Loudon
Scene 3
 "A Song for Dancing"
  L. Roberts, B. Knee
  Danced by the Ballroom Regulars.
 "One By One"
  L. Roberts, B. Knee
  Danced by P. Drylie, H. Parker, the Ballroom Regulars.
 "The Dance Montage"
  Danced by the Ballroom Regulars
 "Dreams"
  L. Roberts
 "Somebody Did Alright for Herself"
  D. Loudon
Scene 5
 "The Tango Contest"
  Danced by M. A. Niles and T. Violino, D. Loudon and V. Gardenia, B. Erwin and G. Kelton, S. M. Grody and D. Evans, L. Sheridan and M. Vita, M. Ray and P. Gladke, A. Keathley and V. Griffin
 "Goodnight Is Not Goodbye"
  L. Roberts, B. Knee
  Danced by the Ballroom Regulars.
Scene 8
 "I've Been Waiting All My Life"
  B. Knee
  Danced by the Ballroom Regulars.
 "I Love to Dance"
  D. Loudon, V. Gardenia
Scene 10
 "More of the Same"
  L. Roberts, B. Knee
  Danced by the Ballroom Regulars.
Scene 12
 "Fifty Percent"
  D. Loudon
Scene 13
 "The Stardust Waltz"
  Danced by the Ballroom Regulars
 "I Wish You a Waltz"
  D. Loudon

1978.28 # A BROADWAY MUSICAL

A Musical about a Broadway Musical, in Two Acts, a Prologue and 9 Scenes[18]. Book by William F. Brown. Music by Charles Strouse. Lyrics by Lee Adams. Production supervised by Gower Champion. (Direction, choreography uncredited). Sets by Peter Wexler. Costumes by Randy Barcelo. Lighting by John DeSantis. Musical conductor, Kevin Farrell. Orchestrations by Robert M. Freedman. Musical supervision and vocal arrangements by Don Pippin. Dance arrangements by Donald Johnston. Co-choreographer, George Bunt. Sound by Abe Jacob. Production co-ordinator, Barbara-Mae Phillips. Associate producer, Maria DiDia. Produced by Norman Kean and Garth H. Drabinsky. Opened and closed 21 December 1978 at the Lunt-Fontanne Theatre after 1 performance.

CAST (in order of appearance): *Policeman:* Nate Barnett. *James Lincoln:* IRVING ALLEN LEE. *Eddie Bell:* WARREN BERLINGER. *Lonnie Paul:* LARRY RILEY. *Melinda Bernard:* Jackee Harry. *Stan Howard:* ALAN WEEKS. *Maggie Simpson:* PATTI KARR. *Stephanie Bell:* GWYDA DONHOWE. *Kumi-Kumi:* Christina Kumi-Kimball. *Smoke & Fire Back-Up Singers:* Maris Clement, Loretta Devine, Jackee Harry. *Richie Taylor's Lawyers:* Sydney Anderson, Michael Gallagher. *Rehearsal Pianist:* Gwen Arment. *Richie Taylor:* LARRY MARSHALL. *Nathaniel:* Nate Barnett. *Richie's Secretary:* Jo Ann Ogawa. *Shirley Wolfe:* ANNE FRANCINE. *Theater Party Associates:* Sydney Anderson, Maris Clement, Loretta Devine. *Male Dancers:* Albert Stephenson, Robert Melvin, Martin Rabbett. *Sylvester Lee:* TIGER HAYNES. *Louie:* Reggie Jackson. *Jake:* Martin Rabbett. *Big Jake:* Albert Stephenson. *Junior:* Robert Melvin.

Ensemble: Sydney Anderson, Gwen Arment, Nate Barnett, Maris Clement, Prudence Darby, Don Edward Detrick, Loretta Devine, Sharon Ferrol, Michael Gallagher, Scott Geralds, Maggy Gorrill, Jackee Harry, Leon Jackson, Reggie Jackson, Carleton Jones, Christina Kumi-Kimball, Michael Kubala, Robert Melvin, Jo Ann Ogawa, Karen Paskow, Martin Rabbett, Albert Stephenson, Marilynn Winbush, Brad Witsger.

Prologue: One year ago, Times Square. *Act 1, Scene 1:* The same day. Eddie Bell's office. *Scene 2:* Six months later. Eddie and Stephanie Bell's apartment. *Scene 3:* Later. Stan Howard's apartment. *Scene 4:* One week later. A midtown Italian restaurant. *Scene 5:* A few minutes later. On a stage in a theatre on West 44th Street.

Act 2, Scene 1: Early one morning a week later. The Federal Theatre, Washington, D.C. *Scene 2:* Technical run-through and opening night in Washington. *Scene 3:* Later on opening night. The Federal Theatre. *Scene 4:* Later. The bar at the Washington Hotel.

ACT 1
Prologue
 "Broadway, Broadway"
  New Kids in Town, N. Barnett, I. A. Lee
Scene 1
 "A Broadway Musical"
  W. Berlinger, I. A. Lee, L. Riley, J. Harry, A. Weeks, P. Karr, Ensemble
Scene 3
 "Smoke and Fire"
  A. Weeks, I. A. Lee, C. Kumi-Kimball, Ensemble
Scene 4
 "Lawyers"
  W. Berlinger, G. DonHowe, S. Anderson, M. Gallagher
Scene 5
 "Yenta Power"
  A. Francine, Theatre Party Associates
 "Let Me Sing My Song"
  L. Marshall
 "A Broadway Musical" (reprise)
  W. Berlinger, G. DonHowe, I. A. Lee, A. Francine, P. Karr, L. Riley, A. Weeks, Ensemble
ACT 2
Scene 1
 "The 1934 Hot Chocolate Jazz Babies Revue"
  T. Haynes, I. A. Lee, Ensemble
Scene 2
 "Let Me Sing My Song" (reprise)
  L. Marshall, Friends
Scene 3
 "It's Time for a Cheer-Up Song"
  A. Weeks, P. Karr, L. Riley, I. A. Lee

[18]Originally produced in New York Off-Off Broadway 10 October 1978 at the Theatre of Riverside Church for 26 performances.

"You Gotta Have Dancing"
  P. Karr, I. A. Lee, Ensemble
Scene 4
"What You Go Through"
  G. DonHowe, W. Berlinger
"Don't Tell Me"
  W. Berlinger
"Together"
  I. A. Lee, W. Berlinger, Staff

1979.01 MONTEITH & RAND

A Comedy Revue in Two Acts[19]. (Devised by John Monteith and Suzanne Rand.) Assisted by bill-boy russell. Lighting by Gilbert V. Hemsley, Jr. Costumes by Donald Brooks. Produced by James Lipton Productions. Opened 2 January 1979 at the Booth Theatre and closed 10 March 1979 after 79 performances. Total, including Off-Broadway run, 110 performances.

CAST: JOHN MONTEITH, SUZANNE RAND.

1979.02 THE GRAND TOUR

A Musical in Two Acts, a Prologue and 13 Scenes. Book by Michael Stewart and Mark Bramble. Based on the play "Jacobowsky and the Colonel" by Franz Werfel and the American play based on the same, by S. N. Behrman. Music and lyrics by Jerry Herman. Directed by Gerald Freedman. Choreography by Donald Saddler. Sets by Ming Cho Lee. Costumes by Theoni V. Aldredge. Lighting by Martin Aronstein. Musical direction by Wally Harper. Orchestrations by Philip J. Lang. Dance music arranged by Peter Howard. Vocal arrangements by Don Pippin. Assistant choreographer, Mercedes Ellington. Sound by Jack Mann. Produced by James M. Nederlander, Diana Shumlin, Jack Schlissel in association with Carole J. Shorenstein and Stewart F. Lane. Opened 11 January 1979 at the Palace Theatre and closed 4 March 1979 after 61 performances.

CAST (in order of appearance): S. L. Jacobowsky: JOEL GREY. Mme. Bouffier: Grace Keagy. Cziesno: Jack Karcher. Jeannot: Mark Waldrop. Colonel Tadeusz Boleslav Stjerbinsky: RON HOLGATE. Szabuniewicz: Stephen Vinovich. Chauffeur: Stan Page. Captain Meuller: George Reinholt. Mme. Vauclain: Chevi Colton. Marianne: FLORENCE LACEY. Conductor: Gene Varrone. Mme. Marville, an Elegant Lady: Travis Hudson. A Peasant Woman with Chickens: Grace Keagy. Jacques, the Ejected Passenger: Bob Morrisey. Hugo, the Hungarian Hercules: Kenneth Kantor. Mme. Manzoni: Chevi Colton. Stiltwalker: Papa Clairon. Bargeman: Kenneth Kantor. Man with flower in his lapel: Jay Stuart. Papa Clairon: Jay Pierce. Claudine: Jo Speros. Bride's Mother: Grace Keagy. Bride's Father: Gene Varrone. Bride's Aunt: Chevi Colton. Groom: Mark Waldrop. Bride: Michelle Marshall. Commissaire of Police: Bob Morrisey. Peddler: Stan Page. Mother Madeleine: Travis Hudson.

Refugees, Soldiers, Guests, Sisters, etc.: Bjarne Buchtrup, Carol Dorian, Kenneth Kantor, Jack Karcher, Debra Lyman, Michelle Marshall, Bob Morrisey, Stan Page, Tian Paul, Jay Pierce, Linda Poser, Theresa Rakov, Paul Solen, Jo Speros, Mark Waldrop, Jeff Veazey, Bonnie Young. Swing Dancers: Bronna Lipton, Jeff Richards.

The action takes place 13-18 June 1940 between Paris and the Atlantic Coast of France.

Act 1, Scene 1: Square outside the Hotel de La Rose. Scene 2: Saint-Cyrille. Scene 3: A local train heading West. Scene 4: Wagons of the Carnival Manzoni. Scene 5: Open spot in the countryside near Rennes. Scene 6: Dressing area of the Carnival Manzoni. Scene 7: Midway of the Carnival Manzoni.

Act 2, Scene 1: A tree-lined canal in the West of France. Scene 2: Cafe of Papa Clairon at St. Nazaire. Scene 3: A country road near St. Nazaire. Scene 4: 23 Rue Mace. Scene 5: Empty street in St. Nazaire. Scene 6: The Old Wharf at St. Nazaire.

ACT 1
Prologue
"I'll Be Here Tomorrow"
  J. Grey
Scene 1
"For Poland"
  R. Holgate, G. Keagy, Parisians
Scene 2
"I Belong Here"
  F. Lacey
"Marianne"
  R. Holgate

Scene 3
"We're Almost There"
  F. Lacey, S. Vinovich, J. Grey, R. Holgate, T. Hudson, G. Varrone, Passengers
Scene 4
"Marianne" (reprise)
  J. Grey
Scene 5
"More and More"/"Less and Less"
  F. Lacey, R. Holgate
Scene 6
"One Extraordinary Thing"
  J. Grey, F. Lacey, R. Holgate, S. Vinovich, the Carnival Manzoni
Scene 7
"One Extraordinary Thing" (reprise)
  J. Grey
ACT 2
Scene 1
"Mrs. S. L. Jacobowsky"
  J. Grey
Scene 2
"Wedding Conversation"
  J. Grey, G. Varrone
"Mazeltov"
  G. Varrone, Wedding Guests
Scene 3
"I Think, I Think"
  R. Holgate
Scene 4
"For Poland" (reprise)
  F. Lacey, T. Hudson, Sisters of Charity
Scene 5
"You I Like"
  R. Holgate, J. Grey
Scene 6
"I Belong Here" (reprise)
  F. Lacey
"I'll Be Here Tomorrow" (reprise)
  J. Grey

1979.03 SARAVÁ

A Musical in Two Acts, 17 Scenes. Book and lyrics by N. Richard Nash. Based on the novel "Dona Flor and Her Two Husbands" by Jorge Amado. Music by Mitch Leigh. Directed and choreographed by Rick Atwell. Sets and costumes by Santo Loquasto. Lighting by David F. Segal. Musical direction and vocal arrangements by David Friedman. Orchestrations by Daniel Troob. Dance arrangements by Dom Salvador. Sound by Robert Kerzman. A Mitch Leigh Production. Produced by Eugene V. Wolsk. Opened in preview 11 January 1979 at the Mark Hellinger Theatre, moved 1 March 1979 to the Broadway Theatre and closed 17 June 1979 after 177 performances[20].

CAST (in order of appearance): Vadinho: P. J. BENJAMIN. Flor: TOVAH FELD-SHUH. Arigof: RODERICK SPENCER SIBERT. Costas: Doncharles Manning. Manuel: Wilfredo Suarez. Dealer: Jack Neubeck. Dionisia: CAROL JEAN LEWIS. Policemen: Lloyd Sannes, Gaetan Young. Dona Paiva: BETTY WALKER. Rosalia: RANDY GRAFF. Antonio: ALAN ABRAMS. Priest: Ken Waller. Teo: MICHAEL INGRAM. Senhor Baldez: Jack Neubeck. Pinho: David Kottke.

The People of Bahia: Steve J. Ace, Frank Cruz, Donna Cyrus, Marlene Danielle, Adrienne Frimet, Brenda Garratt, Trudie Green, Jane Judge, David Kottke, Daniel Lorenzo, Doncharles Manning, Jack Neubeck, Thelma Ann Nevitt, Ivson Polk, Wynonna Smith, Michelle Stubbs, Wilfredo Suarez, Ken Waller, Freida Ann Williams, John Leslie Wolfe, Gaetan Young.

The action takes place in Bahia, Brazil, from Carnival to Carnival.

Act 1, Scene 1: A Street. Scene 2: Barrabas Casino. Scene 3: Kitchen in Flor's House. Scene 4: A Cemetery. Scene 5: Teo's Pharmacy. Scene 6: Bedroom in Flor's House. Scene 7: Dionisia's Candomble. Scene 8: Teo's Pharmacy. Scene 9: Kitchen in Flor's House. Scene 10: A Church.

[19]Originally produced in New York Off-Broadway 27 July 1978 at Theatre East for 31 performances.

[20]Management never designated an opening night; the New York Times reviewed the show 12 February 1979, Variety 14 February 1979, other press followed by 23 February 1979.

Act 2, Scene 1: A Hotel Terrace. *Scene 2*: Flor's House. *Scene 3*: Barrabas Casino. *Scene 4*: Bedroom in Flor's House. *Scene 5*: Dionisia's. *Scene 6*: A Street. *Scene 7*: Finale.

ACT 1
Scene 1
"Saravá"
P. J. Benjamin, T. Feldshuh, Others
Scene 2
"Makulelé"
W. Suarez, D. Manning, P. J. Benjamin, R. S. Sibert
"Vadinho is Gone"
T. Feldshuh
Scene 4
"Hosanna"
T. Feldshuh, Others
Scene 5
"Nothing's Missing"
M. Ingram, T. Feldshuh
Scene 6
"Nothing's Missing" (reprise)
T. Feldshuh
Scene 7
"I'm Looking for a Man"
C. J. Lewis, Others
Scene 8
"A Simple Man"
M. Ingram
Scene 10
"Viva a Vida"
All
ACT 2
Scene 1
"Muito Bom"
T. Feldshuh, M. Ingram, Others
Scene 2
"Nothing's Missing" (reprise)
T. Feldshuh, M. Ingram
Scene 3
"Play the Queen"
T. Feldshuh, P. J. Benjamin, R. S. Sibert, Others
Scene 4
"Which Way Do I Go?"
T. Feldshuh
"Remember"
P. J. Benjamin
"A Simple Man" (reprise)
M. Ingram
Scene 5
"You Do"
C. J. Lewis, Others
Scene 6
"A Single Life"
P. J. Benjamin
"Vadinho Is Gone" (reprise)
T. Feldshuh
Scene 7
"Saravá" (reprise)
All

1979.04 THEY'RE PLAYING OUR SONG

A Musical Comedy in Two Acts, 13 Scenes. Book by Neil Simon. Music by Marvin Hamlisch. Lyrics by Carole Bayer Sager. Directed by Robert Moore. Musical numbers staged by Patricia Birch. Scenery and projections by Douglas W. Schmidt. Costumes by Ann Roth. Lighting by Tharon Musser. Music direction by Larry Blank. Orchestrations by Ralph Burns, Richard Hazard, Gene Page. Sound by Tom Morse. Produced by Emanuel Azenberg. Opened 11 February 1979 at the Imperial Theatre and closed 6 September 1981 after 1082 performances.

CAST (in order of appearance): *Vernon Gersch*: ROBERT KLEIN. *Sonia Walsk*: LUCIE ARNAZ.
The Voices of Vernon Gersch: Wayne Mattson, Andy Roth, Greg Zadikov. *The Voices of Sonia Walsk*: Helen Castillo, Celia Celnik Matthau, Debbie Shapiro. *The Voice of Phil the Engineer*: Philip Cusack. "I Still Believe in Love" reprise sung by Johnny Mathis.

(The action takes place in New York and California at the present time.)

Act 1, Scene 1: Vernon's Apartment—Central Park West, New York City. *Scene 2*: Vernon's Studio—Five days later. *Scene 3*: Le Club. *Scene 4*: Sonia's Apartment—An hour and a half later. *Scene 5*: On the street. *Scene 6*: On the road. *Scene 7*: A beach house in Quogue, Long Island.

Act 2, Scene 1: Vernon's Apartment—A few days later. *Scene 2*: Vernon's Bedroom—Three weeks later. *Scene 3*: Vernon's Bedroom—The middle of the night. *Scene 4*: A Recording Studio—11:00 AM the next morning. *Scene 5*: A Hospital Room—Los Angeles, a few months later. *Scene 6*: Sonia's Apartment—A few months later.

ACT 1
Scene 1
"Fallin'"
R. Klein
Scene 2
"Workin' It Out"
R. Klein, L. Arnaz, Voices
"If He Really Knew Me"
L. Arnaz, R. Klein
Scene 3
"They're Playing Our Song"
R. Klein, L. Arnaz
Scene 4
"If He Really Knew Me" (reprise)
R. Klein, L. Arnaz
"Right"
L. Arnaz, R. Klein, Voices
Scene 7
"Just for Tonight"
L. Arnaz
ACT 2
Scene 1
"When You're in My Arms"
R. Klein, L. Arnaz, Voices
Scene 4
"I Still Believe in Love"
L. Arnaz
Scene 5
"Fill in the Words"
R. Klein, Vocies

1979.05 WHOOPEE!

A Revival of the Musical Comedy in Two Acts, 12 Scenes[21]. Book by William Anthony McGuire. Based on the play "The Nervous Wreck" by Owen Davis (based on a short story "The Wreck" by E. J. Rath.) Music by Walter Donaldson. Lyrics by Gus Kahn. Entire Production directed by Frank Corsaro. Choreography and musical staging by Dan Siretta. Musical direction by Lynn Crigler. Scenery by John Lee Beatty. Costumes by David Toser. Lighting by Peter M. Erhardt. Sound design by Warren E. Jenkins. Production supervisor, Ron Abbott. Production consultant, G. William Oakley. Music research consultant, Alfred Simon. Assistant choreographer, Larry McMillan. Orchestrations and dance arrangements by Russell Warner. Associate producers, Martin Markinson, Joseph Harris, Donald Tick. Produced by Ashton Springer, Frank C. Pierson, Michael Price. Opened 14 February 1979 at the ANTA Theatre and closed 12 August 1979 after 204 performances.

CAST (in order of appearance): *Sheriff Bob*: J. KEVIN SCANNELL. *Mary Custer*: CAROL SWARBRICK. *Judson Morgan*: BOB ALLEN. *Sally Morgan*: BETH AUSTIN. *Henry Williams*: CHARLES REPOLE. *Wanenis*: FRANC LUZ. *Black Eagle*: LEONARD DRUM. *Chester Underwood*: GARRETT M. BROWN. *Harriet*

---

[21]Originally produced in New York 4 December 1928 at the New Amsterdam Theatre for 379 performances.

Underwood: CATHERINE COX. *Jerome Underwood*: PETER BOYDEN. *Mort*: VIC POLIZOS. *Andy McNab*: BILL ROWLEY. *Jim*: Al Micacchion. *Slim*: Steven Gelfer. *Jack*: Rick Pessagno. *Pete*: Paul M. Elkin. *Red Buffalo*: Brent Saunders. *Matape*: Candy Darling. *Leslie*: Susan Stroman. *Becky*: Robin Black. *Tilly*: Diane Epstein. *Olive*: Teri Corcoran. *Ensemble Alternates*: Jo-Ann Cifala, Jonathan Aronson.

Act 1, Scene 1: Mission rest, Arizona. *Scene 2*: En route to Black Top Canyon. *Scene 3*: Black Top Canyon. *Scene 4*: En route to the Bar "M" Ranch. *Scene 5*: The Bar "M" Ranch. *Scene 6*: Near the Reservation. *Scene 7*: Outside the Bar "M" Ranch.

Act 2, Scene 1: Outside the Reservation. *Scene 2*: Back at the Reservation. *Scene 3*: In the Wilderness. *Scene 4*: Outside the Bar "M" Ranch. *Scene 5*: In the Desert.

ACT 1[22]

Scene 1

"Let's All Make Whoopee Tonight"
    Ensemble
"Makin' Whoopee"
    C. Repole, Bridesmaids
"I'm Bringing a Red, Red Rose"
    F. Luz
Scene 2
"Go Get 'Im"
    J. K. Scannell, Ensemble
Scene 3
"Until You Get Somebody Else"
    C. Repole, B. Austin
Scene 4
"Go Get 'Im" (reprise)
    J. K. Scannell, Ensemble
Scene 5
"Love Me or Leave Me"
    C. Swarbrick, C. Repole
Scene 6
"I'm Bringing a Red, Red Rose" (reprise)
    F. Luz, B. Austin
Scene 7
"My Baby Just Cares for Me"
    C. Repole, Ensemble
"Go Get 'Im" (finaletto)
    J. K. SCannell, Ensemble
ACT 2
Scene 2
"Out of the Dawn"
    F. Luz, B. Austin
"The Tapahoe Tap"
    Indian Ensemble
Scene 3
"Reaching for Someone"
    J. K. Scannell
"You"
    C. Cox
Scene 4
"Yes, Sir, That's My Baby"
    C. Repole, Ensemble
Scene 5
"Makin' Whoopee" (reprise)
    C. Repole, Company

---

[22]For the subsequent National Tour, the show was renamed *MAKIN' WHOOPEE!*. Numerous alterations were made and the following musical numbers were added:
"Come West, Little Girl, Come West"
    Mamie Van Doren (Mary Custer), Cowboys
    (replacing "I'm Bring a Red, Red Rose" in Act 1, Scene 1)
"My Heart Is Just a Gypsy"
    Imogene Coca (Harriet), Gypsies
    (added to Act 1, Scene 3 after "Until You Get Somebody Else")
"Harriet's Ecdysiastical Delight" (dance specialty)(Act 2, Scene 3)
    I. Coca

SWEENEY TODD-
THE DEMON BARBER
OF FLEET STREET

1979.06

A Musical Thriller in Two Acts. Book by Hugh Wheeler. Based on a version of "Sweeney Todd" by Christopher Bond (after the original melodrama by George Dibdin-Pitt). Music and lyrics by Stephen Sondheim. Directed by Harold Prince. Dance and movement by Larry Fuller. Production designed by Eugene Lee. Costumes designed by Franne Lee. Lighting designed by Ken Billington. Orchestrations by Jonathan Tunick. Musical director, Paul Gemignani. Sound by Jack Mann. Assistant to Mr. Prince, Ruth Mitchell. Associate producer, Marc Howard. Produced by Richard Barr, Charles Woodward, Robert Fryer, Mary Lea Johnson, Martin Richards in association with Dean and Judy Manos. Opened 1 March 1979 at the Uris Theatre and closed 29 June 1980 after 557 performances.

CAST (in order of appearance): *Anthony Hope*: VICTOR GARBER. *Sweeney Todd*: LEN CARIOU. *Beggar Woman*: MERLE LOUISE. *Mrs. Lovett*: ANGELA LANSBURY. *Judge Turpin*: EDMUND LYNDECK. *The Beadle*: JACK ERIC WILLIAMS. *Johanna*: SARAH RICE. *Tobias Ragg*: KEN JENNINGS. *Pirelli*: JOAQUIN ROMAGUERA. *Jonas Fogg*: Robert Ousley.
    The Company: Duane Bodin, Walter Charles, Carole Doscher, Nancy Eaton, Mary-Pat Green, Cris Groenendahl, Skip Harris, Marthe Ihde, Betsy Joslyn, Nancy Killmer, Frank Kopyc, Spain Logue, Craig Lucas, Pamela McLernon, Duane Morris, Robert Ousley, Richard Warren Pugh, Maggie Task. *Swings*: Heather B. Withers, Robert Hendersen.

The action takes place in London's Fleet Street and environs during the nineteenth century.

ACT 1
"The Ballad of Sweeney Todd"
    Company
"No Place Like London"
    V. Garber, L. Cariou, M. Louise
"The Barber and His Wife"
    L. Cariou
"The Worst Pies in London"
    A. Lansbury
"Poor Thing"
    A. Lansbury
"My Friend"
    L. Cariou, A. Lansbury
"Green Finch and Linnet Bird"
    S. Rice
"Ah, Miss"
    V. Garber, M. Louise
"Johanna"
    V. Garber
"Pirelli's Miracle Elixir"
    K. Jennings, L. Cariou, A. Lansbury, Company
"The Contest"
    J. Romaguera
"Wait"
    A. Lansbury
"Kiss Me"
    S. Rice, V. Garber
"Ladies in Their Sensitivities"
    J. E. Williams
"Quartet"
    S. Rice, V. Garber, J. E. Williams, E. Lyndeck
"Pretty Women"
    L. Cariou, E. Lyndeck
"Epiphany"
    L. Cariou
"A Little Priest"
    L. Cariou, A. Lansbury
ACT 2
"God, That's Good!"
    K. Jennings, A. Lansbury, L. Cariou, M. Louise, Customers
"Johanna" (reprise)
    V. Garber, L. Cariou, S. Rice, M. Louise
"By the Sea"
    A. Lansbury

"Not While I'm Around"
    K. Jennings, A. Lansbury
"Parlor Songs"
    J. E. Williams, A. Lansbury
"City on Fire!"
    Lunatics, S. Rice, V. Garber
Final Sequence
    V. Garber, M. Louise, L. Cariou, E. Lyndeck, A. Lansbury, S. Rice, K. Jennings
"The Ballad of Sweeney Todd" (reprise)
    Company

SPOKESONG,
1979.07   or The Common Wheel

A Play with Songs in Two Acts. Play and lyrics by Stewart Parker. Music by Jimmy Kennedy. Directed by Kenneth Frankel. Set by Marjorie Kellogg. Costumes by Bill Walker. Lighting by John McLain. Musical director and pianist, Tom Fay. Cycle coach, John Jenack. Produced by the Circle-in-the-Square (Theodore Mann, Artistic director; Paul Libin, Managing director) and Long Wharf Theatre (Arvin Brown, Artistic director; M. Edgar Rosenblum, Executive director). Opened 15 March 1979 at the Circle-in-the-Square and closed 20 May 1979 after 77 performances.

CAST (in order of appearance): *The Trick Cyclist:* JOSEPH MAHER. *Frank:* JOHN LITHGOW. *Daisy:* VIRGINIA VESTOFF. *Francis,* Frank grandfather: JOSEF SOMMER. *Kitty,* Francis' wife: MARIA TUCCI. *Julian,* Frank's brother: JOHN HORTON.

The action takes place in the 1970s and the 80 years preceding, in a bicycle shop in Belfast, Northern Ireland.

ACT 1[23]
"Daisy Bell"
    J. Maher, Company
    (*Music and Lyrics by* Harry Dacre.)
"Daisy Bell" (reprise)
    J. Lithgow
"The Parlour Song" (Song of the Spokes)
    J. Sommer
"Cocktail Song" (Energy)
    J. Maher
"Cowboy Song" (Old Bob)
    J. Maher
"Daisy Bell" (reprise)
    J. Maher, Company
ACT 2
"Music Hall Song" (Salome Danced)
    J. Maher, J. Lithgow
"The Parlour Song" (reprise)
    J. Maher
"Army Song"
    J. Maher
"Spinning Song"
    J. Lithgow
    (*Lyrics by* Madelyne Bridges.)
"Army Song" (parody)
    J. Maher
"The Anthem (of the Common Wheel)"
    M. Tucci, J. Sommer
"Daisy Bell" (reprise)
    J. Maher, J. Horton

1979.08   ## ZOOT SUIT

An American Play (Drama with Music) in Two Acts, 2 Prologues and 20 Scenes. Written and directed by Luis Valdez. Choreographic sequences by Patricia Birch. Musical sequences and production by Daniel Valdez. Setting by Thomas A. Walsh from a concept by Roberto Morales, Thomas A. Walsh. Costumes by Peter J. Hall. Lighting by Dawn Chiang. Sound design by Abe Jacob. Production associate, Kenneth S. Brecher. Assistant director, Jack

Bender. Original (Music) arrangements by Dan Kuramoto, Daniel Valdez. Additional orchestrations by Dan Kuramoto. A Mark Taper Forum Production. Produced by The Shubert Organization, Center Theatre Group of Los Angeles and Gordon Davidson in association with Lou Adler. Opened 25 March 1979 at the Winter Garden and closed 29 April 1979 after 41 performances.

CAST (in order of appearance): *El Pachuco:* EDWARD JAMES OLMOS. *Henry Reyna:* DANIEL VALDEZ.
    His Family: Enrique Reyna: Abel Franco. *Dolores Reyna:* Lupe Ontiveros. *Lupe Reyna:* Roberta Delgado Esparza. *Rudy Reyna:* Tony Plana.
    His Friends: George Shearer: CHARLES AIDMAN. *Alice Bloomfield:* Karen Hensel.
    His Gang: Della Barrios: Rose Portillo. *Smiley Torres:* Geno Silva. *Joey Castro:* Mike Gomez. *Tommy Roberts:* Paul Mace. *Elena Torres:* Laura Leyva. *Bertha Villareal:* Angela Moya. *Cholo:* Luis Manuel.
    Los Angelinos: Swabbie: Dennis Stewart. *Manchuka:* Kim Miyori. *Zooter:* Lewis Whitlock. *Little Blue:* Darlene Bryan.
    The Downey Gang: Rafas: Miguel Delgado. *Ragman:* Lee Mathis. *Hobo:* Richard Jay-Alexander. *Guera:* Gela Jacobson. *Blondie:* Helena Andreyko. *Hoba:* Michele Mais.
    The Law: Lieutenant Edwards: Vincent Duke Milana. *Sergeant Smith:* Raymond Barry.
    The Press: Press: Arthur Hammer. *Cub Reporter:* Dennis Stewart. *Newsboy:* Lee Mathis.
    The Court: Judge Charles: Vincent Duke Milana. *Bailiff:* Raymond Barry.
    The Prison: Guard: Vincent Duke Milana.
    The Military: Sailors: Dennis Stewart, Lee Mathis, Raymond Barry. *Marine:* Richard Jay-Alexander.

The action takes place in the Los Angeles area between the fall of 1942 and the fall of 1944, inspired by the infamous Sleepy Lagoon Murder Trial and subsequent Pachuco riots.

Act 1, Scene 1: Zoot Suit (A Barrio Dance). *Scene 2:* The Mass Arrests. *Scene 3:* Pachuco Yo. *Scene 4:* The Interrogation. *Scene 5:* The Press. *Scene 6:* The People's Lawyer. *Scene 7:* The Saturday Night Dance. *Scene 8:* El Dia de la Raza. *Scene 9:* Opening of the Trial. *Scene 10:* Sleepy Lagoon. *Scene 11:* The Conclusion of the Trial.

Act 2, Scene 1: San Quentin. *Scene 2:* The Letters. *Scene 3:* The Incorrigible Pachuco. *Scene 4:* Major George. *Scene 5:* Solitary. *Scene 6:* Zoot Suit Riots. *Scene 7:* Alice. *Scene 8:* The Winning of the War. *Scene 9:* Return to the Barrio.

ACT 1
Scene 1
    "(Put on a) Zoot Suit" (Zoot Suit Theme)
        E. J. Olmos, Dancing Couples
        (*Music and Lyrics by* Daniel Valdez.)
Scene 4
    "Los Chucos Suaves"
        E. J. Olmos, Dancers
        (*Music and Lyrics by* Lalo Guerrero.)
Scene 7
    "Vamos a Bailar"
        E. J. Olmos, Dancing Couples
        (*Music and Lyrics by* Lalo Guerrero.)
ACT 2
Scene 6
    "Chicas Patas Boogie"
        Dancing Couples
        (*Original Lyrics by* Lalo Guerrero.)

1979.09   ## CARMELINA

A Musical in Two Acts, 12 Scenes. Book by Alan Jay Lerner and Joseph Stein. Based on the film "Buona Sera, Mrs. Campbell" (by Melvin Frank, Sheldon Keller, Dennis Norden.) Music by Burton Lane. Lyrics by Alan Jay Lerner. Directed by Jose Ferrer. Choreographed by Peter Gennaro. Sets designed by Oliver Smith. Costumes designed by Donald Brooks. Lighting by (Abe) Feder. Sound designed by John McClure. Orchestrations by Hershy Kay. Musical direction by Don Jennings. Vocal arrangements by Maurice Levine. Dance music arrangements by David Krane. A Whitehead-Stevens Production. Produced by Roger L. Stevens, J. W. Fisher, Joan Cullman and Jujamcyn Productions. Opened 8 April 1979 at the St. James Theatre and closed 21 April 1979 after 17 performances.

CAST (in order of appearance): *Bellini:* Marc Jordan. *Mayor Nunzio Manzoni:* Gonzalo Madurga. *Vittorio Bruno:* CESARE SIEPI. *Rosa:* GRACE KEAGY. *Salvatore:* Ian Towers. *Signora Carmelina Campbell:* GEORGIA BROWN. *Signora Bernardi:* Judy Sabo. *Roberto Bonafaccio:* Joseph d'Angerio. *Father Tommaso:* Frank Bouley. *Gia Campbell:* JOSSIE deGUZMAN. *Walter Braddock:* GORDON RAMSEY. *Steve Karzinski:* HOWARD ROSS. *Carlton Smith:* JOHN MICHAEL KING. *Flo Braddock:*

<hr>

[23]No song list appears in the program. Song titles prepared from the published play text.

VIRGINIA MARTIN. *Mildred Karzinski*: Kita Bouroff. *Katherine Smith*: Caryl Tenney. *Father Federico*: David E. Thomas.

Ensemble: Frank Bouley, Kita Bouroff, Kathryn Carter, Karen DiBianco, Spence Ford, Ramon Galindo, Liza Gennaro, Laura Klein, Michael Lane, Morgan Richardson, Judy Sabo, Charles Spoerri, Caryl Tenney, David E. Thomas, Ian Michael Towers, Kevin Wilson, Lee Winston. *Swing Dancers*: Debra Mathews, Michael Rivera.

The action takes place in 1961 somewhere in Italy.

Act 1, Scene 1: The Piazza of San Forino. *Scene 2*: A short time later in Carmelina's house. *Scene 3*: The wee hours of the following morning. The Piazza. *Scene 4*: Late morning, the following day. *Scene 5*: A short time later. Carmelina's house. *Scene 6*: later. The Piazza. *Scene 7*: Carmelina's house, late that night.

Act 2, Scene 1: Early the following morning. The Piazza. *Scene 2*: Immediately following. Carmelina's house. *Scene 3*: A Church. *Scene 4*: Immediately following. Carmelina's house. *Scene 5*: Immediately following. The Piazza.

ACT 1
Scene 1
  "It's Time for a Love Song"
    C. Siepi
  "Why Him?"
    G. Brown, C. Siepi
  "I Must Have Her"
    C. Siepi
Scene 2
  "Someone in April"
    G. Brown
  "Signora Campbell"
    G. Keagy, G. Brown, F. Bouley, G. Madurga, Townspeople
Scene 3
  "Love Before Breakfast"
    G. Brown, C. Siepi
Scene 4
  "Yankee Doodles Are Coming to Town"
    Townspeople
Scene 6
  "One More Walk Around the Garden"
    G. Ramsey, H. Ross, J. M. King
  "All That He'd Want Me to Be"
    J. deGuzman, Friends
Scene 7
  "It's Time for a Love Song" (reprise)
    C. Siepi
ACT 2
Scene 1
  "Carmelina"
    C. Siepi
  "The Image of Me"
    G. Ramsey, H. Ross, J. M. King
Scene 4
  "I'm a Woman"
    G. Brown
Scene 5
  "The Image of You"
    V. Martin, G. Ramsey
  "It's Time for a Love Song" (reprise)
    G. Brown

THE UTTER GLORY OF MORRISSEY HALL
1979.10

A Musical in Two Acts. Book by Clark Gesner and Nagle Jackson. Music and lyrics by Clark Gesner. Directed by Nagle Jackson. Musical numbers and dances staged by Buddy Schwab. Sets and lighting by Howard Bay. Costumes by David Graden. Musical director, John Lesko. Orchestrations by Jay Blackton, Russell Warner. Dance music arrangements by Allen Cohen. Sound by Charles Bellin. Associate producer, Sandy Stern. Produced by Arthur Whitelaw, Albert W. Selden, H. Ridgely Bullock in association with Marc Howard. Opened and closed 13 May 1979 at the Mark Hellinger Theatre after 1 performance.

CAST: *Administration*: Julia Faysle, Headmistress of Morrissey Hall: CELESTE HOLM. *Elizabeth Wilkins, Secretary*: MARILYN CASKEY. *Staff*: Foresta Studley: PATRICIA FALKENHAIN. *Teresa Winkle*: Laurie Franks. *Mrs. Delmonde*: TAINA ELG. *Miss Newton*: Karen Gibson. *Mr. Weyburn, Groundskeeper*: John Wardwell.

Sixth Form Students: Carswell: Mary Saunders. *Vickers*: Gina Franz. *Boody*: Adrienne Alexander. *Dale*: Jill P. Rose. *Dickerson*: Kate Kelly. *Haverfield*: Polly Pen. *Fifth Form Students*: Alice: Cynthia Parva. *Helen*: Becky McSpadden. *Frances*: Dawn Jeffory. *Angela*: Bonnie Hellman. *Marjorie*: Anne Kaye. *Mary*: Lauren Shub.
Visitors: Richard Tidewell: Willard Beckham. *Charles Hill*: John Gallogly. *Mr. Osgood*: Robert Lanchester.

The action takes place at the present time in the Morrissey Hall School for Girls in England.

ACT 1
  Overture: "At the Fair" from "Country Suite" by Desmond Gorss (1885-1958) arranged and conducted for the Morrissey Hall Concert Orchestra by Evelyn Potts, Director of Music.
  "Promenade"
    Company
  "Proud, Erstwhile, Upright, Fair"
    C. Holm, P. Falkenhain, M. Caskey
  "Elizabeth's Song"
    M. Caskey
  "Way Back When"
    C. Holm, P. Falkenhain
  "Lost"
    The Sixth Form
  "Morning"
    T. Elg, Dancing Class
  "The Letter"
    B. McSpadden, J. Gallogly, Company
  "Oh Sun"
    A. Kaye (St. George), B. Hellman (Dragon), B. McSpadden, D. Jeffory, L. Shub (Dryads), T. Elg
  "Give Me That Key"
    C. Holm, B. McSpadden, M. Caskey
  "Duet"
    M. Caskey, W. Beckham, Company
ACT 2
  "Interlude and Gallop"
    Orchestra, Students
  "You Will Know When the Time Has Arrived"
    L. Franks, M. Saunders, Fifth and Sixth Forms
  "You Would Say"
    B. McSpadden, J. Gallogly, Fifth Form
  "See the Blue"
    C. Holm, Flowers (Girls)
  "Dance of Resignation"
    T. Elg
  "Reflection"
    C. Holm
  "The War" ("Les Preludes" by Franz Liszt.)
    Company
  "Oh, Sun" (reprise), The Ending
    Company

UP IN ONE
1979.11

A Musical Revue in One Act. Conceived by Peter Allen and Craig Zadan. Songs and additional musical material written by Peter Allen with Adrienne Anderson, Jeff Barry, Marvin Hamlisch, Marsha Malamet, Dean Pitchford, Carole Bayer Sager. Additional material by Bruce Vilanch. Directed by Craig Zadan. Choreography by Betsy Haug. Scenery by Douglas W. Schmidt. Lighting by Marilyn Rennagel. Costumes by Charles Suppon. Projections by Douglas W. Schmidt, Wendall K. Harrington. Sound by Tom Morse. Production coordinator, Gregory Connell. Production supervisor, Janet Beroza. Musical direction and arrangements by Marc Shaiman. Special arrangements by Marvin Hamlisch. Assistant director, Neil Meron. A Dee Anthony Production. Executive producer, Vince Mauro. Produced by Ron Delsener. Opened 23 May 1979 at the Biltmore Theatre and closed 30 June 1979 after 46 performances.

CAST: PETER ALLEN, LENORA NEMETZ.

MUSICAL NUMBERS[24] (in alphabetical order)

---

[24]Overture arranged by Marvin Hamlisch. Background Vocals: Janis Cercone, Louis Cortelezzi, Corky Hale, Al Scotti.

"Dixie"
(*Music and Lyrics by* Peter Allen.)
"Don't Cry Out Loud"
(*Music and Lyrics by* Peter Allen and Carole Bayer Sager.)
"Don't Wish Too Hard"
(*Music and Lyrics by* Peter Allen and Carole Bayer Sager.)
"Everything Old Is New Again"
(*Music and Lyrics by* Peter Allen and Carole Bayer Sager.)
"Fly Away" (debut)
(*Music and Lyrics by* Peter Allen and Carole Bayer Sager.)
"Harlem on My Mind" (from *AS THOUSANDS CHEER*)
(*Music and Lyrics by* Irving Berlin.)
"I Could Have Been a Sailor"
(*Music and Lyrics by* Peter Allen.)
"I Could Really Show You Around" (debut)
(*Music and Lyrics by* Peter Allen and Dean Pitchford.)
"I'd Rather Leave While I'm Still in Love"
(*Music and Lyrics by* Peter Allen and Carole Bayer Sager.)
"If You Were Wondering"
(*Music and Lyrics by* Peter Allen.)
"I Go to Rio"
(*Music and Lyrics by* Peter Allen and Adrienne Anderson.)
"I Honestly Love You"
(*Music and Lyrics by* Peter Allen and Jeff Barry.)
"Impatient Heart" (debut)
(*Music and Lyrics by* Peter Allen and Marsha Malamet.)
"I Never Never Thought I'd Break" (debut)
(*Music and Lyrics by* Peter Allen and Dean Pitchford.)
"Just a Gigolo"
(*Music and Lyrics by* Leonello Casucci and Irving Caesar.)
"Love Crazy"
(*Music and Lyrics by* Peter Allen and Adrienne Anderson.)
"Make 'Em Pay" (debut)
(*Music and Lyrics by* Peter Allen and Dean Pitchford.)
"More Than I Like You"
(*Music and Lyrics by* Peter Allen and Carole Bayer Sager.)
"Only Wounded" (debut)
(*Music and Lyrics by* Peter Allen and Carole Bayer Sager.)
"Paris at 21"
(*Music and Lyrics by* Peter Allen.)
"Planes"
(*Music and Lyrics by* Peter Allen and Carole Bayer Sager.)
"Puttin' Out Roots Again"
(*Music and Lyrics by* Peter Allen.)
"6:30 Monday Morning"
(*Music and Lyrics by* Peter Allen.)
"Tenterfield Saddler"
(*Music and Lyrics by* Peter Allen.)
"Two Boys"
(*Music and Lyrics by* Marvin Hamlisch, Carole Bayer Sager, Peter Allen.)
"We've Come to an Understanding"
(*Music and Lyrics by* Peter Allen.)
"What Am I Doing Here?" (debut)
(*Music and Lyrics by* Peter Allen and Dean Pitchford.)
"You Oughta Hear Me Sing" (debut)
(*Music and Lyrics by* Peter Allen and Dean Pitchford.)

1979.12   I REMEMBER MAMA

A Musical in Two Acts, 12 Scenes. Book by Thomas Meehan. Based on the play of the same name by John Van Druten and the stories ("Mama's Bank Account") on which it was based by Kathryn Forbes. Music by Richard Rodgers. Lyrics by Martin Charnin. Additional lyrics by Raymond Jessel. Directed by Cy Feuer. Musical numbers staged by Danny Daniels. Scenery by David Mitchell. Costumes by Theoni V. Aldredge. Lighting by Roger Morgan. Sound by Otts Munderloh. Orchestrations by Philip J. Lang. Musical direction and vocal arrangements by Jay Blackton. Co-producer, Roy Somlyo. Production supervisor Jerry Adler. Produced by Alexander H. Cohen and Hildy Parks. Opened 31 May 1979 at the Majestic Theatre and closed 2 September 1979 after 108 performances.

CAST (in order of appearance): *Katrine*: MAUREEN SILLIMAN. *Christine*: CARRIE HORNER. *Dagmar*: TARA KENNEDY. *Johanne*: KRISTEN VIGARD. *Nils*: IAN ZIERING. *Papa*: GEORGE HEARN. *Mama*: LIV ULLMANN. *Mr. McGuire*: RICHARD ENSSLEN. *Aunt Trina*: ELIZABETH HUBBARD. *Aunt Jenny*: DOLORES WILSON. *Aunt Sigrid*: BETTY ANN GROVE. *Mr. Thorkelson*: ARMIN SHIMERMAN. *Uncle Chris*: GEORGE S. IRVING. *Lucie*: Janet McCall. *Nurse*: Sigrid Heath. *Doctor Anderson*: Stan Page. *Dame Sybil Fitzgibbons*: MYVANWY JEAN.
Steiner Street Neighbors: Austin Colyer, John Dorrin, Mickey Gunnersen, Daniel Harnett, Danny Joel, Jan Kasni, Kevin Marcum, Richard Maxon, Marisa Morell, Frank Pietri, Elissa Wolfe.

Act 1, Scene 1: The kitchen and dining room of the Hansen house on Steiner Street in San Francisco, Spring 1910. *Scene 2*: The Hansen parlor, 21 June 1910, evening. *Scene 3*: The Hansen kitchen, mid-November 1910, early afternoon. *Scene 4*: The hospital, later that day. *Scene 5*: The Hansen kitchen, ten days later, early afternoon. *Scene 6*: Teh Hansen kitchen, early December 1910, a Friday evening.

Act 2, Scene 1: The Hansen back porch, Spring, 1911, evening. *Scene 2*: The Hansen kitchen, later that night and the following morning. *Scene 3*: The Lobby of the Fairmount Hotel, a few hours later. *Scene 4*: Uncle Chris' ranch, mid-May 1911, later afternoon. *Scene 5*: The Hansen kitchen, three days later, evening. *Scene 6*: The Hansen parlor, June 1911.

ACT 1
Scene 1
  "I Remember Mama"
    M. Silliman
  "A Little Bit More"[25]
    L. Ullman, G. Hearn, Children
  "A Writer Writes at Night"
    M. Silliman, L. Ullman
Scene 2
  "Ev'ry Day (Comes Something Beautiful)"
    L. Ullman, Company
  "The Hardangerfjord" (dance)
    Company
  "You Could Not Please Me More"
    G. Hearn, L. Ullman
    (*Choreographed by* Graciela Daniele.)
Scene 3
  "Uncle Chris"[26]
    E. Hubbard, D. Wilson, B. A. Grove
Scene 5
  "Easy Come, Easy Go"[27]
    G. S. Irving, Friends
Scene 6
  "It Is Not the End of the World"
    The Family
ACT 2
Scene 1
  "Mama Always Makes It Better"
    The Children
  "Lars, Lars"[28]
    L. Ullman
Scene 3
  "Fair Trade"
    M. Jean, L. Ullman, Friends
Scene 4
  "It's Going To Be Good To Be Gone"
    G. S. Irving
Scene 5
  "Time"
    L. Ullman
Scene 6
  "I Remember Mama" (reprise)[29]
    M. Silliman

---

[25]Lyrics by Raymond Jessel
[26]Lyrics by Raymond Jessel
[27]Lyrics by Raymond Jessel
[28]Lyrics by Raymond Jessel
[29]Lyrics by Raymond Jessel

1979–1980 SEASON

Jim Dale in BARNUM
Martha Swope/TimePix

1979–1980 SEASON

1979.13 ## A NEW YORK SUMMER

A Musical Revue in One Act, 19 Scenes. Produced and directed by Robert
F. Jani. Creative director, Tom Bahler. Production executive, John Jay
Moore. Executive musical director, Don Pippin. Art director, John William
Keck. Costumes by Frank Spencer; Special costume designs for the
Rockettes by Bob Mackie. Lighting by Billy B. Walker. Dialogue and narra-
tion by Stan Hart. Choreography and staging by Dru Davis, Violet Holmes,
Louis Johnson, Linda Lemac, Howard Parker. Production coordinators,
Charles Gillette, Anthony Salerno. Orchestrations by Elman Anderson,
Billy Byers, Jack Eskew, Mitch Farber, Allen Faust, Michael Gibson,
Quincy Jones, Jay Kennedy, Phil Lang, John Mandel, Peter Matz, Glen
Osser, Larry Wilcox, Ray Wright. Produced by the Radio City Music Hall
Entertainment Center. Opened 1 June 1979 at the Radio City Music Hall
and closed 26 September 1979 after 203 performances.

CAST: KAREN ANDERS, TIM CASSIDY, ANTHONY FALCO, JOHN HALLOW,
JOHN J. MARTIN, CHRISTINA SAFFRAN.

    THE ROCKETTES: Pauline Achillas, Carol Beatty, Catherine Beatty, Dottie Belle,
Susan Boron, Katie Braff, Deniene Bruck, Barbara Ann Cittadino, Eileen Collins,
Susanne Doris, Joyce Dwyer, Jody Erickson, Jacqueline Fancy, Deniene Fenn, Phyllis
Frew, Prudence Gray, Carol Harbich, Ginny Hounsell, Cynthia Hughes, Holly Jones,
Pam Kelleher, Dee Dee Knapp, Judy Little, Leslie Gryszko-McCarthy, Geraldine
McDonough, Barbara Moore, Ann Murphy, Joan Peer, Cindy Peiffer, Sheila Phillips,
Lorraine Salerno, Jereme Sheehan, Terry Spano, Pam Stacey, Juen Taylor, Susan
Theobald, Carol Toman, Rose Ann Woolsey, Phyllis Wujko.

    THE APPLES: Steve (Ace) Williams, Stanley Dalton, Rodney Green, Carl Hardy,
Mercie J. Hinton, Jr., Ivson (Scooter) Polk.

    THE NEW YORKERS: Steve Baumann, Nancy Byne, Lou Ann Csaszar, Scott
Dainton, Marcia-Anne Dobres, Christine Doelger, Cecily Douglas, Jeffrey Dreisbach,
Barry Eric, Sharon Ferrol, Neal Gold, Lisa Grant, Bill Hedge, Deidre Kane, Dirk
Lombard, Michelle Marshall, Tony Moore, Alan Nicholson, Andy Parker, Lorraine
Person, Teresa Puente, Joel Rosina, Tina Sherman, Robin Stone, Chris Wheeler,
Curtis Worthy.

    PRODUCTION DANCERS: Phillip Bond, John Cashman, Jerry James, Mic
Kozyra, Tony Lillo, James Parker, Malcolm Perry, Ken Prescott, Robert Raimondo,
David Roman, Randy Skinner, J. Thomas Smith. THE ICE-SKATERS: Robert
Metcalf, Darlene Gilbert.

MUSICAL NUMBERS

Scene 1

"New York, New York" (from ON THE TOWN)
    The New Yorkers, Entire Company
    (Music by Leonard Bernstein. Lyrics by Betty Comden and Adolph Green.)
"Another Hundred People" (from COMPANY)
    (Music and Lyrics by Stephen Sondheim.)

Scene 2

A Street Scene in Manhattan
    The Cabbie: J. Hallow. Louise: K. Anders. Charlie: J. J. Martin. Beth: C. Saffran.
    The Policeman: A. Falco. Larry: T. Cassidy.

Scene 3

A Visit to the United Nations featuring the Cherry Blossom Doncho
Curtain

The largest silk stage curtain ever woven in Japan was a gift of the people
of Tokyo to the people of New York City under their Sister-City
Affiliation. It was presented on 4 May 1964 as a symbol of friendship. A
masterpiece of the Nishijin weavers of Kyoto, it was made possible by the
generosity of the people of Tokyo and scores of Japanese firms and organ-
izations. The Music Hall is the official custodian of this gift to the City of
New York.

Scene 4

Central Park in Summertime: A Fantasy at the Turn of the Century
"Put on Your Sunday Clothes" (from HELLO, DOLLY!)
    (Music and Lyrics by Jerry Herman.)

Scene 5

Central Park in Wintertime: A Fantasy on Ice
"Sleigh Ride"
    (Music by Leroy Anderson. Lyrics by Mitchell Parish.)

Scene 6

The Folk Art of New York

Scene 7

The Streets of Harlem: The Apples
Dance Music from WEST SIDE STORY (Music by Leonard Bernstein.)

Scene 8

Coney Island: "I Thank Heaven"
    (Music by Tom Bahler. Lyrics by Quincy Jones and Mark Vieha.)

Scene 9

"New York at Night"
    (Music and Lyrics by Tom Bahler and Mark Vieha.)

Scene 10

Broadway — 1979: New York is Dancing:
"I'm Just Wild About Harry" (from EUBIE!)
"Not While I'm Around" (from SWEENEY TODD)
"Yes, Sir, That's My Baby" (from WHOOPEE)
"The Joint Is Jumpin'" (from AIN'T MISBEHAVIN')
"We Go Together" (from, GREASE)
"Sing Sing Sing" (from DANCIN')
"One" (from A CHORUS LINE)
"They're Playing Our Song" (from THEY'RE PLAYING OUR SONG)

Scene 11

Our Salute to Mr. Broadway: George M. Cohan
    L. Grant
"I'm a Yankee Doodle Dandy," "Give My Regards to Broadway," You're a
Grand Old Flag."

Scene 12

Disco! (pre-recorded)
"Countdown" (performed by Dan Hartman from "Instant Reply" album.)
"Singin' in the Rain" (performed by Sheila and B. Devotions)
"Over the Rainbow" (performed by Meco)
"Mac Arthur Park" (performed by Donna Summer from "Live and
More" album)
"La Bamba" (performed by Antonio Rodriguez)
"Brand New Day" (from THE WIZ film)

Scene 13

A Street Scene at Night: "New York Lullaby"
    (Music and Lyrics by Tom Bahler and Mark Vieha.)
    Bag Lady: K. Anders.

Scene 14

Shopping on the Avenue: "Avenue, Fifth Avenue"
    (Music and Lyrics by Tom Bahler and Mark Vieha.)

Scene 15

On Our Way through Rockefeller Center: "A New York Summer"
    (Music and Lyrics by Tom Bahler and Mark Vieha.)

Scene 16

Radio City Music Hall Movie Memories

Scene 17

The Music and Glamour of the Nation's Showplace

Scene 18

50 Years of America's Rockettes:
"Top Hat, White Tie and Tails" (from TOP HAT film)
    (Music and Lyrics by Irving Berlin.)
"Applause" (from APPLAUSE)
    (Music by Charles Strouse. Lyrics by Lee Adams.)

Scene 19

Where in the World But in America: A Finale Tribute to "Lady
America" on the beginning of our second half century as New York's
Entertainment Center
    (New Lyrics set to the Music of "America" by Leonard Bernstein from WEST
    SIDE STORY)Entire Company

BRUCE FORSYTHE
1979.14 ## ON BROADWAY

A One-Man Show in Two Acts. Musical director, Don Hunt. Production
supervisor, Peter Mavoides. Lighting by Richard Nelson. Drummer, Freddie
Adamson. Produced by Lee Guber and Shelly Gross. A Music Fair Concerts
Presentation. Opened 12 June 1979 at the Winter Garden and closed 16
June 1979 after 5 performances.

CAST: BRUCE FORSYTHE.

ACT 1
"Just in Time" (from *BELLS ARE RINGING*)
    (*Music by* Jule Styne. *Lyrics by* Betty Comden and Adolph Green.)
Opening Monologue
"It's Never Too Late"
    (*Music and Lyrics by* Carmen Lombardo and John Jacob Loeb.)
Piano Solo: "Claire de Lune by Debussy"
"Star Dust"
    (*Music by* Hoagy Carmichael. *Lyrics by* Mitchell Parish.)
"Nola"
    (*Music by* Felix Arndt. *Lyrics by* Sammy Skylar.)
"Singin' in the Rain" (from *HOLLYWOOD REVUE OF 1929, SING-IN' THE RAIN* films.)
    (*Music by* Nacio Herb Brown. *Lyrics by* Arthur Freed.)
"Give Me That Old Soft Shoe" (from *THREE TO MAKE READY*)
    (*Music by* Morgan Lewis. *Lyrics by* Nancy Hamilton.)
The Generation Game Sequence (television):
    "The Laughing Policeman"
    (*Music and Lyrics by* Billie Grey.)
    Dance Competition
ACT 2
"My Shining Hour" (from *THE SKY'S THE LIMIT* film)
    (*Music by* Harold Arlen. *Lyrics by* Johnny Mercer.)
Noël Coward Impression
The Most Beautiful Girl in the World (sketch)
La Vie en Rose sketch
Valencia sketch
"It's the Ending of My Day"
Savoir Faire Sketch ("Un Homme et Une Femme")
Impressions: Tom Jones, Frank Sinatra, Sammy Davis, Jr., Anthony Newley

1979.15   GOTTU GO DISCO

An Entertainment in Two Acts, a Prologue and 14 Scenes. Book by John Zodrow. Music and lyrics by Kenny Lehman, John Davis, Ray Chew, Nat Adderley, Jr., Thomas Jones, Wayne Morrison, Steve Boston, Eugene Narmore, Betty Rowland, Jerry Powell. Directed by Larry Forde. Choeographed by Jo Jo Smith, Troy Garza. Scenery design by James Hamilton. Lighting by S. A. Cohen. Artistic direction and costumes by Joe Eula. Musical supervision and direction by Kenny Lehman. Vocal direction by Kenny Lehman, Mitch Kerper. Film sequences by Robert Rabinowitz. Sound design by Lenny Will. Associate artistic director, Ron Ferri. Assistant director, Donnis Honeycutt, Jr. Special effects by Chris Langhart. Produced by Jerry Brandt in association with Roy Rifkind, Julie Rifkind, Bill Spitalsky, WKTU—Radio 92. Opened 25 June 1979 at the Minskoff Theater and closed 30 June 1979 after 8 performances.

CAST (in order of appearance): *Narrator, (Vitus)*: JOE MASIELL. *Cassette*: IRENE CARA. *Billy*: PATRICK JUDE. *Minnie*: Lisa Raggio. *Contact*: Laurie Dawn Skinner. *Antwerp*: PATTI KARR. *Lila*: Jane Holzer. *Cubby*: Charlie Serrano. *Snap-Fish*: RHETTA HUGHES. *Pete*: JUSTIN ROSS. *Marc*: Marc Benecke. *Spinner*: Bob Pettie.
    Singing Ensemble: Robin Lynn Beck, Gloria Covington, Gerri Griffin, Jack Magradey, Billy Newton-Davis. *Dancing Ensemble*: Connie Marie Brazelton, Prudence Darby, Ronald Dunham, Miguel Gonz, Christine Jacobson, Peter Kapetan, Patrick Kinser-Lau, Julia Lema, Bronna Lipton, Mark Manley, Jodi Moccia, Jamie Patterson, Dee Ranzweiler, Adrian Rosario, Willie Rosario, Sue Samuels. *Swing*: Tony Constantine.

Act 1, Scene 1: The Disco Rag Store. *Scene 2*: Streets of New York; A Bridge in Central Park. *Scene 3*: Antwerp's Apartment. *Scene 4*: Roof Top of Antwerp's Apartment. *Scene 5*: Vitus' Office. *Scene 6*: Various Parts of the Disco Rag Store. *Scene 7*: Sidewalk Outside the Dream Castle Disco. *Scene 8*: The Dream Castle Disco.

Act 2, Scene 1: Vitus' Office; The City. *Scene 2*: Antwerp's Apartment, Roof Top and a Park. *Scene 3*: Various Parts of the Disco Rag Store. *Scene 4*: The King and Queen's Dressing Room. *Scene 5*: A Bridge in Central Park. *Scene 6*: The Dream Castle Disco.

ACT 1
Prologue
"Puttin' It On"
    R. L. Beck, Ensemble
    (*Music and Lyrics by* Kenny Lehman and Steve Boston, orchestrated by Kenny Lehman.)
Scene 1
"Disco Shuffle"
    P. Jude, I. Cara

    (*Music and Lyrics by* Ray Chew with assistance by Nat Adderly, Jr.; orchestrated by Ray Chew with vocal arrangements by Nat Adderly, Jr.)
Scene 4
"All I Need"
    I. Cara
    (*Music and Lyrics by* Thomas Jones and Wayne Morrison, orchestrated by Kenny Lehman.)
Scene 5
"It Won't Work"
    J. Masiell
    (*Music, Lyrics and Orchestration by* John Davis.)
Scene 6
"Trust Me"
    C. Serrano, L. D. Skinner
    (*Music and Lyrics by* Kenny Lehman and Steve Boston, orchestrated by Kenny Lehman.)
Scene 7
"In and Out"
    M. Beneche, Entire Company
    (*Music and Lyrics by* Kenny Lehman and Steve Boston, orchestrated by Kenny Lehman.)
Scene 8
"Got Tu Go Disco"
    B. Newton-Davis, Ensemble
    (*Music, Lyrics and Orchestration by* John Davis)
"Pleasure Pusher"
    J. Ross
    (*Music and Lyrics by* Eugene Narmore, orchestrated by Brad Baker.)
"If That Didn't Do It, It Can't Be Done"
    Entire Company
    (*Music and Lyrics by* Ray Chew with assistance by Nat Adderly, Jr.; orchestrated by Ray Chew with vocal arrangements by Nat Adderly, Jr.)
ACT 2
"Inter-mish-un"
    B. Newton-Davis
    (*Music and Lyrics by* Kenny Lehman, Thomas Jones and Wayne Morrison.)
Scene 1
"Hanging Over and Out"
    J. Masiell
    (*Music and Lyrics by* Kenny Lehman and Steve Boston, orchestrated by Kenny Lehman.)
Scene 3
"Chic to Cheap"
    R. Hughes
    (*Music and Lyrics by* Jerry Powell, orchestrated by Brad Baker.)
"Bad, Glad, Good and Had"
    I. Cara
    (*Music, Lyrics and Orchestration by* John Davis)
Scene 5
"Cassie"
    P. Jude
    (*Music and Lyrics by* Ray Chew with assistance by Nat Adderly, Jr.; orchestrated by Ray Chew with vocal arrangements by Nat Adderly, Jr.)
Scene 6
"Takin' the Light"
    I. Cara, P. Jude, G. Griffin, Ensemble
    (*Music and Lyrics by* Kenny Lehman, Thomas Jones and Wayne Morrison, orchestrated by Kenny Lehman.)
"Gettin' to the Top"
    P. Karr
    (*Music, Lyrics and Orchestration by* John Davis)

BROADWAY OPRY '79:
1979.16   A Little Country in the Big City

A Country Music Revue in Two Acts. Creative director, Jonas McCord. Talent coordination, Niles Siegel. Scenery and lighting by Michael J. Hotopp and Paul dePass. Sound by Sound Associates. Associate producers, Spyros Venduras, Joseph D'Alesandro. Produced by Family Affair Enterprises, Inc (David S. Fitzpatrick, Edward J. Lynch, Jr., Executive producers.) Opened 27 July 1979 at the St. James Theatre and closed 2 August 1979 after 6 performances[1].

---

[1]No musical numbers listed in programs.

CAST: TANYA TUCKER, FLOYD CRAMER, DON GIBSON, MICKEY NEW-BURY, WAYLON JENNINGS, THE CRICKETS, THE WAYLORS.

EVERY GOOD BOY DESERVES FAVOUR
1979.17

A Play for Actors and Orchestra in One Act. Play by Tom Stoppard. Music by Andre Previn. From an original concept by Trevor Nunn. Directed by Tom Stoppard. Sets and Costumes by Eldon Elder. Lighting by Thomas Skelton. Orchestra conducted by David Gilbert. Sound by Dennis Roe. Produced by The Kennedy Center (Roger L. Stevens) and the Metropolitan Opera. Opened 30 July 1979 at the Metropolitan Opera House and closed 4 August 1979 after 8 performances.

CAST: *Ivanov:* RENÉ AUBERJONOIS. *Alexander:* ELI WALLACH. *Teacher:* CAROL TEITEL. *Sacha:* BOBBY SCOTT. *Doctor:* REMAK RAMSAY. *Colonel Rozinsky:* CARL LOW.

BUT NEVER JAM TODAY
1979.18

A Musical in Two Acts, 16 Scenes[2]. Book by Vinnette Carroll and Bob Larimer. Adapted from the works of Lewis Carroll. Music by Bert Keyes and Bob Larimer. Lyrics by Bob Larimer. Entire production devised and directed by Vinnette Carroll. Choreography by Talley Beatty. Music direction and incidental music by Donald Johnston. Scenery and costumes by William Schroder. Lighting by Ken Billington. Choral arrangements and vocal preparation by Cleavant Derricks. Production supervisor, Robert L. Borod. Sound design by T. Richard Fitzgerald. Orchestrations by Bert Keyes. Special orchestration by H. B. Barnum, Larry Blank. Dance music by H. B. Barnum. Associate producers, Herb Hugel, Gene Messinger. Produced by Arch Nadler, Anita MacShane and the Urban Arts Theatre. Opened 31 July 1979 at the Longacre Theatre and closed 5 August 1979 after 7 performances.

CAST (in order of appearance): *Alice:* MARILYNN WINBUSH. *Caterpillar:* CLEAVANT DERRICKS. *Persona Non Grata:* LYNNE THIGPEN. *Mushrooms:* Brenda Braxton, Clayton Strange, Sharon K. Brooks, Gary Q. Lewis, Celestine DeSaussure, Jeffrey Anderson-Gunter. *The Black Queen:* LYNNE CLIFTON-ALLEN. *The White Rabbit:* JEFFREY ANDERSON-GUNTER. *The Duchess:* REGINALD VEL JOHNSON. *The Cheshire Cat:* JEFFREY ANDERSON-GUNTER. *Cooks:* Cleavant . Derricks, Sheila Ellis, Celestine DeSaussure. *The Mad Hatter:* JAI OSCAR ST. JOHN. *The March Hare:* SHEILA ELLIS. *The Dormouse:* Celestine DeSaussure. *The White Queen:* Charlene Harris. *Humpty-Dumpty:* REGINALD VEL JOHNSON. *Tweedledum:* JAI OSCAR ST. JOHN. *Tweedledee:* CLEAVANT DERRICKS. *The Two of Spades:* JAI OSCAR ST. JOHN. *The Five of Spades:* SHEILA ELLIS. *The Seven of Spades:* CLEAVANT DERRICKS. *The Queen of Hearts:* CHARLENE HARRIS. *The King of Hearts:* REGINALD VEL JOHNSON. *Guards:* Clayton Strange, Garry Q. Lewis. *The Mock Turtle:* JEFFREY ANDERSON-GUNTER.

Act 1, Scene 1: Down the Rabbit Hole. *Scene 2:* Interview with a Caterpillar (Square 1). *Scene 3:* The Black Queen (Square 2). *Scene 4:* The Kitchen of the Duchess (Square 3). *Scene 5:* The Cheshire Cat. *Scene 6:* A Mad Party (Square 4). *Scene 7:* The White Queen (Square 5). *Scene 8:* Humpty Dumpty. *Scene 9:* Tweedledum and Tweedledee (Square 6).

Act 2, Scene 1: The Queen of Hearts' Croquet Ground. *Scene 2:* The Queen's Dungeon. *Scene 3:* The Mock Turtle (Square 7). *Scene 4:* The Queen's Dungeon. *Scene 5:* An Examination (Square 8). *Scene 6:* Alice's Reward. *Scene 7:* The Daydream Ends.

ACT 1

"Curiouser and Curiouser"
    M. Winbush
"Twinkle Twinkle Little Star"
    C. Derricks, L. Thigpen, Company
"Long Live the Queen"
    L. Clifton-Allen, M. Winbush
"A Real Life Lullaby"
    R. V. Johnson, C. Derricks, S. Ellis, C. DeSaussure
"The More I See People"
    J. Anderson-Gunter
"My Little Room"
    M. Winbush
"But Never Jam Today"
    C. Harris, M. Winbush

---

[2]Originally produced Off-Off Broadway 23 August 1978 at the Urban Arts Corp for 12 performances. An earlier version developed by Vinnette Carroll but written by different authors was produced at New York City Center 23 April 1969 for 1 performance as part of the Black Expo Festival.

"Riding for a Fall"
    L. Thigpen, R. V. Johnson, M. Winbush
"All the Same to Me"
    J. Oscar St. John, C. Derricks
"I've Got My Orders"
    M. Winbush
ACT 2
"God Could Give Me Anything"
    J. O. St. John, S. Ellis, C. Derricks
"But Never Jam Today" (reprise)
    Company, L. Thigpen
"I Like to Win"
    M. Winbush
"And They All Call the Hatter Mad"
    L. Thigpen
"Jumping from Rock to Rock"
    J. Anderson-Gunter, M. Winbush, Company
"They"
    J. O. St. John, S. Ellis, C. Derricks
"Long Live the Queen" (reprise)
    The Company
""I've Got My Orders" (reprise)
    M. Winbush, Company

GILDA RADNER— LIVE FROM NEW YORK
1979.19

An Entertainment (Revue) in Two Acts, 14 Scenes. Written by Anne Beatts, Lorne Michaels, Marilyn Suzanne Miller, Don Novello, Michael O'Donoghue, Gilda Radner, Paul Shaffer, Rosie Shuster, Alan Zweibel. Producer and director, Lorne Michaels. Choreography by Patricia Birch. Musical consultation, Paul Shaffer. Music director, Howard Shore. Production design by Eugene Lee, Akira Yoshimura. Costume design by Franne Lee, Karen Roston. Lighting design by Roger Morgan. Sound design by Abe Jacob. Associate producer, Barbara Burns. Presented by Ron Delsener. Opened 2 August 1979 at the Winter Garden and closed 22 September 1979 after 51 performances.

CAST: GILDA RADNER, BOB CHRISTIANSON, FATHER GUIDO SARDUCCI (Don Novello), PAUL SHAFFER, NILS NICHOLS.
    Rouge: Diana Grasselli, Myriam Valle, Maria Vidal. *The Candy Slice Group:* John Caruso, Paul Shaffer, Howard Shore, G. E. Smith.

MUSICAL NUMBERS AND SKETCHES
Scene 1
    "Let's Talk Dirty to the Animals"
        G. Radner
        (*Music and Lyrics by* Michael O'Donoghue.)
Scene 2
    The Audition: I Love to Be Unhappy
        G. Radner
        (*Music and Lyrics by* Gilda Radner and Paul Shaffer.)
Scene 3
    Father Guido Sarducci: Slide Show
        D. Novello
Scene 4
    The Judy Miller Show (Little Brownie Girl sketch)
Scene 5
    Don Kirschner
    Rhonda Weiss introduction
        (*by* Anne Beatts and Rosie Shuster.)
Scene 6
    Rhonda Weiss and the Rhondettes: "Goodbye Saccharine"
        G. Radner
        (*Music and Lyrics by* Hardwick, Marilyn Suzanne Miller and Paul Shaffer.)
Scene 7
    Father Guido Sarducci: Five Minute University
        D. Novello
Scene 8
    "If You Look Close"/"Gimme Mick"
        G. Radner, Candy Slice Group
        (*Music and Lyrics by* Gilda Radner and Paul Shaffer.)

Scene 9

Lisa Loopner Piano Recital: "The Way We Were" (from film)
G. Radner
(*Sketch by* Anne Beatts and Rosie Shuster. *Music by* Marvin Hamlisch. *Lyrics by* Marilyn and Alan Bergman.)

Scene 10

Father Guido Sarducci: Pay for Your Sins
D. Novello

Scene 11

Emily Litella: Tiny Kingdom (*by* Rosie Shuster)
G. Radner

Scene 12

Nadia Kominich
G. Radner

Scene 13

Roseanne Roseannadanna (*by* Alan Zweibel)
G. Radner

Scene 14

"Honey" (Touch Me with My Clothes On)
G. Radner
(*Music and Lyrics by* Gilda Radner and Paul Shaffer.)

1979.20 ## NAUGHTY MARIETTA

A Revival of the Musical Comedy in Two Acts, 4 Scenes[3]. Music by Victor Herbert. New book and additional lyrics by Frederick S. Roffman (based on the original by Rida Johnson Young) adapted by Jack Eddleman. Directed by Jack Eddleman. Musical numbers staged by Graciela Daniele. Costumes designed by Patricia Zipprodt. Sets designed by Oliver Smith. Lighting designed by Ken Billington. Musical director and conductor, John Mauceri. Chorus master, Lloyd Walser. Production conceived by Frederick S. Roffman. Produced by the New York City Opera. Opened 30 August 1979 at the New York State Theatre and closed 2 September 1979 after 6 performances.

CAST: *Marietta d'Altena*: ELIZABETH HYNES. *Captain Richard Warrington* of Kentucky: HOWARD HENSEL. *Etienne Grandet*: ALAN TITUS. *Adah Le Clercq, his Quadroon Mistress*: SUSANNE MARSEE. *Private Silas Slick of the Rangers*: LARA TEETER. *Lizette*: Dana Krueger. *Acting Governor Grandet, Etienne's Father*: JAMES BILLINGS. *Florenze, His Secretary*: DAVID GATELY. *Sergeant Harry Blake of the Rangers*: DON YULE. *Rudolfo*: HARLAN FOSS. *Pirates*: Taras Kalba, Michael Rubino. *Town crier*: Edward Zimmerman. *Flower Girls*: Susan Delery-Whedon, Sally Lambert. *Nanette*: Cindy Lynn Aaronson. *Felice*: Sally Lambert. *Fanchon*: Leslie Luxemburg. *Knife Grinder*: Barry Carl. *Flower Vendor*: George Bohachevsky. *Bird Vendor*: Louis Perry. *Fruit Vendor*: Robert Brubaker. *Sugar Cane Vendor*: Harris Davis. *Indian*: Don Carlo. *Pierrot*: José Bourbon. *Graziella*: Toni-Ann Gardella. *Major-Domo*: Glenn Rowen. *Spanish Dancer*: Esperanza Galan. *San Domingo Ladies*: Toni-Ann Gardella, Candace Itow, Rebeka Pradera. *Quadroon Waiters*: Taras Kalba, Michael Rubino, Rafael Romero, José Bourbon. *Man at auction*: Mervin Crook. *Turk*: Barry Carl *Ensemble*: New York City Opera Chorus.

1979.21 ## THE MERRY WIDOW

A Revival of the Operetta in Three Acts, 4 Scenes[4]. Original Viennese libretto ('Die lustige witwe') and lyrics by Victor Léon and Leo Stein (after "L'Attaché d'Ambassade" by Henri Meilhac.) Music by Franz Lehár. New English translation and dialogue by Ursula Eggers and Joseph de Rugeris. New lyrics by Sheldon Harnick. This San Diego Opera production directed by Tito Capobianco. Stage director, Antoni Jaworski. Choreographer, Jessica Redel. Production (settings, costumes) design by Carl Toms. Lighting design by Ken Billington. Conductor, Imre Pallo. Produced by the New York City Opera. Opened 5 September 1979 at the New York State Theatre and closed 9 September 1978 after 7 performances.

CAST: *Baron Mirko Zeta*: DAVID RAE SMITH. *Valencienne*: Marianna Christos. *Count Danilo*: ALAN TITUS. *Anna Glawari*: DIANA SOVIERO. *Camille de Rosillon*: BRUCE REED. *Vicomte Cascada*: HARLAN FOSS. *Raoul St. Brioche*: ALAN KAYS. *Bogdanovitch*: Herbert Hunsberger. *Sylviane*: Jane Shaulis. *Kromov*: William

Ledbetter. *Olga*: Penny Orloff. *Pritchitch*: Louis Perry. *Praskovia*: Susan Delery-Whedon. *Njegus*: JAMES BILLINGS. *Lolo*: Candace Itow. *Dodo*: Jane Shaulis. *Jou-Jou*: Penny Orloff. *Frou-Frou*: Toni-Ann Gardella. *Clo-Clo*: Susan Delery-Whedon. *Margot*: Raven Wilkinson. *Ensemble*: New York City Opera Chorus.

1979.22 ## PETER PAN,
or The Boy Who Wouldn't Grow Up

A Revival of the Musical in Three Acts, 9 Scenes[5]. Book by James M. Barrie, (adaptation uncredited). Music by Mark [Moose] Charlap. Lyrics by Carolyn Leigh. Additional music by Jule Styne. Additional lyrics by Betty Comden and Adolph Green. Original production conceived, directed and choreographed by Jerome Robbins. Entire production directed and choreographed by Rob Iscove. Production (scenery) by Peter Wolf. Costumes designed by Bill Hargate. Lighting designed by Thomas Skelton. Musical and vocal direction by Jack Lee. Sound designed by T. Richard Fitzgerald. Special laser effects by Laser Media. Flying by Foy. Produced by Zev Bufman and James M. Nederlander in association with Jack Molthen, Spencer Tandy and J. Ronald Horowitz. Opened 6 September 1979 at the Lunt-Fontanne Theatre and closed 4 January 1981 after 578 performances.

CAST (in order of appearance): *Michael*: Jonathan Ward. *Nana*: James Cook. *Liza*: Maggy Gorrill. *Wendy*: MARSHA KRAMER. *John*: Alexander Winter. *Mrs. Darling*: BETH FOWLER. *Mr. Darling*: GEORGE ROSE. *Peter Pan*: SANDY DUNCAN. *Lion*: Jim Wolfe. *Turtle*: Cleve Asbury. *Kangaroo*: Reed Jones. *Ostrich*: Maggy Gorrill. *Slightly*: Chris Farr. *Curly*: Michael Estes. *First Twin*: Rusty Jacobs. *Second Twin*: Joey Abbott. *Tootles*: Carl Tramon. *Captain Hook*: GEORGE ROSE. *Nibs*: Dennis Courtney. *Captain Hook*: GEORGE ROSE. *Noodler*: Guy Stroman. *Smee*: ARNOLD SOBOLOFF. *Crocodile*: Kevin McCready. *Tiger Lily*: MARIA POGEE. *Starkey*: Jon Vandertholen. *Cecco*: Trey Wilson. *Mullins*: Steven Yuhasz. *Jukes*: Gary Daniel. *Wendy, Grown-up*: Neva Rae Powers. *Jane*: MARSHA KRAMER. *Tinker Bell*: Laser Media, Inc.
Pirates: William Carmichael, James Cook, Gary Daniel, Dianna Hughes, Guy Stroman, Jon Vandertholen, Trey Wilson, Steven Yuhasz. *Indians*: Cleve Asbury, Maggy Gorrill, Sharon-Ann Hill, Reed Jones, C. J. McCaffrey, Kevin McCready, David Storey, Jim Wolfe. *Trees*: C. J. McCaffrey, Kevin McCready, David Storey.

Act 1, Scene 1: Nursery of the Darling Home.

Act 2, Scene 1: Neverland. *Scene 2*: Path to Lagoon. *Scene 3*: Neverland Forest. *Scene 4*: Home Underground.

Act 3, Scene 1: *The Jolly Roger*. *Scene 2*: Neverland. *Scene 3*: Nursery of the Darling Home. *Scene 4*: The Nursery many years later.

ACT 1

Scene 1

"Tender Shepherd"
B. Fowler, M. Kramer, A. Winter, J. Ward
(*Music by* Mark Charlap. *Lyrics by* Carolyn Leigh.)

"I've Got to Crow"
S. Duncan
(*Music by* Mark Charlap. *Lyrics by* Carolyn Leigh.)

"Neverland"
S. Duncan
(*Music by* Jule Styne. *Lyrics by* Betty Comden and Adolph Green.)

"I'm Flying"
S. Duncan, M. Kramer, A. Winter, J. Ward
(*Music by* Mark Charlap. *Lyrics by* Carolyn Leigh.)

ACT 2

Scene 1

"Morning in Neverland"
Never Animals, Lost Boys
(*Music by* Jule Styne. *Lyrics by* Betty Comden and Adolph Green.)

"Pirate Song"
Pirates
(*Music by* Mark Charlap. *Lyrics by* Carolyn Leigh.)

"A Princely Scheme"
G. Rose, Pirates
(*Music by* Mark Charlap. *Lyrics by* Carolyn Leigh.)

"Indians!"
M. Pogee, Indians
(*Dance Arrangement by* Dorothea Freitag.)

"Wendy"
S. Duncan, Lost Boys
(*Music by* Jule Styne. *Lyrics by* Betty Comden and Adolph Green.)

[3]Originally produced in New York 7 November 1910 at the New York Theatre for 136 performances; this version first produced in New York 31 August 1978 at the New York State Theatre for 14 performances. For Synopsis of Scenes and Musical Numbers, see 1978 revival.
[4]Originally produced in New York 21 October 1907 at the New Amsterdam Theatre for 416 performances; this version first produced in New York 2 April 1978 at the New York State Theatre for 8 performances. For Synopsis of Scenes and Musical Numbers, see 1978 revival.

[5]Originally produced in New York 20 October 1954 at the Winter Garden for 152 performances. For this production, "Neverland Waltz," "The Pow Pow Polka," and "To the Ship" were dropped; "Morning in Neverland" was added.

"Another Princely Scheme"
G. Rose, Pirates
(*Music by* Mark Charlap. *Lyrics by* Carolyn Leigh.)
Scene 2
"I Won't Grow Up"
S. Duncan, Lost Boys
(*Music by* Mark Charlap. *Lyrics by* Carolyn Leigh.)
Scene 3
"Mysterious Lady"
S. Duncan, G. Rose, Never Trees
(*Music by* Jule Styne. *Lyrics by* Betty Comden and Adolph Green.)
Scene 4
"Ugg-a-Wugg"
S. Duncan, M. Pogee, Indians, Lost Boys, Darling Children
(*Music by* Jule Styne. *Lyrics by* Betty Comden and Adolph Green.)
"Distant Melody"
M. Kramer
(*Music by* Jule Styne. *Lyrics by* Betty Comden and Adolph Green.)
ACT 3
Scene 1
"Hook's Waltz"
G. Rose, Pirates
(*Music by* Jule Styne. *Lyrics by* Betty Comden and Adolph Green.)
"The Battle"
S. Duncan, G. Rose
(*Music by* Mark Charlap. *Lyrics by* Carolyn Leigh.)
Scene 2
"I've Got to Crow" (reprise)
S. Duncan, Darling Children, Lost Boys
Scene 3
"Tender Shepherd" (reprise)
B. Fowler, M. Kramer, A. Winter, J. Ward
"I Won't Grow Up" (reprise)
The Darling Family, Lost Boys
Scene 4
"Neverland" (reprise)
S. Duncan

1979.23 EVITA

A Musical in Two Acts. Music by Andrew Lloyd Webber. Lyrics by Tim Rice. Directed by Harold Prince. Sets, costumes and projections designed by Timothy O'Brien, Tazeena Firth. Lighting by David Hersey. Sound by Abe Jacob. Choreography by Larry Fuller. Musical director, Rene Wiegert. Orchestrations by Hershy Kay, Andrew Lloyd Webber. Executive producers, R. Tyler Gatchell and Peter Neufeld. Produced by Robert Stigwood in association with David Land. Opened 25 September 1979 at the Broadway Theatre and closed 25 June 1983 after 1568 performances.

CAST (in order of appearance): *Eva:* PATTI LuPONE, Terri Klausner (matinees). *Che:* MANDY PATINKIN. *Peron:* BOB GUNTON. *Peron's Mistress:* Jan Ohringer. *Magaldi:* Mark Syers.
People of Argentina: Seda Azarian, Dennis Birchall, Peppi Borza, Tom Carder, Robin Cleaver, Andy De Gange, Mark East, Teri Gill, Carlos Gorbea, Pat Gorman, Rex David Hays, Terri Klausner, Michael Lichtefeld, Carol Lugenbeal, Paul Lynn, Morgan MacKay, Peter Marinos, Sal Mistretta, Jack Neubeck, Marcia O'Brien, Nancy Opel, Davia Sacks, James Sbano, David Staller, Michelle Stubbs, Robert Tanna, Clarence Teeters, Susan Terry, Phillip Tracy, David Vosburgh, Mark Waldrop, Sandra Wheeler, Brad Witsger, John Leslie Wolfe, Nancy Wood, John Yost. *Children:* Megan Forste, Bridget Francis, Nicole Francis, Michael Pastryk, Christopher Wooten.

The action takes place in Argentina between 1934 and 1952.

ACT 1
"A Cinema in Buenos Aires; July 26, 1952"
Company
"Requiem for Evita"
Company
"Oh What a Circus"
M. Patinkin, Company
"On This Night of a Thousand Stars"
M. Syers
"Eva Beware of the City"
M. Syers, P. LuPone, Family
"Buenos Aires" P. LuPone, Dancers
"Goodnight and Thank You"
M. Patinkin, P. LuPone, Lovers

"The Art of the Possible"
B. Gunton, P. LuPone, Colonels
"Charity Concert"
Company
"I'd Be Surprisingly Good for You"
P. LuPone, B. Gunton
"Another Suitcase in Another Hall"
J. Ohringer
"Peron's Latest Flame"
M. Patinkin, P. LuPone, Company
"A New Argentina"
P. LuPone, B. Gunton, M. Patinkin, Company
ACT 2
"On the Balcony of the Casa Rosada"
B. Gunton, M. Patinkin, Company
"Don't Cry for Me Argentina"
P. LuPone
"High Flying Adored"
M. Patinkin, P. LuPone
"Rainbow High"
P. LuPone, Dressers
"Rainbow Tour"
M. Patinkin, P. LuPone, B. Gunton, Peronists
"The Actress Hasn't Learned (the Lines You'd Like to Hear)"
P. LuPone, M. Patinkin, Company
"And the Money Kept Rolling In (and Out)"
M. Patinkin, Company
"Santa Evita"
Children, Workers
"Waltz for Eva and Che"
P. LuPone, M. Patinkin
"She is a Diamond"
B. Gunton, Officers
"Dice Are Rolling"
B. Gunton, P. LuPone
"Eva's Final Broadcast"
P. LuPone, M. Patinkin
"Montage"
Company
"Lament"
P. LuPone, M. Patinkin

1979.24 THE 1940's RADIO HOUR

A Musical in One Act. (Book) by Walton Jones. Based on an idea by Walton Jones and Carol Lees, as originally presented by the Ensemble Company and Yale Repertory Theatre in New Haven and further developed and presented by the Arena Stage in Washington, D.C. Directed by Walton Jones. Musical numbers staged by Thommie Walsh. Musical supervision and direction by Stanley Lebowsky. Scenic design by David Gropman. Lighting design by Tharon Musser. Costume design by William Ivey Long. Sound design by Otts Munderloh. Orchestrations by Gary S. Fagin. Vocal arrangements by Paul Schierhorn. Produced by Jujamcyn Productions, Joseph Harris, Ira Bernstein and Roger Berlind. Opened 7 October 1979 at the St. James Theatre and closed 6 January 1980 after 105 performances.

CAST (in order of appearance): *Pops Bailey:* Arny Freeman. *Stanley:* John Sloman. *Clifton A. Feddington:* Josef Sommer. *Zoot Doubleman:* Stanley Lebowsky. *Wally Fergusson:* Jack Hallett. *Lou Cohn:* Merwin Goldsmith. *Johnny Cantone:* Jeff Keller. *Ginger Brooks:* Crissy Wilzak. *Connie Miller:* Kathy Andrini. *B. J. Gibson:* Stephen James. *Neal Tilden:* Joe Grifasi. *Ann Collier:* Mary-Cleere Haran. *Geneva Lee Browne:* Dee Dee Bridgewater. *Biff Baker:* John Doolittle.
The Orchestra: Zoot Doubleman: Stanley Lebowsky. *Neeley "Flap" Kovacs:* Mauriuice Mark. *Bonnie Cavanaugh:* Jane Ira Bloom. *Custis Jones:* Billy Butler. *Gus Bracken:* Ray Shenfeld. *Scoops Millikan:* Dennis Elliott. *Moe "Lockjaw" Ambrose:* Josh Edwards. *Biff Baker:* John Doolittle. *Fritz Canigliaro:* Joe Petrizzo. *Charlie "Kid Lips" Snyder:* Dennis Anderson. *Ned "Woof" Bennett:* J. D. Parran. *Totts Schoenfeld:* Mel Rodnon. *Fess "Snookie" Davenport:* Rick Centalonza. *Bob "Bobo" Lewis:* Jon Goldman. *Buzz Cranshaw:* Ron Tooley. *Phil Bentley:* Bruce Samuels. *Pieface Minelli:* Lloyd Michels.

The action takes place in the WOV Broadcast Studios, Algonquin Room on the ground floor of the Hotel Astor in New York City on 21 December 1942 about 8 P.M.

MUSICAL NUMBERS[6]

---

[6]Song titles do not appear in the program. Above list prepared from production manuscript.

"Chattanooga Choo-Choo" (from *SUN VALLEY SERENADE* film)
J. Sommer, M. C. Haran, D. D. Bridgewater, J. Grifasi, S. James, K. Andrini, C. Wilzak, J. Hallett
(*Music by* Harry Warren. *Lyrics by* Mack Gordon.)

Pepsi Cola Radio Jingle
J. Grifasi, S. James, K. Andrini, C. Wilzak, J. Sommer

"Daddy"
The Band, K. Andrini
(*Music and Lyrics by* Bobby Troupe.)

"Our Love Is Here to Stay" (from *THE GOLDWYN FOLLIES*, film)
J. Keller
(*Music by* George Gershwin. *Lyrics by* Ira Gershwin.)

"That Old Black Magic" (from *STAR SPANGLED RHYTHM* film)
M. C. Haran
(*Music by* Harold Arlen. *Lyrics by* Johnny Mercer.)

"Ain't She Sweet"
J. Doolittle, S. James, C. Wilzak, D. D. Bridgewater, All
(*Music by* Milton Ager. *Lyrics by* Jack Yellen.)

"How About You" (from *BABES ON BROADWAY* film)
S. James, K. Andrini
(*Music by* Burton Lane. *Lyrics by* Ralph Freed.)

"Blue Moon"
J. Grifasi
(*Music by* Richard Rodgers. *Lyrics by* Lorenz Hart.)

"Chiquita Banana"
All Girls
(*Music and Lyrics by* Len Mackenzie, Garth Montgomery and William Wirges.)

"Rose of the Rio Grande"
D. D. Bridgewater, Men, Band
(*Music by* Harry Warren and Ross Gorman. *Lyrics by* Edgar Leslie.)

"I'll Never Smile Again" (from *LAS VEGAS NIGHT* film)
J. Grifasi, S. James, M. C. Haran, C. Wilzak, K. Andrini, J. Keller
(*Music and Lyrics by* Ruth Lowe.)

"Boogie Woogie Bugle Boy"
S. James, K. Andrini, C. Wilzak
(*Music and Lyrics by* Don Raye and Hughie Prince.)

"Blues in the Night" (from *BLUES IN THE NIGHT*, film)
C. Wilzak, Men
(*Music by* Harold Arlen. *Lyrics by* Johnny Mercer.)

"Jingle Bells"
J. Doolittle, J. Grifasi, Group
(Bill Finigan, Glenn Miller, Eddie Saracas arrangement)

"I Got It Bad and That Ain't Good" (from *JUMP FOR JOY*)
D. D. Bridgewater
(*Music by* Duke Ellington. *Lyrics by* Paul Francis Webster.)

"At Last" (from *ORCHESTRA WIVES* film)
S. James
(*Music by* Harry Warren. *Lyrics by* Mack Gordon.)

"Little Brown Jug"
(Bill Finigan arrangement for Glenn Miller)

"Have Yourself a Merry Little Christmas" (from *MEET ME IN ST. LOUIS*, film)
M. C. Haran
(*Music and Lyrics by* Hugh Martin and Ralph Blane.)

"Strike Up the Band" (from *STRIKE UP THE BAND*)
Full Company
(*Music by* George Gershwin. *Lyrics by* Ira Gershwin.)

"I'll Be Seeing You" (from *RIGHT THIS WAY*)
Full Company
(*Music by* Sammy Fain. *Lyrics by* Irving Kahal.)

The Mutual Manhattan Variety Cavalcade Theme Band
(*Music by* Stanley Lebowsky.)

1979.25   # SUGAR BABIES

A Burlesque Musical (Revue) in Two Acts, 24 Scenes. Conceived by Ralph G. Allen and Harry Rigby. Sketches by Ralph G. Allen based on traditional material. Music by Jimmy McHugh. Lyrics by Dorothy Fields, Al Dubin. Additional music and lyrics by Arthur Malvin. Staged and choreographed by Ernest Flatt. Sketches directed by Rudy Tronto. Entire production supervised by Ernest Flatt. Scenery and costumes designed by Raoul Pene du Bois. Lighting designed by Gilbert V. Hemsley, Jr. Vocal arrangements by Arthur Malvin. Additional vocal arrangements by Hugh Martin, Ralph Blane. Musical director, Glen Roven. Orchestrations by Dick Hyman. Dance music arranged by Arnold Gross. Associate producers, Jack Schlissel, Thomas Walton Associates, Frank Montalvo. Produced by Terry Allen Kramer and Harry Rigby in association with Columbia Pictures. 8 October 1979 at the Mark Hellinger Theatre and closed 28 August 1982 after 1208 performances.

CAST (in order of appearance): *Mickey:* MICKEY ROONEY. *Scot:* Scot Stewart. *Jillian:* ANN JILLIAN. *Tom:* Tom Boyd. *Peter:* Peter Leeds. *Jack:* Jack Fletcher. *Jimmy:* Jimmy Mathews. *Ann:* ANN MILLER. *Sid:* SID STONE. And Bob Williams.

The Sugar Babies: Laura Booth, Christine Busini, Diane Duncan, Chris Elia, Debbie Gornay, Barbara Hanks, Jeri Kansas, Barbara Mandra, Robin Manus, Faye Fujisaki Mar, Linda Ravinsky, Michele Rogers, Rose Scudder, Patti Winston. *The Gaiety Quartet:* Jonathan Aronson, Eddie Pruett, Michael Radigan, Jeff Veazey. Hank Brunjes (alt.).

ACT 1

Scene 1

A Memory of Burlesque: "A Good Old Burlesque Show"
M. Rooney, His Friends
(*Music by* Jimmy McHugh. *Lyrics by* Arthur Malvin.)

Scene 2

Welcome to the Gaiety: "Let Me Be Your Sugar Baby"
(*Music and Lyrics by* Arthur Malvin.)
P. Leeds, J. Fletcher, Sugar Babies

Scene 3

Meet Me 'Round the Corner[7]
J. Mathews, S. Stewart, P. Leeds, M. Rooney, R. Scudder, C. Elia, M. Rogers, A. Jillian

One of the most famous of all burlesque scenes, originally based on the Homestead Quartet, a minstrel show afterpiece.

Scene 4

Travelin': "In Louisiana"
A. Miller, Sugar Babies, Gaiety Quartet
(*Music by* Jimmy McHugh. *Lyrics by* Arthur Malvin.)

"I Feel a Song Comin' On" (from *EVERY NIGHT AT EIGHT* film)
(*Music by* Jimmy McHugh. *Lyrics by* Dorothy Fields and George Oppenheimer.)

"Goin' Back to New Orleans"[8]
(*Music and Lyrics by* Arthur Malvin.)

Scene 5

The Broken Arms Hotel
J. Fletcher, T. Boyd, M. Rooney, J. Mathews, R. Scudder

Scene 6

Feathered Fantasy (Salute to Sally Rand): "Sally"
S. Stewart, B. Hanks, Sugar Babies
(*Music by* Jimmy McHugh. *Lyrics by* Arthur Malvin.)

Scene 7

The Pitchman
S. Stone

Scene 8

Ellis Island Lament: "Immigration Rose"
M. Rooney, Gaiety Quartet
(*Music by* Jimmy McHugh. *Lyrics by* Eugene West and Irwin Dash.)

Nearly all Columbia Wheel Burlesque Shows had quartets to support the principal comedian in his specialty turn. Among the more prominent examples are the Church City Boys in Louis Robey's 'Knickerbockers' and The Four Harmonists in 'The Girls from Happyland.'

Scene 9

Scenes from Domestic Life
A. Jillian, J. Mathews, J. Fletcher, P. Leeds, T. Boyd, S. Stewart, R. Manus, L. Booth, D. Gornay

Scene 10

Torch Song (after Bobby Clark)[9]: "Don't Blame Me" (from *CLOWNS IN THE CLOVER*, Chicago)
A. Miller, E. Pruett
(*Music by* Jimmy McHugh. *Lyrics by* Dorothy Fields.)

Scene 11

Orientale: Christine Busini introduced by Jack (Fletcher)

---

[7]During the run replaced by:
"I Want a Girl (Just Like the Girl That Married Dear Old Dad)" (Act 1, Scene 3)
J. Mathews, S. Stewart, P. Leeds, M. Rooney, R. Scudder, C. Elia, M. Rogers, A. Jillian
(*Music by* Harry von Tilzer. *Lyrics by* William Dillon.)
[8]Lyrics revised for subsequent National Tour as "Goin' Back to Cucamonga."
[9]Later billed as A Very Moving Love Song (Salute to Ed Wynn).

Little Egypt, the sensation of the Columbian Exposition of 1893 and many imitators on the variety stages as did La Sylphe, a "Salome" dancer who caused a big stir in burlesque in 1908.

Scene 12

The Little Red Schoolhouse
A. Miller, R. Scudder, D. Duncan, J. Mathews, M. Rooney

Scene 13

The New Candy-Coated Craze: "The Sugar Baby Bounce"
A. Jillian, C. Elia, L. Ravinsky
(*Music and Lyrics by* Jay Livingston and Ray Evans.)

There were many sister acts in burlesque. The Watson Sisters owned their own company in the 1890's. The O'Connor Sisters were first featured in Dave Marion's Own show on the Columbia Wheel in 1923. Not many of the sister acts were comprised of real sisters.

Scene 14

Special Added Attraction: Madame Rentz and her All Female Minstrels featuring the Countess Francine. *Introduction:* J. Fletcher.

"Down at the Gaiety Burlesque"/"Mr. Banjo Man"
A. Miller, M. Rooney, J. Mathews, Sugar Babies
(*Music and Lyrics by* Arthur Malvin.)

One of the earliest of all Burlesque Shows was the Rentz Troupe owned by M. B. Leavitt. Minstrel finales remained popular until 1925. Black light was used on the Variety stage as early as 1904, and there were no fewer than five black light numbers in The Radium Girls of 1919.

ACT 2

Scene 1

Candy Butcher
S. Stone, Gaiety Quartet

Scene 2

Girls and Garters:

"I'm Keeping Myself Available for You"
(*Music by* Jimmy McHugh. *Lyrics by* Arthur Malvin.)

"Exactly Like You"
A. Jillian, Sugar Babies
(*Music by* Jimmy McHugh. *Lyrics by* Dorothy Fields.)

The first girl to throw garters at a Burlesque audience appears to have been Millie de Leon, "The Girls in Blue." Her act was a hot number on the circuits during the first decade of this century. As a result of her generosity, she spent several nights in jail.

Scene 3

Justice Will Out[10]
T. Boyd, P. Leeds, M. Rooney, A. Miller

Scene 4

In a Greek Garden (Salute to Rosita Royce):

"Warm and Willing"
A. Jillian
(*Music by* Jimmy McHugh. *Lyrics by* Jay Livingston and Ray Evans.)

Scene 5

Presenting Madame Alla Gazaza
P. Leeds, S. Stone, A. Miller, J. Veazey, M. Rooney, J. Mathews, J. Fletcher, E. Pruett, A. Jillian, J. Aronson, C. Elia

Scene 6

Tropical Madness: "Cuban Love Song"
S. Stewart, M. Rogers
(*Music by* Jimmy McHugh and Herbert Stothart. *Lyrics by* Dorothy Fields.)

Scene 7

Cautionary Tales
R. Scudder, J. Mathews, E. Pruett, M. Radigan, J. Kansas, J. Fletcher, P. Leeds, T. Boyd, S. Stone

Scene 8

Jimmy McHugh Medley[11]:
M. Rooney, A. Miller

---

[10]Revised under the titles The Court of Last Resort and The Court of Last Retort.

[11]Added for National Tour with Carol Channing and Robert Morse:

Early Sophie (A Tribute to the Great Sophie Tucker)
C. Channing

"I'm the Last of the Red Hot Mamas"
(*Music by* Milton Ager. *Lyrics by* Jack Yellen.)

"Every Day Another Tune"
(*Music and Lyrics by* Arthur Malvin.)

"I Can't Give You Anything But Love, Baby"
(*Lyrics by* Dorothy Fields.)

"I'm Shooting High"
(*Lyrics by* Ted Koehler.)

"When You and I Were Young, Maggie Blues"
(*Lyrics by* Jack Frost.)

"On the Sunny Side of the Street"
(*Lyrics by* Dorothy Fields.)

Scene 9

Presenting Bob Williams (Dog Act)[12]

Scene 10

Old Glory: "You Can't Blame Your Uncle Sammy"
Full Company
(*Music by* Jimmy McHugh. *Lyrics by* Al Dubin and Irwin Dash.)

This finale commemorates a famous act, Madame Hilda Case and the Red Raven Cadets, who were headliners on the Empire Circuit in 1905.

1979.26   THE MOST HAPPY FELLA

A Revival of the Musical in Two Acts, 10 Scenes[13]. Book, music and lyrics by Frank Loesser. Based on the play "They Knew What They Wanted" by Sidney Howard. Stage Directed by Jack O'Brien. Choreography by Graciela Daniele. Scenery by Douglas W. Schmidt. Costumes by Nancy Potts. Lighting by Gilbert V. Hemsley, Jr. Orchestrations by Don Walker. Musical direction, Andrew Meltzer. Conductor, Eric Stern. Produced by Sherwin M. Goldman in association with Michigan Opera Theatre (David DiChiera, General director) and Emhan Inc. Opened 11 October 1979 at the Majestic Theatre and closed 25 November 1979 after 53 performances.

CAST (in order of appearance): *The Cashier:* Bill Hastings. *Cleo:* LOUISA FLANINGAM. *Rosabella:* SHARON DANIELS, Linda Michele (matinees). *Waitresses:* Karen Giombetti, Tina Paul, D'Arcy Phifer, Smith Wordes. *Busboy:* Tim Flavin. *The Postman:* Dan O'Sullivan. *Tony:* GIORGIO TOZZI, Frederick Burchinal (matinees). *Marie:* ADRIENNE LEONETTI. *Max:* Steven Alex-Cole. *Herman:* DENNIS WARNING. *Clem:* Dean Badolato. *Jake:* David Miles. *Al:* Kevin Wilson. *Sheriff:* Stephen Dubov. *Joe:* RICHARD MUENZ. *Giuseppe:* Gene Varrone. *Pasquale:* Darren Nimnicht. *Ciccio:* Franco Spoto. *The Doctor:* Joe McGrath. *The Priest:* Lawrence Asher. *Neighbor Ladies:* Melanie Helton, Dee Etta Rowe, Jane Warsaw, Sally Williams. *Brakeman:* Bill Hastings. *Bus Driver:* Michael Capes.

All the Neighbors, and All the Neighbors' Neighbors: Steven Alex-Cole, Lawrence Asher, Dean Badolato, Michael Capes, Richard Croft, Stephen Dubov, Tim Flavin, Karen Giombetti, Bill Hastings, D. Michael Heath, Melanie Helton, David Miles, Tina Paul, D'Arcy Phifer, Patrice Pickering, Candace Rogers, Dee Etta Rowe, Bonnie Simmons, Jane Warsaw, Richard White, Carla Wilkins, Sally Williams, Kevin Wilson, Smith Wordes.

1979.27   STREET SCENE

A Revival of the American Opera (Dramatic Musical) in Two Acts, 3 Scenes[14]. Book by Elmer Rice from his play of the same name. Music by Kurt Weill. Lyrics by Langston Hughes. Directed by Jack O'Brien. Stage Director, Stephen Willems. Conducted by John Mauceri. Scenery designed by Paul Sylbert. Costumes designed by Nancy Potts. Lighting by Gilbert V. Hemsley, Jr. Choreography by Patricia Birch. Chorus master, Lloyd Walser. (Orchestrations by Kurt Weill.) Produced by the New York City Opera. Opened 13 October 1979 at the New York State Theatre and closed 10 November 1979 after 5 performances in repertory.

"Papa, Don't Go Out Tonight"
(*Music by* Milton Ager. *Lyrics by* Jack Yellen.)

"Some of These Days"
(*Music and Lyrics by* Shelton Brooks.)

[12]During run replaced by:

Bon Appetit
Chaz Chase, C. Elia

and subsequently by Michael Davis (Juggling Specialty).

[13]Originally produced in New York 3 May 1956 at the Imperial Theatre for 678 performances. For Synopsis of Scenes and Musical Numbers, see original 1956 production. Originally presented in Three Acts, 11 Scenes.

[14]Originally produced in New York 9 January 1947 at the Adelphi Theatre for 148 performances. For Synopsis of Scenes and Musical Numbers, see original 1947 production.

CAST (in order of appearance): *Greta Fiorentino*: Martha Thigpen. *Emma Jones*: DIANE CURRY. *Olga Olsen*: Rosemarie Freni. *Carl Olsen*: Ralph Bassett. *Neighborhood Woman*: Marie Young. *Shirley Kaplan*: Carol Rosenfeld. *Abraham Kaplan*: Leo Postrel. *Salvation Army Girls*: Kay Schoenfeld, Cindy Lynn Aaronson. *Henry Davis*: Arthur Woodley. *Willie Maurrant*: Timothy Eaton. *Anna Maurrant*: EILEEN SCHAULER. *Sam Kaplan*: ALAN KAYS. *Daniel Buchanan*: Norman Large. *Mrs. Buchanan*: Lila Herbert. *Frank Maurrant*: WILLIAM CHAPMAN. *George Jones*: Robert Paul. *Steve Sankey*: William Ledbetter. *Lippo Fiorentino*: JONATHAN GREEN. *Mrs. Hildebrand*: Sally Lambert. *Jenny Hildebrand*: Kathleen Hegierski. *Graduates*: Denise Adoff, Vanessa Williams. *Charlie Hildebrand*: Matthew McGrath. *Mary Hildebrand*: Dela Bartolini. *Grace Davis*: Kimara Lovelace. *Rose Maurrant*: CATHERINE MALFITANO. *Harry Easter*: HARLAN FOSS. *Mae Jones*: Bronwyn Thomas. *Dick McGann*: Reed Jones. *Vincent Jones*: Bill Herndon. *Dr. Wilson*: Don Carlo. *Officer Murphy*: Edward Zimmerman. *Milkman*: Robert Brubaker. *Joan*: Ann Cawlo. *Myrtle*: Alizon Hull. *Workman*: Harris Davis. *Eddie*: John Henry Thomas. *Sally*: Suzy Block. *Joe*: Raymond Whitney. *Strawberry Seller*: Richard Nelson. *Corn Seller*: Susan Delery-Whedon. *James Henry*: Don Yule. *Fred Cullen*: Irwin Densen. *Old Clothes Man*: Merle Schmidt. *Men*: Frank Tippie, Barry Carl, Herbert Hunsberger. *Grocery Boy*: Marc Mattaliano. *Ambulance Driver*: Louis Perry. *Music Student*: Susan Eagan. *Intern*: James Sergi. *Furniture Mover*: Frank Tippie. *Nursemaids*: Marie Young, Rita Metzger. *Policemen*: Richard Nelson, Don Henderson. *Middle-Aged Couple*: Harriet Greene, Merle Schmidt. *Off Stage Voices*: Vanessa Williams, Anne Cawlo, Lila Herbert.

SNOW WHITE AND THE SEVEN DWARFS

1979.28

A Musical in One Act. Written for the stage by Joe Cook from the Walt Disney film. (Screenplay by Ted Sears, Otto Englander, Earl Hurd, Dorothy Ann Blank, Richard Creedon, Dick Rickard, Merrill De Maris, Webb Smith.) Music by Frank Churchill. Lyrics by Larry Morey. New music for the stage production by Jay Blackton. New lyrics for the stage production by Joe Cook. Directed and choreographed by Frank Wagner. Executive musical director, Don Pippin. Conductor, Don Smith. Orchestrations by Philip J. Lang. Scenic design by John William Keck. Costume design by Frank Spencer. Mask design and animal costumes by Joe Stephen. Lighting director, Ken Billington. Choral arrangements by Jay Blackton and Don Pippin. Produced by Radio City Music Hall (Robert F. Jani, Producer; John J. Moore, Production executive). Opened 18 October 1979 at the Radio City Music Hall, closing 18 November 1979 after 33 performances; resumed after tour 11 January 1980 and closed 9 March 1980 after 70 additional performances. Total: 103 performances.

CAST (in order of appearance): *Chamberlain*: DAVID PURSLEY. *King*: THOMAS RUISINGER. *Queen*: ANNE FRANCINE. *Snow White*: MARY JO SALERNO. *Mirror/Witch*: Charles Hall. *Luna*: YOLANDE BAVAN. *Greta*: Heidi Coe. *Prince Charming*: RICHARD BOWNE. *Mother*: Lauren Lipson. *Huntsman*: BRUCE SHERMAN. *(The Seven Dwarfs)*: *Doc*: DON POTTER. *Happy*: RICHARD DAY. *Grumpy*: BENNY FREIGH. *Sneezy*: LOUIS CARRY. *Bashful*: JAY EDWARD ALLEN. *Sleepy*: JERRY RILEY. *Dopey*: MICHAEL E. KING.

Singers: Ronald Brown, Kenneth Cantor, Peter Constanza, David Dusing, Clifford Fearl, G. Jan Jones, Patricia Landi, Lauren Lipson, Linda Motashami, Dawn Parrish, Caryl Tenney. *Swings*: Tony Gilbert, Marsha Miller. *Dancers*: Conni Brazelton, Beth Buker, Mary-Pat Carey, John Cashman, Danny Clark, Heidi Coe, Joan Cooper, Joy Coronel, Christopher Daniels, Ron Dunham, Alfred Gonzales, Martha Goodman, Jennifer Hammond, Norb Joerder, Janet Marie Jones, David Lee, Kim Leslie, Malcolm Perry, Michael Ragan, Patricia Register, Roger Rouillier, Jerry Sarnat, Hope Sogawa, Reisa Sperling, Thomas J. Stanton, Cassie Stein, Lynn Williford, Kim Woollen. *Swing*: James Paoletti, Jane Wilson.

The action takes place once upon a time in a faraway land.

MUSICAL NUMBERS[15]

"Welcome to the Kingdom"
   Company
   (*Music by* Jay Blackton. *Lyrics by* Joe Cook.)
"Queen's Presentation"
   Company
   (*Music by* Jay Blackton. *Lyrics by* Joe Cook. *Music arranged by* Ronald Melrose.)
"I'm Wishing"
   M. J. Salerno, H. Coe, Villagers
"One Song"
   R. Bowne
"With a Smile and a Song"
   M. J. Salerno, Animals
"Whistle While You Work"
   M. J. Salerno, Animals

[15]For the National Tour an intermission was added after "Will I Ever See Her Again?" For the Tour and return engagement, the ensemble was redivided between the King's Court, Queen's Court and Animals.

"Heigh-Ho"
   The Seven Dwarfs
"Buddle-Uddle-Um-Dum" (The Washing Song)
   The Seven Dwarfs
"Will I Ever See Her Again?"
   R. Bowne
   (*Music by* Jay Blackton. *Lyrics by* Joe Cook.)
"Dwarf's Yodel Song" (The Silly Song)
   M. J. Salerno, The Seven Dwarfs, Animals
"Someday My Prince Will Come"
   M. J. Salerno
"Heigh-Ho" (reprise)
   The Seven Dwarfs
"Here's the Happy Ending" (Finale)
   Company
   (*Music by* Jay Blackton. *Lyrics by* Joe Cook.)

1979.29

STRIDER

A Play With Music in Two Acts[16]. Play by Mark Rozovsky. Adapted from a story ("Kholstomer: The Story of a Horse") by Leo Tolstoy. English stage version by Robert Kalfin. Based on a translation by Tamara Bering Sunguroff. Directed and staged by Robert Kalfin and Lynne Gannaway. Music originally composed by Mark Rozovsky, S. Vetkin. Original Russian lyrics by Uri Riashentsev. Adapter, composer of new additional music, vocal and instrumental arrangements, and Musical director, Norman L. Berman. New English lyrics by Steve Brown. Production design (scenery) by Wolfgang Roth. Costume designs by Andrew B. Marlay. Lighting design by Robby Monk. Sound design by Gary Harris. A Chelsea Theatre Center Production. Produced by Arthur Whitelaw and Miriam Bienstock in association with Lita Starr. Opened 14 November 1979 at the Helen Hayes Theatre and closed 18 May 1980 after 214 performances. Total, including Off-Broadway run, 403 performances.

CAST (in order of speaking): *Vaska/Mr. Willingstone*: ROGER DeKOVEN. *PrinceSerpuhofsky*: GORDON GOULD. *General/Announcer*: RONNIE NEWMAN. *Viazapurikha/Mathieu/Marie*: PAMELA BURRELL. *Strider*: GERALD HIKEN. *Actors*: Katherine Mary-Brown, Jeannine Khoutieff, Vicki Van Grack. *Groom*: SKIP LAWING. *Gypsy*: Nina Dova. *Count Bobrinsky/Darling/The Lieutenant*: BENJAMIN HENDRICKSON. *Feofan/Fritz*: IGORS GAVON. *Bet Taker*: Vincent A. Feraudo. *Vendor*: Charles Walker. *Actors*: John Brownlee, Nancy Kawalek, Tad Ingram. *Gypsies*: Karen Trott, Steven Blane. (Note: *The Herd*: Chorus.)

Pre-show songs performed by Nina Dova, with Karen Trott, Steven Blane, Paul Kreshka, Bill Tynes.

ACT 1[17]

"Oh Jesus—It's Time to Take Out the Nags"
   R. DeKoven
(Only Mortal)
   Chorus
"Song of the Herd"
   Chorus
"Conversation of Strider and the Herd"
   G. Hiken, Chorus
Duet (Warm and Tender)
   P. Burrell, G. Hiken
"Darling's Romance"
   B. Hendrickson
(Oh, Cruel and Hard of Heart Is Man)
   Chorus
"Serpuhovsky's Song"
   G. Gould
(Finale Act I: Along the Blacksmith's Alley)
   G. Hiken, I. Gavon, G. Gould, Company
ACT 2
"Oh, Jesus—It's Time to Take Out the Nags" (reprise)
   R. DeKoven
"Serpuhovsky's Romance"
   G. Gould, Chorus

[16]Originally produced in New York Off-Broadway 31 May 1979 at the Chelsea Theatre Center for 187 performances under the title *STRIDER: THE STORY OF A HORSE*.
[17]No song titles appeared in the program. Above list prepared from published text.

(Oh, Hard Is Life for Man and Horse) reprise
  N. Dova
"Live Long Enough"[18]
  G. Hiken, Chorus
(Strider's Death)
  Entire Company

1979.30   ## BETTE!: DIVINE MADNESS

A Musical Revue in Two Acts. Special material written by Bette Midler, Jerry Blatt, Bruce Vilanch. Staged by Bette Midler and Jerry Blatt. Choreographed by Maria Blakey. Additional choreography by Toni Basil. Musical direction by Tony Berg, Randy Kerber. Lighting designer, Chipmonck. Sound engineer, Bill Darlington. Produced by Ron Delsener. Opened 5 December 1979 at the Majestic Theatre and closed 6 January 1980 after 40 performances.

CAST: BETTE MIDLER, THE STAGGERING HARLETTES (Franny Eisenberg, Linda Hart, Paulette McWilliams), SHABBA-DOO (Adolfo Quinones).

MUSICAL NUMBERS[19]

"Big Noise from Winnetka"
  (*Music and Lyrics by* Gil Rodin, Bob Crosby, Bob Haggart, Ray Bauduc.)
"Paradise"
  (*Music and Lyrics by* Harry Nilsson, Gil Garfield, Perry Botkin, Jr.)
"Shiver Me Timbers"
  (*Music and Lyrics by* Tom Waits)
"The Rose" (from THE ROSE film)
  (*Music and Lyrics by* Amanda McBroom.)
"Fire Down Below"
  (*Music and Lyrics by* Bob Seeger.)
"Stay With Me"
  (*Music and Lyrics by* Jerry Ragovoy and George Weiss.)
"Dolores Delago the Toast of Chicago"
"My Mother's Eyes"
  (*Music and Lyrics by* Tom Jans.)
"Chapel of Love"
  (*Music and Lyrics by* Jeff Barry, Ellie Greenwich, Phil Spector.)
"Boogie Woogie Bugle Boy"
  (*Music and Lyrics by* Don Raye and Hughie Prince.)
"E Street Shuffle"
  (*Music and Lyrics by* Bruce Springsteen.)
"Summer" (The First Time)
  (*Music and Lyrics by* Bobby Goldsboro.)
"Leader of the Pack"
  (*Music and Lyrics by* George Morton, Jeff Barry, Ellie Greenwich.)
Those Wonderful Sophie Tucker Jokes
Hang onto My Rainbow Sleeve
Hobo Pantomime
"I'm Ready to Begin Again"
  (*Music and Lyrics by* Jerry Leiber and Mike Stoller.)
"Do You Wanna Dance?"
  (*Music and Lyrics by* Bobby Freeman.)
"You Can't Always Get What You Want"
  (*Music and Lyrics by* Mick Jagger and Keith Richards.)
"I Shall Be Released"
  (*Music and Lyrics by* Bob Dylan.)

1979.31   ## OKLAHOMA!

A Revival of the Musical Play in Two Acts, 6 Scenes[20]. Book and lyrics by Oscar Hammerstein II. Music by Richard Rodgers. Based on the play "Green Grow the Lilacs" by Lynn Riggs. Directed by William Hammerstein. Choreography by Agnes de Mille, restaged by Gemze de Lappe. Music director, Jay Blackton. Assistant conductor, Robert Stanley. Scenery by Michael J. Hotopp, Paul dePass. Costumes by Bill Hargate. Lighting by Thomas Skelton. Tap sequences by Miriam Nelson. Rope sequences by Montie

---

[18]Added during the run on Broadway.
[19]No list of Musical Numbers appears in the program; above list has been prepared from press materials, recordings and the film of the stage production.
[20]Originally produced in New York 31 March 1943 at the St. James Theatre for 2212 performances. For Synopsis of Scenes and Musical Numbers, see original 1943 production.

Montana. Produced by Zev Bufman and James M. Nederlander in association with Donald C. Carter. Opened 13 December 1979 at the Palace Theatre and closed 31 August 1980 after 301 performances.

CAST (in order of appearance): *Aunt Eller:* MARY WICKES. *Curly:* LAURENCE GUITTARD. *Laurey:* CHRISTINE ANDREAS. *Ike Skidmore:* Robert Ray. *Slim:* Stephen Crain. *Will Parker:* HARRY GROENER. *Jud Fry:* MARTIN VIDNOVIC. *Ado Annie Carnes:* CHRISTINE EBERSOLE. *Ali Hakim:* BRUCE ADLER. *Gertie Cummings:* Martha Traverse. *Curley* (in ballet): DAVID EVANS. *Laurey* (in ballet): LOUISE HICKEY. *Jud* (in ballet): Anthony Santiago. *The Child* (in ballet): Judy Epstein. *Jud's Postcards:* Patti Ross, Ilene Strickler, Susan Whelan. *Andrew Carnes:* Philip Rash. *Cord Elam:* Nick Jolley.

Singers: Sydney Anderson, Stephen Crain, Lorraine Foreman, Nick Holley, John Kildahl, Jessica Molaskey, Joel T. Myers, Philip Rash, Robert Ray, Martha Traverse, M. Lynne Wieneke. *Dancers:* Eric Aaron, Brian Bullard, Phillip Candler, Judy Epstein, David Evans, Tonda Hannum, Louise Hickey, Kristina Koebel, Leslie Morris, Michael Page, Patti Ross, Kevin Ryan, Anthony Santiago, Ilene Strickler, Robert Sullivan, Susan Whelan. *Swings:* Gina Martin, Jerry Ziaja.

1979.32   ## COMIN' UPTOWN

A Musical in Two Acts, 13 Scenes. Book by Philip Rose and Peter Udell. Based on "A Christmas Carol" by Charles Dickens. Music by Garry Sherman. Lyrics by Peter Udell. Directed by Philip Rose. Choreographed by Michael Peters. Scenery designed by Robin Wagner. Costumes designed by Ann Emonts. Lighting designed by Gilbert V. Hemsley, Jr. Sound Designed by Jack Shearing. Musical director, Howard Roberts. Orchestrations and vocal arrangements by Garry Sherman. Dance music arrangements by Timothy Graphenreed. Associate choreographer, Frances Lee Morgan. Associate producers, Leslie K. Bullock, Anthony Weymouth, Kimako. Produced by W. Ridgely Bullock, Albert W. Selden in association with Columbia Pictures. Opened 20 December 1979 at the Winter Garden and closed 27 January 1980 after 45 performances.

CAST (in order of appearance): *Salvation Army Trio:* DEBORAH LYNN BRIDGES, DEBORAH BURRELL, JENIFER LEWIS. *Shoppers:* Harlem Residents. *Scrooge:* GREGORY HINES. *Bob Crachit:* John Russell. *Tenant's Representative:* LARRY MARSHALL. *Mary* (Recreation Center Director): Saundra McClain. *Minister:* Robert Jackson. *Marley:* TIGER HAYNES. *Christmas Past:* LARRY MARSHALL. *Trio:* DEBORAH LYNN BRIDGES, DEBORAH BURRELL, JENIFER LEWIS. *Time:* Frances Lee Morgan. *Mary* (Younger): Loretta Devine. *Young Scrooge:* Duane Davis. *His Assistant:* Vernal Polson. *Reverend Byrd:* Ned Wright. *Gospel Singer:* Esther Marrow. *Deacon:* John Russell. *Mrs. Crachit, Deacon's Wife:* Virginia McKinzie. *Christmas Present:* SAUNDRA McCLAIN. *Crachit Daughters:* Shirley Black-Brown, Allison R. Manson. *Martha Crachit:* Carol Lynn Maillard. *Tiny Tim:* Kevin Babb. *Christmas Future:* ROBERT JACKSON.

Harlem Residents: Kevin Babb, Shirley Black-Brown, Roslyn Burrough, Barbara Christopher, Duane Davis, Ronald Dunham, Milton Grayson, Linda James, Kevin Jeff, Carol Lynn Maillard, Allison R. Manson, Esther Marrow, Frances Lee Morgan, Raymond Patterson, Vernal Polson, Gloria Sauve, Eric Sawyer, Kiki Shepard, Faruma Williams, Ned Wright.

Act 1, Scene 1: Harlem—125th Street. *Scene 2:* Scrooge's Office. *Scene 3:* Scrooge's Bedroom. *Scene 4:* A Street in Harlem. *Scene 5:* Harlem Baptist Church. *Scene 6:* Scrooge's Bedroom. *Scene 7:* The Crachit Dining Room. *Scene 8:* Outside the Crachit House.

Act 2, Scene 1: Scrooge's Bedroom. *Scene 2:* A Cemetary. *Scene 3:* Another Cemetary. *Scene 4:* Scrooge's Bedroom. *Scene 5:* The Crachit Dining Room.

ACT 1
Scene 1
  "Christmas Is Comin' Uptown"
    Christmas Shoppers, D. L. Bridges, D. Burrell, J. Lewis, G. Hines
Scene 2
  "Somebody's Gotta Be the Heavy"
    G. Hines
Scene 3
  "Now I Lay Me Down to Sleep"
    G. Hines
  "Get Your Act Together"
    T. Haynes
  "Lifeline"
    L. Marshall, D. L. Bridges, D. Burrell, J. Lewis
    (*Orchestrated by* Willie Strickland.)
Scene 4
  "What Better Time for Love"
    G. Hines, L. Devine
Scene 5
  "It Won't Be Long"
    E. Marrow, Congregation

Scene 6

"Get Down Brother, Get Down"

S. McClain, D. L. Bridges, D. Burrell, J. Lewis

Scene 7

"Sing a Christmas Song"

J. Russell, V. McKinzie, S. Black-Brown, A. R. Manson, the Carolers

"What Better Time for Love" (reprise)

K. Babb, J. Russell, V. McKinzie, S. Black-Brown, A. R. Manson

Scene 8

"Have I Finally Found My Heart?"

G. Hines

ACT 2

Scene 1

"Nobody Really Do"

R. Jackson, D. L. Bridges, D. Burrell, J. Lewis

"Goin', Gone"

R. Jackson

Scene 2

"Get Down, Brother, Get Down" (reprise)

J. Russell, V. McKinzie, S. Black-Brown, A. R. Manson, Mourners

Scene 3

"One Way Ticket to Hell"

D. L. Bridges, D. Burrell, J. Lewis

"Nobody Really Do" (reprise)

R. Jackson, D. L. Bridges, D. Burrell, J. Lewis

Scene 4

"Born Again"

G. Hines

Scene 5

"Born Again" (reprise)

G. Hines, Company

1979.33 THE BABES IN TOYLAND

An Adaptation of the Musical Comedy in Two Acts, a Prologue and 10 Scenes[21]. Original music by Victor Herbert. (Original book and lyrics by Glenn McDonough.) New book adaptation by Ellis Weiner, based on an original idea by Barry Weissler. New music and lyrics by Shelly Markham and Annette Leisten. Directed by Munson Hicks. Choreographed by Tony Stevens. Scenery and costumes by Michael J. Hotopp and Paul de Pass. Puppets by Sid and Marty Krofft. Lighting by Associated Theatrical Designers. Musical direction, Rock Orchestration by Bob Christiansen. Orchestral arrangements by Kirk Nurock. Dance arrangements by Bob Stecko. Produced by American Entertainment Enterprises (Barry and Fran Weissler). Opened 21 December 1979 at the Felt Forum and closed 1 January 1980 after 16 performances.

CAST (in order of appearance): *Tom*: MARK HOLLERAN. *Sugarbear*: ROGER LAWSON. *Horace*: MICHAEL CALKINS. *'The Puppettes'*: Mona Finstoin, Edward T. Jacobs, Robert Hancock, Lynn Hippen, Steve Mathews, Alan F. Seiffert. *Promoter*: Dan Kruger. *Haystack* (Shaggy Dog): Edward T. Jacobs. *Grandfather*: KEN BONAFONS. *Mary*: DEBBIE McLEOD. *Mother Goose*: S. BARKLEY MURRAY. *Barnaby*: C. A. HUTTON. *Old King Cole*: DAN KRUGER. *Jack Be Nimble*: Alan F. Seiffert. *The Old Woman in the Shoe*: Lynn Hippen. *The Children in the Shoe*: Mona Finstin, Steve Matthews. *Drummer Boy*: Alan F. Seiffert. *Humpty Dumpty*: , Ken Bonafons, Alan F. Seiffert. *The Wall*: Robert Hancock. *Little Bo Peep*: SHARI WATSON. *Vendors*: Roger Lawson, Mark Holleran, Michael Calkins. *The Shrouds*: S. Barkley Murray, Alan F. Seiffert. *The Toy Soldiers*: Mona Finsten, Robert Hancock, Lynn Hippen, Dan Kruger, Steve Mathews, S. Barkley Murray, Alan F. Seiffert. *Puppeteers*: Mona Finstoin, Robert Hancock, Lynn Hippen, Steve Mathews, Alan F. Seiffert. *Computer Bob*: ROBERT HANCOCK. (Note: The Babes are Tom, Sugarbear, Horace, Mary and Haystack.)

Act 1, Scene 1: The Interior of Grandfather's Toyshop. *Scene 2*: The Town Square of Toyland. *Scene 3*: The Interior of the Old Toy Shop. *Scene 4*: Dream Toyland. *Scene 5*: The Dark Interior of Barnaby's Hide-Out Workshop and Prison in the Closed Tunnel of Love.

Act 2, Scene 1: Central Exterior of Toyland in front of Tunnel of Love. *Scene 2*: The Interior of Barnaby's House of Horrors. *Scene 3*: The Interior of Barnaby's House of Horrors. *Scene 4*: Barnaby's Robot-operated computer room. *Scene 5*: Transition from Laboratory to a modern Disco Toyland.

---

[21]First presented in New York as *BABES IN TOYLAND* 13 October 1903 at the Majestic Theatre for 192 performances.

ACT 1

Prologue

"Big Baby"

The Babes, The Puppettes

"It's a Sweet Life"

The Babes

Scene 2

"Something Must Be Done"

D. Kruger, K. Bonafons, A. F. Sieffert, R. Hancock, S. B. Murray, L. Hippen, M. Finston, S. Mathews, the Babes

"Don't Cry, Bo Peep"

The Babes

"Bare Facts"

The Babes

Scene 3

"Step Out in Front"

D. McLeod, the Babes

Scene 4

"Dream Toyland"

Ladies of the Grand Ballet, Vendors

ACT 2

Scene 2

"The Two of Us"

M. Holleran, D. McLeod

Scene 4

"The March of the Wooden Soldiers"

Toy Soldiers

Scene 5

FinaleCompany

1980.01 CANTERBURY TALES

A Revival of the Musical in Two Acts, 10 Scenes and a Prologue[22]. Book by Martin Starkie and Nevill Coghill. Based on Nevill Coghill's translation of Geoffrey Chaucer's "Canterbury Tales." Music by Richard Hill and John Hawkins. Lyrics by Nevill Coghill. Directed by Robert Johanson. Choreography by Randy Hugill. Musical direction, vocal arrangements by John Kroner. Setting by Michael Anania. Costumes by Sigrid Insull. Lighting by Gregg Marriner. An Equity Library Theatre Production. Produced by Burry Fredrik and Bruce Schwartz. Opened 12 February 1980 at the Rialto Theatre and closed 24 February 1980 after 16 performances. Total, including Off-Broadway run, 46 performances.

CAST (in order of appearance): *Chaucer* (January): Earl McCarroll. *Knight*: Robert Stoeckle. *Squire* (Nicholas/Damian/Horse): Robert Tetirick. *Yeoman* (John/King Arthur): Andy Ferrell. *Prioress*: Mimi Sherwin. *Nun* (Proserpina); K. K. Preece. *Molly* (Guenevere): Kaylyn Dillehay. *May*: Tricia Witham. *Alison* (Sweetheart): Krista Neumann. *Friar* (Justinus): Andrew Traines. *Merchant* (Gervase): Vance Mizelle. *Clerk* (Robin/Page/Horse): Richard Stillman. *Cook* (Miller's Wife/Duenna): Polly Pen. *Miller*: Win Atkins. *Steward* (Carpenter/Placebo): Ted Houck, Jr. *Wife of Bath* (Old Woman): Maureen Sadusk. *Summoner* (Absalon/Alan): Kelly Walters. *Pardonner* (Executioner): Martin Walsh. *Host* (Pluto): George Maguire.

The action takes place on a four day Pilgrimage to Canterbury Carhedral, England in the late 1300s.

ACT 1

Prologue

E. McCarroll, Company

Scene 1

"Welcome Song"

G. Maguire, Company

"Goodnight Hymn"

Company

"Canterbury Day"

Company

---

[22]Originally presented in New York 3 February 1969 at the Eugene O'Neill Theatre for 122 performances; this revival previously presented Off-Broadway by the Equity Library Theatre 29 November 1979 at the Master Theatre for 30 performances. For this production, the Mug Dance, "Hymen, Hymen" and "Love Pas de Deux" were dropped. "Pear Tree Quintet" revised as "Pear Tree Sextet." "What Do Women Want?" renamed "What Do Women Most Desire?" Song order rearranged.

Scene 2

"Horse Ride" (Pilgrim Riding Music)
Company

Scene 3

"I Have a Noble Cock"
R. Tetirick

"There's the Moon"
R. Tetirick, K. Neumann

"Darling, Let Me Teach You How to Kiss"
K. Walters

Scene 4

"It Depends on What You're At"
M. Sadusk, K. K. Preece, Company

Scene 5

"Beer Is Best"
W. Atkins, P. Pen, K. Dillehay, K. Walters, A. Ferrell

Scene 6

"Love Will Conquer All"
M. Sherwin, K. K. Preece, Company

"Canterbury Day" (reprise)
Company

ACT 2

Scene 1

"Come On and Marry Me Honey"
M. Sadusk, Company

"Where Are the Girls of Yesterday"
G. Maguire
Danced by K. Neumann, T. Witham, K. Dillehay.

Scene 2

"April Song"
Company

"If She Has Never Loved Before"
E. McCarroll, T. Witham

"I'll Give My Love a Ring"
R. Tetirick, T. Witham

"Pear Tree Sextet"
E. McCarroll, T. Witham, R. Tetirick, G. Maguire, K. K. Preece, V. Mizelle

Scene 3

"What Do Women Most Desire?"
R. Stoeckle, Ladies

"I Am All Ablaze"
R. Stoeckle
Danced by A. Ferrell, K. Dillehay.

Scene 4

"Love Will Conquer All" (reprise)
M. Sherwin, K. K. Preece, Company

1980.02   WEST SIDE STORY

A Revival of the Musical in Two Acts, 15 Scenes[23]. Book by Arthur Laurents. Based on a conception of Jerome Robbins. Music by Leonard Bernstein. Lyrics by Stephen Sondheim. Entire production directed and choreographed by Jerome Robbins. Book Co-directed by Gerald Freedman. Co-choreographer, Peter Gennaro. Choreography reproduced with the assistance of Tom Abbott, Lee Becker Theodore. Scenery designed by Oliver Smith. Costumes designed by Irene Sharaff. Lighting designed by Jean Rosenthal. Musical director, John DeMain. Orchestrations by Leonard Bernstein, with Sid Ramin, Irwin Kostal. Associate producers, Allan Tessler, Steven Jacobson, Stewart F. Lane. Executive producer, Ruth Mitchell. Produced by Gladys Rackmil, The John F. Kennedy Center and James M. Nederlander in association with Zev Bufman Opened 14 February 1980 at the Minskoff Theatre and closed 30 November 1980 after 341 performances.

CAST (in order of appearance): THE JETS: *Riff*, the Leader: JAMES J. MELLON. *Tony*, his friend: KEN MARSHALL. *Action*: Mark Bove. *A-Rab*: Todd Lester. *Baby John*: Brian Kaman. *Snowboy*: Cleve Asbury. *Big Deal*: Reed Jones. *Diesel*: Brent Barrett. *Gee-Tar*: G. Russell Weilandich. *Mouthpiece*: Stephen Bogardus. *Tiger*: Mark Fotopoulos. *Their Girls*: *Graziella*: Georganna Mills. *Velma*: Heather Lea Gerdes.

Minnie: Frankie Wade. *Clarice*: Charlene Gehm. *Pauline*: Nancy Louise Chismar. *Anybodys*: Missy Whitchurch.

THE SHARKS: *Bernardo*, the Leader: HECTOR JAIME MERCADO. *Maria*, his Sister: JOSSIE DE GUZMAN. *Anita*, his Girl: DEBBIE ALLEN. *Chino*, his Friend: Ray Contreras. *Pepe*: Michael Rivera. *Indio*: Darryl Tribble. *Luis*: Adrian Rosario. *Anxious*: Michael DeLorenzo *Nibbles*: Willie Rosario. *Juano*: Michael Franks. *Toro*: Mark Morales. *Moose*: Gary-Michael Davies. *Their Girls*: *Rosalia*: Yamil Borges. *Consuelo*: Nancy Ticotin. *Francisca*: Harolyn Blackwell. *Teresita*: Stephanie E. Williams. *Estella*: Marlene Danielle. *Marguerita*: Amy Lester.

THE ADULTS: *Doc*: SAMMY SMITH. *Schrank*: Arch Johnson. *Krupke*: John Bentley. *Gladhand*: Jake Turner.

1980.03   DIE FLEDERMAUS

A Revival of the Operetta in Three Acts[24]. Original Viennese libretto by Carl Haffner and Richard Genée. Lyrics by Richard Genée. (Based on the comedy "Le Réveillon" by Henri Meilhac and Ludovic Halévy.) English libretto by Ruth and Thomas Martin. Music by Johann Strauss. Production devised and directed by Gerald Freedman. Choreography by Thomas Andrew, restaged by Jessica Redel. Scenery designed by Lloyd Evans Costumes design by Theoni V. Aldredge. Lighting by Hans Sondheimer. Conducted by Imre Pallo. Chorus master, Lloyd Walser. Produced by the New York City Opera. Opened 23 February 1980 at the New York State Theatre and closed 1 March 1980 after 4 performances in repertory.

CAST (in order of appearance): *Alfred*, an itinerant tenor: Gerald Grahame. *Adele*, von Eisenstein's chambermaid: INGA NIELSEN. *Rosalinda von Eisenstein*: MARALIN NISKA. *Gabriel von Eisenstein*: CHARLES ROE. *Dr. Blind*, a lawyer: Norman Large. *Dr. Falke*, a close friend of Eisenstein: DOMINIC COSSA. *Frank*, the prison warden: RICHARD McKEE. *Sally*, Adele's sister: Puli Toro. *Ivan*, servant to Orlofsky: Gary J. Dietrich. *Prince Orlofsky*, a wealthy, bored Russian: DAVID RAE SMITH. *Frosch*, the jailer: Jack Harrold. *Solo Dancers*: Esperanza Galan, Taras Kalba. *Special Guest*: CYNTHIA GREGORY. (Miss Gregory's solo choreographed by Dennis Nahat.) *Ensemble*: New York City Opera Chorus.

1980.04   SILVERLAKE, or A Winter's Tale

A Play with Music (an Opera) in Two Acts, 11 Scenes[25]. Original German libretto ('Der Silbersee') by Georg Kaiser. Music by Kurt Weill. New book by Hugh Wheeler. New lyrics by Lys Symonette. Selections of Weill's incidental music integrated by Lys Symonette. Directed by Harold Prince. Conducted by Julius Rudel. Choreography by Larry Fuller. Scenery and costumes designed by Manuel Lutgenhorst. Lighting designed by Ken Billington. Musical preparation by Robert De Ceunynck, Scott Bergeson. Chorus master, Lloyd Walser. Sound designed by Jack Mann. Produced by the New York City Opera and Gert von Gontard. Opened 20 March 1980 at the New York State Theatre and closed 4 April 1980 after 6 performances in repertory.

CAST (in order of appearance): *Johann*: Harlan Foss. *Dietrich*: Robert McFarland. *Severin*: WILLIAM NEILL. *Heckler*: Edward Zimmerman. *Klaus*: James Clark. *Hans*: Norman Large. *Hunger*: Gary Chryst. *Salesgirls*: Penny Orloff, Jane Shaulis. *Handke*: David Rae Smith. *Officer Olim*: JOEL GREY. *City Inspector*: William Poplaski. *Lottery Agent*: JACK HARROLD. *Doctor*: Richard L. Porter. *Baron Laur*: JACK HARROLD. *Fennimore*: ELIZABETH HYNES. *Liveried Footman*: Gary J. Dietrich. *Frau von Luber*: ELAINE BONAZZI. *Chefs*: Michael Rubino, Rafael Romero. *Ensemble*: New York City Opera Chorus.

The action takes place in and around the mythical village of Silverlake.

Act 1, Scene 1: A Shantytown near Silverlake. *Scene 2*: The Grocery Store in the City. *Scene 3*: By a Country Bridge. *Scene 4*: The Police Station. *Scene 5*: The Hospital. *Scene 6*: Outside the Castle. *Scene 7*: The Castle Dining Room. *Scene 8*: The Great Hall.

Act 2, Scene 1: The Castle Cellars and Attic. *Scene 2*: Various Locations in the Castle. *Scene 3*: On the Road to Silverlake.

ACT 1

Scene 1

Duet of the Woodcutters
H. Foss, R. McFarland

Scene 2

Duet of the Salesgirls
P. Orloff, J. Shaulis

---

[23]Originally produced in New York 26 September 1957 at the Winter Garden for 732 performances. For Synopsis of Scenes and Musical Numbers, see original 1957 production.

[24]First English language production in New York 16 March 1885 at the Casino Theatre for 42 performances. First New York production of this adaptation 20 December 1950 at the Metropolitan Opera House. For Synopsis of Scenes and Musical Numbers, see May 1954 revival.

[25]Musical Numbers and Scenes do not appear in the program, but have been prepared from the recording and libretto.

Scene 4
  In the Police Station: Unseen Chorus
    Chorus
  Tango
    J. Grey, J. Harrold
  Unseen Chorus (reprise)
    Chorus
Scene 5
  Duet in the Hospital
    W. Neill, J. Grey
Scene 7
  Fennimore's Song
    E. Hynes
  The Ballad of Caesar's Death
    E. Bonazzi
  Severin's Revenge Aria
    W. Neill
  Severin-Fennimore Duet
    W. Neill, J. Grey
Scene 8
  Act 1 Finale
    Chorus
ACT 2
Scene 1
  Severin in Chains
    W. Neill
  First Laur and von Luber Duet
    E. Bonazzi, J. Harrold
Scene 2
  Friendship Duet
    J. Grey, W. Neill
  Second Laur and von Luber Duet
    E. Bonazzi, J. Harrold
Scene 3
  Act 2 Finale
    J. Grey, W. Neill, Chorus

1980.05   # REGGAE

A Musical Revelation in Two Acts, 11 Scenes. Concept and production by Michael Butler. Story by Kendrew Lascelles. Book by Melvin Van Peebles, Kendrew Lascelles and Stafford Harrison. Music and lyrics by Ras Karbi, Michael Kamen, Kendrew Lascelles, Stafford Harrison, Max Romeo, Randy Bishop, Jackie Mittoo. Directed by Glenda Dickerson. Additional direction by Gui Andrisano. Choreographer, Mike Malone. Musical director, Mike Malone. Cultural consultant dance, Rex Nettleford. Set design by Ed Burbridge. Costume design by Raoul Pene du Bois. Lighting design by Beverly Emmons. Sound design by Lou Gonzalez. Associate musical director, Michael Tschudin. Executive producer, Woodie King. Produced by Michael Butler and Eric Nazhad with David Cogan. Opened 27 March 1980 at the Biltmore Theatre and closed 13 April 1980 after 21 performances.

CAST (in order of appearance): *Anancy, The Spider*: Alvin McDuffie. *Faith*: SHERYL LEE RALPH. *Esau*: PHILIP MICHAEL THOMAS. *Rockets*: OBBA BABATUNDE. *Mrs. Brown*: Fran Salisbury. *Louise*: Louise Robinson. *Ras Joseph*: CALVIN LOCKHART. *Natty*: RAS KARBI. *Gorson*: Charles Wisnet. *Binghi Maytal*: Sam Harkness.

  Ensemble: Loretta Abbott, Breeha Clarke, Ralph Glenmore, Jeffrey Anderson Gunter, Thomas Pinnock, Louise Robinson, Kiki Shepard, Beth Shorter, Paul Cook'Tartt, Bruce Taylor, Ras-jawara Tesfa, Avon Testamark, Constance Thomas, Juanita Grace Tyler, Byron Utley, Lewis Whitlock.

The action takes place in one day in Jamaica.

Act 1, Scene 1: Jamaican Airport. *Scene 2*: A Mountain Village. *Scene 3*: A Deserted Greathouse on the Road to Kingston. *Scene 4*: Mrs. Brown's Yard. *Scene 5*: A Road through a Forest. *Scene 6*: A Kingston Rehearsal Hall.

Act 2, Scene 1: Ras Joseph's Yard. *Scene 2*: A Kingston Market. *Scene 3*: On the Edge of the Ghetto. *Scene 4*: The Ghetto. *Scene 5*: The Benefit Concert.

ACT I
  "Junkanoo"
    Masquerade Parade
    (*Music by* Michael Kamen.)
Scene 1
  "Jamaica Is Waiting"
    Ensemble
    (*Music and Lyrics by* Ras Karbi, Max Romeo, Michael Kamen.)

Scene 2
  "Rise Tafari"
    Ensemble
    (*Music and Lyrics by* Ras Karbi.)
Scene 3
  "Farmer"
    P. M. Thomas
    (*Music and Lyrics by* Max Romeo.)
  "Hey Man"
    S. L. Ralph, P. M. Thomas
    (*Music and Lyrics by* Ras Karbi and Michael Kamen.)
  "Mash Em Up"
    O. Babatunde, Rude Boys
    (*Music and Lyrics by* Kendrew Lascelles, Ras Karbi, Kackie Mittoo and Michael Kamen.)
Scene 4
  "Mrs. Brown"
    F. Salisbury, L. Robinson, Ensemble
    (*Music and Lyrics by* Stafford Harrison and Max Romeo.)
  "Everything That Touches You"
    F. Salisbury, Mr. Brown
    (*Music and Lyrics by* Michael Kamen.)
Scene 5
  "Mash Ethiopia"
    O. Babatunde, Rude Boys
    (*Music and Lyrics by* Kendrew Lascelles, Stafford Harrison, Ras Karbi, Jackie Mittoo, Michael Kamen.)
  "Star of Zion"
    R. Karbi
    (*Music and Lyrics by* Michael Kamen.)
Scene 6
  "Reggae Music Got Soul"
    S. Harkness, Ensemble
    (*Music and Lyrics by* Jackie Mittoo.)
  "Talkin' 'Bout Reggae"
    S. Harkness, Ensemble
    (*Music and Lyrics by* Kendrew Lascelles, Stafford Harrison, Michael Kamen, Jackie Mittoo.)
  "Everything That Touches You" (reprise)
    S. L. Ralph

ACT 2
Scene 1
  "Rise Up Jah-Jah Children"
    The Rastas, C. Lockhart
    (*Music and Lyrics by* Ras Karbi.)
  "No Sinners in Jah Yard"
    C. Lockhart, The Rastas
    (*Music and Lyrics by* Max Romeo and Ras Karbi.)
Scene 2
  "Banana, Banana, Banana"
    Ensemble
    (*Music and Lyrics by* Ras Karbi and Michael Kamen.)
  "Promised Land"
    R. Karbi
    (*Music and Lyrics by* Ras Karbi.)
Scene 3
  "Rasta Roll Call"
    C. Lockhart, The Rastas
    (*Music and Lyrics by* Ras Karbi.)
  "Ethiopian Pageant"
    Orchestra
    (*Music by* Michael Kamen.)
  "Rastafari"
    Ensemble
    (*Music and Lyrics by* Michael Kamen.)
  "Roots of the Tree"
    C. Lockhart, The Rastas
    (*Music and Lyrics by* Kendrew Lascelles and Ras Karbi.)
  "I and I"
    S. L. Ralph, P. M. Thomas
    (*Music and Lyrics by* Kandrew Lascelles and Max Romeo.)
Scene 4
  "Gotta Take a Chance"
    O. Babatunde, the Rude Boys
    (*Music and Lyrics by* Max Romeo and Michael Kamen.)

"Star of Zion" (reprise)
R. Karbi, S. L. Ralph
"Chase the Devil"
P. M. Thomas
(*Music and Lyrics by* Max Romeo.)
"Now I See It"
S. L. Ralph
(*Music and Lyrics by* Kendrew Lascelles and Randy Bishop.)
Scene 5
"Now I See It" (Reggae)(reprise)
S. L. Ralph, Ensemble
"Everything That Touches You" (reprise)
S. L. Ralph, P. M. Thomas
"Reggaae Music Got Soul" (reprise)
S. L. Ralph, P. M. Thomas, Ensemble
"Jamaica Is Waiting" (reprise)
S. L. Ralph, P. M. Thomas, Ensemble

1980.06 HAPPY NEW YEAR

A Musical in Two Acts. Book by Burt Shevelove. Based on the play "Holiday" by Philip Barry. Music and lyrics by Cole Porter, edited by Buster Davis. Directed by Burt Shevelove. Choreography by Donald Saddler. Musical direction and vocal arrangements by Buster Davis. Orchestrations by Luther Henderson. Additional orchestrations by Daniel Troob. Dance music arrangements by Charles H. Coleman. Production designed by Michael Eagan. Costumes designed by Pierre Balmain. Costumes supervised by John Falabella. Lighting designed by Ken Billington. Sound designed by Tom Morse. Assistant choreographer, Mercedes Ellington. Associate producer, Dorothy Cherry. Produced by Leonard Soloway, Allan Francis, Hale Matthews in association with Marble Arch Productions. Opened 27 April 1980 at the Morosco Theatre and closed 10 May 1980 after 17 performances.

CAST: *The Narrator*: JOHN McMARTIN. *Edward Seton*: WILLIAM ROERICK. *Edward Seton, Jr.* (Ned): RICHARD BEKINS. *Julia Seton*: KIMBERLY FARR. *Linda Seton*: LESLIE DENNISTON. *Johnny Case*: MICHAEL SCOTT.

The Staff: Frazer: Roger Hamilton. *Charles*: Morgan Ensminger. *Anderson*: Morgan Ensminger. *Patrick*: J. Thomas Smith. *George*: Tim Flavin. *Thompson*: Tim Flavin. *Steven*: Richard Christopher. *Victor*: Lara Teeter. *Rose*: Lauren Goler. *Nancy*: Lauren Goler. *Maude*: Mary Sue Finnerty. *Miss Madden*: Mary Sue Finnerty. *Mary*: Mary Sue Finnerty. *Annie*: Bobbie Nord. *Bridget*: Michele Marshall. *Miss Madden*: Mary Sue Finnerty.

Some of the Stork Club Set: Nancy: Lauren Goler. *Mary*: Mary Sue Finnerty. *Joan*: Michelle Marshall. *Gloria*: Bobbie Nord. *Thompson*: Tim Flavin. *Dixon*: lara Teeter. *Anderson*: Morgan Ensminger. *Harrison*: Richard Christopher.

The action takes place on the five floors in the Fifth Avenue townhouse of Edward Seton in New York City.

Act 1: December 1933.

Act 2: January 1934.

ACT 1[26]

"At Long Last Love"[27]
K. Farr, L. Denniston, R. Bekins
"Ridin' High"[28]
M. Scott, K. Farr
"Let's Be Buddies"[29]
M. Scott, L. Denniston
"Boy, Oh Boy"[30]
L. Denniston
"Easy to Love"[31]
The Young Men
"You Do Something to Me"[32]

M. Scott
"Red, Hot and Blue"[33]
L. Denniston, M. Scott, J. T. Smith, Stork Club Set
"Once Upon a Time"[34]
R. Bekins, L. Denniston
ACT 2
"Night and Day"[35]
J. McMartin, M. Scott
"Let's Make It a Night"[36]
L. Denniston, T. Flavin, L. Teeter
"Ours"[37]
K. Farr
"After You, Who?"[38]
M. Scott
"I Am Loved"[39]
K. Farr
"When Your Troubles Have Started"[40]
L. Denniston, R. Bekins
("Boy, Oh, Boy" reprise)
L. Denniston
("Once Upon a Time" reprise)
R. Bekins, L. Denniston

1980.07 BARNUM

A Musical in Two Acts. Book by Mark Bramble. Music by Cy Coleman. Lyrics by Michael Stewart. Directed and staged by Joe Layton. Scenery designed by David Mitchell. Costumes designed by Theoni V. Aldrdge. Lighting designed by Craig Miller. Sound design by Otts Munderloh. Orchestrations by Hershy Kay. Vocal arrangements by Cy Coleman, Jeremy Stone. Music director, Peter Howard. Circus training by The Big Apple Circus/The New York School for Circus Arts. Associate producers, Steven A. Greenberg, Michael Scharf. Produced by Judy Gordon, Cy Coleman, Maurice Rosenfield, Lois F. Rosenfield in association with Irvin Feld and Kenneth Feld. Opened 30 April 1980 at the St. James Theatre and closed 16 May 1982 after 854 performances.

CAST: *Phineas Taylor Barnum*: JIM DALE. *Chairy Barnum*: GLENN CLOSE. *Ringmaster*: WILLIAM C. WITTER. *Chester Lyman*: TERRENCE V. MANN. *Joice Heth*: TERRI WHITE. *Amos Scudder*: Kelly Walters. *Lady Plate Balancer*: Catherine Carr. *Lady Juggler*: Barbara Nadel. *Chief Bricklayer*: Edward T. Jacobs. *White-faced Clown*: Andy Teirstein. *Sherwood Stratton*: Dirk Lumbard. *Mrs. Sherwood Stratton*: Sophie Schwab. *Tom Thumb*: LEONARD JOHN CROFOOT. *Susan B. Anthony*: Karen Trott. *Julius Goldschmidt*: WILLIAM C. WITTER. *Jenny Lind*: MARIANNE TATUM. *One-Man Band*: Steven Michael. *Wilton*: Bruce Robertson. *Edgar Templeton*: Kelly Walters. *Humbert Morrissey*: TERRENCE V. MANN. *Lady Aerialist*: Robbi Morgan. *James A. Bailey*: WILLIAM C. WITTER. And Ringmasters, Clowns, Bricklayers, Acrobats, Tumblers, Gymnasts, Jugglers, The Bridgeport Pageant Choir, Bands of Every Size Shape and Description, the Mob in general, and Characters too numerous to mention.

Commencing one-half hour before the show: Bradley Steven-Fields. *With tours through The Exhibition of Wonders by* Catherine Carr. *And Musical Diversions in the theatre by* Andy Teirstein, Bruce Robertson. *Pianists:* Karen Gustafson, Peter Phillips.

The action takes place all over America and the major capitals of the world from 1835 to 1880.

ACT 1
"There Is a Sucker Born Ev'ry Minute"
J. Dale
"Thank God I'm Old"
T. White, Tambourine Players
"The Colors of My Life"
J. Dale, G. Close
"One Brick at a Time"
G. Close, J. Dale, Bricklayers
"Museum Song"
J. Dale

---

[26]Incidental Music: "Just One of Those Things," "It's De-Lovely," "Take Me Back to Manhattan," "Make It Another Old-Fashioned, Please," "They Couldn't Compare to You," "You've Got That Thing," "Every Time We Say Goodbye," "Let's Do It," "Where Have You Been?," Let's Fly Away," "Girls," "What Is This Thing Called Love?"
[27]Originally from YOU NEVER KNOW, 1938.
[28]Originally from RED, HOT AND BLUE, 1936.
[29]Originally from PANAMA HATTIE, 1940.
[30]Lyrics by Burt Shevelove.
[31]Originally from BORN TO DANCE, film, 1936.
[32]Originally from FIFTY MILLION FRENCHMEN, 1929.

[33]Originally from RED, HOT AND BLUE, 1936.
[34]From an unproduced musical of the same title.
[35]Originally from GAY DIVORCE, 1932.
[36]Intended for SILK STOCKINGS, 1955, unused.
[37]Originally from RED, HOT AND BLUE, 1936.
[38]Originally from YOU NEVER KNOW, 1938.
[39]Originally from OUT OF THIS WORLD, 1950.
[40]Dropped from tryout of RED, HOT AND BLUE, 1936.

"I Like Your Style"
  J. Dale, G. Close
"Bigger Isn't Better"
  L. J. Crofoot
"Love Makes Such Fools of Us All"
  M. Tatum
"Out There"
  J. Dale
ACT 2
"Come Follow the Band"
  The Potomac Marching Band and Washingtonians
"Black and White"
  G. Close, Choir, T. White, J. Dale, Citizens of Bridgeport
"The Colors of My Life" (reprise)
  J. Dale, G. Close
"The Prince of Humbug"
  J. Dale
"Join the Circus"
  W. C. Witter, All Circus Performers, J. Dale
("There Is a Sucker Born Ev'ry Minute" reprise)
  J. Dale

A DAY IN HOLLYWOOD/
1980.08   A NIGHT IN THE UKRAINE

A Musical Double Feature (Two one-act musicals). Book and lyrics by Dick Vosburgh . Music by Frank Lazarus. Directed and choreographed by Tommy Tune. Co-choreographed by Thommie Walsh. Scenery by Tony Walton. Lighting by Beverly Emmons. Costumes by Michel Stuart. Sound design by Otts Munderloh. Musical direction, vocal and dance arrangements by Wally Harper. Co-Producer, Roy Somlyo. Associate producer, Philip M. Getter. Produced by Alexander H. Cohen and Hildy Parks. Opened 1 May 1980 at the John Golden Theatre, moved 17 June 1980 to the Royale Theatre and closed 27 September 1981 after 588 performances.

ACT 1: A DAY IN HOLLYWOOD

A Musical Revue in One Act.

<u>CAST:</u> PRISCILLA LOPEZ, DAVID GARRISON, STEPHEN JAMES, PEGGY HEWETT, FRANK LAZARUS, KATE DRAPER, Niki Harris, Albert Stephenson.

MUSICAL NUMBERS
"Just Go to the Movies"
  (The Company)
  (*Music and Lyrics by* Jerry Herman.)
"Famous Feet"
  (D. Garrison, P. Lopez)
"I Love a Film Cliché"
  (F. Lazarus)
  (*Music by* Trevor Lyttleton. *Additional Music by* Frank Lazarus.)
"Nelson"
  (P. Hewett)
  (*Music and Lyrics by* Jerry Herman.)
"The Best in the World"
  (P. Lopez)
  (*Music and Lyrics by* Jerry Herman.)
"It All Comes Out of the Piano"
  (F. Lazarus)
  (*Lyrics by* Dick Vosburgh and Frank Lazarus.)
Richard A. Whiting Medley:
  (Company)
  "Ain't We Got Fun"
    (*Lyrics by* Gus Kahn and Raymond B. Egan.)
  "Too Marvelous for Words" (from *READY, WILLING AND ABLE* film)
    (*Lyrics by* Johnny Mercer.)
  "(The) Japanese Sandman"
    (*Lyrics by* Raymond B. Egan.)
  "On the Good Ship Lollipop" (from *BRIGHT EYES* film)
    (*Lyrics by* Sidney Clare.)
  "Double Trouble" (from *THE BIG BROADCAST* OF 1936 film)
    (*Music by* Ralph Rainger and Richard A. Whiting. *Lyrics by* Leo Robin.)
  "Louise" (from *INNOCENTS OF PARIS* film)
    (*Lyrics by* Leo Robin.)
  "Sleepy Time Gal" (later used in the film of the same name)
    (*Music by* Ange Lorenzo and Richard A. Whiting. *Lyrics by* Joseph R. Alden and Raymond B. Egan.)

"Beyond the Blue Horizon" (from *MONTE CARLO* film)
  (*Music by* Richard A. Whiting and W. Frank Harling. *Lyrics by* Leo Robin.)
"Thanks for the Memory"
  (S. James, K. Draper)
  (*Music by* Ralph Rainger. *Lyrics by* Leo Robin.)
"Another Memory"
  (S. James, K. Draper)
"Doin' the Production Code"
  (P. Lopez, D. Garrison, F. Lazarus, S. James, P. Hewett, K. Draper)
"A Night in the Ukraine"
  (Company)
ACT 2: A NIGHT IN THE UKRAINE

A Musical in One Act loosely based on "The Bear" by Anton Chekhov.

<u>CAST:</u> *Mrs. Pavlenko,* a rich widow: PEGGY HEWETT. *Carlo,* her Italian footman: FRANK LAZARUS. *Gino,* her gardener: PRISCILLA LOPEZ. *Serge B. Samovar,* a Moscow lawyer: DAVID GARRISON. *Nina,* Mrs. Pavlenko's daughter: KATE DRAPER. *Constantine,* a coachman: STEPHEN JAMES. *Masha,* a maid: Niki Harris. *Sascha,* a manservant: Albert Stephenson.

Scene: The Morning room of the Pavlenko residence in the Ukraine before the Revolution.

MUSICAL NUMBERS
"Samovar the Lawyer"
  (D. Garrison)
"Just Like That"
  (K. Draper, S. James)
"Again"
  (K. Draper, S. James)
"A Duel! A Duel!"
  (P. Hewett, D. Garrison)
"Natasha"
  (D. Garrison)
"A Night in the Ukraine"[41] (reprise)
  (Company)

A ROCKETTE SPECTACULAR
1980.09

A Musical Revue in One Act, 15 Scenes. Dialogue script writer, Stan Hart. Produced and directed by Robert F. Jani. Executive musical director, Don Pippin. Scenery designed by John William Keck. Rockettes choreographed/staged by Violet Holmes. Costumes designed by Frank Spencer. Miss Rogers choreographed/staged by Howard Parker. Lighting designed by Ken Billington. Conductor, Elman Anderson. Musical routing by Ronald Melrose. Orchestrations by Philip J. Lang, Michael Gibson, Elman Anderson, Arthur Harris, Danny Holgate. Produced by Radio City Music Hall Productions, Inc. Opened 2 May 1980 at the Radio City Music Hall and closed 22 June 1980 after 96 performances.

<u>CAST:</u> GINGER ROGERS, Gail Nelson, Jack Blackton.
Dancers: David Brownlee, John Cashman, Ron Crofoot, David Fredericks, Michael Lang, Bobby [Robert] Longbottom, Daryl Murphy, Scott Plank, Patrick Roddy, David Roman, Brent Saunders, David Scala, Lyn Schaal.
THE ROCKETTES: Pauline Achillas, Carol Beatty, Catherine Beatty, Dottie Belle, Karen Berman, Nina Berman, Susan Boron, Deniene Bruck, Barbara Ann Cittadino, Eileen Collins, Brie Daniels, Susanne Doris, Joyce Dwyer, Jacqueline Fancy, Prudence Gray, Carol Harbich, Ginny Hounsell, Cynthia Hughes, Holly Jones, Pam Kelleher, Dee Dee Knapp, Judy Little, Leslie Gryszko McCarthy, Barbara Moore, Ann Murphy, Lynn Newton, Pam Stacey Pasqualino, Joan Peer, Cindy Peiffer, Geraldine Presky, Sheila Rodriguez, Maryellen Scilla, Terry Spano, Lynn Sullivan, Sunny Summers, Susan Theobald, Carol Toman, Darlene Wendy, Rose Ann Woolsey, Phyllis Wujiko. *Organist:* Timothy Stella.

MUSICAL NUMBERS[42]
Scene 1
  The March
    The Rockettes
Scene 2
  In Their Dressing Room
    The Rockettes
Scene 3
  In the Star's Dressing Room
    G. Rogers, G. Nelson

---

[41]Added to program shortly after opening.
[42]Running order was revised during the run.

Scene 4

Rockette Rehearsal
The Rockettes, Their Choreographer

Scene 5

In the Star's Dressing Room
G. Rogers, G. Nelson

Scene 6

"My Big Moment"
G. Rogers, The Dancers
(*Music by* Don Pippin. *Lyrics by* Sammy Cahn.)

Scene 7

"Alike, Alike"
The Rockettes
(*Music by* Don Pippin. *Lyrics by* Sammy Cahn.)

Scene 8

Dance Dance Dance
G. Rogers, J. Blackton, The Dancers
("Come Dance With Me")
(J. Blackton, Dancers)
("I Won't Dance"/"Come Dance With Me" Medley)
G. Rogers, J. Blackton, The Dancers

Scene 9

In the Star's Dressing Room
G. Rogers, G. Nelson

Scene 10

Fifty Years of the Rockettes
The Rockettes

Scene 11

Stage-Struck
G. Nelson
("Star")
(G. Nelson)

Scene 12

Five Minutes 'Til Showtime
The Rockettes

Scene 13

Hoedown
The Rockettes, The Dancers

Scene 14

On Her Own
G. Rogers
(*Vocal Introduction for Miss Rogers*: J. Blackton. *Pianist*: William Roy.)
("My Big Moment" reprise)
("Embraceable You" from *GIRL CRAZY*)
("But Not For Me" from *GIRL CRAZY*)
(*Music by* George Gershwin. *Lyrics by* Ira Gershwin.)
("Forty-Second Street" from *FORTY-SECOND STREET* film and show)
("Shuffle Off to Buffalo" from *FORTY SECOND STREET* film and show)
(*Music by* Harry Warren. *Lyrics by* Al Dubin.)"
("Did You Ever See a Dream Walking?" from *SITTING PRETTY* film)
(*Music by* Harry Revel. *Lyrics by* Mack Gordon.)
("We're in the Money" [The Golddiggers' Song] from *GOLDDIGGERS OF 1933* film including pig-Latin chorus)
(*Music by* Harry Warren. *Lyrics by* Al Dubin.)
("Isn't This a Lovely Day?" from *TOP HAT* film)
(*Music and Lyrics by* Irving Berlin.)
("Let's Call the Whole Thing Off" from *SHALL WE DANCE* film)
("They All Laughed" from *SHALL WE DANCE* film)
("They Can't Take That Away from Me" from *SHALL WE DANCE* film)
(*Music by* George Gershwin. *Lyrics by* Ira Gershwin.)

Scene 15

Finale: "You're at the Music Hall"
Company
(*Music by* Don Pippin. *Lyrics by* Sammy Cahn.)

1980.10 # BLACK BROADWAY

A Musical Revue in Two Acts, 33 Scenes[43]. Orchestrations and musical arrangements by Dick Hyman. Musical director, Frank Owens. Production designer, Leo Gambacorta. Associate producer, John P. Fleming. Sound by Paul Blank—Omnisound. Produced by George Wein in association with Honi Coles, Robert Kimball and Bobby Short. Opened 4 May 1980 at Town Hall and closed 24 May 1980 after 24 performances.

CAST (in alphabetical order): JOHN W. BUBBLES, NELL CARTER, (CHARLES) HONI COLES, ADELAIDE HALL, GREGORY HINES, BOBBY SHORT, ELISABETH WELCH, EDITH WILSON; Charles "Cookie" Cook, Leslie "Bubba" Gaines, Mercedes Ellington, Carla Earle, Terri Griffin, Wyetta Turner.

ACT 1

Overture
(Medley from "*RUNNIN' WILD*": Ginger Brown," "Old-Fashioned Love," Charleston"
(*Music by* James P. Johnson.)

Scene 1

The Story of Black Broadway
B. Short or H. Coles
(*by* George Wein, Dick Hyman, Honi Coles, Robert Kimball.)

Scene 2

"Liza" (Entrance of Copasetics)
G. Hines or H. Coles, C. Cook, B. Gaines
(*Music by* Maceo Pinkard.)
"Blue Turning Gray Over You"
C. Cook
(*Music by* Thoams "Fats" Waller. *Lyrics by* Andy Razaf.)
"I Can't Believe That You're in Love With Me" (from *GAY PAREE*, 1925)
(*Music by* Jimmy McHugh. *Lyrics by* Clarence Gaskill.)
"Perdido"
(*Music by* Juan Tizol. *Lyrics by* Hans Lengsfelder and Ervin Drake.)
"Who"
B Gaines
"Christopher Columbus"
G. Hines or H. Coles, C. Cook, B. Gaines
(*Music by* Leon Berry. *Lyrics by* Andy Razaf.)

Scene 3

"Under the Bamboo Tree" (1902) (from *SALLY IN OUR ALLEY*)
(*Music and Lyrics by* Bob Cole, J. Rosamund Johnson, James Weldon Johnson.)
"(Oh Say,) Wouldn't It Be a Dream" (1905)
(*Music and Lyrics by* Earl Jones and Joe Jordan.)
"Broadway in Dahomey" (from *IN DAHOMEY*, 1903)
B. Short
(*Music and Lyrics by* Alex Rogers, Bert Williams, George Walker.)

Scene 4

"Black and Blue"[44] (from *HOT CHOCOLATES*, 1929)
(*Music by* Thomas "Fats" Waller, Harry Brooks. *Lyrics by* Andy Razaf.)
"He May Be Your Man But He Comes To See Me Sometimes"[45] (from *THE PLANTATION REVUE*, 1922)
E. Wilson
(*Music and Lyrics by* Lemuel Fowler.)

Scene 5

"The Unbeliever" (1920)
B. Short
(*Music and Lyrics by* Chris Smith, Frederick Bryan, Bert Williams.)

Scene 6

The Mayor of Harlem (Patter by Honi Coles)
"Doin' the New Low Down" (from Lew Leslie's *BLACKBIRDS OF 1928*)
G. Hines or H. Coles, C. Cook, B. Gaines, Girls
(*Music by* Jimmy McHugh. *Lyrics by* Dorothy Fields.)

Scene 7

"Creole Love Call"[46] (1928)
(*Music and Lyrics by* Duke Ellington.)

---

[43]First produced in New York 24 June 1979 by the Newport Jazz Festival at Avery Fisher Hall for 1 concert performance. "Program Subject to Change Owing to Magnitude of Production"—Lew Leslie.
[44]Artist introduced song.
[45]Artist introduced song.
[46]Artist introduced song.

"I Must Have That Man"[47] (from Lew Leslie's *BLACKBIRDS OF 1928*)
(*Music by* Jimmy McHugh. *Lyrics by* Dorothy Fields.)
"Diga, Digga Do"[48] (from Lew Leslie's *BLACKBIRDS OF 1928*)
(*Music by* Jimmy McHugh. *Lyrics by* Dorothy Fields.)
"I Can't Give You Anything But Love"[49] (from Lew Leslie's *BLACK-BIRDS OF 1928*)
A. Hall
(*Music by* Jimmy McHugh. *Lyrics by* Dorothy Fields.)

Scene 8
Harlem Medley:
B. Short
"She's Tall, She's Tan, She's Terrific" (from *COTTON CLUB PARADE 1937, 3rd ed.*)
(*Music by* J. Fred Coots. *Lyrics by* Benny Davis.)
"Posin'" (from *GRAND TERRACE REVUE*, 1937)
(*Music by* Saul Chaplin. *Lyrics by* Sammy Cahn.)
"Truckin'" (from *COTTON CLUB PARADE*, 26th ed., 1935)
(*Music by* Rube Bloom. *Lyrics by* Ted Koehler.)
"Breakfast in Harlem"
"Gimme a Pigfoot" (*Music and Lyrics by* Wesley Wilson.)

Scene 9
"Ill Wind" (from *COTTON CLUB PARADE*, 24th ed., 1934)
A. Hall
(*Music by* Harold Arlen. *Lyrics by* Ted Koehler.)

Scene 10
"Between the Devil and the Deep Blue Sea" (from *RHYTHMANIA*, Cotton Club, 1931)
A. Hall, B. Short
(*Music by* Harold Arlen. *Lyrics by* Ted Koehler.)

Scene 11
"As Love As I Live" (from *COTTON CLUB PARADE*, 24th ed., 1934)
B. Short
(*Music by* Harold Arlen. *Lyrics by* Ted Koehler.)

Scene 12
"The Brown-Skin Gal in the Calico Gown" (from *JUMP FOR JOY*, 1941)
B. Short
(*Music by* Duke Ellington. *Lyrics by* Paul Francis Webster.)

Scene 13
"Jump For Joy" (from *JUMP FOR JOY*, 1941)
B. Short, Company
(*Music by* Duke Ellington. *Lyrics by* Paul Francis Webster.)

ACT 2
Scene 1
"Cotton Club Stomp" (from *COTTON CLUB REVUE*, 14th ed., 1929)
Frank Owens and Orchestra
(*Music by* Duke Ellington, Johnny Hodges, Harry Carney.)

Scene 2
"Tan Manhattan" (from *TAN MANHATTAN*, 1940)
G. Hines
Music by Eubie Blake. *Lyrics by* Andy Razaf.)

Scene 3
"Charleston Rag"
G. Hines
(*Music by* Eubie Blake.)

Scene 4
Entrance of Elisabeth Welch to "When Lights Are Low" (1936)
(*Music and Lyrics by* Spencer Williams and Benny Carter.)
"Love for Sale" (from *THE NEW YORKERS*, 1930)
(*Music and Lyrics by* Cole Porter.)
"Solomon"[50] (from *NYMPH ERRANT*, 1933, London)
E. Welch
(*Music and Lyrics by* Cole Porter.)

Scene 5
"Charleston"[51] (from *RUNNIN' WILD*, 1923)
E. Welch
(*Music and Lyrics by* Cecil Mack and James P. Johnson.)

Scene 6
Entrance of Nell Carter to Opening Bars of:
"Ain't Misbehavin'" (from *HOT CHOCOLATES*, 1929)
(*Music by* Thomas "Fats" Waller, Harry Brooks. *Lyrics by* Andy Razaf.)
"I've Got a Feeling I'm Falling" (1929)(from *APPLAUSE*, film)
N. Carter
(*Music by* Thomas "Fats" Waller, Harry Link. *Lyrics by* Billy Rose.)

Scene 7
"Legalize My Name" (from *ST. LOUIS WOMAN*, 1946)
N. Carter
(*Music by* Harold Arlen. *Lyrics by* Johnny Mercer.)

Scene 8
A Tribute to Florence Mills: (Scenes 8 & 9)
"I'm a Little Blackbird Looking for a Bluebird" (from *DIXIE TO BROADWAY*, 1924)
E. Wilson
(*Music by* Grant Clarke, Roy Turk. *Lyrics by* George W. Meyer, Arthur Johnston.)

Scene 9
"Silver Rose" (from Lew Leslie's *BLACKBIRDS OF 1926*, London)
E. Welch
(*Music and Lyrics by* George W. Meyer.)

Scene 10
A Tribute to Ethel Waters: (Scenes 10-16)
"Heat Wave" (from *AS THOUSANDS CHEER*, 1933)
N. Carter
(*Music and Lyrics by* Irving Berlin.)

Scene 11
"You're Lucky to Me" (from Lew Leslie's *BLACKBIRDS OF 1930*)
E. Wilson
(*Music by* Eubie Blake. *Lyrics by* Andy Razaf.)

Scene 12
"Suppertime" (from *AS THOUSANDS CHEER*, 1933)
A. Hall
(*Music and Lyrics by* Irving Berlin.)

Scene 13
"Honey in the Honeycomb" (from *CABIN IN THE SKY*, 1940)
N. Carter
(*Music by* Vernon Duke. *Lyrics by* John Latouche.)

Scene 14
"Stormy Weather" (from *COTTON CLUB PARADE*, 22nd ed., 1933)
E. Welch
(*Music by* Harold Arlen. *Lyrics by* Ted Koehler.)

Scene 15
"Taking a Chance on Love" (from *CABIN IN THE SKY*, 1940)
A. Hall, E. Wilson, E. Welch, N. Carter, G. Hines or H. Coles
(*Music by* Vernon Duke. *Lyrics by* John Latouche and Ted Fetter.)

Scene 16
"Dinah" (from *THE PLANTATION REVUE*, 1925)
G. Hines or B. Short
(*Music by* Harry Akst. *Lyrics by* Sam Lewis, Joe Young.)

Scene 17
"Sweet Georgia Brown" (1925)
G. Hines, Ensemble
(*Music and Lyrics by* Ben Bernie, Maceo Pinkard, Kenneth Casey.)

Scene 18
"It Ain't Necessarily So"[52] (from *PORGY AND BESS*, 1935)
"There's a Boat That's Leavin' Soon for New York"[53] (from *PORGY AND BESS*, 1935)
J. W. Bubbles
(*Music by* George Gershwin. *Lyrics by* Ira Gershwin.)

Scene 19
"Memories of You" (from Lew Leslie's *BLACKBIRDS OF 1930*)
J. W. Bubbles, Entire Company
(*Music by* Eubie Blake. *Lyrics by* Andy Razaf.)

Scene 20
"Jump for Joy" (reprise)
Entire Company

[47]Artist introduced song.
[48]Artist introduced song.
[49]Artist introduced song.
[50]Artist introduced song.
[51]Artist introduced song.

[52]Artist introduced song.
[53]Artist introduced song.

1980.11   MUSICAL CHAIRS

A Musical in Two Acts. Book by Barry Berg, Ken Donnelly, Tom Savage. Based on an original story concept by Larry P. Pontillo. Music and lyrics by Tom Savage. Entire production directed and choreographed by Rudy Tronto. Scenery designed by Ernest Allen Smith. Lighting designed by Peggy Clark. Costumes designed by Michael J. Cesario. Director-assistant choreographer, Susan Stroman. Musical direction, Barry H. Gordon. (Music) arrangements and orchestrations by Ada Janik, Dick Leib. Produced by Lesley Savage and Bert Stratford. Opened 14 May 1980 at the Rialto Theatre and closed 25 May 1980 after 15 performances.

CAST (in order of appearance): *Joe Preston:* RON HOLGATE. *Matty:* Ellen McCabe. *Stage Manager:* Douglas Walker. *Sally's Boyfriend:* Scott Ellis. *Millie:* Enid Blaymore. *Roberta:* GRACE KEAGY. *Brad:* Randall Easterbrook. *Miranda:* Leslie-Ann Wolfe. *Lillian:* PATTI KARR. *Harold:* BRANDON MAGGART. *Gary:* JESS RICHARDS. *Janet:* JOY FRANZ. *Brown Suit:* Edward Earle. *Blue Suit:* Tom Breslin. *Tuxedo:* Rick Emery. *Valerie Brooks:* LEE MEREDITH.

The action takes place at the present time in an Off-Broadway theatre on opening night in a section of the audience.

ACT 1
"Tonight's the Night"
  Company
"My Time"
  R. Holgate
"Who's Who"
  Company
"If I Could Be Beautiful"
  L. Wolfe, Boys
"What I Could Have Done Tonight"
  B. Maggart, J. Franz
"There You Are"
  R. Emery
"Sally"
  S. Ellis, Company
"Other People"
  J. Franz
"My Time" (reprise)
  R. Holgate
"Hit the Ladies"
  P. Karr, Ladies

ACT 2
"Musical Chairs"
  R. Emery, T. Breslin, E. Earle
"Suddenly Love"
  J. Richards
"Better Than Broadway"
  E. Blaymore, G. Keagy
"Every Time the Music Starts"
  R. Easterbrook, Company
"There You Are" (reprise)
  R. Emery, R. Holgate, L. Meredith
"My Time" (reprise)
  R. Holgate

1980.12   BLACKSTONE!

A Magnificent Musical Magic Show in Two Acts. Directed and choreographed by Kevin Carlisle. Scenery designed by Peter Wolf. Costumes designed by Winn Morton. Lighting designed by Martin Aronstein. Magic production designer, Jack Hart. Musical supervisor-conductor, Milton Setzer. Orchestrations by Richard Bellis. Magic direction, Charles Reynolds. Production supervisor, Jackie Schrock. Illusion supervisor, Bill Smith. Produced by Columbia Artists Theatricals Corporation and Blackstone Magik Enterprises, Inc. Opened 19 May 1980 at the Majestic Theatre and closed 17 August 1980 after 104 performances.

CAST: HARRY BLACKSTONE, GAY BLACKSTONE, BECKY GARRETT, Elaine Barnes, Lynn Castles, Karen Curlee, Ann McLean, Robbin McDowell, Mary

McNamara, Reenie Moore, Richard Ruth, Bill Smith, Nikki Summerford, Jim Thompson, John Traub, Michal Weir.

ACT 1
The Vanishing Birdcage
A Salute to Our Heritage
The Wizard
Cassadaga Propaganda
Mysteries of the Orient
Hare
The Incredible Buzzsaw

ACT 2
The Enchanted Garden
Roses for Your Lady
The Wizard Returns
The Extraordinary Floating Lightbulb
Moorish Fantasies
So You Want to Be a Magician
Circus of Mysteries

1980.13   BILLY BISHOP GOES TO WAR

A Play with Music in Two Acts[54]. Written, composed and directed by John Gray, in collaboration with Eric Peterson. (Suggested by the book "Winged Warfare" by Billy Bishop.) Scenery by David Gropman. Lighting by Jennifer Tipton. Sound design by Robert Kerzman. Associate producers, Stephen Graham and Ventures West Capital, Inc. Co-produced by Vancouver East Cultural Centre (Christopher Wootten, Executive Director). First presented in the United States by Arena Stage, Washington, D.C. Produced by Mike Nichols and Lewis Allen. Opened 29 May 1980 at the Morosco Theatre and closed 7 June 1980 after 12 performances. Transferred Off-Broadway 17 June 1980 to the Theatre de Lys and closed 24 August 1980 after 78 additional performances. Total, including Off-Broadway, 90 performances.

CAST: *Billy Bishop, Upperclassman, Adjutant Perrault, Officer, Sir Hugh Cecil, Lady St. Helier, Cedric, Doctor, General John Higgins, Tommy, Lovely Helene, Albert Ball, Walter Bourne, General Hugh M. Trenchard, Servant, King George V:* ERIC PETERSON. *Narrator, Pianist:* JOHN GRAY.

ACT 1
"(We're) Off to Fight the Hun"
  E. Peterson, J. Gray
"Canada at War"
  E. Peterson, J. Gray
"The Good Ship Caledonia"
"Buried Alive in the Mind"
"December Nights"
  E. Peterson, J. Gray
"The RE-7"
"Nobody Shoots No-One in Canada"
  E. Peterson, J. Gray
"Lady St. Helier"
  E. Peterson
"My First Solo Flight"
  E. Peterson
"In the Sky"
  E. Peterson, J. Gray

ACT 2
"As Calm as the Ocean"
"Friends Ain't S'posed to Die"
  E. Peterson, J. Gray
"General Sir Hugh M. Trenchard"
"The Empire Soirée"
  E. Peterson, J. Gray
"(We're) Off to Fight the Hun" (reprise)
  E. Peterson, J. Gray
"In the Sky" (reprise)
  E. Peterson, J. Gray

[54]No songs were listed in the program. Above list prepared from production typescript and recording.

1980–1981 SEASON

Tammy Grimes (foreground) in 42ND STREET
Martha Swope/TimePix

1980–1981 SEASON

YOUR ARMS TOO SHORT TO BOX WITH GOD

1980.14

A Revival of the Soaring Celebration in Songs and Dance (Gospel Musical) in Two Acts[1]. Conceived from the Book of St. Matthew by Vinnette Carroll. Music and lyrics by Alex Bradford. Additional music and lyrics by Micki Grant. Directed by Vinnette Carroll. Choreography by Talley Beatty. Sets and costumes by William Schroder. Lighting by Richard Winkler. Sound by Abe Jacob. Musical direction by Michael Powell. Orchestrations and dance music by H. B. Barnum. First produced at the Urban Arts Theatre; Producing director, Anita MacShane. Production supervisors, Jerry R. Moore, Richard Martini. Artistic production coordinator, Ralph Farrington. Produced by Tom Mallow in association with James Janek. Opened 2 June 1980 at the Ambassador Theatre, moved 16 September 1980 to the Belasco Theatre, and closed 12 October 1980 after 149 performances.

CAST (in alphabetical order): Adrian Bailey, Julius Richard Brown[2], Cleavant Derricks, Sheila Ellis, Ralph Farrington, Jamil K. Garland, Elijah Gill, William-Keebler Hardy, Jr., Jennifer-Yvette Holliday, Linda James, Garry Q. Lewis, Linda Morton, Jai Oscar St. John, Kiki Shepard, Leslie Hardesty Sisson, Ray Stephens, Quincella Swyningan, Faruma S. Williams, Marilynn Winbush, Linda Young. *Swing Dancers*: Adrian Bailey, Linda James.

ACT 1

"Beatitudes"
   Company
   (*Music and Lyrics by* Micki Grant.)
"We're Gonna Have a Good Time"
   J. R. Brown/C. Derricks, Company
   (*Music and Lyrics by* Micki Grant.)
"There's a Stranger in Town"
   S. Ellis, Company
   (*Music and Lyrics by* Alex Bradford.)
"Do You Know Jesus?"/"He's a Wonder"
   J. K. Garland, Company
   (*Music and Lyrics by* Alex Bradford.)
"Just a Little Bit of Jesus Goes a Long Way"
   J. Holliday
   (*Music and Lyrics by* Alex Bradford.)
"We Are the Priests and Elders"
   J. R. Brown, C. Derricks, W. Hardy, Jr., J. O. St. John
   (*Music and Lyrics by* Micki Grant.)
"Something Is Wrong in Jerusalem"
   S. Ellis, Q. Swyningan
   (*Music and Lyrics by* Micki Grant.)
"It Was Alone"/"I Know I Have to Leave Here"
   J. Holliday, Company
   (*Music and Lyrics by* Alex Bradford.)
"Be Careful Whom You Kiss"
   S. Ellis, Q. Swyningan
   (*Music and Lyrics by* Alex Bradford.)
"Trial"
   Company
   (*Music and Lyrics by* Micki Grant.)
"It's Too Late"
   Company
   (*Music and Lyrics by* Micki Grant.)
"Judas Dance" (*Music by* H. B. Barnum.)
   R. Farrington
"Your Arms Too Short to Box With God"
   J. Holliday, Company
   (*Music and Lyrics by* Alex Bradford.)
"Give Us Barabbas"
   Company
   (*Music and Lyrics by* Alex Bradford.)

"See How They Done My Lord"
   S. Ellis, Company
   (*Music and Lyrics by* Alex Bradford.)
"Come on Down"
   L. E. Young, J. K. Garland, J. O. St. John
   (*Music and Lyrics by* Alex Bradford.)
"Can't No Grave Hold My Body Down"
   R. Stephens, Company
   (*Music and Lyrics by* Alex Bradford.)
"Beatitudes" (reprise)
   C. Derricks, Company

ACT 2

"Didn't I Tell You"
   J. R. Brown/C. Derricks
   (*Music and Lyrics by* Alex Bradford.)
"When the Power Comes"
   Company
   (*Music and Lyrics by* Alex Bradford.)
"Everybody Has His Own Way"
   J. R. Brown/C. Derricks, R. Stephens
   (*Music and Lyrics by* Alex Bradford.)
"Down By the Riverside"
   C. Derricks, Company
"I Love You So Much Jesus"
   J. Y. Holliday
   (*Music and Lyrics by* Alex Bradford.)
"The Band"
   Company

1980.15 IT'S SO NICE TO BE CIVILIZED

A Musical in Two Acts[3]. Book, music and lyrics by Micki Grant. Directed by Frank Corsaro. Choreography by Mabel Robinson. Musical director, Coleridge-Taylor Perkinson. Scenery and visuals, Charles E. Hoefler. Lighting by Charles E. Hoefler, Ralph Madero. Costume design by Ruth Morley. Orchestrations by Danny Holgate, Neal Tate. Choral arrangements by Tasha Thomas. Dance arrangements by Carl Maultsby. Sound design by Palmer Shannon. Associate producer, Danny Holgate. Produced by Jay Julien, Arnon Milchan, Larry Kalish. Opened 3 June 1980 at the Martin Beck Theatre and closed 8 June 1980 after 8 performances.

CAST (in order of appearance): *Sharkey*: OBBA BABATUNDE. *Mollie*: VIVIAN REED. *Larry*: Larry Stewart. *Sissy*: Vickie D. Chappell. *LuAnne*: Carol Lynn Maillard. *Grandma*: MABEL KING. *Mr. Anderson*: Stephen Pender. *Blade*: Dan Strayhorn. *Rev. Williams*: Eugene Edwards. *Mother*: Deborah Burrell. *Dancing Bag Lady*: Juanita Grace Tyler.
   Ensemble: Daria Atanian, Paul Binotto, Sharon K. Brooks, P. L. Brown, Jean Cheek, Vondie Curtis-Hall, Paul Harman, Esther Marrow, Wellington Perkins, Dwayne Phelps, Juanita Grace Tyler. *Dance Alternates*: Allison Rene Manson, Steiv Semien.

The action takes place on Sweetbitter Street over a weekend in late summer.

ACT 1

"Step into My World"
   Ensemble
"Keep Your Eye on the Red"
   O. Babatunde
"Wake-up, Sun"
   O. Babatunde, V. Reed
"Subway Rider"
   Ensemble
"God Help Us"
   L. Stewart, C. L. Maillard
"Who's Going to Teach the Children?"
   M. King
"Out on the Street"
   Ensemble
"Welcome, Mr. Anderson"
   D. Strayhorn, Gang
"Why Can't Me and You?"
   S. Pender

---

[1]Originally produced 22 December 1976 at the Lyceum Theatre for 429 performances.
[2]The roles performed by Julius Richard Brown and Cleavant Derricks are alternated.

[3]First produced in New York Off-Off Broadway 22 February 1979 at AMAS Repertory for 12 performances. Directed by Jeffrey Dunn.

"Why Can't Me and You?" (reprise)
   V. D. Chappelle, S. Pender
"Out on the Street" (reprise)
   Ensemble
"When I Rise"
   E. Edwards
"World Keeps Going Round"
   V. Reed, Ensemble
ACT 2
"Antiquity"
   Ensemble
"I've Still Got My Bite"
   M. King
"Look at Us"
   L. Stewart, C. L. Maillard
"Keep Your Eye on the Red"
   O. Babatunde
"The American Dream"
   S. Pender
"Bright Lights"
   V. Reed
"Step into My World" (reprise)
   O. Babatunde, V. Reed
"It's So Nice to be Civilized"
   S. Pender, V. D. Chappell, The Hawks
"Like a Lady"
   V. Reed
"Pass a Little Love Around"
   Ensemble

1980.16 ## THE MUSIC MAN

A Revival of the Musical Comedy in Two Acts, 17 Scenes[4]. Book, music and lyrics by Meredith Willson. Book written in collaboration with Franklin Lacey. Directed and choreographed by Michael Kidd. Sets designed by Peter Wolf. Costumes designed by Stanley Simmons. Lighting designed by Marcia Madeira. Sound designed by Barry Rimler. Orchestrations by Don Walker. Musical and vocal direction by Milton Rosenstock. Produced by James M. Nederlander, Raymond Lussa, Fred Walker. Opened 5 June 1980 at the New York City Center and closed 22 June 1980 after 21 performances.

CAST (in order of appearance): *Travelling Salesmen*: Dennis Holland, Lee Winston, Michael J. Rockne, Randy Morgan, Tom Garrett, Ralph Braun, Andy Hostettler, Larry Cahn. *Charlie Cowell*: JAY STUART. *Conductor*: Peter Wandel. *Harold Hill*: DICK VAN DYKE. *Mayor Shinn*: IGGIE WOLFINGTON. *Ewart Dunlop*: Larry Cahn. *Oliver Hix*: Randy Morgan. *Jacey Squires*: Lee Winston. *Olin Britt*: Ralph Braun. *Marcellus Washburn*: RICHARD WARREN PUGH. *Tommy Djilas*: CALVIN McRAE. *Marian Paroo*: MEG BUSSERT. *Mrs. Paroo*: CAROL ARTHUR. *Amaryllis*: Lara Jill Miller. *Winthrop Paroo*: CHRISTIAN SLATER. *Eulalie MacKecknie Shinn*: JEN JONES. *Zaneeta Shinn*: CHRISTINA SAFFRAN. *Alma Hix*: Marcia Brushingham. *Maud Dunlop*: Mary Gaebler. *Ethel Toffelmier*: P. J. Nelson. *Mrs. Squires*: Mary Roche. *Constable Locke*: Dennis Holland.

River City Townspeople: Victoria Ally, Carol Ann Basch, Dennis Batutis, David Beckett, Mark A. Esposito, Tom Garrett, Liza Gennaro, Dennis Holland, Andy Hostettler, Tony Jaeger, Wendy Kimball, Ara Marx, Darleigh Miller, Gail Pennngton, Rosemary Rado, Michael J. Rockne, Coley Sohn, Peter Wandel.

1980.17 ## FEARLESS FRANK

A Musical in Two Acts. Book and lyrics by Andrew Davies. (Inspired by "My Life and Loves" by Frank Harris.) Music by Dave Brown. Directed by Robert Gillespie. Musical staging by Michael Vernon. Scenery by Martin Tilley. Costumes supervised by Carrie F. Robbins. Lighting by Ruth Roberts. Orchestrations by Michael Reed. Musical direction and additional arrangements by Michael Rose. Associate producers, Norma Adler, Michael A. Riddell. Originally produced at the King's Head Theatre Club in London. Produced by David Black and Robert Fabian in association with

Oscar Lewenstein and Theodore P. Donahue, Jr. Opened 15 June 1980 at the Princess Theatre and closed 25 June 1980 after 12 performances.

CAST: *Frank Harris*: NIALL TOIBIN. *French Waiter, Headmaster, Kendrick, Lord Folkestone, Whistler*: Alex Wipf. *Secretary, Schoolgirl, Jessie, Lilly*: Valerie Mahaffey. *Nellie, Kate, Laura*: Kristen Meadows. *Tobin, Whitehouse, Smith, Chapman, Oscar Wilde*: Steve Burney. *Nursemaid, Actress, Bootblack, Topsy, Newsboy, Enid*: Ann Hodapp. *Cowboy, Carlyle, Mr. Clapton, deMaupassant, Dowson*: OLIVER PIERRE. *Mrs. Mayhew, Mrs. Clapton, Mrs. Clayton*: Evelyn Baron.

And School boys, New Yorkers, Hotel Guests, Cowboys, Cows, Indians, A Crowd, Newsboys, Strollers, Opera Chorus, Harris Detractors, Harris Praisers: The Company.

The action takes place in 1921 in Nice and in the memory of Frank Harris.

ACT 1
"The Man Who Made His Life into a Work of Art"
   N. Toibin, Girls
"The Examination Song, or Get Me on That Boat"
   A. Wipf, S. Burney, N. Toibin
"Come Help Yourself to America, or Frank in the Melting Pot"
   Company
"Halted at the Very Gates of Paradise"—A Song of Frustration
   N. Toibin, Girls
"Dandy Night Clerk, or How to Get On in the Hotel Trade"
   Company
"Riding the Range"—A Song of the Old West
   Company
"Oh Catch Me, Mr. Harris, Cause I'm Falling for You!"
   K. Meadows, A. Hodapp, V. Mahaffey, E. Baron, N. Toibin
"The Greatest Man of All"
   N. Toibin, Company
ACT 2
"My Poor Wee Lassie"—A Scottish Lament
   O. Pierre
"Evening News"—A Song of Success
   Company
"Le Maitre de la Conte, or Maupassant Tells All"
   O. Pierre
"Oh, Mr. Harris, You're a Naughty Man!"
   N. Toibin, E. Baron
"Free Speech, Free Thought, Free Love"
   A. Hodapp, N. Toibin, Company
"Mr. Harris, It's All Over Now!"
   N. Toibin, Company
"Fearless Frank"
   The Company

1980.18 ## MANHATTAN SHOWBOAT

A Musical Revue in One Act, 10 Scenes. Conceived and produced by Robert F. Jani. Original music and lyrics by Donald Pippin, Sammy Cahn and Nan Mason. Executive musical director, Donald Pippin. Production executive, John J. Moore. Choreographed by Linda Lemac, Howard Parker, Debra Pigliavento, Frank Wagner. Principals Staged by Frank Wagner. Rockettes choreographed by Violet Holmes. Dialogue by Stan Hart. Special material, Nan Mason. Musical routining, Stan Lebowsky. Scenery designed by Robert Guerra. Costumes designed by Frank Spencer, Michael Casey. Lighting designed by David F. Segal. Orchestrations by Elman Anderson, Michael Gibson, Arthur Harris, Philip J. Lang. Produced by Radio City Musical Hall Productions, Inc. Opened 30 June 1980 at the Radio City Music Hall and closed 15 October 1980 after 191 performances.

CAST: *Belle*: KAREN ANDERS. *Edgar*: LOUIS CARRY. *Hiram Boggs*: THOMAS RUISINGER. *Tree*: STEVEN WILLIFORD. *Daisy*: Herself (the baby elephant). *P. T. Barnum*: Tony Moore. *Buffalo Bill*: Buddy Crutchfield. *Annie Oakley*: Luu Ann Csaszar. *Annie*: Laurie Stephenson.

THE ROCKETTES: Pauline Achillas, Carol Beatty, Catherine Beatty, Dottie Belle, Karen Berman, Susan Boron, Deniene Bruck, Barbara Ann Cittadino, Eileen Collins, Brie Daniels, Susan DiGilio, Susanne Doris, Jacqueline Fancy, Alexis Ficks, Mary Ann Fiordalisi, Prudence Gray, Carol Harbich, Ginny Hounsell, Cynthia Hughes, Pam Kelleher, Dee Dee Knapp, Judy Little, Leslie Gryszko McCarthy, Barbara Moore, Ann Murphy, Lynn Newton, Pam Stacey Pasqualino, Joan Peer, Cindy Peiffer, Geraldine Presky, Sheila Rodriguez, Maryellen Scilla, Terry Spano, Lynn Sullivan, Sunny Summers, Susan Theobald, Carol Toman, Darlene Wendy, Rose Ann Woolsey, Phyllis Wujko.

THE NEW YORKERS: Pam Cecil, Joanna Coggins, Lou Ann Csaszar, Buddy Crutchfield, Alvin Davis, Rick Emery, Dale Furry, Bobby Grayson, Phil Hall, Nina

---

[4]Originally produced in New York 19 December 1957 at the Majestic Theatre for 1375 performances. For Synopsis of Scenes and Musical Numbers, see original 1957 production. Original Act 1, Scene 2 was divided in two, yielding an extra scene.

Hennessey, Stephen Hope, Deirdre Kane, Dale Kristien, Andrea Lyman, James Mahady, Tony Moore, Sylvia Nolan, Denise O'Neill, Susan Powers, Cleo Price, Jeffory Robinson, Laurie Stephenson, Bob Teterick, Kay Walbye, Scott Whiteleather, Bob Wrenn.

Dancers: Dennis Angulo, Phillip Bond, Ron Chisholm, Angie Daye, Danute Debney, John Michael Doyle, Glenn Ferrugiari, Doug Fogel, Neisha Folkes, Linda Kay Hamil, Kristie Hannum, Edward Henkel, Ogalyn Jolly, Elisa Lenhart, Kim Leslie, Gail Lohla, Cary Lowenstein, Margaret McGee, Terry McLemore, Ron Meier, Lorena Palacios, James Parker, Debra Pigliavento, Michele Pigliavento, Sam Singhaus, Cassie Stein, Alan Stuart, Karen Toto, Barry Weiss.

Organists: Timothy Stella, David Messineo.

SCENES AND MUSICAL NUMBERS

Scene 1

  The Opening
    K. Anders, Her Crew

Scene 2

  The Circus from our Circus Deck

Scene 3

  Nightclubs and Floorshows from our Music Deck

Scene 4

  Vaudeville from our Old Troupers Deck
    (Bridge Lyrics for Medley by Nan Mason.)

Scene 5

  The Sing-A-Long from our Projection Booth Crow's Nest

Scene 6

  The Musical Theatre from our Broadway Deck

Scene 7

  The Great Revues from our Show Deck

Scene 8

  The Rockettes from our Music Hall Deck

Scene 9

  Belle's Turn from the Captain's Brig

Scene 10

  The Grand Finale: The Ship's Company on Parade
  Vocal Solos:
  "A Pretty Girl Is Like a Melody" (from *ZIEGFELD FOLLIES OF 1919*)
    B. Crutchfield
    (*Music and Lyrics by* Irving Berlin.)
  "Love Is a Simple Thing" (from *NEW FACES OF 1952*)
    C. Price
    (*Music by* Arthur Siegel. *Lyrics by* June Carroll.)
  "He Takes Me Off His Income Tax" (from *NEW FACES OF 1952*)
    C. Price
    (*Music by* Arthur Siegel. *Lyrics by* June Carroll.)
  Original Songs included:
  "Manhattan Showboat"
    (*Music by* Donald Pippin. *Lyrics by* Sammy Cahn.)
  "There Are No Girls Quite Like Show Girls"
    (*Music by* Donald Pippin. *Lyrics by* Sammy Cahn.)
  "Right Here"
    (*Music by* Donald Pippin. *Lyrics by* Nan Mason.)

1980.19   CAMELOT

A Revival of the Musical in Two Acts, Two Prologues and 14 Scenes[5]. Book and lyrics by Alan Jay Lerner. Based on the novel "The Once and Future King" by T. H. White. Music by Frederick Loewe. Original New York production staged by Moss Hart. Directed by Frank Dunlop. Choreography by Buddy Schwab. Sets and costumes by Desmond Heeley. Lighting design by Thomas Skelton. Musical director, Franz Allers. Orchestra conductor, James Martin. Orchestrations by Robert Russell Bennett and Philip J. Lang. Production supervisor, Jerry Adler. Artistic consultant, Stone Widney. A Dome/Cutler-Herman Production. Produced by Mike Merrick and Don Gregory by arrangement with James M. Nederlander. Opened 8 July 1980 at the New York State Theatre and closed 23 August 1980 after 56 performances.

CAST (in order of appearance): *Arthur:* RICHARD BURTON. *Sir Sagramore:* Andy McAvin. *Merlyn:* JAMES VALENTINE. *Guenevere:* CHRISTINE EBERSOLE. *Sir Dinadan:* WILLIAM PARRY. *Nimue:* Jeanne Caryl. *Lancelot:* RICHARD MUENZ. *Mordred:* ROBERT FOX. *Dap:* Robert Molnar. *Friar:* JAMES VALENTINE. *Lady Anne:* Nora Brennan. *Lady Sybil:* Deborah Magid. *Sir Lionel:* William James. *King Pellinore:* PAXTON WHITEHEAD. *Horrid:* Bob. *Sir Lionel's Squire:* David Gaines. *Sir Sagramore's Squire:* Steve Soborn. *Sir Dinadan's Squire:* Herndon Lackey. *Knights of the Investiture:* Ken Henley, Gary Jaketic, Jack Sharkey, Ronald Bennett Stratton. *Tom:* THOR FIELDS.

Knights, Lords, Ladies of the Court: Nora Brennan, Jeanne Caryl, Melanie Clements, Stephanie Conlow, Van Craig, John Deyle, Debra Dickinson, Richard Dodd, Cecil Fulfer, Davis Gaines, Lisa Ann Grant, Ken Henley, John Herrera, Gary Jaketic, William James, Kelby Kirk, Herndon Lackey, Deborah Magid, Andy McAvin, Laura McCarthy, Robert Molnar, Steve Osborn, Patrice Pickering, Janelle Price, Nancy Rieth, Patrick Rogers, Deborah Roshe, D. Paul Shannon, Jack Starkey, Ronald Bennett Stratton, Sally Ann Swarm, Sally Williams. *Alternates:* Lynn Keeton, Richard Maxon.

Prologue: A Battlefield near Joyous Gard—A long time ago.

Act 1, Scene 1: A Hilltop near Camelot—Eight years earlier. *Scene 2:* Arthur's Study—Five years later. *Scene 3:* A Roadside near Camelot—A few months later. *Scene 4:* A Park near the Castle—Immediately following. *Scene 5:* A Terrace of the Castle—Two months later. *Scene 6:* The Jousting Fields—The next day. *Scene 7:* The Terrace—Early evening of that day. *Scene 8:* The Great Hall—Immediately following.

Prologue: The Castle Garden—A few years later. *Scene 1:* A Cloister on the castle grounds—Immediately following. *Scene 2:* The Terrace—A few weeks later. *Scene 3:* The Forest—The following day. *Scene 4:* The Queen's Bedchamber—Immediately following. *Scene 5:* Camelot—A month later. *Scene 6:* A Battlefield near Joyous Gard—A few weeks later.

ACT 1

  Prologue
  "Guenevere"
    Ensemble

Scene 1

  "I Wonder What the King is Doing Tonight?"
    R. Burton
  "The Simple Joys of Maidenhood"
    C. Ebersole
  "Camelot"
    R. Burton, C. Ebersole
  "Follow Me"
    J. Caryl

Scene 2

  "Camelot" (reprise)
    R. Burton, C. Ebersole

Scene 3

  "C'est Moi"
    R. Muenz

Scene 4

  "The Lusty Month of May"
    C. Ebersole, Ensemble

Scene 5

  "How to Handle a Woman"
    R. Burton

Scene 6

  "The Jousts"
    R. Burton, C. Ebersole, Ensemble

Scene 7

  "Before I Gaze at You Again"
    C. Ebersole

ACT 2

Scene 1

  "If Ever I Would Leave You"
    R. Muenz
  "The Seven Deadly Virtues"
    R. Fox

Scene 2

  "What Do the Simple Folk Do?"
    C. Ebersole, R. Burton

[5]Originally produced in New York 3 December 1960 at the Majestic Theatre for 873 performances. This revival reduced the number of scenes from 20 to 14. The character of Morgan LeFey has been dropped. Musical Numbers dropped: "Then You May Take Me to the Fair," "The Persuasion." "Guenevere" moved from Act 2, Scene 7 to the beginning of Act 1.

"Fie on Goodness!"
　R. Fox, Knights
Scene 4
"I Loved You Once in Silence"
　C. Ebersole
Scene 5
"Guenevere" (reprise)
　Ensemble
Scene 8
"Camelot" (reprise)
　R. Burton

1980.20　FORTY-SECOND STREET

The Song and Dance Fable of Broadway (A Musical) in Two Acts, 16 Scenes. Lead ins and crossovers (Book) by Michael Stewart and Mark Bramble. Based on the novel of the same name by Bradford Ropes (and the Warner Brothers film adapted from it by Rian James and James Seymour.) Music by Harry Warren. Lyrics by Al Dubin. (Other lyrics by Johnny Mercer and Mort Dixon.) Direction and dances by Gower Champion. Scenery design by Robin Wagner. Costumes designed by Theoni V. Aldredge. Lighting designed by Tharon Musser. Musical direction and vocal arrangements by John Lesko. Orchestrations by Philip J. Lang. Dance arrangements by Donald Johnston. Sound by Richard Fitzgerald. Dance assistants, Karin Baker, Randy Skinner. Produced by David Merrick. Opened 25 August 1980 at the Winter Garden, moved 30 March 1981 to the Majestic Theatre, moved 7 April 1987 to the St. James Theatre and closed 8 January 1989 after 3486 performances.

CAST (in order of appearance): Andy Lee: DANNY CARROLL. Oscar: Robert Colston. Mac: Stan Page. Annie: KAREN PRUNCZIK. Maggie Jones: CAROLE COOK. Bert Barry: JOSEPH BOVA. Billy Lawlor: LEE ROY REAMS. Peggy Sawyer: WANDA RICHERT. Lorraine: Ginny King. Phyllis: Jeri Kansas. Julian Marsh: JERRY ORBACH. Dorothy Brock: TAMMY GRIMES. Abner Dillon: DON CRABTREE. Pat Denning: JAMES CONGDON. Thugs: Stan Page, Ron Schwinn. Doctor: Stan Page.

Ensemble: Carole Banninger, Steve Belin, Robin Black, Joel Blum, Mary Cadorette, Ronny DeVito, Denise DiRenzo, Mark Dovey, Rob Draper, Brandt Edwards, Jon Engstrom, Sharon Ferrol, Cathy Greco, Dawn Herbert, Christine Jacobsen, Jeri Kansas, Ginny King, Terri Ann Kundrat, Shan Martin, Beth McVey, Maureen Mellon, Sandra Menhart, Bill Nabel, Tony Parise, Don Percassi, Jean Preece, Vicki Regan, Lars Rosager, Linda Sabatelli, Nikki Sahagen, Ron Schwinn, Yveline Semeria, Alison Sherve, Robin Stephens, David Storey, Karen Tamburrelli.

The action takes place during 1933 in New York City and Philadelphia.

Act 1, Scene 1: 42nd Street Theatre, New York City. Scene 2: Gypsy Tea Kettle. Scene 3: On Stage. Scene 4: Dorothy Brock's Dressing Room. Scene 5: On Stage. Scene 6: Arch Street Theatre, Philadelphia. Scene 7: Regency Club and Dorothy Brock's Suite at Hotel Stratford. Scene 8; Opening Night, Arch Street Theatre, Philadelphia.

Act 2, Scene 1: Outside Dorothy Brock's Dressing Room, ten minutes later. Scene 2: Dressing Rooms at the Arch Street Theatre. Scene 3: Stage of the Arch Street Theatre. Scene 4: Broad Street Station, Philadelphia. Scene 5: 42nd Street Theater, New York City. Scene 6: Peggy's Dressing Room. Scene 7: Opening Night of "Pretty Lady," 42nd Street Theatre, New York City. Scene 8: Backstage.

ACT 1
Scene 1
"Audition" (42nd Street instrumental)
　D. Carroll, Ensemble
"Young and Healthy"
　L. R. Reams, W. Richert
"Shadow Waltz" (from GOLDDIGGERS OF 1933 film)
　C. Cook, T. Grimes, Girls
"Shadow Waltz" (reprise)
　T. Grimes
Scene 2
"Go into Your Dance" (from GO INTO YOUR DANCE film, 1935)
　C. Cook, W. Richert, K. Prunczik, D. Carroll, G. King, J. Kansas
Scene 3
"You're Getting to Be a Habit With Me"
　T. Grimes, L. R. Reams, W. Richert, Ensemble
Scene 5
"Getting Out of Town" (Excerpt from "Gotta Go to Town" from THE LAUGH PARADE, film)
　J. Congdon, J. Bova, C. Cook, K. Prunczik, T. Grimes, Ensemble
　(Lyrics by Mort Dixon.)

Scene 6
"Dames" (from DAMES film, 1934)
　L. R. Reams, Ensemble
Scene 7
"I Know Now" (from THE SINGING MARINE film, 1937)
　T. Grimes
Scene 8
"I Know Now" (reprise)
　L. R. Reams, Girls
"We're in the Money" (from GOLDDIGGERS OF 1933 film)
　K. Prunczik, W. Richert, G. King, J. Kansas, L. R. Reams, Ensemble
Act One Finale
　T. Grimes, W. Richert, Full Company

ACT 2
Scene 2
"Sunny Side to Every Situation" (from HARD TO GET film, 1938)
　K. Prunczik, Ensemble
　(Lyrics by Johnny Mercer.)
Scene 4
"Lullaby of Broadway" (from GOLDDIGGERS OF 1935 film)
　J. Orbach, Full Company
Scene 6
"About a Quarter to Nine" (from GO INTO YOUR DANCE film, 1935)
　T. Grimes, W. Richert
Scene 7
"Pretty Lady" Overture
　Orchestra
"Shuffle Off to Buffalo"
　K. Prunczik, J. Bova, C. Cook, Girls
"Forty-Second Street"
　W. Richert, L. R. Reams, Ensemble
Scene 8
"Forty Second Street" (reprise)
　J. Orbach

1980.21　THE STUDENT PRINCE

A Revival of the Operetta in Three Acts, a Prologue and 4 Scenes[6]. Music by Sigmund Romberg. Book and lyrics by Dorothy Donnelly. (Based on the play "Old Heidelberg" by Rudolf Bleichmann, adapted from "Alt-Heidelberg" by Wilhelm Meyer-Förster.) Book adaptation by Hugh Wheeler. Conducted by Andrew Meltzer. Directed by Jack Hofsis. Assistant stage Director, Christian Smith. Scenery designed by David Jenkins Costumes designed by Patton Campbell. Lighting designed by Gilbert V. Hemsley, Jr. Choreography by Donald Saddler. Chorus master, Lloyd Walser. Produced by the New York City Opera. Opened 29 August 1980 at the New York State Theatre and closed 7 September 1980 after 13 performances.

CAST (in order of their appearance): Lackeys: Edward Zimmerman, Louis Perry, Harris Davis, Mervin Crook. Dr. Engel, the Prince's Tutor: DOMINIC COSSA. Count von Mark: DAVID RAE SMITH. Secretaries: Sven Leaf, Barry Carl. Prince Karl Franz: JACQUE TRUSSEL. Lutz, valet to the Prince: JAMES BILLINGS. Gretchen, Maid at the Inn: MARTHA THIGPEN. Ruder: Dan Sullivan. Nicholas: Robert LaFosse. Toni, a waiter: Jack Harrold. Hubert: Harlan Foss. Detlef, a student leader: John Lankston. von Asterberg, another student leader: Thomas Jamerson. Lucas, another student leader: Ralph Bassett. Freshman: Louis Perry. Kathie, niece of Ruder: LEIGH MUNRO. Girls: Madeleine Mines, Jean Rawn, Barbara Wright. Students: Dominick Farone, Louis Perry, Merle Schmidt, Spencer Smith. Grand Duchess Anastasia: MURIEL COSTA-GREENSPON. Princess Margaret, fiancée of Prince Karl Franz: KATHRYN BOULEYN. Captain Tarnitz: JOSEPH EVANS. Countess Leydon, lady-in-waiting to the Princess: Jane Shaulis. Huzzars: Richard Nelson, Herbert Hunsberger, Robert Brubaker, Merle Schmidt. Friends of the Huzzars: Madeleine Mines, Jean Rawn, Barbara Wright, Maria Donaldi.
Ensemble: New York City Opera Chorus.

The action takes place in Karlsberg, Germany in the Golden Years.

Prologue: Garden of the Palace at Karlsberg.

---

[6]First produced in New York 2 December 1924 as THE STUDENT PRINCE IN HEIDELBERG at the Jolson Theatre for 608 peformances. This production was made possible by a generous and deeply appreciated gift from The Fan Fox and Leslie R. Samuels Foundation, Inc.

Act 1: Garden of the Inn of the Three Golden Apples in Heidelberg.

Act 2: Prince Karl Franz's rooms at the Inn. Four months later.

Act 3, Scene 1: The Royal Palace at Karlsberg. *Scene 2*: Garden of the Inn of the Three Golden Apples. The next day.

PROLOGUE

"By Our Bearing So Sedate"
  Lackeys
"Golden Days"
  D. R. Smith, J. Trussel

ACT 1

"Garlands Bright With Glowing Flowers"
  M. Thigpen, D. Sullivan, Girls
"To the Inn We're Marching" (Students Marching Song)
  J. Lankston, R. Bassett, T. Jamerson, Students
"Drink, Drink, Drink" (Drinking Song)
  J. Lankston, R. Bassett, T. Jamerson, Students
"Come Boys, Let's All Be Gay, Boys"
  L. Munro, J. Lankston, R. Bassett, T. Jamerson, Students
"Drink, Drink, Drink"/"To the Inn We're Marching" (reprise)
  J. Lankston, R. Bassett, T. Jamerson, Students
"Heidelberg, Beloved Vision of My Heart"
  D. Cossa, J. Trussel, L. Munro, D. Sullivan, M. Thigpen, Girls
"Gaudeamus Igitur"
  Students
"Golden Days" (reprise)
  D. Cossa
"Deep in My Heart, Dear"
  L. Munro, J. Trussel
"Come Sir, Will You Join Our Noble Saxon Corps"
  Students
"Overhead the Moon Is Beaming" (Serenade)
  J. Trussel, Students
"When the Spring Wakens Everything" (Carnival of Springtime)
  Company

ACT 2

"Farmer Jacob Lay Asnoring"
  Students
"Student Life"
  Company
"Golden Days" (reprise)
  J. Trussel, D. Cossa
"Thoughts Will Come to Me"
  J. Trussel, D. Cossa
Finale
  L. Munro, J. Trussel

ACT 3

Scene 1
  Ballet
    Orchestra
  "Just We Two"
    K. Bouleyn, J. Evans, Men
  "What Memories, Sweet Rose"
    Company
Scene 2
  "Let Us Sing a Song"
    Students
  "If He Knew"
    L. Munro, K. Bouleyn
  Finale
    Company

DIE FLEDERMAUS

1980.22

A Revival of the Operetta in Three Acts[7]. Original libretto by Carl Haffner and Richard Genée. Lyrics by Richard Genée. Based on the comedy "Le

Réveillon" by Henri Meilhac and Ludovic Halévy. English libretto by Ruth and Thomas Martin. Production devised and directed by Gerald Freedman. Choreography by Thomas Andrew. Music by Johann Strauss. Scenery designed by Lloyd Evans Costumes design by Theoni V. Aldredge. Lighting by Hans Sondheimer. Conducted by Imre Pallo. Chorus master, Lloyd Walser. Produced by the New York City Opera. Opened 12 September 1980 at the New York State Theatre and closed 20 September 1980 after 4 performances in repertory.

CAST (in order of appearance): *Alfred,* an itinerant tenor: Henry Price. *Adele,* von Eisenstein's chambermaid: INGA NIELSEN. *Rosalinda von Eisenstein:* MARALIN NISKA. *Gabriel von Eisenstein:* ALAN TITUS. *Dr. Blind,* a lawyer: Norman Large. *Dr. Falke,* a close friend of Eisenstein: RICHARD FREDERICKS. *Frank,* the prison warden: HARLAN FOSS. *Sally,* Adele's sister: Puli Toro. *Ivan,* servant to Orlofsky: Gary J. Dietrich. *Prince Orlofsky,* a wealthy, bored Russian: JAMES BILLINGS. *Frosch,* the jailer: Jack Harrold. *Solo Dancers:* Esperanza Galan, Taras Kalba. *Special Guest:* CYNTHIA GREGORY. (Miss Gregory's solo choreographed by Dennis Nahat.)
  Ensemble: New York City Opera Chorus.

CHARLIE AND ALGERNON

1980.23

A Very Special Musical in One Act[8]. Book and lyrics by David Rogers. Based on the novel "Flowers for Algernon" by Daniel Keyes. Music by Charles Strouse. Directed by Louis W. Scheeder. Musical director, Conductor, Liza Redfield. Choreography by Virginia Freeman. Orchestrations by Philip J. Lang. Scenery by Kate Edmunds. Costumes by Jess Goldstein. Lighting by Hugh Lester. Sound by William H. Clements. Produced for the Kennedy Center and the Folger Theatre Group by Michael Sheehan and Louis W. Scheeder. Produced by The Kennedy Center, Isobel Robins Konecky, the Fisher Theater Foundation and the Folger Theatre Group. Opened 14 September 1980 at the Helen Hayes Theatre and closed 28 September 1980 after 17 performances.

CAST (in order of appearance): *Charlie:* P. J. BENJAMIN. *Alice Kinnian:* SANDY FAISON. *Dr. Strauss:* EDWARD EARLE. *Dr. Nemur:* ROBERT SEVRA. *Mrs. Donner:* Nancy Franklin. *Lita:* Loida Santos. *Frank:* Patrick Jude. *Charlie's Mother:* Julienne Marie. *Little Charlie:* Matthew Duda. *Charlie's Father:* Michael Vita.

The action takes place at the present time in Brooklyn and Manhattan.

MUSICAL NUMBERS

"Have I the Right"
  S. Faison, R. Sevra, E. Earle
"I Got a Friend"
  P. J. Benjamin
"I Got a Friend" (reprise)
  P. J. Benjamin, S. Faison
"Some Bright Morning"
  R. Sevra, P. J. Benjamin, E. Earle, S. Faison
"Jelly Donuts and Chocolate Cake"
  N. Franklin, L. Santos, P. Jude
"Hey Look at Me"
  P. J. Benjamin, S. Faison
"Reading"
  P. J. Benjamin, S. Faison
"No Surprises"
  S. Faison
"Midnight Riding"
  P. Jude, L. Santos
"Dream Safe With Me"
  J. Marie
"Not Another Day Like This"
  J. Marie, M. Vita
"Somebody New"
  N. Franklin, P. J. Benjamin
"I Can't Tell You"
  P. J. Benjamin
"Now"
  P. J. Benjamin, S. Faison
"Charlie and Algernon"
  P. J. Benjamin

---

[7]First English language production in New York 16 March 1885 at the Casino Theatre for 42 performances. First New York production of this adaptation 20 December 1950 at the Metropolitan Opera House. For Synopsis of Scenes and Musical Numbers, see May 1954 revival.

---

[8]Previously produced in London under the title *FLOWERS FOR ALGERNON.*

"The Maze"
    P. J. Benjamin
"Whatever Time There Is"
    S. Faison, P. J. Benjamin
"Everything Was Perfect"
    E. Earle, R. Sevra
"Charlie"
    P. J. Benjamin
"I Really Loved You"
    P. J. Benjamin
"Whatever Time There Is" (reprise)
    S. Faison

INSIDEOUTANDALLAROUND

1980.24   with Shelley Berman

A One Man Show in Two Acts. Production supervisor, Kitzi Becker. Production advisor, Richard G. Miller. Produced by Arthur Shafman International, Ltd. Opened 29 September 1980 at the Bijou Theatre and closed 25 October 1980 after 24 performances.

CAST: SHELLEY BERMAN (Comedy monologues).

SILVERLAKE,

1980.25   or A Winter's Tale

A Revival of the Play with Music (Opera) in Two Acts, 11 Scenes[9]. Original German libretto (Der Silbersee) by Georg Kaiser. Music by Kurt Weill. New book by Hugh Wheeler. New lyrics by Lys Symonette. Selections of Weill's incidental music integrated by Lys Symonette. Directed by Harold Prince. Conducted by Julius Rudel. Choreography by Larry Fuller. Scenery and costumes designed by Manuel Lutgenhorst. Lighting designed by Ken Billington. Musical preparation by Robert De Ceunynck, Scott Bergeson. Chorus master, Lloyd Walser. Sound designed by Jack Mann. Produced by the New York City Opera and Gert von Gontard. Opened 11 October 1980 at the New York State Theatre and closed 19 October 1980 after 4 performances in repertory.

CAST (in order of appearance): *Johann:* Harlan Foss. *Dietrich:* Robert McFarland. *Severin:* WILLIAM NEILL. *Heckler:* Edward Zimmerman. *Klaus:* James Clark. *Hans:* Norman Large. *Hunger:* Gary Chryst. *Salesgirls:* Penny Orloff, Jane Shaulis. *Handke:* David Rae Smith. *Officer Olim:* JOHN LANKSTON. *City Inspector:* William Poplaski. *Lottery Agent:* JACK HARROLD. *Doctor:* Richard Nelson. *Baron Laur:* JACK HARROLD. *Fennimore:* KATHLEEN HEGIERSKI. *Liveried Footman:* Gary Dietrich. *Frau von Luber:* MURIEL COSTA-GREENSPON. *Chefs:* Michael Rubino, Rafael Romero. *Ensemble:* New York City Opera Chorus.

BRIGADOON

1980.26

A Revival of the Musical Play in Two Acts, 12 Scenes[10]. Book and lyrics by Alan Jay Lerner. Music by Frederick Loewe. Choreography and musical staging by Agnes de Mille, recreated by James Jamieson. Directed by Vivian Matalon. Scenery designed by Michael J. Hotopp and Paul dePass. Costumes designed by Stanley Simmons. Lighting designed by Thomas Skelton. Musical direction and vocal arrangements by Wally Harper. Orchestrations by Mack Schlefer, Bill Brohn. Sound by T. Richard Fitzgerald. A Wolf Trap Production (Craig Hankenson, Executive producer.) Produced by Zev Bufman and The Shubert Organization. Opened 16 October 1980 at the Majestic Theatre and closed 8 February 1981 after 133 performances.

CAST (in order of appearance): *Tommy Albright:* MARTIN VIDNOVIC. *Jeff Douglas:* MARK ZIMMERMAN. *Angus MacGuffie:* Kenneth Kantor. *Archie Beaton:* Casper Roos. *Sandy Dean:* Michael Cone. *Maggie Anderson:* MARINA EGLEVSKY.

---

[9]Originally produced in New York 20 March 1980 at the New York State Theatre for 6 performances. For Synopsis of Scenes and Musical Numbers, see March 1980 production.

[10]Originally produced in New York 13 March 1947 at the Ziegfeld Theatre for 581 performances. The original production was in Two Acts, 11 Scenes and a Prologue; for this production the book was revised into Two Acts, 12 Scenes, and scene descriptions, the intermission placement and song order have been slightly altered. "My Mother's Wedding Day" was dropped.

Harry Beaton: JOHN CURRY. *Meg Brockie:* ELAINE HAUSMAN *Andrew MacLaren:* Jack Dabdoub. *Fiona MacLaren:* MEG BUSSERT. *Jean MacLaren:* Mollie Smith. *Charlie Dalrymple:* STEPHEN LEHEW. *Mr. Lundie:* Frank Hamilton. *Jane Ashton:* Betsy Craig.

Townsfolk of Brigadoon: Singers: Michael Cone, Betsy Craig, Larry French, Linda Hohenfeld, Michael Hayward-Jones, Joseph Kolinski, Diane Pennington, Cheryl Russell, Linda Wonneberger. *Dancers:* Bill Badolato, Cherie Bower, Amy Danis, Tom Fowler, John Giffin, Mickey Gunnersen, Jennifer Henson, David Hughes, Phil LaDuca, Elena Malfitano, Susie McCarter, Jerry Mitchell, Eric Nesbitt, Holly Reeve, Dale Robbins, Harry Williams. *Swing Dancers/Singers:* Randal Harris, Suzi Winson. *Bagpiper:* Larry Cole.

Act 1, Scene 1: A Hillside in Scotland. *Scene 2:* MacConnachy Square (in the village of Brigadoon). *Scene 3:* A Hillside in Brigadoon. *Scene 4:* The Brockie Shed. *Scene 5:* Outside the MacLaren House.

Act 2, Scene 1: Outside Mr. Lundie's House *Scene 2:* The Glen. *Scene 3:* The Forest. *Scene 4:* Outside the MacLaren House. *Scene 5:* A Hillside in Scotland. *Scene 6:* A Cocktail Bar in New York City. *Scene 7:* A Hillside in Scotland.

ACT 1
Scene 1
"Once in the Highlands"
    Ensemble
"Brigadoon"
    Ensemble
Scene 2
"Down on MacConnachy Square"
    M. Cone, E. Hausman, Townsfolk
"Waitin' for My Dearie"
    M. Bussert, Girls
"I'll Go Home With Bonnie Jean"
    S. Lehew, Men
        Danced by J. Curry, M. Eglevsky Townsfolk.
Scene 3
"The Heather on the Hill"
    M. Vidnovic, M. Bussert
"Rain Exorcism"
    Townsfolk
Scene 4
"The Love of My Life"
    E. Hausman
Scene 5
"Jeannie's Packing Up"
    Danced by Girls
"Come to Me, Bend to Me"
    S. Lehew
        Danced by M. Smith, Girls.
"Almost Like Being in Love"
    M. Vidnovic, M. Bussert
ACT 2
Scene 2
"Wedding Dance"
    M. Smith, S. Lehew, Townsfolk
"Sword Dance"
    J. Mitchell, Sword Dancers, Dancers
Scene 3
"The Chase"
    J. Curry, Men of Brigadoon
"There But For You Go I"
    M. Vidnovic, M. Bussert
Scene 4
"Steps Stately"
    Danced by Townsfolk
"Drunken Reel"
    Danced by Townsfolk
"Funeral Dance"
    Danced by M. Eglevsky
Scene 5
"From This Day On"
    M. Vidnovic, M. Bussert
"Brigadoon" (reprise)
    Ensemble

Scene 6

"Come to Me, Bend to Me" (reprise)
M. Bussert

"The Heather on the Hill" (reprise)
M. Bussert

Scene 7

"From This Day On" (reprise)
M. Vidnovic

"Brigadoon" (reprise)
Ensemble

1980.27 TINTYPES

A Musical (Revue) in Two Acts, 13 Scenes[11]. Conceived by Mary Kyte, Mel Marvin and Gary Pearle. Directed by Gary Pearle. Musical staging by Mary Kyte. Settings by Tom Lynch. Costumes by Jess Goldstein. Lighting by Paul Gallo. Sound design by Jack Mann. Musical and vocal arrangements by Mel Marvin. Orchestrations and vocal arrangements by John McKinney. Production coordinator, Brent Peek. An American National Theatre and Academy Production. Originally produced by the Arena Stage, Washington, D.C. Produced by Richmond Crinkley and Royal Pardon Productions, Ivan Bloch, Larry J. Silva, Eve Skina in association with Joan F. Tobin. Opened 23 October 1980 at the John Golden Theatre and closed 11 January 1981 after 93 performances. Total, including Off-Broadway, 230 performances.

CAST (in alphabetical order): Carolyn Mignini, Lynne Thigpen, Trey Wilson, Mary Catherine Wright, Jerry Zaks. At the Piano: Mel Marvin.

Act 1, Scene 1: Arrivals. *Scene 2:* Ingenuity and Inventions. *Scene 3:* TR (Teddy Roosevelt). *Scene 4:* Wheels. *Scene 5:* The Factory. *Scene 6:* Anna Held. *Scene 7:* Outside Looking In. *Scene 8:* Fitting In.

Act 2, Scene 1: Panama. *Scene 2;* The Ladies. *Scene 3:* Rich and Poor. *Scene 4:* Vaudeville. *Scene 5:* Finale.

ACT 1
Scene 1

"Ragtime Nightingale"
(*Music and Lyrics by* Joseph F. Lamb.)(1915)

"The Yankee Doodle Boy" (from *LITTLE JOHNNY JONES,* 1904)
(*Music and Lyrics by* George M. Cohan.)

"Ta-Ra-Ra Boom-De-Ay!"
(*Music and Lyrics by* Henry J. Sayers.)(1891)

"I Don't Care"
(*Music by* Harry O. Sutton. *Lyrics by* Jean Lenox.)(1905)

"Come Take a Trip in My Airship"
(*Music and Lyrics by* George Evans and Ren Shields.)(1904)

"Kentucky Babe"
(*Music and Lyrics by* Richard H. Buck and Adam Geibel.)(1896)

"A Hot Time in the Old Town Tonight"
(*Music by* Theodore H. Metz. *Lyrics by* Joe Hayden.)(1896)

"Stars and Stripes Forever"
(*Music by* John Philip Sousa.)(1897)

Scene 2

"Electricity"
(*Music by* Karl Hoschna. *Lyrics by* Harry B. Smith.)(1905)

Scene 3

"El Capitan" (from *EL CAPITAN,* 1896)
(*Music by* John Philip Sousa.)

Scene 4

"Pastime Rag"
(*Music by* Artie Matthews.)(1920)

"Meet Me in St. Louis"
(*Music by* Kerry Mills. *Lyrics by* Andrew B. Sterling.)(1904)

"Solace"
(*Music by* Scott Joplin.)

"Waltz Me Around Again Willie" (from *HIS HONOR, THE MAYOR,* 1906)
(*Music by* Ren Shields. *Lyrics by* Will D. Cobb.)

"Wabash Cannonball" (traditional)

"In My Merry Oldsmobile"
(*Music by* Gus Edwards. *Lyrics by* Vincent P. Bryan.)(1905)

Scene 5

"Wayfaring Stranger" (traditional)

"Sometimes I Feel Like a Motherless Child" (traditional)

"Aye, Lye, Lyu Lye" (traditional)

"I'll Take You Home Again Kathleen"
(*Music and Lyrics by* Thomas P. Westendorf.)(1876)

"America the Beautiful"
(*Music and Lyrics by* Katherine Lee Bates and Samuel Ward.)(1910)

"Wait for the Wagon" (traditional)

"What It Takes to Make Me Love You—You've Got It"
(*Music and Lyrics by* J. W. Johnson and James Reese Europe.)(1914)

Scene 6

"The Maiden With the Dreamy Eyes" (from *THE LITTLE DUCHESS,* 1901)
(*Music by* Bob Cole. *Lyrics by* James Weldon Johnson.)

"If I Were on the Stage (Kiss Me Again)" (from *MADEMOSIELLE MODISTE,* 1905)
(*Music by* Victor Herbert. *Lyrics by* Henry Blossom.)

Scene 7

"Shortnin' Bread"
(traditional; *Music by* Reese 'Pree.)(1905)

"Nobody"
(*Music by* Alex Rogers. *Lyrics by* Bert Williams.)
(interpolated into *ZIEGFELD FOLLIES OF 1910*)

Scene 8

"Elite Syncopations"
(*Music by* Scott Joplin.)(1902)

"I'm Goin' to Live Anyhow, 'Til I Die"
(*Music and Lyrics by* Shepard N. Edmonds.)(1900)

ACT 2

"The Ragtime Dance"
(*Music by* Scott Joplin.)(1902)

Scene 1

"I Want What I Want When I Want It" (from *MADEMOISELLE MODISTE,* 1905)
(*Music by* Victor Herbert. *Lyrics by* Henry Blossom.)

Scene 2

"It's Delightful to Be Married" (from *A PARISIAN MODEL,* 1907)
(*Music by* Vincent Scotto. *Lyrics by* Anna Held.)

"Fifty-Fifty"
(*Music and Lyrics by* Jim Burris and Chris Smith.)(1914)

"American Beauty"
(*Music and Lyrics by* Joseph F. Lamb.)(1913)

Scene 3

"Then I'd Be Satisfied With Life" (from *RUNNING FOR OFFICE,* 1903)
(*Music and Lyrics by* George M. Cohan.)

"Narcissus"
(*Music by* Ethelbert Nevin.)(1891)

"Jonah Man"
(*Music and Lyrics by* Alex Rogers.)(1903)

"When It's All Goin' Out and Nothin' Comin' In" (from *SALLY IN OUR ALLEY,* 1902)
(*Music and Lyrics by* Bert Williams and George Walker.)

"We Shall Not Be Moved" (traditional)

Scene 4

"Hello, Ma Baby"
(*Music by* Joseph E. Howard. *Lyrics by* Ida Emerson.)(1899)

"Teddy Da Roose"
(*Music and Lyrics by* Ed Moran and J. Fred Helf.)(1910)

"A Bird in a Gilded Cage"
(*Music by* Arthur J. Lamb and Harry von Tilzer.)(1900)

"Bill Bailey, Won't You Please Come Home"
(*Music and Lyrics by* Hughie Cannon.)(1902)

---

[11]Originally produced in New York Off-Broadway 17 April 1980 at the Theater at St. Peter's Church for 137 performances.

"She's Gettin' More Like the White Folks Every Day"
(*Music and Lyrics by* Bert Williams and George Walker.)(1901)
"You're a Grand Old Flag" (frm *GEORGE WASHINGTON, JR.*)(1906)
(*Music and Lyrics by* George M. Cohan.)
"The Yankee Doodle Boy" (reprise)

Scene 5

"Toyland" (from *BABES IN TOYLAND*, 1903)
(*Music by* Victor Herbert. *Lyrics by* Glen MacDonough.)
"Smiles" (from *THE PASSING SHOW OF 1918*)
(*Music by* Lee G. Roberts. *Lyrics by* J. Will Callahan.)

1980.28
QUICK CHANGE

A Revue in Two Acts, 8 Scenes. Written by Bruce Belland, Roy M. Rogosin, Michael McGiveney. Directed by Roy M. Rogosin. Music by Roy M. Rogosin. Lyrics by Bruce Belland. Costumes by Mary Wills. Set by John Shipley, Chris Flower. Sound by Alan Chapman, Eric Neufeld. Production advisor, Richard G. Miller. Produced by Arthur Shafman International Ltd. Opened 30 October 1980 at the Bijou Theatre and closed 2 November 1980 after 5 performances.

<u>CAST:</u> MICHAEL McGIVENEY, assisted by Judith Hudson, Mark Bodine, Chris Flower.

ACT 1
Scene 1
Carnival
Scene 2
The Triumph of Arthur
Scene 3
The Lady Recites
Scene 4
Bill Sikes (from Charles Dickens' "Oliver Twist" celebrating 75 years of family tradition.)

ACT 2
Scene 1
Pitchman and the Cop
Scene 2
Quicker Than the Eye
Scene 3
A Misunderstood Minority
Scene 4
Shoot-Out at Belle's Saloon

1980.29
PERFECTLY FRANK

A Musical Revue in Two Acts, a Prologue and 11 Scenes. Conceived and written by Kenny Solms. Music and lyrics by Frank Loesser. Scenery and costumes designed by John Falabella. Lighting designed by Ken Billington. Musical director, Yolanda Segovia. Directed by Fritz Holt. Choreography by Tony Stevens. Music consultant, Larry Grossman. Orchestrations by Bill Byers. Dance arrangements by Ronald Melrose. Sound designed by Larry Spurgeon. Associate producer, Vivian Serota. Produced by Gladys Rackmill and Fred Levinson in association with Emhan Inc. Opened 30 November 1980 at the Helen Hayes Theatre and closed 13 December 1980 after 17 performances.

<u>CAST</u> (in alphabetical order): Andra Akers, Wayne Cilento, Jill Cook, Don Correia, David Holliday, David Ruprecht, Virginia Sandifur, Debbie Shapiro, Jo Sullivan, Jim Walton.

Act 1, Scene 1: Screen Test. *Scene 2*: USO Show. *Scene 3*: Dressing Room. *Scene 4*: Understudy Rehearsal. *Scene 5*: Manhattan.

Act 2, Scene 1: Rumble Rumble. *Scene 2*: Marriage. *Scene 3*: Rosabella. *Scene 4*: Dressing Room. *Scene 5*: Blues. *Scene 6*: Finale.

ACT 1[12]
Prologue

---

[12]Song list not included in program, but was prepared from management and press materials.

"Three Cornered Tune" (from *GUYS AND DOLLS*)
Company
"I Hear Music" (from *DANCING ON A DIME* film)
Company
(*Music by* Burton Lane.)

Scene 1

"Kiss the Boys Goodbye" (from *KISS THE BOYS GOODBYE* film)
V. Sandifur
(*Music by* Victor Schertzinger.)
"Snug as a Bug in a Rug" (from *THE GRACIE ALLEN MURDER CASE* film)
V. Sandifur
(*Music by* Matt Malneck.)
"The Moon of Manakoora" (from *THE HURRICANE* film)
V. Sandifur
(*Music by* Alfred Newman.)
"The Boys in the Backroom" (from *DESTRY RIDES AGAIN* film)
V. Sandifur
(*Music by* Frederick Hollander.)

Scene 2

"Murder, He Says" (from *HAPPY GO LUCKY* film)
J. Cook, W. Cilento
(*Music by* Jimmy McHugh)
"Some Like It Hot" (from *SOME LIKE IT HOT* film)
(*Music by* Gene Krupa and Remo Biondi.)
"I Don't Want to Walk Without You" (from *SWEATER GIRL* film)
D. Shapiro
(*Music by* Jule Styne.)
"Roseanna" (from *ROSEANNA McCOY* film)
J. Walton
"I Wish I Didn't Love You So" (from *THE PERILS OF PAULINE* film)
D. Holliday
"Where Are You Now (That I Need You?)" (from *RED, HOT AND BLUE* film)
D. Holliday
"They're Either Too Young or Too Old" (from *THANK YOUR LUCKY STARS*
film)
A. Akers
(*Music by* Arthur Schwartz.)
"What Do You Do in the Infantry?"
A. Akers, Men
"Praise the Lord and Pass the Ammunition"
D. Holliday
"Spring Will Be a Little Late This Year"
J. Sullivan

Scene 3

"I Believe in You" (from *HOW TO SUCCEED IN BUSINESS* . . . .)
D. Ruprecht, Men

Scene 4

"Make a Miracle" (from *WHERE'S CHARLEY?*)
D. Correia, J. Cook
"My Darling, My Darling" (from *WHERE'S CHARLEY?*)
D. Correia, J. Cook

Scene 5

"My Time of Day" (from *GUYS AND DOLLS*)
D. Holliday
"Two Sleepy People" (from *THANKS FOR THE MEMORY* film)
A. Akers, D. Ruprecht
(*Music by* Hoagy Carmichael.)
"No Two People" (from *HANS CHRISTIAN ANDERSEN* film)
D. Correia, J. Cook
"Baby, It's Cold Outside" (from *NEPTUNE'S DAUGHTER* film)
V. Sandifur, J. Walton
"Luck Be a Lady" (from *GUYS AND DOLLS*)
D. Holliday
"Fugue for Tinhorns" (from *GUYS AND DOLLS*)
D. Shapiro, W. Cilento, D. Holliday
"Take Back Your Mink" (from *GUYS AND DOLLS*)
V. Sandifur

"How'dja Like to Love Me?" (from *COLLEGE SWING* film)
  J. Cook
  (*Music by* Burton Lane.)
"The Lady's in Love With You" (from *SOME LIKE IT HOT* film)
  D. Shapiro
  (*Music by* Burton Lane.)
"Guys and Dolls" (from *GUYS AND DOLLS*)
  Company
"I've Never Been in Love Before" (from *GUYS AND DOLLS*)
  D. Holliday, Company

ACT 2

Entr'acte: Medley from *HANS CHRISTIAN ANDERSEN* film

Scene 1

"Rumble, Rumble, Rumble" (from *THE PERILS OF PAULINE* film)
  D. Shapiro, J. Walton, J. Cook

Scene 2

"Standing on the Corner" (from *THE MOST HAPPY FELLA*)
  D. Ruprecht, W. Cilento, J. Walton
"Once in Love With Amy" (from *WHERE'S CHARLEY?*)
  W. Cilento
"Marry the Man Today" (from *GUYS AND DOLLS*)
  V. Sandifur, A. Akers, J. Cook
"Happy To Keep His Dinner Warm" (from *HOW TO SUCCEED IN BUSINESS* . . .)
  V. Sandifur
"Never Will I Marry" (from *GREENWILLOW*)
  J. Walton
"Adelaide's Lament" (from *GUYS AND DOLLS*)
  A. Akers

Scene 3

"Ooh, My Feet!"
"I Like Everybody"
"I Don't Know Nothing About You" (The Letter)
  J. Sullivan, D. Holliday
"Somebody Somewhere"
  J. Sullivan
"Rosabella"
  D. Holliday
"Warm All Over"
  J. Sullivan
"Like a Woman Loves a Man"
  J. Sullivan
"My Heart Is So Full of You"
  D. Holliday
  (all of the above from *THE MOST HAPPY FELLA*)

Scene 4

Central Park Duck
  J. Sullivan

Scene 5

"Can't Get Out of This Mood" (from *SEVEN DAYS LEAVE* film)
  V. Sandifur
  (*Music by* Jimmy McHugh.)
"Luck Be a Lady" Dance (from *GUYS AND DOLLS*)
  D. Shapiro, D. Correia
"Junk Man"
  D. Shapiro
  (*Music by* Joseph Meyer.)

Scene 6

"More I Cannot Wish You" (from *GUYS AND DOLLS*)
  Company
"If I Were a Bell" (from *GUYS AND DOLLS*)
  V. Sandifur, D. Holliday
"Hoop-Dee-Do"
  W. Cilento, V. Sandifur, D. Correia, J. Cook
  (*Music by* Milton Delugg.)
"Just Another Polka"
  Company
  (*Music by* Milton Delugg.)

"The New Ashmolean Marching Society and Students Conservatory Band"
  (from *WHERE'S CHARLEY?*)
  Company
"Bubbles in the Wine"
  D. Ruprecht
  (*Music by* Lawrence Welk.)
"What Are You Doing New Year's Eve?"
  D. Holliday, D. Shapiro
"Sposalizio" (from *THE MOST HAPPY FELLA*)
  Company
"Jingle, Jangle, Jingle" (from *THE FOREST RANGERS* film)
  W. Cilento, D. Correia
  (*Music by* Joseph J. Lilley.)
"Big D" (from *THE MOST HAPPY FELLA*)
  J. Cook, W. Cilento, D. Correia, D. Shapiro
"Anywhere I Wander" (from *HANS CHRISTIAN ANDERSEN* film)
  J. Sullivan
"Sand in My Shoes" (from *KISS THE BOYS GOODBYE* film)
  A. Akers
  (*Music by* Victor Schertzinger.)
"Sing a Tropical Song" (from *HAPPY GO LUCKY* film)
  D. Ruprecht, A. Akers
  (*Music by* Jimmy McHugh.)
"Dolores" (from *LAS VEGAS NIGHTS* film)
  D. Holliday, Men
  (*Music by* Louis Alter.)
"Sit Down You're Rockin' the Boat" (from *GUYS AND DOLLS*)
  Company
"Brotherhood of Man" (from *HOW TO SUCCEED IN BUSINESS* . . .)
  Company
"On a Slow Boat to China"
  V. Sandifur
"Small Fry" (from *SING YOU SINNERS* film)
  J. Cook
  (*Music by* Hoagy Carmichael.)
"A Bushel and a Peck" (from *GUYS AND DOLLS*)
  A. Akers
"Heart and Soul" (from *A SONG IS BORN* film short)
  Company
  (*Music by* Hoagy Carmichael.)

1980.30   ONWARD VICTORIA

A Musical in Two Acts, 17 Scenes[13]. Book and lyrics by Charlotte Anker and Irene Rosenberg. Music by Keith Herrmann. Directed by Julianne Boyd. Musical numbers staged by Michael Shawn. Scenic design by William Rittman. Costumes by Theoni V. Aldredge. Lighting by Richard Nelson. Music direction by Larry Blank. Orchestrations by Michael Gibson. Dance arrangements by Donald Johnston. Vocal arrangements by Keith Herrmann, Larry Blank. Sound design by Lewis Mead. Produced by John N. Hart, Jr. in association with Hugh J. Hubbard and Robert M. Browne. Opened and closed 14 December 1980 at the Martin Beck Theatre after 1 performance.

CAST (in order of appearance): *Little Girl:* Lora Jeanne Martens. *Victoria Woodhull:* JILL EIKENBERRY. *Tennie Claflin:* BETH AUSTIN. *Telegraph Boy:* Marty McDonough. *Jim:* Dan Cronin. *Cornelius Vanderbilt:* TED THURSTON. *Mrs. Fleming:* Carrie Wilder. *Mrs. Baxter:* Karen Gibson. *Mrs. Randolph:* Lora Jeanne Martens. *Fleming:* Gordon Stanley. *Randolph:* Marty McDonough. *Baxter:* John Kildahl. *Woman Investor #1:* Carol Lurie. *Johnson:* Scott Fless. *Perkins:* Ian Michael Towers. *William Evarts:* REX HAYS. *Woman Investor #2:* Dru Alexandrine. *Beth Tilton:* MARTHA JEAN STERNER. *Theodore Tilton:* EDMOND GENEST. *Elizabeth Cady Stanton:* LAURA WATERBURY. *Jim's Girlfriend:* Lauren Goler. *Congressman Butler:* Kenneth H. Waller. *Henry Ward Beecher:* MICHAEL ZASLOW. *Susan B. Anthony:* Dorothy Holland. *Grant Speaker:* Kenneth H. Waller. *Eunice Beecher:* Linda Poser. *Charlie Delmonico:* LENNY WOLPE. *Maginnes:* Kenneth H. Waller. *Anthony Comstock:* JIM JANSEN. *Judge:* Kenneth H. Waller. *Fullerton:* LENNY WOLPE.

The action takes place in New York City and Washington, D.C. during 1871.

---

[13]Originally produced in New York Off-Broadway 22 February 1979 by the Joseph Jefferson Theatre Co. at the Greenwich Mews Theatre for 12 performances.

Act 1, Scene 1: New York City, 1871. *Scene 2*: Commodore Cornelius Vanderbilt's Office. *Scene 3*: Victoria's Salon, six months later. *Scene 4*; Plymouth Church, Brooklyn Heights. *Scene 5*; Woodhull and Claflin's Brokerage. *Scene 6*: Washington, D.C., 24 May 1872. *Scene 7*: Victoria's Campaign Tour. *Scene 8*: Beecher's Study—The next day. *Scene 9*: Victoria's Brokerage/Beecher's Study—Three months later. *Scene 10*: Delmonico's Restaurant—Two hours later.

Act 2, Scene 1: Victoria's Brokerage—The next day. *Scene 2*: Beecher's Study—Two months later. *Scene 3*: Steinway Hall. *Scene 4*: Victoria's Brokerage: Two days later. *Scene 5*: Brokerage/Street/Jail. *Scene 6*: Exterior and Interior of Courtroom—*Scene 7**Scene 8*

ACT 1

Scene 1

"The Age of Brass"
J. Eikenberry, B. Austin, M. Zaslow, J. Jansen, E. Genest, M. J. Sterner, L. Waterbury, D. Holland, Ensemble

Scene 2

"Magnetic Healing"
J. Eikenberry, B. Claflin, T. Thurston

Scene 3

"Curiosity"
R. Hays, M. J. Sterner, E. Genest, L. Waterbury, T. Thurston, Ensemble

Scene 4

"Beecher's Processional"
M. Zaslow, Ensemble

Scene 5

"I Depend on You"
J. Eikenberry, B. Austin

Scene 7

"Victoria's Banner"[14]
J. Eikenberry, B. Austin, L. Waterbury, D. Holland, Ensemble
"Changes"
J. Eikenberry

Scene 9

"A Taste of Forever"
J. Eikenberry, E. Genest

Scene 10

"Unescorted Women"
L. Wolpe, B. Austin, J. Eikenberry, Ensemble

ACT 2

Scene 1

"Love and Joy"
J. Eikenberry, M. Zaslow

Scene 2

"Everyday I Do a Little Something for the Lord"
J. Jansen
"It's Easy for Her"
M. Zaslow

Scene 3

"You Cannot Drown the Dreamer"
J. Eikenberry, L. Waterbury

Scene 4

"Respectable"
B. Austin

Scene 5

"Read It in the Weekly"
J. Eikenberry, M. Zaslow, E. Genest, B. Austin, J. Jansen, Newsboys, Readers

Scene 6

"A Valentine for Beecher"
Ensemble
"Beecher's Defense"
J. Eikenberry
"Another Life"
J. Eikenberry, M. Zaslow
"You Cannot Drown the Dreamer" (reprise)
J. Eikenberry, B. Austin

---

[14]Based on Victoria Woodhull's original campaign lyrics.

THE PIRATES OF PENZANCE,
or The Slave of Duty

1981.01

A Revival of the Comic Opera in Two Acts[15]. Libretto by William S. Gilbert. Music by Arthur Sullivan. Directed by Wilford Leach. Music adapted and conducted by William Elliott. Choreography by Graciela Daniele. Scenery by Bob Shaw and Wilford Leach, supervised by Paul Eads. Costumes by Patricia McGourty. Lighting by Jennifer Tipton. Sound by Don Ketteler. Production supervisor, Jason Steven Cohen. A New York Shakespeare Festival Production. Produced by Joseph Papp. Opened 8 January 1981 at the Uris Theater, moved 12 August 1981 to the Minskoff Theatre, and closed 28 November 1982 after 772 performances.

CAST (in order of appearance): *The Pirate King*: KEVIN KLINE. *Samuel*, his Lieutenant: Stephen Hanan. *Frederic*, the Pirate Apprentice: REX SMITH. *Ruth*, A Pirate Maid-of-all-work: ESTELLE PARSONS. *Major General Stanley's Daughters* (8): *Edith*: Alexandra Korey. *Kate*: Marcie Shaw. *Isabel*: Wendy Wolfe. *Mabel*: LINDA RONSTADT. And Robin Boudreau, Maria Guida, Nancy Heikin, Bonnie Simmons. *Major-General Stanley*: GEORGE ROSE. *Sergeant of Police*: TONY AZITO.
Pirates and Police: Dean Badolato, Mark Beudert, Brian Bullard, Scott Burkholder, Walter Caldwell, Tim Flavin, Ray Gill, George Kmeck, Daniel Marcus, G. Eugene Moose, Joseph Neal, Walter Niehenke, Joe Pichette, Ellis Skeeter Williams, Michael Edwin Willson.

ACT 1

"Pour, O Pour the Pirate Sherry"
K. Kline, S. Hanan, R. Smith, Pirates
"When Frederic Was a Little Lad"
E. Parsons
"Oh, Better Far to Live and Die"
K. Kline, Pirates
"Oh, False One, You Have Deceived Me!"
E. Parsons, R. Smith
"Climbing Over Rocky Mountain"
Daughters
"Stop Ladies, Pray!"
R. Smith, Daughters
"Oh, Is There Not One Maiden Breast"
R. Smith, Daughters
"Poor Wandering One"
L. Ronstadt, Daughters
"What Ought We to Do?"
M. Shaw, A. Korey, Daughters
"How Beautifully Blue the Sky"
L. Ronstadt, R. Smith, Daughters
"Stay, We Must Not Lose Our Senses"
R. Smith, Daughters, Pirates
"Hold, Monsters!"
L. Ronstadt, S. Hanan, G. Rose, Daughters, Pirates
"I Am the Very Modern Model of a Modern Major-General"
G. Rose, Ensemble
"Oh, Men of Dark and Dismal Fate"
Ensemble

ACT 2

"Oh, Dry the Glistening Tear"
L. Ronstadt, Daughters
"Then Frederic"
G. Rose, R. Smith
"When the Foreman Bares His Steel"
T. Azito, L. Ronstadt, Police, Daughters
"Now for the Pirates' Lair!"
R. Smith, K. Kline, E. Parsons
"When You Had Left Our Pirate Fold"
E. Parsons, R. Smith, K. Kline
"My Eyes Are Fully Open" (from *RUDDIGORE*)
R. Smith, E. Parsons, K. Kline

---

[15]First presented in New York 31 December 1879 at the Fifth Avenue Theatre for 91 performances in two engagements. This revival first produced in New York Off-Broadway by the New York Shakespeare Festival 15 July 1980 at the Delacorte Theatre (in Central Park) for 42 performances.

"Away, Away! My Heart's on Fire"
E. Parsons, K. Kline, R. Smith
"All Is Prepared"
L. Ronstadt, R. Smith
"Stay Frederic, Stay!"
L. Ronstadt, R. Smith
"Sorry Her Lot" (from *H.M.S. PINAFORE*)
L. Ronstadt
"No, I Am Brave"
L. Ronstadt, T. Azito, Police
"When a Felon's Not Engaged in His Employment"
T. Azito, Police
"A Rollicking Band of Pirates We"
Pirates, T. Azito, Police
"With Cat-Like Tread Upon Our Prey We Steal"
Pirates, Police, S. Hanan
"Hush, Hush! Not a Word!"
R. Smith, Pirates, Police, G. Rose
"Sighing Softly to the River"
G. Rose, Ensemble
Finale[16]
Ensemble

1981.02 SHAKESPEARE'S CABARET

A Musical Revue in One Act[17]. Concept and music by Lance Mulcahy. (Words by William Shakespeare.) Entire production directed by John Driver. Choreography by Lynne Taylor-Corbett. Scenery and costumes by Frank J. Boros. Lighting by Marc B. Weiss. Orchestrations, vocal arrangements and musical direction by Don Jones. Production advisor, Richard G. Miller. Produced by Arthur Shafman. Opened 21 January 1981 at the Bijou Theatre and closed 8 March 1981 after 54 performances.

CAST (in order of speaking appearance): Patti Perkins, Michael Rupert, Catherine Cox, Larry Riley, Pauletta Pearson, Alan Brasington.

MUSICAL NUMBERS
"If Music and Sweet Poetry Agree" (from *THE PASSIONATE PILGRIM*)
Ensemble
"What Thou See'st When Thou Dost Awake" (*from A MIDSUMMER NIGHT'S DREAM*)
Ensemble
"All That Glitters" (from *THE MERCHANT OF VENICE*)
C. Cox, P. Perkins, P. Pearson
"Why Should This a Desert Be?" (from *AS YOU LIKE IT*)
M. Rupert
"Crabbed Age and Youth" (from *THE PASSIONATE PILGRIM*)
A. Brasington, P. Perkins
"Orpheus and His Lute" (from *HENRY III*)
P. Pearson
"Music With Her Silver Sound" (from *ROMEO AND JULIET*)
C. Cox, M. Rupert, P. Perkins, A. Brasington
"Come Live With Me and Be My Love"
(attributed to Christopher Marlowe, quoted in *TWELFTH NIGHT*)
L. Riley
"Have More Than Thou Showest" (from *KING LEAR*)
M. Rupert, A. Brasington
"Venus and Adonis Suite" (An Erotic Narrative Poem)
Ensemble
Venus sees Adonis bathing naked in the stream. She tries to seduce him. He rejects her. Her premonition of his death. He is killed by the wild boar. Venus mourns his death. She flies off to her home in the skies.
"Tell Me Where Is Fancy Bred?" (from *THE MERCHANT OF VENICE*)
Ensemble

"If Music Be the Food of Love" (from *TWELFTH NIGHT*)
A. Brasington, P. Pearson
"Epitaph for Marina" (from *PERICLES*)
M. Rupert, C. Cox
"The Phoenix and the Turtle"
A. Brasington, P. Perkins, P. Pearson, C. Cox, M. Rupert
"Now" (from *A MIDSUMMER NIGHT'S DREAM*)
L. Riley
"The Willow Song" (from *OTHELLO*)
C. Cox
"Immortal Gods" (from *TIMON OF ATHENS*)
A. Brasington
"Tomorrow Is St. Valentine's Day" (from *HAMLET*)
P. Perkins
"Fathers That Wear Rags" (from *KING LEAR*)
P. Pearson
"The Grave Digger's Song" (from *HAMLET*)
L. Riley
"Now" (reprise)
L. Riley, P. Perkins, P. Pearson, C. Cox, A. Brasington
"Come Unto These Yellow Sands" (from *THE TEMPEST*)
Ensemble
"Shall I Compare Thee to a Summer's Day?" (from *SONNET 18*)
C. Cox, A. Brasington
"Lawn as White as Driven Snow" (from *THE WINTER'S TALE*)
Ensemble
"Rosalynde" (from *AS YOU LIKE IT*)
L. Riley, A. Brasington
"Let the Canakin Clink" (from *OTHELLO*)
Ensemble
"Shakespeare's Epitaph"
Ensemble
"Fear No More the Heat of the Sun" (from *CYMBELINE*)
Ensemble
"Epitaph" (reprise)
Ensemble

1981.03 THE FIVE O'CLOCK GIRL

A Revival of the Musical Comedy in Two Acts, 10 Scenes[18]. Book by Guy Bolton and Fred Thompson. Music and lyrics by Bert Kalmar and Harry Ruby. Entire production directed by Sue Lawless. Musical staging and choreography by Dan Siretta. Scenery by John Lee Beatty. Costumes by Nanzi Adzima. Lighting by Craig Miller. Sound design by Richard Fitzgerald. Music research consultant, Alfred Simon. Orchestrations and dance arrangements by Russell Warner. Assistant choreographer, Larry McMillian. Musical direction by Lynn Crigler. Production consultant, Warren Pincus. A Goodspeed Opera House Production. Produced by Rodger Hess. Opened 28 January 1981 at the Helen Hayes Theatre and closed 8 February 1981 after 14 performances.

CAST (in order of appearance): *Madame Irene*: SHEILA SMITH. *Hudgins*, Mr. Brooks' valet: TED PUGH. *Susan Snow*: PAT STANLEY. *Patricia Brown*: LISBY LARSON. *Gerald Brooks*: ROGER RATHBURN. *Ronnie Webb*: BARRY PRESTON. *Cora Wainwright*: DEE HOTY. *Jasper Cobb*: TIMOTHY WALLACE.
Ensemble: *Jeanie*: Teri Corcoran. *Pete*, the waiter: James Homan. *Rodney*, Madame Irene's escort: Richard Ruth. *Sam*: Rodney Pridgen. *Ethel; Molly* the Maid: Annette Michelle. *Elsie*: Lora Jeanne Martens. *Bunnie*: Jean McLaughlin. *Polly*: Debra Grimm. *Maisie*: Carla Farnsworth-Webb. *Jules*, the Maitre d'*: Jonathan Aronson. *Detective*: G. Brandon Allen. *Bobby, Policeman*: Gary Kirsch.

The action takes place in New York in the 1920's.

Act 1, Scene 1: A Block Party near Beekman Place. *Scene 2*: On the Telephone. *Scene 3*: Gerry's Apartment. *Scene 4*: The Snowflake Cleaners. *Scene 5*: The Kit Kat Club.

Act 2, Scene 1: Outside the Field and Stream Hotel, Southampton, Long Island. *Scene 2*: The Snowflake Cleaners. *Scene 3*: A Street in New York. *Scene 4*: Roof garden between the Apartments of Gerry and Ronnie. *Scene 5*: The Church.

---

[16] The restoration of part of the original New York finale to THE PIRATES OF PENZANCE of 1879 was done by Richard Traubner.
[17] Originally produced 1 February 1980 Off-Broadway at the Colonnades Theatre Lab for 40 performances.

[18] Originally produced in New York as THE 5 O'CLOCK GIRL 10 October 1927 at the 44th Street Theatre for 280 performances.

ACT 1

Scene 1

"In the Old Neighborhood"
S. Smith, Ensemble

Scene 2

"Keep Romance Alive" (from HIPS, HIPS, HOORAY film)
Telephone Girls

"Thinking of You"
L. Larson, R. Rathburn

Scene 3

"I'm One Little Party"
B. Preston, Female Ensemble

"Up in the Clouds"
L. Larson, R. Rathburn, Ensemble

"My Sunny Tennessee" (from MIDNIGHT ROUNDERS OF 1921)
T. Wallace, Ensemble
(Music and Lyrics by Bert Kalmar, Harry Ruby, Herman Ruby.)

"Any Little Thing"
P. Stanley, T. Pugh

Scene 5

"Manhattan Walk" (from GOOD BOY)
S. Smith, B. Preston, D. Hoty, T. Pugh, Ensemble
(Music by Herbert Stothart and Harry Ruby. Lyrics by Bert Kalmar.)

ACT 2

Scene 1

"Long Island Low Down" (from ANIMAL CRACKERS)
S. Smith, Ensemble

"Who Did? You Did!"
L. Larson, R. Rathburn

"Any Little Thing" (reprise)
P. Stanley

Scene 2

"Nevertheless (I'm in Love With You)" (interpolation)
P. Stanley, T. Pugh

Scene 3

"All Alone Monday" (from THE RAMBLERS)
R. Rathburn

Scene 4

"Dancing the Devil Away" (from LUCKY)
B. Preston, Ensemble
(Music by Harry Ruby. Lyrics by Bert Kalmar and Otto Harbach.)

Scene 5

"Up in the Clouds"
L. Larson, R. Rathburn

Finale

Company

1981.04 **PIAF**

A Drama (with Songs) in Two Acts, 24 Scenes, by Pam Gems. Directed by Howard Davies. Setting by David Jenkins. Costumes by Julie Weiss. Lighting by Beverly Emmons. Produced originally in Great Britain by the Royal Shakespeare Company. Production coordinator, Brent Peek. Sound by Jack Mann. Assistant director, Helaine Head. Musical direction and arrangements, Michael Dansicker. Produced by Elizabeth I. McCann, Nelle Nugent, The Shubert Organization, Ray Larsen in association with Warner Theatre Productions, Inc. Opened 5 February 1981 at the Plymouth Theatre and closed 28 June 1981 after 165 performances.

CAST (in order of appearance): Emcee/Manager: David Leary. Piaf: JANE LAPOTAIRE. "Papa" Leplée, owner of Cluny Club: Peter Friedman. Toine: ZOË WANAMAKER. Emil, maitre d' at Cluny Club: Nicholas Woodeson. Legionnaire: Stephen Davies. Thugs (3): Jacques: Lewis Arlt. Eddie: Robert Christian. Little Louis: Michael Ayr. Police Inspector: Kenneth Welsh. Paul, man with rose: David Purdham. German Soldier #1: Lewis Arlt. German Soldier #2: Michael Ayr. Georges: Kenneth Welsh. Butcher: Robert Christian. Pierre, on bicycle; later, Piaf's Agent: Stephen Davies. Marlene: Jean Smart. Marcel: Robert Christian. American Soldier #1: David Purdham. American Soldier #2: Peter Friedman. Barman: Robert Christian. Madeleine: Judith Ivey. Lucien: Michael Ayr. Angelo: Lewis Arlt. Physiotherapist: Kenneth Welsh. Jacko: Nicholas Woodeson. Dope Pusher: Michael Ayr. Nurse: Sherry Steiner. Theo: David Purdham.

The play is a celebration of the life of Edith Piaf from the late 1920's through 1963.

Act 1, Scene 1: The bare stage of the Cluny Club. *Scene 2:* Outside the Cluny Club. *Scene 3:* Piaf's Room. *Scene 4:* The Cluny Club. *Scene 5:* The Street. *Scene 6:* The Cluny Club. *Scene 7:* A Police Station, and afterwards. *Scene 8:* A classy club. *Scene 9:* Piaf's apartment. *Scene 10:* A Street. *Scene 11:* Piaf's Apartment. *Scene 12:* Josephine's Nightclub. *Scene 13:* Piaf and Marcel.

Act 2, Scene 1: A Stage Dressing Room. *Scene 2:* A Bar. *Scene 3:* Piaf's Apartment. *Scene 4:* A Parisian café. *Scene 5:* A Hospital Waiting Room. *Scene 6:* A Rehearsal Studio. *Scene 7:* Piaf's Apartment. *Scene 8:* A Room at the Ritz. *Scene 9:* An empty stage. *Scene 10:* Piaf's Private Room in a Nursing Home. *Scene 11:* Piaf's Room in the South of France.

ACT 1[19]

Scene 2

"Les Mômes de la Cloche"
J. Lapotaire
(Music by Vincent Scotto. Lyrics by Decaye.)

Scene 4

"Les Mômes de la Cloche" (reprise)
J. Lapotaire

Scene 6

"La Ville Inconnue"
J. Lapotaire
(Music by Charles Dumont. Lyrics by Michel Vaucaire.)

Scene 7

"Tu Me Fais Tourner Ma Tête"
J. Lapotaire

Scene 8

"Si Tu Partais"
J. Lapotaire

"L'Accordéoniste" (The Accordionist)
J. Lapotaire
(Music by M. Emer. English Lyrics by Adrian Mitchell.)

Scene 9

"C'est à Hambourg" (Harbour Girl)
J. Lapotaire
(Music and Lyrics by Charles Dumont and Edith Piaf. English Lyrics by Pam Gems and Adrian Mitchell.)

Scene 11

"Milord"
J. Lapotaire, Z. Wanamaker
(Music by Marguerite Monnot. Lyrics by Georges Moustaki.)

"Auprès de Ma Blonde"
J. Lapotaire, Z. Wanamaker

Scene 13

"La Belle Histoire D'Amour
J. Lapotaire
(Music and Lyrics by Edith Piaf and Charles Dumont. English Lyrics by Adrian Mitchell.)

ACT 2

Scene 6

"Deep in the Heart of Texas"
S. Davies
(Music by Don Swander. Lyrics by June Hershey.)

Scene 7

"Le Droit D'Aimer"
J. Lapotaire

Scene 9

"La Goualante du Pauvre Jean" (The Ballad of Poor Old John)
J. Lapotaire
(Music by Marguerite Monnot. Lyrics by René Rouzoud. English Lyrics by Adrian Mitchell.)

Scene 10

"Non, Je Ne Regrette Rien"
J. Lapotaire
(Music by Charles Dumont. Lyrics by Michel Vaucaire.)

---

[19]Scene list and song list prepared from production typescript.

Additional Music used:
"Les Trois Cloches" (The Three Bells)
  (*Music and Lyrics by* Jean Villard {Gilles}. *English Lyrics by* Bert Reisfeld.)
"Bravo Pour Le Clown"
  (*Music and Lyrics by* Henri Contet and Louiguy.)
"Je T'ai Dans le Peau"
"La Vie en Rose"
  (*Music and Lyrics by* Edith Piaf and Louiguy. *English Lyrics by* Mack David.)
"Mon Dieu"
  (*Music and Lyrics by* Charles Dumont and Michel Vaucaire.)
"Hymne à L'Amour" (If You Love Me)
  (*Music by* Marguerite Monnot. *Lyrics by* Edith Piaf. *English Lyrics by* Geoffrey Parsons.)
"Un Sale Petit Brouillard"

JACQUES BREL IS ALIVE AND WELL AND LIVING IN PARIS

1981.05

A Revival of the Musical Entertainment (Revue) in Two Acts[20]. Music by Jacques Brel. Production conception, English lyrics and additional material by Eric Blau. Based on Jacques Brel's lyrics and commentary. Original direction by Moni Yakim. Production supervised by Eric Blau. Produced by Lily Tuner Attractions. Opened 19 February 1981 at Town Hall and closed 8 March 1981 after 21 performances.

CAST: JOE MASIELL, BETTY RHODES, SALLY COOKE, SHAWN ELLIOTT.

SOPHISTICATED LADIES

1981.06

A Musical (Revue) in Two Acts. Music by Duke Ellington. Concept by Donald MacKayle. Directed by Michael Smuin. Musical staging and choreography by Donald MacKayle, Michael Smuin. Co-choreography and tap choreography by Henry LeTang. Musical director, Mercer Ellington. Settings designed by Tony Walton. Costumes designed by Willa Kim. Lighting designed by Jennifer Tipton. Sound designed by Otts Munderloh. Orchestrations by Al Cohn. Musical and dance arrangements by Lloyd Mayers. Vocal arrangements by Malcolm Dodds, Lloyd Mayers. Associate choreographer, Bruce Heath. Assistant choreographer, Mercedes Ellington. Musical consultant and additional arrangements, Paul Chihara. Produced by Roger S. Berlind, Manheim Fox, Sondra Gilman, Burton L. Litwin and Louise Westergaard in association with Belwin Mills Publishing Corporation and Norzar Productions. Opened 1 March 1981 at the Lunt-Fontanne Theatre and closed 2 January 1983 after 767 performances.

CAST: GREGORY HINES, JUDITH JAMISON, PHYLLIS HYMAN, P. J. BENJAMIN, HINTON BATTLE, GREGG BURGE, MERCEDES ELLINGTON, PRISCILLA BASKERVILLE, TERRI KLAUSNER.
Ensemble: Claudia Asbury, Paula Lynn, Wynonna Smith, Adrian Bailey, Michael Lichtefeld, Michael Scott Gregory, T. A. Stephens.

ACT 1[21]
"I've Got To Be a Rug Cutter" (1937)
  H. Battle, G. Burge, M. S. Gregory, M. Lichtefeld
  (*Music and Lyrics by* Duke Ellington.)
"Music Is a Woman" (Based on "Jubilee Stomp" 1928)
  G. Hines, J. Jamison
  (*Music by* Duke Ellington. *Lyrics by* John Guare.)
"The Mooche" (1929)
  H. Battle, C. Asbury, M. Ellington, P. Lynn, W. Smith
  (*Music by* Duke Ellington and Irving Mills.)
"Hit Me With a Hot Note (and Watch Me Bounce)" (1945)
  T. Klausner
  (*Music by* Duke Ellington. *Lyrics by* Don George.)

"I Love You Madly" (1950)
  (*Music and Lyrics by* Duke Ellington.)
"Perdido" (1971)
  J. Jamison, G. Burge, H. Battle
  (*Music and Lyrics by* Juan Tizol, Ervin Drake, Hans Lengsfelder.)
"Fat and Forty"[22]
  P. J. Benjamin
  (*Music and Lyrics by* Al Hibbler and Duke Ellington.)
"It Don't Mean a Thing (If It Ain't Got That Swing)" (1929)
  P. Hyman, G. Burge, G. Hines, A. Bailey, M. Lichtefeld, M. S. Gregory, T. A. Stephens
  (*Music by* Duke Ellington. *Lyrics by* Irving Mills.)
"Bli-Blip" (1941)
  P. J. Benjamin, T. Klausner
  (*Music by* Duke Ellington. *Lyrics by* Duke Ellington and Irving Mills.)
"Cotton Tail" (1940)
  P. J. Benjamin, T. Klausner, Ensemble
  (*Music by* Duke Ellington.)
"Take the "A" Train" (1941)
  P. Hyman, G. Hines
  (*Music by* Billy Strayhorn.)
"Solitude" (1934)
  J. Jamison, P. Baskerville
  (*Music by* Duke Ellington. *Lyrics by* Eddie DeLange and Irving Mills.)
"Don't Get Around Much Anymore" (1942)
  G. Hines
  (*Music by* Duke Ellington. *Lyrics by* Bob Russell.)
"I Let a Song Go Out of My Heart" (from *COTTON CLUB PARADE*, 1938)
  J. Jamison
  (*Music by* Duke Ellington. *Lyrics by* Irving Mills and John Redmond.)
"Caravan" (1937)
  G. Burge, M. Ellington, Ensemble
  (*Music by* Duke Ellington and Juan Tizol. *Lyrics by* Irving Mills.)
"Something to Live For" (1939)
  G. Hines
  (*Music and Lyrics by* Duke Ellington and Billy Strayhorn)
"Old Man Blues" (1930)
  H. Battle, J. Jamison
  (*Music and Lyrics by* Duke Ellington and Irving Mills.)
"Drop Me Off in Harlem" (1933)
  H. Battle, P. J. Benjamin, G. Burge, G. Hines, P. Baskerville, Ensemble
  (*Music by* Duke Ellington. *Lyrics by* Nick Kenny.)
"Rockin' in Rhythm" (*from EARL CARROLL'S VANITIES OF 1932*)
  Company
  (*Music by* Duke Ellington, Irving Mills, Harry Carney.)
ACT 2
"Duke's Place" (1957)
  G. Hines
  (*Music by* Duke Ellington. *Lyrics by* Bill Katz and Robert Thiele.)
"Diminuendo in Blue" (1942)
  G. Hines
  (*Music by* Duke Ellington.)
"In a Sentimental Mood" (1935)
  P. Hyman
  (*Music by* Duke Ellington. *Lyrics by* Manny Kurtz and Irving Mills.)
"I'm Beginning to See the Light" (1944)
  J. Jamison, G. Hines
  (*Music and Lyrics by* Duke Ellington, Don George, Johnnie Hodges, Harry James.)
"Satin Doll" (1958)
  P. J. Benjamin
  (*Music by* Duke Ellington. *Lyrics by* Billy Strayhorn and Johnny Mercer.)
"Just Squeeze Me" (1946)
  T. Klausner
  (*Music by* Duke Ellington. *Lyrics by* Lee Gaines.)
"Dancers in Love" (1945)
  H. Battle, G. Burge, M. Ellington
  (*Music by* Duke Ellington.)

---

[20]Originally produced in New York Off-Broadway 22 January 1968 at the Village Gate for 1847 performances; transferred to Broadway 15 September 1972 at the Royale Theatre for 51 performances. For Synopsis of Musical Numbers, see 1972 production.
[21]Added to Act 1, after "Old Man Blues" for National Tour:
  "Prelude to a Kiss" (1938)
    Paula Kelly
    (*Music by* Duke Ellington. *Lyrics by* Irving Gordon and Irving Mills.)

[22]Replaced during the run and for subsequent tour by:
  "Everything But You" (1945)
    (*Music by* Duke Ellington, Harry James. *Lyrics by* Don George.)

"Echoes of Harlem" (1936)
    H. Battle, G. Burge, Ladies
    (*Music by* Duke Ellington.)
"I'm Just a Lucky So-and-So" (1945)
    G. Hines, Gentlemen
    (*Music by* Duke Ellington. *Lyrics by* Mack David.)
"Hey Baby" (1946)[23]
    P. J. Benjamin, M. Ellington
    (*Music and Lyrics by* Duke Ellington.)
"Imagine My Frustration" (1966)
    T. Klausner, G. Burge
    (*Music and Lyrics by* Duke Ellington, Billy Strayhorn, Gerald Wilson.)
"Kinda Dukish" (1955)
    G. Hines
    (*Music by* Duke Ellington.)
"Ko-Ko" (1939)
    G. Hines, A. Bailey, M. S. Gregory, M. Lichtefeld, T. A. Stephens
    (*Music by* Duke Ellington.)
"I'm Checking Out Goombye" (1939)
    P. Hyman
    (*Music and Lyrics by* Duke Ellington and Billy Strayhorn.)
"Do Nothing 'Til You Hear from Me" (1943)
    G. Hines
    (*Music by* Duke Ellington. *Lyrics by* .Bob Russell)
"I Got It Bad and That Ain't Good" (from *JUMP FOR JOY*, 1941)
    P. Hyman
    (*Music by* Duke Ellington. *Lyrics by* Paul Francis Webster.)
"Mood Indigo" (1931)
    P. Hyman, T. Klausner
    (*Music by* Duke Ellington, Irving Mills, Albany "Barney" Bigard.)
"Sophisticated Lady" (1933)
    G. Hines, J. Jamison, Company
    (*Music by* Duke Ellington. *Lyrics by* Mitchell Parish and Irving Mills.)
"It Don't Mean a Thing" (reprise)
    G. Hines, Company

1981.07 ## BRING BACK BIRDIE

A Musical Comedy in Two Acts, 15 Scenes[24]. Book by Michael Stewart. Music by Charles Strouse. Lyrics by Lee Adams. Production conceived and directed by Joe Layton. Scenery designed by David Mitchell. Costumes designed by Fred Voelpel. Lighting designed by David Hays. Sound designed by Otts Munderloh. Video sequences created by Wakefield Poole, Frank O'Dowd. Musical direction, vocal arrangements by Mark Hummel. Dance music arranged by Daniel Troob. Still photographs by Barbara J. Rossi. orchestral arrangements by Ralph Burns, Stanley Applebaum, Daniel Troob, Philip J. Lang, Jim Tyler, Gary Anderson, Gerald Alters, Scott Kuney, Coleridge-Taylor Perkinson, Charles Strouse. Produced by Lee Guber, Shelly Gross, Slade Brown and Jim Milford. Opened 5 March 1981 at the Martin Beck Theatre and closed 7 March 1981 after 4 performances.

<u>CAST</u> (in order of appearaance): *Storyteller*: Donna Monroe. *Albert*: DONALD O'CONNOR. *Rose*: CHITA RIVERA. *Mtobe*: MAURICE HINES. *Hogan*: Howard Parker. *Albert, Jr.*: Evan Seplow. *Jenny*: Robin Morse. *Gary*: Jeb Brown. *Girl Friends*: Barbara Dare Thomas, Vanessa Bell, Julie Cohen, Christine Langner. *Porter*: Frank DeSal. *Guard*: Howard Parker. *Sunnie*: Betsy Friday. *Tourist*: Bill Bateman. *His Wife*: Zoya Leporska. *Shopping Bag Lady*: Rebecca Renfroe. *Indian Squaw*: Janet Wong. *Indian Brave*: Larry Hyman. *Mae Peterson*, (Delores Zepol): MARIA KARNILOVA. *Mayor C. B. Townshend*, (Conrad Birdie): Marcel Forestieri. *Effie*: Zoya Leporska. *Marshall*: Howard Parker. *"Filth" Group*: Evan Seplow, Jeb Brown, Cleve Asbury, Leon Evans, Mark Frawley. *House Manager*: Peter Oliver Norman. *Chorus Girls*: Betsy Friday, Rebecca Renfroe, Vanessa Bell. *Rose II*: Lynnda Ferguson. *Reverend Sun*: Frank DeSal. *Reporter #1*: Bill Bateman. *Reporter #2*: Donna Monroe. *Reporter #3*: Larry Hyman, Frank DeSal. *Street Cleaner*: Frank DeSal. *Cameraman*: Michael Blevins. *Stage Door Johnnies*: Bill Bateman, Peter Oliver Norman, Cleve Asbury, Frank DeSal. *Birdettes*: Betsy Friday, Rebecca Renfroe, Vanessa Bell. *Walter*: Kevin Petitt.

Act 1, Scene 1: A Darkened Office, (twenty years after 'Bye Bye Birdie'). *Scene 2*: Forest Hills and Environs. *Scene 3*: Peterson Kitchen. *Scene 4*: Port Authority Bus Terminal.

Scene 5: Bent River Junction, Arizona. *Scene 6*: El Coyote Club. *Scene 7*: Office of Mayor. *Scene 8*: University Stadium.

Act 2, Scene 1: University Staadium. *Scene 2*: Reverend Sun's Compound. *Scene 3*: Office of the Mayor. Main Street, Bent River Junction. *Scene 4*: University Stadium Locker Room. *Scene 5*: Rose's Motel .*Scene 6*: Television Studio. *Scene 7*: The Grammy Show.

ACT 1
Scene 1
    "Twenty Happy Years"
        C. Rivera, D. O'Connor
Scene 2
    "Movin' Out"
        R. Morse, J. Brown, Kids
    "Half of a Couple"
        R. Morse, Girl Friends
Scene 3
    "I Like What I Do"
        C. Rivera
Scene 4
    "Bring Back Birdie"
        M. Hines, Company
    "Movin' Out" (reprise)
        Kids
Scene 5
    "Baby You Can Count on Me"
        D. O'Connor
Scene 6
    "A Man Worth Fightin' For"
        C. Rivera, Cowboys
Scene 7
    "You Can Never Go Back"
        M. Forestieri
Scene 8
    "Filth"
        E. Seplow, J. Brown, C. Asbury, L. Evans, M. Frawley
    "Back in Show Biz Again"
        D. O'Connor
ACT 2
Scene 1
    "Middle Age Blues"
        D. O'Connor
Scene 2
    "Inner Peace"
        C. Rivera, F. DeSal, Sunnies
Scene 3
    "There's a Brand New Beat in Heaven"
        M. Hines, The Tucson Tabernacle Choir
    "Twenty Happy Years" (reprise)
        D. O'Connor
    "Well, I'm Not!"
        C. Rivera
Scene 4
    "When Will Grown-Ups Grow Up?"
        Kids
    "Middle Age Blues" (reprise)
        D. O'Connor
Scene 5
    "Young"
        D. O'Connor
Scene 7
    "I Love 'Em All"
        M. Karnilova, Boyfriends
    "Bring Back Birdie" (reprise)
        M. Forestieri, The Birdettes
    "Twenty Happy Years" (reprise)
        D. O'Connor, C. Rivera

---

[23]Dropped for subsequent tour.
[24]Conceived as a sequel by the same authors whose *BYE BYE BIRDIE* opened 14 April 1960 at the Martin Beck Theatre for 607 performances.

1981.08 AMERICA

A Musical Revue in One Act, 11 Scenes. Conceived and produced by Robert F. Jani. Original music and lyrics by Tom Bahler and Mark Vieha. Musical direction and routines by Tom Bahler. Choreography by Violet Holmes, Linda Lemac and Frank Wagner. Principals staged by Frank Wagner. Scenic design by Robert Guerra. Costume design by Michael Casey. Lighting design by Ken Billington. Special material and dialogue by Harvey Jacobs. Orchestrations by Mitch Farber, Robert M. Freedman, Jay Kennedy, Billy May. Synthesizer program and performance by Don Dorsey. Director of the Rockettes, Violet Holmes. Produced by Radio City Music Hall Productions, Inc. Opened 13 March 1981 at the Radio City Music Hall and closed 7 September 1981 after 284 performances.

CAST: THE AMERICANS: Wendy Edmead, Jeff Johnson, Reed Jones, Mark Morales, Iris Revson.
THE ROCKETTES: Pauline Achillas, Carol Beatty, Catherine Beatty, Dottie Belle, Susan Boron, Barbara Ann Cittadino, Eileen Collins, Brie Daniels, Susanne Doris, Jacqueline Fancy, Deniene Fenn, Alexis Ficks, Prudence Gray, Jennifer Hammond, Carol Harbich, Terry Spano Higgins, Ginny Hounsell, Cynthia Hughes, Pam Kelleher, Dee Dee Knapp, Judy Little, Kris Mooney, Barbara Moore, Lynn Newton, Pam Stacey Pasqualino, Kerri Pearsall, Joan Peer, Cindy Peiffer, Gerri Presky, Ann Murphy St. John, Lynn Sullivan, Sunny Summers, Susan Theobald, Carol Toman, Patricia Tully, Darlene Wendy, Rose Ann Woolsey, Phyllis Wujko, Joyce Dwyer (Captain).
THE NEW YORKERS: Michael Booker, Andrew Charles, Buddy Crutchfield, Lou Ann Csaszar, Johnny Driscoll, Catherine Fries, Dale Furry, David Holland, Laurie Jaeger, David Michael Johnson, Rena Phillips, Kitty Preston, Cleo Price, Edward Prostak, Lance Roberts, Danny Robins, Lisa Sherman, Marc Villa.
THE DANCERS: Blake Atherton, David Beckett, Ron Chisholm, Rick Conant, Lloyd Culbreath, Renee DuLaney, Byron Easley, Glenn Ferrugiari, Karen Fraction, Michael Graham, Tony Jaegar, David Lee, Kim Leslie, Bronna Lipton, David Roman, Sam Singhaus, Thomas Stanton, Maureen Stevens, Barry Weiss, Kim Woollen.
THE ORGANISTS: Robert Maidhof, George Wesner.

MUSICAL NUMBERS
Scene 1
The Opening
Let music swell the breeze and ring from all the trees sweet freedom's song.
Scene 2
The Story of America
From school house days.
Scene 3
"Fifty Great Places All in One Place"
(Music and Lyrics by Tom Bahler and Mark Vieha.)
Scene 4
"The Spirit of America"
(Music and Lyrics by Tom Bahler and Mark Vieha.)
Scene 5
A Tour de Force of America
A magical, musical, pictorial entertainement voyage to America's fifty great states.
Scene 6
Hawaii Is the 50th Star
In the flag of the U.S.A.
Scene 7
The Electro-Live-Synthomagnetic Radio City Music Hall Orchestra
Conducted by Kevin Farrell. Assistant Conductor, Paul Bogaev.
Scene 8
Freedom
From Yankee Doodle to Dixie we praise the Lord for our freedom.
Scene 9
A New American Spirit Is Alive
Scene 10
On Parade
(includes "Come Follow the Band" from BARNUM)
(Music by Cy Coleman. Lyrics by Michael Stewart.)
Scene 11
The Finale—America the Beautiful

1981.09 BROADWAY FOLLIES

A Vaudeville Revue in Two Acts, 15 Scenes. Music and lyrics by Walter Marks. Concept and direction by Donald Driver. Choreography by Arthur Faria. Scenery designed by Peter Larkin. Costumes designed by Alvin Colt. Lighting designed by Roger Morgan. Sound designed by Abe Jacob. Musical direction, vocal and dance arrangements by Marvin Laird. Orchestrations by Bill Byers. Talent coordinator, Gilbert Miller. Production supervisor, Robert Strauss. Produced by Edgar Lansbury, Joseph Beruh and James Nederlander. Opened and closed 15 March 1981 at the Nederlander Theatre after 1 performance.

CAST: ROBERT SHIELDS, LORENE YARNELL, TESSIE O'SHEA, Milo & Roger, Scott's Royal Boxers (Katherine and George Scott, Tina Scott), Los Malambos (Guido Lopez, Nicolas Sarrea, Hector Diaz), Michael Davis, Gaylord Maynard & Chief Bearpaw.
Ensemble: Stephen Bourneuf, Kitty Kuhn, Mark Martino, Nancy Meadows, Brad Miskell, Alice Ann Oakes, Aurelio Padron, R. J. Peters, D'Arcy Phifer, Mark Ruhala, Karen Teti, Suzanne Walker.

ACT 1
Scene 1
"Broadway Follies"
Ensemble
Scene 2
Vaudeville
R. Shields, L. Yarnell
Scene 3
Wonderful U
Scott's Royal Boxers, Follies Ensemble
Scene 4
"Piccadilly"
T. O'Shea
Scene 5
The Oasis
Milo & Roger
Scene 6
The Pampas
Los Malambos
Scene 7
The Toyshop
R. Shields, L. Yarnell
Scene 8
"The Paper Bag Rag"
T. O'Shea, Bud's Paper Bag Band

ACT 2
Scene 1
At Home with the Clinkers
R. Shields, L. Yarnell
Scene 2
"The Barnyard"
T. O'Shea, Her Chicks
Scene 3
Specialty
R. Shields
Scene 4
The Saloon
G. Maynard, Belinda, Chief Bearpaw, The Dingbats
Scene 5
Tap My Way to the Stars
L. Yarnell, Ensemble
Scene 6
The Rest of Michael Davis (juggling act)
Scene 7
Grand Parade
Entire Company

WOMAN OF THE YEAR

1981.10

A Musical Comedy in Two Acts, 15 Scenes. Book by Peter Stone. Based on the MGM film of the same name by Ring Lardner, Jr. and Michael Kanin. Music by John Kander. Lyrics by Fred Ebb. Directed by Robert Moore. Musical numbers staged by Tony Charmoli. Settings designed by Tony Walton. Costumes designed by Theoni V. Aldredge. Lighting designed by Marilyn Rennagel. Sound designed by Abe Jacob. Musical direction and vocal arrangements by Donald Pippin. Orchestrations by Michael Gibson. Dance arrangements by Ronald Melrose. Animations by Michael Sporn. Produced by Lawrence Kasha, David S. Landay, James M. Nederlander, Warner Theatre Productions/Claire Nichtern, Carole J. Shorenstein, Stewart F. Lane. Opened 29 March 1981 at the Palace Theatre and closed 13 March 1983 after 770 performances.

CAST (in order of appearance): *Chairperson:* Helon Blount. *Tess Harding:* LAUREN BACALL. *Floor Manager:* Michael O'Gorman. *Chip Salisbury:* Daren Kelly. *Gerald:* RODERICK COOK. *(The Cartoonists {5}): Pinky Peters:* Gerry Vichi. *Phil Witaker:* Tom Avera. *Sam Craig:* HARRY GUARDINO. *Ellis McMaster:* Rex D. Hays. *Abbott Canfield:* Lawrence Raiken. *Murray:* Rex Everhart. *Helga:* Grace Keagy. *Alexi Petrikov:* Eivind Harum. *Cleaning Women:* Helon Blount, Marian Haraldson. *Jan Donovan:* Marilyn Cooper. *Larry Donvan:* Jamie Ross. *(Voice of Katz:* Fred Ebb.)

Chorus: DeWright Baxter, Joan Bell, Helon Blount, Sergio Cal, Donna Drake, Richard Glendon-Larsen, Marian Haraldson, Michael Kubala, Paige Massman, Gene Montoya, Michael O'Gorman, Susan Powers, Daniel Quinn, Robert Warners. *Swings:* Ed Nolfi, Karen Giombetti.

Act 1, Scene 1: Backstage at a Hotel Ballroom. *Scene 2:* A TV Studio and Sam's Studio. *Scene 3:* Tess' Office. *Scene 4:* Sam's Studio. *Scene 5:* The Inkpot. *Scene 6:* Tess' Apartment. *Scene 7:* Around New York .*Scene 8:* Tess' Apartment. *Scene 9:* Tess' Apartment and a Hotel Ballroom.

Act 2, Scene 1: The Street. *Scene 2:* The Inkpot. *Scene 3:* A Ballet Rehearsal Room. *Scene 4:* Sam's Studio. *Scene 5:* Larry's House. *Scene 6:* The TV Studio.

ACT 1[25]

Scene 1

"Woman of the Year"[26]
L. Bacall, Women

Scene 2

"The Poker Game"
H. Guardino, Cartoonists

"See You in the Funny Papers"
H. Guardino

Scene 3

"When You're Right, You're Right"
L. Bacall, R. Cook

Scene 4

"Shut Up, Gerald"
L. Bacall, H. Guardino, R. Cook

"So What Else Is New?"
H. Guardino, F. Ebb

Scene 5

"One of the Boys"
L. Bacall, Cartoonists, R. Everhart, Men

"Table Talk"
L. Bacall, H. Guardino

Scene 6

"The Two of Us"
L. Bacall, H. Guardino

Scene 7

"It Isn't Working"
Cartoonists, D. Kelly, G. Keagy, R. Cook, New Yorkers

Scene 8

"I Told You So"
R. Cook, G. Keagy

Scene 9

"Woman of the Year" (reprise)
L. Bacall

ACT 2[27]

Scene 1

"So What Else Is New?" (reprise)
H. Guardino, F. Ebb

Scene 2

"I Wrote the Book"
L. Bacall, H. Blount, M. Haraldson

Scene 3

"Happy in the Morning"
E. Harum, L. Bacall, Dancers

Scene 4

"Sometimes a Day Goes By"
H. Guardino

Scene 5

"The Grass Is Always Greener"
L. Bacall, M. Cooper

Scene 6

"We're Gonna Work It Out"
L. Bacall, H. Guardino

AAAH OUI GENTY!

1981.11

A Marionette Revue in Two Acts. (Conceived by Philippe Genty.) Production supervisor, Christopher Dunlop. Produced by Arthur Shafman. Opened 9 April 1981 at the Bijou Theatre and closed 3 May 1981 after 29 performances.

CAST: *COMPAGNIE PHILIPPE GENTY:* Mary Genty, Philippe Genty, Michel Guillaume, Jean-Louis Heckel.

ACT 1

Signboard
Clown
Signboard
Pierrot
Drifting

ACT 2

Metamorphosis
Signboard
The Offcier
Signboard
Ostrich Ballet

COPPERFIELD

1981.12

A Musical in Two Acts, 19 Scenes. Book, music and lyrics by Al Kasha and Joel Hirschhorn. Based on the novel "David Copperfield" by Charles Dickens. Direction and choreography by Rob Iscove. Set design by Tony Straiges. Costume design by John David Ridge. Lighting design by Ken Billington. Musical direction, vocal arrangements by Larry Blank. Orchestrations by Irwin Kostal. Dance arrangements, incidental music by Donald Johnston. Sound design by John McClure. A Dome Production. Produced by Don Gregory and Mike Merrick. Opened 16 April 1981 at the ANTA Theatre and closed 26 April 1981 after 13 performances.

CAST (in order of appearance): *Dr. Chilip:* Richard Warren Pugh. *Peggotty:* Mary Stout. *Nurse:* Katharine Buffaloe. *Aunt Betsey Trotwood:* CARMEN MATHEWS. *Young David:* EVAN RICHARDS. *Clara Copperfield:* Pamela McLernon. *Mr. Murdstone:* MICHAEL CONNOLLY. *Jane Murdstone:* Maris Clement. *Mr. Micawber:* GEORGE S. IRVING. *Bootmaker:* David Horwitz. *Butcher:* Bruce

---

[25]The subsequent national tour was re-staged in Two Acts, 14 Scenes, and re-choreographed by Joe Layton. Added to Act 1, Scene 8 after "I Told You So:"

"Who Would Have Dreamed"
Raquel Welch (Tess Harding)

[26]New title song written for the national tour.

---

[27]During the Broadway run, Act 2, Scene 1 was dropped.
For the national tour, the following was added to Act 2, Scene 6 (revised as Scene 5):

"Open the Window, Sam"
L. Bacall

Sherman. *Baker*: Richard Warren Pugh. *Mrs. Micawber*: Linda Poser. *Victoria*: Spence Ford. *Vanessa*: Dana Moore. *Constable*: Michael Danek. *Mick Walker*: Gary Munch. *Mealy Potatoes*: Brian Quinn. *Billy Mowcher*: Christian Slater. *Mr. Quinion*: Ralph Braun. *Mr. Dick*: Lenny Wolpe. *Janet*: Darleigh Miller. *Adult David*: BRIAN MATTHEWS. *Mrs. Heep*: Beulah Garrick. *Uriah Heep*: BARRIE INGHAM. *Mr. Wickfield*: Keith Perry. *Agnes Wickfield*: LESLIE DENNISTON. *Dora Spenlow*: MARY MASTRANTONIO. *Julia Mills*: Katharine Buffaloe. *Ticket Taker*: Michael Gorman.

Ensemble: David Ray Bartee, Ralph Braun, Katharine Buffaloe, Maris Clement, Michael Danek, Spence Ford, Michael Gorman, David Horwitz, Pamela McLernon, Darleigh Miller, Dana Moore, Gary Munch, Keith Perry, Linda Poser, Richard Warren Pugh, Brian Quinn, Lynne Savage, Bruce Sherman, Claude Tessier, Missy Whitchurch. *Swing Dancers*: Heather Lee Gerdes, Daniel Dee.

The action takes place in 1812 and 1822 in England.

Act 1, Scene 1: A stormy December night, 1812. The drawing room of the Copperfield cottage in Blunderstone in Suffolk. *Scene 2*: An afternoon in the autumn, 1822. The garden of the Copperfield cottage. *Scene 3*: The following spring. The drawing room of the Copperfield cottage. *Scene 4*: 6:30 in the morning. The Murdstone and Grinby Warehouse. *Scene 5*: Mid-afternoon, the following summer. *Scene 6*: Immediately following. On the road to Dover. *Scene 7*: A few weeks later. *Scene 8*: A week later. On the road near Aunt Betsey's house. *Scene 9*: Immediately following. The parlor of Aunt Betsey's house. (The same), Ten years later. *Scene 10*: A week later. Mr. Wickfield's sitting room in London. *Scene 11*: The following Sunday. Southwark Fair.

Act 2, Scene 1: Several months later. Mr. Wickfield's office. *Scene 2*: Outside the church. *Scene 3*: Several months later. Mr. Wickfield's sitting room. *Scene 4*: Several weeks later. The home of David and Dora Copperfield. *Scene 5*; A street near the Wickfield house. *Scene 6*: The office of Wickfield and Heep. *Scene 7*: The home of David and Dora Copperfield. *Scene 8*: One year later. The London docks.

ACT 1

Scene 1

"I Don't Want a Boy"
  C. Mathews, M. Stout, Ensemble

Scene 2

"Mama, Don't Get Married"
  E. Richards, P. McLernan, M. Stout

Scene 4

"Copperfield" (TheBottle Song)
  E. Richards, R. Braun, B. Quinn, C. Slater, G. Munch, Ensemble

Scene 5

"Something Will Turn Up"
  G. S. Irving, E. Richards, Creditors, Ensemble
"Something Will Turn Up" (reprise)
  G. S. Irving, E. Richards, Micawber Family

Scene 6

"Anyone"
  E. Richards

Scene 9

"Here's a Book"
  C. Mathews, L. Wolpe, E. Richards

Scene 10

"'Umble"
  B. Ingham, B. Garrick

Scene 11

"The Circle Waltz"
  B. Matthews, M. Mastrantonio, L. Denniston, Ensemble

ACT 2

Scene 1

"Up the Ladder"
  B. Ingham, G. S. Irving
"I Wish He Knew"
  L. Denniston

Scene 2

"The Lights of London"
  B. Matthews, M. Mastrantonio

Scene 3

"'Umble" (reprise)
  B. Ingham

Scene 4

"I Wish He Knew" (reprise)
  L. Denniston

Scene 5

"Something Will Turn Up" (reprise)
  G. S. Irving, B. Matthews

Scene 6

"Villainy Is the Matter"
  B. Matthews, B. Ingham, G. S. Irving, L. Denniston, C. Mathews, L. Wolpe, B. Garrick, M. Stout, L. Poser

Scene 7

"With the One I Love"
  B. Matthews

Scene 8

"Something Will Turn Up" (reprise)
  G. S. Irving, Company

CAN CAN

1981.13

A Revival of the Musical (Comedy) in Two Acts, a Prologue and 17 Scenes[28]. Book (revised) by Abe Burrows. Music and lyrics by Cole Porter. Entire production staged and choreographed by Roland Petit. Directed by Abe Burrows. Scenery designed by David Mitchell. Costumes designed by Franca Squarciapino, supervised by Patricia Adshead. Lighting designed by Thomas Skelton. Musical direction, vocal arrangements by Stanley Lebowsky. Orchestrations by Philip J. Lang. Dance arrangements, new dance music by Donald York. Sound by Larry Spurgeon. Produced by James M. Nederlander, Arthur Rubin, Jerome Minskoff, Stewart F. Lane, Carole J. Shorenstein, Charles D. Kelman. Opened 30 April 1981 at the Minskoff Theatre and closed 3 May 1981 after 5 performances.

CAST (in order of appearance): *Policemen*: Tommy Breslin, John Remme, John Dolf, Dennis Batutis, Kevin McCready. *Bailiff*: Joseph Cusanelli. *Judge Paul Barriere*: DAVID BROOKS. *Court President*: Tom Batten. *Judge Aristede Forestier*: RON HUSMANN. *Claudine*: PAMELA SOUSA. *Hilaire Jussac*: SWEN SWENSON. *Boris Adzinidzinadze*: AVERY SCHREIBER. *Waiter*: John Remme. *La Mome Pistache*: ZIZI JEANMAIRE. *Hercule*: MICHAEL DANTUONO. *Theophile*: MITCHELL GREENBERG. *Etienne*: TOMMY BRESLIN. *Photographer*: James Dunne. *Tabac Waiter*: Joseph Cusanelli. *Monarchist*: Tom Batten. *Jail Guard*: John Remme. *Model*: Deborah Carlson. *Adam*: Darrell Barnett. *Eve*: PAMELA SOUSA. *The Snake*: ZIZI JEANMAIRE, Dennis Batutis, James Horvath, Steven LaChance, Kevin McCready. *Mimi*: Donna King. *Apache Leader*: Luigi Bonino. *Patrons*: Nealey Gilbert, Dennis Batutis. *Chief Justice*: Joseph Cusanelli.

Ensemble: Deborah Carlson, Pam Cecil, Edyie Fleming, Nealey Gilbert, Linda Haberman, Nancy Hess, Brenda Holmes, Donna King, Manette LaChance, Meredith McIver, Gail Pennington, Rosemary Rado, Daryl Richardson, Linda Von Germer, Darrell Barnett, Dennis Batutis, John Dolf, James Dunne, James Hovath, Steven LaChance, Kevin McCready, Gregory Schanuel. *Swings*: Kim M. Noor, Bob Renny.

THE MOONY SHAPIRO SONGBOOK

1981.14

A Musical Comedy in Two Acts[29]. Book by Monty Norman and Julian More. Music by Monty Norman. Lyrics by Julian More. Directed by Jonathan Lynn. Musical numbers staged by George Faison. Setting by Saul Radomsky. Costumes by Franne Lee. Lighting by Tharon Musser. Musical direction by Elman Anderson. Dance arrangements by Timothy Graphenreed. Vocal arrangements by Ray Cook. Associate conductor, Irving Joseph. Musical supervisor, Stanley Lebowsky. Sound by Otts Munderloh. Projections by Wendall Harrington. Originally produced on the London stage by Jack Gill for Stoll Productions, Ltd. by arrangement with The Cambridge Theatre Company, Ltd. Produced by Stuart Ostrow in association with T.A.T. Communications Company. Opened and closed 3 May 1981 at the Morosco Theatre after 1 performance.

CAST: JEFF GOLDBLUM plays Himself, Mr. Shapiro, Rocco the Shoeshine Boy, Talking Picture Star, Louis Da Rosa, French Crooner, Street Trumpeter, Fat German, Member of the Big Band Vocal Group, U.S.O. Entertainer, Marvin, Israeli Dancer, Russian Singer, Lee Pyong-Do, Liverpool Pop Group Drummer.

---

[28]Originally produced in New York 7 May 1953 at the Sam S. Shubert Theatre for 892 performances. For Synopsis of Scenes and Musical Numbers, see original 1953 production. "Every Man Is a Stupid Man," "If You Loved Me Truly" dropped for this production.

[29]Produced in London under the title *SONGBOOK*. The show presents the fictitious life and work of a prolific songwriter in revue form.

JUDY KAYE plays Herself, Reverend Mother, Mrs. Shapiro, Mrs. Kleinberg, Salvation Army Girl, Talking Picture Star, Torch Singer, Another Torch Singer, Busby Berkeley Girl, Bella, Fat German, Member of Big Band Vocal Group, Marlene, U.S.O. Entertainer, Rusty, Israeli Dancer, Kim-Sung, Liverpool Pop Singer, Sheila O'Toole.

TIMOTHY JEROME plays Himself, Moony Shapiro, Mr. Woo, Cop, Fat German, U.S.O. Entertainer, Senator "Beanpole" Pickles.

ANNE McGREEVEY plays Herself, Tilly, Mary Cassidy, Mae Feldman, Astrid Kalmar, Talking Picture Star, Dolly Ralston, Busby Berkeley Girl, French Music Hall Singer, Fat German, Member of Big Band Vocal Group, British Comedienne, U.S.O. Entertainer, Bonny Van Heysen, Debbie Stellman, Jude, Israeli Dancer, Russian Singer, KGB Officer, Lin-Chi, Magda Gyor, Liverpool Pop Group Singer.

GARY BEACH plays Himself, Dead End Kid, Rabbi Kotchinsky, Sailor, U.S. Immigration Officer, Talking Picture Star, First Newsboy, Rudy Vallee, Bum, Dancer, Busby Berkeley Tenor, Waiter, Flower Seller, Fat German, Gestapo Officer, Press Photographer, Member of Big Band Vocal Group, Second Newsboy, Prisoner-of-War Guard, U.S.O. Entertainer, Academy Awards Singer, Alvin Burns, Chuck, Israeli Dancer, Schmuel, Russian Singer, Johnny Bakuba, Bob Dylan, Bob Dylan's Spokesman, Benedict Rickenbaker, Leader of the Liverpool Pop Group, British Trades Union Leader, Bonny's Singing Partner.

Back-Up Singers: Philip Hoffman, Audrey Lavine, Brenda Pressley. *March of Time Announcer:* Philip Hoffman.

ACT 1

"Songbook" (from *BALTIMORE BALLYHOO* film, 1948)
Company
"East River Rhapsody" (from revue *FELDMAN FOLLIES OF 1926*)
G. Beach, Company
"Talking Picture Show" (from *EVERMORE* film, 1928)
J. Goldblum, J. Kaye, A. McGreevey, G. Beach
"Meg" (Trunk Song, 1929)
T. Jerome
"Mister Destiny" (from hit recording, 1930)
J. Kaye
"Your Time Is Different to Mine" (from hit recording, 1932)
J. Kaye
"Pretty Face" (from *PRETTY FACES OF 1934* film)
G. Beach, A. McGreevey, J. Kaye
"Je Vous Aime, Milady" (from hit recording, 1935)
J. Goldblum
"Les Halles" (Cabaret Song, 1935)
A. McGreevey
"Olympics '36" (from hit recording, 1936)
Company
"Nazi Party Pooper" (Trunk Song, 1936)
T. Jerome
"I'm Gonna Take Her Home to Momma" (from hit recording, 1938)
A. McGreevey, J. Kaye, J. Goldblum, G. Beach
War Songs 1939-1945:
"Bumpity-Bump"
A. McGreevey
"The Girl in the Window" (Das Mädchen Am Fenster)
J. Kaye
"Victory"
Company
Academy Award-winning Hollywood Evergreens 1945-1948:
"April in Wisconsin" (from *A YANK AT THE VATICAN* film)/
"It's Only a Show" (from *LET'S DO THE SHOW RIGHT HERE* film)/
"Bring Back Tomorrow" (from *BRING BACK TOMORROW* film)
G. Beach
"Songbook" (reprise)(from *BALTIMORE BALLYHOO*, 1948)
Company

ACT 2

"Happy Hickory" (from musical *HAPPY HICKORY*, 1954)
A. McGreevey
HAPPY HICKORY Rejects (Trunk Songs)—
"When a Brother Is a Mother to His Sister"
T. Jerome
"Climbin'"
A. McGreevey
"Don't Play That Lovesong Anymore"
T. Jerome
Vocal Gems from *HAPPY HICKORY*:
"Happy Hickory" (reprise)
Company
"Lovely Sunday Mornin'"
A. McGreevey, G. Beach

"Rusty's Dream Ballet"
J. Kaye, J. Goldblum
"A Storm in My Heart"
G. Beach, A. McGreevey, J. Goldblum, J. Kaye
"The Pokenhatchit Public Protest Committee"
Company
"Happy Hickory" (reprise)
Company
"I Accuse" (from *RED, WHITE AND BLACK*, 1957)
A. McGreevey, J. Kaye
"Messages I" (Trunk Song, 1958)
J. Goldblum
"Messages II" (Version for Bob Dylan, 1963)
G. Beach
"I Found Love" (from hit recording, 1964)
A. McGreevey, J. Kaye, J. Goldblum, G. Beach
"Don't Play that Lovesong Anymore" (Trunk Song)
J. Kaye
"Golden Oldie" (Trunk Song, 1972)
T. Jerome
"Climbin'" (from hit recording, 1972)
A. McGreevey, G. Beach, J. Goldblum, J. Kaye, T. Jerome
"Nostalgia" (Trunk Song, 1977)
J. Goldblum
Finale
Company

1981.15

INACENT BLACK

A Heaven-Sent Comedy (with songs) in Two Acts, 9 Scenes[30]. Play by A. Marcus Hemphill. Original music and lyrics by (Gene) McFadden, (John) Whitehead and (Melba) Moore. Directed by Mikell Pinkney. Scenic design by Felix E. Cochren. Costume design by Marty Pakledinaz. Lighting design by Tim Phillips. Sound design by Joseph Donohue. Musical conductor, Barry Eastmond. Associate director, Ed Cambridge. Produced by Gloria Hope Sher, Marjorie Moon and Jay J. Cohen in association with Zaida Coles Edley and Spirit Will Productions (a subsidiary of Bedford Stuyvesant Restoration Corporation). Opened 6 May 1981 at the Biltmore Theatre and closed 17 May 1981 after 15 performances.

CAST (in order of appearance): *Helwin Rydell:* Gregory Miller. *Mama Essie Rydell:* BARBARA MONTGOMERY. *Mary Rydell:* Reginald Vel Johnson. *Charles Rydell:* Count Stovall. *Percy Rydell:* Bruce Strickland. *Waitress:* Rosanna Carter. *Inacent Black:* MELBA MOORE. *Pretty Pete:* Ronald "Smokey" Stevens. *Carmen Casteel:* Joyce Sylvester. *Sally-Baby Washington:* Lorey Hayes. *Voice of Hamilton Rydell:* Ed Cambridge.

The action takes place in the spring, 1980, in the Rydell Estate Mansion in Old Westbury, Long Island, and in New York City.

Act 1, Scene 1: Friday, 10:15 A.M. Study of the Rydell Mansion in Old Westbury, Long Island, New York. *Scene 2:* Friday, 1:00 P.M. Coffee Shop at New York Port Authority. *Scene 3:* Friday, 4:00 P.M. Rydell Mansion. *Scene 4:* Saturday, 9:00 A.M. Rydell Mansion. *Scene 5:* Saturday, Noon. Rydell Mansion.

Act 2, Scene 1: Saturday, 2:30 P.M. Near an outside phone booth—New York City. *Scene 2:* Saturday, 3:00 P.M. Central Park—New York City. *Scene 3:* Saturday, 6:00 P.M. Rydell Mansion. *Scene 4:* Sunday, 8:15 P.M. Rydell Mansion.

MUSICAL NUMBERS[31]
"Stand Together"
"He's All That We Need"
"Somebody Told Me"

LENA HORNE:
1981.16 THE LADY AND HER MUSIC

A Musical Revue in Two Acts. Production staged by Arthur Faria. Musical direction by Harold Wheeler. Scenery designed by David Gropman.

---

[30]Originally produced in Brooklyn *as INACENT BLACK AND THE FIVE BROTHERS* by the Billie Holiday Theatre 12 May 1979 for 7 months of performances.
[31]Musical numbers not listed in program; above list prepared from press materials.

Costumes designed by Stanley Simmons. Lighting designed by Thomas Skelton. Musical conductor, Coleridge-Taylor Perkinson. Musical consultants, Luther Henderson, Coleridge Taylor-Perkinson. Miss Horne's Wardobe, Giorgio Sant'Angelo. Assistant conductor, Linda Twine. Produced by James M. Nederlander, Michael Frazier, Fred Walker in association with Sherman Sneed and Jack Lawrence. Opened 12 May 1981 at the Nederlander Theatre and closed 30 June 1982 after 333 performances.

<u>CAST</u>: LENA HORNE.
Lena's Trio: Grady Tate (Drums), Steve Bargonetti (Guitar), Bob Cranshaw (Bass).
The Company: Clare Bathé, Tyra Ferrell, Vondie Curtis-Hall. *Alternates*: Deborah Lynn Bridges, Peter Oliver-Norman.

ACT 1[32]

"From This Moment On" (from *KISS ME KATE* film)
(*Music and Lyrics by* Cole Porter. *Arranged by* Ron Roullier.)

"I Got a Name"
(*Music and Lyrics by* Norman Gimbel, Charles Fox. *Arranged by* Harold Wheeler.)

"I'm Glad There Is You"
(*Music and Lyrics by* Paul Madeira, Jimmy Dorsey. *Arranged by* Lennie Hayton.)

"I Want To Be Happy" (from *NO, NO, NANETTE*)
(*Music by* Vincent Youmans. *Lyrics by* Irving Caesar. *Arranged by* Bob Freedman.)

Cotton Club Revue: (*Arrangements by* Coleridge-Taylor Perkinson.)
"Copper Colored Gal (of Mine)" (from *COTTON CLUB PARADE*, 1936, 27th ed)
(*Music and Lyrics by* Benny Davis and J. Fred Coots.)
"Raisin' the Rent" (from *COTTON CLUB PARADE*, 1933, 22nd ed)
(*Music by* Harold Arlen. *Lyrics by* Ted Koehler.)
"As Long As I Live" (from *COTTON CLUB PARADE*, 1934, 24th ed)
(*Music by* Harold Arlen. *Lyrics by* Ted Koehler.)
"Lady With a Fan" (from *COTTON CLUB PARADE*, 1933, 23rd ed)
(*Music by* Harold Arlen. *Lyrics by* E. Y. Harburg.)

Cotton Club to Hollywood
"Where or When" (from *BABES IN ARMS*)
(*Music by* Richard Rodgers. *Lyrics by* Lorenz Hart. *Arranged by* Harold Wheeler.)

"Can't Help Lovin' Dat Man" (from *SHOWBOAT*)
(*Music by* Jerome Kern. *Lyrics by* Oscar Hammerstein II. *Arranged by* Ron Roullier.)

Hollywood
"Just One of Those Things" (from *JUBILEE*)
(*Music and Lyrics by* Cole Porter. *Arranged by* Ron Roullier.)

"Stormy Weather"
(*Music by* Harold Arlen. *Lyrics by* Ted Koehler. *Arranged by* Bob Freedman.)

"Love" (from *THE ZIEGFELD FOLLIES* film, 1946)
(*Music and Lyrics by* Hugh Martin and Ralph Blane. *Arranged by* Mark Wolfram, Gil Askey, C. T. Perkins.)

Broadway
"Push de Button" (from *JAMAICA*)
(*Music by* Harold Arlen. *Lyrics by* E. Y. Harburg. *Arranged by* Ron Roullier.)

"The Lady Is a Tramp" (from *BABES IN ARMS*)
(*Music by* Richard Rodgers. *Lyrics by* Lorenz Hart. *Arranged by* Mark Wolfram, Gil Askey, C. T. Perkins.)

"Yesterday When I Was Young"
(*Music by* Charles Aznavour. *Lyrics by* Herbert Kretzmer. *Arranged by* Harold Wheeler.)

"Deed I Do"
(*Music by* Walter Hirsch. *Lyrics by* Fred Rose. *Arranged by* Grady Tate and Lena Horne.)

"Life Goes On"
(*Music by* Paul Williams. *Lyrics by* Craig Doerge. *Arranged by* Harold Wheeler.)

ACT 2
"Watch What Happens" (from *THE UMBRELLAS OF CHERBOURG* film)
(*Music by* Michel Legrand. *English Lyrics by* Norman Gimbel. *Arranged by* Gary Anderson.)

"The Surrey With the Fringe on Top" (from *OKLAHOMA!*)
(*Music by* Richard Rodgers. *Lyrics by* Oscar Hammerstein II. *Arranged by* Lennie Hayton.)

"Fly"
(*Music and Lyrics by* Martin Charnin. *Arranged by* Coleridge-Taylor Perkinson.)

"Bewitched" (from *PAL JOEY*)
(*Music by* Richard Rodgers. *Lyrics by* Lorenz Hart. *Arranged by* Harold Wheeler.)

"A Lady Must Live" (from *AMERICA'S SWEETHEART*)
(*Music by* Richard Rodgers. *Lyrics by* Lorenz Hart. *Arranged by* Coleridge-Taylor Perkinson.)

Love This Business
"That's What Miracles Are All About"
(*Music and Lyrics by* Charlie Smalls. *Arranged by* Coleridge-Taylor Perkinson.)

Early Career
"I'm Going to Sit Right Down and Write Myself a Letter"
(*Music by* Fred Ahlert. *Lyrics by* Joe Young. *Arranged by* Coleridge-Taylor Perkinson.)

"Stormy Weather" (reprise)

"If You Believe" (from *THE WIZ*)
(*Music and Lyrics by* Charlie Smalls. *Arranged by* Harold Wheeler and Gary Anderson.)

---

[32]Song list prepared from program and Original Cast live recording. Also performed:
"Better Than Anything"
(*Music and Lyrics by* D. Wheat and William Loughborough.)

1981–1982 SEASON

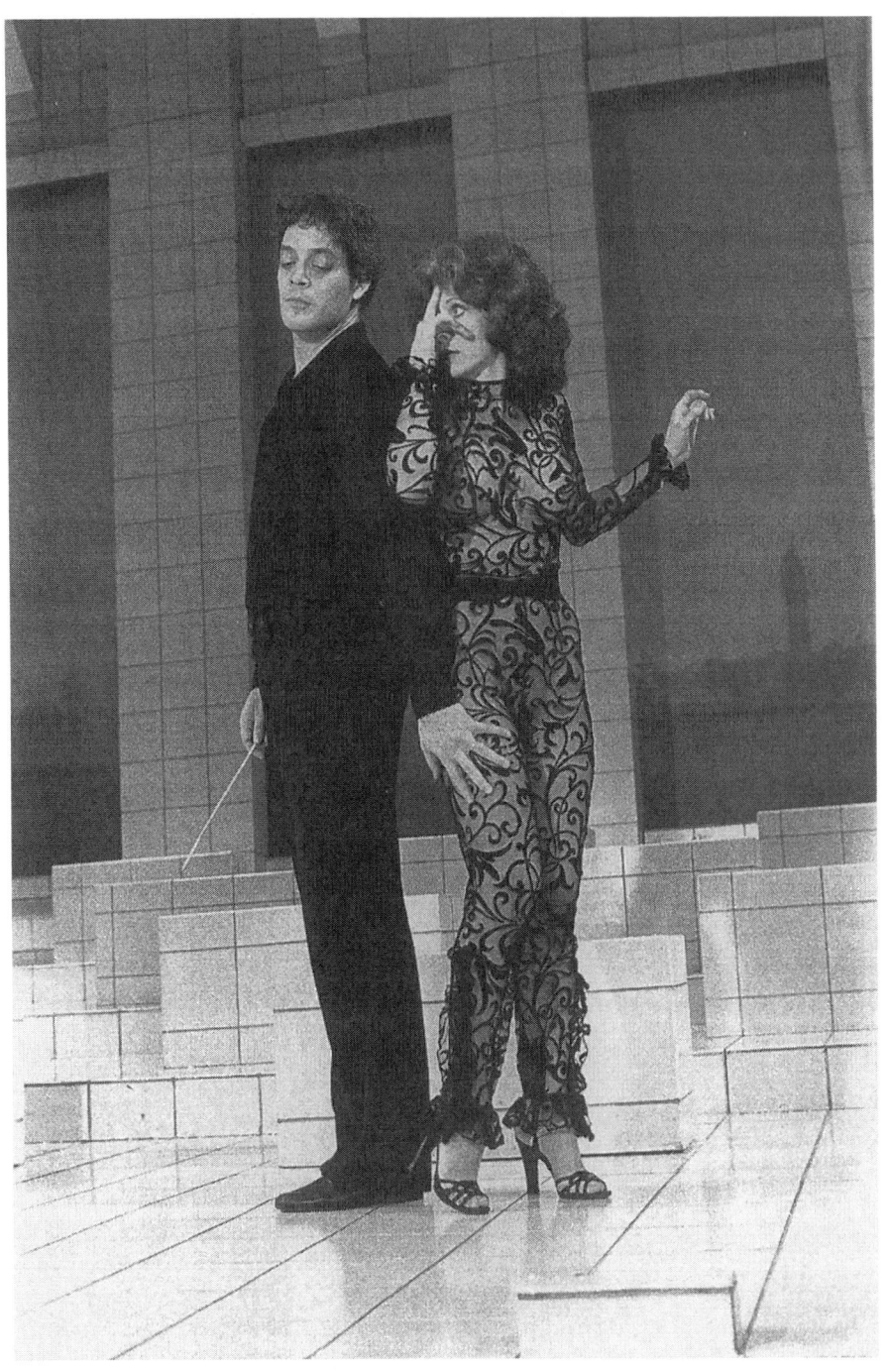

Raul Julia and Anita Morris in NINE
Martha Swope/TimePix

1981–1982 SEASON

1981.17 ## THIS WAS BURLESQUE

A New Edition of the Burlesque Revue in Two Acts, 20 Scenes[1]. Based on Ann Corio's recollections. Entire production supervised and directed by Ann Corio. Choreographer, Fred Albee. Musical conductor, Richard DeMone. Costumes by Rex Huntington. Associate Producer, Glenn Myles. Co-Producer, Jeff Satkin, Inc. Produced by MPI Productions Ltd. (Michael P. Iannucci) Opened 23 June 1981 at the Princess Theatre and closed 17 July 1981 after 28 performances.

CAST: ANN CORIO, CLAUDE MATHIS, TAMI ROCHE (Amtullah Khan), DEXTER MAITLAND, PHIL FORD, JERRY KURLAND, CHARLIE NAPLES, LILI CHANEL, FRANK VOHS, MARILYN SIMON, "PATRICK."
The Burley Cuties: Marilyn Simon, Diane Gallagher, Bonnie Wintz, Sharon Longo, Kathleen DeFreest, Rusty Riegelman, Treva Hill, Christine Chulick, Erin Lareau.

ACT 1
Scene 1
   The Queen of Burlesque
      A. Corio
Scene 2
   "Hello Everybody"
      The Burley Cuties
Scene 3
   Fun in One
      C. Mathis, D. Maitland
Scene 4
   Persian Nights
      F. Vohs, Burley Cuties
Scene 5
   Chaplin Reminiscences
      C. Naples, A. Corio
Scene 6
   An American Beauty
      Shivers Regal, P. Ford, J. Kurland
Scene 7
   Exotic
      L. Chanel
Scene 8
   Two Eggs
      C. Naples, F. Vohs, D. Maitland, A. Corio
Scene 9
   Les Girls
      The Burley Cuties
Scene 10
   The Music Teacher
      C. Mathis, D. Maitland, F. Vohs
Scene 11
   Feature Attraction
      T. Roche
Scene 12
   Act 1 Finale
      Entire Cast
   Candy Butcher
      F. Vohs
ACT 2
Scene 1
   "Powder My Back"
      The Burley Cuties
Scene 2
   "Lucky Pierre"
      C. Mathis, D. Maitland, F. Vohs, A. Corio

Scene 3
   The All-American Male Stripper
      Patrick
Scene 4
   "Charleston"
      T. Roche, The Burley Cuties
Scene 5
   Hall of Fame
      A. Corio
Scene 6
   Crazy House
      Entire Cast
Scene 7
   Memories
      A. Corio
Scene 8
   Grand Finale
      Entire Cast

1981.18 ## FIDDLER ON THE ROOF

A Revival of the Musical in Two Acts, a Prologue and 18 Scenes[2]. Book by Joseph Stein. Based on stories by Sholom Aleichem's stories (Tevye's Daughters) by special permission of Arnold Perl. Music by Jerry Bock. Lyrics by Sheldon Harnick. Entire Production directed and choreographed by Jerome Robbins. Associate director, Ruth Mitchell. Choreography reproduced by Tom Abbott. Settings by Boris Aronson. Costumes by Patricia Zipprodt. Lighting by Ken Billington. Orchestrations by Don Walker. Musical direction by Richard Vitzhum. Vocal arrangements by Milton Greene. Dance music arranged by Betty Walberg. Associate producer, Stella Saltonstall. Produced by Eugene V. Wolsk and James M. Nederlander. Opened 9 July 1981 at the New York State Theatre and closed 23 August 1981 after 53 performances.

CAST (in order of appearance): *Tevye*, the Dairyman: HERSCHEL BERNARDI. *Golde*, his wife: MARIA KARNILOVA. *Their Daughters: Tzeitel*: Lori Ada Jarolslow. *Hodel*: Donalyn Petrucci. *Chava*: Liz Larsen. *Shprintze*: Susan Sheppard. *Beilke*: Eydie Alyson. *Yente*, the Matchmaker: RUTH JAROSLOW. *Motel*, the Tailor: Irwin Pearl. *Perchik*, The Student: Michelan Sisti. *Lazar Wolf*, The Butcher: PAUL LIPSON. *Mordcha*, the Innkeeper: Fyvush Finkel. *Rabbi*: Alvin Meyerovich. *Mendel*, his son: Ken Leroy. *Avram*, the Bookseller: Tog Richards. *Nachum*, the Beggar: Ralph Vucci. *Grandma Tzeitel*: Susan Sheppard. *Fruma-Sarah*: Joyce Martin. *Constable*: Paul E. Hart. *Fyedka*: Joel Robertson. *Shandel*, Motel's Mother: Bess Meisler. *The Fiddler*: Jay Fox. *Yussel*: Stephen Wright.
Villagers: Bradford Dunaway, Jimmy Ferraro, Michael Fogarty, Margo F. Gruber, Michael Lane, Mark Manley, Elaine Manzel, Joyce Martin, Ben Meisler, Robert Parola, Thomas Scalise, Charles Spoerri, Marsha Tamaroff, Susan Tilson, Timothy Tobin, Stephen Wright, Robert Yacko. *Swing Dancers*: Frank Colardo, Debra Timmons.

1981.19 ## MY FAIR LADY

A Revival of the Musical (Comedy) in Two Acts, 18 Scenes[3]. Book and lyrics by Alan Jay Lerner. Based on the play "Pygmalion" by George Bernard Shaw, produced on the screen by Gabriel Pascal. Music by Frederick Loewe. Directed by Patrick Garland. Choreography and musical numbers staged by Crandall Diehl, based on the original by Hanya Holm. Production (settings) designed by Oliver Smith. Costumes designed by Cecil Beaton. Co-costume designer, John David Ridge. Lighting by Ken Billington. Musical arrangements (orchestrations) by Robert Russell Bennett and Philip J. Lang. Sound by John McClure. Musical director, Franz Allers. (Associate producers, Steve Herman, Jon Cutler.) Produced by Don Gregory and Mike Merrick. A Dome/Cutler-Herman Production. Opened 18 August 1981 at the Uris Theatre and closed 29 November 1981 after 119 performances.

---

[1]Originally produced in New York Off-Broadway 6 March 1962 at the Casino East Theatre for 1509 performances; transferred to Broadway 16 March 1965 at the Hudson Theatre for 124 performances.

[2]Originally produced in New York 22 September 1964 at the Imperial Theatre for 3242 performances. For Synopsis of Scenes and Musical Numbers, see original 1964 production. "Chavaleh" appears in the program for this revival.
[3]Originally produced in New York 15 March 1956 at the Mark Hellinger Theatre for 2717 peformances. For Synopsis of Scenes and Musical Numbers, see original 1956 production.

CAST (in order of appearance): *Buskers:* Eric Alderfer, Alan Gilbert, Lisa Guignard. *Mrs. Eynsford-Hill:* Harriet Medin. *Eliza Doolittle:* NANCY RINGHAM. *Freddy Eynsford-Hill:* NICHOLAS WYMAN. *Colonel Pickering:* JACK GWILLIM. *Henry Higgins:* REX HARRISON. *Selsey Man:* Ben Wrigley. *Hoxton Man:* Clifford Fearl. *A Bystander:* Joseph Billone. *Another Bystander:* Ned Coulter. *First Cockney:* John Caleb. *Second Cockney:* Ned Coulter. *Third Cockney:* Ned Peterson. *Fourth Cockney:* Jeffrey Calder. *Bartender:* David Cale Johnson. *Harry:* Ben Wrigley. *Jamie:* Clifford Fearl. *Alfred P. Doolittle:* MILO O'SHEA. *Mrs. Pearce:* Marion Baer. *Mrs. Hopkins:* Mary O'Brien. *Butler:* Frank Bouley. *Servants:* Jeralyn Glass, David Miles, Ellen McLain, Judith Thiergaard. *Mrs. Higgins:* CATHLEEN NESBITT. *Chauffeur:* Alan Gilbert. *Footmen:* John Caleb, Ned Peterson. *Lord Boxington:* Richard Ammon. *Lady Boxington:* Mary O'Brien. *Constable:* Alan Gilbert. *Flower Girl:* Karen Toto. *Zoltan Karpathy:* Jack Sevier. *Major-Domo:* David Cale Johnson. *Queen of Transylvania:* Svetlana McLee Grody. *Ambassador:* Ben Wrigley. *Bartender:* Ned Peterson. *Mrs. Higgins' Maid:* Elizabeth Worthington.

Singing Ensemble: Frank Bouley, Jeffrey Calder, John Caleb, Ned Coulter, Diana Lynne Drew, Julie Ann Fogt, Terri Gervais, Jeralyn Glass, David Cale Johnson, Michael McGifford, Ellen McLain, David Miles, Mary O'Brien, Ned Peterson, Judith Thiergaard. *Dancing Ensemble:* Eric Alderfer, Richard Ammon, Joseph Billone, Arlene Columbo, Ron Crofoot, Raul Gallyot, Alan Gilbert, Svetlana McLee Grody, Lisa Guignard, Scott Harris, Lynn Keeton, Gail Lohla, James Boyd Parker, Karen Paskow, Karen Toto, Elizabeth Worthington. *Alternates:* Scott Harris, Lynne Savage.

1981.20 THE STUDENT PRINCE

A Revival of the Operetta in Three Acts, a Prologue and 4 Scenes[4]. Book and lyrics by Dorothy Donnelly. Book adaptation by Hugh Wheeler. Music by Sigmund Romberg. Conducted by Brain Salesky. Directed by Jack Hofsis. Stage director, Christian Smith. Scenery designed by David Jenkins Costumes designed by Patton Campbell. Lighting designed by Gilbert V. Hemsley, Jr. Choreography by Donald Saddler, restaged by Jessica Redel. Chorus master, Lloyd Walser. Produced by the New York City Opera. Opened 27 August 1981 at the New York State Theatre and closed 30 August 1981 after 6 performances.

CAST (in order of their appearance): *Lackeys:* Edward Zimmerman, Louis Perry, Harris Davis, Mervin Crook. *Dr. Engel,* the Prince's Tutor: DOMINIC COSSA. *Count von Mark:* DAVID RAE SMITH. *Secretaries:* Glenn Rowen, Barry Carl. *Prince Karl Franz:* HENRY PRICE. *Lutz,* valet to the Prince: JACK HARROLD. *Gretchen,* Maid at the Inn: PENNY ORLOFF. *Ruder:* Dan Sullivan. *Nicholas:* Taras Kalba. *Toni,* a waiter: James Billings. *Hubert:* William Ledbetter. *Detlef,* a student leader: John Lankston. *von Asterberg,* another student leader: Thomas Jamerson. *Lucas,* another student leader: Ralph Bassett. *Freshman:* Louis Perry. *Kathie,* niece of Ruder: ELIZABETH HYNES. *Girls:* Madeleine Mines, Jean Rawn, Barbara Wright. *Students:* Rick Christman, Louis Perry, Merle Schmidt, Spencer Smith. *Grand Duchess Anastasia:* MURIEL COSTA-GREENSPON. *Princess Margaret,* fiancée of Prince Karl Franz: NADIA PELLE. *Captain Tarnitz:* WILLIAM EICHORN. *Countess Leydon,* lady-in-waiting to the Princess: Rita Metzger. *Huzzars:* Richard Nelson, Herbert Hunsberger, Robert Brubaker, Merle Schmidt. *Friends of the Huzzars:* Madeleine Mines, Jean Rawn, Barbara Wright, Maria Donaldi. *Ensemble:* New York City Opera Chorus.

1981.21 SONG OF NORWAY

A Revival of the Operetta in Two Acts, 7 Scenes[5]. Book by Milton Lazarus from a play by Homer Curran. Based on the life and music of Edvard Grieg. Musical adaptation and lyrics by Robert Wright and George Forrest. Conceived and originally produced by Edwin Lester. Conductor, Scott Bergeson. Directed by Gerald Freedman. Choreography by Eliot Feld; danced by The Feld Ballet. Scenery designed by David Jenkins. Principal costumes designed by Ann Roth. Costume coordination, Joseph A. Citarella. Lighting designed by Gilbert V. Hemsley, Jr. Chorus master, Lloyd Walser. Assistant stage directors, Jay Lesenger, Gary Dietrich. Additional orchestrations by Scott Bergeson. Special dance orchestrations by Sol Berkowitz. Produced by the New York City Opera. Opened 3 September 1981 at the New York State Theatre and closed 13 September 1981 after 14 performances.

---

[4]First produced in New York as *THE STUDENT PRINCE IN HEIDELBERG* 2 December 1924 at the Jolson Theatre for 608 peformances; this version first presented 29 August 1980 at the New York State Theatre for 13 performances. For Synopsis of Scenes and Musical Numbers, see 1980 revival.

[5]Originally produced in New York 21 August 1944 at the Imperial Theatre for 860 performances. For Synopsis of Scenes and Musical Numbers, see original 1944 production. "Chocolate Pas des Trois" dropped for this production.

CAST (in order of appearance): *Rikard Nordraak:* DAVID EISLER. *Einar:* Mark M. Kelly. *Gunnar:* Jamie Cohen. *Sigrid:* Patricia Ludd. *Eric:* Patrick Cea. *Grima:* Traci Owens. *Christa:* Catherine Ulissey. *Nina Hagerup:* SHERYL WOODS. *Edvard Grieg:* STEPHEN DICKSON. *Freddy,* the Fiddler: JEFF SATINOFF. *Mother Grieg:* MURIEL COSTA-GREENSPON. *Father Grieg:* DAN SULLIVAN. *Father Nordraak:* Ralph Bassett. *Count Peppi Le Loup:* DAVID RAE SMITH. *Louisa Giovanni, Countess Le Loup:* SUSANNE MARSEE. *Villagers:* Jennifer Grissette, Cheryl Jones, Megan Murphy, Traci Owens, Mary Randolph, Catherine Ulissey, Patrick Cea, Timothy Cronin, Thomas Lemanski, David Lukcso, Remus Marcu, Gregory Mitchell. *Elvera:* Madeleine Mines. *Miss Norden:* Rita Metzger. *Miss Anders:* Barbara Wright. *Hedwig:* Madeleine Soyka. *Greta:* Lee Bellaver. *Marghareta:* Diana Skinner. *Henrik Ibsen:* JAMES BILLINGS. *Adelina/Anitra:* Jacqueline O'Dell. *Tito:* Michael Rubino. *Pisoni:* Joaquin Romaguera. *Marcello:* Michael Martorano. *Major Domo:* William Poplaski. *Children:* Anne-Marie Blaber, Eliot Van Buskirk, Emily Van Buskirk. *Waltzing Couples:* Gloria Brisbin, Judith Garfinkel, Cheryl Jones, Megan Murphy, Mary Randolph, Catherine Ulissey, Patrick Cea, Jamie Cohen, Richard Fein, Remus Marcu, Gregory Mitchell, Jeff Satinoff. *Spirit of Grieg:* Richard Fein. *Maidens of Norway:* Gloria Brisbin, Patricia Brown, Judith Garfinkel, Mindy Gars, Jennifer Grissette, Cheryl Jones, Megan Murphy, Jacqueline O'Dell, Traci Owens, Mary Randolph, Joan Tsao, Catherine Ulissey. *Ensemble:* New York City Opera Chorus.

1981.22 DIE FLEDERMAUS

A Revival of the Operetta in Three Acts[6]. (Original libretto by Carl Haffner and Richard Genée. Lyrics by Richard Genée. Based on the comedy "Le Réveillon" by Henri Meilhac and Ludovic Halévy.) English libretto by Ruth and Thomas Martin. Music by Johann Strauss. Production devised and directed by Gerald Freedman. Choreography by Thomas Andrew, restaged by Jessica Redel. Scenery designed by Lloyd Evans Costumes design by Theoni V. Aldredge. Lighting by Hans Sondheimer. Conducted by David Effron. Chorus prepared by Mitchell Krieger. Produced by the New York City Opera. Opened 19 September 1981 at the New York State Theatre and closed 10 October 1981 after 5 performances in repertory.

CAST (in order of appearance): *Alfred,* an itinerant tenor: Jerry Hadley. *Adele,* von Eisenstein's chambermaid: LEIGH MUNRO. *Rosalinda von Eisenstein:* PATRICIA WELLS. *Gabriel von Eisenstein:* JOSEPH EVANS. *Dr. Blind,* a lawyer: Norman Large. *Dr. Falke,* a close friend of Eisenstein: DOMINIC COSSA. *Frank,* the prison warden: SPIRO MALAS. *Sally,* Adele's sister: Puli Toro. *Ivan,* servant to Orlofsky: Gary Dietrich. *Prince Orlofsky,* a wealthy, bored Russian: JAMES BILLINGS. *Frosch,* the jailer: Jack Harrold. *Solo Dancers:* Esperanza Galan, Taras Kalba. *Ensemble:* New York City Opera Chorus.

1981.23 AN EVENING WITH DAVE ALLEN

A One Man Performance in Two Acts. Lighting by John Gleason. Produced by Chartwell Communications, Inc. in association with Theater Now Inc. Opened 20 September 1981 at the Booth Theatre and closed 17 October 1981 after 29 performances.

CAST: DAVE ALLEN. (Comic Monologuist/Stand-up Comedian)

1981.24 MARLOWE

A Rock Musical in Two Acts, 8 Scenes. Book and lyrics by Leo Rost. Music and lyrics by Jimmy Horowitz. Directed and staged by Don Price. Set design by Cary Chalmers. Lighting design by Mitch Acker, Rick Belzer. Costume design by Natalie Walker. Sound design by Peter Fitzgerald. Orchestrations by Jimmy Horowitz. Musical supervision by Larry Fallon. Musical direction, Kinny Landrum. Vocal arrangements by Jimmy Horowitz, Patrick Jude. Choral direction by Billy Cunningham. Fight choreography by Peter Moore. Associate producer, Raymond Serra. A John Annunziato Production. Produced by Tony Conforti; co-produced by Robert R. Blume with Billy Gaff and Howard P. Effron. Opened 12 October 1981 at the Rialto Theatre and closed 22 November 1981 after 48 performances.

CAST (in order of appearance): *Queen Elizabeth I:* Margaret Warncke. *Audrey Walsingham:* Debra Greenfield. *Captain Townshend:* Steve Hall. *Archbishop Parker:* RAYMOND SERRA. *Richard Burbage:* John Henry Kurtz. *William Shakespeare:* Lennie Del Duca, Jr. *Ermelia Bossano:* LISA MORDENTE. *Christopher Marlowe:* PATRICK JUDE. *Ingram Frizer:* Robert Rosen.

---

[6]First English language production in New York 16 March 1885 at the Casino Theatre for 42 performances. First New York production of this adaptation 20 December 1950 at the Metropolitan Opera House. For Synopsis of Scenes and Musical Numbers, see May 1954 revival.

Chorus: Kenneth D. Ard, Marlene Danielle, Robert Hoshour, Renee Dulaney, Timothy Tobin, Teri Gibson, Diane Pennington, Caryn Richmond.

The action takes place in England in 1593. The story of this drama is true and accurate, except for minor adjustments in time for dramatic purpose.

Act 1, Scene 1: Queen Elizabeth's Bed Chamber. 28 May. Late morning. *Scene 2:* Backstage at the Globe Theatre. A few hours later. *Scene 3:* The Mall near St. James Palace. During the Jubilee Festival. *Scene 4:* Sir Walter Raleigh's Observatory. That evening. *Scene 5:* The Privy Council Chamber at St. James Palace. 30 May. Morning.

Act 2, Scene 1: Eleanor Bull's Tavern at Deptford. 30 May. Early evening. *Scene 2:* Deptford Waterfront Docks. 30 May. Later that evening. *Scene 3:* The Courtyard at St. James Palace. A few days later.

ACT 1
  Prologue
    Chroniclers
  "Rocking the Boat"
    R. Serra, M. Warncke, S. Hall, Chorus
  "Because I'm a Woman"
    L. Mordente, L. Del Duca, Jr., J. H. Kurtz
  "Live for the Moment"
    P. Jude, Company
  "Emelia"
    L. Del Duca, Jr., P. Jude
  "I'm Coming 'Round to Your Point of View"
    P. Jude, L. Mordente
  "The Ends Justify the Means"
    R. Rosen, D. Greenfield
  "Higher Than High"
    P. Jude, L. Mordente, J. H. Kurtz, L. Del Duca, Jr., Chorus
  "Rocking the Boat" (reprise)
    Company
ACT 2
  Act 2 Prologue
    Chroniclers
  "Christopher"
    L. Mordente, Chorus
  "So Do I" (Ode to Virginity)
    J. H. Kurtz, Chorus
  "Two Lovers"
    L. Mordente
  "The Funeral Dirge"
    J. H. Kurtz, L. Mordente, L. Del Duca, Jr., R. Rosen, S. Hall, M. Warncke
  "Live for the Moment" (reprise)
    P. Jude, L. Mordente
  "Emelia" (reprise)
    P. Jude, L. Mordente
  "Can't Leave Now"
    P. Jude
  "Christopher" (reprise)
    L. Mordente, L. Del Duca, Jr., Company
  "The Madrigal Blues"
    P. Jude, Company

1981.25   OH, BROTHER!

A Musical Comedy in One Act. Book[7] and lyrics by Donald Driver. (Suggested by William Shakespeare's "The Comedy of Errors" and the comedies of Plautus.) Music by Michael Valenti. Directed and staged by Donald Driver. Scenery designed by Michael J. Hotopp, Paul DePass. Costumes designed by Ann Emonts. Lighting designed by Richard Nelson. Musical direction, vocal and dance arrangements by Marvin Laird. Sound designed by Richard Fitzgerald. Orchestrations by Jim Tyler. Assistant choreographer, Ahmed Hussein. Produced by Zev Bufman, the John F. Kennedy Center, the Fisher Theater Foundation, Joan Cullman, Sidney Shlenker. Opened 10 November 1981 at the ANTA Theatre and closed 11 November 1981 after 3 performances.

CAST (in order of appearance): *Revolutionary Leader:* LARRY MARSHALL. *Revolutionaries:* Mark Martino, Thomas LoMonaco. *Bugler:* Sal Provenza. *Revolutionary Women:* ALYSON REED, Pamela Khoury, Kathy Mahoney-Bennett, Geraldine Hanning, Suzanne Walker, Karen Teti. *Revolutionaries:* Stephen Bourneuf, Michael-Pierre Dean. *Lew:* RICHARD B. SHULL. *A Camel:* Steve Sterner, Eric

_____
[7]Program note: Litigation pending W. Shakespeare and Plautus.

Scheps. *Western Mousada:* HARRY GROENER. *Western Habim:* ALAN WEEKS. *Fatatatatatima:* ALYSON REED. *Eastern Habim:* JOE MORTON. *Eastern Mousada:* DAVID-JAMES CARROLL. *Saroyana:* JUDY KAYE. *Musica:* MARY MASTRANTONIO. *Revolutionaries:* Steve Sterner, Eric Scheps. *Balthazar:* BRUCE ADLER. *Ayatollah:* Thomas LoMonaco. *Lillian:* Geraldine Hanning.

The action takes place at the present time on the Persian Gulf.

MUSICAL NUMBERS
  "We Love an Old Story"
    L. Marshall, Revolutionaries
  "I To the World"
    H. Groener, A. Weeks, D. Carroll, J. Morton
  "How Do You Want Me?"
    J. Kaye
  "That's Him"
    M. Mastrantonio, Revolutionaries
  "Everybody Calls Me by My Name"
    H. Groener, Revolutionaries
  "O.P.E.C. Maiden"
    H. Groener, Revolutionaries
  "A Man"
    D. Carroll
  "How Do You Want Me?" (reprise)
    J. Kaye
  "Tell Sweet Saroyana"
    D. Carroll, A. Weeks, Arabs
  "What Do I Tell People This Time?"
    J. Kaye
  "O.P.E.C. Maiden" (reprise)
    M. Mastrantonio, Women
  "A Loud and Funny Song"
    J. Kaye, M. Mastrantonio, A. Reed
  "The Chase"
    Full Company
  "I To the World" (reprise)
    H. Groener, A. Weeks, D. Carroll, J. Morton
  "Oh, Brother!"
    Full Company

1981.26   CAMELOT

A Return Engagement of the Revival of the Musical in Two Acts, 14 Scenes[8]. Book and lyrics by Alan Jay Lerner. Based on the novel "The Once and Future King" by T. H. White. Music by Frederick Loewe. Directed by Frank Dunlop. Choreography by Buddy Schwab. Sets and costumes by Desmond Heeley. Lighting design by Thomas Skelton. Musical director, Franz Allers. Conductor, Terry James. Orchestrations by Robert Russell Bennett and Philip J. Lang. Sound design by John McClure. Musical consultant, Robert Kreis. Artistic consultant, Stone Widney. A Dome/Cutler-Herman Production. Associate producers, Steve Herman, Jon Cutler. Produced by Mike Merrick and Don Gregory. Opened 15 November 1981 at the Winter Garden and closed 2 January 1982 after 57 performances.

CAST (in order of appearance): *Arthur:* RICHARD HARRIS. *Sir Sagramore:* Andy McAvin. *Merlyn:* James Valentine. *Guenevere:* MEG BUSSERT. *Sir Dinadan:* William Parry. *Nimue:* Jeanne Caryl. *Lancelot:* RICHARD MUENZ. *Mordred:* RICHARD BACKUS. *Dap:* Robert Molnar. *Friar:* Vincenzo Prestia. *Lady Anne:* Sally Williams. *Lady Sybil:* Patrice Pickering. *Sir Lionel:* William James. *King Pellinore:* BARRIE INGHAM. *Horrid:* Daisy. *Sir Lionel's Squire:* Steve Osborn. *Sir Sagramore's Squire:* Randy Morgan. *Sir Dinadan's Squire:* Richard Maxon. *Knights of the Investiture:* Bruce Sherman, Jack Sharkey, Ken Henley, Ronald Bennett Stratton. *Tom:* Thor Fields.

Knights, Lords, Ladies of the Court: Elaine Barnes, Marie Berry, Bjarne Buchtrup, Jeanne Caryl, Melanie Clements, John Deyle, Norb Joerder, Kelby Kirk, Debra Dickinson, Kathy Flynn-McGrath, Ken Henley, William James, Dale Kristien, Lorraine Lazarus, Lauren Lipson, Craig Mason, Richard Maxon, Andy McAvin, Robert Molnar, Randy Morgan, Ann Neville, Steve Osborn, Patrice Pickering, Joel Sager, Mariellen Sereduke, D. Paul Shannon, Bruce Sherman, Jack Starkey, Ronald Bennett Stratton, Nicki Wood. *Alternates:* Ellyn Arons, Gary Wales.

_____
[8]Originally produced in New York 3 December 1960 at the Majestic Theatre for 873 performances; this revival previously produced in New York 8 July 1980 at the New York State Theatre for 56 performances. For Synopsis of Scenes and Musical Numbers, see 1980 revival.

1981.27 MERRILY WE ROLL ALONG

A Musical Comedy in Two Acts, 17 Scenes. Book by George Furth. Based on the play of the same name by George S. Kaufman and Moss Hart. Music and lyrics by Stephen Sondheim. Production directed by Harold Prince. Choreography by Larry Fuller. Scenery designed by Eugene Lee. Costumes designed by Judith Dolan. Lighting designed by David Hersey. Orchestrations by Jonathan Tunick. Musical director, Paul Gemignani. Sound design by Jack Mann. Dance arrangements by Tom Fay, Arnold Gross. Associate producers, Ruth Mitchell, Howard Haines. Produced by Lord Grade, Martin Starger, Robert Fryer, Harold Prince. Opened 16 November 1981 at the Alvin Theatre and closed 28 November 1981 after 16 performances.

CAST (in order of appearance): *Franklin Shephard*: JIM WALTON. *Mary Flynn*: ANN MORRISON. *Charley Kringas*: LONNY PRICE. *Gussie*: TERRY FINN. *Joe*: JASON ALEXANDER. *Beth*: SALLY KLEIN. *Franklin Shephard (at age 43)*: Geoffrey Horne. *Jerome*: David Cady. *Terry*: Donna Marie Elio. *Ms. Gordon*: Maryrose Wood. *Alex*, Talk Show Host: Marc Moritz. *Gwen Wilson*: Tonya Pinkins. *Ted*: David Loud. *Les*: David Shine. *Mr. Spencer*: Paul Hyams. *Mrs. Spencer*: Mary Johansen. *Meg*: Daisy Prince. *Ru*: Forest D. Ray. *Bartender*: Tom Shea. *Evelyn*: Abby Pogrebin. *Valedictorian*: Giancarlo Esposito. *George*, the Headwaiter: James Bonkovsky. *Girl auditioning*: Marianna Allen. *Nightclub Waitress*: Liz Callaway. *Photographer*: Steven Jacob. *Soundman*: Clark Sayre. *Waiter*: Gary Stevens.

The action moves backwards in time from 1980 to 1955.

Act 1, Scene 1: Lake Forest Academy, Lake Forest, Illinois. 1980. *Scene 2*: Franklin Shepard's house, Bel Air, California. 1979. *Scene 3*: 1979-1976. *Scene 4*: The Polo Lounge of the Beverly Hills Hotel, Beverly Hills, California. 1975. *Scene 5*: A TV Studio, New York City. 1973-1969. *Scene 6*: 1973-1969. *Scene 7*: Frank's Apartment. Central Park West, New York City. 1968. *Scene 8*: 1968-1966. *Scene 9*: Outside a courthouse, Centre Street. 1966.

Act 2, Scene 1: Outside a theatre. 1964. *Scene 2*: 1964-1962. *Scene 3*: Joe and Gussie's Apartment, Sutton Place. 1962. *Scene 4*: 1961. *Scene 5*: A small nightclub in Greenwich Village. 1960. *Scene 6*: Frank and Charley's apartment; Joe Josephson's office; Manhattan. 1959-1957. *Scene 7*: A rooftop on West 110th Street. 1957. *Scene 8*: Lake Forest Academy. 1955.

ACT 1
Scene 1
  "Merrily We Roll Along"
    Company
Scene 2
  "Rich and Happy"
    J. Walton, Company
Scene 3
  "Merrily We Roll Along" (reprise)
    Company
Scene 4
  "Like It Was"
    A. Morrison
Scene 5
  "Franklin Shephard, Inc."
    L. Price
Scene 6
  "Merrily We Roll Along" (reprise)
    Company
Scene 7
  "Old Friends"
    J. Walton, L. Price, A. Morrison
Scene 8
  "Merrily We Roll Along" (reprise)
    Company
Scene 9
  "Not a Day Goes By"
    J. Walton
  "Now You Know"
    A. Morrison, Company
ACT 2
Scene 1
  "It's a Hit!"
    J. Walton, A. Morrison, L. Price, J. Alexander
Scene 2
  "Merrily We Roll Along" (reprise)
    Company

Scene 3
  "Good Thing Going"
    L. Price, J. Walton
Scene 4
  "Merrily We Roll Along" (reprise)
    Company
Scene 5
  "Bobby and Jackie and Jack"
    L. Price, S. Klein, J. Walton, D. Loud
  "Not a Day Goes By" (reprise)
    J. Walton, A. Morrison
Scene 6
  "Opening Doors"
    J. Walton, L. Price, A. Morrison, J. Alexander, S. Klein
Scene 7
  "Our Time"
    J. Walton, L. Price, A. Morrison, Company
Scene 8
  "The Hills of Tomorrow"
    Company

1981.28 THE FIRST

A Musical in Two Acts, a Prologue and 17 Scenes. Book by Joel Siegel with Martin Charnin. Music by Bob Brush. Lyrics by Martin Charnin. Entire production staged and directed by Martin Charnin. Musical numbers choreographed by Alan Johnson. Scenery by David Chapman. Costumes by Carrie Robbins. Lighting by Marc B. Weiss. Sound by Louis Shapiro. Consultant, Rachel Robinson. Musical supervision, Orchestrations, dance arrangements by Luther Henderson. Musical conductor, Mark Hummel. Vocal arranger, Joyce Brown. Associate producer, Roger Luby. Produced by Zev Bufman and Neil Bogart, Michael Harvey and Peter A. Bobley. Opened 17 November 1981 at the Martin Beck Theatre and closed 12 December 1981 after 37 performances.

CAST (in order of appearance): *Patsy*, the bartender: Bill Buell. *Leo Durocher*: TREY WILSON. *Clyde Sukeforth*: RAY GILL. *Powers*: Sam Stoneburner. *Thurman*, Brooklyn Eagle Photographer: Thomas Griffith. *Branch Rickey*: DAVID HUDDLESTON. *Cannon*: Jack Hallett. *Holmes*: Stephen Crain. *Sorrentino*, a busboy: Paul Forrest. *People at the Bar* (Bartender, Soldier, and Girl): (D.) Peter Samuel, Bob Morrisey, Kim Criswell. *Jackie Robinson*: DAVID ALAN GRIER. *Third Baseman*: Steven Bland. *Junkyard Jones*: Luther Fontaine. *Catcher*: Michael Edward-Stevens. *Jo-Jo*: Rodney Saulsberry. *Umpire*: Paul Forrest. *Cool Minnie*: CLENT BOWERS. *Softball*: Paul Cook Tartt. *Bucky*: Michael Edward-Stevens. *Equipment Manager*: Steven Bland. *Redcap*: Michael Edward-Stevens. *Rachel Isum*: LONETTE McKEE. *Passengers*: Margaret Lamee, Sam Stoneburner, Rodney Saulsberry, Janet L. Hubert, Thomas Griffith, Kim Criswell, Steven Bland, Bob Morrisey, Stephen Crain, Boncellia Lewis. *Cuban Reporters*: Rodney Saulsberry, Steven Bland. *Swanee Rivers*: Steven Boockvor. *Casey Higgins*: COURT MILLER. *Hatrack Harris*: D. Peter Samuel. *Pee Wee Reese*: Bob Morrisey. *Eddie Stanky*: Stephen Crain. *Dodger Coaches*: Jack Hallett, Bill Buell. *Dodger Rookie*: Thomas Griffith. *Trainer*: Paul Forrest. *Fans*: Boncellia Lewis, Steven Bland, Michael Edward-Stevens, Janet Hubert, Rodney Saulsberry. *Sheriff*: Jack Hallett. *Huey*, a fan: Jack Hallett. *Philadelphia Reporters*: Paul Forrest, Jack Hallett. *Brian Waterhouse*: Bill Buell. *Opal* (on the left): Janet L. Hubert. *Ruby* (on the right): Boncellia Lewis. *Dodger Wives*: Kim Criswell, Margaret Lamee. *Red Barber*: Himself. *Hilda Chester*: Kim Criswell. *Pittsburgh Pirates*: Stephen Crain, Thomas Griffith.

The play dramatizes actual events in the life of Jackie Robinson that occurred between August 1945 and September 1947. Some characters have been created and some chronology and situations have been altered.

Prologue: On the Playing Field.

Act 1, Scene 1: Gallagher's Restaurant, West 52nd Street, New York. *Scene 2*: The Third Base Line; Comiskey Park, Chicago. *Scene 3*: The Locker Room of the Kansas City Monarchs in Chicago. *Scene 4*: Union Station, Chicago. *Scene 5*: Branch Rickey's Office: 215 Montague Street, Brooklyn. *Scene 6*: The Havana Training Camp of the Brooklyn Dodgers. *Scene 7*: Outside a Ballpark; Jacksonville, Florida. *Scene 8*: The Locker Room. *Scene 9*: Branch Rickey's Office. *Scene 10*: The Playing Field.

Act 2, Scene 1: Behind First Base, The Polo Grounds, New York. *Scene 2*: The Dodger Locker Room, Shibe Park, Philadelphia. *Scene 3*: Behind Third Base, Ebbets Field. *Scene 4*: The Front Porch of a Farmhouse, Outside of St. Louis. *Scene 5*: Outside Ebbets Field. *Scene 6*: Inside Ebbets Field. The bottom of the seventh. *Scene 7*: Inside Ebbets Field. The top of the ninth.

ACT 1
Scene 1
  "Jack Roosevelt Robinson"
    D. Huddleston, T. Wilson, R. Gill

Scene 2
  "Dancin' Off Third"
    D. A. Grier, L. Fontaine, the Monarchs
Scene 3
  "The National Pastime"
    C. Bowers, D. A. Grier, L. Fontaine, the Monarchs
Scene 4
  "Will We Ever Know Each Other"
    D. A. Grier, L. McKee
Scene 5
  "The First"
    D. A. Grier
Scene 6
  "Bloat"
    T. Wilson, Reporters, the Dodgers
Scene 7
  "The First" (reprise)
    D. A. Grier
Scene 8
  "It Ain't Gonna Work!"
    C. Miller, the Dodgers
  "The Brooklyn Dodger Strike"
    D. Huddleston, T. Wilson
Scene 9
  "Jack Roosevelt Robinson" (reprise)
    D. Huddleston
  "The First" (reprise)
    L. McKee

ACT 2
Scene 1
  "You Do-Do-Do-It Good!"
    C. Bowers, D. A. Grier, L. Fontaine, the Monarchs, J. Hubert, B. Lewis
Scene 2
  "Is This Year Next Year?"
    S. Stoneburner, Reporters, D. Huddleston, R. Gill, the Dodgers
Scene 3
  "There Are Days And There Are Days"
    L. McKee
Scene 4
  "It's a Beginning"
    D. Huddleston, D. A. Grier
Scene 5
  "The Opera Ain't Over"
    K. Criswell, the Fans, D. A. Grier, the Dodgers, L. McKee, D. Huddleston

1981.29   DREAMGIRLS

A Musical in Two Acts, 20 Scenes. Book and lyrics by Tom Eyen. Music by Henry Krieger. Directed and choreographed by Michael Bennett. Co-choreographer, Michael Peters. Scenic design by Robin Wagner. Costume design by Theoni V. Aldredge. Lighting design by Tharon Musser. Sound design by Otts Munderloh. Musical supervision and orchestrations, Harold Wheeler. Musical director, Yolanda Segovia. Vocal arrangements, Cleavant Derricks. Produced by Michael Bennett, Bob Avian, Geffen Records, the Shubert Organization. Opened 20 December 1981 at the Imperial Theatre and closed 4 August 1985 after 1522 performances.

CAST (in order of appearance): *The Stepp Sisters*: Deborah Burrell, Vanessa Bell, Tenita Jordan, Brenda Pressley. *Charlene*: Cheryl Alexander. *Joanne*: Linda Lloyd. *Marty*: Vondie Curtis-Hall. *Curtis Taylor, Jr.*: BEN HARNEY. *Deena Jones*: SHERYL LEE RALPH. *The M.C.*: Larry Stewart. *Tiny Joe Dixon*: Joe Lynn. *Lorrell Robinson*: LORETTA DEVINE. *C. C. White*: OBBA BABATUNDE. *Effie Melody White*: JENNIFER HOLLIDAY. *Little Albert and the Tru-Tones*: Wellington Perkins, Charles Bernard, Jamie Patterson, Charles Randolph-Wright, Weyman Thompson. *James Thunder Early*: CLEAVANT DERRICKS. *Edna Burke*: Sheila Ellis. *The James Early Band*: Charles Bernard, Jamie Patterson, Wellington Perkins, Scott Plank, Charles Randolph-Wright, Weyman Thompson. *Wayne*: Tony Franklin. *Dave and the Sweethearts*: Paul Binotto, Candy Darling, Stephanie Eley. *Frank*, a press agent: David Thomé. *Michelle Morris*: Deborah Burrell. *Jerry*, a nightclub owner: Joe Lynn. *The Five Tuxedos*: Charles Bernard, Jamie Patterson, Charles Randolph-Wright, Larry Stewart, Weyman Thompson. *Les Style*: Cheryl Alexander, Tenita Jordan, Linda Lloyd, Brenda Pressley. *Film Executives*: Paul Binotto, Scott Plank, Weyman Thompson. *Mr. Morgan*:

Larry Stewart. (N.B. *The Dreamettes, the Dreams* {through Act 1, Scene 11}: J. Holliday, L. Devine, S. L. Ralph. *Deena Jones and The Dreams* thereafter: S. L. Ralph, L. Devine, D. Burrell.)

Announcers, Fans, Reporters, Stagehands, Party Guests, Photographers: Cheryl Alexander, Phylicia Ayers-Allen, Vanessa Bell, Charles Bernard, Paul Binotto, Candy Darling, Ronald Dunham, Stephanie Eley, Sheila Ellis, Tenita Jordan, Linda Lloyd, Joe Lynn, Frank Mastrocola, Jamie Patterson, Wellington Perkins, Scott Plank, Brenda Pressley, David Thomé, Charles Randolph-Wright, Larry Stewart, Weyman Thompson. *Swings*: Brenda Braxton, Milton Craig Nealy.

Act 1: The Early Sixties. *Scene 1*: The Apollo Theatre. *Scene 2*: On the Road. *Scene 3*: A Recording Studio. *Scene 4*: Limbo. *Scene 5*: A Hotel in St. Louis. *Scene 6*: Miami. *Scene 7*: Dressing Room in the Atlantic Hotel. *Scene 8*: Cleveland. *Scene 9*: A TV Studio. *Scene 10*: San Francisco. *Scene 11*: Las Vegas, backstage. *Scene 12*: Las Vegas, on stage.

Act 2: The Early Seventies. *Scene 1*: Las Vegas Hilton. *Scene 2*: Chicago Nightclub. *Scene 3*: Vogue Magazine Photo Call. *Scene 4*: National Democratic Fundraiser. *Scene 5*: A Chicago Recording Studio. *Scene 6*: Los Angeles. *Scene 7*: Chicago. *Scene 8*: New York.

ACT 1
Scene 1
  "I'm Looking for Something"
    D. Burrell, V. Bell, T. Jordan, B. Pressley
  "Goin' Downtown"
    W. Perkins, C. Bernard, J. Patterson, C. Randolph-Wright, W. Thompson
  "Takin' the Long Way Home"
    J. Lynn
  "Move (You're Steppin' on My Heart)"
    J. Holliday, L. Devine, S. L. Ralph
  "Fake Your Way to the Top"
    C. Derricks, J. Holliday, L. Devine, S. L. Ralph, The James Early Band
  "Cadillac Car"
    B. Harney, C. Derricks, O. Babatunde, V. Curtis-Hall, The Company
Scene 2
  "Cadillac Car" (reprise)
    The Company
Scene 3
  "Cadillac Car" (reprise)
    The Company
Scene 4
  "Cadillac Car" (reprise)
    P. Binotto, C. Darling, S. Eley
  "Steppin' to the Bad Side"
    B. Harney, O. Babatunde, C. Derricks, T. Franklin, J. Holliday, L. Devine, S. L. Ralph, the Company
Scene 5
  "Party, Party"
    The Company
Scene 6
  "I Want You Baby"
    C. Derricks, J. Holliday, L. Devine, S. L. Ralph
Scene 7
  "Family"
    O. Babatunde, B. Harney, C. Derricks, S. L. Ralph, L. Devine
Scene 8
  "Dreamgirls"
    J. Holliday, L. Devine, S. L. Ralph
  "Press Conference"
    The Company
  "Only the Beginning"
    B. Harney, S. L. Ralph, J. Holliday
Scene 9
  "Heavy"
    J. Holliday, L. Devine, S. L. Ralph
Scene 10
  "Heavy" (reprise)
    J. Holliday, L. Devine, S. L. Ralph, B. Harney
Scene 11
  "It's All Over"
    B. Harney, J. Holliday, S. L. Ralph, L. Devine, O. Babatunde, D. Burrell, C. Derricks
  "And I Am Telling You I Am Not Going"
    J. Holliday

Scene 12
  "Love Love You Baby"
    L. Devine, S. L. Ralph, D. Burrell

ACT 2
Scene 1
  "Dreams" Medley[9]
    S. L. Ralph, L. Devine, D. Burrell, Company
Scene 2
  "I Am Changing"
    J. Holliday
Scene 3
  "One More Picture Please"
    The Company
  "When I First Saw You"
    B. Harney, S. L. Ralph
Scene 4
  "Got to Be Good Times"
    C. Bernard, J. Patterson, C. Randolph-Wright, L. Stewart, W. Thompson
  "Ain't No Party"
    L. Devine, C. Derricks
  "I Meant You No Harm"
    C. Derricks
  "Quintette"
    S. L. Ralph, L. Devine, O. Babatunde, D. Burrell, C. Derricks
  "The Rap"
    C. Derricks, O. Babatunde, V. Curtis-Hall, D. Thomé, L. Devine, the Company
Scene 5
  "I Miss You Old Friend"
    J. Holliday, V. Curtis-Hall, O. Babatunde, Les Style
  "One Night Only"
    J. Holliday
Scene 6
  "One Night Only" (reprise)
    S. L. Ralph, L. Devine, D. Burrell, Company
Scene 7
  "I'm Somebody"
    S. L. Ralph, L. Devine, D. Burrell
  "Faith in Myself"
    J. Holliday
Scene 8
  "Hard To Say Goodbye, My Love"
    S. L. Ralph, L. Devine, D. Burrell
  ("Dreamgirls" reprise)
    (S. L. Ralph, L. Devine, D. Burrell, J. Holliday)

1982.01   LITTLE ME

A Revival of the Musical Comedy in Two Acts, 19 Scenes[10]. Book (revised) by Neil Simon. Based on the novel of the same name by Patrick Dennis. Music by Cy Coleman. Lyrics by Carolyn Leigh. Directed by Robert Drivas. Choreographed by Peter Gennaro. Sets and costumes by Tony Walton. Lighting by Beverly Emmons. Vocal and dance arrangements by Cy Coleman. Orchestrations by Harold Wheeler. Music director, Donald York. Sound designer, Tom Morse. Produced by Ron Dante, Wayne Rogers, Steven Leber, David Krebs, (J.) McLaughlin, (Marc) Piven, Inc., Warner Theatre Productions, Inc., Emanuel Azenberg. Opened 21 January 1982 at the Eugene O'Neill Theatre and closed 21 February 1982 after 36 performances.

CAST (in order of appearance): Act 1: Announcer: Gibby Brand. Belle (today): JESSICA JAMES. Charlie Drake: Henry Sutton. Belle: MARY GORDON MURRAY. Momma: Mary Small. Ramona: Mary C. Holton. Cerine: Gail Pennington. Bruce: Brian Quinn. Noble Eggleston VICTOR GARBER. Flo Eggleston: JAMES COCO.

Greensleeves: Henry Sutton. Ms. Kepplewhite: Maris Clement. Pinchley Junior: James Brennan. Nurse: Sean Murphy. Amos Pinchley: JAMES COCO. Town Spokesman: Henry Sutton. Court Clerk: Stephen Berger. Attorney: Gibby Brand. Bandleader: Gibby Brand. Henchmen: Bob Freschi, Stephen Berger. Frankie Polo: Don Correia. Val du Val: VICTOR GARBER. Fred Poitrine: VICTOR GARBER. Boom Boom Girls: Bebe Neuwirth, Gail Pennington. Bert: Mark McGrath. Sergeant: Stephen Berger. Preacher: Gibby Brand. German Soldier: Gibby Brand. General: Gibby Brand. Red Cross Nurse: Andrea Green.

Act 2: Captain: Bob Freschi. Steward: David Cahn. Sailor I: Brian Quinn. Sailor II: Mark McGrath. Mr. Worst: JAMES COCO. Assistant Director: Henry Sutton. Otto Schnitzler: JAMES COCO. Pharoah I: Kevin Winkler. Croupier: James Brennan. Doctor: Gibby Brand. Yulnick: Gibby Brand. Prince Cherney: JAMES COCO. Baby Belle: MARY GORDON MURRAY. Noble Junior: VICTOR GARBER.

Townspeople, Skylight patrons, Nurses, Soldiers, Passengers, International set and Peasants: Stephen Berger, Michael Blevins, David Cahn, Maris Clement, Bob Freschi, Andrea Green, Mary C. Holton, Mark McGrath, Gary Mendelson, Sean Murphy, Bebe Neuwirth, Gail Pennington, Susan Powers, Brian Quinn, Kevin Brooks Winkler. Swings: John Hillner, Meredith Murray.

Act 1, Scene 1: The Casa Manana, Hackensack, New Jersey, this evening. Young Belle's home in Twin Jugs, Illinois, years ago. Scene 2: Noble Eggleston's home on Quality Hill. Belle's Shack. Scene 3: Pinchley's Bank. Scene 4: Young Belle's Apartment. Scene 5: The Skylight Roof Cafe. Scene 6: Young Belle's Apartment. Scene 7: Young Belle's Apartment, a few months later. In the trenches in Europe in World War I. Scene 8: A base hospital somewhere in France.

Act 2, Scene 1: The Casa Manana, tonight. On board ship, after World War I. Scene 2: Older Belle recalls her life back in the United States. Scene 3: The Dining Room in the Castle of Phillip Randolph Worst. Scene 4: Hollywood set at Paramour Pictures. Scene 5: Older Belle recalls her life after Hollwood. Scene 6: The Casino at Monte Carlo. Scene 7: The Royal Bedchamber of the Prince Cherny of Rosenzweig. Scene 8: Older Belle recalls her life after the Prince's funeral. The house on Quality Hill. Scene 9: Outside the house on Quality Hill. Scene 10: The house on Quality Hill. Scene 11: The Casa Manana, tonight.

ACT 1
Scene 1
  "Don't Ask a Lady"
    J. James
  "The Other Side of the Tracks"
    M. G. Murray
Scene 2
  "The Rich Kids Rag" (The Birthday Party)
    Company
  "I Love You"
    V. Garber, M. G. Murray, Company
  "The Other Side of the Tracks" (reprise)
    M. G. Murray
Scene 3
  "Deep Down Inside"[11]
    J. Coco, M. G. Murray, Company
Scene 5
  "Boom-Boom"
    V. Garber
  "I've Got Your Number"
    D. Correia
Scene 6
  "Real Live Girl"
    V. Garber
Scene 8
  "Real Live Girl" (reprise)
    Doughboys
ACT 2
Scene 1
  "I Love You" (reprise)
    V. Garber, M. G. Murray
Scene 3
  "I Wanna Be Yours"
    M. G. Murray, J. Coco
Scene 5
  "Little Me"
    J. James, M. G. Murray, M. Small

---

[9]During the run, replaced by a reprise of "Dreamgirls."
[10]Originally produced in New York 17 November 1962 at the Lunt-Fontanne Theatre for 257 performances. "The Truth," "Be a Perfomer!," "Dimples," "Poor Little Hollywood Star" were dropped for this production. "Don't Ask a Lady" and "I Wanna Be Yours" were newly written for this production.

---

[11]Choreography by Bob Fosse recreated from original production.

Scene 7

"Farewell" (The Prince's Goodbye)
J. Coco, G. Brand, H. Sutton, Company

Scene 8

"Here's To Us"
J. James, Company

Scene 11

(Finale)
J. James, Company

THE CURSE OF AN ACHING HEART

1982.02

A Drama (with Music) in One Act, a Prologue and 5 Scenes. Play (and lyrics) by William Alfred. Music by Claibe Richardson. Directed by Gerald Gutierrez. Sets designed by John Lee Beatty. Costumes designed by Nancy Potts. Lighting designed by Dennis Parichy. Sound designed by David Rapkin. Orchestrations by Bruce Pomohac. Associate producers, David Jiranek, Frederick C. Venturelli. Produced by Margot Harley, John Houseman, Everett King, David Weil, Sidney Shlenker. Opened 25 January 1982 at the Little Theatre and closed 21 February 1982 after 32 performances.

CAST (in order of appearance): *Prologue: Frances Walsh*: FAYE DUNAWAY. *Scene 1: Frances Anna Duffy*: FAYE DUNAWAY. *Gertrude "Lulu" Fitter*: Audrie Neenan. *Scene 2: Frances Anna Duffy*: FAYE DUNAWAY. *John Joseph " Jo Jo" Finn*: Bernie McInerney. *Scene 3: Pasquale "Packy" Malardino*: Jon Polito. *Man with newspaper*: Dale Helward. *Herman Crump*: Kurt Knudson. *Martin "Lugs" Walsh*: Terrance O'Quinn. *Fran Duffy*: FAYE DUNAWAY. *Lulu Fitter*: Audrie Neenan. *Minnie Crump*: Francine Beers. *J. Stanislaus McGahey*: Colin Stinton. *Aloysius "Wishy" Burke*: Paul McCrane. *Scene 4: Frances Anna Duffy Walsh*: FAYE DUNAWAY. *Gertrude "Lulu" Fitter Malardino*: Audrie Neenan. *Gertrude Graham Finn*: Beverly May. *Scene 5: Frances Anna Duffy*: FAYE DUNAWAY. *Martin Thomas Walsh*: Raphael Sbarge. *John Joseph " Jo Jo" Finn*: Bernie McInerney.

Prologue: 1942. *Scene 1*: Friday Night Dreams Come True—1923. *Scene 2*: Clothes Make the Woman—1925. *Scene 3*: The Curse of an Aching Heart—1927. *Scene 4*: All Saints, All Souls—1935. *Scene 5*: Holy Saturday—1942.

MUSICAL NUMBERS[12]

Scene 1

"Love to Your Heart's Desire"
F. Dunaway, A. Neenan

Scene 2

"Make It New"
F. Dunaway

Scene 3

"Spring, Spring, Spring"
J. Polito

"Thorspring"
A. Neenan, F. Dunaway

"I Got Eyes for a Girl on the Car"
J. Polito

"Ain't Love Grand"
A. Neenan, J. Polito

JOSEPH AND THE AMAZING TECHNICOLOR DREAMCOAT

1982.03

A Musical in Two Acts and a Prologue[13]. Music by Andrew Lloyd Webber. Lyrics by Tim Rice. Direction and choreography by Tony Tanner. Scenery by Karl Eigsti. Costumes by Judith Dolan. Lighting by Barry Arnold. Sound by Tom Morse. Musical supervision, arrangements and orchestrations by Martin Silvestri, Jeremy Stone. Musical director, David Friedman. Associate producers, Thomas Pennini, Jean Luskin, Jerome Edson. Produced by Zev

Bufman, Susan R. Rose, Melvyn J. Estrin, Sidney Shlenker, Gail Berman by arrangement with The Robert Stigwood Organization Ltd. and David Land. Opened 27 January 1982 at the Royale Theatre and closed 4 September 1983 after 670 performances. Total, including Off-Broadway run: 747 performances.

CAST (in order of appearance): *Narrator*: LAURIE BEECHMAN. *Women's Chorus*: Lorraine Barrett, Karen Bogan, Katharine Buffaloe, Lauren Goler, Randon Lo, Joni Masella, Kathleen Rowe McAllen, Renée Warren. *Jacob*: GORDON STANLEY. *Brothers (11): Reuben*: ROBERT HYMAN. *Simeon*: Kenneth Bryan. *Levi*: STEVE McNAUGHTON. *Napthali*: CHARLIE SERRANO. *Issachar*: Peter Kapetan. *Asher*: David Asher. *Dan*: James Rich. *Zebulon*: Doug Voet. *Gad*: Barry Tarallo. *Benjamin*: PHILIP CARRUBBA. *Judah*: Stephen Hope. *Joseph*: BILL HUTTON. *Ismaelites*: TOM CARDER, DAVID ARDAO. *Potiphar*: DAVID ARDAO. *Mrs. Potiphar*: RANDON LO. *Butler*: Kenneth Bryan. *Baker*: Barry Tarallo. *Pharaoh*: TOM CARDER. *Swings*: Rosalyn Rahn, John Ganzer.

Prologue ("You Are What You Feel")
L. Beechman

ACT 1

"Jacob and Sons"/"Joseph's Coat"
L. Beechman, Brothers, G. Stanley, B. Hutton, Women

"Joseph's Dreams"
L. Beechman, B. Hutton, Brothers

"Poor Poor Joseph"
L. Beechman, Brothers, Women

"One More Angel in Heaven"
S. McNaughton, Brothers

"Potiphar"
L. Beechman, Women, R. Lo, D. Ardao, B. Hutton

"Close Every Door"
B. Hutton, Women

"Stone the Crows"[14]
L. Beechman, T. Carder, B. Hutton, Women, Men

"Pharaoh's Story"
L. Beechman, Women

ACT 2

"Poor, Poor Pharaoh"/"Song of the King"
L. Beechman, T. Carder, Women, Men

"Pharaoh's Dream Explained"
B. Hutton, Women, Men

"Stone the Crows" (reprise)
L. Beechman, T. Carder, B. Hutton, Women, Men

"Those Canaan Days"
R. Hyman, Brothers

"The Brothers Came to Egypt"/"Grovel, Grovel"
L. Beechman, Brothers, B. Hutton, Women

"Who's the Thief?"
B. Hutton, Brothers, Women

"Benjamin Calypso"
C. Serrano, Brothers

"Joseph All the Time"
L. Beechman, B. Hutton, Brothers, Women

"Jacob in Egypt"
B. Hutton, Brothers, Women

"Any Dream Will Do"
B. Hutton, Company

"May I Return to the Beginning"
The Company

PUMP BOYS AND DINETTES

1982.04

A Musical in Two Acts[15]. Conceived and written by the Company (John Foley, Mark Hardwick, Debra Monk, Cass Morgan, John Schimmel, Jim Wann). Scenery by Doug Johnson, Christopher Nowak. Costumes by Patricia McGourty. Lighting by Fred Buchholtz. Sound by Bill Dreisbach.

---

[12]Songs not listed in program. Above list prepared from production typescript.

[13]Originally produced in New York Off-Broadway 18 November 1981 at the Entermedia Theatre for 77 performances. Previously produced Off-Broadway twice at the Brooklyn Academy of Music: 26 December 1976 for 22 performances, and 13 December 1977 for 24 performances.

[14]During the run and for subsequent national tour, replaced by:
"Go, Go Joseph"
L. Beechman, B. Tarallo, K. Bryan, Chorus, B. Hutton, Men

[15]Originally produced Off-Broadway 10 July 1981 at the Westside Arts Theatre for 20 performances, 13 October 1981 at the Colonnades Theatre for 112 performances.

Production coordinator, Sherman Warner. Produced by Dodger Productions (Michael David, Doug Johnson, Rocco Landesman, Des McAnuff, Edward Strong, Sherman Warner), Louis Busch Hager, Marilyn Strauss, Kate Studley, Warner Theatre Productions, Inc. and Max Weitzenhoffer. Opened 4 February 1982 at the Princess Theatre and closed 18 June 1983 after 573 performances.

CAST (in alphabetical order): *Jackson:* John Foley. *L.M.:* Mark Hardwick. *Prudie Cupp:* Debra Monk. *Rhetta Cupp:* Cass Morgan. *Eddie:* John Schimmel. *Jim:* Jim Wann.

ACT 1

"Highway 57"
All
(*Music and Lyrics by* Jim Wann.)
"Taking It Slow"
Pump Boys (Men)
(*Music and Lyrics by* John Foley, Mark Hardwick, John Schimmel, Jim Wann.)
"Serve Yourself"
M. Hardwick
(*Music and Lyrics by* Jim Wann.)
"Menu Song"
Dinettes (Women)
(*Music and Lyrics by* Debra Monk, Cass Morgan.)
"The Best Man"
D. Monk
(*Music and Lyrics by* Jim Wann.)
"Fisherman's Prayer"
Pump Boys
(*Music and Lyrics by* Jim Wann.)
"Caution: Men Cooking"[16]
Pump Boys
(*Music and Lyrics by* Debra Monk, Cass Morgan, Jim Wann, John Foley.)
"Mamaw"
J. Wann
(*Music and Lyrics by* Jim Wann.)
"Be Good or Be Gone"
C. Morgan
(*Music and Lyrics by* Jim Wann.)
"Drinkin' Shoes"
All
(*Music and Lyrics by* Mark Hardwick, Cass Morgan, Debra Monk.)

ACT 2

"Pump Boys"
Pump Boys
(*Music and Lyrics by* Jim Wann.)
"Mona"
J. Foley
(*Music and Lyrics by* Jim Wann.)
"T.N.D.P.W.A.M."
M. Hardwick
(*Music and Lyrics by* Jim Wann.)
"Tips"
Dinettes
(*Music and Lyrics by* Debra Monk, Cass Morgan.)
"Sister"
Dinettes
(*Music and Lyrics by* Cass Morgan.)
"Vacation"
All
(*Music and Lyrics by* Jim Wann.)
"No Holds Barred"
All
(*Music and Lyrics by* Jim Wann, Cass Morgan.)
"Farmer Tan"
M. Hardwick, Dinettes
(*Music and Lyrics by* Jim Wann.)
"Highway 57" (reprise)
All

---

[16]Replaced after opening with:
"Catfish"
Pump Boys
(*Music and Lyrics by* Jim Wann, Bland Simpson.)

"Closing Time"
All
(*Music and Lyrics by* Jim Wann.)

1982.05 LITTLE JOHNNY JONES

A Revival of the Musical (Comedy) in Two Acts, 8 Scenes[17]. Book, music and lyrics by George M. Cohan. Adapted by Alfred Uhry. Entire production directed by Gerald Gutierrez. Scenery designed by Robert Randolph. Costumes designed by David Toser. Lighting designed by Thomas Skelton. Sound designed by Abe Jacob. Choreography and musical staging by Dan Siretta. Musical direction by Lynn Crigler. Additional orchestrations by Eddie Sauter, Mack Schlefer. Dance arrangements by Russell Warner. Vocal arrangements and additional dance arrangements by Robert Fisher. Musical consultant, Alfred Simon. Production associate, Warren Pincus. Production supervisor, Robert Strauss. Originally produced by the Goodspeed Opera House, East Haddam, Connecticut (Michael P. Price, Executive producer). Presented by James M. Nederlander, Steven Leber, David Krebs, and the John F. Kennedy Center. Opened and closed 21 March 1982 at the Alvin Theatre after 1 performance.

CAST (in order of appearance): *Starter at the Hotel Cecil:* JACK BITTNER. *Anthony Anstey*, a racetrack man: PETER VAN NORDEN. *Florabelle Fly*, Society Editor of the *San Francisco Searcher:* JANE GALLOWAY. *Timothy D. McGee*, another racetrack man: TOM ROLFING. *Goldie Gates*, an American copper heiress: MAUREEN BRENNAN. *Sing-Song*, Sports Editor, *Peking Gazette:* Bruce Chew. *Whitney Wilson*, the great unknown: ERNIE SABELLA. *A Bellboy:* Al Micacchion. *Johnny Jones*, an American jockey: DONNY OSMOND. *Mrs. Kenworth*, Goldie's aunt and guardian: ANNA McNEELY. *Announcer at English Derby:* JACK BITTNER. *Captain Squirvy:* JACK BITTNER. *A Newsboy:* David Fredericks.

American Boys, Porters, Sailors: Richard Dodd, David Fredericks, James Homan, Gary Kirsch, Bobby Longbottom, Al Micacchion, David Monzione, Keith Savage. *American Girls:* Colleen Ashton, Terri Corcoran, Susie Fenner, Linda Gradl, Debra Grimm, Lori Lynott, Annette Michelle, Mayme Paul. *Dance Alternates:* Tammy Silva, Jonathan Aronson, Jamie Torcellini.

The action takes place in England, New York and Saratoga in 1904.

Act 1, Scene 1: Exterior of the Hotel Cecil, London, 1904. *Scene 2:* Interior of the Hotel Cecil, immediately following. *Scene 3:* Hyde Park, immediately following. *Scene 4:* The British Derby, that afternoon.

Act 2, Scene 1: Outside the Pier at Southampton, a week later. *Scene 2:* The Pier itself, immediately following. *Scene 3:* A New York Street, two weeks later. *Scene 4:* Saratoga, the Fourth of July.

ACT 1
Scene 1
"The Cecil in London"
J. Bittner, Ensemble
Scene 2
"Then I'd Be Satisfied With Life"
P. Van Norden
"Yankee Doodle Boy"
D. Osmond, Ensemble
Scene 3
"Oh, You Wonderful Boy" (from *THE LITTLE MILLIONAIRE*, 1911)
M. Brennan, J. Galloway, American Girls
Scene 4
"The Voice in My Heart" (from *LITTLE NELLIE KELLY*, 1922)
A. McNeely, Ensemble
"Finaletto"
Company
ACT 2
Scene 1
"Captain of a Ten Day Boat"
J. Bittner, Ensemble
Scene 2
"Goodbye Flo"
J. Galloway, Sailors
"Life's a Funny Proposition"
D. Osmond

---

[17]Originally produced in New York 7 November 1904 at the Liberty Theatre for 52 performances.

"Let's You and I Just Say Goodbye" (from *THE RISE OF ROSIE O'REILLY*, 1923)
    M. Brennan
"Give My Regards to Broadway"
    D. Osmond, Ensemble
Scene 3
    "Extra! Extra!"
        Newsboys
Scene 4
    "American Ragtime" (from *THE AMERICAN IDEA*, 1908)
        J. Galloway, T. Rolfing, D. Osmond, Ensemble
    Finale
        Company

1982.06   ENCORE

Fifty Years of Showstoppers (A Musical Revue) in Two Acts, 11 Scenes. Producer and director, Robert F. Jani. Musical director, Tom Bahler. Scenic designer, Charles Lisanby. Scenic coordinator, Terry Carriker. Production costume designer, Michael Casey. Lighting designer, Ken Billington. Staging and choreography by Adam Grammis, Geoffrey Holder, Frank Wagner, Shozo Nakano, Linda Lemac, Violet Holmes. Conductor, Joseph Klein. Produced by Radio City Music Hall Productions, Inc. Opened 26 March 1982 at the Radio City Music Hall and closed 6 September 1982 after 288 performances.

CAST: WENDY EDMEAD, TOM GARRETT, MICHAEL KUBALA, KUNIKO NARAI, DEBORAH PHELAN, JUSTIN ROSS, LUIS VILLANUEVA, KAREN ZIEMBA.
    THE ROCKETTES: Lois Ann Alston, Kathy Beatty, Dottie Belle, Susan Boron, Elizabeth Chanin, Barbara Ann Cittadino, Susan Cleland, Eileen Marie Collins, Brie Daniels, Susanne Doris, Jackie Fancy, Deniene Fenn, Alexis Ficks, Prudence Gray, Jennifer Hammond, Carol Harbich, Cindy Hughes, Stephanie James, Joan Peer Kelleher, Pam Kelleher, Dee Dee Knapp, Judy Little, Sonya Livingston, Leslie Grysko, McCarthy, Mary McNamara, Lynn Newton, Pam Stacey Pasqualino, Kerri Pearsall, Cindy Peiffer, Gerri Presky, Terry Spano, Lynn Sullivan, Susan Theobald, Carol Toman, Pat Tully, Darlene Wendy, Rose Ann Woolsey, Phyllis Wujko.
    THE NEW YORKERS: John Aller, David Brownlee, Rick Conant, Dale Furry, Edyie Fleming Geistman, Sonya Hensley, David Michael Johnson, Joe Joyce, Connie Kunkle, Rosemary Loar, Keith Locke, Edward Prostak, Susan Streater, Scott Willis.
    Dancers: David Askler, Robert Boling, Leigh Catlett, Cisco X. Drayton, Larry Lynd, Will Mead, Jackie Patterson, David Roman, Stan Shelmire.

ACT 1
Scene 1
    "Encore"
        Full Company
        (*Music by* Stanley Lebowsky. *Lyrics by* Fred Tobias. *Staged and Choreographed by* Adam Grammis assisted by Linda Lemac.)
Scene 2
    Our Scrapbook of Memories
        G. Hounsell
    The Rockette selected to be Radio City Music Hall's Golden Jubilee Ambassador-to-the-World, recalls some of the great moments of the past with the assistance of an animated collage of photos and films.
Scene 3
    The Glory of Easter (*Staged and Choreograped by* Linda Lemac.)
        Full Company
    "The Lord's Prayer"
        (*Music by* Albert Hay Malotte.)
    "Kamenoi Ostrow"
        (*Music by* Anton Rubinstein.)
    Originally presented in 1933 during the first year of the Music Hall, the cathedral spectacle quickly became a world-famous tradition, one of hundreds of lavish musical productions presented on The Great Stage through the years.
Scene 4
    "Ohka-No-Zu" (Cherry Blossom)
        The Rockettes
            The Lions: T. Garrett, M. Kubala. (*Staged and Choreographed by* Shozo Nakano, assisted by Violet Holmes.)
    The famed Doncho Curtain, a special gift to New York City from its sister city, Tokyo, was presented as an act of friendship in 1964. This magnificent curtain, the largest hand-woven silk, theatrical backdrop ever

created, is featured in this international tribute to the Music Hall fiftieth anniversary.
Scene 5
    "Rhapsody in Blue"
        (*Music by* George Gershwin. *Staged and Choreographed by* Geoffrey Holder, assisted by Linda Lemac.)
            Danced by K. Narai, L. Villanueva, The New Yorkers, The Rockettes, The Dancers
    Gershwin himself gave his wholehearted approval to the Music Hall's first opulent staging of his "Rhapsody" in a production by Leon Leonidoff. The dance-realization of this Gershwin classic was so well recived that it has been brought back—and reinterpreted—many times, as in this, our Golden Jubilee production.
Scene 6
    "Showstoppers"
        V. Holmes, The Rockettes
        (*Music by* John Kander. *Lyrics by* Fred Ebb. *Staged and Choreographed by* Frank Wagner and Violet Holmes.)
    Founded by Russell Markert in 1925, the Rockettes quickly established a new style of American dance that has been widely emulated. Only rarely in their 57-year history has an audience had the opportunity to see how the Rockettes rehearse. Here is a backstage glimpse of the world's most famous precision dance troupe in drill with their real-life, present director.

ACT 2
Scene 1
    "Bolero"
        (*Music by* Maurice Ravel. *Staged and Choreographed by* Geoffrey Holder, assisted by Linda Lemac.)
            Danced by K. Narai, L. Villanueva, The Dancers, The Rockettes
    Soon after Arturo Toscanini introduced American audiences to Ravel's "Bolero" in 1929, the peice became a national craze. In February, 1935, barely two months after the Music Hall opened, a production by Leonidoff presented the work for the first time in America in its original dance version. Here, then, is a new interpretation of one of the Hall's most frequently requested favorites.
Scene 2
    Fifty Years of American Popular Music
        W. Edmead, T. Garrett, M. Kubala, D. Phelan, J. Ross, K. Ziemba, The New Yorkers
        (*Staged and Choreographed by* Adam Grammis assisted by Linda Lemac.)
    Whether danced, sung or played—or all three—Music Hall audiences have been treated to the best of America's own popular music during each of the past five decades. Here we relive some of the memorable tunes from past shows, songs that came from the great films, recordings and musicals of the day.
Scene 3
    Dancing in Diamonds (*Staged and Choreographed by* Violet Holmes.)
        "There Are No Girls Like Show Girls"The Rockettes
        (*Music by* Donald Pippin. *Lyrics by* Sammy Cahn.)
        "Encore"The Rockettes
        (*Music by* Stanley Lebowsky. *Lyrics by* Fred Tobias.)
    No anniversary tribute to the Music Hall would be complete without honoring the most sparkling act in show business, the Radio City Music Hall Rockettes. The world's most famous line of precision dancers dress their glamorous best to show you why fifty years of dancing at the Music Hall hasn't been nearly long enough.
Scene 4
    "That's Entertainment" (from *THE BANDWAGON* film)
        The Company
        (*Music by* Arthur Schwartz. *Lyrics by* Howard Dietz. *Staged and Choreographed by* Frank Wagner.)
    Radio City Music Hall is the greatest motion picture palace in the world having introduced more great stars and films to American audiences than any other theatre. The history of the Hall traces the story of entertainment itself—whole worlds of delight on stage and film that have sustained—and enlivened—the country's spirits for half a century.
Scene 5
    A Salute to the Music Hall: "You're at the Music Hall"
        Full Company
        (*Music by* Donald Pippin. *Lyrics by* Sammy Cahn.)

THE GRAND DUCHESS OF GÉROLSTEIN

1982.07

A Revival of the Opéra-bouffe in Three Acts, 4 Scenes[18]. Original (French) libretto ("La Grande-Duchesse de Gérolstein") by Henri Meilhac and Ludovic Halévy. Music by Jacques Offenbach. English adaptation by Ruth and Thomas Martin. Directed by Jack Hofsis. Conducted by Antonio de Almeida. Choreography by Christopher Chadman. Scenery and costumes designed by John Conklin. Lighting designed by Gilbert V. Helmsley, Jr. Chorus master, Lloyd Walser. Produced by the New York City Opera. Opened 15 April 1982 at the New York State Theatre and closed 24 April 1982 after 5 performances in repretory[19].

CAST (in order of appearance): *Fritz:* HENRY PRICE. *Wanda:* LEIGH MUNRO. *General Boom:* CLAUDE CORBEIL. *Baron Puck:* JAMES BILLINGS. *Nepomuc:* William Ledbetter. *The Grand Duchess:* MURIEL COSTA-GREENSPON. *Prince Paul:* JACK HARROLD. *Notary:* Don Yule. *Baron Grog:* JONATHAN GREEN. *Ensemble:* New York City Opera Chorus.

Act 1: A Military Encampment in a small town of a European Duchy.

Act 2: A Hall in the Palace of the Grand Duchess.

Act 3, Scene 1: The Bridal Suite in the Right Wing. *Scene 2:* A Banquet Hall in the Palace.

IS THERE LIFE AFTER HIGH SCHOOL?

1982.08

A Musical in Two Acts. Book by Jeffrey Kindley. Suggested by the book of the same title by Ralph Keyes. Music and lyrics by Craig Carnelia. Entire production staged by Robert Nigro. Set design by John Lee Beatty. Costumes designed by Carol Oditz. Lighting design by Beverly Emmons. Sound design by Tom Morse. Musical direction and orchestrations by Bruce Coughlin. World premiere at Hartford Stage Company, Hartford, Connecticut. Associate producer, Robert Feiden. Produced by Clive Davis, Francois de Menil, Harris Maslansky, Twentieth-Century Fox Theater Productions, Inc. Opened 7 May 1982 at the Ethel Barrymore Theater and closed 16 May 1982 after 12 performances.

CAST (in alphabetical order): Raymond Baker, Cynthia Carle, Alma Cuervo, Sandy Faison, Harry Groener, Philip Hoffman, David Patrick Kelly, Maureen Silliman, James Widdoes.

ACT 1
"The Kid Inside"
    Entire Company
"Things I Learned in High School"
    H. Groener
"Second Thoughts"
    R. Baker, S. Faison, D. P. Kelly, M. Silliman, J. Widdoes
"Nothing Really Happened"
    A. Cuervo, Women
"Beer"
    R. Baker, H. Groener, D. P. Kelly
"For Them"
    P. Hoffman, Company
"Diary of a Homecoming Queen"
    M. Silliman

ACT 2
"Thousands of Trumpets"
    J. Widdoes, Company
    Drum Major: H. Groener.
"Reunion"
    Entire Company
"High School All Over Again"
    D. P. Kelly
"Fran and Janie"
    S. Faison, M. Silliman

"I'm Glad You Didn't Know Me"
    C. Carle, P. Hoffman

NINE

1982.09

A Musical in Two Acts. Book by Arthur Kopit. (Based on an English) Adaptation from the Italian (screenplay for "8 1/2" by Federico Fellini, Tullio Pinelli, Ennio Flaiano) by Mario Fratti. Music and lyrics by Maury Yeston. Directed by Tommy Tune. Scenery by Lawrence Miller. Costumes by William Ivey Long. Lighting by Marcia Madeira. Musical supervision and orchestrations by Jonathan Tunick. Musical director, Wally Harper. Choral composition and musical continuity by Maury Yeston. Artistic associate, Thommie Walsh. Sound by Jack Mann. Initial staged reading, Composer/Librettist Conference, Eugene O'Neill Memorial Theater Center. Associate producer, Mark Beigelman. Presented in association with Shulamith and Michael N. Appell, Jerry Wexler and Michael Kleinman Productions. Produced by Michel Stuart, Harvey J. Klaris, Roger S. Berlind, James M. Nederlander, Francine LeFrak, Kenneth D. Greenblatt. Opened 9 May 1982 at the 46th Street Theatre and closed 4 February 1984 after 732 performances.

CAST: *Guido Contini:* RAUL JULIA. *Guido at an early age:* Cameron Johann. *Luisa:* KAREN AKERS. *Carla:* ANITA MORRIS. *Claudia:* SHELLY BURCH. *Guido's Mother:* TAINA ELG. *Liliane LaFleur:* LILIANE MONTEVECCHI. *Lina Darling:* Laura Kenyon. *Stephanie Necrophorus:* STEPHANIE COTSIRILOS. *Our Lady of the Spa:* KATE DEZINA. *Mama Maddelena, Chief of Chambermaids:* CAMILLE SAVIOLA. *Seraghina:* KATHI MOSS.

The Italians: Maria: Jeanie Bowers. *Francesca:* Kim Criswell. *A Venetian Gondolier:* Colleen Dodson. *Giulietta:* Louise Edeiken. *Annabella:* Nancy McCall. *Diana:* Cynthia Meryl. *Renata:* Rita Rehn.

The Germans: Gretchen von Krupf: Lulu Downs. *Heidi von Sturm:* Linda Kerns. *Olga von Sturm:* Dee Etta Rowe. *Ilsa von Hesse:* Alaina Warren Zachary.

Young Guido's Schoolmates: Evans Allen, Jadrien Steele, Patrick Wilcox.

(The action takes place in a health spa near Venice and in the mind of Guido Contini.)

ACT 1
"Overture Delle Donne"
    Company
"Spa Music"
"Not Since Chaplin"
"Guido's Song"
    R. Julia
"Coda di Guido"
    Company
"The Germans at the Spa"
    C. Saviola, Italians, Germans
"My Husband Makes Movies"
    K. Akers
"A Call from the Vatican"
    A. Morris
"Only With You"
    R. Julia
"Folies Bergere"
    L. Montevecchi, S. Cotsirilos, Company
"Nine"
    T. Elg, Company
"Ti Voglio Bene"/"Be Italian"
    K. Moss, Boys, Company
"The Bells of St. Sebastian"
    R. Julia, Boys, Company

ACT 2[20]
"A Man Like You"/"Unusual Way"/"Grand Canal"
    S. Burch, R. Julia
"The Grand Canal:"
    R. Julia, Company
"Contini Submits"/"The Grand Canal"/"Tarantella"/"Every Girl in Venice"/"Marcia Di Ragazzi"/"Recitativo"/"Amor"/"Recitativo"/"Only You"/Finale

---

[18]First performed in English in New York 17 June 1868 at the New York Theatre for 33 performances.
[19]Note: The Act 2 Finale and the Duchess' Aria which opens Act 3 were recently discovered in France. The current production marks the first time they have been performed since the premiere of the opera in Paris in 1867.

---

[20]Added for the National Tour, before "The Grand Canal" in Act 2:
    "Now's the Moment"
        Sergio Franchi (Guido Contini)

"Simple"
A. Morris
"Be On Your Own"
K. Akers
"I Can't Make This Movie"
R. Julia
"Getting Tall"
C. Johann
"Nine"/"Long Ago"/"Nine" (reprise)
R. Julia

DO BLACK PATENT LEATHER SHOES REALLY REFLECT UP?

1982.10

A Musical in Two Acts, 14 Scenes. Book by John R. Powers, based on his novel of the same name. Music and lyrics by James Quinn, Alaric Jans. Directed by Mike Nussbaum. Musical numbers staged by Thommie Walsh. Settings by James Maronek. Costumes by Nancy Potts. Lighting by Marilyn Rennagel. Sound by Richard Fitzgerald. Orchestrations and musical supervision by Jerome Jay Dryer. Musial direction and vocal arrangements by Larry Hochman. Dance arrangements by Peter Larson. Production supervisor, William Gardner. Associate choreographer, Ronna Kaye. Produced by Mavin Productions Inc., Libby Adler Mages, Daniel A. Golman. Opened 27 May 1982 at the Alvin Theatre and closed 30 May 1982 after 5 performances.

CAST (in order of appearance): *Eddie Ryan*: RUSS THACKER. *Secretary*: Amy Miller. *Becky Bakowski*: MAUREEN MOORE. *Sister Melanie*: Amy Miller. *Sister Lee*: Ellen Crawford. *Father O'Reilly*: ROBERT FITCH. *Virginia Lear*: Vicki Lewis. *Felix Lindor*: Don Stitt. *Mike Depki*: Peter Heuchling. *Nancy Ralansky*: Karen Tamburrelli. *Mary Kenny*: Christine Gradl. *Louie Schlang*: Jason Graae. *Sister Helen*: Elizabeth Hansen. *Sister Monica Marie*: Catherine Fries.

Act 1: Elementary School. *Scene 1*: St. Bastion's School: The Present. *Scene 2*: Second Grade at St. Bastion's. *Scene 3*: Confession at St. Bastion's Church. *Scene 4*: The Playground—Fifth Grade. *Scene 5*: Fifth Grade at St. Bastion's. *Scene 6*: Confession at St. Bastion's Church. *Scene 7*: Eighth Grade at St. Bastion's.

Act 2: High School. *Scene 1*: The Freshman Mixer in the Gym of St. Patrick Bremmer High School for Boys. *Scene 2*: The Front Yard of Becky's House—A year later. *Scene 3*: Confession at St. Bastion's Church. *Scene 4*: The Athletic Fields of St. Patrick Bremmer & St. Ann's High Schools—Senior Year. *Scene 5*: The Night of the Senior Prom. *Scene 6*: Becky's Hospital Room. *Scene 7*: The Present.

ACT 1

Scene 1
"Get Ready, Eddie"
The Company
Scene 2
"The Greatest Gift"
E. Hansen, the Kids
Scene 4
"It's the Nuns"
The Kids, the Nuns
"Little Fat Girls"
M. Moore, R. Thacker
Scene 5
"Cookie Cutters"
E. Crawford, M. Moore
Scene 6
"Patron Saints"
R. Fitch, R. Thacker, the Kids, the Nuns
Scene 7
"Private Parts"
R. Fitch, the Boys
"How Far Is Too Far"
The Girls, the Boys
Finale Act 1
The Company

ACT 2

Scene 1
"Doo-waa, Doo-wee"
J. Graae, the Company
"I Must Be in Love"
R. Thacker
Scene 2
"Friends, the Best Of"
M. Moore, R. Thacker
Scene 4
"Mad Bombers and Prom Queens"
D. Stitt, V. Lewis, the Kids
Scene 5
"Late Bloomer and Prom Montage"
R. Thacker, the Kids
Scene 6
"Friends, the Best Of" (reprise)
M. Moore, R. Thacker
Scene 7
"Thank God"
The Company

THE BEST LITTLE WHOREHOUSE IN TEXAS

1982.11

A Return Engagement of the Musical Comedy in Two Acts, a Prologue and 16 Scenes[21]. Book by Larry L. King and Peter Masterson. (Based on a short story by Larry L. King.) Music and lyrics by Carol Hall. Directed by Peter Masterson and Tommy Tune. Musical numbers staged by Tommy Tune. Sets by Marjorie Bradley Kellogg. Costumes by Ann Roth. Lighting by Dennis Parichy. Musical supervision, direction and vocal arrangements by Robert Billig. Associate choreographer, Thommie Walsh. Associate producers, Bonnie Champion, Danny Kreitzberg. Produced by Stevie Phillips in association with Universal Pictures. Opened 31 May 1982 at the Eugene O'Neill Theatre and closed 24 July 1982 after 63 performances.

CAST (in order of appearance): *Band*: Craig Chambers (guitar, narrator), Racine Romaguera (bass), Harvey Shapiro (steel guitar), Pete Blue (piano), Chuck Zeuren (drums), Marty Laster (fiddle). *Girls*: Merilee Magnuson, Mimi Bessette, Roxie Lucas, Ruth Gottschall, Valerie Leigh Bixler. *Cowboys*: Beau Allen, Don Bernhardt, Michael Boyd. *Farmer*: Andy Parker. *Shy Kid*: Eric Aaron. *Miss Wulla Jean*: Louise Quick. *Travelling Salesman*: Patrick Hamilton. *Slick Dude*: Roger Berdahl. *Choir*: Don Bernhardt, Karen Sutherland, Diana Broderick, Merilyn J. Johnson, Clare Fields, George Dvorsky. *Angel*: Susann Fletcher. *Shy*: CHERYL EBARB. *Jewel*: DELORES HALL. *Mona Stangley*: CARLIN GLYNN. *The Girls at Miss Mona's*: Linda Lou: Valerie Leigh Bixler. *Dawn*: Mimi Bessette. *Ginger*: Roxie Lucas. *Beatrice*: Clare Fields. *Taddy Jo*: Merilee Magnuson. *Ruby Rae*: Diana Broderick. *Eloise*: Karen Sutherland. *Durla*: Ruth Gottschall.
Leroy Sliney: Roger Berdahl. *The Dogettes*: Don Bernhardt, George Dvorsky, Andy Parker, Joel Anderson. *Melvin P. Thorpe*: CLINTON ALLMON. *Soundman*: Roger Berdahl. *Melvin Thorpe Singers*: Karen Sutherland, Beau Allen, Diana Broderick, Clare Fields, Eric Aaron, Merilee Magnuson. *Sheriff Ed Earl Dodd*: GIL ROGERS *Cameraman*: Eric Aaron. *C. J. Scruggs*: Patrick Hamilton. *Mayor Rufus Poindexter*: J. FRANK LUCAS. *Edsel Mackey*: Robert Moyer. *Doatsey Mae*: BECKY GELKE. *Townspeople*: Beau Allen, Karen Sutherland, Patti D'Beck, Clare Fields, Eric Aaron, Merilee Magnuson. *TV Announcer*: Larry L. King. *Angelette Imogene Charlene*: Mimi Bessette. *Angelettes*: Merilee Magnuson, Ruth Gottschall, Karen Sutherland, Diana Broderick, Valerie Leigh Bixler. *Chip Brewster*: Patrick Hamilton. *Senator Wingwoah*: J. FRANK LUCAS. *Aggie #17*: Michael Boyd. *Aggie #71*: Beau Allen *Aggie #11*: Joel Anderson. *Scandinavian Placekicker—Aggie #1*: Roger Berdahl. *Aggie #21*: Eric Aaron. *Aggie #7*: Don Bernhardt. *Aggie #12*: George Dvorsky. *Aggie #77*: Andy Parker. *Aggie Specialty Dancer*: Tom Cashin. *Photographers*: Beau Allen, Eric Aaron, Michael Boyd, Don Bernhardt. *Reporter #1*: Becky Gelke. *Reporter #2*: Beau Allen. *Governor's Aide*: Joel Anderson. *Governor*: PATRICK HAMILTON. *Reporter #3*: Beau Allen. *Alternate Dancer*: Patti D'Beck.

---

[21]Originally produced in New York Off-Broadway 17 April 1978 at the Entermedia Theatre for 85 performances; transferred to Broadway 19 June 1978 at the 46th Street Theatre for 1584 performances. For Synopsis of Scenes and Musical Numbers, see original 1978 production. For this production, Act 1 ended with Act 1, Scene 10 and "The Aggie Song;" Scene 11 was dropped. "Bus from Amarillo" was moved to Act 2, Scene 4, to follow the reprise of "Hard Candy Christmas."

1982–1983 SEASON

Natalia Makarova and Dina Merrill in ON YOUR TOES
Martha Swope/TimePix

1982–1983 SEASON

1982.12   ### BLUES IN THE NIGHT

A Musical (Revue) in Two Acts[1]. Conceived and directed by Sheldon Epps. Set design by John Falabella. Costume design by David Murin. Lighting design by Ken Billington. Conductor, Charles Coleman. Musical director, supervisor, vocal arrangements by Chapman Roberts. Co-musical director, arrangements and orchestrator, Sy Johnson. Sound by Bill Merrill, Tay McLaren. Associate producer, Joshua Silver. Produced by Mitchell Maxwell, Alan J. Schuster, Fred H. Krones, M2 Entertainment. Opened 2 June 1982 at the Rialto Theatre and closed 18 July 1982 after 53 performances.

CAST (in order of singing appearance): *Woman #1*: LESLIE UGGAMS. *Woman #2*: DEBBIE SHAPIRO. *Woman #3*: JEAN DuSHON. *Saloon Singer*: Charles Coleman.

The action takes place in a Chicago hotel during 1938.

ACT 1

"Blue Blue"
  The Company
  (*Music and Lyrics by* Bessie Smith.)
"Four Walls (and One Dirty Window) Blues"
  C. Coleman
  (*Music and Lyrics by* Willard Robison)
"I've Got a Date With a Dream" (from *MY LUCKY STAR* film)
  L. Uggams, D. Shapiro
  (*Music by* Harry Revel. *Lyrics by* Mack Gordon.)
"These Foolish Things (Remind Me of You)" (from *NEW FACES*, London)
  L. Uggams
  (*Music by* Harry Link, Jack Strachey. *Lyrics by* Holt Marvell [Eric Maschwitz].)
"New Orleans Hop Scop Blues"
  J. DuShon
  (*Music and Lyrics by* George W. Thomas.)
"It Makes My Love Come Down"
  L. Uggams, D. Shapiro, J. DuShon
  (*Music and Lyrics by* Bessie Smith.)
"Copenhagen"
  D. Shapiro
  (*Music by* Charlie Davis. *Lyrics by* Walter Melrose.)
"Wild Women Don't Have the Blues"
  C. Coleman
  (*Music and Lyrics by* Ida Cox.)
"Lover Man"
  L. Uggams
  (*Music and Lyrics by* Jimmy Davis, Roger "Ram" Ramirez, Jimmy Sherman.)
"Take Me for a Buggy Ride"
  J. DuShon
  (*Music and Lyrics by* Leola and Wesley Wilson.)
"Willow Weep for Me"
  D. Shapiro
  (*Music and Lyrics by* Ann Ronnell.)
"Kitchen Man"
  J. DuShon
  (*Music and Lyrics by* Andy Razaf and Alex Bellenda.)
"Low"
  L. Uggams
  (*Music and Lyrics by* Vernon Duke, Milton Drake, Ben Oakland.)
"Take It Right Back"
  L. Uggams, D. Shapiro, J. DuShon
  (*Music and Lyrics by* H. Grey.)
ACT 2
"Wild Women Don't Have the Blues" (reprise)
  The Band
"Blues in the Night" (from *BLUES IN THE NIGHT* film)
  L. Uggams, D. Shapiro
  (*Music by* Harold Arlen. *Lyrics by* Johnny Mercer.)

---

[1]Originally produced Off-Broadway 26 March 1980 at the Production Company for 51 performances.

"Dirty No Gooder Blues"
  J. DuShon
  (*Music and Lyrics by* Bessie Smith.)
"When a Woman Loves a Man"
  C. Coleman
  (*Music by* Bernard Hanighen and Gordon Jenkins. *Lyrics by* Johnny Mercer.)
"Am I Blue?" (from *ON WITH THE SHOW* film)
  L. Uggams, D. Shapiro, J. DuShon
  (*Music by* Harry Akst. *Lyrics by* Grant Clarke.)
"Rough and Ready Man"
  L. Uggams
  (*Music and Lyrics by* Alberta Hunter.)
"Reckless Blues"
  D. Shapiro
  (*Music and Lyrics by* Bessie Smith.)
"Wasted Life Blues"
  J. DuShon
  (*Music and Lyrics by* Bessie Smith.)
"Baby Doll"
  C. Coleman
  (*Music and Lyrics by* Bessie Smith.)
"Nobody Knows You When You're Down and Out"
  L. Uggams, D. Shapiro, J. DuShon
  (*Music and Lyrics by* Jimmy Cox.)
"I Gotta Right to Sing the Blues" (from *EARL CARROLL'S VANITIES*, 1932)
  L. Uggams, D. Shapiro, J. DuShon
  (*Music by* Harold Arlen. *Lyrics by* Ted Koehler.)
"Blue Blue"/"Blues in the Night" (reprise)
  L. Uggams, D. Shapiro, J. DuShon

1982.13   ### PLAY ME A COUNTRY SONG

A Musical in Two Acts. Book by Jay Broad. Music and lyrics by John R. Briggs, Harry Manfredini. Directed by Jerry Adler. Choreography by Margo Sappington. Scenic design by David Chapman. Costume design by Carol Oditz. Lighting design by Marc B. Weiss. Musical direction, vocal arrangements by Phil Hall. Sound design by Robert Kerzman. Developmental supervision, Milton Moss. Associate producer, Cheryl Raab. Produced by Frederick R. Selch. Opened and closed 27 June 1982 at the Virginia Theatre after 1 performance.

CAST (in order of appearance): *Norm*: Reed Jones. *Ellen*: Mary Gordon Murray. *Tony*: Stephen Crain. *Fred*: Jay Huguely. *Howard*: Ronn Carroll. *Lizzie*: Louisa Flaningam. *Frances*: Karen Mason. *Penny*: Mary Jo Catlett. *Buster*: Kenneth Ames. *Meg*: Candace Tovar. *Jerome*: René Clemente. *Hank*: Rick Thomas.

ACT 1
"Sail Away"
  M. G. Murray
"Rodeo Dreams"
  R. Jones
"Why Does a Woman Leave Her Man"
  J. Huguely
"Eighteen-Wheelin' Baby"
  C. Tovar, L. Flaningam, M. J. Catlett, M. G. Murray
"Waitin' Tables"
  L. Flaningam, Company
"Playing For Position"
  R. Clements, K. Ames
"Just Thought I'd Call"
  R. Thomas
"Sing-a-Long"
  K. Mason, R. Carroll, Company
"Sail Away"/"If You Don't Mind"
  M. G. Murray, S. Crain
"Play Me a Country Song"
  Company
ACT 2
"Coffee Beer and Whiskey"
  J. Huguely, Company
"Only a Fool"
  C. Tovar, R. Thomas

421

"You Can't Get Ahead"
M. J. Catlett
"You Have to Get It Out to Get Away"
M. G. Murray
"Big City"
K. Ames
"My Sweet Woman"
J. Huguely, Men
"All of My Dreams"
L. Flaningam, Women
"Rodeo Rider"
S. Crain, Company

SEVEN BRIDES FOR SEVEN BROTHERS

1982.14

A Musical in Two Acts, 19 Scenes. Book by Lawrence Kasha and David S. Landay. Music by Gene de Paul. Lyrics by Johnny Mercer. New songs by Al Kasha and Joel Hirschhorn. Based on the MGM film (screenplay by Frances Goodrich, Albert Hackett, Dorothy Kinsley) and the short story "The Sobbin Women" by Stephen Vincent Benet on which it was based. Choreography and musical staging by Jerry Jackson. Directed by Lawrence Kasha. Sets by Robert Randolph. Costumes by Robert Fletcher. Lighting by Thomas Skelton. Sound by Abe Jacob. Musical director, Richard Parrinello. Orchestrations by Irwin Kostal. Dance arrangements by Robert Webb. Associate producers, Martin Gould, Bernard Hodes. Produced by Kaslan Productions (Lawrence Kasha-David S. Landay). Opened 8 July 1982 at the Alvin Theatre and closed 11 July 1982 after 5 performances.

CAST (in order of appearance): (*The Seven Brothers*): Adam: DAVID-JAMES CAR-ROLL. *Benjamin*: D. Scot Davidge. *Ephraim*: Jeffrey Reynolds. *Caleb*: Lara Teeter. *Daniel*: Jeff Calhoun. *Frank*: Michael Ragan. *Gideon*: CRAIG PERALTA. *Mr. Bixby*: Fred Curt. *Mrs. Bixby*: Jeanne Bates. *Preacher*: Jack Ritschel. *Mr. Perkins*: Gino Gaudio. *Lumbermen*: James Horvath, Russell Giesenschlag, Don Steffy, Gary Moss, Clark Sterling, Kevin McCready. *Indian*: Conley Schnaterbeck. (*The Seven Brides*): *Milly*: DEBBIE BOONE. *Ruth*: Sha Newman. *Martha*: Laurel van der Linde. *Sarah*: Linda Hoxit. *Liza*: Jan Mussetter. *Alice*: NANCY FOX. *Dorcas*: Manette LaChance. *Jeb*: Russell Giesenschlag. *Zeke*: Kevin McCready. *Carl*: Don Steffy. *Matt*: Gary Moss. *Luke*: James Horvath. *Joel*: Clark Stering. *Dorcas' Sister*: Marylou Hume. *Mrs. Perkins*: Marykatherine Somers. *Townsboy*: David Pavlosky.

Townspeople: Jeanne Bates, Cheryl Randall, Fred Curt, Gino Gaudio, Russell Giesenschlag, James Horvath, Marylou Hume, Kevin McCready, Gary Moss, David Davlovsky, Jack Ritschel, Conley Schnaterbeck, Sam Singhaus, Marykatherine Somers, Don Steffy, Clark Sterling, Stephanie Stromer.

The action takes place in the Pacific Northwest during the 1850's.

Act 1, Scene 1: On the Road. *Scene 2*: The Town Square. *Scene 3*: The Restaurant. *Scene 4*: The Pontipee House. *Scene 5*: The Pontipee House. Later the same evening. *Scene 6*: The Pontipee House. The next morning. *Scene 7*: Church Yard. *Scene 8*: The Road Home. *Scene 9*: The Pontipee House. *Scene 10*: The Barn.

Act 2, Scene 1: The Town. *Scene 2*: Echo Pass. *Scene 3*: The Pontipee Yard. *Scene 4*: The Barn. *Scene 5*: The Pontipee Yard. *Scene 6*: The Trapping Cabin. *Scene 7*: The Pontipee House. *Scene 8*: The Woods. *Scene 9*: Church Yard.

ACT 1
Scene 1
"Bless Your Beautiful Hide"
D. Carroll
Scene 3
"Wonderful Wonderful Day"
D. Boone, Brides, Townspeople
Scene 4
"One Man"
D. Boone
(*Music and Lyrics by* Al Kasha and Joel Hirschhorn.)
Scene 6
"Goin' Courting"
D. Boone, The Brothers
Scene 7
"Social Dance"
D. Boone, D. Carroll, Brides, Brothers, Suitors, Townspeople
Scene 9
"Love Never Goes Away"
D. Carroll, D. Boone, C. Peralta
(*Music and Lyrics by* Al Kasha and Joel Hirschhorn.)

Scene 10
"Sobbin' Women"
D. Carroll, Brothers

ACT 2
Scene 2
"The Townsfolk's Lament"
Suitors, Townspeople
(*Music and Lyrics by* Al Kasha and Joel Hirschhorn.)
Scene 3
"A Woman Ought To Know Her Place"
D. Carroll
(*Music and Lyrics by* Al Kasha and Joel Hirschhorn.)
Scene 4
"We Gotta Make It Through the Winter"
The Brothers
(*Music and Lyrics by* Al Kasha and Joel Hirschhorn.)
"You Gotta Make It Through the Winter" (reprise)
D. Boone, Brides
Scene 5
"Spring Dance"
Brides, Brothers
Scene 6
"A Woman Ought To Know Her Place" (reprise)
D. Carroll, C. Peralta
Scene 7
"Glad That You Were Born"
D. Boone, Brides, Brothers
(*Music and Lyrics by* Al Kasha and Joel Hirschhorn.)
Scene 9
"Wedding Dance"
D. Boone, D. Carroll, Brides, Brothers, Townspeople

MANHATTAN RHYTHM

1982.15

A Dance Revue in Two Acts, 8 Scenes. Conceived and staged by Jon Devlin. Additional choreography by Jay Norman, Mary Delia Quigley, Harry Bell. Musical arrangements by Richard Dimino; additional horn arrangements by Smithcox Organization. Costumes by David Toser. Lighting by David Adams. Sound by Gary Harris. Fantasy creatures, Richard Tautkus. Produced by Barbara Moore. Opened 21 July 1982 at the Savoy Theatre and closed 14 August 1982 after 27 performances.

CAST: JON DEVLIN AND HIS COMPANY: *Female Dancers*: Virginia Clark East, Lyn Gendron, Anne Marie Giambattista, Kim Kuhlman, Diana Laurenson (Dance Captain), Linda Paul, Lisa Rudy, Lauren Salerno. *Male Dancers*: Louis Albert, Richard Loreto, Ralph Rodriguez, Steven Van Dyke (Dance Captain). *Singers*: Armour Gomez, Teri Hiatt, Karen Quackenbush, Bonnie Sue Taylor.

Act 1, Scene 1: Jazz. *Scene 2*: Big Band 40's. *Scene 3*: Broadway. *Scene 4*: Disc Space Fantasy.

Act 2, Scene 1: Rock n' Roll n' Rock Medley. *Scene 2*: Latin. *Scene 3*: Country/Western. *Scene 4*: Top Hits.

ACT 1
Scene 1
Opening
The Company
"Love For Sale"
T. Hiatt
Danced by J. Devlin, L. Rudy, A. M. Giambattista, D. Laurenson, K. Kuhlman, V. C. East, S. Van Dyke, R. Loreto, L. Albert.
"Manhattan Rhythm Blues"
Danced by J. Devlin, L. Gendron.
"All Blues"
Dance Solo: A. M. Giambattista.
Danced by V. C. East, L. Rudy, D. Laurenson, L. Salerno, L. Paul, K. Kuhlman.
"Take Five"
Danced by S. Van Dyke, R. Loreto, L. Albert.
"Walkin' Sally"
Danced by D. Laurenson, L. Paul, A. M. Giambattista.
Scene 2
"One O'Clock Jump"/"In the Mood"
T. Hiatt

Danced by J. Devlin. *Backup Vocals*: B. S. Taylor, A. Gomez, K. Quackenbush.

"Fifty-Seventh Street"
Danced by L. Albert, K. Kuhlman, S. Van Dyke, D. Laurenson, R. Rodriguez, A. M. Giambattista, L. Paul, L. Gendron.

Scene 3

Crossover
V. C. East

Medley
K. Quackenbush, B. S. Taylor, A. Gomez
Danced by A. M. Giambattista, L. Salerno, R. Loreto, R. Rodriguez, S. Van Dyke.
(Additional Choreography by Mary Delia Quigley.)

"You Can Dance"
T. Hiatt
Danced by S. V. Dyke, R. Rodriguez.
(Additional Choreography by Harry Bell.)

Scene 4

Star Trek Medley/Star Wars Cantina
Danced by L. Gendron, R. Loreto, L. Salerno, L. Albert, D. Laurenson, A. M. Giambattista, L. Rudy, S. Van Dyke, R. Rodriguez.

ACT 2

Scene 1

Rock n' Roll n' Rock Medley
The Company
(Additional Choreography by Jay Norman.)

Scene 2

Mambo/Cha-Cha/Mambo
Danced by A. M. Giambattista, D. Laurenson, V. C. East, L. Salerno, J. Devlin, L. Gendron.

Merengue
Danced by A. M. Giambattista, L. Gendron, V. C. East, L. Salerno.

Spanish Cape
Danced by J. Devlin.

Tango
Danced by J. Devlin, D. Laurenson.

Samba
Danced by The Compnay.
Duo: J. Devlin, A. M. Giambattista.

Scene 3

"Hey Good Lookin'"
B. S. Taylor

"Lady"
A. Gomez

"9 to 5"
K. Quackenbush

"Never Ending Love"
The Company

Scene 4

"Guilty"
T. Hiatt, A. Gomez

"Physical"
Danced by B. S. Taylor, S. Van Dyke, R. Rodriguez.

"Out Here on My Own"
T. Hiatt

"Fame"
Danced by D. Laurenson, A. M. Giambattista, L. Gendron, V. C. East.

"Celebration"
The Company
(Additional Choreography by Jay Norman.)

1982.16 THE MERRY WIDOW

A Revival of the Operetta in Three Acts, 4 Scenes[2]. Music by Franz Lehár. Original German libretto (Die Lustige Witwe) by Victor Léon and Leo

---

[2]Originally produced in New York 21 October 1907 at the New Amsterdam Theatre for 416 performances. For Synopsis of Scenes and Musical Numbers, see original 1907 production. Interpolated into this production:
"One Love in a Lifetime" (from *GIUDITTA*)
(Music by Franz Lehár. Original Lyrics by Paul Knepler and Fritz Löhner. New English Lyrics by Scott Bergeson.)

Stein (after "L'Attaché d'Ambassade.") English version by Adrian Ross. Directed by Bill Gile. Choreography by Donald Saddler. Scenery designed by Helen Pond and Herbert Senn. Costumes designed by Suzanne Mess. Lighting designed by Gilbert V. Helmsley, Jr. Conductor, Scott Bergeson. Produced by the New York City Opera. Opened 7 September 1982 at the New York State Theatre and closed 13 November 1982 after 13 performances in repertory.

CAST (in order of appearance): *Baron Popoff*: JACK HARROLD. *Natalie*: Susanne Marsee. *M. de St. Brioche*: WILLIAM EICHORN. *Marquis de Cascada*: Thomas Jamerson. *Sylviane*: Bonnie Kirk. *Olga*: Janis Eckhart. *General Novikovich*: Douglas Perry. *Vicomte Camille de Jolidon*: JOSEPH EVANS. *Counsellor Khadja*: William Ledbetter. *Nisch*: James Billings. *Sonia*: ELIZABETH HYNES. *Prince Danilo*: ALAN TITUS. *Head Waiter*: Robert Brubaker. *Zozo*: Susan Elizabeth Scott. *Lolo*: Rebeka Pradera. *Dodo*: Esperanza Galan. *Jou-Jou*: Candace Itow. *Frou-Frou*: Victoria Rinaldi. *Clo-Clo*: Kate Langan. *Margot*: Tamara Mark. *Chorus of Marsovian and Parisian Society, Dancers, Servants and Waiters*: New York City Opera Chorus.

1982.17 YOUR ARMS TOO SHORT TO BOX WITH GOD

A Revival of the Gospel Musical in Two Acts[3]. Conceived from the Book of St. Matthew by Vinnette Carroll. Music and lyrics by Alex Bradford and Micki Grant. Entire production directed by Vinnette Carroll. Choreography by Talley Beatty, restaged by Ralf Paul Haze. Sets and costumes by William Schroder. Lighting by Richard Winkler. Sound by R. Shepard, Jim Esher. Musical direction, arrangements by Michael Powell. Orchestrations and dance music by H. B. Barnum. Associate producer, Jerry R. Moore. Co-producers, Anita MacShane, The Urban Arts Theatre. Produced by Barry and Fran Weissler. Opened 9 September 1982 at the Alvin Theatre and closed 7 November 1982 after 69 performances.

CAST: PATTI LaBELLE, AL GREEN, Julius Richard Brown, Nora Cole, Jamil K. Garland, Eijah Gill, L. Michael Gray, Ralf Paul Haze, Cynthia Henry, The Bobby Hill, Rufus E. Jackson, Elmore James, Linda James, Tommi Johnson, Janice Nunn Nelson, Dwayne Phelps, Quincella, Kiki Shepard, Leslie Hardesty Sisson, Marilynn Winbush.

ACT 1

"Beatitudes"
Company
(Music and Lyrics by Micki Grant.)

"We're Gonna Have a Good Time"
P. LaBelle, Company
(Music and Lyrics by Micki Grant.)

"Me and Jesus"
A. Green, Company
(Music and Lyrics by Micki Grant.)

"There's a Stranger in Town"
A. Green
(Music and Lyrics by Alex Bradford.)

"Running for Jesus"
J. N. Nelson, Company
(Music and Lyrics by Inez Andrews.)

"We Are the Priests and Elders"
J. R. Brown, T. B. Hill, L. M. Gray, E. James
(Music and Lyrics by Micki Grant.)

"Something Is Wrong in Jerusalem"
N. Cole, Quincella
(Music and Lyrics by Micki Grant.)

"It Was Alone"/"I Know I Have to Leave Here"
E. Gill, T. Johnson, Company
(Music and Lyrics by Alex Bradford.)

"Be Careful Whom You Kiss"
E. Gill, R. P. Haze, N. Cole, Quincella
(Music and Lyrics by Alex Bradford.)

"Trial"
Company
(Music and Lyrics by Micki Grant.)

"It's Too Late"
Company
(Music and Lyrics by Micki Grant.)

---

[3]Originally produced in New York 22 December 1976 at the Lyceum Theatre for 429 performances.

"Judas' Dance"
    R. P. Haze
    (*Music and Lyrics by* H. B. Barnum.)
"Your Arms Too Short to Box With God"
    P. LaBelle, Company
    (*Music and Lyrics by* Alex Bradford.)
"Give Us Barrabas"
    Company
    (*Music and Lyrics by* Alex Bradford.)
"See How They Done My Lord"
    N. Cole, Company
    (*Music and Lyrics by* Alex Bradford.)
"Come on Down"
    M. M. Gray, J. K. Garland, L. James
    (*Music and Lyrics by* Alex Bradford.)
"Veil of the Temple"
    P. LaBelle, Company
"Can't No Grave Hold My Body"
    L. M. Gray, Quincella, E. Gill, Company
    (*Music and Lyrics by* Alex Bradford.)
"Beatitudes" (reprise)
    P. LaBelle, A. Green, Company

ACT 2
"Didn't I Tell You"
    A. Green, Company
    (*Music and Lyrics by* Alex Bradford.)
"Couldn't Keep It to Myself"
    A. Green, Company
    (*Music and Lyrics by* Alex Bradford.)
"When the Power Comes"
    A. Green, Company
    (*Music and Lyrics by* Alex Bradford.)
"Everybody Has His Own Way"
    A. Green, J. R. Brown, T. B. Hill, T. Johnson
    (*Music and Lyrics by* Alex Bradford.)
"Down By the Riverside"
    L. M. Gray, A. Green, Company
"I Love You So Much Jesus"
    P. LaBelle
    (*Music and Lyrics by* Alex Bradford.)
"As Long as I Live"
    T. Johnson
    (*Music and Lyrics by* Alex Bradford.)
"On That Day"
    T. B. Hill, Company
    (*Music and Lyrics by* Alex Bradford.)
"The Band"
    Company
    (*Music and Lyrics by* Alex Bradford.)

1982.18   A DOLL'S LIFE

A Musical in Two Acts, 16 Scenes. Book[4] and lyrics by Betty Comden and Adolph Green. Music by Larry Grossman. Production directed by Harold Prince. Musical director, Paul Gemignani. Orchestrations by Bill Byers. Choreography by Larry Fuller. Scenery designed by Timothy O'Brien, Tazeena Firth. Costumes designed by Florence Klotz. Lighting designed by Ken Billington. Sound by Jack Mann. Produced by James M. Nederlander, Sidney Shlenker, Warner Theatre Productions, Inc., Joseph Harris, Mary Lea Johnson, Martin Richards, Robert Fryer in association with Harold Prince. Opened 23 September 1982 at the Mark Hellinger Theatre and closed 26 September 1982 after 5 performances.

CAST: *Nora*: BETSY JOSLYN. *Actor, Torvald, Johan*: GEORGE HEARN. *Otto*: PETER GALLAGHER. *Eric*: EDMUND LYNDECK. *Astrid*: Barbara Lang. *Audition Singer, Selma, Jacqueline*: Penny Orloff. *Conductor, Mr. Gustafson, Escamillo, Audition Singer, Loki, Mr. Zetterling*: Norman A. Large. *Stage Hand, Dr. Berg, Audition Singer, Ambassador*: David Vosburgh. *Stage Manager, Hamsun, Petersen, Warden, Nilson*: Michael Vita. *Dowager*: Diane Armistead. *Musician, Mr. Kloster*: Gordon Bovinet. *Camilla Forrester*: Willi Burke. *Assistant Stage Manager, Helga*: Patti

Cohenour. *Prison Guards*: John Corsaut, David Cale Johnson. *Helmer's Maid, Waitress*: Carol Lurie. *Musician, Waiter*: Larry Small. *Waiter, Audition Singer, Muller*: Paul Straney. *Maid, The Widow*: Olga Talyn. *Ivar*: Jim Wagg. *Emmy*: Kimberly Stern. *Bob*: David Seaman. *Woman in White*: Lisa Peters. *Woman in Red*: Peri Gill. *Woman in Black*: Patricia Parker. *Man in Black*: David Evans.

The action takes place at a rehearsal of Ibsen's "A DOLL'S HOUSE: in 1982.

Act 1, Scene 1: A Rehearsal of Ibsen's "A Doll's House"—1982. *Scene 2*: The Train. *Scene 3*: The Cafe Europa. *Scene 4*: Street Outside the Cafe Europa. *Scene 5*: Otto's Room. *Scene 6*: Backstage at the Opera. *Scene 7*: An Opera Reading. *Scene 8*: Otto's Room. *Scene 9*: Cannery. *Scene 10*: Prison. *Scene 11*: The Opera House.

Act 2, Scene 1: Eric's Bedroom. *Scene 2*: Billiard Room. *Scene 3*: Billiard Room. The next morning. *Scene 4*: The Grand Cafe. Spring, Fall, Winter. *Scene 5*: The Living Room.

ACT 1
Scene 1
    Prologue
        B. Joslyn, Company
Scene 2
    "A Woman Alone"
        B. Joslyn, P. Gallagher, N. A. Large, Company
Scene 3
    "Letter to the Children"
        B. Joslyn
    "New Year's Eve"
        E. Lyndeck, G. Hearn, D. Vosburgh, N. A. Large
Scene 5
    "Stay with Me, Nora"
        P. Gallagher, B. Joslyn
Scene 7
    The Opera Audition:
        "Arrival"
            B. Lang
        "Loki and Baldur"
            P. Gallagher, (Audition) Singers
        "You Interest Me"
            G. Hearn
        "Departure"
            B. Lang, Company
Scene 8
    "Letter from Klemnacht"
        B. Lang
    "Learn to Be Lonely"
        B. Joslyn
Scene 9
    "Rats and Mice and Fish"
        Women
Scene 10
    "Jailer, Jailer"/"Letter to the Children" (reprise)
        B. Joslyn, Women
Scene 11
    Excerpts from 'Loki and Baldur'
        Company
    "Rare Wines"
        E. Lyndeck, G. Hearn
ACT 2
Scene 1
    "No More Mornings"
        B. Joslyn
Scene 2
    "There She Is"
        G. Hearn, E. Lyndeck, P. Gallagher
    "Power"
        B. Joslyn
Scene 3
    "Letter to the Children" (reprise)
        B. Joslyn
    "At Last"
        G. Hearn
Scene 4
    "The Grand Cafe"
        Company

---

[4]Conceived by its authors as a response to the play "A Doll's House" by Henrik Ibsen.

Scene 5
Finale
Company

1982.19 CATS

A Musical in Two Acts, a Prologue and 20 Scenes. Based on T.S. Eliot's "Old Possum's Book of Practical Cats."[5] Music by Andrew Lloyd Webber. Directed by Trevor Nunn. Associate director, choreography by Gillian Lynne. (Scenic and costume) Design by John Napier. Lighting by David Hersey. Sound design by Martin Levan. Musical director, Rene Wiegert. Production musical director, Stanley Lebowsky. Orchestrations by David Cullen, Andrew Lloyd Webber. Executive producers, R. Tyler Gatchell Jr., Peter Neufeld. Produced by Cameron Mackintosh, The Really Useful Company (Limited), David Geffen, The Shubert Organization. Opened 7 October 1982 at the Winter Garden and closed 10 September 2000 after 7485 performances.

CAST (in amphibolical order): *Alonzo*: Hector Jaime Mercado. *Bustopher Jones, Asparagus, Growltiger*: Stephen Hanan. *Bombalurina*: Donna King. *Carbucketty*: Steven Gelfer. *Cassandra*: René Ceballos. *Coricopat, Mungojerrie*: René Clemente. *Demeter*: Wendy Edmead. *Etcetera, Rumpleteazer*: Christine Langner. *Grizabella*: BETTY BUCKLEY. *Jellylorum, Griddlebone*: Bonnie Simmons. *Jennyanydots*: Anna McNeely. *Mistoffolees*: Timothy Scott. *Munkustrap*: Harry Groener. *Old Deuteronomy*: Ken Page. *Plato, Macavity, Rumpus Cat*: Kenneth Ard. *Pouncival*: Herman W. Sebek. *Rum Tum Tugger*: Terrence Mann. *Sillabub*: Whitney Kershaw. *Skimbleshanks*: Reed Jones. *Tantomile*: Janet L. Hubert. *Tumblebrutus*: Robert Hoshour. *Victoria*: Cynthia Onrubia.
The Cats Chorus: Walter Charles, Susan Powers, Carol Richards, Joel Robertson.

Act 1: "When cats are maddened by the midnight dance"

Act 2: "Why will the summer day delay—when will time flow away"

ACT 1
Prologue
"Jellicle Songs for Jellicle Cats"
The Company
(*Additional Material written by* Trevor Nunn and Richard Stilgoe.)
Scene 1
"The Naming of Cats"
The Company
Scene 2
"Invitation to the Jellicle Ball"
Victoria: C. Onrubia. *Mistoffolees*: T. Scott.
Scene 3
"The Old Gumbie Cat"
Jennyanydots: A. McNeely. *Cassandra*: R. Ceballos. *Bombalurina*: D. King. *Jellylorum*: B. Simmons.
Scene 4
"Rum Tum Tugger"
T. V. Mann
Scene 5
"Grizabella, the Glamour Cat"
Grizabella: B. Buckley. *Dememter*: W. Edmead. *Bombalurina*: D. King.
Scene 6
"Bustopher Jones"
Bustopher: S. Hanan. *Jennyanydots*: A. McNeely. *Jellylorum*: B. Simmons. *Bombalurina*: D. King.
Scene 7
"Mungojerrie and Rumpleteazer"
Mistoffolees: T. Scott. *Mungojerrie*: R. Clemente. *Rumpleteazer*: C. Langner.

Scene 8
"Old Deuteronomy"
Munkustrap: H. Groener. *The Rum Tum Tugger*: T. V. Mann. *Old Deuteronomy*: K. Page.
Scene 9
"The Awful Battle of the Pekes and Pollicles" together with "The Marching Song of the Pollicle Dogs"
Munkustrap: H. Groener. *The Rumpus Cat*: K. Ard.
Scene 10
"The Jellicle Ball"
The Company
Scene 11
"Memory"
Grizabella: B. Buckley.
(*Lyrics by* Trevor Nunn, based on poems by T. S. Eliot.)
ACT 2
Scene 1
"The Moments of Happiness"
Old Deuteronomy: K. Page.
Scene 2
"Gus: The Theatre Cat"
Jellylorum: B. Simmons. *Asparagus*: S. Hanan.
Scene 3
"Growltiger's Last Stand"
Growltiiger: S. Hanan. *Griddlebone*: B. Simmons. *The Crew*: H. Groener, R. Jones, T. V. Mann, T. Scott. *Siamese Acrobat*: S. Gelfer.
Scene 4
"Skimbleshanks"
Skimbleshanks: R. Jones.
Scene 5
"Macavity"
Demeter: W. Edmead. *Bombalurina*: D. King. *Alonzo*: H. J. Mercado. *Macavity*: K. Ard. *Munkustrap*: H. Groener.
Scene 6
"Mr. Mistoffolees"
Mistoffolees: T. Scott. *The Rum Tum Tugger*: T. V. Mann.
Scene 7
"Memory" (reprise)
Grizabella: B. Buckley.
Scene 8
"The Journey to the Heavyside Layer"
The Company
Scene 9
"The Ad-Dressing of Cats"
Old Deuteronomy: K. Page.

1982.20 CANDIDE

A Revival of the Musical in Two Act, 23 Scenes[6]. Book[7] adapted from Voltaire's satire (of the same name) by Hugh Wheeler. (Original Book by Lillian Hellman.) Music by Leonard Bernstein. Lyrics by Richard Wilbur. Additional lyrics by Stephen Sondheim and John Latouche. Directed by Harold Prince. Choreography by Patricia Birch. Scenery designed by Clarke Dunham. Costumes designed by Judith Dolan. Lighting designed by Ken Billington. Conducted by John Mauceri. Orchestrations by Leonard Bernstein and Hershy Kay. Chorus master, David Leighton. Set graphics by Donald Beckman. Produced by the New York City Opera. Opened 13 October 1982 at the New York State Theatre and closed 2 November 1982 after 7 performances in repertory.

CAST (in order of appearance): *Voltaire*: JOHN LANKSTON. *Candide*: DAVID EISLER. *Huntsman*: Don Yule. *Paquette*: DEBORAH DARR. *Baroness*: Bonnie Kirk. *Baron*: JACK HARROLD. *Cunegonde*: ERIE MILLS. *Maximilian*: SCOTT REEVE.

---

[5]A Note on the Text: Most of the poems comprising "Old Possum's Book of Practical Cats" (1939) have been set to music complete and in their originally published form; a few have been subject to a minor revision of tense or pronoun, and eight lines have been added to "The Song of the Jellicles."

However, some of our lyrics, notably "The Marching Song of the Pollicle Dogs" and the story of "Grizabella" were discovered among the unpublished writings of Eliot.

The prologue is based on ideas and incorporates lines from another unpublished poem, entitled "Pollicle Dogs and Jellicle Cats." Growltiger's aria is taken from an Italian translation of "Practical Cats."

"Memory" includes lines from and is suggested by "Rhapsody on a Windy Night," and other poems of the Prufrock period. All other words in the show are taken from the Collected Poems. —Trevor Nunn

[6]Original production first produced in New York 1 December 1956 at the Martin Beck Theatre for 73 performances; revised version first produced Off-Broadway 11 December 1973 at the Chelsea Theater Center, Brooklyn Academy of Music for 48 performances; transferred 5 March 1974 to the Broadway Theatre for 740 performances.
[7]Hugh Wheeler and Harold Prince made further small changes to the 1974 script for this new 'Opera House' version.

Servant of Maximilian: JAMES BILLINGS. *Dr. Pangloss:* JOHN LANKSTON. *Bulgarian Soldiers:* Don Yule, JAMES BILLINGS. *Westphalian Soldiers:* Andy Roth, William Ledbetter. *Don Isaachar, the Jew:* JAMES BILLINGS. *Grand Inquisitor:* JACK HARROLD. *Calliope Player:* Bonnie Kirk. *Heresy Agent:* Ralph Bassett. *Inquisition Agents:* Gary Dietrich, William Poplaski. *Judge:* JAMES BILLINGS. *Old Lady:* MURIEL COSTA-GREENSPON. *Dons:* Robert Estner, Andy Roth, Michael Rubino, Don Yule, William Ledbetter, Ralph Bassett. *Businessman:* JOHN LANKSTON. *Governor:* JOHN LANKSTON. *Governor's Aide:* Andy Roth. *Slave Driver:* JACK HARROLD. *Father Bernard:* JAMES BILLINGS. *Sailors:* Gary Dietrich, William Poplaski, Andy Roth, Jeffrey Smith. *Pirates:* John Henry Thomas, William Ledbetter. *Pink Sheep:* Ivy Austin, Rhoda Butler. *Lion:* James Sergi. *Pasha-Prefect:* JACK HARROLD. *First Gambler:* JAMES BILLINGS. *Second Gambler (Police Chief):* JOHN LANKSTON. *Sage:* JOHN LANKSTON.

(The action takes place in Westphalia and throughout the world in the eighteenth century. Scenes overlap and are played simultaneously.)

Scene 1: Dr. Voltaire's Traveling Freak Show. *Scene 2:* The Castle and Gardens. *Scene 3:* A Desolate Heath. *Scene 4:* The Baronial Chapel. *Scene 5:* A Meadow by Moonlight and The Battlefield. *Scene 6:* Cunegonde's Room. *Scene 7:* Destroyed Village. *Scene 8:* Central Square in Lisbon. *Scene 9:* A Lisbon Street. *Scene 10:* Cunegonde's Room. *Scene 11:* A Room in the Inn at Cadiz. *Scene 12:* Central Plaza at Cadiz.

Act 2, Scene 1: Plaza Grande, Cartagena. *Scene 2:* A Ship at Sea. *Scene 3:* Montevideo Cathedral. *Scene 4:* A Jungle. *Scene 5:* Eldorado and a Jungle. *Scene 6:* A Jungle and Sheep Meadow. *Scene 7:* Ballroom in Cartagena and The Dock. *Scene 8:* A Desert Island. *Scene 9:* A Hall in the Palace. *Scene 10:* The Cave of the Wisest Man. *Scene 11:* Candide's Farm.

ACT 1

"Life Is Happiness Indeed"
  D. Eisler, E. Mills, S. Reeve, D. Darr

("Fanfare" instrumental)

"The Best of All Possible Worlds"
  J. Lankston, D. Eisler, E. Mills, S. Reeve, D. St. Darr

"Oh Happy We"
  D. Eisler, E. Mills

(Candide Begins His Travels)

"It Must Be So" (Candide's Meditation)
  D. Eisler

(Westphalian Fanfare, Chorale, Battle Music)
  (Chorus)

"It Must Be So" (instrumental reprise)

"Glitter and Be Gay"
  E. Mills

"Dear Boy"
  J. Lankston, Men's Chorus

"Auto da Fé" (What a Day)
  Company

"Candide's Lament" (This World)
  D. Eisler

"You Were Dead, You Know"
  D. Eisler, E. Mills

"I Am Easily Assimilated"
  M. Costa-Greenspon, Dons

Quartet Finale
  D. Eisler, E. Mills, M. Costa-Greenspon, J. Lankston, Chorus

ACT 2

"Ballad of the New World"
  D. Eisler, Chorus

"My Love"
  J. Lankston, S. Reeve

(Barcarolle)

"Alleluia"
  S. Reeve, E. Mills, J. Lankston, Chorus

("Eldorado" instrumental)

"Sheep Song"
  I. Austin, R. Butler, J. Sergi, D. Darr, D. Eisler, Chorus

"Governor's Waltz"

"Bon Voyage" (Schottische)
  J. Lankston, Company

"Quiet"
  M. Costa-Greenspon, D. Darr, D. Eisler

"The Best of All Possible Worlds" (reprise)
  M. Costa-Greenspon, D. Eisler, D. Darr

("Constantinople" instrumental)

"What's the Use"
  J. Harrold, J. Billings, J. Lankston

"You Were Dead, You Know" (reprise)
  D. Eisler, E. Mills

"Make Our Garden Grow"
  Company

THE GRAND DUCHESS OF GEROLSTEIN
1982.21

A Revival of the Opéra-bouffe in Two Acts, 4 Scenes[8]. Original (French) libretto (La Grande-Duchesse de Gérolstein) by Henri Meilhac and Ludovic Halévy. Music by Jacques Offenbach. English adaptation by Ruth and Thomas Martin. Directed by Jack Hofsiss. Conducted by Scott Bergeson. Choreography by Christopher Chadman. Scenery and costumes designed by John Conklin. Lighting designed by Gilbert V. Helmsley, Jr. Chorus master, David Leighton. Produced by the New York City Opera. Opened 23 October 1982 (matinee) at the New York State Theatre and closed 3 November 1982 after 3 performances in repertory.

CAST (in order of appearance): *Fritz:* CAROLL FREEMAN. *Wanda:* CLAUDETTE PETERSON. *General Boom:* SPIRO MALAS. *Baron Puck:* JAMES BILLINGS. *Nepomuc:* WILLIAM LEDBETTER. *The Grand Duchess:* SUSANNE MARSEE. *Prince Paul:* RON [Ronald] RAINES. *Baron Grog:* NICO CASTEL. *Ensemble:* New York City Opera Chorus.

ROCK 'N' ROLL! THE FIRST 5,000 YEARS
1982.22

A Rock Musical Revue in Two Acts. Conceived by Bob Gill and Robert Rabinowitz. Musical continuity and supervision by John Simon. Special consultant, Dick Clark. Directed and choreographed by Joe Layton. Scenery by Mark Ravitz. Costumes by Franne Lee. Lighting by Jules Fisher. Sound by Bran Ferren. Orchestrations, dance and vocal arrangements by John Simon. Musical direction by Andrew Dorfman. Media by Gill & Rabinowitz. Co-choreographer, Jerry Grimes. Associate producers, Charles Koppelman, Martin Bandier. Produced by Jules Fisher and Annie Fargue in association with Dick Clark, Inc., Fred Disipio. Opened 24 October 1982 at the St. James Theater and closed 31 October 1982 after 9 performances.

CAST: Rob Barnes, Joyce Leigh Bowden, Ka-Ron Brown, Sandy Dillon, Andrew Dorfman, Rich Hebert, Lon Hoyt, William Gregg Hunter, Bill Jones, Jenifer Lewis, Dave MacDonald, Wendy Leigh MacKenzie, Karen Mankes, Bob Miller, Michael Pace, Raymond Patterson, Marion Ramsey, Jim Riddle, Shaun Solomon, Tom Teeley, Russell Velazquez, Barbara Walsh, Patrick Weathers, Carl E. Weaver, Lillias White.

ACT 1

"Love Is a Many Splendored Thing" (from the film)
  Frank Sinatra (recording)
  (*Music by* Sammy Fain. *Lyrics by* Paul Francis Webster.)

"Tutti Frutti"
  C. Weaver, Compnay
  (*Music and Lyrics by* Richard Penniman, D. La Bostrie, Joe Lubin.)

"Rock Around the Clock"
  J. Riddle, Company
  (*Music and Lyrics by* Max Friedman and Jimmy DeKnight.)

"Blueberry Hill"
  W. G. Hunter, Company
  (*Music and Lyrics by* Al Lewis, Larry Stock, Vincent Rose.)

"Wake Up Little Susie"
  R. Velazquez, T. Teeley, Company
  (*Music and Lyrics by* Boudleaux and Felice Bryant.)

"Great Balls of Fire"
  T. Teeley, Company
  (*Music and Lyrics by* Otis Blackwell and Jack Hammer.)

"Johnny B Goode"
  C. E. Weaver, Company
  (*Music and Lyrics by* Chuck Berry.)

---

[8]First performed in English in New York 17 June 1868 at the New York Theatre for 33 performances. For Synopsis of Scenes and Musical Numbers, see 1982 revival.

"Heartbreak Hotel"
P. Weathers, Company
(*Music and Lyrics by* Mae Boren Axton, Tommy Durden, Elvis Presley.)
"Hound Dog"
P. Weathers, Company
(*Music and Lyrics by* Jerry Lieber and Mike Stoller.)
"Love Me Tender"
P. Weathers, Company
(*Music and Lyrics by* Vera Matson and Elvis Presley.)
"Why Do Fools Fall in Love"
C. E. Weaver, R. Barnes, S. Solomon, W. G. Hunter, R. Patterson, Company
(*Music and Lyrics by* Frank Lymon and Morris Levy.)
"Sh-Boom" (Life Could Be a Dream)
D. MacDonald, Company
(*Music and Lyrics by* James Edwards, Carl Feaster, James Keyes, Floyd F. McRae.)
"Will You Still Love Me Tomorrow"
M. Ramsey, Company
(*Music and Lyrics by* Gerry Goffin and Carole King.)
"Da Doo Ron Ron"
W. L. MacKenzie, Company
(*Music and Lyrics by* Jeff Barry, Ellie Greenwich, Phil Spector.)
"The Twist"
R. Patterson, Company
(*Music and Lyrics by* Hank Ballard.) *Featured Dancer*: K. Brown.
"Land of a Thousand Dances"
W. G. Hunter, Company.
(*Music and Lyrics by* Chris Kenner and Antoine Domino.) *Featured Dancer*: K. Brown.
"I'll Be There"
R. Barnes, Company
(*Music and Lyrics by* Hal Davis, Berry Gordy, Bob West, Willie Hutch.)
"You Keep Me Hanging On"
J. Lewis, L. White, M. Ramsey, Company
(*Music and Lyrics by* Eddie Holland, Lamont Dozier, Bryant Holland.)
"Proud Mary"
M. Ramsey, Company
(*Music and Lyrics by* John C. Fogerty.)
"A Hard Day's Night" (from film)
J. Riddle, R. Velazquez, T. Teeley, B. Miller, Company
{*Music and Lyrics by* John Lennon and Paul McCartney.}
"I Got You Babe"
K. Mankes, M. Pace, Company
(*Music and Lyrics by* Sonny Bono.)
"Good Vibrations"
R. Hebert, C. E. Weaver, J. Riddle, Company
(*Music and Lyrics by* Brian Wilson and Mike Love.)
"Here Comes the Sun"
T. Teeley, Company
(*Music and Lyrics by* George Harrison.)
"The Sunshine of Your Love"
T. Teeley, R. Velazquez, Company
(*Music and Lyrics by* Jack Bruce, Eric Clapton, Peter Brown.)
"Blowin' in the Wind"
P. Weathers, Company
(*Music and Lyrics by* Bob Dylan.)
"Like a Rolling Stone"
P. Weathers, Company
(*Music and Lyrics by* Bob Dylan.)
"Whiter Shade of Pale"
D. MacDonald, Company
(*Music and Lyrics by* Keith Reid and Gary Brooker.) *Featured Dancer*: K. Brown.
"Mrs. Robinson"
R. Velazquez, T. Teeley, Company
(*Music and Lyrics by* Paul Simon.) *Featured Dancer*: K. Brown.
"White Rabbit"
B. Walsh, K. Mankes, W. L. MacKenzie, Company
(*Music and Lyrics by* Grace Slick.)
"Respect"
L. White, Company
(*Music and Lyrics by* Otis Redding.)
"The Night They Drove Old Dixie Down"
P. Weathers, Company
(*Music and Lyrics by* J. Robbie Robertson.)

"People Got to be Free"
R. Velazquez, Company
(*Music and Lyrics by* Edward Brigate, Felix Cavaliere.)
"Cry Baby"
S. Dillon, Company
(*Music and Lyrics by* Burt Russell and Norman Meade.)
"Forever Young"
B. Walsh, Company
(*Music and Lyrics by* Bob Dylan.)
"Everybody's Talking"
M. Pace, Company
(*Music and Lyrics by* Fred Neil.)
"Joy to the World"
R. Velazquez, Company
(*Music and Lyrics by* Hoyt Axton.)
"Both Sides Now"
W. L. MacKenzie, Company
(*Music and Lyrics by* Joni Mitchell.)
"Higher and Higher"
R. Patterson, Company
(*Music and Lyrics by* Renard Miner, Gary Jackson, Carl Smith.)

ACT 2

"Tubular Bells" (instrumental)
B. Miller, Company
(*Music by* Mike Oldfield.)
"I Feel the Earth Move"
J. L. Bowden, Company
(*Music and Lyrics by* Carole King.)
"Satisfaction"
D. MacDonald, Company
(*Music and Lyrics by* Mick Jagger and Keith Richard.)
"When Will I Be Loved"
J. L. Bowden, Company
(Music and Lyrics by Phil Everly.)
"My Generation"
J. Riddle, Company
(*Music and Lyrics by* Peter Townshend.)
"You've Got a Friend"
M. Pace, Company
(*Music and Lyrics by* Carole King.)
"Nothing from Nothing"
W. G. Hunter, Company
(*Music and Lyrics by* Billy Preston and Bruce Fisher.) *Featured Dancer*: K. Brown.
"Say It Loud I'm Black and Proud"
R. Barnes, Company
(*Music and Lyrics by* James Brown.)
"Summer in the City"
J. Riddle, Company
(*Music and Lyrics by* John Sebastian, Steve Boone, Mark Sebastian.) *Featured Dancer*: K. Brown.
"Whole Lotta Love"
R. Velazquez, J. Riddle, Company
(*Music and Lyrics by* John Baldwin, John Bonham, James Patrick Page.)
"Star Spangled Banner" (instrumental)
T. Teeley
(*Music arranged by* Jimi Hendrix.)
"Boogie Woogie Bugle Boy"
J. L. Bowden, Company
(*Music and Lyrics by* Don Raye and Hughie Prince.)
"I Feel Like I'm Gonna Die Rag"
D. MacDonald, Company
(*Music and Lyrics by* Joe McDonald.)
"American Pie"
R. Hebert, Company
(*Music and Lyrics by* Don McLean.)
"Imagine"
T. Teeley, Company
{*Music and Lyrics by* John Lennon.}
"School's Out"
D. MacDonald, Company
(*Music and Lyrics by* Alice Cooper and Michael Bruce.)
"Rock and Roll All Night"
J. Riddle, Company
(*Music and Lyrics by* Paul Stanley and Gene Simmons.)

427

"Benny and the Jets"
L. Hoyt, Company
(*Music and Lyrics by* Elton John, Bernie Taupin.)

"Space Oddity"
M. Pace, R. Velazquez, Company
(*Music and Lyrics by* David Bowie.)

"Take a Walk on the Wild Side"
P. Weathers, Company
(*Music and Lyrics by* Lou Reed.)

"Everybody Is a Star"
C. E. Weaver, L. White, R. Patterson, W. G. Hunter, Company
(*Music and Lyrics by* Sylvester Stewart.) *Featured Dancer:* K. Brown.

"Stayin' Alive" (from *SATURDAY NIGHT FEVER* film)
L. Hoyt, M. Pace, R. Hebert, Company
(*Music and Lyrics by* Barry Gibb, Robin Gibb, Maurice Gibb.)

"Love to Love You Baby"
J. Lewis, Company
(*Music and Lyrics by* Peter Bellote, Giorgio Morder, Donna Summer.)

"I Will Survive"
L. White, Company
(*Music and Lyrics by* Dino Fekaris, Frederick J. Perren.)

"On the Run" (instrumental)
A. Dorfman, R. Velazquez
(*Music by* Roger Waters, David Gilmour, Rick Wright. *Lyrics by* Roger Waters.)

"Jocko Homo"
D. MacDonald, Company
(*Music and Lyrics by* Mark Mothersbaugh.)

"Message in a Bottle"
L. Hoyt, Company
(*Music and Lyrics by* Sting Summer.)

"Our Lips Are Sealed"
K. Mankes, Company
(*Music and Lyrics by* Jane Weidlin and Terry Hall.)

"Concrete Shoes"
S. Dillon, S. Solomon, Company
(*Music and Lyrics by* Rod Swenson.)

"Rock and Roll Music"
Company
(*Music and Lyrics by* Chuck Berry.)

HERMAN VAN VEEN: ALL OF HIM

1982.23

A Musical Show (One-Man Musical Revue) in Two Acts. Concept by Herman van Veen, Michel Lafaille. English adaptation and lyrics by Christopher Adler. Translations by Patricia Braun. Directed by Michel Lafaille. Set designed by Gerard Jongerius, Ed DeBoer. Costumes designed by Ellen van der Horst. Lighting designed by Rob Munnik. Sound designed by Hans van der Linden. Musical direction, Eric van der Wurff. English associate producer, Patricia Braun. Produced by Joost Taverne, Michael Frazier, Ron van Eeden in association with Harlekyn U.S.A. Company. Opened 8 December 1982 at the Ambassador Theatre and closed 12 December 1982 after 6 performances.

CAST: HERMAN VAN VEEN.

MUSICAL NUMBERS (in alphabetical order)
{*All Lyrics by* Herman van Veen except where noted.}

"A Girl"
(*Music by* Herman van Veen and Erik van der Wurff.)

"A Loose Woman"
(*Music by* Herman van Veen. *Original {Dutch}Lyrics by* Willem Wilmink. *English Lyrics by* Christopher Adler.)

"Cranes"
(*Music traditional with adaptation by* Herman van Veen. *Original {Dutch} Lyrics by* Willem Wilmink. *English Lyrics by* Christopher Adler.)

"Do You Remember"
(*Music by* Herman van Veen. *Original {Dutch} Lyrics by* Hans Lodeizen. *English Lyrics by* Christopher Adler.)

"Hello"
(*Music by* Herman van Veen and Erik van der Wurff.)

"Heroes"
(*Music by* Chris Pilgrim. *Original {Dutrch} Lyrics by* Rob Chrispijn. *English Lyrics by* Christopher Adler.)

"Hole-in-One"
(*Music by* Erik van der Wurff and Herman van Veen.)

"I Don't Want Any Help"
(*Music by* Erik van der Wurff and Herman van Veen. *Original {Dutch} Lyrics by* Herman van Veen. *English Lyrics by* Christopher Adler.)

"I Won't Let That Happen to Him"
(*Music by* Georges Delerue.)

"Jacob Is Dead"
(*Music by* Herman van Veen.)

"Kitchen Sink"
(*Music by* Erik van der Wurff and Herman van Veen. *Original {Dutch} Lyrics by* Herman van Veen. *English Lyrics by* Christopher Adler.)

"Ode to Suicide"
(*Music by* Joop Stokkermans. *Original {Dutch} Lyrics by* Guus Vleugel. *English Lyrics by* Christopher Adler.)

"Parade of Clowns"
(*Music by* Erik van der Wurff and Herman van Veen. *Original {Dutch} Lyrics by* Ron Chrisijn. *English Lyrics by* Christopher Adler.)

"Sarabande"
(*Music by* J. B. Senaille, Herman van Veen and Erik van der Wurff.)

"Station"
(*Music by* Erik van der Wurff and Herman van Veen.)

"Tell Me Who I Was"
(*Music by* Phillipe-Gerard. *Original French Lyrics by* Gébé. *Dutch Lyrics by* Willem Wilmink. *English Lyrics adapted from the Dutch by* Christopher Adler.)

"The Back of Life"
(*Music by* Herman van Veen. *Original {Dutch} Lyrics by* Willem Wilmink. *English Lyrics by* Christopher Adler.)

"The Fence"
(*Music by* Erik van der Wurff.)

"The Interveiw"
(*Music by* Erik van der Wurff and Herman van Veen.)

"The Rules of the Asylum"
(*Music by* Herman van Veen. *Original {Dutch} Lyrics by* Rob Chrispijn.)

"Time Passed Her By"
(*Original Music and {Dutch} Lyrics by* Jean Ferrat. *English Lyrics by* Christopher Adler.)

"What a Day"
(*Music by* Erik van der Wurff.)

ALICE IN WONDERLAND

1982.24

A Revival of the Fantasy by Lewis Carroll, adapted for the stage in Two Acts by Eva Le Gallienne and Florida Freibus[9]. Music by Richard Addinsell. Set design by John Lee Beatty. Costume design by Patricia Zipprodt. Lighting design by Jennifer Tipton. Puppets by The Puppet People. Music adapted and supervised by Jonathan Tunick. Movement by Bambi Linn. Illustrated by John Tenniel. Sound by Jack Mann. Musical conductor, Les Scott. Special effects by Chic Silber. Entire production conceived and directed by Eva Le Gallienne. Co-directed by John Strasberg. An Eva LeGallienne Production. Produced by Sabra Jones, Anthony D. Marshall in association with WNET/Thirteen. Opened 23 December 1982 at the Virginia Theatre and closed 9 January 1983 after 21 performances.

CAST (in order of appearance): *Singers:* Nancy Killmer, Marti Morris. *Alice:* KATE BURTON. *Small White Rabbit:* Mary Stuart Masterson. *Mouse:* John Remme. *Lory:* John Miglietta. *Duck:* Nicholas Martin. *Dodo:* James Valentine. *Eaglet:* Rebecca Armen. *White Rabbit:* Curt Dawson. *Caterpillar:* John Heffernan. *Fish Footman:* Geddeth Smith. *Frog Footman:* Claude-Albert Saucier. *Duchess:* Edward Zang. *Cook:* Richard Sterne. *Voice of Cheshire Cat:* Geddeth Smith. *March Hare:* Josh Clark. *Mad Hatter:* MacIntyre Dixon. *Dormouse:* Nicholas Martin. *Two of Spades:* Geoff Garland. *Five of Spades:* Rober Ott Boyle. *Seven of Spades:* Steve Massa. *Three of Clubs:* Skip Harris. *Seven of Clubs:* Cliff Rakerd. *Ace of Hearts:* Geddeth Smith. *Two of Hearts:* Rebecca Armen. *Three of Hearts:* John Remme. *Four of Hearts:* Mary Stuart Masterson. *Five of Hearts:* Claude-Albert Saucier. *Six of Hearts:* Marti Morris. *Seven of Hearts:* John Miglietta. *Eight of Hearts:* Nancy Killmer. *Nine of Hearts:* Richard Sterne. *Ten of Hearts:* John Heffernan. *Knave of Hearts:* John Seidman. *Queen of Hearts:* Brian Reddy. *King of Hearts:* Richard Woods. *Gryphon:* Edward Hibbert. *Mock Turtle:* James Valentine. *Red Queen:* Mary Louise Wilson. *Train Guard:* Nicholas Martin. *Man in

---

[9]First presented *as ALICE IN WONDERLAND AND THROUGH THE LOOKING GLASS* in New York 12 December 1932 at the Civic Repertory Theatre for 127 performances. For Synopsis of Scenes and Musical Numbers, see original 1932 production.

White Paper: Geddeth Smith. *Goat*: Claude-Albert Saucier. *Tweedledum*: Robert Ott Boyle. *Tweedledee*: John Remme. *White Queen*: EVA Le GALLIENNE, Joan White, alt. *Sheep*: John Heffernan. *Voice of Humpty Dumpty*: Richard Woods. *White Knight*: Curt Dawson. *Front of Horse*: Josh Clark. *Back of Horse*: Cliff Rakerd. *Old Frog*: Edward Hibbert. *Voice of Leg of Mutton*: Steve Massa.

1983.01   MERLIN

A Musical in Two Acts, 12 Scenes. Book by Richard Levinson, William Link. Songs (Music) and incidental music by Elmer Bernstein. Lyrics by Don Black. Magic illusions, Doug Henning. Directed by Ivan Reitman. Choreography by Christopher Chadman, Billy Wilson. Scenic design by Robin Wagner. Costume design by Theoni V. Aldredge. Lighting design by Tharon Musser. Sound design by Abe Jacob. Orchestrations by Larry Wilcox. Music direction, vocal arrangements by David Spear. Dance arrangements by Mark Hummel. Magic consultant, Charles Reynolds. Production supervisor, Jeff Hamlin. Associate producer, Joe Medjuck. Produced by Ivan Reitman, Columbia Pictures Stage Productions, Inc., Marvin A. Krauss, James M. Nederlander. Opened 13 February 1983 at the Mark Hellinger Theatre and closed 7 August 1983 after 199 performances.

CAST (in order of appearance): *Old Merlin*: George Lee Andrews. *Creatures of the Glade*: Robin Cleaver, Ramon Galindo, Todd Lester, Claudia Shell, Robert Tanna. *Young Merlin*: Christian Slater. *The Wizard*: EDMUND LYNDECK. *Merlin*: DOUG HENNING. *Philomena*: Rebecca Wright. *The Queen*: CHITA RIVERA. *The Queen's Companion*: Gregory Mitchell. *Prince Fergus*: NATHAN LANE. *Merlin's Vision*: Debby Henning. *Ariadne*: Michelle Nicastro. *Acolyte*: Alan Brasington. *Earth*: Peggy Parten. *Air*: Robyn Lee. *Fire*: Spence Ford. *Water*: Debby Henning. *Ladies of the Court*: Pat Gorman, Leslie Hicks, Robyn Lee, Peggy Parten, Iris Revson. *Manservant*: Alan Brasington. *Old Soldier*: George Lee Andrews. *Arthur*: Christian Slater.

Ladies of the Ensemble: Robin Cleaver, Spence Ford, Pat Gorman, Andrea Handler, Debby Henning, Leslie Hicks, Sandy Laufer, Robyn Lee, Peggy Parten, Iris Revson, Claudia Shell. *Men of the Ensemble*: David Asher, Ramon Galindo, Todd Lester, Joe Locarro, Fred C. Mann III, Gregory Mitchell, Andrew Hill Newman, Eric Roach, Robert Tanna, Robert Warners.

The action takes place in the time of sorcery.

Act 1, Scene 1: Merlin's Glade. *Scene 2*: The Palace of the Queen. *Scene 3*: The Glade. *Scene 4*: A Crystal Grove. *Scene 5*: A River. *Scene 6*: The Hall of the Angels.

Act 2, Scene 1: A Far Away Village. *Scene 2*: The Palace. *Scene 3*: A Marsh. *Scene 4*: the Palace Ramparts. *Scene 5*: The Queen's Dungeon. *Scene 6*: On the Way to London.

ACT 1
Scene 1
"It's About Magic"
G. L. Andrews, C. Slater, D. Henning, R. Wright, Ensemble
Scene 2
"I Can Make It Happen"
C. Rivera
Scene 3
"Beyond My Wildest Dreams"
M. Nicastro
"Something More"
D. Henning, M. Nicastro
Scene 4
"The Elements"
D. Henning, E. Lyndeck, Ensemble
Scene 5
"Fergus' Dilemma"
N. Lane, Ladies of the Court
Scene 6
"Nobody Will Remember Him"
C. Rivera, E. Lyndeck

ACT 2
Scene 1
"Put a Little Magic in Your Life"
G. L. Andrews, D. Henning, R. Wright, Ensemble
"He Who Knows the Way"
E. Lyndeck
Scene 2
"I Can Make It Happen" (reprise)
C. Rivera
Scene 3
"He Who Knows the Way" (reprise)
E. Lyndeck

Scene 4
"We Haven't Fought a Battle in Years"
N. Lane, Soldiers
Scene 5
"Satan Rules"
C. Rivera
"Nobody Will Remember Him" (reprise)
C. Rivera
Scene 6
"He Who Knows the Way" (reprise)
D. Henning, E. Lyndeck, C. Slater

1983.02   ON YOUR TOES

A Revival of the Musical Comedy in Two Acts, 12 Scenes[10]. Book by Richard Rodgers, Lorenz Hart and George Abbott. Lyrics by Lorenz Hart. Music by Richard Rodgers. Directed by George Abbott. Original choreography by George Balanchine. Additional ballet choreography by Peter Martins. Musical numbers choreographed by Donald Saddler. Production (scenic and costume) design by Zack Brown. Lighting by John McLain. Musical director, conductor, John Mauceri. Original orchestrations by Hans Spialek. Coordinating producer, Charlene Harrington. Produced by Alfred de Liagre, Jr., Roger L. Stevens, John Mauceri, Donald R. Seawell, André Pastoria. Opened 6 March 1983 at the Virginia Theatre and closed 20 May 1984 after 505 performances.

CAST (in order of appearance): *Phil Dolan II*: Eugene J. Anthony. *Lil Dolan*: Betty Ann Grove. *Phil Dolan III, Junior*: Philip Arthur Ross. *Stage Manager*: Dirk Lumbard. *Lola*: Mary C. Robare. *Phil Dolan III, Junior (15 years later)*: LARA TEETER. *Miss Pinkerton*: Michaela K. Hughes. *Sidney Cohn*: Peter Slutsker. *Frankie Frayne*: CHRISTINE ANDREAS. *Joe McCall*: Jerry Mitchell. *Vera Barnova*: NATALIA MAKAROVA. *Anushka*: Tamara Mark. *Peggy Porterfield*: DINA MERRILL. *Sergei Alexandrovitch*: GEORGE S. IRVING. *Konstantine Morrosine*: GEORGE DE LA PEÑA. *Oscar*: Eugene J. Anthony. *Stage Doorman*: David Gold. *A Woman Reporter*: Betty Ann Grove. *Dimitri*: Chris Peterson. *Ivan*: Don Steffy. *Louie*: George Kmeck.

Princess Zenobia Ballet: *Princess Zenobia*: NATALIA MAKAROVA. *Beggar*: GEORGE DE LA PEÑA. *Kringa Khan*: George Kmeck. *Ali Shar*: Eugene J. Anthony. *Ahmud Ben B'Du*: David Gold.

Hank Jay Smith: Michael Vita.

On Your Toes Ballet: *Ballet Leaders*: Alexander Filipov, Starr Danias. *Tap Leaders*: Dirk Lumbard, Dana Moore.

Cop: Michael Vita. *Messenger Boy*: Dean Badolato.

Slaughter on Tenth Avenue Ballet: *Hoofer*: LARA TEETER. *Strip Tease Girl*: NATALIA MAKAROVA. *Big Boss*: Michael Vita.

Cop: Jerry Mitchell.

Ensemble: Melody A. Dye, Michaela K. Hughes, Tamara Mark, Dana Moore, Mary C. Robare, Marcia Lynn Watkins, Leslie Woodies, Sandra Zigars, Dean Badolato, Alexander Filipov, Wade Laboissonniere, Dirk Lumbard, Robert Meadows, Jerry Mitchell, Chris Peterson, Don Steffy, Kirby Tepper, David Gold, Georeg Kmeck.

Act 1, Scene 1: A Vaudeville Stage, about 1920. *Scene 2*: The Vaudeville Dressing Room. *Scene 3*: A Classroom of Knickerbocker University—WPA Extension. *Scene 4*: Vera's Apartment, the next morning. *Scene 5*: The Schoolroom. *Scene 6*: The Bare Stage, Cosmopolitan Opera House, the next morning. *Scene 7*: Cosmopolitan Opera House. "Princesse Zenobia" Ballet.

Act 2, Scene 1: The Bare Stage, Cosmopolitan Opera House. *Scene 2*: The Classroom. *Scene 3*: The Bare Stage, Cosmopolitan Opera House. *Scene 4*: The Stage Door, Cosmopolitan Opera House. *Scene 5*: Stage of the Cosmopolitan Opera House. "Slaughter on Tenth Avenue" Ballet.

ACT 1
Scene 1
"Two A Day for Keith"
E. J. Anthony, B. A. Grove, P. A. Ross
Scene 3
"Questions and Answers" (The Three B's)
L. Teeter, Students
"It's Got To Be Love"
C. Andreas, L. Teeter, Students

---

[10]Originally produced in New York 11 April 1936 at the Imperial Theatre for 315 performances. For this revival, "The Heart Is Quicker Than the Eye" was moved from Act 1 to Act 2. "The Seduction" and a reprise of "Quiet Night" were added, and the song and scene order, scene descriptions were slightly revised.

Scene 4
  "Too Good for the Average Man"
    G. S. Irving, D. Merrill
  "The Seduction"
    N. Makarova, L. Teeter
Scene 5
  "There's a Small Hotel"
    C. Andreas, L. Teeter
Scene 7
  "La Princesse Zenobia" Ballet

ACT 2
Scene 1
  "The Heart Is Quicker Than the Eye"
    D. Merrill, L. Teeter
  "Glad To Be Unhappy"
    C. Andreas
Scene 2
  "Quiet Night"
    M. Vita, Ensemble
  "On Your Toes"
    C. Andreas, Ensemble
Scene 4
  "Quiet Night" (reprise)
    G. S. Irving
Scene 5
  "Slaughter on Tenth Avenue" Ballet
    (Finale)
    (Entire Company)

1983.03   CHARLES AZNAVOUR

A Solo Performance in Two Acts[11]. Music director, Aldo Frank. Sound, Robert Kerzman. Wardrobe by Ted Lapidus. Musical coordinator, Bob Cranshaw. Produced by Ron Delsener and Levon Sayan. Opened 14 March 1983 at the Lunt-Fontanne Theater and closed 26 March 1983 after 14 performances.

CAST: CHARLES AZNAVOUR.
  Background vocalists: Diana Green, Ednah Holt, Carol Steele.

MUSICAL NUMBERS
(All music and lyrics by Charles Aznavour except where noted.)
  "Le Temps"
    (*Music by* Davis.)
  "In Your Room"
    (*Music and Lyrics by* Charles Aznavour and Buddy Kaye.)
  "I Didn't See the Time Go By"
    (*Music and Lyrics by* Charles Aznavour and Herbert Kretzmer.)
  "Etre"
    (*Music by* Georges Garaventz.)
  "Happy Anniversary"
    (*English Lyrics by* Herbert Kretzmer.)
  "In Times To Be"
    (*French Lyrics by* Jacques Plante. *English Lyrics by* Herbert Kretzmer.)
  "L'amour bon dieu"
  "I Act As If"
    (*Lyrics by* Jacques Plante. *English Lyrics by* Dee Shipman.)
  "To Be a Soldier"
    (*Music and Lyrics by* Charles Aznavour and Herbert Kretzmer.)
  "Nous n'avons pas d'enfant"
    (*Music by* Georges Garaventz.)
  "I'll Be There"
    (*Music by* Georges Garaventz. *Lyrics by* Charles Aznavour and Herbert Kretzmer.)
  "Les comediens"
    (*Lyrics by* Jacques Plante.)
  "She"

"Take Me Along"
"The Happy Days"
"Mon ami mon Judas"
"And I in My Chair"
  (English Lyrics by D. Newberg.)
"Isabelle"
"You've Let Yourself Go"
  (*English Lyrics by* Marcel Stellman.)
"Mon emouvant amour"
"Ave Maria"
  (*Music by* Georges Garaventz.)
"What Makes a Man"
"La Boheme"
  (*Lyrics by* Jacques Plante.)
"The Old Fashioned Way"
  (*Music by* Georges Garaventz.)
"Yesterday When I Was Young"
  (*English Lyrics by* Herbert Kretzmer.)
"You've Got to Learn"
"La Mama"
  (*Music by* Robert Gall.)
"Mourir d'aimer"
"Qui, de t'avoir aimee"
"Que c'est triste Venise"
  (*Music by* F. Dorin.)
"Non je n'ai rien oublie"
  (*Music by* Georges Garaventz.)
"Ils sont tombes"
"The First Dance"

1983.04   PORGY AND BESS

A Revival of the Folk Opera in Two Acts, 9 Scenes[12]. Libretto by DuBose Heyward adapted from the play "Porgy" by DuBose and Dorothy Heyward. Music by George Gershwin. Lyrics by DuBose Heyward and Ira Gershwin. Directed by Jack O'Brien Assistant director, production supervisor, Helaine Head. Scenery designer, Douglas W. Schmidt. Costume designer, Nancy Potts. Lighting designer, Gilbert V. Hemsley, Jr. Musical director C. William Harwood. Choreographer, George Faison. Production coordinator, M. Jane Weaver. Assistant conductor, Edward Strauss. Associate conductor, John Miner. Associate producer, Virginia Hymes. Produced by Radio City Music Hall Productions, Inc. (Bernard Gersten, Executive producer) and Sherwin M. Goldman Productions. Opened 7 April 1983 at the Radio City Music Hall and closed 15 May 1983 after 45 performances.

CAST (in order of appearance): *Jasbo Brown:* Edward Strauss. *Clara:* PRISCILLA BASKERVILLE or LUVENIA GARNER. *Mingo:* Timothy Allen. *Jake:* Alexander Smalls or James Tyeska. *Sportin' Life:* LARRY MARSHALL. *Robbins:* Tyrone Jolivet. *Serena:* SHIRLEY BAINES, REGINA McCONNELL, WILMA SHAKESNIDER or VERONICA TYLER. *Jim:* Donald Walter Kase. *Peter,* (the Honey Man): Mervin Bertel Wallace. *Lily:* Y. Yvonne Matthews. *Maria:* LORETTA HOLKMANN or GWENDOLYN SHEPHERD. *Scipio:* Akili Prince. *Porgy:* ROBERT MOSLEY, JR., MICHAEL V. SMARTT, JONATHAN SPRAGUE or JAMES TYESKA. *Crown:* GREGG BAKER or GEORGE ROBERT MERRITT. *Bess:* PRISCILLA BASKERVILLE, HENRIETTA ELIZABETH DAVIS, NAOMI MOODY or DAISY NEWMAN. *Detective:* Larry Storch. *Policeman:* William Moize. *Undertaker:* Joseph S. Eubanks. *Annie:* Lou Ann Pickett. *Frazier:* Raymond H. Bazemore. *Strawberry Woman:* Denice Woods. *Crab Man:* Thomas J. Young. *Nelson:* Everett McCorvey. *Coroner:* Richert Easley.
  Ensemble (Residents of Catfish Row): Loretta Abbott, Timothy Allen, Earl L. Baker, Emerson Battles, Raymond H. Bazemore, Shirley Black-Brown, Roslyn Burrough, Vertrelle Cameron, Seraiah Carol, Duane Clenton Carter, Dabriah Chapman, Louise Coleman, Janice D. Dixon, Cisco Xavier Drayton, Alberta M. Driver, Joseph S. Eubanks, Karen E. Eubanks, Lori Eubanks, Beno Foster, Jerry Godfrey, Earl Grandison, Milton B. Grayson, Jr., Elvira Green, Lawrence Hamilton, Gurcell Henry, Lisa D. Holkmann, Janice T. Hutson, David-Michael Johnson, Leavata Johnson, Tyrone Jolivet, Dorothy L. Jones, Donald Walker Kase, Roberta Alexandra Laws, Eugene Little, Ann Marie Mackey, Barbara Mahajan, Amelia Marshall, Richard Mason, Y. Yvonne Matthews, Everett McCorvey, John McDaniels, William Moize, Byron Onque, H. William Penn, Marenda Perry, Lou Ann Pickett, Herbert Lee Rawlings, Jr., Roumel Reaux, David Robertson, Lattilia Ronrico, Renee L. Rose, Myles

---

[11]Charles Aznavour previously appeared on Broadway 14 October 1965 at the Ambassador Theatre for 29 performances, and 4 February 1970 at the Music Box Theatre for 23 performances.

---

[12]First produced in New York 10 October 1935 at the Alvin Theatre for 124 performances.

Gregory Savage, Sheryl Shell, Kiki Shepard, Chuck Thorpes, Mervin Bertel Wallace, Pamela Warrick-Smith, Cornelius White, Rodney Wing, Denice Woods, Thomas J. Young, and Diallobe Dorsey, Angela Holcomb, Robert Kryser, Jason Little, Noelle Richards, Kevin L. Stroman, Charee Adia Thropes, Tarik Winston.

The action takes place in Charleston, South Carolina, in the early 1930's.

Act 1, Scene 1: Catfish Row, a summer evening. *Scene 2*: Serena's Room, the following night. *Scene 3*: Catfish Row, a month later. *Scene 4*: Kittiwah Island, late afternoon.

Act 2, Scene 1: Catfish Row, before dawn, a week later. *Scene 2*: Serena's Room, the dawn of the following day. *Scene 3*: Catfish Row, the next night. *Scene 4*: Catfish Row, the next afternoon. *Scene 5*: Catfish Row, a week later.

ACT 1

Scene 1

"Brown Blues"
Piano
"Summertime"
P. Baskerville
"A Woman Is A Sometime Thing"
A. Smalls, Men
"Here Come De Honey Man"
M. B. Wallace
"They Pass By Singing"
R. Mosley, Jr.
"Oh Little Stars"
R. Mosley, Jr.

Scene 2

"Gone, Gone, Gone"
Ensemble
"Overflow"
Ensemble
"My Man's Gone Now"
S. Baines,
"Leavin' For the Promise' Lan'"
P. Baskerville, Ensemble

Scene 3

"It Takes a Long Pull to Get There"
A. Smalls, Men
"I Got Plenty o' Nuttin'"
R. Mosley, Jr., Ensemble
"Struttin' Style"
L. Holkmann
"Buzzard Song"
R. Mosley, Jr., Ensemble
"Bess, You Is My Woman Now"
R. Mosley, Jr., P. Baskerville
"Oh, I Can't Sit Down"
Ensemble

Scene 4

"I Ain't Got No Shame"
Ensemble
"It Ain't Necessarily So"
L. Marshall, Ensemble
"What You Want With Bess?"
P. Baskerville, G. Baker

ACT 2

Scene 1

"Oh, Doctor Jesus"
S. Baines, L. Holkmann, M. B. Wallce, Y. Y. Matthews, R. Mosley, Jr.
"I Loves You, Porgy"
R. Mosley, Jr., P. Baskerville

Scene 2

"Oh, He'venly Father"
Ensemble
"Oh, de Lawd Shake de Heavens"
Ensemble
"Oh, Dere's Somebody Knockin' at De Do'"
Ensemble
"A Red Headed Woman"
G. Baker, Ensemble

Scene 3

"Clara, Clara"
Ensemble

Scene 4

"There a Boat Dat's Leavin' Soon for New York"
L. Marshall, P. Baskerville
"Good Mornin', Sistuh!"
Ensemble

Scene 5

"Oh, Bess, Oh Where's My Bess"
R. Mosley, Jr., S. Baines, Y. Y. Matthews
"Oh Lawd, I'm On My Way"
R. Mosley, Jr. . Ensemble

1983.05 # SHOWBOAT

A Revival of the Musical (Play) in Two Acts, 15 Scenes[13]. Book and lyrics by Oscar Hammerstein II. Based on the novel of the same name by Edna Ferber. Music by Jerome Kern. Directed by Michael Kahn. Choreography by Dorothy Danner. Scenery designed by Herbert Senn, Helen Pond. Costumes designed by Molly Maginnis. Lighting designed by Thomas Skelton. Musical director, John DeMain. Conductor, Jack Everly. Sound by Richard Fitzgerald. A Houston Grand Opera Production. Executive producers, Robert A. Buckley, Douglas Urbanski. Produced by James M. Nederlander, John F. Kennedy Center (Roger L. Stevens, Chairman), Denver Center (Donald R. Seawell, Chairman). Opened 24 April 1983 at the Uris Theatre and closed 26 June 1983 after 73 performances.

<u>CAST</u> (in order of their appearance): *Windy (McLain)*: Richard Dix. *Steve*: Wayne Turnage. *Pete*: Glenn Martin. *Queenie*: KARLA BURNS. *Parthy Ann Hawkes*: AVRIL GENTLES. *Captain Andy*: DONALD O'CONNOR. *Ellie*: PAIGE O'HARA. *Frank*: PAUL KEITH. *Mahoney*: Randy Hansen. *Julie*: LONETTE McKEE. *Gaylord Ravenal*: RON RAINES. *(Sheriff Ike) Vallon*: Jacob Mark Hopkin. *Magnolia*: SHERYL WOODS. *Joe*: BRUCE HUBBARD. *Backwoodsman*: Lewis White. *Jeb*: James Gedge. *Barkers*: Lewis White, Randy Hansen, James Gedge. *La Belle Fatima*: Lynda Karen. *Old Sport*: Larry Hansen. *Landlady*: Mary Rocco. *Jim*: Jacob Mark Hopkin. *Jake*: Randy Hansen. *Young Man with Guitar*: Larry Hansen. *Charlie*: P. L. Brown. *Mother Superior*: Linda Milani. *Young Kim*: Tracy Paul. *Lottie*: Gloria Parker. *Dolly*: Dale Kristien. *Old Lady on Levee*: Mary Rocco. *Older Kim*: Karen Culliver. *Radio Announcer's Voice*: Hal Douglas.

Chorus: Women: Vanessa Ayers, Joanna Beck, Karen Culliver, Olivia Detante, Kim Fairchild, Cheryl Freeman, Lynda Karen, Dale Kristien, Linda Milani, Gloria Parker, Veronica Rhodes, Mary Rocco, Molly Wassermann, Carrie Wilder. *Swings*: Jeane July, Suzanne Ishee. *Men*: P. L. Brown, Michael-Pierre Dean, Merwin Foard, Joe Garcia, James Gedge, Michael Gray, Larry Hansen, Randy Hansen, Jacob Mark Hopkin, Glenn Martin, Randy Morgan, Dennis Perren, Leonard Piggee, Alton Spencer, Robert Vincent, Lewis White, Wardell Woodard. *Swings*: Tom Garrett, Ed Battle.

Act 1, Scene 1: The Levee at Natchez on the Mississippi, in the 1880s. *Scene 2*: Kitchen pantry of the *Cotton Blossom*. . Five minutes later. *Scene 3*: Outside a river front gambling saloon. Simultaneously. *Scene 4*: Auditorium and Stage of the *Cotton Blossom*. . One hour later. *Scene 5*: Box office, on foredeck. Three weeks later. *Scene 6*: Auditorium and stage during the Third Act of "The Parson's Bride," that night. *Scene 7*: The top deck. Later that night. *Scene 8*: The Levee at Greenville. Next morning.

Act 2, Scene 1: The Midway Plaisance, Chicago World's Fair, 1893. *Scene 2*: A room on Ontario Street, 1904. *Scene 3*: Rehearsal room, Trocadero Music Hall. A few days later. *Scene 4*: St. Agatha's Convent. About the same time. *Scene 5*: Trocadero Music Hall, New Year's Eve, ringing in the year 1905. *Scene 6*: The deck of the *Cotton Blossom*, 1927. *Scene 7*: The levee at Greenville, the next night.

ACT 1

"Cotton Blossom"
Stevedores, Townspeople
"Show Boat Parade and Ballyhoo"
D. O'Connor, the Showboat Troupe, Townspeople
"Only Make Believe"
R. Raines, S. Woods
"Ol' Man River"
B. Hubbard, Stevedores
"Can't Help Lovin' Dat Man"
L. McKee, R. Le Noire, S. Woods, B. Hubbard, Ensemble
"Life Upon the Wicked Stage"
P. O'Hara, Ensemble
"I Might Fall Back on You"
P, Keith, P. O'Hara

---

[13]First presented December 27, 1927 at the Ziegfeld Theatre for 572 performances. This production was made possible in part through a major grant from Citibank•Citicorp and a generous gift from Mrs. Edgar Tobin.

"Queenie's Ballyhoo"
  R. Le Noire, D. O'Connor, Ensemble
"You Are Love"
  S. Woods, R. Raines
Finale
  Entire Ensemble

ACT 2
"At the Fair"
  Sightseers, Barkers
"Why Do I Love You?"
  S. Woods, R. Raines, D. O'Connor, A. Gentles, Ensemble
"Bill" (*Lyrics by* P. G. Wodehouse.)
  L. McKee
"Can't Help Lovin' Dat Man" (reprise)
  S. Woods
Service and Scene Music-St. Agnes Convent
"Only Make Believe" (reprise)
  R. Raines
"Goodbye, My Lady Love" — Cakewalk
  P. Keith, P. O'Hara
  (*Music and Lyrics by* Joseph E. Howard.)
Magnolia's Debut at the Trocadero Music Hall:
"After the Ball"
  S. Woods, Ensemble
  (*Music and Lyrics by* Charles K. Harris.)
"Ol' Man River" (reprise)
  B. Hubbard
"You Are Love" (reprise)
  R. Raines
"Hey Feller"
  K. Burns, Ensemble
Finale (Act 2)
  Entire Ensemble

1983.06   MY ONE AND ONLY

A Musical in Two Acts, 15 Scenes. Book by Peter Stone and Timothy S. Mayer[14]. Music by George Gershwin. Lyrics by Ira Gershwin. Staged and choreographed by Thommie Walsh and Tommy Tune. Associate choreographer, Baayork Lee. Associate director, Phillip Oesterman. Scenic design by Adrianne Lobel. Costume design by Rita Ryack. Lighting design by Marcia Madeira. Sound design by Otts Munderloh. Musical concept, dance arrangements by Wally Harper. Orchestrations by Michael Gibson. Musical and vocal direction, Jack Lee. Dance arrangements by Peter Larson. Musical consultant, Michael Feinstein. A King Street Production (Bernard Carragher, Obie Bailey, Bernard Bailey). Associate producer, Jonathan Farkas. Produced by Paramount Theatre Productions, Francine LeFrak, Kenneth-Mark Productions (Kenneth D. Greenblatt, Mark S. Schwartz), in association with Jujamcyn Theatres, Tams-Witmark Music Library, Lewis Allen. Opened 1 May 1983 at the St. James Theatre and closed 5 March 1985 after 767 performances.

CAST (in order of appearance): *The New Rhythm Boys*: David Jackson, Ken Leigh Rogers, Ronald Dennis. *Captain Billy Buck Chandler*: TOMMY TUNE. *Mickey*: DENNY DILLON. *Prince Nicolai Erraclyovitch Tchatchavadze*: BRUCE McGILL. *Fish* (6): *Flounder*: Nana Visitor. *Sturgeon*: Susan Hartley. *Minnow*: Stephanie Eley. *Prawn*: Jill Cook. *Kipper*: Niki Harris. *Anchovie*: Karen Tamburrelli. *Edith Herbert*: TWIGGY. *Right Reverend J. D. Montgomery*: ROSCOE LEE BROWNE. *Reporter*: Jill Cook. *Mr. Magix*: CHARLES "HONI" COLES. *Ritz Quartet*: Casper Roos, Paul David Richards, Carl Nicholas, Will Blankenship. *Stage Doorman*: Paul David Richards. *Mrs. O'Malley*: Ken Leigh Rogers. *Conductor*: Adrian Bailey. *Dancing Gentlemen*: Adrian Bailey, Bar Dell Conner, Ronald Dennis, David Jackson, Alde Lewis, Jr., Bernard Manners, Ken Leigh Rogers. *Achmed*: BRUCE McGILL. *Swings*: Merilee Magnuson, Melvin Washington.

Act 1, Scene 1: Pennsylvania Station, 1 May 1927. *Scene 2*: Billy's Hangar. *Scene 3*: Mr. Magix' Emporial. *Scene 4*: Club Havana. *Scene 5*: Cinema. *Scene 6*: Central Park. *Scene 7*: The Hangar. *Scene 8*: A Deserted Beach.

Act 2, Scene 1: Aquacade. *Scene 2*: Mr. Magix' Emporial. *Scene 3*: Pennsylvania Station. *Scene 4*: The Hangar. *Scene 5*: Club Oasis. *Scene 6*: The Uptown Chapel. *Scene 7*: Bows and Finale.

---

[14]Adapted from the musical "Funny Face," book by Fred Thompson and Paul Gerard Smith.

ACT 1
Scene 1
"I Can't Be Bothered Now" (from *A DAMSEL IN DISTRESS* film)
  The New Rhythm Boys, T. Tune, Twiggy, B. McGill, D. Dillon, Ensemble
"Blah, Blah, Blah" (from *DELICIOUS* film)
  T. Tune
Scene 2
"Boy Wanted" (from *A DANGEROUS MAID*)
  Twiggy, J. Cook
"Soon" (from *STRIKE UP THE BAND*)
  T. Tune
Scene 3
"High Hat" (from *FUNNY FACE*)/"Sweet and Low-Down" (from *TIP-TOES*)
  H. Coles, T. Tune, the New Rhythm Boys, Ensemble
Scene 4
"Blah, Blah, Blah" (reprise)
  Twiggy
"Just Another Rhumba"[15] (unused, *THE GOLDWYN FOLLIES* film, 1938)
  R. L. Browne, Ensemble
Scene 5
"He Loves and She Loves" (from *FUNNY FACE*)
  T. Tune, Twiggy
"He Loves and She Loves" (reprise)
  Ritz Quartette
Scene 7
"I Can't Be Bothered Now" (reprise)
  The New Rhythm Boys
Scene 8
"'S Wonderful" (from *FUNNY FACE*)
  T. Tune, Twiggy
"'S Wonderful" (reprise)
  Ritz Quartette
"Strike Up the Band" (from *STRIKE UP THE BAND*)
  T. Tune
ACT 2
Scene 1
"In the Swim" (from *FUNNY FACE*)/"What Are We Here For" (from *TREASURE GIRL*)
  Fish, B. McGill
"Nice Work If You Can Get It" (from *A DAMSEL IN DISTRESS* film)
  Twiggy
Scene 2
"My One and Only" (from *FUNNY FACE*)
  H. Coles, T. Tune
  (*Special Material by* Charles "Honi" Coles.)
Scene 4
"Funny Face" (from *FUNNY FACE*)
  D. Dillon, B. McGill
Scene 5
"My One and Only" (reprise)
  T. Tune
Scene 6
"Kickin' the Clouds Away" (from *TELL ME MORE!*)
  R. L. Browne, Ensemble
  (*Lyrics by* Buddy DeSylva and Ira Gershwin. *Dance Arrangements by* Peter Howard.)
"How Long Has This Been Going On?" (from *ROSALIE*, dropped from *FUNNY FACE*)
  Twiggy, T. Tune
Scene 7
"Strike Up the Band" (reprise)
  Company

---

[15]Dropped after opening.

THE FLYING
1983.07 KARAMAZOV BROTHERS

An Entertainment in Two Acts. (Conceived by the Cast.) Setting and costumes by Robert Fletcher. Lighting by Marc B. Weiss. Sound by Robert Kerzman. Associate Producers, Harold Thau, Robert Courson. Produced by Mace Neufeld and Viacom International, Inc. Opened 10 May 1983 at the Ritz Theatre and closed 19 June 1983 after 47 performances.

CAST: *Dmitri*: Paul David Magid. *Alyosha*: Randy Nelson. *Fyodor*: Timothy Daniel Furst. *Smerdyakov*: Sam Williams. *Ivan*: Howard Jay Patterson.
    Kamikaze Ground Crew (band): Douglas Wieselman, Mike van Liew, Gina Leishman, Bud Chase, Alex Willows.

The action takes place at the present time on the stage of a prestigious Broadway theatre.
    "Ivan's Antique Store" and "The Chumleighland March" (*Music by* Thaddeus Spae.)
    All other music by Douglas Wieselman.

DANCE A LITTLE CLOSER
1983.08

A Musical in Two Acts, 9 Scenes. Book and lyrics by Alan Jay Lerner. Based on the play "Idiot's Delight" by Robert E. Sherwood. Music by Charles Strouse. Directed by Alan Jay Lerner. Musical staging and choreography by Billy Wilson. Scenery by David Mitchell. Costumes by Donald Brooks. Lighting by Thomas Skelton. Orchestrations by Jonathan Tunick. Musical direction by Peter Howard. Dance music by Glen Kelly. Sound design by John McClure. Production supervisor, Stone Widney. Associate producer, Paul N. Temple. Produced by Frederick Brisson, Jerome Minskoff, James Nederlander, the John F. Kennedy Center (Roger L. Stevens, Chairman). Opened and closed 11 May 1983 at the Minskoff Theatre after 1 performance.

CAST (in order of appearance): *Roger Butterfield*: Don Chastain. *Harry Aikens*: LEN CARIOU. *The Delights (3)*: *Shirley*: Diane Pennington. *Bebe*: Cheryl Howard. *Elaine*: Alyson Reed. *Johannes Hartog*: David Sabin. *Contessa Carla Pirianno*: Elizabeth Hubbard. *Captain Mueller*: Noel Craig. *Charles Castleton*: Brent Barrett. *Edward Dunlop*: Jeff Keller. *Bellboy*: Philip Mollet. *Waiter*: Brian Sutherland. *Reverend Oliver Boyle*: I. M. Hobson. *Hester Boyle*: Joyce Worsley. *Heinrich Walter (Halloway)*: Joseph Kolinski. *Cynthia Brookfield-Bailey*: LIZ ROBERTSON. *Dr. Josef Winkler*: GEORGE ROSE. *Pas de Deux*: *Harry's Double*: Brian Sutherland. *Cynthia's Double*: Robin Stephens. *Rink Attendant*: James Fatta. *Ice Skater*: Colleen Ashton. *Violinist*: James Fatta. *Harry, Harry, Harry, Harry*: Peter Wandel, Philip Mollet, Brian Sutherland, James Fatta.
    Hotel Guests: Colleen Ashton, Candy Cook, Mary Dale, James Fatta, Philip Mollet, Linda Poser, Robin Stephens, Brian Sutherland, Peter Wandel. *Swings*: Joanne Genelle, Mark Lamanna.

The action takes place during "the avoidable future" at the Barclay-Palace Hotel on a hillside in the Austrian Alps.

Act 1, Scene 1: The nightclub of the Barclay-Palace Hotel New Year's Eve, shortly before midnight. *Scene 2*: The main entrance lounge of the hotel 2 A.M. that night. *Scene 3*: The Winkler Suite later that night. *Scene 3A*: Harry's Memory. *Scene 4*: A Bedroom in a mid-Western hotel ten years earlier. *Scene 5*: The skating rink at the Hotel New Year's Day morning. *Scene 6*: The nightclub of the hotel that evening.

Act 2, Scene 1: The main entrance lounge of the hotel the following morning. *Scene 2*: Cynthia's memory. *Scene 3*: The main entrance lounge of the hotel immediately following.

ACT 1
Scene 1
    "It Never Would've Worked"
      L. Cariou, the Delights

"Happy, Happy New Year"
    L. Cariou, the Delights, Guests
Scene 2
    "No Man Is Worth It"
      L. Robertson
    "What Are You Going to Do About It?"
      L. Cariou, J. Kolinski
Scene 3
    "A Woman Who Thinks I'm Wonderful"
      G. Rose
Scene 3A
    "Pas de Deux"
      (*Danced by*) B. Sutherland, R. Stephens
Scene 4
    "There's Never Been Anything Like Us"
      L. Cariou
    "Another Life"
      L. Robertson
Scene 5
    "Why Can't the World Go and Leave Us Alone?"
      B. Barrett, J. Keller
    "He Always Comes Home to Me"
      L. Robertson
Scene 6
    "I Got a New Girl"
      L. Cariou, the Delights
    "Dance a Little Closer"
      L. Cariou, L. Robertson, Guests
    "There's Always One You Can't Forget"
      L. Cariou

ACT 2
Scene 1
    "Homesick"
      The Delights
    "Mad"
      L. Cariou, the Delights
    "I Don't Know"
      L. Cariou, I. M. Hobson, E. Hubbard, the Delights, B. Barrett, J. Keller, L. Robertson
    "Auf Wiedersehen"
      G. Rose
    "I Never Want To See You Again"
      L. Cariou
Scene 2
    "On Top of the World"
      L. Robertson, Men
Scene 3
    "I Got a New Girl" (reprise)
      L. Cariou, L. Robertson
    "Dance a Little Closer" (reprise)
      L. Cariou, L. Robertson

1983–1984 SEASON

George Hearn in LA CAGE AUX FOLLES
Martha Swope/TimePix

1983–1984 SEASON

1983.09   ## 5.6.7.8 . . . DANCE!

A Musical Revue in Two Acts, 10 Scenes. Written by Bruce Vilanch. Original songs by David Zippel and Wally Harper. Directed and choreographed by Ron Field. Associate director, David Rubinstein. Associate choreographer, Marianne Selbert. Musical director, Thomas Helm. Scenery by Tom H. John. Costumes by Lindsay W. Davis. Lighting by Richard Nelson. Film sequences by Christopher Dixon. Musical supervisor, Wally Harper. Orchestrations by Bill Byers. Dance arrangements by Mark Hummel and Donald York. Production coordinator, Stephen Nisbet. Director of the Rockettes, Violet Holmes. Produced by Radio City Music Hall Productions, Inc. (Bernard Gersten, Executive Producer). Opened 15 June 1983 at the Radio City Music Hall and closed 5 September 1983 after 149 performances.

CAST: SANDY DUNCAN, DON CORREIA, BILL IRWIN, ARMELIA McQUEEN, KEN SACHA, MARGE CHAMPION.
THE ROCKETTES: Joyce Dwyer, Carol Harbich, Joan Peer Kelleher, Gerri Presky, Susan Boron, Dee Dee Knapp, Deniene Fenn, Barbara Ann Moore, Judy Little, Phyllis Wujiko, Barbara Ann Cittadino, Leslie McCarthy, Eileen M. Collins, Cindy Peiffer, Pauline A. Tzikas, Cynthia Hughes, Susanne Doris, Carol Toman, Pam Kelleher, Jackie Fancy, Ginny Hounsell, Prudence Gray Demmler, Terry Spano, Dottie Belle, Sonya Livingston, Rose Anne Woolsey, Susan Theobald, Carol Beatty, Catherine Beatty, Brie Daniels, Lynn Newton, Darlene Wendy, Lynn Sullivan, Alexis Ficks, Jennifer Hammond, Kerri Pearsall, Patricia Tully, Susan Cleland, Elizabeth Chanin.
Dancers: Robin Alpert, Christine Colby, Carol Estey, Edyie Fleming, Blanche, Sonya Hensley, Jodi Moccia, Gayle Samuels, Gregory Brock, Ciscoe Bruton II, Daniel Esteras, Douglas Graham, Michael Lafferty, Dan McCoy, Rodney Pridgen, Adrian Rosario.
Singers: Freida A. Williams, Holly Lipton Nash, Lois Sage, Roger Berdahl, Michael Halpern, Wayne Mattson, Wes Skelley, Paul Solen.

ACT 1
Scene 1
   5-6-7-8 . . . Dance!:
     S. Duncan, the Rockettes, Dancers, Singers
   Half-Hour
     (Film Sequence by Christopher Dixon.)
   "Five, Six, Seven, Eight . . . Dance!"
     (Music by Wally Harper. *Lyrics by* David Zippel.)
   "Life Is a Dance"
     (Music by Gavin Christopher.)
   Dance
     (Music by Paul Jabara.)
Scene 2
   5-6-7-8 . . . Band!:
     S. Duncan, Dancers
   "It's Better with a Band"
     (Music by Wally Harper. *Lyrics by* David Zippel.)
Scene 3
   5-6-7-8 . . . Husband!:
   Meet Don
     (Film Sequence by Christopher Dixon.)
   "I've Got Your Number" (from *LITTLE ME*)
     D. Correia, Dancers, the Rockettes
     (Music by Cy Coleman. *Lyrics by* Carolyn Leigh.)
   "You Musn't Kick It Around" (from *PAL JOEY*)
     D. Correia, Dancers, the Rockettes
     (Music by Richard Rodgers. *Lyrics by* Lorenz Hart.)
   "It Only Happens When I Dance With You" (from *EASTER PARADE* film)
     (Music and Lyrics by Irving Berlin.)
       S. Duncan, D. Correia, the Rockettes, Dancers
Scene 4
   5-6-7-8 . . . Protest!:
     A. McQueen, the Rockettes
   "Singers' Protest"
     (Music by Wally Harper. *Lyrics by* David Zippel.)

"One Step" (from *HOW DO YOU DO, I LOVE YOU* and *STARTING HERE, STARTING NOW*)
     (Music by David Shire. *Lyrics by* Richard Maltby, Jr.)
Scene 5
   5-6-7-8 . . . Victory!:
     The Company
   "It Had to Be You"
     (Music by Isham Jones. *Lyrics by* Gus Kahn.)
   "Bad Habits"
     (Music and Lyrics by Billy Field and Tom Price.)
   "It's Not What You Weigh"
     (Music by Wally Harper. *Lyrics by* David Zippel.)
   "Sing, Sing, Sing"
     (Music by Louis Prima.)
   "Make Way for Tomorrow" (from *COVER GIRL* film)
     (Music by Jerome Kern. *Lyrics by* Ira Gershwin and E. Y. Harburg.)

ACT 2
Scene 1
   5-6-7-8 . . . Marilyn!:
     S. Duncan, D. Correia, the Rockettes, Singers
   Don's Fantasy
     (Film Sequence by Christopher Dixon.)
   "Cheek to Cheek" (from *TOP HAT* film)
     (Music by Irving Berlin.)
   "I Go to Rio!"
     (Music and Lyrics by Peter Allen and Adrienne Anderson.)
   "I'm Flying" (from *PETER PAN*)
     (Music by Mark [Moose] Charlap. *Lyrics by* Carolyn Leigh.)
Scene 2
   5-6-7-8 . . . Sandy!:
     S. Duncan, Male Dancers
   "She Just Loves Las Vegas"
     (Music by Wally Harper. *Lyrics by* David Zippel.)
   "Dance With Me"
     (Music and Lyrics by R. Parker, Jr. and David Rubinson.)
   "Neverland" (from *PETER PAN*)
     (Music by Jule Styne. *Lyrics by* Betty Comden and Adolph Green.)
Scene 3
   5-6-7-8 . . . Audition!:
     B. Irwin
   "Tea for Two" (from *NO, NO NANETTE*)[instrumental]
     (Music by Vincent Youmans.)
Scene 4
   5-6-7-8 . . . Inspirations!:
   Dance Teams Medley:
     Company
     "I Love to Dance" (from *BALLROOM*)
       (Music by Billy Goldenberg. *Lyrics by* Marilyn and Alan Bergman.)
     "Tres Moutarde"
       (Music by Cecil Macklin.)
     "La Cumparsita"
       (Music by G. H. Matos Rodriguez.)
     "The Continental" (from *THE GAY DIVORCEE* film)
       (Music by Con Conrad.)
     "Our Love Is Here to Stay" (from *THE GOLDWYN FOLLIES* film)
       (Music by George Gershwin. *Lyrics by* Ira Gershwin.)
   "Where Did You Learn to Dance" (from *I LOVE MELVIN* film)
     S. Duncan, M. Champion
     (Music by Josef Myrow. *Lyrics by* Mack Gordon.)
   "I Love to Dance" (reprise)
     M. Champion, D. Correia, Dancers
Scene 5
   5-6-7-8 . . . Finale:
     Company
   "Broadway Rhythm" (from *BROADWAY MELODY OF 1936* film)
     (Music by Nacio Herb Brown. *Lyrics by* Arthur Freed.)
   "Body Language"
     (Music and Lyrics by Steve Sperry and Barry Fasman.)
   "Five, Six, Seven, Eight . . . Dance!" (reprise)

MAME

1983.10

A Revival of the Musical in Two Acts, 16 Scenes[1]. Book by Jerome Lawrence and Robert E. Lee. Based on the novel "Auntie Mame" by Patrick Dennis and the play of the same name by Lawrence and Lee. Music and lyrics by Jerry Herman. Directed by John Bowab. Choreography by Diana Baffa-Brill, based on the original by Onna White. Production supervisor, Jerry Herman. Scenery by Peter Wolf, based on the originals by William and Jean Eckart. Costumes by Robert Mackintosh. Lighting by Thomas Skelton. Sound by Christine Voellinger. Musical director, Jim Coleman. Vocal arrangements by Donald Pippin. Orchestrations by Philip J. Lang. Executive producer, Michael Lynne. Associate producer, Manny Kladitis. Produced by the Mitch Leigh Company. Opened 24 July 1983 at the Gershwin Theatre and closed 28 August 1983 after 41 performances.

CAST (in order of appearance): *Patrick Dennis, age 10:* Roshi Handwerger. *Agnes Gooch:* JANE CONNELL. *Vera Charles:* ANNE FRANCINE *Mame Dennis:* ANGELA LANSBURY. *Ralph Devine:* Jacob Mark Hopkin. *Bishop:* Merwin Foard. *M. Lindsay Woolsey:* Donald Torres. *Ito:* SAB SHIMONO. *Doorman:* Brian McAnally *Elevator Boy:* Marshall Hagins. *Messenger:* David Miles. *Dwight Babcock:* WILLARD WATERMAN. *Bubbles the Clown:* Ken Henley. *Dance Teacher:* Louise Kirtland. *Bird Dancers:* Suzanne Ishee, Patrick Sean Murphy. *Leading Man:* Kenneth Kantor. *Stage Manager:* Rchard Poole. *Madame Branislowski:* Fran Stevens. *Gregor:* Ken Henley. *Beauregard Jackson Pickett Burnside:* Scot Stewart. *Uncle Jeff:* Kenneth Kantor. *Cousin Fan:* Carol Lurie. *Sally Cato:* Barbara Lang. *Mother Burnside:* Fran Stevens. *Patrick Dennis, age 19-29:* Byron Nease. *Junior Babcock:* Patrick Sean Murphy. *Mrs. Upson:* Louise Kirtland. *Mr. Upson:* John C. Becher. *Gloria Upson:* Michaela K. Hughes. *Pegeen Ryan:* Ellyn Arons. *Peter Dennis:* Daniel Mahon.

Mame's Friends: Ellyn Arons, Alyson Bristol, Merwin Foard, Marshall Hagins, Ken Henley, Jacon Mark Hopkin, Michaela Hughes, Suzanne Ishee, Kenneth Kantor, Harry Kingsley, Melinda Koblick, David Loring, Carol Lurie, Brian McNally, David Miles, Patrick Sean Murphy, Viewma Negromonte, Michele Pigliavento, Cissy Rebich, Richard Poole, Joseph Rich, Mollie Smith.

LA CAGE AUX FOLLES

1983.11

A Musical in Two Acts, 10 Scenes. Book by Harvey Fierstein. Based on the play of the same name by Jean Poiret. Music and lyrics by Jerry Herman. Directed by Arthur Laurents. Choreography by Scott Salmon. Settngs designed by David Mitchell. Costumes designed by Theoni V. Aldredge. Lighting designed by Jules Fisher. Sound designed by Peter Fitzgerald. Musical direction, vocal arrangements by Donald Pippin. Orchestrations by Jim Tyler. Dance music arrangements by Gordon Lowry Harrell. Assistant choreographer, Richard Balestrino. Executive producers, Barry Brown and Fritz Holt. Produced by Allan Carr, with Kenneth D. Greenblatt, Marvin A. Krauss, Stewart F. Lane, James M. Nederlander, Martin Richards, in association with Jonathan Farkas, John J. Pomerantz, Martin Heinfling. Opened 21 August 1983 at the Palace Theatre and closed 14 November 1987 after 1761 performances.

CAST (in order of appearance): *Georges:* GENE BARRY. *Les Cagelles (12): Chantal:* David Cahn. *Monique:* Dennis Callahan. *Dermah:* Frank DiPasquale. *Nicole:* John Dolf. *Hanna:* David Engel. *Mercedes:* David Evans. *Bitelle:* Linda Haberman. *Lo Singh:* Eric Lamp. *Odette:* Dan O'Grady. *Angelique:* Deborah Phelan. *Phaedra:* David Scala. *Clo-Clo:* Sam Singhaus.

Francis: Brian Kelly. *Jacob:* William Thomas, Jr. *Albin:* GEORGE HEARN. *Jean-Michel:* John Weiner. *Anne:* Leslie Stevens. *Jacqueline:* Elizabeth Parrish. *M. Renaud:* Walter Charles. *St. Tropez Townspeople (8): Mme. Renaud:* Sydney Anderson. *Paulette:* Betsy Craig. *Hercule:* Jack Neubeck. *Etienne:* Jay Pierce. *Babette:* Marie Santell. *Colette:* Jennifer Smith. *Tabarro:* Mark Waldrop. *Pepe:* Ken Ward.

Edouard Dindon: Jay Garner. *Marie Dindon:* Merle Louise. *Swing Performers:* Robert Bruback, Drew Geraci, Jan Leigh Herndon, Leslie Simons.

The action takes place in summer in St. Tropez, France, at the present time.

Act 1, Scene 1: Outside, then inside, the club "La Cage aux Folles." Late afternoon. *Scene 2:* The Apartment of Georges and Albin; onstage at "La Cage aux Folles." *Scene 3:* Offstage at "La Cage aux Folles:" the apartment. *Scene 4:* The Promenade and a Cafe in St. Tropez. *Scene 5:* Offstage and Onstage at "La Cage aux Folles." *Scene 6:* Offstage and Onstage at "La Cage aux Folles."

Act 2, Scene 1: The Promenade and the Cafe in St. Tropez. *Scene 2:* The Apartment. *Scene 3:* Chez Jacqueline, an elegant restaurant. *Scene 4:* The Apartment; the club "La Cage aux Folles."

[1]Originally produced in New York 24 May 1966 at the Winter Garden for 1508 performances. For Synopsis of Scenes and Musical Numbers, see original 1966 production.

ACT 1
Scene 1
  "We Are What We Are"
    Les Cagelles
Scene 2
  "A Little More Mascara"
    G. Hearn, Friends
Scene 3
  "With Anne on My Arm"
    J. Weiner
  "With You on My Arm" (reprise)
    G. Barry, G. Hearn
Scene 4
  "The Promenade"
    Townspeople
  "Song on the Sand"
    G. Hearn
Scene 5
  "La Cage aux Folles"
    G. Hearn, Les Cagelles
Scene 6
  "I Am What I Am"
    G. Hearn
ACT 2
Scene 1
  "Song on the Sand" (reprise)
    G. Barry, G. Hearn
  "Masculinity"
    G. Barry, G. Hearn, Townspeople
Scene 2
  "Look Over There"
    G. Barry
  "Cocktail Counterpoint"
    G. Barry, J. Garner, M. Louise, W. Thomas
Scene 3
  "The Best of Times"
    G. Hearn, E. Parrish, Patrons
Scene 4
  "Look Over There" (reprise)
    J. Weiner
  Grand Finale
    (Entire Company)

THE MERRY WIDOW

1983.12

A Revival of the Operetta in Three Acts[2]. (Music by Franz Lehár. Original German libretto (Die Lustige Witwe) by Victor Léon and Leo Stein (after "L'Attaché d'Ambassade.") English version by Adrian Ross. Directed by Ronald Bentley. Choreography by Donald Saddler. Scenery designed by Helen Pond and Herbert Senn. Costumes designed by Suzanne Mess. Lighting designed by Gilbert V. Helmsley, Jr. Conductor, Eric Knight. Chorus master, Joseph Colaneri. Produced by the New York City Opera. Opened 2 October 1983 at the New York State Theatre and closed 13 November 1983 after 6 performances in repertory.

CAST (in order of appearance): *Baron Popoff:* JACK HARROLD. *Natalie:* Susanne Marsee. *M. de St. Brioche:* WILLIAM EICHORN. *Marquis de Cascada:* Thomas Jamerson. *Sylviane:* Debra Vanderlinde. *Olga:* Joyce Castle *General Novikovich:* Jonathan Green. *Vicomte Camille de Jolidon:* Alan Kays. *Counsellor Khadja:* William Ledbetter. *Nisch:* Gerald Isaac. *Sonia:* KAREN HUFFSTODT. *Prince Danilo:* CRIS GROENENDAAL. *Head Waiter:* Mervin Crook. *Zozo:* Anny DeGange. *Lolo:* Joan Mirabella. *Dodo:* Esperanza Galan. *Jou-Jou:* Candace Itow. *Frou-Frou:* Victoria Rinaldi. *Clo-Clo:* Raven Wilkinson. *Margot:* Jean Barber. *Chorus of Marsovian and Parisian Society, Dancers, Servants and Waiters:* New York City Opera Chorus.

[2]Originally produced in New York 21 October 1907 at the New Amsterdam Theatre for 416 performances. For Synopsis of Scenes and Musical Numbers, see original 1907 production. Interpolated into this production:
  "Girls Were Made to Love and Kiss" (from *PAGANINI*)
    (*Music by* Franz Lehar. *Original German Lyrics by* Paul Knepler and Bela Jenbach. *English Lyrics by* A. P. Herbert.)

1983.13 CANDIDE

A Revival of the Musical in Two Act, 23 Scenes[3]. (New) Book adapted from Voltaire's satire (of the same name) by Hugh Wheeler. (Original book by Lillian Hellman.) Music by Leonard Bernstein. Lyrics by Richard Wilbur. Additional lyrics by Stephen Sondheim and John Latouche. Directed by Harold Prince. Stage director, Arthur Masella. Choreography by Patricia Birch. Scenery designed by Clarke Dunham. Costumes designed by Judith Dolan. Lighting designed by Ken Billington. Conducted by Scott Bergeson. Orchestrations by Leonard Bernstein and Hershy Kay. Chorus prepared by Mitchell Krieger. Produced by the New York City Opera. Opened 16 October 1983 (matinee) at the New York State Theatre and closed 30 October 1983 after 5 performances in repertory.

CAST (in order of appearance): *Voltaire:* JOHN LANKSTON. *Candide:* CRIS GROENENDAAL. *Huntsman:* Don Yule. *Paquette:* MARIS CLEMENT. *Baroness:* Bonnie Kirk. *Baron:* JACK HARROLD. *Cunegonde:* CLAUDETTE PETERSON. *Maximilian:* SCOTT REEVE. *Servant of Maximilian:* JAMES BILLINGS. *Dr. Pangloss:* JOHN LANKSTON. *Bulgarian Soldiers:* Don Yule, JAMES BILLINGS. *Westphalian Soldiers:* Andy Ferrell, William Ledbetter. *Don Isaachar, the Jew:* JAMES BILLINGS. *Grand Inquisitor:* JACK HARROLD. *Calliope Player:* Bonnie Kirk. *Heresy Agent:* Ralph Bassett. *Inquisition Agents:* Gary Dietrich, William Selissen. *Judge:* JAMES BILLINGS. *Old Lady:* MURIEL COSTA-GREENSPON. *Dons:* Vasilis Iraclides, Brian Kaman, Michael Rubino, Don Yule, William Ledbetter, Ralph Bassett. *Businessman:* JOHN LANKSTON. *Governor:* JOHN LANKSTON. *Governor's Aide:* Andy Ferrell. *Slave Driver:* JACK HARROLD. *Father Bernard:* JAMES BILLINGS. *Sailors:* Gary Dietrich, William Selissen, Andy Ferrell, Travis Wright. *Pirates:* John Henry Thomas, William Ledbetter. *Pink Sheep:* Ivy Austin, Rhoda Butler. *Lion:* Robert Brubaker. *Pasha-Prefect:* JACK HARROLD. *First Gambler:* JAMES BILLINGS. *Second Gambler (Police Chief):* JOHN LANKSTON. *Sage:* JOHN LANKSTON.

1983.14 ZORBA

A Revival of the Musical in Two Acts, 15 Scenes[4]. Book (revised) by Joseph Stein. Adapted From the novel "Zorba the Greek" by Nikos Kazantzakis. Music by John Kander. Lyrics by Fred Ebb. Directed by Michael Cacoyannis. Choreographed by Graciela Daniele. Scenic design by David Chapman. Costumes designed by Hal George. Lighting designed by Marc B. Weiss. Sound system designed by T. Richard Fitzgerald. Musical direction by Randolph Mauldin. Orchestrations by Don Walker. Dance arrangements by Tom Fay. Associate producer, Alecia Parker. Produced by Barry and Fran Weissler, Kenneth-John Productions (Kenneth D. Greenblatt, John J. Pomerantz). Opened 16 October 1983 at the Broadway Theatre and closed 2 September 1984 after 362 performances.

CAST (in order of appearance): *The Woman:* DEBBIE SHAPIRO. *Konstandi, Turkish Dancer, Russian Admiral:* Frank DeSal. *Thanassai, French Admiral, Monk:* John Mineo. *Constable:* Raphael LaManna. *Athena, Crow:* Suzanne Costallos. *Niko:* ROBERT WESTENBERG. *Zorba:* ANTHONY QUINN. *Despo, Crow:* Panchali Null. *Marika, Crow:* Angelina Fiordellisi. *Katina:* Susan Terry. *Vassilakas:* Chip Cornelius. *Marinakos, Monk:* Peter Marinos. *Mimiko:* Aurelio Padron. *Katapolis, Monk:* Peter Kevoian. *Yorgo, Italian Admiral:* Richard Warren Pugh. *Sophia, Crow:* Pamela Trevisani. *Mavrodani:* Charles Karel. *Pavli:* Thomas David Scalise. *Manolakas:* Michael Dantuono. *The Widow:* TARO MEYER. *Priest, English Admiral:* Paul Straney. *Madame Hortense:* LILA KEDROVA. *Marsalias, Monk:* Rob Marshall. *Anagnosti:* Tim Flavin. *Maria, Cafe Whore:* Karen Giombetti.

The action takes place in Piraeus, Greece and the island of Crete.

Act 1, Scene 1: A Market Place, Piraeus. *Scene 2:* A Café, Piraeus. *Scene 3:* A Crete Village. *Scene 4:* Hortense's Garden. *Scene 5:* Interior of Hortense's Inn. *Scene 6:* The Mine Site. *Scene 7:* A Village Street. *Scene 8:* A Bar in Piraeus. *Scene 9:* A Village Street.

Act 2, Scene 1: Hortense's Garden. *Scene 2:* The Widow's House. *Scene 3:* The Church Square. *Scene 4:* Entrance to the Mine. *Scene 5:* Hortense's Bedroom. *Scene 6:* The Port, Piraeus.

---

[3]Original production first produced in New York 1 December 1956 at the Martin Beck Theatre for 73 performances; revised version first produced Off-Broadway 11 December 1973 at the Chelsea Theater Center, Brooklyn Academy of Music for 48 performances; transferred 5 March 1974 to the Broadway Theatre for 740 performances. For Synopsis of Scenes and Musical Numbers, see 1982 revival.
[4]Originally produced in New York 17 November 1968 at the Imperial Theatre for 305 performances. For this revival, the book was revised from 17 to 15 Scenes; Belly Dance, and Bells, were dropped. Added were "Woman," "That's a Beginning" and Easter Dance.

ACT 1
Scene 1
"Life Is"
D. Shapiro, Company
Scene 2
"The First Time"
A. Quinn
Scene 3
"The Top of the Hill"
D. Shapiro, Chorus
Scene 4
"No Boom Boom"
L. Kedrova, Admirals, A. Quinn, R. Westenberg
Scene 5
"Vive La Difference"
The Admirals,
Scene 6
"Mine Song"
Company
Scene 7
"The Butterfly"
T. Meyer, R. Westenberg, D. Shapiro
"Goodbye, Canavaro"
L. Kedrova, A. Quinn, R. Westenberg
Scene 8
"Grandpapa"
A. Quinn, D. Shapiro, Chorus
(*Additional Choreography* by Theodore Pappas.)
Scene 9
"Only Love"
L. Kedrova
"The Bend of the Road"
D. Shapiro
"Only Love" (reprise)
D. Shapiro
ACT 2
Scene 1
"Y'assou"
Company
"Woman"
A. Quinn
Scene 2
"Why Can't I Speak?"/"That's a Beginning"
T. Meyer, R. Westenberg, D. Shapiro
Scene 3
Easter Dance
Company
Scene 4
Miners' Dance
The Men
Scene 5
"The Crow"
D. Shapiro, Crows, Monks
"Happy Birthday"
L. Kedrova
Scene 6
"I Am Free"
A. Quinn

1983.15 AMEN CORNER

A Musical in Two Acts, 6 Scenes. Book by Philip Rose, Peter Udell. Based on the play "The Amen Corner" by James Baldwin. Music by Garry Sherman. Lyrics by Peter Udell. Directed by Philip Rose. Choreography by Al Perryman. Scenery by Karl Eigsti. Costumes by Felix E. Cochren. Lighting by Shirley Prendergast. Orchestratons by Garry Sherman, Dunn Pearson. Vocal arrangements by Garry Sherman. Dance arrangements by Dunn Pearson, George Butcher. Musical direction by Margaret Harris. Sound by Peter Fitzgerald. Associate producer, Philip Rose. Produced by Prudhomme Productions (Edward Mann, Judith Henry, Joel Goldstein, Gil

Gerard). Opened 10 November 1983 at the Nederlander Theatre and closed 4 December 1983 after 29 performances.

CAST (in order of speaking): *Margaret Alexander, Pastor of the Church:* RHETTA HUGHES. *Sister Moore, elder of the Church:* Jean Check. *Odessa, Margaret's older sister:* RUTH BROWN. *David, Margaret's son:* KEITH LORENZO AMOS. *Sister Boxer, elder of the Church:* Helena-Joyce Wright. *Brother Boxer, elder of the Church:* Chuck Cooper. *Luke, Margaret's husband:* ROGER ROBINSON.

Members of the Congregation: Loretta Abbott, Leslie Dockery, Cheryl Freeman, Gene Lewis, Denise Morgan, Lewis Robinson, Renee Rose, Vanessa Shaw, Jeffery V. Thompson. *Dancers:* Loretta Abbott (Captain), Leslie Dockery, Renee Rose. *Swings:* Venida Evans, Leonard Piggee.

The action takes place in a sanctified storefront church in Harlem and in the adjoining apartment early in the 1960's.

Act 1, Scene 1: Church, Sunday morning. *Scene 2:* Apartment. Later that morning. *Scene 3:* Apartment, late afternoon the following Saturday. *Scene 4:* Church, same afternoon. *Scene 5:* Apartment, same afternoon.

Act 2: Apartment, early Sunday morning.

ACT 1

Scene 1
"Amen Corner"
    R. Hughes
Scene 2
"That Woman Can't Play No Piano"
    K. L. Amos, Friends
"In the Real World"
    C. Cooper
"You Ain't Gonna Pick Up Where You Left Off"
    R. Hughes, R. Robinson
Scene 3
"In the Real World" (reprise)
    H. Wright
"We Got a Good Thing Goin'"
    R. Robinson, K. L. Amos
Scene 4
"In His Own Good Time"
    H. Wright, C. Cooper, J. Cheek, R. Brown, Congregation
Scene 5
"Heat Sensation"
    R. Robinson
"Everytime We Call It Quits"
    R. Robinson

ACT 2
"Somewhere Close By"
    R. Brown
"Leanin' on the Lord"
    H. Wright, C. Cooper, J. Cheek, R. Brown, Congregation
"I'm Already Gone"
    K. L. Amos
"Love Dies Hard"
    R. Hughes
"Everytime We Call It Quits" (reprise)
    R. Robinson, R. Hughes
"Rise Up and Stand Again"
    R. Hughes

1983.16 LA TRAGÉDIE DE CARMEN

An Adaptation of Georges Bizet's opera 'Carmen' in One Act (in French). (Original Libretto by Henri Meilhac and Ludovic Halévy, based on the novel "Carmen" by Prosper Merimée.) Adaptation by Marius Constant, Jean-Claude Carrière, Peter Brook. Directed by Peter Brook. Musical director, Marius Constant. Scenery by Jean-Guy Lecat. Costumes by Chloé Obolensky. Conductors, Randall Behr, Roger Cantrell. Artistic advisor, Bernard Lefort. Associate director, Maurice Benichou. As originally presented in Paris at The Bouffes du Nord by the Théâtre National de L'Opéra de Paris and the Centre International de Créations Théâtrales, Micheline Rozan, Producer. Co-Producer, Roy A. Somlyo. Produced by Alexander H. Cohen and Hildy Parks in association with James Nederlander, Jr. and Arthur Rubin. Opened 17 November 1983 at the Vivian Beaumont Theater and closed 28 April 1984 after 187 performances[5].

---

[5]On 19 March 1984 an English language version titled simply *CARMEN* by Sheldon Harnick was added to the performance schedule in rotating

CAST: *Carmen:* Cynthia Clarey or Hélèle Delavault or Emily Golden or Eva Saurova or Patricia Schuman. *Don José:* Evan Bortnick or Laurence Dale or Howard Hensel or James Hoback or Peter Puzzo. *Micaëla:* Anne Christine Biel or Véronique Dietschy or Agnès Host or Beverly Morgan. *Escamillo:* Carl Johan Falkman or Jake Gardner or Ronald Madden or John Rath. *Lillas Pastia:* Andreas Katsulas or Alain Maratrat. *Lieutenant Zuniga, Old Woman:* Jean-Paul Denizon or Andreas Katsulas. *Garcia, Carmen's husband:* Tapa Sudana or Andreas Katsulas.

MARILYN:
1983.17 AN AMERICAN FABLE

A Musical in Two Acts, 16 Scenes. Libretto (Book) by Patricia Michaels. Music and lyrics by Jeanne Napoli, Doug Frank, Gary Portnoy, Beth Lawrence, Norman Thalheimer. Directed and Choreographed by Kenny Ortega. Scenery design by Tom H. John. Costume design by Joseph G. Aulisi. Lighting design by Marcia Madeira. Sound design by T. Richard Fitzgerald. Musical supervision, direction, vocals and orchestral arrangements by Steven Margoshes. Orchestrations by Bill Brohn. Dance arrangements and additional orchestrations by Donald Johnston. Additional dance arrangements by Ronald Melrose. Consultant producer, Janet Robinson. Music consultants, Fred Bestall, Lance Reynolds. Assistant director, Greg Smith. Assistant choreographer, Veda Jackson. Associate producers, Peter Duke, Paul Faske, France Weiner. Produced by Malcolm Cooke, William May, Dolores Quinton, James Kabler, Joseph DioGuardi, John Ricciardelli, Arnold Bruck, Tom Kaye, Leo Rosenthal, Harper Sibley, June Curtis, Renee Blau in association with Jerome Minskoff. Opened 20 November 1983 at the Minskoff Theatre and closed 3 December 1983 after 16 performances.

CAST (in order of appearance): *Young Norma Jean:* KRISTI COOMBS. *Destiny:* PEGGIE BLUE, MICHAEL KUBALA, T. A. [Ty] STEPHENS. *Norma Jean/Marilyn Monroe:* ALYSON REED. *Jim Dougherty:* GEORGE DVORSKY. *Pat:* Debi Monahan. *Factory Girls:* Melissa Bailey, Deborah Dotson, Jodi Marzorati, Mary Testa, Dooba Wilkins. *Photographer:* JAMES HASKINS. *Servicemen:* Gary-Michael Davies, Mark Ziebell. *Agent:* MITCHELL GREENBERG. *Studio Head:* ALAN NORTH. *Director:* Gary-Michael Davies. *Assistant Director:* Ty Crowley. *Camera Man:* Ed Forsyth. *Hairdresser:* Deborah Dotson. *Designer:* Michael Rivera. *Hedda:* Mary Testa. *Louella:* Melissa Bailey. *Joe DiMaggio:* SCOTT BAKULA. *Sis:* LISE LANG. *Tommy:* WILLY FALK. *Coach/Companion:* Dooba Wilkins. *Arthur Miller:* WILL GERARD. *Strasberg:* Steve Schocket. *Acting Coach:* Ty Crowley.

Ensemble: Melissa Bailey, Eileen Casey, Andrew Charles, Kevin Cort, Ty Crowley, Gary-Michael Davies, Deborah Dotson, Mark Esposito, Ed Forsyth, Marcial Gonzalez, Christine Gradl, Marguerite Lowell, Jodi Marzorati, Debi Monahan, Michael Rivera, Steve Schocket, Mary Testa, Dooba Wilkins, Mark Ziebell. *Swings:* Ivson Polk, Maryellen Scilla.

The action takes place from 1934 to 1962 in Hollywood and New York City.

Act 1, Scene 1: Under the Hollywood Hills, 1934-1942. *Scene 2:* The Parachute Factory, 1945. *Scene 3:* Overseas. *Scene 4:* Studio's Executive Office. *Scene 5:* The Soundstage, 1948-1953. *Scene 6:* Outside the Studio. *Scene 7:* The Soundstage, 1955. *Scene 8:* Marilyn's Dressing Room. *Scene 9:* DiMaggio's Restaurant. *Scene 10:* Premier Night.

Act 2, Scene 1: Marilyn's Bedroom. *Scene 2:* Soundstage. *Scene 3:* New York City, 1956-1960. *Scene 4:* New York Penthouse. *Scene 5:* New York to Hollywood. *Scene 6:* Soundstage.

ACT 1

Scene 1
"A Single Dream"
    K. Coombs, P. Blue, M. Kubala, T. A. Stephens
    (*Music and Lyrics by* Jeanne Napoli and Doug Frank.)
"Jimmy Jimmy"
    P. Blue, M. Kubala, T. A. Stephens, A, Reed, G. Dvorsky, D. Monahan, Ensemble
    (*Music and Lyrics by* Jeanne Napoli and Doug Frank.)
"Church Doors"
    P. Blue, M. Kubala, T. A. Stephens
    (*Music and Lyrics by* Beth Lawrence and Norman Thalheimer.)
Scene 2
"Swing Shift"
    Factory Girls
    (*Music and Lyrics by* Beth Lawrence and Norman Thalheimer.)
Scene 3
"The Golden Dream"
    G. Dvorksy, Servicemen
    (*Music and Lyrics by* Beth Lawrence and Norman Thalheimer.)

repertory with the original French language version. The production was performed as an opera with no individual musical numbers listed

Scene 4

"When You Run the Show"
A. North, M. Greenberg
(*Music and Lyrics by* Beth Lawrence and Norman Thalheimer.)

Scene 5

"Gossip"
M. Testa, M. Bailey
(*Music and Lyrics by* Komack and Doug Frank.)

"Cold Hard Cash"
A. Reed, Men
(*Music by* Wally Harper. *Lyrics by* David Zippel.)

Scene 6

"I'm a Fan"
W. Falk, L. Lang
(*Music and Lyrics by* Beth Lawrence and Norman Thalheimer.)

Scene 7

"Finally"
S. Bakula, A. Reed
(*Music and Lyrics by* Beth Lawrence and Norman Thalheimer.)

"Church Doors" (reprise)
P. Blue, M. Kubala, T. A. Stephens

Scene 10

"It's a Premiere Night"
The Company
(*Music and Lyrics by* Beth Lawrence and Norman Thalheimer.)

"A Single Dream" (reprise)
A. Reed

ACT 2

Scene 1

"We'll Help You Through the Night"
P. Blue, M. Kubala, T. A. Stephens
(*Music and Lyrics by* Jeanne Napoli, Dawson, Turner.)

Scene 2

"Run Between the Raindrops"
A. Reed
(*Music and Lyrics by* Jeanne Napoli and Gary Portnoy.)

"You Are So Beyond"
W. Falk
(*Music and Lyrics by* Jeanne Napoli and Doug Frank.)

Scene 3

"Cultural Pursuits"
A. Reed, W. Gerard, Ensemble
(*Music and Lyrics by* Doug Frank.)

"Church Doors" (reprise)
P. Blue, M. Kubala, T. A. Stephens

Scene 4

"Don't Hang Up the Telephone"
S. Bakula
(*Music and Lyrics by* Jeanne Napoli and Gary Portnoy.)

Scene 5

"All Roads Lead to Hollywood"
A. Reed, Company
(*Music and Lyrics by* Beth Lawrence and Norman Thalheimer.)

Scene 6

"My Heart's an Open Door"
A. Reed, S. Bakula
(*Music and Lyrics by* Beth Lawrence and Norman Thalheimer.)

"Miss Bubbles"
A. Reed, Men's Ensemble
(*Music and Lyrics by* Jeanne Napoli, Doug Frank and Gary Portnoy.)

"The Best of Me"
A. Reed
(*Music and Lyrics by* Beth Lawrence and Norman Thalheimer.)

"A Single Dream" (reprise)
A. Reed

Finale: "We Are the Ones"
The Company
(*Music and Lyrics by* Beth Lawrence and Norman Thalheimer.)

1983.18   DOONESBURY

A Musical in Two Acts, 13 Scenes. Book and lyrics by Garry Trudeau, based on his comic strip of the same name. Music by Elizabeth Swados. Directed by Jacques Levy. Choreography by Margo Sappington. Scenery designed by Peter Larkin. Costumes designed by Patricia McGourty. Lighting designed by Beverly Emmons. Sound designed by Tom Morse. Orchestrations by Elizabeth Swados. Arrangements and musical direction by Jeff Waxman. Produced by James Walsh in association with Universal Pictures. Opened 21 November 1983 at the Biltmore Theatre and closed 19 February 1984 after 104 performances.

CAST (in order of appearance): *Roland:* Reathel Bean. *Mike Doonesbury:* Ralph Bruneau. *Mark:* Mark Linn-Baker. *B.D.:* Keith Szarabajka. *Boopsie:* Laura Dean. *Zonker:* Albert Macklin. *Duke:* Gary Beach. *Honey:* Lauren Tom. *J.J.:* Kate Burton. *Joanie:* Barbara Andres. *Provost:* Peter Shawn. *Voice of President Reagan:* Reathel Bean.

The action takes place on Graduation weekend in Walden, an off-off-campus house.

Act 1, Scene 1: Walden, Living Room. *Scene 2*: Walden, Back Porch. *Scene 3*: Los Angeles County Courtroom. *Scene 4*: Walden, Living Room. *Scene 5*: Los Angeles County Courtroom. *Scene 6*: Walden, Living Room. *Scene 7*: WBBY, Radio Station. *Scene 8*: Walden Living Room.

Act 2, Scene 1: Walden, Living Room. *Scene 2*: Walden, Front Yard. *Scene 3*: Walden Puddle. *Scene 4*: Walden, Living Room. *Scene 5*: Commencement Exercises.

ACT 1[6]

Scene 1

"Graduation"
R. Bean, R. Bruneau, K. Szarabajka, L. Dean, M. Linn-Baker, A. Macklin

"Just One Night"
R. Bruneau

Scene 2

"I Came to Tan"
A. Macklin, Ensemble

Scene 3

"Guilty"
G. Beach, Ensemble

Scene 4

"I Can Have It All"
L. Dean, Ensemble

Scene 6

"Get Together"
K. Burton, R. Bruneau

Scene 7

"Baby Boom Boogie Boy"
M. Linn-Baker, R. Bean, Ensemble

Scene 8

"Another Memorable Meal"
R. Bruneau, K. Szarabajka, L. Dean, M. Linn-Baker, A. Macklin, K. Burton, B. Andres

ACT 2

Scene 1

"Just a House"
Ensemble

Scene 2

"Complicated Man"
L. Tom, L. Dean

Scene 3

"Real Estate"
G. Beach, A. Macklin

Scene 4

"Mother"
K. Burton, B. Andres

"It's the Right Time to be Rich"
K. Szarabajka, R. Bean

---

[6]For subsequent national tour, "Just One Night" moved from Act 1, Scene 1, to Act 1, Scene 6, replacing "Get Together." Added to Act 1, Scene 5:

"The Chairman's Song"
The Chairman, Duke, Honey, Ensemble

"Muffy and the Topsiders"
L. Dean, R. Bruneau, M. Linn-Baker, A. Macklin
"Just One Night" (reprise)
R. Bruneau, K. Burton
Scene 5
"Graduation" (reprise)
Ensemble

1983.19   BABY

A Musical in Two Acts, 24 Scenes. Book by Sybille Pearson. Based on a story developed with Susan Yankowitz. Music by David Shire. Lyrics by Richard Maltby, Jr. Directed by Richard Maltby, Jr. Musical staging by Wayne Cilento. Scenery by John Lee Beatty. Costumes by Jennifer von Mayrhauser. Lighting by Pat Collins. Film design by John Pieplow. Film sequences by Lennart Nilsson, Bo G. Erikson, Carl O. Lofman, Swedish Television. Orchestrations by Jonathan Tunick. Music direction, Peter Howard. Sound design by Jack Mann. Sound Textures, Electronic programming by Dan Wyman. Associate producers, Ronald Licht, Robert A. Stewart, J. C. Associates, Elaine Yaker, Karen Howard, Lillian Steinberg. Produced by James B. Freydberg, Ivan Bloch, Kenneth-John Productions (Kenneth D. Greenblatt, John J. Pomerantz), Suzanne J. Schwartz in association with Manuscript Productions. Opened 4 December 1983 at the Ethel Barrymore Theater and closed 1 July 1984 after 241 performances.

CAST (in order of appearance): *Lizzie Fields:* LIZ CALLAWAY. *Danny Hooper:* TODD GRAFF. *Arlene MacNally:* BETH FOWLER. *Alan MacNally:* JAMES CONGDON. *Pam Sakarian:* CATHERINE COX. *Nick Sakarian:* MARTIN VIDNOVIC. *Nurse:* Barbara Gilbert. *Doctor:* John Jellison. *Mr. Weiss:* Philip Hoffman. *Dean Webber:* Dennis Warning. *Mr. Hart:* Dennis Warning. *Intern:* Lon Hoyt. *First Woman:* Judith Thiergaard. *Second Woman:* Lisa Robinson. *Third Woman:* Kirsti Carnahan. *Fourth Woman:* Barbara Gilbert. *Fifth Woman:* Judith Thiergaard. *Sixth Woman:* Kim Criswell.
People in the Town: Kirsti Carnahan, Kim Criswell, Barbara Gilbert, Philip Hoffman, Lon Hoyt, John Jellison, Lisa Robinson, Judith Thiergaard, Dennis Warning. *Swings:* Judith Bliss, Michael Waldron.

The action takes place at the present time from March through November.

Act 1, Scene 1: A College Town. March to early April. *Scene 2:* Danny and Lizzie's Apartment. Early April. *Scene 3:* Alan and Arlene's Bedroom. *Scene 4:* Nick and Pam's Bedroom. *Scene 5:* A Doctor's Writing Room. Mid-April. *Scene 6:* The Track. *Scene 7:* On the Campus. *Scene 8:* A Doctor's Office. Early May. *Scene 9:* A Baseball Field. *Scene 10:* Alan and Arlene's Bedroom. *Scene 11:* A Bus Station. Mid-May. *Scene 12:* Alan and Arlene's House. *Scene 13:* Nick and Pam's Bedroom. *Scene 14:* Graduation. Early June. *Scene 15:* Danny and Lizzie's Apartment. Mid-July.

Act 2, Scene 1: The Town. Late August. *Scene 2:* A Doctor's Office. Early September. *Scene 3:* On the Campus. *Scene 4:* Nick and Pam's Bedroom. *Scene 5:* Alan and Arlene's Porch. *Scene 6:* Danny and Lizzie's Apartment. Mid-September. *Scene 7:* Nick and Pam's Bedroom. Mid-October. *Scene 8:* Alan and Arlene's Porch. *Scene 9:* All Three Bedrooms. Mid-November.

ACT 1[7]
Scene 1
"We Start Today"
T. Graff, L. Callaway, J. Congdon, B. Fowler, M. Vidnovic, C. Cox, People in the Town
Scene 2
"What Could Be Better?"
T. Graff, L. Callaway
Scene 3
"The Plaza Song"
J. Congdon, B. Fowler
Scene 4
"Baby, Baby, Baby"
M. Vidnovic, C. Cox, J. Congdon, B. Fowler, T. Graff, L. Callaway
Scene 5
"I Want It All"
C. Cox, L. Callaway, B. Fowler
Scene 6
"At Night She Comes Home to Me"
M. Vidnovic, T. Graff

Scene 7
"What Could Be Better?" (reprise)
T. Graff, L. Callaway
Scene 9
"Fatherhood Blues"
T. Graff, J. Congdon, M. Vidnovic, P. Hoffman, D. Warning
Scene 13
"Romance"
M. Vidnovic, C. Cox
"I Chose Right"
T. Graff
Scene 14
"We Start Today" (reprise)
Ensemble
Scene 15
"The Story Goes On"
L. Callaway
ACT 2
Scene 1
"The Ladies Singin' Their Song"
L. Callaway, the Women in the Town
Scene 2
"Baby, Baby, Baby" (reprise)
B. Fowler
Scene 4
"Romance" (reprise)
M. Vidnovic, C. Cox
Scene 5
"Easier to Love"
J. Congdon
Scene 6
"Two People in Love"
T. Graff, L. Callaway
Scene 7
"With You"
M. Vidnovic, C. Cox
Scene 8
"And What If We Had Loved Like That"
J. Congdon, B. Fowler
Scene 9
"We Start Today" (reprise)
T. Graff, L. Callaway, M. Vidnoiv, C. Cox, J. Congdon, B. Fowler
"The Story Goes On" (reprise)
Company

1983.20   PEG

A Musical Autobiography in Two Acts. Story and new lyrics by Peggy Lee. New music by Paul Horner. Directed by Robert Drivas. Creative consultant, Cy Coleman. Musical direction, Larry Fallon. Scenery designed by Tom H. John. Costumes designed by Florence Klotz. Lighting designed by Thomas Skelton. Sound consultant, Phil Ramone. Vocal arrangements by Ray Charles. Sound design by Jan Nebozenko. Orchestrations by Artie Butler, Larry Fallon, Dominic Frontiere, Bill Holman, Gordon Jenkins, Philip J. Lang, Johnny Mandel, Billy May, Leon Pendarvis, Don Sebesky, Larry Wilcox, Torrie Zito, (Benny Carter, Randy Newman). (Choral arrangements by Ray Charles.) Produced by Zev Bufman, Marge and Irv Cowan, Georgia Frontiere. Opened 14 December 1983 at the Lunt-Fontanne Theater and closed 17 December 1983 after 5 performances.

CAST: PEGGY LEE.
Quartet: Michael Renzi (Piano), Grady Tate (Drums), Jay Leonhart (Bass), Bucky Pizzarelli (Guitar).

ACT 1
"Fever"
(*Music and Lyrics by* Johnny Davenport and Eddie Cooley.)
"Soul"
(*Music by* Paul Horner. *Lyrics by* Peggy Lee. *Orchestration by* Don Sebesky. *Choral Arrangement by* Ray Charles.)

---

[7]In the subsequent tour and other regional productions, the song "Patterns' sung by Arlene (B. Fowler) was restored to Act 1.

"Daddy Was a Railroad Man"
 (*Music by* Paul Horner. *Lyrics by* Peggy Lee. *Orchestration by* Larry Wilcox. *Choral Arrangement by* Ray Charles.)

"Mama"
 (*Music by* Paul Horner. *Lyrics by* Peggy Lee. *Orchestration by* Gordon Jenkins. *Choral Arrangement by* Ray Charles.)

"That Old Piano"
 (*Music by* Paul Horner. *Lyrics by* Peggy Lee. *Orchestration by* Billy May.)

"One Beating a Day"
 (*Music by* Paul Horner. *Lyrics by* Peggy Lee. *Orchestration by* Leon Pendarvis. *Choral Arrangement by* Ray Charles.)

"That's How I Learned to Sing the Blues"
 (*Music by* Paul Horner. *Lyrics by* Peggy Lee. *Orchestration by* Billy May. *Choral Arrangement by* Ray Charles.)

"Goody Goody"
 (*Music by* Matt Malneck. *Lyrics by* Johnny Mercer. *Orchestration by* Mike Renzi. *Choral Arrangement by* Ray Charles.)

"Sometimes You're Up"
 (*Music by* Paul Horner. *Lyrics by* Peggy Lee. *Orchestration by* Philip J. Lang. *Choral Arrangement by* Ray Charles.)

"He'll Make Me Believe That He's Mine"
 (*Music by* Paul Horner. *Lyrics by* Peggy Lee. *Orchestration by* Johnny Mandel.)

"Why Don't You Do Right?"
 (*Music and Lyrics by* Joe McCoy. *Orchestration by* Bill Holman. *Choral Arrangement by* Ray Charles.)

ACT 2

"I Love Being Here With You"
 (*Music and Lyrics by* Peggy Lee. *Orchestration by* Larry Wilcox.)

"The Other Part of Me"
 (*Music by* Paul Horner. *Lyrics by* Peggy Lee. *Orchestration by* Dominic Frontiere. *Choral Arrangement by* Ray Charles.)

"I Don't Know Enough About You"
 (*Music and Lyrics by* Peggy Lee and Dave Barbour. *Orchestration by* Tore Zito.)

"Angels on Your Pillow"
 (*Music by* Paul Horner. *Lyrics by* Peggy Lee. *Orchestration by* Don Sebesky.)

"It's a Good Day"
 (*Music and Lyrics by* Peggy Lee and Dave Barbour *Orchestration by* Larry Fallon. *Choral Arrangement by* Ray Charles.)

"Manana"
 (*Music and Lyrics by* Peggy Lee and Dave Barbour. *Orchestration by* Leon Pendarvis. *Choral Arrangement by* Ray Charles.)

"What Did Dey Do to My Goil?"
 (*Music by* Paul Horner. *Lyrics by* Peggy Lee. *Orchestration by* Philip J. Lang. *Choral Arrangement by* Ray Charles.)

"Stay Away from Louisville Lou"
 (*Music by* Paul Horner. *Lyrics by* Peggy Lee. *Orchestration by* Billy May.)

"No More Rainbows"
 (*Music by* Paul Horner. *Lyrics by* Peggy Lee. *Orchestration by* Artie Butler. *Choral Arrangement by* Ray Charles.)

"Flowers and Flowers"
 (*Music by* Paul Horner. *Lyrics by* Peggy Lee. *Orchestration by* Tore Zito. *Choral Arrangement by* Ray Charles.)

"Lover" (from *LOVE ME TONIGHT* film)
 (*Music by* Richard Rodgers. *Lyrics by* Lorenz Hart. *Orchestration by* Sy Oliver.)

"Big Spender" (from *SWEET CHARITY*)
 (*Music by* Cy Coleman. *Lyrics by* Dorothy Fields. *Orchestration by* Bill Holman and Dave Grusin.)

"I'm a Woman"
 (*Music and Lyrics by* Jerry Lieber and Mike Stoller. *Orchestration by* Benny Carter.)

"Is That All There Is?"
 (*Music and Lyrics by* Jerry Lieber and Mike Stoller. *Orchestration by* Randy Newman.)

"There Is More"
 (*Music by* Paul Horner. *Lyrics by* Peggy Lee. *Orchestration by* Don Sebesky. *Choral Arrangement by* Ray Charles.)

Bows and Exit Music
 (*Orchestration by* Philip J. Lang.)

1983.21   THE TAP DANCE KID

A Musical in Two Acts, 15 Scenes. Book by Charles Blackwell. Based on the novel "Nobody's Family Is Going to Change" by Louise Fitzhugh. Music by Henry Krieger. Lyrics by Robert Lorick. Directed by Vivian Matalon.

Dances and musical staging by Danny Daniels. Musical supervision, orchestra and vocal arrangements by Harold Wheeler. Scenic production by Michael J. Hotopp and Paul DePass. Costumes by William Ivey Long. Lighting by Richard Nelson. Musical And vocal direction by Don Jones. Dance music arrangements by Peter Howard. Sound design by Jack Mann. Assistant choreographer, D. J. Giagni. Scenic photography by Mark Feldstein. Associate producers, Mark Beigelman, Richard Chwatt. Produced by Stanley White, Evelyn Barron, Harvey J. Klaris, Michel Stuart in association with Michel Kleinman Productions. Opened 21 December 1983 at the Broadhurst Theatre, moved 27 March 1984 to the Minskoff Theatre and closed 11 March 1985 after 669 performances.

CAST (in order of appearance): *Willie:* ALFONSO RIBEIRO. *Ginnie:* HATTIE WINSTON. *Dulcie:* BARBARA MONTGOMERY. *Emma:* MARTINE ALLARD. *William:* SAMUEL E. WRIGHT. *Dipsey:* HINTON BATTLE. *Mona:* Karen Paskow. *Carole:* JACKIE LOWE. *Daddy Bates:* ALAN WEEKS. *Winslow:* Michael Blevins. *Joe:* Jackie Patterson. *Offstage Voice:* Lloyd Culbreath.
  Little Rio Dancers and New Yorkers: Leah Bass, Kevin Berdini, Michael Blevins, Karen Curlee, Suzzanne Douglas, Rick Emery, Karen E. Fraction, D. J. Giagni, J. J. Jepson, Karen Paskow, Rodney Alan McGuire, Jackie Patterson, Mayme Paul, Jamie M. Pisano, Ken Prescott, Oliver Woodall, James Young. *Swings:* Llloyd Culbreath, Linda Von Germer.

The action takes place at the present time in New York City's Roosevelt Island and Manhattan.

Act 1, Scene 1: Dining Room. *Scene 2:* Dipsey's Loft. *Scene 3:* William's Study. *Scene 4:* Playground. *Scene 5:* Manhattan. *Scene 6:* The Fabulous Westway Hotel Ballroom. *Scene 7:* William's Study. *Scene 8:* Terrace.

Act 2, Scene 1: Dining Room. *Scene 2:* Playground. *Scene 3:* Dipsey's Loft. *Scene 4:* Willie's Bedroom. *Scene 5:* Manhattan. *Scene 6:* Dispey's Loft. *Scene 7:* Street.

ACT 1[8]

Scene 1

"Another Day"[9]
 H. Winston, M. Allard, A. Ribeiro

Scene 3

"Four Strikes Against Me"
 M. Allard

"Class Act"
 H. Winston, H. Battle, A. Weeks

Scene 4

"They Never Hear What I Say"
 M. Allard, A. Ribeiro

"Dancing Is Everything"
 A. Ribeiro

Scene 5

"Crosstown"
 A. Ribeiro, New Yorkers

Scene 6

"Fabulous Feet"
 H. Battle, J. Lowe, Dancers

"I Could Get Used to Him"
 J. Lowe, Dancers

---

[8]For the subsequent national tour, substantial changes were made to the book and score as follows: Production re-directed by by Jerry Zaks.

New Act 1, Scene 1

"Dipsey's Comin' Over"
 Dulé Hill (Willie)

New Act 1, Scene 2: Rehearsal Studio

"High Heels"
 H. Battle, Theresa Hayes (Carole), Dancers

"Something Better, Something More"
 H. Battle

Act 2, Scene 2 and 3 reversed

New Act 2, Scene 4: Rehearsal Studio

"Dipsey's Vaudeville"
 Dancers, H. Battle, T. Hayes

"I Remember How It Was" (moved from Scene 3)

Former Scene 4 now Scene 5

New Act 2, Scene 6 (replacing former Scenes 5 and 6): A Theatre.

[9]Dropped for subsequent tnational tour.

Scene 8
  "Man in the Moon"
    H. Battle
ACT 2
Scene 1
  "Like Him"
    M. Allard, H. Winston
Scene 2
  "Someday"
    M. Allard, A. Ribeiro
Scene 3
  "My Luck Is Changing"
    H. Battle
  "I Remember How It Was"
    H. Winston
Scene 4
  "Lullabye"
    H. Winston
  "Tap Tap"
    A. Weeks, A. Ribeiro, H. Battle
Scene 5
  "Dance If It Makes You Happy"
    A. Ribeiro, H. Battle, A. Weeks, J. Lowe, Dancers
Scene 6
  "William's Song"
    S. E. Wright
Scene 7
  "Class Act" (Finale)
    The Family

1984.01 THE RINK

A Musical in Two Acts. Book by Terrence McNally. Music by John Kander. Lyrics by Fred Ebb. Directed by A. J. Antoon. Choreography by Graciela Daniele. Scenery designed by Peter Larkin. Costumes designed by Theoni V. Aldredge. Lighting designed by Marc B. Weiss. Sound designed by Otts Munderloh. Musical director, Paul Gemignani. Dance arrangements by Tom Fay. Orchestrations by Michael Gibson. Assistant choreographer, Tina Paul. Associate producer, Tina Chen. Executive producer, Robin Ullman. Produced by Jules Fisher, Roger Berlind, Joan Cullman, Milbro Productions (Jim Milford, Slade Brown), Kenneth-John Productions (Kenneth D. Greenblatt-John Pomerantz) in association with Jonathan Farkas and Jujamcyn Theatres. Opened 9 February 1984 at the Martin Beck Theatre and closed 4 August 1984 after 204 performances.

CAST (in order of appearance):*Angel:* LIZA MINNELLI. *Little Girl:* Kim Hauser. *The Wreckers* (6): *Lino:* Jason Alexander. *Buddy:* Mel Johnson, Jr. *Guy:* Scott Holmes. *Lucky:* Scott Ellis. *Tony:* Frank Mastrocola. *Ben:* Ronn Carroll. *Anna:* CHITA RIVERA. *Dino:* Scott Holmes. *Dino's Father:* Ronn Carroll. *Lenny:* Jason Alexander. *Hiram:* Mel Johnson, Jr. *Tom:* Frank Mastrocola. *Sugar:* Scott Ellis. *Punk:* Frank Mastrocola. *Punk:* Scott Ellis. *Punk:* Jason Alexander. *Mrs. Silverman:* Ronn Carroll. *Mrs. Jackson:* Mel Johnson, Jr. *Arnie:* Scott Ellis. *Charlie:* Mel Johnson, Jr. *Uncle Fausto:* Jason Alexander. *Suitor:* Scott Ellis. *Suitor:* Mel Johnson, Jr. *Suitor:* Frank Mastrocola. *Father Rocco:* Scott Holmes. *Bobby Perillo:* Scott Ellis. *Sister Philomena:* Ronn Carroll. *Peter Reilly:* Frank Mastrocola. *Junior Miller:* Mel Johnson, Jr. *Debbie Duberman:* Scott Holmes. *Danny:* Scott Ellis.

The action takes place in a roller rink somewhere on the Eastern seaboard during the 1970's.

ACT 1
  "Colored Lights"
    L. Minnelli
  "Chief Cook and Bottle Washer"
    C. Rivera
  "Don't Ah Ma Me"
    C. Rivera, L. Minnelli
  "Blue Crystal"
    S. Holmes
  "Under the Roller Coaster"
    L. Minnelli
  "Not Enough Magic"
    S. Holmes, L. Minnelli, C. Rivera, S. Ellis, M. Johnson, Jr., F. Mastrocola, J. Alexander, R. Carroll

  "We Can Make It"
    C. Rivera
  "After All These Years"
    The Wreckers
  "Angel's Rink and Social Center"
    L. Minnelli, the Wreckers
  "What Happened to the Old Days?"
    C. Rivera, R. Carroll, M. Johnson, Jr.
  "Colored Lights" (reprise)
    L. Minnelli
ACT 2[10]
  "The Apple Doesn't Fall Very Far"
    C. Rivera, L. Minnelli
  "Marry Me"
    J. Alexander
  "We Can Make It" (reprise)
    C. Rivera
  "Mrs. A"
    C. Rivera, L. Minnelli, J. Alexander, Suitors
  "The Rink"
    The Wreckers
  "Wallflower"
    C. Rivera, L. Minnelli
  "All the Children in a Row"
    L. Minnelli, S. Ellis

1984.02 THE HUMAN COMEDY

A Musical in Two Acts, 17 Scenes[11]. Libretto by William Dumaresq. Based on the novel of the same name by William Saroyan. Music by Galt MacDermott. Directed by Wilford Leach. Scenery by Bob Shaw. Costumes by Rita Ryack. Lighting by James F. Ingalls. Sound by Tom Morse. Music director, orchestrator, Galt MacDermott. Conductor, Tania León. Projections, Wendall Harrington. A New York Shakespeare Festival Production. Associate producer, Jason Steven Cohen. Produced by Joseph Papp and the Shubert Organization. Opened 5 April 1984 at the Royale Theatre and closed 15 April 1984 after 13 performances.

CAST (in order of singing): *Trainman:* David Lawrence Johnson. (*The Family,* 4): *Ulysses Macauley:* JOSH BLAKE. *Mrs. Kate Macauley:* BONNIE KOLOC. *Homer Macauley:* STEPHEN GEOFFREYS. *Bess Macauley:* MARY [Elizabeth] MASTRANTONIO. *Helen:* Anne Marie Bobby. *Miss Hicks:* Laurie Franks. *Spangler:* REX SMITH. *Thief:* Christopher Edmonds. *Mr. Grogan:* GORDON CONNELL. *Felix:* Daniel Noel. *Beautiful Music:* Debra Byrd. *Mary Arena:* Caroline Peyton. *Mexican Woman:* Olga Merediz. *Voice Of Matthew Macauley:* Grady Mulligan. *Marcus Macalay:* Don Kehr. *Tobey:* JOSEPH KOLINSKI. *Soldiers:* Kenneth Bryan, Louis Padilla, Michael Willson. *A Neighbor:* Kathleen Rowe McAllen. *Diana Steed:* Laeta Galloway. *Minister:* Walter Hudson. *Townspeople:* Marc Stephen Delgatto, Lisa Kirchner, Vernon Spencer, Dan Tramon.

The action takes place in 1943 in a little town in California.

Act 1, Scene 1: At a Train Crossing. *Scene 2:* At Home. *Scene 3:* At School. *Scene 4:* At the Telegraph Office. *Scene 5:* Message. *Scene 6:* At Home. *Scene 7:* Message. *Scene 8:* At the Telegraph Office. *Scene 9:* At Home.

Act 2, Scene 1: At the Debarkation Center. *Scene 2:* At Home. *Scene 3:* War Front. *Scene 4:* Home Front. *Scene 5:* At War and at Home. *Scene 6:* At the Telegraph Office. *Scene 7:* In the Park. *Scene 8:* Home.

ACT 1
  "In a Little Town in California"
    Company
Scene 1
  "Hi Ya Kid"
    D. L. Johnson, J. Blake
Scene 2
  "We're a Little Family"
    B. Koloc, S. Geoffreys, J. Blake, M. E. Mastrantonio

---

[10]Added to the close of Act 2 after opening:
  "Coda"
    C. Rivera, L. Minnelli
[11]Originally produced in New York Off-Broadway 20 December 1983 at the Public Theatre/Anspacher for 79 performances.

Scene 3
  "The Assyrians"
    A. M. Bobby, L. Franks
  "Noses"
    S. Geoffreys
Scene 4
  "You're a Little Young for the Job"
    R. Smith, S. Geoffreys
  "I Can Carry a Tune"
    S. Geoffreys
  "Happy Birthday"
    S. Geoffreys
  "Happy Anniversary"
    S. Geoffreys, R. Smith, G. Connell
  "I Think the Kid Will Do"
    G. Connell, R. Smith
  "Beautiful Music"
    D. Byrd, Company
  "Cocoanut Cream Pie"
    G. Connell, S. Geoffreys
  "When I Am Lost"
    S. Geoffreys, D. Byrd, Company
Scene 5
  "I Said, Oh No"
    M. E. Mastrantonio, C. Peyton, O. Merediz
Scene 6
  "Daddy Will Not Be Walking Through The Door"
    B. Koloc
  "The Birds in the Sky"
    M. E. Mastrantonio
  "Remember Always to Give"
    B. Koloc
  "Long Past Sunset"
    D. Kehr
Scene 7
  "Don't Tell Me"
    C. Peyton, D. Kehr, the Family, Company
Scene 8
  "The Fourth Telegram"
    R. Smith, G. Connell
  "Give Me All the Money"
    C. Edmonds, R. Smith
Scene 9
  "Everything Is Changed"
    S. Geoffreys, B. Koloc
  "The World Is Full of Loneliness"
    B. Koloc
  "Hi Ya Kid" (reprise)
    D. L. Johnson, J. Blake, Company
ACT 2
Scene 1
  "How I Love Your Thingamajig"
    Soldiers
  "Everlasting"
    J. Kolinski
  "An Orphan, I Am"
    J. Kolinski
  "I'll Tell You About My Family"
    D. Kehr
Scene 2
  "I Wish I Were a Man"
    C. Peyton
Scene 3
  "Marcus, My Friend"
    J. Kolinski
  "My Sister Bess"
    D. Kehr
Scene 4
  "I've Known a Lot of Guys"
    L. Galloway

"Diana"
    R. Smith
Scene 5
  "Dear Brother"
    S. Geoffreys, D. Kehr
  "The Birds in the Trees"/"A Lot of Men" (reprise)
    L. Galloway, R. Smith
  "Parting"
    B. Koloc, Wives, Sweethearts, Mothers, Freinds, Soldiers
Scene 6
  "Mr. Grogan, Wake Up"
    S. Geoffreys
  "Hello Doc"
    R. Smith
Scene 7
  "What Am I Supposed to Do?"
    S. Geoffreys, R. Smith
Scene 8
  "Long Past Sunset"
    B. Koloc, Company
  "I'm Home"
    J. Kolinski
  "Somewhere, Someone"
    M. E. Mastrantonio
  "I'll Always Love You"
    C. Peyton, Company
  "Hi Ya Kid" (reprise)
    D. L. Johnson, J. Blake, Company
  "Fathers and Mothers (And You and Me)"
    Company

DIE FLEDERMAUS

1984.03

A Revival of the Operetta in Three Acts, in German[12]. Original libretto by Carl Haffner and Richard Genée. Lyrics by Richard Genée. Based on the comedy "Le Réveillon" by Henri Meilhac and Ludovic Halévy. Music by Johann Strauss. Produced (Staged) by Karl Dönsch. Sets by Pantelis Dessyllas. Costumes by Fred Adlmüller and Alice Maria Schlesinger. Choreography by Gerhard Senft. Chorus master, Franz Gerstacker. Lighting, Mark W. Stanley. Conductors, Franz Bauer-Theussl, Rudolf Bibl. A Vienna Volksoper Production. Produced by Kazuko Hillyer International. Opened 10 April 1984 at the New York State Theatre and closed 20 April 1984 after 5 performances in repertory.

CAST: *Gabriel von Eisenstein*, a man of leisure: PETER MINICH. *Rosalinda*, his wife: BARBARA DANIELS. *Frank*, the prison governor: Karl Dönsch. *Prinz Orlofsky*: DAGMAR KOLLER. *Alfred*, tenor, one of Rosalinda's former suitors: ADOLPH DAL-LAPOZZA. *Dr. Falke*, a Notary: RUSSELL SMYTHE. *Dr. Blind*, a Solicitor: Rudolf Wasserlof. *Adele*, Rosalinda's maid: ELISABETH KALES. *Ida*, her sister: Guggi Loewinger. *Frosch*, the prison warden: Ossy Kolman.
  Ballet: Polka: "Thunder and Lightning (op. 314): Christina Klein, Elisabeth Stelzer, Istvan Bernath and the corps de ballet. Waltz: "Blue Danube" (op. 314): Melitta Ogrisse, Ivan Jakus, and the corps de ballet. *Chorus*: Vienna Volsoper Chorus.

THE MERRY WIDOW

1984.04

A Revival of the Operetta (DIE LUSTIGE WITWE) in Three Acts, 4 Scenes, in German[13]. Music by Franz Lehár. Original German book and lyrics by Victor Léon and Leo Stein (after "L'Attaché d'Ambassade" by Henri Meilhac.) Produced (Staged) by Robert Herzl. Choreography by Gerhard Senft. Settings by Pantelis Dessyllas. Costumes by Barbara Bilabel, Alice Maria Schlesinger. Lighting, Mark W. Stanley. Conductors, Franz Bauer-Theussl, Rudolf Bibl. Chorus master, Franz Gerstacker. A Vienna Volksoper Production. Produced by Kazuko Hillyer International. Opened

---

[12]First English language production in New York 16 March 1885 at the Casino Theatre.
[13]Originally produced in New York in English 21 October 1907 at the New Amsterdam Theatre for 416 performances.

11 April 1984 at the New York State Theatre and closed 21 April 1984 after 5 performances in repertory.

CAST: *Baron Mirko Zeta,* Pontevedrinian Ambassador in Paris: KARL DÖNSCH. *Valencienne,* his wife: MELANIE HOLIDAY. *Count Danilo Danilowitsch,* Secretary of the Pontevedrinian Embassy: EBERHARD WAECHTER. *Hanna Glawari,* the Widow: IRJANA IROSCH. *Camille de Rosillon:* RICHARD KARCZYKOWSKI. *Vicomte Cascada:* Peter Drahosch. *Raoul de St. Brioche:* HEINZ HELLBERG. *Bogdanowitsch,* Pontevedrinian Consul: WOLFGANG DAUSCHA. *Sylviane,* his wife: Renate Krula. *Kromow,* Councellor: Hans Kraemmer. *Olga,* his wife: Magdalena Emesz. *Pritschitsch,* Military attaché: Wolfgang Jeschek. *Praskowia,* his wife: Sonja Mottl. *Njegus,* Major-domo of the Pontevedrinian Embassy: ERICH KUCHAR.

Ballet: Act 2, "Kolo": Melitta Ogrise, Elisabeth Stelzer, Istvan Bernath, Zdislav Zelinka and the corps de ballet. Act 3, "Zwanzinette": Christina Klein, Zdislav Zelinka, Lili Clemente, Felicitas Prikopa, Istvan Bernath, Istvan Varga. "Nachledil-March": Gabriella Masek, Percy Kofranek, Peter Gavrikov, men of the corps de ballet. "Can Can": Corps de de ballet. *Chorus:* Vienna Volksoper Chorus.

1984.05   CZARDAS PRINCESS

A Revival of the Operetta, DIE CSÁRDÁSFÜRSTIN,{The Gypsy Princess} in Three Acts[14], in German. Original (Viennese) book and lyrics by Leo Stein and Bela Jenbach. Music by Emmerich Kálmán. Produced (staged) by Robert Herzl. Sets by Pantelis Dessyllas. Costumes by Silvia Strahammer. Choreography by Michael Maurer. Lighting Mark W. Stanley. Chorus master, Karl Heinz Dold. Conductors, Franz Bauer-Theussl, Rudolf Bibl. A Vienna Volksoper Production. Produced by Kazuko Hillyer International. Opened 12 April 1984 at the New York State Theatre and closed 20 April 1984 after 4 performances in repertory.

CAST: *Leopold Maria, Prince von und Lippert-Weylersheim:* RUDOLF WASSERLOF. *Anhilte,* his wife: Sonja Mottl. *Edwin Ronald,* his son: FRANZ WAECHTER. *Countess Anastasia,* his niece: ELISABETH KALES. *Baron Eugen von Rohnsdorff, army captain, his nephew:* PETER DRAHOSCH. *Count Boni Kácsiánu:* JACK POPPELL. *Feri von Kerekes,* called 'Feri bácsi': SÁNDOR NÉMETH. *Sylva Varescu, a cabaret singer:* MELENA RUDIFERIA. *Wilhlem von Billing,* ambassador: Wolfgang Dauscha. *Siggi Gross,* manager of the Orpheum in Budapest: Helmut Randers. *Sandor von Kiss,* a Notary, syndic of the Orpheum: Rudolf Katzboeck. *Max,* head-waiter of the Grand Hotel, Vienna: Josef Forstner.

Chorus: Vienna Volksoper Chorus.

ACT 1

"Heia, heia in den Bergen ist mein Heimatland"

"Alle sind wir Sünder"

"Sylva, ich will nur dich-Ja Mädchen gibt es wunderfeine"

"Aus ist's mit der Liebe-Ganz ohne Weiber geht die Chose nicht"

"O jag' dem Glück nicht nach"

"Ich Edwin Ronald-Hochzeitstanz-Ja so ein Teufelsweib"

ACT 2

"Erstrahlen die Lichter"

"Ich warte auf das grosse Wunder-Machen wir's den Schwalben nach"

"Heller Jubel"

"Liebchen, mich reisst es"

"Mädel guck-Das ist die Liebe"

"Tanzen möcht' ich-Tausend kleine Engel singen"

"Verzeih' Papa-Lieben sich zwei Menschenkinder"

ACT 3

"Nimm, Zigeunder, deine Geige-Jaj Mamám, Bruderherz ich kauf mir die Welt"

"Mädel guck-Das ist die Liebe"

"Tausend kleine Engel singen"

SHIRLEY MacLAINE
1984.06   ON BROADWAY

A Musical Entertainment (Revue) in One Act. Original music and lyrics by Marvin Hamlisch, Christopher Adler. Additional material by Larry

Grossman, Buz Kohan. Staged and choreographed by Alan Johnson. Lighting design by Ken Billington. Costumes by Pete Menefee. Musical director, Jack French. Associate lighting designer, Jeffrey Schissler. Producer, Michael Flowers. Presented by Guber/Gross Productions (Lee Guber, Shelly Gross) and The Nederlander Organization. Opened 19 April 1984 at the Gershwin Theatre and closed 27 May 1984 after 46 performances.

CAST: SHIRLEY MacLAINE. *Company:* Mark Reina, Larry Vickers, Jamilah Lucas, Antonette Yuskis. *Swing:* Gary Flannery.

MUSICAL NUMBERS[15]

"Now"

Harold Arlen Medley (with a little Gershwin):
   "If I Only Had a Brain"
   "Get Happy"
   "I've Got the World on a String"
   "S'Wonderful"

Hooker Medley:
   "If They Could See Me Now"

"In the Movies"

Monologues from 3 of Shirley's non-musical films:
   "Terms of Endearment"
   "Some Came Running"
   "The Turning Point"

Tribute to the dance styles of Bob Fosse, Michael Kidd and new black choreographers (George Faison, Billy Wilson, Geoffrey Holder)

Anecdotes about mountain climbing in the Himalayas

"Life Is Just a Bowl of Cherries" (from *GEORGE WHITE'S SCANDALS OF 1931*)
   (*Music by* Ray Henderson. *Lyrics by* Lew Brown and Buddy DeSylva.)

"Nobody Does It Better" (from *SEESAW*)
   (*Music by* Cy Coleman. *Lyrics by* Dorothy Fields.)

"A Cockeyed Optimist" (from *SOUTH PACIFIC*)
   (*Music by* Richard Rodgers. *Lyrics by* Oscar Hammerstein II.)

"Imagine"
   (Music and Lyrics by John Lennon.)

1984.07   OLIVER!

A Revival of the Musical in Two Acts, 12 Scenes[16]. Book, music and lyrics by Lionel Bart. Based on the novel "Oliver Twist" by Charles Dickens. Directed by Peter Coe. (Production) Designed by Sean Kenny. Lighting design by Andrew Bridge. Sound design by Jack Mann. Orchestrations by Eric Rogers. Musical Director, John Lesko. Associate director, Geoffrey Ferris. Executive producers, R. Tyler Gatchell, Jr., Peter Neufeld. Produced by Cameron Mackintosh, Carole J. Shorenstein, James M. Nederlander by arrangement with The Southbrook Group. Opened 29 April 1984 at the Mark Hellinger Theatre and closed 13 May 1984 after 17 performances.

CAST: *Oliver Twist:* BRADEN DANNER.

At the Workhouse: Mr. Bumble, the Beadle: MICHAEL McCARTY. *Mrs. Bumble,* the Matron: ELIZABETH LARNER. *Old Sally,* a Pauper: Susan Willis.

At the Undertaker's: Mr. Sowerberry, the Undertaker: RODERICK HORN. *Mrs. Sowerberry,* his wife: FRANCES CUKA. *Charlotte,* their daughter: Andi Henig. *Noah Claypole,* their apprentice: Alan Braunstein.

At the Thieves' Kitchen: Fagin: RON MOODY. *The Artful Dodger:* DAVID GARLICK. *Nancy:* PATTI LuPONE. *Bet:* Sarah E. Litzsinger. *Bill Sykes:* GRAEME CAMPBELL. *Bullseye:* Vito, Buffy.

At the Brownlow's: Mr. Brownlow: MICHAEL ALLINSON. *Dr. Grimwig:* Louis Beachner. *Mrs. Bedwin:* ELIZABETH LARNER.

Workhouse Boys and Fagin's Gang: Robert David Cavanaugh, Samir Chowdhury, Ruben Cuevas, Roshi Handwerger, Cameron Johann, Mark Manasseri, Michael Manasseri, Kipp Marcus, Shawn Morgal, Brian Noodt, Roy Nygaard, R. D. Robb, Dennis Singletary, Zachary A. Stier. *Londoners:* Diane Armistead, Louis Beachner, Alan Braunstein, Frances Cuka, W. P. Dremak, Gregg Edelman, Tony Gilbert, Eleanor Glockner, Beth Guiffre, Jan Horvath, Michael McCarty, William McClary, Marcia Mitzman, Martin Moran, Barbara Moroz, Cheryl Russell, Clark Sayre, Jane Strauss, Susan Willis.

---

[14]First produced in New York in English as "The Riviera Girl" 24 September 1917 for 78 performances.

[15]Note: No song list included in program. Above list prepared from press files and recordings.

[16]Originally produced in New York 6 January 1963 at the Imperial Theatre for 774 performances. For Synopsis of Scenes and Musical Numbers, see original 1963 production.

SUNDAY IN THE PARK WITH GEORGE

1984.08

A Musical in Two Acts[17]. Book by James Lapine[18]. Music and Lyrics by Stephen Sondheim. Directed by James Lapine. Scenery by Tony Straiges. Costumes by Patricia Zipprodt, Ann Hould-Ward. Set and costume designs adapted from the Georges Seurat painting entitled "Sunday Afternoon on the Island of the Grand Jatte." Lighting by Richard Nelson. Special effects, Bran Ferren. Sound by Tom Morse. Movement by Randolyn Zinn. Musical direction, Paul Gemignani. Orchestrations by Michael Starobin. Produced by The Shubert Organization and Emanuel Azenberg by arrangement with Playwrights Horizons. Opened 2 May 1984 at the Booth Theatre and closed 13 October 1985 after 604 performances.

CAST (in order of appearance): *Act 1: George*, an artist: MANDY PATINKIN. *Dot*, his mistress: BERNADETTE PETERS. *An Old Lady*: BARBARA BRYNE. *Her Nurse*: Judith Moore. *Franz*, a servant: Brent Spiner. *A Boy Bathing in the river*: Danielle Ferland. *A Young Man sitting on the bank*: Nancy Opel. *A Man lying on the bank*: Cris Groenendaal. *Jules*, another artist: CHARLES KIMBROUGH. *Yvonne*, his wife: DANA IVEY. *A Boatman*: William Parry. *Celeste #1*: Melanie Vaughan. *Celeste #2*: Mary D'Arcy. *Louise*, the daughter of Jules and Yvonne: Danielle Ferland. *Frieda*, a cook: Nancy Opel. *Louis*, a baker: Cris Groenendaal. *A Soldier*: Robert Westenberg. *A Man with bicycle*: John Jellison. *A Little Girl*: Michele Rigan. *A Woman with baby carriage*: Sue Anne Gershenson. *Mr.*: Kurt Knudson. *Mrs.*: Judith Moore.

Act 2: George, an artist: MANDY PATINKIN. *Marie*, his grandmother: BERNADETTE PETERS. *Dennis*, a technician: Brent Spiner. *Bob Greenberg*, the museum director: CHARLES KIMBROUGH. *Naomi Eisen*, a composer: DANA IVEY. *Harriet Pawling*, a patron of the arts: Judith Moore. *Billy Webster*, her friend: Cris Groenendaal. *A Photographer*: Sue Anne Gershenson. *A Museum Assistant*: John Jellison. *Charles Redmond*, a visiting curator: WILLIAM PARRY. *Alex*, an artist: Robert Westenberg. *Betty*, an artist: Nancy Opel. *Lee Randolph*, the museum's publicist: Kurt Knudson. *Blair Daniels*, an art critic: BARBARA BRYNE. *A Waitress*: Melanie Vaughan. *Elaine*: Mary D'Arcy.

Act 1 takes place on a series of Sundays from 1884 to 1886 and alternates between a park on an island in the Seine just outside of Paris, and Georges' studio. Act 2 takes place in 1984 at an American art museum, and on the island in the Seine.

ACT 1

"Sunday in the Park With George"
    B. Peters
"No Life"
    C. Kimbrough, D. Ivey
"Color and Light"
    B. Peters, M. Patinkin
"Gossip"
    M. Vaughan, M. D'Arcy, W. Parry, J. Moore, B. Bryne, C. Kimbrough, D. Ivey
"The Day Off"
    M. Patinkin, J. Moore, B. Spiner, N. Opel, W. Parry, R. Westenberg, M. Vaughan, M. D'Arcy, D. Ivey, D. Ferland, C. Kimbrough, C. Groenendaal
"Everybody Loves Louis"
    B. Peters
"Finishing the Hat"
    M. Patinkin
"We Do Not Belong Together"
    B. Peters, M. Patinkin
"Beautiful"

B. Bryne, M. Patinkin
"Sunday"
    Company

ACT 2
"It's Hot Up Here"
    Company
"Chromolume #7"
    M. Patinkin, B. Peters
"Putting It Together"
    M. Patinkin, Company
"Children and Art"
    B. Peters
"Lesson #8"
    M. Patinkin
"Move On"
    M. Patinkin, B. Peters
"Sunday" (reprise)
    Company

THE WIZ

1984.09

A Revival of the Musical in Two Acts, a Prologue and 15 Scenes[19]. Book by William F. Brown. Based on the novel "The Wizard of Oz" by L. Frank Baum. Music and lyrics by Charlie Smalls. Direction and costume design by Geoffrey Holder. Choreography and musical numbers staged by George Faison. Scenery designed by Peter Wolf. Lighting designed by Paul Sullivan. Orchestrations by Harold Wheeler. Musical direction and vocal arrangements by Charles Coleman. Dance arrangements by Timothy Graphenreed. Sound by Gary M. Stocker. Produced by Tom Mallow, James Janek and the Shubert Organization. Opened 24 May 1984 at the Lunt-Fontanne Theater and closed 3 June 1984 after 13 performances.

CAST (in order of appearance): *Aunt Em*: PEGGIE BLUE. *Toto*: Toto. *Dorothy*: STEPHANIE MILLS. *Uncle Henry*: David Weatherspoon. *Tornado*: Daryl Richardson. *Munchkins*: Carol Dennis, Ada Dyer, Lawrence Hamilton, Sam Harkness, David Weatherspoon. *Addaperle*: JUANITA FLEMING. *Yellow Brick Road*: Alfred L. Dove, Germaine Edwards, Dwight Leon, David Robertson. *Scarecrow*: CHARLES VALENTINO. *Sunflowers*: Carol Dennis, Ada Dyer, Sam Harkness, David Weatherspoon. *Crows*: Paula Anita Brown, Marvin Engran, Jasmine Guy. *Tinman*: HOWARD PORTER. *Lion*: GREGG BAKER. *Strangers*: Carol Dennis, Sam Harkness, David Weatherspoon. *Kalidahs*: Marvin Engran, Jasmine Guy, Lawrence Hamilton, Raymond C. Harris, Gigi Hunter, Martial Roumain. *Poppies*: Sharon Brooks, Paula Anita Brown, Carla Earle, Tanya Gibson, Gigi Hunter, Daryl Richardson. *Chief of Field Mice*: Ada Dyer. *Field Mice*: Lawrence Hamilton, David Weatherspoon. *Royal Gatekeeper*: Sam Harkness. *Head of the Society of Emerald City*: Sharon Brooks.

Emerald City Citizens: Paula Anita Brown, Roslyn Burrough, Carol Dennis, Alfred L. Dove, Ada Dyer, Carla Earle, Germaine Edwards, Marvin Engran, Tanya Gibson, Jasmine Guy, Lawrence Hamilton, Sam Harkness, Raymond C. Harris, Gigi Hunter, Dwight Leon, Daryl Richardson, David Robertson, Martial Roumain, David Weatherspoon.

The Wiz: CARL HALL. *Evillene*: ELLA MITCHELL. *Lord High Underling*: Lawrence Hamilton. *Soldier Messenger*: Marvin Engran. *Winged Monkey*: Germaine Edwards. *Glinda*: ANN DUQUESNAY.

---

[17]Orginally produced in New York Off-Broadway 9 July 1983 at Playwrights Horizons for 25 performances.
[18]Although suggested by the life of Georges Seurat and by his painting "A Sunday Afternoon on the Island of La Grande Jatte," all characters in "Sunday in the Park With George" are products of the authors' imaginations.

---

[19]Originally produced in New York 5 January 1975 at the Majestic Theatre for 1672 performances. For Synopsis of Scenes and Musical Numbers, see original 1975 production. For this production, the original Act 2, Scene 4 (Emerald City Gate), was dropped.

Stubby Kaye in GRIND
Martha Swope/TimePix

1984–1985 SEASON

1984.10 ## GOTTA GETAWAY!

A Magical Musical Voyage (Revue) in Two Acts, 11 Scenes. Conceived and created by Stephen Nisbet, James Lecesne. Writer, James Lecesne. Directed and choreographed by Larry Fuller. Co-choreographer, Marianne Selbert. Producer-Artistic director, Patricia Morinelli. Associate producer, Stephen Nisbet. Original music by Marc Elliot, Chip Orton, Gene Palumbo, Marc Shaiman, Eric Watson. Musical director, Gene Palumbo. Orchestrations by Michael Gibson, Bill Brohn. Conductor, Robert Billig. Vocal arrangements, Gene Palumbo, Robert Billig. Dance arrangements by Michael Rice. Scenery by Eduardo Sicangco. Costumes by Michael Casey. Lighting by Clarke W. Thornton. Music video by Neil Wagman. Produced by Radio City Music Hall Productions, Inc. Opened 13 June 1984 at the Radio City Music Hall and closed 3 September 1984 after 149 performances.

CAST: LILIANE MONTEVECCHI, TONY AZITO, LORETTA DEVINE, ALYSON REED, RON and JOY HOLIDAY.

THE ROCKETTES: Pauline Achillas, Carol Beatty, Katherine Beatty, Dottie Belle, Susan Boron, Elizabeth Chanin, Barbara Ann Cittadino, Susan Cleland, Eileen Collins, Brie Daniels, Prudence Gray Demmler, Susanne Doris, Jackie Fancy, Deniene Fenn, Alexis Ficks, Carol Harbich, Jennifer Hammond, Ginny Hounsell, Cindy Hughes, Joan Peer Kelleher, Pam Kelleher, DeeDee Knapp, Judy Little, Sonya Livingston, Leslie Gryszko McCarthy, Mary McNamara, Barbara Moore, Lynn Newton, Kerri Pearsall, Gerri Presky, Terry Spano, Pamela Stacy Pasqualino, Lynn Sullivan, Susan Theobald, Carol Toman, Patricia Tully, Rose Ann Woolsey, Darlene Wendy.

Cruisettes: Arminae Azarian, Ellia English, Connie Kunkle, Jacqueline Reilly, Freida Williams.

Stewards: Ciscoe Bruton, John Clonts, Joe DeGunther, Brian Feehan, Darrell Greene, Marc Hunter, David Michael Johnson, Robert Kellett, Lacy Darryl Phillips, Jeff Shade, Paul Solen, Alan Stuart, John M. Wiltberger.

Act 1, Scene 1: Bon Voyage. *Scene 2:* Shipshape. *Scene 3:* 50,000 Leagues under the Sea. *Scene 4:* The Poop Deck. *Scene 5:* Island Hopping.

Act 2, Scene 1: Ohh, La La Paris. *Scene 2:* Up in the Air. *Scene 3:* A Wild Holiday. *Scene 4:* The Forbidden City. *Scene 5:* The Stardeck. *Scene 6:* Land Ho.

ACT 1
Scene 1
"Gotta Getaway"
    L. Montevecchi, A. Reed, L. Devine, T. Azito
    (*Video Sequence Directed by* Neil Wagman.)
"Gotta Getaway"
    A. Reed, L. Devine, T. Azito
    (*Music and Lyrics by* Glenn Roven.)
"I'm Throwing a Ball Tonight" (from *PANAMA HATTIE*)
    L. Montevecchi, A. Reed, L. Devine, T. Azito, The Rockettes, Cruisettes, Stewards
    (*Music and Lyrics by* Cole Porter.)
"Use Your Imagination" (from *OUT OF THIS WORLD*)
    L. Montevecchi
    (*Music and Lyrics by* Cole Porter.)
Scene 2
"Too Marvelous for Words" (from *READY, WILLING AND ABLE* film)
    (*Music by* Richard A. Whiting. *Lyrics by* Johnny Mercer.)
"This Heart of Mine" (from *ZIEGFELD FOLLIES* film)
    A. Reed, J. Clonts, R. Kellett, B. Feehan, M. Hunter, Stewards
    (*Music by* Harry Warren. *Lyrics by* Arthur Freed.)
Scene 3
"Bubble Bubble"
    L. Devine, The Rockettes, Cruisettes
    (*Music by* Gene Palumbo. *Lyrics by* Chip Orton.)
    Mermen: C. Bruton, D. Greene, J. Shape, L. Philips. *Divers:* T. Azito, D. M. Johnson, A. Stuart. *Sea Nymphs:* R. Woolsey, G. Hounsell, S. Cleland, J. Hammond. *Seaweed:* M. McNamara, J. Little, K. Beatty. *Mermaids:* B. Chanin, S. Livingston, P. Tully, L. Sullivan, T. Spano.
Scene 4
"La Cumparsita"
    L. Montevecchi, J. DeGunther
    (*Music by* G. H. Matos Rodriguez. *Original Choreography by* George Reich.)
Scene 5
"Here in Minipoora"
    T. Azito, L. Devine, A. Reed, The Rockettes, Stewards, Cruisettes
    (*Music and Lyrics by* Marc Elliot and Marc Shaiman.)

"Hot VooDoo" (from *BLONDE VENUS* film)
    L. Montevecchi, Full Company
    (*Music by* Sam Coslow. *Lyrics by* Ralph Rainger.)
    Dancing Trees: C. Beatty, P. Stacey, L. Newton.
ACT 2
Scene 1
"Hello Beautiful"
    T. Azito, Folies Showgirls
    (*Music and Lyrics by* Walter Donaldson.)
    Showgirls: B. Daniels, T. Spano, C. Hughes, B. A. Cittadino, K. Pearsall, C. Beatty, P. Tully, L. G. McCarthy, L. Newton, R. Woolsey, S. Cleland, P. G. Demler.
"Le Dernier Pierrot"
    L. Montevecchi
    (*Music by* Pierre Porte. *Lyrics by* Pascal Sevran.)
"Folies Bergeres" (from *NINE*)
    L. Montevecchi, The Rockettes, Stewards
    (*Music and Lyrics by* Maury Yeston.)
"(I'll Build a) Stairway to Paradise" (from *GEORGE WHITE'S SCANDALS OF 1922*)
    L. Montevecchi, T. Azito, The Rockettes, Stewards
    (*Music by* George Gershwin. *Lyrics by* Buddy DeSylva and Ira Gershwin.)
Scene 2
"Higher and Higher"
    The Cruisettes: A. Azarian, E. English, J. Reilly, F. Williams.
    (*Music and Lyrics by* Gary Jackson, Carl Smith, Raynard Miner.)
Scene 3
    The Holidays (Dancers, Acrobats, Animal Trainers)
    R. Holiday, J. Holiday, Cats
Scene 4
"Come to the Supermarket in Old Peking" (from *ALADDIN*, TV Musical)L. Devine
    (*Music and Lyrics by* Cole Porter.)
"Peking Ballet"
    A. Reed, J. Shade, The Stewards, Rockettes
    (*Original Ballet Music by* Eric Watson. *Masks by* Willa Shalit.)
Scene 5
"Once You've Seen a Rainbow"
    A. Reed, L. Devine, L. Montevecchi
    (*Music and Lyrics by* Gene Palumbo and Chip Orton.)
Scene 6
"Manhattan"
    T. Azito, The Stewards
    (*Music and Lyrics by* Marc Elliot and Marc Shaiman.)
"Take Good Care of That Lady"
    L. Devine, A. Reed, L. Montevecchi, T. Azito, Full Company
    (*Music and Lyrics by* Marc Elliot and Marc Shaiman.)

1984.11 ## CANDIDE

A Revival of the Musical in Two Act, 23 Scenes[1]. (New) Book adapted from Voltaire's satire (of the same name) by Hugh Wheeler. (Original book by Lillian Hellman.) Music by Leonard Bernstein. Lyrics by Richard Wilbur. Additional lyrics by Stephen Sondheim and John Latouche. Directed by Harold Prince. Stage directors, Arthur Masella and Albert Sherman. Choreography by Patricia Birch. Scenery designed by Clarke Dunham. Costumes designed by Judith Dolan. Lighting designed by Ken Billington. Conducted by John Mauceri. Orchestrations by Leonard Bernstein and Hershy Kay. Chorus Master, Joseph Colaneri. Produced by the New York City Opera. Opened 18 July 1984 at the New York State Theatre and closed 22 July 1984 after 7 performances.

CAST (in order of appearance): *Voltaire:* JOHN LANKSTON. *Candide:* DAVID EISLER. *Huntsman:* Don Yule. *Paquette:* DEBORAH DARR. *Baroness:* Carol Sparrow. *Baron:* JACK HARROLD. *Cunegonde:* LEIGH MUNRO. *Maximilian:* SCOTT REEVE. *Servant of Maximilian:* JAMES BILLINGS. *Dr. Pangloss:* JOHN

---

[1]Original production first produced in New York 1 December 1956 at the Martin Beck Theatre for 73 performances; revised version first produced Off-Broadway 11 December 1973 at the Chelsea Theater Center, Brooklyn Academy of Music for 48 performances; transferred 5 March 1974 to the Broadway Theatre for 740 performances. For Synopsis of Scenes and Musical Numbers, see 1982 revival.

LANKSTON. *Bulgarian Soldiers:* Don Yule, JAMES BILLINGS. *Westphalian Soldiers:* Scott Evans, William Ledbetter. *Don Isaachar, the Jew:* JAMES BILLINGS. *Grand Inquisitor:* JACK HARROLD. *Calliope Player:* Carol Sparrow. *Heresy Agent:* Ralph Bassett. *Inquisition Agents:* Gary Dietrich, Michael Martorano. *Judge:* JAMES BILLINGS. *Old Lady:* MURIEL COSTA-GREENSPON. *Dons:* Vasilis Iracledes, Scott Evans, Richard Smith, Don Yule, William Ledbetter, Ralph Bassett. *Businessman:* JOHN LANKSTON. *Governor:* JOHN LANKSTON. *Governor's Aide:* Scott Evans. *Slave Driver:* JACK HARROLD. *Father Bernard:* JAMES BILLINGS. *Sailors:* Gary Dietrich, Michael Martorano, Scott Evans, Travis Wright. *Pirates:* John Henry Thomas, William Ledbetter. *Pink Sheep:* Ivy Austin, Susan Delery-Whedon. *Lion:* Robert Brubaker. *Pasha-Prefect:* JACK HARROLD. *First Gambler:* JAMES BILLINGS. *Second Gambler (Police Chief):* JOHN LANKSTON. *Sage:* JOHN LANKSTON.

THE MIKADO,
1984.12   or The Town of Titipu

A Revival of the Comic Opera in Two Acts[2]. Libretto by William S. Gilbert. Music by Arthur Sullivan. Directed by Lofti Mansouri. Choreography by Patricia Birch. Scenery and costumes designed by Thierry Bosquet. Lighting designed by John Gleason. Conducted by David Stahl. Chorus master, Jospeh Colaneri. Produced by the New York City Opera. Opened 6 September 1984 at the New York State Theatre and closed 9 September 1984 after 6 performances in repertory.

CAST (in order of appearance): *Pooh-Bah, Lord High Everything Else:* RICHARD McKEE. *Pish-Tush,* a Noble Lord: Dominic Cossa. *Nanki-Poo,* his son, disguised as a wandering minstrel in love with Yum-Yum: BRUCE REED. *Ko-Ko, Lord High Executioner of Titipu:* JAMES BILLINGS. *Yum-Yum, Pitti-Sing, Peep-Bo,* three sisters, wards of Ko-Ko: ELIZABETH HYNES, CYNTHIA ROSE, LOUISA JONASON. *Katisha:* ELAINE BONAZZI. *The Mikado of Japan:* WILLIAM WILDERMANN. *Chorus of School Girls, Nobles, Guards and Coolies:* New York City Opera Chorus.

SWEENEY TODD-
THE DEMON BARBER
1984.13   OF FLEET STREET

A Revival of the Musical Thriller in Two Acts[3]. Book by Hugh Wheeler. Based on a version of "Sweeney Todd" by Christopher Bond (after the original melodrama by George Dibdin-Pitt). Music and Lyrics by Stephen Sondheim. Directed by Harold Prince. Choreography by Larry Fuller. Scenery designed by Eugene Lee. Costumes designed by Franne Lee. Lighting designed by Ken Billington. (Orchestrations by Jonathan Tunick.) Conductor, Paul Gemignani. Assistant to Mr. Prince, Arthur Masella. Assistant stage directors, Raymond Menard, Albert Sherman. Produced by the New York City Opera. Opened 11 October 1984 at the New York State Theatre and closed 16 November 1984 after 13 performances. in repertory.

CAST (in order of appearance): *Anthony Hope:* CRIS GROENENDAAL. *Sweeney Todd:* TIMOTHY NOLEN. *Beggar Woman:* ADAIR LEWIS. *Mrs. Lovett:* ROSALIND ELIAS. *Judge Turpin:* WILLIAM DANSBY. *The Beadle:* JOHN LANKSTON. *Johanna:* LEIGH MUNRO. *Tobias Ragg:* PAUL BINOTTO. *Pirelli:* JEROLD SIENA. *Jonas Fogg:* William Ledbetter. *Ensemble:* New York City Opera Chorus.

1984.14   ## THE THREE MUSKETEERS

A Revival of the Musical Adventure in Two Acts, 17 Scenes[4]. (Original) Book by William Anthony McGuire. New version by Mark Bramble. Based on the novel of the same name by Alexandre Dumas. Music by Rudolf Friml. Lyrics by P. G. Wodehouse and Clifford Grey. Directed by Joe Layton. Choreography by Lester Wilson. Fights by Steve Dunnington. Scenery designed by Nancy Winters. Costumes designed by Freddy Wittop.

Lighting designed by Ken Billington. Sound designed by Jan Nebozenko. Music adapted, arranged and supervised by Kirk Nurock. Conductor, Gordon Lowry Harrell. Orchestrations by Larry Wilcox. Vocal and fight arrangements by Kirk Nurock. Dance arrangements by Wally Harper, Mark Hummel. Produced by Irvin Feld, Kenneth Feld, Ina Lea Meibach, Jerome Minskoff. Opened 11 November 1984 at the Broadway Theatre and closed 18 November 1984 after 9 performances.

CAST (in order of appearance): *Queen Anne of France:* Darlene Anders. *Lady Constance Bonacieux:* LIZ CALLAWAY. *Cardinal Richelieu:* ED DIXON. *Sergeant Jussac:* Raymond Patterson. *Innkeeper:* J. P. Dougherty. *The Duke of Buckingham:* Joseph Kolinski. *The Compte de la Rochefort:* Michael Dantuono. *Milady de Winter:* MARIANNE TATUM. *D'Artagnan:* MICHAEL PRAED. *Athos:* CHUCK WAGNER. *Aramis:* BRENT SPINER. *Porthos:* RON TAYLOR. *Selenus:* J. P. Dougherty. *Laundress:* Susan Goodman. *de Beauvarais:* Steve Dunnington. *Captain Treville:* Peter Samuel. *King Louis XIII:* Roy Brocksmith. *Tavern Wench:* Susan Goodman. *Chambermaid:* Elisa Fiorillo. *Patrick:* Perry Arthur. *Major Domo:* J. P. Dougherty.

Cardinal's Guards: Bill Badolato, Steve Dunnington, Craig Heath Nim, Steve Marder, Mark McGrath, Sal Viviano, Faruma Williams. *Citizens of Poissy, Paris, Calais, The King's Musketeers, and Characters Too Numerous to Mention:* Janet Aldrich, Perry Arthur, Bill Badolato, Tina Belis, Steven Blanchard, Steve Dunnington, Elisa Fiorillo, Terri Garcia, Susan Goodman, Patty Holley, Jeff Johnson, Steve Marder, Mark McGrath, Craig Heath Nim, Susan Postel, Wynonna Smith, Sal Viviano, Faruma Williams, Sandra Zigars. *Swings:* De Dwight Baxter, Kirsti Carnahan, Craig Frawley, Jacqueline Smith-Lee.

The action takes place in 1626 in France and England.

Act 1, Scene 1: France. April, 1626. *Scene 2:* Poissy, A Market Town outside Paris. *Scene 3:* Paris, the Night of All Fool's Eve. *Scene 4:* Garden of the Convent of Carmier. *Scene 5:* Streets of Paris. *Scene 6:* The Laundry at Number 7 Rue de Colombier. *Scene 7:* The Cardinal's Chamber in the Louvre. *Scene 8:* Gardens of the Tuileries. *Scene 9:* Palace Corridor into the Great Hall. *Scene 10:* On the Road to Calais.

Act 2, Scene 1: The Golden Lily Tavern, Calais. *Scene 2:* Streets of Calais and the Ship to England. *Scene 3:* The Duke of Buckingham's Castle in England. *Scene 4:* Milady's Bedroom at the Golden Lily Tavern, Calais. *Scene 5:* The Road to Paris. *Scene 6:* All over Paris. *Scene 7:* The Hotel de Ville.

ACT 1
Scene 1
  Prologue
    C. Wagner, B. Spiner, R. Taylor, R. Brocksmith, P. Samuel, D. Anders, L. Callaway, R. Patterson, J. P. Dougherty, J. Kolinski, M. Dantuono, M. Tatum, M. Praed
Scene 2
  "Gascony Bred"
    M. Praed, J. P. Dougherty, All
  "All for One"
    C. Wagner, B. Spiner, R. Taylor
  "Only a Rose"
    M. Praed, L. Callaway
  "My Sword and I"
    M. Praed, All
Scene 3
  Carnival of Fools
    Full Company
Scene 4
  "L'Amour Toujours L'Amour"
    J. Kolinski, D. Anders
Scene 5
  "Come to Us"
    M. Tatum, R. Patterson
Scene 6
  "March of the Musketeers"
    C. Wagner, B. Spiner, R. Taylor, M. Praed, All
Scene 7
  "Bless My Soul"
    E. Dixon, M. Tatum, M. Dantuono
Scene 8
  "Only a Rose" (reprise)
    L. Callaway, M. Praed, All
Scene 10
  Act 1 Finale
    M. Praed, C. Wagner, B. Spiner, R. Taylor, Full Company
ACT 2
Scene 1
  "Vive la France"
    R. Brocksmith, Company
  "The Actor's Life"
    C. Wagner, B. Spiner, R. Taylor, M. Praed

---

[2]First presented in New York 20 July, 10-29 August 1885 at the Union Square and People's Theatres for 22 performances. First authorized production presented 19 August 1885 at the Fifth Avenue Theatre by Richard D'Oyly Carte for 250 performances. For Synopsis of Scenes and Musical Numbers, see 19 August 1885 D'Oyly Carte production.

[3]Originally produced in New York 1 March 1979 at the Uris Theatre for 557 performances. For Synopsis of Scenes and Musical Numbers, see original 1979 production.
Restored for this production:
  "Johanna" (Act 1, after "The Contest")
    W. Dansby

[4]Originally produced in New York 13 March 1928 at the Lyric Theatre for 318 performances.

"My Belle"
 M. Praed, L. Callaway
Scene 2
 "The Chase"
 Full Company
 "My Belle" (reprise)
 M. Praed, C. Wagner, B. Spiner, R. Taylor
Scene 3
 "Dreams"
 J. Kolinski
Scene 4
 "L'Amour Toujours L'Amour" (reprise)
 M. Tatum
Scene 5
 "All for One" (reprise)
 C. Wagner, B. Spiner, R. Taylor, M. Praed
Scene 6
 "Gossip"
 C. Wagner, B. Spiner, R. Taylor, M. Praed, M. Tatum, R. Patterson, E. Dixon,
 L. Callaway, P. Samuel, R. Brocksmith, D. Anders, Full Company
Scene 7
 Finale
 Full Company

1984.15 HAARLEM NOCTURNE

A Musical (Revue) in One Act[5]. Conceived by André de Shields. Written and directed by André DeShields, Murray Horwitz. Musical direction, orchestrations, vocal arrangements by Marc Shaiman. Scenic design by David Chapman. Costume design by Jean-Claude Robin. Lighting design by Marc B. Weiss. Sound design by Bill Dreisbach. Associate producer, Alecia Parker. Produced by Barry and Fran Weissler by special arrangement with Black Goat Entertainment. Opened 18 November 1984 at the Latin Quarter and closed 30 December 1984 after 49 performances.

CAST: ANDRÉ DeSHIELDS, DEBRA BYRD, ELLIA ENGLISH, MARC SHAIMAN, FREIDA WILLIAMS.

MUSICAL NUMBERS
 "Love in the Morning"
 A. DeShields, Ladies
 (*Music and Lyrics by* Steven Lemberg.)
 "Wishful Thinking"
 A. DeShields, Ladies
 (*Music and Lyrics by* Kenny Moore, Martri McCall and Zedrick Turnbough.)
 "New York Is a Party"
 A. DeShields, Ladies
 (*Music by* Marc Shaiman. *Lyrics by* Robert I.)
 "Jungle Hip Hop"
 A. DeShields, Ladies
 (*Music and Lyrics by* André DeShields.)
 "Sweet Dreams Are Made of This"
 The Ladies
 (*Music by* Annie Lennox. *Lyrics by* D. A. Stewart.)
 "What Becomes of the Broken-Hearted"
 A. DeShields, Ladies
 (*Music and Lyrics by* W. Witherspoon, P. Riser, J. Dean.)
 "Love's Sad Glance"
 The Ladies
 (*Music by* Marc Shaiman. *Lyrics by* Ula Hedwig.)
 "Secret Love"
 D. Byrd, The Ladies
 (*Music by* Kenny Moore. *Lyrics by* Alex Brown.)
 "Say It Again"
 F. Williams, Ladies
 (*Music and Lyrics by* Dennis Andreopolous.)
 "Heads or Tails"
 A. DeShields, Ladies
 (*Music and Lyrics by* Dennis Andreopolous.)
 "Hit the Road Jack"
 E. English, A. DeShields, Ladies
 (*Music and Lyrics by* Percy Mayfield.)

"Waterfaucet Blues"
 E. English
 (Traditional blues; *Music and Lyrics adapted by* Micki Grant.)
"Streetcorner Symphony"
 A. DeShields, Ladies
 ("The Way We Were," *Music by* Marvin Hamlisch. Lyrics by Marilyn and Alan Bergman. "Release Yourself" *Lyrics by* Larry Graham.)
"Bad Boy"
 A. DeShields, Ladies
 (*Music and Lyrics by* Lil Armstrong.)
"Symphony Rap"
 A. DeShields, Ladies
 (*Music and Lyrics by* André DeShields.)
"Mary Mack"
 A. DeShields, F. Williams, Ladies
 (traditional children's song)
Pastiche
 The Ladies
 ("Locomotion" by Carole King, Gerry Goffin; "My Boyfriend's Back" by Bob Feldman, Gerald Goldstein, Richard Gottehrer; "Chapel of Love" by Jeff Barry, Ellie Greenwich, Phil Spector; "Soldier Boy" by Florence Green, Luther Dixon; "Come and Get These Memories" by Eddie Holland, Lamont Dozier, Brian Holland; "Da Doo Run Run" by Jeff Barry, Ellie Greenwich, Phil Spector; "Wishing and Hoping" by Burt Bacharach, Hal David; "He's So Fine" by Ronald Mack; "My Sweet Lord" by George Harrison; "Please Mr. Postman" by Brian Holland, Robert Bateman, Freddie Gorman; "Tell Him" by Burt Russell; "Baby Love" by Eddie Holland, Brian Holland, Lamont Dozier; "And Then He Kissed Me" by Jeff Barry, Ellie Greenwich, Phil Spector; "Leader of the Pack" by Jeff Barry, Ellie Greenwich, Phil Spector; "The Shoop Shoop Song" by Rudy Clark; "He's Sure the Boy I Love" by Cynthia Weil, Barry Mann; "My Boyfriend's Back"; I Can Never Go Home Anymore" by George Morton; "He's a Rebel" by Gene Pitney; "The Girl I'm Gonna Marry" by Ellie Greenwich, Tony Powers, Phil Spector; "Not Too Young to Get Married" by Jeff Barry, Ellie Greenwich, Phil Spector, Thomas Elliott; "Memories" by Andrew Lloyd Webber, Trevor Nunn.)
"Lush Life"
 A. DeShields
 (*Music and Lyrics by* Billy Strayhorn.)
"Haarlem Nocturne"
 The Ladies
 (*Music by* Earle Hagen. *Lyrics by* Dick Rogers.)
"B.Y.O.B."
 A. DeShields, Ladies
 (*Music and Lyrics by* André DeShields.)
"Now Is the Time"
 A. DeShields, Ladies
 (*Music and Lyrics by* André DeShields.)

1984.16 DOUG HENNING AND HIS WORLD OF MAGIC

A Magic Revue in Two Acts. Conceived and directed by Doug Henning. Staged and choreographed by Charlene Painter. Music composed and directed by Peter Matz. Costumes by Jeff Billings; Additional costumes by Bill Hargate. Set by Bill Bohnert. Lighting design by Michael McGiveney. Music designer and coordinator, Jim Steinmeyer. Head illusion engineer and additional illusions, William Kennedy. Illusions design and construction, John Gaughan. Magical consultant, Charles Reynolds. Animal trainer, Rick Glassey. Produced by James M. Nederlander and Arthur Rubin. Opened 11 December 1984 at the Lunt-Fontanne Theatre and closed 27 January 1985 after 60 performances.

CAST: DOUG HENNING, DEBBY HENNING, Victor Heineman, D. J. Mergenthaler, Gina Rose, Kathleen White.

The production includes illusions and magic that Doug Henning has performed in the theatre (The Magic Show, Merlin) and on television during the past ten years, such as 'The Tunnel of Awe' and 'The Miracle Levitation Vanish.' Others include conjuring a 450-pound tiger and a Burmese panther, and sleight-of-hand magic visible to the audience on giant television screens. Mr. Henning saws two women in half, transports himself from inside a sack to the inside of a stuffed animal.

1985.01 THE KING AND I

A Revival of the Musical Play in Two Acts, 17 Scenes[6]. Book and lyrics by Oscar Hammerstein II. Music by Richard Rodgers. Based on the novel

---

[5]Originally produced Off-Broadway 19 January 1984 at B.Y.O.B. Cabaret Downstairs at La Mama.

[6]Originally produced in New York 29 March 1951 at the St. James Theatre for 1246 performances. For Synopsis of Scenes and Musical Numbers, see original 1951 production. Yul Brynner also appeared in a revival of *THE KING AND I* 2 May 1977 at the Uris Theatre for 719 performances.

"Anna and the King of Siam" by Margaret Landon. Original choreography by Jerome Robbins; choreography reproduced by Rebecca West. Directed by Mitch Leigh. Settings designed by Peter Wolf. Costumes by Stanley Simmons, based on the original costumes designed by Irene Sharaff. Lighting designed by Ruth Roberts. (Orchestrations uncredited.) Production supervisor, Conwell Worthington II. Musical director, Richard Parrinello. Sound designed by Scott Marcellus. Associate producer, Manny Kladitis. Executive producer, Milton Hershon. Produced by the Mitch Leigh Company. Opened 7 January 1985 at the Broadway Theatre and closed 30 June 1985 after 191 performances.

CAST (in order of appearance): *Louis Leonowens:* Jeffrey Bryan Davis. *Captain Orton:* Burt Edwards. *Anna Leonowens:* MARY BETH PEIL. *The Interpreter:* Jae Woo Lee. *The Kralahome:* JONATHAN FARWELL. *The King:* YUL BRYNNER. *Lead Royal Dancer:* Kathy Lee Brynner. *Lun Tha:* Sal Provenza. *Tuptim:* PATRICIA WELCH. *Lady Thiang:* IRMA-ESTEL LaGUERRE. *Prince Chulalongkorn:* Araby Abaya. *Princess Ying Yaowalak:* Yvette Laura Martin. *Fan Dancer:* Patricia Weber. *Sir Edward Ramsay:* Edward Crotty.

The Small House of Uncle Thomas (ballet): Uncle Thomas: Hope Sogawa. *Little Eva:* Evelina Deocares. *Topsy:* Deborah Harada. *Eliza:* Kathy Lee Brynner. *King Simon:* Rebecca West. *Angel:* Patricia Weber.

The Royal Dancers and Wives: Marla F. Bingham, Young-Hee Cho, Carolyn DeLany, Evelina Deocares, Deborah Harada, Valerie Lau-Kee, Suzen Murakoshi, Hope Sogawa, Sylvia Yamada. *Princesses and Princes:* Max Barabas, Michael Bulos, Amy Chin, Lisa Chui, Mark Damrongsri, Kate Gwon, Tracie Mon-Ting Lee, Michelle Nigalan, Steven Tom, Luke Trainer, Annie Woo. *Nurses and Amazons:* Alis-Elaine Anderson, Joyce Campana, Mariann Cook, Janet Jordan. *Priests and Slaves:* Cornel Chan, Kaipo Daniels, Gary Bain Domasin, Stanley Earl Harrison, Thomas Heath, Andre Lengyel, Ron Stefan.

1985.02   # HARRIGAN 'N HART

A Musical in Two Acts, 16 Scenes. Book by Michael Stewart. Based on material compiled by Nedda Harrigan Logan and "The Merry Partners" by E. J. Kahn, Jr. (New) Music by Max Showalter. (New) Lyrics by Peter Walker. Songs of the Period by Edward Harrigan (Lyrics) and David Braham (Music). Entire production directed by Joe Layton. Choreographed by D. J. Giagni. Scenic design by David Mitchell. Costume design by Ann-Hould Ward. Lighting design by Richard Nelson. Music supervision, orchestrations and arrangements by John McKinney. Musical director, Peter Howard. Sound design by Otts Munderloh. Originally produced by the Goodspeed Opera House (Michael P. Price, Executive director). Produced by Elliott Martin, Arnold Bernhard and The Shubert Organization. Opened 31 January 1985 at the Longacre Theatre and closed 3 February 1985 after 5 performances.

CAST (in order of appearance): *Stetson:* Mark Fotopoulos. *Edward Harrigan:* HARRY GROENER. *Tony Hart:* MARK HAMILL. *Archie White:* Clent Bowers. *Old Colonel:* Cleve Asbury. *The Colonel's Wife:* Barbara Moroz. *Eleanor:* Roxie Lucas. *Andrew LeCouvrier:* Mark Fotopoulos. *Martin Hanley:* Oliver Woodall. *Sam Nichols:* Clent Bowers. *Alfred J. Dugan:* Christopher Wells. *Felix Barker:* Clent Bowers. *Judge:* Mark Fotopoulos. *Annie Braham Harrigan:* Tudi Roche. *Johnny Wild:* Mark Fotopoulos. *Billy Gross:* Cleve Asbury. *Chester Fox:* Kenston Ames. *Lily Fay:* Merilee Magnuson. *Elsie Fay:* Barbara Moroz. *Ada Lewis:* Roxie Lucas. *Mrs. Annie Yeamons:* ARMELIA McQUEEN. *Jennie Yeamons:* Amelia Marshall. *Harry Mack:* Christopher Wells. *Photographer:* Kenston Ames. *Judge Hilton:* Christopher Wells. *Nat Goodwin:* Cleve Asbury. *Captain:* Mark Fotopoulos. *Newsboy:* Kenston Ames. *Newsgirl:* Amelia Marshall. *Belle:* Barbara Moroz. *Gerta Granville:* CHRISTINE EBERSOLE. *Adelaide Harrigan:* Merilee Magnuson. *Uncle Albert:* Clent Bowers. *Newspaperman:* Kenston Ames. *William Gill:* Mark Fotopoulos. *Doctor:* Christopher Wells. *Nurse:* Merilee Magnuson. *Swings:* Michael Gorman, Alison Mann.

The action takes place from 1871 to 1888.

Act 1, Scene 1: Stetson's American Music Hall, Galesburg, Illinois, 1871. *Scene 2*: New York City. *Scene 3*: The Theatre Comique. *Scene 4*: U. S. Courthouse, Worcester, Massachusetts. *Scene 5*: The Theatre Comique. *Scene 6*: The Theatre Comique. *Scene 7*: Outside the New Theatre Comique, Opening Night. *Scene 8*: Old Nieuw Amsterdam. *Scene 9*: A Restaurant, later that evening. *Scene 10*: The New Theatre Comique.

Act 2, Scene 1: New York City and the Park Theatre. *Scene 2*: Harrigan's Tour, 1880 to 1886. *Scene 3*: Backstage, Wallack's Theatre. *Scene 4*: New York City. *Scene 5*: New York Hospital. *Scene 6*: The Park Theatre, 22 March 1888

ACT 1
Scene 1
"Put Me in My Little Bed"
M. Hamill
"Wonderful Me"
H. Groener, M. Hamill
Scene 3
"Mulligan Guard"
H. Groener, M. Hamill
(*Music by* David Braham. *Lyrics by* Edward Harrigan.)

Scene 4
"Put Me in My Little Bed" (reprise)
M. Hamill
Scene 5
"I Love to Follow a Band"
H. Groener, Company
(*Music by* David Braham. *Lyrics by* Edward Harrigan.)
"Such an Education Has My Mary Ann"
H. Groener, M. Hamill, Company
(*Music by* David Braham. *Lyrics by* Edward Harrigan.)
"Maggie Murphy's Home"
T. Roche, H. Groener, C. Bowers, Company
(*Music by* David Braham. *Lyrics by* Edward Harrigan.)
"McNally's Row of Flats"
A. McQueen, Company
(*Music by* David Braham. *Lyrics by* Edward Harrigan.)
"Something New, Something Different"
H. Groener, M. Hamill, Company
Scene 6
"That's My Partner"
H. Groener, M. Hamill
Scene 8
"She's Our Gretel"
H. Groener, M. Hamill, A. McQueen, Company
(*Music by* David Braham. *Lyrics by* Edward Harrigan.)
Scene 9
"What You Need Is a Woman"
C. Ebersole
Scene 10
"Knights of the Mystic Star"
A. McQueen, Company
(*Music by* David Braham. *Lyrics by* Edward Harrigan.)
"Girl of the Mystic Star"
C. Ebersole, Men
(*Music by* David Braham. *Lyrics by* Edward Harrigan.)
"Mulligan Guard" (reprise)
H. Groener, M. Hamill

ACT 2
Scene 1
"Skidmore Fancy Ball"
C. Bowers, C. Wells, M. Fotopoulos, C. Asbury
(*Music by* David Braham. *Lyrics by* Edward Harrigan.)
"Sweetest Love"
R. Lucas, B. Moroz
(*Music by* David Braham. *Lyrics by* Edward Harrigan.)
"The Old Barn Floor"
M. Fotopoulos, A. Marshall, K. Ames, M. Magnuson
"Silly Boy"
C. Ebersole, C. Asbury, C. Wells
(*Music by* David Braham. *Lyrics by* Edward Harrigan.)
"Mulligan Guard" (reprise)
H. Groener, M. Hamill, Company
"We'll Be There"
H. Groener, M. Hamill, Company
Scene 2
"Ada with the Golden Hair"
T. Roche, M. Fotopoulos, C. Asbury
(*Music by* David Braham. *Lyrics by* Edward Harrigan.)
"That Old Featherbed"
C. Wells, M. Magnuson, B. Moroz
(*Music by* David Braham. *Lyrics by* Edward Harrigan.)
"Sam Johnson's Colored Cakewalk"
C. Bowers, A. Marshall
(*Music by* David Braham. *Lyrics by* Edward Harrigan.)
"Dip Me in the Golden Sea"
H. Groener, A. McQueen, Company
(*Music by* David Braham. *Lyrics by* Edward Harrigan.)
"That's My Partner" (reprise)
H. Groener
Scene 3
"I've Come Home to Stay"
M. Hamill
(*Music by* David Braham. *Lyrics by* Edward Harrigan.)

"If I Could Trust Me"
M. Hamill
Scene 4
"Maggie Murphy's Home" (reprise)
O. Woodall, M. Magnuson, A. McQueen, R. Lucas
"I've Come Home to Stay" (reprise)
M. Hamill, Girls
Scene 5
"I Need This One Chance"
C. Ebersole
Scene 6
"I Love to Follow a Band" (reprise)
T. Roche, Company
"Mulligan Guard" (reprise)
H. Groener, M. Hamill, A. McQueen
"Something New, Something Different" (reprise)
H. Groener, M. Hamill, Company

1985.03   LEADER OF THE PACK

A Musical (Revue) in One Act[7]. Music and lyrics by Ellie Greenwich and Friends. Liner notes (Book) by Anne Beatts. Additional material by Jack Heifner. Based on the original play by Melanie Mintz. Directed and choreographed by Michael Peters. Settings designed by Tony Walton. Costumes designed by Robert de Mora. Lighting designed by Pamela Cooper. Musical director and musical adapter, Jimmy Vivino. Vocal arrangements by Marc Shaiman. Dance arrangements by Timothy Graphenreed. Sound designed by Abe Jacob. Produced by The Pack (Elizabeth I. McCann, Nelle Nugent, Francine LeFrak, Clive Davis, John Hart Associates, Inc., Rodger Hess, Richard Kagan). Opened 8 April 1985 at the Ambassador Theater and closed 21 July 1985 after 120 performances.

CAST (in order of appearance): *Darlene Love:* DARLENE LOVE. *Annie Golden:* ANNIE GOLDEN. *Young Ellie Greenwich (1960's):* DINAH MANOFF. *Rosie,* Ellie's Mother: Zora Rasmussen. *Shelley:* Barbara Yeager. *Mickey:* Jasmine Guy. *Jeff Barry:* PATRICK CASSIDY. *Gus Sharkey:* DENNIS BAILEY. *D. J. Voice:* Peter Neptune. *Waitress:* Jasmine Guy. *Lounge Singer:* Pattie Darcy. *Dance Couple:* Shirley Black-Brown, Keith McDaniel. *Gina:* Gina Taylor. *Ellie Greenwich (1980's):* ELLIE GREENWICH.
Girls and Guys: Shirley Black-Brown, Pattie Darcy, Christopher Gregory, Jasmine Guy, Danny Herman, Lon Hoyt, Keith McDaniel, Jodi Moccia, Peter Neptune, Zora Rasmussen, Joey Sheck, Gina Taylor, Barbara Yeager.

The action takes place here and now . . . and in the days of beehives and 45s.

MUSICAL NUMBERS
"Be My Baby"
A. Golden, Girls
(*Music and Lyrics by* Ellie Greenwich, Jeff Barry, Phil Spector.)
"Wait 'Til My Bobby Gets Home"
D. Love, Company
(*Music and Lyrics by* Ellie Greenwich, Jeff Barry, Phil Spector.)
"A . . . . My Name Is Ellie"
D. Manoff
(*Music and Lyrics by* Ellie Greenwich.)
"Jivette Boogie Beat"
D. Manoff, B. Yeager, J. Guy
(*Music and Lyrics by* Ellie Greenwich.)
"Why Do Lovers Break Each Others Hearts"
D. Love, Company
(*Music and Lyrics by* Ellie Greenwich, Tony Powers, Phil Spector.)
"Today I Met the Boy I'm Gonna Marry"
D. Love, Company
(*Music and Lyrics by* Ellie Greenwich, Tony Powers, Phil Spector.)
"I Wanna Love Him So Bad"
D. Manoff, Girls
(*Music and Lyrics by* Ellie Greenwich, Jeff Barry, Phil Spector.)
"Do Wah Diddy"
P. Cassidy, Guys
(*Music and Lyrics by* Ellie Greenwich, Jeff Barry.)
"And Then He Kissed Me"
D. Manoff, Girls
(*Music and Lyrics by* Ellie Greenwich, Jeff Barry, Phil Spector.)

"Hanky Panky"
P. Cassidy, Guys
(*Music and Lyrics by* Ellie Greenwich, Jeff Barry.)
"Not Too Young (to Get Married)"
D. Love, Girls
(*Music and Lyrics by* Ellie Greenwich, Jeff Barry, Phil Spector.)
"Chapel of Love"
Entire Company
(*Music and Lyrics by* Ellie Greenwich, Jeff Barry, Phil Spector.)
"Baby I Love You"
A. Golden, Girls
(*Music and Lyrics by* Ellie Greenwich, Jeff Barry, Phil Spector.)
"Leader of the Pack"
A. Golden, Company
(*Music and Lyrics by* Ellie Greenwich, Jeff Barry, George "Shadow" Morton.)
"Look of Love"
P. Darcy
(*Music and Lyrics by* Ellie Greenwich, Jeff Barry.)
"Christmas—Baby Please Come Home"
D. Love, Girls
(*Music and Lyrics by* Ellie Greenwich, Jeff Barry, Phil Spector.)
"I Can Hear Music"
A. Golden, P. Darcy, K. McDaniel, L. Hoyt
(*Music and Lyrics by* Ellie Greenwich, Jeff Barry, Phil Spector.)
"Rock of Rages"
D. Manoff
(*Music and Lyrics by* Ellie Greenwich, Jeff Kent.)
"Keep It Confidential"
G. Taylor, Company
(*Music and Lyrics by* Ellie Greenwich, Jeff Kent, Ellen Foley.)
"Da Doo Ron Ron"
E. Greenwich, Guys
(*Music and Lyrics by* Ellie Greenwich, Jeff Barry, Phil Spector.)
"What a Guy"
E. Greenwich, Company
(*Music and Lyrics by* Ellie Greenwich, Jeff Barry, Phil Spector.)
"Maybe I Know"
E. Greenwich, Girls
(*Music and Lyrics by* Ellie Greenwich, Jeff Barry.)
"River Deep, Mountain High"
D. Love, Company
(*Music and Lyrics by* Ellie Greenwich, Jeff Barry, Phil Spector.)
"We're Gonna Make It (After All)"
E. Greenwich, D. Love, A. Golden, Company
(*Music and Lyrics by* Ellie Greenwich.)

1985.04   TAKE ME ALONG

A Revival of the Musical in Two Acts, 15 Scenes[8]. Book (revised) by Joseph Stein and Robert Russell. Based on the play "Ah, Wilderness!" by Eugene O'Neill. Music and lyrics by Bob Merrill. Directed by Thomas Gruenewald. Choreography and musical staging by Dan Siretta. Scenery by James Leonard Joy. Costumes by David Toser. Lighting by Craig Miller. Musical direction by Lynn Crigler. Dance arrangements by Allen Cohen. Orchestrations by Philip J. Lang. Additional orchestrations by Lynn Crigler, Allen Cohen. Sound by Jan Nebozenko. A Goodspeed Opera House Production (Michael P. Price, Executive director). Produced by the John F. Kennedy Center. Opened and closed 14 April 1985 at the Martin Beck Theatre after 1 performance.

CAST (in order of appearance): *Nat Miller,* Editor of the Centerville Globe: ROBERT NICHOLS. *Essie Miller,* Nat's wife: BETTY JOHNSON. *Arthur Miller,* Richard's older brother, at Yale: STEPHEN McDONOUGH. *Mildred Miller,* the youngest Miller: ALYSON KIRK. *Lily Miller,* Nat's sister: BETH FOWLER. *Muriel Macomber,* Macomber's daughter and friend to Richard: TARYN GRIMES. *Richard Miller,* Nat's younger son: GARY LANDON WRIGHT. *David Macomber,* dry goods store owner: Richard Korthaze. *Sid Davis,* Essie's brother: KURT KNUDSON. *Belle,* a travelling artiste for hire: NIKKI SAHAGEN. *Wint,* Arthur's friend: Joel Whittaker. *Bartender:* David Vosburgh. *The Salesman:* John Witham.
Trolley Conductors, Firemen, Townsfolk, Bar Patrons, Ladies of the Evening: Kathy Andrini, Blake Atherton, Michael Kelly Boone, Ed Brazo, Richard Dodd, Andy Hostettler, Richard Korthaze, Patrick S. Murphy, Mercedes Perez, Keith Savage, David Vosburgh, Joel Whittaker, Betty Winsett, John Witham.

The action takes place in Centerville, Connecticut, in 1906.

---
[7]Originally produced Off-Broadway 17 January 1984 at the Bottom Line.

[8]Originally produced in New York 22 October 1959 at the Sam S. Shubert Theatre for 448 performances. Dropped for this production were: "For Sweet Charity," "The Beardsley Ballet" and "Pleasant Beach House" (Wint's Song).

Act 1, Scene 1: The Miller Home. *Scene 2*: The Macomber Yard. *Scene 3*: The Centerville Car Barn. *Scene 4*: The Miller Home. *Scene 5*: The Picnic Grounds. *Scene 6*: The Miller Home. *Scene 7*: The Miller Home.

Act 2, Scene 1: The Pleasant Beach House. *Scene 2*: The Miller Home. *Scene 3*: The Miller Home. *Scene 4*: Richard's Bedroom. *Scene 5*: The Dock. *Scene 6*: The Miller Home. *Scene 7*: The Miller Home. *Scene 8*: The Centerville Car Barn.

ACT 1
Scene 1
   "Marvelous Fire Machine" (The Parade)
      R. Nichols, Ensemble
   "Oh, Please"
      B. Johnson, R. Nichols
   "Oh, Please" (reprise)
      B. Johnson, R. Nichols, B. Fowler, S. McDonough, A. Kirk
Scene 2
   "I Would Die"
      G. L. Wright, T. Grimes
Scene 3
   "Sid, Ole Kid"
      K. Knudson, N. Sahagen, Townspeople
Scene 4
   "Staying Young"
      R. Nichols
   "I Get Embarrassed"
      K. Knudson, B. Fowler
   "We're Home"
      B. Fowler
   "Take Me Along"
      K. Knudson, R. Nichols
Scene 5
   "Take Me Along" (reprise)
      Company
   "The Only Pair I've Got"[9]
      N. Sahagen, Ensemble
   "In the Company of Men"[10]
      K. Knudson, R. Nichols, Male Ensemble
Scene 6
   "Knights on White Horses"[11]
      B. Fowler, B. Johnson
Scene 7
   "That's How It Starts"
      G. L. Wright

ACT 2
Scene 1
   "If Jesus Don't Love Ya"[12]
      G. L. Wright, N. Sahagen, Ensemble
Scene 2
   "Oh, Please" (reprise)
      R. Nichols, B. Johnson
Scene 3
   "Promise Me a Rose" (A Slight Detail)
      B. Fowler,
   "Staying Young" (reprise)
      R. Nichols
Scene 4
   "Little Green Snake"
      K. Knudson
Scene 5
   "Nine O'Clock"
      G. L. Wright
   "Nine O'Clock" (reprise)
      G. L. Wright, T. Grimes
Scene 6
   "But Yours"
      K. Knudson, B. Fowler

---

[9]Newly written for this production.
[10]Newly written for this production.
[11]Newly written for this production.
[12]Newly written for this production.

Scene 8
  Finale
      B. Fowler, K. Knudson

1985.05

GRIND

A Musical in Two Acts, a Prologue and 23 Scenes. Book by Fay Kanin. Music by Larry Grossman. Lyrics by Ellen Fitzhugh. Directed by Harold Prince. Choreographed by Lester Wilson. Scenery designed by Clarke Dunham. Costumes designed by Florence Klotz. Lighting designed by Ken Billington. Musical director, Paul Gemignani. Orchestrations by Bill Byers. Additional orchestrations by Jim Tyler, Harold Wheeler. Dance music arrangements by Tom Fay. Sound by Otts Munderloh. Assistant choreographer, Larry Vickers. Executive producers, Ruth Mitchell and Sam Crothers. Produced by Kenneth D. Greenblatt, John J. Pomerantz, Mary Lea Johnson, Martin Richards, James M. Nederlander, Harold Prince, Michael Frazier in association with Susan Madden Samson and Jonathan Farkas. Opened 16 April 1985 at the Mark Hellinger Theatre and closed 22 June 1985 after 79 performances.

CAST (in order of appearance): *Leroy*: BEN VEREEN. *Harry*: LEE WALLACE. *Gus*: STUBBY KAYE. *Solly*: JOEY FAYE. *Vernelle*: Marion Ramsey. *(Earle's Pearls, 4)*: *Ruby*: Hope Clarke. *Fleta*: Valarie Pettiford. *Kitty*: Candy Brown. *Linette*: Wynonna Smith. *Maybelle*: Carol Woods. *Mechanical Man*: Jackie Jay Patterson. *Knockabouts*: Leonard John Crofoot, Ray Roderick, Kelly Walters, Steve Owsley, Malcolm Perry. *Romaine*: Sharon Murray. *Satin*: LEILANI JONES. *Louis, the Stage Manager*: Brian McKay. *Mike, the Doorman*: Oscar Stokes. *Stooge*: Leonard John Crofoot. *Doyle*: TIMOTHY NOLEN. *Grover*: Donald Acree. *Mrs. Faye*: Ruth Brisbane. *Toughs*: Leonard John Crofoot, Ray Roderick, Kelly Walters, Steve Owsley, Malcolm Perry.

The action takes place in and around Harry Earle's Burlesque Theatre in Chicago, Illinois during 1933.

Prologue: Harry Earle's Burlesque Theatre.

Act 1, Scene 1: Backstage. *Scene 2*: Onstage. *Scene 3*: In the Wings. *Scene 4*: Onstage. *Scene 5*: The Alley next to the Theatre. *Scene 6*: Girls' Dressing Room; Backstage. *Scene 7*: The Alley. *Scene 8*: Onstage. *Scene 9*: The Alley. *Scene 10*: Backstage. *Scene 11*: Mrs. Fay's Kitchen. *Scene 12*: On the Street.

Act 2, Scene 1: Backstage. *Scene 2*: Onstage. *Scene 3*: Stage Right Wing. *Scene 4*: Onstage. *Scene 5*: Backstage. *Scene 6*: Backstage. *Scene 7*: The Alley. *Scene 8*: Satin's Room. *Scene 9*: Onstage. *Scene 10*: Backstage. *Scene 11*: Onstage.

ACT 1
  Prologue
    "This Must Be the Place"
      Company
Scene 2
   "Cadava"
      J. Faye, S. Kaye, S. Murray
Scene 4
   "A Sweet Thing Like Me"
      L. Jones, Earle's Pearls
Scene 5
   "I Get Myself Out"
      S. Kaye
Scene 6
   "My Daddy Always Taught Me to Share"
      B. Vereen
Scene 7
   "All Things to One Man"
      L. Jones
Scene 8
   "The Line"
      B. Vereen, Earle's Pearls
Scene 9
   "Katie My Love"
      T. Nolen
Scene 10
   "The Grind"
      S. Kaye, Company
   "Yes, Ma'am"
      T. Nolen
Scene 11
   "Why, Mama, Why"
      L. Jones, B. Vereen
Scene 12
   "This Crazy Place"
      B. Vereen, Company

ACT 2

Scene 1

"From the Ankles Down"
B. Vereen, Earle's Pearls

"Who Is He?"
L. Jones

"Never Put It in Writing"
S. Kaye

"I Talk, You Talk"
T. Nolen

Scene 4

"Timing"
S. Murray, J. Faye

Scene 5

"These Eyes of Mine"
C. Woods, Company

Scene 6

"New Man"
B. Vereen
(*Dance Music Arranged by* Gordon Lowry Harrell.)

Scene 8

"Down"
T. Nolen

Scene 9

"A Century of Progress"
B. Vereen, L. Jones, Earle's Pearls

Scene 11

Finale
Company

BIG RIVER:
1985.06 The Adventures of Huckleberry Finn

A Musical in Two Acts, 18 Scenes. Book by William Hauptman. Adapted from the novel "The Adventures of Huckleberry Finn" by Mark Twain. Music and lyrics by Roger Miller. Production staged by Des McAnuff. Scenery by Heidi Landesman. Costumes by Patricia McGourty. Lighting by Richard Riddell. Sound by Otts Munderloh. Musical supervision by Daniel Troob. Orchestrations by Steven Margoshes and Danny Troob. Dance and incidental music by John Richard Lewis. Musical direction and vocal arrangements by Linda Twine. Choreography by Janet Watson. Stage movement and fights by B. H. Barry. Originally produced by The American Repertory Theatre, Cambridge, Massachusetts (Robert Brustein, Artistic director); subsequently produced by The LaJolla Playhouse, LaJolla, California (Des McAnuff, Artistic director). Associate producers, Arthur Katz, Emily Landau, Frederic H. Mayerson, TM Productions, Inc. Produced by Rocco Landesman, Heidi Landesman, Rick Steiner, M. Anthony Fisher and Dodger Productions. Opened 25 April 1985 at the Eugene O'Neill Theatre and closed 20 September 1987 after 1005 performances.

CAST (in order of appearance): *In St. Petersburg, and later on the Illinois shore and Jackson's Island: Mark Twain*: GORDON CONNELL. *Huckleberry Finn*: DANIEL H. JENKINS. *Widow Douglas*: Susan Browning. *Miss Watson*: Evalyn Baron. *Jim*: RON RICHARDSON. *Tom Sawyer*: John Short. *Ben Rogers*: William Youmans. *Jo Harper*: Andi Henig. *Simon*: Aramis Estevez. *Dick*: Michael Brian. *Pap Finn*: John Goodman. *Judge Thatcher*: Ralph Byers. *Woman in Shanty*: Evalyn Baron.
On the River, south of St. Louis: Slaves and Overseers on a Flatboat: Carol Dennis, Elmore James, Jennifer Leigh Warren, Franz Jones, Aramis Estevez, John Goodman, William Youmans, Michael Brian.
On the River, near Cairo, Illinois: Three Men on a Skiff: Ralph Byers, Reathel Bean, Elmore James.
On the Riverbank in Kentucky: The King: BOB GUNTON. *The Duke*: RENE AUBERJONOIS. *Soldiers and Citizens*: The Company.
In Bricktown, Arkansas: Hank: William Youmans. *Andy*: Michael Brian. *Lafe*: Reathel Bean. *Townspeople*: The Company.
In Hillsboro, Arkansas: A Young Fool: William Youmans. *Mary Jane Wilkes*: PATTI COHENOUR. *Susan Wilkes*: Peggy Harmon. *Joanna Wilkes, a hare-lip*: Andi Henig. *Bill, a servant*: Franz Jones. *Counselor Robinson*: Reathel Bean. *Alice, their slave*: Carol Dennis. *Alice's daughter*: Jennifer Leigh Warren. *Mourners*: The Company. *Sheriff Bell*: John Goodman. *Harvey Wilkes*: Ralph Byers. *Man in the Crowd*: Michael Brian. *Harmonia Player*: Evalyn Baron. *Mourners and Mob*: The Company.
On a Farm near Hilsboro: Sally Phelps: Susan Browning. *Silas Phelps*: Ralph Byers. *Doctor*: Gordon Connell. *Hired Hands*: Reathel Bean, Michael Brian, John Goodman.

The action takes place along the Missippi River Valley, sometime in the 1840's.

Act 1, Scene 1: The Widow Douglas' home in St. Petersburg, Missouri. *Scene 2*: A Cave by the River. *Scene 3*: The Widow Douglas' home. *Scene 4*: A Cabin on the Illinois shore. *Scene 5*: The Cabin; Jackson's Island. *Scene 6*: A Cabin on the Missouri shore; a Raft on the River. *Scene 7*: On the Raft in the moonlight, approaching Cairo, Illinois. *Scene 8*: On the Riverbank in Kentucky; on the Raft downriver.

Act 2, Scene 1: On the Raft in Tennessee. *Scene 2*: In Bricktown, Arkansas. *Scene 3*: On the Raft in a nearby cove. *Scene 4*: In Hillsboro, Arkansas; the Wilkes' Farm near Hillsboro. *Scene 5*: Next day at the Farm. *Scene 6*: The Farm; the Cemetery. *Scene 7*: To the Shore and the Raft. *Scene 8*: A Country Road; the Phelps Farm near Hillsboro. *Scene 9*: The Phelps Farm, that night; the Raft. *Scene 10*: The Phelps Farm.

ACT 1

Scene 1

"Do You Want to Go to Heaven"
The Company

Scene 2

"The Boys"
J. Short, the Gang

"Waiting for the Light to Shine"
D. H. Jenkins

Scene 4

"Guv'ment"
J. Goodman

Scene 5

"Hand for the Hog"
J. Short

"I Huckleberry Me"
D. H. Jenkins

Scene 6

"Muddy Water"
R. Richardson, D. H. Jenkins

Scene 7

"Crossing Over"
Slaves, Overseer

"River in the Rain"
D. H. Jenkins, R. Richardson

Scene 8

"When the Sun Goes Down in the South"
R. Auberjonois, B. Gunton, D. H. Jenkins

ACT 2

Scene 2

"The Royal Nonesuch"
R. Auberjonois, Company

Scene 3

"Worlds Apart"
R. Richardson, D. H. Jenkins

Scene 4

"Arkansas"
W. Youmans

"How Blest We Are"
J. L. Warren, Company

"You Ought To Be Here With Me"
P. Cohenour, P. Harmon, A. Henig

Scene 5

"How Blest We Are" (reprise)
C. Dennis

"Leaving's Not the Only Way to Go"
P. Cohenour, R. Richardson, D. H. Jenkins

Scene 7

"Waiting for the Light to Shine" (reprise)
D. H. Jenkins

Scene 8

"Free at Last"
R. Richardson

Scene 10

"River in the Rain" (reprise)
D. H. Jenkins, R. Richardson

"Muddy Water" (reprise)
The Company

1985–1986 SEASON

Betty Buckley (left) in DROOD
Martha Swope/TimePix

1985–1986 SEASON

1985.07   ## TANGO ARGENTINO

A Dance Revue in Two Acts. Conceived and directed by Claudio Segovia, Héctor Orezzoli. Choreography by Juan Carlos Copes. Musical directors, José Libertella, Luis Stazo, Osvaldo Berlingieri. Scenery and costumes by Héctor Orezzoli, Claudio Segovia. Originally commissioned by the Festival d'Automne, Paris. Produced by Mel Howard and Donald K. Donald. Opened 25 June 1985 at the New York City Center and closed 30 June 1985 after 7 performances; re-opened 9 October 1985 at the Mark Hellinger Theater and closed 30 March 1986 after 199 performances. Total: 206 performances.

CAST: *Singers:* Raúl Lavié, Jovita Luna, Elba Berón, Alba Solís.
  Dancers: Naanim Timoyko (soloist), Juan Carlos Copes, María Nieves, Nélida and Nelson, Gloria and Eduardo, Mayoral and Elsa María, Virulazo and Elvira, The Dinzels (Gloria, Rodolfo), Maria and Carlos Rivarola.
  Musicians: Sexteto Mayor: José Libertella (bandoneón); Luis Stazo (bandoneón); Mario Abramovich (violin); Eduardo Walczak (violin); Oscar Palermo (piano); Osvaldo Aulicino (bass). And: Osvaldo Berlingieri (piano); Oscar Ruben Gonzalez (bandoneón, flute); Rodolfo Fernandez (violin); Juan Schiaffino (violin); Dino Carlos Quarleri (violoncello); Lisandro Adrover (bandoneón).

ACT 1[1]
  "Quejas de Bandoneon"
    (*Music by* J. de Dios Filiberto.)
  "El Apache Argentino"
    (*Music by* M. Aróztegui, A. Mathón.)
  Ballet
  Two thugs entwine and dance the tango.
  "El Esquinazo"
    (*Music by* A. Villoldo.)
  Ballet
  Couples of "outsiders" dance the "milonga."
  "Milonga del Tiempo Heroico"
    (*Music by* F. Canaro.)
    J. C. Copes, M. Nieves

[1]The program which appears below is from the Broadway engagement at the Mark Hellinger. The running order and selection of music was subject to change during the run and subsequent national tour. The City Center engagement was produced in association with the 55th Street Dance Theatre Foundation, Inc. The program and cast changes appear below.
  Appearing at City Center, and not at the Mark Hellinger:
    Singers: Roberto Goyeneche, María Graña. *Added for Broadway:* Alba Solís.
    Dancers: Virulazo and Elvira. *Musicians:* unchanged.
    Music dropped after City Center engagement:
  "Cancion Desesperada"
    (*Music and Lyrics by* E. S. Discépolo.)
    M. Graña
  I am a desperate song.
  "Caseron de Tejas"
    (*Music and Lyrics by* S. Piana, C. Castillo.)/
  "Sin Palabras"
    (*Music and Lyrics by* M. Mores, E. S. Discépolo.)
    M. Graña
  The piano music will drift in from the dimly lit room, to sing the pure tenderness of the waltz.
  "Malena"
    (*Music and Lyrics by* L. Demare, C. Castillo.)
    R. Goyeneche
  Malena grieves like a bandoneón.
  "El Motivo"
    (*Music and Lyrics by* J. C. Cobián, P. Contursi.)
    R. Goyeneche
  The nostalgia of those days of pleasure and love has lost its flavor, today it invites tears.

"La Puñalada"
  (*Music by* P. Castellanos, E. C. Flores.)
  O. Berlingieri, Orchestra
"La Morocha"
  (*Music by* E. Saborido, A. Villoldo.)
  Gloria, M. Rivarola
Two young girls dance the tango "discreetly."
"El Choclo"
  (*Music and Lyrics by* A. Villoldo, E. S. Discépolo.)
  E. Berón
"With this tango, the tango was born and, weeping, fled the mud, searching for the sky . . . "
"La Cumparsita"
  (*Music by* G. H. Matos Rodriguez.)
  M. Rivarola, C. Rivarola
European dance hall
"Mi Noche Triste"
  (*Music and Lyrics by* S. Castriotta, P. Contursi.)
  R. Lavié
For me there is no consolation and that's why I get drunk, to forget our love.
"Orgullo Criollo"
  (*Music by* J. DeCaro, P. Laurenz.)
  Virulazo, Elvira
    Choreography: Virulazo.
"De Mi Barrio"
  (*Music and Lyrics by* R. Goyeneche.)
  J. Luna
"Bandoneones"
  J. Libertella, L. Stazo, L. Adrover, O. R. González
"Milonguita"
The story of the young girl of the barrio who, seduced by a ruffian, follows the road of her ruin.
"Milonguita"
  (*Music by* E. Delfino, S. Linning.)
"Divina"
  (Music by J. Mora, J. de la Calle.)
"Melenita de Oro"
  (*Music by* E. Delfino, S. Linning.)
"Re-fa-si"
  (*Music by* E. Delfino.)
    Milonguita: N. Timoyko. *The Ruffian:* J. C. Copes. *The Ruffian's Accomplice:* Nélida. *The Bridegroom:* Nelson. *The Cabaret's Customers:* Eduardo, Mayoral, C. Rivarola. *The Prostitutes:* Gloria, E. Maria, G. Dinzel, M. Rivarola.
"Nostalgias"
  (*Music by* J. C. Cobian, E. Cadícamo.)
  Sexteto Mayor
Bandoneon, groan your gray tando, perhaps you also suffer from love.
"Cuesta Abajo"
  (Music and Lyrics by Gardel, Le Pera.)
  R. Lavié
I carry my shame everywhere, shame to have been and pain of being no more.
"El Entrerriano"
  (*Music by* R. Mendizabal.)
  G. Dinzel, R. Dinzel.
    Choreography: R. Dinzel.
"Canaro en Paris"
  (*Music by* Scarpino, Caldarella.)
  O. Berlingieri, Orchestra
"Taquito Militar"
  (*Music by* M. Mores.)
  J. C. Copes, M. Nieves, Nélida and Nelson, Gloria and Eduardo
ACT 2
"Milongueando en El 40"
  (*Music by* Armando Pontier.)
  Gloria and Eduardo
    Choreography: Eduardo.
"Uno"
  (*Music and Lyrics by* E. S. Discépolo, M. Mores.)
  A. Solís

One is so alone with her pain, one is so blind in her sorrow.

"La Ultima Curda"
(*Music and Lyrics by* A. Troilo, C. Castillo.)
A. Solís

Life is an absurd wound.

"La Yumba"
(*Music by* O. Pugliese.)
Mayoral, E. María
Choreography: Mayoral.

"Nunca Tuvo Novio"
(*Music and Lyrics by* E. Cadícamo, A. Bardi.)
R. Lavié, O. Berlingieri, Orchestra

Poor and alone, you are without illusion, without faith.

"Jealousy" [Celos]
(*Music by* J. Gade.)
Nélida and Nelson
Choreography: Nélida and Nelson.

"Desencuentro"
(*Music and Lyrics by* A. Troilo, C. Castillo.)
E. Berón

Your luck is so bad that when you want to put the last bullet in your pistol in your head—it won't fire.

"Tanguera"
(*Music by* M. Mores)
Orchestra

"Verano Porteño"
(*Music by* Astor Piazzolla.)
J. C. Copes, M. Nieves

"Balada Para Mi Muerte"
(*Music and Lyrics by* Astor Piazzolla and H. Ferrer.)
J. Luna

I'll toss the cloak of dawn around my shoulders, my next to last whiskey will age in its glass, my death, in love, will arrive on a tango step, and I will die precisely at six o'clock.

"Adios Nonino"
(*Music by* Astor Piazzolla.)
Sexteto Mayor

"Danzarin"
(*Music by* J. Plaza.)

"Quejas de Bandoneon"
(*Music by* J. de Dios Filiberto.)
Ballet

The dance floor fills with the sound of the orchestra, and under the spotlights, the marionettes embrace.

1985.08   SINGIN' IN THE RAIN

A Musical in Two Acts, 17 Scenes. Adaptation (book) by Betty Comden and Adolph Green. Based on their screenplay for the MGM film of the same name. Music by Nacio Herb Brown. Lyrics by Arthur Freed. Directed and choreographed by Twyla Tharp with some original choreography by Gene Kelly and Stanley Donen. Scenery by Santo Loquasto. Costumes by Ann Roth. Lighting by Jennifer Tipton. Sound by Sound Associates. Film sequences by Gordon Willis. Music supervision and arrangements by Stanley Lebowsky. Music director, Robert Billig. Orchestrations by Larry Wilcox. Associate Producer, Eugene V. Wolsk. Produced by Maurice Rosenfield, Lois F. Rosenfield, and Cindy Pritzker, Inc. Opened 2 July 1985 at the Gershwin Theatre and closed 18 May 1986 after 367 performances.

CAST (in order of appearance): *Dora Bailey*: Melinda Gilb. *Cosmo Brown*: PETER SLUTSKER. *Lina Lamont*: FAYE GRANT. *Don Lockwood*: DON CORREIA. *R. F. Simpson*: HANSFORD ROWE. *Roscoe Dexter*: RICHARD FANCY. *Rod*: Robert Radford. *Kathy Selden*: MARY D'ARCY. *Sid Phillips*: Martin Van Treuren. *Phoebe Dinsmore*: Jacque Dean. *Diction Coach*: Austin Colyer. *Sound Engineer*: John Spalla. *Ticket Taker*: Martin Van Treuren. *A Warner Brother*: Austin Colyer. *Zelda Zanders*: Mary Ann Kellogg.
Ensemble: Ray Benson, John Carrafa, Richard Colton, Austin Colyer, Jacqe Dean, Diane Duncan, Yvonne Dutton, Craig Frawley, Melinda Gilb, Katie Glasner, Barbara Hoon, David-Michael Johnson, Mary Ann Kellogg, Raymond Kurshals, Alison Mann, Barbara Moroz, Kevin O'Day, Robert Radford, Tom Rawe, Gene Sager, John Spalla, Amy Spencer, Cynthia Thole, Martin Van Treuren, Shelley Washington, Laurie Williamson. *Swings*: Cheri Butcher, Brad Moranz, David Askler.
Cast in Film Sequences: "The Royal Rascal": *Philippe*: D. Correia. *Jeanette*: F. Grant. *Enemies of the King*: R. Benson, C. Frawley, G. Sager, M. Van Treuren.

"Talking Picture Demonstration": *Man on Screen*: J. Spalla.
"The Dueling Cavalier" and "The Dancing Cavalier": *Yvonne*: F. Grant. *Lady-in-Waiting*: C. Thole. *Ladies of the Court*: D. Duncan, A. Mann, B. Moroz. *Pierre*: D. Correia. *Manservant*: G. Sager. *Villain*: M. Van Treuren.

The action takes place in Hollywood in the 1920's.

Act 1, Scene 1: The Premiere of "The Royal Rascal." Grauman's Chinese Theatre, September, 1927. *Scene 2*: Altoona, Pennsylvania—a vaudeville theatre, ten years earlier. *Scene 3*: Grauman's Chinese Theatre, onstage and backstage, at the premiere. *Scene 4*: Hollywood Boulevard, later that evening. *Scene 5*: The Coconut Grove party after the premiere. *Scene 6*: The Studios of Monumental Pictures. Silent Stage, 7 October, 1927. *Scene 7*: Shooting "The Duelling Cavalier," a silent film. *Scene 8*: An empty soundstage. *Scene 9*: Diction lessons. *Scene 10*: Shooting "The Duelling Cavalier" as a talking picture. *Scene 11*: Conversion of "The Duelling Cavalier" to a Musical. The Glendale Theatre, sneak preview of "The Dueling Cavalier" as a talkie, January 1928. *Scene 12*: Don's home, later that evening. *Scene 13*: A street near Kathy's house.

Act 2, Scene 1: Filming musical numbers at Warner Brothers Studio. *Scene 2*: Monumental Pictures' recording studio. (a.) The next day. (b.) Later that week. *Scene 3*: Title production number in "The Dancing Cavalier." *Scene 4*: Grauman's Chinese Theatre, the premiere of "The Dancing Cavalier."

ACT 1[2]
Scene 2
"Fit as a Fiddle"[3]
D. Correia, P. Slutsker
(*Music and Lyrics by* Arthur Freed, Al Hoffman, Al Goodhart.)
Scene 4
"Beautiful Girl" (from *GOING HOLLYWOOD* film)
D. Correia, Fans
Scene 5
"I've Got a Feelin' You're Foolin'" (from *BROADWAY MELODY OF 1936* film)
M. D'Arcy, Coconut Grove Coquettes
Scene 6
"Make 'Em Laugh"
P. Slutsker
"Hub Bub"
P. Slutsker, Studio Stage Hands
(*Music by* Stanley Lebowsky.)
Studio Stage Hands: J. Carrafa, R. Colton, R. Kurshals, K. O'Day, R. Radford, T. Rawe.
Scene 8
"You Are My Lucky Star" (from *BROADWAY MELODY OF 1936* film)
D. Correia, M. D'Arcy
Scene 9
"Moses Supposes"[4]
D. Correia, P. Slutsker
(*Music by* Roger Edens. *Lyrics by* Betty Comden and Adolph Green.)
Scene 12
"Good Mornin'"[5] (from *BABES IN ARMS* film)
D. Correia, M. D'Arcy, P. Slutsker
Scene 13
"Singin' in the Rain"[6] (from *HOLLYWOOD REVUE OF 1929* film)
D. Correia

---

[2]All of the songs listed below appeared in the original MGM film, with the exception of "Hub Bub," "Rag Doll," "Temptation," "Takin' Miss Mary to the Ball," "Love Is Where You Find It," and "Blue Prelude" which were added for this production. A substantially revised production (Two Acts, 19 Scenes) was mounted for a national tour under the direction of Lawrence Kasha, choreography by Peter Gennaro, sets by Peter Wolf, costumes by Robert Fletcher, lighting by Thomas Skelton. All of the song additions which appear in the note above were dropped. Added to Act 2, Scene 3 was:
"What's Wrong with Me?" (from *THE KISSING BANDIT* film)
Jennifer Smith (Lina Lamont)
(*Music by* Nacio Herb Brown. *Lyrics by* Edward Heyman.)
[3]As choreographed by Gene Kelly and Stanley Donen in the film.
[4]As choreographed by Gene Kelly and Stanley Donen in the film.
[5]As choreographed by Gene Kelly and Stanley Donen in the film.
[6]As choreographed by Gene Kelly and Stanley Donen in the film.

ACT 2
Scene 1

"(The) Wedding of the Painted Doll" (from *BROADWAY MELODY* film)
> D. Duncan, Y. Dutton, K. Glasner, K. O'Day, A. Spencer, C. Thole.

"Rag Doll"
> R. Colton, B. Hoon, R. Kurshals.

"Temptation" (from *GOING HOLLYWOOD* film)
> M. Gilb
>> *Dancers:* M. A. Kellogg, R. Radford, S. Washington.

"Takin' Miss Mary to the Ball" (from *ON AN ISLAND WITH YOU* film)
> (*Lyrics by* Edward Heyman.) R. Benson, A. Mann
>> *Dancing Horse:* J. Carrafa, T. Rawe.

"Love Is Where You Find It" (from *THE KISSING BANDIT* film)
> (*Lyrics by* Earl Brent.) Ensemble

Scene 2

"Would You?" (from *SAN FRANCISCO* film)
> M. D'Arcy

Scene 3

"Broadway Rhythm" (from *BROADWAY MELODY OF 1936* film)
> The Company

"Blue Prelude"
> The Company
> (*Music and Lyrics by* Joe Bishop and Gordon Jenkins.)
> *Court at Frolic:* R. Benson, J. Carraf, R. Colton, K. Glasner, B. Hoon, M. A. Kellogg, R. Kurshals, R. Radford, T. Rawe, A. Spencer, C. Thole, S. Washington. *Pierre:* D. Correia. *Manservant:* G. Sager. *Villain:* M. Van Treuren. *Ladies of the Court:* D. Duncan, A. Mann, B. Moroz. *Apache Dancers:* J. Carrafa, R. Colton, Y. Dutton, K. Glasner, B. Hoon, M. A. Kellogg, R. Kurshals, K. O'Day, T. Rawe, A. Spencer. *Chanteuse:* L. Williamson. *Danseuse:* S. Washington. *Savate Fighters:* R. Benson, R. Kurshals. *Peasants:* A. Colyer, J. Dean, C. Frawley, M. Gilb, D. Johnson, J. Spalla.

Scene 4

"Would You?" (reprise)
> M. D'Arcy

"You Are My Lucky Star" (reprise)
> D. Correia, M. D'Arcy, Company

"Singin' in the Rain" (reprise)
> The Company

1985.09 THE STUDENT PRINCE

A Revival of the Operetta in Three Acts, a Prologue and 4 Scenes[7]. Music by Sigmund Romberg. Book and lyrics by Dorothy Donnelly. (Based on the play "Old Heidelberg" by Rudolf Bleichmann, adapted from "Alt-Heidelberg" by Wilhelm Meyer-Förster.) Book adaptation by Hugh Wheeler. Conducted by Paul Gemignani. Directed by Jack Hofsis. Stage director, Christian Smith. Scenery designed by David Jenkins Costumes designed by Patton Campbell. Lighting designed by Gilbert V. Hemsley, Jr. Choreography by Donald Saddler. Chorus master, Joseph Colaneri. Produced by the New York City Opera. Opened 5 July 1985 at the New York State Theatre and closed 21 July 1985 after 9 performances in repertory.

CAST (in order of their appearance): *Lackeys:* Edward Zimmerman, Louis Perry, George Wyman, Neil Eddinger. *Dr. Engel*, the Prince's Tutor: ADIB FAZAH. *Count von Mark:* DAVID RAE SMITH. *Secretaries:* Glenn Rowen, Jonathan Guss. *Prince Karl Franz:* JERRY HADLEY. *Lutz*, valet to the Prince: JACK HARROLD. *Gretchen*, Maid at the Inn: CAROL SPARROW. *Ruder:* Joseph McKee. *Nicholas:* Douglas Hamilton. *Toni*, a waiter: James Billings. *Hubert:* William Ledbetter. *Detlef*, a student leader: Stephen O'Mara. *von Asterberg*, another student leader: Robert Brubaker. *Lucas*, another student leader: Wilbur Pauley. *Freshman:* Louis Perry. *Kathie*, niece of Ruder: ELIZABETH HYNES. *Girls:* Madeleine Mines, Paula Hostetter, Beth Pensiero. *Grand Duchess Anastasia:* MURIEL COSTA-GREENSPON. *Princess Margaret*, fiancée of Prince Karl Franz: CYNTHIA ROSE. *Captain Tarnitz:* Cris Groenendaal. *Countess Leydon*, lady-in-waiting to the Princess: Jane Shaulis. *Huzzars:* George Wyman, Glenn Rowan, Neil Eddinger, Gregory Moore. *Friends of the Huzzars:* Madeliene Mines, Paula Hostetter, Beth Pensiero, Jill Bosworth. *Ensemble:* New York City Opera Chorus.

---

[7]First produced in New York as "The Student Prince in Heidelberg" 2 December 1924 at the Jolson Theatre for 608 performances. For Synopsis of Scenes and Musical Numbers, see 1980 revival.

1985.10 THE MIKADO, or The Town of Titipu

A Revival of the Comic Opera in Two Acts[8]. Libretto by William S. Gilbert. Music by Arthur Sullivan. Directed by Lofti Mansouri. Stage director, Christian Smith. Choreography by Patricia Birch. Scenery and costumes designed by Thierry Bosquet. Lighting designed by John Gleason. Conducted by David Stahl. Chorus master, Jospeh Colaneri. Produced by the New York City Opera. Opened 13 July 1985 (matinee) at the New York State Theatre and closed 16 October 1985 after 12 performances in repertory.

CAST (in order of appearance): *Nanki-Poo*, his son, disguised as a wandering minstrel in love with Yum-Yum: DAVID EISLER. *Pish-Tush*, a Noble Lord: David Hamilton. *Pooh-Bah*, Lord High Everything Else: JOSEPH McKEE. *Ko-Ko*, Lord High Executioner of Titipu: JACK HARROLD. *Yum-Yum, Pitti-Sing, Peep-Bo*, three sisters, wards of Ko-Ko: CLAUDETTE PETERSON, DIANNE IAUCO, CAROL SPARROW. *Katisha:* JOYCE CASTLE. *The Mikado of Japan:* WILLIAM WILDERMANN. *Chorus of School Girls, Nobles, Guards and Coolies:* New York City Opera Chorus.

1985.11 THE MERRY WIDOW

A Revival of the Operetta in Three Acts and a Prologue[9]. Music by Franz Lehár. Original German book (Die Lustige Witwe) and lyrics by Victor Léon and Leo Stein after "L'Attaché d'Ambassade" by Henri Meilhac. English version by Adrian Ross. Directed by Ronald Bentley. Conducted by Imre Pallo. Set designers, Helen Pond and Herbert Senn. Costume designer, Suzanne Mess. Lighting designer, Gilbert V. Hemsley, Jr. Chorus master, Joseph Colaneri. Produced by the New York City Opera Company. Opened 30 August 1985 at the New York State Theatre and closed 3 November 1985 after 12 performances in repertory.

CAST (in order of appearance): *Baron Popoff:* JACK HARROLD. *Natalie:* Susanne Marsee. *General Novikovich:* Douglas Perry. *Counsellor Khadja:* William Ledbetter. *Marquis de Cascada:* William Parcher. *Sylviane:* Ruth Golden. *M. de St. Brioche:* JOHN LANKSTON. *Olga:* Jane Bunnell. *Vicomte Camille de Jolidon:* MARK THOMSEN. *Nisch:* James Billings. *Sonia:* LEIGH MUNRO. *Count Danilo:* ALAN TITUS. *Head Waiter:* Mervin Crook. *Zozo:* Ivy Austin. *Lolo:* Joan Mirabella. *Dodo:* Esperanza Galan. *Jou-Jou:* Candace Itow. *Frou-Frou:* Victoria Rinaldi. *Clo-Clo:* Victoria Rinaldi. *Margot:* Jean Barber. *Chorus of Marsovian and Parisian Society, Dancers, Servants and Waiters:* New York City Opera Chorus.

1985.12 SONG & DANCE

A Musical in Two Acts. Music by Andrew Lloyd Webber. Lyrics by Don Black. American adaptation, additional lyrics and direction by Richard Maltby, Jr. Choreography by Peter Martins. Entire production supervised by Richard Maltby, Jr. and Peter Martins. Orchestrations by Andrew Lloyd Wbber and David Cullen. Musical advisor, David Caddick. Musical supervision and direction, John Mauceri. Associate tap choreographer, Gregg Burge. Settings by Robin Wagner. Costumes by Willa Kim. Lighting by Jules Fisher. Sound by Martin Levan. Executive producers, R. Tyler Gatchell, Jr., Peter Neufeld. A Cameron Mackintosh/Shubert Organization Production. Produced by Cameron Mackintosh, Inc., The Shubert Organization, F. W. M. Producing Group by arrangement with The Really Useful Company, (Inc). Opened 18 September 1985 at the Royale Theater and closed 8 November 1986 after 474 performances.

CAST: *Act 1: Emma:* BERNADETTE PETERS.

The action takes place at the present time in New York and Los Angeles.

ACT 1: SONG

"Take That Look Off Your Face"

---

[8]First presented in New York 20 July, 10-29 August 1885 at the Union Square and People's Theatres for 22 performances. First authorized production presented 19 August 1885 at the Fifth Avenue Theatre by Richard D'Oyly Carte for 250 performances. For Synopsis of Scenes and Musical Numbers, see 19 August 1885 D'Oyly Carte production.

[9]Original New York production first presented 21 October 1907 at the New Amsterdam Theatre for 416 performances. For Synopsis of Scenes and Musical Numbers, see original 1907 production.

Interpolated into this production:
"Girls Were Made to Love and Kiss" (from *PAGANINI*)
> (*Music by* Franz Lehar. *Original German Lyrics by* Paul Knepler and Bela Jenbach. *English Lyrics by* A. P. Herbert.)

"Let Me Finish"

"So Much to Do in New York"

"First Letter Home"

"English Girls"

"Capped Teeth and Caesar Salad"

"You Made Me Think You Were in Love"

"So Much to Do in New York" (reprise)

"Second Letter Home"

"Unexpected Song"

"Come Back with the Same Look in Your Eyes"

"Take That Look Off Your Face" (reprise)

"Tell Me on a Sunday"

"I Love New York"

"So Much to Do in New York" (reprise)

"Married Men"

"Third Letter Home"

"Let Me Finish" (reprise)

"What Have I Done?"

Finale (Take That Look Off Your Face)

ACT 2: DANCE

CAST: *Act 2: Joe:* CHRISTOPHER D'AMBOISE.
The Women: Charlotte d'Amboise, Denise Faye, Cynthia Onrubia, Mary Ellen Stuart. *The Men:* Gregg Burge, Gen Horiuchi, Gregory Mitchell, Scott Wise.
A city street: Man from the streets: Gregg Burge. *A street outside a disco: Woman in gold:* Mary Ellen Stuart. *Her Two Escorts:* Scott Wise, Gregory Mitchell. *A bar: Woman in blue:* Charlotte d'Amboise. *A Customer:* Gen Horiuchi. *Two Singles:* Cynthia Onrubia, Denise Faye. *Wall Street: Woman in Grey Flannel:* Cynthia Onrubia.

The action takes place at the present time in New York.

Scene 1: A New York subway station. *Scene 2:* The city. *Scene 3:* A street outside a disco. *Scene 4:* Billboards. *Scene 5:* A bar. *Scene 6:* A city street. *Scene 7:* Wall Street. *Scene 8:* A park. *Scene 9:* Fifth Avenue. *Scene 10:* A department store fashion show. *Scene 11:* New York.

1985.13 KISMET

A Revival of the Musical Play (Musical Arabian Night) in Two Acts, 15 Scenes[10]. Book by Charles Lederer and Luther Davis. Based on the play of the same name by Edward Knoblock. Music based on themes by Alexander Borodin. Musical adaptation and lyrics by Robert Wright and George Forrest. Directed by Frank Corsaro. Conducted by Scott Bergeson. Set and costume designer, Lawrence Miller. Lighting designer, Mark W. Stanley. Chorus master, Joseph Colaneri. Produced by the New York City Opera. Opened 3 October 1985 at the New York State Theatre and closed 17 November 1985 after 13 performances in repertory.

CAST (in order appearance): *Imam of The Mosque:* James Clark. *Silk Dancers:* Ashley Janeway, Jean Barber, Malcolm Grant, Terry Lacy. *Muezzins:* Louis Perry, Glenn Rowen, Bernard Waters, George Wyman. *Beggars:* Don Yule, Robert Brubaker. *Dervishes:* Vasilis Iracledes, Richard Smith. *Omar:* JAMES BILLINGS. *A Public Poet,* later called *Hajj:* THEODORE BAERG. *Marsinah, His Daughter:* MICHEL McBRIDE. *Businessman:* William Ledbetter. *Hassan-Ben:* Ralph Bassett. *Jawan:* JOHN LANKSTON. *Bangle Man:* James Clark. *Silk Merchants:* Louis Perry, Bernard Waters. *Brave Merchant:* Harris Davis. *Young Women:* Madeleine Mines, Mary Ann Rydzeski. *Pearl Merchant:* William Ledbetter. *Slave Merchant:* Mervin Crook. *Informer:* William Ledbetter. *Policemen:* Ralph Bassett, Robert Brubaker. *Chief of Police:* Don Yule. *Wazir of Police:* RICHARD McKEE. *Wazir's Guards:* Jeff Davis, Eric Miller, Donald R. Richardson, Elliot Santiago, Frank Sollito. *Slave Girls:* Jean Barber, Stephanie Godino, Ashley Janeway. *Harem Girl:* Deborah Saverance. *Lalume:* JOYCE CASTLE. *Princesses of Ababu:* Shannon Bresnahan, Joan Mirabella, Victoria Rinaldi. *The Caliph:* MARK THOMSEN. *Widow Yussef:* Jane Shaulis. *Ayah to Lalume:* Mary Ann Rydzeski. *Princess Zubbediya of Damascus:* Esperanza Galan. *Ayah to Zubbediya:* Jane Shaulis. *Princess Samaris of Bangalore:* Candace Itow. *Prosecutor:* James Clark. *Spies:* Ralph Bassett, Robert Brubaker, William Ledbetter. *Guest:* Louis Perry. *Ensemble:* New York City Opera Chorus.

1985.14 LA GATTA CENERENTOLA

Favola in musica (a fable in music) in Three Acts [Cinderella the Cat], in Italian. Book, music and lyrics by Roberto De Simone. Directed by Roberto de Simone. Scenery by Mauro Carosi. Costumes by Odette Nicoletti. Musical director, Renato Piemontese. Produced by the Italian Government with special assistance from the America-Italy Society in celebration of the City of New York's Italian Cultural Month. Opened 19 October 1985 at the Vivian Beaumont Theatre and closed 20 October 1985 after 2 performances.

CAST (from the Ente Teatro Cronaca of Naples): *Jesce sole:* Antonella D'Agostino. *La donna della cabala:* Ofelia De Simone. *La zingara:* Ofelia De Simone. *Il canto dei turchi:* Virgilio Villani. *Bene mio:* Virgilio Villani. *La voce del rosario:* Virgilio Villani. *Asso di bastoni:* Virgilio Villani. *Il ballo di S. Giovanni:* Lello Giulivo, Giuseppe De Vittorio. *La gatta cenerentola:* VALERIA BAIANO. *La matrigna:* RINO MARCELLI. *La pettinatrice* (a door-to-door Neapolitan hair-dresser): Isa Danielli. *La sorella Patrizia:* Giuseppe De Vittorio. *La sarta orfana di madre:* Patrizia Spinosi. *Il monacello* (a magic Neapolitan figure): Giovanni Mauriello. *Cuccurucú:* Giovanni Mauriello. *Il femminella:* Giovanni Mauriello. *Vurria addeventare:* Gianni Lamagna. *La cameriere di Palazzo Reale:* Anna Incoronato, Patrizia Spinosi, Adria Mortari, Anna Spagnuolo, Antonella D'Agostino. *La voce castrata:* Gianfranco Mari. *Il militaire francese:* Gianfranco Mari. *Il militaire spagnuolo:* Lello Giulivo. *La canzone dei militari:* Luciano Catapano, Gianni Lamagna. *L'angoscia, la crisi e la violenza delle lavandaie:* Isa Danielli.

ACT 1[11]

"Jesce Sole"

"E' Nata"

"Villanella di Cenerentola"

"Canzoni dei Sette Mariti"

"Canzone delle Sei Sorelle"

"Duetto (mamma mamma che bella cosa)"

"Rosario"

"Canzone del Monacello"

ACT 2

"Villanella a Ballo (vurria addeventare)"

"Moresca"

"Madrigale"

"Tarantella (oi mamma ca mò vene)"

ACT 3

"Coro dei Soldati"

"1°Coro Delle Lavandaie"

"2°Coro Delle Lavandaie"

"Canzone della Zingara"

"Il Suicidio del Femminella"

"Jesce Sole"

"Scena Delle Ingiurie"

Finale

1985.15 MAYOR

A Musical in Two Acts, 19 Scenes[12]. Book by Warren Leight. Based on the book "Mayor" by Edward I. Koch. Music and lyrics by Charles Strouse. Directed by Jeffrey B. Moss. Choreography by Barbara Siman. Sets and costumes designed by Randy Barcelo. Lighting designed by Richard Winkler. Musical director and arranger, Michael Kosarin. Orchestrations by Christopher Bankey. Sound by Lewis Mead. Assistant choreographer, Laurie Brongo. Associate producer, Sam Crothers. Produced by Martin Richards, Jerry Kravat, Mary Lea Johnson with the New York Music Company. Opened 23 October 1985 at the Latin Quarter and closed 5 January 1986 after 70 performances. Total, including Off-Broadway run: 268 performances.

CAST (in alphabetical order): Douglas Bernstein, Marion J. Caffey, Nancy Giles, Ken Jennings, Ilene Kristen, Kathryn McAteer, John Sloman, Lenny Wolpe (as the Mayor).

The action takes place at the present time in New York City.

---

[10]Originally produced in New York 3 December 1953 at the Ziegfeld Theatre for 583 performances. For Synopsis of Scenes and Musical numbers, see original 1953 production.

[11]No songs listed in program. List prepared from Italian cast recording.
[12]Originally produced in New York Off-Broadway 13 May 1985 at the Top of the Village Gate for 198 performances.

Act 1, Scene 1: Gracie Mansion. *Scene 2*: Midtown Street. *Scene 3*: City Hall. *Scene 4*: Street. *Scene 5*: Outside Third Avenue Tunnel. *Scene 6*: Limbo. *Scene 7*: An Office. *Scene 8*: Street.

Act 2, Scene 1: Central Park. *Scene 2*: Offices at City Hall. *Scene 3*: City Hall. *Scene 4*: On the Subway. *Scene 5*: Gracie Mansion—At a Mirror. *Scene 6*: Posh Grand Ballroom—Helmsley Palace Hotel. *Scene 7*: Street, outside the Helmsley Palace Hotel—Night. *Scene 8*: Gracie Mansion—the Mayor's Bedroom. *Scene 9*: Limbo. *Scene 10*: Mayor's Bedroom. *Scene 11*: Limbo.

ACT 1

Scene 1

"Mayor"
Mayor: L. Wolpe

Scene 2

"You Can Be a New Yorker Too!"
Businessman: J. Sloman. *Out of Towner*: D. Bernstein. *Bicycle Messenger*: M. J. Caffey. And Company.

Scene 3

Board of Estimate
Mayor: L. Wolpe. *Carol Bellamy*: K. McAteer. *Leona Helmsley*: I. Kristen. *Harrison J. Goldin*: D. Bernstein. *Security Guard*: M. J. Caffey.

"You're Not the Mayor"
Carol Bellamy: K. McAteer. *Security Guard*: M. J. Caffey. *Aide*: K. Jennings.

"Mayor" (reprise)
Mayor: L. Wolpe.

Scene 4

Critics
K. Jennings, M. J. Caffey, K. McAteer

"March of the Yuppies"
N. Giles, J. Sloman, D. Bernstein, Company

Scene 5

The Ribbon Cutting

"Hootspa"
Mayor: L. Wolpe. *John V. Lindsay*: J. Sloman. *Abe Beame*: K. Jennings.

Scene 6

Alternate Side
K. McAteer

Scene 7

"Coalition"
M. J. Caffey, I. Kristen, D. Bernstein

Scene 8

("Coalition" reprise)
M. J. Caffey, I. Kristen, D. Bernstein

"What You See Is What You Get"
Sue Simmons: N. Giles. *Mayor*: L. Wolpe. And Company.

ACT 2

Scene 1

In the Park
Company

"Ballad"
I. Kristen, J. Sloman

Scene 2

On the Telephone
Mayor: L. Wolpe. *Carol Bellamy*: K. McAteer.

Scene 3

"I Want to Be the Mayor"
Harrison J. Goldin: D. Bernstein.

Scene 4

Subway: "The Last 'I Love New York' Song"
Company

Scene 5

"Ballad" (reprise)
(*Lyrics by* Warren Leight.)
Mayor: L. Wolpe.

Scene 6

Testimonial Dinner: "Good Times"
Mayor: L. Wolpe. *John Cardinal O'Connor*: D. Bernstein. *Bess Myerson*: N. Giles. *Leona Helmsley*: I. Kristen. *Harry Helmsley*: J. Sloman. *David Rockefeller*: K. Jennings. *Waiter*: M. J. Caffey.

Scene 7

"We Are One" (I'll Never Leave You)
Homeless People: M. J. Caffey, K. McAteer. *Leona Helmsley*: I. Kristen. *Harry Helmsley*: J. Sloman.

Scene 8

"How'm I Doin'?"
Mayor: L. Wolpe. And Company.

Scene 10

"Mayor" (reprise)
Mayor: L. Wolpe.

Scene 11

"My City"
Company

1985.16 PIPINO IL BREVE

A Musical [Pippin the Short] in Three Acts, in Italian, performed with Puppets. Book, music and lyrics by Tony Cucchiara. Directed by Giuseppe DiMartino. Produced by the Italian Government with special assistance from the America-Italy Society in celebration of the City of New York's Italian Cultural Month. Opened 25 October 1985 at the Vivian Beaumont Theatre and closed 26 October 1985 after 2 performances.

CAST: *Pipino il Breve, Berta la piedona, Belisenda, Filippo, Falista, Marante, Belisario di Magonza, Bernardo di Chiaramonte, Morando de Ribera, Aquilone di Baviera, Lamberto, La lamentatriceII cantastorie*: Teatro Stabile di Catania of Sicily.

MUSICAL NUMBERS[13]

"Figlia"
"Chilpericu III"
"Di Berta e Pipinu Cuntamu La Storia"
"La Partenza di L'Ambasceria"
"Figlia"
"La Me Ventura"
"U Corredu"
"Duetto d'Amore"
"Chistu Succedi da Mill'anni"
"Matruzza Mia"
"Viva Viva La Regina"
"Picchi' Chiangi Sta Beddra Rigina"
"Berta Filava"
"Viva Carlu Magnu"

1985.17 THE NEWS

A Musical in Two Acts. Story (Book) by Paul Schierhorn, David Rotenberg, R. Vincent Park. Music and lyrics by Paul Schierhorn. Directed by David Rotenberg. Choreography by Wesley Fata. Scenery by Jane Musky. Costumes by Richard Hornung. Lighting by Norman Coates. Sound by Gary Scott Peck/ATI. Conductor, John Rinehimer. (Musical) Arrangements by John Rinehimer, Paul Schierhorn. Supervisor, Orchestrator, John Rinehimer. Originally presented at the Burt Reynolds Jupiter Theatre (Karen Poindexter, Managing director). Associate producers, Patricia Bayer, Annette R. McDonald, Quentin H. McDonald. Produced by Zev Bufman, Kathleen Lindsey, Nicholas Neubauer, R. Vincent Park, Martin and Janice Barandes. Opened 7 November 1985 at the Helen Hayes Theatre and closed 9 November 1985 after 4 performances.

CAST (in order of appearance): *Reporter*: Cheryl Alexander. *Circulation Editor*: Frank Baier. *Executive Editor*: JEFF CONAWAY. *Killer*: ANTHONY CRIVELLO. *City Editor*: Michael Duff. *Feature Editor*: Jonathan S. Gerber. *Talk Show Host*: Anthony Hoylen. *Reporter*: Patrick Jude. *Girl*: LISA MICHAELIS. *Reporter*: Charles Pistone. *Sports Editor*: John Rinehimer. *Style Editor*: Peter Valentine. *Managing Editor*: Billy Ward.

---

[13]Taken from cast recording.

The action takes place in the City Room of a large metropolitan newspaper, the bedroom of a 15-year old girl, a one room apartment, and a city street.

ACT 1

"I Am the News"
J. Conaway, Company

"They Write the News"
J. Conaway

"Mirror, Mirror"
L. Michaelis

"Front Page Exposé"
J. Conaway, Reporters

"Dad"
L. Michaelis

"Hot Flashes" (I)
Reporters

"She's on File"
J. Conaway

"Super Singo"
J. Conaway, Reporters

"Dear Felicia"
J. Conaway, F. Baier

"Horoscope"
C. Alexander, P. Jude, C. Pistone, Band

"Hot Flashes" (II)
Band, Reporters

"Classifieds"/"Personals"
Band, Reporters, L. Michaelis, A. Crivello

"Wonderman"
L. Michaelis

"Shooting Stars"
A. Crivello

"What's the Angle"
Reporters, J. Conaway

"The Contest"
J. Conaway, Reporters, J. S. Gerber, Band

"Dear Editor"
A. Crivello

"Editorial"
J. Conaway, Reporters, A. Crivello, Band

ACT 2

"Hot Flashes" (Financial)
Band

"Talk to Me"
A. Crivello, L. Michaelis

"Pyramid Lead"
J. Conaway, Reporters

"Beautiful People"
J. Conaway, C. ALexander, A. Crivello, Reporters, Band

"Hot Flashes" (III)
Reporters, Band

"Sports"
Reporters, Band

"Open Letter"
J. Conaway, A. Crivello, Company

"Mirror, Mirror" (reprise)
L. Michaelis

"Ordinary, Extraordinary Day"
A. Crivello, L. Michaelis

"What's the Angle" (reprise)
Reporters, Band

"Violent Crime"
J. Conaway, L. Michaelis, Reporters

"What in the World"
P. Jude, Reporters, Band

"Acts of God" (Births, Death and the Weather)
Company

THE MYSTERY OF EDWIN DROOD

1985.18

A Musical in Two Acts, 12 Scenes[14]. Book, music and lyrics by Rupert Holmes. Suggested by the unfinished novel of the same name by Charles Dickens. Directed by Wilford Leach. Choreography by Graciela Daniele. Scenery by Bob Shaw. Costumes by Lindsay W. Davis. Lighting by Paul Gallo. Sound by Tom Morse. Magic lantern projections by James Cochrane. Orchestrations by Rupert Holmes. Musical direction by Michael Starobin. A New York Shakespeare Festival. Associate producer, Jason Steven Cohen. Opened 2 December 1985 at the Imperial Theatre and closed 16 May 1987 after 608 performances.

CAST[15] (in order of appearance): *Mayor Thomas Sapsea/Mr. William Cartwright, Your Chairman*: GEORGE ROSE. *Stage Manager and Barkeep/Mr. James Throttle*: Peter McRobbie. *John Jasper/Mr. Clive Paget*: HOWARD MCGILLIN. *The Reverend Crisparkle/Mr. Cedric Moncrieffe*: GEORGE N. MARTIN. *Edwin Drood/Miss Alice Nutting*: BETTY BUCKLEY. *Rosa Bud/Miss Deidre Peregrine*: PATTI COHENOUR. *Alice/Miss Isabel Yearsley*: Judy Kuhn. *Beatrice/Miss Florence Gill*: Donna Murphy. *Helena Landless/Miss Janet Conover*: JANA SCHNEIDER. *Neville Landless/Mr. Victor Grinstead*: JOHN HERRERA. *Durdles/Mr. Nick Cricker*: JEROME DEMPSEY. *Deputy/Master Nick Cricker*: STEPHEN GLAVIN. *The Princess Puffer/Miss Angela Prysock*: CLEO LAINE. *Shade of Jasper/Mr. Harry Sayle*: Nicholas Gunn. *Shade of Drood/Mr. Montague Pruitt*: Brad Miskell. *Clients of Princess Puffer (2): Mr. Alan Eliot*: Herndon Lackey. *Mr. Christopher Lyon*: Rob Marshall. *Succubae (4): Miss Gwendolyn Pynn*: Francine Landes. *Miss Sarah Cook*: Karen Giombetti. *Miss Florence Gill*: Donna Murphy. *Miss Isabel Yearsley*: Judy Kuhn. *Satyr/Master Nick Cricker*: STEPHEN GLAVIN. *Servants (3): Mr. Philip Bax*: JOE GRIFASI. *Miss Violet Balfour*: Susan Goodman. *Miss Gwendolen Pynn*: Francine Landes. *Harold/Mr. James Throttle*: Peter McRobbie. *Julian/Mr. Alan Eliot*: Herndon Lackey. *Horace/Mr. Brian Pankhurst*: Charles Goff. *Bazzard/Mr. Philip Bax*: JOE GRIFASI.

Citizens of Cloisterham: Karen Giombetti, Charles Goff, Susan Goodman, Nicholas Gunn, Judy Kuhn, Herndon Lackey, Francine Landes, Rob Marshall, Peter McRobbie, Brad Miskell, Donna Murphy, Joe Pichette.

The action takes place at the Music Hall Royale this evening. Opening comments by Your Chairman, Mr. William Cartwright, immediately followed by the Music Hall Royale's presentation of "The Mystery of Edwin Drood."

Act 1: The Situation. Scene 1: The home of John Jasper at Minor Canon Corner in the cathedral city of Cloisterham, (England). A morning in late December. *Scene 2*: The conservatory at the Nun's House, a seminary for young women in Cloisterham High Street. Later that morning. *Scene 3*: Cloisterham High Street, outside the residence of Mayor Thomas Sapsea. The following afternoon. *Scene 4*: The opium den of Princess Puffer in the East End of London. Dawn, the next day. *Scene 5*: Cloisterham High Street. That afternoon. *Scene 6*: The crypts of Cloisterham Cathedral. Late that night. *Scene 7*: The ruins of Cloisterham. Christmas Eve. *Scene 8*: The home of John Jasper. A short time later. *Scene 9*: Minor Canon Corner. Christmas day and night.

Act 2: The Sleuths. Scene 1: Cloisterham Station. Six months later. *Scene 2*: Cloisterham High Street. *Scene 3*: The Voting; the Solution.

ACT 1

"There You Are"
G. Rose, Company

Scene 1

"A Man Could Go Quite Mad"
H. McGillin

"Two Kinsmen"
B. Buckley, H. McGillin

Scene 2

"Moonfall"
P. Cohenour

"Moonfall" (reprise)
P. Cohenour, J. Schneider, J. Kuhn, D. Murphy

Scene 4

"The Wages of Sin"
C. Laine

---

[14]Originally produced Off-Broadway 4 August 1985 at the Delacorte Theatre, Central Park, for 27 performances. Late in the Broadway run the title of the show was altered to DROOD.
[15]The theatrical characters from "The Mystery of Edwin Drood" appear in regular typeface; the Victorian music hall actors' names performing "The Mystery of Edwin Drood" appear in italics.

"Jasper's Vision"
N. Gunn, B. Miskell, Succubae, S. Glavin
Scene 5
"Ceylon"
B. Buckley, P. Cohenour, J. Schneider, J. Herrera, Ensemble
"Both Sides of the Coin"
H. McGillin, G. Rose, Ensemble
Scene 7
"Perfect Strangers"
B. Buckley, P. Cohenour
Scene 8
"No Good Can Come from Bad"
J. Herrera, B. Buckley, P. Cohenour,
J. Schneider, G. N. Martin, H. McGillin, J. Grifasi
Scene 9
"The Name of Love"/"Moonfall" (reprise)
P. Cohenour, H. McGillin, Ensemble

ACT 2
Scene 1
"Settling Up the Score"
Dick Datchery, C. Laine, Ensemble
Scene 2
"Off to the Races"
G. Rose, J. Dempsey, S. Glavin, Ensemble
"Don't Quit While You're Ahead"
C. Laine, Company
Scene 3
(The Voting: "Settling Up the Score" reprise)
Company
"The Garden Path to Hell"
C. Laine
("The Solution")
Entire Company

1985.19   JERRY'S GIRLS

A Broadway Entertainment (Musical Revue) in Two Acts[16]. Music and lyrics by Jerry Herman. Staged and directed by Larry Alford. Choreography by Wayne Cilento. Concepts by Larry Alford, Wayne Cilento, Jerry Herman. Scenery designed by Hal Tine. Costumes designed by Florence Klotz. Lighting designed by Tharon Musser. Sound designed by Peter Fitzgerald. Dance arranger, Mark Hummel. Musical supervisor, Donald Pippin. Orchestrations by Christopher Bankey, Joseph Gianono, Jim Tyler. Musical director, Janet Glazener. Produced by Zev Bufman, Kenneth-John Productions (Kenneth D. Greenblatt, John J. Pomerantz). Opened 18 December 1985 at the St. James Theatre and closed 20 April 1986 after 139 performances.

CAST (in order of appearance): (Ensemble:) Ellyn Arons, Kirsten Childs, Kim Crosby, Anita Ehrler, Terri Homberg, Robin Kersey, Joni Masella, Deborah Phelan. DOROTHY LOUDON, LESLIE UGGAMS, CHITA RIVERA.
Swing: Jacquey Maltby. Onstage Pianist: Sue Anderson.

ACT 1
"It Takes a Woman" (from HELLO, DOLLY!)
Ensemble
"It Takes a Woman" (reprise)
Ensemble
"Just Leave Everything to Me" (from HELLO, DOLLY! film)
D. Loudon
"Put on Your Sunday Clothes" (from HELLO, DOLLY!)
D. Loudon, Ensemble
"It Only Takes a Moment" (from HELLO, DOLLY!)
L. Uggams
"Wherever He Ain't" (from MACK AND MABEL)
C. Rivera

---

[16]Originally produced Off-Broadway in an earlier version 17 August 1981 at Ted Hook's Onstage for 101 performances.

"We Need a Little Christmas" (from MAME)
E. Arons, K. Childs, K. Crosby, A. Ehrler, D. Phelan
"Tap Your Troubles Away" (from MACK AND MABEL)
D. Loudon, C. Rivera, L. Uggams, Ensemble
"I Won't Send Roses" (from MACK AND MABEL)
L. Uggams
Vaudeville Medley:
"Two-a-Day" (from PARADE)
D. Loudon
"Bosom Buddies" (from MAME)
C. Rivera, L. Uggams
"The Man in the Moon" (from MAME)
D. Loudon
"So Long Dearie" (from HELLO, DOLLY!)
C. Rivera
"Take It All Off" (from JERRY'S GIRLS)
K. Crosby, T. Homberg, R. Kersey, J. Masella, D. Loudon
"Two-a-Day" (reprise)
D. Loudon, C. Rivera, Ensemble
"Shalom" (from MILK AND HONEY)
L. Uggams
"Milk and Honey" (from MILK AND HONEY)
L. Uggams, E. Arons, K. Childs, K. Crosby, T. Homberg, R. Kersey, D. Phelan
"Before the Pararde Passes By" (from HELLO, DOLLY!)
C. Rivera
"Have a Nice Day" (cut from LA CAGE AUX FOLLES)
D. Loudon, E. Arons, K. Childs, K. CRosby, T. Homberg, R. Phelan, J. Masella
"Showtune" (from PARADE)
C. Rivera, Ensemble
"If He Walked into My Life" (from MAME)
L. Uggams
"Hello, Dolly!" (from HELLO, DOLLY!)
D. Loudon, L. Uggams, C. Rivera, Ensemble

ACT 2
Movies Medley:
"Just Go to the Movies"
E. Arons, K. Childs, K. Crosby, T. Homberg, D. Phelan
(from A DAY IN HOLLYWOOD/A NIGHT IN THE UKRAINE)
"Movies Were Movies" (from MACK AND MABEL)
L. Uggams
"Look What Happened to Mabel" (from MACK AND MABEL)
C. Rivera
"Nelson"
D. Loudon
(from A DAY IN HOLLYWOOD/A NIGHT IN THE UKRAINE)
"Just Go to the Movies" (reprise)
"I Don't Want to Know" (from DEAR WORLD)
C. Rivera
"It's Today" (from MAME)
L. Uggams, E. Arons, K. Crosby,
A. Ehrler, T. Homberg, R. Kersey, J. Masella, D. Phelan
"Mame" (from MAME)
D. Loudon, E. Arons, K. Crosby,
A. Ehrler, T. Homberg, R. Kersey, J. Masella, D. Phelan
"Kiss Her Now" (from DEAR WORLD)
L. Uggams, K. Childs
"The Tea Party" (from DEAR WORLD):
"Dickie"
D. Loudon
"Voices"
L. Uggams
"Thoughts"
C. Rivera
"Time Heals Everything" (from MACK AND MABEL)
D. Loudon
"That's How Young I Feel" (from MAME)
C. Rivera, A. Ehrler, J. Masella

"My Type" (from *NIGHTCAP*)
  D. Loudon
LA CAGE AUX FOLLES Medley:

"La Cage Aux Folles"
  C. Rivera, K. Childs, A. Ehrler, T. Homberg, R. Kersey, J. Masella, D. Phelan
"Song on the Sand"
  D. Loudon, K. Childs, T. Homberg, R. Kersey, D. Phelan
"I Am What I Am"
  L. Uggams
"The Best of Times"
  D. Loudon, C. Rivera, L. Uggams, Ensemble

1985.20 WIND IN THE WILLOWS

A Musical in Two Acts, 15 Scenes. Book by Jane Iredale. Based on the novel of the same name by Kenneth Grahame. Music by William Perry. Lyrics by Roger McGough, William Perry. Staged by Tony Stevens. Choreography by Margery Beddow. Scenery by Sam Kirkpatrick. Costumes by Freddy Wittop. Lighting by Craig Miller. Sound by Jack Mann. Musical supervision by Jonathan Tunick. Orchestrations by William D. Brohn. Dance and incidental music by David Krane. Musical director and vocal arrangements by Robert Rogers. Production supervisor, Stephen Zweigbaum. Asisstant choreographer, James Brennan. Fights by Conal O'Brien. Originally produced by the Folger Theatre, Washington, D.C. Produced by RLM Productions, Inc. (Michael Bright, Richard Ericson, Laura Harris, Renny Serre) and Liniva Productions, Inc. Opened 20 December 1985 at the Nederlander Theatre and closed 22 December 1985 after 4 performances.

CAST (in order of appearance): *Mole*: VICKI LEWIS. *Mother Rabbit*: Nora Mae Lyng. *Father Rabbit*: John Jellison. *Rat*: DAVID (James) CARROLL. *Toad*: NATHAN LANE. *Chief Stoat*: Donna Drake. *Badger*: IRVING BARNES. *Chief Weasel*: P. J. BENJAMIN. *Wayfarer Rat*: Jackie Lowe. *Police Sergeant*: Scott Waara. *Court Clerk*: Kenston Ames. *Judge*: John Jellison. *Prosecutor*: Michael Byers. *Jailer's Daughter*: Nora Mae Lyng. *Jailer*: Michael Byers.

Ensemble: Kenston Ames, Shell M. Benjamin, Michael Byers, Jackie Lowe, Marguerite Lowell, Nora Mae Lyng, Mary C. Robare, Jamie Rocco, Ray Roderick, Scott Waara. *Swings*: Teresa Payne-Rohan, Kevin Winkler.

Act 1, Scene 1: A Meadow in Spring. *Scene 2*: The River. *Scene 3*: The Wild Wood. *Scene 4*: The Lawns of Toad Hall. *Scene 5*: Rat's Dock in Summer. *Scene 6*: The Wild Wood. *Scene 7*: The Car Park at the Red Lion Inn. *Scene 8*: A Meadow in Autumn.

Act 2, Scene 1: The Courtroom. *Scene 2*: Rat's Dock in Autumn. *Scene 3*: Toad Hall. *Scene 4*: A Jail Cell. *Scene 5*: The Woods. *Scene 6*: Rat's Dock. *Scene 7*: The Grand Dining Room at Toad Hall.

ACT 1

Scene 1

"The World Is Waiting for Me"
  V. Lewis

Scene 2

"When Springtime Comes to My River"
  D. Carroll
"Messing About in Boats"
  D. Carroll, V. Lewis

Scene 3

"Evil Weasel"
  P. J. Benjamin, D. Drake, Weasels, Stoats

Scene 4

"That's What Friends Are For"
  N. Lane, D. Carroll, V. Lewis, the Rabbits

Scene 6

"Follow Your Instinct"
  V. Lewis, the Rabbits, Weasels, Stoats

Scene 7

"The Gasoline Can-Can"
  N. Lane, the Rabbits
"You'll Love It in Jail"
  P. J. Benjamin, D. Drake, N. Lane, the Policemen

Scene 8

"Mediterranean"
  J. Lowe
"The Day You Came into My Life"
  V. Lewis

ACT 2

Scene 1

"S-S-S-Something Comes over Me"
  N. Lane

Scene 2

"I'd Be Attracted"
  V. Lewis, D. Carroll
"When Springtime Comes to My River" (reprise)
  D. Carroll
"The Day You Came into My Life" (reprise)
  V. Lewis

Scene 3

"Moving Up in the World"
  P. J. Benjamin, D. Drake, Weasels, Stoats

Scene 4

"Brief Encounter"
  N. Lane, N. M. Lyng

Scene 5

"Where Am I Now?"
  N. Lane
"The Wind in the Willows"
  The Company

Scene 6

"That's What Friends Are For" (reprise)
  N. Lane, D. Carroll, I. Barnes, The Rabbits

Scene 7

"Come What May"
  The Company

1985.21 THE ROBERT KLEIN SHOW!

An Entertainment (Revue) in Two Acts. Written and conceived by Robert Klein. Musical director, Bob Stein. Produced by Circle-in-the-Square (Theodore Mann, Artistic director; Paul Libin, Producing Director). Opened 20 December 1985 at the Circle-in-the-Square and closed 4 January 1986 after 16 performances.

CAST: ROBERT KLEIN, KENNY RANKIN.

1986.01 JEROME KERN GOES TO HOLLYWOOD

A Musical Revue in Two Acts. Conceived by David Kernan. Written by Dick Vosburgh. Music by Jerome Kern. Lyrics by Oscar Hamerstein II, Dorothy Fields, Ira Gershwin, Otto Harbach, Johnny Mercer, E. Y. Harburg, Jimmy McHugh, P. G. Wodehouse, Buddy DeSylva, Gus Kahn, Bernard Dougall, Herbert Reynolds. Directed by David Kernan. Set design by Colin Pigott. Costume design by Christine Robinson. Lighting design by Ken Billington. Musical director, Peter Howard. Sound design by Tony Meola. Musical consultant, Clive Chaplin. Additional staging, Irving Davies. Produced by Arthur Cantor, Bonnie Nelson Schwartz by arrangement with Peter Wilson and Showpeople. Opened 23 January 1986 at the Ritz Theatre and closed 1 February 1986 after 13 performances.

CAST (in alphaabetical order): ELAINE DELMAR, SCOTT HOLMES, LIZ ROBERTSON, ELISABETH WELCH.

ACT 1[17]

"The Song Is You" (from *MUSIC IN THE AIR*, 1934)
  Ensemble
  (*Lyrics by* Oscar Hammerstein II.)

---

[17]Dates that appear below are the year the song first appeared on screen.

"I've Told Every Little Star" (from *MUSIC IN THE AIR*, 1934)
Ensemble
(*Lyrics by* Oscar Hammerstein II.)

"Let's Begin" (from *ROBERTA*, 1935)
E. Delmar
(*Lyrics by* Otto Harbach.)

"I Won't Dance" (from *ROBERTA*, 1935)
L. Robertson
(*Lyrics by* Otto Harbach, Oscar Hammerstein II, Jimmy McHugh, Dorothy Fields.)

"Californ-i-ay" (from *CAN'T HELP SINGING*, 1944)
(*Lyrics by* E. Y. Harburg.)
E. Delmar, S. Holmes, L. Robertson

"I'll Be Hard to Handle" (from *ROBERTA*, 1935)L. Robertson
(*Lyrics by* Bernard Dougall.)

"Smoke Gets in Your Eyes" (from *ROBERTA*, 1935)
E. Welch
(*Lyrics by* Otto Harbach.)

"Yesterdays" (from *ROBERTA*, 1935)
S. Holmes, L. Robertson
(*Lyrics by* Otto Harbach.)

"Bojangles of Harlem" (from *SWING TIME*, 1936)
E. Delmar, S. Holmes, L. Robertson
(*Lyrics by* Dorothy Fields.)

"I'm Old-Fashioned" (from *YOU WERE NEVER LOVELIER*, 1942)
E. Delmar
(*Lyrics by* Johnny Mercer.)

"Make Believe" (from *SHOW BOAT*, 1936)
L. Robertson
(*Lyrics by* Oscar Hammerstein II.)

"Why Do I Love You?" (from *SHOW BOAT*, 1951)
L. Robertson
(*Lyrics by* Oscar Hammerstein II.)

"I Have the Room Above Her" (from *SHOW BOAT*, 1936)
S. Holmes
(*Lyrics by* Oscar Hammerstein II.)

"I Still Suits Me" (from *SHOW BOAT*, 1936)
S. Holmes, E. Welch
(*Lyrics by* Oscar Hammerstein II.)

"Day Dreaming" (1941)
E. Delmar, S. Holmes, L. Robertson
(*Lyrics by* Gus Kahn.)

"I Dream Too Much" (from *I DREAM TOO MUCH*, 1935
(*Lyrics by* Dorothy Fields.)
E. Delmar, S. Holmes, L. Robertson

"Can I Forget You?" (from *HIGH, WIDE AND HANDSOME*, 1937)
(*Lyrics by* Oscar Hammerstein II.)
E. Delmar, S. Holmes, L. Robertson

"Pick Yourself Up" (from *SWING TIME*, 1936)
E. Delmar, L. Robertson
(*Lyrics by* Dorothy Fields.)

"She Didn't Say Yes" (from *THE CAT AND THE FIDDLE*, 1934)
E. Welch
(*Lyrics by* Otto Harbach.)

"The Folks Who Live on the Hill" (from *HIGH, WIDE AND HANDSOME*, 1937)
(*Lyrics by* Oscar Hammerstein II.)
S. Holmes

"Long Ago and Far Away" (from *COVER GIRL*, 1944)
Ensemble
(*Lyrics by* Ira Gershwin.)

ACT 2

"The Show Must Go On" (from *COVER GIRL*, 1944)
Ensemble
(*Lyrics by* Ira Gershwin.)

"Don't Ask Me Not to Sing" (from *ROBERTA*, 1935)
S. Holmes
(*Lyrics by* Otto Harbach.)

"The Way You Look Tonight" (from *SWING TIME*, 1936)
S. Holmes
(*Lyrics by* Dorothy Fields.)

"A Fine Romance" (from *SWING TIME*, 1936)
E. Delmar, S. Holmes
(*Lyrics by* Dorothy Fields.)

"Lovely to Look At" (from *ROBERTA*, 1935)
E. Welch
(*Lyrics by* Dorothy Fields, Jimmy McHugh.)

"Just Let Me Look at You" (from *JOY OF LIVING*, 1938)
L. Robertson
(*Lyrics by* Dorothy Fields.)

"Who?" (from *SUNNY*, 1930)
Ensemble
(*Lyrics by* Otto Harbach and Oscar Hammerstein II.)

"Remind Me" (from *ONE NIGHT IN THE TROPICS*, 1940)
E. Delmar
(*Lyrics by* Dorothy Fields.)

"The Last Time I Saw Paris" (from *LADY BE GOOD*, 1940)
S. Holmes
(*Lyrics by* Oscar Hammerstein II.)

"Ol' Man River" (from *SHOW BOAT*, 1929)
E. Delmar, S. Holmes, L. Robertson
(*Lyrics by* Oscar Hammerstein II.)

"Why Was I Born?" (from *SWEET ADELINE*, 1935)
E. Welch
(*Lyrics by* Oscar Hammerstein II.)

"Bill" (from *SHOW BOAT*, 1936)
L. Robertson
(*Lyrics by* P. G. Wodehouse, Oscar Hammerstein II.)

"Can't Help Lovin' Dat Man" (from *SHOW BOAT*, 1936)
E. Delmar
(*Lyrics by* Oscar Hammerstein II.)

"All the Things You Are" (from *BROADWAY RHYTHM*, 1943)
(*Lyrics by* Oscar Hammerstein II.)
E. Delmar, S. Holmes, L. Robertson

"I've Told Every Little Star" (reprise)
E. Welch

"They Didn't Believe Me" (from *TILL THE CLOUDS ROLL BY*, 1946)
Ensemble
(*Lyrics by* Herbert Reynolds.)

"Till the Clouds Roll By" (from *TILL THE CLOUDS ROLL BY*, 1946)
Ensemble
(*Lyrics by* Guy Bolton and P. G. Wodehouse.)

"Look for the Silver Lining" (from *SALLY*, 1929)
Ensemble
(*Lyrics by* Buddy deSylva.)

"Make Way for Tomorrow" (from *COVER GIRL*, 1944)
Ensemble
(*Lyrics by* E. Y. Harburg, Ira Gershwin.)

1986.02 ## UPTOWN ... IT'S HOT!

A Musical (Revue) in Two Acts, 5 Scenes and a Prologue. Conceived, directed and choreographed by Maurice Hines. Narrations written by Jeffery V. Thompson, Marion Ramsey. Scenery designed by Tom McPhillips. Costumes designed by Ellen Lee. Lighting designed by Marc B. Weiss. Musical direction and supervision, Frank Owens. Dance arrangements by Frank Owens and Thom Bridwell. Production supervisor, Beverley Randolph. Assistant choreographer, Mercedes Ellington. Associate producer, Stanley Kay. Produced by Allen Spivak and Larry Magid. Opened 28 January 1986 at the Lunt-Fontanne Theatre and closed 16 February 1986 after 24 performances.

CAST: MAURICE HINES, MARION RAMSEY, JEFFERY V. THOMPSON, LAWRENCE HAMILTON, TOMMI JOHNSON, ALISA GYSE.
Ensemble: Sheila D. Barker, Toni-Maria Chalmers, Leon Evans, Michael Franks, Robert H. Fowler, Lovette George, Ruthanna Graves, Yolanda Graves, Emera Hunt, Leslie Williams-Jenkins, Lisa Ann Malloy, Delphine T. Mantz, Gerry McIntyre, Christopher T. Moore, Elise Neal, Leesa M. Osborn, Marishka Shanice Phillips, R. LaChanze Sapp, Cheryl Ann Scott, Darious Keith Williams.

Act 1, Scene 1: 1930s. *Scene 2:* 1940s.

Act 2, Scene 1: 1950s and 1960s. *Scene 2:* 1970s. *Scene 3:* 1980s.

ACT 1

Prologue

J. V. Thompson, A. Gyse, L. Hamilton,
T. Johnson, M. Ramsey, M. Hines, Men Ensemble

Scene 1

"Swing That Music"

M. Ramsey
(*Music and Lyrics by* Louis Armstrong and H. Gerlach.)

"Cotton Club Stomp"

M. Ramsey, Ensemble
(*Music by* Duke Ellington.)

Three Gents:

L. Hamilton, C. T. Moore, R. H. Fowler

"Daybreak Express"

(*Music by* Duke Ellington.)

"Tap Along with Me"

(*Music by* F. Owens.)

"Dinah"

(*Music by* Harry Akst. *Lyrics by* Sam M. Lewis, Joe Young.)

That Shot 'Em!

(*Adaptation by* Marion Ramsey, Jefffery V. Thompson.)
J. V. Thompson, M. Ramsey, T. Johnson, R. H. Fowler

Stormy Weather Medley:

M. Hines, A. Gyse

"When Your Lover Has Gone"

(*Music and Lyrics by* E. A. Swan.)

"Ill Wind"

(from *COTTON CLUB PARADE*, 1934)
(*Music by* Harold Arlen. *Lyrics by* Ted Koehler.)

"Body and Soul"

(from *THREE'S A CROWD*)
(*Music by* Johnny Green. *Lyrics by* Edward Heyman, Robert Sour, Frank Eyton.)

"Stormy Weather"

(*Music by* Harold Arlen. *Lyrics by* Ted Koehler.)

"Diga Diga Doo" (from *BLACKBIRDS OF 1928*)

(*Music by* Jimmy McHugh. *Lyrics by* Dorothy Fields.)
M. Ramsey, G. McIntyre, D. T. Mantz, Ensemble

"Lady Be Good"

M. Hines
(*Music by* George Gershwin.)

Cab Calloway and the Nicholas Brothers:

"Jim Jam Jumpin'"

T. Johnson, L. Evans, D. K. Williams
(*Music by* Cab Calloway.)

Scene 2

Big Band Tribute

Chick Webb Theme Song: "Let's Get Together"

Orchestra
(*Music by* Chick Webb.)

"A-Tisket, A-Tasket"

A. Gyse
(*Music and Lyrics by* Ella Fitzgerald and Van Alexander.)

Jitterbuggin': "Jumpin' at the Woodside"

M. Hines,
M. Ramsey, J. V. Thompson, L. Hamilton, D. T. Mantz, S. Barker,
Ensemble
(*Music by* Count Basie.)

ACT 2

Scene 1

Doo Woppers: "Why Do Fools Fall in Love"

A. Gyse, L. Hamilton, T. Johnson
(*Music and Lyrics by* Frank Lymon and Morris Levy.)

The Apollo: Master of Ceremonies

J. V. Thompson

The Gospel Caravan:

"His Eye Is on the Sparrow" (traditional)

L. Hamilton

"Amazing Grace" (traditional)

A. Gyse

"Just a Closer Walk with Thee" (traditional)

T. Johnson

"Old Landmark"

L. Hamilton, A. Gyse, T. Johnson, R. L. Sapp, Ensemble
(*Music and Lyrics by* M. A. Brunner.)

Good Mornin' Judge

(*Adaptation by* Jeffery V. Thompson.)
Judge Pigmeat: J. V. Thompson. *De District Attorney:* M. Ramsey. *The Defendant:* A. Gyse. *Sonny Rayburn:* M. Hines.

Rock & Roll Medley:

"You Send Me"

T. Johnson
(*Music and Lyrics by* L. C. Cooke.)

"Blueberry Hill"

J. V. Thompson
(*Music and Lyrics by* Al Lewis, Larry Stock, Vincent Rose.)

"Tutti Frutti"

G. McIntyre
(*Music and Lyrics by* Richard Penniman, D. LaBostrie, Joe Lubin.)

"Johnny B. Goode"

L. Hamilton, Ensemble Men
(*Music and Lyrics by* Chuck Berry.)

Battle of the Groups:

"Will You Still Love Me Tomorrow?"

T. Chalmers, L. Williams-Jenkins, D. T. Mantz, C. A. Scott
(*Music and Lyrics by* Gerry Goffin and Carole King.)

"Be My Baby"

A. Gyse, S. D. Barker, E. Neal
(*Music and Lyrics by* Phil Spector, Ellie Greenwich, Jeff Barry.)

"Don't Mess with Bill"

R. L. Sapp, L. A. Mallory, L. M. Osborn
(*Music and Lyrics by* W. Smokey Robinson.)

"Dancin' in the Streets"

Y. Graves, L. George, E. Hunt
(*Music and Lyrics by* Marvin Gaye, I. Hunter, W. Stevenson.)

"Stop! in the Name of Love"

M. Ramsey, R. Graves, M. S. Phillips
(*Music and Lyrics by* Brian Holland, Lamont Dozier, Eddie Holland.)

"Ain't Too Proud to Beg"

L. Hamilton, D. K. Williams, L. Evans, T. Johnson, G. McIntyre
(*Music and Lyrics by* Eddie Holland, Norman Whitfield.)

"Proud Mary"

M. Ramsey, R. Graves, M. S. Phillips, C. A. Scott
(*Music and Lyrics by* John C. Fogerty.)

Scene 2

Station WHOT

J. V. Thompson

Stevie Wonder Medley

(*Music and Lyrics by* Stevie Wonder and Leon Evans):

"Superstition"

Ensemble Dancers

"Keep on Running"

M. Hines (Devil)

"Higher Ground"

A. Gyse (Victim)

"Do I Do"

L. Hamilton (Angel)

Scene 3

Radio Playoffs

M. Ramsey, L. Hamilton, R. L. Sapp, L. Evans, G. McIntyre,
M. Hines

"Express"

M. Ramsey, J. V. Thompson, Ensemble Dancers
(*Music and Lyrics by* B. T. Express.)

Rappers

L. Hamilton, J. V. Thompson

"1999"

Full Company
(*Music and Lyrics by* Prince.)

THE AMERICAN DANCE MACHINE

1986.03

A Theatre Dance Revue in Two Acts, 15 Scenes[18]. Entire production concieved, supervised and directed by Lee Theodore. Musical director and orchestrator, James Raitt. Lighting designer, Curt Osterman. Produced by the American Dancemachine, Inc. in association with 55th Street Dance Theater Foundation, Inc. Opened 4 February 1986 at the New York City Center and closed 16 February 1986 after 16 performances.

CAST: DICK CAVETT (Special Guest Host), HAROLD CROMER, TINKA GUTRICK, KELBY KIRK, AJA MAJOR, Newton Cole, Joe Deer, Dan Fletcher, Kim Freshwater, Camille Ross, David Storey, Dannul Dailey, Jennifer Dempster, Brian Duguay, Diana Losk, Michael Lott, Mark Curtis Smith, Donna Smythe, Lynn Sterling, 'Ali Theodore, Kyle Williams.

ACT 1

Scene 1

"The Whip Dance" (from *DESTRY RIDES AGAIN*, 1959)
M. Lott, N. Cole, M. C. Smith
(*Choreography by* Michael Kidd, reconstructed by Swen Swenson. *Music and Lyrics by* Harold Rome.)

Scene 2

"Popularity" (from *GEORGE M!*, 1968)
D. Fletcher, Ensemble
(*Choreography by* Joe Layton. *Music and Lyrics by* George M. Cohan.)

Scene 3

"June Is Bustin' Out All Over" (from *CAROUSEL*, 1945)
C. Ross, Female Ensemble
(*Choreography by* Agnes deMille, reconstructed by Gemze deLappe. *Music by* Richard Rodgers. *Lyrics by* Oscar Hammerstein II.)

Scene 4

"Shriners' Ballet" (from *BYE BYE BIRDIE*, 1960)
T. Gutrick, Male Ensemble
(*Choreography by* Gower Champion, reconstructed by Edmond Kresley. *Music by* Charles Strouse. *Lyrics by* Lee Adams.)

Scene 5

"Won't You Charleston With Me?" (from *THE BOY FRIEND*, 1970 revival)
A. Major, B. Duguay
(*Choreography by* Buddy Schwab, reconstructed by Eleanor Treiber. *Music and Lyrics by* Sandy Wilson.)

Scene 6

"The Telephone Dance" (from *CABARET*, 1966)
T. Gutrick, D. Dailey, Ensemble
(*Choreography by* Ron Field, reconstructed by Marianne Seibert. *Music by* John Kander. *Lyrics by* Fred Ebb.)

Scene 7

"The Clog Dance" (from *WALKING HAPPY*, 1966)
D. Fletcher, Male Ensemble
(*Choreography and Reconstruction by* Danny Daniels. *Introduction by* Joe Deer. *Music by* James Van Heusen. *Lyrics by* Sammy Cahn. *Dance Arrangement by* Ed Scott.)

Scene 8

"Floyd's Guitar Blues" (from the Katherine Dunham Repertory)
T. Gutrick, J. Deer
(*Choreography by* Katherine Dunham, reconstructed by Glory Van Scott. *Music by* Floyd Smith.)

Scene 9

"Charlie's Place" (from *OVER HERE*, 1974)
A. Major, D. Storey, Ensemble
(*Choreography and Reconstruction by* Patricia Birch. *Music and Lyrics by* Richard Sherman and Robert Sherman.)

Intermission: Historical material performed by Harold Cromer, arranged by Harold Cromer in collaboration with Albert Murray. "Mr. Bojangles" score composed by Jerry Jeff Walker.

ACT 2

Scene 1

"If the Rain's Gotta Fall" (from *HALF A SIXPENCE*, 1965)
K. Kirk, Ensemble
(*Choreography by* Onna White, reconstructed by Eleanor Treiber and Tom Panko. *Music and Lyrics by* David Heneker.)

Scene 2

"Satin Doll" (from *THE ED SULLIVAN SHOW*, TV, 1962)
K. Williams, C. Ross, L. Sterling

"Me and My Gal" (from *THE ED SULLIVAN SHOW*, TV, 1962)
T. Gutrick, A. Theodore
(*Choreography by* Carol Haney, reconstructed by Buzz Miller. *Music by* Duke Ellington, Billy Strayhorn, Johnny Mercer. *Arrangement by* Luther Henderson.)

Scene 3

"Little Old New York" (from *TENDERLOIN*, 1960)
A. Major, K., Freshwater, Ensemble
(*Choreography by* Joe Layton, reconstructed by Joe Layton and Lee Theodore. *Music by* Jerry Bock. *Lyrics by* Sheldon Harnick.)

Scene 4

"Come to Me, Bend to Me" (from *BRIGADOON*, 1947)
K. Kirk

"The Funeral Dance" (from *BRIGADOON*, 1947)
T. Gutrick, Female Ensemble
(*Choreography by* Agnes deMille, reconstructed by Gemze deLappe. *Music by* Frederick Loewe. *Lyrics by* Alan Jay Lerner.)

Scene 5

"You Can Dance with Any Girl at All" (from *NO, NO, NANETTE*, 1971 revival)
A. Major, K. Kirk
(*Choreography by* Donald Saddler, reconstructed by Donald Saddler. *Music by* Vincent Youmans. *Lyrics by* Irving Caesar and Otto Harbach.)

Scene 6

"The Aggie Song" (from *THE BEST LITTLE WHOREHOUSE IN TEXAS*, 1978)
N. Cole, Male Ensemble
(*Choreography by* Tommy Tune, reconstructed by Jerry Yoder. *Music and Lyrics by* Carol Hall.)

BRIGADOON

1986.04

A Revival of the Musical Play in Two Acts, Eleven Scenes[19]. Book and lyrics by Alan Jay Lerner. Music by Frederick Loewe. Original dances by Agnes de Mille, recreated by James Jamieson. Directed by Gerald Freedman. Set and costume designer, Desmond Heeley. Lighting designer, Duane Schuler. Conductor, Paul Gemignani. Chorus master, Joseph Colaneri. Sound consultant, Farrel Becker. Produced by the New York City Opera. Opened 1 March 1986 at the New York State Theatre and closed 30 March 1986 after 40 performances[20].

CAST (in order of appearance): *Tommy Albright*: RICHARD WHITE or JOHN LESLIE WOLFE. *Jeff Douglas*: TONY ROBERTS. *Maggie Anderson*: TINKA GUTRICK. *Archie Beaton*: William Ledbetter. *Angus MacGuffie*: Don Yule. *Meg Brockie*: JOYCE CASTLE or MARCIA MITZMAN. *Stuart Dalrymple*: Robert Brubaker. *Sandy Dean*: Gregory Moore. *Harry Beaton*: LUIS PEREZ. *Andrew MacLaren*: David Rae Smith. *Fiona MacLaren*: SHERYL WOODS or BEVERLY LAMBERT. *Jean MacLaren*: Camille Ross. *Charlie Dalrymple*: CRIS GROENEN-DAAL or DAVID EISLER. *Fish Monger*: Stephanie Godino. *Mr. Lundie*: James Billings. *Sword Dancers*: Terry Lacy, Joe Deer. *Bagpiper*: Stephen Fox. *Frank*: Ralph Bassett. *Jane Ashton*: Alison Bevan.

Townsfolk of Brigadoon: Singers: *New York City Opera Chorus*: Marilyn Armstrong, Lee Belaver, George Bohachevsky, Jill Bosworth, Don Carlo, Mervin Crook, Harris Davis, Neil Eddinger, Harriet Green, Jonathan Guss, Don Henderson, Lila Herbert, Ron Hilley, Paula Hostetter, Rita Metzger, Madeline Mines, Gregory Moore, Beth Pensiero, Louis Perry, J. Randolph Peyton, Bridget Ramos, Frank Ream, Glenn Rowen, Mary Ann Rydzeski, Deborah Saverance, Susan Schafer, Carolyn Sielski, Frank Tippie,

---

[18]A previous edition was presented Off-Broadway 14 June 1978 at the Century Theatre for 198 performances. Between 1978 and 1986 the company toured widely with an changing repertory.

[19]Originally produced in New York 13 March 1947 at the Ziegfeld Theatre for 581 performances. For Synopsis of Scenes and Musical Numbers, see original 1947 production.
[20]Orchestrations uncredited.

Catherine Williams, George Wyman, Marie Young, Edward Zimmerman. *New York City Opera Dancers*: Jean Barber, Savia Berger, Jose Bourbon, Kathy Bradney, Joe Deer, Esperanza Galan, Stephanie Godino, Malcolm Grant, Vasilis Iracledes, Candace Itow, Ashley Janeway, Terry Lacy, Marc Mahler, Fritz Masten, Joan Mirabella, Louis Navarette, Daniel Pelzig, Deirdre Sheehan, Richard Smith, Anina von Molnar.

THE FLYING KARAMAZOV BROTHERS

1986.05

Juggling and Cheap Theatrics (A Vaudeville Revue) in Two Acts. Conceived, written and directed by the Flying Karamazov Brothers. Sets by Seiza de Tarr. Lighting by Eben Sprinsock. Produced by Lincoln Center Theatre (Gregory Mosher, Artistic director; Bernard Gersten, Executive producer). Opened 1 April 1986 at the Vivian Beaumont Theatre and closed 20 April 1986 after 24 performances; re-opened (Off Broadway) 23 April 1986 at the Mitzi Newhouse Theater and closed 4 May 1986 after 16 additional performances. Total: 40 performances.

CAST: *Fyodor*: TIMOTHY DANIEL FURST. *Dmitri*: PAUL DAVID MAGID. *Alyosha*: RANDY NELSON. *Ivan*: HOWARD JAY PATTERSON. *Smerdyakov*: SAM WILLIAMS.

BIG DEAL

1986.06

A Musical in Two Acts, 24 Scenes. (Book) Written by Bob Fosse. Based on the film "Big Deal on Madonna Street," (Screenplay by Susi Cecchi D'Amico, Mario Monicelli, Agenore Incrocci and Furio Scarpelli.) Directed and choreographed by Bob Fosse. Scenery by Peter Larkin. Costumes by Patricia Zipprodt. Lighting by Jules Fisher. Orchestrations by Ralph Burns. Sound by Abe Jacob. Associate choreographer, Christopher Chadman. Music arranged and conducted by Gordon Lowry Harrell. Executive producer, Jules Fisher. Produced by The Shubert Organization, Roger Berlind, Jerome Minskoff in association with Jonathan Farkas. Opened 10 April 1986 at the Broadway Theatre and closed 8 June 1986 after 70 performances.

CAST (in order of appearance): *Lilly*: LORETTA DEVINE. *First Narrator*: Wayne Cilento. *Second Narrator*: Bruce Anthony Davis. *Kokomo*: Gary Chapman. *Otis*: Alde Lewis, Jr. *Charley*: CLEAVANT DERRICKS. *Pearl*: Valarie Pettiford. *Slick*: Larry Marshall. *Sunnyboy*: Mel Johnson, Jr. *Willie*: ALAN WEEKS. *Judge and Bandleader*: Bernard J. Marsh. *Band Singer*: Valarie Pettiford. *Phoebe*: Desiree Coleman. *Dancin' Dan*: Gary Chapman. *First Shadow*: Valarie Pettiford. *Second Shadow*: Barbara Yeager. *Little Willie*: Roumel Reaux. *Announcer*: Candace Tovar.
Dancers: Ciscoe Bruton II, Lloyd Culbreath, Kim Darwin, Cady Huffman, Amelia Marshall, Frank Mastrocola, Stephanie Pope, Roumel Reaux, George Russell, Candace Tovar. *Alternates*: Bryant Baldwin, Diana Laurenson, Vince Cole. *On-Stage Band*: Brian Brake (drums), Leonard Oxley (piano), William Shadel (clarinet), Joe Mosello (trumpet), Earl May (bass), Britt Woodman (trombone).

The action takes place in the 1930's on the South Side of Chicago, Illinois.

Act 1, Scene 1: Prologue. *Scene 2*: Locker Room and Fight Arena. *Scene 3*: The Judge's Chambers. *Scene 4*: Prsion Yard. *Scene 5*: Gem Theatre. *Scene 6*: The Men's Room at the Gem Theatre. *Scene 7*: A Camera Store. *Scene 8*: Cottage Grove Avenue. *Scene 9*: Pool Hall. *Scene 10*: Cottage Grove Avenue. *Scene 11*: Paradise Ballroom. *Scene 12*: Alley Outside Dancehall.

Act 2, Scene 1: Prologue. *Scene 2*: Slick's Apartment. *Scene 3*: Willie's House. *Scene 4*: A Pawnshop. *Scene 5*: Slick's Apartment. *Scene 6*: Charlie's Room. *Scene 7*: Lily's Rented Room. *Scene 8*: Refreshment Stand of Gem Theatre. *Scene 9*: Lily's Rented Room. *Scene 10*: The Robbery. *Scene 11*: The Fantasies. *Scene 12*: A Street.

ACT 1
Scene 1

"Life Is Just a Bowl of Cherries" (from *GEORGE WHITE'S SCANDALS OF 1931*)
(*Music by* Ray Henderson. *Lyrics by* Buddy DeSylva, Lew Brown.)
L. Devine
"For No Good Reason at All"
W. Cilento, B. A. Davis
(*Music and Lyrics by* Abel Baer, Samuel W. Lewis, Joe Young.)
Scene 2
"Charley My Boy"
C. Derricks
(*Music and Lyrics by* Ted Fiorito and Gus Kahn.)

Scene 3
"I've Got a Feelin' You're Foolin'" (from *BROADWAY MELODY OF 1936*, film)
G. Chapman, C. Derricks, B. J. Marsh, W. Cilento, B. A. Davis
(*Music by* Nacio Herb Brown. *Lyrics by* Arthur Freed.)
Scene 4
"Ain't We Got Fun"
The Prisoners
(*Music by* Richard A. Whiting. *Lyrics by* Gus Kahn and Raymond Egan.)
Scene 5
"For No Good Reason at All" (reprise)
W. Cilento, B. A. Davis, The Dancers
Scene 8
"Chicago"
W. Cilento, B. A. Davis
(*Music and Lyrics by* Fred Fisher.)
Scene 9
"Pick Yourself Up" (from *SWING TIME* film)
C. Derricks, A. Weeks, L. Marshall, M. Johnson, Jr., A. Lewis, Jr.
(*Music by* Jerome Kern. *Lyrics by* Dorothy Fields.)
Scene 10
"I'm Just Wild About Harry" (from *SHUFFLE ALONG*)
L. Devine
(*Music by* Eubie Blake. *Lyrics by* Noble Sissle.)
Scene 11
"Beat Me Daddy Eight to the Bar"
B. J. Marsh, Band, Dancers
(*Music and Lyrics by* Don Raye, Hughie Prince, Eleanor Sheehy.)
"The Music Goes 'Round and 'Round"
B. J. Marsh, Band
(*Music by* Edward Farley and Michael Riley. *Lyrics by* Red Hodgson.)
Scene 12
"Life Is Just a Bowl of Cherries" (reprise)
L. Devine

ACT 2
Scene 1
"Now's the Time to Fall in Love"
W. Cilento, B. A. Davis, Dancers
(*Music and Lyrics by* Al Sherman and Al Lewis.)
Scene 2
"Ain't She Sweet"
M. Johnson, Jr., D. Coleman, W. Cilento, B. A. Davis, Dancers
(*Music by* Milton Ager. *Lyrics by* Jack Yellen.)
Scene 3
"Everybody Loves My Baby"
A. Weeks, W. Cilento, B. A. Davis
(*Music and Lyrics by* Jack Palmer and Spencer Williams.)
"Me and My Shadow"
G. Chapman, V. Pettiford, B. Yeager
(*Music by* Al Jolson and Dave Dreyer. *Lyrics by* Billy Rose.)
Scene 5
"Love Is Just Around the Corner" (from *HERE IS MY HEART*, film)
W. Cilento, B. A. Davis
(*Music by* Lewis E. Gensler. *Lyrics by* Leo Robin.)
Scene 7
"Just a Gigolo"
B. J. Marsh, C. Derricks
(*Music by* Leonello Casucci. *Original German Lyrics by* Julius Brammer. *English Lyrics by* Irving Caesar.)
"Who's Your Little Who-Zis?"
B. J. Marsh, V. Pettiford
(*Music by* Hal Goering and Ben Bernie. *Lyrics by* Walter Hirsch.)
Scene 9
"Yes Sir, That's My Baby"
C. Derricks
(*Music by* Walter Donaldson. *Lyrics by* Gus Kahn.)
"Button Up Your Overcoat" (from *FOLLOW THRU*)
L. Devine
(*Music by* Ray Henderson. *Lyrics by* Buddy DeSylva, Lew Brown.)

Scene 11

    "Daddy, You've Been a Mother to Me"
      A. Weeks, R. Reaux
      (Music and Lyrics by Fred Fisher.)

    "Hold Tight—Hold Tight"
      A. Lewis, Jr., Ladies
      (Music and Lyrics by Leonard Ware, Willie Spottswood, Ed Robinson, Ben Smith, Sidney Bechet.)

    "Happy Days Are Here Again" (from *CHASING RAINBOWS*, film)
      L. Marshall, D. Coleman, M. Johnson, Jr., Company
      (Music by Milton Ager. *Lyrics by* Jack Yellen.)

    "I'm Sitting on Top of the World"
      C. Derricks, Company
      (Music by Ray Henderson. *Lyrics by* Samuel L. Lewis, Joseph Young.)

Scene 12

    "Life Is Just a Bowl of Cherries' (reprise)
      L. Devine

1986.07   # SWEET CHARITY

A Revival of the Musical in Two Acts, a Prologue and 19 Scenes[21]. Book (revised) by Neil Simon. Based on the film "Le Notte di Cabiria" [Nights of Cabiria], screenplay by Federico Fellini, Tullio Pinelli, Ennio Flaiano. Music by Cy Coleman. Lyrics by Dorothy Fields. Original production conceived, staged and choreographed by Bob Fosse. Scenery and lighting by Robert Randolph. Costumes by Patricia Zipprodt. Musical direction by Fred Werner. Orchestrations by Ralph Burns. Sound by Otts Munderloh. Production manager, Phil Friedman. Assisant to Mr. Fosse, Gwen Verdon. Directed and choreographed by Bob Fosse. Produced by Jerome Minskoff, James M. Nederlander, Arthur Rubin, Joseph Harris. Opened 27 April 1986 at the Minskoff Theatre and closed 15 March 1987 after 368 performances.

<u>CAST</u> (in order of appearance): *Charity:* DEBBIE ALLEN. *Dark Glasses:* David Warren Gibson. *Married Couple:* Quin Baird, Jan Horvath. *First Young Man:* Jeff Shade. *Woman with hat:* CELIA TACKABERRY. *Ice Cream Vendor:* Kelly Patterson. *Young Spanish Man:* Adrian Rosario. *A Cop:* Tanis Michaels. *Helene:* ALLISON WILLIAMS. *Nickie:* BEBE NEUWIRTH. *Herman:* LEE WILKOF. *Panhandler:* CELIA TACKABERRY. *Doorman:* Tom Wierney. *Ursala:* CARRIE NYGREN. *Vittorio Vidal:* MARK JACOBY. *Waiter:* Tom Wierney. *Manfred:* Fred C. Mann III. *Receptionist:* Celia Tackaberry. *Old Maid:* Jan Horvath. *Oscar:* MICHAEL RUPERT. *Daddy Johann Sebastian Brubeck:* IRVING ALLEN LEE. *Brother Harold:* Tanis Michaels. *Brother Ray:* Stanley Wesley Perryman. *Rosie:* Dana Moore. *Mike:* Michael Davis. *Good Fairy:* CELIA TACKABERRY.

    Singers and Dancers of Times Square: Quin Baird, Christine Colby, Alice Everett Cox, David Warren Gibson, Kim Morgan Greene, Jan Horvath, Jane Lanier, Fred C. Mann III, Alison Reneé Manson, Tanis Michaels, Dana Moore, Kelly Patterson, Stanley Wesley Perryman, Mimi Quillin, Adrian Rosario, Jeff Shade, Tom Wierney. *Alternates:* Michelle O'Steen, Chet Walker.

---

[21]Originally produced in New York 29 January 1966 at the Palace Theatre for 608 performances. For Synopsis of Scenes and Musical Numbers, see original 1966 production. "You Should See Yourself" retained for this production; "Charity's Soliloquy" (Act 1, Scene 3) dropped. New music written for "I'm the Bravest Individual" (Act 1, Scene 8) and the title song, "Sweet Charity" (Act 2, Scene 5).

1986–1987 SEASON

Teresa Stratas in RAGS
Martha Swope/TimePix

1986–1987 SEASON

CANDIDE

1986.08

A Revival of the Musical in Two Act, 23 Scenes[1]. (New) Book adapted from Voltaire's satire (of the same name) by Hugh Wheeler. (Original book by Lillian Hellman.) Music by Leonard Bernstein. Lyrics by Richard Wilbur. Additional lyrics by Stephen Sondheim and John Latouche. Directed by Harold Prince. Stage director, Arthur Masella. Choreography by Patricia Birch. Scenery designed by Clarke Dunham. Costumes designed by Judith Dolan. Lighting designed by Ken Billington. Conducted by Scott Bergeson. Orchestrations by Leonard Bernstein and Hershy Kay. Additional orchestrations by John Mauceri. Chorus master, Joseph Colaneri. Produced by the New York City Opera. Opened 1 July 1986 at the New York State Theatre and closed 6 July 1986 after 8 performances; re-opened 11 November 1986 and closed 16 November 1986 after an additional 8 performances. Total: 16 performances.

CAST (in order of appearance): *Voltaire:* JOHN LANKSTON. *Candide:* DAVID EISLER. *Huntsman:* Don Yule. *Paquette:* DEBORAH DARR. *Baroness:* Ruth Golden. *Baron:* JACK HARROLD. *Cunegonde:* ERIE MILLS. *Maximilian:* SCOTT REEVE. *Servant of Maximilian:* JAMES BILLINGS. *Dr. Pangloss:* JOHN LANKSTON. *Bulgarian Soldiers:* Don Yule, JAMES BILLINGS. *Westphalian Soldiers:* William Ledbetter, Andy Roth. *Don Issachar, the Jew:* JAMES BILLINGS. *Grand Inquisitor:* JACK HARROLD. *Calliope Player:* Ruth Golden. *Heresy Agent:* Ralph Bassett. *Inquisition Agents:* Gary Dietrich, Douglas Hamilton. *Judge:* JAMES BILLINGS. *Old Lady:* MURIEL COSTA-GREENSPON. *Dons:* Vasilis Iracledes, Scott Evans, Richard Smith, Don Yule, William Ledbetter, Ralph Bassett. *Businessman:* JOHN LANKSTON. *Governor:* JOHN LANKSTON. *Governor's Aide:* Andy Roth. *Slave Driver:* JACK HARROLD. *Father Bernard:* JAMES BILLINGS. *Sailors:* Gary Dietrich, Douglas Hamilton, Andy Roth, Scott Evans. *Pirates:* John Henry Thomas, William Ledbetter. *Pink Sheep:* Ivy Austin, Rhoda Butler. *Lion:* Robert Brubaker. *Pasha-Prefect:* JACK HARROLD. *First Gambler:* JAMES BILLINGS. *Second Gambler (Police Chief):* JOHN LANKSTON. *Sage:* JOHN LANKSTON.

KISMET

1986.09

A Revival of the Musical Play (Musical Arabian Night) in Two Acts, 15 Scenes[2]. Book by Charles Lederer and Luther Davis. Based on the play of the same name by Edward Knoblock. Music based on themes by Alexander Borodin. Musical adaptation and lyrics by Robert Wright and George Forrest. Directed by Frank Corsaro. Choreographer, Randolyn Zinn. Conducted by Paul Gemignani. Set and costume designer, Lawrence Miller. Lighting designer, Mark W. Stanley. Chorus master, Joseph Colaneri. Produced by the New York City Opera. Opened 8 July 1986 at the New York State Theatre and closed 13 July 1986 after 8 performances.

CAST (in order appearance): *Imam of The Mosque:* James Clark. *Silk Dancers:* Ashley Janeway, Jean Barber, Terry Lacy, Fritz Masten. *Muezzins:* Louis Perry, Frank Ream, Glenn Rowen, George Wyman. *Beggars:* Don Yule, Robert Brubaker. *Dervishes:* Vasilis Iracledes, Richard Smith. *Omar:* JAMES BILLINGS. *A Public Poet,* later called *Hajj:* TIMOTHY NOLEN. *Marsinah, His Daughter:* DIANA WALKER. *Businessman:* William Ledbetter. *Hassan-Ben:* Ralph Bassett. *Jawan:* JOHN LANKSTON. *Swains:* Terry Lacy, Fritz Masten.. *Bangle Man:* James Clark. *Silk Merchants:* Louis Perry, Frank Ream. *Brave Merchant:* Harris Davis. *Young Women:* Madeleine Mines, Mary Ann Rydzeski. *Pearl Merchant:* William Ledbetter. *Slave Merchant:* Mervin Crook. *Informer:* William Ledbetter. *Policemen:* Ralph Bassett, Robert Brubaker. *Chief of Police:* Don Yule. *Wazir of Police:* JACK HARROLD. *Wazir's Guards:* Jeff Davis, Eric Miller, Donald R. Richardson, Elliot Santiago, Frank Sollito. *Slave Girls:* Jean Barber, Savia Berger, Ashley Janeway. *Harem Girl:* Rebecca Rosales. *Lalume:* SUSANNE MARSEE. *Princesses of Ababu:* Stephanie Godino, Joan Mirabella, Victoria Rinaldi. *The Caliph:* CRIS GROENENDAAL. *Widow Yussef:* Rebecca Russell. *Ayah to Lalume:* Mary Ann Rydzeski. *Princess Zubbediya of Damascus:* Esperanza Galan. *Ayah*

to Zubbediya: Rebecca Russell *Princess Samaris of Bangalore:* CANDACE ITOW. *Prosecutor:* James Clark. *Spies:* Ralph Bassett, Robert Brubaker, William Ledbetter. *Guest:* Louis Perry. *Ensemble:* New York City Opera Chorus.

DIE FLEDERMAUS

1986.10

A Revival of the Operetta in Three Acts[3]. Original libretto by Carl Haffner and Richard Genée. Lyrics by Richard Genée. Based on the comedy "Le Réveillon" by Henri Meilhac and Ludovic Halévy.) English version by Ruth and Thomas Martin. Music by Johann Strauss. Devised and directed by Gerald Freedman. Stage director, Christian Smith. Set designer, Lloyd Evans. Costume designer, Thierry Bosquet. Choreographer, Thomas Andrew. Lighting designer, Hans Sondheimer. Conductor, Imre Pallo. Produced by the New York City Opera. Opened 18 July 1986 at the New York State Theatre and closed 8 November 1986 after 9 performances in repertory.

CAST (in order of appearance): *Alfred,* an itinerant tenor: MICHAEL COUSINS. *Adele,* Rosalinda's chambermaid: CLAUDETTE PETERSON. *Rosalinda von Eisenstein:* LEIGH MUNRO. *Gabriel von Eisenstein:* THEODORE BAERG. *Dr. Blind,* a lawyer: Jerold Siena. *Dr. Falke,* a close friend of Eisenstein: WILLIAM PARCHER. *Frank,* the prison warden: Richard McKee. *Sally,* Adele's sister: Alison Bevan. *Ivan,* servant to Orlofsky: Larry Becker. *Prince Orlofsky,* a wealthy bored Russian: JAMES BILLINGS. *Guest Artist:* Patricia McBride. *Solo Dancer:* Esperanza Galan. *Frosch,* the jailer: Jack Harrold. *Ensemble:* New York City Opera Chorus.

HONKY TONK NIGHTS,
or How Billy Sampson and Company Left Hell's Kitchen for the Promised Land and What They Found There

1986.11

A Musical Comedy in Two Acts. Book and lyrics by Ralph Allen, David Campbell. Music by Michael Valenti. Direction and choreography by Ernest O. Flatt. Associate choreographer, Toni Kaye. Scenery by Robert Cothran. Costumes by Mardi Phillips. Lighting by Natasha Katz. Sound by Jack Mann. Musical direction, vocal arrangements by George Broderick. Orchestrations by Jim Tyler. Dance arrangements by David Krane. Produced by Edward H. Davis and Allen M. Shore in association with Marty Feinberg and Schellie Archbold. Opened 7 August 1986 at the Biltmore Theatre and closed 9 August 1986 after 4 performances.

CAST (in order of appearance): *Barney Walker:* JOE MORTON. *Billy Sampson:* IRA HAWKINS. *Armistead Sampson:* DANNY STRAYHORN. *Lily Meadows:* TERESA BURRELL. *George Gooseberry:* REGINALD VelJOHNSON. *Ruby Bush:* Yolanda Graves. *Ivy Vine:* Kyme. *Countess Aida:* Susan Beaubian. *Kitty Stark:* Robin Kersey. *Montgomery Boyd:* M. Demby Cain. *Winston Grey:* Keith Rozie. *Sparks Roberts:* Lloyd Culbreath. *Patron:* Charles Bernard Murray.

Sampson Philharmonia: George Broderick, Kaman Adilifu, John Gale, Robert Keller, David Krane, Gregory Maker, James Sedlar, Andrew Stein, Quinten White.

Act 1: Sampson's Music Hall, on a winter evening. New York City's Hell's Kitchen, 1912.

Act 2: The Promised Land Saloon, summer, 1922, Harlem.

ACT 1

"The Honky Tonk Nights Rag, or Professor Walker and His Solo Symphony"
    The Sampson Philharmonia
"Honky Tonk Nights"
    I. Hawkins and His Company
"Hot and Bothered"
    T. Burrell
"Roll With the Punches"
    J. Morton, D. Strayhorn, S. Beaubian, Kyme, R. Kersey, Y. Graves
"Lily of the Alley"
    D. Strayhorn, K. Rozie, M. D. Cain, L. Culbreath, J. Morton, T. Burrell
"Choosing a Husband's a Delicate Thing"
    D. Strayhorn, J. Morton, R. VelJohnson

---

[1]Original production first produced in New York 1 December 1956 at the Martin Beck Theatre for 73 performances; revised version first produced Off-Broadway 11 December 1973 at the Chelsea Theater Center, Brooklyn Academy of Music for 48 performances; transferred 5 March 1974 to the Broadway Theatre for 740 performances. For Synopsis of Scenes and Musical Numbers, see 1982 revival.

[2]Originally produced in New York 3 December 1953 at the Ziegfeld Theatre for 583 performances. For Synopsis of Scenes and Musical numbers, see original 1953 production.

[3]First English language production in New York 16 March 1885 at the Casino Theatre for 42 performances. First New York production of this adaptation 20 December 1950 at the Metropolitan Opera House. For Synopsis of Scenes and Musical Numbers, see May 1954 revival.

"Little Dark Bird"
 T. Burrell
"Withered Irish Rose"
 J. Morton, D. Strayhorn, R. VelJohnson, M. D. Cain, T. Burrell
"Tapaholics"
 L. Culbreath, Kyme, M. D. Cain
"Eggs"
 J. Morton, T. Burrell
"A Ticket to the Promised Land"
 The Sampson Company

ACT 2
"The Promised Land"
 The Pyromaniacs
"Stomp the Blues Away"
 The Sampson Company
"I've Had It"
 J. Morton, T. Burrell
"The Sampson Beauties"
 Kyme, R. Kersey, Y. Graves
"The Reform Song"
 J. Morton, R. VelJohnson, D. Strayhorn
"I Took My Time"
 T. Burrell
"The Brothers Vendetto"
 J. Morton, R. VelJohnson, D. Strayhorn
"A Man of Many Parts"
 J. Morton
Finale
 The Sampson Company

1986.12 ME AND MY GIRL

A Musical Comedy in Two Acts, a Prologue and 9 Scenes. Book and lyrics by L. Arthur Rose and Douglas Furber. Music by Noel Gay. Book revised by Stephen Fry; contributions to revisions by Mike Ockrent. Directed by Mike Ockrent. Choreography by Gillian Gregory. Set design by Martin Johns. Costume designs by Ann Curtis. Lighting design by Chris Ellis, Roger Morgan. Musical direction by Stanley Lebowsky. Sound design by Tom Morse. Orchestrations and dance arrangements by Chris Walker. Produced by Richard Armitage, Terry Allen Kramer, James M. Nederlander, Stage Promotions Limited & Co. Opened 10 August 1986 at the Marquis Theatre and closed 31 December 1989 after 1420 performances.

CAST (in order of appearance): *Lady Jacqueline Carstone*: JANE SUMMERHAYS. *The Honorable Gerald Bolingbroke*: NICK ULLETT. *Lord Battersby*: Eric Hutson. *Lady Battersby*: Justine Johnston. *Herbert Parchester*: TIMOTHY JEROME. *Sir Jasper Tring*: Leo Leyden. *Maria, Duchess of Dene*: JANE CONNELL. *Sir John Tremayne*: GEORGE S. IRVING. *Charles Heathersett, the Butler*: THOMAS TONER. *Bill Snibson*: ROBERT LINDSAY. *Sally Smith*: MARYANN PLUNKET. *Pub Pianist*: John Spalla. *Mrs. Worthington-Worthington*: Gloria Hodes. *Lady Diss*: Elizabeth Larner. *Lady Brighton*: Susan Cella. *Bob Barking*: Kenneth H. Waller. *Telegraph Boy*: Bill Brassea. *Mrs. Brown*: Elizabeth Larner. *Constable*: Eric Johnson.

Ensemble: Cleve Asbury, Bill Brassea, Jonathan Brody, Frankie Cassidy, Susan Cella, Sheri Cowart, Bob Freschi, Ann-Marie Gerard, Larry Hensen, Ida Henry, Randy Hills, Gloria Hodes, K. Craig Innes, Eric Johnson, Michael Hayward-Jones, Barry McNabb, Donna Monroe, Barbara Moroz, Cindy Oakes, William Ryall, John Spalla, Cynthia Thole, Mike Turner, Kenneth H. Waller. *Swings*: Corinne Melancon, Tony Parise.

The action takes place in the late 1930's, in and around Hareford Hall, Hampshire, Mayfair and Lambeth.

Prologue: Mayfair.

Act 1, Scene 1: Hareford Hall, Hampshire. *Scene 2*: The Kitchen. *Scene 3*: The Drawing Room. *Scene 4*: The Hareford Arms. *Scene 5*: The Terrace.

Act 2, Scene 1: The Garden at Hareford Hall. The next afternoon. *Scene 2*: The Library. *Scene 3*: Lambeth. *Scene 4*: Hareford Hall.

ACT 1
Scene 1
 "A Weekend at Hareford"
  Ensemble
 "Thinking of No-One But Me"
  J. Summerhays, N. Ullett

"The Family Solicitor"
 T. Jerome, G. S. Irving, J. Connell, N. Ullett, E. Hutson, J. Johnston
"Me and My Girl"
 R. Lindsay, M. Plunkett
Scene 2
 "An English Gentleman"
  T. Toner, Staff
Scene 3
 "You Would If You Could"
  J. Summerhays, R. Lindsay
 "Hold My Hand" (from *HOLD MY HAND*, London)
  R. Lindsay, M. Plunkett, Dancers
Scene 4
 "Once You Lose Your Heart"
  M. Plunkett
Scene 5
 "Preparation Fugue"
  The Company
 "The Lambeth Walk"
  R. Lindsay, M. Plunkett, Company

ACT 2
Scene 1
 "The Sun Has Got His Hat On"[4]
  N. Ullett, J. Summerhays, Ensemble
 "Take It on the Chin"
  M. Plunkett
Scene 2
 "Once You Lose Your Heart" (reprise)
  M. Plunkett
 "Song of Hareford"
  J. Connell, R. Lindsay, Ensemble
 "Love Makes the World Go Round" (from *THESE FOOLISH THINGS*, London)
  R. Lindsay, G. S. Irving
Scene 3
 "Leaning on a Lamppost" (from *FEATHER YOUR NEST*, film)
  R. Lindsay, Ensemble
Scene 4
 Finale
  The Company

1986.13 RAGS

A Musical in Two Acts, 22 Scenes. Book by Joseph Stein. Music by Charles Strouse. Lyrics by Stephen Schwartz. Directed by Gene Saks. Musical staging by Ron Field. Sets designed by Beni Montresor. Costumes designed by Florence Klotz. Lighting designed by Jules Fisher. Sound designed by Peter Fitzgerald. Musical direction and additional arrangements by Eric Stern. Orchestrations by Michael Starobin. Production supervisor, Robert V. Straus. Associate producer, Madeline Lee Gilford. Produced by Lee Guber, Martin Heinfling, Marvin A. Krauss. Opened 21 August 1986 at the Mark Hellinger Theatre and closed 23 August 1986 after 4 performances.

CAST (in order of appearance): *Homesick Immigrant*: Andy Gale. *Rebecca Hershkowitz*: TERESA STRATAS. *David Hershkowitz*: JOSH BLAKE. *Guards*: John Aller, Peter Samuel. *The Americans*: Michael Cone, Michael Davis. *Bella Cohen*: JUDY KUHN. *Avram Cohen*: DICK LATESSA. *Anna Blumberg*: EVALYN BARON. *Jack Blumberg*: MORDECAI LAWNER. *Ben*: LONNY PRICE. *Recruiters*: Andy Gale, Stan Rubin. *Nathan's Landlady*: Irma Rogers. *Millie, her neighbor*: Bonnie Schon. *Editor of newspaper*: Stan Rubin. *Social Worker*: Joanna Glushak. *Klezmorim*: Teddy Bragin (tuba), Sean Mahony (trombone), Bruce Engel (trumpet), Harold Seletsky (clarinet), Marshall Coid (violin). *Mr. Bronstein*: Stan Rubin. *Sweatshop Workers (3)*: *Rosa*: Audrey Lavine. *Esther*: Joan Finkelstein. *Sam*: Gabriel Barre. *Saul, a union organizer*: TERRENCE MANN. *Cigar Boss*: Peter Samuel. *Rachel Halpern*: MARCIA LEWIS. *An Avid Shopper*: Joanna Glushak. *Mr. Rosen*: John Aller. *Hamlet*: Peter Samuel. *Ophelia*: Joanna Glushak. *Gertrude*: Irma Rogers. *Rosencrantz*: Michael Cone. *Laertes*: Gabriel Barre. *Frankie*: Michael Cone. *Mike*: Michael Davis. *"Big Tim" Sullivan*: REX EVERHART. *Mr. Harris*: LARRY KERT. *Irish Tenor on Recording*: Michael Cone. *Ragman*: Gabriel Barre. *Wealthy New Yorkers*: Bill Hastings, John Aller,

---

[4]An interpolation, not in the original English 1937 production.

Michael Davis, Joan Finkelstein, Joanna Glushak, Wendy Kimball, Robert Radford, Peter Samuel, Catherine Ulissey. *Man on Stilts*: Gabriel Barre. *Thugs*: Andy Gale, Peter Samuel. *A Passerby*: Stan Rubin. *Morris*. a little boy: Devon Michaels. *His Mother*: Bonnie Schon. *Violinist*: Marshall Coid. *His Mother*: Irma Rogers. *Irish Girl*: Wendy Kimball. *Her Mother*: Audrey Lavine. *Italian Tenor*: Andy Gale. *His Mother*: Joanna Glushak. *Mrs. Sullivan*: Bonnie Schon. *Herschel Cohen*: John Aller. *Swings*: Patti Mariano, Cissy Rebich, Mark Fotopoulos.

The action takes place during 1910 on the Lower East Side of New York City.

Act 1, Scene 1: Ellis Island, April 1910. *Scene 2*: Battery Park, immediately following. *Scene 3*: East Side Streets and Blumberg Tenement Apartment. That afternoon. *Scene 4*: East Broadway and Offices of the Lower East Side. The next few days. *Scene 5*: A Street and Sweatshops. A few days later. *Scene 6*: Outside Bronstein's Sweatshop. Later that day and weeks following. *Scene 7*: A Yiddish Theatre. A few weeks later. *Scene 8*: Suffolk Street and under the Brooklyn Bridge. Later that night. *Scene 9*: McCarthy's Bar. *Scene 10*: The Blumberg Apartment. Evening, 3 July. *Scene 11*: Suffolk Street and Above Fourteenth Street. Immediately following. *Scene 12*: The Street Market. 4 July. *Scene 13*: The Blumberg Apartment. Immediately following.

Act 2, Scene 1: The Rooftop. Evening, 4 July. *Scene 2*: The Rooftop. Later that night. *Scene 3*: The Street Market. The next day. *Scene 4*: A few days later. *Scene 5*: The Lower East Side Democratic Club. A week later. *Scene 6*: The Blumberg Apartment. Some time later. *Scene 7*: Bronstein's Sweatshop. *Scene 8*: Union Square, A Protest Demonstration. Later that day. *Scene 9*: Suffolk Street and Battery park. A few weeks later.

ACT 1

Scene 1

"I Remember"
A. Gale

Scene 2

"Greenhorns"
M. Cone, New Immigrants

Scene 3

"Brand New World"
T. Stratas, J. Blake

Scene 4

"Children of the Wind"
T. Stratas, D. Latessa, J. Blake

Scene 5

"Penny a Tune"
M. Lewis, Klezmorim, Peddlers, Workers

Scene 6

"Easy for You"
T. Mann, T. Stratas, J. Blake

Scene 7

"Hard to Be a Prince"
P. Samuel, Company

Scene 8

"Blame It on the Summer Night"
T. Stratas, Clarinetist

Scene 9

"What's Wrong with That?"
M. Cone, M. Davis, R. Everhart, L. Kert

Scene 10

"For My Mary"
M. Cone, L. Price

Scene 11

"Rags"
J. Kuhn, D. Latessa

Scene 12

"On the Fourth of July"
Picnickers (Company)

Scene 13

"To America"
T. Stratas, L. Kert

ACT 2

Scene 1

"Yankee Boy"
L. Kert, Neighbors

Scene 2

"Uptown"
L. Kert, T. Stratas

"Wanting"
T. Stratas, T. Mann

Scene 3

"Three Sunny Rooms"
M. Lewis, D. Latessa

Scene 4

"The Sound of Love"
L. Price, J. Blake, Shoppers

"For My Mary" (reprise)
J. Kuhn, L. Price

Scene 5

"Democratic Club Dance"
T. Stratas, R. Everhart, L. Kert, B. Schon, Democrats

Scene 7

"Bread and Freedom"
A. Lavine, T. Stratas, J. Finkelstein, G. Barre

Scene 8

"Dancing with the Fools"
T. Stratas, L. Kert, Strikers

Scene 9

Finale
T. Stratas, J. Blake, The Americans, New Immigrants

1986.14   THE NEW MOON

A Revival of the Operetta in Two Acts, 7 Scenes[5]. Book by Oscar Hammerstein II, Frank Mandel and Laurence Schwab. Music by Sigmund Romberg. Lyrics by Oscar Hammerstein II. New adaptation of the book and lyrics by Robert Johanson. Conductor, Jim Coleman. Director and choreographer, Robert Johanson. Set designer, Michael Anania. Costume designer, Andrew Marlay. Lighting designer, Mark W. Stanley. Chorus master, Joseph Colaneri. Produced by the New York City Opera. Opened 26 August 1986 at the New York State Theatre and closed 7 September 1986 after 16 performances.

CAST (in order of appearance): *Julie*, Marianne's maid: JOYCE CAMPANA. *Alexander*, Bondservant to Beaunoir: GERALD ISAAC. *M. Beaunoir*, Marianne's father, owner of *The New Moon*: Jack Harrold. *Captain Duval*, Commander of *The New Moon*, suitor to Marianne: Joseph McKee. *Vicomte Ribaud*, the great French detective: DAVID RAE SMITH. *Fouchette*, informer for Ribaud: Allen Riberdy. *Robert Mission*, Bondservant to Beaunoir, formerly a nobleman: RICHARD WHITE or DAVIS GAINES. *Besac*, Boatswain on *The New Moon*: Richard McKee. *Jacques*, ship's carpenter on *The New Moon*: Michael Brown. *Marianne Beaunoir*, Beaunoir's daughter: LEIGH MUNRO or MARYANNE TALESE. *Proprietor*: Harris Davis. *Spaniard*: Terry Lacy. *Flower Dancer*: Esperanza Galan. *Philippe Dupres*, French exile, Robert's comrade: MICHAEL COUSINS or MARK THOMSEN. *Clotilde Lombaste*, leader of the brides bound for Martinique: MURIEL COSTA-GREENSPON. *Admiral de Jean*, commander of the new French Navy: John Lankston. *Servants, Courtiers, Ladies, Sailors, Pirates, Tavern Wenches, Brides and French Soldiers*: New York City Opera Chorus.

The action takes place in New Orleans, Louisiana, 1792.

Act 1, Scene 1: Ballroom of M. Beaunoir. *Scene 2*: Cafe Creole, shortly thereafter. *Scene 3*: Ballroom of M. Beanoir, later that night.

Act 2, Scene 1: Deck of *The New Moon*, three days later. *Scene 2*: Isle of Pines, one year later. *Scene 3*: Marianne's cabin, immediately thereafter. *Scene 4*: The stockade, the next morning.

ACT 1[6]

Scene 1

Opening
J. Campana, Servants, Courtiers

---

[5]First presented in New York 19 September 1928 at the Imperial Theatre for 509 performances. The original production was performed in Three Acts, 8 Scenes.

[6]No song list was included in the program for this production. The list below was prepared from Robert Johanson's previous production of THE NEW MOON at Papermill Playhouse.

"Marianne"
    R. White
"Marianne" (reprise)
    L. Munro, M. Brown, Sailors
"The Girl on the Prow"
    L. Munro, R. McKee, Sailors
"Gorgeous Alexander"
    G. Isaac, J. Campana, Servants
"An Interrupted Love Song"
    J. McKee
"Marianne" (reprise)
    R. White
Scene 2
"Tavern Song"
    Sailors, Wenches
"Softly, as in a Morning Sunrise"
    M. Cousins, Men
"Stouthearted Men"
    R. White, M. Cousins, Men
Scene 3
"One Kiss"
    L. Munro, Ladies
"Wanting You"
    L. Munro, R. White
Finale
    Ensemble

ACT 2
Scene 1
"Chanty"
    R. McKee, Sailors
"Funny Little Sailor Man"
    M. Costa-Greenspon, R. McKee, Sailors, Brides
"Lover Come Back to Me"
    L. Munro
"Stouthearted Men" (reprise)
    R. White, Ensemble
Scene 2
"Lover Come Back to Me" (reprise)
    R. White, M. Cousins, L. Munro
Scene 3
"Love Is Quite a Simple Thing"
    J. Campana, M. Costa-Greenspon
"One Kiss" (reprise)
    L. Munro, R. White
Scene 4
Finale
    Ensemble

ROWAN ATKINSON AT THE ATKINSON

1986.15

An Evening of Comedy in Two Acts. Written by Richard Curtis, Rowan Atkinson, Ben Elton. Music by Howard Goodall. Directed by Mike Ockrent. Musical director, Steven Margoshes. (Set) Design by Will Bowen. Lighting design by Mark Henderson. Sound design by Tony Meola. Production supervisor, Mitchell Erickson. Produced by Arthur Cantor in association with Caroline Hirsch, Peter Wilson, Tony Aljoe. Opened 14 October 1986 at the Brooks Atkinson Theatre and closed 18 October 1986 after 6 performances.

CAST: ROWAN ATKINSON, ANGUS DEAYTON.

The "Schoolmaster" monologue was written by Richard Sparks.

RAGGEDY ANN

1986.16

A Musical Adventure in Two Acts. Book by William Gibson. (Based on characters created by Johnny Gruelle in the "Raggedy Ann Stories.") Music and lyrics by Joe Raposo. Directed and choreographed by Patricia Birch. Set design by Gerry Hariton, Vicki Baral. Costume design by Carrie Robbins.

Lighting design by Marc B. Weiss. Sound design by Abe Jacob. Flying by Foy. Musical supervision, dance arrangements by Louis St. Louis. Orchestrations by Stan Applebaum. Musical directors, Ross Allen, Roy Rogosin. Conductor, Ross Allen. Originally produced for the stage by Empire State Institute for the Performing Arts (Patricia B. Snyder, Producing director). Produced by Jon Silverman Associates, Ltd., the (John F.) Kennedy Center, the Empire State Institute for the Performing Arts, Donald K. Donald, in association with CBS. Opened 16 October 1986 at the Nederlander Theatre and closed 19 October 1986 after 5 performances.

CAST (in order of appearance): *Doctors:* Dick Decareau, Joe Barrett, Richard Ryder. *Poppa:* BOB MORRISEY. *Marcella:* LISA RIEFFEL. *Raggedy Ann:* IVY AUSTIN. *Raggedy Andy:* SCOTT SCHAFER. *Baby Doll:* CAROLYN MARBLE. *Panda:* MICHELAN SISTI. *General D:* LEO BURMESTER. *Bat:* GAIL BENEDICT. *Wolf:* GORDON [JOSEPH] WEISS. *Camel with the wrinkled knees:* JOEL AROESTE. *Mommy:* ELIZABETH AUSTIN.

Company: Melinda Buckley, Gregory Butler, Anny DeGange, Susann Fletcher, Michaela Hughes, Steve Owsley, Andrea Wright. *Swing:* Helena Andreyko.

The action takes place sometime earlier in this century on the New York riverfront.

ACT 1
"Gingham and Yarn"
    Company
"Carry On"
    B. Morrisey
"Diagnosis"
    D. Decareau, J. Barrett, R. Ryder
"The Light"
    Dolls, L. Rieffel
"Make Believe"
    I. Austin, L. Burmester
"Blue"
    J. Aroeste, I. Austin
"Make Believe" (reprise)
    S. Schafer, L. Rieffel, Dolls, Company
"Make Believe" (reprise)
    I. Austin, L. Rieffel
"Something in the Air"
    Company
"Delighted"
    Clouds
"So Beautiful"
    I. Austin, L. Rieffel, Clouds
"A Heavenly Chorus"
    Yellow Yum Yum
"The Shooting Star"
    E. Austin, B. Morrisey, The Rat in the Rolls Royce
"The Wedding"
    Company
"Rag Dolly"
    I. Austin

ACT 2
"Gingham and Yarn" (reprise)
    Company
"You'll Love It"
    G. Benedict, S. Schafer, the Batettes
"A Little Music"
    L. Rieffel, J. Aroeste, I. Austin, Dolls
"Gone"
    Dolls, Company
"Why Not"
    E. Austin
"What Did I Lose?"
    E. Austin
"Somewhere"
    I. Austin
"Welcome to L.A."
    Nurses
"Diagnosis" (reprise)
    Doctors
"I Come Riding"
    L. Burmester

"Gingham and Yarn" (reprise)
    Company
"Rag Dolly" (Finale)
    Company

1986.17 FLAMENCO PURO

A Dance Revue in Two Acts. Conceived, directed and designed by Claudio Segovia and Hector Orezzoli. Sound by F. Richard Fitzgerald. Associate producer, Marilynn LeVine. Produced by Mel Howard and Donald K. Donald. Opened 19 October 1986 at the Mark Hellinger Theatre and closed 30 November 1986 after 53 performances.

CAST (in alphabetical order): *Dancers*: Manuela Carrasco, José Cortés (El Biencasao), Antonio Montoya (El Farruco), Pilar Montoya (La Faraona), Rosario Montoya (La Farruquita), Eduardo Serrano (El Guito), Angelita Vargas.
    Singers: Juan José Amador, Diego Camacho (El Boquerón), Adela Chaqueta, Enrique (El Extremeño), Fernanda de Utrera, Juan Fernández (El Moreno), Antonio Núñez (El Chocolate).
    Guitarists: Joaquin Amador, Ramón Amador, Agustin Carbonell (El Bola), José Carmona Carmona (El Habichuela), Juan Carmona Carmona (El Habichuela), José Miguel Carmona Niño.

ACT 1
"Bulerias"
    The Entire Company
My sorrow is great/My fatigue is great/I'll take them to the grave with me/And say nothing to anyone.
Sallow, with rings under her eyes?/Don't ask her what's wrong/She is truly in love.
I am brown and poor/Even browner is Cinnamon.
"Martinete"
    A. Núñez
A primal scream, with artifice is "truth in a clenched fist."
"Toque"
    Pepe Habichuela
"Cana"
    (*Danced by*) M. Carrasco, P. Montoya, R. Montoya, A. Vargas
        Singers: Enrique, D. Cumacho, J. Fernández. *Guitars*: A. Carbonell, Juan C. Carmona, J. Amador.
Cafe Cantate:
    "Alegrias"A. Chaqueta
My child has a balcony
Which faces the rising sun
The sun rises, my child rises
And God's grace rises too.
I spread my hair out on a branch
On a branch
And the name of the person who will unravel it
Is Manuel
"Romeras"
    (*Danced by*) J. Cortés
"Garrotin"
    (*Danced by*) A. Vargas
"Romance"
    (*Danced by*) M. Carrasco
"Farruca"
    (*Danced by*) E. Serrano
"Alegrias"
    (*Danced by*) R. Montoya
        Singers: D. Camacho, Enrique, J. J. Amador, J. Fernández. *Guitars*: J. Amador, R. Amador, A. Carbonell, J. M. Carmona.
"Fandangos"
    F. de Utrera, A. Núñez, Juan Carmona Carmona, José Carmona Carmona
I am not afraid of death/Because death is a natural thing/ I am more afraid of life/Because I don't know where it will lead me/With this head of mine.
If I call you sun I abuse you/If I call you moon I wound you/And when I call you morning star/It seems as if I am killing you/Would you like, perhaps, for me to call you sky?
"Tarantos"
    The Entire Company

Don't be afraid Señora
It's just a miner singing
A miner with a sore throat
Because of the dust in his path
I lost my handkerchief
While leaving the mine
And who has found it?
A gypsy that I love
And he doesn't want to give it back.

ACT 2
"Tangos"
    (*Danced by*) A. Chaqueta, R. Montoya, P. Montoya
        Singers: Enrique, J. Fernández, J. J. Amador. *Guitars*: A. Carbonell, J. M. Carmona.
Hold your tongue, Hold your tongue
Because I have hidden things about you.
Little secrets that no one knows.
All black eyes/Are to be taken prisoner tomorrow.
Yours are so black/You must cover your face with a veil.
"Tientos"
    (*Danced by*) A. Vargas
        Guitars: José Carmona Carmona, Juan Carmona Carmona. *Singer*: D. Camacho.
Listening to her I trembled/She told me my fortune.
But what she didn't tell me
Is that I have begun to hate my love/for the rest of my life.
What kind of bird is singing on the green olive?
Tell him to stop!
He's hurting my ears.
"Soleares"
    F. de Utrera
        Guitar: José Carmona Carmona. *Danced by* E. Serrano. *Guitars*: A. Carbonell, Juan Carmona Carmona. *Singers*: Enrique, J. J. Amador. *Danced by* M. Carrasco. *Guitars*: J. Amador, R. Amador. *Singers*: Enrique, J. J. Amador.
Perhaps I was born on a Tuesday
Because this bad luck of mine
Follows me everywhere.
"Seguiriya"
    (*Danced by*) A. Montoya, A. Núñez
        Guitars: José Carmona Carmona, R. Amador. *Singer*: J. Fernández.
Ay, Don't knock at this door
For the love of God don't knock
The gypsy inside
Is dead by my fault.
"Bulerias"
    Entire Company

1986.18 INTO THE LIGHT

A Musical in Two Acts, a Prologue, 13 Scenes and an Epilogue. Book by Jeff Tambornino. Music by Lee Holdridge. Lyrics by John Forster. Directed by Michael Maurer. Choreography by Mary Jane Houdina. Scenery, projections by Neil Peter Jampolis, Hervig Libowitzky. Costumes by Karen Roston. Lighting by Neil Peter Jampolis. Sound design by Jack Mann. Musical direction by Peter Howard. Orchestrations by Ira Hearshen. Laser design by Marilyn Lowey. Special laser effects by Laser Media. Synthesizer programming by Jeff Waxman. Produced by Joseph Z. Nederlander, Richard Kughn, Jerrold Perenchio. Opened 22 October 1986 at the Neil Simon Theatre and closed 26 October 1986 after 6 performances.

CAST (in order of speaking): *Friend*: ALAN MINTZ. *Mathew Prescott*: DANNY GERARD. *Kate Prescott*: SUSAN BIGELOW. *James Prescott*: DEAN JONES. *Colonel*: Ted Forlow. *Major*: David Young. *Father Frank Girella*: WILLIAM PARRY. *Peter Vonn*: LENNY WOLPE. *Nathan Gelb*: Peter Walker. *Vijay Bannerjee*: Mitchell Greenberg. *Phyllis Terwilliger*: Kathryn McAteer. *Paul Cooper*: Alan Brasington. *Don Cesare*: CASPER ROOS. *Archbishop Parisi*: TOM BATTEN. *Signor Bocciarelli*: Gordon Stanley.
    Ensemble: Michael Duran, David Young, Deborah Carlson, Terri Homberg, Valerie DePena. *Swings*: Cheri Butcher, Ron Chisholm.

The action takes place at the present time during late summer in Los Alamos, New Mexico, and in Turin, Italy.

473

Act 1, Scene 1: James Prescott's office and the Prescott home. *Scene 2*: The lab at Los Alamos. *Scene 3*: The Prescott home. late at night. *Scene 4*: The next morning. *Scene 5*: Turin, Italy. The Council Chambers of Il Centro di Sindonologia. *Scene 6*: The Precott home. *Scene 7*: The airport and lab at Los Alamos.

Act 2, Scene 1: Turin, Italy. *Scene 2*: Turin, Italy. *Scene 3*: The Prescott home. *Scene 4*: The testing room, St. John's Cathedral. *Scene 5*: Albergo Excelsiore. *Scene 6*: The testing room.

ACT 1

Prologue: "Poltergeists"
D. Gerard, S. Bigelow

Scene 1

"Neat/Not Neat"
D. Jones, W. Parry, S. Bigelow
"It Can All Be Explained"
D. Jones, W. Parry

Scene 2

"The Data"
D. Jones, Team

Scene 3

"A Talk About Time"
D. Jones, K. Bigelow

Scene 4

"Trading Solos"
W. Parry, D. Gerard, A. Mintz

Scene 5

"Let There Be Light"
D. Jones, C. Roos, W. Parry, G. Stanley, T. Batten

Scene 6

"Wishes"
D. Gerard

Scene 7

"The Three of Us"
S. Bigelow, D. Jones
"Rainbow Logic"
D. Jones

ACT 2

Scene 1

"Fede Fede"
C. Roos, T. Batten, Team

Scene 2

"To Measure the Darkness"
D. Jones, S. Bigelow

Scene 4

"The Testing"
D. Jones, Team

Scene 5

"The Rose and I"
S. Bigelow

Scene 6

"The Testing" continued
D. Jones, Team
"Measure the Darkness" (reprise)
D. Jones
"Be There"
D. Jones, D. Gerard
Epilogue: "Into the Light"
Company

1986.19   OH, COWARD!

A Revival of the Musical Revue in Two Acts, 18 Scenes[7]. Words and music by Noël Coward. Devised and Directed by Roderick Cook. Settings by Helen Pond, Herbert Senn. Costumes by David Toser. Lighting by F. Mitchell Dana. Musical director, Dennis Buck. Musical arrangements by

---

[7]Originally produced Off-Broadway 4 October 1972 at the New Theatre for 295 performances.

Rene Wiegert. Executive producer, Richard Seader. Produced by Raymond J. Greenwald. Opened 17 November 1986 at the Helen Hayes Theater and closed 3 January 1987 after 56 performances.

CAST: RODERICK COOK, CATHERINE COX, PATRICK QUINN.

Act 1, Scene 1: Introduction. *Scene 2*: Oh Coward! *Scene 3*: England. *Scene 4*: Family Album. *Scene 5*: Music Hall. *Scene 6*: If Love Were All. *Scene 7*: Travel. *Scene 8*: Finale Act 1.

Act 2, Scene 1: Mad Dogs and Englishmen. *Scene 2*: A Marvelous Party. *Scene 3*: Design for Dancing. *Scene 4*: You Were There. *Scene 5*: Theatre. *Scene 6*: Love. *Scene 7*: Women. *Scene 8*: World Weary. *Scene 9*: Let's Do It. *Scene 10*: Finale.

ACT 1

Scene 1

The Boy Actor
C. Cox, P. Quinn, R. Cook

Scene 2

"Something to Do With Spring" (from *WORDS AND MUSIC*, London)
"Bright Young People" (from *COCHRAN'S 1931 REVUE*, London)
"Poor Little Rich Girl" (from *ON WITH THE DANCE*, London)
"Zigeuner" (from *BITTER SWEET*)
"Let's Say Goodbye" (from *WORDS AND MUSIC*, London)
"This Is a Changing World" (from *PACIFIC 1860*, London)
"We Were Dancing" (from *TONIGHT AT 8:30*)
"Dance Little Lady" (from *THIS YEAR OF GRACE*)
"(A) Room with a View" (from *THIS YEAR OF GRACE*)
"Sail Away" (from *ACE OF CLUBS*, London; *SAIL AWAY!*)
C. Cox, P. Quinn, R. Cook

Scene 3

"London Is a Little Bit of All Right" (from *THE GIRL WHO CAME TO SUPPER*)
P. Quinn
"The End of the News" (from *SIGH NO MORE*)
C. Cox, R. Cook
"The Stately Homes of England" (from *OPERETTE*, London; *SET TO MUSIC*)
P. Quinn, R. Cook
"London Pride"
C. Cox

Scene 4

Auntie Jessie
R. Cook
"Uncle Harry" (from *PACIFIC 1860*, London)
C. Cox, P. Quinn

Scene 5

Introduction
R. Cook
"Chase Me Charlie" (from *ACE OF CLUBS*, London)
C. Cox
"Saturday Night at the Rose and Crown"
(from *THE GIRL WHO CAME TO SUPPER*)
C. Cox, P. Quinn, R. Cook
"Island of Bollamazoo" (from *OPERETTE*, London)
P. Quinn
"What Ho, Mrs. Brisket" (from *THE GIRL WHO CAME TO SUPPER*)
R. Cook
"Has Anybody Seen Our Ship?" (from *TONIGHT AT 8:30*)
C. Cox, P. Quinn, R. Cook
"Men About Town" (from *TONIGHT AT 8:30*)
P. Quinn, R. Cook

Scene 6

"If Love Were All" (from *BITTER SWEET*)

Scene 7

Too Early or Too Late
R. Cook
"Why Do the Wrong People Travel?" (from *SAIL AWAY!*)
C. Cox, P. Quinn

"The Passenger's Always Right" (from *SAIL AWAY!*)
C. Cox, P. Quinn, R. Cook

Scene 8

"Mrs. Worthington"
C. Cox, P. Quinn, R. Cook

ACT 2

Scene 1

"Mad Dogs and Englishmen" (from *WORDS AND MUSIC*
London; *THIRD LITTLE SHOW*)
C. Cox, P. Quinn, R. Cook

Scene 2

"The Party's Over Now" (from *WORDS AND MUSIC*, London;
SET TO MUSIC)
R. Cook

Scene 3

"Dance Little Lady" (from *THIS YEAR OF GRACE*)
C. Cox, P. Quinn, R. Cook

Scene 4

"You Were There" (from *TONIGHT AT 8:30*)
P. Quinn

Scene 5

"Three White Feathers" (from *WORDS AND MUSIC*, London)
C. Cox, R. Cook
The Star, P. Quinn
The Critic, R. Cook
The Elderly Actress, C. Cox

Scene 6

Gertie
R. Cook
Loving
P. Quinn
I Am No Good at Love
R. Cook
Sex Talk
P. Quinn
A Question of Lighting
P. Quinn, R. Cook
"Mad About the Boy" (from *WORDS AND MUSIC*, London;
SET TO MUSIC)
C. Cox

Scene 7

Introduction
R. Cook
"Nina" (from *SIGH NO MORE*, London)
P. Quinn
"Mrs. Wentworth-Brewster" (A Bar on the Piccola Marina)
R. Cook

Scene 8

"World Weary" (from *THIS YEAR OF GRACE*)
C. Cox, P. Quinn, R. Cook

Scene 9

"Let's Do It"
(*Music by* Cole Porter.) C. Cox, P. Quinn, R. Cook

Scene 10

"Where Are the Songs We Sung?" (from *OPERETTE*,
London)
P. Quinn
"Someday I'll Find You" (from *PRIVATE LIVES*)
R. Cook
"I'll Follow My Secret Heart" (from *CONVERSATION PIECE*)
C. Cox
"If Love Were All" (reprise)
C. Cox, P. Quinn, R. Cook
"Play, Orchestra, Play" (from *TONIGHT AT 8:30*)
C. Cox, P. Quinn, R. Cook
"I'll See You Again" (from *BITTER SWEET*)
C. Cox, P. Quinn, R. Cook

1986.20 # SMILE

A Musical in Two Acts. Book and lyrics by Howard Ashman. Based on the film of the same name with screenplay by Jerry Belson. Music by Marvin Hamlisch. Directed by Howard Ashman. Musical staging by Mary Kyte. Scenic design by Douglas W. Schmidt. Costume design by William Ivey Long. Lighting design by Paul Gallo. Sound design by Otts Munderloh. Musical director, Paul Gemignani. Orchestrations by Sid Ramin, Bill Byers, Dick Hazard, Torrie Zito. Vocal arrangements by Buster Davis. Associate producers, Barbara Livitz, Ronald and Barbara Balser. Produced by Lawrence Gordon, Richard Kagan, Sidney Shlenker. Opened 24 November 1986 at the Lunt-Fontanne Theatre and closed 3 January 1987 after 48 performances.

CAST: *Contestants: Robin Gibson*, Antelope Valley: ANNE MARIE BOBBY. *Doria Hudson*, Yuba City: JODI BENSON. *Sandra-Kay Macafee*, Bakersfield: VEANNE COX. *Maria Gonzales*, Salinas: CHERYL-ANN ROSSI. *Shawn Christianson*, La Jolla: TIA RIEBLING. *Valerie Sherman*, Sacramento: LAUREN GOLER. *Heidi Anderson*, Anaheim: Deanna D. Wells. *Patti-Lynn Bird*, El Centro: Mana Allen. *Debralee Davis*, Eureka: Andrea Leigh-Smith. *Kate Gardner*, Fresno: Mia Malm. *Linda Lee*, San Francisco: Valerie Kau-Lee. *Kimberly Lyons*, Palo Alto: Julie Tussey. *Gina Minelli*, San Luis Obispo: Donna Marie Elio. *Dana Simpson*, Sausalito: Renée Veneziale. *Connie-Sue Whipple*, Visalia: Cindy Oakes. *Cookie Wilson*, Carson: Nikki Rene. *Joanne Marshal*, last year's winner: Mia Malm.
Adults: Brenda DiCarlo Freelander: MARSHA WATERBURY. *Big Bob Freelander:* JEFF McCARTHY. *Tommy French*, the pageant choreographer: MICHAEL O'GORMAN. *Dale Wilson-Shears*, chairman of the Young American Miss Foundation: RICHARD WOODS. *Ted Farley*, an Emcee: DICK PATTERSON. *Carol*, Brenda's assistant: Ruth Williamson. *Tony*, a volunteer: Jeffrey Wilkins. *Robin's Mom, Judge, Volunteer*: Laura Gardner. *Photographer, Judge, Volunteer*: K. C. Wilson.
Kids: Little Bob Freelander: Tommy Daggett. *Freddy*: Andrew Cassese.
Swings: Michael Bologna, Susan Dow, Linda Hess, Woody Howard, Joyce Nolen.

Act 1: Santa Rosa Junior College, (Santa Rosa, California). Three days last summer.

Act 2: Santa Rosa Junior College. Saturday night.

ACT 1

Prologue
The Contestants
"Orientation/Postcard #1"
M. Waterbury, A. M. Bobby, Contestants
"Disneyland"
J. Benson
"Shine"
The Contestants, M. O'Gorman, M. Waterbury
"Postcard #2"
A. M. Bobby
"Nerves"
The Contestants
"Young and American" (Preliminary Night)
The Contestants
"Until Tomorrow Night"
The Contestants, M. Waterbury, J. McCarthy

ACT 2

"Postcard #3/Dressing Room Scene"
A. M. Bobby, J. Benson, D. Patterson, Contestants
"Smile"
D. Patterson, Contestants
"In Our Hands"
The Contestants
"Pretty as a Picture"
D. Patterson, J. McCarthy, A. M. Bobby, Contestants

THE WORLD ACCORDING TO ME

1986.21

A One Man Comedy Revue in Two Acts. Created and written by Jackie Mason. Supervised by Ron Clark. Scenery and lighting by Neil Peter Jampolis. Sound by Bruce D.Cameron. Associate producer, Jyll Rosenfeld. Produced by Nick Vanoff. Opened 22 December 1986 at the Brooks Atkinson Theater and closed 2 January 1988 after 367 performances.

CAST: JACKIE MASON (stand-up comedy, monologues, impressions.

THE MIKADO,
1987.01　or The Town of Titipu

A Revival of the Comic Opera in Two Acts[8]. Libretto by William S. Gilbert. Music by Arthur Sullivan. Directed and choreographed by Brian Macdonald. Set design by Susan Benson and Douglas McLean. Costumes designed by Susan Benson. Lighting designed by J. Michael Whitfield. Musical direction, additional musical arrangements by Berthold Carriere. Orchestra of the New York Opera Repertory Theater. A Stratford Festival of Canada Production. Produced by Ed and David Mirvish and Brian Macdonald. Opened 13 January 1987 at the New York City Center and closed 18 January 1987 after 7 performances; re-opened 2 April 1987 at the Virginia Theatre and closed 3 May 1987 after 38 additional performances. Total: 45 performances.

<u>CAST</u>: *The Mikado of Japan*: AVO KITTASK. *Nanki-Poo*, his son, disguised as a wandering minstrel in love with Yum-Yum: JOHN KEANE. *Ko-Ko*, Lord High Executioner of Titipu: ERIC DONKIN. *Pooh-Bah*, Lord High Everything Else: RICHARD McMILLAN. *Pish-Tush*, a Noble Lord: Paul Massel. *Yum-Yum, Pitti-Sing, Peep-Bo*, three sisters, wards of Ko-Ko: MARIE BARON, KAREN WOOD, KAREN SKIDMORE. *Katisha*, an elderly lady in love with Nanki-Poo: ARLENE MEADOWS. *Tumbler*: David Gonzales.

Chorus of School Girls, Nobles, Guards and Coolies: Stephen Beamish, Timothy Cruickshank, Aggie Cekuta Elliot, Glori Gage, Paul Gatchell, Larry Herbert, Deborah Joy, Devid Keeley, Calla Krause, Richard March, Janet Martin, Dale Mieske, Lyndsay Richardson, Bradley C. Rudy, Joy Thompson-Allen, Marcia Tratt, Jim White.

1987.02　## STARDUST

A Musical Revue in Two Acts[9]. Lyrics by Mitchell Parish. Music by Hoagy Carmichael, Benny Goodman, Duke Ellington, Leroy Anderson, others. Based on an idea by Burton L. Litwin and Albert Harris. Conceived and directed by Albert Harris. Musical staging by Patrice Soreiro. Musical supervision and direction, vocal arrangements, orchestrations by James Raitt. Scenery by David Jenkins. Costumes by Mardi Philips. Lighting by Ken Billington. Sound by Gary Harris. Associate producer, Richard Jay Smith. Tap dance created and staged by Henry LeTang. Produced by Burton L. Litwin, Howard Rose, Martin I. Rein, Louise Westergaard in association with Paula Hutter Gilliam[10]. Opened 19 February 1987 at the Biltmore Theatre and closed 17 May 1987 after 118 performances. Total including Off-Broadway run: 177 performances.

<u>CAST</u> (in alphabetical order): MICHELE BAUTIER, MAUREEN BRENNAN, KIM CRISWELL, ANDRE DeSHIELDS, JASON GRAAE, JIM WALTON.

ACT 1
"Carolina Rolling Stone"
　J. Graae, Company
　(*Music by* Eleanor Young, Harry D. Squires. 1921)
"Riverboat Shuffle"
　A. DeShields, Company
　(*Music by* Hoagy Carmichael, Dick Voynow, Irving Mills. 1924)
"One Morning in May"[11]
　M. Brennan
　(*Music by* Hoagy Carmichael. 1933)
"Sweet Lorraine"
　J. Walton
　(*Music by* Cliff Burwell. 1928)
"Sentimental Gentleman from Georgia"
　M. Bautier, M. Brennan, K. Criswell

(*Music by* Frank Perkins. 1932)
"Sophisticated Lady"
　M. Bautier
　(*Music by* Duke Ellington. *Co-Lyricist*: Irving Mills. 1933)
"Dixie After Dark"
　A. DeShields, J. Walton
　(*Music by* Ben Oakland, Irving Mills. 1934)
"Stairway to the Stars"
　K. Criswell
　(*Music by* Matty Malneck, Frank Signorelli. 1935)
"Wealthy, Shmelthy, as Long as You're Healthy"
　J. Graae
　(*Music by* Sammy Fain. 1935)
The 1930's Unrequited Love Montage:
"Hands Across the Table" (from *CONTINENTAL VARIETIES*)
　M. Bautier
　(*Music by* Jean Delettre. 1934)
"You're So Indiff'rent"
　J. Graae
　(*Music by* Sammy Fain. 1935)
"It Happens to the Best of Friends"
　K. Criswell
　(*Music by* Rube Bloom. 1934)
"I Would If I Could But I Can't"
　J. Walton
　(*Music by* Bing Crosby, Alan Grey. 1933.
"The Scat Song"
　A. DeShields, M. Brennan
　(*Music by* Frank Perkins, Cab Calloway. 1932)
"Sidewalks of Cuba" (from *COTTON CLUB PARADE OF 1934*)
　K. Criswell, J. Graae
　(*Music by* Ben Oakland, Irving Mills. 1934)
"Evenin'"[12]
　M. Bautier
　(*Music by* Harry White. 1934)
"Deep Purple"
　A. DeShields, Company
　(*Music by* Peter DeRose. 1934)

ACT 2
"Sophisticated Swing"
　K. Criswell, M. Brennan, J. Walton
　(*Music by* Will Hudson. 1936)
"Midnight at the Onyx"
　A. DeShields, M. Brennan, J. Walton
　(*Music by* Will Hudson. 1937)
"Tell Me Why"
　(J. Graae)
　(*Music by* Michael Edwards, Sigmund Spaeth. 1945)
"Does Your Heart Beat for Me?"
　J. Graae
　(*Music by* Russ Morgan, Arnold Johnson. 1936)
"Stars Fell on Alabama"
　J. Walton, M. Brennan
　(*Music by* Frank Perkins. 1934)
"Don't Be That Way"
　A. DeShields, M. Bautier
　(*Music by* Benny Goodman, Edgar Sampson. 1935)
"Organ Grinder's Swing"
　A. DeShields, J. Graae, J. Walton
　(*Music by* Will Hudson. *Co-Lyricist*: Irving Mills. 1936)
"Moonlight Serenade"
　Company
　(*Music by* Glenn Miller. 1939)
"Star Dust"
　M. Bautier

---

[8]First presented in New York 20 July, 10-29 August 1885 at the Union Square and People's Theatres for 22 performances. First authorized production presented 19 August 1885 at the Fifth Avenue Theatre by Richard D'Oyly Carte for 250 performances. For Synopsis of Scenes and Musical Numbers, see 19 August 1885 D'Oyly Carte production. Added to the Ensemble for the Broadway run: Elizabeth Adams, David Playfair, Gerald Smuin, , Steve Yorke. Dropped from Ensemble for Broadway run: Calla Krause, Dale Mieske, Bradley C. Rudy. Added for Broadway run: Conductor, Fen Watkin. Additional Tumbler {Acrobat}: Walter Quigley.
[9]Originally produced Off-Broadway 11 November 1986 at Theater Off Park for 59 peformances.
[10]Late in Broadway run William H. Kessler joined as a co-producer.
[11]Dropped late in Broadway run.

---

[12]Replaced late in run by:
"The Lamp Is Low" M. Bautier
　(*Music by* Peter DeRose, Bert Shefter, adapted from Maurice Ravel's 'Pavanne pour une Infante Defunte.' 1939)

(Music by Hoagy Carmichael. 1929)
Your Cavalcade of Hits: *Host*: A. DeShields.
"Belle of the Ball"
J. Graae, M. Brennan
(Music by Leroy Anderson. 1951)
"The Syncopated Clock"
M. Brennan, J. Graae, K. Criswell, J. Walton
(Music by Leroy Anderson. 1946)
"Take Me in Your Arms"
M. Brennan
(Music by Fred Markush. 1932)
"Ciao, Ciao, Bambino"
K. Criswell
(Music by Domenico Modugno. 1959)
"Sleigh Ride"
M. Brennan, J. Graae, K. Criswell, J. Walton
(Music by Leroy Anderson. 1949)
"Volare"
J. Walton, Company
(Music by Domenico Modugno. 1958)
"Your Cavalcade of Hits" Theme
Music by James Raitt. *Lyrics by* Jay Jeffries.
"Happy Cigarettes" Theme
Music by James Raitt. *Lyrics by* Peter Jablonski.
"Ruby" (from *RUBY GENTRY*, film)
A. DeShields
(Music by Heinz Roemheld. 1953)
"Forgotten Dreams"
Company
(Music by Leroy Anderson. 1954)
"Star Dust" (reprise)
Company

1987.03 SOUTH PACIFIC

A Revival of the Musical Play in Two Acts, 23 Scenes[13]. Book by Oscar Hammerstein II and Joshua Logan. Adapted from James A. Michener's novel "Tales of the South Pacific." Music by Richard Rodgers. Lyrics by Oscar Hammerstein II. Direction and musical staging by Gerald Freedman. Scenery and costumes by Desmond Heeley. Lighting by Duane Schuler. Choreography by Janet Watson. Sound by Thomas Maher. Musical director, Paul Gemignani. Orchestrations by Robert Russell Bennett. Produced by the New York City Opera. Opened 28 February 1987 at the New York State Theatre and closed 26 April 1987 after 68 performances.

CAST (in order of appearance): *Ngana*: Lynn Chen or Allegra Forste. *Jerome*: Robin Ria or Peter Yarin. *Henry*: Thomas Ikeda. *Ensign Nellie Forbush*: SUSAN BIGELOW or MARCIA MITZMAN. *Emile DeBecque*: JUSTINO DIAZ or STANLEY WEXLER. *Bloody Mary*: MURIEL COSTA-GREENSPON or CAMILLE SAVIOLA. *Bloody Mary's Assistant*: Raven Wilkinson. *Luther Billis*: TONY ROBERTS. *Lt. Joseph Cable, U.S.M.C.*: RICHARD WHITE or CRIS GROENENDAAL. *Capt. George Brackett, U.S.N.*: JAMES BILLINGS. *Cmdr. William Harbison, U.S.N.*: Daren Kelly or Joseph Culliton. *Lt. Buzz Adams*: Ralph Bassett. *Seaman Tom O'Brien*: Terry Lacy. *Cpl. Hamilton Steeves, U.S.M.C.*: Ron Hilley. *Abner*: Charles Mandracchia. *Sgt. Kenneth Johnson*: Gregory Moore. *Radio Operator Bob McCaffrey*: Jonathan Guss. *Stewpot*: John Welch. *Professor*: Jeff Blumenkrantz. *Private Victor Jerome*: Andrew Cuk. *Pvt. Sven Larsen*: Edward Zimmerman. *Yeoman Herbert Quale*: Frank Ream. *Sgt. Jack Waters*: Louis Perry. *Seabee Richard West*: Robert Brubaker. *Seabee Morton Wise*: William Dyszel. *Staff-Sgt. Thomas Hassinger*: David Frye. *Seabee Joseph Grant*: Don Yule. *Lt. Genevieve Marshall*: Michele McBride. *Ensign Lisa Minelli*: Ivy Austin. *Ensign Connie Walewska*: Deborah Darr. *Ensign Janet MacGregor*: Janet Villas. *Ensign Bessie Noonan*: Paula Hostetter. *Ensign Rita Adams*: Deanna Wells. *Ensign Sue Yaeger*: Tina Johnson. *Ensign Cora MacRae*: Sylvia Rhyne. *Ensign Dinah Murphy*: Kay Schoenfeld. *Liat*: ANN YEN or ADRIENNE TELEMAQUE. *Marcel*: Henry Ravelo.

---

[13]First produced in New York 7 April 1949 at the Majestic Theatre for 1925 performances. For Synopsis of Scenes and Musical Numbers, see original 1949 production. For this production, the Act 1 Finale was listed under the title"This Is How It Feels"/"I'm Gonna Wah That Man Right Out-a My Hair" (reprise); The Soft Shoe Dance (Act 2, Scene 1) dropped.

1987.04 LES MISÉRABLES

A Musical in Two Acts, a Prologue and 4 Scenes. Original French text by Alain Boublil and Jean-Marc Natel. Additional material by James Fenton. Based on the novel of the same name by Victor Hugo. Music by Claude-Michel Schönberg. (English) Lyrics by Herbert Kretzmer. Directed and adapted by Trevor Nunn and John Caird. Orchestral score by John Cameron. Musical supervision and direction by Robert Billig. Sound by Andrew Bruce/Autograph. (Settings) Designed by John Napier. Lighting by David Hersey. Costumes by Andreane Neofitou. Executive producers, Martin McCallum, Richard-Jay Alexander. Original London production produced by Cameron Mackintosh and the Royal Shakespeare Company. Produced by Cameron Mackintosh in association with the John F. Kennedy Center. Opened 12 March 1987 at the Broadway Theatre, moved 16 October 1990 to the Imperial Theatre, and is still running at this time!

CAST (in order of appearance): *Prologue, 1815*: Jean Valjean: COLM WILKINSON. *Javert*: TERRENCE MANN. *Chain Gang*: Kevin Marcum, Paul Harman, Anthony Crivello, John Dewar, Joseph Kolinski, Leo Burmester, David Bryant, Alex Santoriello, Michael Maguire. *Farmer*: Jesse Corti. *Labourer*: Alex Santoriello. *Innkeeper*: John Norman. *Innkeeper's Wife*: Susan Goodman. *The Bishop of Digne*: Norman Large. *Constables*: Marcus Lovett, Steve Shocket.
Montreuil-sur-Mer, 1823: *Fantine*: RANDY GRAFF. *Foreman*: Paul Harman. *Workers*: Jesse Corti, John Dewar. *Women Workers*: Cindy Benson, Marcie Shaw, Jane Bodle, Joanna Glushak. *Factory Girl*: Ann Crumb. *Sailors*: Jospeh Kolinski, Kevin Marcum, John Dewar. *Whores*: Susan Goodman, Joanna Glushak, Jane Bodle, Kelli James, Ann Crumb, Frances Ruffelle, Judy Kuhn, Gretchen Kingsley-Weihe. *Old Woman*: Cindy Benson. *Crone*: Marcie Shaw. *Pimp*: Steve Shocket. *Bamatabois*: Anthony Crivello. *Fauchelevent*: Steve Shocket.
Montfermeil, 1823: *Young Cosette*: Donna Vivino. *Madame Thénardier*: JENNIFER BUTT. *Thénardier*: LEO BURMESTER. *Young Eponine*: Chrissie McDonald. *Drinker*: Jesse Corti. *Young Couple*: Alex Santoriello, Gretchen Kingsley-Wiehe. *Drunk*; John Norman. *Diners*: Norman Large, Joanna Glushak. *Other Drinkers*: Steve Shocket, Anthony Crivello, Kevin Marcum, Ann Crumb, Susan Goodman, Cindy Benson. *Young Man*: Joseph Kolinski. *Young Girls*: Jane Bodle, Kelli James. *Old Couple*: Marcie Shaw, John Dewar. *Travelers*: Paul Harman, Marcus Lovett.
Paris, 1832: *Gavroche*: Braden Danner. *Old Beggar Woman*: Susan Goodman. *Young Prostitute*: Ann Crumb. *Pimp*: John Norman. *Eponine*: FRANCES RUFFELLE. *Thénardier's Gang (4)*: *Montparnasse*: Alex Santoriello. *Babet*: Marcus Lovett. *Brujon*: Kevin Marcum. *Claquesous*: Steve Schocket. *Enjolras*: MICHAEL MAGUIRE. *Marius*: DAVID BRYANT. *Cosette*: JUDY KUHN. *Combeferre*: Paul Harman. *Feuilly*: Joseph Kolinski. *Courfeyrac*: Jesse Corti. *Joly*: John Dewar. *Grantaire*: Anthony Crivello. *Lesgles*: Norman Large. *Jean Prouvaire*: John Norman.

Prologue: Digne, (France). 1815.

Act 1, Scene 1: Montreuil-sur-Mer, 1823. *Scene 2*: Montfermeil, 1823. *Scene 3*: Paris, 1832.

Act 2: Paris, 1832.

ACT 1
Prologue
Prologue
The Company
"Soliloquy"
C. Wilkinson
"At the End of the Day"
Unemployed, Factory Workers
Scene 1
"I Dreamed a Dream"
R. Graff
"Lovely Ladies"
Ladies, Clients
"Who Am I?"
C. Wilkinson
"Come to Me"
R. Graff, C. Wilkinson
"Castle on a Cloud"
D. Vivino
"Master of the House"
L. Burmester, J. Butt, Customers
"Thénardier Waltz (of Treachery)"
L. Burmester, J. Butt, C. Wilkinson
Scene 2
"Look Down"
B. Danner, Beggars

"Stars"
 T. Mann
"Red and Black"
 M. Maguire, D. Bryant, Students
"Do You Hear the People Sing?"
 M. Maguire, Students, Citizens
Scene 3
"In My Life"
 J. Kuhn, C. Wilkinson, D. Bryant, F. Ruffelle
"A Heart Full of Love"
 J. Kuhn, D. Bryant, F. Ruffelle
"One Day More"
 The Company

ACT 2
"On My Own"
 F. Ruffelle
"A Little Fall of Rain"
 F. Ruffelle, D. Bryant
"Drink with Me to Days Gone By"
 A. Crivello, Students, Women
"Bring Him Home"
 C. Wilkinson
"Dog Eats Dog"
 L. Burmester
"Soliloquy" (Javert's Suicide)
 T. Mann
"Turning"
 Women
"Empty Chairs at Empty Tables"
 D. Bryant
"Wedding Chorale"
 Guests
"Beggars at the Feast"
 L. Burmester, J. Butt
Finale
 The Company

1987.05   STARLIGHT EXPRESS

A Musical in Two Acts. Music by Andrew Lloyd Webber. Lyrics by Richard Stilgoe. Directed by Trevor Nunn. Choreographed by Arlene Phillips. (Sets, costumes) Designed by John Napier. Lighting by David Hersey. Sound by Martin Levan. Musical director, Paul Bogaev. Musical direction and supervision, David Caddick, Andrew Lloyd Webber. Orchestrations by David Cullen, Andrew Lloyd Webber. Production advisor, Arthur Cantor. Originally produced on the London stage by The Really Useful Company. Executive producer, Gatchell & Neufeld Ltd. Produced by Martin Starger and Lord Grade in association with MCA Music Entertainment Group, Stage Promotions (Four)/Strada Holdings, Weintraub Entertainment Group, Inc. Opened 15 March 1987 at the Gershwin Theatre and closed 8 January 1989 after 761 performances.

CAST (in order of appearance): *Bobo:* A. C. Ciulla. *Expresso:* Philip Clayton. *Weltschaft:* Michael Berglund. *Turnov:* William (Christopher) Frey. *Hashamoto:* D. Michael Heath. *Prince of Wales:* Sean McDermott. *Greaseball:* ROBERT TORTI. *Greaseball's Gang:* Todd Lester, Sean Grant, Ronald Garza, Angel Vargas, Joey McKneely, Gordon Owens. *Rusty:* GREG MOWRY. *Pearl:* REVA RICE. *Dinah:* JANE KRAKOWSKI. *Ashley:* ANDREA McARDLE. *Buffy:* JAMIE BETH CHANDLER. *Rocky I:* Frank Mastrocola. *Rocky II:* Sean Grant. *Rocky III:* Ronald Garza. *Rocky IV:* Angel Vargas. *Dustin:* MICHAEL SCOTT GREGORY. *Flat-Top:* Todd Lester. *Red Caboose:* BERRY K. BERNAL. *Krupp:* Joey McKneely. *Wrench:* Christina Youngman. *Joule:* Nicole Picard. *Volta:* Mary Ann Lamb. *Purse:* Gordon Owens. *Electra:* KEN ARD. *Poppa:* STEVE FOWLER. *Belle:* Janet Williams Adderley.
 Voice of the Boy: Braden Danner. *Voice of the Mother:* Melanie Vaughan. *Starlight Chorus:* Paul Binotto, Lon Hoyt, Melanie Vaughan, Mary Windholtz. *Swing:* Anthony Calde.

(The action takes place in the imagination of the boy.)

ACT 1[14]
"Rolling Stock"
 R. Torti, Greaseball's Gang
"Engine of Love"[15]
 G. Mowry, R. Rice, J. Krakowski, A. McArdle, J. B. Chandler
"Lotta Locomotion"
 J. Krakowski, A. McArdle, J. B. Chandler, G. Mowry
"Freight"
 The Company
"AC/DC"
 K. Ard, J. McKneely, C. Youngman, N. Picard, M. A. Lamb, G. Owens, Company
"Pumping Iron"
 R. Torti, R. Rice, J. Krakowski,
  A. McArdle, J. B. Chandler, N. Picard, M. A. Lamb, C. Youngman
"Freight" (reprise)
 The Company
"Make Up My Heart"
 R. Rice
"Race One"
 R. Torti and J. Krakowski, M. Berglund and N. Picard,
  W. Frey and B. K. Bernal, K. Ard and R. Rice
"There's Me"
 B. K. Bernal, J. Krakowski
"Poppa's Blues"
 S. Fowler, F. Mastrocola, S. Grant, R. Garza, A. Vargas, G. Mowry
"Belle"
 J. W. Adderley, S. Fowler, F. Mastrocola, S. Grant,
  R. Garza, A. Vargas, G. Mowry, M. S. Gregory, T. Lester
"Race Two"
 A. C. Ciulla and J. B. Chandler, K. Rose and M. A. Lamb,
  P. Clayton and A. McArdle, S. Fowler and M. S. Gregory
"Laughing Stock"
 The Company
"Starlight Express"
 G. Mowry
ACT 2[16]
"Silver Dollar"
 The Company
"U.N.C.O.U.P.L.E.D."
 J. Krakowski, A. McArdle, J. B. Chandler
"Rolling Stock" (reprise)
 J. Krakowski, A. McArdle, J. B. Chandler
"Wide Smile, High Style, That's Me"
 B. K. Bernal, K. Ard, J. McKneely, C. Youngman, N. Picard, M. A. Lamb, G. Owens
"First Final"
 R. Torti and R. Rice, K. Ard and J. Krakowski,
  K. Rose and M. A. Lamb, S. Fowler and B. K. Bernal
"Right Place, Right Time"
 F. Mastrocola, S. Grant, R. Garza, A. Vargas
"I Am the Starlight"
 G. Mowry, S. Fowler

---

[14]The subsequent national tour, subtitled "Tracking Across America" made the following revisions:
 "Taunting Rusty" (added after "Engine of Love") Greaseball and Gang
 "Belle" was dropped.
 "Silver Dollar" was replaced by "The Rap."
 The national tour was directed and choreographed by Arlene Phillips, tour lighting by Rick Belzer and Ted Mather, associate scenic designer Raymond Huessy, produced by James M. Nederlander, Columbia Artists Management, Inc., Concert Productions International and Pace Theatrical Group.
[15]Devised from an original lyric by Peter Reeves.
[16]During the Broadway run, the song order in Act 2 was revised as follows: "Chase" was dropped; after "Final Selection," the order was "One Rock & Roll Too Many," "Only You," and "Light at the End of the Tunnel."

478

"Final Selection"
G. Mowry, M. S. Gregory, J. Krakowski, K. Ard, R. Rice, R. Torti, B. K. Bernal
"Only You"
R. Rice, G. Mowry
"Chase"
The Company
"One Rock & Roll Too Many"
R. Torti, K. Ard, B. K. Bernal
"Light at the End of the Tunnel"
The Company

BARBARA COOK:
1987.06 A CONCERT FOR THE THEATRE

A One Woman Show in Two Acts. Music arranged and conducted by Wally Harper. Scenery by John Falabella. Costumes by Joseph G. Aulisi. Lighting by Richard Winkler. Sound by Fred Miller. Keyboard coordinator, John Clifton. Associate producer, Perry B. Granoff. Produced by Jerry Kravat, The Shubert Organization, Emanuel Azenberg. Opened 15 April 1987 at the Ambassador Theater and closed 26 April 1987 after 13 performances.

CAST: BARBARA COOK.
Musicians: Wally Harper (piano), John Beal (bass), Charles Loeb (guitar), John Redsecker (drums), David Carey (percussion), Mack Schlefer (keyboard), John Clifton (keyboard), Lawrence Feldman (reeds).

MUSICAL NUMBERS
"Sing a Song with Me"
(*Music by Wally Harper. Lyrics by Paul Zakrzewski.*)
"Let Me Sing a Simple Song"
(from *MASS*)
(*Music by Leonard Bernstein. Lyrics by Stephen Schwartz.*)
"Come Rain or Come Shine" (from *ST. LOUIS WOMAN*)
(*Music by Harold Arlen. Lyrics by Johnny Mercer.*)
"The Man I Love" (dropped from *LADY BE GOOD* and *STRIKE UP THE BAND*)
(*Music by George Gershwin. Lyrics by Ira Gershwin.*)
"A Foggy Day" (from *A DAMSEL IN DISTRESS* film)
(*Music by George Gershwin. Lyrics by Ira Gershwin.*)
"Sweet Georgia Brown"
(*Music and Lyrics by Maceo Pinkard, Ben Bernie, Kenneth Casey.*)

"If Love Were All" (from *BITTER SWEET*)
(*Music and Lyrics by Noël Coward.*)
"Them There Eyes"
(*Music and Lyrics by Maceo Pinkard, Ben Bernie, Kenneth Casey.*)
"Widescreen"
(*Music and Lyrics by Rupert Holmes.*)
"Stars"
(*Music and Lyrics by Laura Nyro.*)
"Wait Till You See Him" (from *BY JUPITER*)
(*Music by Richard Rodgers. Lyrics by Lorenz Hart.*)
"I Love a Piano" (from *STOP! LOOK! LISTEN!*)
(*Music and Lyrics by Irving Berlin.*)
"I See Your Face Before Me" (from *BETWEEN THE DEVIL*)
(*Music by Arthur Schwartz. Lyrics by Howard Dietz.*)
"Change Partners" (from *CAREFREE* film)
(*Music and Lyrics by Irving Berlin.*)
"Mr. Snow" (from *CAROUSEL*)
(*Music by Richard Rodgers. Lyrics by Oscar Hammerstein II.*)
"Dear Friend"/"Ice Cream" (from *SHE LOVES ME*)
(*Music by Jerry Bock. Lyrics by Sheldon Harnick.*)
"Till There Was You" (from *THE MUSIC MAN*)
(*Music and Lyrics by Meredith Willson.*)
"An Ingenue"
(*Music by Wally Harper. Lyrics by David Zippel.*)
"I Can Cook Too" (from *ON THE TOWN*)
(*Music by Leonard Bernstein. Lyrics by Betty Comden and Adolph Green.*)
"He Was Too Good To Me" (from *SIMPLE SIMON*)
(*Music by Richard Rodgers. Lyrics by Lorenz Hart.*)
"Losing My Mind" (from *FOLLIES*)
(*Music and Lyrics by Stephen Sondheim.*)
"Carolina in the Morning" (from *THE PASSING SHOW OF 1922*)
(*Music by Walter Donaldson. Lyrics by Gus Kahn.*)
"Why Did I Choose You?" (from *THE YEARLING*)
(*Music by Michael Leonard. Lyrics by Herbert Martin.*)
"In Between Goodbyes"
(*Music by Wally Harper. Lyrics by David Zippel.*)

Joanna Gleason in INTO THE WOODS
Martha Swope/TimePix

1987–1988 SEASON

1987.07   DREAMGIRLS

A Revival of the Musical in Two Acts, 20 Scenes[1]. Book and lyrics by Tom Eyen. Music by Henry Krieger. Directed and choreographed by Michael Bennett. Co-choreographer, Michael Peters. Scenic design by Robin Wagner. Costume design by Theoni V. Aldredge. Lighting design by Tharon Musser. Sound design by Otts Munderloh. Musical supervision and orchestrations, Harold Wheeler. Musical coordinator, Yolanda Segovia. Musical director, Marc Falcone. Vocal arrangements, Cleavant Derricks. Production supervised by Bob Avian. Produced by Marvin A. Krauss and Irving Siders. Opened 28 June 1987 at the Ambassador Theatre and closed 29 November 1987 after 177 performances.

CAST (in order of appearance): _The Stepp Sisters_: Susan Beaubian, Rhetta Hughes, R. LaChanze Sapp, Lorraine Velez. _Charlene_: Yvette Louise Cason. _Joanne_: Lynda McConnell. _Marty_: Roy L. Jones. _Curtis Taylor, Jr._: WEYMAN THOMPSON. _Deena Jones_: ALISA GYSE. _The M.C._: Vernon Spencer. _Tiny Joe Dixon_: Leonard Piggee. _Lorrell Robinson_: ARNETIA WALKER. _C. C. White_: KEVYN MORROW. _Effie Melody White_: LILLIAS WHITE. _Little Albert and the Tru-Tones_: Bobby Daye, Robert Clater, Matthew Dickens, Germaine Edwards, Robert Fowler. _James Thunder Early_: HERBERT L. RAWLINGS, JR. _Edna Burke_: Fuschia Walker. _The James Early Band_: Robert Clater, Bobby Daye, Matthew Dickens, Germaine Edwards, Robert Fowler, David Thomé. _Wayne_: Milton Craig Nealy. _Dave and the Sweethearts_: Stephen Bourneuf, Shirley Tripp, Lorraine Velez. _Frank_, a press agent: Tim Cassidy. _Dwight_, a TV Director: David Thomé. _TV Stage Manager_: Stephen Bourneuf. _Michelle Morris_: Susan Beaubian. _Jerry_, a nightclub owner: Leonard Piggee. _Carl_, a piano player: Robert Fowler. _The Five Tuxedos_: Robert Clater, Bobby Daye, Matthew Dickens, Germaine Edwards, Robert Fowler. _Les Style_: Yvette Louise Cason, Rhetta Hughes, Lynda McConnell, R. LaChanze Sapp. _Film Executives_: Matthew Dickens, Robert Fowler, David Thomé. _Mr. Morgan_: Vernon Spencer. _Security Guard_: Leonard Piggee.

Party Guests, Photographers: Stephen Bourneuf, Yvette Louise Cason, Tim Cassidy, Robert Clater, Bobby Daye, Matthew Dickens, Germaine Edwards, Robert Fowler, Rhetta Hughes, Lynda McConnell, Milton Craig Nealy, Leonard Piggee, R. LaChanze Sapp, Vernon Spencer, David Thomé, Shirley Tripp, Fuschia Walker. _Swings_: Brenda Braxton, Graciela Simpson, Phillip Gilmore, Darryl Eric Tribble. (N.B. _The Dreamettes, the Dreams_ {through Act 1, Scene 11}: L. White, A. Walker, A. Gyse. _Deena Jones and The Dreams_ thereafter: A, Gyse, A. Walker, S. Beaubian.)

1987.08   THE STUDENT PRINCE

A Revival of the Operetta in Three Acts, a Prologue and 4 Scenes[2]. Music by Sigmund Romberg. Book and lyrics by Dorothy Donnelly. (Based on the play "Old Heidelberg" by Rudolf Bleichmann, adapted from "Alt-Heidelberg" by Wilhelm Meyer-Förster.) Book adaptation by Hugh Wheeler. Conducted by Jim Coleman. Directed by Jack Hofsis. Stage director, Christian Smith. Scenery designed by David Jenkins. Costumes designed by Patton Campbell. Lighting Designed by Gilbert V. Hemsley, Jr. Choreography by Donald Saddler, restaged by Jessica Redel. Chorus Master, Joseph Colaneri. Produced by the New York City Opera. Opened 7 July 1987 at the New York State Theatre and closed 8 November 1987 after 14 performances in repertory.

CAST (in order of their appearance): _Lackeys_: Edward Zimmerman, Louis Perry, George Wyman, Neil Eddinger, Glenn Rowen, Gregory Moore. _Dr. Engel_, the Prince's Tutor: BRIAN STEELE or CHESTER LUDGIN. _Count von Mark_: DAVID RAE SMITH. _Secretaries_: Glenn Rowen, Jonathan Guss. _Prince Karl Franz_: JOHN STEWART or JON GARRISON. _Lutz_, valet to the Prince: JAMES BILLINGS or JACK HARROLD. _Gretchen_, Maid at the Inn: SUSANNE MARSEE. _Ruder_: Joseph McKee. _Nicholas_: Douglas Hamilton. _Toni_, a waiter: Jack Harrold or James Billings. _Hubert_: William Ledbetter. _Detlef_, a student leader: Stanley Cornett. _von Asterberg_, another student leader: Robert Brubaker. _Lucas_, another student leader: Robert Ferrier. _Freshman_: Louis Perry. _Kathie_, niece of Ruder: CLAUDETTE PETERSON or LEIGH MUNRO. _Girls_: Madeleine Mines, Paula Hostetter, Beth Pensiero, Jill

Bosworth. _Grand Duchess Anastasia_: MURIEL COSTA-GREENSPON. _Princess Margaret_, fiancée of Prince Karl Franz: LISBETH LLOYD or CYNTHIA ROSE. _Captain Tarnitz_: CRIS GROENENDAAL. _Countess Leydon_, lady-in-waiting to the Princess: Rebecca Russell. _Huzzars_: Edward Zimmerman, Louis Pewrry, George Wyman, Neil Eddinger, Glenn Rowen, Gregory Moore. _Friends of the Huzzars_: Madeleine Mines, Paula Hostetter, Beth Pensiero, Jill Bosworth. _Ensemble_: New York City Opera Chorus.

1987.09   SWEENEY TODD–THE DEMON BARBER OF FLEET STREET

A Revival of the Musical Thriller in Two Acts[3]. Book by Hugh Wheeler. Based on a version of "Sweeney Todd" by Christopher Bond (after the original melodrama by George Dibdin-Pitt). Music and lyrics by Stephen Sondheim. Directed by Harold Prince. Choreography by Larry Fuller, recreated by William Kirk. Production designed by Eugene Lee. Costumes designed by Franne Lee. Lighting designed by Ken Billington. Orchestrations by Jonathan Tunick. Musical director, Paul Gemignani. Stage director, Arthur Masella. Produced by the New York City Opera. Opened 29 July 1987 at the New York State Theater and closed 4 October 1987 after 11 performances in repertory.

CAST (in order of appearance): _Anthony Hope_: CRIS GROENENDAAL. _Sweeney Todd_: STANLEY WEXLER or TIMOTHY NOLEN. _Beggar Woman_: BROOKS ALMY or IVY AUSTIN. _Mrs. Lovett_: MARCIA MITZMAN or JOYCE CASTLE. _Judge Turpin_: JOSEPH McKEE or WILL ROY. _The Beadle_: JOHN LANKSTON. _Johanna_: SUSAN POWELL or LEIGH MUNRO. _Tobias Ragg_: ROBERT JOHANSON. _Pirelli_: JEROLD SIENA. _Jonas Fogg_: William Ledbetter. _The Company_: New York City Opera Chorus.

1987.10   THE DESERT SONG

A Revival of the Operetta {Musical} in Two Acts, 7 Scenes[4]. Book and lyrics by Otto Harbach and Oscar Hammerstein II. New adaptation of book and lyrics by Robert Johanson. Music by Sigmund Romberg. Directed and choreographed by Robert Johanson. Conductor, Jim Coleman. Costume designer, Suzanne Mess. Set design, Michael Anania. Lighting design, Mark W. Stanley. Chorus master, Joseph Colaneri. Produced by the New York City Opera. Opened 25 August 1987 at the New York State Theatre and closed 6 September 1987 after 16 performances.

CAST (in order of appearance): _Sid El Kar_: MICHAEL COUSINS or JOHN STEWART. _Hassi_: KENNETH KANTOR. _Hadji_: William Ledbetter. _Neri_: Joyce Campana. _Red Shadow/Pierre Birabeau_: RICHARD WHITE. _Benjamin Kidd_: PHILIP WILLIAM McKINLEY. _Azuri_: LOUISE HICKEY. _Captain Paul Fontaine_: THEODORE BAERG or CRIS GROENENDAAL. _Sergeant LaVergne_: David Frye. _Susan_: LILLIAN GRAFF. _Edith_: Paula Hostetter. _General Birabeau_: DAVID RAE SMITH. _Margot Bonvalet_: LINDA MICHELE or JANE THORNGREN. _Ali Ben Ali_: RAYMOND BAZEMORE. _Clementina_: JOYCE CAMPANA. _Nogi_: Robert Brubaker. _Ensemble_: New York City Opera Chorus.

The action takes place in Morocco in the 1930's.

Act 1, Scene 1: Retreat of the "Red Shadow" in the Riff Mountains. _Scene 2_: Near the desert, outside General Birabeau's house. _Scene 3_: The garden of General Birabeau's home, the same day.

Act 2, Scene 1: The Great Hall of Ali Ben Ali. The following day. _Scene 2_: The room of the Silken Couch. _Scene 3_: The edge of the desert. _Scene 4_: Back at General Birabeau's, two nights later.

ACT 1[5]

Scene 1

"High on a Hill"
    M. Cousins, Riffs
"The Riff Song"
    R. White, Riffs

---

[1]Originally produced in New York 20 December 1981 at the Imperial Theatre for 1522 performances. For Synopsis of Scenes and Musical Numbers, see original 1981 production.
[2]First produced in New York as "The Student Prince in Heidelberg" 2 December 1924 at the Jolson Theatre for 608 peformances; this adaptation first produced in New York 29 August 1980 at the New York State Theatre for 13 performances. For Synopsis of Scenes and Musical Numbers, see 1980 revival.

[3]Originally produced in New York 1 March 1979 at the Uris Theatre for 557 performances. For Synopsis of Scenes and Musical Numbers, see original 1979 production.
[4]Originally produced in New York 30 November 1926 at the Casino Theatre for 471 performances.
[5]No song list was included in the program for this production. The list below was prepared from Robert Johanson's previous production of THE DESERT SONG at Papermill Playhouse.

"My Margot"
 T. Baerg, Soldiers
Scene 2
 "Why Did We Marry Soldiers?"
  L. Graff, Women
Scene 3
 "French Military Marching Song"
  L. Michele, Company
 "Romance"
  L. Michele, Women
 "I Want a Kiss"
  L. Michele, T. Baerg
 "It"
  P. W. McKinley, L. Graff
 "The Desert Song"
  R. White, L. Michele
 Finale, Act 1
  Full Company

ACT 2
Scene 1
 "Song of the Brass Key"
  J. Campana, Harem Girls
 "One Good Boy Gone Wrong"
  P. W. McKinley, J. Campana
 "Eatern Western Love"
  R. Bazemore, M. Cousins
 "One Alone"
  R. White, Men
Scene 2
 "The Sabre Song"
  L. Michele
 "The Desert Song" (reprise)
  R. White, L. Michele
Scene 3
 "One Alone" (reprise)
  R. White, L. Michele, M. Cosuins, T. Baerg, R. Bazemore, Men
Scene 4
 "It" (reprise)
  P. W. McKinley, L. Graff
 "Dance of Triumph"
  L. Hickey
 Finale, Act 2
  Full Company

1987.11   DIE FLEDERMAUS

A Revival of the Operetta in Three Acts[6]. Music by Johann Strauss. Original libretto by Carl Haffner and Richard Genée. Lyrics by Richard Genée. Based on the comedy "Le Réveillon" by Henri Meilhac and Ludovic Halévy. English libretto by Ruth and Thomas Martin. Production devised and directed by Gerald Freedman. Stage director, Christian Smith. Choreography by Thomas Andrew. Scenery designed by Lloyd Evans Costumes design by Thierry Bosquet. Lighting design by Hans Sondheimer. Conducted by Imre Pallo. Chorus master, Joseph Colaneri. Produced by the New York City Opera. Opened 26 September 1987 at the New York State Theatre and closed 31 October 1987 (matinee) after 5 performances in repertory.

CAST (in order of appearance): *Alfred*, an itinerant tenor: Michael Cousins. *Adele*, Rosalinda's chambermaid: CLAUDETTE PETERSON. *Rosalinda von Eisenstein*: LEIGH MUNRO. *Gabriel von Eisenstein*: THEODORE BAERG. *Dr. Blind*, a lawyer: Jonathan Green. *Dr. Falke*, a close friend of Eisenstein: WILLIAM PARCHER. *Frank*, the prison warden: JOSEPH McKEE. *Sally*, Adele's sister: Alison Bevan. *Ivan*, servant to Orlofsky: Larry Becker. *Prince Orlofsky*, a wealthy, bored Russian: JAMES BILLINGS. *Guest Artist*: PATRICIA McBRIDE. *Solo Dancer*: Esperanza Galan. *Frosch*, the jailer: Jack Harrold. *Ensemble*: New York City Opera Chorus.

---

[6]First English Language Production in New York 16 March 1885 at the Casino Theatre for 42 performances. First New York production of this adaptation 20 December 1950 at the Metropolitan Opera House. For Synopsis of Scenes and Musical Numbers, see May 1954 revival.

1987.12   ROZA

A Musical in Two Acts. Book and lyrics by Julian More. Based on the novel "La Vie Devant Soi" by Romain Gary. Music by Gilbert Becaud. Directed by Harold Prince. Musical staging by Patricia Birch. Costumes by Florence Klotz. Scenery by Alexander Okun. Lighting by Ken Billington. Sound by Otts Munderloh. Musical direction, vocal and dance arrangements by Louis St. Louis. Orchestrations by Michael Gibson. Production consultant, Mervyn Nelson. Executive producer, Ruth Mitchell. Associate producer, Allen M. Shore. Produced by The Producers Circle Company (Mary Lea Johnson, Martin Richards, Martin Richards, Sam Crothers) and the Shubert Organization by arrangement with Les Editions Musicales et Artistiques (EMA). Opened 1 October 1987 at the Royale Theatre and closed 11 October 1987 after 12 performances.

CAST (in order of appearance): *Madame Roza*: GEORGIA BROWN. *Max*: Al DeCristo. *Raoul*: Ira Hawkins. *Madame Bouaffa*: Michele Mais. *Jasmine*: Yamil Borges. *Hamil*: Neal Ben-Ari. *Doctor Katz*: Jerry Matz. *Madame Katz*: Marcia Lewis. *Michel*: David Shoichi Chan. *Banania*: Mandla Msomi. *Salima*: Monique Cintron. *Young Momo*: Max Loving. *Lola*: BOB GUNTON. *Young Moise*: Stephen Rosenberg. *Woman*: Thuli Dumakude. *Man*: Richard Frisch. *Moise*: Joey McKneely. *Momo*: Alex Paez. *Yussef Kadir*: Neal Ben-Ari.

The action takes place in a house in Belleville, an immigrant quarter of Paris, inhabited by many different ethnic groups.

Act 1: 1970.

Act 2: 1974.

ACT 1
 "Happiness"
  G. Brown
 "Max's Visit"
  A. DeCristo, G. Brown
 "Different"
  B. Gunton, G. Brown, M. Lewis, M. Mais, Y. Borges
 "Is Me"
  M. Loving, S. Rosenberg, M. Cintron,
   D. S. Chan, M. Msomi, M. Mais, Y. Borges
 "Get the Lady Dressed"
  G. Brown, B. Gunton, M. Loving,
   S. Rosenberg, M. Cintron, D. S. Chan, M. Msomi
 "Hamil's Birthday"
  Company
 "Bravo Bravo"
  G. Brown
 "Moon Like a Silver Window"
  M. Loving, A. Paez, Company
ACT 2
 "Merci"
  A. Paez, J. McKneely
 "House in Algiers"
  G. Brown
 "Yussef's Visit"
  N. Ben-Ari, G. Brown, A. Paez, J. McKneely, B. Gunton
 "Life Is Ahead of Me"
  A. Paez
 "Sweet Seventeen"
  M. Mais, Y. Borges, A. Paez, J. McKneely
 "Lola's Ceremony"
  B. Gunton, Company
 "Don't Make Me Laugh"
  G. Brown, B. Gunton
 "Live a Little"
  G. Brown
 Finale
  Company

1987.13   MORT SAHL ON BROADWAY

A One Man Show in One Act. Lighting by Roger Morgan. Executive producer, Marvin A. Krauss. Produced by James L. Nederlander and Arthur Rubin. Opened 11 October 1987 at the Neil Simon Theatre and closed 1 November 1987 after 25 performances.

CAST: MORT SAHL.

1987.14 LATE NITE COMIC

A Musical in Two Acts, 21 Scenes. Book by Allan Knee. Music and lyrics by Brian Gari. Directed by Philip Rose[7]. Choreographed by Dennis Dennehy. Scenery designed by Clarke Dunham. Costumes designed by Gail Cooper-Hecht. Lighting designed by Ken Billington. Musical direction by Gregory J. Dlugos. Orchestrations by Larry Hochman. Vocal and dance arrangements by James Raitt. Sound designed by Abe Jacob. Produced by Rory Rosegarten. Opened 15 October 1987 at the Ritz Theatre and closed 17 October 1987 after 4 performances.

CAST: *David Ackerman*: ROBERT LuPONE. *Gabrielle*: TERESA TRACY. *Susan, Hooker*: Pamela Blasetti. *Club Owner, Hooker*: Kim Freshwater. *Jenny, Hooker*: Lauren Goler. *Cecil, Club Owner, Voice of God, Krazy Korn Emcee*: Patrick Hamilton. *Hooker*: Judine Hawkins. *Tanya, Delilah*: Aja Major. *Club Owner, Mike, Las Vegas Emcee*: Michael McAssey. *Hooker, Metropolitan Ballerina*: Sharon Moore. *Nat, Bartender, David's Alter Ego, Metropolitan Male Dancer*: Mason Roberts. *Clara, Hooker*: Susan Santoro. *Club Owner, Bartender, Busboy*: Don Stitt.

Ensemble: Pamela Blasetti, Kim Freshwater, Lauren Goler, Judine Hawkins, Aja Major, Sharon Moore, Susan Santoro, Don Stitt. *Swings*: Danielle P. Connell, Barry Finkel.

The action takes place at the present time in New York and Las Vegas.

Act 1, Scene 1: A piano lounge. *Scene 2*: Comedy Clubs. *Scene 3*: Streets of New York. *Scene 4*: David's Apartment. *Scene 5*: Streets of New York. *Scene 6*: David's Apartment. *Scene 7*: Streets of New York. *Scene 8*: David's Apartment. *Scene 9*: Streets of New York. *Scene 10*: Krazy Korn Club. *Scene 11*: David's Apartment.

Act 2, Scene 1: Mr. Ribs' Club. *Scene 2*: A Hooker's Bar. *Scene 3*: Club Dressing Room. *Scene 4*: Bloomingdale's. *Scene 5*: Apartment Stoop. *Scene 6*: Metropolitan Opera House. *Scene 7*: Streets of New York. *Scene 8*: David's Apartment. *Scene 9*: The Comedy Circuit. *Scene 10*: Las Vegas.

ACT 1
Scene 1
  "Gabrielle"
    R. LuPone
Scene 2
  "The Best in the Business"
    R. LuPone, Club Owners
Scene 4
  "Clara's Dancing School"
    T. Tracy, S. Santoro
  "This Lady Isn't Right for Me"
    R. LuPone, A. Major, L. Goler, P. Blasetti, T. Tracy
Scene 7
  "Having Someone"
    R. LuPone, Club Owners
Scene 8
  "Stand-Up"
    R. LuPone
Scene 9
  "The Best in the Business" (reprise)
    R. LuPone
Scene 10
  "Late Nite Comic"
    R. LuPone
  "Stand-Up" (reprise)
    R. LuPone
Scene 11
  "It Had to Happen Sometime"
    R. LuPone, T. Tracy
  "When I Am Movin'"
    T. Tracy
  "Think Big"
    R. LuPone, M. Roberts
ACT 2
Scene 2
  "Relax With Me, Baby"
    R. LuPone, M. Roberts, Hookers

Scene 6
  "Dance"
    R. LuPone, T. Tracy, Ensemble
Scene 9
  "Late Nite Comic" (reprise)
    R. LuPone
Scene 10
  "It's Such a Different World"
    R. LuPone, Vegas Girls, Vegas Guys
  "It Had to Happen Sometime" (reprise)
    R. LuPone, T. Tracy
  "Gabrielle"/"Yvonne"
    R. LuPone

1987.15 ANYTHING GOES

A Revival of the Musical Comedy in Two Acts, 13 Scenes[8]. Original book by Guy Bolton and P. G. Wodehouse, Howard Lindsay and Russel Crouse. New book by Timothy Crouse and John Weidman. Music and lyrics by Cole Porter. Settings and costumes by Tony Walton. Lighting by Paul Gallo. Musical director, Edward Strauss. Orchestrations by Michael Gibson. Dance arrangements by Tom Fay. Sound by Tony Meola. Choreographed by Michael Smuin. Directed by Jerry Zaks. Produced by Lincoln Center Theater (Gregory Mosher, Artistic director; Bernard Gersten, Executive producer). Opened 19 October 1987 at the Vivian Beaumont Theatre and closed 3 September 1989 after 804 performances.

CAST (in order of appearance): *Louie*: Eric Y. L. Chan. *Elisha Whitney*: REX EVERHART. *Fred*: Steve Steiner. *Billy Crocker*: HOWARD McGILLIN. *Reno Sweeney*: PATTI LuPONE. *Young Girl*: Michele Pigliavento. *Sailor*: Alec Timerman. *Captain*: David Pursley. *Purser*: Gerry Vichi. *Reporter #1*: Robert Kellett. *Photographer*: Gerry McIntyre. *Reporter #2*: Larry Cahn. *Purity*: Daryl Richardson. *Chastity*: Maryellen Scilla. *Virtue*: Jane Lanier. *Minister*: Richard Korthaze. *Luke*: Stanford Egi. *John*: Toshi Toda. *Hope Harcourt*: KATHLEEN MAHONY-BENNETT. *Mrs. Evangeline Harcourt*: ANNE FRANCINE. *Lord Evelyn Harcourt*: ANTHONY HEALD. *G-Man #1*: Dale Hensley. *G-Man #2*: Leslie Feagan. *Erma*: LINDA HART. *Moonface Martin*: BILL McCUTCHEON. *Woman in Bathchair*: Jane Seaman. *Her Niece*: Alice Ann Oakes. *Countess*: Pat Gorman. *Thuggish Sailors*: Mark Chmiel, Dan Fletcher, Darryl Phillips. *Ship's Crew and Passengers*: Ensemble.

Chanty Quartet: Steve Steiner, Larry Cahn, Dale Hensley, Leslie Feagan. *Dancing Ensemble*: Eric Y. L. Chan, Mark Chmiel, Dan Fletcher, Robert Kellett, Jane Lanier, Gerry McIntyre, Alice Ann Oakes, Lacy Darryl Phillips, Michele Pigliavento, Daryl Richardson, Maryellen Scilla, Alec Timerman, Barbara Yeager. *Swings*: Robert Ashford, Amy O'Brien.

Act 1, Scene 1: A Bar. *Scene 2*: The Ships' Deck. *Scene 3*: The Ship's Deck. *Scene 4*: Mr. Whitney's Cabin. *Scene 5*: The Ship's Deck. *Scene 6*: Lord Evelyn's Stateroom. *Scene 7*: The Ships' Deck. *Scene 8*: The Ships' Deck.

Act 2, Scene 1: The Ships' Nightclub. *Scene 2*: The Brig. *Scene 3*: The Ships' Deck. *Scene 4*: The Brig. *Scene 5*: The Ships' Deck.

ACT 1
  ("Anything Goes")
    (Recording sung by Cole Porter)
Scene 1
  "I Get a Kick Out of You"
    P. LuPone
  "(There's) No Cure Like Travel"
    (dropped from original production)
    A. Timerman, M. Pigliavento, Ship's Crew
Scene 2
  "Bon Voyage"
    Company
Scene 3
  "You're the Top"
    P. LuPone, H. McGillin
  "Easy to Love"
    (from BORN TO DANCE, film) H. McGillin

---

[7]Succeeded by Tony Stevens, uncredited.

[8]Originally produced in New York 21 November 1934 at the Alvin Theater for 420 performances.

Scene 4

"I Want to Row with the Crew"
(from *PARANOIA*, Yale) R. Everhart

Scene 5

"Sailor's Chanty" (There'll Always Be a Lady Fair)
Chanty Quartet

"Friendship"
(from *DUBARRY WAS A LADY*) P. LuPone, B. McCutcheon

Scene 7

"It's Delovely"
(from *RED HOT AND BLUE*) H. McGillin, K. Mahony-Bennett

Scene 8

"Anything Goes"
P. LuPone, Company

ACT 2

Scene 1

"Public Enemy #1"
Company

"Blow, Gabriel, Blow"
P. LuPone, Company

"Goodbye, Little Dream, Goodbye"
(from *O MISTRESS MINE*, London)
K. Mahoney-Bennett

Scene 2

"Be Like the Bluebird"
B. McCutcheon

"All Through the Night"
H. McGillin, K. Mahony-Bennett, Men

Scene 3

"The Gypsy in Me"
A. Heald

Scene 5

"Buddie, Beware"
L. Hart, Sailors

"I Get a Kick Out of You" (reprise)
Company

CABARET

1987.16

A Revival of the Musical in Two Acts[9]. Book (revised) by Joe Masteroff. Based on the play ("I Am a Camera") by John Van Druten and stories ("The Berlin Stories") by Christopher Isherwood. Music by John Kander. Lyrics by Fred Ebb. Directed by Harold Prince. Dances and cabaret numbers staged by Ron Field. Scenic design, David Chapman based on original set design by Boris Aronson. Costume design by Patricia Zipprodt. Lighting design by Marc B. Weiss. Sound design by Otts Munderloh. Musical director, Donald Chan. Musical supervisor, Donald Pippin. Orchestrations by Don Walker. Additional orchestrations by Michael Gibson. Dance arrangements by Ronald Melrose. Associate producer, Alecia Parker, in association with Phil Witt. Produced by Barry and Fran Weissler. Opened 29 October 1987 at the Imperial Theatre, moved 9 February 1988 to the Minskoff Theatre and closed 4 June 1988 after 262 performances.

CAST (in order of appearance): *The Emcee (Master of Ceremonies)*: JOEL GREY. *Clifford Bradshaw*: GREGG EDELMAN. *Ernst Ludwig*: DAVID STALLER. *Customs Official*: David Vosburgh. *Fraulein Schneider*: REGINA RESNIK. *Fraulein Kost*: NORA MAE LYNG. *Herr Schultz*: WERNER KLEMPERER. *Telephone Girl*: Ruth Gottschall. *Sally Bowles*: ALYSON REED. *Girl Orchestra*: Sheila Cooper (tenor sax),

---

[9]Originally produced in New York 20 November 1966 at the Broadhurst Theatre for 1166 performances. For Synopsis of Scenes and Musical Numbers, see original 1966 production. Dropped from this production:
"Meeskite."
Added for this production:
"Don't Go" (replacing "Why Should I Wake Up?")
G. Edelman
"I Don't Care Much" (added Act 2, after "What Would You Do?")
J. Grey

Barbara Merjan (drums), Panchali Null (trombone), Eve Potfora (piano). *Two Ladies*: Ruth Gottschall, Sharon Lawrence. *Maitre D'*: David Vosburgh. *Max*: Jon Vandertholen. *Kissing Couple*: Mark Dovey, Sharon Lawrence. *German Sailors*: Jim Wolfe, Mark Dovey, Greg Schanuel. *Frau Wendel*: Mara Landi. *Kit Kat Girls*: Laurie Crochet, Noreen Evans, Caitlin Larsen, Sharon Lawrence, Mary Rotella. *First Waiter*: Stan Chandler. *Bobby*: Michelan Sisti. *Victor*: Lars Rosager.

Ensemble: Stan Chandler, Laurie Crochet, Bill Derifield, Mark Dovey, Noreen Evans, Karen Fraction, Laura Franks, Ruth Gottschall, Caitlin Larsen, Sharon Lawrence, Mary Munger, Pachali Null, Steve Potfora, Lars Rosager, Mary Rotella, Gregory Schanuel, Michelan Sisti, Jon Vandertholen, David Vosburgh, Jim Wolfe. *Swings*: Candy Cook, Aurelio Padron.

DON'T GET GOD STARTED

1987.17

A Musical in Two Acts. Written by Ron Milner. Story and idea development by Barry Hankerson, Ron Milner. Music and lyrics by Marvin Winans. Directed by Ron Milner. Scenic design by Llewellen Harrison. Costume design by Victoria Shaffer. Lighting design by Shirley Prendergast. Sound by Scott Marcellus. Vocal and musical arranger, Ronald Winans. Musical director, Steven Ford. Additional staging by Conni Marie Brazelton. Artistic consultant, Woodie King, Jr. Associate producers, Reuben Cannon, Bernard Parker. Produced by Barry Hankerson, Quentin Perry and Jeffrey Day Sharp. Opened 29 October 1987 at the Longacre Theatre and closed 10 January 1988 after 86 performances.

CAST: *Female Lead Vocalist*: VANESSA BELL ARMSTRONG. *Wise Old Man, The Reverend*: Ernie Banks. *Claudette, Sister Needlove*: Conni Marie Brazelton. *Wise Old Woman*: Marilyn Coleman. *Jack, Silk*: GIANCARLO ESPOSITO. *Sylvia, Barbara Ann*: CHIP FIELDS. *Male Lead Vocalist*: BE BE WINANS. *Robert, Lawrence, Buzz*: Marvin Wright-Bey.

Choir: Donald Albert, Margaret Bell, Susan Dawn Carson, Victor Trent Cook, Starletta DuPois, Patty Heaton, Keith Laws, Andrea McClurkin, Nadine Middlebrook Norwood, Stefone Pettis, Sylvia Simmons, Monique Williams, Angie Winans, Debbie Winans, Ronald Wyche.

ACT 1

"Cry Loud (Lift Your Voice Like a Trumpet)"
V. B. Armstrong, B. B. Winans

"Slipping Away from You"
V. B. Armstrong, B. B. Winans

"After Looking for Love"
V. B. Armstrong

"Change Your Nature"
B. B. Winans

"What's Wrong with Our Love"
V. B. Armstrong, B. B. Winans

"Don't Turn Your Back"
V. B. Armstrong

"Turn Us Again"
V. B. Armstrong, B. B. Winans

ACT 2

"Abide With Me" (Hymn)
B. B. Winans

"Let the Healing Begin"
V. B. Armstrong, B. B. Winans, Choir

"Renew My Mind"
Choir

"Denied Stone"
V. B. Armstrong, B. B. Winans

"He'll Make It Alright"
Choir

"Can I Build My Home in You"/"Bring Back the Days of Yea and Nay"
V. B. Armstrong, B. B. Winans

"Always"
V. B. Armstrong

"I Made It" (reprise)
V. B. Armstrong, B. B. Winans

"Millions"

"Still in Love with You"
B. B. Winans

"It's Alright Now" (reprise)
Choir

1987.18 # INTO THE WOODS

A Musical in Two Acts. Book by James Lapine[10]. Music and lyrics by Stephen Sondheim. Directed by James Lapine. Musical staging by Lar Lubovitch. Settings designed by Tony Straiges. Costumes by Ann Hould-Ward, based on original concepts by Patricia Zipprodt and Ann Hould-Ward. Lighting by Richard Nelson. Magic consultant, Charles Reynolds. Sound by Alan Stieb, James Brousseau. Orchestrations by Jonathan Tunick. Originally produced by the Old Globe Theatre, San Diego, California. Executive producer, Michael David. Associate producers, Gregory Mosher, Paula Fisher, David B. Brode, The Mutual Benefit Companies/Fifth Avenue Productions. Produced by Heidi Landesman, Rocco Landesman, Rick Steiner, M. Anthony Fisher, Frederic H. Mayerson, Jujamcyn Theatres. Opened 5 November 1987 at the Martin Beck Theatre and closed 3 September 1989 after 764 performances.

CAST (in order of appearance): *Narrator*: TOM ALDREDGE. *Cinderella*: Kim Crosby. *Jack*: Ben Wright. *Baker*: CHIP ZIEN. *Baker's Wife*: JOANNA GLEASON. *Cinderella's Stepmother*: Joy Franz. *Florinda*: Kay McClelland. *Lucinda*: Lauren Mitchell. *Jack's Mother*: Barbara Bryne. *Little Red Ridinghood*: Danielle Ferland. *Witch*: BERNADETTE PETERS. *Cinderella's Father*: Edmund Lyndeck. *Cinderella's Mother*: Merle Louise. *Mysterious Man*: TOM ALDREDGE. *Wolf*: ROBERT WESTENBERG. *Rapunzel*: Pamela Winslow. *Rapunzel's Prince*: Chuck Wagner. *Grandmother*: Merle Louise. *Cinderella's Prince*: ROBERT WESTENBERG. *Steward*: Philip Hoffman. *Giant*: Merle Louise. *Snow White*: Jean Kelly. *Sleeping Beauty*: Maureen Davis.

ACT 1

Prologue: "Into the Woods"
    Company
"Hello, Little Girl"
    R. Westenberg, D. Ferland
"I Guess This Is Goodbye"
    B. Wright
"Maybe They're Magic"
    J. Gleason
"I Know Things Now"
    D. Ferland
"A Very Nice Prince"
    K. Crosby, J. Gleason
"Giants in the Sky"
    B. Wright
"Agony"
    R. Westenberg, C. Wagner
"It Takes Two"
    C. Zien, J. Gleason
"Stay With Me"
    B. Peters
"On the Steps of the Palace"
    K. Crosby
"Ever After"
    T. Aldredge, Company
ACT 2
Prologue: "So Happy"
    Company
"Agony" (reprise)
    R. Westenberg, C. Wagner
"Lament"
    B. Peters
"Any Moment"
    R. Westenberg, J. Gleason
"Moments in the Woods"
    J. Gleason
"Your Fault"
    B. Wright, C. Zien, B. Peters, K. Crosby, D. Ferland
"Last Midnight"
    B. Peters
"No More"
    C. Zien, T. Aldredge

---

[10]Inspired by the Fairy Tales of Jacob and Wilhelm Grimm.

"No One Is Alone"
    K. Crosby, D. Ferland, C. Zien, B. Wright
Finale: "Children Will Listen"
    B. Peters, Company

1987.19 # TEDDY AND ALICE

A Musical in Two Acts, a Prelude and 15 Scenes. Book by Jerome Alden. Music by John Philip Sousa. Adaptations and original music by Richard Kapp. Lyrics by Hal Hackady. Artistic consultant, Alan Jay Lerner. Directed by John Driver. Choreography by Donald Saddler. Additional musical staging by D. J. Giagni. Scenery design by Robin Wagner. Costume design by Theoni V. Aldredge. Lighting design by Tharon Musser. Sound design by Peter Fitzgerald. Orchestrations by Jim Tyler. Vocal arrangements, music supervisor, Donald Pippin. Dance arrangements by Gordon Lowry Harrell. Musical director, Larry Blank. Originally produced at the Tampa Bay Performing Arts Center. Associate producers, Glen Cross, Clarice Swan Fitzgerald, Wilmor Four in association with Jon Cutler. Produced by Hinks Shimberg. Opened 12 November 1987 at the Minskoff Theatre and closed 17 January 1988 after 77 performances.

CAST (in order of appearance): *James Amos*: Tony Floyd. *Belle Hagner*: Karen Ziemba. *J. P. Morgan*: David Green. *Harriman*: John Witham. *Henry Cabot Lodge*: Raymond Thorne. *Elihu Root*: Gordon Stanley. *William Howard Taft*: Michael McCarthy. *Theodore 'Teddy' Roosevelt*: LEN CARIOU. *Edith Roosevelt*: BETH FOWLER. *Ted Roosevelt, Jr.*: Robert D. Cavanaugh. *Kermit Roosevelt*: Seth Granger. *Ethel Roosevelt*: Sarah Reynolds. *Archie Roosevelt*: Richard H. Blake. *Quentin Roosevelt*: John Daman. *Ida Tarbel*: Mary Jay. *Wheeler*: John Remme. *Officer O'Malley*: Christopher Wells. *Alice Roosevelt*: NANCY HUME. *Eleanor Roosevelt*: Nancy Opel. *Nick Longworth*: RON RAINES. *Franklin Roosevelt*: Alex Kramarevsky. *Admiral Murphy*: David Green. *Samuel Gompers*: John Witham. *Elliott Roosevelt*: Ken Hilliard. *Ghost*: Pamela McLernon.
    Servants, Reporters, Tea Party Ladies, Marines, Ambassadors: Ellyn Aarons, Ruth Bormann, Kathleen Gray, Ken Hilliard, Alex Kramarevsky, Mark Lazore, Keith Locke, Pamela McLernon, Elizabeth Mozer, Keith Savage, Jeff Shade. *Swings*: Kaylyn Dillehay, Travis Layne Wright.

Act 1, Scene 1: Interior of the White House, Fall 1901, shortly after President McKinley's assassination. *Scene 2*: White House Yard. *Scene 3*: The President's Office. *Scene 4*: Alice's Dressing Room, different day. *Scene 5*: Presidential Bedroom Suite. *Scene 6*: Rose Garden of the White House, later that evening. *Scene 7*: Public Area in the White House, later that evening. *Scene 8*: North Portico of the White House, three weeks later. *Scene 9*: Republican National Convention, Summer 1904.

Act 2, Scene 1; Main Entrance Hall, Summer 1904. *Scene 2*: Area of Birch Trees near the White House, same day. *Scene 3*: Election Day. *Scene 4*: The President's Office. *Scene 5*: Campsite near the White House in the Woods. *Scene 6*: East Room of the White House.

ACT 1

Prelude: "The Thunderer"
    Orchestra
Scene 1
"This House"
    L. Cariou, Family, Friends, Staff, Reporters
Scene 2
"But Not Right Now"
    N. Hume
Scene 3
"She's Got to Go"
    M. McCarty, G. Stanley, R. Thorne
Scene 4
"The Fourth of July"
    N. Hume, N. Opel
Scene 5
"Charge"
    L. Cariou, B. Fowler, R. D. Cavanaugh,
    S. Granger, S. Reynolds, R. D. Blake, J. Daman
"Battlelines"
    B. Fowler
Scene 6
"The Coming-Out Party Dance"
    L. Cariou, N. Hume, R. Raines, B. Fowler, Guests
"Leg O' Mutton"
    N. Hume, R. Raines, Guests

"Not Love"
R. Raines, M. McCarty, G. Stanley, R. Thorne

Scene 7

"Her Father's Daughter"
L. Cariou

"Perfect for Each Other"
R. Raines

Scene 8

"He's Got to Go" (reprise)
M. McCarty, G. Stanley, R. Thorne, R. Raines

Scene 9

"Wave the Flag"
L. Cariou, B. Fowler, N. Opel, R. D. Cavanaugh, S. Granger,
S. Reynolds, R. H. Blake, J. Daman, J. Witham, D. Green, Hecklers,
Supporters

ACT 2

Scene 1

"(The) Fourth of July" (reprise)
L. Cariou

"(The) Fourth of July" (reprise)
N. Hume, N. Opel, B. Fowler, Ladies

Scene 2

"Nothing to Lose"
R. Raines, N. Hume

Scene 3

"Election Eve"
M. McCarty, G. Stanley, R. Thorne, J. Witham, D. Green, Reporters

Scene 4

"Perfect for Each Other" (reprise)
N. Hume

Scene 5

"Can I Let Her Go?"
L. Cariou

Scene 6

"Private Thoughts"
M. McCarty, G. Stanley, R. Thorne, B. Fowler, R. D. Cavanaugh, S. Reynolds,
S. Granger, R. H. Blake, J. Daman, Servants, Staff, Reporters

"This House" (reprise)
L. Cariou, B. Fowler, Guests

1987.20   PENN & TELLER

A Magic Revue in Two Acts, 12 Scenes[11]. Directed by Art Wolff. Set by John Lee Beatty. Lighting by Dennis Parichy. Sound by Chuck London Media/Stuart Werner. Director of Covert Activities, Marc Garland. Produced by Richard Frankel, Thomas Viertel, Steven Baruch. Opened 1 December 1987 at the Ritz Theatre and closed 20 March 1988 after 130 performances.

CAST: PENN JILLETTE, TELLER.

ACT 1

Casey at the Bat
A Card Trick
Cups and Balls
Suspension
Domestication of Animals
East Indian Needle Mystery
Quote of the Day

ACT 2

Another Card Trick
MOFO the Psychic Gorilla
How We Met
Shadows
10 in 1

---

[11]A previous edition of "Penn & Teller" appeared Off-Broadway 18 April 1985 at the Westside Arts/Downstairs Theatre for 666 performances.

1988.01   THE PHANTOM OF THE OPERA

A Musical in Two Acts, a Prologue and 19 Scenes. Book by Richard Stilgoe, Andrew Lloyd Webber. (Based on the novel of the same name [Le Fantôme de l'Opéra] by Gaston Leroux.) Music by Andrew Lloyd Webber. Lyrics by Charles Hart. Additional lyrics by Richard Stilgoe. Directed by Harold Prince. Musical staging and choreography by Gillian Lynne. Production design (sets and costumes) by Maria Björnson. Lighting by Andrew Bridge. Sound by Martin Levan. Musical supervision and direction by David Caddick. Orchestrations by David Cullen, Andrew Lloyd Webber. Produced by Cameron Mackintosh and the Really Useful Company. Opened 26 January 1988 at the Majestic Theater and is still running at the present time!

CAST: *The Phantom of the Opera*: MICHAEL CRAWFORD. *Christine Daaé*: SARAH BRIGHTMAN, PATTI COHENOUR (alt.) *Raoul*, Vicomte de Chagny: STEVE BARTON. *Carlotta Guidicelli*: JUDY KAYE. *Monsieur André*: Cris Groenendaal. *Monsieur Firmin*: Nicholas Wyman. *Madame Giry*: Leila Martin. *Ubaldo Piangi*: David Romano. *Meg Giry*: Elisa Heinsohn. *Monsieur Reyer*: Peter Kevoian. *Auctioneer*: Richard Warren Pugh. *Porter, Marksman*: Jeff Keller. *Monsieur Lefèvre*: Kenneth H. Waller. *Joseph Buquet*: Philip Steele. *Don Attilio* ("Il Muto"), *Passarino*: George Lee Andrews. *Slave Master* ("Hannibal"): Luis Perez. *Flunky, Stagehand*: Barry McNabb. *Policeman*: Charles Rule. *Page* ("Don Juan Triumphant"): Olga Talyn. *Potter, Fireman*: William Scott Brown. *Page* ("Don Juan Triumphant"): Candace Rogers-Adler. *Wardrobe Mistress, Confidante* ("Il Muto"): Mary Leigh Stahl. *Princess* ("Hannibal"): Rebecca Luker. *Madame Firmin*: Beth McVey. *Innkeeper's Wife* ("Don Juan Triumphant"): Jan Horvath.

The Ballet Chorus of the Opéra Populaire: Irene Cho, Nicole Fosse, Lisa Lockwood, Lori MacPherson, Dodie Petit, Catherine Ulissey. *Ballet Swing*: Denny Berry. *Swings*: Frank Mastrone, Alba Quezada.

The action takes place in the Paris Opéra House in 1911, and Paris in 1881.

Prologue: The stage of the Paris Opéra House, 1911.

Act 1: Paris, 1881. *Scene 1*: The dress rehearsal of 'Hannibal.' *Scene 2*: After the gala. *Scene 3*: Christine's dressing room. *Scene 4*: The Labyrinthe underground. *Scene 5*: Beyond the lake. *Scene 6*: Beyond the lake, the next morning. *Scene 7*: Backstage. *Scene 8*: The Managers' office. *Scene 9*: A performance of 'Il Muto.' *Scene 10*: The roof of the Opéra House.

Act 2: Six months later. *Scene 1*: The staircase of the Opéra House, New Year's Eve. *Scene 2*: Backstage. *Scene 3*: The Managers' office. *Scene 4*: A rehearsal for 'Don Juan Triumphant.' *Scene 5*: A graveyard in Peros. *Scene 6*: The Opéra House stage before the Premiere. *Scene 7*: 'Don Juan Triumphant.' *Scene 8*: The Labyrinthe underground. *Scene 9*: Beyond the lake.

ACT 1

Scene 1

"Think Of Me"
J. Kaye, S. Brightman, S. Barton

Scene 2

"Angel of Music"
S. Brightman, E. Heinsohn

Scene 3

"Little Lotte"/"The Mirror" (Angel of Music)
S. Barton, S. Brightman, M. Crawford

Scene 4

"The Phantom of the Opera"
M. Crawford, S. Brightman

Scene 5

"The Music of the Night"
M. Crawford

Scene 6

"I Remember"/"Stranger Than You Dreamt It"
S. Brightman, M. Crawford

Scene 7

"Magical Lasso"
P. Steele, E. Heinsohn, L. Martin, Ballet Girls

Scene 8

"Notes"/"Prima Donna"
N. Wyman, C. Groenendaal, S. Barton,
J. Kaye, L. Martin, E. Heinsohn, M. Crawford

Scene 9

"Poor Fool, He Makes Me Laugh"
J. Kaye, Company

Scene 10

"Why Have You Brought Me Here"/"Raoul, I've Been There"
S. Barton, S. Brightman

"All I Ask of You"
S. Barton, S. Brightman

"All I Ask of You" (reprise)
M. Crawford

ACT 2
Scene 1

"Masquerade"/"Why So Silent"
Full Company

Scene 3

"Notes"/"Twisted Every Way"
C. Groenendaal, N. Wyman, J. Kaye,
D. Romano, S. Barton, S. Brightman, L. Martin, M. Crawford

Scene 5

"Wishing You Were Somehow Here Again"
S. Brightman

"Wandering Child"/"Bravo Bravo" (Bravo, Monsieur)
M. Crawford, S. Brightman, S. Barton

Scene 7

"The Point of No Return"
M. Crawford, S. Brightman

Scene 8

"Down Once More"/"Track Down This Murderer"
Full Company

1988.02 SARAFINA!

A Musical in Two Acts[12]. (Book) Written by Mbongeni Ngema. Music and lyrics by Mbongeni Ngema. Additional songs by Hugh Masekela. Musical arrangements by Mbongeni Ngema and Hugh Masekela. Conceived and directed by Mbongeni Ngema. Set and costumes by Sarah Roberts. Lighting by Mannie Manim. Conductor, additional choreography by Ndaba Mhlongo. Sound by Tom Sorce. First presented by the Committed Artists and the Market Theatre at the Market Theatre, Johannesburg, (South Africa) June 1987. A Committed Artists Production. Produced by Lincoln Center Theatre (Gregory Mosher, Artistic director; Bernard Gersten, Executive producer) in association with Lucille Lortel, The Shubert Organization. Opened 28 January 1988 at the Cort Theatre and closed 2 July 1989 after 597 performances.

CAST: Magundane: Ntomb'khona Dlamini. Scabha: Khumbuzile Dlamini. Colgate: Pat Mlaba. Teaspoon: Lindiwe Dlamini. Crocodile: Dumisani Dlamini. Silence: Congo Hadebe. Stimela Sase-Zola: Nhlanhla Ngema. S'Ginci, Police Sergeant: Mhlathi Khuzwayo. Sarafina: Leleti Khumalo. Mistress It's a Pity: Baby Cele. Dumadu: Nonhlanhla Mbambo. China: Linda Mchunu. Lindiwe: Lindiwe Hlengwa. Zandile: Zandile Hlengwa. Siboniso: Siboniso Khumalo. Timba: Cosmas Sithole. Priest: Thandani Mavimbela. Charnele: Charnele Dozier Brown. Mubi: Mubi Mofokeng. Nandi: Nandi Ndlovu. Thandekile: Thandekile Nhlanhla. Police Lieutenant: Pumi Shelembe. Kipizane: Kipizane Skweyiya. Thandi: Thandi Zulu.

Musicians: Master Mathibe, Eddie Mathibe (keyboards), Makate Peter Mofolo , Ray Molefe (trumpets), Douglas Mnisi (lead guitar), Bruce Mwansla (drums), S'Manga Nhlebela (bass).

The action takes place at Morris Isaacson High School in Soweto, South Africa in 1976.

ACT 1

"Zibuuylle Emasisweni" (It's Finally Happening)
Company

"Niyayibona Lento Engiyibonayo" (Do You See What I See)
Company

"Sarafina"
M. Khuzwayo, N. Ngema
(Music and Lyrics by Hugh Masekela.)

"The Lord's Prayer"
B. Cele, Company

"Yes! Mistress It's a Pity"
B. Cele, Company
(Music and Lyrics by Hugh Masekela and Mbongeni Ngema.)

"Give Us Power"
T. Zulu, N. Dlamini, B. Cele, Company

"Afunani Amaphoyisa eSoweto" (What Is the Army Doing in Soweto?)
Company

"Nkosi Sikeleli'Afrika"
Company

"Freedom Is Coming Tomorrow"
Company

Entr'acte: "Excuse Me Baby Please, Please If You Don't Mind Baby, Thank You"
Band
(Music and Lyrics by Hugh Masekela.)

ACT 2

"Meeting Tonight"
T. Nhlanhla, Company
(Music and Lyrics by Hugh Masekela.)

"We Are Guerillas"
T. Nhlanhla, Company

"Uyamemeza Ungoma"
T. Zulu

"We Will Fight for Our Land"
T. Mavimbela, T. Zulu, D. Dlamini, Company

"Mama"
N. Dlamini, T. Nhlanhla, B. Cele, Company

"Sechaba"
Company
(Music and Lyrics by Hugh Masekela.)

"Isizwe" (The Nation Is Dying)
T. Nhlanhla

"Goodbye"
B. Cele
(Music and Lyrics by Hugh Masekela.)

"Kilimanjaro"
Company

"Africa Burning in the Sun"
Company
(Music and Lyrics by Hugh Masekela.)

"Stimela Sasezola"
N. Ngema, Company

"Olayithi" (It's All Right)
Company

"Bring Back Nelson Mandela"
L. Khumalo, Company
(Music and Lyrics by Hugh Masekela.)

"Wololo!"
Company

RODNEY DANGERFIELD ON BROADWAY

1988.03

A Comedy Revue in Two Acts. Production designer, Steven A. Cohen. Sound designer, Peter Fitzgerald. Produced by James M. Nederlander. Opened 2 February 1988 at the Mark Hellinger Theatre and closed 7 February 1988 after 6 performances.

CAST: RODNEY DANGERFIELD, Bob Nelson.

THE MUSIC MAN

1988.04

A Revival of the Musical (Comedy) in Two Acts, 17 Scenes[13]. Book, music and lyrics by Meredith Willson. Book written in collaboration with Franklin Lacey. Directed by Arthur Masella. Choreographed by Marcia Milgrom Dodge. Sets designed by David Jenkins. Costumes designed by Andrew Marlay. Lighting designed by Duane Schuler. Orchestrations by Don Walker. Chorus master, Joseph Colaneri. Conductor, Donald Pippin.

---

[12]Originally produced Off-Broadway 25 October 1987 at the Mitzi Newhouse Theatre for 81 performances.

[13]Originally produced in New York 19 December 1957 at the Majestic Theatre for 1375 performances. For Synopsis of Scenes and Musical Numbers, see original 1957 production. Original Act 1, Scene 2 has been divided in two, yielding an extra scene.

Produced by the New York City Opera. Opened 26 February 1988 at the New York State Theatre and closed 10 April 1988 after 51 performances.

CAST (in order of appearance): *Travelling Salesmen:* WIlliam Ledbetter, James Clark, Robert Brubaker, Stanley Wexler, Jonathan Green. *Newpaper Readers:* Louis Perry, Neil Eddinger. *Charlie Cowell:* Rex D. Hays. *Conductor:* Ralph Bassett or John Henry Thomas. *Harold Hill:* BOB GUNTON. *Mayor Shinn:* RICHARD McKEE. *Eulalie MacKecknie Shinn:* MURIEL COSTA-GREENSPON. *Zaneeta Shinn:* JILL POWELL. *Gracie Shinn:* Alexandra Steinberg. *Alma Hix:* Bridget Ramos. *Ethel Toffelmier:* Ivy Austin. *Maud Dunlop:* Lee Belaver. *Mrs. Squires:* Rita Metzger. *Jacey Squires:* Jonathan Green. *Marcellus Washburn:* JAMES BILLINGS. *Ewart Dunlop:* James Clark. *Oliver Hix:* Robert Brubaker. *Olin Britt:* Don Yule. *Marian Paroo:* LEIGH MUNRO. *Mrs. Paroo:* BROOKS ALMY. *Amaryllis:* Allegra Victoria Forste *Winthrop Paroo:* JOEL CHAIKEN. *Tommy Djilas:* STEVEN M. SCHULTZ *Constable Locke:* William Ledbetter. *River City Townspeople:* New York City Opera Chorus.

1988.05 THE GOSPEL AT COLONUS

A Musical in Two Acts[14]. Book and lyrics by Lee Breuer. Based on an adaptation of Sophocles' "Oedipus at Colonus" in the version by Robert Fitzgerald and incorporates passages from both Sophocles' "Oedipus Rex" and "Antigone" in the versions by Dudley Fitts and Robert Fitzgerald. Music by Bob Telson. Directed by Lee Breuer. Production and set design by Alex Yerxa. Costume design by Ghretta Hynd. Lighting design by Julie Archer. Sound design by David Hewitt, Ron Lorman. Originally produced by the Brooklyn Academy of Music Next Wave Festival. Executive producers, Michael David, Edward Strong, Sherman Warner. Produced by Dodger Productions, Liza Lorwin, Louis Busch Hager, Playhouse Square Center (Cleveland, Ohio), Fifth Avenue Productions (Karen Walter Goodwin, Elizabeth Williams). Opened 24 March 1988 at the Lunt-Fontanne Theatre and closed 15 May 1988 after 61 performances.

CAST: *Messenger,* a visiting pastor who narrates the role of Oedipus and performs the role of Messenger as a sermon: MORGAN FREEMAN. *Oedipus,* a soloist and gospel quintet who sing portions of the role of Oedipus: CLARENCE FOUNTAIN AND THE FIVE BLIND BOYS OF ALABAMA (Bobby Butler, Jimmy L. Carter, J. T. Clinkscales, Reverend Olice Thomas, Joseph Watson). *Antigone,* an evangelist who performs the role of Antigone and selected choral material: ISABELL MONK. *Theseus,* the assistant pastor of the church who performs the role of Theseus: Reverend Earl F. Miller. *Ismene:* Jevetta Steele and the J. D. Steele Singers (J. D. Steele, Fred Steele, Janice Steele, Jevetta Steele). *Creon,* a deacon of the church who performs the role of Creon: Robert Earl Jones. *Polyneices,* a member of the congregation who performs the role of Polyneices: Kevin Davis. *Choragos:* Martin Jacox, J. J. Farley and the Soul Stirrers (Jackie Banks, Martin Jacox, Ben Odom, Willie Rogers). *The Singer:* Sam Butler, Jr. *The Choir Soloist:* Carolyn Johnson-White. *Guest Choir Director:* J. D. Steele.

Chorus: The Institutional Radio Choir: *Altos:* Betty Cooper, Angie Haddock, Vincent Haddock, Jr., Crystal Johnson, Selene Jones, Shellie Jordan, O'Jean Lilly, Janet Napper, Pamela Poitier, Francine Tompkins, Candace White. *Sopranos:* Regina Berry, Katie Braan, Deborah Britt, Sharon K. Driskill, Mary Fischer, Josie Johnson, Carolyn Johnson-White, Ernestine King, Kecia Lewis-Evans. *Tenors:* Charles Bellamy, Lindwood Chamberlain, George Cooper, Hayward Jerome Gregory, Kevin Jackson, Roscoe Robinson, Billy Steele, Ezekiel Tobby, Carl Williams, Jr., Jeff Young.

ACT 1
The Welcome and Quotations
  M. Freeman
The Invocation ("Live Where You Can")
  Choir, J. Steele (Soloist)
Recapitulation from Oedipus the King
  I. Monk, E. F. Miller
Oedipus and Antigone enter Colonus
  I. Monk, M. Freeman
Ode to Colonus ("Fair Colonus")
  W. Rogers (Solist)
"Stop! Do Not Go On"
  S. Butler, Jr. (Soloist), J. J. Farley and the Soul Stirrers
Bridge
  C. Fountain and the Five Blind Boys of Alabama
Choral Dialogue: ("Who is This Man?")
  M. Jacox, M. Freeman
Ismene Comes to Colonus: "How Shall I See Through My Tears?"
  The J. D. Steele Singers, Jevetta Steele (Soloist)

Narrative of Ismene
  I. Monk
Tableau, Polyneices and Eteocles
  J. D. Steele, F. Steele
The Rite
  I. Monk, M. Freeman, C. Fountain
Tableau, Antigone and Ismene
  Janice Steele, Jevetta Steele
Dialogue: Chorus Questions Oedipus
  M. Jacox, M. Freeman
The Prayer: ("A Voice Foretold")
  C. Fountain and the Five Blind Boys of Alabama, S. Butler, Jr.
Oedipus Is Welcomed in Colonus
Peroration
  E. F. Miller
Jubilee ("No Never")
  M. Jacox, the Soul Stirrers
Bridge
  C. Fountain and the Five Blind Boys of Alabama, Choir, Ensemble
Creon Comes to Colonus and the Seizure of the Daughters
  R. E. Jones, M. Freeman, C. Fountain and the Five Blind Boys of Alabama
Oedipis Curses Creon (Suite, "All My Heart's Desire")
  C. Fountain and the Five Blind Boys of Alabama, Choir, R. E. Jones, M. Freeman
Choral Ode ("Numberless Are the World's Wonders")
  J. D. Steele Singers (J. D. Steele, Janice Steele, Soloists), Choir
ACT 2
Oedipus Laments ("Lift Me Up")
  C. Fountain and the Five Blind Boys of Alabama
Polyneices' Testimony and Supplication, Oedipus' Curse
  K. Davis, M. Freeman, C. Fountain
"Evil"
  S. Butler, Jr.
"You Break My Heart"
  J. D. Steele, F. Steele, B. Odom
Poem ("Love Unconquerable")
  I. Monk
Preaching with Tuned Response
  M. Freeman, C. Fountain
Special Effect ("Ah! Heaven's Height Has Cracked!")
The Teachings
  M. Freeman, E. F. Miller
The Descent of Oedipus
"Oh Sunlight of No Light"
  S. Butler, Jr.
"Eternal Sleep"
  W. Rogers, the Soul Stirrers
Mourning
  I. Monk, E. F. Miller, Jevetta Steele, Jancie Steele
Doxology, the Paen ("Lift Him Up")
  Choir (C. Johnson-White, Soloist)
The Sermon
  M. Freeman
Closing Hymn ("Now Let the Weeping Cease")
  W. Rogers, the Soul Stirrers, Choir, Ensemble
Benediction
  M. Freeman

1988.06 OBA OBA

A Brazilian Extravaganza (Musical Revue) in Two Acts, 13 Scenes. Conceived by Franco Fontana. Musical direction by Wilson Mauro. Choreographer, Roberto Abrahão. Assistant choreographers, Soraya Bastos, Luis Bocanha. Technical consultant, Mario Ruffa. Sound by Peter Fitzgerald. Lighting consultant, Steve Cochrane. Co-producer, Dino Cuzzoni. Produced by Franco Fontana. Opened 29 March 1988 at the Ambassador Theatre and closed 8 May 1988 after 48 performances.

CAST: ELIANA ESTVÃO, NILZE CARVALHO, TOCO PRETO, JAIME SANTOS, Bebeto, Beiçola, Borracha, Brechó, Chita, Claudia Jacomo, Claudinho

---

[14]Previously produced in Brooklyn 8 November 1983 at the Brooklyn Academy of Music/Carey Playhouse for 30 performances.

Nascimento, Cobra Mansa, Concheta, Gerson do Pandeiro, José Roberto Ferreira, Ledinha da Mangueira, Lindete Souza, Lucia Helena Máximo, Luis Bernardo, Luis Bocanha, Marcia Souza, Marcos Negão, Marquinho da Dona Geralda, Marta Sargentelli, Miguel do Repinique, Milani Nicolau, Olga Maria, Paulo Xavier, Pedro Pottier, Roberto Silva, Rosemary Silva, Soninha Toda Pura, Soraya Bastos, Tomé de Bebedouro, Vivian Machado Soares, Waldir Cavalcanti, Wilmar Vieira, Wilson Mauro.

Ensemble: Claudio Sargentelli, Cristino Ricardo, Dalto Macedo, Garcia de Aragão, Iole Fernandes, Lucelita Barros, Maria Elza de Jesus, Monica Gonçalves, Nino, Ondina Lopes, Vera Lima.

ACT 1

Scene 1

"Xica da Silva"
    R. Silva, W. Vieira, Company

The story opens when Brazil is still a land of slaves ruled by the Portuguese. Through her feminine charms the beautiful Xica da Silva wins the heart of the nobleman João Fernandes. As a result she gains her freedom and earns a place in the Portuguese court. As time goes by, Xica becomes a lady and the nobleman bcomes her slave.

Scenes 2 and 4

Homage to Baião and Chorinho
    N. Carvalho, T. Preto

Some classics of these two particular kinds of popular music featuring the most expressive Brazilian instruments, the badolim and the cavaquinho, a small guitar with four chords. Pieces such as "Tico, Tico," "Urubu Malandro" and two famous compositions by Waldir Azevedo, "Brasilierinho" and "Delicado," have made Baião and Chorinho famous throughout the world.

Scene 3

"Samba de Roda"
    T. Preto, G. Pandeiro, M. Nicolau, C. Jacomo,
    Concheta, L. da Mangueira, L. Souza, M. Sargentelli,
    O. Maria, R. Silva, S. T. Pura, V. M. Soares

This is a typical dance born in Bahia's public squares and markets. A festive competition among the women of the town. This coquettish contest displays their superiority in performing this particular type of samba.

Scene 5

Homage to the Northeast
    J. Santos, Company

The most evocative music and songs of this marvelous, but desolately poor territory, moves from the resigned lamentations of the Acordeon to the explosive reactions of the people who find in song and dance the strength and joy of life.

Scene 6

"Brazil Capela"
    E. Estevao

Scene 7

Homage to the Bossanova and Brazilian Music of the Seventies
    E. Estevao, N. Carvalho, W. Mauro, W. Cavalcanti

A medley dedicated to that great musical phenomenon of the Sixties that made artists like Tom Jobim, Baden Powell, Vincius de Moraes and songs like "Manhã de Carnaval," "Samba de uma nota so" and "Garota de Ipanema" world-famous.
    E. Estevao, M. Sargentelli, O. Maria, S. T. Pura, S. Bastos

A medley dedicated to the artists who still follow the great tradition of Brazilian music, and brilliantly insert their work into the present international musical language, thus mantaing the worldwide prestige of Brazilian popular music.

Scene 8

Tribute to the 'Brazilian Bombshell' Carmen Miranda
    N. Carvalho, E. Estevao, L. Souza, Company

ACT 2

Scene 1

"Macumba"
    L. de Mangueira, L. Souza, Bebeto,
    G. do Pandeiro, O. Maria, L. Bocanha, J. R. Ferrera, M. Sargentelli, Company

This religious African cult with its dances and its saints (Orixa) including the magical appearance of Iemanjā, Queen of the Seas and Fertility.

Scene 2

Afro-Brazilian Folk Songs and Dances:

Berimbau Medley
    L. Bocanha, G. do Pandeiro, Brechó, C. Nascimento,
    L. Bernardo, R. Silva, T. de Bebedouro, W. Cavalcanti, W. Mauro, J. Santos

Capoeira of Angola
    Bebeto, Bericola, Borracha, Chita, C. Mansa,
    L. Bocanha, M. Negão, C. Jacomo, Concheta, L. Souza, M. Souza,
    M. Sargentelli, O. Maria, R. Silva, S. T. Pura, S. Bastos, V. M. Soares

A tribute to the first struggles against the white masters wherein the slaves used their hands and feet as their only weapon. (Capoeira, which later became a dance.)

Maculele
    Brecho, C. Jacomo, C. Nascimento, J. R. Ferreira, L. Souza,
    L. H. Máximo, L. Bernardo, M. Souza, M. Sargentelli, P. Xavier,
    R. Silva, S. Bastos, T. de Bebedouro, W. Cavalcanti, W. Vieira

Dances that require agility and skill and are carried out with small batons accompanied by the lively rhythm of tambores and agogo.

Acrobatic Capoeira
    Bebeto, Beicola, Borracha, Chita, Cobra Mansa, L. Bocanha, M. Negão

Scene 3

Rhythm Beaters
    G. do Pandeiro, Bebeto, Borracha, L. Bocanha,
    M. da Dona Geralda, M. do Repinique, M. Nicolau, P. Pottier

Various instruments are at first played separately, in order to stress their peculiarities, and then all together in a sweeping progress of rhythm.

Scene 4

Show of Samba Dancers
    O. Maria, R. Silva, S. T. Pura

An exaltation of the beauty and charm of the Brazilian Mulatto women through the sensual progress of their samba.

Scene 5

Grand Carnival
    Company

The most popular themes of the various carnivals, featuring a parade of the artists who then allow the audience to participate in the great and collective festivities.

1988.07   MAIL

A Musical in Two Acts and a Prologue. Book and lyrics by Jerry Colker. Music by Michael Rupert. Directed by Andrew Cadiff. Choreography by Grover Dale. Scenery and projections by Gerry Hariton, Vicki Baral. Costume design by William Ivey Long. Lighting by Richard Nelson. Sound design by Tom Morse. Multi-image production by Nelson & Sixta. Musical supervision, Paul Gemignani. Orchestrations by Michael Gibson. Musical direction, vocal and dance arrangements by Tom Fay. Assistant choreographer, Stephen Jay. Originally produced by the Pasadena Playhouse, State Theatre of California, Inc. Associate producer, Kenneth Biller. Produced by Michael Frazier, Susan Dietz, Stephen Wells and the John F. Kennedy Center/ANTA (Donald R. Seawell). Opened 14 April 1988 at the Music Box Theatre and closed 14 May 1988 after 36 performances.

CAST (in order of appearance): *Alex*: MICHAEL RUPERT. *Dana*: MARA GETZ. *Radio Announcer*: Rick Stockwell. *Radio Singer*: Mary Bond Davis. *LIFE Execs*: Alan Muraoka, Robert Loftin, Rick Stockwell. *Franklin*: BRIAN MITCHELL. *Sandi*: ANTONIA ELLIS. *Max*: ROBERT MANDAN. *Kathy Sue Binger*: Michelle Pawk. *Billy Ray Binger*: Rick Stockwell. *Assistants*: Alan Muraoka, Robert Loftin. *Power Ladies*: Louise Hickey, Michele Pawk. *Mama Utility*: Mary Bond Davis. *Con Ed Men*: Alan Muraoka, Rick Stockwell, Robert Loftin. *Democratic Party Delegate*: Michelle Pawk. *Brunhilda*: Mary Bond Davis. *Hunter*: Rick Stockwell. *Gypsy*: Louise Hickey. *Boy Scout*: Robert Loftin. *I.R.S. Auditor*: Alan Muraoka. *Operator*: Mary Bond Davis. *Candi Suwinski*: Michelle Pawk. *Harmony Steinberg*: Louise Hickey. *Craterface Callahan*: Robert Loftin. *Takeuchi Fujimoto*: Alan Muraoka. *Mr. Stansbury*: Rick Stockwell. *Lois T. Wertshafter*: Mary Bond Davis. *Pitchman*: Rick Stockwell.
    Pitchpeople: Mary Bond Davis, Robert Loftin, Alan Muraoka, Michele Pawk, Rick Stockwell, Louise Hickey. *Swings*: Stephen Jay, Rachelle Ottley.

Prologue: 6:00 A. M. one winter morning. A Manhattan apartment.

Act 1: 11:15 P. M., four months later. The same apartment.

Act 2: The same.

PROLOGUE

"Monolithic Madness"
    M. Rupert

ACT 1

"Gone So Long"
   M. B. Davis
"Hit the Ground Running"
   M. Getz, M. Rupert
"It's Your Life"
   A. Muraoka, R. Loftin, R. Stockwell
"Cookin' with Steam"
   B. Mitchell
   (*Music by* Brian Mitchell and Michael Rupert. *Lyrics by* Jerry Colker. Recorded track arranged and played by Brian Mitchell.)
"It's Just a Question of Technique"
   A. Ellis, M. Rupert
"It's None of My Business"
   R. Mandan
"Crazy World"
   M. Getz
"Ambivalent Rag"
   M. Rupert
"It's Your Life" II
   A. Muraoka, R. Loftin, R. Stockwell
"You Better Get Outta Town"
   M. Pawk, R. Stockwell, A. Muraoka, R. Loftin
"We're Gonna Turn Off Your Juice"
   L. Hickey, M. Pawk, M. B. Davis, A. Muraoka, R. Stockwell, R. Loftin
"The World Set on Fire by a Black and a Jew"
   B. Mitchell, M. Rupert
"Where Are You/Where Am I?"
   M. Getz
"Family Ties"
   R. Mandan
"One Lost Weekend"
   A. Ellis, M. Rupert, M. Getz
"Junk Mail"/"Disconnected"
   Ensemble
"Helplessness at Midnight"
   M. B. Davis
"What Have You Been Doing for the Past Ten Years?"
   M. Rupert, Ensemble
"A Blank Piece of Paper"
   M. Rupert

ACT 2

"Sweepstakes"
   M. Rupert, R. Stockwell, Pitchpeople
"It's Getting Harder to Love You"
   M. Getz, Pitchwomen
"Publish Your Book"
   A. Ellis, M. Rupert, Pitchpeople
"Ambivalent Rag" II
   M. Rupert
"Pages of My Diary"
   M. Getz, M. Rupert, Pitchwomen
"One Step at a Time"/"Ambivalent Rag" III
   M. Rupert, Pitchpeople
"Don't Count on It"
   A. Ellis, M. Rupert
"Friends for Life"
   B. Mitchell, M. Rupert
"Twenty-Nine Years Ago"
   R. Mandan, M. Rupert
"Crazy World" (reprise)
   M. Rupert
"Sweepstakes" (reprise)
   Pitchpeople
"A Blank Piece of Paper" (reprise)
   M. Rupert
"Crazy World" (Finale)
   M. Rupert, M. Getz

MICHAEL FEINSTEIN IN CONCERT

1988.08

A One Man Show in Two Acts. Conceived by Michael Feinstein, Christopher Chadman. Special material, Bruce Vilanch. Staged by Christopher Chadman. Musical director, Elliot Finkel. Set designed by Andrew Jackness. Lighting designed by Beverly Emmons. Sound designed by Tom Sorce. Orchestrations by Ian Finkel. Special arrangements by David Spear. Associate producers, Jonthan Scharer, Peter Kapp. Produced by Ron Delsener. Opened 19 April 1988 at the Lyceum Theatre and closed 12 June 1988 after 57 performances.

CAST: MICHAEL FEINSTEIN.
   Musicians: Eliot Finkel (pianist, conductor), David Finck (bass), Ian Finkel (percussion), Luther Rix (drums), Don de Marco (guitar), Ralph Olsen (woodwinds).

ACT 1

"Isn't It Romantic?" (from *LOVE ME TONIGHT*, film)
   (*Music by* Richard Rodgers. *Lyrics by* Lorenz Hart.)
"Taking a Chance on Love" (from *CABIN IN THE SKY*)
   (*Music by* Vernon Duke. *Lyrics by* John Latouche and Ted Fetter.)
"You Keep Coming Back Like a Song"(from *BLUE SKIES*, film)
"Be Careful, It's My Heart" (from *HOLIDAY INN*, film)
"It Only Happens When I Dance with You" (from *EASTER PARADE*, film)
"Alexander's Ragtime Band"
   (*Music and Lyrics by* Irving Berlin.)
"Lydia, the Tattooed Lady" (from *MARX BROTHERS AT THE CIRCUS*, film)
   (*Music by* Harold Arlen. *Lyrics by* E. Y. Harburg.)
"Our Love Is Here to Stay" (from *THE GOLDWYN FOLLIES*, film)
"Fascinatin' Rhythm" (from *LADY, BE GOOD*)
"I Got Rhythm" (from *GIRL CRAZY*)
   (*Music by* George Gershwin. *Lyrics by* Ira Gershwin.)
"Sail Away" (from *SAIL AWAY* and *ACE OF CLUBS*, London)
   (*Music and Lyrics by* Noël Coward.)
"Sing a Tropical Song" (from *HAPPY GO LUCKY*, film)
   (*Music by* Jimmy McHugh. *Lyrics by* Frank Loesser.)
"Another Song about Paris"
   (*Music and Lyrics by* Dave Frischberg.)
"Rhode Island Is Famous for You" (from *INSIDE U.S.A.*)
   (*Music by* Arthur Schwartz. *Lyrics by* Howard Dietz.)
"Never Never Land" (from *PETER PAN*)
   (*Music by* Jule Styne. *Lyrics by* Betty Comden and Adolph Green.)
"Wasn't It Romantic?"
   (*Music by* Hugh Martin. *Lyrics by* Marshall Barer.)

ACT 2

"I Want to Hear a Yankee Doodle Tune"
   (*Music and Lyrics by* George M. Cohan.)
"Will You Remember Me" (dropped from *LADY, BE GOOD*)
   (*Music by* George Gershwin. *Lyrics by* Ira Gershwin.)
"Loopin' the Loop" (dropped from *CHICAGO*)
   (*Music by* John Kander. *Lyrics by* Fred Ebb.)
"I Won't Send Roses"/"Time Heals Everything" (from *MACK AND MABEL*)
   (*Music and Lyrics by* Jerry Herman.)
"Can Can" (from *CAN CAN*)
   (*Music and Lyrics by* Cole Porter.)
"I Can Dream, Can't I?"/"I'll Be Seeing You" (from *RIGHT THIS WAY*)
   (*Music by* Sammy Fain. *Lyrics by* Irving Kahal.)
"Old Friends" (from *MERRILY WE ROLL ALONG*)
   (*Music and Lyrics by* Stephen Sondheim.)
"Wanna Sing a Show Tune"
   (*Music and Lyrics by* Ray Jessel.)
Harry Warren medley:
   (*All Music by* Harry Warren.)
   "I Found a Million Dollar Baby" (from *BILLY ROSE'S CRAZY QUILT*)
      (*Lyrics by* Billy Rose, Mort Dixon.)
   "Would You Like to Take a Walk?"
      (from *SWEET AND LOW, BILLY ROSE'S CRAZY QUILT*)
      (*Lyrics by* Billy Rose, Mort Dixon.)

"You're My Everything" (from *THE LAUGH PARADE*)
  (*Lyrics by* Mort Dixon, Joe Young.)
"Jeepers Creepers" (from *GOING PLACES*, film)
  (*Lyrics by* Johnny Mercer.)
"You Must Have Been a Beautiful Baby" (from *HARD TO GET*, film)
  (*Lyrics by* Johnny Mercer.)
"There Will Never Be Another You" (from *ICELAND*, film)
  (*Lyrics by* Mack Gordon.)
"About a Quarter to Nine"
(from *GO INTO YOUR DANCE*, film; *42nd STREET*, musical)
  (*Lyrics by* Al Dubin.)
"Lulu's Back in Town" (from *BROADWAY GONDOLIER*, film)
  (*Lyrics by* Al Dubin.)
"I Got a Gal in Kalamazoo" (from *ORCHESTRA WIVES*, film)
  (*Lyrics by* Mack Gordon.)
"Latin from Manhattan" (from *GO INTO YOUR DANCE*, film)
  (*Lyrics by* Al Dubin.)
"Forty-Second Street" (from *FORTY-SECOND STREET*, film and show)
  (*Lyrics by* Al Dubin.)
"An Affair to Remember" (from film of the same name)
  (*Lyrics by* Harold Adamson and Leo McCarey.)
"The More I See You" (from *BILLY ROSE'S DIAMOND HORSESHOE*, film)
  (*Lyrics by* Mack Gordon.)
"You'll Never Know" (from *HELLO, FRISCO HELLO!*, film)
  (*Lyrics by* Mack Gordon.)
"September in the Rain" (from *MELODY FOR TWO*, film)
  (*Lyrics by* Al Dubin.)
"I Had the Craziest Dream" (from *SPRINGTIME IN THE ROCKIES*, film)
  (*Lyrics by* Mack Gordon.)
"No Love, No Nothin'" (from *THE GANG'S ALL HERE*, film)
  (*Lyrics by* Leo Robin.)
"I Only Have Eyes for You" (from *DAMES*, film)
  (*Lyrics by* Al Dubin.)
"I Wanna Be a Dancin' Man"
(from *THE BELLE OF NEW YORK*, film; *DANCIN'*, show)
  (*Lyrics by* Johnny Mercer.)
"The Lady in the Tutti Frutti Hat" (from *THE GANG'S ALL HERE*, film)
  (*Lyrics by* Leo Robin.)
"On the Atcheson, Topeka and the Santa Fe" (from *THE HARVEY GIRLS*, film)
  (*Lyrics by* Johnny Mercer.)
"Lullaby of Broadway"
(from *GOLDDIGGERS OF 1935*, film; *42nd STREET*, show)
  (*Lyrics by* Al Dubin.)
"I Love a Piano" (from *STOP! LOOK! LISTEN!*)
  (*Music and Lyrics by* Irving Berlin.)
"Along the Way"
  (*Music by* Jule Styne. *Lyrics by* Bob Merrill.)

1988.09   # CHESS

A Musical in Two Acts, 2 Prologues and 23 Scenes. Book by Richard Nelson. Based on an idea by Tim Rice. Music by Benny Andersson, Björn Ulvaeus. Lyrics by Tim Rice. Directed by Trevor Nunn. Dance staging by Lynne Taylor-Corbett. Scenic design by Robin Wagner. Costume design by Theoni V. Aldredge. Lighting design by David Hersey. Sound design by Andrew Bruce. Musical director and supervisor, Paul Bogaev. Orchestrations and (musical) arrangements by Anders Eljas. Executive producers, (Tyler) Gatchell & (Peter) Neufeld, Ltd. Produced by The Shubert Organization, 3 Knights Ltd. (Benny Andersson, Tim Rice, Björn Ulvaeus), Robert Fox, Ltd. Opened 28 April 1988 at the Imperial Theatre and closed 25 June 1988 after 68 performances.

CAST (in order of appearance): *Gregor Vassey*: Neal Ben-Ari. *Young Florence*: Gina Gallagher. *Freddie*: PHILIP CASNOFF. *Florence*: JUDY KUHN. *Anatoly*: DAVID CARROLL. {David-James Carroll}. *Molokov*: Harry Goz. *Nickolai*: Kurt Johns. *Walter*: Dennis Parlato. *Arbiter*: Paul Harman. *Svetlana*: Marcia Mitzman. *Joe and Harold*, Embassy Officials: Richard Muenz, Eric Johnson.
  Ensemble: John Aller, Neal Ben-Ari, Suzanne Briar, Steve Clemente, Katherine Lynne Condit, Ann Crumb, David Cryer, R. F. Daley, Deborah Geneviere, Kurt Johns, Eric Johnson, Paul Laureano, Rosemary Loar, Judy McLane, Jessica Molaskey, Richard Muenz, Kip Niven, Francis Ruivivar, Alex Santoriello, Wysandria Woolsey. *Swings*: Karen Babcock, Craig Wells.

Prologue: Budapest, Hungary, 1956.

Act 1, Scene 1: A large meeting room in the Bangkok Hilton Hotel, Thailand, the present time. *Scene 2*: Hotel hallway and Anatoly's hotel suite. *Scene 3*: Freddie's suite. *Scene 4*: The Chess trade show. *Scene 5*: The Chess Board Arena, and later, elevators,

and Anatoly's office. *Scene 6*: Freddie's suite. *Scene 7*: The streets of Bangkok. *Scene 8*: The Generous Sole Restaurant, and Terrace. *Scene 9*: The Chess Board Arena and later, Florence's hotel room. *Scene 10*: Underground parking square below the Arena. *Scene 11*: A small baggage room at the airport and later, a concourse in the airport.

Prologue: Kennedy Airport, New York, eight weeks later.

Act 2, Scene 1: Budapest, Hungary, eight weeks later. *Scene 2*: A chapel of a large cathedral. *Scene 3*: Freddie's suite. *Scene 4*: A walk along the Danube outside the hotel after dinner. *Scene 5*: Svetlana's hotel room. *Scene 6*: Outside the Chess Arena building. *Scene 7*: The Lobby of the Chess Arena. *Scene 8*: An elegant restaurant. *Scene 9*: Freddie's suite. *Scene 10*: The walk along the Danube. *Scene 11*: Anatoly's dressing room. *Scene 12*: A room at the Budapest Airport and later, a hangar.

PROLOGUE
  "The Story of Chess"
    N. Ben-Ari

ACT 1[15]
Scene 1
  "Press Conference" (What a Scene, What a Joy)
    P. Casnoff, J. Kuhn, Reporters
Scene 2
  "Where I Want to Be"
    D. Carroll
Scene 3
  "How Many Women" (Argument)
    J. Kuhn, P. Casnoff
Scene 4
  "Merchandisers' Song"
    D. Parlato, Merchandisers
  "U.S vs. U.S.S.R."
    H. Goz, American and Soviet Delegates
Scene 5
  "Chess Hymn"
    P. Harman, Company
  Quartet ("A Model of Decorum and Tranquility")
    H. Goz, J. Kuhn, P. Harman, D. Carroll
Scene 6
  "You Want to Lose Your Only Friend?"
    J. Kuhn, P. Casnoff
  "Someone Else's Story"
    J. Kuhn
Scene 7
  "One Night in Bangkok"
    P. Casnoff, Company
Scene 8
  "Terrace Duet"
    J. Kuhn, D. Carroll
Scene 9
  "So You Got What You Want"
    P. Casnoff, J. Kuhn

---

[15]For the National tour presented under the auspices of Tom Mallow in association with William H. Kessler, Michael M. Weatherly, Robert R. Larsen and Pace Theatrical Group, the book was revised by Robert Coe. A new physical production (Sets, David Mitchell; Costumes, Susan Hilferty; Lighting, Ken Billington; Sound, Gary Stocker) was assembled under the direction of Des McAnuff, with choreography by Peter Anastos, additional choreography by Wayne Cilento. The song order was altered substantially. Added were:
  "The Russian and Molokov" (added to Act 1, Scene 3)
    John Herrera (Anatoly), David Hurst (Molokov)
  "Who'd Ever Think It" (Act 1, Scene 8)
    Stephen Bogardus (Freddie), Carolee Carmello (Florence)
  "The Reporters" (Act 1, final scene before 'Anthem')
    Ensemble
  "Someone Else's Story" (reprise replaced "Anthem" at end of show)
    C. Carmello
Subsequent tours and revivals implemented a variety of changes to the text and score too numerous to detail here.

"Nobody's Side"
  J. Kuhn
Scene 11
  "Anthem"
    D. Carroll
PROLOGUE[16]
  "Arbiter's Song"
    P. Harman, Company
ACT 2
Scene 1
  "Hungarian Folk Song"
    Company
Scene 2
  "Heaven Help My Heart"
    J. Kuhn
Scene 3
  "No Contest" (Winning)
    P. Casnoff, D. Parlato
Scenes 4 and 5
  "You and I"
    D. Carroll, J. Kuhn, M. Mitzman
Scene 6
  "A Whole New Board Game"
    P. Casnoff
Scene 7
  "Let's Work Together"
    D. Parlato, H. Goz
Scene 8
  "I Know Him So Well"
    J. Kuhn, M. Mitzman
Scene 9
  "Pity the Child"
    P. Casnoff
Scene 10
  "Lullaby" ("Apukad Eros Kezen")
    N. Ben-Ari, J. Kuhn
Scene 11
  "Endgame"
    D. Carroll, P. Casnoff, Company
Scene 12
  "You and I" (reprise)
    D. Carroll, J. Kuhn
  "Anthem" (reprise)
    J. Kuhn

1988.10 ROMANCE ROMANCE

Two Musicals each in One Act[17]. Book and lyrics by Barry Harman. Music by Keith Herrmann. Directed by Barry Harman. Choreographed by Pamela Sousa. Scenic design by Steven Rubin. Costume design by Steven Jones. Lighting design by Craig Miller. Sound design by Peter Fitzgerald. Musical director, Kathy Sommer. Vocal and dance arrangements by Keith Herrmann. Orchestrations by Michael Starobin. Additional orchestrations by Daniel Troob, Joseph Gianono. Produced by Dasha Epstein, Harve Brosten, Jay S. Bulmash, in association with George Krynicki and Marvin A. Krauss. Opened 1 May 1988 at the Helen Hayes Theater and closed 15 January 1989 after 297 performances.

ACT 1: The Little Comedy

Based on the short story by Arthur Schnitzler (as translated by George Edward Reynolds).

---

[16]Dropped after the opening.
[17]Originally produced Off-Broadway 30 October 1987 at the Actors Outlet Theatre for 37 performances.

CAST: *Alfred von Wilmers*: SCOTT BAKULA. *Josefine Weninger*: ALISON FRASER. *"Him"*: Robert Hoshour. *"Her"*: Deborah Graham.

The action takes place in Vienna at the turn of the century.

MUSICAL NUMBERS
  "The Little Comedy"
    S. Bakula, A. Fraser
  "Goodbye, Emil"
    A. Fraser
  "It's Not Too Late"
    S. Bakula, A. Fraser
  "Great News"
    S. Bakula, A. Fraser
  "Oh, What a Performance!"
    S. Bakula, A. Fraser
  "I'll Always Remember the Song"
    S. Bakula, A. Fraser
  "Happy, Happy, Happy"
    S. Bakula
  "Women of Vienna"
    S. Bakula
  "Yes, It's Love"
    A. Fraser
  "A Rustic Country Inn"
    S. Bakula, A. Fraser
  "The Night It Had to End"
    A. Fraser
  "The Little Comedy" (Finale)
    S. Bakula, A. Fraser

ACT 2: Summer Share

Based on the play "Pain de Menage" by Jules Renard (as translated by Max Gulack).

CAST: *Lenny*: Robert Hoshour. *Barb*: Deborah Graham. *Sam*: SCOTT BAKULA. *Monica*: ALISON FRASER.

The action takes place in the Hamptons during August of the current year.

MUSICAL NUMBERS
  "Summer Share"
    All
  "Think of the Odds"
    D. Graham, R. Hoshour
  "It's Not Too Late" (reprise)
    S. Bakula, A. Fraser
  "Plans A & B"
    A. Fraser, R. Hoshour
  "Let's Not Talk About It"
    S. Bakula, D. Graham
  "So Glad I Married Her"
    All
  "Small Craft Warnings"
    D. Graham, R. Hoshour
  "How Did I End Up Here?"
    A. Fraser
  "Words He Doesn't Say"
    S. Bakula
  "My Love for You"
    R. Hoshour, D. Graham
  "Moonlight Passing Through a Window"
    S. Bakula
  "Now"
    A. Fraser
  "Romantic Notions"
    S. Bakula, D. Graham, R. Hoshour, A. Fraser
  "Romance, Romance"
    All

THE WORLD ACCORDING TO ME

1988.11

A Return Engagement of the One Man Comedy Revue in Two Acts[18]. Written and created by Jackie Mason. Supervised by Ron Clark. Scenery and lighting by Neil Peter Jampolis. Sound by Bruce Cameron. Associate producer, Jyll Rosenfeld. Produced by Nick Vanoff. Opened 3 May 1988 at the Brooks Atkinson Theatre and closed 31 December 1988 after 203 performances. Total including first engagement: 570 performances.

CAST: JACKIE MASON (stand-up comedy, monologues, impressions).

Act 1: Current events and cultural experiences.

Act 2: The ever-popular Gentiles and Jews.

CARRIE

1988.12

A Musical in Two Acts, a Prologue and 13 Scenes. Book by Lawrence D. Cohen. Based on the novel of the same name by Stephen King. Music by Michael Gore. Lyrics by Dean Pitchford. Directed by Terry Hands. Choreography by Debbie Allen. Set design by Ralph Koltai. Costume design by Alexander Reid. Lighting design by Terry Hands. Sound design by Martin Levan. Assistant director, Louis W. Scheeder. Orchestrations by Anders Eljas, Harold Wheeler, Michael Starobin. Music supervisor, Harold Wheeler. Musical director, Paul Schwartz. A Friedrich Kurz/Royal Shakespeare Company Production. Produced by Friedrich Kurz in association with Whitecap Productions (Lawrence D. Cohen, Michael Gore) and Martin Barandes. Opened 12 May 1988 at the Virginia Theatre and closed 15 May 1988 after 5 performances.

CAST: *Margaret White*: BETTY BUCKLEY. *Carrie White*: LINZI HATELEY. *Chris*: Charlotte d'Amboise. *Tommy*: Paul Gyngell. *Miss Gardner*: Darlene Love. *Billy*: Gene Anthony Ray. *Sue*: Sally Ann Triplett.
  Ensemble: Jamie: Jamie Beth Chandler. *Cathy*: Catherine Doffey. *Michèle*: Michèle du Verney. *Shelley*: Michelle Hodgson. *Rose*: Rosemarie Jackson. *Kelly*: Kelly Littlefield. *Maddy*: Madeleine Loftin. *Michelle*: Michelle Nelson. *Mary Ann*: Mary Ann Oedy. *Squeeze*: Suzanne Maria Thomas. *Gary*: Gary Co-Burn. *Kevin*: Kevin Coyne. *David*: David Danns. *Matthew*: Matthew Dickens. *Eric*: Eric Gilliom. *Kenny*: Kenny Linden. *Joey*: Joey McKneely. *Mark*: Mark Santoro. *Chris*: Christopher Solari. *Scott*: Scott Wise. *Swing Dancers*: Mary Ann Lamb, Darryl Eric Tribble.

The action takes place at the present time.

Prologue: The Gynasium.

Act 1, Scene 1: The Showers. *Scene 2*: The Locker Room. *Scene 3*: The White Home. *Scene 4*: The Drive-In. *Scene 5*: The White Home. *Scene 6*: The Gymnasium. *Scene 7*: The Night Spot. *Scene 8*: The White Home.

Act 2, Scene 1: The Pig Farm. *Scene 2*: The Gymnasium. *Scene 3*: Carrie's Room. *Scene 4*: The Prom. *Scene 5*: Epilogue.

PROLOGUE
  "In"
    D. Love, Girls

ACT 1
Scene 1
  "Dream On"
    Girls, L. Hateley

Scene 2
  "Carrie"
    L. Hateley
Scene 3
  "Open Your Heart"
    B. Buckley, L. Hateley
  "And Eve Was Weak"
    B. Buckley, L. Hateley
Scene 4
  "Don't Waste the Moon"
    S. A. Triplett, P. Gyngell, C. Solari, G. A. Ray, Girls, Boys
Scene 5
  "Evening Prayers"
    L. Hateley, B. Buckley
Scene 6
  "Unsuspecting Hearts"
    D. Love, L. Hateley
Scene 7
  "Do Me a Favor"
    S. A. Triplett, P. Gyngell, C. Solari, G. A. Ray, Girls, Boys
Scene 8
  "I Remember How Those Boys Could Dance"
    B. Buckley

ACT 2
Scene 1
  "Out for Blood"
    C. Solari, G. A. Ray, Boys
Scene 2
  "It Hurts To Be Strong"
    S. A. Triplett
Scene 3
  "I'm Not Alone"
    L. Hateley
  "When There's No One"
    B. Buckley
Scene 4
  "Wotta Night!"
    Girls, Boys
  "Unsuspecting Hearts" (reprise)
    D. Love, L. Hateley
  "Heaven"
    P. Gyngell, S. A. Triplett, D. Love, L. Hateley, B. Buckley, Girls, Boys
  "Alma Mater"
    Girls, Boys, D. Love
  "The Destruction"
    L. Hateley
Scene 5
  "Carrie" (reprise)
    B. Buckley

---

[18]Originally produced in New York 22 December 1986 at the Brooks Atkinson Theatre for 367 performances.

1988–1989 SEASON

Mary Ann Lamb, Barbara Yaeger, and JoAnn Hunter in JEROME ROBBINS' BROADWAY
Martha Swope / TimePix

1988–1989 SEASON

AN EVENING WITH ROBERT KLEIN

1988.13

A Revue in One Act[1]. Conceived and written by Robert Klein. Musical director, Bob Stein. Presented by Circle-in-the-Square Theatre (Theodore Mann, Artistic director; Paul Libin, Producing director). Opened 19 June 1988 at the Circle-in-the-Square Theatre and closed 27 June 1988 after 3 performances.

<u>CAST</u>: ROBERT KLEIN.
  Vocalists: Betsy Bircher, Catherine Russell.

THE MERRY WIDOW

1988.14

A Revival of the Operetta in Three Acts[2]. Music by Franz Lehár. Original Viennese libretto 'Die lustige witwe' by Victor Léon and Leo Stein (after "L'Attaché d'Ambassade" by Henri Meilhac.) English version by Adrian Ross. Original production (stage direction) by Ronald Bentley. Choreographer, Sharon Halley. Set designers, Helen Pond and Herbert Senn. Costume designer, Suzanne Mess. Lighting designer, Ken Tabachnick. Conductor, Imre Pallo. Assistant stage director, Cynthia Edwards. Chorus master, Joseph Colaneri. Produced by the New York City Opera. Opened 6 July 1988 at the New York State Theatre and closed 25 August 1988 after 5 performances in repertory.

<u>CAST</u> (in order of appearance): *Baron Popoff*: RICHARD MCKEE. *Natalie*: Ruth Golden. *General Novikovich*: John Lankston. *Counsellor Khadja*: Michael Willson. *Marquis de Cascada*: Robert Ferrier. *Sylviane*: Michele McBride. *M. de St. Brioche*: MICHAEL REES DAVIS. *Olga*: Joyce Campana. *Vicomte Camille de Jolidon*: Paul Austin Kelly. *Nisch*: James Billings. *Sonia*: LEIGH MUNRO. *Count Danilo*: RICHARD WHITE. *Head Waiter*: Jonathan Guss. *Zozo*: Ivy Austin. *Lolo*: Joan Mirabella. *Dodo*: Esperanza Galan. *Jou-Jou*: Candace Itow. *Frou-Frou*: Victoria Rinaldi. *Clo-Clo*: Ashley Janeway. *Margot*: Jean Barber. *Chorus of Marsovian and Parisian Society, Dancers, Servants and Waiters*: New York City Opera Chorus.

CANCIONES DE MI PADRE

1988.15 (Songs for My Father)

A Romantic Evening in Old Mexico (Musical Revue) in Two Acts, 7 Scenes. (Conceived by Linda Ronstadt.) Directed and choreographed by Michael Smuin. Setting designed by Tony Walton. Costumes by Arturo Ceballos; Manuel. Lighting designed by Jules Fisher. Conductor, Ruben Fuentes. Sponsor, Tecate Imported Beer. Produced by Ira Koslow for Asher/Frost Management. Opened 12 July 1988 at the Minskoff Theatre and closed 30 July 1988 after 18 performances.

<u>CAST</u>: LINDA RONSTADT, DANIEL VALDEZ (vocals).
  MARIACHI VARGAS DE TECALITLAN: Jose Martinez Baravas, Mario A. Santiago Miranda, Juan Manuel Biurquis Isiano, Daniel Martinez Rodriguez, Idlefonso Moya Escobedo, Francisco Javier Gonzalez Bautista (violins), Federico Torres Martinez, Rigoberto Mercado Alvarez (trumpets), Natividad Santiago Gonzalez, Victor Cardenas Garcia, Rafael Palomar Ruelas (guitar), Arturo Mendoza Villaluazo, Rubén Fuentes, Pepe Martinez, Juan Pinzon. Silvestre Vargas, Ruben Fuentes, Jose "Pepe" Martinez (directors), Arturo Mendoza (coordinator).
  BALLET FOLKLORICO DE LA FONDA, GILBERTO PUENTE (guitar), SAL LOPEZ, URBANIE LUCERO, Mary Louise Diaz, Elsa Annette Estrada, Luis Valdez, Lalo Garcia (dancers).

The setting is a romantic evening in old Mexico.

---

[1]A previous production THE ROBERT KLEIN SHOW opened 20 December 1985 at the Circle-in-the-Square for 16 performances.
[2]Originally produced in New York 21 October 1907 at the New Amsterdam Theatre for 416 performances. For Synopsis of Scenes and Musical Numbers, see original 1907 production. Interpolated into this production:
  "Girls Were Made to Love and Kiss" (from PAGANINI)
    (*Music by* Franz Lehar. *Original German Lyrics by* Paul Knepler and Bela Jenbach. *English Lyrics by* A. P. Herbert.)

Act 1, Scene 1: First Mariachi section. *Scene 2*: Traditional Dances—Jalisco costumes. *Scene 3*: Revolutionary section.

Act 2, Scene 1: Mariachi Vargas. *Scene 2*: Ballad section. *Scene 3*: Traditional dances. *Scene 4*: Town courtyard.

ACT 1
Scene 1
  "Fanfarria"Mariachi Vargas
  "Los Laureles" (The Laurels)
    (*Music and Lyrics by* Consuelo Velásquez, José López.)
  "Por Un Amor" (For a Love)
    (*Music and Lyrics by* Gilberto Parra.)
  "La Cigarra" (The Cicada)
    (*Music and Lyrics by* Ray Pérez Y Soto.)
  "Tú Sólo Tú" (You Only You)
    (*Music and Lyrics by* Felipe Valdez Leal.)
    L. Ronstadt, I. Moya
    Violin Solos: Jose Martinez, Juan Manuel Biurquix.
  "Cancion Mexicana" (Mexican Cancion)
    (*Music and Lyrics by* Lalo Guerrero.)
Scene 2
  "La Negra"
    M. L. Diaz, E. Estrada, U. Lucero, L. Garcia, S. Lopez, L. Valdez
  "El Gusto"
    M. L. Diaz, E. Estrada, U. Lucero, L. Garcia, S. Lopez, L. Valdez
  "El Caballito"
    S. Lopez, M. L. Diaz
Scene 3
  "El Tren Sone"
    Mariachi Vargas
  "La Rielera" (The Railroad Woman)
  "Corrido de Cananea" (Ballad of Cananea)
    (L. Ronstadt)
    (Traditional; *Music and Lyrics adapted by* Rubén Fuentes.)
  "(El) Adios del Soldado" (The Soldier's Farewell)
    L. Ronstadt, D. Valdez
    (*Music and Lyrics by* Valdez Leal.)
      Chorus: M. Santiago, I. M. Escobedo. *Violin Solos*: J. Martinez, J. M. Biurquix.
  "Yo Soy el Corrido" (I Am the Ballad)
    L. Ronstadt, D. Valdez
  "El Sol Que Tú Eres" (The Sun That You Are)
    L. Ronstadt, D. Valdez
    (Traditional; *Music and Lyrics adapted by* Daniel Valdez.)
  "La Rielera" (reprise)
  "Viva México"
    Company

ACT 2
Scene 1
  "Fiesta En Jalisto"
  "Las Bodas de Luiz Alonso"
Scene 2
  "Hay Unos Ojos" (There Are Some Eyes)
    (L. Ronstadt)
    (Traditional; *Music and Lyrics adapted by* Rubén Fuentes.)
      Violin Solos: J. Martinez, J. M. Biurquix.
  "Rogaciano el Huapanguero" (Rogaciano the singer of huapangos)
    L. Ronstadt, D. Martinez, I. Moya
    (*Music and Lyrics by* Valeriano Trejo.)
  "Dos Arbolitos" (Two Little Trees)
    L. Ronstadt, D. Martinez, I. Moya
    (*Music and Lyrics by* Chuco Martinez Gil.)
      Violin Solos: J. Martinez, J. M. Biurquix.
  "La Barca de Guaymas" (The Boat from Guaymas)
    L. Ronstadt, I. Moya, R. Palaomar
    (Traditional, *Music and Lyrics adapted by* Rubén Fuentes.)
      Violin Solos: J. Martinez, J. M. Biurquix.
  "Amorcito Corazon" (Sweet Love)
    D. Valdez

495

Scene 3

"La Bamba"
 Dance Company in Vera Cruz costumes
"Malguena Salerosa"
 G. Puente
"(El) Jarabe Tapatio"
 Dance Company in China Poblana costumes
"El Cascabel"
 Mariachi Vargas

Scene 4

"Y Andale" (Get On With It)
 L. Ronstadt, D. Martinez
 (*Music and Lyrics by* Minerva Elizondo.)
"(El) Crucifijo de Piedra" (The Crucifix of Stone)
 (*Music and Lyrics by* Hermanos Cantorale.)
"La Calandria" (The Lark)
 L. Ronstadt, D. Martinez, I. Moya
 (*Music and Lyrics by* Nicandro Castillo.)
"La Charreada" (A show of skills of the charro, a gentleman cowboy)
 (L. Ronstadt)
 (*Music and Lyrics by* Felipe Bermejo.)
"Cancion Mixteca" (Song from Mixteca)
 (*Music and Lyrics by* Lopez Alaves.)
"Volver, (Volver)" (Return, Return)(from *CHULAS FRONTERAS* film)
 Company
 (*Music and Lyrics by* F. Maldonado.)

1988.16 THE NEW MOON

A Revival of the Operetta in Two Acts, 7 Scenes[3]. Book by Oscar Hammerstein II, Frank Mandel and Laurence Schwab. Music by Sigmund Romberg. Lyrics by Oscar Hammerstein II. New adaptation of the book and lyrics by Robert Johanson. Conductor, Jim Coleman. Director and choreographer, Robert Johanson. Set designer, Michael Anania. Costume designer, Andrew Marlay. Lighting designer, Mark W. Stanley. Chorus master, Joseph Colaneri. Assistant stage directors, Albert Sherman and Laura Alley. Assistant choreographer, Sharon Halley. Produced by the New York City Opera. Opened 19 July 1988 at the New York State Theatre and closed 24 July 1988 after 7 performances.

CAST (in order of appearance): *Julie*, Marianne's maid: JOYCE CAMPANA. *Alexander*, Bondservant to Beaunoir: GERALD ISAAC. *M. Beaunoir*, Marianne's father, owner of *The New Moon*: James Billings. *Captain Duval*, Commander of *The New Moon*, suitor to Marianne: Joseph McKee. *Vicomte Ribaud*, the great French detective: DAVID RAE SMITH. *Fouchette*, informer for Ribaud: Allen Riberdy. *Robert Mission*, Bondservant to Beaunoir, formerly a nobleman: RICHARD WHITE or WILLIAM PARCHER. *Besac*, Boatswain on*The New Moon*: Kenneth Kantor. *Jacques*, ship's carpenter on *The New Moon*: David Frye. *Marianne Beaunoir*, Beaunoir's daughter: LEIGH MUNRO or JANE THORNGREN. *Proprietor*: Harris Davis. *Spaniard*: Terry Lacy. *Flower Dancer*: Esperanza Galan. *Philippe Dupres*, French exile, Robert's comrade: MICHAEL COUSINS or MICHAEL REES DAVIS. *Clotilde Lombaste*, leader of the brides bound for Martinique: MURIEL COSTA-GREENSPON. *Admiral de Jean*, commander of the new French Navy: John Lankston. *Servants, Courtiers, Ladies, Sailors, Pirates, Tavern Wenches, Brides and French Soldiers*: New York City Opera Chorus.

1988.17 AIN'T MISBEHAVIN'

A Revival of the Musical Revue in Two Acts, 22 Scenes[4]. Based on the music of Thomas "Fats" Waller. Conceived and directed by Richard Maltby, Jr. Based on an idea by Murray Horwitz and Richard Maltby, Jr. Musical staging and choreography by Arthur Faria. Music supervision by Luther Henderson. Associate director, Murray Horwitz. Orchestrations and arrangements by Luther Henderson. Vocal and musical concepts, Jeffrey Gutcheon. Vocal arrangements by William Elliott, Jeffrey Gutcheon. Sets by John Lee Beatty. Costumes by Randy Barcelo. Lighting by Pat Collins. Sound by Tom Morse. Originally produced (Off-Broadway) by the Manhattan Theatre Club. Produced by The Shubert Organization, Emanuel Azenberg, Dasha Epstein, Roger Berlind. Opened 15 August 1988 at the Ambassador Theatre and closed 15 January 1989 after 176 performances.

CAST: NELL CARTER, ANDRE DE SHIELDS, ARMELIA MCQUEEN, KEN PAGE, CHARLAINE WOODARD. *Conductor and Pianist*: LUTHER HENDERSON.

1988.18 NAUGHTY MARIETTA

A Revival of the Musical Comedy in Two Acts, 3 Scenes[5]. Music by Victor Herbert. Book and lyrics adapted by Theodore Pappas based on the original by Rida Johnson Young. Director and choreographer, Theodore Pappas. Costumes designed by Andrew Marlay. Sets designed by Oliver Smith. Lighting designed by Ken Tabachnick. Conductor, Scott Bergeson. Chorus master, Joseph Colaneri. Produced by the New York City Opera. Opened 30 August 1988 at the New York State Theatre and closed 11 September 1988 after 14 performances.

CAST (in order of appearance): *Watchman*: Jonathan Guss. *Flower Girl*: Rebecca Rosales. *Fanchon*: Christine Meadows. *Nanette*: Paula Hostetter. *Felice*: Madeleine Mines. *Etienne Grandet*, alias Bras Pique: RICHARD WHITE. *Adah* (Le Clercq): SUSANNE MARSEE. *Manuel*: Ralph Bassett. *Pirate*: John Henry Thomas. *Town crier*: William Ledbetter. *Silas Slick*: JACK KENNY. *Harry Blake*: DON YULE. *Captain Richard Warrington*: MICHAEL REES DAVIS. *Lizette*: Ivy Austin. *American Indian*: David Gramlich. *Lieutenant Governor Grandet*: JOSEPH MCKEE. *Florence*: JOHN LANKSTON. *Marietta d'Altena*: CHERYL PARRISH. *Rudolfo*: JAMES BILLINGS. *Graziella*: Esperanza Galan. *Men*: Neil Eddinger, Louis Perry.
 Ensemble: New York City Opera Chorus.

Act 1: A Town Square in New Orleans, 1780.

Act 2, Scene 1: Rudolfo's Theater, ten days later.*Scene 2*: A Men's Club, later that evening.

ACT 1

 Opening Chorus
  Ensemble
 "Tramp, Tramp, Tramp"
  M. R. Davis Rangers
 "Taisez-Vous"
  Rangers, Casquette Girls
 "Naughty Marietta"
  C. Parrish
 "It Never, Never Can Be Love"
  C. Parrish, M. R. Davis
 "If I Were Anyone Else But Me"
  J. Kenny, I. Austin
 "'Neath the Southern Moon"
  S. Marsee
 "Italian Street Song"
  C. Parrish, Ensemble
 Finale
  Principals, Chorus

ACT 2

 "All I Crave Is More of Life"
  C. Parrish
 "You Marry a Marionette"
  R. White
 Intermezzo
  Orchestra
 "At the Ball"
  Male Ensemble
 "Loves of New Orleans"
  Ensemble

---

[3]First presented in New York 19 September 1928 at the Imperial Theatre for 509 performances. For Synopsis of Scenes and Musical Numbers, see 1986 revival.

[4]Originally produced in New York 9 May 1978 at the Longacre Theatre for 1604 performances, transferring from its Off-Broadway debut 8 February 1978 at the Manhattan Theatre Club for 28 performances. For Synopsis of Scenes and Musical Numbers, see original 1978 production.

---

[5]Originally produced in New York 7 November 1910 at the New York Theatre for 136 performances.

"Mister Right"
    I. Austin
"A Royal Whipping Boy"
    J. Kenny
"Live for Today"
    C. Parrish, S. Marsee, M. R. Davis, R. White, Ensemble
"I'm Falling in Love With Someone"
    M. R. Davis
"Ah, Sweet Mystery of Life"
    C. Parrish, M. R. Davis
Finale Ultimo
    C. Parrish, M. R. Davis, R. White, Chorus

MICHAEL FEINSTEIN
IN CONCERT:
1988.19   ISN'T IT ROMANTIC

A One Man Show in Two Acts. Special material, Bruce Vilanch. Production staged and supervised by Christopher Chadman. Musical director, conductor, Joel Silberman. Set designed by Andrew Jackness. Lighting designed by Beverly Emmons. Sound designed by Daryl Bornstein. Orchestrations by Ian Finkel. Additional orchestrations by Joseph Gianono, Larry Hochman, Pete Levin, Johnny Mandel, John Oddo. Special arrangements by Stan Freeman and Joel Silberman. Produced by Ron Delsener, Jonathan Scharer. Opened 5 October 1988 at the Booth Theatre and closed 6 November 1988 after 39 performances[6].

CAST: MICHAEL FEINSTEIN.
    Musicians: Joel Silberman (pianist, conductor), David Finck (bass), Ian Finkel (xylophone), Dave Ratajczak (drums), John Basile (guitar), Ralph Olsen (woodwinds).

1988.20   LEGS DIAMOND

A Musical in Two Acts, 21 Scenes. Book by Harvey Fierstein, Charles Suppon. Based on the Warner Brothers film "The Rise and Fall of Legs Diamond" (screenplay by Joseph Landon). Music and lyrics by Peter Allen. Directed by Robert Allan Ackerman. Musical numbers choreographed by Alan Johnson. Scenery designed by David Mitchell. Costumes designed by Willa Kim. Lighting designed by Jules Fisher. Sound designed by Peter Fitzgerald. Black art effects consultant, Ted Shapiro. Musical director, vocal arrangements by Eric Stern. Orchestrations by Michael Starobin. Dance music arrangements by Mark Hummel. Associate producer, Kathleen Raitt. Produced by James M. Nederlander, James L. Nederlander, Arthur Rubin, The Entertainment Group (Howard Perloff, Eddie Bruce, Joey Roberts, Marc Rose, Ken Silver), George M. Steinbrenner III, in association with Jonathan Farkas and Marvin A. Krauss (Executive producer). Opened 26 December 1988 at the Mark Hellinger Theatre and closed 19 February 1989 after 64 performances.

CAST (in order of appearance): *Jack Diamond*: PETER ALLEN. *Convicts*: Adrian Bailey, Quin Baird, Frank Cava, Norman Wendall Kauahi, Bobby Moya, Paul Nunes, Keith Tyrone. *Prison Guards*: Stephen Bourneuf, Rick Manning. *Madge*: Brenda Braxton. *Cigarette Girl*: Deanna Dys. *Bones*: Christian Kauffmann. *Augie*: Raymond Serra. *Kiki Roberts*: Randall Edwards. *Devane*: Pat McNamara. *Hotsy Totsy Announcer*: Mike O'Carroll. *Flo*: JULIE WILSON. *Hotsy Totsy Girls*: Carol Ann Baxter, Colleen Dunn, Deanna Dys, Gwendolyn Miller, Wendy Waring. *Moran*: Jim Fyfe. *Arnold Rothstein (A.R.)*: JOE SILVER. *Tropicana Announcer*: James Brandt. *Tuxedo Dancers*: Stephen Bourneuf, Jonathan Cerullo, K. Craig Innes, Kevin Weldon. *Latin Dancers*: Frank Cava, Norman Wendall Kauahi, Bobby Moya, Paul Nunes, Keith Tyrone. *Champagne Girls*: Carol Ann Baxter, Gwendolyn Miller. *Showgirls*: Colleen Dunn, Wendy Waring. *Gangsters*: Quin Baird, Stephen Bourneuf, James Brandt, Jonathan Cerullo, Rick Manning, Bobby Moya, Paul Nunes, Mike O'Carroll. *Taxi Dancers*: Frank Cava, K. Craig Innes, Bobby Moya. *Boys from Bay Ridge*: Adrian Bailey, Rick Manning, Bobby Moya. *Mourner*: Ruth Gottschall. *Burlesque Women*: Gwendolyn Miller, Wendy Waring. *Barber*: Mike O'Carroll. *Chinese Waiter*: Norman Wendall Kauahi. *A.R.'s Gang*: Adrian Bailey, Quin Baird, Jonathan Cerullo, Rick Manning, Bobby Moya. *Jack's Gang*: Stephen Bourneuf, Frank Cava, K. Craig Innes, Norman

Wendall Kauahi, Paul Nunes, Keith Tyrone. *Policeman*: Paul Nunes. *Jack Diamond's Secretary*: Shelley Wald. *FBI Men*: James Brandt, Rick Manning.
    Swings: Dan O'Grady, Jennifer Rymer, Steven Scionti.

The action takes place in and around New York during the 1920's.

Act 1, Scene 1: Pennsylvania State Prison, 1921. *Scene 2*: Pennsylvania Station, New York City. *Scene 3*: The Hotsy Totsy Club and Grill. *Scene 4*: The Backroom of The Hotsy Totsy Club. *Scene 5*: Hotsy Totsy Club Alley. *Scene 6*: The Stage of The Tropicana. *Scene 7*: Times Square. *Scene 8*: The Backroom of the Hotsy Totsy Club. *Scene 9*: Flo's Office. *Scene 10*: The Hotsy Totsy Club and Grill. *Scene 11*: Taxi Dancers' Dressing Room. *Scene 12*: Around New York. *Scene 13*: The Hotsy Totsy Club and Grill.

Act 2, Scene 1: A Funeral Parlor. *Scene 2*: The Streets of New York. *Scene 3*: The Hotsy Totsy Stage and The Tropicana Stage. *Scene 4*: The Ladies' Powder Room of The Hotsy Totsy Club. *Scene 5*: The Backroom of The Hotsy Totsy Club. *Scene 6*: The Hotsy Totsy Stage. *Scene 7*: The Diamond Building. *Scene 8*: The Hotsy Totsy Club and Grill.

ACT 1
Scene 1
    "When I Get My Name in Lights"
        P. Allen, Ensemble
Scene 3
    "Speakeasy"
        Ensemble
    "Applause"
        J. Wilson, The Hotsy Totsy Girls
    "Knockers"
        P. Allen, The Hotsy Totsy Girls
Scene 6
    "I Was Made for Champagne"
        R. Edwards, The Tropicana Dancers
    "Tropicana Rhumba"
        P. Allen, R. Edwards
Scene 7
    "Sure Thing Baby"
        P. Allen
Scene 8
    "Speakeasy Christmas"
        The Hotsy Totsy Girls
    "Charge It to A.R."
        J. Silver, R. Serra, J. Fyfe, C. Kauffmann, Gangsters
Scene 9
    "Only an Older Woman"
        P. Allen, J. Wilson
Scene 10
    "Taxi Dancers' Tango"
        P. Allen, Ensemble
Scene 12
    "Only Steal from Thieves"
        P. Allen, R. Edwards, Gangsters
Scene 13
    "When I Get My Name in Lights" (reprise)
        P. Allen, Company
ACT 2
Scene 1
    "Cut of the Cards"
        P. Allen, Company
Scene 2
    "Gangland Chase"
        P. Allen, Gansters
Scene 3
    "Now You See Me, Now You Don't"
        P. Allen, R. Edwards, Ensemble
Scene 4
    "The Man Nobody Could Love"
        R. Edwards, J. Wilson, B. Braxton

---

[6]No musical numbers listed in program. Michael Feinstein previously appeared in concert at the Lyceum Theatre 19 April 1988 for 57 performances.

Scene 6
  "The Music Went Out of My Life"
    J. Wilson
Scene 7
  "Say It Isn't So"
    P. Allen, Company
Scene 8
  "All I Wanted Was the Dream"
    P. Allen

1989.01   H.M.S. PINAFORE

A Revival of the Comic Opera in Two Acts[7]. Libretto by William S. Gilbert. Music by Arthur Sullivan. Directed by Christopher Renshaw. Choreographed by Stuart Hopps. Conducted by David White. (Settings and costumes) Designed by Tim Goodchild. Original lighting design by Mick Hughes; lighting design by Colin Scott. The New Sadler's Wells Opera production. Produced by the City Center 55th Street Theatre Foundation, Inc., by arrangement with Sadler's Wells Trust, Ltd. Opened 17 January 1989 at the New York City Center and closed 29 January 1989 after 16 performances.

CAST: *The Rt. Hon. Sir Joseph Porter, K.C.B., First Lord of the Admiralty*: NICKOLAS GRACE. *Captain Corcoran, Commander of the H.M.S. Pinafore*: GORDON SANDISON. *Ralph Rackstraw*, Able Seaman: HUGH HETHERINGTON. *Dick Deadeye*, Able Seaman: THOMAS LAWLOR. *Bill Bobstay*, Boatswain: Steven Page. *Bob Becket*: Jeremy Jacka. *Josephine*, the Captain's Daughter: ROSEMARY ASHE. *Little Buttercup*, a Bumboat woman: LINDA ORMINSTON. *Cousin Hebe*, Sir Joseph's First Cousin: Joan Davies.
  First Lord's Sisters, Cousins, Aunts, Sailors, Marines, etc.: Brigitta Angsmyr, Jane Cammack, Joan Carroll, David Dyer, Michael Fitchew, George Freeburn, Ann Gall, Claire Hayes, Jeremy Jacka, Robert Jon, Fiona Lamont, Guy Matthews, Tim Menah, Sally-Anne Middleton, Michael Neill, Anne O'Neill, Ian Platt, Elisabeth Stirling, Susan Stubbs, Colin Trickett.

1989.02   BLACK AND BLUE

A Musical Revue in Two Acts. Entire production conceived and directed by Claudio Segovia and Héctor Orrezoli. Choreographers, Cholly Atkins, Henry LeTang, Frankie Manning, Fayard Nicholas. Musical supervision, arrangements, orchestrations by Sy Johnson. Additional arrangements and orchestrations by Luther Henderson. Scenery, costumes designed, and lighting conceived by Claudio Segovia and Héctor Orezzoli. Lighting by Neil Peter Jampolis, Jane Reisman. Sound designed by Abe Jacob. Assistant choreographer, Dianne Walker. Conductor, Leonard Oxley. Associate producer, Marilynn LeVine. Produced by Mel Howard and Donald K. Donald. Opened 26 January 1989 at the Minskoff Theatre and closed 20 January 1991 after 829 performances.

CAST: *The Singers*: RUTH BROWN, LINDA HOPKINS, CARRIE SMITH.
  The Hoofers: Bunny Briggs, Ralph Brown, Lon Chaney, Tina Pratt, Jimmy Slyde, Dianne Walker.
  The Dancers: Rashamella Cumbo, Tanya Gibson, Germaine Goodson, Angela Hall, Kyme, Valerie Macklin, Deborah Mitchell, Valerie E. Smith, Frederick J. Boothe, Eugene Fleming, Ted Levy, Bernard Manners, Van Porter, Kevin Ramsey, Ken Roberson, Melvin Washington, Ivery Wheeler.
  The Younger Generation: Cyd Glover, Savion Glover, Dormeshia Sumbry.
  The Musicians: Martin Aubert, Bill Easley, Stephen Furtaldo, Sir Roland Hanna, Haywood Henry, Virgil Jones, Al McKibbon, Leonard Oxley, Jerome Richardson, Grady Tate, Emery Thompson, Claude Williams, Britt Woodman.

ACT 1
  Blues: "I'm a Woman"
    L. Hopkins, Ruth Brown, C. Smith
    (*Music and Lyrics by* McDaniel.)
  Hoofers a Cappella
    Ralph Brown, B. Manners, S. Glover, B. Briggs, T. Levy, J. Slyde, L. Chaney
  "Royal Garden Blues"
    Musicians
    (*Music and Lyrics by* Spencer Williams and Clarence Williams.)

---

[7]Originally presented in New York 15 January 1879 at the Standard Theatre for 175 performances. For Synopsis of Scenes and Musical Numbers, see original 1879 production.

"St. Louis Blues"
  Ruth Brown
  (*Music and Lyrics by* W. C. Handy.)
    Featured Musicians: R. Hanna, H. Henry, B. Woodman, E. Thompson, G. Tate, M. Aubert.
"Everybody Loves My Baby"
  The Dancers
  (*Music and Lyrics by* Jack Palmer and Spencer Williams. *Choreography by* Henry LeTang. *Arrangements and orchestrations by* Luther Henderson.)
"After You've Gone"
  L. Hopkins, B. Manners, Male Dancers
  (*Music by* Henry Creamer. *Lyrics by* Turner Layton.)
"If I Can't Sell It I'll Keep Sittin' on It"
  Ruth Brown
  (*Music by* Alexander Hill. *Lyrics by* Andy Razaf.)
"I Want a Big Butter and Egg Man"
  C. Smith, E. Fleming, K. Ramsey, T. Levy
  (*Music and Lyrics by* Percy Venable and Louis Armstrong.)
    Featured Musicians: R. Hanna, E. Thompson.
"Rhythm Is Our Business"
  S. Glover, C. Glover, D. Sumbry
  (*Music by* Jimmie Lunceford and Saul Chaplin. *Lyrics by* Sammy Cahn. *Choreography by* Henry LeTang.)
"Mystery Song"
  T. Gibson, R. Cumbo, Valerie E. Smith
  (*Music by* Duke Ellington. *Lyrics by* Irving Mills.)
"Stompin' at the Savoy"
  J. Slyde
  (*Music by* Benny Goodman, Chick Webb, Edgar Sampson. *Lyrics by* Andy Razaf.)
"I've Got a Right to Sing the Blues" (from *EARL CARROLL'S VANITIES OF 1932*)
  (*Music by* Harold Arlen. *Lyrics by* Ted Koehler.)
    C. Smith
"Black and Tan Fantasy"
  B. Briggs, Dancers
  (*Music by* Duke Ellington and Bubber Miley.)
    Choreography by Frankie Manning.
"Come Sunday"
  L. Hopkins
  (*Music and Lyrics by* Duke Ellington.)
"Daybreak Express"
  Musicians
  (*Music by* Duke Ellington.)
"'Tain't Nobody's Bizness If I Do"
  Ruth Brown, L. Hopkins
  (*Music and Lyrics by* Porter Grainger, Clarence Williams, Graham Prince.)
    Featured Musician: R. Hanna.
"That Rhythm Man" (from *HOT CHOCOLATES*)
  Dancers
  (*Music by* Fats Waller and Harry Brooks. *Lyrics by* Andy Razaf. *Arrangements and orchestrations by* Luther Henderson.)

ACT 2
  "Swinging" to "Wednesday Night Hop"
    Dancers
    (*Music by* Johnson; Johnakins-Kirk.)
  "Cry Like a Baby"
  "I'm Getting 'Long Alright"
    L. Hopkins
    (*Music and Lyrics by* R. Sharp and C. Singleton.)
  "Memories of You" (from *BLACKBIRDS OF 1930*)
    D. Walker, B. Manners, K. Ramsey
    (*Music by* Eubie Blake. *Lyrics by* Andy Razaf.)
    Choreography by Cholly Atkins.
  "Body and Soul" (from *THREE'S A CROWD*)
    Ruth Brown
    (*Music by* Johnny Green. *Lyrics by* Edward Heyman, Robert Sour, Frank Eyton.)
  "I'm Confessing (That I Love You)"
    Kyme, B. Manners, F. Boothe, T. Levy, K. Ramsey
    (*Music by* Al. J. Neiberg. *Lyrics by* Don Daugherty and Ellis Reynolds.)
    Choreography by Cholly Atkins. *Featured Musicians*: C. Williams, M. Aubert.

"East St. Louis Toodle-oo"
Ralph Brown, L. Chaney
(*Music by* Duke Ellington, {Bubber Miley}.)

"Am I Blue?" (from *ON WITH THE SHOW* film)
C. Smith
(*Music by* Harry Akst. *Lyrics by* Grant Clarke.)
Featured Musican: C. Williams.

"I Can't Give You Anything But Love" (from *BLACKBIRDS OF 1928*)
A. Hall, E. Fleming, Dancers
(*Music by* Jimmy McHugh. *Lyrics by* Dorothy Fields. *Choreography by* Henry LeTang.)

"In a Sentimental Mood"
B. Briggs
(*Music by* Duke Ellington.)
Featured Musician: J. Richardson.

"Black and Blue" (from *HOT CHOCOLATES*)
Ruth Brown, L. Hopkins, C. Smith, J. Slyde, B. Briggs
(*Music by* Fats Waller and Harry Brooks. *Lyrics by* Andy Razaf.)

Finale
S. Glover, C. Glover, D. Sumbry,
J. Slyde, B. Briggs, Ralph Brown, L. Chaney, D. Walker, Dancers
(*Arrangements and orchestrations by* Luther Henderson.)

1989.03 JEROME ROBBINS' BROADWAY

A Musical Revue in Two Acts, a Prologue and 12 Scenes. Entire production directed and choreographed by Jerome Robbins. Dialogue, music and lyrics by James M. Barrie, Irving Berlin, Leonard Bernstein, Jerry Bock, Sammy Cahn, Moose Charlap, Betty Comden, Larry Gelbart, Morton Gould, Adolph Green, Oscar Hammerstein II, Sheldon Harnick, Arthur Laurents, Carolyn Leigh, Stephen Longstreet, Hugh Martin, Jerome Robbins, Richard Rodgers, Burt Shevelove, Stephen Sondheim, Joseph Stein, Jule Styne. Co-director, Grover Dale. Production scenic designer, Robin Wagner. Scenery by Boris Aronson, Jo Mielziner, Oliver Smith, Robin Wagner, Tony Walton. Supervising costume designer, Joseph G. Aulisi. Costumes by Joseph G. Aulisi, Alvin Colt, Raoul Pene du Bois, Irene Sharaff, Tony Walton, Miles White, Patricia Zipprodt. Musical director, Paul Gemignani. Assistants to the choreographer, Cynthia Onrubia, Victor Castelli, Jerry Mitchell. Sound by Otts Munderloh. Lighting designed by Jennifer Tipton. Orchestrations by Sid Ramin, William D. Brohn. Musical continuity by Scott Frankel. Narrative continuity by Jason Alexander. Produced by The Shubert Organization, Roger Berlind, Suntory International Corporation, Byron Goldman, Emanuel Azenberg, in association with Pace Theatrical Group. Opened 26 February 1989 at the Imperial Theatre and closed 1 September 1990 after 634 performances.

CAST (in alphabetical order): JASON ALEXANDER, Richard Amaro, Dorothy Benham, Jeffrey Lee Broadhurst, Christophe Caballero, Mindy Cartwright, Irene Cho, Jamie Cohen, CHARLOTTE D'AMBOISE, Camille de Ganon, Donna Di Meo, Donna Marie Elio, Mark Esposito, SUSANN FLETCHER, Scott Fowler, Angelo H. Fraboni, Ramon Galindo, Nicholas Garr, Gregorey Garrison, Carolyn Goor, Michael Scott Gregory, Andrew Grose, Alexia Hess, NANCY HESS, Louise Hickey, Eric A. Hoisington, Barbara Hoon, JoAnn M. Hunter, Scott Jovovich, Pamela Khoury, SUSAN KIKUCHI (dance captain), MICHAEL KUBALA, ROBERT LA FOSSE, Mary Ann Lamb, JANE LANIER, David Lowenstein, Michael Lynch, Greta Martin, JOEY McKNEELY, Julio Monge, Troy Myers, Maria Neenan, Steve Ochoa, Kelly Patterson, LUIS PEREZ, FAITH PRINCE, James Rivera, Tom Robbins, George Russell (dance captain), Greg Schanuel, DEBBIE SHAPIRO, Renée Stork, Mary Ellen Stuart, Linda Talcott, Leslie Trayer, Ellen Troy, Andi Tyler, SCOTT WISE, Elaine Wright, Barbara Yeager, Alice Yearsley.

ACT 1

Overture—Prologue
The Setter: J. Alexander.

("Gotta Dance" from *LOOK MA, I'M DANCIN'*")
M. Lynch, Company
(*Music and Lyrics by* Hugh Martin.)

("Papa, Won't You Dance With Me?" from *HIGH BUTTON SHOES*)
(*Music by* Jule Styne. *Lyrics by* Sammy Cahn.) D. Shapiro, Company

("Shall We Dance?" from *THE KING AND I*)
Company
(*Music by* Richard Rodgers. *Lyrics by* Oscar Hammerstein II.)

Scene 1

"New York, New York"
"Sailors on the Town"
"Ya Got Me"
(from *ON THE TOWN*,1944)
Gaby: R. La Fosse. *Chip*: S. Wise. *Ozzie*: M. Kubala. *Hildy*: D. Shapiro. *Claire*: M. E. Stuart. *Dolores Dolores*: N. Hess. *Emcee*: J. Alexander. *First Workman*: D. Lowenstein. *Sailors, Workmen, Dance Hall Hostesses, Passers-by, etc.*: Company.
Book based on an idea by Jerome Robbins. Music by Leonard Bernstein. Book and lyrics by Betty Comden and Adolph Green. Scenery by Oliver Smith. Costumes by Alvin Colt.

Scene 2

"Charleston" From *BILLION DOLLAR BABY* (1945)
Cop: D. Lowenstein. *Doorman*: M. Lynch. *Three Flappers*: B. Yeager, M. A. Lamb, J. M. Hunter. *Socialites*: J. Lanier, N. Garr. *A Timid Girl*: S. Fletcher. *Good Time Charlie*: T. Meyers. *Collegiates*: E. Wright, A. H. Fraboni. *Younger Generation*: C. Caballero, L. Talcott. *Older Generation*: B. Hoon, S. Fowler. *Two Gangsters*: M. S. Gregory, S. Jovovich. *Two Bootleggers*: A. Grose, J. Monge.
Book and lyrics by Betty Comden and Adolph Green. Music by Morton Gould. Scenery by Oliver Smith. Costumes designed by Irene Sharaff.

Scene 3

"Comedy Tonight" From *A FUNNY THING HAPPENED ON THE WAY TO THE FORUM* (1962)
Pseudolus: J. Alexander. *First Protean*: S. Wise. *Second Protean*: J. McKneely. *Third Protean*: M. Kubala. *The Company*: C. d'Amboise, D. Benham, S. Fletcher, M. S. Gregory, A. Grose, R. La Fosse, M. A. Lamb, D. Lowenstein, M. Lynch, J. Noseworthy, K. Patterson, L. Perez, T. Robbins, G. Schanuel, D. Shapiro.
Book by Burt Shevelove and Larry Gelbart. Music and lyrics by Stephen Sondheim. Scenery and costumes by Tony Walton. Dance music arranged by Betty Walberg. Staged by Jerome Robbins.

Scene 4

"I Still Get Jealous" From *HIGH BUTTON SHOES* (1947)
Ma: F. Prince. *Pa*: J. Alexander.
Book by Stephen Longstreet. Music by Jule Styne. Lyrics by Sammy Cahn. Scenery by Oliver Smith. Costumes by Miles White.

Scene 5

"Suite of Dances" From *WEST SIDE STORY* (1957)
(Prologue; The Dance at the Gym; Cool; America; The Rumble; Somewhere.)
Tony: R. La Fosse. *Maria*: A. Hess. *Riff*: S. Wise. *Bernardo*: N. Garr. *Anita*: C. d'Amboise. *Rosalia*: D. Shapiro. *Graziella*: D. Di Meo. *"Somewhere" Soloist*: D. Benham. *The Jets*: J. McKneely, C. Caballero, S. Fowler, A. H. Fraboni, M. S. Gregory, A. Grose, E. A. Hoisington, T. Meyers, J. Noseworthy, K. Patterson, G. Schanuel. *Their Girls*: L. Hickey, B. Hoon, M. A. Lamb, M. Neenan, M. E. Stuart, L. Talcott, L. Trayer, A. Yearsley. *The Sharks*: J. Cohen, M. Esposito, S. Jovovich, D. Lowenstein, M. Lynch, J. Monge, S. Ochoa, J. Rivera. *Their Girls*: I. Cho, D. M. Elio, N. Hess, J. M. Hunter, R. Stork, A. Tyler, E. Wright, B. Yeager.
Based on a conception of Jerome Robbins. Book by Arthur Laurents. Music by Leonard Bernstein. Lyrics by Stephen Sondheim. Scenery by Oliver Smith. Costumes designed by Irene Sharaff. Co-choreographer, Peter Gennaro. Directed and choreographed by Jerome Robbins.

ACT 2

Scene 1

"The Small House of Uncle Thomas" From *THE KING AND I* (1951)
Narrator: B. Yeager. *Eliza*: S. Kikuchi. *King Simon*: J. McKneely. *Little Eva*: L. Talcott. *Topsy*: J. M. Hunter. *Uncle Thomas*: B. Hoon. *Angel/George*: I. Cho. *Royal Dancers*: C. Caballero, D. Di Meo, M. Esposito, E. A. Hoisington, M. Neenan, S. Ochoa, R. Stork, A. Tyler, E. Wright, A. Yearsley. *Royal Singers*: D. Benham, D. M. Elio, L. Trayer, N. Hess, L. Hickey, M. E. Stuart. *Propmen*: J. Cohen, A. H. Fraboni, S. Fowler, N. Garr, S. Jovovich, J. Rivera.
Book and lyrics by Oscar Hammerstein II. Music by Richard Rodgers. Based upon the novel "Anna and the King of Siam" by Margaret Landon. Scenery by Jo Mielziner. Costumes designed by Irene Sharaff. Dance music arranged by Trude Rittman.

Scene 2

"You Gotta Have a Gimmick" From *GYPSY* (1959)
Cigar: J. Alexander. *Louise*: M. A. Lamb. *Tessie*: F. Prince. *Mazeppa*: D. Shapiro. *Electra*: S. Fletcher.
Book by Arthur Laurents. Music by Jule Styne. Lyrics by Stephen Sondheim. Suggested by the memoirs of Gypsy Rose Lee. Scenery by Jo Mielziner. Costumes by Raoul Pene du Bois.

Scene 3

"I'm Flying" From *PETER PAN* (1954)

(Charlap-Leigh)

Peter Pan: C. d'Amboise. *Wendy*: D. Di Meo. *Michael*: L. Talcott. *John*: S. Ochoa.

Book by James M. Barrie. Music by Moose Charlap and Jule Styne. Lyrics by Carolyn Leigh, Betty Comden and Adolph Green. New scenery by Robin Wagner. New costumes by Joseph Aulisi. Flying by Foy.

Scene 4

"On a Sunday by the Sea" From *HIGH BUTTON SHOES* (1947)

Book by Stephen Longstreet. Music by Jule Styne. Lyrics by Sammy Cahn.

Scene 5

"Mr. Monotony" From *MISS LIBERTY* (1949), *CALL ME MADAM* (1950), dropped.

Singer: D. Shapiro. *First Dancer*: L. Perez. *Second Dancer*: J. Lanier. *Third Dancer*: R. La Fosse.

Music and Lyrics by Irving Berlin. New costumes by Joseph Aulisi. Dance music arranged by Genevieve Pitot.

Scene 6

("Tradition;" "The Dream;" "Sunrise, Sunset;" "Wedding Dance.") From *FIDDLER ON THE ROOF* (1964)

Tevye: J. Alexander. *Golde*: S. Fletcher. *Motel Kamzoil*: M. Lynch. *Tzeitel*: A. Tyler. *Grandma Tzeitel*: B. Hoon. *Fruma-Sarah*: N. Hess. *Lazar Wolf*: T. Robbins. *The Rabbi*: T. Meyers. *The Fiddler*: J. McKneely. *Bottle Dancers*: C. Caballero, M. Esposito, S. Jovovich, G. Schanuel. *Villagers, Wedding Guests*: Company.

Book by Joseph Stein. Music by Jerry Bock. Lyrics by Sheldon Harnick. Based on Sholom Aleichem's stories by special arrangement of Arnold Perl. Scenery by Boris Aronson. Costumes by Patricia Zipprodt. Dance music arranged by Betty Walberg.

Scene 7

"Some Other Time"

"New York, New York" (reprise)

Finale from *ON THE TOWN* (1944)

Gaby: R. La Fosse. *Chip*: S. Wise. *Ozzie*: M. Kubala. *Hildy*: D. Shapiro. *Claire*: M. E. Stuart. *Ivy*: A. Hess. *Three Sailors*: C. Caballero, K. Patterson, M. S. Gregory. And the Full Company.

Setting for "Broadway at Night" designed by Robin Wagner.

1989.04   THE PAJAMA GAME

A Revival of the Musical Comedy in Two Acts, 17 Scenes[8]. Book by George Abbott and Richard Bisssell. Based on the novel "7 1/2 Cents" by Richard Bissell. Music and lyrics by Richard Adler and Jerry Ross. Director and choreographer, Theodore Pappas. Conductor, Peter Howard. Set designer, Michael Anania. Costume designer, by Marjorie McCown. Lighting designer, Ken Tabachnick. Chorus Master, Joseph Colaneri. Produced by the New York City Opera. Opened 3 March 1989 at the New York State Theatre and closed 16 April 1989 after 51 performances.[9]

CAST (in order of appearance): *Hines*: AVERY SALTZMAN. *Prez*: David Green. *Joe*: Jim Borstelmann. *Hasler*: Steve Pudenz. *Gladys*: LENORA NEMETZ. *Mae*: Susan Nicely. *Brenda*: Joyce Campana. *Poopsie*: Lillian Graff. *Sid Sorokin*: RICHARD MUENZ. *Charlie*: Louis Perry. *First Helper*: Scott Robertson. *Second Helper*: David Koch. *Mabel*: Brooks Almy. *Babe Williams*: JUDY KAYE. *Max*: Don Yule. *Pat*: Paula Hostetter. *Pop*: William Ledbetter. *Steam Heat Boys*: Jim Borstelmann, David Koch.

Ensemble: New York City Opera Chorus.

1989.05   CHU CHEM

The First Chinese-Jewish Musical in Two Acts[10]. Book by Ted Allan. Music by Mitch Leigh. Lyrics by Jim Haines, Jack Wohl. Entire production staged

---

[8]Originally produced in New York 13 May 1954 at the St. James Theatre for 1063 performances. For Synopsis of Scenes and Musical Numbers, see original 1954 production. The action was reset to June 1957.
[9]Orchestrations uncredited.
[10]Originally produced in New York Off-Broadway 22 December 1988 at the Jewish Repertory Theatre for 20 performances. An earlier version starring Menasha Skulnick and Molly Picon was presented in Philadelphia in December 1966 but closed before reaching New York.

by Albert Marre. Scenery by Robert Mitchell. Costumes by Kenneth M. Yount. Lighting by Jason Sturm. Sound by Gary M. Stocker. Musical, vocal direction by Don Jones. Orchestrations by Michael Gibson. Production supervisor, Dwight Frye. A Jewish Repertory Theatre Production. Produced by The Mitch Leigh Company and William D. Rollnick. Opened 7 April 1989 at the Ritz Theatre and closed 14 May 1989 after 45 performances.

CAST: *The Oriental Company*: *The Prince*: KEVIN GRAY. *The Elder*: Alvin Lum. *Hong Ho, the Governor*: Chev Rodgers. *The Prince's Brother*: Hechter Ubarry. *Dah-ah-Dil, Concubine, Villager*: Zoie Lam. *The Prompter*: Timm Fujii. *Na Mi, Concubine, Villager*: Simone Gee. *Lei-An, Concubine, Villager*: Keelee Seetoo. *Shu-Wo, Propman, Villager*: Kenji Nakao. *Ho-Ke, Propman, Villager*: Jason Ma. *Nu-Wo, Propman, Villager*: Paul Nakauchi. *Chueh-Wu, Propman, Guard*: Nephi Jay Wimmer. *The Westerners*: *Chu Chem*: MARK ZELLER. *Lotte*: EMILY ZACHARIAS. *Jacob*: Irving Burton.

The action takes place some six hundred years ago in China.

ACT 1

"Orient Yourself"

Oriental Company

"What Happened, What?"

M. Zeller, I. Burton

"Welcome"

Villagers

"You'll Have to Change"

E. Zacharias

"Love Is"

K. Gray

"I'll Talk to Her"

M. Zeller, K. Gray, H. Ubarry

"Shame on You"

M. Zeller, K. Gray, Concubines

"It Must be Good for Me"

E. Zacharias

"I'll Talk to Her" (reprise)

M. Zeller, K. Gray

"You'll Have to Change" (reprise)

K. Gray

"The River"

E. Zacharias, K. Gray, Propmen

"We Dwell in Our Hearts"

M. Zeller, E. Zacharias, K. Gray

ACT 2

"Re-Orient Yourself"

Oriental Company

"What Happened, What?" (reprise)

I. Burton

"I Once Believed"

E. Zacharias

"It's Possible"

M. Zeller

"Our Kind of War"

Company

"Boom!"

C. Rodgers

Finale

Company

1989.06   THE WIZARD OF OZ

A Musical Spectacle in Two Acts. Based on the novel of the same name by L. Frank Baum and the MGM film adaptation by Noel Langley, Florence Ryerson, Edgar Allan Woolf. Book by Michel M. Grilikhes. Original music by Harold Arlen. Original lyrics by E. Y. Harburg. Original incidental music by Herbert Stothart. Directed and produced by Michel M. Grilikhes. Dances by Onna White. Costumes by Bill Campbell. Art director, Jeremy Railton. Scenery designed by Stephen Ehlers. Musical supervisor, Tom Worrall. Dimensional sound by John Neal. Associate choreographer, Jim Tyler. Dance arrangements by Jackie Shaw O'Neill. Sponsors, Purina Dog Chow, Downy Fabric Softener. Produced by M.M.G. Arena Productions.

Opened 22 March 1989 at Radio City Music Hall and closed 9 April 1989 after 37 performances.

CAST: *Dorothy*: GRACE GREIG. *Aunt Em, Glinda*: LINDA JOHNSON. *Uncle Henry*: John Sovec. *Zeke, Cowardly Lion*: GUY ALLEN. *Hunk, Scarecrow*: JOE MCDONOUGH. *Hickory, Tin Woodsman*: JOE GIUFFRE. *Miss Gulch, Wicked Witch of the West*: POLLY SEALE. *Professor Marvel, Wizard, Gate Keeper*: BART WILLIAMS. *Toto*: Toby, Coby, Patrick, Darrin, or Misty.

MUSICAL NUMBERS[11]
"Over the Rainbow"
"Munchkinland"
"Ding Dong! The Witch Is Dead"
"Follow the Yellow Brick Road"
"If I Only Had a Brain"
"If I Only Had a Heart"
"Lions and Tigers and Bears"
"If I Only Had the Nerve"
"Optimistic Voices"
"The Merry Old Land of Oz"
"If I Were King of the Forest"
"Courage"
"There's No Place Like Home"
Finale

1989.07 ## WELCOME TO THE CLUB

A Musical in Two Acts. Book by A. E. Hotchner. Music by Cy Coleman. Lyrics by Cy Coleman and A. E. Hotchner. Directed by Peter Mark Schifter. Musical numbers staged by Patricia Birch. Scenery designed by David Jenkins. Costumes designed by William Ivey Long. Lighting designed by Tharon Musser. Sound designed by Otts Munderloh. Orchestrations by Doug Katsaros. Vocal arrangements by Cy Coleman, David Pogue. Musical director, David Pogue. Associate producer, Robert R. Larsen. Produced by Cy Coleman, A. E. Hotchner, William H. Kessler, Jr., Michael M. Weatherly in association with Raymond J. Greenwald. Opened 13 April 1989 at the Music Box Theatre and closed 22 April 1989 after 13 performances.

CAST (in order of appearance): *Arlene Meltzer*: MARILYN SOKOL. *Milton Meltzer*: AVERY SCHREIBER. *Gus Bottomly*: Bill Buell. *Aaron Bates*: Scott Wentworth. *Bruce Aiken*: Samuel E. Wright. *Kevin Bursteter*: Scott Waara. *Betty Bursteter*: Jodi Benson. *Carol Bates*: Marcia Mitzman. *Eve Aiken*: Terri White. *Winona Shook*: Sally Mayes.

The action takes place at the present time in a section of a New York City jail exclusively reserved for alimony delinquents.

ACT 1
"A Place Called Alimony Jail"
    Husbands, Wives
"Pay the Lawyer"
    Husbands
"Mrs. Meltzer Wants the Money Now!"
    M. Sokol, Husbands
"That's a Woman"
    S. Wentworth, M. Mitzman, Wives
"Piece of Cake"
    T. White, S. E. Wright
"Rio"
    A. Schreiber, M. Sokol, Wives, B. Buell
"Holidays"
    M. Sokol
"The Trouble with You"
    S. Wentworth, M. Mitzman, Husbands, Wives
"Mother-in-Law"
    Husbands
"At My Side"
    S. E. Wright, S. Waara

ACT 2
"Southern Comfort"
    S. Mayes, S. Wentworth, Wives, Husbands
"The Two of Us"
    S. E. Wright, A. Schreiber
"It's Love! It's Love!"
    B. Buell, Husbands.
"The Name of Love"
    M. Mitzman
"Miami Beach"
    M. Sokol, Husbands
"Guilty"
    S. Mayes
"Love Behind Bars"
    S. Mayes, S. Wentworth, Wives
"At My Side" (reprise)
    S. Waara, J. Benson
"It Wouldn't Be You"
    Husbands, Wives

1989.08 # BARRY MANILOW AT THE GERSHWIN

A Musical Revue in Two Acts. Written by Ken and Mitzie Welch, Roberta Kent, Barry Manilow. Concept by Ernie Chambers, Jack Feldman, Roberta Kent, Barry Manilow, Bruce Sussman. Production created and directed by Joe Gannon. Production (set, costumes) designer, Jeremy Railton. Lighting designer, J. T. McDonald. Music directors, Bud Harner, Ron Pedley. Original production created and produced by Joe Gannon. Presented by Garry C. Kief, James M. Nederlander, James L. Nederlander, Arthur Rubin. Opened 18 April 1989 at the Gershwin Theatre and closed 10 June 1989 after 44 performances[12].

CAST: BARRY MANILOW.
    Musicians: Vanessa Brown (percussion, vocals), Debra Byrd (vocals), Billy Kidd (keyboards, vocals), Marc Levine (bass guitar, vocals), Joe Melotti (keyboards, vocals), John Pondel (guitar, vocals), Dana Robbins (woodwinds, vocals), Bud Harner (drums), Ron Pedley (keyboards).

1989.09 # STARMITES

A Musical in Two Acts, a Prologue, 9 Scenes and an Epilogue[13]. Book by Stuart Ross and Barry Keating. Music and lyrics by Barry Keating. Directed and staged by Larry Carpenter. Choreography by Michele Asaf. Assistant choreographer, T. C. Charlton. Sets by Lowell Detweiler. Costumes by Susan Hirschfeld. Lighting by Jason Kantrowitz. Sound by John Kilgore. Musical direction, dance arrangements by Henry Aronson. Orchestrations, sound effects by James McElwane. Vocal arrangements, associate musical director, Dianne Adams. Associate producers, Peter Bogyo, John Burt, Severn Sandt. Produced by Hinks Shimberg, Mary Keil, Steven Warnick. Opened 27 April 1989 at the Criterion Center Stage Right and closed 18 June 1989 after 60 performances.

CAST (in order of appearance): *On Earth*: *Eleanor*: LIZ LARSEN. *Mother*: SHARON MCKNIGHT.
    Innerspace: *Shak Graa*: Ariel Grabber. *Spacepunk*: BRIAN LANE GREEN. *Trinkulus*: GABRIEL BARRE.
    Starmites: *Ack Ack Ackerman*: Bennett Cale. *Herbie Harrison*: Victor Trent Cook. *Dazzle Razzledorf*: Christopher Zelno. *Diva*: SHARON MCKNIGHT. *Bizarbara*: LIZ LARSEN.
    Banshees: *Shotzi*: Mary Kate Law. *Canibelle*: Gwen Stewart. *Balbraka*: Freida Williams. *Maligna*: Janet Aldrich. *Droids*: John-Michael Flate, Ric Ryder.

The action takes place now on Earth and in Innerspace.

Prologue: Eleanor's Bedroom, Planet Earth.

---

[11]The cast performed to pre-recorded dialogue and music from the 1939 film, whose songs are listed below.

[12]Musical numbers not listed in program.
[13]Originally produced Off-Broadway 23 October 1980 at the Ark Theatre for 20 performances; subsequently produced 24 April 1987 by Musical Theatre Works at the CSC Theatre for 16 performances.

Act 1, Scene 1: A Sacrificial Lab in Innerspace. *Scene 2*: Shriekwood Forest. *Scene 3*: Castle Nemesis: The Great Hall. *Scene 4*: The Castle Mortuary. *Scene 5*: Castle Nemesis: The Great Hall.

Act 2, Scene 1: Castle Nemesis: The Great Hall. *Scene 2*: The Chamber of Psychosorcery. *Scene 3*: Castle Nemesis: The Great Hall. *Scene 4*: A Sacrificial Lab in Innerspace.

Epilogue: Eleanor's Bedroom, Planet Earth.

ACT 1
  Prologue
    "Superhero Girl"
      L. Larsen
  Scene 1
    "Starmites"
      Starmites, B. L. Green
    "Trink's Narration"
      G. Barre, Starmites
    "Afraid of the Dark"
      B. L. Green, Starmites, L. Larsen, G. Barre
  Scene 2
    "Little Hero"
      L. Larsen
    "Attack of the Banshees"
      Banshees
  Scene 3
    "Hard to Be Diva"
      S. McKnight, Banshees
  Scene 4
    "Love Duet"
      B. L. Green, L. Larsen
  Scene 5
    "The Dance of Spousal Arousal"
      Banshees, L. Larsen
    Finaletto
      Company

ACT 2
  Scene 1
    "Bizarbara's Wedding"
      L. Larsen, Banshees
    "Milady"
      B. L. Green, Starmites
  Scene 2
    "Beauty Within"
      S. McKnight, L. Larsen
  Scene 3
    "The Cruelty Stomp"
      G. Barre, Company
    "Reach Right Down"
      Starmites, S. McKnight, Banshees
  Scene 4
    "Immolation"
      L. Larsen, A. Grabber, B. L. Green
    "Starmites"/"Diva" (reprise)
      S. McKnight, Starmites, Banshees
  Epilogue
  Finale
    Company

GHETTO:
The Last Performance
in the Vilna Ghetto

1989.10

A Drama with Music in Two Acts, 22 Scenes. Play by Joshua Sobol. Translated (from the Hebrew) by David Lan. English lyrics by Jeremy Sams. Directed by Gedalia Besser. Musical direction, orchestrations, arrangements

of authentic ghetto songs by William Schimmel. Movement by Nir Ben Gal, Liat Dror. Fight direction, B. H. Barry. Set by Adrian Vaux. Costumes by Edna Sobol. Lighting by Kevin Rigdon. This translation was commissioned by the Royal National Theatre of Great Britain. Produced by Circle in the Square (Theodore Mann, Artistic director; Paul Libin, Producing director). Opened 30 April 1989 at the Circle in the Square and closed 28 May 1989 after 33 performances.

CAST (in order of appearance): *Srulik*, a ventriloquist: AVNER EISENBERG. *Kittel*: STEPHEN MCHATTIE. *Hayyah*: HELEN SCHNEIDER. *The Dummy*: Gordon Joseph Weiss. *Gens*: GEORGE HEARN. *The Hassid*: Jerry Matz. *Weiskopf*: DONAL DONNELLY *Kruk*: JARLATH CONROY. *Haiken*: Marshall Coid. *Reed Player*: David Hopkins. *Guitar Player*: Barry Mitterhoff. *Accordion Player*: William Swindler. *Miriam*: Julie Goell. *Ooma, Dr. Weiner*: Alma Cuervo. *The Rich Man*: Richard M. Davidson. *Dr. Gottlieb*: Jerry Matz. *A Judge*: David Rosenbaum. *Luba*: Andrea Clark Libin. *Yankel*: Jon Rothstein. *Yitzhak Geivish*: Matthew P. Mutrie. *Elia Geivish*: Jonathan Mann. *Dessler*: William Verderber. *Jewish Policeman Averbuch*: Ahvi Spindell. *Jewish Policeman Levas*: Angelo Ragonesi. *A Woman*: Julie Anne Eigenberg. *German Soldiers*: Brain Maffitt, Spike McClure.

The action opens in an apartment in Tel Aviv in 1983, and thereafter takes place in and around the theatre in the Vilna ghetto under the Nazi occupation from September 1941 to its liquidation two years later.

ACT 1[14]
Scene 2
  "Unter Daine Vaisse Shteren" (In the sky the stars all glisten . . .)
    H. Schneider
  "Hot Zich Mir Di Shich Zerissn" (Someone stole my overcoat . . .)
    A. Eisenberg, H. Schneider, G. D. Weiss
Scene 9
  "Vei Zu Di Teg" (Ah my children, my children . . .)
    Actors
  "Swanee" (from *SINBAD*)
    H. Schneider
    (*Music by* George Gershwin. *Lyrics by* Irving Caesar.)
Scene 11
  "Shtiler, Shtiler" (Go to sleep my little flower . . .)
Scene 12
  "Lullaby" (Hush my child, the winds are blowing . . .)
    A. Cuervo

ACT 2
Scene 1
  "Yidishe Brigades" (Forget the sun—forget the flowers . . .)
    Company
  "Isrulik" (I'm Isrulik—the orphan of the ghetto . . .)
    J. Mann
Scene 3
  "Isrulik" (reprise)
    A. Cuervo, Company
Scene 4
  "Friling" (I walk through the ghetto alone and forsaken . . .)
    H. Schneider
  "Je t'aime—c'est fou" (Je suis peut etre mal foutoe . . .)
    H. Schneider
    (*Music by* Jeremy Sams. *Lyrics by* Joshua Sobol.)
  "Mir Lebn Eibik" (We'll live forever—year after year . . .)
    Company
Scene 5
  "Dremlen Feigl" (Birds are dreaming in the treetops . . .)
    H. Schneider
Scene 8
  "Mayday Song" (We've dragged through the mud . . .)
    H. Schneider
  "Zog Nit Keinmol" (Never say the final journey is at hand . . .)

---

[14]No song list appears in the program. The list below was prepared from the production typescript.

Scene 11

"Pak Zich Ain" (Move along, move along, every Jew knows this song . . .)
G. J. Weiss

1989.11 LEGENDS IN CONCERT

A Musical Revue in Two Acts[15]. Created and directed by John Stuart. Choreography by Inez Mourning. Musical director, Kerry McCoy. Lighting, production consultatnt, Dennis Condon. Costumes by Betty Lurenz. Technical consultant, Ron Popp. Multi-media design, Media Innovations/Joseph Jarred. Lasers, Mark Fisher. Supervisor in charge of production, Steve Yuhasz. Associate producers, Don Saxon, Robert R. Blume, Malcolm Allen. Produced by John Stuart. Opened 4 May 1989 at the Academy Theatre and closed 28 May 1989 after 22 performances.

CAST (in order of appearance): *Jack Benny*: Eddie Carroll. *Al Jolson*: Clive Baldwin. *Buddy Holly*: George Trullinger. *Liberace*: Daryl Wagner. *Marilyn Monroe*: Katie LaBourdette. *Nat King Cole*: Donny Ray Evins. *Judy Garland*: Julie Sheppard. *John Lennon*: Randy Clark. *Another Guest*: Tony Roi.

Singer/Dancers: Renee Chambers, Troy Christian, Vincent D'Elia, Elena Ferrante, Debby Kole, Gary La Rosa, Michael Roberts, Marrielle Monte.

---

[15]An evening of impersonations. No musical numbers were listed in the program.

Danny Strayhorn, David Jackson, and Jane Krakowski in GRAND HOTEL
Martha Swope/TimePix

1989–1990 SEASON

ELVIS:
1989.12 ## A ROCKIN' REMEMBRANCE

A Musical Biography of Elvis Presley in Two Acts, a Prologue and 10 Scenes. (Book) Written by Robert Rabinowitz. Entire production directed and choreographed by Patricia Birch. Scenery designed by Douglas W. Schmidt. Costumes designed by Jeanne Button. Lighting designed by Jules Fisher, Peggy Eisenhauer. Sound designed by Otts Munderloh. Media film designed and directed by Robert Rabinowitz. Film sequences produced by Chrisann Verges. Projection supervision, Bran Ferren. Musical supervisors, Phil Ramone, Robby Merkin. Musical director, Terry Mike Jeffrey. Orchestrations and vocal arrangements by Robby Merkin. Assistant director, John Mineo. Produced by Jules Fisher, Rodger Hess, Magic Promotions Inc., Pace Theatrical Group, Concert Productions International, Marvin A. Krauss, Act III Communications Inc., Joseph Rascoff, Julian and Jean Aberbach, Mark Levy, in association with the estate of Elvis Presley. Presented by Madison Square Garden Enterprises. Opened 6 June 1989 at the Beacon Theatre and closed 30 June 1989 after 31 performances.

CAST: *Young Elvis*: TERRY MIKE JEFFREY. *Heyday Elvis*: JOHNNY SEATON. *Older Elvis*: JULIAN WHITAKER. *Principal Dancers*: Dannul Dailey, Tinka Gutrick.
   Company (in alphabetical order): Helena Andreyko, Darren Dollar, James Ellis, Collette Hill, Debbie Jeffrey, Leonard Joseph, Paul Mahos, Pat Moya, David Mullen, Kaye Pryor, Carol Denise Smith, Trish Vevera, Patrick Weathers. *Swing*: Harrison Beal.

Prologue: America Sends Mixed Signals.

Act 1, Scene 1: The Eisenhower Years. The last throes of innocence. *Scene 2*: Elvis finds his fans and his fans find a new rebel hero and an independent lifestyle. *Scene 3*: Graceland. *Scene 4*: Dreams and nightmares.

Act 2, Scene 1: The unreal world of Hollywood clashes with the real world of the Sixties. *Scene 2*: "Here I am strange and afraid in a world I never made." *Scene 3*: Las Vegas I. A New Elvis. *Scene 4*: A Carousel. *Scene 5*: Las Vegas II and after. *Scene 6*: A new beginning.

PROLOGUE
   "By and By" (traditional)
      D. Jeffrey
   "Let the Good Times Roll"
      J. Ellis
      (*Music and Lyrics by* Leonard Lee.)
   "Boogie-Woogie Bugle Boy"
      (Andrews Sisters)
      (*Music and Lyrics by* Don Raye and Hughie Prince.)
   "(Gimme That) Old Time Religion" (traditional)
"Oh, Happy Days"
      L. Joseph, Company
      (*Music and Lyrics by* Edwin Hawkins.)

ACT 1
Scene 1
   "That's All Right Mama"
      T. M. Jeffrey, K. Freeman, K. McCann, W. Pryor
      (*Music and Lyrics by* Arthur Crudup.)
   "Blue Moon of Kentucky"
      T. M. Jeffrey, Company
      (*Music and Lyrics by* Bill Monroe.)
   "I Don't Care if the Sun Don't Shine"
      T. M. Jeffrey, Company
      (*Music and Lyrics by* Mack David.)
   "Mystery Train"
      T. M. Jeffrey, Company
      (*Music and Lyrics by* Herman Parker, Jr. and Sam C. Phillips.)
   "Heartbreak Hotel"
      J. Seaton, Company
      (*Music and Lyrics by* Mae Boren Axton, Tommy Burden and Elvis Presley.)
   "Mama Don't Allow"
      P. Mahos
      (Traditional; *Additional Lyrics by* Robby Merkin.)
   "Can't Nobody Do Me Like Jesus"
      L. Joseph, C. Hill, D. Jeffrey, K. Pryor
      (Traditional; *Additional Lyrics by* Robby Merkin.)

Scene 2
   "All Shook Up"
      J. Seaton
      (*Music and Lyrics by* Otis Blackwell and Elvis Prelsey.)
   "Don't Be Cruel"
      J. Seaton
      (*Music and Lyrics by* Otis Blackwell and Elvis Prelsey.)
   "Shake, Rattle and Roll"
      J. Seaton, Company
      (*Music and Lyrics by* Charles Calhoun.)
   "Treat Me Nice"
      J. Seaton, T. Gutrick
      (*Music and Lyrics by* Jerry Lieber and Mike Stoller.)
   "Hound Dog"
      J. Seaton, Company
      (*Music and Lyrics by* Jerry Lieber and Mike Stoller.)
   "In the Garden" (traditional)
      C. Hill, K. Pryor, D. Jeffrey, P. Moya
      Saxophone Solo: T. M. Jeffrey.
Scene 3
   "Baby Let's Play House"
      J. Seaton, Company
      (*Music and Lyrics by* Arthur Gunter.)
   "Teddy Bear"
      J. Seaton, Company
      (*Music and Lyrics by* Bernie Lowe and Kal Mann.)
   "Hot Dog Buddy"
      J. Seaton, Company
      (*Music and Lyrics by* Bill Haley.)
   "Return to Sender"
      J. Seaton, Company
      (*Music and Lyrics by* Otis Blackwell and Winfield Scott.)
   "Long Tall Sally"
      J. Seaton, Company
      (*Music and Lyrics by* Robert Blackwell, Enotris Johnson, Richard Penniman.)
   "Great Balls of Fire"
      J. Seaton, Company
      (*Music and Lyrics by* Jack Hammer.)
   "The Great Pretender"
      J. Seaton, Company
      (*Music and Lyrics by* Buck Ram.)
Scene 4
   "Love Me Tender"
      J. Seaton
      (*Music and Lyrics by* Vera Matson and Elvis Presley.)
   "I Want You, I Need You, I Love You"
      J. Seaton, D. Dailey, D. Mullen, P. Mahos, D. Dollar
      (*Music and Lyrics by* Ira Kosloff and Maurice Mysels.)
   "It's Now or Never"
      J. Seaton, D. Dailey, T. Gutrick
      (*Music and Lyrics by* Wally Gold and Aaron Schroeder.)
   "A Big Hunk of Love"
      J. Seaton, D. Dailey
      (*Music and Lyrics by* Aaron Schroeder and Sid Wyche.)

ACT 2
   "Amazing Grace"
      T. M. Jeffrey (off-stage)
      (*Music and Lyrics by* Elvis Presley.)
Scene 1
   "Jailhouse Rock"
      J. Seaton, Company
      (*Music and Lyrics by* Jerry Lieber and Mike Stoller.)
   "Wear My Ring Around Your Neck"
      J. Seaton, P. Weathers, Company
      (*Music and Lyrics by* Bert Carroll, Russell Moody.)
   "Surrender"
      J. Seaton, P. Weathers, Company
      (*Music and Lyrics by* Doc Pomus, Mort Shuman.)
   "Mean Woman Blues"
      J. Seaton, P. Weathers, Company
      (*Music and Lyrics by* Claude DeMetrius.)

"You're the Devil in Disguise"
J. Seaton, P. Weathers, Company
(*Music and Lyrics by* Bernie Baum, Bill Giant, Florence Kaye.)

"G. I. Blues"
J. Seaton, P. Weathers, Company
(*Music and Lyrics by* Roy C. Bennett and Sid Tepper.)

"Rock-a-Hula Baby"
J. Seaton, Company
(*Music and Lyrics by* Fred Wise, Ben Weisman, Dolores Fuller.)

"Bossa Nova Baby"
T. M. Jeffrey, T. Gutrick, D. Dailey
(*Music and Lyrics by* Jerry Lieber and Mike Stoller.)

"Blue Hawaii" (from the films *BLUE HAWAII, WAIKIKI WEDDING*)
(*Music by* Ralph Rainger. *Lyrics by* Leo Robin.) J. Seaton, C. Hill

"Backlash Blues"
J. Seaton, C. Hill
(*Music and Lyrics by* Nina Simone and Langston Hughes.)
Drum Solo: W. Pryor.

Scene 2

"Are You Lonesome Tonight?"
J. Whitaker, T. M. Jeffrey
(*Music and Lyrics by* Lou Handman and Roy Turk.)
Monologue: J. Seaton.

Scene 3

"2001: Thus Spake Zarathustra"
J. Seaton, Company
(*Music by* Richard Strauss.)

"CC Rider"
J. Seaton, Company
(*Music and Lyrics by* Elvis Presley.)

"Burning Love"
J. Seaton, Company
(*Music and Lyrics by* Denis Linde.)

"Can't Help Falling in Love"
J. Seaton, Company
(*Music and Lyrics by* Luigi Creatore, Hugo Peretti, George Weiss.)

Scene 4

"My Way"
J. Whitaker
(*Music and Lyrics by* Paul Anka.)

Scene 5

"Battle Hymn" (traditional)
T. M. Jeffrey, Company (off-stage)

"Suspicious Minds"
J. Whitaker, Company
(*Music and Lyrics by* Mark James.)

"If I Can Dream"
J. Whitaker, Company
(*Music and Lyrics by* W. Earl Brown.)

"Blue Suede Shoes"
J. Whitaker
(*Music and Lyrics by* Carl Lee Perkins.)

Scene 6

"Precious Memories"
D. Jeffrey, C. D. Smith

"Blue Suede Shoes" (reprise)
J. Seaton

THE MERRY WIDOW

1989.13

A Revival of the Operetta in Three Acts, 4 Scenes[1]. Music by Franz Lehár. Original German book and lyrics by Victor Léon and Leo Stein (after "L'Attaché d'Ambassade.") English version by Adrian Ross. This San Diego Opera production directed by Tito Capobianco. Original production (direction) by Ronald Bentley. Stage director, Cynthia Edwards. Choreographer, Sharon Halley. Set designers, Helen Pond and Herbert Senn. Lighting design by Ken Tabachnick. Conductor, Imre Pallo. Chorus master, Joseph

Colaneri. Produced by the New York City Opera. Opened 8 July 1989 at the New York State Theatre and closed 1 August 1989 after 4 performances in repertory.

CAST (in order of appearance): *Baron Popoff:* RICHARD MCKEE. *Natalie:* Ruth Golden. *General Novikovich:* JOHN LANKSTON. *Counsellor Khadja:* Michael Willson. *Marquis de Cascada:* ROBERT FERRIER. *Sylviane:* Lisbeth Lloyd. *M. de St. Brioche:* RICHARD BYRNE. *Olga:* Joyce Campana. *Vicomte Camille de Jolidon:* PAUL AUSTIN KELLY. *Nisch:* JAMES BILLINGS. *Count Danilo:* RICHARD MUENZ. *Sonia:* MICHELE MCBRIDE. *Head Waiter:* Jonathan Guss. *Zozo:* Ivy Austin. *Lolo:* Joan Mirabella. *Dodo:* Esperanza Galan. *Jou-Jou:* Candace Itow. *Frou-Frou:* Victoria Rinaldi. *Clo-Clo:* Stephanie Godino. *Margot:* Jean Barber. *Ensemble:* New York City Opera Chorus.

CANDIDE

1989.14

A Revival of the Musical in Two Act, 23 Scenes[2]. (New) Book adapted from Voltaire's satire (of the same name) by Hugh Wheeler. (Original book by Lillian Hellman.) Music by Leonard Bernstein. Lyrics by Richard Wilbur. Additional lyrics by Stephen Sondheim and John Latouche. Directed by Harold Prince. Stage director, Albert Sherman. Choreography by Patricia Birch. Scenery designed by Clarke Dunham. Costumes designed by Judith Dolan. Lighting designed by Ken Billington. Conducted by Scott Bergeson. Orchestrations by Leonard Bernstein and Hershy Kay; additional orchestrations by John Mauceri. Chorus master, Joseph Colaneri. Produced by the New York City Opera. Opened 18 July 1989 at the New York State Theatre and closed 10 September 1989 (matinee) after 14 performances.

CAST (in order of appearance): *Voltaire:* JOHN LANKSTON. *Candide:* MARK BEUDERT. *Huntsman:* Don Yule. *Paquette:* MARIS CLEMENT. *Baroness:* Christine Meadows *Baron:* Richard McKee. *Cunegonde:* CYNDIA SIEDEN. *Maximilian:* JAMES JAVORE. *Servant of Maximilian:* James Billings. *Dr. Pangloss:* JOHN LANKSTON. *Bulgarian Soldiers:* Don Yule, James Billings. *Westphalian Soldiers:* William Ledbetter, Jose Traba. *Don Isaachar, the Jew:* JAMES BILLINGS. *Grand Inquisitor:* RICHARD MCKEE. *Calliope Player:* Christine Meadows. *Old Lady:* MURIEL COSTA-GREENSPON. *Dons:* Daniel Albert, William Ward, Joey R. Smith, Don Yule, William Ledbetter, Ralph Bassett. *Businessman:* John Lankston. *Governor:* JOHN LANKSTON. *Governor's Aide:* Daniel Albert. *Slave Driver:* Richard McKee. *Father Bernard:* James Billings. *Sailors:* Gary Dietrich, Kirk Griffith, Jose Traba, Daniel Albert. *Pirates:* John Henry Thomas, William Ledbetter. *Pink Sheep:* Andrea Green, Karen Ziemba. *Lion:* Michael Willson *Pasha-Prefect:* RICHARD MCKEE. *First Gambler:* JAMES BILLINGS. *Second Gambler (Police Chief):* JOHN LANKSTON. *Sage:* JOHN LANKSTON.

THE MIKADO,
or The Town of Titipu

1989.15

A Revival of the Comic Opera in Two Acts[3]. Libretto by William S. Gilbert. Music by Arthur Sullivan. Director, Lotfi Mansouri. Stage director, David Pfeiffer. Conductor, Peter Howard. Choreographer, Patricia Birch. Set and costume designer, Thierry Bosquet. Lighting designer, John Gleason. Chorus master, Joseph Colaneri. Produced by the New York City Opera. Opened 29 July 1989 at the New York State Theatre and closed 18 August 1989 after 4 performances in repertory.

CAST (in order of appearance): *Nanki-Poo*, his son, disguised as a wandering minstrel in love with Yum-Yum: PAUL AUSTIN KELLY. *Pish-Tush*, Noble Lord: William Parcher. *Pooh-Bah*, Lord High Everything Else: JOSEPH MCKEE. *Ko-Ko*, Lord High Executioner of Titipu: JAMES BILLINGS. *Yum-Yum, Pitti-Sing, Peep-Bo*, three sisters, wards of Ko-Ko: LISA SAFFER, CHRISTINE MEADOWS, BARBARA SHIRVIS. *Katisha:* JANE SHAULIS. *The Mikado of Japan:* RICHARD MCKEE. *Chorus of School Girls, Nobles, Guards and Coolies:* New York City Opera Chorus.

---

[1]Originally produced in New York 21 October 1907 at the New Amsterdam Theatre for 416 performances. For Synopsis of Scenes and Musical Numbers, see 1907 production.

---

[2]Original production first produced in New York 1 December 1956 at the Martin Beck Theatre for 73 performances; revised version first produced Off-Boadway 11 December 1973 at the Chelsea Theater Center, Brooklyn Academy of Music for 48 performances; transferred 5 March 1974 to the Broadway Theatre for 740 performances; this version first produced 13 October 1982 at the New York State Theatre for 7 performances in repertory. For Synopsis of Scenes and Musical Numbers, see 1982 revival.
[3]First presented in New York 20 July, 10-29 August 1885 at the Union Square and People's Theatres for 22 performances. First authorized production presented 19 August 1885 at the Fifth Avenue Theatre by Richard D'Oyly Carte for 250 performances. For Synopsis of Scenes and Musical Numbers, see 19 August 1885 D'Oyly Carte production.

MANDY PATINKIN IN CONCERT:
1989.16 ## DRESS CASUAL

A One Man Musical Revue in One Act[4]. Lighting by Richard Nelson. Produced by Ron Delsener. Opened 1 August 1989 at the Helen Hayes Theatre and closed 16 September 1989 after 49 performances.

CAST: MANDY PATINKIN.
Piano: Paul Ford.

MUSICAL NUMBERS[5]
"Soliloquy" (from *CAROUSEL*)
 (*Music by Richard Rodgers. Lyrics by Oscar Hammerstein II.*)
Medley from *PAL JOEY*
 ("Great Big Town" [Chicago]; "You Mustn't Kick It Around"; "I Could Write a Book"; "Happy Hunting Horn"; "What Do I Care for a Dame?;" "Do It the Hard Way"; "I'm Talking to My Pal"[6])
 (*Music by Richard Rodgers. Lyrics by Lorenz Hart.*)
"Buddy's Blues" (from *FOLLIES*)
 (*Music and Lyrics by Stephen Sondheim.*)
"When the Red, Red Robin Comes Bob, Bob, Bobbin' Along"
 (*Music and Lyrics by Harry Woods.*)
"And the Band Played On"
 (*Music by John F. Palmer. Lyrics by Charles B. Ward.*)
"Over the Rainbow" (from *THE WIZARD OF OZ* film)
 (*Music by Harold Arlen. Lyrics by E. Y. Harburg.*)
"Pennies from Heaven" (from *PENNIES FROM HEAVEN* film)
 (*Music by Arthur Johnston. Lyrics by Johnny Burke.*)
"Top Hat, White Tie and Tails" (from *TOP HAT* film)
 (*Music and Lyrics by Irving Berlin.*)
"Puttin' on the Ritz"
 (*Music and Lyrics by Irving Berlin.*)
"Alexander's Ragtime Band"
 (*Music and Lyrics by Irving Berlin .*)
"Sonny Boy" (from *THE SINGING FOOL* film)
 (*Music and Lyrics by Al Jolson, Buddy DeSylva, Lew Brown, Ray Henderson.*)
"No One Is Alone" (from *INTO THE WOODS*)
 (*Music and Lyrics by Stephen Sondheim.*)
"No More" (from *INTO THE WOODS*)
 (*Music and Lyrics by Stephen Sondheim.*)
"A-Tisket, A-Tasket" (from *COTTON CLUB PARADE* 1938)(5th edition)
 (*Music and Lyrics by Ella Fitzgerald, Al Feldman.*)
"Coffee in a Cardboard Cup" (from *70 GIRLS 70*)
 (*Music by John Kander. Lyrics by Fred Ebb.*)

1989.17 ## SHENANDOAH

A Revival of the Musical in Two Acts, 18 Scenes and a Prologue[7]. Book by James Lee Barrett, Peter Udell and Philip Rose. Based on the film of the same name by James Lee Barrett. Music by Gary Geld. Lyrics by Peter Udell. Directed by Philip Rose. Choreography by Robert Tucker. Original set design by Kert Lundell, adapted by Reginald Bronskill. Costumes by Guy Geoly. Lighting by Stephen Ross. Musical direction by David Warrack. Produced by Howard Hurst, Sophie Hurst, Peter Ingster. Opened 8 August 1989 at the Virginia Theatre and closed 2 September 1989 after 31 performances.[8]

CAST (in order of appearance): *Charlie Anderson:* JOHN CULLUM. *Jacob:* BURKE LAWRENCE. *James:* CHRISTOPHER MARTIN. *Nathan:* Nigel Hamer. *John:* Stephen McIntyre. *Jenny:* TRACEY MOORE. *Henry:* Robin Blake. *Robert,* the boy: Jason Zimbler. *Anne:* CAMILLA SCOTT. *Gabriel:* Roy McKay. *Reverend Byrd:* Donald Saunders. *Sam:* THOMAS CAVANAGH. *Sergeant Johnson:* Jim Selman. *Lieutenant:* Casper Roos. *Tinkham:* Richard Liss. *Carol:* Jim Bearden. *Corporal:* Stephen Simms. *Marauder:* Sam Mancuso. *Engineer:* Donald Saunders. *Confederate Snipers:* David Connolly, Gerhard Kruschke.

Ensemble: Henry Alessami, Jim Bearden, Mark Bernkoff, David Connolly, Lesley Corne, Mark Ferguson, Brian Gow, Jennifer Griffin, Gerhard Kruschke, Richard Liss, Robert Longo, Sam Mancuso, Casper Roos, Fernando Santos, Jim Selman, Stephen Simms. *Swing:* Paul Malloy.

1989.18 ## THE DESERT SONG

A Revival of the Musical in Two Acts, 7 Scenes[9]. Book and lyrics by Otto Harbach and Oscar Hammerstein II. Music by Sigmund Romberg. New adaptation of book and lyrics by Robert Johanson. Director and choreographer, Robert Johanson. Conductor, James Allen Gahres. Co-choreographer, Sharon Halley. Set designer, Michael Anania. Costume designer, Suzanne Mess. Lighting designer, Mark W. Stanley. Chorus master, Joseph Colaneri. Produced by the New York City Opera. Opened 29 August 1989 at the New York State Theatre and closed 3 September 1989 after 7 performances.

CAST (in order of appearance): *Sid El Kar:* MICHAEL COUSINS. *Hassi:* ERICK DEVINE. *Hadji:* William Ledbetter. *Neri:* Joyce Campana. *Benjamin Kidd:* PHILIP WILLIAM MCKINLEY. *Azuri:* LOUISE HICKEY. *Captain Paul Fontaine:* LOUIS OTEY. *Sergeant La Vergne:* David Frye. *Susan:* LILLIAN GRAFF. *Edith:* Paula Hostetter. *Margot Bonvalet:* MICHELE MCBRIDE. *General Birabeau:* RON PARADY. *Pierre Birabeau,* Red Shadow: RICHARD WHITE. *Ali Ben Ali:* RAYMOND BAZEMORE. *Clementina:* JOYCE CAMPANA. *French Girls, Spanish Cabaret Girls and Soldiers' Wives, Native Dancers, Servants and Soldiers:* New York City Opera Chorus.

The action takes place in Morocco in the 1930s.

Act 1, Scene 1: Retreat of the Red Shadow in the Riff Mountains. *Scene 2:* Near the desert, outside General Birabeau's house. *Scene 3:* The garden of General Birabeau's home, the same day.

Act 2, Scene 1: The Great Hall of Ali Ben Ali. The following day. *Scene 2:* The room of the Silken Couch. *Scene 3:* The edge of the desert. *Scene 4:* Back at General Birabeau's, two nights later.

ACT 1[10]
Scene 1
"High on a Hill"
 M. Cousins, Riffs
"The Riff Song"
 R. White, Riffs
"My Margot"
 L. Otey, Soldiers
Scene 2
"Why Did We Marry Soldiers?"
 L. Graff, Women
Scene 3
"French Military Marching Song"
 M. McBride, Company
"Romance"
 M. McBride, Women
"I Want a Kiss"
 M. McBride, L. Otey
"It"
 P. W. McKinley, L. Graff
"The Desert Song"
 R. White, M. McBride
Finale, Act 1
 Full Company
ACT 2
Scene 1
"Song of the Brass Key"
 J. Campana, Harem Girls
"One Good Boy Gone Wrong"
 P. W. McKinley, J. Campana

---

[4]Originally produced Off-Broadway 27 February 1989 at the Public Theatre for 6 performances.
[5]Not in performance order.
[6]Dropped from original production of PAL JOEY.
[7]Originally produced in New York 7 January 1975 at the Alvin Theatre for 1050 performances. For Synopsis of Scenes and Musical Numbers, see original 1975 production. Act 1 was set in Spring, Act 2 in Autumn.
[8]Dance arrangements, orchestrations uncredited.

[9]Originally produced in New York 30 November 1926 at the Casino Theatre for 471 performances.
[10]No song list appears in program; this list prepared from the Papermill Playhouse production where this adaptation premiered. Dropped for this production: "I'll Be a Buoyant Girl," "Then You'll Know," "Let Love Go," "One Flower in Your Garden," "Farewell," and "All Hail to the General," "Let's Have a Love Affair;" also Act 2, Scene 2.

"Eastern Western Love"
R. Bazemore, M. Cousins
"One Alone"
R. White, Men
Scene 2
"The Saber Song"
M. McBride
"The Desert Song" (reprise)
R. White, M. McBride
Scene 3
"One Alone" (reprise)
R. White, M. McBride, M. Cousins, L. Otey, R. Bazemore, Men
Scene 4
"It" (reprise)
P. W. McKinley, L. Graff
Dance of Triumph
J. Campana
Finale, Act 2
Full Company

SWEENEY TODD-
THE DEMON BARBER
OF FLEET STREET

1989.19

A Revival of the Musical Thriller in Two Acts[11]. Book by Hugh Wheeler. Based on a version of "Sweeney Todd" by Christopher Bond (after the original melodrama by George Dibdin-Pitt). Music and lyrics by Stephen Sondheim. Directed by Susan H. Schulman. Choreography by Michael Lichtefeld. Scenic design by James Morgan. Costumes designed by Beba Shamash. Lighting designed by Mary Jo Dondlinger. Musical direction and design, David Krane. Assistant musical director, Jan Rosenberg. Originally directed on Broadway by Harold Prince. Produced Off-Off Broadway by the York Theatre Company (Janet Hayes Walker, Producing Director). Produced by the Circle in the Square Theatre (Theodore Mann, Artistic director; Paul Libin, Producing director.) Opened 14 September 1989 at the Circle in the Square Theatre and closed 25 February 1990 after 189 performances.

CAST (in order of appearance): *Jonas Fogg*: Tony Gilbert. *Policeman*: David E. Mallard. *Bird Seller*: Ted Keegan. *Dora*: Sylvia Rhyne. *Mrs. Mooney*: Mary Philips. *Anthony Hope*: Jim Walton. *Sweeney Todd*: BOB GUNTON. *Beggar Woman*: SuEllen Estey. *Mrs. Lovett*: BETH FOWLER. *Judge Turpin*: David Barron. *The Beadle*: Michael McCarty. *Johanna*: Gretchen Kingsley. *Tobias Ragg*: Eddie Korbich. *Pirelli*: Bill Nabel.

1989.20   ## DANGEROUS GAMES

A Musical in Two Acts (2 One-Act Musicals)[12]. Book by Jim Lewis and Graciela Daniele. Music by Astor Piazzolla. Lyrics by William Finn. Conceived, choreographed and directed by Graciela Daniele. Co-choreographer, Tina Paul. Scenic design, Tony Straiges. Costume design, Patricia Zipprodt. Lighting design, Peggy Eisenhauer. Sound design, Otts Munderloh. Musical direction and arrangements by James Kowal. Musical consultant and arrangements by Rodolfo Alchourron. Fight direction by B. H. Barry (Tango), Luis Perez (Orfeo). Originally produced by the American

[11]Originally produced in New York 1 March 1979 at the Uris Theatre for 557 performances; this revival first produced Off-Off Broadway 31 March 1989 at the York Theatre for 24 performances. For Synopsis of Scenes and Musical Numbers, see original 1979 production. Omitted from this production: "The Barber and His Wife," "Quartet (Act 1)." Restored for this production:
"Johanna" (Act 1, after "The Contest")
D. Barron
(Not the same song as "Johanna" as sung by J. Walton above.)
Added to this production:
"Wigmaker Sequence" (Act 2, after "By the Sea")
J. Walton, B. Gunton, Quintet
The last two musical numbers have been retitled "The Judge's Return" and Final Scene.
[12]No individual song titles given in the program.

Music Theatre Festival, Philadelphia; Spoleto Festival USA, Charleston, and La Jolla Playhouse, San Diego. Produced by Jules Fisher, James M. Nederlander, Arthur Rubin in association with Mary Kantor. Opened 19 October 1989 at the Nederlander Theatre and closed 21 October 1989 after 4 perfomances.

ACT 1: Tango

CAST: *Tango*: *Delia*, the Madam: Dana Moore. *The Men (3)*: *Felipe*: Philip Jerrry. *Ricardo*: Richard Amaro. *Carlos*: Ken Ard. *The Women (4)*: *Renata*: René Ceballos. *Diana*: Diana Laurenson. *Maria*: Malinda Shaffer. *Adriana*: Adrienne Hurd-Sharlein. *The Brothers (2)*: *Juan*: John Mineo. *Gregorio*: Gregory Mitchell, Luis Perez (alt.). *Cristina*, the new whore: Tina Paul, Elizabeth Mozer (alt.).

ACT 2: Orfeo

CAST: *Orfeo*: Gregory Mitchell, Luis Perez (alt.). *Dicha*: René Ceballos. *Aurora*, a child: Danyelle Weaver. *Pluton*: Ken Ard. *Nora/Lascivia*: Tina Paul, Elizabeth Mozer (alt.). *Antares/Altivo*: John Mineo. *Mira/Codicia*: Dana Moore. *Lyrae/LaGula*: Malinda Shaffer. *Cleo/Envidia*: Diana Laurenson. *Alberio/Ira*: Marc Villa. *Ursula/Malicia*: Adrienne Hurd-Sharlein. *Leon/Mentira*: Phillip Jerry. *Arturo/Charon/Perez*: Richard Amaro. *Bombo Player*: Adrian Brito. *Swings*: Frank Cava; Mamie Duncan-Gibbs.
Quintet: Rodolfo Alchourron (guitar), Jorge Alfano (bass, bamboo flute), Miguel Arrabal (bandoneon), Jon Kass (violin), James Kowal (piano, conductor), René Ceballos (offstage vocals).

"Desaparecidos" is the Spanish word for "the ones who have disappeared," and refers specifically to those individuals arrested by the Argentina military dictatorship (who are never heard from again).

Dedicated to the "desaparecidos" of Argentina and numerous other countries around the world. "Orfeo" is an attempt to give new meaning to the age-old myth of Orpheus and Eurydice. In the original myth, Orpheus, whose job it is to raise the sun, falls in love with Eurydice. But Eurydice dies. Orpheus' love for Eurydice is so great that he goes after her to Hell. He plays his magic lute so beautifully that Pluto, King of Hell, permits Orpheus to take Eurydice back to the living. But on one condition: Orpheus must not turn around and look at Eurydice before leaving Hell. He turns around to look at Eurydice too early, and loses Eurydice forever.

In "Orfeo," the story is reset in Argentina, and told through the eyes of a young girl whose parents have "been disappeared." Pursued by the same man who kidnapped her parents, Aurora manages to escape and falls asleep. In her dream version of the myth, the child comes to understand that only by confronting the truth head-on will she ever be able to wake up from this all-too-real nightmare.

1989.21   ## TAKARAZUKA

A Musical Revue (from Japan) in Two Acts, 11 Scenes. Artistic directors, Shinju Ueda, Hirotoshi Ohara. Composers and arrangers, Takio Terada, Kenji Yoshizaki, Kaoru Irie, Kazuakira Hashimoto, Toshiko Yonekawa. Conductor, Kazuakira Hashimoto. Choreographers, Yoshijiro Hanayagi, Mayumi Nishizaki, Eiken Fujima, Hagi Hanayagi, Kiyomi Hayama, Taku Yamada, Roger Minami. Set design by Hideo Ishihama, Toshiaki Sekiya. Costume design by Harumi Tokoro, Kikue Nakagawa, Ikuei Touda. Lighting design by Naoji Imai, supervised by Ken Billington. Assistant directors, Masazumi Tani, Masaya Ishida. President, Haruhiko Saka. Produced by Kohei Kobayashi. Opened 25 October 1989 at the Radio City Music Hall and closed 29 October 1989 after 6 performances.

CAST: YURI MATSUMOTO, JUNKO TAKARA, AKIRA BAN, MIZUKI OURA, KAE SEGAWA, MITO HIBIKI, YU SHION, AI KODAMA, MIRA ANJU, YUKI AMAMI.
(Company:) Yu Asuka, Yo Natsumi, Miya Aoi, Manami Kozue, Yuka Shima, Nachi Mineoka, Kanade Nazuki, Hikaru Senju, Mitsuru Aiko, Aya Maiki, Mayu Omine, Michuru Namine, Naoki Ema, Chitose Kagami, Chie Kinami, Risa Wakao, Ayu Mitsuki, Natsuki Yuma, Fubuki Takane, Rio Hanbusa, Katusra Godai, Nari Asaoka, Ai Otohara, Ginka Itsuki, Yuka Shino, Yuzumi Mari, Mami Natsuki, Hajime Wako, Reo Kazami, Maika Tomo, Ko Minoru, Ayano Ogishiro, Yoko Hana, Shun Tasai, Yura Natsukawa, Mire Aika, Chikoto Yumeno, Mitsuki Mario, Satomi Akino, Tatsuki Koju, Konomi Akane, Yuki Maori, Aki Itsumine, Serika Moemi, Kei Miyabi, Shoko Kirihara, Jun Shibuki, Akari Michi, Rei Natsushiro, Hibiki Takumi, Mai Gojo.

ACT 1: Takarazuka Dance Festival
Scene 1
Prologue/"Takarazuka March" (Ondo Takarazuka Koshinkyoku)
M. Oura, Y. Matsumoto, Company
(Composer/Arranger: Takio Terada. Lyricist: Ken Kumon. Choreographer: Eiken Fujima.)

A medley of traditional Japanese dances set to modern music in celebration of Takarazuka.

Scene 2

"Snow, Moon and Flower" (Utsukushiki Nippon)
Y. Shion, M. Hibiki, A. Kodama, R. Natsushiro, Company
(*Composer*: Takio Terada. *Arranger*: Kaoru Irie. *Lyricist*: Shinji Ueda. *Choreographer*: Yoshijiro Hanayagi.)

A selection of delicate dances that celebrate the transient beauty of snow, moon and flowers as the seasons change.

Scene 3

"Icy Moon" (Koreru Tsuki)
M. Oura, M. Hibiki, A. Kodama, A. Ban, Company
(*Composer*: Takio Terada. *Arranger*: Kaoru Irie. *Lyricist*: Shinji Ueda. *Choreographer*: Yoshijiro Hanayagi.)

A Noh dancer performs ritualistically before statues of the Buddha and summons spirits whose dances and costumes are reminiscent of Japan in the eighth century.

Scene 4

"Swirling Snow" (Yuki Shimaki)
A. Mitsuki, Y. Matsumoto, Company
(*Composer*: Takio Terada. *Arranger*: Kaoru Irie. *Lyricist*: Shinji Ueda. *Choreographer*: Yoshijiro Hanayagi.)

A traveller rests against a torii gate to reflect on her life. A vision of a young and beautiful self rises from the snow and dances for a lover who will never return.

Scene 5

"The Cherry Flower" (Sakura/Sakura Gensokyoku)
M. Kozue, Company
(*Composers/Arrangers*: Toshiko Yonekawa, Takio Terada. *Choreographer*: Mayumi Nishizaki.)

Koto players and dancers perform in a tribute to the national flower of Japan.

ACT 2: Takarazuka Forever, a Grand Revue

Scene 1

Prologue (*Choreographer*: Roger Minami.)
"Takarazuka Forever"
A. Kodama, Company
(*Composer/Arranger*: Kenji Yoshizaki. *Lyricist*: Hirotoshi Ohara.)
Dance
M. Oura, Company
"A Pretty Girl Is Like a Melody"
M. Oura, Y. Amani, Company
(*Composer/Lyricist*: Irving Berlin. *Arranger*: Kenji Yoshizaki.)

Scene 2

Flower Fantasy (*Choreographer*: Taku Yamada.)
"I'll String Along with You"
Y. Shion, M. Kozue, Company
(*Composer*: Harry Warren. *Arranger*: Kazuakira Hashimoto. *Lyricist*: Al Dubin.)
"I Only Have Eyes for You"
A. Kodama, A. Ban, K. Segawa, M. Anju, M. Hibiki, Y. Shima, Y. Shino
(*Composer*: Harry Warren. *Arranger*: Kazuakira Hashimoto. *Lyricist*: Al Dubin.)

Scene 3

Arabian Dream (*Choreographer*: Kiyomi Hayama.)
"Too Close for Comfort" (from MR. WONDERFUL)
J. Takara, Y. Ammi, Company
(*Composer*: Jerry Bock. *Arranger*: Kenji Yoshizaki. *Lyricists*: Larry Holofcener, George Weiss.)
Dance/Polovtsian (from "Prince Igor")
M. Oura, A. Kodama, Company
(*Composer*: Alexander Borodin. *Arranger*: Takio Terada.)

Scene 4

Keep Young and Beautiful (*Choreographer*: Taku Yamada.)
"American Beauty Rose"
Y. Shion, Company
(*Composer*: Read Evans, Hal David, Arthur Altman. *Arranger*: Kenji Yoshizaki.)
"Keep Young and Beautiful"
M. Hibiki, Company
(*Composer*: Harry Warren. *Arranger*: Kazuakira Hashimoto. *Lyricist*: Al Dubin.)
"You Stepped Out of a Dream"
M. Oura, Company

(*Composer*: Nacio Herb Brown. *Arranger*: Kazuakira Hashimoto. *Lyricist*: Gus Kahn.)
"The Lady Is a Tramp"
M. Oura, M. Hibiki, Company
(*Composer*: Richard Rodgers. *Arranger*: Kazuakira Hashimoto. *Lyricist*: Lorenz Hart.)

Scene 5

Piano Fantasy
"Play a Simple Melody"
Y. Shion
(*Composer/Lyricist*: Irving Berlin. *Arranger*: Kazuakira Hashimoto. *Choreographer*: Kiyomi Hayama.)
"Shaking the Blues Away"
M. Oura, Company
(*Composer/Lyricist*: Irving Berlin. *Arranger*: Kazuakira Hashimoto. *Choreographer*: Roger Minami.)
"Rhapsody in Blue"
M. Oura, M. Hibiki, K. Segawa, M. Anju, Company
(*Composer*: George Gershwin. *Arranger*: Kenji Yoshizaki. *Choreographer*: Roger Minami.)

Scene 6

Finale (*Choreographer*: Kiyomi Hayama.)
"The Words Are in My Heart"
N. Mineoka, Company
(*Composer*: Harry Warren. *Arranger*: Kazuakira Hashimoto. *Lyricist*: Al Dubin.)
"In the Cool, Cool, Cool of the Evening"
Y. Shion, M. Hibiki, Company
(*Composer*: Hoagy Carmichael. *Arranger*: Kazuakira Hashimoto. *Lyricist*: Johnny Mercer.)
"Something's Gotta Give"
M. Oura, K. Segawa, M. Anju, N. Yuma, Y. Amami
(*Composer/Lyricist*: Johnny Mercer. *Arranger*: Kazuakira Hashimoto.)
"Takarazuka Forever" (reprise)
M. Oura, M. Hibiki, A. Kodama, Y. Shion, N. Mineoka, Company

SID CAESAR & COMPANY:
Does Anybody Know
1989.22 What I'm Talking About?

A Musical Revue in Two Acts[13]. Directed by Martin Charnin. Original songs by Martin Charnin. Scenery and lighting by Neil Peter Jampolis. Costumes by Karen Roston. Sound by Bruce Cameron. Musical director, Elliot Finkel. Originally presented by Art D'Lugoff at the Village Gate. Associate producers, J. Scott Broder, Sonny Bloch., Robert Courson. Produced by Ivan Bloch and Harold Thau in association with Larry Spellman. Opened 1 November 1989 at the John Golden Theatre and closed 5 November 1989 after 5 performances.

CAST: SID CAESAR, Lee Delano, Linda Hart, Lubitza [Luba] Gregus, Peter Shawn, Laura Turnbull, Erick Devine, Carolyn Michel.

SCENES AND MUSICAL NUMBERS
Sleep
S. Caesar
A Boy at His First Dance
S. Ceasar
A Man Walking Down the Aisle
S. Ceasar
Zero Hour
S. Caesar
A Man with His Wife Arguing to the First Movement of Beethoven's Fifth Symphony
S. Caesar, L. Turnbull
The Last Angry Bull
S. Caesar, L. Gregus, L. Delano, L. Hart, P. Shawn, L. Turnbull, E Devine, C. Michel
At the Movies
S. Caesar, L. Hart, L. Delano, P. Shawn

---
[13]Originally produced Off-Broadway 22 June 1989 at the Vilage Gate for 72 performances.

We Aren't Fooling Anyone
  Company
The World Through the Eyes of a Baby
  S. Caesar
The Penny Candy Gum Machine
  S. Caesar
The Grieg Piano Concerto
  S. Caesar
The Professor
  S. Caesar, L. Delano
"Make a New Now, Now!"
  S. Caesar, Company

1989.23   MEET ME IN ST. LOUIS

A Musical in Two Acts, 14 Scenes. Based on "The Kensington Stories" by Sally Benson and the MGM motion picture "Meet Me in St. Louis." Book by Hugh Wheeler. Music and lyrics by Hugh Martin and Ralph Blane. Directed by Louis Burke. Choreography by Joan Brickhill. Assistant director, Lonnie Chase. Associate choreographer, Herman-Jay Muller. Production (settings, costumes) design by Keith Anderson. Lighting by Ken Billington. Musical supervisor, Milton Rosenstock. Musical director, Bruce Pomohac. Orchestrations by Michael Gibson. Dance arranger, James Raitt. Sound by Alan Stieb, James Brousseau. Vocal arrangers, Hugh Martin, Bruce Pomohac. Ice choreographer, Michael Tokar. Associate producers, Loren Krok, P. K. Sloman, L. Everett Chase. Produced by Brickhill-Burke Productions (Louis Burke, Joan Brickhill), Christopher Seabrooke and EPI Products. Opened 2 November 1989 at the Gershwin Theater and closed 10 June 1990 after 253 performances.

CAST (in order of appearance): *Lon Smith:* Michael O'Steen. *Randy Travis:* Brian Jay. *Katie:* BETTY GARRETT. *Motorman:* Jim Semmelman. *Tootie Smith:* COURTNEY PELDON. *Mrs. Smith:* CHARLOTTE MOORE. *Grandpa Prophater:* MILO O'SHEA. *Esther Smith:* DONNA KANE. *Rose Smith:* Juliet Lambert. *John Truitt:* Jason Workman. *Agnes Smith:* Rachael Graham. *Mr. Alonzo Smith:* GEORGE HEARN. *Warren Sheffield:* Peter Reardon. *Ida Boothby:* Naomi Reddin. *Douglas Moore:* Gregg Whitney. *Eve Finley:* Shauna Hicks. *Dr. Bond:* Gordon Stanley. *Lucille Ballard:* Karen Culliver. *Clinton A. Badger:* Craig A. Meyer.

Ensemble: Kevin Backstrom, Dan Buelow, Victoria Lynn Burton, Karen Culliver, Deanna Dys, H. David Gunderman, Shauna Hicks, K. Craig Innes, Brian Jay, Rachel Jones, Nancy Lemenager, Joanne McHugh, Frank Maio, Carol Lee Meadows, Craig A. Meyer, Christopher Lee Michaels, Ron Morgan, Georga L. Osborne, Rachelle Ottley, Christina Pawl, Naomi Reddin, Carol Schuberg, Jim Semmelman, Ken Shepski, Gordon Stanley, Sean Frank Sullivan, Cynthia Thole, Gregg Whitney, Kyle Whyte, Lee Wilson.

The action takes place in and around the Smith family home, 5135 Kensington Avenue, St. Louis—from summer 1903 to the spring of 1904 and the opening of the Louisiana Purchase Exposition.

Act 1, Scene 1: Street outside the Smith Family Home—Summer 1903. *Scene 2:* Interior of the Smith House. *Scene 3:* Lon's Princeton Party. *Scene 4:* Preparing for Hollywood. *Scene 5:* The Girls' Bedroom and the Smith Home. *Scene 6:* Esther's Dream. *Scene 7:* The Bedroom again—the next morning.

Act 2, Scene 1: The Frozen Pond—before Thanskgiving. *Scene 2:* The Smith Home—preparing for Thanksgiving. *Scene 3:* Tree-Trimming Time. *Scene 4:* Snowy Men—Christmas Eve. *Scene 5:* The Ball and Portico Outside. *Scene 6:* Back Home—later that evening. *Scene 7:* The Louisiana Purchase Exposition—Spring 1904.

ACT 1[14]
Scene 1

"Meet Me in St. Louis"
  Ensemble

(*Music by* Kerry Mills. *New Lyrics by* Hugh Martin and Ralph Blane.)
Scene 2
"Meet Me in St. Louis" (reprise)
  M. O'Shea, C. Peldon
"The Boy Next Door"
  D. Kane
"Be Anything But a Girl"[15]
  M. O'Shea, R. Graham, C. Peldon
Scene 3
"Skip to My Lou"
  J. Lambert, D. Kane, M. O'Steen,
    G. Whitney, J. Workman, P. Reardon, Company
  (Traditional; *New Lyrics by* Hugh Martin and Ralph Blane.)
"Under the Bamboo Tree" (If You Lak-a Me Like I Lak-a You) (from *SALLY IN OUR ALLEY*)
  D. Kane, C. Peldon
  (*Music and Lyrics by* Bob Cole and J. Rosamund Johnson.)
"Banjos"[16]
  M. O'Steen, Company
Scene 4
"Ghosties and Ghoulies and Things That Go Bump in the Night"[17]
  B. Garrett, R. Graham, C. Peldon, Neighborhood Kids
"Halloween Ballet"[18]
  Company
Scene 5
"Wasn't It Fun?"[19]
  G. Hearn, C. Moore
Scene 6
"The Trolley Song"
  D. Kane, Company

ACT 2
Scene 1
"Ice"[20]
  J. Lambert, P. Reardon, G. Whitney, Company
  Featured Skaters: R. Ottley, R. Morgan
"Raving Beauty"[21] (from *BEST FOOT FORWARD*, 1963 revival)
  P. Reardon, G. Whitney, J. Lambert
Scene 2
"A Touch of the Irish"[22]
  B. Garrett, D. Kane, J. Lambert
"You Are For Loving" (from *BEST FOOT FORWARD*, 1963 revival)
  J. Workman, D. Kane
Scene 3
"A Day in New York"
  G. Hearn, Family
Scene 5
"The Ball"[23]
  M. O'Shea, Company
"Diamonds in the Starlight"[24]
  J. Workman, D. Kane
Scene 6
"Have Yourself a Merry Little Christmas"
  D. Kane
Scene 7
"Paging Mr. Sousa"[25]
  G. Hearn, Company

---

[14]For subsequent national tour, the show was substantially revised; Act 1, Scenes 1 and 7 were dropped, and the Ice Skating sequence (Act 2, Scene 1) was reset inside the Smith Family Home. Added for the national tour:
  "Whenever I'm With You" (Act 1, Scene 3)
    Billy Barnes (Grandpa), Family
  "You'll Hear a Bell" (Act 1, Scene 3)
    Jo Ann Cunningham (Mrs. Smith)
  "Over the Bannister" (Act 1, Scene 5)
    Stuart Larson (John Tuitt)
  "What's His Name?" (Act 2, Scene 3)
    Barbara Sharma (Katie)

[15]Dropped for national tour.
[16]For national tour, moved to Act 2, Scene 4.
[17]Dropped for national tour.
[18]Dropped for national tour.
[19]For national tour, moved to Act 2, Scene 3.
[20]Dropped for national tour.
[21]Dropped for national tour.
[22]Dropped for national tour.
[23]Dropped for national tour.
[24]Dropped for national tour.
[25]Dropped for national tour.

Finale
  Company

1989.24 ## 3 PENNY OPERA

A Revival of the Musical in Three Acts, a Prologue and 9 Scenes[26]. Book and lyrics by Bertolt Brecht. (Newly) Translated by Michael Feingold. Music by Kurt Weill. Directed by John Dexter. Musical staging by Peter Gennaro. Music director, Julius Rudel. Scenery and costumes by Jocelyn Herbert. Lighting by Andy Phillips, Brian Nason. Sound by Peter Fitzgerald. Additional orchestrations, musical continuity by Julius Rudel. Associate producers, Margo Lion, Hiroshi Sugawara, Lloyd Philips, Kiki Mayake, Nancy Ellison. Produced by Jerome Hellman in association with Haruki Kadokawa and James M. Nederlander. Opened 5 November 1989 at the Lunt-Fontanne Theatre and closed 31 December 1989 after 65 performances.

CAST (in order of appearance): *A Ballad Singer*: Ethyl Eichelberger. *Jenny Diver*, a whore: SUZZANNE DOUGLAS. *Jonathan Jeremiah Peachum*, head of a gang of beggars: ALVIN EPSTEIN. *Filch*, beggar: Jeff Blumenkrantz. *Mrs. Peachum*: GEORGIA BROWN. *Polly Peachum*, their daughter: MAUREEN MCGOVERN. *Macheath*, head of a gang of crooks: STING. *Macheath's Gang (6): Matt of the Mint*: JOSH MOSTEL. *Crook-Finger Jack*: Mitchell Greenberg. *Sawtooth Bob*: David Schechter. *Ed*: Philip Carroll. *Walter (called "Walt Dreary")*: Tom Robbins. *Jimmy*: Alex Santoriello. *Tiger Brown*, Chief of London Police: LARRY MARSHALL. *Whores (6): Dolly*: Anne Kerry Ford. *Betty*: Jan Horvath. *Vixen*: Teresa de Zarn. *Molly*: Nancy Ringham. *Suky Tawdry*: K. T. Sullivan. *Old Whore*: Fiddle Viracola. *Smith*, a police constable : David Pursley. *Policemen*: MacIntyre Dixon, Michael Piontek. *Lucy*, Brown's daughter: KIM CRISWELL.

Beggars, Bystanders: Philip Carroll, MacIntyre Dixon, Michael Piontek, David Schechter, Steven Major West.

The action takes place in London during the nineteenth century.

Prologue: Street Fair in Soho.

Act 1, Scene 1: Peachum's Shop. Wednesday morning. *Scene 2*: A deserted stable. 5:00 p.m. *Scene 3*: Peachum's Shop. Thursday morning.

Act 2, Scene 1: The stable. Thursday afternoon. *Scene 2*: A whorehouse in Turnbridge. Later that afternoon. *Scene 3*: Old Bailey Jail. Immediately afterward.

Act 3, Scene 1: Peachum's shop. Late that night. *Scene 2*: Lucy's Room in the Old Bailey. *Scene 3*: Macheath's Cell in the Old Bailey. 6:00 a.m. Friday.

ACT 1
  Prologue
    "Ballad of Mack the Knife (Moritat)"
      E. Eichelberger
  Scene 1
    "Peachum's Morning Hymn"
      A. Epstein
    "Why-Can't They Song"
      A. Epstein, G. Brown
  Scene 2
    "Wedding Song"
      Gang
    "Pirate Jenny"
      M. McGovern
    "Soldiers' Song"
      Sting, L. Marshall
    "Wedding Song" (reprise)
      Gang
    "Love Song"
      Sting, M. McGovern
  Scene 3
    "Barbara Song"
      M. McGovern
    First 3 Penny Finale
      M. McGovern, A. Epstein, G. Brown

ACT 2
Scene 1
  "Melodrama and Polly's Song"
    Sting, M. McGovern
  Interlude
  "Ballad of the Prisoner of Sex"
    G. Brown
Scene 2
  "Pimp's Ballad" (Tango)
    Sting, S. Douglas
Scene 3
  "Ballad of Living in Style"
    Sting
  "Jealousy Duet"
    K. Criswell, M. McGovern
  Second 3 Penny Finale
    Sting, G. Brown, Chorus
ACT 3
Scene 1
  "Ballad of the Prisoner of Sex" (reprise)
    G. Brown
  "Song of Futility"
    A. Epstein
Scene 2
  "Lucy's Aria"
    K. Criswell
  Interlude
  "Solomon Song"
    S. Douglas
Scene 3
  "Call from the Grave"
    Sting
  "Epitaph"
    Sting
  "March to the Gallows"
    Orchestra
  Third 3 Penny Finale
    Entire Company

1989.25 ## PRINCE OF CENTRAL PARK

A Musical in Two Acts. Book by Evan H. Rhodes, based on his novel of the same name. Music by Don Sebesky. Lyrics by Gloria Nissenson. Directed and choreographed by Tony Tanner. Scenery and costumes by Michael Bottari, Ronald Case. Lighting by Norman Coates. Musical direction, vocal arrangements by Joel Silberman. Sound by Daryl Bornstein. Associate choreographer, Stephen Bourneuf. Supervisor, orchestrator, Don Sebesky. Dance arrangements by Henry Aronson. Originally produced at Jan McArt's Cabaret Theatre, Key West, Florida; subsequently produced at the Al Hirschfeld Theatre, Miami Beach, Florida. Associate producer, Belle M. Deitch. Executive producer, Karen Poindexter. Produced by Abe Hirschfeld and Jan McArt. Opened 9 November 1989 at the Belasco Theater and closed 11 November 1989 after 4 performances.

CAST (in order of appearance): *Jay-Jay*: RICHARD H. BLAKE. *School Guard*: Sel Vitella. *Street People*: John Hoshko, Adrian Bailey. *Agnes*: Bonnie Perlman. *Officer Washinski*: Ruth Gottschal!. *Bag Lady*: Marilyn Hudgins. *Anna Squagliatoria*: Bonnie Perlman. *May Berg*: Anne-Marie Gerard. *Aerobics Instructor*: Stephen Bourneuf. *Margie Miller*: JO ANNE WORLEY. *Sally*: CHRIS CALLEN. *Officer Simpson*: Adrian Bailey. *Stock Broker*: John Hoshko. *Fist*: Sean Grant. *Bird Brain*: Jason Ma. *Feather*: Alice Yearsley. *Elmo*: ANTHONY GALDE. *Park Ranger Rupp*: Sel Vitella. *Carpenter*: Terry Eno. *Young Richard*: John Hoshko. *Young Margie* Ruth Gottschall. *Ballet Dancer*: Alice Yearsley. *Floor Walker*: Marilyn Hudgins. *Maitre d'*: Terry Eno. *Waiter*: Sel Vitella. *Twitchy*: Anne-Marie Gerard. *Aerobics Students*: Adrian Bailey, Terry Eno, Ruth Gottschall, Anne-Marie Gerard, John Hoshko, Sel Vitella.

Tap Dancers: Adrian Bailey, Stephen Bourneuf, Ruth Gottschall, John Hoshko, Jason Ma, Bonnie Perlman, Alice Yearsley. *Swings*: Terry Iten, Jody Keith Barrie.

The action takes place in and around New York City's Central Park at the present time.

---

[26]Originally produced as "The 3-Penny Opera" in New York 13 April 1933 at the Empire Theatre for 12 performances. An Off-Broadway revival (in an adaptation by Marc Blitzstein) at the Theatre de Lys 10 March 1954 for 94 performances, and its return engagement 30 September 1955 for 2611 performances established the show's international reputation.

ACT 1

"Here's Where I Belong"
R. H. Blake, Ensemble

"All I've Got Is Me"
R. H. Blake

"New Leaf"
J. A. Worley, Aerobics Club

"Follow the Leader"
A. Galde, Gang, R. H. Blake

Montage: "Here's Where I Belong"
Ensemble

"We Were Dancing"
J. A. Worley, J. Hoshko, R. Gottschall

"One of a Kind"
J. A. Worley, R. H. Blake

"I Fly By Night"
A. Galde, Gang

"Zap"
J. A. Worley, R. H. Blake, Ensemble

ACT 2

"Good Evening"
Ensemble

"All I've Got Is Me" (reprise)
J. A. Worley, R. H. Blake

"They Don't Give You Life at Sixteen"
A. Galde, Ensemble

"Red"
J. A. Worley, Ensemble

"I Fly By Night" (reprise)
A. Galde, Gang, R. H. Blake

"The Prince of Central Park"
R. H. Blake

"One of a Kind" (reprise)
J. A. Worley

1989.26 GRAND HOTEL

A Musical in One Act, 20 Scenes. Book by Luther Davis, based on the novel of the same name by Vicki Baum, by arrangement with Turner Entertainment Co., owner of the MGM film. Music and lyrics by Robert Wright and George Forrest. Additional music and lyrics by Maury Yeston. Directed and choreographed by Tommy Tune. Setting design by Tony Walton. Costume design by Santo Loquasto. Lighting design by Jules Fisher. Sound design by Otts Munderloh. Orchestrations by Peter Matz. Musical and vocal direction by Jack Lee. Music supervision and additional music by Wally Harper. Associate director, Bruce Lumpkin. Production associate, Kathleen Raitt. Associate producers, Sandra Greenblatt, Martin R. Kaufman, Kim Poster. Produced by Martin Richards, Mary Lea Johnson, Sam Crothers, Sander Jacobs, Kenneth D. Greenblatt, Paramount Pictures, Jujamcyn Theatres in association with Patty Grubman and Marvin A. Krauss. Opened 12 November 1989 at the Martin Beck Theatre, moved 3 February 1992 to the Gershwin Theatre, and closed 19 April 1992 after 1018 performances.

CAST (in order of appearance): *Colonel Dr. Otternschlag*: JOHN WYLIE. *The Doorman*: Charles Mandracchia. *The Countess*: Yvonne Marceau. *The Gigolo*: Pierre Dulaine. *Madame Peepee*: Kathi Moss. *Rohna, the Grand Concierge*: REX D. HAYS. *Bellboys (4): Georg Strunk*: Ken Jennings. *Kurt Krönenberg*: Keith Crowningshield. *Hanns Bittner*: Gerrit de Beer. *Willibald*, captain: J. J. Jepson. *Erik*, Front Desk: BOB STILLMAN. *The Telephone Operators (3): Hildegarde Bratts*: Jennifer Lee Andrews. *Siegfriede Holzheim*: Suzanne Henderson. *Wolffe Bratts*: Lynette Perry. *The Chauffeur*: Ben George. *Zinnowitz*, the lawyer: Hal Robinson. *General Director Preysing*, Saxonia Mills: TIMOTHY JEROME. *Flaemmchen*, the Typist: JANE KRAKOWSKI. *Otto Kringelein*, the Bookkeeper: MICHAEL JETER. *Raffaela*, the confidante: KAREN AKERS. *Sandor*, the Impresario: Mitchell Jason. *(Victor) Witt*, Company Manager: Michel Moinot. *Elizaveta Grushinskaya*, the Ballerina: LILIANE MONTEVECCHI. *Felix von Gaigern*, the Baron: DAVID (James) CARROLL. *The Jimmys*: David Jackson, Danny Strayhorn. *The Scullery Workers (4): Ernst Schmidt*: Henry Grossman. *Franz Kohl*: William Ryall. *Werner Holst*: David Elledge. *Gunther Gustaffson*: Walter Willison. *Hotel Courtesan*: Suzanne Henderson. *Trudie*, the maid: Jennifer Lee Andrews.

Swings: Michael DeVries, Niki Harris, Glenn Turner.

The action takes place in the Grand Hotel in Berlin, 1928.

Scene 1: The Grand Hotel Lobby and far below in the Scullery. *Scene 2*: The Moroccan Coffee Bar. *Scene 3*: A corner of The Grand Ballroom. *Scene 4*: The Ladies Powder Room. *Scene 5*: Men's Washroom and The Hotel Bar. *Scene 6*: The Baron's Room. *Scene 7*: The Yellow Pavilion. *Scene 8*: The Hotel Conference Room. *Scene 9*: Backstage at the Opera House. *Scene 10*: The Financial Corner of the Hotel Lobby. *Scene 11*: The Roof of the Grand Hotel .*Scene 12*: Grushinskaya's Suite. *Scene 13*: Raffalela's Room. *Scene 14*: The Hotel Conference Room and just inside the ever-revolving door. *Scene 15*: Raffaela's Room. *Scene 16*: Grishinskaya's Suite. *Scene 17*: The Hotel Bar. *Scene 18*: A Cross Corridor upstairs in the Hotel/ The Doctor's Room/Presying's Room/Flemmchen's adjoining room/Kringelein's Room/The Bedchamber of The Countess and The Gigolo. *Scene 19*: Grushinskaya's Suite/Kringelein's Room/Preysing's Room. *Scene 20*: The Lobby of the Grand Hotel.

MUSICAL NUMBERS

The Presentation of the Company:

"The Grand Parade"
J. Wylie, Company
(*Additional music and lyrics by* Maury Yeston.)

Scene 1

"As It Should Be"
D. Carroll
(*Lyrics revised by* Maury Yeston.)

"Some Have, Some Have Not"
Scullery Workers
(*Lyrics revised by* Maury Yeston.)

"At the Grand Hotel"
M. Jeter
(*Additional music and lyrics by* Maury Yeston.)

"Table with a View"
M. Jeter
(*Lyrics revised by* Maury Yeston.)

Scene 2

"Maybe My Baby Loves Me"
D. Jackson, D. Strayhorn, J. Krakowski

Scene 3

"Fire and Ice"
L. Montevecchi, Ensemble
(*Lyrics revised by* Maury Yeston.)

"Twenty-two Years"
K. Akers
(*Additional music and lyrics by* Maury Yeston.)

"Villa on a Hill"
K. Akers

Scene 4

"I Want to Go to Hollywood"
J. Krakowski
(*Additional music and lyrics by* Maury Yeston.)

Scene 5

"Everybody's Doing It"
H. Robinson
(*Additional music and lyrics by* Maury Yeston.)

"The Crooked Path"
T. Jerome
(*Lyrics revised by* Maury Yeston.)

Scene 6

"As It Should Be" (reprise)
D. Carroll
(*Lyrics revised by* Maury Yeston.)

Scene 7

"Who Couldn't Dance with You?"
J. Krakowski, D. Carroll, M. Jeter

Scene 8

"The Boston Merger"
H. Robinson, T. Jerome, Shareholders
(*Lyrics revised by* Maury Yeston.)

Scene 9

"No Encore"
L. Montevecchi

Scene 11

"Fire and Ice" (reprise)
Company
(*Lyrics revised by* Maury Yeston.)

Scene 12

"Love Can't Happen"
D. Carroll, L. Motevecchi
(*Additional music and lyrics by* Maury Yeston.)

Scene 13

"What She Needs" (What You Need)
K. Akers
(*Lyrics revised by* Maury Yeston.)

Scene 16

"Bonjour Amour"
L. Montevecchi
(*Additional music and lyrics by* Maury Yeston.)

Scene 17

"Happy"
D. Jackson, D. Strayhorn
"We'll Take a Glass Together"
M. Jeter, D. Carroll
(*Lyrics revised by* Maury Yeston.)

Scene 18

"I Waltz Alone"
J. Wylie
(*Lyrics revised by* Maury Yeston.)
"Roses at the Station"
D. Carroll
(*Additional music and lyrics by* Maury Yeston.)

Scene 19

"How Can I Tell Her?"
K. Akers
(*Lyrics revised by* Maury Yeston.)

Scene 20

"As It Should Be" (reprise)
B. Stillman, Company
(*Lyrics revised by* Maury Yeston.)
"Some Have, Some Have Not" (reprise)
Scullery Workers
(*Lyrics revised by* Maury Yeston.)
"The Grand Parade"
Company
(*Additional music and lyrics by* Maury Yeston.)
The Grand Finale:
"The Grand Waltz"
Entire Company

1989.27   GYPSY

A Revival of the Musical Fable in Two Acts[27]. Book by Arthur Laurents. Suggested by the memoirs (of the same name) by Gypsy Rose Lee. Directed by Arthur Laurents. Original production directed and choreographed by Jerome Robbins; choreography reproduced by Bonnie Walker. Music by Jule Styne. Lyrics by Stephen Sondheim. Scenery design by Kenneth Foy. Costume design by Theoni V. Aldredge. Lighting design by Natasha Katz. Sound design by Peter Fitzgerald. Musical director, Eric Stern.

---

[27]Originally produced in New York 21 May 1959 at the Broadway Theatre for 702 performances. For Synopsis of Scenes and Musical Numbers, see original 1959 production. For this revival, several songs were retitled in the program:

"May We Entertain You" (Act 1, Scene 1) retitled "Let Me Entertain You."

"Mr. Goldstone, I Love You" (Act 1, Scene 6) retitled "Mr. Goldstone."

"Let Me Entertain You" (Act 2, Scene 4) retitled "The Strip."

Dropped: Traveling (Act 1, Scene 3), "Small World" (reprise) (Act 2, Scene 4).

Orchestrations by Sid Ramin, Rob(John Kander. Produced by Barry Brown in association with Tokyo E and Pace Theatrical Group. Open(Theatre and closed 6 January 1991 engagement 28 April 1991 at the N (see separate entry in 1990-1991 seas

CAST (in order of appearance): *Uncle Clarence* (and his classic clarinet): Bobby J *Louise*: Kristen Mahon. *Baby June*: Chri *Peewee*. *Pop*: Ronn Carroll. *Newsboys*: D Cistone, Jason Miner. *Weber*: Mace Barre CHRISTA MOORE. *June*: Tracy Venne Moore. *L.A.*: Craig Waletzko. *Kansas*: Ne(Alec Timerman. *Mr. Goldstone*: John I *Hollywood Blondes (5)*: Barbara Folts, Teri Robin Robinson. *Agnes*: Lori Ann Mahl. *P,* Erwin. *Mazeppa*: Jana Robbins. *Electra*: Ai Ginger Prince. *Phil*: Mace Barrett. *Bouger* Graves, Eric H. Kaufman.

VICTOR I
                             ON BRO/

1989.28

A Musical Entertainment in Two Ac Assistant to Mr. Borge, Jim Colias. Pro Inc. (Shelly Gross) Opened 5 Decem Theatre and closed 10 December 1989 a

CAST: VICTOR BORGE.

---

[28]Victor Borge has appeared previously in Broa(
  Comedy in Music, 2 October 1953, John Go
  performances.

  Comedy in Music, Opus 2, 9 November 196(192 performances.

  Comedy with Music, 3 October 1977, Imperi(performances.

CITY OF AI

1989.29

A Musical in Two Acts, 37 Scenes. Bool Coleman. Lyrics by David Zippel. Di Musical numbers staged by Walter Painter, Costume design by Florence Klotz. Light design by Peter Fitzgerald, Bernard Fox. O arrangements by Cy Coleman, Varon G(Gordon Lowry Harrell. Fight staging by Vanoff, Roger Berlind, Jujamcyn Th Corporation, The Shubert Organization. O Virginia Theatre and closed 19 January 199.

MOVIE CAST (in order of appearance): *Stone* James Hindman, Tom Galantich. *Oolie*: RAND HOTY. *Big Six*: Herschel Sparber. *Sonny*: Raymor *The Angel City Four*: Peter Davis, Amy Jane Londo(Shawn Elliott. *Officer Pasco*: Tom Galantich. *Bob(Irving*: RENE AUBERJONOIS. *Peter Kingsley*: I Carmello. *Luther Kingsley*: Keith Perry. *Dr. Mandr* Rachel York. *Mahoney*: James Hindman. *Yamato*: I Evan Thompson. *Margie*: Eleanor Glockner. *Bootsi(*
HOLLYWOOD CAST (in order of appearan(*Buddy Fidler*: RENE AUBERJONOIS. *Shoeshine* MCCLELLAND. *Barber*: James Cahill. *Donna*: I Glockner. *Jimmy Powers*: Scott Waara. *The Angel (* London, Gary Kahn, Jackie Presti. *Carla Haywood*: I Hindman. *Pancho Vargas*: Shawn Elliott. *Werner Kr* Doug Tompos. *Avril Raines*: Rachel York. *Gene*: To Alvin Lum. *Stand-In*: Carolee Carmello. *Hairdresser:* Herschel Sparber, Raymond Xifo.
Swings: Chrissy Faith, Marcus Neville.

The action takes

Act 1, Scene 1: L
Writer's Cell, M
Office. *Scene 6:*
Scene 8: Buddy
Scene 11: Bobb
Mansion. *Scene*
Scene 17: Don
Morgue. *Scene*

Act 2, Scene 1:
Jail. *Scene 4*: O
Scene 7: Buddy
Bedroom. *Scen*
The Red Room
Soundstage, M

ACT 1
Prelude: 7
Angel C

Scene 2
"Double 7
J. Naug|

Scene 4
"Double 7
R. Aub(

Scene 6
"What Y(
K. Mc(

Scene 7
"Ya Gott
S. Waa

Scene 8
"The Bu
R. Au|

Scene 10
"With F
K. M(

Scene 14
"Tennis
J. N|

Scene 15
"Ev'ryb
J. N|

Scene 16
"Lost a
R. Y

Scene 2|
"All Y|
S. E

"You'|
G.

ACT 2
Scene 1
"Stay|
S.

Scene 4
"You
R.

Scene |
"You
R

Scene
"It N
K

Scene
"W|
J

place in Los Angeles during the late 1940's.

A. County Hospital. *Scene 2*: Stone Office, one week earlier. *Scene 3*:
ster Pictures Studio. *Scene 4*: Buddy Fidler's Office. *Scene 5*: Stone's
Stine's Bedroom, The Garden of Allah. *Scene 7*: Stone's Bungalow.
s Office. *Scene 9*: Stone's Bungalow. *Scene 10*: A Cocktail Lounge.
's Dressing Room. *Scene 12*: Writer's Cell. *Scene 13*: The Kingsley
14: The Solarium. *Scene 15*: The Search. *Scene 16*: Stone's Bungalow.
a's Bedroom. *Scene 18*: Stone's Bungalow. *Scene 19*: L.A. County
0: Buddy's Office. *Scene 21*: The Morgue.

Recording Studio. *Scene 2*: A Bel-Air Bedroom. *Scene 3*: L.A. County
lie's Bedroom. *Scene 5*: Donna's Bedroom. *Scene 6*: A Bel-Air Garden.
s Study. *Scene 8*: The Jail. *Scene 9*: Buddy's Study. *Scene 10*: Alaura's
11: Buddy's Office. *Scene 12*: Stine's Apartment, New York. *Scene 13*:
Scene 14: The Kingsley Solarium. *Scene 15*: Writer's Cell. *Scene 16*: A
ster Pictures Studio.

heme from "City of Angels"
ty 4

alk"
ton, D. Hoty

alk" (reprise)
rjonois, G. Edelman

u Don't Know About Women"
lelland, R. Graff

Look Out for Yourself"
ra, The Angel City 4

ddy System"
erjonois, R. Graff

very Breath I Take"
Clelland

Song"
ighton, D. Hoty

ody's Gotta Be Somewhere"
ughton, The Angel City 4

nd Found"
rk

Have to Do Is Wait"
lliott, A. Lum, J. Hindman, T. Galantich
Nothing Without Me"
Edelman, J. Naughton

With Me"
Vaara, The Angel City 4

Can Always Count on Me"
Graff

Can Always Count on Me" (reprise)
Graff

2

eeds Work"
McClelland

3

h Every Breath I Take" (reprise)
Naughton, K. McClelland

Scene 15
"Funny"
G. Edelman
Scene 16
"You're Nothing Without Me" (reprise)
J. Naughton, G. Edelman, K. McClelland

1990.01   JUNON AND AVOS-THE HOPE

A Soviet Rock Musical in Two Acts, a Prologue and Epilogue (in Russian).
Book and lyrics by Andrey Voznesensky. Music by Alexis Ribnikov. Directed
by Mark Zakharov. Choreography by Vladimir Vassiliev. Sets by Oleg
Sheintsiss. Costumes by Valentina Komolova. Sound by Abe Jacob. English
narrative written by Susan Silver and Albert Todd. America producer, Lucy
Jarvis. Presented by Pierre Cardin, by special arrangement with Lencom
Theatre and the Theatre Union of the U.S.S.R. Opened 7 January 1990 at
the New York City Center and closed 4 February 1990 after 35 performances.

CAST: *Count Nikolai Rezanov*, Chamberlain of Emperor Alexander I: NIKOLAI
KARACHENTSEV. *Conchita*, Maria de la Concepcione de Arguello: YELENA
SHANINA. *First Conjurer*: Yury Naumkin. *Second Conjurer*: Gennady Trofimov.
Burning Heretic, Fernando Lopez, the Theatrical Narrator: ALEXANDER ABDULOV.
Vision of a woman with an infant: Ludmilla Porgina. *Count Alexey Rumiantsev/The
Governor of San Francisco*: Vladimir Shiryayev. *Naval Officers*: Vladimir Belousov,
Boris Chunayev, Vladimir Kuznetsov, Rady Ovchinnikov. *Padre Abella*: Villor
Kuznetsov. *Interpreter*: Rady Ovchinnikov. *Spanish Ladies*: Irena Alfiorova, Tatiana
Derbeneva, Ludmilla Porgina, Alexandra Zakharova, Tatiana Rudina, Ludmilla
Artemieva. *Conchita's Messenger*: Yury Zelenin. *The Singing Monk*: Alexander Sado.
    *The Russian Sailors, Spaniards, the Shareholders of the Russian-American Company,
the monks, chimeras and others*: Vladislav Victor Rakov, Alexander Sririn, Nikolai
Shusharin, Alexander Karnaushkin, Igor Fokin, Andrey Leonov, Sergey Chonishvilli,
Oleg Ruduk, Leonid Luvinsky, Leonid Gromov, Denis Karasiov.
    The Choir: *Sopranos*: Irena Musayelian, Valentina Prokhorova, Zinaida Morozova,
Natlia Mishenko. *Altos*: Irena Kushnarenko, Valeria Zhivova, Lilia Semashko, Yelena
Rudnitskaya. *Tenor*: Vladimir Tursky. *Basses*: Alexey Larin, Valdimir Prokhorov, Sergey
Stepanchenko.
    Rock Group Araks: *Keyboards*; Sergey Rudnitsky. *Bass Guitar*: Seregy Rizhov. *Vocals*:
Alexander Sado, Nikolai Parfenyuk, Pavel Smeian. *Guitar/Violin/Cello*: Sergey
Berezkin. *Drums*: Anatoly Abromov. *Brass*: Yakov Levda, Victor Denisov.
    Storyteller (Narration in English): PHILIP CASNOFF.

The action takes place in Russia and San Francisco from 1806 to 1842.

MUSICAL NUMBERS[29]
  "I Will Never See You Again, I Will Never Forget You"
  "Avos" (the hope for good luck)
  "The White Wild Rose"
  "Hallelejuah to Love"

1990.02   THE SOUND OF MUSIC

A Revival of the Musical (Play) in Two Acts, 19 Scenes[30]. Book by Howard
Lindsay and Russel Crouse. Suggested by the book "The Trapp Family
Singers" by Maria Augusta Trapp. Music by Richard Rodgers. Lyrics by
Oscar Hammerstein II. Directed by James Hammerstein. Musical staging by
Joel Bishoff. Set and lighting designer, Neil Peter Jampolis. Costume design-
er, Suzanne Mess. Conductor, Richard Parrinello. Orchestrations by Robert
Russell Bennett. Sound by Abe Jacob. Chorus master, Joseph Colaneri.
Produced by the New York City Opera in association with James M.
Nederlander. Opened 8 March 1990 at the New York State Theatre and
closed 22 April 1990 after 54 performances.

CAST (in order of appearance): *Maria Rainer*, a Postulant at Nonnberg Abbey:
DEBBY BOONE. *Sister Berthe*, Mistress of Novices: Jill Bosworth *Sister Margaretta*,
Mistress of Postulants: Michele McBride. *The Mother Abbess*: CLAUDIA
CUMMINGS. *Sister Sophia*: Robin Tabachnik. *Captain Georg von Trapp*:

---

[29]Performed as an opera without individual scenes or musical numbers listed. The plot synopsis however included the following song titles.
[30]Originally produced in New York 16 November 1959 at the Lunt-
Fontanne Theatre for 1443 performances. For Synopsis of Scenes and
Musical Numbers, see original 1959 production.

514

LAURENCE GUITTARD. *Franz*, the butler: David Rae Smith. *Frau Schmidt*, the housekeeper: Ellen Tovatt. *Children of Captain von Trapp (7)*: *Liesl*: EMILY LOESSER. *Friedrich*: Richard H. Blake. *Louisa*: Kelly Karbacz. *Kurt*: Ted Huffman. *Brigitta*: Kia Graves. *Marta*: Lauren Gaffney. *Gretl*: Mary Mazzello. *Rolf Gruber*: Marc Heller. *Elsa Schraeder*: MARIANNE TATUM. *Ursula*: Bridget Ramos. *Max Detweiler*: WERNER KLEMPERER. *Herr Zeller*: Louis Perry. *Baron Elberfeld*: William Ledbetter. *Postulant*: Barbara Shirvis. *Admiral von Schreiber*: Glenn Rowen.

Neighbors of Captain von Trapp, Nuns, Novices, Postulants, Contestants in the Festival Concert: New York City Opera Chorus.

1990.03 ## OBA OBA '90

A New Edition of the Brazilian Extravaganza (Revue) in Two Acts, 13 Scenes[31]. (Conceived and directed by Franco Fontana.) Musical director, Wilson Mauro. Choreographer, Roberto Abrahão. Lighting consultant, Giancarlo Campora. Produced by Franco Fontana. Opened 15 March 1990 at the Marquis Theatre and closed 22 April 1990 after 45 performances.

<u>CAST</u>: SONIA SANTOS, JAIME SANTOS, TOCO PRETO, PAULO RAMOS.
(in alphabetical order): Aderson Cirne, Amilton Lino, Andrea Candida, Bananal, Betho Filho, Branca de Neve, Carlos Leça, Carlos Oliveira, Cesar de Alabama, Claudia Capoeira, Curimã, Delma de Oliviera, Edgar Pretinho, Edilson Nery, Edmilson Nery, Edson Escovão, Eliane Garcia, Elisangela Maia, Evelyn Eduardo, Formiguinha, Gerson Galante, Glaucia Ribeiro, Heron DeAngola, Ivon Rosas, Janete Santos, Jorge Rum, Julio Peluchi, Katia Rio, Maguila Meneses, Malaguti, Mara Boeing, Maranhão, Marcelo Boim, Mario Capoeira, Marquinho da Dona Geralda, Marta Jacintho, Mauro Boim, Meia-Noite, Mirna Montenegro, Monica Acioli, Norberto Queiroz, Pé de Cão, Pelé, Pena Rodrigues, Renny Flores, Robertinho da Cuica, Rui Lima, Val Ventilador, Velly Bahia, Vivian M. Soares, Wilson Mauro.

ACT 1

Scene 1

Liberation from Slavery
The suffering of black slaves in prison. Their consciousness of their condition. The final unification of all blacks until freedom was achieved.

Scenes 2 and 4

Homage to "Chorinho"
Some classics of this particular kind of popular music feature the most expressive Brazilian instrument, the cavaquinho, a small guitar with four chords. Pieces such as "Carinhoso," "Urubu Malandro" and "Tico Tico" have made Chorinho famous throughout the world.

Scene 3

Samba de Roda-Lambada
This is a typical dance born in Bahia's public squares and markets—a festive competition among the women of the town. This coquettish contest displays their superiority in performing this particular type of samba. Lambada is a sexy popular dance from northeast Brazil that is becoming very popular and successful all over the world.

Scene 5

Homage to the Northeast
The most evocative music and songs of this marvelous, but desolately poor, territory move from the resigned lamentations of the Acordeom to the explosive reactions of the people who find in song and dance the strength and joy of life.

Scene 6

Brazil Capela

Scene 7

Homage to the Bossa Nova and the Seventies
The Bossa Nova—a medley dedicated to that great musical phenomenon of the sixties that made artists Tob Jobim, Baden Powell and Vinicius de Moraes and the songs "Wave," Samba de uma nota so" and "Garota de Ipanema" world-famous. The Seventies—a medley dedicated to the music of the seventies that made famous artists Jorge Ben and Sergio Mendess and the songs "Mais Que Nada," "Taj Mahal" and Pais Tropical."

Scene 8

Tribute to the 'Brazilian Bombshell' Carmen Miranda

ACT 2

Scene 1

Macumba

[31]First produced in New York 29 March 1988 at the Ambassador Theatre for 46/53? performances.

The religious African cult with its dances and its saints (Orixa) including the magical appearance of Iemanja, Queen of the Seas and Fertility.

Scene 2

Afro-Brazilian Folk Songs and Dances; Berimbau Medley

Capoeira of Angola:
A tribute to the struggles against the white masters wherein the slaves used their hands and feet as their only weapon (Capoeira, which later became a dance).

Maculele:
Dances that require agility and skill and are carried out with small batons accompanied by the lively rhythm of tambores and agogo.

Acrobatic Capoeira

Scene 3

Rhythm Beaters
Various instruments are at first played separately, in order to stress their peculiarities, and then all together in a sweeping progress of rhythm.

Scene 4

Show of Samba Dancers
An exaltation of the beauty and charm of the Brazilian mulatto women through the sensual progress of their samba.

Scene 5

Grand Carnival
The most popular themes of the various carnivals, featuring a parade of the artists who then allow the audience to participate in the great and collective festivals.

1990.04 ## ASPECTS OF LOVE

A Musical in Two Acts, a Prologue and 34 Scenes. Book adaptation by Andrew Lloyd Webber. Based on the novel of the same name by David Garnett. Music by Andrew Lloyd Webber. Lyrics by Don Black and Charles Hart. Directed by Trevor Nunn. Choreography by Gillian Lynne. Production design (costumes, settings) by Maria Björnson. Lighting by Andrew Bridge. Sound by Martin Levan. Production musical director, Paul Bogaev. Orchestrations by David Cullen, Andrew Lloyd Webber. Produced by The Really Useful Company (Bridget Hayward, producer). Opened 8 April 1990 at the Broadhurst Theatre and closed 2 March 1991 after 377 performances.

<u>CAST</u>: *Rose Vibert*, a French actress: ANN CRUMB. *Alex Dillingham*, a young Englishman: MICHAEL BALL. *George Dillingham*, Alex's uncle, an English painter: KEVIN COLSON. *Giulietta Trapani*, an Italian sculptress: KATHLEEN ROWE MCALLEN. *Marcel Richard*, an actor manager: WALTER CHARLES. *Jenny Dillingham*, age 12: Deanna du Clos. *Jenny Dillingham*, age 14: Danielle du Clos. *Elizabeth*, George's housekeeper: Suzanne Briar. *Hugo Le Muenier*, Rose's friend: Don Goodspeed. *Jerome*, George's gardener: Philip Clayton.

At the Cafe: *Actors*: Philip Clayton, John Dewar, Marcus Lovett, Kurt Johns. *Actresses*: Elinore O'Connell, Lisa Vroman, Wysandria Woolsey. *Stage Manager*: Don Goodspeed. *Assistant Stage Manager*: Jane Todd Baird. *Waiter*: Gregory Mitchell. *Man on Date*: Eric Johnson. *His Date*: Suzanne Briar.

At the Fairground: *First Barker*: Eric Johnson. *Second Barker*: Kurt Johns. *Alex's Friends*: Don Goodspeed, Philip Clayton. *Their Girlfriends*: Elinore O'Connell, Lisa Vroman. *Alex's Date*: Jane Todd Baird. *War Veteran*: John Dewar. *His Wife*: Suzanne Briar. *Local Men*: Marcus Lovett, Gregory Mitchell. *Local Woman*: Wysandria Woolsey. *In Venice*: *Gondolier*: Kurt Johns. *Hotel Cashier*: Lisa Vroman. *Nun*: Elinore O'Connell. *Doctor*: John Dewar. *Hotleier*: Eric Johnson. *Pharmacist*: Wysandria Woolsey. *Registrar*: Eric Johnson. *Assistant Registrar*: John Dewar.

In Rose's Dressing Room: *Rose's Friends*: Jane Todd Baird, Suzanne Briar, Philip Clayton, John Dewar, Kurt Johns, Eric Johnson, Marcus Lovett, Gregory Mitchell, Elinore O'Connell, Lisa Vroman, Wysandria Woolsey.

At the Circus: *Clowns*: Gregory Mitchell, Marcus Lovett, Philip Clayton, John Dewar. *Knife Thrower*: Kurt Johns. *His Assistant*: Wysandria Woolsey.

At the Wake: *The Young Peasant*: Gregory Mitchell.

Swings: Wiley Kidd, Brad Oscar, Anne Marie Runolfsson.

The action takes place on the (European) continent between 1947-1964.

Prologue: On the Terrace at Pau, 1964.

Act 1, Scene 1: France, 1947. A Small Theatre in Montpellier. *Scene 2*: A Cafe in Montpellier. *Scene 3*: The Railway Station. *Scene 4*: In a Train Compartment. *Scene 5*: The House at Pau. *Scene 6*: A Sculpture Exhibition in Paris. *Scene 7*: In many rooms in the House at Pau. *Scene 8*: On the Terrace. *Scene 9*: Outside the bedroom. *Scene 10*: Up in the Pyrenees. *Scene 11*: The House at Pau. *Scene 12*: The Railway Station. *Scene 13*: Two Years pass . . . A Fairground in Paris. *Scene 14*: George's Flat in Paris. *Scene 15*:

Giulietta's Studio in Venice. *Scene 16*: A Registry Office. *Scene 17*: A Military Camp in Malaya.

Act 2, Scene 1: Thirteen years later ... A Grand Theatre in Paris. *Scene 2*: At the Stage Door. *Scene 3*: George's House in Pau. *Scene 4*: A Cafe in Venice/The House at Pau. *Scene 5*: The Garden at Pau. *Scene 6*: The Countryside around the House. *Scene 7*: Two years pass ... The Garden at Pau. *Scene 8*: On the Terrace., *Scene 9*: Up in the Pyrenees. *Scene 10*: In the Vineyard at Pau. *Scene 11*: A Circus in Paris. *Scene 12*: Outside the Circus. *Scene 13*: Jenny's Bedroom in Paris. *Scene 14*: The Vineyards at Pau. *Scene 15*: A Hayloft. *Scene 16*: On the Terrace.

ACT 1
Prologue
"Love Changes Everything"
M. Ball
Scene 2
"Parlez-vous français?"
A. Crumb, M. Ball, Ensemble
Scene 4
"Seeing Is Believing"
M. Ball, A. Crumb
Scene 6
"A Memory of a Happy Moment"
K. Colson, K. R. McAllen
Scene 10
"Chanson d'enfance"
A. Crumb
Scene 13
"Everybody Loves a Hero"
Barkers, Ensemble
Scene 14
"She'd Be Far Better Off with You"
M. Ball, K. Colson, A. Crumb, S. Briar
Scene 15
"Stop. Wait. Please."
K. R. McAllen, K. Colson, Ensemble

ACT 2
Scene 1
"Leading Lady"
W. Charles, Ensemble
Scene 3
"Other Pleasures"
K. Colson
Scene 4
"There Is More to Love"
K. R. McAllen, A. Crumb
Scene 5
"Mermaid Song"
D. Du Clos, M. Ball
Scene 8
"The First Man You Remember"
K. Colson, D. Du Clos
Scene 11
"The Journey of a Lifetime"
Company
Scene 12
"Falling"
K. Colson, A. Crumb, M. Ball, D. Du Clos
Scene 14
"Hand Me the Wine and the Dice"
K. R. McAllen, Ensemble
Scene 16
"Anything But Lonely"
A. Crumb

TRULY BLESSED:
A Musical Celebration of Mahalia Jackson

1990.05

A Musical in Two Acts, 14 Scenes. Written, conceived, original music and lyrics by Queen Esther Marrow. Additional music and lyrics, original (musical) arrangements by Reginald Royal. Directed by Robert Kalfin. Choreography by Larry Vickers. Musical supervision and orchestrations by Joseph Joubert. Scenery and lighting design by Fred Kolo. Costume design by Andrew B. Marlay. Sound design by Peter Fitzgerald. Production supervisor, Mortimer Halpern. Originally produced by Ford's Theatre, Washington, D.C. Produced by Howard Hurst, Philip Rose, Sophie Hurst in association with Frankie Hewitt. Opened 22 April 1990 at the Longacre Theatre and closed 20 May 1990 after 33 performances.

CAST: *Mahalia Jackson*: QUEEN ESTHER MARROW.
Ensemble: Carl Hall, Lynette G. DuPré, Doug Eskew, Gwen Stuart.

Act 1, Scene 1: Opening. *Scene 2*: New Orleans. *Scene 3*: Going to Chicago. *Scene 4*: The Church. *Scene 5*: Touring. *Scene 6*: On the Backsteps. *Scene 7*: Mayor Daley and the Rally. *Scene 8*: Mr. Sigmund Galloway. *Scene 9*: On Top of the World.

Act 2, Scene 1: Carnegie Hall. *Scene 2*: The March on Washington. *Scene 3*: Mahalia in the Berkshires. *Scene 4*: In the Holy Land. *Scene 5*: Epilogue and Celebration.

ACT 1
"I Found the Answer"
(*Music and Lyrics by* Johnny Lange.)
"St. Louis Blues"
(*Music and Lyrics by* W. C. Handy.)
"It's Amazing What God Can Do"
(*Music and Lyrics by* Reginald Royal.)
Medley: "On the Battlefield for My Lord"/"Glory Hallelujah"
"He May Not Come When You Want Him"
"Lord, I'm Determined"
(*Music and Lyrics by* Queen Esther Marrow.)
"Happy Days Are Here Again" (from *CHASING RAINBOWS* film)
(*Music by* Milton Ager. *Lyrics by* Jack Yellen.)
"Precious Lord"
(*Music and Lyrics by* Thomas A. Dorsey.)
"Jesus Remembers When Others Forget"
(*Music by* Joseph Joubert. *Lyrics by* Thomas A. Dorsey.)
"Thank You for the Change in My Life"
(*Music and Lyrics by* Queen Esther Marrow.)
"Come on Children, Let's Sing"

ACT 2
"Even Me"
(*Arranged by* Roberta Martin.)
"Didn't It Rain"
Spiritual Medley:
"Wade in the Water"
"Old Ship of Zion"
"Battle Hymn of the Republic"
(Traditional; *Lyrics by* Julia Ward Howe.)
"I've Been Buked"
"Soon I Will Be Done"
"His Gift to Me"
(*Music and Lyrics by* Reginald Royal.)
"Move on up a Little Higher"
(*Music and Lyrics by* Mahalia Jackson.)
"Rusty Bell"
"Truly Blessed"
(*Music and Lyrics by* Reginald Royal.)
"He's Got the Whole World in His Hands"
(Traditional; *adapted by* Geoff Love.)

A CHANGE IN THE HEIR

1990.06

A Musical Comedy in Two Acts and a Prologue. Book by George H. Gorham and Dan Sticco. Music by Dan Sticco. Lyrics by George H. Gorham. Directed and choreographed by David H. Bell. Sets by Michael Anania. Costumes by David Murin. Lighting by Jeff Davis. Musical director and dance arrangements by Rob Bowman. Orchestrations by Robby Merkin. World premiere originally produced by New Tuners, Theatre, Chicago. Produced by Stewart F. Lane. Opened 29 April 1990 at the Edison Theater and closed 13 May 1990 after 17 performances.

CAST (in order of appearance): *Aunt Julia*: BROOKS ALMY. *Giles*: Brian Sutherland. *Edwin*: J. K. Simmons. *Nicholas*: David Gunderman. *Countess*: Connie Day. *Lady Enid*: Mary Stout. *Prince Conrad*: JUDY BLAZER. *Princess Agnes*: JEFFREY HERBST. *Martha*: Jan Neuberger. *Lady Elizabeth*: Jennifer Smith.

Prologue: Once upon a time, long, long ago, in a castle far, far away.

Act 1: Twenty years later, Friday and Saturday.

Act 2: Sunday morning.

ACT 1
  Prologue
    Company
  "Here I Am"
    J. Blazer
  "The Weekend"
    B. Almy, C. Day, J. Neuberger, M. Stout, J. K. Simmons, B. Sutherland
  "Look at Me"
    J. Herbst, J. Blazer
  "Take a Look at That"
    J. Herbst, J. Smith
  "The Quintet"
    J. K. Simmons, M. Stout, J. Herbst, C. Day, J. Blazer
  "Can't I?"
    J. Blazer
  "When"
    B. Almy, J. Neuberger
  "A Fairy Tale"
    J. Herbst, J. Blazer
  "An Ordinary Family"
    Company
ACT 2
  "Happily Ever After After All"
    J. Herbst
  "Can't I?" (reprise)
    J. Blazer
  "Duet"
    J. Herbst, J. Blazer
  "Hold That Crown"
    B. Almy
  "By Myself"
    J. Blazer, Company
  Finale
    Company

Keith Carradine in THE WILL ROGERS FOLLIES
Martha Swope/TimePix

1990–1991 SEASON

A LITTLE NIGHT MUSIC

1990.07

A Revival of the Musical in Two Acts, a Prologue and 15 Scenes[1]. Book by Harold Wheeler. Suggested by a film ("Smiles of a Summer Night") by Ingmar Bergman. Music and lyrics by Stephen Sondheim. Directed by Scott Ellis. Choreography by Susan Stroman. Sets designed by Michael Anania. Costumes designed by Lindsay W. Davis. Lighting designed by Dawn Chiang. Conductor, Paul Gemignani. Orchestrations by Jonathan Tunick. Sound by Abe Jacob. Produced by the New York City Opera. Opened 3 August 1990 at the New York State Theatre and closed 7 November 1990 after 11 performances in repertory.

CAST (in order of appearance): *Mrs. Segstrom*: Susanne Marsee. *Mr. Lindquist*: Ron Baker. *Mrs. Nordstrom*: Lisa Saffer. *Mrs. Anderssen*: Barbara Shirvis. *Mr. Erlanson*: Michael Rees Davis. *Frederika Armfeldt*: Danielle Ferland. *Madame Armfeldt*: REGINA RESNICK. *Frid*, her butler: DAVID COMSTOCK. *Henrik Egerman*: KEVIN P. ANDERSON. *Anne Egerman*: BEVERLY LAMBERT. *Fredrik Egerman*: GEORGE LEE ANDREWS. *Petra*: SUSAN TERRY. *Desirée Armfeldt*: SALLY ANN HOWES. *Malla*, her maid: Raven Wilkinson. *Bertrand*, a page: Michael Rees Davis. *Count Carl-Magnus Malcolm*: MICHAEL MAGUIRE. *Countess Charlotte Malcolm*: MAUREEN MOORE. *Osa*: Judith Jarosz. *Serving Gentlemen*: Michael Cornell, Ernest Foederer, Kent A. Heacock, Ronald Kelly, Brian Michels, Brian Quirk, Christopher Sheperd, John Henry Thomas.

STREET SCENE

1990.08

A Revival of the American Opera (Dramatic Musical) in Two Acts, 3 Scenes[2]. Book by Elmer Rice from his play of the same name. Music by Kurt Weill. Lyrics by Langston Hughes. Production directed by Jack O'Brien, restaged by Jay Lesenger. Conducted by Chris Nance. Scenery designed by Paul Sylbert. Costumes designed by Marjorie McCown. Lighting by Gilbert V. Hemsley, Jr. Choreography by Patricia Birch. Chorus Master, Joseph Colaneri. (Orchestrations by Kurt Weill.) Produced by the New York City Opera. Opened 7 September 1990 at the New York State Theatre and closed 29 September 1990 after 6 performances in repertory.

CAST (in order of appearance): *Greta Fiorentino*: Rachel Rosales. *Emma Jones*: JOYCE CASTLE. *Olga Olsen*: Susanne Marsee. *Carl Olsen*: Robert Ferrier. *Neighborhood Woman*: Lisa Jablow. *Shirley Kaplan*: Elinor Basescù. *Abraham Kaplan*: David Rae Smith. *Salvation Army Girls*: Deborah Williams, Kathleen Smith. *Henry Davis*: Eugene Perry. *Willie Maurrant*: Keith Cacciola-Morales. *Anna Maurrant*: MARGARET CUSACK. *Sam Kaplan*: KEVIN P. ANDERSON. *Daniel Buchanan*: Peter Blanchet. *Mrs. Buchanan*: Lila Herbert. *Frank Maurrant*: WILLIAM PARCHER. *George Jones*: William Ledbetter. *Steve Sankey*: Richard Maynard. *Lippo Fiorentino*: JONATHAN GREEN. *Mrs. Hildebrand*: Jennifer Lane. *Jenny Hildebrand*: Robin Tabachnik. *Graduates*: Alexis Martin, Karla Simmons. *Charlie Hildebrand*: Derek Dreyer. *Mary Hildebrand*: Rachel Samberg. *Grace Davis*: Melissa Martin. *Rose Maurrant*: SHERYL WOODS. *Harry Easter*: HARLAN FOSS. *Mae Jones*: Jeanette Palmer. *Dick McGann*: John MacInnis. *Vincent Jones*: David Comstock. *Dr. Wilson*: Don Henderson. *Officer Murphy*: David Frye. *Milkman*: Ian D. Klapper. *Joan*: Allegra Victoria Forste. *Myrtle*: Francesca LaGuardia. *Workman*: Louis Perry. *Eddie*: Gregory Moore. *Sally*: Kelley Faulkner. *Joe*: Michael Cole. *Strawberry Seller*: Marty Singleton. *Corn Seller*: Rita Metzger. *James Henry*: Don Yule. *Fred Cullen*: Jonathan Guss. *Old Clothes Man*: Don Henderson. *Grocery Boy*: Kent A. Heacock. *Ambulance Driver*: Ronald Kelley. *Music Student*: Jane Cummins. *Intern*: John Henry Thomas. *Furniture Movers*: Glenn Rowen, Webster Latimer. *Nursemaids*: Lee Bellaver, Susan Ward. *Policemen*: Michael Putsch, Neil Eddinger. *Middle-Aged Couple*: Harris Davis, Rita Metzger.

MICHAEL FEINSTEIN IN CONCERT: PIANO AND VOICE

1990.09

A One Man Show in Two Acts[3]. Special material, Bruce Vilanch. Production staged and supervised by Christopher Chadman. Musical director, Ian Finkel. Lighting by David Agress. Sound designed by Daryl Bornstein. Johnny Mercer material arranged by Stan Freeman. Produced by Ron Delsener. Opened 2 October 1990 at the John Golden Theatre and closed 27 October 1990 after 30 performances.

CAST: MICHAEL FEINSTEIN[4].

Musicians: Ian Finkel (xylophone), David Fink (bass), Martin Fischer (drums), Bruce Uchitel (guitar).

ACT 1
"I Hear Bells" (from *LOVE MATCH*)
   (*Music by* David Shire. *Lyrics by* Richard Maltby, Jr.)
"Manhattan" (from *GARRICK GAIETIES OF 1925*)
   (*Music by* Richard Rodgers. *Lyrics by* Lorenz Hart.)
"Make Believe" (from *SHOWBOAT*)
   (*Music by* Jerome Kern. *Lyrics by* Oscar Hammerstein II.)
"I Have Dreamed" (from *THE KING AND I*)
   (*Music by* Richard Rodgers. *Lyrics by* Oscar Hammerstein II.)
"Sweet and Low Down" (from *TIP TOES*)
   (*Music by* George Gershwin. *Lyrics by* Ira Gershwin.)
"The Man I Love"[5] (alternate lyric as "The Girl I Love")
   (*Music by* George Gershwin. *Lyrics by* Ira Gershwin.)
"I'll Build a Stairway to Paradise" (from *GEORGE WHITE'S SCANDALS* 1922)
   (*Music by* George Gershwin. *Lyrics by* B. G. DeSylva.)
"Sister Susie's Sewing Shirts for Soldiers"
   (*Music by* Hermann Darewski. *Lyrics by* R. P. Weston.)
"Where Do You Start"
   (*Music by* Johnny Mandel. *Lyrics by* Marilyn and Alan Bergman.)
"Let Me Love You"
   (*Music and Lyrics by* Bart Howard.)
"Wait Till You See Her" (from *BY JUPITER*)
   (*Music by* Richard Rodgers. *Lyrics by* Lorenz Hart.)
"The Most Beautiful Girl in the World" (from *JUMBO*)
   (*Music by* Richard Rodgers. *Lyrics by* Lorenz Hart.)
"Lover" (from *LOVE ME TONIGHT* film)
   (*Music by* Richard Rodgers. *Lyrics by* Lorenz Hart.)
BURTON LANE Medley:
   "Babes on Broadway" (from *BABES ON BROADWAY* film)
      (*Music by* Burton Lane. *Lyrics by* E. Y. Harburg, Ralph Freed.)
   "How About You?" (from *BABES ON BROADWAY* film)
      (*Music by* Burton Lane. *Lyrics by* E. Y. Harburg, Ralph Freed.)
   "Anything Can Happen in New York" (from *BABES ON BROADWAY* film)
      (*Music by* Burton Lane. *Lyrics by* E. Y. Harburg, Ralph Freed.)
   "On a Clear Day You Can See Forever" (from show of same name)
      (*Music by* Burton Lane. *Lyrics by* Alan Jay Lerner.)
"No One Is Alone" (from *INTO THE WOODS*)
   (*Music and Lyrics by* Stephen Sondheim.)

ACT 2
"The Old Music Master" (from *TRUE TO LIFE* film)
   (*Music by* Hoagy Carmichael. *Lyrics by* Johnny Mercer.)
Tin Pan Alley/Broadway Medley:
   "Are You Havin' Any Fun?" (from *GEORGE WHITE'S SCANDALS* 1939)
      (*Music by* Sammy Fain. *Lyrics by* Jack Yellen.)
   "On the Sunny Side of the Street" (*LEW LESLIE'S INTERNATIONAL REVUE*)
      (*Music by* Jimmy McHugh. *Lyrics by* Dorothy Fields.)

---

[1]Originally produced in New York 25 February 1973 at the Sam S. Shubert Theatre for 601 performances. For Synopsis of Scenes and Musical Numbers, see original 1973 production.

[2]Originally produced in New York 9 January 1947 at the Adelphi Theatre for 148 performances. For Synopsis of Scenes and Musical Numbers, see original 1947 production.

---

[3]Michael Feinstein appeared on Broadway in his previous one man shows:
   MICHAEL FEINSTEIN IN CONCERT, 19 April 1988, Lyceum, 62.
   MICHAEL FEINSTEIN IN CONCERT: ISN'T IT ROMANTIC?, 5 October 1988, Booth, 38.

[4]On opening night, composer Burton Lane joined the performance as a special guest star.

[5]Dropped from *LADY, BE GOOD, STRIKE UP THE BAND* and *ROSALIE*.

"The Best Things in Life Are Free" (from *GOOD NEWS*)
(*Music by* Ray Henderson. *Lyrics by* Buddy G. DeSylva, Lew Brown.)
"I Can't Give You Anything But Love" (from *BLACKBIRDS OF 1928*)
(*Music by* Jimmy McHugh. *Lyrics by* Dorothy Fields.)
"Love Will Find a Way" (from *SHUFFLE ALONG*)
(*Music by* Eubie Blake. *Lyrics by* Noble Sissle.)
"Whatever Happened to Melody?"
(*Music and Lyrics by* Cynthia Thompson, Ray Jessel and Bryn Celli Ddu.)
"Holiday for Strings"
(*Music by* David Rose. *Lyrics by* Sammy Gallop.)
"Rhode Island Is Famous for You" (from *INSIDE U.S.A.*)
(*Music by* Arthur Schwartz. *Lyrics by* Howard Dietz.)
"Killing Time"
(*Music by* Jule Styne. *Lyrics by* Carolyn Leigh)
"The Music That Makes Me Dance" (from *FUNNY GIRL*)
(*Music by* Jule Styne. *Lyrics by* Bob Merrill.)
Johnny Mercer Medley:
"Too Marvelous for Words" (from *READY, WILLING, AND ABLE* film)
(*Music by* Richard Whiting. *Lyrics by* Johnny Mercer.)
"Lazybones"
(*Music and Lyrics by* Johnny Mercer and Hoagy Carmicahael.)
"Hooray for Hollywood" (from *HOLLYWOOD HOTEL* film)
(*Music by* Richard Whiting. *Lyrics by* Johnny Mercer.)
"I'm Old-Fashioned" (from *YOU WERE NEVER LOVELIER* film)
(*Music by* Jerome Kern. *Lyrics by* Johnny Mercer.)
"The Girl Friend of the Whirling Dervish" (from *GARDEN OF THE MOON* film)
(*Music by* Harry Warren. *Lyrics by* Johnny Mercer.)
"Glow Worm"
(*Music by* Paul Lincke. *Lyrics by* Lilla Cayley Robinson, Johnny Mercer.)
"Satin Doll"
(*Music by* Billy Strayhorn and Duke Ellington. *Lyrics by* Johnny Mercer.)
"Laura" (from *LAURA* film)
(*Music by* David Raksin. *Lyrics by* Johnny Mercer.)
"Dream"
(*Music and Lyrics by* Johnny Mercer.)
"Come Rain or Come Shine" (from *ST. LOUIS WOMAN*)
(*Music by* Harold Arlen. *Lyrics by* Johnny Mercer.)
"Where Would I Be Without You"
"I Love a Piano" (from *STOP! LOOK! LISTEN!*)
(*Music and Lyrics by* Irving Berlin.)

BUGS BUNNY
1990.10 ON BROADWAY

A Musical Revue in Two Acts. Created and conducted by George Daugherty. Music by Carl Stalling and Milt Franklyn, based upon the works of von Suppé, Rossini, Wagner, J. Strauss, Donizetti and Liszt. Animation directed by Chuck Jones, Friz Freleng, Robert McKimson, Robert Clampett. Voice characterizations by Mel Blanc and Arthur Q. Bryan. Scenic design by Michael Giaimo. Art direction by Darrel Van Citters. Lighting design by Bob Jared. Executive producer for the Nederlander Corporation, Peter H. Russell. Executive producer, Steven Goldberg. Produced by Warner Brothers, in association with Industrial FX Productions Inc. (Producer, George Daugherty.) Opened 4 October 1990 at the Gershwin Theatre and closed 7 October 1990 after 5 performances.

CAST: BUGS BUNNY, ELMER FUDD, PORKY PIG, DAFFY DUCK, Giovanni Jones, Granny, Baby Daffy Duck.

ACT 1

The Merrie Melodies Theme
The Ride of the Valkyries
(*Music by* Richard Wagner.)
Baton Bunny
(*Guest Conductor:* Bugs Bunny.)
(*Music by* Franz von Suppé. Based upon "Morning, Noon and Night in Vienna." Animation directed by Chuck Jones.)
Excerpt from "What's Up, Doc?"
(*Animation directed by* Robert McKimson. *Musical Direction by* Carl W. Stalling.)
Hungarian Rhapsody No. 2
(*Music by* Franz Liszt.)
High Note
(*Original score by* Milt Franklyn after Johann Strauss. Based upon "The Blue Danube." *Animation directed by* Chuck Jones.)

A Salute to Carl Stalling
(*Music by* Carl W. Stalling. Score from "Jumping Jupiter.")
The Rabbit of Seville
Bugs Bunny, Elmer Fudd
(*Music by* Gioacchino Rossini, arranged by Milt Franklyn. Based upon "The Barber of Seville" Overture. *Animation directed by* Chuck Jones. *Voice characterization by* Mel Blanc and Arthur Q. Bryan.)

ACT 2

Excerpt from "This Is a Life?"
Bugs Bunny, Daffy Duck, Elmer Fudd, Granny
(*Music by* Milt Franklyn. *Animation Direction by* Friz Freleng. *Voice characterization by* Mel Blanc.)
A Corny Concerto
Bugs Bunny, Porky Pig, Baby Daffy Duck
(*Music by* Carl W. Stalling. Based upon "Tales of the Vienna Woods" and "The Blue Danube" by Johann Strauss. *Animation Direction by* Robert Clampett.)
Morning, Noon and Night in Vienna
Rhapsody Rabbit
Bugs Bunny
(*Music by* Franz Liszt. Based on the Second Hungarian Rhapsody. Music originally arranged by Carl W. Stalling. *Animation Direction by* Friz Freleng. *Voice characterization by* Mel Blanc.)
Long-Haired Hare
Bugs Bunny, Giovanni Jones
(*Original Score by* Carl W. Stalling, after Wagner, Donizetti and Rossini. *Animation Directed by* Chuck Jones. *Voice characterization by* Mel Blanc.)
What's Opera, Doc?
Bugs Bunny, Elmer Fudd
(*Music by* Richard Wagner, arranged by Milt Franklyn. Based upon music from "The Flying Dutchman," "Die Walküre," Siegfreid" and "Tannhauser." *Directed by* Chuck Jones. *Voice characterizations by* Mel Blanc and Arthur Q. Bryan.)

JACKIE MASON:
1990.11 BRAND NEW

A One Man Comedy Revue in Two Acts[6]. Production design and lighting by Neil Peter Jampolis. Sound design by Bruce Cameron. Opening sequence directed by David Niles. Executive producer, Jyll Rosenfeld. Produced by Old Friends Group (Michael Simoff, Eric P. Aschenberg). Opened 17 October 1990 at the Neil Simon Theatre and closed 30 June 1991 after 216 performances.

CAST: JACKIE MASON (stand-up comedy, monologues, impressions).

1990.12 ONCE ON THIS ISLAND

A Musical in One Act[7]. Book and lyrics by Lynn Ahrens. Based on the novel "My Love, My Love" by Rosa Guy. Music by Stephen Flaherty. Directed and choreographed by Graciela Daniele. Set by Loy Arcenas. Costumes by Judy Dearing. Lighting by Allen Lee Hughes. Sound by Scott Lehrer. Orchestrations by Michael Starobin. Musical director, Steve Marzullo. Associate choreographer, Willie Rosario. Vocal and dance arrangements, musical continuity by Stephen Flaherty. Percussion concepts, Norbert Goldberg. Produced by The Shubert Organization, Capital Cities/ABC Inc., Suntory International Corporation, and James Walsh in association with Playwrights Horizons. Opened 18 October 1990 at the Booth Theatre and closed 1 December 1991 after 469 performances.

CAST (in alphabetical order): *The Storytellers: Daniel:* JERRY DIXON. *Erzulie, Goddess of Love:* Andrea Frierson. *Mama Euralie:* Sheila Gibbs. *Ti Moune:* LaCHANZE. *Asaka, Mother of the Earth:* Kecia Lewis-Evans. *Little Ti Moune:* Afi

---

[6]Previously produced Off-Broadway 27 January 1990 at the Public Theatre for 18 performances, and 5 May 1990 for 12 additional performances. Previous editions of Jackie Mason's one man show have been presented 22 December 1986 at the Brooks Atkinson Theatre for 367 performances; 3 May 1988 at the Brooks Atkinson for 203 performances.
[7]Originally produced Off-Broadway 6 May 1990 at Playwrights Horizons for 60 performances.

McClendon. *Armand*: Gerry McIntyre. *Agwe, God of Water*: Milton Craig Nealy. *Andrea*: Nikki Rene. *Papa Ge*: Demon of Death: Eric Riley. *Tonton Julian*: Ellis E. Williams.

The action takes takes place on an island in the French Antilles at night, in a storm.

MUSICAL NUMBERS

"We Dance"
 Storytellers
"One Small Girl"
 S. Gibbs, E. E. Williams, A. McClendon, Storytellers
"Waiting for Life"
 La Chanze, Storytellers
"And the Gods Heard Her Prayer"
 K. Lewis-Evans, M. C. Nealy, E. Riley, A. Frierson
"Rain"
 M. C. Nealy, Storytellers
"Pray"
 La Chanze, E. E. Williams, S. Gibbs, Guard, Storytellers
"Forever Yours"
 La Chanze, J. Dixon, E. Riley
"The Sad Tale of the Beauxhommes"
 G. McIntyre, Storytellers
"Ti Moune"
 S. Gibbs, E. E. Williams, La Chanze
"Mama Will Provide"
 K. Lewis-Evans, Storytellers
"Waiting for Life" (reprise)
 La Chanze
"Some Say"
 Storytellers
"The Human Heart"
 A. Frierson, Storytellers
"Pray" (reprise)
 Storytellers
"Some Girls"
 J. Dixon
"The Ball"
 N. Rene, J. Dixon, La Chanze, Storytellers
"Forever Yours" (reprise)
 E. Riley, La Chanze, A. Frierson, Storytellers
"A Part of Us"
 S. Gibbs, A. McClendon, E. E. Williams, Storytellers
"Why We Tell the Story"
 Storytellers

THE MIKADO,
or The Town of Titipu

1990.13

A Revival of the Comic Opera in Two Acts[8]. Libretto by William S. Gilbert. Music by Arthur Sullivan. Production (direction), Lofti Mansouri. Conductor, Chris Nance. Stage director, David Pfeiffer. Set and costume designer, Thierry Bosquet. Lighting designer, John Gleason. Choreographer, Patricia Birch. Chorus master, Joseph Colaneri. Produced by the New York City Opera. Opened 20 October 1990 at the New York State Theatre and closed 9 November 1990 after 5 performances in repertory.

CAST (in order of appearance): *Nanki-Poo*: CARROLL FREEMAN. *Pish-Tush*: WILLIAM PARCHER. *Pooh-Bah*: JOSEPH McKEE. *Ko-Ko*: JAMES BILLINGS. *Yum-Yum*: LISA SAFFER. *Pitti-Sing*: BRONWYN THOMAS. *Peep-Bo*: MICHELE MCBRIDE. *Katisha*: JOSEPH GAYER. *The Mikado of Japan*: RICHARD McKEE. *Chorus of School Girls, Nobles, Guards and Coolies*: New York City Opera Chorus.

---

[8]First presented in New York 20 July, 10-29 August 1885 at the Union Square and People's Theatres for 22 performances. First authorized production presented 19 August 1885 at the Fifth Avenue Theatre by Richard D'Oyly Carte for 250 performances. For Synopsis of Scenes and Musical Numbers, see 19 August 1885 D'Oyly Carte production.

1990.14

OH, KAY!

A Revival of the Musical Comedy in Two Acts, 8 Scenes[9]. Book by Guy Bolton and P. G. Wodehouse, adaptation by James Racheff. Concept, direction and choreography by Dan Siretta. Musical direction, vocal and additional dance arrangements by Tom Fay. Orchestrations by Arnold Goland. Dance arrangements by Donald Johnston. Scenic design by Kenneth Foy. Costume design by Theoni V. Aldredge. Lighting design by Craig Miller. Sound by Jan Nebozenko. Associate producer, Leo K. Cohen. Executive producer, Natalie Lloyd. Inspired by the Goodspeed Opera House (East Haddam, Connecticut) and Birmingham (Michigan) productions. Produced by David Merrick. Opened 1 November 1990 at the Richard Rodgers Theatre and closed 5 January 1991 after 77 performances. (Reopened 2-16 April 1991 at the Lunt-Fontanne Theatre with a revised cast for 16 additional previews, but closed before its scheduled re-opening[10].)

CAST (in order of appearance): *Billy Lyles*: GREGG BURGE. *Dolly Greene*: Kyme. *Duke*: Stanley Wayne Mathis. *Nick*: David Preston Sharpe. *Joe*: Fracaswell Hyman. *Waiter, Jake*: Frantz Hall. *Larry Potter*: Kevin Ramsey. *Shorty*: HELMAR AUGUSTUS COOPER. *Sam*: David Preston Sharpe. *B.J.*: Keith Robert Bennett. *Floyd*: Frederick J. Boothe. *Zeke*: Ken Roberson. *Jimmy Winter*: BRIAN MITCHELL. *Constance DuGrasse*: Tamara Tunie Bouquett. *Chauffeur*: Byron Easley. *Kay Jones*: ANGELA TEEK. *Janson*: Mark Kenneth Smaltz. *Reverend Alphonse DuGrasse*: Alexander Barton. *Duo Pianists*: Donald Johnston, Robert Colston.
 Ensemble: Keith Robert Bennett, Jacquelyn Bird, Frederick J. Boothe, Cheryl Burr, Byron Easley, Robert H. Fowler, Karen E. Fraction, Frantz Hall, Garry Q. Lewis, Greta Martin, Sharon Moore, Elise Neal, Ken Roberson, David Preston Sharp, Allyson Tucker, Mona Wyatt.

The action takes place in Harlem in 1926.

Act 1, Scene 1: Onstage at the Paradise Club. *Scene 2*: Backstage at the Paradise Club. *Scene 3*: Jimmy Winter's townhouse, late that night. *Scene 4*: Jimmy Winter's townhouse, the next morning.

Act 2, Scene 1: Jimmy's Terrace, that afternoon. *Scene 2*: Onstage at the Paradise Club. *Scene 3*: Backstage at the Paradise Club. *Scene 4*: Onstage at the Paradise Club.

ACT 1
Scene 1
"Slap That Bass" (from *SHALL WE DANCE* film)
 G. Burge, Kyme, Ensemble
Scene 3
"When Our Ship Comes Sailing In"[11]
 S. W. Mathis, H. A. Cooper, Male Ensemble
"Dear Little Girl"
 B. Mitchell, H. A. Cooper
"Maybe"
 B. Mitchell, A. Teek
Scene 4
"You've Got What Gets Me" (from *GIRL CRAZY* film)
 G. Burge, Kyme
"Do, Do, Do"
 B. Mitchell, A. Teek
"Clap Yo' Hands"
 K. Ramsey, Ensemble

---

[9]Originally produced in New York 8 November 1926 at the Imperial Theater for 256 performances.
[10]For revised version, the creative credits remained the same, except that the set design was uncredited. The new cast appears below with cast changes marked with an *. The roles of Duke, Joe, Waiter, Jake, Sam, Floyd were eliminated.

CAST (in order of appearance): *Billy Lyles*: GREGG BURGE. *Dolly Greene*: Kyme. *Kay Jones*: RAE DAWN CHONG*. *Nick*: David Preston Sharpe. *Zeke*: Ken Roberson. *Larry Potter*: Kevin Ramsey. *Shorty*: HELMAR AUGUSTUS COOPER. *B.J.*: Keith Robert Bennett. *Jimmy Winter*: RON RICHARDSON*. *Constance DuGrasse*: Natalie Oliver*. *Chauffeur*: Byron Easley. *Janson*: Mark Kenneth Smaltz. *Reverend Alphonse DuGrasse*: Alexander Barton. *Duo Pianists*: David Evans*, Robert Colston.
 Ensemble: added were Frederick J. Boothe (previously in a featured role), Melissa Haizlip, Sara Beth Lane, Ken Leigh Rogers; dropped was Mona Wyatt.

Added to Act 2, Scene 1, after "Fidgety Feet":
 "Ask Me Again" (reprise)
 R. Richardson
[11]Dropped from original 1926 production.

ACT 2
Scene 1
  "Oh, Kay!"
    G. Burge, A. Teek, Ensemble
    (*Lyrics by* Ira Gershwin and Howard Dietz.)
  "Ask Me Again" (interpolation)
    A. Teek
  "Fidgety Feet"
    S. W. Mathis, Ensemble
  "Someone to Watch Over Me"
    A. Teek
Scene 2
  "Heaven on Earth"
    K. Ramsey, S. W. Mathis, G. Burge
    (*Lyrics by* Ira Gershwin and Howard Dietz.)
Scene 4
  "Show Me the Town"[12]
  "Sleepless Nights"
    A. Teek, G. Burge, Kyme, K. Ramsey, Ensemble
  "Someone to Watch Over Me" (reprise)
    B. Mitchell, A. Teek

BUDDY:
1990.15 THE BUDDY HOLLY STORY

A Musical in Two Acts. Based on the life and career of Buddy Holly. (Book) Written by Alan Janes, from an idea by Laurie Mansfield. (Music and lyrics by Buddy Holly and various writers.) Directed by Rob Bettinson. (Set) Designed by Andy Walmsley. Costumes by Bill Butler, Carolyn Smith. Lighting by Graham McLusky. Musical director, Paul Jury. Musical consultant, Bruce Welch. Sound by Rick Price. All jingles composed by Paul Jury. Executive producer, Brian Sewell. Associate producer, Contracts International, Ltd. Produced by Paul Elliott, Laurie Mansfield and Greg Smith (for International Artistes), David Mirvish. Opened 4 November 1990 at the Sam S. Shubert Theatre and closed 19 May 1991 after 225 performances.

CAST (in order of appearance): *Act 1: Hipockets Duncan*: Fred Sanders. *Jingle Singers*: Jo Lynn Burks, Caren Cole, Liliane Stilwell. *The Hayriders*: Melanie Doane, Kevin Fox, Tom Nash, Steve Steiner, Don Stitt. *Engineer (KDAV)*: Philip Anthony. *Buddy Holly*: PAUL HIPP. *Joe B. Mauldin*: Bobby Prochaska. *Jerry Allison*: Russ Jolly. *Boppers and Autograph Hunters*: Jill Hennessy, Paul McQuillan, Ken Triwush. *Decca Session Musicians*: Kevin Fox, Tom Nash, Ken Triwush, Steve Steiner. *Decca Producer*: David Mucci. *Decca Engineers*: Paul McQuillan, Don Stitt. *Norman Petty*: Kurt Ziskie. *Vi Petty*: Jo Lynn Burks. *Fourth Cricket*: Ken Triwush. *DJ (WCLS)*: David Mucci. *DJ (WWOL)*: Philip Anthony. *DJ (WDAS)*: Demo Cates. *DJ (KPST)*: Don Stitt. *Candy*: Melanie Doane. *Couples in Woods*: Jo Lynn Burks, Caren Cole, Kevin Fox, Jill Hennessy, Liliane Stilwell, Ken Triwush. *Apollo Singers*: Sandra Caldwell, Denese Matthews, Lorraine Scott. *Musicians at Apollo*: Demo Cates, Alvin Crawford, Jerome Smith, Jr., James H., Wiggins, Jr. *Performer at Apollo*: Jerome Smith, Jr. *DJ at Apollo*: Don Stitt. *Man at Apollo*: Demo Cates.
  Act 2: Jingle Singers, WWOL: Sandra Caldwell, Denese Matthews, Lorraine Scott. *Maria Elena*: Jill Hennessy. *Murray Deutch*: Steve Steiner. *Shirley*: Caren Cole. *Maria Elena's Aunt*: Liliane Stilwell. *English DJ*: Paul McQuillan. *Photographers*: Members of the Company. *Peggy Sue*: Melanie Doane. *DJ (KRWP)*: Kurt Ziskie. *Clearlake MC*: Don Stitt. *The Big Bopper*: David Mucci. *Dion*: Paul McQuillan. *The Belmonts*: Russ Jolly, Tom Nash. *Richie Valens*: Philip Anthony. *Tommy*: Ken Triwush. *Mary Lou Sokoloff*: Caren Cole. *Jack Daw*: Steve Steiner. *The Snowbirds*: Jo Lynn Burks, Caren Cole, Melanie Doane, Jill Hennessy, Liliane Stilwell. *Band and Back-Up Singers at Clearlake*: Members of the Company.

The action covers the life of Buddy Holly with a re-creation of his last concert in Clear Lake, Iowa on 2 February 1959.

ACT 1[13]
  "Texas Rose"
    (*Music and Lyrics by* Paul Jury.)
  "Flower of My Heart"
    (*Music and Lyrics by* Paul Jury.)
  "Ready Teddy"
    (*Music and Lyrics by* John Marascolo and Robert Blackwell.)

  "That's All Right"
    (*Music and Lyrics by* Arthur Crudup.)
  "That'll Be the Day"
    (*Music and Lyrics by* Jerry Allison, Buddy Holly, Norman Petty.)
  "Blue Days, Black Nights"
    (*Music and Lyrics by* Ben Hall.)
  "Changing All These Changes"
    (*Music and Lyrics by* J. Denny.)
  "Peggy Sue"
    (*Music and Lyrics by* Jerry Allison, Buddy Holly, Norman Petty.)
  "(I'm) Looking for Someone to Love"
    (*Music and Lyrics by* Buddy Holly, Norman Petty.)
  "Mailman Bring Me No More Blues"
    (*Music and Lyrics by* Ruth Roberts, Bill Klatz, Stanley Clayton.)
  "Maybe Baby"
    (*Music and Lyrics by* Buddy Holly, Norman Petty.)
  "Everyday"
    (*Music and Lyrics by* Charles Hardin, Norman Petty.)
  "Sweet Love"
    (*Music and Lyrics by* Paul Jury and Caren Cole.)
  "You Send Me"
    (*Music and Lyrics by* Sam Cooke.)
  "Not Fade Away"
    (*Music and Lyrics by* Charles Hardin and Norman Petty.)
  "Words of Love"
    (*Music and Lyrics by* Buddy Holly.)
  "Oh Boy"
    (*Music and Lyrics by* Norman Petty, Sonny West, Bill Tilghman.)
ACT 2
  "Listen to Me"
    (*Music and Lyrics by* Charles Hardin and Norman Petty.)
  "Well All Right"
    (*Music and Lyrics by* Jerry Allison, Buddy Holly, Norman Petty, Joe Maudlin.)
  "It's So Easy to Fall in Love"
    (*Music and Lyrics by* Buddy Holly, Norman Petty.)
  "Think It Over"
    (*Music and Lyrics by* Jerry Allison, Buddy Holly, Norman Petty.)
  "True Love Ways"
    (*Music and Lyrics by* Buddy Holly, Norman Petty.)
  "Why Do Fools Fall in Love"
    (*Music and Lyrics by* Frank Lymon, Morris Levy.)
  "Chantilly Lace"
    (*Music and Lyrics by* J. P. Richardson.)
  "Peggy Sue Got Married"
    (*Music and Lyrics by* Buddy Holly.)
  "Heartbeat"
    (*Music and Lyrics by* Bob Montgomery, Norman Petty.)
  "La Bamba"
    (*Traditional, adapted by* Richie Valens.)
  "Raining in My Heart"
    (*Music and Lyrics by* Felice and Boudleaux Bryant.)
  "It Doesn't Matter Anymore"
    (*Music and Lyrics by* Paul Anka.)
  "Rave On"
    (*Music and Lyrics by* Norman Petty, Bill Tilghman, Sonny West.)
  "Johnny B. Goode"
    (*Music and Lyrics by* Chuck Berry.)

1990.16 THOSE WERE THE DAYS

An English-Yiddish Musical Revue in Two Acts. Concept and continuity by Zalmen Mlotek, Moishe Rosenfeld. (Music and lyrics by M. Warshavsky, M. Gebirtig, A. Lebedeff, Itsik Manger, W. Younin, J. Rumshinsky, Mani Lieb, Gene Raskin, Mel Tolkin, Ben Bonus, Ben Yomen, Hymie Jacobson, Chana Mlotek, Gioacchino Rossini, R. Abelson, M. Rosenfeld, Jack Yellen, Lew Pollack, Jacob Jacobs, Sholom Secunda, Sammy Cahn, Saul Chaplin, Bella Meisel, Herman Yablokoff, Nellie Cashman, Samuel Steinberg. Scenes by I. L. Peretz, Sholom Aleichem, and others. Additional material by Ernesto Lecuona, Jacques Offenbach, Miriam Makeba, Frank Loesser, Manos

---
[12]Dropped from original 1926 production, restored here for the first time.
[13]Publishers, not authors or vocalists, listed in the program.

Hadjidakis, Billy Towne, Bruce Adler, Robert Abelson, Mina Bern, Eleanor Reissa.) Directed and choreographed by Eleanor Reissa. Musical director, Zalmen Mlotek. Costumes by Gail Cooper-Hecht. Lighting by Tom Sturge. Sound by Jim Badrak, Alan Gregorie. Produced by Moe Septee in association with Victor H. Potamkin, Zalmen Mlotek, Moishe Rosenfeld. Opened 7 November 1990 at the Edison Theatre and closed 24 February 1991 after 126 performances.

CAST: BRUCE ADLER, MINA BERN, ELEANOR REISSA, ROBERT ABELSON, LORI WILNER, The Golden Land Klezmer Orchestra.

Act 1: The Shtetl.

Act 2: The Music Hall.

ACT 1
Prologue—Nigunim (melodies)
Company
"Lomir Loybn" (Let Us Praise)(folksong)
"Sha Shtil" (The Rabbi's Coming)(folksong)
"Oyfn Pripetshik" (At the Fireplace)
B. Adler
(*Music and Lyrics by* M. Warshavsky.)
On a Moonlit Night (based on a story by I. L. Peretz)
E. Reissa, L. Wilner
"Ver Der Ershter Vet Lahkn" (Who Will Laugh First?)
E. Reissa, L. Wilner
(*Music and Lyrics by* M. Gebirtig.)
"Motele"
R. Abelson, E. Reissa
(*Music and Lyrics by* M. Gebirtig.)
"Hudl Mitn Shtrudl" (Hudl with the Shtrudl)
B. Adler
(*Music and Lyrics by* A. Lebedeff.)
Kasrilevke Restoran (A Restaurant in Kasrilevke)
B. Adler, R. Abelson, M. Bern
(Based on a story by Sholom Aleichem)
"Di Dinst" (The Maid)(folksong)
E. Reissa
Shalakh-Mones (Gifts for Purim)
E. Reissa, L. Wilner
(Based on a story by Sholom Aleichem)
"Yosl Ber"
B. Adler, L. Wilner, E. Reissa
(*Music*, Folk-melody. *Lyrics by* Itsik Manger.)
"Halevay Volt Ikh Singl Geven" (I Wish I Were Single Again)
R. Abelson, M. Bern
(American folksong adapted by W. Younin.)
"Shloymele-Malkele"
L. Wilner, B. Adler
(Music by J. Rumshinsky.)
"Mamenyu Tayere" (Dear Mama)
L. Wilner, M. Bern
(*Music*, Folk-melody. *Lyrics by* Mani Leib, from the repertoire of Menashe Oppenheim.)
"Nokhumke, Mayn Zun" (Nochum, My Son)(folksong)
R. Abelson, B. Adler
"Saposhkelekh" (The Boots)
E. Reissa
(*Folksong*, from the research of Michael Alpert.)
"The Wedding"
Company
"Khosn-Kale mazl-Tov" (Congratulations to the Bride and Groom) (folksong)
"Di Rod" (The Circle)
(*Music and Lyrics by* M. Warshavsky.)
"Der Ayznban" (The Train) (folksong)
"Yoshke Fort Avek" (Yoshke's Going Away) (folksong)
"Mayn Alte Heym"
(from the "Forbidden Songs" of Soviet Jews as recorded by David Eshet)
ACT 2
"Those Were the Days"
E. Reissa, R. Abelson
(*Music and Lyrics by* Gene Raskin.)

Shpil Gitar (Play Guitar)
L. Wilner
"The Palace of the Czar"
B. Adler
(*Music and Lyrics by* Mel Tonkin.)
"Shabes, Shabes, Shabes" (Welcoming the Sabbath)
M. Bern
(*Music by* Ben Yomen. *Lyrics by* Ben Bonus.)
Chelm
Company
"Litvak/Galitsyaner"
B. Adler, E. Reissa
(*Music and Lyrics by* Hymie Jacobson.)
Di Mame (The Mother)
M. Bern
"Yiddish International Radio Hour"
Company
(*Yiddish Lyrics by* Chana Mlotek.)
"Figaro's Aria" (from The Barber of Seville)
R. Abelson
(*Music by* Giaocchino Rossini. *Yiddish Lyrics by* Ron Abelson, Moishe Rosenfeld.)
"My Yiddishe Mame"
E. Reissa
(*Music by* Lew Pollack. *Lyrics by* Jack Yellen.)
"Hootsatsa"
B. Adler
(Based on a song by Fishl Kanapoff.)
"Bei Mir Bistu Schoen" (To Me, You're Beautiful)
E. Reissa, L. Wilner, B. Adler
(*Music by* Sholom Secunda. *Yiddish Lyrics by* Jacob Jacobs. *English Adaptation by* Sammy Cahn, Saul Chaplin.)
"In an Orem Shtibele" (In a Poor Little House)(folksong)
M. Bern
"A Khanzndl Oyf Shabes" (A Cantor for the Sabbath)(folksong)
R. Abelson
"Papirosn" (Cigarettes)
L. Wilner
(*Music and Lyrics by* Bella Meisel, Herman Yablokoff.)
"Yosl, Yosl"
E. Reissa
(*Music by* Samuel Steinberg. *Lyrics by* Nellie Cashman.)
"Rumania, Rumania"
B. Adler
(*Music and Lyrics by* A. Lebedeff, Sholom Secunda.)
"Those Were the Days" (Finale)
Company

SHOGUN: THE MUSICAL

1990.17

A Musical in Two Acts. Book and lyrics by John Driver. Based on the novel "Shogun" by James Clavell. Music by Paul Chihara. Directed and choreographed by Michael Smuin. Scenery designed by Loren Sherman. Costumes designed by Patricia Zipprodt. Lighting designed by Natasha Katz. Sound by Tony Meola. Orchestrations by David Cullen, Steven Margoshes. Musical director, Edward G. Robinson. Fight instructor, Masahiro Kunii. Co-choreographer, Kirk Peterson. Assistant director, J. Steven White. Production supervision, Jeremiah J. Harris. Co-producers, Hiroshi Sugawara, Lloyd Phillips. Produced by James Clavell, Joseph Harris, Haruki Kadokawa. Opened 20 November 1990 at the Marquis Theater and closed 20 January 1991 after 72 performances.

CAST (in order of appearance): *John Blackthorne*an English sea captain of the *Erasmus*: PHILIP CASNOFF. *The Crew of the Erasmus (3):* Roper: Ron Navarre. *Pieterzoon:* Lee Lobenhofer. *Sonk:* Terry Lehmkuhl. *Father Alvito*, a Portuguese priest: John Herrera. *Lord Buntaro*, Daimyo of Anjiro Province, married to Lady Mariko: Joseph Foronda. *Omi*, a Samurai in love with Kiku: Eric Chan. *A Captured Samurai:* Tito Abeleda. *Gyoko*, Madam of the Tea House, owner of Kiku's contract: Freda Foh Shen. *Kiku*, courtesan of the first class: JoAnn M. Hunter. *First Samurai Guard:* Darren Lee. *Second Samurai Guard:* Marc Oka. *Third Samurai Guard:* Owen Johnston. *Lord Toranaga*, Overlord of Central Province, second most powerful Daimyo in Japan, member of Council of Regents: FRANCIS RUIVIVAR. *Sazuko*, Toranaga's youngest consort: Jenny Woo. *Osagi*, son of Lord Toranaga: Jason Ma. *Lady Mariko* educated by the Jesuits, married to Lord Buntaro: JUNE ANGELA. *Captain General Ferriera,* Portuguese Captain of the Black Ship: Lee Lobenhofer. *The Courtier of Osaka*: Darren Lee. *Catholic Daimyos*: Cholsu Kim, Marc Oka, Kenji Nakao. *Lord Ishido*, the most powerful Daimyo in Japan: Alan Muraoka. *A Ninja*: Andrew Pacho. *Fujiko*, widow of Osagi, consort to Blackthorne: Leslie Ishii. *Ishido's Head Samurai*: Tito Abeleda. *Osaka Guards*: Kenji Nakao, Andrew Pacho. *Ishido's General*, Challenger to Omi at river crossing: Jason Ma. *Chimmoko*, maid to Lady Mariko: Kiki Moritsugu. *An Acolyte*: Jason Ma. *Slatterns of the Hovel*: Tina Horii, Linda Igarashi, Chi-En Telemaque. *The Red Guards of Osaka Castle*: Marc Oka, Alan Ariano. *Ninja Attackers*: Cheri Nakamura, Andrew Pacho, Darren Lee, Owen Johnston, Tito Abeleda, Jason Ma, Terry Lehmkuhl, Cholsu Kim, Ron Navarre. *Taiko Drummers*: Jason Ma, Marc Oka, Leslie Ishii, Lee Lobenhofer.

Swings and Other Dancers: Ted Hewlett, Herman Sebek, Victoria Lee, Lyd-Lyd Gaston.

The action takes place in Japan between April and July 1600.

ACT 1

"Karma"
  Orchestra
"Night of Screams"
  P. Casnoff, Sailor, Ensemble
"This Is Samurai"
  Samurai
"How Nice to See You"
  F. Ruivivar, J. Foronda, J. Herrera, J. Angela
"Impossible Eyes"
  J. Angela, P. Casnoff
"He Let Me Live"
  J. Angela
"Honto"
  P. Casnoff
"Assassination"
  J. Herrera, L. Lobenhofer
"Shogun"
  Hostages
"Royal Blood"
  A. Muraoka, F. Ruivivar
"An Island"
  F. Ruivivar
"No Word for Love"
  J. Angela
"Mad Rum Below/Escape"
  P. Casnoff, Ensemble
"Karma" (reprise)
  F. Ruivivar, Ensemble
"Born to Be Together"
  J. Angela, P. Casnoff

ACT 2

"Fireflies"
  Ensemble, J. Angela, P. Casnoff
"Sail Home"
  P. Casnoff
"Rum Below"
  P. Casnoff, F. Ruivivar, Ensemble
"Pillowing"
  F. Foh Shen, J. M. Hunter, Ladies
"Born to Be Together" (reprise)
  J. Angela, P. Casnoff
"No Man"
  P. Casnoff
"Cha-No-Yu"
  J. Angela, J. Foronda
"Absolution"
  J. Herrera, J. Ma, Ensemble, J. Angela
"Poetry Competition"
  A. Muraoka, J. Woo, J. Angela
"Death Walk"
  Ensemble, P. Casnoff
"One Candle"
  J. Angela, P. Casnoff
"Ninja Raid"
  Orchestra

"One Candle" (reprise)
  J. Angela, P. Casnoff
"Winter Battle"
  Orchestra
"Resolutions"
  F. Ruivivar, Ensemble
"Trio"
  F. Ruivivar, P. Casnoff, J. Angela
Finale
  Ensemble

1990.18 FIDDLER ON THE ROOF

A Revival of the Musical in Two Acts, Two Prologues, an Epilogue and 17 Scenes[14]. Book by Joseph Stein. Based on stories by Sholom Aleichem's stories (Tevye's Daughters) by special permission of Arnold Perl. Music by Jerry Bock. Lyrics by Sheldon Harnick. Original production directed and choreographed by Jerome Robbins. Direction reproduced by Ruth Mitchell. Choreography reproduced by Sammy Dallas Bayes. Scenery by Boris Aronson. Costumes based on original designs by Patricia Zipprodt. Lighting by Ken Billington. Sound by Peter Fitzgerald. Orchestrations by Don Walker. Musical direction, vocal arrangements by Milton Greene. Associate producer, Alecia Parker. Produced by Barry and Fran Weissler and Pace Theatrical Group, in association with C. Itoh & Co., Ltd./Tokyo Broadcasting System International, Inc., A. Deshe (Pashanel). Opened 18 November 1990 at the Gershwin Theatre and closed 16 June 1991 after 241 performances.

CAST (in order of appearance): *Tevye*, the Dairyman: TOPOL. *Golde*, his wife: MARCIA LEWIS. *Their Three Daughters*: *Tzeitel*: Sharon Lawrence. *Hodel*: Tia Riebling. *Chava*: Jennifer Prescott. *Shprintze*: Kathy St. George. *Beilke*: Judy Dodd. *Motel*, the Tailor: Jack Kenny. *Perchik*, the Student: Gary Schwartz. *Fyedka*: Ron Bohmer. *Lazar Wolf*, the Butcher: Mark Zeller. *Mordcha*, the Innkeeper: David Masters. *Nachum*, the Beggar: Michael J. Farina. *Yente*, the Matchmaker: RUTH JAROSLOW. *Rabbi*: Jerry Matz. *Avram*, the Bookseller: Jerry Jarrett. *Constable*: Mike O'Carroll. *Mendel*, the Rabbi's son: David Pevsner. *The Fiddler*: Stephen Wright. *Grandma Tzeitel*: Kathy St. George. *Fruma-Sarah*: Jeri Sager. *Shandel*, Motel's Mother: Panchali Null. *Bottle Dancers*: Kenneth M. Daigle, David Enriquez, Craig Gahnz, Keith Keen. *Russian Dancers*: Brian Arsenault, Michael Berresse, Brian Henry.

Villagers: Brian Arsenault, Michael Berresse, Joanne Borts, Stacey Lynn Brass, Gerry Burkhardt, Lisa Cartmell, Kenneth M. Daigle, David Enriquez, Craig Gahnz, Brian Henry, Todd Heughens, Keith Keen, Brad Little, Panchali Null, Marty Ross, Jeri Sager, Beth Thompson, Jeffrey Wilkins, Lou Williford. *Alternate Villagers*: James Horvath, Lori Ada Jaroslow, Laura Patinkin, Gary John La Rosa. *Swings*: Chris Jamison, Newton Cole.

AN EVENING WITH HARRY CONNICK JR. AND HIS ORCHESTRA
1990.19

A One Man Musical Revue in Two Acts. Directed by Joe Layton. Conductor, Marc Shaiman. Musical director, Benjamin Jonah Wolfe. Scenery design by John Falabella. Lighting designer, Marilyn Lowey. Wardrobe by Alexander Julian. Executive producer, Ann Marie Wilkins. Presented by Radio City Music Hall Productions (Ed Micone, Scott Sanders, producers) and James L. Nederlander. Opened 23 November 1990 at the Lunt-Fontanne Theatre and closed 8 December 1990 after 13 performances[15].

CAST: HARRY CONNICK JR.
Musicians: Marc Shaiman (conductor), Benjamin Jonah Wolfe (bass), Shannon Powell (drums), Leroy Jones (trumpet), Jerry Weldon (tenor saxophone), Lucien Barbarin (trombone), Russell Malone (guitar), Craig Klein (trombone), Mark Mullins (trombone), Jeremy Davenport (trumpet), Roger Ingram (trumpet), Dan Miller (trumpet), Ned Goold (tenor saxophone), Brad Leali (alto saxophone), William Campbell (alto saxophone), Dave Schumacher (baritone saxophone).

---

[14]Originally produced in New York 22 September 1964 at the Imperial Theatre for 3242 performances. For Synopsis of Scenes and Musical Numbers, see original 1964 production. "Chavaleh" appears in the program for this revival.
[15]Musical numbers not listed in program.

1990.20

PETER PAN

A Revival of the Musical in Three Acts, Seven Scenes[16]. Book by James M. Barrie[17]. Music by Mark Charlap. Lyrics by Carolyn Leigh. Additional music by Jule Styne. Additional lyrics by Betty Comden and Adolph Green. Original production conceived, directed and choreographed by Jerome Robbins. Directed by Fran Soeder. Choreographed by Marilyn Magness. Neverland sets by James Leonard Joy; (original scenery by The Edgewood Organization). Costumes designed by Mariann Verheyen. Lighting designed by Natasha Katz. Musical supervision and direction by Kevin Farrell. New orchestrations by Brian W. Tidwell. Additional (music) arrangements by M. Michael Fauss, Kevin Farrell. Sound designed by Peter Fitzgerald. Flying by Foy. A McCoy-Rigby Entertainment Production. Produced by James M. Nederlander, Arthur Rubin, Thomas P. McCoy, Keith Stava, P.P. Investments, Jon B. Platt. Opened 13 December 1990 at the Lunt-Fontanne Theatre and closed 20 January 1991 after 45 performances.

CAST (in order of appearance): *Wendy Darling*: CINDY ROBINSON. *John Darling*: BRITT WEST. *Michael Darling*: CHAD HUTCHISON. *Liza*: Anne McVey. *Nana*: Bill Bateman. *Mrs. Darling*: LAUREN THOMPSON. *Mr. Darling*: STEPHEN HANAN. *Peter Pan*: CATHY RIGBY. *Never Bear*: Adam Ehrenworth. *Curly*: Alon Williams. *First Twin*: Janet Kay Higgins. *Second Twin*: Courtney Wyn. *Slightly*: Christopher Ayres. *Tootles*: Julian Brightman. *Mr. Smee*: DON POTTER. *Cecco*: Calvin Smith. *Gentleman Starkey*: Carl Packard. *Noodler*: Barry Ramsey. *Bill Jukes*: Andy Ferrara. *Captain Hook*: STEPHEN HANAN. *Crocodile*: Barry Ramsey. *Tiger Lily*: HOLLY IRWIN.

Pirates and Indians: Bill Bateman, Andy Ferrara, Anne McVey, Christian Monte, Carl Packard, Barry Ramsey, Joseph Savant, Calvin Smith, Timothy Talman, David Thome, John Wilkerson.

Wendy, Grown-up: LAUREN THOMPSON. *Jane*: CINDY ROBINSON.

Act 1: The Nursery of the Darling Residence.

Act 2, Scene 1: Neverland. *Scene 2*: Cavern (Marooner's Rock). *Scene 3*: The Home Underground.

Act 3, Scene 1: The Pirate Ship *Scene 2*: The Nursery of the Darling Residence. *Scene 3*: The Nursery many years later.

ACT 1

"Tender Shepherd"
    L. Thompson, C. Robinson, B. West, C. Hutchison

"I've Got to Crow" (I Gotta Crow)
    C. Rigby

"Neverland"
    C. Rigby
    (*Music by* Jule Styne. *Lyrics by* Betty Comden and Adolph Green.

"I'm Flying"
    C. Rigby, C. Robinson, B. West, C. Hutchison

ACT 2

Scene 1

"Pirate March"
    S. Hanan, Pirates

"A Princely Scheme" (Hook's Tango)
    S. Hanan, Pirates
    (*Music by* Trude Rittman. *Lyrics by* Carolyn Leigh.

"Indians!"
    H. Irwin, Indians

"Wendy"
    C. Rigby, Boys
    (*Music by* Jule Styne. *Lyrics by* Betty Comden and Adolph Green.

"Tarantella" (Another Princely Scheme)
    S. Hanan, Pirates

Scene 2

"I Won't Grow Up"
    C. Rigby, C. Robinson, Lost Boys

Scene 3

"Ugg-aWugg"

---

[16]Originally produced in New York 20 October 1954 at the Winter Garden for 152 performances. For this production, "Neverland Waltz," "The Pow Pow Polka," "Dangerous Lady," "To the Ship," "The Battle," "Morning in Neverland" dropped from the program; the 9 Scenes of previous productions consolidated into 7 Scenes.

[17]Book adaptation uncredited.

C. Rigby, H. Irwin, C. Robinson, Boys, Indians
    (*Music by* Jule Styne. *Lyrics by* Betty Comden and Adolph Green.

"Distant Melody"
    C. Rigby
    (*Music by* Jule Styne. *Lyrics by* Betty Comden and Adolph Green.

ACT 3

Scene 1

"(Captain) Hook's Waltz"
    S. Hanan, Pirates
    (*Music by* Jule Styne. *Lyrics by* Betty Comden and Adolph Green.

"I've Got to Crow" (reprise)
    C. Rigby, Company

Scene 2

"Tender Shepherd" (reprise)
    C. Robinson, B. West, C. Hutchison

"I Won't Grow Up" (reprise)
    The Darling Family, Lost Boys

Scene 3

"Neverland" (reprise)
    C. Rigby

1991.01

MULE BONE

A Comedy with Songs in Two Acts, 2 Prologues and 3 Scenes. Play by Langston Hughes and Zora Neale Thurston. (Based on her short story "The Bone of Contention.") Prologue and epilogue by George Houston Bass. Music by Taj Mahal. (Lyrics by Langston Hughes.) Directed by Michael Schultz. Sets by Edward Burbridge. Costumes by Lewis Brown. Lighting by Allen Lee Hughes. Sound by Serge Ossorguine. Musical supervisor, Taj Mahal. Fights by Ron Van Clief. Dances staged by Dianne McIntyre. Produced by Lincoln Center Theatre (Gregory Mosher, Director; Bernard Gersten, Executive producer). Opened 14 February 1991 at the Ethel Barrymore Theatre and closed 14 April 1991 after 67 performances.

CAST (in order of appearance): *Zora*: Joy Lee. *Dave Carter*: Eric Ware. *Jim*: KENNY NEAL. *Daisy*: Akosua Busia. *Deacon Hambo*: Sonny Jim Gaines. *Old Man Brazzle*: Clebert Ford. *Lum Boger*: Paul S. Eckstein. *Lige Mosely*: Reggie Montgomery. *Robena*: Pauline Meyer. *Joe Lindsay*: Allie Woods, Jr. *Walter Thomas*: Donald Griffin. *Mayor Joe Clark*: SAMUEL E. WRIGHT. *Sister Blunt*: Ebony Jo-Ann. *Senator*: Pee Wee Love. *Teets*: Joy Lee. *Bootsie*: Vanessa Williams. *Mattie Clark*: Myra Taylor. *Luther*: Bron Wright. *Matilda*: Shareen Powlett. *Willie Lewis*: Robert Earl Jones. *Tony Taylor*: Mansoor Najeeullah. *Sister Taylor*: Marilyn Coleman. *Reverend Simms*: Leonard Jackson. *Jesse, Julius*: T. J. Jones. *Katie Pitts*: Theresa Merritt. *Sister Lewis*: Frances Foster. *Sister Thomas*: Fanni Green. *Sister Hambo*: Edwina Lewis. *Sister Lindsay*: Peggy Pettitt. *Reverend Singletary*: Arthur French.

The action takes place in Eatonville, Florida, on Saturday, 8 November during the 1920's.

Prologue: Just outside of Eatonville.

Act 1: Joe Clark's General Store.

Prologue: A barn. Dave Carter's house. Saturday night.

Act 2, Scene 1: Macedonia Baptist Church. The following Monday. *Scene 2*: A high stretch of railroad tracks a mile out of town. The same day. late afternoon.

ACT 1

"Jubilee" (Opening Theme)

"Graveyard Mule" (Hambone Rhyme)
    (*Lyrics by* George Houston Bass.)

"Me and the Mule"

"Song for a Banjo Dance"

"But I Rode Some"

"Hey Hey Blues"

"Shake That Thing"
    (*Music by* "Poppa" Charlie Jackson.)

ACT 2

"Crossing" (Lonely Day)

"Bound No'th Blues"

Finale

PENN & TELLER:
1991.02 THE REFRIGERATOR TOUR

An Evening of Magic and Mayhem in Two Acts. (Conceived by Penn & Teller. Original music by Gary Stockdale.) Set by John Lee Beatty. Lighting by Dennis Parichy. Sound by T. Richard Fitzgerald, Craig Van Tassell. Director of covert activities, Robert P. Libbon. Director of internal affairs, Mike Wills. Associate producer, Marc Routh. Produced by Richard Frankel, Thomas Viertel and Steven Baruch. Opened 3 April 1991 at the Eugene O'Neill Theatre and closed 29 June 1991 after 103 performances[18].

CAST: PENN JILLETTE, TELLER, Carol Jenkins.

ACT 1

Amana Damocles

A Card Trick

"Liftoff to Love/Ripoff of Love"
(*Written by* Gary Stockdale, Penn Jillette and Teller. *Performed by* Gary Stockdale.)

Two Modern Fakir Tricks

Quotation of the Day

Two Houdini Tricks

ACT 2

Mofo, the Psychic Gorilla

By Buddha, This Duck Is Immortal!

Cuffed to a Creep

"Burnin' Luv"
(*Written by* Gary Stockdale.)

Shadows

King of Animal Traps

1991.03 MISS SAIGON

A Musical in Two Acts, 6 Scenes. Book by Alain Boublil, Claude-Michel Schönberg. Additional material by Richard Maltby, Jr. Music by Claude-Michel Schönberg. Lyrics by Richard Maltby, Jr., Alain Boublil, adapted from original French lyrics by Alain Boublil. Directed by Nicholas Hytner. Musical staging by Bob Avian. Production (settings) designed by John Napier. Costumes by Andreane Neofitou, Suzy Benzinger. Lighting by David Hersey. Sound by Andrew Bruce. Orchestrations by William D. Brohn. Musical supervision, David Caddick, Robert Billig. Conductor, Robert Billig. Associate director, Mitchell Lemsky. Associate producer, Martin McCallum. Executive producers, Mitchell Lemsky, Richard Jay-Alexander. Produced by Cameron Mackintosh. Opened 11 April 1991 at the Broadway Theatre and closed 28 January 2001 after 4125 performances.

CAST (in order of appearance): *Saigon, 1975: The Engineer:* JONATHAN PRYCE. *Kim:* LEA SALONGA, KAM CHENG (alt.). *Gigi:* Marina Chapa. *Mimi:* Sala Iwamatsu. *Yvette:* Imelda de los Reyes. *Yvonne:* JoAnn M. Hunter. *Bar Girls:* Raquel C. Brown, Annette Calud, Mirla Criste, Jade Stice, Melanie Mariko Tojio. *Chris:* WILLY FALK. *John:* HINTON BATTLE. *Marines:* Paul Dobie, Michael Gruber, Leonard Joseph, Paul Matsumoto, Sean McDermott, Thomas James O'Leary, Gordon Owens, Christopher Pecaro, Matthew Pedersen, Kris Phillips, W. Ellis Porter, Alton F. White, Bruce Winant. *Barmen:* Zar Acayan, Alan Ariano, Jason Ma. *Vietnamese Customers:* Tony C. Avanti, Eric Chan, Francis J. Cruz, Darren Lee, Ray Santos, Nephi Jay Wimmer. *Thuy:* BARRY BERNAL. *Embassy Workers, Inhabitants of Saigon, Vendors:* Company.
Ho Chi Minh City, April 1978: Ellen: LIZ CALLAWAY. *Tam:* Brian R. Baldomero or Philip Lyle Kong. *Guards:* Tony C. Avanti, Francis J. Cruz. *Assistant Commissar:* Eric Chan. *Dragon Acrobats:* Darren Lee, Michael Gruber, Nephi Jay Wimmer. *Soldiers:* Zar Acayan, Alan Ariano, Jason Ma, Paul Matsumoto, Ray Santos, Nephi Jay Wimmer. *Citizens of Ho Chi Minh City, Refugees:* Company.
U.S.A., September 1978: Conference Delegates: Company.
Bangkok, October 1978: Hustlers: Zar Acayan, Jason Ma, Paul Matsumoto, Ray Santos, Nephi Jay Wimmer. *Owner of the Moulin Rouge:* Francis J. Cruz. *Inhabitants of Bangkok, Bar Girls, Vendors, Tourists:* Company.

Saigon, April 1975: Schultz: Thomas James O'Leary. *Antoine:* Alton F. White. *Reeves:* Bruce Winant. *Gibbons:* Paul Dobie. *Troy:* Leonard Joseph. *Nolen:* Gordon Owens. *Huston:* Matthew Pedersen. *Frye:* Sean McDermott. *Marines, Vietnamese Civilians:* Company.
Bangkok, October 1978: Inhabitants of Bangkok, Customers of the Moulin Rouge: Company.
Swings: Sylvia Dohi, Henry Menendez, Todd Zamarripa.

Act 1, Scene 1: Saigon, 1975. *Scene 2:* Ho Chi Minh City (formerly Saigon), April 1978.

Act 2, Scene 1: U.S.A., September 1978. *Scene 2:* Bangkok, October 1978. *Scene 3:* Saigon, April 1975. *Scene 4:* Bangkok, October 1978.

ACT 1
Scene 1
"The Heat Is On in Saigon"
    J. Pryce, Girls, Marines, Company
"The Movie in My Mind"
    M. Chapa, L. Salonga, Girls
"The Transaction"
    H. Battle, J. Pryce, W. Falk, Company
"Why God Why?"
    W. Falk
"Sun and Moon"
    L. Salonga, W. Falk
"The Telephone"
    H. Battle, W. Falk, J. Pryce
"The Ceremony"
    L. Salonga, W. Falk, Girls
"The Last Night of the World"
    L. Salonga, W. Falk
Scene 2
"The Morning of the Dragon"
    Company, B. K. Bernal, J. Pryce
"I Still Believe"
    L. Salonga, L. Callaway
"Back in Town"
    L. Salonga, J. Pryce, B. K. Bernal
"You Will Not Touch Him"
    L. Salonga, B. K. Bernal
"If You Want to Die in Bed"
    J. Pryce
"I'd Give My Life for You"
    L. Salonga, Company

ACT 2
Scene 1
"Bui-Doi"
    H. Battle, Company
Scene 2
"What a Waste"
    J. Pryce, Company
"Please"
    H. Battle, L. Salonga
Scene 3
"The Guilt Inside Your Head" (The Fall of Saigon, April 1975)
    B. K. Bernal, L. Salonga, W. Falk, H. Battle, Company
Scene 4
"Sun and Moon" (reprise)
    L. Salonga
"Room 317"
    L. Callaway, L. Salonga
"Now That I've Seen Her"
    L. Callaway
"The Confrontation"
    L. Callaway, W. Falk, H. Battle
"The American Dream"
    J. Pryce, Company
"Little God of My Heart"
    L. Salonga, B. R. Baldomero

---

[18]Reopened Off-Broadway as PENN & TELLER ROT IN HELL 30 July 1991 at the John Houseman Theatre closing 19 January 1992 after 200 performances.

LIZA MINNELLI: STEPPING OUT AT RADIO CITY

1991.04

A Musical Revue in Two Acts. Special musical material, John Kander and Fred Ebb. Directed by Fred Ebb. Musial director, Bill LaVorgna. Choreography by Susan Stroman; additional choreography by Lisa Mordente. Musical supervision, Marvin Laird, Glen Roven. Vocal arranger, Billy Stritch. Scenic designer, Michael J. Hotopp. Costume designer, Julie Weiss. Lighting designer, David Agress. Sound designer, Hank Catteneo. Musical arrangements by Marvin Laird, Artie Schreck, Mike Abene, Ralph Burns, Torrie Zito, Glen Roven, Russell Kassoff, Billy Stritch, Peter Howard, Pet Shop Boys. Executive producers, Eliot Weisman, Premiere Artists Services, Inc. Produced by Radio City Music Hall Productions (Scott Sanders, Ed Micone). Opened 23 April 1991 at the Radio City Music Hall and closed 12 May 1991 after 15 performances; returned 24 January 1992 to Radio City Music Hall and closed 1 February 1992 after 7 additional performances. Total: 22 performances.

CAST: LIZA MINNELLI.

Ensemble (in alphabetical order): Mamie Duncan-Gibbs, Sherry Dundish, Roxanne Dundish, Ruth Gotschall, Joanne McHugh, Joanna Noble, Jeanette Palmer (swing), Irma Rogers, Jessica Sheridan, Dorothy Stanley, Terri White, Monica Wemitt, Tara Young.

Act 1: Liza in Concert.

Act 2: Liza and Friends.

ACT 1

"The Nearness of You"
   (*Music by* Hoagy Carmichael. *Lyrics by* Ned Washington.)
"Teach Me Tonight"
   (*Music by* Gene de Paul. *Lyrics by* Sammy Cahn.)
"Who Would Have Dreamed?"
"Cottage for Sale"
   (*Music by* Willard Robison. *Lyrics by* Larry Conley.)
"Some People" (from *GYPSY*)
   (*Music by* Jule Styne. *Lyrics by* Stephen Sondheim.)
"Sara Lee"
   (*Music by* John Kander. *Lyrics by* Fred Ebb.)
"Sorry I Asked"
   (*Music by* John Kander. *Lyrics by* Fred Ebb.)
"Similar Features"
"Le Temps"
"Quiet Love"
"What Makes a Man a Man"
"Sailor Boy"
"Live Alone and Like It"
   (*Music and Lyrics by* Stephen Sondheim.)
"Seeing Things" (from *THE HAPPY TIME*)
   (*Music by* John Kander. *Lyrics by* Fred Ebb.)
Vincent Minnelli Tribute
"Stepping Out" (from *STEPPING OUT*, film)
   (*Music by* John Kander. *Lyrics by* Fred Ebb.)
"Losing My Mind" (from *FOLLIES*)
   (*Music and Lyrics by* Stephen Sondheim.)
"(But) The World Goes Round" (from *NEW YORK, NEW YORK* film)
   (*Music by* John Kander. *Lyrics by* Fred Ebb.)
"All By Myself"
   (*Music and Lyrics by* Irving Berlin.)

ACT 2

"Hey Liza It's Me"
   (*Music by* John Kander. *Lyrics by* Fred Ebb.)
Men Medley with the Demon Divas:
   "Natural Man"
"The Man I Love"
   (*Music by* George Gershwin. *Lyrics by* Ira Gershwin.)
"Not for the Life of Me"
"Drum Dance"
"Old Friend"

"My Buddy"
Bob Fosse Tribute
Medley:
   "Pack Up Your Troubles (in Your Old Kit Bag)"
      (*Music by* Felix Powell. *Lyrics by* George Asaf.)
   "It's a Long Way To Tipperary"
      (*Music and Lyrics by* Jack Judge and Harry M. Williams.)
   "Imagine"
      (*Music and Lyrics by* John Lennon.)
Group Stepping Out
"New York, New York" (from *NEW YORK, NEW YORK* film)
   (*Music by* John Kander. *Lyrics by* Fred Ebb.)

THE SECRET GARDEN

1991.05

A Musical in Two Acts, a Prologue and 18 Scenes. Book and lyrics by Marsha Norman. Based on the novel of the same name by Frances Hodgson Burnett. Music by Lucy Simon. Directed by Susan H. Schulman. Choreography by Michael Lichtefeld. Scenery by Heidi Landesman. Costumes by Theoni V. Aldredge. Lighting by Tharon Musser. Sound by Otts Munderloh. Orchestrations by William D. Brohn. Musical direction, vocal arrangements by Michael Kosarin. Dance arrangements by Jeanine Levenson. Associate producers, Greg C. Mosher, Rhoda Mayerson, Playhouse Square Center (Lawrence J. Wilker, President), Dorothy and Wendell Cherry, Margo Lion, 126 Second Avenue Corporation (Hal Luftig, Alan D. Perry). Produced by Heidi Landesman, Rick Steiner, Frederic H. Mayerson, Elizabeth Williams, Jujamcyn Theatres/TV Asahi, Dodger Productions (Michael David, Doug Johnson, Rocco Landesman, Des McAnuff, Edward Strong, Sherman Warner). Opened 25 April 1991 at the St. James Theatre and closed 3 January 1993 after 706 performances.

CAST: *Lily*: REBECCA LUKER. *Mary Lennox*: DAISY EAGAN, Kimberly Mahon (alt.)

In Colonial India, 1906: Fakir: Peter Marinos. *Ayah*: Patricia Phillips. *Rose*, Mary's mother: Kay Walbye. *Captain Albert Lennox*, Mary's father: Michael DeVries. *Lieutenant Peter Wright*: Drew Taylor. *Lieutenant Ian Shaw*: Paul Jackel. *Major Holmes*: Peter Samuel. *Claire*, his wife: Rebecca Judd. *Alice*, Rose's friend: Nancy Johnston.

At Misselthwaite Manor, North Yorkshire, England, 1906: Archibald Craven, Mary's uncle: MANDY PATINKIN. *Dr. Neville Craven*, his brother: ROBERT WESTENBERG. *Mrs. Medlock*, the housekeeper: BARBARA ROSENBLAT. *Martha*, a chambermaid: ALISON FRASER. *Dickon*, her brother: JOHN CAMERON MITCHELL. *Ben*, the gardener: TOM TONER. *Colin*: JOHN BABCOCK. *Jane*: Teresa De Zarn. *William*: Frank DiPasquale. *Betsy*: Betsy Friday. *Timothy*: Alec Timerman. *Mrs. Winthrop*: Nancy Johnston.

Swings: Kevin Ligon, Bill Nolte, Jane Seaman, Jennifer Smith.

The action takes place in 1906.

Opening (Prologue): India; The Library at Misselthwaite Manor; A Train Platform in Yorkshire; The Door to Misselthwaite Manor; Mary's Room; The Gallery.

Act 1, Scene 1: Mary's Sitting Room. *Scene 2*: The Ballroom. *Scene 3*: In the Maze/The Greenhouse; The Edge of the Moor. *Scene 4*: Archibald's Library. *Scene 5*: The Gallery. *Scene 6*: The Hallway. *Scene 7*: Colin's Room. *Scene 8*: On the Grounds/The Door to the Garden.

Act 2, Scene 1: The Tea Party Dream/The Other Side of the Door. *Scene 2*: Archibald's Dressing Room. *Scene 3*: Colin's Room. *Scene 4*: The Greenhouse. *Scene 5*: Colin's Room. *Scene 6*: In the Maze/The Garden. *Scene 7*: The Library. *Scene 8*:Mary's Room/Paris. *Scene 9*: Archibald's Rooms in Paris. *Scene 10*: The Garden.

ACT 1[19]
Opening
   "Opening Dream"
      R. Luker, P. Marinos, D. Eagan, Company
   "There's a Girl"
      Company
   "House Upon the Hill"
      Company

---

[19]Added to Act 1, beginning of Scene 6 for national tour:
   "I Heard Someone Crying" (reprise)
      [Mary Lennox], Company

"I Heard Someone Crying"
    D. Eagan, M. Patinkin, R. Luker, Company
Scene 1
  "A Fine White Horse"
    A. Fraser
Scene 2
  "A Girl in the Valley"
    R. Luker, M. Patinkin, Dancers
Scene 3
  "It's a Maze"
    T. Toner, D. Eagan, J. C. Mitchell
  "Winter's on the Wing"
    J. C. Mitchell
  "Show Me the Key"
    D. Eagan, J. C. Mitchell
Scene 4
  "A Bit of Earth"
    M. Patinkin
Scene 5
  "Storm I"
    Company
  "Lily's Eyes"
    M. Patinkin, R. Westenberg
Scene 6
  "Storm II"
    D. Eagan, Company
Scene 7
  "Round-Shouldered Man"
    J. Babcock
Scene 8
  "Final Storm"
    Company

ACT 2
Scene 1
  "The Girl I Meant to Be"
    D. Eagan, Company
Scene 2
  "Quartet"
    M. Patinkin, R. Westenberg, K. Walbye, R. Luker
Scene 3
  "Race You to the Top of the Morning"
    M. Patinkin
Scene 4
  "Wick"
    J. C. Mitchell, D. Eagan
Scene 5
  "Come to My Garden"
    R. Luker, J. Babcock
Scene 6
  "Come Spirit, Come Charm"
    D. Eagan, A. Fraser, J. C. Mitchell, P. Marinos, P. Phillips, R. Luker, Company
  "A Bit of Earth" (reprise)
    R. Luker, K. Walbye, M. DeVries
Scene 7
  "Disappear"
    R. Westenberg
Scene 8
  "Hold On"
    A. Fraser
  "Letter Song"
    D. Eagan, A. Fraser
Scene 9
  "Where in the World"
    M. Patinkin
  "How Could I Ever Know?"
    R. Luker, M. Patinkin
Scene 10
  Finale
    Company

1991.06   GYPSY

A Return Engagement of the Revival of the Musical Fable in Two Acts[20]. Book by Arthur Laurents. Suggested by the memoirs (of the same name) by Gypsy Rose Lee. Directed by Arthur Laurents. Original choreography of Jerome Robbins, reproduced by Bonnie Walker. Music by Jule Styne. Lyrics by Stephen Sondheim. Scenery design by Kenneth Foy. Costume design by Theoni V. Aldredge. Lighting design by Natasha Katz. Sound by Peter Fitzgerald. Musical direction by Michael Rafter. Orchestrations by Sid Ramin with Robert Ginzler. Dance music arranged by John Kander. Produced by Barry and Fran Weissler, Kathy Levin, Barry Brown, in association with Tokyo Broadcasting System International and Pace Theatrical Group. Opened 28 April 1991 at the Minskoff Theater and closed 28 July 1991 after 105 performances. Total including first engagement: 581 performances.

CAST (in order of appearance): *Uncle Jocko*: Stan Rubin. *George*: Victor Raider-Wexler. *Clarence (and His Classic Clarinet)*: Bobby John Carter. *Balloon Girl*: Jeana Haege. *Baby Louise*: Kristen Mahon. *Baby June*: Susan Cremin. *Rose*: TYNE DALY. *Pop*: Ronn Carroll. *Newsboys*: Bobby John Carter, Thomas Fox, Danny Cistone, Tony Yazbeck. *Weber*: Richard Levine. *Herbie*: JONATHAN HADARY. *Louise*: CRISTA MOORE. *June*: TRACY VENNER. *Tulsa*: ROBERT LAMBERT. *Yonkers*: Bruce Moore. *L.A.*: Craig Waletzko. *Kansas*: Paul Geraci. *Flagstaff*: Kevin Petitto. *St. Paul*: Cory English. *The Cow*: Crista Moore, Barbara Folts, Robin Robinson, Cory English, Kevin Petitto. *Kringelein*: Stan Rubin. *Mr. Goldstone*: Victor Raider-Wexler. *Miss Cratchitt*: Barbara Erwin. *Hollywood Blondes (5)*: Teri Furr, Barbara Folts, Nancy Melius, Michele Pigliavento, Robin Robinson. *Agnes*: Lori Ann Mahl. *Pastey*: Jeff Brooks. *Tessie Tura*: BARBARA ERWIN. *Mazeppa*: JANA ROBBINS. *Electra*: ANNA McNEELY. *Cigar*: Ronn Carroll. *Maid*: Ginger Prince. *Phil*: Richard Levine. *Bougeron-Couchon*: Jeff Brooks. *Swings*: Laurie Crochet, George Smyros.

THE WILL ROGERS FOLLIES:
1991.07   A Life in Revue

A Musical in Two Acts, a Prelude and 12 Scenes. Book by Peter Stone. Inspired by the words of Will and Betty Rogers. Music by Cy Coleman. Lyrics by Betty Comden and Adolph Green. Directed and choreographed by Tommy Tune. Settings design by Tony Walton. Costume design by Willa Kim. Lighting design by Jules Fisher. Sound design by Peter Fitzgerald. Projection design by Wendall K. Harrington. Orchestrations by Billy Byers. Musical direction by Eric Stern. Associate director, Phillip Oesterman. Associate choreographer, Jeff Calhoun. Produced by Pierre Cossette, Martin Richards, Sam Crothers, James M. Nederlander, Stewart F. Lane, Max Weitzenhoffer, in association with Japan Satellite Broadcasting. Opened 1 May 1991 at the Palace Theatre and closed 5 September 1993 after 983 performances.

CAST (in order of appearance): *Ziegfeld's Favorite*: CADY HUFFMAN. *Will Rogers*: KEITH CARRADINE. *Unicyclist*: Vince Bruce. *Wiley Post*: PAUL UKENA. JR. *Clem Rogers*: DICK LATESSA. *Will's Sisters*: Roxane Barlow, Maria Calabrese, Colleen Dunn, Dana Moore, Wenda Waring, Leigh Zimmerman. *Betty Blake*: DEE HOTY. *The Wild West Show (Trainers)*: Tom and Bonnie Brackney, with B.A., Cocoa, Gigi, Rusty, Trixie, Zee. *Betty's Sisters*: Roxane Barlow, Maria Calabrese, Colleen Dunn, Dana Moore, Wenda Waring, Leigh Zimmerman. *Will Rogers, Jr.*: Rick Faugno. *Mary Rogers*: Tammy Minoff. *James Rogers*: Lance Robinson. *Freddy Rogers*: Gregory Scott Carter. *Roper*: Vince Bruce.
    The Will Rogers Wranglers: John Ganun, Troy Britton Johnson, Jerry Mitchell, Jason Opsahl. *The New Ziegfeld Girls*: Roxane Barlow, Maria Calabrese, Ganine Derleth, Rebecca Downing, Colleen Dunn, Sally Mae Dunn, Toni Georgiana, Eileen Grace, Luba Gregus, Tonia Lynn, Dana Moore, Aimee Turner, Jillana Urbina, Wendy Waring, Christina Youngman, Leigh Zimmerman. *The Voice of Mr. Ziegfeld*: Gregory Peck. *Swings*: Mary Lee DeWitt, Jack Doyle, Angie L. Schworer.

The action takes place in the Palace Theatre at the present time.

Act 1, Scene 1: The Follies. *Scene 2*: The Ranch. *Scene 3*: The Moon. *Scene 4*: The Follies. *Scene 5*: The St. Louis Exposition. *Scene 6*: Vaudeville. *Scene 7*: The Follies.

Act 2, Scene 1: The Follies. *Scene 2*: The Convention. *Scene 3*: The Hollywood Ranch. *Scene 4*: The Bare Stage. *Scene 5*: The Finale.

---

[20]Originally produced in New York 21 May 1959 at the Broadway Theatre for 702 performances; this production originally opened 16 November 1989 at the St. James Theatre for 476 performances. For Synopsis of Scenes and Musical Numbers, see original 1959 production and 1989 revival.

ACT 1
Prelude
    "Let's Go Flying"
        (Chorus)
Scene 1
    "Will-a-Mania"
        C. Huffman, Company
    "Give a Man Enough Rope"
        K. Carradine, The Will Rogers Wranglers
Scene 2
    "It's a Boy"
        D. Latessa, Will's Sisters
    "So Long Pa"
        K. Carradine
Scene 3
    "My Unknown Someone"
        D. Hoty
Scene 5
    "We're Heading for a Wedding"
        K. Carradine, D. Hoty
Scene 6
    "The Big Time"
        K. Carradine, D. Hoty, the Children
    "My Big Mistake"
        D. Hoty
Scene 7
    "The Powder Puff Ballet" (My Big Mistake)
        The New Ziegfeld Girls

"Marry Me Now"/"I Got You"
    K. Carradine, D. Hoty
Wedding Finale
    (Company)
ACT 2
Scene 1
    "Give a Man Enough Rope" (reprise)
        K. Carradine, The Will Rogers Wranglers
    "Look Around"
        K. Carradine
Scene 2
    "Favorite Son"
        K. Carradine, Chorus
Scene 3
    "No Man Left for Me"
        D. Hoty
    "Presents for Mrs. Rogers"
        K. Carradine, The Will Rogers Wranglers, The New Ziegfeld Girls
Scene 4
    "Will-a-mania" (reprise)
        K. Carradine, D. Latessa
    "Without You" ("I Got You" reprise)
        D. Hoty
Scene 5
    "Never Met a Man I Didn't Like"
        K. Carradine, Company

Gregory Hines and Stanley Wayne Mathis in JELLY'S LAST JAM
Martha Swope/TimePix

1991–1992 SEASON

1991.08 ## A LITTLE NIGHT MUSIC

A Revival of the Musical in Two Acts, a Prologue and 15 Scenes[1]. Book by Harold Wheeler. Suggested by a film ("Smiles of a Summer Night") by Ingmar Bergman. Music and Lyrics by Stephen Sondheim. Directed by Scott Ellis. Choreography by Susan Stroman. Sets designed by Michael Anania. Costumes designed by Lindsay W. Davis. Lighting designed by Dawn Chiang. Conductor, Paul Gemignani. (Orchestrations by Jonathan Tunick.) Sound designed by Abe Jacob. Produced by the New York City Opera. Opened 9 July 1991 at the New York State Theatre and closed 10 August 1991 after 7 performances in repertory.

CAST (in order of appearance): *Mrs. Segstrom*: Susanne Marsee. *Mr. Lindquist*: Ron Baker. *Mrs. Nordstrom*: Lisa Saffer. *Mrs. Anderssen*: Barbara Shirvis. *Mr. Erlanson*: Peter Blanchet. *Frederika Armfeldt*: Danielle Ferland. *Madame Armfeldt*: ELAINE BONAZZI. *Frid*, her butler: David Fuller. *Henrik Egerman*: KEVIN P. ANDERSON. *Anne Egerman*: BEVERLY LAMBERT. *Fredrik Egerman*: GEOERGE LEE ANDREWS. *Petra*: JOANNA GLUSHAK. *Desirée Armfeldt*: SALLY ANN HOWES. *Malla*, her maid: Raven Wilkinson. *Bertrand*, a page: Peter Blanchet. *Count Carl-Magnus Malcolm*: MICHAEL MAGUIRE. *Countess Charlotte Malcolm*: MAUREEN MOORE. *Osa*: Judith Jarosz. *Serving Gentlemen*: Kent A. Heacock, Ronald Kelly, Jeff Kensmoe, Ian D. Klapper, Brian Michaels, Brian Quirk, John Henry Thomas, Mike Timoney.

1991.09 ## THE MOST HAPPY FELLA

A Revival of the Musical in Three Acts, 10 Scenes[2]. Book, music and lyrics by Frank Loesser. Based on the play "They Knew What They Wanted" by Sidney Howard. Directed by Arthur Allan Seidelman. Conducted by Chris Nance. Choreography by Dan Siretta. Set designer, Michael Anania. Costume designer, Beba Shamash. Lighting designer, Mark W. Stanley. Sound designer, Abe Jacob. Orchestrations by Don Walker. Chorus master, Joseph Colaneri. Produced by the New York City Opera. Opened 4 September 1991 at the New York State Theatre and closed 18 October 1991 after 10 performances in repertory.

CAST (in order of appearance): *The Cashier*: William Ledbetter. *Cleo*: KAREN ZIEMBA or JOANNA GLUSHAK. *Rosabella*: ELIZABETH WALSH or MICHELE MCBRIDE. *Waitresses*: Jean Barber, Joan Mirabella, Deidre Sheehan. *Busboys*: Dean Dufford, Michael Langlois. *The Postman*: William Ledbetter. *Tony*: LOUIS QUILICO or JOHN FIORITO. *Marie*: ELAINE BONAZZI or SUSANNE MARSEE. *Max*: Ron Hilley. *Herman*: LARA TEETER or BRIAN QUINN. *Clem*: Gregory Moore. *Jake*: David Frye. *Al*: Jonathan Guss. *Joe*: BURKE MOSES or JOHN LESLIE WOLFE. *Giuseppe*: Arthur Rubin. *Pasquale*: Richard Byrne. *Ciccio*: John Lankston. *The Doctor*: Peter Blanchet. *The Priest*: Don Yule. *Tessie*: Alice Roberts. *Gussie*: Zachary London. *Artie*: Jonathan Zwi. *Neighbors*: Harris Davis, Michael Langlois, Louis Perry, Phillip Sneed, William Ward, Edward Zimmerman. *Neighbor Ladies*: Lee Bellaver, Esperanza Galan, Stephanie Godino, Rita Metzger. *Station Attendant*: James Russell.

1991.10 ## BARRY MANILOW'S SHOWSTOPPERS

A Musical Revue in Two Acts. Written by Mitzie Welch, Ken Welch, Barry Manilow. Directed by Kevin Carlisle. Creative consultant, Roberta Kent. Set design by Jim Youmans. Costume design by Phillip Dennis. Lighting by Don Holder. Sound design by Jon Weston. Musical director, Kevin Bassinson. Vocal director, Debra Byrd. Produced by Kevin Carlisle, Ken Welch, Mitzie Welch and Garry Kief. Opened 25 September 1991 at the Paramount Theatre (at Madison Square Garden) and closed 28 September 1991 after 4 performances.

CAST: BARRY MANILOW, Kevin Brackett, Donna Cherry, Craig Meyer, Michelle Nicastro, Debra Byrd.

In addition to Mr. Manilow's repertoire [see below], the following songs may be included in tonight's performance:

---

[1]Originally produced in New York 25 February 1973 at the Sam S. Shubert Theatre for 601 performances. For Synopsis of Scenes and Musical Numbers, see original 1973 production.
[2]Originally produced in New York 3 May 1956 at the Imperial Theatre for 678 performances. For Synopsis of Scenes and Musical Numbers, see original 1956 production. For this production, Act 2, Scenes 1 and 2 have been combined.

MUSICAL NUMBERS[3]
"All I Need Now Is the Girl" (from *GYPSY*)
  (*Music by* Jule Styne. *Lyrics by* Stephen Sondheim.)
"But the World Goes 'Round" (from *AND THE WORLD GOES ON*)
  (*Music by* John Kander. *Lyrics by* Fred Ebb.)
"Dancing in the Dark" (from *THE BANDWAGON*)
  (*Music by* Arthur Schwartz. *Lyrics by* Howard Dietz.)
"Fascinating Rhythm" (from *LADY BE GOOD*)
  (*Music by* George Geshwin. *Lyrics by* Ira Gershwin.)
"Fugue for Tinhorns" (from *GUYS AND DOLLS*)
  (*Music and Lyrics by* Frank Loesser.)
"Give My Regards to Broadway" (from *LITTLE JOHNNY JONES*)
  (*Music and Lyrics by* George M. Cohan.)
"Guys and Dolls" (from *GUYS AND DOLLS*)
  (*Music and Lyrics by* Frank Loesser.)
"I'll Be Seeing You" (from *RIGHT THIS WAY*)
  (*Music by* Sammy Fain. *Lyrics by* Irving Kahal.)
"Let Freedom Ring" (from *WE THE PEOPLE*, CBS Television Special)
  (*Music by* Barry Manilow. *Lyrics by* Bruce Sussman and Jack Feldman.)
"Luck Be a Lady" (from *GUYS AND DOLLS*)
  (*Music and Lyrics by* Frank Loesser.)
"Memory" (from *CATS*)
  (*Music by* Andrew Lloyd Webber. *Lyrics by* T. S. Eliot.)
"Never Met a Man I Didn't Like" (from *THE WILL ROGERS FOLLIES*)
  (*Music by* Cy Coleman. *Lyrics by* Betty Comden and Adolph Green.)
"Old Friends" (from *MERRILY WE ROLL ALONG*)
  (*Music and Lyrics by* Stephen Sondheim.)
"Once in Love with Amy" (from *WHERE'S CHARLEY?*)
  (*Music and Lyrics by* Frank Loesser.)
"Real Live Girl" (from *LITTLE ME*)
  (*Music by* Cy Coleman. *Lyrics by* Carolyn Leigh.)
"The Kid Inside" (from *IS THERE LIFE AFTER HIGH SCHOOL?*)
  (*Music and Lyrics by* Craig Carnelia.)
"Where or When" (from *BABES IN ARMS*)
  (*Music by* Richard Rodgers. *Lyrics by* Lorenz Hart.)
"Who Needs to Dream" (from *COPACABANA*, CBS Television Film)
  (*Music by* Barry Manilow and Artie Butler. *Lyrics by* Bruce Sussman and Jack Feldman.)
"You Can Have the TV" (from *NOTES*)
  (*Music and Lyrics by* Craig Carnelia.)

REPERTOIRE[4]
"I Got Rhythm" (from *GIRL CRAZY*)
  (*Music by* George Gershwin. *Lyrics by* Ira Gershwin.)
"Rhapsody in Blue"
  (*Music by* George Gershwin.)
"Trying to Get the Feeling Again"
  (*Music and Lyrics by* David Pomeranz.)
"Tonight" (from *WEST SIDE STORY*)
  (*Music by* Leonard Bernstein. *Lyrics by* Stephen Sondheim.)
"Somewhere in the Night"
  (*Music by* Richard Kerr. *Lyrics by* Will Jennings.)
"Cabaret" (from *CABARET*)
  (*Music by* John Kander. *Lyrics by* Fred Ebb.)
"Daybreak"
  (*Music and Lyrics by* Barry Manilow and Adrienne Anderson.)
"76 Trombones" (from *THE MUSIC MAN*)
  (*Music and Lyrics by* Meredith Willson.)
"It's a Miracle"
  (*Music and Lyrics by* Barry Manilow and Marty Panzer.)
"Even Now"
  (*Music by* Barry Manilow. *Lyrics by* Marty Panzer.)
"Mandy" (from *YIP YIP YAPHANK, ZIEGFELD FOLLIES OF 1919*)
  (*Music and Lyrics by* Irving Berlin.)
"Read 'Em and Weep"
  (*Music and Lyrics by* Jim Steinman.)

---

[3]Not in performance order.
[4]These songs represent Barry Manilow's current repertoire, as recorded on the album of the same name.

"NYC Rhythm"
  (*Music and Lyrics by* Barry Manilow.)
"I Am Your Child"
  (*Music and Lyrics by* Barry Manilow.)

ANDRÉ HELLER'S WONDERHOUSE

1991.11

An Entertainment in One Act. Entire production created, designed and directed by André Heller. Assistant director, Ivana De Vert. Rideau de Scène, Erté. Costumes by Susanne Schmoegner. Lighting by Pluesch. Sound by T. Richard Fitzgerald. English language adaptation by Mel Howard. Incidental music arranged and orchestrated by Andrew Powell. Band conductor, J. Leonard Oxley. Executive producer, Norman Rothstein. Originally produced in Europe by Peter Schwenkow and Stefan Seigner in association with Vereinigte Buehnen Wien. Produced by Mel Howard in association with Jean D. Weill. Opened 20 October 1991 at the Broadhurst Theatre and closed 27 October 1991 after 9 performances[5].

CAST: *Igor*: BILLY BARTY. *Olga*: PATTY MALONEY. *The Stagehand*, Gunila Carina Evalena Winniwingquist: GUNILLA WINGQUIST. *Guests*: RAO, CARLO OLDS, MACAO, BARONESS JEANNETTE LIPS VON LIPSTRILL, OMAR PASHA, MARION AND ROBERT KONYOT, EZIO BEDIN, MILO and ROGER, Aroon Kalan (assistant to Milo and Roger).

The action takes place in the old Wonderhouse Theatre at present.

BRIGADOON

1991.12

A Revival of the Musical Play in Two Acts, 11 Scenes[6]. Book and lyrics by Alan Jay Lerner. Music by Frederick Loewe. Original dances by Agnes deMille, recreated by James Jamieson. Directed by Gerald Freedman. Set and costume designer, Desmond Heeley. Lighting designer, Duane Schuler. Conductor, Paul Gemignani. Orchestrations by Ted Royal. Chorus master, Joseph Colaneri. Sound by Abe Jacob. Produced by the New York City Opera. Opened 7 November 1991 at the New York State Theatre and closed 17 November 1991 after 12 performances.

CAST (in order of appearance): *Tommy Albright*: JOHN LESLIE WOLFE or GEORGE DVORSKY. *Jeff Douglas*: TONY ROBERTS. *Maggie Anderson*: JOAN MIRABELLA. *Archie Beaton*: William Ledbetter. *Angus MacGuffie*: Don Yule. *Meg Brockie*: JOYCE CASTLE or LOUISA FLANIGAM. *Stuart Dalrymple*: Richard Byrne. *Sandy Dean*: Gregory Moore. *Harry Beaton*: SCOTT FOWLER. *Andrew MacLaren*: David Rae Smith. *Fiona MacLaren*: MICHELE MCBRIDE or ELIZABETH WALSH. *Jean MacLaren*: Camille de Ganon. *Charlie Dalrymple*: DAVID EISLER or ROBERT TATE. *Fish Monger*: Stephanie Godino. *Mr. Lundie*: Ron Randell. *Sword Dancers*: Joe Deer, William Ward. *Bagpiper*: Stephen Fox. *Frank*: Jonathan Guss. *Jane Ashton*: Leslie Farrell. *Townsfolk of Brigadoon*: New York City Opera Chorus, New York City Opera Dancers.

PETER PAN

1991.13

A Return Engagement of the Revival of the Musical in Three Acts, 7 Scenes[7]. Book by James M. Barrie[8]. Music by Mark [Moose] Charlap. Lyrics by Carolyn Leigh. Additional music by Jule Styne. Additional lyrics by Betty Comden and Adolph Green. Original production conceived, directed and choreographed by Jerome Robbins. Directed by Fran Soeder, restaged by Bill Bateman. Choreographed by Marilyn Magness. Scenery designed by Michael J. Hotopp, Paul dePass, James Leonard Joy. Costumes designed by Mariann Verheyen. Lighting designed by Natasha Katz. Musical director, Brian W. Tidwell. Musical supervisor, Kevin Farrell. Additional (musical) arrangements by M. Michael Fauss, Kevin Farrell. Sound designed by Peter Fitzgerald. Flying by Foy. Produced by Thomas P. McCoy, Keith Stava, P.P. Investments, Jon B. Platt. Opened 27 November 1991 at the Minskoff Theatre and closed 5 January 1992 after 48 performances.

CAST (in order of appearance): *Wendy Darling*: CINDY ROBINSON. *John Darling*: DAVID BURDICK. *Michael Darling*: JOEY CEE. *Liza*: Anne McVey. *Nana*: Bill Bateman. *Mrs. Darling*: LAUREN THOMPSON. *Mr. Darling*: J. K. SIMMONS. *Peter Pan*: CATHY RIGBY. *Curly*: Alon Williams. *First Twin*: Janet Kay Higgins. *Second Twin*: Courtney Wyn. *Slightly*: Christopher Ayres. *Tootles*: Julian Brightman. *Mr. Smee*: DON POTTER. *Cecco*: Calvin Smith. *Gentleman Starkey*: Carl Packard. *Captain Hook*: J. K. SIMMONS. *Crocodile*: Barry Ramsey. *Tiger Lily*: MICHELLE SCHUMACHER. *Pirates and Indians*: Bill Bateman, Andy Ferrara, Anne McVey, Charlie Mateus, Carl Packard, Barry Ramsey, Joseph Savant, Calvin Smith, David Thome, John Wilkerson.
Wendy, Grown-up: LAUREN THOMPSON. *Jane*: CINDY ROBINSON.
Ensemble Swing: Jim Alexander.

CATSKILLS ON BROADWAY

1991.14

An Evening of Comedy in One Act, 4 Scenes. Conceived by Freddie Roman. Entire production supervised by Larry Arrick. Set design by Lawrence Miller. Lighting design by Peggy Eisenhauer. Sound design by Peter Fitzgerald. Musical director, Barry Levitt. Opening musical sequence arranged by Don Pippin. Projection design by Wendall K. Harrington. Creative consultant, Richard Vos. Associate producer, Sandra Greenblatt. Presented by Kenneth D. Greenblatt, Stephen D. Fish, and 44 Productions (Michael G. Miller, Jeff Schwartz). Opened 5 December 1991 at the Lunt-Fontanne Theatre and closed 3 January 1993 after 452 performances.

CAST (in order of appearance): FREDDIE ROMAN, MARILYN MICHAELS, DICK CAPRI, MAL Z. LAWRENCE.

SCENES

  Freddie Roman (stand-up comedy)

  Marilyn Michaels (impressions, songs)

  Dick Capri (stand-up comedy)

  Mal Z. Lawrence (stand-up comedy)

NICK & NORA

1991.15

A Musical in Two Acts, 14 Scenes. Book by Arthur Laurents. Based on characters created by Dashiell Hammett and "The Thin Man" motion pictures owned by Turner Entertainment Co. Music by Charles Strouse. Lyrics by Richard Maltby, Jr. Directed by Arthur Laurents. Scenic design by Douglas W. Schmidt. Costume design by Theoni V. Aldredge. Lighting design by Jules Fisher. Choreography by Tina Paul. Orchestrations by Jonathan Tunick. Musical and vocal direction by Jack Lee. Dance and incidental music by Charles Strouse. Dance and incidental music arrangements by Gordon Lowry Harrell. Sound design by Peter Fitzgerald. Animals by William Berloni Theatrical Animals, Inc. Production supervisor, Janet Beroza. Assistant choreographer, Luis Perez. Associate musical director, Patrick Scott Brady. Produced by Terry Allen Kramer, Charlene and James M. Nederlander, Daryl Roth, Elizabeth Ireland McCann, in association with James Pentecost and Charles Suisman. Opened 8 December 1991 at the Marquis Theater and closed 15 December 1991 after 9 performances.

CAST (in order of appearance): *Asta*: Riley. *Nora Charles*: JOANNA GLEASON. *Nick Charles*: BARRY BOSTWICK. *Tracy Gardner*: CHRISTINE BARANSKI. *Yukido*: THOM SESMA. *Mavis*: Kathy Morath. *Delli*: Kristen Wilson. *Max Bernheim*: REMAK RAMSAY. *Victor Moisa*: CHRIS SARANDON. *Spider Malloy*: JEFF BROOKS. *Lorraine Bixby*: FAITH PRINCE. *Edward J. Connors*: KIP NIVEN. *Lieutenant Wolfe*: MICHAEL LOMBARD. *Maria Valdez*: YVETTE LAWRENCE. *Lily Connors*: DEBRA MONK. *Selznick*: Hal Robinson. *Monsignor Flaherty*: John Jellison. *Mariachi*: Tim Connell, Kris Phillips. *Waitress*: Kristen Wilson.
Swings: Mark Hoebee, Cynthia Thole.

The action takes place in Hollywood, 1937.

Act 1, Scene 1: Nick & Nora's bungalow, The Garden of Allah. *Scene 2*: The Studio. *Scene 3*: Lorraine's (Max's version). *Scene 4*: The Studio. *Scene 5*: Nick & Nora's bungalow. *Scene 6*: Lorraine (Victor's version). *Scene 7*: Beverly Hills. *Scene 8*: Lorraine's.

Act 2, Scene 1: Victor's villa. *Scene 2*: Nick & Nora's bungalow. *Scene 3*: Lorraine's (Maria's version). *Scene 4*: Lorraine's. *Scene 5*: The Big Bamboo. *Scene 6*: Tracy's terrace.

ACT 1
Scene 1
  "Is There Anything Better Than Dancing?"
    B. Bostwick, J. Gleason, C. Baranski
Scene 2
  "Everybody Wants to Do a Musical"
    C. Baranski

---

[5]No musical numbers listed in program.
[6]Originally produced in New York 13 March 1947 at the Ziegfeld Theatre for 581 performances. For Synopsis of Scenes and Musical Numbers, see original 1947 production.
[7]Originally produced in New York 20 October 1954 at the Winter Garden for 152 performances; this production previously presented in New York 13 December 1990 at the Lunt-Fontanne Theatre for 45 performances. For Synopsis of Scenes and Musical Numbers, see 1990 revival.
[8]Adaptation uncredited.

Scene 3
  "Not Me"
    R. Ramsay, F. Prince, K. Niven
Scene 4
  "Swell"
    B. Bostwick, J. Brooks, J. Gleason, C. Sarandon
Scene 5
  "As Long as You're Happy"
    B. Bostwick, J. Gleason
  "People Get Hurt"
    D. Monk
Scene 6
  "Men"
    F. Prince, C. Sarandon, K. Niven, C. Baranski
Scene 7
  "May the Best Man Win"
    B. Bostwick, J. Gleason, C. Baranski
  "Detectiveland"
    Company
Scene 8
  "Look Who's Alone Now"
    B. Bostwick

ACT 2
Scene 1
  "Class"
    C. Sarandon
Scene 2
  "Let's Go Home"
    J. Gleason
Scene 4
  "A Busy Night at Lorraine's"
    B. Bostwick, J. Gleason, J. Brooks, Suspects
Scene 5
  "Boom Chicka Boom"
    Y. Lawrence, T. Connell, K. Phillips
Scene 6
  "Let's Go Home" (reprise)(Married Life)
    B. Bostwick, J. Gleason

1992.01   THE MOST HAPPY FELLA

A Revival of the Musical in Two Acts, 11 Scenes[9]. Book, music and lyrics by Frank Loesser. Based on the play "They Knew What They Wanted" by Sidney Howard. Entire production directed by Gerald Gutierrez. Choreography by Liza Gennaro. Sets by John Lee Beatty. Costumes by Jess Goldstein. Lighting by Craig Miller. Duo piano arrangements by Robert Page under the supervision of Frank Loesser. Musical direction, Tim Stella. Artistic associate, Jo Sullivan. Originally produced by the Goodspeed Opera House Production. Produced by The Goodspeed Opera House, Center Theater Group/Ahmanson Theatre, Lincoln Center Theatre, The Shubert Organization, and Japan Satellite Broadcasting/Stagevision. Opened 13 February 1992 at the Booth Theatre and closed 30 August 1992 after 229 performances.

CAST (in order of appearance): *The Cashier*: Tad Ingram. *Cleo*: LIZ LARSON. *Rosabella*: SOPHIE {Schwab} HAYDEN. *Postman*: TAD INGRAM. *Tony*: SPIRO MALAS. *Herman*: SCOTT WAARA. *Clem*: Bob Freschi. *Jake*: John Soroka. *Al*: Ed Romanoff. *Marie*: CLAUDIA CATANIA. *Max*: Bill Badolato. *Joe*: CHARLES PISTONE. *Pasquale*: Mark Lotito. *Ciccio*: BUDDY CRUTCHFIELD. *Giuseppe*: BILL NABEL. *The Priest*: Bill Badolato. *Doctor*: TAD INGRAM.

The Folks of San Francisco and Napa Valley: John Aller, Anne Allgood, Bill Badolato, Molly Brown, Kyle Craig, Mary Helen Fisher, Bob Freschi, Ramon Galindo, T. Doyle Leverett, Ken Nagy, Gail Pennington, Ed Romanoff, Jane Smulyan, John Soroka, Laura Streets, Thomas Titone, Melanie Vaughan. *Swings*: Robert Ashford, Keri Lee.

1992.02   CRAZY FOR YOU

A Musical Comedy in Two Acts, 17 Scenes. Book by Ken Ludwig. Co-conceived by Ken Ludwig and Mike Ockrent, inspired by material (the musical "Girl Crazy," with original book) by Guy Bolton and John McGowan. Music by George Gershwin. Lyrics by Ira Gershwin, (Gus Kahn, Desmond Carter). Directed by Mike Ockrent. Choreography by Susan Stroman. Scenic design by Robin Wagner. Costume design by William Ivey Long. Lighting design by Paul Gallo. Sound design by Otts Munderloh. Orchestrations by William D. Brohn, (Sid Ramin). Musical director, Paul Gemignani. Musical consultant, Tommy Krasker. Dance and incidental music arranged by Peter Howard. Fights by B. H. Barry. Associate director, Steven Zweigbaum. Associate producers, Richard Godwin, Valerie Gordon. Produced by Roger Horchow and Elizabeth Williams. Opened 19 February 1992 at the Sam S. Shubert Theatre and closed 7 January 1996 after 1622 performances.

CAST (in order of appearance): *Tess*: BETH LEAVEL. *Patsy*: STACEY LOGAN. *Bobby Child*: HARRY GROENER. *Bela Zanger*: BRUCE ADLER. *Sheila*: Judine Hawkins Richard. *Mitzi*: Paula Leggett. *Susie*: Ida Henry. *Louise*: Jean Marie. *Betsy*: Peggy Ayn Maas. *Margie*: Salomé Mazard. *Vera*: Louise Ruck. *Elaine*: Pamela Everett. *Irene Roth*: MICHELE PAWK. *Mother*: JANE CONNELL. *Perkins*: Gerry Burkhardt. *Cactus*: Gerry Burkhardt. *Moose, Mingo, Sam*: THE MANHATTAN RHYTHM KINGS: Brian M. Nalepka, Tripp Hanson, Hal Shane. *Junior*: Casey Nicholaw. *Pete*: Fred Anderson. *Jimmy*: Michael Kubala. *Billy*: Ray Roderick. *Wyatt*: Jeffrey Lee Broadhurst. *Harry*: Joel Goodness. *Polly Baker*: JODI BENSON. *Everett Baker*: RONN CARROLL. *Lank Hawkins*: JOHN HILLNER. *Eugene*: STEPHEN TEMPERLEY. *Patricia*: AMELIA WHITE.

Ensemble: Fred Anderson, Jeffrey Lee Broadhurst, Gerry Burkharrdt, Pamela Everett, Joel Goodness, Tripp Hanson, Ida Henry, Michael Kubala, Paula Leggett, Stacey Logan, Penny Ayn Maas, Jean Marie, Salomé Mazzard, Brian M. Nalepka, Casey Nicholaw, Judine Hawkins Richard, Ray Roderick, Louise Ruck, Hal Shane. *Swings*: Ken Lundie, Chris Peterson, Maryellen Scilla.

Act 1, Scene 1: Backstage at the Zangler Theatre, New York City, in the 1930s. *Scene 2*: 42nd Street, outside the theatre. *Scene 3*: Main Street, Deadrock, Nevada. *Scene 4*: Lank's Saloon. *Scene 5*: In the Desert. *Scene 6*: The Gaiety Theatre. *Scene 7*: Main Street, Deadrock, three days later. *Scene 8*: The Lobby of the Gaiety Theatre, two weeks later. *Scene 9*: The Stage of the Gaiety Theatre. *Scene 10*: The Gaiety Theatre Dressing Rooms, opening night. *Scene 11*: Main Street, Deadrock.

Act 2, Scene 1: Lank's Saloon, later that evening. *Scene 2*: Lank's Saloon, the next morning. *Scene 3*: The Gaiety Theatre, backstage. *Scene 4*: The Auditorium of the Gaiety Theatre. *Scene 5*: New York, six weeks later. *Scene 6*: Main Street, Deadrock, six days later.

ACT 1
Scene 1
  "K-ra-azy for You" (from TREASURE GIRL)
    H. Groener
Scene 2
  "I Can't Be Bothered Now" (from A DAMSEL IN DISTRESS film)
    H. Groener, Girls
Scene 3
  "Bidin' My Time" (from GIRL CRAZY)
    T. Hanson, B. M. Nalepka, H. Shane
  "Things Are Looking Up" (from A DAMSEL IN DISTRESS film)
    H. Groener
Scene 4
  "Could You Use Me?" (from GIRL CRAZY)
    J. Benson, H. Groener
Scene 5
  "Shall We Dance?" (from SHALL WE DANCE film)
    J. Benson, H. Groener
Scene 7
  "Someone to Watch Over Me" (from OH, KAY!)
    J. Benson
Scene 9
  "Slap That Bass" (from SHALL WE DANCE film)
    H. Groener, B. M. Nalepka, B. Leavel, S. Logan, Company
    (Orchestrations by Sid Ramin)
  "Embraceable You" (from GIRL CRAZY)
    J. Benson, H. Groener
Scene 10
  "Tonight's the Night"[10]
    Company
    (Lyrics by Ira Gershwin and Gus Kahn.)
Scene 11
  "I Got Rhythm" (from GIRL CRAZY)
    J. Benson, H. Groener, Company

---

[9]Originally produced in New York 3 May 1956 at the Imperial Theatre for 678 performances. For Synopsis of Scenes and Musical Numbers, see original 1956 production.

[10]Previously unused.

ACT 2

Scene 1

"The Real American Folk Song Is a Rag" (from *LADIES FIRST*)
T. Hanson, B. M. Nalepka, H. Shane

"What Causes That?" (from *TREASURE GIRL*)
H. Groener, B. Adler

Scene 2

"Naughty Baby"[11]
M. Pawk, J. Hillner
(*Lyrics by* Ira Gershwin and Desmond Carter.)

Scene 4

"Stiff Upper Lip" (from *A DAMSEL IN DISTRESS* film)
H. Groener, J. Benson, S. Temperley, A. White, Company

"They Can't Take That Away from Me" (from *SHALL WE DANCE* film)
H. Groener

"But Not For Me" (from *GIRL CRAZY*)
J. Benson

Scene 5

"Nice Work If You Can Get It" (from *A DAMSEL IN DISTRESS* film)
H. Groener, Girls

Scene 6

Finale
Company

1992.03   FIVE GUYS NAMED MOE

A Musical (Revue) in Two Acts, based on the music made popular by Louis Jordan. Book by Clarke Peters. Music and lyrics by Louis Jordan, (Leo Hickman, Dallas Bartley, Larry Wynn, Jerry Bresler, Morry Lasco, Dick Adams, Fleecie Moore, Claude Demetriou, Jon Hendricks, Lora Lee, Johnny Burke, Jimmy Van Heusen, Sid Robin, Bill Davis, Don Wolf, Johnny Lange, Hy Heath, Joe Willoughby, Dr. Walt Merrick, Ellis Walsh, Busby Meyers, R. McCoy, C. Singleton, Browley Bri, Sam Theard, Spencer Lee, Joan Whitney, Alex Kramer, Jo Greene, Vaughn Horton, Denver Darling, Milton Gabler, Joseph Meyer, Buddy Bernier, Robert Emmerich, S. Austin.) Directed and choreographed by Charles Augins. (Setting) Designed by Tim Goodchild. Costumes by Noel Howard. Lighting by Andrew Bridge. Sound by Tony Meola/Autograph. Orchestrations by Neil McArthur. Vocal arrangements, musical supervision by Chapman Roberts. Musical direction, musical supervision, Reginald Royal. Executive producer, Richard Jay Alexander. Originally produced at The Theatre Royal, Stratford East (England). Produced by Cameron Mackintosh. Opened 8 April 1992 at the Eugene O'Neill Theatre and closed 2 May 1993 after 445 performances.

CAST (in order of appearance): *Nomax*: JERRY DIXON. *Big Moe*: DOUG ESKEW. *Four-Eyed Moe*: MILTON CRAIG NEALY. *No Moe*: KEVIN RAMSEY. *Eat Moe*: JEFFREY D. SAMS. *Little Moe*: GLENN TURNER.

ACT 1

"Early in the Morning"
(*Music and Lyrics by* Louis Jordan, Leo Hickman, Dallas Bartley.)

"Five Guys Named Moe"
(*Music and Lyrics by* Larry Wynn and Jerry Bresler.)

"Beware Brother Beware"
(*Music and Lyrics by* Morry Lasco, Dick Adams, Fleecie Moore.)

"I Like 'em Fat Like That"
(*Music and Lyrics by* Claude Demetriou and Louis Jordan.)

"Messy Bessy"
(*Music and Lyrics by* Jon Hendricks.)

"Pettin' and Pokin'"
(*Music and Lyrics by* Lora Lee.)

"Life Is So Peculiar" (from *MR. MUSIC* film)
(*Music and Lyrics by* Johnny Burke and James Van Heusen.)

"I Know What I've Got"
(*Music and Lyrics by* Sid Robin and Louis Jordan.)

"Azure Te"
(*Music and Lyrics by* Bill Davis and Don Wolf.)

"Safe, Sane and Single"
(*Music and Lyrics by* Louis Jordan, Johnny Lange, Hy Heath.)

"Push Ka Pi Shi Pie"
(*Music and Lyrics by* Joe Willoughby, Louis Jordan, Dr. Walt Merrick.)

ACT 2

"Saturday Night Fish Fry"
(*Music and Lyrics by* Ellis Walsh, Louis Jordan.)

"What's the Use of Getting Sober"
(*Music and Lyrics by* Busby Meyers.)

"If I Had Any Sense"
(*Music and Lyrics by* Rose Marie McCoy, Charles. Singleton.)

"Dad Gum Your Hide Boy"
(*Music and Lyrics by* Browley Bri.)

The Cabaret:

"Let the Good Times Roll"
(*Music and Lyrics by* Fleecie Moore, Sam Theard.)

"Reet, Petite and Gone"
(*Music and Lyrics by* Spencer Lee, Louis Jordan.)

"Caldonia"
(*Music and Lyrics by* Fleecie Moore.)

"Ain't Nobody Here But Us Chickens"
(*Music and Lyrics by* Joan Whitney, Alex Kramer.)

"Don't Let the Sun Catch You Crying"
(*Music and Lyrics by* Jo Greene.)

"Choo, Choo, Ch'boogie"
(*Music and Lyrics by* Vaughn Horton, Denver Darling, Milton Gabler.)

"Look Out Sister"
(*Music and Lyrics by* Sid Robin, Louis Jordan.)

Medley:

"Hurry Home"
(*Music and Lyrics by* Joseph Meyer, Buddy Bernier, Robert Emmerich.)

"Is You Is or Is You Ain't Ma' Baby?" (from *FOLLOW THE BOYS* film)
(*Music and Lyrics by* Billy Austin, Louis Jordan.)

"Five Guys Named Moe" (Finale)

1992.04   GUYS AND DOLLS

A Revival of the Musical Fable of Broadway in Two Acts, 17 Scenes[12]. Book by Jo Swerling and Abe Burrows. Based on a story and characters by Damon Runyon. Music and lyrics by Frank Loesser. Directed by Jerry Zaks. Choreographed by Christopher Chadman. Settings by Tony Walton. Costumes by William Ivey Long. Lighting by Paul Gallo. Orchestrations by George Bassman, Ted Royal, Michael Starobin, (Michael Gibson, Danny Troob). Dance music by Mark Hummel. Sound by Tony Meola. Assistant choreographer, Linda Haberman. Associate producers, Playhouse Square Center (Cleveland), David B. Brode. Executive producer, David Strong Warner, Inc. Produced by Dodger Productions, Roger Berlind, Jujamcyn Theatres/TV Asahi, Kardana Productions, Inc. and the John F. Kennedy Center. Opened 14 April 1992 at the Martin Beck Theatre and closed 8 January 1995 after 1143 performances.

CAST (in order of appearance): *Nicely-Nicely Johnson*: WALTER BOBBIE. *Benny Southstreet*: J. K. SIMMONS. *Rusty Charlie*: Timothy Shew. *Sister Sarah Brown*: JOSIE DE GUZMAN. *Arvide Abernathy*: JOHN CARPENTER. *Agatha*: Eleanor Glockner. *Calvin*: Leslie Feagan. *Martha*: Victoria Clark. *Harry the Horse*: Ernie Sabella. *Lieut. Brannigan*: STEVE RYAN. *Nathan Detroit*: NATHAN LANE. *Angie the Ox*: Michael Goz. *Miss Adelaide*: FAITH PRINCE. *Sky Masterson*: PETER GALLAGHER. *Joey Biltmore*: Michael Goz. *Hot Box Master of Ceremonies*: Stan Page. *Mimi*: Denise Faye. *General Matilda B. Cartwright*: RUTH WILLIAMSON. *Big Jule*: Herschel Sparber. *Drunk*: Robert Michael Baker. *Waiter*: Kenneth Kantor. *Crapshooter Dance Lead*: Scott Wise.

Other Guys: Robert Michael Baker, Gary Chryst, Lloyd Culbreath, R. F. Daley, Randy André Davis, David Elder, Cory English, Mark Esposito, Leslie Feagan, Michael Goz, Kenneth Kantor, Carlos Lopez, John MacInnis, Stan Page, Timothy Shew, Scott Wise. *Other Dolls*: Tina Marie DeLeone, Denise Faye, JoAnn M. Hunter, Nancy Lemenager, Greta Martin, Pascale Faye-Williams. *Swings*: Larry Cahn, Susan Misner, Steven Sofia.

1992.05   METRO

A Musical in Two Acts, 17 Scenes. Original (Polish) book and lyrics by Agata Miklaszewska and Maryna Miklaszewska. English book by Mary Bracken Phillips and Janusz Józefowicz. Music by Janusz Stokłosa. English lyrics by Mary Bracken Phillips. Direction and choreography by Janusz Józefowicz. Scenery by Janusz Sosnowski. Costumes by Juliet Polcsa, Marie

---

[11]Previously unused.

[12]First presented in New York 24 November 1950 at the 46th Street Theatre for 1200 performances. For Synopsis of Scenes and Musical Numbers, see original 1950 production. "Travelling Light" omitted for this production.

Anne Chiment. Lighting by Ken Billington. Sound by Jaroslaw Regulski. Laser effects by Mike Deissler. Musical direction, vocal and orchestral arrangements by Janusz Stoklosa. American dance supervisor, Cynthia Onrubia. Executive producer, Donald C. Farber. Originally produced at the Dramatyczny Theatre in Warsaw, Poland. Produced by Wiktor Kubiak. Opened 16 April 1992 at the Minskoff Theatre and closed 26 April 1992 after 13 performances.

CAST: *Anka:* KATARZYNA GRONIEC, Robyn Griggs (alt.) *Jan:* ROBERT JANOWSKI, Rohn Seykell (alt.). *Edyta:* Edyta Górniak. *Max:* Mariusz Czajka. *Philip:* Olek Krupa, Janusz Józefowicz (alt.). *Viola:* Violetta Klimczewska. *Iwona:* Iwona Runowska.

Ensemble: Krzysztof Adamski, Monika Ambroziak, Andrew Appolonow, Jacek Badurek, Alicja Borkowska, Michal Chamera, Pawel Cheda, Magdalena Depczyk, Jaroslaw Derybowski, Wojciech Dmochowski, Malgorzata Duda, Katarzyna Galica, Katarzyna Gawel, Denisa Geislerova, Lidia Groblewska, Piotr Hajduk, Joanna Jagla, Jaroslaw Janikowski, Adam Kamien´, Grzegorz Kowalczyk, Andrzej Kubicki, Katarzyna Lewandowska, Barbara Melzer, Michal Milowicz, Radoslaw Natkan´ski, Polina Oziernych, Marek Palucki, Beata Pawlik, Katarzyna Skarpetowska, Igor Sorine, Ewa Szawlowska, Marc Thomas, Ilona Trybula, Beata Urban´ska, Kamila Zapytowska.

Act 1, Scene 1: A Theatre somewhere in Europe. *Scene 2:* A Metro somewhere in Europe. *Scene 3:* The Theatre. *Scene 4:* The Metro. *Scene 5:* The Theatre. *Scene 6:* The Metro. *Scene 7:* Audition results. *Scene 8:* Tower of Babel.

Act 2, Scene 1: The Metro. *Scene 2:* Philip's Office. *Scene 3:* Abandoned subway station. *Scene 4:* The Metro. *Scene 5:* The Metro. *Scene 6:* The Metro. *Scene 7:* Pieniadze. *Scene 8:* The Metro. *Scene 9:* The Metro.

ACT 1[13]
Scene 2
  "Metro"
    R. Janowski, Company
Scene 3
  "My Fairy Tale"
    Basia, A. Borkowska, D. Geislerova
    Dancers: I. Runowska, L. Groblewska, V. Klimczewska.
Scene 4
  "But Not Me"
    R. Janowski, Company
Scene 5
  "Windows"
    K. Groniec
Scene 7
  "Bluezwis"
    R. Janowski, W. Dmochowski, Company
  "Love Duet I"
    K. Groniec, R. Janowski
Scene 8
  "Tower of Babel"
    Company
ACT 2
Scene 1
  "Benjamin Franklin"
    R. Janowski, Company
Scene 3
  "Uciekali"
    R. Janowski, Company
Scene 5
  "Waiting"
    E. Gorniak, K. Groniec, Dancers
Scene 7
  "Pieniadze"
    Company
Scene 8
  "Love Duet II"
    K. Groniec, R. Jankowski
Scene 9
  "Dreams Don't Die"
    K. Groniec

THE HIGH ROLLERS
1992.06 SOCIAL AND PLEASURE CLUB

A Musical Revue in Two Acts. Conceived by Judy Gordon. Directed and choreographed by Alan Weeks. Arrangements, musical direction, orchestrations by Allen Toussaint. Scenery by David Mitchell. Costumes by Theoni

---

[13]Final running order for opening night as per program insert.

V. Aldredge. Lighting by Beverly Emmons. Sound by Peter Fitzgerald. Music advisors, Jerry Wexler, Charles Neville. Associate director, Bruce Heath. Production supervisor, Mary Porter Hall. Associate producers, Nicholas Evans, Donald Tick, Mary Ellen Ashley, Irving Welzer. Produced by Judy Gordon, Dennis Grimaldi, Allen M. Shore, Martin Markinson. Opened 22 April 1992 at the Helen Hayes Theatre and closed 2 May 1992 after 14 performances.

CAST (in order of appearance): *Wonder Boy #1:* Keith Robert Bennett. *Queen:* DEBORAH BURRELL-CLEVELAND. *King:* Lawrence Clayton. *Jester:* Eugene Fleming. *Sorcerer:* Michael McElroy. *Enchantress:* VIVIAN REED. *Princess:* Nikki Rene. *Wonder Boy #2:* Tarik Winston. And ALLEN TOUSSAINT.

The High Roller Band: Allen Toussaint (conductor, piano), Carl Maultsby (associate conductor), Frank Canino (bass), Gary Keller (saxophone), Joel Helleny (trombone), Steve Johns (drums), Darryl Shaw (trumpet), Bob Rose (guitar).

The action takes place in the High Rollers Social and Pleasure Club, New Orleans, with a side trip to the Bayou at the time of Mardi Gras.

ACT 1
  "Tu Way Pocky Way"
    E. Fleming
    (Traditional; arranged by the Wild Magnolias.)
  "Open Up"
    Band
  "Mr. Mardi Gras"
    Company
    (*Music and Lyrics by* Allen Toussaint.)
  Piano Solo
    A. Toussaint
  "Chicken Shack Boogie"
    E. Fleming, Company
    (*Music and Lyrics by* Lola Ann Callum and Amos Milburn.)
  "Lady Marmalade"
    V. Reed, M. McElroy, Company
    (*Music and Lyrics by* Kenny Nolan.)
  "Don't You Feel My Leg"
    D. Burrell-Cleveland, L. Clayton, E. Fleming, M. McElroy
    (*Music and Lyrics by* Danny Barker and Blue Lu Barker.)
  "You Can Have My Husband" (Don't Mess with My Man)
    V. Reed
    (*Music and Lyrics by* Dorothy Labostrie.)
  "Fun Time"
    K. R. Bennett, T. Winston
    (*Music and Lyrics by* Allen Toussaint.)
  Rock Medley:
    Company
    "It Will Stand"
      (*Music and Lyrics by* Norman Johnson.)
    "Mother-in-Law"
      (*Music and Lyrics by* Allen Toussaint.)
    "Working in a Coal Mine"
      (*Music and Lyrics by* Allen Toussaint.)
    "Lipstick Traces (on a Cigarette)"
      (*Music and Lyrics by* Naomi Neville.)
    "Rockin' Pneumonia"
      (*Music and Lyrics by* Huey P. Smith.)
    "(Sittin' in) Ya Ya"
      (*Music and Lyrics by* Lee Dorsey, Clarence Lewis, Morgan Robinson.)
  "Feet Don't Fail Me Now" (My Feet Can't Fail Me Now)
    K. R. Bennett, T. Winston
    (*Music and Lyrics by* Mad Musicians.)
  "Ooh Poo Pa Doo"
    E. Fleming
    (*Music and Lyrics by* Jesse Hill.)
  "Dance the Night (Away with You)"
    (*Music and Lyrics by* Doc Pomus and Mac Rebennack.)
  "Such a Night"
    L. Clayton, D. Burrell-Cleveland
    (*Music and Lyrics by* Mac Rebennack.)
  "All These Things"
    V. Reed, M. McElroy
    (*Music and Lyrics by* Naomi Neville.)
  "Mellow Sax"
    N. Rene, G. Keller (saxophone), Company
    (*Music and Lyrics by* Roy Montrell.)
  "Sea Cruise"
    V. Reed, D. Burrell-Cleveland, N. Rene
    (*Music and Lyrics by* Huey P. Smith.)

"Jambalaya (on the Bayou)"
E. Fleming, Company
(*Music and Lyrics by* Hank Williams.)

ACT 2
"Tu Way Pocky Way" (reprise)
E. Fleming
"Bourbon Street Parade"
Company
(*Music and Lyrics by* Paul Barbarin.)
"(I Ain't Gonna Give Nobody None o' This) Jelly Roll"
K. R. Bennett, T. Winston
(*Music and Lyrics by* Spencer Williams, Clarence Williams.)
"Heebie Jeebie Dance"
N. Rene, D. Burrell-Cleveland, V. Reed
(*Music by* Boyd Atkins.)
"I Like It Like That"
E. Fleming, Company
(*Music and Lyrics by* Chris Kenner.)
"Fiyou on the Bayou" (Fire on the Bayou)
Company
(*Music and Lyrics by* Arthur Neville, Jr., Leo Nocentelli.)
"Marie Laveau"
V. Reed
(*Music and Lyrics by* Shel Silverstein, Baxter Taylor III.)
"Walk on Gilded Splinters"
Company
(*Music and Lyrics by* Mac Rebennack.)
"Black Widow Spider"
L. Clayton
(*Music and Lyrics by* Mac Rebennack.)
"Tell It Like It Is"
(*Music and Lyrics by* Lee Diamond, George Davis.)
"You're the One"
D. Burrell-Cleveland, L. Clayton
(*Music and Lyrics by* Adolph Smith, Cosmo Matassa.)
"Let the Good Times Roll"
Company
(*Music and Lyrics by* Leonard Lee.)
"Challenge Dance"
E. Fleming, L. Clayton, M. McElroy, K. R. Bennett, T. Winston
"Mos Scoscious"
M. McElroy, N. Rene
(*Music and Lyrics by* Mac Rebennack.)
"We All Need Love"
V. Reed
(*Music and Lyrics by* Allen Toussaint.)
"Tu Way Pocky Way" (reprise)
E. Fleming
"Injuns Here We Come"
K. R. Bennett, Company
(*Music and Lyrics by* The Wild Magnolias and Wilson Turbinton.)
"Golden Crown"
Company
(*Music and Lyrics by* Theodore Dollis.)
"Jockomo"
Company
(*Music and Lyrics by* James Crawford.)
"Hey Mama"
Company
"(When the) Saints Go Marchin' In"
Company

MAN OF LA MANCHA
1992.07

A Revival of the Musical Play in One Act[14]. Book by Dale Wasserman. Suggested by the life and work ("Don Quixote") of Miguel de Cervantes y Saavedra. Music by Mitch Leigh. Lyrics by Joe Darion. Entire production

[14]First produced in New York 22 November 1965 at the ANTA Washington Square Theatre for 2328 performances. For Synopsis of Scenes and Musical Numbers, see original 1965 production.

staged by Albert Marre. Sets by Howard Bay. Costumes by Howard Bay and Patton Campbell. Lighting by Gregory Allen Hirsch. Sound by Jon Weston. Musical director, Brian Salesky. Dance arrangements by Neil Warner. Executive producer, Manny Kladitis. Produced by The Mitch Leigh Company. Opened 24 April 1992 at the Marquis Theatre and closed 26 July 1992 after 108 performances[15].

CAST: *Cervantes/Don Quixote*: RAUL JULIA. *Aldonza/Dulcinea*: SHEENA EASTON. *Sancho*: TONY MARTINEZ. *Governor/Pedro*, the Head Muleteer: CHEV RODGERS. *The Padre*: DAVID WASSON. *Dr. Carrasco*: IAN SULLIVAN. *The Innkeeper*: DAVID HOLLIDAY. *Antonia*: VALERIE DE PENA. *The Housekeeper*: MARCELINE DECKER. *The Barber*: Ted Forlow. *Paco*, a Muleteer/*The Mule*: Hechter Ubarry. *Juan*, a Muleteer/*The Horse*: Jean-Paul Richard. *Manuel*, a Muleteer: Luis Perez. *Tenorio*, a Muleteer: Gregory Mitchell. *Jose*, a Muleteer: Bill Santora. *Jorge*, a Muleteer: Chet D'Elia. *Maria*, the Innkeeper's Wife: Tanny McDonald. *Fermina*, a slavey/*Moorish Dancer*: Joan Susswein Barber. *Captain of the Inquisition*: Jon Vandertholen. *Guitarists*: Robin Polseno, David Serva. *Guards*: Chet D'Elia, Darryl Ferrera. *Swing*: Rick Manning.

JELLY'S LAST JAM
1992.08

A Musical in Two Acts, 12 Scenes. Book by George C. Wolfe. (Suggested by the life and music of Jelly Roll Morton.) Music by Jelly Roll Morton; additional music composed by Luther Henderson. Lyrics by Susan Birkenhead. Directed by George C. Wolfe. Choreography by Hope Clarke. Tap choreography by Gregory Hines, Ted L. Levy. Musical adaptation, orchestrations, musical supervision by Luther Henderson. Musical director, Linda Twine. Scenic design by Robin Wagner. Costumes designed by Toni-Leslie James. Lighting design by Jules Fisher. Sound design by Otts Munderloh. Mask and puppet design by Barbara Pollitt. Associate producers, Peggy Hill Rosencranz, Marilyn Hall, Dentsu Inc. Executive producer, David Strong Warner, Inc. Produced by Margo Lion and Pamela Koslow in association with Polygram Diversified Entertainment, 126 Second Avenue Corporation/Hal Luftig, Rodger Hess, Jujamcyn Theatres/TV Asahi, and Herb Alpert. Opened 26 April 1992 at the Virginia Theatre and closed 5 September 1993 after 569 performances.

CAST (in order of appearance): *Chimney Man*: KEITH DAVID. *The Hunnies*: Mamie Duncan-Gibbs, Stephanie Pope, Allison M. Williams. *The Crowd*: Ken Ard, Adrian Bailey, Sherry D. Boone, Brenda B. Braxton, Mary Bond Davis, Ralph Deaton, Melissa Haizlip, Cee-Cee Harshaw, Ted L. Levy, Stanley Wayne Mathis, Victoria Gabrielle Platt, Gil Pritchett III, Michelle M. Robinson. *Jelly Roll Morton*: GREGORY HINES.
The People of His Past: Young Jelly: SAVION GLOVER. *The Sisters*: Victoria Gabrielle Platt, Sherry D. Boone. *The Ancestors*: Adrian Bailey, Mary Bond Davis, Ralph Deaton, Ann Duquesnay, Melissa Haizlip. *Miss Mamie*: Mary Bond Davis. *Buddy Bolden*: Ruben Santiago-Hudson. *Too-Tight Nora*: Brenda Braxton. *Three Finger Jake*: Gil Pritchett III. *Gran Mimi*: Ann Duquesnay. *Jack the Bear*: STANLEY WAYNE MATHIS. *Foot-in-Yo-Ass Sam*: Ken Ard. *Anita*: TONYA PINKINS. *The Melrose Brothers*: Don Johanson, Gordon Joseph Weiss. *Swings*: Ken Roberson, Janice Lorraine-Holt.
Jelly's Red Hot Peppers: Brian Grice (drums), Ben Brown (bass), Steve Bargonetti (banjo), Virgil Jones (trumpet), Britt Woodman (trombone), Bill Easley (clarinet).

The action takes place in The Jungle Inn, a lowdown club somewhere 'tween Heaven 'n' Hell on the eve of Jelly Roll Morton's death.

Act 1, Scene 1: The Jam. *Scene 2*: In the Beginning. *Scene 3*: Goin' Uptown. *Scene 4*: The Journey to Chicago. *Scene 5*: Chicago! *Scene 6*: Jelly 'n' Anita. *Scene 7*: The Midnite Inn.

Act 2, Scene 1: The Chimney Man Takes Charge. *Scene 2*: The New York Suite. *Scene 3*: The Last Chance. *Scene 4*: Central Avenue. *Scene 5*: The Last Rites.

ACT 1
Scene 1
"Jelly's Jam" (adapted from "King Porter Stomp")
The Hunnies, The Crowd
"In My Day" (adapted from "Wild Man Blues")
G. Hines, The Hunnies
Scene 2
"The Creole Way"
(*Music by* Luther Henderson.)
A. Bailey, M. B. Davis, R. Deaton, A. Duquesnay, M. Haizlip, S. Glover
"The Whole World's Waitin' to Sing Your Song"
(adapted from "My Little Dixie Home")
"Street Scene" (*Music by* Luther Henderson.)
G. Hines, S. Glover, The Street Crowd

[15]Orchestrations uncredited.

Scene 3
"Michigan Water" (traditional)
M. B. Davis, R. Santiago-Hudson
The Banishment:
"Get Away Boy" (*Music by* Luther Henderson.)
"Lonely Boy Blues" (traditional)
A. Duquesnay, S. Glover, G. Hines
Scene 4
"Somethin' More" (adapted from "Pretty Lil")
G. Hines, S. W. Mathis, K. David, The Hunnies, The Crowd
"That's How You Jazz"
G. Hines, S. W. Mathis, The Dance Hall Crowd
Scene 5
"The Chicago Stomp" (adapted from "Burnin' the Iceberg")
G. Hines, The Red Hot Peppers, K. David, The Hunnies, The Chicago Crowd
Scene 6
"Play the Music for Me" (adapted from "Dead Man Blues")
T. Pinkins
"Lovin' Is a Lowdown Blues" (adapted from "Jungle Blues")
The Hunnies
Scene 7
"Dr. Jazz"
G. Hines, The Crowd
(*Music by* King Oliver and Walter Melrose.)

ACT 2
Scene 2
"Good Ole New York" (adapted from "Hyena Stomp")
K. David, The Hunnies, G. Hines, The New York Crowd
"Too Late, Daddy"
G. Hines, The Harlem Crowd
(*Music by* Luther Henderson.)
"That's the Way We Do Things in New Yawk"
(adapted from "Shreveport Stomp") G. Hines, D. Johanson, G. J. Weiss
Jelly's Isolation Dance
G. Hines, S. Glover
Scene 3
"The Last Chance Blues" (adapted from "Blue Blood Stomp")
G. Hines, T. Pinkins
Scene 5
"The Last Rites" (includes "Creole Boy")
G. Hines, K. David, The People of His Past
(*Music by* Luther Henderson, Jelly Roll Morton.)

1992.09   FALSETTOS

A Musical in Two Acts[16]. Book by William Finn and James Lapine. Music
and lyrics by William Finn. Directed by James Lapine. Set design by
Douglas Stein. Costume design by Ann Hould-Ward. Lighting design by
Frances Aronson. Sound design by Peter Fitzgerald. Musical arrangements
by Michael Starobin. Musical direction, Scott Frankel. Associate producer,
Alecia Parker. Produced by Barry and Fran Weissler, in association with
James and Maureen O'Sullivan Cushing and Masakazu Shibaoka Broadway
Pacific. Opened 29 April 1992 at the John Golden Theatre and closed 27
June 1993 after 487 performances.

CAST (in order of appearance): *Marvin:* MICHAEL RUPERT. *Whizzer:* STEPHEN
BOGARDUS. *Mendel:* CHIP ZIEN. *Jason:* JONATHAN KAPLAN, ANDREW
HARRISON LEEDS (alt.). *Trina:* BARBARA WALSH. *Charlotte:* HEATHER
MACRAE. *Cordelia:* CAROLEE CARMELLO.

Act 1: 1979.

Act 2: 1981.

ACT 1
"Four Jews in a Room Bitching"
S. Bogardus, M. Rupert, J. Kaplan, C. Zien
"A Tight Knit Family"
M. Rupert, C. Zien

---

[16]Act 1 previously presented Off-Broadway as MARCH OF THE
FALSETTOS 9 April 1981 at Playwrights Horizons and the Westside Arts
Theatre for 298 performances, and Act 2 as FALSETTOLAND 28 June 1990
at Playwrights Horizons and the Lucille Lortel Theatre for 238 performances.

"Love Is Blind"
M. Rupert, J. Kaplan, S. Bogardus, C. Zien, B. Walsh
"Thrill of First Love"
M. Rupert, S. Bogardus
"Marvin at the Psychiatrist" (A Three-Part Mini-Opera)
J. Kaplan, C. Zien, S. Bogardus, M. Rupert
"Everyone Tells Jason to See a Psychiatrist"
J. Kaplan, M. Rupert, B. Walsh, S. Bogardus
"This Had Better Come to a Stop"
M. Rupert, S. Bogardus, J. Kaplan, B. Walsh, C. Zien
"I'm Breaking Down" (from *IN TROUSERS*)
B. Walsh
"Jason's Therapy"
C. Zien, B. Walsh, S. Bogardus, M. Rupert, J. Kaplan
"A Marriage Proposal"
C. Zien, B. Walsh, J. Kaplan
"A Tight Knit Family" (reprise)
M. Rupert, C. Zien
"Trina's Song"
B. Walsh
"March of the Falsettos"
C. Zien, M. Rupert, J. Kaplan, S. Bogardus
"Trina's Song" (reprise)
B. Walsh
"The Chess Game"
M. Rupert, S. Bogardus
"Making a Home"
C. Zien, J. Kaplan, B. Walsh, S. Bogardus
"The Games I Play"
S. Bogardus, C. Zien, B. Walsh, J. Kaplan
"Marvin Goes Crazy"
M. Rupert, C. Zien, J. Kaplan, B. Walsh, S. Bogardus
"I Never Wanted to Love You"
M. Rupert, C. Zien, J. Kaplan, B. Walsh, S. Bogardus
"Father to Son"
M. Rupert, J. Kaplan

ACT 2
"Welcome to Falsettoland"
Company
"The Year of the Child"
Company
"Miracle of Judaism"
Company
"Sitting Watching Jason (Play Baseball)"
Company
"A Day in Falsettoland"
Company
"Everyone Hates His Parents"
C. Zien, J. Kaplan, M. Rupert, B. Walsh
"What More Can I Say"
M. Rupert, S. Bogardus
"Something Bad Is Happening"
H. MacRae, C. Carmello
"Holding to the Ground"
B. Walsh
"Days Like This I Almost Believe in God"
Company
"Cancelling the Bar Mitzvah"
J. Kaplan, C. Zien, B. Walsh
"Unlikely Lovers"
M. Rupert, S. Bogardus, H. MacRae, C. Carmello
"Another Miracle of Judaism"
J. Kaplan
"You Gotta Die Sometime"
S. Bogardus
"Jason's Bar Mitzvah"
Company
"What Would I Do?"
M. Rupert, S. Bogardus

1992–1993 SEASON

Chita Rivera in KISS OF THE SPIDER WOMAN
Martha Swope/TimePix

1992–1993 SEASON

1992.10   110 IN THE SHADE

A Revival of the Musical in Two Acts, 11 Scenes[1]. Book by N. Richard Nash. Based on his play "The Rainmaker." Music by Harvey Schmidt. Lyrics by Tom Jones. Original direction by Joseph Anthony. Dances and musical numbers originally staged by Agnes de Mille. Directed by Scott Ellis. Choreographed by Susan Stroman. Set designer, Michael Anania. Costume design, Lindsay W. Davis. Lighting design, Jeff Davis. Sound design, Abe Jacob. Conductor, Paul Gemignani. Orchestrations by Hershy Kay; additional orchestrations by William D. Brohn. (Original dance music by William Goldenberg); additional dance music arrangements by Peter Howard. Chorus master, Joseph Colaneri. Fight coordinator, Steve Hall. Dialect coach, K. C. Ligon. Produced by the New York City Opera. Opened 18 July 1992 at the New York State Theatre and closed 15 November 1992 after 12 performances in repertory

CAST (in order of appearance): *Tommy:* Robert Mann Keyser. *Dance Couple:* Jennifer Paulson Lee, John Scott. *File:* RICHARD MUENZ. *Jimmy Curry:* DAVID AARON BAKER. *Noah Curry:* WALTER CHARLES. *H.C. Curry:* HENDERSON FORSYTHE. *Lizzie Curry:* KAREN ZIÉMBA. *Snookie Updegraff:* CRISTA MOORE. *Bill Starbuck:* BRIAN SUTHERLAND. *Townspeople:* New York City Opera Chorus.

The action takes place in a western state during a 24-hour period, on a summer day in a time of drought.

Act 1, Scene 1: A fence and a windmill. *Scene 2:* The depot. *Scene 3:* A street in Three Point, File's office. *Scene 4:* The park. *Scene 5:* Outside the Curry house. *Scene 6:* An open space.

Act 1, Scene 1: The park. *Scene 2:* Starbuck's truck. *Scene 3:* A picnic area. *Scene 4:* An open space. *Scene 5:* A fence and a windmill.

ACT 1
  "Gonna Be Another Hot Day"
    R. Muenz, Townspeople
  "Lizzie's Coming Home"
    D. A. Baker, W. Charles, H. Forsythe
  "Love, Don't Turn Away"
    K. Ziémba
  "Overhead"[2]
    Townspeople
  "Poker Polka"
    D. A. Baker, W. Charles, H. Forsythe, R. Muenz
  "Why Can't They Leave Me Alone"[3]
    R. Muenz
  "Come on Along"[4]
    Townspeople
  "Rain Song"
    B. Sutherland, Townspeople
  "You're Not Foolin' Me"
    K. Ziémba, B. Sutherland
  "Cinderella"[5]
    Children
  "Raunchy"
    K. Ziémba
  "A Man and a Woman"
    R. Muenz, K. Ziémba
  "Old Maid"
    K. Ziémba

---

[1]Originally produced in New York 24 October 1963 at the Broadhurst Theatre for 330 performances. Dropped from the original production was "Hungry Men."
[2]Newly written song for this production.
[3]Newly written song for this production.
[4]Newly written song for this production.
[5]Newly written song for this production.

ACT 2
  "Come on Along" (reprise)
    Townspeople
  "Everything Beautiful Happens at Night"
    Townspeople
  "Shooting Star"[6]
    B. Sutherland
  "Melisande"
    B. Sutherland
  "Simple Little Things"
    K. Ziémba
  "Little Red Hat"
    D. A. Baker, C. Moore
  "Is It Really Me?"
    K. Ziémba, B. Sutherland
  "Wonderful Music"
    B. Sutherland, R. Muenz, K. Ziémba
  Finale: "Rain Song"
    Company

1992.11   ANNA KARENINA

A Musical in Two Acts, a Prologue and 19 Scenes. Book and lyrics by Peter Kellogg. Based on the novel of the same name by Leo Tolstoy. Music by Daniel Levine. Directed by Theodore Mann. Musical sequences staged by Patricia Birch. Musical direction and dance music arrangements by Nicholas Archer. Scenic design by James Morgan. Costume design by Carrie Robbins. Lighting design by Mary Jo Dondlinger. Sound design by Fox and Perla. Orchestrations by Peter Matz. Associate choreographer, Jonathan Cerullo. Produced by Circle in the Square Theatre (Theodore Mann, Artistic director; Robert A. Buckley, Managing director; Paul Libin, Consulting producer). Opened 26 August 1992 at the Circle in the Square Theatre and closed 11 October 1992 after 46 performances.

CAST (in order of appearance): *Count Alexis Vronsky:* SCOTT WENTWORTH. *Anna Karenina:* ANN CRUMB. *Constantine Levin:* GREGG EDELMAN. *Train Conductor:* David Pursley. *Prince Stephen Oblonsky, "Stiva":* JERRY LANNING. *Princess Kitty Scherbatsky:* MELISSA ERRICO. *Dunyasha,* Kitty's maid: Naz Edwards. *Korsunsky,* Master of Ceremonies: Gabriel Barre. *Men at the Ball:* Larry Hansen, Ray Wills. *Guard at the Station:* Larry Hansen. *Masha,* woman at the station: Amelia Prentice. *Seryozha Karenin,* Anna's son: ERIC HOUSTON SAARI. *Annushka,* Karenin's maid: Darcy Pulliam. *Nicolai Karenin,* Anna's husband: JOHN CUNNINGHAM. *Fyodor,* a servant: David Pursley. *Basso:* David Pursley. *Princess Elizabeth Tversky,* Betsy: Jo Ann Cunningham. *Woman at Party:* Naz Edwards. *Finance Minister:* Ray Wills. *Man at Party:* Gabriel Barre. *Prince Yashvin,* a Captain: Ray Wills. *Vasily,* Vronsky's servant: Larry Hansen. *Levin's Foreman:* David Pursley. *Peasant:* Gabriel Barre. *Gina:* Amelia Prentice.

  Swings: Jonathan Cerullo, Audrey Lavine. *Extras:* Jeremy Black, Billy Hipkins.

The action takes place in the 1870's.

Act 1: Russia.

Act 2: Russia and Italy.

Prologue: St. Petersburg Train Station.

Act 1, Scene 1: Moscow Train Station, next morning. *Scene 2:* Kitty Scherbatsky's house, later the same day. *Scene 3:* A Ball, a few days later. *Scene 4:* A small station between Moscow and St. Petersburg, the next night. *Scene 5:* Anna's House in St. Petersburg. *Scene 6:* Prince Tversky's home, that night. *Scene 7:* Croquet Lawn, several weeks later. *Scene 8:* Kitty's House. *Scene 9:* A small dance in St. Petersburg. *Scene 10:* On the way home. *Scene 11:* Anna's House. *Scene 12:* Vronsky's apartment.

Act 2, Scene 1: Anna's House, three months later. *Scene 2:* Levin's Estate and Italy. *Scene 3:* A Villa in Rome. *Scene 4:* Kitty's House. *Scene 5:* A Hotel in Moscow. *Scene 6:* Karenin's House. *Scene 7:* St. Petersburg Train Station.

ACT 1
Prologue
  "On a Train"
    A. Crumb, S. Wentworth, G. Edelman, Chorus

---

[6]Newly written song for this production.

539

Scene 1

"There's More to Life Than Love"
J. Lanning, A. Crumb

Scene 2

"How Awful"
M. Errico

"Would You?"
G. Edelman

"In a Room"
G. Edelman, M. Errico, A. Crumb, S. Wentworth

Scene 3

Waltz and Mazurka
A. Crumb, M. Errico, S. Wentworth, J. Lanning, Chorus

Scene 5

"Nothing Has Changed"
A. Crumb

Scene 6

"Lowlands"
D. Pursley

Scene 7

"Rumors"
Chorus

Scene 8

"How Many Men?"
M. Errico

Scene 9

"We Were Dancing"
S. Wentworth

Scene 10

"I'm Lost"
A. Crumb

Scene 11

"Karenin's List"
J. Cunningham

Scene 12

"Waiting for You"
A. Crumb, S. Wentworth

ACT 2

Scene 1

"This Can't Go On"
A. Crumb, S. Wentworth, J. Cunningham

Scene 2

"Peasants' Idyll"
Chorus

"That Will Serve Her Right"
G. Edelman

Scene 3

"Everything's Fine"
A. Crumb, S. Wentworth

Scene 4

"Would You?" (reprise)
G. Edelman, M. Errico

Scene 5

"Everything's Fine" (reprise)
A. Crumb

Scene 6

"Only at Night"
J. Cunningham

Scene 7

Finale
A. Crumb, Chorus

MUSIC OF
ANDREW LLOYD WEBBER

1992.12

A Musical Revue in Two Acts. Directed by Arlene Phillips. Production (scenic) designer, Marc B. Weiss. Costume coordinator, Frank Krenz. Sound designer, Martin Levan. Production musical supervisor, Michael Reed. Musical director, Paul Bogaev. Produced by Broadway in Concert, Inc. (LIVENT), Pace Theatrical Group by arrangement with The Really Useful Company and Superstar Ventures. Opened 22 September 1992 at the Radio City Music Hall and closed 4 October 1992 after 14 performances.

CAST: MICHAEL CRAWFORD, TIM DONOGHUE, WILLY FALK, MARK HARDY, JULIET LAMBERT, JIMMY LOCKETT, DONNA LEE MARSHALL, GARY MAUER, CATHY PORTER, TAMI TAPPAN, TY TAYLOR, ELIZABETH WARD, GAY WILLIS, LAURIE BEECHMAN, LUANN ARONSON, Ensemble.

ACT 1

Jesus Christ Superstar Overture
Orchestra

"Jesus Christ Superstar" (from *JESUS CHRIST SUPERSTAR*)
(*Lyrics by* Tim Rice.) W. Falk, Company

"Potiphar" (from *JOSEPH AND THE AMAZING TECHNICOLOR DREAMCOAT*)
(*Lyrics by* Tim Rice.) D. L. Marshall, W. Falk, M. Hardy, J. Lockett, T. Taylor

"Close Every Door" (from *JOSEPH AND THE AMAZING TECHNICOLOR DREAMCOAT*)
(*Lyrics by* Tim Rice.) T. Donoghue

"A Pharaoh's Story" (from *JOSEPH AND THE AMAZING TECHNICOLOR DREAMCOAT*)
(*Lyrics by* Tim Rice.) L. Beechman

"Starlight Express" (from *STARLIGHT EXPRESS*)
(*Lyrics by* Richard Stilgoe.) G. Mauer, J. Lockett

"Unexpected Song" (from *SONG & DANCE*)
(*Lyrics by* Don Black.) L. Aronson

"Another Suitcase in Another Hall" (from *EVITA*)
(*Lyrics by* Tim Rice.) L. Aronson

"Memory" (from *CATS*)
(*Text and additional lyrics by* Trevor Nunn after T. S. Eliot.) L. Beechman

"Mr. Mistoffelees" (from *CATS*)
(*Text by* T. S. Eliot.) T. Taylor, Company

"Jellicle Ball" (from *CATS*)
(*Orchestration by* David Cullen.) Orchestra

"Amigos Para Siempre" (Friends for Life)
(*Lyrics by* Don Black.) G. Willis, W. Falk

"I Don't Know How to Love Him" (from *JESUS CHRIST SUPERSTAR*)
(*Lyrics by* Tim Rice.) C. Porter

"Everything's Alright" (from *JESUS CHRIST SUPERSTAR*)
(*Lyrics by* Tim Rice.) C. Porter, G. Mauer, T. Taylor

"Gethsemane" (from *JESUS CHRIST SUPERSTAR*)
(*Lyrics by* Tim Rice.) M. Crawford

ACT 2

Evita Suite Orchestra

"Don't Cry for Me Argentina" (from *EVITA*)
(*Lyrics by* Tim Rice.) E. Ward

"And the Money Kept Rolling In" (from *EVITA*)
(*Lyrics by* Tim Rice.) M. Crawford, Company

"Pie Jesu" (from *REQUIEM*)
G. Willis, T. Tappan, Company

The Phantom of the Opera Overture
Orchestra

"Think of Me" (from *THE PHANTOM OF THE OPERA*)
(*Lyrics by* Charles Hart. *Additional Lyrics by* Richard Stilgoe.) J. Lambert

"The Phantom of the Opera" (from *THE PHANTOM OF THE OPERA*)

(*Lyrics by* Charles Hart. *Additional Lyrics by* Richard Stilgoe and Mike Batt.)
M. Crawford, J. Lambert

"All I Ask of You" (from *THE PHANTOM OF THE OPERA*)
(*Lyrics by* Charles Hart. *Additional Lyrics by* Richard Stilgoe.)
M. Crawford, C. Porter

"Wishing You Were Somehow Here Again" (from *THE PHANTOM OF THE OPERA*)
(*Lyrics by* Charles Hart. *Additional Lyrics by* Richard Stilgoe.) J. Lambert

"Masquerade" (from *THE PHANTOM OF THE OPERA*)
(*Lyrics by* Charles Hart. *Additional Lyrics by* Richard Stilgoe.) Company

"The Music of the Night" (from *THE PHANTOM OF THE OPERA*)
(*Lyrics by* Charles Hart. *Additional Lyrics by* Richard Stilgoe.) M. Crawford

1992.13   OBA OBA '93

A New Edition of the Brazilian Musical Revue in Two Acts, 13 Scenes[7]. (Conceived and directed by Franco Fontana) Musical direction, Wilson Mauro. Choreography by Roberto Abraho. Produced by Franco Fontana. Opened 1 October 1992 at the Marquis Theatre and closed 11 November 1992 after 45 performances.[8]

CAST: ELIANA ESTAVO, Ailto Souza, Ana Careca, Ana Paula Dos Reis, Angela Mara, Arlindo Pipiu, Carlos Leca, Carlos Oliveira, Carlos Silva, Casemiro Raposo, Chico Filho, Claudia Lisboa, Claudio Nascimento, Claudio Sampaio, Claudio Santos, Cobrinha Mansa, Christiane Moreira, Edgar Aguiar, Edval Boa Morte, Eliane Garcia Emerson Bernardes, Formiguinha, Gamo, Giovani Ramos, Ilson Helvecio, Iris Da Rocha, Jaime Santos, Jones Santana, Jorge Boa Morte, Jorge Rum, Julio Peluchi, Lu Viana, Luciano Ribeiro, Mac, Marcia Labios de Mel, Marcio Do Repenique, Marquinho Da Geralda, Mauricio De Souza, Mercia Alexandre, Messias Bastos, Monica Acioli, Nelaci Costa, Nilton Maravilha, Patricia Dantas, Patricia Moreira, Paulo W. Takase, R. Malaguti, Ray Do Pandeiro, Ratinho, Rita De Cassia Nobre, Roberto Silva, Rodman Clayson, Rose Perola, Sergio Rocha, Sete Mola, Sonia Regina Maraes, Toco Preto, Valeria Matos, Wellington Gusmao, Wilson Mauro.

Scene 1

Origins of Brazil

Before the Portuguese people came to Brazil, it was a jungle full of beautiful nature—wonderful flora and fauna—and the only human beings living there were the native Indians. These people lived completely free in this natural paradise until Europeans came to Brazil with African slaves. Today, Brazil is touted as the world's cultural melting pot—and the apparently seamless integration of blacks, native Indians and white Europeans to create "the Brazilian" is witness to that. But it was not always so. Until the liberation of slaves, proclaimed by Princess Isabel of Portugal in 1888, the pain of blacks captive in Brazil was unmatched elsewhere in the Americas. Even after gaining their freedom, Afro-Brazilians had to struggle within a society full of discrimination. It was only through the attempted unification of all blacks that they began to rebuild and recovered their culture, brutally interrupted by slavery. This opening act portrays the stages of black culture in Brazil, from the early days of slavery to the redemption.

Scene 2

Homage to "Chorinho"

Chorinho is a Portuguese word that literally means "little cry." One would not guess that meaning, however, by listening to this lively rhythm that flourished in the turn of the nineteenth century in urban areas of Brazil, especially Sao Paulo and Rio de Janeiro. The cavaquinho, a type of ukelele, which is the centerpiece of any typical chorinho band, requires an amazing level of dexterity by the player. The cavaquinho sounds like a high-pitched lament, a little cry indeed, even when it is played in cheerful songs such as "Tico Tico No Fuba" or "Urubu Malandro," both of which were written by Brazil's most important chorinho composer, Zequinha de Abreu.

Scene 3a

Samba de Roda

In the public squares of Sao Salvador, the beautiful and mystic capital of Bahia, one may inadvertently run into an improvised competition of bliss and grace among women. The natives refer to this competition as Samba de Roda, roughly translated as "Samba in a Circle," a popular Bahia tradition whose roots are lost in the past. This competition is one of joy, with the girls taking turns flaunting their natural talents.

Scene 3b

Lambada

Another popular dance comes from Belem at the border of the Eastern Amazon: the now world-famous Lambada. Unlike Samba de Roda which is unqiuely Brazilian, the Lambada shares common ground with Caribbean culture; the rhythm bears a striking resemblance to Santo Domingo's merengue. The dance—voluptuous, sensual and downright carnal—is a lifesize reflection of one of the strongest aspects of Brazilian culture, one that can be found throughout the giant country: the lust for love.

Scene 3c

Samba Reggae

This dance was born just a few months ago in the town of Salvador, Bahia. In this short time, there has been an explosion of popularity of this dance, which is now becoming the rage throughout cities in Brazil. The rhythm which underscores this dance combines the traditional samba with reggae music from the Caribbean. This is the first time that this dance form is being presented in the United States.

Scene 4

Homage to the Northeast

It has been said that despite personal and national tragedies, Brazilians have a natural joie de vivre. From the desolate and poor Northeast—where droughts may last for many years in a row, destroying crops and spreading hunger—comes songs of lament seasoned with ever-lasting hope. Eventually, the mourn of the accordion resolves in an outburst of a people that learned to extract the good from bad situations and dance with candid jubilation.

Scene 5

Brazil Cappela

Ary Barroso's "Aquarela do Brazil"—"Brazilian Colors" in English—has become a classic that has risen to the level of an "alternative" Brazilian national anthem. The poetic lyrics rhapsodize about the exuberant natural splendors of Brazil. So strong is the chant that it demands no more than the superb voice of Eliana Estevao to bring it to life.

Scene 6

Homage to the Bossa Nova and the Seventies

The Bossa Nova is undisputed as the most precious artistic gift Brazil has given to the world. This musical revolution started in the mid-1950s with a handful of young composers in Rio de Janeiro and it spread throughout the world to such an extent that virtually all modern pop music—from jazz to heavy metal—shows some level of Bossa Nova influence, with its new concepts of harmonization, rhythmic division and melody writing. At the center of it all, one man guided the legion of followers that even today continues growing—Antonio Carlos Jobim. The composer of the revolutionary "Desafinado," the delightful "Girl from Ipanema" and dozens of other tunes that worked their way up the jazz and pop charts, Jobim is one of the most appreciated musicians in the world today.

Scene 7

Tribute to Carmen Miranda—the 'Brazilian Bombshell'

The first wave of Brazilian music ever to reach the United States came through the body and soul of Carmen Miranda. Born in Portugal, Carmen became an emblem of Brazil and managed to represent a comprehensive culture which encompassed the much wider and larger Hispanic community of Latin America. Her 'chica-chica-boom,' peculiar arm dance, colorful clothes and fruit basket hat are easily recognized in the U.S. But behind the outrageous facade was an authentic singer whose interpretations still rank among the best ever.

---

[7]Previous editions presented in New York 29 March 1988 at the Ambassador Theatre for 46 performances; 15 March 1990 at the Marquis Theatre for 45 performances.
[8]Settings and costumes uncredited.

ACT 2

Scene 1

Macumba

Brazil is the largest Catholic country in the world, but it is also true that many Brazilians are devoted to a second religion: the Macumba. Macumba is a type of voodoo, equivalent to Santeria in Cuba and Puerto Rico, and it has its roots in the same boats that brought the African slaves to Brazil and those other Caribbean countriies. The saints of Macumba (Oxossi, Yemanja, Xango, Obatala, and others) represent a blending of Catholic divinities with primitive African gods in an ambiance of magic and mystery that commences as the drums start echoing and a trance takes over the stage. As they say in the Macumba worship places, "Sarava!"

Scene 2

Afro-Brazilian Folk Songs and Dances — Berimbau Medley

Capoeira of Angola:

Capoeira is one of the principal elements of black culture in Brazil, where it arrived with the first boats coming from Angola. Deprived by their masters of carrying any kind of weapons, the slaves kept the tradition of capoeira as a means of conquering, and then defending, their freedom in the new land. To elude their white masters, blacks disguised capoeira in a dance to the rhythm of berimbau, pandeiro, ganga and caxixi. The berimbau is one of the many intriguing musical instruments developed by black culture in Brazil. It consists of a wood arch, bent by a string of metal wire; the resulting tension gives the wire a distinctive sound that can be "tuned" when pressed with a round metal chip by one hand and struck with a wood stick by the other. The sound is transmitted to an open, hollow coconut shell connected to the string through another piece of wire. A small caxixi — a device which produces a shaker-like sound — completes the set. The player hits the single string with the wood stick, tunes it with the metal chip, shakes the caxixi and presses the coconut shell back and forth against his thorax, and the resulting sound creates an atmosphere that can become a musical event in itself, or the background to a capoeira dance.

Maculele:

The dance of the Maculele, like Capoeira, was born in Bahia from the traditions brought by African slaves. Also like Capoeira, the dance is a practical disguise of a type of martial art. The batons used by the dancers can be replaced by swords and other types of mortal weapons, making it a very dangerous dance. Today, there are several Maculele groups, not only in Bahia, but in many other areas of Brazil, including the industrialized Sao Paulo.

Acrobatic Capoeira:

For the capoerista, the practice is more than a dance and more than a martial art — it is a philosophy, a way of life. The acrobatic capoeira here takes the form of a jogo, an exceedingly dangerous contest in which the opponents attempt to best one another combining traditional moves and individual improvisations. Oba Oba's capoeiristas, recruited among the best in the country, perform incredible acrobatic feats that are at once mighty and gracious.

Scene 3

Partido Alto

One of the most genuine expressions of Brazilian urban music in Partido Alto. Literally, the name means "High Party," in reference to the most distinguished members of a school of samba. Those are usually from the Ala de Compositores, a group of composers in charge of preparing the songs that will be sung during Carnival. They get together to improvise verses around some theme of the moment. A similar variation of Partido Alto is the Pagode — roughly meaning 'mockery' — in which sambistas joke around in a type of jam session with plenty of room for improvisation. As one would expect, in both cases the rhythm is the same that marks the Carnival parades — only a bit slower and with a more important role reserved to the acoustic guitar and the cavaquinho. In a typical Partido Alto or Pagode, a chorus is repeated by all members of the group and the improvised verses are sung alternately by each individual. Sometimes the verses express a duel between two members of the group, the winner being the one who has the last word.

Scene 4

Rhythm Beaters

The magic of the samba is rooted in many different percussion instruments: the humorous cuica — a drum that has the unique characteristic of being played from the inside, where a piece of wood attached to the skin is rubbed by the skillful hands of the player; the surdo — a huge drum that produces the bass-beat; the tamborins — high-pitched, small drums that are played with a stick; and finally, the father of it all, the pandeiro. The pandeiro, known to Americans as tambourine, is the central instrument of any samba group. Its round shape and leather skin remind its players of a soccer ball and it is almost inevitable that the two Brazilian passions — soccer and samba — come together in the performance.

Scene 5

Show of Samba Dancers

Joining the rhythm beaters are a group of mulatto women in a joyous display of samba dancing. The mulatto is perhaps the best expression of a possible "Brazilian race." Resulting from a mixture of the white Portuguese with the black Africans, the mulatto has more than just skin color to prove such inheritance. The duality of the African and the European continents is merged into the mulatto, transforming one single body into the conveyor of master and slave, pose and humbleness, sorrow and happiness, sensuality and innocence, and, most of all, beauty and strength.

Scene 6

Grand Carnival

Carnival is undoubtedly the greatest popular party in the whole world. It developed out of a Portuguese tradition of pagan parties which marked the four days preceding the grieving sobriety of Lent. In Brazil, Carnival has become a tapestry into which millions of lives are woven during day-to-day preparations. Carnival takes place 40 days before Lent; it starts on a Friday evening and lasts through the following Ash Wednesday. During these five nights and four days, certain morals take a vacation and perhaps the world becomes a better place in which to live. Although it is celebrated throughout the country, it is in Rio de Janeiro that the Carnival became the symbol that the world has learned to admire. In Oba Oba, the traditional parade of Rio de Janeiro's Schools of Samba is recreated to give a truthful taste of Brazil.

1992.14   REGINA

A Revival of the Musical Drama (Opera) in Three Acts, a Prologue and 4 Scenes[9]. Text and music by Marc Blitzstein. Based on the play "The Little Foxes" by Lillian Hellman. Directed by Rosalind Elias. Conducted by Laurie Ann Hunter. Set design by James Leonard Joy. Costume design by Joseph A. Citarella. Lighting design by Jeff Davis. Chorus master, Joseph Colaneri. (Orchestrations by Marc Blitzstein.) Produced by the New York City Opera. Opened 9 October 1992 at the New York State Theatre and closed 24 October 1992 after 4 performances in repertory.

CAST (in order of appearance): Addie, Regina's housekeeper: DENISE WOODS. Cal, Regina's houseman: MICHAEL LOFTON. Alexandra Giddens, Zan, Regina's daughter: ELIZABETH FUTRAL. Birdie Hubbard, Oscar's wife: SHERYL WOODS. Oscar Hubbard, Regina's brother: RON BAKER. Leo Hubbard, Birdie and Oscar's son: JOHN DANIECKI. Regina Giddens: LEIGH MUNRO. William Marshall, a businessman from Chicago: PAUL AUSTIN KELLY. Benjamin Hubbard, Regina's brother: ANDREW WENTZEL. Horace Giddens, Regina's husband: LEROY LEHR. Townspeople: New York City Opera Chorus.

1992.15   GYPSY PASSION

A Return Engagement of the Flamenco Musical Revue in Two Acts, 8 Scenes[10]. (Conceived) and directed by Tomas Rodriguez-Pantoja.

---

[9]Originally produced in New York 31 October 1949 at the 46th Street Theatre for 56 performances. For Synopsis of Scenes and Musical Numbers, see original 1949 production.

[10]Originally produced in New York 22 April 1992 at Town Hall for 15 performances.

Traditional music and lyrics from Spanish Gypsy Life. Artistic and musical director, Manuel Morao. Choreography by Gitanos de Jerez. Scenery by David Sumner. Costumes by Mercedes Muñiz. Lighting by Tom Sturge. Sound by Otts Munderloh. Production supervisor, Carlos Gorbea. Produced by Roy A. Somlyo and Andalucia Productions for the Government of Andalucia, Spain. Opened 17 November 1992 at the Plymouth Theatre and closed 2 January 1993 after 54 performances. Total including prior Town Hall engagement: 69 performances.

CAST: *First Generation*: MANUEL MORAO, Lorenzo Galvez, Manuel Moneo, Juana la del Pipa. *Second Generation*: Antonio el Pipa, Sara Baras, Concha Vargas, Juan Antonio Ogalla, Pepe de la Joaquina, Luis Moneo, Antonio Moreno, Carmen de la Jeroma. *Third Generation*: Manuela Nuñez, Mercedes Ruiz, Patricia Valdés, Estephania Aranda. And Maria Gonzalez.

Act 1, Scene 1: The Patriarch. *Scene 2*: The Forest outside Seville. *Scene 3*: In Seville, the next day. *Scene 4*: Seville, the market place.

Act 2, Scene 1: Romance. *Scene 2*: The Wedding. *Scene 3*: At work. *Scene 4*: Finale.

ACT 1

Scene 1

"Toná"
M. Morao (singer)

The chief of the gypsies, the oldest and wisest of the tribe, tells the story of his people in song.

Scene 2

"Villancico"
Entire Company
"Soleá"
J. la del Pipa (singer), C. Vargas (dancer),
M. Morao, L. Moneo, A. Moreno (guitarists)
"Cantiña"
P. de la Juaquina (singer), A. el Pipa (dancer),
M. Morao, L. Moneo, A. Moreno (guitarists)
"Tangos"
J. la del Pipa (singer/dancer)
"Tanguillos"
J. la del Pipa (singer/dancer), M., Nuñez, M. Ruiz, P. Valdés,
E. Aranda (dancers), M. Morao, L. Moneo, A. Moreno (guitarists)
"Seguirillas"
M. Moneo (singer), S. Baras (dancer), M. Morao, L. Moneo, A. Moreno (guitarists)

Gypsies prepare to spend the night in a gypsy camp, before going to the city market in the morning to trade their handicrafts. The birth of a child heightens the joy and excitement in the camp.

Scene 3

"Zapateado"
Entire Company
"Taranto"
L. Galvez, J. A. Ogalla, C. de la Jeroma (dancers), M. Morao (guitarist)

After conducting their business, the adults go to a tavern where they sing and dance the Flamenco.

Scene 4

"Bulerias"
P. de la Joaquina, J. la del Pipa (singers), M. Nuñez, M. Ruiz, P. Valdés, E. Aranda (dancers), L. Moneo, A. Moreno (guitarists)

After the business is conducted, the children express their emotions in a natural and spontaneous way.

ACT 2

Scene 1

"Alegrias"
P. de la Joaquina (singer), A. el. Pipa, S. Baras, J. A. Ogalla, C. de la Jeroma (dancers), M. Morao, L. Moneo, A. Moreno (guitarists)

Two young adults who have fallen in love express their emotions in song and dance.

Scene 2

"Alboreá"
Entire Company
"El Polo de Tobalo"

P. de la Joaquina (singer), A. el Pipa, S. Baras (dancers), M. Morao, L. Moneo, A. Moreno (guitarists)

The young lovers receive their families' approval to marry. The marriage ceremony takes place with the traditional gypsy rites and the new couple promises to perpetuate the gypsy heritage.

Scene 3

"Martinetes"
L. Galvez, M. Moneo, P. de la Joaquina (singers), A. el Pipa, S. Baras (dancers)

The new husband must work long hours in his father's blacksmith shop to support his bride.

Scene 4

"Bulerias" (reprise/finale)
Entire Company

Always a unique and happy people devoted to tradition, the gypsies embrace their treasured Flamenco in an affirmation of joy and celebration of life.

1992.16   3 FROM BROOKLYN

A Musical Revue in One Act. Conceived and directed by Sal Richards. Original music and lyrics by Sandi Merle and Steve Michaels. Musical director, Steve Michaels. Set design, Charles E. McCarry. Lighting design, Phil Monat. Sound design, Raymond D. Schilke. Produced by Michael Frazier, Larry Spellman, Don Ravella. Opened 19 November 1992 at the Helen Hayes Theatre and closed 27 December 1992 after 45 performances.

CAST: SAL RICHARDS, ROSLYN KIND, (BOBBY) ALTO & (BUDDY) MANTIA, ADRIANNE TOLSCH, RAYMOND SERRA (Cosmo the Cabbie). *THE BQE DANCERS*: Guy Richards, John Michaels, Damon Rusignola.

The action takes place on a street in Brooklyn at the present time.

MUSICAL NUMBERS[11]
"People" (from *FUNNY GIRL*)
R. Kind
(*Music by* Jule Styne. *Lyrics by* Bob Merrill.)
"I've Gotta Be Me" (from *GOLDEN RAINBOW*)
R. Kind
(*Music and Lyrics by* Walter Marks.)
"Take a Trip"
R. Kind
"Meadowlark" (from *THE BAKER'S WIFE*)
R. Kind
(*Music and Lyrics by* Stephen Schwartz.)
"3 from Brooklyn"
(Company)
(*Music by* Steve Michaels. *Lyrics by* Sandi Merle.)

1992.17   MY FAVORITE YEAR

A Musical in Two Acts, 15 Scenes. Book by Joseph Daugherty. Based on the film of the same name; screenplay by Norman Steinberg, Dennis Palumbo, from a story by Dennis Palumbo. Music by Stephen Flaherty. Lyrics by Lynn Ahrens. Directed by Ron Lagomarsino. Musical staging by Thommie Walsh. Sets by Thomas Lynch. Costumes by Patricia Zipprodt. Lighting by Jules Fisher. Sound by Scott Lehrer. Musical director, Ted Sperling. Orchestrations by Michael Starobin. Dance music arrangements by Wally Harper. Fight director, B. H. Barry. Produced by Lincoln Center Theatre (Andre Bishop, Artistic director; Bernard Gersten, Executive producer) in association with AT&T OnStage. Opened 10 December 1992 at the Vivian Beaumont Theatre and closed 10 January 1993 after 37 performances.

CAST (in order of appearance): *Benjy Stone*: EVAN PAPPAS. *King Kaiser*: TOM MARDIROSIAN. *Sy Benson*: JOSH MOSTEL. *K. C. Downing*: LANNYL STEPHENS. *Alice Miller*: ANDREA MARTIN. *Herb Lee*: ETHAN PHILLIPS. *Belle Steinberg Carroca*: LAINIE KAZAN. *Leo Silver*: PAUL STOLARSKY. *Alan Swann*: TIM CURRY. *Rookie Carroca*: THOMAS IKEDA. *Tess*: Katie Finneran. *Uncle Morty*: David Lipman. *Aunt Sadie*: Mary Stout.

---

[11]Not in performance order.

Ensemble: Leslie Bell, Maria Calabrese, Kevin Chamberlin, Colleen Dunn, Katie Finneran, James Gerth, Michael Gruber, David Lipman, Roxie Lucas, Nora Mae Lyng, Michael McGrath, Alan Muraoka, Jay Poindexter, Russell Ricard, Mary Stout, Thomas Titone, Bruce Winant, Christina Youngman. *Swings*: Robert Ashford, Aimee Turner.

The action takes place in New York City in 1954.

Act 1, Scene 1: The Broadcast Studio. *Scene 2*: The Writers' Office, morning. *Scene 3*: The Writers' Office, later that day. *Scene 4*: Swann's Waldorf Suite. *Scene 5*: Streets of New York. *Scene 6*: The Broadcast Studio. *Scene 7*: The Ladies' Room. *Scene 8*: The Broadcast Studio. *Scene 9*: Belle's Apartment.

Act 2, Scene 1: Central Park. *Scene 2*: The Plaza Hotel. *Scene 3*: Swann's Waldorf Suite. *Scene 4*: The Broadcast Studio. *Scene 5*: Swann's Dressing Room. *Scene 6*: The Broadcast Studio.

ACT 1

Scene 1

"Twenty Million People"
E. Pappas, Company

Scene 2

"Larger Than Life"
E. Pappas

Scene 3

"The Musketeer Sketch"
E. Pappas, J. Mostel, T. Mardirosian, A. Martin, L. Stephens, P. Stolarsky, E. Phillips

Scene 4

"Waldorf Suite"
E. Pappas
"Rookie in the Ring"
L. Kazan

Scene 5

"Manhattan"
T. Curry, E. Pappas, Ensemble
(*Orchestration by* Danny Troob.)

Scene 6

"Naked in Bethesda Fountain"
J. Mostel, A. Martin, P. Stolarsky, E. Phillips, L. Stephens
"The Gospel According to King"
T. Mardirosian, T. Curry, Company
"The Musketeer Sketch Rehearsal"
E. Pappas, T. Curry, Ensemble

Scene 7

"Funny/The Duck Joke"
L. Stephens, A. Martin

Scene 8

"The Musketeer Sketch Rehearsal" (Part 2)
T. Mardirosian, T. Curry, Ensemble

Scene 9

"Welcome to Brooklyn"
D. Lipman, T. Ikeda, L. Kazan, M. Stout, E. Pappas, T. Curry, Neighbbors
"If the World Were Like the Movies"
T. Curry

ACT 2

Scene 1

"Exits"
T. Curry

Scene 3

"Shut Up and Dance"
L. Stephens, E. Pappas

Scene 4

"Professional Showbizness Comedy"
A. Martin, T. Mardirosian, Ensemble

Scene 5

"The Lights Come Up"
T. Curry, E. Pappas

Scene 6

"Maxford House"
Maxford House Girls
"The Musketeer Sketch Finale"
Company
"My Favorite Year"
E. Pappas, Company

TOMMY TUNE
TONITE!

1992.18

A Song and Dance Act (Musical Revue) in One Act. Directed by Jeff Calhoun. Choreographic contributions by Charles "Honi" Coles, Tripp Hanson, Allan Johnson, Leslie J. Lockery, Ann Reinking, Hal Shane, Ron Young. Setting design by Tony Walton. Costume design by Willa Kim. Lighting design by Jules Fisher, Peggy Eisenhauer. Sound design by David Dansky. Musical direction, Michael Biagi. (Musical) arrangements and/or orchestrations by Michael Biagi, Randall Biagi, Wally Harper, Bob Holloway, Dick Lieb, Peter Matz, Michael Reeder, Alex Rybeck, Don Sebesky, Harold Wheeler. Overture arranged by Mark Hummel, orchestrated by Don Sebesky. Associate producers, Phillip Oesterman, David Wolfe. Produced by Pierre Cossette, James M. Nederlander, William E. Simon. Opened 27 December 1992 and closed 3 January 1993 after 10 performances.

CAST: TOMMY TUNE, Robert Fowler, Frantz Hall.

MUSICAL NUMBERS

"Tap Your Troubles Away" (from *MACK AND MABEL*)
(*Music and Lyrics by* Jerry Herman.)
"Let's Face the Music and Dance" (from *FOLLOW THE FLEET* film)
(*Music and Lyrics by* Irving Berlin.)
"A Song for Dancing" (from *BALLROOM*)
(*Music by* William Goldenberg. *Lyrics by* Marilyn and Alan Bergman.)
"Dancing in the Dark" (from *THE BANDWAGON*)
(*Music by* Arthur Schwartz. *Lyrics by* Howard Dietz.)
"Everything Old Is New Again"
(*Music by* Peter Allen. *Lyrics by* Carole Bayer Sager.)
"You're the Top" (from *ANYTHING GOES*)
(*Music and Lyrics by* Cole Porter.)
"Puttin' on the Ritz" (from *PUTTIN' ON THE RITZ* film)
(*Music and Lyrics by* Irving Berlin.)
"Someone to Watch Over Me" (verse only) (from *OH, KAY!*)
(*Music by* George Gershwin. *Lyrics by* Ira Gershwin.)
"Star Dust" (verse only)
(*Music by* Hoagy Carmichael. *Lyrics by* Mitchell Parish.)
"Blue Skies" (from *BETSY*
(*Music and Lyrics by* Irving Berlin.)
"The Old Soft Shoe" (from *THREE TO MAKE READY*)
(*Music by* Morgan Lewis. *Lyrics by* Nancy Hamilton.)
"Once in Love With Amy" (from *WHERE'S CHARLEY?*)
(*Music and Lyrics by* Frank Loesser.)
"I'm Building Up to an Awful Let-Down" (from *RISE AND SHINE*, London)
(*Music by* Fred Astaire. *Lyrics by* Johny Mercer.)
"They Can't Take That Away from Me" (from *SHALL WE DANCE* film)
(*Music by* George Gershwin. *Lyrics by* Ira Gershwin.)
"Taking a Chance on Love" (from *CABIN IN THE SKY*)
(*Dance music only by* Vernon Duke.)
"In the Still of the Night" (from *ROSALIE* film)
(*Music and Lyrics by* Cole Porter.)
"You Go to My Head"
(*Music by* J. Fred Coots. *Lyrics by* Haven Gillespie.)
Recollections of the Variety Arts Studios and Broadway
"Broadway Melody" (from *THE BROADWAY MELODY* {1929})
(*Music by* Nacio Herb Brown. *Lyrics by* Arthur Freed.)

"Please Don't Monkey With Broadway"
(from *BROADWAY MELODY OF 1940* film)
(*Music and Lyrics by* Cole Porter.)
"Sam the Old Accordion Man"
(*Music and Lyrics by* Walter Donaldson.)
"When the Midnight Choo-Choo Leaves for Alabam'"
(*Music and Lyrics by* Irving Berlin.)
"Strike Up the Band" (from *STRIKE UP THE BAND*)
(*Dance Music only by* George Gershwin.)
"Shanghai Lil" (from *FOOTLIGHT PARADE* film)
(*Music by* Harry Warren. *Lyrics by* Al Dubin.)
"Top Hat, White Tie and Tails" (from *TOP HAT* film)
(*Music and Lyrics by* Irving Berlin.)
Finale

1993.01   FOOL MOON

A Comedy Performance Revue in Two Acts. Created by Bill Irwin and David Shiner. (Original music and lyrics by the Red Clay Ramblers.) Set design by Douglas Stein. Costume design by Bill Kellard. Lighting design by Nancy Schertler. Sound design by Tom Morse. Flying by Foy. Producing associate, Nancy Harrington. Produced by James B. Freydberg, Kenneth Feld, Jeffrey Ash, Dori Berinstein. Opened 25 February 1993 at the Richard Rodgers Theatre and closed 5 September 1993 after 207 performances.

CAST (in order of appearance): DAVID SHINER, BILL IRWIN.
THE RED CLAY RAMBLERS: Clay Buckner (fiddle, harmonica), Chris Frank (piano, tuba, accordion, ukelele), Jack Herrick (trumpet, bass, banjolin, tin whistle, concertina), Tommy Thompson (banjos), Rob Ladd (drums).

ACT 1
Opening
  D. Shiner, B. Irwin, Red Clay Ramblers, 2 Ushers
"Fire and Sugar" (traditional)
  Red Clay Ramblers
Encounter
  D. Shiner, B. Irwin
"Old Jim Canaan's"
  Red Clay Ramblers
  (*Music and Lyrics by* Reverend Robert Wilkins.)
Dance Solo
  D. Shiner
Dance to the Left
  B. Irwin, Stage Manager
Big Night Out
  D. Shiner, B. Irwin, an Audience Member

ACT 2
"I Crept into the Crypt (and Cried)"
  Red Clay Ramblers
  (*Music and Lyrics by* Elizabeth Anderson.)
Improvisation in Public
  D. Shiner, an Audience Memeber
Harlequin/Pantalone
  B. Irwin, Red Clay Ramblers, D. Shiner
"Hiawatha's Lullaby"
  Red Clay Ramblers
  (*Music by* Walter Donaldson. *Lyrics by* Joe Young.)
"Tea for Two" (from *NO, NO NANNETTE*)
  D. Shiner, B. Irwin
  (*Music by* Vincent Youmans. *Lyrics by* Irving Caesar.)
Conductor
  B. Irwin, Red Clay Ramblers
Cinema
  D. Shiner, 4 Audience Members
"Valley of the Dry Bones" (traditional; a capella)
  Red Clay Ramblers, D. Shiner, B. Irwin
Dance/"Fire and Sugar" (reprise)
  B. Irwin, D. Shiner, Red Clay Ramblers

1993.02   THE GOODBYE GIRL

A Musical in Two Acts, 21 Scenes. Book by Neil Simon. (Based on his screenplay for the film of the same name.) Music by Marvin Hamlisch. Lyrics by David Zippel. Directed by Michael Kidd. Musical staging by Graciela Daniele. Scenery and costumes by Santo Loquasto. Lighting by Tharon Musser. Sound design by Tom Clark. Musical direction, Jack Everly. Assistant choreographer, Willie Rosario. Orchestrations by Billy Byers, Torrie Zito. Conductor, Jack Everly. Production supervisor, Peter Lawrence. Dance musical arranged by Mark Hummel. Associate producer, Kaede Seville. Produced by Office Two-One Inc., Gladys Nederlander, Stewart F. Lane, James M. Nederlander, Richard Kagan, Emanuel Azenberg. Opened 4 March 1993 at the Marquis Theatre and closed 15 August 1993 after 188 performances.

CAST (in order of appearance): *Lucy:* TAMMY MINOFF. *Paula:* BERNADETTE PETERS. *Billy:* Scott Wise. *Donna:* Susann Fletcher. *Jenna:* Cynthia Onrubia. *Cynthia:* Erin Torpey. *Melanie:* Lisa Molina. *Mrs. Crosby:* CAROL WOODS. *Elliott:* MARTIN SHORT. *Mark:* John Christopher Jones. *Stage Manager:* Darlesia Cearcy. *First Man at Theatre:* Larry Sousa. *Woman at Theatre:* Mary Ann Lamb. *Second Man at Theatre:* Rick Crom. *Cast of 'Richard III':* Barry Bernal, Darlesia Cearcy, Jamie Beth Chandler, Dennis Daniels, Denise Faye, Nancy Hess, Joe Locarro, Rick Manning, Cynthia Onrubia, Linda Talcott, Scott Wise. *Audience at 'Richard III':* Rick Crom, Ruth Gottschall, Sean Grant, Mary Ann Lamb, Larry Sousa. *Mark's Mother:* Ruth Gottschall. *TV Stage Manager:* Rick Crom. *Ricky Simpson Announcer:* Rick Crom. *Ricky Simpson:* John Christopher Jones. *Swings:* Ned Hannah, Michele Pigliavento.

Act 1, Scene 1: Paula's apartment. *Scene 2:* A dance studio. *Scene 3:* In front of Paula's building. *Scene 4:* Paula's apartment. *Scene 5:* Paula's apartment. *Scene 6:* An off-off-Broadway theater. *Scene 7:* Central Park. *Scene 8:* Paula's apartment. *Scene 9:* An off-off-Broadway theater.

Act 2, Scene 1: Paula's apartment. *Scene 2:* Paula's apartment. *Scene 3:* The Ricky Simpson Show. *Scene 4:* Paula's apartment. *Scene 5:* Paula's apartment. *Scene 6:* The rooftop of Paula's building. *Scene 7:* Paula's apartment. *Scene 8:* A schoolyard. *Scene 9:* The lake in Central Park. *Scene 10:* A TV Studio. *Scene 11:* Paula's apartment. *Scene 12:* In front of Paula's building.

ACT 1
Scene 1
  "This Is as Good as It Gets"
    B. Peters, T. Minoff
  "No More"
    B. Peters
Scene 2
  "A Beat Behind"
    B. Peters, S. Wise, Ensemble
Scene 3
  "This Is as Good as It Gets" (reprise)
    T. Minoff, L. Molina, E. Torpey
Scene 4
  "My Rules"/("Elliot Garfield Grant")
    M. Short, B. Peters
  "Good News, Bad News"
    M. Short, B. Peters, T. Minoff
Scene 5
  "Good News, Bad News" (reprise)
    C. Woods
Scene 7
  "Footsteps"
    B. Peters, T. Minoff
Scene 8
  "How Can I Win?"
    B. Peters
Scene 9
  "Richard Interred"
    M. Short, B. Peters, T. Minoff, J. C. Jones, C. Woods, S. Fletcher, Ensemble
ACT 2
Scene 1
  "How Can I Win?" (reprise)
    B. Peters

Scene 2
"Good News, Bad News" (reprise)
M. Short
Scene 3
"Too Good to Be Bad"
B. Peters, S. Fletcher, C. Onrubia
Scene 4
"2 Good 2 B Bad" (reprise)
C. Woods
Scene 5
"Who Would've Thought?"
B. Peters, M. Short, T. Minoff, L. Molina, E. Torpey
Scene 6
"Paula" (An Improvised Love Song)
M. Short, B. Peters
Scene 8
"Who Would've Thought?" (reprise)
T. Minoff, L. Molina, E. Torpey
Scene 9
"I Can Play This Part"
M. Short
Scene 10
"Jump for Joy"
B. Peters, Ensemble
Scene 11
"What a Guy"
B. Peters
Scene 12
Finale
B. Peters, M. Short, T. Minoff

THE WIZ

1993.03

A Revival of the Musical in Two Acts, a Prologue and 16 Scenes[12]. Book by William F. Brown. Based on the novel "The Wonderful Wizard of Oz" by L. Frank Baum. Music and lyrics by Charlie Smalls. Directed and choreographed by George Faison. Scenic design by Randel Wright. Costumes by Jonathan Bixby. Lighting by Jonathan McLain. Musical direction and dance arrangements by Timothy Graphenreed. Sound by Abe Jacob. Produced by Atlanta's Theatre of the Stars (Christopher B. Manos, producer) and Robert L. Young and Associates, in association with The National Black Arts Festival. Opened 16 March 1993 at the Beacon Theater and closed 28 March 1993 after 16 performances.

CAST (in order of appearance): *Aunt Em*: TONI SEAWRIGHT. *Toto*: Mischief. *Dorothy*: STEPHANIE MILLS. *Uncle Henry*: Maurice Lautner. *Tornado*: Evelyn Thomas. *Munchkins*: Inaya Jafan Davis, Bobby Daye, Kellie Turner, Virginia Ann Woodruff. *Addaperle*: EBONY JO-ANN. *Yellow Brick Road*: Christopher Davis, James A. Ervin, Cornell Ivey, Neil Whitehead. *Scarecrow*: GARRY Q. LEWIS. *Crows*: Evelyn Ebo, Gina Reneé Ellis, Roland Hayes, Frederick Moore, April Nixon, John Eric Parker, Katherine J. Smith. *Tinman*: EUGENE FLEMING. *Lion*: H. CLENT BOWERS. *Kalidahs*: Evelyn Ebo, Roland Hayes, Frederick Moore, April Nixon, Katherine J. Smith, Evelyn Thomas, Rachel Tecora Tucker. *Poppies*: Evelyn Ebo, Gina Reneé Ellis, April Nixon, Katherine J. Smith, Rachel Tecora Tucker. *Field Mice*: Inaya Jafan Davis, Cornell Ivey, John Eric Parker, Virginia Ann Woodruff. *Gatekeeper*: Bobby Daye. *The Wiz*: ANDRE DE SHIELDS. *Evillene*: ELLA MITCHELL. *Lord High Underling*: Maurice Lautner. *Soldier Messenger*: Roland Hayes. *Winged Monkey*: Cornell Ivey.
Winged Monkeys: Christopher Davis, Evelyn Ebo, James A. Ervin, Roland Hayes, Frederick Moore, April Nixon, John Eric Parker, Katherine J. Smith, Rachel Tecora Tucker, Neil Whitehead. *Emerald City Citizens*: Christopher Davis, Inaya Jafan Davis, Bobby Daye, Evelyn Ebo, Gina Reneé Ellis, James A. Ervin, Roland Hayes, Cornell Ivey, Maurice Lautner, Frederick Moore, April Nixon, John Eric Parker, Katherine J. Smith, Evelyn Thomas, Rachel Tecora Tucker, Kellie Turner, Neil Whitehead, Virginia Ann Woodruff. *Glinda*: TONI SEAWRIGHT. *Swings*: Raymond C. Harris, Maureen Brown.

---

[12]Originally produced in New York 5 January 1975 at the Majestic Theatre for 1672 performances. For Synopsis of Scenes and Musical Numbers, see original 1975 production. For this production, reprises of "Ease on Down the Road" for Dorothy, Scarecrow, Tinman, Lion (Scene 4 only) and "Yellow Brick Road" were added at the end of Act 1, Scenes 3 and 4.

THE SONG OF JACOB ZULU

1993.04

A Drama with Music in Two Acts by Tug Yourgrau. Original music composed by Ladysmith Black Mambazo. Lyrics by Tug Yourgrau and Ladysmith Black Mambazo. Directed by Eric Simonson. Set design by Kevin Rigdon. Costume design, Erin Quigley. Lighting design, Robert Christen. Sound design, Rob Milburn. Dialect coach, Gillian Lane-Plescia. Fight director, Ned Mochel. Produced by the Steppenwolf Theatre, Randall Arney, Stephen Eich, Albert Poland, Susan Liederman, Bette Cerf Hill, in association with Maurice Rosenfield. Opened 24 March 1993 at the Plymouth Theatre and closed 9 May 1993 after 53 performances.

CAST (in alphabetical order): *Marty Frankel*: Gerry Becker. *Mrs. Zulu, Mrs. Mgobese, Ma Buthelezi*: Pat Bowie. *Judge Neville*: Robert Breuler. *John Dawkins, Dr. Shaw*: David Connelly. *Martin Zulu, Zebulun, Guerrilla*: Leelai Demoz. *Jacob Zulu*: K. TODD FREEMAN. *Mrs. Sabelo, Beauty Dlamini, Guerrilla*: Erika L. Heard. *Mr. Vilakazi, Fumani, Guerrilla*: Danny Johnson. *Policeman, Mbongeni, Michael Dube, Guerrilla, Philip Zulu*: Gary DeWitt Marshall. *Reverend Zulu, Mr. X, Itshe*: ZAKES MOKAE. *Magistrate, Mr. Van Heerden, Mr. Jeppe*: Don Oreskes. *Aunt Miriam, Student, Ruth Dube*: Tania Richard. *Interpreter, Policeman, Student, Jacob's Superior*: Seth Sibanda. *Anthony Dent, Lieutenant Malan*: Alan Wilder. *Michael Jeppe, Lieutenant Kramer*: Nicholas Cross Wodtke. *Policeman, Uncle Mdishwa, Teacher, Percy, Commissar*: Cedric Young.
Chorus Leader: JOSEPH SHABALA. *Chorus*: LADYSMITH BLACK MAMBAZO: Jabulani Dubazana, Abednego Mazibuko, Albert Mazibuko, Geophrey Mdletshe, Russel Mthembu, Inos Phungula, Jockey Shabalala, Ben Shabalala, Joseph Shabalala.

Act 1, Scene 1: Shaka's Rock Shopping Mall, Natal, South Africa. 24 December 1985. *Scene 2*: Interrogation Room at a Jail in Pietermaritzburg. 29 December 1985. *Scene 3*: Visitors room, Eshowe Courthouse Jail. 6 February 1986. *Scene 4*: Eshowe Courtroom. Immediately afterward. *Scene 5*: The Jail Visitors Room. 7 February 1986. *Scene 6*: The Courtroom. Later the same day. *Scene 7*: A kraal, a traditional home, in Zululand; A Hospital in Pietermaritzburg. 8 February 1986. *Scene 8*: The Visitors Room. Later the same day. *Scene 9*: The Courtroom., 9 February 1986. *Scene 10*: The main room of the Zulu home in Imbali. Afternoon, the same day. *Scene 11*: A street near Imbali High School; one week later. A field on the edge of Imbali, two months later. A street in Imbali, later that afternoon. *Scene 12*: The main room of the Zulu home in Imbali. October 1984. *Scene 13*: Interrogation room at a jail in Pietermaritzburg; three days later. A street near Imbali High School; one week later. The Zulu home, one week later. Outside a store in Imbali, late October 1984. *Scene 14*: Outside the house in Imbali, later the same night. The South African border with Swaziland.

Act 2, Scene 1: Ma Buthelezi's home near Piet Retief, near the Swaziland border. Late evening in October 1984. The South African/Swazi border later that night. *Scene 2*: A street in Matola, asuburb of Maputo, Mozambique, two days later; before sunset. *Scene 3*: An Umkhonto we Sizwe training camp in Angola. October 1985; across the border in South Africa, mid-November 1985. *Scene 4*: The Courtroom, 10 February 1986; the same, morning of 11 February 1986. *Scene 5*: Jacob's cell, that evening. *Scene 6*: The courtroom, 12 February 1986; Pretoria Central Prison, 29 April 1986.

ACT 1[13]

Scene 1
"Lalelani!" (Listen!)
Scene 2
You are the one . . .
Scene 3
Cabanga! Imagine, imagine, imagine . . .
Jesus is my Savior . . .
Scene 4
"Ayikanoni!" (The time is not right!)
Blood river, Blood river. .
Scene 5
Oh, Jacob!
Scene 7
Our brother acts so strangely
Scene 8
"Ingane yeZulu!" (Child of Heaven!)
Scene 9
Boycott Bantu Education . . .

---

[13]List of musical numbers taken from published text (Arcade Publishing Co., New York, 1993).

Scene 11

The mouth is still, but the blood will tell . . .

Scene 12

Oh, Zulu, Zulu! Children of Heaven . . .

Scene 14

"Baba nomana" (Oh, Papa and Mama)

ACT 2

Scene 1

Wo ngaze ngahamba, ngahamba wema (I am wandering and roving all over)

It is dark in my mind, it is dark in my heart . . .

Scene 3

Wo ngaze ngahamba, ngahamba wema (reprise)

Scene 4

"Ingane yeZulu!" (Child of Heaven!)(reprise)

Scene 5

Uyezwa uyezwa uyezka na! (Do you hear, do you hear . . .)

Child of Heaven

Scene 6

Wozani! Wozani sihambe (Come see the wounds of Christ in heaven..)

"Lalelani!" (Listen!) (reprise)

"Nkosi Sikelel' iAfrika" (God Bless Africa)

(*Music and Lyrics by* Enoch Sontonga; translated by Rev. Philip Notombela, Tug Yourgrau.)

1993.05   AIN'T BROADWAY GRAND

A Musical in Two Acts, 18 Scenes. Book by Thomas Meehan and Lee Adams. (Inspired by the Michael Todd biography "A Valuable Property" by Michael Todd, Jr. and Susan McCarthy Todd.) Music by Mitch Leigh. Lyrics by Lee Adams. Directed by Scott Harris. Choreography by Randy Skinner. Scenery designed by David Mitchell. Costumes designed by Suzy Benzinger. Lighting designed by Ken Billington. Sound by Otts Munderloh. Musical direction, Nicholas Archer. Musical supervision, vocal arrangements by Neil Warner. Orchestrations by Chris Bankey. Dance arrangements by Scot Woolley. A Tra La La Inc. Production. Produced by Arthur Rubin. Opened 18 April 1993 at the Lunt-Fontanne Theatre and closed 9 May 1993 after 25 performances.

CAST (in order of appearance): *Bobby Clark:* GERRY VICHI. *Gypsy Rose Lee:* DEB-BIE SHAPIRO GRAVITTE. *Mike Todd:* MIKE BURSTYN. *Harriet Popkin:* Alix Korey. *Lou, the Stage Manager:* Bill Nabel. *Murray Pearl:* Mitchell Greenberg. *Reuben Pelish:* David Lipman. *Joan Blondell:* MAUREEN McNAMARA. *Marvin Fischbein:* Gabriel Barre. *Waldo Klein:* Bill Kux. *Wally Farfle:* Scott Elliott. *Dexter Leslie:* Richard B. Shull. *Jaeger:* Merwin Goldsmith. *Lindy's Waiters:* Bill Corcoran, Jerold Goldstein, Bill Nabel. *Thelma:* Caitlin Carter. *Floyd:* Patrick Wetzel. *Rocco:* Luis Perez. *Frankie, the Bartender:* Scott Fowler. *Herbie, the Office Boy:* Jerold Goldstein.

'Of The People,' Part 1: *The President and His Cabinet:* Timothy Albrecht, Bill Corcoran, Scott Elliott, Scott Fowler, Jerold Goldstein, Joe Istre, Rod McCune, Bill Nabel, Luis Perez, Mimi Cichanowicz Quillin, Patrick Wetzel. *Riverside Drive Streetwalker:* Beverly Britton. *Lili:* Ginger Prince. *Sheryl:* Jennifer Frankel. *Linda:* Mimi Cichanowicz Quillin.

'Of the People,' Part 2: *The President and His Cabinet:* Leslie Bell, Beverly Britton, Caitlin Carter, Colleen Dunn, Jennifer Frankel, Lauren Golar-Kosarin, Elizabeth Mills, Ginger Prince, Mimi Chicanowicz Quillin, Carol Denise Smith. *Ensemble:* Timothy Albrecht, Leslie Bell, Beverly Britton, Caitlin Carter, Bill Corcoran, Colleen Dunn, Scott Elliott, Scott Fowler, Jennifer Frankel, Jerold Goldstein, Lauren Goler-Kosarin, Joe Istre, Rod McCune, Elizabeth Mills, Bill Nabel, Luis Perez, Ginger Prince, Mimi Cichanowicz Quillin, Carol Denise Smith, Patrick Wetzel. *Swings:* Kelli Barclay, James Horvath, Lynn Sullivan.

The action takes place in the summer and early fall, 1948.

Act 1, Scene 1: The stage of the Alvin Theatre. *Scene 2:* Backstage at the Alvin Theatre. *Scene 3:* Backstage at a production meeting. *Scene 4:* Lindy's Restaurant. *Scene 5:* The Bar at "21." *Scene 6:* Todd's office. *Scene 7:* 'Of the People' show curtain. *Scene 8:* The Oval Office. *Scene 9:* The stage of the Colonial Theatre, Boston.

Act 2, Scene 1: The street in front of Lindy's. *Scene 2:* Todd's suite, Ritz-Carlton Hotel, Boston. *Scene 3:* Riverside Drive, near Grant's tomb. *Scene 4:* A costume shop. *Scene 5:*

Rehearsal backstage at the Alvin Theatre. *Scene 6:* The Beverly Hills Hotel, Beverly Hills, California. *Scene 7:* Behind the curtain at the Alvin Theatre. *Scene 8:* The Oval Office. *Scene 9:* Backstage at the Alvin Theatre.

ACT 1

Scene 1

"Girls Ahoy!"

G. Vichi, D. S. Gravitte, Ensemble

Scene 2

"Ain't Broadway Grand"

M. Burstyn, A. Korey, M. Greenberg, D. Lipman, Ensemble

"Class"

M. Burstyn, Chorus Girls

Scene 3

"The Theatre, the Theatre"

G. Barre, B. Kux

"Ain't Broadway Grand" (reprise)

M. Burstyn, A. Korey, M. Greenberg, R. B. Shull, G. Barre, B. Kux, S. Elliott, Ensemble

Scene 4

"Lindy's"

M. Goldsmith, Waiters, Company

"It's Time to Go"

D. S. Gravitte, Ensemble

Scene 5

"Waiting in the Wings"

M. McNamara

"You're My Star"

M. Burstyn, Ensemble

Scene 8

"A Big Job"

President, Ensemble

Scene 9

"Ain't Broadway Grand" (reprise)

Company

ACT 2

Scene 1

"Ain't Broadway Grand" (reprise)

M. Goldsmith, Waiters

Scene 2

"They'll Never Take Us Alive"

M. Burstyn, A. Korey, M. Greenberg

Scene 3

"On the Street"

M. Burstyn

"The Man I Married"

M. McNamara, Female Ensemble

Scene 4

"Maybe, Maybe Not"

D. S. Gravitte

Scene 5

"Tall Dames and Low Comedy"

G. Vichi, Ensemble

Scene 6

"He's My Guy"

M. McNamara

Scene 8

"A Big Job" (reprise)

President, Ensemble

Scene 9

"You're My Star" (reprise)

M. Burstyn

"Ain't Broadway Grand" (reprise)

Company

1993.06 (THE WHO'S) TOMMY

A Musical in Two Acts, 22 Scenes[14]. Book by Pete Townshend and Des McAnuff. Music and lyrics by Pete Townshend. Additional music and lyrics by John Entwistle and Keith Moon. Directed by Des McAnuff. Choreographed by Wayne Cilento. Scenery by John Arnone. Costumes by David C. Woolard. Lighting by Chris Parry. Projections by Wendall K. Harrington. Sound by Steve Canyon Kennedy. Musical supervision and direction, Joseph Church. Video by Batwin + Robin Productions, Inc. Orchestrations by Steven Margoshes. Special effects, Gregory Meeh. Flying by Foy. Fight direction by Steve Rankin. Technical supervision by Gene O'Donovan. Executive producers, David, Strong, Warner, Inc., Scott Zeiger/Gary Gunas. Associate producer, John F. Kennedy Center. Executive producers, David, Strong, Warner, Inc. and Scott Zeiger/Gary Gunas. Produced by Pace Theatrical Group and Dodger Productions with Kardana Productions, Inc. Opened 22 April 1993 at the St. James Theatre and closed 17 June 1995 after 900 performances.

CAST (in order of appearance): *Mrs. Walker*: MARCIA MITZMAN. *Captain Walker*: JONATHAN DOKUCHITZ. *Uncle Ernie*: PAUL KANDEL. *Minister*: Bill Buell. *Mr. Simpson*: Bill Buell. *Minister's Wife*: Jody Gelb. *Nurse*: Lisa Leguillou. *Officer #1*: Michael McElroy. *Officer #2*: Timothy Warmen. *Allied Soldier #1*: Donnie Kehr. *Allied Soldier #2*: Michael Arnold. *Lover*: Lee Morgan. *Tommy, age 4*: Carly Jane Steinborn or Crysta Macalush. *Tommy*: MICHAEL CERVERIS. *Judge*: Tom Flynn. *Tommy, age 10*: Buddy Smith. *Cousin Kevin*: Anthony Barrile. *Kevin's Mother*: Maria Calabrese. *Kevin's Father*: Tom Flynn. *Local Lads, later Security Guards*: Michael Arnold, Paul Dobie, Christian Hoff, Donnie Kehr, Michael McElroy, Timothy Warmen. *Local Lasses*: Maria Calabrese, Tracy Nicole Chapman, Pam Klinger, Lisa Leguillou, Alice Ripley, Sherie Scott. *Hawker*: Michael McElroy. *Harmonica Player*: Lee Morgan. *The Gypsy*: Cheryl Freeman. *First Pinball Lad*: Donnie Kehr. *Second Pinball Lad*: Christian Hoff. *Specialist*: Norm Lewis. *Specialist's Assistant*: Alice Ripley. *News Vendor*: Tom Flynn. *Sally Simpson*: Sherie Scott. *Mrs. Simpson*: Pam Klinger. *Mr. Simpson*: Bill Buell. *D.J.*: Tom Flynn.

Ensemble: Michael Arnold, Bill Buell, Maria Calabrese, Tracy Nicole Chapman, Paul Dobie, Tom Flynn, Jody Gelb, Chistian Hoff, Donnie Kehr, Pam Klinger, Lisa Leguillou, Norm Lewis, Michael McElroy, Lee Morgan, Alice Ripley, Sherie Soctt, Timothy Warmen. *Swings*: Victoria Lecta Cave, Romain Frugé, Todd Hunter, Trecy Langran.

Act 1, Scene 1: 22 Heathfield Gardens, London, England/POW Camp, Germany, 1941. *Scene 2*: Hospital/POW Camp, 1945. *Scene 3*: 22 Heathfield Gardens. *Scene 4*: English Courtroom. *Scene 5*: Hospital. *Scene 6*: Church/The home of the relatives, 1950. *Scene 7*: 22 Heathfield Gardens. *Scene 8*: 22 Heathfield Gardens/A youth club. *Scene 9*: Psychiatric clinic. *Scene 10*: 22 Heathfield Gardens. *Scene 11*: The Isle of Dogs. *Scene 12*: Amusement Arcade.

Act 2, Scene 1: The Sunlight Laundry. *Scene 2*: Research Laboratory. *Scene 3*: The Street/22 Heathfield Gardens. *Scene 4*: 22 Heathfield Gardens. *Scene 5*: The Streets of London, 1961-1963. *Scene 6*: Holiday Camp. *Scene 7*: The Simpsons'. *Scenes 8, 9, and 10*: Heathfield Gardens.

ACT 1

Overture: 1941
  Company
Scene 1
  "Captain Walker"
    Officers
Scene 2
  "It's a Boy"
    Nurses, M. Mitzman
  "We've Won"
    J. Dokuchitz, Allied Soldiers
Scene 3
  "Twenty-One"
    M. Mitzman, L. Morgan, J. Dokuchitz
  "Amazing Journey"
    M. Cerveris
Scene 5
  "Sparks" (instrumental)

"Amazing Journey" (reprise)
  M. Cerveris
Scene 6
  "Christmas"
    J. Dokuchitz, M. Mitzman, B. Buell, J. Gelb, Ensemble
  "See Me, Feel Me"
    M. Cerveris
Scene 7
  "Do You Think It's Alright"
    J. Dokuchitz, M. Mitzman
  "Fiddle About"
    P. Kandel, Ensemble
    (*Music and Lyrics by* John Entwistle.)
  "See Me, Feel Me" (reprise)
    M. Cerveris
Scene 8
  "Cousin Kevin"
    P. Kandel, Ensemble
    (*Music and Lyrics by* John Entwistle.)
  "Sensation"
    M. Cerveris, Ensemble
Scene 9
  "Sparks" (reprise, instrumental)
Scene 10
  "Eyesight to the Blind"
    M. McElroy, L. Morgan, Ensemble
    (Additional material *Music and Lyrics by* Sonny Boy Williamson.)
Scene 11
  "Acid Queen"
    C. Freeman
Scene 12
  "Pinball Wizard"
    Local Lads, A. Barrile, Ensemble

ACT 2

Underture (Entr'acte): 1960
  (Ensemble)
Scene 1
  "There's a Doctor"
    J. Dokuchitz, M. Mitzman
Scene 2
  "Go to the Mirror"
    N. Lewis, A. Ripley, J. Dokuchitz, M. Mitzman
  "Listening to You"
    M. Cerveris, C. J. Steinborn, B. Smith
Scene 3
  "Tommy Can You Hear Me"
    Local Lads
Scene 4
  "I Believe My Own Eyes"
    J. Dokuchitz, M. Mitzman
  "Smash the Mirror"
    M. Mitzman
  "I'm Free"
    M. Cerveris
Scene 5
  "Miracle Cure"
    T. Flynn, Local Lads
  "Sensation" (reprise)
    M. Cerveris, Ensemble
  "I'm Free"/"Pinball Wizard" (reprise)
    M. Cerveris, Company
Scene 6
  "Tommy's Holiday Camp"
    P. Kandel
    (*Music and Lyrics by* Keith Moon.)

---

[14]A ballet adaptation of TOMMY performed to the pre-recorded score by The Who was performed 3 May 1972 at the New York City Center by Les Ballets Canadiennes for 31 performances; see entry in that season.

Scene 7

"Sally Simpson"

A. Barrile, Security Guards, S. Scott, B. Buell, P. Klinger

Scene 8, 9, 10

"Welcome"

M. Cerveris, Ensemble

"We're Not Going to Take It"

M. Cerveris, Ensemble

"See Me, Feel Me"/"Listening to You" (reprises)/Finale

M. Cerveris, Company

BLOOD BROTHERS

1993.07

A Musical in Two Acts. Book, music and lyrics by Willy Russell. Directed by Bill Kenwright and Bob Tomson. Set and costume design by Andy Walmsley. Lighting design by Joe Atkins. Sound design by Paul Astbury. Production musical direction, Rod Edwards. Musical direction, Rick Fox. (Musical) arrangemnts, Del Newman. Associate producer, Jon Miller. Technical supervision, Gene O'Donovan. Produced by Bill Kenwright. Opened 25 April 1993 at the Music Box Theatre and closed 30 April 1995 after 839 performances.

CAST (in order of appearance): *Mrs Johnstone:* STEPHANIE LAWRENCE. *Narrator:* WARWICK EVANS. *Mrs. Lyons:* BARBARA WALSH. *Mr. Lyons:* Ivar brogger. *Mickey:* CON O'NEILL. *Eddie:* MARK MICHAEL HUTHINSON. *Sammy:* James Clow. *Linda:* JAN GRAVESON. *Perkins:* Sam Samuelson. *Donna Marie, Miss Jones:* Regina O'Malley. *Policeman, Teacher:* Robin Haynes. *Brenda:* Anne Torsiglieri.

Other Parts: Ivar Brogger, Kerry Butler, James Clow, Robin Haynes, Philip Lehl, Regina O'Malley, Sam Samuelson, John Schiappa, Anne Torsiglieri, Douglas Weston.

The action takes place in Liverpool, England.

ACT 1

"Marilyn Monroe"

S. Lawrence

"My Child"

S. Lawrence, B. Walsh

"Easy Terms"

S. Lawrence

"Shoes Upon the Table"

W. Evans

"Easy Terms" (reprise)

S. Lawrence

"Kids Game"

J. Clow, J. Graveson, C. O'Neill, Ensemble

"Shoes Upon the Table" (reprise)

W. Evans

"Shoes Upon the Table" (reprise)

W. Evans

"Bright New Day" (Prelude)

S. Lawrence

"Long Sunday Afternoon"/"My Friend"

C. O'Neill, M. M. Hutchinson

"Bright New Day"

S. Lawrence, Full Company

ACT 2

"Marilyn Monroe" (reprise)

S. Lawrence

"Shoes Upon the Table" (reprise)

W. Evans

"That Guy"

C. O'Neill, M. M. Hutchinson

"Shoes Upon the Table" (reprise)

W. Evans

"I'm Not Saying a Word"

M. M. Hutchinson

"Take a Letter, Miss Jones"

I. Brogger, R. O'Malley, Ensemble

"Marilyn Monroe" (reprise)

S. Lawrence

"Light Romance"

S. Lawrence, W. Evans

"Madman"

W. Evans

"Tell Me It's Not True"

S. Lawrence, Full Company

TANGO PASIÓN

1993.08

A Dance Musical in Two Acts, and a Prologue. Entire production conceived by Mel Howard. Choreography by Hector Zaraspe. Orchestrations, arrangements, musical direction and original music, José Libertella, Luis Stazo. Sets based on paintings by Ricardo Carpani. Costume and scenic design by John Falabella. Lighting by Richard Pilbrow, Dawn Chiang. Sound design by Jan Nebozenko. Originally presented at the Coconut Grove Playhouse, Miami, Florida (Arnold Mittelman, Producing artistic director). Executive producer, Norman Rothstein. Produced by Mel Howard, Donald K. Donald and Irving Schwartz. Opened 28 April 1993 at the Longacre Theatre and closed 2 May 1993 after 5 performances.

CAST (in order of appearance): *Ricardo,* the artist: Alberto del Solar. *Pedro Montero:* Jorge Torres. *Lila Quintana:* Pilar Alvarez. *Lucas,* the Maitre d': Osvaldo Cliento. *Juan Larossa:* Gustavo Russo. *Señorita Virginia:* Veronica Gardella. *Carmela,* the Waitress: Alejandra Mantinan. *Julio Camargo:* Marcelo Bernadaz. *Dr. Bertolini:* Luis Castro. *Señora Rosalinda Bertolini:* Claudia Mendoza. *Carlos Bronco:* Armando Orzuza. *Señora Dora Bronco:* Daniela Arcuri. *Grisel,* Carlos' Mistress: Graciela Garcia. *Romero Brandán,* the Spoiler: Jorge Romano. *Rosendo Frías,* Pool Player: Fernando Jimenez. *Angela,* Rosendo's Girlfriend: Judit Aberastain. *Rodolfo,* the Club Singer: Daniel Bouchet. *Flora Rosa,* the Club Singer: Yeni Patiño. *Zully,* the Lieutenant's Date: Viviana Laguzzi. *The Lieutenant:* Juan Corvalan. *Ludmilla Orlinskaya,* the European Movie Star: Gunilla Wingquist.

Sexteto Mayor: José Libertella, Luis Stazo (bandoneon), Mario Abramovich, Eduardo Walczak (violin), Oscar Palermo (piano), Osvaldo Aulicino (bass). And Tomás Giannini (bandoneon), Juan Zunini (keyboards, synthesizer), Jorge Orlando (percussion). *Dancing Couples:* Armando & Daniela, Fernando & Judit, Gustavo & Alejandra, Jorge & Pilar, Juan & Viviana, Luis & Claudia, Marcelo & Veronica, Osvaldo & Graciela. *Other dancers:* Jorge Romano, Gunila Wingquist. *Singers:* Daniel Bouchet, Alberto del Solar, Yeni Patiño.

Prologue: The present.

Act 1: The late 1940's.

Act 2: The present.

ACT 1[15]

How could I forget you, my Cafetín of Buenos Aires?

"Mi Buenos Aires Querido" (Gardel)

"Payadora" (Plaza)

Company

"Cafetín de Buneos Aires" (Mores, Discépolo)

A. del Solar (singer)

Sitting at your tables which ask no questions, I wept the bitter tears of my first heartbreak ...

"El Internado" (Canaro)

Armando & Daniela (dancers)

"El Moleston" (Libertella, Stazo)

Romano (dancer)

"Taquito Militar" (Mores)

Romano & Graciela (dancers)

"Nostalgias" (Cadicamo, Cabián)

D. Bouchet (singer)

I lift my glass and make a toast to the cruel misfortunes of love ...

"Chique" (Brignolo)

Luis & Claudia (dancers)

"Uno" (Mores)

Y. Patiño (singer)

One crawls and slithers between thorns simply trying to feel love ...

"La Cumparsita" (Rodríguez)

---

[15]Opening night song list prepared as per program insert.

"Recitado"
A. del Solar
I wasted my life shuffling empty dreams ...
"Canto"
D. Bouchet
If only you knew how much I still love you ...
"Danza"
Juan & Viviana
"Copete" (Anon.)
Fernando & Judit (dancers)
"Milonga del 900" (Piana)
Gustavo, Fernando, Marcelo, Osvaldo, Armando, Juan (dancers)
"La Tablada" (Canaro)
Osvaldo & Graciela
"Ojos Negros" (Anon.)
Gunilla, Osvaldo, Alberto
"Hotel Victoria" (Latasa)
Yeni, Juan, Osvaldo, Romano, Armando, Gustavo (dancers)
"El Firulete" (Mores)
Armando, Daniela, Gustvao, Alejandra, Luis, Claudia, Juan, Viviana
"Ojos Negros" (reprise)
Luis, Gunilla, Juan (dancers)
"Orgullo Criollo" (Decaro, Laurenz)
Gustavo & Alejandra
"Preludio a Francini" (Abramovich, Stazo)
Luis & Claudia
"El Dia Que Me Quieras" (Gardel, Le Pera)
D. Bouchet, Y. Patiño (singers)
The soft sound of your breathing caresses my daydreams ...
"Milonga de Mis Amores" (Laurenz)
Fernando & Judit (dancers)
"Responso" (Troilo)
Romano & Claudia (dancers)
"Re Fa Si" (Delfino)
Company
"Canaro en Paris" (Scarpino)
Sexteto Mayor, Company

ACT 2
I am because you have dreamed me.
"Rapsodia de Arrabal" (Libertella)
A. del Solar, Jorge & Pilar
"Bailonga" (Mores)
Company
"Melancolico" (Plaza)
Armando, Daniela, Osvaldo, Graciela (dancers)
"A Media Luz" (Donato)
Y. Patiño, D. Bouchet (singers), Luis, Gunilla, Alejandra, Judit, Claudia, Verónica (dancers)
When the lights are low, love casts a magic spell ...
"Seleccion de Milongas" (Castellanos, Villoldo, Laurenz)
Juan, Gustavo, Fernando, Romano (dancers)
"Asi Se Baila El Tango" (Marvil)
A. del Solar (singer)
This is how you tango; the arm, like a serpent, coils, around the waist ...
"Quejas de Bandoneon" (Filiberto)
Jorge & Pilar (dancers)
"Celos" (Gadé)
Sexteto Mayor
"Balada Para Un Loco" (Piazzolla, Ferrer)
Luis, Pilar, Gunilla (dancers), A. del Solar (singer)
Love me just as I am: loco, loco, loco!
"Melancolico Buenos Aires" (Piazzolla)
Marcelo & Verónica (dancers)
"Libert Tango" (Piazzolla)
Graciela, Viviana, Alejandra, Judit, Osvaldo, Juan, Gustavo, Fernando (dancers)
"Verano Porteño" (Piazzolla)
Juan, Jorge (dancers)

"Fuga Y Misterio" (Piazzolla)
Marcelo, Luis, Gustavo, Viviana (dancers)
"Adios Nonino" (Piazzolla)
Sexteto Mayor
Provocacion:
"Paris Otoñal" (Libertella)/
"Balada Para Mi Vida" (Libertella, Ferrer)
Jorge, Pilar, Company (dancers), A. del Solar, Y. Patiño, D. Bouchet (singers)
We will be lovers forever, passionate for eternity, two fires of God ...
"Onda 9" (Piazzolla)
Company

KISS OF
THE SPIDER WOMAN

1993.09

A Musical in Two Acts, a Prologue and 19 Scenes. Book by Terrence McNally, based on the novel of the same name by Manuel Puig. Music by John Kander. Lyrics by Fred Ebb. Directed by Harold Prince. Choreography by Vincent Patterson; additional choreography by Rob Marshall. Scenic design and projections, Jerome Sirlin. Costumes designed by Florence Klotz. Lighting design by Howell Binkley. Sound design by Martin Levan. Musical supervision, conductor, Jeffrey Huard. Orchestrations by Michael Gibson. Dance music by David Krane. Produced by Livent (U.S.) Inc. (Garth Drabinsky, Myron I. Gottlieb). Opened 3 May 1993 at the Broadhurst Theatre and closed 1 July 1995 after 906 performances.

CAST (in order of appearance): *Molina*: BRENT CARVER. *Warden*: HERNDON LACKEY. *Valentin*: ANTHONY CRIVELLO. *Esteban*: Philip Hernandez. *Marcos*: Michael McCormick. *Spider Woman, Aurora*: CHITA RIVERA. *Aurora's Men, Prisoners*: Keith McDaniel, Robert Montano, Dan O'Grady, Raymond Rodriguez. *Molina's Mother*: MERLE LOUISE. *Marta*: KIRSTI CARNAHAN. *Escaping Prisoner*: Colton Green. *Religious Fanatic, Prisoner*: John Norman Thomas. *Amnesty International Observer, Prisoner Emilio*: Joshua Finkel. *Prisoner Fuentes*: Gary Schwartz. *Gabriel, Prisoner*: Jerry Christakos. *Window Dresser at Montoya's, Prisoner*: Aurelio Padron.
Swings: Gregory Mitchell, Colton Green.

The action takes place in a prison in Latin America sometime in the recent past.

Prologue: A Prison. *Act 1, Scene 1*: The Prison; Molina's Cell. *Scene 2*: The Prison. *Scene 3*: Molina and Valentin's Cell. *Scene 4*: The Prison. *Scene 5*: The Cell. *Scene 6*: The Prison. *Scene 7*: Warden's Office. *Scene 8*: The Prison; the Cell. *Scene 9*: The Cell. *Scene 10*: The Infirmary. *Scene 11*: The Cell. *Scene 12*: Molina's movie; the Cell.

Act 2, Scene 1: The Cell. *Scene 2*: Limbo; Warden's Office. *Scene 3*: The Cell. *Scene 4*: Kiss of the Spider Woman. *Scene 5*: The Cell. *Scene 6*: The Prison; Warden's Office; Molina's Apartment; A Park; Molina's Mother's Apartment. *Scene 7*: The Interrogation Room; A Theatre.

ACT 1
Prologue
C. Rivera, Prisoners
Scene 1
"Her Name Is Aurora"
B. Carver, C. Rivera, Aurora's Men, Prisoners
Scene 2
"Over the Wall"
Prisoners
Scene 3
"Bluebloods"
B. Carver
"Dressing Them Up"/"I Draw the Line"
B. Carver, A. Crivello
"Dear One"
M. Louise, K. Carnahan, A. Crivello, B. Carver
Scene 4
"Over the Wall" II
Prisoners, B. Carver, A. Crivello
Scene 5
"Where You Are"
C. Rivera, Aurora's Men, Prisoners

Scene 6
  "Over the Wall" III-"Marta"
    A. Crivello, Prisoners
Scene 7
  "Come"
    C. Rivera
Scene 8
  "I Do Miracles"
    C. Rivera, K. Carnahan
Scene 9
  "Gabriel's Letter"/"My First Woman"
    J. Christakos, A. Crivello
Scene 10
  "Morphine Tango"
    Orderlies
  "You Could Never Shame Me"
    M. Louise
  "A Visit"
    C. Rivera, B. Carver
Scene 11
  "She's a Woman"
    B. Carver
Scene 12
  "Gimme Love"
    C. Rivera, B. Carver, Aurora's Men

ACT 2
Scene 1
  "Russian Movie"/"Good Times"
    C. Rivera, B. Carver, A. Crivello
  "The Day After That"
    A. Crivello, Families of the Disappeared
Scene 2
  "Mama, It's Me"
    B. Carver
Scene 3
  "Anything for Him"
    C. Rivera, B. Carver, A. Crivello
Scene 4
  "Kiss of the Spider Woman"
    C. Rivera
Scene 6
  "Over the Wall" IV-"Lucky Molina"
    H. Lackey, Prisoners
Scene 7
  "Only in the Movies"
    B. Carver, People in His Life (Company)

Sally Murphy and Michael Hayden in CAROUSEL
Joan Marcus/Photofest

1993–1994 SEASON

1993.10   SHE LOVES ME

A Revival of the Musical (Comedy) in Two Acts[1]. Book by Joe Masteroff. Based on the play "Illatszertár" [Parfumerie] by Miklos Laszlo. Music by Jerry Bock. Lyrics by Sheldon Harnick. Directed by Scott Ellis. Musical staging by Rob Marshall. Settings by Tony Walton. Costume design by David Charles, Jane Greenwood. Lighting design by Peter Kaczorowski. Sound by Tony Meola. Musical direction by David Loud. Orchestrations[2] by Fred Matosich, Jr., Don Walker (original orchestrations). Produced by The Roundabout Theatre Company (Todd Haimes, Artistic director; Gene Feist, Founding director). Opened 10 June 1993 at the Criterion Center Stage Right and closed 1 August 1993 after 61 performances; reopened 7 October 1993 at the Brooks Atkinson Theatre under the commercial auspices of James M. Nederlander, Elliott Martin, with Herbert Wasserman, Freddy Bienstock, Roger L. Stevens and closed 19 June 1994 after an additional 294 performances. Total: 355 performances.

CAST (in order of appearance): *Ladislav Sipos*: LEE WILKOF. *Arpad Laszlo*: BRAD KANE. *Ilona Ritter*: SALLY MAYES. *Steven Kodaly*: HOWARD McGILLIN. *Georg Nowack*: BOYD GAINES. *Mr. Maraczek*: LOUIS ZORICH. *First Customer*: Tina Johnson. *Second Customer*: Kristi Lynes. *Third Customer*: Trisha Gorman. *Fourth Customer*: Cynthia Sophiea. *Fifth Customer*: Laura Waterbury. *Amalia Balash*: JUDY KUHN[3]. *Keller*: Nick Corley. *Headwaiter*: JONATHAN FREEMAN. *Busboy*: Joey McKneely.

Ensemble: Bill Badolato, Peter Boynton, Nick Corley, Trisha Gorman, Tina Johnson, Kristi Lynes, Joey McKneely, Cynthia Sophiea, Laura Waterbury. *Swings*: Mary Illes, Mason Roberts.

1993.11   CAMELOT

A Revival of the Musical in Two Acts, 16 Scenes[4]. Book and lyrics by Alan Jay Lerner. Based on the novel "The Once and Future King" by T. H. White. Music by Frederick Loewe. Original New York production staged by Moss Hart. Directed and choreographed by Norbert Joerder. Scenic production supervision and additional design by Neil Peter Jampolis. Costume supervision and additional design by Franne Lee. Sound design by Tom Morse. Musical director, conductor, John Visser. Produced by Music Fair Productions, Inc. (Shelly Gross, Executive producer). Opened 21 June 1993 at the Gershwin Theatre and closed 7 August 1993 after 56 performances[5].

CAST (in order of appearance): *Sir Dinadan*: RICHARD SMITH. *Sir Lionel*: Virl Andrick. *Merlyn*: JAMES VALENTINE. *Arthur*: ROBERT GOULET. *Sir Sagramore*: Cedric C. Cannon. *Lady Anne*: Jean Mahlmann. *Guenevere*: PATRICIA KIES. *Nimue*: Vanessa Shaw. *Lancelot*: STEVE BLANCHARD. *Dap*: Newton R. Gilchrist. *Pellinore*: JAMES VALENTINE. *Mordred*: TUCKER MCCRADY. *Tom of Warwick*: CHRIS VAN STRANDER.

Ensemble: Virl Andrick, Steve Asciolla, Greg Brown, Cedrick C. Cannon, Ben Starr Coates, William Thomas Evans, Newton R. Gilchrist, Lisa Guignard, Theresa Hudson, Brian Jefferey Hurst, Donald Ives, Ted Keegan, Karen Longwell, Jean Malhlmann, Raymond Sage, Barbara Scanlon, Vanessa Shaw, Richard Smith, Verda Lee Tudor, Kimberly Wells. *Swings*: Tina Belis, Michael J. Novin.

Act 1, Scene 1: A hilltop near Camelot—a long time ago. *Scene 2*: The forest—immediately following. *Scene 3*: Arthur's Study—Five years later. *Scene 4*: A roadside near Camelot—A few months later. *Scene 5*: A park near the Castle. *Scene 6*: Arthur's study—A few weeks later. *Scene 7*: The grandstand of the jousting field. *Scene 8*: Arthur's study. *Scene 9*: The Great Hall.

---

[1]Originally produced in New York 23 April 1963 at the Eugene O'Neill Theatre for 301 performances. For Synopsis of Scenes and Musical Numbers, see original 1963 production. A shortened version of "Thank You, Madam" was performed at the close of "Sounds While Selling." "Tango Tragique" was omitted from this production, but performed as an instrumental during the scene. "A Romantic Atmosphere" orchestrated by David Krane. "Days Gone By" (reprise) dropped from Act 2.
[2]David Krane joined Frank Matosich, Jr. in revising Don Walker's orchestrations.
[3]Succeeded by DIANE FRATANTONI for the commercial transfer.
[4]Originally produced in New York 3 December 1960 at the Majestic Theatre for 873 performances.
[5]Orchestrations uncredited.

Act 2, Scene 1: The Castle Garden—A few years later. *Scene 2*: The Terrace—A few weeks later. *Scene 3*: Near the Forest of Morgan Le Fey—A few days later. *Scene 4*: The Forest of Morgan Le Fey—Immediately following. *Scene 5*: Corridor—That night. *Scene 6*: The Queen's Bedchamber—Immediately following. *Scene 7*: Camelot—Several days later. *Scene 8*: A Battlefield near Joyous Gard—A few weeks later.

ACT 1[6]
Scene 1
    "I Wonder What the King is Doing Tonight?"
        R. Goulet
    "The Simple Joys of Maidenhood"
        P. Kies
    "Camelot"
        R. Goulet, P. Kies
    "Camelot" (reprise)
        R. Goulet, P. Kies
Scene 2
    "Follow Me"
        M. Smith
Scene 3
    "Camelot" (reprise)
        R. Goulet, P. Kies
Scene 4
    "C'est Moi"
        S. Blanchard
Scene 5
    "The Lusty Month of May"
        P. Kies, Ensemble
Scene 6
    "How to Handle a Woman"
        R. Goulet
Scene 7
    "The Jousts"
        R. Goulet, P. Kies, Ensemble
Scene 8
    "Before I Gaze at You Again"
        P. Kies

ACT 2
Scene 1
    "Madrigal"
        Court Dancers, Musicians
    "If Ever I Would Leave You"
        S. Blanchard
    "The Seven Deadly Virtues"
        T. McCrady
Scene 2
    "Fie on Goodness!"
        T. McCrady, Knights
Scene 3
    "What Do the Simple Folk Do?"
        P. Kies, R. Goulet
Scene 5
    "I Loved You Once in Silence"
        P. Kies
Scene 6
    "Guenevere"
        Ensemble
Scene 7
    "Camelot" (reprise)
        R. Goulet

1993.12   THE STUDENT PRINCE

A Revival of the Operetta in Three Acts, a Prologue and 4 Scenes[7]. Music by Sigmund Romberg. Book and lyrics by Dorothy Donnelly. Book adaptation

---

[6]For this production, "Then You May Take Me to the Fair" and "The Persuasion" were omitted; "The Madrigal" was added.
[7]First produced in New York 2 December 1924 at the Jolson Theatre for 608 performances; this adaptation first produced by the NYC Opera 29 August 1980. For Synopsis of Scenes and Musical Numbers, see 1980 revival.

by Hugh Wheeler. Conducted by Scott Bergeson. Production (original direction) by Jack Hofsis. Stage director, Christian Smith. Scenery designed by David Jenkins. Costumes designed by Patton Campbell. Lighting designed by Gilbert V. Hemsley, Jr. Choreography by Donald Saddler, restaged by Jessica Redel. Chorus master, Joseph Colaneri. Produced by the New York City Opera. Produced by the New York City Opera. Opened 14 August 1993 at the New York State Theatre and closed 28 August 1993 after 15 performances.

CAST (in order of their appearance): Lackeys: Steven Raiford, Louis Perry, Edward Zimmerman, Ron Hilley. Dr. Engel, the Prince's Tutor: LOUIS OTEY. Count von Mark: DAVID RAE SMITH. Secretaries: Michael Lockley, Jonathan Guss. Prince Karl Franz: MICHAEL REES DAVIS. Lutz, valet to the Prince: JAMES BILLINGS. Gretchen, Maid at the Inn: SANDRA RUGGLES. Ruder: Joseph McKee. Nicholas: Gunnar Waldman. Toni, a waiter: Jonathan Green. Hubert: William Ledbetter. Detlef, a student leader: Gordon Gietz. von Asterberg, another student leader: Ron Baker. Lucas, another student leader: David Langan. Freshman: Steven Raiford. Kathie, niece of Ruder: MICHELE PATZAKIS. Girls: Madeleine Mines, Paula Hostetter, Jill Bosworth, Beth Pensiero. Grand Duchess Anastasia: MURIEL COSTA-GREENSPON. Princess Margaret, fiancée of Prince Karl Franz: MICHELE MCBRIDE. Captain Tarnitz: JEFF MATSEY. Countess Leydon, lady-in-waiting to the Princess: Dulcy Reyes. Huzzars: James Russell, Michael Lockley, Daniel Shigo, Richard Pearson. Friends of the Huzzars: Madeleine Mines, Paula Hostetter, Beth Pensiero, Jill Bosworth. Ensemble: New York City Opera Chorus.

THE MIKADO,
1993.13   or The Town of Titipu

A Revival of the Comic Opera in Two Acts[8]. Libretto by William S. Gilbert. Music by Arthur Sullivan. Stage director, Christian Smith. Choreography by Patricia Birch, restaged by Helen Andreyko. Conductor, Steven Mosteller. Scenery and costumes by Thierry Bousquet. Lighting by John Gleason. Chorus master, Joseph Colaneri. Produced by the New York City Opera. Opened 12 September 1993 at the New York State Theatre and closed 19 October 1993 after 7 performances in repertory.

CAST: The Mikado of Japan: RICHARD MCKEE. Nanki-Poo, his son, disguised as a wandering minstrel in love with Yum-Yum: PAUL AUSTIN KELLY. Ko-Ko, Lord High Executioner of Titipu: JAMES BILLINGS. Pooh-Bah, Lord High Everything Else: JOSEPH MCKEE. Pish-Tush, Noble Lord: Jeff Matsey. Yum-Yum, Pitti-Sing, Peep-Bo, three sisters, wards of Ko-Ko: ABBIE FURMANSKY, SANDRA GELB, FRANCES PALLOZZI. Katisha: CHRISTENE PALMER, BETTI LLOYD-JONES. Chorus of School Girls, Nobles, Guards and Coolies: New York City Opera Chorus.

CINDERELLA
1993.14

A Musical in Two Acts, a Prologue and 10 Scenes. Book and lyrics (for television) by Oscar Hammerstein II. Book adapted by Steve Allen, adapted for the stage by Robert Johanson. Music by Richard Rodgers. Directed and choreographed by Robert Johanson. Co-choreographer, Sharon Halley. Set designer, Henry Bardon. Costume designer, Gregg Barnes. Lighting designer, Jeff Davis. Sound designer, Abe Jacob. Conductor, Eric Stern. Orchestrations by Robert Russell Bennett. Chorus master, Joseph Colaneri. Assistant stage director, Paul L. King. Produced by the New York City Opera. Opened 9 November 1993 at the New York State Theatre and closed 21 November 1993 after 14 performances.

CAST (in order of appearance): Fairy Godmother: SALLY ANN HOWES. Royal Herald: Ron Baker. Little Girl: Abigail Mentzer. Cinderella's Stepmother: NANCY MARCHAND. Cinderella's Stepsisters (2): Joy: ALIX KOREY. Portia: JEANETTE PALMER. Cinderella: CRISTA MOORE. Dog: Andrew Pacho. Cat: Debbi Fuhrman. Queen: MARIA KARNILOVA. King: GEORGE S. IRVING. Royal Chef: Jonathan Green. Royal Steward: John Lankston. Prince: GEORGE DVORSKY. Youngest Fairy: Stephanie Godino. Tiara Fairy: Shawn Stephens. Ensemble: New York City Opera Chorus.

Prologue: A Public Square.

Act 1, Scene 1: The Kitchen. Scene 2: Royal Dressing Room. Scene 3: Back in the Kitchen. Scene 4: A Magical Place.

Act 2, Scene 1: The Palace Ballroom. Scene 2: A Garden at the Palace. Scene 3: The Palace Ballroom. Scene 4: Back in the Kitchen. Scene 5: Garden at the Palace. Scene 6: The Palace Ballroom.

ACT 1[9]
Prologue
   "The Prince Is Giving a Ball"
      R. Baker, Townspeople
Scene 1
   "In My Own Little Corner"
      C. Moore
Scene 2
   "The Prince Is Giving a Ball" (reprise)
      Townspeople
   "Your Majesties"
      G. S. Irving, M. Karnilova, J. Lankston, J. Green, Ensemble
   "The Loneliness of Evening"[10]
      G. Dvorsky
   "My Best Love"[11]
      G. S. Irving, G. Dvorsky
Scene 3
   "Impossible"
      C. Moore, S. A. Howes
Scene 4
   "The Gavotte"
      Ensemble

ACT 2
Scene 1
   "Ten Minutes Ago"
      C. Moore, G. Dvorsky
Scene 2
   "Stepsisters' Lament"
      A. Korey, J. Palmer
Scene 3
   "Waltz for a Ball"
      Ensemble
   "If I Weren't King"[12]
      G. S. Irving
   "Do I Love You Because You're Beautiful?"
      C. Moore, G. Dvorsky
Scene 4
   ("When You're Driving Through the Moonlight")
      C. Moore, N. Marchand, A. Korey, J. Palmer
   "A Lovely Night"
      C. Moore, N. Marchand, A. Korey, J. Palmer
Scene 6
   Finale
      Company

JOSEPH AND THE AMAZING TECHNICOLOR DREAMCOAT
1993.15

A Revival of the Musical in Two Acts, a Prologue and 21 Scenes[13]. Music by Andrew Lloyd Webber. Lyrics by Tim Rice. Based on the Old Testament story. Directed by Stephen Pimlott. Choreography by Anthony Van Laast. (Scenery and costume) Design by Mark Thompson. Lighting design by Andrew Bridge. Sound design by Martin Levan. Musical direction by Patrick Vaccariello. Musical supervision by Michael Reed. Orchestrations by John Cameron. An Andrew Lloyd Webber Production. Produced by James M. Nederlander and Terry Allen Kramer. Opened 10 November 1993 at the Minskoff Theatre and closed 29 May 1994 after 231 performances.

CAST: Joseph: MICHAEL DAMIAN. Narrator: KELLI RABKE. Pharaoh: ROBERT TORTI. Jacob/Potiphar/Guru: CLIFFORD DAVID. Butler: Glenn Sneed. Baker: Bill Nolte. Mrs. Potiphar: JULIE BOND. Apache Dancers: Tina Ou, Tim Schultheis.

[9]Musical numbers not listed in programs.
[10]Dropped from SOUTH PACIFIC before its opening.
[11]Dropped from FLOWER DRUM SONG before its opening.
[12]Newly interpolated.
[13]Originally produced in New York Off-Broadway 18 November 1981 at the Entermedia Theatre for 77 performances; transferred 27 January 1982 to the Royale Theatre for 670 performances. Total: 747 performances. Previously produced Off-Broadway twice at the Brooklyn Academy of Music: 26 December 1976 for 22 performances, and 13 December 1977 for 24 performances.

[8]First presented in New York 20 July, 10-29 August 1885 at the Union Square and People's Theatres for 22 performances. First authorized production presented 19 August 1885 at the Fifth Avenue Theatre by Richard D'Oyly Carte for 250 performances. For Synopsis of Scenes and Musical Numbers, see 19 August 1885 D'Oyly Carte production.

Brothers and Wives: Reuben: MARC KUDISCH. *Reuben's Wife*: Michelle Murlin. *Simeon*: Neal Ben-Ari. *Simeon's Wife*: Mindy Franzese. *Levi*: ROBERT TORTI. *Levi's Wife*: Jocelyn Vodovoz Cook. *Napthali*: DANNY BOLERO. *Napthali's Wife*: Mamie Duncan-Gibbs. *Issachar*: Bill Nolte. *Issachar's Wife*: Jacquie Porter. *Asher*: Timothy Smith. *Asher's Wife*: Lisa Akey. *Dan*: Joseph Savant. *Dan's Wife*: Sarah Miles. *Zebulun*: Tim Schultheis. *Zebulun's Wife*: Diana Brownstone. *Gad*: Glenn Sneed. *Gad's Wife*: Gina Trano. *Benjamin*: TY TAYLOR. *Benjamin's Wife*: Tina Ou. *Judah*: Gerry McIntyre. *Judah's Wife*: Susan Carr George.

Swings: Ron Kellum, Andrew Makay, Janet Rothermel, Kelli Severson, Gina Trano, Matthew Zarley.

Children's Choirs: The Carolabbe Chorus, La Petite Musicale, Long Island Performing Arts Center Choir, The William F. Halloran Vocal Ensemble.

ACT 1
Prologue ("You Are What You Feel")
    K. Rabke
Scene 1
    "Any Dream Will Do"
        M. Damina, Children
Scene 2
    "Jacob and Sons"/"Joseph's Coat"
        K. Rabke, Brothers, Wives, Children, C. David, M. Damian
Scene 3
    "Joseph's Dreams"
        K. Rabke, M. Damian, Brothers, Female Ensemble
Scene 4
    "Poor Poor Joseph"
        K. Rabke, Brothers, Children
Scene 5
    "One More Angel in Heaven"
        M. Kudisch, M. Murlin, K. Rabke, Brothers, Wives, C. David, Children
Scene 6
    "Potiphar"
        K. Rabke, Ensemble, J. Bond, C. David, M. Damian
Scene 7
    "Close Every Door"
        M. Damian, Children
Scene 8
    "Go, Go, Go Joseph"
        K. Rabke, G. Sneed, B. Nolte, Ensemble, C. David, Children
ACT 2
Scene 1
    "Pharaoh's Story"
        K. Rabke, Children
Scene 2
    "Poor, Poor Pharaoh"/"Song of the King"
        K. Rabke, G. Sneed, C. David, Children, Men
Scene 3
    "Pharaoh's Dream Explained"
        M. Damian, Ensemble, Children
Scene 4
    "Stone the Crows"
        K. Rabke, C. David, Children, M. Damian, Female Ensemble
Scene 5
    "Those Canaan Days"
        P. Harman, C. David, Brothers, Apache Dancers
Scene 6
    "The Brothers Came to Egypt"/"Grovel, Grovel"
        K. Rabke, Brothers, M. Damian, Female Ensemble, Children
Scene 7
    "Who's the Thief?"
        M. Damian, Brothers, Female Ensemble, Children
Scene 8
    "Benjamin Calypso"
        G. McIntyre, Brothers, Female Ensemble, Children
Scene 9
    "Joseph All the Time"
        K. Rabke, M. Damian, Children, Brothers, Female Ensemble
Scene 10
    "Jacob in Egypt"
        K. Rabke, M. Damian, Children, Ensemble
Scene 11
    "Any Dream Will Do"
        M. Damian, K. Rabke, Ensemble, C. David, Children

Scene 12
    "Close Every Door" (reprise)
        M. Damian, Children
Scene 13
    "Joseph Megamix"
        The Company

A GRAND NIGHT FOR SINGING

1993.16

A Musical Revue in Two Acts[14]. Conceived and directed by Walter Bobbie. Music by Richard Rodgers. Lyrics by Oscar Hammerstein II. Settings by Tony Walton. Costume design by Martin Pakledinaz. Lighting design by Natasha Katz. Sound by Tony Meola. Orchestrations by Michael Gibson, Jonathan Tunick. Musical direction and arrangements by Fred Wells. Additional staging by Pamela Sousa. Produced by The Roundabout Theatre Company (Todd Haimes, Artistic director; Gene Feist, Founding director). Opened 17 November 1993 at the Criterion Center Stage Right and closed 2 January 1994 after 52 performances.

CAST (in order of appearance): MARTIN VIDNOVIC, JASON GRAAE, VICTORIA CLARK, ALYSON REED, LYNNE WINTERSTELLER

ACT 1
    "Carousel Waltz" (from *CAROUSEL*)/
        "So Far" (from *ALLEGRO*)/
    "It's a Grand Night For Singing" (from *STATE FAIR* film)
        Company
    "The Surrey with the Fringe on the Top" (from *OKLAHOMA!*)
        J. Graae
    "Stepsisters' Lament" (from *CINDERELLA*)
        L. Wintersteller, V. Clark
    "We Kiss in a Shadow" (from *THE KING AND I*)
        M. Vidnovic
    "Hello, Young Lovers" (from *THE KING AND I*)
        Company
    "A Wonderful Guy" (from *SOUTH PACIFIC*)
        A. Reed
    "I Cain't Say No" (from *OKLAHOMA!*)
        V. Clark
    "Maria" (from *THE SOUND OF MUSIC*)
        J. Graae
    "Do I Love You Because You're Beautiful?" (from *CINDERELLA*)
        L. Wintersteller
    "Honey Bun" (from *SOUTH PACIFIC*)
        M. Vidnovic, Company
    "The Gentleman Is a Dope" (from *ALLEGRO*)
        A. Reed
    "Don't Marry Me" (from *FLOWER DRUM SONG*)
        M. Vidnovic, J. Graae, L. Wintersteller, V. Clark
    "I'm Gonna Wash That Man Right Outa My Hair" (from *SOUTH PACIFIC*)
        A. Reed, L. Wintersteller, V. Clark
    "If I Loved You" (from *CAROUSEL*)
        V. Clark
    "Shall We Dance?" (from *THE KING AND I*)
        L. Wintersteller, J. Graae
    "That's the Way It Happens" (from *ME AND JULIET*)
        A. Reed, J. Graae
    "All at Once You Love Her" (from *PIPE DREAM*)
        M. Vidnovic, J. Graae
    "Some Enchanted Evening" (from *SOUTH PACIFIC*)
        Company
ACT 2
    "Oh, What a Beautiful Mornin'" (from *OKLAHOMA!*)
        M. Vidnovic
    "Wish Them Well" (from *ALLEGRO*)
        Company

---

[14]Originally produced Off-Broadway as a nightclub revue 2 March-10 April 1993 at Rainbow and Stars for 60 performances.

"The Man I Used To Be" (from *PIPE DREAM*)
V. Clark, A. Reed, J. Graae
(*Dance arrangements by* Wally Harper.)

"It Might As Well Be Spring" (from *STATE FAIR*)
L. Wintersteller

"Kansas City" (from *OKLAHOMA!*)
Company

"When the Children Are Asleep" (from *CAROUSEL*)

"I Know It Can Happen Again" (from *ALLEGRO*)

"My Little Girl" (excerpt from "Soliloquy," from *CAROUSEL*)
Company

"It's Me" (from *ME AND JULIET*)
A. Reed, J. Graae, M. Vidnovic
(*Dance arrangements by* Wally Harper.)

"Love, Look Away" (from *FLOWER DRUM SONG*)
V. Graae

"When You're Driving Through the Moonlight" (from *CINDERELLA*)

"A Lovely Night" (from *Cinderella*)
V. Clark, M. Vidnovic, A. Reed, J. Graae

"Something Wonderful" (from *THE KING AND I*)
L. Wintersteller

"This Nearly Was Mine" (from *SOUTH PACIFIC*)
M. Vidnovic

"Impossible" (from *CINDERELLA*)

"I Have Dreamed" (from *THE KING AND I*)
Company

1993.17 CYRANO: THE MUSICAL

A Musical in Two Acts, 3 Scenes. Based on the play "Cyrano de Bergarac" by Edmond Rostand. (Original Dutch) Book and lyrics by Koen van Dijk. Music by Ad van Dijk. English lyrics by Peter Reeves; additional lyrics by Sheldon Harnick. Directed by Eddy Habbema. Scenery designed by Paul Gallis. Costumes designed by Yan Tax. Lighting designed by Reinier Tweebeeke. Sound designed by Rogier van Rossum. Associate set design, Duke Durfee. Associate costume design, Marcia K. McDonald. Associate lighting design, Brian Nason. Associate sound design, Steve Canyon Kennedy. Orchestrations by Don Sebesky, Tony Cox. Special effects, Gregory Meeh. Associate director, Eleanor Fazan. Fight director, Malcolm Ranson. Executive producer, Robin DeLevita. Produced by Joop van den Ende in association with Peter Kulok. Opened 21 November 1993 at the Neil Simon Theatre and closed 20 March 1994 after 137 performances.

CAST (in order of appearance): *Man:* Geoffrey Blaisdell. *Le Bret:* PAUL SCHOEFFLER. *Ragueneau:* ED DIXON. *Christian:* PAUL ANTHONY STEWART. *DeGuiche:* TIMOTHY NOLEN. *Roxane:* ANNE RUNOLFSSON. *Valvert:* Adam Pelty. *Chaperone:* Joy Hermalyn. *Montfleury:* Mark Agnes. *Cyrano:* BILL VAN DIJK, Jordan Bennett (alternate). *Captain de Castel Jaloux:* Geoffrey Blaisdell. *Mother Superior:* Elizabeth Acosta. *Novice:* Michele Ragusa.
Opera Audience, Cadets, Precieuses, Chefs, Waitresses, Nuns: Elizabeth Acosta, Mark Agnes, Carina Andersson, Christopher Eaton Baily, James Barbour, Geoffrey Blaisdell, Michelle Dawson, Jeff Gardner, Daniel Guzman, Joy Hermalyn, Bjørn Johnson, Peter Lockyer, Stuart Marland, Kerry O'Malley, Adam Pelty, Tom Polum, Michele Ragusa, Sam Scalamoni, Robin Skye, Tami Tappan, Ann van Cleave, Charles West. *Swings:* Ted Keegan, Rose McGuire, Christian Nova.

Act 1: Paris, 1640.

Act 2, Scene 1: A besieged camp near Arras, a few month later. *Scene 2:* Paris, seven years later.

ACT 1

Prologue
G. Blaisdell, P. Schoeffler, E. Dixon, Ensemble

"Opera, Opera"
Ensemble

"Aria"
M. Agnes, B. Van Dijk, Ensemble

"One Fragment of a Moment"
P. A. Stewart, A. Runolfsson

"Confrontation"
Ensemble

"The Duel"
B. Van Dijk, Ensemble

"Where's All This Anger Coming From"
P. Schoeffler, B. Van Dijk

"Loving Her"
B. Van Dijk, P. A. Stewart

"A Message from Roxane"
J. Hermalyn, B. Van Dijk

"Ragueneau's Patisserie"
E. Dixon, Chefs, Waitresses

"Roxane's Confession"
A. Runolfsson, B. Van Dijk

"What a Reward"
T. Nolen, P. Schoeffler, E. Dixon

"Hate Me"
B. Van Dijk

"Courage Makes a Man"
Cadets, G. Blaisdell

"Cyrano's Story"
B. Van Dijk, P. A. Stewart

"A Letter for Roxane"
B. Van Dijk, P. A. Stewart

"I Have No Words"
P. A. Stewart

"Two Musketeers"
B. Van Dijk, P. A. Stewart

"An Evening Made for Lovers"
Ensemble

"Balcony Scene"
A. Runolfsson, P. A. Stewart, B. Van Dijk

"Poetry"
B. Van Dijk, A. Runolfsson

"Moonsong"
B. Van Dijk

"Stay With Me!"
Ensemble

ACT 2
Scene 1

"Every Day, Every Night"
B. Van Dijk, P. A. Stewart, Cadets

"A White Sash"
T. Nolen, B. Van Dijk, Cadets

"When I Write"
B. Van Dijk

"Two Musketeers" (reprise)
P. A. Stewart, B. Van Dijk

"Rhyming Menu"
A. Runolfsson, E. Dixon, Ensemble

"Even Then"
A. Runolfsson

"Tell Her Now"
P. A. Stewart, B. Van Dijk

"The Evening"
B. Van Dijk, Cadets

"Even Then" (reprise)
A. Runolfsson, B. Van Dijk

"The Battle"
Ensemble

"Everything You Wrote"
A. Runolfsson

Scene 2

"He Loves To Make Us Laugh"
Nuns, E. Acosta

"A Visit from DeGuiche"
T. Nolen, A. Runolfsson, E. Acosta

"Opera, Opera" (reprise)
Ensemble

"An Old Wound"/"The Letter"/"Moonsong"
B. Van Dijk, A. Runolfsson

1993.18

MY FAIR LADY

A Revival of the Musical (Comedy) in Two Acts, 18 Scenes[15]. Book and lyrics by Alan Jay Lerner. Based on the play "Pygmalion" by George Bernard Shaw, produced on the screen by Gabriel Pascal. Music by Frederick Loewe. Directed by Howard Davies. Choreography by Donald Saddler. Scenic design based on original designs by Ralph Koltai. Costume design by Patricia Zipprodt. Lighting design by Natasha Katz. Sound design by Peter Fitzgerald. Musical and vocal direction, Jack Lee. Production supervisor, Craig Jacobs. Associate producer, Alecia Parker. Produced by Barry and Fran Weissler, Jujamcyn Theatres in association with Pace Theatrical Group, Tokyo Broadcasting System International and Martin Rabbett. Opened 9 December 1993 at the Virginia Theatre and closed 1 May 1994 after 165 performances.

CAST (in order of appearance): *Eliza Doolittle*: MELISSA ERRICO. *Freddy Eynsford-Hill*: ROBERT SELLA. *Mrs. Eynsford-Hill*: Lisa Merrill McCord. *Colonel Pickering*: PAXTON WHITEHEAD. *Professor Henry Higgins*: RICHARD CHAMBERLAIN. *The 'Loverly Quartet'*: Jeffrey Wilkins, Bruce Moore, Michael Gerhart, Jamie Mackenzie. *George the Bartender*: Bill Ullman. *Jamie*: Michael J. Farina. *Harry*: James Young. *Mrs. Pearce*: GLYNIS BELL. *Butler*: Jeffrey Wilkins. *Alfred P. Doolittle*: JULIAN HOLLOWAY. *Servants*: Edwardyne Cowan, Michael Gerhart, Marilyn Kay Huelsman, Corinne Melançon, Meg Tolin. *Charles*, the Chauffeur: Michael Gerhart. *Mrs. Higgins*: DOLORES SUTTON. *Lord Boxington*: Jeffrey Wilkins. *Lady Boxington*: Marnee Hollis. *Policeman*: Ron Schwinn. *Flower Girl*: Corinne Melançon. *Footman*: Ben George. *Professor Zoltan Karpathy*: James Young. *Queen of Transylvania*: Patti Karr. *Mrs. Higgins' Maid*: Sue Delano.

Ensemble: Edwardyne Cowan, Laurie Crochet, Alexander de Jong, Sue Delano, Rebecca Downing, Michael J. Farina, Ben George, Michael Gerhart, Marnee Hollis, Marilyn Kay Huelsman, Patti Karr, Tom Kosis, John Vincent Leggio, Jamie MacKenzie, Lisa Merrill McCord, Corinne Melançon, Bruce Moore, Ron Schwinn, Meg Tolin, Bill Ullman, Jeffrey Wilkins, James Young. Swings: Newton Cole, Wendy Oliver, John Scott.

The action takes place in London in 1912.

Act 1, Scene 1: Outside Covent Garden. *Scene 2*: The Pub—Tottenham Court Road. *Scene 3*: Higgins' Laboratory. *Scene 4*: Higgins' Laboratory. *Scene 5*: Higgins' Laboratory—The Lessons. *Scene 6*: The Bed. *Scene 7*: Outside Ascot. *Scene 8*: Ascot. *Scene 9*: Wimpole Street. *Scene 10*: Higgins' Laboratory.

Act 2, Scene 1: The Ballroom. *Scene 2*: Higgins' Laboratory. *Scene 3*: Wimpole Street. *Scene 4*: Covent Garden. *Scene 5*: Higgins' Laboratory. *Scene 6*: The Garden of Mrs. Higgins. *Scene 7*: Wimpole Street. *Scene 8*: Higgins' Laboratory.

ACT 1
Scene 1
"Why Can't the English?"
    R. Chamberlain
"Wouldn't It Be Loverly"
    M. Errico, Quartet
Scene 2
"With a Little Bit of Luck"
    J. Holloway, J. Young, M. J. Farina, Company
Scene 3
"I'm an Ordinary Man"
    R. Chamberlain
Scene 5
"Just You Wait"
    M. Errico
"The Servants' Chorus"
    Servants
"The Rain in Spain"
    R. Chamberlain, M. Errico, P. Whitehead
Scene 6
"I Could Have Danced All Night"
    M. Errico
Scene 8
"Ascot Gavotte"
    Company
Scene 9
"On the Street Where You Live"
    R. Sella

---

[15]Originally produced in New York 15 March 1956 at the Mark Hellinger Theatre for 2717 peformances. For this production, Street Entertainers (Act 1, Scene 1) and "With a Little Bit of Luck" (reprise) were dropped. The Ballroom Scene/"Embassy Waltz" was moved from the close of Act 1 to the Opening of Act 2.

ACT 2
Scene 1
"The Embassy Waltz"
    Company
Scene 2
"You Did It"
    R. Chamberlain, P. Whiehead, Servants
"Just You Wait" (reprise)
    M. Errico
Scene 3
"On the Street Where You Live" (reprise)
    R. Sella
"Show Me" M. Errico
Scene 4
"Wouldn't It Be Loverly" (reprise)
    Company
"Get Me to the Church on Time"
    J. Holloway, Company
Scene 5
"Hymn to Him"
    R. Chamberlain
Scene 6
"Without You"
    M. Errico
Scene 7
"I've Grown Accustomed to Her Face"
    R. Chamberlain

1993.19

THE RED SHOES

A Musical in Two Acts, 19 Scenes. Book by Marsha Norman. Based on the film of the same name, screenplay by Emeric Pressburger. Music by Jule Styne. Lyrics by Marsha Norman and Paul Stryker [Bob Merrill]. Directed by Stanley Donen. Choreographed by Lar Lubovitch. Scenery by Heidi Landesman. Costumes by Catherine Zuber. Lighting by Ken Billington. Sound by Tony Meola. Musical direction and vocal arrangements by Don Pippin. Ballet and dance music arrangements by Gordon Harrell. Orchestrations by Sid Ramin, William D. Brohn. Flying by Foy. Associate producer, Jujamcyn/The Broadway Fund. Produced by Martin Starger in association with MCA/Universal and James M. Nederlander. Opened 16 December 1993 at the Gershwin Theatre and closed 19 December 1993 after 5 performances.

CAST (in order of appearance): *Grisha Ljubov*: GEORGE DE LA PEÑA. *Irina Boronskaya*: LESLIE BROWNE. *Ivan Boleslavsky*: Jon Marshall Sharp. *Livy*: Robert Jensen. *Sergei Ratov*: TAD INGRAM. *Dmitri*: Charles Goff. *Boris Lermontov*: STEVE BARTON. *Julian Craster*: HUGH PANARO. *Lady Ottoline Neston*: Pamela Burrell. *Victoria Page*: MARGARET ILLMAN, Amy Wilder (alternate). *Miss Hardiman*: Lydia Gaston. *Miss Lovat*: Laurie Gamache. *Dr. Copelias*: Daniel Wright. *James* ("Les Sylphides"): Scott Fowler. *Marguerite*: Jamie Chandler-Torns. *The Priest*: Robert Jensen. *Jean Louis*: Scott Fowler, Don Bellamy (alternate). *The Angel*: Jeff Lander.

The Company of The Ballet Lermontov: Jennifer Alexander, Anita Intrieri, Don Bellamy, Robert Jensen, Mucuy Bolles, Christina Johnson, Jamie Chandler-Torns, Jeff Lander, Geralyn Del Corso, Christina Marie Norrup, Scott Fowler, Oscar Ruge, Antonia Franceschi, Laurie Gamache, Jonathan Riseling, Lydia Gaston, Joan Tsao, Nina Goldman, James Weatherstone, Daniel Wright. Swings: Kellye Gordon, James Hadley, Alexies Sánchez, Catherine Ulissey, Aliceann Wilson.

The action takes place in the world of The Ballet Lermontov in London, Paris and Monte Carlo, in 1921–1922.

Act 1, Scene 1: Covent Garden Opera House—London. *Scene 2*: Lady Neston's Town House—Mayfair, London. *Scene 3*: Covent Garden Rehearsal Hall. *Scene 4*: Julian's Hotel Room—Paris. *Scene 5*: Paris Opera House—Lermontov's Office. *Scene 6*: Paris Opera House—On stage. *Scene 7*: Paris Opera House—Rehearsal hall and on stage. *Scene 8*: Monte Carlo Opera House—Vicky's Dressing Room. *Scene 9*: Lermontov's Villa—Monte Carlo. *Scene 10*: Monte Carlo Opera House—On stage. *Scene 11*: A Promenade—Monte Carlo. *Scene 12*: A Restaurant—Monte Carlo. *Scene 13*: Monte Carlo Opera House—On stage.

Act 2, Scene 1: Monte Carlo Opera House—Rehearsal Hall. *Scene 2*: Monte Carlo Opera House—Lermontov's Office. *Scene 3*: Vicky and Julian's flat—London/Monte Carlo Opera House—Lermontov's Office. *Scene 4*: Monte Carlo Opera House—Backstage. *Scene 5*: Monte Carlo Opera House—Vicky's Dressing Room. *Scene 6*: Monte Carlo Opera House—The Ballet of the Red Shoes.

ACT 1
Scene 1
"Swan Lake"
    L. Browne, J. M. Sharp, G. De La Peña, Company

"I Make the Rules"
S. Barton, G De La Peña
Scene 3
"The Audition"
M. Illman
"Corps de Ballet"
G. De La Peña, Company
Scene 4
"When It Happens to You"
H. Panaro
Scene 6
"Top of the Sky"
S. Barton, M. Illman
Scene 7
Ballet Montage (Swan Lake, Coppelia, Sleeping Beauty, Les Sylphides, Swan Lake)
M. Illman, Company
Scene 9
"It's a Fairy Tale"
S. Barton, H. Panaro, G. De La Peña, T. Ingram, C. Goff
Scene 11
"Be Somewhere"
H. Panaro
Scene 12
"The Rag"
G. De La Peña, Company
Scene 13
"Am I To Wish Her Love"
S. Barton, M. Illman

ACT 2
Scene 1
"Do Svedanya"
G. De La Peña, T. Ingram, Company
Scene 2
"Come Home"
S. Barton
Scene 3
"When You Dance for a King"
S. Barton, M. Illman
Scene 6
The Ballet of the Red Shoes
The Girl: M. Illman. *The Shoemaker:* G. De La Peña. *The Young Man:* S. Fowler.

DAMN YANKEES

1994.01

A Revival of the Musical in Two Acts[16]. Book by George Abbott and Douglass Wallop[17]. Based on the novel "The Year the Yankees Lost the Pennant" by Douglass Wallop. Music and lyrics by Richard Adler and Jerry Ross. Directed by Jack O'Brien. Choreographed by Rob Marshall. Scenic design by Douglas W. Schmidt. Costume design by David C. Woolard. Lighting design by David F. Segal. Sound design by Jonathan Deans. Special effects design by Gregory Meeh. Orchestrations by Douglas Besterman. Dance arrangements by Tom Fay; additional dance arrangements by David Krane. Vocal arrangements and musical supervision by James Raitt. Assistant director, Will Roberson. Assistant choreographer, Kathleen Marshall. Originally produced by The Old Globe Theatre, San Diego, California. Associate producers, Thomas Hall, Jennifer Manocherian, Jonathan Pillot, Andrea Pines, TDI, Mark Balsam, Meyer Ackerman, Julian Schlossberg, Workin' Man Films, Inc. Produced by Mitchell Maxwell, PolyGram Diversified Entertainment, Dan Markley, Kevin McCollum, Victoria Maxwell, Fred H. Krones, Andrea Nasher, The (Richard) Frankel•(Thomas) Viertel•(Steven) Baruch Group, Paula Heil Fisher, Julie Ross, in association with Jon B. Platt, Alan J. Schuster and Peter Breger. Opened 3 March 1994 at the Marquis Theatre, closing 1 January 1995 after 342 performances; re-opened 28 February 1995 at the Marquis Theatre and closed 6 August 1995 after 184 additional performances. Total: 526 performances.

CAST (in order of appearance): *Meg Boyd:* LINDA STEPHENS. *Joe Boyd:* DENNIS KELLY. *Sister:* Susan Mansur. *Gloria Thorpe:* VICKI LEWIS. *Applegate:* VICTOR GARBER. *Joe Hardy:* JARROD EMICK. *Rocky:* Scott Wise. *Smokey:* Jeff Blumenkrantz. *Sohovik:* Gregory Jbara. *Mickey:* John Ganun. *Vernon:* Joey Pizzi. *Del:* Scott Robertson. *Ozzie:* Michael Winther. *Bubba:* Cory English. *Henry:* Bruce Anthony Davis. *Bomber:* Michael Berresse. *Van Buren:* DICK LATESSA. *Betty:* Paula Leggett Chase. *Donna:* Nancy Ticotin. *Kitty:* Cynthia Onrubia. *Photographer:* Amy Rider. *Rita:* Amy Rider. *Welch:* Terrence P. Currier. *Lola:* BEBE NEUWIRTH. (Note: The Senators include Rocky, Smokey, Sohovik, Mickey, Vernon, Del, Ozzie, Bubba, Henry, Bomber.)
Swings: Mark Santoro, Robyn Peterman.

(The action takes place the year the Yankees lost the pennant in the 1950s.)

ACT 1
"Six Months Out of Every Year"
L. Stephens, D. Kelly, S. Mansur, V. Lewis, Husbands, Wives
"Goodbye, Old Girl"
D. Kelly, J. Emick
"Blooper Ballet"[18]
The Senators
"Heart"
D. Latessa, The Senators
"Shoeless Joe from Hannibal, Mo."
V. Lewis, The Senators
"Shoeless Joe from Hannibal, Mo." (reprise)
V. Lewis, J. Emick, Ensemble
"A Little Brains—A Little Talent"
B. Neuwirth
"A Man Doesn't Know"
L. Stephens, J. Emick
"Whatever Lola Wants (Lola Gets)"
B. Neuwirth

ACT 2
"Who's Got the Pain?"
B. Neuwirth, The Senators
"The Game"
The Senators
"Near To You"
J. Emick, S. Bolin
"Those Were the Good Old Days"
V. Garber
"Two Lost Souls"
B. Neuwirth, V. Garber
"A Man Doesn't Know" (reprise)
L. Stephens, D. Kelly
Finale: "Heart" (reprise)
Company

CAROUSEL

1994.02

A Revival of the Musical Play in Two Acts, 9 Scenes[19]. Book and lyrics by Oscar Hammerstein II. Based on Ferenc Molnar's play "Liliom" as adapted by Benjamin F. Glazer. Music by Richard Rodgers. Directed by Nicholas Hytner. Choreography by Sir Kenneth MacMillan, staged by Jane Elliott. Sets and costumes by Bob Crowley. Lighting by Paul Pyant. Sound by Steve Canyon Kennedy. Musical director, Eric Stern. Orchestrations by William D. Brohn. Fight direction by David Leong. Dances for the original Theatre Guild production by Agnes de Mille. Originally produced by The Royal National Theatre (Great Britain). Produced by the Lincoln Center Theatre (André Bishop, Artistic director; Bernard Gersten, Executive producer), by arrangement with The Royal National Theatre, Cameron Mackintosh and The Rodgers and Hammerstein Organization. Opened 24 March 1994 at the Vivian Beaumont Theatre and closed 17 January 1995 after 322 performances.

---

[16]Originally produced in New York 5 May 1955 at the 46th Street Theatre for 1019 performances. Song order, vocals and reprises have been substantially revised from the original; "Who's Got the Pain?" moved from the end of Act 1 to the opening of Act 2.

[17]Uncredited book revisions by George Abbott and Jack O'Brien.

[18]New for this production.

[19]First produced in New York 19 April 1945 at the Majestic Theatre for 890 performances. For Synopsis of Scenes and Musical Numbers, see original 1945 production. For this production, "The Carousel Waltz" became the Prologue. "The Highest Judge of All" was omitted from this production.

CAST (in order of appearance): *Carrie Pipperidge*: AUDRA ANN MC DONALD. *Julie Jordan*: SALLY MURPHY. *Mrs. Mullin*: KATE BUDDEKE. *Billy Bigelow*: MICHAEL HAYDEN. *Policeman*: Taye Diggs. *David Bascombe*: Robert Breuler. *Nettie Fowler*: SHIRLEY VERRETT. *Enoch Snow*: EDDIE KORBICH. *Jigger Craigin*: FISHER STEVENS. *Innkeeper*: Rebecca Eichenberger. *Captain*: Brian d'Arcy James. *Heavenly Friend*: Lauren Ward. *Starkeeper*: JEFF WEISS. *Louise*: SANDRA BROWN. *Fairground Boy*: JON MARSHALL SHARP. *Enoch Snow, Jr.*: Duane Boutté. *Margaret Snow*: Lovette George. *Other Snow Children*: Philipp Lee Carabuena, Cece Cortes, Lyn Nagel, Cindy Robinson, Tiffany Sampson, tse-Mach Washington.

Principal: Brian d'Arcy James. *Dr. Selden*: Jeff Weiss. *Robert Allen*: Steven Ochoa. *Hannah Bentley*: Cindy Robinson. *Peter Bentley, Jr.*: Tony Capone. *Abbie Chase*: Natascia A. Diaz. *Charles "Chip" Chase*: Alexies Sânchez. *Jonathan Chase*: Robert Cary. *Virginia Frazer*: Rebecca Eichenberger. *Buddy Hamlin*: Devin Richards. *Cyrus Hamlin*: Taye Diggs. *Arminy Livermore*: Paula Newsome. *Hudson Livermore*: Brian d'Arcy James. *William Osgood*: Rocker Verastique. *Orrin Peesley*: Duane Boutté. *Susan Peters*: Linda Gabler. *Myrtle Robbins*: Lacey Hornkohl. *Ella Sanborn*: Alexia Hess. *Jenny Sanborn*: Lauren Ward. *Martha Sewell*: Keri Lee. *Liza Sinclair*: Endalyn Taylor-Shellman. *Penny Sinclair*: Lovette George. *Henry Sears*: Jeffrey James. *Abner Sperry*: Michael O'Donnell. *Ben Sperry*: Glen Harris. *Sadie Sperry*: Dana Stackpole.

Louise's Friends: Robert Cary, Glen Harris, Steven Ochoa, Michael O'Donnell, Alexie Sanchez, Rocker Verastique. *Swings*: Robert Cary, Lisa Mayer, Donna Rubin, Thomas Titone, Reggie Valdez.

JACKIE MASON:
1994.03 POLITICALLY INCORRECT

A One Man Comedy Revue in Two Acts[20]. Written and created by Jackie Mason. Production design and lighting by Neil Peter Jampolis. Sound design by Bruce Cameron. Produced by Jyll Rosenfeld. Opened 5 April 1994 at the John Golden Theatre and closed 4 June 1995 after 347 performances.

CAST: JACKIE MASON (stand-up comedy, monologues, impressions).

(DISNEY'S)
1994.04 BEAUTY AND THE BEAST

A Musical in Two Acts. Book by Linda Woolverton (based on her screenplay for the Walt Disney animated film of the same name). Music by Alan Menken. Lyrics by Howard Ashman and Tim Rice. Directed by Robert Jess Roth. Choreography by Matt West. Scenic design by Stan Meyer. Costume design by Ann Hould-Ward. Lighting design by Natasha Katz. Sound design by T. Richard Fitzgerald. Illusions by Jim Steinmeyer, John Gaughan. Prosthetics, John Dods. Musical direction and incidental music arrangements by Michael Kosarin. Orchestrations by Danny Troob. Musical supervision and vocal arrangements by David Friedman. Fight director, Rick Sordelet. Dance arrangements by Glen Kelly. Produced by Walt Disney Productions (Ron Logan, Robert McTyre, Theatrical Production Division). Opened 18 April 1994 at the Palace Theatre and closed 5 September 1999 after 2250 performances; re-opened 12 November 1999 at the Lunt-Fontanne Theatre (see separate entry in 1999-2000 season) and is still running at this time!

CAST (in order of appearance): *Enchantress*: Wendy Oliver. *Young Prince*: Harrison Beal. *Beast*: TERRENCE MANN. *Belle*: SUSAN EGAN. *Lefou*: KENNY RASKIN. *Gaston*: BURKE MOSES. *Three Silly Girls*: Sarah Solie Shannon, Paige Price, Linda Talcott. *Maurice*: TOM BOSLEY. *Cogsworth*: HEATH LAMBERTS. *Lumiere*: GARY BEACH. *Babette*: STACEY LOGAN. *Mrs. Potts*: BETH FOWLER. *Chip*: BRIAN PRESS. *Madame de la Grande Bouche*: ELEANOR GLOCKNER. *Monsieur D'Arque*: Gordon Stanley.

Townspeople, Enchanted Objects: Joan Barber, Roxane Barlow, Harrison Beal, Michael-Demby Cain, Kate Dowe, David Elder, Merwin Foard, Gregorey Garrison, Jack Hayes, Kim Huber, Elmore James, Rob Lorey, Patrick Loy, Barbara Marineau, Joanne McHugh, Anna McNeeley, Bill Nabel, Wendy Oliver, Vince Pesce, Paige Price, Sarah Solie Shannon, Gordon Stanley, Linda Talcott, Wysandra Woolsey. *Voice of Prologue Narrator*: David Ogden Stiers. *Swings*: Alisa Klein, Dan Mojica, Joan Barber, Kate Dowe, Gregorey Garrison, Rob Lorey.

ACT 1[21]

Prologue
  Enchantress

"Belle"
  S. Egan, B. Moses, K. Raskin, Silly Girls, Townspeople
"No Matter What"
  T. Bosley, S. Egan
  (*Lyrics by* Tim Rice.)
"No Matter What" (reprise)
  T. Bosley
"Me"
  B. Moses, S. Egan
  (*Lyrics by* Tim Rice.)
"Belle" (reprise)
  S. Egan
"Home"
  S. Egan
  (*Lyrics by* Tim Rice.)
"Home" (reprise)
  B. Fowler
"Gaston"
  K. Raskin, B. Moses, Silly Girls, Tavern Patrons
"Gaston" (reprise)
  B. Moses, K. Raskin
"How Long Must This Go On?"
  T. Mann
  (*Lyrics by* Tim Rice.)
"Be Our Guest"
  G. Beach, B. Fowler, H. Lamberts, E. Glockner, B. Press, S. Logan, Enchanted Objects
"If I Can't Love Her"
  T. Mann
  (*Lyrics by* Tim Rice.)

ACT 2[22]

Wolf Chase
"Something There"
  S. Egan, T. Mann, G. Beach, B. Fowler, H. Lamberts
"Human Again"
  G. Beach, E. Glockner, H. Lamberts, B. Fowler, S. Logan, B. Press, Enchanted Objects
"Maison des Lunes"
  B. Moses, K. Raskin, G. Stanley
  (*Lyrics by* Tim Rice.)
"Beauty and the Beast"
  B. Fowler
"If I Can't Love Her" (reprise)
  T. Mann
"The Mob Song"
  B. Moses, K. Raskin, G. Stanley, Townspeople
"The Battle"
  Company
"Transformation"
  T. Mann, D. Eagan
  (*Lyrics by* Tim Rice.)
"Beauty and the Beast" (reprise)
  Company

1994.05 PASSION

A Musical in One Act, 16 Scenes. Book by James Lapine, based on the film "Passione D'Amore" by Ettore Scola, and the novel on which it was based, "Fosca" by I. U. Tarchetti. Music and lyrics by Stephen Sondheim. Directed by James Lapine. Set design by Adrianne Lobel. Costume design by Jane Greenwood. Lighting design by Beverly Emmons. Sound design by Otts Munderloh. Musical direction by Paul Gemignani. Orchestrations by Jonathan Tunick. Associate director, Jane Comfort. Produced by The Shubert Organization, Capital Cities/ABC, Roger Berlind, and Scott Rudin, by arrangement with Lincoln Center Theatre. Opened 9 May 1994 at the Plymouth Theatre and closed 7 January 1995 after 280 performances.

---

[20]Previous editions of Jackie Mason's one man show have been presented as THE WORLD ACCORDING TO ME 22 December 1986 at the Brooks Atkinson Theatre for 367 performances; returned 3 May 1988 at the Brooks Atkinson for 203 performances; JACKIE MASON: BRAND NEW 17 October 1990 at the Neil Simon Theatre for 216 performances.
[21]All lyrics by Howard Ashman except where noted.

[22]In September 1998 the following new song was added for Toni Braxton as Belle, before "The Mob Song":
  "A Change in Me"
    T. Braxton
    (*Lyrics by* Tim Rice.)

CAST (in order of speaking): *Clara*: MARIN MAZZIE. *Giorgio (Bachetti)*: JERE SHEA. *Colonel Ricci*: GREGG EDELMANN. *Doctor Tambourri*: TOM ALDREDGE. *Lieutenant Torasso*: Francis Ruivivar. *Sergeant Lombardi*: Marcus Olson. *Lieutenant Barri*: William Parry. *Major Rizzolli*: Cris Groenendaal. *Private Augenti*: George Dvorsky. *Fosca*: DONNA MURPHY. *Fosca's Mother*: Linda Balgord. *Fosca's Father*: John Leslie Wolfe. *Ludovic*: Matthew Porretta. *Mistress*: Juliet Lambert.

The action takes place in Milan and a remote military outpost, in 1863.

Scene 1: Clara's bedroom in Milan. *Scene 2*: The Officers' Dining Quarters in a remote part of Italy; Outdoors; the Dining Quarters. *Scene 3*: The Castle Garden. *Scene 4*: The Dining Quarters. *Scene 5*: The Courtyard; Fosca's Drawing Room/Clara's Bedroom. *Scene 6*: Fosca's Drawing Room; the Doctor's Office. *Scene 7*: Fosca's Bedroom. *Scene 8*: The Billiard Room; flashback to Fosca's past. *Scene 9*: The Mountainside, a distance from the outpost. *Scene 10*: The Parade Ground; Giorgio's bedroom. *Scene 11*: A Train compartment to Milan; back at the Courtyard. *Scene 12*: A Bench near the Milan Train Station. *Scene 13*: A Christmas party at the Dining Quarters. *Scene 14*: Fosca's Bedroom. *Scene 15*: An Open Field. *Scene 16*: A hospital; Giorgio's past.

MUSICAL NUMBERS[23]

Scene 1
  "Happiness"
    M. Mazzie, J. Shea
Scene 2
  "First Letter"
    M. Mazzie, J. Shea, T. Aldredge, G. Edelman
  "Second Letter"
    M. Mazzie, J. Shea
  "Third Letter"
    M. Mazzie, J. Shea, Soldiers
  "Fourth Letter"
    M. Mazzie, J. Shea
  "I Read"
    D. Murphy
  Transition
    J. Shea, Men
Scene 3
  "Garden Sequence"
    J. Shea, D. Murphy
Scene 4
  Transition
    Soldiers
Scene 5
  "Trio"
    D. Murphy, J. Shea, M. Mazzie
  Transition
    Attendants
Scene 6
  Solders' Gossip
    Soldiers
Scene 7
  "I Wish I Could Forget You"
    D. Murphy, J. Shea
Scene 8
  "Soldiers' Gossip" (1)
    Soldiers
  Flashback
    D. Murphy, G. Edelman, L. Balgord, J. L. Wolfe, M. Porretta, J. Lambert
Scene 9
  "Sunrise Letter"
    M. Mazzie, J. Shea
  "Is This What You Call Love?"
    J. Shea
Scene 10
  "Soldiers' Gossip" (2)
    Soldiers
Scene 11
  Transition
    C. Groenendaal
  "Forty Days"
    M. Mazzie

"Loving You"
  D. Murphy
Transition
  Woman, Man
"Soldiers' Gossip" (3)
  Soldiers
Scene 12
  Letter from Clara
    M. Mazzie
Scene 13
  Christmas Carol (in Italian)
    F. Ruivivar
  "Farewell Letter"
    M. Mazzie, J. Shea
Scene 14
  "No One Has Ever Loved Me"
    J. Shea, D. Murphy
Scene 16
  Finale
    Company

THE BEST LITTLE WHOREHOUSE GOES PUBLIC

1994.06

A Musical Comedy in Two Acts, a Prologue and 15 Scenes[24]. Book by Larry L. King and Peter Masterson. Music and lyrics by Carol Hall. Directed by Peter Masterson and Tommy Tune. Choreography by Jeff Calhoun, Tommy Tune. Scenery designed by John Arnone. Costumes designed by Bob Mackie. Lighting designed by Jules Fisher, Peggy Eisenhauer. Sound by Tony Meola. Musical and vocal direction, Karl Jurman. Musical supervision, vocal and dance arrangements by Wally Harper. Orchestrations by Peter Matz. Musical advisor, Robert Billig. Video by Batwin + Robin Productions, Inc. Associate director, Phillip Oesterman. Associate choreographer, Niki Harris. Production supervisor, Gene O'Donovan. Produced by Stevie Phillips and MCA/Universal. Opened 10 May 1994 at the Lunt-Fontanne Theatre and closed 21 May 1994 after 15 performances.

CAST (in order of appearance): *Showroom Headliner*: Troy Britton Johnson. *Showroom Patrons*: Gerry Burkhardt, Laurel Lynn Collins, Sally Mae Dunn, Tom Flagg, Joe Hart, Don Johanson, Mark Manley, Mary Frances McCatty, Casey Nicholaw, Louise Ruck, William Ryall, Shaver Tillitt, Jillana Urbina, Richard Vida, Theara J. Ward. *Street Whores*: Pamela Everett, Ganine Giorgione, Amy Heggins, Lainie Sakakura, Christina Youngman. *Ralph J. Bostick*: Danny Rutigliano. *Comedian*: JIM DAVID. *Las Vegas Legends*: Mary Frances McCatty, Don Johanson, Laurel Lynn Collins, Gerry Burkhardt, Sally Mae Dunn, Theara J. Ward, William Ryall. *I.R.S. Director*: KEVIN COONEY. *Schmidt, his assistant*: DAVID DOTY. *Terri Clark*: GINA TORRES. *Mona Stangley*: DEE HOTY. *A Client of the Whorehouse*: Joe Hart. *Sam Dallas*: SCOTT HOLMES. *B. S. Bullshit*: DAVID DOTY. *Senator A. Harry Hardast*: RONN CARROLL. *Lotta Lovingood*: Pamela Everett. *The President of the United States*: DAVID DOTY. *His Hairdresser*: JIM DAVID.
The Working Girls and the Wall Street Wolves: Gerry Burkhardt, Laurel Lynn Collins, Sally Mae Dunn, Pamela Everett, Tom Flagg, Ganine Giorgione, Joe Hart, Amy N. Heggins, Don Johanson, Troy Britton Johnson, Mark Manley, Mary Frances McCatty, Casey Nicholaw, Louise Ruck, Danny Rutigliano, William Ryall, Lainie Sakakura, Shaver Tillitt, Jillana Urbina, Richard Vida, Theara J. Ward, Christina Youngman. *Swings*: Niki Harris, Vincent D'Elia.

Prologue: The showroom, Las Vegas.

Act 1, Scene 1: Conference Room, I.R.S., Washington, D.C. *Scene 2*: Cactus Motel, somewhere in Texas. *Scene 3*: In the shadows of the Washington Monument. *Scene 4*: In the kitchen of the whorehouse, Nevada. *Scene 5*: The parlor of the whorehouse and Wall Street, New York.

Act 2, Scene 1: On the information highway. *Scene 2*: Air Force One—on the tarmac, LAX. *Scene 3*: I.R.S. Director's Georgetown home. *Scene 4*: Sam Dallas' apartment, Washington, D.C. *Scene 5*: An I.R.S. corridor. *Scene 6*: The hearing. *Scene 7*: Larry King Live. *Scene 8*: Sam Dallas' dressing room, Washington, D.C. *Scene 9*: The Stallion Fields Whorehouse, Nevada. *Scene 10*: The steps of our nation's Capitol.

---

[23]Neither a Synopsis of Scenes nor list of Musical Numbers appear in the program. Above list was prepared from the published text and cast recording.

[24]Conceived by the same authors as a sequel to their Broadway musical "The Best Little Whorehouse in Texas" which opened 19 June 1978 at the 46th Street Theatre for 1584 performances.

ACT 1
Prologue
"Let the Devil Take Us"
Las Vegas Legends, Showroom Patrons, Street Whores, D. Rutigliano
Scene 2
"Nothin' Like a Picture Show"
D. Hoty
"I'm Leavin' Texas"
D. Hoty, Texans
Scene 4
"It's Been a While"
S. Holmes, D. Hoty
Scene 5
"Brand New Start"
S. Holmes, D. Hoty, G. Torres, K. Cooney, D. Doty, Working Girls, Wall Street Wolves

ACT 2
Scene 1
"The Smut Song"
R. Carroll
"Call Me"
D. Hoty, Girls, Couch Potatoes (Men)
Scene 4
"Change in Me"
S. Holmes
Scene 6
"Here for the Hearing"
Ladies, Senators
Scene 7
"Piece of the Pie"
D. Hoty, S. Holmes, Ladies
Scene 8
"Change in Me" (reprise)
S. Holmes
Scene 10
"If We Open Our Eyes"
Entire Company

GREASE

1994.07

A Revival of the Musical (Comedy) in Two Acts, 13 Scenes[25]. Book, music and lyrics by Jim Jacobs and Warren Casey. Directed and choreographed by Jeff Calhoun. Scenic design by John Arnone. Costume design by Willa Kim. Lighting design by Howell Brinkley. Sound design by Tom Morse. Musical direction, vocal and dance music arrangements by John McDaniel. Orchestrations by Steven Margoshes. Associate choreographer, Jerry Mitchell. Associate producer, Alecia Parker. A Tommy Tune Production. Produced by Barry and Fran Weissler and Jujamcyn Theatres, in association with Pace Theatrical Group and TV Asahi. Opened 11 May 1994 at the Eugene O'Neill Theatre and closed 23 February 1997 after 1150 performances; re-opened 8 April 1997 at the Eugene O'Neill Theatre and closed 25 January 1998 after an additional 353 performances. Total: 1503 performances.

<u>CAST</u> (in order of appearance): *Vince Fontaine*: Brian Bradley. *Miss Lynch*: MARCIA LEWIS. *Patty Simcox*: Michelle Blakeley. *Eugene Florczyk*: Paul Castree. *Jan*: Heather Stokes. *Marty*: Megan Mullally. *Betty Rizzo*: ROSIE O'DONNELL. *Doody*: SAM HARRIS. *Roger*: Hunter Foster. *Kenickie*: Jason Opsahl. *Sonny Latierri*: Carlos Lopez. *Frenchy*: Jessica Stone. *Sandy Dumbrowski*: SUSAN WOOD. *Danny Zuko*: RICKY PAULL GOLDIN. *The Heartbeats*: Katy Grenfell, Janice Lorraine Holt, Lorna Shane. *The Straight A's*: Clay Adkins, Patrick Boyd, Denis Jones. *The Dream Mooners*: Patrick Boyd, Katy Grenfell. *Cha-Cha DeGregorio*: Sandra Purpuro. *Teen Angel*: BILLY PORTER.

Ensemble: Clay Adkins, Melissa Bell, Patrick Boyd, Katy Grenfell, Ned Hannah, Janice Lorraine Holt, Denis Jones, Allison Metcalf, H. Hylan Scott II, Lorna Shane. *Swings*: Patti D'Beck, Brian-Paul Mendoza.

(The action takes place in the late 1950s.)

Act 1, Scene 1: Rydell High. *Scene 2*: Cafeteria. *Scene 3*: School Hallway. *Scene 4*: Marty's Bathroom. *Scene 5*: Street Corner. *Scene 6*: Bleachers. *Scene 7*: School Yard. *Scene 8*: The Lockers.

---

[25]Originally produced in New York Off-Broadway 14 February 1972 at the Eden Theatre for 128 performances; transferred 7 June 1972 to the Broadhurst Theatre for a total of 3388 performances, including Off-Broadway run.

Act 2, Scene 1: Rydell High Boy's Gym. *Scene 2*: Outside the Burger Palace. *Scene 3*: Twi-Light Drive-In. *Scene 4*: Rizzo's Rec Room. *Scene 5*: Burger Palace.

ACT 1[26]
Scene 1
"Alma Mater"[27]
M. Lewis, Company
"We Go Together"
Pink Ladies, Burger Palace Boys
Scene 2
"Summer Nights"
S. Wood, R. P. Goldin, Pink Ladies, Burger Palace Boys
Scene 3
"Those Magic Changes"
S. Harris, Company
Scene 4
"Freddy, My Love"
M. Mullally, Pink Ladies
Scene 5
"Greased Lightnin'"
J. Opsahl, Burger Palace Boys
"Greased Lightnin'" (reprise)
R. O'Donnell, Burger Palace Boys
Scene 6
"Rydell Fight Song"[28]
S. Wood, M. Blakely, Cheerleading Squad
Scene 7
"Mooning"
H. Foster, H. Stokes
"Look at Me, I'm Sandra Dee"
R. O'Donnell
Scene 8
"Since I Don't Have You"[29]
S. Wood
(*Music and Lyrics by* Joseph Rock, James Beaumont and the Skyliners.)
"We Go Together" (reprise)
Company

ACT 2
Scene 1
"Shakin' at the High School Hop"
The Four Straight A's
"It's Raining on Prom Night"
S. Wood, The Four Straight A's
"Born to Hand-Jive"
P. Castree, M. Lewis, Company
Scene 2
"Beauty School Dropout"
B. Porter, J. Stone, Company
Scene 3
"Alone at a Drive-In Movie"
R. P. Goldin
Scene 4
"Rock 'N' Roll Party Queen"
S. Harris, J. Opsahl
"There Are Worse Things I Could Do"
R. O'Donnell
"Look at Me, I'm Sandra Dee" (reprise)
S. Wood, R. O'Donnell
Scene 5
Finale[30]
Company

---

[26]Pink Ladies include Rizzo, Frenchy, Marty, Jan. Burger Palace Boys include Kenickie, Doody, Roger, Sonny. For this revival, the role of Johnny Casino and the reprise of "Shakin' at the High School Hop" were dropped.
[27]Revised as an "a cappella" version of "We Go Together."
[28]Not in the original production, but added for this production.
[29]Not in the original production, but added for this production.
[30]Includes "All Choked Up."

Alan Campbell and Betty Buckley in SUNSET BOULEVARD
Joan Marcus/Photofest

1994.08 SHOWBOAT

A Revival of the Musical (Play) in Two Acts, 20 Scenes[1]. Music by Jerome Kern. Book and lyrics by Oscar Hammerstein II. Based on the novel of the same name by Edna Ferber. Directed by Harold Prince. Choreography by Susan Stroman. Production (scenery) design by Eugene Lee. Costumes designed by Florence Klotz. Lighting design by Richard Pilbrow. Orchestrations by Robert Russell Bennett, William D. Brohn. Production musical supervisor, Jeffrey Huard. Dance music arranged by David Krane. Sound design by Martin Levan. Assistant to Mr. Prince, Ruth Mitchell. Produced by LIVENT (U.S.) Inc. (Garth Drabinsky, Chairman and Chief executive officer; Myron I. Gottlieb, President.) Opened 2 October 1994 at the Gershwin Theatre and closed 5 January 1997 after 946 performances.

CAST (in order of their appearance): *Steve*: DOUG LABRECQUE. *Queenie*: GRETHA BOSTON. *Pete*: David Bryant. *Parthy Ann Hawkes*: ELAINE STRITCH. *Windy (McLain)*: Ralph Williams. *Cap'n Andy*: JOHN McMARTIN. *Ellie*: DOROTHY STANLEY. *Frank*: JOEL BLUM. *Julie*: LONNETTE McKEE. *Gaylord Ravenal*: MARK JACOBY. *(Sheriff Ike) Vallon*: Jack Dabdoub. *Magnolia*: REBECCA LUKER. *Joe*: MICHEL BELL. *Dealer*: Bob Walton. *Jeb*: David Earl Hart. *Backwoodsman*: Mike O'Carroll. *Young Kim*: Larissa Auble. *Ethel*: Danielle Greaves. *Landlady*: Lorraine Foreman. *Mother Superior*: Sheila Smith. *Jim*: Mike O'Carroll. *Jake*: Bob Walton. *Charlie*: Michael Scott. *Lottie*: Louise-Marie Mennier. *Dottie*: Karen Curlee. *Drunk*: David Bryant. *Radio Announcer*: Michael Scott. *Kim*: Tammy Amerson. *Old Lady on Levee*: Sheila Smith.

Ensemble: Van Abrahams, Timothy Albrecht, Derin Altay, Kevin Bagby, Hal Beasley, Timothy Robert Blevins, David Bryant, Joseph Cassidy, Roosevelt André Credit, Karen Curlee, Jack Dabdoub, Debbie de Coudreaux, Lorraine Foreman, Jose Garcia, Ron Gibbs, Steve Girardi, Danielle Greaves, Jeff Hairston, Lorna Hampson, Linda Hardwick, Pamela Harley, David Earl Hart, Richard L. Hobson, Michel LaFlèche, Karen Lifshey, Kim Lindsay, Jesse Means II, Louise-Marie Mennier, Kiri-Lyn Muir, Panchali Null, Mike O'Carroll, Amy Jo Phillips, Catherine Pollard, Jimmy Rivers, Michael Scott, Jill Slyter, Bob Walton, Laurie Walton, Cheryl Warfield, Jo Ann Hawkins White, Dathan B. Williams, Gay Willis, Lonel Woods, Darlene B. Young. *Swings*: Dannis Daniels, David Dannehl, Tari Kelly, Richie McCall, Kimberley Michaels, Louise St. Cyr. *Children*: Larissa Auble, Kimberly Jean Brown, Joran Corneal, Edwin Hodge. *Band on the Cotton Blossom*: Derin Altay (cymbals), Bob Walton (glockenspiel), Paul Gallo (clarinet), Dan Levine (trombone), Michael Scott (bass drums), Nathan Durham (tuba), Brian Miller (flute).

Act 1, Scene 1: The Levee at Natchez on the Mississippi River in 1887. *Scene 2*: Kitchen pantry of the *Cotton Blossom*. Five minutes later. *Scene 3*: Natchez. Outside a riverfront gambling saloon. *Scene 4*: Auditorium of the *Cotton Blossom*. *Scene 5*: The windows of Magnolia's cabin and Ravenal's room. *Scene 6*: Fort Adams. Box office on the foredeck of the *Cotton Blossom*. *Scene 7*: Auditorium and stage of the *Cotton Blossom*. *Scene 8*: Upper deck of the *Cotton Blossom*. *Scene 9*: The Levee in Natchez.

Act 2, Scene 1: The levee in Natchez. Exterior of the *Cotton Blossom*. (1889). *Scene 2*: Magnolia's room on the *Cotton Blossom*. *Scene 3*: Montage I. Chicago (1889); On the Dock at Natchez (1899); Chicago, outside the Palmer House Hotel (1899). *Scene 4*: Chicago. A room in a boarding house. *Scene 5*: Chicago. St. Agatha's Convent. *Scene 6*: Chicago. Rehearsal at the Trocadero Night Club. *Scene 7*: Entrance to the Palmer House Hotel, New Year's Eve, 1899. *Scene 8*: Trocadero Night Club. *Scene 9*: Montage II (1900-1921). The Levee at Natchez. The streets of Chicago. The revolving door of the Palmer House Hotel. *Scene 10*: The levee at Natchez (1927). *Scene 11*: Later on the levee.

ACT 1

Scene 1
  "Cotton Blossom"
    Stevedores, Gals, Townspeople
  "Cap'n Andy's Ballyhoo"
    J. McMartin, E. Stritch, the Showboat Troupe, Stevedores, Gals, Townspeople
  "Where's the Mate for Me?"
    M. Jacoby
  "Make Believe"
    M. Jacoby, R. Luker
  "Ol' Man River"
    M. Bell, Stevedores

Scene 2
  "Can't Help Lovin' Dat Man"
    L. McKee, G. Boston, M. Bell, R. Luker, Ensemble
Scene 3
  "Till Good Luck Comes My Way"
    M. Jacoby, D. Bryant, J. Blum, Townsmen
Scene 4
  "Mis'ry's Comin' Aroun'"
    G. Boston, Stevedores, Gals
Scene 5
  "I Have the Room Above Her"
    M. Jacoby, R. Luker
Scene 6
  "Life Upon the Wicked Stage"
    D. Stanley, Townswomen
  "Queenie's Ballyhoo"
    G. Boston, Stevedores, Gals
Scene 8
  "You Are Love"
    M. Jacoby, R. Luker
Scene 9
  Act 1 Finale: "The Wedding Celebration"
    Company

ACT 2
Scene 2
  "Why Do I Love You?"
    E. Stritch, Company
Scene 3
  "Dandies on Parade"
    City Folk
Scene 5
  "Alma Redemptoris Mater" (Hymn)
    Choir
  "Ol' Man River" (reprise)
    M. Bell
Scene 6
  "Bill"
    L. McKee
    (*Lyrics by P. G. Wodehouse, revised by Oscar Hammerstein II.*)
  "Can't Help Lovin' Dat Man" (reprise)
    R. Luker
Scene 8
  "Goodbye, My Lady Love"
    J. Blum, D. Stanley
    (*Music and Lyrics by Joseph E. Howard.*)
  "After the Ball" (from *A TRIP TO CHINATOWN*)
    R. Luker, Ensemble
    (*Music and Lyrics by Charles K. Harris.*)
Scene 9
  "Ol' Man River" (reprise)
    M. Bell
Scene 10
  "Dance Away the Night"
    R. Luker
Scene 11
  "Kim's Charleston"
    T. Amerson, E. Stritch, Company
  Act 2 Finale
    M. Bell, Company

1994.09 WONDERFUL TOWN

A Revival of the Musical Comedy in Two Acts, 13 Scenes[2]. Book by Joseph Fields and Jerome Chodorov. Based on the play "My Sister Eileen" by

---

[1] First presented in New York 27 December 1927 at the Ziegfeld Theatre for 572 performances.

[2] Originally produced in New York 25 February 1953 at the Winter Garden for 559 performances. For Synopsis of Scenes and Musical Numbers, see original 1953 production. "Conquering New York" Ballet dropped from this production.

Joseph Fields and Jerome Chodorov (and the stories of the same name by
Ruth McKinney). Music by Leonard Bernstein. Lyrics by Betty Comden
and Adolph Green. Directed by Richard Sabellico. Conductor, Eric Stern.
Choreographer, Tina Paul. Set designer, Michael Anania. Costume design-
er, Gail Baldoni. Lighting designer, Jeff Davis. Sound designer, Abe Jacob.
Chorus master, Joseph Colaneri Assistant stage director, Paul L. King.
(Orchestrations uncredited.) Produced by the New York City Opera.
Opened 8 November 1994 at the New York State Theatre and closed 20
November 1994 after 14 performances.

CAST (in order of their appearance): *Tour Guide*: William Ledbetter. *Appopolous*:
LARRY BLOCK. *Lonigan*: Don Yule. *Helen*: MEGHAN STRANGE. *Wreck*:
TIMOTHY WARMEN. *Violet*: Amanda Green. *Speedy Valenti*: Carlos Lopez. *Eileen
Sherwood*: CRISTA MOORE. *Ruth Sherwood*: KAY MCCLELLAND. *Fletcher*: Gary
Jackson. *Drunks*: Mason Roberts, Louis Perry. *Eskimo Pie Man*: Mason Roberts. *Robert
Baker*: RICHARD MUENZ. *Associate Editors*: John Lankston, William Ledbetter.
Rexford: Gary Jackson. *Mr. Mallory*: Louis Perry. *Danny*: Jeffrey Weber. *Party Guest*:
Marilyn Armstrong. *Trent*: Daniel Shigo. *Mrs. Wade*: Susan Browning. *Frank
Lippencott*: DON STEPHENSON. *Chef*: William Ledbetter. *Waiter*: Daniel Shigo.
Delivery Boy: Larry Sousa. *Chick Clark*: STEPHEN BERGER. *Shore Patrolman*: Ron
Hilley. *First Cadet*: Larry Sousa. *Second Cadet*: Mason Roberts. *Brazilian Ambassador*:
John Lankston. *Solo Policeman*: John Lankston. *Policemen*: Ron Hilley, Louis Perry,
William Ledbetter, Jeffrey Weber. *Ruth's Escort*: Gary Jackson. *Flower Sellers*: Paula
Hostetter, Melissa Maravell. *Customer*: Beth Pensiero. *Children*: Zoe Startz Barton,
Simon Behr, Dov Lebowitz-Nowak, Sebastian Perez, Jacqueline Rosenfield, Rachel
Rosenfield.

1994.10   SUNSET BOULEVARD

A Musical in Two Acts, 21 Scenes. Book and lyrics by Don Black and
Christopher Hampton. Based on the film and screenplay of the same name
by Billy Wilder. Music by Andrew Lloyd Webber. Directed by Trevor Nunn.
Musical staging by Bob Avian. Production (settings) design by John Napier.
Costume design by Anthony Powell. Lighting design by Andrew Bridge.
Sound design by Martin Levan. Musical supervision and direction by David
Caddick. Musical director, Paul Bogaev. Orchestrations by David Cullen
and Andrew Lloyd Webber. Associate production design, Peter David
Gould. Production supervision, Peter Lawrence. Produced by The Really
Useful Company (Edgar Dobie, President). Opened 17 November 1994 at
the Minskoff Theatre and closed 22 March 1997 after 977 performances.

CAST: *Norma Desmond*: GLENN CLOSE. *Joe Gillis*: ALAN CAMPBELL. *Max von
Mayerling*: GEORGE HEARN. *Betty Schaefer*: ALICE RIPLEY. *Cecil B. DeMille*:
Alan Oppenheimer. *Artie Green*: Vincent Tumeo.
 (Ensemble): *First Harem Girl, Beautician*: Sandra Allen. *Young Writer, Salesman,
DeMille's Assistant*: Bryan Batt. *Heather, Second Masseuse*: Susan Dawn Carson. *Cliff,
Salesman, Young Guard*: Matthew Dickens. *Third Harem Girl (Jean), Beautician, Hedy
Lamarr*: Colleen Dunn. *Morino, Salesman, Hog Eye*: Steven Stein-Grainger. *Lisa,
Doctor*: Kim Huber. *First Financeman, Film Actor, Salesman*: Rich Hebert. *Katherine,
Psychiatrist*: Alicia Irving. *Second Harem Girl, Beautician*: Lada Boder. *Mary, First
Masseuse*: Lauren Kennedy. *Sheldrake, Police Chief*: Sal Mistretta. *John, Salesman,
Victor Mature*: Mark Morales. *Myron, Manfred*: Rick Podell. *Second Financeman,
Salesman, Party Guest*: Tom Alan Robbins. *Jonesy, Sammy, Salesman*: David Eric.
Choreographer, Salesman: Rick Sparks. *Joanna, Astrologer*: Wendy Walter.

The action takes place in Los Angeles, 1949-1950.

Act 1, Scene 1: Exterior/Dawn, the House on Sunset. *Scene 2*: Exterior/Day, Paramount
Studios. *Scene 3*: Exterior/Day, on the road. *Scene 4*: Exterior/Day, the Garage on
Sunset. *Scene 5*: Interior/Day and Evening, the house on Sunset. *Scene 6*:
Interior/Night, Norma's Guest House. *Scene 7*: Interior/Evening, Schwab's Drugstore.
Scene 8: Exterior/Night, the Terrace on Sunset. *Scene 9*: Interior/Evening, the House
on Sunset. *Scene 10*: Interior/Day, the House on Sunset. *Scene 11*: Interior/Night, the
House on Sunset. *Scene 12*: Interior/Night, Artie Green's Apartment. *Scene 13*:
Interior/Night, the House on Sunset.

Act 2, Scene 1: Exterior/Day, Norma's Swimming Pool. *Scene 2*: Exterior/Day,
Paramount Studio. *Scene 3*: Interior/Night, Betty's office at Paramount. *Scene 4*:
Interior/Day, the House on Sunset. *Scene 5*: Interior/Exterior/Night, Betty's
office/Paramount backlot. *Scene 6*: Exterior/Night, the House on Sunset. *Scene 7*:
Exterior/Interior/Night, the House on Sunset. *Scene 8*: Exterior/Interior/Dawn, the
House on Sunset.

ACT 1
Scene 1
 Prologue
  A. Campbell
Scene 2
 "Let's Have Lunch"
  A. Campbell, Ensemble

Scene 5
 "Surrender"
  G. Close
 "With One Look"
  G. Close
 "Salome"
  G. Close, A. Campbell
Scene 6
 "The Greatest Star of All"
  G. Hearn
Scene 7
 "Every Movie's a Circus"
  A. Campbell, A. Ripley, V. Tumeo, Ensemble
 "Girl Meets Boy"
  A. Campbell, A. Ripley
Scene 9
 "New Ways to Dream"
  G. Close
Scene 10
 "The Lady's Paying"
  R. Podell, G. Close, A. Campbell, Salesmen
Scene 11
 "The Perfect Year"
  G. Close, A. Campbell
Scene 12
 "This Time Next Year"
  A. Campbell, A. Ripley, V. Tumeo, Ensemble

ACT 2
Scene 1
 "Sunset Boulevard"
  A. Campbell
 "The Perfect Year" (reprise)
  G. Close
Scene 2
 "As If We Never Said Goodbye"
  G. Close
 "Surrender" (reprise)
  A. Oppenheimer
Scene 3
 "Girl Meets Boy" (reprise)
  A. Ripley, A. Campbell
Scene 4
 "Eternal Youth Is Worth a Little Suffering"
  Norma's Consultants
Scene 5
 "Too Much in Love to Care"
  A. Ripley, A. Campbell
Scene 6
 "New Ways to Dream" (reprise)
  G. Hearn
Scene 7
 "Sunset Boulevard" (reprise)
  A. Campbell, A. Ripley
Scene 8
 "The Greatest Star of All" (reprise)
  G. Hearn, G. Close
 "Surrender" (reprise)
  G. Close

THE FLYING KARAMAZOV BROTHERS DO THE IMPOSSIBLE!

1944.11

A Comedy Revue in Two Acts. (Conceived by the Flying Karamazov
Brothers.) Musical direction by Doug Wieselman. Produced by An
Imagination Company, Ltd., Herb Goldsmith Productions Ltd, and
Jujamcyn Theatres. Opened 20 November 1994 at the Helen Hayes Theatre
and closed 1 January 1995 after 50 performances.

CAST: *Dmitri Karamazov:* PAUL MAGID. *Ivan Karamazov:* HOWARD JAY PATTERSON. *Rakitin Karamazov:* MICHAEL PRESTON. *Smerdyakov Karamazov:* SAM WILLIAMS. The Kamakaze Ground Crew.

1994.12

A CHRISTMAS CAROL

A Musical in One Act, 14 Scenes. Book by Mike Ockrent and Lynn Ahrens. Based on the novel of the same name by Charles Dickens. Music by Alan Menken. Lyrics by Lynn Ahrens. Directed by Mike Ockrent. Choreographed by Susan Stroman. Setting design by Tony Walton. Costume design by William Ivey Long. Lighting design by Jules Fisher and Peggy Eisenhauer. Sound design by Tony Meola. Projections by Wendall K. Harrington. Flying by Foy. Production supervisor, Gene O'Donovan. Associate director, Steven Zweigbaum. Associate choreographer, Chris Peterson. Musical direction by Paul Gemignani. Orchestrations by Michael Starobin. Dance arrangements and incidental music by Glen Kelly. Executive producer, Dodger Productions. Producer, Tim Hawkins. Presented by Nickleodeon Family Classics and Madison Square Garden. Opened 1 December 1994 at the Paramount Theatre, Madison Square Garden and closed 1 January 1995 after 71 performances[3].

CAST (in order of their appearance): *Punch and Judy Man:* Christopher Sieber. *Punch and Judy Woman:* Donna Lee Marshall. *Organ Grinder:* Robert Ousley. *Grave Digger:* Bill Nolte. *Mr. Smythe:* JOSEPH KOLINSKI. *Jack Smythe:* Andy Jobe. *Grace Smythe:* Lindsay Jobe. *Scrooge:* WALTER CHARLES. *Crachit:* NICK CORLEY. *Charity Men:* Robert Ousley, Martin Van Treuren, Walter Willison. *Old Joe:* Ken McMullen. *Match Girl:* Arlene Pierret. *Street Urchins and Children:* Matthew F. Byrne, Jacy de Filippo, Justin Bartholomew Kamen, Olivia Oguma, Christopher Mark. *Sandwich Board Man:* MICHAEL MANDELL. *Fred:* ROBERT WESTENBERG. *Jonathan:* Jason Fuchs. *Lamplighter:* KEN JENNINGS. *Blind Hag:* Andrea Frierson Toney. *Mrs. Mops:* Darcy Pulliam. *Ghost of Jacob Marley:* JEFF KELLER. *Ghost of Christmas Past:* KEN JENNINGS. *Judge:* Michael H. Ingram. *Scrooge at 8:* David Gallagher. *Fan at 6:* Mary Elizabeth Albano. *Scrooge's Mother:* Andrea Frierson Toney. *Scrooge's Father:* Michael X. Martrin. *Mr. Kent:* Ken McMullen. *Scrooge at 12:* Ramzi Khalaf. *Fan at 10:* Jacy de Filippo, Olivia Oguma. *Fezziwig:* Gerry Vichi. *Scrooge at 18:* Michael Christopher Moore. *Marley, as a young man:* Christopher Sieber. *Mrs. Fezziwig:* Mary Stout. *Emily:* Emily Skinner. *Ghost of Christmas Present:* MICHAEL MANDELL. *Tiny Tim:* Matthew Mezzacappa. *Mrs. Crachit:* Joy Hermalyn. *The Crachit Children:* Mary Elizabeth Albano, Betsy Chang, David Gallagher, Sean Thomas Morrissey. *Sally, Fred's wife:* Natalie Toro. *Undertakers:* Michael X. Martin, Christopher Sieber. *Ghost of Christmas Future:* Theara J. Ward.

Business Men, Ghosts, Gifts and the People of London: Mary Elizabeth Albano, Joan Barber, Renée Bergeron, Christophe Caballero, Betsy Chang, Candy Cook, Madeleine Doherty, Mark Dovey, Donna Dunmire, Andrea Frierson Toney, David Gallagher, Melissa Haizlip, Joy Hermalyn, Michael H. Ingran, Don Johanson, Eric H. Kaufman, John-Charles Kelly, Ramzi Khalaf, David Lowenstein, Seth Malkin, Donna Lee Marshall, Michael X. Martin, Carol Lee Meadows, Michael Christopher Moore, Sean Thomas Morrissey, Ken McMullen, Karen Murphy, Bill Nolte, Robert Ousley, Tom Pardoe, Gail Pennington, Angela Piccinni, Arlene Pierret, Darcy Pulliam, Josef Reiter, Pamela Remler, Sam Reni, Eric Riley, Rommy Sandhu, Christopher Sieber, Emily Skinner, Erin Stoddard, Mary Stout, Tracy Terstriep, Natalie Toro, Martin Van Treuren, Gerry Vichi, Theara J. Ward, Walter Willison. *Angels:* Blessed Sacrament Chorus of Staten Island, Public School 26 Chorus, Righteousness Unlimited, William F. Halloran Vocal Ensemble-School 22. *Swings:* Leslie Bell, Matthew F. Byrne, Jacy de Filippo, Mark S. Hoebee, Michael Hayward-Jones, Justine Bartholomew Kamen, Olivia Oguma, Christopher Mark Petrizzo, P. J. Smith, Matthew J. Vargo, Billy Vitelli, Cynthia Thole, Whitney Webster.

The action takes place in London, 1880.

Scene 1: A Graveyard near St. Paul's Cathedral, Christmas Eve. *Scene 2:* The Royal Exchange. *Scene 3:* The Street. *Scene 4:* Scrooge's House. *Scene 5:* Scrooge's Bed Chamber. *Scene 6:* The Law Courts. *Scene 7:* The Factory. *Scene 8:* Fezziwig's Banking House. *Scene 9:* Montage. *Scene 10:* A Starry Night. *Scene 11:* All Over London. *Scene 12:* The Graveyard. *Scene 13:* Scrooge's Bed Chamber. *Scene 14:* The Street, Christmas Day.

MUSICAL NUMBERS
Scene 1
"The Years Are Passing By"
B. Nolte
Scene 2
"Jolly, Rich and Fat" (A Jolly Good Time)
Charity Men, Smythe Family, Businessmen, Wives, Children

[3]The production played an irregular schedule of multiple daily performances.

"Nothing to Do With Me"
W. Charles, N. Corley
Scene 3
"Street Song" (Nothing to Do With Me)
People of London, W. Charles, R. Westenberg, J. Fuchs, M. Mandell, K. Jennings, A. F. Toney, A. Jobe
Scene 4
"Link By Link"
J. Keller, W. Charles, Ghosts
Scene 5
"The Lights of Long Ago" (Part 1)
K. Jennings
Scene 6
"God Bless Us, Everyone"
A. F. Toney, M. E. Albano, D. Gallagher
Scene 7
"A Place Called Home"
R. Khalaf, J. de Filippo/O. Oguma, W. Charles
Scene 8
"Mr. Fezziwig's Annual Christmas Ball"
G. Vichi, M. Stout, Guests
"A Place Called Home" (reprise)
E. Skinner, M. C. Moore, W. Charles
Scene 9
"The Lights of Long Ago" (Part 2)
M. C. Moore, C. Sieber, E. Skinner, People from Scrooge's Past
Scene 10
"Abundance and Charity"
M. Mandell, W. Charles, Christmas Presents
Scene 11
"Christmas Together"
M. Mezzacappa, N. Corley, J. Hermalyn, Crachit Children, R. Westenberg, N. Toro, W. Charles, People of London
Scene 12
"Dancing on Your Grave"
Grave Diggers, T. J. Ward, Monks, Businessmen, D. Pulliam, M. X. Martin, C. Sieber, K. McMullen, J. Kolinski, N. Corley
"Yesterday, Today and Tomorrow"
W. Charles, Angels, People of London
Scene 13
"The Years Are Passing By" (reprise)
J. Fuchs
Scene 14
"Nothing to Do With Me" (reprise)
W. Charles
"Christmas Together" (reprise)
People of London
"God Bless Us, Everyone" (Finale)
Company

1994.13

COMEDY TONIGHT

A Comedy Revue in One Act. (Assembled by Alexander H. Cohen.) Special material for Ms. Loudon contributed by Bruce Vilanch. Directed by Alexander H. Cohen. Musical staging by Albert Stephenson. Sets by Ray Klausen. Costumes by Alvin Colt. Lighting by Richard Nelson. Sound by Bruce D. Cameron. Musical director, Peter Howard. Associate producer, Hildy Parks. Produced by Alexander H. Cohen and Max Cooper. Opened 18 December 1994 at the Lunt-Fontanne Theatre and closed 24 December 1994 after 8 performances.

CAST: JOY BEHAR, MICHAEL DAVIS, DOROTHY LOUDON, MORT SAHL.
SCENES

Joy Behar (stand-up comedy)

Michael Davis (juggling and comedy)

Dorothy Loudon (songs and comedy):
"Fifty Percent" (from *BALLROOM*)
(*Music by* William Goldenberg. *Lyrics by* Marilyn and Alan Bergman.)
Mort Sahl (political satire and comedy)

YOUNG MAN, OLDER WOMAN

1995.01

A Musical Comedy in Two Acts. Book by Doug and Helen Smith. Songs by Millie Jackson, PJaye Scott, Douglas Knyght-Smith, Reynaldo Rey, Jolyon Skinner. (Directed by Millie Jackson. Produced by Millie Jackson.) Opened 10 January 1995 at the Beacon Theatre and closed 5 February 1995 after 28 performances.[4]

CAST: *Millie*: MILLIE JACKSON. *Reynaldo*: REYNALDO REY. *Doctor Lester*, the Psychiatrist: Douglas Knyght. *Connie Vertible*, Dr. Lester's nurse: Kenneth "Chocolate Thunder" Montague. *Millie's Daughter*: Keisha Jackson. *Background Singers*.

MUSICAL NUMBERS
    "Baby I'm Ready Now"
        (*Music and Lyrics by* Millie Jackson, PJaye Scott, Douglas Knyght-Smith.)
    "Living with a Stranger"
        (*Music and Lyrics by* PJaye Scott, Douglas Knyght-Smith.)
    "The Weight of Love"
        (*Music and Lyrics by* Millie Jackson, Reynaldo Rey.)
    "You Gonna Miss Me"
        (*Music and Lyrics by* PJaye Scott, Douglas Knyght-Smith.)
    "Don't Wanna B N Luv"
        (*Music and Lyrics by* PJaye Scott, Douglas Knyght-Smith.)
    "When a Woman Makes Up her Mind"
        (*Music and Lyrics by* PJaye Scott, Douglas Knyght-Smith.)
    "I Wish It Would Rain Down"
        (*Music and Lyrics by* Phil Collins.)
    "Someday We'll All Be Free"
        (*Music and Lyrics by* Donny Hathaway.)
    "Taking My Life Back"
        (*Music and Lyrics by* Millie Jackson, Jolyon Skinner.)
    "People in My Head"
        (*Music and Lyrics by* Millie Jackson, PJaye Scott, Douglas Knyght-Smith.)
    "Young Man, Older Woman"
        (*Music and Lyrics by* Millie Jackson, Jolyon Skinner.)

JESUS CHRIST SUPERSTAR

1995.02

A Revival of the Musical in Two Acts[5]. Music by Andrew Lloyd Webber. Lyrics by Tim Rice. Directed and choreographed by Tony Christopher. Scenery by Bill Stabile. Costumes by David Paulin. Lighting by Rick Belzer. Sound by Jonathan Deans. Musical director, Craig Barna. Special effects, Gregg Stephens. Associate choreographer, Larry Vickers. Executive producer, Forbes Candlish. Produced by Landmark Entertainment Group, Magic Promotions & Theatricals, TAP Productions. Opened 17 January 1995 at the Paramount Theatre, Madison Square Garden and closed 29 January 1995 after 16 performances.

CAST: *Jesus of Nazareth*: TED NEELEY. *Judas Iscariot*: CARL ANDERSON. *Mary Magdalene*: SYREETA WRIGHT. *Caiaphas*: David Bedella. *Annas*: Danny Zolli. *First Priest*: Mark Slama. *Second Priest*: Michael Guarnera. *Third Priest*: Gary Bankston. *Simon (Zealotes)*: Lawrence Clayton. *Pontius Pilate*: DENNIS DEYOUNG. *Tormentors*: Carol Bentley, Shannon Falank, Kristen Young. *Peter*: Mike Eldred. *King Herod*: Douglass Fraser. *Maid by the Fire*: Karen Byers. *Soldier by the Fire*: Mark C. Reis. *Old Man by the Fire*: Pressley Sutherland. *Soul Sisters*: Karen Byers, J. Kathleen Lamb, Hillary Turk. *Apostles, Their Women, The People of Bethany and Jerusalem*: Gary Bankston, Carol Bentley, Kevin Bernard, Karen Byers, Phil Dominguez, Mike Eldred, Shannon Falank, Robert H. Fowler, Michael Guarnera, Vanessa A. Jones, Eileen Kaden, J. Kathleen Lamb, Mark C. Reis, Mark Slama, Pressley Sutherland, Hillary Turk, Kritsen Young. *Swings*: Michelle DeJean, Jill B. Gounder, Hans Kriefall, Cindi Parise, Larry Vickers.

---

[4]No program available. Details prepared from recordings, press materials.

[5]First produced in New York 12 October 1971 at the Mark Hellinger Theatre for 711 performances. For Synopsis of Scenes and Musical Numbers, see original 1971 production.

SMOKEY JOE'S CAFE: The Songs Of Leiber And Stoller

1995.03

A Musical Revue in Two Acts. Words and music by Jerry Leiber and Mike Stoller. Directed by Jerry Zaks. Musical staging by Jerry McKneely. Original concept by Stephen Helper and Jack Viertel. Co-conceived with additional musical staging by Otis Sallid. Scenery design by Heidi Landesman. Costume design by William Ivey Long. Lighting design by Timothy Hutton. Sound design by Tony Meola. Orchestrations by Steven Margoshes. Arranged and conducted by Louis St. Louis. Production supervisor, Steven Beckler. Associate producers, Marc Routh, Rhoda Mayerson, Thomas Glaser. Produced by Richard Frankel, Thomas Viertel, Steven Baruch, Jujamcyn Theatres/Jack Viertel, Rick Steiner, Frederic H. Mayerson, Center Theatre Group/Ahmanson Theatre/Gordon Davidson. Opened 2 March 1995 at the Virginia Theatre and closed 16 January 2000 after 2036 performances.

CAST (in alphabetical order): KEN ARD, ADRIAN BAILEY, BRENDA BRAXTON, VICTOR TRENT COOK, B. J. CROSBY, PATTIE DARCY JONES, DELEE LIVELY, FREDERICK B. OWENS, MICHAEL PARK.

ACT 1[6]
    "Neighborhood"
        Company
        (*Music and Lyrics by* Jerry Leiber, Mike Stoller, Ralph Dino.)
    "Young Blood"
        A. Bailey, with F. B. Owens, K. Ard, V. T. Cook
        (*Music and Lyrics by* Jerry Leiber, Mike Stoller, Doc Pomus.)
    "Falling"
        D. Lively
    "Ruby Baby"
        M. Park, with A. Bailey, F. B. Owens, K. Ard, V. T. Cook
    "Dance With Me"
        K. Ard, B. J. Crosby, with A. Bailey, F. B. Owens, K. Ard, V. T. Cook
        (*Music and Lyrics by* Jerry Leiber, Mike Stoller, Louis Lebish, George Treadwell, Irv Nathan.)
    "Neighborhood" (reprise)
        B. J. Crosby, B. Braxton, D. Lively, P. D. Jones
    "Keep On Rollin'"
        V. T. Cook, with A. Bailey, K. Ard, F. B. Owens
    "Searchin'"
        V. T. Cook, A. Bailey, K. Ard, F. B. Owens
    "Kansas City"
        B. J. Crosby, P. D. Jones, M. Park
    "Trouble"
        D. Lively, B. Braxton
    "Love Me/Don't"
        A. Bailey, P. D. Jones
    "Fools Fall in Love"
        B. J. Crosby
    "Poison Ivy"
        K. Ard, with A. Bailey, F. B. Owens, V. T. Cook
    "Don Juan"
        B. Braxton
    "Shoppin' for Clothes"
        V. T. Cook, F. B. Owens, with A. Bailey, K. Ard, M. Park
        (*Music and Lyrics by* Jerry Leiber, Mike Stoller, Kent Harris.)
    "I Keep Forgettin'"
        P. D. Jones
    "On Broadway"
        A. Bailey, F. B. Owens, K. Ard, V. T. Cook
        (*Music and Lyrics by* Jerry Leiber, Mike Stoller, Barry Mann, Cynthia Weil.)
    "D. W. Washburn"
        V. T. Cook, Company
    "Saved"
        B. J. Crosby, Company

---

[6]All music and lyrics by Jerry Leiber and Mike Stoller, except where noted below.

ACT 2

"That Is Rock & Roll"
Company

"Yakety Yak"
Company

"Charlie Brown"
Company

"Stay a While"
L. St. Louis, David Keyes (synthesizer)

"Pearl's a Singer"
P. D. Jones
(*Music and Lyrics by* Jerry Leiber, Mike Stoller, Ralph Dino, John Sembello.)

"Teach Me How to Shimmy"
M. Park, D. Lively, with A. Bailey, V. T. Cook

"You're the Boss"
F. B. Owens, B. Braxton

"Smokey Joe's Café"
F. B. Owens, Company

"Loving You"
K. Ard, Company

"Treat Me Nice"
V. T. Cook

"Hound Dog"
B. J. Crosby

"Little Egypt"
F. B. Owens, with A. Bailey, K. Ard, M. Park, V. T. Cook

"I'm a Woman"
B. J. Crosby, B. Braxton, D. Lively, P. D. Jones

"There Goes My Baby"
A. Bailey, with F. B. Owens, K. Ard, M. Park, V. T. Cook
(*Music and Lyrics by* Jerry Leiber, Mike Stoller, Benjamin Nelson, Lover Patterson, George Treadwell.)

"Love Potion #9"
A. Bailey, with F. B. Owens, K. Ard, M. Park, V. T. Cook

"Some Cats Know"
B. Braxton

"Jailhouse Rock"
M. Park, Company

"Fools Fall in Love" (reprise)
B. J. Crosby

"Spanish Harlem"
K. Ard, B. Braxton
(*Music and Lyrics by* Phil Spector, Jerry Leiber.)

"I (Who Have Nothing)"
V. T. Cook
(*Music and Lyrics by* Jerry Leiber, Mike Stoller, Carlo Donida.)

"Neighborhood" (reprise)
P. D. Jones

"Stand By Me"
A. Bailey, Company
(*Music and Lyrics by* Jerry Leiber, Mike Stoller, Ben E. King.)

"That Is Rock & Roll" (Finale)
Company

MAMA I WANT TO SING PART 2

1995.04

A Gospel Musical in Two Acts[7]. Book and lyrics by Vy Higginsen and Ken Wydro. Original music by Wesley Naylor. Music arranged and conducted by Wesley Naylor. Set design by Charles McClannahan. Lighting design by Marshall Williams. Directed by Ken Wydro. Choreography by Cisco Drayton. Produced by Vy Higginsen and Ken Wydro. Opened 7 March 1995 at the Paramount Theatre, Madison Square Garden, and closed 12 March 1995 after 8 performances.

---

[7]Originally opened Off-Broadway 25 March 1990-30 March 1991 at the Heckscher Theatre in repertory with "Mama I Want to Sing, Part 1."

CAST: *Doris Winter:* DESIREE COLEMAN-JACKSON. *Mama Winter:* SHIRLEY CAESAR. *Sister Carrie:* VANESSA BELL ARMSTRONG. *Reverend Julian Simmons:* MARK KIBBLE. *Minister of Music:* Pierre Cook. *Little Doris:* Knoelle Higginson Wydro. *Narrator:* Hazel Smith. And the Mt. Calvary Choir.
The New York Reach Ensemble: Sopranos: Anissia Bunton, Marilyn Davis, Kim Summerson, Michelle C. White, Jannis Winstead. Altos: Shannon Cooper, Robin Cunningham, Kimberly Marshall, Diane Spann-Miller, Anita Wells. Tenors: Daryl Banks, Tyrone Flowers, Willie Heard, Damon Horton, Ronnie McLeod. *The Halos:* Kim Summerson, Diane Spann-Miller, Anita Wells.

ACT 1

Choir Rehearsal
P. Cook, Mt. Calvary Choir

"The Spirit of Your Father"
S. Caesar

"The Lord Is Blessing Me"
M. Kibble, Mt. Calvary Choir

"Faith"
V. B. Armstrong, Mt. Calvary Choir

"Sermon"
M. Kibble

"Because He Lives"
D. Coleman-Jackson, Mt. Calvary Choir

"Something Pretty"
D. Coleman-Jackson, M. Kibble

"Finding a Man Ain't Easy"
V. B. Armstrong, S. Caesar, D. Coleman-Jackson

"We Belong Together"
D. Coleman-Jackson, M. Kibble

"Bless You, My Children"
S. Caesar, Mt. Calvary Choir

ACT 2

"Stay Close to the Music"
D. Coleman-Jackson, The Halos

"Long Distance Love"
Las Vagas Hotel, Julian's Apartment, New York

"New Life on the Planet"
D. Coleman-Jackson

"Mt. Calvary Baptism Day"
Baptism at Mt. Calvary

"Sister Carrie's Song"
V. B. Armstrong, Mt. Calvary Choir

"The Promise of the Future"
M. Kibble

"To Love Is To Serve"
D. Coleman-Jackson, M. Kibble

"Please Understand"
D. Coleman-Jackson

"Something to Remember Me By"
V. B. Armstrong

"Where Is My Mommy, Please"
K. H. Wydro, S. Caesar

"Alone on the Road"
S. Caesar

"Going Home"
S. Caesar

Finale Medley
Company

HOW TO SUCCEED IN BUSINESS WITHOUT REALLY TRYING

1995.05

A Revival of the Musical (Comedy) in Two Acts[8]. Book by Abe Burrows, Jack Weinstock and Willie Gilbert. Based on the novel of the same name by

---

[8]Originally opened in New York 14 October 1961 at the 46th Street Theatre for 1417 performances. For Musical Numbers, see original 1961 production. For this production, "Cinderella Darling" was dropped from the opening of Act 2 and replaced by:
"How to Succeed" (reprise)
V. Clark, K. Lynes, Women

Shepherd Mead. Music and lyrics by Frank Loesser. Scenery design by John Arnone. Costume design by Susan Hilferty. Lighting design by Howell Binkley. Directed by Des McAnuff. Choreography by Wayne Cilento. Video design by Batwin + Robin Productions, Inc. Sound design by Steve Canyon Kennedy. Music direction and vocal arrangements by Ted Sperling. Orchestrations by Danny Troob; additional orchestrations by David Siegel, Robert Ginzler. Dance arrangements by Jeanine Tesori. Incidental music arranged by Ted Sperling. Executive producer, Dodger Productions. Associate producer, Whistlin' Dixie. Originally produced by LaJolla Playhouse, LaJolla, California (Michael Greif, artistic director; Terrence Dwyer, managing director). Produced by Dodger Productions (Michael David, Doug Johnson, Des McAnuff, Rocco Landesman, Edward Strong, Sherman Warner), Kardana Productions, Inc. (John N. Hart, Jr., Mort Swinsky), The John F. Kennedy Center (James D. Wolfensohn, chairman; Lawrence J. Wilker, president), the Nederlander Organization (James M. Nederlander). Opened 23 March 1995 at the Richard Rodgers Theatre and closed 14 July 1996 after 548 performances.

CAST (in order of their appearance): *Voice of the Narrator:* Walter Cronkite. *J. Pierrepont Finch:* MATTHEW BRODERICK. *Milt Gatch:* Tom Flynn. *Jenkins:* Jay Aubrey Jones. *Davis:* William Ryall. *Bert Bratt:* JONATHAN FREEMAN. *Tackaberry:* Martin Moran. *J. B. Biggley:* RONN CARROLL. *Rosemary Pilkington:* MEGAN MULLALLY. *Smitty:* VICTORIA CLARK *Bud Frump:* JEFF BLUMENKRANTZ. *Miss Krumholtz:* Kristi Lynes. *Office Boy:* Randl Ask. *Security Guard:* Kevin Bogue. *Henchmen:* Jack Hayes, Jerome Vivona. *Miss Jones:* LILLIAS WHITE. *Twimble:* GERRY VICHI. *Hedy La Rue:* LUBA MASON. *Toynbee:* Tom Flynn. *Scrubwomen:* Rebecca Holt, Carla Renata Williams. *Dance Soloist:* Nancy Lemenager. *Ovington:* Randl Ask. *TV Announcer:* Randl Ask. *Wickets and Wickettes:* Kevin Bogue, Maria Calabrese, Jack Hayes, Nancy Lemenager, Kristi Lynes, Aiko Nakasone, Jerome Vivona, Carla Renata Williams. *Wally Womper:* GERRY VICHI.

Ensemble: Randl Ask, Kevin Bogue, Maria Calabrese, Tom Flynn, Jack Hayes, Rebecca Holt, Jay Aubrey Jones, Nancy Lemenager, Martin Moran, Aiko Nakasone, William Ryall, Jerome Vivona, Carla Renata Williams. *Swings:* Jeffry Denman, Tom Flagg, Pamela Gold.

The action takes place in 1961 at the World Wide Wicket Company in New York City.

1995.06 THE MERRY WIDOW

A Revival of the Operetta in Three Acts, 4 Scenes[9]. Music by Franz Lehár. Original German book and lyrics by Victor Léon and Leo Stein (after "L'Attaché d'Ambassade.") (New) English book adaptation by Robert Johanson. (New) English lyrics by Albert Evans. Production director, Robert Johanson. Choreographer, Sharon Halley. Set design by Michael Anania. Costume design by Gregg Barnes. Lighting design by Mark W. Stanley. Sound design by Abe Jacob. Chorus master, Joseph Colaneri. Conductor, Eric Stern. Produced by the New York City Opera. Opened 26 March 1995 at the New York State Theatre and closed 22 April 1995 after 7 performances in repertory.

CAST: *Baron Mirko Zeta:* GEORGE S. IRVING. *Valencienne:* Elizabeth Futral. *Kromov:* Joseph McKee. *Olga:* Beth McVey. *Bogdanovitch:* JOHN LANKSTON. *Sylviane:* Suzanne Ishee. *Njegus:* ROBERT CREIGHTON. *Camille de Rosillon:* CARLO SCIBELLI. *Vicomte Cascada:* JEFFREY LENTZ. *Raoul de St. Brioche:* JAMES BOBICK. *Hanna (Glawari):* JANE THORNGREN. *Count Danilo:* MICHAEL HAYES. *Lolo:* Jean Barber. *Dodo:* Stephanie Godino. *Jou-Jou:* Christiane Farr. *Frou-Frou:* Kathy Meyer. *Clo-Clo:* Debbi Fuhrman. *Margot:* Joan Mirabella. *Young Danilo:* John MacInnis. *Young Hanna:* Christane Farr. *Ensemble:* New York City Opera Chorus.

Act 1: The Marsovian Embassy. Paris, early 1900's.

Act 2: The Garden of Mme. Glawari's villa.

Act 3: Chez Maxim.

ACT 1[10]

"For Marsovia"
  G. S. Irving, E. Futral, J. Lentz, J. Bobick, C. Scibelli, Marsovians, Parisians
"A Respectable Wife"
  E. Futral, C. Scibelli

"Gentlemen, I Pray" (The Widow's Entrance)
  J. Thorngren, Men
"Maxim's"
  M. Hayes, R. Creighton, Grisettes
"The Quarrel"
  J. Thorngren, M. Hayes
Finale, Act 1
  J. Thorngren, M. Hayes, Full Company

ACT 2
"Marsovian Dances"
  Company
"Vilia"
  J. Thorngren, Company
"Women"
  M. Hayes, G. S. Irving, R. Creighton, J. Lankston, J. McKee, J. Bobick, J. Lentz, C. Scibelli
"Marsovian Dances" (reprise)
  J. Thorngren, M. Hayes, Dancers
"Romance"
  E. Futral, C. Scibelliil
"Summerhouse Quintet"
  J. Thorngren, M. Hayes, E. Futral, C. Scibelli, G. S. Irving
Finale, Act 2
  J. Thorngren, M. Hayes, Company

ACT 3
"Cakewalk"
  Full Company
"Another Frenchman" (Njegus' Song)
  R. Creighton, Women
"I'll Remember"[11]
  E. Futral, C. Scibelli
"Cancan"
  J. Thorngren, Grisettes, Company
"Yours Is My Heart"[12]
  M. Hayes
"The Merry Widow Waltz"
  M. Hayes, J. Thorngren
Finale, Act 3
  Company

1995.07 GENTLEMEN PREFER BLONDES

A Revival of the Musical Comedy in Two Acts, 11 Scenes[13]. Book by Joseph Fields and Anita Loos[14], adapted from her novel of the same name. Music by Jule Styne. Lyrics by Leo Robin. Directed by Charles Repole. Choreographed by Michael Lichtefeld. Scenery and costume designed by Eduardo Sicangco. Lighting design by Kirk Bookman. Sound design by T. Richard Fitzgerald. Orchestrations by Douglas Besterman. Musical supervision and vocal arrangements by Michael O'Flaherty. Dance music by Gordon Harrell. Musical director, Andrew Wilder. Associate producer, Sue Frost. Executive producer, Manny Kladitis. Produced by National Actors

---

[9]Originally produced in New York 21 October 1907 at the New Amsterdam Theatre for 416 performances.
[10]No song list appears in the New York City Opera program. Song list prepared from the previous Papermill Playhouse production where this adaptation premiered.

---

[11]Interpolation "Meine Lippen, sie kuessen so heiss" from GIUDITTA.
[12]Interpolation "Dein ist mein ganzes Herz" (Yours Is My Heart) from THE LAND OF SMILES.
[13]Originally produced in New York 8 December 1949 at the Ziegfeld Theatre for 740 performances.
[14]Book revisions were uncredited. The book was drastically revised, songs reassigned, dropped and moved within the show, which was revised from 12 to 11 scenes. "Homesick Blues" was retitled "Homesick." The "Sunshine" song lyrics were largely dropped and its music formed the basis for the dance sequence "Sunshine Montage." "You Say You Care" was excised from the plot and became incidental music in the final scene for the Park Casino Trio. The following musical numbers were dropped:
  "Bye Bye Baby" (reprises), the Practice Scherzo, "In the Champs de Mers" (dance), "House on Rittenhouse Square," "Coquette" and "Button Up with Esmond."

Theatre (Tony Randall, Founder and artistic direction) in association with The Goodspeed Opera House (Michael P. Price, Executive producer). Opened 10 April 1995 at the Lyceum Theatre and closed 30 April 1995 after 24 performances.

CAST (in order of their appearance): *Dorothy Shaw*: KAREN PRUNZIK. *Lorelei Lee*: K. T. SULLIVAN. *Gus Esmond*: ALLEN FITZPATRICK. *Lady Phyllis Beekman*: CAROL SWARBRICK. *Sir Francis Beekman*: DAVID PONTING. *Mrs. Ella Spofford*: SUSAN RUSH. *Henry Spofford*: GEORGE DVORSKY. *Josephus Gage*: JAMIE ROSS. *Steward*: Dick Decareau. *Frank*: Craig Waletzko. *George*: Ken Nagy. *Mime*: Joe Bowerman. *Robert Lemanteur*: Craig Waletzko. *Louie Lemanteur*: John Hoshko. *Tango Couples*: Paula Grider, Joe Bowerman, Lisa Hanna, Ken Nagy, Richard Costa, Lorinda Santos. *Park Casino Trio*: Angela Bond, John Hoshko, Craig Waletzko. *Mr. Esmond, Sr.*: Dick Decareau.

Ensemble: Angela Bond, Joe Bowerman, Richard Costa, Paula Grider, Lisa Hanna, Bryan S. Haynes, John Hoshko, Ken Nagy, Wendy Roberts, Lorinda Santos, Craig Waletzko. *Swings*: Melissa Bell, Marty McDonough.

Time: 1926.

Act 1, Scene 1: Onstage and backstage at Club Purgatory, New York City. *Scene 2*: The French Line Pier in New York, midnight sailing. *Scene 3*: The Sun Deck of the *Ile de France*, three days out. *Scene 4*: Lorelei's Suite on the *Ile de France*, later that day. *Scene 5*: Paris. *Scene 6*: Lorelei's suite at The Ritz in Paris, evening.

Act 2, Scene 1: Onstage at the Club Cocteau in Paris, the next evening. *Scene 2*: Dorothy's dressing room backstage, immediately following. *Scene 3*: Streets of Paris, in front of the Café Rouge. *Scene 4*: Lorelei's Suite, 3 A.M. *Scene 5*: The Central Park Casino, New York, 10 days later.

ACT 1
Scene 1
  Opening
    K. Prunzik, Men
  "It's High Time"
    K. T. Sullivan, K. Prunzik
Scene 2
  "It's High Time" (reprise)
    Company
  "Bye, Bye Baby"
    A. Fitzpatrick, K. T. Sullivan, Company
Scene 3
  "I'm Just A Little Girl from Little Rock"
    K. T. Sullivan
  "I'm Atingle, I'm Aglow"
    J. Ross, K. T. Sullivan, K. Prunzik, S. Rush

  "I Love What I'm Doing"
    K. Prunzik, Olympic Men
Scene 4
  "Just a Kiss Apart"
    G. Dvorsky, K. Prunzik
  "It's Delightful Down in Chile"
    D. Ponting, K. T. Sullivan
Scene 5
  "Sunshine Montage"
    J. Bowerman, Company
Scene 6
  "I'm Atingle, I'm Aglow" (reprise)
    J. Ross, Company
  Finale Act 1
    K. T. Sullivan

ACT 2
Scene 1
  "Mamie Is Mimi"
    K. Prunzik, Company
Scene 2
  "Diamonds Are a Girl's Best Friend"
    K. T. Sullivan
Scene 3
  "A Ride on a Rainbow" (from *RUGGLES OF RED GAP*, television)
    G. Dvorsky, K. Prunzik, Tango Couples
Scene 4
  "Gentlemen Prefer Blondes"
    K. T. Sullivan, A. Fitzpatrick
  "Homesick"
    A. Fitzpatrick, K. T. Sullivan, K. Prunzik, G. Dvorsky, S. Rush, J. Ross
Scene 5
  "I Love What I'm Doing" (reprise)
    Trio
  "You Say You Care"
    Trio
  "Keeping Cool With Coolidge"
    Company
  Finale
    Company

1995–1996 SEASON

Julie Andrews (center) and Members of the Company of VICTOR/VICTORIA
Joan Marcus/Photofest

1995–1996 SEASON

1995.08 ## BUTTONS ON BROADWAY

Celebrating his 60th Anniversary in Show Business (A One Man Show in Two Acts). Musical director, Bryan Louiselle. Scenic design by Nancy Thun. Lighting design by Ken Billington. Sound design by Lewis Mead. Produced by Don Gregory. Opened 8 June 1995 at the Ambassador Theatre and closed 16 July 1995 after 33 performances.

CAST: RED BUTTONS (comedy, impressions, a few songs[1]).

CHRONICLE OF
1995.09 ## A DEATH FORETOLD

A Musical in One Act. Based on the novel (of the same name) by Gabriel García Márquez. Adapted by Graciela Daniele and Jim Lewis. Music by Bob Telson. Additional material by Michael John LaChiusa. Conceived, directed and choreographed by Graciela Daniele. Sets by Christopher Barreca. Costumes by Toni-Leslie James. Lighting by Jules Fisher, Beverly Emmons. Sound by Tony Meola. Musical director, dance music arrangements by Steve Sandberg. (Music) Arrangements by Bob Telson. Associate choreographer, Willie Rosario. Sponsored by A&T. Production made possible by grants from The Rockefeller Foundation, The Gilman and Gonzalez-Falla Theatre Foundation, Inc. Produced by Linclon Center Theatre (André Bishop, Artistic director; Bernard Gersten, Executive producer), by arangement with INTAR Hispanic American Arts Center. Opened 15 June 1995 at the Plymouth Theatre and closed 16 July 1995 after 37 performances[2].

CAST: *Santiago Nasar*: GEORGE DE LA PEÑA. *Cristo*, his friend: JULIO MONGE. *Placida*, Santiago's mother: YOLANDE BAVAN. *Victoria*, the cook: Myra Lucretia Taylor. *Divina*, her daughter: Monica McSwain. *Angela Vicario*: SAUNDRA SANTIAGO. *Pura Vicario*, her mother: Ivonne Coll. *Pablo Vicario*, Angela's brother: LUIS PEREZ. *Pedro Vicario*, Angela's brother: GREGORY MITCHELL. *Bayardo San Roman*: ALEXANDRE PROIA. *Clotilde*, the bodega keeper: TONYA PINKINS. *Flora*, Santiago's fiancée: Lisa Leguillou. *Faustino*, a butcher: Lazaro Perez. *Xius*, a widower: Norberto Kerner. *Colonel Aponte*: Nelson Roberto Landrieu. *Father Amador*: Jaime Tirelli. *Margot*, a novice: René M. Ceballos. *Maria*: Denise Faye.

Place and time: An isolated Latin American town in the past and present.

THE MIKADO,
1995.10 ## or The Town of Titipu

A Revival of the Comic Opera in Two Acts[3]. Libretto by William S. Gilbert. Music by Arthur Sullivan. Production (direction), Lofti Mansouri. Stage director, Christian Smith. Conductor, Randall Craig Fleischer. Set and costume designer, Thierry Bosquet. Lighting designer, John Gleason. Choreographer, Patricia Birch; choreography re-staged by Helena Andreyko. Chorus master, Joseph Colaneri. Produced by the New York City Opera. Opened 23 September 1995 at the New York State Theatre and closed 4 November 1995 after 4 performances in repertory; returned 3 March 1996 and closed 18 April 1996 after 4 additional performances. Total this season: 8 performances.

CAST (in order of appearance): *Nanki-Poo*: MATTHEW CHELLIS. *Pish-Tush*: JAMES BOBICK. *Pooh-Bah*: JOSEPH MCKEE. *Ko-Ko*: JAMES BILLINGS. *Yum-Yum*: BARBARA SHIRVIS. *Pitti-Sing*: ANGELA HORN. *Peep-Bo*: DIANNA HELDMAN. *Katisha*: JOYCA CASTLE. *The Mikado of Japan*: RICHARD MCKEE. *Chorus of School Girls, Nobles, Guards and Coolies*: New York City Opera Chorus.

---

[1]Included "Sam, You Made the Pants Too Long"

[2]No individual scenes or musical numbers were listed.

[3]First presented in New York 20 July, 10-29 August 1885 at the Union Square and People's Theatres for 22 performances. First authorized production presented 19 August 1885 at the Fifth Avenue Theatre by Richard D'Oyly Carte for 250 performances. For Synopsis of Scenes and Musical Numbers, see 19 August 1885 D'Oyly Carte production.

1995.11 # COMPANY

A Revival of the Musical Comedy in Two Acts, 11 Scenes[4]. Book by George Furth. Music and lyrics by Stephen Sondheim. Directed by Scott Ellis. Choreographed by Rob Marshall. Set by Tony Walton. Costumes by William Ivey Long. Lighting by Peter Kaczorowski. Sound by Tony Meola. Projections by Wendall K. Harrington. Musical direction by David Loud. Orchestrations by Jonathan Tunick. Fights by David Leong. Assistant choreographer, Sarah Miles. Originally produced (and directed) on Broadway by Harold Prince. Original dance arrangements by Wally Harper. Original 'Tick Tock' dance music arrangements by David Shire. Produced by The Roundabout Theatre Company (Todd Haimes, Artistic director; Ellen Richard, Managing director). Opened 5 October 1995 at the Criterion/Stage Right and closed 3 December 1995 after 68 performances.

CAST: *Robert*: BOYD GAINES. *Sarah*: KATE BURTON. *Harry*: ROBERT WESTENBERG. *Susan*: PATRICIA BEN PETERSON. *Peter*: JONATHAN DOKUCHITZ. *Jenny*: DIANA CANOVA. *David*: JOHN HILLNER. *Amy*: VEANNA COX. *Paul*: DANNY BURSTEIN. *Joanne*: DEBRA MONK. *Larry*: TIMOTHY LANDFIELD. *Marta*: LA CHANZE. *Kathy*: CHARLOTTE D'AMBOISE. *April*: JANE KRAKOWSKI.

1995.12 # PATTI LUPONE ON BROADWAY

A One Woman Show in Two Acts. Conceived and directed by Scott Wittman. Written by Jeffrey Richman. Musical director, Dick Gallagher. Musical arrangements, John McDaniel. Lighting by John Hastings. Sound by Otts Munderloh. Additional musical arrangements by Steven D. Bowen, Dick Gallagher, Glen Roven, Marc Shaiman, Jonathan Tunick. Produced by Jujamcyn Theatres (James H. Binger, Chairman; Rocco Landesman, Preident; Paul Libin, Producing Director; Jack Viertel, Creative Director). Opened 12 October 1995 at the Ritz Theatre and closed 25 November 1995 after 46 performances.

CAST: PATTI LUPONE.
The Mermen: Byron Motley, Josef Powell, Gene Van Buren, John West.

MUSICAL NUMBERS[5]
"I Get a Kick Out of You" (from *ANYTHING GOES*)
 (*Music and Lyrics by* Cole Porter.)
"I'm a Stranger Here Myself" (from *ONE TOUCH OF VENUS*)
 (*Music by* Kurt Weill. *Lyrics by* Ogden Nash.)
"It Never Was You" (from *KNICKERBOCKER HOLIDAY*)
 (*Music by* Kurt Weill. *Lyrics by* Maxwell Anderson.)
"Everything Happens to Me"
 (*Music by* Matt Dennis. *Lyrics by* Tom Adair.)
"Lush Life"
 (*Music and Lyrics by* Billy Strayhorn.)
"Ain't Nobody Here But Us Chickens" (interpolated into *FIVE GUYS NAMED MOE*)
 (*Music and Lyrics by* Alex Kramer and Joan Whitney.)
"I've Got the Sun in the Morning" (from *ANNIE GET YOUR GUN*)
 (*Music and Lyrics by* Irving Berlin.)
"Dirty Hands! Dirty Face!" (from *BOMBO*)
 (*Music by* James V. Monaco. *Lyrics by* Al Jolson, Grant Clarke and Edgar Leslie.)
"(And) His Rocking Horse Ran Away" (from *AND THE ANGELS SING* film)
 (*Music by* Johnny Burke. *Lyrics by* Jimmy Van Heusen.)
"My Ship" (from *LADY IN THE DARK*)
 (*Music by* Kurt Weill. *Lyrics by* Ira Gershwin.)
"Surabaya Johnny" (from *HAPPY END*)
 (*Music by* Kurt Weill. *Lyrics by* Bertolt Brecht.)

---

[4]Originally produced in New York 26 April 1970 at the Alvin Theatre for 690 performances. For Synopsis of Scenes and Musical Numbers, see original 1970 production. The Vocal Minority were dropped for this revival. Added for this production:
 "Marry Me a Little" (Act 1 closing)
 B. Gaines

[5]Miss LuPone accompanied by The Mermen on "Ain't Nobody Here But Us Chickens," "I Got the Sun in the Morning," "Sleepy Man," "Anything Goes," "Moonshine Lullaby," and "Heaven."

"Calling You" (from film *BAGDAD CAFE*)
  (*Music and Lyrics by* Bob Telson.)
"Get Here"
  (*Music and Lyrics by* Brenda Russell.)
"Come to the Supermarket in Old Peking" (from TV musical *ALADDIN*)
  (*Music and Lyrics by* Cole Porter.)
"Being Alive" (from *COMPANY*)
  (*Music and Lyrics by* Stephen Sondheim.)
"Looking for Love on Broadway"
  (*Music and Lyrics by* James Taylor.)
"Don't Cry for Me Argentina" (from *EVITA*)
  (*Music by* Andrew Lloyd Webber. *Lyrics by* Tim Rice.)
"Sleepy Man" (from *THE ROBBER BRIDEGROOM*)
  (*Music by* Robert Waldman. *Lyrics by* Alfred Uhry.)
"Meadowlark" (from *THE BAKER'S WIFE*)
  (*Music and Lyrics by* Stephen Schwartz.)
"As Long as He Needs Me" (from *OLIVER!*)
  (*Music and Lyrics by* Lionel Bart.)
"Nickel Under Your Foot" (from *THE CRADLE WILL ROCK*)
  (*Music and Lyrics by* Marc Blitzstein.)
"I Dreamed a Dream" (from *LES MISERABLES*)
  (*Music by* Claude-Michel Schönberg. *Lyrics by* Alain Boublil and Herbert Kretzmer.)
"Anything Goes" (from *ANYTHING GOES*)
  (*Music and Lyrics by* Cole Porter.)
"Moonshine Lullaby" (from *ANNIE GET YOUR GUN*)
  (*Music and Lyrics by* Irving Berlin.)
"Heaven"
  (*Music and Lyrics by* Julie Gold.)
"Lost in the Stars" (from *LOST IN THE STARS*)
  (*Music by* Kurt Weill. *Lyrics by* Maxwell Anderson.)
"Bewitched" (from *PAL JOEY*)
  (*Music by* Richard Rodgers. *Lyrics by* Lorenz Hart.)

1995.13
HELLO, DOLLY!

A Revival of the Musical Comedy in Two Acts, 13 Scenes[6]. Book by Michael Stewart. Based on the play "The Matchmaker" by Thornton Wilder. Music and lyrics by Jerry Herman. Original production directed and choreographed by Gower Champion. Directed and staged by Lee Roy Reams. Associate choreographer, Bill Bateman. Set design by Oliver Smith. Costume design by Jonathan Bixby. Lighting design by Ken Billington. Sound design by Peter Fitzgerald. Musical director and conductor, Jack Everly. Musical supervision, Tim Stella. Orchestrations by Philip J. Lang. Dance arrangements by Peter Howard. Production supervisor, Jerry Herman. Scenic supervision by Rosaria Sinisi. Produced by Manny Kladitis, Magic Promotion and Theatricals (Lee D. Marshall, Joe Marsh, Glenn Bechdel), Pace Theatrical Group (Allen Becker, Brian Becker, Miles Wilkin, Scott Zeiger). Opened 19 October 1995 at the Lunt-Fontanne Theatre and closed 28 January 1996 after 116 performances.

CAST (in the order of appearance): *Mrs. Dolly Gallagher Levi*: CAROL CHANNING. *Ernestina*: Monica M. Wemitt. *Ambrose Kemper*: James Darrah. *Horse*: Sharon Moore, Michele Tibbitts. *Horace Vandergelder*: JAY GARNER. *Ermengarde*: Christine DeVito. *Cornelius Hackl*: MICAHEL DEVRIES. *Barnaby Tucker*: CORY ENGLISH. *Minnie Fay*: LORI ANN MAHL. *Irene Molloy*: FLORENCE LACEY. *Mrs. Rose*: Elizabeth Green. *Rudolph*: Steve Pudenz. *Stanley*: Julian Brightman. *Judge*: Bill Bateman. *Court Clerk*: Halden Michaels.

Townspeople, Waiters, Etc.: John Bantay, Desta Barbieri, Bill Bateman, Kimberly Bellmann, Bruce Blanchard, Stephen Bourneuf, Julian Brightman, Holly Cruikshank, Simone Gee, Jason Gillman, Milica Govich, Elizabeth Green, Donald Ives, Dan LoBuono, Jim Madden, Halden Michaels, Sharon Moore, Michael Quinn, Robert Randle, Mitch Rosengarten, Mary Setrakian, Clarence M. Sheridan, Randy Slovacek, Roger Preston Smith, Ashley Stover, Michele Tibbitts. *Swings*: Kevin M. Burrows, Jennifer Joan Joy, John Salvatore, Matthew A. Sipress.

---

[6]Originally produced in New York 16 January 1964 at the St. James Theatre for 2844 performances. For Synopsis of Scenes and Musical Numbers, see original 1964 production. As in previous revivals, "Come and Be My Butterfly" was not performed. Act 1, Scene 3, and Act 2, Scene 4, were eliminated. "The Polka Contest" followed "Hello, Dolly!" in Act 2, Scene 3.

1995.14
SWINGING ON A STAR

A Musical Revue in Two Acts, 7 Scenes. Lyrics by Johnny Burke. Music by Johnny Burke, Erroll Garner, Robert Haggart, Arthur Johnston, James Monaco, Harold Spina, Jimmy Van Heusen. Written and directed by Michael Leeds. Choreographed by Kathleen Marshall. Scenery designed by James Youmans. Costumes designed by Judy Dearing. Lighting designed by Richard Nelson. Orchestrations and vocal arrangements by Barry Levitt. Dance arrangements by Peter Howard. Additional orchestrations by Brian Besterman. Sound designer, T. Richard Fitzgerald. Video and projections by Batwin + Robin Productions, Inc. Assistant musical director and additional arrangements by Ron Drotos. Production coordinator, Todd Little. Musical direction by Barry Levitt. Originally produced by the Goodspeed Opera House, George Street Playhouse. Produced by Richard Seader, Mary Burke Kramer, Paul B. Berkowsky. Opened 22 October 1995 at the Music Box Theatre and closed 14 January 1996 after 97 performances.

CAST (in alphabetical order): TERRY BURRELL, LEWIS CLEALE, KATHY FITZGERALD, EUGENE FLEMING, ALVALETA GUESS, LORI HART, MICHAEL MCGRATH.

Act 1, Scene 1: Speakeasy, Chicago. *Scene 2*: Depression, The Bowery. *Scene 3*: Radio Show, New York City. *Scene 4*: USO Show, the Pacific Islands.

Act 2, Scene 1: Ballroom, Hotel Roosevelt, Akron, Ohio. *Scene 2*: Road to Paramount Studios, Hollywood. *Scene 3*: Supper Club, the Present.

ACT 1
Scene 1
"You're Not the Only Oyster in the Stew"
  A. Guess, L. Hart, K. Fitzgerald
  (*Music by* Harold Spina.)
"Chicago Style" (from *ROAD TO BALI* film)
  E. Fleming, L. Hart, K. Fitzgerald, M. McGrath
  (*Music by* Jimmy Van Heusen.)
"Ain't It a Shame About Mame" (from *RHYTHM ON THE RIVER* film)
  E. Fleming, T. Burrell
  (*Music by* James Monaco.)
"What's New"
  L. Hart
  (*Music by* Robert Haggart.)
"Doctor Rhythm" (dropped from *DOCTOR RHYTHM* film)
  A. Guess, E. Fleming
  (*Music by* James Monaco.)
  (*Choreographed by* Kathleen Marshall and Eugene Fleming.)
  The Waiter: M. McGrath. *Mame*: T. Burrell. *Escort*: L. Cleale. *Cleo*: A. Guess. *Jeannie*: L. Hart. *Flora*: K. Fitzgerald. *Ben*: E. Fleming.
Scene 2
"Pennies from Heaven" (from *PENNIES FROM HEAVEN* film)
  L. Cleale
  (*Music by* Arthur Johnston.)
"When Stanislaus Got Married" (from *AND THE ANGELS SING* film)
  M. McGrath, A. Guess, L. Hart, E. Fleming, T. Burrell
  (*Music by* Jimmy Van Heusen.)
"His Rocking Horse Ran Away" (from *AND THE ANGELS SING* film)
  K. Fitzgerald
  (*Music by* Jimmy Van Heusen.)
"Annie Doesn't Live Here Anymore"
  L. Cleale, M. McGrath, E. Fleming
  (*Music by* Harold Spina. *Lyrics by* Joe Young, Johnny Burke.)
  The Homeless Man: L. Cleale. *The Street People*: A. Guess, L. Hart, E. Fleming, T. Burrell. *The Polish Gentleman*: M. McGrath. *The Housewife*: K. Fitzgerald. *The Suitors*: L. Cleale, M. McGrath, E. Fleming.
Scene 3
"Annie Doesn't Live Here Anymore" (reprise)
  M. McGrath, L. Hart, L. Cleale, E. Fleming, A. Guess, T. Burrell
"Scatterbrain" (from *SCATTERBRAIN* film)
  M. McGrath
  (*Music by* Keene Bean, Frankie Masters.)
"One, Two, Button Your Shoe" (from *PENNIES FROM HEAVEN* film)
  L. Hart, M. McGrath
  (*Music by* Arthur Johnston.)
"Whoopsie Daisy Day"
  L. Cleale, E. Fleming, A. Guess, T. Burrell
  (*Music by* Johnny Burke.)

"What Does It Take To Make You Take to Me?"
K. Fitzgerald
(*Music by* Jimmy Van Heusen.)

"Irresistible"
L. Cleale, K. Fitzgerald, E. Fleming, A. Guess, T. Burrell.
(*Music by* Harold Spina.)

"An Apple for the Teacher" (from *THE STAR MAKER* film)
All
(*Music by* Arthur Johnston.)
The Burkettes: E. Fleming, A. Guess, T. Burrell.
The Announcer: L. Cleale. *Buddy*: M. McGrath.
Betty: L. Hart. *Vicky Voyay*: K. Fitzgerald.

Scene 4

"Thank Your Lucky Stars and Stripes" (from *PLAYMATES* film)
M. McGrath, E. Fleming
(*Music by* Jimmy Van Heusen.)

"Personality" (from *ROAD TO UTOPIA* film)
K. Fitzgerald, L. Hart, T. Burrell
(*Music by* Jimmy Van Heusen.)

"There's Always the Blues"
A. Guess
(*Music by* Joe Bushkin.)

"Polka Dots and Moonbeams"
L. Cleale
(*Music by* Jimmy Van Heusen.)

"Swinging on a Star" (from *GOING MY WAY* film)
All
(*Music by* Jimmy Van Heusen.)

"(Thank Your Lucky) Stars and Stripes" (reprise)
All
Don Carter: M. McGrath. *Buzz Albright*: E. Fleming. *Miss South Dakota*:
K. Fitzgerald. *Miss North Carolina*: L. Hart. *Miss Rhiengold*: T. Burrell. *Lena
George*: A. Guess. *Eddie*: L. Cleale.

ACT 2

Scene 1

"Don't Let That Moon Get Away" (from *SING YOU SINNERS* film)
E. Fleming
(*Music by* James Monaco.)

"All You Want to Do Is Dance"(from *DOUBLE FOR NOTHING* film)
(*Music by* Arthur Johnston.)

"You Danced with Dynamite"
K. Fitzgerald, M. McGrath
(*Music by* Jimmy Van Heusen.)

"Imagination"
T. Burrell, E. Fleming, L. Hart
(*Music by* Jimmy Van Heusen.)

"It Could Happen to You" (from *AND THE ANGELS SING* film)
A. Guess
(*Music by* Jimmy Van Heusen.)
The Manager: L. Cleale. *The Coat Check Girl*: L. Hart.
The Waiter: E. Fleming. *The Vocalist*: T. Burrell. *The Man*:
M. McGrath. *The Date*: K. Fitzgerald. *The Woman Alone*: A. Guess.

Scene 2

"Apalachicola" (from *ROAD TO RIO* film)
L. Cleale, M. McGrath, K. Fitzgerald
(*Music by* Jimmy Van Heusen.)

"You Don't Have to Know the Language" (from *ROAD TO RIO* film)
L. Cleale, M. McGrath, K. Fitzgerald, L. Hart, T. Burrell
(*Music by* Jimmy Van Heusen.)

"Going My Way" (from *GOING MY WAY* film)
L. Cleale
(*Music by* Jimmy Van Heusen.)

"Shadows on the Swanee"
A. Guess, L. Cleale, M. McGrath
(*Music by* Harold Spina. *Lyrics by* Joe Young, Johnny Burke.)

"Rhythm on the River" (from *RHYTHM ON THE RIVER* film)
All
(*Music by* James Monaco.)

"Road to Morocco" (from *ROAD TO MOROCCO* film)
L. Cleale, M. McGrath, K. Fitzgerald
(*Music by* Jimmy Van Heusen.)
Assistant Director: E. Fleming. *Bing*: L. Cleale. *Bob*: M. McGrath. *Dorothy*: K.
Fitzgerald. *Girls*: L. Hart, T. Burrell. *Southern Woman*: A. Guess.

Scene 3

"But, Beautiful" (from *ROAD TO RIO* film)
T. Burrell
(*Music by* Jimmy Van Heusen.)

"Moonlight Becomes You" (from *ROAD TO MOROCCO* film)
L. Cleale
(*Music by* Jimmy Van Heusen.)

"Sunday, Monday or Always" (from *DIXIE* film)
A. Guess
(*Music by* Jimmy Van Heusen.)

"Misty"
E. Fleming
(*Music by* Erroll Garner.)

"Here's That Rainy Day" (from *CARNIVAL IN FLANDERS*)
K. Fitzgerald
(*Music by* Jimmy Van Heusen.)

"Pennies from Heaven" (reprise)
All

"Swinging on a Star" (reprise)
All
The Lovers: L. Hart and L. Cleale, A. Guess and M. McGrath, T. Burrell and
E. Fleming, K. Fitzgerald.

1995.15 ## VICTOR/VICTORIA

A Musical Comedy in Two Acts, 16 Scenes. Book by Blake Edwards. (Based on the musical film of the same name, screenplay by Blake Edwards, which was based on the German Ufa film "Viktor und Viktoria" conceived by Hans Hoemburg and written by Rheinhold Schuenzer.) Music by Henry Mancini. Lyrics by Leslie Bricusse. Directed by Blake Edwards. Choreographed by Rob Marshall. Additional musical material by Frank Wildhorn. Scenic design by Robin Wagner. Costume design by Willa Kim. Lighting design by Jules Fisher and Peggy Eisenhauer. Sound design by Peter Fitzgerald. Orchestrations by Billy Byers. Dance and incidental music by David Krane. Fight staging by B. H. Barry. Music direction and vocal arrangements by Ian Fraser. Assistant director, Kirsten Sanderson. Assistant choreographers, Cynthia Onrubia and Sarah Miles. Executive producers, Edwards-Adams Theatrical Inc., Metropolitan Theatrical Entertainment Inc. Co-producers, Robin De Levita, Jeff Rowland. Associate producers, Joop Van Den Ende, Tina Vanderheyden, TDI, Ogden Entertainment. Produced by Blake Edwards, Tony Adams, John Scher, Endemol Theater Productions, Inc., Polygram Broadway Ventures, Inc. Opened 25 October 1995 at the Marquis Theatre and closed 27 July 1997 after 738 performances[7].

CAST (in order of appearance): *Carroll Todd* (Toddy): TONY ROBERTS. *Les Boys*: Michael Demby-Cain, Angelo Fraboni, Darren Lee, Michael O'Donnell, Vince Pesce, Arte Phillips, Rocker Verastique. *Richard Di Nardo*: MICHAEL CRIPE. *Henri Labisse*: ADAM HELLER. *Gregor*: Casey Nicholaw. *Madame Roget*: Jennifer Smith. *Victoria Grant* (Victor): JULIE ANDREWS. *Choreographer*: Christopher Innvar. *Miss Selmer*: Cynthia Sophiea. *André Cassell*: RICHARD B. SHULL. *Jazz Singer*: Devin Richards. *Jazz Hot Musicians*: Michael Demby-Cain, Arte Phillips, Rocker Verastique. *Jazz Hot Ensemble*: Roxane Barlow, Caitlin Carter, Pascale Faye, Angelo Fraboni, Amy Heggins, Darren Lee, Aixa M. Rosario Medina, Casey Nicholaw, Michael O'Donnell, Cynthia Onrubia, Vince Pesce. *Norma Cassidy*: RACHEL YORK. *King Marchan*: MICHAEL NOURI. *Squash* (Mr. Bernstein): GREGORY JBARA. *Louis Says Ensemble*: Roxane Barlow, Michael-Demby Cain, Caitlin Carter, Pascale Faye, Angelo Fraboni, Amy Heggins, Darren Lee, Aixa M. Rosario Medina, Michael O'Donnell, Cynthia Onrubia, Vince Pesce, Arte Phillips, Devlin Richards, Jennifer Smith, Cynthia Sophiea, Rocker Verastique. *Chambermaid*: Jennifer Smith. *Apache Dancers*: Angelo Fraboni, Darren Lee, Michael O'Donnell, Vince Pesce, Arte Phillips, Rocker Verastique. *Street Singer*: Tara O'Brien. *Norma's Girls*: Roxane Barlow, Caitlin Carter, Pascale Faye, Amy Heggins, Aixa M. Rosario Medina, Cynthia Onrubia. *Sal Adretti*: Ken Land. *Clam*: Mark Lotito. *Juke*: Casey Nicholaw.
Ensemble: Roxane Barlow, Michael-Demby Cain, Caitlin Carter, Pascale Faye, Angelo Fraboni, Amy Heggins, Darren Lee, Aixa M. Rosario Medina, Tara O'Brien, Michael O'Donnell, Cynthia Onrubia, Vince Pesce, Arte Phillips, Devlin Richards, Jennifer Smith, Rocker Verastique. *Swings*: Mark S. Hoebee, Elizabeth Mozer, Scott Taylor.

---

[7]Subsequent national tour produced by NETworks, in association with the Jeriko Touring Company. Directed by Mark Hoebee, choreographed by Dan Mojica.

Act 1, Scene 1: Small Square/Chez Lui. *Scene 2*: Small Square/Toddy's Flat. *Scene 3*: Backstage at Cassell's. *Scene 4*: Cassell's Nightclub. *Scene 5*: Backstage at Cassell's. *Scene 6*: Left Bank Cafe. *Scene 7*: Paris Hotel Suites.

Act 2, Scene 1: Cassell's Nightclub. *Scene 2*: Victoria's Dressing Room. *Scene 3*: Paris Hotel Suites. *Scene 4*: Chez Lui. *Scene 5*: Small Square. *Scene 6*: Paris Hotel Suites. *Scene 7*: Chicago Speakeasy. *Scene 8*: Paris Hotel Suites. *Scene 9*: Cassell's Nightclub.

ACT 1
Scene 1
    "Paris By Night"
        T. Roberts, Les Boys
Scene 2
    "If I Were a Man"[8]
        J. Andrews
    "Trust Me"
        T. Roberts, J. Andrews
        (*Music by* Frank Wildhorn.)
Scene 4
    "Le Jazz Hot"
        J. Andrews, Ensemble
Scene 6
    "The Tango"
        J. Andrews, R. York
Scene 7
    "Paris Makes Me Horny"[9]
        R. York
    "Crazy World"[10]
        J. Andrews
ACT 2
Scene 1
    "Louis Says"[11]
        J. Andrews, Ensemble
        (*Music by* Frank Wildhorn.)
Scene 3
    "King's Dilemma"
        M. Nouri
Scene 4
    "Apache"
        Les Boys
    "You & Me"
        T. Roberts, J. Andrews
Scene 5
    "Paris By Night" (reprise)
        T. O'Brien
Scene 6
    "Almost a Love Song"
        M. Nouri, J. Andrews
Scene 7
    "Chicago, Illinois"
        R. Yorke, Girls
Scene 8
    "Living in the Shadows"
        J. Andrews
        (*Music by* Frank Wildhorn.)
Scene 9
    "Victor/Victoria"
        J. Andrews, T. Roberts, Company
    "Who Can I Tell?"
        Liza Minnelli (Victoria Grant)
        (*Music and Lyrics by* Leslie Bricusse.)

---

[8]Dropped during the run.
[9]Dropped for subsequent national tour.
[10]Replaced in January 1997 by:
    "Who Can I Tell?"
        Liza Minnelli (Victoria Grant)
        (*Music and Lyrics by* Leslie Bricusse.)
[11]"Louis Says" and the entire Act 2, Scene 1 dropped during the run.

1995.16

FOOL MOON

A Revival of the Comedy Performance Revue in Two Acts[12]. Created by Bill Irwin and David Shiner. (Original music and lyrics by the Red Clay Ramblers.) Set design by Douglas Stein. Costume design by Bill Kellard. Lighting design by Nancy Schertler. Sound design by Tom Morse. Flying by Foy. Producing associate, Nancy Harrington. Associate producer, Daniel F. Kearns. Produced by James B. Freydberg, Kenneth Feld, Jeffrey Ash, Dori Berinstein. Opened 29 October 1995 at the Ambassador Theatre and closed 7 January 1996 after 81 performances.

<u>CAST</u> (in order of appearance): DAVID SHINER, BILL IRWIN.
    THE RED CLAY RAMBLERS: Clay Buckner (fiddle), Chris Frank (piano, accordion, trombone, ukelele), Jack Herrick (bass, trumpet, mellophone, banjolin, tin whistle), Mark Roberts (banjo, flute, oboe, tin whistle, keyboard), Rob Ladd (drums, ukelele).

ACT 1[13]
    Opening
        D. Shiner, B. Irwin, Red Clay Ramblers, 2 Ushers
    "Fire and Sugar" (traditional)
        Red Clay Ramblers
    Encounter
        D. Shiner, B. Irwin
    "Wa-Hoo"[14]
        Red Clay Ramblers
    Dance Solo
        D. Shiner
    Dance to the Left
        B. Irwin, Stage Manager
    Big Night Out
        D. Shiner, B. Irwin, an Audience Member
ACT 2
    "Pal-Yat-Chee"[15]
        Red Clay Ramblers
    Improvisation in Public
        D. Shiner, an Audience Memeber
    Harlequin/Pantalone
        B. Irwin, Red Clay Ramblers, D. Shiner
    "Hiawatha's Lullaby"
        Red Clay Ramblers
        (*Music by* Walter Donaldson. *Lyrics by* Joe Young.)
    "Tea for Two" (from *NO, NO NANETTE*)
        D. Shiner, B. Irwin
        (*Music by* Vincent Youmans. *Lyrics by* Irving Caesar.)
    Conductor
        B. Irwin, Red Clay Ramblers
    Cinema
        D. Shiner, 4 Audience Members
    "Valley of the Dry Bones" (traditional; a capella)
        Red Clay Ramblers, D. Shiner, B. Irwin
    "Melancholy Moon Song"[16]
        Red Clay Ramblers, B. Irwin, D. Shiner
    "Fire and Sugar" (reprise)
        B. Irwin, D. Shiner, Red Clay Ramblers

THE MANY VOICES
OF DANNY GANS

1995.17

A One Man Revue in One Act. Production supervisor, Chip Lightman. Lighting, John Featehrstone, Fred Irish, Norm Schwab. Sound, On Stage Audio. Produced by the Nederlander Organization. Opened 8 November 1995 at the Neil Simon Theatre and closed 12 November 1995 after 6 performances.

---

[12]Originally produced in New York 25 February 1993 at the Richard Rodgers Theatre for 207 performances.
[13]Scenes and Musical Numbers not identified in programs; list prepared from producers' materials.
[14]Not in previous 1992 production.
[15]Not in previous 1992 production.
[16]Not in previous 1992 production.

CAST: DANNY GANS (impressionist). *The Band:* Pat Caddick (keyboards, vocals), Rapahel Erardy (drums, vocals); Tim Manfredi (keyboards, guitar, vocals).

1995.18 CINDERELLA

A Revival of the Musical in Two Acts, a Prologue and 10 Scenes[17]. Book and lyrics (for television) by Oscar Hammerstein II. Book adapted (for the stage) by Steve Allen, Robert Johanson. Music by Richard Rodgers. Directed and choreographed by Robert Johanson. Co-choreographer, Sharon Halley. Scenery by Henry Bardon. Costumes by Gregg Barnes. Lighting by Jeff Davis. Sound by Abe Jacob. Conductor, Rob Fisher. Orchestrations by Robert Russell Bennett. Chorus master, Joseph Colaneri. Produced by the New York City Opera. Opened 9 November 1995 at the New York State Theatre and closed 19 November 1995 after 12 performances.

CAST (in order of appearance): *Fairy Godmother:* SALLY ANN HOWES. *Royal Herald:* Stephen Howell. *Little Girl:* Elizabeth Dietrich. *Cinderella's Stepmother:* JEAN STAPLETON. *Cinderella's Stepsisters (2):* Joy: ALIX KOREY. *Portia:* JEANETTE PALMER. *Cinderella:* REBECCA BAXTER. *Dog:* Andrew Pacho. *Cat:* Debbi Fuhrman. *Queen:* JANE POWELL. *King:* GEORGE S. IRVING. *Royal Chef:* Joel Sorenson. *Royal Steward:* John Lankston. *Prince:* GEORGE DVORSKY. *Youngest Fairy:* Stephanie Godino. *Tiara Fairy:* Irina Dvorovenko. *Ensemble:* New York City Opera Chorus.

1995.19 A CHRISTMAS CAROL

A Revival of the Musical in One Act, 13 Scenes[18]. Book by Mike Ockrent and Lynn Ahrens. Based on the novel of the same name by Charles Dickens. Music by Alan Menken. Lyrics by Lynn Ahrens. Directed by Mike Ockrent. Choreographed by Susan Stroman. Setting design by Tony Walton. Costume design by William Ivey Long. Lighting design by Jules Fisher and Peggy Eisenhauer. Sound design by Tony Meola. Projections by Wendall K. Harrington. Flying by Foy. Production supervisor, Gene O'Donovan. Associate director, Steven Zweigbaum. Associate choreographer, Chris Peterson. Musical direction by Paul Gemignani. Orchestrations by Michael Starobin and Douglas Besterman. Dance arrangements and incidental music by Glen Kelly. Executive producer, Dodger Productions. Producer, Tim Hawkins. Presented by Madison Square Garden. Opened 30 November 1995 at the Paramount, Madison Square Garden and closed 31 December 1995 after 70 performances[19].

CAST (in order of appearance): *Beadle:* David Lowenstein. *Mr. Smythe:* JAMES JUDY. *Grace Smythe:* Cara Horner, Joanna Howard. *Scrooge:* TERRENCE MANN. *Cratchit:* NICK CORLEY. *Charity Men:* Robert Ousley, Wayne W. Pretlow, Walter Willison. *Old Joe:* Ken McMullen. *Street Urchins and Children:* Matthew Ballinger, Zachary Petkanas, Paul Franklin Dano, Christopher Mark Petrizzo, Olivia Oguma, Diana Mary Rice. *Mrs. Cratchit:* Robin Baxter. *Tiny Tim:* Zachary London, Chris Marquette. *Poulterer:* Walter Willison. *Sandwichboard Man:* BEN VEREEN. *Fred:* STEVE BLANCHARD. *Jonathon:* Jason Fuchs, Evan J. Newman. *Lamplighter:* KEN JENNINGS. *Blind Hag:* Nicole Arrington. *Mrs. Mops:* Karen Murphy. *Ghost of Jacob Marley:* PAUL KANDEL. *Ghost of Christmas Past:* KEN JENNINGS. *Lights of Christmas Past:* Matthew Baker, Sean Thomas Morrissey, Rommy Sandhu, Tom Pardoe. *Judge:* Michael H. Ingram. *Scrooge at 8 years:* Matthew Ballinger, Zachary Petkanas. *Fan at 6:* Diana Mary Rice, Olivia Oguma. *Scrooge's Mother:* Barbara Marineau. *Scrooge's Father:* Michael X. Martin. *Mr. Hawkins:* Kenneth McMullen.

---

[17]Originally produced in New York 9 November 1993 at the New York State Theatre for 14 performances. For Synopsis of Scenes and Musical Numbers, see original 1993 production.

[18]Originally produced in New York 1 December 1994 at the Paramount, Madison Square Garden for 71 performances. For Synopsis of Scenes and Musical Numbers, see original 1994 production.

[19]The production played an irregular schedule of multiple daily performances. For this revival the following changes were made:
Scene 1 and "The Years Are Passing By" were dropped.
Added to Scene 2 (former Scene 3) before "Street Song":
   "You Mean More to Me"
      N. Corley, Z. London or C. Marquette
   "The Years Are Passing By" (reprise) in former Scene 13 (new Scene 12) was replaced by:
   "London Town Carol"
      J. Fuchs or E. J. Newman

Scrooge at 12 years: Paul Franklin Dano, Christopher Mark Petrizzo. *Fan at 10 years:* Eliza Atkins Clark, Nathalie Paulding. *Fezziwig:* Michael Cone. *Scrooge at 18 years:* Tom Stuart. *Young Marley:* Ken Barnett. *Mrs. Fezziwig:* Joy Hermalyn. *Emily:* Emily Skinner. *Ghost of Christmas Present:* BEN VEREEN. *The Crachit Children:* Eliza Atkins Clark, Nathalie Paulding, Anthony Roth Costanzo, Bobby Steggert, Sean Thomas Morrissey. *Sally, Fred's wife:* Stephanie Bast. *Ignorance:* Matthew Ballinger, Zachary Petkanas. *Undertakers:* Michael X. Martin, Ken Barnett. *Ghost of Christmas Future:* Theara J. Ward.

Business Men, Gifts, Ghosts and the People of London: Farah Alvin, Nicole Arrington, Matthew Baker, Ken Barnett, Stephanie Bast, Robin Baxter, Amy B. Blake, Steve Blanchard, Brad Bradley, Michael Cone, Candy Cook, Donna Dunmire, Peter Gregus, Jeffrey Hankinson, Melissa Haizlip, Joy Hermalyn, Michael H. Ingram, James Judy, David Lowenstein, Barbara Marineau, Michael X. Martin, Dana Lynn Mauro, Carol Lee Meadows, Sean Thomas Morrissey, Kenneth McMullen, Karen Murphy, Robert Ousley, Tom Pardoe, Gail Pennington, Angela Piccinni, Wayne W. Pretlow, Josef Reiter, Eric Riley, Pamela Remler, Sam Reni, Rommy Sandhu, Emily Skinner, Erin Stoddard, Tom Stuart, Tracy Terstreip, Theara J. Ward, Walter Willison. *Swings:* Rachel Black, Jillian Bowen, Rob Donohoe, Mathis M. Fender, Nicholas Gould, Jack Ingram, Dana Leigh Jackson, Don Johanson, Nicole Napolitano, Christian Stuck, Cynthia Thole, Matthew J. Vargo, Jeff Williams. *Angels:* P.S. 26 Chorus, Bronx; William Alexander Middle School 51, Brooklyn; Roy H. Mann Concert Choir, Brooklyn; Park Middle School Chorus, Scotch Plains, New Jersey. *The Red Children's Cast:* Matthew Ballinger, Jason Fuchs, Joanna Fuchs, Joanna Howard, Chris Marquette, Nathalie Paulding, Christopher Mark Perizzo, Diana Mary Rice, Bobby Steggert. *The Green Children's Cast:* Eliza Atkins Clark, Anthony Roth Constanzo, Paul Franklin Dano, Cara Horner, Zach London, Evan J. Newman, Olivia Oguma, Zachary Petkanas.

1996.01 RIVERDANCE

A Dance Revue in Two Acts. Music by Bill Whelan. Poetry by Theo Dorgan. Directed by John McColgan. Choreography by Michael Flatley, Jean Butler, Colin Dunne, Tara Little, Moscow Folk Ballet Company, Maria Pages, Tarik Winston. Scenery and painted projections by Robert Ballagh. Costumes by Jen Kelly. Lighting by Rupert Murray. Sound by Michael O'Gorman. Orchestrations by Nick Ingman, Bill Whelan. Projections by Chris Slinsgby. Produced by Moya Doherty. Opened 13 March 1996 at the Radio City Music Hall and closed 17 March 1996 after 8 performances.[20]

CAST: *Narrator:* JOHN KAVANAGH. *Solo Dancers:* JEAN BUTLER, COLIN DUNNE, MARIA PAGES, TARIK WINSTON, DANIEL WOOTEN. *Solo Singer:* IVAN THOMAS. Company of 30.

1996.02 THE MERRY WIDOW

A Revival of the Operetta in Three Acts, 4 Scenes[21]. Music by Franz Lehár. Original German book and lyrics by Victor Léon and Leo Stein (after "L'Attaché d'Ambassade.") (New) English book adaptation by Robert Johanson. (New) English lyrics by Albert Evans. Production director, Robert Johanson. Choreographer, Sharon Halley. Set design by Michael Anania. Costume design by Gregg Barnes. Lighting design by Mark W. Stanley. Sound design by Abe Jacob. Chorus master, Joseph Colaneri. Conductor, Alexander Sander. Produced by the New York City Opera. Opened 23 March 1996 at the New York State Theatre and closed 19 April 1996 after 6 performances in repertory.

CAST (in order of appearance): *Baron Mirko Zeta, Marsovian Ambassador to Paris:* GEORGE S. IRVING. *Valencienne, his wife:* Patricia Johnson. *Kromov, Masovian General:* Joseph McKee. *Olga, wife of Kromov:* Beth McVey. *Bogdanovich, Marsovian Consul:* JOHN LANKSTON. *Sylviane, wife of Bogdanovich:* Suzanne Ishee. *Njegus, aide to Baron Zeta:* ROBERT CREIGHTON. *Camille de Rosillon, Valencienne's admirer, a Parisian:* CARLO SCIBELLI. *Vicomte Cascada, an eligible Parisian:* MATTHEW CHELLIS. *Raoul de St. Brioche, another eligible Parisian:* SHON SIMS. *Hanna, the widow Glawari:* JANE THORNGREN. *Count Danilo, nephew of the King of Marsovia:* MICHAEL HAYES. *Lolo:* Jean Barber. *Dodo:* Stephanie Godino. *Jou-Jou:* Julie Stahl. *Frou-Frou:* Kathy Meyer. *Clo-Clo:* Debbi Fuhrman. *Margot:* Joan Mirabella. *Young Hanna:* Julie Stahl. *Young Danilo:* Marty McDonough. *Chorus of Marsovian and Parisian Society, Dancers, Servants and Waiters:* New York City Opera Chorus.

---

[20]For Synopsis of Scenes and Musical Numbers, see return engagement 2 October 1996.

[21]Originally produced in New York 21 October 1907 at the New Amsterdam Theatre for 416 performances.

1996.03 ## LOVE THY NEIGHBOR

A One Man Comedy Revue in Two Acts[22]. Written and created by Jackie Mason. Production design and lighting by Neil Peter Jampolis. Sound design by Charles McIntyre. Executive producer, Jyll Rosenfeld. Produced by Abe Hirschfeld. Opened 24 March 1996 at the Booth Theatre and closed 5 January 1997 after 236 performances.

CAST: JACKIE MASON (stand-up comedy, monologues, impressions).

1996.04 ## STATE FAIR

A Musical in Two Acts, 18 Scenes. Book by Tom Briggs and Louis Mattioli, based on the screenplay for the film "State Fair" by Oscar Hammerstein II and the novel of the same name by Philip Stong. Music by Richard Rodgers. Lyrics by Oscar Hammerstein II. Co-directed by James Hammerstein and Randy Skinner. Choreography by Randy Skinner. Scenic design by James Leonard Joy. Costume design by Michael Bottari and Ronald Case. Lighting design by Natasha Katz. Sound design by Brian Ronan. Musical direction and vocal arrangements by Kay Cameron. Orchestrations by Bruce Pomohac. Dance arrangements by Scot Woolley. Produced by David Merrick, the Theatre Guild, Philip Langner, Robert Franz, Natalie Lloyd, Jonathan C. Herzog, Meredith Blair, Gordon Smith. Executive producer, Thomas Viertel. Associate producers, Mark N. Sirangello and the PGI Entertainment Company. Pre-Broadway National Tour (also) produced by Sonny Everett, Bonnie Nelson Schwartz, Matt Garfield, Ron Kumin; Associate producers, David Young and Norma Langworthy, by arrangement with Celia Lipton Productions, Inc, in association with the North Carolina School of the Arts Foundation. Opened 27 March 1996 at the Music Box Theatre and closed 30 June 1996 after 118 performances.

CAST (in order of appearance): *Abel Frake*: JOHN DAVIDSON. *Gus*, the Frake's hired man: James Patterson. *Melissa Frake*, Abel's wife: KATHRYN CROSBY. *Wayne Frake*, their son: BEN WRIGHT. *Dave Miller*, the local storekeeper: Charles Goff. *Eleanor*, Wayne's girlfriend: Susan Haefner. *Margy Frake*, Wayne's sister: ANDREA MCARDLE. *Harry*, Margy's boyfriend: Peter Benson. *Uncle Sam*: Michael Lee Scott. *Fair Announcer*: J. Lee Flynn. *Midway Cow*: Kelli Barclay. *Midway Pig*: Jackie Angelescu. *The Houp-La Barker*: Tim Fauvell. *Emily Arden*: DONNA MCKECHNIE. *The Astounding Stralenko*: Steve Steiner. *Vivian*, a cooch dancer: Tina Johnson. *Jeanne*, a cooch dancer: Leslie Bell. *Mrs. Edwin Metcalf* of Pottsville: Jacquiline Rohrbacker. *Pat Gilbert*, a newspaper reporter: SCOTT WISE. *Charlie*, a newspaper photographer: Darrian C. Ford. *Lem*, a farmer: John Wilkerson. *Clay*, a farmer: J. Lee Flynn. *Hank Munson*, a farmer: Newton R. Gilchrist. *The Chief of Police*: Steve Steiner. *Violet*, his daughter: Jackie Angelescu. *The Fairtones*: Ian Knauer, James Patterson, Michael Lee Scott, Scott Willis. *Judge Heppenstahl*: Charles Goff.
  Barkers, Vendors, Judges, Fairgoers: Kelli Barclay, Leslie Bell, Linnea Dakin, Suellen Estey, Tim Fauvell, Amy Gage, Susan Haefner, Tina Johnson, Ian Knauer, James Patterson, Michael Lee Scott, Mary C Sheehan, Steve Steiner, Scott Willis. *Roustabouts*: Michael Lee Scott, Scott Willis. *Swings*: Julie Lira, John Scott.

The action takes place over five days in late August of 1946 on the Frake Farm in Brunswick, Iowa and at the State Fair in Des Moines.

Act 1, Scene 1: The Frake Farm, a Tuesday afternoon in late August. *Scene 2*: On the Road to Des Moines. Wednesday morning before dawn. *Scene 3*: The Midway at the Hoop-La Booth. Later that morning. *Scene 4*: The Midway at the Temple of Wonder. Later that morning. *Scene 5*: The Beer Tent. That afternoon. *Scene 6*: Outside the Dairy Pavilion. Later that afternoon. *Scene 7*: The Starlight Dance Meadow. That evening. *Scene 8*: Camper's Hill. Thursday morning. *Scene 9*: Exhibition Hall. That afternoon. *Scene 10*: A Nearby Hillside. Early that night. *Scene 11*: The Starlight Dance Meadow. Later that night.

Act 2, Scene 1: Outside the Livestock Pavilion. Friday afternoon. *Scene 2*: Outside the Dairy Pavilion. Early that night. *Scene 3*: The Starlight Dance Meadow. Immediately following. *Scene 4*: The Hillside. Later that night. *Scene 5*: Camper's Hill. Later that night. *Scene 6*: On the Midway. Immediately following. *Scene 7*: The Frake Farm. Saturday night after supper.

ACT 1
Scene 1
  Opening ("Our State Fair")[23]
    J. Davidson, K. Crosby, B. Wright
  "It Might As Well Be Spring"[24]
    A. McArdle
Scene 2
  "Driving at Night"
    J. Davidson, K. Crosby, B. Wright, A. McArdle
Scene 3
  "Our State Fair" (reprise)
    Ensemble
Scene 4
  "That's For Me"[25]
    B. Wright
Scene 5
  "More Than Just a Friend"[26] (Sweet Hog of Mine)
    J. Davidson, N. R. Gilchrist, J. Sloman, J. L. Flynn
    (*Lyrics by* Richard Rodgers.)
Scene 6
  "Isn't It Kinda Fun?"[27]
    S. Wise, A. McArdle
Scene 7
  "You Never Had It So Good"
    D. McKechnie, the Fairtones
Scene 8
  "It Might As Well Be Spring" (reprise)
    A. McArdle
  "When I Go Out Walking With My Baby"
    J. Davidson, K. Crosby
Scene 10
  "So Far" (from *ALLEGRO*)
    B. Wright, D. McKechnie
Scene 11
  "It's a Grand Night for Singing"[28]
    Company

ACT 2
Scene 1
  "The Man I Used To Be" (from *PIPE DREAM*)
    S. Wise, T. Johnson, L. Bell
  "All I Owe Ioway"[29]
    J. Davidson, Company
Scene 2
  "The Man I Used To Be" (reprise)
    S. Wise
  "Isn't It Kinda Fun?" (reprise)
    A. McArdle
Scene 3
  "That's the Way It Happens" (from *ME & JULIET*)
    D. McKechnie, the Fairtones
Scene 5
  "Boys and Girls Like You and Me"
    J. Davidson, K. Crosby
Scene 6
  "The Next Time It Happens" (from *PIPE DREAM*)
    A. McArdle

---

[22]Previous editions of Jackie Mason's one man show have been presented as THE WORLD ACCORDING TO ME 22 December 1986 at the Brooks Atkinson Theatre for 367 performances; returned 3 May 1988 at the Brooks Atkinson for 203 performances; JACKIE MASON: BRAND NEW 17 October 1990 at the Neil Simon Theatre for 216 performances; JACKIE MASON: POLITICALLY INCORRECT, 5 April 1994 at the John Golden Theatre for 347 performances.

[23]Songs included in the original 1945 film.
[24]Songs included in the original 1945 film.
[25]Songs included in the original 1945 film.
[26]Written for the 1962 film.
[27]Songs included in the original 1945 film.
[28]Songs included in the original 1945 film.
[29]Songs included in the original 1945 film.

1996.05 THE KING AND I

A Revival of the Musical Play in Two Acts[30]. Book and lyrics by Oscar Hammerstein II. Music by Richard Rodgers. Based on the novel "Anna and the King of Siam" by Margaret Landon. Musical staging by Lar Lubovitch. (Original) Choreography by Jerome Robbins, supervised by Susan Kikuchi. Directed by Christopher Renshaw. Scenic design by Brian Thomson. Costume design by Roger Kirk. Lighting design by Nigel Levings. Orchestrations by Robert Russell Bennett. Additional orchestrations by Bruce Coughlin. Musical director, Michael Rafter. Musical supervisor, Eric Stern. Sound by Tony Meola and Lewis Mead. Produced by Dodger Productions, The John F. Kennedy Center, James M. Nederlander, Perseus Productions with John Frost and the Adelaide Festival Centre in association with The Rodgers and Hammerstein Organization. Opened 11 April 1996 at the Neil Simon Theatre and closed 22 February 1998 after 781 performances[31].

CAST (in order of appearance): *Captain Orton*: John Curless. *Louis Leonowens*: Ryan Hopkins. *Anna Leonowens*: DONNA MURPHY. *The Interpreter*: Alan Muraoka. *The Kralahome*: RANDALL DUK KIM. *The King of Siam*: LOU DIAMOND PHILLIPS. *Lun Tha*: JOSE LLANA. *Tuptim*: JOOHEE CHOI. *Lady Thiang*: TAEWON KIM. *Prince Chulalongkorn*: John Chang. *Princess Yaowlak*: Lexine Bondoc. *Sir Edward Ramsay*: Guy Paul.

Royal Wives, Slaves, Courtiers, Guards, Monks, English Guests, Market People: Tito Abeleda, John Bantay, Camille M. Brown, Benjamin Bryant, Meng-Chen Chang, Kam Cheng, Vivien Eng, Lydia Gaston, Margaret Ann Gates, C. Sean Kim, Shawn Ku, Doan Mackenzie, Paolo Montalban, Alan Muraoka, Paul Nakauchi, Tina Ou, Andrew Pacho, Mami Saito, Lainie Sakakura, Carol To, Yolanda Tolentino, Tran T. Thuc Hanh, Yan Ying, Kayoko Yoshioka, Greg Zane. *The Royal Children*: Kelly Jordan Bit, Lexine Bondoc, Kailip Boonrai, Jacqueline Te Lem, Erik Lin-Greenberg, Kenji Miyata, Brandon Marshall Ngai, Amy Y. Tai, Jenna Noelle Ushkowitz, Shelby Rebecca Wong, Jeff G. Yalun.

The Small House of Uncle Thomas (ballet): Eliza: Yan Ying. *Simon of Legree*: Tito Abeleda. *Angel George*: Meng-Chen Chang. *Little Eva*: Tran T. Thuc Hanh. *Topsy*: Tina Ou. *Uncle Thomas*: Mami Saito. *Dogs*: John Bantay, Doan Mackenzie, Greg Zane. *Guards*: Andrew Pacho, C. Sean Kim, Shawn Ku. *Propmen*: Benjamin Bryant, Paolo Montalban, Alan Muraoka, Paul Nakauchi. *Archers*: Camille M. Brown, Vivien Eng, Lainie Sakakura, Kayoko Yoshioka. *Singers*: Kam Cheng, Margaret Ann Gates, Carol To, Yolanda Tolentino.

1996.06 A FUNNY THING HAPPENED ON THE WAY TO THE FORUM

A Revival of the Musical Comedy in Two Acts[32]. Book by Burt Shevelove and Larry Gelbart. Based on the plays ("The Haunted House," "Mostellaria", etc.) of Plautus. Music and lyrics by Stephen Sondheim. Directed by Jerry Zaks. Choreographed by Rob Marshall. Set and costume design by Tony Walton. Lighting by Paul Gallo. Sound by Tony Meola. Musical director, Eddie Strauss. Orchestrations by Jonathan Tunick. Dance music arrangements by David Chase. Associate producer, Marc Routh. Produced by Jujamcyn Theatres, Scott Rudin/Paramount Pictures, The Viertel-Baruch-Frankel Group (Tom Viertel-Steven Baruch-Richard Frankel), Roger Berlind, Dodger Productions. Opened 18 April 1996 at the St. James Theatre and closed 4 January 1998 after 715 performances.

CAST (in order of appearance): *Prologus*, an actor: NATHAN LANE. *The Proteans*: Brad Aspel, Cory English, Ray Roderick. *Hero*, son of Senex and Domina: JIM STANEK. *Philia*, a virgin: JESSICA BOEVERS. *Senex*, a citizen of Rome: LEWIS J. STADLEN. *Domina*, his wife: MARY TESTA. *Hysterium*, slave to Senex and Domina:

MARK LINN-BAKER. *Lycus*, a buyer and seller of courtesans: ERNIE SABELLA. *Pseudolus*, slave to hero: NATHAN LANE. *Tintinabula*, a courtesan: Pamela Everett. *Panacea*, a courtesan: Leigh Zimmerman. *The Geminae*, courtesans: Susan Misner, Lori Werner. *Vibrata*, a courtesan: Mary Ann Lamb. *Gymnasia*, a courtesan: Stephanie Pope. *Erronius*, an citizen of Rome: WILLIAM DUELL. *Miles Gloriosus*, a warrior: CRIS GROENENDAAL.

1996.07 BRING IN 'DA NOISE, BRING IN 'DA FUNK

A Rap/Tap Discourse on the Staying Power of the Beat (Musical Revue), in Two Acts, 6 Scenes[33]. Choreographer, Savion Glover. Based on an idea by Savion Glover and George C. Wolfe. Book by Reg E. Gaines. Music by Daryl Waters, Zane Mark and Ann Duquesnay. Conceived and directed by George C. Wolfe. Scenic design by Riccardo Hernandez. Costume design by Paul Tazewell. Lighting design by Jules Fisher, Peggy Eisenhauer. Sound design by Dan Moses Schreier. Projection design by Batwin + Robin Productions, Inc. Music supervision and orchestrations by Daryl Waters. Music direction by Zane Mark. Vocal arrangements by Ann Duquesnay. Dramaturg, Shelby Jiggetts. Produced by the Joseph Papp Public Theater/New York Shakespeare Festival (George C. Wolfe, Producer; Rosemarie Tichler, Artistic producer; Laurie Beckelman, Executive director; Joey Parner, Executive producer), by special arrangement with The Shubert Organization. Associate producer, Wiley Hausam. Opened 24 April 1996 at the Ambassador Theatre and closed 10 January 1999 after 1123 performances.

CAST (in order of appearance): SAVION GLOVER, BAAKARI WILDER, JIMMY TATE, VINCENT BINGHAM, JEFFREY WRIGHT, ANN DUQUESNAY, JARED CRAWFORD, RAYMOND KING, DULÉ HILL.

Act 1, Scene 1: In 'Da Beginning. *Scene 2*: Som'thin from Nuthin'. *Scene 3*: Urbanization.

Act 2, Scene 1: Where's the Beat? *Scene 2*: Street Corner Symphony. *Scene 3*: Noise/Funk.

ACT 1

Scene 1

"Bring in 'Da Noise, Bring in 'Da Funk"
   Company
"The Door to Isle Gorée"
   J. Wright
"Slave Ships"
   A. Duquesnay, S. Glover

Scene 2

"Som'thin from Nuthin'"/"The Circle Stomp"
   B. Wilder, D. Hill, J. Tate, V. Bingham, A. Duquesnay, J. Wright
"The Pan Handlers"
   J. Crawford, R. King

Scene 3

"The Lynching Blues"
   B. Wilder, A. Duquesnay, Company
"Chicago Bound"
   S. Glover, A. Duquesnay, Company
"Shifting Sounds"
   J. Wright
"Industrialization"
   S. Glover, B. Wilder, J. Tate, V. Bingham, J. Crawford, R. King
"The Chicago Riot Rag"
   S. Glover, B. Wilder, J. Tate, V. Bingham, J. Crawford
"I Got the Beat"/"Dark Tower"
   A. Duquesnay, J. Wright, Company
"The Whirligig Stomp"
   Company

[30]Originally produced in New York 29 March 1951 at the St. James Theatre for 1246 performances. For Synopsis of Scenes and Musical Numbers, see original 1951 production.

[31]Added to this production were two new dance numbers, choreography by Lar Lubovitch, with Richard Rodgers' melodies arranged by Eric Stern:

"Royal Dance Before the King" (Act 1, before "My Lord and Master")
   Company
"Procession of the White Elephant" (Act 2, after "Shall We Dance")
   Company
"Western People Funny" was dropped from this production.
"The Royal Bangkok Academy" (though not in the program) was performed in a shortened form.

[32]Originally produced in New York 8 May 1962 at the Alvin Theatre for 964 performances. For Synopsis of Scenes and Musical Numbers, see original 1962 production. Dropped for this production: "Pretty Little Picture."

[33]Originally produced Off-Broadway 18 November 1995-28 January 1996 in the Newman Theatre at the Joseph Papp Public Theater/New York Shakespeare Festival for 85 performances.

ACT 2

Scene 1

Where's the Beat?:
  The Voice: J. Wright. *The Chanteuse*: A. Duquesnay. *The Kid*: D. Hill. *Grin & Flash*: J. Tate, V. Bingham. *Uncle Huck-A-Buck*: B. Wilder. *Li'l Darlin'*: S. Glover.

"Now That's Tap"
  J. Tate, V. Bingham

"The Uncle Huck-A-Buck Song"
  B. Wilder, S. Glover, Company

"Kid Go!"
  D. Hill, Company

"The Lost Beat Swing"
  A. Duquesnay, Company

"Green, Chaney, Buster, Slyde"
  S. Glover

Scene 2

"1956—Them Conkheads"
  A. Duquesnay, Company

"1967—Hot Fun"
  A. Duquesnay, J. Wright, Company

"1977—Blackout"
  S. Glover, B. Wilder, J. Tate, V. Bingham

"1987—Gospel/Hip Hop Rant"
  J. Wright, S. Glover, A. Duquesnay

Scene 3

"Drummin'"
  J. Crawford, R. King

"Taxi"
  S. Glover, J. Tate, B. Wilder, V. Bingham

"Conversations"
  J. Crawford, R. King, S. Glover, J. Tate, B. Wilder, V. Bingham

"Hittin'"
  S. Glover, B. Wilder, J. Tate, V. Bingham, J. Crawford, R. King, J. Wright

"Bring in 'Da Noise, Bring in 'Da Funk" (reprise)
  Company

1996.08

BIG

A Musical in Two Acts, 14 Scenes. Book by John Weidman. Based on the Twentieth Century Fox film of the same name with screenplay by Gary Ross and Anne Spielberg. Music by David Shire. Lyrics by Richard Maltby, Jr. Directed by Mike Ockrent. Choreography by Susan Stroman. Scenic design by Robin Wagner. Costume design by William Ivey Long. Lighting design by Paul Gallo. Sound by Steve Canyon Kennedy. Special effects design by Gregory Meeh. Orchestrations by Douglas Besterman. Dance music arranged by David Krane. Additional vocal arrangements by Patrick Scott Brady. Magic consultant, Charles Reynolds. Electronic music designed by Brian Besterman. Musical direction by Paul Gemignani. Associate director, Steven Zweigbaum. Assistant choreographer, Ginger Thatcher. Co-produced by Pachyderm Entertainment, Fuji Television Network, Inc./Kyodo Tokyo, Inc. Associate producer, Daniel F. Kearns. Producing associate, Michelle Leslie. Produced by James B. Freydberg, Kenneth Feld, Laurence Mark and Kenneth D. Greenblatt in association with F.A.O. Schwarz, Fifth Avenue. Opened 28 April 1996 at the Sam S. Shubert Theatre and closed 13 October 1996 after 193 performances.

CAST (in order of appearance): *Cynthia Benson*: Lizzy Mack. *Young Josh*: PATRICK LEVIS. *Tiffany*: Samantha Robyn Lee. *Maggie*: Lori Aine Bennett. *Mrs. Baskin*: BARBARA WALSH. *Mr. Baskin*: John Sloman. *Mr. Kopecki*: Ray Wills. *Billy*: BRETT TABISEL. *Mrs. Kopecki*: Donna Lee Marshall. *Carnival Man*: Clent Bowers. *Derek*: Alex Sanchez. *Zoltar*: Himself. *Josh Baskin*: DANIEL JENKINS. *Panhandler*: Ray Wills. *Arcade Man*: Frank Mastrone. *Derelict*: John Sloman. *Matchless*: Frank Vlastnik. *Paul*: GENE WEYGANDT. *Susan*: CRISTA MOORE. *MacMillan*: JON CYPHER. *Starfighter*: Brandon Espinoza. *F.A.O. Sales Executive*: Joan Barber. *Birnbaum*: Frank Vlastnik. *Lipton*: Frank Mastrone. *Barrett*: Clent Bowers. *Miss Watson*: Jan Neuberger. *Deathstarettes*: Joyce Chittick, CJay Hardy. *Larry Johnson*: John Sloman. *Nick*: Ray Wills. *Tom*: John Sloman. *Diane*: Donna Lee Marshall. *Abigail*: Jill Matson. *Skatephone*: Spencer Liff. *Kid with Walkman*: Enrico Rodriguez. *Skateboard Romeo*: Graham Bowen.
  Parents, Shoppers, Executives and Office Staff: Joan Barber, Clent Bowers, Joyce Chittick, CJay Hardy, Donna Lee Marshall, Frank Mastrone, Jill Matson, Jan Neuberger, Alex Sanchez, John Sloman, Frank Vlastnik, Ray Wills. *The Big Kids*: Lori Aine Bennett, Graham Bowen, Brandon Espinoza, Samantha Robyn Lee, Spencer Liff, Lizzy Mack, Enrico Rodriguez. *Swings*: Stacey Todd Holt, Joseph Medeiros, Corinne Melancon, Kari Pickler.

Act 1, Scene 1: The Neighborhood, New Jersey. *Scene 2*: The Baskin Home. *Scene 3*: Port Authority Bus Terminal. *Scene 4*: F.A.O.Schwarz. *Scene 5*: The Offices of MacMillan Toys. *Scene 6*: Josh's Loft. *Scene 7*: A New York Restaurant.

Act 2, Scene 1: The Mall. *Scene 2*: Susan's Office. *Scene 3*: The Offices of MacMillan Toys. *Scene 4*: An Eastside Apartment. *Scene 5*: The Roof Terrace. *Scene 6*: The Neighborhood. *Scene 7*: A Warehouse.

ACT 1

Scene 1

"Can't Wait"
  P. Levis, B. Walsh, B. Tabisel, Kids, Parents

"Talk to Her"
  B. Tabisel, P. Levis

"The Carnival"
  Company

Scene 2

"This Isn't Me"
  D. Jenkins

Scene 3

"I Want To Go Home"
  D. Jenkins

Scene 4

"The Time of Your Life"
  The Kids

"Fun"
  J. Cypher, D. Jenkins, Company

Scene 5

"Dr. Deathstar"
  J. Chittick, C. Hardy

"Josh's Welcome"
  C. Moore, G. Weygandt, Executives

"Here We Go Again"
  C. Moore

Scene 6

"Stars, Stars, Stars"
  D. Jenkins, C. Moore

Scene 7

"Tavern Foxtrot"
  G. Weygandt, Company

"Cross the Line"
  D. Jenkins, Kids, Company

ACT 2

Scene 1

"It's Time"
  B. Tabisel, Kids

"Stop, Time"
  B. Walsh

"Happy Birthday, Josh"
  Kids

Scene 2

"Dancing All the Time"
  C. Moore

"I Want to Know"
  P. Levis

Scene 3

"Coffee, Black"
  D. Jenkins, J. Cypher, J. Neuberger, F. Vlastnik, C. Bowers, F. Mastrone, Executives and Staff

Scene 4

"The Real Thing"
  R. Wills, J. Sloman, D. L. Marshall, J. Matson

Scene 5

"One Special Man"
  C. Moore

Scene 6
   "When You're Big"
      D. Jenkins
   "Skateboard Romance"
      Kids
Scene 7
   "I Want to Go Home"/"Stars, Stars, Stars" (reprise)
      D. Jenkins, C. Moore

1996.09   RENT

A Musical in Two Acts[34]. Book, music and lyrics by Jonathan Larson,[35] (inspired by Giaccomo Puccini's "La Bohème," libretto by Luigi Illica and Giuseppe Giacosa, after Henri Murger's "Scènes de la Vie de Bohème.") Directed by Michael Greif. Choreography by Marlies Yearby. Set design by Paul Clay. Costume design by Angela Wendt. Lighting design by Blake Burba. Sound design by Kurt Fischer. Music supervision and additional arrangements by Tim Weil. Musical arranger, Steve Skinner. Film by Tony Gerber. Produced by Jeffrey Seller, Kevin McCollum, Allan S. Gordon and New York Theatre Workshop. Opened 29 April 1996 at the Nederlander Theatre and is still running at this time!

CAST (in order of appearance): *Roger Davis:* ADAM PASCAL. *Mark Cohen:* ANTHONY RAPP. *Tom Collins:* JESSE L. MARTIN. *Benjamin Coffin III:* TAYE DIGGS. *Joanne Jefferson:* FREDI WALKER. *Angel Schunard:* WILSON JERMAINE HEREDIA. *Mimi Marquez:* DAPHNE RUBIN-VEGA. *Maureen Johnson:* IDINA MENZEL. *Mark's Mom, Alison, others:* Kristen Lee Kelly. *Christmas caroler, Mr. Jefferson, a pastor, and others:* Byron Utley. *Mrs. Jefferson, woman with bags, and others:* Gwen Stewart. *Gordon, the man, Mr. Grey and others:* Timothy Britten Parker. *Man with squeegee, a waiter, and others:* Gilles Chiasson. *Paul, a cop, and others:* Rodney Hicks. *Alexi Darling, Roger's mom, and others:* Aiko Nakasone.
   Swings: Yassmin Alers, Darius de Haas, Shelley Dickinson, David Driver, Mark Setlock, Simone.

ACT 1
   "Tune Up"/"Voice Mail #1"
      A. Rapp, A. Pascal, K. L. Kelly, J. L. Martin, T. Diggs
   "Rent"
      Company
   "You Okay Honey?"
      W. J. Heredia, J. L. Martin
   "One Song Glory"
      A. Pascal
   "Light My Candle"
      A. Pascal, D. Rubin-Vega
   ("Voice Mail #2")
      (B. Utley, G. Stewart)
   "Today 4 U"
      W. J. Heredia
   "You'll See"
      T. Diggs, A. Rapp, J. L. Martin, A. Pascal, W. J. Heredia
   "Tango: Maureen"
      A. Rapp, F. Walker

   "Life Support"
      R. Hicks, T. B. Parker, Company
   "Out Tonight"
      D. Rubin-Vega
   "Another Day"
      A. Pascal, D. Rubin-Vega, Company
   "Will I?"
      Company
   "On the Street" (X-M Bells #2/Bummer)
      Company
   "Santa Fe"[36]
      J. L. Martin, Company
   "We're Okay"
      F. Walker
   "I'll Cover You"
      W. J. Heredia, J. L. Martin
   "Christmas Bells"
      Company
   "Over the Moon"
      I. Menzel
   "La Vie Bohème"/"I Should Tell You"[37]
      Company
ACT 2
   "Seasons of Love"
      Company
   "Happy New Year"/"Voice Mail #3"
      D. Rubin-Vega, A. Pascal, A. Rapp, I. Menzel, F. Walker, J. L. Martin, W. J. Heredia, K. L. Kelly, A. Nakasone, T. Diggs
   "Take Me or Leave Me"
      I. Menzel, F. Walker
   "Without You"
      A. Pascal, D. Rubin-Vega
   "Voice Mail #4"
      A. Nakasone
   "Contact"
      Company
   "I'll Cover You" (reprise)
      J. L. Martin, Company
   "Halloween"
      A. Rapp
   "Goodbye, Love"
      A. Rapp, D. Rubin-Vega, A. Pascal, I. Menzel, F. Walker, J. L. Martin, T. Diggs
   "What You Own"
      B. Utley, A. Rapp, J. L. Martin, T. Diggs, A. Pascal
   "Voice Mail #5"
      A. Nakasone, Mimi's Mom, B. Utley, K. L. Kelly
   Finale/"Your Eyes"
      A. Pascal, Company

---

[34]Originally produced by the New York Theatre Workshop as a work in progress 29 October–6 November 1995 and then Off-Broadway 13 February–31 March 1996 for 51 performances. Dropped from Off-Broadway production:
   "Door"/"Wall"
      A. Rapp, A. Pascal
[35]In late 1998, dramaturge Lynn Thomson was granted co-authorship credit by court settlement.

---

[36]Additional lyrics by Billy Aronson.
[37]Additional lyrics by Billy Aronson.

1996–1997 SEASON

Michael Mulheren, Henry Stram, Ted Sperling, Brian d'Arcy James, David Elder, and Martin Moran in TITANIC
Joan Marcus/Photofest

1996–1997 SEASON

1996.10 ## FOUR SAINTS IN THREE ACTS

A Revival of the Opera in a Prelude and Four Acts[1]. Words by Gertrude Stein. Music by Virgil Thomson. Scenario by Maurice Grosser. Production conceived, designed and directed by Robert Wilson. Conductor, Dennis Russell Davies. Costumes designed by Francesco Clemente. Lighting designed by Jennifer Tipton, Robert Wilson. Chorus master, Richard Bado. Text edited for projection by Francis Rizzo. Produced by Lincoln Center Festival 96 (John Rockwell, Director). Opened 1 August 1996 at the New York State Theatre and closed 3 August 1996 after 4 performances[2].

CAST (in order of vocal appearance): *St. Stephen:* John McVeigh. *St. Settlement:* Nicole Heaston. *St. Plan:* Eric Owens. *St. Sarah:* Jill Grove. *Commère:* MARIETTA SIMPSON. *Compère:* WILBUR PAULEY. *St. Theresa I:* ASHLEY PUTNAM. *St. Theresa II:* SUZANNA GUZMAN. *St. Ignatius:* SANFORD SYLVAN. *St. Cecilia:* Jonita Lattimore. *St. Celestine:* Beth Clayton. *St. Lawrence:* Chuck Winkler. *St. Chavez:* Gran Wilson. *St. Jan:* Brett Scharf. *St. Genevieve:* Audrey Vallance. *St. Anne:* Barbie Brandon. *St. Answers:* Mark Swindler. *St. Placide, St. Vincent, St. Eustace:* Eric Edlund. *St. Absalom, St. Phillip:* Matthew A. Kreger. *Acrobat:* John M. Phillips.

Houston Grand Opera Chorus: Barbie Brandon, Sandra Tye Campbell, Beth Clayton, Kelley Leigh Cooksey, Eric Edlund, Lisa Fjoslien, Jill Grove, Derek W. Henry, Matthew A. Kreger, Kimberly Lane, Jonita Lattimore, Kathleen M. Manley, John McVeigh, Kevin M. Moody, Eric Owens, Bret Scharf, Marc Shreiner, Susan Stone, Nark Swindler, Denise Thorson, Audrey Vallance, Nathan Wight, Chuck Winkler, James Marley Winslow.

Prelude: A choral introduction to all the Saints.

Act 1: On the steps of Avila Cathedral. "A Pageant, or Sunday School Entertainment."

Act 2: A garden party in the country near Barcelona.

Act 3: A monastery garden on the coast near Barcelona.

Act 4: The Saints in heaven.

H.M.S. PINAFORE,

1996.11 ## or The Lass That Loved a Sailor

A Revival of the Comic Opera in Two Acts[3]. Libretto by William S. Gilbert. Music by Arthur Sullivan. Directed by James Billings. Choreographer, Jessica Redel. Conductor, John McGlinn. Set designer, Michael Anania. Costume designer, Joseph A. Citarella. Lighting designer, Jeff Davis. Chorus master, Joseph Colaneri. Produced by the New York City Opera. Opened 20 September 1996 at the New York State Theatre and closed 9 November 1996 after 9 performances in repertory.

CAST (in order of appearance): *Captain Corcoran,* Commanding the *H.M.S. Pinafore:* VICTOR BENEDETTI. *Bill Bobstay,* Boatswain's Mate: James Bobick. *Bob Becket,* Carpenter's Mate: Don Yule. *Little Buttercup,* (Mrs. Cripps), a Portsmouth Bumboat Woman: DIANA DANIELE. *Dick Deadeye,* Able Seaman: JOSEPH MCKEE. *Ralph Rackstraw,* Able Seaman: GEORGE DYER. *Josephine,* the Captain's Daughter: BARBARA SHIRVIS. *The Rt. Hon. Sir Joseph Porter,* K.C.B., First Lord of the Admiralty: JAMES BILLINGS. *Cousin Hebe,* Sir Joseph's First Cousin: Angela Horn.

First Lord's Sisters, his Cousins, his Aunts, Sailors, Marines: New York City Opera Chorus: Marilyn Armstrong, Lee Bellaver, George Bohachevsky, Jill Bosworth, Frank Burzio, Mervin Crook, Harris Davis, Neil Eddinger, Bernadette Fiorella, Don Henderson, Bridget R. Hendrix, Ron Hilley, Gregory Hostetler, Paula Hostetter, Katherine Keyes, April Lindevald, Melissa Maravell, Andrea Miller, Madeleine Mines, Roger Ohlsen, Beth Pensiero, Louis Perry, Mary Ann Rydzeski, Daniel Shigo, Boyd Schlaefer, Phillip Sneed, Matthew Surapine, Verda Lee Tudor, Jeffrey Weber, Leslie Wilk, Deborah Williams, Edward Zimmerman. *New York City Opera Dancers:* Joan Barber, Martha Chapman-Verges, Gregorio DeSilva, Erica Fischbach, Esperanza Galan, Gary Giffune, Stephanie Godino, Randall Graham, Tyler Ingram, Susannah Israel, Candace Itow, Violetta Klimczewska, Ruth-Ellen Kroll, Terry Lacy, Fritz

---

[1]First produced in New York 20 February 1934 at the 44th Street Theatre for 32 performances; re-opened 2 April 1934 at the Empire Theatre for an additional 16 performances. Total: 48 performances.
[2]Performed as an opera with no intermission; no individual musical numbers listed.
[3]Originally presented in New York 15 January 1879 at the Standard Theatre for 175 performances. For Synopsis of Scenes and Musical Numbers, see original 1879 production.

Masten, Joan Mirabella, John Radwick, Brandon L. Saxon, Deirdre Sheehan, Philipp Verges, Yurly Vodolaga, William Ward.

1996.12 ## RIVERDANCE

A Return Engagement of the Dance Revue in Two Acts, 13 Scenes[4]. Music by Bill Whelan. Poetry by Theo Dorgan. Directed by John McColgan. Choreography by Michael Flatley, Jean Butler, Colin Dunne, Tara Little, Moscow Folk Ballet Company, Paula Nic Cionnaith, Maria Pagés, Tarik Winston. Scenery and painted projections by Robert Ballagh. Costumes by Jen Kelly. Lighting by Rupert Murray. Sound by Michael O'Gorman. Orchestrations by Nick Ingman, Bill Whelan. Projection design by Chris Slinsgby. Produced by Abhann Productions Ltd. (Moya Doherty, producer). Opened 2 October 1996 at the Radio City Music Hall and closed 20 October 1996 after 21 performances.

CAST: *Narrator:* JOHN CAVANAGH. *Solo Dancers:* COLIN DUNNE, EILEEN MARTIN, MARIA PAGES. With TARIK WINSTON, EILEEN IVERS, IVAN THOMAS, DANIEL B. WOOTEN, HERBIN VAN CAYSEELE. *Solo Singers:* KATIE MCMAHON, MORGAN CROWLEY.

Irish Dance Troupe: Sarah Berry, Dearbhail Bates, Natalie Biggs, Lorna Bradley, Martin Brennan, Rachel Byrne, Yzanne Cloonan, Andrea Curley, Jo Ellen Forsyth, Fiona Gallagher, Susan Ginnety, Deirdre Goulding, Paula Goulding, Conor Hayes, Miceál Hopkins, Donnacha Howard, Kellie Hughes, Ciara Kennedy, Sinéad Lightley, Eileen Martin, Stephen McAteer, Sorcha McCaul, Kevin McCormack, Jonathan McMorrow, Aoibheann O'Brien, Niamh O'Brien, Cormac Ó Sé, Ursula Quigley, Joan Rafter, Pat Roddy, Sheila Ryan, Anthony Savage, Glenn Simpson, Claire Usher, J. R. Vancheri, Raymond Walls, Leanda Ward. *Moscow Folk Ballet:* Svetlana Kossoroukova, Ilia Stretsov, Tatiana Nedostop, Marina Taranda, Iouri Oustiougov, Serguei Iakoubov, Iouri Shishkine, Olena Krutsenko. *Riverdance Singers:* Derek Byrne, Patrick Connolly, Jennifer Curran, Tony Davoren, Maire Lang, Kay Lynch, Lorraine Nolan, Cathal Synnott (choirmaster). *Drummers:* Abraham Doron, Vinny Ozborne, Andrew Reilly, Derek Tallon.

ACT 1

Scene 1

Introduction

"Reel Around the Sun"
(*Choreographed by* Michael Flatley.)
Cornora; The Chroos Reel; Reel Around the Sun.

Scene 2

"The Heart's Cry"

Scene 3

Women of Ireland:
(*Choreographed by* Jean Butler.)
The Countess Cathleen; Women of Sidhe.

Scene 4

"Caoineadh Chú Chulainn" (Lament)

Scene 5

Thunderstorm
(*Choreographed by* Michael Flatley.)

Scene 6

"Shivna"
(*Choreographed by* Moscow Folk Ballet Company.)

Scene 7

Firedance
(*Choreographed by* Maria Pagés.)

Scene 8

Slip into Spring—The Harvest

Scene 9

Riverdance: "Cloudsong," "Dance of the Riverwoman," Earthrise, Riverdance
(*Choreographed by* Mavis Ascott; *Irish Step Dance Choreography by* Michael Flatley; *Female Solo Choreography by* Jean Butler.)

ACT 2

Scene 1

Introduction

---

[4]First produced in New York 13 March 1996 at the Radio City Music Hall for 8 performances

American Wake (Nova Scotia Set, "Lift the Wings")
(*Choreographed by* Michael Flatley, Paula Nic Cionnath.)

Scene 2

The Harbour of the New World:

"Heal Their Hearts"—Freedom

Trading Tips
(*Choreographed by* Colin Dunne, Tarik Winston.)

Morning in Macedonia (The Russian Dervish)
(*Choreographed by* Moscow Folk Ballet Company.)

Oscail an Doras (Open the Door)

Heartbeat of the World—Andalucia
(*Choreographed by* Maria Pagés, Colin Dunne.)

Scene 3

"Home and the Heartland"
(*Choreographed by* Michael Flatley, Colin Dunne, Jean Butler.)

Scene 4

Riverdance International

1996.13 BRIGADOON

A Revival of the Musical Play in Two Acts, 11 Scenes[5]. Book and lyrics by Alan Jay Lerner. Music by Frederick Loewe. Original dances by Agnes de Mille. Choreography recreation and additional choreography by Gemze de Lappe. Stage director, Christian Smith. Original set and costume designer, Desmond Heeley. Lighting designer, Duane Schuler. Conductor, John McGlinn. Orchestrations by Ted Royal. Dance arrangements by Trude Rittman. Vocal arrangements by Frederick Loewe. Sound design, Abe Jacob. Chorus master, Joseph Colaneri. Produced by the New York City Opera. Opened 13 November 1996 at the New York State Theatre and closed 24 November 1996 after 14 performances.

CAST (in order of appearance): *Tommy Albright:* BRENT BARRETT. *Jeff Douglas:* SEAN DONNELLAN. *Maggie Anderson:* LESLIE BROWNE. *Archie Beaton:* William Ledbetter. *Angus MacGuffie:* James Bobick. *Meg Brockie:* JUDY KAYE. *Stuart Dalrymple:* Joel Sorenson. *Sandy Dean:* Ron Hilley. *Harry Beaton:* ROBERT LAFOSSE *Andrew MacLaren:* Don Yule. *Fiona MacLaren:* REBECCA LUKER. *Jean MacLaren:* Elizabeth Ferrell. *Charlie Dalrymple:* GEORGE DYER. *Mr. Lundie:* George Hall. *Sword Dancers:* Philipp Verges, William Ward. *Bagpiper:* Stephen Frank. *Frank:* Jon Brent Curry. *Jane Ashton:* Stacy Lee Tilton.

Townsfolk of Brigadoon: New York City Opera Chorus: same as H.M.S. PINAFORE above. *New York City Opera Dancers:* same as H.M.S. PINAFORE above.

1996.14 CHICAGO

A Revival of the Musical (Vaudeville) in Two Acts[6]. Book by Fred Ebb and Bob Fosse. Based on the play of the same name by Maurine Dallas Watkins. Music by John Kander. Lyrics by Fred Ebb. Original production directed and choreographed by Bob Fosse. Directed by Walter Bobbie. Choreographed by Ann Reinking in the style of Bob Fosse. Scenic design by John Lee Beatty. Costume design by William Ivey Long. Lighting design by Ken Billington. Music director, Rob Fisher. Original orchestrations by Ralph Burns. Dance music arranged by Peter Howard. Sound design by Scott Lehrer. Script adaptation by David Thompson. Associate producer, Alecia Parker. Presesnted in association with Pace Theatrical Group.

Produced by Barry and Fran Weissler in association with Kardana Productions Inc. Opened 14 November 1996 at the Richard Rodgers Theatre, moved 12 February 1997 to the Sam S. Shubert Theatre and is still running at this time!

CAST (in order of appearance): *Velma Kelly:* BEBE NEUWIRTH. *Roxie Hart:* ANN REINKING. *Fred Casely:* Michael Berresse. *Sergeant Fogarty:* Michael Kubala. *Amos Hart:* JOEL GREY. *Liz:* Denise Faye. *Annie:* Mamie Duncan-Gibbs. *June:* Mary Ann Lamb. *Hunyak:* Tina Paul. *Mona:* Caitlin Carter. *Matron "Mama" Morton:* MARCIA LEWIS. *Billy Flynn:* JAMES NAUGHTON. *Mary Sunshine:* D. SABELLA. *Go-to-Hell Kitty:* Leigh Zimmerman. *Harry:* Rocker Verastique. *Aaron:* David Warren-Gibson. *The Judge:* Jim Bortselmann. *Martin Harrison:* Bruce Anthony Davis. *Court Clerk:* John Mineo.

1996.15 A CHRISTMAS CAROL

A Revival of the Musical in One Act, 13 Scenes[7]. Book by Mike Ockrent and Lynn Ahrens. Based on the novel of the same name by Charles Dickens. Music by Alan Menken. Lyrics by Lynn Ahrens. Directed by Mike Ockrent. Choreographed by Susan Stroman. Setting design by Tony Walton. Costume design by William Ivey Long. Lighting design by Jules Fisher and Peggy Eisenhauer. Sound design by Tony Meola. Projections by Wendall K. Harrington. Flying by Foy. Associate director, Steven Zweigbaum. Associate choreographer, Chris Peterson. Musical direction by Paul Gemignani. Orchestrations by Michael Starobin and Douglas Besterman. Dance arrangements and incidental music by Glen Kelly. Executive producer, Dodger Productions. Producer, Tim Hawkins. Presented by Madison Square Garden. Opened 26 November 1996 at the (Paramount) Theatre, Madison Square Garden and closed 5 January 1997 after 90 performances.

CAST (in order of appearance): *Beadle:* David Lowenstein. *Mr. Smythe:* JAMES JUDY. *Grace Smythe:* Jennifer Blain, Cara Horner. *Scrooge:* TONY RANDALL. *Crachit:* NICK CORLEY. *Charity Men:* Michael H. Ingram, Keith Byron Kirk, Seth Malkin. *Old Joe:* Don Mayo. *Street Urchins:* Matthew Hoffman, Christopher Mark Petrizzo, Zachary Stefan Petkanas, Gemini Quintos, Diana Mary Rice, Evan Silverberg. *Mrs. Crachit:* Robin Baxter. *Tiny Tim:* Matthew Ballinger, Pierce Cravens. *Poulterer:* Michael H. Ingram. *Sandwichboard Man:* BEN VEREEN. *Jonathon:* Jason Fuchs, Evan J. Newman. *Lamplighter:* KEN JENNINGS. *Blind Hag:* Joan Barber. *Fred:* GREG ZERKLE. *Mrs. Mops:* Corinne Melancon. *Ghost of Jacob Marley:* PAUL KANDEL. *Ghost of Christmas Past:* KEN JENNINGS. *Lights of Christmas Past:* Matthew Baker, Christopher F. Davis, Sean Thomas Morrissey, David Rosales. *Judge:* Michael H. Ingram. *Scrooge at 8 years:* Zachary Stefan Petkanas, Evan Silverberg. *Fan at 6:* Gemini Quintos, Diana Mary Rice. *Scrooge's Mother:* Joan Barber. *Scrooge's Father:* Michael X. Martin. *Mr. Hawkins:* Don Mayo. *Scrooge at 12 years:* Matthew Hoffman, Christopher Mark Petrizzo. *Fan at 10 years:* Eliza Atkins Clark, Elizabeth Lundberg. *Fezziwig:* Ray Friedeck. *Scrooge at 18 years:* Michael Moore. *Young Marley:* Ken Barnett. *Mrs. Fezziwig:* Joy Hermalyn. *Emily:* Emily Skinner. *Fiddler:* Brad Bradley. *Ghost of Christmas Present:* BEN VEREEN. *The Crachit Children:* Eliza Atkins Clark, Matthew Hoffman, Elizabeth Lundberg, Sean Thomas Morrissey, Christopher Mark Petrizzo. *Sally, Fred's wife:* Whitney Webster. *Ignorance:* Zachary Stefan Petkanas, Evan Silverberg. *Undertakers:* Ken Barnett, Michael X. Martin. *Ghost of Christmas Future:* VALENTINA KOZLOWA.

Business Men, Gifts, Ghosts and the People of London: Matthew Baker, Joan Barber, Ken Barnett, Robin Baxter, Leslie Bell, Carol Bentley, Brad Bradley, Betsy Chang, Candy Cook, Rosa Curry, Christopher F. Davis, Ray Friedeck, Peter Gregus, Jeffrey Hankinson, Joy Hermalyn, Michael H. Ingram, James Judy, Louisa Kendrick, Carrie Kenneally, Keith Byron Kirk, David Lowenstein, Jason Ma, Seth Malkin, Donna Lee Marshall, Michael X. Martin, Dana Lynn Mauro, Don Mayo, Elizabeth Mills, Corinne Melancon, Michael Moore, Seth Thomas Morrissey, Adam Pelty, Gail Pennington, Angela Piccinni, Pamela Remler, Samuel Reni, David Rosales, Emily Skinner, Whitney Webster, Greg Zerkle. *Swings:* Rachel Black, Rob Donohoe, Jesse

---

[5]Originally produced in New York 13 March 1947 at the Ziegfeld Theatre for 581 performances. For Synopsis of Scenes and Musical Numbers, see original 1947 production.

[6]Originally produced in New York 3 June 1975 at the 46th Street Theatre for 947 performances. For Synopsis of Scenes and Musical Numbers, see original 1975 production. This revival was based on the Encore Series concert production 2-4 May 1996 at the New York City Center for 4 performances with much the same cast and creative team. For this production, "Chicago After Midnight" was dropped. "Nowadays" (reprise/"R.S.V.P."/"Keep It Hot") were replaced by:

"Honey Rag"
A. Reinking, B. Neuwirth

Finale
Company

[7]Originally produced in New York 1 December 1994 at the Paramount, Madison Square Garden for 71 performances. For Synopsis of Scenes and Musical Numbers, see original 1994 production. For this year's and the 1995 revival the following changes were made:

Scene 1 and "The Years Are Passing By" were dropped.

Added to Scene 2 (former Scene 3) before "Street Song":

"You Mean More to Me"
N. Corley, M. Ballinger or P. Cravens

"The Years Are Passing By" (reprise) in former Scene 13 (new Scene 12) was replaced by:

"London Town Carol"
J. Fuchs or E. J. Newman

Note: The production played an irregular schedule of multiple daily performances.

Adam Eisenberg, Nicholas Gould, Dana Leigh Jackson, Don Johanson, Robin Lewis, Grace Ann Pisani, Jordan Siwek, Lindsay Sperber, Cynthia Thole, Brandon Urbanowitz, Jeff Williams. *Angels:* Bergen Beach School, P.S. 26 Chorus, Terrill Middle School, P.S. 250 Concert Choral *The Red Children's Cast:* Jennifer Blain, Pierce Cravens, Jason Fuchs, Matthew Hoffman, Elizabeth Lundberg, Grace Ann Pisani, Gemini Quintos, Evan Silverberg, Jordan Siwek. *The Green Children's Cast:* Matthew Ballinger, Eliza Atkins Clark, Nicholas Gould, Cara Horner, Evan Jay Newman, Zachary Stefan Petkanas, Christopher Mark Petrizzo, Diana Mary Rice, Lindsay Sperber, Brandon Urbanowitz.

1996.16 JUAN DARIÉN

A Revival of the Carnival Mass in One Act[8], 14 Scenes, a Prologue and an Epilogue. Conceived by Julie Taymor and Elliot Goldenthal. Music and original lyrics by Elliot Goldenthal. Based on a tale by Horacio Quirogà. Directed by Julie Taymor. Sets and costumes by G. W. Mercier and Julie Taymor. Puppetry and masks by Julie Taymor. Lighting design by Donald Holder. Sound by Tony Meola. Musical direction by Richard Cordova. Produced by Lincoln Center Theatre Co. (André Bishop, Artistic director; Bernard Gersten, Executive producer) in association with Music-Theatre Group (Lyn Austin, Diane Wondisford, Producers). Opened 24 November 1996 at the Vivian Beaumont Theatre and closed 5 January 1997 after 49 performances.

CAST: *Plague Victims:* The Company. *Mother (Dancer):* ARIEL ASHWELL. *Mother (Vocalist):* ANDREA FRIERSON TONEY. *Hunter:* Kristofer Batho. *Mr. Bones:* BRUCE TURK. *Shadows:* The Company, led by Stephen Kaplin. *Juan (Puppet):* Kristofer Batho, Andrea Kane, Barbara Pollitt. *Juan (Boy):* DANIEL HODD. *Schoolteacher:* BRUCE TURK. *Schoolchildren:* The Company. *Drunken Couple:* Kristofer Batho, Andrea Kane. *Señor Toledo:* Martín Santangelo. *Circus Tigers:* The Company. *Circus Barker, Street Singer:* DAVID TONEY. *Old Woman:* Ariel Ashwell. *Green Dwarf:* Andrea Kane, Sophia Salguero. *Marie Posa:* Sophia Salguero. *Ballad of Return Soloist:* IRMA-ESTEL LAGUERRE.

The action takes place in a South American jungle and a nearby village.

Prologue: Darkness; A Church in the Jungle. *Scene 1:* The Jungle. *Scene 2:* The Plague; A Village in Mourning. *Scene 3:* A Prayer Answered; The Transformation. *Scene 4:* The Nurturing; Juan's Ritual Baptism. *Scene 5:* Night in the Village. *Scene 6:* Journey to School; The Parting. *Scene 7:* School: Discipline, Fact. *Scene 8:* The Mother Dies. *Scene 9:* The Carnival. *Scene 10:* Discovery; Suspicion. *Scene 11:* The Interrogation; Schoolroom 2. *Scene 12:* The Torture and Retransformation of Juan Darién. *Scene 13:* The Jaguars' Congress; Retribution. *Scene 14:* The Mother's Grave and the Return to the Jungle. *Epilogue:* The Jungle.

MUSICAL NUMBERS[9]

Prologue

Agnus Dei
  Chorus

Lacrymosa
  Chorus, A. Ashwell, A. F. Toney

Mr. Bones Fanfare (dance)
  B. Turk

Jaguar Cub Approach
  A. Ashwell, A. F. Toney

Mr. Bones' Two-Step (dance)
  B. Turk

The Hunter's Entrance

Gloria
  Chorus, A. Ashwell, A. F. Toney

Initiation

A Round at Midnight

Sanctus
  A. Ashwell, A. F. Toney

School
  D. Hodd

Recordare
  A. Ashwell, A. F. Toney, D. Hodd, Chorus

Carnaval
  D. Toney

Lullabye
  D. Toney
  (*Lyrics* by Elliot Goldenthal.)

Trance
  D. Hodd
  (*Lyrics* by Horacio Quirogà.)

Dies Irae
  D. Toney, Chorus, D. Hodd, A. Ashwell, A. F. Toney

Lacrymosa II/Retribution
  Chorus, D. Hodd, A. Ashwell, A. F. Toney

"The Ballad of Return"
  I. LaGuerre
  (*Lyrics* by Elliot Goldenthal.)

1996.17 GREASE

A Revival of the Musical (Comedy) in Two Acts, 12 Scenes[10]. Book, music and lyrics by Jim Jacobs and Warren Casey. Directed and choreographed by Jeff Calhoun. Scenic design by John Arnone. Costume design by Willa Kim. Lighting design by Howell Brinkley. Sound design by Tom Morse. Musical supervision, vocal and dance music arrangements by John McDaniel. Musical direction, John Samorian. Orchestrations by Steven Margoshes. Associate choreographer, Jerry Mitchell. Associate producer, Alecia Parker. A Tommy Tune Production. Produced by Barry and Fran Weissler and Jujamcyn Theatres, in association with Pace Theatrical Group and TV Asahi. Opened 29 November 1996 at the New York City Center and closed 1 December 1996 after 5 performances.

CAST (in order of appearance): *Vince Fontaine:* PETER SCOLARI. *Miss Lynch:* MIMI HINES. *Sonny:* Stephen Gnojewski. *Kenickie:* Steve Geyer. *Frenchy:* Alisa Klein. *Doody:* Roy Chicas. *Betty Rizzo:* JASMINE GUY. *Marty:* Cathy Trien. *Roger:* David Josefsberg *Jan:* Farah Alvin. *Danny Zuko:* ADRIAN ZMED. *Eugene Florczyk:* Christopher Youngsman. *Patty Simcox:* Stephanie Seeley. *Sandy Dumbrowski:* Christiane Noll. *The Heartbeats:* Denise Boccanfuso, Stefani Rae, Joelle Letta. *The Dream Mooners:* Shannon Bailey, Stefani Rae. *The Straight A's:* Shannon Bailey, Christopher Youngsman, Alan Jenkins, Daniel Paulus. *Cha-Cha DeGregorio:* Lori Lynch. *Teen Angel:* Kevin Anthony.
  Ensemble: Shannon Bailey, Denise Boccanfuso, Ashton Byrum, Scot Fedderly, Alan Jenkins, Michelle Kittrell, Joelle Letta, Daniel Paulus, Stefani Rae, Mary Ruvolo. *Swings:* Thomas Scott, Jeanna Schweppe, Timothy Edward Smith. {Note: Pink Ladies include Rizzo, Frenchy, Marty, Jan. Burger Palace Boys include Kenickie, Doody, Roger, Sonny.}

1996.18 ONCE UPON A MATTRESS

A Revival of the Musical Comedy in Two Acts[11]. Book (revised) by Jay Thompson, Marshall Barer and Dean Fuller. (Based on the story "The Princess and the Pea" by Hans Christian Andersen.) Music by Mary Rodgers. Lyrics by Marshall Barer. Directed by Gerald Gutierrez. Choreographed by Liza Gennaro. Scenery by John Lee Beatty. Costumes by Jane Grrenwood. Lighting by Pat Collins. Sound by Tom Morse. Musical direction and vocal arrangements by Eric Stern. Orchestrations by Bruce Coughlan. Dance arrangements by Tom Fay. Executive producer, Dodger Management Group. Produced by Dodger Productions and Joop Van Den

---

[8]Originally produced in New York Off-Broadway 4 March 1988 at St. Clement's Theatre for 23 performances; revived 26 December 1989 at St. Clement's Theatre for 48 performances.

[9]Musical Numbers not listed in the program. Above listing prepared from libretto in the theatre program and the recording of the original concert version.

[10]Originally produced in New York Off-Broadway 14 February 1972 at the Eden Theatre for 128 performances; transferred 7 June 1972 to the Broadhurst Theatre for a total of 3388 performances, including Off-Broadway run. This version originally produced 11 May 1994 at the Eugene O'Neill Theatre for 1503 performances; this national touring company played simultaneously with the Broadway company of GREASE! at the Eugene O'Neill for 3 days. For this touring production, Act 2, Scenes 4 and 5 have been combined, eliminating the Burger Palace set.

[11]Originally produced Off-Broadway 11 May 1959 at the Phoenix Theatre for 216 performances; transferred to Broadway 25 November 1959 at the Alvin Theatre for an additional 244 performances. Total: 460 performances. For Musical Numbers, see original 1959 production. For this production, a new song was added to Act 2, after "Quiet":

"Goodnight, Sweet Princess"
  D. A. Baker

Ende. Opened 19 December 1996 at the Broadhurst Theatre and closed 1 June 1997 after 187 performances.

CAST: *King Sextimus*: HEATH LAMBERTS. *Queen Aggravain*: MARY LOU ROSATO. *Prince Dauntless*: DAVID AARON BAKER. *Winnifred*, Princess of Farfelot: SARAH JESSICA PARKER. *Sir Harry*, Knight of the Herald: LEWIS CLEALE. *Lady Larken*, a Lady in Waiting: JANE KRAKOWSKI. *Jester*: DAVID HIBBARD. *Master Merton*, confidante to the Queen: Tom Alan Robbins. *The Nightingale of Samarkand*, a royal pet: Ann Brown. *The Royal Cellist*: Laura Bontrager. *The Royal Ballet*: Arte Phillips, Pascale Faye. *Minstrel*, a travelling player: LAWRENCE CLAYTON. *Player Queen*: David Jennings. *Player Prince*: David Elder. *Player Princess*: Bob Walton. *Other Players*: Arte Phillips, Nick Cokas, Stephen Reed.

Knights, Lords and Ladies attending the Queen: Nick Cokas, David Elder, David Jennings, Sebastian LaCause, Jason Psahl, Arte Phillips, Stephen Reed, Bob Walton, Ann Brown, Maria Calabrese, Thursday Farrar, Pascale Faye, Janet Metz, Tina Ou, Aixa M. Rosario Medina, Jennifer Smith. *Swings*: Pamela Gould, Thomas Titone.

The action takes place in and about the castle in the spring, 1428.

1997.01 MANDY PATINKIN IN CONCERT

A One Man Show in One Act. At the piano, Paul Ford. Produced by Dodger Endemol Theatricals[12]. Opened 1 March 1997 at the Lyceum Theatre and closed 23 March 1997 after 17 performances[13].

CAST: MANDY PATINKIN.

MUSICAL NUMBERS[14]

"Beat Out Dat Rhythm on a Drum" (from *CARMEN JONES*)
  (*Music by* Georges Bizet. *Lyrics by* Oscar Hammerstein II.)
"School Days"
  (*Music by* Gus Edwards. *Lyrics by* Will D. Cobb.)
"Time in a Bottle"
  (*Music and Lyrics by* Jim Croce.)
"Inchworm" (from *HANS CHRISTIAN ANDERSEN* film)
  (*Music and Lyrics by* Frank Loesser.)
"The Wrong Note Rag" (from *WONDERFUL TOWN*)
  (*Music by* Leonard Bernstein. *Lyrics by* Betty Comden and Adolph Green.)
"A-Tisket, A-Tasket"
  (*Music and Lyrics by* Van Alexander and Ella Fitzgerald.)
"You Are Beautiful" (from *FLOWER DRUM SONG*)
  (*Music by* Richard Rodgers. *Lyrics by* Oscar Hammerstein II.)
"Not a Day Goes By" (from *MERRILY WE ROLL ALONG*)
  (*Music and Lyrics by* Stephen Sondheim.)
"Sam, You Made the Pants Too Long"
  (*Music by* Isham Jones. *Lyrics by* Sam M. Lewis, Milton Berle, Fred Whitehouse.)
"Cohen Owes Me $97"
  (*Music and Lyrics by* Irving Berlin.)
"Loving You" (from *PASSION*)
  (*Music and Lyrics by* Stephen Sondheim.)
"If I Loved You" (from *CAROUSEL*)
  (*Music by* Richard Rodgers. *Lyrics by* Oscar Hammerstein II.)
"When I Grow Too Old to Dream" (from *THE NIGHT IS YOUNG* film)
  (*Music by* Sigmund Romberg. *Lyrics by* Oscar Hammerstein II.)
"Remember" (*A LITTLE NIGHT MUSIC*)
  (*Music and Lyrics by* Stephen Sondheim.)
"Ya Got Trouble" (from *THE MUSIC MAN*)
  (*Music and Lyrics by* Meredith Willson.)
"Frankfurter Sandwiches"
  (*Music and Lyrics by* Al Dubin, Harry Pease and Ed G. Nelson.)
"Honey Bun" (from *SOUTH PACIFIC*)
  (*Music by* Richard Rodgers. *Lyrics by* Oscar Hammerstein II.)

"And the Band Played On"
  (*Music by* John Palmer. *Lyrics by* Charles B. Ward.)
"Marie"
  (*Music and Lyrics by* Randy Newman.)
"Once Upon a Time" (from *ALL AMERICAN*)
  (*Music by* Charles Strouse. *Lyrics by* Lee Adams.)
"Taxi"
  (*Music and Lyrics by* Harry Chapin.)
"Soliloquy" (from *CAROUSEL*)
  (*Music by* Richard Rodgers. *Lyrics by* Oscar Hammerstein II.)
"Waters of March"
  (*Music and Lyrics by* Antonio Carlos Jobim.)
"How Glory Goes" (from *FLOYD COLLINS*)
  (*Music and Lyrics by* Adam Guettel.)
"Bring Him Home" (from *LES MISERABLES*)
  (*Music by* Alain Boublil, Claude-Michel Schönberg. *Lyrics by* Herbert Kretzmer.)
"Carefully Taught" (from *SOUTH PACIFIC*)
  (*Music by* Richard Rodgers. *Lyrics by* Oscar Hammerstein II.)
"Children Will Listen" (from *INTO THE WOODS*)
  (*Music and Lyrics by* Stephen Sondheim.)
"Pennies from Heaven" (from *PENNIES FROM HEAVEN* film)
  (*Music by* Arthur Johnston. *Lyrics by* Johnny Burke.)
"Oh, What a Circus" (from *EVITA*)
  (*Music by* Andrew Lloyd Webber. *Lyrics by* Tim Rice.)
"Experiment" (from *NYMPH ERRANT*)
  (*Music and Lyrics by* Cole Porter.)
"Over the Rainbow" (from *THE WIZARD OF OZ* film)
  (*Music by* Harold Arlen. *Lyrics by* E. Y. Harburg.)
"White Christmas" (from *HOLIDAY INN* film)
  (*Music and Lyrics by* Irving Berlin.)
"God Bless America"
  (*Music and Lyrics by* Irving Berlin.)
"As Time Goes By" (from *EVERYBODY'S WELCOME*)
  (*Music and Lyrics by* Herman Hupfeld.)
  (*Yiddish Lyrics [for 3 songs above] by* Henry Sapoznik.)
"Rockabye Your Baby with a Dixie Melody" (from *SINBAD*)
  (*Music by* Jean Schwartz. *Lyrics by* Sam M. Lewis, Joe Young.)

THE MIKADO,
1997.02 or The Town of Titipu

A Revival of the Comic Opera in Two Acts[15]. Libretto by William S. Gilbert. Music by Arthur Sullivan. Production (direction), Lotfi Mansouri. Stage direction, Christian Smith. Conductor, Randall Craig Fleischer. Set and costume designer, Thierry Bosquet. Lighting designer, John Gleason. Choreographer, Patricia Birch. Chorus master, Gary Wedow. Produced by the New York City Opera. Opened 8 March 1997 at the New York State Theatre and closed 23 April 1997 after 6 performances in repertory.

CAST (in order of appearance): *Nanki-Poo*: MATTHEW CHELLIS. *Pish-Tush*: SHON SIMS. *Pooh-Bah*: JOSEPH MCKEE. *Ko-Ko*: JAMES BILLINGS. *Yum-Yum*: BARBARA SHIRVIS. *Pitti-Sing*: ANGELA HORN. *Peep-Bo*: DEANE MEEK. *Katisha*: CYNTHIA MUNZER. *The of Japan*: RICHARD MCKEE. *Chorus of School Girls, Nobles, Guards and Coolies*: New York City Opera Chorus.

1997.03 PLAY ON!

A Musical in Two Acts. Book by Cheryl L. West. (Based loosely on "Twelfth Night" by William Shakespeare.) Songs (music) by Duke Ellington. Conceived and directed by Sheldon Epps. Choreographed by Mercedes Ellington. Arrangements, musical supervision, orchestrations by Luther Henderson. Scenic design, James Leonard Joy. Costume design, Marianna Elliott. Lighting design, Jeff Davis. Sound design, Jeff Ladman. Creative

---

[12]Billed as a benefit engagement for 5 charities: Association to Benefit Children; Crohn's and Colitis Foundation; National Dance Institute; Peace Now; Physicians for Human Rights.
[13]Played an irregular schedule of 5 performances a week.
[14]No songs listed in program. Not in performance order; not all songs performed at all performances.

[15]First presented in New York 20 July, 10-29 August 1885 at the Union Square and People's Theatres for 22 performances. First authorized production presented 19 August 1885 at the Fifth Avenue Theatre by Richard D'Oyly Carte for 250 performances. For Synopsis of Scenes and Musical Numbers, see 19 August 1885 D'Oyly Carte production.

consultant, Louis Johnson. Creative historic consultant, Frankie Manning. Musical director, J. Leonard Oxley. Originally produced at the Old Globe Theatre, San Diego, California. Associate producers, Leon Memoli, David Levy, Nancy Eichorn, Louis F. Raizin, James L. Simon, Fred H. Krones. Produced by Mitchell Maxwell, Eric Nederlander, Thomas Hall, Hal Luftig, Bruce Lucker, Mike Skipper, Victoria Maxwell, in association with Kery Davis, Alan J. Shuster. Opened March 20 1997 at the Brooks Atkinson Theatre and closed 11 May 1997 after 61 performances.

CAST (in order of appearance): *Vy*: CHERYL FREEMAN. *Jester*: ANDRÉ DESHIELDS. *Sweets*: LARRY MARSHALL. *Miss Mary*: YVETTE CASON. *CC*: Crystal Allen. *Duke*: CARL ANDERSON. *Rev*: LAWRENCE HAMILTON. *Lady Liv*: TONYA PINKINS.

Denizens of Harlem: Ronald "Cadet" Bastine, Jacqueline Bird, Wendee Lee Curtis, Byron Easley, Alan H. Green, Frantz G. Hall, Gil P., Lacy Darryl Phillips, Lisa Scialabba, Erika Vaughn, Karen Callaway Williams. *Swings*: Germaine Goodson, Bryan S. Haynes, Stacie Precia, William Wesley.

Time: The Swingin' '40's.

Location: The Magical Kingdom of Harlem.

Act 1, Scene 1: Grand Central Station. *Scene 2*: 125th Street. *Scene 3*: The Duke's Apartment. *Scene 4*: The Cotton Club. *Scene 5*: Lady Liv's Dressing Room. *Scene 6*: The Cotton Club. *Scene 7*: *Scene 8*: The Cotton Club. *Scene 9*: *Scene 10*: The Cotton Club.

Act 2, Scene 1: The Cotton Club. *Scene 2*: Lady Liv's Dressing Room. *Scene 3*: The Cotton Club. *Scene 4*: Outside of the Cotton Club. *Scene 5*: The Cotton Club. *Scene 6*: Lady Liv's Apartment. *Scene 7*: Outside of the Cotton Club. *Scene 8*: The Duke's Apartment. *Scene 9*: 125th Street.

ACT 1

Scene 1

"Take the A Train"
C. Freeman, Ensemble
(*Music and Lyrics by* Billy Strayhorn.)

Scene 2

"Drop Me Off in Harlem"
C. Freeman, Denizens of Harlem
(*Music by* Duke Ellington. *Lyrics by* Nick Kenny.)

"I've Got to Be a Rug Cutter"
A. DeShields, C. Freeman, Cotton Club Dancers
(*Music and Lyrics by* Duke Ellington.)

Scene 3

"I Let a Song Go Out of My Heart"
C. Anderson
(*Music and Lyrics by* Duke Ellington, Irving Mills, Henry Nemo, John Redmond.)

Scene 4

"C Jam Blues"
Cotton Club Dancers
(*Music by* Duke Ellignton.)

"Mood Indigo"
T. Pinkins
(*Music and Lyrics by* Duke Ellington, Irving Mills, Albany Bigard.)

Scene 5

"Don't Get Around Much Anymore"
C. Freeman, T. Pinkins
(*Music by* Duke Ellington. *Lyrics by* Bob Russell.)

"Don't You Know I Care"
L. Hamilton
(*Music by* Duke Ellington. *Lyrics by* Mack David.)

Scene 6

"It Don't Mean a Thing If It Ain't Got That Swing"
A. DeShields, Y. Cason, L. Marshall, L. Hamilton
(*Music by* Duke Ellington. *Lyrics by* Irving Mills.)

Scene 7

"I Got It Bad and That Ain't Good" (from JUMP FOR JOY)
C. Anderson, C. Freeman
(*Music by* Duke Ellington. *Lyrics by* Paul Francis Webster.)

"Hit Me With a Hot Note and Watch Me Bounce"
C. Freeman, Duke's Band
(*Music by* Duke Ellington. *Lyrics by* Don George.)

Scene 9

"I'm Just a Lucky So and So"

A. DeShields, Cotton Club Dancers
(*Music by* Duke Ellington. *Lyrics by* Mack David.)

Scene 10

"Everything But You"
T. Pinkins, C. Freeman
(*Music and Lyrics by* Duke Ellington, Don George, Harry James.)

"Solitude"
C. Freeman, C. Anderson, T. Pinkins, L. Hamilton
(*Music and Lyrics by* Duke Ellington, Eddie DeLange, Irving Mills.)

ACT 2

Scene 1

"Black Butterfly"
Lady Liv's Escorts
(*Music and Lyrics by* Duke Ellington, Ben Carruthers, Irving Mills.)

"I Ain't Got Nothin' But the Blues"
T. Pinkins
(*Music by* Duke Ellington. *Lyrics by* Don George.)

Scene 3

"I'm Beginning to See the Light"
L. Hamilton, Cotton Club Dancers
(*Music by* Duke Ellington, Don George, Harry James, Johnny Hodges.)

"I Got It Bad and That Ain't Good" (reprise)
L. Hamilton

Scene 4

"I Didn't Know About You"
C. Freeman
(*Music by* Duke Ellington. *Lyrics by* Bob Russell.)

Scene 5

"Rocks in My Bed"
L. Marshall, A. DeShields
(*Music and Lyrics by* Duke Ellington.)

Scene 6

"Something to Live For"
L. Hamilton, T. Pinkins
(*Music by* Duke Ellington. *Lyrics by* Billy Strayhorn.)

Scene 7

"Love You Madly"
Y. Cason, L. Marshall
(*Music and Lyrics by* Duke Ellington.)

Scene 8

"Prelude to a Kiss"
C. Freeman, C. Anderson
(*Music and Lyrics by* Duke Ellington, Irving Gordon, Irving Mills.)

Scene 9

"In a Mellow Tone"
C. Freeman, C. Anderson, T. Pinkins, L. Hamilton, Denizens of Harlem
(*Music by* Duke Ellington. *Lyrics by* Milt Gabler.)

1997.04   ANNIE

A Revival of the Musical in Two Acts, 13 Scenes[16]. Book by Thomas Meehan. Based on the "Little Orphan Annie" comic strip (by Harold Gray). Music by Charles Strouse. Lyrics by Martin Charnin. Musical numbers choreographed by Peter Gennaro. Directed by Martin Charnin. Settings by Kenneth Foy. Costumes by Theoni V. Aldredge. Lighting by Ken Billington. Sound by T. Richard Fitzgerald. Musical direction and supervision by Keith Levinson. (Original orchestrations by Philip J. Lang.) Associate producers, Tamar Climan and Herb Goldsmith. Produced by Timothy Childs, Rodger Hess and Jujamcyn Theatres, in association with Terri B. Childs and Al

---

[16]Originally opened 21 April 1977 at the Alvin Theatre for 2377 performances. For Synopsis of Scenes and Musical Numbers, see original 1977 production. For this production, a new song was added to Act 1, Scene 7, before "Easy Street":

"You Make Me Happy"
N. Carter, C. Dunn

After the opening, Act 1, Scene 3 was dropped, including "We'd Like to Thank You, (Herbert Hoover)."

Nocciolino. Opened 26 March 1997 at the Martin Beck Theatre and closed 19 October 1997 after 240 performances.

CAST (in order of appearance): *Annie:* BRITTNY KISSINGER. *Molly:* Christiana Anbri. *Pepper:* Cassidy Ladden. *Duffy:* Mekenzie Rosen-Stone. *July:* Casey Tuma. *Tessie:* Lyndsey Watkins. *Kate:* Melissa O'Malley *Miss Hannigan:* NELL CARTER. *Bundles McCloskey:* Michael E. Gold. *Apple Seller:* Brad Wills. *Dog Catchers:*Tom Treadwell, Sutton Foster. *Sandy:* Cindy Lou. *Sergeant Thayer:* Michael E. Gold. *Lieutenant Ward:* Drew Taylor. *Sophie, the Kettle:* Barbara Tirrell. *Fred:* Tom Treadwell. *Grace Farrell:* COLLEEN DUNN. *Drake:* MichaelJohn McGann. *Mrs. Pugh:* Barbara Tirrell. *Cecille:* Sutton Foster. *Mrs. Greer:* Elizabeth Richmond. *Annette:* Kelley Swaim. *Oliver Warbucks:* CONRAD JOHN SCHUCK. *A Star to Be:* Sutton Foster. *Rooster Hannigan:* JIM RYAN. *Lily:* KAREN BYERS-BLACKWELL. *Bert Healy:* MichaelJohn McGann. *Fred McCracken:* Brad Wills. *Jimmy Johnson:* Tom Treadwell. *Sound Effects Man:* Michael E. Gold. *Bonnie Boylan:* Elizabeth Richmond. *Connie Boylan:* Kelley Swaim. *Ronnie Boylan:* Sutton Foster. *Oxydent "Hour of Smiles" Producer:* Jennifer L. Neuland. *H.V. Kaltenborn's Voice:* Bryan Young. *F.D.R.:* RAYMOND THORNE. *Ickes:* Brad Wills. *Howe:* Tom Treadwell. *Hull:* Drew Taylor. *Perkins:* Barbara Tirrell. *Morganthau:* MichaelJohn McGann. *Honor Guard:* Michael E. Gold. *Justice Brandeis:* Drew Taylor.

Hooverville-ites, Warbucks' Staff, New Yorkers: Sutton Foster, Michael E. Gold, MichaelJohn McGann, Jennifer L. Neuland, Elizabeth Richmond, Kelley Swaim, Drew Taylor, Barbara Tirrell, Tom Treadwell, Brad Wills.

1997.05

DREAM

A Musical Revue in Two Acts, 5 Scenes. Based on the lyrics of Johnny Mercer. Music by Harold Arlen, Rube Bloom, Hoagy Carmichael, Walter Donaldson, Duke Ellington, Ziggy Elman, Bernie Hanighen, Jerome Kern, Matt Malneck, Henry Mancini, Johnny Mercer, David Raksin, Victor Schertzinger, Billy Strayhorn, James Van Heusen, Harry Warren, Richard Whiting. Conceived by Louise Westergaard and Jack Wrangler. Directed and choreographed by Wayne Cilento. Scenic design, David Mitchell. Costume design, Ann Hould-Ward. Lighting design, Ken Billington. Sound design, Peter Fitzgerald. Musical supervision and vocal arrangements, Donald Pippin. Musical direction and vocal arrangements, Bryan Louiselle. Dance music arrangements, Jeanine Tesori. Orchestrations by Dick Lieb. Originally staged and developed at Tennessee Repertory Theatre, Nashville, Tennessee (Mac Pirkle, Artistic director; Brian J. Laczko, Managing director). Associate producers, Nicole Michelle Cuillo, Nancy LaVista, L. Michael Post, Elisa Sterling. Produced by Louise Westergaard, Mark Schwartz Bob Cuillo, Roger Dean, Obie Bailey, Stephen O'Neil, Abraham Salaman. Opened 3 April 1997 at the Royale Theatre and closed 6 July 1997 after 109 performances.

CAST: LESLEY ANN WARREN, JOHN PIZZARELLI, MARGARET WHITING, BROOKS ASHMANSKAS, JONATHAN DOKUCHITZ, CHARLES MCGOWAN, JESSICA MOLASKEY, DARCIE ROBERTS, Todd Bailey, Angelo Fraboni, Amy Heggins, Jennifer Lamberts, Nancy Lemenager, Susan Misner, Kevyn Morrow, Timothy Edward Smith, Ray Kennedy (John Pizzarelli Trio, piano), Martin Pizzarelli (John Pizzarelli Trio, bass). *Understudies/Swings:* Jeffrey Denman, Jody Ripplinger, Bill Szobody, Deborah Yates.

Act 1, Scene 1: Savannah—The Age of Innocence. *Scene 2:* Magnicificent Obsession—The Age of Decadence. *Scene 3:* Rainbow Room.

Act 2, Scene 1: Hollywood Canteen. *Scene 2:* Academy Awards.

ACT 1
Scene 1
"Dream"
 D. Roberts, J. Molaskey, N. Lemenager, Company
 (*Music by* Johnny Mercer.)
"Lazybones"
 A. Heggins, K. Morrow, J. Dokuchitz, Company
 (*Music by* Hoagy Carmichael.)
"On Behalf of the Travelling Salesmen"
 B. Ashmanskas, T. E. Smith
 (*Music by* Walter Donaldson.)
"Pardon My Southern Accent"
 L. A. Warren
 (*Music by* Matt Malneck.)
"You Must Have Been a Beautiful Baby" (from *HARD TO GET* film)
 C. McGowan, D. Roberts
 (*Music by* Harry Warren.)
"Have You Got Any Castles, Baby?" (from *VARSITY SHOW* film)
 J. Dokuchitz, L. A. Warren, Company
 (*Music by* Richard Whiting.)

"Goody, Goody"
 L. A. Warren, Company
 (*Music by* Matt Malneck.)
"Skylark"
 J. Molaskey
 (*Music by* Hoagy Carmichael.)
"The Dixieland Band"
 J. Dokuchitz, Company
 (*Music by* Bernie Hanighen.)
Scene 2
"I Had Myself a True Love"
 "I Wonder What Became of Me" (from *ST. LOUIS WOMAN*)
 L. A. Warren, D. Roberts
 (*Music by* Harold Arlen.)
"Jamboree Jones Jive"
 John Pizzarelli Trio, Company
 (*Music by* Johnny Mercer.)
"Fools Rush In"
 John Pizzarelli Trio, Company
 (*Music by* Rube Bloom.)
"Come Rain or Come Shine" (from *ST. LOUIS WOMAN*)
 B. Ashmanskas
 (*Music by* Harold Arlen.)
"Out of This World" (from film of the same name)
 D. Roberts
 (*Music by* Harold Arlen.)
"I Remember You" (from *THE FLEET'S IN* film)
 J. Molaskey
 (*Music by* Victor Schertzinger.)
"Blues in the Night" (from film of the same name)
 L. A. Warren
 (*Music by* Harold Arlen.)
"One for My Baby" (from *THE SKY'S THE LIMIT* film)
 M. Whiting
 (*Music by* Harold Arlen.)
Scene 3
"You Were Never Lovelier" (from film of the same name)
 J. Dokuchitz
 (*Music by* Jerome Kern.)
"Satin Doll"
 S. Misner, Men
 (*Music by* Billy Strayhorn and Duke Ellington.)
"I'm Old Fashioned" (from You Were Never Lovelier film)
 D. Roberts, J. Dokuchitz
 (*Music by* Jerome Kern.)
"Dearly Beloved" (from You Were Never Lovelier film)
 J. Dokuchitz, D. Roberts
 (*Music by* Jerome Kern.)
"This Time the Dream's on Me" (from Blues In The Night film)
 L. A. Warren, J. Pizzarelli, M. Whiting
 (*Music by* Harold Arlen.)
"Something's Gotta Give" (from Daddy Long Legs film)
 J. Molaskey
 (*Music by* Johnny Mercer.)
"Too Marvelous for Words" (from Ready, Willing and Able film)
 C. McGowan, Company
 (*Music by* Richard Whiting.)

ACT 2
Scene 1
"I Thought About You"
 J. Pizzarelli
 (*Music by* James Van Heusen.)
"And the Angels Sing"
 Orchestra
 (*Music by* Ziggy Elman.)
"The Fleet's In" (from film of the same name)
 Men
 (*Music by* Victor Schertzinger.)
"G.I. Jive"
 L. A. Warren, J. Molaskey, N. Lemenager
 (*Music by* Johnny Mercer.)
"I'm Doin' It for Defense" (from Star Spangled Rhythm film)
 D. Roberts
 (*Music by* Harold Arlen.)

"Tangerine" (from *THE FLEET'S IN* film)
B. Ashmanskas, Company
(*Music by* Victor Schertzinger.)
"Day In—Day Out"
M. Whiting
(*Music by* Rube Bloom.)
"Jeepers Creepers" (from *GOING PLACES* film)
John Pizzarelli Trio, Company
(*Music by* Harry Warren.)
"That Old Black Magic" (from *STAR SPANGLED RHYTHM* film)
L. A. Warren
(*Music by* Harold Arlen.)
"Laura" (from film of the same name)
J. Dokuchitz
(*Music by* David Raksin.)
"You Go Your Way"
Company
(*Music by* Johnny Mercer.)
"My Shining Hour" (from *THE SKY'S THE LIMIT* film)
M. Whiting, Company
(*Music by* Harold Arlen.)
Scene 2
"Hooray for Hollywood" (from *HOLLYWOOD HOTEL* film)
B. Ashmanskas, A. Fraboni, K. Morrow, T. E. Smith
(*Music by* Richard Whiting.)
"Accentuate the Positive" (from *HERE COME THE WAVES* film)
B. Ashmanskas, A. Fraboni, K. Morrow, T. E. Smith, N. Lemenager
(*Music by* Harold Arlen.)
"In the Cool, Cool of the Evening" (from *HERE COMES THE GROOM* film)
M. Whiting, John Pizzarelli Trio, Company
(*Music by* Hoagy Carmichael.)
"Charade" (from film of the same name)
(*Music by* Henry Mancini.)
"The Days of Wine and Roses" (from film of the same name)
J. Dokuchitz, J. Molaskey, Company
(*Music by* Henry Mancini.)
"Moon River" (from *BREAKFAST AT TIFFANY'S* film)
L. A. Warren
(*Music by* Henry Mancini.)
"On the Atchison, Topeka and the Santa Fe" (from *THE HARVEY GIRLS* film)
(*Music by* Harry Warren.) Company

1997.06 # TITANIC

A Musical in Two Acts, a Prologue and Twenty-Three Scenes. Story and book by Peter Stone. Music and lyrics by Maury Yeston. Directed by Richard Jones. Choreographed by Lynne Taylor-Corbett. Scenic and costume design, Stewart Laing. Lighting design, Paul Gallo. Sound design, Steve Canyon Kennedy. Orchestrations by Jonathan Tunick. Music supervision and direction, Kevin Stites. Executive producer, Dodger Management Group. Produced by Dodger Endemol Productions, Richard Pechter, The John F. Kennedy Center for the Performing Arts. Opened 23 April 1997 at the Lunt-Fontanne Theatre and closed 28 March 1999 after 804 performances.

CAST: *Officers and Crew of the R.M.S. Titanic: Captain E. J. Smith:* JOHN CUNNINGHAM. *First Officer William Murdoch:* David Costabile. *Second Officer Charles Lightoller:* John Bolton. *Third Officer William Pitman:* Matthew Bennett. *Frederick Barrett, Stoker:* Brian d'Arcy James. *Harold Bride, Radioman:* Martin Moran. *Henry Etches, First Class Steward:* Allan Corduner. *Frederick Fleet, Lookout:* David Elder. *Quartermaster Robert Hichens:* Adam Alexi-Malle. *Fourth Officer Joseph Boxhall:* Andy Taylor. *Chief Engineer Joseph Bell:* Ted Sperling. *Wallace Hartley, Orchestra Leader:* Ted Sperling. *Bandsman Bricoux:* Adam Alexi-Malle. *Bandsman Taylor:* Andy Taylor. *Stewardess Robinson:* Michele Ragusa. *Stewardess Hutchinson:* Stephanie Park. *Bellboy:* Mara Stephens.
Passengers aboard R.M.S. Titanic: First Class: J. Bruce Ismay: DAVID GARRISON. *Thomas Andrews:* MICHAEL CERVERIS. *Isidor Straus:* LARRY KEITH. *Ida Straus:* ALMA CUERVO. *J. J. Astor:* WILLIAM YOUMANS. *Madeline Astor:* Lisa Datz. *Benjamin Guggenheim:* Joseph Kolinski. *Mme. Aubert:* Kimberly Hester. *John B. Thayer:* Michael Mulheren. *Marion Thayer:* Robin Irwin. *George Widener:* Henry Stram. *Eleanor Widener:* Jody Gelb. *Charlotte Cardoza:* Becky Ann Baker. *J. H. Rogers:* Andy Taylor. *The Major:* Matthew Bennett. *Edith Corse Evans:* Mindy Cooper. And David Elder, Erin Hill, Theresa McCarthy, Charles McAteer, Jennifer Piech, Clarke Thorell.
Second Class: Charles Clarke: DON STEPHENSON. *Caroline Neville:* JUDITH BLAZER. *Edgar Beane:* BILL BUELL. *Alice Beane:* VICTORIA CLARK. And John Bolton, Mindy Cooper, David Costabile, David Elder.

Third Class: Kate McGovern: Jennifer Piech. *Kate Murphey:* Theresa McCarthy. *Kate Mullins:* Erin Hill. *Jim Farrell:* Clarke Thorell. And Adam Alexi-Malle, Becky Ann Baker, Matthew Bennett, Mindy Cooper, Alma Cuervo, Liza Datz, Jody Gelb, Kimberly Hester, Robin Irwin, Larry Keith, Joseph Kolinski, Michael Mulheren, Charles McAteer, Ted Sperling, Mara Stephens, Henry Stram, Andy Taylor, William Youmans.
On Shore: Frank Carlson: Henry Stram.
Swings: Melissa Bell, Kay Walbye, Jonathan Brody, John Jellison, Drew McVety.

The action takes place between 10-15 April 1912. All characters and events are based on fact.

Prologue: Harland & Wolff, Shipbuilders, Aberdeen, Scotland.

Act 1, Scene 1: Southampton: The Ocean Dock. *Scene 2:* Aboard the R.M.S. *Titanic.* The stern. *Scene 3:* The Dock. *Scene 4:* The Bridge and Boiler Room #6. *Scene 5:* The Saloon ("D") Deck. *Scene 6:* The First Class Dining Saloon. *Scene 7:* The Bridge. *Scene 8:* The Middle ("F") Deck. *Scene 9:* The Third Class Commissary. *Scene 10:* The Radio Room. *Scene 11:* The Boat Deck: First Class Promenade. *Scene 12:* "A" Deck. *Scene 13:* The Bridge: then The Promenade ("B") Deck, The Saloon ("D") Deck, The Middle ("F") Deck; The First Class Smoke Room and The Crow's Nest.

Act 2, Scene 1: First, Second, Third Class Corridors, and The Bridge. *Scene 2:* The First Class Grand Salon. *Scene 3:* ("E") Deck: A Stairwell. *Scene 4:* The Boat Deck. *Scene 5:* The Radio Room. *Scene 6:* At the Lifeboats. *Scene 7:* Portholes. *Scene 8:* The Upper Promenade ("A") Deck. *Scene 9:* The First Class Smoke Room. *Scene 10:* The Aftermath.

The Decks:

Boat Deck: The Bridge, the Radio Room, the Life Boats
Upper Promenade (A) Deck: First Class Promenade, First Class Reading and Writing Room, First Class Smoke Room
Promenade (B) Deck: First Class Promenade
Upper (C) Deck: Second Class Promenade
Saloon (D) Deck: First Class Dining Saloon; Second Class Promenade
Main (E) Deck: Second Class Cabins
Middle (F) Deck: Third Class Dining Saloon; Third Class Promenade
Lower (G) Deck: Third Class (Steerage) Dormitories
Orlop (H) Deck: Boiler Room #6

Act 1
Prologue: "In Every Age"
M. Cerveris
The Launching:
"How Did They Build Titanic?"
B. James
"There She Is"
B. James, M. Moran, D. Elder
"Loading Inventory"
J. Cunningham, Stevedores, Ship's Personnel
"The Largest Moving Object"
D. Garrison, J. Cunningham, M. Cerveris
"I Must Get On That Ship"
M. Bennett, Second and Third Class Passengers
"The First Class Roster"
M. Bennett, V. Clark
"Godspeed Titanic"
The Company
"Barrett's Song"
B. James
"What a Remarkable Age This Is!"
A. Corduner, Staff and First Class Diners
"To Be a Captain"
D. Costabile
"Lady's Maid"
J. Piech, T. McCarthy, E. Hill, Steerage
"The Proposal"
B. James
"The Night Was Alive"
M. Moran
"Hymn"
The Company
"Doing the Latest Rag"
T. Sperling, A. Alexi-Malle, A. Taylor, Company

"I Have Danced"
V. Clark, B. Buell

"No Moon"
D. Elder, Company

"Autumn"
T. Sperling

ACT 2

"Wake up, Wake up!"
A. Corduner, Stewards, Company

"Dressed in Your Pajamas in the Grand Salon"
The Company

"The Staircase"
C. Thorell, J. Piech, T. McCarthy, E. Hill

"The Blame"
D. Garrison, M. Cerveris, J. Cunningham

To the Lifeboats:

"Getting in the Lifeboat"
M. Mulheren, R. Irwin

"I Must Get on That Ship" (reprise)
D. Costabile, J. Bolton, A. Corduner, M. Stephens, Passengers

"Lady's Maid" (reprise)
C. Thorell

"Canons"
Company

"The Proposal" (reprise)
B. James

"The Night Was Alive" (reprise)
M. Moran

"We'll Meet Tomorrow"
D. Stephenson

"Still"
L. Keith, A. Cuervo

"To Be a Captain" (reprise)
A. Corduner

"Mr. Andrews' Vision"
M. Cerveris

"In Every Age" (reprise)
The Company

Finale
The Company

1997.07

STEEL PIER

An American Fable (Musical) in Two Acts, 20 Scenes. Book by David Thompson. Music by John Kander. Lyrics by Fred Ebb. Conceived by Scott Ellis, Susan Stroman and David Thompson. Directed by Scott Ellis. Choreography by Susan Stroman. Setting design, Tony Walton. Costume design, William Ivey Long. Lighting design, Peter Kaczorowski. Sound design, Tony Meola. Dance and incidental music arrangements, Glen Kelly. Projections, Wendall K. Harrington. Orchestrations by Michael Gibson. Musical direction and vocal arrangements by David Loud. Associate producer, Pace Theatrical Group. Produced by Roger Berlind. Opened 24 April 1997 at the Richard Rodgers Theatre and closed 28 June 1997 after 76 performances.

CAST (in order of appearance): *Bill Kelly*: DANIEL MCDONALD. *Rita Racine*: KAREN ZIEMBA. *Shelby Stevens*: DEBRA MONK. *Mick Hamilton*: GREGORY HARRISON. *Mr. Walker*: Ronn Carroll. *Buddy Becker*: Joel Blum. *Bette Becker*: Valerie Wright. *Johnny Adel*: Timothy Warmen. *Dora Foster*: Alison Bevan. *Happy McGuire*: Jim Newman. *Precious McGuire*: Kristen Chenoweth. *Luke Adams*: John C. Havens. *Mick's Picks*: Mary Illes, Rosa Curry, Sarah Solie Shannon. *Corky*: Casey Nicholaw. *Dr. Johnson*: John MacInnes. *Sonny*: Gregory Mitchell. *Preacher*: Adam Pelty. *The Flying Dunlaps*: Leigh-Anne Wencker, Jack Hayes, JoAnn M. Hunter, Robert Fowler, John MacInnis.

Steel Pier Marathon Couples: *Couple #39*: K. Ziemba, D. McDonald. *Couple #32*: D. Monk, J. C. Havens. *Couple #17*: V. Wright, J. Blum. *Couple #4*: K. Chenoweth, J. Newman. *Couple #26*: A. Bevan, T. Warmen. *Couple #46*: J. M. Hunter, G. Mitchell. *Couple #8*: D. L. Mauro, A. Blankenbuehler. *Couple #50*: E. Mills, J. Hayes. *Couple #68*: L. Wencker, R. Fowler. *Couple #71*: I. Gilliams, A. Pelty. *Couple #51*: S. S. Shannon, C. Nicholaw. *Couple #54*: M. Illes, B. Bradley. *Couple #65*: R. Curry, J. MacInnis. *Couple #18*: L. Wencker, J. Hayes. *Couple #41*: I. Gilliams, J. MacInnis. *Couple #11*: R. Curry, R. Fowler. *Couple #30*: E. Mills, A. Pelty. *Couple #25*: K. Chenoweth, G. Mitchell. *Couple #19*: M. Illes, C. Nicholaw. *Couple #14*: L. Wencker, B. Bradley. *Couple #40*: I. Gilliams, R. Fowler. *Couple #55*: S. S. Shannon, B. Bradley. *Couple #34*: R. Curry, J. Hayes. *Couple #62*: M. Illes, T. Warmen. *Swings*: Julio Augustin, Leslie Bell, Angelique Ilo, Scott Taylor.

Place: Steel Pier, Atlantic City, New Jersey. *Time*: August, 1933.

Act 1, Scene 1: The Beach/The Boardwalk. *Scene 2*: The Steel Pier Ballroom. *Scene 3*: Mick Hamilton's Office. *Scene 4*: The Rest Stations. *Scene 5*: The Steel Pier Ballroom. *Scene 6*: Behind the Bandstand. *Scene 7*: The Steel Pier Ballroom. *Scene 8*: Mick Hamilton's Office. *Scene 9*: The Steel Pier Ballroom. *Scene 10*: The Diving Horse Tank. *Scene 11*: The Steel Pier Ballroom/The Trenton Air Show.

Act 2, Scene 1: The Rest Stations. *Scene 2*: A Corridor near the Dance Floor. *Scene 3*: The Steel Pier Ballroom. *Scene 4*: Outside the Steel Pier Ballroom. *Scene 5*: The Rooftop of the Ballroom. *Scene 6*: The Steel Pier Ballroom. *Scene 7*: The Women's Rest Station. *Scene 8*: The Steel Pier Ballroom. *Scene 9*: The Women's Rest Station/Outside the Steel Pier.

ACT 1

Scene 1

"Waiting to Ride"
K. Ziemba

Scene 2

"Everybody Dance"
G. Harrison, M. Illes, R. Curry, S. S. Shannon

"Second Chance"
D. McDonald

Scene 4

"In Here"
D. Monk, J. Blum, J. Newman, V. Wright, J. C. Havens, K. Ziemba, T. Warmen, K. Chenoweth, A. Bevan, D. McDonald

Scene 5

"Montage I"
The Company

Scene 6

"Winning"
G. Harrison, Company

Scene 7

"Dance with Me"/"The Last Girl"
G. Harrison, K. Ziemba, D. McDonald, Company

"Montage II"
The Company

Scene 9

"Everybody's Girl"
D. Monk

Scene 10

"Wet"
K. Ziemba, D. McDonald

Scene 11

"Lovebird"
K. Ziemba

"Everybody Dance" (reprise)
G. Harrison, Company

ACT 2

Scene 1

"Leave the World Behind"
D. McDonlad, K. Ziemba, Company

Scene 3

"Montage III"
The Company

Scene 4

"Somebody Older"
D. Monk

Scene 5

"Running in Place"
K. Ziemba

Scene 6

"Lookin' for Love"
G. Harrison

"Two Little Words"
  K. Chenoweth, M. Illes, R. Curry, S. S. Shannon
"First You Dream"
  D. McDonald, K. Ziemba
Scene 8
  "Steel Pier"
  G. Harrison, K. Ziemba, M. Illes, R. Curry, S. S. Shannon
Scene 9
  "Steel Pier" (reprise)
  The Company

1997.08 ## THE LIFE

A Musical in Two Acts. Book by David Newman, Ira Gasman and Cy Coleman. Based on an original idea by Ira Gasman. Music by Cy Coleman. Lyrics by Ira Gasman. Directed by Michael Blakemore. Choreographed by Joey McKneely. Scenic design by Robin Wagner. Costumes design by Martin Pakledinaz. Lighting design by Richard Pilbrow. Sound design by Peter Fitzgerald. Music direction by Gordon Lowry Harrell. Orchestrations by Don Sebesky and Harold Wheeler. Dance and vocal arrangements by Cy Coleman and Doug Katsaros. Originally produced in New York City by Westbeth Theater Center (Arnold Engelman, Producing director). Produced by Roger Berlind, Martin Richards, Cy Coleman and Sam Crothers. Opened 26 April 1997 at the Ethel Barrymore Theatre and closed 7 June 1998 after 465 performances.

CAST (in order of appearance): *Jojo:* SAM HARRIS. *Carmen:* Lynn Sterling. *Chichi:* Sharon Wilkins. *Frenchie:* Katy Grenfell. *Tracy:* Judine Richárd. *Bobby:* Mark Bove. *Oddjob:* Michael Gregory Gong. *Silky:* Rudy Roberson. *Slick:* Mark Anthony Taylor. *Memphis:* CHUCK COOPER. *April:* Felicia Finley. *Snickers:* GORDON JOSEPH WEISS. *Lacy:* VERNEL BAGNERIS. *Queen:* PAMELA ISAACS. *Sonja:* LILLIAS WHITE. *Fleetwood:* KEVIN RAMSEY. *Mary, (Angel):* BELLAMY YOUNG. *Doll House Dancer:* Stephanie Michels. *Street Evangelists:* Judine Richárd, Rudy Roberson, Mark Anthony Taylor. *Cop:* Mark Bove. *Shoeshine:* Michael Gregory Gong. *Lou:* RICH HEBERT. *Shatellia:* Mark Anthony Taylor. *Enrique:* Rudy Roberson. *Monte Hustlers:* Mark Bove, Michael Gregory Gong, Mark Anthony Taylor.

Ensemble: Mark Bove, Felicia Finley, Chris Ghelfi, Michael Gregory Gong, Katy Grenfell, Stephanie Michels, Judine Richárd, Rudy Roberson, Lynn Sterling, Mark Anthony Taylor, Sharon Wilkins. *Swing:* Tracy Nicole Chapman.

Place: 42nd Street, (New York City.) *Time:* Then.

ACT 1
  "Check It Out!"
    The Company
  "Use What You Got"
    S. Harris, Company
  "A Lovely Day to Be Out of Jail"
    P. Isaacs, L. White
  "A Piece of the Action"
    K. Ramsey
  "The Oldest Profession"
    L. White
  "Don't Take Much"
    C. Cooper
  "Go Home"
    P. Isaacs, B. Young
  "You Can't Get to Heaven"
    P. Isaacs, L. White, Street Evangelists
  "My Body"
    K. Grenfell, S. Wilkins, J. Richárd, L. Sterling, L. White, P. Isaacs, F. Finley
  "Why Don't They Leave Us Alone"
    M. G. Gong, M. Bove, R. Roberson, M. A. Taylor, G. J. Weiss, F. Finley, L. Sterling, S. Wilkins, K. Grenfell, P. Isaacs, L. White, J. Richárd
  "Easy Money"
    B. Young, S. Harris, K. Ramsey
  "He's No Good"
    P. Isaacs
  "I'm Leaving You"
    P. Isaacs
  "The Hookers' Ball"
    V. Bagneris, Company
ACT 2
  "Step Right Up"
    R. Roberson, M. A. Taylor, M. G. Gong, M. Bove

"Mr. Greed"
  S. Harris, M. Bove, M. G. Gong, R. Roberson, M. A. Taylor
"My Way or the Highway"
  C. Cooper, P. Isaacs
"People Magazine"
  R. Hebert, B. Young
"We Had a Dream"
  P. Isaacs
"Use What You Got" (reprise)
  B. Young, R. Hebert, S. Harris
"'Someday' Is For Suckers"
  L. White, K. Grenfell, F. Finley, M. A. Taylor, L. Sterling, J. Richárd, S. Wilkins
"My Friend"
  P. Isaacs, L. White
"We Gotta Go"
  K. Ramsey, P. Isaacs
"Check It Out!" (reprise)
  Company

1997.09 ## JEKYLL & HYDE

A Musical in Two Acts, 26 Scenes. Based on the novel "The Strange Case of Dr. Jekyll and Mr. Hyde" by Robert Louis Stevenson. Conceived for the stage by Steve Cuden and Frank Wildhorn. Book and lyrics by Leslie Bricusse. Music by Frank Wildhorn. Scenic design by Robin Phillips and James Noone. Costume design by Ann Curtis. Lighting design by Beverly Emmons. Properties and set dressing by Christina Poddubiuk. Sound design by Karl Richardson and Scott Stauffer. Orchestrations by Kim Scharnberg. Musical director, Jeremy Roberts. Musical conductor, Jason Howland. Vocal arrangements by Jason Howland and Ron Melrose. Musical supervisor, Jeremy Roberts. Special effects design by Gregory Meeh. Fight coordinator, J. Allen Suddeth. Choreography by Joey Pizzi. Directed by Robin Phillips. Previous developmental productions by the Alley Theatre (Houston), 5th Avenue Musical Theatre (Seattle), and Theatre Under the Stars (Houston). Associate producer, Bill Young. Executive producer, Gary Gunas (PACE). Produced by PACE Theatrical Group (Allen Becker, Brian Becker, Miles Wilkin, Scott Zieger) and Fox Theatricals (Michael Leavitt, David Fay, Leon Strauss, Robert Baudendistel, Harvey Harris), in association with Jerry Frankel, Magicworks Entertainment (Joe Marsh, Lee Marshall, Brad Krassner) and the Landmark Entertainment Group (Tony Christopher, Gary Goddard). Opened 28 April 1997 at the Plymouth Theatre and closed 7 January 2001 after 1543 performances[17]

CAST (in order of appearance): *John Utterson:* GEORGE MERRITT. *Sir Danvers Carew:* BARRIE INGHAM. *Dr. Henry Jekyll:* ROBERT CUCCIOLI, ROBERT EVAN (Wednesday, Saturday matinees). *An Old Man,* in the mental hospital: David Chaney. *Mental Patients:* David Koch, Bill E. Dietrich. *Doctor:* Donald Grody. *Attendants:* Frank Mastrone, Charles E. Wallace. *Nurses:* Emily Scott Skinner, Jodi Stevens. *Kate,* a cockle seller: Leah Hocking. *Alice,* a scullery maid: Emily Scott Skinner. *Molly,* a fish gutter: Jodi Stevens. *Bet,* a scullery maid: Jodi Stevens. *Polly,* a scrubber woman: Bonnie Schon. *Mike,* a clerk: John Treacy Egan. *Albert,* a barman: Frank Mastrone. *Davie,* a barrow boy: David Chaney. *Ned,* a sailor: David Koch. *Bill,* a docker: Bill E. Dietrich. *Jack,* a beggar: Charles E. Wallace. *Mr. Simon Stride:* Raymond Jaramillo McLeod. *Rupert,* Bishop of Basingstoke: Michael Ingram. *The Right Honorable Archibald Proops:* Brad Oscar. *Lord Savage:* Martin Van Truren. *Lady Beaconsfield:* Emily Zacharias. *General Lord Glossop:* Geoffrey Blaisdell. *Emma Carew,* Jekyll's fiancée: CHRISTIANE NOLL. *First Gentleman:* Frank Mastrone. *Second Gentleman:* Brad Oscar. *Manservant at Sir Danvers':* David Chaney. *Under Footman:* Charles E. Wallace. *Grooms:* Bill E. Dietrich, John Treacy Egan. *Housemaids:* Emily Scott Skinner, Jodi Stevens. *Guinevere,* manageress of "The Red Rat": Emily Zacharias. *Lucy,* the main attraction at "The Red Rat": LINDA EDER. *Three Toughs,* of "The Red Rat": Bill E. Dietrich, David Koch, Charles E. Wallace. *Two Whores:* Emily Scott Skinner, Bonnie Schon. *Siegfried,* The Pianist at "The Red Rat": Geoffrey Blaisdell. *The Spider,* proprietor of "The Red Rat": Martin Van Treuren. *Sir Douglas:* Michael Ingram. *Sir Peter:* Brad Oscar. *Lord G:* Donald Grody. *Poole,* Jekyll's manservant: Donald Grody. *Edward Hyde,* Jekyll's "other half": ROBERT CUCCIOLI, ROBERT EVAN (Wednesday, Saturday matinees). *Dog:* B.J. A *Young*

---

[17]Subsequent national tour directed by David Warren, choreographed by Jerry Mitchell. Direction and scenic design based on Robin Phillips' original Broadway production. Dropped for subsequent tour were: "Good 'n' Evil," "His Work and Nothing More," "No One Knows Who I Am," "Obsession," "Dear Lord and Father of Mankind."

Girl, managed by Gwinny: Jodi Stevens. *A Newsboy*: Bill E. Dietrich. *A Priest*, at the Bishop's funeral: Frank Mastrone. *Mr Bisset*, an apothecary: David Chaney. *Policemen*: Michael Ingram, Geoffrey Blaisdell. *A Maitre d'Hotel*, at a social club: David Chaney. *A Doorman*, at the same: Charles E. Wallace. *Barrow Boys*: Michael Ingram, Brad Oscar, Geoffrey Blaisdell. *Boy Soprano*, at the wedding: LINDA EDER. *Bridesmaids*: Emily Scott Skinner, Jodi Stevens. *Priest at wedding*: David Chaney. *Curate*: Charles E. Wallace. *Choir Boy*: Bill E. Dietrich. *Swings*: Paul Hadobas, Rebecca Spencer.

(The action takes place in nineteenth century London.)

Act 1, Scene 1: A London Street. *Scene 2:* The Violent Ward, St. Jude's Hospital. *Scene 3:* A London Square. *Scene 4:* St. Jude's Hospital. *Scene 5:* The sidewalk, Regent's Park. *Scene 6:* Sir Danvers Carew's Home, Regent's Park. *Scene 7:* Dock Side, London's East End. *Scene 8:* Backstage at The Red Rat. *Scene 9:* The Red Rat. *Scene 10:* Harley Street. *Scene 11:* Dr. Jekyll's Consulting Room. *Scene 12:* Dr. Jekyll's Laboratory. *Scene 13:* The East End. *Scene 14:* Harley Street. *Scene 15:* Dr. Jekyll's Consulting Room, The Carew House. *Scene 16:* Dr. Jekyll's Consulting Room. *Scene 17:* The Embankment, Westminster.

Act 2, Scene 1: A London Street, Outside the Cathedral, A Pharmacy, Harley Street, Supper Club Entrance in the West End, Platform at Victoria Station. *Scene 2:* Dr. Jekyll's Laboratory. *Scene 3:* The Carew House, The River Bank. *Scene 4:* The Bridge, London's East End. *Scene 5:* Dr. Jekyll's Laboratory. *Scene 6:* Lucy's Room, above The Red Rat. *Scene 7:* Dr. Jekyll's Laboratory. *Scene 8:* Westminster. *Scene 9:* St. Anne's Church, Westminster.

ACT 1[18]

---

[18]National tour restaged in Two Acts, a Prologue and Sixteen Scenes, with scene and song changes as follows:

Prologue: A London Street. *Act 1, Scene 1:* The Violent Ward, St. Jude's Hospital. *Scene 2:* A London Square. *Scene 3:* St. Jude's Hospital. *Scene 4:* Sir Danvers Carew's Home, Regent's Park. *Scene 5:* The Red Rat. *Scene 6:* Outside Dr. Jekyll's Laboratory. *Scene 7:* The Streets of London. *Scene 8:* Jekyll's Study. *Scene 9:* Shabby Street near The Red Rat.

Act 2, Scene 1: London Montage. *Scene 2:* Dr. Jekyll's Laboratory. *Scene 3:* Outside The Red Rat. *Scene 4:* Dr. Jekyll's Laboratory. *Scene 5:* Lucy's Room, above The Red Rat. *Scene 6:* Dr. Jekyll's Laboratory. *Scene 7:* St. Anne's Church, Westminster.

ACT 1
Scene 1
  "Lost in the Darkness"
    [Dr. Jekyll]
  "I Need to Know"
    [Dr. Jekyll]
Scene 2
  "Façade"
    [Ensemble]
Scene 3
  "Board of Governors" (Jekyll's Plea)
    [Dr. Jekyll, Board of Governors]
  "Pursue the Truth"
    [Dr. Jekyll, John Utterson]
Scene 4
  "The Engagement Party"
    [Sir Danvers, Simon Stride, Emma Carew]
  "Take Me As I Am"
    [Dr. Jekyll, E. Carew]
  "Letting Go"
    [Sir Danvers, E. Carew]
Scene 5
  "Bring on the Men"
    [Lucy, Ensemble]
Scene 6
  "This Is the Moment"
    [Dr. Jekyll]
  "The Transformation"
    [Dr. Jekyll]
    (*Lyrics by* Steve Cuden, Leslie Bricusse and Frank Wildhorn.)
Scene 7
  "Alive!"
    [Edward Hyde, Lucy]
    (*Lyrics by* Steve Cuden, Leslie Bricusse and Frank Wildhorn.)

Scene 2
  "Lost in the Darkness"
    R. Cuccioli (Jekyll)
Scene 3
  "Façade"
    Ensemble
Scene 4
  "Jekyll's Plea"
    R. Cuccioli (Jekyll), Board of Governors
Scene 5
  "Façade" (reprise)
    Ensemble
Scene 6
  "Emma's Reasons"
    R. J. McLeod, C. Noll
  "Take Me As I Am"
    R. Cuccioli (Jekyll), C. Noll
Scene 7
  "Façade" (reprise)
    Ensemble
Scene 8
  "No One Knows Who I Am"
    C. Noll

Scene 8
  "Sympathy, Tenderness"
    [Lucy]
  "Someone Like You"
    [Lucy]
Scene 9
  "Alive!" (reprise)[Edward Hyde]

ACT 2
Scene 1
  "Murder, Murder!"
    [Ensemble]
    (*Lyrics by* Steve Cuden, Leslie Bricusse and Frank Wildhorn.)
Scene 2
  "Once Upon a Dream"
    [Emma Carew]
    (*Lyrics by* Steve Cuden, Leslie Bricusse and Frank Wildhorn.)
  "Streak of Madness"
    [Emma Carew, Dr. Jekyll]
  "In His Eyes"
    [Lucy, Emma Carew]
Scene 3
  "(It's a) Dangerous Game"
    [Lucy, Edward Hyde]
  "Façade" (reprise)
    [Spider, Ensemble]
Scene 4
  "The Way Back"
    [Dr. Jekyll]
Scene 5
  "A New Life"
    [Lucy]
  "Sympathy, Tenderness"
    [Edward Hyde]
Scene 6
  "Confrontation"
    [Dr. Jekyll and Edward Hyde]
Scene 7
  "Facade" (reprise)
    [Ensemble]
  "Final Transformation"
    [Dr. Jekyll]

Scene 9
  "Good 'N' Evil"
    L. Eder
Scene 11
  "This Is the Moment"
    R. Cuccioli (Jekyll)
Scene 13
  "Alive!"
    R. Cuccioli (Hyde)
Scene 15
  "His Work, and Nothing More"
    R. Cuccioli (Jekyll), G. Merritt, B. Ingram, C. Noll
Scene 16
  "Someone Like You"
    L. Eder
Scene 17
  "Alive!"
    R. Cuccioli (Hyde), Ensemble
ACT 2
Scene 1
  "Murder, Murder!"
    B. E. Dietrich, Ensemble
Scene 2
  "Once Upon a Dream"
    C. Noll
  "Obsession"
    R. Cuccioli (Jekyll)
Scene 3
  "In His Eyes"
    L. Eder, C. Noll
Scene 4
  "(It's a) Dangerous Game"
    R. Cuccioli (Hyde), L. Eder
Scene 5
  "The Way Back"
    R. Cuccioli (Jekyll)
Scene 6
  "A New Life"
    L. Eder
  "Sympathy, Tenderness"
    R. Cuccioli (Hyde)
Scene 7
  "Lost in the Darkness" (reprise)
    R. Cuccioli (Jekyll)
  "Confrontation"
    R. Cuccioli (as Jekyll and Hyde)
Scene 8
  "Facade" (reprise)
    Ensemble
Scene 9
  "Dear Lord and Father of Mankind"
    L. Eder (Boy Soprano)

1997.10 CANDIDE

A Revival of the Musical in Two Act[19]. Book adapted from Voltaire's satire (of the same name) by Hugh Wheeler[20]. Music by Leonard Bernstein. Lyrics by Richard Wilbur. Additional lyrics by Stephen Sondheim and John Latouche. Directed by Harold Prince. Choreography by Patricia Birch. Scenery designed by Clarke Dunham. Costumes designed by Judith Dolan.

[19]This revival first produced on Broadway 8 March 1974 at the Broadway Theatre for 740 performances; original production 1 December 1956 at the Martin Beck Theatre for 73 performances. For Synopsis of Scenes and Musical Numbers, see 1974 revival.
[20]Original book by Lillian Hellman.

Lighting designed by Ken Billington. Sound designed by Jonathan Deans. Music continuity and additional orchestrations by John Mauceri. Musical supervision and direction by Eric Stern. Orchestrations by Leonard Bernstein and Hershy Kay. Produced by LIVENT (U.S.) Inc. (Garth Drabinsky, Chairman). Opened 29 April 1997 at the Gershwin Theatre and closed 27 July 1997 after 103 performances.

CAST (in order of appearance): *Voltaire:* JIM DALE. *Candide:* JASON DANIELEY. *Paquette:* STACEY LOGAN. *Baroness Von Thunder:* Julie Johnson. *Baron Von Thunder:* MAL Z. LAWRENCE. *Cunegonde:* HAROLYN BLACKWELL, GLENDA BALKAN (alt.). *Maximilian:* BRENT BARRETT. *Hugo,* Maximilian's Servant: ARTE JOHNSON. *Old Lady:* ANDREA MARTIN. *Dr Pangloss:* JIM DALE. *Governor:* JIM DALE. *Radu,* A Bulgarian Soldier: ARTE JOHNSON. *Second Bugarian Soldier:* Paul Harman. *Don Isaachar, The Rich Jew:* ARTE JOHNSON. *Grand Inquisitor:* MAL Z. LAWRENCE. *Heresy Agent:* David Girolmo. *Judge Gomez:* ARTE JOHNSON. *Businessman:* JIM DALE. *Governor:* JIM DALE. *Governor's Aide:* Allen Hidago. *Columbo, A Slave Driver:* MAL Z. LAWRENCE. *Father Bernard:* ARTE JOHNSON. *Sheep One:* Nanne Puritz. *Sheep Two:* D'Vorah Bailey. *Lion:* Seth Malkin. *Pasha-Prefect of Constantinople:* MAL Z. LAWRENCE. *Turhan Bey, A Constantinople Gambler:* ARTE JOHNSON. *Second Gambler* (Police Chief): JIM DALE. *Sage:* JIM DALE. *Ensemble:* D'Vorah Bailey, Mary Kate Boulware, Diana Brownstone, Alvin Crawford, Chrisopher F. Davis, Sherrita Duran, Deanna Dys, David Girolmo, Paul Harman, Joy Hermalyn, Allen Hidalgo, Wendy Hilliard, Elizabeth Jimenez, Julie Johnson, Ken Krugman, Chad Larget, Shannon Lewis, Seth Malkin, Andrew Pacho, Nanne Puritz, Owen Taylor, Eric Van Hoven. *Swings:* Matthew Aibel, Rachel Coloff, Joseph P. McDonnell, Starla Pace.

ACT 1
  "Life Is Happiness Indeed"
    J. Dale, J. Danieley, H. Blackwell, B. Barrett, S. Logan
    (*Lyrics by* Stephen Sondheim.)
  "(The) Best of All Possible Worlds"
    J. Dale, J. Danieley, H. Blackwell, B. Barrett, S. Logan, Ensemble
  "Oh Happy We"
    J. Danieley, H. Blackwell
  "It Must Be So"
    J. Danieley
  "Westphalian Chorale"
    Ensemble
    (*Lyrics by* Leonard Bernstein.)
  "Glitter and Be Gay"
    H. Blackwell
  "Auto-da-fé" (What a Day)
    Full Company
    (*Lyrics by* John Latouche, Stephen Sondheim.)
  "Candide's Lament" (This World)
    J. Danieley
    (*Lyrics by* Stephen Sondheim.)
  "You Were Dead, You Know"
    J. Danieley, H. Blackwell
    (*Lyrics by* John Latouche.)
  "I Am (So) Easily Assimilated"
    A. Martin, Dons, Company
    (*Lyrics by* Leonard Bernstein.)
  Quartet Finale
    J. Danieley, H. Blackwell, J. Dale, A. Martin, Ensemble

ACT 2
  "Ballad of the New World"
    J. Danieley, Ensemble
  "My Love"
    J. Dale, B. Barrett
    (*Lyrics by* John Latouche, Richard Wilbur.)
  "Alleluia"
    Ensemble
  "Sheep Song"
    N. Puritz, D. Bailey, S. Malkin, S. Logan
    (*Lyrics by* Stephen Sondheim.)
  "Bon Voyage" (Schottische)
    J. Dale, Company
  "Quiet"
    A. Martin, J. Danieley, S. Logan
  "(The) Best of All Possible Worlds" (reprise)
    J. Danieley, S. Logan, A. Martin, N. Puritz, D. Bailey
  "What's the Use"
    M. Z. Lawrence, A. Johnson, J. Dale, Ensemble

"You Were Dead, You Know" (reprise)
J. Danieley, H. Blackwell
"Make Our Garden Grow"
Full Company

1997.11 THE WIZARD OF OZ

A Musical Spectacle in One Act, 16 Scenes[21]. Based on the novel of the same name by L. Frank Baum and the MGM film adaptation by Noel Langley, Florence Ryerson, Edgar Allan Woolf. Book by John Kane for the Royal Shakespeare Company. Music by Harold Arlen. Lyrics by E. Y. Harburg. Background music by Herbert Stothart. Directed by Robert Johanson. Choreographed by Jamie Rocco. Scenic design by Michael Anania. Costume design by Gregg Barnes. Lighting design by Timothy Hunter. Sound design by David R. Paterson. Musical director, Jeffrey Rizzo. Production originally presented at the Papermill Playhouse, New Jersey. Produced by Madison Square Garden Productions (Tim Hawkins, producer). Opened 15 May 1997 at the Theatre at Madison Square Garden and closed 8 June 1997 after 45 performances[22].

CAST (in order of appearance) In Kansas: *Dorothy*: JESSICA GROVÉ. *Toto*: Plenty. *Aunt Em*: JUDITH MCCAULEY. *Uncle Henry*: Roger Preston Smith. *Hunk*: LARA TEETER. *Hickory*: MICHAEL GRUBER. *Zeke*: KEN PAGE. *Almira Gulch*: ROSEANNE (BARR). *Professor Marvel*: GERRY VICHI.
In Oz: *Glinda, the Good Witch*: JUDITH MCCAULEY. *Mayor of Munchkinland*: Louis Carry. *Barristers*:Wendy Coates, Jonas Moscartolo. *Coroner*: Derrick McGinty. *The Wicked Witch of the West*: ROSEANNE (BARR). *The Scarecrow*: LARA TEETER. *The Tinman*: MICHAEL GRUBER. *The Cowardly Lion*: KEN PAGE. *The Wizard of Oz*: GERRY VICHI. *Nikko*, Commander of the Flying Monkeys: Martin Klebba. *Winkie General*: Roger Preston Smith.
Munchkins, Crows, Apple Trees, Poppies, Citizens of Oz, Flying Mionkeys and Winkies: Vivian Y. Bayubay, Maggie Keenan Bolger, Patrick Boyd, Kai Braithwaite, Lindsy Canuel, Casey Colgan, Christine DeVito, Chantele M. Doucette, Peter William Dunn, Danielle Lee Greaves, Gail Cook Howell, Heidi Karol Johnson, Martin Klebba, Benjamin E. Lear, Don Mayo, M. Kathryn Quinlan, Gemini Quintos, D. J. Salisbury, Dana Scarborough, Samantha Sensale, Evan Silverberg, Andrea Szucs, Christopher Trousdale, Wendy Watts. *Swings*: Lenny Daniel, Jamie Waggoner. *Children's Choirs*: Oaks School #3 (Oceanside, New York), Public School 312 (Brooklyn, New York), Public School 95 (Queens, New York), Terrill Middle School (Scotch Plains, New Jersey).

Scene 1: The Gale's Farm in Kansas. *Scene 2*: Professor Marvel's Wagon. *Scene 3*: The Gale's Farm. *Scene 4*: Munchkinland. *Scene 5*: A Cornfield. *Scene 6*: An Apple Orchard. *Scene 7*: A Wild Forest. *Scene 8*: A Field of Poppies. *Scene 9*: Outside the Gates of the Emerald City. *Scene 10*: Inside the Emerald City. *Scene 11*: The Wizard's Chamber. *Scene 12*: The Haunted Forest. *Scene 13*: Inside the Witch's Castle. *Scene 14*: The Wizard's Chamber. *Scene 15*: Inside the Emerald City. *Scene 16*: The Gale's Farm in Kansas.

MUSICAL NUMBERS
Scene 1
"Over the Rainbow"
J. Grové
Scene 3
The Cyclone
Scene 4
"Come Out, Come Out"
J. McCauley, J. Grové, Munchkins
"Ding Dong! The Witch Is Dead"
J. McCauley, L. Carry, W. Coates, J. Moscartolo, D. McGinty, Munchkins
"Follow the Yellow Brick Road"
J. Grové, Munchkins
Scene 5
"If I Only Had a Brain"
L. Teeter, J. Grové, Crows
"We're Off to See the Wizard"
J. Grové, L. Teeter
Scene 6
"If I Only Had a Heart"
M. Gruber, J. Grové, L. Teeter, Apple Trees

"We're Off to See the Wizard" (reprise)
J. Grové, L. Teeter, M. Gruber
Scene 7
"Lions and Tigers and Bears"
J. Grové, L. Teeter, M. Gruber
"If I Only Had the Nerve"/"We're Off to See the Wizard" (reprise)
K. Page, J. Grové, M. Gruber, L. Teeter
Scene 8
"Poppies"/"Optimistic Voices"
J. McCauley, J. Grové, L. Teeter, M. Gruber, K. Page, Roseanne, Poppies
Scene 9
"Optimistic Voices" (reprise)
Female Chorus
Scene 10
"(The) Merry Old Land of Oz"
J. Grové, L. Teeter, M. Gruber, K. Page, Guard, Citizens of Oz
"(If I Were) King of the Forest"
K. Page, J. Grové, M. Gruber, L. Teeter
Scene 12
"March of the Winkies"
Winkies
Scene 13
"Ding Dong! The Witch Is Dead" (reprise)
Winkies, J. Grové, K. Page, L. Teeter, M. Gruber
Scene 15
"Over the Rainbow" (reprise)
J. McCauley
Scene 16
Finale
Company

1997.12 KING DAVID

A Musical Concert in Two Acts, Ten Scenes. Book and lyrics by Tim Rice. Based on the story of the shepherd boy who was chosen to be King of Israel. Music by Alan Menken. Directed by Mike Ockrent. Scenic design by Tony Walton. Costume design by William Ivey Long. Lighting design by David Agress. Sound design by Jonathan Deans. Musical direction, vocal and incidental music arrangements by Michael Kosarin. Orchestrations by Douglas Besterman. Co-producer, Ritza B. Barath. Produced by Walt Disney Theatrical Productions and André Djaoui. Opened 18 May 1997 at the New Amsterdam Theatre and closed 23 May 1997 after 6 performances.

CAST (in order of appearance): *David*: MARCUS LOVETT. *Bathsheba*: ALICE RIPLEY. *Young Solomon*: Daniel James Hodd. *Joab*: STEPHEN BOGARDUS. *Samuel*: PETER SAMUEL. *Saul*: MARTIN VIDNOVIC. *Agag*: Timothy Robert Blevins. *Jesse*: Michael Goz. *Abner*: TIMOTHY SHEW. *Jonathan*: ROGER BART. *Michal*: JUDY KUHN. *Goliath*: BILL NOLTE. *Young Absalom*: Dylan Lovett. *Absalom*: ANTHONY GALDE. *Uriah*: Peter C. Ermides. *Abishag*: Kimberly JaJuan.
Ensemble: Mark Agnes, Joan Barber, Stephanie Bast, Robin Baxter, Kristen Behrendt, Timothy Robert Blevins, Benjamin Brecher, Timothy Breese, Kirsti Carnahan, Nick Cavarra, Philip A. Chaffin, Michael DeVries, Peter C. Ermides, Hunter Foster, Ray Friedeck, Anthony Galde, Michael Goz, Ellen Hoffman, Kimberly JaJuan, James Javore, Keith Byron Kirk, Ann Kittredge, David Lowenstein, Barbara Marineau, Donna Lee Marshall, Michael X. Martin, Karen Murphy, Bill Nolte, Ilysia Pierce, Ron Sharpe, Timothy Shew, Rachel Ulanet, Andrew Varela, Melanie Vaughan, Sally Wilfert, Laurie Williamson.

Act 1, Scene 1: Prologue. *Scene 2*: Samuel. *Scene 3*: Saul. *Scene 4*: Goliath. *Scene 5*: Jonathan. *Scene 6*: Exile.

Act 2, Scene 1: David the King. *Scene 2*: Bathsheba. *Scene 3*: Absalom. *Scene 4*: David's Final Days.

ACT 1
Scene 1
Prologue
M. Lovett, A. Ripley, D. J. Hodd, S. Bogardus, Chorus
Scene 2
"Israel and Saul"
S. Bogardus, P. Samuel, M. Vidnovic, Chorus
"Samuel Confronts Saul"
M. Vidnovic, P. Samuel, T. R. Blevins, Chorus

---

[21]THE WIZARD OF OZ was previously produced in a different adaptation 22 March 1989 at Radio City Music Hall for 37 performances.
[22]Performed an irregular performance schedule of 12 performances a week.

"Samuel Anoints David"
S. Bogardus, P. Samuel, M. Goz, M. Lovett, Chorus
Scene 3
"The Enemy Within"
M. Vidnovic, Chorus
"There is a View . . . "
S. Bogardus, T. Shew, M. Vidnovic, Chorus
"Psalm 8"
M. Lovett
"Genius from Bethlehem"
M. Vidnovic, M. Lovettt, T. Shew, S. Bogardus, R. Bart, J. Kuhn
Scene 4
"The Valley of Elah"
B. Nolte, T. Shew, S. Bogardus, M. Lovett, M. Vidnovic, Soldiers
"Goliath of Gath"
B. Nolte, M. Lovett, S. Bogardus, Soldiers, Chorus
"Sheer Perfection"
S. Bogardus, M. Vidnovic, M. Lovett, J. Kuhn
Scene 5
"Saul Has Slain His Thousands"
S. Bogardus, Chorus
"You Have It All"
M. Vidnovic, R. Bart, M. Lovett
"Psalm 23"
M. Vidnovic, M. Lovett
"You Have It All"/"Sheer Perfection" (reprises)
R. Bart, S. Bogardus, J. Kuhn, M. Lovett
Scene 6
"Hunted Partridge on the Hill"
S. Bogardus, M. Vidnovic, J. Kuhn, M. Lovett, Men
"The Death of Saul"
M. Vidnovic, R. Bart, P. Samuel, Chorus
"How Are the Mighty Fallen"
M. Lovett, Chorus

ACT 2
Scene 1
"This New Jerusalem"
M. Lovett, A. Galde, R. Bart, S. Bogardus, Chorus

"David and Michal"
M. Lovett, S. Bogardus, J. Kuhn
"The Ark Brought to Jerusalem"
M. Lovett, Chorus
"Never Again"
J. Kuhn, M. Lovett
Scene 2
"How Wonderful the Peace"
A. Galde, S. Bogardus, M. Lovett, Chorus
"Off Limits"
A. Ripley, M. Lovett, S. Bogardus
"Warm Spring Night"
M. Lovett
"When in Love"
A. Ripley
"Uriah's Fate Sealed"
M. Lovett, S. Bogardus, A. Ripley, Chorus
"Atonement"
M. Lovett, M. Vidnovic, P. Samuel, A. Ripley, Chorus
Scene 3
"The Caravan Moves On"
S. Bogardus, A. Galde, M. Lovett, M. Vidnovic, P. Samuel, Men
"Death of Absalom"
S. Bogardus, A. Galde
"Absalom My Absalom"
M. Lovett
Scene 4
"Solomon"
D. J. Hodd, S. Bogardus, M. Lovett, A. Ripley
"David's Final Hours"
J. Kuhn, M. Lovett, S. Bogardus, A. Ripley, B. Nolte, M. Vidnovic, R. Bart, P. Samuel, Chorus
"The Long Long Day"
M. Lovett
"This New Jerusalem"
D. J. Hodd, Company

1997–1998 SEASON

Emily Skinner and Alice Ripley in SIDE SHOW
Joan Marcus/Photofest

1997–1998 SEASON

1997.13   ## FOREVER TANGO

A Dance Revue in Two Acts. Created and directed by Luis Bravo. Musical direction and arrangements by Lisandro Adrover. Choreography by the dancers. Costume design, Argemira Affonso. Lighting design, Luis Bravo. Sound design, Tom Craft. Associate producer, Joe Watson. Produced by Steven Baruch, Richard Frankel, Thomas Viertel, Marc Routh, Jujamcyn Theatres, Interamerica, Inc. Opened 19 June 1997 at the Walter Kerr Theatre, closing 5 April 1998; moved 15 April 1998 to the Marquis Theatre, and closed 1 August 1998 after 453 performances.

CAST: *Dancers*: Miriam Larici, Diego DiFalco, Luis Castro and Claudia Mendoza, Carlos Gavito and Marcela Durán, Jorge Torres and Karina Piazza, Carlos Vera and Laura Marcarie, Guillermo Merlo and Cecilia Saia, Gabriel Ortega and Sandra Bootz, Pedro Calveyra and Nora Robles, Carolina Zokalski. *Singer*: Carlos Morel.
Musicians: *Bandoneóns*: Lisandro Adrover, Hector Del Curto, Carlos Niesi, Victor Lavallen. *Violins*: Humberto Ridolfi, Rodion Boshoer. *Viola*: Oscar Hasbun. *Cello*: Dino Quarleri. *Bass*: Silvio Acosta. *Piano*: Fernando Marzan. *Keyboard*: Mario Araolaza.

ACT 1

"Preludio del Bandoneón y la Noche"
> M. Larici, D. DiFalco
> *Conception*: Luis Bravo.
> A metaphorical scene composed and written from the mind of a bandoneón virtuoso. The image presented is of a bandoneón in search of passion. The metaphor represents both. The bandoneón—personified by the male dancer—gives birth to the woman, his dream and his ideal. She is born of his dream, but is lost and becomes the night, where he pursues her.

Overture
> Forever Tango Orchestra
> (*Music by* Lisandro Adrover.)

"El Suburbio"

This typical scene of the 1880s takes place in a brothel located between the barrio and the city where people of all classes meet. The choreography of the fight, as the two "compadritos" fight for a woman, asserts their power.

"A Los Amigos"
> Forever Tango Orchestra
> (*Music by* A. Pontier.)

"Derecho Viejo"
> K. Piazza, J. Torres
> (*Music by* E. Arolas.)
> A scene in the famous Hansen House in the early 1900s as the tango began to spread throughout Buenos Aires. People of all classes gathered to dance the prohibited "tango" at one of the city's most reputable dance spots.

"El Dia Que Me Quieras"
> C. Morel
> (*Music and Lyrics by* C. Gardel and A. Lepera.)
> The song is the romantic wish of the singer wishing for his unachievable dream. Carlos Gardel, Argentina's most famous singer, made this one of the tango's most popular songs of the 1930s.

"La Mariposa"
> L. Macarie, C. Vera
> (*Music by* O. Pugliese.)

"Comme Il Faut"
> S. Bootz, G. Ortega
> (*Music by* E. Arolas.)
> The tango, prohibted in Buenos Aires, was introduced to Parisian high society in the 1930s. Only after it was accepted by Parisian aristocracy was it finally welcomed by Buenos Aires' "good families." The tango eventually broke the barrier that separated Buenos Aires' rich elite from the lower classes near the port. The scene reflects years when the tango won legitimacy in Buenos Aires as it became the craze of Paris salons.

"Berretín"
> Forever Tango Orchestra
> (*Music by* P. Laurenz.)
> A piece to the essential emotion of the tanguero. The love that can not be because it does not exist. The infatuation.

"La Tablada"
> C. Mendoza, L. Castro
> (*Music by* F. Canaro.)
> This dance is in the typical style of the pretentious Argentine middle class. More than a tango, it is a playful exaggeration. By the 1920s, the street tough of the turn of century known as the compadron, had been replaced by the compadrito—a middle class imitation. The narcissistic gestures of the male dancer and his exaggerated "macho" act were part of the role but also underlined by his obsessive insecurity. The woman, in turn, plays the coquette.

"Milongueando En El '40"
> C. Saia, G. Merlo
> (*Music by* A. Pontier.)

"S.V.P."
> M. Durán, C. Gavito
> (*Music by* Astor Piazzolla.)
> Like the initial dream, this dance is a testimony to the encounter—or disencounter between man and woman. The dancers search for each other with the intensity born of passion. Yet, they walk away from each other at the end of the dance, in this allegory of the duality of passion and lust, search, and desperation and loss that is the tango, leaving us with the sense of incompleteness of the porteño.

"Responso"
> Forever Tango Orchestra
> (*Music by* A. Troilo.)

"Azabache"
> (Entire) Company
> (*Music by* E. M. Fracini.)
> In the early 1900s, the residents of San Telmo gathered to dance "Candombes." Descendants of African slaves brought to Rio de la Plata by the Conquistadores in the 1700s stayed behind, mixing their rhythms in this precursor of the milonga and the tango.

ACT 2

"Tanguera"
> N. Robles, P. Calveyra
> (*Music by* M. Mores.)
> From the 1950s, she was the woman with an attitude where only the most brazen dared to show their lust for life and their carnality dancing a tango.

"A Evaristo Carriego"
> M. Durán, C. Gavito
> (*Music by* E. Rovira.)
> The eternal fantasy. The impossibility of an older man with a younger woman. They meet again, and finally, he seduces her. This is the ultimate conquest. She has given herself to him, submitted to his will. Yet he is empty, incomplete. Having lost the challenge of her seduction, he remains aloof and distant. Once again—like the tango—he is alone.

"Payadora"
> Forever Tango Orchestra
> (*Music by* J. Plaza.)

"Quejas De Bandoneón"
> L. Marcarie, C. Vera
> (*Music by* J. de Dios Filiberto.)
> Bandoneón, instrument of tears and pain, solitude and melancholy. Its high wailing laments fill the nights of arrabales in Buenos Aires.

"Gallo Ciego"
> K. Piazza, J. Torres
> (*Music by* A. Bardi.)

"Balda Para un Loco"
> C. Morel
> (*Music by* Astor Piazzolla. *Lyrics by* H. Ferrer.)
> The eternal "crazy." Always in love; with a flower, with a cloud, with a wisp of air—he is the kite taken by the wind, floating in every direction and searching ... searching for what? The perfect flower, the music of a garbage can, a street horn or ... perhaps ... just to turn the corner and run in "Her." A toast to the "crazy!"

"La Cumparista"
> C. Saia, G. Merlo; K. Piazza, J. Torres; M. Durán, C. Gavito
> (*Music by* G. M. Rodriguez.)
> Three couples in this tribute to the most famous of all tangos.

"Jealousy"
> Forever Tango Orchestra
> (*Music by* Jacob Gade.)

"Felicia"
C. Mendoza, L. Castro
(*Music by* E. Saborido.)
The is a tribute to the "compadrito" born of Italian culture. Like the wise guys of the New York streets, these characters were also important to the Buenos Aires tango scene. The eternal cat and mouse game between man and woman.

"Adiós Nonino"
Forever Tango Orchestra
(*Music by* Astor Piazzolla.)
Astor Piazzolla wrote this mournful tribute to his father, Nonino, upon his death. It was first played during his funeral.

"Libertango"
C. Saia, G. Merlo
(*Music by* Astor Piazzolla.)

Romance del Bandoneón y la Noche: "Tus Ojos de Cielo"
M. Larici, D. DiFalco
(*Music by* Lisandro Adrover. *Conception:* Luis Bravo.)
And the metaphor continues between the bandoneón and its passion for the night. In the end, she returns to her origins in the emotions of the bandoneón.

"Lo Que Vendrá" (Finale)
(Dance) Company
(*Music by* Astor Piazzolla.)

1997.14 UMABTHA: THE ZULU MACBETH

A Revival of the Zulu Musical in Two Acts[1]. Written and directed by Welcome Msomi. Music by Welcome Msomi with traditional songs. Assistant director and vocal arranger, Thuli Dumakude. Choreographed by Thuli Dumakude, Mduduzi Zwane, Mafika Mgwazi. Original lighting by Mannie Manim; lighting for this production by France Mavana and Denis Hutchinson. Sound by Emmanuel McGarth. A Production of the Johannesburg Civic Theater. Produced by Lincoln Center Festival 97. Opened 21 July 1997 at the New York State Theatre and closed 27 July 1997 after 7 performances.

CAST: *Mabatha* (Macbeth), the King's cousin: THABANI PATRICK TSHANINI. *Ka Madonsela* (Lady Macbeth): DIEKENTSENG MNISI. *Dangane* (Duncan), the King: LAWRENCE MASONDO. *Donebane* (Donalbain), the Prince: BUYANI SHANGASE. *Makhiwane* (Malcolm), the Prince: MARTIN JWARA. *Mafudu* (Macduff), the King's cousin: Qond'okwakhe Mngwengwe. *Bhangane* (Banquo), the King's Induna/*Isipoki* (Spirit): Qed'umunyu Zungu. *Folose* (Fleance), Bhangane's son/*Isipoki* (Spirit): Shaun Dugen. *Isangoma 1, 2, 3* (Witches): S'bongile Ngqulunga, Promise S'thembile Jali, Mary-Anne Busi Mchunu.
Ka Makhawulana (Lady Macduff), Maludu's wife: Philile Sibiya. *Indodana* (Mafudu's son): Skhumbuzo Nsele. *Sidakwa*: Skhumbuzo Nsele. *The King's Guard*: Skhumbuzo Nsele. *Isipoki* (Spirit): Skhumbuzo Nsele. *Hoshweni* (Ross)/*Isipoki* (Spirit): Zam'akhule Ngiba. *Linalo* (Lennox)/*Isipoki* (Spirit): Cyprian Nzama. *Anganao* (Angus)/ *Inceku/Isipoki/uMbulali II*: Thakozani Makhoba. *Inceku/Dance Captain*: Mduduzi Zwane. *Imbongi*, the King's praise singer/*Isipoki*: Pa Vusi Chili. *Inyanga/Isipoki*: Thal'ithemba Mthembu. *Isalukozi*, the nurse: Thokozile Gumede. *Msimbithi*, the messenger: Philani Radebe. *KaMadonsela understudy I/Intombi* (Maiden): Bulelwa Maqungo. *KaMadonsela understudy II/Intombi* (Maiden): Gcinile Nkosi. *Mabatha understudy/Inceku* (King's servant): Vumisani Ndlavu. *Mafudu understudy/Inceku* (King's servant): Xolani Ncobeni.
Izintombi (Maidens): Thembelihle Chiliza, Bongiwe Hlophe, Nomthandaze Langa, Lady-Fair Mngadi, Thandekile Msomi, Ntombifuthi Nzama, Winile Sibiya. *Drummers*: William Lembede, Bernard Hlophe, Jacob Makatsanyane, David Msimango, Bong'nkosi Nxumalo. *Igoso*, Captain of the Warriors: Mafika Ngwazi. *Iphini* (understudies): Joseph Mngumi, Prince Gambushe, Zafuka Qwatubane. *Umbulali I* (Murderer)/*Ibutho* (Warrior): Mbongwa Njilo. *Umbali II* (Murderer)/ *Ibutho* (Warrior): Bhekisisa Mthembu. *Amabutho*, Warriors: Bhekumuthi Cele, Magazine Amon Cele, Mazwi Cele, Kufakwakhe Dlamini, France Duna, Zwelibanzi Gansa, Mbokodo Mhlongo, Sipho Mngadi, Bhekuyise Mnyandu, Mkhanyiselwa Mvundla, Xolani Ngubane, Alpheus Ngwazi, Nkosibuka Qumbisa.

MUSICAL NUMBERS[2]
"Bayeza Abangoma"
"Wathukuthela"

---

[1]A Production of the Johannesburg Civic Theatre (South Africa). Previously produced in New York Off-Broadway 9 April 1979 at the Entermedia Theatre for 41 performances. The 1979 production was performed in Two Acts, 21 Scenes.
[2]No Scenes or Musical Numbers listed in programs. List of musical numbers prepared from 1979 production and recordings.

"Wangishiya U Mabatha"
"Washumlilo"
"Qon Qo Qo"
"Umngcwabo"
"Udumo Lonke Mbathazeli"
"Kwasa Kusile"
"Shayani Izandla"
"Indlu Kamalandela"
"Bhula Wenyanga"
"Obani Labaya"

1997.15 1776

A Revival of the Musical in Two Acts, 7 Scenes[3]. Book by Peter Stone. Based on a conception of Sherman Edwards (about the making of the Declaration of Independence). Music and lyrics by Sherman Edwards. Directed by Scott Ellis. Musical staging by Kathleen Marshall. Settings designed by Tony Walton. Costumes designed by William Ivey Long. Lighting designed by Brian Nason. Sound designed by Brian Ronan. Orchestrations by Brian Besterman. Dance arrangements by Peter Howard. Musical direction by Paul Gemignani. Dialects by K. C. Ligon. Produced by the Roundabout Theatre Company (Todd Haimes, Artistic director; Ellen Richard, General manager). Opened 14 August 1997 at the Criterion Center Stage Right and closed 16 November 1997 after 109 performances; re-opened 3 December 1997 at the Gershwin Theatre under the commercial auspices of James M. Nederlander, Stewart F. Lane, Rodger Hess, Bill Haber, Robert Halmi, Jr., Dodger Endemol Theatrical Productions and Hallmark Entertainment, and closed 14 June 1998 after 224 additional performances. Total: 333 performances.

CAST: *Members of the Continental Congress: John Hancock*, President: Richard Poe. *Dr. Josiah Bartlett*, New Hampshire: Michael X. Martin. *John Adams*, Massachusetts: BRENT SPINER. *Stephen Hopkins*, Rhode Island: TOM ALDREDGE. *Roger Sherman*, Connecticut: John Herrera. *Lewis Morris*, New York: Tom Riis Farrell. *Robert Livingston*, New York: Daniel Marcus. *Reverend Jonathan Witherspoon*, New Jersey: Jerry Lanning. *Benjamin Franklin*, Pennsylvania: PAT HINGLE. *John Dickinson*, Pennsylvania: MICHAEL CUMPSTY. *James Wilson*, Pennsylvania: Michael Winther. *Caesar Rodney*, Delaware: Michael McCormick. *Colonel Thomas McKean*, Delaware: Bill Nolte. *George Read*, Delaware: Kevin Ligon. *Samuel Chase*, Maryland: Ric Stoneback. *Richard Henry Lee*, Virginia: Merwin Foard. *Thomas Jefferson*, Virginia: Paul Michael Valley. *Joseph Hewes*, North Carolina: David Lowenstein. *Edward Rutledge*, South Carolina: GREGG EDELMAN. *Dr. Lyman Hall*, Georgia: Brian Sutherland.
Charles Thomson, Congressional Secretary: Guy Paul. *Andrew McNair*, Congressional Custodian: MacIntyre Dixon. *A Leather Apron*: Joseph Cassidy. *Courier*: Dashiell Eaves. *Abigail Adams*: Linda Emond. *Martha Jefferson*: Lauren Ward. *Painter*: Ben Sheaffer.

1997.16 THE LAST EMPRESS

A Musical in Two Acts, a Prologue, Epilogue and 13 Scenes, in Korean. Book by Mun Yul Yi. Adaptation by Kwang Lim Kim. Music by Hee Gab Kim. Lyrics by In Ja Yang. Directed by Ho Jin Yun. Choreography by Byung Goo Seo. Costume design by Hyun Sook Kim. Scenic design by Dong Woo Park. Lighting design by Hyung O Choi. Sound by Ki Young Kim. Musical direction by Kolleen Park. Orchestrations and additional music by Peter Casey. Executive producer, Young Hwan Kim. Associate producers, Sang Ryul Lee, Su Mun Lee, Young il Yang, Woo Jong Lee. Produced by Arts Communications Seoul Company (A-Com). Opened 15 August 1997 at the New York State Theater and closed 24 August 1997 after 12 performances[4].

CAST: *Queen Min*, Ja-young Min: WONJUNG KIM, TAEWON KIM (alternate). *Taewongun*, King Kojung's Father: JAE HWAN LEE. *King Kojung*: HEE SUNG YU. *Inoue*, Ambassador of Japan: HEE JUNG LEE. *Itoh Hirobumi*, Prime Minister of Japan: MU YEOL CHOI. *Kye Hun Hong*, General Hong: MIN SOO KIM. *Miura*

---

[3]Originally produced in New York 16 March 1969 at the 46th Street Theatre for 1217 performances. For Synopsis of Scenes and Musical Numbers, see original 1969 entry. For this revival, an intermission was added after Scene 5; the reprise of "Yours, Yours, Yours" in the final scene was renamed "Compliments."
[4]Returned 31 July-23 August 1998 to the New York State Theatre for 29 additional performances; see separate entry in following season.

Goroh, Ambassador of Japan: SUNG KI KIM. *Chillyunggun*, Shaman: HYUN DONG KIM. *Four Japanese Merchants*: Hak Jun Kim, Do Kyung Kim, Ho Jin Kim, Sang Hoe Park. *Park, Kim*, Court Ladies: Young Ju Jeong, He Jung Kim. *Weber*, Russian Envoy: David DeWitt. *Sontag*, Russian Lady: Mary Jo Todaro. *Young Queen*: Anne Chun. *Prince*: Hyun Dong Kim. *Foreign Envoys*: Tom Schmid, Eric Morgan, Claire Beckman, Samantha Camp.

Chorus/Dancers: So Youn An, Geon Ryeong Bae, Eun Jung Cho, Im Su Choi, Se Hwan Choi, Jeong Ju Doh, Soon Chul Hyun, Young Ju Jeong, Woo Jeong Jeoung, Do Hyeong Kim, Hakjun Kim, Hak Muk Kim, Ho Jin Kim, Hyun Dong Kim, Soo Jin Kim, Young Ju Kim, Young Ok Kim, Min Kyeng Kwak, He Jeong Lee, Jae Gu Lee, Ji Eun Lee, Ji Youn Lee, Kyoung Woo Lee, Sung Ho Lee, Hyo Jung Moon, Sang Hoe Park, Seung Jun Seo, Hyo In Shin, Chan Youn.

ACT 1
Prologue
"Japan's Choice"
Scene 1
"The Day We Greet the New Queen"
Scene 2
"Taewongun's Regency"
"King & Courtesans"
"Your Highness Is Beautiful"
"Look on Me"
Scene 3
"Marketplace"
"Four Japanese Merchants"
"Fight at the Marketplace"
"I Am Hong Kye-Hun"
"A Wish for a Prince"
"The Shaman"
"Knock Knock"/"Song of the Soldiers"
Scene 4
"Grow Big and Strong, Dear Prince"
"You Are the King of Chosun"
"Until the World Needs Me Again"
Scene 5
"Kojong's Imperial Conference"
"It's All a Scheme"
"Seven Foreign Envoys"
"Four Japanese"
"Itoh's Ambition"
Scene 6
"Uprising of the Old Line Units"
"Military Mutiny of 1882"
"Back at the Seat of Power"
"I Miss You, My Dear Queen"
"We Shall Return"
"Wu Chang-Ching and Taewongun"
Scene 7
"Taewongun Is Taken to China"
"Inoe Threatens King Kojong"
"Queen Min's Return"
"We Shall Rise Again"
"Meeting of Japan's Chosun Policy"

ACT 2
Scene 1
"Dancing at the Grand Banquet"
"Come Celebrate Our Reforms"
"Elizabeth I of Chosun"
"Negotiations at the Grand Banquet"
"New Morning Is Dawning in Chosun"
"Isn't It Strange, Snowflakes Are Falling"
Scene 2
"You Shall Drink Miura's Wine"
"Tripartite Intervention and the Atami House Conspiracy"

"Isn't It Strange, Snowflakes Are Falling" (reprise)
Scene 3
"Chosun Is Tangun's Land"
"Miura's Audience with the King"
Scene 4
"The French Lesson"
"When the Wine Gets Cold"
"Welcome, Ladies"
"Ritual for Murder"
Scene 5
"Prince and Queen"
"Where Was It That We Met"
"You Are My Destiny"
"Take Away the Darkening Sky"
Scene 6
"Do Not Hurt the Queen"
"The Last of Hyong Kye-Hun"
"Queen Min Chased by the Beasts"
"Find the Queen, Kill the Fox"
"How Will I Live Now"
Epilogue
"Rise, People of Chosun"

1997.17 # SIDE SHOW

A Musical in Two Acts, Five Scenes. Book and lyrics by Bill Russell[5]. Music by Henry Krieger. Directed and choreographed by Robert Longbottom. Scenic design by Robin Wagner. Costume design by Gregg Barnes. Lighting design by Brian MacDevitt. Sound design by Tom Clark. Orchestrations by Harold Wheeler. Musical direction, dance and vocal arrangements by David Chase. Associate producer, Ginger Montel. Produced by Emanuel Azenberg, Joseph Nederlander, Herschel McKenna, Janice McKenna and Scott Nederlander. Opened 16 October 1997 at the Richard Rodgers Theatre and closed 3 January 1998 after 90 performances.

CAST (in alphabetical order): *Reptile Man*: Barry Finkel. *Bearded Lady*: Andy Gale. *Roustabout*: Billy Hartung. *Snake Girl*: Emily Hsu. *Fortune Teller*: Alicia Irving. *Fakir*: Devavand N. Janki. *The Boss*: KEN JENNINGS. *Jake*: NORM LEWIS. *Sixth Exhibit*: Judy Malloy. *Sheik*: David Masenheimer. *Terry Connor*: JEFF MCCARTHY. *Roustabout*: David McDonald. *Geek*: Philip Officer. *Buddy Foster*: HUGH PANARO. *Dolly Dimples*: Verna Pierce. *Violet Hilton*: ALICE RIPLEY. *Roustabout*: Jim T. Ruttman. *Daisy Hilton*: EMILY SKINNER. *Harem Girl*: Jenny-Lynn Duckling. *Harem Girl*: Susan Taylor. *Roustabout*: Timothy Warmen. *Harem Girl*: Darlene Wilson.

Reporters, Vaudevillians, the Follies Company, Party Guests, Radio Show Singers, the Movie Crew, Hawkers: Side Show Cast. *Swings*: John Paul Almon, Kelly Cole, John Frenzer, Michelle Millerick, J. Robert Spencer.

Act 1, Scene 1: The Midway. *Scene 2*: Vaudeville.

Act 1, Scene 1: The Follies. *Scene 2*: On the Road. *Scene 3*: The Texas Centennial.

ACT 1
Scene 1
"Come Look at the Freaks"
    K. Jennings, Company
"Like Everyone Else"
    E. Skinner, A. Ripley
"You Deserve a Better Life"
    J. McCarthy
"Crazy, Deaf and Blind"
    K. Jennings
"The Devil You Know"
    N. Lewis, Attractions
"More Than We Bargained For"
    J. McCarthy, H. Panaro

---

[5]Inspired by the lives of Daisy and Violet Hilton, Siamese twins who earned their living as musical performers in sideshows, carnivals, and vaudeville.

"Feelings You've Got to Hide"
E. Skinner, A. Ripley
"When I'm By Your Side"
E. Skinner, A. Ripley
"Say Goodbye to the Freak Show"
Company
Scene 2
"Overnight Sensation"
J. McCarthy, Reporters
"Leave Me Alone"
E. Skinner, A. Ripley
"We Share Everything"
E. Skinner, A. Ripley, Vaudevillians
"The Interview"
E. Skinner A. Ripley, Reporters
"Who Will Love Me As I Am"
E. Skinner, A. Ripley

ACT 2
Scene 1
"Rare Songbirds on Display"
Company
"New Year's Day"
J. McCarthy, H. Panaro, N. Lewis, E. Skinner, A. Ripley, Company
"Private Conversation"
J. McCarthy
Scene 2
"One Plus One Equals Three"
H. Panaro, E. Skinner, A. Ripley
"You Should Be Loved"
N. Lewis
"They Hardly Know I'm Around"
A. Ripley, H. Panaro, E. Skinner
"Tunnel of Love"
J. McCarthy, H. Panaro, E. Skinner, A. Ripley
Scene 3
"Beautiful Day for a Wedding"
K. Jennings, Hawkers
"She's Gone"
A. Ripley
"Marry Me, Terry"
E. Skinner
"I Will Never Leave You"
E. Skinner, A. Ripley
Finale
Company

1997.18 TRIUMPH OF LOVE

A Musical Comedy in Two Acts. Book by James Magruder. Based on (his own translation of) the French play of the same name by Pierre Marivaux. Music by Jeffrey Stock. Lyrics by Susan Birkenhead. Directed by Michael Mayer. Choreographed by Doug Varone. Set design by Heidi Ettinger. Costume design by Catherine Zuber. Lighting design by Paul Gallo. Sound design by Brian Ronan. Musical supervisor/arrangements, Michael Kosarin. Orchestrations by Bruce Coughlin. Music direction, Patrick Brady. Produced by Margo Lion, Metropolitan Entertainment Group (Jeff Rowland), Jujamcyn Theatres, in association with Pace Theatrical Group, The Baruch-Frankel-Viertel Group[6], Alex Hitz. Associate producers, Charles Kelman, Productions Inc., Marc Routh. Opened 23 October 1997 at the Royale Theatre and closed 4 January 1998 after 84 performances.

CAST (in order of appearance): Agis, a student of reason: Christopher Sieber. Hesione, his aunt, a philosopher: BETTY BUCKLEY. Dimas, the gardener: Kevin Chamberlin. Harlequin, the valet: Roger Bart. Hermocrates, a philosopher, brother to Hesione: F. MURRAY ABRAHAM. Princess Léonide: SUSAN EGAN. Corine, her maid servant: NANCY OPEL.

The action takes place in the garden retreat of the philosopher Hermocrates, an eighteenth century Greco-French topiary labyrinth.

---

[6]Steve Baruch, Richard Frankel, Thomas Viertel.

ACT 1
"This Day of Days"
B. Buckley, R. Bart, K. Chamberlin, C. Sieber, F. M. Abraham
"Anything"
S. Egan
"The Bond That Can't Be Broken"
S. Egan, C. Sieber
"Mr. Right"
N. Opel, R. Bart
(Music by Van Dyke Parks.)
"You May Call Me Phocion"
S. Egan, B. Buckley
"Mr. Right" (reprise)
N. Opel, K. Chamberlin
"Emotions"
F. M. Abraham, S. Egan
"The Sad and Sordid Saga of Cécile"
S. Egan, C. Sieber, N. Opel, R. Bart, K. Chamberlin
"Serenity"
B. Buckley
"Issue in Question"
C. Sieber
"Teach Me Not to Love You"
The Company
ACT 2
"Have a Little Faith"
N. Opel, S. Egan, R. Bart, K. Chamberlin
(Music by Michael Kosarin.)
"The Tree"
B. Buckley, F. M. Abraham
"What Have I Done?"
S. Egan
"Henchmen Are Forgotten"
R. Bart, K. Chamberlin, N. Opel
"Love Won't Take No for an Answer"
F. M. Abraham, B. Buckley, C. Sieber
"This Day of Days" (reprise)
S. Egan, C. Sieber, N. Opel, R. Bart, K. Chamberlin

1997.19 THE SCARLET PIMPERNEL

A Musical Adventure in Two Acts. Book and lyrics by Nan Knighton. Based on the novel of the same name by Baroness Orczy[7]. Music by Frank Wildhorn. Directed by Peter Hunt. Choreographed by Adam Pelty. Scenery by Andrew Jackness. Costumes by Jane Greenwood. Lighting by Natasha Katz. Sound by Karl Richardson. Fight director, Rick Sordelet. Orchestrations by Karl Richardson. Musical direction and vocal arrangements by Ron Melrose. Produced by Pierre Cossette, Bill Haber, Hallmark Entertainment, Ted Forstmann, with Kathleen Raitt. Opened 9 November 1997 at the Minskoff Theatre; closed 3-9 October 1998 for revision; resumed 10 October 1998 (see detail below) and closed 30 May 1999 after 640 performances[8].

CAST (in order of appearance): Madame St. Cyr: Marine Jahan. St. Cyr: Timothy Shew. Marie: Elizabeth Ward. Tussaud: Philip Hoffman. Dewhurst: James Judy. Chauvelin: TERRENCE MANN. Percy (Blakeney): DOUGLAS SILLS. Marguerite (St. Just): CHRISTINE ANDREAS. Lady Digby: Sandy Rosenberg. Lady Llewellyn: Pamela Burrell. Armand St. Just: GILLES CHIASSON. Ozzy: Ed Dixon. Farleigh: Allen Fitzpatrick. Leggett: Bill Bowers. Elton: Adam Pelty. Hal Hastings: William Thomas Evans. Ben: Dave Clemmons. Neville: R. F. Daley. Robespierre: David Cromwell. Grappin: Ken Labey. Coupeau: Eric Bennyhoff. Mercier: Jeff Gardner. Jessup: James Dybas. Prince of Wales: David Cromwell. French Mob and Soldiers/British Guest and Servants: Stephanie Bast, Nick Cavarra, Sutton Foster, Melissa Hart, Lauri Landry, Alison Lory, Don Mayo, Kevyn Morrow, Katie Nutt, Terry Richmond, Craig Rubano, Charles West. Fisherman: David Cromwell. Swings: Paul Castree, Sarah Knapp, Catherine LaValle, Ed Sala.

The action takes place from May into July, 1794, in England and France.

---

[7]Pen name for Mrs. Montague Barstow.
[8]Played a return engagement 10 September 1999 at the Neil Simon Theatre for 132 additional performances; for detail of revised production, see entry in 1999-2000 season.

ACT 1

"Madame Guillotine"
French Chorus
"Believe"
D. Sills, C. Andreas, British Chorus
"Vivez!"
C. Andreas, S. Rosenberg, P. Burrell, D. Sills, et al
"Prayer"
D. Sills
"Into the Fire"
D. Sills, His Men
"Falcon in the Dive"
T. Mann
'When I Look at You"
C. Andreas
"The Scarlet Pimpernel"
D. Sills, C. Andreas, G. Chiasson, S. Rosenberg, P. Burrell,
Servants
"Where's the Girl?"
T. Mann
"When I Look at You" (reprise)
D. Sills
"The Creation of Man"
D. Sills, D. Cromwell, Percy's Men
"The Riddle"
T. Mann, C. Andreas, D. Sills, et al

ACT 2

"They Seek Him Here"
D. Sills, D. Cromwell, S. Rosenberg, P. Burrell, et al
"Only Love"
C. Andreas
"She Was There"
D. Sills
"Storybook"
C. Andreas {Leontine}, French Chorus
"Where's the Girl?" (reprise)
T. Mann
"Lullaby"
Chorus Solos {Helene, Chloe}
"You Are My Home"
C. Andreas, G. Chiasson, French Prisoners
"Believe" (reprise)
Company

Reconstructed version previewed from 10 October 1998, opened 4 November 1998 at the Minskoff Theatre. (All credits same as above except the following.) Directed and choreographed by Robert Longbottom. Assistant choreographers, Tom Kosis and Darlene Wilson. Dance arrangements by David Chase. Executive producer, Tim Hawkins. Produced by Radio City Entertainment and Ted Forstmann, by arrangement with Pierre Cossette, Bill Haber, Hallmark Entertainment and Kathleen Raitt.

CAST (in order of appearance): *Marguerite (St. Just):* RACHEL YORK. *Chauvelin:* REX SMITH. *Percy (Blakeney):* DOUGLAS SILLS. *Marie:* Elizabeth Ward. *Armand St. Just:* JAMES BOHANEK. *Tussaud:* Philip Hoffman. *Coupeau:* Timothy Eric Hart. *Mercier:* Jeff Gardner. *Ozzy:* Harvey Evans. *Farleigh:* Tom Zemon. *Dewhurst:* James Judy. *Jessup:* James Dybas. *Ben:* Ken Land. *Hastings:* William Thomas Evans. *Neville:* Stephen Hope. *Leggett:* Douglas Storm. *Hal:* Michael Hance. *Robespierre:* David Cromwell. *Lady Digby:* Sandy Rosenberg. *Lady Llewellyn:* Pamela Burrell. *Prince of Wales:* Davd Cromwell. *Jailer:* T. Doyle Leverett.

French Mob and Soldiers/British Guest and Servants: Stephanie Bast, Nick Cavarra, Michael Halling, Marine Jahan, John Lathan, Alison Lory, Mark McGrath, Katie Nutt, Jessica Philips, Terry Richmond, Craig Rubano, Cynthia Sophiea, Charles West. *Swings:* Drew Garaci, Stephen Hope, Sarah Knapp, James Van Treuren.

The action takes place from May into July, 1794, in England and France.

ACT 1[9]

"Storybook"
R. York, French Ensemble
"Madame Guillotine"
R. Smith

[9]Dropped from first production: "Vivez," "Believe," "Only Love," and Lullaby. Added for reconstructed version: Wedding Dance, The Rescue, The Gavotte, The Duel, "I'll Forget You," "She Was There."

"Believe"
D. Sills, R. York, British Chorus
"You Are My Home"
D. Sills, R. York
Wedding Dance
Ensemble
"Prayer"
D. Sills
"Into the Fire"
D. Sills, the League
The Rescue
Ensemble
"Falcon in the Dive"
R. Smith
"When I Look at You"
R. York
"Where's the Girl?"
R. Smith
"You Are My Home" (reprise)
R. York, J. Bohanek
"The Creation of Man"
D. Sills, the League
"The Riddle"
R. Smith, R. York, D. Sills, et al

ACT 2

"The Scarlet Pimpernel"
D. Sills, R. York, Ball Guests
"They Seek Him Here"
D. Sills, S. Rosenberg, P. Burrell, D. Cromwell, et al
The Gavotte
Ensemble
"She Was There"
D. Sills
"Storybook" (reprise)
R. York, French Girls
"Where's the Girl?" (reprise)
R. Smith
"Into the Fire" (reprise)
The League
"I'll Forget You"
R. York
The Duel
D. Sills, R. Smith, R. York
"When I Look at You" (reprise)
D. Sills, R. York
"Into the Fire" (reprise)
Company

1997.20   THE LION KING

A Musical in Two Acts, 20 Scenes. Book by Roger Allers and Irene Mecchi. Based on the Disney film of the same name, screenplay by Irene Mecchi, Jonathan Roberts and Linda Woolverton. Music by Elton John. Lyrics by Tim Rice. Additional music and lyrics by Lebo M, Mark Mancina, Jay Rifkin, Julie Taymor, Hans Zimmer. Directed by Julie Taymor. Choreographed by Garth Fagan. Scenic design by Richard Hudson. Costume design by Julie Taymor. Mask and puppet design by Julie Taymor and Michael Curry. Lighting design by Donald Holder. Sound design by Tony Meola. Musical director, Joseph Church. Orchestrations by Robert Elhai, David Metzger, Bruce Fowler. Associate producer, Donald Franz. Produced by Walt Disney Theatrical Productions. Opened 13 November 1997 at the New Amsterdam Theatre and is still running at this time!

CAST (in order of appearance): *Rafiki:* TSIDII LE LOKA. *Mufasa:* SAMUEL E. WRIGHT. *Sarabi:* Geena Breedlove. *Zazu:* GEOFF HOYLE. *Scar:* JOHN VICKERY. *Young Simba:* SCOTT IRBY-RANNIAR. *Young Nala:* KAJUANA SHUFORD. *Shenzi:* TRACY NICOLE CHAPMAN. *Banzai:* STANLEY WAYNE MATHIS. *Ed:* KEVIN CAHOON. *Timon:* MAX CASELLA. *Pumbaa:* TOM ALAN ROBBINS. *Simba:* JASON RAIZE. *Nala:* HEATHER HEADLEY.

Ensemble Singers: Eugene Barry-Hill, Gina Breedlove, Ntomb'khona Dlamini, Sheila Gibbs, Lindiwe Hlengwa, Christopher Jackson, Vanessa A. Jones, Faca Kulu, Ron Kunene, Philip Dorian McAdoo, Sam McKelton, Lebo M, Nandi Morake. *Ensemble Dancers:* Camille M. Brown, Iresol Cardona, Mark Allan Davis, Lana

Gordon, Timothy Hunter, Michael Joy, Aubrey Lynch II, Karine Plantadit-Bageot, Endalyn Taylor-Shellman, Levensky Smith, Ashi K. Smythe, Christine Yasunaga. *Swings:* Lindiwe Dlamini, Sonya Leslie, Peter Anthony Moore, Nhlanhla Ngema, Rachel Tecora Tucker, Frank Wright II.

Act 1, Scene 1: Pride Rock. *Scene 2:* Scar's Cave. *Scene 3:* Rafiki's Tree. *Scene 4:* The Pridelands. *Scene 5:* Scar's Cave. *Scene 6:* The Pridelands. *Scene 7:* Elephant Graveyard. *Scene 8:* Under the Stars. *Scene 9:* Elephant Graveyard. *Scene 10:* The Gorge. *Scene 11:* Pride Rock. *Scene 12:* Rafiki's Tree. *Scene 13:* The Desert/The Jungle.

Act 2, Scene 1: Scar's Cave. *Scene 2:* The Pridelands. *Scene 3:* The Jungle. *Scene 4:* Under the Stars. *Scene 5:* Rafiki's Tree. *Scene 6:* The Jungle. *Scene 7:* Pride Rock.

ACT 1
Scene 1
  "Circle of Life"
    T. LeLoka, Ensemble
Scene 4
  "The Morning Report"
    G. Hoyle, S. Irby-Ranniar, S. E. Wright
Scene 6
  "I Just Can't Wait To Be King"
    S. Irby-Ranniar, K. Shuford, G. Hoyle, Ensemble
Scene 7
  "Chow Down"
    T. N. Chapman, S. W. Mathis, K. Cahoon
Scene 8
  "They Live in You"
    S. E. Wright, Ensemble
Scene 9
  "Be Prepared"
    J. Vickery, T. N. Chapman, S. W. Mathis, K. Cahoon, Ensemble
Scene 11
  "Be Prepared" (reprise)
    J. Vickery, Ensemble
Scene 13
  "Hakuna Matata"
    M. Casella, T. A. Robbins, S. Irby-Ranniar, J. Raise, Ensemble
ACT 2
Entr'acte
  "One By One"
    Ensemble
Scene 1
  "The Madness of King Scar"
    J. Vickery, G. Hoyle, S. W. Mathis, T. N. Chapman, K. Cahoon, H. Headley
Scene 2
  "Shadowland"
    H. Headley, T. LeLoka, Ensemble
Scene 4
  "Endless Night"
    J. Raize, Enseble
Scene 6
  "Can You Feel the Love Tonight"
    M. Casella, T. A. Robbins, J. Raize, H. Headley, Ensemble
  "He Lives in You" (reprise)
    T. LeLoka, J. Raize, Ensemble
Scene 7
  "King of Pride Rock"/"Circle of Life" (reprise)
    Ensemble

1997.22   A CHRISTMAS CAROL

A Revival of the Musical in One Act, 13 Scenes[10]. Book by Mike Ockrent and Lynn Ahrens. Based on the story of the same name by Charles Dickens. Music by Alan Menken. Lyrics by Lynn Ahrens. Directed by Mike Ockrent.

---

[10]Originally produced in New York 1 December 1994 at the Paramount, Madison Square Garden for 71 performances. For Synopsis of Scenes and Musical Numbers, see original 1994 production. For this year's and the 1995 and 1996 revivals the following changes were made:

Choreographed by Susan Stroman. Setting design by Tony Walton. Costume design by William Ivey Long. Lighting design by Jules Fisher and Peggy Eisenhauer. Sound design by Tony Meola. Projections by Wendall K. Harrington. Flying by Foy. Associate director, Steven Zweigbaum. Associate choreographer, Chris Peterson. Musical direction by Paul Gemignani. Orchestrations by Michael Starobin and Douglas Besterman. Dance arrangements and incidental music by Glen Kelly. Executive producer, Dodger Productions. Producer, Tim Hawkins. Presented by Madison Square Garden. Opened 18 November 1997 at the (Paramount) Theatre, Madison Square Garden and closed 4 January 1998 after 96 performances.

CAST (in order of appearance): *Beadle:* Del-Bourree Bach. *Mr. Smythe:* CHRIS VASQUEZ. *Grace Smythe:* Tavia Riveé Jefferson, Olivia Oguma *Scrooge:* HAL LINDEN, RODDY MCDOWALL. *Crachit:* TED GROSS. *Charity Men:* Roland Rusinek, Wayne Pretlow, Erik Stein. *Old Joe:* Kenneth McMullen. *Street Urchins:* Paul Franklin Dano, Anthony Blair Hall, Zoe Petkanas, Gemini Quintos, Joseph Louis Santos III, Evan Silverberg. *Mrs. Crachit:* Robin Baxter. *Tiny Tim:* Christopher Cordell, Patrick J. P. Duffey. *Poulterer:* Roland Rusinek. *Sandwichboard Man:* KEN PAGE. *Jonathon:* Adam Barruch, Christopher Marquette. *Lamplighter:* JOEL BLUM. *Blind Hag:* Debra Cardona. *Fred:* PAUL JACKEL. *Mrs. Mops:* Marilyn Pasekoff. *Ghost of Jacob Marley:* PAUL KANDEL. *Ghost of Christmas Past:* JOEL BLUM. *Lights of Christmas Past:* Matthew Baker, Christopher F. Davis, Sean Haythe, Sean Thomas Morrissey. *Judge:* Roland Rusinek. *Scrooge at 8 years:* Anthony Blair Hall, Joseph Louis Santos III. *Fan at 6:* Zoe Petkanas, Gemini Cardona. *Scrooge's Mother:* Debra Cardona. *Scrooge's Father:* Wayne Schroder. *Mr. Hawkins:* Kenneth McMullen. *Scrooge at 12 years:* Paul Franklin Dano, Evan Silverberg. *Fan at 10 years:* Elizabeth Lundberg, Jenell Slack. *Fezziwig:* Ray Friedeck. *Scrooge at 18 years:* Tom Stuart. *Young Marley:* Ken Barnett. *Mrs. Fezziwig:* Joy Hermalyn. *Emily:* Kate Dawson. *Fiddler:* Brad Bradley. *Ghost of Christmas Present:* KEN PAGE. *The Crachit Children:* Paul Franklin Dano, Elizabeth Lundberg, Sean Thomas Morrissey, Jenell Slack, Evan Silverberg. *Sally, Fred's wife:* Whitney Webster. *Ignorance:* Anthony Blair Hall, Joseph Louis Santos III. *Want:* Zoe Patkanas, Gemini Quintos. *Undertakers:* Ken Barnett, Wayne Schroder. *Ghost of Christmas Future:* CHRISTINE DUNHAM.

Business Men, Gifts, Ghosts and the People of London: Del-Bourree Bach, Matthew Baker Ken Barnett, Robin Baxter, Leslie Bell, Carol Bentley, Renée Bergeron, Brad Bradley, Debra Cardona, Candy Cook, Christopher F. Davis, Kate Dawson, Ray Friedrick, Peter Gregus, James Hadley, Sean Smythe, Joy Hermalyn, Paul Jackel, Louisa Kendrick, Carrie Kenneally, Donna Lee Marshall, Kenneth McMullen, Aiza M. Rosaio-Medina, Elizabeth Mills, Sean Thomas Morrissey, Christopher Nilsson, Marilyn Pasekoff, Meredith Patterson, Wayne Pretlow, Gail Pennington, Josef Reiter, Pamela Remler, Samuel Reni, Ronald Rusinek, Vikki Schnurr, Erik Stein, Tom Stuart, Chris Vasquez, Whitney Webster. *Swings:* Rachel Black, Alex Brumel, Dana Chechile, Alexander Dollin, Rob Donohoe, Carissa Farina, Brett Figliozzi, Matt L. Hedge, Yvonne Meyer, Rommy Sandhu, Scott Taylor, Cythia Thole, Jeff Williams. *Angels:* Park Middle School, M. S. 330; South Side Middle School, P.S. 95. *Red Children's Cast:* Adam Barruch, Alex Brumel, Dana Chechile, Christopher Cordell, Paul Franklin Dano, Anthony Blair Hall, Matt L. Hedge, Elizabeth Lundberg, Olivia Oguma, Zoe Petkanas.*Green Children's Cast:* Alexander Dollin, Patrick J. P. Duffey, Carissa Farina, Brett Figliozzi, Tavia Riveé Jefferson, Christopher Marquette, Gemini Quintos, Joseph Louis Santos III, Evan Silverberg, Jenell Slack.

1997.21   STREET CORNER SYMPHONY

A Retro Musical (Revue) in One Act. Conceived and staged by Marion J. Caffey. Scenic design by Neil Peter Jampolis. Costume design by Jonathan Bixby. Lighting design by Jules Fisher and Peggy Eisenhauer. Sound design by Jonathan Deans. Vocal arrangements by Michael McElroy. Musical supervision, orchestrations and dance music arrangements by Daryl Waters. Musical director, Lon Hoyt. Associate producer, Sharleen Cooper Cohen. Produced by Kenneth Waissman and Brian Bantry[11]. Opened 24 November 1997 at the Brooks Atkinson Theatre and closed 1 February 1998 after 80 performances.

Scene 1 and "The Years Are Passing By" were dropped.
Added to Scene 2 (former Scene 3) before "Street Song":
  "You Mean More to Me"
    N. Corley, M. Ballinger or P. Cravens
"The Years Are Passing By" (reprise) in former Scene 13 (new Scene 12) was replaced by:
  "London Town Carol"
    J. Fuchs or E. J. Newman
Note: The production played an irregular schedule of multiple daily performances.
[11]Kenneth Waissman withdrew as co-producer after the opening.

CAST (in order of appearance): *Clarence*: EUGENE FLEMING. *The Narrator/Cynthia*: CAROL DENNIS. *Jessie-Lee*: JOSE LLANA. *Sukki*: CATHERINE MORIN. *C.J.*: C. E. SMITH. *Debbie*: DEBRA WALTON. *Chip*: VICTOR TRENT COOK. *Susan*: STACY FRANCIS.

Scene: The Neighborhood—The 1960s. The Fantasy Concert—The 1970s.

MUSICAL NUMBERS

"Dancing in the Street"
　　The Guys
　　(*Music and Lyrics by* Marvin Gaye, William Stevenson and Ivy Jo Hunter.)
"Dance to the Music"
　　Company
　　(*Music and Lyrics by* Sylvester Stewart.)
"The Way You Do the Things You Do"
　　V. T. Cook, E. Fleming, the Guys
　　(*Music and Lyrics by* William Robinson and Robert Rogers.)
"I Wanna Know Your Name"
　　V. T. Cook, Company
　　(*Music and Lyrics by* Kenneth Gamble and Leon Huff.)
"My Boyfriend's Back"
　　C. Morin, D. Walton, S. Francis
　　(*Music and Lyrics by* Robert Feldman, Gerald Goldstein and Richard Gottehrer.)
"It's in His Kiss" (Shoop Shoop Song)
　　S. Francis, C. Morin, D. Walton
　　(*Music and Lyrics by* Rudy Clark.)
"Try a Little Tenderness"
　　E. Fleming
　　(*Music and Lyrics by* Harry Woods, Jimmy Campbell and Reg Connelly.)
"Respect"
　　C. Dennis, the Girls
　　(*Music and Lyrics by* Otis Redding.)
"Baby Workout"
　　J. Llana, D. Walton, Company
　　(*Music and Lyrics by* Alonzo Tucker and Jackie Wilson.)
"Dance Chant"
　　Company
　　(Based on an idea of and inspired by Andre De Shields.)
"Baby Workout" (reprise)
　　J. Llana, D. Walton, Company
"Unchained Melody" (from *UNCHAINED MELODY* film)
　　C. E. Smith
　　(*Music by* Alex North. *Lyrics by* Hy Zaret.)
"Psychedelic Shack"
　　Company
　　(*Music and Lyrics by* Norman J. Whitfield and Barrett Strong.)
"Cloud Nine"
　　Company
　　(*Music and Lyrics by* Norman J. Whitfield and Barrett Strong.)
"I Want to Take You Higher"
　　Company
　　(*Music and Lyrics by* Sylvester Stewart.)
"Ohio"
　　J. Lana, Company
　　(*Music and Lyrics by* Neil Young.)
"Machine Gun"
　　J. Llana
　　(*Music and Lyrics by* Jimi Hendrix.)
"American Pie"
　　C. Dennis
　　(*Music and Lyrics by* Don McLean.)
"Love's in Need of Love Today"
　　C. Dennis
　　(*Music and Lyrics by* Stevie Wonder.)
"Get Ready"
　　V. T. Cook, Company
　　(*Music and Lyrics by* William Robinson, Jr.)
"Want Ads"
　　S. Francis, C. Morin, D. Walton
　　(*Music and Lyrics by* J. Perry, B. Perkins and G. Johnson.)
"Love Train"
　　E. Fleming, the Guys
　　(*Music and Lyrics by* Kenneth Gamble and Leon Huff.)

"Oh Girl"
　　J. Llana, the Guys
　　(*Music and Lyrics by* Eugene Record.)
"Betcha By Golly Wow"
　　V. T. Cook, the Guys
　　(*Music and Lyrics by* Thomas Bell and Linda Creed.)
"Heaven Must Be Missing an Angel"
　　The Guys
　　(*Music and Lyrics by* Frederick J. Perren and Kenneth St. Lewis.)
"The Tracks of My Tears"
　　S. Francis
　　(*Music and Lyrics by* Marvin Tarplin, Warre Moore and William Robinson, Jr.)
"Can I?"
　　V. T. Cook
　　(*Music and Lyrics by* Herman Griffth and Hal Davis.)
"Midnight Train to Georgia"
　　C. Dennis, with E. Fleming, J. Llana, C. E. Smith
　　(*Music and Lyrics by* James D. Weatherly.)
"Mr. and Mrs. Jones"
　　The Guys
　　(*Music and Lyrics by* Kenneth Gamble, Leon Huff and Cary Gilbert.)
"Proud Mary"
　　D. Walton, C. Morin, S. Francis
　　(*Music and Lyrics by* John Fogerty.)
"Hold On I'm Coming"
　　C. E. Smith, E. Fleming
　　(*Music and Lyrics by* Isaac Hayes, Jr. and David Porter.)
"Soul Man"
　　C. E. Smith, E. Fleming
　　(*Music and Lyrics by* Isaac Hayes and David Porter.)
"End of the Road"
　　C. Dennis, Company
　　(*Music and Lyrics by* Antonio Reid, Daryl Simmons and Kenneth Edmonds.)
"Love Train" (reprise)
　　Company

1998.01　　RAGTIME

A Musical in Two Acts, 18 Scenes, a Prologue and Epilogue. Book by Terrence McNally. Based on the novel of the same name by E. L. Doctorow. Music by Stephen Flaherty. Lyrics by Lynn Ahrens. Directed by Frank Galati. Musical staging by Graciela Daniele. Production design by Eugene Lee. Costume design by Santo Loquasto. Lighting design by Jules Fisher and Peggy Eisenhauer. Sound design by Jonathan Deans. Musical director, David Loud. Orchestrations by William David Brohn. Dance music arranged by David Krane. Vocal arrangements by Stephen Flaherty. Projections designed by Wendall K. Harrington. Magic illusions by Franz Harary. Associate choreographger, Willie Rosario. Produced by LIVENT (US) Inc.[12] (Garth Drabinksy, Chairman; Myron I. Gottlieb, President). Opened 18 January 1998 at the Ford Center for the Performing Arts and closed 16 January 2000 after 861 performances.

CAST (in order of appearance): *The Little Boy*: Alex Strange. *Father*: MARK JACOBY. *Mother*: MARIN MAZZIE. *Mother's younger brother*: STEVEN SUTCLIFFE. *Grandfather*: Conrad McLaren. *Coalhouse Walker*: BRIAN STOKES MITCHELL. *Sarah*: AUDRA MCDONALD. *Booker T. Washington*: Tommy Hollis. *Tateh*: PETER FRIEDMAN. *The Little Girl*: Lea Michele. *Harry Houdini*: Jim Corti. *J. P. Morgan*: Mike O'Carroll. *Henry Ford*: Larry Daggett. *Emma Goldman*: JUDY KAYE. *Evelyn Nesbit*: LYNNETTE PERRY. *Stanford White*: Kevin Bogue. *Harry K. Thaw*: Colton Green. *Admiral Peary*: Rod Campbell. *Matthew Henson*: Duane Martin Foster. *Judge*: Mike O'Carroll. *Foreman*: Conrad McLaren. *Reporter*: Jeffrey Kuhn. *Kathleen*: Anne Kanengeiser. *Policeman*: Larry Dagget. *Doctor*: Bruce Winant. *Dirty Old Man*: Bruce Winant. *Policeman*: Colton Green. *Sarah's Friend*: Vanessa Townsell-Crisp. *Trolley Conductor*: Gordon Stanley. *Willie Conklin*: David Mucci. *Fireman*: Jeffrey Kuhn. *Brigit*: Anne. L. Nathan. *Conductor*: Joe Locarro. *Town Hall Bureaucrat*: Larry Dagget. *Second Bureaucrat*: Anne Kanengeiser. *Clerk*: Jeffrey Kuhn. *White Lawyer*: Brce Winant. *Black Lawyer*: Duane Martin Foster. *Reporters*: Rod Campbell, Godon Stanley. *Welfare Official*: Anne Kanengeiser. *Baron's Assistant*: Anne L. Nathan. *Gang Member*: Duane Martin Foster. *Pas de Deux*: Monica L. Richards, Keith LaMelle Thomas. *Charles S. Whitman*: Gordon Stanley. *Little Coalhouse*: (to be announced).

The Ensemble: Shaun Amyot, Darlene Bel Grayson, Kevin Bogue, Sondra M. Bonitto, Jamie Chandler-Torns, Ralph Deaton, Rodrick Dixon, Bernard Dotson, Donna Dunmire, Adam Dyer, Duane Martin Foster, Patty Goble, Colton Green, Elisa

[12]In September 1999 SFX Entertainment Group acquired the assets of LIVENT and became the show's producer.

Heinshohn, Anne Kanengeiser, Jeffrey Kuhn, Joe Langworth, Joe Locarro, Anne L. Nathan, Pachali Null, Mimi Quillen, Monica L. Richards, Orgena Rose, Gordon Stanley, Angela Teek, Keith LaMelle Thomas, Allyson Tucker, Leon Williams, Bruce Winant. *Swings:* Karen Andrew, John D. Baker, Mark Cassius, Dioni Michelle Collins, Mary Sharon Dziedzic, Valerie Hawkins, Kennl Hobson, Todd Thurston.

Act 1, Scene 1: Dock in the New York Harbor/At sea. *Scene 2:* A vaudeville theater, New York City. *Scene 3:* Mother's garden, New Rochelle. *Scene 4:* Ellis Island/Lower East Side. *Scene 5:* The Tempo Club/Harlem/Ford's assembly line. *Scene 6:* Railroad station, New Rochelle. *Scene 7:* Emerald Isle Firehouse. *Scene 8:* Mother's house, New Rochelle. *Scene 9:* A hillside above New Rochelle. *Scene 10:* A union hall in New York City/Lawrence, Massachusetts/A train. *Scene 11:* New Rochelle and New York City.

Act 2, Scene 1: The streets of New Rochelle/Mother's house. *Scene 2:* The Polo Grounds. *Scene 3:* Mother's house. *Scene 4:* Atlantic City/Million Dollar Pier/Boardwalk. *Scene 5:* Harlem/Coalhouse's hideout. *Scene 6:* The beach, Atlantic City. *Scene 7:* The Morgan Library, New York City.

ACT 1

Prologue
"Ragtime"
Company

Scene 1
"Goodbye, My Love"
M. Mazzie
"Journey On"
M. Jacoby, P. Friedman, M. Mazzie

Scene 2
"The Crime of the Century"
L. Perry, S. Sutcliffe, Ensemble

Scene 3
"What Kind of Woman"
M. Mazzie

Scene 4
"A Shtetl Iz Amereke"
P. Friedman, L. Michele, Immigrants
"Success"
P. Friedman, M. O'Carroll, J. Corti, Ensemble

Scene 5
"Gettin' Ready Rag"
B. S. Mitchell, Ensemble
"Henry Ford"
L. Daggett, B. S. Mitchell, Ensemble

Scene 6
"Nothing Like the City"
P. Friedman, M. Mazzie, A. Strange, L. Michele

Scene 8
"Your Daddy's Son"
A. McDonald
"New Music"
M. Jacoby, M. Mazzie, S. Sutcliffe, B. S. Mitchell, A. McDonald, Ensemble

Scene 9
"Wheels of a Dream"
B. S. Mitchell, A. McDonald

Scene 10
"The Night That Goldman Spoke at Union Square"
S. Sutcliffe, J. Kaye, Ensemble
"Lawrence, Massachusetts"
Ensemble
"Gliding"
P. Friedman

Scene 11
"Justice"
B. S. Mitchell, Ensemble
"President"
A. McDonald
"Till We Reach That Day"
V. Townsell-Crisp, B. S. Mitchell, J. Kaye, S. Sutcliffe, M. Mazzie, P. Friedman, Ensemble

ACT 2

Entr'acte
"Harry Houdini, Master Escapist"
A. Strange, J. Corti

Scene 1
"Coalhouse's Soliloquy"
B. S. Mitchell
"Coalhouse Demands"
Company

Scene 2
"What a Game"
M. Jacoby, A. Strange, Ensemble

Scene 3
"Atlantic City"
L. Perry, J. Corti
"New Music" (reprise)
M. Jacoby

Scene 4
"Atlantic City" (Part 2)
Ensemble
"The Crime of the Century"/"Harry Houdini, Master Escapist" (reprise)
L. Perry, J. Corti
"Buffalo Nickel Photoplay, Inc."
Baron Ashkenazy
"Our Children"
M. Mazzie, Baron Ashkenazy

Scene 5
"Sarah Brown Eyes"
B. S. Mitchell, A. McDonald
"He Wanted to Say"
J. Kaye, S. Sutcliffe, B. S. Mitchell, Coalhouse's Men

Scene 6
"Back to Before"
M. Mazzie

Scene 7
"Look What You've Done"
T. Hollis, B. S. Mitchell, Coalhouse's Men
"Make Them Hear You"
B. S. Mitchell

Epilogue
"Ragtime"/"Wheels of a Dream" (reprise)
Company

1998.02 # CAPEMAN

A Musical in Two Acts, 9 Scenes. Music, book and lyrics by Paul Simon. Book and lyrics by Derek Walcott. Directed and choreographed by Mark Morris[13]. Sets and costumes by Bob Crowley. Lighting by Natasha Katz. Sound by Peter J. Fitzgerald. Projections by Wendell K. Harrington. Orchestrator, Stanley Silverman. Musical director, Oscar Hernandez. Co-producer, Stephen Eich. Produced by Plenaro Productions (Dan Klores, Brad Grey, Edgar Dobie), James L. Nederlander, in association with Dreamworks Records and King World Productions Inc. Opened 29 January 1998 at the Marquis Theatre and closed 28 March 1998 after 68 performances.

CAST (in order of appearance): *Children's Choir:* Evan Newman, Sebastian Pérez, Khalid Rivera, Amanda Vacharat, Tara Ann Villaneuva. *Salvador Agrón,* (ages 36 to 42): RUBEN BLADES. *Carlos Apache:* Julio Monge. *Angel Soto:* Raymond Rodriguez. *Sal Agrón,* (ages 16 to 20): MARC ANTHONY. *Frenchy Cordero:* Ray Rodríguez-Rosa. *Babu Charlie Cruz:* Lugo. *Tony Hernandez:* Renoly Santiago. *Reverend González:* Philip Hernández. *Bernadette:* Sophia Salguero. *Yolanda:* Natascia A. Díaz. *Cookie:* Élan. *Salvi Agrón* (age 7): Evan Newman. *Aurea Agrón* (age 8): Tara Ann Villaneuva. *Esmeralda Agrón:* EDNITA NAZARIO. *Carmen:* Claudette Sierra. *Santero/Lazarus:* Nestor Sanchez. *Doo-Wop Group:* Milton Cardona, Ray De La Paz, Myrna Lynn Gomila, Roger Mazzeo, Frank Negrón, Yassmin Alers, Kia Joy Goodwin. *Mrs. Young:* Cass Morgan. *Mrs. Krzesinski:* Luba Mason. *Aurea Agrón* (age 30): Michelle Ríos. *Wahzinak:* Sara Ramirez. *First Inmate:* John Lathan. *The Warden:* John Jellison. *Virgil, a guard:* Stephen Lee Anderson. *The Master of Ceremonies:* Ray De La Paz.

Parade Attendants, Vendors, Parade Officials, People at the Asilo, Guests, Celebrants, People on New York Street, Inmates, Guards, Immigrants, Party Guests, Three Kings, Sales Clerks, Boys, Orphans, Border Patrol: Yassmin Alers, Stephen Lee Anderson,

---

[13]Additional directorial assistance by Jerry Zaks; choreographic assistance by Joey McNeeley.

Milton Cardona, René M. Ceballos, Tony Chiroldes, Ray De La Paz, Élan, José Joaquín García, Kia Joy Goodwin, Elise Hernández, John Jellison, Lugo, Luba Mason, Roger Mazzeo, Claudia Montiel, Marisol Morales, Frank Negrón, Evan Newman, Sebastian Perez, Mark Price, Sara Ramirez, Khalid Rivera, Ray Rodríguez-Rosa, Raymond Rodriguez, Ramón Saldaña, Claudette Sierra, Amanda Vacharat, Tara Ann Villanueva. *Swings:* Lada Boder, Osborn Focht, Jason Martinez.

Act 1, Scene 1: New York City, 1979. *Scene 2:* Puerto Rico, early 1950s. *Scene 3:* New York City, 1959. *Scene 4:* New York City, 1962.

Act 2, Scene 1: New York City, 1963. *Scene 2:* Various prisons in New York state, 1963-76. *Scene 3:* Fishkill Prison, 1976-77. *Scene 4:* The desert, Arizona, 1977. *Scene 5:* New York City, 1979.

ACT 1
Scene 1
  "El Coquí"
    Children's Choir, R. Blades
  "Puerto Rican Day Parade"
    Parade Singers, Ensemble
  "Born in Puerto Rico"
    R. Baldes, M. Anthony, J. Monge, R. Rodriguez, R. Rodríguez-Rosa, Lugo, R. Santiago, P. Hernández, N. Sanchez
Scene 2
  "In Mayagüez"
    R. Blades, E. Nazario, Nuns, Children
  "Carmen"
    E. Nazario, C. Sierra
  "The Santero"
    N. Sanchez, E. Nazario, Celebrants
  "Chimes"
    E. Nazario
  "Christmas in the Mountains"
    Three Kings, C. Sierra, E. Nazario, Guests
Scene 3
  "Satin Summer Nights"
    M. Anthony, S. Salguero, Élan, R. Santiago, Doo-Wop Group
  "Bernadette"
    M. Anthony, S. Salguero, Doo-Wop Group
  "The Vampires"
    R. Santiago, M. Anthony, J. Monge, R. Rodriguez, R. Rodríguez-Rosa, Lugo, Doo-Wop Group
  "Shopliftin' Clothes"
    M. Anthony, R. Santiago, Sales Clerks, J. Monge, Doo-Wop Group
  "Dance to a Dream"
    J. Monge, N. A. Díaz, S. Salguero, M. Anthony
  "Quality"
    S. Salguero, N. Díaz, Élan, R. Blades, Doo-Wop Group
  "Manhunt"
    R. Blades, J. Monge, M. Anthony, R. Santiago, Ensemble
  "Can I Forgive Him"
    E. Nazario, C. Morgan, L. Mason
  "Adios Hermanos"
    M. Anthony, R. Blades, M. Ríos, R. Santiago, S. Salguero, N. Díaz, N. Sanchez, Ensemble
Scene 4
  "Jesús Es Mi Señor"
    Congregants, P. Hernández, E. Nazario, M. Ríos, S. Salguero, N. Díaz, N. Sanchez

ACT 2
Scene 1
  "Sunday Afternoon"
    E. Nazario
Scene 2
  "Time is an Ocean"
    M. Anthony, R. Blades, E. Nazario
Scene 3
  "Wahzinak's First Letter"
    S. Ramirez
  "Killer Wants to Go to College"
    J. Lathan, J. Jellison, Inmates
  "Virgil"
    S. L. Anderson, J. Jellison

"My Only Defense"
  M. Anthony
"Wahzinak's Letter (Duet)"
  R. Blades, S. Ramirez
"Virgil and the Warden"
  J. Lathan, R. Blades, J. Jellison
Manhunt (Instrumental)
"Trailways Bus"
  N. Sanchez, S. Ramirez, R. Blades, Border Patrolman
Scene 4
  "The Mission"
    R. Blades, N. Sanchez
  "El Malecón"
    R. Blades
  "Children's Chimes"
    E. Newman, T. A. Villaneuva, P. Hernández, Orphans
  "You Fucked Up My Life"
    R. Rodriguez, Lugo, M. Anthony, R. Santiago, R. Rodríguez-Rosa, R. Blades, Doo-Wop Group
  "Lazarus"/"Last Drop of Blood"
    N. Sanchez, R. Blades, C. Morgan, Ensemble
  "Wahzinak's Last Letter"
    S. Ramirez
Scene 5
  "El Coquí" (reprise)
    Children's Choir, R. Blades
  "Tony Hernandez"
    R. Blades, R. Santiago
  "Carlos and Yolanda"
    R. De La Paz, M. Ríos, R. Blades, J. Monge, N. Díaz, Ensemble
  "Sal's Last Song"
    R. Blades, E. Nazario
  "Esmeralda's Dream"
    E. Nazario, M. Anthony, Doo-Wop Group

1998.03   THE SOUND OF MUSIC

A Revival of the Musical (Play) in Two Acts[14]. Book by Howard Lindsay and Russel Crouse. Suggested by the book "The Trapp Family Singers" by Maria Augusta Trapp. Music by Richard Rodgers. Lyrics by Oscar Hammerstein II. Directed by Susan Schulman. Choreography by Michael Lichtefeld. Scenery by Heidi Ettinger. Costumes by Catherine Zuber. Lighting by Paul Gallo. Sound design by Tony Meola. Orchestrations by Bruce Coughlin. Dance and incidental music arrangements by Jeanine Tesori. Original orchestrations by Robert Russell Bennett. Original choral and dance arrangements by Trude Rittmann. Musical direction by Michael Rafter. Associate producers, James D. Stern, Pace Theatrical Group. Produced by Hallmark, Steven Baruch, Richard Frankel, Thomas Viertel, Jujamcyn Theaters, in association with the Rodgers and Hammerstein Organzation, Charles Kelman Productions, Simone Genatt Haft, Marc Routh, Jay Binder, Robert Halmi, Jr. Opened 12 March 1998 at the Martin Beck Theatre and closed 20 June 1999 after 533 performances.

CAST (in order of appearance): *Sister Margaretta,* Mistress of Postulants: Jeanne Lehman. *Sister Berthe,* Mistress of Novices: Gina Ferrall *The Mother Abbess:* PATTI COHENOUR. *Sister Sophia:* Ann Brown. *Maria Rainer,* a Postulant at Nonnberg Abbey: REBECCA LUKER. *Captain Georg von Trapp:* MICHAEL SIBERRY. *Franz,* the butler: John Curless. *Frau Schmidt,* the housekeeper: Patricia Conolly. *Children of Captain von Trapp* (7): *Liesl:* SARA ZELLE. *Friedrich:* Ryan Hopkins. *Louisa:* Natalie Hall. *Kurt:* Matthew Ballinger. *Brigitta:* Tracy Alison Walsh. *Marta:* Andrea Bowen. *Gretl:* Ashley Rose Orr. *Rolf Gruber:* Dashiell Eaves. *Ursula,* a maid: Lynn C. Pinto. *Elsa Schraeder:* JAN MAXWELL. *Max Detweiler:* FRED APPLEGATE. *Herr Zeller:* Timothy Landfield. *Baron Elberfeld:* Gannon McHale. *Baroness Elberfeld:* Martha Hawley. *A New Postulant:* Laura Benanti. *Admiral von Schreiber:* Reno Roop.
  Neighbors and Servants of Captain von Trapp, Nuns, Novices, Postulants, Priests, Clerics, Nazis, Contestants in the Festival Concert: Anne Allgood, Joan Barber, Laura

---

[14]Originally produced in New York 16 November 1959 at the Lunt-Fontanne Theatre for 1443 performances. For Synopsis of Scenes (dropped for this revival), see original 1959 production. Dropped for this production: "An Ordinary Couple." The order of songs has been rearranged to correspond more closely to the film version.

Benanti, Ann Brown, Patricia Connoly, Gina Ferrall, Natalie Hgall, Martha Hawley, Kelly Cae Hogan, Siri Howard, Matt Loney, Patricia Phillips, Lynn C. Pinto, Reno Roop, Kristie Dale Sanders, Ben Sheaffer, Sara Zelle. *Swings*: Tad Ingram, Betsi Morrison, Margaret Shafer.

ACT 1

Preludium
 P. Cohenour, J. Lehmann, G. Ferrall, A. Brown, Nuns, Novices, Postulants
"The Sound of Music"
 R. Luker
"Maria"
 P. Cohenour, J. Lehmann, G. Ferrall, A. Brown
"I Have Confidence"[15]
 R. Luker
 (*Lyrics by* Richard Rodgers.)
"Do-Re-Mi"
 R. Luker, Children
"(You Are) Sixteen Going on Seventeen"
 S. Zelle, D. Eaves
"My Favorite Things"
 R. Luker, P. Cohenour
"How Can Love Survive?"
 J. Maxwell, F. Applegate
"The Sound of Music" (reprise)
 M. Siberry, Children, R. Luker
"So Long, Farewell"
 Children
"Morning Hymn"
 P. Cohenour, Nuns, Novices, Postulants
"Climb Every Mountain"
 P. Cohenour

ACT 2

Opening, Act 2
 F. Applegate, Children
"No Way to Stop It"
 J. Maxwell, F. Applegate, M. Siberry
"Something Good"[16]
 R. Luker, M. Siberry
Wedding Processional
 P. Cohenour, Nuns, Novices, Postulants
"Sixteen Going on Seventeen" (reprise)
 R. Luker, S. Zelle
"The Lonely Goatherd"
 R. Luker, M. Siberry, Children
"Edelweiss"
 M. Siberry, R. Luker, Children
"So Long, Farewell" (reprise)
 R. Luker, M. Siberry, Children
Finale Ultimo
 P. Cohenour, Nuns, Novices, Postulants

1998.04 CABARET

A Revival of the Musical in Two Acts[17]. Book (revised) by Joe Masteroff. Based on the play ("I Am a Camera") by John Van Druten and stories ("The Berlin Stories") by Christopher Isherwood. Music by John Kander. Lyrics by Fred Ebb. Directed by Sam Mendes. Co-directed and choreographed by Rob Marshall. Set designed by Robert Brill. Costumes designed by William Ivey Long. Lighting designed by Peggy Eisenhauer and Mike Baldassari. Sound designed by Brian Ronan. Musical director, Patrick Vaccariello. Orchestrations by Michael Gibson. Dance music arranged by David Krane. Original dance music arranged by David Baker. Produced by the Roundabout Theatre Company. Opened 19 March 1998 at the Kit Kat Klub (Henry Miller's Theatre); suspended 21 July 1998 and resumed 20 August 1998; moved 13 November 1998 to Studio 54 and is still running at this time!

CAST (in order of appearance): *Emcee*: ALAN CUMMING. *The Kit Kat Girls (6)*: *Rosie*: Christina Pawl. *Lulu*: Erin Hill. *Frenchie*: Joyce Chittick. *Texas*: Leenya Rideout. *Fritzie*: Michele Pawk. *Helga*: Kristin Olness. *The Kit Kat Boys (4)*: *Bobby*: Michael O'Donnell. *Victor*: Brian Duguay. *Hans*: Bill Szobody. *Herman*: Fred Rose. *Sally Bowles*: NATASHA RICHARDSON. *Clifford Bradshaw*: JOHN BENJAMIN HICKEY. *Ernst Ludwig*: DENIS O'HARE. *Customs Official*: Fred Rose. *Fraulein Schneider*: MARY LOUISE WILSON. *Fraulein Kost*: MICHELLE PAWK. *Rudy*: Bill Szobody. *Herr Schultz*: RON RIFKIN. *Gorilla*: Joyce Chittick. All other parts played by members of the company. *Swings*: Linda Romoff, Vance Avery.

The action takes place in Berlin, Germany, 1929-30.

ACT 1[18]

"Wilkommen"
 A. Cumming, The Kit Kat Klub
"So What?"
 M. L. Wilson
"Don't Tell Mama"
 N. Richardson, the Kit Kat Girls
"Mein Herr"[19] (from film *CABARET*)
 N. Richardson, the Kit Kat Girls
"Perfectly Marvelous"
 J. B. Hickey, N. Richardson
"Two Ladies"
 A. Cumming, E. Hill, M. O'Donnell
"It Couldn't Please Me More"
 M. L. Wilson, R. Rifkin
"Tomorrow Belongs to Me"
 A. Cumming
"Maybe This Time"[20] (from film *CABARET*)
 N. Richardson
"Money" (The Money Song)
 A. Cumming, the Kit Kat Girls
"Married"
 M. L. Wilson, R. Rifkin
"Tomorrow Belongs to Me" (reprise)
 M. Pawk, D. O'Hare, Company

ACT 2

"Kick Line" (dance)
 The Kit Kat Club
"Married" (reprise)
 R. Rifkin
"If You Could See Her"
 A. Cumming, J. Chittick
"What Would You Do?"
 M. L. Wilson
"I Don't Care Much" (from film *CABARET*)
 A. Cumming
"Cabaret"
 N. Richardson
Finale
 Company

1998.05 HIGH SOCIETY

A Musical Comedy in Two Acts, 16 Scenes. Book by Arthur Kopit. Based on the the play "The Philadelphia Story" by Philip Barry and the Turner Entertainment Company film "High Society." Music and lyrics by Cole Porter. Additional lyrics by Susan Birkenhead. Directed by Christopher Renshaw[21]. Musical staging by Lar Lubovitch[22]. Scenery by Loy Arcenas. Costumes by Jane Greenwood. Lighting by Howell Binkley. Sound by Tony Meola. Musical direction by Paul Gemignani. Dance music arrangements by Glen Kelly. Ocrhestrations by William David Brohn. Associate producer,

---

[15]Written for the film version.
[16]Written for the film version. Replaced "(An) Ordinary Couple" from the original production.
[17]Originally produced in New York 20 November 1966 at the Broadhurst Theatre for 1166 performances. For Synopsis of Scenes and Musical Numbers, see original 1966 production.

---

[18]Dropped for this revival: "Meeskite."
[19]Replaced "Telephone Song."
[20]Replaced "Why Should I Wake Up?"
[21]Program credit to the contrary, Des McAnuff assumed the direction during previews.
[22]Program credit to the contrary, Wayne Cilento assumed the choreography duing previews.

Kevin C. Whitman. Produced by Lauren Mitchell and Robert Gallus, Hal Luftig and Richard Samson, Dodger Endemol Theatricals in association with Bill Haber. Originally produced by American Conservatory Theater, San Francisco (Carey Perloff, Artistic director; Heather Kitchen, Managing director). Opened 27 April 1998 at the St. James Theatre and closed 30 August 1998 after 144 performances.

CAST (in order of appearance): *Polly*, Downstairs Maid: Jennifer Smith. *Arthur*, Butler: Glenn Turner. *Chester*, House Man: Barry Finkel. *Sunny*, Scullery Maid: Kisha Howard. *Stanley*, House Boy: Jeff Skowron. *Patsy*, Cook: Betsy Joslyn. *Peg*, Upstairs Maid: Dorothy Stanley. *Edmund*, Major Domo: William Ryall. *Margaret Lord*: LISA BANES. *Dinah Lord*: ANNA KENDRICK. *Tracy Lord*: MELISSA ERRICO. *Uncle Willie*: JOHN MCMARTIN. *C. K. Dexter Haven*: DANIEL MCDONALD. *Mike Connor*: STEPHEN BOGARDUS. *Liz Imbrie*: RANDY GRAFF. *George Kittredge*: MARC KUDISCH. *Seth Lord*: Daniel Gerroll. *Swings*: Vince Pesce, Solie Shannon.

The action takes place on a glorious weekend in June 1938 in Oyster Bay, Long Island.

Act 1, Scene 1: The Lord's Estate. *Scene 2*: Tracy's Room. *Scene 3*: The Veranda. *Scene 4*: The Nursery. *Scene 5*: The Grounds. *Scene 6*: The South Parlor. *Scene 7*: The Pavilion. *Scene 8*: The Pool.

Act 2, Scene 1: Uncle Willie's House, very early Sunday morning. *Scene 2*: Uncle Willie's Ballroom. *Scene 3*: Dexter's House. *Scene 4*: Uncle Willie's Kitchen. *Scene 5*: Uncle Willie's Grounds. *Scene 6*: The Lord's Pool. *Scene 7*: The Lord's Garden. *Scene 8*: The Terrace, the next morning.

ACT 1

Scene 1

"High Society"[23]
The Household Staff

Scene 2

"Ridin' High" (from *RED, HOT AND BLUE*)
M. Errico, Household Staff

Scene 3

"(I'm) Throwing a Ball Tonight"[24] (from *PANAMA HATTIE*)
L. Banes, M. Errico, J. McMartin, A. Kendrick

Scene 4

"Little One"
D. McDonald, A. Kendrick

Scene 5

"Who Wants To Be a Millionaire?"
S. Bogardus, R. Graff

Scene 6

"I Love Paris" (from *CAN CAN*)
A. Kendrick, M. Errico

Scene 7

"She's Got That Thing" (from *FIFTY MILLION FRENCHMEN*)
J. McMartin, D. McDonald, Company

Scene 8

"Once Upon a Time"[25]
M. Errico

"True Love"
D. McDonald, M. Errico

ACT 2

Scene 1

"High Society"[26] (reprise)
Household Staff

Scene 2

"Let's Misbehave"[27] (from *PARIS*)
M. Errico, J. McMartin, Company

"I'm Getting Myself Ready for You" (from *THE NEW YORKERS*)
J. McMartin, R. Graff

Scene 3

"Once Upon a Time"[28] (reprise)
D. McDonald

"Just One of Those Things" (from *JUBILEE*)
D. McDonald

Scene 4

"Well, Did You Evah?"[29]
Household Staff, M. Errico, J. McMartin, R. Graff

Scene 5

"You're Sensational"
S. Bogardus

"Say It with Gin" (from *THE NEW YORKERS*)
J. McMartin

"Ridin' High" (reprise)
L. Banes

Scene 6

"It's All Right with Me" (from *CAN CAN*)
M. Errico

Scene 7

"He's a Right Guy" (from *SOMETHING FOR THE BOYS*)
R. Graff

Scene 8

"(I Love You) Samantha"
D. McDonald

"True Love" (reprise)
M. Errico, D. McDonald

1998.06 THE WIZARD OF OZ

A Revival of the Musical Spectacle in One Act, 16 Scenes[30]. Based on the novel of the same name by L. Frank Baum and the MGM film adaptation by Noel Langley, Florence Ryerson, Edgar Allan Woolf. Book by John Kane (for the Royal Shakespeare Company), adapted by Robert Johanson. Music by Harold Arlen. Lyrics by E. Y. Harburg. Background music by Herbert Stothart. Directed by Robert Johanson. Choreographed by Jamie Rocco; associate choreographer, Donna Drake. Scenic design by Michael Anania. Costume design by Gregg Barnes. Lighting design by Timothy Hunter. Sound design by David R. Paterson, Mark Menard. Flying by Foy. Animals by William Berloni. Special effects by Ian O'Connor. Musical direction and additional orchestration by Jeff Rizzo. Production originally presented at the Papermill Playhouse, New Jersey (Angelo Del Rossi, Producer) Produced by Madison Square Garden Productions (Tim Hawkins, producer); presented by Cold-Eeze. Opened 6 May 1998 at the Theatre at Madison Square Garden and closed 31 May 1998 after 38 performances[31].

CAST (in order of appearance) In Kansas: *Dorothy*: JESSICA GROVÉ. *Toto*: Plenty. *Aunt Em*: JUDITH MCCAULEY. *Uncle Henry*: Bob Dorian. *Hunk*: LARA TEETER. *Hickory*: DIRK LUMBARD. *Zeke*: KEN PAGE. *Almira Gulch*: EARTHA KITT. *Professor Marvel*: MICKEY ROONEY.
In Oz: *Glinda*, the Good Witch: JUDITH MCCAULEY. *Mayor of Munchkinland*: Eugene Pidgeon. *Barristers*: Steve Babiar, Wendy Coates. *Coroner*: P.J. Terranova. *Lollipop Guild*: Martin Klebba, Mark Povinelli, Deborah Wilson. *The Wicked Witch of the West*: EARTHA KITT. *The Scarecrow*: LARA TEETER. *Crows*: Renee Bonadio, Christine DeVito, Martin Klebba. *Crow Voices*: D'Ambrose Boyd, Casey Colgan, Daniel Herron, D. J. Salisbury, Russell Warfield. *The Tinman*: DIRK LUMBARD. *Apple Trees*: Casey Colgan, Daniel Herron, D.J. Salisbury. *Apple Tree Voices*: Gail Cook Howell, Heidi Karol Johnson, Angela Robinson. *The Cowardly Lion*: KEN PAGE. *The Wizard of Oz*: MICKEY ROONEY. *Nikko*, Commander of the Flying Monkeys: Martin Klebba. *Winkie General*: Bob Dorian.
Munchkins, Crows, Apple Trees, Poppies, Citizens of Oz, Flying Monkeys and Winkies: Steve Babiar, Renee Bonadio, D'Ambrose Boyd, Bill Brassca, Wendy Coates, Casey Colgan, Christine DeVito, Kassandra Marie Hazard, Kristopher Michael Hazard, Daniel Herron, Gail Cook Howell, Shauna Markey, Andrea McCormick, Caroline McMahon, Eugene Pidgeon, Mark Povinelli, Angela Robinson, Mary Ruvolo, D. J. Salisbury, Kristi Sperling, Andrea Szücs, Leslie Stump-Vanderpool, P.J. Terranova, Russell Warfield, Wendy Watts, Deborah Wilson. *Swings*: Lenny Daniel, Donna Drake, Ron Gibbs, Jamie Waggoner. *Children's Choirs*.

---

[23]New lyrics by Susan Birkenhead.
[24]New lyrics by Susan Birkenhead.
[25]New lyrics by Susan Birkenhead.
[26]New lyrics by Susan Birkenhead.
[27]Additional lyrics by Susan Birkenhead.
[28]New lyrics by Susan Birkenhead.

[29]New lyrics by Susan Birkenhead.
[30]This adaptation previously produced in New York 15 May 1997 at the Theatre at Madison Square Garden for 45 performances. THE WIZARD OF OZ was previously produced in a different adaptation 22 March 1989 at Radio City Music Hall for 37 performances.
[31]Performed an irregular performance schedule of 12 performances a week.

1998–1999 SEASON

Members of the Company of FOSSE
Joan Marcus/Photofest

1998–1999 SEASON

AN EVENING WITH JERRY HERMAN

1998.07

A Musical Revue in Two Acts. Music and lyrics by Jerry Herman. Directed by Lee Roy Reams. Set design, Kenneth Foy. Lighting design, Ken Billington. Sound design, Peter Fitzgerald. Produced by Manny Kladitis and Jon Wilner, in association with Magicworks Entertainment and PACE Theatrical Group, Inc. Opened 28 July 1998 at the Booth Theatre and closed 23 August 1998 after 28 performances.

CAST: JERRY HERMAN (piano, vocals), LEE ROY REAMS (vocals), FLORENCE LACEY (vocals), Jered Egan (bass).

ACT 1

"Shalom" (from *MILK AND HONEY*)
F. Lacey, L. R. Reams

"Put On Your Sunday Clothes" (from *HELLO, DOLLY!*)
L. R. Reams

"It Only Takes a Moment" (from *HELLO, DOLLY!*)
L. R. Reams

"Before the Parade Passes By" (from *HELLO, DOLLY!*)
L. R. Reams

"So, Long Dearie" (from *HELLO, DOLLY!*)
F. Lacey

"Ribbons Down My Back" (from *HELLO, DOLLY!*)
F. Lacey

"Dancing" (from *HELLO, DOLLY!*)
F. Lacey

"Penny in My Pocket" (dropped from *HELLO, DOLLY!*)
L. R. Reams

"Hello, Dolly!" (from *HELLO, DOLLY!*)
F. Lacey, L. R. Reams, J. Herman

"It's Today" (from *MAME*)
L. R. Reams

"Gooch's Song" (from *MAME*)
J. Herman

"We Need a Little Christmas" (from *MAME*)
F. Lacey, J. Herman

"If He Walked into My Life" (from *MAME*)
F. Lacey

"Mame" (from *MAME*)
F. Lacey, L. R. Reams, J. Herman

ACT 2

"I Don't Want to Know" (from *DEAR WORLD*)
F. Lacey

"Movies Were Movies" (from *MACK AND MABEL*)
F. Lacey, L. Reams, J. Herman

"I Won't Send Roses" (from *MACK AND MABEL*)
L. R. Reams

"Hundreds of Girls" (from *MACK AND MABEL*)
J. Herman

"Time Heals Everything" (from *MACK AND MABEL*)
F. Lacey

"Tap Your Troubles Away" (from *MACK AND MABEL*)
L. R. Reams

"Movies Were Movies" (reprise)
F. Lacey, L. R. Reams, J. Herman

"I Belong Here" (from *THE GRAND TOUR*)
F. Lacey

"Mrs. S. L. Jacobowsky" (from *THE GRAND TOUR*)
L. R. Reams

"I'll Be Here Tomorrow" (from *THE GRAND TOUR*)
J. Herman

"La Cage Aux Folles" (from *LA CAGE AUX FOLLES*)
L. R. Reams

"Song on the Sand" (from *LA CAGE AUX FOLLES*)
F. Lacey

"I Am What I Am" (from *LA CAGE AUX FOLLES*)
L. R. Reams

"The Best of Times" (from *LA CAGE AUX FOLLES*)
F. Lacey, L. R. Reams, J. Herman

"The Best Christmas of All"[1] (from *MRS SANTA CLAUS*, Television)
F. Lacey, L. R. Reams

THE LAST EMPRESS

1998.08

A Revised Version of the Musical in Two Acts, a Prologue, Epilogue and 13 Scenes, in Korean[2]. Book by Mun Yol Yi. Adaptation by Kwang Lim Kim. Music by Hee Gab Kim. Lyrics by In Ja Yang. Directed by Ho Jin Yun. Choreography by Byung Goo Seo. Costume design by Hyun Sook Kim. Scenic design by Dong Woo Park. Lighting design by Hyung O Choi. Sound design by Ki Young Kim. Musical direction by Kolleen Park. Orchestrations and additional music by Peter Casey. Executive producer, Young Hwan Kim. Associate producers, Sang Ryul Lee, Su Mun Lee, Young Il Yang, Mun Yol Yi, Hee Hwan Lee, Woo Jong Lee. Produced by Arts Communications Seoul Company (A-Com). Opened 4 August 1998 at the New York State Theater and closed 23 August 1998 after 24 performances.

CAST: *Queen Min*, Ja-young Min: TAEWON YI KIM, WONJUNG KIM(alternate). *Taewongun*, King Kojung's Father (Regent): SUNG HOON LEE. *King Kojung*: HEE SUNG YU. *Inoue*, Ambassador of Japan: HEE JUNG LEE. *Itoh Hirobumi*, Prime Minister of Japan: YOUNG CHAE CHOI. *Kye Hun Hong*, General Hong: MIN SOO KIM. *Miura Goroh*, Ambassador of Japan: SUNG KI KIM. *Yuan Shi Kai*, Ambassador of China: SUNG HO LEE. *Chillyunggun*, Shaman: HYUN DONG KIM. *Park, Kim*, Court Ladies: Young Joo Jeong, Hyo Jung Moon. *German Envoy*: Peter Marinos. *(Lady) Sontag*, Russian Lady: Mary Jo Todaro. *French Envoy*: Paul Taylor. *Lady Underwood*: Marci Reid. *Weber*, Russian Envoy: Al Bundonis. *Prince*: Jung Hoon Woo. *(Child*: Eun Soo Jang. *Royal Tutor*: Kyoung Woo Lee. *Japanese Military Officer*: Hak Muk Kim.)

Chorus/Dancers: So Youn An, Ji Soo Choi, So Young Choi, Jeong Ju Doh, Eun Kyoung Han, Mi Kyung Jung, Do Hoon Kim, Do Hyeong Kim, Tai Hyun Kim, Ho Jin Kim, Sang Jin Kim, Young Ju Kim, Sun Mi Kim, Hak Muk Kim, Bong Soo Kim, So Yeoun Kim, So Young Kim, Sang Yun Kim, Yu Lim Kwak, Ji Eun Lee, Soo Hyoung Lee, Kyoung Woo Lee, Ji Youn Lee, Sang Ho Park, Yong Park, Sang Ryu, Beom Seok Seo, Eun Kyoung Yoon, Chan Yun.

ACT 1
Prologue

"Japan Has Chosen"
S. K. Kim, Japanese Assassins

Scene 1

"The Day We Greet the New Queen"
Sung Hoon Lee, H. S. Yu, T. Y. Kim, The Company

Scene 2

"Regency of the King's Father"
Sung Hoon Lee, Subjects

"Soft is the Spring Breeze"
H. S. Yu, Court Ladies

"Your Highness Is So Beautiful"
Court Ladies

"There Is a Star in My Heart"
T. Y. Kim

"The Examination for State Military Service"
M. S. Kim, Sung Hoon Lee, H. S. Yu, Applicants

"A Wish for a Prince"
T. Y. Kim, H. S. Yu, Sung Hoon Lee, Court Ladies, Subjects

"Shaman Rite (for Child Bearing)"
H. D. Kim, Shamans

Scene 3

"Open Up the Door"
Sung Hoon Lee, Foreigners

"Song of the Soldiers"
Soldiers, People

Battle Against the Foreigners

Scene 4

"Grow Big and Strong, Dear Prince"
Court Ladies

---

[1]Dropped during the run and replaced by:
"You I Like" (from *THE GRAND TOUR*)
J. Herman, L. R. Reams, F. Lacey
[2]First produced in New York 15 August 1997 at the New York State Theater for 12 performances.

"You Are the King of Chosun"
T. Y. Kim, H. S. Yu, Court Ladies
"Until the World Needs Me Again"
Sung Hoon Lee
Scene 5
"Kojong's Imperial Conference"
H. S. Yu, Subjects
"It's All a Scheme"
T. Y. Kim
"Seven Foreign Envoys"
Foreign Envoys
Scene 6
"New Army Unit, Old Army Unit"
Soldiers, Japanese Merchants
Military Mutiny of 1882
"Back at the Seat of Power"
Sung Hoon Lee
"I Miss You, My Dear Queen"
H. S. Yu
"We Shall Return to the Palace"
T. Y. Kim, H. S. Yu, M. S. Kim
Scene 7
"Regent and Chinese"
Sung Hoon Lee, Sung Ho Lee
"Regent Is Taken to China"
Sung Hoon Lee
"Inoue Threatens King Kojong"
H. J. Lee
"Queen Min's Return"
The Company
"We Shall Rise Again"
T. Y. Kim, H. S. Yu, M. S. Kim, The Company
"Meeting on Japan's Chosun Policy"
Y. J. Choi, S. K. Kim, Japanese Cabinet Members

ACT 2
Scene 1
Dance at the Grand Banquet
"Come Celebrate Our Reforms"
T. Y. Kim, H. S. Yu
"Queen Elizabeth of Chosun"
Wives of the Foreign Envoys
"Negotiations at the Grand Banquet"
H. J. Lee, T. Y. Kim, Foreign Envoys
"The Sun Is Rising in Chosun"
The Company
"Isn't It Strange, Snowflakes Are Falling"
E. S. Jang
Scene 2
"You Shall Drink the Wine Offered by Miura"
T. Y. Kim
"Tripartite Intervention and the Atami House Conspiracy"
T. Y. Kim, H. S. Yu, A. Bundonis, P. Marinos, P. Taylor, S. K. Kim, Assassins
"Isn't It Strange, Snowflakes Are Falling" (reprise)
E. S. Jang
Scene 3
"New Era for the Prince"
K. W. Lee, T. Y. Kim, H. S. Yu
"Miura's Audience with the King"
S. K. Kim, T. Y. Kim, H. S. Yu
Scene 4
"The Situation Has Quickly Been Changed"
S. K. Kim
"The Queen Is Studying French Today"
M. J. Todaro
"By the Time This Drink Gets Cold"
S. K. Kim, Assassins
"Welcome"
Wives of the Foreign Envoys, T. Y. Kim
Ritual for 'Fox Hunt'
Scene 5
"The Prince and Queen"
J. H. Woo, T. Y. Kim

"Where Was It That We Met"
T. Y. Kim, M. S. Kim
"You Are My Destiny"
M. S. Kim
"Thunder and Lightning"
J. H. Woo, T. Y. Kim
"Light Up My Darkest Night"
T. Y. Kim
Scene 6
"Do Not Harm the Queen"
Sung Hoon Lee, H. M. Kim
"The Last of General Hong"
M. S. Kim
"The Queen Is Hunted Down"
T. Y. Kim, Y. J. Jeong
"Find the Queen, Kill the Fox"
Assassins, Court Ladies
"How Will I Live From Now On?"
J. H. Woo
"The World After the Death"
H. S. Yu, Sung Hoon Lee
Epilogue
"Rise, People of Chosun"
T. Y. Kim, The Company

1998.09   RIVERDANCE

A Return Engagement of the Dance Revue in Two Acts, 13 Scenes[3]. Music by Bill Whelan. Poetry by Theo Dorgan. Directed by John McColgan. Choreography by Michael Flatley, Jean Butler, Colin Dunne, Tara Little, Moscow Folk Ballet Company, Paula Nic Cionnaith, Maria Pagés, Tarik Winston. Scenery and painted projections by Robert Ballagh. Costumes by Jen Kelly. Lighting by Rupert Murray. Sound by Michael O'Gorman. Orchestrations by Nick Ingman, Bill Whelan. Projection design by Chris Slinsgby. Musical director, Eoghan O'Neill. Produced by Abhann Productions Ltd. (Moya Doherty, producer). Opened 24 September 1998 (matinee) at the Radio City Music Hall and closed 11 October 1998 after 23 performances.

CAST: *Narrator:* JOHN CAVANAGH. *Solo Dancers:* EILEEN MARTIN, PAT RODDY. *Solo Singers:* KATIE MCMAHON.
   Irish Dance Troupe: Andrea Curley (Dance Captain), Dearbhail Bates (Assistant Dance Captain), Sarah Berry, Tara Barry, Natalie Biggs, Lorna Bradley, Martin Brennan, Rachel Byrne, Zeph Caissie, Melissa Convery, Jo Ellen Forsyth, Susan Ginnety, Paula Goulding, Sinéad Green, Gary Healy, Donnacha Howard, Sean Kelliher, Nicola Leonard, Matt Martin, Sorcha McCaul, Jonathan McMorrow, Paula McNelis, Joe Moriarty, Niall Mulligan, Aoibheann O'Brien, Niamh O'Brien, Ursula Quigley, Katie Regan, Ann Ryan, Lisa Ryan, Sheila Ryan, Anthony Savage, Anthony Sharkey, Ryan Sheridan, Claire Usher, Leanda Ward. *Firedance/Andalucia:* Nuria Brisa, Marta Jiménez Luis, Aranxta Jurado. *Moscow Folk Ballet:* Serguei Iakoubov, Svetlana Kossoroukova, Olena Krutsenko, Tatiana Nedostop, Iouri Oustiougov, Iouri Shishkine, Ilia Stretsov, Marina Taranda. *Riverdance Singers:* Derek Byrne, Derek Collins, Patrick Connolly, Jennifer Curran, Tony Davoren (Soloist—Oscail an Doras), Johanna Higgins, Maire Lang, Denise O'Kane, Cathal Synnott (choirmaster). *Trading Taps:* Robert Reed, Toby Harris, Donnell A. Russell. *Heal Their Hearts:* Charles Gray. *Slip into Spring/Home and the Heartland:* Eileen Ivers (Fiddle Player). *Drummers:* Abraham Doron, Vinny Ozborne, Darren Smith, David Tilly.

1998.10   SWAN LAKE

A Ballet in Two Acts, a Prologue and 11 Scenes. Music by Peter Ilyich Tchaikovsky. Directed and choreographed by Matthew Bourne. (Scenery and costumes) Designed by Lez Brotherson. Lighting by Rick Fisher. Musical director, David Frame. Orchestrations by David Cullen. Sound by Mark Menard. Conductor, David Frame. Associate conductor, Jack Buckhannan. Executive Management (North America), Martin McCallum and Alan Wasser. Produced by Adventures in Motion Pictures (Katharine Doré, Producing Director) and Cameron Mackintosh. Opened 8 October 1998 at the Neil Simon Theatre and closed 24 January 1999 after 124 performances.

---

[3]First produced in New York 13 March 1996 at the Radio City Music Hall for 8 performances, returned 2 October 1996 to the Radio City Music Hall for 21 performances. For Synopsis of Scenes and Musical Numbers, see October 1996 engagement.

CAST: *The Swan*: ADAM COOPER, WILL KEMP. *The Prince*: SCOTT AMBLER, BEN WRIGHT. *The Queen*: ISABEL MORTIMER, MARGUERITE PORTER. *The Prince's Girlfriend*: EMILY PIERCY. *The Private Secretary*: BARRY ATKINSON. *The Young Prince*: ANDREW WALKINSHAW. *Company*: Detlev Alexander, Jacqueline Anderson, Sarah Barron, Wilson E. Batista, Andrew Corbett, Saranne Curtin, Matthew Dalby, Vicky Evans, Ramon Flowers, Christopher Freeman, Jeffrey Lane Freeze, Nina Goldman, Gino Grenek, Heather Habens, Ben Hartley, Floyd Hendricks, Hans-Werner Klohe, Martin Lofsnes, Michela Meazza, Mark Mitchell, Neil Penlington, Arthur Pita, Colin Ross-Waterson, Tom Searle, Kirsty Tapp, Alan Vincent, Tom Ward, Ewan Wardrop, William Yong.

Prologue: The Prince's Bedroom.

Act 1, Scene 1: The Prince's Bedroom. *Scene 2*: The Palace. *Scene 3*: The Opera House. The Ballet. *Scene 4*: The Prince's Private Quarters. *Scene 5*: The Street. *Scene 6*: A Seedy Club [Club Swank]. *Scene 7*: The Street. *Scene 8*: A City Park.

Act 2, Scene 1: The Palace Gates. *Scene 2*: The Royal Ball. *Scene 3*: The Prince's Bedroom.

ACT 1
Scene 1
Maids, Valet and Footmen: The Company.
Scene 2
Cadets, Dignitaries, Officals, Soldiers, etc.: The Company.
Scene 3
The Queen's Escort: N. Penlington. *The Moth Maiden*: M. Meazza. *The Nobleman*: E. Wardrop. *Butterfly Maidens*: S. Barron, S. Curtin, H. Habens, I. Mortimer. *Evil Forest Troll*: D. Alexander. *His Attendants*: J. Anderson, V. Evans.
Scene 6
Club Owner: A. Vincent. *Barmaid*: J. Anderson. *Fan Dancer*: H. Habens. *Hostesses*: S. Barron, S. Curtin. *Party Girls*: V. Evans, I. Mortimer. *East End Gangsters*: B. Hartley, M. Lofsnes. *Sailors*: D. Alexander, H. Klohe. *Barflies*: A. Corbett, N. Goldman, C. Ross-Waterson. *Pop Idol*: N. Penlington. *Pimp*: A. Pita. *Juvenile Delinquent*: A. Walkinshaw.
Scene 8
Swans: The Company. *Duet*: A. Cooper or S. Ambler, W. Kemp or B. Wright. *Cygnets*: D. Alexander, W. E. Batista, R. Flowers, B. Hartley. *Solo*: W. Kemp or B. Wright. *Big Swans*: A. Corbett, H. Klohe, A. Pita, A. Vincent.

ACT 2
Scene 1
Doorman, Royal Spotters, Autograph Hunters, Paparazzi: The Company.
Scene 2
The German Princess: H. Habens. *The Spanish Princess*: J. Anderson. *The Hungarian Princess*: S. Barron. *Princess of Monaco*: I. Mortimer. *The Italian Princess*: S. Curtin. *The French Princess*: N. Goldman. *The Romanian Princess*: V. Evans. *The Royal Escorts*: The Company.
The Russian Dance: A. Cooper or W. Kemp, S. Barron, V. Evans, H. Habens.
The Spanish Dance: D. Alexander, J. Anderson, the Company.
The Neapolitan Dance: S. Curtin, E. Wardrop, the Company.
Czardas: A. Cooper or W. Kemp, S. Ambler or B. Wright, N. Goldman, E. Piercy, the Company.
Scene 3
Doctor, Nurses, Swans: The Company.

MANDY PATINKIN IN CONCERT: MAMALOSHEN
1998.11

A One-Man Revue of Yiddish Song in One Act[4]. (Conceived by Mandy Patinkin.) Piano, Lawrence Yurman. Violin, Saeka Matsuyama. Musical arrangements by Paul Ford and Eric Stern. Scenic consultant, Eric Renschler. Lighting design, Eric Cornwell. Sound design, Otts Munderloh. Produced by Dodger Endemol Theatricals[5]. Opened 13 October 1998 at the Belasco Theatre and closed 7 November 1998 after 28 performances.[6]

CAST: MANDY PATINKIN.

MUSICAL NUMBERS[7]
"Rozhinkes Mit Mandlen" (Raisins and Almonds)
A mother rocks her child, wishes him everything
(*Music and Lyrics by* Abraham Goldfaden, Henry Lefkowitch, Stanley Lionel.)
"Mayn Mirl" (Maria)(from *WEST SIDE STORY*)
(*Music by* Leonard Bernstein. *English lyrics by* Stephen Sondheim.)
"Yome, Yome . . . " (Traditional)
A mother questions her daughter.
"Belz"
Remembering a little town called Belz
(*Music and Lyrics by* Alexander Olshanetsky and Jacob Jacobs.)
"Tsen Kopikes" (Ten Kopecks)(Traditional)
A guy wants ten pennies to romance his girl.
"Supercalifragilisticexpialidocious" (from *MARY POPPINS*, film)
(*Music and English Lyrics by* Richard M. Sherman and Robert B. Sherman.)
"The Hokey Pokey"
(*Music and Lyrics by* Charles Mack, Taft Baker and Roland LaPrise.)
"Papirosin" (Cigarettes)
A boy sells cigarettes to survive the war.
(*Music and Lyrics by* Herman Yablokoff.)
"Motl Der Opreyter"
A sweatshop worker struggles to support his family.
(*Music and Lyrics by* Chaim Towber and H. Solomonson.)
"Unter Dayne Vayse Shtern" (Under Your White Stars)
A holocaust song.
(*Music and Lyrics by* Abraham Sutzkever and Abraham Brudno.)
"Lid Fun Titanic" (Song of the Titanic)
A ship is lost at sea—hope survives.
(*Music and Lyrics by* Joshua Rayzner.)
"Hey, Tsigelekh" (Hey, Little Goats)
The diaspora.
(*Music and Lyrics by* Mordecai Gebirtig.)
"Take Me Out to the Ball Game"
(*Music by* Albert Von Tilzer. *English Lyrics by* Jack Norworth.)
"God Bless America"
(*Music and English Lyrics by* Irving Berlin.)
"Der Alter Tzigayner" (The Old Gypsy)
The old gypsy fiddler plays an unfogettable tune.
(*Music by* Abraham Ellstein. *Lyrics by* Jacob Jacobs.)
"White Christmas" (from film of the same name)
(*Music and English Lyrics by* Irving Berlin.)
"Oyfn Pripetshik"
Children learn their ABC's at the fireplace.
(*Music and Lyrics by* Mark M. Warshawsky.)
"American Tune"
Our journey to America.
(*Music and American Lyrics by* Paul Simon.)

AZNAVOUR ON BROADWAY
1998.12

A One-Man Show in Two Acts. Musical director, Russell Kassoff. Mr. Aznavour's clothing by Francesco Smalto. Produced by Delsenerslater/SFX Entertainment (Ron Delsener-Slater) by special arrangement with Lévon Sayan. Opened 20 October 1998 at the Marquis Theatre and closed 15 November 1998 after 24 performances.

CAST: CHARLES AZNAVOUR.

MUSICAL NUMBERS[8]
"Je Bois"
"Sa Jeunesse"
"Yesterday, When I Was Young"
(*Music and French lyrics by* Charles Aznavour. *English lyrics by* Herbert Kretzmer.)
"La Mamma"
"What Makes a Man"

---

[4]Mamaloshen means "mother tongue" in Yiddish.
[5]Dodger Productions: Michael David, Doug Johnson, Des McAnuff, Rocco Landesman, Edward Strong and Sherman Warner. Endemol Theatre Productions: Joop van den Ende and Robin de Levita.
[6]Previously produced Off-Broadway at the Angel Orensantz Centre 21 July 1998- 22 August 1998 for 30 performances. Program note: "Special thanks to Judy Blazer and her glorious voice and to Zalman Mlotek and his wonderful Yiddish Chorale" (performances on tape).

[7]Dropped after Off-Broadway engagement: "A Day in the Park."
[8]Musical numbers not listed in programs.

1998.13 FOOTLOOSE

A Musical in Two Acts, 18 Scenes. Book by Dean Pitchford and Walter Bobbie. Based on the film of the same name, screenplay by Dean Pitchford. Music by Tom Snow. Lyrics by Dean Pitchford. Additional songs by Kenny Loggins and Eric Carmen. Directed by Walter Bobbie. Choreographed by A. C. Ciulla. Scenery designed by John Lee Beatty. Costumes designed by Toni-Leslie James. Lighting designed by Ken Billington. Sound designed by Tony Meola. Orchestrations by Danny Troob. Music supervision and vocal arrangements by Doug Katsaros. Dance music arrangements by Joe Baker. Produced by Madison Square Garden Productions (Tim Hawkins, Producer) and Dodger Endemol Productions[9]. Opened 22 October 1998 at the Richard Rodgers Theatre and closed 2 July 2000 after 737 performances.

CAST (in order of appearance): *Ren McCormack*: JEREMY KUSHNIER. *Ethel McCormack*: CATHERINE COX. *Shaw Moore*: STEPHEN LEE ANDERSON. *Vi Moore*: DEE. HOTY. *Ariel Moore*: JENNIFER LAURA THOMPSON. *Lulu Warnicker*: Catherine Campbell. *Wes Warnicker*: Adam LeFevre. *Eleanor Dunbar*: Donna Lee Marshall. *Doreen*: Donna Lee Marshall. *Coach Dunbar*: JOHN HILLNER. *Rusty*: STACY FRANCIS. *Urleen*: Kathy Deitch. *Wendy Jo*: Rosalind Brown. *Chuck Cranston*: BILLY HARTUNG. *Lyle*: Jim Ambler. *Travis*: Bryant Carroll. *Cop*: Nick Sullivan. *Country Fiddler*: Nick Sullivan. *Betty Blast*: Robin Baxter. *Irene*: Robin Baxter. *Willard Hewitt*: TOM PLOTKIN. *Saloon Keeper*: John Deyle *Principal Clerk*: John Deyle. *Cowboy Bob*: Artie Harris. *Jeter*: Artic Harris. *Bickle*: Hunter Foster. *Garvain*: Paul Castree.

Ensemble: Billy Angell, Angela Brydon, Paul Castree, Hunter Foster, Kristen Leigh Gorski, Artie Harris, Sean Haythe, Lori Holmes, Daniel Karaty, Katharine Leonard, Mark Myars, JoAnna Ross, Serena Soffer, Ron Todorowski. *Swings*: Ben Cameron, Sean Haythe, Paige Hinton, Jeanine Meyers, Orfeh.

Scene: Somewhere in the heartland of America in the recent past.

Act 1, Scene 1: City of Chicago; Town of Bomont, Church. *Scene 2*: Church Yard. *Scene 3*: Burger Blast Restaurant. *Scene 4*: High School Hallway. *Scene 5*: Street Corner; Principal's Office; Warnicker Home. *Scene 6*: Moore Home. *Scene 7*: Burger Blast Restaurant. *Scene 8*: Plains of Bomont. *Scene 9*: Moore Home. *Scene 10*: High School Gymnasium.

Act 2, Scene 1: The "Bar-B-Q" Country & Western Bar. *Scene 2*: Moore Home. *Scene 3*: Lot behind the Feed and Fuel. *Scene 4*: The Potawney Bridge. *Scene 5*: Bomont Town Hall. *Scene 6*: Church. *Scene 7*: Church Yard. *Scene 8*: High School Gymnasium.

ACT 1

Scene 1

"Footloose"
  J. Kushnier, Company
  (*Music by* Kenny Loggins. *Lyrics by* Kenny Loggins, Dean Pitchford.)
"On Any Sunday"[10]
  S. L. Anderson, Company

Scene 3

"The Girl Gets Around"
  B. Hartung, J. L. Thompson, B. Carroll, J. Ambler
  (*Music by* Sammy Hagar.)

Scene 4

"I Can't Stand Still"[11]
  J. Kushnier

Scene 5

"Somebody's Eyes"
  S. Francis, R. Brown, K. Deitch, Company

Scene 6

"Learning To Be Silent"[12]
  D. Hoty, C. Cox

Scene 7

"Holding Out for a Hero"
  J. L. Thompson, S. Francis, R. Brown, K. Deitch
  (*Music by* Jim Steinman.)

Scene 9

"Somebody's Eyes" (reprise)
  S. Francis, R. Brown, K. Deitch
"Heaven Help Me"
  S. L. Anderson

Scene 10

"I'm Free"
  (*Music by* Kenny Loggins.)
"Heaven Help Me"/"On Any Sunday" (reprise)
  J. Kushnier, S. L. Anderson, Company

ACT 2

Scene 1

"Still Rockin'"/"Let's Make Believe We're in Love?"[13]
  R. Baxter, Country Kickers
"Let's Hear It for the Boy"
  S. Francis, Company

Scene 2

"Can You Find It in Your Heart?"[14]
  D. Hoty

Scene 3

"Mama Says"[15]
  T. Plotkin, the Boys

Scene 4

"Almost Paradise"
  J. Kushnier, J. L. Thompson
  (*Music by* Eric Carmen.)

Scene 5

"Dancing Is Not a Crime"[16]
  J. Kushnier, the Boys

Scene 6

"I Confess"[17]
  S. L. Anderson
"On Any Sunday" (reprise)
  Company

Scene 7

"Can You Find It in Your Heart?" (reprise)
  S. L. Anderson

Scene 8

"Footloose" (reprise)
  Company

1998.14 SANDRA BERNHARD: I'M STILL HERE DAMN IT!

A One-Woman Show in One Act[18]. (Conceived and written by Sandra Bernhard.) Director, Marty Callner. Scenic consultant, Paul Holt. Lighting consultant, Allen Branton. Sound consultant, Nelson-O'Reilly Productions, Inc. Special material, musical director, Mitchell Kaplan. Produced by Contemporary Productions (An SFX Entertainment Company) and Arielle Tepper. Opened 5 November 1998 at the Booth Theatre and closed 3 January 1999 after 51 performances.

CAST: SANDRA BERNHARD.
  The Band: Mitchell Kaplan (keyboards), Denise Fraser (drums, percussion), Dan Petty (guitar), Michael Stanzilis (bass guitar), Soumaya Akaaboune (gembe, vocals).

MUSICAL NUMBERS[19]

"Walk Tall"
  (*Music and Lyrics by* Mitchell Kaplan and Sandra Bernhard.)
"On the Runway"
  (*Music and Lyrics by* Mitchell Kaplan, Sandra Bernhard and Derrick Smit.)
"Nightingale"
  (*Music and Lyrics by* Mitchell Kaplan and Sandra Bernhard.)
"God Is Good"
  (*Music and Lyrics by* Mitchell Kaplan and Sandra Bernhard.)
"Midnight Train to Georgia"
  (*Music and Lyrics by* Jim Weatherly.)

---

[9]Dodger Productions: Michael David, Doug Johnson, Des McAnuff, Rocco Landesman, Edward Strong and Sherman Warner. Endemol Theatre Productions: Joop van den Ende and Robin de Levita.
[10]Newly written for the stage, and not in the original film.
[11]Newly written for the stage, and not in the original film.
[12]Newly written for the stage, and not in the original film.
[13]Newly written for the stage, and not in the original film.
[14]Newly written for the stage, and not in the original film.
[15]Newly written for the stage, and not in the original film.
[16]Newly written for the stage, and not in the original film.
[17]Newly written for the stage, and not in the original film.
[18]Previously produced Off-Broadway 11 November 1997 at the Westbeth Theatre Center.
[19]Musical numbers not listed in programs. List prepared from press materials, reviews, recordings; not in performance order.

1998.15

LITTLE ME

A Revival of the Musical Comedy in Two Acts[20]. Book (revised) by Neil Simon. Based on the novel of the same name by Patrick Dennis. Music by Cy Coleman. Lyrics by Carolyn Leigh. Directed and choreographed by Robert Marshall. Set design by David Gallo. Costume design by Anne Hould-Ward. Lighting design by Kenneth Posner. Sound design by Brian Ronan. Orchestrations by Harold Wheeler. Musical director, David Chase. Dance music arranged by David Krane. Projection design by Jan Hartley. Associate director and choreographer, Cynthia Onrubia. Produced by Roundabout Theatre Company (Todd Haimes, Artistic Director; Ellen Richard, Managing Director). Opened 12 November 1998 at the Roundabout Theatre/Stage Right and closed 7 February 1999 after 101 performances.

CAST (in order of appearance): *Belle:* FAITH PRINCE. *Belle's Boys:* Michael Arnold, Jeffrey Hankinson, Ned Hannah, Denis Jones. *Momma:* RUTH WILLIAMSON. *Ramona:* Andrea Chamberlain. *Bruce:* MICHAEL MCGRATH. *Cerine:* Cynthia Onrubia. *Noble Eggleston* MARTIN SHORT. *Mrs. Eggleston:* RUTH WILLIAMSON. *Greensleeves:* Michael McEachran. *Maid:* Christine Pedi. *Lucky:* MICHAEL PARK. *Miss Kepplewhite:* Christine Pedi. *Pinchley Junior:* Brooks Ashmanskas. *Nurse:* Kimberly Lyon. *Amos Pinchley:* MARTIN SHORT. *Kleeg:* Peter Benson. *Newsboys:* Michael Arnold, Jeffrey Hankinson. *Bernie Buchsbaum:* MICHAEL MCGRATH. *Benny Buchsbaum:* MARTIN SHORT. *Attorney:* Peter Benson. *Chain Gang:* Michael Arnold, Jeffrey Hankinson, Ned Hannah, Denis Jones. *Maitre D':* Peter Benson. *Boom Boom Girls:* Kimberly Lyon, Joanne McHugh, Cynthia Onrubia. *Val du Val:* MARTIN SHORT. *Colette:* Roxane Barlow. *Kitty:* Cynthia Onrubia. *Suzie:* Joanne McHugh. *Roxane:* Roxane Barlow. *Christine:* Christine Pedi. *Bert:* MICHAEL MCGRATH. *Soldier:* Denis Jones. *Fred Poitrine:* MARTIN SHORT. *Sergeant:* Michael McEachran. *Preacher:* Peter Benson. *German Soldier:* MICHAEL MCGRATH. *General:* Peter Benson. *Army Nurse:* Christine Pedi. *Captain:* Peter Benson. *Steward:* Brooks Ashmanskas. *First Sailor:* Ned Hannah. *Second Sailor:* Jeffrey Hankinson. *Assistant Director:* Brooks Ashmanskas. *Secretary:* Christine Pedi. *Otto Schnitzler:* MARTIN SHORT. *Movie "King":* Michael McEachran. *Victor:* Peter Benson. *Prince Cherney:* MARTIN SHORT. *Yulnick:* MICHAEL MCGRATH. *Casino Woman:* Christine Pedi. *Doctor:* Brooks Ashmanskas. *Justices:* Denis Jones, Jeffrey Hankinson. *The Drunk:* MARTIN SHORT. *Party Guests, Rich Kids, Drifter's Row Townspeople, Courtroom Dancers, Skylight Roof Patrons, Nurses, Soldiers, Medics, Passengers, Biblical Slaves, Casino Patron Patrons and Mourners.* *Swings:* Joey Pizzi, Josh Prince, Courtney Young.

Scenes: The Present: Southampton, 1962. The Past: Venezuela, Illinois; Chicago; Somewhere in France; On the North Atlantic; Hollywood; Monte Carlo; A Principality in Middle Europe.

ACT 1[21]

"Little Me"
F. Prince, Belle's Boys

"The Other Side of the Tracks"
F. Prince

"Rich Kids Rag" (The Birthday Party)
Rich Kids, M. Short [Noble]

"I Love You"
M. Short [Noble], F. Prince, Company

"The Other Side of the Tracks" (reprise)
F. Prince

"Deep Down Inside"
F. Prince, M. Short [Pinchley], Company

"Be a Performer"
M. McGrath, M. Short [Bernie], F. Prince

"Dimples"
F. Prince, Her Chain Gang

"Boom-Boom"
M. Short [Val du Val], Boom Boom Girls

"I've Got Your Number"
M. Park

"Real Live Girl"
M. Short [Fred Poitrine]

"Real Live Girl" (reprise)
M. Short [Fred Poitrine], Soldiers

Finale (Act 1)
F. Prince

ACT 2

"I Love Sinking You"
F. Prince, M. Short [Fred Poitrine], Company

"Poor Little Hollywood Star"
F. Prince

"(The Prince's) Goodbye" (Farewell)
M. Short [Prince Cherney], M. McGrath, Company

"Here's To Us"
F. Prince, Company

1998.16

ON THE TOWN

A Revival of the Musical Comedy in Two Acts, 17 Scenes[22]. Book and lyrics[23] by Betty Comden and Adolph Green. Book based on an idea by Jerome Robbins. Music by Leonard Bernstein. Directed by George C. Wolfe. Choreographed by Keith Young. Set design by Adrianne Lobel. Costume design by Paul Tazewell. Lighting design by Paul Gallo. Sound design by Jon Weston. Musical direction by Kevin Stites. Orchestrations by Bruce Coughlin. Produced by The Joseph Papp Public Theater/New York Shakespeare Festival (George C. Wolfe, Producer; Rosemarie Tichler, Artistic Producer; Mark Litvin, Managing Director). Opened 22 November 1998 at the Gershwin Theatre and closed 17 January 1999 after 65 performances.

CAST (in order of appearance): *Workman:* Gregory Emanuel Rahming. *Quartet:* Tom Aulino, Christopher F. Davis, Blake Hammond, John Jellison. *Ozzie:* ROBERT MONTANO. *Chip:* JESSE TYLER FERGUSON. *Gabey:* PERRY LAYLON OJEDA. *Flossie:* Linda Mugleston. *Flossie's Friend:* Chandra Wilson. *Subway Bill Poster:* John Jellison. *Little Old Lady:* MARY TESTA. *Mannequins:* Dottie Earle, Jennifer Frankel, Amy Heggins, Judine Richard. *Miss Turnstiles Announcers:* Nora Cole, Gregory Emanuel Rahming. *Ivy Smith:* TAI JIMENEZ. *Policeman:* Christopher F. Davis. *Mr. S. Uperman:* Blake Hammond. *Hildy Esterhazy:* LEA DELARIA. *Waldo Figment:* Tom Aulino. *Claire DeLoone:* SARAH KNOWLTON. *Primitive Man and Woman:* Stephen Campanella, Judine Richàrd. *Pas de Deux Dancers:* Kristine Bendul, Darren Gibson. *Madame Maude P. Dilly:* MARY TESTA. *Women of Carnegie Hall:* Nora Cole, Linda Mugleston, Chandra Wilson. *Pitkin W. Bridgework:* JONATHAN FREEMAN. *Lucy Schmeeler:* ANNIE GOLDEN. *Diamond Eddie's Girls:* Kristine Bendul, Jennifer Frankel, Amy Heggins, Keenah Reid, Judine Richàrd. *Master of Ceremonies:* Blake Hammond. *Diana Dream/Dolores Dolores:* Nora Cole. *Rajah Bimmy:* John Jellison.

Dance Ensemble: Brad Aspel, Tom Aulino, Kristine Bendul, Stephen Campanella, R. J. Durell, Dottie Earle, Jennifer Frankel, Edgard Gallardo, Darren Gibson, Amy Heggins, John Jellison, Darren Lee, Keenah Reid, Judine Richard. *The People of New York:* Tom Aulino, Blake Hammond, John Jellison, Linda Mugleston, Gregory Emanuel Rahming, Chandra Wilson. *Swings:* Kim Craven, Sloan Just, Rommy Sandhu, Scott Spahr.

The action takes place in New York City in June, 1944.

Act 1, Scene 1: The Brooklyn Navy Yard. *Scene 2:* A Subway Train in Motion. *Scene 3:* A New York Street. *Scene 4:* Presentation of Miss Turnstiles. *Scene 5:* A Taxi Cab. *Scene 6:* The Museum of Natural History. *Scene 7:* A Busy New York Street. *Scene 8:* A Corridor and Studio in Carnegie Hall. *Scene 9:* Central Park. *Scene 10:* Claire's and Hildy's Apartments. *Scene 11:* Times Square.

Act 2, Scene 1: Night Clubs, (a) Diamond Eddie's Club, (b) The Congacabana, (c) The Slam Bang Club. *Scene 2:* The Subway Train to Coney Island. *Scene 3:* The Dream Coney Island. *Scene 4:* Subway Platform. *Scene 5:* The Real Coney Island. *Scene 6:* The Brooklyn Navy Yard.

ACT 1

Scene 1

"I Feel Like I'm Not Out of Bed"
G. E. Rahming, Quartet

"New York, New York"
R. Montano, J. T. Ferguson, P. L. Ojeda, Full Company

Scene 3

"Gabey's Coming"
R. Montano, J. T. Ferguson, P. L. Ojeda, Mannequins

Scene 4

"Presentation of Miss Turnstiles" (Ballet)
N. Cole, G. E. Rahming, T. Jimenez, Dance Ensemble

---

[20]Originally produced in New York 17 November 1962 at the Lunt-Fontanne Theatre for 257 performances.
[21]Not used in this production: "The Truth" (original 1962 production), and "I Wanna Be Yours" and "Don't Ask a Lady" (both from the 1982 revival). "I Love Sinking You" is a revised version of "I Love You."

[22]Originally produced in New York 28 December 1944 at the Adelphi Theatre for 462 performances. For Synopsis of Scenes and Musical Numbers, see original 1944 production. This revival originated in an open air production 17-31 August 1997 at the Delacorte Theatre (Off-Broadway) for 14 performances. For this revival, the previously unused "Gabey's Comin'" was added to Act 1, Scene 3.
[23]Additional lyrics by Leonard Bernstein.

Scene 5
"Come Up to My Place"
    L. DeLaria, J. T. Ferguson
Scene 6
"(I Get) Carried Away"
    S. Knowlton, R. Montano, S. Campanella, J. Richàrd
Scene 7
"Lonely Town"
    P. L. Ojeda, Dance Ensemble
Scene 8
"Carnegie Hall Pavane" (Do, Do, Re, Do)
    T. Jimenez, M. Testa, Women of Carnegie Hall
Scene 9
"Lucky to Be Me"
    P. L. Ojeda, Ensemble
Scene 10
"I Understand"
    J. Freeman
"I Can Cook Too"
    L. DeLaria
Scene 11
"Times Square Ballet"
    Full Company
ACT 2
Scene 1a
"So Long Baby"
    Diamond Eddie's Girls
"I Wish I Was Dead" (I'm Blue)
    N. Cole [Diana Dream]
Scene 1b
"I Wish I Was Dead" (I'm Blue)
    N. Cole [Dolores Dolores]
"You Got Me"
    L. DeLaria, S. Knowlton, R. Montano, J. T. Ferguson
Scene 1c
"I Understand"
    J. Freeman, A. Golden
Scene 2
Subway Ride
    P. L. Ojeda, People of New York
Scene 3
Imaginary Coney Island (Ballet)
    P. L. Ojeda, T. Jimenez, Dance Ensemble
Scene 4
"Some Other Time"
    S. Knowlton, L. DeLaria, R. Montano, J. T. Ferguson
Scene 5
"The Real Coney Island"
    J. Jellison
Scene 6
"I Feel Like I'm Not Out of Bed" (reprise)
    G. E. Rahming
"New York, New York" (reprise)
    Entire Company

1998.17   FOOL MOON

A Revival of the Comedy Performance Revue in Two Acts[24]. Created by Bill Irwin and David Shiner. (Original music and lyrics by the Red Clay Ramblers.) Set design by Douglas Stein. Costume design by Bill Kellard. Lighting design by Nancy Schertler. Sound design by Tom Morse. Flying by Foy. Producing associate, Nancy Harrington. Associate producer, Sammi Rose Cannold. Produced by James B. Freydberg, Jeffrey Ash, Dori Berinstein, CTM Productions (David Jiranek, David Weil and Cricket Hooper). Opened 22 November 1998 at the Brooks Atkinson Theatre and closed 3 January 1999 after 49 performances.

---

[24]Originally produced in New York 25 February 1993 at the Richard Rodgers Theatre for 207 performances, and 29 October 1995 at the Ambassador Theatre for 81 performances.

CAST (in order of appearance): DAVID SHINER, BILL IRWIN.
    THE RED CLAY RAMBLERS: Clay Buckner (fiddle, harmonica), Chris Frank (piano, accordion, trombone, ukelele, tuba, guitar), Jack Herrick (bass, trumpet, mandolin, tin whistle, concertina), Mark Roberts (banjo, flute, oboe, tin whistle, keyboard), Rob Ladd (drums, ukelele).
ACT 1[25]
Opening
    D. Shiner, B. Irwin, Red Clay Ramblers, 2 Ushers
"Fire and Sugar" (traditional)
    Red Clay Ramblers
Encounter
    D. Shiner, B. Irwin
"Wa-Hoo"[26]
    Red Clay Ramblers
Dance Solo
    D. Shiner
Dance to the Left
    B. Irwin, Stage Manager
Big Night Out
    D. Shiner, B. Irwin, an Audience Member
ACT 2
"Pal-Yat-Chee"[27]
    Red Clay Ramblers
    (*Music and Lyrics by* Eddie Maxwell and Spike Jones.)
Improvisation in Public
    D. Shiner, an Audience Memeber
Harlequin/Pantalone
    B. Irwin, Red Clay Ramblers, D. Shiner
"Hiawatha's Lullaby"
    Red Clay Ramblers
    (*Music by* Walter Donaldson. *Lyrics by* Joe Young.)
"Tea for Two" (from NO, NO NANETTE)
    D. Shiner, B. Irwin
    (*Music by* Vincent Youmans. *Lyrics by* Irving Caesar.)
Conductor
    B. Irwin, Red Clay Ramblers
Cinema
    D. Shiner, 4 Audience Members
"Valley of the Dry Bones" (traditional; a capella)
    Red Clay Ramblers, D. Shiner, B. Irwin
"Melancholy Moon Song"[28]
    Red Clay Ramblers, B. Irwin, D. Shiner
"Fire and Sugar" (reprise)
    B. Irwin, D. Shiner, Red Clay Ramblers

PETER PAN,
1998.18   or The Boy Who Wouldn't Grow Up

A Revival of the Musical in Three Acts, 7 Scenes[29]. Book by James M. Barrie[30]. Music by Moose [Mark] Charlap. Lyrics by Carolyn Leigh. Additional music by Jule Styne. Additional lyrics by Betty Comden and Adolph Green. Original Broadway production conceived, directed and choreographed by Jerome Robbins. Directed by Glenn Casale. Choreographed by Patti Columbo. Scenery designed by John Iacovelli. Costumes designed by Shigeru Yaji. Lighting designed by Martin Aronstein. Sound designed by Francois Bergeron. Musical direction and vocals arrangements by Craig

---

[25]Scenes and Musical Numbers not identified in programs; list prepared from producers' materials. Also performed:
    "Old Jim Canaan's" (by Reverend Robert Wilkins.)
    "Take Five" (by Paul Desmond)
    Love Theme from Romeo And Juliet(film)
        (*Music by* Nino Rota.)
[26]Not in previous 1993 production.
[27]Not in previous 1993 production.
[28]Not in previous 1993 production.
[29]Originally produced in New York 20 October 1954 at the Winter Garden for 152 performances. This adaptation previously presented in New York 13 December 1990 at the Lunt-Fontanne Theatre for 45 performances, and 27 November 1991 at the Minskoff Theatre for 48 performances. For Synopsis of Scenes and Musical Numbers, see 1990 revival.
[30]Musical libretto uncredited.

Barna. Flying illusions by ZFX, Inc. Produced by (Thomas P.) McCoy-Rigby Entertainment, The Nederlander Organization and La Mirada Theatre for the Performing Arts, in association with Albert Nocciolino, Larry Payton and J. Lynn Singleton. Opened 23 November 1998 at the Minskoff Theatre and closed 3 January 1999 after 48 performances; returned 7 April 1999 to the Gershwin Theatre and closed 29 August 1999 after 168 additional performances. Total: 216 performances.

CAST (in order of appearance): *Mrs. Darling*: BARBARA MCCULLOH. *Wendy Darling*: ELISA SAGARDIA. *John Darling*: CHASE KNIFFEN. *Michael Darling*: DRAKE ENGLISH. *Liza*: Dana Solimando. *Nana*: Buck Mason. *Mr. Darling*: PAUL SCHOEFFLER. *Peter Pan*: CATHY RIGBY. *Curly*: Alon Williams. *First Twin*: Janet Higgins. *Second Twin*: Doreen Chila. *Slightly*: Scott Bridges. *Tootles*: Aileen Quinn. *Mr. Smee*: MICHAEL NOSTRAND. *Cecco*: Tony Spinosa. *Gentleman Starkey*: Sam Zeller. *Noodler*: Randy Davis. *Bill Jukes*: Buck Mason. *Captain Hook*: PAUL SCHOEFFLER. *Crocodile*: Buck Mason. *Tiger Lily*: DANA SOLIMANDO. *Mermaid*: Barbara McCulloh. *Pirates and Indians*: Kim Arnett, Randy Davis, Jeffrey Elsass, Casey Miles Good, Buck Mason, Brian Shepard, Roger Preston Smith, Tony Spinosa, Sam Zeller.
    Wendy, Grown-up: BARBARA MCCULLOH. *Jane*: AILEEN QUINN.
    General Understudy: Michelle Berti. *Swing*: William Alan Coats.

1998.19   CHRISTMAS FROM THE HEART

A Christmas Entertainment in One Act, 3 Scenes. Book by Kenny Rogers and Kelly Junkermann Rogers. Music and lyrics by Kenny Rogers, Warren Hartman and Steve Glassmeyer. Beacon Theatre Production directed by Larry Pellegrini. Musical staging by Dani Davis and Adam Pelty. Set design by George Xenos. Costumes design by Frank Krenz and Juan DeArmas. Lighting design by Jeff Metter. Sound design by Keith Bugos. Orcestrator/Musical director, Warren Hartman. Executive producers, Robert Halmi, Jr. and Larry Levinson. Produced by Hallmark Entertainment. Opened 24 November 1998 at the Beacon Theatre and closed 3 January 1999 after 47 performances.

CAST: The Grown-Ups: *Hank Longley*: KENNY ROGERS. *Roscoe Baxter*: Martin Epstein. *Katie*: Jillian Arciero. *Agnes*: Charlotte Franklin. *Rosemary's Mom/Nativity Teacher*: Cara D'Emanuele-Sanders. *Patterson*: James Broderick. *Doug*: Doug Dean. *Mary Claire*: Ellie Dvorkin. *Mary's Assistant*: Johnny Tammaro, Jr.
    The Kids: *Rosemary*: Taylor Burgos. *Tray*: Shaw Leggett. *Beckie*: Francesca Mari. *Maleek*: Jeremy Maleel Leggett. *Percival*: Evan Broder. *Kurt*: James Kurlinski.
    The Toys: *Jack*: Drew DiStefano. *Bruno*: Steve Calzaretta. *Rags*: Mamie Parris. *Riches*: Topher Goodman. *Foxy*: Kathy Connolly. *Cheeseball*: Heather Feeney. *Sarge*: Stephen G. Kennedy. *Giselle*: Jacqueline Maloney. *Ballerina*: Matina Parisi.
    Christmas Sprites: Johnny Tammaro, Jr., Steve Calzaretta, Topher Goodman, Derek Staranowski, Marnie Parris, Ellie Dvorkin, Robin Higginbotham, Julie Foldesi. *Ensemble*: Johnny Tammaro, Jr., Ellie Dvorkin, Robin Higginbotham, Derek Staranowski, Julie Foldesi. *Choir*: The Voice of Praise Choir.

Scene 1: Merryville Town Park. *Scene 2*: Merryville Church. *Scene 3*: Hank Longley's Toy Shoppe.

MUSICAL NUMBERS
Scene 1
  "Frosty the Snowman"
    The Kids
  "Winter Wonderland" (from *ZIEGFELD FOLLIES OF 1934*)
    K. Rogers, Ensemble
  "Let It Snow, Let It Snow, Let It Snow"
    K. Rogers
    (*Music by* Jule Styne. *Lyrics by* Sammy Cahn.)
  "The Christmas Song"
    K. Rogers
    (*Music and Lyrics by* Mel Tormé and Robert Wells.)
  "White Christmas" (from *WHITE CHRISTMAS* film)
    K. Rogers
    (*Music and Lyrics by* Irving Berlin.)
  "(The) Twelve Days of Christmas"
    K. Rogers, Special Guests
  "It's Not Just Christmas"
    K. Rogers
    (*Music and Lyrics by* Debi Smith-Cochran, Anathale G. Sandlin, Bill Swindell, Tina Murrah-Swindell.)
Scene 2
  "The Chosen One" "Away in the Manger," "O Holy Night," "Silent Night," "The First Noel," "We Three Kings," "Joy to the World"
    (Traditional; *music arranged by* Kenny Rogers, Warren Hartman.)
Scene 3
  "Merry Christmas"
    Ensemble
    (*Music and Lyrics by* Kenny Rogers, Warren Hartman and Steve Glassmeyer.)

"I Want To Be a Christmas Present"
    The Toys
    (*Music and Lyrics by* Kenny Rogers, Warren Hartman and Steve Glassmeyer.)
"Heroes"
    K. Rogers
    (*Music and Lyrics by* Kenny Rogers, Warren Hartman and Steve Glassmeyer.)
"Money Isn't What Really Matters"
    K. Rogers, The Kids
    (*Music and Lyrics by* Kenny Rogers, Warren Hartman and Steve Glassmeyer.)
"Love Me Just For Me"
    J. Maloney
"If I Only Had Your Heart"
    K. Rogers, J. Maloney
    (*Music and Lyrics by* Kenny Rogers, Warren Hartman and Steve Glassmeyer.)
"Mr. Perfect"
    The Toys
    (*Music and Lyrics by* Kenny Rogers, Warren Hartman and Steve Glassmeyer.)
"I Promise You"
    K. Rogers
    (*Music and Lyrics by* Kenny Rogers, Warren Hartman and Steve Glassmeyer.)
"The Toy Shoppe"
    Ensemble
    (*Music and Lyrics by* Kenny Rogers, Warren Hartman and Steve Glassmeyer.)
"'Til the Season Comes 'Round Again" (Finale)
    K. Rogers
    (*Music and Lyrics by* John Barlow Jarvis and Randy Goodrum.)

1998.20   A CHRISTMAS CAROL

A Revival of the Musical in One Act, 13 Scenes[31]. Book by Mike Ockrent and Lynn Ahrens. Based on the story of the same name by Charles Dickens. Music by Alan Menken. Lyrics by Lynn Ahrens. Directed by Mike Ockrent. Choreographed by Susan Stroman. Setting design by Tony Walton. Costume design by William Ivey Long. Lighting design by Jules Fisher and Peggy Eisenhauer. Sound design by Tony Meola. Projections by Wendall K. Harrington. Flying by Foy. Associate director, Steven Zweigbaum. Associate choreographer, Chris Peterson. Musical direction by Paul Gemignani. Orchestrations by Michael Starobin and Douglas Besterman. Dance arrangements and incidental music by Glen Kelly. Executive producer, Dodger Endemol Theatricals. Producer, Tim Hawkins. Presented by American Express/Madison Square Garden. Opened 2 December 1998 at the (Paramount) Theatre, Madison Square Garden and closed 27 December 1998 after 57 performances.

CAST (in order of appearance): *Beadle*: Del-Bourree Bach. *Mr. Smythe*: CHRIS VASQUEZ. *Grace Smythe*: Netousha Harris, Tavia Riveé Jefferson. *Scrooge*: ROGER DALTREY. *Crachit*: TODD GROSS. *Charity Men*: David Aaron Damane, Roland Rusinek, Wayne Schroder. *Old Joe*: Kenneth McMullen. *Street Urchins*: Dana Chechile, Carissa Farina, Dennis Michael Hall, Jesse McCartney, Gabriel Millman, Stephen Scarpulla. *Mrs. Crachit*: Rachel Black. *Tiny Tim*: Anthony Blair Hall, Christian Valiando. *Poulterer*: Roland Rusinek. *Sandwichboard*: ROZ RYAN. *Jonathon*: Adam Barruch, Kennedy Kanagawa. *Lamplighter*: KEN JENNINGS. *Blind Hag*: Debra Cardona. *Fred*: JOHN SLOMAN. *Mrs. Mopps*: Marilyn Pasekoff. *Ghost of Jacob Marley*: PAUL KANDEL. *Ghost of Christmas Past*: KEN JENNINGS. *Lights of Christmas Past*: Matthew Baker, Ronald Cadet Bastine, Keith Fortner, Michael Lomeka. *Judge*: Roland Rusinek. *Scrooge at 8 years*: Dennis Michael Hall, Stephen Scarpulla. *Scrooge's Mother*: Debra Cardona. *Scrooge's Father*: Wayne Schroder. *Mr. Hawkins*: Kenneth McMullen. *Scrooge at 12 years*: Jesse McCartney, Gabriel Millman. *Fan*: Dana Chechile, Carissa Farina. *Fezziwig*: Daniel Marcus. *Scrooge at 18 years*: Joe Cassidy. *Young Marley*: Ken Barnett. *Mrs. Fezziwig*: Joy Hermalyn. *Emily*:

---

[31]Originally produced in New York 1 December 1994 at the Paramount Theatre, Madison Square Garden for 71 performances. For Synopsis of Scenes and Musical Numbers, see original 1994 production. For this year's and the 1995, 1996 and 1997 revivals the following changes were made:
  Scene 1 and "The Years Are Passing By" were dropped.
  Added to Scene 2 (former Scene 3) before "Street Song":
  "You Mean More to Me"
    T. Gross, A. B. Hall or C. Valiando.
"The Years Are Passing By" (reprise) in former Scene 13 (new Scene 12) was replaced by:
  "London Town Carol"
    A. Barruch or K. Kanagawa
Note: The production played an irregular schedule of multiple daily performances.

Kristin Huxhold. *Ghost of Christmas Present*: ROZ RYAN. *The Crachit Children*: Dana Chechile, Carissa Farina, Jesse McCartney, Gabriel Millman. *Sally, Fred's wife*: La Tanya Hall. *Ignorance*: Dennis Michael Hall, Stephen Scarpulla. *Want*: Netousha Harris, Tavia Riveé Jefferson. *Undertakers*: Ken Barnett, Wayne Schroder. *Ghost of Christmas Yet-To-Be*: CHRISTINE DUNHAM.

Business Men, Gifts, Ghosts and the People of London: Lori Alexander, Del-Bourree Bach, Matthew Baker, Ken Barnett, Ronlad Cadet Bastine, Hayes Bergman, Rachel Balck, Liam Burke, Joe Cassidy, Debra Cardona, Candy Cook, David Aaron Damane, Juliet Fischer, Keith Fortner, Peter Gregus, La Tanya Hall, Joy Hermalyn, Kristin Huxhold, Carrie Kinneally, Kate Levering, Michael Lomeka, Daniel Marcus, Kenneth McMullen, Marilyn Pasekoff, Gail Pennington, Meredith Patterson, Pamela Remler, Roland Rusinek, Yasuko Tamaki, Vikki Schnurr, Wayne Schroder, John Sloman, Chris Vasquez. *Swings*: Ron Bagden, Jane Brockman, Ann Kittredge, Robin Lewis, Angela Piccinni, Scott Taylor, Cynthia Thole, Jeff Williams. *Angels*: Terrill Middle School Broadway Chorus, P.S./M.S. 330 Glee Club, South Side Middle School Select Chorus, Eastwood International Children's Choir. *Red Children's Cast*: Adam Barruch, Carissa Farina, Anthony Blair Hall, Dennis Michael Hall, Netousha Harris, Gabriel Millman. *Green Children's Cast*: Dana Chechile, Kennedy Kanagawa, Tavia Riveé Jefferson, Jesse McCartney, Stephen Scarpulla, Chritian Valiando. *Swings*: Barry Cavanagh, Bret Fox, Chloé Zeitounian.

1998.21   PARADE

A Musical in Two Acts. Book by Alfred Uhry. Music and lyrics by Jason Robert Brown. Co-conceived and directed by Harold Prince. Choreographed by Patricia Birch. Settings by Riccardo Hernandez. Costumes by Judith Dolan. Lighting by Howell Binkley. Sound by Jonathan Deans. Musical supervision and direction, Eric Stern. Orchestrations by Don Sebesky. Produced by Lincoln Center Theater Company (André Bishop, Artistic director; Bernard Gersten, Executive producer), in association with LIVENT (US) Inc. Opened 17 December 1998 at the Vivian Beaumont Theatre and closed 28 February 1999 after 84 performances.

CAST (in order of appearance): *Young Soldier*: JEFF EDGERTON. *Aide*: Don Stephenson. *Assistant*: Melanie Vaughan. *Old Soldier*: DON CHASTAIN. *Lucille Frank*: CAROLEE CARMELLO. *Leo Frank*: BRENT CARVER. *Hugh Dorsey*: HERNDON LACKEY. *Governor Slaton*: JOHN HICKOK. *Frankie Epps*: KIRK MCDONALD. *Mary Phagan*: CHRISTY CARLSON ROMANO. *Iola Stover*: Brooke Sunny Moriber. *Jim Conley*: RUFUS BONDS, JR. *J. N. Starnes*: Peter Samuel. *Officer Ivey*: Tad Ingram. *Newt Lee*: RAY ARANHA. *Prison Guard*: Randy Redd. *Mrs. Phagan*: JESSICA MOLASKEY. *Lizzie Phagan*: Robin Skye. *Floyd MacDaniel*: J. B. ADAMS. *Britt Craig*: EVAN PAPPAS. *Tom Watson*: JOHN LESLIE WOLFE. *Angela*: Angela Lockett. *Riley*: J. C. Montgomery. *Luther Rosser*: J. B. ADAMS. *Fiddlin' John*: JEFF EDGERTON. *Judge Roan*: DON CHASTAIN. *Nurse*: Adinah Alexander. *Monteen*: Abbi Hutcherson. *Essie*: Emily Klein. *Mr. Peavy*: Don Stephenson.

Ensemble: Adinah Alexander, Duane Boutté, Diana Brownstone, Thursday Farrar, Will Gartshore, Abbi Hutcherson, Tad Ingram, Emily Klein, Angela Lockett, Megan McGinniss, J. C. Montgomery, Brooke Sunny Moriber, Randy Redd, Joel Robertson, Peter Samuel, Don Stephenson, Bill Szobody, Anne Torsiglieri, Melanie Vaughan, Wysandria Woolsey.

(The action takes place in Marietta and Atlanta, Georgia and environs in 1913.)

ACT 1

"The Old Red Hills of Home" (Prologue)
    J. Edgerton, D. Chastain, Ensemble

"The Dream of Atlanta" (Anthem)
    Ensemble

"How Can I Call This Home?"
    B. Carver, Ensemble

"The Picture Show"
    K. McDonald, C. C. Romano

"Leo at Work/What Am I Waiting For?"
    B. Carver, C. Carmello

"I am trying to remember . . ." (Interrogation)
    R. Aranha, J. Molaskey

"Big News!"
    E. Pappas

"There Is a Fountain"/"It Don't Make Sense"[32]
    K. McDonald, Ensemble

"Watson's Lullaby"
    J. L. Wolfe

"Somethin' Ain't Right"
    H. Lackey

"Real Big News"
    E. Pappas, Reporters, Ensemble

---

[32]Incorporating "There Is a Fountain," traditional hymn by William Cowper, melody by Lowell Mason, 1772.

"You Don't Know This Man"
    C. Carmello

The Trial (Finale Act 1):

"It Is Time Now"
    J. Edgerton, J. L. Wolfe, Ensemble

"Twenty Miles from Marietta"
    H. Lackey

Frankie's Testimony
    K. McDonald, C. C. Romano, J. L. Wolfe

"The Factory Girls/Come Up to My Office"
    B. S. Moriber, E. Klein, A. Hutcherson, B. Carver

Newt Lee's Testimony
    R. Aranha, Ensemble

"My Child Will Forgive Me"
    J. Molaskey

"That's What He Said"
    R. Bonds, Jr.

"It's hard to speak my heart" (Leo's Statement)
    B. Carver

Closing Statement and Verdict
    Ensemble

ACT 2

"It Goes On and On"
    E. Pappas

"A Rumblin' and a Rollin'"
    J. C. Montgomery, A. Lockett, R. Aranha, R. Bonds, Jr.

"Do It Alone"
    C. Carmello

"Pretty Music"
    J. Hickok

"Letter to the Governor"
    D. Chastain

"This Is Not Over Yet"
    B. Carver, C. Carmello, Factory Girls, R. Aranha

"Feel the Rain Fall" (Blues)
    R. Bonds, Ensemble

"Where Will You Stand When the Flood Comes?"
    J. L. Wolfe, H. Lackey, Ensemble

"All the Wasted Time"
    B. Carver, C. Carmello

Finale
    Ensemble

THE FLYING KARAMAZOV BROTHERS:

1998.22   Sharps, Flats and Accidentals

A Vaudeville Revue in Two Acts[33]. Written, directed and produced by the Flying Karamazov Brothers. Music by Doug Wieselman. Ballet choreography by Doug Elkins. Dance costumes by Susan Hilferty. Lighting by David Hutson. Produced by Interpresario and Anne Geenen Productions Inc. in association with Alice Tully Hall. Opened 18 December 1998 at Alice Tully Hall and closed 3 January 1999 after 18 performances.

CAST: *Dimitri*: PAUL MAGID. *Ivan*: HOWARD JAY PATTERSON. *Rakitin*: MICHAEL PRESTON. *Fyodor*: TIM FURST.

1999.01   FOSSE

A Celebration in Song and Dance (a Musical Revue) in Three Acts, Five Parts. Choreography by Bob Fosse. Conceived by Richard Maltby, Jr., Chet Walker and Ann Reinking. Artistic advisor, Gwen Verdon. Choreography recreated by Chet Walker. Co-directed and co-choreographed by Ann Reinking. Production directed by Richard Maltby, Jr. Scenery and costume design by Santo Loquasto. Lighting design by Andrew Bridge. Sound design

---

[33]THE FLYING KARAMAZOV BROTHERS have appeared in their own revues three times before on Broadway (as well as off Broadway and on tour): 10 May 1983 at the Ritz Theatre for 47 performances; 1 April 1986 at the Vivian Beaumont Theatre for 40 performances, and in THE FLYING KARAMAZOV BROTHERS DO THE IMPOSSIBLE! 20 November 1994 at the Helen Hayes Theatre for 50 performances.

by Jonathan Deans. Musical director, Patrick S. Brady. Orchestrations by Ralph Burns and Douglas Besterman. Produced by Livent (U.S.) Inc.[34] Opened 14 January 1999 at the Broadhurst Theatre and closed 25 August 2001 after 1100 performances.

CAST: VALARIE PETTIFORD, JANE LANIER, EUGENE FLEMING, DESMOND RICHARDSON, SERGIO TRUJILLO, KIM MORGAN GREENE, MARY ANN LAMB, DANA MOORE, ELIZABETH PARKINSON, SCOTT WISE, Julio Agustin, Brad Anderson, Andy Blankenbuehler, Marc Calamia, Holly Cruikshank, Lisa Gajda, Scott Jovovich, Christopher R. Kirby, Dede LaBarre, Shannon Lewis, Mary MacLeod, Brad Musgrove, Michael Paternostro, Rachelle Rak, Lainie Sakakura, Alex Sanchez. *Swings*: Bill Burns, Susan Lamontagne, Deborah Leamy, Sean Palmer, Josh Rhodes, J. Kathleen Watkins. (*Music specialties*: Perry Cavari (drums), Mike Hall (bass), Jim Pugh (trombone), Glenn Drewes (trumpet), Walt Weiskopf (clarinet), Jon Werking (piano).)

ACT 1
Prologue:
"Life Is Just a Bowl of Cherries"[35] (from *BIG DEAL*, 1986)
 V. Pettiford
 (*Music by* Ray Henderson. *Lyrics by* Lew Brown, B. G. DeSylva.)
Fosse's World
 B. Musgrove, J. Lanier, Entire Company
 (*Music by* Gordon Lowry Harrell, including "Calypso" by G. Harrell, and "Snake in the Grass" by Frederick Loewe from *THE LITTLE PRINCE*. film, 1974. *Staged by* Ann Reinking. *Dance elements inspired by* THE LITTLE PRINCE and signature Fosse styles which appeared in *DAMN YANKEES, REDHEAD, NEW GIRL IN TOWN, LITTLE ME, SWEET CHARITY, HOW TO SUCCEED IN BUSINESS WITHOUT REALLY TRYING, CABARET, CHICAGO*)
"Bye Bye Blackbird" (from *LIZA WITH A "Z"*, television, 1972)
 V. Pettiford, J. Agustin, A. Blankenbuehler, M. Calamia, H. Cruikshank, L. Gajda, S. Jovovich, D. LaBarre, M. A. Lamb, S. Lewis, M. MacLeod, D. Moore, E. Parkinson, M. Paternostro, R. Rak, D, Richardson, L. Sakakura, S. Trujillo
 (*Music by* Ray Henderson. *Lyrics by* Mort Dixon.)
Part 1: [Chicago - Influences]
From the Edge (from *DANCIN'*, 1978)
 B. Anderson, C. K. Kirby, A. Sanchez
 (*Music by* Gordon Lowry Harrell.)
Percussion 4 (from *DANCIN'*, 1978)
 D. Richardson
 (*Music by* Gordon Lowry Harrell.)
"Big Spender" (from *SWEET CHARITY*, 1966)
 V. Pettiford, J. Lanier, K. M. Greene, D. LaBarre, M. A. Lamb, S. Lewis, M. MacLeod, D. Moore, E. Parkinson, R. Rak
 (*Music by* Cy Coleman. *Lyrics by* Dorothy Fields.)
"Crunchy Granola Suite" (from *DANCIN'*)
 B. Anderson, E. Fleming
 Danced by J. Agustin, M. Calamia, H. Cruikshank, L. Gajda, S. Jovovich, C. R. Kirby, D. LaBarre, M. A. Lamb, S. Lewis, M. MacLeod, E. Parkinson, M. Paternostro, D. Richardson, L. Sakakura, A. Sanchez.
 (*Music and Lyrics by* Neil Diamond.)
Part 2: [Hollywood]
Transition: "Hooray for Hollywood"
 (*Music by* Richard Whiting. *Lyrics by* Johnny Mercer.)
"From This Moment On" (from *KISS ME, KATE*, film, 1953)
 M. A. Lamb or L. Sakakura (mats.), A. Blankenbuehler
 (*Music and Lyrics by* Cole Porter. The first 45 seconds of film choreography by Bob Fosse; originally danced by Bob Fosse and Carol Haney.)
Alley Dance (from *MY SISTER EILEEN*, film, 1955)
 "Got No Room for Mr. Gloom"
 S. Wise or B. Musgrove (mats.), S. Jovovich
 (*Music by* Jule Styne. *Lyrics by* Leo Robin.)
Transition: Dance elements inspired by *RED HEAD* (1959)
 Company
Walking the Cat (*Music by* Patrick S. Brady. *Staged by* Ann Reinking.)
 "I Wanna Be a Dancin' Man"[36] (from *DANCIN'*, 1978)
 E. Fleming, V. Pettiford, J. Lanier, S. Wise, and B. Anderson, A. Blankenbuehler, M. Calamia, L. Gajda, K. M. Greene, C. R. Kirby, M. A. Lamb, S. Lewis, M. McLeod, D. Moore, B. Musgrove, E. Parkinson, A. Sanchez, S. Trujillo.
 (*Music by* Harry Warren. *Lyrics by* Johnny Mercer. *Dedicated to* Fred Astaire.)

ACT 2
Part 3: [New York]
"Shoeless Joe from Hannbal Mo" (from *DAMN YANKEES*, 1955)
 J. Agustin, B. Anderson, A. Blankenbuehler, M. Calamia, E. Fleming, C. R. Kirby, A. Sanchez, S. Trujillo, M. Paternostro, M. Wise
 Pitcher: A. Sanchez. *Batters*: B. Anderson, S. Wise. *Bunter*: J. Agustin.
 (*Music and Lyrics by* Richard Adler and Jerry Ross.)
Transition: Dance elements inspired by *NEW GIRL IN TOWN* (1957)
 A. Sanchez
Nightclubs: The Dance Team of Bob Fosse and Mary Ann Niles:
"Dancing in the Dark"
 (*Music by* Arthur Schwartz. *Lyrics by* Howard Dietz.)
"I Love a Piano" (from *STOP! LOOK! LISTEN!*, 1916)
 (*Music and Lyrics by* Irving Berlin.) S. Lewis, R. Rak
 Danced by S. Wise; E. Parkinson and S. Jovovich; L. Sakakura and A. Blankenbuehler; J. Lanier, M. Paternostro and A. Sanchez; J. Agustin, B. Anderson, M. Calamia, H. Cruikshank, D. LaBarre, M. A. Lamb, M. MacLeod, S. Trujillo.
 Dance elements inspired by Fosse/Niles or Fosse appearances on such television shows as Your Hit Parade (1950), the Morey Amsterdam Show (1949), the Colgate Comedy Hour (1951), the motion picture *THE AFFAIRS OF DOBIE GILLIS* (1953), Cavalcade of Stars (1951), The Ed Sullivan Show (1956).
 Music arranged by Patrick S. Brady. *Staged by* Ann Reinking.
"Steam Heat"
 J. Lanier, M. Paternostro, A. Sanchez
 (*Music and Lyrics by* Richard Adler and Jerry Ross.)
"I Gotcha" (from the *LIZA WITH A "Z"*, TV, 1972.)
 S. Lewis, B. Musgrove, C. R. Kirby
 (*Music and Lyrics by* Joseph Arrington, Jr. [Joe Tex].)
"Rich Man's Frug" (from *SWEET CHARITY*, 1966)
 L. Gajda; B. Musgrove, and A. Blankenbuehler; J. Agustin, B. Anderson, M. Calamia, H. Cruikshank, S. Jovovich, C. R. Kirby, D. LaBarre, S. Lewis, M. MacLeod, R. Rak, L. Sakakura, S. Trujillo
 The Aloof; The Heavyweight; The Big Finish.
 (*Music by* Cy Coleman.)
Transition: My Silky Thoughts
 (*Music by* Patrick Brady.)
Cool Hand Luke (from The Bob Hope Special, TV, October 1968)
 E. Parkinson, D. Richardson and C. R. Kirby
 (*Music by* Lalo Schifrin. *Choreographed for* Gwen Verdon, with Lee Roy Reams and Buddy Vest.)
Transition: "Big Noise from Winnetka"[37] (from *DANCIN'*, 1978)
 (*Music by* Ray Bauduc, Bob Haggart. *Lyrics by* Bob Crosby, Gil Rodin.)
"Dancing Dan"[38] (Me and My Shadow) (from *BIG DEAL*, 1986)
 (*Music by* Dave Dryer and Al Jolson. *Lyrics by* Billy Rose.)
 E. Fleming, K. M. Greene, D. Moore
"Nowadays"/"The Hot Honey Rag" (from *CHICAGO*, 1975)
 V. Pettiford, J. Lanier
 (*Music by* John Kander. *Lyrics by* Fred Ebb.)

ACT 3
Part 4: [Complexities]
"Glory" (from *PIPPIN*, 1972)
 E. Fleming
 Danced by C. R. Kirby, J. Agustin, B. Anderson, A. Blankenbuehler, M. Calamia, S. Jovovivh, M. A. Lamb, B. Musgrove, E. Parkinson, M. Paternostro, L. Sakakura, A. Sanchez.
 (*Music and Lyrics by* Stephen Schwartz.)
"Manson Trio" (from *PIPPIN*, 1972)
 E. Fleming, D. LaBarre, M. McLeod
 (*Music and Lyrics by* Stephen Schwartz.)
"Mein Herr" (from *CABARET*, film, 1972)
 V. Pettiford, and H. Cruikshank, L. Gajda, K. M. Greene, S. Lewis, D. Moore, R. Rak
 (*Music by* John Kander. *Lyrics by* Fred Ebb.)
"Take Off with Us" (Three Pas de Deux from *ALL THAT JAZZ*, film, 1979)
 M. Calamia and L. Sakakura; M. A. Lamb and E. Parkinson; B. Musgrove and D. Richardson
 (*Music by* Stanley R. Lebowsky. *Lyrics by* Fred Tobias.)
"Razzle Dazzle" (from *CHICAGO*, 1975)
 S. Wise, K. M. Greene, D. Moore
 (*Music by* John Kander. *Lyrics by* Fred Ebb.)

[34]In September 1999 SFX Entertainment Group acquired the assets of LIVENT and became the show's producer.
[35]Song first introduced to Broadway by Ethel Merman in *GEORGE WHITE'S SCANDALS* (1931).
[36]Song first introduced on film by Fred Astaire in *THE BELLE OF NEW YORK*, 1951.

[37]First introduced by its authors on film in *LET'S MAKE MUSIC* in 1941.
[38]First introduced as a popular song by Al Jolson and Ted Lewis in 1927.

"Who's Sorry Now?"[39] (from *ALL THAT JAZZ*, film, 1979)
    H. Cruikshank, L. Gajda, D. LaBarre, M. A. Lamb, S. Lewis, M. MacLeod,
    E. Parkinson, R. Rak, L. Sakakura
    (*Music by* Harry Ruby. *Lyrics by* Ted Snyder and Bert Kalmar.)
"There'll Be Some Changes Made"[40] (from *ALL THAT JAZZ*, film, 1979)
    J. Lanier, K. M. Greene, D. Moore
    (*Music by* W. Benton Overtsreet. *Lyrics by* Billy Higgins.)
"Mr. Bojangles"[41] (from *DANCIN'*, 1978)
    A. Blankenbuehler
    Mr. Bojangles: S. Trujillo. *The Spirit*: D. Richardson.
    (*Music and Lyrics by* Jerry Jeff Walker.)
"Life Is Just a Bowl of Cherries" (reprise)
    V. Pettiford
Part 5: Finale
Benny Goodman's "Sing Sing Sing"[42] (from *DANCIN'*, 1978)
    (*Music and Lyrics by* Louis Prima.)/
"Christopher Columbus"
    (*Music and Lyrics by* Andy Razaf and Leon Berry.) Entire Company
    Drums: P. Cavari. *Bass*: M. Hall. *Trombone solo*: J. Pugh.
    Danced by H. Cruikshank, C. R. Kirby, D. Richardson.
    Trumpet solo: G. Drewes.
    Danced by E. Parkinson.
    Clarinet solo: W. Weiskopf.
    Danced by V. Pettiford, J. Lanier, M. MacLeod, D. Moore, K. M. Greene,
    M. A. Lamb, R. Rak, J. Agustin, B. Anderson, M. Calamia, C. Kirby,
    A. Sanchez, S. Trujillo, M. Paternostro.
    Piano solo: J. Werking.
    Danced by S. Wise, E. Fleming.

1999.02   (DEIN PERRY'S) STEEL CITY

A Dance Revue in One Act[43]. Conceived, directed and choreographed by
Dein Perry. Music (and lyrics) by Tim Finn. Sets designed by Brian
Thomson. Costumes by Michael Wilkinson. Lighting by Trudy Dalgleish.
Sound by Darryl Lewis. Produced by Garry Van Egmond for Theaters and
Concerts International. Opened 26 January 1999 at Radio City Music Hall
and closed 30 January 1999 after 7 performances.

CAST: DEIN PERRY, Paul Davis, Nathan Sheens, Lee McDonald, Grant Turner,
Sheldon Perry, Brian Burke, Dan Clemente, Steven Grace, Andrew Harrison, Nigel
Long, Sean Mulligan, Shane Preston, Glen Rhule, Dean Street, Aaron Sweetman,
Melissa Gibson, Brooke Henderson, Leah Howard, Rebecca Jeffs, Rachel Schmaltz,
Ann Tsirigotis.

MUSICAL NUMBERS
    "Steel City"
    Truss Dance
    "Spirit Level"
    "Old Car"
    "Drop Out"
        (*Music and Lyrics by* Tim Finn and M. Azcona.)
    "Walking"
    "Smoke Duet"
    "Rock & Roll Girl"
    "Absail"
    "Forklifts"
    "Where I Live"
        (*Music and Lyrics by* Tim Finn and M. Chunn.)
    "New Car"
    "Road Trip"
        (*Music and Lyrics by* Tim Finn and M. Azcona.)
    "Glide"
Finale

**YOU'RE A GOOD MAN,
CHARLIE BROWN**

1999.03

A Revival of the Musical Entertainment in Two Acts[44]. Book[45], music and
lyrics by Clark Gesner. Based on the comic strip "Peanuts" by Charles M.
Schulz. Directed by Michael Mayer. Choreography by Jerry Mitchell.
Scenic design by David Gallo. Costume design by Michael Krass. Lighting
design by Kenneth Posner. Sound design by Brian Ronan. Musical direction
by Kimberly Grigsby. Music supervision, arrangements and additional mate-
rial by Andrew Lippa. Orchestrations by Michel Gibson. Produced by
Michael Leavitt, Fox Theatricals, and Jerry Frankel, Arthur Whitelaw, Gene
Persson, in association with Larry Payton. Opened 4 February 1999 at the
Ambassador Theatre and closed 13 June 1999 after 150 performances.

CAST (in order of appearance): *Sally*: KRISTIN CHENOWETH. *Schroeder*:
STANLEY WAYNE MATHIS. *Linus*: B. D. WONG. *Snoopy*: ROGER BART. *Lucy*:
ILANA LEVINE. *Charlie Brown*: ANTHONY RAPP.

Time: An average day in the life of Charlie Brown.

ACT 1
    "You're a Good Man, Charlie Brown"[46]
        Company
    "Schroeder"
        I. Levine, S. W. Mathis
    "Snoopy"
        R. Bart
    "My Blanket and Me"
        B. D. Wong, Company
    "The Kite"
        A. Rapp
    "The Doctor Is In" (Dr. Lucy)
        I. Levine, A. Rapp
    "Beethoven Day"
        S. W. Mathis
        (*Music and Lyrics by* Andrew Lippa.)
    "Rabbit Chasing"
        K. Chenoweth, R. Bart
    "Book Report"
        A. Rapp, I. Levine, B. D. Wong, S. W. Mathis
ACT 2
    "The Red Baron"
        R. Bart
    "My New Philosophy"
        K. Chenoweth, S. W. Mathis
        (*Music and Lyrics by* Andrew Lippa.)
    "T.E.A.M." (The Baseball Game)
        A. Rapp, Entire Company
    "Glee Club Rehearsal"
        Entire Company
    "Little Known Facts"
        I. Levine, B. D. Wong, A. Rapp
    "Suppertime"
        R. Bart
    "Happiness"
        Entire Company

1999.04   ANNIE GET YOUR GUN

A Revival of the Musical in Two Acts[47]. Music and lyrics by Irving Berlin.
Book by Herbert and Dorothy Fields, revised by Peter Stone. Directed by
Graciela Daniele. Choreographed by Graciela Daniele and Jeff Calhoun.

---

[39]First introduced as a popular song in vaudeville by Gus Van and Joe
Schenck in 1923.
[40]First introduced as a popular song in vaudeville by Billy Higgins in 1924.
[41]First introduced as a popular song by its author in 1968
[42]First introduced on film in *AFTER THE THIN MAN* in 1936.
[43]Production originated in Australia prior to a 40-city American and
Canadian tour. No program found; song list prepared from Australian com-
pact disc (Sony/Columbia), not in performance order.

[44]Originally produced in New York Off-Broadway 7 March 1967 at the
Theatre 80 St. Marks for 1,597 performances. Subsequently revived on
Broadway 1 June 1971 at the John Golden Theatre for 31 performances.
[45]Original book credited to John Gordon, a pseudonym for Clark Gesner
and the collective company of the Original Off-Broadway Cast who devised
the show. Book revisions uncredited.
[46]Additional material by Andrew Lippa.
[47]First produced in New York 16 May 1946 at the Imperial Theatre for
1147 performances.

Scenic design by Tony Walton. Costume design by William Ivey Long. Lighting design by Beverly Emmons. Sound by G. Thomas Clark. Musical director and dance music arrangements by Marvin Laird. Orchestrations by Bruce Coughlin. Supervising music director, vocal and incidental music arranger, John McDaniel. Associate producers, Alecia Parker, Judith Ann Abrams. Produced by Barry and Fran Weissler, in association with Kardana, Michael Watt, Irving Welzer and Hal Luftig. Opened 4 March 1999 at the Marquis Theatre and closed 1 September 2001 after 1046 performances.

CAST (in order of appearance): *Buffalo Bill* (Colonel William F. Cody): RON HOLGATE. *Frank Butler:* TOM WOPAT. *Dolly Tate:* VALERIE WRIGHT. *Tommy Keeler:* ANDREW PALERMO. *Winnie Tate:* NICOLE RUTH SNELSON. *Mac*, the Propman: Kevin Bailey. *Charlie Davenport:* PETER MARX. *Foster Wilson:* RONN CARROLL. *Chief Sitting Bull:* GREGORY ZARAGOZA. *Annie Oakley:* BERNADETTE PETERS. *Kids (3): Jessie Oakley:* Cassidy Ladden. *Nellie Oakley:* Mia Walker. *Little Jake:* Trevor McQueen Eaton. *Running Deer:* Kevin Bailey. *Eagle Feather:* Carlos Lopez. *Dining Car Waiter:* Brad Bradley. *Sleeping Car Porter:* Patrick Wetzel. *Pawnee Bill* (Major Gordon Lillie): RONN CARROLL. *Messenger:* Kevin Bailey. *Band Leader:* Marvin Laird. *Mrs. Schuyler Adams:* Julia Fowler. *Silvia Potter-Porter:* Jenny-Lynn Suckling.

Ensemble: Shaun Amyot, Kevin Bailey, Brad Bradley, Randy Donaldson, Madeleine Ehlert, Julia Fowler, Kisha Howard, Adrienne Hurd, Keri Lee, Carlos Lopez, Desiree Parkman, Eric Sciotto, Kelli Bond Severson, Timothy Edward Smith, Jenny-Lynn Suckling, David Villela, Patrick Wetzel. *Swings:* Leasen Beth Almquist, Patti D'Beck, Rick Spaans.

ACT 1[48]

"There's No Business Like Show Business"
 T. Wopat, Company

"Doin' What Comes Naturally"
 B. Peters, Kids, R. Carroll [Foster Wilson]

"The Girl That I Marry"
 T. Wopat, B. Peters

"You Can't Get a Man with a Gun"
 B. Peters

"There's No Business Like Show Business" (reprise)
 T. Wopat, R. Holgate, P. Marx, B. Peters

"I'll Share It All With You"
 A. Palermo, N. R. Snelson, Company

"Moonshine Lullaby"
 B. Peters, Kids, Ensemble Trio

"There's No Business Like Show Business" (reprise)
 B. Peters

"They Say It's Wonderful"
 B. Peters, T. Wopat

"My Defenses Are Down"
 T. Wopat, Young Men

The Trick
 B. Peters, Company

Finale Act 1: "You Can't Get a Man with a Gun" (reprise)
 B. Peters

ACT 2

"The European Tour"
 B. Peters, Company

"(I Got) Lost in His Arms"
 B. Peters

"Who Do You Love, I Hope"
 A. Palermo, N. R. Snelson, Company

"I Got the Sun in the Morning"
 B. Peters, Company

"An Old-Fashioned Wedding"
 B. Peters, T. Wopat

"The Girl That I Marry" (reprise)
 T. Wopat

"Anything You Can Do"
 B. Peters, T. Wopat

"They Say It's Wonderful"
 B. Peters, T. Wopat, Company

Finale Ultimo
 Company

---

[48]For subsequent national tour, Jeff Calhoun was credited as both director and choreographer. "I'll Share It All with You" and "The European Tour" were both dropped.

1999.05 BAND IN BERLIN

A Musical in One Act. (Book) Written and conceived by Susan Feldman[49]. Production staged and choreographed and co-conceived by Patricia Birch. Directed by Patricia Birch and Susan Feldman. Set design by Douglas W. Schmidt. Costume design by Jonathan Bixby, Gregory Gale. Lighting design by Kirk Bookman. Sound design by David Schnirman. Musical director, Wilbur Pauley. Media design, Richard Law. Filmmakers, Anthony Chase, Eric Rodine. Puppet design by Stephen Kaplin. Assistant director/choreographer, Jonathan Stuart Cerullo. Keyboard arrangements by Robert Wolinsky. Associate producers, Marsha Dubrow, Gilford/Freeley, Kathleen O'Grady, Geoffrey Shearing, Joseph S. Steinberg. Produced by Robert V. Strauss, Jeffrey Ash, Randall L. Wreghitt, Gayle Francis in association with Marcia Roberts, DLT Entertainment/ADF Enterprises, by special arrangement with Art at St. Ann's and American Music Theater Festival (Philadelphia). Opened 7 March 1999 at the Helen Hayes Theatre and closed 21 March 1999 after 17 performances.

CAST: *Roman Cykowski*, on film and voice-over: HUBERT RUBENS. (HUDSON SHAD): *Ari Leshnikoff*, First Tenor: MARK BLEEKE. *Erich Collin*, Second Tenor: TIMOTHY LEIGH EVANS. *Harry Frommermann*, Lyric Baritone: HUGO MUNDAY. *Roman Cykowski*, Baritone: PETER BECKER. *Robert Biberti*, Bass: WILBUR PAULEY. *Erwin Bootz*, Pianist: ROBERT WOLINSKY.

Time and Place: Memories of Germany 1927-1935.

MUSICAL NUMBERS[50]
Overture
 "Schlaf Mein Neüer Liebling" (Good Night, Sweetheart)
  (*Music by* Ray Noble. *German Lyrics by* Beda [Fritz Löhner].)
Prologue
 "Ein Neüer Frühling Wird In Die Heimat Kommen" (A New Spring Will Come to the Homeland)
  (*Music and German Lyrics by* Will Meisel, Willy Engelberger and Fritz Rotter.)
The Beginning
 "Schöne Isabella Aus Kastilien" (Dearest Isabella from Castille)
  (*Music and German Lyrics by* Erwin Bootz and Gerd Karlick. *English lyrics by* Wilbur Pauley.)
 "My Little Green Cactus" (Meine kleine Gruner Kaktus)
  (*Music and Lyrics by* Dorian and Horda [Bert Reisfeld and Rolf Marbot].)
 "Quand Il Pleut"/"Stormy Weather"
  (*Music by* Harold Arlen. *English Lyrics by* Ted Koehler.)
The Rise
 "Wochenend und Sonnenschein" (Happy Days Are Here Again)
  (*Music by* Milton Ager. *English Lyrics by* Jack Yellen. *German Lyrics by* Charles Amberg.)
 "Veronika, Der lenz ist Da" (Spring Is Here)
  (*Music by* Walter Jurmann. *German Lyrics by* Fritz Rotter. *English Lyrics by* Wilbur Pauley.)
 "Die Dorfmusik" (Village Music)
  (*Music and Lyrics by* Fryberg, von Donop and Kirsten.)
 "Tea for Two" (from NO, NO, NANETTE)
  (*Music by* Vincent Youmans. *Lyrics by* Irving Caesar.)
World Tour
 "Wie Wär's Mal Mit Lissabon?" (What's Happening in Lisbon?)
  (*Music and Lyrics by* Werner Bochman and Lehnow.)
 It Don't Mean a Thing If It Ain't Got That Swing"
  (*Music by* Duke Ellington. *Lyrics by* Irving Mills.)
 "Creole Love Call"
  (*Music and Lyrics by* Duke Ellington.)
 Overture to THE BARBER OF SEVILLE
  (*Music by* Giaccomo Rossini.)
Performing Under the Third Reich
 "Night and Day"/"Nuit et Jour" (from THE GAY DIVORCE)
  (*Music and Lyrics by* Cole Porter. *French Lyrics by* Emila Renaud.)
 "Ein Neuer Frühling Wird In Die Heimat Kommen" (A New Spring Will Come to the Homeland) (reprise)
 "Eine Kleine Frühlingsweise" (A Little Spring Melody)
  (*Music by* Anton Dvorak. *German Lyrics by* Langsfelder.)

---

[49]Based on the true story of the Comedian Harmonists, a German vocal sextet whose sudden rise to fame in the 1920s was cut short by the Third Reich.
[50]All music numbers performed by Hudson Shad in German, English and/or French with piano accompaniment.

"Der Onkel Bumba Aus Columba Tanzt Nur Rumba" (When Yuba Plays the Rumba on His Tuba)(from *THE THIRD LITTLE SHOW*)
(*Music and English Lyrics by* Herman Hupfeld. *German Lyrics by* Fritz Rotter and A. Robinson.)

Swansong Tour

"Whistle While You Work" (from *SNOW WHITE AND THE SEVEN DWARFS* film)
(*Music by* Frank Churchill. *Lyrics by* Larry Morey.)

"Die Liebe Kommt Die Liebe Geht" (Love Comes, Love Goes)
(*Music by* Fritz Kreisler. *German Lyrics by* Ernst Marischka. *English Lyrics by* Wilbur Pauley.)

"Baby, (Wo Ist Mein Baby)"
(*Music by* Friedrich Holländer. *Lyrics by* Mehring.)

"Der Alte Cowboy" (The Last Round-Up) (from *ZIEGFELD FOLLIES OF 1934*)
(*Music and English Lyrics by* Billy Hill. *German Lyrics by* Walter.)

Epilogue

"Auf Wiederseh'n, My Dear"
(*Music and English Lyrics by* Al Hoffman, Al Goodheart, Ed Nelson, Milton Ager. *German Lyrics by* Charles Amberg.)

1999.06 ROLLIN' ON THE T.O.B.A.

A Tribute to the Last Days of Black Vaudeville (Musical Revue) in Two Acts, 11 Scenes. Conceived by Ronald "Smokey" Stevens and Jaye Stewart, featuring excerpts from "The Simple Stories" by Langston Hughes. Additional material by Irvin S. Bauer. Set design by Larry W. Brown. Costume design by Michele Reisch. Lighting design by Jon Kusner. Sound design by Shabach Audio. Musical direction and orchestrations by David Alan Bunn. Choreographed by Leslie Dockery. Directed by Ronald "Smokey" Stevens and Leslie Dockery. Associate producers, Martin Shugrue, Carriene Nevin. Produced by John Grimaldi, Ashton Springer, Frenchmen Productions, Inc. Opened 24 March 1999 at the Kit Kat Club (Henry Miller's Theatre) and closed 4 April 1999 after 14 performances[51].

<u>CAST</u> (in order of appearance): *Stevens:* RONALD "SMOKEY" STEVENS. *Stewart:* RUDY ROBERSON. *Bertha Mae Little:* SANDRA REAVES-PHILLIPS.

The action takes place on the T. O. B. A.[52] circuit in 1931.

Act 1, Scene 1: On the Train. *Scene 2:* Monogram Theatre. *Scene 3:* Bertha's Phone Call. *Scene 4:* Dressing Room. *Scene 5:* Royal Theatre. *Scene 6:* Bertha's Letter/On the Train. *Scene 7:* Booker T. Theatre.

Act 2, Scene 1: Regal Theatre. *Scene 2:* Bertha's Show/The Regal Theatre. *Scene 3:* On the Train. *Scene 4:* On the Train.

ACT 1

Overture

"Rollin' on the T.O.B.A."
Entire Company
(*Music and Lyrics by* Ronald "Smokey" Stevens, Sandra Reaves-Phillips, Chapman Roberts, Benny Key and David Alan Bunn.)

Scene 1

Toast to Harlem
R. Roberson, R. S. Stevens

Scene 2

"Bill Robinson Walk"
R. S. Stevens
(*Music by* Bill "Bojangles" Robinson.)

Evolution
(*by* Flournoy Miller and Aubrey Lyles)

"Ugly Chile"
R. Roberson, R. S. Stevens
(*Music by* Clarence Williams. *Lyrics by* Johnny Mercer.)

Scene 3

"Travelin' Blues"
S. Reaves-Phillips
(*Music and Lyrics by* Ronald "Smokey" Stevens and Sandra Reaves-Phillips.)

Scene 4

Lincoln West
(*by* Gwendolyn Brooks)
The Liar (Staggerlee)
(*by* Terrence Cooper) R. Roberson, R. S. Stevens

Scene 5

"(Saturday Night) Fish Fry"
R. Roberson, R. S. Stevens
(*Music and Lyrics by* Ellis Walsh and Louis Jordan.)

Scene 6

"St. Louis Blues"
S. Reaves-Phillips
(*Music and Lyrics by* W. C. Handy.)

Scene 7

"The Poker Game"
R. S. Stevens
(*Sketch by* Bert Williams, set to music "Black and Tan Fantasy" by Duke Ellington.)

"Nobody" (interpolated into *ZIEGFELD FOLLIES OF 1910*)
R. S. Stevens
(*Music and Lyrics by* Bert Williams.)

"Huggin' and Chalkin'"
R. Roberson
(*Music and Lyrics by* Kermit Goell and Clancy Hayes.)

"Sexy Blues"/"You've Taken My Blues and Gone"
S. Reaves-Phillips
(*Music and Lyrics by* Sandra Reaves-Phillips, Chapman Roberts and Ronald "Smokey" Stevens; *Sketch by* Langston Hughes.)

The Car Crash and Broken Dialogue
(*by* Flournoy Miller and Aubrey Lyles)
R. Roberson, R. S. Stevens

Conversationalization
(*by* Flournoy Miller and Aubrey Lyles)
R. Roberson, R. S. Stevens

"Let the Good Times Roll"
Entire Company
(*Music and Lyrics by* Sam Theard and Fleecie Moore.)

ACT 2

Scene 1

"(New Orleans) Hop Scop Blues"
R. S. Stevens
(*Music by* Clarence Williams.)

The Chess Game
R. Roberson, R. S. Stevens
(Sketch set to "Funeral March of the Marionettes," *Music by* Charles Gounod.)

Scene 2

"Take Me as I Am"
S. Reaves-Phillips
(*Music by* Sandra Reaves-Phillips.)

"One Hour Mama"
S. Reaves-Phillips
(*Music and Lyrics by* Porter Grainger.)

"Million Dollar Secret"
S. Reaves-Phillips
(*Music and Lyrics by* Helen Humes and Jules Bihari.)

Freddie and Flo
(*by* Butterbeans and Susie) S. Reaves-Phillips, R. Roberson

"A Good Man is Hard to Find"
S. Reaves-Phillips
(*Music and Lyrics by* Eddie Green.)

"Take Me as I Am" (reprise)
S. Reaves-Phillips

Scene 3

Simple on Integration
(*by* Langston Hughes) R. Roberson, R. S. Stevens

Soul Food
(*by* Langston Hughes) R. Roberson, R. S. Stevens, S. Reaves-Phillips

Scene 4

Banquet in Honor
(*by* Langston Hughes) R. Roberson, R. S. Stevens

I'm Still Here
(*by* Langston Hughes)

---

[51]First produced by the AMAS Musical Theatre (Rosetta LeNoire, Founder and Artistic Director), and subsequently Off-Broadway 28 January-7 March 1999 at the 47th Street Theatre for 45 performances.

[52]Theatre Owners' Booking Association controlled a circuit of exclusively black theatres.

Trouble in Mind
  (*by* Richard Jones) R. Roberson, R. S. Stevens, S. Reaves-Phillips
"Rollin' on the T. O. B. A." (reprise)
  Entire Company

1999.07

MARLENE

A Musical Play in Two Acts. Play by Pam Gems. Directed by Sean Matthias. Set designer, John Arnone. Costume designer, David C. Woolard. Lighting designer, Marc Jonathan. Sound designer, Peter J. Fitzgerald. Musical direction, Kevin Amos. Associate producers, Alice Chebba Walsh, Mary Ellen Ashley, Anne L. Bernstein, Kimberly Vaughn, Richard Samson, Jennifer Lee, Herb Goldsmith Productions. Produced by Ric Wanetik and Frederic B. Vogel. Opened 11 April 1999 at the Cort Theatre and closed 2 May 1999 after 25 performances.

CAST (in order of appearance): *Mutti*: Mary Diveny. *Vivian (Hoffman)*: Margaret Whitton. *Marlene Dietrich*: SIÂN PHILLIPS.

Scene: A theatre in Paris. 1969.

ACT 1[53]

"You Do Something to Me" (from *FIFTY MILLION FRENCHMEN*)
  (*Music and Lyrics by* Cole Porter.)
"Look Me Over Closely"
  (*Music and Lyrics by* Terry Gilkyson.)
"Illusions" (from *ILLUSIONS* film)
  (*Music and Lyrics by* Frederick Holländer.)
"Johnny, (wenn Du Geburtstag hast)"(Jonny) (from *SONG OF SONGS* film)
  (*Music and Lyrics by* Frederick Holländer.)
"(Ich bin die fesche) Lola" (from *THE BLUE ANGEL* film)
  (*Music and Lyrics by* Frederick Holländer.)
"I Wish You Love" (Que Reste-til de Nos Amours)
  (*Music and French lyrics by* Charles Trenet . *English lyrics by* Albert Beach.)

ACT 2

"Mein Blondes Baby"
  (*Music and Lyrics by* Peter Kreueder and Fritz Rotter.)
"Warum" (Frag' Nicht Warum Ich Gehe)
  (*Music by* Robert Stolz. *Lyrics by* Walter Reisch and A. Robinson.)
"The Laziest Girl in Town" (from *STAGE FRIGHT* film)
  (*Music and Lyrics by* Cole Porter.)
"The Boys in the Back Room" (See What the Boys in the Back Room Will Have) (from *DESTRY RIDES AGAIN,* film)
  (*Music by* Frederick Holländer. *Lyrics by* Frank Loesser.)
"Lili Marlene"
  (*Music by* Norbert Schultze. *Original German lyrics by* Hans Leip. *English lyrics by* Tommie Connor.)
"Honeysuckle Rose" (from *LOAD OF COAL* revue)
  (*Music by* Fats Waller. *Lyrics by* Andy Razaf.)
"Where Have All the Flowers Gone?"
  (*Music and Lyrics by* Pete Seeger.)
"La vie en Rose"
  (*Music and French Lyrics by* Edith Piaf and Louiguy.)
"Falling in Love Again" (Ich bin von Kopf bis Fuss auf Liebe eingestellt) (from *THE BLUE ANGEL,* film)
  (*Music by* Frederick Holländer. *Lyrics by* Sammy Lerner.)

1999.08

THE CIVIL WAR

An American Musical Event (a Musical) in Two Acts. Book and lyrics by Frank Wildhorn, Jack Murphy and Gregory Boyd[54]. Music by Frank Wildhorn. Directed by Jerry Zaks. Musical staging by Luis Perez. Scenic design by Douglas W. Schmidt. Costume design by William Ivey Long. Lighting design by Paul Gallo. Sound design by Karl Richardson. Projections by Wendall K. Harrington. Orchestrations by Kim Scharnberg. Musical director, Jeff Lams. Musical supervision, Jason Howland. Vocal director, Dave Clemmons. Battles by David Leong. Originally commis-

sioned and produced by Alley Theatre, Houston, Texas. Executive producer, Gary Gunas, PACE Theatrical Group. Associate producers, I. W. Marks, Michael Skipper and Chris Edgecomb. Produced by Pierre Cossette, PACE Theatrical Group/SFX Entertainment, Bomurwil Productions, Kathleen Raitt, and Jujamcyn Theatres. Opened 22 April 1999 at the St. James Theatre and closed 13 June 1999 after 61 performances.

CAST: Union Army: *Captain Emmet Lochran*: Michael Lanning. *Sergeant Patrick Anderson*: Rod Weber. *Sergeant Byron Richardson*: Royal Reed. *Corporal William McEwen*: Gilles Chiasson. *Private Conrad Bock*: Ron Sharpe. *Private Charles Spencer*: Bart Shatto. *Private Nathaniel Taylor*: John Sawyer.

Of the Confederate Army: *Captain Billy Pierce*: Gene Miller. *Sergeant Virgil Franklin*: Dave Clemmons. *Corporal John Beauregard*: Mike Eldred. *Corporal Henry Stewart*: David M. Lutken. *Private Darius Barksdale*: Anthony Galde. *Private Cyrus Stevens*: Jim Price. *Private Sam Taylor*: Matt Bogart.

Frederick Douglass: Keith Byron Kirk. *Clayton Toler*: Michel Bell. *Bessie Tholer*: Cheryl Freeman. *Benjamin Reynolds*: Lawrence Clayton. *Exter Thomas*: Wayne W. Pretlow. *Harriet Jackson*: Capathia Jenkins. *Liza Hughes*: Cassandra White.

Autolycus Fell: Leo Burmester. *Auctioneer's Assistant*: Dave Clemmons. *Sarah McEwen*: Irene Molloy. *Violet*: Hope Harris. *Mabel*: Beth Leavel. *Mrs. Bixby*: Beth Leavel. *Nurse*: Hope Harris. *Voice of President Lincoln*: David M. Lutken. *Pit Singers*: David Michael Felty, Hope Harris, Monique Midgette, Raun Ruffin. *Swings*: David Michael Felty, Monique Midgette, Chris Roberts, Raun Ruffin.

(The action is set during the American Civil War 1861-1865.)

ACT 1[55]

"A House Divided"
  The Citizens
"Freedom's Child"
  K. B. Kirk, other Abolitionists
"By the Sword"/"Sons of Dixie"
  The Armies
"Tell My Father"
  M. Bogart
"The Peculiar Institution"
  The Enslaved
"If Prayin' Were Horses"
  M. Bell, C. Freeman
"Greenback"
  L. Burmester, B. Leavel, H. Harris
"Missing You (My Bill)"
  I. Molloy
"Judgement Day"
  G. Miller, M. Lanning, M. Bogart, the Armies
"Father, How Long?"
  M. Bell
"Someday"
  C. Jenkins, C. Freeman, Others
"I'll Never Pass This Way Again"
  D. M. Lutken
"How Many Devils?"
  The Armies

ACT 2

"Virginia"
  G. Miller
"Candle in the Window"
  C. Jenkins
"Oh! Be Joyful!"
  L. Burmester, R. Reed, R. Sharpe, B. Shatto
"The Hospital"
  B. Leavel, H. Harris, Union Soldiers, M. Bell
"If Prayin' Were Horses" (reprise)
  M. Bell, C. Freeman
"River Jordan"
  L. Clayton, others
"Sarah"
  G. Chiasson

---

[53]Some songs performed in excerpt form. All vocals by Siân Phillips.
[54]Authors' note: Many voices inspired the writing of *THE CIVIL WAR*: Sojourner Truth and Abraham Lincoln; Walt Whitman, Sullivan Ballou and Frederick Douglass; Hanna Ropes and R. E. Lee; Henry Kyd Douglas (2nd Virginia) and Henry Pearson (6th New Hampshire), among others.

---

[55]The subsequent national tour presented by Networks (SFX Entertainment) was directed by Stephen Rayne. Musical staging, by Ken Roberson; Costumes by Christine Hanak; Lighting by Howell Binkley; Sound by Duncan Edwards, other credits unchanged. The order of musical numbers was substantially revised; added were "Brother My Brother," "Old Gray Coat," "I Never Knew His Name," and "The Day the Sun Stood Still."

"The Honor of Your Name"
  I. Molloy
"Greenback" (reprise)
  L. Burmester, H. Harris
"Northbound Train"
  M. Lanning
"Last Waltz for Dixie"
  G. Miller, Confederate Soldiers
"The Glory"
  M. Lanning, K. B. Kirk, L. Clayton, Full Company

IT AIN'T NOTHIN' BUT THE BLUES

1999.09

A Musical (Revue) in Two Acts. Written by Charles Bevel, Lita Gaithers, Randal Myler, Ron Taylor, Dan Wheetman. Based on an original idea by Ron Taylor. Directed by Randal Myler. Movement, Donald McKayle. Set design, Robin Sanford Roberts. Costume design by Enid Turnbull. Lighting design, Don Darnutzer. Sound design, Jon Weston. Musical direction, Dan Wheetman. Vocal direction, Lita Gaithers. Associate producers, Electric Factory Concerts, Adam and David Friedson, Richard Martini, Marcia Roberts, Murray Schwartz. Associate producer, Ron Taylor. Produced by Eric Krebs, Jonathan Reinis, Lawrence Horowitz, Anita Waxman, Elizabeth Williams, CTM Productions, Anne Squadron, in association with Lincoln Center Theater Company. A production of the Crossroads Theater Company, San Diego Repertory Theatre and Alabama Shakespeare Festival. Opened 24 April 1999 at the Vivian Beaumont Theatre, closing 29 August 1999, moved 9 September 1999 to the Ambassador Theatre and closed 2 January 2000 after 276 performances.[56]

CAST (*The Ensemble*): "MISSISSIPPI" CHARLES BEVEL, GRETHA BOSTON, CARTER CALVERT, ELOISE LAWS, GREGORY PORTER, RON TAYLOR, DAN WHEETMAN.
  The Band: Kevin Cooper, Jim Ehinger, Debra Laws, Tony Matthews, Charlie Rhythm, Daryll Whitlow.

ACT 1[57]
"Odun De" (Music traditional[58].)
  Company
"Niwah Wechi" (Music traditional[59].)
  E. Laws, Company
"Blood Done Signed My Name" (Music traditional.)
  R. Taylor, G. Boston
"Raise Them Up Higher" (Music traditional.)
  C. Bevel
"Danger Blues" (Music traditional.)
  E. Laws
"Black Woman" (Music traditional.)
  G. Porter
"I'm Gonna Do What the Spirit Say Do" (Music traditional.)
  G. Boston
"I've Been Living with the Blues"
  Company
  (*Music and Lyrics by* Sonny Terry and Brownie McGhee.)
"Blues Man"
  R. Taylor
  (*Music and Lyrics by* Z. Z. (Arzelle) Hill.)

---

[56]First produced in New York Off-Broadway 26 March-11 April 1999 at the New Victory Theatre for 15 performances. Returned (Off-Broadway) 28 August 2000 to B.B. King Blues Club for a 6 performances/week run.
[57]Dropped after New Victory Theatre engagement:
  "Gabrielle" (Act 1)
  D. Wheetman, R. Taylor
    (*Music and Lyrics by* Dan Wheetman.)
  "Goin' to Lousianne" (Act 1)
    R. Taylor
    (*Music and Lyrics by* Ron Taylor.)
  "How Can I Keep from Singing" (Music traditional.) (Act 1)
    C. Calvert
  "Go Tell It on the Mountain" (Music traditional.)(Act 1)
    E. Laws
[58]Special thanks to Adetunji Joda.
[59]Special thanks to Donald McKayle.

"My Home's Across the Blue Ridge Mountains" (Music traditional.)
  C. Calvert
"'T' for Texas"
  D. Wheetman
  (*Music and Lyrics by* Jimmie Rogers.)
"Who Broke the Lock?" (Music traditional.)
  G. Porter, C. Bevel
"My Man Rocks Me" (Music traditional.)
  E. Laws
"St. Louis Blues"
  G. Boston
  (*Music and Lyrics by* W.C. Handy.)
"Now I'm Gonna Be Bad"
  C. Calvert
  (*Music and Lyrics by* Dan Wheetman.)
"Walking Blues"
  C. Bevel
  (*Music and Lyrics by* Ron Taylor.)
"Come On In My Kitchen"
  G. Porter
  "(*Music and Lyrics by* Robert L. Johnson.)
"Cross Road Blues"
  C. Bevel
  (*Music and Lyrics by* Robert L. Johnson.)
"I Know I've Been Changed" (Music traditional.)
  G. Boston
"Child of the Most High King"
  R. Taylor, Men
  (Music traditional, arranged by Ron Taylor.)
"Children, Your Line Is Dragging"
  G. Porter
  (Music traditional, arranged by Fisher Thompson, Sr.)
"Catch on Fire"
  Company
  (Music traditional, arranged by Lita Gaithers.)

ACT 2
"Let the Good Times Roll"
  R. Taylor
  (*Music and Lyrics by* Sam Theard and Fleecie Moore.)
"Sweet Home Chicago"
  G. Porter, C. Bevel
  (*Music and Lyrics by* Robert L. Johnson.)
"Wang Dang Doodle"
  G. Boston, C. Calvert, E. Laws
  (*Music and Lyrics by* Willie Dixon.)
"Someone Else Is Stepping In"
  E. Laws
  (*Music and Lyrics by* Denise LaSalle.)
"Please Don't Stop Him"
  G. Boston
  (*Music and Lyrics by* Herb J. Lance and John Wallace; *additional lyrics and arrangements by* Lita Gaithers.)
"I'm Your Hootchie Coochie Man"
  R. Taylor
  (*Music and Lyrics by* Willie Dixon, arranged by Ron Taylor.)
"Crawlin' King Snake"
  G. Porter
  (*Music and Lyrics by* John Lee Hooker.)
"Mind Your Own Business"
  D. Wheetman
  (*Music and Lyrics by* Hank Williams, Sr.)
"Walking After Midnight"
  C. Calvert
  (*Music by* Alan Block. *Lyrics by* Don Hecht.)
"I Can't Stop Lovin' You"
  C. Bevel
  (*Music and Lyrics by* Don Gibson.)
"The Thrill Is Gone"
  R. Taylor
  (*Music and Lyrics by* Roy Hawkins and Rick Darnell.)
"I Put a Spell on You"
  E. Laws
  (*Music and Lyrics by* Jay Hawkins.)
"Fever"
  C. Calvert
  (*Music and Lyrics by* John Davenport and Eddie Cooley.)

"Candy Man" (Music traditional.)
D. Wheetman
"Goodnight, Irene"
C. Bevel, D. Wheetman
(*Music and Lyrics by* Huddie Ledbetter and John A. Lomax.)
"Strange Fruit"
G. Boston
(*Music and Lyrics by* Lewis Allan.)
"Someday We'll All Be Free"
C. Bevel, G. Porter
(*Music and Lyrics by* Donny Hathaway and Edward Howard, arranged by Charles Bevel.)
"Members Only"
Company
(*Music and Lyrics by* Larry Addison, arranged by Ron Taylor.)
"Let the Good Times Roll" (reprise)
Company

THE GERSHWINS'
FASCINATING RHYTHM

1999.10

A Musical (Revue) in One Act. Music by George Gershwin. Lyrics by Ira Gershwin. Conceived for the stage by Mel Marvin and Mark Lamos. Choreographed by David Marques. Directed by Mark Lamos. Source material by Deena Rosenberg. Scneic design, Michael Yeargan. Costume design, Paul Tazewell. Lighting design, Peggy Eisenhauer. Sound design, Abe Jacob. Orchestrations, Larry Hochman. Music direction and supervision, Cynthia Kortman. Musical/vocal arranger, Mel Marvin. Additional arrangements, Paul J. Ascenzo, Joseph Church. First produced at the Hartford Stage Company, and subsequently at the Arizona Theatre Company. Associate producers, Magicworks/SFX Entertainment and Jerry Frankel. Produced by Music Makers Inc. [Mitch Leigh], Columbia Artists, Manny Kladitis. Opened 25 April 1999 at the Longacre Theatre and closed 9 May 1999 after 17 performances.

CAST: MICHAEL BERESSE, DARIUS de HAAS, ADRIANE LENOX, ORFEH, SARA RAMIREZ, PATRICK WILSON, Chris Ghelfi, Tim Hunter, Karen Lifshey, Jill Nicklaus. *Swings:* Brian J. Marcum, Kenya U. Massey.

MUSICAL NUMBERS

"Fascinating Rhythm" (from *LADY, BE GOOD!*)
Company
"I've Got a Crush on You" (from *TREASURE GIRL; STRIKE UP THE BAND*)
S. Ramirez, M. Beresse
"Oh, Lady, Be Good!" (from *LADY, BE GOOD!*)
D. de Haas
"High Hat" (from *FUNNY FACE*)
P. Wilson, S. Ramirez
"Clap Yo' Hands" (from *OH, KAY!*)
Orfeh, Company
"(My) Cousin in Milwaukee" (from *PARDON MY ENGLISH*)
"The Lorelei" (from *PARDON MY ENGLISH*)
A. Lenox, Orfeh
"The Man I Love" (dropped from *STRIKE UP THE BAND*, 1927[60])
"Soon" (from *STRIKE UP THE BAND*)
S. Ramirez, P. Wilson
"Love Is Here to Stay" (pas de deux)
J. Nicklaus, M. Beresse
"Little Jazz Bird" (from *LADY, BE GOOD!*)
D. de Haas
"Isn't It a Pity" (from *PARDON MY ENGLISH*)
S. Ramirez, K. Lifshey
"I Love to Rhyme" (from *GOLDWYN FOLLIES*, film)
"Blah, Blah, Blah" (from *DELICIOUS*, film)
"I Got Rhythm" (from *GIRL CRAZY*)
M. Beresse, Company
"Embraceable You" (from *GIRL CRAZY*)
P. Wilson, C. Ghelfi, T. Hunter, K. Lifshey, J. Nicklaus
"Let's Call the Whole Thing Off" (from *SHALL WE DANCE*, film)
D. de Haas, Orfeh

"Nice Work If You Can Get It" (from *A DAMSEL IN DISTRESS*, film)
A. Lenox
"But Not for Me" (from *GIRL CRAZY*)
P. Wilson
"Just Another Rhumba" (from *GOLDWYN FOLLIES*, film, unused)
S. Ramirez, M. Beresse
"Someone to Watch Over Me" (from *OH, KAY!*)
D. de Haas, K. Lifshey, Orfeh, S. Ramirez, P. Wilson
"The Half of It, Dearie, Blues" (from *LADY, BE GOOD!*)
A. Lenox
"Love Is Here to Stay" (from *GOLDWYN FOLLIES*, film)
S. Ramirez
"How Long Has This Been Going On" (from *ROSALIE*)
P. Wilson
"Home Blues" (from *SHOW GIRL*)
S. Ramirez, P. Wilson
(*Lyrics by* Ira Gershwin and Gus Kahn, set to the Homesickness Theme from 'An American in Paris.')
"Who Cares?" (from *OF THEE I SING*)
M. Beresse. Company
"They Can't Take That Away from Me" (from *SHALL WE DANCE*, film)
Company
"Hang on to Me" (from *LADY, BE GOOD!*)
Company

THE WIZARD OF OZ

1999.11

A Return Engagement of the Musical Spectacle in One Act, 16 Scenes[61]. Based on the novel of the same name by L. Frank Baum and the MGM film adaptation by Noel Langley, Florence Ryerson, Edgar Allan Woolf. Book by John Kane (for the Royal Shakespeare Company), adapted by Robert Johanson. Music by Harold Arlen. Lyrics by E. Y. Harburg. Background music by Herbert Stothart. Directed by Robert Johanson; assistant director, Ron Gibbs. Musical staging by Jamie Rocco; associate choreographer, Donna Drake. Dance and vocal arrangements by Peter Howard. Scenic design by Michael Anania. Costume design by Gregg Barnes. Lighting design by Steve Cochrane. Sound design by David R. Paterson, Mark Menard. Flying by Foy. Animals by William Berloni. Special effects by Ian O'Connor. Musical direction and additional orchestration by Jeff Rizzo. Production originally presented at the Papermill Playhouse, New Jersey (Angelo Del Rossi, Producer). Produced by Madison Square Garden Productions (Tim Hawkins, producer). Opened 6 May 1999 at the Theatre at Madison Square Garden and closed 16 May 1999 after 22 performances[62].

CAST (in order of appearance) In Kansas: *Dorothy:* JESSICA GROVÉ. *Toto:* Plenty. *Aunt Em:* JUDITH MCCAULEY. *Uncle Henry:* Tom Urich. *Hunk:* CASEY COLGAN. *Hickory:* DIRK LUMBARD. *Zeke:* FRANCIS RUIVIVAR. *Almira Gulch:* JOANNE WORLEY. *Professor Marvel:* MICKEY ROONEY.
In Oz: *Glinda, the Good Witch:* JUDITH MCCAULEY. *Lollipop Guild:* Ethan Crough, Martin Klebba, David Steinberg. *Mayor of Munchkinland:* Eugene Pidgeon. *Barristers:* Wendy Coates, Wendy Watts. *Coroner:* Bill Rolon. *The Wicked Witch of the West:* JOANNE WORLEY. *The Scarecrow:* CASEY COLGAN. *Crows:* Shauna Markey, Mary Ruvolo, Martin Klebba. *Crow Voices:* Lenny Daniel, Trent Armand Kendall, Danny Vaccaro. *The Tinman:* DIRK LUMBARD. *Apple Trees:* Lenny Daniel, Bill Rolon, Danny Vaccaro. *Apple Tree Voices:* Karen Babcock, Gail Cook Howell, Christi Moore. *The Cowardly Lion:* FRANCIS RUIVIVAR. *The Wizard of Oz:* MICKEY ROONEY. *Nikko,* Commander of the Flying Monkeys: Martin Klebba. *Winkie General:* Tom Urich.
Munchkins, Poppies, Citizens of Oz, Jitterbugs, Flying Monkeys and Winkies: Karen Babcock, Steve Babiar, Bill Brassea, Alvin Brown, Kelly Burnette, Wendy Coates, Ethan Crough, Lenny Daniel, Gail Cook Howell, Trent Armand Kendall, Martin Klebba, Shauna Markey, Caroline McMahon, Christi Moore, Eugene Pidgeon, Allison Queal, Bill Rolon, Mary Ruvolo, David Steinberg, Danny Vaccaro, Wendy Watts, Deborah Y. Wilson. *Swings:* Ron Gibbs, Kevin Steele, Jamie Waggoner, Emily Westhafer. *Dance Captain:* Ron Gibbs.

[60]Also intended for but unused in *LADY, BE GOOD!* and *ROSALIE.*

[61]This adaptation previously produced in New York 15 May 1997 at the Theatre at Madison Square Garden for 45 performances, and 6 May 1998 at the Theatre at Madison Square Garden for 38 performances. THE WIZARD OF OZ was previously produced on stage in New York in a different adaptation 22 March 1989 at Radio City Music Hall for 37 performances.
[62]Performed an irregular performance schedule of 11 performances a week.

Adam Pascal and Heather Headley in AIDA
Joan Marcus/Photofest

1999–2000 SEASON

1999.12 ## KAT AND THE KINGS

A Musical in Two Acts from South Africa. Book and lyrics by David Kramer. Music and arrangements by Taliep Petersen. Direction by David Kramer. Choreography by Jody J. Abrahams and Loukmaan Adams. Set and costume design by Saul Radomsky. Lighting design by Howard Harrison. Sound design by Orbital Sound/Sebastian Frost. Musical supervision by Gary Hind. Musical direction by Jeff Lams. Produced by Harriet Newman Leve, Judith and David Rosenbauer, in association with Richard Frankel, Marc Routh, Willette Klausner, Kardana-Swinsky Productions, David Kramer, Taliep Petersen, Renaye Kramer, by special arrangement with Paul Elliott, Nick Salmon, Lee Menzies. Opened 19 August 1999 at the Cort Theatre and closed 2 January 2000 after 157 performances.

CAST (in order of appearance): *Kat Diamond*: TERRY HECTOR. *Lucy Dixon*: KIM LOUIS. (*The Kings (4)*): *Young Kat Diamond*: JODY J. ABRAHAMS. *Bingo* LOUKMAAN ADAMS. *Ballie*: JUNAID BOOYSEN. *Magoo*: ALISTAIR IZOBELL.

Act 1: Cape Town, South Africa, 1999. District Six, 1957.

Act 2: Cape Town, South Africa, 1999/1959. Durban, South Africa, 1959.

ACT 1

"Memory"
 K. Louis, the Kings
"American Thing"
 T. Hector, Company
"My Lucky Day"
 J. J. Abrahams, T. Hector
"Mavis"
 T. Hector, L. Adams, J. J. Abrahams, J. Booysen, A. Izobell
"Boetie Guitar"
 T. Hector, The Kings
"Cavalla Kings"
 K. Louis, The Kings
"If Your Shoes Don't Shine"
 T. Hector
"Dress to Kill"
 K. Louis, The Kings
"Shine"
 K. Louis, The Kings
"The Tafelberg Hotel"
 K. Louis, The Kings
"Lonely Girl"
 L. Adams, A. Izobell, T. Hector, J. J. Abrahams, J. Booysen
"Josephine"
 J. Booysen, The Kings
"Wild Time"
 Company

ACT 2

"Happy to Be Nineteen"
 Company
"Lonely Girl" (reprise)
 L. Adams, The Kings
"Oo Wee Bay Bee"
 J. J. Abrahams, The Kings
"Only If You Have a Dream"
 K. Louis, A. Izobell
"The Last Thing You Need"
 J. J. Abrahams, L. Adams, A. Izobell, J. Booysen
"Stupid Boy"
 T. Hector
The Claridges Hotel Medley:
"Cavalla Kings" intro
 The Kings
"The Singing Sensation"
 J. J. Abrahams, K. Louis, The Kings

"The Bell Hop"
 L. Adams, The Kings
"Blind Date"
 A. Izobell
"Lonely Girl" (reprise)
 K. Louis, The Kings
"The Invisible Dog"
 L. Adams, The Kings
"Hey Baby"
 J. J. Abrahams, The Kings
"Cavalla Kings" (reprise)
 K. Louis, The Kings
Skeleton Dance
 The Kings
"Lagunya"
 L. Adams, J. Booysen, J. J. Abrahams, A. Izobell
"Lucky Day" (reprise)
 J. J. Abrahams, T. Hector
Finale:
"The Singing Sensation" (reprise)
 J. J. Abrahams, The Kings
"Hey Baby" (reprise)
 A. Izobell, The Kings
"We Were Rocking"
 T. Hector, Company
"Lagunya" (reprise)
 L. Adams, Company
"Wild Time" (reprise)
 Company

1999.13 ## THE SCARLET PIMPERNEL

A Return Engagement of the Musical Adventure in Two Acts[1]. Book and lyrics by Nan Knighton. Based on the novel of the same name by Baroness Orczy[2]. Music by Frank Wildhorn. Directed and choreographed by Robert Longbottom. Scenery by Andrew Jackness. Costumes by Jane Greenwood. Lighting by Natasha Katz. Sound by Karl Richardson. Fight director, Rick Sordelet. Orchestrations by Kim Scharnberg. Musical direction and vocal arrangements by Ron Melrose. Musical supervision, Jason Howland. Assistant choreographers, Tom Kosis and Darlene Wilson. Dance arrangements by David Chase. Executive producer, Tim Hawkins. Produced by Radio City Entertainment and Ted Forstmann. Opened 10 September 1999 at the Neil Simon Theatre and closed 2 January 2000 after 132 performances. Total, including previous engagement: 772 performances.

CAST (in order of appearance): *Marguerite (St. Just)*: CAROLEE CARMELLO. *Chauvelin*: MARC KUDISCH. *Percy (Blakeney)*: RON BOHMER. *Marie*: Elizabeth Ward Land. *Armand St. Just*: KIRK McDONALD. *Tussaud*: David Masenheimer. *Coupeau*: Stephonne Smith. *Mercier*: David St. Louis. *Ozzy*: Harvey Evans. *Elton*: Russell Garrett. *Dewhurst*: Ken Land. *Jessup*: Charles West. *Ben*: James Hindman. *Farleigh*: Matthew Shepard. *Hal*: Danny Gurwin. *Robespierre*: David Cromwell. *Prince of Wales*: Davd Cromwell.
 Opera Dancers, Soldiers, Prisoners, British Guests and Servants: Emily Hsu, Alicia Irving, David Masenheimer, Robb McKindles, Katie Nutt, Elizabeth O'Neill, Jessica Phillips, Terry Richmond, Laura Schutter, Charles West. *Swings*: Peter Flynn, Drew Geraci, Cynthia Leigh Heim, Jennifer Smith, James Van Teuren.

(The action takes place from May into July, 1794, in England and France.)

ACT 1[3]

---

[1]Originally produced in New York 9 November 1997 at the Minskoff Theatre; revised version opened 10 October 1998, closing after 640 performances. This third engagement reflected minor changes in the script and score, a smaller cast and orchestra.
[2]Pen name for Mrs. Montague Barstow.
[3]Dropped from first production: "Vivez," "Believe," "Only Love," and Lullaby. Added for reconstructed version: Wedding Dance, The Rescue, The Gavotte, The Duel, "I'll Forget You," "She Was There." Dropped for this return engagement: "Believe," "You Are My Home" (reprise), All Act 2 reprises.

"Storybook"
C. Carmello, French Ensemble
"Madame Guillotine"
M. Kudisch
"You Are My Home"
R. Bohmer, C. Carmello
Wedding Dance
Ensemble
"Prayer"
R. Bohmer
"Into the Fire"
R. Bohmer, the League
The Rescue
Ensemble
"Falcon in the Dive"
M. Kudisch
"When I Look at You"
C. Carmello
"Where's the Girl?"
M. Kudisch
"The Creation of Man"
R. Bohmer, the League
"The Riddle"
M. Kudisch, C. Carmello, R. Bohmer

ACT 2
"The Scarlet Pimpernel"
R. Bohmer, C. Carmello, Ball Guests
"They Seek Him Here"
R. Bohmer
The Gavotte
The Company
"She Was There"
R. Bohmer
"I'll Forget You"
C. Carmello
The Duel
R. Bohmer, M. Kudisch, C. Carmello
"Into the Fire" (reprise)
Company

DAME EDNA:
THE ROYAL TOUR

1999.14

An Entertainment in Two Acts. Devised and written (and directed) by Barry Humphries. Music and lyrics by Barry Humphries. Additional material by Ian Davidson. Scenic design by Kenneth Foy. Costume design by Stephen Adnitt. Lighting design by Jason Kantrowitz. Sound design by Peter Fitzgerald. Musical arrangements by Andrew Ross. Artistic associate, Cynthia Onrubia. Associate producers, Skylight Productions, Adam Friedson, David Friedson, Allen Spivak/Larry Magid, Richard Martini. Produced by Leonard Soloway, Chase Mishkin, Steven M. Levy and Jonathan Reinis. Opened 17 October 1999 at the Booth Theatre and closed 2 July 2000 after 297 performances.

CAST: *Dame Edna Everage:* DAME EDNA (Barry Humphries). *The Fingers on the Keyboards:* Andrew Ross. *The Gorgeous Ednaette #1:* Roxane Barlow. *An Equally Gorgeous Ednaette #2:* Tamlyn Brooke Shusterman.

MUSICAL NUMBERS[4]
"It's Edna-Time"
"Look at Me When I'm Talking to You"
"Call Me Old-Fashioned (I'm a Broadway Star)"
"Any Friend of Kenny's Is a Friend of Mine"
(Friends of Kenny)
"Come On Possums, Wave Your Gladiola"

[4]Musical numbers not listed in programs.

1999.15 # SATURDAY NIGHT FEVER

A Musical in Two Acts, 19 Scenes. Based on the Paramount/RSO Picture, based on a story by Nik Cohn. Screenplay by Norman Wexler. Stage adaptation by Nan Knighton, in collaboration with Arlene Phillips, Paul Nicholas and Robert Stigwood. Songs by the Bee Gees[5]. Directed and choreographed by Arlene Phillips. Scenic designer, Robin Wagner. Costumes designed by Andy Edwards. Broadway Costumes designed by Suzy Benzinger. Lighting by Andrew Bridge. Sound by Mick Potter. Musical director, Martyn Axe. Orchestrations by Nigel Wright. Dance and vocal arrangements by Phil Edwards. Associate producers, Manny Kladitis and David Rocksavage. Produced by Robert Stigwood. Opened 21 October 1999 at the Minskoff Theatre and closed 30 December 2000 after 500 performances.

CAST: *Tony Manero:* JAMES CARPINELLO. *Stephanie Mangano:* PAIGE PRICE. *Annette:* ORFEH. *Bobby C:* PAUL CASTREE. *Joey:* SEAN PALMER. *Double J:* ANDY BLANKENBUEHLER. *Gus:* RICHARD H. BLAKE. *Monty:* BRYAN BATT. *Frank Manero:* Casey Nicholaw. *Flo Manero/Lucille:* Suzanne Costallos. *Frank Junior:* Jerry Tellier. *Fusco/Al:* Frank Mastrone. *Jay Langhart/Becker:* David Coburn. *Chester:* Andre Ward. *Cesar:* Michael Balderrama. *Vinnie:* Chris Ghelfi. *Sal:* Danial Jerod Brown. *Dino:* Brian J. Marcum. *Lou:* Rick Spaans. *Dom:* Miles Alden. *Roberto:* Ottavio. *Antonio:* Disco Fernandez. *Ike:* David Robertson. *Shirley:* Karine Plantadit-Bageot. *Maria:* Natalie Willes. *Connie:* Jeanine Meyers. *Doreen:* Angelo Pupello. *Linda Manero/patti:* Aliane Baquerot. *Gina:* Rebecca Sherman. *Sophia:* Paula Wise. *Donna:* Shannon Beach. *Rosalie:* Deanna Dys. *Lola:* Jennifer Newman. *Inez:* Danielle Jolie. *Lorelle:* Stacey Martin. *Kenny:* Kristoffer Cusick. *Nick:* Karl duHoffmann. *Rocker:* Roger Lee Israel. *Natalie:* Anne Nicole Biancofiore. *Ann Marie:* Marcia Urani. *Angela:* Gina Philistine.

Swings: Anne Nicole Biancofiore, Kristoffer Cusick, Karl duHoffmann, David Eggers, Roger Lee Israel, Gina Philistine, Amanda Plesa, Marcia Urani.

Time: 1976.or whenever you were 19. *Place:* New York City (Brooklyn and Manhattan.)

Act 1, Scene 1: The Neighborhood. Bay Ridge, Brooklyn. *Scene 2:* The Manero House. *Scene 3:* Outside 2001 Odyssey – Saturday Night. *Scene 4:* Inside 2001 Odyssey – Saturday Night. *Scene 5:* The Neighborhood Paint Store. *Scene 6:* The Manero House. *Scene 7:* Dale Dance Studios. *Scene 8:* The Neighborhood. *Scene 9:* Inside 2001 Odyssey – Saturday Night.

Act 2, Scene 1: The Verrazano Narrows Bridge – Saturday Night. *Scene 2:* Dale Dance Studios. *Scene 3:* The Neighborhood. *Scene 4:* Stephanie's Apartment – Manhattan. *Scene 5:* Bench overlooking Bridge. *Scene 6:* The Neighborhood. *Scene 7:* Inside 2001 Odyssey – Saturday Night. The Dance Competition. *Scene 8:* Exterior 2001 Odyssey – Saturday Night. *Scene 9:* The Verrazano Narrows Bridge – Saturday Night. *Scene 10:* Park Bench near the Bridge.

ACT 1[6]
Scene 1
"Stayin' Alive"
J. Carpinello, the Company
Scene 3
"Boogie Shoes"
J. Carpinello, the Faces
(*Music and Lyrics by* Harry Casey and Richard Finch.)
Scene 4
"Disco Inferno"
B. Batt, the Company
(*Music and Lyrics by* Leroy Green and Ron 'Have Mercy' Kersey.)
"Night Fever"
J. Carpinello, the Company
Scene 7
"Disco Duck"
B. Batt
(*Music and Lyrics by* Rick Dees.)
"More Than a Woman"
J. Carpinello, P. Price

[5]Brothers Gibb: Barry, Robin and Maurice.
[6]Additional music credits:
"A Fifth of Beethoven"
(*Music by* Walter Murphy.)
"Also Spake Zarathustra"
(*Music by* Richard Strauss.)
"Night on Disco Mountain"
(*Music by* David Shire.)

Scene 8

"If I Can't Have You"
Orfeh

Scene 9

"It's My Neighborhood"
The Company

"You Should Be Dancin'"
J. Carpinello, the Company

ACT 2

Scene 1

"Jive Talkin'"
J. Carpinello, Orfeh, the Faces, the Company

Scene 2

"First and Last"
P. Castree

"Tragedy"
P. Castree

Scene 4

"What Kind of Fool"
P. Price
(*Music and Lyrics by* Barry Gibb and Albhy Galuten.)

Scene 7

"Nights on Broadway"
Orfeh, P. Price, the Company

The Dance Competition:

"Open Sesame"
Danced by A. Ward, K. Plantadit-Bageot
(*Music and Lyrics by* Robert Bell, Ronald Bell, George Brown, Charles Smith, Dennis Thomas.)

"More Than a Woman"
Danced by J. Carpinello, P. Price

"Salsation"
Danced by M. Balderrama, N. Willes
(*Music by* David Shire.)

Scene 8

"Immortality"
J. Carpinello

Scene 10

"How Deep Is Your Love"
J. Carpinello, P. Price

(DISNEY'S) BEAUTY AND THE BEAST

1999.16

A Return Engagement of the Musical in Two Acts[7]. Book by Linda Woolverton (based on her screenplay for the Walt Disney animated film of the same name). Music by Alan Menken. Lyrics by Howard Ashman and Tim Rice. Directed by Robert Jess Roth. Choreography by Matt West. Scenic design by Stanley A. Meyer. Costume design by Ann Hould-Ward. Lighting design by Natasha Katz. Sound design by Jonathan Deans. Illusion design by Jim Steinmeyer, John Gaughan. Prosthetics, John Dods. Musical direction and incidental music arrangements by Michael Kosarin. Orchestrations by Danny Troob. Musical supervision and vocal arrangements by David Friedman. Fight director, Rick Sordelet. Dance arrangements by Glen Kelly. Associate producers, Tony McLean and Pam Young. Produced by Walt Disney Theatrical Productions (Peter Schneider, Thomas Schumacher). Opened 12 November 1999 at the Lunt-Fontanne Theatre and is still running at this time!

CAST (in order of appearance): *Enchantress*: Lisa Mayer. *Young Prince*: Michael Lang. *Beast*: STEVE BLANCHARD. *Belle*: ANDREA McARDLE. *Bookseller*: Glenn Rainey. *Lefou*: JAY BRIAN WINNICK. *Gaston*: PATRICK RYAN SULLIVAN. *Three Silly Girls*: Lauren Goler-Kosarin, Linda Talcott Lee, Amanda Watkins. *Maurice*: J. B.

---

[7]Originally opened 18 April 1994 at the Palace Theatre and closed 5 September 1999 after 2250 performances. For Musical Numbers, see original 1994 production. The added song "A Change in Me" was retained for this engagement.

ADAMS. *Wolves*: Robert H. Fowler, Jennifer Hampton, Michael Lang, Lisa Mayer. *Cogsworth*: JEFF BROOKS. *Lumiere*: PATRICK PAGE. *Babette*: PAM KLINGER. *Mrs. Potts*: BARBARA MARINEAU. *Chip*: RICKY ASHLEY, MATTHEW DOTZMAN. *Madame de la Grande Bouche*: JUDITH MOORE. *Salt and Pepper*: Robert H. Fowler, Joseph Savant. *Doormat*: Michael Lang. *Cheesegrater*: Kevin M. Burrows. *Monsieur D'Arque*: Glenn Rainey.

Townspeople, Enchanted Objects: Kevin Berdini, Kevin M. Burows, Karl Christian, Kate Dowe, Barbara Folts, Robert H. Fowler, Lauren Goler-Kosarin, Jennifer Hampton, Michael Lang, Robin Lewis, Anna McNeely, William Paul Michals, Lisa Mayer, Bill Nabel, Glenn Rainey, Joseph Savant, Marguerite Shannon, Linda Talcott Lee, Rachel Ulanet, Amanda Watkins. *Voice of Prologue Narrator*: David Ogden Stiers. *Swings*: Karl Christian, Kate Dowe, Barbara Folts, Robin Lewis.

ABBY'S SONG

1999.17

A Musical in Two Acts and a Prologue. Book and lyrics by Mary Pat Kelly. Music by Elliot Willensky. Directed and choreographed by Randy Skinner. Set design, Bill Clarke. Costume design, David C. Woolard. Lighting design, Nancy Schertler. Sound design, Scott Lehrer. Orchestrations, Michael Gibson. Musical direction, vocal and dance arrangements, Stephen Bates. Produced by Spirit Lake Productions, Mickey Kelly, Susan Kelly Panian and Michael Kelly. Opened 14 November 1999 at the New York City Center and closed 28 November 1999 after 16 performances.

CAST (in order of appearance). *The Mentor*: PAUL SORVINO. *Danny* (a young angel): David A. Tay. *Judith*: JUDY MALLOY. *Bertha*: Jacquiline Rohrbacker. *Leah*: Monica L. Patton. *Ethan*: Sebastian Sozzi. *Becky*: Maggie Panian. *Susannah*: Courtney Leigh. *Lilly*: Ally Hilfiger. *John*: JOHN WILKERSON. *Josh*: Daniel Elborne. *Bennie*: Michael-Leon Wooley. *Abby*: JACKIE ANGELESCU. *Ruben*: John Paul Almon.

A story that has grown old lives again when it's retold.

Time: The present. *Place*: Whispering Pines, Montana.

PROLOGUE

"An Ordinary Town"
P. Sorvino

ACT 1

"Woman's Work"
J. Malloy, M. L. Patton, J. Rohrbacker, M. Panian, A. Hilfiger, C. Leigh

"Fly a Rainbow"
J. Angelescu

"Fly a Rainbow" (reprise)
J. Angelescu, D. A. Tay

"More Than Ever"
J. Wilkerson, J. Malloy

"The Wolf Song"
M. Wooley, J. Wilkerson, D. Elborne, S. Sozzi

"I Am Home"
J. P. Almon, M. L. Patton

"Another Girl Who's Just Like Me"
J. Angelescu, M. Panian, A. Hilfiger, C. Leigh, J. Malloy, M. L. Patton

"There's a Price"
J. Rohrbacker, J. Malloy

"You Just Gotta Be You"
D. A. Tay, J. Angelescu

"She Left Without a Word"
J. Malloy

ACT 2

"A Little Girl in the Night"
J. Angelescu, Ensemble

"Beyond"
Men, Boys

"I Did It"
J. Angelescu

"An Angel Has a Message"
D. A. Tay, J. Angelescu

"A Mother's Heart"
J. Malloy, M. L. Patton, J. Rohrbacker

"Pass the Wine"
Men and Boys

"The Revelation"
D. A. Tay, J. Angelescu, Men and Boys

"How Do You Follow a Star"
  J. Angelescu, S. Sozzi
"Who is This Child"
  J. Angelescu, J. Wilkerson
"Abby's Song"
  Ensemble
"Fly a Rainbow" (reprise)
  J. Angelescu, Ensemble
"One Small Voice"
  Ensemble

1999.18   TANGO ARGENTINO

A Revival of the Dance Revue in Two Acts[8]. Entire production conceived and directed by Claudio Segovia, Héctor Orezzoli. Choreographic conception, Claudio Segovia. Choreography by the dancers. Musical directors, Osvaldo Berlingieri, Julio Oscar Pane. Scenery, costumes design and lighting conceived by Claudio Segovia and Héctor Orezzoli. Lighting consultatnt, Marcelo Cuervo. Sound design, Gastón Brisky. Executive producers, Daniel Grinbank, Fernando Moya, Isabel Chaput. Produced by DG Producciones, a CIE-R&P Company (Daniel Grinbank, President). Opened 17 November 1999 at the Gershwin Theatre and closed 9 January 2000 after 63 performances.

CAST: *Singers:* Raúl Lavié, María Graña, Jovita Luna, Alba Solís.
  Dancers: Nélida and Nelson, Héctor and Elsa María Mayoral, Carlos and Inés Bórquez, Norma and Luis Pereyra, Carlos Copello and Alicia Monti, Roberto Herrera and Lorena Yácono, Guillermina Quiroga, Vanina Bilous, Antonio Cervila Jr., Johana Copes. *Guest Artists:* Juan Carlos Copes, María Nieves, Pablo Verón.
  Musicians: Osvaldo Berlingieri (piano); Christian Zárate (piano); Roberto Pansera (bandoneón); Horacio Romo (bandoneón); Rubén Oscar Gonzalez (bandoneón, percussion, flute); Pablo Agri (violin); Pablo Aznarez (violin); Raúl Di Renzo (violin); Gustavo Roberto Mulé (violin); Walter Sebastián Prusac (violin); Leonardo Suarez Paz (violin); Dino Carlos Quarleri (violoncello); Enrique Guerra (contrebass).

ACT 1
  "Quejas de Bandoneon"
    (*Music by* J. de Dios Filiberto.)
  "El Apache Argentino"
    (*Music by* M. Aróztegui, A. Mathón.)
    A. Cervila Jr., P. Verón, L. Pereyra, J. C. Copes, C. Borquez, C. Copello
  "El Porteñíto"
    (*Music by* A. Villoldo.)
    G. Quiroga, N. Pereyra, A. Monti, J. Copes, I. Borquez
  "El Esquinazo"
    (*Music by* A. Villoldo.)
    P. Verón, G. Quiroga
  "La Puñalada"
    (*Music by* P. Castellanos, E. C. Flores.)
  "El Choclo"
    (*Music by* A. Villoldo, E. S. Discépolo.)
    Orchestra
  "La Cumparsita"
    (*Music by* G. H. Matos Rodriguez.) P. Verón,
    G. Quiroga
  "Mi Noche Triste"
    (*Music and Lyrics by* S. Castriotta, P. Contursi.)
    R. Lavié
  "El Entrerriano"
    (*Music by* R. Mendizábal.)
    N. Pereyra, L. Pereyra
  "De Mi Barrio"
    (*Music and Lyrics by* R. Goyeneche.)
    J. Luna
  "Chiqué"
    J. C. Copes, J. Copes
  "Bandoneones"
    R. Pansera, H. Romo, R. González, A. Zárate

Milonguita:
  V. Bilous, Nelson, Nélida, A. Cervila Jr.,
  E. Maria, N. Pereyra, I. Bórquez, A. Monti,
  G. Quiroga, J. Copes, H. Mayoral, L. Pereyra,
  C. Bórquez, P. Véron, C. Copello
"Milonguita"
  (*Music by* E. Delfino, S. Linning.)
"Divina"
  (*Music by* J. Mora, J. De la Calle.)
"Melenita de Oro"
  (*Music by* E. Delfino, S. Linning.)
"Re-fa-si"
  (*Music by* E. Delfino.)
"Nostalgias"
  (*Music by* J. C. Cobian, E. Cadícamo.)
  Orchestra
"La Yumba"
  (*Music by* O. Pugliese.)
  I. Bórquez, C. Bórquez
"Cautivo" [song]
  M. Graña
"Recuerdo"
  (*Music by* O. Pugliese.)
  C. Copello, A. Monti
"Canaro en Paris"
  (*Music by* A. Scarpino, J. Caldarella.)
  Orchestra
"Nocturna"
  (*Music by* J. Plaza.)
  N. Pereyra, L. Pereyra, I. Bórquez, C. Bórquez,
  C. Copello, A. Monti, A. Cervila Jr., J. Copes, R. Herrera,
  L. Yácono
ACT 2
  "Milongueando en El 40"[9]
    R. Herrera, L. Yácono
  "Uno"
    (*Music and Lyrics by* E. S. Discépolo, M. Mores.)
  "La Ultima Curda" [song][10]
    A. Solís
  "Milonguero Viejo"
    H. Mayoral, E. M. Mayoral
  "Celos" (Jealousy)
    (*Music by* J. Gade.)
    Nélida and Nelson
  "Naranjo en Flor"
    (*Music and Lyrics by* H. Y. V. Espósito.)
    R. Lavié
  "Tanguera"
    (*Music by* M. Mores.)
    P. Véron, G. Quiroga
  "La Mariposa"
    Orchestra
  "Patetico"
    J. C. Copes, M. Nieves
  "Cancion Desesperada" [song]
    M. Graña
  "Verano Porteño"
    (*Music by* Astor Piazzolla.)
    V. Bilous, A. Cervila Jr.
  "Balada Para Mi Muerte"
    (*Music and Lyrics by* Astor Piazzolla and H. Ferrer.)
    Orchestra
  "Danzarin"
    (*Music by* J. Plaza.)
  "Quejas de Bandoneon"
    (*Music by* J. De Dios Filiberto.)
    Dancers

---

[8]First produced in New York 25 June 1985 at the New York City Center for 7 performances; re-opened 9 October 1985 at the Mark Hellinger Theatre and closed 30 March 1986 after 199 performances. Total: 206 performances

[9]In previous production, the music was credited to Armando Pontier.
[10]In previous production, the music was credited to A. Troilo, C. Castillo.

1999.19   KISS ME, KATE

A Revival of the Musical Comedy in Two Acts, 17 Scenes[11]. Book by Sam and Bella Spewack[12]. (Based on William Shakespeare's "The Taming of the Shrew.") Music and lyrics by Cole Porter. Directed by Michael Blakemore. Choreographed by Kathleen Marshall. Scenery by Robin Wagner. Costumes by Martin Pakledinaz. Lighting by Peter Kaczorowski. Sound design by Tony Meola. Musical director, Paul Gemignani. Orchestrations by Don Sebesky. Produced by Roger Berlind and Roger Horchow. Opened 18 November 1999 at the Martin Beck Theatre and closed 30 December 2001 after 881 performances.

CAST (in order of appearance): *Hattie*: ADRIANE LENOX. *Paul*: STANLEY WAYNE MATHIS. *Ralph* (Stage Manager): Eric Michael Gillett. *Lois Lane*: AMY SPANGLER. *Bill Calhoun*: MICHAEL BERRESSE. *Lilli Vanessi*: MARIN MAZZIE. *Fred Graham*: BRIAN STOKES MITCHELL. *Harry Trevor*: John Horton. *Pops* (Stage Doorman): Robert Ousley. *Cab Driver*: Jerome Vivona. *First Man*: LEE WILKOF. *Second Man*: MICHAEL MULHEREN. *Harrison Howell*: Ron Holgate.
"Taming of the Shrew" Players: *Bianca* (Lois Lane): AMY SPANGLER. *Baptista* (Harry Trevor): MICHAEL BERRESSE. *Gremio* (First Suitor): Kevin Neil McCready. *Hortensio* (Second Suitor): Darren Lee. *Lucentio* (Bill Calhoun): MICHAEL BERRESSE. *Katharine* (Lilli Vanessi): MARIN MAZZIE. *Petruchio* (Fred Graham): BRIAN STOKES MITCHELL. *Nathaniel*: Jerome Vivona. *Gregory*: Vince Pesce. *Philip*: Blake Hammond. *Haberdasher*: Michael X. Martin.
Ensemble: Eric Michael Gillet, Patty Goble, Blake Hammond, JoAnn M. Hunter, Nancy Lemenager, Darren Lee, Michael X. Martin, Kevin Neil McCready, Carol Lee Meadows, Elizabeth Mills, Linda Mugleston, Robert Ousley, Vince Pesce, Cynthia Sophiea, Jerome Vivona.

Act 1, Scene 1: The stage of Ford's Theatre, Baltimore. June. 1948. *Scene 2*: The Backstage Corridor. *Scene 3*: Fred and Lilli's Dressing Rooms. *Scene 4*: Padua. *Scene 5*: Street in Padua (Piazza). *Scene 6*: The Backstage Corridor. *Scene 7*: Fred and Lilli's Dressing Rooms. *Scene 8*: A Country Road in Padua. *Scene 9*: The Church in Padua.

Act 2, Scene 1: Immediately following. The Theatre Alley. *Scene 2*: Before the Curtain. *Scene 3*: Petruchio's House. *Scene 4*: The Backstage Corridor. *Scene 5*: Fred and Lilli's Dressing Rooms. *Scene 6*: The Backstage Corridor. *Scene 7*: Before the Curtain. *Scene 8*: Baptista's House, Padua.

ACT 1
Scene 1
   "Another Op'nin', Another Show"
     A. Lenox, Company
Scene 2
   "Why Can't You Behave?"
     A. Spangler, M. Berresse
Scene 3
   "Wunderbar"
     M. Mazzie, B. S. Mitchell
   "So in Love"
     M. Mazzie
Scene 4
   "We Open in Venice"
     B. S. Mitchell, M. Mazzie, A. Spangler, M. Berresse
Scene 5
   "Tom, Dick or Harry"
     A. Spangler, M. Berresse, K. N. McCready, D. Lee
   "I've Come to Wive It Wealthily in Padua"
     B. S. Mitchell, Men
   "I Hate Men"
     M. Mazzie
   "Were Thine That Special Face"
     B. S. Mitchell
Scene 8
   "Cantiamo D'Amore" (I Sing of Love)
     Ensemble
Scene 9
   "Kiss Me, Kate"
     B. S. Mitchell, M. Mazzie, Singing Ensemble

ACT 2
Scene 1
   "Too Darn Hot"
     S. W. Mathis, Ensemble
Scene 3
   "Where Is the Life That Late I Led?"
     B. S. Mitchell
Scene 4
   "Always True to You (in My Fashion)"
     A. Spangler
Scene 5
   "From This Moment On"[13]
     R. Holgate, M. Mazzie
Scene 6
   "Bianca"
     M. Berresse, Ensemble
   "So in Love" (reprise)
     B. S. Mitchell
Scene 7
   "Brush Up Your Shakespeare"
     L. Wilkof, M. Mulheren
Scene 8
   Pavane
     A. Spangler, M. Berresse, Ensemble
   "I Am Ashamed That Women Are So Simple"
     M. Mazzie
   "Kiss Me, Kate" (Finale)
     Company

1999.20   PUTTING IT TOGETHER

A Musical Review in Two Acts[14]. Music and Lyrics by Stephen Sondheim. Directed by Eric D. Schaeffer. Choreographed by Bob Avian. (Scenery and costumes) Designed by Bob Crowley. Lighting designed by Howard Harrison. Projections designed by Wendall K. Harrington. Miss Burnett's Costumes by Bob Mackie. Sound designed by Andrew Bruce, Mark Menard. Orchestrations by Jonathan Tunick. Musical director, Paul Raiman. Associate director/choreographer, Jodi Moccia. Executive producers, David Caddick and Martin McCallum. Produced by Cameron Mackintosh, in association with the Mark Taper Forum (Gordon Davidson, Artistic Director). Opened 21 November 1999 at the Ethel Barrymore Theatre and closed 20 February 2000 after ?99 performances.

CAST: *The Wife*: CAROL BURNETT. *The Husband*: GEORGE HEARN. *The Younger Man*: JOHN BARROWMAN. *The Younger Woman*: RUTHIE HENSHALL. *The Observer*: BRONSON PINCHOT. *The Wife*, (alternate) at certain performances: KATHIE LEE GIFFORD.

ACT 1
   "Invocation and Instructions to the Audience"
   (from THE FROGS)
     B. Pinchot
   "Putting It Together"
   (from SUNDAY IN THE PARK WITH GEORGE)
     The Company
   "Rich and Happy"
   (from MERRILY WE ROLL ALONG)
     The Company
   "Do I Hear a Waltz?"
   (from DO I HEAR A WALTZ)
     C. Burnett, G. Hearn

---

[11]Originally produced on Broadway 30 December 1948 at the New Century Theatre for 1077 performances.
[12]Uncredited revisions by John Guare.

[13]Originally from the film KISS ME, KATE; dropped from OUT OF THIS WORLD prior to opening.
[14]Original English 1992 production devised by Stephen Sondheim and Julia McKenzie. Previously produced in an earlier version in New York Off-Broadway 2 March-23 May 1993 at the Manhattan Theatre Club for 96 performances. The author and producer have purposely chosen the spelling of the word "review."

"Merrily We Roll Along" #1 (from MERRILY WE ROLL ALONG)
  B. Pinchot
"Lovely" (from A FUNNY THING HAPPENED ON THE WAY TO THE FORUM)
  The Company
"Hello Little Girl" (from INTO THE WOODS)
  G. Hearn, R. Henshall
"My Husband the Pig" (from A LITTLE NIGHT MUSIC, unused)
  C. Burnett
"Everyday a Little Death" (from A LITTLE NIGHT MUSIC)
  C. Burnett, R. Henshall
"Everybody Ought to Have a Maid" (from A FUNNY THING HAPPENED ON THE WAY TO THE FORUM)
  B. Pinchot, C. Burnett
"Have I Got a Girl for You?" (from COMPANY)
  J. Barrowman, G. Hearn
"Pretty Women" (from SWEENEY TODD-THE DEMON BARBER OF FLEET STREET)
  J. Barrowman, G. Hearn
"Sooner or Later" (from DICK TRACY, film)
  R. Henshall
"Bang!" (from A LITTLE NIGHT MUSIC, unused)
  J. Barrowman, B. Pinchot, R. Henshall
"Country House" (from FOLLIES, London)
  C. Burnett, G. Hearn
"Unworthy of Your Love" (from ASSASSINS)
  J. Barrowman, R. Henshall
"Merrily We Roll Along" #2 (from MERRILY WE ROLL ALONG)
  B. Pinchot
"Could I Leave You?" (from FOLLIES)
  C. Burnett
"Rich and Happy" (reprise)
  The Company

ACT 2

"Back in Business" (from DICK TRACY, film)
  The Company
"It's Hot Up Here" (from SUNDAY IN THE PARK WITH GEORGE)
  The Company
"The Ladies Who Lunch" (from COMPANY)
  C. Burnett
"The Road You Didn't Take" (from FOLLIES)
  G. Hearn
"Live Alone and Like It" (from DICK TRACY, film)
  J. Barrowman
"More" (from DICK TRACY, film)
  R. Henshall
"There's Always a Woman" (from ANYONE CAN WHISTLE, unused)
  C. Burnett, R. Henshall
"Buddy's Blues" (from FOLLIES)
  B. Pinchot
"Good Thing Going" (from MERRILY WE ROLL ALONG)
  G. Hearn
"Marry Me a Little" (from COMPANY)
  J. Barrowman
"Not Getting Married Today" (from COMPANY)
  R. Henshall
"Merrily We Roll Along" #3 (from MERRILY WE ROLL ALONG)
  The Company
"Being Alive" (from COMPANY)
  The Company
"Like It Was" (from MERRILY WE ROLL ALONG)
  C. Burnett
Finale—"Old Friends" (from MERRILY WE ROLL ALONG)
  The Company

1999.21   # A CHRISTMAS CAROL

A Revival of the Musical in One Act, 13 Scenes[15]. Book by Mike Ockrent and Lynn Ahrens. Based on the story of the same name by Charles Dickens. Music by Alan Menken. Lyrics by Lynn Ahrens. Directed by Mike Ockrent. Choreographed by Susan Stroman. Setting design by Tony Walton. Costume design by William Ivey Long. Lighting design by Jules Fisher and Peggy Eisenhauer. Sound design by Tony Meola. Projections by Wendall K. Harrington. Flying by Foy. Associate directors, Ray Roderick, Steven Zweigbaum. Associate choreographer, Chris Peterson. Musical direction by Paul Gemignani. Orchestrations by Michael Starobin and Douglas Besterman. Dance arrangements and incidental music by Glen Kelly. Executive producer, Dodger Endemol Theatricals. Producer, Tim Hawkins. Presented by American Express/Madison Square Garden. Opened 30 November 1999 at the (Paramount) Theatre, Madison Square Garden and closed 30 December 1999 after 64 performances.

CAST (in order of appearance): *Beadle:* Del-Bourree Bach. *Mr. Smythe:* CHRIS VASQUEZ. *Grace Smythe:* Brittany Alexander Campbell, Marissa Gould. *Scrooge:* TONY ROBERTS. *Bob Crachit:* NICK CORLEY. *Charity Men:* Don Mayo, Roland Rusinek, Wayne Schroder. *Old Joe:* Kenneth McMullen. *Street Urchins:* Andrew Keenan-Bolger, Lexine Bondoc, Johnny Cennicola, Kennedy Kanagawa, Tristin Mays, Jimmy Walsh. *Mrs. Crachit:* Whitney Webster. *Tiny Tim:* Dennis Michael Hall, Patrick Stogner. *Poulterer:* Roland Rusinek. *Sandwichboard Man:* REGINALD VelJOHNSON. *Jonathon:* Matt Bowles, Marshall Pailet. *Lamplighter:* DIDI CONN. *Blind Hag:* Joan Barber. *Fred:* JAMES JUDY. *Mrs. Mopps:* Marilyn Pasekoff. *Ghost of Jacob Marley:* PAUL KANDEL. *Ghost of Christmas Past:* DIDI CONN. *Lights of Christmas Past:* Leo Alvarez, Keith Fortner, Michael Lomeka, David Rosales. *Judge:* Roland Rusinek. *Scrooge at 8 years:* Johnny Cennicola, Jimmy Walsh. *Scrooge's Mother:* Joan Barber. *Scrooge's Father:* Wayne Schroder. *Mr. Hawkins:* Kenneth McMullen. *Scrooge at 12 years:* Andrew Keenan-Bolger, Kennedy Kanagawa. *Fan:* Lexine Bondoc, Tristin Mays. *Fezziwig:* Daniel Marcus. *Scrooge at 18 years:* Joe Cassidy. *Young Marley:* Ken Barnett. *Mrs. Fezziwig:* Debra Cardona. *Emily:* Kristin Huxhold. *Ghost of Christmas Present:* REGINALD VelJOHNSON. *The Crachit Children:* Andrew Keenan-Bolger, Lexine Bondoc, Kenendy Kanagawa, Tristin Mays. *Sally, Fred's wife:* La Tanya Hall. *Ignorance:* Johnny Cennicola, Jimmy Walsh. *Want:* Brittany Alexander Campbell, Marissa Gould. *Undertakers:* Ken Barnett, Wayne Schroder. *Ghost of Christmas Yet-To-Be:* CHRISTINE DUNHAM.

Business Men, Gifts, Ghosts and the People of London: Lori Alexander, Leo Alvarez, Del-Bourree Bach, Joan Barber, Ken Barnett, Hayes Bergman, Liam Burke, Debra Cardona, Joe Cassidy, Candy Cook, Juliet Fischer, Keith Fortner, La Tanya Hall, Kristin Huxhold, James Judy, Carrie Kenneally, Jessica Kostival, Michael Lomeka, Daniel Marcus, Don Mayo, Kenneth McMullen, Marilyn Pasekoff, Meredith Patterson, Gail Pennington, Josef Reiter, David Rosales, Wendy Rosoff, Roland Rusinek, Vikki Schnurr, Wayne Schroder, Erin Stoddard, Chris Vasquez, Whitney Webster. *Swings:* Ron Bagden, Jane Brockman, Jeffrey Hankinson, Ann Kittredge, Adam Pelty, Angela Piccinni, Rommy Sandhu, Cynthia Thole. *Angels:* P.S. 390 and 330 La Petite Musicale, Park Middle School Broadway Chorus, South Side Middle School Chorale, YPC Jubilee Chorus. *Red Children's Cast:* Marissa Gould, Kennedy Kanagawa, Tristin Mays, Marshall Pailet, Patrick Stogner, Jimmy Walsh. *Green Children's Cast:* Andrew Keenan-Bolger, Lexien Bondoc, Matt Bowles, Brittany Alexander Campbell, Johnny Cennicola, Dennis Michael Hall. *Swings:* Patrick Dunn, Bret Fox, Molly Jobe.

1999.22   # MARIE CHRISTINE

A Musical in Two Acts and a Prelude. Words and music by Michael John LaChiusa[16]. Directed and choreographed by Graciele Daniele. Sets by

---

[15]Originally produced in New York 1 December 1994 at the Paramount Theatre, Madison Square Garden for 71 performances. For Synopsis of Scenes and Musical Numbers, see original 1994 production. For this year's and the 1995, 1996, 1997 and 1998 revivals the following changes were made:
Scene 1 and "The Years Are Passing By" were dropped.
Added to Scene 2 (former Scene 3) before "Street Song":
  "You Mean More to Me"
    T. Gross, A. B. Hall or C. Valiando
"The Years Are Passing By" (reprise) in former Scene 13 (new Scene 12) was replaced by:
  "London Town Carol"
    A. Barruch or K. Kanagawa
Note: The production played an irregular schedule of multiple daily performances.
[16]Freely adapted from the legend of Medea.

Christopher Barreca. Costumes by Toni-Leslie James. Lighting by Jules Fisher and Peggy Eisenhauer. Sound by Scott Stauffer. Musical director, David Evans. Orchestrations by Jonathan Tunick. Associate choreographer, Willie Rosario. Fight director, Luis Perez. Produced by Lincoln Center Theater Company (André Bishop, Artistic director; Bernard Gersten, Executive producer). Opened 2 December 1999 at the Vivian Beaumont Theatre and closed 9 January 2000 after 44 performances.

CAST: *Prisoner #1*: Jennifer Leigh Warren. *Prisoner #2*: Andrea Frierson-Toney. *Prisoner #3*: Mary Bond Davis. *Marie Christine L'Adrese*: AUDRA McDONALD, Sherry Boone (alt.). *Marie Christine's Mother*: VIVIAN REED. *Serpent*: Donna Dunmire. *Dante Keyes*: ANTHONY CRIVELLO. *Celeste*, a maid: Lovette George. *Ozelia*, A Maid: Rosena M. Hill. *Jean L'Adrese*: KEITH LEE GRANT. *Paris L'Adrese*: DARIUS deHAAS. *Lisette*, Marie Christine's maid: KIMBERLY JaJUAN. *Joachim*, a valet: André Garner. *Osmond*, a valet: Jim Weaver. *Monsieur St. Vinson*: Jim Weaver. *Monsieur Archambeau*: André Garner. *Beatrice*, Jean's fiancée: Joy Lynn Matthews. *Children*: Powers Pleasant, Zachary Thornton, Joshua Walter. *Magdalena*: MARY TESTA. *Petal*, Magdalena's "daughter": Janet Metz. *Duchess*, Magdalena's "daughter": Kim Huber. *Gates*: SHAWN ELLIOTT. *Bartender*: Peter Samuel. *Bar Patron*: Michael Babin. *Leary*: Michael McCormick. *McMahon*: Mark Lotito. *Esau Parker*: Peter Samuel. *Olivia Parker*: Janet Metz. *Grace Parker*: Kim Huber. *Old Dante*: Michael Babin. *Helena*, Gates' daughter: Donna Dunmire. *Chaka* (drums): David Pleasant.

Ensemble: Franz C. Alderfer, Ana Marie Andricain, Michael Babin, Brent Black, Donna Dunmire, André Garner, Lovette George, Rosena M. Hill, Kim Huber, Mark Lotito, Joy Lynn Matthews, Michael McCormick, Janet Metz, Monique Midgette, Peter Samuel, Jim Weaver.

Prelude: A Prison. *Act 1*: 1894. A park on Lake Pontchartrain outside of New Orleans. Marie Christine's home on Mandolin Street in New Orleans and its interiors, as well as its garconniere and ballroom. A pier.

Act 2: 1899. A saloon in the First Ward, Chicago. An alleyway. A small house and its interior; Interior of a church.

ACT 1

"Before the Morning"
    Women
"Mamzell' Marie"
    Company
"Ton Grandpere est le soleil"
    V. Reed
"Beautiful"
    A. McDonald
"The Map of Your Heart"
    D. deHaas, K. L. Grant, A. McDonald
"Way Back to Paradise"
    A. McDonald, K. JaJuan
"To Find a Lover"
    A. McDonald, Company
"The Adventure Never Ends"/"Nothing Beats Chicago"/
"Ocean Is Different"/"Danced with a Girl"
    A. Crivello
"Tou Mi Mi"
    K. JaJuan
"Miracles and Mysteries"
    V. Reed, Prisoners
"I Don't Hear the Ocean"
    A. Crivello, A. McDonald
"Bird Inside the House"
    Maids and Valets
"All Eyes Look Upon You"
    K. L. Grant
"A Month Ago"
    Maids
"Danced with a Girl" (reprise)
    A. Crivello
"We're Gonna Go to Chicago"
    A. Crivello, A. McDonald
"Dansez Calinda"
    K. JaJuan
"I Will Give"
    A. McDonald, Prisoners
Finale of Act 1
    D. deHaas, Company

ACT 2

Opening/"I Will Love You"
    Prisoners, A. Crivello, A. McDonald
"Cincinnati"
    M. Testa, J. Metz, K. Huber
"You're Looking at the Man"
    M. McCormick, M. Lotito, A. Crivello
"The Scorpion"
    A. Crivello, A. McDonald
"Lover Bring Me Summer"
    J. Metz, K. Huber
"Old Dante'
    M. Babin
"Tell Me"
    A. McDonald
"Paradise Is Burning Down"
    M. Testa
"Prison in a Prison"
    A. McDonald, Prisoners, D. Dunmire, A. Crivello
"Better & Best"
    M. McCormick, M. Lotito
"Good Looking Woman"
    S. Elliott, M. McCormick, M. Lotito
"No Turning Back"
    D. deHaas, V. Reed, K. L. Grant, K. JaJuan
"Beautiful" (reprise)
    A. McDonald
"A Lovely Wedding"
    M. Testa
"I Will Love You" (reprise)
    A. McDonald
"Your Name"
    A. Crivello
Finale of Act 2
    Women

1999.23 # MINNELLI ON MINNELLI

A Musical Revue in Two Acts. [Liza sings songs from the movies of Vincente Minnelli.] Directed by Fred Ebb. Choreographed by John DeLuca. Scenery by John Arnone. Costumes by Bob Mackie. Lighting by Howell Binkley. Sound by Peter J. Fitzgerald. Projections by Batwin+Robin. Film sequence prepared by Jack Haley, Jr. Musical arrangements and supervision, Marvin Hamlisch and Billy Stritch. Vocal arranger, Billy Stritch. Dance arrangements, David Krane, Peter Howard. Orchestrations by Michael Abene, William David Brohn, Jorge Calendrelli, Ned Ginsburg, Russell Kassoff, Peter Matz, Don Sebesky, Jonathan Tunick, Torrie Zito. Musical director, Bill LaVorgna. Executive producers, Gary Labriola and Edward J. Micone, Jr. Produced by Radio City Entertainment, LM Concerts, Scott Nederlander and Stewart F. Lane. Opened 8 December 1999 at the Palace Theatre and closed 2 January 2000 after 19 performances.[17]

CAST: LIZA MINNELLI, Jeffrey Broadhurst, Stephen Campanella, Billy Hartung, Sebastian LaCause, Jim Newman; Alex Timmerman [swing].

ACT 1

"If I Had You" (Incidental music THE CLOCK, film)
    L. Minnelli
    (*Music and Lyrics by* Ted Shapiro, Jimmy Campbell and
    Reg Connelly.)
"Taking a Chance on Love" (from CABIN IN THE SKY, film[18])
    L. Minnelli
    (*Music by* Vernon Duke. *Lyrics by* Jonathan Latouche and
    Ted Fetter.)

---

[17]Played an irregular holiday performance schedule of approximately 5 performances weekly.
[18]Previously introduced in the stage production of CABIN IN THE SKY in 1940.

"Cabin in the Sky" (from CABIN IN THE SKY, film[19])
    L. Minnelli
    (*Music by* Vernon Duke. *Lyrics by* Jonathan Latouche.)
"Happiness Is Just a Thing Called Joe" (from CABIN IN THE SKY, film)
    L. Minnelli
    (*Music by* Harold Arlen. *Lyrics by* E. Y. Harburg.)
"Love" (from ZIEGFELD FOLLIES, film, 1946)
    L. Minnelli
    (*Music and Lyrics by* Hugh Martin and Ralph Blane.)
"Limehouse Blues" (from ZIEGFELD FOLLIES, film[20], 1946)
    L. Minnelli, Men
    (*Music by* Philip Braham. *Lyrics by* Douglas Furber.)
"Meet Me in St. Louis" (from MEET ME IN ST. LOUIS, film)
    L. Minnelli, Men
    (*Music by* Kerry Mills. *Lyrics by* Andrew B. Sterling.)
"Under the Bamboo Tree" (from MEET ME IN ST. LOUIS, film[21])
    L. Minnelli, Men
    (*Music by* J. Rosamund Johnson. *Lyrics by* Bob Cole.)
"The Boy Next Door" (from MEET ME IN ST. LOUIS, film)
    L. Minnelli
    (*Music and Lyrics by* Hugh Martin and Ralph Blane.)
"Skip to My Lou" (from MEET ME IN ST. LOUIS, film)
    Men
    (*Traditional; Music and Lyrics by* Hugh Martin and Ralph Blane.)
"Have Yourself a Merry Little Christmas " (from MEET ME IN ST. LOUIS, film)
    L. Minnelli
    (*Music and Lyrics by* Hugh Martin and Ralph Blane.)
"That's Entertainment" (from THE BANDWAGON, film)
    Men
    (*Music by* Arthur Schwartz. *Lyrics by* Howard Dietz.)
"I Guess I'll Have to Change My Plan" (from THE BANDWAGON, film[22])
    L. Minnelli, J. Newman
    (*Music by* Arthur Schwartz. *Lyrics by* Howard Dietz.)
"By Myself" (from THE BANDWAGON, film[23])
    Men
    (*Music by* Arthur Schwartz. *Lyrics by* Howard Dietz.)
"That's Entertainment" (reprise)
    Men
"Triplets" (from THE BANDWAGON, film[24])
    L. Minnelli, B. Hartung, J. Broadhurst
    (*Music by* Arthur Schwartz. *Lyrics by* Howard Dietz.)
"Dancing in the Dark" (from THE BANDWAGON, film[25])
    J. Newman, S. LaCause, S. Campanella
    (*Music by* Arthur Schwartz. *Lyrics by* Howard Dietz.)
"A Shine on Your Shoes" (from THE BANDWAGON, film[26])
    L. Minnelli, Men
    (*Music by* Arthur Schwartz. *Lyrics by* Howard Dietz.)

ACT 2

Medley:Men

"This Heart of Mine" (from ZIEGFELD FOLLIES, film, 1946)
    (*Music by* Harry Warren. *Lyrics by* Arthur Freed.)
"Just in Time" (from BELLS ARE RINGING, film[27])
    (*Music by* Jule Styne. *Lyrics by* Betty Comden and Adolph Green.)

"I'll Build a Stairway to Paradise" (from AN AMERICAN IN PARIS, film[28])
    (*Music by* George Gershwin. Lyrics by Buddy G. DeSylva and Ira Gershwin.)
"Be a Clown" (from THE PIRATE, film)
    (*Music and Lyrics by* Cole Porter.)
"'S Wonderful" (from AN AMERICAN IN PARIS, film[29])
    (*Music by* George Gershwin. *Lyrics by* Ira Gershwin.)
"Liza" (All the Clouds'll Roll Away) (from SHOW GIRL)
    (*Music by* George Gershwin. *Lyrics by* Gus Kahn and Ira Gershwin.)
Childhood Reminiscences
    L. Minnelli
"An American in Paris Ballet" (Film excerpt)
    (*Music by* George Gershwin.)
"I Got Rhythm" (from AN AMERICAN IN PARIS, film[30])
    L. Minnelli
    (*Music by* George Gershwin. *Lyrics by* Ira Gershwin.)
"Baubles, Bangles and Beads" (from KISMET, film[31])
    L. Minnelli, Men
    (*Music and Lyrics by* Robert Wright and George Forrest, based on themes of Alexander Borodin.)
"The Night They Invented Champagne" (from GIGI, film)
    L. Minnelli, Men
    (*Music by* Frederick Loewe. *Lyrics by* Alan Jay Lerner.)
"I Remember It Well" (from GIGI, film)
    L. Minnelli
    (*Music by* Frederick Loewe. *Lyrics by* Alan Jay Lerner. *Additional lyrics by* Fred Ebb.)
"On a Clear Day You Can See Forever" (from ON A CLEAR DAY YOU CAN SEE FOREVER, film[32])
    Men
    (*Music by* Burton Lane. *Lyrics by* Alan Jay Lerner.)
"Come Back to Me" (from ON A CLEAR DAY YOU CAN SEE FOREVER, film[33])
    Men
    (*Music by* Burton Lane. *Lyrics by* Alan Jay Lerner.)
"What Did I Have That I Don't Have" (from ON A CLEAR DAY YOU CAN SEE FOREVER, film[34])
    L. Minnelli
    (*Music by* Burton Lane. *Lyrics by* Alan Jay Lerner.)
Film montage from MADAME BOVARY, THE BAD AND THE BEAUTIFUL, BRIGADOON (The Chase), GIGI (end)
"The Trolley Song" (from MEET ME IN ST. LOUIS, film[35])
    L. Minnelli, Men
    (*Music and Lyrics by* Hugh Martin and Ralph Blane.)
"If It Wasn't for You (There Wouldn't Be Me)"
    L. Minnelli
    (*Music by* John Kander. *Lyrics by* Fred Ebb.)

1999.24   SWING!

A Musical (Dance Revue) in Two Acts. Original concept, Paul Kelly. Directed and choreographed by Lynne Taylor-Corbett. Production supervisor, Jerry Zaks. Scenic design by Thomas L. Lynch. Costume design by William Ivey Long. Lighting design by Kenneth Posner. Sound design by

[19]Previously introduced in the stage production of CABIN IN THE SKY in 1940.
[20]Previously introduced to the stage in the London revue A TO Z, then in New York in CHARLOT'S REVUE OF 1924.
[21]Previously introduced to the stage in SALLY IN OUR ALLEY, 1902.
[22]Previously introduced to the stage in THE LITTLE SHOW, 1929.
[23]Previously introduced to the stage in BETWEEN THE DEVIL, 1937.
[24]Previously introduced to the stage in BETWEEN THE DEVIL, 1937.
[25]Previously introduced to the stage in the stage production of THE BANDWAGON, 1931.
[26]Previously introduced to the stage in FLYING COLORS, 1932.
[27]Previously introduced to the stage in BELLS ARE RINGING, 1956.

[28]Previously introduced to the stage in GEORGE WHITE'S SCANDALS OF 1922.
[29]Previously introduced to the stage in FUNNY FACE, 1927.
[30]Previously introduced to the stage in GIRL CRAZY, 1930.
[31]Previously introduced to the stage in KISMET, 1953.
[32]Previously introduced to the stage in ON A CLEAR DAY YOU CAN SEE FOREVER in 1965.
[33]Previously introduced to the stage in ON A CLEAR DAY YOU CAN SEE FOREVER in 1965.
[34]Previously introduced to the stage in ON A CLEAR DAY YOU CAN SEE FOREVER in 1965.
[35]Liza Minnelli accompanied her mother Judy Garland in the film clip of "The Trolley Song."

Peter Fitzgerald. Musical director, Jonathan Smith. Orchestrations by Harold Wheeler. Music supervisor, Michael Rafter. Music direction, Jonathan Smith. Aerial flying by ANTIGRAVITY, Inc. Associate producers, TV/Asahi/Hankyu, MARS Theatrical Productions, Judith Marinoff. Produced by Marc Routh, Richard Frankel, Stephen Baruch, Thomas Viertel, Lorie Cowen Levy/Stanley Shopkorn, Jujamcyn Theaters, in association with BB Promotion, Dede Harris/Jeslo Productions, Libby Adler Mages/Mari Glick, James D. Stern/Douglas L. Meyer and PACE Theatrical Group/SFX. Opened 9 December 1999 at the St. James Theatre and closed 14 January 2001 after 461 performances.

CAST: ANN HAMPTON CALLAWAY, EVERETT BRADLEY, LAURA BENANTI, Laureen Baldovi, Kristine Bendul, Carol Bentley, Caitlin Carter, Geralyn Del Corso, Desirée Duarte, Beverly Durand, Erin East, Scott Fowler, Ryan Francois, Kevin Michael Gaudin, Edgar Godineaux, Aldrin Gonzalez, Janine LaManna, Carlos Sierra-López, Rod McCune, J. C. Montgomery, Arte Phillips, Robert Royston, Jenny Thomas, Keith Lamelle Thomas, Maria Torres, CASEY MacGILL AND THE GOTHAM CITY GATES, MICHAEL GRUBER. *Swings:* Kristine Bendul, Desirée Duarte, Erin East, Kevin Michael Gaudin, Rod McCune.

The Gotham City Gates: Conductor, Piano/Keyboard: Jonathan Smith. *Guitars:* Dan Hovey. *Bass Piano/Keyboard:* Conrad Korsch. *Drums/Percussion:* Scott Neumann. *Woodwinds:* Matt Hong, Lance Bryant. *Associate Conductor, Trumpet:* Douglas Oberhamer. *Trombone:* Steve Armour.

ACT 1[36]

"It Don't Mean a Thing (If It Ain't Got That Swing)"
C. MacGill, The Band
(*Music by* Duke Ellington. *Lyrics by* Irving Mills. *Musical arrangements by* Jonathan Smith and Steve Armour.)

"Airmail Special"
Company
(*Music by* Benny Goodman, James R. Mundy and Charles Christian. *Musical arrangements by* Ian Herman.)

"Jersey Bounce"
(*Music by* B. Plater, T. Bradshaw, E. Johnson, B. Feyhe and Duke Ellington. *Musical arrangements by* Ian Herman.)

"Opus One"
(*Music by* D. George, J. Hodges and H. James. *Musical arrangements by* Ian Herman.)

"Jumpin at the Woodside"
R. Francois, J. Thomas, Company[37]
(*Music by* Count Basie.)

"Bounce Me, Brother (with a Solid Four)" (from BUCK PRIVATES film)
A. H. Callaway, Company
(*Music and Lyrics by* Don Raye and Hughie Prince. *Musical arrangements by* Jonathan Smith.)

"Two and Four"
L. Benanti, C. MacGill, The Band
(*Music and arrangement by* Ann Hampton Callaway.)

"Hit Me with a Hot Note and Watch Me Bounce"
(*Music by* Duke Ellington. *Lyrics by* D. George. *Vocal arrangements by* Michael Rafter.)

"Rhythm"
C. MacGill, M. Gruber, Company
(*Music by* Casey MacGill.)

"Throw That Girl Around"
E. Bradley, Company
(*Music and Lyrics by* Everett Bradley, Ilene Reid and Michael Heitzman. *Dance arrangements by* Everett Bradley and Lynne Taylor-Corbett.)

"Show Me What You Got"
(*Music by* Everett Bradley and Jonathan Smith. *Dance arrangements by* Everett Bradley and Lynne Taylor-Corbett.)
West Coast Couple: B. Durand, A. Gonzalez. *Latin Couple:* C. Sierra-López, M. Torres.

[36]All musical arrangements by Jonathan Smith except as noted. Additional musical quotations excerpted from:
"It Had to Be You"
(*Music by* Isham Jones. *Lyrics by* Gus Kahn.)
"The Jumpin' Jive" (Jump, Jive and Wail)
(*Music and Lyrics by* Cab Calloway, Frank Froeba and Jack Palmer.)
[37]Ryan Francois and Jenny Thomas perform their own choreography.

"Bli-Blip" (from JUMP FOR JOY)
A. H. Callaway, E. Bradley
(*Music by* Duke Ellington. *Lyrics by* Sid Kuller. *Vocal arrangements by* Everett Bradley and Ann Hampton Callaway.)

"Billy-A-Dick"
M. Gruber, Company
(*Music by* Hoagy Carmichael. *Lyrics by* Paul Francis Webster. *Additional lyrics by* Sean Martin Hingston.)

"Harlem Nocturne"
C. Carter, C. Korsch
(*Music by* Earle Hagen and Dick Rogers. *Musical arrangements by* Jon C. Cowherd.)

"Kitchen Mechanics' Night Out"
C. MacGill, R. Francois, J. Thomas, Company
(*Music and Lyrics by* Casey MacGill, Jonathan Smith, Lynne Taylor-Corbett and Paul Kelly.)

"Shout and Feel It"
R. Francois, J. Thomas
(*Music by* Count Basie. *Choreographed by* Ryan Francois and Jenny Thomas.)

"Boogie Woogie Bugle Boy (of Company B)" (from BUCK PRIVATES film)
E. Bradley, K. L. Thomas, E. Godineaux, with D. Oberhamer, L. Bryant, M. Hong
(*Music and Lyrics by* Don Raye and Hughie Prince. *Musical arrangements by* Jonathan Smith and Everett Bradley.)

The U.S.O.:
"G.I. Jive"
L. Benanti, G. DelCorso, C. Carter
(*Music and Lyrics by* Johnny Mercer. *Musical arrangements by* Jonathan Smith and Michael Rafter.)

"A String of Pearls"
A. Gonzales, K. L. Thomas, M. Gruber, Company
(*Music by* Jerry Gray. *Lyrics by* Eddie DeLange.)

"I Got a Gal in Kalamazoo"
(*Music by* Harry Warren. *Lyrics by* Mack Gordon.)

"Candy"
(*Music and Lyrics by* Mack David, Joan Whitney and Alex C. Kramer.)

"I'm Gonna Love You Tonight"
L. Benanti, M. Gruber, Company
(*Music by* Casey MacGill. *Lyrics by* Jack Murphy. *Additional lyrics by* Lynne Taylor-Corbett. *Vocal arrangements by* Michael Rafter.)

"I'll Be Seeing You" (from RIGHT THIS WAY)
A. H. Callaway, S. Fowler, C. Bentley
(*Music by* Sammy Fain. *Lyrics by* Irving Kahal. *Vocal arrangements by* Ann Hampton Callaway. *Dance arrangements by* Ian Herman.)

"In the Mood"
Company
(*Music by* Joe Garland. *Lyrics by* Andy Razaf.)

"Don't Sit Under the Apple Tree"
(*Music and Lyrics by* Lew Brown, Sam H. Stept and Charlie Tobias.)

ACT 2

"Swing, Brother, Swing"
A. H. Callaway, L. Benanti, E. Bradley, M. Gruber, C. MacGill, Company[38]
(*Music and Lyrics by* Walter Bishop, Lewis Raymond and Clarence Williams. *Vocal arrangements by* Casey MacGill.)

"Caravan"
The Gotham City Gates
(*Music by* Juan Tizol and Duke Ellington. *Lyrics by* Irving Mills.)

"Dancers in Love"
G. DelCorso, K. L. Thomas
(*Music by* Duke Ellington.)

"Cry Me a River"
L. Benanti, S. Armour
(*Music and Lyrics by* Arthur Hamilton. *Trombone arrangements by* Steve Armour.)

"Blues in the Night"
A. H. Callaway, C. Carter, E. Godineaux
(*Music by* Harold Arlen. *Lyrics by* Johnny Mercer.)

[38]Scott Fowler performs his own choreography.

"Take Me Back to Tulsa"/"Stay a Little Longer"
E. Bradley, M. Gruber, C. MacGill, Company
(*Music by* James Robert Wills and Tommy Duncan.)

"Boogie Woogie Country"
M. Gruber, R. Royston, L. Baldovi, Company[39]
(*Music by* Jack Murphy and Jonathan Smith.)

"All of Me"
E. Bradley, A. H. Callaway
(*Music by* Gerald Marks. *Lyrics by* Seymour Simons. *Vocal arrangements by* Ann Hampton Callaway. *Musical arrangements by* Ann Hampton Callaway and Jon C. Cowherd.)

"I Won't Dance" (from ROBERTA, film)
(*Music by* Jerome Kern. *Lyrics by* Dorothy Fields. *Additional lyrics by* Ann Hampton Callaway. *Vocal arrangements by* Ann Hampton Callaway. *Musical arrangements by* Ann Hampton Callaway and Jon C. Cowherd.)

"Bill's Bounce"
A. Gonzalez, S. Fowler, B. Durand, C. Bentley
(*Music by* Bill Elliott.)

"Stompin' at the Savoy"
A. H. Callaway
(*Music by* Benny Goodman, Edgar M. Sampson, Chick Webb. *Lyrics by* Andy Razaf. *Additional lyrics by* Ann Hampton Callaway. *Vocal arrangements by* Ann Hampton Callaway and Yaron Gershovsky.)

Finale:

"Swing, Brother, Swing" (reprise)
Company

"Sing, Sing, Sing"
(*Music and Lyrics by* Louis Prima, Andy Razaf, L. Berry.)

"It Don't Mean a Thing (If It Ain't Got That Swing)" (reprise)
(*Vocal arrangements by* Yaron Gershovsky. *Musical arrangements by* Ryan Francois and Jonathan Smith.)

MUCH ADO ABOUT EVERYTHING

1999.25

A One-Man Comedy Revue in Two Acts[40]. Written and directed by Jackie Mason. Lighting designer, Stan Crocker. Sound designer, Christopher Cronin. Associate producers, Howard Weiss, Henry Handler, Jam Theatricals (Arny Granat, Jerry Mickelson, Steve Traxler). Executive producers, Jyll Rosenfeld and Fred Krohn. Produced by Raoul Lionel Felder and Jon Stoll. Opened 30 December 1999 at the John Golden Theatre and closed 30 July 2000 after 183 performances.

CAST: JACKIE MASON (stand-up comedy, monologues, impressions).

JAMES JOYCE'S THE DEAD

2000.01

A Musical Play in One Act, Four Scenes[41]. Book by Richard Nelson (adapted from the last chapter of James Joyce's "The Dubliners"). Music by Shaun Davey. Lyrics[42] conceived and adapted by Richard Nelson and

---

[39]Robert Royston and Laureen Baldovi perform their own choreography.
[40]Previous editions of Jackie Mason's one man show have been presented as THE WORLD ACCORDING TO ME 22 December 1986 at the Brooks Atkinson Theatre for 367 performances; returned 3 May 1988 at the Brooks Atkinson for 203 performances; JACKIE MASON: BRAND NEW 17 October 1990 at the Neil Simon Theatre for 216 performances; JACKIE MASON: POLITICALLY INCORRECT, 5 April 1994 at the John Golden Theatre for 347 performances; LOVE THY NEIGHBOR 24 March 1996 at the Booth Theatre for 236 performances. This edition addressed such topics as the Internet, cell phones, Y2K, Bill Gates, plus 20 minutes of vintage Jackie Mason.
[41]Previously produced in New York Off-Broadway 28 October–28 November 1999 at Playwrights Horizons for 32 performances.
[42]Authors' note: The lyrics to some of these songs have been or adapted from or inspired by a number of eighteenth and nineteenth century Irish poems by Oliver Goldsmith, Lady Sydney Morgan, Michael William Balfe, William Allingham and from an anonymous nineteenth century music hall song. Other lyrics are adapted from Joyce or are original. Lyrics of D'Arcy's Aria were translated into Italian by Ali Davey. Mary Jane's academy piece and additional arrangements by Deborah Abramson. Other party pieces and underscore pieces in Scene 3 derive from works by Thomas Moore.

Shaun Davey. Sets by David Jenkins. Costumes by Jane Greenwood. Lighting by Jennifer Tipton. Sound by Scott Lehrer. Orchestrations by Shaun Davey. Musical direction by Charles Prince. Choreographed by Seán Curran. Directed by Richard Nelson. Produced by Gregory Mosher and Arielle Tepper, in association with Playwrights Horizons (Tim Sanford, Artistic Director). Opened 11 January 2000 at the Belasco Theatre and closed 16 April 2000 after 112 performances.

CAST: *The Hostesses* (3): *Aunt Julia Morkan, a music teacher:* SALLY ANN HOWES. *Aunt Kate Morkan, her sister (also a music teacher):* MARNI NIXON. *Mary Jane Morkan, their niece (also a music teacher):* EMILY SKINNER. *The Family* (2): *Gabriel Conroy, Julia and Kate's nephew:* CHRISTOPHER WALKEN. *Gretta Conroy, Gabriel's wife:* BLAIR BROWN. *The Guests* (5): *Mr. Browne, a friend of the Aunts:* BRIAN DAVIES. *Freddy Malins:* STEPHEN SPINELLA. *Mrs. Malins, Freddy's mother:* PADDY CROFT. *Miss Molly Ivors:* ALICE RIPLEY. *Bartell D'Arcy, an opera singer:* JOHN KELLY.
The Help (5): *Lily, the maid:* Brooke Sunny Moriber. *Michael, a music student of Mary Jane's:* Dashiell Eaves. *Rita, another student of Mary Jane's:* Daisy Eagan. *Cellist, a music student of Julia's:* Daniel Barrett. *Violinist, a music student of Kate's:* Louise Owen.
Ghost: Young Julia Morkan: DAISY EAGAN.

Setting: The Misses Morkans' annual Christmas-time party. Dublin, near the turn of the century.

Scene 1: The drawing room of the Misses Morkans' flat. *Scene 2:* The drawing room arranged for dinner. *Scene 3:* Aunt Julia's bedroom. *Scene 4:* A room in the Gresham Hotel.

MUSICAL NUMBERS

Scene 1
"Killarney's Lakes"
E. Skinner, M. Nixon, D. Eagan
"Kate Kearney"
D. Eaves, E. Skinner, Company
"Parnell's Plight"
A. Ripley, D. Eaves, C. Walken, B. Brown, Company
"Adieu to Ballyshannon"
C. Walker, B. Brown
"When Lovely Lady"
S. A. Howes, M. Nixon
"Three Jolly Pigeons"
S. Spinella, B. Davies, Company
"Goldenhair"
B. Brown, C. Walken

Scene 2
"Three Graces"
G. Conroy, Company
"Naughty Girls"
S. A. Howes, M. Nixon, E. Skinner, Company
"Wake the Dead"
S. Spinella, Company

Scene 3
"D'Arcy's Aria"
J. Kelly
"Queen of Our Hearts"
B. Davies, S. Spinella, C. Walken, J. Kelly, D. Eaves
"When Lovely Lady" (reprise)
S. A. Howes, D. Eagan

Scene 4
"Michael Furey"
B. Brown
"The Living and the Dead"
C. Walken, Company

SQUONK

2000.02

BigSmörgåsbørdWünderWerk (A Musical Entertainment) in One Act. Created by Steve O'Hearn and Jackie Dempsey in collaboration with the original NY Squonk Ensemble, Casi Pacilio, Kevin Kornicki, Jana Losey and T. Weldon Anderson. Directed by Tom Diamond. Music by Jackie Dempsey with Squonk. Image book, Steve O'Hearn. Lyrics by Jana Losey with Jackie Dempsey. Sets, puppets and costumes by Steve O'Hearn. Lighting by Tim Saternow. Sound, Bernard Fox. Projections by Steve

O'Hearn, with Casi Pacilio and Nick Fox-Geig. Musical direction by Jackie Dempsey. Associate producers, Mastantuono/Palumbo, Eric Falkenstein. Produced by William Repicci, Michael Minichiello, Lauren Doll, Cookie Centracco, Chris Groenewold. Opened 29 February 2000 at the Helen Hayes Theatre and closed 26 March 2000 after 32 performances[43].

CAST (in order of appearance): Jackie Dempsey (keyboard, accordion), Kevin Kornicki (electronic and acoustic percussion, sound textures), Steve O'Hearn (flutes, electronic winds, many-belled trumpet), T. Weldon Anderson (double bass), Jana Losey (vocals).

MUSICAL NUMBERS

Scene 1

tarantella tourner
what stirs

Scene 2

tutti di frutti
gadabout

Scene 3

fête de la tête
eat you up

Scene 4

jardin du jewels
sighs of her eyes

Scene 5

gigue giocoso
dance of the seven vowels

Scene 6

ballata bel canto
whirring of the wheel

Scene 7

tasto solo
tines

Scene 8

voce solomente
spoon

Scene 9

pas de deux
one bite too

Scene 10

basso virtuoso
blade

Scene 11

dansa de la lumiere
in the kitchen of the mountain king

Scene 12

torso con brio
touched

Scene 13

balletto di bocca buffo
dance of the jawbone glee club

Scene 14

diva du jour
whirl din din din

Scene 15

requiem de l'eau
caught

Scene 16

arioso splashetto
drank big drink

Scene 17

duettino pianissimo
in wavelet white

Scene 18

finale toronado
everything stirs

DANCING ON DANGEROUS GROUND

2000.04

An Irish Dance Drama in Two Acts. (Based on the Celtic legend "The Hunt for Dairmuid and Grania.") Original choreography by Jean Butler and Colin Dunne. Music composed by Seamus Egan and performed by Solas. Narrative and lyrics by Johnny Cunningham. Additional Irish Dance choreography by Michael Smith. Directed by Jeremy Sturt. Settings and costumes designed by Tim Hatley. Lighting design by Tom Kenny. Produced by Tricky Feat Ltd., Radio City Entertainment, Electric Factory Concerts, Artiste Management Productions and Creative Management Ltd[44]. Opened 8 March 2000 at Radio City Music Hall and closed 12 March 2000 after 7 performances.

CAST: *Grania*: JEAN BUTLER. *Diarmuid*: COLIN DUNNE. *Finn McCool*: Tony Kemp. *Deirdru*, friend of Grania: Sorcha McCaul. *Oisin*, son of Finn: Glenn Simpson. *Grania's Bodyguards*: Bobby Fox, Ciaran Maguire, Brian Swanton.

Finn McCool's Court, The Fianna/Women of the Court: Mary Ann Bakke, Aisling Barr, Angela Burns, Cara Butler, Marc Daniels, Michael Donegan, Colleen Farrell, Jo Ellen Forsyth, Sinead Gibbons, Roisin Alana Gilfedder, Tara Hegarty, Joel Hanna, Catriona Kelly, Maria Kirby, Leanna Leonard, Ryan McCaffery, Laura Minogue, Ronan Morgan, Mark O'Donnell, Aisling O'Dwyer, Martin Percival, Stephen Scarriff, Martina Stewart, J. R. Vancheri. *The Voice of Finn*: Stanley Townshend.

Solas: Seamus Egan, John Doyle (guitar), Mick McAuley (accordion, tin whistle), Deirdre Scalon (vocals), Ray Fean (percussion). *Soundtrack Musicians*: Noel Eccles (percussion), Dave West (keyboards), Kieran O'Hare (Uilleann pipes), Eoghan O'Neill (bass guitar).

ACT 1

"Finn's Prologue" (Truth is the hardest tale to tell)

From out of Ireland's mythic past comes Finn McCool, the leader of the Fianna. His story unfolds bringing forth Diarmuid and Grania, his fellow players in legend.

At the Court of Finn McCool

We join the court of Finn and meet his household, including Finn's great friend and colleague, Diarmuid, who is revered as the finest of the Fianna. There is an air of joyful anticipation among the court as Grania, Finn's betrothed, is soon to make her appearance.

Grania's Arrival

Grania enters Finn's court for the first time and meets her future husband. Her solo dance for Finn reflects her delight with her betrothed and her respect and admiration for him which is mirrored by his evident affection for her.

The Training

In another part of Finn's fortress home Diarmuid puts the Fianna through its paces in a series of training exercises. With their commander, Finn, in attendance, they display the precision of their skills and Diarmuid shows why he is regarded as being matchless among his peers.

The Gift of the Bodyguards

As a visible token of his love and esteem for Grania, Finn presents her with his warrior son, Oisin, and three other members of his elite military force who are to form her personal retinue of bodyguards.

The Female State of Mind

Led by Grania's friend and confidante, Deirdru, the women of the court take part in a light-hearted dance which expresses their delight at Grania's introduction to the court. Grania acknowledges the compliment by briefly joining their dance under Finn's watchful and admiring gaze.

The Hooley

The off-duty Fianna members join their women-folk for a lively and up-beat dance session on the eve of wedding celebrations that gather momentum with the approach of nightfall.

Diarmuid's Reflection

An encounter with a fiddle player beguiles Diarmuid into a more relaxed and mellow mood, encouraging him into dropping his guard and showing the playful and fun-loving side of his character.

---

[43]Previously produced Off-Off Broadway 2-28 August 1999 at P.S. 122.

[44]Tricky Feat Ltd. (Ian Allen, Jean Butler, Colin Dunne, Harvey Goldsmith, Producers); Radio City Entertainment (Edward J. Micone, Jr., Executive Vice President and Executive Producer of RCE; Bob Garcia, Vice President Entertainment Finance of RCE); Electric Factory Concerts (Allen Spivak, Larry Magid, Producers).

Meeting in a late-night bar

The arrival of more musicans and party-goers draws Diarmuid into a late-night bar where amidst an ever more boisterous and rowdy session of music and dance he is unexpectedly confronted by another man's bride-to-be.

On Dangerous Ground

Oblivious to their surrounding and companions, Diarmuid's and Grania's smoldering attraction for one another catches fire in a sexy and seductive dance. As their passion threatens to flare over they are drawn back into the company of their fellow revelers, but with their hearts still racing and with eyes only for each other.

ACT 2

At the Wedding of Finn and Grania

Finn's joy as he takes Grania's hand in marriage is tempered by the dread expressed in his later doubts and misgivings;
'Yet though she placed her hand in mine she would not share my glance
And a fear came over me
For her soul seemed to dance with another.'
However, the wedding festivities and dancing continue unabated, but with Diarmuid an increasingly central and provocative figure to whom Grania is constantly drawn.

Grania's Betrayal

With all thoughts of her new husband now obliterated by her wanton passion for Diarmuid, Grania conspires to free herself from her marital vows by enlisting Dierdru aqnd the women of the court to ply Finn and the Fianna with adulterated wine. As Finn and his men sink into comatose sleep, Grania and Diarmuid steal away into the night.

The Lovers in Flight

The lovers have fled deep into the forest and in this secure retreat share some tender moments of a romantic idyll. But both Diarmuid and Grania know that the tranquility of their newfound sanctuary is a temporary lull before the terror of the pursuit that must surely come.

The Fianna Awaken

Arising slowly from long hours of drugged slumber, the Fianna members struggle to shake off their stupor and their stiffness, but succeed in regaining their composure and military bearing before throwing off the ties that bind them.

Finn's Cry for War

Enraged by Grania's betrayal and his womenfolk's part in the flown lovers' act of treachery, Finn calls the Fianna to arms to answer his call for vengeance and, as punishment, compels the women of the court to make ready to join their men in the hunt for the fugitive couple.

The Pursuit and a Death

Driven on the by vengeful Finn, the Fianna remorselessly hunts down the outlawed lovers and at the height of their pursuit Diarmuid and Grania become separated. One by one Diarmuid's every escape route is sealed off until Finn and the pursuers close in on their former comrade with fatal consequences.

Grania's Lament

The Fianna and the women of the court melt away as Grania cradles the body of her one true love. Turning to Finn for consolation she finds only rejection. Utterly alone with her grief she dances herself into a state of inconsolable surrender.

Epilogue

As the dance returns Diarmuid and Grania to their rightful place in legend, Finn concludes our story with words that are full of insight, but also of regret:
'Only the past I hold, for the heart I can't possess
And the heart is every moment our destiny and our time
Till the rivers run backward and the moon no longer turns the tide
So hear me as I tell my truth
All is for love, and all is forever.'

2000.03 PORGY AND BESS

A Revival of the Folk Opera in Two Acts[45]. Book by DuBose Heyward adapted from the play "Porgy" by DuBose and Dorothy Heyward. Music by George Gershwin. Lyrics by DuBose Heyward and Ira Gershwin. Production directed by Tazewell Thompson. Choreography by Julie Arenal. Sets by Douglas W. Schmidt. Costumes by Nancy Potts. Lighting by Robert Wierzel. Fight director, Roddy Kinter. Conductors, John DeMain, Richard Bado. Produced by the New York City Opera (Paul Kellogg, Artistic and General Director). Opened 7 March 2000 at the New York State Theatre and closed 25 March 2000 after 10 performances in repertory.

CAST (in order of appearance): *Jasbo Brown:* Gerald Steichen. *Clara:* ANITA JOHNSON. *Mingo:* Robert Mack. *Jake:* Kenneth Floyd. *Sportin' Life:* DWAYNE CLARK. *Robbins:* Michael Austin. *Serena:* ANGELA SIMPSON or MONIQUE McDONALD. *Jim:* Edward Pleasant. *Peter:* Bert Lindsey. *Lily:* Shirley Russ. *Maria:* SABRINA ELAYNE CARTEN. *Scipio:* Nkosane Jackson. *Porgy:* ALVY POWELL or RICHARD HOBSON. *Crown:* TIMOTHY ROBERT BLEVINS or LESTER LYNCH. *Bess:* MARQUITA LISTER or KISHNA DAVIS. *Detective:* Wynn Harmon. *Policemen:* Michael Hajek, Charles Mandracchia. *Undertaker:* Bryan Jackson. *Annie:* Jeanette Blakeney. *Frazier:* Marvin Lowe. *Strawberry Woman:* Adina Aaron. *Crab Man:* Duane Martin Foster. *Nelson:* E. Mani Cadet. *Coroner:* John Henry Thomas.

(Residents of Catfish Row) Ensemble: Adina Aaron, Jeanette Blakeney, Bert Boone, Elaugh Butler, E. Mani Cadet, Aixa Cruz-Falú, David Aron Damane, Jean Derricotte-Murphy, Devonne Douglas, Mia Douglas, Rochelle Ellis, Duane Martin Foster, Anne Fridal, Chinyelu Ingram, Clinton Ingram, Bryan Jackson, Nicola James, Quanda Johnson, Naomi Elizabeth Jones, Pamela E. Jones, Jason Phillip Knight, Bert Lindsey, Lisa Lockhart, Marvin Lowe, Robert Mack, Edward Pleasant, Dorian Gray Ross, Elizabeth Lyra Ross, Leonard Rowe, Shirley Russ, Martín Solá, Lucy Salome Sträuli, Marcelin Summers, Everett Suttle, Kellie Turner. *Children:* Khalif Diouf, Ayanna Francis, Leilani Irvin, Nkosane Jackson, Kayla Leacock, Grace Price, Afrika Rhames, Khadijha Stewart, Lacey Thomas, Jamal Russ, Verne Watley.

2000.05 RIVERDANCE ON BROADWAY

A Revival of the Dance Revue in Two Acts, 22 Scenes[46]. Music and lyrics by Bill Whelan. Directed by John McColgan. Set design, Robert Ballagh. Lighting design,Rupert Murray. Costume design, Joan Bergin. Sound design, Michael O'Gorman. Orchestrations by Bill Whelan, Nick Ingman, David Downes. Musical director, Cathal Synnott. Original principal Irish dance choreographer, Michael Flatley. Original choreography by Mavis Ascott, Jean Butler, Colin Dunne, Carol Leavy Joyce, Andrei Kisselev, Moscow Folk Ballet Company, Maria Pagés, Tarik Winston. Executive producer, Julian Erskine. Produced by Abhann Productions Ltd. (Moya Doherty, producer). Opened 16 March 2000 at the Gershwin Theatre and closed 26 August 2001 after 605 performances.

CAST: *Solo Dancers:* PAT RODDY, EILEEN MARTIN, MARIA PAGÉS. *Solo Singers:* TSIDII LE LOKA, BRIAN KENNEDY. *Narrator:* LIAM NEESON (voice on tape).

The Riverdance Irish Dance Troupe: Dearbhail Bates, Sarah Berry, Tara Barry, Natalie Biggs, Lorna Bradley, Martin Brennan, Zeph Caissie, Suzanne Cleary, Andrea Curley, Marty Dowds, Lindsay Doyle, Shannon Doyle, Susan Ginnety, Paula Goulding, Conor Hayes, Gary Healy, Matt Martin, Tokiko Masuda, Sinéad McCafferty, Holly McGlinchy, Jonathan McMorrow, Joe Moriarty, Niall Mulligan, Catherine O'Brien, David O'Hanlon, Debbie O'Keeffe, Ursula Quigley, Kathleen Ryan, Anthony Savage, Rosemarie Schade, Ryan Sheridan, Claire Usher, Leanda Ward, Margaret Williams.

The Riverdance Orchestra: Cathal Synnott (Musical director/keyboards), Athena Tergis (Fiddle), Ivan Goff (Uilleann pipes/low whistle), Kenneth Edge (Soprano and alto saxophones), Nikola Parov (Gadulka, Kaval, Gaida and Bouzouki), Eilís Egan (Accordion), Des Moore (Electric and acoustic guitars), Noel Heraty (Percussion), Desi Reynolds (Drums and percussion), Tony Steele (Bass guitar), Robbie Harris (Bodhrán, Darrabukkas, Dunbeg, and Ouda).

The Riverdance Singers: Sara Clancy (soloist), Patrick Connolly, Brian Dunphy, Joanna Higgins, Darren Holden, Michael Londra, Tara O'Beirne, Sherry Steele, Ben Stubbs, Yvonne Woods.

Moscow Folk Ballet Company: Denis Boroditski, Andrei Kisselev, Yulia Koryagina, Olena Krutsenko, Svetlana Malinina, Ilia Streltsov, Vitaly Verterich, Yana Volkova.

The Riverdance Tappers: Walter "Sundance" Freeman, Channing Cook Holmes, Karen Callaway Williams.

The Amanzi Singers: Notombikhona Dlamini, Fana Kekana, Ntombifuthi Pamella Mhlongo, Francina Moliehi Mokubetsi, Keneilwe Margaret Motsage, Isaac Mthethwa, Andile Selby Ndebele, Mbuso Dick Shange.

The Riverdance Drummers: Darren Andrews, Abe Doron, Eamon Ellams, Gary Grant.

ACT 1

Scene 1

Invocation: "Hear My Cry"
B. Kennedy

---

[45]First produced in New York 10 October 1935 at the Alvin Theatre for 124 performances. For Synopsis of Scenes and Musical Numbers, see original 1935 production. This production was reduced from Three Acts to Two, with its one intermission following the original Act Two, Scene 2.

[46]First produced in New York 13 March 1996 at Radio City Music Hall for 8 performances, returned 2 October 1996 to Radio City Music Hall for 21 performances; returned 24 September 1998 to Radio City Music Hall for an additional 23 performances.

Scene 2
"Reel Around the Sun"
P. Roddy, The Irish Dance Troupe
Scene 3
"The Heart's Cry"
The Riverdance Singers
Scene 4
"The Countess Cathleen"
E. Martin, The Irish Dance Troupe
Scene 5
"Caoineadh Chú Chulainn" (Lament)
I. Goff
Scene 6
"Thunderstorm"
P. Roddy, The Irish Dance Troupe
Scene 7
"Shivna"
Moscow Folk Ballet, The Riverdance Singers
Scene 8
"Firedance"
M. Pagés, The Irish Dance Troupe
Scene 9
"At the Edge of the World"
B. Kennedy
Scene 10
"Slip into Spring–The Harvest"
The Riverdance Orchestra
Scene 11
"Riverdance"
P. Roddy, E. Martin,
The Riverdance Singers and Drummers, The Irish Dance Troupe

ACT 2
Scene 1
"American Wake"
The Company
Scene 2
"Lift the Wings"
B. Kennedy, S. Clancy
Scene 3
Harbour of the New World:
Trading Taps
W. S. Freeman, C. C. Holmes, K. C. Williams
"Amanzi"
Amanzi Singers
"I Will Set You Free"
T. Le Loka, Amanzi Singers
"Let Freedom Ring"
T. Le Loka, Amanzi Singers
Scene 4
"Morning in Macedonia"
The Riverdance Orchestra
Scene 5
"The Russian Dervish"
Moscow Folk Ballet Company
Scene 6
"Heartbeat of the World—Andalucia"
M. Pagés, N. Heraty, P. Roddy
Scene 7
"Rí Rá"
E. Martin, The Irish Dance Troupe,
Moscow Folk Ballet Company, The Riverdance Singers and
Drummers
Scene 8
"Homecoming"
A. Tergis, M. Pagés, R. Harris

Scene 9
Anthem: "Endless Journey"
T. Le Loka, B. Kennedy,
Amanzi and Riverdance Singers, The Irish Dance Troupe
Scene 10
"Heartland"
P. Roddy, E. Martin, The Irish Dance Troupe
Scene 11
Finalé
The Company

2000.06   # AIDA

A Musical in Two Acts. Book by Linda Woolverton, Robert Falls and David Henry Hwang, suggested by the opera[47]. Music by Elton John. Lyrics by Tim Rice. Directed by Robert Falls. Choreographed by Wayne Cilento. Scenic and costume design by Bob Crowley. Lighting design by Natasha Katz. Sound design by Steve C. Kennedy. Fight direction by Rick Sordelet. Musical arrangements by Guy Babylon, Paul Bogaev. Orchestrations by Steve Margoshes, Guy Babylon and Paul Bogaev. Dance arrangements by Bob Gustafson. Musical direction and vocal arrangements by Paul Bogaev. Associate producer, Marshall B. Purdy. Produced by Hyperion Theatricals[48] (Peter Schneider, Thomas Schumacher, Producers). Opened 23 March 2000 at the Palace Theatre and is still running at this time!

<u>CAST</u> (in order of appearance): *Amneris:* SHERIE RENÉ SCOTT. *Radames:* ADAM PASCAL. *Aida:* HEATHER HEADLEY. *Mereb:* DAMIAN PERKINS. *Zoser:* JOHN HICKOK. *Pharaoh:* DANIEL ORESKES. *Nehebka:* Schele Williams. *Amonasro:* TYREES ALLEN.
    Ensemble: Robert M. Armitage, Troy Allan Burgess, Franne Calma, Bob Gaynor, Kisha Howard, Tim Hunter, Youn Kim, Kyra Little, Nekya Unique Massey, Corinne McFadden, Phineas Newborn III, Jody Ripplinger, Raymond Rodriguez, Eric Sciotto, Samuel N. Thiam, Jerald Vincent, Schele Williams, Natalia Zisa. *Swings:* Chris Payne Dupré, Kelli Fournier, Timothy Edward Smith, Endalyn Taylor-Shellman.

(The story is set in ancient Egypt.)

ACT 1
"Every Story Is a Love Story"
S. R. Scott, Company
"Fortune Favors the Brave"
A. Pascal, Soldiers
"The Past is Another Land"
H. Headley
"Another Pyramid"
J. Hickok, Ministers
"How I Know You"
D. Perkins, H. Headley
"My Strongest Suit"
S. R. Scott, Women of the Palace
"Enchantment Passing Through"
A. Pascal, H. Headley
"My Strongest Suit" (reprise)
S. R. Scott, H. Headley
"The Dance of the Robe"
H. Headley, S. Williams, Nubians
"Not Me"
A. Pascal, D. Perkins, H. Headley, S. R. Scott
"Elaborate Lives"
A. Pascal, H. Headley
"The Gods Love Nubia"
H. Headley, J. Hickok, Nubians

ACT 2
"A Step Too Far"
S. R. Scott, A. Pascal, H. Headley

---

[47]The opera AIDA was composed by Giuseppe Verdi to a libretto by Antonio Ghislanzoni and Camille duLocke.
[48]Hyperion is a division of Walt Disney Theatrical Productions.

"Easy as Life"
  H. Headley
"Like Father Like Son"
  J. Hickok, A. Pascal, Ministers
"Radames' Letter"
  A. Pascal
"How I Know You" (reprise)
  D. Perkins
"Written in the Stars"
  H. Headley, A. Pascal
"I Know the Truth"
  S. R. Scott
"Elaborate Lives" (reprise)
  H. Headley, A. Pascal
"Every Story Is a Love Story" (reprise)
  S. R. Scott

CONTACT

2000.07

A Dance Play in Two Acts, Three Parts, by Susan Stroman and John Weidman[49]. Written by John Weidman. Directed and choreographed by Susan Stroman. Sets by Thomas Lynch. Costumes by William Ivey Long. Lighting by Peter Kaczorowski. Sound by Scott Stauffer. Associate choreographer, Chris Peterson. Produced by Lincoln Center Theater Company (André Bishop, Artistic Director; Bernard Gersten, Executive Producer). Opened 30 March 2000[50] at the Vivian Beaumont Theater and is still running at this time!

CAST (in alphabetical order): JASON ANTOON, John Bolton, Tomé Cousin, Holly Cruikshank, Pascle Faye, BOYD GAINES, Nina Goldman, Peter Gregus, Shannon Hammons, Jack Hayes, SEÁN MARTIN HINGSTON, Stacey Todd Holt, Angelique Ilo, DAVID MacGILLIVRAY, STEPHANIE MICHELS, Mayumi Miguel, Dana Stackpole, SCOTT TAYLOR, Rocker Verastique, Robert Wersinger, DEBORAH YATES, KAREN ZIEMBA. *Swings*: Steve Geary, Joanne Manning.

ACT 1

Part I: SWINGING[51]

A Servant, an Aristocrat, a Girl on a Swing

Scene: A forest glade, 1767.

CAST: *Two Frenchmen*: S. M. Hingston, S. Taylor. *Girl on the Swing*: S. Michels.

MUSIC
  "My Heart Stood Still"
    Stephane Grappelli
    (*Music by* Richard Rodgers.)
  Anitra's Dance (from PEER GYNT SUITE No. 1)
  Waltz Eugene (from EUGENE ONEGIN, Opus 24)
  La Farandole (from L'Arlesienne Suite No. 2)
    New York Philharmonic, conducted by Leonard Bernstein

Part II: DID YOU MOVE?

A Wife, a Husband, a Headwaiter

Scene: An Italian restaurant, Queens, 1954.

CAST: *A Wife*: K. Ziemba. *A Husband*: J. Antoon. *A Headwaiter*: D. MacGillivray. *Restaurant Patrons*: T. Cousin, N. Goldman, P. Gregus, D. Stackpole. *Waiters*: S. Taylor, R. Wersinger. *Photographer*: P. Faye. *Cigarette Girl*: S. Hammons. *Uncle Vinnie*: S. M. Hingston. *Headwaiter*: D. MacGillivray. *Busboy*: R. Verastique.

MUSIC
  "You're Nobody til Somebody Loves You"
    Dean Martin
    (*Music and Lyrics by* Russ Morgan, Larry Stock and James Cavanaugh.)

[49]All the music in CONTACT was pre-recorded.
[50]First produced Off-Broadway 7 October 1999-7 January 2000 at the Mitzi Newhouse Theater for 109 performances.
[51]Inspired by the painting, The Swing, circa 1768, by Jean-Honoré Fragonard.

"Powerful Stuff"
  The Fabulous Thunderbirds
  (*Music and Lyrics by* Wally Wilson, Michael Henderson and Robert S. Field.)
"Put a Lid on It"
  Squirrel Nutzippers
  (*Music by* Tom Maxwell.)
"Sweet Lorraine"
  Stephane Grappelli
  (*Music and Lyrics by* Clifford Burwell and Mitchell Parish.)
"Runaround Sue"
  Dion
  (*Music by* Ernest Maresca, Dion DiMucci.)
"Beyond the Sea"
  Royal Crown Revue, conducted by Arte Butler
  (*Music by* Charles Trenet and Jack Lawrence.)

ACT 2

Part III: CONTACT

An Advertising Executive, a Bartender, a Girl in a Yellow Dress

Scene: (An apartment and a bar.) New York City, 1999.
  CAST: *Michael Wiley*: B. Gaines. *Bartender, Voice Messages*: J. Antoon. *Girl in the Yellow Dress*: D. Yates. *Jack*: J. Hayes. *Johnny*: S. M. Hingston. *Joe*: R. Wersiger. *Clubgoers*: T. Cousin, P. Faye, N. Goldman, P. Gregus, S. Hammons, S. T. Holt, S. Michels, M. Miguel, D. Stackpole, S. Taylor, R. Verastique. *Swings* (for all 3 Parts): S. Geary, A. Ilo, D. MacGillivray, J. Manning.

MUSIC
  "See What I Mean?"
    Al Cooper and His Savoy Sultans
    (*Music by* J. Chapman.)
  "Simply Irresistible"
    Robert Palmer
    (*Music by* Robert Palmer.)
  "Do You Wanna Dance?"
    Beach Boys
    (*Music and Lyrics by* Bobby Freeman.)
  "Topsy"
    Royal Crown Revue
    (*Music by* William Edgar Battle and Eddie Durham.)
  "Sing Sing Sing"
    Benny Goodman and His Orchestra
    (*Music by* Louis Prima, arranged by Benny Goodman.)
  "Christopher Columbus"
    Benny Goodman and His Orchestra
    (*Music and Lyrics by* Andy Razaf.)
  "Moondance"
    Van Morrison
    (*Music by* Van Morrison.)

THE WILD PARTY

2000.08

A Musical in One Act, 5 Scenes. Book by Michael John LaChiusa and George C. Wolfe. Music and lyrics by Michael John LaChiusa. Based on the poem of the same name by Joseph Moncure March. Directed by George C. Wolfe. Choreographed by Joey McKneely. Scenic design, Robin Wagner. Costume design, Toni-Leslie James. Lighting design, Jules Fisher and Peggy Eisenhauer. Sound design, Tony Meola. Musical director, Todd Ellison. Orchestrations by Bruce Coughlin. Associate producer, Wiley Hausam. Produced by the Joseph Papp Public Theatre/New York Shakespeare Festival (George C. Wolfe, Producer), Scott Rudin/Paramount Pictures, Roger Berlind, (Elizabeth) Williams/(Anita) Waxman. Opened 13 April 2000 at the Virginia Theatre and closed 11 June 2000 after 68 performances.

CAST (in order of appearance): *Queenie*: TONI COLLETTE. *Burrs*: MANDY PATINKIN. *Jackie*: Marc Kudisch. *Miss Madelaine True*: Jane Summerhays. *Sally*: Sally Murphy. *Eddie Mackrel*: Norm Lewis. *Mae*: Leah Hocking. *Nadine*: Brooke Sunny Moriber. *Phil D'Armano*: Nathan Lee Graham. *Oscar D'Amano*: Michael McElroy. *Dolores*: EARTHA KITT. *Gold*: Adam Grupper. *Goldberg*: Stuart Zagnit. *Black*: YANCEY ARIAS. *Kate*: TONYA PINKINS.

Time: New York, New York. 1928.

Scene 1: The Vaudeville. *Scene 2*: Promenade of Guests. *Scene 3*: The Party. *Scene 4*: After Midnight Dies. *Scene 5*: Finale.

MUSICAL NUMBERS

Scene 1

"Queenie Was a Blonde"/"Marie Is Tricky"/"Wild Party"
T. Collette, M. Patinkin, Company

Scene 2

"Dry"
M. Patinkin, M. Kudisch, J. Summerhays, S. Murphy, N. Lewis, L. Hocking, N. L. Graham, M. McElroy. E. Kitt

"Welcome to My Party"
T. Collette

"Like Sally"
J. Summerhays

"Breezin' Through Another Day"
M. Kudisch

"Uptown"
N. L. Graham, M. McElroy

"Eddie & Mae"
N. Lewis, L. Hocking

"Gold & Goldberg"
A. Grupper, S. Zagnit

"Moving Uptown"
E. Kitt

Scene 3

"Black Bottom"
T. Collette, Company

"Best Friend"
T. Collette, T. Pinkins

"A Little M-M-M"
N. L. Graham, M. McElroy

"Tabu/Taking Care of the Ladies"
M. McElroy, Y. Arias, Company

"Wouldn't It Be Nice?"
M. Patinkin

"Lowdown-Down"
T. Collette

"Gin"
M. Patinkin, Company

"Wild"
Company

"Need"
J. Summerhays, Company

"Black Is a Moocher"
T. Pinkins

"People Like Us"
T. Collette, Y. Arias

Scene 4

"After Midnight Dies"
S. Murphy

"Godlen Boy"
N. Lewis, N. Graham, M. McElroy

"The Movin' Uptown Blues"
A. Grupper, S. Zagnit

"The Lights of Broadway"
B. S. Moriber

"More"
M. Kudisch

"Love Ain't Nothin'/Welcome to Her Party/What I Need"
T. Pinkins, M. Patinkin, T. Collette

"How Many Women in the World?"
M. Patinkin

"When It Ends"
E. Kitt

Scene 5

"This is What It Is"
T. Collette

Finale
T. Collette, M. Patinkin, Company

2000.09 JESUS CHRIST SUPERSTAR

A Revival of the Musical in Two Acts[52]. Music by Andrew Lloyd Webber. Lyrics by Tim Rice. Directed by Gale Edwards. Choreography by Anthony Van Laast. Scenic design by Peter J. Davison. Costume design by Roger Kirk. Lighting design by Mark McCullough. Sound design by Richard Ryan. Musical supervisor, Simon Lee. Associate musical supervisor, Kristen Blodgett. Musical director, Patrick Vaccariello. Assistant choreographer, Denny Berry. Orchestrations by Andrew Lloyd Webber. Produced by The Really Useful Superstar Company and Nederlander Producing Company of America Inc. Opened 16 April 2000 at the Ford Center for the Performing Arts and closed 3 September 2000 after 161 performances.

CAST: *Jesus of Nazareth*: GLENN CARTER. *Judas Iscariot*: TONY VINCENT. *Mary Magdalene*: MAYA DAYS. *Pontius Pilate*: KEVIN GRAY. *King Herod*: PAUL KANDEL. *Simon Zealotes*: MICHAEL K. LEE. *Caiaphas*: FREDERICK B. OWENS. *Annas*: RAY WALKER. *Peter*: RODNEY HICKS.

Apostles/Disciples: Christian Borle, Lisa Brescia, D'Monroe, Manoel Feliciano, Somer Lee Graham, J. Todd Howell, Daniel C. Levine, Anthony Manough, Joseph Melendez, Eric Millegan, Michael Seelbach, Alexander Selma, David St. Louis, Shayna Steele, Max Von Essen, Joe Wilson, Jr., Andrew Wright. *Soul Girls/Disciples*: Merle Dandridge, Deidre Goodwin, Lana Gordon. *Priests*: Hank Campbell, Devin Richards, Timothy Warmen. *Swings*: Bernard Dotson, Jessica Phillips, Adam Simmons. *Profiteers, Lepers, Roman Guards, The Mob, Herod's Court and Paparazzi*: Members of the Company.

2000.10 THE GREEN BIRD

A Comedy with Music in Two Acts[53]. (Original Italian) Play by Carlo Gozzi, translated by Albert Bermel and Ted Emery. Original music composed and orchestrated by Elliot Goldenthal. Additional text by Eric Overmeyer. Scenic design by Christine Jones. Costume design by Constance Hoffman. Lighting design by Donald Holder. Sound design, Jon Weston. Mask and puppet design, Julie Taymor. Music director, Richard Martinez. Vocal director, Joe Church. Musical staging by Daniel Ezralow. Directed by Julie Taymor. Produced by Ostar Enterprises Inc. (Robert E. Wankel, Executive Vice President), with Theater for a New Audience (Jeffrey Horowitz, Artistic Director) and Nina Lannan. Opened 18 April 2000 at the Cort Theatre and closed 4 June 2000 after 55 performances.

CAST (in order of appearance): *Brighella*: Reg. E. Cathey. *Pantalone*: Andrew Weems. *Smeraldina*: DIDI CONN. *Truffaldino*: NED EISENBERG. *Barbarina*: Katie MacNichol. *Renzo*: SEBASTIAN ROCHÉ. *The Green Bird*: BRUCE TURK. *Ninetta*: KRISTINE NIELSEN. *Voice of Calmon*: Andrew Weems. *Tartaglia*: DEREK SMITH. *Tartagliona*: EDWARD HIBBERT. *Beautician*: Andrew Weems. *Pompea*: Lee Lewis. *Pierrot*: Andrew Weems. *Voice of Serpentina*: Lee Lewis.

Singing Apples: Sophia Salguero (soloist), Meredith Patterson, Sarah Jane Nelson. *Dancing Waters*: Erico Villanueva (soloist), Ramon Flowers. *Servants/Marching Band/Puppeteers*: Ken Barnett, Ramon Flowers, Sarah Jane Nelson, Meredith Patterson, Sophia Salguero, Erico Villanueva.

The action is set in the imaginary city of Monterotondo, Serpentina's garden, the ogre's mountain lair and other suitably fabulous places.

ACT 1[54]

"Truffaldino's Sausage Shop"

"O Greedy People" (The Apples That Sing)
S. Salguero, S. J. Nelson, M. Patterson
(*Lyrics by* Carlo Gozzi and Albert Bermel.)

---

[52]First produced in New York 12 October 1971 at the Mark Hellinger Theatre for 711 performances. For Synopsis of Scenes and Musical Numbers, see original 1971 production. For this production, the following were added to the list of musical numbers:

"Everything's Alright" (reprise)

(Act 1, after "The Temple")
M. Days, G. Carter

"Blood Money" (added at the close of Act 1, to accompany "Damned for All Time")

[53]An earlier production of this play under the direction of Julie Taymor was presented Off-Broadway 7 March 1996 at the New Victory Theater for 15 performances.

[54]Musical numbers (except for "Oh Foolish Heart") not listed in programs. List prepared from press office materials and Original Cast Recording from DRG Records.

"Tartaglia's Lament"
D. Smith

"The Bickering"

"Calmon, King of Statues"

"Joy to the King"
S. Salguero
(*Lyrics by* Carlo Gozzi and Albert Bermel.)

Ninetta's Hope

"Renzo and Pompea Duet"
S. Roche, L. Lewis
(*Lyrics by* Albert Bermel.)

"Barbarina's Lament"
K. MacNichol

The Waters That Dance

"Serpentina's Garden"
A. Weems

Under Bustle Funk

Green Bird Descent

The Magic Feather

The King's Lament (violin solo)

Accordions and Palace Rhumba

ACT 2

Prologue (Radio Waves)

Acids and Alkalis

Apple Aria (instrumental)

"Oh Foolish Heart" (Finale)
Full Company
(*Lyrics by* David Suehsdorf.)

2000.11

THE MUSIC MAN

A Revival of the Musical Comedy in Two Acts, 18 Scenes[55]. Book, music and lyrics by Meredith Willson. Story by Meredith Willson and Franklin Lacey. Direction and choreography by Susan Stroman. Scenery designed by Thomas Lynch. Costumes designed by William Ivey Long. Lighting designed by Peter Kaczorowski. Sound designed by Jonathan Deans. Musical supervision and direction by David Chase. Orchestrations by Doug Besterman. Dance and incidental music by David Krane. Associate choreographer, Tara Young, Associate director, Ray Roderick. Produced by Dodger Theatricals, John F. Kennedy Center for the Performing Arts, Elizabeth Williams/Anita Waxman, Kardana-Swinsky Productions, Lorie Cowen Levy/Dede Harris. Opened 27 April at the Neil Simon Theatre and closed 30 December 2001 after 685 performances.

CAST (in order of appearance): *Conductor:* Andre Garner. *Charlie Cowell:* RALPH BYERS. *Travelling Salesmen:* Liam Burke, Kevin Bogue, E. Clayton Cornelious, Michael Duran, Blake Hammond, Michael McGurk, Dan Sharkey, John Sloman. *Harold Hill:* CRAIG BIERKO. *Olin Britt:* Michael-Leon Wooley. *Amaryllis:* Jordan Puryear. *Maud Dunlop:* Martha Hawley. *Ewart Dunlop:* Jack Doyle. *Mayor Shinn:* PAUL BENEDICT. *Alma Hix:* Leslie Hendrix. *Ethel Toffelmier:* Tracy Nicole Chapman. *Oliver Hix:* John Sloman. *Jacey Squires:* Blake Hammond. *Marcellus Washburn:* MAX CASELLA. *Tommy Djilas:* CLYDE ALVES. *Marian Paroo:* REBECCA LUKER. *Mrs. Paroo:* KATHERINE McGRATH. *Winthrop Paroo:* MICHAEL PHELAN. *Eulalie Mackecknie Shinn:* RUTH WILLIAMSON. *Zaneeta Shinn:* KATE LEVERING. *Gracie Shinn:* Ann Whitlow Brown. *Mrs. Squires:* Ann Brown. *Constable Locke:* Kevin Bogue.

Residents of River City: Cameron Adams, Kevin Bogue, Sara Brenner, Chase Brock, Liam Burke, E. Clayton Cornelious, Michael Duran, Andre Garner, Ellen Harvey, Mary Illes, Joy Lynn Matthews, Michael McGurk, Robbie Nicholson, Ipsita Paul, Pamela Remler, Dan Sharkey, Lauren Ullrich, Travis Wall. *Swings:* Jennie Ford, Leigh Heim, Jason Snow, Jeff Williams.

Act 1, Scene 1: A Railway Coach, morning, 3 July, 1912. *Scene 2:* Train Depot. River City, Iowa. *Scene 3:* The Center of Town. *Scene 4:* A Street. *Scene 5:* The Paroo's House. *Scene 6:* Madison Gymnasium. 4 July. *Scene 7:* The Center of Town. *Scene 8:* A Street just off the Center of Town. *Scene 9:* Madison Library. *Scene 10:* A Street, the

following Saturday, late afternoon. *Scene 11:* The Paroos' Porch, immediately following. *Scene 12:* The Edge of Town, noon, the following Saturday.

Act 2, Scene 1: Madison Gymnasium, the following Tuesday evening. *Scene 2:* The Front of the Hotel, the following Wednesday evening. *Scene 3:* The Paroos' Porch, immediately following. *Scene 4:* Madison Park. *Scene 5:* The Footbridge. *Scene 6:* The Center of Town, immediately following.

ACT 1

Scene 1

"Rock Island"
R. Byers, Travelling Salesmen

Scene 3

"Iowa Stubborn"
Townspeople of River City

"(Ya Got) Trouble"
C. Bierko, Townspeople

Scene 5

"Piano Lesson"
R. Luker, K. McGrath, K. Puryear

"Goodnight, My Someone"
R. Luker

Scene 6

"Seventy Six Trombones"
C. Bierko, Boys, Girls

Scene 7

"Sincere"
M. Wooley, J. Sloman, J. Doyle, B. Hammond

Scene 8

"The Sadder-But-Wiser Girl"
C. Bierko, M. Casella

"Pickalittle (Talkalittle)"
L. Hendrix, T. N. Chapman, R. Williamson, M. Hawley, A. Brown, Ladies of River City

"Goodnight Ladies"
M. Wooley, J. Sloman, J. Doyle, B. Hammond

Scene 9

"Marian the Librarian"
C. Bierko, Boys, Girls

Scene 11

"Gary, Indiana"
C. Bierko, K. McGrath

"My White Knight"
R. Luker

Scene 12

"The Wells Fargo Wagon"
M. Phelan, Townspeople

ACT 2

Scene 1

"It's You"
M. Wooley, J. Sloman, J. Doyle, B. Hammond, C. Bierko, Townspeople

"Pickalittle" (reprise)
R. Williamson, M. Hawley, T. N. Chapman, L. Hendrix, A. Brown, Ladies of River City

Scene 2

"Lida Rose"
M. Wooley, J. Sloman, J. Doyle, B. Hammond

"Will I Ever Tell You?"
R. Luker

Scene 3

"Gary, Indiana" (reprise)
M. Phelan, K. McGrath, R. Luker

Scene 4

"Shipoopi"
M. Casella, C. Bierko, Townspeople

Scene 5

"Till There Was You"
R. Luker

[55]Originally produced in New York 19 December 1957 at the Majestic Theatre for 1375 performances. For Synopsis of Scenes and Musical Numbers, see original 1957 production. Original Act 1, Scene 2 was divided in two, yielding an extra scene.

"Seventy Six Trombones"/"Goodnight, My Someone" (reprise)
    C. Bierko, R. Luker
"Till There Was You" (reprise)
    C. Bierko
Scene 6
  Finale
    Company

2000.12   DIRTY BLONDE

A Play (with Songs) in One Act[56]. Play by Claudia Shear, conceived by Claudia Shear and James Lapine. Directed by James Lapine. Musical staging, John Carrafa. Scenic design, Douglas Stein. Costume design, Susan Hilferty. Lighting design, David Lander. Sound design, Dan Moses Schreier. Arrangements, musical direction by Bob Stillman. Produced by The Shubert Organization, Chase Mishkin, Ostar Enterprises, ABC, Inc., in association with the New York Theatre Workshop. Opened 1 May 2000 at the Helen Hayes Theatre and closed 4 March 2001 after 352 performances.

CAST (in order of appearance): *Frank Wallace, Ed Hearn and others*: BOB STILLMAN. *Jo, Mae (West)*: CLAUDIA SHEAR. *Charlie and others*: KEVIN CHAMBERLIN.

MUSICAL NUMBERS[57]
  "Dirty Blonde"
    (*Music and Lyrics by* Bob Stillman.)

"A Guy What Takes His Time" (from SHE DONE HIM WRONG, film)
    (*Music and Lyrics by* Ralph Rainger.)
"Cuddle Up and Cling to Me"
    (*Music by* Henry I. Marshall. *Lyrics by* Stanley Murphy.)
"I Found a New Way to Go to Town" (from I'M NO ANGEL, film)
    (*Music by* Harvey Brooks. *Lyrics by* Gladys Dubois and Ben Ellison.)
"I'm No Angel" (from I'M NO ANGEL, film)
    (*Music by* Harvey Brooks. *Lyrics by* Gladys Dubois and Ben Ellison.)
"I Love It"
    (*Music by* Harry Von Tilzer. *Lyrics by* E. Ray Goetz.)
"I Want You, I Need You" (from I'M NO ANGEL, film)
    (*Music by* Harvey Brooks. *Lyrics by* Ben Ellison.)
"I Wonder Where My Easy Rider's Gone" (from SHE DONE HIM WRONG, film)
    (*Music and Lyrics by* Shelton Brooks.)
"Oh My, How We Posé" (from McALLISTER'S LEGACY)
    (*Music by* David Braham. *Lyrics by* Edward Harrigan.)
"Perfect Love"
    (*Music and Lyrics by* Garret Frerichs and Oezlem Cetin.)

---

[56]Previously produced Off-Broadway 13 January-13 February 2000 at the New York Theatre Workshop for 33? performances.
[57]Not in performance order. "Dirty Blonde" is the only new song written especially for this production.

2000–2001 SEASON

Carolee Carmello, Lonny Price, and Randy Graff in A CLASS ACT
Joan Marcus/Photofest

2000-2001 SEASON

2000.13   PENN & TELLER

A New Edition of the Comedy Revue in Two Acts. Written by Penn Gillette and Teller. Directed by Ken Krashner Lewis and Nathan Santucci. Opened 6 June 2000 at the Beacon Theatre and closed 11 June 2000 after 8 performances.

CAST: PENN GILLETTE; TELLER.

2000.14   BORSCHT BELT BUFFET ON BROADWAY

A Musical Revue in One Act. Staged by Dan Siretta. Musical director, Zalmen Mlotek. Associate producers, Arnold Graham, Howard Rapp. Produced by NYK Productions, Inc. Opened 24 October 2000 at Town Hall and closed 6 November 2000 after 16 performances.

CAST: BRUCE ADLER, DAVID "Dudu" FISHER, MAL Z. LAWRENCE.

MUSICAL NUMBERS, SPECIALTIES[1]

"Borscht Belt Buffet"
    B. Adler, D. Fisher, M. Z. Lawrence
Hebrew language sketch
    B. Adler, D. Fisher, M. Z. Lawrence
Bruce Adler Specialty
["It Don't Mean a Thing If It Ain't Got That Swing" (Jewish Be-bop version)
"Style"
"Makin' Whoopee" (from WHOOPEE)(Eddie Cantor impression)
"If I Were the King of the Forest" (Bert Lahr impression)
"You Gotta Start Each Day with a Song" (Jimmy Durante impression)
"Bessie Mae" (Menasha Skulnick impression)
"Singin' in the Rain" (Gene Kelly impression)
"Rockabye Your Baby with a Dixie Melody" (Al Jolson impression)
"The Candy Man" (Sammy Davis impression)
"The Birth of the Blues" (Sammy Davis impression)
"The Palace of the Czar" (from THOSE WERE THE DAYS) (Danny Kaye impression)
Yiddish language sketch
"Oh They Call Me Kullman with a capital K"
Cowboy Medley
"Huz-zah-zah"]
"Romania"
    B. Adler, D. Fisher, M. Z. Lawrence
"Dudu" Fisher Specialty
["Shalom" (from MILK AND HONEY, in Hebrew)
"Memory" (from CATS)
"Kol Nidre" (interspersed with musical quotes from LES MISERABLES)
(concluding with "Who Am I?" and "Bring Him Home")
"All I Ask of You" (from THE PHANTOM OF THE OPERA)
"The Phantom of the Opera" (from THE PHANTOM OF THE OPERA)
Broadway Medley (performed in Hebrew)
"Maria" (from WEST SIDE STORY)
"The Music of the Night" (from THE PHANTOM OF THE OPERA)
"Sunrise, Sunset" (from FIDDLER ON THE ROOF)
"Send in the Clowns" (from A LITTLE NIGHT MUSIC)
"Don't Cry for Me, Argentina" (from EVITA)
"Oklahoma" (from OKLAHOMA!)

"All That Jazz" (from CHICAGO)
"Edelweiss" (from THE SOUND OF MUSIC)
"Climb Every Mountain" (from THE SOUND OF MUSIC)
"The Impossible Dream" (from MAN OF LaMANCHA)]
The Audition
    B. Adler, D. Fisher, M Z. Lawrence
Mal. Z. Lawrence Specialty
Florida, Lancaster (Penn.), Atlantic City, Catskills sketches
Vocal Medley (including "Killing Me Softly" and "Knock Three Times")
Bruce Springsteen
"Borscht Belt on Broadway" (Finale)
    B. Adler, D. Fisher, M. Z. Lawrence

2000.15   THE FULL MONTY

A Musical in Two Acts. Book by Terrence McNally (based on the film of the same name with screenplay by Simon Beaufoy). Music and Lyrics by David Yazbek. Directed by Jack O'Brien. Choreographed by Jerry Mitchell. Scenic design by John Arnone. Costume design by Robert Morgan. Lighting design by Howell Binkley. Sound design by Tom Clark. Orchestrations by Harold Wheeler. Dance arrangements by Zane Mark. Music direction/Vocal and Incidental Music Arrangements by Ted Sperling. Produced by Fox Searchlight Pictures, Lindsey Law, Thomas Hall. Opened 26 October 2000 at the Eugene O'Neill Theatre, still running at time of this writing.

CAST (in order of appearance): *Georgie Bukatinsky*: ANNIE GOLDEN. *Buddy "Keno" Walsh*: Denis Jones. *Reg Willoughby*: TODD WEEKS. *Jerry Lukowski*: PATRICK WILSON. *Dave Bukatinsky*: JOHN ELLISON CONLEE. *Malcolm MacGregor*: JASON DANIELY. *Ethan Girard*: ROMAIN FRUGÉ. *Nathan Lukowski*: Nicholas Cutro or Thomas Michael Fiss. *Susan Hershey*: Laura Marie Duncan. *Joanie Lish*: Jannie Jones. *Estelle Genovese*: Liz McConahay. *Pam Lukowski*: LISA DATZ. *Teddy Slaughter*: Angelo Fraboni. *Molly MacGregor*: Patti Perkins. *Harold Nichols*: MARCUS NEVILLE. *Vicki Nichols*: EMILY SKINNER. *Jeanette Burmeister*: KATHLEEN FREEMAN. *Noah "Horse" T. Simmons*: ANDRÉ DeSHIELDS. *Moving Man*: C. E. Smith. *Police Sergeant*: C. E. Smith. *Social Worker*: Jannie Jones. *Minister*: Jay Douglas. *Tony Giordano*: Jimmy Smagula. *Swings*: Sue-Anne Morrow, Jason Opsahl, Matthew Stocke, Ronald Wyche.

The action is set in Buffalo, New York, at the present time.

ACT 1
"Scrap"
    P. Wilson, J. E. Conlee, M. Neville, J. Daniely, R. Frugé, T. Weeks, Men
"It's a Woman's World"
    A. Golden, L. M. Duncan, J. Jones, L. McConahay
"Man"
    P. Wilson, J. E. Conlee
"Big Ass Rock"
    P. Wilson, J. E. Conlee, J. Daniely
"Life with Harold"
    M. Neville, E. Skinner
"Big Black Man"
    A. DeShields, the Guys
"You Rule My World"
    J. E. Conlee, M. Neville
"Michael Jordan's Ball"
    The Guys

ACT 2
"Jeanette's Showbiz Number" (Things Could Be Better)
    K. Freeman, the Guys
"Breeze Off the River"
    P. Wilson
"The Goods"
    P. Wilson, J. E. Conlee, M. Neville, J. Daniely, R. Frugé, A. DeShields, the Women
"You Walk with Me"
    J. Daniely, R. Frugé
"You Rule My World" (reprise)
    A. Golden, E. Skinner
"Let It Go"
    P. Wilson, R. Frugé, J. Daniely, J. E. Conlee, A. DeShields, M. Neville, the Company

---

[1]Musical numbers and specialties not listed in programs.

2000.16 MATTERS OF THE HEART

A One-Woman Concert in Two Acts. Conceived and directed by Scott Wittman. Additional dialogue by John Weidman. Musical direction and arrangements by Dick Gallagher. Lighting by John Hastings. Sound by Mark Fiore. Gowns designed by Oscar de la Renta. Produced by Lincoln Center Theatre (André Bishop, Artistic Director, and Bernard Gersten, Executive Producer). Opened 13 November 2000 at the Vivian Beaumont Theatre and closed 17 December 2000 after 11 performances[2].

CAST: PATTI LuPONE.

ACT 1[3]

"Love Makes the World Go Round" (Theme from CARNIVAL)
(*Music and Lyrics by* Bob Merrill.)
"I'm in Love with a Wonderful Guy" (from SOUTH PACIFIC)
(*Music by* Richard Rodgers. *Lyrics by* Oscar Hammerstein II.)
"God Only Knows"
(*Music and Lyrics by* Brian Wilson.)
"Easy to Be Hard" (from HAIR)
(*Music by* Galt MacDermott. *Lyrics by* James Rado and Gerome Ragni.)
"The Last Time I Saw Richard"
(*Music and Lyrics by* Joni Mitchell.)
"Where Love Resides"
(*Music and Lyrics by* Jimmy Webb.)
"Shattered Illusions"
(*Music and Lyrics by* Adele Anderson and Dillie Keane.)
"Unexpressed"
(*Music and Lyrics by* John Bucchino.)
"Not a Day Goes By" (from MERRILY WE ROLL ALONG)
(*Music and Lyrics by* Stephen Sondheim.)
"Playbill"
(*Music and Lyrics by* John Bucchino.)
"Alone Again (Naturally)"
(*Music and Lyrics by* Gilbert O'Sullivan.)
"Better Off Dead"
(*Music and Lyrics by* Randy Newman.)
"Air That I Breath"
(*Music and Lyrics by* Albert Hammond and Michael Hazelwood.)
"Sand and Water"
(*Music and Lyrics by* Beth Nielson Chapman.)
"Being Alive" (from COMPANY)
(*Music and Lyrics by* Stephen Sondheim.)

ACT 2

"When the World Was Young"
(*Music by* Angele Vannier and Phillipe Bosch. *Lyrics by* Johnny Mercer.)/
"I Never Do Anything Twice" (from THE SEVEN PERCENT SOLUTION, film)
(*Music and Lyrics by* Stephen Sondheim.)
"Back to Before"
(*Music by* Stephen Flaherty. *Lyrics by* Lynn Ahrens.)
"Real Emotional Girl"
(*Music and Lyrics by* Randy Newman.)
"My Father"
(*Music and Lyrics by* Judy Collins.)
"Look Mummy, No Hands"
(*Music and Lyrics by* Dillie Keane.)
"Time After Time"
(*Music and Lyrics by* Cyndi Lauper and Rob Hyman.)
"Another Auld Lang Syne"
(*Music and Lyrics by* Dan Fogelberg.)
"Hello, Young Lovers" (from THE KING AND I)
(*Music by* Richard Rodgers. *Lyrics by* Oscar Hammerstein II.)
"My Best to You"
(*Music and Lyrics by* Gene Willadsen and Isham Jones.)

2000.17 THE ROCKY HORROR SHOW

A Revival of the Rock Musical in Two Acts[4]. Book, music and lyrics by Richard O'Brien. Directed by Christopher Ashley. Choreographed by Jerry Mitchell. Scenic design by David Rockwell. Costume design by David C. Woolard. Lighting design by Paul Gallo. Sound design by Richard Fitzgerald/Domonic Sack. Video design by Batwin + Robin Productions. Musical direction and vocal arrangements by Henry Aronson. New orchestrations by Doug Katsaros. Original orchestrations by Richard Hartley. Produced by Jordan Roth, by arrangement with Christopher Malcolm, Howard Panter and Richard O'Brien for the Rocky Horror Company, Ltd. Opened 15 November 2000 at the Circle-in-the-Square Theatre; closed 23 September 2001; re-opened 30 October 2001 and closed 6 January 2002 after 436 performances.

CAST (in order of appearance): *Usherette*: DAPHNE RUBIN-VEGA. *Usherette*: JOAN JETT. *Janet Weiss*: ALICE RIPLEY. *Brad Majors*: JARROD EMICK. *Narrator*: DICK CAVETT. *Riff Raff*: RAÚL ESPARZA. *Magenta*: DAPHNE RUBIN-VEGA. *Columbia*: JOAN JETT. *Frank 'N' Furter*: TOM HEWITT. *Rocky*: SEBASTIAN LaCAUSE. *Eddie*: LEA DeLARIA. *Dr. Scott*: LEA DeLARIA. *Phantoms*: Kevin Cahoon, Deidre Goodwin, Aiko Nakasone, Mark Price, Jonathan Sharp, James Stovall. *Swings*: John Jeffrey Sharp, Kristen Lee Kelly.

Time: Then and Now. *Place*: Here and There.

ACT 1

"Science Fiction Double Feature"
D. Ruben-Vega, J. Jett [Usherettes], Phantoms
"Damn It, Janet"
J. Emick, A. Ripley, Phantoms
"Over at the Frankenstein Place"
J. Emick, A. Ripley, R. Esparza, Phantoms
"The Time Warp"
R. Esparza, D. Ruben-Vega, J. Jett, D. Cavett, Company
"Sweet Transvestite"
T. Hewitt, J. Emick, R. Esparza, D. Ruben-Vega, J. Jett, Phantoms
"The Sword of Damocles"
S. LaCause, D. Cavett, Company
"I Can Make You a Man" (Charles Atlas Song)
T. Hewitt, Company
"Hot Patootie" (What Ever Happened to Saturday Night)
L. DeLaria [Eddie], Company
"I Can Make You a Man" (reprise)
T. Hewitt, Company

ACT 2

"Touch-A-Touch-A-Touch Me"
A. Ripley, D. Ruben-Vega, J. Jett, Phantoms
"Once in a While"
J. Emick, Phantoms
"Eddie's Teddy"
L. DeLaria [Dr. Scott], D. Cavett, J. Jett, T. Hewitt, Company
"Planet Shmanet – Wise Up Janet Weiss"
T. Hewitt, Company
"Floorshow/Rose Tint My World" (It Was Great When It All Began)
J. Jett, S. LaCause, J. Emick, A. Ripley, T. Hewitt, R. Esparza, Company
"I'm Going Home"
T. Hewitt, Company
"Super Heroes"
J. Emick, A. Ripley, D. Cavett, Phantoms
"Science Fiction Double Feature" [reprise]
D. Ruben-Vega, J. Jett, Phantoms

2000.18 SEUSSICAL

A Musical in Two Acts. Conceived by Eric Idle, Lynn Ahrens and Stephen Flaherty, from the works of Dr. Seuss [Theodore Geisel]. Book by Lynn Ahrens and Stephen Flaherty. Music by Stephen Flaherty. Lyrics by Lynn Ahrens. Directed by Frank Galati, (Rob Marshall). Choreographed by Kathleen Marshall. Scenery by Eugene Lee, (Tony Walton). Costumes by William Ivey Long. Lighting by Natasha Katz. Sound by Jonathan Deans.

---

[2]Played an irregular schedule of Sunday evening and Monday performances concurrent with the run of CONTACT.
[3]Not in performance order.

[4]Previously produced in New York 10 March 1975 at the Belasco Theatre for 45 performances. The 1975 production was presented in One Act, 11 Scenes, a Prologue and Epilogue.

Orchestrations by Douglas Besterman. Musical director, David Holcenberg. Dance arranger, David Chase. Vocal arranger, Stephen Flaherty. Executive Producers, Gary Gunas and Alecia Parker. Produced by SFX Theatrical Group, Barry and Fran Weissler and Universal Studios, in association with Hal Luftig, Mort Swinsky and Michael Watt. Opened 30 November 2000 at the Richard Rodgers Theatre and closed 20 May 2001 after 197 performances.

CAST: *The Cat in the Hat*: DAVID SHINER. *Horton the Elephant*: KEVIN CHAMBERLIN. *Gertrude McFuzz*: JANINE LaMANNA. *Mayzie LaBird*: MICHELE PAWK. *JoJo*: ANTHONY BLAIR-HALL, Andrew Keenan-Bolger (alt.). *Sour Kangaroo*: Sharon Wilkins. *The Mayor of Whoville*: Stuart Zagnit. *Mrs. Mayor*: Alice Playten. *Cat's Helpers*: Joyce Chittick, Jennifer Cody, Justin Greer, Mary Ann Lamb, Darren Lee, Jerome Vivona. *General Genghis Khan Schmitz*: Erick Devine. *Bird Girls*: Natascia A. Diaz, Sara Gettelfinger, Catrice Joseph. *Wickersham Brothers*: David Engel, Tom Plotkin, Eric Jordan Young. *The Grinch*: William Ryall. *JoJo's Teacher*: Monique L. Midgette. *JoJo's Principal*: Casey Nicholaw. *Vlad Vladikoff*: Darren Lee. *Judge Yertle the Turtle*: Devin Richards. *Marshal of the Court*: Ann Harada.

Citizens of the Jungle of Nool, Whos, Mayor's Aides, Fish, Cadets, Hunters, Circus McGurkus Animals and Performers: Joyce Chittick, Jennifer Cody, Erich Devine, Natascia Diaz, David Engel, Sara Gettelfinger, Justin Greer, Ann Harada, Catrice Joseph, Eddie Korbich, Mary Ann Lamb, Darren Lee, Monique L. Midgette, Casey Nicholaw, Tom Plotkin, Devin Richards, William Ryall, Jerome Vivona, Sharon Wilkins, Eric Jordan Young. *Swings*: Shaun Amyot, Jenny Hill, Michelle Kittrell, David Lowenstein.

ACT 1

"Oh, the Thinks You Can Think!"
D. Shiner, the Company

"Our Story Begins"
D. Shiner

"Horton Hears a Who"
K. Chamberlin, Bird Girls, Citizens of the Jungle of Nool

"Biggest Blame Fool"
S. Wilkins, K. Chamberlin, D. Engel, T. Plotkin, E. J. Young, Bird Girls, J. LaManna, M. Pawk, Citizens of the Jungle of Nool, D. Shiner

"Here on Who"
S. Zagnit, A. Playten, W. Ryall, Whos, K. Chamberlin

"A Day for the Cat in the Hat"
D. Shiner, A. B. Hall, Cat's Helpers

"It's Possible" (In McElligott's Pool)
A. B. Hall, D. Shiner, the Fish

"How to Raise a Child"
S. Zagnit, A. Playten

"The Military"
E. Devine, S. Zagnit, A. Playten, A. B. Hall, Cadets

"Alone in the Universe"
A. B. Hall, K. Chamberlin

"The One Feather Tail of Miss Gertrude McFuzz"
J. LaManna

"Amayzing Mayzie"
M. Pawk, J. LaManna, Bird Girls

"Amayzing Gertrude"
J. LaManna, D. Shiner, Bird Girls

"Monkey Around"
D. Engel, T. Plotkin

"Chasing the Whos"
K. Chamberlin, S. Wilkins, Bad Girls, D. Engel, T. Plotkin, D. Shiner, D. Lee, the Whos

"How Lucky You Are"
D. Shiner

"Notice Me, Horton"
J. LaManna, K. Chamberlin

"How Lucky You Are" (reprise)
M. Pawk, K. Chamberlin, D. Shiner

Act 1 Finale
Full Company

ACT 2

"How Lucky You Are" (reprise)
D. Shiner

"Our Story Resumes"
D. Shiner, K. Chamberlin, S. Zagnit, A. Playten, J. LaManna, Bird Girls

"Egg, Nest and Tree"
S. Wilkins, Bird Girls, D. Engel, T. Plotkin, D. Shiner, Cat's Helpers, Hunters

"The Circus McGurkus"
D. Shiner, K. Chamberlin, Circus McGurkus Animals and Performers

"The Circus on Tour"
K. Chamberlin

"Mayzie in Palm Beach"
M. Pawk, D. Shiner, K. Chamberlin

"Solla Sollew"
K. Chamberlin, Circus McGurkus Animals and Performers, S. Zagnit, A. Playten, A. B. Hall

"The Whos' Christmas Pageant"
W. Ryall, the Whos

"A Message from the Front"
E. Devine, S. Zagnit, A. Playten, Cadets

"Alone in the Universe" (reprise)
A. B. Hall, K. Chamberlin

"Havin' a Hunch"
D. Shiner, A. B. Hall, Cat's Helpers

"All for You"
J. LaManna, Bird Girls

"The People Versus Horton the Elephant"
K. Chamberlin, S. Wilkins, D. Engel, T. Plotkin, A. Harada, D. Richards, Bird Girls, J. LaManna, S. Zagnit, A. Playten, A. B. Hall, Whos, D. Shiner

Finale/"Oh, the Thinks You Can Think!" (reprise)
Full Company

2000.19   # A CHRISTMAS CAROL

A Revival of the Musical in One Act, 13 Scenes[5]. Book by Mike Ockrent and Lynn Ahrens. Based on the novel of the same name by Charles Dickens. Music by Alan Menken. Lyrics by Lynn Ahrens. Direction by Mike Ockrent. Choreographed by Susan Stroman. Setting design by Tony Walton. Costume design by William Ivey Long. Lighting design by Jules Fisher and Peggy Eisenhauer. Sound design by Tony Meola. Projections by Wendall K. Harrington. Flying by Foy. Associate director, Ray Roderick. Associate choreographer, Chris Peterson. Musical direction by Paul Gemignani. Orchestrations by Michael Starobin and Douglas Besterman. Dance arrangements and incidental music by Glen Kelly. Executive producer, Howard Kolins. Producer, Marshall Jones. Presented by American Express. Opened 30 November 2000 at the (Paramount) Theatre, Madison Square Garden and closed 31 December 2000 after 63 performances.

CAST (in order of appearance): *Beadle*: Del-Bourree Bach. *Mr. Smythe*: ERIC PINNICK. *Grace Smythe*: Catherine Marie Downey, Amelia Harris. *Scrooge*: FRANK LANGELLA. *Bob Cratchit*: NICK CORLEY. *Charity Men*: Roland Rusinek, Wayne Schroder, Erik Stein. *Old Joe*: Kenneth McMullen. *Street Urchins*: Johnny Cenicola, Patrick Dunn, Nicholas Jonas, Lindsey Pickering, Justin Riordan, Lily Havala Wen. *Mrs. Cratchit*: Whitney Webster. *Tiny Tim*: Patrick Stogner, Jimmy Walsh. *Poulterer*: Roland Rusinek. *Sandwichboard Man*: D'AMBROSE BOYD. *Jonathon*: Gerard Canonico, Scott Owen Cumberbatch. *Lamplighter*: KEN JENNINGS. *Blind Hag*: Joan Barber. *Fred*: JAMES JUDY. *Mrs. Mopps*: Marilyn Pasekoff. *Ghost of Jacob Marley*: PAUL KANDEL. *Ghost of Christmas Past*: KEN JENNINGS. *Lights of Christmas Past*: Leo Alvarez, James Hadley, Deon Ridley, David Rosales. *Judge*: Roland Rusinek. *Scrooge at 8*: Nicholas Jonas, Justin Riordan. *Scrooge's Mother*: Joan Barber. *Scrooge's Father*: Wayne Schroder. *Mr. Hawkins*: Kenneth McMullen. *Scrooge at 12*: Johnny Cenicola, Patrick Dunn. *Fan*: Lindsey Pickering, Lily Havala Wen. *Fezziwig*: Daniel Marcus. *Scrooge at 18*: Joe Cassidy. *Young Marley*: Ken Barnett. *Mrs. Fezziwig*: Kelly Ellenwood. *Emily*: Kate Dawson. *Ghost of Christmas Present*: D'AMBROSE

---

[5]Originally produced in New York 1 December 1994 at the Paramount Theatre, Madison Square Garden for 71 performances. For Synopsis of Scenes and Musical Numbers, see original 1994 production. For this year's and the 1995, 1996, 1997, 1998, and 1999 revivals the following changes were made:

Scene 1 and "The Years Are Passing By" were dropped.
Added to Scene 2 (former Scene 3) before "Street Song":
"You Mean More to Me"
   T. Gross, A. B. Hall or C. Valiando
"The Years Are Passing By" (reprise) in former Scene 13 (new Scene 12) was replaced by:
"London Town Carol"
   A. Barruch or K. Kanagawa
Note: The production played an irregular schedule of multiple daily performances.

BOYD. *The Cratchit Children*: Johnny Cenicola, Patrick Dunn, Lindsey Pickering, Lily Havala Wen. *Sally, Fred's wife*: La Tanya Hall. *Ignorance*: Nicholas Jones, Justin Riordan. *Want*: Amelia Harris, Catherine Marie Downey. *Undertakers*: Ken Barnett, Wayne Schroder. *Ghost of Christmas Yet-To-Be*: CHRISTINE DUNHAM.

Business Men, Gifts, Ghosts and the People of London: Leo Alvarez, Del-Bourree Bach, Joan Barber, Ken Barnett, Hayes Bergman, Joe Cassidy, Candy Cook, James Hadley, La Tanya Hall, Amy Heggins, James Judy, Donna Kapral, Carrie Kenneally, Natalie King, Daniel Marcus, Kenneth McMullen, Patrick Mullaney, Shaun R. Parry, Marilyn Pasekoff, Gail Pennington, Erick Pinnick, Deon Ridley, David Rosales, Parisa Ross, Roland Rusinek, Wayne Schroder, Debra Denys Smith, Erik Stein, Yasuko Tamaki, Whitney Webster, Mindy Franzese Wild. *Swings*: Jane Brockman, Rob Donohoe, Donna Dunmire, Jeffrey Hankinson, Ann Kittredge, Cynthia Thole, Matthew J. Vargo, Craig Waletzko. *Angels*: Terrill Middle School Broadway Chorus, YPC Jubilee Chorus, La Petite Musicale, South Side Middle School Chorale. *Red Children's Cast*: Scott Owen Cumberbatch, Catherine Marie Downey, Patrick Dunn, Lindsey Pickering, Justin Riordan. *Green Children's Cast*: Gerard Canonico, Johnny Cenicola, Amelia Harris, Nicholas Jonas, Lily Havala Wen. *Children Swings*: Harley Adams, Allison Fischer, Kenny Gureck.

2000.20 JANE EYRE

A Musical in Two Acts. Book and additional lyrics by John Caird. Based on the novel of the same name by Charlotte Brontë. Music and lyrics by Paul Gordon. Directed by John Caird and Scott Schwartz. Settings by John Napier. Costumes by Andreane Neofitou. Lighting by Jules Fisher and Peggy Eisenhauer. Sound design by Mark Menard and Tom Clark. Dance and movement by Jayne Patterson. Projections design by John Napier, Lisa Podgur Cuscuna, Jules Fisher and Peggy Eisenhauer. Musical director, vocal and incidental music arrangements by Steve Tyler. Orchestrations by Larry Hochman. Produced by Annette Niemtzow, Janet Robinson, Pamela Koslow and Margaret McFeeley Golden, in association with Jennifer Manocherian and Carolyn Kim McCarthy. Opened 10 December 2000 at the Brooks Atkinson Theatre and closed 10 June 2001 after 210 performances.

CAST (in order of appearance): *Jane Eyre*: MARLA SCHAFFEL. *Young Jane*: Lisa Musser. *Young John Reed*: Lee Zarrett. *Mrs. Reed*: Gina Ferrall. *Mr. Brocklehurst*: Don Richard. *Miss Scatcherd*: Marguerite MacIntyre. *Marigold*: MARY STOUT. *Helen Burns*: Jayne Patterson. *Schoolgirls*: Nell Balaban, Andrea Bowen, Elizabeth DeGrazia, Bonnie Gleicher, Rita Glynn, Gina Lamparella. *Mrs. Fairfax*: MARY STOUT. *Robert*: Bruce Dow. *Adele*: Andrea Bowen. *Grace Poole*: Nell Balaban. *Edward Fairfax Rochester*: JAMES BARBOUR. *Bertha*: Marguerite MacIntyre. *Blanche Ingram*: ELIZABETH DeGRAZIA. *Lady Ingram*: Gina Ferrall. *Mary Ingram*: Jayne Patterson. *Young Lord Ingram*: Lee Zarrett. *Mr. Eshton*: Stephen R. Buntrock. *Amy Eshton*: Nell Balaban. *Louisa Eshton*: Gina Lamparella. *Colonel Dent*: Don Richard. *Mrs. Dent*: Marguerite MacIntyre. *Richard Mason*: Bill Nolte. *The Gypsy*: Marje Bubrosa [JAMES BARBOUR]. *Vicar*: Don Richard. *St. John Rivers*: STEPHEN R. BUNTROCK.

Swings: Sandy Binion, Bradley Dean, Erica Schroeder.

The action is set in England in the 1840s at Gateshead Hall, Lowood School, Thornfield Hall and the surrounding Yorkshire Moors.

ACT 1

"The Orphan"
  M. Schaffel
"Children of God"
  School Girls, D. Richard, G. Ferrall, M. MacIntyre, Ensemble
"Forgiveness"
  J. Patterson, L. Musser, M. Schaffel
"The Graveyard"
  M. Schaffel, L. Musser, Ensemble
"Sweet Liberty"
  M. Schaffel, Ensemble
"Perfectly Nice"
  M. Stout, A. Bowen, M. Schaffel
"As Good as You"
  J. Barbour
"Secret Soul"
  M. Schaffel, J. Barbour
"The Finer Things"
  E. DeGrazia
"Oh How You Look in the Light"
  J. Barbour, E. DeGrazia, Ensemble
"The Pledge"
  M. Schaffel, J. Barbour
"Sirens"
  J. Barbour, M. Schaffel, M. MacIntyre

ACT 2

"Things Beyond This Earth"
  Ensemble
"Painting Her Portrait"
  M. Schaffel
"In the Light of the Virgin Morning"
  M. Schaffel, E. DeGrazia
"The Gypsy"
  M. Bubrosa
"The Proposal"
  M. Schaffel, J. Barbour
"Slip of a Girl"
  M. Stout, M. Schaffel, B. Dow, A. Bowen
"The Wedding"
  Ensemble
"Wild Boy"
  J. Barbour, M. Schaffel, M. MacIntyre, Ensemble
"Sirens" (reprise)
  M. Schaffel, J. Barbour
"Farewell Good Angel"
  J. Barbour
"My Maker"
  M. Schaffel, Ensemble
"Forgiveness" (reprise)
  G. Ferrall, M. Schaffel, Ensemble
"The Voice Across the Moors"
  S. R. Buntrock, M. Schaffel, J. Barbour
"Poor Sister"
  B. Nolte, M. Schaffel
"Brave Enough for Love"
  M. Schaffel, J. Barbour, Ensemble

2001.01 A CLASS ACT

A Musical in Two Acts, 17 Scenes[6]. Music and lyrics by Edward Kleban. Book by Linda Kline and Lonny Price. Directed by Lonny Price. Choreographed by Marguerite Derricks. Scenic design by James Noone. Costume design by Carrie Robbins. Lighting design by Kevin Adams. Sound design by Acme Sound Partners. Musical direction, additional arrangements by David Loud. Incidental music by Todd Ellison. Orchestrations by Larry Hochman. Production consultant, Lori Steinberg. Executive producer, East Egg Entertainment. Executive producer, East Egg Entertainment. Associate producers, Robyn Goodman, Tokyo Broadcasting System/Kumiko Yoshii. Marty Bell, Chase Mishkin and Arielle Tepper present the Manhattan Theatre Club Production. Opened 11 March 2001 at the Ambassador Theatre and closed 10 June 2001 after 105 performances.

CAST[7] (in order of appearance): *Lucy et al*: DONNA BULLOCK. *Bobby, (Michael Bennett) et al*: DAVID HIBBARD. *Ed (Kleban) et al*: SARA RAMIREZ. *Lehman (Engel) et al*: PATRICK QUINN. *Charley, (Marvin Hamlisch) et al*: JEFF BLUMENKRANTZ. *Mona et al.*: NANCY KATHRYN ANDERSON. *Sophie*: RANDY GRAFF.

Act 1, Scene 1: The Shubert Theatre, 1988. *Scene 2*: Hillside Hospital, 1958. *Scene 3*: The Shubert Theatre, 1988. *Scene 4*: The BMI Workshop, 1966. *Scene 5*: Ed's Apartment, 1966. *Scene 6*: Recording Studio/Columbia Records, 1966-1971. *Scene 7*: Outside the Royal Alexandra Theatre, Toronto, 1972.

Act 2, Scene 1: The Shubert Theatre, 1988; Manhattan, 1973. *Scene 2*: Sophie's Laboratory, 1972. *Scene 3*: Central Park, 1973. *Scene 4*: Michael Bennett's Studio, 1973. *Scene 5*: The Public Theatre, 1974-1975. *Scene 6*: Manhattan, 1975-1985. *Scene 7*: Sophie's Laboratory, 1985. *Scene 8*: The BMI Musical Theatre Workshop, 1986. *Scene 9*: St. Vincent's Hospital, 1987. *Scene 10*: The Shubert Theatre, 1988.

---

[6]First produced in New York Off-Broadway 9 November-10 December 2000 at Manhattan Theater Club's City Center Stage II for 38 performances.
[7]At the Manhattan Theatre Club, the following played roles but did not transfer to Broadway: *Felicia*: JULIA MURNEY. *Lehman*: JONATHAN FREEMAN. *Lucy*: CAROLEE CARMELLO. *Charley*: RAY WILLS. Choreography by Scott Wise. Dropped before Broadway were:
  "Making Up Ways" (Act 1, Scene 5)
    L. Price
  "When the Dawn Breaks" (Act 2, Scene 8)
    L. Price

ACT 1
Scene 1
  "Light on My Feet"
    L. Price, Company
    (*Additional lyrics by* Brian Stein.)
Scene 2
  "The Fountain in the Garden"
    Company
  "One More Beautiful Song"
    L. Price, R. Graff
Scene 4
  "Fridays at Four"
    Company
  "Bobby's Song"
    D. Hibbard
  "Charm Song"
    P. Quinn, Company
  "Paris Through the Window"
    L. Price, D. Hibbard, J. Blumenkrantz
    (*Additional lyrics by* Glenn Slater.)
Scene 5
  "Mona"
    N. K. Anderson
Scene 6
  "Under Separate Cover"
    D. Bullock, R. Graff, L. Price
  "Don't Do It Again"
    S. Ramirez, L. Price
  "Gaugin's Shoes"
    L. Price, Company
  "Don't Do It Again" (reprise)
    P. Quinn
Scene 7
  "Follow Your Star"
    R. Graff, L. Price
ACT 2
Scene 1
  "Better"[8]
    L. Price, Company
Scene 2
  "Scintillating Sophie"
    L. Price
  "Next Best Thing to Love"
    R. Graff
Scene 4
  "Broadway Boogie Woogie"
    D. Bullock
Scene 5
  A CHORUS LINE excerpts ("At the Ballet," "One," "What I Did for
  Love")
    Company
    (*Music by* Marvin Hamlisch.)
Scene 6
  "Better" (reprise)
    L. Price, Company
  "I Choose You"
    L. Price, D. Bullock
  "The Nightmare"
    L. Price
Scene 7
  "Say Something Funny"
    Company
Scene 8
  "I Won't Be There"
    L. Price

[8]Previously interpolated into the Off-Broadway revue THE MADWOMAN
OF CENTRAL PARK WEST.

Scene 9
  "Self-Portrait"
    L. Price
Scene 10
  "Self-Portrait" (reprise)
    Company

2001.02   FOLLIES

A Revival of the Musical in Two Acts[9]. Book by James Goldman. Music and
lyrics by Stephen Sondheim. Directed by Matthew Warchus. Choreography
by Kathleen Marshall. Set design by Mark Thompson. Costume design by
Theoni V. Aldredge. Lighting design by Hugh Vanstone. Sound design by
Jonathan Deans. Original dance music arranged by John Berkman.
Additional dance music arranged by David Chase. Associate choreographer,
Joey Pizzi. Associate director, Thomas Caruso. Orchestrations by Jonathan
Tunick. Musical direction by Eric Stern. Executive producer, Frank P.
Scardino. Produced by the Roundabout Theatre (Todd Haimes, Artistic
Director; Ellen Richard, Managing Director; Julia C. Levy, Executive
Director). Opened 5 April 2001 at the Belasco Theatre and closed 14 July
2001 after 116 performances.

CAST (in order of appearance): *Dimitri Weismann:* LOUIS ZORICH. *Showgirls:*
Jessica Leigh Brown, Colleen Dunn, Amy Heggins, Wendy Waring. *Sally Durant
Plummer:* JUDITH IVEY. *Sandra Crane:* Nancy Ringham. *Dee Dee West:* Dorothy
Stanley. *Stella Deems:* CAROL WOODS. *Sam Deems:* Peter Cormican. *Solange
LaFitte:* JANE WHITE. *Roscoe:* Larry Raiken. *Heidi Schiller:* JOAN ROBERTS. *Emily
Whitman:* MARGE CHAMPION. *Theodore Whitman:* DONALD SADDLER.
Carlotta Campion: POLLY BERGEN. *Hattie Walker:* BETTY GARRETT. *Phyllis
Rogers Stone:* BLYTHE DANNER. *Benjamin Stone:* GREGORY HARRISON. *Buddy
Plummer:* TREAT WILLIAMS. *Young Phyllis:* Erin Dilly. *Young Sally:* Lauren Ward.
Young Dee Dee: Roxane Barlow. *Young Emily:* Carole Bentley. *Young Carlotta:* Sally
Mae. Dunn. *Young Sandra:* Dottie Earle. *Young Solange:* Jacqueline Hendy. *Young
Heidi:* Brooke Sunny Moriber. *Young Hattie"* Kelli O'Hara. *Young Stella:* Allyson
Tucker. *Young Ben:* Richard Roland. *Young Buddy:* Joey Sorge. *Young Theodore:* Rod
McCune. *Kevin:* Stephen Campanella. "Margie": Roxane Barlow. "Sally": Jessica
Leigh Brown.
  Ladies and Gentlemen of the Ensemble: Roxane Barlow, Carole Bentley, Jessica
Leigh Brown, Stephen Campanella, Colleen Dunn, Sally Mae Dunn, Dottie Earle,
Aldrin Gonzalez, Amy Heggins, Jacqueline Hendy, Rod McCune, Kelli O'Hara, T.
Oliver Reid, Alex Sanchez, Allyson Tucker, Matt Wall, Wendy Waring. *Swings:* Nadine
Isenegger, Parisa Ross, Jeffrey Hankinson.

2001.03   BELLS ARE RINGING

A Revival of the Musical Comedy in Two Acts[10]. Book and lyrics by Betty
Comden and Adolph Green. Music by Jule Styne. Directed by Tina
Landau. Choreography by Jeff Calhoun. Settings by Riccardo Hernandez.
Costumes designed by David C. Woolard. Lighting by Donald Holder.
Sound design, Acme Sound Partners. Musical Direction and Vocal
Arrangements, David Evans. Orchestrations by Don Sebesky. Dance Music
Arrangements, Mark Hummel. Associate producers, Alan S. Kopit, Richard
Berger. Produced by Mitchell Maxwell, Mark Balsam, Victoria Maxwell,
Robert Barandes, Richard Bernstein, Mark Goldberg, James L. Simon, in
association with Fred H. Krones and Momentum Productions, Inc. Opened
12 April 2001 at the Plymouth Theatre closed 10 June 2001 after 69
performances.

CAST (in order of appearance): *TV Announcer:* Shane Kirkpatrick. *Telephone Girls:*
Caitlin Carter, Joan Hess, Emily Hsu, Alice Rietveld. *Sue:* BETH FOWLER. *Gwynne:*
Angela Robinson. *Ella Peterson:* FAITH PRINCE. *Carl:* Julio Agustin. *Inspector
Barnes:* ROBERT ARI. *Francis:* JEFFREY BEAN. *Sandor:* DAVID GARRISON. *Jeff
Moss:* MARC KUDISCH. *Larry Hastings:* David Brummel. *Louie:* Greg Reuter. *Padie,*

[9]Originally produced in New York 4 April 1971 at the Winter Garden for
522 performances. For Synopsis of Musical Numbers, see original 1971
production. First produced in New York in One Act without intermission,
this revival added an intermission after "Too Many Mornings." Bolero
d'Amour was revised as Danse d'Amour.
[10]First produced in New York 29 November 1956 at the Sam S. Shubert
Theatre for 924 performances. Comden & Green revised the book, the
order of songs was revised, and the reprise of "Long Before I Knew You"
was reassigned to Jeff (M. Kudisch) and dropped from the program listing.
"Better Than a Dream," added during the New York run and for national
tour and film version, was retained.

the Street Sweeper: Roy Harcourt. *Ludwig Smiley*: Lawrence Clayton. *Charlie Bessemer*: Josh Rhodes. *Dr. Kitchell*: Martin Moran. *Blake Barton*: Darren Ritchie. *Joey*: Shane Kirkpatrick. *Olga*: Caitlin Carter. *Corvello Mob Men*: David Brummel, Greg Reuter. *Maid*: Linda Romoff. *Paul Arnold*: Lawrence Clayton. *Bridgette*: Joan Hess. *Waiter*: Josh Rhodes. *Man on Street*: Josh Rhodes. *Madame Grimaldi*: Joanne Baum. *Mrs. Mallet*: Joan Hess.

Ensemble: Julio Agustin, Joanne Baum, David Brummel, Caitlin Carter, Lawrence Clayton, Roy Harcourt, Joan Hess, Emily Hsu, Shane Kirkpatrick, Greg Reuter, Josh Rhodes, Alice Rietveld, Darren Ritchie, Angela Robinson, Linda Romoff, *Dancers*: Caitlin Carter, Roy Harcourt, Joan Hess, Emily Hsu, Shane Kirkpatrick, Greg Reuter, Josh Rhodes. *Swings*: James Hadley, Stacey Harris, Marc Oka, Kelly Sullivan.

Time: 1956. *Place*: New York City.

ACT 1

"Bells Are Ringing"
    Telephone Girls
"It's a Perfect Relationship"
    F. Prince
"Independent"
    M. Kudisch, Dancers
"You've Got to Do It"
    M. Kudisch
"It's a Simple Little System"
    D. Garrison, Ensemble
"It's Better Than a Dream"
    F. Prince, M. Kudisch
"Hello, Hello There"
    L. Clayton, F. Prince, M. Kudisch, Ensemble
"I Met a Girl"
    M. Kudisch, Ensemble
"Is It a Crime?"
    F. Prince, R. Ari, J. Bean
"Long Before I Knew You"
    F. Prince, M. Kudisch

ACT 2

"Mu-Cha-Cha"
    J. Agustin, F. Prince, A. Robinson, Dancers
"Just in Time"
    M. Kudisch, F. Prince, Ensemble
    (*Original dance arrangements by* John Morris.)
"Drop That Name"
    F. Prince, Ensemble
"The Party's Over"
    F. Prince
"Salzburg"
    B. Fowler, D. Garrison
"The Midas Touch"
    M. Moran, Dancers
"I'm Goin' Back"
    F. Prince
Finale
    The Company

2001.04

BLAST

A Music Revue in Two Acts. Directed by James Mason. Choreography by Jim Moore, George Pinney, John Vanderkolff. Music director, James Prime. Scene and costume design, Mark Thompson. Lighting design, Hugh Vanstone. Orchestrations by James Prime. Sound design, Mark Hood, Bobby Aitken, Tom Morse. Tour direction, Dodger Touring, Big League Theatricals. Associate Producer, Donnie Vandoren. Executive producer, Dodger Management Group. Presented by Cook Group Incorporated and Star of Indiana. Opened 17 April 2001 at the Broadway Theatre and closed 23 September 2001 after 173 performances.

CAST [in alphabetical order]: Trey Allgood III (Visual Ensemble, Voice), Rachel J. Anderson (French Horn, Mellophone, Voice), Nicholas E. Angelis (Snare Drum, Percussion, Voice), Matthew A. Banks (Tuba, Euphonium, Voice), Kimberly Beth Baron (French Horn, Mellophone, Keyboard, Voice), Wesley Bullock (Cornet, Trumpet, Didgerydoo, Voice), Mark Burroughs (Tuba), Jesus Cantu, Jr. (Trumpet, Coronet, Keyboard, Voice, Percussion), Jodina Rosario Carey (Visual Ensemble, Voice), Robert Carmical (Trombone, Baritone, Voice), Alan "Otto" Compton (Percussion, Voice), Dayne Delahoussaye (French Horn, Mellophone, Voice), Karen Duggan (Visual Ensemble, Voice), John Elrod (Trombone, Euphonium, Voice),

Brandon J. Epperson (Trombone, Didgerydoo, Bass Trombone, Voice), Kenneth Frisby (Visual Ensemble, Voice), J. Derek Gipson (Trumpet, Piccolo Trumpet, Cornet, Voice), Trevor Lee Gooch (Tuba, Didgerydoo, Percussion, Voice), Casey Marshall Gooding (Trumpet, Piccolo Trumpet, Cornet, Didgerydoo, Voice), Bradley Kerr Green (Trombone, Conductor, Trombonium, Didgerydoo, Voice), Benjamin Taber Griffin (Trombone, Bass Trombone, Euphonium, Trombonium, Didgerydoo, Voice), Benjamin Raymond Handel (Percussion, Voice), Benjamin W. Harloff (Trumpet, Piccolo Trumpet, Flugelhorn, Cornet, Mellophone, Voice), Joe Haworth (Euphonium, Percussion, Voice), Darren M. Hazlett (Percussion, Didgerydoo, Voice), Tim Heasley (Trombone, Percussion, Voice), Freddy Hernandez, Jr. (Trumpet, Mellophone, Didgerydoo, Voice), George Hester (Trumpet, Cornet, Mellophone, Voice), Jeremiah Todd Huber (Visual Ensemble, Percussion, Voice), Martin A. Hughes (Visual Ensemble, Voice), Naoki Ishikawa (Percussion, Voice), Stacy J. Johnson (Visual Ensemble, Voice), Sanford R. Jones (Tuba, Didgerydoo, Voice), Anthony F. Leps (Trumpet, Cornet, Mellophone, Didgerydoo, Percussion, Voice), Ray Linkous (Conductor, Tuba, Didgerydoo, Voice), Jean Marie Mallicoat (Euphonium, Didgerydoo, Percussion, Voice), Jack Mansager (Percussion, Voice), Brian Mayle (Didgerydoo, Percussion, Voice), Dave Millen (Trumpet, Voice), Jim Moore (Visual Ensemble, Voice), Westley Morehead (Trombone, Trombonium, Didgerydoo, Voice), David Nash (Percussion, Voice), Jeffrey A. Queen (Snare Drum, Percussion, Voice), Douglas Raines (Percussion, Didgerydoo, Voice), Chris Rasmussen (Percussion, Voice), Joseph J. Reinhart (Trumpet, Cornet, Voice), Jamie L. Roscoe (Visual Ensemble, Voice), Jennifer Ross (Visual Ensemble, Voice), Christopher Eric Rutt (French Horn, Mellophone, Didgerydoo, Percussion, Voice), Christopher J. Schletter (Trombone, Trombonium, Euphonium, Voice), Andrew Schnieders (Percussion, Voice), Jonathan L. Schwartz (Visual Ensemble, Voice), Greg Seale (Percussion, Voice), Andy Smart (Trumpet, Didgerydoo, Voice), Radiah Y. Stewart (Visual Ensemble, Voice), Bryan Anthony Sutton (Visual Ensemble, Voice), Sean Terrell (Trumpet, Didgerydoo, Voice), Andrew James Toth (Visual Ensemble, Voice), Joni Paige Viertel (French Horn, Mellophone, Didgerydoo, Voice), Kristin Whiting (Visual Ensemble, Voice).

ACT 1

Bolero
    (*Music by* Maurice Ravel.)
Color Wheel
    (*Music by* J. Lee.)
Split Commentaries
    (*Music by* Josh Talbot.)
Everybody Loves the Blues
    (*Music by* Maynard Ferguson and Nicholas Lane.)
Loss
    (*Music by* Don Ellis.)
"Simple Gifts" (from Old American Songs, Set 1)/Appalachian Spring
    (*Music by* Aaron Copland.)
Battery Battle
    (*Music by* T. Hannum, J. Lee and P. Rennick.)
Medea
    (*Music by* Samuel Barber.)
The Promise of Living (from THE TENDER LAND)
    (*Music by* Aaron Copland.)

ACT 2

Color Wheel Too
    (*Music by* John Vanderkolff.)
Gee, Officer Krupke (from WEST SIDE STORY)
    (*Music by* Leonard Bernstein.)
Lemontech
    (*Music by* Jonathan Vanderkolff.)
Tangerinamadidge
    (*Music by* James Mason and Jonathan Vanderkolff.)
Land of Make Believe
    (*Music by* Chuck Mangione.)
Spiritual of the Earth:
    Marimba Spiritual
        (*Music by* Minoru Miki.)
    Earth Beat
        (*Music by* Michael Spiro.)
    Malagueña
        (*Music by* Ernesto Lecuona.)

2001.05

THE PRODUCERS

A Musical in Two Acts, 18 Scenes. Book by Mel Brooks and Thomas Meehan (based on Mel Brooks' film). Music and lyrics by Mel Brooks. Direction and choreography by Susan Stroman. Scenery designed by Robin Wagner. Costumes designed by William Ivey Long. Lighting designed by

Peter Kaczorowski. Sound designed by Steven C. Kennedy. Orchestrations by Douglas Besterman. Music direction and vocal arrangements, Patrick S. Brady. Musical arrangements and supervision, Glen Kelly. Associate director, Steven Zweigbaum. Associate producers, Frederic H. and Rhoda Mayerson, Lynn Landis. Produced by Rocco Landesman, SFX Theatrical Group, Frankel-Baruch-Viertel-Routh Group[11], Bob and Harvey Weinstein, Rick Steiner, Robert F. X. Sillerman and Mel Brooks, in association with James D. Stern/Douglas Meyer. Opened 19 April 2001 at the St. James Theatre, still running at time of this writing.

CAST (in order of appearance): *The Usherettes*: Bryn Dowling, Jennifer Smith. *Max Bialystock*: NATHAN LANE. *Leo Bloom*: MATTHEW BRODERICK. *Hold-me Touch-me*: Madeleine Doherty. *Mr. Marx*: Ray Wills. *Franz Liebkind*: BRAD OSCAR. *Carmen Ghia*: ROGER BART. *Roger De Bris*: GARY BEACH. *Bryan*: Peter Marinos. *Kevin*: Ray Wills. *Scott*: Jeffry Denman. *Shirley*: Kathy Fitzgerald. *Ulla*: CADY HUFFMAN. *Lick-me Bite-me*: Jennifer Smith. *Kiss-me Feel-me*: Kathy Fitzgerald. *Jack Lepidus*: Peter Marinos. *Donald Dinsmore*: Jeffry Denman. *Jason Green*: Ray Wills. *Lead Tenor*: Eric Gunhus. *Sergeant*: Ray Wills. *O'Riley*: Matt Loehr. *O'Rourke*: Abe Sylvia. *O'Houllihan*: Robert H. Fowler. *Guard*: Jeffry Denman. *Bailiff*: Abe Sylvia. *Judge*: Peter Marinos. *Foreman of the Jury*: Kathy Fitzgerald. *Trustee*: Ray Wills.

Ensemble: Jeffry Denman, Madeleine Doherty, Bryn Dowling, Kathy Fitzgerald, Robert H. Fowler, Ida Gilliams, Eric Gunhus, Kimberly Hester, Naomi Kakuk, Matt Loehr, Peter Marinos, Angie L. Schworer, Jennifer Smith, Abe Sylvia, Tracy Terstriep, Ray Wills. *Swings*: Jim Borstelmann, Adrienne Gibbons, Jamie LaVerdiere, Brad Musgrove, Christina Marie Norrup.

Act 1: New York, 1959. *Scene 1*: Shubert Alley. *Scene 2*: Max's Office, 16 June 1959. *Scene 3*: The Chambers Street Offices of Whitehall and Marx. *Scene 4*: Max's Office. *Scene 5*: The Rooftop of a Greenwich Village Apartment (on Jane Street). *Scene 6*: The Living Room of Renowned Theatrical Director Roger Debris' Elegant Upper East Side Townhouse on a Sunny Tuesday afternoon in June. *Scene 7*: Max's Office. *Scene 8*: Little Old Lady Land.

Act 2, Scene 1: Max's Office, late morning, a few weeks later. *Scene 2*: The Bare Stage of a Broadway Theatre. *Scene 3*: Shubert Alley. *Scene 4*: The stage of The Shubert Theatre. *Scene 5*: Max's Office, later that night. *Scene 6*: The Holding Cell of a New York Courthouse, ten days later. *Scene 7*: A New York Courtroom. *Scene 8*: Sing Sing. *Scene 9*: The Stage of the Shubert Theatre. *Scene 10*: Shubert Alley. *Curtain Call*.

ACT 1

Scene 1

"Opening Night"
Ensemble

"The King of Broadway"
N. Lane, Ensemble

Scene 2

"We Can Do It"
N. Lane, M. Broderick

Scene 3

"I Wanna Be a Producer" ["Unhappy"]
M. Broderick, the Accountants

Scene 4

"We Can Do It" (reprise)
N. Lane, M. Broderick

Scene 5

"In Old Bavaria"
B. Oscar

"Der Guten Tag Hop Clop"
B. Oscar, N. Lane, M. Broderick

Scene 6

"Keep It Gay"
G. Beach, R. Bart, P. Marinos, R. Wills, J. Denman, K. Fitzgerald, N. Lane, M. Broderick

Scene 7

"When You Got It, Flaunt It"
C. Huffman

Scene 8

"Along Came Bialy"
N. Lane, Little Old Ladies

Act One Finale
N. Lane, M. Broderick, B. Oscar, C. Huffman, G. Beach, R. Bart, P. Marinos, R. Wills, J. Denman, K. Fitzgerald

ACT 2

Scene 1

"That Face"
M. Broderick, C. Huffman, N. Lane

Scene 2

"Haben Sie Gehoert Das Deutsche Band?" (Have You Ever Heard the German Band?)
R. Wills, B. Oscar

Scene 3

"Opening Night" (reprise)
B. Dowling, J. Smith

"You Never Say 'Good Luck' on Opening Night"
G. Beach, N. Lane, R. Bart, B. Oscar, M. Broderick

Scene 4

"Springtime for Hitler"
E. Gunhus, G. Beach, C. Huffman, Ensemble

Scene 5

"Where Did We Go Right?"
N. Lane, M. Broderick

Scene 6

"Betrayed"
N. Lane

Scene 7

"'Till Him"
M. Broderick, N. Lane

Scene 8

"Prisoners of Love"
The Convicts

Scene 9

"Prisoners of Love" (continued)
G. Beach, C. Huffman, Ensemble

Scene 10

"Prisoners of Love" (reprise); "Leo and Max"
N. Lane, M. Broderick

Curtain Call

"Goodbye!"
The Company

THE ADVENTURES OF TOM SAWYER

2001.06

A Musical in Two Acts, 14 Scenes. Book by Ken Ludwig, based on the novel of the same name by Mark Twain. Music and Lyrics by Don Schlitz. Directed by Scott Ellis. Choreographed by David Marques. Scenic design by Heidi Ettinger. Costume design by Anthony Powell. Lighting design by Kenneth Posner. Sound design by Lew Mead. Musical director, Paul Gemignani. Orchestrations by Michael Starobin. Dance and incidental music by David Krane. Fight director, Rick Sordelet. Produced by James M. Nederlander, James L. Nederlander and Watt/Dobie Productions. Opened 26 April 2001 at the Minskoff Theatre and closed 13 May 2001 after 21 performances.

CAST (in order of appearance): *Tom Sawyer*: JOSHUA PARK. *Ben Rogers*: Tommar Wilson. *George Bellamy*: Joe Gallagher. *Lyle Bellamy*: Blake Hackler. *Joe Harper*: Erik J. McCormack. *Alfred Temple*: Pierce Cravens. *Amy Lawrence*: Ann Whitlow Brown. *Lucy Harper*: Mekenzie Rosen-Stone. *Susie Rogers*: Èlan. *Sabina Temple*: Nikki M. James. *Sally Bellamy*: Stacia Fernandez. *Sereny Harper*: Donna Lee Marshall. *Lucinda Rogers*: Amy Jo Phillips. *Naomi Temple*: Sally Wilfert. *Aunt Polly*: LINDA PURL. *Sid Sawyer*: MARSHALL PAILET. *Doc Robinson*: Stephen Lee Anderson. *Reverend Sprague*: TOMMY HOLLIS. *Lanyard Bellamy*: RICHARD POE. *Gideon Temple*: Ric Stoneback. *Lemuel Dobbins*: JOHN CHRISTOPHER JONES. *Muff Potter*: TOM ALDREDGE. *Huckleberry Finn* JIM POULOS. *Injun Joe*: KEVIN DURANT. *Judge Thatcher*: JOHN DOSSETT. *Becky Thatcher*: KRISTEN BELL. *Widow Douglas*: JANE CONNELL. *Pap*: Stephen Lee Anderson. *Swings*: Patrick Boll, Michael Burton, John Herrera, Kate Reinders, Elise Santora.

The action takes place in St. Petersburg, Missouri, in 1844.

Act 1, Scene 1: A Meadow and the town of St. Petersburg. *Scene 2*: The fence in front of Tom's house. *Scene 3*: The graveyard. *Scene 4*: On the way to church. *Scene 5*: Outside the schoolhouse. *Scene 6*: Inside the schoolhouse. *Scene 7*: The alley behind the jail. *Scene 8*: Inside the courthouse.

[11]Richard Frankel, Steve Baruch, Tom Viertel, Mark Routh.

Act 2, Scene 1: The school and the town. *Scene 2*: Tom's bedroom. *Scene 3*: Widow Douglas' front porch. *Scene 4*: The picnic grounds, Cardiff Hill. *Scene 5*: McDougal's Cave. *Scene 6*: Inside and outside the church.

ACT 1

Scene 1

"Hey, Tom Sawyer"
J. Park, L. Purl, J. C. Jones, T. Hollis, Townspeople

Scene 2

"Here's My Plan"
J. Park
"Smart Like That"
J. Park, T. Wilson, Boys

Scene 3

"Hands All Clean"
K. Durand
"The Vow"
J. Park, K. Poulos

Scene 4

"Ain't Life Fine"
Townspeople

Scene 5

"It Ain't Just Me"
J. Poulos

Scene 6

"To Hear You Say My Name"
J. Park, K. Bell

Scene 7

"Murrel's Gold"
K. Durand, T. Aldredge, J. Park, J. Poulos

Scene 8

"The Testimony"
J. Park, Townspeople

ACT 2

Scene 1

"Ain't Life Fine" (reprise)
Townspeople

Scene 2

"This Time Tomorrow"
L. Purl

Scene 3

"I Can Read"
J. Poulos, J. Connell

Scene 4

"You Can't Can't Dance"
J. Dossett, L. Purl, Townspeople
"Murrel's Gold" (reprise)
K. Durand

Scene 5

"Angel's Lost"
L. Purl, J. Dossett, Townspeople
"Light"
J. Park
"Angel's Lost" (reprise)
K. Bell

Scene 6

"Light" (reprise)
Townspeople

Finale

J. Park, J. Poulos, K. Bell, Boys, Girls

2001.07   GEORGE GERSHWIN ALONE

A Play with Music in Two Acts. Play by Hershey Felder. Music by George Gershwin. Lyrics by Ira Gershwin. Directed by Joel Zwick. Settings by Yael Pardess. Sound by John Gottlieb. Produced by Richard Willis, Martin Markinson, HTG Productions. Opened 30 April 2001 at the Helen Hayes Theatre and closed 22 July 2001 after 96 performances.

CAST: *George Gershwin*: HERSHEY FELDER.

MUSICAL NUMBERS

"Swanee" (interpolated into SINBAD)
    (*Lyrics by* Irving Caesar.)
"Embraceable You" (from GIRL CRAZY)
"Someone to Watch Over Me" (from OH KAY!)
"Bess, You is My Woman Now" (from PORGY AND BESS)
    (*Lyrics by* DuBose Heyward and Ira Gershwin.)
"An American in Paris"
"Rhapsody in Blue"

2001.08   42nd STREET

A Revival of the Song and Dance Fable of Broadway (A Musical) in Two Acts, 16 Scenes[12]. Book by Michael Stewart and Mark Bramble. Based on the novel of the same name by Bradford Ropes (and the Warner Brothers film adapted from it by Rian James and James Seymour.) Music by Harry Warren. Lyrics by Al Dubin. (Other lyrics by Johnny Mercer and Mort Dixon.) Original direction and dances by Gower Champion. Staged by Mark Bramble. Musical staging and new choreography by Randy Skinner. Scenery design by Douglas W. Schmidt. Costume design by Roger Kirk. Lighting design by Paul Gallo. Sound design by Peter Fitzgerald. Musical direction by Todd Ellison. Musical adaptation, arrangements and additional orchestrations by Donald Johnston. Orchestrations by Philip J. Lang. Executive producer, Dodger Management Group. Produced by Dodger Theatricals, Joop van den Ende and Stage Holding. Opened 2 May 2001 at the Ford Center for the Performing Arts and is still running at this writing.

CAST (in order of appearance): *Andy Lee*: MICHAEL ARNOLD. *Oscar*: BILLY STRITCH. *Mac*: ALLEN FITZPATRICK. *Annie*: MYLINDA HULL. *Diane*: Tamlyn Brooke Shusterman. *Maggie Jones*: MARY TESTA. *Bert Barry*: JONATHAN FREEMAN. *Billy Lawlor*: DAVID ELDER. *Peggy Sawyer*: KATE LEVERING. *Phyllis*: Catherine Wreford. *Lorraine*: Megan Sikora. *Julian Marsh*: MICHAEL CUMPSTY. *Dorothy Brock*: CHRISTINE EBERSOLE. *Abner Dillon*: MICHAEL McCARTY. *Pat Denning*: RICHARD MUENZ. *Waiters*: Brad Aspel, Mike Warshaw, Shonn Wiley. *Thugs*: Allen Fitzpatrick, Jerry Tellier. *Doctor*: ALLEN FITZPATRICK. (*Standby*: BETH LEAVEL.)

Ensemble: Brad Aspel, Becky Bersteler, Randy Bobish, Chris Clay, Michael Clowers, Maryam Myika Day, Alexander deJong, Amy Dolan, Isabelle Flachsmann, Jennifer Jones, Dontee Kiehn, Renée Klapmeyer, Jessica Kostival, Keirsten Kupiec, Todd Lattimoore, Melissa Rae Mahon, Michael Malone, Jennifer Marquardt, Meredith Patterson, Darin Phelps, Wendy Rosoff, Megan Schenck, Kelly Sheehan, Tamlyn Brooke Shusterman, Megan Sikora, Erin Stoddard, Yasuko Tamaki, Jonathan Taylor, Jerry Tellier, Elisa van Duyne, Erika Vaughn, Mike Warshaw, Merrill West, Shonn Wiley Catherine Wreford. *Swings*: Kelli Barclay, Melissa Giattino, Brian J. Marcum, Luke Walrath.

2001.09   CINDERELLA

A Revival of the Musical in Two Acts, a Prologue and 13 Scenes[13]. Book and lyrics by Oscar Hammerstein II. Music by Richard Rodgers. Adapted for the

---

[12]First produced in New York 25 August 1980 at the Winter Garden for 3486 performances. For Synopsis of Scenes and Musical Numbers, see original 1980 production. For this revival the following changes were made:

"Shadow Waltz" (reprise, dropped from Act 1, Scene 1)

"I Only Have Eyes for You" (from DAMES film)(Added to Act 1, Scene 7, replacing "I Know Now")
    C. Ebersole

"Getting Out of Town" (reprise, added to Act 2, Scene 4)
    J. Freeman, M. Testa, Full Company

"Montage" (Added to Act 2, Scene 5)
    M. Cumpsty, M. Arnold, K. Levering, Ensemble

"With Plenty of Money and You" (from GOLD DIGGERS OF 1937 film) (Added to Act 2, Scene 7, after Overture)
    K. Levering, Men

Finale (Act 2, Scene 8)
    Full Company

[13]First produced for television in 31 March 1957; this production was adapted from the 2 November 1998 telecast. A previous stage adaptation was presented in New York 9 November 1993 at the New York State Theatre for 14 performances.

stage by Tom Briggs from the teleplay by Robert L. Freedman. Directed by Gabriel Barre. Choreographed by Ken Roberson. Scenic design by James Youmans. Costume design by Pamela Scofield. Lighting design by Tim Hunter. Sound design by Duncan Edwards. Special effects by Gregory Meeh. Puppets designed by Integrity Designworks. Music Director/Conductor, John Mezzio. Orchestrations by David Siegel. Original orchestrations by Robert Russell Bennett. Musical supervision and arrangements by Andrew Lippa. Executive producer, Ken Gentry. Presented by Radio City Entertainment; National Tour presented by Marshalls. Produced by NETworks. Opened 3 May 2001 at the Theatre at Madison Square Garden and closed 13 May 2001 after 16 performances.

CAST: *The Fairy Godmother*: EARTHA KITT. *Cinderella*: JAMIE-LYNN SIGLER. *Prince Christopher*: PAOLO MONTALBAN. *The Stepmother*: EVERETT QUINTON. *Cinderella's Stepsisters (2)*: *Grace*: NATASHA YVETTE WILLIAMS. *Joy*: ALEXANDRA KOLB. *Lionel*, the Court Herald: Victor Trent Cook. *Queen Constantina*: Leslie Becker. *King Maximilian*: Ken Prymus. *4 White Mice*: Kip Driver, Kevin Duda, Jason Ma, Jason Robinson. *Charles*, a cat: Patrick Wetzel. *A Dove*: André Ward.

Villagers, Merchants, Maidens and Palace Guests: Joanne Borts, Natalie Cortez, Kip Driver, Kevin Duda, Davis Kirby, Amy Nicole Krawcek, Jason Ma, Christy Morton, Kerri Nowe, Monica Patton, Karine Plantadit-Bageot, Christeena Michelle Riggs, Jason Robinson, Jessica Rush, Jonathan Stahl, Kate Strohbehn, Keith L. Thomas, Ron J. Todorowski, André Ward, Patrick Wetzel. *Swings*: Lyn Philistine, Todd L. Underwood.

The action takes place once upon a time in a kingdom far away.

Act 1, Scene 1: The Village Square. *Scene 2*: The Stepmother's Manor House, immediately following. *Scene 3*: The Royal Parlor, immediately following. *Scene 4*: The Manor House, one week later. *Scene 5*: The Pumpkin Patch behind the Manor House. *Scene 6*: Outside the Royal Palace, immediately following.

Act 2, Scene 1: The Royal Ballroom. *Scene 2*: The Royal Gardens, immediately following. *Scene 3*: Outside the Royal Palace, immediately following. *Scene 4*: The Manor House, later that night. *Scene 5*: Throughout the Kingdom, the following day and night. *Scene 6*: The Manor House, the following morning. *Scene 7*: The Wedding Finale.

ACT 1

Prologue
    E. Kitt, J. Sigler, Ensemble
Scene 1
    "The Sweetest Sounds" (from NO STRINGS)
        J. Sigler, P. Montalban
        (*Lyrics by* Richard Rodgers.)
    "The Prince Is Giving a Ball"
        V. T. Cook, E. Quinton, N. Y. Williams, A. Kolb, Villagers
Scene 2
    "In My Own Little Corner"
        J. Sigler, Animals
Scene 3
    "The Sweetest Sounds" (reprise)
        J. Sigler, P. Montalban

Scene 4
    "In My Own Little Corner" (reprise)
        J. Sigler
Scene 5
    "Fol-de-Rol" (Godmothers' Song)
        E. Kitt
    "Impossible"
        E. Kitt, J. Sigler
    "The Transformation"
        E. Kitt, J. Sigler, Animals
    "It's Possible!"
        J. Sigler, E. Kitt, Horses, Coachman, Footman

ACT 2

Scene 1
    "(The) Gavotte"
        P. Montalban, Maidens, Other Guests
    "The Cinderella Waltz" (Waltz for a Ball)
        J. Sigler, P. Montalban, Guests
    "Ten Minutes Ago"
        P. Montalban, J. Sigler, Company
Scene 2
    "Stepsisters' Lament"
        N. Y. Williams, A. Kolb
    "Do I Love You Because You're Beautiful?"
        P. Montalban, J. Sigler
Scene 3
    "Ten Minutes Ago" (reprise)
        P. Montalban
Scene 4
    "When You're Driving Through the Moonlight"
        J. Sigler, E. Quinton, N. Y. Williams, A. Kolb, E. Quinton
    "A Lovely Night"
        J. Sigler, E. Quinton, N. Y. Williams, A. Kolb, Animals
    "A Lovely Night" (reprise)
        J. Sigler
Scene 5
    "The Search"
        V. T. Cook, P. Montalban, Maidens
Scene 7
    "There's Music in You" (Finale Ultimo)(from MAIN STREET TO BROADWAY film)
        E. Kitt, Company

INDEX OF SHOWS

Note: Variant show titles have been indexed for ease of use, so that both PO-CA-HON-TAS and POCAHONTAS, FOLLIES OF 1907 and ZIEGFELD FOLLIES OF 1907, BEAUTY AND THE BEAST and DISNEY'S BEAUTY AND THE BEAST will be found. If a show's title changed during the course of its run, that will be both footnoted and cross-indexed (THE MYSTERY OF EDWIN DROOD, 1985, became DROOD!; PIGGY, 1927, became I TOLD YOU SO).

651

INDEX OF SHOWS

Nimble Nip!, or, Ogre Ugliphiz, Fairy Silvereyes & the Princess with the Strawberry Mask 1875.39
Nina Rosa 1930.27
Nine 1982.09
Nine Fifteen Revue 1930.06
1940! or, .Crummles in Search of Novelty 1840.02
1940's Radio Hour, The 1979.24
90 in the Shade 1915.01
97 or 79 1884.24
Niniche 1885.59
Nisida 1880.66
No Foolin' 1926.18
No More Peace 1938.02
No Other Girl 1924.22
No Strings 1962.03
No for an Answer 1941.01
No, No, Nanette 1925.30, 1971.03
Noble Rouge, A 1929.30
Nobody Home 1915.07
Noces d'Olivette, Les 1881.53
Noces de Jeannette, Les 1861.05, 1866.27, 1872.01
Noël Coward's Sweet Potato 1968.19
Norma on the Half Shell 1867.11
Norman Leslie 1836.01
Normandy Wedding, A 1898.12
Norma; or, Titiens in a Minstrel Band 1876.07
Not Yet, But Soon 1907.12
Nothing But Love 1919.29
Nothing Venture Nothing Have, or, a Courtship in 1640 1859.17
Notoriety 1894.49
Novelty 1856.01
Nowhere to Go But Up 1962.24

O'Brien Girl, The 1921.32
O'Flynn, The 1934.41
O'Neill of Derry 1907.56
O'Nero, or, the Lady of Lions 1890.45
O'Reagans, The 1886.52, 1889.11
Oba Oba 1988.06
Oba Oba '90 1990.03
Oba Oba '93 1992.13
Object of Interest, An 1869.44
Octoroons 1899.31
Odds and Ends of 1917 1917.29
L'Oeil Crevé 1869.03, 1874.07
Of Thee I Sing 1931.48, 1933.13, 1952.07
Of V We Sing 1942.05
Off the Earth 1895.03
Office Boy, The 1903.34
Ogallallas, The 1894.08
Oh Captain! 1958.02
Oh Justine 1917.31
Oh What a Lovely War 1964.28
Oh! Calcutta! 1971.04, 1976.27
Oh! Oh! Delphine! 1912.34
Oh! Oh! Nurse 1925.44
Oh! What a Night 1885.69
Oh, Boy! 1917.06
Oh, Brother! 1981.25
Oh, Coward! 1986.19
Oh, Ernest! 1927.20
Oh, I Say! 1913.29
Oh, Kay! 1926.36, 1928.01, 1990.14
Oh, Lady! Lady! 1918.03
Oh, Look! 1918.07
Oh, My Dear! 1918.37
Oh, Please! 1926.46
Oh, What a Girl! 1919.19
Oily Vet, or, the Wilful Maid and the Sad Sea Dog 1881.12

Oklahoma! 1943.04, 1951.16, 1953.09, 1958.07, 1963.06, 1965.38, 1969.12, 1979.31
Old Bill, M.P. 1926.38
Old Dame Trot and Her Comical Cat 1865.01
Old Dutch 1909.30
Old Homestead, The 1887.02, 1887.42, 1888.25, 1889.43, 1890.36, 1894.52, 1898.45, 1899.32, 1904.32, 1907.43, 1908.32
Old Lady, The/Dreams of Three 1919.17
Old Lavender 1877.24, 1885.49, 1888.14, 1893.46
Old Limerick Town 1902.36
Old Town, The 1910.02
Oliver! 1963.01, 1965.23, 1984.07
Olivette 1880.69, 1881.03, 1881.14, 1881.38, 1881.56, 1882.11, 1882.32, 1882.37, 1882.47, 1882.52, 1882.72, 1883.25, 1884.03, 1884.28, 1896.21, 1899.14
Olympiana, or, a Night With Mitchell 1857.04
On Broadway 1896.39
On Your Toes 1936.05, 1954.12, 1983.02
On a Clear Day You Can See Forever 1965.31
On the Frontier 1888.30
On the Town 1944.33, 1971.15, 1998.16
On the Track! 1871.17
On the Twentieth Century 1978.02
On the Yellowstone 1884.10
Once Over Lightly 1942.33
Once Upon a Mattress 1959.26, 1996.18
Once on This Island 1990.12
Ondina!, or, the Spirit of the Waters 1861.06
One Horse Town, A 1906.28
110 in the Shade 1963.26, 1992.10
One Kiss 1923.44
One Round of Pleasure 1897.25
One Touch of Venus 1943.19
One for the Money 1939.12
One of the Old Stock 1888.31
Only Fools are Sad 1971.17
Only Girl, The 1914.27, 1934.14
Onward Victoria 1980.30
Oolah, The 1889.24
Opera Ball, The 1912.08
Operation Sidewinder 1970.04
Optimists, The 1928.04
Orange Blossoms 1922.33
Orchid, The 1907.15
Orchids Preferred 1937.06
Oriental America, or, In the Isle of San Domingo 1896.46
Origin of the Cakewalk, or, Clorindy 1898.41
Orphée Aux Enfers 1867.05, 1868.13, 1868.28, 1869.10
Orpheus (Burlesque) 1893.01
Orpheus and Eurydice 1883.65
Orpheus in der Unterwelt 1861.02, 1866.33
Orpheus in the Underworld 1956.09
Other Way, The 1899.30
Otoyo 1903.19
Otto, a German 1878.15, 1880.51
Our Belle Hélene 1890.13
Our Bridget's Dreams 1903.30
Our Goblins, or, Fun on the Rhine 1880.32, 1881.16
Our Irish Visitors 1886.46, 1887.23
Our Japanese Embassy 1860.04
Our Jennie 1887.51
Our Miss Gibbs 1910.21
Our Nell 1922.46
Out of This World 1950.20
Over Here! 1974.05
Over the Garden Wall 1885.03, 1886.62
Over the River 1912.02
Over the Top 1917.31

Ovid's Metamorphoses 1971.08
Oxygen 1886.32
Oxygen! or, Gas in Burlesque Metre 1877.23
Oy Is Dus A Leben! 1942.28
Oyster Man, The 1907.55

Pa 1887.09
Pacific Mail, The 1894.39
Pacific Overtures 1976.02
Pacific Paradise 1972.20
Padlocks of 1927 1927.31
Paese Dei Campanelli, Il 1935.02
Page's Revel; or, the Summer Night's Bivouac 1869.02
Paint Your Wagon 1951.24
Painting the Town 1906.39
Pair of Pinks, A 1904.11
Pajama Game, The 1954.05, 1957.08, 1973.15, 1989.04
Pal Joey 1940.22, 1952.01, 1961.15, 1963.17, 1976.19
Panama Hattie 1940.19
Panhandle Pete 1906.31
Panjandrum 1893.16
Pansy 1929.21
Paola, or, the First of the Vendettas 1889.36
Papa's Boy 1905.24
Papa's Darling 1914.26
Papa's Wife 1899.38
Parade (Moross) 1935.03
Parade (J.R. Brown) 1998.21
Paradise Alley 1924.07
Paradise of Mahomet, The 1911.03
Pardon My English 1933.01
Pardon Our French 1950.14
Paris 1928.33
Paris '90 1952.04
Paris and Helen, or, the Grecian Elopement 1868.08
Paris by Night 1904.23
Paris, or, the Apple of Discord 1870.42
Parisian Folly, A 1874.10
Parisian Model, A 1906.45, 1908.04
Parisiana 1928.09
Paris; or, the Judgement 1869.21
Park 1970.12
Park Avenue 1946.20
Parlor Match, A 1890.32, 1892.45, 1896.31
Parlor Match, A, or, Turning a Crank 1884.48
Parlor Match, a, Up to Now 1892.18
Party With Betty Comden & Adolph Green, A 1958.21, 1977.02
Pas Sur la Bouche 1929.16
Passing Show of 1894, The 1894.21
Passing Show of 1912, The/The Ballet of 1830 1912.24
Passing Show of 1913, The 1913.18
Passing Show of 1914, The 1914.16
Passing Show of 1915, The 1915.11
Passing Show of 1916, The 1916.11
Passing Show of 1917, The 1917.08
Passing Show of 1918, The 1918.20
Passing Show of 1919, The 1919.30
Passing Show of 1921, The 1920.47
Passing Show of 1922, The 1922.34
Passing Show of 1923, The 1923.17
Passing Show of 1924, The 1924.29
Passing Show of 1926, The 1926.15
Passion 1994.05
Passionnément! 1929.11
Passions of 1926 1926.15
Pat's New Wardrobe 1888.42, 1889.25
Pat's Wardrobe 1886.61
Patchwork 1875.16

INDEX OF SONGS

Note: All songs which appear in quotation marks in the text have been indexed (for example, "Erbie Fitch's Twitch" or "Which Switch Is the Switch, Miss, for Ipswich?"), including variant titles which appear in parentheses alongside the original title. Thus the song "Merely Marvelous" as it appears in the program for REDHEAD will also appear in the index as "I Feel Merely Marvelous" since its sheet music was published under that title; in the body of the book, it will also appear as "(I Feel) Merely Marvelous." The original SHOW BOAT program contains both "Ol' Man River" and "Old Man River." Generic entries like Song, Specialty, Finale, Dance, Trio are not indexed. Overtures and Entr'actes are not listed in the book, whether or not listed in the program, as they were as often performed as not.

Anna, What's Wrong? 1913.23
Anna, zu Dir ist mein liebster Gang 1885.01
Annabel was Fairest 1902.04
Annabelle Jerome 1911.42
Annabelle Lee 1923.31
Anne of Green Gables 1971.21
Annette 1930.15
Annexation 1907.13
Annie 1924.38, 1977.06
Annie Dear, Good Bye 1869.20
Annie Doesn't Live Here Anymore 1995.14
Annie Laurie 1871.16, 1891.37, 1920.24, 1921.02, 1936.03
Annie Laurie Rag 1924.35
Annie More 1901.08
Annie O' the Banks O' Dee 1866.22, 1866.26
Annie o' the banks O'Dee 1862.06
Annie's Thing 1971.01
Anniversary, The 1973.08
Another Auld Lang Syne 2000.16
Another Autumn 1951.24
Another cheer 1868.01
Another Day 1967.06, 1983.21, 1996.09
Another Girl Who's Just Like Me 1999.17
Another Hundred People 1970.13, 1977.05, 1979.13
Another Life 1980.30, 1983.08
Another Little Coon in Town 1894.34
Another Little Cup of Tea 1960.18
Another Little Girl 1915.07
Another Love Affair 1932.14
Another Memorable Meal 1983.18
Another Memory 1980.08
Another Miracle of Judaism 1992.09
Another Op'nin', Another Show 1948.32, 1999.19
Another Pair of Shoes 1897.55
Another Princely Scheme 1954.13, 1979.22, 1990.20
Another Pyramid 2000.06
Another Situation 1906.44
Another Song About Paris 1988.08
Another Spring 1974.11
Another Suitcase in Another Hall 1979.23, 1992.12
Another Time, Another Place 1961.24
Another Wide River to Cross 1880.32
Anstatt-Dass-Song, Der 1965.04
Answer 1908.22
Answer is No, The 1932.08
Answer Me 1911.18
Answer My Heart 1933.06
Answers That You Don't Expect to Get 1906.14
Antes de la Corrida Del Toro 1922.32
Anthem 1988.09
Anthem of the Common Wheel, The 1979.07
Anthem of the Milk White Flag 1894.37
Anti-Cigarette Society, The 1897.39
Antici-tici-pation 1895.43
Antics of the Comics 1911.26
Antidote of a doting mother, The 1873.05
Antique et fort viel adage, Un 1887.35
Antique Spanish 1917.33
Antiques 1923.07
Antiquity 1980.15
Antoine 1907.38
Antoinette 1901.18, 1914.27
Antonio 1905.48
Antony and Cleopatra 1891.15
Anushka 1922.06
Anvedi Si Che Paciocca 1964.03
Anvil 1880.24
Any Afternoon 1920.32
Any Afternoon About Five 1953.02
Any Bonds for Sale 1938.08
Any Bonds Today 1938.08
Any Dream Will Do 1982.03, 1993.15
Any Friend of Kenny's is a Friend of Mine 1999.14
Any Girl 1918.25, 1921.33
Any Kind of a Daddy Will Do 1919.32
Any Kind of Man 1918.30
Any Kinder Coon 1899.31
Any Little Girl 1907.58
Any Little Girl Will Fall 1923.02
Any Little Melody 1920.19
Any Little Thing 1927.52, 1981.03
Any Little Tune 1926.28

Any Millenniums Today, Lady? 1973.08
Any Moment 1987.18
Any Night on Broadway 1916.11
Any Night on Old Broadway 1921.25
Any Old Iron 1960.17
Any Old Nag at All 1908.21
Any Old Night is a Wonderful Night 1915.07
Any Old Place in Yankee Land is Good Enough for Me 1908.08
Any Old Place With You 1908.07, 1919.14
Any Old Port in a Storm 1909.16
Any Old Thing 1903.16
Any Old Time at All 1906.37, 1907.28, 1918.19, 1923.06
Any Old Time With You 1915.12
Any Old Tree 1904.54
Any Old Tune 1911.45
Any Place I Hang My Hat is Home 1946.08
Any Place the Old Flag Flies 1911.33
Any Place Would be Wonderful With You 1920.18
Any Sort of Girl 1904.03
Any Step 1926.14
Any Time 1927.30
Any Time at All 1910.10
Any Time is Love Time 1921.35
Any Time New York Goes Dry 1919.01
Any Time's Kissing Time 1917.24, 1919.20
Any Time, Any Place, Anywhere 1916.07
Any Way the Wind Blows 1933.16
Anya 1965.35
Anybody's Man Will be My Man 1925.18
Anyone 1981.12
Anyone Can Whistle 1964.15, 1977.05
Anyone Who do's That Can't be so Dumb 1927.05
Anyone Would Love You 1959.11
Anything 1997.18
Anything But Lonely 1990.04
Anything Can Happen 1935.18, 1948.23
Anything Can Happen in New York 1948.04, 1990.09
Anything for Him 1993.09
Anything for You 1962.01
Anything Goes 1934.36, 1978.26, 1987.15, 1995.12
Anything Goes When You Sing Calypso 1947.19
Anything is Possible 1968.06, 1973.02
Anything You Can Do 1946.12, 1966.12, 1999.04
Anything You Liked 1920.14
Anything You Want to do, Dear 1920.38
Anything Your Heart Desires 1928.34
Anytime 1962.17, 1978.01
Anytime, Anywhere, Anyhow 1925.26
Anyway, We've had Fun 1930.39
Anywhere I Wander 1980.29
Anywhere the Wind Blows 1975.09
Anywhere You Are 1974.01
Apache 1995.15
Apache Argentine 1924.47
Apache Argentino, El 1985.07, 1999.18
Apaches, The 1953.07
Apaga La Luz 1970.01
Apalachicola 1995.14
Apassionette 1934.15
Aphrodite 1971.02
Aphrodite Waltz 1919.38
Aphronightie 1919.43
Apollon 1946.21
Apologia 1940.08
Apology 1961.26
Appalachian Spring 2001.04
Appearances Were Against Her 1896.26
Appendectomy 1978.11
Appendectomy II 1978.11
Apperances are Oft Deceitful 1904.51
Applause 1970.09, 1979.13, 1988.20
Apple and the Bough, The 1930.14
Apple Blossom Victory 1978.06
Apple Doesn't Fall Very Far, The 1984.01
Apple for the Teacher, An 1995.14
Apple Jack 1948.23
Apple Mary Maguire 1904.49
Apple Tree, The 1966.18
Apples, Bananas and You 1923.36
Appointments 1973.11
Apres la Guerre 1919.40

Apres les penibles voyages 1887.35
April Blossoms 1923.05
April Face 1952.05
April Fool 1925.17
April in Fairbanks 1956.08
April in Harrisburg 1940.23
April in Paris 1964.02
April in Wisconsin 1981.01
April Showers 1921.34, 1940.10, 1962.17
April Snow 1945.03
April Song 1969.04, 1980.01
Apukad Eros Kezen 1988.09
Aquarius 1968.11
Arab Love Song, The 1908.36
Arab Maid With Midnight Eyes 1927.34
Arabian Fox Trot, The 1917.13
Arabian Nights 1929.28
Araby 1920.02
Araminta to Herself 1951.17
Arbiter's Song 1988.09
Arcadians, The 1902.30
Arcady 1921.34, 1923.12
Arcady is Ever Young 1910.05
Archers' Song 1925.32
Archie 1902.01
Are Then the Vows so Lately Spoken 1891.11
Are We Downhearted, No 1964.28
Are We Strong? 1972.23
Are We Widows, Wives or What? 1912.17
Are You a Man 1974.12
Are You a Single or Married Man? 1906.15
Are You Done, Mr. Dunn 1897.33, 1900.24
Are You Going to Dance? 1912.33
Are You Happy? 1947.10
Are You Havin' Any Fun? 1990.09
Are You Having Any Fun? 1939.25
Are You Insured? 1885.29
Are You Lonesome Tonight? 1978.01, 1989.12
Are You Love? 1931.39
Are You On? 1888.32, 1903.19
Are You Ready, Gyp Watson? 1959.11
Are You Satisfied? 1926.16
Are you sure 1887.44
Are You Sure? 1960.20
Are You the Girl That Dined With Me? 1907.33
Are You There? 1927.08, 1947.10
Are You With It? 1945.18
Areito 1939.18
Aren't We All 1924.04
Aren't You Glad? 1956.04
Aren't You the Girl I Met at Sherry's? 1907.45
Aren't You the Girl I Met at Sherrys? 1907.42
Aren't You Wonderful! 1936.02, 1936.17
Argentina 1922.27
Argentine 1923.03, 1927.19
Argentine Arago, The 1923.10
Argentine Tango 1957.14
Argentines, the Portuguese and Greeks, The 1919.06
Argentines, the Portuguese and the Greeks, The 1919.32
Argufyin' 1927.32
Argument, The 1962.14
Ari's Promise 1971.02
Aria 1948.27, 1966.03, 1993.17
Ariella 1907.52
Arieni 1977.01
Aristocracy 1911.46
Aristocracy, The 1900.59
Aristocratic Annie 1905.43
Arithmetic Dancing Bee 1925.26
Ark Brought to Jerusalem, The 1997.12
Arkansas 1985.06
Arlee 1907.26
Arm in Arm 1963.21
Armadillo Idyll 1966.32
Armadillo, The 1973.08
Armchair Golfer, The, or Whimpers of a Shortchanged Viewer 1973.08
Armored Knight, The 1899.40
Armorer's Song 1896.02, 1896.45
Armorer's Song, The 1929.43, 1944.25
Armors, The 1872.23
Armour 1950.14

Bernadette 1998.02
Bernice 1922.22
Berretin 1997.13
Berry-Pickers 1934.32
Berta e Pipinu Cuntamu La Storia, Di 1985.16
Berta Filava 1985.16
Bertha, the Sewing Machine Girl 1937.14
Bertie 1924.38, 1925.10, 1925.24
Bertie the Bounder 1910.21
Beside the Babbling Brook 1923.33
Beside the Star of Glory 1925.06
Bess You is My Woman Now 1958.10, 1974.09
Bess, You is My Woman Now 1935.13, 1983.04,
    2001.07
Bessie Clayton 1908.21
Bessie Mae 2000.14
Best Brittany, The 1909.29
Best Christmas of All, The 1998.07
Best Dance I've had Tonight, The 1923.05
Best Dance of All, The 1937.11
Best Friend 2000.08
Best Gold 1960.07
Best I Ever Get is the Worst of It, The 1922.02
Best I Get is 'Much Obliged to You', The 1907.41
Best in the Business, The 1987.14
Best in the Trade, The 1924.22
Best in the World, The 1980.08
Best Little Lover in Town, The 1927.08
Best Little Sweetheart of All, The 1915.17
Best Man Never Gets the Worst of It, The 1918.33
Best Man, The 1982.04
Best Night of My Life, The 1970.09
Best of All Possible Worlds, The 1956.15, 1974.06,
    1982.20, 1997.10
Best of Everything, The 1919.12
Best of Good Friends 1922.40
Best of Me, The 1983.17
Best of Times, The 1983.11, 1985.19, 1998.07
Best of What This Country's Got, The 1958.20
Best Queen of All, The 1913.31
Best Songs of All, The 1925.07
Best Thing for You Would be Me, The 1950.15
Best Thing of All, The 1949.16
Best Things in Life are Free, The 1927.41, 1974.26,
    1975.22, 1990.09
Best Time of the Day, The 1949.01
Best Toast of All, The 1914.28
Best Waltz of All, The 1915.04
Best Woman in the World, The 1969.11
Best Years of His Life, The 1941.04
Bet on the One You Fancy 1923.47
Betcha by Golly Wow 1997.21
Betcha I Make Good 1942.35
Betrayed 2001.05
Betrothal Kiss, The 1913.14
Betsy Ross 1922.01
Betsy's the Belle of Bathers 1908.17
Better 2001.01
Better & Best 1999.22
Better All the Time 1964.35
Better be Good to Me 1928.30
Better Days 1971.14
Better Far 1969.15
Better Get Out of Here 1948.26, 1974.25
Better Late Than Never 1903.06, 1940.16
Better Not Try It 1930.35
Better Off Dead 2000.16
Better Place to Be 1975.05
Better Than a Dream 2001.03
Better Than Broadway 1980.11
Better Times 1922.30, 1927.53
Betty Lee 1924.47
Betty Lou 1930.29
Betty Martin 1890.23
Betty's Advice 1910.21
Betty, be Good 1920.15
Betty, the One Best Bet 1908.15
Between the Devil and the Deep Blue Sea 1942.11,
    1980.10
Between Those Two 1870.38
Between Us All is O'er 1905.46
Between You, Me and the Lamp Post 1940.16
Bevo 1918.21

Beware 1919.29, 1923.37
Beware Brother Beware 1992.03
Beware my hate 1880.24
Beware of an Innocent Maid 1899.29
Beware of Lips That Say, 'Cherie' 1947.13
Beware of Love 1894.08, 1915.33
Beware of the Brigand Bold 1904.03
Beware of the Girl With a Fan 1925.22
Beware of the Rose 1926.09, 1926.35
Beware of the Sirens So Fair 1911.27
Beware you saucy minx 1887.43
Bewitched 1962.17, 1981.16, 1995.12
Bewitched, Bothered and Bewildered 1940.22, 1975.13
Beyond 1999.17
Beyond My Wildest Dreams 1983.01
Beyond the Blue Horizon 1980.08
Beyond the Gates of Paradise 1900.46
Beyond the Sea 2000.07
Beyond the Seas 1895.04
Bhula Weyyanga 1997.14
Bianca 1948.32, 1999.19
Bible Stories 1904.43
Bickering, The 2000.10
Bicycle 1936.03
Bicycle Built for Two 1944.32
Bicycle Built for Two, A 1936.03
Bicycle Girl, The 1895.36
Bicycle Song, The 1964.16
Bid Me Forget 1914.09
Bid Me Goodbye and Go 1889.05
Biddle-be-boo 1919.24
Bidelia 1903.27, 1903.30
Bidin' My Time 1930.31, 1992.02
Bie Mir Bistu Schoen 1990.16
Biff! Bang! 1903.10
Big Ass Rock 2000.15
Big Baby 1979.33
Big Back Yard, The 1945.03, 1947.11
Big Banshee, The 1906.19, 1908.13
Big Beat, The 1974.05
Big Bill 1957.05
Big Black Man 2000.15
Big Bottom Betty 1976.33
Big Boy 1930.24
Big Boy, I Gotta Belong to You 1929.52
Big Brass Band from Brazil, The 1947.20
Big Brass Band, The 1916.07
Big Broad Smile 1942.19
Big Brother 1938.14
Big Brother to Me 1930.05
Big Brown Boo Lo Eyes 1908.22
Big Casino 1921.18
Big Chief Oi, Oi 1908.37
Big Chief Smoke 1908.05
Big City 1949.05, 1982.13
Big Clown Balloons, The 1963.21
Big D 1956.04, 1980.29
Big Department Store, The 1898.56
Big Drum, Little Drum 1919.08
Big Fish, Little Fish 1970.05
Big Four, The 1949.02
Big Future 1972.10
Big Guitar, The 1966.30
Big Hats, The 1908.19
Big Hearted Baby 1928.47
Big Hunk of Love, A 1989.12
Big Indian and Little Maid, The 1904.39
Big Indian and the Little Maid, The 1904.39
Big Indian Chief 1904.04
Big Injun 1905.02
Big Job, A 1993.05
Big Meeting Tonight 1963.13
Big Mole 1949.15, 1972.06
Big Movie Show in the Sky, The 1949.17
Big News! 1998.21
Big Noise from Winnetka 1978.05, 1979.30, 1999.01
Big Offensive 1919.08
Big Old River 1945.08
Big One, A 1965.37
Big Papoose is on the Lose 1930.09
Big Parade, The 1945.09
Big Pound Cake 1902.29
Big Red Shawl, The 1909.10

Big Shoe Act 1888.39
Big Show, The 1918.25
Big Spender 1966.01, 1983.20, 1999.01
Big Time 1956.02, 1974.18
Big Time Buck White Chant 1969.15
Big Time, The 1991.07
Big Town 1944.29
Big Trouble 1967.16
Big, Black Coon, The 1891.14, 1892.06
Big, Black Giant, The 1953.08
Bigger and Better Than Ever 1929.35
Bigger isn't Better 1980.07
Biggest Aspidistra in the World, The 1942.14
Biggest Blame Fool 2000.18
Biggest Thing in My Life, The 1926.04
Bilbao Song, The 1977.08
Bilbo's Song 1966.32
Bile ole possum down 1894.44
Bill 1927.67, 1946.01, 1964.02, 1966.14, 1974.09,
    1983.05, 1986.01, 1994.08
Bill and Coo 1911.08, 1920.37
Bill Bailey 1965.05
Bill Bailey, Won't You Please Come Home 1980.27
Bill of Fare, The 1879.35
Bill of Right, The 1940.21
Bill Robinson Walk 1999.06
Bill Simmons 1906.17
Bill's Bounce 1999.24
Billet Doux, A 1900.47
Billet-Doux, A 1901.21
Billeting of the Hussars, The 1929.05
Billie 1928.31, 1968.07
Billie's Blues 1948.13
Billiken Man, The 1909.11
Bills 1918.42
Billy 1904.33
Billy and Furgie 1880.37
Billy Barlow 1862.01
Billy Baxter's Swing Song 1905.51
Billy Gray, U.S.A., O.K. 1903.04
Billy Joe Ju 1969.03
Billy Jones 1894.50
Billy Nubbs, the Poet 1876.11
Billy of the Olden Days 1897.21
Billy Rose Buys the Metropolitan Opera House!
    1944.29
Billy the Bubbler 1915.29
Billy, You're off Again 1899.19
Billy-A-Dick 1999.24
Bim-Bam-Bom 1971.17
Bimbo 1904.07
Biminy 1924.18, 1925.10
Bing! Bang! Boom 1888.18
Bingen on the Rhine 1871.16
Bingo 1904.07
Bird Ballet, The 1925.25
Bird in a Gilded Cage, A 1980.27
Bird Inside the House 1999.22
Bird of Beauty, The 1862.06
Bird of Paradise 1975.02
Bird of Passage, A 1949.15
Bird Song 1903.36
Bird Talk 1913.33
Bird That Came in Spring, The 1877.25
Bird Upon the Tree 1959.04
Bird Watcher's Song 1947.16
Bird, a Bottle and a Cigarette, A 1898.47
Birdie 1905.36, 1917.03
Birdie, A 1923.47
Birdies 1928.06
Birdies in the Tree, The 1918.02
Birds and Flowers 1872.23
Birds and the Bees, The 1945.03
Birds are Dreaming in the Treetops 1989.10
Birds Fly South, The 1908.43
Birds in the bush 1887.43
Birds in the Sky, The 1984.02
Birds in the Spring 1930.43
Birds in the Trees 1908.25
Birds in the Trees, The 1984.02
Birds of Paradise 1902.22
Birds of Plumage 1923.17
Birds on High 1926.51
Birth of a Chicken, The 1915.16

Bobby and Me 1928.37
Bobby's Nightmare 1928.41
Bobby's Song 2001.01
Bobo's 1977.16
Bodas de Luiz Alonso, Las 1988.15
Body and Soul 1930.32, 1954.11, 1986.02, 1989.02
Body Beautiful, The 1958.01
Body Language 1983.09
Boetie Guitar 1999.12
Boffola 1955.12
Bogie Boo, The 1912.31
Bogie Man, The 1892.29, 1905.17
Boheme, La 1965.30, 1970.01, 1974.19, 1983.03
Bohemia 1900.08, 1903.34, 1912.26, 1916.07
Bohemia Good-Bye 1909.23
Bohemia is the Life for Me 1906.39
Bohemia, Good-Bye 1908.24
Bohemian Artist, The 1899.30
Bohemian Polka 1964.25
Bohmische Polka 1964.25
Bois d'Amour, The 1909.29
Bois de Boulogne, The 1902.20
Bojangles of Harlem 1986.01
Bokhara 1921.06
Bold Banditti, The 1907.59
Bold Brigade, The 1879.15
Bold Dragon, The 1899.06
Bold Dragoon, The 1860.03, 1898.60
Bold Gendarmes' Dance, The 1908.31
Bold Hussars, The 1901.13
Bold Musketeers 1921.15
Bold Pierre 1896.28
Bold Vicious Man 1873.28
Bold-faced ranger 1894.15
Bolerdo d'Amour 1971.05
Bolero 1881.12, 1922.36, 1931.26, 1932.04, 1982.06, 2001.04
Bolero on Rye 1976.09
Bolero, The 1906.07, 1907.07
Bolshie Quartet, The 1924.01
Bom, Bom, Bom 1879.42
Bom-Bom-Beedle-Um-Bo 1924.32
Bombay Bombashay, The 1920.25
Bon Bon Buddie 1908.08
Bon et doux vin de France, Le 1929.11
Bon Jour 1896.28, 1960.20
Bon Jour Monsieur 1897.40
Bon Jour, Marie 1919.21
Bon Soir, Paris 1948.24
Bon Vivant 1964.04
Bon Voyage 1934.36, 1935.03, 1956.15, 1974.06, 1982.22, 1987.15, 1997.10
Bonbonera 1932.19
Bond That Can't be Broken, The 1997.18
Bonds 1970.15
Bonga Boo 1924.30
Bongo on the Congo 1924.08
Bongo, Bongo, Bongo 1947.20
Bongo-Boola 1952.08
Bonita 1927.55
Bonita Cachelti 1905.34
Bonjour Amour 1989.26
Bonjour Follies 1964.22
Bonjour Monsieur 1896.51
Bonjour, Bonsoir 1929.16
Bonjour, General Bombardos 1883.51
Bonne heure, on vous voit mieux, A la 1885.57
Bonne Nuit, Merci 1929.41
Bonnet Shop 1903.33
Bonnie Banks 1939.19
Bonnie Blue Flag 1927.42, 1975.22
Bonnie Briar Bush 1907.14
Bonnie Little Johnnie 1899.12
Bonnie Prince Charlie 1855.01
Bonnie, My Highland Lassie 1908.38
Bons Moments, Les 1970.01
Bonus Blues, The 1922.03
Boo Ra Boo 1902.40, 1908.03
Boo to a Goose 1956.13
Boo-Hoo 1920.12
Boo-Hoo-Hoo 1910.26
Boo-Hoo-Tee-Hee 1908.18
Boo-Ra-Boo 1902.34

Boodle, the Boodle for Me, The 1884.41
Boogie Boo 1910.26
Boogie Boo, The 1909.05
Boogie Shoes 1999.15
Boogie Woogie Bugle Boy 1973.14, 1975.12, 1979.24, 1979.30, 1982.22
Boogie Woogie Bugle Boy of Company B 1999.24
Boogie Woogie Country 1999.24
Boogie-Woogie Bugle Boy 1989.12
Book of Life, The 1972.10
Book Report 1971.11, 1999.03
Book-Maker, The 1892.05
Bookies and Cookies 1925.01
Boola Bola 1912.25
Boola Boo 1917.05
Boola-Boola 1917.17
Boolyvar de Paree, The 1898.63
Boom Chicka Boom 1991.15
Boom Ditty Boom 1971.07
Boom Whee! 1920.45
Boom! 1989.05
Boom, A 1897.52
Boom-Boom 1962.27, 1982.01, 1998.15
Boomerang 1918.35, 1931.31
Boomerang Baby 1967.13, 1968.20
Boomps-a-Daisy 1938.08
Boop-Boop-Poop-a-Doop 1930.09
Boosters 1922.08
Bootblack Quartette 1897.55
Boots 1918.20
Boots and Shoes 1914.32
Boots, The 1990.16
Booze 1973.10
Booze of Auld Lang Syne, The 1923.01
Bored 1969.02
Boring Straight Song 1964.29
Born Again 1963.25, 1979.32
Born All Over Again 1944.27
Born and Bred in Brooklyn 1923.46
Born and Bred in Old Kentucky 1925.01
Born in Puerto Rico 1998.02
Born Lover 1975.06
Born to be Hand-Jive 1972.12
Born to be Together 1990.17
Born to Hand-Jive 1994.07
Borneo 1905.22
Borrow from Me 1912.38
Borscht Belt Buffet 2000.14
Borscht Belt on Broadway 2000.14
Bosom Buddies 1966.10, 1985.19
Bosphorous 1911.12
Boss is Dead, The 1965.30
Boss Tweed 1945.03
Bossa Nova Baby 1989.12
Boston 1931.47
Boston Beguine 1952.09
Boston in the Spring 1938.12
Boston Merger, The 1989.26
Boston Post Road 1928.17
Botany Bay 1886.45, 1886.53
Both Blind and poor dears 1859.14
Both Sides Now 1982.22
Both Sides of the Coin 1985.18
Bottle and a Bird, A 1900.40
Bottle Imp, The 1908.34
Bottle of Canada Dry, A 1925.25, 1925.48
Bottle Song, The 1981.12
Bottle Up a Pretty Girl 1920.22
Bottleneck 1959.11
Bottles 1907.63
Bottom of the Sea, The 1892.29
Bottoms Up 1929.35, 1942.15
Boublitchki 1929.05
Bouboulina 1968.30
Boudior Dolls 1930.06
Bought and Paid For 1914.04
Boukra Fill Mish Mish 1945.17
Boule' Miche 1909.23
Boule' Miche, The 1908.24
Boulevard Glide, The 1909.07
Boulevardiers, The 1904.23
Bounce Me 1926.12
Bounce Me, Brother With a Solid Four 1999.24

Bound No'th Blues 1991.01
Bound to be a Sailor Boy 1866.16, 1867.18
Bounding Brothers of Barbary, The 1891.46
Bouquet in Bloom, A 1894.37
Bouquet of Fond Memories 1929.21
Bouquet of Girls 1922.15
Bouquet, La 1929.16
Bourbon Street Parade 1992.06
Bourgeoise et bourgeois 1877.32
Boutiuque, A la 1884.43
Bow Bow 1938.10
Bow Down Sinners 1936.30
Bow Down! 1895.08
Bow With Air Ceremonious 1899.06
Bow Wow 1870.01
Bow ye Venal Servile Train 1860.03
Bow, Students, Bow! 1882.63
Bow-Legged Sal 1941.12
Bow-Wow 1928.04
Bowed with tribulation 1896.13
Bowery Girls, The 1894.50
Bowery of Today, The 1923.02
Bowery, The 1892.38, 1893.23, 1930.39
Bowl of Roses, A 1907.56
Bowlene 1976.34
Bowler Hat, A 1976.02
Box Office Tells the Story, The 1908.16
Boxing at Shadows 1929.33
Boxing Bout 1930.19
Boy and a Girl, A 1955.14
Boy and Girl 1902.30
Boy and Man 1964.03
Boy for Sale 1963.01
Boy Friend Back Home, The 1929.45
Boy Friend, The 1954.09
Boy from, The 1977.05
Boy Guessed Right the Very First Time, The 1898.46
Boy I Left Behind Me, The 1942.15
Boy I Love, The 1899.19
Boy in the Blue Uniform 1927.03
Boy Like That, A 1957.12, 1977.05
Boy Like You, A 1947.02
Boy Most Likely to Succeed 1956.08
Boy Next Door, The 1989.23, 1999.23
Boy Oh Boy 1976.09
Boy Scouts, The 1913.01
Boy Talk 1965.36
Boy Wanted 1983.06
Boy was Dancing, A 1959.15
Boy With the Fiddle, The 1971.14
Boy With the Violin, The 1913.19
Boy! What Love has Done to Me 1930.31
Boy, a Girl, a Moon, A 1937.06
Boy, I Give You Now 1931.06
Boy, Oh Boy 1980.06
Boys 1913.26
Boys and girls come out to play 1862.02
Boys and Girls Come Out to Play 1971.20
Boys and Girls Like You and Me 1996.04
Boys and Girls of DeVere's, The 1922.43
Boys and the Girls, The 1896.41
Boys Before the Mast, The 1902.21
Boys from the South 1975.04
Boys in Blue 1935.03
Boys in Gray 1927.42
Boys in the Back Room, The 1999.07
Boys in the Backroom, The 1980.29
Boys of the 71st, The 1898.56
Boys of the Empire, The 1898.41
Boys of the Household Brigade 1894.33
Boys of Yankee Land, The 1898.43
Boys Together 1891.14
Boys Who Fight the Flames 1908.09
Boys Will be Boys 1903.02, 1909.07
Boys Will be Boys and Girls Will be Girls 1907.11
Boys, be Proud You're a Usaac 1918.14
Boys, Boys, Boys 1883.04, 1914.06, 1922.18, 1964.44
Boys, The 1985.06
Bracelet Number 1929.28
Bracelets 1927.58
Brad 1946.21
Bradshaw 1901.19
Braes o' Ballachloe 1925.21

Brag and Bluster, The - it's Painful to the Yankee Soul 1912.40
Bragging Song 1921.17
Brahn Boots 1960.17
Braid the raven hair 1885.47, 1885.51
Braid the Raven Hair 1939.15, 1939.17
Brain Wafers 1897.25
Brakeman's Chorus 1888.05
Brand New Day 1979.13
Brand New Day, A 1978.22
Brand New Dress, A 1969.17
Brand New Soldier Tune, A 1912.29
Brand New Start 1994.06
Brand New World 1986.13
Brannigan's Band 1877.05
Bras d'Antonie, Les 1964.39
Brass Band, The 1911.23
Brat, The 1906.15
Brava! Well Done! 1881.36
Brave Blue Coats 1864.12
Brave Deserve the Fair, The 1929.46
Brave Enough for Love 2000.20
Brave Hussar, The 1900.40
Brave Huzzar, The 1914.28
Brave Margot 1958.06
Brave Old City of New York, The 1971.20
Brave Soldier Boy, The 1895.17, 1903.40
Brave Volunteers you must enroll 1864.12
Bravo Antonio! 1917.29
Bravo Bravo 1987.12, 1988.01
Bravo Pour Le Clown 1981.04
Bravo, Bravo 1927.17
Bravo, Bravo, Novelistro 1964.35
Bravo, Giovanni 1962.14
Brazil 1943.02
Brazil Capela 1988.06
Brazilian Jubilee 1915.23
Brazilian Nuts 1942.18
Breachy's Law 1962.14
Bread and Butter and Sugar 1926.02
Bread and Freedom 1986.13
Bread and Gravy 1953.12
Bread Brigade, The 1864.12
Bread, Cheese and Kisses 1897.40, 1917.10
Break into Your Heart 1924.11
Break it Up 1942.29
Break it Up, Cinderella 1940.09
Break That Party 1972.10
Break the News to Mother 1898.61
Break'n th' Rhythm 1929.21
Break-Me-Down, The 1928.34
Break-Neck Quadrille, The 1913.10
Breakaway, The 1908.12
Breakfast 1963.16
Breakfast Dance 1930.06
Breakfast in Bed 1927.01, 1927.68
Breakfast in Harlem 1980.10
Breakin' 'Em Down 1924.27
Breakin' a Leg 1922.22
Breaking into the Movies 1921.17
Breaking the Ice 1947.12
Breaking Up a Rhythm 1933.15
Breath from Bohemia, A 1915.20
Breath of May, The 1894.08
Breathe Soft, Wind of the South 1898.46
Breathing the Air 1974.12
Breeze in the Trees 1919.19
Breeze Kissed Your Hair, The 1931.37
Breeze Off the River 2000.15
Breezes That Blow 1911.05
Breezin' Through Another Day 2000.08
Breezy 1947.20
Brendas 1946.20
Brenton Boat Song 1893.40
Brewster the Millionaire 1907.41
Brickerty-Brackerty-Tootsies 1917.35
Bridal Bevy, The 1914.10
Bridal Chorus 1896.45
Bridal March, The 1887.48
Bridal Moon 1868.03
Bridal Song 1905.53
Bridal Song, The 1895.06
Bridal Veil, The 1887.05, 1920.08

Bride and Groom 1926.36
Bride Bells 1928.37
Bride Sings, The 1967.08
Bride was Dressed in White, The 1928.44
Bride's Song 1903.33
Bride, The 1923.22
Bridegroom and bride 1890.02
Brides and Grooms 1902.03
Bridesmaid's Sextette 1910.21
Bridesmaids 1918.42
Bridesmaids' Chorus 1895.25
Bridge 1908.10
Bridge of Caulaincourt, The 1960.13
Bridge Over the River Kwai 1973.13
Bridge to Nowhere, The 1969.08
Bridget McShane 1921.25
Bridget Salome 1907.24
Brief Encounter 1985.20
Brief Guide to New York, A 1973.08
Brigadoon 1947.07, 1980.26
Brigand Chief 1904.03
Brigands' Chorus, The 1914.09
Bright and Black 1976.11
Bright Champagne 1868.19
Bright College Days 1952.10
Bright Day's Dawning 1916.05
Bright Eyes 1920.33
Bright Lights 1917.01, 1980.15
Bright Morning Star 1915.28
Bright New Day 1993.07
Bright star of love 1898.25
Bright wine and love 1887.43
Bright Young People 1986.19
Brighten Up and be a Little Sunbeam 1948.28
Brightly dawns our wedding day 1885.47, 1885.51
Brighton Beach Rag, The 1912.29
Brindisi 1860.05, 1866.11
Brindle's Farm 1924.21
Bring 'Em Back 1920.39
Bring All the Boys Back Home 1971.18
Bring Along the Camera 1911.11
Bring Along Your Dancing Shoes 1914.22
Bring Back Birdie 1981.07
Bring Back My Blushing Rose 1921.21
Bring Back Nelson Mandela 1988.02
Bring Back That Old Yama Dance to Me 1918.13
Bring Back the Days of Yea and Nay 1987.17
Bring Back Those Wonderful Days 1919.15
Bring Back Tomorrow 1981.14
Bring Back Your Heart to Me 1924.05
Bring Back Your Love 1913.05
Bring Him Home 1987.04, 1997.01, 2000.14
Bring Him My Love Thoughts 1921.14
Bring in 'Da Noise, Bring in 'Da Funk 1996.07
Bring in the prisoner 1896.26
Bring Me a Blonde 1918.14
Bring Me a Radio 1924.32
Bring Me a Rose 1910.05
Bring Me Back My Butterfly 1919.25
Bring Me Back to My Childhood Days 1896.33
Bring Me My Bride 1962.12
Bring Me Roses 1935.19
Bring on the Concubines 1944.16
Bring on the Follies Girls 1931.19
Bring on the Girls 1918.20, 1922.19, 1923.20, 1923.22, 1957.01, 1977.05
Bring on the Men 1997.09
Bring on the Pepper 1922.39
Bring the Brightest of Faces 1888.18
Bring Your Darling Daughter 1961.27
Bringing Up Daughter 1957.14
Brinkley Coon, The 1909.16
Briskly beat the Hollow Drum 1853.01
Britannia Rules the Waves 1928.42, 1937.14
British Maidens 1929.20
British Peer, The 1883.04
British tar is a soaring soul, A 1879.05
British Waiter, The 1884.57
Brittany 1913.20, 1924.32
Briv, A 1970.17
Broad Highway 1924.23
Broad Highway, The 1934.17
Broadcast a Jazz 1924.32

Broadminded 1946.06, 1956.13
Broads Ain't People 1961.21
Broads of Broadway 1926.22
Broadway 1922.03
Broadway at Night 1989.03
Broadway Baby 1971.05, 1977.05
Broadway Battle Cry, The 1924.16
Broadway Beauty Show, The 1897.34
Broadway Belles 1919.13
Broadway Blossom 1945.20
Broadway Blossoms 1958.20, 1958.21
Broadway Blues, The 1920.45
Broadway Boogie Woogie 2001.01
Broadway Butterflies, The 1891.14
Broadway Butterfly 1919.03
Broadway Cabaret, The 1912.02
Broadway Cinderella, A 1920.28
Broadway Coon, The 1899.33
Broadway Favorites 1905.44
Broadway Follies 1981.09
Broadway Girl 1918.13
Broadway Glide, The 1912.38
Broadway in Dahomey 1904.26, 1980.10
Broadway in Paree, A 1914.01
Broadway Indians 1923.38
Broadway isn't Broadway Since They Close at One O'Clock 1917.08
Broadway Lament 1910.10
Broadway Love Song 1949.12
Broadway Mammy 1929.24
Broadway Mammy Blues 1925.20
Broadway Melody 1992.18
Broadway Musical, A 1978.28
Broadway Nights from the Roof Garden 1929.28
Broadway of My Heart, The 1971.09
Broadway Pirates 1921.25
Broadway Reverie 1931.19
Broadway Rhythm 1983.09, 1985.08
Broadway Rose 1923.42
Broadway Sam 1915.12
Broadway School Days 1916.11
Broadway Show, The 1907.42
Broadway Swell and Bowery Bum 1920.27
Broadway Tipperary 1914.34
Broadway to Madrid 1926.23
Broadway Triangle, The 1914.22
Broadway Wedding Bells 1921.27
Broadway Whirl, The 1921.19
Broadway Zoo, The 1962.17
Broadway's Boudoir 1924.33
Broadway's Not a Bad Place After All 1918.19
Broadway, Broadway 1978.28
Broadway, My Street 1971.07
Broadway, My Sweet 1929.27
Broadway, the Heart of the World 1927.46
Broken Blossoms 1919.39
Broken Bus, The 1948.24
Broken Cavalier, The 1884.57
Broken Heart of the Wages of Sin, The 1970.10
Broken Hearted Romeo 1941.07
Broken Hearts 1923.34
Broken Komona, The 1956.08
Broken Nose, The 1871.19
Broken Pianolita, The 1948.24
Broken Rhythm 1926.37
Broken String Blues 1957.09
Broken-Hearted 1927.37
Bronco Busters 1930.31
Bronx Express, The 1927.47
Brook of Haugtussa Cycle, The 1944.21
Brooklyn 1912.44
Brooklyn Baseball Cantata 1940.18, 1942.05
Brooklyn Dodger Strike, The 1981.28
Brooklyn U.S.A. 1945.01
Broom Buy a Broom 1840.03
Broomstick Witches, The 1904.25
Broth of a Boy, A 1914.29
Brother Bill 1903.17
Brother Dear 1877.20
Brother Masons, The 1905.23
Brother new, A 1882.44
Brother the Men 1869.47
Brother Trucker 1978.12

Dreamland Dimple, The 1901.18
Dreamless Rest 1897.32
Dreams 1892.06, 1910.29, 1919.41, 1926.06, 1978.27, 1981.29, 1984.14
Dreams Ago 1950.06
Dreams Come True 1945.20
Dreams Don't Die 1992.05
Dreams for Sale 1922.19, 1926.29
Dreams of Delight! 1921.12
Dreams of the Past 1914.16
Dreams of Tomorrow 1921.38
Dreamy Days 1928.04
Dreamy Eyes 1924.42
Dreamy Florence 1919.30
Dreamy Montmartre 1927.15
Dreary, Dreary, Rainy Days 1925.18
Dremlen Feigl 1989.10
Dresden China Belle, The 1920.29
Dresden China Girl, The 1899.41
Dresden China Love Affair, A 1896.45
Dresden China Plate, The 1908.41
Dresden Northwest Mounted, The 1933.01
Dress to Kill 1999.12
Dress, Dress, Dress 1918.20
Dressed in Your Pajamas in the Grand Salon 1997.06
Dressing 1924.06
Dressing Room Echoes 1906.39
Dressing Them Up 1993.09
Drift With Me 1917.02
Drifting 1978.10
Drifting Along With the Tide 1921.22
Drifting On 1920.01
Drigo Serenade 1915.26
Drigo's Polka 1920.33
Drill of the Coquette Corps 1908.42
Drill of the Seventh 1911.33
Drill Song 1961.11
Drill, The 1925.25
Drill, Ye Tarriers, Drill 1888.32, 1888.34
Drink 1944.29
Drink and be Jolly T-Day 1908.30
Drink and be Merry 1913.27
Drink and Let's be Gay 1900.16
Drink of All Nations, The 1902.43
Drink Out the Cold Drinks 1918.32
Drink Some Tea 1917.30
Drink to the Health of This Great Man 1909.30
Drink Up 1906.39
Drink With Me 1907.57
Drink With Me the Night Away 1907.05
Drink With Me to Days Gone By 1987.04
Drink's Song 1966.15
Drink, Drink, Drink 1913.35, 1980.21
Drinkin' Again 1973.14
Drinkin' Shoes 1982.04
Drinking Again 1975.12
Drinking Chorus 1879.15
Drinking Game, The 1964.03
Drinking Song 1869.47, 1881.22, 1885.70, 1896.44, 1896.50, 1905.40, 1924.45, 1925.32, 1930.40, 1932.05, 1968.22
Drinking Song, A 1971.17
Drinking Song, The 1879.64, 1963.20
Drinks of the Day 1897.32
Drittes Dreigroschen-Finale 1965.04
Driving at Night 1996.04
Droit D'Aimer, Le 1981.04
Drole de musique 1964.39
Drop a Nickel in the Slot 1890.03
Drop for me, A 1859.14
Drop in on Me at Luncheon 1905.03
Drop Me a Line 1920.31
Drop Me Off in Harlem 1981.06, 1997.03
Drop Out 1999.02
Drop That Name 1956.14
Drop Your Kerchief 1929.35
Dropsy Cure Weather 1971.16
Drown in the Mantling Glass 1862.03
Drowsily, Dreamily 1901.27
Drowsy Waters, The 1912.03
Drucilla 1914.21
Drug Store Girls 1931.08
Drugstore Scene 1937.08

Drugstore Song, The 1946.10
Drum Dance 1991.04
Drum Major as is a Drum Major, A 1870.33
Drum Major Jimmy 1894.22
Drummed Out 1908.42
Drummin' 1996.07
Drums in My Heart 1932.03
Drums of Kane 1930.29
Drums of the Nations, The 1912.39
Drums, The 1902.41, 1917.11
Drunken Reel 1980.26
Drunken Sailor, The 1922.21
Dry 2000.08
Dry Bones 1955.13, 1963.10
Dry Goods Clerk, The 1871.12
Dub-Derro 1921.18
DuBarry was a Lady 1939.30
Dubbing, The 1965.34
Dublin Boy 1881.39
Dublin Night 1959.04
Dublin Rag, The 1910.22
Dublin Saunter 1963.30
Dublin Town 1960.12
Dublinola 1924.29
Duc de Rivoli 1937.17
Duchess of Central Park, The 1900.40
Duchess of Dreams, The 1916.20
Duchess of Table D'Hote, The 1908.19
Duck Joke, The 1992.17
Duck-Foot Sue 1876.30
Ducks and Geese 1922.04
Ducks Call it Luck, The 1927.39
Dudah 1869.42
Dude All Dude 1972.18
Dudelet in the Front, The 1898.56
Dudes and the Slipper, The 1888.39
Dudes of New York, The 1896.34
Dudu 2000.14
Due Hut Mir Kainer Nit Gezugt 1970.17
Duel!, A Duel!, A 1980.08
Duel, The 1911.11, 1911.12, 1947.18, 1976.33, 1993.17
Duello, The 1941.12
Duet 1925.48, 1979.10, 1990.06
Duet des Domestiques 1929.14
Duet for One 1976.11
Duet of Rachel and Jacob 1937.01
Duetto d'Amore 1985.16
Duetto mamma mamma che bella cosa 1985.14
Dugan Kid Who Lives in Hogan's Alley, The 1896.38
Duke and Duchess hither wend their way, The 1893.02
Duke's Place 1981.06
Dulcinea 1965.34
Dull and Gay 1930.08, 1931.08
Dumb Girl 1931.05
Dumb Luck 1924.27
Dumbells May be Foolish 1924.42
Dumber They Come They Better I Like 'Em, The 1923.47
Dunnerwetter 1910.22
Duo de la Capa 1917.33
Durch die weiten Felder... 1920.46
Dusky Debutante 1938.04
Dusky Lil from Louisville 1898.67
Dusky Love 1928.10
Dusky Maiden 1902.38
Dusky Salome, The 1908.44
Dust Chasers 1924.05
Dust in Your Eyes 1933.20
Dusty Fustchuns 1970.04
Dutch Cadets, The 1900.59
Dutch Comedians 1898.47
Dutch's Song 1976.04
Dutchess of Central Park, The 1902.09
Dutiful Wife, A 1907.48, 1943.09
Dva Kuma 1977.13
Dwarf's Yodel Song 1979.28
Dying Cowboy, The 1938.12
Dying Flamingo, The 1931.09
Dying Swan, The 1916.10, 1937.06
Dynamic 1954.17

'E Didn't Know Exactly What to Say 1899.19

E Didn't Seem to Know Just Wot to Soy 1900.47
E L 'Omo Mio 1964.03
E Oho Te Whaanau 1972.20
E Pare Ra 1972.20
E Street Shuffle 1979.30
E' Nata 1985.14
E-Gypsy-Ann 1923.11
Each Frenchman is surely aware 1888.07
Each Little Jack 1923.04
Each One has a Way of His Own 1907.33
Each Pearl a Thought 1913.29
Each Tomorrow Morning 1969.05
Eadie was a Lady 1932.25
Eager Beaver 1962.03
Eager Hounds, The 1884.57
Eagle and Me, The 1944.23
Eagle high on cloudland soaring 1894.15
Eagle of Battle, The 1868.02
Eagle Rock, The 1914.16
Earl is Crazy 1971.10
Earl was Ahead 1971.10
Early and late, with soldierly gait 1888.07
Early Hours of the Morn 1914.01
Early in the Morning 1866.18, 1926.12, 1992.03
Early to Bed 1943.07
Earth and Other Minor Things, The 1973.12
Earth and the Sky, The 1953.17
Earth Beat 2001.04
Earth is green and fair to see, The 1881.04
Earth, The 1972.18
Ease Along 1921.27
Ease on Down the Road 1975.01
Easier to Love 1983.19
Easiest Way's Always the Best, The 1882.45
East and West Side 1898.61
East Coast Blues 1931.31
East Indian Maid 1919.43
East Lynne 1923.32
East River Hoe Down 1951.19
East River Rhapsody 1981.14
East Side Lil 1905.41
· East Side Walk 1905.41
East St. Louis Toodle-O 1930.38
East St. Louis Toodle-Oo 1930.13
East St. Louis Toodle-oo 1989.02
East Wind 1931.39
Easter Greetings 1941.13
Easter Parade 1927.47, 1933.22
Eastern and Western Love 1926.42, 1946.03
Eastern Western Love 1987.10
Easy 1955.11, 1972.15, 1978.05
Easy as Life 2000.06
Easy Boss, The 1897.25
Easy Come, Easy Go 1918.06, 1979.12
Easy Dawson March 1905.26
Easy Does It 1949.12
Easy for You 1986.13
Easy Goin' Man 1970.06
Easy Money 1901.17, 1997.08
Easy Pickins 1921.36
Easy Street 1906.06, 1977.06
Easy Terms 1993.07
Easy to be Hard 1968.11, 2000.16
Easy to be Lonely 1971.10
Easy to Love 1948.13, 1980.06, 1987.15
Easy to Remember 1975.13
Easy to Take 1966.05
Eat a Little Something 1962.05
Eat It 1972.18
Eat Your Nice Lily, Unicorn 1963.16
Ebb and Flow 1900.39
Ebeneezer McAfee III 1964.04
Ebenezer Brown 1905.10
Ebenezer Frye 1907.27
Ebony Rag 1922.22
Eccentricities 1907.04, 1938.03
Eccentrique 1873.29, 1897.19
Echo 1892.31, 1897.19, 1907.01, 1920.12, 1946.20
Echo Duet 1918.18
Echo of a Song, The 1937.06
Echo of My Heart 1908.27
Echo Song 1877.43, 1882.28, 1882.75, 1897.21, 1972.03

Felicia 1997.13
Felicida 1964.02
Feline Wisdom 1937.11
Fellatio 101 1976.20
Feller That Looks Like Me, The 1866.22
Fellow Like Me, A 1924.40
Fellow Needs a Girl, A 1947.17
Fellow That Played the Drum, The 1894.21
Fellow Who Might be Galloping, The 1900.51,
 1902.05, 1920.09
Fellow Who Might, The 1900.51, 1902.05
Female Drummer, A 1898.78
Feminine Rhythm 1930.20
Femininity 1958.02
Femme de Chambre, The 1897.37
Femme en naissent, A la 1887.35
Femmes 1935.19
Femmes Fatales 1958.18
Fence, The 1982.23
Fencing 1925.23
Fencing Girl, The 1911.29
Fencing Girls, The 1901.25, 1907.24
Fencing Song 1894.28
Fenian Ball, The 1866.26
Ferban 1915.17
Fergus' Dilemma 1983.01
Feria, La 1934.32
Fermons les yeux 1878.08
Fern wie aus vergang'nen Tagen... 1920.46
Ferry boat, The 1887.04
Festa 1917.23
Festa, La 1955.04
Festival 1972.09
Festival Nights 1919.03
Festival of Mourning 1905.53
Festival, The 1948.24
Festive Continong, The 1896.48
Fetch the Cat 1870.20
Fete a Loulou, La 1959.15
Fetes d'Hebe, Les 1933.24
Fetter Mord'che Heist, Der 1968.22
Feudin' and Fightin' 1944.30
Feuds of a nation's strife, The 1844.01
Feuilles Mortes, Les 1959.15
Feux Follets 1978.26
Fever 1983.20, 1999.09
Few Foolish Ideas, A 1898.61
Few Steps in Front of the Curtain, A 1924.37
Fiasco 1969.17
Fickle Finger of Fate 1964.44
Fickle Weather Vane, The 1906.07
Fiddle about 1972.08
Fiddle About 1993.06
Fiddle and I 1899.11, 1901.04
Fiddle Dee Dee 1901.18, 1937.11
Fiddle-dee-dee March 1900.38
Fiddler and the Fighter, The 1964.21
Fiddler Must be Paid, The 1911.07
Fiddlers' Green, The 1969.08
Fidgety Feet 1926.36, 1990.14
Fie on Goodness! 1960.21, 1980.19
Fie Upon You! Fie! 1885.58
Fie, Upon You! Fie! 1878.02
Field and Forest, The 1903.10
Field of Cloth of Gold, The 1976.08
Fiesta 1927.55, 1932.07
Fiesta En Jalisto 1988.15
Fiesta in Madrid 1935.11, 1969.11
Fiesta in Rio 1975.12
Fifer of the Old Drum Corps, The 1902.42
Fifteen Glorious Years 1965.39
Fifteen Minutes 1906.39
Fifteen Minutes a Day 1924.40, 1933.06
Fifth Avenue 1901.12, 1915.27, 1949.01
Fifth Avenue Brigade, The 1908.18, 1908.19
Fifth Avenue Stride, The 1924.16
Fifth Commandment, The 1931.29
Fifth of Beethoven, A 1977.09, 1999.15
Fifty Great Places All in One Place 1981.08
Fifty Million Years Ago 1969.02
Fifty Percent 1978.27
Fifty Ways to Leave Your Lover 1976.32
Fifty-Fifty 1980.27

Fifty-Fifty I'll Fifty-Fifty With You 1919.32
Fifty-Seven Ways to Catch a Man 1904.18
Fifty-Seventh Street 1982.15
Fig Leaf Number 1920.22
Fig Leaves are Falling, The 1969.01
Figaro's Aria 1990.16
Fight at the Marketplace 1997.16
Fight Over Me 1925.30
Fight Song, The 1962.04
Fight Them Like Your Dear Old Dad 1905.34
Fight, The 1964.32, 1969.11
Fighters of Flames are We 1905.25
Fighting for Pharaoh 1972.13
Fighting Kid, The 1908.28
Fighting Man, A 1900.12
Fighting Regiment, The 1910.23
Fights, The 1959.14
Figlia 1985.16
Fiji 1906.04, 1919.03
Fiji Island 1945.07
Fiji Mick 1888.30
Fiji Serenade 1887.29
Filipino Maid, The 1902.05
Fill ev'ry Glass, for Wine inspires us 1750.01
Fill every glass 1854.06
Fill Every Glass 1957.02
Fill High! Drink Deep! 1895.08
Fill in the Words 1979.04
Fill Up Again Warriors 1899.06
Fill up and let us drink 1880.18
Fill up on Champagne and pate de foie gras 1885.45
Fill Up the Loving Cup 1896.41
Fill Up Your Tankards 1903.07
Fill, my jolly Boys 1859.05
Fille de Levy, La 1935.19
Fille de madame Angot, La 1926.47
Fille de Mme. Angot, La 1877.43
Filles qui, la nuit..., Les 1934.32
Filth 1981.07
Fin de Siecle 1929.31
Final Report 1975.07
Final Selection 1987.05
Final Song 1939.23
Final Storm 1991.05
Finale 1948.30
Finaletto 1923.10, 1945.09, 1947.11, 1982.05
Finally 1983.17
Financial Viking, The 1916.14
Financier's Song 1938.02
Find a Good Time 1925.07
Find Me a Hero 1978.11
Find Me a Primitive Man 1929.45, 1975.22
Find Out What They Like and How They Like It
 1978.09
Find the Queen, Kill the Fox 1997.16, 1998.08
Find the Right Girl 1922.40
Find Your Own Cricket 1970.21
Find Yourself a Man 1964.11
Finders is Keepers and I Found You 1920.36
Finding a Man Ain't Easy 1995.04
Finding Words for Spring 1965.02
Findjan 1960.18
Fine and Dandy 1930.28
Fine Art of Strip Teasing, The 1936.17
Fine Feathers 1917.23, 1921.25, 1923.21, 1926.37
Fine Old English Gentleman, The 1871.16
Fine Romance, A 1986.01
Fine Strawberries 1911.13
Fine White Horse, A 1991.05
Fine, Thank You, Fine 1969.07
Finer Things, The 2000.20
Finery 1932.06
Finesse 1909.14
Fingers and Toes 1978.10
Fini 1953.17
Finish 1907.46
Finish, The 1898.70
Finishing School 1907.46
Finishing the Hat 1984.08
Finnan Haddie 1929.17
Finnegan's Wake 1866.19
Fioretta 1929.08
Fire and Ice 1989.26

Fire and Mist 1923.04
Fire and Sugar 1993.01, 1995.16, 1998.17
Fire Belles 1911.35
Fire Down Below 1979.30
Fire Ladies' Ball, The 1911.35
Fire on Goodness! 1993.11
Fire on the Bayou 1992.06
Fire Water 1907.07
Fire-Fly 1869.40
Firedance 2000.05
Fireflies 1910.10, 1990.17
Firefly 1916.05
Firefly and the Rose, The 1905.55
Firefly Ballet 1900.07
Firefly, The 1905.40, 1923.08
Fireman's Bride, The 1945.03, 1947.11
Fireman's Flame, The 1937.12
Fireman's Parade, The 1905.26
Fireman's Picnic, The 1909.16
Fireworks 1929.49, 1960.23
Fireworks, The 1938.06
First Act, Second Act, Third Act 1917.36
First and Last 1999.15
First and Only 1907.25
First Blossom Ballet, The 1925.52
First Campaign Song 1969.03
First Class Number One Bum 1970.08
First Class Roster, The 1997.06
First Dance, The 1911.39, 1983.03
First Day of May, The 1917.06
First Final 1987.05
First Gray Hair 1911.46
First I met was a young lieutenant, The 1894.28
First Impression 1937.14
First is Last, The 1924.17
First Kiss of Love 1926.24
First Kiss, The 1907.07
First Lady of the Land, The 1931.21, 1976.11
First Lady, The 1962.20
First Letter 1994.05
First Letter Home 1985.12
First Love 1880.69, 1884.57, 1886.50, 1918.35,
 1921.33
First Love Days 1911.35
First Love is the Best Love of All 1915.12
First Man You Remember, The 1990.04
First Mate Martin 1929.31
First Nighters 1917.35
First Nighters, The 1924.07
First Noel, The 1998.19
First Prize at the Fair 1948.14
First Regression 1965.31
First Rose of Summer, The 1919.09
First Spring Day, The 1933.15
First Submarine Boat, The 1902.08
First Thing in the Morning 1932.08
First Thing Monday Mornin' 1970.05
First time at the Looking-Glass, The 1750.01
First Time for Me, The 1930.11
First Time I Spoke of You, The 1957.17
First Time I was Yours in the Dark, The 1950.16
First Time We Rode on the Cars, The 1905.30
First Time, The 1968.30, 1979.30, 1983.14
First We Throw Moe Out 1926.51
First Wench Done Turned White 1896.49
First You Do the Rag, Then You Bombashay, Dat's How
 de Rag-Time Dance is Done 1899.12
First You Dream 1997.07
First you're born 1894.15
First, Last and Only 1926.06
First, The 1981.28
Firulete, El 1993.08
Fischerine du Kleinere 1888.34
Fish Chorus 1907.55
Fisherman's Prayer 1982.04
Fisherwoman's Song, The 1880.18
Fishes in the Sea 1903.22
Fishing 1904.22, 1907.10, 1912.30
Fishing Fleet is Homeward Bound, The 1914.13
Fishing Maidens, The 1894.17
Fishmonger, The 1926.35
Fit as a Fiddle 1985.08
Five Growing Boys 1970.07

Fugue for Four Girls 1970.20
Fugue for Tinhorns 1950.17, 1980.29, 1991.10
Full Blown Roses 1925.31
Full Moon Union, 1st Degree!, The 1893.27
Full Moons, The 1880.09
Fun 1996.08
Fun in the Country 1953.02
Fun Life 1959.12
Fun on a Motor 1902.35
Fun Time 1992.06
Fun to be Fooled 1934.19
Fundamental Character 1948.15
Funeral Dance 1980.26
Funeral Dance, The 1986.03
Funeral Dirge, The 1981.24
Funeral March 1950.10
Funeral March of the Marionettes 1999.06
Funeral Procession 1945.20
Funeral Tango 1972.16
Funky Girl on Motherless Broadway 1971.13
Funky Monkeys 1975.01
Funnies, The 1933.22
Funny 1989.29, 1992.17
Funny Bunny Hug 1944.32
Funny Face 1927.59, 1974.09, 1983.06
Funny Family, The 1902.08
Funny Funeral, A 1965.19
Funny Honey 1975.14
Funny Little Man, A 1897.33, 1900.24
Funny Little Sailor Man 1928.29, 1986.14
Funny Little Something 1918.25
Funny Side of That, The 1897.13, 1930.12
Funny Thing Happened, A 1962.05
Funzapoppin 1949.06
Furs and Frills 1917.21
Further it is from Tipperary, The 1917.29
Furthermore, An' 1928.33
Fussin', Feudin' and Fightin' 1944.30
Future Stars 1942.35
Futurist Girl, The 1914.15
Futurist Rag, The 1920.43
Futurist Twirl, The 1913.26
Futuristic Melody 1921.18
Futuristic Rhythm 1928.50
Fuzzy Wuzzy 1909.05

G-Man 1937.14
G.I. Blues 1989.12
G.I. Jive 1997.05, 1999.24
G.O.P. 1905.03, 1905.33
Ga-Ga 1929.07
Gabey's Comin' 1998.16
Gabie 1899.35, 1902.38, 1963.13
Gabriel 1927.27
Gabriel's Letter 1993.09
Gabrielle 1969.17, 1987.14
Gaby 1916.02
Gaby Glide, The 1911.43, 1912.09
Gaelic Air 1963.30
Gaiety Dance, The 1909.13
Gaiety, The 1965.33
Gaily marches the soldier 1897.17
Gaily Over the Bounding Billows 1904.17
Gaily the Troubadour 1880.24
Gaily, Gaily, Gaily 1890.12
Gaily, the minstrel boy 1859.08
Gainesboro Glide, The 1925.12
Gaite Parisienen 1977.09
Gal With the Hood On 1866.26
Gallagher, Let Her Go 1888.30
Gallant Thunderbomb, The 1881.07, 1882.20
Gallant Would-be-General, A 1900.57
Galli Curci Rag, The 1918.20
Gallo Ciego 1997.13
Gallop, Gallop 1910.09
Gallop, The 1928.48
Gallopin' Dominoes 1926.19
Galloping Cavalree, The 1912.47
Galloping Major 1916.12
Galloping Through the Park 1933.21
Gallous Old Goddess of Greece, The 1910.10
Galop 1904.22
Gamble on Me 1915.12

Gamblers, The 1959.27
Gambling 1929.38
Game of Cards, A 1915.04
Game of Eyes 1914.08
Game of Golf, The 1908.05
Game of Hearts, A 1906.26
Game of Love 1913.24, 1922.18, 1947.04
Game of Love, A 1904.39
Game of Love, The 1901.16, 1956.16
Game of Morra, The 1964.03
Game of Poker, A 1959.27
Game of War, The 1968.24
Game Sports, The 1894.26
Game That Ends With a Kiss, A 1919.02
Game What They're At, The 1877.43
Game, The 1955.08, 1994.01
Games I Play, The 1992.09
Games We Used to Play, The 1904.37
Gamesters and Lawyers are Jugglers alike, The 1750.01
Gang's All Here, The 1931.05
Gangland Chase 1988.20
Gangster Influence, The 1934.06
Gant's Waltz 1978.10
Gantry's Reaction 1970.02
Gap in the Hedge, The 1924.09
Garbage 1969.05
Garcon dansait, Un 1961.25
Garcon, S'il vous plait 1931.48
Garde of Your Dreams, The 1918.19
Garden Gate 1914.18
Garden Guaracha 1970.21
Garden in the Sky 1944.27
Garden in the Sun, A 1970.06
Garden of Beautiful Girls 1928.23
Garden of Birds, The 1914.12
Garden of Dreams 1903.36, 1907.59
Garden of Eden, The 1953.07
Garden of Flowers, The 1912.45
Garden of Girls, The 1912.43
Garden of Kama, The 1923.31
Garden of Love 1923.18, 1924.13
Garden of Love, The 1905.46
Garden of Make Believe 1920.41
Garden of Memories, A 1926.14
Garden of Used to Be, The 1924.32
Garden of Versailles 1947.12
Garden of Yesterday, The 1912.07
Garden of Youth, The 1903.19
Garden Path to Hell, The 1985.18
Garden Sequence 1994.05
Garden That Blooms for You, The 1908.31
Garden, The 1974.23
Gardeners, The 1872.23
Gardens of Paradise 1915.02
Gardiens du palais 1887.35
Garibaldi Band 1919.11
Garlands Bright 1924.45
Garlands Bright With Glowing Flowers 1980.21
Garotin Song 1917.25
Garrison Ball, The 1892.45, 1908.13
Garrotin 1986.17
Garter Song 1867.10, 1869.42
Gary Owen 1978.05
Gary, Indiana 1957.18, 2000.11
Gas Mask 1919.08
Gascony Bred 1984.14
Gashlycrumb Tinies, The 1978.24
Gasman Cometh, The 1966.32
Gasoline Can-Can, The 1985.20
Gassed Last Night 1964.28
Gaston 1994.04
Gastronome, A la 1924.41
Gates of Cairo, The 1920.34
Gates of Heaven, The 1935.04
Gateway of the Temple of Minerva, The 1942.15
Gather Roses While You May 1925.50
Gather the Rose 1927.65
Gather Ye Autographs 1935.14
Gather Ye Rosebuds 1909.19
Gathering of the Clans 1911.44
Gathering of the Clans, The 1910.19
Gathering of the Slaves, The 1917.37
Gathering Shells by the Seashore 1876.14

Gathering Shells on the Seashore 1876.04
Gathering the Myrtle With Mary 1886.44, 1890.06
'Gator and the Coon, The 1905.31
Gaucho Love Song, A 1930.27
Gaudeamus Igitur 1980.21
Gaugin's Shoes 2001.01
Gavotte 1924.45, 1925.31, 1939.30, 1945.14
Gavotte, The 1993.14, 1997.19, 2001.09
Gay and Merry Play, The 1906.40
Gay Bohemi-ah 1895.43
Gay Brazilian 1921.25
Gay Butterfly on the Wheel 1922.15
Gay Butterfly, A 1912.02
Gay Castinets, The 1902.33
Gay Cavalier 1860.05
Gay Cavalier, The 1891.03
Gay Divorcee, The 1904.55
Gay Excursion, A 1913.22
Gay Fleurette 1903.24
Gay Fusilier, The 1907.52
Gay Gendarme, The 1897.37
Gay Georgette 1899.29
Gay Hussar, The 1885.03, 1895.26
Gay Hussars, The 1909.15
Gay Life, The 1914.30
Gay Little Wives 1935.14
Gay Lothario, A 1904.09
Gay New York 1906.10
Gay Nineties 1938.08
Gay Paree 1894.17
Gay Parisienne, The 1896.31
Gay Photographer, The 1880.42, 1882.39
Gay Soldier Boy 1913.21
Gay Soubrettes, The 1898.10
Gay Tom-tit, The 1895.43
Gay Young Farmer, The 1960.17
Gayest Manhattan 1898.01
Gayest Old Sport, The 1897.34
Gayety 1902.02
Gaze on her portrait 1881.04
Gaze on This Face, so Noble 1930.12
Gazooka, The 1936.02, 1936.17
Gee Chee 1926.19
Gee Mom, I Want to Go Home 1943.23
Gee! But This is a Lonesome Town 1908.05
Gee! What a Wonderful Mate You'll Be 1917.16
Gee! Wouldn't That be Great 1904.27
Gee, Ain't I Glad I'm Home 1907.57
Gee, Ain't I Glad I'm Single 1908.38
Gee, But I'd Like to be Bad 1926.29
Gee, But I'd Like to Furnish a Flat for You 1910.16
Gee, But it's Good to be Here 1956.16
Gee, But it's Great to be Alive 1928.37
Gee, But it's Great to be Here 1976.24
Gee, But it's Great to Meet a Girl from Home 1919.40
Gee, But This is a Lonesome Town 1905.55
Gee, But You Look Awfully Good to Me 1908.36
Gee, I Certainly Hate These Trousers 1907.63
Gee, I Wish I had a Girl 1921.20
Gee, I Wish I had Someone to Rock Me in the Cradle of
   Love 1978.21
Gee, I'm Glad I'm No One Else But Me 1971.21
Gee, I'm so Good it's too Bad 1930.06
Gee, Officer Krupke 1957.12, 2001.04
Gee, We Get Along 1925.35
Gee, You Must be in Love 1924.24
Geht's und verkauft's mei G'wand 1964.25
Geisha 1970.21
Geisha are we 1896.27
Geisha's Lament, The 1926.11
Geisha's Life, A 1896.27
Gem of the Orient 1894.22
Gemissante, La 1933.24
Gems of the Night 1912.42
Gen d'Arms Duet 1873.17
Gendarme 1938.07
Gendarme, The 1937.16
Genealogy 1928.36
General Bingham's Squad 1906.22
General Boom 1904.22
General Boomerang 1898.17
General Election 1834.01
General Four Flush 1903.20

General Hard Tack 1904.20
General has relented, The 1897.17
General Jackson had a Snuff-Box 1857.06
General la corvee est faite! 1883.51
General Sir Hugh M. Trenchard 1980.13
General Siss-Boom-ah 1899.31
General Store 1971.21
General's Gone to a Party, The 1933.25
General's Song, The 1940.17, 1969.03
Generalonely 1970.04
Generosity 1888.44
Genevieve 1870.01, 1879.52, 1898.03
Genius from Bethlehem 1997.12
Gentle Annie 1939.21
Gentle Buffoon, The 1974.12
Gentle Faces 1885.64, 1887.13
Gentle Jenny Gray 1862.06
Gentle Lover 1976.03
Gentle Moon 1914.20
Gentle River 1910.04
Gentle Sighs 1971.01
Gentle Zerlina 1864.13
Gentleman Friend 1948.04
Gentleman is a Dope, The 1947.17, 1993.16
Gentleman Jimmy 1959.25
Gentleman of Leisure 1894.06
Gentleman's Gentleman, A 1909.01, 1965.28, 1968.02
Gentleman, Un 1955.14
Gentlemanly Brigands, The 1911.47
Gentlemen 1910.21, 1923.44
Gentlemen Don't Fall Wildly in Love 1959.06
Gentlemen from Ireland, A 1888.15
Gentlemen of Japan 1933.27
Gentlemen of the Press 1906.02, 1930.05, 1957.17
Gentlemen Prefer Blondes 1925.45, 1926.18, 1926.25,
    1949.18, 1995.07
Gentlemen Shoppers 1960.04
Gentlemen, Be Seated 1963.22
Gentlemen, do Not Fight 1886.62
Gentlemen, How Kind 1978.07
Gently 1911.11
Gently the Breeze of Summer 1902.18
Gently, gently, evidently, we are safe so far 1884.09
Genuine Plastic 1972.07
George and Mary 1930.18, 1930.33
George L. 1966.18
Georgia Land 1912.14
Georgia Rose 1921.26
Georgia Shows 'Em How 1975.09
Georgianna Dunn 1906.13
Georgie 1891.39, 1923.07
Georgy 1970.03
Geraniums in the Winder 1945.05
German 5th, The 1877.05
German Cooking 1913.18
German Prince May Wed Me Since, A 1903.21
German Singing Society, The 1898.08
German Swell 1892.31
German Swell, The 1888.30
German Troubles 1894.17
German Warble 1890.29
Germans at the Spa, The 1982.09
Gershwiana 1932.04
Gertie, the Stool Pigeon's Daughter 1942.05
Gertrude Hoffmann Glide, The 1912.43
Geshray of de Vilde Katchke 1951.21
Gesticulate 1953.16, 1978.03
Gesundheit 1892.31
Get a Girlie 1916.23
Get a Load of That 1947.02
Get a Load of This 1926.39
Get a Move On 1913.04
Get Away Boy 1992.08
Get Away for a Day in the Country 1947.16
Get Away from it All 1935.12
Get Away from My Window 1929.18
Get Away, I'm a Married Man 1911.39
Get Away, Young Man 1943.07
Get Back 1974.24, 1977.10
Get Down 1969.15
Get Down Brother, Get Down 1979.32
Get Happy 1930.06, 1951.15, 1984.06
Get Here 1995.12

Get Him on a Moonlight Night 1923.04
Get Him Up 1919.19
Get Hot Foot 1933.16
Get in a Bathing Suit 1923.21
Get Me on That Boat 1980.17
Get Me Out 1952.13
Get Me to the Church on Time 1956.01, 1974.22,
    1993.18
Get Next to the Man With a Pull 1901.16
Get on the Merry Go Round 1908.28
Get on With It 1988.15
Get Out and Get Under 1913.30
Get Out of Town 1938.13
Get Ready 1997.21
Get Ready, Eddie 1982.10
Get Rich Quick Wallingford 1912.29
Get the Hook 1911.17
Get the Lady Dressed 1987.12
Get the Money 1905.48
Get Them All Over at Once 1924.31
Get Together 1923.10, 1983.18
Get Up Jack, John Sit Down 1893.46
Get Up on a New Routine 1929.19
Get Up, Jack; John, Sit Down 1885.49
Get Yer Program for de Big Fight 1943.24
Get Your Act Together 1979.32
Get Your Man 1928.14
Get Your Partner for the Barn Dance 1908.27
Get Your Woman 1925.16
Get Yourself a Geisha 1935.12
Gethsemane 1971.12, 1992.12
Gettin' a Man 1959.27
Gettin' Back to Me 1970.03
Gettin' Off 1930.29
Gettin' Ready Rag 1998.01
Gettin' to the Top 1979.15
Gettin' Together 1929.21
Gettin' Up Mornin' 1931.11
Getting Better 1974.24
Getting in the Lifeboat 1997.06
Getting into the Talkies 1929.29
Getting Married Today 1970.13, 1977.05
Getting Oriental Over You 1944.15
Getting Out of Town 1980.20
Getting Tall 1982.09
Getting the Beautiful Girls 1928.23
Getting to Know You 1951.12, 1963.07
Gevald 1968.22
Gevald Aria 1968.22
Ghetto Glide, The 1912.36
Ghetto Life 1972.13
Ghost Ensemble 1923.39
Ghost of a Coon, The 1899.33
Ghost of Deacon Brown, The 1907.22
Ghost of Kelly, The 1910.19
Ghost of Little Egypt, The 1931.34
Ghost of Old Black Joe 1919.26
Ghost of Old Black Joe, The 1928.09
Ghost of the Ukelele, The 1916.23
Ghost Quintette 1912.26
Ghost Recitative 1923.39
Ghost That Never Walked, The 1904.15
Ghost Town 1934.40
Ghosties and Ghoulies and Things That Go Bump in
    the Night 1989.23
Ghostly Vengeance, We Invoke Thee 1890.03
Ghosts 1917.12
Gianetta 1864.22
Gianina 1919.35
Giannina Mia 1912.46
Giants in the Sky 1987.18
Giava, La 1935.02
Gibson Bathing Girls, The 1907.24
Gibson Coon, The 1908.22
Gibson Girl, The 1906.29, 1906.45
Giddy Up, Giddy Up, Dearie 1913.19
Giddyup Back 1930.28
Gideon Briggs, I Love You 1960.05
Gift Today, A 1962.05
Gigi 1973.12
Gigolette 1925.42
Gigolo 1926.13, 1927.50
Gilbert & Sullivan Blues, The 1945.08

Gilbert and Filbert 1914.18, 1975.22
Gilding the Guild 1925.17
Gilet Raye 1961.25
Gimme Love 1993.09
Gimme Mick 1979.19
Gimme That Old Time Religion 1989.12
Gimme the Shimmy 1950.12
Gimmie a Pigfoot 1975.20, 1980.10
Gimmie Some 1964.32
Gimmie This - Gimme This - Gimme That 1919.19
Gin 2000.08
Gin Rummy, I Love You 1942.19
Gin-Gin-Ginger Boy 1905.56
Gina 1941.01
Ginette 1928.07
Ginger 1912.45, 1915.17, 1917.35, 1922.18, 1923.37
Ginger Brown 1980.10
Ginger Cake and Frosted Cake 1921.20
Gingerbread Bcy, The 1903.27
Gingerbread Doll, The 1898.63
Gingerbrown 1923.39
Gingerena 1923.11
Gingham and Yarn 1986.16
Gingham Girl 1922.28
Gingham Girl, A 1922.28
Gip-Gip 1927.47
Gipsy Song 1897.40, 1917.10
Gipsy Warned Me, The 1922.05
Girl 'n' Girls 'n' Girls 1956.08
Girl and the Gum Tree, The 1888.15
Girl at the Helm, The 1905.03
Girl Behind the Gun, The 1918.28
Girl Behind the Man Behind the Gun, The 1908.03
Girl Belongs to You 1920.19
Girl by the Saskatchewan, The 1911.11
Girl for Each Month of the Year, A 1915.16
Girl for Me, The 1917.31
Girl Friend of the Whirling Dervish, The 1990.09
Girl Friend, The 1926.07, 1974.09, 1975.13
Girl Friends 1970.17
Girl from Broadway, The 1907.04
Girl from Casimo 1923.05
Girl from Everywhere, A 1906.29
Girl from Gay Paree, The 1895.34
Girl from Mars, The 1902.27
Girl from Paree, A 1915.20
Girl from Paris, The 1896.48, 1898.10
Girl from Rector's, The 1917.08
Girl from the Golden West, A 1922.23
Girl from Utah 1914.18
Girl Gets Around, The 1998.13
Girl has a Sailor in Every Port, A 1921.34
Girl He Couldn't Kiss, The 1914.09
Girl He Left Behind Him, The 1904.05
Girl I Can't Forget, The 1912.42, 1918.15
Girl I Knew, The 1909.03
Girl I Know, A 1904.42, 1907.16
Girl I Left in Boston Town, The 1905.20
Girl I Marry, The 1922.01
Girl I Meant to Be, The 1991.05
Girl I Might Have Been, The 1929.20
Girl I Never Met, The 1920.36
Girl I Used to Know, The 1904.02
Girl I Want to Call Wife 1919.33
Girl I Would Have Left Behind, The 1894.51
Girl I'll Call My Sweetheart Must Look Like You, The
    1912.06
Girl I'm Gonna Marry, The 1984.15
Girl I've Never Met, The 1923.27
Girl in Blue, The 1903.15
Girl in Every Port 1919.03
Girl in His Arms, The 1958.20
Girl in Pink, The 1911.24
Girl in the Baby-Blue Tights, The 1906.29
Girl in the Clogs and Shawl, The 1914.18
Girl in the Gingham Gown, The 1913.22
Girl in the Mirror, The 1968.13
Girl in the Show, The 1961.01
Girl in the Valley, A 1991.05
Girl in the White Silk Dress, The 1898.41
Girl in the Window, The 1981.14
Girl in Your Arms 1926.03
Girl in Your Arms, A 1921.07

Let's Get Together 1986.02
Let's Give a Cheer 1928.25
Let's Go 1918.09, 1919.14, 1919.40, 1965.29
Let's Go and Sit on the Piazza 1907.46
Let's Go Back to the Waltz 1962.20
Let's Go Down to the Shop 1918.11
Let's Go Eat Worms in the Garden 1930.28
Let's Go Flying 1991.07
Let's Go Home 1969.17, 1991.15
Let's Go Lovin' 1932.13
Let's Go Out in the Open Air 1931.21
Let's Go to Fairyland 1919.22
Let's Go to Town 1928.10
Let's Go too Far 1944.15
Let's Have a Good Time 1924.13, 1925.35
Let's Have a Love Affair 1926.42
Let's Have a Party 1950.06
Let's Have a Rattling Good Time 1920.47
Let's Have Another Cup of Coffee 1932.05
Let's Have Lunch 1994.10
Let's Hear it for Me 1977.09
Let's Hear it for the Boy 1998.13
Let's Hold Hands 1934.40
Let's Improvise 1961.26
Let's Keep it That Way 1943.20
Let's Kiss and Make Up 1922.41, 1927.59
Let's Laugh and be Merry 1927.43
Let's Make a Little Home for the Old Folks 1887.02
Let's Make a Night of It 1917.06
Let's Make Hey, Hey While the Sun is Shinin' 1929.52
Let's Make it a Night 1980.06
Let's Make it Forever 1952.13
Let's Make Love 1908.37
Let's Make Memories Tonight 1939.24
Let's Make Up 1921.13
Let's Marry 1920.01
Let's Merge 1929.44
Let's Misbehave 1998.05
Let's Not Get Married 1922.33
Let's Not Have a Kissless Day 1916.21
Let's Not Talk About It 1988.10
Let's Not Talk About Love 1941.08
Let's Not Waste a Moment 1961.20
Let's Play Hookey 1922.26
Let's Play Hookie 1918.18
Let's Pretend 1908.07, 1919.37, 1920.21, 1921.06, 1927.20
Let's Pretend We're Free 1920.15
Let's Put it to Music 1938.07
Let's Quietly Steal Away 1885.58, 1888.13, 1896.35
Let's Raise Hell 1931.31
Let's Say Good Night Till it's Morning 1925.33
Let's Say Goodbye 1986.19
Let's Say Goodnight With a Dance 1941.11
Let's scuttle 1887.43
Let's See What Happens 1968.02
Let's Sing Yiddish 1966.21
Let's Sit and Talk About You 1928.50
Let's Steal a Tune from Offenbach 1940.21
Let's Step Out 1929.45
Let's Stroll Along and Sing a Song 1927.04
Let's Swing It 1935.04
Let's Take a Walk Around the Block 1934.19
Let's Take Advantage of Now 1934.35
Let's Take an Old-Fashioned Walk 1907.20, 1949.08
Let's Take Him Home in Triumph 1911.40
Let's take this book before us 1885.28
Let's Talk About the Weather 1936.01
Let's Talk Dirty to the Animals 1979.19
Let's Twist Again 1977.10
Let's Wander Off Nowhere 1907.44
Let's Work Together 1988.09
Let's You and I Just Say Goodbye 1923.46, 1982.05
Let-A-Go Your Heart 1961.07
Letter Boxes Just Placed in New York 1917.03
Letter Chansonette 1904.30
Letter Duet 1916.01, 1930.03, 1952.15
Letter for Roxane, A 1993.17
Letter from Klemnacht 1982.18
Letter from Papa, The 1898.73
Letter Song 1912.27, 1919.41, 1926.41, 1929.39, 1930.03, 1930.15, 1991.05
Letter Song, The 1909.22, 1912.17, 1925.07, 1947.06

Letter to His Dad, A 1891.02
Letter to the Children 1982.18
Letter to the Governor 1998.21
Letter to the President 1935.03
Letter Trio 1916.21
Letter Writing Song 1903.37
Letter You Shouldn't Have Sent, The 1911.25
Letter, A 1970.17
Letter, The 1880.46, 1909.22, 1940.08, 1948.23, 1956.04, 1979.10, 1980.29, 1993.17
Letters 1904.24, 1908.17, 1965.02
Letters from Home 1909.23
Letters That Never Were Written, The 1912.37
Letting Go 1997.09
Levee Along Broadway, The 1915.17
Levee Ladies 1937.09
Levee Land 1922.18
Levee Lou 1928.09
Levi is a Grand Old Name 1913.30
Li'l Augie is a Natural Man 1946.08
Li'l Gal 1930.16
Liable to Catch On 1940.12
Liar's Song, The 1950.10
Liasons 1973.04
Libby 1922.28
Libertad 1861.03
Libertango 1997.13
Liberty 1925.21
Liberty Bell 1918.10
Liberty Girl, The 1900.59
Liberty Hall 1899.19, 1912.15
Liberty Tango 1993.08
Lichtenburg 1950.15
'Licious Meal, A 1876.30
Lick, and a Riff, and a Slow Bounce, A 1943.16
Licorice Lize 1899.29
Lid Fun Der Goldener Paveh, Das 1968.22
Lid Fun Titanic 1998.11
Lida Rose 1957.18, 2000.11
Lido Shores 1929.22
Lido, The 1928.42
Liebchen, mich reisst es 1984.05
Liebe, Liebe Freundlin 1870.27
Lieben Dich 1968.06
Lieber Augustin 1913.23
Liebeslied 1976.10
Liebeslied/Love Song 1965.04
Liebestraum 1924.32
Lied Ist Aus, Das 1968.20
Lied von der Unzulanglichkeit menschichen Strebens, Das 1965.04
Lieutenants of the Lord 1977.08
Life 1972.19
Life All Free from Care 1904.37
Life and Love 1919.01
Life as a Twosome 1928.17, 1928.40, 1928.45
Life Begins 1934.19
Life Begins at City Hall 1934.19
Life Begins at Sweet Sixteen 1935.18
Life Can be Beautiful 1965.01
Life Can be Funny 1973.02
Life Could be a Dream 1982.22
Life Could be so Beautiful 1935.03
Life Does a Man a Favor When it Gives Him Simple Joys 1958.02
Life Does a Man a Favor When it Leads Him Down to the Sea 1958.02
Life Does a Man a Favor When it Puts Him in Paree 1958.02
Life Goes On 1981.16
Life has Just Begun 1915.20
Life in Kansas 1903.03, 1904.13, 1904.44
Life in the Country 1910.04
Life in the Morning 1929.41
Life in the Old Dog Yet 1918.28
Life in the Shop 1966.21
Life in Town 1924.30
Life Is 1968.30, 1983.14
Life is a Carousal 1920.29
Life is a Dance 1983.09
Life is a Dirty Business 1946.18
Life is a Gamble 1921.34
Life is a Game of Bluff 1916.19

Life is a Game of Chance 1912.43
Life is a Game of Checkers 1909.10
Life is a Garden 1914.28
Life is a One-Way Street 1969.14
Life is a Revel 1901.09
Life is a Riddle 1911.36
Life is a See-Saw 1906.44, 1907.59
Life is a Toyshop 1899.25
Life is a Woman 1978.18
Life is Ahead of Me 1987.12
Life is All Sunshine With You 1921.11
Life is But Short at Best 1897.17
Life is Happiness Indeed 1974.06, 1982.20, 1997.10
Life is Just a Bowl of Cherries 1931.30, 1974.26, 1984.06, 1986.06, 1999.01
Life is Just a Joke 1914.33
Life is Just a Merry-Go-Round 1910.17
Life is Like a Punch and Judy Show 1920.36
Life is Like a Toy Balloon 1925.47
Life is Like a Train 1978.02
Life is Lonely 1914.09
Life is Love 1929.02
Life is Love and Laughter 1908.06
Life is Not an Airy Bubble 1903.40
Life is Short, My Dear Friends 1905.46
Life is so Peculiar 1992.03
Life is Such a Stupid Bore 1892.20
Life is too Short 1964.35
Life is too Short to be Wasting Your Time 1904.18
Life is What We Make It 1898.01
Life is What We Make it After All 1910.13
Life itself is at the best 1844.01
Life of a Bold Dragoon, The 1891.46
Life of a Bold Free Lance, The 1903.37
Life of a Nurse, The 1929.07
Life of a Rose, The 1923.17, 1923.18
Life of a Rover, The 1892.52
Life of a Woman, The 1972.07
Life of Love, The 1905.20
Life of Sin 1934.40
Life of the Party, The 1925.47, 1968.01
Life on the Stage 1905.22
Life Oriental 1911.03
Life seems only sunshine 1889.10
Life Support 1996.09
Life Upon the Wicked Stage 1927.67, 1946.01, 1966.14, 1983.05, 1994.08
Life was Pie for the Pioneer 1940.10
Life was Worth While 1920.24
Life Wins 1972.25
Life With Father 1942.15
Life With Harold 2000.15
Life With Rocky, A 1945.20
Life's a Bubble 1895.44
Life's a Bumper 1853.01
Life's a Dance 1917.02, 1937.15
Life's a Dress Parade 1914.01
Life's a Funny Present 1944.27
Life's a Funny Proposition 1904.42, 1982.05
Life's a Game at Best 1917.07
Life's a Game of Cards 1894.31
Life's a Holiday 1970.03
Life's a Masquerade 1905.29
Life's a Race 1919.22
Life's a Tale 1917.20
Life's Highway 1908.33
Life, long life 1840.03
Life, Unbar the Door 1933.24
Lifeline 1976.16, 1979.32
Lifetime Love, A 1964.18
Liffey Waltz, The 1959.04
Lift 'Em Up and Put 'Em Down 1943.24
Lift Him Up 1988.05
Lift Me Up 1988.05
Lift the Cup 1902.21
Lift the Wings 1996.12, 2000.05
Lift Your Eyes to Mine 1916.01
Lift Your Voice Like a Trumpet 1987.17
Liftoff to Love/Ripoff of Love 1991.02
Light 2001.06
Light at the End of the Tunnel 1987.05
Light Fantastic, The 1951.10
Light is My Heart 1910.05

Love is Blind 1890.26, 1992.09
Love is Coming Back 1975.04
Love is Divine 1891.20
Love is Elusive 1904.09, 1908.17
Love is Enough 1925.21
Love is Good for You 1962.02
Love is Hell 1958.02
Love is Here to Stay 1999.10
Love is in the Air 1925.14, 1977.05
Love is Just a Fairy Tale 1918.02
Love is Just Around the Corner 1986.06
Love is Just the Same 1902.15
Love is Just the Same Old Game in Every Land 1913.16
Love is King 1904.34, 1908.26, 1922.17
Love is Like a Blushing Rose 1927.05
Love is Like a Butterfly 1915.04
Love is Like a Cigarette 1908.24, 1909.23, 1911.31
Love is Like a Dainty Flower 1895.25
Love is Like a Firefly 1912.46, 1924.09
Love is Like a Little Rubber Band 1911.32
Love is Like a Pinwheel 1924.13
Love is Like a Red, Red Rose 1910.25
Love is Like a Violin 1914.04
Love is Like That 1928.46, 1930.18
Love is Like the Rose 1911.37
Love is Lord 1881.16
Love is Lost 1892.20
Love is Lost, Love is Gone 1977.01
Love is Love Where the Cherry Blossoms Fall 1919.04
Love is Made of Smiles and Tears 1881.04
Love is Merest Folly 1899.34
Love is My Enemy 1945.04
Love is My Friend 1940.22
Love is My Inspiration 1932.18
Love is never blind! 1882.60
Love is Not for a Day 1907.13, 1925.02
Love is Not for a Daytime 1893.16
Love is Not Love 1973.07
Love is Only What You Made, Love 1934.43
Love is Queen of the Sea 1902.21
Love is Quite a Simple Thing 1928.29, 1986.14
Love is Simply Heavenly 1957.09
Love is Spring 1894.45
Love is Such a Cheat 1943.14
Love is Such a Funny Little Feeling 1913.19
Love is Sweeping the Country 1931.48
Love is the Best of All 1915.24
Love is the Bunk 1923.42
Love is the Funniest Thing 1954.01
Love is the Joy of Living 1912.37
Love is the Mountain 1928.47
Love is the Prize 1976.01
Love is the Queen of the Sea 1902.21
Love is the Reason 1915.04, 1951.14
Love is the Sovereign of My Heart 1947.14
Love is the Sun 1928.12
Love is the Tenderest of Themes 1896.45
Love is the Theme of My Dream 1911.30
Love is to All a Dainty Dream 1895.25
Love is Trouble 1952.15
Love is Tyrant so I Bid You Beware 1899.34
Love is Very Different 1917.25
Love is Very Wonderful 1919.22
Love is Victor 1908.03
Love is What I Never Knew 1956.07
Love is Where You Find It 1985.08
Love isn't Everything 1966.29
Love it Hurts so Good 1950.02
Love Land 1913.25
Love Lasts a Day 1926.31
Love laughs at locksmiths 1859.12
Love Laughs at Locksmiths 1904.05
Love Let Me Know 1961.21
Love Letter to Manhattan 1950.19
Love Letters 1899.15, 1899.25, 1916.12, 1929.46
Love Life of a Gondolier, The 1966.03
Love Light in Your Eyes, The 1900.12
Love Like Ours, A 1935.19
Love Lives On 1932.10
Love Long 1947.14
Love Look Away 1958.19
Love Lorn Lilly, The 1900.07
Love Lorn Lobster 1897.09

Love Lost and Found 1879.15
Love Love Love 1947.19
Love Love You Baby 1981.29
Love Lurks Around unknown 1883.66
Love Lust Poem 1976.27
Love Makes Such Fools of Us All 1980.07
Love Makes the World Go 1962.03
Love Makes the World Go Round 1906.44, 1909.17, 1919.35, 1937.02, 1961.10, 1986.12, 2000.16
Love Makes the World Go Round, Boys 1896.28
Love Maketh the Heart a Garden Fair 1907.51
Love Match Test 1889.41
Love May be a Mystery 1916.01
Love May Come Again 1894.08
Love May Come and Love May Go 1902.04
Love Me 1910.26, 1921.08, 1922.44, 1926.46, 1934.27, 1971.18
Love Me and the World is Mine 1905.47
Love Me as You Used to Do 1907.04
Love Me at Twilight 1916.09
Love Me Baby Mine 1909.10
Love Me Best of All 1917.09
Love Me for Old Love's Sake 1894.37
Love Me Forever 1922.42, 1931.40
Love Me in a Viennese Melody 1913.30
Love Me in the Spring 1918.34
Love Me in the Winter 1906.50
Love Me Just a Little Bit 1916.22
Love Me Just Because 1909.02
Love Me Just for Me 1998.19
Love Me Just Like Romeo Loved His Juliet 1909.18
Love Me Like a Real, Real Man 1912.39
Love Me Little, Love Me Long 1891.39, 1902.07
Love Me Lize 1901.04
Love Me Love 1896.51
Love Me More, Love Me Less 1932.08
Love Me or Leave Me 1928.47, 1930.08, 1931.08, 1975.22, 1979.05
Love Me Over Dearie 1911.12
Love Me Tender 1982.22, 1989.12
Love Me Tomorrow 1940.17
Love Me Tonight 1920.32, 1925.32, 1975.13
Love Me While the Lovin' is Good 1913.18
Love Me While the Snow Flakes Fall 1920.33
Love Me While You're Gone 1925.18
Love Me With All Your Heart 1976.32
Love Me, Don't You? 1926.34
Love Me, Honey, Do 1896.02
Love Me, Love Me, Won't You? 1913.33
Love Me, Love My Dog 1905.57, 1915.05, 1949.17
Love Me, Sweetheart Mine 1920.11
Love Me/Don't 1995.03
Love Mill, The 1918.04
Love Mississippi 1972.14
Love Monopoly, The 1916.19
Love Moon 1914.23
Love Must be Blind 1904.37
Love Ne'er Came Nigh' 1894.45
Love Nest, The 1920.38
Love Never Changes 1920.07
Love Never Dies 1911.44
Love Never Goes Away 1982.14
Love Never Went to College 1939.27, 1975.13
Love of a Prince, The 1869.14
Love of Golden Years 1970.18
Love of Long Ago 1922.34
Love of Mine 1919.04
Love of My Life, The 1947.07, 1980.26
Love of the Lorelei, The 1914.30
Love of the Shamrock, The 1879.63
Love or Money 1973.02
Love or Reason 1945.08
Love Parade, The 1931.37
Love Pas de Deux 1969.04
Love Potion #9 1995.03
Love Potion, The 1932.10
Love Power 1972.13
Love Reigns! 1886.15
Love Remains the Same 1896.11
Love Revolution 1977.04
Love Rules the World 1926.24
Love Serves in a Candy Store 1879.03
Love shall guide me 1879.38

Love Sneaks Up on You 1955.10
Love Song 1885.65, 1948.25, 1966.19, 1969.02, 1972.22, 1989.24
Love Song of Montosol 1886.43
Love Song of the Espada 1893.16
Love Song of Today, The 1923.34
Love Song of Yesterday, The 1923.34
Love Song, The 1925.02
Love Songs are Made in the Night 1943.05
Love Spans the World 1922.05
Love Spats 1912.33
Love Spell, The 1913.10
Love Stolen 1975.18, 1976.31
Love Story 1973.17
Love Swept Like a Storm 1952.13
Love Test, The 1922.11
Love That is True 1897.37
Love That Man 1950.19
Love That's Sincere 1911.36
Love the Magician 1896.10
Love the Wife of Your Neighbor 1922.35
Love the World Over is Much the Same 1913.14
Love Thought Garden 1927.45
Love Thoughts 1926.30
Love Through the Ages 1923.22
Love Time 1909.05, 1921.35
Love to Love You Baby 1982.22
Love to Your Heart's Desire 1982.02
Love Today 1923.42
Love Train 1997.21
Love Tunes 1922.23
Love Turned the Light Out 1940.17
Love Unconquerable 1988.05
Love Under the Republicans (or Democrats) 1973.08
Love Up a Tree 1908.13
Love Was 1966.30
Love was Just a Game 1975.23
Love Waves 1911.40
Love Where are You Now 1932.19
Love While You May 1922.40
Love Will Always be the Same 1944.20
Love Will Always Find a Way 1921.06
Love Will Bring You Happiness 1923.11
Love Will Call 1920.25
Love Will Conquer All 1969.04, 1980.01
Love Will Find a Way 1918.27, 1921.16, 1952.08, 1976.04, 1990.09
Love Will Find Out the Way 1959.06
Love Will Find the Way 1890.26
Love Will Find You 1920.09, 1934.29
Love Will Find You Some Day 1925.02
Love will guide me 1887.40
Love Will Keep Us Young 1925.44
Love Will Make or Break a Man 1909.26
Love Will See Us Through 1971.05
Love Will Win 1912.26
Love with doubt can never dwell 1881.04
Love Won't Take No for an Answer 1997.18
Love! Love! 1896.27
Love's a Game 1920.09
Love's a Most Exacting Master 1894.47
Love's a Race 1909.21
Love's a Riddle 1939.29
Love's Advent 1901.18
Love's Agony 1928.04
Love's Alphabet 1912.37
Love's Answer 1888.05
Love's Art 1923.37
Love's Awakening 1915.04
Love's Bouquet 1908.27
Love's Call 1926.15
Love's Charming Art 1911.32
Love's Conquests 1911.46
Love's Corporation 1922.24
Love's Cruel Dart 1866.07
Love's Dear Eyes 1894.07
Love's Dream 1888.43
Love's Dream After the Ball 1895.27
Love's Dream is O'er 1897.19
Love's Dream is Over 1908.42
Love's Eternal Song 1907.08
Love's Ever New 1918.11
Love's Fairy Tales 1913.02

Many a New Day 1943.04
Many Moons Ago 1959.26
Many the Beasts 1972.23
Many Things that Ought Not to Be 1876.30
Many Ways to Skin a Cat 1964.04
Many Years Ago 1899.01
Many Years Ago I Strode 1902.25
Many years ago, when I was young and charming, A 1879.05
Many Young Men from Now 1968.23
Many, Many Ways to Say Good-By 1904.53
Manzanillo, The 1894.47
Maori 1908.08
Map of Your Heart, The 1999.22
Marabella 1947.19
Maracatu 1950.07
Marathon 1972.16
Marathon Dance, The 1945.20
Marathoners, The 1945.20
Marce du Biable 1880.24
Marceline's Meat Sauce 1907.59
Marcelle 1920.22
March Ahead 1977.08
March Gypsies 1929.04
March No. 1918.35
March of Foreign Commissioners 1910.21
March of the 'Frisco Chinks 1907.16
March of the Allies, The 1900.42
March of the Amazons 1866.18
March of the Bridegrooms 1913.10
March of the City Troops 1897.55
March of the Continentals, The 1917.13
March of the Dwarfs 1944.21
March of the Enchantress 1917.35
March of the Falsettos 1992.09
March of the Flags 1904.15
March of the Frisco Chinks 1904.42
March of the Gladiators 1920.10
March of the Gods, The 1910.10
March of the Guards 1950.10
March of the Heroes 1902.06
March of the King's Amazons 1909.26
March of the Militant Suffragettes 1912.40
March of the Musketeers 1928.12, 1984.14
March of the New York Dailies 1898.01
March of the Newspapers 1897.14
March of the Plumbers 1888.44
March of the Rangers 1927.08
March of the Rice and Old Shoes 1930.14
March of the Royal Amazons 1896.35
March of the Royal Siamese Children 1951.12
March of the States, The 1915.25
March of the Toreadors 1911.18
March of the Toys 1905.55, 1917.26, 1924.18, 1929.48
March of the Trollgers 1944.21
March of the Watch 1893.40
March of the Winkies 1997.11
March of the Wooden Soldiers 1979.33
March of the Yuppies 1985.15
March of Time, The 1930.22
March On 1905.56, 1925.02, 1925.06
March on for Tennessee 1952.15
March On! 1930.10
March to the Gallows 1989.24
March to Zion, The 1937.01
March With Me 1924.01, 1925.42, 1928.02
March, March, March 1978.22
Marche de menilmontant, La 1947.05
Marches des Pompiers 1916.07
Marching 1908.17
Marching Away 1897.40, 1917.10
Marching By 1932.06
Marching Down This Road 1944.32
Marching Song of the Pollice Dogs, The 1982.19
Marching Through Georgia 1922.25, 1924.37
Marching Through Port Arthur 1904.13
Marchons d'un air conquerant 1883.51
Marchosito 1917.25
Marcia Di Ragazzi 1982.09
Marcus, My Friend 1984.02
Mardi Gras 1954.19
Mardi Gras Day in New Orleans 1935.04
Mardi Gras, The 1909.23

Margaret 1898.10
Margate Sands 1904.08
Margie 1920.33
Margineers, The 1930.09
Margot 1926.42, 1946.03
Marguerite 1887.02, 1893.43, 1894.17
Maria 1934.38, 1938.07, 1957.12, 1959.24, 1962.17, 1993.16, 1998.03, 1998.11, 2000.14
Marian 1926.03
Marian the Librarian 1957.18, 2000.11
Mariana 1922.36, 1926.35
Marianne 1928.29, 1972.07, 1979.02, 1986.14
Marice, La 1947.18
Marie 1909.17, 1997.01
Marie Antoinette 1899.30
Marie Cahill's Congo Love Song 1903.07
Marie from Paree 1907.35
Marie is Tricky 2000.08
Marie Laveau 1992.06
Marie Odile 1915.16
Marie vision, La 1961.25
Marie's Law 1959.25
Marie's Mink Coat 1959.15, 1961.25
Marie, Marie 1908.39, 1967.13, 1968.20
Marie-Vision, La 1959.15
Marieka 1972.16
Mariette 1924.46
Marilyn Monroe 1993.07
Marimba Spiritual 2001.04
Marina 1914.28
Marine's Hymn, The 1946.13
Mariner in his barque, The 1848.04
Marineritos, Los 1969.11
Marinesca 1892.52
Marion Lee 1866.19
Marionette Song 1931.43
Marionette Song, The 1910.35
Marionettes 1916.08, 1925.39
Marionettes, The 1915.23
Mariposa, La 1997.13, 1999.18
Marital Infidelity 1961.16
Marital Malignity 1914.04
Marjolaine 1922.04
Marjorie Waltz 1924.21
Mark his approach with thunder 1860.01
Mark His Bright and Flashing Eye 1912.40
Mark of a Man, The 1976.11
Mark Twain 1953.17, 1955.03
Marked Millions 1928.19
Market Day 1925.08
Market Day in the Village 1936.22
Market on Saturday Night 1883.26
Market on Saturday Night, The 1882.79
Market Place, The 1872.23
Marketing, Marketing 1971.01
Marketplace 1997.16
Marlborough Goes to the Wars 1922.06
Marlborough s'en va-t-en guerre 1922.06
Marquis de Boulogne-sur-Mer 1895.44
Marquis is a Good Old Soul, The 1882.33
Marriage 1964.22
Marriage al la Mode 1965.31
Marriage C.O.D. 1922.38
Marriage Game 1905.37
Marriage is a Lottery 1904.09
Marriage is Not What it Used to Be 1913.14
Marriage is Sublime 1903.04
Marriage Knot, The 1919.27
Marriage Market, The 1913.26
Marriage of the Daffodil and the Daisy, The 1903.18
Marriage of the Lily and the Rose, The 1919.22
Marriage Proposal, A 1992.09
Marriage Type Love 1953.08
Marriageable Daughter, A 1880.10
Married 1966.24, 1998.04
Married Couple Seeks Married Couple 1977.04
Married Life 1917.05
Married Life Blues 1923.07
Married Man, A 1965.02
Married Men 1985.12
Married Men and Single Men 1929.03
Married on Michaelmas' Day 1870.44
Marry a Sunshine Girl 1912.45

Marry Me 1914.03, 1984.01
Marry Me a Little 1977.05, 1995.11, 1999.20
Marry Me and See 1916.08
Marry Me Now 1991.07
Marry Me, Terry 1997.17
Marry the Family 1935.03
Marry the Girl Myself 1967.02
Marry the Man Today 1950.17, 1980.29
Marry With Me 1971.16
Marrying for Love 1950.15
Marsch und Palotas 1920.46
Marseilles 1919.03
Marseilles, La 1930.39
Marsellaise, The 1871.16
Marta 1993.09
Martha 1896.45
Martha Spanks the Grand Pianner 1902.19
Martial Music of the Fife and Drum, The 1902.02
Martinete 1986.17
Martinetes 1992.15
Marvelous Dancing 1894.17
Marvelous Fire Machine 1959.22, 1985.04
Marvelous Weekend, A 1976.15
Marvels of Hypnotism, The 1895.17
Marvin at the Psychiatrist 1992.09
Marvin Goes Crazy 1992.09
Mary 1897.56, 1910.21, 1919.41, 1920.38, 1923.27, 1968.07
Mary and Doug 1920.18
Mary and John 1892.05
Mary Ann 1906.30, 1910.19, 1913.27
Mary Ann Malone 1889.05
Mary Ann O'San 1915.05
Mary Ann O'Shea 1917.18
Mary Ann, She's All My Own 1906.20
Mary Ann, Where are You? 1911.42
Mary Black 1901.17
Mary Brown 1917.03
Mary Canary 1904.13, 1904.41
Mary Carey 1908.21, 1911.42
Mary Ellen Brown 1897.26, 1897.54
Mary from Maryland 1903.41
Mary from Tipperary 1904.47
Mary Green 1892.38
Mary had a Lamb That Little Lamb was Me 1915.04
Mary had a Little Lamb 1895.06
Mary has a Little Fair 1927.07
Mary is a Grand Old Name 1906.02
Mary Jane 1899.18, 1902.02
Mary Jane Marie 1897.34
Mary Jane McKane 1923.45
Mary Kelly's Beau 1880.36
Mary Lou 1976.32
Mary Mack 1908.28, 1984.15
Mary Make Believe 1928.42
Mary Margaret's House in the Country 1973.03
Mary Mary 1903.31, 1929.48
Mary McGee 1907.32
Mary to the Market Went 1925.36
Mary was a Housemaid 1899.35
Mary Wise 1907.12
Mary! My Heather Belle 1908.10
Mary's a Grand Old Name 1968.07
Mary's Gone wid' a Coon 1881.47
Mary's Got a Beau 1904.17
Mary's Lamb 1906.26
Mary's Little Lamb 1908.30
Mary, be Wary 1902.24
Mary, Dear! I Miss You Most of All 1926.29
Mary, Get the Supper 1880.25
Mary, Mary 1946.14, 1971.20
Mary, Mary, Quite Contrary 1929.33
Mary, My Prairie Fairy 1906.04
Mary, Queen of Scots 1920.25
Maryland 1896.26
Mascot of the Troop, The 1905.57
Masculinity 1951.17, 1983.11
Masetto's Song 1975.23
Mash Em Up 1980.05
Mash Ethiopia 1980.05
Mash Notes 1926.04
Mashing Eyes 1889.33
Mask, The 1880.04

My Yiddish Colleen 1910.18
My Yiddisha Mammy 1922.15
My Yiddishe Mame 1990.16
My Yokohama Girl 1917.08
My Young Man 1896.26
My Yukon Belle 1904.58
My Zebra Lady Fair 1915.16
My Zoo 1902.01
Myltil and Tyltil 1920.14
Myrella 1912.26
Myron Brown, Farewell 1905.35
Mysterioso 1920.01
Mysterious Kiss, The 1913.10
Mysterious Lady 1954.13, 1977.02, 1979.22
Mysterious Maid 1906.21, 1907.20
Mystery Moon 1930.21
Mystery of History, The 1906.18
Mystery Play, The 1922.43
Mystery Song 1989.02
Mystery Train 1989.12
Mystic Hussars, The 1923.40
Mystic Poet, hear our prayer 1881.37
Mystical Maidens are We 1900.37

N Everything 1918.05
N'est Pas 1898.05
N'fait's pas ca! J'suis tres bonn' fille 1886.19
N'imaginez pas qu'il me coute 1929.11
N.Y.C. 1951.10, 1977.06
Na also schreib' und tu' nicht schmieren 1964.25
Na Botta E Via 1964.03
Nadia 1977.01
Nadjy 1888.45
Nag! Nag! Nag! 1962.18
Naga Saki 1927.62
Nagnu Bekol 1968.04
Najla's Song 1951.15
Naked in Bethesda Fountain 1992.17
Naked Truth, The 1920.28
Name and Day 1893.19
Name it and it's Yours 1939.14
Name of Kelly, The 1922.43·
Name of Love, The 1985.18, 1989.07
Name the Day 1920.05
Name's LaGuardia, The 1959.25
Namely You 1956.12
Names I Love to Hear 1922.46
Naming of Cats, The 1982.19
Nana, La 1949.07
Nancy 1896.02, 1902.06, 1910.11
Nancy and I 1897.25
Nancy Brown 1902.16
Nancy Clancy 1904.39
Nancy Hogan's Ball 1897.26
Nancy Hogan's Ball! 1897.54
Nancy Teel 1894.44
Nancy's Farewell 1919.27
Nanette 1919.32, 1931.16, 1952.11
Nanette and Rin Tin Tin 1919.03
Nanking Blues 1920.24
Nanny 1928.05
Nanon Waltz 1885.08
Nanty 1952.09
Nanty Puts Her Hair Up 1952.09
Napenee 1904.28
Napoleon 1861.04, 1909.05, 1917.01, 1934.40, 1957.16
Napoleon Bonaparte 1905.45
Napoleon's a Pastry 1937.15
Naranjo en Flor 1999.18
Narcissus 1980.27
Nargileh 1930.20
Nasty Way He Sez It, The 1891.14
Natacha 1926.23
Natalie 1966.20
Natasha 1972.17, 1980.08
Nathalie 1968.21
Nathan Marching Song 1962.01
Nation is Dying, The 1988.02
Nation's Fate, A 1897.17
National Airs 1918.35
National Guard, The 1890.39
National Hymn 1910.24

National Pastime, The 1981.28
Native Glens 1889.36
Native Plantation Song 1912.03
Native Women 1915.04
Natives 1906.26
Natural Allies 1962.24
Natural Man 1974.01, 1991.04
Nature 1924.21
Nature Class 1905.44
Nature Divine 1915.28
Nature Hunt Ballet 1971.21
Nature Played a Dirty Trick on You 1931.36
Nature's Repose 1896.45
Natuscha 1947.14
Naught's a Naught 1949.16
Naughty Baby 1992.02
Naughty Boy 1910.29, 1929.31
Naughty Boys 1900.03
Naughty Cipriano/That Waltz Espagnol 1926.09, 1926.35
Naughty Continong, The 1894.46
Naughty Cupid 1909.12
Naughty Eyes 1920.19, 1925.35
Naughty Girl 1888.42, 1889.25
Naughty Girl from Paris 1896.49
Naughty Girls 2000.01
Naughty Kid Song 1907.19
Naughty Little Clock, The 1899.06
Naughty Little Fly 1902.21
Naughty Little Lady, O 1907.26
Naughty Little Step 1925.26
Naughty Lola 1967.13, 1968.20
Naughty Marietta 1910.35, 1978.19, 1988.18
Naughty Nineties, The 1927.23
Naughty Nobleman, The 1922.45
Naughty Riquette 1926.26
Naughty Scarecrow, The 1904.23
Naughty Sporty Boys 1894.35
Naughty! Naughty! Naughty! 1916.23
Naughty, Naughty Man 1866.18, 1870.44
Naughty, Naughty Men 1885.29
Naughty-Boy 1927.54
Naughty-Naught 1937.02, 1946.19
Navajo 1903.07
Naval Manoeuvres 1913.26
Naviganti 1880.42
Navy Foxtrot Man, The 1919.09
Navy of To-Day's All Right, The 1917.29
Navy, The 1902.03
Nay, Nay Pauline 1914.17
Nazi Party Pooper 1981.14
Ndinosara Nani? 1966.03
Ne Comptez Pas Sur Moi... Pour Me Montrer Toute Nue 1958.18
Ne dis pas toujours 1934.32, 1935.19
Ne parlez pas de mon courage 1878.08
Ne'er did we such a rascal see 1895.17
Neapoli 1902.08
Neapolitan Jazz 1919.30
Neapolitan Love Song 1915.24
Near Future, The 1919.15
Near Him at Last 1894.47
Near Them 1883.12
Near to You 1955.08, 1994.01
Nearer My God to Thee 1887.02
Nearest and Dearest 1880.69
Nearing the Day 1922.41
Nearly True to You 1922.12
Nearness of You, The 1991.04
Neat to be a Newsboy 1978.12
Neat/Not Neat 1986.18
Neath Italian Skies 1921.34, 1923.12
Neath My Lattice 1900.37
Neath Oriental Skies 1902.11
Neath the Blue Neapolitan Skies 1900.25
Neath the Casement 1920.41
Neath the Cherry Blossom Moon 1927.14
Neath the Old Cherry Tree 1907.53
Neath the Old Palm Tree 1907.33
Neath the Shade of the Old Apple Tree 1922.27
Neath the Southern Moon 1978.19, 1988.18
Neath the Southern Moon for Thee 1910.35
Neath Thy Window 1899.28

Neath Thy Window, Senorita 1903.27
Necessity 1947.03
Nectar for the Gods 1911.07
Need 2000.08
Needles 1926.12
Negotiations at the Grand Banquet 1997.16, 1998.08
Negra, La 1988.15
Negresco 1929.51
Negro Love Song, A 1966.15
Neige 1964.22
Neighborhood 1995.03
Neighborhood Song, The 1964.44
Nell Brinkley Girl, The 1908.19
Nellie After Five 1892.54
Nellie Bly 1946.04
Nellie Kelly 1902.15, 1924.16
Nellie Kelly, I Love You 1922.43, 1968.07
Nellie Kept on Smiling 1896.06
Nellie to Me is a Queen 1894.17
Nellie's Blue Eyes 1885.06
Nelly Bly 1864.13
Nelly Brady 1886.60
Nelson 1980.08, 1985.19
Nena 1926.09, 1926.35
Nenette and Rintintin 1918.33
Nerve 1900.38
Nerves 1986.20
Nervous 1974.04
Nervous Blues 1921.26
Nesting in a New York Tree 1904.42, 1907.16
Nesting Place 1922.04
Nesting Time in Flatbush 1917.06
Nestle by My Side 1907.13
Neuftette 1928.04
Neurotic You and Psychopathic Me 1948.30
Nevada Hoe Down 1954.17
Nevada Moonlight 1931.28
Never 1978.02
Never a Dull Moment 1939.13
Never a Law to Prevent It 1885.08
Never a moment left for leisure 1888.18
Never Again 1900.41, 1912.08, 1915.05, 1927.38, 1939.07, 1965.30, 1997.12
Never Be-Devil the Devil 1961.08
Never Before 1958.20
Never Borrow Trouble 1908.17
Never Breathe a Word of This 1901.07
Never Breathe a Word of This to Mother 1906.21
Never Count Your Chicks Before They're Hatched 1913.26
Never Ending Love 1982.15
Never Felt This Way Before 1953.03
Never for You 1928.29
Never Give Anything Away 1953.07
Never had an Education 1933.03
Never had to Work 1902.35
Never in the Wide, Wide World 1902.04
Never Land 1950.08
Never Let Her Go 1948.18
Never Marry a Dancer 1934.38
Never Marry a Girl With Cold Feet 1907.32
Never Mention Love When We're Alone 1914.30
Never Met a Girl Like You 1923.46
Never Met a Man I Didn't Like 1991.07, 1991.10
Never Mind the Singing - Just Dance, My Dear 1911.41
Never Mind the Why and Wherefore 1945.09
Never mind the why or wherefore 1879.05
Never Mind, Bo-Peep, We Will Find Your Sheep 1929.48
Never More 1919.39
Never More Removing 1787.01
Never Never Land 1958.20, 1958.21, 1977.02, 1988.08
Never Never Land, The 1907.11
Never on Sunday 1962.17, 1967.05
Never Put it in Writing 1985.05
Never Say the Final Journey is at Hand 1989.10
Never Say the World was Made to Cry 1926.14
Never Take a Step too Far 1913.14
Never Take the Horseshoe from the Door 1880.09
Never Talk to Me of Waltzing 1860.05
Never too Late for Love 1954.15
Never Trouble Trouble 1927.20

On Sunday Morning 1897.07
On Ten Square Miles by the Potomac River 1976.11
On That Day 1965.35, 1976.35, 1982.17
On That Day of Days 1970.08
On That Matter No One Budges 1931.48
On the 'Phone 1906.48
On the Atcheson, Topeka and the Santa Fe 1988.08
On the Atchison, Topeka and the Santa Fe 1997.05
On the Avenue 1902.33, 1911.40
On the Balcony of the Casa Rosada 1979.23
On the Banks of the Bronx 1919.27
On the Banks of the Schnitza-Komisski 1920.44
On the Banks of the Wabash Far Away 1920.04
On the Battlefield for My Lord 1990.05
On the Beach 1889.36, 1900.42, 1927.20, 1954.09
On the Beach at Gay Manhattan 1899.29
On the Beach at Narragansett 1897.39
On the Beach at Waiki-ki 1915.32
On the Boardwalk 1910.16
On the Boat 1913.18
On the Border Line 1929.49
On the Boulevard 1903.28
On the Bounding Main 1902.11
On the Bowery 1891.39, 1894.07, 1894.35
On the Brim of Her Old-Fashioned Bonnet 1921.18
On the Campus 1927.41
On the Charts 1971.01
On the Congo 1911.34
On the Corner of the Rue Cambon 1969.17
On the Crest of a Wave 1928.22
On the Day I Marry 1912.48
On the day I was wedded 1890.02
On the Deep Blue Sea 1922.04
On the Dial 1899.39
On the Dummy Line 1897.45
On the Farm 1911.27, 1957.07
On the Fourth of July 1986.13
On the Gay Luneta 1907.22
On the Go 1903.39
On the Golden Trail 1928.44
On the Good Ship Lollipop 1980.08
On the Grand Old Sands 1907.24
On the Grassy Banks of Scheldt 1882.75
On the Ground 1913.36
On the Harlem When the Moon Shines Bright 1889.37
On the Heights of Glentann There's No Voice 1902.25
On the Honeymoon Express 1913.06
On the Lake, or the New Year Festival 1904.40
On the Levee 1928.10, 1932.08
On the Links 1906.10
On the Lonely Lagoon 1914.07
On the Moonlit Swanee 1922.44
On the Mountain 1916.15
On the Other Hand 1934.06
On the Other Side of the Wall 1903.37
On the Parthenon 1956.09
On the Piazza 1907.46
On the Quiet 1912.14
On the Radio 1924.32
On the Right Track 1972.22
On the River Nile 1917.34
On the Riviera 1922.33
On the Road to Calais 1918.05
On the Road to Monterey 1909.10
On the Run 1982.22
On the Runway 1998.14
On the S.S. Bernard Cohn 1965.31
On the Sands of the Negev 1960.18
On the Sea 1886.15
On the Shore at Le Lei Wi 1915.31
On the Shores of Sheepshead Bay 1909.04
On the Side 1903.02
On the Side of the Angels 1959.25
On the Sly 1879.35
On the Stage 1898.61, 1901.09, 1903.37, 1912.07
On the Steps of the Palace 1987.18
On the Street 1993.05, 1996.09
On the Street Where You Live 1956.01, 1993.18
On the Strict Q.T. 1877.23
On the Subway 1966.21
On the Sunny Side of the Street 1930.09, 1979.25, 1990.09
On the Track 1897.40, 1917.10

On the Train of a Wedding Gown 1916.24
On the Twentieth Century 1978.02
On the Washington Train 1924.41
On the Waterfront 1977.09
On the Way to Sloppy Joe's 1946.15
On the Way to Spain 1925.12
On the Willows 1976.17
On the Winning Side 1972.02
On the Yellowstone 1897.33
On the Z-R-3 1925.01
On This Festal Day 1902.18
On This Night of a Thousand Stars 1979.23
On This Rock 1971.20
On this Solemnity 1882.75
On This Wedding Day 1964.18
On Thru the Night 1932.06
On Thy Lattice 1899.40
On to Africa 1933.03
On to Chicago 1894.38
On to Conquer 1915.04
On to Hollywood 1926.29
On to Paris 1887.50, 1903.40, 1930.37
On to Paris a la Automobile 1904.39
On to Petrograd 1916.17
On to the Hall 1886.32
On to Victory 1906.18, 1918.32
On Top 1929.06, 1938.03
On Top of the World 1983.08
On Trial for My Life 1975.07
On Union Square 1886.42
On Wings of Doubt 1918.40
On With the Dance 1914.17, 1920.44, 1925.17, 1930.08, 1931.08
On With the Game 1923.47
On With the Rehearsal 1910.09
On With the Show 1954.17
On y revient toujours 1895.43
On yonder rock reclining 1864.13
On Your Toes 1936.05, 1936.12, 1952.11, 1975.13, 1983.02
On, admirable art! 1894.15
On, Comrades 1925.39
On, How I Adore Your Name 1966.09
On, on, On 1972.23
On, Students, on! 1882.63
On, Yes! Oh, Yes! 1894.38
Ona Hundred Different Ships 1909.26
Once 1925.14, 1927.59
Once a Fisherman Went to Sea 1912.30
Once a King 1861.03
Once a King there chanced to be 1866.34
Once a Prince there chanced to be, who to marry had a mind 1888.39
Once a Year Day 1954.05
Once Again 1882.39
Once I Loved the Girl Cecelia 1901.24
Once in 2.7 Years 1968.08
Once in a Blue Moon 1923.40, 1927.12
Once in a Lifetime 1928.23, 1962.18, 1974.11, 1974.22, 1978.18
Once in a While 1888.44, 1890.12, 1891.14, 1908.30, 1975.08, 2000.17
Once in Love With Amy 1948.26, 1974.25, 1980.29, 1991.10, 1992.18
Once in September 1927.01
Once in the Highlands 1947.07, 1980.26
Once Knew a Fella 1959.11
Once More to Dream 1907.14
Once More to Find Her 1866.34
Once the Man You Laughed At 1967.18
Once There was a Melody 1971.17
Once Too Often 1904.01
Once Upon a Dream 1997.09
Once Upon a Time 1884.57
Once upon a time 1887.43
Once Upon a Time 1895.25, 1916.19, 1918.29, 1919.35, 1922.47, 1939.12, 1947.14, 1962.04, 1978.11, 1980.06, 1997.01, 1998.05
Once Upon a Time and Long Ago 1958.20, 1958.21
Once Upon a Time Today 1950.15
Once Upon the Natchez Trace 1976.31
Once was Enough for Him 1886.15
Once You Lose Your Heart 1986.12

Once You've Seen a Rainbow 1984.10
Once-in-a-While 1934.38
Onda 9 1993.08
Ondo Takarazuka Koshinkyoku 1989.21
One 1937.03, 1975.15, 1979.13, 2001.01
One - Two - Three 1917.16
One Alone 1926.42, 1946.03, 1987.10
One and One Make One 1906.19
One and Only 1915.04
One auf of de Boys 1878.15
One Baby 1927.09
One Beating a Day 1983.20
One Big Happy Family 1974.03
One Big Union for Two 1937.14
One Boy 1960.06
One Boy's Enough for Me 1927.29
One Brick at a Time 1980.07
One Brief Moment 1939.13
One Bumper at Parting 1860.03
One by One 1978.27, 1997.20
One Candle 1990.17
One Coro Delle Lavandaire 1985.14
One Day 1918.15
One Day a Little Maid 1893.40
One Day in May 1923.08
One Day it Will Come to Pass 1965.39
One day King Papagallo sent a note 1898.25
One Day Margot, or Three to One 1891.36
One Day More 1987.04
One Day We Dance 1960.22
One Day, a Captain Bold 1881.22
One day, the J. LeHay of This town 1895.29
One Dozen Roses 1942.16
One Extraordinary Thing 1979.02
One Feather Tail of Miss Gertrude McFuzz, The 2000.18
One Flag 1971.02
One Flower Grows Alone in Your Garden 1926.42, 1946.03
One Foot, Other Foot 1947.17
One for All 1930.30
One for Another 1896.30
One for My Baby 1997.05
One Fragment of a Moment 1993.17
One Galician Miss 1931.29
One Girl 1923.32
One Girl Boy, The 1921.03
One Girl Man 1928.31
One Girl, The 1907.47, 1928.44, 1929.22
One Golden Hour 1926.34
One Good Boy Gone Wrong 1946.03, 1973.09, 1987.10
One Good Friend 1927.64
One Good Man Gone Wrong 1926.42
One Good Time 1923.10
One Hallow'een 1970.09
One Hand, One Heart 1957.12
One Heart 1933.16
One Heart to Thee 1899.06
One Horse Shay 1858.04
One Hour Ahead of the Posse 1955.12
One Hour Mama 1999.06
One Hour, Sweetheart, With You! 1918.26
One Hundred Easy Ways 1953.09
One Hundred Years from Now 1903.14
One I Love, The 1913.26
One I Love, the Other I Abhor 1902.37
One I Love, Two I Love 1919.14
One I'm Looking For, The 1926.27
One in a Million 1931.36, 1934.15, 1969.14
One in a Million Like You 1912.38
One in the Game of Love 1915.28
One Indispensable Man, The 1938.11
One is a Lonely Number 1950.03, 1952.13
One Kind Word 1959.04
One Kiss 1923.44, 1928.12, 1928.29, 1986.14
One Last Kiss 1960.06
One Last Love Song 1945.11
One Last Waltz 1923.22
One Leg too Few 1973.13
One Life to Live 1941.04
One Little Angry Word 1899.08
One Little Baby 1906.03

Pluto's Partner I 1898.48
Plymouth Rock 1921.21
Po Karekare Ana 1972.20
Po' Li'l Black Chile 1926.31
Po' Lil' Frenchie 1940.01
Po, Po, Po 1967.05
Po-lo-ma 1878.05
Poaching 1907.32
Pobre chica, la que tiene que servir 1969.11
Pocahontas 1907.24
Pocapdedious 1973.07
Pocketful of Dreams 1950.12
Pocketful of Miracles 1974.10
Poeme Erotique 1944.21
Poems 1976.02
Poet and Peasant 1942.12
Poetry 1993.17
Poetry and All That Jazz 1960.01
Poetry Competition 1990.17
Poetry in Motion 1944.19
Poetry of Motion, The 1925.14
Poi Ball 1925.23
Point of No Return, The 1988.01
Point Venice 1923.07
Poison Ivy 1995.03
Pokenhatchit Public Protest Committee, The 1981.14
Poker Game 1927.55
Poker Game, The 1981.10, 1999.06
Poker Love 1906.37
Poker Polka 1963.26, 1992.10
Poker Polka, The 1950.14
Polar Bear Strut, The 1926.17
Police Report, A 1834.01
Policeman Song 1881.06
Policeman's Ball, The 1949.08
Policeman's Lot is a Happy One, A 1912.24
Policeman's song 1882.44
Policeman's Song 1938.10
Policemen 1880.59
Policeology 1919.01
Policy Players Ball, The 1899.31
Political Whip, The 1873.10
Politics 1949.17
Politics and Poker 1959.25
Polk Salad Annie 1978.01
Polka 1851.03, 1948.27
Polka Dot, The 1924.08, 1929.29
Polka Dots and Moonbeams 1995.14
Polka, The 1959.27
Polly 1902.08, 1929.02
Polly Believes in Preparedness 1917.01
Polly from Hollywood 1924.44
Polly of Hollywood 1927.10
Polly Poll 1917.16
Polly Pretty Polly 1917.37
Polly Put the Kettle On 1923.47
Polly Wolly Doodle 1944.32
Polly's Lied 1976.10
Polly's Song 1966.19
Polly, will you try me 1859.08
Polly, won't you try me now 1858.04
Pollyanna 1927.20
Polo 1887.32, 1904.03
Polo de Tobalo, El 1992.15
Polonaise 1945.14, 1964.25
Poltergeists 1986.18
Polyglot Trio 1883.04
Polythene Pam 1974.24
Pom-Pom 1916.04
Pomme d'Or 1917.28
Pomme est un fruit plein de seve, La 1878.08
Pomp and Circumstance 1935.12
Pompadour 1933.03
Pompanola 1928.37
Pompeii Restored 1872.23
Pompey's Complaint 1787.01
Poncho De Panther from Brazil 1943.24
Ponies on Parade 1925.48
Pony Boy 1924.47
Poogie Woo 1924.17
Pooh Pooh 1880.47
Pool 1877.22
Pool of Love 1927.34

Pool Room Papa 1929.23
Poontang 1976.20
Poor as a Church Mouse 1944.27
Poor Baby 1970.13
Poor Butterfly 1916.15, 1916.20, 1921.02
Poor Cadets, The 1913.02
Poor Cinderella 1881.11, 1927.09
Poor Cock Robin 1879.64
Poor Everybody Else 1973.06
Poor Florodora Girl 1920.18
Poor Fool, He Makes Me Laugh 1988.01
Poor Irish Minstrel, The 1882.69, 1886.51
Poor Jerusalem 1971.12
Poor Jud 1943.04
Poor Little Country Maid, The 1895.27
Poor Little Fluttering Moths 1901.17
Poor Little Foolish Man 1907.37
Poor little Gipsey, A 1853.01
Poor Little Girl Like Me, A 1908.44
Poor Little Hollywood Star 1962.27, 1998.15
Poor Little Man 1888.18
Poor Little Marie 1926.18
Poor Little Marionette, The 1905.49
Poor Little Mary 1894.38, 1895.02
Poor Little Me 1884.48, 1918.19, 1945.18
Poor Little Person 1967.14
Poor Little Pierrette 1954.09
Poor Little Red Papoose 1904.39
Poor Little Red Pappoose 1906.01
Poor Little Rich Girl 1925.42, 1975.22, 1986.19
Poor Little Rich Girl's Dog 1917.19
Poor Little Rich Little Me 1920.35
Poor Little Ritz Girl 1920.25
Poor Little Shy Little, Demure Little Me 1932.15
Poor Little Wall Flower 1923.07
Poor Man 1948.18
Poor Marat in Your Bathtub Seat 1965.39
Poor Married Man, The 1888.20
Poor O'Hoolihan Held the Fuse 1898.43
Poor Old Dad in New York for the Summer 1909.17
Poor Old Florodora Girl 1920.35
Poor Old King Carrot 1872.23
Poor Old Marat 1965.39
Poor Old Solomon 1910.20
Poor Old World 1923.46
Poor Pierrot 1894.33, 1925.34, 1926.09, 1926.35,
  1931.37
Poor Poor Joseph 1982.03, 1993.15
Poor Relations 1889.36
Poor Shepherds We 1900.50
Poor Sister 2000.20
Poor Soldier, The 1860.03
Poor Thing 1979.06
Poor Tied Up Darlin' 1975.18, 1976.31
Poor Uncle Gasazus 1914.13
Poor Unfortunate Sister Anne 1903.04
Poor Wand'ring One 1879.72
Poor Wandering One 1938.10, 1981.01
Poor Wicked Man, The 1881.07
Poor Winter Garden Girl 1920.20
Poor Working Girl, A 1909.12
Poor Workingman 1920.30
Poor young thing 1887.04
Poor, Poor Pharaoh 1982.03, 1993.15
Pop goes his Weasel 1864.13
Pop, Pop, Pop 1898.55
Pop, Pop, Pop! 1900.57
Poppa's Blues 1987.05
Poppies 1960.17, 1997.11
Poppy 1914.15
Poppy Chorus 1903.03, 1904.13, 1904.44
Poppy Dear 1923.27
Poppy Land 1921.19
Poppy the Dream Girl 1925.12
Poppyland 1919.43
Popsey Wopsey 1912.26
Popular Airs, The 1894.51
Popular art of the day, The 1895.43
Popular Girl, A 1910.34
Popular Pauline 1905.44
Popular Pests, The 1919.15
Popular Pop, The 1914.26
Popular Song, A 1910.02, 1922.08

Popular Songs 1906.25
Popular Tune, A 1902.04
Popularity 1922.48, 1924.21, 1968.07, 1986.03
Por Un Amor 1988.15
Porcelain Maid 1922.39
Porgy 1928.18, 1930.34
Port of the World 1931.29
Portenito, El 1999.18
Porter! Porter! 1923.13
Porterology 1925.18
Porto Banos 1920.13
Porto Rico 1911.20
Porto Rico Girls 1899.31
Portofino 1958.04
Portrait Parade 1926.32
Portrait, The 1910.03
Posin' 1980.10
Posing 1910.11
Posing for Venus 1912.34
Possessors of a Magic Art 1875.19
'Possum Chase, De 1899.35
Possum Rag 1911.08
Possum Trot 1929.01
Post Card Beau, A 1911.35
Post Office 1922.48
Postage-Stamp Principality 1956.16
Postcard #2 1986.20
Postcard #3/Dressing Room Scene 1986.20
Poster Diversity 1904.24
Poster Girl 1926.01
Posterity is Just Around the Corner 1931.48
Posterland 1917.31
Posty and a Maid, A 1921.25
Pot Pourri 1919.19
Pot-Pourri 1917.21
Pot-Pourri 1958.06
Potash and Perlmutter Ball, The 1917.37
Potato Bug, The 1917.13
Potato Song, The 1903.02
Potatoes a pound 1880.18
Potekha 1977.13
Potiphar 1982.03, 1992.12, 1993.15
Potpourri 1925.25
Pottawattomie 1939.27
Poules, Les 1965.05
Pour elles, c'est un jour de fete 1883.51
Pour J'en-Ai-Marre 1922.34
Pour la chapelle qu'ono s'apprete 1887.36
Pour le tresor que to nous abandonnes 1878.12
Pour les compter, mes amoureux 1886.19
Pour oh pour the Prowler's whiskey 1881.06
Pour plaire, en nos regouts 1887.36
Pour sortir en tout saison 1929.11
Pour te faire plaisir 1929.15
Pour toi 1929.14
Pour trouver un mari 1929.10
Pour un joyeux repas 1884.43
Pour voir Irma 1887.35
Pour, O Pour the Pirate Sherry 1981.01
Pour, Oh Pour the Pirate Sherry 1879.72
Pourquoi prendre ce front severe 1884.43
Pourquoi rever? 1934.32
Pourquoi vous chagriner 1884.43
Pousse Cafe 1912.13
Poverty Program 1971.20
Poverty Row 1936.06
Poverty's Tears Ebb and Flow 1885.49, 1893.46
Pow Wow Polka, The 1954.13
Pow! Bam! Zonk! 1966.06
Powder My Back 1965.05, 1981.17
Powder Puff 1926.01
Powder Puff Ballet, The 1991.07
Powder Your Nose 1900.56
Power 1982.18
Power behind the throne 1879.35
Power of Gold, The 1878.02
Power of Love 1862.09
Power of Love, The 1863.06, 1870.44, 1881.12
Power of Negative Thinking, The 1956.09
Power of the Human Eye, The 1898.60
Power of the Press, The 1904.55
Powerful Stuff 2000.07
Powers of Goodness 1882.60

Pox Upon the Traitor's Brow, A 1965.29
Practical 1953.02
Practical Patriots, The 1913.27
Practising Up on You 1930.32
Prairie Frolic, A 1918.19
Prairie Mary 1907.53
Praise the Lord and Pass the Ammunition 1980.29
Praises of Cupid, The 1879.38
Prast-Chi - Prast Chi 1925.29
Prater, The 1908.06
Pray 1990.12
Pray Excuse 1910.24
Pray for the Lights to Go Out 1976.04
Pray for the soul's repose 1855.06
Pray Tell Me 1912.04
Pray, Daddy, please to moderate 1859.08
Pray, excuse me 1887.04
Pray, Pretty Maid 1906.49
Pray, Tell Me Why? 1881.22
Prayer 1948.27, 1970.08, 1972.09, 1972.14, 1997.19, 1999.13
Prayer to God 1970.17
Prayer to St. Valentine, A 1907.06
Pre-Eminently Handsome 1890.26
Pre-Historic Man 1912.40
Preach Them Blues 1975.20
Precious Jewels 1920.19
Precious Lord 1990.05
Precious Memories 1989.12
Precision 1958.18
Prefect punctuality, a virtue rare 1888.18
Prehistoric Complaint 1966.32
Preliminary Skirmish 1919.10
Prelude 1969.08
Prelude to a Kiss 1981.06, 1997.03
Preludes, Les 1979.10
Preludio a Francini 1993.08
Preludio del Bandoneon y la Noche 1997.13
Prenez mes roses 1934.32, 1935.19
Preparation Fugue 1986.12
Preparation, The 1969.17
Prepare the Dolls 1910.24
Prepare Ye the Way of the Lord 1976.17
Prepossessing Maid 1904.04
Preposterous 1968.08
Present for Gilbert 1956.13
Presentation of Miss Turnstiles 1998.16
Presentation of Princesses 1953.16
Presenting Clara Spencer 1960.01
Presents for Mrs. Rogers 1991.07
President 1998.01
President am I 1901.27
President Jefferson Sunday Luncheon Party March, The 1976.11
President's Daughter, The 1970.18
Presidente, El 1920.13
Press Conference 1981.29, 1988.09
Press Me to Thee 1912.03
Pretend You're Living 1975.23
Pretending 1909.30
Pretty 1947.19
Pretty am I, so Pretty 1960.18
Pretty Ankle 1923.13
Pretty as a Butterfly 1886.32
Pretty as a Picture 1876.31, 1879.32, 1883.07, 1913.24, 1944.23, 1947.04, 1986.20
Pretty Baby 1914.23, 1916.11
Pretty Baby Doll from Paree 1918.12
Pretty Betsy Brown 1901.25
Pretty Betty, if you love me 1869.43
Pretty Bird 1888.34
Pretty Bobolink 1892.31
Pretty City Girl 1923.07
Pretty Dance is Like a Violin, A 1921.17
Pretty Daughter of Mine 1945.09
Pretty Drummer 1922.06
Pretty Edelweiss 1915.28
Pretty Face 1981.14
Pretty Flowers from Me to You 1923.38
Pretty Girl 1923.37, 1924.11, 1928.23
Pretty Girl is Like a Melody, A 1919.15, 1965.05, 1980.18, 1989.21
Pretty Girl Milking Her Cow 1860.05

Pretty Girl, A 1891.11
Pretty Girl, A Summer Night A 1904.17
Pretty Gitana 1848.04
Pretty Isabella and Her Umbrella 1897.42
Pretty Jemima 1870.01
Pretty Kitty 1957.05
Pretty Lady 1976.02, 1977.05, 1980.20
Pretty Lips 1882.39
Pretty Little Bathers 1902.42
Pretty Little Boys 1880.10
Pretty Little Chichis 1913.10
Pretty Little China Girl 1897.39
Pretty Little Cinderella 1920.02
Pretty Little Dark Blue Eyes 1884.23
Pretty Little Girl Inside, The 1910.19
Pretty Little Girl That I Know 1900.03
Pretty Little Girls Like You 1919.11
Pretty Little Heather Bell 1907.58
Pretty Little Japanese Lady 1908.20
Pretty Little Laundry Girls 1885.29
Pretty Little Maid of Zanzibar, The 1905.35
Pretty Little Maiden on the Screen 1912.30
Pretty Little Mayflower Girl 1916.03
Pretty Little Picture 1962.12
Pretty little Quaker, The 1885.51
Pretty Little Shoe 1881.11
Pretty Little So-and-So 1927.11
Pretty Little Squaw from Utah, The 1904.22
Pretty Little Stranger 1927.09
Pretty Little Sunshine 1911.28
Pretty Lulu Lu 1902.42
Pretty Maid Adelaide 1903.14
Pretty Maid Milking Her Cow 1888.28
Pretty Maid, A 1888.09
Pretty Maiden 1905.36
Pretty Malindy 1923.11
Pretty Milliners, The 1911.12
Pretty Ming Toy 1920.25
Pretty Mollie Shannon She's the Real, Real Thing 1901.25
Pretty Mrs. Smith 1914.21
Pretty Music 1998.21
Pretty New England Pink 1902.21
Pretty Page, My 1869.42
Pretty Pair, The 1873.28
Pretty Part for Me to Play, A 1909.19
Pretty Patty Moss 1938.06
Pretty Peggy 1902.24, 1923.21
Pretty Pin-Up 1978.06
Pretty Polly 1904.31, 1920.02, 1922.40
Pretty Polly Hopkins 1877.25, 1879.03
Pretty Polly Palmer 1896.44
Pretty Polly Primrose 1903.17
Pretty Polly, say 1750.01, 1854.06
Pretty Pond Lillies 1884.48
Pretty Primrose 1906.32
Pretty Punchinello 1909.07
Pretty Soft, Pretty Sweet 1928.10
Pretty Suzette 1897.37
Pretty Things 1924.28
Pretty Tillie, if you Love me 1869.07
Pretty to Walk With 1957.16
Pretty Typewriters, The 1894.17
Pretty Up, Pretty Up, Pretty Baby 1919.26
Pretty Widow, The 1894.07
Pretty Wilhelmina 1877.28
Pretty Woman 1979.06
Pretty Women 1999.26
Pretty Young Widow, The 1891.39, 1894.21, 1894.35
Pretty, Petite and Sweet 1928.34
Prevalent Condition of the Mind, The 1921.06
Priam's Little Congai 1929.20
Pricklepear Bloom, The 1975.18, 1976.31
Pride and Joy 1964.29
Pride and Pet of the Lane, The 1905.21
Pride Goes Before a Fall 1896.41
Pride of the London Stage 1896.24
Priere 1948.12
Priglio Don't Know 1937.11
Prim and Proper 1971.09
Prima Donna 1988.01
Prima Donna Waltz 1855.11
Prima Donna, The 1907.10

Prima Donnas, The 1912.44
Primavera, La 1879.38
Primitive Ebony, The 1932.19
Primrose Path, The 1914.24, 1920.19, 1923.13
Primrose Way, The 1915.12
Prince and Queen 1997.16
Prince and Queen, The 1998.08
Prince Charming 1919.19, 1922.26, 1925.21, 1934.15
Prince here you see, A 1862.08
Prince is a Coming, The 1861.03
Prince is Giving a Ball, The 1993.14, 2001.09
Prince Leander is His Name 1870.20, 1876.06
Prince Leander is My Name 1868.03
Prince of Bohemia, The 1910.04
Prince of Borneo 1906.13
Prince of Borneo, The 1909.07
Prince of Central Park, The 1989.25
Prince of Good Fellows 1903.36
Prince of Humbug, The 1980.07
Prince of My Dreams 1912.40
Prince of Philadelphia, The 1953.10
Prince of Wales, The 1922.34, 1924.31
Prince's Farewell, The 1962.27
Prince's Goodbye, The 1982.01, 1998.15
Princely Scheme, A 1954.13, 1979.22, 1990.20
Princess Beautiful 1922.15
Princess Can't be Found, Sir, The 1912.47
Princess I, A 1896.10
Princess Nicotine 1923.42
Princess of Far Away 1912.39
Princess of Mulberry Bend, The 1899.03
Princess of My Dreams 1921.21
Princess of Pure Delight, The 1941.04
Princess of Trebizonde, The 1895.36
Princess Virtue 1921.11
Princess We Adore, The 1901.27
Princess Who Never Smiled, The 1924.48
Princess Zenobia, La 1936.05, 1983.02
Printemps 1907.10
Priorities 1942.05
Priscilla 1902.29
Prisms 1968.13
Prison in a Prison 1999.22
Prisoner of Love, A 1912.41
Prisoner's Song 1927.37
Prisoner's Song, The 1926.37
Prisoner, Prisoner, Run Along 1918.36
Prisoners in Niggertown 1968.11
Prisoners of Love 2001.05
Prisoners, Stand Up! 1912.40
Prisonniere, La 1927.23
Pristi, sapristi 1878.08
Prithee, Pretty Maiden, Willow, Willow, Waly 1881.37
Private Affair, A 1899.38
Private Conversation 1997.17
Private Dining Room, The 1973.08
Private Parts 1982.10
Private Thoughts 1987.19
Private Tommy Atkins 1894.33, 1894.46, 1900.43
Prize for That, A 1904.03
Probably 1971.10
Problem After Problem 1978.11
Procession, The 1926.09, 1926.35
Processional 1934.43, 1943.10
Processional March 1899.39
Procurer's Ballad, The 1965.04
Prodigal Daughter 1949.02
Prodigal Son, The 1891.27
Profession of a Manicure, The 1906.17
Professional Beauty, A 1883.04
Professional Showbizness Comedy 1992.17
Professions 1897.20
Professor and His Pupil 1905.34
Professor and His Pupil, The 1904.58
Professor and the Students, The 1974.26
Professor Walker and His Solo Symphony 1986.11
Professor Won't You Teach Me All You Know? 1899.38
Progress 1948.25, 1968.05
Progress is the Root of All Evil 1956.12
Progressive Poker Game, The 1898.50
Progressive Poker Party 1905.07
Prohibition 1919.15
Prohibition Ball 1919.08

Shame! Shame! 1844.01
Shamrock Blooms White, The 1894.22
Shamrock of Erin, The 1905.30
Shamrock, The 1880.39
Shandon Belles 1910.04
Shangaane 1977.01
Shanghai Lil 1992.18
Shangri-La 1956.07
Shanty Town Romance 1978.06
Sharlee 1923.42
Sharper Than the Serpent's Fang 1904.17
Shattered Illusions 2000.16
Shauny O'Shay 1948.08
Shav Ain Eleich 1968.04
Shavian Shivers 1930.18, 1930.33
Shayani Izandla 1997.14
She 1974.19, 1983.03
She Alone Could Understand 1920.42
She Always Does Exactly as She's Told 1897.14
She Always Told the Truth 1906.26
She and He 1955.14
She and I Together 1895.30
She Came in Through the Bathroom Window 1974.24
She Came, She Saw, She Canned 1940.10
She Can Love True 1870.20
She Can't Lick Me 1888.05
She Could Shake the Maracas 1939.27, 1975.13
She Did it All Herself 1902.16
She Did the Fandango 1938.06
She Didn't Know 1906.41
She Didn't Know Enough About the Game 1902.35
She Didn't Say 'Yes' 1931.37
She Didn't Say Yes 1986.01
She Didn't Seem to Care 1911.42
She Didn't Understand 1899.25
She Doctor 1975.23
She Doesn't Exist at All 1916.07
She Don't Wanna 1927.37
She Done Him Wrong 1939.14
She Fainted Away in My Arms 1878.04, 1878.12, 1879.63
She Gonna Come Home Wit' Me 1956.04
She Got Him 1941.12
She Hadda Go Back 1963.21
She has No Past 1897.21, 1897.21
She is a Diamond 1979.23
She is My Picnic Girl 1896.02
She is seen 1862.03
She is so Good 1870.27
She is the Belle of New York 1897.39, 1897.39
She is the One Girl 1911.27
She Just Loves Las Vegas 1983.09
She Just Suites Me 1904.46
She Just Suits Me 1905.31
She Just Walks On 1898.38, 1899.19
She Knew a Thing or Two 1908.29
She Knows It 1920.36
She Left Without a Word 1999.17
She Likes Baseball 1968.31
She Lives on Murray Hill 1882.74
She Loved Me, And 1976.20
She Loves Me 1925.35, 1963.14
She Loves Me, She Loves Me Not 1921.37
She Loves Thee 1938.06
She Loves You 1977.10
She Married a Minstrel 1891.32
She May Have Seen Better Days 1927.48
She Never Did the Same Thing Twice 1897.20
She Never Loved a Man as Much as That 1900.41
She Only had a Dollar in Her Purse 1898.56
She Passed My Way 1972.24
She Reads the New York Papers Every Day 1902.40
She Says She's Possessed 1892.42
She Sells Sea Shells 1909.07
She Touched Me 1965.29
She Trimmed Them All so Neatly 1910.34
She Used to Take Me on Her Knee 1898.47, 1902.34
She Walks Like This 1903.16
She Wanted Something to Play With 1896.05
She was a Cau-, She was a Shun 1885.26
She was a Maid of Sweet Simplicit-ee 1898.48
She was Bred in Old Kentucky 1898.66, 1898.70, 1919.16

She was Bred in Old Virginia 1899.23
She was Not Like Other Maidens 1907.27
She was Only a Farmer's Daughter 1919.41
She was Right 1894.35
She was the Miller's Daughter 1903.22
She was There 1997.19, 1999.13
She was Very Dear to Me 1921.23
She wasn't You 1965.31
She will of me a martyr make 1864.12
She Would be a Novelty 1894.17
She'd be Far Better Off With You 1990.04
She'll Do 1902.40
She's a Daisy 1879.09
She's a gal of mine 1869.43
She's a Lady With Money 1905.29
She's a Nut 1978.02
She's a Spectable Married Collud Lady 1898.28
She's a Star 1976.07
She's a Thoroughbred 1898.69
She's a Woman 1993.09
She's Acquitted 1888.13
She's Acquitted, He's Outwitted 1878.02, 1885.58, 1896.35
She's All Right 1903.17, 1904.40
She's an English Girl 1904.29
She's Artistic 1920.29
She's Exciting 1950.04
She's Funny That Way 1928.22
She's Gettin' More Like the White Folks Every Day 1980.27
She's Gone 1916.04, 1997.17
She's Got Everything 1956.08
She's Got That Thing 1998.05
She's Got the Lot 1960.13
She's Got to Go 1987.19
She's Innocent 1921.10
She's Just a Baby 1921.22
She's Just a Little Bit Different from the Others That I Know 1904.37
She's Just Another Girl 1956.16
She's Leaving Home 1974.24
She's Like the Violets Blue 1894.20
She's Ma Daisy 1928.05, 1930.17
She's My Daisy 1908.38
She's My Girl 1897.43, 1903.17
She's My Love 1961.10
She's My Tiger Lily 1900.15
She's No Longer a Gypsy 1970.09
She's Not Thinking of Me 1973.12
She's on File 1985.17
She's on Her Way 1926.32
She's Our Gretel 1985.02
She's Roses 1965.29
She's Salvation Sal 1919.08
She's saved! She's saved! 1878.02
She's Saved! She's Saved! 1885.58, 1888.13, 1896.35
She's Such a Comfort to Me 1929.51
She's Tall, She's Tan, She's Terrific 1980.10
She's Taught Me to Play the Piano 1880.25
She's the Apple of My Eye 1907.39
She's the Image of Her Mother in a Thousand Different Ways 1885.69
She's the Only Girl for Me 1910.12
She's too Far Above Me 1965.14
She's Venus de Milo to Me 1918.31
Sheath Gown in Darktown, The 1908.08
Sheathe the Sword 1896.41
Sheelah, Weave the Spell 1888.40
Sheep Song 1982.20, 1997.10
Sheep's Song 1974.06
Sheer Perfection 1997.12
Sheik of Alabam' Weds a Brown-Skin-Vamp, The 1923.39
Sheik of Araby, The 1922.15
Sheik, The 1922.15
Sheikin Fool 1930.40
Shelling Green Peas 1960.17
Sheltered from the Noonday Glare 1901.19
Sheperdess Interlude, The 1925.03
Shepherd Gavotte, The 1914.22
Shepherd Song, The 1944.06
Shepherd's Delight, The 1963.28
Shepherd's Song 1961.20

Shepherd, The 1937.03
Sheriff's Song 1902.04
Sherry 1967.02
Sheyibone Beis Hamikdosh 1967.03
Sheyn bin ich, sheyn 1960.18
Shifting of the Sign, The 1898.63
Shifting Sounds 1996.07
Shika, Shika 1954.15
Shilgia 1968.04
Shiloh 1963.22
Shimmering Nile, The 1916.07
Shimmering, Glimmering Nile, The 1918.15
Shimmy - Shaking - Love 1919.34
Shimmy a la Egyptian 1919.30
Shimmy All the Blues Away 1920.06
Shimmy Nods 1920.23
Shimmy Sisters, The 1918.20
Shimmy Town 1919.15
Shimmy Valentine 1920.22
Shinbone Alley 1957.05
Shine 1937.09, 1986.20, 1999.12
Shine 'Em Up! 1927.32
Shine it On 1977.16
Shine on Harvest Moon 1927.12, 1974.01
Shine on Your Shoes, A 1932.17, 1972.05, 1999.23
Shine on, Bright Star 1900.43
Shine on, Harvest Moon 1908.19, 1908.39, 1955.03
Shine on, Little Son 1920.22
Shine on, Right Sunlight 1899.22
Shine on, Silvery Moon 1902.21
Shine, Shine, Shine 1905.47
Ship has Sailed, The 1939.24
Ship I Love, The 1894.17
Ship of Zion 1940.01
Ship Went Sailing, The 1892.19
Ship Without a Sail, A 1929.42, 1975.13
Ship's Concert in the Eighties, A 1934.42
Ship's the Girl for Me, My 1902.03
Shipboard Frolics 1910.13
Shipbuilders' Song, The 1900.50
Shipoopi 1957.18, 2000.11
Shipping News, The 1890.33
Ships in the Night 1916.04
Ships That Pass in the Night 1919.11
Shir Hatan Biem 1968.20
Shir Hattan 1967.13
Shir La Shalom 1972.17
Shirt Song 1882.76
Shirts by Millions 1933.25
Shiver Me Timbers 1975.12, 1979.30
Shivna 1996.12, 2000.05
Shloymele-Malkele 1990.16
Shnyderisher Gezong 1966.21
Sho-Gun of Ka-Choo, The 1904.37
Shoe Shine Boy 1970.17
Shoe-Clap-Platter 1929.46
Shoein' the Mare 1934.19
Shoeless Joe from Hannbal Mo 1999.01
Shoeless Joe from Hannibal Mo 1994.01
Shoeless Joe from Hannibal, Mo 1955.08
Shoemaker Rum 1881.12
Shoener Charley 1877.28
Shoes 1924.36, 1934.40, 1942.34
Shoes of Husband Number One as Worn by Number Two, The 1915.24
Shoes Upon the Table 1993.07
Shogun 1990.17
Sholem Aleichem 1931.29, 1951.20
Shonnie Vas a Nice Young Man 1873.19
Shoo Fly 1869.42
Shoo Fly, don't bodder me 1869.43
Shoo-Fly 1870.07
Shoop Shoop Song, The 1984.15
Shoot Dat Pistol 1927.30
Shooters, The 1880.10
Shooting Craps 1897.07
Shooting Gallery 1940.04
Shooting Show Girls and French Chauffeurs 1911.34
Shooting Star 1920.05, 1992.10
Shooting Star, The 1986.16
Shooting Stars 1925.44, 1985.17
Shop 1917.01

Sweetest Love 1885.49, 1985.02
Sweetest Maid of All 1908.06
Sweetest Melody 1920.47
Sweetest of the Roses 1928.35
Sweetest of Williams 1871.16
Sweetest Part of Loving is to Dream, The 1905.33
Sweetest Song in the World, The 1942.14
Sweetest Sounds, The 1962.03, 1962.17, 2001.09
Sweetest Story Ever Told 1894.37
Sweetest Story Ever Told, The 1895.44
Sweetest Words That Ere Were Said, The 1907.30
Sweetheart 1889.39, 1908.29, 1909.22, 1913.06, 1915.21, 1921.38, 1923.03, 1931.08
Sweetheart - -Will You Answer Yes 1921.37
Sweetheart Goodbye 1890.30
Sweetheart Lane 1922.32
Sweetheart Let Us Dance the Boston 1914.06
Sweetheart Love Ne'er Grows Old 1894.37
Sweetheart Lue 1905.05
Sweetheart Mine 1903.27
Sweetheart of All the Words of Love 1900.01
Sweetheart of Mine 1924.42
Sweetheart of My Own, A 1917.22
Sweetheart of Mystery 1923.16
Sweetheart of Our Student Corps 1929.17
Sweetheart of Your Dream, The 1926.24
Sweetheart Shop Wedding, A 1920.29
Sweetheart Shop, The 1920.29
Sweetheart Time 1912.14, 1926.03
Sweetheart Tree, The 1974.22
Sweetheart, Farewell 1923.11
Sweetheart, I Love But Thee 1896.31
Sweetheart, I'm Waiting 1896.13
Sweetheart, if Thou be Nigh! 1884.57
Sweetheart, Let's Go a Walking 1912.30
Sweethearts 1894.38, 1896.06, 1913.24, 1918.07, 1927.08, 1947.04
Sweethearts in Every Town 1905.28, 1906.24
Sweethearts of the Team, The 1939.27
Sweethearts, Wives and Good Fellows 1912.15
Sweetie 1907.34, 1920.39, 1923.20
Sweetie Dear 1906.14
Sweetie Mine 1930.29
Sweetness 1911.20, 1918.13
Sweetness of Love 1938.03
Sweets to the Sweet 1919.14
Swell 1991.15
Swell Girls 1894.37
Swell Song 1877.23
Swell With the Glass in His Eye, The 1885.51
Swell, The 1879.63, 1880.39
Swellest Cullud Lady of Them All, The 1897.34
Swellest Thing in Town, The 1897.30, 1897.40
Swellest Thing, The 1898.78
Swells of the Ocean 1883.04
Swept Away 1961.09
Swift as Dart 1868.02
Swim Out 1884.65, 1886.35
Swimming Master, The 1901.25
Swing Along 1904.26
Swing Low, Sweet Harriet 1943.20
Swing Low, Sweet Chariot 1976.04
Swing Mikado, The 1939.15
Swing on the Corner 1949.06
Swing Shift 1983.17
Swing Song 1918.06, 1963.29, 1963.29
Swing Struck 1939.14
Swing That Music 1986.02
Swing That Swing 1935.14
Swing Wedding 1937.09
Swing With Me 1881.11
Swing Your Bag 1970.10
Swing Your Lady, Mr. Hemingway 1943.05
Swing Your Projects 1961.28
Swing Your Tails 1930.25
Swing! 1953.03
Swing, Brother, Swing 1999.24
Swing, My Petty One, Swing 1902.03
Swing, The 1920.23
Swingaroo Trio, The 1939.26
Swingin' a Dream 1939.29
Swinging 1989.02
Swinging a Dance 1966.30

Swinging in the Lane 1892.19
Swinging on a Gospel Gate 1886.28
Swinging on a Star 1995.14
Swinging on the Gate 1926.02
Swinging Round the Circle 1869.06
Swinging the Bhumba 1942.35
Swinging, Swinging 1888.34
Swings, The 1910.18
Swingy Little Thingy 1933.16
Swirling Snow 1989.21
Swiss Boy 1860.05
Swiss Echo Song 1920.02
Swiss Miss 1924.43
Swiss Mountain Song 1866.26
Swiss Porters 1904.39
Switchblade Bess 1961.01
Switzer's Home, The 1883.07
Switzerland 1913.30
Sword Dance 1980.26
Sword Dance, The 1947.07
Sword in hand, man to man 1880.04
Sword is My Sweetheart True, The 1910.07
Sword of Damocles, The 1975.08, 2000.17
Sword Quadrille, The 1880.59
Sword Song, The 1901.06
Sword, Rose and Cape 1961.10
Swordfight 1976.03
Sylphide, La 1861.06
Sylphides Avec la Bumpe, Les 1942.18
Sylva, ich will nur dich-Ja Madchen gibt es wunderfeine 1984.05
Sylvia the Gibson Girl 1905.27
Sylvie 1955.03
Symbol of Fire 1950.09
Sympathetic Someone 1925.38
Sympathetic Sue 1909.06
Sympathy 1909.22, 1912.46, 1926.03, 1947.06
Sympathy, Tenderness 1997.09, 1997.09
Symphonic Pantomime 1941.12
Symphonic Poem 1923.08
Symphonie des smelles de bois, La 1947.05, 1948.12
Symphony 1971.18
Symphony in Dress 1920.22
Symphony in Smoke, A 1953.10
Symphony Rap 1984.15
Syncopassion 1926.22
Syncopate 1922.29
Syncopated Clock, The 1987.02
Syncopated Cocktail, A 1919.15
Syncopated Harp 1917.04
Syncopated Heart 1920.01
Syncopated Pipes of Pan 1924.32
Syncopated Sandy 1897.45
Syncopated Strain 1923.11
Syncopated Vamp, The 1920.18
Syncopated Walk, The 1914.31
Syncopatia Land 1913.05
Syncopating Baby 1925.24
Syncopation 1915.27
Syncopation Stenos 1921.16
Syndicate Song, The 1961.16
Synergy 1970.04
Syren and Friar, The 1869.14
Syren and the Friar, The 1870.20
Syringa Tree 1922.04
System 1922.38, 1924.03

T & A 1976.16
T Aint Nobody's Biz-ness if I Do 1978.09
T'Ain't Nobody's Bizness if I Do 1975.20
T'Avoir Aimer, De 1970.01
T'es pianiste de Varsovie 1968.21
T'es venu de loin 1966.20
'T' for Texas 1999.09
T'morra', T'morra' 1944.23
T.C.A. Dance 1957.10
T.E.A.M. 1971.11, 1999.03
T.N.D.P.W.A.M. 1982.04
T.S.O.P. 1974.22
Ta bouche 1929.14
Ta Ra Ra 1964.22
Ta Ra Ra Boom De Ay 1929.41
Ta Ta, My Dainty Little Darling 1906.48

Ta Ta, Ol' Bean 1930.06
Ta Voo 1920.47
Ta! Ta! Ma Bonnie Maggie Darlin' 1930.17
Ta, Ta, Old Bean 1931.36
Ta-hoo 1920.47
Ta-Ra-Ra Boom-De-Ay! 1980.27
Ta-ra-ra-boom-de-ay 1892.38, 1893.23
Ta-ra-ra-Boom-de-re 1891.32
Ta-Ta, Little Girl 1911.32
Tablada, La 1993.08, 1997.13
Table Bay 1966.03
Table for Two, A 1917.08
Table Talk 1981.10
Table With a View 1989.26
Tabloid Papers 1926.21
Taboo 1912.05
Tabor and Drum 1893.02
Tabu/Taking Care of the Ladies 2000.08
Tact 1900.51, 1902.05, 1920.09, 1922.02
Tactics 1971.02
Tactless Little Troubadour 1956.09
Taewongun is Taken to China 1997.16
Taewongun's Regency 1997.16
Tafelberg Hotel, The 1999.12
Taffy 1971.20
Tag Day 1922.44
Tahiti 1926.03
Tahiti Sweetie 1926.03
Tail of a Kite, The 1906.39
Tail of a Whale, The 1905.32
Tailor Made 1887.29
Tailor Made Babies 1929.25
Tailor Man, A 1910.36
Tailor Motel Kamzoil, The 1964.27
Tailor's Drinking Song 1968.22
Tailor's Dummy 1905.55
Tailor's Megilla, The 1968.22
Tailor's Song, The 1968.22
Tain't Gwine to be No Rain 1908.08
Tain't Nobody's Bizness 1976.16
Tain't Nobody's Bizness if I Do 1989.02 see T'a
Tainted Gold 1905.54
Taisez-Vous 1910.35, 1978.19, 1988.18
Tait Song 1974.26
Takarazuka Forever 1989.21
Takarazuka March 1989.21
Take 'Em to the Door Blues 1925.26
Take a Bow 1944.19
Take a Chance 1923.37
Take a Chance Little Girl and Learn to Dance 1918.34
Take a Chance With Me 1921.02
Take a Crank Letter 1949.17
Take a Day Off, Mary Ann 1891.25, 1891.37, 1891.46
Take a Job 1960.22
Take a Letter to the King 1930.30
Take a Letter, Miss Jones 1993.07
Take a Little Baby Home With You 1925.23
Take a Little One Step 1924.02
Take a Little One-Step 1971.03
Take a Little Perfume 1913.33
Take a Little Sip 1971.16
Take a Little Walk 1925.43
Take a Little Wife 1922.39
Take a Look at Me Now 1910.12, 1921.12
Take a Look at That 1990.06
Take a Maid 1907.30
Take a pair of sparkling eyes 1890.02
Take a Pair of Sparkling Eyes 1938.10
Take a Poem 1942.05
Take a Step With Me 1914.04
Take a Swing With Me 1917.22
Take a Tip from Venus 1909.13
Take a Trip 1992.16
Take a Trip in My Auto 1905.33
Take a Trip to Candyland 1917.22
Take a Trip to Harlem 1930.34
Take a Trip to the Seaside 1910.23
Take a Walk on the Wild Side 1982.22
Take a Walk With Me 1925.02
Take and Take and Take 1937.13
Take Away the Darkening Sky 1997.16
Take Back Your Mink 1950.17, 1980.29
Take Care of This House 1976.11

Tar's Song 1892.18
Tar's Song, The 1891.14
Tarantella 1870.22, 1892.21, 1898.46, 1899.39, 1901.19, 1906.49, 1928.26, 1954.13, 1982.09, 1990.20
Tarantella oi mamma ca mo vene 1985.14
Tarantella Rhythm 1934.20
Taranto 1992.15
Tarantos 1986.17
Tarantula 1952.13
Tarantula, The 1969.11
Tarde del Corpus, La 1926.09
Tarradiddle 1897.32
Tartaglia's Lament 2000.10
Tartar 1925.52
Tartar Legend, A 1928.45
Tartar Song, The 1928.30
Tartarin Now Comes 1893.40
Tartarin, the Terrible 1893.40
Tarts and Flowers 1934.15
Taste 1968.03
Taste of Forever, A 1980.30
Taste of the Sea 1934.42
Tattooed Man, The 1897.42
Tattoos, The 1964.39
Taunting Rusty 1987.05
Tausend kleine Engel singen 1984.05
Tavern Foxtrot 1996.08
Tavern Song 1928.29, 1986.14
Tax the Bachelors 1910.01
Taxi 1975.05, 1996.07, 1997.01
Taxi Dancers' Tango 1988.20
Taxi Drivers Lament 1926.17
Taxicab, The 1908.19
Tbiliso 1977.13
Tchastushky 1924.48
Te Deum 1925.32, 1928.12, 1976.08
Tea 1927.20
Tea and Cake Walk 1903.22
Tea and Toast and Kisses 1880.10
Tea Blossom 1926.35
Tea for Two 1925.30, 1942.10, 1942.16, 1971.03, 1973.13, 1983.09, 1993.01, 1995.16, 1998.17, 1999.05
Tea Garden, The 1923.22
Tea in Chicago 1954.16
Tea in the Orient 1918.33
Tea Kettel Song 1905.12
Tea Kettle, The 1924.06
Tea Leaves 1914.20
Tea Party, The 1918.32, 1969.05, 1985.19
Tea Song 1936.28
Tea Time Tap 1927.52
Tea, Tea, Tea 1904.40
Teach Me Everything You Know 1912.13
Teach Me How 1923.37
Teach Me How to Kiss 1921.20
Teach Me How to Kiss, Dear 1897.39
Teach Me How to Love 1915.32
Teach Me How to Shimmy 1995.03
Teach Me Not to Love You 1997.18
Teach Me to Dance 1923.23
Teach Me to Dance Like Grandma 1928.42, 1968.19
Teach Me to Forget 1911.36
Teach Me to Smile 1915.20
Teach Me Tonight 1974.10, 1991.04
Teach the Young Idea How to Shoot 1904.37
Teach Us the Subtle Art of Kissing 1903.14
Teacher, Teacher! 1919.09
Teachers on Parade 1968.06
Teaching McFadden to Waltz 1910.33
Teacup and a Spoon, A 1920.12
Tear the Town Apart 1972.04
Teas for Two 1947.19
Teasin' Baby 1928.10
Teasing 1911.12
Teasing Mama 1928.10
Tecla's Mood 1945.14
Teddy Bear 1989.12
Teddy Bears 1907.03
Teddy Da Roose 1980.27
Teddy Girl, The 1907.27

Teddy the Jungle Man 1909.05
Teddy Toddle, The 1921.36
Teddy-Bear and the Bee, The 1907.61
Tee Oodle Um Bum Bo 1919.12
Teedelum, Tadelum 1897.25
Teenie, Eenie, Weenie 1914.28
Teeter Totter Tessie 1939.12
Telegrams, the Actor's Great Ball 1876.30
Telegraph Boy, The 1879.64
Telephone Dance, The 1986.03
Telephone Duet 1914.04
Telephone Fighters, The 1899.19
Telephone Girl, The 1897.54, 1917.08
Telephone Girlie 1971.03
Telephone Hour, The 1960.06
Telephone Song 1912.15, 1966.24
Telephone Tango 1956.13
Telephone Your Riskey Issey 1910.18
Telephone, The 1991.03
Telescope, The 1880.46
Television's Tough on Love 1950.09
Tell Her 1956.08, 1966.09, 1973.07
Tell Her in the Springtime 1924.44
Tell Her Now 1993.17
Tell Her While the Waltz is Playing 1922.28
Tell Him 1984.15
Tell him thus the love lingers in the heart 1855.03
Tell Him to Come/Hurry Mateo 1926.09, 1926.35
Tell Him, Rose, That I'll Return 1894.47
Tell it All 1904.54
Tell it All Over Again 1914.27
Tell it Like it Is 1992.06
Tell it to the Marines 1928.16
Tell Me 1902.22, 1904.10, 1917.02, 1919.26, 1925.39, 1999.22
Tell Me a Bedtime Story 1923.32
Tell Me Again 1907.61, 1927.43
Tell Me Again, Sweetheart 1902.04
Tell Me Cigarette 1927.14
Tell Me Daisy 1921.31
Tell Me Honey 1902.02
Tell Me How 1954.17
Tell Me it's Not True 1993.07
Tell Me Jo 1961.25
Tell Me More 1925.14
Tell Me Mother 1932.04
Tell Me Not That You are Forgetting 1925.02
Tell Me on a Sunday 1985.12
Tell Me Ruby, Will You be True? 1895.02
Tell Me Something About Yourself 1932.13
Tell Me the French Word for Squeeze Me 1914.14
Tell Me the Story 1946.07
Tell me true, love 1882.63
Tell Me Truly 1924.07, 1928.23
Tell Me What is Love 1929.41
Tell Me What the Rain is Saying 1971.17
Tell Me What Your Eyes Were Made For 1924.39
Tell Me What's the Matter Lovable Eyes 1922.15
Tell Me Where I Shall Find Him 1900.41
Tell Me Where is Fancy Bred? 1981.02
Tell Me where My Wife has gone 1869.07
Tell Me Who I Was 1982.23
Tell Me Who You Are 1928.35
Tell Me Why 1918.07
Tell Me Why, Why, Why 1904.08
Tell Me With Smiles 1923.12
Tell Me, Crystal Ball 1918.33
Tell Me, Daisy 1886.15, 1920.15
Tell Me, Dusky Maiden 1901.27
Tell me, girl 1878.16
Tell Me, Honey 1892.45
Tell Me, Kind Spirit 1920.06
Tell Me, Little Gypsy 1920.18
Tell Me, Lovers, I Pray 1896.45
Tell Me, Pretty Maiden 1900.51, 1902.05, 1920.09, 1933.21, 1938.09
Tell Me, What This Can Be 1930.43
Tell My Father 1999.08
Tell My Why 1987.02
Tell Sweet Saroyana 1981.25
Tell the Band to Play an Irish Tune 1906.22
Tell the Doc 1927.59
Tell the World I'm Through 1927.52

Tell Them Yer Baby's Comin' to Town 1896.31, 1896.37
Tell Tony and Rosabella Goodbye for Me 1956.04
Tell Us What's the Row 1908.44
Tell Us, Jolly Sailors 1902.29
Tell Us, Pretty Ladies 1900.38
Tell-Tale Eyes 1903.24
Telling Fortunes 1923.03
Temperament 1919.05
Temperamental Dances 1912.47
Temperance Crowd, The 1893.30
Temple Bells 1912.30
Temple of Fortune 1902.42
Temple of Love 1870.38
Temple, The 1971.12
Tempo 1961.17
Tempo Di Gavotte 1913.02
Temporary Widow, The 1913.02
Temporary Wives 1920.37
Temps, Le 1965.30, 1974.19, 1983.03, 1991.04
Tempt Me Not 1939.27
Temptation 1920.15, 1920.27, 1985.08
Temptation Rag 1910.18, 1944.32
Temptation Strut, The 1926.14
Temptation Waltz 1915.20
Temptation, The 1904.36
Ten Cents a Dance 1930.08, 1931.08, 1975.13
Ten Commandments of Love, The 1919.12
Ten Dirty Little Fingers 1918.18
Ten Kopecks 1998.11
Ten Little Bridesmaids 1915.07, 1917.29
Ten Little Gentlemen of Spooney Town 1902.44
Ten Minutes Ago 1993.14, 2001.09
Ten Minutes in Bed 1930.38
Ten O'Clock 1914.07, 1970.17
Ten O'Clock Town 1937.07
Ten Plagues, The 1972.09
Ten Years in the Country 1930.18
Tender Feeling of Heart, A 1787.01
Tender Shepherd 1954.13, 1979.22, 1990.20
Tender Spot, A 1964.05
Tender Trap, The 1974.10
Tenderloin Celebration, The 1960.19
Tenderloin, The 1897.25
Tenderly 1976.32
Tendresse, La 1965.08
Tengu 1974.12
Tennessee 1904.43, 1924.30
Tennessee Dan 1931.04
Tennessee, I Hear You Calling 1914.22
Tennis 1909.21, 1912.25, 1930.23
Tennis Champs 1926.13
Tennis Song 1989.29
Tennis Song, The 1976.33
Tennis Terpsichorean 1921.25
Tennis Tournament 1913.05
Tenor, all singers above, A 1894.15
Tenterfield Saddler 1979.11
Tenth and Greenwich 1971.13
Terence's Farewell to Kathleen 1858.03
Teresa, Little Word 1893.02
Terminate 1975.02
Terminix 1972.02
Terpsichore, the Goddess of Dance 1923.04
Terpsichorean Trifle, A 1898.78
Terrace Duet 1988.09
Terre Haute High 1972.25
Terre, terre, droit devant nous! 1929.11
Terres et des coupons, Des 1929.14
Terrible Man, The 1873.28
Terribly Attractive 1939.13
Terrific Band and a Real Nice Crowd, A 1978.27
Terror, Terror 1895.21
Teru, Teru 1948.24
Terzetto Buffo 1910.22
Tessie, You are the Only, Only, Only 1902.35
Test Song 1892.42
Testament 1933.07
Testimony, The 2001.06
Testing, The 1986.18
Tete a l'ombre, La 1961.25
Tete a Tete 1941.11
Tete a Tete With You, A 1916.25

That's the Way of a Sailor 1902.15
That's the Way to Treat a Little Doggie 1911.15
That's the Way to Win a Girl 1914.17
That's the Way We do Things in New Yawk 1992.08
That's What a Fellow Does When He's in Love 1908.13
That's What Friends are For 1985.20
That's What Harlem is to Me 1976.04
That's What He Did 1933.25
That's What He Said 1998.21
That's What I Need Tonight 1972.24
That's What I Told Him Last Night 1950.04
That's What I'd Like for Christmas 1965.28
That's What it is to be Young 1965.19
That's What Life is All About 1976.32
That's What Men are For 1918.34
That's What Miracles are All About 1981.16
That's What My Organ Plays 1908.12
That's What Puzzles the Quaker 1880.10
That's What the Bible Say 1976.35
That's What the Dickie Birds Say 1884.66
That's What the Papers Say 1905.37
That's What the Rose Said to Me 1907.24
That's What the Wild Waves are Saying 1892.29
That's What Young Ladies Do 1966.09
That's What, by Gosh! 1896.37
That's Where a Man Fits In 1955.25
That's Where She Sits All Day 1903.03
That's Where the Laugh Comes In! 1873.19
That's Where We Come In 1934.01
That's Why Darkies Were Born 1931.30
That's Why I Never Married 1907.46, 1911.02
That's Why I Want to Go Home 1947.13
That's Why Lots of People Marry 1910.27
That's Why the Danube is Blue 1907.10
That's Why They Call Me Shine 1911.20
That's Why They Call Us Johns 1924.07
That's Why We Misbehave 1929.33
That's Why We're Dancing 1930.09
That's You 1932.19
That's Your Funeral 1963.01
Theatre is a Lady 1952.20
Theatre, the Theatre, The 1993.05
Theatre/Theatre 1972.18
Theatrical Blues, The 1920.08
Theda Bara 1920.19
Their Courage High, You May Defy 1902.25
Their Eyes, their lips, their Busses 1750.01
Their Fathers Fought at Ramillies 1902.25
Their Hearts are Over Here 1917.37
Them There Eyes 1948.13
Them was the Childhood Days 1912.39
Theme from 2001 1978.01
Theme of the Megilla 1968.22
Theme Song, The 1929.19
Then 1925.47, 1936.29
Then All Come Along 1912.34
Then Away We Go 1903.04
Then Came the War 1930.35
Then Comes the Dawning 1922.33
Then Frederic 1981.01
Then He Kissed Me, And 1984.15, 1985.03
Then I am rich 1859.13
Then I may sing and play? 1894.15
Then I Will Live Love for Thee 1894.40
Then I'd be Satisfied With Life 1901.07, 1902.35, 1980.27, 1982.05
Then I'll Have Time for You 1929.03
Then I'll Marry You 1918.40
Then I'm Yours 1951.10
Then Love Began 1920.27
Then Love Me Some Mo 1927.40
Then Off We Go 1896.48
Then one of us 1890.02
Then Say Good Bye! 1894.17
Then Shout Hurrah 1921.40
Then They Winked the Other Eye 1890.29, 1890.30
Then With a Cachuca, Fandango and Bolero 1899.06
Then You Go 1909.21
Then You May Take Me to the Fair 1960.21
Then You Swing, Swing, Swing 1911.23
Then You Were Never in Love 1940.10
Then You Will Know 1926.42, 1946.03
Then you'll remember me 1844.01

Then You're in Love 1924.25
Then, Frederic, let your escort lion-hearted 1879.72
Then, if I Understand Right 1900.39
Then, take me, Clifford 1887.08
Thenardier Waltz of Treachery 1987.04
Theodora 1902.22
Theodore 1907.41
Theophilus 1910.22
Ther's Rhythm in That Heart of Mine 1936.31
There 1956.02
There a Boat Dat's Leavin' Soon for New York 1983.04
There a Boat That's Leavin' Soon for New York 1935.13
There Ain't No Color Line Around the Rainbow 1943.14
There Ain't No Flies on Me 1957.07
There Ain't No Harm in What You Do 1913.19
There Ain't No Love 1930.33
There Ain't No Sweet Man Worth the Salt of My Tears 1929.04
There are 57 Ways to Win a Man 1911.43
There are Bet and Bell 1887.04
There are Brigands in Every Station 1879.71
There are cases 1895.26
There are Days and There are Days 1981.28
There are Fairies at the Bottom of My Garden 1931.14
There are Fairies at the Bottom of Our Garden 1952.11
There are ladies who dwell 1863.04
There are Lots of Things Teacher Does Not Know 1905.50
There are No Girls Like Show Girls 1982.06
There are No Girls Quite Like Show Girls 1980.18
There are Some Eyes 1988.15
There are some things in this wide world 1895.17
There are Some Things We Can Never Forget 1923.44
There are Such Things 1974.09
There are Times 1924.01, 1925.42, 1952.11
There are Tricks in All Trades 1902.43
There are Worse Things I Could Do 1972.12, 1994.07
There are Yanks 1944.01
There But for You Go I 1947.07, 1980.26
There Came a Vision 1911.46
There Comes a Night 1908.15
There Comes a Some Day 1921.03
There Goes My Baby 1995.03
There grew a little flower 'neath a great oak tree 1887.10
There had to be the Waltz 1938.15
There He Goes 1910.13
There He Goes, Mr. Phileas Fogg 1946.13
There I Go Dreaming Again 1932.07
There I'd Be 1945.20
There in the Dark 1969.08
There is a beauty, in the bellow of the blast 1885.47
There is a Birthday 1974.23
There is a flower that bloometh 1848.04
There is a Fountain/it Don't Make Sense 1998.21
There is a Garden in Loveland 1925.06
There is a Girl 1921.33
There is a Santa Claus 1936.12
There is a Soul Mate 1911.36
There is a Star in My Heart 1998.08
There is a Sucker Born Ev'ry Minute 1980.07
There is a Time 1965.30, 1974.01
There is a View... 1997.12
There is Beautiful You Are 1966.09
There is Beauty in the Bellows of the Blast 1939.15
There is Gold Along the Rivers 1907.26
There is Life Everywhere 1924.48
There is More 1983.20
There is More to Love 1990.04
There is no human joy 1855.03, 1855.06
There is No Land Like England 1892.14
There is No Other Way 1976.02
There is No Place Like Home 1908.23
There is no such thing as a Bogie man 1902.32
There is Nothin' Like a Dame 1949.04
There is Nothing too Good for You 1923.18
There is Only One Paris for That 1960.13
There is Somebody Waiting for Me 1928.05
There is Something About You That I Love, Love, Love 1904.22
There is the Key 1904.01
There Isn't Anything That Can't be Cured 1906.30
There isn't One Girl 1924.08

There lived a king, as I've been told 1890.02
There Must be Someone for Me 1944.02
There Must be Something Better Than Love 1950.04
There Must be Something Wrong About My Face 1900.16
There Never was a Baby Like My Baby 1951.19
There Never was a Town Like Paris 1926.37
There Never was a White Hope Whose Christian Name was Cohen 1912.36
There Never was a Woman 1958.14
There Once was a Man 1954.05
There Once was a Small Street Arab 1900.37
There Once was a Time 1886.45
There Once was a Witch 1892.42
There Once was an Owl 1903.37
There Really isn't Any More to Tell 1911.29
There Really Must be Something Nice About Me 1903.22
There she goes with horses prancing 1878.16
There She Is 1982.18, 1997.06
There so Much More 1931.04
There the bells go 1884.14
There was a Fairy Queen 1870.20
There was a Fellow and a Girl 1940.21
There was a Little Man 1971.20
There was a little sailor lad 1888.07
There was a Time 1890.02, 1915.02, 1924.40
There was a Time When on Broadway 1898.50
There was Life, There was Love, There was Laughter 1945.04
There was no ray of light! 1884.14
There was Once a Little Soldier 1902.25
There was Once a Little Village by the Sea 1934.34
There was the Punch 1923.02
There Were Actors Then 1908.07
There When I Need Him 1977.16
There Will be a Girl 1932.15
There Will Never be Another You 1988.08
There You Are 1932.10, 1980.11, 1985.18
There You Have New York Town 1912.24
There'll Always be a Lady Fair 1934.36
There'll Always be an England 1944.29
There'll be a Hot Time in the Old Town To-Night 1896.52, 1897.40
There'll be a Hot Time in the Old Town Tonight 1927.48, 1930.16, 1975.20
There'll be Life, Love and laughter 1945.04
There'll be Lovers as Long as the World Goes Round 1884.41
There'll be Murder Tonight 1895.27
There'll be Some Changes Made 1976.04, 1999.01
There'll be Trouble 1947.02
There'll Have to be Changes Made 1952.15
There'll Never be Another Girl Like Daisy 1917.20
There's "Yes" in the Air 1943.07
There's a Big Cry Baby in the Moon 1908.05
There's a Boat Dat's Leavin' Soon for New York 1958.10
There's a Boat That's Leavin' Soon for New York 1980.10
There's a Brand New Beat in Heaven 1981.07
There's a Brand New Hero 1917.36, 1976.25
There's a Broadway Up in Heaven 1935.11
There's a Certain Kind o' Jingle to My Spurs 1951.05
There's a Chapter 1917.25
There's a Chill in the Air 1934.20
There's a Circus in Town 1969.16
There's a Coach Comin' In 1951.24
There's a Comin' Together 1970.03
There's a Doctor 1993.06
There's a doctor I've found 1972.08
There's a Girl 1991.05
There's a Girl in Havana 1911.35
There's a Great Day Coming, Manana 1940.10
There's a Happy Land 1911.13
There's a Happy Land in the Sky 1943.01
There's a Hill Beyond a Hill 1951.22
There's a Lad That I Know 1896.41
There's a Land in the Silvery Shimmery Moon 1892.55
There's a Legend That is Famous 1889.38
There's a Light in Your Eyes 1918.28
There's a Little Bit of Everything on Broadway 1915.02
There's a Little Fighting Blood in Me 1905.39
There's a little group of isles 1894.15

Tiger, Tiger 1966.18
Tigers' Chorus, The 1883.52
Tight Knit Family, A 1992.09
Tight Rope Walker, The 1902.08
Til the Big Fat Moon Falls Down 1958.20
'Til the Season Comes 'Round Again 1998.19
Till Good Luck Comes My Way 1927.67, 1994.08
Till Him 2001.05
Till I Come Home to You 1918.14
Till I Met You 1929.46
Till My Luck Comes Rolling Along 1922.43
'Till on my venture bold 1887.04
Till the Clouds Roll By 1917.06, 1986.01
Till the Day of My Majority 1903.21
Till the End of Time 1924.05
Till the Liberty Bell Rings Out 1918.10
Till the Light Fades 1890.33
Till the Real Thing Comes Along 1931.11
Till the Volunteers Return 1902.44
Till Then 1969.06
Till There was You 1957.18, 2000.11
Till Tomorrow 1959.25
Till We Meet Again 1877.22, 1894.31
Till We Reach That Day 1998.01
Till You Try 1916.05
Tiller Girls, The 1924.36
Tiller, Foster, Hoffman, Hale and Albertina Rasch 1929.29
Tillie of Longacre Square 1925.27
Tillie Titwillow 1916.03
Tim's Songs and Jokes 1895.44
Time 1958.10, 1979.12
Time After Time 1974.10, 2000.16
Time Ain't Very Long 1927.32
Time and a Half for Overtime 1924.02
Time and Tide 1896.15
Time and Time Again 1935.13, 1942.35
Time Brings About a Change 1972.13
Time for Jukin 1939.24
Time for Love 1926.03
Time for Singing, A 1966.09
Time for Tea 1952.09
Time for the King 1910.03
Time has Changed so Many Customs in the Last Decade 1912.20
Time has come, The 1887.44
Time Heals Everything 1974.18, 1985.19, 1988.08, 1998.07
Time in a Bottle 1997.01
Time is a Gypsy 1934.01
Time is an Ocean 1998.02
Time is Flying 1904.52, 1913.37
Time is Money 1897.25
Time is Not Right, The 1993.04
Time is Now, The 1960.12, 1965.30
Time is Ripe for Loving, The 1976.33
Time is Standing Still 1941.12
Time Marches On 1936.02, 1936.17
Time of Day 1980.02
Time of Dolls is Past, The 1910.24
Time of Our Life, The 1972.21
Time of Your Life 1941.03
Time of Your Life, The 1996.08
Time on My Hands 1930.39
Time Passed Her By 1982.23
Time Stands Still 1948.18
Time Step 1960.07
Time there was when earthly joy 1893.02
Time to Let Go 1968.08
Time to Love, The 1903.39
Time to Sing 1941.09
Time to Take a Drink 1920.31
Time Warp 1975.08
Time Warp, The 2000.17
Time was, when Love and I were well acquainted 1879.10
Time Wasted 1923.23
Time will come, The 1870.20
Time Will Come, The 1894.45
Time Will Tell 1922.31
Time, Oh, Time 1914.03
Time, the Place and the Girl, The 1905.57
Time-Clock Slaves 1923.45

Timely Topics 1898.70
Times are Gettin' Hard, Boys 1963.19
Times Have Changed 1969.11
Times Square 1922.45
Times Square Arguments, The 1915.02
Times Square Ballet 1971.15, 1998.16
Times up to now, to the gate 1877.39
Timid and Graceful 1880.69
Timid Bird 1884.57
Timid Frieda 1972.16
Timing 1985.05
Timothy D. Sullivan Chowder Party, The 1899.19
Tin Gee Gee, The 1900.44
Tin Pan Alley 1953.17
Tin Wedding Whistle 1973.08
Ting Tang Kee 1904.18
Ting-a-Ling 1915.17, 1925.45
Ting-a-Ling Dearie 1963.20
Ting-a-ling-a-ling 1920.37
Ting-a-Ling-a-Ling Ping Pong 1905.37
Tinker Song, The 1944.25
Tinker, Tailor 1907.32
Tinkers' Song, The 1891.29, 1929.43
Tinkle Tune 1923.36
Tinkle-inkle-inkle 1918.12
Tinkle-Tinkle 1929.29
Tiny Room 1948.08
Tiny Touch, A 1913.04
Tip Top Toreador 1920.47
Tip Your Hat 1938.01
Tip Your Hat to Hatty 1919.44
Tip Your Hat to the American Millionairess 1912.15
Tip Your Hat to Uncle Sammy 1905.32
Tip-a-Top 1912.04
Tip-Toe 1919.07
Tip-Toe Tip-Tap 1929.26
Tip-Toes 1925.49
Tip-Top 1920.36
Tipferl aus dem I, Das 1880.60
Tippecanoe 1902.15
Tipperary 1907.34
Tipperary Nora 1906.29
Tippy Tippy Toes 1960.22
Tips 1903.33, 1982.04
Tips of Gay Paree, The 1900.38
Tipsey Song, The 1871.16
Tipsy Swell and the Messenger Boy, The 1908.15
Tiptoe 1911.39
Tira a Campa 1964.03
Tirade, The 1954.03
Tirana, La 1917.25, 1917.33
Tired Business Man, The 1920.01
Tired of it All 1928.41
Tired of Love 1930.25
Tired of the South 1935.11
Tirollallero 1964.03
Tirrallallera 1964.03
'Tis a Glorious Thing to Plot 1888.38
'Tis a gossip too 1887.04
'Tis a Shame I Declare 1860.03
'Tis a Very Ticklish Question 1888.19
Tis an Irish Girl I Love, and She's Just Like You 1912.06
'Tis Astounding 1906.01
Tis Better to Have Loved and Lost Than Never to Have Loved at All 1902.02
Tis Boulotte 1875.19
'Tis done! I am a bride! 1888.35
'Tis Dreadful 1906.01
'Tis Eventide 1897.48
'Tis for a Land of Roses 1888.19
'Tis gone - the past was all a dream 1844.01
'Tis hard to put the hand 1864.13
'Tis He! 1881.36
Tis I Alone Can Tell 1884.28,
'Tis I Alone Can Tell 1885.08
'Tis I! 1884.57
Tis in Vain That I Try to Forget You 1920.15
'Tis Joy to Meet 1882.33
Tis Love 1927.55
'Tis Love has Caused All Mortal Trouble 1881.11
'Tis most perplexing 1888.07
Tis Noon of Tropic Day 1909.04
'Tis Not on Hills 1880.47

'Tis Oanita 1868.02
Tis of Thee 1940.18
Tis Pity, Tis True 1976.03
Tis Sad to Leave 1934.17
'Tis Sad to Leave a Business Grand 1845.01
'Tis sad to leave our fatherland 1844.01
'Tis Sad to Love in Vain 1895.06
'Tis shameful thus to treat you 1877.20
'Tis she! A happy fate 1878.16
'Tis she! Mystery stranger 1888.07
Tis Summer 1912.30
'Tis the Borgia 1873.05
Tis the End 1915.30
'Tis the harp in the air 1848.04
'Tis the Hour 1904.51
Tis the Luck of the Irish 1948.21
'Tis the Spirit Not the Letter 1896.10
'Tis Time 1879.42
'Tis Time to Say Good Night 1880.38
'Tis Twelve, I think 1879.10
'Tis Very Awkward 1882.33
'Tis very hard to choose 1895.26
'Tis Woman that seduces all Mankind 1750.01
'Tis woman that seduces all mankind 1854.06
Tis Woman That Seduces All Mankind 1957.02
Tis You I Love 1902.02
Tisket a Tax It, A 1939.19
Tisket, A-Tasket, A 1997.01
Tit for Tat 1888.28
Tit Willow 1886.11
Tit, Tat, Toe 1876.32
Titina 1924.36, 1925.05, 1925.10, 1925.24
Titled Widows All are We 1894.45
Titles 1908.19
Titsy Bitsy Girl, The 1908.25
Tittle Tattle 1904.55
Titwillow 1939.15, 1939.17
Tizan 1904.17
Tkambuzza 1965.32
TNT 1946.24
To a slow and stately measure 1882.63
To a Small Boy Standing on My Shoes While I am Wearing Them 1973.08
To Adjust is a Must 1957.17
To America 1986.13
To Anacreon in Heav'n 1976.11
To and Fro 1895.08
To Arms 1906.49
To Arms! 1879.15
To Arms! Hear the Cry 1904.50
To arms! To arms! 1886.49
To be a Captain 1997.06
To be a Little Singing Girl 1899.34
To be a Lone Widow 1891.11
To be a Soldier 1983.03
To be Able to Feel 1975.01
To be Alone With You 1964.33
To be an Actor 1907.40, 1908.12
To be Artistic 1967.14
To be Beautiful 1905.02
To be Continued 1910.20
To be or Not to Be 1933.22
To be or Not to be in Love 1955.12
To be Together is the Thing 1919.31
To be Truly Refined 1902.43
To be With Thee 1902.03
To be Worthy of You 1919.36
To bed so soon, Good night 1887.44
To Blazassus 1907.55
To Bring Up a Girl 1909.28
To Call Thee Mine 1903.36
To Day 1899.29
To Death: a Valentine 1956.09
To Die of Love 1974.19
To do What We Like 1938.19
To Drik We Have No Fear 1907.05
To Dwell Beside Us Evermore 1882.18
To Each His Dulcinea 1965.34
To Educate These Young Ladies 1881.11
To Erminie 1886.30
To Every Man His Dreams 1965.34
To Find a Lover 1999.22
To Follow Every Fancy 1916.06

Twilight Song 1919.31
Twilight Voices 1925.39
Twill Never be the Same 1950.10
Twilly of Fifth Avenue 1924.38
Twin Butterflies That Fitfully Fall 1903.21
Twin Duet, The 1897.37
Twin Soliloquies 1949.04
Twinkle 1918.40
Twinkle in Your Eye, A 1938.05
Twinkle in Your Eye, The 1922.28
Twinkle Little Star 1919.28
Twinkle Twinkle 1896.06
Twinkle Twinkle Little Star 1979.18
Twinkle, Twinkle 1880.18, 1917.30, 1926.39
Twinkle, Twinkle, Little Star 1904.23
Twinkling Star 1907.58
Twinkling stars are laughing Love 1869.43
Twist Canotier, Le 1963.02
Twist Her Mind 1976.03
Twist My Arm 1955.12
Twist, The 1982.22
Twisted Every Way 1988.01
Twit, Twit, Twit 1918.20
Twixt Love and Duty 1917.28
Twixt You and Me 1879.50
Two a Day for Keith 1936.05, 1983.02
Two a Day on the Milky Way 1957.01
Two and Four 1999.24
Two and Two 1883.12
Two are Company 1926.26
Two are One 1922.08
Two Bad Men are We 1877.43
Two Big Eyes 1915.26
Two birdies with their feathers 1889.10
Two Bold Bad Men 1898.22
Two Boys 1928.37, 1979.11
Two by Four 1926.03
Two by Two 1970.19
Two Can Play at That Game 1916.01
Two Cockatoos 1911.44
Two Coro Delle Lavandiare 1985.14
Two Dandy Darkies 1914.34
Two Dead Game Sports 1899.18
Two Dolls and the Glory of France, The 1903.40
Two Enemies 1889.09
Two Enemies, The 1889.41
Two Eves, The 1881.36
Two Eyes 1903.07
Two Eyes of Blue 1902.35
Two Eyes of Brown 1903.32
Two Faced Woman 1972.05
Two Faces in the Dark 1959.01
Two Fellows and a Girl 1926.12
Two Gendarmes, The 1904.22
Two Get Together 1934.40
Two Giddy Goats 1909.29
Two Girls from the Chorus 1923.46
Two Guitars 1934.32, 1965.30
Two Happy Gods 1895.26
Two Happy Tadpoles 1916.25
Two Heads 1976.31
Two Heads are Better Than One 1896.29, 1912.45, 1915.21
Two Hearts Beat as One 1906.31, 1908.21
Two Hearts in Gypsy Time 1951.10
Two Hearts Made One 1902.18
Two in a Crowd 1935.19
Two in a Taxi 1940.07
Two in Love 1929.39
Two is Company 1900.57, 1915.22, 1918.39, 1927.34
Two is Company - Three is None 1902.25
Two is Plenty 1908.06
Two Kinsmen 1985.18
Two Ladies 1966.24, 1998.04
Two Ladies and a Man 1936.27
Two Ladies in de Shade of de Banana Tree 1954.19
Two Laughing Irish Eyes 1915.24
Two Letters 1880.19
Two Lips are Roses 1923.08
Two Lips are Waiitng in Tulip Town 1912.16
Two Lips from Georgia 1919.26
Two Little Babes in the Wood 1924.32

Two Little Blue Birds 1925.33
Two Little Cannibal Ladies 1912.40
Two Little Chicks 1902.30
Two Little Dolls 1895.17
Two Little Doves 1903.38
Two Little Girls and a Boy 1923.22
Two Little Girls in Blue 1893.30, 1894.07, 1921.10
Two Little Hearts 1912.15
Two Little Love Bees 1910.37
Two Little Love Birds 1921.06
Two Little Lovebirds 1904.35
Two Little Pals 1923.36
Two Little Ruby Rings 1922.26
Two Little Sausages 1908.25
Two Little Ships 1927.01
Two Little Stars 1926.31
Two Little Tramps from Jail 1886.32
Two Little Trees 1988.15
Two Little Wooden Shoes 1922.23
Two Little Words 1997.07
Two Lives, The 1883.04
Two Lost Souls 1955.08, 1994.01
Two Lovely Black Eyes 1960.17
Two Lovers 1981.24
Two Lovers Once Wooed the Same Maiden 1894.47
Two Loves 1955.19
Two Loving Arms 1927.54
Two Loving Birds 1930.17
Two Make a Home 1923.27
Two Months Have Passed 1882.45
Two Musketeers 1993.17
Two of Us, The 1928.31, 1948.08, 1968.07, 1977.05, 1979.33, 1981.10, 1989.07
Two Old Sports 1894.51
Two People in Love 1983.19
Two Perfect Lovers 1930.20
Two Pictures 1894.07
Two Playhouses, The 1914.34
Two Rivers, The 1881.07, 1882.20
Two Rubes 1920.18
Two Sides of a Story 1894.17
Two Sleepy People 1978.09, 1980.29
Two Thousand and one: Thus Spake Zarathustra 1989.07
Two to One 1919.37
Two Tramps 1892.19
Two Unfortunate Orphans 1931.04
Two wise men, The 1883.66
Two Years in the Making 1958.14
Two's Company 1890.23, 1974.13
Two's Company, Three's a Crowd 1919.35, 1921.35
Two-a-Day 1985.19
Two-Day for Keith 1975.13
Two-Faced Woman 1932.17
Two-Headed Nightingale, The 1908.34
Twould Never Never Do 1884.37
Tycoon March 1886.15
Tyler My Boy 1959.14
Tympany Dance 1886.15
Typewriter Girls, The 1898.08
Typewriter Song, The 1921.37
Typewriting 1909.21
Typical Day, A 1956.12
Typical Mashers, The 1889.37
Typical Opening Chorus, The 1915.02
Typical Self-Made American 1930.02
Typical Topical Tunes 1918.07
Typical tune of Zanzibar, A 1896.13
Typically English 1962.18, 1978.18
Typische Deutsche 1962.18, 1978.18
Tyrolean 1885.03
Tyrolean Duet 1892.45
Tyrolean Maid 1906.49
Tyroliene 1868.08
Tyrolienne 1869.43, 1873.02
Tyup 1922.41
Tzigane Song 1895.12

U Corredu 1985.16
U, Dearie 1909.30
U.N.C.O.U.P.L.E.D. 1987.05
U.S. Black Marines, The 1886.52

U.S. March 1899.12
U.S. Volunteers, The 1904.23
U.S. vs. U.S.S.R. 1988.09
U.S.A. 1903.28, 1904.14
U.S.A. Limited, The 1913.22
Ua Like No a Like 1912.03
Uber die Unsicherheit menschlicher Verhaltnisse 1965.04
Uciekali 1992.05
Udumo Lonke Mbathazeli 1997.14
Ugg-a-Wugg 1954.13, 1979.22
Ugg-aWugg 1990.20
Ugly Chile 1999.06
Uh-Huh, Oh-Yeah! 1958.01
Uh-Oh! 1963.08
Uh-Uh 1924.30
Uia Mai Koia 1972.20
Ukelele Lady 1924.46
Ukelele Lorelei 1925.14
Uking the Uke 1924.33
Ukrainian Song, The 1922.37
Uli, ali ola, e! 1881.04
Ultima Curda, La 1985.07, 1999.18
Ultra Peacock Strut, The 1923.23
Um-Um-Da-Da 1924.46
Umble 1981.12
Umbrellas of Cherbourg, The 1974.20
Umngcwabo 1997.14
Ump-pum Man, The 1903.27
Umpty Umpty Aye 1895.43
Un Garcon Dansait 1959.15
Un Jour Tu Verras 1958.06
Un mari semblable merite 1877.32
Un Mejor Dia Vendra 1978.12
Un Oncore 1904.26
Un par un 1974.19
Un peu d'Amour 1919.12
Un Sale Petit Brouillard 1981.04
Unaccustomed as I Am 1927.23, 1930.33, 1930.37
Unafraid 1965.17
Unbeliever, The 1980.10
Unborn Love, The 1970.05
Uncertainty of Human Conditions, The 1965.04
Unchain the dogs of war 1898.25
Unchained Melody 1955.13, 1997.21
Uncle Chris 1979.12
Uncle Harry 1986.19
Uncle John Tappit 1907.51
Uncle Reilly 1890.49
Uncle Sam 1899.33
Uncle Sam and Columbia 1892.45
Uncle Sam Land 1907.53
Uncle Sam Rag, The 1959.01
Uncle Sam's Best Girl 1907.25
Uncle Sam's Boys in Blue 1900.38
Uncle Sam's Lullaby 1939.24
Uncle Sam's Marines 1904.25
Uncle Says I Musn't, so I Won't 1910.22
Uncle Tom and Old Black Joe 1921.16
Uncle Tom Cabin Blues 1924.46
Uncle Tom Combination, The 1893.10
Uncle Tom's Saloon 1922.16
Uncle Tom's Wedding 1870.38
Uncle-Huck-A-Buck Song, The 1996.07
Und der Deutscher Lied 1894.13
Und nun sagen Sie geschwind 1885.01
Undecided Blues, The 1925.05
Under a Gay Sombrero 1914.19
Under a One-Man Top 1924.03
Under a Panama 1904.13
Under a Spell 1958.04
Under an Oak 1894.45
Under Any Old Flag at All 1907.57
Under Cover 1903.26
Under Fire 1916.02
Under Grecian Skies 1920.03
Under My Umbrella 1925.44
Under Our Lovely Umbrellas 1904.15
Under Separate Cover 2001.01
Under the Bamboo Tree 1902.23, 1902.42, 1903.01, 1917.26, 1946.21, 1980.10, 1989.23, 1999.23
Under the Bargain Tree 1908.07

Under the China Moon 1913.16
Under the Clock at the Astor 1931.13
Under the Clover Moon 1927.19
Under the Deodar 1902.30
Under the Double Eagle 1978.05
Under the Elms at Old New Haven 1901.17
Under the Goo Goo Tree 1904.15
Under the Honeymoon 1908.44
Under the Jessamine 1920.12
Under the Jungle Moon 1907.33
Under the Love Tree 1912.14
Under the Mazuma Tree 1908.12
Under the Midsummer Moon 1927.43
Under the Mistletoe Bough 1902.04, 1903.39
Under the Moon 1919.42
Under the Mulberry Tree 1903.29
Under the Palm Tree Shade 1905.31
Under the pump 1887.44
Under the Ragtime Flag 1912.25
Under the Roller Coaster 1984.01
Under the Ropes 1967.06
Under the Sea 1906.46, 1915.16, 1916.24
Under the Shade of the Palm 1900.51, 1902.05
Under the Shade of the Sheltering Palms 1920.09
Under the Sleeping Volcano 1949.12
Under the Statler Clock 1931.36
Under the Tree 1969.02
Under the Willow She's Sleeping 1939.21
Under the Willow Tree 1917.08
Under the Yum-Yum Tree 1910.12
Under Two Flags 1901.12
Under Wicket 1905.36
Under Your White Stars 1998.11
Under-World, The 1908.42
Underneath a Big Umbrella 1919.14
Underneath a Japanese Moon 1914.15
Underneath it All 1970.07
Underneath the Dixie Moon 1920.10
Underneath the Palms 1922.34
Underneath the Table 1923.22
Understand Don't You See, don't you know 1889.46
Understudy Dance Specialty, The 1926.29
Undertakers' Frolic, The 1899.11
Underture 1972.08
Underworld: an Expose, The 1956.09
Undiscovered Son, The 1978.11
Undo 1972.18
Undressing Girls With My Eyes 1976.09
Une Demoiselle Sur Une Balancoire 1959.15
Une fois seule avec le comte 1885.59
Une Nuit Paris 1913.30
Une servante qui m'importe 1878.08
Unescorted Women 1980.30
Unexpected Song 1985.12, 1992.12
Unexpectedly 1922.25
Unexpressed 2000.16
Unfair 1959.25
Unfaithful One Will Die, The 1977.01
Unfortunate Baron and I 1879.38
Unfortunate Rosie 1928.09
Unhappy 1917.13, 2001.05
UNICEF Song 1960.10
Uniform, The 1937.16
Union Label 1940.21
Union League, The 1933.25
Union Square 1906.19, 1933.25
United Nations 1943.11
United We Stand 1906.07
Universe in Mourning 1972.14
Unlikely Lovers 1992.09
Unlucky Blues 1921.27
Unlucky in Love 1924.44
Unmistakable Sign 1957.14
Unnecessary Town 1956.12
Uno 1923.06, 1925.05, 1985.07, 1993.08, 1999.18
Unofficial Spokesman, The 1930.02
Unprotected Spinster, The 1882.17
Unrequited 1925.21
Unrequited love 1880.46
Unrequited Love 1920.31, 1947.14
Unsuspecting Hearts 1988.12
Untalented Relative, The 1962.02

Unter Daine Vaisse Shteren 1989.10
Unter Dayne Vayse Shtern 1998.11
Unter der Linden 1907.37
Until the Real Thing Comes Along 1974.10
Until the World Needs Me Again 1997.16, 1998.08
Until Then 1908.08
Until Today 1966.30
Until Tomorrow Night 1986.20
Until We Meet Again 1905.44
Until We Say Goodbye 1928.12
Until You Get Somebody Else 1928.47, 1979.05
Until You Say Goodbye 1920.27
Until You Say Yes 1922.31
Unto the Castle Gates I'll Guide You 1877.39
Unto Your Heart 1929.17
Untrue Pigeon, The 1978.11
Unusual Way 1982.09
Unveiling of a Broadway Girl, The 1922.17
Unveiling of the Statue, The 1907.52
Unworthy of Your Love 1999.20
Up Above the Stars 1919.13
Up Among the Chimney Pots 1930.06
Up and at 'Em 1933.25
Up and Down the Boardwalk 1905.23, 1905.37
Up and Down, Over the Town 1907.15
Up Chickamauga Hill 1936.28
Up from the Gutter 1945.03
Up Helm! 1886.50
Up High 1938.08
Up in a Balloon 1869.11, 1909.17
Up in the Air 1919.26
Up in the Clouds 1922.01, 1927.52, 1981.03, 1981.03
Up in the Elevated Railway 1954.01
Up in the Sky 1930.24, 1947.10
Up in the Tenderloin 1894.49
Up on High 1927.36
Up on Our Toes 1923.19
Up on the Hudson Shore 1913.05
Up on the Roof 1900.40
Up She Goes 1922.41
Up the Ladder 1981.12
Up There 1923.44
Up to Date 1889.54
Up to G 1869.40
Up to His Old Tricks 1974.13
Up Where the People Are 1960.20
Up with the banner 1844.01
Up With the Stars 1922.41
Up with the Sun 1864.22
Up! Up! Up! In My Aeroplane 1909.13
Up, Corsairs, have at them 1887.43
Up, Down, Left, Right 1917.36
Up, Up, Help a Fellow Up 1907.49
Up-to-Date Chansonettes, The 1896.34
Up-to-Date Policeman, The 1897.04
Upon a Moonlight Night in May 1946.16
Upon my word, Miss 1893.02
Upon Our Little Farm 1893.19
Upon our sea-girt land 1894.15
Upon Paul's Steeple 1881.11, 1881.27
Upon the sea 1887.43
Upon the Stage Let's Have a Fling 1896.48
Upper Broadway After Dark 1902.24
Upper Crust, The 1922.48
Uprising of the Old Line Units 1997.16
Ups and Downs 1925.06, 1930.20
Ups-a-Daisy 1928.35
Upsi-Daisy 1911.36
Upside Down 1921.33
Upside-Down Thief, The 1965.29
Upstairs 1968.31
Upstairs Over a Speakeasy 1929.24
Uptown 1973.14, 1986.13, 2000.08
Uptown Downtown 1897.54
Urban Renewal 1971.20
Uriah's Fate Sealed 1997.12
Uriti 1962.14
Uriti Kitchen 1962.14
Us on a Bus 1936.07
Usaac 1918.14
Use of French, The 1898.17
Use What You Got 1997.08

Use Your Imagination 1950.20, 1984.10
Use Your Judgement 1921.17
Use Your Noggin 1966.27
Useful Phrases 1961.18, 1968.19
Useless Song 1966.19
Usher 1927.27
Usher from the Mezzanine, The 1964.21
Ushing Ain't the Only Thing We Do 1916.15
Usual Opening Chorus, The 1920.33
Uthando Luphelile 1977.01
Utopia 1927.16
Utsukushiki Nippon 1989.21
Uyamemeza Ungoma 1988.02
Uz-Guz-Goozle-Um 1911.14
V.I.P. 1960.23
Va petite Mousse 1878.08
Va-Pas T'Imaginer 1958.06
Vacation 1982.04
Vacation in the Store 1949.01
Vadinho is Gone 1979.03
Vagabond Boy 1872.34
Vagrant Fancies 1909.15
Vagrant Stream, The 1907.08
Vagrants of Erin, The 1897.12
Vait Sare and hear von little story 1840.03
Val-De-Ri, Val-De-Ra 1955.13
Vale of Dreaming, The 1913.02
Valencia 1926.14
Valentine 1932.04, 1947.05, 1948.12, 1963.02, 1965.03
Valentine for Beecher, A 1980.30
Valentine's Day Card 1941.13
Valet, The 1906.25
Valiant Solders 1870.27
Valking Dat Broadway Down 1870.24
Valley of Dreams 1920.26
Valley of Dreams, The 1920.08
Valley of Elah, The 1997.12
Valley of Hokus Po, The 1904.52
Valley of the Dry Bones 1993.01, 1995.16, 1998.17
Vals de Espana 1948.24
Valse 1909.03, 1972.24
Valse Amoreuse 1931.09
Valse Anglaise 1956.13
Valse au L'Air 1919.06
Valse Julian 1911.30
Valse Milieu 1960.13
Vamos a Bailar 1979.08
Vamp a Little Lady 1918.07, 1919.16
Vamp, The 1919.18
Vampire Dance 1919.03
Vampires, The 1998.02
Vamps, They 1955.25
Van der ershter vet lachn 1960.18
Van Vattel's Vengeance 1882.75
Vandal of Music, The 1936.06
Vanderbilt Cup 1906.05
Vanderdecken 1904.03
Vandyke and Klondyke 1900.40
Vanilla Ice Cream 1963.14
Vaniteaser 1928.23
Vanities 1919.21
Vanities Girls 1924.31
Vanity 1920.13
Vanity Box, The 1922.05
Vanity Drives Them All to Me 1890.26
Variations 1890.23, 1938.08
Variety 1900.20, 1901.08
Varinoe 1906.14
Various Types of Mashers 1898.58
Varsity Drag 1974.26, 1977.09
Varsity Drag, The 1927.41
Varsovienne 1938.06
Vashti's Farewell 1968.22
Vashti's Kloglid 1968.22
Vassar Girl Finds Job 1937.14
Vassar Waiters - Jubilee 1884.65
Vaterland, Oh, Vaterland 1870.08
Vaterland, Vaterland 1870.27
Vaudeville Ain't Dead 1951.19
Vaudeville Duet 1902.21
Vaudeville is Back 1942.10

Voice With the Smile Wins, The 1917.29
Voices 1969.05, 1985.19
Voices of My Homeland 1933.23
Voices of Youth 1921.11
Voici la minut' deelicate.. 1885.59
Voici la petite chanteuse 1884.50
Voici le Cheese-Knife 1868.05
Voici Madame Grivolin 1887.36
Voila le plus clair de l'affair 1885.56
Vois-tu, j'ai le coeur trop sensible 1877.32
Volare 1987.02
Volga Boat Song 1924.35
Volga Boat Song, The 1924.48
Volga Boatman 1942.16
Volga Boatmen's Song, The 1932.09
Volunteer Fireman, The 1906.48
Volunteers 1904.34
Volunteers, The 1901.19
Volver, Volver 1988.15
Voodoo 1927.33
Voodoo in Haiti 1945.07
Voodoo King, The 1906.08
Voodoo Man 1907.58, 1923.07
Voodoo Night 1947.19
Voodoo of the Zulu Isle 1926.01
Voodoo Pageant 1933.22
Voodoo Venus, The 1888.39
Vordevelle 1918.25
Vote for Lincoln 1961.11
Voting Blues 1950.19
Voting, The 1985.18
Votre femme m'a dit 'je t'aime! 1884.50
Voulez Vous 1920.20
Voulez-vous, Mrs. Yifnif? 1940.21
Vous etes surpris, mes amis 1887.36
Vous ne pouvez la regarder sans rire 1885.56
Vous pouvez, mon cher ami 1886.09
Vous qui voulez des servantes 1878.08
Vous savez ce qu'on dit? 1887.36
Vow, The 2001.06
Voyageur's Song 1919.42
Voyageuse, La 1934.32, 1935.19
Vu Iz Yoysher? 1970.17
Vurria 1932.19

Wa-Hoo 1995.16, 1998.17
Wabash Cannonball 1980.27
Wabash Moon 1927.13
WAC and the Sniper, The 1943.11
Wade in the Water 1990.05
Wading 1909.07
Wading We Go 1901.25
Wages of Sin, The 1951.10, 1985.18
Waggle o' the Kilt 1930.17
Wagon Wheels 1934.01
Wah Wah 1972.18
Wah-Wah 1927.13
Wahzinak's First Letter 1998.02
Wahzinak's Last Letter 1998.02
Wahzinak's Letter 1998.02
Waialae 1912.03
Waikki, I Hear You Calling Me 1922.15
Wail of the Chorus Girl, The 1917.08
Wail of the Tale of the Long Long Trail, The 1919.31
Wail of Their Sweeties 1926.15
Wailana 1912.03
Wait 1935.19, 1971.01, 1979.06
Wait 'Til My Bobby Gets Home 1985.03
Wait 'Til We're Sixty-Five 1965.31
Wait 'Till You See Me in the Morning 1940.09
Wait a Little While 1974.03
Wait for Me 1919.14, 1971.19
Wait for Me Marlena 1974.05
Wait for the Happy Ending 1929.29
Wait for the Little Fairy 1879.38
Wait for the Moon 1924.32
Wait for the Wagon 1854.04, 1980.27
Wait for Tomorrow 1945.14
Wait Til the Clouds Roll By 1884.61
Wait Till I Get on My Robes 1880.24
Wait Till the Cows Come Home 1917.22
Wait Till the Silver Moon Rolls By 1917.35

Wait Till Tomorrow 1917.17
Wait till we see the sweet bye and bye 1893.17
Wait Till You See Her 1942.15, 1975.13, 1990.09
Wait Until My Ship Comes In 1921.34
Wait Until the Sun 1974.23
Wait Until You See My Madeleine 1920.28
Wait! 1934.32
Waiter Girl, The 1906.40
Waiter's Gallop, The 1964.01
Waiter's Song 1885.45
Waiter, the Porter and the Upstairs Maid, The 1940.16
Waiters 1927.17
Waiters' Chorus, The 1893.10
Waiters, The 1906.39
Waiters, The, or Two More to Come 1883.63
Waitin' 1954.19
Waitin' for My Dearie 1947.07, 1980.26
Waitin' for the Evening Train 1963.25
Waitin' Tables 1982.13
Waiting 1920.38, 1992.05
Waiting All the Time for You 1926.04
Waiting Around the Corner 1918.03
Waiting for a Certain Girl 1906.36
Waiting for Charley 1885.06
Waiting for Charlie 1887.05
Waiting for Life 1990.27
Waiting for Me 1898.17, 1907.01, 1912.17
Waiting for the Bride 1907.10
Waiting for the Girls Upstairs 1971.05, 1977.05
Waiting for the Light to Shine 1985.06
Waiting for the Robert E. Lee 1912.09, 1912.29, 1962.17
Waiting for the Sun to Come Out 1920.29
Waiting for the Train 1925.49
Waiting for You 1904.34, 1912.04, 1918.27, 1918.39, 1971.03, 1992.11
Waiting in a Queue 1928.42
Waiting in the Wings 1993.05
Waiting Maid, The 1891.39
Waiting Room 1956.13
Waiting to Ride 1997.07
Waiting, Waiting 1960.22
Wake Me Up a Star 1937.07
Wake Out 1878.04
Wake Out! 1873.19
Wake the Dead 2000.01
Wake Up and Dream 1929.51
Wake Up Father Time 1920.26
Wake Up Little Susie 1982.22
Wake Up! It's Cake Walk Day 1915.23
Wake Up, Little Hepzibah 1913.01
Wake Up, Sleepy Moon 1934.18
Wake Up, Wake Up! 1997.06
Wake, Lady, Wake 1866.07, 1866.21
Wake, The 1952.05
Wake, then, awake! 1895.26
Wake, wake Dinah 1873.04
Wake-Up Sun 1980.15
Wakin' Up the Folks Downstairs 1930.34
Waking Early at Dawn 1868.03
Waking Up Sun 1968.05
Waldorf 1899.12
Waldorf Suite 1992.17
Walk Along John 1871.16
Walk Around 1872.04, 1872.25
Walk Away 1967.16
Walk Down the Avenue With Me 1917.35
Walk Him Up the Stairs 1970.05
Walk into Heaven 1971.16
Walk Like a Sailor 1955.04
Walk On 1963.20
Walk on Gilded Splinters 1992.06
Walk Sweet 1956.07
Walk Tall 1998.14
Walk This Way 1910.01
Walk Together, Children 1930.19
Walk up, walk up 1898.63
Walk up, walk up! 1895.32
Walk, Girls, Walk 1897.03
Walk, Mister, Walk 1903.10, 1904.16, 1905.16
Walk, Walk, Walk 1912.41
Walk, You Sucker, Walk 1901.04

Walker Walk, The 1969.14
Walkin' Along Mindin' My Business 1940.10
Walkin' Sally 1982.15
Walkin' the Track 1926.12
Walking 1905.28, 1906.24, 1999.02
Walking After Midnight 1999.09
Walking Among My Yesterdays 1968.01
Walking Away Whistling 1960.05
Walking Blues 1999.09
Walking by the River 1942.13
Walking Delegate 1911.17
Walking Dogs Around 1926.16
Walking Family, The 1906.39
Walking Happy 1966.27, 1974.10
Walking Home With Angeline 1922.46
Walking Home With Josie 1925.38
Walking in Space 1968.11
Walking in the Starlight 1872.34
Walking Music Store, The 1915.30
Walking My Baby Back Home 1938.19
Walking on a Wire 1911.01
Walking on Air 1931.31
Walking Papers 1977.16
Walking Step Walkover 1915.29
Walking the Deck 1934.20
Walking the Lake 1915.23
Walking Tour, The 1908.10
Walking Walkover, The 1916.07
Walks 1904.07, 1905.29
Walks and Talks 1899.29
Walkure, Die 1990.10
Walkurye 1932.14
Wall Street Blues 1924.11
Wall Street Broker, The 1884.42
Wall Street Reel 1962.02
Wall Street Zoo 1926.30
Walla Walla Boola, The 1963.29
Walla-Walla 1924.17
Wallflower 1911.27, 1924.15, 1984.01
Walter Lee Younger and Son 1973.10
Walter's Dancing School 1897.34
Waltz 1916.05, 1963.12
Waltz and Two-Step 1908.10
Waltz away! Happy day! 1887.12
Waltz by Strauss, A 1964.25
Waltz Caprice 1911.27, 1944.21
Waltz Ensemble 1924.45
Waltz Entrancing 1915.28
Waltz Eternal 1944.21
Waltz Fantasie 1936.27
Waltz for a Ball 1993.14
Waltz for Eva and Che 1979.23
Waltz Huguette 1925.32
Waltz I Heard in a Dream, The 1952.04
Waltz Me Around Again Willie 1980.27
Waltz Me Around Again, Willie 1906.20
Waltz Me Down in the Alley, Sally 1902.15
Waltz Me Up to the Alter, Waiter 1912.16
Waltz of Long Ago, The 1923.32
Waltz of Love, The 1925.10, 1925.24, 1936.22
Waltz of Memory, The 1940.16
Waltz of the Mazy 1897.30
Waltz of the Season 1915.18
Waltz of the Wild, The 1911.40
Waltz Time 1923.01
Waltz Time Girl, The 1912.41
Waltz was Born in Vienna, A 1936.01
Waltz was Made for Lovers, The 1922.35
Waltz With Me 1908.09, 1930.15
Waltz With Me 'Till I'm Dreamy 1908.23
Waltz Without a Kiss, The 1912.17
Waltz, Interlude 1948.27
Waltz, The 1905.50, 1938.03
Waltz, Waltz, Waltz 1904.23
Waltz, You Siren of Melody 1914.09
Waltzing in the Moonlight 1941.09
Waltzing in the Shadow 1963.22
Waltzing in Venice 1952.09
Waltzing is Passing from Land to Land 1921.13
Waltzing Lieutenant, The 1910.18
Waltzing With Jane 1904.15
Walzer von Strauss, A 1964.25

What'd Yo' do Wid' de Letter Mr. Johnson? 1901.25
What'll I do to McAdoo 1898.03
What'll They Think of Next 1940.09
What's a Girl Supposed to Do 1945.12
What's a Kiss 1904.51
What's a Kiss Among Friends? 1927.16
What's a Maiden 1905.36
What's a Nice Girl Like Her 1971.18
What's a Sailor Got? 1945.17
What's a Show 1951.10
What's A-Gonna be Next? 1921.21
What's Become of the Bowery? 1928.09
What's de matter, Susey? 1873.05
What's Goin' on Here? 1951.24
What's Going on Inside? 1969.16
What's Gonna be Tomorrow 1964.18
What's Gonna Happen to Me 1971.01
What's Good About Good Morning? 1946.19
What's Good for General Bullmoose 1956.12
What's Happening in Lisbon? 1999.05
What's He Like? 1945.17
What's His Name? 1989.23
What's in a Kiss 1885.53, 1886.51, 1888.12
What's in a Kiss? 1891.07
What's in a Name 1950.10
What's in a Name? 1920.08, 1931.29
What's in a Name? Here's What's in a Name, or, I
    Wonder What Became of John and , 1973.08
What's in it for Me? 1962.05
What's in it for You? 1960.19
What's in Store for You 1925.19
What's it All About? 1902.40, 1922.21
What's it Coming To? 1928.09
What's Mine is Thine 1940.18
What's Mine is Yours 1944.01
What's My Man Gonna be Like? 1930.35
What's New 1995.14
What's New at the Zoo 1960.23
What's New in New York 1944.15
What's New? 1924.10
What's on the Penny 1940.16
What's Out There for Me? 1969.14
What's Passing Here 1884.57
What's Sauce for the Gander is Sauce for the Goose
    1911.25
What's she saying 1878.16
What's the Angle 1985.17
What's the Buzz 1971.12
What's the Difference 1931.42
What's the Latest News from Town? 1903.02
What's the Matter 1904.01
What's the Matter With Buffalo? 1964.18
What's the Matter With Ham? 1895.15
What's the Matter With Hannah 1900.15
What's the Matter With Letty? 1919.37
What's the Matter With My Man in the Moon 1904.28
What's the Matter With Our City? 1948.23
What's the Matter With Our Team? 1906.30
What's the Matter With the Moon To-Night? 1902.37
What's the Matter With Women Now? 1920.40
What's the Matter With You? 1916.11
What's the Proletariat? 1933.25
What's the Reason? 1928.14
What's the Use 1909.02, 1982.20
What's the use 1997.10
What's the Use of Dreaming 1908.13
What's the Use of Dreaming? 1906.19
What's the Use of Getting Sober 1992.03
What's the Use of Going to Bed 1911.01
What's the Use of Hanging Around With You? 1930.02
What's the Use of Love? 1903.16
What's the Use of Loving Only One Girl? 1917.32
What's the Use of Moonlight? 1911.36
What's the Use of Talking? 1926.13
What's the Use of Wond'rin' 1945.05
What's the Use? 1907.44, 1918.37, 1924.34, 1956.15
What's the Younger Generation Coming To? 1946.22
What's this rumor? 1884.14
What's to Lose 1959.12
What's Wrong With Me? 1959.15, 1961.24, 1961.25,
    1985.08
What's Wrong With Our Love 1987.17

What's Wrong With That? 1986.13
What's Wrong With This Picture? 1925.47
What, Ho! Guards Within 1894.47
What, Marry That Gal! 1898.50
What-a-Ya-Say 1943.18
What-d'ye-say? 1926.29
What? She Your Wife! 1880.69
Whatever 1959.14
Whatever Became of Old Temple 1964.33
Whatever Happened to Melody? 1990.09
Whatever Happened? 1959.14
Whatever has Become of Him? 1884.42
Whatever it is, I've Got It 1928.48
Whatever Lola Wants 1955.08
Whatever Lola Wants Lola Gets 1994.01
Whatever That May Be 1961.08
Whatever the Hue of Your Eyes 1901.08
Whatever Time There Is 1980.23
Whatever Turns You On 1976.20
Whatever's the row? 1884.14
Whats ee I? 1859.18
Whatsoever may be won 1882.75
Wheatless Days 1918.03
Wheel of Fate 1920.19
Wheel the Baby Out 1881.09
Wheels 1928.23
Wheels of a Dream 1998.01
Wheels of Steel 1930.28
When 1950.19, 1990.06
When a Black Man's Blue 1930.29
When a Brother is a Mother to His Sister 1981.14
When a Fella Needs a Friend 1962.24
When a Fellow Loves a Girl 1910.03
When a Fellow Meets a Flapper 1929.02
When a Fellow's on the Level With a Girl That's on the
    Square 1907.57
When a Felon's Not Engaged in His Employment
    1879.72, 1981.01
When a gentleman supposes 1895.29
When a Girl 1918.33
When a Girl Doesn't Know What She Is 1900.34
When a Girl Forgets to Scream 1936.27
When a Girl is Born to be a Lady 1907.27
When a Girl Leads the Band 1910.11
When a Girl's About to Marry 1915.24
When a Good King Reigns 1896.10
When a Good Man Takes to Drink 1945.18
When a Good Soldier 1870.27
When a Hick Chick Meets a City Slicker 1945.17
When a Lady Leads the Band 1902.33
When a Little Farm We Keep 1859.09, 1878.20
When a Lover is Poor 1866.07
When a Maid Comes Knocking at Your Heart 1912.46
When a Maiden is Wooed by a Man 1904.01
When a maiden loves she sits and sighs 1888.35
When a Maiden Must Decide 1942.33
When a Maiden Weds 1891.29, 1929.43, 1944.25
When a Maiden Won't 1907.07
When a maiden's of pure affection 1890.44
When a Man Cries 1972.19
When a man has been a naughty Baronet 1887.10
When a Man is Married 1882.33
When a Man is Single 1916.25
When a Man is Twenty-One 1897.39
When a Man's in Love 1901.18
When a Masculine Stranger Goes By 1894.33
When a merry maiden marries 1890.02
When a Nigger Keeps You Guessing 1897.45
When a Pansy was a Flower 1930.38
When a Pullet is Plump 1917.24
When a Pullet is Plump, it's Tender 1919.20
When a Small own Girl Meets a Small Town Boy
    1917.34
When a Wife Gets Fat 1920.07
When a Wife's in her Pout 1750.01
When a Woman Exits Laughing 1920.38
When a Woman has a Baby 1947.02
When a Woman Loves a Man 1982.12
When a Woman Makes Up Her Mind 1995.01
When a wooer goes a-wooing 1888.35
When a Youth and a Maid Pine and Love 1895.38
When Alfred's Friends Their King Forsook 1902.25

When all around in slumber lies 1887.12
When all around our path is dreary 1855.06
When all night long a chap remains 1882.78
When all the world's asleep 1859.15
When am I Going to Meet Your Mother? 1953.17
When an anger spreads his wing 1884.09
When an Englishman Marries a Parisian 1914.22
When an Interfering Person 1900.51
When Another Cherub Songs 1900.54
When Antello Plays the Cello 1911.02
When as sovereign here I reign 1888.18
When ashore 1880.04
When Baya's Raven Tresses 1893.40
When Black Sallie Sings Pagliacci 1919.25
When Bloom the Roses 1895.27
When Britain truly ruled the waves 1882.78
When Broadway and the Bowery Meet 1888.15
When Buffalo Bill and His Wild West Show First Came
    to Baltimore 1907.55
When Bullets we trade in 1863.01
When but a maid 1894.15
When Caruso Comes to Town 1920.47
When Charlie Plays the Slide Trombone 1902.06
When Ching-a-Lung Hit High 1889.01
When Chloe awakens 1840.03
When Chloe Sings a Song 1899.30, 1912.07
When countryman has a day to himself 1882.20
When Cupid Calls 1916.01
When Cupid Comes a Tapping at the Door 1899.06
When Cupid Entertains 1913.14
When Cupid Hunting Goes 1900.46
When Cupid is the Postman 1908.35
When Dad was Twenty-One 1925.12
When Dancing's a Profession 1919.24
When darkly looms the day 1882.78
When daylight's going 1859.18
When de Reszke Strikes High C 1891.43
When de Wheel Goes Roun' and Roun' 1899.31
When Did I Fall in Love 1959.25
When do We Dance? 1925.49
When Does This Feeling Go Away? 1951.13
When Dreams Come True 1913.19, 1921.27
When Each Day 1918.27
When Enoch, He Knocked, She Knocked Enoch
    1894.35
When Ere You Leave 1896.41
When Evening Shadows Fall 1924.32
When Everything is Hunky-Dory 1929.32
When Eyes Like Yours Look into Eyes Like Mine
    1908.23
When Eyes Meet Eyes 1902.22
When Eyes Meet Eyes, When Lips Meet Lips 1922.09
When first eighteen 1859.16
When first I heard 1863.01
When First I Put This Uniform On 1881.37
When First I Saw My Lady's Face 1976.33
When first my old, old love I knew 1875.35
When First You Left Our Pirate Fold 1879.72
When Foreign Princes Come to Visit Us 1963.29
When fortune parts 1886.40
When Fortune Smiles 1907.05, 1916.08
When Fred'ric was a Little Lad 1879.72
When Freddy was a little boy 1881.06
When Fredric was a Little Lad 1981.01
When from His Couch Uprising 1888.19
When Gaby Did the Gaby Glide 1913.05
When Gemini Meets Capricorn 1962.05
When gentlemen a-courting go 1859.15
When Gentlemen Disagree 1921.04
When Gentlemen Grew Whiskers and Ladies Grew Old
    1927.09
When George Crossed the Delaware 1929.20
When George the Third was King 1869.47, 1903.12
When Girls Command the Army 1908.40
When Grammercy Square was Uptown 1921.04
When Grandma was a Girl 1915.02
When Granny is Elected 1900.03
When Greek Meets Greek 1932.19
When Grown Up Ladies Act Like Babies I've Gotta Love
    'Em, That's All 1914.22
When he holds up his Hand arraign'd for his Life
    1750.01

Where or When 1937.04, 1975.13, 1975.22, 1981.16, 1991.10
Where Shall I Find Him? 1961.18
Where shall I take my Bride? 1870.26
Where Shall I Turn? 1939.21
Where Shall We Go 1920.15
Where Shall We Go Tonight? 1922.16
Where the Bamboo Babies Grow 1922.15
Where the Bee lurks 1862.02
Where the Bee Sucks there lurk I 1880.19
Where the Black-Eyed Susans Grow 1916.03, 1916.25, 1952.11
Where the Blue of the Night Meets the Gold of the Day 1976.32
Where the Cotton Blossoms Grow 1918.04
Where the Edelweiss is Blooming 1912.25
Where the Fairest Flowers are Blooming 1903.37
Where the Flag is Waving 1905.50
Where the Ganges Flows 1923.16
Where the Gigantic Ocean Atlantic 1902.01
Where the Honeymoon Alone Can See 1922.02
Where the Hudson River Flows 1925.31
Where the Lances Gleam 1894.08
Where the Lanterns Gleam 1922.12
Where the Morning Glories Grow 1976.32
Where the pocketbook expert is not a snatching 1881.06
Where the Red, Red Roses Grow 1913.05
Where the River Shannon Flows 1907.28
Where the Sparrows and Chippies Parade 1888.27
Where the Sunset Meets the Sea 1928.47
Where the Sweet Magnolia Grows 1887.48
Where the Willow Makes a Shade 1888.15
Where To 1938.08
Where Tomorrow Begins 1920.45
Where was I When They Passed Out the Luck? 1970.07
Where was I? 1966.27
Where was it That We Met 1997.16, 1998.08
Where We Can be in Love 1925.19
Where Were You? 1920.21
Where Were You? Where was I? 1928.31
Where Would I be Without You 1990.09
Where Would You be Without Me? 1965.19
Where Would You Get Your Coat? 1929.45
Where You Are 1930.20, 1944.14, 1946.05, 1963.25, 1993.09
Where You Carved Your Name 1928.22
Where You Go Will I Go 1906.47
Where You Go, I Go 1933.01
Where You Lead 1930.26
Where'd Marilla Come From? 1971.21
Where's (What's Keeping) My Prince Charming? 1931.11
Where's All This Anger Coming From 1993.17
Where's Charley? 1948.26, 1974.25
Where's Mama? 1910.08
Where's My Bess 1935.13, 1942.03
Where's my duck-a-deary? 1893.02
Where's My Happy Ending? 1931.31
Where's My Shoe? 1963.14
Where's My Sweet and Pretty Man? 1920.06
Where's My Wife? 1945.19
Where's North? 1971.18
Where's That Cat? 1876.37
Where's That Rainbow? 1926.50, 1975.13
Where's That Steamboat Going 2001.06
Where's the Boy I Saved for a Rainy Day? 1940.23
Where's the Boy? Here's the Girl! 1928.43
Where's the Bridegroom? 1911.42
Where's the Girl 1997.19
Where's the Girl for Me? 1915.01
Where's the Girl? 1999.13
Where's the Little Boy for Me? 1916.22
Where's the Mate for Me? 1927.67, 1994.08
Where's the Police? 1857.04
Where, Oh Where 1947.10
Where, Oh Where Can I Find Love? 1933.16
Where, Oh, Where 1950.20
Where-Has-My-Hubby-Gone-Blues 1971.03
Where? 1959.04
Whereas 1967.14
Wherefore and the Why, The 1904.55
Wherefore Art Thou Juliet 1936.01

Wherever He Ain't 1974.18, 1985.19
Wherever I May Go 1954.17
Wherever There's Music and Beautiful Girls 1918.07
Wherever They Fly the Flag of Old England 1946.13
Wherever You Are 1927.48
Wherever You Go 1972.09
Which Door? 1966.18
Which is Brown? 1899.08
Which is the Right Life? 1929.51
Which My Sally Didn't Love Me True 1883.04, 1888.11
Which One Shall We Marry? 1906.26
Which Shall I Choose? 1912.09
Which Shall it Be? 1927.64
Which Way do I Go? 1979.03
Which way shall I turn me? - How can I decide? 1750.01
Which Witch? 1953.17
Whichaway'd They Go? 1949.17
Whichness of the Whatness, The 1922.10
Whiffenpoof Song 1974.09
Whiffenpoof Song, The 1943.23
Whiffer's Song 1940.01
While All are Asleep 1917.30
While all the town is sleeping 1884.14
While I' am Waiting 1905.46
While in My Submarine 1905.33
While My Wife's Away 1921.11
While pensive I thought of my love 1860.01
While Strolling Through the Park 1944.32
While the City Sleeps 1964.32
While the Four Winds Blow 1897.40, 1917.10
While There's a Song to Sing 1947.14
While There's Still Time 1972.01
While They Were Dancing Around 1913.05
While this heart 1859.18
While this heart with joy revealing 1873.04
While Wheeling With the Girl You Love 1896.37
While You are Young 1931.01
While You Love Me 1934.29
While You're Thinking 1902.41, 1917.11
Whilst roughest Mountain Tops 1834.03
Whimsical Girl was I, A 1890.23
Whip Dance 1926.18
Whip Dance, The 1986.03
Whip Hand, The 1921.14
Whip, The 1923.46
Whip-poor-Will 1920.44
Whipo-Poor-Wills 1898.55
Whipperwill 1923.06
Whippoorwill Never Again for Me 1911.24
Whippoorwill Waltz, The 1948.16
Whippoorwill, The 1880.24
Whirl of the Opera, The 1914.01
Whirl of the World, The 1914.01
Whirled into Happiness 1925.07
Whirligig 1899.39
Whirligig Stomp, The 1996.07
Whirling Waters, The 1912.03
Whirlwind Trot 1917.01
Whirlwind Whirl, The 1917.32
Whiskerettes 1902.21
Whiskers 1923.31
Whiskers' Dance 1969.08
Whiskey in the Jug 1856.01
Whiskey, You're the Devil 1893.10
Whisper Alone to Me 1894.17
Whisper in My Ear 1920.23
Whisper to Me 1924.38
Whisper Words of Love 1895.25
Whisper Yes or No, Love 1876.05
Whisper, O Whisper Me, Soft in My Ears 1894.41
Whispered Love 1888.39
Whispering Breeze 1902.39
Whispering Song, The 1926.20
Whispering Trees 1926.15
Whist! Sweet Idle Moon 1894.47
Whist! The Boogie Man 1880.09
Whistle 1914.02, 1926.39
Whistle and I'll Come to Meet You 1920.19
Whistle and I'll Come to You 1915.02
Whistle and the Girls Come Running 'Round 1911.45

Whistle as You Walk Out 1907.59
Whistle Away Your Blues 1925.47
Whistle It 1906.33, 1912.14, 1945.16
Whistle When You Walk Out 1906.44
Whistle When You Want Me 1914.33
Whistle When You're Lonely 1908.05, 1910.20
Whistle While You Work 1979.28, 1999.05
Whistle While You Work, Boys 1930.15
Whistle Works, A 1963.20
Whistling Bill 1902.23
Whistling Colored Boy 1896.02
Whistling Cowboy Joe 1913.18
Whistling Dago, The 1894.06
Whistling Dan 1915.01
Whistling Extraordinary 1894.07, 1894.35
Whistling it All Over Town 1921.20
Whistling March, The 1884.60
Whistling Sue 1903.35
Whistling Superlative 1894.37
Whistling Yankee Girl, The 1906.45
White and Brown Girl 1904.40
White and Gold Ballet 1955.10
White and the Pink, The 1938.06
White and the Red, Huzzah!, The 1894.40
White Boys 1968.11
White Cargo 1925.47
White Christmas 1997.01, 1998.11, 1998.19
White Cliffs of Dover, The 1974.09
White Cockade, The 1883.07
White Fete, The 1911.41
White Folks Call it Chanticler, But it's Just Plain Chicken to Me 1910.18
White Grass 1968.20
White Heat 1931.16, 1972.05
White Horse Inn 1936.22
White Horse, The 1970.20
White Lies 1903.10
White Lies, Black Lies 1912.20
White Light Alley 1911.05
White Light Lane 1910.13
White Lights 1927.53
White Lights Were Coming 1929.28
White Lilacs 1928.26
White Man's Hope, The 1912.20
White Rabbit 1982.22
White Rose, Red Rose 1926.15
White Sash, A 1993.17
White Squall, The 1869.14
White Wash 1907.55
White Wild Rose, The 1990.01
White Wings 1936.03
White Wings, They Never Grow Weary 1930.16
White Witch of Jamaica, The 1956.08
Whitehouse Glide, The 1913.18
Whiter Shade of Pale 1982.22
Whitewash Man, The 1909.09
Whither Thou Goest 1966.30
Whizzin Away Along de Track 1943.24
Who 1924.44, 1970.01, 1980.10
Who am I Thinking Of? 1925.04
Who am I? 1926.27, 1950.08, 1987.04, 2000.14
Who are drivers lacking 1878.16
Who are wanting maidens able 1878.16
Who are We Kidding 1963.12
Who are You Now? 1964.11
Who are you, Sir? 1879.21
Who Ate Napoleons With Josephine When Napoleon was Away? 1920.03
Who Bites the Holes in Schweitzer Cheese? 1925.44
Who Broke the Lock? 1999.09
Who Can I Turn To When Nobody Needs Me? 1965.19
Who Can I Turn To? 1974.11, 1974.22
Who can it be? 1882.60
Who Can Tell Where She Dwells? 1894.40
Who Can Tell? 1919.27
Who Can This Be 1930.12
Who Can? You Can? 1961.27
Who Cares 1921.34
Who Cares for a Name 1923.03
Who Cares for Love? 1969.11
Who Cares? 1914.26, 1917.03, 1920.23, 1930.23, 1931.48, 1999.10

Note: All principal performers listed in a musical's program cast list have been indexed here. In order to contain the index size, ensemble or chorus persons have not been indexed, except where they also appear with a given character name, or else if their subsequent fame warrants their inclusion.

927

Mears, John Henry 1919.18, 1919.43, 1921.19, 1927.09
Mears, Miss 1886.32
Mears, Paul 1935.11
Mears, Poppy 1935.11
Mears, Stanard 1918.13, 1926.02
Meat Loaf 1975.08, 1976.03
Meauberts, Messr. 1861.02
Meazza, Michela 1998.10
Mebus, Gus 1901.04
Mecchi, Irene 1997.20
Meco 1979.13
Mecusker, Inez 1897.15
Medcraft, Russell 1921.24, 1925.47, 1941.08
Medceyum, Amelia 1883.33
Mederick, Mons. 1868.13
Medeyum, Amelia 1882.24
Medford, Kay 1951.24, 1953.17, 1955.11, 1957.11, 1960.06, 1963.17, 1964.11
Media House Production, A 1976.04
Media Innovations 1989.11
Medica, Leon 1971.10
Medic, Miriam 1918.11
Medin, Harriet 1981.19
Medina, Aixa M. Rosario 1995.15
Medina, Benigno 1942.14
Medina, Louisa H. 1836.01
Medina, Mlle. 1870.44, 1871.27
Medinger, Kate 1888.30
Medjuck, Joe 1983.01
Medley, Lottie 1900.58, 1907.16
Medlin, Janet 1947.04
Medoff, Sam 1945.17
Medrano, Roberta 1924.15
Medwin, Charles 1888.38, 1888.41
Mee, Rose 1900.45
Meech, Clifford W. 1905.42
Meech, George T. 1913.26, 1914.24, 1918.01
Mceh, Gregory 1993.06, 1993.17, 1994.01, 1996.08, 1997.09, 2001.09
Meehan, Aileen 1924.22, 1925.26, 1926.12
Mcehan, Danny 1958.20, 1964.11
Meehan, Frank 1896.14, 1918.17
Meehan, Ginger 1930.18, 1930.33
Meehan, Harry 1896.14, 1905.23, 1908.33, 1936.03, 1937.02, 1937.12, 1938.11, 1945.03, 1947.11
Meehan, John 1921.22, 1923.46, 1924.22, 1976.18
Mechan, Jr., John 1927.29, 1942.31, 1944.16
Meehan, Sarah 1884.27
Meehan, Thomas 1977.06, 1979.12, 1993.05, 1997.04, 2001.05
Meehan, William E. 1907.16
Meek, Deanne 1997.02
Meek, Donald 1917.36, 1919.29, 1927.50
Meek, Frederick 1902.18
Meek, Kate 1877.02
Meek, William 1928.25
Meeker, George 1895.15, 1905.10, 1927.09
Meeker, Jess 1951.18
Meeker, Jesse 1950.15
Meeker, Maybelle 1909.11
Meeker, Willie 1905.10
Meers, Thelma 1932.08
Meffert, Emmy 1885.01
Megley, Macklin 1922.29, 1936.27, 1938.04
Megna, John 1960.05
Megrew, Janet 1920.13
Mcgvinet-Ukhutsesi, Tiemuraz 1977.13
Mehan, Dodd 1931.06
Mehl, Brynar 1966.12, 1966.16, 1969.12
Mehl, Charlene 1963.08, 1964.21
Mehlinger, Artie 1913.18, 1915.16, 1919.26
Mcibach, Ina Lea 1984.14
Meier, Johanna 1974.16, 1975.16, 1976.23, 1977.11, 1978.20
Meiggs, H.B. 1894.42
Meighan, James 1927.42
Meighan, T.W. 1857.04, 1857.06
Meilhac 1945.06, 1946.09
Meilhac, Henri 1867.24, 1868.07, 1868.08, 1868.15, 1868.18, 1868.24, 1868.25, 1868.27, 1869.01, 1869.16, 1869.18, 1870.03, 1870.40, 1870.41, 1870.45, 1871.03, 1871.07, 1871.23, 1871.25, 1871.28, 1872.03, 1872.20, 1872.28, 1872.29, 1872.33, 1872.39, 1873.01, 1873.15, 1873.16, 1873.21, 1875.19, 1875.22, 1875.23, 1876.24, 1876.25, 1876.27, 1877.06, 1877.10, 1877.13, 1877.14, 1877.30, 1877.31, 1877.34, 1877.38, 1878.06, 1878.07, 1878.14, 1879.15, 1879.18, 1879.19, 1879.36, 1879.39, 1879.45, 1879.47, 1879.51,

1879.55, 1879.57, 1879.61, 1879.69, 1880.27, 1880.52, 1880.60, 1882.35, 1882.68, 1882.75, 1883.27, 1884.01, 1884.05, 1884.20, 1884.34, 1884.46, 1885.14, 1885.52, 1885.55, 1885.68, 1886.08, 1886.09, 1886.18, 1886.19, 1886.20, 1886.21, 1887.50, 1889.23, 1890.01, 1890.11, 1891.17, 1894.48, 1895.09, 1896.12, 1899.10, 1899.13, 1900.02, 1907.48, 1912.27, 1921.29, 1925.46, 1926.48, 1929.39, 1929.47, 1931.27, 1933.23, 1941.10, 1942.21, 1942.32, 1943.09, 1943.24, 1944.24, 1945.02, 1953.06, 1953.15, 1954.06, 1954.10, 1955.17, 1956.06, 1956.10, 1957.04, 1957.13, 1958.15, 1959.16, 1962.21, 1964.06, 1964.30, 1964.31, 1965.25, 1965.27, 1974.14, 1974.16, 1975.16, 1976.23, 1976.26, 1977.11, 1978.07, 1978.20, 1979.21, 1980.03, 1980.22, 1981.22, 1982.07, 1982.21, 1983.16, 1984.03, 1984.04, 1985.11, 1986.10, 1987.11, 1988.14
Meir, Golda 1971.17
Meisel, Bella 1990.16
Meisel, Will 1999.05
Meiser, Edith 1925.17, 1926.13, 1926.50, 1930.18, 1941.08, 1944.02, 1960.20
Meisler, Bess 1981.18
Meisner, Sanford 1925.17, 1936.28
Meiss, Edwin 1936.12
Meissener, Nell 1900.37
Meisslinger, Louise 1895.28
Meister, Barbara 1960.14, 1960.15, 1959.18, 1961.03, 1961.05, 1966.08, 1966.13
Meister, Fred 1964.25
Meister, Mirzl 1892.31
Meister, Mrs., Toni 1898.53
Meister, Toni 1890.31, 1891.33, 1892.43, 1893.29, 1894.01, 1894.30, 1897.35
Mejia, Carlos 1927.55
Mekka, Eddie 1975.07
Melancon, Corinne 1993.18, 1996.15
Melanie, Mlle. 1862.05
Melbane, May 1902.32
Melbourne, Ada 1876.36
Melbourne, Lillian 1891.18
Melbourne, Madge 1903.20, 1908.03, 1908.27
Melbourne, Richard 1915.17
Melburn, Arline 1927.01
Mele, Louise 1924.42
Melendez, Guadalupe 1917.16
Melendy, E.G. 1907.21
Melesville 1866.27, 1882.45, 1884.08
Melfi, Leonard 1971.04, 1976.27
Melford, Austin 1923.36, 1928.04
Melford, Mark 1886.59, 1887.52
Meli, Gloria 1949.04
Melihac, Henri 1868.16
Melin, Florence 1889.04
Melino, Van J. 1922.01
Melius, Nancy 1989.27, 1991.06
Mella, Fred 1947.18
Mella, Signora 1898.38
Mellen, Dan H. 1903.09
Meller, Harro 1952.08
Meller, Raquel 1926.09, 1926.35
Meller, Tina 1929.51
Melles, Sadie 1910.11, 1912.15
Mellette, Helen 1920.47
Mellette, Rosalie 1920.47
Mellin, Florence 1888.20
Mellini, D. 1894.30
Mellish, Fuller 1924.45, 1926.34, 1927.42
Mellish, Harold 1926.50
Mellish, Jr., Fuller 1926.50, 1928.16
Mellish, Mary 1925.06
Mellner, Frl. 1882.68
Mello, Albert 1966.29, 1970.21
Mellon, Edward 1918.14
Mellon, James J. 1980.02
Mellor, James 1965.39
Mellor, Tom 1911.32, 1912.44, 1930.13
Mellow, Stephen 1968.06
Melmoth, Mrs. 1793.01, 1796.01
Melnick, Daniel 1946.21, 1965.01
Melnotte, K. 1871.18
Melnotte, Katie 1870.33
Melody, Charles 1917.16, 1918.23
Melody, Deanna 1966.12, 1966.16
Melotti, Joe 1989.08
Melrose, Ada 1885.35, 1892.15, 1892.59
Melrose, Bert 1933.14
Melrose, Frank 1895.40, 1897.29
Melrose, Howard 1975.09

Melrose, John 1895.40
Melrose, Kitty 1909.21
Melrose, Ron 1997.09, 1997.19, 1999.13
Melrose, Ronald 1977.16, 1979.28, 1980.09, 1980.29, 1981.10, 1983.17, 1987.16
Melrose, Wally 1895.40
Melrose, Walter 1939.29, 1982.12, 1992.08
Mels, Fred 1924.18
Mels, Irving 1920.47, 1921.31
Melton, A. 1879.04
Melton, Katherine 1906.42
Meltzer, Andrew 1979.26, 1980.21
Melville, A.E. 1904.18
Melville, Alan 1952.09, 1953.17, 1960.07
Melville, Belle 1881.02, 1881.13
Melville, Bert 1919.31, 1921.24
Melville, Bert D. 1914.04
Melville, Emelie 1877.35, 1882.15
Melville, Emilie 1866.13, 1866.16, 1866.17, 1877.36, 1882.16
Melville, Frank 1905.17, 1906.46, 1908.26
Melville, Frederick 1896.32
Melville, George 1906.46, 1908.26, 1910.23
Melville, George D. 1889.50, 1890.25, 1891.41, 1899.04
Melville, Herman 1969.08
Melville, Janet 1907.03
Melville, Julia 1864.02
Melville, June 1952.09
Melville, Lloyd 1897.29
Melville, Messr. 1861.03, 1882.04, 1882.20
Melville, Miss 1855.11
Melville, Mrs. George D. 1890.25
Melville, Nellie 1922.30
Melville, Rose 1899.11
Melvin, Crissie 1924.11
Melvin, Joseph 1948.04
Melvin, Louise 1885.16
Melvin, Mabel 1904.14
Melvin, Maureen 1955.15, 1955.20, 1955.24
Melvin, Murray 1964.28
Melvin, Robert 1978.28
Melvinc, Mable 1908.12
Melvyn, Miss 1860.06
Memoli, Leon 1997.03
Menahemi, Elis 1972.17
Menard, Mark 1998.06, 1998.10, 1999.11, 1999.20, 2000.20
Menard, Raymond 1984.13
Mence, Len 1926.34, 1927.63, 1929.31, 1937.17, 1939.28, 1951.12
Mence, Leonard 1937.01
Menchen Electrical Company 1904.41
Menchen, Joseph 1900.12, 1902.15, 1903.36, 1904.15, 1904.20, 1905.15, 1906.10
Menchen, Joseph C. 1902.19
Mencher, Murray 1935.04
Menching, Joseph 1902.38
Mende, William 1938.15, 1946.10, 1948.18
Mendel, Herr 1883.08
Mendelsohn, Daniel 1941.05
Mendelsohn, Edward 1921.30
Mendelsohn, Jack 1942.20
Mendelsohn, Joseph 1923.15
Mendelssohn 1862.09, 1880.55
Mendelssohn, Felix 1939.29
Mendelvitch, Rodion 1915.11
Mendes, John 1942.20
Mendes, Sam 1998.04
Mendez, Julio 1946.21
Mendez, Lucila 1923.24
Mendez, Lucilla 1924.40
Mendez, Lucille 1925.34
Mendez, Philipo 1943.02
Mendick, Charles 1941.01
Mendizabal, R. 1985.07, 1999.18
Mendoza, Arturo 1988.15
Mendoza, Claudia 1993.08, 1997.13
Mendoza, David 1940.16, 1942.19, 1944.20, 1946.14, 1947.12, 1948.19, 1949.05
Mendoza, Fred 1887.05, 1891.41
Mendoza, Norma 1915.29
Mendum, Georgie Drew 1908.23, 1910.20, 1915.08
Menefee, Pete 1975.20, 1984.06
Menendez, Carlos 1964.02
Menendez, Rosendo Gali 1974.14
Menette, Ada 1890.25
Meng, Constance 1964.02
Menges, Herr 1879.62
Menken, Alan 1994.04, 1994.12, 1995.19, 1996.15, 1997.12, 1997.22, 1998.20, 1999.16, 1999.21, 2000.19
Menlin, Ving 1943.18
Mennier, Louise-Marie 1994.08

Menotti, Gian-Carlo 1947.10, 1948.29, 1950.05, 1950.13, 1952.12, 1954.18, 1958.17, 1959.07, 1960.03, 1962.06, 1965.07, 1965.26, 1966.04, 1966.17, 1974.08, 1975.11, 1976.31, 1978.08
Menowitz, Fred 1970.02
Menteer, Gary 1970.21, 1974.26
Menter, Mack 1891.40
Mention, Michael 1964.39
Menton, Olive 1907.41
Mentzer, Abigail 1993.14
Menz, Clifford 1935.17
Menzel, Idina 1996.09
Menzeli, Lola 1920.46
Menzelli, Elizabeth 1876.16, 1880.07
Menzelli, Helen 1876.16
Menzelli, Helene 1878.03
Menzies, Angus 1939.07
Menzies, Lee 1999.12
Menzies, Lillian 1893.27, 1893.36, 1896.35
Menzies, Pony 1900.35
Meo, Julie 1928.13
Meola, Tony 1986.01, 1986.15, 1987.15, 1990.17, 1992.04, 1993.10, 1993.16, 1993.19, 1994.06, 1994.12, 1995.03, 1995.09, 1995.11, 1995.19, 1996.05, 1996.06, 1996.15, 1996.16, 1997.07, 1997.20, 1997.22, 1998.03, 1998.05, 1998.13, 1998.20, 1999.19, 1999.21, 2000.08, 2000.19
Meorz, Otto C.A. 1914.17
Merande, Doro 1965.21
Merano, Cora 1929.25
Mercado, Hector 1977.12
Mercado, Hector Jaime 1972.14, 1975.09, 1976.35, 1982.19
Mercedes 1938.04
Mercedes, E. 1927.62
Mercenary, Mary 1904.25
Mercer, Beryl 1922.42
Mercer, Frances 1939.28, 1943.01
Mercer, Johnny 1930.18, 1930.33, 1932.20, 1939.14, 1939.29, 1940.09, 1940.16, 1942.10, 1942.18, 1942.24, 1946.08, 1949.17, 1951.23, 1956.02, 1956.12, 1959.27, 1962.17, 1963.02, 1964.04, 1965.08, 1967.11, 1967.13, 1968.20, 1973.14, 1974.09, 1975.12, 1976.32, 1978.05, 1979.14, 1979.24, 1980.08, 1980.20, 1981.06, 1982.12, 1982.14, 1983.20, 1984.10, 1986.01, 1986.03, 1988.08, 1989.06, 1989.21, 1990.09, 1992.18, 1997.05, 1999.01, 1999.06, 1999.24, 2000.16, 2001.08
Mercer, Mabel 1908.27, 1950.05, 1952.12, 1960.03, 1962.06, 1966.04, 1966.17, 1974.08, 1975.11
Mercer, Marian 1962.02, 1968.31, 1978.18
Mercer, Ruby 1931.46, 1936.27, 1941.10, 1942.22
Mercer, Vera 1918.05
Mercer, Will 1904.21
Merchant, Jan 1978.13
Mercier, G.W. 1996.16
Mercier, Rene 1927.39
Mercoolova 1958.20
Mercoolova, Asia 1958.02
Mercouri, Melina 1967.05, 1972.23
Merdith, H. 1868.22
Meredith, Ann 1911.24
Meredith, Burgess 1932.28, 1933.07, 1950.01, 1960.04
Meredith, F.S. 1876.35
Meredith, Gene 1938.08
Meredith, Harry 1880.41, 1881.02, 1894.36
Meredith, Hoyt 1928.14, 1929.28
Meredith, J.C. 1902.38
Meredith, Jane 1912.03
Mcredith, Lee 1980.11
Meredith, Letta 1894.21, 1894.34
Mcredith, Lottie 1896.46
Meredith, Lucille 1886.12
Meredith, Madeline 1929.28
Meredith, Maude 1901.22
Meredith, Morley 1960.10
Meredith, Pearl 1898.41
Meredith, Suzanne 1946.18
Meredith, William 1921.24
Merediz, Olga 1984.02
Mergenthaler, D.J. 1984.16
Merian, Leon 1955.02
Meriden, Messr. 1879.56
Merighi, C. 1911.16
Merighi, Guiseppe 1911.19

983

Printed in the USA/Agawam, MA
November 28, 2011